lonely pl

DUR

D0190131

China

Hēilóngjiāng
p186

Jílín
p175

Xīnjiāng
p799

Inner Mongolia
p875

Běijīng
p64

Liáoníng
p157

Tiānjīn & Héběi
p133

Níngxià
p864

Shānxī
p358

Shāndōng
p201

Qīnghǎi
p891

Gānsù
p832

Shaanxi
(Shǎnxī)
p379

Hénán
p420

Jiāngsū
p236

Shànghǎi
p290

Tibet
p909

Sìchuān
p730

Chóngqìng
p782

Húběi
p440

Ānhuī
p400

Zhèjiāng
p263

Húnán
p471

Jiāngxī
p454

Fújiàn
p337

Guìzhōu
p638

Yúnnán
p666

Guǎngxī
p610

Guǎngdōng
p557

Hong Kong
p499

Hǎinán
p594

Macau
p536

Piera Chen, Mega
Trent Holde
Emily Matchar, E
Christo

PLAN YOUR TRIP

LÌJIĀNG P693

BĚIJĪNG P64

EFIRED/SHUTTERSTOCK ©

ZHAO JIAN KANG/SHUTTERSTOCK ©

ON THE ROAD

Contents

ON THE ROAD

ZHU DIFENG/SHUTTERSTOCK ©

HONG KONG P499

Contents

UNDERSTAND

SURVIVAL GUIDE

SPECIAL FEATURES

Welcome to China

China. The name alone makes you want to get packing. It's going places, so jump aboard, go along for the ride and see where it's headed.

Breathtaking Antiquity

Its modern face is dazzling, but China is no one-trick pony. The world's oldest continuous civilisation isn't all smoked glass and brushed aluminium and while you won't be tripping over artefacts – three decades of round-the-clock development and rash town planning have taken their toll – rich seams of antiquity await. Serve it all up according to taste: collapsing sections of the Great Wall, temple-topped mountains, villages that time forgot, languorous water towns, sublime Buddhist grottoes and ancient desert forts. Pack a well made pair of travelling shoes and remember the words of Laotzu: 'a journey of a thousand miles begins with a single step'.

Stupendous Scenery

Few countries do the Big Outdoors like the Middle Kingdom. China's landscapes span the range from alpha to omega: take your pick from the sublime sapphire lakes of Tibet or the impassive deserts of Inner Mongolia, island-hop in Hong Kong or bike between fairy-tale karst pinnacles around Yángshuò; swoon before the rice terraces of the south, take a selfie among the gorgeous yellow rapeseed of Wùyuán or hike the Great Wall as it meanders across mountain peaks; get lost in green forests of bamboo or, when your energy fails you, flake out on a distant beach and listen to the thud of falling coconuts.

Cuisine

The Chinese live to eat and with 1.4 billion food-loving people to feed, coupled with vast geographic and cultural variations in a huge land, expect your tastebuds to be tantalised, tested and treated. Wolf down Peking duck in Běijīng, melt over a Chóngqìng hotpot or grab a seasoned *ròujiāmó* (shredded pork in a bun) before climbing Huá Shān. Gobble down a steaming bowl of Lánzhōu noodles in a Silk Road street market, raise the temperature with some searing Húnán fare or flag down the dim sum trolley down south. Follow your nose in China and you won't want to stop travelling.

Diversity

China is vast. Off-the-scale massive. A riveting jumble of wildly differing dialects and climatic and topographical extremes, it's like several different countries rolled into one. Take your pick from the tossed-salad ethnic mix of the southwest, the yak-butter-illuminated temples of Xiàhé, a journey along the dusty Silk Road, spending the night at Everest Base Camp or getting into your glad rags for a night on the Shànghǎi tiles. You're spoilt for choice: whether you're an urban traveller, hiker, cyclist, explorer, backpacker, irrepressible museum-goer or faddish foodie, China's diversity is second to none.

Why I Love China

By Damian Harper, Writer

A passion for Chinese martial arts saw me enrolling for a four-year degree in Chinese at university in London back in the 1990s. They were fun days, when travelling China was testing but exciting in equal measure. Hot spots like Píngyáo were unheard of and Shànghǎi's Pǔdōng was a cocktail-free flatland. I could say it's the fantastic food, the awesome landscapes, the thrill of train travel, the delightful people or pitching up in a small town I've never been to before, and I wouldn't be lying. But it's the Chinese language I still love most of all.

For more about our writers, see p1056

Above: Traditional dancers leaving the stage at the Summer Palace (p91), Běijīng

China

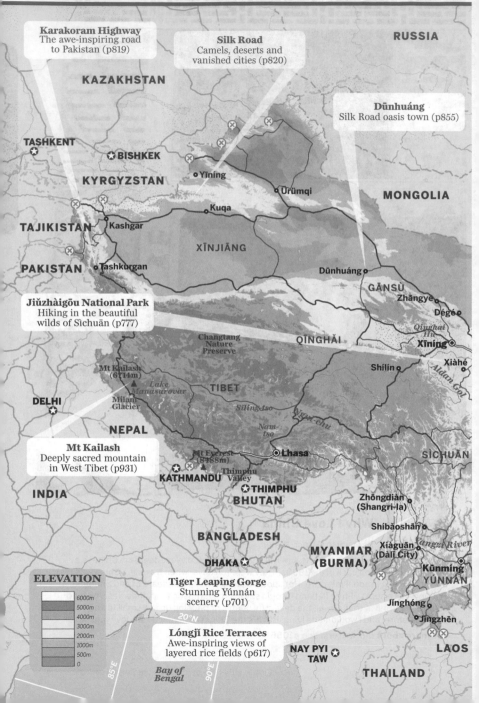

Karakoram Highway
The awe-inspiring road
to Pakistan (p819)

Silk Road
Camels, deserts and
vanished cities (p820)

Dūnhuáng
Silk Road oasis town (p855)

RUSSIA

KAZAKHSTAN

TASHKENT

BISHKEK

KYRGYZSTAN

Yīníng

Ūrümqi

MONGOLIA

TAJIKISTAN

Kashgar

Kuqa

PAKISTAN

Tashkurgan

XĪNJIĀNG

Dūnhuáng

GĀNSÙ

Zhāngyè

Dégê

Jiǔzhàigōu National Park
Hiking in the beautiful
wilds of Sìchuān (p777)

Chāngtáng
Nature
Preserve

QĪNGHǍI

Qinghai
Hú

Xīníng

Mt Kailash
(6714m)

Lake
Manasarovar

Shílín

Xiàhé

Aldan Gol

TIBET

Siling Tso

Milam
Glacier

DELHI

NEPAL

Nam-
tso

Ngan-chu

Mt Kailash
Deeply sacred mountain
in West Tibet (p931)

Mt Everest
(8488m)

Lhasa

SÌCHUĀN

KATHMANDU

Thimphu
Valley

INDIA

THIMPHU

BHUTAN

Zhōngdiàn
(Shangri-la)

BANGLADESH

Shíbǎoshān

DHAKA

MYANMAR
(BURMA)

Xiàguān
(Dàli City)

Yangzi River

Kūnmíng

YÚNNÁN

ELEVATION

6000m
5000m
4000m
3000m
2000m
1000m
500m
0

Tiger Leaping Gorge
Stunning Yúnnán
scenery (p701)

Jīnghóng

Jingzhēn

20°N

Lóngjǐ Rice Terraces
Awe-inspiring views of
layered rice fields (p617)

NAY PYI
TAW

LAOS

85°E

90°E

Bay of
Bengal

THAILAND

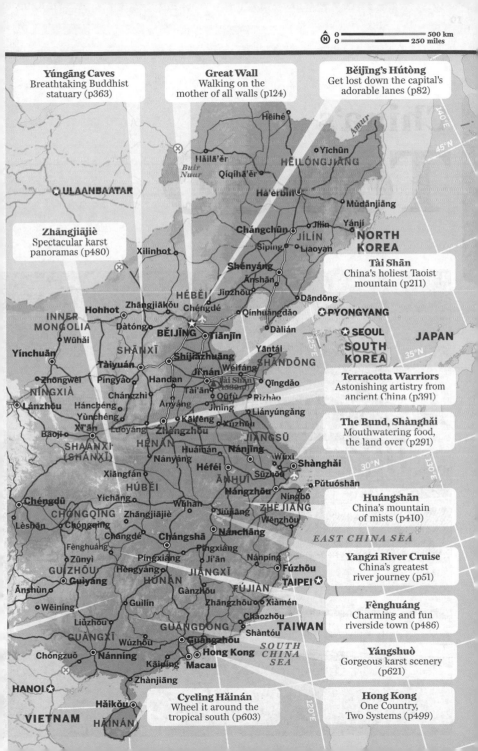

Yúngāng Caves
Breathtaking Buddhist
statuary (p363)

Great Wall
Walking on the
mother of all walls (p124)

Běijīng's Hútòng
Get lost down the capital's
adorable lanes (p82)

Zhāngjiājiè
Spectacular karst
panoramas (p480)

Tài Shān
China's holiest Taoist
mountain (p211)

Terracotta Warriors
Astonishing artistry from
ancient China (p391)

The Bund, Shànghǎi
Mouthwatering food,
the land over (p291)

Huángshān
China's mountain
of mists (p410)

Yangzi River Cruise
China's greatest
river journey (p51)

Fènghuáng
Charming and fun
riverside town (p486)

Yángshuò
Gorgeous karst scenery
(p621)

Cycling Hǎinán
Wheel it around the
tropical south (p603)

Hong Kong
One Country,
Two Systems (p499)

0 | 500 km
0 | 250 miles

Hēihé

Hǎilǎ'ěr
Buïr
Nuur
Qíqíhǎ'ěr

Yīchūn

HĒILÓNGJIĀNG

ULAANBAATAR

Hā'ěrbīn

Mǔdānjiāng

Chángchūn
Jílín
Yánjí

JÍLÍN
NORTH
KOREA

Xilinhot
Shěnyáng
Ānshān

Sìpíng
Liaoyan

Hohhot
Zhāngjiākǒu
Chéngdé

HÉBĚI
Jǐnzhōu

Dāndōng

PYONGYANG

INNER
MONGOLIA
Dàtóng
Qínhuángdǎo
Dàlián

SEOUL
SOUTH
KOREA
JAPAN

Yínchuān
Wūhǎi

BĚIJĪNG
Tiānjīn

Yāntái

SHĀNXĪ
Shíjiāzhuāng
Jǐ'nán
SHĀNDŌNG

Tàiyuán
Weifang

Zhōngwèi
Píngyáo
Handan
Tài Shān
1532m
Qīngdǎo

NÍNGXIÀ
Chángzhì
Tài'ān
Qūfù
Rìzhào

Lánzhōu
Hánchéng
Ānyáng
Jíníng

Yùnchéng
Kāifēng
Liányúngǎng

Bǎojī
Xī'ān
Luòyáng
Zhèngzhōu
Xúzhōu

SHAANXI
(SHǍNXĪ)
HÉNÁN
JIĀNGSŪ

Huáiyīn
Nánjīng
Wúxī

Xiāngfán
Nányáng
Héféi
Sūzhōu
Shànghǎi

HÚBĚI
ĀNHUĪ

Chéngdū
Yíchāng
Wǔhàn
Hángzhōu
Níngbō
Pǔtuóshān

CHÓNGQÌNG
Zhāngjiājiè
Jiǔjiāng
ZHÈJIĀNG

Lèshān
Chóngqìng
Chángdé
Chángshā
Nánchāng
Wēnzhōu

Fènghuáng
Píngxiāng
Jí'ān
Nánpíng

Zūnyí
Héngyáng
JIĀNGXĪ
Fúzhōu

GUÌZHŌU
HÚNÁN
FÚJIÀN
TAIPEI

Ānshùn
Guìyáng
Gànzhōu

Wēiníng
Guìlín
Zhāngzhōu
Xiàmén

Liǔzhōu
GUǍNGDŌNG
Cháozhōu

GUǍNGXĪ
Wúzhōu
Guǎngzhōu
Shàntóu
TAIWAN

Chóngzuǒ
Nánníng
Hong Kong
SOUTH
CHINA
SEA

Kāipíng
Macau

HANOI
Zhànjiāng

Hǎikǒu
VIETNAM
HǍINÁN

EAST CHINA SEA

SOUTH CHINA SEA

Amur

China's
Top 30

Forbidden City

1 Not a city and no longer forbidden, Běijīng's enormous palace (p68) is the be-all-and-end-all of dynastic grandeur with its vast halls and splendid gates. No other place in China teems with so much history, legend and good old-fashioned imperial intrigue. You may get totally lost here but you'll always find something to write about on the first postcard you can lay your hands on. The complex also heads the list with one of China's most attractive admission prices and almost endless value-for-money sightseeing.

Great Wall

2 Spotting it from space is both tough and pointless: the only place you can truly put the Great Wall (p124) under your feet is in China. Select the Great Wall according to taste: perfectly chiselled, dilapidated, stripped of its bricks, overrun with saplings, coiling splendidly into the hills or returning to dust. The fortification is a fitting symbol of those perennial Chinese traits: diligence, mass manpower, ambitious vision and engineering skill (coupled with a distrust of the neighbours).

Below: Bādáling Great Wall (p132)

SEAN PAVONE/SHUTTERSTOCK ©

FEIYUEZHANG.IE/SHUTTERSTOCK ©

The Bund, Shànghǎi

3 More than just a city, Shànghǎi is the country's neon-lit beacon of change, opportunity and modernity. Its sights set squarely on the not-too-distant future, Shànghǎi offers a taste of all the superlatives China can dare to dream up, from the world's highest observation deck to its fastest commercially operating train. Whether you're just pulling in after an epic 44-hour train trip from Xīnjiāng or it's your first stop, you'll find plenty to indulge in here. Start with the Bund (p291), Shànghǎi's iconic riverfront area.

The Lí River & Cycling Yángshuò

4 It's hard to exaggerate the beauty of Yángshuò (p621) and the Lí River area around Yángshuò, renowned for classic images of mossy-green jagged limestone peaks providing a backdrop for tall bamboo fronds leaning over bubbling streams, wallowing water buffaloes and farmers sowing rice paddies. Ride a bamboo raft along the river and you'll understand why this stunning rural landscape has inspired painters and poets for centuries. Another popular way to appreciate the scenery is a bike tour along the Yùlóng River.

Left: Lí River, Guilín (p612)

Dūnhuáng

5 Where China starts transforming into a lunar desertscape in the far west, the handsome oasis town of Dūnhuáng is a natural staging post for dusty Silk Road explorers. Mountainous sand dunes swell outside town while Great Wall fragments lie scoured by abrasive desert winds, but it is the magnificent grottoes (p858) at Mògāo that truly dazzle. Mògāo is the cream of China's crop of Buddhist caves, and its statues are ineffably sublime and some of the nation's most priceless cultural treasures.

Above: Crescent Moon Lake (p860)

8

China's Cuisine

6 Say *zàijiàn* (goodbye) to that Chinatown schlock and *nǐhǎo* (hello) to a whole new world of food and flavour (p965). For Peking duck and dumplings galore, Běijīng's a good place to start, but you don't have to travel far to find that China truly is your oyster, from the liquid fire of a Chóngqìng hotpot to the dainty dim sum of Hong Kong. You'll see things you've never seen before, eat things you've never heard of and drink things that could lift a rocket into orbit.

Top left: Dim sum, Hong Kong (p523)

Hiking Lóngjǐ Rice Terraces

7 After a bumpy bus ride to northern Guǎngxī, you'll be dazzled by one of China's most archetypal and photographed landscapes: the splendidly named Lóngjǐ (Dragon's Backbone) Rice Terraces (p617). A region that's a beguiling patchwork of minority villages and layers of waterlogged terraces climbing the hillsides, you'll be enticed into a game of village-hopping. The most invigorating walk between Píng'ān and Dàzhài villages offers the most spine-tingling views. Visit after the summer rains when the fields are glistening with reflections.

Terracotta Warriors

8 Standing silent guard over their emperor for more than two millennia, the terracotta warriors (p391) are one of the most extraordinary archaeological discoveries ever made. It's not just that there are thousands of the life-sized figures lined up in battle formation; it's the fact that no two of them are alike – each one is animated with a distinct expression. This is an army and one made up entirely of individuals. Gazing at these skilfully sculpted faces brings the past alive with a unique intensity.

Zhāngjiājiè

9 Claimed by some to be the inspiration behind Pandora's floating mountains in the hit film *Avatar*, Zhāngjiājiè's otherworldly rock towers (p482) do indeed seem like they come from another planet. Rising from the misty subtropical forests of northwest Húnán, more than 3000 karst pinnacles form a landscape so surreal it is, arguably, unmatched by any other in China. Raft along a river, hike to your heart's content, walk along a petrifying glass walkway, or just spend hours filling up the memory card on your camera.

French Concession, Shànghǎi

10 The French Concession (p299) is Shànghǎi sunny-side up, at its coolest, hippest and most alluring. Once home to the bulk of Shànghǎi's adventurers, revolutionaries, gangsters, prostitutes and writers – though ironically many of them weren't French – the former concession (also called Frenchtown) is the most graceful part of Pǔxī. The Paris of the East turns on its European charms to maximum effect here, where leafy streets and 1920s villas meet art deco apartment blocks, elegant restaurants and chic bars.

LZF/GETTY IMAGES ©

GIFTOGRAPHY/SHUTTERSTOCK ©

PAVEL ILYUKHIN/SHUTTERSTOCK ©

OOMEZORA/GETTY IMAGES ©

CULVANUIT SWDPV/GETTY IMAGES ©

Huángshān & Hui Villages

11 Shrouded in mist and light rain more than 200 days a year, and maddeningly crowded most of the time, Huángshān has an appeal that attracts millions of annual visitors. Perhaps it's the barren landscape, or an otherworldly vibe on the mountain. Mist rolls in and out at will; spindly bent pines stick out like lone pins across sheer craggy granite faces. Not far from the base are the perfectly preserved Hui villages including Xīdì (p406) and Hóngcūn. Unesco, Ang Lee and Zhang Yimou were captivated – you will be too. Mist on Huángshān (p410)

Cruising up Victoria Harbour

12 A buzzer sounds, you bolt for the gangplank. A whistle blows, your boat chugs forward. Beyond the waves, one of the world's most famous views unfolds – Hong Kong's skyscrapers in their steel and neon brilliance, against a backdrop of mountains. You're on the Star Ferry (p515), a legendary service that's been carrying passengers between Hong Kong Island and Kowloon Peninsula since the 19th century. Ten minutes later, a hemp rope is cast, then a bell rings, and you alight. At only HK$2, this is possibly the world's best-value cruise.

Hiking in Jiǔzhàigōu National Park

13 Exploring the forested valleys of Jiǔzhàigōu National Park (p777) – past bluer-than-blue lakes and small Tibetan villages, in the shadow of snow-brushed mountains – was always a highlight of any trip to Sìchuān province, but the excellent ecotourism scheme in the restricted Zhārú Valley means travellers can hike and camp their way around this stunning part of southwest China. Guides speak English and all camping equipment is provided, so all you need to bring is your sense of adventure and a spare set of camera batteries.

14

KITCHARKON/GETTY IMAGES ©

15

KEREN SU/GETTY IMAGES ©

Fènghuáng

14. Houses perched precariously on stilts, ancestral halls, crumbling temples and gate towers set amid a warren of back alleys full of shops selling mysterious foods and medicines – it's enough on its own to make the ancient town of Fènghuáng (p486) an essential stop. Add in the seductive setting on either side of the Tuó River and the chance to stay at an inn right by the water, and you have one of the most evocative towns in the land.

The Silk Road

15. There are other Silk Road cities in countries such as Uzbekistan and Turkmenistan, but an impressive length of the historic route runs through China, dotted with west and northwest China's pervasive Muslim heritage and fragments from earlier Buddhist civilisations along its trail. You may not be setting off on horse or camel-back from Xī'ān, but hopping on a bus still allows you to follow the route as ancient traders once did. Far-off Kashgar (p814) is the ultimate Silk Road town and remains a unique melting pot of peoples.
Above: Grand Sunday Bazaar (p814), Kashgar

16

17

Píngyáo

16 Time-warped Píngyáo (p371) is a true gem: an intact, walled Chinese town with an unbroken sense of continuity to its Qing dynasty heyday. Píngyáo ticks most of your China boxes with a flourish: imposing city walls, atmospheric alleys, ancient shopfronts, traditional courtyard houses, some excellent hotels, hospitable locals and all in a compact area. You can travel the length and breadth of China and not find another town like it. Step back in time and spend a few days here – it's unique.

Yúngāng Caves

17 Buddhist art taken to sublime heights, these 5th-century caves (p363) house some of the most remarkable statues in all of China. Carved out of the harsh yellow earth of Shānxī and surrounded by superb frescoes, the statues inside the caves represent the highpoint of the Tuoba people's culture and draw on influences from as far away as Greece and Persia. Marvel at how the pigment clinging to some of them has miraculously survived 1500-odd years, and admire how sacred the statuary remains to Buddhist worshippers today.

Tiger Leaping Gorge

18 Picture snow-capped mountains rising on either side of a gorge so deep that you can be 2km above the river rushing across the rocks far below. Then imagine winding up and down trails that pass through tiny farming villages, where you can rest while enjoying views so glorious they defy superlatives. Cutting through remote northwest Yúnnán for 16km, Tiger Leaping Gorge (p701) is a simply unmissable experience. Hikers returning from the gorge invariably give it glowing reviews.

Běijīng's Hútòng

19 To get under the skin of the capital, you need to get lost at least once in its enchanting, ancient alleyways (p83). *Hútòng* are Běijīng's heart and soul; it's in these alleys that criss-cross the centre of the city that you'll discover the capital's unique street life. Despite its march into the 21st century, Běijīng's true charms – heavenly courtyard architecture, pinched lanes and a strong sense of community – are not high-rise. It's easy to find that out; just check into a courtyard hotel and true Běijīng will be right on your doorstep.

Karakoram Highway

20 The Karakoram Highway (p819) is one of the most dramatic roads in the world, linking the ancient Silk Road city of Kashgar with Pakistan over the Khunjerab Pass. A trip here takes you past soaring snowcapped peaks, plate glass lakes backed by sand dunes and verdant valleys where yaks and horses graze and lonely yurts dot the horizon. Even if you don't plan to continue into Pakistan, journeying to the town of Tashkurgan will easily rank as one of your most extraordinary experiences in China.

Labrang Monastery

21 If you can't make it to Tibet, visit the Gānsù province town of Xiàhé, a more accessible part of the former Tibetan region of Amdo. One moment you are in Han China, the next you are virtually in Tibet. Here, Labrang Monastery (p839) attracts legions of suntanned Tibetan pilgrims who perambulate single-mindedly around the huge monastery's prayer wheel-lined *kora* (pilgrim path). As a strong source of spiritual power, the monastery casts its spell far and wide, and with great hiking opportunities plus an intriguing ethnic mix, it's a fascinating corner of China.

Yuányáng Rice Terraces

22 Hewn out of hills that stretch off into the far distance, the rice terraces of Yuányáng (p680) are testimony to the wonderfully intimate relationship the local Hani people have with the sublime landscape they live in. Rising like giant steps, the intricate terraces are a stunning sight at any time of year. But when they are flooded in winter and the sun's rays are dancing off the water at sunrise or sunset, they're absolutely mesmerising and some of the most photogenic spectacles that China has to offer.

Grand Buddha, Lè Shān

23 You can read all the stats you like about Lè Shān's Grand Buddha statue (p750) – yes, its ears really are 7m long! – but until you descend the steps alongside the world's tallest Buddha statue and stand beside its feet, with its toenails at the same level as your eyes, you can't really comprehend just how vast it is. Still not impressed? Consider this, then: the huge stone statue was carved painstakingly into the riverside cliff face more than 1200 years ago.

Fújiàn's Tŭlóu Roundhouses

24 Rising up in colonies from the hilly borderlands of Fújiàn and Guǎngdōng, the stupendous *tŭlóu* roundhouses (p347) house entire villages, even though occupant numbers are way down these days. The imposing and well-defended bastions of wood and earth – not all circular it must be added – can be most easily found in the Fújiàn counties of Nánjìng and Yŏngdìng. Do the right thing and spend the night in one: this is a vanishing way of life, the pastoral setting is quite superb and the architecture is unique.

23

24

LMSPENCER/SHUTTERSTOCK ©

FOTOTRAV/GETTY IMAGES ©

Mystic Tài Shān

25 A visit to China just isn't complete without scaling a sacred mountain or two, and antediluvian Tài Shān (p211) in Shāndōng province is the granddaddy of them all. Climb the Taoist mountain and you'll live to 100, they say, even if you feel you are going to drop dead with exhaustion on the gruelling Path of 18 Bends (lightweights can hitch a ride on the cable car instead). The views are outstanding and with Tài Shān's mountainous aspect in the east, summit sunrises are the order of the day.

Yangzi River Cruise

26 Snow melting from the world's 'third pole' – the high-altitude Tibet–Qīnghǎi plateau – is the source of China's mighty, life-giving Yangzi. The country's longest river, the Yangzi surges west–east across the nation before pouring into the Pacific Ocean. It reaches a crescendo with the Three Gorges, carved out through the millennia by the inexorable persistence of the powerful waters. The gorges are a magnificent spectacle and a Yangzi River cruise (p51) is a rare chance to hang up your travelling hat, take a seat and leisurely watch the drama unfold.

Diāolóu in Kāipíng

27 If you only have time for one attraction in Guǎngdōng, Kāipíng's *diāolóu* (p576) should be it. Approximately 1800 outlandishly designed watchtowers and fortified residences are scattered higgledy-piggledy in the farmland in Kāipíng, a town not far from Guǎngzhōu. These sturdy bastions built in the early 20th century may not be what you'd typically expect in the Middle Kingdom, but they inspire awe with their eccentric fusion of foreign and domestic architectural styles. Greek, Roman, Gothic, Byzantine and baroque – you name it, they've got it.

28

PHILIP YUAN/SHUTTERSTOCK ©

Mt Kailash, Western Tibet

28 Worshipped by more than a billion Buddhists and Hindus, Asia's most sacred mountain (p931) rises from the Barkha plain like a giant four-sided 6714m-high *chörten* (stupa). Throw in stunning nearby Lake Manasarovar and a basin that forms the source of four of Asia's greatest rivers, and it's clear that this place is special. Travelling here to one of the world's most beautiful and remote corners brings a bonus: the three-day pilgrim path around the mountain erases the sins of a lifetime.

Lhasa

29 The holy city of Lhasa (p915) is the perfect introduction to Tibet, and just arriving here can make the hairs stand up on the back of your neck. The spectacular prayer halls of the Potala Palace, the medieval Jokhang Temple and the monastic cities of Drepung and Sera are the big draws, but don't miss the less-visited chapels and pilgrim paths. The whitewashed alleys of the old town hold the real heart of the Tibetan quarter, and you could spend hours here wandering around backstreet handicraft workshops, hidden temples and local teahouses.

Top Right: Potala Palace (p915)

Cycling Hǎinán

30 The same blue skies and balmy weather that make China's only tropical island (p603) ideal for a do-nothing holiday, make it superb for exploring on a bicycle. Hit the east for picturesque rice-growing valleys, spectacular bays and China's finest beaches. And don't miss the sparsely populated central highlands, a densely forested region that's home to the island's original settlers, the Li and the Miao. Here, even the road more frequently taken is still not taken by many at all.

Below right: Sānyà (p605), Hǎinán

29

30

Need to Know

For more information, see Survival Guide (p995)

Currency
yuán (元; ¥)

Language
Mandarin, Cantonese

Visas
Needed for all visits to China except Hong Kong, Macau and 72-hour-and-under trips to Shànghǎi, Běijīng, Chángshā, Chéngdū, Chóngqìng, Dàlián, Guǎngzhōu, Guìlín, Harbin, Kūnmíng, Qīngdǎo, Shěnyáng, Tiānjīn, Wǔhàn, Xiàmén and Xī'ān.

Money
ATMs in big cities and towns. Credit cards less widely used; always carry cash.

Mobile Phones
A mobile phone should be the first choice for calls, but ensure your mobile is unlocked for use in China if taking your own. SIM cards can be bought at the arrivals area at major airports.

Time
GMT/UTC plus eight hours

When to Go

- Warm to hot summers, mild winters
- Mild to hot summers, cold winters
- Mild summers, very cold winters
- Desert, dry climate
- Cold climate

Beijing
GO Sep–Oct

Shànghǎi
GO Oct

Chéngdū
GO Mar–May

Kūnmíng
GO Dec–Jan

Hong Kong
GO Nov–Feb

High Season (May–Aug)

➡ Prepare for summer downpours and crowds at traveller hot spots.

➡ Accommodation prices peak during the first week of the May holiday period.

Shoulder (Feb–Apr, Sep & Oct)

➡ Expect warmer days in spring, cooler days in autumn.

➡ In the north this is the optimal season, with fresh weather and clear skies.

➡ Accommodation prices peak during holidays in early October.

Low Season (Nov–Feb)

➡ Domestic tourism is at a low ebb, but things are busy and expensive for Chinese New Year.

➡ Weather is bitterly cold in the north and at altitude, and only warm in the far south.

Useful Websites

Lonely Planet (lonelyplanet.com/china) Destination information, hotel bookings, traveller forum and more.

Ctrip (www.english.ctrip.com) Hotel booking, air and train ticketing.

Chinasmack (www.chinasmack.com) Human-interest stories and videos.

Popupchinese (www.popupchinese.com) Excellent podcasts (great for learning Chinese).

Far West China (www.farwestchina.com) Indispensable resource for Silk Roaders.

Important Numbers

Ambulance	120
Fire	119
Police	110
Country code (China/Hong Kong/Macau)	86/852/853
International access code	00
Directory assistance	114

Exchange Rates

Australia	A$1	¥5.28
Canada	C$1	¥5.24
Euro	€1	¥7.29
Hong Kong	HK$1	¥0.89
Japan	¥100	¥6.07
New Zealand	NZ$1	¥6.07
UK	UK£1	¥8.58
US	US$1	¥6.88

For current exchange rates, see www.xe.com.

Daily Costs

Budget: Less than ¥200

➡ Dorm bed: ¥40–60

➡ Food markets, street food: ¥40

➡ Bike hire or other transport: ¥20

➡ Free museums

Midrange: ¥200–1000

➡ Double room in a midrange hotel: ¥200–600

➡ Lunch and dinner in local restaurants: ¥80–100

➡ Drinks in a bar: ¥60

➡ Taxis: ¥60

Top end: More than ¥1000

➡ Double room in a top-end hotel: ¥600 and up

➡ Lunch and dinner in excellent local or hotel restaurants: ¥300

➡ Shopping at top-end shops: ¥300

➡ Two tickets to Chinese opera: ¥300

Opening Hours

China officially has a five-day working week; Saturday and Sunday are public holidays.

Banks Open Monday to Friday 9am to 5pm (or 6pm); may close for two hours in the afternoon. Many also open Saturday and maybe Sunday. Same for offices and government departments.

Bars Open in the late afternoon, shutting around midnight or later.

Post offices Generally open daily.

Restaurants Open from around 10.30am to 11pm; some shut at around 2pm and reopen at 5pm or 6pm.

Shops Open daily 10am to 10pm. Same for department stores and shopping malls.

Arriving in China

Capital Airport (Běijīng; p1009) Airport Express train services run every 10 minutes. The airport bus runs to central Běijīng every 10 to 20 minutes. A taxi will cost ¥90 to ¥120.

Pǔdōng International Airport (Shànghǎi; p1009) Maglev trains run every 20 minutes. Metro Line 2 links the airport with Hóngqiáo Airport. Airport buses run every 15 to 30 minutes. A taxi to central Shànghǎi will cost ¥160.

Hong Kong International Airport (p1009) Airport Express trains run every 10 minutes. A taxi to Central will cost about HK$300.

Getting Around

Despite being a land of vast distances, it's quite straightforward to navigate your way terrestrially around China by rail and bus if you have time. Transport in China needs considerable preplanning due to the distances involved and periodic shortages of tickets.

Air Affordable and excellent for long distances, but delays are common.

Bus Cheaper and slower than trains but crucial for remote destinations.

Car China is too large and there are too many restrictions to make this a viable option.

Train Very reasonably priced – apart from high-speed rail, which is more expensive – and very efficient.

For much more on **getting around**, see p1012

First Time China

For more information, see Survival Guide (p995)

Checklist

☐ Check the validity of your passport

☐ Make any necessary bookings (for accommodation and travel)

☐ Secure your visa and additional permits well in advance

☐ Check what clothing you will need

☐ Check the airline baggage restrictions

☐ Organise travel insurance

☐ Check if you can use your mobile/cell phone

☐ Work out your itinerary

☐ Inform your credit/debit-card company

What to Pack

☐ Passport

☐ Credit card

☐ Phrasebook

☐ Money belt

☐ Travel plug

☐ Medical kit

☐ Insect repellent

☐ Mobile-phone charger

☐ Sunscreen

☐ Sunhat and shades

☐ Waterproof clothing

☐ Torch

☐ Pocketknife

☐ Earplugs

Top Tips for Your Trip

➡ Be patient and understand that many things you may take for granted – orderly queues, international levels of English ability, personal space – may not exist.

➡ Although they are not that user friendly, choosing to take local buses instead of taxis could mean you're the only foreigner on board and a local could well strike up a conversation with you.

➡ Treat China as an adventure and learning curve, rather than purely as a holiday.

➡ Dining in local street markets is a great way to eat out of your comfort zone and discover the full, variety of Chinese cooking.

What to Wear

You can pretty much wear casual clothes throughout your entire journey in China, unless dining in a smart restaurant in Shànghǎi, Běijīng or Hong Kong, when you may need to dress less casually. In general, trousers (pants) and shirts or tees for guys, and dresses, skirts or trousers for women will serve you well nationwide; shorts and short sleeves are generally fine in summer, but don long trousers and long sleeves in the evenings to keep mosquitoes at bay. A sunhat can be invaluable. A thin waterproof coat and sturdy shoes are a good idea for hiking and sightseeing. Winter is a different ball game up north and especially at altitude: you'll need several layers, thick shirts, jerseys and warm coats, jackets, gloves, socks and a hat.

Sleeping

It's generally always a good idea to book your accommodation in advance, especially in the high season and when visiting big ticket destinations, such as Hángzhōu, at weekends. See p996 for more accommodation information.

Hotels From two-star affairs with very limited English and simple rooms to international-level, five-star towers and heritage hotels.

Hostels Exist across China in growing numbers, usually offering dorm beds and double rooms and dispensing useful travel advice.

Homestays In rural locations, you can often find double rooms in converted houses, with meals provided.

Money

Credit cards Credit and debit cards are increasingly accepted in tourist towns and big cities, particularly Visa and MasterCard. Ask if bars and restaurants take cards before ordering.

ATMs There are 24-hour ATMs available at Bank of China and Industrial and Commercial Bank of China (ICBC) branches.

Changing money You can change money at hotels, large branches of Bank of China, some department stores and international airports. Some towns don't have any money-changing facilities, so make sure you carry enough cash.

Bargaining

Haggling is standard procedure in markets and shops (outside of department stores and malls) where prices are not clearly marked. There's no harm in coming in really low, but remain polite at all times. In touristy markets in Shànghǎi and Běijīng, vendors can drop as low as 25% of the original price.

Tipping

Tipping is never done at cheap restaurants in mainland China. Smart, international restaurants will encourage tipping, but it is not obligatory and it's uncertain whether wait staff receive their tips at the end of the night.

Hotel restaurants automatically add a 15% service charge; some high-end restaurants may do the same.

Etiquette

China is a pretty relaxed country regarding etiquette, but be aware of a few things:

Greetings and goodbyes Shake hands, but never kiss someone's cheek. Say 'Nǐhǎo' for hello and 'Zàijiàn' (or increasingly just 'Bye bye') for goodbye

Asking for help To ask for directions start with 'Qǐng wèn....' ('Can I ask...'); say 'Duìbuqǐ' ('Sorry') to apologise.

Religion Dress sensitively when visiting Buddhist (especially in Tibet) and Taoist temples, churches and mosques.

Eating and drinking Help fill your neighbour's plate at the dinner table; toast the host and others at the table; at the start of dinner, wait till toasting starts before drinking from your glass; offer your cigarettes around if you smoke; always offer to buy drinks in a bar but never fight over the drink/food tab if someone else wants to pay (but do offer at least once).

Gestures Don't use too many hand movements or excessive body language.

Booking Ahead

Reserving a room, even if only for the first night of your stay, is the best way to ensure a smooth start to your trip. These phrases should see you through a call if English isn't spoken.

Hello	你好	Nǐhǎo
I would like to book a room	我想订房间	Wǒ xiǎng dìng fángjiān
a single room	单人间	dānrén jiān
a double room	双人间	shuāngrén jiān
My name is...	我叫...	Wǒ jiào...
from... to... (date)	从...到...	cóng... dào...
How much is it per night/person?	每天/个人多少钱?	Měi tiān/gè rén duōshǎo qián?
Thank you	谢谢你	Xièxie nǐ

Language

It is entirely possible to travel around China hardly hearing any English at all. Tourist-industry employees across the land are more likely to speak English; in the big cities such as Shànghǎi, Běijīng and, of course, Hong Kong, English is more widely spoken and understood, but generally only among educated Chinese. In smaller towns and the countryside, English is often of little or no use: the vast majority of Chinese do not speak the language at all.

If You Like...

The Great Wall

The Wall most famously belongs to Běijīng, but fragments leave a ragged band across much of north China, trailing from the North Korean border to the wind-scoured deserts of China's wild northwest.

Jiànkòu Běijīng's prime chunk of ruin, a sublime portrait of disintegrating brickwork, overgrown with saplings and immersed in a magnificent mountain panorama. (p127)

Gǔběikǒu Trekking options galore at this Great Wall crossroads accessible from Běijīng. (p127)

Zhuàngdàokǒu Little-visited length of wall near Běijīng packing supreme views and hiking opportunities. (p128)

Huánghuā Chéng Excellent hiking opportunities along some of the most authentic sections of wall to be found around Běijīng. (p130)

Jiāyùguān Fort Confront weathered slogans from Mao's Cultural Revolution lashed by the Gānsù desert winds. (p852)

Bā Táizi Sublime Gothic church tower ruin alongside a similarly dilapidated length of the Great Wall, outside Dàtóng. (p364)

Fantastic Food

With its novel flavours, unexpected aromas and tastes, China is a true culinary adventure. Head west for zing, zest and spice, north for hearty and salty flavours, east for fresh and lightly flavoured seafood, and south for dim sum.

Peking duck Once bitten, forever smitten, and only true to form in Běijīng. (p103)

Chóngqìng hotpot Sweat like you're in a sauna over China's most volcanic culinary creation. (p790)

Xiǎolóngbāo Shànghǎi's bite-sized snack packs a lot of flavour (but watch out for the super heated meat juice). (p318)

Dim Sum Head to Hong Kong for the very best in China's bite-size delicacies. (p523)

Hiking

Despite urban encroachment, China is one of the world's most geographically varied and largest nations, with stupendous hiking opportunities amid breathtaking scenery.

Tiger Leaping Gorge Yúnnán's best-known and most enticing hike is not for the faint-hearted. (p701)

Lóngjǐ Rice Terraces Work your way from Dàzhài to Píng'ān through some of China's most mesmerising scenery. (p617)

Wùyuán Follow the old postal roads from village to village in the drop-dead gorgeous Jiāngxī countryside. (p466)

Lángmùsì Excellent options in most directions from the charming monastic town on the Gānsù–Sìchuān border. (p845)

Yàdīng Nature Reserve Follow a Tibetan pilgrimage route on two- to eight-day tracks around magnificent peaks. (p770)

Ganden to Samye An 80km, four- to five-day high-altitude hike between these two Tibetan monasteries. (p495)

Extremes

China has more than enough extremes to satisfy thrill-seekers, or just the plain inquisitive. From the world's highest mountain to the world's fastest trains and the world's furthest city from the sea, take your pick from China's extremes.

Běihóngcūn China's northernmost village in Hēilóngjiāng, where winter temperatures are glacial. (p199)

Turpan China's hottest spot and the world's second-lowest depression, where the thermometer has topped 48°C. (p808)

Shànghǎi Maglev The world's fastest commercially operating Maglev system train has a top operational speed of 431 km/h (268 mph; p334)

Everest Base Camp Rise early for dramatic images of the world's highest mountain in the morning sun. (p929)

Ürümqi Journey along the Silk Road and stop by the world's most remote city from the sea. (p802)

Imperial Architecture

Crumbling dynasties have deposited an imposing trail of antiquity across north China, from vast imperial palaces to the noble ruins of the Great Wall and altars reserved for the emperor.

Forbidden City China's standout imperial residence in Běijīng, home to two dynasties of emperors and their concubines. (p68)

Summer Palace An epic display of traditional Chinese aesthetics with crucial ingredients: hills, lakes, bridges, pavilions, temples and tantalising sunsets. (p91)

Imperial Palace Manchu splendour in Shěnyáng within the former Manchurian heartland of Liáoníng province. (p170)

Xī'ān Shaanxi home of the Terracotta Warriors, an imposing Ming city wall and traces of the city's astonishing Tang apogee. (p381)

Chéngdé Summer bolt-hole of the Qing emperors, with palatial remains and a riveting brood of Tibetan-style temples. (p147)

Top: Woman in traditional Miao dress
Bottom: Summer Palace (p91), Běijīng

Ancient Settlements

Traditional China can be glimpsed in its picturesque, ancient villages and towns. Ming and Qing dynasty architecture, narrow lanes and superlative feng shui combine in a pastoral aesthetic complemented by a relaxed rural tempo.

Píngyáo China's best-looking, best-preserved walled town – by a long shot – warrants thorough exploration. (p371)

Fènghuáng Make sure you overnight in this fantastic historic town on the Tuó River for its beautiful evening lights. (p486)

Wùyuán Take time off to village-hop in the gorgeous Jiāngxī countryside and dream of abandoning urban China for good. (p463)

Fújiàn Tǔlóu Explore the fortress-like earthen 'roundhouses' of Fújiàn, distinctive for their imposing enormity. (p347)

Xīnyè This effortlessly charming village is designed with an eye for traditional Chinese harmony and balance. (p281)

Sacred China

From the esoteric mysteries of Tibetan Buddhism to the palpable magic of its holy Taoist mountains and its disparate collection of Christian churches, mosques and shrines, China's sacred realm is the point at which the supernatural and natural worlds converge.

Pǔníng Temple, Chéngdé Be rendered speechless by China's largest wooden statue, a towering effigy of the Buddhist Goddess of Mercy. (p150)

Labrang Monastery Tap into the ineffable rhythms of southern Gānsù's place of pilgrimage for legions of Tibetans. (p839)

Gyantse Kumbum An overwhelming sight and monumental experience, the nine-tiered *chörten* is Tibet's largest stupa. (p925)

Dà Zhào Hohhot's riveting and colossal Tibetan Buddhist temple at the heart of the Inner Mongolian capital. (p878)

Wǔdāng Shān Commune with the spirit of Taoist martial arts in the birthplace of taichi. (p449)

Museums

Urbanisation means that museum collections can be the clearest window onto China's past, and they are ubiquitous, covering everything from ethnic clothing to clocks, Buddhist artefacts and vanished civilisations.

Palace Museum The official and highly prosaic name for the Forbidden City, China's supreme link to its dynastic past. (p68)

Shànghǎi Museum A dazzling collection of ceramics, paintings, calligraphy and much more at the heart of Shànghǎi. (p294)

Alashan Museum Terrific museum and collection of artefacts and objects relating to Ālāshān and Mongolian culture. (p888)

Hong Kong Museum of History Entertaining, resourceful and informative. (p513)

Nánjīng Museum A lavish celebration of Chinese culture's big hitters, with astounding exhibitions. (p239)

Stunning Scenery

You haven't really experienced China until you've had your socks blown off by one of its scenic marvels. China's constructed splendours give cities such as Shànghǎi head-turning cachet, but nature steals the show.

Yángshuò You've probably seen the karst topography before in picture-perfect photographs; now see the real thing. (p621)

Huángshān When suffused in spectral mists, China's Yellow Mountain enters a different dimension of beauty. (p410)

Jiǔzhàigōu National Park Turquoise lakes, waterfalls, snowcapped mountains and green forests: all this and more. (p777)

Chìshuǐ Trek past waterfalls and through ancient forests dating to the Jurassic. (p657)

Yuányáng Rice Terraces Be transfixed by the dazzling display of light and water. (p680)

Urban Extravaganzas

Among China's most dynamic cities is Shànghǎi, where glittering skyscrapers overlook Maglev trains, and cashed-up consumers shop in chic malls, drink at elegant cocktail bars and dine at fashionable restaurants.

Shànghǎi The city that everyone – architects, fashionistas, cocktail connoisseurs, foodies, urban travellers, interior designers – is talking about. (p290)

Hong Kong Poised between China and the West, the ex-British colony continues

Yuányáng Rice Terraces (p680)

to plough its own distinctive furrow. (p499)

Běijīng China's leading city; a riveting blend of ancient capital and modern metropolis. (p64)

Hángzhōu One of China's most attractive cities with the sublime and romantic West Lake at its heart. (p265)

Ethnic Minorities

Han China hits the buffers around its far-reaching borderlands, where a colourful patchwork of ethnic minorities preserves distinct cultures, languages, architectural styles and livelihoods.

Tibet Explore this vast region in the west of China or chart an itinerary through the easier-to-access regions outside the Tibetan heartland. (p909)

Déhāng This Miao village in hilly Húnán finds itself delightfully embedded in some breathtaking scenery. (p485)

Lìjiāng Yúnnán's famous home of the blue-clothed Naxi folk. (p693)

Kashgar Dusty Central Asian outpost and Uighur China's most famous town, on the far side of the Taklamakan Desert. (p814)

Bayanhot Easily reached just over the border from Níngxià, this town is a fascinating introduction to west Inner Mongolia and its awesome desertscapes. (p888)

Boat Trips

China is cut by some dramatic and breathtaking rivers, including the mighty Yangzi. Hop on a riverboat

and ease into a totally different experience of China's landscapes.

Three Gorges China's most awesome river panorama. (p53)

Lí River The hypnotising karst landscapes of northeast Guǎngxī. (p616)

Star Ferry, Hong Kong The short but iconic ferry hop across Victoria Harbour from Tsim Sha Tsui. (p515)

Evening river cruise, Chóngqìng Before getting all misty on the Yangzi, experience Chóngqìng's nocturnal, neon performance. (p788)

Qīngyuǎn boat trip, Guǎngdōng Lazily float along the Běi River, past secluded Fēilái Temple and Fēixiá monastery. (p580)

Month by Month

January

North China is a deep freeze but the south is less bitter; preparations for the Lunar New Year get underway well in advance of the festival, which arrives any time between late January and March.

🎊 Spring Festival

The Lunar New Year is family-focused, with dining on dumplings and gift-giving of *hóngbāo* (red envelopes stuffed with money). Most families feast together on New Year's Eve, then China goes on a big week-long holiday. Expect fireworks, parades, temple fairs and lots of colour.

🎊 Harbin Ice & Snow Festival

Hēilóngjiāng's good-looking capital Harbin is aglow with rainbow lights refracted through fanciful buildings and statues carved from blocks of ice. It's peak season and outrageously cold.

☉ Yuányáng Rice Terraces

The watery winter is the optimum season for the rice terraces' spectacular combination of liquid and light. Don't forget your camera, or your sense of wonder.

February

North China remains shockingly icy and dry but things are slowly warming up in Hong Kong and Macau. The Lunar New Year could well be underway, but sort out your tickets well in advance.

🎊 Monlam Great Prayer Festival

Held during two weeks from the third day of the Tibetan New Year and celebrated with spectacular processions (except in Lhasa or the Tibet Autonomous Region); huge silk *thangka* (sacred art) are unveiled and, on the last day, a statue of the Maitreya Buddha is conveyed around.

🎊 Lantern Festival

Held 15 days after the Spring Festival, this was traditionally a time when Chinese hung out highly decorated lanterns. Píngyáo in Shānxī is an atmospheric place to soak it up (sometimes held in March).

March

China comes to life after a long winter, although it remains glacial at high altitudes. The mercury climbs in Hong Kong and abrasive dust storms billow into Běijīng, scouring everything in their path. It's still low season.

🎊 Běijīng Book Bash

Curl up with a good book at the Bookworm cafe for Běijīng's international literary festival, and lend an ear to lectures from international and domestic authors at one of China's best bookshops. (p106)

☉ Fields of Yellow

Delve into south Chinese countryside to be bowled over by a landscape

saturated in bright-yellow rapeseed. In some parts of China, such as lovely Wùyuán in Jiāngxī province, it's a real tourist draw.

April

Most of China is warm and it's a good time to be on the road. The Chinese take several days off for the Qīngmíng festival, a traditional date for honouring their ancestors and now an official holiday.

A Good Soaking

Flush away the dirt, demons and sorrows of the old year and bring in the fresh at the Dai New Year, with its water-splashing festival in Xīshuāngbǎnnà. Taking an umbrella is pointless.

Paean to Peonies

Wángchéng Park in Luòyáng bursts into full-coloured bloom with its peony festival: pop a flower garland on your head and join in the floral fun.

Third Moon Festival

This Bai ethnic minority festival is another excellent reason to pitch up in the lovely north Yúnnán town of Dàlǐ. It's a week of horse racing, singing and merrymaking from the 15th day of the third lunar month (usually April) to the 21st.

Formula One

Petrolheads and aficionados of speed, burnt rubber and hairpin bends flock to Shànghǎi for some serious motor racing at the track near Āntíng. Get your hotel room booked early: it's

Top: Ice & Snow Festival, Harbin (p188)
Bottom: Spring Festival decorations, Tàiyuán (p368)

one of the most glamorous events on the Shànghǎi calendar.

May

Mountain regions, such as Sìchuān's Jiǔzhàigōu National Park, are in full bloom. For the first four days of May China is on holiday (Labour Day). Buddha's Birthday falls on the 8th day of the fourth lunar month, usually in May.

✦ Buddha's Birthday in Xiàhé

A fascinating time to enjoy the Tibetan charms of Gānsù province's Xiàhé, when Buddhist monks make charitable handouts to beggars and the streets throng with pilgrims.

✦ Circling the Mountain Festival

On Pǎomǎ Shān, Kāngdìng's famous festival celebrates the birthday of Sakyamuni, the historical Buddha, with a magnificent display of horse racing, wrestling and a street fair.

✦ Great Wall Marathon

Experience the true meaning of pain. Not for the infirm or unfit. See www.great-wall-marathon.com for more details.

June

Most of China is hot and getting hotter. Once-frozen areas, such as Jílín's Heaven Lake, are accessible – and nature springs instantly

to life. The great China peak tourist season is cranking up.

✦ Festival of Aurora Borealis

The Northern Lights are sometimes visible from Mòhé in Hēilóngjiāng, in the ultra-far north of China not far from the Russian border. Even if you don't get to see the (often elusive) multicoloured glow, the June midnight sun is a memorable experience.

☆ Dragon Boat Festival

Head to Zhènyuǎn or the nearest large river and catch all the water-borne drama of dragon-boat racers in this celebration of one of China's most famous poets. The Chinese traditionally eat *zòngzi* (triangular glutinous rice dumplings wrapped in reed leaves).

✦ Dhama Festival

This three-day festival in Gyantse in Tibet kicks off on 20 June for horse racing, wrestling, archery, yak races and more.

✦ Shangri-la Horse Racing Festival

In mid- to late June, the north Yúnnán town of Shangri-la (Zhōngdiàn) lets go of the reins with this celebration of horse racing, coupled with singing, dancing and merriment on the southeastern fringes of Tibet.

☆ Tǎgōng Horse Festival

Celebrated on varying dates each year based on the Tibetan calendar, this festival on a hilltop

overlooking the town's two monasteries and surrounding mountain peaks is a breathtaking display of Tibetan horsemanship.

July

Typhoons can wreak havoc with travel itineraries down south, lashing the Guǎngdōng and Fújiàn coastlines. Plenty of rain sweeps across China: the 'plum rains' give Shànghǎi a big soaking, and the grasslands of Inner Mongolia and Qīnghǎi turn green.

✦ Torch Festival, Dàlǐ

Held on the 24th day of sixth lunar month (usually July), this festival is held throughout Yúnnán by the Bai and Yi minorities. Making for great photos, flaming torches are paraded at night through streets and fields, and go up outside shops around town.

✦ Mongolian Merrymaking, Naadam

Mongolian wrestling, horse racing, archery and more during the weeklong Naadam festival on the grasslands of Inner Mongolia at the end of July, when the grass is at its summer greenest.

♟ Dàlián International Beer Festival

Xīnghǎi Square in the Liáoníng port city is steeped in the aroma of hops and ale and strewn with beer tents in this 12-day celebration of more than 400 international and Chinese beers from a plethora of breweries.

August

The temperature gauge of Yangzi's 'three ovens' – Chóngqìng, Wǔhàn and Nánjīng – gets set to blow. Rainstorms hit Běijīng, which is usually 40°C plus; so is Shànghǎi. So head uphill to Lúshān, Mògānshān, Huáng Shān or Guōliàngcūn.

🎭 Lǐtáng Horse Festival

Occasionally cancelled in recent years (restrictions on travel may suddenly appear) and also shrunk from one week to one day, this festival in West Sìchuān is a breathtaking display of Tibetan horsemanship, archery and more.

🍺 Qīngdǎo International Beer Festival

Slake that chronic summer thirst with a round of beers and devour a plate of mussels in Shāndōng's best-looking port town, a former German concession and home of the famous Tsingtao beer brand.

September

Come to Běijīng and stay put – September is part of the fleetingly lovely *tiāngāo qìshuǎng* ('the sky is high and the air is fresh') autumnal season – an event in itself. It's also a pleasant time to visit the rest of north China.

🏃 Tài Shān International Climbing Festival

Held annually since 1987, this festival at the sacred Taoist mountain of Tài Shān in Shāndōng draws hundreds of trail runners, mountain bikers, climbers and worshippers of all ages and abilities.

🎭 Mid-Autumn Festival

Also called the moon festival; celebrated by devouring daintily prepared moon cakes – stuffed with bean paste, egg yolk, walnuts and more. With a full moon, it's a romantic occasion for lovers and a special time for families. On the 15th day of the eighth lunar month.

☉ International Qiántáng River Tide Observing Festival

The most popular time to witness the surging river tides sweeping at up to 40km/h along the Qiántáng River in Yánguān is during the mid-autumn festival, although you can catch the wall of water during the beginning and middle of every lunar month.

🎭 Confucius' Birthday

Head to the Confucius Temple in Qūfù for the 28 September birthday celebrations of axiom-quipping philosopher, sage and patriarch Confucius.

October

The first week of October can be hellish if you're on the road: the National Day weeklong holiday kicks off, so everywhere is swamped. Go midmonth instead, when everywhere is deserted.

🍴 Hairy Crabs in Shànghǎi

Now's the time to sample delicious hairy crabs in Shànghǎi; they are at their best – male and female crabs eaten together with shots of lukewarm Shàoxīng rice wine – between October and December.

🎭 Miao New Year

Load up with rice wine and get on down to Guìzhōu for the ethnic festivities in the very heart of the minority-rich southwest.

🎭 Kurban Bairam (Gǔěrbāng Jié)

Catch the four-day celebrations of the Muslim festival of sacrifice in communities across China; the festival is at its liveliest and most colourful in Kashgar.

November

Most of China is getting pretty cold as tourist numbers drop and holidaymakers begin to flock south for sun and the last pockets of warmth.

🏃 Surfing Hǎinán

The peak surfing season kicks off in Rì Yuè Bay (Sun & Moon Bay) in Hǎinán, where the island's best surf rolls in. Hordes of Chinese flee the cold mainland for these warmer climes.

Itineraries

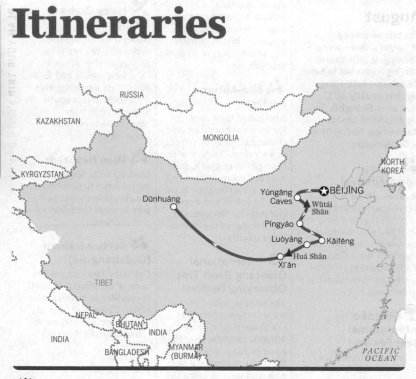

Northern Tour

China's richest seam of historic antiquity runs through rugged, dry north China. This route takes in the north's signature sights, all the way from Běijīng and the Great Wall via the Terracotta Warriors to the Silk Road of the distant northwest.

Běijīng is fundamental to this tour, so give yourself five days to do the Forbidden City, size up the Great Wall, the Summer Palace and and the city's *hútòng* (narrow alleyways). The splendour of the **Yúngāng Caves** outside the rebuilt ancient city of Dàtóng should put you in a Buddhist mood, sharpened by a few nights on monastic **Wǔtái Shān**. Make a three-day stopover in **Píngyáo**, an age-old walled town, followed by the historic walled city of **Kāifēng** in Hénán, once the traditional home of China's small community of Chinese Jews; move on to **Luòyáng** and the Buddhist spectacle of the Lóngmén Caves and the Shàolín Temple, also within reach. Four days' sightseeing in **Xī'ān** brings you face-to-face with the Army of Terracotta Warriors and gives you time for the Taoist mountain of **Huà Shān**. Xī'ān traditionally marked the start of the Silk Road which you can follow through Gānsù province all the way to the oasis town of **Dūnhuáng**, and beyond.

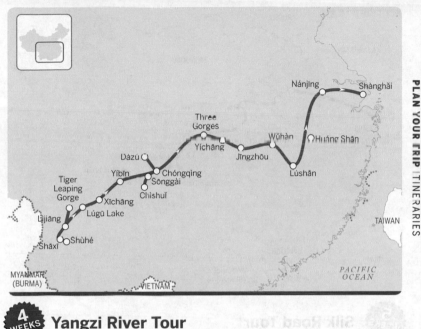

4 WEEKS Yangzi River Tour

This epic tour follows the astonishingly long Yangzi river, from the foothills of the Himalayas to the bustling boom town of Shànghǎi.

After exploring north Yúnnán's ancient Naxi town of **Lìjiāng**, pick up the trail of the Jīnshā River (Gold Sand River, which spills down from Tibet and swells into the Yangzi River) on a breathtaking multiday hike along **Tiger Leaping Gorge**. Rest your worn-out legs before discovering the scattered villages and old towns around Lìjiāng, including **Shāxī** and **Shùhé** on the old Tea Horse Road, and being blown away by the magnificent views of Yùlóng Xuěshān. Also consider (warmer months only) a trip from Lìjiāng northeast towards west Sìchuān and the gorgeous **Lúgū Lake** on the provincial border, where you can spend several days unwinding by the lakeside. During the winter months this entire area is snowbound, so you may have to fly on from Lìjiāng. Daily minibuses do the seven-hour run from Lúgū Hú to **Xīchāng** in Sìchuān, from where you can reach **Yíbīn** and then **Chóngqìng**; alternatively, return to Lìjiāng to fly to Chóngqìng, home of the spicy and searing Chóngqìng hotpot and gateway to the Three Gorges. Detour by bus to the stunning landscapes and natural beauty of **Chìshuǐ** on the Guìzhōu border to relax, unwind and explore the region before returning by bus to urban Chóngqìng. You'll need around three days in Chóngqìng for the sights in town and for a journey to the Buddhist Caves at **Dàzú** and a trip to the Yangzi River village of **Sōnggài** to keep a perspective on historic, rural China. Then hop on a cruise vessel or passenger boat (or even a bus followed by hydrofoil) to **Yíchāng** in Húběi through the magnificent **Three Gorges**. Journey from Yíchāng to the Yangzi River city of **Wǔhàn** via the walled town of **Jīngzhōu**, where it's worth spending the night. After two days in Wǔhàn, jump on a bus to **Lúshān** in Jiāngxī province, from where you can reach **Nánjīng** or make your way to **Huáng Shān** in the Yangzi River province of Ānhuī. Alternatively, travel direct to Nánjīng and thread your way to **Shànghǎi** via a delightful string of canal towns – Sūzhōu, Tónglǐ, Lùzhí and Zhūjiājiǎo. Explore Shànghǎi and consider launching yourself into the East–Southwest Rural Tour (p44).

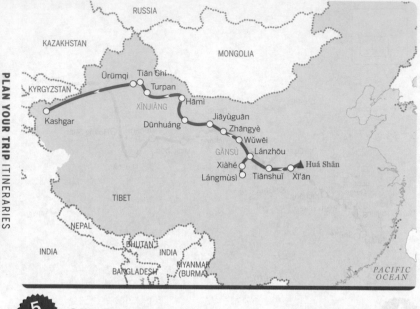

5 WEEKS Silk Road Tour

This breathtaking journey takes you from the must-see Terracotta Warriors via the Buddhist heritage of Gānsù to the vast desert distances of Xīnjiāng and far-flung Kashgar.

From the southernmost extents of the Silk Road at **Xī'ān**, discover one of imperial China's most iconic remains at the Army of Terracotta Warriors and, for a major workout, climb the precipitous Taoist mountain of **Huá Shān** – just don't look down. Back in Xī'ān, explore the Muslim Quarter to feast on local Hui specialities – one of the culinary high points of China travel – and climb atop the imposing city walls. Hop aboard the train to **Lánzhōu** but get off in southeast Gānsù at **Tiānshuǐ** for the remarkable Buddhist grottoes at verdant Màijī Shān. From Lánzhōu you have the option to disengage temporarily from the Silk Road to ramble along the fringes of the Tibetan world in the Buddhist monastic settlements of **Xiàhé** and **Lángmùsì**. The Hèxī Corridor draws you on to the ancient Great Wall outpost of **Jiāyùguān**, via the Silk Road stopover town of **Wǔwēi**, and the Great Buddha Temple with its outsize effigy of a reclining Sakyamuni in **Zhāngyè**. Stand on the wind-blasted ramparts of Jiāyùguān Fort, the last major stronghold of imperial China, and tramp alongside westerly remnants of the Great Wall. The delightful oasis outpost of **Dūnhuáng** is one of China's tidiest and most pleasant towns, with the mighty sand dunes of the Singing Sands Mountains pushing up from the south, a scattered array of sights in the surrounding desert and some excellent food. The town is also the hopping-off point for China's splendid hoard of Buddhist art, the spellbinding Mògāo Grottoes. From Dūnhuáng you can access the mighty northwestern Uighur province of Xīnjiāng via the melon town of **Hāmì** before continuing to **Turpan** and **Ürümqi**; consider also spending the night in a yurt or camping on the shores of mountainous **Tiān Chí**. Thread your way through a string of Silk Road towns by rail to the Central Asian outpost of **Kashgar**, or reach the distant Uighur town via the Marco Polo–journeyed southern Silk Road along the cusp of the Taklamakan Desert. From Kashgar, hatch exciting plans to conquer the Karakoram Hwy or, in the other direction, work out how to get back into China proper.

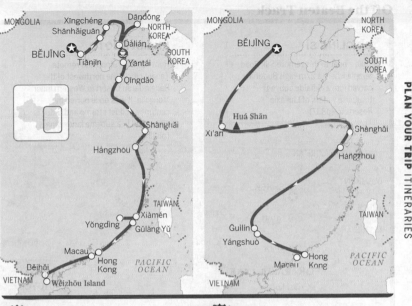

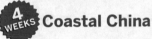 **Coastal China**

 Big Ticket Tour

This coastal tour journeys through China's largest collection of concession-era heritage as well as big-ticket port towns, all set to a sublime maritime backdrop.

From **Běijīng**, zip to **Tiānjīn** en route to the Ming dynasty garrison town of **Shānhǎiguān** on the edge of Manchuria. Beyond the ancient port town of **Xīngchéng** and around the coast lies urbane **Dàlián** and trips to the North Korean border at **Dāndōng**, or the ferry crossing to **Yāntái** en route to a two-day sojourn around breezy **Qīngdǎo**. Cashing in on dashing **Shànghǎi** is crucial – allow five to six days to tick off surrounding sights, including a trip to the cultured former southern Song dynasty capital of **Hángzhōu**. Work your way south around the coast to **Xiàmén** (Amoy) to capture some of the magic of **Gǔlàng Yǔ**, using the port town as a base to explore the roundhouses around **Yǒngdìng**. Conclude the tour feasting on dim sum and getting in step with the rhythms of **Hong Kong** before surrendering to the Portuguese lilt of **Macau**, or go further along the coast to the sleepy port town of **Běihǎi** in Guǎngxī and bounce over the sea in a boat to the volcanic outpost of **Wéizhōu Island**.

Tick off the top sights on this varied tour that covers everything from antiquity to some of China's most awesome landscapes and the modern allure of Hong Kong.

Give yourself four days for **Běijīng**'s mandatory highlights before zipping by high-speed G-class train across north China to **Xī'ān** to inspect the Terracotta Warriors, walk around the city's formidable Ming dynasty walls and climb the granite peaks of Taoist **Huá Shān**. Then climb aboard the overnight high-speed sleeper, which pulls into pulsating **Shànghǎi** before 8am. After three days of sightseeing, museum-going, shopping and sizing up the sizzling skyscrapers of Pǔdōng, detour for a day to the former southern Song dynasty capital of **Hángzhōu**, before flying from either Hángzhōu or Shànghǎi to **Guìlín** for some of China's most serene and ageless panoramas, the breathtaking karst landscapes of **Yángshuò**. For a fitting and natural conclusion to your journey, fly straight from Guìlín to **Hong Kong**, or to Guǎngzhōu or Shēnzhèn to make your way south across the border to the former British territory. Squeeze in a day for exploring **Macau** to add a Portuguese complexion to your voyage.

Off the Beaten Track

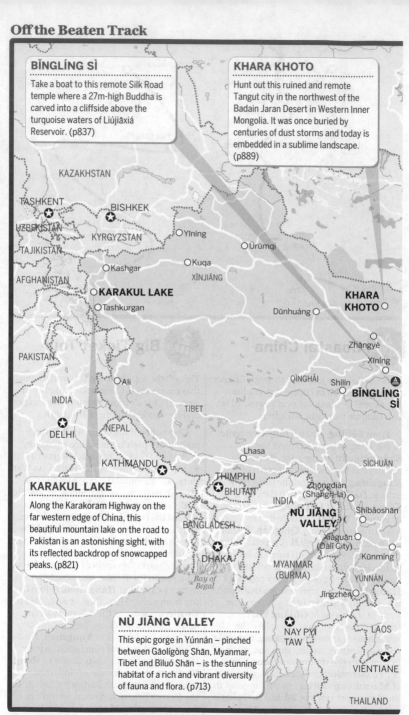

BĬNGLÍNG SÌ

Take a boat to this remote Silk Road temple where a 27m-high Buddha is carved into a cliffside above the turquoise waters of Liújiāxiá Reservoir. (p837)

KHARA KHOTO

Hunt out this ruined and remote Tangut city in the northwest of the Badain Jaran Desert in Western Inner Mongolia. It was once buried by centuries of dust storms and today is embedded in a sublime landscape. (p889)

KARAKUL LAKE

Along the Karakoram Highway on the far western edge of China, this beautiful mountain lake on the road to Pakistan is an astonishing sight, with its reflected backdrop of snowcapped peaks. (p821)

NÙ JIĀNG VALLEY

This epic gorge in Yúnnán – pinched between Gāolígòng Shān, Myanmar, Tibet and Bìluó Shān – is the stunning habitat of a rich and vibrant diversity of fauna and flora. (p713)

BĀ TÁIZI

A short journey by bus from Dàtóng brings you to the ruined spire of the 19th-century Holy Mother Church, standing sublimely next to a dilapidated stretch of the Great Wall that reaches off into the Shānxī hills beyond. (p364)

KOGURYO SITES

Scattered outside Jí'ān, the ruins, stone pyramids and tombs of the ancient Korean Koguryo kingdom dot a striking landscape of remote fields, terraces and green hills. (p181)

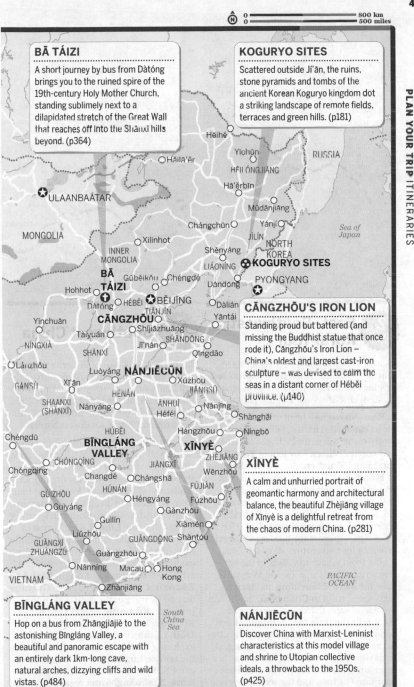

CĀNGZHŌU'S IRON LION

Standing proud but battered (and missing the Buddhist statue that once rode it), Cāngzhōu's Iron Lion – China's oldest and largest cast-iron sculpture – was devised to calm the seas in a distant corner of Héběi province. (p140)

XĪNYÈ

A calm and unhurried portrait of geomantic harmony and architectural balance, the beautiful Zhèjiāng village of Xīnyè is a delightful retreat from the chaos of modern China. (p281)

BĪNGLÁNG VALLEY

Hop on a bus from Zhāngjiājiè to the astonishing Bīngláng Valley, a beautiful and panoramic escape with an entirely dark 1km-long cave, natural arches, dizzying cliffs and wild vistas. (p484)

NÁNJIĒCŪN

Discover China with Marxist-Leninist characteristics at this model village and shrine to Utopian collective ideals, a throwback to the 1950s. (p425)

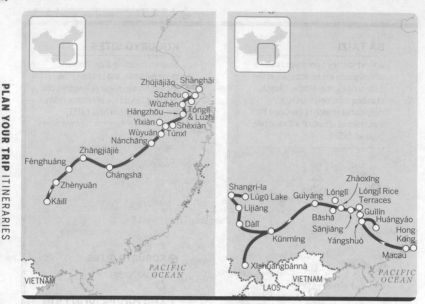

2 WEEKS East–Southwest Rural Tour

Flee the big cities and go rural on this tour that takes you through some of China's best-looking villages and water towns as well as choice scenic areas and sublime panoramas.

From **Shànghǎi**, head to **Zhūjiājiǎo** for its canalside charms, followed by the pretty water towns and villages of Jiāngsū and north Zhèjiāng – including **Tónglǐ**, **Lùzhí** and **Wūzhèn**. From either **Sūzhōu** or **Hángzhōu**, bus it to **Túnxī** in Ānhuī province to spend several days exploring the delightful ancient Huīzhōu villages of Hóngcūn, Xīdì in **Yīxiàn** and **Shèxiàn** and to scale gorgeous Huáng Shān. Hop on a bus again to cross the border to Jiāngxī province for two or three days' fabulous hiking from village to village in the gorgeous rural landscape around **Wùyuán**. Take the bus to **Nánchāng** and then a high-speed train to **Chángshā**, the Húnán provincial capital, from where you can fly or take the train to the stunning karst panoramas of **Zhāngjiājiè**. Jump on a bus to the funky rivertown of **Fènghuáng**, from where it's a hop, skip, and a bus-then-train jump via Huáihuà through the back-door into Guìzhōu and the scenic riverside town of **Zhènyuǎn**. **Kǎilǐ** and the rest of the province lies beyond.

3 WEEKS Southwest China

Embark on this tour of China's southwest for vibrant ethnic colour, some outstanding landscapes, an array of ancient towns and villages, all the bubbly magic of Hong Kong and a profusion of hiking opportunities around China's southwest borders.

Four days' wining and dining in **Hong Kong** and **Macau** should whet your appetite, before you head inland to **Guìlín** and three days' immersion in the dreamy karst landscape of **Yángshuò**. Join a local tour from Yángshuò to delightful **Huángyáo** before backtracking to Guìlín and journeying north to the **Lóngjǐ Rice Terraces** and the wind-and-rain bridges and ethnic hues of **Sānjiāng**. Creep over the border to explore the minority-rich villages of eastern Guìzhōu, including **Lóngjǐ**, **Bāshā** and **Zhàoxīng**, before continuing to **Guìyáng** and on by train to the capital of Yúnnán province, **Kūnmíng**. Spend a few days in Kūnmíng before heading north to explore **Dàlǐ**, **Lìjiāng** and **Shangri-la**. Consider exploring the border area with Sìchuān at the remote **Lúgū Hú**, from where you can enter Sìchuān. In the other direction, the fertile **Xīshuāngbǎnnà** region lies in the deep south of the province, where Yúnnán's Southeast Asian virtues comes to the fore.

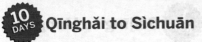

Qīnghǎi to Sìchuān

10 DAYS

An epic journey along the outer fringes of Han China, through a region deeply coloured with Tibetan culture, this colossal, rough-and-ready journey draws you through stunning landscapes from Xīníng to Chéngdū.

Do this trip only in summer (it's too cold even in spring); take cash and lots of food with you (you can't change money). Prepare also for bus breakdowns, simple accommodation and high altitudes. The bus journey from **Xīníng** to **Sharda** in the former Tibetan kingdom of Nangchen, where monasteries and dramatic scenery await, takes 20 to 24 hours. From Sharda you can continue to Sìchuān by looping back to the Tibetan trading town of **Yùshù**. You can also fly direct (or bus it) from Xīníng to Yùshù to continue to Sìchuān from there. Buses from Yùshù run through some stunning scenery to **Mǎnígāngē** (with a fantastic side trip to **Dégé** and **Yarchen Gar**), the Tibetan town of **Gānzī** (check ahead to see it's open) and on past **Tǎgōng** to **Kāngdìng** along the Sìchuān–Tibet Hwy, from where you can head west towards Tibet or east to **Chéngdū**. Direct buses also run from Yùshù to Chéngdū.

Tibet Fringes Tour

3 WEEKS

An arduous undertaking at the best of times, Tibet is a land periodically inaccessible to foreigners. This tour immerses you in more accessible areas around its long edges.

Only undertake the tour in the warmer summer months; other times can be dangerous. From **Lánzhōu** in Gānsù province, head southwest to **Lángmùsì** and **Xiàhé**, before passing awesome scenery by bus or taxi into **Qīnghǎi** via the monastery town of **Tóngrén**. Pick up a *thangka* (Tibetan sacred art) and continue by bus to **Xīníng**, then fly to **Chéngdū** in Sìchuān and take the bus to **Kāngdìng**, or fly to Kāngdìng via Chéngdū. The long, overland bus route from Xīníng to Kāngdìng is also possible via Yùshù in south Qīnghǎi. (Allow an extra week if taking this route.) From Kāngdìng you can journey by bus west to the stupendous scenery around **Lǐtáng**, with some breathtaking hiking opportunities, or travel south by minivan to **Xiāngchéng** and on to **Shangri-la** and the gorgeous Tibetan region of north Yúnnán. From Shangri-la take a bus to high-altitude **Déqīn**, enveloped in gorgeous mountain scenery.

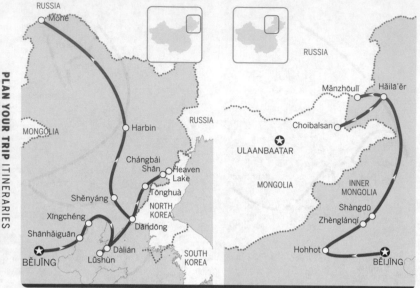

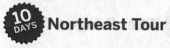

Northeast Tour
10 DAYS

Hop aboard this tour through the less-visited northeast for raw scenic beauty, borderland towns, modern, dapper towns and intriguing traces of imperial Manchurian heritage.

Start in **Běijīng**, then spend a few days exploring the historic walled coastal towns of **Shānhǎiguān** and **Xīngchéng** en route to stylish **Dàlián**. You'll need several days for Dàlián's sights, including the historic port of **Lǔshùn**. Border watchers will be keen to get to **Dāndōng**, on the border with North Korea. Take a boat tour along the Yālù River, dine on North Korean food and visit Tiger Mountain Great Wall. Consider a trip by rail and bus to **Heaven Lake** in **Chángbái Shān** (the largest nature reserve in China) via **Tōnghuà**. Straddling the North Korea border, the volcanic lake is a stunning sight (only accessible mid-June to September). Alternatively, take the train to **Shěnyáng** and visit its Qing dynasty Imperial Palace and the tomb of Huang Taiji, founder of the Qing dynasty. Hop on a bus or a train to **Harbin** to wonder at the city's Russian and Jewish ancestry. If you've really picked up momentum and can't stop, carry on to China's 'North Pole Village' to try to catch the aurora borealis in **Mòhé** or to bask in the summer's midnight sun.

Běijīng to Mongolia
1 WEEK

For a taste of Inner Mongolia's ranging grasslands, esoteric temples, imperial ruins and Russian borderland regions, head towards Mongolia on this one-week tour.

After sightseeing, wining and dining in **Běijīng**, jump aboard a train to **Hohhot** in Inner Mongolia where a late-July arrival should coincide with the Naadam festivities at Gegentala to the north, when the grasslands are turning green. Explore Hohhot's lamaseries and temples and make a trip to the grasslands outside town for a taste of the epic Inner Mongolian prairie. From Hohhot you can either take the train direct to Ulaanbaatar in Mongolia; or an alternative route to Mongolia is to first journey by bus from Hohhot to **Zhènglánqí** and **Shàngdū** – vanished site of Kublai Khan's celebrated palace at Xanadu – and then on to **Hǎilā'ěr** in the far north of Inner Mongolia, towards the border with Mongolia and Russia. The grasslands outside Hǎilā'ěr are a real highlight, so consider spending the night under the stars in a yurt on the prairie. If you are Russia-bound, you can enter the country via the nearby trading town of **Mǎnzhōulǐ** on the border. Alternatively, jump aboard a flight to **Choibalsan** in eastern Mongolia.

Plan Your Trip

Eat & Drink Like a Local

China has a broad range of eating options from street food to fine dining; if you don't speak Chinese, you'll find photo menus are common. In most areas it's possible to hunt down mouth-watering specialities from other regions.

Food Experiences

Cheap Treats

Snacking your way around China is a fine way to sample the different flavours of the land while on the move. Most towns have a super market or a night market (夜市; *yèshì*), a great place for good-value snacks and meals; you can either take it away or park yourself on a wobbly stool and grab a beer.

Street markets such as Kāifēng's boisterous night market abound with choices you may not find in restaurants. Vocal vendors will be forcing their tasty creations on you but you can also see what other people are buying and what's being cooked up; all you have to do is join the queue and point.

Dare to Try

➡ Stinky tofu (*chòu dòufu*), a form of fermented tofu that has an aroma somewhere between unwashed socks and rotting vegetation.

➡ Cantonese snake soup (*shé gēng*), served at **Ser Wong Fun** (蛇王芬; ☑852 2543 1032; 30 Cochrane St, Soho; meals HK$70; ⊘11am-10.30pm; Ⓜ Central, exit D1) in Hong Kong.

➡ Bowls of pigs brain (脑花; *nǎohuā*), a side dish at *shāokǎo* barbeque spots in Chóngqìng (p790).

➡ Fried centipedes, Hángzhōu (p271) street food.

➡ Scorpions on skewers, Wángfǔjǐng Snack Street (p103) in Běijīng.

➡ Donkey meat in a flaky bread pocket (驴肉火烧; *lúròu huǒshāo*), a Héběi (p133) speciality.

Meals of a Lifetime

➡ Jīngzūn Peking Duck (p106), Běijīng

➡ Georg (p105), Běijīng

➡ Luk Yu Tea House (p524), Hong Kong

➡ António (p551), Macau

➡ Ultraviolet (p319), Shànghǎi

➡ Fú Hé Huì (p323), Shànghǎi

➡ Green Tea Restaurant (p271), Hángzhōu

➡ Taste of Tibet (p760), Kāngdìng

Local Specialities

Běijīng & the North

Besides being the most obvious place to seek out authentic Peking duck (北京烤鸭; *Běijīng kǎoyā*), Běijīng is where you'll find the best restaurants for it.

For the most scrumptious *jiǎozi* (dumplings), head north and northeast. If you like them crispy, get them *guōtiē* (fried). Shànghǎi's delicious interpretation is *xiǎolóngbāo* – steamed and scalding.

In the north, also fill up on a tasty dish of *húntún* (wontons) stuffed with juicy leeks and minced pork, or *Měnggǔ huǒguō* (Mongolian hotpot), a hearty brew of mutton, onions and cabbage.

Shaanxi

Stop by Xī'ān for warming servings of *yángròu pàomó* (mutton broth and shredded flat bread).

Look for *ròujiāmó* (肉夹馍; fried pork or beef in pitta bread, sometimes with green peppers and cumin), *ròuchuàn* (肉串; kebabs) and yummy *yángròu pàomó* (羊肉泡馍; lamb broth poured over breadcrumbs).

Gānsù

The province's most famous export is Lánzhōu beef noodles (牛肉拉面; *niúròu lāmiàn*) – hand-pulled noodles in spicy soup – which are available in small restaurants and shops all over Gānsù.

Xīnjiāng

To sample the full range of Uighur food, make your way to Kashgar, where you'll have your pick of street food and night markets.

Fruit is a big deal in Xīnjiāng, from Hāmì's *tawuz* (watermelon) to Turpan's *uzum* (grapes) and *yimish* (raisins). Market heave with fruit from July to September.

Shànghǎi

In case you're pining for something sweet, head to Shànghǎi for delicious *mìzhī xūnyú* (honey-smoked carp), and where you can also dine on more savoury helpings of steaming *xiǎolóngbāo* dumplings – which require considerable dexterity to consume without meat juices jetting to all compass points.

Look out for the characters 本帮菜 (*běnbāngcài*) on restaurant shopfronts and in menus, which refers to authentic Shànghǎi homestyle cooking.

Sìchuān

Some like it hot, and little comes hotter than the fiery flavours of Sìchuān. Begin with mouth-numbing *mápó dòufu* (spicy beancurd dish), followed by the celebrated *gōngbǎo jīdīng* (spicy chicken with peanuts). If the smoke isn't now coming out of your ears, *shuǐzhǔ yú* (fish smothered in chilli) should have you breathing fire.

Chóngqìng

Chóngqìng hotpot is ideal for banishing the bitter cold of a northern winter, while in its home town – one of China's 'three furnaces' on the Yangzi River – old folk devour the spiciest of hotpots in summer with little regard for the sweltering weather.

Yúnnán

Yúnnán specialities include *qìguōjī* (汽锅鸡; slow-cooked, herb-infused chicken), *guòqiáo mǐxiàn* (过桥米线; across-the-bridge noodles) and *rǔbǐng* (辱饼; goat's cheese).

Téngchōng is famous for its cured ham, known as *huǒtuǐ* (火腿), as well as having all the great Yúnnán vegies and mushrooms, and there are many restaurants in the region to sample them at.

In Lìjiāng, make sure to try the cuisine of the local Naxi minority, while Shangri-la is a great place to sample Tibetan cooking.

Húnán

Húnán is no province for lightweight, dainty palates. A firecracker of a cuisine, Xiāngcài (湘菜; Húnán food) is one of the most potent of Chinese cooking styles, with ample use of chilli and piquant herbs. It eschews the numbing heat of Sìchuān cooking and instead goes for a sharp, full-flavoured spiciness.

Hong Kong, Macau & Guǎngzhōu

Dim sum is steamed up across China, but like the Cantonese dialect, it's best left to the masters of the south to get it right. Hong Kong, Macau and Guǎngzhōu should be your first stops.

While in Macau, taste the Macanese dish *porco à alentejana,* a mouthwatering casserole of pork and clams.

Chóngqìng hotpot

Hǎinán

Hǎinán specialties include *dōngshān yáng* (东山羊; mountain goat, stewed, roasted or cooked in coconut milk), *chǎobīng* (炒冰; blended tropical fruit that is 'fried' on a cold plate until it turns thick like sorbet) and *jiājī yā* (加积鸭; steamed duck).

How to Eat & Drink

Where to Eat

Chinese eateries come in every conceivable shape, size and type: from shabby, hole-in-the-wall noodle outfits with flimsy PVC furniture, blaring TV sets and well worn plastic menus to gilded, banquet-style restaurants where elegant cheongsam-clad waitresses show you to your seat, straighten your chopsticks and bring you a warm hand towel and a gold-embossed wine list. In between are legions of very serviceable midrange restaurants serving cuisine from across China.

As dining in China is such a big, sociable and often ostentatious affair, many Chinese banqueting-style restaurants have huge round tables, thousand-candle-power electric lights and precious little sense of intimacy or romance. Overattentive and ever-present staff can add to the discomfort for foreigners.

When to Eat

The Chinese eat early. Lunch usually commences from around 11.30am, either self-cooked or a takeaway at home, or in a streetside restaurant. Dinner kicks off from around 6pm. Reflecting these dining times, some restaurants open at around 11am, close for an afternoon break at about 2.30pm, open again around 5pm and then close in the late evening. Street-food vendors then take over the duty of feeding the late-night hungry folk.

Menus

In Běijīng, Shànghǎi and other large cities, you may be proudly presented with an English menu (英文菜谱; *Yīngwén càipǔ*). In smaller towns and out in the sticks, don't expect anything other than a Chinese-language menu and hovering waitstaff with no English-language skills. The best is undoubtedly the ever-handy photo menu. If you like the look of what

COOKING COURSES

Want to learn how to make Chinese cuisine while on your travels? Popular cooking classes can be found at The Hutong (p97) and Black Sesame Kitchen (p97) in Běijīng and the Kitchen At... (p310) in Shànghǎi.

More options include:

Chinese Cooking Workshop (www.chinesecookingworkshop.com; 108-109, 2 Dongping Rd, Shànghǎi; 东平路2号; courses from ¥150-200; MHengshan Rd, Shanghai Library) Learn different Chinese cooking styles from dim sum to Sichuanese. It also offers market tours and courses for kids.

Home's Cooking (www.homescookingstudio.com; Hong Kong; classes HK$600) This highly rated cooking class, run out of the owner's home, offers three-hour morning or afternoon sessions. Students cook a three-course Chinese meal: think spring rolls, lotus-leaf chicken and ginger pudding. Classes include a trip to a local wet market and lunch or dinner.

Martha Sherpa (852 2381 0132; www.marthasherpa.com; Flat F, 14th fl, Wah Lai Mansion, 62-76 Marble Rd, North Point, Hong Kong; courses HK$1680; MNorth Point, exit A2) Expert Cantonese home-cook Martha Sherpa (her last name comes from her Nepali husband) has taught the likes of former Australian PM Julia Gillard how to cook dim sum and Hong Kong favourites. Small group classes cover topics like wok cookery, dim sum and vegetarian Chinese. Half-day, full-day and evening classes are available.

Classes can also be found in Dàlǐ (p684), Yángshuò (p621), and Lhasa (p920).

---

other diners are eating, just point at it and say 'wǒ yào nàge' (我要那个; 'I want that') – a very handy phrase. Alternatively, pop into the kitchen and point out the meats and vegetables you would like to eat.

Eating with Kids

Similar to travelling with children in China, dining out with kids can be a challenge. Budget eateries won't have kids' menus; nor will they have booster seats. Smarter restaurants may supply these but it can be touch-and-go. In large cities you will be able to find more restaurants switched on to the needs of families; Western restaurants especially may have a play area, kids' menu, activities, booster seats and other paraphernalia.

Vegetarian Travellers

If you'd rather chew on a legume than a leg of lamb, it can be hard to find truly vegetarian dishes. China's history of famine and poverty means the consumption of meat has always been a sign of status, and is symbolic of health and wealth. Eating meat is also considered to enhance male virility, so vegetarian men raise eyebrows. Partly because of this, there is virtually no vegetarian movement in China, although Chinese people may forgo meat for Buddhist reasons. For the same reasons, they may avoid meat on certain days of the month but remain carnivorous at other times.

You will find that vegetables are often fried in animal-based oils; vegetable soups are often made with chicken or beef stock, so simply choosing 'vegetable' items on the menu is ineffective. A dish that you are told does not contain meat may still mean it is riddled with tiny pieces of meat. In Běijīng and Shànghǎi you will, however, find a generous crop of vegetarian restaurants to choose from, alongside outfits such as Element Fresh, which has a decent range of healthy vegetarian options.

Out of the large cities, your best bet may be to head to a sizeable active Buddhist temple or monastery, where Buddhist vegetarian restaurants are often open to the public. Buddhist vegetarian food typically consists of 'mock meat' dishes created from tofu, wheat gluten, potato and other vegetables. Some of the dishes are almost works of art, with vegetarian ingredients sculpted to look like spare ribs or fried chicken. Sometimes the chefs go to great lengths to create 'bones' from carrots and lotus roots.

If you want to say 'I am a vegetarian' in Chinese, the phrase to use is 'wǒ chī sù' (我吃素).

Plan Your Trip

Cruising the Yangzi

Taking a boat down the Yangzi River (长江; Cháng Jiāng) – China's longest and most scenic waterway – is all about the journey rather than the destination. It isn't just an escape from marathon train journeys and agonising bus rides, but a chance to kick back as an astonishing panorama slides by at a sedate pace which allows time for contemplation and relaxation. Cruising the Yangzi is a truly unique experience, one that gets you up close with mostly domestic travellers allowing time for real interaction. Jump aboard.

The River

The journey puts you adrift on China's mightiest – and the world's third-longest – river, the gushing 6300km Yangzi River. Starting life as trickles of snow melt in the Tánggǔlā Shān of southwestern Qīnghǎi, the river then spills from Tibet, swells through seven Chinese provinces, sucks in water from hundreds of tributaries and rolls powerfully into the Pacific Ocean north of Shànghǎi.

The Route

Apocryphally the handiwork of the Great Yu, a legendary architect of the river, the gorges – Qútáng, Wū and Xīlíng – commence just east of Fèngjié in Chóngqìng province and level out west of Yíchāng in Húběi province, a distance of around 200km. The principal route for those cruising the Yangzi River is therefore between the cities of Chóngqìng and Yíchāng.

The route can be travelled in either direction, but most passengers journey downstream from Chóngqìng. Travelling upstream does ensure a less crowded boat, but somehow feels less dramatic.

If you buy your ticket from an agency, ensure you're not charged upfront for the

When to Go

Dec–Mar
The low season; rates are cheaper and the journey is more serene.

Apr & May
The best weather, with fewer crowds than summer.

Jun–Aug
Chinese summer holidays mean crowded, kid-filled boats.

Oct & Nov
Cooler climes but the crowds are back.

Yangzi River (Cháng Jiāng)

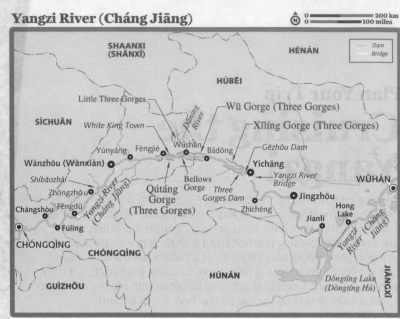

sights along the way, as you may not want to visit them all. Some of the sights are underwhelming and entrance fees are as steep as the surrounding inclines. The only ticket truly worth buying in advance is for the popular and worthwhile Little Three Gorges tour, which is often full.

Chóngqìng to Wànzhōu

The initial stretch is slow going and unremarkable, although the dismal view of factories gradually gives way to attractive terraced countryside and the occasional small town.

Passing the drowned town of Fúlíng (涪陵), the first port of call is **Fēngdū** (丰都), 170km from Chóngqìng city. Long nicknamed the City of Ghosts (鬼城; Guǐchéng), the town is just that: inundated in 2009, its residents were moved across the river. This is the stepping-off point for crowds to clamber up **Míng Mountain** (名山; Míng Shān; adult ¥120, cable car ¥20), with its theme-park crop of ghost-focused temples.

Drifting through the county of Zhōngzhōu, the boat takes around three hours to arrive at **Shíbǎozhài** (石宝寨, Stone Treasure Stockade; adult ¥70; ⏰8am-4pm) on the northern bank of the river. A 12-storey, 56m-high wooden pagoda built on a huge, river-water-encircled rock bluff,

the structure dates to the reign of Qing dynasty emperor Kangxi (1662–1722). Your boat may stop for rapid expeditions up to the tower and for climbs into its interior.

Most morning boats moor for the night at partially inundated **Wànzhōu** (万州; also called Wànxiàn). Travellers aiming to get from A to B as fast as possible while taking in the gorges can skip the Chóngqìng to Wànzhōu section by hopping on a 3½-hour bus and then taking a passenger ship from the Wànzhōu jetty.

Wànzhōu to Yíchāng

Boats departing from Wànzhōu soon pass the relocated **Zhāng Fēi Temple** (张飞庙, Zhāngfēi Miào; ¥40). Quick disembarkations can be made here, allowing a visit to the ancient but much-restored temple, which was moved 30km upstream in 2002 and now sits opposite **Yúnyáng** (云阳). A modern, utilitarian and unremarkable town strung out along the northern bank of the river, Yúnyáng is typical of many of the new settlements created in the wake of the building of the Three Gorges Dam. Past here, boats drift on past ragged islets, some carpeted with small patchworks of fields, and alongside riverbanks striated with terraced slopes, rising like green ribbons up the inclines.

The ancient town of **Fèngjié** (奉节), capital of the state of Kui during the periods known as the 'Spring and Autumn' (722–481 BC) and 'Warring States' (475–221 BC), overlooks Qútáng Gorge, the first of the three gorges. The town – where most ships and hydrofoils berth – is also the entrance point to half-submerged **White Emperor City** (白帝城, Báidìchéng; ¥120), where the King of Shu, Liu Bei, entrusted his son and kingdom to Zhu Geliang, as chronicled in *The Romance of the Three Kingdoms*.

Qútáng Gorge (瞿塘峡; Qútáng Xiá), also known as Kui Gorge (夔峡; Kuí Xiá), rises dramatically into view, towering into huge vertiginous slabs of rock, its cliffs jutting out in jagged and triangular chunks. The shortest and narrowest of the three gorges, 8km-long Qútáng Gorge is over almost as abruptly as it starts, but is considered by many to be the most awe-inspiring. The gorge offers a dizzying perspective onto huge strata despite having some of its power robbed by the rising waters. On the northern bank is **Bellows Gorge** (风箱峡; Fēngxiāng Xiá), where nine coffins were discovered, possibly placed here by an ancient tribe.

After Qútáng Gorge, the terrain folds into a 20km stretch of low-lying land before boats pull in at the riverside town of **Wūshān** (巫山), situated high above the river. Most boats stop at Wūshān for five to six hours so passengers can transfer to smaller boats for trips along the **Little Three Gorges** (小三峡, Xiǎo Sānxiá; ticket ¥200) on the **Dàníng River** (大宁河; Dàníng Hé). The landscape is gorgeous and you're right up close to it, and many travellers insist that the narrow gorges are more impressive than their larger namesakes. Some tours include a 40-minute ride on local fishing boats here too.

Back on the Yangzi River, boats pull away from Wūshān to enter the penultimate Wū Gorge, under a bright-red bridge. Some of the cultivated fields on the slopes overhanging the river reach almost illogical angles.

Wū Gorge (巫峡; Wū Xiá) – the Gorge of Witches – is stunning, cloaked in green and carpeted in shrubs, its sides frequently disappearing into ethereal layers of mist. About 40km in length, its towering cliffs are topped by sharp, jagged peaks on the northern bank. A total of 12 peaks cluster on either side, including **Goddess Peak** (神女峰; Shénnǚ Fēng) and **Peak of the Immortals** (集仙峰, Jíxiān Fēng). If you're fortunate, you'll catch the sunrise over Goddess Peak.

Boats continue floating eastward out of Wū Gorge and into Húběi province, along a 45km section before reaching the last of the three gorges. At this time, many boats offer the option of a two-hour trip on motorised dragon boats along **Jiǔwǎn Stream** (九畹溪; Jiǔwǎn Xī) and nearby tributaries of the Yangzi. Some travellers enjoy the experience, although the scenery isn't as inspiring as that of the Little Three Gorges.

At 80km, **Xīlíng Gorge** (西陵峡; Xīlíng Xiá) is the longest and perhaps least spectacular gorge; sections of the gorge in the west have been submerged. Note the slow moving cargo vessels, including long freight ships loaded with mounds of coal, ploughing downriver to Shànghǎi. The gorge was traditionally the most hazardous, where hidden shoals and reefs routinely holed vessels, but it has long been tamed, even though river traffic slows when the fog reduces visibility.

Apart from the top-end luxury cruises, tour boats no longer pass through the monumental **Three Gorges Dam**, although many tours offer the option of a visit to the dam by bus. The passenger ferries and hydrofoils tend to finish (or begin)

EFFECTS OF THE THREE GORGES DAM

The dwarfing chasms of rock, sculpted over aeons by the irresistible volume of water, are the Yangzi River's most fabled stretch. Yet the construction of the controversial and record-breaking Three Gorges Dam (三峡大坝; Sānxiá Dàbà) cloaked the gorges in as much uncertainty as their famous mists: have the gorges been humbled or can they somehow shrug off the rising waters?

In brief, the gorges have been undoubtedly affected by the rising waters. The peaks are not as towering as they once were, nor are the flooded chasms through which boats travel as narrow and pinched. The effect is more evident to seasoned boat hands or repeat visitors. For first-timers the gorges still put on a dramatic show.

their journey at **Tàipíng Creek Port** (太平溪港; Tàipíngxī Gǎng), upstream from the dam. From here, two types of shuttle bus wait to take you into Yíchāng (one hour). One is free and takes you to the old ferry port (老码头; lǎo mǎtóu) in the centre of town. The other costs ¥10 and drops you at Yíchāng East Train Station (火车东站; Huǒchē Dōngzhàn). Ordinary tourist boats tend to use **Máopíng Port** (茅坪港; Máopíng Gǎng), from where you can at least see the dam, and which is also connected to Yíchāng via shuttle buses.

Boats

There are three categories of boats: luxury cruises, tourist boats and passenger ships.

Luxury Cruises

The most luxurious passage is on one of the international-standard cruise ships (豪华游轮; háohuá yóulún), where maximum comfort and visibility accompany a leisurely agenda. Trips normally depart Chóngqìng mid-evening and include shore visits to all the major sights (Three Gorges Dam, Little Three Gorges etc), allowing time to tour the attractions (often secondary to the scenery). Cabins have air-con, TV (perhaps satellite), fridge/minibar and sometimes more. These vessels are aimed at both Chinese and Western tourists and are ideal for travellers with time, money

BEST TOP-END CRUISES

Viking River Cruises (www.vikingrivercruises.com; from US$3010) Very luxurious cruise, offering five-day cruises from Chóngqìng to Wǔhàn, as part of a larger 13-day tour of China.

Century Cruises (www.centuryrivercruises.com; from US$450) Claims to be the most luxurious cruise service on the Yangzi. Ships are new, service is first class and facilities are top notch.

Victoria Cruises (www.victoriacruises.com; from US$550) Comfortable four-day trips between Chóngqìng and Yíchāng. Older boats than some other operators, but has excellent English-speaking guides.

and negligible Chinese skills. The average duration for such a cruise is three nights and three to four days.

Top-end cruises feature daily buffet meals, generally including both Western and Chinese food. Seating is assigned, and meals are included in your ticket price. There will also be on-board bars and lounges, sometimes featuring cabaret shows and the like. Cabins are like comfy hotel rooms, complete with private balconies and daily maid service.

Tourist Boats

Typically departing from Chóngqìng around 9pm, ordinary tourist cruise ships (普通游轮; pǔtōng yóulún) usually take just under 40 hours to reach Yíchāng (including three nights on-board). Some boats stop at all the sights; others stop at just a few. They are less professional than the luxury tour cruises and are squarely aimed at domestic travellers (Chinese food, little English spoken).

Expect early starts: the public-address system starts going off after 6am. Cabins in all classes are fairly basic – hard beds in 2nd and 3rd class – but come with air-con and a TV and usually have a small attached bathroom with a shower (although that doesn't mean hot water). Many travellers now book packages that take you first by bus from Chóngqìng to Wànzhōu, where you board a vessel for the rest of the trip. This reduces the journey by one night.

In theory, you can buy tickets on the day of travel, but booking one or two days in advance is recommended. Fares vary, although not by much, depending whether you buy your ticket from a hostel, agency or direct from the ticket hall, so it's worth shopping around to check. If buying a ticket through an agent, ensure you know exactly what the price includes. Note that the following prices include admission to the most popular stops along the way (including the Little Three Gorges).

Special class (特等; tèděng) ¥1780, two-bed cabin

1st class (一等; yīděng) ¥1100, two-bed cabin

2nd class (二等; èrděng) ¥900, four-bed cabin

3rd class (三等; sānděng) ¥750, six-bed cabin

Tourist boats have restaurants serving standard Chinese fare, often not included in the ticket price.

Above: Wǔ Gorge (p53)
Right: Xīlíng Gorge (p53)

Passenger Ships

Straightforward passenger ships *(客船; kè chuán)* are cheap, but can be disappointing because you sail through two of the gorges in the dead of night. Stops are frequent, but hasty, and they pass by the tourist sights. Journeys between Chóngqìng and Yíchāng take around 36 hours; between Fèngjié and Yíchāng, around 12 hours. Toilets are shared, and soon get pretty grotty. There are no showers, but there are sinks and power sockets in the twin cabins (as well as TVs, which usually don't work). Passenger boats have on-board Chinese-style canteens. Meals are decent and cheap but there is no choice of dishes, so take along your own food and drinks in case you don't like what's on offer.

Eastbound boats leave Chóngqìng at 10pm and Fèngjié at 9pm. For westbound journeys, shuttle buses, which connect with the boats, leave Yíchāng's old ferry port at 7.30pm; the boat leaves at 9pm.

Tickets can usually be bought on the day of travel.

Chóngqìng to Yíchāng fares:

1st class (一等; *yīděng*) ¥884, twin cabin

2nd class (二等; *èrděng*) ¥534, twin cabin

3rd class (三等; *sānděng*) ¥367, four- to six-bed dorm

4th class (四等; *sìděng*) ¥224, eight-bed dorm

Fèngjié to Yíchāng fares:

1st class ¥343

2nd class ¥212

3rd class ¥147

4th class ¥119

Tickets

In Chóngqìng or Yíchāng, most hotels, hostels and travel agents can sell you a trip on either the luxury cruise ships or the ordinary tourist boats. In either city, passenger ferry tickets have to be bought at the ferry-port ticket halls, which also sell ordinary tourist-boat tickets.

The price of your ticket will include the one-hour shuttle bus ride to/from the old ferry port in the centre of Yíchāng from/to one of the two newer ferry ports, about 45km upstream, where almost all boats now leave from or terminate.

Chóngqìng

Travelling With Hostel (p789) mostly sells tickets for the ordinary tourist boats, but can arrange luxury cruises too. Helpful and excellent English skills.

Harbour Plaza Travel Centre (p793) specialises in luxury cruises, but also sells ordinary tourist-boat tickets. Staff are friendly and speak OK English.

Chóngqìng Ferry Port Ticket Hall (p794) is the cheapest place to buy ordinary tourist-boat tickets, and the only place that sells passenger ferry tickets; no English is spoken.

Yíchāng

China International Travel Service (p453)

Three Gorges Tourist Centre (p453)

Yangtze River International Travel (p453)

Fèngjié

Fèngjié Ferry Port Ticket Hall (奉节港售票厅, Fèngjié Gǎng Shòupiàotīng) sells passenger-ferry tickets in either direction. Don't expect to be able to board tourist boats from here because tickets usually sell out in Chóngqìng or Yíchāng.

Regions at a Glance

The high-altitude, far west of China, including Tibet, Qīnghǎi and west Sìchuān, gradually and fitfully steps down to level out as it nears the prosperous and well irrigated canal-town provinces of Jiāngsū and Zhèjiāng, and the dazzling metropolis of Shànghǎi in the east. The lion's share of scenic marvels and hiking territory belongs to the mountainous interior of China, while in the mighty northwest, peaks and deserts meet in dramatic fashion. Minority culture is a speciality of the west and southwest, and of the remote border regions. Different cuisines range across the entire nation, from the hardy northeast to the warm jungles of the far southwest.

Běijīng

History
Temples
Food

Běijīng's imperial pedigree (and the Great Wall) assures it a rich vein of dynastic history, balanced by splendid seams of temple and *hútòng* (narrow alleyway) architecture. Wining and dining is a further attraction as the capital is home to a resourceful restaurant scene.

p64

Tiānjīn & Héběi

History
Temples
Outdoors

Tiānjīn's spruced-up foreign concession streetscapes echo stylish Shànghǎi, and some standout pagodas and temples can be found in Héběi, where the rural side of China – peppered with rustic village getaways – comes to the fore.

p133

Liáoníng

Festivals
History
Minority Culture

In history-rich Liáoníng, imperial relics contend with the legacy of Russian and Japanese colonialism. The North Korean border at Dāndōng is a sobering contrast to the wild beer festival at Dàlián.

p157

Jílín

Landscapes
Culture
Skiing

Boasting China's largest nature reserve, and a top ski destination, Jílín exerts a pull on the nature lover. On the trail of the exotic? Head to Jí'ān for the ruins of the ancient Korean Koguryo empire.

p175

Hēilóngjiāng

Festivals
Culture
Nature

Fire and ice are the highlights in this province where volcanic explosions have left one of China's most mesmerising landscapes, and the winter's bitter climate provides the raw materials for a spectacular ice-sculpture festival.

p186

Shāndōng

History
Mountains
Seaside

Shāndōng groans under the weight of its historical heavy-hitters: Confucius' home and tomb at Qūfù and sacred Tài Shān. Then, of course, there's the home of Tsingtao beer, Qīngdǎo, a breezy, laid-back modern and sophisticated port city.

p201

Jiāngsū

Canal Towns
Outdoors
History

Jiāngsū's awash with cute-as-pie canal towns – all reachable as day trips from neighbouring Shànghǎi. The provincial capital, Nánjīng, has history in spades, with its fabulous Ming wall and epic past as former national capital.

p236

Zhèjiāng

Canal Towns
Outdoors
Islands

Flushed with water and vaulted with bridges, the canal town of Wūzhèn is full of traditional charm. Hángzhōu is one of China's most appealing cities, while stunning pastoral escapes abound further south, including the gorgeous villages of Xīnyè and Zhūgě.

p263

Shànghǎi

Architecture
Food
Urban Style

Shànghǎi exudes a unique style unlike anywhere else in China. There's plenty to do, from nonstop shopping and skyscraper-hopping to standout art, fantastic eats and touring the city's elegant art-deco heritage.

p290

Fújiàn

Architecture
Food
Islands

Fújiàn is Hakka heartland and home to the intriguing *tǔlóu* – massive packed stone, wood and mud structures once housing hundreds of families. Gǔlàng Yǔ, a tiny, hilly island off Xiàmén, is decorated with crumbling colonial villas.

p337

Shānxī

History
Culture
Mountains

Repository to the superlative Buddhist grottoes at Yúngāng, Shānxī also brings you the beautiful Buddhist mountain, Wǔtái Shān; the intact walled city of Píngyáo; the rebuilt city fortifications of Dàtóng; and time worn sections of the Great Wall.

p358

Shaanxi

Historic Sites
Museums
Mountains

Archaeological sites lie scattered across the plains surrounding Shaanxi's magnificent walled capital, Xī'an, where museums galore await. Blow off all that ancient dust with a trip to Huá Shān, one of China's five holy Taoist peaks.

p379

Ānhuī

Villages
Mountains
Outdoors

The charming Unesco-listed Hui villages of Hóngcūn and Xīdì are some of China's best preserved. But let's not forget that astonishing mountain, Huáng Shān, whose soaring granite peaks and ethereal mist have inspired legions of poets and painters.

p400

Hénán

History
Temples
Mountains

Hénán's overture of dynastic antiquity is balanced by some excellent mountain escapes and the quirky allure of Nánjiēcūn, China's last Maoist collective. The province's *wǔshù* (martial arts) credentials come no better: the Shàolín Temple is here.

p420

Húběi

Scenic Wonders
History
Rivers

Slashed by the mighty Yangzi River, history-rich Húběi is one of the gateways to the Three Gorges, but Taoist martial artists may find themselves mustering on Wǔdāng Shān, home of taichi and scenic views.

p440

Jiāngxī

Scenery
Mountains
Ancient Villages

Communists herald it as the mythic starting point of the Long March, but it's the spectacular mountain scenery and hiking trails past preserved villages and terraced fields that should pop Jiāngxī into your travel plans.

p454

Húnán

Ancient Towns
Minority Villages
Mountains

Home to one of China's most enjoyable ancient towns, Fènghuáng – beautifully illuminated come nightfall – as well as the sacred mountain of Héng Shān, the other-worldly karst peaks of Zhāngjiājiè, and secluded Miao and Dong villages.

p471

Hong Kong

Food
Shopping
Scenery

This culinary capital offers the best of China and beyond, while a seductive mix of vintage and cutting-edge fashion attracts armies of shoppers. Meanwhile, leafy mountains, shimmering waters, skyscrapers and tenements make an unlikely but poetic match.

p499

Macau

Food
Architecture
Casinos

Marrying flavours from five continents, Macanese cooking is as unique as the cityscape, where Taoist temples meet baroque churches on cobbled streets with Chinese names. It's also a billionaire's playground where casino resorts and other luxuries vie for space.

p536

Guǎngdōng

Food
History
Architecture

A strong gastronomic culture offers travellers the chance to savour world-renowned Cantonese cuisine. Guǎngdōng's seafaring temperament has brought the region diverse, exotic architectural styles, including the World Heritage–listed watchtowers of Kāipíng.

p557

Hǎinán

Beaches
Cycling
Surfing

When it comes to golden-sand beaches and warm clear waters, this tropical island doesn't disappoint. An ideal cycling destination, Hǎinán attracts in-the-know adventurers with its good roads, balmy winters and varied landscape.

p594

Guǎngxī

Scenery
Outdoors
Cycling

Famed for the dreamy karst landscapes of Yángshuò, Guǎngxī also offers lush green valleys, charming folksy villages and countless walking, cycling and rafting opportunities, as well as Wéizhōu Island, a short trip from sleepy Běihǎi.

p610

Guìzhōu

Festivals
Minority Villages
Waterfalls

With more folk festivals than anywhere else in China, you can party here with the locals year-round. For nature lovers, there's an abundance of waterfalls; for old-town watchers, there's lovely Zhènyuǎn.

p638

Yúnnán

Ancient Towns
Mountains
Minority Villages

Yúnnán has it all: towering Himalayan mountains, tropical jungle, sublime rice terraces and over half of China's minority groups; plus historic, little-visited villages including Nuòdèng and Hēijǐng, gorgeous and ancient Lìjiāng, fantastic trekking and great food.

p666

Sìchuān

Mountains
Scenery
Cuisine

One province; three regions. Stay in central or southern Sìchuān for steamy bamboo forests and Ming dynasty villages. Head north for stunning lakes among alpine-like mountain scenery. Venture west for remote Tibetan plateau grasslands and towering peaks.

p730

Chóngqìng

Cuisine
Ancient Villages
River Trips

A unique city with a unique location, hilly Chóngqìng hugs cliffs overlooking the Yangzi, bursts with old-China energy, offers some fascinating day trips and is home to hotpot – the spiciest dish on the planet.

p782

Xīnjiāng

History
Minority Culture
Nature

Bazaars, kebabs and camels are just a few of the icons that hint at your arrival in Central Asia. Ancient Silk Road towns include Turpan, Kashgar and Hotan; hikers gravitate to Kanas Lake and the Tiān Shān range.

p799

Gānsù

Silk Road
Tibetan Culture
Buddhism

Gānsù is about diversity: colourful Tibetan regions in the southwest, the dunes of Taklamakan in the northwest, and a rich accumulation of Silk Road culture through the middle. Think deserts, mountains, Buddhist temples, camels, yaks, pilgrims and nomads.

p832

Níngxià

History
Minority Culture
Activities

In the designated home-land of the Muslim Hui, visit the great tombs of the Xixia, nomadic rock art and the enormous Buddhas of Xūmí Shān. For camel trekking or sliding down sand dunes, head for the Tengger Desert.

p864

Inner Mongolia

Remote Journeys
Food
Activities

Ride a famed Mongolian horse at a yurt camp near Hohhot and Hǎilā'ěr and sit down to a Mongolian hotpot. Further-flung west-ern Inner Mongolia is a stunning landscape of tow-ering sand dunes, desert lakes and ancient ruins.

p875

Qīnghǎi

Monasteries
Scenery
Culture

Vast and remote, the best parts of Qīnghǎi – way up on the Tibetan plateau – are for those who like their travel rough. Need a hot shower and a coffee every morning? Go somewhere else.

p891

Tibet

Monasteries
Scenery
Culture

The 'Roof of the World' is a stunningly beautiful high plateau of turquoise lakes, desert valleys and Himalayan peaks, dotted with monasteries, yaks and sacred Buddhist sites. Tight and ever-changing travel regulations can eas-ily derail travel plans.

p909

On the Road

Běijīng

Includes ➡

Best Places to Eat

➡ Dàlǐ Courtyard (p105)

➡ Běijīng Dàdǒng Roast Duck Restaurant (p104)

➡ In & Out (p106)

➡ Duck de Chine (p106)

➡ Bǎihé Vegetarian Restaurant (p104)

Best Places to Sleep

➡ Temple Hotel (p100)

➡ Qiánmén Hostel (p102)

➡ Courtyard 7 (p101)

➡ Opposite House Hotel (p101)

➡ Aman at Summer Palace (p102)

Why Go?

Inextricably linked to past glories (and calamities) yet hurtling towards a power-charged future, Běijīng (北京), one of history's great cities, is as complex as it is compelling.

Few places on earth can match the extraordinary historical panorama on display here – there are six Unesco World Heritage Sites in this city alone, just one less than the whole of Egypt. But this is also where China's future is being shaped: Běijīng is the country's political nerve centre, a business powerhouse and the heartbeat of China's rapidly evolving cultural scene.

Yet for all its gusto, Běijīng dispenses with the persistent pace of Shànghǎi or Hong Kong. The remains of its historic *hútòng* (alleyways) still exude a unique village-within-a-city vibe, and it's in these most charming of neighbourhoods that locals shift down a gear and find time to sit out front, play chess and watch the world go by.

When to Go
Běijīng

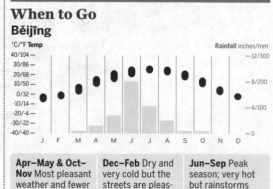

Apr–May & Oct–Nov Most pleasant weather and fewer tourists.

Dec–Feb Dry and very cold but the streets are pleasantly quiet.

Jun–Sep Peak season; very hot but rainstorms offer respite.

History

Although seeming to have presided over China since time immemorial, Běijīng (literally, 'Northern Capital') – positioned outside the central heartland of Chinese civilisation – only emerged as a cultural and political force that would shape the destiny of China with the 13th-century Mongol occupation of China.

Chinese historical sources identify the earliest settlements in these parts from 1045 BC. In later centuries Běijīng was successively occupied by foreign forces: it was established as an auxiliary capital under the Khitan, nomadic Mongolic people who formed China's Liao dynasty (AD 907–1125). Later the Jurchens, Tungusic people originally from the Siberian region, turned the city into their Jīn dynasty capital (1115–1234), during which time it was enclosed within fortified walls, accessed by eight gates.

But in 1215 the army of the great Mongol warrior Genghis Khan razed Běijīng, an event that was paradoxically to mark the city's transformation into a powerful national capital. Apart from the first 53 years of the Ming dynasty and 21 years of Nationalist rule in the 20th century, it has enjoyed this status to the present day.

The city came to be called Dàdū (大都; Great Capital), also assuming the Mongol name Khanbalik (the Khan's town). By 1279, under the rule of Kublai Khan, grandson of Genghis Khan, Dàdū was the capital of the largest empire the world has ever known.

The basic grid of present-day Běijīng was laid during the Ming dynasty, and Emperor Yongle (r 1403–24) is credited with being the true architect of the modern city. Much of Běijīng's grandest architecture, such as the Forbidden City and the iconic Hall of Prayer for Good Harvests in the Temple of Heaven Park, date from his reign.

The Manchus, who invaded China in the 17th century to establish the Qing dynasty, essentially preserved Běijīng's form. In the last 120 years of the Qing dynasty, though, Běijīng was subjected to power struggles, invasions and ensuing chaos. The list is long: the Anglo-French troops who in 1860 burnt the Old Summer Palace to the ground; the corrupt regime of Empress Dowager Cixi; the catastrophic Boxer Rebellion; the Japanese occupation of 1937; and the Nationalists. Each and every period left its undeniable mark, although the shape and symmetry of Běijīng was maintained.

Modern Běijīng came of age when, in January 1949, the People's Liberation Army (PLA) entered the city. On 1 October of that year Mao Zedong proclaimed a 'People's Republic' from the Gate of Heavenly Peace to an audience of some 500,000 citizens.

Like the emperors before them, the communists significantly altered the face of Běijīng. The *páilóu* (decorative archways) were destroyed and city blocks pulverised to widen major boulevards. From 1950 to 1952, the city's magnificent outer walls were levelled in the interests of traffic circulation. Soviet experts and technicians poured in, bringing their own Stalinesque touches.

The past quarter of a century has transformed Běijīng into a modern city, with skyscrapers, shopping malls and an ever-expanding subway system. The once flat skyline is now crenellated with vast apartment blocks and office buildings. Recent years have also seen a convincing beautification of Běijīng, from a toneless and unkempt city to a greener, cleaner and more pleasant place, albeit one heavily affected by ever-increasing pollution.

Sadly, as Běijīng continues to evolve, it is slowly shedding its links to the past. More than 4 million sq metres of old *hútòng* courtyards have been demolished since 1990; around 40% of the total area of the city centre. Preservation campaign groups have their work cut out to save what's left.

Language

Fewer people than you think speak English in Běijīng, and most people speak none at all (taxi drivers, for example). However, many people who work in the tourist industry do

---

PRICES

Sleeping

Price ranges for a standard double room per night:

$ less than ¥400

$$ ¥400–¥1000

$$$ more than ¥1000

Eating

Price ranges for a meal for one person:

$ less than ¥40

$$ ¥40–100

$$$ more than ¥100

Běijīng Highlights

❶ Great Wall
(p124) Hiking your way along an unrestored 'wild' section of China's most famous icon.

❷ Forbidden City
(p68) Marvelling at the might and splendour of the world's largest palace complex and home to 24 consecutive emperors of China.

❸ Hútòng Losing yourself in the city's warren of historic *hútòng* (alleyways), or following our walking tour (p82).

❹ Parks Wandering around Běijīng's host of splendid royal parks, the highlight of which is the unmissable Temple of Heaven Park (p84).

❺ Summer Palace
(p91) Enjoying a taste of imperial high life by wandering the sumptuous gardens, temples, pavilions and corridors.

❻ Peking duck
Scoffing the capital's signature dish in the restaurants where it originated (p105).

❼ Drum & Bell Towers Climbing the magnificent Drum Tower (p79) or its charming counterpart, the Bell Tower (p79), and looking over the grey-tiled rooftops in the alleys below.

❽ Back-alley bars Downing a beer or catching some live music. Great Leap Brewing (p108) is a good place to start.

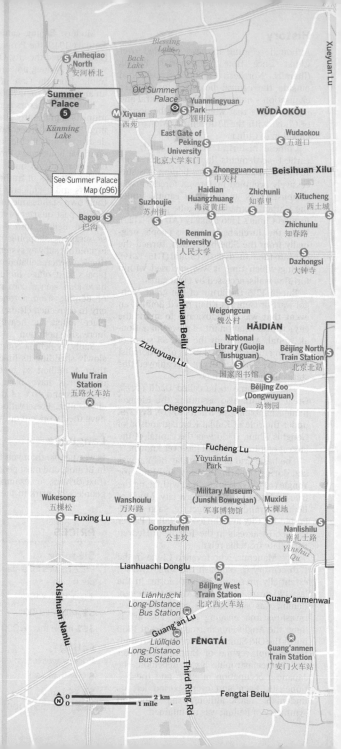

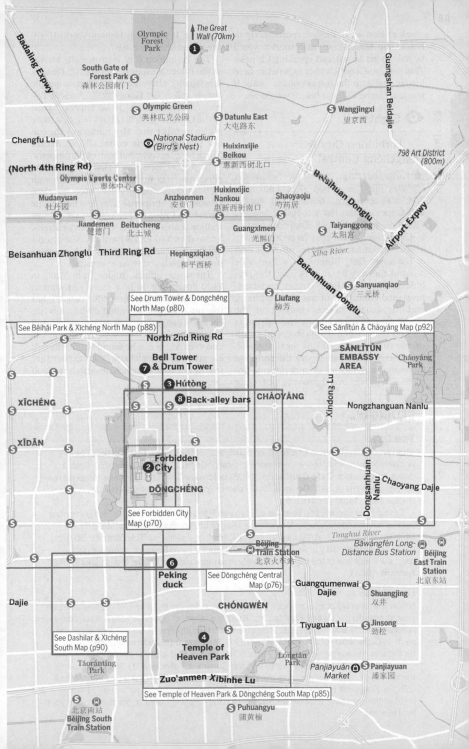

The Great Wall (70km)
①

Olympic Forest Park

Badaling Expwy

South Gate of Forest Park
森林公园南门

Olympic Green
奥林匹克公园

Datunlu East
大屯路东

Wangjingxi
望京西

Chengfu Lu

National Stadium (Bird's Nest)

Huixinxijie Beikou
惠新西街北口

798 Art District (800m)

Guangshan Beidajie

(North 4th Ring Rd)

Olympic Sports Center
奥体中心

Mudanyuan
牡丹园

Anzhenmen
安贞门

Huixinxijie Nankou
惠新西街南口

Shaoyaoju
芍药居

Beisihuan Donglu

Jiandemen
健德门

Beitucheng
北土城

Guangximen
光熙门

Taiyanggong
太阳宫

Airport Expwy

Beisanhuan Zhonglu   **Third Ring Rd**

Hepingxiqiao
和平西桥

Xiha River

Beisanhuan Donglu

Sanyuanqiao
三元桥

Liufang
柳芳

See Drum Tower & Dōngchéng North Map (p80)

See Běihǎi Park & Xīchéng North Map (p88)

North 2nd Ring Rd

See Sānlǐtún & Cháoyáng Map (p92)

SĀNLǏTÚN EMBASSY AREA

Cháoyáng Park

Bell Tower & Drum Tower
⑦

③ **Hútòng**

⑧ **Back-alley bars**

CHÁOYÁNG

XĪCHÉNG

Xindong Lu

Nongzhanguan Nanlu

XĪDĀN

② **Forbidden City**

DŌNGCHÉNG

Dongsanhuan Nanlu

Chaoyang Dajie

See Forbidden City Map (p70)

Tonghui River

⑥ **Peking duck**

Běijīng Train Station
北京火车站

See Dōngchéng Central Map (p76)

Bāwángfén Long-Distance Bus Station

Běijīng East Train Station
北京东站

Dajie

CHÓNGWÉN

Guangqumenwai Dajie

Shuangjing
双井

Tiyuguan Lu

Jinsong
劲松

See Dashilar & Xīchéng South Map (p90)

④ **Temple of Heaven Park**

Lóngtán Park

Panjiāyuán Market

Panjiayuan
潘家园

Táoróngtíng Park

Zuo'anmen Xibinhe Lu

See Temple of Heaven Park & Dōngchéng South Map (p85)

北京南站
Běijīng South Train Station

Puhuangyu
蒲黄榆

speak at least some English (particularly in hotels and hostels), so, as a tourist, you'll be able to get by without speaking Chinese. That said, you'll enrich your experience here hugely, and gain the respect of the locals, if you learn some Chinese before you come.

Sights

Forbidden City & Dōngchéng Central

★**Forbidden City** HISTORIC SITE
(紫禁城, Zǐjìn Chéng; Map p70; ☎010 8500 7114; www.dpm.org.cn; Nov-Mar ¥40, Apr-Oct ¥60, Clock Exhibition Hall ¥10, Hall of Jewellery ¥10, audio guide ¥40; ⏰8.30am-5pm Apr-Oct, to 4.30pm Nov-Mar, last entry 1hr prior to closing, closed Mon Sep-Jun; [S] Line 1 to Tian'anmen West or Tian'anmen East) Ringed by a 52m-wide moat at the very heart of Běijīng, the Forbidden City is China's largest and best-preserved collection of ancient buildings, and the largest palace complex in the world. So called because it was off limits for 500 years, when it was steeped in stultifying ritual and Byzantine regal protocol, the other-worldly palace was the reclusive home to two dynasties of imperial rule until the Republic overthrew the last Qing emperor. It has been Unesco World Heritage-listed site since 1987.

The Forbidden City is prosaically known as the Palace Museum (故宫博物馆; Gùgōng Bówùguǎn), although most Chinese people simply call it Gù Gōng (故宫; Ancient Palace). 'Forbidden City' is an approximation of the Chinese 紫禁城 (Zǐjìn Chéng), a more poetic moniker that also references the colour purple and the cosmically significant North Star, the 'celestial seat' of the emperor.

In former ages the price for uninvited admission was instant execution, although mere mortals wouldn't have even got close because the Imperial City enclosing the Forbidden City with yet another set of huge walls was also off limits to ordinary citizens. These days ¥40 or ¥60 will do. Allow yourself the best part of a day for exploration or several trips if you're an enthusiast.

There are official guides from ¥200 to ¥400 depending on how much you want to cover (inclusive for up to five people), but the automatically activated audio tours are cheaper (¥40; more than 40 languages) and more reliable. Restaurants, a cafe, toilets and even ATMs can be found within the palace grounds. Wheelchairs (¥500 deposit) are free to use, as are pushchairs/strollers (¥300 deposit).

BĚIJĪNG IN...

Two Days

Stroll around the incense smoke–filled courtyards of the **Lama Temple** (p79) before hopping over the road to the even more laid-back **Confucius Temple** (p79). Grab a coffee and lunch at **Cafe Confucius** (p108) before walking through the *hútòng* (narrow alleyways) to the ancient **Drum & Bell Towers** (p79) and finishing off the day with a meal in **Dàlǐ Courtyard** (p105).

Get up early to enjoy the **Temple of Heaven Park** (p84) at its magical, early-morning best: filled with opera-singing locals rather than photo-snapping tourists. Make it juicy lamb kebabs for lunch at **Yīzhēn Yuán** (p105) before walking via **Tiān'ānmén Sq** (p74) to the **Forbidden City** (p68). Finish the day by tucking into Běijīng's signature dish – roast duck – at one of the city's most celebrated restaurants – **Lìqún Roast Duck Restaurant** (p105).

Four Days

Follow the itinerary above, but save plenty of energy for the trip of a lifetime on day three: your journey to the **Great Wall** (p124). There are plenty of options, from a quick half-day jaunt at touristy **Bādálǐng** (p132) to a strenuous hike along wild, unrestored sections such as **Gǔběikǒu** (p127) or **Jiànkòu** (p127). **Mùtiányù** (p126) makes a good option for families. Pack a picnic and don't expect to get back to the city until nightfall.

Hop on the subway on day four to visit the **Summer Palace** (p91). You could spend the day here or make side trips to the **Botanic Gardens** (p95), **Old Summer Palace** (p97) or **Fragrant Hills Park** (p95), all of which are close. Return for an early evening meal so that you have time to catch a show (p110) – Peking opera or acrobatics – on your final evening.

DON'T MISS

The **Clock Exhibition Hall** (钟表馆, Zhōngbiǎo Guǎn, ¥10, ⊙ 8.30am-4pm summer, to 3.30pm winter) is one of the unmissable highlights of the Forbidden City. Located in the **Hall for Ancestral Worship** (奉先殿; Fèngxiān Diàn), the exhibition contains an astonishing array of elaborate timepieces, many of which were gifts to the Qing emperors from overseas. Exquisitely wrought, fashioned with magnificently designed elephants and other creatures, they all display astonishing artfulness and attention to detail. Time your arrival for 11am or 2pm to see the **clock performance** in which choice timepieces strike the hour and give a display to wide-eyed children and adults.

➡ Entrance

Tourists must enter through the **Meridian Gate** (午门; Wǔ Mén), a massive U-shaped portal at the south end of the complex, which in former times was reserved for the use of the emperor. Gongs and bells would sound imperial comings and goings, while lesser mortals used lesser gates: the military used the west gate, civilians the east gate and servants the north gate. The emperor also reviewed his armies from here, passed judgement on prisoners, announced the new year's calendar and oversaw the flogging of troublesome ministers. Up top is the **Meridian Gate Gallery**, which hosts temporary cultural exhibitions for both traditional Chinese arts and from abroad.

Through the Meridian Gate, you enter an enormous courtyard, and cross the **Golden Stream** (金水; Jīn Shuǐ) – shaped to resemble a Tartar bow and spanned by five marble bridges – on your way to the magnificent **Gate of Supreme Harmony** (太和门; Tàihé Mén). This courtyard could hold an imperial audience of 100,000 people. For an idea of the size of the restoration challenge, note how the crumbling courtyard stones are stuffed with dry weeds, especially on the periphery.

➡ First Side Galleries

Before you pass through the Gate of Supreme Harmony to reach the Forbidden City's star attractions, veer off to the east and west of the huge courtyard to visit the **Calligraphy and Painting Gallery** inside the **Hall of Martial Valor** (武英殿; Wǔ Yīng Diàn) and the particularly good **Ceramics Gallery**, housed inside the creaking **Hall of Literary Glory** (文化殿; Wén Huà Diàn).

➡ Three Great Halls

Raised on a three-tier marble terrace with balustrades are the Three Great Halls, the glorious heart of the Forbidden City. The recently restored **Hall of Supreme Harmony** (太和殿; Tàihé Diàn) is the most important and largest structure in the Forbidden City.

Built in the 15th century and restored in the 17th century, it was used for ceremonial occasions, such as the emperor's birthday, the nomination of military leaders and coronations. Inside the Hall of Supreme Harmony is a richly decorated **Dragon Throne** (龙椅; Lóngyǐ), from which the emperor would preside over trembling officials. The entire court had to touch the floor nine times with their foreheads (the custom known as kowtowing) in the emperor's presence. At the back of the throne is a carved Xumishan, the Buddhist paradise, signifying the throne's supremacy.

Behind the Hall of Supreme Harmony is the smaller **Hall of Middle Harmony** (中和殿; Zhōnghé Diàn), which was used as the emperor's transit lounge. Here he would make last-minute preparations, rehearse speeches and receive close ministers. On display are two Qing dynasty sedan chairs, the emperor's mode of transport around the Forbidden City. The last of the Qing emperors, Puyi, used a bicycle and altered a few features of the palace grounds to make it easier to get around.

The third of the Great Halls is the **Hall of Preserving Harmony** (保和殿; Bǎohé Diàn), used for banquets and later for imperial examinations. The hall has no support pillars. To its rear is a 250-tonne marble imperial carriageway carved with dragons and clouds, which was transported into Běijīng on an ice path. The emperor used to be carried over this carriageway in his sedan chair as he ascended or descended the terrace. The outer housing surrounding the Three Great Halls was used for storing gold, silver, silks, carpets and other treasures.

A string of side halls on the eastern and western flanks of the Three Great Halls usually, but not always, house a series of excellent exhibitions, ranging from scientific instruments and articles of daily use to objects presented to the emperor by visiting dignitaries. One contains an interesting diorama of the whole complex.

Forbidden City

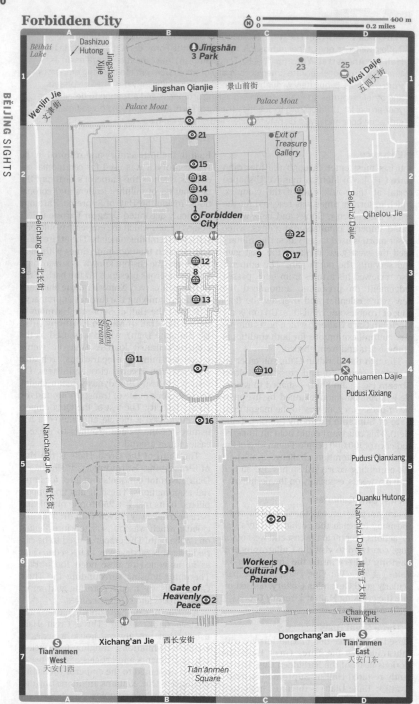

400 m
0.2 miles

Běihǎi Lake

Dashizuo Hutong

Jingshan Xijie

Jǐngshān 3 Park

23

25

Wusi Dajie 五四大街

Wenjin Jie 文津街

Jingshan Qianjie 景山前街

Palace Moat

Palace Moat

6

21

Exit of Treasure Gallery

Beichang Jie 北长街

15

18

14

19

5

Beichizi Dajie

Qihelou Jie

1 **Forbidden City**

22

9

17

12

8

13

Golden Stream

11

7

10

24

Donghuamen Dajie

Pudusi Xixiang

16

Pudusi Qianxiang

Nanchang Jie 南长街

Duanku Hutong

Nanchizi Dajie 南池子大街

20

Workers Cultural Palace

4

Gate of Heavenly Peace

2

Changpu River Park

Tian'anmen West 天安门西

Xichang'an Jie 西长安街

Dongchang'an Jie

Tian'anmen East 天安门东

Tiān'ānmén Square

Forbidden City

➡ Lesser Central Halls

The basic configuration of the Three Great Halls is echoed by the next group of buildings. Smaller in scale, these buildings were more important in terms of real power, which in China traditionally lies at the back door.

The first structure is the **Palace of Heavenly Purity** (乾清宫; Qiánqīng Gōng), a residence of Ming and early Qing emperors, and later an audience hall for receiving foreign envoys and high officials.

Immediately behind it is the **Hall of Union** (交泰殿; Jiāotài Diàn), which contains a clepsydra – a water clock made in 1745 with five bronze vessels and a calibrated scale. There's also a mechanical clock built in 1797 and a collection of imperial jade seals on display. The **Palace of Earthly Tranquillity** (坤宁宫; Kūnníng Gōng) was the imperial couple's bridal chamber and the centre of operations for the palace harem.

➡ Imperial Garden

At the northern end of the Forbidden City is the **Imperial Garden** (御花园; Yù Huāyuán), a classical Chinese garden with 7000 sq metres of fine landscaping, including rockeries, walkways, pavilions and ancient cypresses. Before you reach the **Gate of Divine Prowess** (神武门; Shénwǔ Mén), the Forbidden City's north exit, and **Shùnzhēn Gate** (顺贞门; Shùnzhēn Mén), which leads to it, note the pair of bronze elephants whose front knees bend in an anatomically impossible fashion, signifying the power of the emperor.

➡ Treasure Gallery

In the northeastern corner of the complex is a mini Forbidden City known as the **Treasure Gallery** (珍宝馆; Zhēn Bǎo Guǎn; ¥10), or Complete Palace of Peace and Longevity (宁寿全宫; Níng Shòu Quán Gōng). During the Ming dynasty, the Empress Dowager and the imperial concubines lived here. Today it comprises a number of atmospheric halls, pavilions, gardens and courtyard buildings that hold a collection of fine museums.

The complex is entered from the south – not far from the Clock Exhibition Hall (p69). Just inside the entrance, you'll find the beautiful glazed **Nine Dragon Screen** (九龙壁; Jiǔlóng Bì; included in through ticket), one of only three of its type left in China.

Visitors work their way north, exploring a number of peaceful halls and courtyards before being popped out at the northern end of the Forbidden City. Don't miss the **Pavilion of Cheerful Melodies** (畅音阁; Chàngyīn Gé), a three-storey wooden opera house, which was the palace's largest theatre. Note the trap doors that allowed actors to make dramatic stage entrances.

➡ Western & Eastern Palaces

A dozen smaller palace courtyards lie to the west and east of the three lesser central halls. It was in these smaller courtyard buildings that most of the emperors actually lived and many of the buildings, particularly those to the west, are decked out in imperial furniture. Those that are open to the public have cultural exhibitions displaying anything from temple musical instruments to ceremonial bronze vessels and ceramics.

Forbidden City

WALKING TOUR

After entering through the imperious Meridian Gate, resist the temptation to dive straight into the star attractions and veer right for a peek at the excellent **1 Ceramics Gallery** housed inside the creaking Hall of Literary Glory.

Walk back to the central complex and head through the magnificent Gate of Supreme Harmony towards the Three Great Halls: first, the largest – the **2 Hall of Supreme Harmony**, followed by the **3 Hall of Middle Harmony** and the **4 Hall of Preserving Harmony**, behind which slopes the enormous Marble Imperial Carriageway.

Turn right here to visit the fascinating **5 Clock Exhibition Hall** before entering the **6 Complete Palace of Peace & Longevity**, a mini Forbidden City constructed along the eastern axis of the main complex. It includes the beautiful **7 Nine Dragon Screen** and, to the north, a series of halls, housing some excellent exhibitions and known collectively as The Treasure Gallery. Don't miss the **8 Pavilion of Cheerful Melodies**, a wonderful three-storey opera house.

Work your way to the far north of this section, then head west to the **9 Imperial Garden**, with its ancient cypress trees and pretty pavilions, before exiting via the garden's West Gate (behind the Thousand Year Pavilion) to explore the **10 Western Palaces**, an absorbing collection of courtyard homes where many of the emperors lived during their reign.

Exit this section at its southwest corner before turning back on yourself to walk north through the Gate of Heavenly Purity to see the three final Central Halls – the **11 Palace of Heavenly Purity**, the **12 Hall of Union** and the **13 Palace of Earthly Tranquility** – before leaving via the North Gate.

Water Vats
More than 300 copper and brass water vats dot the palace complex. They were used for fighting fires and in winter were prevented from freezing over by using thick quilts.

ENTRANCE/EXIT

You must enter through the south gate (Meridian Gate), but you can exit via south, north or east.

← Ticket Offices →

Guardian Lions
Pairs of lions guard important buildings. The male has a paw placed on a globe (representing the emperor's power over the world). The female has her paw on a baby lion (representing the emperor's fertility).

Kneeling Elephants
At the northern entrance of the Imperial Garden are two bronze elephants kneeling in an anatomically impossible fashion, which symbolise the power of the emperor; even elephants kowtowed before him.

Nine Dragon Screen
One of only three of its type left in China, this beautiful glazed dragon screen served to protect the Hall of Imperial Supremacy from evil spirits.

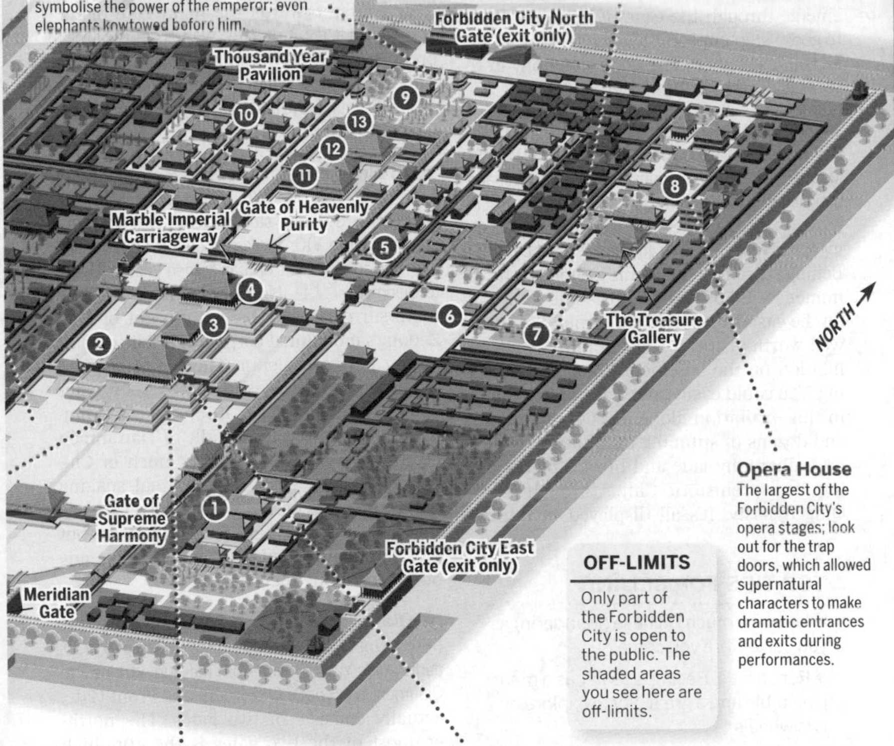

Forbidden City North Gate (exit only)

Thousand Year Pavilion

⑨

⑩ ⑬ ⑫ ⑪

Gate of Heavenly Purity

Marble Imperial Carriageway

④ ⑤ ⑧

③ ⑥ ⑦

② The Treasure Gallery

NORTH →

Gate of Supreme Harmony

①

Forbidden City East Gate (exit only)

Meridian Gate

OFF-LIMITS
Only part of the Forbidden City is open to the public. The shaded areas you see here are off-limits.

Opera House
The largest of the Forbidden City's opera stages; look out for the trap doors, which allowed supernatural characters to make dramatic entrances and exits during performances.

Dragon-Head Spouts
More than a thousand dragon-head spouts encircle the raised marble platforms at the centre of the Forbidden City. They were – and still are – part of the drainage system.

Roof Guardians
The imperial dragon is at the tail of the procession, which is led by a figure riding a phoenix followed by a number of mythical beasts. The more beasts, the more important the building.

★Tiān'ānmén Square SQUARE

(天安门广场, Tiān'ānmén Guǎngchǎng; Map p76; [S]Line 1 to Tian'anmen West, Tian'anmen East, or Line 2 to Qianmen) [FREE] Flanked by stern 1950s Soviet-style buildings and ringed by white perimeter fences, the world's largest public square (440,000 sq metres) is an immense flatland of paving stones at the heart of Běijīng. If you get up early, you can watch the flag-raising ceremony at sunrise, performed by a troop of People's Liberation Army (PLA) soldiers drilled to march at precisely 108 paces per minute, 75cm per pace. The soldiers emerge through the Gate of Heavenly Peace to goose-step impeccably across Chang'an Jie; all traffic is halted. The same ceremony in reverse is performed at sunset.

★National Museum of China MUSEUM

(中国国际博物馆, Zhōngguó Guójì Bówùguǎn; Map p76; http://en.chnmuseum.cn; Guangchangdongce Lu, Tiān'ānmén Sq, 天安门，广场东侧路; audio guide ¥30; ⏲9am-5pm Tue-Sun, last entry 4pm; [S] Line 1 to Tian'anmen East, exit D) [FREE] Běijīng's premier museum is housed in an immense 1950s communist-style building on the eastern side of Tiān'ānmén Sq, and is well worth visiting. The **Ancient China** exhibition on the basement floor is outstanding. You could easily spend a couple of hours in this exhibition alone. It contains dozens and dozens of stunning examples of ceramics, calligraphy jade and bronze pieces dating from prehistoric China through to the Qing dynasty. It's all displayed beautifully in modern, spacious, low-lit exhibition halls. You'll need your passport to gain entry.

★Workers Cultural Palace PARK

(劳动人民文化宫, Láodòng Rénmín Wénhuà Gōng, Imperial Ancestral Temple; Map p70; ☎tennis court 010 6512 2856; park entrance ¥2, Sacrificial Hall ¥15; ⏲6.30am-7.30pm; [S] Line 1 to Tian'anmen East, exit A) Despite the prosaic name and its location at the very heart of town, this reclusive park, between Tiān'ānmén Sq and the Forbidden City, is one of Běijīng's best-kept secrets. Few visitors divert here from their course towards the main gate of the Forbidden City, but this was the emperor's premier place of worship and contains the **Sacrificial Hall** (Front Hall, 太庙, Tài Miào; Map p70; ¥15); as exquisite as any temple you'll find in Běijīng.

★Chairman Mao Memorial Hall MAUSOLEUM

(毛主席纪念堂, Máo Zhǔxí Jìniàntáng; Map p76; Tiān'ānmén Sq; bag storage ¥10, electonics storage per device ¥10; ⏲7am-noon Tue-Sun; [S] Line 1 to Tian'anmen West or Tian'anmen East or Line 2 to Qianmen) [FREE] No doubt one of Běijīng's more surreal spectacles is the sight of Mao Zedong's embalmed corpse on public display within his mausoleum. The Soviet-inspired memorial hall was constructed soon after Mao died in September 1976, and is a prominent landmark in the middle of Tiān'ānmén Sq. He is still revered across much of China, as evidenced by the perpetual snaking queues of locals here clutching flowers to pay their respects; some are reduced to tears but most are in high spirits, treating it like any other stop along their Běijīng tour.

★Qiánmén HISTORIC SITE

(前门, Front Gate, Zhèngyáng Mén; Map p76; ¥20, audio guide ¥20; ⏲9am-4pm Tue-Sun; [S] Line 2 to Qianmen, exit B or C) Qiánmén, aka Front Gate, actually consists of two gates. The northernmost of the two gates is the 40m-high **Zhèngyáng Gate** (正阳门城楼; Zhèngyáng Mén Chénglóu), which dates from the Ming dynasty and which was the largest of the nine gates of the Inner City Wall separating the inner, or Tartar (Manchu) city, from the outer, or Chinese city. With the disappearance of the city walls, the gate sits out of context, but it can be climbed for decent views of the square and of Arrow Tower, immediately to the south.

★Gate of Heavenly Peace HISTORIC SITE

(天安门, Tiān'ānmén; Map p70; Xichang'an Jie, 西长安街; ¥15, bag storage ¥3-6; ⏲8.30am-4.30pm,

TOP TIPS FOR BĚIJĪNG

➡ Learn as much Chinese (Mandarin) as you can before you come.

➡ Rent a bike. Běijīng is as flat as a mahjong table and a great city to explore on two wheels.

➡ Have the name and address of wherever you're going each day written down in Chinese characters before you go out. And always bring your hotel business card with you, so you can find your way home.

➡ Try as wide a variety of Chinese food as you can. Běijīng has every culinary base covered, from Peking duck to spicy Sìchuānese, so grab some chopsticks and tuck in. Oh, and don't listen to anyone who tells you to avoid the street food – terrible advice.

to 4pm Nov-Mar; [S] Line 1 to Tian'anmen West, exit B or Line 1 to Tian'anmen East, exit A) Characterised by a giant framed portrait of Mao Zedong, and guarded by two pairs of Ming stone lions, the double-eaved Gate of Heavenly Peace, north of Tiān'ānmén Sq, is a potent national symbol. Built in the 15th century and restored in the 17th century, the gate was formerly the largest of the four gates of the Imperial City Wall, and it was from this gate that Mao proclaimed the People's Republic of China on 1 October 1949. Today's political coterie watches mass troop parades from here.

★ Jǐngshān Park PARK

(景山公园, Jǐngshān Gōngyuán; Map p70; Jingshan Qianjie, 景山前街; adult/child ¥10/5; ⌚6.30am-9pm; [S] Lines 6, 8 to Nanluoguxiang, exit A) The dominating feature of Jǐngshān – one of the city's finest parks – is one of central Běijīng's few hills; a mound that was created from the earth excavated to make the Forbidden City moat. Called Coal Hill by Westerners during Legation days, Jǐngshān also serves as a feng shui shield, protecting the palace from evil spirits – or dust storms – from the north. Clamber to the top for a magnificent panorama of the capital and princely views over the russet roofing of the Forbidden City.

Galaxy Soho ARCHITECTURE

(银河Soho, Yínhé Soho; Map p76; Chaoyangmennei Dajie, 朝阳门内大街; [S] Lines 2, 6 to Chaoyangmen, exit G) Along with the CCTV Tower and the Bird's Nest, Běijīng's striking Galaxy Soho has announced itself as one the capital's modern architectural landmarks. Opened in 2012, it stands in direct juxtaposition to the adjoining *hútòng* housing (which controversially was cleared for its development). It was designed by acclaimed British-Iraqi architect Zaha Hadid (1950–2016), and is characterised by its flowing, sleek contours and an interconnected design with adjoining walkways and space-age Modernist facade.

Zhìhuà Temple BUDDHIST TEMPLE

(智化寺, Zhìhuà Sì; Map p76; 5 Lumicang Hutong, 禄米仓胡同5号; adult ¥20, audio guide ¥10, Wed free; ⌚8.30am-4.30pm, closed Mon; [S] Lines 1, 2 to Jianguomen, exit A or Lines 2, 6 to Chaoyangmen, exit G) Běijīng's surviving temple brood has endured casual restoration that often buried authenticity. But this rickety nonactive temple, hidden down a rarely visited *hútòng*, is thick with the flavours of old Peking, having eluded the Dulux treatment that invariably precedes entrance-fee inflation and stomping tour groups.

[i] BĚIJĪNG MUSEUM PASS

If you're staying in the capital for a while, the **Běijīng Museum Pass** (☎010 6222 3793; www.bowuguan.com.cn; annual pass ¥120) – website and phone service in Chinese only – is a decent investment that will save you both money and queuing for tickets. For ¥120 you get either complimentary access or discounted admission (typically 50%) to 112 tourist attractions, including some 61 museums, plus temples and tourist sights in and around Běijīng. Attractions covered include the Great Wall at Bādálǐng, Front Gate, the Drum Tower, the Bell Tower, the Confucius Temple, the Botanic Gardens, the Railway Museum, Dōngyuè Temple, White Cloud Temple and Zhìhuà Temple. Not all the sights are worth visiting, but you only have to visit a small selection to make it worth the money. The pass comes in the form of a booklet (Chinese with minimal English), valid from 1 January to 31 December in any one year. The pass, which is harder to obtain as the year goes on, can be picked up from participating museums and most post offices; see its website for locations.

Shǐjiā Hútòng Museum MUSEUM

(史家胡同博物馆, Shǐjiā Hútòng Bówùguǎn; Map p76; 24 Shijia Hutong, 史家胡同24号; ⌚9.30am-4.30pm Tue-Sun; [S] Line 5 to Dengshikou) [FREE] Within a pleasant, renovated double courtyard, which used to be a local kindergarten, is this small museum that explains the history of Shǐjiā Hútòng, and of Běijīng's *hútòng* districts in general. There are interesting large-scale models, old photos and a range of artefacts, all with excellent English captions throughout.

Great Hall of the People NOTABLE BUILDING

(人民大会堂, Rénmín Dàhuìtáng; Map p88; Renda Huitang W Rd; adult ¥30, bag deposit ¥2-5; ⌚8.15am-4pm, times vary; [S] Line 1 to Qianmen, exit A, or Line 1 to Tian'anmen West, exit C) On the western side of Tiān'ānmén Sq, on a site previously occupied by Taichang Temple, the Jinyiwei (Ming dynasty secret service) and the Ministry of Justice, the Great Hall of the People is the venue of the legislature, the National People's Congress (NPC). The 1959 Soviet-style architecture (which features on the ¥100 note) is monolithic and intimidating, and a fitting symbol of China's

Dōngchéng Central

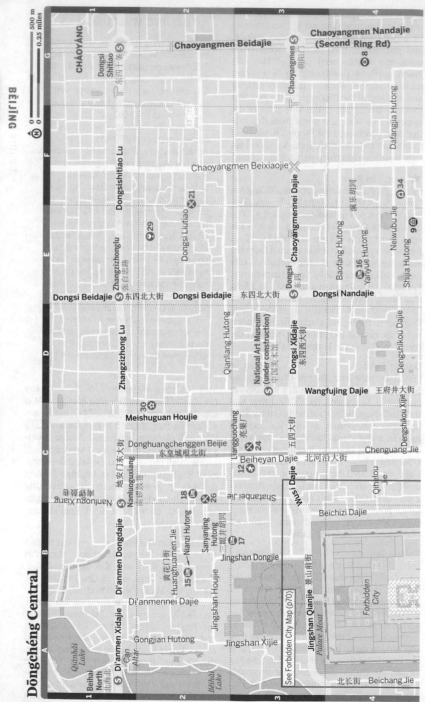

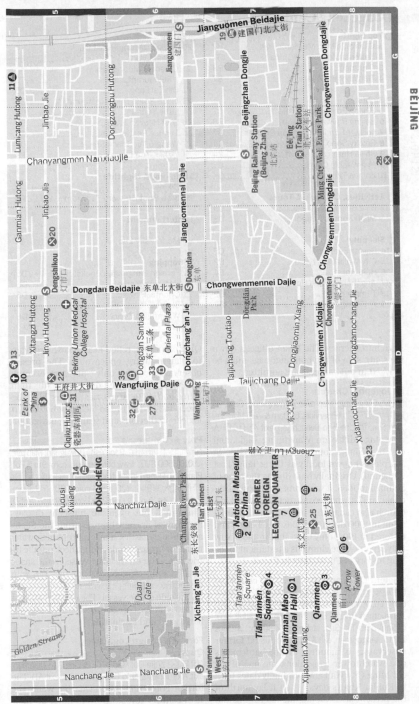

BĚIJĪNG

Jianguomen Beidajie 建国门北大街
19 建国门北大街

Jianguomen 建国门

Beijingzhan Dongjie

Beijing Railway Station (Beijing Zhan) 北京火车站

Ēēīng

Train Station 北京火车站

Ming City Wall Ruins Park

Chongwenmen Dongdajie

28

Lumicang Hutong   11

Jinbao Jie

Dongzongbu Hutong

Chaoyangmen Nanxiaojie

Ganmian Hutong

Jinbao Jie

20

Dengshikou 灯市口

Dongdan Beidajie 东单北大街   Dongdan 东单   Chongwenmennei Dajie

Xitangzi Hutong

Jinyu Hutong

Peking Union Medical College Hospital 协和医院

Dongdan Santiao

东单三条

35   Oriental Plaza

33   Dongchang'an Jie

Dongdan Park

Taijichang Toutiao

Chongwenmen Xidajie   Chongwenmen 崇文门

Dongdamochang Jie

13

Peak of China

10

22

王府井大街   Wangfujing Dajie

Ciqiku Hutong 瓷器库胡同   31

32   27

Wangfujing 王府井

Taijichang Dajie

东交民巷

Donglaomin Xiang

Xidamochang Jie

23

DŌNGCHÉNG

Pucusi Xixiang

14

Nanchizi Dajie

Changpu River Park

Tian'anmen East 天安门东

National Museum of China 2

FORMER FOREIGN LEGATION QUARTER

7

东交民巷

5

25

Zhengyi Lu 正义路

Golden Stream

Duan Gate

Xichang'an Jie

Tian'anmen West 天安门西

Nanchang Jie

Nanchang Jie

Tian'anmen Square

Tiān'ānmén Square 4

Chairman Máo Memorial Hall 1

Xijiaomin Xiang

Qianmen 3

Qianmen 前门

Arrow Tower 前门东大街

6

5

Dōngchéng Central

huge bureaucracy. The ticket office is down the south side of the building; bags must be checked in but cameras are admitted.

St Joseph's Church CHURCH
(东堂, Dōng Táng; Map p76; 74 Wangfujing Dajie, 王府井大街74号; ⏲services 6.30am & 7am Mon-Sat, 7am Sun; [S] Line 5 to Dengshikou, exit A) [FREE] A crowning edifice on Wangfujing Dajie, and one of Běijīng's four principal churches, St Joseph's is known locally as Dōng Táng (East Cathedral). Originally built during the reign of Shunzhi in 1655, it was damaged by an earthquake in 1720 and reconstructed. The luckless church also caught fire in 1807, was destroyed again in 1900 during the Boxer Rebellion and restored in 1904, only to be shut in 1966. Now fully repaired, the church is a testament to the long history of Christianity in China.

Ancient Observatory OBSERVATORY
(古观象台, Gǔ Guānxiàngtái; Map p92; Erhuandong Lu, Jianguomen Qiao, 二环东路建国门桥, Jianguomen Bridge, East 2nd Ring Rd; adult ¥20; ⏲9am-5pm Tue-Sun, last entry 4.30pm; [S] Lines 1, 2 to Jianguomen, exit A) This unusual former observatory is mounted on the battlements of a watchtower lying along the line of the old Ming City Wall and originally dates back to Kublai Khan's days, when it lay north of the present site. Kublai, like later Ming and Qing emperors, relied heavily on astrologers to plan military endeavours. The present observatory – the only surviving example of several constructed during the Jin, Yuan, Ming and Qing dynasties – was built between 1437 and 1446 to facilitate both astrological predictions and seafaring navigation.

Poly Art Museum MUSEUM
(保利艺术博物馆, Bǎolì Yìshù Bówùguǎn; Map p92; ☎010 6500 8117; www.polymuseum.com; 9th fl, Poly Plaza, 14 Dongzhimen Nandajie, 东直门南大街14号保利大厦9层; ¥20, audio guide ¥10; ⏲9.30am-5pm, closed Sun; [S] Line 2 to Dongsi Shitiao, exit D) This small but exquisite museum displays an array of ancient bronzes from the Shang and Zhou dynasties, a magnificent high-water mark for bronze production. Check out the intricate scaling on the '*Zūn* vessel in the shape of a Phoenix' (倗季凤鸟尊) or the '*Yǒu* with Divine Faces' (神面卣), with its elephant head on the side of the vessel. The detailed animist patterns on the *Gangbo You* (棡柏卣) are similarly vivid and fascinating.

Former Foreign Legation Quarter HISTORIC BUILDING
(租界区, Zūjiè Qū; Map p76; [S] Line 2 to Qianmen, exit A or Lines 2, 5 to Chongwenmen, exit A1) The former Foreign Legation Quarter, where the 19th-century foreign powers flung up their

embassies, schools, post offices and banks, lies east of Tiān'ānmén Sq. Apart from the **Běijīng Police Museum** (北京警察博物馆, Běijīng Jǐngchá Bówùguǎn; Map p76; ☎010 8522 5018; 36 Dongjiaomin Xiang, 东交民巷36号; adult ¥5, through ticket ¥20; ⌚9am-4pm Tue-Sun, last entry 3.30pm; [S]Line 2 to Qianmen, exit A) and a complex of trendy restaurants facing onto a grass quadrangle, accessed from the south, you can't enter most of the buildings. Many are now used as government buildings, but a stroll along the streets here (Dongjiaomin Xiang, Taijichang Dajie and Zhengyi Lu) gives you a hint of the area's former European flavour.

Drum Tower & Dōngchéng North

★Drum Tower HISTORIC SITE

(鼓楼, Gǔlóu; Map p80; Gulou Dongdajie, 鼓楼东大街; ¥20, both towers through ticket ¥30; ⌚9am-5pm, last entry 4.40pm; [S]Line 8 to Shichahai, exit A2) Along with the older-looking Bell Tower, which stands behind it, the magnificent red-painted Drum Tower used to be the city's official timekeeper, with drums and bells beaten and rung to mark the times of the day. Originally built in 1272, the Drum Tower was once the heart of the Mongol capital of Dàdū, as Běijīng was then known. It was destroyed in a fire before a replacement was built, slightly to the east of the original location, in 1420. The current structure is a Qing dynasty version of that 1420 tower.

★Bell Tower HISTORIC SITE

(钟楼, Zhōnglóu; Map p80; Gulou Dongdajie, 鼓楼东大街; ¥20, both towers through ticket ¥30; ⌚9am-5pm, last tickets 4.40pm; [S]Line 8 to Shichahai, exit A2) The modest, grey-stone structure of the Bell Tower is arguably more charming than its resplendent other half, the Drum Tower, after which this area of Běijīng is named. It also has the added advantage of being able to view its sister tower from a balcony.

★Lama Temple BUDDHIST TEMPLE

(雍和宫, Yōnghé Gōng; Map p80; www.yonghegong.cn; 12 Yonghegong Dajie, 北新桥雍和宫大街12号; ¥25, English audio guide ¥50; ⌚9am-4.30pm; [S]Lines 2, 5 to Yonghegong-Lama Temple, exit C) This exceptional temple is a glittering attraction in Běijīng's Buddhist firmament. If you only have time for one temple (the Temple of Heaven isn't really a temple) make it this one, where riveting roofs, fabulous frescoes, magnificent decorative arches, tapestries, eye-popping carpentry, Tibetan prayer wheels, tantric statues and a superb pair of Chinese lions mingle with dense clouds of incense.

The most renowned Tibetan Buddhist temple outside Tibet, the Lama Temple was converted to a lamasery in 1744 after serving as the former residence of Emperor Yong Zheng. While the temple is an active place of worship, and you may occasionally see pilgrims prostrating themselves in submission at full length within its halls, the temple is mostly visited by tourists these days.

Resplendent within the **Hall of the Wheel of the Law** (Fǎlún Diàn), the fourth hall you reach from the entrance, is a substantial bronze statue of a benign and smiling Tsong Khapa (1357-1419), founder of the Gelugpa or Yellow Hat sect, robed in yellow and illuminated by a skylight.

The fifth hall, the **Wànfú Pavilion** (Wànfú Gé), houses a magnificent 18m-high statue of the Maitreya Buddha in his Tibetan form, clothed in yellow satin and reputedly sculpted from a single block of sandalwood. Each of the Bodhisattva's toes is the size of a pillow. Behind the statue is the Vault of Avalokiteshvara, from where a diminutive and blue-faced statue of Guanyin peeks out. The Wànfú Pavilion is linked by an overhead walkway to the **Yánsuí Pavilion** (Yánsuí Gé), which encloses a huge lotus flower that revolves to reveal an effigy of the Longevity Buddha.

Don't miss the collection of bronze Tibetan Buddhist statues within the **Jiètái Lóu**, a small side hall. Most effigies date from the Qing dynasty, from languorous renditions of Green Tara and White Tara to exotic, tantric pieces (such as Samvara) and figurines of the fierce-looking Mahakala. Also peruse the collection of Tibetan Buddhist ornaments within the **Bānchán Lóu**, another side hall, where an array of *dorje* (Tibetan sceptres), mandalas and tantric figures are displayed along with an impressive selection of ceremonial robes in silk and satin.

The street outside the temple entrance heaves with shops piled high with statues of Buddha, talismans, Buddhist charms, incense and keepsakes, picked over by a constant stream of pilgrims.

Confucius Temple & Imperial College CONFUCIAN TEMPLE

(孔庙、国子监, Kǒng Miào & Guózǐjiàn; Map p80; 13 Guozijian Jie, 国子监街13号; ¥30, audio guide ¥30; ⌚8.30am-6pm May-Oct, to 5pm Nov-Apr, last entry 1hr before closing; [S]Lines 2, 5 to Yonghegong-Lama Temple, exit C) An incense stick's toss away from the Lama Temple, China's second-largest Confucian temple has had a refit in

Drum Tower & Dōngchéng North

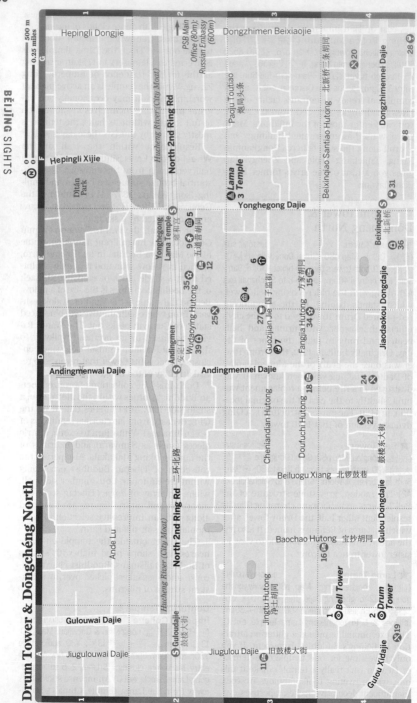

Hepingli Dongjie

Dongzhimen Beixiaojie

北新桥三条胡同 Beixinqiao Santiao Hutong

Dongzhimennei Dajie

28

20

8

31

PSB Main
Office (80m);
Russian Embassy
(600m)

炮局头条 Paoju Toutiao

North 2nd Ring Rd

Hucheng River (City Moat)

Hepingli Xijie

Dìtán Park

Lama
Temple 3

Yonghegong Dajie

Beixinqiao 北新桥

36

Yonghegong:
Lama Temple

9 5

12 五道营胡同 Wudaoying Hutong

6

4

35

25

27 国子监街 Guozijian Jie

7

方家胡同 Fangjia Hutong

15

34

Jiaodaokou Dongdajie

Andingmen
安定门

Andingmenwai Dajie

Andingmennei Dajie

North 2nd Ring Rd
三环北路

39

Cheniandian Hùtòng

Doufuchi Hutong

18

24

21

鼓楼东大街

Hucheng River (City Moat)

Beiluogu Xiang 北锣鼓巷

Gulou Dongdajie

Baochao Hutong 宝抄胡同

16

Jingtu Hutong 净土胡同

Gulouwai Dajie

Guloudajie
鼓楼大街

Bell Tower

Drum
Tower

1

2

Jiugulouwai Dajie

Jiugulou Dajie 旧鼓楼大街

11

Ande Lu

19

Gulou Xidajie

500 m
0.25 miles

N
0
0

Drum Tower & Dōngchéng North

HÚTÒNG TOURS

Exploring Běijīng's *hútòng* (narrow alleyways) is an unmissable experience. Go on a walking or cycling tour and delve deep into this alternately ramshackle and genteel, but always magical, world. Best of all, just wander off the main roads in the centre of Běijīng into the alleyways that riddle the town within the 2nd Ring Rd. Getting lost is part of the fun of exploring the *hútòng*, and you don't have to worry about finding your way back because you'll never be far from a main road.

Good places to plunge into are the alleys to the west of Hòuhǎi Lakes, the area around Nanluogu Xiang, the roads branching west off Chaoyangmen Beixiaojie and Chaoyangmen Nanxiaojie, east of Wangfujing Dajie, and the lanes southwest of Tiān'ānmén Sq.

Hiring a bike is by far the best way to explore this historic world. But if you want to join a tour, the **China Culture Center** (p98) runs regular tours, or can arrange personalised tours. Call for further details, or check the website. **Bike Běijīng** (p98) also does guided *hútòng* tours. Many hotels run tours of the *hútòng*, or will point you in the direction of someone who does. Alternatively, any number of pedicab touts infest the roads around Hòuhǎi Lakes, offering 45-minute or one-hour tours. Such tours typically cost ¥60 to ¥120 per person. If you want an English-speaking rickshaw rider, the Běijīng Tourist Information Centre opposite the north gate of Běihǎi Park can find you one.

recent years, but the almost otherworldly sense of detachment is seemingly impossible to shift. A mood of impassiveness reigns and the lack of worship reinforces a sensation that time has stood still. However, in its tranquillity and reserve, the temple can be a pleasant sanctuary from Běijīng's often congested streets – a haven of peace and quiet.

Antediluvian *bìxì* (mythical tortoiselike dragons) glare from repainted pavilions while lumpy and ossified ancient cypresses claw stiffly at the Běijīng air. There's the Qianlong Stone Scriptures, a stone 'forest' of 190 stelae recording the 13 Confucian classics in 630,000 Chinese characters at the temple rear. Also inscribed on stelae are the names of successful candidates of the highest level of the official Confucian examination system.

Next to the Confucius Temple, but within the same grounds, stands the Imperial College, where the emperor expounded the Confucian classics to an audience of thousands of kneeling students, professors and court officials – an annual rite. Built by the grandson of Kublai Khan in 1306, the former college was the supreme academy during the Yuan, Ming and Qing dynasties. On the site is a marvellous, glazed, three-gate, single-eaved decorative archway called a *liúli páifāng* (glazed archway). The **Biyong Hall** (辟雍大殿, Pìyōng Dàdiàn) beyond is a twin-roofed structure with yellow tiles surrounded by a moat and topped with a splendid gold knob. Its stupendous interior houses a vermillion and gold lectern. The side pavilions house several interesting museums on Confucianism and the academy itself.

Some of Běijīng's last remaining *páilou* (decorated archways) bravely survive in the tree-lined street outside (Guozijian Jie) and the entire area of *hútòng* here is now dotted with small cafes, cute restaurants and boutique shops, making it an ideal place to browse in low gear. At the western end of Guozijian Jie stands a diminutive **Fire God Temple** (火神庙, Huǒshén Miào; Map p80; Guozijian Jie, 国子监街; [S] Lines 2, 5 to Yonghegong-Lama Temple, exit C), built in 1802 and now occupied by Běijīng residents.

Běijīng Cultural & Art Centre GALLERY
(北京文化艺术中心, Běijīng Wénhuà Yìshù Zhōngxīn, BCAC; Map p80; ☎ 010 8408 4977; www.bcac.org.cn; 3 Wudaoying Hutong, 五道营胡同3号; ¥10; ⏲ 10am-8pm Tue-Sun; [S] Lines 2, 5 to Yonghegong-Lama Temple, exit D) In a beautiful *hútòng* courtyard building along one of Beijing's coolest streets, this not-for-profit art gallery has three slick exhibition spaces that cover anything from contemporary and traditional arts to design, fashion and architecture. It generally shows a mix of local and international artists.

Arrow Factory GALLERY
(箭厂空间, Jiànchǎng Kōngjiān; Map p80; www.arrowfactory.org.cn; 38 Jianchang Hutong, off Guozijian Jie, 国子监街，箭厂胡同38号; ⏲ 24hr; [S] Lines 2, 5 to Yonghegong Lama Temple or Line 2 to Andingmen) This tiny, 15-sq-metre, storefront gallery occupies a former vegetable shop and is now an independently run art space for avant-garde installations and modern-art projects designed to be viewed from the street, 24 hours a day, seven days a week. You can't

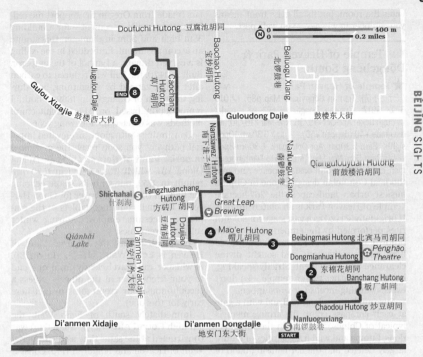

⚡ City Walk
Historic Hútòng Around Nanluogu Xiang

START NANLUOGUXIANG SUBWAY STATION
END DRUM & BELL TOWERS
LENGTH 2KM; ONE HOUR

Běijīng's *hútòng* are the heart and soul of the city.

Exit Nanluoguxiang subway station and turn right into Chaodou Hutong (炒豆胡同). Starting at No 77, the next few courtyards once made up the **❶ former mansion of Seng Gelinqin**, a Qing dynasty army general. Note the enormous *bǎogǔshí* (drum stones) at the entranceway to No 77, followed by more impressive gateways at Nos 75, 69, 67 and 63. After No 53, turn left up an unmarked winding alleyway then left onto Banchang Hutong (板厂胡同).

At No 19, turn right through an unusual **❷ hallway gate**, a connecting passageway leading to Dongmianhua Hutong (东棉花胡同). Turn right here, then left down an unnamed alley, which is signposted to Pénghāo Theatre.

Turn left onto Beibingmasi Hutong (北兵马司胡同) and cross Nanluogu Xiang into historic **❸ Mao'er Hutong** (帽儿胡同). Admire the entranceways, or if the gates are open, step into the charming courtyards at Nos 5 and 11. Further on, No 37 was the **❹ former home of Wan Rong**, who would later marry China's last emperor, Puyi.

Next, turn right down Doujiao Hutong (豆角胡同) and wind your way (past Great Leap Brewing) to Fangzhuanchang Hutong (方砖厂胡同) then Nanxiawazi Hutong (南下洼子胡同), with its small **❺ fruit & veg street market**, and continue north to Gulou Dongdajie (鼓楼东大街). Turn left here and then, just before you reach the imperious red-painted **❻ Drum Tower** (p79), turn right into Caochang Hutong (草厂胡同). Continue down the lane, then take the second left: you'll see the magnificent grey-brick **❼ Bell Tower** (p79) in front of you. Follow this wonderfully winding alley to the back of the Bell Tower, then walk around the tower to the recently redeveloped **❽ Drum & Bell Square**.

enter the room, but its all-glass front means you can peer in whenever you walk past.

Temple of Heaven Park & Dōngchéng South

★Temple of Heaven Park PARK
(天坛公园, Tiāntán Gōngyuán; Map p85; ☎010 6702 9917; Tiantan Donglu, 天坛东路; park/through ticket Apr-Oct ¥15/35, Nov-Mar ¥10/30, audio guide ¥40 (deposit ¥50); 🕒park 6.30am-10pm, sights 8am-5.30pm Apr-Oct, park 6.30am-8pm, sights 8am-5pm Nov-Mar; [S] Line 5 to Tiantandongmen, exit A) A tranquil oasis of peace and methodical Confucian design in one of China's busiest urban landscapes, the 267-hectare Temple of Heaven Park is absolutely unique. It originally served as a vast stage for solemn rites performed by the emperor of the time (known as the Son of Heaven), who prayed here for good harvests and sought divine clearance and atonement. Strictly speaking, it's an altar rather than a temple – so don't expect burning incense or worshippers.

Surrounded by a long wall and with a gate at each compass point, the arrangement is typical of Chinese parks, with the imperfections, bumps and wild irregularities of nature largely deleted and the harmonising hand of man accentuated in obsessively straight lines and regular arrangements. This effect is magnified by Confucian objectives, where the human intellect is imposed on the natural world, fashioning order and symmetry. The resulting balance and harmony have an almost haunting – but slightly claustrophobic – beauty. Police whir about in electric buggies as visitors stroll among old buildings, groves of ancient trees and birdsong. Around 4000 ancient, knotted cypresses (some 800 years old, their branches propped up on poles) poke towards the Běijīng skies within the grounds.

Seen from above, the temple halls are round and the bases square, in accordance with the notion 'Tiānyuán Dìfāng' (天圆地方) – 'Heaven is round, Earth is square'. Also observe that the northern rim of the park is semicircular, while its southern end is square. The traditional approach to the temple was from the south, via Zhāohēng Gate (昭亨门; Zhāohēng Mén); the north gate is an architectural afterthought. The highlight of the park, and an icon of Běijīng in its own right, is the **Hall of Prayer for Good Harvests** (祈年殿, Qínián Diàn; ¥20; 🕒8am-5pm), an astonishing structure with a triple-eaved purplish-blue umbrella roof mounted on a three-tiered marble terrace. The wooden pillars (made from Oregon fir) support the ceiling without nails or cement – for a building 38m high and 30m in diameter, that's quite an accomplishment. Embedded in the ceiling is a carved dragon, a symbol of the emperor. Built in 1420, the hall was reduced to carbon after being zapped by a lightning bolt during the reign of Guangxu in 1889; a faithful reproduction based on Ming architectural methods was erected the following year.

Continuing south along an elevated imperial pathway, you soon reach the octagonal **Imperial Vault of Heaven** (皇穹宇; Huáng Qióng Yǔ), which was erected in 1530 and rebuilt in 1752, but with its shape echoing the lines of the Hall of Prayer for Good Harvests. The hall contained tablets of the emperor's ancestors, employed during winter solstice ceremonies.

Wrapped around the Imperial Vault of Heaven is **Echo Wall** (回音壁; Huíyīn Bì). A whisper can travel clearly from one end to your friend's ear at the other – unless a cacophonous tour group joins in (get here early for this one).

Immediately south of Echo Wall, the 5m-high **Round Altar** (圜丘; Yuán Qiū) was constructed at the same time as the Imperial Vault of Heaven and rebuilt in 1740. Consisting of white marble arrayed in three tiers, its geometry revolves around the imperial number nine. Odd numbers possess heavenly significance, with nine the largest single-digit odd number. Symbolising heaven, the top tier is a huge mosaic of nine rings, each composed of multiples of nine stones, so that the ninth ring equals 81 stones. The stairs and balustrades are similarly presented in multiples of nine. Sounds generated from the centre of the upper terrace undergo amplification from the marble balustrades (the acoustics can get noisy when crowds join in).

Off to the eastern side of the Hall of Prayer for Good Harvests, and with a green-tiled two-tier roof, the **Animal Killing Pavilion** (宰牲亭, Zǎishēng Tíng) was the venue for the slaughter of sacrificial oxen, sheep, deer and other animals. Today it stands locked and passive but can be admired from the outside. Stretching out from here runs a **Long Corridor** (长廊; Cháng Láng), where locals sit and deal cards, listen to the radio, play keyboards, practise Peking opera, try dance moves and play *jiànzi*, a game similar to hacky-sack but played with a weighted shuttlecock. Just north of here is a large and very popular exercise park.

Temple of Heaven Park & Dōngchéng South

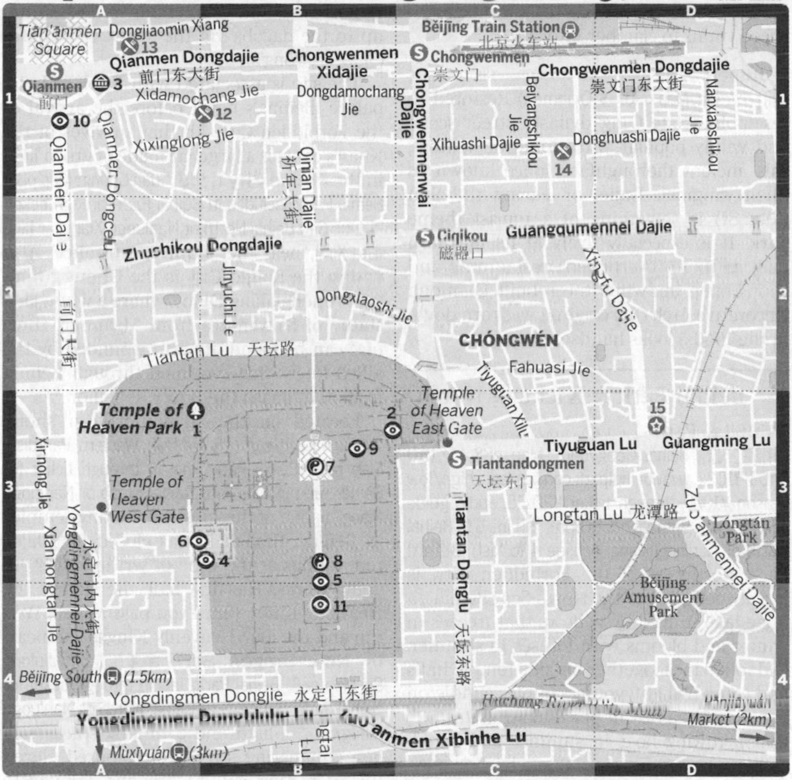

Temple of Heaven Park & Dōngchéng South

Top Sights
1 Temple of Heaven Park........................A3

Sights
2 Animal Killing Pavilion........................B3
3 Běijīng Railway Museum........................A1
4 Divine Music Administration........................B3
5 Echo Wall........................B3
6 Fasting Palace........................A3
7 Hall of Prayer for Good Harvests........................B3
8 Imperial Vault of Heaven........................B3
9 Long Corridor........................B3
10 Qianmen Dajie........................A1
11 Round Altar........................B4

Eating
12 Lìqún Roast Duck Restaurant........................B1
13 Lost Heaven........................A1
14 Yīzhēn Yuán........................C1

Entertainment
15 Red Theatre........................D3

In the west of the park, sacrificial music was rehearsed at the **Divine Music Administration** (神乐署, Shényuè Shǔ, ¥10), while feral cats inhabit the dry moat of the green-tiled **Fasting Palace** (斋宫; Zhāi Gōng).

The **East Gate** (天坛东门, Tiāntán Dóngmén; Map p85; Tiantan Donglu, 天坛东路; [S]Tiantandongmen) is the most popular place to enter the park but queues for tickets are shorter at the **West Gate** (天坛西门, Tiāntán Xīmén; Map p85; Tianqiao Nandajie, 天桥南大街).

Běijīng Railway Museum MUSEUM
(北京铁路博物馆, Běijīng Tiělù Bówùguǎn; Map p76; ☎010 6705 1638; 2a Qianmen Dongdajie, 前门东大街2a号; ¥20; 🕒9am-5pm Tue-Sun; [S]Qianmen) Located in the historic former Qiánmén Railway Station, which once connected Běijīng to Tiānjīn, this museum offers an engaging history of the development of the capital and China's railway system, with plenty of photos and models. Its lack of space, though, means it doesn't have many

actual trains, although there is a life-size model of the cab of one of China's high-speed trains to clamber into (¥10).

Qianmen Dajie
HISTORIC SITE

(前门大街; Map p90; S Qianmen) Restored to resemble a late Qing dynasty street scene and wildly popular with domestic visitors, this ancient thoroughfare (once known as Zhengyangmen Dajie, or Facing the Sun Gate St) is something of a tourist theme park. It is especially lively at its northern end, as more (overpriced) restaurants and shops open up, while the rebuilt Qiánmén Decorative Arch (the original was torn down in the 1950s) looks handsome.

◉ Běihǎi Park & Xīchéng North

★ Běihǎi Park
PARK

(北海公园, Běihǎi Gōngyuán; Map p88; ☎ 010 6403 1102; www.beihaipark.com.cn/en; high/low season ¥10/5, through ticket ¥20/15, audio guide ¥60; ⊙ 6am-9pm, sights to 5pm; S Line 6 to Beihai North or Nanluoguxiang, or Line 4 to Xisi) Běihǎi Park, northwest of the Forbidden City, is largely occupied by the North Sea (Běihǎi), a huge lake fringed by willows that freezes in winter and blooms with lotuses in summer. Old folk dance together outside temple halls and come twilight, young couples cuddle on benches. It's a restful place to stroll around, rent a rowing boat in summer and watch calligraphers practising characters on paving slabs with fat brushes and water.

Topping Jade Islet (琼岛; Qióngdǎo) on the lake, the 36m-high Tibetan-style White Dagoba (白塔, Báitǎ; Map p88; Běihǎi Park; included in through ticket for Běihǎi Park; ⊙ 9am-5pm; S Line 6 to Beihai North or Nanluogu Xiang, or

Line 4 to Xisi) was built in 1651 for a visit by the Dalai Lama, and was rebuilt in 1741. Climb up to the dagoba via the Yǒng'ān Temple (永安寺; Yǒng'ān Sì).

The site is associated with Kublai Khan's palace, Běijīng's navel before the arrival of the Forbidden City. All that survives of the Khan's court is a large jar made of green jade in the Round City (团城, Tuán Chéng; Map p88; Běihǎi Park; included in through ticket; S Line 6 to Beihai North or Nanluogu Xiang, or Line 4 to Xisi), near the southern entrance. Also within the Round City is the Chengguang Hall (Chéngguāng Diàn), where a white jade statue of Sakyamuni from Myanmar (Burma) can be found, its arm wounded by the allied forces that swarmed through Běijīng in 1900 to quash the Boxer Rebellion.

Located on the lake's northern shore, Xītiān Fánjìng (西天梵境, Western Paradise; Map p88; Běihǎi Park; incl in through ticket for Běihǎi Park; S Line 6 to Beihai North or Nanluogu Xiang) is one of the most interesting temples in Běijīng, though it was closed for major renovations at the time of writing with on-going works. The first hall, the Hall of the Heavenly Kings, takes you past Mílèfó, Wei-tuo and the four Heavenly Kings. The near-by Nine Dragon Screen (九龙壁, Jiǔlóng Bì; Map p88; Běihǎi Park; incl in through ticket for Běihǎi Park; S Line 6 to Beihai North or Nanluogu Xiang), a 5m-high and 27m-long spirit wall, is a glimmering stretch of coloured glazed tiles depicting coiling dragons, similar to its counterpart in the Forbidden City. West, along the shore, is the unique Xiaoxitian (Little Western Heaven, 小西天; Map p88; Běihǎi Park; included in through ticket for Běihǎi Park; S Line 6 to Beihai North or Nanluogu Xiang), the

GOING UNDERGROUND

The hordes of skateboarding teens, couples and families who crowd out Xidan Culture Square – Xīchéng's busiest shopping and entertainment square – may not know it, but the space beneath them (which until recently was the 77th St shopping mall) was once part of what was possibly the world's largest bomb shelter. In 1969, alarmed at the prospect of pos-sible nuclear war with either the Soviet Union or the US, Mao Zedong ordered that a huge warren of underground tunnels be burrowed underneath Běijīng. The task was completed Cultural Revolution–style – by hand – with the finishing touches made in 1979, just as the US reopened its embassy in the capital and the Russians were marching into Afghanistan.

Legend has it that one tunnel stretched all the way to Tiānjīn (a mere 130km away), while another runs to the Summer Palace. Nowadays it is believed that some tunnels are still used for clandestine official purposes, while the rest of the underground city has been rendered unsafe by the construction boom that has gone on above it since the 1990s. But a few portions of the complex have been turned over for commercial use, like the 77th St mall, a fitting metaphor for the way China has embraced consumerism and left Maoism far behind.

WORTH A TRIP

798 ART DISTRICT

A vast area of disused factories built by the East Germans, **798 Art District** (798艺术新区, Qī Jiǔ Bā Yìshù Qū; cnr Jiuxianqiao Lu & Jiuxianqiao Beilu, 酒仙桥路; 🕐galleries 10am-6pm, most closed Mon; 🚌403, 909, [S] Line 14 to Jiangtai, exit A), also known as Dàshānzi (大山子), is Běijīng's main concentration of contemporary art galleries. The industrial complex celebrates its proletarian roots in the communist heyday of the 1950s via the retouched red Maoist slogans decorating gallery walls and statues of burly, lantern-jawed workers dotting the lanes. The giant former factory workshops are ideally suited to multimedia installations and other ambitious projects.

You could easily spend half a day wandering around the complex. There are signboards with English-language maps to guide you around.

Some of the bigger galleries and highlights include:

798 Art Factory (798艺术工厂, 798 Yìshù Gōngchǎng; ☎186 1132 2248; 4 Jiuxianqiao Lu, 酒仙桥路4号大山子艺术区; 🕐10am-6pm) A Bauhaus hangar-like space with its ceiling decorated in 1950s Maoist slogans, and original machinery scattered among changing art exhibitions by Chinese and foreign artists.

Faurschou Foundation Beijing (林冠基金会北京, Línguān Jījīn Huì Běijīng; www.faurschou.com; 2 Jiuxuanquao Lu, 酒仙桥路2号798艺术区; 🕐10am-6pm) A Danish gallery, which has exhibitions by internationally acclaimed artists. Past shows include the likes of Lucien Freud, Ai Wei Wei, Andy Warhol and Yoko Ono.

Springs Centre of the Arts (泉空间, Quán Kōngjiān; ☎010 5762 6373; www.springsart.com; 2 Jiuxianqiao Lu, 酒仙桥路2号大山子艺术区; ¥10; 🕐10am-6pm Tue-Sun) Exhibits headliner artists from both China and abroad.

UCCA (Ullens Center for Contemporary Art, 尤伦斯当代艺术中心, Yóulúnsī Dāngdài Yìshù Zhōngxīn; ☎010 5780 0200; http://ucca.org.cn/en/; 4 Jiuxianqiao Lu, 酒仙桥路4号大山子艺术区; ¥10-60; 🕐10am-7pm Tue-Sun) Another big-money gallery with immense, modern exhibition halls. Attached is cool **UCCA Design Store** (尤伦斯当代艺术中心, Yóulúnsī Dāngdài Yìshù Zhōngxīn; ☎010 5780 0224; http://ucca.org.cn/en/uccastore/; 🕐10am-6pm Tue-Sun).

Xin Dong Cheng Space for Contemporary Art (程昕东国际当代艺术空间, Chéngxīndōng Guójì Dāngdài Yìshù Kōngjiān; 4 Jiuxianqiao Lu, 酒仙桥路4号大山子艺术区; 🕐10am-6.30pm Tue-Sun) Showcases young avant-garde Chinese artists in a lovely space;

Zhu Bingren Art Museum (朱炳仁美术博物馆, Zhūbǐngrén Měishù Bówùguǎn; www.cu100.com, 大山子艺术区; 🕐10am-6pm) Features the copper and bronze sculpture of renowned Shandong artist Zhu Bingren.

Mansudae Art Studio (万寿台创作社, Wànshòutái Chuàngzuò Shè; ☎010 5978 9317; www.mansudaeartstudio.com; 2 Jiuxianqiao Lu, 酒仙桥路2号大山子艺术区; 🕐10am-6pm Tue-Sun), Exhibits North Korean artists and sells Democratic People's Republic of Korea (DPRK) collectibles. Pyongyang-based.

There are also plenty of quirky open-air sculptures scattered around the site. The caged dinosaurs out front of 798 Art Factory are popular, while original socialist realism sculptures in the southwest of the complex include a headless Chairman Mao statue. Nearby are shipping containers used as a canvas by graffiti artists. The area around 798 Live House is the best for stencils, murals and other street art.

largest square pavilion-style palace in China. Its centrepiece features a rather garish diorama of Mt Sumeru with Bodhisattva seated at its peak along with arhats on rocks.

Attached to the North Sea, the South (Nánhǎi) and Middle (Zhōnghǎi) Seas to the south lend their name to Zhōngnánhǎi (literally 'Middle and South Seas'), the heavily-guarded compound less than a mile south of the park where the Chinese Communist Party's top leadership live.

★Hòuhǎi Lakes — LAKE

(后海, Hòuhǎi; Map p88; [S] Line 6 to Beihai North, exit B, or Line 8 to Shichahai, exit A1, or Line 2 to Jishuitan, exit B) [FREE] Also known as Shíchàhǎi (什刹海) but mostly just referred to collectively as Hòuhǎi, the Hòuhǎi Lakes

Běihǎi Park & Xīchéng North

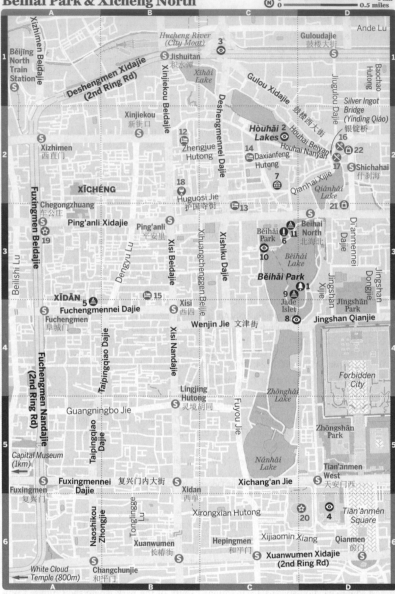

are comprised of three lakes: Qiánhǎi (Front Lake), Hòuhǎi (Back Lake) and Xīhǎi (West Lake). Together they are one of the capital's favourite outdoor spots, heaving with locals and out-of-towners in the summer especially, and providing great people-spotting action.

Prince Gong's Residence HISTORIC BUILDING
(恭王府; Gōngwáng Fǔ; Map p88; ☏010 8328 8149; 14 Liuyin Jie; ¥40, tours incl short opera show & tea ceremony ¥70; ⊗8am-5pm Apr-Oct, 9am-4pm Nov-Mar; ⓢLine 6 to Beihai North, exit B) The historic courtyard home of Prince Gong's (aka Prince Kung) mansion is one of Běijīng's

Běihǎi Park & Xīchéng North

Top Sights
1 Běihǎi Park ... D3
2 Hòuhǎi Lakes ... C2

Sights
3 Déshèngmén Gateway ... C1
4 Great Hall of the People ... D6
5 Miàoyīng Temple White Dagoba ... A4
6 Nine Dragon Screen ... C3
7 Prince Gong's Residence ... C2
8 Round City ... C4
9 White Dagoba ... C3
10 Xiǎoxītiān ... C3
11 Xītiān Fánjìng ... C3

Sleeping
12 Graceland Yard ... B2
13 Shíchàhǎi Sandalwood Boutique Hotel ... C3
14 Shíchàhǎi Shadow Art Hotel ... C2
15 Siheju Courtyard Hostel ... B3

Eating
16 4corners ... D2
17 Kǎo Ròu Jì ... D2

Drinking & Nightlife
18 NBeer Pub ... B2

Entertainment
19 Mei Lanfang Grand Theatre ... A3
20 National Centre for the Performing Arts ... D6

Shopping
21 Three Stone Kite Shop ... D3
22 Yandai Xiejie ... D2

largest private residential compounds. It remains one of the capital's more attractive retreats, decorated with rockeries, plants, pools, pavilions and elaborately carved gateways, although it can get very crowded with tour groups. It's reputed to be the model for Chinese writer Cáo Xuěqín's 18th-century classic *Dream of the Red Mansions*.

★Capital Museum — MUSEUM

(首都博物馆, Shǒudū Bówùguǎn; ☎010 6339 3339; www.capitalmuseum.org.cn; 16 Fuxingmenwai Dajie, 复兴门外大街16号; ⏰9am-5pm Tue-Sun, last entry 4pm; [S]Line 1 to Muxidi, exit C1) [FREE] Behind the good looks of this sleek museum are some first-rate galleries, including a mesmerising collection of ancient Buddhist statues and a lavish exhibition of Chinese porcelain. There is also an interesting chronological history of Běijīng, an exhibition that is dedicated to cultural relics of Peking opera, a fascinating Běijīng Folk Customs exhibition, and displays of ancient bronzes, jade, calligraphy and paintings. Bring your passport or photo ID for free entry and audio guide.

Come out of exit C1 of Muxidi subway station, and the museum is on your right (200m).

Miàoyīng Temple White Dagoba — BUDDHIST TEMPLE

(妙应寺白塔, Miàoyīng Sì Báitǎ; Map p88; ☎010 6616 0211; 171 Fuchengmennei Dajie, 阜成门内大街171号; adult ¥20; ⏰9am-5pm Tue-Sun; [S]Line 2 to Fuchengmen, exit B, or Line 4 to Xisi, exit A) Originally built in 1271, the serene Miàoyīng Temple slumbers beneath its huge, distinctive, chalk-white Yuan dynasty pagoda, which towers over the surrounding *hútòng*. It was, when it was built, the tallest structure in Dàdū (the Yuan dynasty name for Běijīng), and even today it is the tallest Tibetan-style pagoda in China. The highlights of a visit here include the diverse collection of Buddhist statuary.

White Cloud Temple — TAOIST TEMPLE

(白云观, Báiyún Guān; ☎010 6346 3887; 9 Baiyunguan Jie, 白云路白云观街9号; adult ¥10; ⏰8.30am-4.30pm May-early Oct, to 4pm early Oct-Apr; [S]Line 1 to Muxidi, exit C1) Once the Taoist centre of northern China, this temple was founded in AD 739, although most of the temple halls date from the Qing dynasty. It's a lively, huge and fascinating complex of shrines and courtyards, tended by Taoist monks with their hair gathered into topknots.

Déshèngmén Gateway — LANDMARK

(德胜门, Déshèngmén; Map p88) A monumental landmark along the 2nd Ring Road is this Ming dynasty city gate and watchtower, which made up part of Běijīng's northern wall. The remaining structure is the archery tower, built in 1437, which stands over the city's northern moat. On the north side is where buses leave for the Ming Tombs and Bādálǐng Great Wall section..

Dashilar & Xīchéng South

Xiānnóng Altar & Běijīng Ancient Architecture Museum — MUSEUM

(先农坛、北京古代建筑博物馆, Xiānnóngtán & Běijīng Gǔdài Jiànzhú Bówùguǎn; Map p90; ☎010 6304 5608; 21 Dongjing Lu, 东经路21号; ¥15, audio guide ¥10; ⏰9am-4pm Tue-Sun; [S]Line 4 to Taoranting) This altar – to the west of the

Dashilar & Xīchéng South

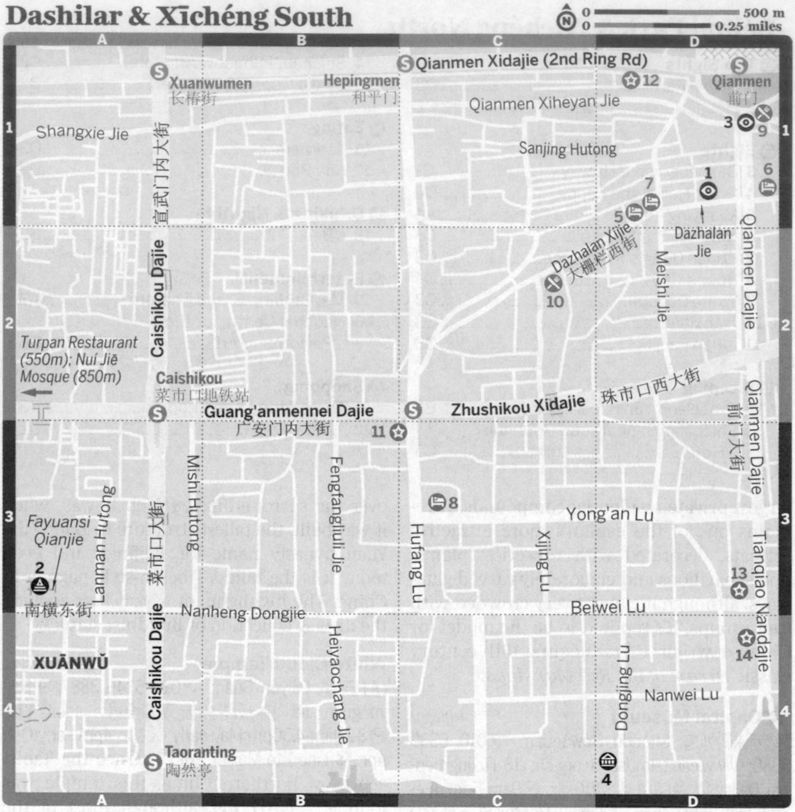

Temple of Heaven (p84) – was the site of solemn imperial ceremonies and sacrificial offerings. Here you'll find the excellent Běijīng Ancient Architecture Museum, which informatively narrates the elements of traditional Chinese building techniques. The museum is spread over the four 15th-century halls which face one another across the large courtyard. Each features different exhibits, but the centrepiece is the magnificent **Jupiter Hall** (太岁殿; Tàisuì Diàn), with exquisite detail in its ceiling.

Dashilar AREA

(大栅栏, Dàzhàlan; Map p90; Dazhalan Jie, 大栅栏街; [S] Line 2 to Qianmen, exit B or C) This centuries-old pedestrianised shopping street, also known as Dazhalan Jie, is just west of Qianmen Dajie. While a misjudged make over has sadly robbed it of much of its charm, many of the shops have been in business here for hundreds of years and still draw many Chinese tourists. Some specialise in esoteric goods – ancient herbal remedies, handmade cloth shoes – and most make for intriguing window-shopping.

Fǎyuán Temple BUDDHIST TEMPLE

(法源寺, Fǎyuán Sì; Map p90; 7 Fayuansi Qianjie, 法源寺前街7号; adult ¥5; ⏰8.30-4pm; [S] Lines 4, 7 to Caishikou, exit D) Infused with an air of reverence and devotion, this lovely temple dates back to the 7th century. The temple follows the typical Buddhist layout, with drum and bell towers. Do hunt out the unusual copper-cast Buddha, seated atop four further Buddhas ensconced on a huge bulb of myriad effigies in the Pilu Hall (the fourth hall).

Niújiē Mosque MOSQUE

(牛街礼拜寺, Niújiē Lǐbài Sì; ☎010 6353 2564; 18 Niu Jie, 牛街18号; adult ¥10, Muslims free; ⏰8.30am-sunset; [S] Lines 4, 7 to Caishikou, exit D) Dating back to the 10th century, this unique mosque blends traditional Chinese temple design with Middle Eastern flourishes. It's Běijīng's largest mosque and centre for its community of 10,000 or so Huí Chinese Muslims

Dashilar & Xīchéng South

Sights
1 Dashilar D1
2 Fǎyuán Temple A3
3 Qianmen Dajie D1
4 Xiānnóng Altar & Běijīng Ancient Architecture Museum D4

Sleeping
5 365 Inn D1
6 Emperor D1
7 Qiánmén Hostel D1
8 Qiánmén Jiànguó Hotel C3

Eating
9 Capital M D1
10 Liú Family Noodles C2

Entertainment
11 Húguǎng Guild Hall B3
12 Lao She Teahouse D1
Líyuán Theatre .... (see 8)
13 Tiānqiáo Acrobatics Theatre D3
14 Tiānqiáo Performing Arts Centre D4

who live nearby. Look out for the **Building for Observing the Moon** (望月楼; Wàngyuèlóu), from where the lunar calendar was calculated. Also note the spirit wall on Nui Jie that guards the entrance, a feature of all Chinese temples regardless of denomination.

Sānlǐtún & Cháoyáng

Bird's Nest ARCHITECTURE
(北京国家体育场, Běijīng Guójiā Tǐyùchǎng, Beijing National Stadium; http://cyvu.org/english/; Beijing Olympic Park, 奥林匹克公园; ¥50; ⌚9am-6.30pm Apr-Oct, to 5pm Nov-Mar,; [S] Line 8 to Olympic Sports Center, exit B2) The centerpiece from the 2008 Olympics is the National Stadium, known colloquially as the Bird's Nest (鸟巢; Niǎocháo). It's one primarily for lovers of contemporary architecture, or those interested in sporting history. Otherwise, walking around the desolate Olympic Sports Centre midweek is rather like being stuck in one of those zombie movies where humans have all but been wiped out. Nevertheless, it remains an iconic piece of architecture designed by Swiss firm Herzog & de Meuron in consultancy with controversial Běijīng-born artist Ai Wei Wei.

CCTV Headquarters ARCHITECTURE
(央视大楼, Yāngshì Dàlóu; Map p92; 32 Dongsanhuan Zhonglu, 东三环中路32号; [S] Line 10 to Jintaixizhao, exit C) Shaped like an enormous pair of trousers, and known locally as Dà Kùchǎ (大裤衩; Big Pants), the astonishing CCTV Tower is an architectural fantasy that appears to defy gravity. It's made possible by an unusual engineering design that creates a three-dimensional cranked loop, supported by an irregular grid on its surface. Designed by Rem Koolhaas and Ole Scheeren, the building is an audacious statement of modernity (despite its nickname) and a unique addition to the Běijīng skyline.

Rìtán Park PARK
(日坛公园, Rìtán Gōngyuán; Map p92; 6 Ritan Beilu, 日坛北路6号; ⌚6am-9pm; [S] Lines 2, 6 to Chaoyangmen, exit A or Lines 1, 2 to Jianguomen, exit B) [FREE] Meaning 'Altar of the Sun', Rìtán ('rer-tan') is a real oasis in the heart of Běijīng's business district. It's a nice place to stroll and take in the atmosphere of this beautifully landscaped park where you'll see locals dancing, singing, flying kites, playing table tennis and hanging out. It dates back to 1530 and was one of a set of imperial parks that covered each compass point – others include the Temple of Heaven and Temple of Earth (Dìtán Park).

Dōngyuè Temple TAOIST TEMPLE
(东岳庙, Dōngyuè Miào; Map p92; 141 Chaoyangmenwai Dajie, adult ¥10, with guide ¥40; ⌚8.30am-4.30pm Tue-Sun, last entry 4pm; [S] Lines 2, 6 to Chaoyangmen, exit A, or Line 6 to Dongdaqiao, exit A) Dedicated to the Eastern Peak (Tài Shān) of China's five Taoist mountains, the morbid Taoist shrine of Dōngyuè Temple is an unsettling, albeit fascinating, experience and one of the capital's most unusual temples. An active place of worship tended by top-knotted Taoist monks, the temple's roots go all the way back to the Yuan dynasty. It's most notable for its long corridor exhibiting a series of comically macabre displays of statues representing different 'departments' from the Taoist underworld.

Summer Palace & Hǎidiàn

★ **Summer Palace** HISTORIC SITE
(颐和园, Yíhé Yuán; Map p96; 19 Xinjian Gongmen, 新建宫门19号; Apr-Oct ¥30, through ticket ¥60, Nov-Mar ¥20, through ticket ¥50, audio guide ¥40; ⌚7am-7pm, sights 8am-5pm summer, 8.30am-4.30pm winter; [S] Xiyuan or Beigongmen) As mandatory a Běijīng sight as the Great Wall or the Forbidden City, the Summer Palace

Sānlǐtún & Cháoyáng

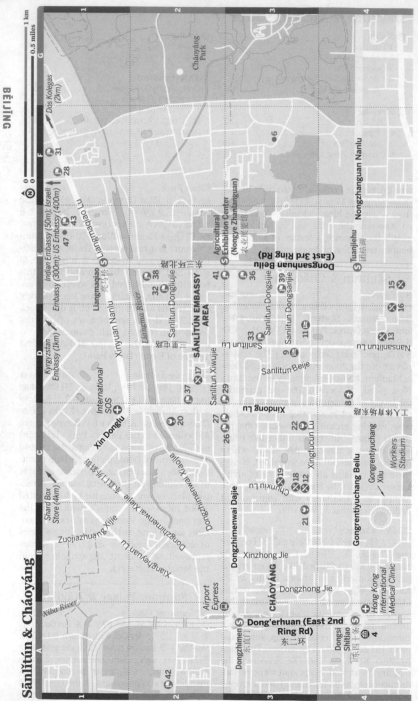

Dos Kolegas (2km)

Indian Embassy (50m); Israeli Embassy (300m); US Embassy (400m)

Kyrgyzstan Embassy (1km)

Shard Box Store (4km)

Cháoyáng Park

Liangmaqiao Lu

Xinyuan Nanlu

Liangmaqiao
亮马桥

Liangma River

Sanlitun Dongliujie

Agricultural Exhibition Center (Nongye Zhanlanguan)
农业展览馆

Dongsanhuan Beilu (East 3rd Ring Rd)

Nongzhanguan Nanlu

Tuanjiehu
团结湖

SĀNLĬTÚN EMBASSY AREA

Sanlitun Dongsijie

Sanlitun Dongsanjie

International SOS

Xin Donglu

Sanlitun Xiwujie

Sanlitun Lu

Sanlitun Beijie

Nansanlitun Lu

Zuojiazhuang Xijie

Dongzhimenwai Xiejie

Dongzhimenwai Xiejie

Xiangheyuan Lu

Xiba River

Airport Express

Dongzhimen
东直门

Dongzhimenwai Dajie

Xinong Lu

Xingfucun Lu

Chunxiu Lu

Xinzhong Jie

Dongzhong Jie

CHÁOYÁNG

Dong'erhuan (East 2nd Ring Rd)
东二环

Hong Kong International Medical Clinic

Gongrentiyuchang Beilu

Gongrentiyuchang
Xilu

Workers Stadium

工人体育场北路

Dongsi Shitiao
东四十条

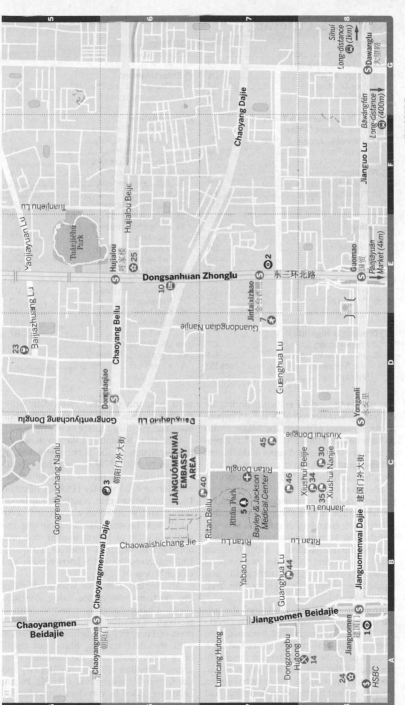

Sìhuī
Long-distance (1km)
Ⓢ Dawanglu 大望路

Bāwángfén
Long-distance (400m)

Jianguo Lu

Chaoyang Dajie

Guomao
Ⓢ 国贸
Panjiāyuán
Market (4km)

Tuánjiéhú Lu

Tuánjiéhú
Park

Hujialou Beijie

Hujialou
呼家楼
☆ Ⓢ 25 ★

Dongsanhuan Zhonglu 10 ⑪ 东三环北路 Ⓢ

Jintaixizhao
Ⓢ 金台夕照 ● 2

Baijiazhuang Lu 23 ⓘ

Chaoyang Beilu

Guandongdian Nanjie 7 ✪

Guanghua Lu

Dongdaqiao
Ⓢ

Gongrentiyuchang Donglu

Chaoyangmenwai Dajie

Gongrentiyuchang Nanlu

JIĀNGUÓMÉNWÀI
EMBASSY
AREA
● 3 朝阳门外大街 Panjiāhuō Lu

Ⓢ Yonganli
永安里

Xiushui Dongjie

45 ●

Ritan Donglu
Bayley & Jackson
Medical Center ➕ 46 ● 34 ● 30 ●
Ritan Park Xiushui Beijie
5 ★ 35 ● Xiushui Nanjie
Ⓒ 40 Ritan Beilu Jianhua Lu

Ritan Lu Ritan Lu

Chaowaishichang Jie

Yabao Lu

Guanghua Lu 44 ●

Jianguomenwai Dajie
建国门外大街

Chaoyangmen
Beidajie Ⓢ Chaoyangmen
朝阳门

Jianguomen Beidajie

Lumicang Hutong

Dongzongbu
Hutong 14 ✖

Jianguomen
Ⓢ 建国门 1 ◉

24 ☆ Ⓢ
HSBC

Sānlǐtún & Cháoyáng

was the playground for emperors fleeing the suffocating summer torpor of the old imperial city. A marvel of design, the palace – with its huge lake and hilltop views – offers a pastoral escape into the landscapes of traditional Chinese painting. It merits an entire day's exploration, although a (high-paced) morning or afternoon exploring the temples, gardens, pavilions, bridges and corridors may suffice.

The domain had long been a royal garden before being considerably enlarged and embellished by Emperor Qianlong in the 18th century. He marshalled a 100,000-strong army of labourers to deepen and expand **Kūnmíng Lake** (昆明湖; Kūnmíng Hú), and reputedly surveyed imperial navy drills from a hilltop perch.

Anglo-French troops vandalised the palace during the Second Opium War (1856–60). Empress Dowager Cixi launched into a refit in 1888 with money earmarked for a modern navy; the marble boat at the northern edge of the lake was her only nautical, albeit quite unsinkable, concession. Foreign troops, angered by the Boxer Rebellion, had another go at torching the Summer Palace in 1900, prompting further restoration work. By 1949 the palace had once more fallen into disrepair, eliciting a major overhaul.

Glittering Kūnmíng Lake swallows up three-quarters of the park, overlooked by **Longevity Hill** (万寿山; Wànshòu Shān). The principal structure is the **Hall of Benevolence & Longevity** (仁寿殿, Rénshòu Diàn), by the east gate, housing a hardwood throne and attached to a courtyard decorated with bronze animals, including the mythical *qílín* (a hybrid animal that only appeared on earth at times of harmony). Unfortunately, the hall is barricaded so you can only peer in.

An elegant stretch of woodwork along the northern shore, the **Long Corridor** (长廊, Cháng Láng) is trimmed with a plethora of paintings, while the slopes and crest of Longevity Hill behind are adorned with Buddhist temples. Slung out uphill on a north–south axis, the **Buddhist Fragrance Pavilion** (佛香阁, Fóxiāng Gé) and the **Cloud Dispelling Hall** (排云殿, Páiyún Diàn) are linked by corridors. Crowning the peak is the **Buddhist Temple of the Sea of**

Wisdom (智慧海, Zhìhuì Hǎi), tiled with effigies of Buddha, many with obliterated heads.

Cixi's **marble boat** (清晏舫, Qīngyuàn Chuán) sits immobile on the north shore, south of some fine **Qing boathouses** (船坞, Chuán Wù). When the lake is not frozen, you can traverse Kūnmíng Lake by ferry to **South Lake Island** (南湖岛; Nánhú Dǎo), where Cixi went to beseech the **Dragon King Temple** (龙王庙, Lóngwáng Miào) for rain in times of drought. A graceful 17-arch bridge spans the 150m to the eastern shore of the lake. In warm weather **pedal boats** (脚踏船, Jiǎotà Chuán; Map p96; 4-/6-person boat per hour ¥80/100; ⏰ 0am– 4pm Apr-Oct) are also available from the dock.

Try to do a circuit of the lake along the **West Causeway** (西堤, Xīdī) to return along the east shore (or vice versa). It gets you away from the crowds, the views are gorgeous and it's a great cardiovascular workout. Based on the Su Causeway in Hángzhōu, and lined with willow and mulberry trees, the causeway kicks off just west of the boathouses.

With its delightful hump, the grey- and white-marble **Jade Belt Bridge** (玉带桥, Yùdài Qiáo) dates from the reign of emperor Qianlong and crosses the point where the **Jade River** (玉河, Yù Hé) enters the lake (when it flows).

Towards the **North Palace Gate** (北宫门, Běigōngmén; Ⓢ Beigongmen), **Sūzhōu Street** (苏州街; Sūzhōu Jiē) is an entertaining and light-hearted diversion of riverside walkways, shops and eateries, which are designed to mimic the famous Jiāngsū canal town.

Běijīng Botanic Gardens　　　　GARDENS
(北京植物园, Běijīng Zhíwùyuán; adult ¥5, through ticket ¥50; ⏰ 6am-8pm Apr-Oct, last entry 7pm, 7.30am-5pm Nov-Mar, last entry 4pm; Ⓢ Xiyuan or Yuanmingyuan, then 🚌 331) Exploding with blossom in spring, the well tended Běijīng Botanic Gardens, set against the backdrop of the Western Hills and about 1km northeast of Fragrant Hills Park, makes for a pleasant outing among bamboo fronds, pines, orchids, lilacs and China's most extensive

---

WORTH A TRIP

FRAGRANT HILLS PARK

Easily within striking distance of the Summer Palace are Běijīng's Western Hills (西山; Xī Shān), **Fragrant Hills Park** (香山公园, Xiāng Shān Gōngyuán; ¥10 Apr-Oct, ¥5 Nov-Mar; ⏰ 6am-6.30pm Apr-Oct, to 6pm Nov-Mar; Ⓢ Xiyuan or Yuanmingyuan, then 🚌 331) is another former villa-resort of the emperors. The part of Xī Shān closest to Běijīng is known as Fragrant Hills Park. Beijingers flock here in autumn when the maple leaves saturate the hillsides in great splashes of red.

Scramble up to the top of **Incense-Burner Peak** (Xiānglú Fēng), or take the **chairlift** (one-way/return ¥80/160, ⏰ 9am-4pm). From the peak you get an all-embracing view of the countryside, and you can leave the crowds behind by hiking further into the Western Hills.

Near the north gate of Fragrant Hills Park, but still within the park, is the excellent **Azure Clouds Temple** (碧云寺, Bìyún Sì; adult ¥10; ⏰ 9am-4.30pm; 🚌 331, Ⓢ Xiyuan or Yuanmingyuan), which dates back to the Yuán dynasty. The **Mountain Gate Hall** (Shānmén) contains two vast protective deities: Heng and Ha, beyond which is a small courtyard and the drum and bell towers, leading to a hall with a wonderful statue of Mílèfó – it's bronze, but coal-black with age. Only his big toe shines from numerous inquisitive fingers.

The **Sun Yatsen Memorial Hall** (Sūn Zhōngshān Jìniàn Tāng) contains a statue and a glass coffin donated by the USSR on the death of Mr Sun (the Republic of China's first president) in 1925. At the very back is the marble **Vajra Throne Pagoda** (Jīngāng Bǎozuò Tǎ), where Sun Yatsen was interred after he died, before his body was moved to its final resting place in Nánjīng. The **Hall of Arhats** (Luóhàn Tāng) is well worth visiting; it contains 500 statues of *luóhàn* (those freed from the cycle of rebirth), each crafted with an individual personality.

Southwest of the Azure Clouds Temple is the Tibetan-style **Temple of Brilliance** (Zhāo Miào), and not far away is a glazed-tile pagoda. Both survived visits by foreign troops intent on sacking the area in 1860, and then in 1900.

There are dozens of restaurants and snack stalls on the approach road to the north gate, making this your best bet for lunch out of any of the sights in this part of the city.

At the time of writing it was expected that sometime in the future the subway will extend here via the Summer Palace and Botanic Gardens.

Summer Palace

BĚIJĪNG SIGHTS

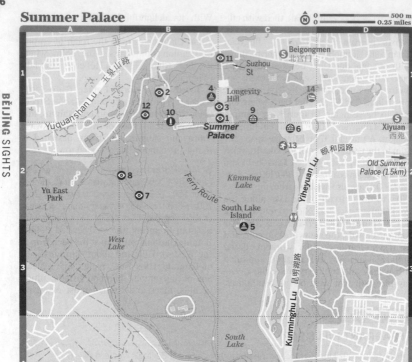

Summer Palace

botanic collection. Containing a rainforest house, the standout **Běijīng Botanical Gardens Conservatory** (Běijīng Zhíwùyuán Wēnshì; with Běijīng Botanical Gardens through ticket ¥50; ◷8am-4.30pm Apr-Oct, 8.30am-4pm Nov-Mar; ◻331, Ⓢ Xiyuan or Yuanmingyuan, then) bursts with 3000 different varieties of plants.

About a 15-minute walk from the front gate (follow the signs), but still within the grounds of the gardens, is **Sleeping Buddha Temple** (卧佛寺, Wòfó Sì; adult ¥5, or entry with through ticket; ◷8am-4.30pm summer, 8.30am-4pm winter). The temple, first built during the Tang dynasty, houses a huge reclining effigy of Sakyamuni weighing 54 tonnes; it's said to have 'enslaved 7000 people' in its casting. Sakyamuni is depicted on the cusp of death, before his entry into nirvana. On each side of Buddha are arrayed some sets of gargantuan shoes, gifts to Sakyamuni from various emperors in case he went for a stroll.

On the eastern side of the gardens is the **Cao Xueqin Memorial** (曹雪芹纪念馆, Cáo

Xuěqín Jìniàn Guǎn; 39 Zhengbalqi Cun, 正白旗村; ⊙ 8.30am-4.30pm Apr-Oct, 9am-4pm Nov-Mar; 🚻; 🚇 331, 🅂 Xiyuan or Yuanmingyuan, then) **FREE**, where Cao Xueqin lived in his latter years. Cao (1715–63) is credited with penning the classic *Dream of the Red Mansions*, a vast and prolix family saga set in the Qing period. Making a small buzz in the west of the gardens is the little **China Honey Bee Museum** (中国蜜蜂博物馆, Zhōngguó Mìfēng Bówùguǎn, ⊙ 8.30am to 4.30pm Mar-Oct)

Old Summer Palace
HISTORIC SITE
(圆明园, Yuánmíng Yuán; 🚇 010 6261 6375; 28 Qinghun Xilu, 清华西路28号; adult ¥10, through ticket ¥25, map ¥6; ⊙ 7am-6pm Apr-Oct, to 5.30pm Nov-Mar; 🅂 Yuanmingyuan) Located northwest of the city centre, the Old Summer Palace was laid out in the 12th century. The ever-capable Jesuits were subsequently employed by Emperor Qianlong in the 18th century to fashion European-style palaces for the gardens, incorporating elaborate fountains and baroque statuary. In 1860, during the Second Opium War, British and French troops torched and looted the palace, an event forever inscribed in Chinese history books as a low point in China's humiliation by foreign powers.

Most of the wooden palace buildings were burned down in the process and little remains, but the hardier Jesuit-designed European Palace buildings were made of stone, and a melancholic tangle of broken columns and marble chunks survives. Note: to see these remains, you need to buy the more expensive 'through ticket'.

The subdued marble ruins of the **Palace Buildings Scenic Area** (Xīyánglóu Jǐngqū) can be mulled over in the **Eternal Spring Garden** (Chángchūn Yuán) in the northeast of the park, near the east gate. There were once more than 10 buildings here, designed by Giuseppe Castiglione and Michael Benoist. The buildings were only partially destroyed during the 1860 Anglo-French looting and the structures apparently remained usable for quite some time afterwards. However, the ruins were gradually picked over and carted away by local people all the way up to the 1970s.

The **Great Fountain Ruins** (Dàshuǐfǎ) themselves are considered the best-preserved relics. Built in 1759, the main building was fronted by a lion-head fountain. Standing opposite is the **Guānshuǐfǎ**, five large stone screens embellished with European carvings of military flags, armour, swords and guns. The screens were discovered in the grounds

of Peking University in the 1970s and later restored to their original positions. Just east of the Great Fountain Ruins stood a four-pillar archway, chunks of which remain.

West of the Great Fountain Ruins are the vestiges of the **Hǎiyàntáng Reservoir** (Hǎiyàntáng Xùshuǐchí Tǎijī), where the water for the impressive fountains was stored in a tower and huge water-lifting devices were employed. The metal reservoir was commonly called the Tin Sea (Xīhǎi). Also known as the Water Clock, the **Hǎiyàntáng**, where 12 bronze human statues with animal heads jetted water for two hours in a 12-hour sequence, was constructed in 1759. The 12 animal heads from this apparatus ended up in collections abroad and Bēijīng is attempting to retrieve them (four can now be seen at the Poly Art Museum; p78). Just west of here is the **Fāngwàiguàn**, a building that was turned into a mosque for an imperial concubine. An artful reproduction of a former labyrinth called the **Garden of Yellow Flowers** is also nearby.

The palace gardens cover a huge area – 2.5km from east to west – so be prepared for some walking. Besides the ruins, there's the western section, the **Perfection & Brightness Garden** (Yuánmíng Yuán) and, in the southern compound, the **10,000 Springs Garden** (Wànchūn Yuán).

Bus 331 goes from the south gate (which is by exit B of Yuanmingyuan subway station) to the east gate of the Summer Palace before continuing to the Botanic Gardens and eventually terminating at Fragrant Hills Park.

🍴 Courses

★ Black Sesame Kitchen
COOKING
(黑芝麻厨房, Hēi Zhīma Chúfáng; Map p70; 🚇 136 9147 4408; www.blacksesamekitchen.com; 28 Zhong Lao Hutong, 中老胡同28号; ⊙ cooking classes 11am Wed & Sun, dinner 7pm Tue & Fri; 🅂 Lines 6, 8 to Nanluoguxiang, exit A) Runs popular cooking classes with a variety of recipes from across China. Booking is essential; walk-in guests are not encouraged as this is a residential courtyard. You can also eat here at one of its communal dinners (set menu ¥300 per person, including wine and beer) – it gets rave reviews – but again you must book.

★ The Hutong
COOKING
(Map p80; 🚇 159 0104 6127; www.thehutong. com; 1 Jiudaowan Zhongxiang Hutong, off Shique Hutong, 北新桥石雀胡同九道弯中巷胡同1号; classes for members/non-members ¥260/300;

⊘ 9.30am-10pm; S Line 5 to Beixinqiao, exit C) Down a maze of narrow alleys, the Hutong is a highly recommended Chinese-culture centre, run by a group of extremely knowledgable locals and expats. Classes are held in a peaceful converted courtyard, and focus on cooking and guided tours. See its website for the schedule.

Mílún Kungfu School   MARTIAL ARTS

(弥纶传统武术学校, Mílún Chuántǒng Wǔshù Xuéxiào; Map p76; ☑138 1170 6568; www.kungfuinchina.com; 36 Ganyu Hutong, 甘雨胡同36号; per class ¥150, 10-class card ¥1100; ⊘7-8.30pm Mon & Wed; S Line 5 to Dengshikou, exit A) Runs classes in various forms of traditional Chinese martial arts (from Shàolín kung fu to kickboxing) in a historic courtyard near Wángfǔjǐng shopping district. In summer, typically in August, classes are held in Rìtán Park. Has set-time drop-in classes, but can arrange individual schedules too. Instruction is in Chinese, but with an English translator. Taichi classes are also available.

China Culture Center   CULTURAL PROGRAMS

(Kent Center; Map p92; ☑weekdays 010 6432 9341, weekends 010 8420 0671; www.chinaculturecenter.org; Victoria Gardens D4, Chaoyang Gongyuan Xilu, 朝阳公园西路, 维多利亚花园D4; S Line 14 to Zaoying or Line 10 to Tuanjiehu, exit C) Offers a range of cultural programs taught in English and aimed squarely at foreign visitors and expats. The club also conducts popular tours around Běijīng and expeditions to other parts of China.

Culture Yard   LANGUAGE

(天井越洋, Tiānjǐng Yuèyáng; Map p80; ☑010 8404 4166; www.cultureyard.net; 10 Shique Hutong, 石雀胡同10号; ⊘9am-9pm Mon-Fri, 10am-4pm Sat; S Line 5 to Beixinqiao, exit C) Tucked away down a hútòng, this cultural centre focuses on Chinese culture. Its main program is a six-week course (¥4500), but you can tailor courses to suit your needs. Its 'Survival Chinese' course is ideal for tourists.

🏃 Activities

★ Bike Běijīng   CYCLING

(康多自行车租赁, Kāngduō Zìxíngchē Zūlìn; Map p76; ☑010 6526 5857; www.bikebeijing.com; 81 Beiheyan Dajie, 北河沿大街81号; ⊘8am-8pm; S Lines 6, 8 to Nanluoguxiang, exit B, or Line 5 to Zhangzizhonglu, exit D) Rents a range of good-quality bikes, offering mountain bikes (¥200), road bikes (¥400) and ordinary city bikes (¥100); helmets inclusive. It also runs popular guided bike tours around the city (half-day tours from ¥300 to ¥400 per person, depending on group size) and beyond, including bike-and-hike trips to the Great Wall (¥1800 per person, including hotel pick-up and lunch).

Koryo Tours   TRAVEL AGENCY

(Map p92; ☑Běijīng 010 6416 7544; www.koryogroup.com; 27 Beisanlitun Nan; S Line 2 to Dongsi Shitiao, exit C, or Line 10 to Tuanjiehu, exit A) Long-established and reputable outfit that organises highly rated tours to North Korea.

Běijīng Hikers   HIKING

(☑010 6432 2786; www.beijinghikers.com; Galaxy Building, bldg A, room 4012, 10 Jiuxianqiao Zhonglu, 星科大厦A座4012室, 酒仙桥中路10号; per person from ¥380; ⊘9am-6pm) Long-established outfit that organises some breathtaking hikes out of town on weekends, with a focus on the Great Wall. It can also arrange private trips.

Dragonfly Therapeutic Retreat   MASSAGE

(Map p92; ☑010 8529 6331; www.dragonfly.net.cn; Kerry Centre basement, 1 Guanghua Lu, 嘉里中心光华路1号; 1hr massage from ¥188; ⊘10am-11pm; S Line 10 to Jintaixizhao, exit A) Swish, professional operation.

🛏 Sleeping

Hostels are best value, with traveller-friendly facilities and staff with good English-language skills. Courtyard hotels are wonderfully atmospheric, and plant you right in the thick of the hútòng action, but they lack the facilities (pool, gym etc) of top-end hotels in similar price brackets.

You can book rooms directly through hotel websites, or over the phone.

🛏 Forbidden City & Dōngchéng Central

★ City Walls Courtyard   HOSTEL $

(城墙旅舍, Chéngqiáng Lǚshè; Map p76; ☑010 6402 7805; www.beijingcitywalls.com; 57 Nianzi Hutong, 碾子胡同57号; dm/s/tw ¥100/260/420; ✳@🛜; S Lines 6, 8 to Nanluoguxiang, exit A) Hidden among a maze of hútòng is this attractive choice within a fabulous location – hidden away from more touristy areas in one of the city's most historic neighbourhoods. Private rooms and dorms all have private bathrooms; spacious four-bed dorms are especially great value. The main selling point is its traditional courtyard decorated with eclectic knick-knacks, plants and couches to enjoy cheap large beers (¥4), ground coffee (¥10) and meals.

It's led by the personable Rick, along with other friendly, helpful staff. There are bikes for rent, and tickets for tours and cultural shows.

To get here, from Jǐngshān Houjie, look for the *hútòng* opening just east of Jǐngshān Table Tennis Park. Walk up the *hútòng* and follow it around to the right and then left; the hostel is on the left-hand side.

Dragon King Hostel   HOSTEL $

(万里路青年酒店东四九条店, Wànlǐlù Qīngnián Jiǔdiàn Dōngsì Jiǔtiáo Diàn; Map p80; ☑010 8400 2660; www.9dragons.hostel.com; 78 Dongsi Jiutiao, 东四九条78号; dm ¥80-100, d ¥300, ❂❸; ⓢLine 5 to Zhangzizhonglu, exit C) Down a *hútòng* featuring some rowdy local restaurants, Dragon King is classic Běijīng with its historic building festooned with Chinese lanterns. There are rough edges, but the good outweighs the bad, especially its central location close to all the action. Dorm beds have curtains for privacy, while private rooms have plenty of space. Its cosy backpacker-style pub does cheap beer and food.

Běijīng Feel Inn   HOSTEL $

(非凡客栈, Fēifán Kèzhàn; Map p76; ☑139 1040 9166, 010 6528 7418; www.beijingfeelinn.com; 2 Ciqiku Hutong, off Nanheyan Dajie, 南河沿大街, 磁器库胡同2号; dm ¥50-60, r from ¥268; ❂@❸; ⓢLine 1 to Tian'anmen East, exit A) A small, understated hostel with a hidden, backstreet location, Feel Inn is tucked away among the *hútòng* containing the little-known Pǔdù Temple, and yet is just a short walk from big-hitters such as the Forbidden City, Tiān'ānmén Sq and the shops on Wangfujing Dajie. Has simple, clean rooms, a small bar-restaurant and wi-fi throughout. It rents bikes for ¥30 per day.

★ Jǐngshān Garden Hotel   HUTONG HOTEL $$

(景山花园酒店, Jǐngshān Huāyuán Jiǔdiàn; Map p76; ☑010 8404 7979; www.jingshangardenhotel.com; 68 Sanyanjing Hutong, off Jingshan Dongjie, 景山东街，三眼井胡同68号; r incl breakfast ¥550-650; ❂@❸; ⓢLines 6, 8 to Nanluoguxiang, exit A) This delightful, unfussy, two-storey guesthouse has bright, spacious rooms surrounding a peaceful, flower-filled courtyard. First-floor rooms are pricier, but larger and brighter than the ground-floor ones, and some have *slight* views of Jǐngshān Park from their bathrooms. It also has an upstairs Sìchuān restaurant.

Walking down Sanyuanjing Hutong from the direction of Jǐngshān Park, turn right down the first alleyway, and the hotel is at the end.

Húlú Hotel   HUTONG HOTEL $$

(壶庐宾馆, Húlú Bīnguǎn; Map p76; ☑010 6543 9229; www.thehuluhotel.com; 91 Yanyue Hutong, off Dongsi Nandajie, 东四南大街，演乐胡同91号; r ¥718-900; ⓢLine 5 to Dengshikou, exit A, or Lines 5, 6 to Dongsi, exit C) Hulu's converted *hútòng* space is minimalist throughout, with cool grey-painted wood beams, slate-tiled bathrooms and a cleverly renovated courtyard that combines its old-Běijīng roots with a modern, comfortable design. The atmosphere is laid-back, and the young staff speak excellent English. There are three grades of room (size increases with price), all of which have large double beds – no twins.

There's a homely cafe at reception that does breakfast, coffee and bar drinks. The small, leafy rooftop terrace is just the place to relax.

★ W Běijīng   BOUTIQUE HOTEL $$$

(北京长安街 W 酒店; Map p76; ☑010 6515 8855; www.whotels.com/beijing; 2 Jianguomennan Jie, 建国门南大街2号; r from ¥2000; ⓢLines 1, 2 to Jianguomen, exit B) The W is all about flashy installations that feel more nightclub than hotel. Rooms are full of gadgetry, from remote-control rotating sofas and touch-screen colour-adjustment wheels to spotlight projectors and automatic sliding curtains. They have circular stand-alone bath-tubs and large windows. A major downside, though, is its out-of-the-way location beside a big highway.

★ Temple Hotel HUTONG HOTEL $$$

(东景缘, Dōngjǐng Yuán; Map p76; ☑010 8401 5680; www.thetemplehotel.com; 23 Shatan Beijie, off Wusi Dajie, 五四大街, 沙滩北街23号; d/ste from ¥2000/4500; ❋ 🌐 🛜; Ⓢ Lines 6, 8 to Nanluoguxiang, exit B or Lines 5, 6 to Dongsi, exit E) Unrivalled by anything else on the Běijīng hotel scene, this unique heritage hotel forms part of a renovation project that was recognised by Unesco for its conservation efforts. A team spent five years renovating what was left of Zhìzhù Sì (智珠寺; Temple of Wisdom), a part-abandoned, 250-year-old Buddhist temple, and slowly transformed it into one of the most alluring places to stay in the capital.

Drum Tower & Dōngchéng North

★ Běijīng Drum Tower International Youth Hostel HOSTEL $

(鼓韵青年旅舍, Gǔyùn Qīngnián Lǚshè; Map p80; ☑010 8401 6565; www.24hostel.com; 51 Jiugulou Dajie, 旧鼓楼大街 51号; dm/d from ¥88/288; ❋ @ 🛜; Ⓢ Lines 2, 8 to Guloudajie, exit G) A large, dependable hostel, the Drum's point of difference is its capsule bunk beds (from ¥88), which are equipped with lockable doors. They offer complete privacy so it's a step up from the usual dorms, but their cramped interior won't suit claustrophobes. Private rooms, on the other hand, are massive and have plenty of natural light.

There's a peaceful rooftop terrace with magnificent views over the Drum Tower, and a cool cafe downstairs.

Nostalgia Hotel HOTEL $

(时光漫步怀旧主题酒店, Shíguāng Mànbù Huáijiù Zhǔtí Jiǔdiàn; Map p80; ☑010 6403 2288; www.nostalgiahotelbeijing.com; 46 Fangjia Hutong, 安定门内大街, 方家胡同46号; r from ¥428; ❋ @ 🛜; Ⓢ Line 5 to Beixinqiao, exit A) A good-value option if you don't fancy staying in a youth hostel, this large, funky hotel is housed in a small arts zone on trendy Fangjia Hutong. Rooms live up to its name, decorated with a Chinese retro theme and knick-knacks throughout. The bathrooms sparkle.

Staff on reception speak English, and there's lift access. There's a breakfast room, but no restaurant. To find it, enter the small arts zone named after its address (46 Fangjia Hutong) and walk to the far left corner of the complex.

Confucius International Youth Hostel HOSTEL $

(雍圣轩青年酒店, Yōngshèngxuān Qīngnián Jiǔdiàn; Map p80; ☑010 6402 2082; www.confucious.hostel.com; 38 Wudaoying Hutong, 雍和宫大街, 五道营胡同38号; dm/s/d ¥80/180/238; Ⓢ Lines 2, 5 to Yonghegong-Lama Temple, exit D) One of the cheapest places that's open to foreigners in this area, Confucius is all about its awesome location along this ultra-hip strip. It has a handful of simple, no-frills rooms off a small, covered courtyard, but there's no restaurant, bar or place to hang out.

Peking Youth Hostel HOSTEL $

(北平国际青年旅社, Běipíng Guójì Qīngnián Lǚshè; Map p80; ☑010 6401 3961, 010 8403 9098; www.peking.hostel.com; 113 Nanluogu Xiang, 南锣鼓巷113号; dm/tw from ¥180/500; ❋ @ 🛜; Ⓢ Lines 6, 8 to Nanluoguxiang, exit E) Slick, colourful, but rather cramped rooms are located round the back of the flower-filled Peking Cafe, which opens out onto Nanluogu Xiang. Prices reflect the sought-after (though, these days, frenetic) location rather than the size or quality of the rooms. All the usual youth-hostel services are dished up, including bike hire and trips to the Great Wall. Enter via Yu'er Hutong.

★ Orchid COURTYARD HOTEL $$

(兰花宾馆, Lánhuā Bīnguǎn; Map p80; ☑010 5799 0806; www.theorchidbeijing.com; 65 Baochao Hutong, 鼓楼东大街宝钞胡同65号; d ¥805-1800; ❋ @ 🛜; Ⓢ Lines 2, 8 to Guloudajie, exit F, or Line 8 to Shichahai, exit A2) Opened by a Canadian guy and a Tibetan girl, this place may lack the history of other courtyard hotels, but it's been renovated into a beautiful space, with a peaceful courtyard and some rooftop seating with distant views of the Drum and Bell Towers. Rooms are doubles only, and are small, but are tastefully decorated and come with Apple TV home-entertainment systems, complimentary loan of mobile phones and bike rental.

There are also self-contained apartments with cooking facilities, and it has the well regarded Toast (p104) restaurant.

It does Great Wall tours (from ¥1100 including lunch, admission and transport), and can organise taxis for city tours. Hard to spot, the Orchid is down an unnamed, shoulder-width alleyway opposite Mr Shi's Dumplings.

Yo-Yo Hotel HOTEL $$

(Map p80; ☑134 6636 4309, 010 5703 7655; yanjiao@yoyozhu.com; 187 Andingmennei Dajie, 安定门内大街187号; r from ¥309; ❋ 🛜; Ⓢ Line

2 to Andingmen) Stumbling distance from all of Beijing's coolest *hútòng* bars, and many major sights, this budget hotel is an excellent choice location-wise. It has a Southeast Asia–backpacker-kinda vibe, so there are some rough edges, but it's comfortable with boutiquey touches, and there's a cafe-bar upstairs. No English.

Courtyard 7　　　　　HUTONG HOTEL $$$
(四合院酒店, Sìhéyuàn Jiǔdiàn; Map p80; ☑010 6406 0777; www.courtyard7.com, 7 Qiangulouyuan Hutong, off Nanluogu Xiang, 鼓楼东大街南锣鼓巷前的鼓楼苑胡同7号; r incl breakfast ¥900-1200; ❄@🖳; Ⓢ Lines 6, 8 to Nanluoguxiang, exit E) Immaculate rooms, decorated in traditional Chinese furniture, face onto a series of different-sized, 400-year-old courtyards, which over the years have been home to government ministers, rich merchants and even an army general. Despite the historical narrative, rooms still come with modern comforts such as underfloor heating, wi-fi and cable TV. Standard rooms are less atmospheric so upgrade to the superior rooms surrounding the courtyard.

🛏 Temple of Heaven Park & Dōngchéng South

Emperor　　　　　　　　HOTEL $$
(皇家驿站, Huángjiā Yìzhàn; Map p90; ☑010 6701 7790; www.theemperor.com.cn; 87 Xianyukou St, Qianmen Commercial Centre, 前门商业区鲜鱼口街87号; r ¥700; ❄🖳🖳; Ⓢ Qianmen) Brand new, this modernist hotel comes with a spa and a rooftop pool that enables you to laze in the sun while enjoying fine views over nearby Tiān'ānmén Sq. The cool, all-white rooms aren't huge, but the price is reasonable for a hotel of this quality and the location is perfect. Service is attentive and the atmosphere laid-back.

🛏 Sānlǐtún & Cháoyáng

Yoyo Hotel　　　　　　　HOTEL $
(优优客酒店, Yōuyōu Kèjiǔdiàn; Map p92; ☑010 6417 3388; www.yoyohotel.cn; Bldg 10 Dongsanjie Erjie, 三里屯北路东三街二街中10楼; r ¥369-399; ❄@🖳; Ⓢ Line 10 to Tuanjiehu, exit A) There's a boutique feel here, but the rooms, especially bathrooms, are tiny. Nevertheless, they are excellent value for the location and fine if you're not planning on spending too much time in the hotel. Staff members speak some English and are friendly considering how rushed off their feet they usually are.

★**Rosewood Běijīng**　　BOUTIQUE HOTEL $$$
(北京瑰丽酒店, Běijīng Guīlì Jiǔdiàn; Map p92; ☑010 6597 8888; www.rosewoodhotels.com/en/beijing; Jing Guang Centre, East 3rd Middle Ring Rd, 呼家楼京广中心; r from ¥2000; ❄🖳🖳; Ⓢ Line 10 to Jintaixizhao, exit A, or Lines 6, 10 to Hujialou, exit D) The elegant Rosewood fits modern luxury within a traditional Chinese design that incorporates decorative arts and a subtle yin-and-yang theme throughout. Its entry gate leaves a striking first impression with two large Jiao Tu (Sons of Dragon) sculptures that guard the hotel. The art-filled rooms are massive, with designer furniture, TV mirrors and automatic blinds that open to views of the iconic CCTV building.

As well as the **Mei Bar** (魅酒吧, Mèi Jiǔbā; Map p92; http://mei-bar.com; 5th fl, Rosewood Beijing, Jing Guang Centre, 呼家楼京广中心,北京瑰丽酒店5层; ⏱6pm-2am Mon-Sat, 5pm-midnight Sun; 🖳; Ⓢ Line 10 to Jintaixizhao, exit A or Lines 6, 10 to Hujialou, exit D), its classy **Country Kitchen** restaurant is acclaimed for its Peking duck. There's also its elegant **Sense Spa**, and a glassed-roof swimming pool, candlelit at night and surrounded by lush plants.

★**Opposite House Hotel**　BOUTIQUE HOTEL $$$
(瑜舍, Yúshè; Map p92; ☑010 6417 6688; www.theoppositehouse.com; Bldg 1, Village, 11 Sanlitun Lu, 三里屯路11号院1号楼; r from ¥2500; ♨❄@🖳; Ⓢ Line 10 to Tuanjiehu, exit A, or Agricultural Exhibition Center, exit D2) With see-all open-plan bathrooms, American oak bath-tubs, lovely mood lighting, underfloor heating, sliding doors, complimentary beers, TVs on extendable arms and a metal basin swimming pool, this trendy Swire-owned boutique hotel is top-drawer chic. The location is ideal for shopping, restaurants and drinking. No obvious sign. Just walk into the striking green glass cube of a building and ask.

🛏 Běihǎi Park & Xīchéng North

Siheju Courtyard Hostel　　HOSTEL $
(Map p88; ☑186 1145 8911; 12 Xisi Beiertiao, 西四北二条12号; dm ¥130, r ¥450-700; Ⓢ Line 4 to Xisi, exit A) Down an atmospheric *hútòng*, you'll definitely feel like you're in Běijīng at this wonderful little hostel full of traditional charm and character. Rooms are clean, beds are comfortable and dorms have their own bathrooms. Staff are super friendly and speak good English. To find it, walk north on Xisi Beidajie from Xisi metro; it's two *hútòng* up on the left.

★Graceland Yard COURTYARD HOTEL $$
(觉品酒店, Juepin Jiudian; Map p88; ☎010 8328 8366; www.graceland-yardhotel.com; 9 Zhengjue Hutong, 正觉胡同9号; s/d/ste ¥666/799/999; [@][wifi]; [S]Line 2 to Jishuitan, exit C) Graceland is an exquisitely renovated courtyard hotel, housed within the grounds of the abandoned, 500-year-old Zhèngjué Temple. Each of the eight rooms is slightly different – there are singles, doubles, twins, a couple of fabulous loft rooms and a suite – but each is decorated with style, using traditional Buddhist-themed furnishings. There's no restaurant – not even breakfast – but you're not short of eateries in the surrounding *hútòng*.

Shíchàhǎi Sandalwood Boutique Hotel HÚTÒNG HOTEL $$$
(什刹海紫檀酒店, Shíchàhǎi Zǐtán Jiǔdiàn; Map p88; ☎010 8322 6686; www.sch-hotel.com; 42 Xinghua Hutong, 兴华胡同42号; r ¥600-1300; [❄][wifi]; [S]Line 6 to Beihai North, exit A) A five minute walk from its sister hotel **Shíchàhǎi Shadow Art Hotel** (什刹海皮影酒店, Shíchàhǎi Píyǐng Jiǔdiàn; Map p88; ☎136 8303 2251, 010 8328 7847; www.shichahaitour.com; 24 Songshu Jie, 松树街24号; tw & d incl breakfast ¥630-994; [S]Line 6 to Beihai North, exit A), the Sandalwood has an atmospheric *hutong* location and decor full of traditional charm. Good deals are available from online booking sites. Note the cheapest rooms don't have windows.

EATING BY NEIGHBOURHOOD

Forbidden City & Dōngchéng Central (p103) Foreign places, dumpling joints and Sìchuān.

Drum Tower & Dōngchéng North (p104) Courtyard restaurants, vegetarian and hotpot on Ghost St.

Temple of Heaven Park & Dōngchéng South (p105) Peking duck and Western food.

Sānlǐtún & Cháoyáng (p106) Largest selection of foreign and fusion restaurants.

Běihǎi Park & Xīchéng North (p106) Local and foreign places around Hòuhǎi Lakes.

Dashilar & Xīchéng South (p107) Muslim food around Nuijie Mosque.

Summer Palace & Hǎidiàn (p107) Korean and Japanese eateries in Wǔdàokǒu.

Dashilar & Xīchéng South

Qiánmén Hostel HOSTEL $
(前门客栈, Qiánmén Kèzhàn; Map p90; ☎010 6313 2370, 010 6313 2369; www.qianmenhostel.net; 33 Meishi Jie, 煤市街33号; dm ¥60-80, r without/with bathroom ¥200/280; [❄][@][wifi]; [S]Line 2 to Qianmen, exit B or C) A five-minute trot southwest of Tiān'ānmén Sq, this heritage hostel with a cool courtyard offers a relaxing environment with able staff. The rooms are simple and not big but, like the dorms, they are clean, as are the shared bathrooms. Despite the busy location, this is an easy place to switch off and appreciate the high ceilings, original woodwork and charming antique buildings.

An affable old-hand, hostel owner Genghis Kane does his best to keep his standards high. Great Wall tours can be arranged.

365 Inn HOSTEL $
(Map p90; ☎010 6308 5956; 55 Dazhalan Xijie, 大栅栏西街55号; dm ¥55-100, d ¥200-250; [❄][@][wifi]; [S]Line 2 to Qianmen, exit B or C) An old-school backpackers, 365 Inn has a social atmosphere with a downstairs pub that makes it one of Běijīng's best for meeting fellow travellers. It also scores points for its prime location that brings you walking distance to most sights. Dorms are your typical crammed-in bunk beds, though private rooms are surprisingly spacious. Reception's often understaffed, but the team are friendly and helpful.

Qiánmén Jiànguó Hotel HOTEL $$
(前门建国饭店, Qiánmén Jiànguó Fàndiàn; Map p90; ☎010 6301 6688; www.hotelsjianguo.com/qianmenhotel; 175 Yong'an Lu, 永安路 175号; r from ¥800; [⊖][❄][@][wifi]; [S]Line 7 to Hufangqiao, exit C) Elegant in parts and popular with tour groups, this refurbished hotel with a vague Peking-opera theme has pushed up its prices to reflect its makeover. Business is brisk, so the staff are on their toes, and the rooms are spacious, bright and well maintained and a reasonable deal with the generous discounts (up to 50% off). Some English spoken.

You can find the Líyuán Theatre (p111) to the right of the domed atrium at the rear of the hotel.

Summer Palace & Hǎidiàn

★Aman at Summer Palace HERITAGE HOTEL $$$
(颐和安缦, Yíhé Ānmàn; Map p96; ☎010 5987 9999; www.amanresorts.com; 1 Gongmen Qianjie, 宫门前街1号; r ¥3000, courtyard r ¥4800, ste ¥5600-8400; [⊖][❄][@][wifi][pool]; [S]Xiyuan) Hard to fault this

exquisite hotel, a candidate for best in Běijīng. It's located around the corner from the Summer Palace (p91) – parts of the hotel date to the 19th century and were used to house distinguished guests waiting for audiences with Empress Cixi. The big rooms are superbly appointed, and contained in a series of picture-perfect pavilions set around courtyards.

✗ Eating

Běijīng is a magnificent place for culinary adventures. With upwards of 60,000 restaurants here, you can enjoy the finest local dishes, as well as eating your way through every region of China. Some of your most memorable Běijīng experiences will take place around the dining table. So do as the locals do – grab those chopsticks and dive in.

✗ Forbidden City & Dōngchéng Central

★ Crescent Moon Muslim Restaurant   XINJIANG $
(新疆弯弯月亮维吾尔穆斯林餐厅,   Xīnjiāng Wānwānyuèliàng Wéiwú'ěr Mùsīlín Cāntīng; Map p76; 16 Dongsi Liutiao Hutong, 东四六条胡同16号, 东四北大街; dishes from ¥18; ⊙11am-11pm; ❄🤖; Ⓢ Line 5 to Zhangzizhonglu, exit C) You can find a Chinese Muslim restaurant on almost every street in Běijīng. Most are run by Huí Muslims, who are Hàn Chinese, rather than ethnic-minority Uighurs from the remote western province of Xīnjiāng. Crescent Moon is the real deal – owned and staffed by Uighurs, it attracts many Běijīng-based Uighurs and people from Central Asia, as well as a lot of Western expats.

It's more expensive than most other Xīnjiāng restaurants in Běijīng, but the food is consistently good, and it has an English menu. The speciality is the barbecued leg of lamb (¥128). The lamb skewers (¥6) are also delicious, and there's naan bread (¥5), homemade yoghurt (¥12) and plenty of noodle options (¥18 to ¥25).

Chuān Bàn   SICHUAN $
(川办餐厅; Map p92; 28 Dongzongbu Hutong, off Chaoyangmen Nanxiaojie, 朝阳门南小街东总部胡同28号; dishes from ¥20; ⊙11am-2pm & 5-9pm Mon-Fri, 11am-11pm Sat & Sun; Ⓢ Lines 1, 2 to Jianguomen, exit A) Every Chinese province has its own official building in Běijīng, complete with a restaurant for cadres and locals working in the capital who are pining for a taste of home. Often they're the most authentic places for regional cuisines. This restaurant

in the Sìchuān Government Offices is always crowded and serves up just about every variety of Sìchuān food you could want.

Wángfǔjǐng Snack Street   STREET FOOD $
(王府井小吃街, Wángfǔjǐng Xiǎochījiē; Map p76; west off Wangfujing Dajie, 王府井大街西侧; dishes & snacks ¥10; ⊙9.30am-10pm; Ⓢ Line 1 to Wangfujing, exit C2) Fronted by an ornate archway, this pedestrianised lane is lined with cheap and cheerful food stalls that are always busy. There are dishes from all over China, including málà tàng (a spicy soup from Sìchuān) and zhájiàngmiàn (Beijing noodles in fried bean sauce), savoury pancakes, oodles of noodles and novelty items such as scorpion skewers. Not all stalls have prices listed, but most things cost around ¥10 for a portion.

★ Little Yúnnán   YUNNAN $$
(小云南, Xiǎo Yúnnán; Map p76; 🕿010 6401 9498; 28 Donghuang Chenggen Beijie, 东皇城根北街28号; mains ¥26-60; ⊙10am-10pm; Ⓢ Lines 6, 8 to Nanluoguxiang, exit B or Line 5 to Zhangzizhonglu, exit D) Run by young, friendly staff and housed in a cute courtyard conversion, Little Yúnnán is one of the more down-to-earth Yúnnán restaurants in Běijīng. The main room has a rustic feel to it, with wooden beams, flooring and furniture. The tables up in the eaves are fun, and there's also some seating in the small open-air courtyard by the entrance.

Dishes include some classic southwest China ingredients, with some tea-infused creations as well as river fish, mushroom dishes, fried goat's cheese and là ròu (腊肉; cured pork – south China's answer to bacon). It also serves a variety of Yúnnán wines (rice, pine and plum), rice-wine-based cocktails and the province's local beer.

Din Tai Fung   DUMPLING $$
(鼎泰丰, Dǐng Tài Fēng; Map p76; 🕿010 6512 8019; www.dintaifung.com.cn; 6th fl, Beijing apm shopping mall, 138 Wangfujing Dajie, 王府井大街138号apm6楼; 5/10 dumplings from ¥25/49; ⊙11.30am-2.30pm & 5-10pm Mon-Thu, 11am-10pm Fri-Sun; ❄🤖; Ⓢ Line 1 to Wangfujing, exit C2 or Line 5 to Dengshikou) One of several Běijīng branches of this world-famous Taiwanese dumpling house.

★ Temple Restaurant Bites   EUROPEAN $$$
(TRB; Map p70; 🕿010 8400 2232; www.trb-cn.com; 95 Donghuamen Dajie, 东华门大街95号; 3/4/5 courses ¥198/258/298; ⊙11.30am-10.30pm Mon-Fri, 10.30am-10pm Sat & Sun; Ⓢ Line 1 to Tian'anmen East, exit A) A peerless location, housed in a Qing dynasty building beside the Forbidden

City moat, Ignace Lecleir's new offering is a more casual version of his upmarket **Temple Restaurant** (嵩祝寺餐厅, Sōngzhù Sì Cāntīng; Map p76; ☎010 8400 2232; www.trb-cn.com; Sōngzhù Temple, 23 Shatanbei Jie, off Wusi Dajie, 五四大街沙滩北街23号, 嵩祝寺; 3/4/5/6 courses ¥388/488/588/688; 🕐11am-3pm & 5.30-11pm; ❄📶; [S] Lines 6, 8 to Nanluoguxiang, exit B or Lines 5, 6 to Dongsi, exit E). The service is flawless, and the contemporary European food – salmon, lobster, pigeon, veal – is sheer quality. Here you order by customising your own meals, picking three or more items from whatever section of the menu takes your fancy.

Reservations are recommended, especially if you want a table overlooking the moat (the walls beside it are lit up in the evening). There's rooftop terrace seating in the warmer months.

★Běijīng Dàdǒng Roast Duck Restaurant PEKING DUCK $$$

(北京大董烤鸭店, Běijīng Dàdǒng Kǎoyādiàn; Map p76; ☎010 8522 1111; 5th fl Jinbao Place, 88 Jinbao Jie, 金宝街88号金宝汇购物中心5层; roast duck half/whole ¥134/268; 🕐11am-10pm; ❄📶; [S] Line 5 to Dengshikou, exit C) Ultramodern Dàdǒng sells itself on being the only restaurant that serves Peking duck with all the flavour of the classic imperial dish, but less fat – the leanest roast duck in the capital. For some, it's hideously overpriced and far from authentic. For others, it's the best roast-duck restaurant in China.

🍴 Drum Tower & Dōngchéng North

★Punk Rock Noodles NOODLES $

(鼓楼吃面, Gǔlóu Chīmiàn; Map p80; ☎010 8402 3180; 25 Donggong Jie, Loudong Dajie, 鼓楼东大街东公街25号; noodles from ¥25; 🕐noon-2am; [S] Line 5 to Beixinqiao, exit A) Run by owner Ma Yue, and her merry staff of punk rockers, this restaurant is equally popular with workers and students as it with skinheads, all drawn by the delicious hand-pulled noodles. It also does inventive dishes such as 'Punk's Not Dead' with sliced ox tongue, enjoyed by hard-core punk band the Exploited upon their visit. Tables are decked out in gingham and walls decorated in punk memorabilia.

It's a good place for a drink too, especially for its cocktail happy hour (¥10, 9-10pm).

Zhāng Māma SICHUAN $

(张妈妈特色川味馆, Zhāng Māma Tèsè Chuānwèiguǎn; Map p80; 76 Jiaodaokou Nandajie, 交道口南大街76号; mains ¥10-20; 🕐11am-10.30pm; [S] Line 5 to Beixinqiao, exit A) The original Zhāng Māma, on nearby Fensiting Hutong, was such a hit with Beijingers that the owners were forced to also open this new, larger branch with two floors. At the smaller, original branch you have to wait up to an hour for a table. Here, they've cut that down to about 15 minutes. It's worth the wait. This is arguably Běijīng's best-value Sichuanese restaurant.

The speciality is *málà xiāngguō* (麻辣香锅; ¥48 to ¥58), a fiery, chilli-laced broth with either chicken (香锅鸡; *xiāngguō jī*), prawns (香锅虾; *xiāngguō xiā*) or ribs (香锅排骨; *xiāngguō páigǔ*) simmering away inside, and with a variety of vegetables added into the mix. One pot is enough for two or three people. Also worth trying here is the *dàndàn miàn* (担担面; spicy dry noodles; ¥8) and the rice meals; the classic being the *gōngbào jīdīng gàifàn* (宫爆鸡丁盖饭; spicy chicken with peanuts; ¥12), which is lip-tinglingly delicious, thanks to the generous sprinkling of Sìchuān peppercorns. No English menu, so don't be shy about pointing to what fellow diners are eating. Chances are it'll be spicy, but delicious.

Bǎihé Vegetarian Restaurant CHINESE $$

(百合素食, Bǎihé Sùshí; Map p80; 23 Caoyuan Hutong, 东直门内北小街草园胡同甲23号; mains ¥25-60, tea per cup/pot from ¥25/45; 🕐11am-10pm; 🌿; [S] Lines 2, 13 to Dongzhimen, exit A, or Line 5 to Beixinqiao, exit B) This peaceful, tastefully furnished, courtyard restaurant, which also serves as a delightful teahouse, has a wonderful air of serenity – it's not uncommon to see monks from nearby Lama Temple (p79) coming here for a pot of tea. The all-vegetarian menu (with English translations) includes imaginative mock-meat dishes as well as more conventional vegetable dishes and a range of tasty noodles.

With courteous service, this is one of Běijīng's more soothing dining experiences. There's also a separate and extensive tea menu – customers are welcome to come here just to sample the tea. To get here, walk north on Dongzhimen Beixiaojie from the junction with Ghost Street for 100m, then turn left into the first *hútòng*. The restaurant is on the right, although the sign is in Chinese only.

Toast MIDDLE EASTERN $$

(Map p80; ☎010 8404 4818, 010 5799 0806; www.theorchidbeijing.com; 65 Baochao Hutong, Dulou Dongdajie, 鼓楼东大街宝钞胡同65号; mains from ¥88; 🕐10am-2.30pm & 6-10pm Wed-Mon; [S] Lines 2, 8 to Guloudajie, exit F or Line 8 to Shichahai, exit A2) Located at the boutique Orchid (p100) hotel is this stylish restaurant with a quality menu of Middle Eastern/North African/Indian-influenced cuisine. Dishes are shared plates and range from homemade bread and dips to poached egg *kofte*, roasted lamb ribs with hummus, and spicy clams. It's popular also for its quality breakfast and brunch menus, and rooftop cocktails when the sun's out.

Stuff'd   INTERNATIONAL $$

(塞, Sāi; Map p80; 010 6407 6308; www.stuff-d. com; 9 Jianchang Hutong, off Guozijian Jie, 国子监街, 箭厂胡同9号; sausages from ¥30, pies ¥68, pizzas ¥68; 11.30am midnight Sun-Thu, to 1am Fri & Sat; ; Line 2 to Andingmen or Lines 2, 5 to Yonghegong-Lama Temple, exit D) Handmade sausages and home brewed beer (¥40). What more could you want? Set up by Arrow Factory brewery (which has a taproom out the back), this rustic space has a warm, cosy feel; almost like an English pub, only housed within a restored Chinese *píngfáng* (bungalow). The menu is all about the sausages and ale, but there are also pies and pizza.

★ Georg   INTERNATIONAL $$$

(Map p80; 010 8408 5300; www.thegeorg.com/en; 45 Dongbuyaqiao Hutong, 东不压桥胡同45号; cafe mains ¥58-78, tasting plates from ¥130, set menu ¥150; restaurant 6.30-10.30pm Tue-Sun, cafe from 10.30am daily; ; Lines 6, 8 to Nanluoguxiang, exit E, or Line 8 to Shichahai, exit C) In a city glaringly short on international fine dining, the Georg delivers with its gastronomic menu of fusion cuisine. It's an enterprise by Copenhagen designer Georg Jensen, creating a refined, intimate space with Danish design and heritage silverware. Tasting plates with a Scandinavian twist are creative and original.

Given the work put into the menu, it is very good value for less than ¥450 a head. Its Living Room cafe is open during the day with a more casual menu of brisket sandwiches, home-cured duck prosciutto, cheesecake and high tea. The location along a picturesque river is a nice area to stroll.

There's a Georg Jensen showroom on the 2nd floor with high-end silverware and jewellery. The **Beijing Centre for the Arts** (www. beijingcenterforthearts.com) gallery is next door.

Dàlǐ Courtyard   YUNNAN $$$

(大理, Dàlǐ; Map p80; 010 8404 1430; 67 Xiaojingchang Hutong, Gulou Dongdajie, 鼓楼东大街小经厂胡同67号; set menu ¥150; noon-2pm & 6-10pm; Line 2 to Andingmen, exit D, or Line 5 to Beixinqiao, exit A) The charming *hútòng* setting in a restored courtyard makes this one of Běi-

jīng's more pleasant places to eat, especially in summer (in winter they cover the courtyard with an unattractive temporary roof). It specialises in the subtle flavours of Yúnnán cuisine. There's no menu. Instead, you pay ¥150 (drinks are extra), and enjoy whatever inspires the chef that day. He rarely disappoints.

From Gulou Dongdajie, turn north onto Xiaojingchang Hutong and look for the red lanterns down the first alley on the left.

✕ Temple of Heaven Park & Dōngchéng South

Yīzhēn Yuán   MUSLIM $

(伊珍源饭庄; Map p76; 010 6712 9856; 80 Xihuashi Dajie, 西花市大街80号; mains from ¥22; 10.30am-9pm; Chongwenmen) A good spot for a lunch break in the area, this Muslim eatery offers juicy *yángròu chuàn* (羊肉串; lamb skewers, ¥5) and decent naan bread, as well as noodle and vegie dishes. No English spoken, but it does have a picture menu.

★ Lost Heaven   YUNNAN $$

(花马天堂, Huāmǎ Tiāntáng; Map p76; 010 8516 2698; www.lostheaven.com.cn; 23 Qianmen Dongdajie, 前门东大街23号; dishes ¥50-130; 11am-2pm & 5.30-10.30pm; Line 2 to Qianmen, exit A) The Běijīng branch of the famed Shànghǎi restaurant, Lost Heaven specialises in the folk cuisine of Yúnnán province. While the spices have been toned down, the flavours remain subtle and light and are guaranteed to transport you to China's balmy southwest. The location in the elegant former Legation Quarter is an added bonus, and there's an outside roof terrace for the summer.

★ Capital M   MEDITERRANEAN $$$

(M餐厅, M Cāntīng; Map p90; 010 6702 2727; www.m-restaurantgroup.com/capitalm; 3rd fl, 2 Qianmen Dajie, 前门步行街2号; mains from ¥208; 11.30am-3pm & 5.30-10.30pm; ; Qianmen) The terrace of this swish but relaxed restaurant, with its unfussy menu of Mediterranean favourites, offers fine views over Qiánmén Gate and Tiān'ānmén Sq. The weekday lunch menu is decent value (¥188). Book ahead.

★ Liqún Roast Duck Restaurant   PEKING DUCK $$$

(利群烤鸭店, Lìqún Kǎoyādiàn; Map p76; 010 6705 5578, 010 6702 5681; 11 Beixiangfeng Hutong, 前门东大街正义路南口北翔凤胡同11号; roast duck for 2/3 people ¥240/285; 11am-10pm; Qianmen) As you walk in to this compact courtyard restaurant, you're greeted by the fine sight of rows of ducks on hooks glowing in the ovens. The delectable duck on offer is in such high demand that it's essential to call ahead to reserve both a bird and a table (otherwise, turn up off-peak and be prepared to wait an hour).

Inside, it's a little tatty and service can be chaotic, but the food more than makes up for that. Buried away in a maze of *hútòng* in east Qiánmén that have somehow survived demolition, look for the red-neon duck sign that points the way to the restaurant.

🍴 Sānlǐtún & Cháoyáng

★In & Out YUNNAN $

(一坐一忘, Yī Zuò Yī Wàng; Map p92; ☎010 8454 0086; 1 Sanlitun Beixiaojie, 三里屯北小街1号; mains ¥28-60; 🕐11am-10pm; [S] Line 2 to Agricultural Exhibition Centre) This fashionable, but laid-back and friendly restaurant specialises in the many cuisines of the ethnic minority groups in southwestern Yúnnán province. The flavours are authentic and, given its popularity, the prices are surprisingly reasonable, unless you go for the mushroom dishes (Yúnnán mushrooms are prized across Asia).

Morning NOODLES $

(过早, Guò Zǎo; Map p92; 10 Chunxiu Lu, 春秀路10号; mains from ¥20; 🕐11am-2.30pm & 5-9.30pm; [S] Line 2 to Dongzhimen, exit C, or Dongsi Shitiao, exit B) A slick, modern space with blonde wood and designer furniture seems incongruous for a restaurant that specialises in cheap, old-school Húběi noodles, and it serves to make Morning all the cooler. Come for the traditional dry noodles, topped with pork mince and thick sesame paste that you'll need to stir through vigorously before you slurp it down.

★Home Plate BBQ BARBECUE $$

(本垒美式烤肉, Běnlěi Měishì Kǎoròu; Map p92; ☎400 096 7670; www.homeplatebbq.com; Lot 10, Courtyard 4, off Gongrentiyuchang Beilu, 三里屯机电院10号; burgers from ¥45; 🕐11am-1am; [S] Line 10 to Tuanjiehu, exit A or D) Serving up some of the finest southern American barbecue in town is this Texas-owned restaurant-bar that's all about slow-cooked meats, burgers and craft beer. Come here for bone-lickin' ribs, plates of barbecued pulled pork, smoky chicken and beef brisket cooked for 12 hours.

★Jīngzūn Peking Duck PEKING DUCK $$

(京尊烤鸭, Jīngzūn Kǎoyā; Map p92; ☎010 6417 4075; 6 Chunxiu Lu, 春秀路6号; mains ¥26-98; 🕐11am-10pm; [S] Line 2 to Dongsi Shitiao, exit B) Very popular place to sample Běijīng's signature dish. Not only is the Peking duck here extremely good value at ¥138/79 for a whole/half bird, but you can also sit outside on its atmospheric wooden-decked terrace decorated with red lanterns. Otherwise, head upstairs to its booth seating overlooking the leafy street. It has its own draft beer too.

Bookworm CAFE $$

(书虫, Shūchóng; Map p92; ☎010 6586 9507; www.beijingbookworm.com; Bldg 4, Nansanlitun Lu, 南三里屯路4号楼; mains from ¥60; 🕐9am-midnight; 📶; [S] Line 10 to Tuanjiehu, exit A or D) A combination of a bar, cafe, restaurant, library and bookshop, the Bookworm is a Běijīng institution and one of the epicentres of the capital's cultural life. Much more than just an upmarket cafe, there are 16,000-plus books here you can browse while sipping your coffee. For freelancers, it's one of the city's best workspaces. The food is reasonably priced, if uninspired, but there's a decent wine list.

Nàjiā Xiǎoguǎn CHINESE $$

(那家小馆, Map p92, ☎010 6567 3663, 10 Yong'an Xili, off Jianguomenwai Dajie, Chunxiu Lu, 建国门外大街永安西里10号, mains ¥40-90, 🕐11.30am-9pm, [S] Line 1 to Yonganli, exit A2) There's a touch of the traditional Chinese teahouse to this excellent restaurant, housed in a reconstructed two-storey interior courtyard, and bubbling with old-Peking atmosphere. The menu is based on an old imperial recipe book known as the Golden Soup Bible, and the dishes are consistently good (and fairly priced considering the quality).

Duck de Chine PEKING DUCK $$$

(全鸭季, Quányājì; Map p92; ☎010 6521 2221; Courtyard 4, 1949 Hidden City, off Gongrentiyuchang Beilu, 工体北路4号; mains ¥78-488; 🕐11am-2pm & 5.30-10pm; [S] Line 10 to Tuanjiehu, exit A or D) Housed in a reconstructed industrial-style courtyard complex known as 1949, this very slick and stylish operation incorporates both Chinese and French duck-roasting methods to produce some stand-out duck dishes, including a leaner version of the classic Peking roast duck (¥268); no half serving available. The mix of expats and moneyed locals who flock here argue it's the best bird in town.

🍴 Běihǎi Park & Xīchéng North

★4corners INTERNATIONAL $

(四角餐厅, Sìjiǎo Cāntīng; Map p80; ☎010 6401 7797; http://these4corners.com; 27 Dashibei Hutong, 大石碑胡同27号; dishes from ¥40; 🕐11am-late Tue-Sun; [S] Line 8 to Shichahai, exit A2) Given this *hútòng* bar-restaurant is run by a Canadian-Vietnamese expat, it makes total sense it's known for its *pho* (Vietnamese noodle soup) and *poutine* (a Canadian dish of French fries and cheese curds with gravy). Everything is made from scratch, including the curds for its poutine and baked baguettes for the *bánh mì* (Vietnamese sandwiches), and everything is gluten-free. Its courtyard bar is also one of the area's best spots for a drink, with Běijīng craft beers on tap and quality cocktails.

Check its website for nightly events including live music, Tuesday quiz, Wednesday 'story-telling' nights and Thursday open mic.

Kǎo Ròu Jì CHINESE, MUSLIM $$

(烤肉季; Map p80; Qianhai Dongyan, 前海东沿银锭桥; mains ¥40-80; ⏲1st fl 11am-11pm, 2nd fl 11am-2pm & 5-9pm; [S] Line 8 to Shichahai, exit A2) This restaurant serves roast duck (including half portions for ¥92), and a range of China-wide dishes, but it's the mutton that everyone comes for – and the lake views from the 2nd floor.

This place has been around for years and its choice location, overlooking Qiánhǎi Lake, makes it as popular as ever. It's pricier than it should be, but the atmosphere is fun, and ordering is easy. Bag a table by the window on the 2nd floor, and order the roast mutton (¥108), a hot plate from heaven. Fill up on freshly roasted sesame-seed buns (¥2 each), called 'sesame cakes' on the menu.

🍴 Dashilar & Xīchéng South

Liú Family Noodles NOODLES $

(刘家人刀削面, Liú Jiārén Dāoxiāomiàn; Map p90; 6 Tieshuxie Jie, 铁树斜街6号; noodles from ¥12; ⏲11am-3pm & 5-10pm; [S] Line 7 to Hufangqiao or Line 2 to Qianmen, exit B or C) A rarity in this area: a restaurant that welcomes foreigners without trying to overcharge them. On the contrary, the prices couldn't be much lower, while the friendly owner is keen to practise her (limited) English. Choose from a selection of tasty noodle and cold dishes. To find it, look for the black sign with 'Best Noodles in China' written in English.

Turpan Restaurant XINJIANG $$

(吐鲁番餐厅, Tǔlǔfān Cāntīng; ☎010 8316 4691; 6 Niu Jie, 牛街6号; kebabs from ¥12, dishes from ¥35; ⏲5am-9am, 10.30am-2.30pm & 4.30-9pm; [S] Lines 4, 7 to Caishikou, exit D) This huge place attracts the local Huí hordes, who flock here for the big, juicy and succulent lamb kebabs (nothing like the tiny skewers sold on the streets). Then there's the array of authentic Uighur dishes from far-off Xīnjiāng, such as salted beef rolls with sweet yam (¥46), as well as a selection of Halal choices.

🍴 Summer Palace & Hǎidiàn

Khan Baba PAKISTANI $$

(汗吧吧餐厅, Hàn Bābā Cāntīng; ☎010 5692 7068; www.khanbababeijing.com; 2/f Jixin Plaza, Zhanchunyuanxi Lu, 展春园西路蓟鑫大厦北侧2层; mains ¥42-58; ⏲11.30am-3pm & 5.30-10.30pm; [S] Wudaokou) Fine and friendly Pakistani-run restaurant with a loyal and ever-increasing following of both foreigners and locals. The large menu ranges across India too, with a good choice of both meat and vegie curries. The weekday lunchtime buffet (¥55) is an excellent deal, allowing you to sample any number of dishes. It has great kebabs too.

Xiǎodiàolítāng BEIJING $$

(小吊梨汤; ☎010 6264 8616; 66 Baofusi, 保福寺66号; dishes from ¥22; ⏲11am-3pm & 5-9pm; [S] Zhichunli) This place specialises in Guanfu Cài, the cuisine associated with Qing dynasty mandarins. It's basically a more refined take on traditional Běijīng dishes. Unsurprisingly, given the restaurant's name, pear soup – *lítāng* – accompanies each meal, and a lot of the dishes on the picture menu incorporate pears, such as shrimp and fried pears (¥38). It's popular: expect to queue at lunchtime.

Everything here is MSG-free. The restaurant is tucked away to the side of the Zhongguancun Sports & Culture Centre.

🍷 Drinking & Nightlife

It's amazing to contemplate, as you sip a martini in the latest hot spot or dance to a big-name European DJ, but until 30 years ago there weren't any bars or nightclubs, outside a few hotels, in Běijīng at all. Now, as more and more locals take to partying after dark, the capital is home to an increasing number of sophisticated nightspots.

🍷 Forbidden City & Dōngchéng Central

★Oasis Cafe CAFE

(绿洲咖啡, Lǜzhōu Kāfēi; Map p70; 2 Jingshan Qianjie, 景山前街2号; coffee from ¥15; ⏲9am-7pm; [S] Lines 6, 8 to Nanluoguxiang, exit A or Line 5, 6 to Dongsi, exit E) Oasis' award-winning owner/barista/coffee roaster, Duan, really knows his stuff. Not only does he nail the V60 drip-coffee pour overs, but he knocks out one of the best flat whites in the city. Its attached restaurant is also a great place for a feed, specialising in cheap traditional Běijīng dishes, including hand-pulled noodles and meat-filled *shāobǐng* (烧饼, sesame-seed rolls; ¥5).

Its location just up from the Forbidden City makes it the ideal spot to take a break after a long day of sightseeing.

★ Slow Boat Brewery Taproom BAR

(悠航鲜啤, Yōuháng Xiānpí; Map p76; www.slowboatbrewery.com; 56-2 Dongsi Batiao, 东四八条56一2号; draft beer ¥25-55; ⏲5pm-midnight Mon-Fri, 2pm-2am Sat, 11.30am-10pm Sun; 📶; [S] Line 5 to Zhangzizhonglu, exit C) One of the original breweries to get Běijīng's craft-beer scene kicking, Slow Boat continues to conjure up some of the city's finest. Well hidden away down a residential side street, it's a cool little bar in a converted *hútòng* house, with a selection of around 15 Slow Boat beers on tap. Get the critically acclaimed Fry Burger stuffed with fries.

Signature beers include the Captain's Pale Ale and Monkey's Fist IPA, but there's a long list of core and seasonal North American-style beers to make your way through. Check the website for specials. Its flagship brewpub opened in **Sānlǐtún** (Map p92; www.slowboatbrewery.com; 6 Sanlitun Nanlu; [S] Line 10 to Tuanjiehu, exit A or D) in 2016.

Biking Cafe CAFE

(双行咖啡, Shuāngxíng Kāfēi; Map p76; ☎010 6455 3909; www.bikingcafe.com; 81 Beiheyan Dajie, 北河沿大街81号; coffee from ¥25; ⏲8am-9pm; 📶; [S] Lines 6, 8 to Nanluoguxiang, exit B or Line 5 to Zhangzizhonglu, exit D) Sharing space with Bike Beijing (p98) is this mellow cafe that does speciality hand-drip coffees, toasted sandwiches and breakfasts specifically designed for cyclists. There are Belgian beers waiting in the fridge upon your return. With its unhurried pace and abundance of power points, it's also well suited as a work space.

Drum Tower & Dōngchéng North

★ Capital Spirits COCKTAIL BAR

(首都酒坊, Shǒudū Jiǔfāng; Map p80; www.capitalspiritsbj.com; 3 Daju Hutong, 大菊胡同3号; cocktails from ¥40; ⏲8pm-12.30am Tue-Sun; 📶; [S] Line 5 to Beixinqiao, exit C) Much maligned by non-Chinese drinkers, *báijiǔ* (白酒; literally 'white alcohol', a face-numbing spirit) is often compared to consuming paint stripper. However, that's until you sample some of the top-shelf stuff, and that's where Capital Spirits step in with an entire speakeasy bar dedicated to quality *báijiǔ*s. On a mission to dispel its poor reputation, here pro bartenders mix up *báijiǔ* cocktails along with tasting flights of four varietals (¥40) from across China.

Once you've figured out your tastes – which vary markedly according to distillery processes – there's a whole choice of flights to follow. The *báijiǔ* cocktails are definitely worth trying, from the Báijiǔ Sour to the Ma-La Rita margarita infused with Sìchuān peppercorns. If you're up for shots, there's a range of infused *báijiǔ,* from jalapeno to bottled snakes.

It's down a residential noncommerical *hútòng* within a nondescript building without signage and you can only enter from the back door; it's 20m from Dongzhimen Nanxiaojie. The tasting gift packs (¥260) make good souvenirs. Cash only.

★ Distillery COCKTAIL BAR

(Map p80; www.capitalspiritsbj.com/#the-distillery; 23 Xinsi Hutong, 辛寺胡同23号; cocktails ¥40-60; ⏲8pm-12.30am Mon-Sat; 📶; [S] Line 5 to Zhangzizhonglu, exit B) Down a residential *hútòng* alley, hidden behind a nondescript facade, is this fantastic bar that's so much your quintessential speakeasy that it even makes its own hooch. It's a classy dark-lit space, where they distill their own gin and vodka on-site, to mix up a great menu of original and classic cocktails.

It's run by the same team as Capital Spirits, and a free rickshaw runs between the two on Friday and Saturdays evenings.

★ Great Leap Brewing BREWERY

(GLB #6, 大跃啤酒, Dàyuè Píjiǔ; Map p80; www.greatleapbrewing.com; 6 Doujiao Hutong, 豆角胡同6号; beer per pint ¥25-50; ⏲2-11pm Sun-Thu, to midnight Fri & Sat; [S] Line 8 to Shichahai, exit C) Běijīng's original microbrewery, this refreshingly simple courtyard bar, set up by American beer enthusiast Carl Setzer, is housed in a hard-to-find, but beautifully renovated, 100-year-old Qing dynasty courtyard and serves up a wonderful selection of unique ales made largely from locally sourced ingredients. Sip on familiar favourites such as pale ales and porters, or choose from China-inspired tipples like Honey Ma, a brew made with lip-tingling Sìchuān peppercorns.

Cafe Confucius CAFE

(秀冠咖啡, Xiù Guàn Kāfēi; Map p80; 25 Guozijian Jie, 国子监街25号; ⏲8.30am-8.30pm; 📶; [S] Lines 2, 5 to Yonghegong-Lama Temple, exit C) This smart and friendly cafe has an

CRAFT BEERS & BARBEQUE

A revolution began in Běijīng in 2010. For once, it didn't concern politics. Instead, it was all about beer. When **Great Leap Brewing** (GLB #12, 大跃啤酒, Dàyuè Píjiǔ; Map p92; ☎010 5712 4376; www.greatleapbrewing.com; Ziming Mansion, Unit 101, 12 Xinzhong Jie, 新中街乙12号紫铭大厦101室; beers ¥25-50, burgers from ¥40; 🕐11am-1am Sun-Thu, to 2am Fri & Sat; 📶; [S] Line 2 to Dongsi Shitiao, exit B) and Slow Boat Brewery started making their own ales from 100% local ingredients, it marked the emergence of the capital's very own craft breweries. Now, at least five microbreweries are operating in Běijīng.

Great Leap, Slow Boat Brewery, Jing A Brewing, and **Arrow Factory Brewing** (箭厂啤酒, Jiàn Píjiǔchǎng; Map p92; ☎010 8532 5335; www.arrowfactorybrewing.com; 1 Xindong Lu, on Liangmaqiao Lu, 新东路1号外交公寓亮马河南岸; 🕐11.30am-midnight Tue-Thu, to 2am Fri & Sat; 📶; [S] Line 10 to Agricultural Exhibition Center) are by far the best of the North American expat brewers, but Chinese microbreweries such as NBeer and **Panda Brew** (Map p80; www.pandabrew.com.cn; 14 Dongsi Beidajie, 东四北大街14号; beers from ¥40; 🕐10am-1am; 📶; [S] Line 5 to Beixinqiao, exit C), among others, have risen to the challenge and produce equally impressive ales

And with craft beers increasingly popular with both locals and foreigners, there are more and more places around town where you can sample their ales.

understated Buddhist theme with a good tea selection, speciality coffee, lassis, juices, and Western and Chinese dishes.

Sānlǐtún & Cháoyáng

★Jing A Brewing MICROBREWERY

(京A Brewing Co.; Map p92; www.jingabrewing.com; Courtyard 4, 1949 Hidden City, off Gongrentiyuchang Beilu, 工体北路4号院; beers ¥40-60; 🕐5pm-1am Mon-Thu, 4pm-2am Fri, 11am-2am Sat, 11am-midnight Sun; 📶; [S] Line 10 to Tuanjiehu, exit A or D) Though Jing A has been brewing in Běijīng at **Big Smoke** (Map p92; ☎010 6416 5195; 1/F Lee World Bldg, Xingfucun Zhong Lu, 幸福村中路57号利世商务楼一层; dishes from ¥36; 🕐11am-midnight Mon-Thu, to 1am Fri & Sat, to 10pm Sun; [S] Line 2 to Dongsi Shitiao, exit B) for some time, now it's finally opened its own taproom. Set within the classy red-brick 1949 precinct, the bar has earned its reputation as a producer of some of Běijīng's best (and most experimental) beers, with a fantastic selection of ales using local ingredients.

There are 15 beers on tap, featuring a mix of core and seasonal ales, and a few guest breweries. Signature beers include the Flying Fist IPA and Worker's Pale Ale, but keep an eye out for the Airpocalypse IPA, the price of which fluctuates in accordance to the air pollution index – the more polluted, the cheaper it is! Happy hour is ¥10 off beers to 7pm.

There's good food too, from kimchi Ruben sandwiches to pan-fried Yunnan cheese and air-dried Sichuan pork.

★Parlor COCKTAIL BAR

(香, Xiāng; Map p92; ☎010 8444 4135; 39-9 Xingfu'ercun, Xindong Lu, 新东路幸福二村39-9号; cocktails from ¥65; 🕐6pm-late; [S] Line 2 to Dongsi Shitiao, exit B) Discretely positioned away from Sānlǐtún's main strip, Parlor aims to re-create the atmosphere of an old-school Shànghǎi speakeasy. Here you'll get bartenders in bow ties mixing originals and classics, a solid wooden bar counter and the roaring 1920s decor. To find it, walk to the end of an alley leading into a car park just before the Bank of China on Xingfu'ercun and look for the wooden door and sign.

Běihǎi Park & Xīchéng North

★NBeer Pub BAR

(牛啤堂, Niú Pí Táng; Map p88; ☎010 8328 8823; www.nbcraftbrewing.com; Huguo Xintiandi, 85 Huguosi Dajie, 护国寺大街85号护国新天地一层; bottles from ¥25, draft ¥35-50; 🕐3pm-2am; 📶; [S] Lines 4, 6 to Ping'anli, exit B) In a scene dominated by North American expats, NBeer is an all-Chinese affair that produces some of Běijīng's best beers. It has a massive 37 ales on tap behind a bar made from Lonely Planet guidebooks! The majority are brewed onsite and include a variety of IPAs, pale ales, stouts and European-style ales. It also boasts the biggest fridge of beers in Běijīng.

The food is also good, including excellent cheeseburgers and enormous, juicy kebabs. Visit before 7pm for 30% discounts on all draft beers.

It's on the ground floor of a multifloor complex known as Xīntiāndì, at the western end of Huguosi Dajie. You can sometimes sit on the patio out the back in summer and spy **Jīngāng Hall** (金刚殿; Jīngāng Diàn), originally built in 1284 and the only surviving feature of Hùguó Temple, which this *hútòng* is named after.

☆ Entertainment

Běijīng is the cultural capital of China and by far the best place to be if you're interested in seeing anything from ballet and contemporary dance, to jazz or punk bands. Then there are the traditional local pastimes such as Peking opera *(jīngjù)* and acrobatic shows, as well as movies, theatre and Běijīng's various sports teams.

★ DDC   LIVE MUSIC
(黄昏黎明俱乐部, Huánghūn Límíng Jùlèbù, Dusk Dawn Club; Map p76; ☑ 010 6407 8969; https://site. douban.com/237627; 14 Shanlao Hutong, 山老胡同 14号; tickets free-¥60; ☺ noon-1am; Ⓢ Lines 6, 8 to Nanluoguxiang, exit B, or Line 5 to Zhangzizhonglu, exit D) One of the capital's current favourite spots to catch Chinese indie, punk and metal bands, DDC is an intimate space located down a nondescript *hútòng*. Its courtyard bar is also a good place for a drink, with a wide selection of Běijīng craft beers (from ¥30), on tap (including a few of their own brews) and cheap cocktails (from ¥35) at its bar made up of Lonely Planet guidebooks.

★ Hot Cat Club   LIVE MUSIC
(热力猫俱乐部, Rèlìmāo Jùlèbù; Map p80; 46 Fangjia Hutong, 方家胡同46号; ☺ 10am-midnight; Ⓢ Line 2 to Andingmen) Hot Cat Club is one of the city's most popular venues with its sticky-carpet pub feel and nightly roster of local and foreign guitar-slinging bands playing everything from rock 'n' roll to electronica. Gigs are usually free, but there are a few paid events. Walk behind the stage to access the grungy beer garden.

★ School Bar   CONCERT VENUE
(Map p80; ☑ 010 6402 8881; https://site.douban. com/school; 53 Wudaoying Hutong, 东城区五道营胡同53号; tickets around ¥50; ☺ 6pm-2am; Ⓢ Lines 2, 5 to Yonghegong-Lama Temple, exit D) Another reason why hip Wudaoying Hutong is too cool for school, this divey band venue is the best spot to tap into the capital's underground scene. Run by a couple of veteran Běijīng punks, it hosts quality gigs from local and touring punk, garage, indie and noise to hard-core and metal bands.

National Centre for the Performing Arts   CLASSICAL MUSIC
(国家大剧院, Guójiā Dàjùyuàn; Map p88; ☑ 010 6655 0000; www.chncpa.org/ens; 2 Xichang'an Jie, 西长安街2号; tickets ¥80-880; ☺ performances 7.30pm; Ⓢ Line 1 to Tian'anmen West, exit C) Sometimes called the National Grand Theatre, this spectacular Paul Andreu–designed dome, known to Beijingers as the 'Alien Egg', attracts as many architectural tourists as it does music fans. But it's *the* place to listen to classical music from home and abroad. You can also watch ballet, opera and classical Chinese dance here.

Cháng'ān Grand Theatre   PEKING OPERA
(长安大戏院, Cháng'ān Dàxìyuàn; Map p92; ☑ 010 6510 1310; Chang'an Bldg, 7 Jianguomennei Dajie, 建国门内大街7号; tickets ¥50-800; ☺ performances 7.30pm; Ⓢ Lines 1, 2 to Jianguomen, exit A) This large theatre, with its distinctive model of a Peking-opera mask standing outside, offers a genuine experience, with the audience chatting among themselves during the daily performances of Peking-opera classics – this is a place for connoisseurs, although there are usually English captions on a screen to one side of the stage. Matinées, when they have them, usually start at 2pm; evening shows at 7.30pm. Most shows last for around two hours. Buy tickets in person from the ticket office here. Shows rarely sell out, but the cheaper seats often do. Note, there are sometimes days that have no performances.

Modernsky Lab   LIVE MUSIC
(Map p76; ☑ 010 5876 0143; http://m.modern sky.com; basement fl, D 5-108 Galaxy Soho, 朝阳门银河SOHO, D座B1层5-108; Ⓢ Lines 2, 6 to Chaoyangmen, exit G) One of Běijīng's newest venues, Modernsky is run by a local music label of the same name, and has shows by local indie, rock and electro bands. It's in the basement of the Galaxy Soho building.

Cháoyáng Theatre   ACROBATICS
(朝阳剧场, Cháoyáng Jùchǎng; Map p92; ☑ 010 6507 2421; www.bjcyjc.com/en; 36 Dongsanhuan Beilu, 东三环北路36号; tickets ¥200-880; ☺ performances 3.50pm, 5.30pm & 7pm; Ⓢ Lines 6, 10 to Hujialou, exit C1) The Cháoyáng Theatre hosts visiting acrobatic troupes from around China who fill the stage with plate spinning and hoop jumping. It's an accessible place for foreign visitors, and tickets are available from its box office, but often bookable through your hotel.

Mei Lanfang Grand Theatre   PEKING OPERA
(梅兰芳大戏院, Méi Lánfāng Dàxìyuàn; Map p88; ☑ 010 5833 1288; www.bjmlfdjy.cn; 32 Ping'anli Xida-

jie, 平安里西大街32号; tickets ¥30-300; ⊙ performances 7.30pm; Ⓢ Lines 2, 6 to Chegongzhuang, exit C) Named after China's most famous practitioner of Peking opera, this theatre opened its doors in 2007 and has since become one of the most popular and versatile venues in town. Performances start at 7.30pm daily. Tickets have to be bought from the ticket office in the lobby between 9.30am and 8pm.

East Shore Jazz Café
JAZZ

(东岸, Dōng'àn; Map p80; ✆ 010 8403 2131; 2nd fl, 2 Shichahai Nanyan, 地安门外大街 什刹海南沿2号楼2层, 地安门邮局西侧; beers from ¥30, cocktails from ¥45; ⊙ 3pm-2am; Ⓢ Line 6 to Beihai North, exit B, or Line 8 to Shichahai, exit A1) Rock star Cui Jian's saxophonist, whose quartet plays here, opened this chilled venue just off Di'anmen Waidajie and next to Qiánhǎi Lake. It's a place to hear the best local jazz bands, with live performances from Wednesdays to Sundays (from 10pm), in a laid-back, comfortable atmosphere.

Líyuán Theatre
PEKING OPERA

(梨园剧场, Líyuán Jùchǎng; Map p90; ✆ 010 6301 6688; Qianmen Jianguo Hotel, 175 Yong'an Lu, 永安路175号前门建国饭店; tickets ¥280-480, with tea ¥580; ⊙ performances 7.30pm; Ⓢ Line 7 to Hufangqiao, exit C) This touristy theatre, in the lobby of the Qiánmén Jiànguó Hotel (p102), has daily performances for Peking-opera newbies. If you want to, you can enjoy an overpriced tea ceremony while watching. The setting isn't traditional: it resembles a cinema auditorium (the stage facade is the only authentic touch), but it's a gentle introduction to the art form.

Tiānqiáo Performing Arts Centre
THEATRE

(天桥艺术中心, Tiānqiáo Yìshù Zhōngxīn; Map p90; ✆ 400 635 3355; www.tartscenter.com; 9 Tianqiao Nandajie, 天桥南大街9号; ⊙ box office 9.30am-8.30pm; Ⓢ Line 7 to Zhushikou) Officially opened in late 2015, Beijing's new modern performing-arts centre comprises four theatres that host both foreign (*My Fair Lady, Phantom of the Opera*) and Chinese musicals and productions.

Lao She Teahouse
PERFORMING ARTS

(老舍茶馆, Lǎoshě Cháguǎn; Map p90; ✆ 010 6303 6830; www.laosheteahouse.com; 3rd fl, 3 Qianmen Xidajie, 前门西大街3号3层; evening tickets ¥180-580; ⊙ performances 7.50pm; Ⓢ Line 2 to Qianmen, exit C) Lao She Teahouse, named after the celebrated writer, has daily and nightly shows, mostly in Chinese, which blend any number of traditional Chinese performing arts. The evening performances of Peking opera, folk art and music, acrobatics and magic (7.50pm to 9.20pm) are the most popular. But there are also tea ceremonies, frequent folk-music performances and daily shadow-puppet shows.

Tiānqiáo Acrobatics Theatre
ACROBATICS

(天桥杂技剧场, Tiānqiáo Zájì Jùchǎng; Map p90; ✆ 010 6303 7449; 95 Tianqiao Shichang Lu Jie, 天桥市场街95号; tickets ¥180-380; ⊙ performances 5.30pm; Ⓢ Line 7 to Zhushikou) West of the Temple of Heaven Park, this 100-year-old theatre offers one of Běijīng's best acrobatic displays, a one-hour show performed by the Běijīng Acrobatic Troupe. Less touristy than the other venues, the theatre's small size means you can get very close to the action. The high-wire display is awesome. The entrance is on Beiwei Lu, along the eastern side of the building.

Húguǎng Guild Hall
PEKING OPERA

(湖广会馆, Húguǎng Huìguǎn; Map p90; ✆ 010 6351 8284; 3 Hufang Lu, 虎坊桥路3号; tickets ¥180-680, opera museum ¥10; ⊙ performances 8pm, opera museum 9am-5.30pm; Ⓢ Line 7 to Hufangqiao, exit C) The most historic and atmospheric place in town for a night of Peking opera. The interior is magnificent, coloured in red, green and gold, and decked out with tables and a stone floor, while balconies surround the canopied stage. Opposite the theatre, there's a very small opera museum displaying operatic scores, old catalogues and other paraphernalia.

There are also colour illustrations of the *liǎnpǔ* (types of Peking-opera facial make-up). The theatre dates back to 1807 and, in 1912, was where the Kuomintang (KMT), led by Dr Sun Yatsen, was founded. Shows here attract a lot of domestic tour groups. There are few English captions, but it's not hard to follow what's going on.

The restaurant here is also very good, and inexpensive, making for a nice pre- or post-theatre meal.

Red Theatre
ACROBATICS

(红剧场, Hóng Jùchǎng; Map p85; ✆ 010 6714 2473; 44 Xingfu Dajie, 幸福大街44号; tickets ¥200-880; ⊙ performance 7.30pm; Ⓢ Tiantandongmen) The daily show is *The Legend of Kung Fu*, which follows one boy's journey to becoming a warrior monk. Slick, high-energy fight scenes are interspersed with more soulful dance sequences, plus plenty of 'how do they do that' balancing on spears and other body-defying acts. To find the theatre, look for the all-red exterior set back from the road.

Shopping

Whether you're a diehard shopaholic or a casual browser, you'll be spoiled for choice in Běijīng. Join the locals in their favourite pastime at any number of shiny shopping malls, markets and specialist shopping streets. Then there are the pavement vendors and itinerant hawkers. All ensure that keeping your cash in your pocket is increasingly difficult.

Forbidden City & Dōngchéng Central

Locals, out-of-towners and tourists haunt Wangfujing Dajie, a prestigious, partly pedestrianised shopping street that's been given a much-needed makeover in recent years and now sports some slick shopping malls and top-name brands, as well as plenty of tacky souvenir outlets.

★Slow Lane TEA, CLOTHING
(细活裡, Xì Huó Lǐ; Map p76; 13 Shijia Hutong, 史家胡同13号; ⏲10am-8pm; [S]Line 5 to Dengshikou, exit C) Secreted away down historic Shijia Hutong, this quietly seductive shop sells beautiful, handmade teaware and quality tea as well as elegant clothing, much of which is made from Tibetan yak wool. Teasets start from around ¥680.

Wangfujing Dajie SHOPPING STREET
(王府井; Map p76; Wangfujing Dajie; [S]Line 1 to Wangfujing, exit C2 or B) Prestigious, but these days rather old-fashioned, this part-pedestrianised shopping street not far from Tiān'ānmén Sq is generally known as Wángfǔjǐng. It boasts a strip of stores selling well known, midrange brands, and a number of tacky souvenir outlets. At its south end, **Oriental Plaza** (东方广场, Dōngfāng Guǎngchǎng; Map p76; ☎010 8518 6363; 1 Dongchang'an Jie, 东长安街1号; ⏲10am-10.30pm; [S]Line 1 to Wangfujing, exit B) is a top-quality, modern shopping mall. Further north, just before the pedestrianised section ends, is the well stocked **Foreign Languages Bookstore** (外文书店, Wàiwén Shūdiàn; Map p76; 235 Wangfujing Dajie, 王府井大街235号; ⏲9.30am-9pm; [S]Line 5 to Dengshikou).

Háoyuán Market GIFTS & SOUVENIRS
(豪园市场, Háoyuán Shìchǎng; Map p76; west off Wangfujing Dajie, 王府井大街西侧; [S]Line 1 to Wangfujing, exit C2) Branching off from Wángfǔjǐng Snack Street is this small, bustling souvenir market. It has lots of Mao memorabilia, pandas and Buddhas, as well as other tacky tourist tat, but if you're pushed for time and need a last-minute present, you might find something. Haggling is imperative.

Drum Tower & Dōngchéng North

The wildly popular *hútòng* of Nanluogu Xiang contains an eclectic mix of clothes and gifts, sold in trendy boutique shops. It can be a pleasant place to shop for souvenirs, but avoid summer weekends when the shopping frenzy reaches fever pitch and you can hardly walk down the street for the crowds. At its northern end, Gulou Dongdajie has for a while now been a popular place for young Beijingers to shop for vintage clothing, skater fashion and music gear.

Yonghegong Dajie, the road the Lama Temple is on, is chock-full of Buddhist-themed shops, selling prayer flags, incense sticks and Buddha figurines to a backdrop of Tibetan-mantra music.

★Plastered 8 CLOTHING
(创可贴T-恤, Chuàngkětiē Tìxù; Map p80; ☎010 5762 6146; www.plasteredtshirts.com; 61 Nanluogu Xiang, 南锣鼓巷61号; ⏲9.30am-10.30pm; [S]Lines 6, 8 to Nanluoguxiang, exit E) British-owned, this iconic Nanluogu Xiang T-shirt shop prints ironic takes on Chinese culture onto its good-quality T-shirts and tops (from ¥168). Also stocks decent smog masks (from ¥225).

Opposite the entrance to the shop is a rare surviving (but very faded) slogan from the Cultural Revolution era, which exhorts the people to put their trust in the People's Liberation Army.

Pottery Workshop CERAMICS
(Map p80; ☎153 1380 5178; 80 Wudaoying Hutong, 五道营胡同80号; ⏲noon-9pm; [S]Line 2 to Andingmen or Lines 2, 5 to Yonghegong-Lama Temple, exit D) Featuring the work from a collective of six young artists, this wonderful, but small, ceramics store has a beautiful range of handmade, hand-painted tea cups, teasets, vases and incense-holders. There's a good variation in techniques and glazes, and all are made in Jǐngdézhèn – the pottery centre of China.

Nanluogu Xiang STREET
(南锣鼓巷; Map p80; Nanluogu Xiang; [S]Lines 6, 8 to Nanluoguxiang, exit E) Once neglected and ramshackle, strewn with spent coal briquettes in winter, and silent bar the hacking coughs of shuffling old-timers and the jangling of bicycle bells, the funky north–south alleyway of Nanluogu Xiang (literally 'South Gong and Drum Alley', and roughly

pronounced 'nan-law-goo-syang') has been undergoing an evolution since 1999 when **Pass By Bar** (过客, Guòkè; Map p80; 108 Nanluogu Xiang, 南锣鼓巷108号; ◎10am-2am; 🛜; ⓢLines 6, 8 to Nanluoguxiang, exit E) first threw open its doors. The alley was the subject of a complete makeover in 2006, and another in 2016. Today, it's an insatiably hectic strip of snack vendors, wi-fi cafes, bars, restaurants, hotels and trendy shops

It is also a victim of its own success, though. Come here on a summer weekend to experience more people than you thought could possibly fit onto one street! But don't miss exploring the quieter alleys, which house Qing dynasty courtyards as well as hidden cafes, shops, restaurants and bars.

🔒 Sānlǐtún & Cháoyáng

The Cháoyáng district has some of the swankiest malls in town, as well as many of the most popular markets for visitors, including the Silk Market and Alien's Street Market, two multifloor indoor clothes and souvenir markets that are heaving at weekends. Key areas for purchases are Sānlǐtún and Guómào, but there are shops of all descriptions spread across the district. Pānjiāyuán Market is on the edge of Cháoyáng and is the city's premier souvenir market 798 Art District (p87) is home to some boutique art stores that have some good shopping.

★ Shard Box Store   JEWELLERY
(慎德阁, Shèndégé; 📞010 5135 7638; shardboxs@hotmail.com; 2 Jiangtai Rd, 将台路2号; ◎9am-7pm; ⓢLine 14 to Jiangtai) Using porcelain fragments from Ming- and Qing-dynasty vases that were destroyed during the Cultural Revolution, this fascinating family-run store creates beautiful and unique shard boxes, bottles and jewellery. The boxes range from the tiny (¥50), for storing rings or cufflinks, to the large (¥780). It also repairs and sells jewellery, both handmade and sourced from Tibet and Mongolia. Check out the photos of the former US presidents who've visited here.

It's located behind the Holiday Inn Lido.

★ Pānjiāyuán Market   ANTIQUES, MARKET
(潘家园古玩市场, Pānjiāyuán Gǔwán Shìchǎng; west of Panjiayuan Qiao, 潘家园桥西侧; ◎8.30am-6pm Mon-Fri, 4.30am-6pm Sat & Sun; ⓢLine 10 to Panjiayuan, exit B) Hands down the best place in Běijīng to shop for yìshù (arts), gōngyì (crafts) and gǔwán (antiques). Some stalls open every day, but the market is at its biggest and most lively on weekends, when

you can find everything from calligraphy and cigarette-ad posters to Buddha heads, ceramics, Qing dynasty–style furniture and Tibetan carpets. It's also one of the best places to pick up authentic Cultural Revolution propaganda posters.

Pānjiāyuán hosts around 3000 dealers and up to 50,000 visitors a day, all scoping for antiques. The serious collectors are early birds, swooping here at dawn to snare precious relics. If you want to join them, an early start is essential. You probably aren't going to find that rare Qianlong dòucǎi stem cup or late Yuan dynasty qīnghuā vase, but what's on view is still a compendium of post-1950 Chinese curios and an A to Z of Middle Kingdom knick-knacks. The market is chaotic and can be difficult if you find crowds or hard bargaining intimidating. Ignore the 'don't pay more than half' rule here – some vendors might start at 10 times the real price. Make a few rounds to compare prices and weigh it up before forking out for something.

To get here, come out of exit B at Panjiayuan subway station, then walk west for 200m to find the main entrance to the market.

🔒 Běihǎi Park & Xīchéng North

Yandai Xiejie   GIFTS & SOUVENIRS
(烟袋斜街; Map p80; Yandai Xiejie, off Di'anmen Neidajie, 地安门内大街烟袋斜街; ⓢLine 8 to Shichahai, exit A2) If nearby Nanluogu Xiang is too hectic for you, you can find some of the same here, on a smaller scale. It's still busy at weekends, but more manageable.

Shops here, on this rebuilt 'old-Běijīng' hútòng, which leads down to the lakes, are almost exclusively souvenir shops but it's more fun shopping here than in one of the city's big, multifloor souvenir markets. Walk south from the Drum Tower, along Di'anmenwai Dajie, and it's the first hútòng on the right.

Three Stone Kite Shop   ARTS & CRAFTS
(三石斋风筝, Sānshízhái Fēngzhēng; Map p80; 📞010 8404 4505; www.cnkites.com; 25 Di'anmen Xidajie, 地安门西大街甲25号; ◎9am-9pm; ⓢLines 6, 8 to Nanluoguxiang, exit F) The great-grandfather of the owner of this friendly store used to make the kites for the Chinese imperial household. Most of the kites here are handmade and hand-painted, although the selection is limited these days, now that the owner uses half his shop to display other, admittedly attractive, souvenirs.

Kites start from around ¥150. You can also find all the gear for kite flying, as well as miniature framed kites, which make pretty gifts.

🔒 Dashilar & Xīchéng South

Dashilar and Xīchéng South are among the capital's finest neighbourhoods for shopping. Apart from Dashilar (p90) itself, Liulichang (meaning 'glazed-tile factory') is Běijīng's best-known antiques street, even if the goods on sale are largely fake. The street is something of an oasis in the area and worth delving into for its quaint, albeit dressed-up, village-like atmosphere. At the western end of **Liulichang Xijie** (琉璃厂, Liúlíchǎng; Liulichang Xijie, 琉璃厂西街; ⊙9am-6pm; Ⓢ Hepingmen), a collection of more informal shops flog bric-a-brac. For boutiques, keep an eye on the *hútòng* around Yangmeizhu Byway with this street emerging as a bit of a hot spot for art and design.

ℹ️ Information

CHILDREN

The Chinese have a deep and uncomplicated love of children and openly display their affection for them. Běijīng may have less child-friendly facilities than equivalent-sized cities in the West, but the locals will go out of their way to accommodate your kids.

DANGERS & ANNOYANCES

Generally speaking, Běijīng is very safe compared to other similarly sized cities. Serious crime against foreigners is rare, although on the rise.

➡ Guard against pickpockets, especially on public transport and in crowded places such as train stations.

➡ Use a money belt to carry valuables, particularly on buses and trains.

➡ Hotels are usually secure places to leave your stuff and older establishments may have an attendant watching who goes in and out.

➡ Staying in dormitories carries its own risks, and while there have been some reports of thefts by staff, the culprits are usually other guests. Use lockers as much as possible.

EMERGENCY
Ambulance ☑120
Fire ☑119
Police ☑110

INTERNET ACCESS

Internet cafes (网吧; *wǎngbā*) are generally easy to find, although some are tucked away down side streets and above shops. They are generally open 24 hours. Standard rates are ¥3 to ¥5 per hour, although there are usually different priced zones within each internet cafe – the common area (pǔtōng qū) is the cheapest. Many internet cafes do not allow the use of a USB stick.

Internet cafes are required to see your passport before allowing you to go online, and you may be photographed at the front desk.

Almost all cafes and most Western-style bars offer free wi-fi. Be prepared for occasionally slow connections and the sudden disappearance of sites for periods of time.

Almost all hotels and guesthouses provide either wi-fi or broadband internet access (or both), although some charge a daily rate. Youth hostels have free wi-fi as well as computer terminals, but levy a small internet charge (around ¥10 per hour) to use them.

MEDICAL SERVICES

A consultation with a doctor in a private clinic will cost ¥500 and up, depending on where you go. It will cost ¥10 to ¥50 in a state hospital.

Bayley & Jackson Medical Center (庇利积臣医疗中心, Bìlì Jīchén Yīliáo Zhōngxīn; Map p92; ☑010 8562 9998; www.bjhealthcare.com; 7 Ritan Donglu; ⊙dental 9am-4pm Mon-Fri, medical 8.30am-6pm Mon-Sat; Ⓢ Line 1 to Yonganli, exit A1 or Line 6 to Dongdaqiao, exit D) Full range of medical and dental services; attractively located in a courtyard next to Rìtán Park. Dental check-up ¥456; medical consultation ¥500.

Běijīng Union Hospital (PUMCH, 协和医院, Xiéhé Yīyuàn; Map p76; ☑010 6915 6699, emergency 010 6915 9180; www.pumch. cn; 1 Shuaifuyuan, 东城区 王府井帅府园1号; ⊙24hr; Ⓢ Lines 1, 5 to Dongdan, exit A) A recommended hospital, open 24 hours and with a full range of facilities for inpatient and outpatient care, plus a pharmacy. Head to International Medical Services, a wing reserved for foreigners which has English-speaking staff and telephone receptionists.

Hong Kong International Medical Clinic (北京香港国际医务诊所, Běijīng Xiānggǎng Guójì Yīwù Zhěnsuǒ; Map p92; ☑010 6553 2288; www.hkclinic.com/en; 9th fl, Office Tower, Hong Kong Macau Center, Swissôtel, 2 Chaoyangmen Beidajie, 朝阳门北大街2号 港澳中心·瑞士酒店办公楼9层, Cháoyáng; ⊙9am-9pm, dental 9am-7pm; Ⓢ Line 2 to Dongsi Shitiao, exit C) Well trusted dental and medical clinic with English-speaking staff. Includes obstetric and gynaecological services and facilities for ultrasonic scanning. Immunisations can also be performed. Prices are more reasonable than at International SOS. Full medical check-ups start from ¥3000 for men, ¥3500 for women and ¥2200 for children. Dental check-up ¥350; medical consultation ¥690. Has night staff on duty too, so you can call for advice round the clock.

International SOS (国际SOS医务诊所, Guójì SOS Yīwù Zhěnsuǒ; Map p92; ☑24hr alarm centre 010 6462 9100, clinic appointments 010 6462 9112, dental appointments 010 6462 0333; www.internationalsos.com; Suite 105, Wing 1, Kunsha Bldg, 16 Xinyuanli, off Xin

Donglu, Cháoyáng; ⏰8am-8pm; Ⓢ Line 10 to Liangmaqiao, exit D) Offering 24 hour emergency medical care, with a high-quality clinic with English-speaking staff. Dental check-up ¥620; medical consultation ¥1320.

MONEY

Most ATMs (取款机; *qǔkuǎnjī*) in Běijīng accept foreign credit cards and bank cards connected to Plus, Cirrus, Visa, MasterCard and Amex; a small withdrawal charge will be levied by your bank. Most large banks change money. Credit and debit cards are now used more widely than before, especially in hotels, shopping malls and upmarket restaurants, but cash remains king in Běijīng, so carry money with you at all times.

Banks

Bank of China (中国银行; Zhōngguó Yínháng; Map p76; ☑ 010 6513 2214; 19 Dong'anmen Dajie, 东安门大街19号) One of dozens of branches around Běijīng with money-changing facilities.

HSBC (汇丰银行; Huìfēng Yínháng; Map p92; www.hsbc.com.cn; 1st fl, Block A, COFCO Plaza, 8 Jianguomennei Dajie, Dōngchéng; ⏰9am-5pm Mon-Fri, 10am-6pm Sat) One of 26 branches and ATMs in the capital.

OPENING HOURS

China officially has a five-day working week, but much remains open at weekends.

Banks, offices and government departments Normally 9am to 5pm or 6pm (some close for two hours at midday), Monday to Friday. Some banks open weekends.

Museums Most close Mondays. Museums stop selling tickets half an hour before closing.

Parks 6am to 9pm or later, shorter hours in winter.

Shops 10am to 9pm.

Restaurants 11am to 11pm, some close 2pm to 5.30pm. Some open for breakfast (6am–8.30am).

Internet cafes Usually 24/7.

Bars To 2am, sometimes later. Some bars close one day of the week.

POST

Large post offices are generally open daily between 9am and 6pm. You can post letters via your hotel reception desk, or at green post boxes around town.

Letters and parcels marked 'Poste Restante, Běijīng Main Post Office' will arrive at the **International Post Office** (Zhōngguó Yóuzhèng; Map p92; ☑ 010 6512 8114; Jianguomen Beidajie, 建国门北大街; ⏰8.30am-6pm; Ⓢ Lines 1, 2 to Jianguomen, exit B), 200m north of Jianguomen station. Outsized parcels going overseas should be sent from here (packaging can be bought at the post office); smaller parcels (up to around 20kg) can go from smaller post offices. Both outgoing and incoming packages will be opened and inspected. If you're sending a parcel, don't seal the package until you've had it inspected.

Letters take around a week to reach most overseas destinations. China charges extra for registered mail, but offers cheaper postal rates for printed matter, small packets, parcels, bulk mailings and so on.

Express Mail Service (EMS; 快递; *kuàidi*) is available for registered deliveries to domestic and international destinations from most post offices around town. Prices are very reasonable.

PUBLIC SECURITY BUREAU

The Foreign Affairs Branch of the local **PSB** (北京公安局出入境管理处, Běijīngshì Gōng'ānjú Chūrùjìng Guǎnlǐchù, Map p80; ☑ 010 8402 0101, 010 8400 2101; www.bjgaj.gov.cn; 2 Andingmen Dongdajie, 东城区安定门东大街2号; ⏰9am-5pm Mon-Sat; Ⓢ Line 2, 5 to Yonghegong-Lama Temple, exit B) – the police force – handles visa extensions. The visa office is on the 2nd floor, accessed from the North 2nd Ring Rd. Allow around seven working days to get your visa extension. You can also apply for a residence permit here.

TOURIST INFORMATION

Tourist information offices are aimed at domestic tourists. Foreigners are better off using hotels or, better still, hostels.

Běijīng Tourist Information Centers (北京旅游咨询, Běijīng Lǚyóu Zīxún Fúwù Zhōngxīn; ⏰9am-5pm) have free tourist maps and brochures. There are branches at Běijīng train station and Capital Airport.

USEFUL WEBSITES

Beijinger (www.thebeijinger.com) Eating and entertainment listings, blog posts and forums.

Timeout Běijīng (www.timeoutbeijing.com) The best listings mag and a useful, well designed website.

GAY & LESBIAN TRAVELLERS

Although the Chinese authorities take a dim view of homosexuality, which was officially classified as a mental disorder until 2001, a low-profile gay and lesbian scene exists in Běijīng. For an informative and up-to-date lowdown on the latest gay and lesbian hot spots in Běijīng, have a look at Utopia (www.utopia-asia.com). Another useful publication is the *Spartacus International Gay Guide* (Bruno Gmunder Verlag), a bestselling guide for gay travellers.

Běijīng Cream (http://beijingcream.com) Lighthearted Běijīng-based blog covering China-wide current affairs.

Sinica Podcast (http://popupchinese.com) Popular, uncensored current-affairs podcast based in Běijīng.

Air Pollution (http://aqicn.org/city/beijing) Real-time Air Quality Index (AQI) for Běijīng (and other cities).

Běijīng Cultural Heritage Protection Center (www.bjchp.org) Info on protecting Běijīng's *hútòng* (alleyways).

Thorn Tree (www.lonelyplanet.com/thorntree) China branch of our long-standing travel forum includes plenty of Běijīng info.

ℹ️ Getting There & Away

Rail and air connections link the city to virtually every point in China, and fleets of buses head to abundant destinations from Běijīng. Most travellers coming from overseas fly into the city, arriving at Běijīng Capital International Airport. Using the nation's capital as a starting point to explore the rest of the country makes perfect sense.

AIR

Běijīng Capital International Airport

Currently the world's second-busiest airport, **Běijīng Capital International Airport** (北京首都国际机场, Běijīng Shǒudū Guójì Jīchǎng, PEK; 📞 010 6454 1100; www.en.bcia.com.cn) has three terminals. **Terminal 3** (三号航站楼; *sān hào hángzhànlóu*) deals with most long-haul flights, although international flights also use **Terminal 2** (二号航站楼; *èr hào hángzhànlóu*). Both are connected to the slick Airport Express, which links to Běijīng's subway system. The smaller **Terminal 1** (一号航站楼; *yī hào hángzhànlóu*) is a 10-minute walk from Terminal 2. Free 24-hour shuttle buses connect all three terminals.

Nányuàn Airport

The very small **Nányuàn Airport** (南苑机场, Nányuàn Jīchǎng, NAY; 📞 010 6797 8899; Jingbeixi Lu, Nányuàn Zhèn, Fēngtái District, 丰台区南苑镇警备西路, 警备东路口) feels more like a provincial bus station than an airport, but it does service quite a few domestic routes. Airport facilities are limited to a few shops and snack stalls, and don't expect to hear much English.

BOAT

The nearest major port is **Tiānjīn International Cruise Home Port** (天津国际游轮母港, Tiānjīn Guójì Yóulún Mǔgǎng). Express trains leave from **Běijīng south train station** (p118) to Tiānjīn every half-hour (¥54 to ¥93, 30 minutes). From there, take subway Line 9 to Citizen Plaza station (市民广场; Shìmín Guǎngchǎng; ¥12, one hour),

then take bus 513 to the last stop (东疆游轮母港; Dōngjiāng Yóulún Mǔgǎng; ¥2, 40 minutes, 7am to 5pm).

At the time of writing, ferry services to Dàlián (大连; ¥260 to ¥880, 12 hours, 8pm) in Liáoníng province were running only between June and October, but check as the service is frequently suspended. It leaves on even-numbered days (the return comes back on odd numbers). Boarding starts at 6pm and tickets can be bought on the day of travel. You can also catch a ferry from here to Incheon (¥888 to ¥1590, 24 hours) in South Korea. Ferries leave twice a week, on Sundays and Thursdays; departure times vary. Check www.jinchon.cn for more details.

CAR & MOTORCYCLE

It is possible to drive to Běijīng from other countries, either by car or motorbike, but it requires permits that take a couple of months to arrange and travel by car or motorbike comes with many conditions.

BUS

There are numerous long-distance bus stations, but no international bus routes to Běijīng.

Bāwángfén long-distance bus station (八王坟长途客运站, Bāwángfén Chángtú Kèyùnzhàn; 17 Xidawang Lu) is in the east of town, 500m south of Dawanglu subway station. Destinations include the following:

Bāotóu 包头; ¥181, 12 hours, 6pm

Chángchūn 长春; ¥288 to ¥362, 12 hours, 6pm and 9pm

Dàlián 大连; ¥326, 8½ hours, 10am, noon and 10pm

Harbin 哈尔滨; ¥375, 14 hours, 5.30pm

Shěnyáng 沈阳; ¥165 to ¥227, nine hours, regular (8am to 10.30pm)

Tiānjīn 天津; ¥35, two hours, regular (7.30am and 6.30pm)

Sihui long-distance bus station (四惠长途汽车站, Sìhuì Chángtú Qìchēzhàn; Jianguo Lu) is in the east of town, 200m east of Sihui subway station. Destinations include the following:

Bāotóu 包头; ¥180, 12 hours, 10.30am

Chéngdé 承德; ¥85, four hours, regular (6am to 5.50pm)

Dāndōng 丹东; ¥270, 12 hours, 4pm and 5.40pm

Jìxiàn 蓟县; ¥30, two hours, regular (5.10am to 7.30pm)

Liùlǐqiáo long-distance bus station (六里桥长途站, Liùlǐqiáo Chángtúzhàn) is in the southwest of town, adjacent to Liuliqiao subway station. Destinations include the following:

Dàtóng 大同; ¥133 to ¥150, 4½ hours, regular (7.10am to 6pm)

Héféi 合肥; ¥380, 13 hours, 1.45pm

Luòyáng 洛阳; ¥148, 10 hours, 5pm and 7.30pm

Shíjiāzhuāng 石家庄; ¥83, 3½ hours, regular (6.30am to 6.30pm)

Xiàmén 厦门; ¥580, 30 hours, 11am

Xī'ān 西安; ¥278, 12 hours, 5.45pm

Zhèngzhōu 郑州; ¥130 to ¥158, 8½ hours, regular (8.30am to 9pm)

Liánhuāchí long-distance bus station (莲花池长途汽车站, Liánhuāchí Chángtú Qìchēzhàn) is a short walk north of Liùlǐqiáo long-distance bus station and close to Liuliqiao subway station. Destinations include the following:

Ānyáng 安阳; ¥100, 6½ hours, six daily (8am to 5.30pm)

Luòyáng 洛阳; ¥150, 11 hours, 5pm and 6.30pm

Yán'ān 延安; ¥256, 14 hours, 2.30pm

Zhàogōngkǒu long-distance bus station (赵公口汽车站, Zhàogōngkǒu Qìchēzhàn) is in the south, 10 minutes' walk west of Liujiayao subway station. Destinations include the following:

Shànghǎi 上海; ¥340, 16 hours, 4.30pm

Jǐnán 济南; ¥129, 5½ hours, regular (6am to 7.30pm)

TRAIN

Běijīng has three major train stations for long-distance travel (Běijīng station, Běijīng west station and Běijīng south station). Běijīng north station is used much less.

There are international train routes to and from Mongolia, North Korea, Russia and Vietnam, as well as trains to and from Hong Kong and Lhasa in Tibet.

The most central of Běijīng's four main train stations, **Běijīng Railway Station** (北京火车站, Běijīng Huǒchēzhàn; ☏ 010 5101 9999; Ⓢ Beijing train station), which has its own subway stop, is mainly for T-class trains (tèkuài), slow trains and trains bound for the northeast; most fast trains heading south now depart from Běijīng south train station and Běijīng west train station. Slower trains to Shànghǎi also go from here.

Approximate travel times and typical train fares are as follows:

Dàlián 大连; Z-series, soft sleeper ¥372, 10½ hours (8.27pm)

Dàlián 大连; K-series, hard sleeper ¥239 to ¥244, 12 hours (4.46am and 8.06pm)

Dàtóng 大同; K-series, hard seat ¥99, six hours (2.49am, 10.57am and 3.45pm)

Harbin 哈尔滨; D-series, soft seat ¥306 to ¥313, 10 hours (6.58am, 10.02am, 1.51pm and 3.15pm)

Harbin 哈尔滨; T-series, hard sleeper, ¥261 to ¥268, 12 hours (5.10am, noon, 6.57pm and 9.24pm)

Jílín 吉林; Z-series, hard sleeper ¥244, 12 hours (4.55pm)

Shànghǎi 上海; T-series, soft sleeper ¥476 to ¥879, 14 hours (7.33pm)

The gargantuan **Běijīng West Station** (北京西站, Běijīng Xī Zhàn; ☏ 010 5182 6253; Ⓢ Beijing West Railway Station) accommodates fast Z-series trains, such as the following (fares are soft sleeper unless indicated):

Chángshā 长沙; ¥504, 13 hours (regular)

Fúzhōu 福州; ¥673, 20 hours (2.45pm)

Hànkǒu (Wǔhàn) 汉口; ¥409, 10 hours (11.32am, 5.43pm and 6.02pm)

Kowloon (Hong Kong) 九龙; ¥707 to ¥738, 24 hours (train Q97, 1.08pm)

Lánzhōu 兰州; 7- and T-series, hard sleeper ¥322 to ¥363, 17 hours (five daily)

Nánchāng 南昌; Z-, T- and K-series, hard sleeper ¥296 to ¥322, 11½ hours (eight daily)

Wǔchāng (Wǔhàn) 武昌; T- and K-series, hard sleeper ¥261, 10 hours (seven daily)

Xī'ān 西安; Z- and T-series, hard sleeper ¥214 to ¥268, 11 to 12 hours (six daily)

Other typical train fares for hard sleeper tickets, and travel times:

Chángshā 长沙; T- and K-series, ¥322, 14 hours (regular)

Chéngdū 成都; Z-, I- and K-series, ¥399 to ¥456, 26 to 31 hours (7.53am, 11.32am, 11.46am, 4.32pm and 10.16pm)

Chóngqìng 重庆; T- and K-series, ¥381 to ¥389, 25 to 30 hours (7.16am, 10.31am, 3.12pm and 9.23pm)

Guǎngzhōu 广州; T- and K-series, ¥426, 21 hours (5.15am)

Guìyáng 贵阳; T- and K-series, ¥434 to ¥463, 29 hours (4.10pm, 9.13pm and 9.23pm)

Kūnmíng 昆明; Z-series, ¥536, 38 hours (8.55am and 1.06pm)

Shēnzhèn 深圳; K-series, ¥434, 24 to 29 hours (11.21pm)

Shíjiāzhuāng 石家庄; D-series, 2nd-class seat ¥86, two hours (7.58am, 1.18pm, 3.29pm and 9.16pm)

Ūrümqi 乌鲁木齐; Z-series, ¥536, 34 hours (10am)

Xīníng 西宁; T-series, ¥353, 20 to 24 hours (1.12pm)

Yíchāng 宜昌; G-series, 2nd-class seat ¥605, 21½ hours (8.30am, 9.32am and 12.51pm)

TRAIN TO TIBET

For Lhasa (拉萨, Lāsà) in Tibet (西藏, Xīzàng), the Z21 (hard seat/hard sleeper/soft sleeper ¥360/720/1144, 44 hours) leaves Běijīng west train station at 8.10pm, taking just under two days. In the return direction, the Z22 departs Lhasa at 3.30pm and arrives at Běijīng west train station at 8.20am.

The ultramodern **Běijīng South Station** (北京南站, Běijīng Nánzhàn; [S] Beijing South Railway Station), which is linked to the subway system on Line 4, accommodates very high-speed 'bullet' trains to destinations such as the following:

Fúzhōu 福州; D-series, ¥765 to ¥2389, 15 hours (regular)

Hángzhōu 杭州; G-series, 2nd-class seat ¥538, six hours (regular)

Jǐ'nán 济南; G-series, 2nd-class seat ¥184, 1½ hours (regular)

Nánjīng 南京; G-series, 2nd-class seat ¥443, four hours (regular)

Qīngdǎo 青岛; G-series, 2nd-class seat ¥249 to ¥314, five hours (regular)

Shànghǎi (Hóngqiáo station) 上海虹桥; G-series, 2nd-class seat ¥553, 5½ hours (regular)

Sūzhōu 苏州; G-series, 2nd-class seat ¥523, five hours (regular)

Tiānjīn 天津; C-series, 1st/2nd-class ¥54/93, 30 minutes (regular)

The smaller **Běijīng North Station** (北京北站, Běijīng Běizhàn; [J] 010 5186 6223; [S] Lines 2, 4, 13 to Xizhimen, exit A1) can be accessed from Xizhimen subway station.

Bādǎlǐng Great Wall 八达岭; hard seat ¥6, 75 minutes, regular (6.12am to 1.35pm)

Hohhot 呼和浩特; K-series, hard sleeper ¥72 to ¥222, nine hours (7.29pm and 11.47pm)

🛈 Getting Around

TO/FROM CAPITAL AIRPORT

The **Airport Express** (机场快轨, Jīchǎng Kuàiguǐ; Map p92; 1 way ¥25; [S] Lines 2, 13 to Dongzhimen, exit B), also written as ABC (Airport Běijīng City), is quick and convenient and links terminals 2 and 3 to Běijīng's subway system at Sanyuanqiao station (Line 10) and Dōngzhímén station (Lines 2 and 13). Train times are as follows: Terminal 3 (6.21am to 10.51pm); Terminal 2 (6.35am to 11.10pm); Dōngzhímén (6am to 10.30pm).

There are 17 different routes for the airport **shuttle bus** (机场巴士, Jīchǎng Bāshì; one way ¥15.50-30), including those listed here. They all leave from all three terminals and run from around 5am to midnight. Note that you may have to show a valid photo ID when buying your ticket.

Line 1 To Fāngzhuāng (方庄), via Dàbèiyáo (大北窑) for the CBD (国贸; guó mào)

Line 2 To Xīdàn (西单)

Line 3 To Běijīng train station (北京站; Běijīng Zhàn), via Dōngzhímén (东直门), Dōngsì Shítiáo (东四十条) and Cháoyángmén (朝阳门)

Line 7 To Běijīng west train station (西站; xī zhàn)

Line 10 To Běijīng south train station (南站; nán zhàn)

Coach service to Tiānjīn (天津; ¥82, 2½ hours, hourly 7.30am to 11pm)

A taxi should cost ¥90 to ¥120 from the airport to the city centre; bank on it taking 40 minutes to one hour to get into town. Ignore unofficial drivers who may approach you as you exit customs and join the line for an official cab. When you get into the taxi, make sure the driver uses the meter (打表; dǎ biǎo). Have the name of your hotel written down in Chinese to show the driver. Very few drivers speak any English.

TO/FROM NÁNYUÀN AIRPORT

The shuttle bus (机场巴士; jīchǎng bāshì) goes to Xīdàn (西单; ¥18, 1½ hours, 9am to last flight arrival) via Qiánmén (前门). You can pick up the subway at either destination.

A taxi costs around ¥60 to ¥70 to the Tiān'ānmén Sq area. Ignore drivers who approach you. Use the taxi queue. Make sure the driver uses the meter (打表; dǎ biǎo).

BICYCLE

Cycling is the most enjoyable way of getting round Běijīng. The city is as flat as a mah-jong table and almost every road has a bike lane, even if cars invade them. The quiet, tree-lined hútòng (alleys) are particularly conducive to cycling.

The following are good options for renting bicycles (租自行车; zū zìxíngchē):

Bike Běijīng (p98)

Giant (捷安特, Jié' àntè; Map p80; [J] 010 6403 4537; www.giant.com.cn; 4-18 Jiaodaokou Dongdajie, 交道口东大街4-18号; ⊙9am-7pm; [S] Line 5 to Beixinqiao, exit A)

Natooke (耍 (自行车店), Shuǎ (Zìxíngchē Diàn); Map p80; [J] 010 8402 6925; www. natooke.com; 19-1 Wudaoying Hutong, 五道营胡同19−1号; ⊙11am-7pm; [S] Lines 2, 5 to Yonghegong-Lama Temple, exit D)

Bike stands around the Hòuhǎi Lakes also rent bikes (per hour ¥10). Hostels typically charge ¥30 to ¥50 per day for a standard town bike.

Bike-Sharing Scheme

Běijīng has a bike-sharing scheme for both locals and foreigners. To use the bikes, you must have an ordinary Běijīng travel card (refundable deposit ¥20) that is activated for bike-rental use.

To do that, head to either exit A2 of Tiāntán Dōngmén subway station or exit A of Dōngzhímén subway station. Both desks are only open Monday to Friday from 9.30am to 11.30am and from 2pm to 4pm. You will need your passport and to fill out an English-language application form.

You have to pay a ¥200 deposit to activate the card for bike use, and then ensure it has at least ¥30 on it.

Bike-sharing kiosks are dotted around the city. Swipe your card at one of them to get a bike; then swipe it again when you put it back. Note that when swiping your card, don't remove it until you hear a click. Bike use is free for the first hour, so if you use them cleverly, swapping bikes at another kiosk before your hour is up, it means free bikes. After the first hour, it's ¥1 per hour to begin with, before it starts rising in price to ¥2, ¥3 or ¥4 per hour, depending on how long you keep the bike for.

BUS

Běijīng's buses (公共汽车; gōnggòng qìchē) have always been numerous and cheap (from ¥2), but they're now easier to use for non-Chinese speakers, with swipe cards, announcements in English and bus-stop signs written in pinyin as well as Chinese characters. Nevertheless, it's still a challenge to get from A to B successfully, and the buses are as packed as ever, so you rarely see foreigners climbing aboard.

If you use a travel card, you get 50% discount on all journeys.

Useful Routes

1 Runs along Chang'an Jie, Jianguomenwai Dajie and Jianguomennei Dajie: Sihuìzhàn, Bāwángfén, Yǒngānlǐ, Dōngdān, Xīdān, Mùxīdì, Jūnshì Bówùguǎn, Gōngzhǔfén, Mǎquányíng

4 Runs along Chang'an Jie, Jianguomenwai Dajie and Jianguomennei Dajie: Gōngzhǔfén, Jūnshì Bówùguǎn, Mùxīdì, Xīdān, Tiān'ānmén West, Dōngdān, Yǒngānlǐ, Bāwángfén, Sihuìzhàn

5 Déshèngmén, Diànmén, Běihǎi Park, Xīhuámén, Zhōngshān Park, Qiánmén

15 Běijīng Zoo, Fùxīngmén, Xīdān, Hépíngmén, Liúlíchǎng, Tiānqiáo

20 Běijīng south train station, Tiānqiáo, Dashilar, Tiān'ānmén Sq, Wángfǔjǐng, Dōngdān, Běijīng train station

44 Outer ring Xīzhímén, Fùchéngmén, Fùxīngmén, Chángchūnjiē, Xuānwǔmén, Qiánmén, Tàijíchǎng, Chóngwénmén, Dōngbiánmén, Cháoyángmén, Dōngzhímén, Āndìngmén, Déshèngmén, Xīnjiēkǒu

52 Běijīng west train station, Mùxīdì, Fùxīngmén, Xīdān, Gate of Heavenly Peace, Dōngdān, Běijīng train station, Jiànguómén

103 Běijīng train station, Dēngshìkǒu, China Art Gallery, Forbidden City (north entrance), Běihǎi Park, Fùchéngmén, Běijīng Zoo

332 Běijīng Zoo, Wèigōngcūn, Renmin Daxue, Zhongguancūn, Hǎidiàn, Běijīng University, Summer Palace

These double-decker routes may also be useful:

2 Qiánmén, north on Dongdan Beidajie, Dongsi Nandajie, Dongsi Beidajie, Lama Temple, Zhōnghuá Mínzú Yuán (Ethnic Minorities Park), Asian Games Village

3 Jijia Miao (the southwest extremity of the 3rd Ring Rd), Grand View Garden, Lèyóu Hotel, Jìnguāng New World Hotel, Tuánjiéhú Park, Agricultural Exhibition Center, Lufthansa Center

4 Běijīng Zoo, Exhibition Center, 2nd Ring Rd, Holiday Inn Downtown, Yuètán Park, Fuxingmen Dajie flyover, Qianmen Xidajie, Qiánmén

TRANSPORT IN A NUTSHELL

Bus Very cheap but crowded, slow and difficult for non-Chinese-speakers to use.

Car and motorcycle Challenging and hazardous for foreigners unused to Chinese road conditions and driving.

Cycling Běijīng is flat, making cycling easy, although the roads can be dangerous for cyclists.

Rickshaw Foreigners are routinely overcharged and we do not recommend using them.

Subway Easy to use and the quickest way to get around Běijīng. Trains start running from 5am to 6am and stop at around 11pm.

Taxi Cheap by Western standards, but often snarled in heavy traffic.

CAR & MOTORCYCLE

China does not recognise the International Driving Permit, but it is relatively straightforward to obtain a temporary driving licence that allows you to drive in Běijīng and the surrounding area. The Vehicle Administration Office at Terminal 3 at Běijīng Capital International Airport issues temporary licences, and you can also rent cars at Terminal 3 and other locations around town from Hertz.

A separate licence is needed to drive a motorbike and it is generally not possible to rent motorbikes in Běijīng as the capital, like many Chinese cities, has restrictions on where motorbikes can be driven. No licence is required to drive a scooter, or electric bike, but they are not normally available for hire. Given the relatively low cost of hiring a car with a driver, or a taxi for the day, few visitors self-drive. Some recommended options are listed on p127.

TAXI

Taxis (出租车; chūzūchē) are everywhere, although finding one can be a problem during rush hour, rainstorms and between 8pm and 10pm – prime time for people heading home after eating out.

Flag fall is ¥13, and lasts for 3km. After that it's ¥2 per kilometre. Rates increase slightly at night.

It's rare for drivers to speak any English, so it's important to have the name and address of where you want to go written down in Chinese characters. Remember to keep your hotel's business card on you so you can always get home.

Most Běijīng taxi drivers are honest and use the meter (打表; dǎ biǎo). If they refuse, get out and find another cab. The exception is for long, out-of-town trips to, say, the Great Wall, where prices are agreed (but not paid for) beforehand.

TRAIN (SUBWAY)

Massive and getting bigger every year, with another 12 lines set to be in operation by 2021, the **Běijīng subway system** (地铁, Dìtiě; www.bjsubway.com; per trip ¥3-8; ⏰6am-11pm) is modern, safe, cheap and easy to use. It does get crowded, though. Fares are ¥3 to ¥8, depending on how far you are travelling. Get hold of a travel card (refundable deposit ¥20) if you don't want to queue for tickets each time you travel. The travel card also gets you a 50% discount on all bus journeys within the municipality of Běijīng.

To recognise a subway station (地铁站; *dì tiě zhàn*), look for the subway symbol, which is a blue English capital 'D' with a circle around it.

The Metroman smartphone app reveals the Běijīng subway map in all its ever-expanding glory, with stations listed in both English and Chinese.

AROUND BĚIJĪNG

For the Great Wall and day trips around Beijing, see p124.

Ming Tombs 十三陵

The **Ming Tombs** (Shísān Líng; ☎010 6076 1643; Changchi Lu, Chāngpíng, 昌平区昌赤路; per site ¥20-60, through ticket Nov-Mar ¥100, Apr-Oct ¥135; ⏰8am-5.30pm; 🚌872, [S]Ming Tombs) are the final resting place of 13 of the 16 Ming emperors (the first Ming emperor, Hongwu, is buried in Nánjīng, which means 'Southern Capital' and was the first capital of the Ming dynasty). Billed with the Great Wall as Běijīng's winning double act, the imperial graveyard can be a dormant and lifeless spectacle, unless you pack a penchant for ceremonial tomb architecture or Ming imperial genealogy.

The Ming Tombs follow a standard imperial layout. In each tomb the plan consists of a main gate (祾恩门, *líng'ēn mén*), leading to the first of a series of courtyards and the main hall (祾恩殿; *líng'ēn diàn*). Beyond this lie gates or archways leading to the **Soul Tower** (明楼; Míng Lóu), behind which rises the burial mound (tumulus). Three tombs have been opened to the public: Cháng Líng, Dìng Líng and Zhāo Líng. The road leading up to the tombs is a 7km stretch called the **Spirit Way** (神道, Shéndào; Apr-Oct ¥30, Nov-Mar ¥20; 🚌872). Commencing with a triumphal arch, the path enters the **Great Palace Gate** (大宫门; Dàgōng Mén), where officials once had to dismount, and passes a giant *bìxì* (mythical tortoiselike dragon), which bears the largest **stele** (碑亭, Bēi Tíng; included in Ming Tombs through ticket; 👪) in China. A guard of 12 sets of stone animals and officials ensues.

Sights

Cháng Líng — TOMB

(长陵; ¥45 Apr-Oct/¥30 Nov-Mar, audio guide ¥50; 🚌872) The resting place of the first of the 13 emperors to be buried at the Ming Tombs, Cháng Líng contains the body of Emperor Yongle (1402–24), his wife and 16 concubines. It's the largest, most impressive and most important of the tombs.

Beyond this lie gates leading to the **Soul Tower** (明楼; Míng Lóu), behind which rises the burial mound surrounded by a fortified wall (宝成; *bǎo chéng*). Seated upon a three-tiered marble terrace, the standout structure in this complex is the **Hall of Eminent Favours** (灵恩殿; Líng'ēn Diàn), containing a recent statue of Yongle, various artefacts excavated from Dìng Líng, and a breathtaking interior with vast *nánmù* (cedar wood) columns. As with all three tombs here, you can climb the Soul Tower at the back of the complex for fine views of the surrounding hills.

Dìng Líng — TOMB

(定陵; Apr-Oct ¥60, Nov-Mar ¥40, audio guide ¥50) Dìng Líng, the resting place of Emperor Wanli (1572–1620) and his wife and concubines, is at first sight less impressive than Cháng Líng because many of the halls and gateways have been destroyed. Many of the priceless artefacts were ruined after being left in a huge, unsealed storage room that leaked water. What treasures that were left – including the bodies of Emperor Wanli and his entourage – were looted and burned by Red Guards during the Cultural Revolution.

This is the only tomb where you can climb down into the vast burial chambers. Learn from signs dotted around the tomb how archaeologists found their way in, by following instructions they discovered on a carved tablet.

The small **Museum of the Ming Tombs** (明十三陵博物馆, Míng Shísānlíng Bówùguǎn; incl in Dìng Líng ticket), just inside the complex, contains a few precious remaining artefacts, plus replicas of destroyed originals.

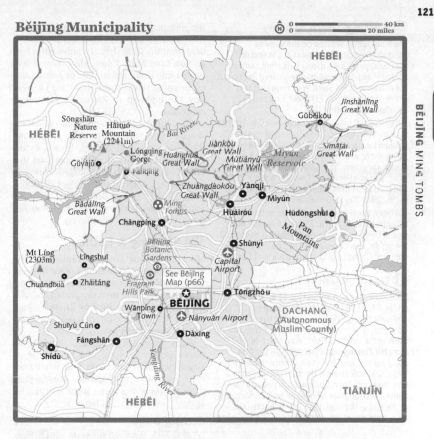

Zhāo Líng TOMB

(昭陵; Apr-Oct ¥30, Nov-Mar ¥20) Zhāo Líng is the smallest of the main three Ming Tombs, and many of its buildings are recent rebuilds. It's much less visited than the others, though, so is more peaceful, and the **fortified wall** (宝成; *bǎo chéng*) surrounding the burial mound is unusual in both its size and form. The tomb, which is the resting place of Emperor Longqing (1537–72), is at the end of the small village of Zhāolíng (昭陵村; Zhāolíng Cūn).

🛏 Sleeping & Eating

There are no hotels or guesthouses in Cháng Líng, Dìng Líng or Zhāo Líng, but you're only a bus ride or a (long) subway trip from central Běijīng, where there are options galore.

For a major attraction, there are surprisingly few eating options in and around the Ming Tombs. Both Dìng Líng and Cháng Líng have a sole restaurant close to their respective ticket offices, and they are your best bet. There are also snack stands at Cháng Líng and you can pick up basic food supplies at a couple of shops in the village of Zhāo Líng.

Nóngjiāfàn Kuàicān CHINESE $

(农家饭快餐; mains ¥18-68; ⊗8.30am-5.30pm) Nóngjiāfàn Kuàicān is a small restaurant in the car park at Dìng Líng (no English sign or menu). Dishes include *xīhóngshì jīdàn miàn* (西红柿鸡蛋面; egg and tomato noodles; ¥18), *zhájiàng miàn* (炸酱面; Běijīng-style pork noodles; ¥20), *huíguō ròu* (回锅肉; spicy cured pork; ¥32), *gōngbào jīdīng* (宫爆鸡丁; spicy chicken with peanuts; ¥24) and *yúxiāng ròusī* (鱼香肉丝; sweet and spicy shredded pork; ¥24).

Míng Cháng Líng Restaurant CHINESE $

(明长陵餐厅, Míng Cháng Líng Cāntīng; Cháng Líng Ming Tomb; dishes from ¥18; ⊗8.30am-4.30pm) Simple but clean restaurant, with an English menu, just beside the Cháng Líng ticket office.

ℹ️ Getting There & Away

The Ming Tombs are now on the subway, although the station is almost at the end of the Chángpíng Line – a long haul from central Běijīng – and is inconveniently located 3km from the entrance to the Spirit Way, requiring you either to take a taxi (¥13) there, or a bus (¥2) and then walk another 1km.

If you're catching the bus, take exit C out of the station, turn right and then turn right again at Nanjian Lu; the bus stop for the 昌53 is around 100m ahead on the right. The 昌 character stands for Cháng, as in Chángpíng. Get off at Jiàntóu Lùkŏu (涧头路口), walk ahead for 200m and then turn left at Changchi Lu; the entrance to the Spirit Way is 10 minutes ahead.

A more direct way to get there is on bus 872 (¥9, one hour, 7.10am to 7.10pm) from the north side of Déshèngmén Gateway (p89). It passes all the sights, apart from Zhāo Líng, before terminating at Cháng Líng. Last bus back is at 6pm.

ℹ️ Getting Around

It's easy to bus-hop around the Ming Tombs. Get off the 872 at **Dà Gōng Mén bus stop** (大宫门), and walk through the triple-arched Great Palace Gate (大宫门) that leads to the Spirit Way. After walking the length of Spirit Way, catch bus 67 from **Hú Zhuāng bus stop** (胡庄) – the first bus stop on your right – to its **terminus** at Zhāo Líng (¥2); walk straight through the village to find the tomb. Then, coming back the way you came, catch another 67 (¥2), or walk (1.5km; left at the end of the road, then left again) to Dìng Líng, from where you can catch bus 314 to Cháng Líng (¥2).

Chuāndĭxià 爨底下

📱 010 / POP 93

Nestled in a valley 90km west of Běijīng and overlooked by towering peaks, the Ming dynasty village of Chuāndĭxià (entrance ¥35) is a gorgeous cluster of historic courtyard homes with old-world charm. The backdrop is lovely: terraced orchards and fields with ancient houses and alleyways rising up the hillside and temples in the surrounding area. Two hours is more than enough to wander around the village because it's not big, but staying the night allows you to soak up its historic charms without the distraction of all those day trippers.

👁 Sights

The main attractions in Chuāndĭxià are the courtyard homes and the cobbled steps and alleyways that link them up. Great fun can be had just wandering the village and pok-

ing your head into whichever ancient doorways take your fancy. Most of the homes date from the Qing dynasty, although a few remain from Ming times. Many have been turned into small restaurants or guesthouses, meaning you can eat, drink tea or even stay the night in a 500-year-old Chinese courtyard.

Chuāndĭxià is also a museum of Maoist slogans, especially up the incline among the better-preserved houses. Look for the very clear, red-painted slogan just past the Landlord's Courtyard (the village's principal courtyard), which reads: 用毛泽东思想武装我们的头脑 (*yòng Máozédōng sīxiǎng wǔzhuāng wǒmen de tóunǎo*; use Mao Zedong thought to arm our minds).

🛏 Sleeping & Eating

More than half the houses in Chuāndĭxià are now guesthouses, so finding a place to sleep isn't a problem (although very few stay open in winter, when the mercury plummets). All the inns can be identified by English signs, even if their owners rarely speak any English. All serve meals too.

Signs are clearly labelled in English, so places are easy to spot. Your best bet is to simply wander round and find what best suits you. Most restaurants have English menus. Specialities here include walnuts, apricots and roast leg of lamb.

Gǔchéngbǎo Inn   INN $
(古城堡客栈, Gǔchéngbǎo Kèzhàn; 📱136 9135 9255; Mon-Thu r ¥120, Fri-Sun ¥180, without bathroom ¥100, mains ¥20-60; ⊙closed Nov-Mar; 🛜) This 400-year-old building is perched high above much of the village and enjoys fine views from its terrace restaurant. Rooms are in the back courtyard and are basic but charming. Each room has a traditional stone *kàng* (raised heated-platform) bed, which sleeps up to four people and can be fire-heated in winter.

The shared bathroom has no shower, but one new room comes with a small one. Gǔchéngbǎo Inn is in the top left-hand corner of the village as you look up from just past the right-hand bend in the road.

Cuànyùn Inn   CHINESE $$
(爨前客栈, Cuànyùn Kèzhàn; 23 Chuāndĭxià Village, 爨底下村23号; mains ¥20-60; ⊙6.30am-8.30pm, closed Nov-Mar; 🛜) The best place to sample roast leg of lamb (烤羊腿, *kǎo yáng tuǐ*; ¥200). On the right of the main road as you enter the village. It has a photo menu.

ℹ Getting There & Away

Bus 892 leaves frequently from a bus stop 400m west of Píngguǒyuán subway station (use exit D and turn right; the bus stop is just past the first big set of traffic lights under the highway) and goes to Zhāitáng (斋堂; ¥15, two hours, 6.30am to 5.50pm), from where you'll have to take a taxi (¥20) for the last 6km to Chuāndǐxià. There's one direct bus to Chuāndǐxià which leaves Píngguǒyuán at 7am. The direct bus back to Píngguǒyuán leaves Chuāndǐxià at 6.50am. There are also two buses from Chuāndǐxià to Zhāitáng (¥2, 9.30am and 3.30pm). The last bus from Zhāitáng back to Píngguǒyuán leaves at 5pm. If you miss that, it's around ¥200 for a taxi.

Wǎnpíng Town 宛平城

♪ 010 / POP 51,346

The star attraction here is the famous 900-year-old Marco Polo Bridge, but the unexpected bonus is the chance to see, at one end of the bridge, the enormous, war-torn, Ming dynasty walls of the once heavily guarded Wǎnpíng Town (Wǎnpíng Chéng). Then there's also the well presented, if clumsily named, Museum of the War of Chinese People's Resistance Against Japanese Aggression.

◎ Sights

Marco Polo Bridge BRIDGE
(卢沟桥, Lúgōu Qiáo; ¥20; ⊘ 7am-8pm Apr-Oct, to 6pm Nov-Mar; ⓢ Changchunjie then 🚍662) Described by the great traveller himself, this 266m-long, multiarched granite bridge is the oldest bridge in Běijīng and is decorated beautifully with 485 individually carved stone lions, each one different. Dating from 1189, although widened in 1969, it spans the Yǒngdìng River, and was once the main route into the city from the southwest.

Despite the praises of Marco Polo, the bridge wouldn't have have rated more than a footnote in Chinese history were it not for the famed Marco Polo Bridge Incident, which ignited a full-scale war with Japan. On 7 July 1937, Japanese troops illegally occupied a railway junction outside Wǎnpíng. Japanese and Chinese soldiers started shooting, and that gave Japan enough of an excuse to attack and occupy Běijīng. Bullet holes from the incident are still visible on the southern wall of the the the Old Town.

Wǎnpíng Old Town WALLS
(宛平城, Wǎnpíng Chéng; ⓢ Dawayao or Changchunjie, then 🚍662) FREE An astonishing sight, given that you are still within the confines of Běijīng's 5th Ring Rd, this double-gated, Ming dynasty walled town is still lived in today. Although few of its original buildings still stand (residents live in newish brick bungalows these days), its 2km-long, 6m-high, battle-scarred town walls date from 1640.

You can't walk on the walls, but you can walk around them or inside; enter via the West Gate, which is beside Marco Polo Bridge, or the East Gate, at the other end of the town's only proper road.

Museum of the War of Chinese People's Resistance Against Japanese Aggression MUSEUM
(中国人民抗日战争纪念馆, Zhōngguó Rénmín Kàng Rì Zhànzhēng Jìniànguǎn; ♪ 010 6377 7088; Chengnei Jie, 城内街; entry with passport free, audio guide ¥120; ⊘ 9am-4.30pm Tue-Sun; ⓢ Dawayao) FREE This modern museum, on the north side of the main road in Wǎnpíng Town, is dedicated to the July 7th Incident (as it's called here) and the ensuing war with Japan. It's obviously biased but some thought has gone into the presentation and there are tons of exhibits and good English captions.

🛏 Sleeping & Eating

There are no hotels or hostels within Wǎnpíng Town, but you're just a subway ride away from central Běijīng, where there are endless sleeping options.

There are a handful of restaurants on Chengnei Jie, the main road, just inside the east gate of Wǎnpíng Town, and a few more just outside it.

Chuān Xiāng Chuān Qíng Shífǔ SICHUAN $$
(川香川情食府; ♪ 010 8389 3301; 1 Chengnei Jie, 城内街1号; dishes ¥22-68; ⊘ 10am-10pm) Reliable and reasonably priced Sìchuān restaurant just inside the east gate of Wǎnpíng Town. It gets busy at lunchtime. No English is spoken, but there is a picture menu.

ℹ Getting There & Away

Bus 662 comes here from Chángchūnjiē subway station (Line 2). Come out of exit A1 and the bus stop is in front of you on the right. Get off the bus at Lú Gōu Xīn Qiáo (卢沟新桥) bus stop (¥2, 40 minutes) then turn right, beside a petrol station, and bear left to follow the road to the Marco Polo Bridge and the West Gate (400m).

Dāwàyáo subway station (Line 14) is about a 1km walk from the East Gate of Wǎnpíng Town. Come out of exit A, turn left at the junction and walk alongside the highway for about 600m before turning right down Chengnei Jie (城内街), which leads to the walls.

The Great Wall

Best Places to Sleep

➡ Commune by the Great Wall (p132)

➡ Brickyard Eco Retreat (p126)

➡ Great Wall Box House (p127)

➡ Zǎoxiāng Yard (p128)

➡ Ténglóng Hotel (p131)

He who has not climbed the Great Wall is not a true man.
Mao Zedong

China's greatest engineering triumph and must-see sight, the Great Wall (万里长城; Wànlǐ Chángchéng) wriggles haphazardly from its scattered Manchurian remains in Liáoníng province to wind-scoured rubble in the Gobi desert and faint traces in the unforgiving sands of Xīnjiāng.

The most renowned and robust examples of the Wall undulate majestically over the peaks and hills of Běijīng municipality, but the Great Wall can be realistically visited in many north China provinces. It is mistakenly assumed that the wall is one continuous entity; in reality, the edifice exists in chunks interspersed with natural defences (such as precipitous mountains) that had no need for further bastions.

Great Wall History

The Great Wall, one of the most iconic monuments on earth, stands as an awe-inspiring symbol of the grandeur of China's ancient history. Dating back 2000-odd years, the Wall snakes its way through 17 provinces, principalities and autonomous regions. But nowhere is better than Běijīng for mounting your assault on this most famous of bastions.

Official Chinese history likes to stress the unity of the Wall through the ages. In fact, there are at least four distinct Walls. Work on the 'original' was begun during the Qin dynasty (221–207 BC), when China was unified for the first time under Emperor Qin Shihuang. Hundreds of thousands of workers, many of them political prisoners, laboured for 10 years to construct it. An estimated 180 million cu metres of rammed earth was used to form the core of this Wall, and legend has it that the bones of dead workers were used as building materials too.

After the Qin dynasty fell, work on the Wall continued during the Han dynasty (206 BC–AD 220). Little more was done until almost 1000 years later, during the Jin dynasty (1115–1234), when the impending threat of Genghis Khan spurred further construction. The Wall's final incarnation, and the one most visitors see today, came during the Ming

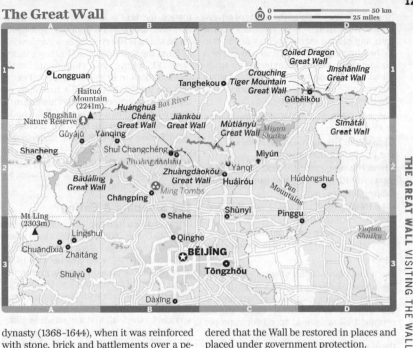

dynasty (1368–1644), when it was reinforced with stone, brick and battlements over a period of 100 years and at great human cost to the two to three million people who toiled on it. During this period it was home to around one million soldiers.

The Wall rarely stopped China's enemies from invading. It was never one continuous structure; there were inevitable gaps and it was through those that Genghis Khan rode in to take Běijīng in 1215.

While the Wall was less than effective militarily, it was very useful as a kind of elevated highway for transporting people and equipment across mountainous terrain. Its beacon tower system, using smoke signals generated by burning wolves' dung, quickly transmitted news of enemy movements back to the capital. But with the Manchus installed in Běijīng as the Qing dynasty (1644–1911) and the Mongol threat long gone, there was little need to maintain the Wall, and it fell into disrepair.

The Wall's decline accelerated during the war with Japan and then the civil war that preceded the founding of the new China in 1949. Compounding the problem, the communists didn't initially have much interest in the Wall. In fact, Mao Zedong encouraged people living near it to use it as a source of free building materials, something that still goes on unofficially today. It wasn't until 1984 that Mao's successor Deng Xiaoping ordered that the Wall be restored in places and placed under government protection.

But classic postcard images of the Wall – flawlessly clad in bricks and undulating over hills into the distance – do not reflect the truth of the bastion today. While the sections closest to Běijīng and a few elsewhere have been restored to something approaching their former glory, huge parts of the Wall are either rubble or, especially in the west, simply mounds of earth that could be anything.

Visiting the Wall

The heavily reconstructed section at Bādálǐng is the most touristy part of the Wall. Mùtiányù and Jīnshānlǐng are also restored sections. These can feel less than authentic, but have the advantage of being much more accessible (with cable cars, handrails etc). Huánghuā Chéng and Zhuàngdàokǒu are part-restored, part-'wild' and offer some short but challenging hikes. Unrestored sections of 'Wild Wall' include Gǔběikǒu and Jiànkòu, but there are many others. All of these can be reached using public transport (you can even get to Bādálǐng by train), although some people choose to hire a car (p127) to speed things up. Staying overnight by the Wall is recommended.

Tours run by hostels, or by specialist tour companies, are far preferable to those run by ordinary hotels or general travel companies.

Not only do they cater to the needs of adventurous Western travellers, they don't come with any hidden extras, such as a side trip to the Ming Tombs (a common add-on) or a tiresome diversion to a gem factory or traditional Chinese medicine centre. The following reputable companies and associations run trips to the Wall that we like.

Bespoke Běijīng (☏ 010 6400 0133; www.bespoke travelcompany.com) High-end trips and tours.

Great Wall Hiking (www.greatwallhiking.com) For locally run hiking trips.

China Hiking (☏ 156 5220 0950; www.chinahik ing.cn) Affordable hiking and camping trips.

Běijīng Hikers (p98)

Bike Běijīng (☏ 010 6526 5857; www.bikebeijing. com) For cycling trips.

Běijīng Sideways (☏ 139 1133 4947; www. beijingsideways.com) For trips in a motorbike sidecar.

You'll find places to stay at some parts of the Wall close to Běijīng – notably Mùtiányù – but most guesthouses and hotels cluster around the more remote sections, where staying overnight allows you to spend some proper time at the Wall. Gǔběikǒu, Jiànkòu, Zhuàngdàokǒu and Huánghuā Chéng all have reasonable sleeping options. Remember, that most places close from November to March.

Bādálǐng can be accessed by both bus and train. You get to Mùtiányù, Jīnshānlǐng, Zhuàngdàokǒu, Gǔběikǒu, Jiànkòu and Huánghuā Chéng by a combination of buses, or a bus and a taxi or minivan. A number of taxi operators make day trips to the Wall, as do some ordinary Běijīng taxi drivers. Agree on the price beforehand.

Mùtiányù 慕田峪

Location 70km from Běijīng

Price Adult ¥45

Hours 7am to 7pm April to October, 7.30am to 6.30pm November to March

Mùtiányù is a recently renovated stretch of Wall that sees a lot of tourists and is fairly easy to reach from Běijīng. It's also well set up for families, with a cable car, a chairlift and a hugely popular toboggan ride. Fewer tour groups come here than go to Bādálǐng, so the crowds are much more manageable.

Famed for its Ming-era guard towers and excellent views, this 3km-long section of wall is largely a recently restored Ming dynasty structure that was built upon an earlier Northern Qi dynasty edifice. With 26 watch-

towers, the wall is impressive and manageable and, although it's popular, most souvenir hawking is reserved to the lower levels.

From the ticket office at Mùtiányù, shuttle buses (¥15 return, 7.20am to 7pm April to October, 8.20am to 6pm November to December) run the 3km to the wall, where there are three or four stepped pathways leading up to the wall itself, plus a **cable car** (缆车, Lǎn Chē; 1 way/return ¥80/100, kids half-price), a **chairlift** (索道, Suǒdào; combined ticket with toboggan ¥80), called a 'ropeway' on the signs here, and a **toboggan ride** (滑道, Huá Dào; 1 way ¥80), making this ideal for those who can't manage too many steps, or who have kids in tow.

🛏 Sleeping & Eating

Brickyard Eco Retreat   GUESTHOUSE $$$
(瓦厂, Wǎ Chǎng; ☏ 010 6162 6506; www.brickyard atmutianyu.com; Běigōu Village, Huáiróu District, 怀柔区渤海镇北沟村; r incl breakfast ¥1040-4746; ✳🛜) 🅿 A 1960s glazed-tile factory renovated into a beautiful guesthouse, sporting lovingly restored rooms, each with views of the Great Wall. Rates include use of a spa, and shuttle services to the Wall and surrounding villages. Brickyard is in Běigōu Village (北沟村; Běigōu Cūn), about 2km from the Mùtiányù Great Wall. Reservations are essential.

Yì Sōng Lóu Restaurant   CHINESE $$
(翼松楼餐厅, Yì Sōng Lóu Cāntīng; mains ¥22-80; ⏱8.30am-5pm) Restaurant up by the main entrance to Mùtiányù Great Wall. It does OK Chinese food.

ℹ Getting to Mùtiányù

Bus From Běijīng's Dōngzhímén Wai bus stand, bus 867 makes a special detour to Mùtiányù twice every morning (¥16, 2½ hours, 7am and 8.30am, 15 March to 15 November only) and returns from Mùtiányù twice each afternoon (2pm and 4pm). Otherwise, go via Huáiróu: from Dōngzhímén Transport Hub (Dōngzhímén Shūniǔzhàn) take bus 916快 (the character is 'kuài', and means 'fast') to Huáiróu (¥11, one hour, 6.30am to 7.30pm). Get off at Míngzhū Guǎngchǎng (明珠广场) bus stop, where private taxis and minivans wait to take passengers to Mùtiányù (per person ¥20, 30 minutes). Note that after around 1pm, you'll probably have to charter your own car or van (¥60 one way). Return minivans start drying up at around 6pm. The last 916快 back to Běijīng leaves Huáiróu at around 7pm. If you miss that, catch a taxi from Huáiróu to Shùnyì subway station (顺义地铁站; Shùnyì Dìtiě Zhàn; about ¥100) on Line 15, or all the way back to Dōngzhímén (¥220).

Taxi A taxi costs around ¥600 to ¥700 for a return day trip from Běijīng.

Gŭběikŏu 古北口

Location 130km from Běijīng
Price through ticket (Great Wall and town) ¥45, town only ¥20

The historic, far-flung town of Gŭběikŏu is just a village these days, but was once an important, heavily guarded gateway into Běijīng from northeast China. The village, split into two sections by a ridge, with the Great Wall running along it and a small tunnel running through it, contains plenty of old courtyard homes (plus lots of rebuilt ones) and half a dozen small temples. Various stretches of the Wall meet in and around the village, in a kind of Great Wall crossroads with lots of hiking options. One short stony stretch of wall dates from the far-off Northern Qi dynasty (AD 550–577). The other stretches are Ming. There are well worn dirt pathways on or beside them, so hiking here isn't as dangerous as it can be at other unrestored sections of the Wall. You should still take great care, though.

There are two main sections of Wall here: the **Coiled Dragon** (蟠龙, Pán Lóng), which runs along the ridge that cuts Gŭběikŏu village in two and which eventually leads to Jīnshānlǐng Great Wall, and **Crouching Tiger Mountain** (卧虎山, Wò Hǔ Shān), on the other side of the Cháo Hé River (walk through the tunnel, cross the river bridge, and follow the steps you'll soon see on your right). Both make for fabulous hiking, although Crouching Tiger is extraordinarily steep. There are other short splintered sections of Wall, like the one that runs down from Coiled Dragon, past Great Wall Box House. The Wall here is less well defined than at other locations across Běijīng, but the scenery is lush, making for pleasant hiking. Pathways along the Coiled Dragon section have yellow spraypaint markers left over from a Great Wall marathon a few years back, so navigation is less confusing than it might otherwise be.

Most guesthouses in Gŭběikŏu, and their attached restaurants, shut down between November and March.

🛏 Sleeping

★ **Great Wall Box House**　GUESTHOUSE $
(团园客栈, Tuán Yuán Kèzhàn; ☑ 010 8105 1123; http://en.greatwallbox.com; No 18 Dongguan, Gŭběikŏu Village, 古北口镇东关甲18号; weekday/weekend incl dinner 6-bed dm ¥180/200, 4-bed ¥180/200, deluxe d ¥1200/1350; ☉ mid-Mar–mid-Nov; ⊜🐕🛜) Run by the friendly, English-speaking Joe, this wonderful place is housed

TAXIS & CAR HIRE

Miles Meng (☑ 137 1786 1403, www.beijing englishdriver.com) Friendly, reliable, English-speaking driver.

Mr Sun (孙先生, Sūn Xiānsheng, ☑ 136 5109 3753) Only speaks Chinese but is dependable and can find other drivers if he's busy. Round trips to the Great Wall from ¥600.

Hertz (赫兹, Hèzī, ☑ 400 888 1336, www. hertz.cn, ☉ 8am-8pm Mon-Fri, 9am-6pm Sat & Sun) Car with driver (代驾; dàijià) from ¥1100 per day.

in a 100-year-old courtyard building that was once an abandoned chessboard factory. Rooms surround a long, garden-courtyard, and are large (the dorm is enormous), bright, comfortable and spotlessly clean. Incredibly, a small, overgrown section of the Great Wall runs along one side of the property.

ⓘ Getting to Gŭběikŏu

Bus Take bus 980快 from Dōngzhímén Transport Hub (Dōngzhímén Shūniǔzhàn) to its terminus at Mìyún bus station (密云汽车站; Mìyún qìchēzhàn; ¥17, 100 minutes, 6am to 8pm). Then, turn right out of the bus station, cross the main road and turn right and walk for 200m to find the stop for bus 25, which runs to Gŭběikŏu (¥10, 70 minutes). To catch the bus back to Mìyún from Gŭběikŏu, walk through the tunnel by the entrance to the village, cross the road and the bus stop is 400m ahead of you. The last bus 25 back to Mìyún leaves at 4.35pm. The last bus 980 back to Dōngzhímén is at 6.30pm.
Taxi Taxis cost ¥1000 to ¥1200 return for a day trip from Běijīng.

Jiànkòu 箭扣

Location 100km from Běijīng
Price ¥25
Hours No official opening hours

For stupefying hikes along perhaps Běijīng's most incomparable section of 'Wild Wall', head to the rear section of the Jiànkòu Great Wall (后箭扣长城; Hòu Jiànkòu Chángchéng), accessible from Xīzhàzi village (西栅子村; Xīzhàzi Cūn), via the town of Huáiróu. Tantalising panoramic views of the Great Wall spread out in either direction from here, as the crumbling brickwork meanders dramatically along a mountain ridge; the setting is truly sublime. But this is completely unrestored wall, so it is both dangerous and, strictly speaking, illegal to hike along it. On summer weekends especially, crowds can render it even more risky. Footwear with very good grip is required, and never attempt to traverse this section in the rain, particularly during thunderstorms.

Xīzhàzi village is actually a collection of five hamlets (*duì*, 队) strung out along a valley. To the left of the valley is a forested ridge, along the top of which runs the Great Wall. You can access the Wall from a number of points along this valley. If you're aiming to hike all the way to Mùtiányù Great Wall, turn left when you hit the Wall. The Wall here has various features that have been given names according to their appearance. They include: the **Ox Horn** (牛角边, Niú Jiǎo Biān; 90 minutes walk to Mùtiányù), which performs a great sweeping, 180-degree u-turn; the **Sharp North Tower** (正北楼, Zheng Bei Lou; 3½ hours to Mùtiányù), which is the highest tower you can view to your left when standing in hamlet No 5; the **Arrow Nock** (剪扣, Jiànkòu; six hours), a low pass in the ridge; and **Upward Flying Eagle** (鹰飞到仰, Ying Fei Dao Yang; nine hours), consisting of three beacon towers, two of which (the wings) stand on the highest point of the mountain above the lower, middle one (the eagle's head).

The H25 bus terminates at the end of the valley road, at hamlet No 5 (五队; *wǔ duì*). From here you can access pathways to Upward Flying Eagle (beyond the village) and Arrow Nock (back towards hamlet No 4). Before the bus gets that far, though, it passes through a decorative archway at the entrance to the valley. Here you'll have to get out to buy an entrance ticket to the scenic area (¥25). Hamlet No 1 (一队; *yī duì*) is just through this archway, to your left. You can walk from here to the Ox Horn in about 90 minutes.

🛏 Sleeping

Zhào Shì Shān Jū   GUESTHOUSE $
(赵氏山居; ☐010 6161 1762, 135 2054 9638; www.jkwall.com; r ¥120-420; ❈📶) The last property in the valley (Hamlet No 5 of Xīzhàzi village), this is a favourite for Chinese hikers (not much English is spoken here and the website is in Chinese only). There is a large shaded terrace dining area with fine Great Wall views. Rooms are neat and clean, and sleep two to seven people. Most have attached bathrooms.

Keep walking along the main road beyond where the bus terminates, and you'll see it up on your right. The food menu (mains ¥20 to ¥60) has photos.

Yáng Èr   GUESTHOUSE $
(杨二; ☐010 6161 1794, 136 9307 0117; Xīzhàzi Village No 1, 西栅子村一队; r ¥120; ❈📶) This is the first village guesthouse you come to as you enter Hamlet No 1 of Xīzhàzi Village. Rooms are set around a vegetable-patch courtyard, and are simple, but have private bathrooms. The food menu (mains ¥25 to ¥50) includes some photos. No English.

ℹ Getting to Jiànkòu

Bus Take bus 916快 from the Dōngzhímén Transport Hub to its terminus at Huáiróu bus station (怀柔汽车站, *Huáiróu qìchēzhàn*; ¥12, 90 minutes, 6.30am to 7.30pm). Turn left out of the station, right at the crossroads and take bus 862 from the first bus stop to Yújiāyuán (于家园; ¥2, five stops), then take the H25 to Xīzhàzi (西栅子; 70 minutes, ¥8). Note, the H25 only runs twice a day; at 11.30am and 4.30pm. The return H25 bus leaves Xīzhàzi at 6.30am and 1.15pm, so you can't do this in a day trip on public transport alone.

Taxi It costs around ¥700 to ¥900 for a return day trip from Běijīng. From Huáiróu to Xīzhàzi village, expect to pay at least ¥120 one way.

Zhuàngdàokǒu   撞道口

Location 80km from Běijīng
Price No entrance fee
Hours No official opening hours

Zhuàngdàokǒu, a small village just over the hill to the east of Huánghuā Chéng, has access to a rarely visited and completely unrestored section of 'Wild Wall'. It's also possible to hike over to Huánghuā Chéng on a restored section from here, although few people do this, which is surprising, considering how straightforward it is. The 'wild' section, towards the reservoir at Shuǐ Chángchéng, is crumbling away and overgrown with small trees and shrubs, but it is still possible to hike along. Just take extreme care.

🛏 Sleeping

Zǎoxiāng Yard   GUESTHOUSE $
(枣香庭院, Zǎoxiāng Tíngyuàn; ☐135 2208 3605; r ¥80-150; 📶) This modest guesthouse is housed in a 70-year-old courtyard building, which has some traditional features such as wooden window frames and paper windowpanes, as well as a terrace to eat on. There are 12 rooms, eight with private bathrooms. The owners are pleasant and the food is decent (mains ¥20 to ¥65; English menu).

It's on your right on the main road, just before where the bus drops you off.

CAMPING ON THE GREAT WALL

Although, strictly speaking, camping on the Great Wall is not allowed, many people do it; some of the watchtowers make excellent bases for pitching tents, or just laying down a sleeping bag. Remember, though; don't light fires and don't leave anything behind. You'll find fun places to camp at Zhuàngdàokǒu, Jiànkòu and Gǔběikǒu.

There are plenty of places to buy camping equipment in Běijīng, but one of the best in terms of quality and choice is **Sanfo** (三夫户外, Sānfū Hùwài; ☑ 010 6201 5550; www.sanfo. com/en; 3-4 Madian Nancun, 北三环中路马甸南村4之3—4号; ⊙ 9am-9pm; Ⓢ Line 10 to Jiandemen, exit D). There are branches across the city, but this location on a side road of the middle section of the North 3rd Ring Rd stands out because it has three outlets side by side, as well as a few smaller cheaper camping shops next door. Turn right out of Exit D of Jiandemen subway station (Line 10) and walk south for about 800m, then cross under the 3rd Ring Rd and the camping shops will be on your right.

There's a smaller, easier-to-get-to **branch** (www.sanfo.com; 9-4 Fuchengmen Dajie, 阜城门大街9—4号; ⊙ 10am-8.30pm; Ⓢ Line 2 to Fuchengmen, exit C), about 200m south of Fuchengmen subway station.

ⓘ Getting to Zhuàngdàokǒu

Bus From Dōngzhímén Transport Hub (Dōngzhímén Shūniǔzhàn) take bus 916快 to Huáiróu (¥12, one hour, 6.30am to 7.30pm). Get off at Nánhuáyuán Sānqū (南花园三区) bus stop, then walk straight ahead about 200m (crossing one road), until you get to the next bus stop, which is called Nánhuáyuán Sìqū (南花园四区). Note that the bus you need, the H21, is not listed on the bus stop. Catch the H21 to Shuǐ Chángchéng (水长城), which stops at Zhuàngdàokǒu (¥8, one hour, every 30 minutes until 6.30pm). The last 916快 bus from Huáiróu back to Běijīng leaves Huáiróu at around 7pm. A taxi from Huáiróu to Zhuàngdàokǒu will cost ¥100.

Taxi A taxi costs around ¥700 to ¥800 for a return day trip from Běijīng.

Jīnshānlǐng 金山岭

Location 142km from Běijīng
Price Summer/winter ¥65/55
Hours 8am to 5pm

The Jīnshānlǐng section of the Great Wall is a completely restored and, in places, very steep stretch, but it's so far from Běijīng that it sees far-fewer tourists than other fully restored sections. It contains some unusual features such as Barrier Walls (walls within the Wall), and each watchtower comes with an inscription, in English, detailing the historic significance of that part of the Wall. The landscape here can be drier and starker than at, say, Jiànkòu or even nearby Gǔběikǒu, but it's arguably more powerful, and it leaves you in no doubt that this is remote territory.

Hiking (in either direction) on the restored section of the Wall here is straightforward. There's an east gate and a west gate (about 2km apart), which means you can do a round

trip (90 minutes) without backtracking; from the east gate, turn right at the Wall to find the west gate, then right again once back down on the road. At the time of writing, though, the east gate was closed, so you can only get onto the Wall from the west gate. If you need it, there's a **cable car** (缆车, Lǎn Chē; 1 way/ return ¥40/80; ⊙ 8am-5pm Apr-Oct, to 4.30pm Nov-Mar) by the west-gate ticket office. If you want to find some unrestored sections, turn right when you hit the Wall and just keep going. This stretch eventually leads to Gǔběikǒu (6½ hours), although you have to leave the Wall for an hour or two in order to walk around the boundary of a small military camp.

🛏 Sleeping & Eating

Accommodation options are limited. There are a few guesthouses strung out along the road that runs between the east gate and west gate. A simple room with bathroom is ¥100 to ¥120. But be prepared for a walk to the ticket office.

There are restaurants around the west gate, and on the road that leads from the east gate to the west gate. Most shut down from November to March. Mains cost from ¥20 to ¥80.

Jīnshān Fànguǎn CHINESE $$
(金山饭馆; West Gate of Jīnshānlǐng Great Wall, 金山岭长城内; dishes ¥20-80; ⊙ 9am-8pm Apr-Oct, to 4pm Nov-Mar) One of the few restaurants by the west gate of Jīnshānlǐng Great Wall that stays open in winter. It has an English menu.

ⓘ Getting to Jīnshānlǐng

A number of hostels in Běijīng run recommended trips by minibus to Jīnshānlǐng for the four-hour hike to Sīmǎtái. Buses usually leave at around 6am or 7am. They drop you at Jīnshānlǐng, then

TOP GREAT WALL HIKES

Zhuàngdàokǒu to Huánghuā Chéng

One hour (plus 20-minute climb to the Wall) It's a mostly restored part of the Wall, and comes with stunning views of the Wall by a reservoir once you reach the summit of your climb. Access the Wall from Zhuàngdàokǒu village; turn right at the end of the village, by the small river, then follow the river (keeping it on your left) before turning right, up the hill between the houses, to climb a stony pathway. When you reach the Wall, turn right and keep going until you reach the last watchtower, where a path to the right leads down to the main road by the reservoir. Don't attempt to descend to the road via the last stretch of Wall here, as it is suicidally steep. You can pick up buses, such as the H14, to Huáiróu from here (until 6pm).

Zhuàngdàokǒu to Shuǐ Chángchéng

Two hours (plus 20-minute climb to the Wall) Climb up to the Wall from Zhuàngdàokǒu village, and turn left at the Wall to be rewarded with this dangerous but fabulous stretch of crumbling bastion. The Wall eventually splits at a corner tower: turn left. Then, soon after you reach another tower from where you can see the reservoir far below you, the Wall crumbles down the mountain, and is impassable. Instead of risking your life, take the path that leads down to your left, just before the tower. This path eventually links up with the Wall again, but you may as well follow it all the way down to the road from here, where you'll be able to catch the H21 bus back to Huáiróu from the lower one of the two large car parks.

The Coiled Dragon Loop

2½ hours This scenic but manageable hike starts and finishes in the town of Gǔběikǒu and follows a curling stretch of the Wall known as the Coiled Dragon. From the Folk Customs Village (the southern half of Gǔběikǒu), walk up to the newly reconstructed **Gǔběikǒu Gate** (古北口关, Gǔběikǒu Guān) but turn right up a dirt track just before the gateway. You should start seeing yellow-painted blobs, left over from an old marathon that was run here: follow them. The first section of Wall you reach is a very rare stony stretch of **Northern Qi Dynasty Wall** (1500 years old). It soon joins up with the Ming dynasty bricked version, which you should continue to walk along (although at one stage, you need to follow yellow arrows down off the Wall to the left, before rejoining it later). Around 90 minutes after you set off, you should reach a big sweeping right-hand bend in the Wall (the coil), with three towers on top. The first and third of these towers are quite well preserved, with walls, windows and part of a roof (great for camping in). At the third tower (called **Jiangjun Tower**),

pick you up four hours later in Sīmǎtái. The entire journey from Běijīng and back takes up to 12 hours. Expect to pay around ¥300 per person.

Bus From April to November, direct buses run from Wàngjīng West subway station (Line 13) to the Jīnshānlǐng ticket office. Come out of Exit C of the subway station and look over your right shoulder to see the red sign for the 'Tourist Bus to Jīnshānlǐng Great Wall' (金山岭长城旅游班车; Jīnshānlǐng Chángchéng lǚyóu bānchē) on the other side of the road. The bus leaves at 8am and returns to Běijīng at 3pm (¥32, 100 minutes). Otherwise, catch a bus to Luánpíng (滦平; ¥32, 90 minutes, 7.30am to 4pm) from the forecourt behind the red sign for the tourist bus, which will drop you at a service station on the highway close to Jīnshānlǐng. Taxis wait at the bus drop-off to drive the 9km to the west gate (¥100). If you want them to wait, expect to pay ¥200. Buses return to Běijīng from the service station. The last bus back leaves at 4.20pm.

Taxi A taxi costs around ¥1000 to ¥1200 for a return day trip from Běijīng.

Huánghuā Chéng 黄花城

Location 77km from Běijīng
Price ¥3 (unofficial)
Hours No official opening hours

Less touristy than other parts of the Great Wall close to Běijīng, Huánghuā Chéng is an extremely rewarding, and impossibly steep, section of the Wall. Undulating across the hillsides of a small reservoir and offering spectacular views of the surrounding area, it has undergone only partial restoration and is refreshingly free of the hawkers who can make visits to other sections a trying experience. There are good opportunities for hikes too.

Strikingly free of crowds, Huánghuā Chéng allows visitors to admire this classic and well preserved example of Ming defence, with its high and wide ramparts, intact parapets and sturdy beacon towers, in relative isolation. The patchy and periodic restoration work on

turn left, skirting right around it, then walk down the steps before turning right at a point marked with a yellow 'X' (the marathon went straight on here). Follow this pathway all the way back to Gǔbèikǒu (30 minutes), turning right when you reach the road.

Jiànkòu to Mùtiányù

Two hours (plus one-hour climb to the Wall) Unrivalled for pure Wild Wall scenery, the Wall at Jiànkòu is very tough to negotiate. This short stretch, which passes through the 180-degree u-turn known as the Ox Horn, is equally hairy, but it soon links to an easier, restored section at Mùtiányù. Access the Wall from hamlet No 1 in Xīzhàzi village (西栅子村一队, Xīzhàzi Cūn Yīduì). It takes an hour to reach the Wall from the village; from the sign that says 'this section of the Great Wall is not open to the public', follow a narrow dirt path uphill and through a lovely pine forest. When you reach a small clearing, go straight on (and down slightly), rather than up to the right. Later, when you hit the Wall, turn left. You'll climb/clamber up to, and round, the Ox Horn before descending (it's very slippery here) all the way to Mùtiányù, where cable cars, toboggan rides and transport back to Běijīng await.

Gǔbèikǒu to Jīnshānlǐng

6½ hours This daylong adventure takes in some ancient stone Wall, some crumbling unrestored brick Wall and some picture-perfect, recently renovated Wall, as well as a 90-minute detour through the countryside. Bring plenty of water and enough food for lunch. Follow the first part of our Coiled Dragon Loop hike, but instead of leaving the Wall just after **Jiangjun Tower**, continue along the Wall for another hour until you reach the impressive **24-Window Tower** (there are only 15 windows left these days). Here, follow the yellow arrows off the Wall, to avoid a military zone up ahead, and walk down through the fields for about 25 minutes. Take the first right, at another yellow arrow, beside a vegetable plot, and climb the path back towards the Wall. After about half an hour you'll pass **Qing Yun Farmhouse**, where you may be able to buy food and drinks (but don't bank on it). It's a 25-minute climb up to the Wall from here (at the fork, the left path is easier). At the Wall, walk through the cute doorway to get up around the other side of the tower, then continue along the Wall to the restored section at Jīnshānlǐng. You'll have to buy a ticket from someone at **Xiliang Zhuandao Tower**, from where it's about 30 minutes to **Little Jinshan Tower** (for the path, or cable car, down to the west gate), or about 90 minutes to **East Tower with Five Holes** (for the path down to the east gate, from where it's a 30-minute walk to the bus back to Běijīng).

the Wall here has left its crumbling nobility and striking authenticity largely intact, with the ramparts occasionally dissolving into rubble and some of the steps in ruins.

From the road, you can go either west (left) towards Zhuàngdàokǒu or east (right) up the stupidly steep section, which rises from the reservoir and eventually leads to Jiànkòu (after about two days). For the eastern route, cross the small dam, pay the enterprising local who sells unofficial ¥3 entrance tickets, and follow the path beside the reservoir. Walk up the steps just after the small shop-cum-cafe until you reach a metal ladder which is used to access the Wall. The Wall climbs abruptly uphill through a series of further watchtowers before going over, dipping down, then climbing again, even more steeply than before.

To head west, climb the path that leads up to the Wall from behind Ténglóng Hotel and which ends at a watchtower which leads onto the Wall itself. The Wall on this side of the road is almost as steep as on the eastern side and, in places, equally smooth and slippery. The views from the top are stunning, though, and you can continue from here to Zhuàngdàokǒu village (45 minutes); turn left off the Wall at its lowest point.

🛏 Sleeping

Ténglóng Hotel   GUESTHOUSE **$**
(滕龙饭店, Ténglóng Fàndiàn; ☏ 010 6165 1929; r with/without bathroom ¥120/60; 🕾) One of a number of small guesthouses in Huánghuā Chéng. Most are on the river side of the road, but this friendly place, accessed via steps on your left just before the Wall, clings to the hillside on the other side and offers fine views of the Wall. Rooms are basic, but clean and sleep three to four people.

No English is spoken, but the restaurant, with terrace seating, has an English menu (mains ¥20 to ¥60).

ℹ️ Getting to Huánghuā Chéng

Bus From Dōngzhímén Transport Hub (Dōngzhímén Shūniǔzhàn) take bus 916快 to Huáiróu (¥12, one hour, 6.30am to 7.30pm). Get off at Nánhuáyuán Sānqū (南花园三区) bus stop, then walk straight ahead about 200m (crossing one road), until you get to the next bus stop, called Nánhuáyuán Siqū (南花园四区). From here take the H14 bound for Èr Dào Guān (二道关) and get off at Huánghuā Chéng (¥8, one hour, until 6.30pm). It only runs about once an hour; taxi drivers hover by the bus stop to test your patience (¥100 one way). Returning from Huánghuā Chéng, you can catch either the H14 or the H21, which passes the bus station in Huáiróu, where the 916快 originates. The last 916快 from Huáiróu back to Běijīng leaves Huáiróu at around 7pm.

Taxi A taxi is around ¥700 to ¥800 return for a day trip from Běijīng.

Bādálǐng   八达岭

Location 70km from Běijīng
Price Apr–Oct ¥40, Nov–Mar ¥35
Hours Summer 6am–7pm, winter 7am–6pm

The mere mention of Bādálǐng sends a shudder down the spine of hard-core Wall walkers, but this is the easiest part of the Wall to get to – you can even get here by train – and as such, if you are really pushed for time, this may be your only option. You'll have to put up with huge crowds of domestic tourists, a lot of souvenir hawkers and a Wall that was completely renovated in the 1980s and so lacks a true sense of historical authenticity. But the Bādálǐng Wall is highly photogenic, authentically steep, has good facilities (restaurants, disabled access, cable cars etc) and can be visited on a half-day trip from Běijīng.

Běijīng's most visited chunk of brick-clad bastion ticks all the iffy Great Wall boxes in one flourish: souvenir stalls, T-shirt flogging hawkers, restaurants, heavily restored brickwork, little authenticity, guardrails and mobs of sightseers. On the plus side, the scenery is raw and striking and the Wall, which snakes off in classic fashion into the hills, is extremely photogenic. It dates to Ming times (1368–1644), but underwent particularly heavy restoration work during the 1950s and 1980s, when it was essentially rebuilt.

The **China Great Wall Museum** (中国长城博物馆, Zhōngguó Chángchéng Bówùguǎn; included with ticket to Bādálǐng section of Wall; ⊙9am–4pm Tue–Sun; 🚌877) offers a comprehensive history of the Wall, from its origins as an earthen embankment in the far-off Qin dynasty (221–207 BC) to the Ming-era battlements you see today. There are decent English captions and it's a good way to get a sense of just how astonishing and extensive a structure the Wall is. The museum is just south of the east car park.

There is a **cable car** (缆车, Lǎn Chē; 1 way/return ¥80/100; ⊙8am–4.30pm) from the bottom of the west car park, and a **toboggan ride** (¥80/100 one-way/return; called a 'sliding car' on the signs here), which descends to the east car park. There is also disabled access. ATMs can be found in the west car park.

🛏️ Sleeping & Eating

Commune by the Great Wall LUXURY HOTEL **$$$**
(长城脚下的公社, Chángchéng Jiǎoxià de Gōngshè; ☎010 8118 1888; www.communebythegreatwall.com; r from ¥2500; ✳@🛜❄) Positioned at the Shuǐguān Great Wall off the Badaling Hwy, the Commune may have a proletarian name but the design and presentation are purely for the affluent. There is a kids club. Reservations are essential.

Àtài Bāozi CHINESE **$**
(阿泰包子; ¥20-32; ⊙7am–4pm) Just up from the east car park at Bādálǐng, this place has a picture menu and does OK dumplings, as well as rice and noodle dishes.

ℹ️ Getting to Bādálǐng

The 877 bus (¥12, one hour, 6am to 5pm) leaves for Bādálǐng from the northern side of the Déshèngmén Gateway (p89), about 400m east of Jīshuǐtán subway station. It goes to the east car park at Bādálǐng. From there, walk uphill a little, turn left through a covered souvenir-shop strip, then left again at the end and uphill to the ticket office, which is between two large fortified archways. Buses return to Běijīng from just south of where they drop you: you'll see the queue of people waiting for them. The last bus back leaves at 5pm (4.30pm November to March).

Expect to pay around ¥600 to ¥700 for a round-trip taxi.

Getting here by train is the cheapest and most enjoyable option. Bādálǐng train station is a short walk downhill from the west car park; come out of the train station and turn left for the Wall (about 1km).

Trains (¥6, 70 to 80 minutes) leave from Běijīng north train station (p118), which is connected to Xīzhímén subway station, at the following times from Tuesday to Thursday: 6.12am, 8.34am, 10.57am and 12.42pm; and at the following times from Friday to Monday: 6.12am, 7.58am, 9.02am, 10.57am and 1.14pm and 1.35pm.

On your return, trains leave from Bādálǐng train station at 1.40pm, 3.08pm, 5.30pm, 7.34pm and 9.33pm (Tuesday to Thursday); 1.33pm, 3.43pm, 4.14pm, 5.30pm, 7.55pm and 9.31pm (Friday to Monday).

Tiānjīn & Héběi

Best Places to Eat

➡ Lerthai Center (p143)

➡ Dà Qīng Huā (p152)

➡ Hànná Shān Kǎoròu (p152)

Best Places to Sleep

➡ Qǐ Wàng Lóu (p151)

➡ Holiday Inn (p143)

➡ Děngfēnglái Youth Hostel (p142)

Why Go?

Běijīng's breadbasket, Héběi (河北) is a slow-moving panorama of grazing sheep, brown earth and fields of corn and wheat. Cosmopolitan Tiānjīn may put on a dazzling show, but the true charms of this region are its time-worn, earthy textures and its deep-rooted historical narrative.

Héběi offers the ideal chance to disengage from Běijīng's modernity and frantic urban tempo, and experience a more timeless China without having to travel too far. Wander through ancient settlements and walled towns, skirt the wild edges of the former Manchuria and journey to the majestic 18th-century summer retreat of the Qīng emperors in Chéngdé.

There are temples to explore, rarely visited stretches of the Great Wall and remote towns and villages whose ancient rhythms and rural seclusion make them the perfect retreats for those prepared to venture slightly off the beaten track.

When to Go

Tiānjīn

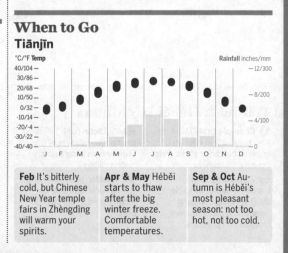

Feb It's bitterly cold, but Chinese New Year temple fairs in Zhèngdìng will warm your spirits.

Apr & May Héběi starts to thaw after the big winter freeze. Comfortable temperatures.

Sep & Oct Autumn is Héběi's most pleasant season: not too hot, not too cold.

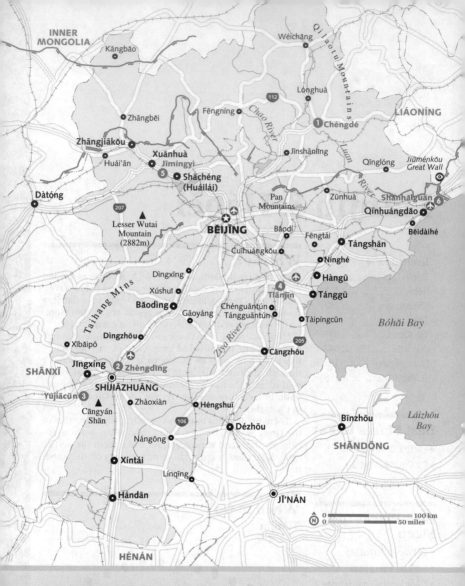

Tiānjīn & Héběi Highlights

1 Chéngdé (p147) Visiting the staggering collection of imperial buildings at the Qing dynasty's summer resort.

2 Zhèngdìng (p145) Exploring the remarkable, 1500-year-old Lóngxìng Temple and other ancient temples and pagodas.

3 Yújiācūn (p147) Walking the cobbled streets of this little-known Ming dynasty 'stone village'.

4 Tiānjīn (p135) Enjoying the cultural riches of the former foreign concession port.

5 Jīmíngyì (p155) Venturing off the beaten track to China's oldest surviving postal station.

6 Shānhǎiguān (p152) Hiking the crumbling, less visited stretches of the Great Wall outside this Ming garrison town.

ℹ Getting There & Around

Běijīng and Tiānjīn both have international airports and are the most convenient bases for exploring Héběi. Shíjiāzhuāng is also a well connected transport hub. High-speed bullet trains will whizz you between cities, but buses are best for reaching smaller towns and villages.

TIĀNJĪN 天津

♪ 022 / POP 10.9 MILLION

Forever being compared to Běijīng (if anything, it's more like Shànghǎi), the former foreign concession port of Tiānjīn is a large, booming, yet laid-back city, with a pleasant river promenade and some charming, European-flavoured neighbourhoods. It's an easy day trip from the capital, but you may want a long weekend to explore the city properly.

History

Tiānjīn rose to prominence as a grain-storage point during the Mongol Yuan dynasty. The city found itself at the intersection of both inland and port navigation routes, and by the 15th century the town had become a walled garrison.

During the foreign concession era, the British and French settled in, joined by the Japanese, Germans, Austro-Hungarians, Italians and Belgians between 1895 and 1900. Each concession was a self-contained world, with its own prison, school, barracks and hospital. During the Boxer Rebellion, the foreign powers levelled the walls of the old Chinese city.

In August 2015 a series of massive chemical explosions – the largest was the equivalent of 430 tonnes of TNT – decimated the Tiānjīn container port, roughly 47km west of the city. In total, 173 people died and an estimated US$6 billion dollars in insurance claims have been filed. Much of the infrastructure around the port, including the western end of metro line 9, remains closed.

◎ Sights

Tiānjīn has a growing number of first-rate cultural venues, though they are fairly spread out. Top on the list for visitors are the Wǔdàdào and Old Town neighbourhoods. The Tiānjīn Museum, though a bit far from the city centre, is also an excellent destination. Architecture buffs can stroll along Jiefang Beilu, the treaty port's former banking street.

★ **Tiānjīn Museum** MUSEUM
(www.tjbwg.com; 62 Pingjiang Lu, 平江道62号; ◎9am-4.30 Tue-Sun) FREE Tiānjīn's premier cultural venue, this three-floor museum has over 200,000 pieces in its collection, ranging from oracle bones and an excellent inkstone exhibit to various artefacts and documents related specifically to the city's historical development. The 3rd floor, which focuses on Tiānjīn's development as a modern city from the Opium War onward, is a highlight.

Part of a cultural complex that includes a handful of other museums, this area is located well south of the city centre. At the time of writing, the easiest way here was to take the metro to the Nanlou station (line 1) and then take a taxi (¥10). However, new lines 5 and 6 will both stop here once they are complete.

Treaty Port Area ARCHITECTURE
(Jiefang Beilu, 解放北路) South of the station across Liberation Bridge was the British concession. The rebuilt riverside facade is an impressive sight at night, but walk further south along Jiefang Beilu to see original, imposing, hundred-year-old European buildings, which once housed the city's international banks. Names are posted on plaques outside each building; many still house banks today. One building of particular note is the **former Qing dynasty post office** (109 Jiefang Beilu, 解放北路109号) FREE, which now has a historic stamp collection on display.

Mínyuán Plaza STADIUM
(民园广场, Mínyuán Guǎngchǎng; 83 Chongqing Dao, 重庆道83号; ◎8.30am-6.30pm) The centrepiece of the Wǔdàdào neighbourhood, Mínyuán Plaza was rebuilt in 2012 on the site of a 90-year-old stadium that was originally designed by former British Olympian

---

PRICE INDICATORS

Sleeping
Prices given are for a double room.
$ less than ¥250
$$ ¥250–¥500
$$$ more than ¥500

Eating
Prices given are for a meal for one.
$ less than ¥40
$$ ¥40–¥80
$$$ more than ¥80

Eric Liddell. It now functions as a giant park of sorts – you can still run laps if you want – with a visitors center, two small museums (of limited interest), and a host of cafes and restaurants.

China House
MUSEUM

(瓷房子, Cí Fángzi; 72 Chifeng Dao, 赤峰道72号; ¥35; ⊙9am-6pm) Tiānjīn's tackiest sight by a long shot, the China House is Zhang Lianzhi's ode to both porcelain and questionable taste. Vases and mosaic-like shards are embedded in every conceivable vertical surface here, making for a truly bizarre facade. Snap your selfie from the outside and move on – the interior is essentially more of the same.

St Joseph's Church
CHURCH

(西开天主教堂, Xīkāi Tiānzhǔ Jiàotáng; Binjiang Dao, 滨江道; ⊙5.30am-4.30pm Mon-Sat, 5am-8pm Sun) Erected by the French in 1917, this domed Catholic church is the largest church in Tiānjīn. Its fine brick exterior is a marked contrast to the shopping malls surrounding it; the interior is more decorative than most Chinese churches.

Folk Art Museum
MUSEUM

(民俗博物馆, Mínsú Bówùguǎn; Tianhou Temple exit; ⊙9am-4pm Tue-Sun; Ⓜ Dongnanjiao) FREE You know all those souvenirs for sale on the Ancient Culture Street (p137)? Well, this collection of handicrafts is the real deal – historic clothing, paintings, ceramics and even an enormous abacus. It's located just past the exit of the Tianhou Temple, up a flight of stairs on your left. No English.

Tiānhòu Temple
TEMPLE

(天后宫, Tiānhòu Gōng; Ancient Culture Street, 古文化街; ¥10; ⊙8.30am-4.30pm Tue-Sun) This busy temple, with its healthy mix of Taoist, Buddhist and Confucian deities, is dedicated to Tianhou (Empress of Heaven). Goddess of the sea and the protector of sailors, she is also popularly known as Mazu and Niangniang. The main hall is the Niangniang Palace, which features an effigy of Tianhou in a glass case, flanked by ferocious-looking weapons and attendant monsters.

Also look for the small Folk Art Museum (p136), just past the temple's exit on the left and up a flight of stairs.

Monastery of Deep Compassion
BUDDHIST TEMPLE

(大悲禅院, Dàbēi Chányuàn; 40 Tianwei Lu, 天纬路40号; ¥5; ⊙9am-6pm Apr-Oct, to 4pm Nov-Mar) Tiānjīn's most important Buddhist temple was built in three stages from 1436 to 1734. While most of the architecture has since been rebuilt, it's a very large and active place and enthralling to wander. Don't miss the huge, multi-armed statue of Guanyin (the Buddhist Goddess of Mercy) – whose eyes seem to follow you around – standing in the Great Compassion Hall in a side courtyard. Admission includes three incense sticks; pick them up to the right of the Hall of Heavenly Kings.

The monastery is close to the **Tiānjīn Eye** (天津之眼, Tiānjīn Zhī Yǎn; Yongle Qiao, 永乐桥; adult/child ¥70/35; ⊙9.30am-9.30pm Tue-Sun, 5-9.30pm Mon), on the east side of the river.

ERIC LIDDELL

Olympic champion, rugby international and devout Christian, Scotsman Eric Liddell is best known as the subject of the 1981 Oscar-winning film *Chariots of Fire,* but few know about his connection to Tiānjīn. He was born here in 1902 before being educated in Scotland; he then embarked on a short but astonishing sporting career. He was capped seven times by the Scotland rugby union team and won gold in the 400m at the 1924 Paris Olympics. Famously, he pulled out of his favoured event – the 100m – because, as a Christian, he refused to run on a Sunday. A year later, he returned to Tiānjīn to follow his true passion as a Christian missionary, and he stayed in China until his death in 1945 in a Japanese internment camp in Shāndōng province.

While in Tiānjīn, he lived at 38 Cambridge Rd – now **Chongqing Dao** (李爱锐旧居, Lǐ Àiruì Jiùjū; 38 Chongqing Dao, 重庆道38号); look for the plaque – and he helped build the Mínyuán Stadium, also in Cambridge Road, in 1926. It's said that he based its design on Stamford Bridge (Chelsea Football Club's home ground and his favourite running track back in Britain). The stadium was demolished in 2012 before being reincarnated as **Mínyuán Plaza** (p135). It still has a running track (which is free to use), but the building itself is now a leisure and restaurant complex from where tourists can rent bicycles or hop on horse-drawn carriages for tours of the surrounding concession-era streets.

Guǎngdōng Guild Hall   HISTORIC BUILDING
(广东会馆, Guǎngdōng Huìguǎn; 31 Nanmenli Dajie, 南门里大街31号; ¥10; ⊙9am-4.30pm; Ⓜ Gulou)
The Guǎngdōng Guild Hall (1907) is one of the few buildings of any genuine age in the Old Town. It's a lovely courtyard complex, centered on a beautiful, ornate, wooden hall where popular Peking opera performances are held on Sunday afternoons (¥20 to ¥50, 2.30 to 4pm). Don't miss poking your head into the back courtyard, with its fading murals by the south entrance. It's opposite the Drum Tower, to the southeast.

Confucius Temple   CONFUCIAN TEMPLE
(文庙, Wén Miào; 1 Dongmennei Dajie, 东门内大街 1号; ¥30; ⊙9am-4.30pm Tue-Sun; Ⓜ Dongnanjiao)
Tiānjīn's quiet Confucius Temple is actually a two-for-one, with the provincial temple on the east side (dating from 1436) and the county temple on the west side (dating from 1734). Although most everything has been rebuilt, the county side has some exhibits on the history and main tenets of Confucianism, all set to *qin* music flowing beneath the cypress trees.

Shi Family Residence   HISTORIC BUILDING
(石家大院, Shí Jiā Dàyuàn; 47 Yangliuqing Guyi Jie, 杨柳青估衣街47号; ¥27; ⊙9am-5pm Apr-Oct, to 4.30pm Nov-Mar) The marvellous Shi family residence is a vast warren of courtyards and enclosed gardens. Formerly belonging to a prosperous merchant family, the restored residence (originally built in 1875) contains a theatre and 278 rooms, some of which are furnished. It's in Yángliǔqīng suburb, 20km west of central Tiānjīn. Take bus 153 (¥2, 90 minutes) from Tiānjīn's west train station, which is on the metro. A taxi can also get you there for about ¥70 one way.

🏃 Activities

Bicycle Rental   CYCLING
(租自行车, Zū Zìxíngchē; Mínyuán Plaza, 民园广场; cycle hire per day ¥15; ⊙8.30am-6.30pm) The quiet, tree-lined streets of Wǔdàdào are ideal for cycling. Rent bikes for the day at the visitor center in the Mínyuán Plaza (p135).

Hǎi River Boat Tours   BOATING
(per person day/evening ¥80/100; ⊙9am-5pm, 7.30pm & 8.30pm) Cruises along the Hǎi River are very popular, especially at night. There are three main boat docks: by the main train station (p142), by Ancient Culture Street and by the Tiānjīn Eye. During the day you can get on and off, but at night you'll only be allowed to disembark where you got on. The round trip takes about 50 minutes.

OLD TOWN
Originally enclosed by a wall, Tiānjīn's reconstructed Old Town has two main tourist areas: the rebuilt **Drum Tower** (鼓楼, Gǔ Lóu; Chengxiang Zhonglu, 城厢中路; ⊙9am-11.30am & 1.30-4.30pm; Ⓜ Gulou) **FREE**, formerly the town centre; and the pedestrian **Ancient Culture Street** (古文化街, Guwenhua Jie; Ⓜ Dongnanjiao), nearly 1km west, which is packed with souvenirs and shoppers.

Horse-Drawn Carriages   TOURS
(马车, Mǎ Chē; Minyuan Plaza, 民园广场; per person ¥80) These horse-drawn-carriage rides offer a 25-minute tour of Wǔdàdào; they're much more of a draw for Chinese tourists, though. The horses appear to be treated fairly.

✪ Festivals & Events

Great Wall Marathon   SPORTS
(www.great-wall-marathon.com; ⊙May) This certifiably insane adventure marathon includes 5164 steps along a gorgeous (and very steep) Huángyáguān stretch of the Great Wall, 150km from Tiānjīn. If you're not a glutton for punishment, no need to do the full thing: a half-marathon and 8.5km fun run are held on the same day.

🛏 Sleeping

Tiānjīn has a good selection of midrange and luxury hotels. Budget accommodation fills up fast, however – make reservations well in advance.

★ Three Brothers Youth Hostel   HOSTEL $
(戈萨国际青年旅舍, Gēsà Guójì Qīngniánlǚshè; ☏022 2723 9777; gesahostel@163.com; 141 Chongqing Dao, 重庆道141号; dm ¥60-100, d ¥238; ✳@☎; ☐951 to Guilin Lu) Friendly hostel, with a laid-back atmosphere and a pleasant location right in the middle of historic Wǔdàdào. The small, covered front yard of the 90-year-old building has been turned into a cafe area; simple but clean rooms are upstairs at the back. Take bus 951 from the main train station and get off at Guilin Lu, which intersects Chongqing Dao.

Cloudy Bay Hostel   HOSTEL $
(云雾之湾, Yúnwù Zhīwān; ☏022 2723 0606; cloudybayhostel@hotmail.com; 120 Harbin Dao, 哈尔滨道120号; dm ¥60-100; Ⓜ Heping Rd) Young and friendly, Cloudy Bay is housed in a four-storey building that's been renovated

Central Tiānjīn

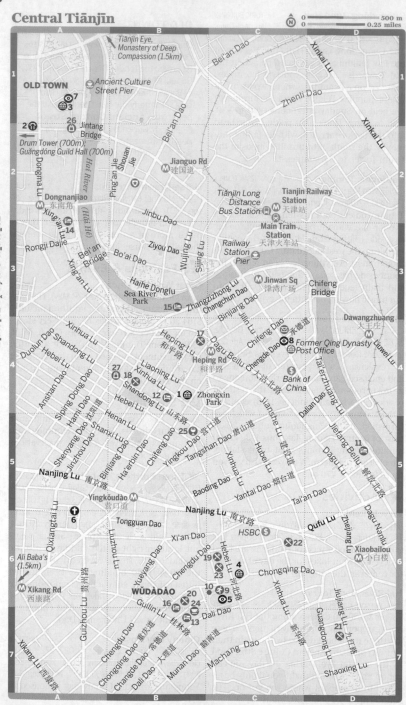

OLD TOWN

Tiānjīn Eye,
Monastery of Deep
Compassion (1.5km)

Bei'an Dao

Ancient Culture
Street Pier

Jintang
Bridge

Drum Tower (700m);
Guǎngdōng Guild Hall (700m)

Jianguo Rd
建国道

Jinbu Dao

Ziyou Dao

Tiānjīn Long
Distance
Bus Station

Tianjin Railway
Station
天津站

Main Train
Station
天津火车站

Railway
Station
Pier

Dongnanjiao
东南角

Xing'an Lu

Rongji Dajie

Bei'an
Bridge

Bo'ai Dao

Haihe Donglu

Sea River
Park

Zhangzizhong Lu

Changchun Dao

Binjiang Dao

Jinwan Sq
津湾广场

Chifeng
Bridge

Dawangzhuang
大王庄

Xinhua Lu

Shandong Lu

Duolun Dao

Hebei Lu

Anshan Dao

Siping Dong Dao

Hami Dao

Shenyang Dao

Jinzhou Dao

Shanxi Luo

Binjiang Dao

Ha'erbin Dao

Henan Lu

Hebei Lu

Shandong Lu

Xinhua Lu

Liaoning Lu

Heping Lu
和平路

Heping Rd
和平路

Dagu Beilu

Chengde Dao

Chifeng Dao

Former Qing Dynasty
Post Office

Bank of
China

Zhongxin
Park

Chifeng Dao

Yingkou Dao

Tangshan Dao

Xinhua Lu

Hubei Lu

Jianshe Lu 建设道

Dalian Dao

Tai'erzhuang Lu

Juwei Lu

Jielang Beilu

Dagu Lu

Baoding Dao

Yantai Dao 烟台道

Tai'an Dao

Nanjing Lu
南京路

Yíngkǒudào
营口道

Nanjing Lu
南京路

Qufu Lu

Xiaobailou
小白楼

Ali Baba's
(1.5km)

Xikang Rd
西康路

Tongguan Dao

Xi'an Dao

Chengdu Dao

HSBC

Chongqing Dao

Qixiangtai Lu

Liuzhou Lu

Yueyang Dao

Chengdu Dao

Hebei Lu 河北路

Xinhua Lu

Zhejiang Lu

Jiujiang Lu 九江路

Guangdong Lu

WǓDÀDÀO

Guilin Lu 桂林路

Dali Dao

Chengdu Dao

Chongqing Dao 重庆道

Changde Dao 常德道

Dali Dao 大理道

Munan Dao 睦南道

Machang Dao

Shaoxing Lu

Xikang Lu 西康路

Dongma Lu

Hai River

(Hǎi Hé)

Ping'an Jie

Ping'an Shouan Jie

Wujing Lu

Silili Lu

Jilin Lu

Dagu Nanlu

Central Tiānjīn

Greek-island-style: whitewashed walls, blue trim and splashes of mosaic tiling. The theme carries over into the cool rooftop terrace, although stops short of Mediterranean views. Apart from one private room (¥280), all rooms are dorms (six to eight beds), including a female-only dorm. English is limited.

Orange Hotel HOTEL $$

(桔子酒店, Júzi Jiǔdiàn; ☑ 022 2734 8333; www.orangehotel.com.cn; 7 Xing'an Lu, 兴安路7号; r from ¥338, with river view from ¥428; 🌫 🖥; Ⓜ Dongnanjiao) Good value with stylish, unfussy rooms, some of which have river views. It's a bit tricky to find: it's accessed from behind another building, via an alley running off Xing'an Lu. Convenient location next to the Dongnanjiao metro. Online discounts drop prices by ¥100.

★ Min Yuan 33 BOUTIQUE HOTEL $$$

(民园三三, Mínyuán Sānsān; ☑ 022 2331 1626; www.minyuan33.com; 31-33 Changde Dao, 常德道 31-33号; r ¥910-1300; 🌫 🖥) Located in a beautifully renovated stretch of hundred-year-old town houses known as the Minyuan Terrace, this Tiānjīn trendsetter has minimalist, all-white rooms that feature stripped-wood furniture and flooring, and tons of space.

The same owners run the Malaysian restaurant **Cafe Sambal** and the cosy cafe 31 Cups (p140), both of which are in the same complex.

★ Astor Hotel HOTEL $$$

(利顺德大饭店, Lìshùndé Dàfàndiàn; ☑ 022 5852 6888; www.starwoodhotels.com; 33 Tai'erzhuang Lu, 台儿庄路33号; d from ¥780; 🌫 🖥 @ 🖥 🖥) China's oldest foreign-run hotel, the Astor dates back to 1863, when it was opened by British missionary John Innocent. Although it's not as luxurious as some of the city's international chains, there's an undeniable character to the place that's hard to find elsewhere.

Make sure you reserve a room in the historic wing, rather than the modern wing – you'll be rewarded with a four-poster bed, parquet flooring and bundles of charm. The **Astor House Museum** (¥50; 11am to 8pm), with its attendant memorabilia, is free for guests.

St Regis Tiānjīn HOTEL $$$

(天津瑞吉金融街酒店, Tiānjīn Ruìjí Jīnróngjiē Jiǔdiàn; ☑ 022 5830 9999; www.starwoodhotels.com; 158 Zhangzizhong Lu, 张自忠路158号; d from ¥817; 🌫 🌫 @ 🖥 🖥; Ⓜ Heping Rd) The last word in luxury in Tiānjīn, the St Regis has a prime riverside location, with alfresco seating on the back terrace – perfect for enjoying its signature Lapsang Souchong Bloody Mary. The heated pool, spa treatments and personal butler service promise serious R & R, while the staff are well attuned to the expectations of international visitors.

✗ Eating

Jīnfú Lóu DUMPLING $

(金福楼; 143 Chongqing Dao, 重庆道143号; meals around ¥10; ◷ 7am-2pm; ✍) Simple but clean dumpling joint run by a friendly guy who doesn't speak English, but does have an English menu. There's only five things on it, mind you, and they're all dumplings (including vegetarian options). There's no English sign, but it's next to the easily spotted Three Brothers Youth Hostel (p137).

In and Out
YUNNAN **$$**

(一坐一忘餐厅, Yī Zuò Yī Wàng Cāntīng; ☎ 022 5870 1999; Xiānnóng Block, 55 Luoyang Dao, 洛阳道55号先农大院内; dishes ¥28-118; ⊙11am-10pm; 🛜) Photos of lush rice terraces and elderly Dai women shouldering woven baskets effortlessly transport you – and all the local 30-somethings who pack the place out – to the land south of the clouds, where pineapple rice, across-the-bridge noodles and other Yúnnán classics tempt with promises of a temporary escape from the big city. Top choice in the Xiānnóng Block.

YY Beer House – Wǔdàdào
THAI **$$**

(粤园泰餐厅, Yuèyuán Tàicāntīng; ☎ 022 5835 2835; 1 Hunan Lu, 湖南路1号; dishes ¥28-68; ⊙11am-10pm) This cosy, atmospheric Thai restaurant has an enviable location at the entrance to the Xiānnóng Block, with a few outdoor stools to perch at while you enjoy an eponymous beer (¥35).

Gǒubùlǐ (main branch)
DUMPLING **$$**

(狗不理, 77 Shandong Lu, 山东路77号; dishes ¥38-128; ⊙7.30am-9pm; 🍴) Tiānjīn's most famous restaurant chain is a mixed bag. While the trademark *bāozi* (steamed dumplings) are big, juicy and delicious, locals will also tell you they're overpriced (¥46 for eight). Nonetheless, it's been in business since 1858, they've got vegetarian options and there's an English picture menu. Another **branch** (金塔店, Jīntǎ; 34 Dagu Beilu, 大沽北路34号; dishes ¥38-128; ⊙7.30am-9pm; 🍴; Ⓜ Heping Rd) is a short walk away.

Shāguō Lǐ
CHINESE **$$**

(砂锅李; ☎ 022 2326 0075; 46 Jiujiang Lu, 九江路46号; dishes ¥36-80; ⊙11.30am-2.30pm & 5.30-8.30pm; Ⓜ Xiaobailou) Of all Tiānjīn's restaurants, this is one the locals consistently

recommend. They flock here for the speciality – pork spare ribs in a sweet barbecue sauce, so tender that they pull apart at the touch of a chopstick. The small portion (¥68) is easily enough for two people.

YY Beer House
THAI **$$**

(粤园泰餐厅, Yuèyuán Tàicāntīng; ☎ 022 2339 9634; 3 Aomen Lu, 澳门路3号; dishes ¥28-68; ⊙11am-10pm; Ⓜ Xiaobailou) Despite the name, this cosy, atmospheric place is actually a Thai restaurant with a wide range of flavourful dishes from the land of smiles. It does, however, have some craft beers (¥35) too. It's tucked away down a quiet street behind Nanjing Lu. A new, smaller branch has opened up in Wǔdàdào.

🍷 Drinking & Nightlife

While you won't be clubbing till dawn in Tiānjīn, there are a handful of welcoming, laid-back bars throughout the city, as well as atmospheric cafes in the Wǔdàdào area.

31 Cups
CAFE

(31杯咖啡, Sānshíyī Bēi Kāfēi; 29 Changde Dao, 常德道29号; ⊙11am-11pm; 🛜) The inviting courtyard of this cool Wǔdàdào cafe is hard to resist – and once you see the menu of milkshakes, tiramisu and evening cocktails, you may find it hard to leave.

Le Procope Lounge
COCKTAIL BAR

(普寇酒廊, Pǔkòu Jiǔláng; ☎ 022 2711 9858; cnr Shandong Lu & Chengde Dao, 山东路与承德道交口; ⊙7.30pm-3am) Distressed urban flair, single-malt whiskys and craft cocktails are the thing at this cool, candlelit lounge.

Ali Baba's
BAR

(阿里巴巴, Ālǐ Bābā; ☎ 186 3092 0830; Bldg 4, Weihua Nanli, off Tong'an Dao, 同安道卫华南里小区4号楼; ⊙11am-3am; Ⓜ Wujiayao) One of Tiānjīn's longest-running bars, this expat-friendly, slightly gritty student hang-out has an unlikely location hidden away in the middle of an apartment block – but it's ever popular. It offers food too.

Come out of Exit A2 of Wujiayao subway station and walk north along Qixiangtai Lu for about 300m, then turn left down Tong'an Dao. After passing the road called Wujiaya Si Haolu, take the first lane on your left. Ali Baba's is up on the right.

🔒 Shopping

Binjiang Dao, between Nanjing Lu and Dagu Beilu, is one huge, long pedestrianised shopping strip.

WǓDÀDÀO

The area of Wǔdàdào (五大道; Five Great Avenues) is rich in the villas and pebble-dash former residences of the well to-do of the early 20th century. It consists of five roads in the south of the city – Machang Dao, Changde Dao, Munan Dao, Dali Dao and Chengdu Dao – and the streetscapes are European, lined with charming houses dating from the 1920s and before.

Filled with tiny cafes and boutiques, this is the most enjoyable part of the city for exploration on foot or by bike.

In markets, look out for *Tiānjīn nírén* (天津泥人) – these chubby clay figurines are the city's trademark souvenir. You can get them at the Ancient Culture Street, as well as in the lobby of the main branch of the restaurant Gǒubùlǐ (p140).

Shěnyángdào Antiques Market   MARKET
(沈阳道古物市场, Shěnyángdào Gǔwù Shìchǎng; cnr Shenyang Dao & Shandong Lu, 沈阳道与山东路交叉口; ⊙8am-5pm) Best visited on Sunday, this antiques market is great for rifling through stamps, silverware, porcelain, clocks, Mao badges and Cultural Revolution memorabilia.

ⓘ Information

There are foreign-friendly ATMs inside and outside the train station.

Bank of China (中国银行, Zhōngguó Yínháng; 80-82 Jiefang Beilu, 解放北路80-82号)

China Post (中国邮政,, Zhōngguó Yóuzhèng; 89 Jiefang Beilu, 解放北路89号)

HSBC (汇丰银行, Huìfēng Yínháng; 75 Nanjing Lu, 南京路75号) There's an HSBC ATM inside the International Building.

Public Security Bureau (PSB, 公安局出入境管理局, Gōng'ānjú Chūrùjìng Guǎnlǐjú; ☑ 022 2445 8825; 19 Shou'an Jie, 寿安街19号)

Tiānjīn International SOS Clinic (天津国际紧急救援诊所, Tiānjīn Guójì Jǐnjí Jiùyuán Zhěnsuǒ, ☑ 022 2352 0143; Sheraton Tianjin Hotel, Zijinshan Lu, 紫金山路喜来登大酒店) Located in the Sheraton, about 1km southeast of the Tianta metro station.

ⓘ Getting There & Away

AIR

Tiānjīn Bīnhǎi International Airport (天津滨海国际机场, Tiānjīn Bīnhǎi Guójì Jīchǎng; ☑ 022 96777; www.tbia.cn) is 15km east of the city centre and has flights to all major cities in China, plus a few international destinations, including Bangkok, Singapore, Tokyo and Seoul. Buy tickets through www.elong.net or www.english.ctrip.com.

BOAT

The nearest passenger port is the **Tiānjīn International Cruise Home Port** (天津国际邮轮母港, Tiānjīn Guójì Yóulún Mǔgǎng; ☑ 022 2560 5128; www.tichp.com), 70km east of the city.

This port is primarily for cruise passengers who are making a stopover in Tiānjīn or Běijīng (180km). Be aware that this is a very inconvenient place to disembark, with no easy way to get to either city from the port. The simplest way to get to Běijīng is to arrange for a private car or bus (eg through www.tour-beijing.com) to pick you up and take you directly there (three hours).

There are two bullet trains per day between the nearby ghost city of Yùjiābǎo and Běijīng South (于家堡; also written 'Yujiapu'; ¥75, one hour), but tickets can be hard to come by. Taxis charge ¥300 to get from the port to this station. There are also numerous bullet trains running from Tiānjīn and Tánggǔ (塘沽) to Běijīng; arrange for a private shuttle to take you directly to these stations.

BUS

Tiānjīn's main **long distance bus station** (天津通莎客运站, Tiānjīn Tōngshā Kèyùnzhàn), located at the train station's north entrance, serves destinations in Héběi, Shāndōng and Liáoníng, plus 12 other provinces. Check train schedules before hopping on a bus – trains are usually faster and more comfortable.

Běijīng (Sihui bus station) ¥35, 3½ hours, hourly

Cāngzhōu ¥47, three hours, nine daily

Chéngdé ¥137, five hours, three daily (7am, 8am, 3pm)

Dàtóng ¥159, seven hours, two daily (9am, 3pm)

Jǐ'nán ¥140, five hours, three daily (8.30am, 9.30am, 10.30am)

Qīngdǎo ¥179, eight hours, one daily (8.15am)

Shíjiāzhuāng ¥125, 4½ hours, three daily (9.30am, 11.30am, 3pm)

TRAIN

Tiānjīn has four train stations: main, north, south and west, all of which are connected to the metro system. Most trains leave from the main train station, though it's not uncommon for similar routes to also run from the south and west stations.

Bullet trains between here and Běijīng make day trips extremely feasible. No need to prebook (except on holidays and Sunday evenings); just turn up and buy a ticket on the next available train. You'll rarely have to wait more than an hour. The last train back to Tiānjīn leaves Běijīng at 10.43pm.

Note that for some destinations, such as Xī'ān, it can be quicker to take bullet trains from Běijīng.

Services from the main train station (天津站; Tiānjīn Zhàn):

Běijīng South C train ¥55, 30 minutes, frequent service

Qīngdǎo G train ¥259, 4½ hours, three daily (2.43pm, 3.53pm, 6.04pm)

Shànghǎi Hóngqiáo G train ¥517, six hours, seven daily

Shānhǎiguān G train ¥130, 1½ hours, five daily

Shíjiāzhuāng G train ¥132, two hours, 10 daily

Wǔhàn G train ¥493, six to seven hours, two daily (10.58am and 11.47am)

Xī'ān hard sleeper ¥326, 18 hours, four daily

Services from the south train station (天津南站; Tiānjīn Nánzhàn):

Hángzhōu East G train ¥495, 5½ hours, six daily

Qīngdǎo G train ¥259, 4½ hours, six daily

Shànghǎi Hóngqiáo G train ¥509, five hours, 10 daily

ⓘ Getting Around

TO/FROM THE AIRPORT
Metro line 2 runs from the city centre all the way to the airport (¥4).

An **airport shuttle bus** (机场巴士; *jīchǎng bāshì*; ¥15, 40 minutes, every 30 minutes 6.30am to 6pm) leaves from the **long distance bus station** (p141), at the north exit of the main train station.

Taxis to the airport cost around ¥60.

PUBLIC TRANSPORT
Local buses (tickets ¥2 to ¥4) run from 5am to 11pm.

Tiānjīn's easy-to-use metro (地铁; *dìtiě*; tickets ¥2 to ¥5) runs from around 6.30am to 10pm. Ticket machines have bilingual instructions. Four lines were in operation at the time of writing; two new lines are expected to be open by 2017.

TAXI
Flag fall is ¥8 for the first 3km, then ¥1.70 per kilometre thereafter; there's also a ¥1 pollution tax.

ⓘ SLEEPING IN HÉBĚI

Héběi has very limited sleeping options for foreigners, and non-Chinese citizens are barred from staying in the vast majority of hotels in most cities. Keep this in mind before jumping on that great online deal: a hotel may not tell you they don't accept foreigners until you show up at the front desk – even if you've reserved in advance. Rural homestays are a good option for budget travellers.

HÉBĚI 河北
POP 73.3 MILLION

Shíjiāzhuāng 石家庄
☑ 0311 / POP 4.3 MILLION

An archetypal Chinese city and the provincial capital of Héběi, Shíjiāzhuāng is a frantic, prosperous and sprawling railway-junction settlement with little sense of history. It does, however, make a comfortable base from which to explore gems such as Zhèngdìng, Cāngyán Shān and Yújiācūn.

⊙ Sights

Héběi Provincial Museum MUSEUM
(河北省博物馆, Héběi Shěng Bówùguǎn; Fanxi Lu, 范西路; ⊙9am-5pm Tue-Sun, last entry 4pm) **FREE** Wandering the cavernous halls of the provincial museum will take you deep into the multilayered realms of Chinese history, with most exhibits focusing on archaeological excavations that date as far back as the Shang dynasty (1600–1046 BC). As fascinating as the trove of funeral figurines, jade burial suits and bronze vessels are, however, the real star is the Quyang Stone Carvings collection, which features masterful ancient statuary – mostly Buddhist – carved from Héběi's Quyuan marble.

The museum is divided in two: the old building (the Zhongshan Donglu side) houses temporary exhibits; the new building houses the permanent collection.

Make sure you bring your passport, as it's required for entry.

🛏 Sleeping

Only a handful of hotels here take foreigners, and even quality domestic chains will turn you away. Be particularly cautious about using booking websites for Shíjiāzhuāng, as it's likely you won't find out that you'll be refused until you turn up in the lobby. International chains, of course, are a sure bet.

Děngfēnglái Youth Hostel HOSTEL $
(等风来青年旅舍, Děngfēnglái Qīngnián Lǚshè; ☑0311 8382 1323; Apt 602, Door 3, Bldg 3, Shuijing Licheng apartment block, Xinshi Zhonglu, 新石中路水晶郦城3楼3号门602室; dm from ¥35; 🛜) More of a homestay with bunk beds than an actual hostel, this is the only budget accommodation in town that takes foreigners. The owners speak no English, but rooms are very clean and the grandmother sometimes cooks up simple meals for guests.

Shíjiāzhuāng

Note that while it is within walking distance of the train station, it's not particularly easy to find. The Shuijing Licheng apartment block is located at the bottom of the station's northwest entrance ramp. Once you've found that, enter the complex, turn right at the second row of buildings, and go to the end. Door 3 is the last one on your left.

⭐ **Holiday Inn**   HOTEL **$$**
(萬象天成假日酒店, Wànxiàng Tiānchéng Jiàrì Jiǔdiàn; ☏ 0311 6779 9999; www.ihg.com; 15 Yuhua Xilu, 裕华西路15号; r from ¥373; ❋ ❀ 🖥 ♨) Far and away the best-value hotel in Shíjiāzhuāng, the Holiday Inn offers supremely comfortable rooms in a swish downtown tower. Glass-walled bathrooms come with a rain shower and deep soaker tub. There's a pillow menu for those with allergies, a top-floor pool and gym, and staff speak decent English.

Silver Spring Hotel   HOTEL **$$**
(银泉酒家, Yínquán Jiǔjiā; ☏ 0311 8598 5888; 12 Zhanqian Jie, 站前街12号; d from ¥288; ❋ @ 🖥) Smart, good-value midrange hotel with welcoming staff and bright, modern rooms. You get good discounts if you buy a lifetime membership card (会员卡; huìyuán kǎ) for ¥28.

World Trade Plaza Hotel   HOTEL **$$$**
(世贸广场酒店, Shìmào Guǎngchǎng Jiǔdiàn; ☏ 0311 8667 8888; www.wtphotels.com; 303 Zhongshan Donglu, 中山东路303号; d ¥600-900; ❀ ❋ @ 🖥) Once Shíjiāzhuāng's finest hotel, the World Trade Plaza is still plenty comfortable, if not quite at the same level as the newer competition. Rooms are big and spick and span, and some floors were entirely renovated in 2014. There are Chinese and Western restaurants on-site, as well as a fitness centre.

Shíjiāzhuāng

◎ Sights
1 Hébĕi Provincial Museum D2

🛏 Sleeping
2 Holiday Inn A2
3 Silver Spring Hotel A2
4 World Trade Plaza Hotel D1

✗ Eating
57°C湘 .... (see 5)
Chéngdó Huìguǎn .... (see 3)
5 Lerthai Center C1

✗ Eating

Nan Xiaojie is an excellent spot to look for a meal, with a tremendous variety of small restaurants and outdoor seating. Across the tracks, the slick new Lerthai Center contains dozens of restaurants.

57°C湘   HUNAN **$**
(Wǔshíqī Dù Xiāng; ☏ 0311 6803 7202; 4th fl, Lerthai Center, Zhongshan Donglu, 中山东路勒泰中心四楼; dishes ¥19-39; ⊙ 11am-10pm) Get your chilli duck or cumin-rubbed lamb fried up in front of you at this entertaining Húnán-meets-teppanyaki crossover. Be forewarned that it's a very energetic place – every so often the music gets cranked up a notch, the waitstaff don sunglasses and proceed to get down to electro pop. English menu.

Lerthai Center   FOOD HALL **$$**
(勒泰中心, Lètài Zhōngxīn; Zhongshan Donglu, 中山东路; meals from ¥30) You can't miss at this slick new mall, with dozens of restaurants ranging from Shanghainese and hotpot to pizza and Korean BBQ. Freshly made juice

ZHÀOZHŌU BRIDGE

China's oldest bridge still standing, the **Zhàozhōu Bridge** (赵州桥, Zhàozhōu Qiáo; ¥40) has spanned the Jiǎo River (Jiǎo Hé) for 1400 years. As the world's first segmental arch bridge (ie its arch is a segment of a circle, as opposed to a complete semicircle), it predates other bridges of its type throughout the world by 800 years. In fine condition, and part of a riverside, landscaped park, it is 50.82m long and 9.6m wide, with a span of 37m.

Twenty-two stone posts are topped with carvings of dragons and mythical creatures, with the centre slab featuring a magnificent *tāotiè* (an offspring of a dragon).

The bridge is in Zhàoxiàn County, about 40km southeast of Shíjiāzhuāng and 2km south of Zhàoxiàn town. To get here from Shíjiāzhuāng, head to the **south bus station**, then take a bus to Zhàoxiàn (赵县; ¥11, one hour, frequent). Get off at Shí Tǎ (石塔), a slim stone pagoda in the middle of the road, where you turn right to walk the final 2km, or else take dinky local bus 2 (¥1). The last bus back to Shíjiāzhuāng swings past Shí Tǎ at about 7pm.

---

will keep you hydrated, while the exterior patios are an inviting place to sit on a summer night. If you're feeling indecisive, the hybrid teppanyaki–Húnán 57°C湘 (p143) has an English menu.

Chéngdé Huìguǎn
HEBEI $$

(承德会馆; 12 Zhanqian Jie, 站前街12号; dishes ¥10-98; ⏰11am-2pm & 5.30-9pm) Specialising in northern Héběi cuisine, this fine place is actually two restaurants in one. The right side has more atmosphere, with faux courtyard decor, while a more proletarian canteen-like restaurant is on the left. Picture menu.

ℹ Information

Internet cafes are numerous and relatively easy to find.

Bank of China (中国银行, Zhōngguó Yínháng; Jinqiao Beidajie, 金桥北大街) Located behind Starbucks, inside the building. No exterior sign.

China Post (中国邮政, Zhōngguó Yóuzhèng; 3 Jianshe Nandajie, 建设南大街3号)

Public Security Bureau (PSB, 公安局, Gōng'ānjú; ☎0311 8686 2511; 66 Yuannan Lu, 元南路66号)

ℹ Getting There & Away

AIR

Shíjiāzhuāng's airport is 40km northeast of town, and has flights to all major cities in China.

BUS

The following are just some of the numerous services that leave from the **long-distance bus station** (石家庄客运总站; Shíjiāzhuāng Kèyùn Zǒngzhàn; Zhanqian Jie, 站前街). It is likely that the bus station will move to the new train-station area in the near future, although there has been no official confirmation yet.

Běijīng ¥95, four hours, hourly (7am to 6pm)

Chéngdé ¥160, seven hours, four daily (8am, 9.30am, 11.30am and 2.30pm)

Jǐ'nán ¥115, four hours, every 40 minutes (7.20am to 5.30pm)

Tiānjīn ¥120 to ¥130, four hours, hourly (8am to 6pm)

Bus services to Zhèngdìng and Zhàozhōu Bridge depart from **south bus station** (石家庄南焦客运站, Shíjiāzhuāng Nánjiāo Kèyùnzhàn; ☎0311 8657 3806; Yuxiang Jie, 裕翔街), 6km southeast of the centre; to get there from central Shíjiāzhuāng, take bus 30 from Zhongshan Lu.

Services to Cāngyán Shān and Yújiācūn depart from the **Xīwáng bus station** (西王客运站, Xīwáng Kèyùnzhàn; Xinhua Lu, 新华路), 6km west of town. Get there on bus 9, which runs up Zhonghua Nandajie from the train station and then west on Xinhua Lu (allow 30 to 45 minutes).

TRAIN

If you don't mind waiting an hour or so, there's no need to book for Běijīng; just turn up at the station and buy a ticket.

Shíjiāzhuāng's new **train station** (石家庄火车站, Shíjiāzhuāng huǒchēzhàn; Zhonghuanan Dajie, 中华南大街) is about 3km south of the more central former train station (老火车站; lǎo huǒchēzhàn), still an important landmark. A few trains also stop at or depart from **Shíjiāzhuāng north train station** (石家庄北站, Shíjiāzhuāng Běizhàn; Taihua Jie, 泰华街). If you're not in a hurry, there are still a handful of cheaper, much slower trains also running out of the city.

A sample of the many routes running through Shíjiāzhuāng:

Běijīng West G train ¥129, 1½ hours, frequent service

Chéngdé Hard seat/sleeper ¥75/150, 10 hours, five daily

Dàtóng Hard sleeper ¥150 to ¥178, six to 10 hours, five daily (two from Shíjiāzhuāng North)

Guǎngzhōu South G train ¥786, eight hours, six daily

Jǐ'nán Hard seat ¥47, 4½ hours, four daily (from Shíjiāzhuāng North)

Luòyáng (Lóngmén) G train ¥250, three hours, six daily

Shànghǎi Z-class hard sleeper ¥303, 12 hours, two daily (from Shíjiāzhuāng North)

Shānhǎiguān G train ¥255, 2½ hours, five daily

Tiānjīn G train ¥123, two hours, frequent service

Xī'ān North G train, ¥409, 4½ hours, nine daily

Zhèngzhōu East G train ¥190, two hours, frequent service

🛈 Getting Around

The **airport bus** (机场大巴; *jīchǎng dàbā*; ¥20, 90 minutes, 4.30am to 8.30pm) leaves every 30 minutes from the train station.

Taxis are ¥8 at flag fall and the easiest way to get around town. Numerous shared rides (both private and taxi) ferry passengers between the train and various bus stations; the standard fare is ¥10 per person. Don't expect these drivers to use the meter.

Shíjiāzhuāng's first metro (line 1) is due to open in 2017, running east–west along Zhongshan Lu. Two more lines are slated to open in 2020.

Zhèngdìng 正定

♪ 0311 / POP 130,300

Its streets littered with temple remains, the once walled town of Zhèngdìng is an appetising – albeit incomplete – slice of old China. From atop Zhèngdìng's reconstructed South Gate, you can see the silhouettes of four distinct pagodas jutting above the sleepy town. Affectionately known as the town of 'nine buildings, four pagodas, eight great temples and 24 golden archways', Zhèngdìng has tragically lost many of its standout buildings and archways (Píngyáo, it isn't), but enough remains to lend the place an air of faded grandeur. And in Lóngxīng Temple, Zhèngdìng can lay claim to having one of the finest temples in northern China.

Zhèngdìng is an easy day trip from Shíjiāzhuāng.

◉ Sights

Bus 177 from Shíjiāzhuāng stops at all the sights, but you may as well start at the best of the lot – Lóngxīng Temple, aka Dàfó Temple – then slowly walk your way back to South Gate.

From Lóngxīng Temple, turn right and walk about 500m to reach Tiānníng Temple (on your right). From here, continue along the same road, then at the crossroads turn left down Yanzhao Nandajie to reach Kāiyuán Temple (on your right). From here, continue another 500m south down Yanzhao Nandajie, then turn left down Linji Lu to reach Línjì Temple. Walking further south on Yanzhao Nandajie, you'll soon reach Guānghuì Temple (on your left) and, finally, South Gate.

⭐ **Lóngxīng Temple**   BUDDHIST TEMPLE
(隆兴寺, Lóngxīng Sì; Zhongshan Donglu, 中山东路; ¥50) Considering its age – almost 1500 years old – we think this is one of the most impressive temples in northern China. It's certainly Zhèngdìng's star attraction. Popularly known as Dàfó Temple (大佛寺; Dàfó Sì), or 'Great Buddha Temple', the complex contains an astonishing array of Buddhist statuary, housed in some stunning temple halls. Dating way back to AD 586, the temple has been much restored and stands divided from its spirit wall by Zhongshan Donglu.

Tiānníng Temple   BUDDHIST TEMPLE
(天宁寺, Tiānníng Sì; Zhongshan Donglu, 中山东路; ¥15) The remains of this temple contain the 41m-high Tang dynasty **Lofty Pagoda** (凌霄塔; Língxiāo Tǎ), also called Mùtǎ or Wooden Pagoda. Originally dating from AD 779, the pagoda was restored in 1045, but is still in fine condition.

Kāiyuán Temple   BUDDHIST TEMPLE
(开元寺, Kāiyuán Sì; Yanzhao Nandajie, 燕赵南大街; ¥20) This temple originally dates from AD 540 but was destroyed in 1966, the first year of the Cultural Revolution. Little remains apart from a bell tower and the dirt-brown **Xūmí Pagoda** (须弥塔; Xūmí Tǎ), a well preserved, nine-storey structure (dating from 636 AD) topped with a spire. Its arched doors and carved stone doorway are particularly attractive, as are the carved figures on the base. You can enter a shrine at the bottom of the pagoda, but you can't climb up.

Línjì Temple   BUDDHIST SITE
(临济寺, Línjì Sì; Linji Lu, 临济路) **FREE** This active monastery is notable for its tall, elegant, carved-brick **Chénglíng Pagoda** (澄灵塔; also called the Green Pagoda), topped with an elaborate lotus plinth plus ball and spire. In the Tang dynasty, the temple was home to one of Chan (Zen) Buddhism's most eccentric and important teachers, Linji Yixuan, who penned the now-famous words, 'If you meet the Buddha on the road, kill him!'

Guānghuì Temple   BUDDHIST TEMPLE
(广惠寺, Guānghuì Sì; Yanzhao Nandajie, 燕赵南大街; ¥15) Nothing remains of this temple except

OFF THE BEATEN TRACK

CĀNGZHŌU'S IRON LION

Standing proud in a long-forgotten corner of southeast Héběi, **Cāngzhōu's Iron Lion** (沧州铁狮子, Cāngzhōu Tiě Shīzi; ¥30) is the oldest and largest cast-iron sculpture in China. Cast way back in AD 953, it weighs in at around 40 tonnes, and stands almost 6m tall, but unsurprisingly for a creature that is more than 1000 years old, it is but a shadow of its former self. The lion lost its tail in the 17th century; its snout and belly were damaged in a storm 200 years later; and the bronze statue of the Bodhisattva Manjusri, which once sat on top of the lotus flower on its back, was stolen centuries ago.

Despite today being almost 100km from the coast, Cāngzhōu was once a large seaport, which suffered from flooding and tsunamis. The Iron Lion was built to protect the city from sea spirits, and was known back then as Zhen Hai Hou (镇海吼), the Roaring Sea Calmer.

Admission includes entry to a nearby abandoned temple, called the **Iron Money Warehouse** (铁钱库; Tiě Qián Kù). Unfortunately, it is relatively empty, aside from a large lump of Song dynasty coins excavated nearby. The lane opposite the museum leads through farmland, and across a river to the southern section of the old, earthen city wall, 1.5km away. It's still around 5m tall here, and you can walk along it in places. It once stretched for almost 10km around the city.

You can make a day trip here from either Běijīng or Tiānjīn. High-speed trains to Cāngzhōu west station (沧州西站; Cāngzhōu Xī Zhàn) run roughly half-hourly from Běijīng south train station (¥95, one hour, last train back 10.30pm) and roughly hourly from Tiānjīn South Train Station (¥50, 45 minutes, last train back 9pm). From Cāngzhōu west station, take bus 16 or 31 to Cāngzhōu main train station (火车站; huǒchēzhàn; ¥1; 40 minutes), then bus 901 (¥2, 45 minutes). Tell the driver you want *tiě shīzi* (tee-ai shur zuh) and he'll show you where to get off. Then follow the signposted lane beside the bus stop and the Iron Lion will soon be on your right, with the Iron Money Warehouse museum on your left.

Huá Pagoda (华塔; Huá Tā), dating from around AD 800. It's an unusual, Indian-style pagoda decorated with lions, elephants, sea creatures and *púsà* (Bodhisattvas, who are those worthy of nirvana who remain on earth to help others attain enlightenment).

Chánglè Gate   GATE
(长乐门, Chánglè Mén; Yanzhao Nandajie, 燕赵南大街; ¥15) Although not immediately obvious, Zhèngdìng was once a walled city. These days much of what remains of its 24km-long city wall is just an earthen mound, but at the southern end of Yanzhao Nandajie is Chánglè Gate, commonly called Nán Mén (South Gate), which has been rebuilt to give you some idea of the city wall's former magnificence.

🛏 Sleeping & Eating

Given its proximity to Shíjiāzhuāng, there is no need to spend the night here.

There are plenty of noodle and dumpling eateries along Zhongshan Donglu and Yanzhao Nandajie (past Kāiyuán Temple). Expect to pay about ¥10 for a simple meal.

Also look out for *lǘ ròu huǒshāo* (驴肉火烧; donkey-meat pastry pockets), a Héběi speciality.

ℹ Information

There's an **Industrial & Commercial Bank** (ICBC, 工商银行, Gōngshāng Yínháng; cnr Zhongshan Donglu & Yanzhao Nandajie, 中山东路与燕赵南大街交叉口) with an ATM a couple of hundred metres past Tiānníng Temple.

ℹ Getting There & Away

Zhèngdìng is generally an easy day trip from Shíjiāzhuāng. From the ring road just north of the **south bus station** (p144), take bus 177 (¥2, one hour, 6.50am to 7pm), which passes through South Gate and the other temples before reaching Lóngxīng Temple (Dàfó Temple; 大佛寺; Dàfó Sì).

From Lóngxīng Temple, you can then walk to all the other temples before catching bus 177 back to Zhèngdìng from South Gate. At the time of writing, much of Nanzhao Nandajie was closed to vehicle traffic as a result of massive road repairs; if these are still ongoing, you'll have to get off before the South Gate and walk a ways into town.

A shared taxi to Zhèngdìng from the south bus station will cost ¥20 per person; otherwise, you should be able to hire a driver for ¥60.

ℹ Getting Around

Zhèngdìng is not huge and walking is easy as sights are largely clustered together.

Bus 177 runs past Lóngxīng Temple, down Zhongshan Donglu and then Yanzhao Nandajie.

Taxi flag fall within Zhèngdìng is ¥5; three-wheel motorcycle rides cost ¥4 for anywhere in town.

Yújiācūn 于家村

POP 1600

Hidden in the hills near the Héběi–Shānxī border is the peaceful little settlement of **Yújiācūn** (admission ¥30). Nearly everything, from the houses to furniture inside, was originally made of stone – hence its nickname, Stone Village. As such, Yújiācūn is remarkably well preserved: bumpy little lanes lead past traditional Ming- and Qing-dynasty courtyard homes, old opera stages and tiny temples.

◎ Sights

Yújiācūn is dissected by a small village road, where the bus will drop you off. The ticket office, the Stone Museum and Xīngshuǐ Yuàn guesthouse are to the right of the road; all the other sights listed are to the left.

There are a number of historic buildings worth hunting down, including the **Guānyīn Pavilion** (观音阁; Guānyīn Gé) and the **Zhēnwǔ Temple** (真武庙; Zhēnwǔ Miào). Near the primary school is the **Stone Museum** (石头博物馆; Shítou Bówùguǎn), displaying local items made of stone.

You may have to get someone at the ticket office to open the sights you wish to see, as their doors are often padlocked.

Qīngliáng Pavilion HISTORIC BUILDING
(清凉阁, Qīngliáng Gé) Completed in 1581, this three-storey pavilion was supposedly the work of one thoroughly crazed individual – Yu Xichun, who wanted to be able to see Běijīng from the top. It was, according to legend, built entirely at night, over a 16-year period, without the help of any other villagers.

Yu Ancestral Hall TEMPLE
(于氏宗祠, Yúshì Zōngcí) Yújiācūn is a model Chinese clan village, where 95% of the inhabitants all share the same surname of Yu (于). One of the village's more unusual sights is the town ancestral hall, where you'll find the 24-generation family tree, reaching back over 500 years. There are five tapestries, one for the descendants of each of the original Yu sons who founded the village.

🛏 Sleeping

Given the mission it took to get here, you'll want to stay the night – it's definitely worth it. As the sun sets, the sounds of village life – farmers chatting after a day in the fields, hens clucking, kids at play – are miles away from the raging pace of modern Chinese cities.

Xīngshuǐ Yuàn GUESTHOUSE $
(兴水院; ☑ 0311 8237 6517, 134 7311 0485; Yújiācūn, 于家村; per person ¥40) One of a handful of village guesthouses in Yújiācūn, this typically simple courtyard guesthouse has rooms in an old stone building, although the main house itself is a white-tiled renovation. No English is spoken, but you'll get a friendly welcome.

❶ Getting There & Away

From Shíjiāzhuāng's **Xīwáng bus station** (p144), take one of the frequent buses to the small town of Jǐngxíng (井陉; ¥12, one hour, 6.30am to 7pm), from where you can catch a bus to Yújiācūn (¥7, one hour, 7.30am to 6.20pm).

Tell the driver on the Jǐngxíng bus that you want to go to Yújiācūn and you'll be dropped off by the place where the Yújiācūn buses leave from.

Note that the last bus back from Yújiācūn leaves at 4.30pm – all the more reason to stay the night.

Chéngdé 承德

☑ 0314 / POP 479,703

Built on the banks of the Wǔliè River and surrounded by forested hills, Chéngdé is a small, pleasant city that just happens to have an extraordinary history.

This was the summer playground of the emperors of the Qing dynasty; beginning with Emperor Kangxi, the Qing Court would flee here to escape the torpid summer heat of the Forbidden City (and occasionally the threat of foreign armies), as well as to be closer to their northern hunting grounds.

The Bìshǔ Shānzhuāng (Fleeing-the-Heat Mountain Villa) is a grand imperial palace and the walled enclosure it lies within houses China's largest regal gardens. Beyond the grounds is a remarkable collection of politically chosen temples, built to host dignitaries such as the sixth Panchen Lama. The Imperial Villa, the gardens and the temples are all, quite rightly, Unesco-protected.

History

In 1703, when an expedition passed through the Chéngdé valley, Emperor Kangxi was so enamoured with the surroundings that he had a hunting lodge built, which gradually grew into the summer resort. Rèhé – or Jehol (Warm River; named after a hot spring here) – as Chéngdé was then known, grew in importance and the Qing court began to spend more time here, sometimes up to

TIĀNJĪN & HÉBĚI YÚJIĀCŪN

Chéngdé

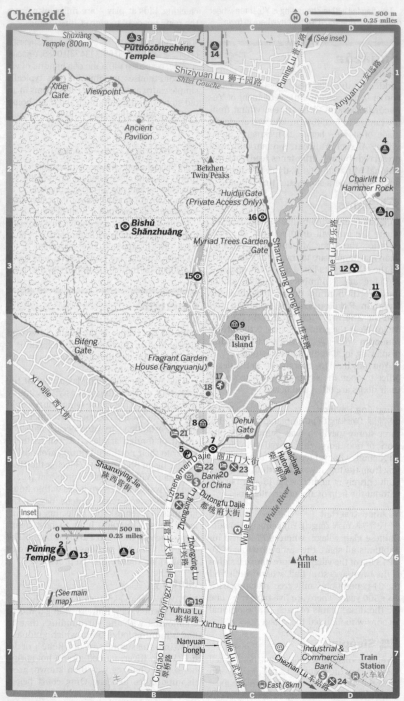

Shūxiàng Temple (800m)

Pǔtuózōngchéng Temple

3

14

Shiziyuan Lu 狮子园路
Shizi Gouche

Puning Lu 普宁路

Anyuan Lu 安远路

(See inset)

Xibei Gate

Viewpoint

Ancient Pavilion

Beizhen Twin Peaks

4

Chairlift to Hammer Rock

10

Bishǔ Shānzhuāng
1

Huidiji Gate (Private Access Only)

16

Myriad Trees Garden Gate

Shanzhuang Donglu 山庄东路

Pule Lu 普乐路

12

11

15

Ruyi Island

9

Bifeng Gate

Fragrant Garden House (Fangyuanju)

17

18

Xi Dajie 西大街

Shaanxiying Jie 陕西营街

8

Dehui Gate

21

5

7

Lizhengmen Dajie 丽正门大街

22

20

23

Bank of China

25

Dutongfu Dajie 都统府大街

Chaichang Hutong 柴场胡同

Wulie River

Zhongxing Lu

Nanyingzi Dajie 南营子大街

Zhonggong Lu 中兴路

Wulie Lu

Wulie River

Arhat Hill

Inset

0 — 500 m
0 — 0.25 miles

Pǔníng Temple
2

13

6

(See main map)

19

Yuhua Lu 裕华路

Xinhua Lu

Nanyuan Donglu

Cuiqiao Lu 翠桥路

Wulie Lu 武烈路

@ Chezhan Lu 车站路

Industrial & Commercial Bank

$

24

Train Station 火车站

East (8km)

0 — 500 m
0 — 0.25 miles
N

Chéngdé

several months a year, with some 10,000 people accompanying the emperor on his seven-day expedition from Běijīng.

The emperors also convened in Jehol with the border tribes – undoubtedly more at ease here than in Běijīng – who posed the greatest threats to the Qīng frontiers: the Mongols, Tibetans, Uighurs and, eventually, the Europeans. The resort reached its peak under Emperor Qianlong (1735–96), who commissioned many of the outlying temples to overawe visiting leaders.

Emperor Xianfeng died here in 1861, permanently warping Chéngdé's *feng shui* and tipping the Imperial Villa towards long-term decline.

◎ Sights

★**Bìshǔ Shānzhuāng**   HISTORIC SITE
(避暑山庄, Imperial Villa; Lizhengmen Dajie, 丽正门大街; summer/winter ¥145/90; ⏰7am-5.30pm Apr-Oct, 8am-4.30pm Nov-Oct) The imperial summer resort is composed of a main palace

complex with vast, parklike gardens, all enclosed by a handsome 10km-long wall. The entrance price is steep (as it is with all the main sights here in Chéngdé), and it gets packed with tourists here in summer, but the splendid gardens provide ample opportunity to take a quiet walk away from the crowds.

A huge spirit wall shields the resort entrance at Lizhengmen Dajie. Through **Lìzhèng Gate**, the **Main Palace** is a series of nine courtyards and five elegant, unpainted halls, with a rusticity complemented by towering pine trees. The wings in each courtyard have various exhibitions (porcelain, clothing, weaponry), and most of the halls are decked out in period furnishings.

The first hall is the refreshingly cool **Hall of Simplicity and Sincerity**, built of an aromatic cedar called *nánmù*, and displaying a carved throne draped in yellow silk. Other prominent halls include the emperor's study (Study of Four Knowledges) and living quarters (Hall of Refreshing Mists and Waves). On the left hand side of the latter is the imperial bedroom. Two residential areas branch out from here: the empress dowager's **Pine Crane Palace** (松鹤斋, Sōnghè Zhāi) to the east, and the smaller **Western Apartments**, where the concubines (including a young Cixi) resided.

Exiting the Main Palace brings you to the gardens and forested hunting grounds, with landscapes borrowed from famous southern scenic areas in Hángzhōu, Sūzhōu and Jiāxīng, as well as the Mongolian grasslands.

The double-storey **Misty Rain Tower** (烟雨楼, Yānyǔ Lóu), on the northwestern side of the main lake, served as an imperial study. Further north is the **Wénjīn Pavilion** (文津阁, Wénjīn Gé), built in 1773. Don't miss the wonderfully elegant 250-year-old **Yǒngyòusì Pagoda** (永佑寺塔, Yǒngyòusì Tǎ), which soars above the fragments of its vanished temple in the northeast of the complex.

Most of the compound is taken up by lakes, hills, forests and plains. There are magnificent views of some of the outlying temples from the northern wall.

Just beyond the Main Palace is the starting point for bus tours of the gardens. Further on you'll find a place for boat rentals.

Almost all of the forested section is closed from November to May because of fire hazard in the dry months, but fear not: you can still turn your legs to jelly wandering around the rest of the park.

Tourists can exit by any of the gates, but entry tickets are available for purchase only at Lìzhèng Gate.

TIĀNJĪN & HÉBĚI CHÉNGDÉ

Guāndì Temple TAOIST TEMPLE

(关帝庙, Guāndì Miào; 18 Lizhengmen Dajie, 丽正门大街18号; ¥20; ☉8am-6pm Apr-Oct, to 5pm Nov-Oct) The heavily restored Guāndì Temple was first built during the reign of Yongzheng, in 1732. For years the temple housed residents but is again home to a band of Taoist monks, garbed in distinctive jackets and trousers, their long hair twisted into topknots. Note the original 300-year-old beamwork in the ceiling of the final hall.

Eight Outer Temples

Skirting the northern and eastern walls of the Bìshǔ Shānzhuāng, the **Eight Outer Temples** (外八庙, *wài bā miào*) were, unusually, designed for diplomatic rather than spiritual reasons. Some were based on actual Tibetan Buddhist monasteries, but the emphasis was on appearance: smaller temple buildings are sometimes solid, and the Tibetan facades (with painted windows) are often fronts for traditional Chinese temple interiors. The surviving temples and monasteries were all built between 1713 and 1780; the prominence given to Tibetan Buddhism was as much for the Mongols (fervent Lamaists) as the Tibetan leaders.

Three of these temples are currently closed to the public: **Pǔrén Temple** (普仁寺, Pǔrén Sì), **Pǔshàn Temple** (溥善寺, Pǔshàn Sì) and **Shūxiàng Temple** (殊像寺, Shūxiàng Si). **Guǎngyuán Temple** (广缘寺, Guǎngyuán Sì), southeast of Pǔníng Temple is unrestored and inaccessible.

★ Pǔníng Temple BUDDHIST TEMPLE

(普宁寺, Pǔníng Sì; Puning Lu, 普宁路; Apr-Oct ¥80, Nov-Mar ¥60; ☉8am-5.30pm Apr-Oct, 8.30am-5pm Nov-Mar) With its squeaking prayer wheels and devotional intonations of its monks, this is Chéngdé's only active temple. It was built in 1755 in anticipation of Qianlong's victory over the western Mongol tribes in Xīnjiāng. Supposedly modelled on the earliest Tibetan Buddhist monastery (Samye), the first half of the temple is distinctly Chinese, with Tibetan buildings at the rear.

Enter the temple grounds to a stele pavilion with inscriptions by the Qianlong emperor in Chinese, Manchu, Mongol and Tibetan. The halls behind are arranged in typical Buddhist fashion, with the **Hall of Heavenly Kings** (天王殿, Tiānwáng Diàn) and beyond, the **Mahavira Hall** (大雄宝殿, Dàxióng Bǎodiàn), where three images of the Buddhas of the three generations are arrayed. Some very steep steps rise up behind

(the temple is arranged on a mountainside) leading to a gate tower, which you can climb.

On the terrace at the top of the steps is the dwarfing **Mahayana Hall**. On either side are stupas and square, block-like Tibetan-style buildings, decorated with attractive water spouts. Some buildings have been converted to shops, while others are solid, serving a purely decorative purpose.

The mind-bogglingly vast gilded **statue of Guanyin** (the Buddhist Goddess of Mercy) towers within the Mahayana Hall. The effigy is astounding: over 22m high, it's the tallest of its kind in the world and radiates a powerful sense of divinity. Hewn from five different kinds of wood (pine, cypress, fir, elm and linden), Guanyin has 42 arms, with each palm bearing an eye and each hand holding instruments, skulls, lotuses and other Buddhist devices. Tibetan touches include the pair of hands in front of the goddess, below the two clasped in prayer, the right one of which holds a sceptre-like *dorje* (*vajra* in Sanskrit), a masculine symbol, and the left a *dril bu* (bell), a female symbol. On Guanyin's head sits the Teacher Longevity Buddha. To the right of the goddess stands a huge male guardian and disciple called Shàncái, opposite his female equivalent, Lóngnǔ (Dragon Girl). Unlike Guanyin, they are both coated in ancient and dusty pigments. On the wall on either side are hundreds of small effigies of Buddha.

Occasionally, tourists are allowed to climb up to the 1st-floor gallery for a closer inspection of Guanyin.

Housed within the grounds, on the east side, is the **Pǔyòu Temple** (普佑寺, Pǔyòu Sì; ☉8am-6pm). It is dilapidated and missing its main hall, but it has a plentiful contingent of merry gilded *luóhàn* (Buddhists who have achieved nirvana) in the side wings, although a fire in 1964 incinerated many of their confrères.

Pǔníng Temple has a number of friendly lamas who manage their domain, so be quiet and respectful at all times.

Take bus 6 (¥1) from in front of Mountain Villa Hotel (p151).

★ Pǔtuózōngchéng Temple BUDDHIST TEMPLE

(普陀宗乘之庙, Pǔtuózōngchéng Zhīmiào; Shiziyuan Lu, 狮子园路; Apr-Oct ¥80, Nov-Mar ¥60; ☉8am-5pm Apr-Oct, 8.30am-5pm Nov-Mar) Chéngdé's largest temple is a not-so-small replica of Lhasa's Potala Palace and houses the nebulous presence of Avalokiteshvara (Guanyin). A marvellous sight on a clear day, the temple's red walls stand out against its mountain backdrop. Enter to a huge stele pavilion, followed by a large triple archway topped with five small stupas in red, green, yellow, white and black.

Fronted by a collection of prayer wheels and flags, the **Red Palace** contains most of the main shrines and halls. Look out for the marvellous sandalwood pagodas in the front hall. Both are 19m tall and contain 2160 effigies of the Amitabha Buddha.

Among the many exhibits on view are displays of Tibetan Buddhist objects and instruments, including a *kapala* bowl, made from the skull of a young girl. The main hall is located at the very top, surrounded by several small pavilions and panoramic views.

The admission ticket includes the neighbouring Temple of Sumeru, Happiness and Longevity. Bus 118 (¥1) goes here from in front of Mountain Villa Hotel.

Temple of Sumeru, Happiness & Longevity   BUDDHIST TEMPLE

(须弥福寿之庙, Xūmífúshòu Zhīmiào; Shiziyuan Lu, 狮子园路; Apr-Oct ¥80, Nov-Mar ¥60; ⊙8am-5pm Apr-Oct, 8.30am-5pm Nov-Mar) This huge temple was built in honour of the sixth Panchen Lama, who stayed here in 1781. Incorporating Tibetan and Chinese architectural elements, it's an imitation of the Panchen's home monastery Tashilhunpo in Shigatse, Tibet. Note the eight huge, glinting dragons (each said to weigh over 1000kg) that adorn the roof of the main hall. The admission price includes entry to the neighbouring Pǔtuózōngchéng Temple.

Bus 118 (¥1) goes here from in front of Mountain Villa Hotel.

Pǔlè Temple   BUDDHIST TEMPLE

(普乐寺, Pǔlè Sì; Pule Lu, 普乐路; ¥50; ⊙8am-5pm Apr-Oct, 8.30am-4.30pm Nov-Mar) This peaceful temple was built in 1776 for the visits of minority envoys from the west (Kazakhs and Uighurs among them). At the rear of the temple is the unusual Round Pavilion, modelled on the Hall of Prayer for Good Harvests at Běijīng's Temple of Heaven Park. Inside is an enormous wooden mandala – a geometric representation of the Buddhist universe.

Admission also includes entry to **Hammer Rock** (磬锤峰; Qìngchuí Fēng) and **Ānyuǎn Temple** (安远庙; Ānyuǎn Miào; Pule Lu, 普乐路; ¥50; ⊙8am-5pm Apr-Oct, 8.30am-4.30pm Nov-Mar). It's a 60-minute walk to the club-shaped rock, which is visible for miles around and said to resemble a kind of musical hammer. It's a pleasant hike offering

commanding views of the area. If you don't fancy walking, take the **chairlift** (one way/return ¥50/80; ⊙7.30am-5.30pm) instead.

Bus 10 (¥1), from in front of Mountain Villa Hotel, will take you close to the chairlift for Hammer Rock, where you buy the entrance ticket for all three sites.

🏃 Activities

Boat Rental   BOATING

(出租小船, Chūzū Xiǎochuán; boat hire per hour ¥60-90, deposit ¥300) Offers boats for rent by the hour so you can explore the lake in the grounds of the imperial summer palace, Bìshǔ Shānzhuāng (避暑山庄; Imperial Villa).

Bus Tours   BUS

(环山车, huánshān chē; per person ¥50) If you'd rather not walk through the vast grounds of the Bìshǔ Shānzhuāng (避暑山庄; Imperial Villa), one-hour bus tours of the gardens (with three short stops) are also available.

🛏 Sleeping

Chéngdé does not offer great sleeping options. The hotels that accept foreigners mostly feel like relics from the state-run era, only with better service. Modern chains were off limits at the time of writing. Most hotels here include breakfast in their rates.

First Met Hostel   HOSTEL $

(初见客栈, Chūjiàn Kèzhàn; ☑186 3148 1357; 2nd fl, No 4 Bldg, Yùhuá Zònghé Market, Yuhua Lu, 裕华路裕华综合市场4号楼2楼; dm/s ¥55/77; 🐱) This makeshift hostel has a pleasant setting on the roof of a low building, sharing the space with a pergola, small garden and a few other apartments. The friendly owner speaks some English; rooms come with toast and a fried egg for breakfast. To find it, enter the 'market' courtyard, turn left at the exterior stairs and go up two flights.

Mountain Villa Hotel   HOTEL $$

(山庄宾馆, Shānzhuāng Bīnguǎn; ☑0314 209 5511; 11 Lizhengmen Dajie, 丽正门路11号; common/standard/deluxe r ¥280/380/480; 🐱🐱) This huge hotel offers pole position for a trip to Bìshǔ Shānzhuāng. The standard and deluxe rooms are comfortable enough, but like most of Chéngdé's hotels, they have begun to show some wear and tear. The cheapest rooms are in a building out the back, but are older and not great value. Some English is spoken here.

⭐ Qí Wàng Lóu   HOTEL $$$

(绮望楼; ☑0314 218 2288; www.qiwanglou.com; 1 Bifengmen Donglu, 碧峰门东路1号; r from ¥1280;

⊖❄) Qī Wàng Lóu boasts a serene setting alongside the Imperial Villa's walls, accentuated by lovely courtyard gardens. This is far and away the most tasteful hotel in town, with museum-quality reproduced Chinese masterpieces hanging in all the rooms. Nicer rooms have balconies, but don't go for anything on the 1st floor, as it is partially underground.

Yìyuán Bīnguǎn HOTEL $$$
(易园宾馆; ☑ 0314 589 1111; 7 Lizhengmen Dajie, 丽正门大街7号; r ¥780-880; ❄❄❄) Rooms here are modern and functional, although the cheapest ones are quite small and come without windows. The main draw is the excellent location in the centre of town; the reasonable prices – expect to pay around ¥228 – sweeten the deal. Buses 13 and 29 come here from the train and bus stations.

✖ Eating

Dà Qīng Huā DUMPLING $
(大清花; Lizhengmen Dajie, 丽正门大街; mains from ¥20; ◷10.30am-9.30pm; ☑) The finest dumpling house in Chéngdé, this excellent establishment has a big choice of juicy *jiǎozi* (boiled dumplings; ¥14 to ¥28 per serving) with some unusual fillings, including veg options; pan-fried dumplings also available. There's a huge range of other dishes too – even some 'emperor dishes' (such as venison).

There's another **branch** (大清花; 241 Chezhan Lu, 车站路241号; mains from ¥20; ◷10.30am-9.30pm; ☑) by the train station.

Hànná Shān Kǎoròu KOREAN $$
(汉拿山烤肉; ☑0314 761 1888; 2nd fl, 5 Liushui Gou, 流水沟5号2楼; grills ¥23-158, stone-bowl dishes ¥23-28; ◷11am-9pm) Seek out this popular Korean restaurant for grill-your-own meats (¥15 fee for coals and sauce bar); kimchi, stone-bowl rice dishes, buckwheat noodles and other delicacies from the peninsula. It's up on the 2nd floor; the not-so-obvious entrance is on Zhongxing Lu. Picture menu.

❶ Information

Bank of China (中国银行, Zhōngguó Yínháng; 4 Dutongfu Dajie, 都统府大街4号) Also on Lizhengmen Dajie; has 24-hour ATMs.

Chāojí Internet Cafe (超级网吧, Chāojí Wǎngbā; Chezhan Lu, 车站路; per hour ¥3; ◷24hr)

China Post (中国邮政, Zhōngguó Yóuzhèng; cnr Lizhengmen Dajie & Dutongfu Dajie, 丽正门大街与都统府大街交叉口; ◷8am-6pm)

Industrial & Commercial Bank (ICBC, 工商银行, Gōngshāng Yínháng; Chezhan Lu, 车站路)

Public Security Bureau (PSB, 公安局, Gōng'ānjú; ☑0314 202 2352; 9 Wulie Lu, 武烈路9号; ◷8.30am-5pm Mon-Fri)

❶ Getting There & Away

BUS
Buses for Chéngdé leave Běijīng hourly from Liùlǐqiáo bus station (¥85, 3½ hours, 5.40am to 6.40pm). From Chéngdé, they leave every half-hour for Běijīng (¥85, 3½ hours, 6.20am to 6.40pm) from the train station square.

Services from Chéngdé's **east bus station** (汽车东站; *qìchē dōngzhàn*), 8km south of town, include the following:

Běijīng ¥85, 3½ hours, half-hourly (6am to 6pm)
Dàlián ¥219, 16 hours, 3pm (every other day)
Qínhuángdǎo (for Shānhǎiguān) ¥110, three hours, six daily (7.30am, 8.05am, 8.30am, 10am, 1pm and 4pm)
Tiānjīn ¥120, four hours, two daily (8.50am and 2pm)

TRAIN
The two fastest trains from Běijīng train station (hard seat ¥35 to ¥40) take 4½ to five hours and leave at 7.56am and 12.20pm. Return services leave Chéngdé at 5.45am, 1.13pm (Běijīng East) and 7.15pm.

Shěnyáng Hard sleeper ¥166, 12½ hours, two daily (7.02am and 5.31pm)
Shíjiāzhuāng Hard sleeper ¥150, nine to 12½ hours, five daily

❶ Getting Around
A taxi from the train station to the Bìshǔ Shānzhuāng should cost around ¥10; from the bus station into town should cost around ¥20 to ¥25.

Buses 13, 24 and 29 link the east bus station with the train station; 13 and 29 carry on to Guāndì Temple.

Shānhǎiguān 山海关
☑ 0335 / POP 18,638

The drowsy walled town of Shānhǎiguān is the fabled point where the Great Wall snakes out of the hills to meet the sea.

The area holds real interest for Wall enthusiasts: in addition to its claim as the eastern end of the Ming Wall, there's an excellent museum and opportunity to explore large stretches of wild, unrestored Wall, climbing up and over the rugged, scrubland hills.

Bear in mind, however, that the town itself feels a bit soulless. With few residents remaining and no economy in the old town apart from tourism, what's left is something that feels mostly like a theme park, but without the rides.

Shānhǎiguān

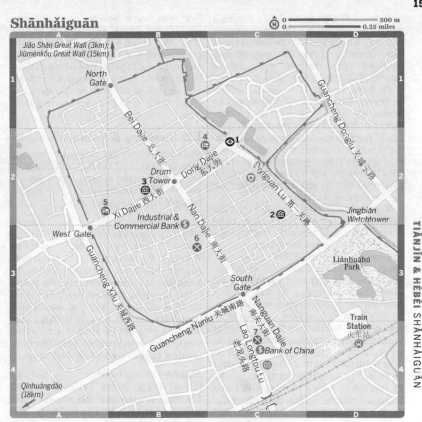

History

Guarding the narrow plain leading to northeastern China, the Ming garrison town of Shānhǎiguān and its wall were developed to seal off the country from the Manchu, whose troublesome ancestors ruled northern China during the Jin dynasty (1115–1234). This strategy succeeded until 1644, when Chinese rebels seized Běijīng and General Wu Sangui opted to invite the Manchu army through the impregnable pass to help suppress the uprising. The plan worked so well that the Manchus proceeded to take over the entire country and establish the Qing dynasty.

⊙ Sights

After full-scale demolition along the main streets, Shānhǎiguān has been busy recreating new diversions in town, such as the imperial military compound, **Zŏng Bīng Fŭ** (总兵府; Xi Dajie, 西大街; ¥80; ⊙8am-5.30pm). These sights are all fairly half-baked,

Shānhǎiguān

⊙ Sights
1 First Pass Under Heaven C2
2 Great Wall Museum C2
3 Zŏng Bīng Fŭ B2

⊜ Sleeping
4 Jīngshān Hotel B2
5 Shānhǎi Holiday Hotel A2

⊗ Eating
6 Lánzhōu Zhèngzōng Niúròu
  Lāmiàn B3
7 Yŏu Gùshì De Jiǎozi C4

however – stick to the main attractions, all of which involve the Wall. Ticket prices for all sights drop considerably in the off season.

★**Jiǎo Shān Great Wall**   WALLS
(角山; ¥40, with chairlift ¥50; ⊙7am-sunset) Although a heavily restored section of the Great Wall, Jiǎo Shān nevertheless offers a great

opportunity to hike up the Wall's first high peak – a telling vantage point over the narrow tongue of land below and one-time invasion route for northern armies. It's a steep 30-minute clamber from the base, or else the old chairlift (索道; *suǒdào*) can haul you up.

To leave behind the crowds, continue beyond the cable-car station to **Qīxián Monastery** (栖贤寺; Qīxián Sì) or even further to **Sweet Nectar Pavilion** (甘露亭; Gānlù Tíng). Better yet, climb up onto the closed section (accessed from paths on the side) and you'll be able to follow the crumbling Wall all the way up past several peaks. Explorers won't be able to resist – but use caution and don't go it alone.

To get here you'll need to take a taxi (¥20 flat rate), but it's an easy 3km walk (or cycle) north of town. Just follow the road straight on from Shānhǎiguān's North Gate.

More fun than just following the road, though, is to approach Jiǎo Shān on an original, overgrown stretch of **earthen Great Wall**, which still creeps its way through farmland from Shānhǎiguān to Jiǎo Shān. Most of its Ming brickwork has long since been pillaged, but there's still a scattering of bricks, including a couple of collapsed watchtowers. To take this route, walk straight on from North Gate and then take the first right on the main road to the Wall (you can't miss it). Turn left up the pathway beside the iron bridge and clamber up. You can walk on this earthen Wall all the way Jiǎo Shān (you'll need to climb over onto a restored section across the highway); at the end, walk down to the ticket office to enter Jiǎo Shān.

Old Dragon Head
HISTORIC SITE

(老龙头, Lǎolóngtóu; ¥50; ⏱7.30am-6.30pm) Famous across China (although a little over-hyped), Old Dragon Head, 4km south of Shānhǎiguān, is where the Great Wall meets the sea. It's photogenic for sure, but bear in mind that what you see now was reconstructed in the late 1980s – the original wall crumbled away long ago. Bus 25 (¥1) goes here from Shānhǎiguān's South Gate.

Great Wall Museum
MUSEUM

(长城博物馆, Chángchéng Bówùguǎn; Diyiguan Lu, 第一关路; ⏱9am-4pm Tue-Sun) **FREE** This impressive museum provides a thorough chronological history of the Wall, going into architectural features and including interesting scale models of the walled town and surrounding Great Wall locations. Plenty of photos and artefacts, as well as English captions.

First Pass Under Heaven
HISTORIC SITE

(天下第一关, Tiānxià Dìyī Guān; Dong Dajie, 东大街; ¥40; ⏱7am-5.30pm) The Great Wall's main gate as it snaked down the mountains and to the sea, the First Pass served as Shānhǎiguān's east gate and principal watchtower. Two storeys tall, with double eaves and 68 arrow-slit windows, it's a towering 13.7m high, with an enceinte extending east.

🛏 Sleeping & Eating

Shānhǎiguān sleeping options are extremely limited. There are few hotels to begin with, and only a handful of those accept foreigners. For international options, stay in Qínhuángdǎo (秦皇岛), 18km away.

Jīngshān Hotel
HOTEL $$$

(景山宾馆, Jīngshān Bīnguǎn; ☎0335 513 2188/46; 1 Dong Dajie, 东大街1号; tw/tr from ¥580/680; 🖥) Housed in a pleasant, reconstructed, two-storey courtyard complex, the Jīngshān – the town's most agreeable hotel – is just steps from the First Pass Under Heaven. Rooms here are airy and comfortable, though don't expect anything too fancy – the hot-water pressure, for instance, ensures you won't be washing your hair here. Discounts can drop rates as low as ¥150. No English.

Shānhǎi Holiday Hotel
HOTEL $$$

(山海假日酒店, Shānhǎi Jiàrì Jiǔdiàn; ☎0335 535 2888; www.shanhai-holiday.com; Bei Madao, 北马道; d & tw ¥880; 🖥) This traditional-style four-star hotel is housed in a large complex with several buildings, and is trying hard to impress, with staff dressed in traditional Manchu clothing. Unfortunately, the rooms we saw were in so-so condition. Discounted rates hover around ¥268.

Yǒu Gùshì De Jiǎozi
DUMPLING $

(有故事的饺子; Lao Longtou Lu, 老龙头路; dumplings ¥9-26, dishes ¥8-48; ⏱10am-9pm) Come evening, venture outside the city walls to this popular, modern eatery, where a team of *jiǎozi* specialists make the goods by hand in the open kitchen. In addition to the dumplings, there's a good range of fried Chinese dishes on the picture menu.

Lánzhōu Zhèngzōng Niúròu Lāmiàn
NOODLES $

(兰州正宗牛肉拉面; Nan Dajie, 南大街; dishes ¥6-17; ⏱7am-6pm) Does a range of tasty noodle dishes, including pulled noodles with beef (牛肉拉面; *niúròu lāmiàn* – the restaurant speciality), with lamb (羊肉拉面; *yángròu lāmiàn*), with Chinese cabbage (青菜拉

面; *qīngcài lāmiàn*) and with egg (鸡蛋拉面; *jīdàn lāmiàn*). Has photos of much of the menu plastered across two walls. No English.

ℹ Information

Bank of China (中国银行, Zhōngguó Yínháng; Lao Longtou Lu, 老龙头路; ⊗ 8.30am-5.30pm) Foreign-exchange facility.

China Post (中国邮政, Zhōngguó Yóuzhèng; Lao Longtou Lu, 老龙头路; ⊗ 8.30am-6pm)

Industrial & Commercial Bank (ICBC, 工商银行, Gōngshāng Yínháng; Nan Dajie, 南大街) Has ATM.

Public Security Bureau (PSB, 公安局, Gōng'ānjú; ☑ 0335 505 1163; Diyiguan Lu, 第一关路) Opposite the entrance to First Pass Under Heaven, on the corner of a small alleyway.

ℹ Getting There & Around

AIR
Qínhuángdǎo's small airport has flights to Dàlián, Shànghǎi, Qīngdǎo and Xī'ān.

BUS
To get to Shānhǎiguān from Qínhuángdǎo's bus or train station, take bus 8 (¥1) from outside the train station for one stop – you can also walk it if you can communicate in Chinese – then cross the road and take bus 33 (¥2, 30 minutes) going the opposite direction to Shānhǎiguān's South Gate (南门; Nán Mén).

There's no long-distance bus station in Shānhǎiguān. Qínhuángdǎo's **bus station** (車皇岛汽车站; *Qínhuángdǎo qìchēzhàn*), where the nearest long-distance buses arrive, is diagonally opposite its train station.

Buses from Qínhuángdǎo's bus station include the following:

Běijīng (Bāwángfén) ¥105, 3½ hours, three daily (8am, 10am and 3.30pm)
Běijīng Capital Airport ¥140, four hours, hourly (5am to 5pm)
Chéngdé ¥110, three hours, six daily (8am, 9am, 10am, 11am, 1pm and 5pm)
Dàlián ¥150, seven hours, 10.50am (every other day)

TAXIS
Taxis in Shānhǎiguān are ¥5 flag fall. Motorrickshaws shouldn't cost more than ¥5 for trips within town, though drivers will invariably try to charge you ¥10.

TRAIN
There are over a dozen D-class bullet trains linking Běijīng Main Station and Shānhǎiguān (¥93, 2½ hours) throughout the day.

Alternatively, even more high-speed trains go from Běijīng to the nearby city of Qínhuángdǎo (秦皇岛; ¥88, 2½ hours), 18km from Shānhǎiguān.

Trains also run to Qínhuángdǎo from Tiānjīn (¥120, 1¼ hours) and Shěnyáng (¥118, 2½ hours).

Jīmíngyì   鸡鸣驿

☑ 0313 / POP 1000

The sleepy hamlet Jīmíngyì is a delightful surprise to find amid the scruffy northern Héběi countryside. This walled town, established during the Yuan dynasty (1206–1368), is China's oldest surviving post station, a historic reminder of a system that endured for 2000 years and enabled the officials in the Forbidden City to keep in touch with their far-flung counterparts around China. Whipped by dust storms in the spring and with archaic, fading Mao-era slogans still visible on walls, Jīmíngyì sees few visitors and feels much further from the gleaming capital than the 140km distance would suggest.

During the Ming and Qing dynasties, Jīmíngyì had considerably more bustle and wealth, as evidenced by its numerous surviving temples and town wall. Many of its courtyard houses remain, though in dilapidated condition.

There's been a flurry of activity recently, with local government attempts to boosts Jīmíngyì's appeal as a tourist destination.

◉ Sights

Meandering along the warren of Jīmíngyì's baked-mud walls and courtyard houses takes you past ancient stages and scattered temples, some of which contain Ming and Qing murals (not all are in good condition). Admission to the village costs ¥40.

God of Wealth Temple   TAOIST TEMPLE
(财神庙, Cáishén Miào) Pop into this tiny edifice to pray for fabulous riches or to check out the fabulous Ming mural, uncovered in 2012. It depicts an ancient bank (票号; *piàohào*); if you look closely you'll also see five foreigners and a *qílín* (麒麟; a mythical Chinese animal) in the lower left-hand corner, on their way to China to do business.

Jīmíngyì Museum   MUSEUM
(鸡鸣驿博物馆, Jīmíngyì Bówùguǎn) Opened in 2015, this tiny museum near the East Gate contains a few photos, artefacts and the like. There's little English signage, though it's worth a peek. Admission is included with entry to the town.

Temple of Eternal Tranquility BUDDHIST TEMPLE
(永宁寺, Yǒngníng Sì; ¥60) The largest and oldest temple in the area sits atop **Cock's Crow Mountain** (鸡鸣山; Jīmíng Shān), which overlooks the town to the northwest. It's still an active monastery and a large and

WORTH A TRIP

JIŬMÉNKŎU GREAT WALL

In a mountain valley 15km north of Shānhǎiguān stretches **Jiŭménkŏu Great Wall** (九门口长城; ¥80), the only section of the Great Wall ever built over water. Normally the Wall stopped at rivers, as they were considered natural defence barriers on their own. At Jiŭménkŏu Great Wall, however, a 100m span supported by nine arches crosses the Jiŭjiāng River, which we can only guess flowed at a much faster and deeper rate than it does today (or else the arches would function more like open gates).

Much effort has gone into restoring this formidable-looking bridge and on both sides the Wall continues its run up the steep, rocky hillsides. Heading left, you can quickly see where the Wall remains unrestored on the opposite side. Sadly, access to this area is blocked but the distant sight of crumbling stone watchtowers truly drives home the terrible isolation that must have been felt by the guardians of frontier regions such as this.

No buses head to the Wall from Shānhǎiguān. A taxi costs around ¥35 one way; ask the drivers gathered outside the **South Gate**. A return trip will cost more like ¥80 to ¥100, including waiting time.

lively festival is held here during April each year. It's only accessible from the town of Xià Huāyuán (下花园); figure on a 90-minute hike. You can also take a taxi up for ¥30.

Jīmíngyì City Walls   HISTORIC SITE
(城墙, Chéng Qiáng) Ascend the **East Gate** or **West Gate** and circle the walls for fine views of the town, the surrounding fields and Cock's Crow Mountain (鸡鸣山; Jīmíng Shān), standing to the northwest.

Tàishān Temple   TAOIST TEMPLE
(泰山行宫, Tàishān Xínggōng) This temple is dedicated to Bìxiá, the goddess of Tài Shān. The paintings here, Jīmíngyì's largest collection of Ming murals, depict the life of the goddess. They were whitewashed – some say for protection – during the Cultural Revolution. A professor from Qīnghuá University helped to uncover them; you can still see streaks of white in places.

**Temple of the
God of Literature**   CONFUCIAN TEMPLE
(文昌宫, Wénchāng Gōng) This simple Ming dynasty temple is dedicated to the god of literature, whom scholars called upon to help with the imperial exams. Like many Confucian temples, it also served as the local school.

🛏 Sleeping & Eating

It's possible to visit Jīmíngyì as a day trip from Běijīng, but spending the night allows you time to enjoy the slower pace of rural life. Sleeping options are limited to *nóngjiāyuàn* (农家院; village guesthouses) on Yicheng Yijie (驿城一街), the road running between the East and West Gates. Expect to pay around ¥60 for a room.

Village guesthouses are the only places serving food inside the city walls. Bear in mind they do eat donkey (驴肉; *lǘròu*) in these parts.

Bǎilè Kèzhàn   GUESTHOUSE $
(百乐客栈; ☎137 8533 9336; rooms ¥60-80; 🌐) Simple but clean restaurant and guesthouse with small, tidy rooms off a tiny courtyard. Has a common shower room. The restaurant menu (mains ¥10 to ¥35) is in Chinese only. You'll find standard dishes such as *zhájiàng miàn* (炸酱面; pork and beanpaste noodles), *xīhóngshì chǎojīdàn* (西红柿炒鸡蛋; scrambled eggs and tomatoes) and *suānlà tǔdòusī* (酸辣土豆丝; shredded fried potato). It's located not far from the West Gate.

ℹ Getting There & Away

Jīmíngyì can be reached from the small mining town of Xià Huāyuán (下花园), 5km away. The easiest way there is to hop on a train from Běijīng Main (¥23.50, three hours, 7.43am) or Běijīng West (¥21.50, 2¼ hours, 10.32am). From the train station, flag down a passing small bus to Shāchéng (沙城), which goes past Jīmíngyì (5 minutes, ¥3). Afternoon trains back to Běijīng leave at 3.55pm (for Běijīng Main) and 4.34pm (for Běijīng West).

Taking a bus offers more flexibility than the train, though you'll want decent navigational/Chinese skills to find it. First, head to Zhuxinzhuang metro station at the end of line 8. Exit the station and walk 300m south to bus 899, which serves Xià Huāyuán (¥24; 2¼ hours; 5.30am to 5.30pm). From the Xià Huāyuán station, take a taxi into town (¥10) and flag down the Shāchéng bus, or simply taxi it all the way to Jīmíngyì – drivers start at ¥30, though you should be able to bargain down to ¥20. The last bus back to Běijīng leaves at 5pm.

Liáoníng

POP 43.9 MILLION

Best Places to Eat

➜ Měijīn Hotpot (p171)

➜ Tiāntiān Yúgǎng (p162)

➜ Handu Restaurant (p162)

Best Places to Sleep

➜ Dàlián Noah's Ark Golden Beach Hostel (p160)

➜ Aloft Dalian (p161)

➜ UniLoft Hostel (p160)

Why Go?

History and hedonism run side by side in Liáoníng (辽宁). Walled Ming dynasty cities rub up against booming beach resorts, while imperial palaces sit in the centre of bustling modern cities. Nothing quite captures the fun and distinction, however, as much as seaside Dàlián, with its golden coastline and summer beer festival, and former battlegrounds where Russian and Japanese armies wrestled for control of the region in the early 20th century. In Dāndōng, regional tensions of recent history are causing some spine-tingling at the border with North Korea. The Yālù River here brings you within glimpsing distance of the hermit kingdom from a boat deck or halfway across a bridge.

When to Go
Dàlián

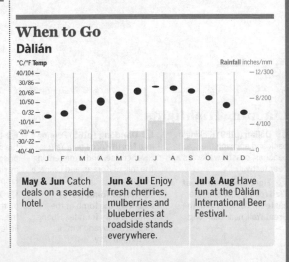

May & Jun Catch deals on a seaside hotel.

Jun & Jul Enjoy fresh cherries, mulberries and blueberries at roadside stands everywhere.

Jul & Aug Have fun at the Dàlián International Beer Festival.

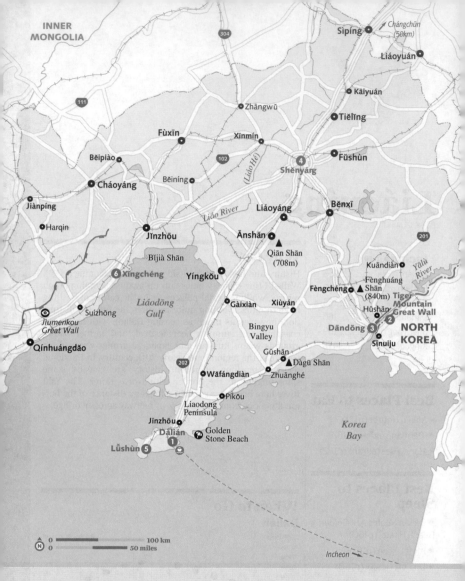

Liáoníng Highlights

1 **Dàlián** (p159) Kicking back and enjoying the beaches, coastal walkways and beer festival.

2 **Tiger Mountain Great Wall** (p166) Climbing the easternmost stretch of the Great Wall, near Dāndōng.

3 **Dāndōng** (p165) Peering into North Korea on a Yālù River cruise, and experiencing the mix of Korean and Chinese culture.

4 **North Tomb** (p171) Exploring the tomb of the Qing dynasty founder, Huang Taiji, in Shěnyáng's mini Forbidden City.

5 **Lǚshùn** (p164) Wandering the old battlefields, graves and prison of Lǚshùn, fought over by rival Japanese and Russian Empires.

6 **Xīngchéng** (p173) Lazing on the beach and strolling the old walled city of historic, little-visited Xīngchéng.

History

The region formerly known as Manchuria, including the provinces of Liáoníng, Jílín and Hēilóngjiāng, plus parts of Inner Mongolia, is now called Dōngběi (the Northeast).

The Manchurian warlords of this northern territory established the Qing dynasty, which ruled China from 1644 to 1911. From the late 1800s to the end of WWII, when Western powers were busy carving up pieces of China for themselves, Manchuria was occupied alternately by the Russians and the Japanese. Today there is a push to transform the flagging steel industry carried over from the 1950s into a tech hub.

ⓘ Getting There & Around

Shěnyáng and Dàlián have domestic and international airports. Dāndōng has an airport with infrequent domestic flights.

Boats connect Dàlián with Shāndōng province and South Korea.

Buses are a slower alternative to high-speed trains but can outpace regular trains.

Rail lines criss-cross the region; fast D and G trains link Shěnyáng with cities south to Dàlián and Dāndōng; north to Harbin and Qíqíhā'ěr; and east to Chángchūn, Jílín City and Yánjí.

Dàlián 大连

⬛ 0411 / POP 6.69 MILLION

Perched on the Liáodōng Peninsula and bordering the Yellow Sea, Dàlián is one of the most relaxed and liveable cities in the northeast, if not all of China. Tree-lined hilly streets with manageable traffic and fresh air, a surfeit of early 20th-century architecture and an impressive coastline, complete with swimming beaches, are just some of its charms. Toss in a decent restaurant-and-bar scene and serious shopping, and that frequent Dàlián epithet, the 'Hong Kong of the North', looks like more than just bluster.

Dàlián is a fine place to unwind for a few days. But after lazing on the beaches and strolling along the southwest coastline, pay a visit to the historic port town of Lǚshùn. The old battlefields and cemeteries offer a rare first-hand glimpse into some of the north's most turbulent days.

⊙ Sights

Xīnghǎi Square SQUARE
(星海广场, Xīnghǎi Guǎngchǎng; Map p164) FREE
This square, which sports some gaudy architecture, is the site of Dàlián's popular beer fes-

tival, and is a good place to people-watch, fly a kite, or just stroll about. Nearby is a small beach and amusement park.

From the train station, take tram 201 (¥2; to its west terminus), or faster metro Line 2 (¥1; stop Xi'an 西安路), then tram 202 (¥2) three stops. Last return tram 11pm. A taxi is about ¥20.

Fisherman's Wharf VILLAGE
(渔人码头, Yúrén Mǎtóu; Map p164; 66 Bīnhǎi Donglu, 滨海东路66号) FREE This seaside community was built in the style of an American East Coast village from the early 20th century. It makes a great backdrop for photos, has a row of pleasant coffee and wine shops, and features a perfect replica of the 1853 German Bremen Port Lighthouse, built with bricks from razed local villages.

Fùjiāzhuāng Beach BEACH
(傅家庄海滩, Fùjiāzhuāng Hǎitān) Fùjiāzhuāng is a popular beach set in a deep bay. Junks float just offshore, small broken islands dot the horizon, and loads of families come here for no other reason than to have fun. Bus 5 leaves from Jiefang Lu (¥1, 20 to 30 minutes) and drops you off across from the beach.

Jīnshí Tān BEACH
(金石滩, Golden Pebble Beach) FREE The coast around Jīnshí Tān, 50km northeast of the city, has been turned into a domestic tourism mecca with a number of theme parks and rock formations commanding inflated entrance fees. The long pebbly beach itself is free and quite pretty, set in a wide bay with distant headlands.

To get here take the light rail, known by the locals as Line 3 (轻轨三号线, Qīngguǐ Sānhàoxiàn), from the depot on the east side of Triumph Plaza, behind the Dàlián

PRICE INDICATORS

The following price indicators are used in this chapter:

Sleeping

$ Less than ¥200

$$ ¥200–¥400

$$$ More than ¥400

Eating

$ Less than ¥40

$$ ¥40–¥80

$$$ More than ¥80

LIÁONÍNG DÀLIÁN

Train Station (¥8, 50 minutes) to its terminus 'Jin Shi Tan'. The ticket machine is Chinese only, but just select the most expensive ticket, then the number of tickets and insert your money. From the beach station it's a 10-minute walk to the beach, or catch a hop-on/off tourist shuttle bus (¥20), which winds round the coast first before dropping you off at the beach. Tickets for the shuttle bus are from the visitor centre (open 8.30am to 5pm) to the right of the train station as you exit, sometimes with English-speaking staff if you need help.

Zhongshan Square HISTORIC BUILDING
(中山广场, Zhōngshān Guǎngchǎng) This is Dàlián's hub, a 223m-wide square with 10 lanes radiating out from a central roundabout designed by the Russians in 1889. With the exception of the Dalian Financial Building, all the other grand structures hail from the early 20th century when Dàlián was under the control of the Japanese. Styles range from art deco to French Renaissance.

The **Dàlián Bīnguǎn**, a dignified hotel built in 1914 and called then the Dalian Yamato Hotel, appeared in the movie *The Last Emperor*.

🛏 Sleeping

Reservations are highly recommended in the summer months, when prices may be 50% more than listed here. The area around the train station's north exit has a number of budget hotels, but it's a noisy, frenetic place. Touts will find you if you do need a room: rates start at ¥100 a night. Better, quieter options are a few blocks southeast of the station.

BEER MANIA

For 12 days every July into August, Dàlián stages the **Dàlián International Beer Festival**, resembling Munich's Oktoberfest. Beer companies from across China and around the world set up tents at the vast Xīnghǎi Sq, near the coast, and locals and visitors (usually about 300,000) flock to sample the brews, gorge on snacks from around China, listen to live music and generally make whoopee.

Entrance tickets are a low ¥20 (¥30 on opening day) and there are typically 30 beer vendors offering over 400 brands for sampling.

★ **UniLoft Hostel** HOSTEL $
(大连联合庭院青旅酒店, Dàlián Liánhé Tíngyuàn Qīnglǚ Jiǔdiàn; Map p164; ☎ 0411 8369 7877; 17-1 Yinghua Jie, 英华街17-1号; dm ¥39-49, d with/without bathroom ¥139/119; P ⊜ ❄ @ ☎) The sleek industrial space resembles a modern museum, and the cleverly sectioned-off beds give privacy alongside clean, comfy mattresses. Opening a window shutter in the small doubles reveals views right onto the lounge area, but they are still an excellent deal for budget yet stylish digs. An in-house cafe makes up for the few surrounding eating options. UniLoft is behind a raised carpark.

A taxi from the train station is ¥10.

★ **Dàlián Noah's Ark Golden Beach Hostel** HOSTEL $
(大连挪亚方舟国际青年旅舍, Dàlián Nuóyà Fāngzhōu Guójì Qīngnián Lǚshè; Map p164; ☎ 0411 3968 4088; www.yhachina.com/ls.php?id=339; 57 Binhai Xilu, 滨海西路57号; dm ¥60-80, tw ¥280; ⊙ closed winter; @ ☎) There's nothing remotely biblical about the hostel: the architecture, a whitewashed edifice built against a hill and facing the sea, evokes Santorini. Rooms are simple but charming: consider staying in a greenhouse-type glasshouse at the top of the compound! The 2nd-level lounge area is a great spot to have a beer and stare out to sea. Room rates are 70% higher for non-YHA members.

Getting here is tough. Take bus 5 near the train station at Qīngníwā Qiáo (青泥洼桥) to the last stop. Walk ahead five minutes through a parking lot and down a slope towards Golden Sand Beach (金沙滩; Jīn Shā Tān), pay ¥2 entry and continue towards the seashore and follow it to the right. Pack light as it's a 1km walk. Note: you have to pay the ¥2 entry daily if you go in and out of the area.

Dàlián South Mountain Youth Hostel HOSTEL $
(大连南山国际青年旅舍, Dàlián Nánshān Guójì Qīngnián Lǚshè; Map p164; ☎ 0411 8263 1189; dlnanshan@126.com; 114 Mingze Jie, 明泽街114号; dm ¥50-65, d/tw ¥168/188; ❄ @ ☎) Tucked away in a quiet hillside neighbourhood is this friendly little hostel with clean, comfortable dorms (but only two bathrooms!). Facilities include self-service laundry and kitchen, as well as computer use and wi-fi. The southwest coastline is a 15-minute bus ride away, numerous parks are within walking distance and the train station can be reached quickly by taxi (¥10).

Dàlián

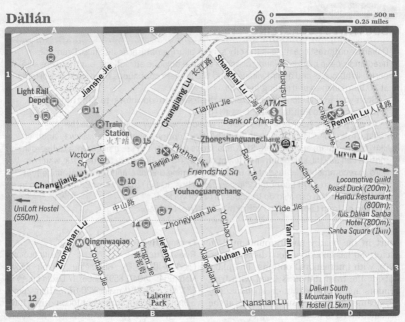

If you want to catch a bus here contact the hostel for directions.

Ibis Dàlián Sanba Hotel HOTEL $$
(大连三八宜必思酒店, Dàlián Sānbā Yìbìsī Jiǔdiàn; Map p164; ☎0411 3986 5555; www.ibishotel.com.cn; 49 Wuwu Iu 中山区八五路49号, d & tw ¥229; ❄@) This business hotel is in a fantastic location surrounded by restaurants and markets, yet only a five-minute walk from parks and quiet tree-lined streets. Public buses (bus 710) connect the hotel to the train station and southwestern coast. Rooms are clean and modern and the English-speaking staff are fairly attentive. For best rates book online.

It's located just off Sanba Sq. A taxi from the train station here costs ¥12.

★ **Aloft Dalian** HOTEL $$$
(大连雅乐轩酒店, Dàlián Yǎlèxuān Jiǔdiàn; ☎0411 3907 1111; www.alofthotels.com/dalian; 18-1 Luxun Lu, 鲁迅路18-1号; r ¥1720-2220; ❄@) This swish hotel is borne aloft thanks to a hip charisma lacking in other international chain hotels. Its colourfully decorated rooms are large with good views and plush beds, and the staff are friendly to a fault. The in-house restaurant and lounge area are good too. Discounts tame rack rates to a more reasonable ¥500 range.

Dàlián

◎ Sights
1 Zhongshan Square C2

🛏 Sleeping
2 Aloft Dalian D2

🍴 Eating
3 Tianjin Jie Night Market B2
4 Tiāntiān Yúgǎng D1

ℹ Transport
5 Bus to Dāndōng B2
6 Bus to Ferry B2
7 Bus to Fùjiāzhuāng Beach B2
8 Bus to Lǚshùn A1
9 Bus to North Train Station A1
10 Bus to Shěnyáng B2
11 Bus to Zhuānghé A1
12 Civil Aviation Administration
    of China A3
13 Da-in Ferry D1
14 Qīngníwá Qiáo Bus Stop B3
15 Tourist Bus Stop B2

🍴 Eating

Plenty of small restaurants are on the roads leading off Zhongshan Sq and Friendship Sq. Friendship Sq has numerous malls with food courts on the higher floors. The food

DON'T MISS

SOUTHWEST COASTLINE

Dàlián's southwest coastline is the city's most alluring natural destination. Dramatic headlands, deep bays and sandy beaches are the obvious attractions, but there are also parks, lighthouses and quaint villages, and the longest continuous boardwalk (reportedly at 20.9km) in the world joining them all.

Start your exploration either by taking the tram from downtown to **Xīnghǎi Sq** (p159), or a bus to **Fùjiāzhuāng Beach** (p159).

A very pleasant boardwalk (it's really a wooden walkway built alongside the main coastal road) joins Fùjiāzhuāng and Xīnghǎi Sq. Continue on the same walkway another 8km to the square at Lǎohǔtān. Statue fanatics who want to see a huge work of tigers in motion can pay the steep entrance fee of over ¥200 for this glitzy theme park, which is hard to recommend because of its use of performing dolphins and seals, a practice that some view as cruel. At Lǎohǔtān you can catch bus 30 (¥1) to Sanba or Zhongshan Sq in central Dàlián. You can also do the coastal route via taxi.

Head on from Lǎohǔtān to **Fisherman's Wharf** (p159).

court in the nearby underground mall in Victory Sq has good food too (dishes ¥10 to ¥20), with international options. The plaza outside the train station is lined with fruit vendors and shops selling cheap *bāozi* (包子; steamed buns). Find supermarkets at the basement level of malls.

Tianjin Jie Night Market   MARKET $
(夜市, Yèshì) Stretching several blocks along Tianjin Jie from the train station to a giant incense-bowl sculpture, this outdoor market, open during the evenings, offers outdoor venues to eat barbecued seafood and other snacks with a beer. There's also a smaller (but better) market around Sanba Sq near the Carrefour Supermarket with outdoor barbecue stalls and seating, in addition to an abundance of fruit stands.

Handu Restaurant   KOREAN $$
(韩都, Hándū; Map p164; 49-1 Wuwu Lu, 五五路 49-1号; dishes ¥15-90; ⊙11am-10pm) In the Sanba Sq area, this fabulous two-storey Korean restaurant decked out in luxe wood and granite fittings lets you barbecue your own meats at the table. There's also a selection of one-dish meals such as *bibimbap* (rice, vegetables and eggs served in a claypot) for those who don't wish to go the whole hog.

Tiāntiān Yúgǎng   SEAFOOD $$$
(天天鱼港; 10 Renmin Lu, 人民路10号; dishes ¥25-100; ⊙11am-10pm) Choose your meal from the near museum-level variety of aquatic creatures at this upscale seafood restaurant. Most dishes are set out in refrigerated displays, making this a rare easy seafood-eating experience in China.

**Locomotive Guild
Roast Duck**   PEKING DUCK $$$
(火车头果木烤鸭, Huǒchētóu Guǒmù Kǎoyā; Map p164; ☑0411 8597 6666; 17 Luxun Lu, 鲁迅路17号; duck ¥197, mains ¥20-67; ⊙11am-2pm & 5-9pm) We're not sure what locomotives have to do with duck, but the birds here are roasted in a wood-fired oven to delicate crispness before being deftly sliced and presented to your table. Live seafood is also available for those who prefer fish over fowl. Picture menu available.

🍷 Drinking & Nightlife

Dàlián has the most happening bar and club scene of any city in the northeast. Most of the action is on Wuwu Lu, which runs off Sanba Sq. Check out *Focus on Dalian* (www.focusondalian.com) for the latest.

❶ Information

There are ATMs all around town. Zhongshan Sq has a number of large bank branches including a **Bank of China** (中国银行, Zhōngguó Yínháng; 9 Zhongshan Sq), where you can change currency.

The 72-Hour Visa-Free Transit policy allows passport holders of many countries a stopover in Dàlián without arranging a visa before arrival. See p1007 for more information.

❶ Getting There & Away

AIR

Dàlián International Airport (大连周水子国际机场) is 12km from the city centre and well connected to most cities in China and the region. Tickets can be purchased at the **Civil Aviation Administration of China** (CAAC, 中国民航, Zhōngguó Mínháng; ☑0411 8361 2888; Zhongshan Lu) or any of the travel offices nearby. In addition to the domestic destinations listed here, there are also flights to Khabarovsk, Vladivostok, Hong Kong and Tokyo. Dàlián Jīnzhōuwān Airport is built on an artificial island and is being phased in as the main airport.

Běijīng ¥760, one to 1½ hours
Harbin ¥1050, 1½ hours

BOAT

There are several daily boats to Yāntái (¥180 to ¥500, five to eight hours) and Wēihǎi (¥190 to ¥500, seven to eight hours) in Shandong. Buy tickets at the passenger ferry terminal in the northeast of Dàlián or from one of the many counters in front of the train station. To the ferry terminal, take bus 13 (¥1) from the southeast corner of Shengli Guangchang and Zhongshan Lu near the train station.

BUS

Long-distance buses leave from various points around the train station. It can be tricky to find the correct ticket booths, and they do occasionally move.

Dāndōng (丹东) ¥105, four hours, nine daily, 6.20am to 2.30pm. Buses leave from stand No 2 on Shengli Guangchang just south of Changjiang Lu.
Lǚshùn (旅顺) ¥7, 1½ hours, every 20 minutes. Buses leave from the back of the train station, across the square.
Shěnyáng (沈阳) ¥100, five hours, every two hours. Buses depart from south of Victory Sq.
Zhuānghé (庄河) ¥45, 2½ hours, frequent. Buses leave from in front of the ticket office on Jianshe Jie, the first street behind the train station.

TRAIN

Buy your ticket as early as possible. Most high-speed D and G trains leave from the north station. Get a bus (¥5, regular, 30 minutes) there from behind the light-rail station. At the main train station, the attendant at ticket window 1 speaks English.

Běijīng hard seat/sleeper ¥142/276, 11 to 15 hours
Běijīng (D/G train) ¥261/400, 6½/five hours

ⓘ BORDER CROSSING: DÀLIÁN TO SOUTH KOREA

The Korean-run **Da-in Ferry** (☑Dàlián 0411 8270 5082, Incheon 032 891 7100, Seoul 822 3218 6500; www.dainferry. co.kr; 17th fl, 68 Renmin Lu, 人民路68号, 宏誉商业大厦17楼) to Incheon in South Korea departs from Dàlián on Monday, Wednesday and Friday at 4.30pm (¥980 to ¥1900, 16 hours).

Chángchūn (G train) ¥304, three hours
Harbin (G train) ¥404, 3½ to 4½ hours
Shěnyáng (G train) ¥174, 1½ to two hours

ⓘ Getting Around

Dàlián's central district is not large and can be covered on foot.

TO/FROM THE AIRPORT

A shuttle bus (¥5) runs to the train station; bus 701 (¥1; no change given) does also, continuing to Zhongshan Sq. A taxi to/from the city centre costs ¥30 to ¥60 depending on the time of day.

BUS

Buses (¥1) are plentiful and stops have English signboards explaining the route. There's a tourist bus (¥10, hourly, 8.30am to 4.30pm) in front of the train station in summer. It does a hop-on, hop-off loop of the city and the southwestern coast. From the train station, bus 710 passes Sanba Sq; while bus 701 passes Zhongshan Sq.

TAXI

Fares start at ¥10; most trips are less than ¥20.

TRAIN

Dàlián has a modern, efficient subway metro system with two main lines running north–south and east–west. The most useful route for a visitor runs from Zhongshan Sq to the train station, which is actually an easily walkable distance.

TRAM

Dàlián has a slow but stylish tram with two lines: the 201 (¥2) and the 202 (¥1). No 201 runs past the train station on Changjiang Lu, while 202 runs out to the ocean and Xīnghǎi Sq (you must take 201 or the faster metro first and transfer).

Around Dàlián

Lǚshùn   旅顺

☑ 0411 / POP 324,700

With its excellent port and strategic location on the northeast coast, Lǚshùn (formerly Port Arthur) was the focal point of both Russian and Japanese expansion in the late 19th and early 20th centuries. The bloody Russo-Japanese War (1904–05) finally saw the area fall under Japanese colonial rule, which would continue for the next 40 years.

Lǚshùn is worth a visit during any trip to Dàlián. While developers are piling on the high-rise apartments, Lǚshùn is still a relaxed town built on the hills. Most sites are related to military history, but there's an excellent museum on Liáoníng, as well as a number of scenic lookouts and parks.

Greater Dàlián

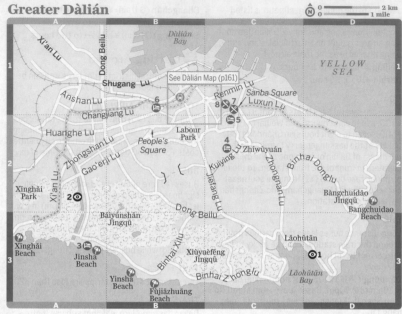

⊙ Sights

★ Lǚshùn Prison
HISTORIC SITE

(旅顺日俄监狱旧址博物馆, Lǚshùn Rì'é Jiānyù Jiùzhǐ Bówùguǎn; ⊙9am-4.30pm, last entry 3.30pm) FREE Lǚshùn's best sight is a cluster of restored red-brick buildings that functioned as a prison from 1902 to 1945. It may have changed hands from the Russians to the Japanese, but its purpose remained unchanged: more than 450,000 prisoners came through its cells. Sombre displays, including an unearthed wooden-barrel coffin

containing an executed inmate, paint a picture of a working early 20th-century jail.

English captions illuminate the plight of prisoners, torture methods, work camps and more. Entry is by free official ushers only.

Bus 3 (¥1) from opposite the bus station terminates outside the prison in 15 minutes.

Lǚshùn Museum
MUSEUM

(旅顺博物馆, Lǚshùn Bówùguǎn; ⊙9am-4pm Tue-Sun) FREE The history of Liáoníng province is covered in this stylish old museum in two early 20th-century buildings. Among the thousands of artefacts on display are ancient bronzes, coins and paintings, as well as several mummies and a quirky chopstick collection. The English captions are good.

The area around the museum has a number of other old buildings from the Japanese colonial era and is a great spot for photographs, especially in spring.

Take bus 4 or 33 (¥1) from outside the bus terminal to the stop 列宁街 (Liening Jie) and walk 450m east.

Báiwáng Shān
HISTORIC SITE

(白王山; ¥40) Head to the top of this hill opposite the bus station for panoramic views out to the bay and across the ever-expanding city. The phallic-shaped monument is **Báiwáng Shān Tǎ** (白王山塔), a pagoda erected by the Japanese in 1909 after they took

Lǔshùn. Climb to the top up the stairs (made in the USA) for ¥10.

Lǔshùn Railway Station   HISTORIC BUILDING
(旅顺火车站, Lǔshùn Huǒchēzhàn) Built in 1903 during Russia's brief control of the area, this handsome station was rebuilt in 2005 following the original design. It's worth a visit en route to other sights.

Bus 18 (¥1) passes here from outside the bus terminal in about 20 minutes.

Soviet Martyrs Cemetery   CEMETERY
(苏军烈士陵园, Sūjūn Lièshì língyuán; ⊙8.30am 4.30pm) FREE The largest cemetery in China for foreign-born nationals honours Soviet soldiers who died in the liberation of northeast China at the end of WWII, as well as pilots killed during the Korean War. Designed by Soviet advisers, the cemetery is heavy with communist-era iconography. A giant rifle-holding soldier guards the front, while inside are memorials to the sacrifice of Soviet soldiers and rows of neatly tended gravestones. Bus 11 (¥1) passes here from outside the bus terminal in about 25 minutes.

🍴 Sleeping & Eating

Most people make a day trip of the area from Dàlián, which has much better and more plentiful options. If you do get stuck, there are budget options opposite Lǔshùn bus station, and a chain hotel at the end of the road south.

People come to Lǔshùn for the sights and not for the eating, which doesn't stand out, good or bad. Bring your own snacks and wait for Dàlián for more restaurant and street-food choices.

ⓘ Getting There & Away

Buses to Lǔshùn (¥7, 1½ hours) leave every 20 minutes from a stop across the square at the back of the Dàlián Train Station. Buy your ticket from the booth before lining up. Buses run back and forth between Lǔshùn and Dàlián from early morning to evening.

ⓘ Getting Around

BUS

Most of Lǔshùn's sights can be easily covered by local buses (¥1), which leave from across the road outside Lǔshùn bus station.

TAXI

As soon as you exit the bus station at Lǔshùn, taxis will cry out for your business. A few hours touring the sights will cost ¥150 (excluding ¥10 car-parking fees at some sights). If the driver

doesn't have one, pick up a bilingual English-Chinese map at the station news-stand to help you negotiate. It is also possible to just flag down taxis as needed. Resist any attempts by taxi drivers to steer you towards sights with admission ¥100 upwards: they are overpriced and underwhelming.

Bīngyù Valley   冰峪沟

If you can't travel south to Guìlín, Bīngyù Valley (Bīngyù Gōu; admission ¥168) offers a taste of what you're missing. About 250km northeast of Dàlián, the valley has tree-covered limestone cliffs set alongside a river. From the entrance, a boat takes you along a brief stretch of the river, where rock formations rise steeply along the banks, before depositing you at a dock. From there, hire a little boat or bamboo raft and paddle around the shallow waters, or follow short trails along the river and up to lookouts.

The park is increasingly popular with tour groups, who come for the zip lines, tame amusement-park rides, and even jet-skiing. Given the rather small area that you can explore, it can be tough to find any tranquillity in this otherwise-lovely environment.

In summer, **day tours** run from Dalian's train-station area, leaving at 7.30am and returning around 8pm. Buy your ticket (¥230 including transport, lunch and admission fees) the day before from the tourism vans across from the light rail depot in the back train-station area. Your hotel should be able to get you discounted rates. Note that tours sometimes do reverse itineraries (with the boat ride coming last) and you'll find precious little time alone. There are also (optional) add-ons such as cable-car rides and electric-car transport. These aren't terrible but can easily double your tour costs.

It's not really worth coming out here on your own, but you can do so by taking the bus to Zhuānghé from Dàlián and transferring to a bus headed for Bīngyù Gōu. Accommodation is available within the park, but is overpriced for what you get.

Dāndōng   丹东
📞 0415 / POP 865,600

The principal gateway to North Korea (Cháoxiǎn) from China, Dāndōng has a buzz that's unusual for a Chinese city of its size. Separated from the Democratic People's Republic of Korea (DPRK) by the Yālù River (Yālù Jiāng), Dāndōng thrives on trade, both illegal and legal, with North Korea.

It handles more than 50% of the DPRK's imports/exports and its increasing wealth means that there are now flashy malls stocking luxury brands and even a fast rail connection under construction.

For most visitors to Dāndōng, this is as close as they will get to the DPRK. While you can't see much, the contrast between Dāndōng's lively, built-up riverfront and the desolate stretch of land on the other side of the Yālù River speaks volumes about the dire state of the North Korean economy and the restrictions under which its people live.

⊙ Sights

Dāndōng is relatively compact and easy to walk around. The river is about 800m southeast of the train station straight down Shiwei Lu (and parallel streets), while the main shopping district is just east of the station.

Tiger Mountain Great Wall   WALLS
(虎山长城, Hūshān Chángchéng; ¥60, museum ¥10, buy ticket at main entrance booth; ⊙8am-5pm) About 20km northeast of Dāndōng, this steep, restored stretch of the Wall, known as Tiger Mountain Great Wall, was built during the Ming dynasty and runs parallel to the North Korean border. Unlike other sections of the Wall, this one sees comparatively few tourists. The Wall ends at a small museum with a few weapons, vases and wartime dioramas.

From here two routes loop back to the entrance. Heading straight ahead on the road is the easy way back. But there's nothing to see. It's better to climb back up the stairs a short way and look for a path on the right that drops and then literally runs along the cliff face! There are some good scrambles and in 20 minutes or so you'll get to a point called Yībùkuà – 'one step across' – marking an extremely narrow part of the river between the two countries. Not far past this you'll reach an area where you can walk back to the entrance.

Buses to the Wall (¥6.50, 40 minutes) run about every hour from Dāndōng's long-distance bus station. A taxi from town will cost ¥35 and you can usually flag a share taxi back for ¥10.

Jīnjiāng Pagoda   PAGODA
(锦江塔, Jǐnjiāng Tǎ) FREE The highest point for kilometres, this pagoda sits atop Jīnjiāng Shān in the park of the same name. The views across to North Korea are unparalleled and the park itself (a former military zone) is a well tended expanse of forested slopes, a pretty pond and walking paths. You can take a taxi to the entrance or easily walk there in 20 minutes from the train station, though it's another steep 1km uphill to the pagoda.

Broken Bridge   BRIDGE
(鸭绿江断桥, Yālùjiāng Duànqiáo; 58 Binjiang Zhonglu, 滨江中路58号; ¥30; ⊙8am-5pm, last entry 4.30pm) In 1950, during the Korean War, American troops 'accidentally' bombed the original steel-span bridge between North Korea and China. The North Koreans dismantled the bridge less than halfway across the river, leaving a row of support columns. You can wander along the remaining section of the shrapnel-scarred bridge and get within a good toss of a baseball of the North

---

FREE TRADE AMONG COMMUNIST ALLIES

It's no exaggeration to say that without China, the North Korean regime would not survive. China has been trading with the Democratic People's Republic of Korea (DPRK) since the 1950s and is now the country's largest trading partner. Almost half of all the DPRK imports come directly from China, and China is the largest provider of humanitarian assistance to the Hermit Kingdom. That China supports its neighbour for its own geopolitical reasons is no surprise – that it does so for economic reasons probably is. The honeymoon may be over, as tensions have grown ever since China signed UN sanctions against North Korea's nuclear testing. However, put simply, Chinese leaders in the northern provinces still insist they need market reforms across the border if they are to see their own long-term development plans fully realised.

Dāndōng is the hub of Sino–North Korean trade, and a free-trade zone between the two countries has been established in North Korea's northeastern cities of Rajin and Sŏnbong. The area is now known as Rason and is also a warm-water port. Another area where the two nations have made progress is in expanding working visas. In 2013 some 93,300 North Koreans were granted visas for employment in China. This translated to a 17% increase from 2012 and continues to increase further.

Dāndōng

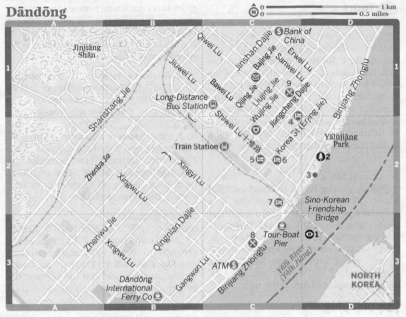

Korean shoreline, where there is a disused amusement park.

Korea Street
STREET

(高丽街, Gāolí Jiē; Erjing Jie, 二经街) Dāndōng may sell Korean culture at the river, but this street is the epicentre of South and North Korean daily life in the city. Local Koreans visit the hairdressers and grocery stores here, and visitors and locals alike eat at the Korean restaurants, which range from quick eats to seafood barbecue restaurants for large groups.

Korea Street is actually Erjing Jie (二经街) and runs parallel to the river a few blocks north. The pretty Korean-style arches mark the entrance at the corner off Shiwei Lu (十纬路).

Yālù Jiāng Park
PARK

For views of the border, stroll along the narrow riverfront Yālù Jiāng Park, which faces the North Korean city of Sinuiju. You can have your photo taken (¥10 each) in Korean costumes and sometimes catch locals dancing, playing music or singing.

Museum to Commemorate US Aggression
MUSEUM

(抗美援朝纪念馆, Kàngměi Yuáncháo Jìniànguǎn; ☑ 0415 215 0510; www.kmycjng.com; 68 Shanshang Jie, 山上街68号; ☉ 9am-4pm Tue-Sun) FREE With everything from statistics

to shells, this comprehensive museum offers Chinese and North Korean perspectives – they take the view that they won it – on the war with the US-led UN forces (1950–53). There are good English captions here, which offer a thought-provoking alternative view to the West's. The adjacent North Korean War Memorial Column was built 53m high, symbolising the year the Korean War ended. A taxi to the museum costs ¥12 from downtown.

LIÁONÍNG DĀNDŌNG

☞ Tours

Boat Cruise   BOATING
(观光船, Guānguāng Chuán; boats ¥60, speedboats ¥80; ⏱ 7am-6pm) To get close to North Korea, take a 30- to 40-minute boat cruise from the tour-boat piers on either side of the border bridges. You have to wait for boats to fill up with passengers (on average 30 minutes), but the pace allows you to take more in than on the smaller, splashy speedboats. In summer you might see kids splashing in the river, or fishermen and boat crews moored on the other side.

Speedboat Tours   BOATING
(快艇码头, Kuàitǐng Mǎtóu; per speedboat ¥180) About 23km northeast of Dāndōng is a small dock where you can board a speedboat (seats eight) for a thrilling, wet 30-minute ride up the Yālù River. Close to shore, the driver will take you close to a portion of river where you are between two DPRK banks – the mainland on the left and a DPRK military-occupied island on the right.

🛏 Sleeping

There are many hotels in Dāndōng, most for around ¥200 a night. High-summer rates may be 30% to 50% more than the prices

---

VISITING THE HERMIT KINGDOM

Most tours to the Democratic People's Republic of Korea (DPRK) start with a flight from Běijīng or Shěnyáng into Pyongyang, but Jílín and Liáoníng offer a more interesting alternative launching pad. You can visit the Special Economic Zone of Rason from Yánjí in Jílín province or consider taking a train from Dāndōng all the way to Pyongyang. The following tour agencies organise visas and offer trips designed for Westerners. Check the websites for costs and itineraries. Note that some travel restrictions apply to American tourists (who must fly in) and Japanese tourists.

Explore North Korea (www.explore northkorea.com) Dāndōng-based agency.

Koryo Tours (p1011) Large, long-running Běijīng-based agency.

Young Pioneer Tours (www.young pioneertours.com) Offers alternative itineraries into Rason, Namyang, Hoeryong city and Onsong county.

---

given here. Anywhere between the train station and the river is a convenient place to base yourself. Unlike in other Chinese cities, staying in the train-station surrounds is not a hectic experience.

Yìhǎi Business Hotel   BOUTIQUE HOTEL $
(艺海商务宾馆, Yìhǎi Shāngwù Bīnguǎn; 12-11 Shiwei Lu, 十纬路12-11号; d incl breakfast ¥218) The faux-antique Chinese-meets-baroque styling of the halls and large rooms, some with bath-tubs, creates a romantic, or over the top, atmosphere depending on your tastes. Either way, staying at Yìhǎi is comfortable and anything but boring or strictly 'business'. It's a short walk to the river or train station. Discounts available.

Lǜyuàn Bīnguǎn   HOTEL $
(绿苑宾馆, ☎ 0415 212 7777; fax 0415 210 9888; cnr Shiwei Lu & Sanjing Jie, 三经街十纬路交界处; dm/s without bathroom ¥60/¥138, d & tw with bathroom from ¥168; ❄@🛜) There are reasonable singles and three- and four-bed dorms at this long-running guesthouse on busy Shiwei Lu.

Life's Business Hotel   BUSINESS HOTEL $$
(莱弗仕商务快捷酒店, Láifúshì Shāngwù Kuàijié Jiǔdiàn; ☎ 0415 213 9555; www.lifeshotel.com; 29 Liuwei Lu, 六纬路29号; r ¥168-298; ❄@🛜) Life's is a smart business hotel popular with North Korean businessmen and within walking distance of the riverfront, restaurants and a Tesco supermarket. Rooms are tidy and comfortable with the ones on higher floors affording river views. Cheaper rooms have no windows.

Zhong Lian Hotel   HOTEL $$$
(中联大酒店, Zhōng Lián Dà Jiǔdiàn; ☎ 0415 233 3333; www.zlhotel.com; 62 Binjiang Zhong Lu, 滨江中路62号; d/tw incl breakfast ¥478/598; ❄@🛜) Directly across from the Broken Bridge is this solid midrange option with large rooms, an even larger marble lobby and English-speaking staff. The pricier rooms offer great views of the bridge and river. Discounts available.

🍴 Eating

On summer nights, barbecue smoke drifts over Dāndōng as street corners become impromptu restaurants serving fresh seafood and bottles of Yālù River beer. One of the best places for barbecue is in the tents on the corner of Bawei Lu and Qijing Jie. More conventional restaurants, including a range of Korean, hotpot and DIY barbecue, line the riverfront on either side of the bridges, and Korea Street (p167) parallel to the river a few blocks north.

Tóudào Wonton CHINESE $
(头道美味馄饨馆, Tóudào Měiwèi Húntún Guǎn; ☑ 0415 212 2500; 37-12 Jiangcheng Dajie cnr Liuwei Lu, 江城大街12号, 六纬路的路口; mains ¥9-16; ☺ 6am-11pm) Locals come to this nothing-fancy place for the good, homemade pork-filled wontons (馄饨; *húntún*) in soup and *lěng miàn* (冷面; cold noodle soup with meat and shredded vegetables) from the picture board. There are side dishes on display too, such as *shíbàn huángguā* (pickled cucumber).

Opposite a Tesco supermarket.

Sōngtáoyuán Fàndiàn NORTH KOREAN $$
(松涛园饭店; 5 Binjiang Zhonglu, 滨江中路5号; dishes ¥18-108; ☺ 11am-3pm & 5-10pm) A big part of the experience for many travellers to this region is eating at a North Korean restaurant with reputedly real North Korean waitresses. This locally recommended place sits appropriately enough just a few hundred metres from the Broken Bridge (directly beside SPR Coffee) and has a range of traditional dishes. There's a full picture menu to help you decide.

Drinking & Nightlife

Drinking with a Korean meal is common practice. Korean beers and the potent spirit *soju* are popular choices in any of the restaurants in and around Korea Street (p167), where there are also a few nondescript bars, which close before midnight.

Information

Bank of China (中国银行, Zhōngguó Yínháng; 60 Jinshan Dajie, 锦山大街60号) Has ATM and will change currency. Another ATM (77-1 Binjiang Zhonglu, 滨江中路77-1号) is closer to the river at 77-1 Binjiang Zhonglu.
Public Security Bureau (PSB, 公安局, Gōng'ānjú; ☑ 0415 210 3138; 15 Jiangcheng Dajie)

Getting There & Away

AIR
Dāndōng airport has infrequent flights to a few cities in China; most travellers arrive by bus or train.

BUS
The **long-distance bus station** (cnr Shiwei Lu & Jinshan Dajie) is near the train station.
Dàlián ¥105, 3½ hours, 15 daily (5.30am to 2.30pm)
Ji'ān ¥87, seven hours, 8.30am

ⓘ BORDER CROSSING: DĀNDŌNG TO SOUTH KOREA

Dāndōng International Ferry Co (丹东国际航运有限公司, Dāndōng Guójì Hángyùn Yǒuxiàn Gōngsī; ☑ 0411 315 2666; www.dandongferry.co.kr; cnr Xingwu Lu & Gangwan Lu; ☺ 8am-5pm) runs a boat to Incheon in South Korea on Tuesday and Thursday at 6pm and Sunday at 4pm (¥1110 to ¥1810, 16 hours). Buy tickets at the company's office on Xingwu Lu. A bus to the ferry terminal leaves two hours before departure (¥20) on the respective departure days from the train station.

Shěnyáng ¥87, three hours, every 30 minutes (5.40am to 6.30pm)
Tōnghuà ¥84, seven hours, 6.30am and 8.50am

TRAIN
The train station is in the centre of town. A lofty Mao statue greets arriving passengers. There are much slower versions of the following trains, but the cost saving is minimal. The attendant at ticket window 1 speaks English.
Dàlián (D/G) ¥109, two to 2½ hours, 10 daily
Shěnyáng (D/G) ¥70, 1½ hours, every 30 minutes

Shěnyáng 沈阳

☑ 024 / POP 6.25 MILLION

The capital of Liáoníng province, prosperous Shěnyáng has made enormous strides in overcoming its reputation as a postindustrial 'rust-belt' city. True, Shěnyáng is still a sprawling metropolis, but the metro is easy to navigate, and there's a buzz on the streets and in the designer malls as locals grow confident, positive and urbane.

For the traveller, Shěnyáng boasts its very own Imperial Palace, a tomb complex and decent museums, as well as several fine parks. Given its strategic location as a transport hub for the north of China, Shěnyáng is well worth a stopover on your journey.

History

Shěnyáng's roots go back to 300 BC, when it was known as Hou City. By the 11th century it was a Mongol trading centre, before reaching its historical high point in the 17th century when it was the capital of the Manchu empire. With the Manchu conquest of

Shěnyáng

Shěnyáng

◎ Top Sights
1 Shěnyáng Imperial Palace..................D3

🛏 Sleeping
2 Liáoníng Bīnguǎn.................................A3
3 Shèntiě Shěnzhàn Bīnguǎn.............A3
4 Vienna International Hotel.................A3

✘ Eating
5 Carrefour Supermarket......................C1
6 Korea Town...A2
7 Lǎobiàn Dumplings............................D2
8 Měijīn Hotpot.....................................A3
9 View & World Vegetarian
    Restaurant..B3

🍷 Drinking & Nightlife
10 Lenore's..B3
11 Stroller's...B3

ℹ Transport
12 China Travel Service of Shenyang......C2

Běijīng in 1644, Shěnyáng became a secondary capital under the Manchu name of Mukden, and a centre of the ginseng trade.

Throughout its history Shěnyáng has rapidly changed hands, dominated by warlords, the Japanese (1931), the Russians (1945), the Kuomintang (1946) and finally the Chinese Communist Party (CCP; 1948).

◉ Sights

From the Main Train Station, it's worth strolling along Zhongshan Lu and around Zhongshan Sq, which has the largest Mao statue in China, for the many historical buildings from the early 20th century.

★ Shěnyáng Imperial Palace   HISTORIC SITE
(沈阳故宫, Shěnyáng Gùgōng; 171 Shenyang Lu, 沈阳路171号; ¥60; ⊙ 8.30am-5.30pm, from 1pm Mon, last entry 4.45pm) This impressive palace complex resembles a small-scale Forbidden City. Constructed between 1625 and 1636 by Manchu emperor Nurhachi (1559–1626) and his son, Huang Taiji, the palace served as the residence of the Qing dynasty rulers until 1644. The central courtyard buildings include ornate ceremonial halls and imperial living quarters, including a royal baby cradle. In all, there are 114 buildings, not all of which are open to the public.

Zhong Jie metro station (exit B) is a few minutes north.

Běilíng Park   PARK
(北陵公园, Běilíng Gōngyuán; 🛉) With its pine trees and large lake, this park is an excellent place to escape Shěnyáng's hubbub. Locals come here to promenade, sing or just kick back with their families. Beiling Gongyuan metro station is directly outside the park.

★ **North Tomb** HISTORIC SITE

(北陵, Běilíng; 12 Taishan Lu, 泰山路12号; ¥50; ⊙7am-6pm) One of Shěnyáng's highlights is this extensive tomb complex, the burial place of Huang Taiji (1592–1643), founder of the Qing dynasty. The tomb's animal statues lead up to the central mound known as the Luminous Tomb (Zhāo Líng). In many ways a better-preserved complex than Shěnyáng's Imperial Palace, the tomb site is worth a few hours examining the dozens of buildings with their traditional architecture and ornamentation.

The North Tomb sits a few kilometres north of town inside expansive Běilíng Park.

🛏 Sleeping

Shěntiě Shěnzhàn Bīnguǎn HOTEL $

(沈铁沈站宾馆, Railway Station Hotel; ☎024 2358 5888; 2 Shengli Dajie, 胜利大街2号; r without bathroom ¥60-80, tw with bathroom ¥148 168; ✳@) A convenient if ageing place next to the Main Train Station. Note that some of the cheaper rooms have no windows.

Vienna International Hotel HOTEL $$

(维也纳国际酒店, Wéiyěnà Guójì Jiǔdiàn; ☎024 8360 8888; 58 Minzu Beijie, 民族北街58号; d & tw ¥348-438, ste ¥538) The Vienna is a neat little hotel tucked down a small road 150m east of the Main Train Station. Smart, clean and bright rooms paired with good service make this a good midrange option. Discounts of 40% with ¥198 membership; coupons for ¥168 doubles sometimes distributed outside.

Liáoníng Bīnguǎn HOTEL $$$

(辽宁宾馆, Liaoning Hotel; ☎024 2383 9104; 97 Zhongshan Lu, 中山路97号; r incl breakfast from ¥458; ✳@✿) This grand dame dates back to 1927 and is perched across from Mao's statue at busy Zhongshan Sq. The Chairman himself stayed here and it retains many of its period details – the marbled lobby and central stairwell are particularly impressive. Rooms are comfortable but could use an update. The outdoor patio serves beer on sunny days. Discounts up to 50% available.

🍴 Eating

Both the north and main train stations are cheap-restaurant zones. You'll also find lots of reasonably priced restaurants around the Imperial Palace. Most have picture menus. For a kimchi fix head to **Korea Town** (西塔, Xītǎ; Xita Jie, 西塔街) on Xita Jie. There are supermarkets at the base of most malls, and a **Carrefour Supermarket** (家乐福, Jiālèfú; 39

Beizhan Yilu, 北站一路39号; ⊙8.30am-9.30pm) is beside the long-distance bus station.

★ **Měijīn Hotpot** HOTPOT $$

(美津火锅, Měijīn Huǒguō; cnr Taiyuan Jie & Bei Sanma Lu, 太原街北三马路的路口; ingredients ¥3-22; ⊙10.30am-2am) This popular hotpot chain teems with the energy of dozens of diners chowing down on everything from vegies to meat and noodles. Friendly staff can help explain ingredients on the incredibly diverse English menu.

Lǎobiàn Dumplings DUMPLING $$

(老边饺子馆, Lǎobiàn Jiǎoziguǎn; 2nd fl, 208 Zhong Jie, 中街路208号2楼; dumplings ¥16-60; ⊙10am-10pm; ✳✿🖬) Shěnyáng's most famous restaurant has been packing in the locals since 1829. It might be resting on its laurels a little, but punters continue to flock here for the boiled, steamed and fried dumplings in an array of flavours: from abalone to cabbage and even curry and plenty of vegetarian options in the picture menu. The restaurant is on the 2nd floor of the Lǎobiàn Hotel, just across from the B1 exit of Zhong Jie metro station.

View & World Vegetarian Restaurant VEGETARIAN $$

(宽巷子素菜馆, Kuān Xiàngzi Sùcàiguǎn; ☎024 2284 1681; 202 Shiyi Wei Lu, 十一纬路202号; dishes ¥12-168; ⊙10am-10.30pm; 🖬) Peking duck and meatballs are on the menu here, but there won't be any actual meat on your plate. Everything is meat-free at this classy nearly vegan paradise, which claims to be the only non-MSG restaurant in all of northeast China (an astonishing claim if true).

The restaurant is on one of Shěnyáng's busy eating streets and you'll find much to sample nearby, including real Peking duck, if you so desire.

THE 'MUKDEN INCIDENT'

By 1931 Japan was looking for a pretext to occupy Manchuria. The Japanese army took matters into its own hands by staging an explosion on the night of 18 September at a tiny section of a Japanese-owned railway outside Mukden, the present-day city of Shěnyáng. Almost immediately, the Japanese attacked a nearby Chinese army garrison and then occupied Shěnyáng the following night. Within five months, they controlled all of Manchuria and ruled the region until the end of WWII.

Drinking & Nightlife

There are bars ranging from glossy to homely on Zhongshan Lu east of Zhongshan Sq. Join the loud crowds in Korea Town (p171) on Xita Jie for some cheap and potent *soju*.

Lenore's   BAR
(丽纳尔斯咖啡馆和酒吧, Lìnà'ěrsī Kāfēiguǎn Hé Jiǔbà; ☑024 2285 7983; 60 Beiwu Malu, 北五马路60号; drinks ¥28-48; ☺11am-midnight; ☞) A rarity in Shenyang: a cafe/bar with real personality. The homely vintage design and friendly English-speaking staff draw a youthful crowd for good cocktails, wine, local and imported beers, coffee, and a Chinese take on Western food (¥25-48). Softly spoken Michael in his cowboy hat is a real, inviting character.

Stroller's   BAR
(流浪者餐厅, Liúlàngzhě Cāntīng; ☑024 2287 6677; 36 Beiwu Jing Jie, 北五经街36号; drinks from ¥25, food ¥40-170; ☺11.30am-2am; ☞) This long-running atmospheric pub is especially popular with expats and has a decent imported beer selection and the usual pub grub. Take Exit B of Nan Shichang Station, cross the road and head up the side street 150m.

Shopping

Zhong Jie   SHOPPING STREET
(中街, Zhōng Jiē) This street, near the Imperial Palace, is a popular pedestrianised shopping zone. It stretches across both sides of Chaoyang Jie. Expect glossy malls with all manner of shops (local and international) and restaurants.

Taiyuan Jie   SHOPPING STREET
(太原街步行街, Tàiyuán Jiē Bùxíng Jiē) Near the Main Train Station is Taiyuan Jie, one of Shěnyáng's major shopping streets, with department stores and an extensive underground shopping street (mostly small clothing boutiques).

Information

ATMs can be found all over the city and around Zhongshan Sq.

The Bank of China has ATMS and currency exchange at **Government Sq** (253 Shifu Dalu) and **Zhonghua Lu** (中国银行, Zhōngguó Yínháng; 96 Zhonghua Lu, 中化路96号).

North Korean Consulate (☑024 8685 2742; 37 Beiling Dajie, 北陵大街37号) North Korea visas are more likely to be obtained at the North Korean embassy in Běijīng.

Public Security Bureau (PSB, 公安局, Gōng'ānjú; ☑024 2253 4850; Zhongshan

Guangchang, 中山广场) There's also a visa office opposite the entrance of the North Tomb.

The 72-Hour Visa-Free Transit policy allows passport holders of many countries a stopover in Shěnyáng without arranging a visa before arrival. See p1007 for more information.

Getting There & Away

Large hotels can help book airline and train tickets, as can the **China Travel Service of Shenyang** (沈阳市中国旅行社, Shěnyáng Shì Zhōngguó Lǚxíngshè; ☑137 0000 0681; 1 Shifu Dalu, 市府大路1号; ☺8.30am-5pm).

AIR

Shěnyáng Táoxiān International Airport keeps growing its destinations, with flights to South Korea, Japan, Thailand, Australia, Germany and Russia as well as the following domestic cities:
Běijīng ¥900, 1½ hours
Shànghǎi ¥1000, two hours

BUS

The **south long-distance bus station** (沈阳长途客运南站, Shěnyáng Chángtú Kèyùn Nánzhàn) is adjacent to the Main Train Station from the east exit. The **north long-distance express bus station** (沈阳快速客运站, Shěnyáng Kuàisù Kèyùn Zhàn; 120 Huigong Jie, 惠工街120号) is south of Beizhan Lu, about a five-minute walk from the North Train Station and next to the Carrefour Supermarket. Schedules are available at the information counter as you walk in. You are much better off taking a train to Běijīng. Buses service the following destinations from the north bus station unless stated otherwise:
Běijīng ¥140, eight hours, 9am (south station at 2pm)
Chángchūn ¥66, 3½ hours, at least hourly (7am to 5pm)
Dàlián ¥94, 4½ hours, every 1½ hours (9am to 4.30pm)
Dāndōng ¥76, 3½ hours, every 30 minutes (7am to 7pm)
Harbin ¥129, 6½ hours, six daily, 8am-3.30pm
Xīngchéng ¥77, 4½ hours, 8.50am and 3.40pm

TRAIN

Shěnyáng's major train stations are the North Train Station (沈阳北站; Shěnyáng Běi Zhàn) and Main Train Station (沈阳站; Shěnyáng Zhàn; also known by the old 'South Station' name Shěnyáng Nánzhàn). Many trains arrive at one station, stop briefly, then travel to the next. It may be different when departing – always confirm which station you need. Buy sleeper or G/D train tickets (to Běijīng or Shànghǎi) as far in advance as possible. Bus 262 runs between the North and Main Train Stations, or take the metro.

From the main train station:

Báihé (for Chángbái Shān) Hard/soft sleeper ¥179/274, 13 to 14 hours, two daily (6.54pm and 8.18pm)

Běijīng (D/G train) ¥206/295, five/four hours, frequent

Dàlián (D, G train) ¥174, two hours

Dāndōng (D, G train) ¥70 1½ hours, frequent

Harbin (D, G train) ¥247, two to three hours

Xīngchéng Hard seat ¥54, four to five hours

From the north train station:

Běijīng (D/G train) ¥206/295, five/four hours, frequent

Běijīng Hard seat/sleeper ¥98/193, nix to 10 hours

Chángchūn (D/G train) ¥115/136, 2½/1½ hours

Dàlián (D, G train) ¥176, two hours

Dāndōng (D, G train) ¥73, 1½ hours, four daily

Harbin (D/G train) ¥166/245, 3/2½ hours

❶ Getting Around

TO/FROM THE AIRPORT

The airport is 25km south of the city. **Shuttle buses** (cnr Zhonghua Lu & Heping Dajie, 中化路和平大街的路口; ¥17) leave from an alley just before the intersection of Zhonghua Lu and Heping Dajie, and from the Shěnyáng south long-distance bus station, or Shěnyáng north long-distance bus station. Taxis cost ¥80.

Most travellers won't venture south of the river, but if you do, the modern Line 2 tram is a leisurely way to travel between the airport and the Olympic Centre.

BUS

Buses are cheap, frequent and cover the city, but the Metro is easier to navigate.

SUBWAY

With only two lines (Line 1 running east–west and Line 2 running north–south) and one connecting station, the clean and relaxed Shěnyáng Metro system is easy to figure out, even with the planned expansions. There are stops at both the north and main train stations as well as the North Tomb and Zhong Jie (for the Imperial Palace). The average ride costs ¥2 to ¥4. Stations have public toilets.

TAXI

Taxi flagfall starts at ¥9.

Xīngchéng 兴城

☏ 0429 / POP 560,000

Despite having a bevy of talking points – it's one of only four Ming dynasty cities to retain its complete outer walls, it has the oldest surviving temple in all of northeast-ern China and it's an up-and-coming beach resort – Xīngchéng has stayed well off most travellers' radars. Yes, it's still a bit dusty and rough round the edges, but conditions are improving and historians and aficionados will have a field day here.

◉ Sights

★ Xīngchéng Old City HISTORIC SITE

(兴城古城, Xīngchéng Gǔ Chéng; ⏱24hr, sights 8am-5pm) FREE Standing like a miniature of the better-known ancient city of Píngyáo (albeit less polluted or glossy...in a good way), this walled city dates back to 1430 and is the principal reason to visit Xīngchéng.

In addition to the **City Walls** (城墙, Chéngqiáng; Old City; ¥25; ⏱8am-5pm), the **Drum Tower** (钟鼓楼, Zhōng Gǔlóu; Old City; ¥20; ⏱8am-5pm), which sits slap in the middle of the Old City with 360-degree views, and the watchtower, on the southeastern corner of the city, are all intact. You can do a complete circuit of the walls in around an hour.

The Old City is home to around 3000 people with stores for daily life. Also inside the Old City is the **Gao House** (将军府, Jiāngjūn Fǔ; Old City; admission ¥10; ⏱8am-5pm), the former residence of General Gao Rulian, who is one of Xīngchéng's most famous sons. The impressive and well maintained **Confucius Temple** (文庙, Wénmiào; Old City; ¥35; ⏱8am-5pm), built in 1430, is reputedly the oldest temple in northeastern China.

You can enter the Old City by any of four gates, but the easiest one to find is the South Gate (南门; Nánmén), which is just off Xinghai Nan Jie Duan at a large intersection. There are signs in English and Chinese pointing the way and maps at each gate. If you plan on seeing everything, buy the ¥100 pass that grants admission to every paid sight within the walled town.

Xīngchéng Beach BEACH

(海滨浴场, Hǎibīn Yùchǎng) Xīngchéng's beach is pretty enough, with OK sands and calm waters, neat paths, a small park, pagoda over the water, and a boardwalk in some parts.

Bus 1 (¥1) travels from the bus station through Xinghai Lu to the beach (9km from the city centre) in about 30 minutes. A taxi to the area costs ¥15 to ¥20.

⌂ Sleeping

Cheap hotels immediately around the train station won't accept foreigners. The beach is a good place to stay in summer with many of the larger hotels accepting foreigners. Note that rooms in ordinary beach hotels go for hundreds a night during the peak season. When it's cold, you're better off staying closer to the train station near restaurants.

7 Days Inn
HOTEL $

(7天酒店温泉街店; ☎ 0429 5167 878; 109 Xinghai Nanjie, 兴海南街109号; d ¥197; [P] ❄ @ 🖝) One of the few modern, budget options between the train station and Xīngchéng Beach (with Bus 1 outside). Rooms are large and clean with flat-screen TVs, and higher levels are peaceful, despite facing busy Xinghai Nanjie. There are KTV joints and a few late-night budget restaurants nearby. Discounts available.

Hǎiyì Holiday Hotel
HOTEL $$

(海逸假日酒店, Hǎiyì Jiàrì Jiǔdiàn; ☎ 0429 541 0000; 21 Haibin Lu, 海滨路21号; r & cabins ¥350-400; ❄ @) Set just off the beach beside a park, Hǎiyì has decent (if small) rooms and a good in-house restaurant. Better yet, stay in one of the cute cabins clustered under leafy trees. Off-peak discounts bring rooms to the ¥200 range, even cheaper without a window. To get here, turn left when you hit the beach strip and walk 300m.

Jīn Zhǒng Zi Bīnguǎn
HOTEL $$

(金种子宾馆, ☎ 0429 352 1111; 9 Xinghai Lu Yi Duan, 兴海路一段9号; r from ¥398; ❄ @ 🖝) Right in the heart of the city on a busy intersection of Xinghai Lu Yi Duan and Xinghai Nanjie, this hotel offers comfortable rooms and a good attached restaurant (dishes from ¥16 to ¥36). With the standard discount, a double goes for around ¥200.

✗ Eating

Seafood is big here. At beachfront restaurants you can pick your crustacean or fish from the tanks. Prices vary according to the season, so ask before eating. Most beach hotels have restaurants with picture menus and fair prices.

Many hotel restaurants serve an excellent range of seafood, meat and vegetable dishes. The busy street leading from the South Gate to the main Xinghai Nanjie is lined with stalls serving noodles, barbecued meats and vegetables. In winter most restaurants not attached to hotels stay closed.

Sìchuān Málà Noodles
SICHUAN $

(四川麻辣面, Sìchuān Málà Miàn; ☎ 0429 3915 583; 93 Xinghai Nanjie, 兴海南街93号; mains ¥7-12) From outside this simple restaurant, you may not realise that there is very good

Sìchuān style *málà miàn* (spicy and numbing noodle soup) on offer. The photo board looks like there are lots of options, but it's just variations of meat or seafood. They make their own dumplings too. It's opposite a dozen flashing KTV signs.

Happy Family Mall
FOOD HALL $

(大家庭, Dàjiātíng; cnr Xinghai Nanjie & Yan Hui Lu, 兴海南路和延辉路的路口; dishes from ¥10; ⊙9am-9pm; ❄) For respite from the busy intersection near the South Gate, head to the food court on the 5th floor of the Happy Family Mall where you'll find delicious handmade *bāozi* and other Chinese staples.

❶ Getting There & Away

Xīngchéng is a frequent stop on the Běijīng–Harbin line. It can be easier to get a bus than a train to Běijīng (all but the 2.04pm take over seven hours or run in the wee hours), but head to Jǐnzhōu south station for comfortable D trains to major cities. Note that buses and trains from Xīngchéng go to the main station in the nearby city of Jǐnzhōu; there are buses (¥5, 30 minutes) to the south station out front.

BUS

Xīngchéng's bus station (兴城市客运站; Xīngchéngshì Kèyùn Zhàn) is just to the left of the train station.

Běijīng ¥127, five hours, 9am

Dàlián ¥124, five hours, 9.30am

Jǐnzhōu Slow/fast bus ¥19/21, two/1½ hours, every 30 minutes (6.30am to 3.50pm)

Shěnyáng ¥72, 3½ hours, five daily

TRAIN

Běijīng Seat/sleeper ¥65/125, five to eight hours, five daily

Jǐnzhōu Seat ¥13, one hour, regular

Shānhǎiguān Seat ¥19, 1½ hours, regular

Shěnyáng Seat ¥47, four to five hours, regular

❶ Getting Around

You can catch a ferry (round trip/including Chinese-speaking guide & local transport ¥90/175) to Júhuā Island. Ferries depart the northern end of Xīngchéng Beach at 8.30am, 10am, 11.30am, 2pm, 3pm and 4pm. Return trips are at 1pm, 2.30pm, 3.30pm and 5pm. Frequency drops outside of these summer hours.

Bus 1 (¥1) is the only local bus you're likely to need. It runs from out front of the train and bus stations, along Xinghai Nanjie near Xīngchéng Old City South Gate, terminating at Xīngchéng Beach on the 35-minute trip.

A taxi from the train station to the beach costs ¥15 to ¥20.

Jílín

POP 27.46 MILLION

Best Places to Eat

➡ Quánzhōu Bànfàn Guǎn (p180)

➡ Sān Qiān Lǐ Cold Noodles (p181)

➡ Sānyú Zhúyuàn (p185)

Best Places to Sleep

➡ Days Hotel Landscape Resort (p179)

➡ Lánjīng Spa Holiday Inn (p179)

➡ Sōngyuàn Hotel (p184)

Why Go?

A flirty province, Jílín (吉林) teases with the ancient and the modern, the artificial and the supernatural. Travellers tired of great walls and imperial facades can explore Japanese-influenced architecture on the trail of the puppet emperor Puyi and the ruins of an ancient Korean kingdom. In fact, much of the far-eastern region comprises the little-known Korean Autonomous Prefecture, home to more than one million ethnic Koreans. Kimchi and cold noodles dominate the menu here and there's an easy acceptance of outsiders.

Although known for its motor cities and smokestack towns, Jilin is also a popular ski destination and boasts China's largest nature reserve. So go for the contrasts? No, go for the superlatives. Heaven Lake, a stunning, deep-blue volcanic crater lake within the country's largest reserve, is one of China's most mesmerising natural wonders. Yes, Jílín can be a little rough around the edges at times, but its rewards are pure polished jewels.

When to Go
Chángchūn

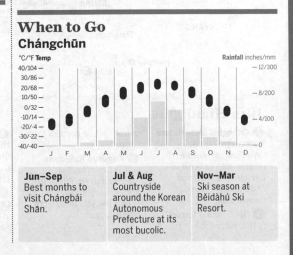

Jun–Sep
Best months to visit Chángbái Shān.

Jul & Aug
Countryside around the Korean Autonomous Prefecture at its most bucolic.

Nov–Mar
Ski season at Běidàhú Ski Resort.

History

Korean kings once ruled parts of Jílín, and the discovery of important relics from the ancient Koguryo kingdom (37 BC–AD 668) in the small southeastern city of Jí'ān has resulted in the area being designated a World Heritage Site by Unesco.

The Japanese occupation of Manchuria in the early 1930s pushed Jílín to the world's centre stage. Chángchūn became the capital of what the Japanese called Manchukuo, with Puyi (the last emperor of the Qing dynasty) given the role of figurehead of the puppet government. In 1944 the Russians wrested control of Jílín from the Japanese and, after stripping the area of its industrial base, handed the region back to Chinese control. For the next several years Jílín would pay a heavy price as one of the front lines in the civil war between the

Jílín Highlights

1 Chángbái Shān Nature Reserve (p177) Visiting China's largest nature reserve, with its waterfalls, birch forests and, most of all, the aptly named Heaven Lake.

2 Běidàhú Ski Resort (p183) Hitting the slopes at one of China's premier skiing spots.

3 Koguryo Kingdom (p181) Exploring the mysterious remains of this ancient kingdom in Jí'ān, just across the Yālù River from North Korea.

4 Imperial Palace of the Manchu State (p183) Shadowing the trail of Puyi, the last emperor of China, at this palace in Chángchūn.

5 Yánjí (p180) Savouring China's ethnic Korean culture in the capital of the Korean Autonomous Prefecture.

Kuomintang and the Chinese Communist Party (CCP).

Jílín's border with North Korea has dominated the region's more recent history. As of 2012, there were an estimated 200,000 North Korean refugees in China. The Chinese government has not looked favourably on these migrants, refusing to grant them protected refugee status and has deported those discovered by the authorities.

A goal has been set to begin transforming Jílín into a biopharmaceutical powerhouse. The first milestone will be the industry contributing 7% to Jílín's total GDP by 2020.

Climate

Jílín is bitterly cold during its long winter, with heavy snow, freezing winds and temperatures as low as -20°C. In contrast, summer is pleasantly warm, especially along the coastal east, but short. Rainfall is moderate.

ⓘ Getting There & Around

The airport connects Chángbái Shān with Chángchūn and other major Chinese cities.

The rail and bus network connects all major cities and towns. High-speed D and G trains link Chángchūn with cities south to Shěnyáng, Dàlián and Dāndōng; north to Harbin and Qíqíhā'ěr; and east to Chángchūn, Jílín City and Yánjí.

Chángbái Shān 长白山

Chángbái Shān (Ever-White Mountains), China's largest nature reserve, covers 2100 sq km (densely forested) on the eastern edge of Jílín. By far the region's top attraction, the park's greenery and open space offers a welcome contrast to Jílín's industrial cities.

The centrepiece of Chángbái Shān is the spellbinding **Heaven Lake**, whose white frozen surface melts into azure waters stretching across an outsized volcanic crater straddling the China–North Korea border come summer. Heaven Lake's beauty and mystical reputation, including its Loch Ness–style monster (guàiwu), lures visitors from all over China, as well as many South Koreans. For the latter, the area is known as Mt Paekdu, or Paekdusan. North Korea claims that Kim Jung-il was born here (although he's believed to have entered the world in Khabarovsk, Russia).

At lower elevations, the park's forests are filled with white birch, Korean pines and hundreds of varieties of plants, including the much-prized Chángbái Shān ginseng. Above

2000m the landscape changes dramatically into a subalpine zone of short grasses and herbs. Giant patches of ice cover parts of the jagged peaks even in mid-June, and mountain streams rush down the treeless, rocky slopes. With the lake at an altitude of nearly 2200m, visitors should be prepared for lower temperatures. It might be sunny and hot when you enter the reserve, but at higher altitudes strong winds, rain and snow are possible.

Though you can visit most of the year, the best time to see the crater (and be assured the roads are open) is from June to early September.

About 15km from the local airport, **Wanda Chángbái Shān International Resort** (万达长白山国际度假区, Wàndá Chángbái Shān Guójì Dùjià Qū; ☑0400 098 7666; www.wanda-group.com/2013/videos_0721/1.html; 455 Baiyun Lu, 白云路455号) has 20 runs over two mountains with some decent hiking in summer. Certainly, the skiing is superlative in the winter.

Accommodation is widely available and most travellers stay in the scruffy gateway towns of Báihé and Sōngjiānghé.

The gateway town for the Northern Slope is Báihé; for the Western Slope it is Sōngjiānghé. It is possible to take buses or trains here from Chángchūn, Yánjí, Tōnghuà and Shěnyáng.

Chángbáishān Airport, halfway between the reserve and Sōngjiānghé, has flights to/from Shànghǎi, Chángchūn and Běijīng.

Báihé 白河

☑ 0433

The views of Chángbái Shān from the Northern Slope (北坡; Běi Pō) are the best and most popular. The gateway town for this area, where travellers have to stay, is **Èrdào Báihé** (二道白河), generally known as Báihé.

The town continues developing with roads and new buildings being upgraded to meet the increased tourist traffic.

◉ Sights

You can see all of the sights on the Northern Slope in a day.

Heaven Lake   LAKE

(天池, Tiān Chí) The jewel of the area, this heavenly blue lake seems impossibly elevated by a ring of 16 mountainous peaks. The dormant crater lake, 13km in circumference, was formed around AD 969. A fixed route takes you around part of the crater lip with panoramic views of its glorious mirrored surface, at such an altitude (2194m) that it feels other-worldly. Legend has it that the lake is home to a large, but shy, beastie with the magical power to blur any photo taken of him.

Chángbái Waterfall   WATERFALL

(长白瀑布, Chángbái Pùbù) From the bus stop, walk up to a small hot spring where you can soak your feet or buy delicious spring-boiled eggs. Past that a 1km trail leads to the viewpoint for the magnificent 68m Chángbái Waterfall. In the past you could follow the dramatic-looking caged trail beside the falls up to the base of the Heaven Lake, but that route is now officially sealed. Don't bother trying to sneak in; park staff will quickly call you back.

Small Heaven Lake   LAKE

(小天池, Xiǎo Tiān Chí) Grab a bus from the Chángbái Waterfall to Small Heaven Lake. Nowhere near the size or majesty of the main crater lake, this is instead a placid lake (or large pond) worth circling. You could venture off into the surrounding forests for a short hike, but don't get lost and be careful not to cross into North Korea! A boardwalk takes you along a fissure stream to the Green Deep Pool.

Green Deep Pool   LAKE

(绿渊潭, Lǜ Yuān Tán) This large, aptly named pool of water, fed by Chángbái Waterfall, is 450m ahead of the Small Heaven Lake. The beautiful milky green pool is great for photos, but not for swimming in. Cross the bus parking lot and head up the stairs to reach it. Buses run from the waterfall down to the main junction and the Underground Forest, a woodland area with a 3km boardwalk (allow at least 1½ hours) to the forest base and back.

🛏 Sleeping & Eating

On your arrival at the train or bus station, touts for cheap guesthouses will likely approach. Many of these guesthouses can be found in the small lanes around town. Private rooms without bathroom go for ¥30 to ¥80. The more expensive rooms sometimes have their own computer.

JÍLÍN CHÁNGBÁI SHĀN

THE LITTLE-KNOWN KOREAN AUTONOMOUS PREFECTURE

Ask people to list some of China's ethnic minorities and you will hear talk of Tibetans, Uighur, Mongolians, Hui and perhaps the Li or Dai. Mention that China also has almost two million ethnic Koreans, and that the majority live in their own autonomous prefecture along the North Korean border, and you'll likely get some astonished looks.

The Yánbiān Korean Autonomous Prefecture (延边朝鲜族自治州, Yánbiān Cháoxiǎnzú Zìzhìzhōu) is the only minority prefecture in the north of China. While established in 1955, in part as a reward for Koreans who fought on the side of the communists during the Civil War, the region has in fact been settled by Koreans since the 1880s. Today, street signs are officially bilingual, much of the population is bilingual (thanks to state-sponsored Korean-language schools), TV shows and newspapers are in Korean, and fusion food is ubiquitous.

Over the past decades, however, the percentage of ethnic Koreans has dropped: from 60% in the 1950s to 38% today. In part this reflects the Chinese government's desire to stamp out any potential for irredentism (many Koreans refer to Yánbiān as the 'third Korea', after the South and North) by encouraging Han migrants. More positively, it seems to indicate that the well educated ethnic population experiences little to no discrimination in seeking employment or advancement outside the prefecture. Yánbiān may occupy a quarter of all Jílín province (it's about half the size of South Korea) but opportunities are limited.

For those doing an extensive tour of northern China, consider looping up through Yánbiān as you go from Dāndōng or Chángbáishān to Harbin. The regional capital, Yánjí (p180), is an attractive laid-back place, loaded with excellent Korean food, and the high-speed trains zoom through the bucolic landscape to Harbin in four hours.

There are small restaurants in all areas of Báihé. Overpriced snacks are also sold inside the park on the Northern Slope, but there are no restaurants, so it pays to bring your own supplies.

Woodland Youth Hostel
HOSTEL $

(望松国际青年旅舍, Wàngsōng Guójì Qīngnián Lǚshè; ☑ 0433 571 0800; cbs800@126.com; Wenhua Lu, 文化路; dm/tw ¥45/100; ❀ @ ☺) Set in a former hotel, the friendly Woodland offers same-sex dorms, clean twins and the usual hostel amenities such as a restaurant (dishes from ¥18 to ¥88), laundry, wi-fi and travel information. The hostel runs its own return shuttle to the North and Western slopes (¥30 and ¥70 respectively) and also sometimes offers overnight camping trips in the park.

To get here from the train or bus station, take a taxi (¥8) or ask about free daytime pick-up.

Lánjǐng Spa Holiday Inn
HOTEL $$$

(蓝景温泉度假酒店, Lánjǐng Wēnquán Dùjià Jiǔdiàn; ☑ 0433 574 5555, 0433 505 2222; r from ¥1500; ❀ @) The top accommodation in the area, this 200-room European-style lodge (with obligatory touches of Chinese kitsch) is just 500m from the north gate entrance but is quietly secluded in a wooded setting off the main road. In addition to multiple food and beverage outlets, the inn features a high-end hot-spring spa with indoor and outdoor facilities. Large discounts available.

❶ Information

The **Bank of China** (中国银行, Zhōngguó Yínháng; Baishan Jie, 白山街) is on the main street in Báihé towards the end of town. It has an ATM.

❶ Getting There & Away

Public transport for the Northern Slope only goes as far as Báihé.

Buses leave from the long-distance bus station (kèyùnzhàn). From the train station head to the main road; the station is across and to the left. Buses include the following:

Chángchūn ¥133, 6½ hours, 6.10am and 5pm

Sōngjiānghé ¥11, two hours, 9.10am, 12.30pm and 2pm

Yánjí ¥53, 3½ hours, five daily

Trains from Báihé include the following:

Shěnyáng Hard/soft sleeper ¥172/263, 13½ hours, two daily (5.35pm and 7.10pm)

Sōngjiānghé Seat ¥11, two hours, five daily

Tōnghuà Hard seat/sleeper ¥32/86, six to seven hours, four daily

❶ Getting Around

From Báihé train or bus station, a tourist bus (¥45) will drop you off at the flashy main entrance of the Northern Slope where you buy tickets (¥125) before proceeding to queue for a tourist shuttle (¥85) to the main transport junction/parking lot. From here you can catch a vehicle for the final 16km trek to Heaven Lake, or a shuttle to the Changbai Waterfall and other sights. Unlimited park bus rides are all included in the park's obligatory ¥85 tourist-shuttle fee, but the Heaven Lake vehicle is another ¥80 return.

From the Woodland Youth Hostel, you can take the hostel's own return shuttle (¥30, departs 8am and returns 4.30pm) to the Northern Slope entrance.

A taxi from the train station into town costs ¥10. Taxi rides within town districts cost ¥5.

Taxis charge ¥60 to ¥70 (per car) for the one-way trip from Báihé to the Northern Slope entrance. Returning, it's usually easy to share a taxi back (per person ¥20), but not if you leave after 5.30pm.

Sōngjiānghé
松江河

☑ 0439

Chángbái Shān's Western Slope (西坡; Xī Pō) offers much the same experience as the Northern Slope. The set-up is fancier, but as in the north, you have little chance of getting away from the crowds.

Sōngjiānghé is the jumping-off point for trips to the Western Slope, 40km southeast. The town is sometimes ignored by visitors who base themselves in Báihé and make day trips to this side of the reserve. They miss blankets of summer flowers and picturesque forests on the approach from this side.

The view from the crater is the main attraction, though Chángbái Shān Canyon really deserves more fame. There is a ¥125 admission fee for the reserve.

Filled with dramatic rock formations, the 70km-long, 200m-wide and 100m-deep **Chángbái Shān Canyon** (长白山大峡谷, Chángbái Shān Dàxiágǔ) has an easy 40-minute route along a boardwalk that follows the canyon rim through the forest.

Sōngjiānghé offers midrange accommodation similar to Báihé, while closer to the reserve a number of resorts have popped up in recent years, including **Days Hotel Landscape Resort** (蓝景戴斯度假酒店, Lánjǐngdàisī Dùjià Jiǔdiàn; ☑ 0433 633 7999; r from ¥850; ❀ @ ☺), a stylish lodge with a lobby fireplace, high-end eating and drinking venues, and wood, glass and stone decor.

Chángbáishān Airport, halfway between the reserve and Sōngjiānghé, has flights

JÍLÍN CHÁNGBÁI SHĀN

to/from Shànghǎi (¥1400, 2½ hours), Chángchūn (¥1000, 45 minutes) and Běijīng (¥1400, two hours). Buses and trains from Sōngjiānghé run to Tōnghuà and Shěnyáng.

Woodland Youth Hostel (p179) in Báihé has a return shuttle to the Western Slope for ¥70 (1½ hours). Taxis also run the route for ¥200 one way. Transport within the reserve costs ¥85.

Yánjí　延吉

☑ 0433 / POP 432,000

The relaxed and youthful capital of China's Korean Autonomous Prefecture, Yánjí has one foot across the nearby border with North Korea. About a third of the population is ethnic Korean and it's common to both hear people speaking Korean – even switching from Mandarin midsentence – and to see Korean written everywhere, from billboards to official road signs. From this fusion springs delicious food, as most northeasterners will tell you, especially budget eats. Yánjí's well regarded university and a sprawling high school fuel a cool, young cafe vibe, while Yánjí's air quality is as equally fresh, with locals claiming it is cleaner than Hainan's.

Yánjí is also a launching point for tours into Rason in North Korea.

◉ Sights & Activities

The Bù'ěrhǎtōng River (布尔哈通河; Bù'ěrhātōng Hé) that bisects the city has pleasant parks and walkways running alongside that are worth strolling on. By night the colourfully lit bridges attract young people coming to hang out.

Mào'ér Mountain　MOUNTAIN
(帽儿山, Mào'ér Shān) FREE The clear favourite of Yánjí families, especially on weekends, this relatively small mountaintop is dotted with young people lounging in the woods in tents or hammocks (¥40 to buy, or ¥10 per day) or walking the 60- to 90-minute return loop to the peak. The whole way is boardwalked, and the locals in all-white outfits and high heels reflects what an easygoing ascent it is, though the last section is quite steep. The views of Yánjí are the best around, and the air is as fresh as locals claim of the city, though not crystal clear.

🛏 Sleeping

The best area to stay in is within a few blocks of the commercial district – along Guangming Lu near the corner with Renmin Lu –

though it can be noisy from 8am till 9pm. It quickly gets quieter towards the river, yet the north bus station is within walking distance. There are a few budget hotels around the scruffy train station. Isolated Yánjí West train station has nothing built-up nearby.

Green Tree Inn　BUSINESS HOTEL $
(格林豪泰时代广场酒店; ☑ 0433 253 2998; 56-1 Jiefang Lu, 解放路56-1号; d & tw ¥138-258, tr ¥288; ☞) Occupying three high floors in the handy commercial district, this business hotel branch is a mixed bag with some tired but good-value rooms that face a shopping square and can get noisy from 8am to 9pm. Dearer rooms have small sitting rooms, newer furnishings and feel more professional.

Baishan Hotel　HOTEL $$$
(白山大厦, Báishān Dàshà; ☑ 0433 258 8888; www.baishan-hotel.com; 66 Youyi Lu, 友谊路66号; d & tw ¥888-1088; ❀@☞) Just a stone's throw away from the river, the Baishan Hotel is an imposing piece of utilitarian architecture with large, comfortable rooms and friendly, efficient staff. The attached ground-floor restaurant has a large selection of excellent Korean and Chinese dishes (from ¥10). Ask for a river-facing room. Discounts knock prices down to the ¥438 range.

🍴 Eating

Head to Guangming Lu near the corner of Renmin Lu for a busy pedestrian street with plenty of restaurants and a street market. Excellent Korean food can be easily found in the surrounding streets and alleys for blocks around. Plenty of cool Korean-run coffee shops line Aidan Lu near the corner of Juzi Lu or Renmin Lu, around the north bus station (客运北站; kèyùn běi zhàn), with decent Western food and wi-fi.

Quánzhōu Bànfàn Guǎn　KOREAN $
(全州拌饭馆; 142 Shenhua Jie, 参花街142号; mains ¥22-46; ☺24hr; P❀☞) A large, well regarded restaurant for its excellent options – mainly jiàngtāng (酱汤; a bubbling pot of pork and potatoes in a miso broth), or bànfàn (拌饭; bibimbap; rice, vegetables and eggs served in a clay pot). Sit at tables or on a heated-floor booth. Off Renmin Lu, west riverside. Picture menu.

Rotti Bun　CAFE $
(2nd fl, 696 Aidan Lu, 爱丹路696号益华广场2楼; coffee ¥18-26; ☺9am-midnight; ❀☞) A lovely, modern cafe with a Korean, designer slant. There are spaces, mezzanines and closed-off

rooms galore, making for a comfy place to spend hours writing postcards, social-media posts or memoirs on the free-use Macs or wifi. You'll need as much time to get through the bucket-sized, sweet Korean desserts.

Sān Qiān Lǐ Cold Noodles KOREAN $
(三千里冷面部, Sānqiānlǐ Lěng Miànbù; 56 Xinhua Jie, 新华街56号; cold noodles ¥15; ⊙ 9am-8pm) One of the best places to slurp down a Yánjí Korean speciality, *lěng miàn* (冷面; cold noodles). Order and almost immediately a large bowl of chewy bean thread noodles is served in a cold beef broth that is addictively savoury and sweet with a fresh topping of shredded cucumber and cabbage.

🍸 Drinking & Nightlife

Nàjiā Coffee BAR
(那家咖啡, Nàjiā Kāfēi; ☑ 0433 256 1859; 2nd fl, 696 Aidan Lu, 爱丹路696号益华广场2楼; ⊙ 9am-midnight) A trendy cafe with a smoky bar side, Nàjiā is an impressive, large space with huge curved windows and a mezzanine, great for watching the well dressed sip imported beers, or the traffic and neon outside.

ℹ️ Information

ATMs are all over the city, including a 24-hour ATM at the **ICBC** (中国工商银行, Zhōngguó Gōngshāng Yínháng) three blocks up from the train station at the corner of Changbaishan Xilu and Zhanqian Jie.

ℹ️ Getting There & Away

The Yánjí train station and Yánjí long-distance bus station are south of the river, while the commercial district and north bus station are near each other north.

Buses to Chángchūn (¥116, 5½ hours, hourly, 6am to 5pm) leave from in front of the train station or north bus station.

The **Yánjí long-distance bus station** (延吉公路客运总站, Yánjí Gōnglù Kèyùn Zǒngzhàn; 2319 Changbaishan Xilu, 长白山西路2319号) serves the following destinations:

Èrdào Báihé ¥45, four hours, six daily (6.40am to 2.30pm)

Húnchūn ¥30, two hours, every 30 minutes (7am to 3.50pm)

Mǔdānjiāng ¥74, 4½ hours, four daily (6.30am, 9.50am, 12.10pm and 4.30pm)

Yánjí's **north bus station** (延吉客运北站, Yánjí Kèyùn Běi Zhàn; 743 Aidan Lu, 爱丹路743号; ⊙ 5.30am-6.30pm) serves Mǔdānjiāng (¥74, five hours; 6.50am, 10.20am, 12.40pm and 4.50pm)

Train service includes the following:

Chángchūn Hard seat/sleeper ¥70/129, eight to nine hours, five daily

ℹ️ Getting Around

Shared taxis outside Yánjí West train station will take you to Yánjí train station or commercial district for ¥10 per passenger. Bus 4 (¥1) also runs to Yánjí train station. Taxi fares start at ¥5; most rides around the commercial district cost less than ¥10.

Bus 60 (¥1) links the train station, commercial district and two bus stations.

Jí'ān 集安

(☑ 0433 / POP 240,000

This small city, just across the Yālù River from North Korea, was once part of the Koguryo (高句丽, Gāogōulì) kingdom, a Korean dynasty that ruled areas of northern China and the Korean peninsula from 37 BC to AD 668. Jí'ān's extensive Koguryo pyramids, ruins and tombs resulted in Unesco designating it a World Heritage Site in 2004. Archaeologists have unearthed remains of three cities plus some 40 tombs around Jí'ān and the town of Huánrén (in Liáoníng province).

With a drive to capitalise on its Korean heritage's tourism potential, modern-day Jí'ān has transformed itself into one of northern China's more pleasant towns, with well tended parks, leafy streets and a renovated riverfront area where you can gaze across to North Korea. Add in the town's mountain backdrop, excellent Korean food, friendly locals and scenic train or bus rides getting here, and it's a great little stopover on a loop through Dōngběi.

◉ Sights

The main sights other than the river park are scattered on the outskirts of the city and you'll need to hire a taxi. Expect to pay at least ¥100 for a three-hour circuit. You'll need to negotiate further if you want to linger at the sights.

The Unesco World Heritage site, **Koguryo Mountain Cities**, is a collection of tombs and the archaeological remains from three main fortress cities. The site is spread around the very lovely green hills surrounding Jí'ān. Despite their historical significance, most of the city remains don't have a terrible amount of detail to examine. Many of the tombs are cairns – essentially heaps of stones piled above burial sites – while others are stone pyramids. But there is something magical about the open fields and high terraces they were constructed on that makes you want to linger.

The most impressive fortress city, Wándū Mountain City, is enough to give an idea of what is on offer. It takes two hours to wander the expansive grounds.

If you are keen to explore more, a ¥100 combo ticket gets you into the three most important mountain cities and a tomb site; you can also buy separate tickets for each sight for ¥30.

★ Wándū Mountain City   RUINS
(丸都山城, Wándū Shānchéng; Shancheng Lu, 山城路; ¥30) First built in AD 3, this city became capital of the Koguryo kingdom in 209, after the fall of the first capital, Guonei city (on the site of present-day Jí'ān). There's little left of the original buildings, but the layout has been cleared and it's immensely enjoyable scrambling about the terraces and taking in the views that surely must have been a deciding factor in establishing the capital here.

Wándū is a 6.5km drive west of the train station.

Cemetery of Noblemen at Yúshān   TOMB
(禹山贵族墓地, Yúshān Guìzú Mùdì; ¥30) Scattered about a small gated park lie the stone crypts of various Koguryo-kingdom noblemen. You can enter and explore Tomb No 5 (wait for the guide) via a creepy descent underground. As your eyes adjust to the light in the chilly stone chamber, look for paintings of dragons, white tigers, black tortoises and lotus flowers on the walls and ceilings.

Jí'ān Museum   MUSEUM
(集安博物馆, Jí'ān Bówùguǎn; Jianshe Jie, 建设街; ¥30; ⊙8.30am-4pm) The sleek museum sports a brown stone base and a glass top with sails that open up like leaves. It features a small display of artefacts from the Koguryo era with good English captions. A lovely park with stone fountains, landscaped gardens, cobbled walkways, lotus ponds and statues is located just next to the museum.

Riverside Plaza   WATERFRONT
This lively modern waterfront park features riverside decks where you can view North Korea across the Yālù River. You can also take a boat ride along the river (¥50, 40 minutes). The park is stretched out along Yanjiang Lu, south of the main Shengli Lu.

Hǎotàiwáng Stele   TOMB
(好太王碑, Hǎotàiwáng Bēi; ¥30) Inscribed with 1775 Chinese characters, the Hǎotàiwáng Stele, a 6m-tall stone slab that dates to AD 415, records the accomplishments of Koguryo king Tan De (374–412), known as Hǎotàiwáng. The surface is blackened from a botched restoration effort when it was rediscovered in 1877: to remove the moss covering the surface, locals smeared it with cow dung and set it alight. Tan De's tomb (labelled 'Tàiwáng Tomb') is on the same site.

Jiāngjūnfén (General's Tomb)   TOMB
(将军坟; ¥30) One of the largest pyramid-like structures in the region, the 12m-tall Jiāngjūnfén was built during the 4th century for a Koguryo ruler. The nearby smaller tomb is the resting place of a family member. The site is set among the hills 4km northeast of town.

🛏 Sleeping & Eating

There are a dozen guesthouses with very basic rooms for ¥50 to ¥80 and a couple of better business-hotel options that are more likely to accept foreigners for ¥170 to ¥200 on Shengli Lu (outside the bus station) and on Yanjiang Lu (outside the train station). Chinese chain-hotel options are at the northern, river-park end of Liming Jie.

Head to the markets east and west of Liming Jie for fruit, dumplings, bread and barbecue. Tuanjie Lu (the parallel road north of Shengli Lu) is home to Chinese greasy spoons, while Liming Jie offers a number of hotpot and barbecue spots. Jianshe Lu near Shengli Lu has several clean Chinese fast-food joints.

Lùmíng Bīnguǎn   HOTEL $
(路明宾馆; ☑0435 622 1293; 653 Shengli Lu, 胜利路653号; d/tw ¥138-158; ❄@☎) Friendly staff and well kept rooms make this Jí'ān's best option. It's 500m east of the bus station on the north side of Shengli Lu just before you reach Liming Jie. Look for the English sign reading 'Guesthouse' above the entrance. Some rooms have their own computer.

ℹ Information

Bank of China (中国银行, Zhōngguó Yínháng; 336 Shengli Lu, 胜利路336号) Located at the corner of Shengli Lu and Li Ming Jie; 24-hour ATM.

ℹ Getting There & Away

The main routes to Jí'ān (not to be confused with the identically pronounced 吉安 in distant Jiāngxī province) are via Tōnghuà and Báihé (the gateway to Chángbái Shān) to the north, and Shěnyáng and Dāndōng in Liáoníng province to the west and south. If you're travelling to Báihé by bus, you need to change in Tōnghuà. Trains are less useful as there's only one per day to Tōnghuà (¥8.50, three hours) at 11am.

Shengli Lu runs east–west through town, with the **long-distance bus station** (集安市客运总站; Jí'ānshì Kèyùnzǒng Zhàn; 1028 Shengli Lu) at the west end. The **train station** (Yanjiang Lu) is 2.9km east, where Shengli Lu changes name to Yanjiang Lu.

Bus services include the following destinations:

Chángchūn ¥140, 5½ hours, three daily (5.30am, 6.25am and 2.50pm)

Dāndōng ¥95 to ¥104, six hours, two daily (7.30am and 9.20am)

Èrdào Báihé (via Tōnghuà) ¥98, six hours, 7.30am and 1.35pm

Chényáng ¥90 to ¥125, six hours, three daily (6.20am, 11.20am and 2.55pm)

Tōnghuà ¥35, two hours, hourly (5am to 5pm)

Běidàhú Ski Resort 北大湖滑雪场

Since it hosted the 2007 Asian Winter Games, **Běidàhú Ski Resort** (Běidàhú Huáxuěchǎng, 北大湖滑雪场; www.beidahuski.com) has established itself as one of China's premier ski resorts. Located in a tiny village 53km south of Jílín City, the resort has runs on two mountains ranging from beginner to advanced. Though it hasn't turned a profit since 2009, Běidàhú has seen continual growth with new runs and the opening of China's second Club Med resort. For more on skiing in Běidàhú, including tour, transport and accommodation information, see China Ski Tours (www.chinaskitours.com).

Chángchūn 长春

📶 0431 / POP 7.64 MILLION

The Japanese capital of Manchukuo between 1933 and 1945, Chángchūn was also the centre of the Chinese film industry in the 1950s and '60s. Visitors expecting a Hollywood-like backdrop of palm trees and beautiful people will be disappointed, though. Chángchūn is now better known as China's motor city, the largest automobile-manufacturing base in the country.

But for people on the trail of Puyi, China's last emperor, it's an essential stop. Its crossroad position, linking three provinces on the high-speed railway, makes Chángchūn a useful stopoff.

◉ Sights

There are a few historic buildings dating back to the early 20th century, mostly along and off Renmin Dajie.

★ **Imperial Palace of the Manchu State** MUSEUM

(Puppet Emperor's Palace, 伪满皇宫博物院, Wěimǎn Huánggōng Bówùyuàn; 5 Guangfu Beilu, 光复北路5号; ¥80; ☉ 8.30am-4.50pm, last entry 40min before closing) This is the former residence of Puyi, the Qing dynasty's final emperor, the basis for Bernardo Bertolucci's film *The Last Emperor* (1987). His study, bedroom, temple, his wife's quarters and opium den, as well as his concubine's rooms, have all been elaborately re-created. His American car is also on display, but it's the exhibition on his extraordinary life, told in part with a fantastic collection of photos, that is most enthralling. An English audio guide costs ¥20. A taxi from the train station costs ¥7.

Chángchūn World Sculpture Park SCULPTURE

(长春世界雕塑公园, Chángchūn Sìjiè Diāodù Gōngyuán; Renmin Dajie, 人民大街; ¥30, shuttle vehicles per person ¥10; ☉ 8am-5pm, 📷 66) Nestled amid 90 hectares of neat parklands with an artificial lake in the far south of the city, the Chángchūn World Sculpture Park hosts an impressive array of sculptures from Chinese and international artists. The huge park is one of Chángchūn's unsung sights and worth sniffing out. A taxi from People's Sq will cost about ¥30.

🛏 Sleeping

There are budget hotels within walking distance of the train station and long-distance bus station at the north end of the city, with broadband-enabled rooms going for between ¥130 and ¥180. If you plan on more than an overnight in Chángchūn, however, the southern end is by far a more pleasant neighbourhood to stay in.

Home Inn HOTEL $

(如家快捷酒店, Rújiā Kuàijié Jiǔdiàn; 📶 0431 8986 3000; 20 Changbai Lu, 长白路20号; r ¥159-209; ❄✳@) If you need a spotlessly clean option near the train station, this branch of the well run nationwide chain is a good choice. Rooms have broadband internet and there's also a computer in the lobby for guest use.

Jinjiang Inn HOTEL $$

(锦江之星, Jínjiāng Zhīxīng; 📶 0431 8914 1666; 4 Mingde Lu, 明德路4号; d ¥198-248; ✳@🛜) This branch of the smart hotel chain is just a block from Renmin Jie and a short walk from good eating and drinking around Tongzhi Jie. The small rooms are super quiet thanks to double glazing and being nestled back from the road.

Chángchūn

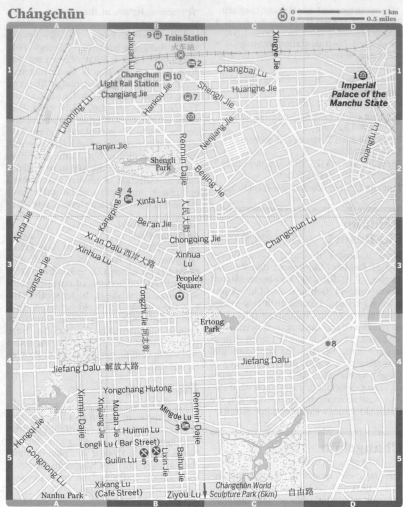

★**Sōngyuàn Hotel**   HOTEL **$$$**

(松苑宾馆, Sōngyuàn Bīnguǎn; ☎0431 8272
7001; 1169 Xinfa Lu, 新发路1169号; d & tw ¥498-
998; ❇@🛜) Nestled within its own park
grounds, the Sōngyuàn was a former army
commander's residence. Today, its heritage
buildings now host tourists in plush, well
decorated rooms. Friendly staff and sever-
al good in-house restaurants (Japanese and
international) seal the deal. The downside
is a slightly inconvenient location. A taxi
from the train station costs ¥7.

✘ Eating

The area surrounding Tongzhi Jie between
Longli Lu and Ziyou Lu is one of the most
popular parts of Chángchūn and is packed
with inexpensive restaurants, music and
clothing shops. Tree-lined Xikang Lu
(west of Tongzhi Jie) is now an unofficial
cafe street. Most of the dozen or so cafes
have wi-fi and offer sandwiches and oth-
er simple meals. Guilin Lu is lined with
cheap eateries and is locally famous for its
street food.

Chángchūn

M+M   NOODLES **$**

(面面, Miàn Miàn; 2447 Tongzhi Jie, 同志街2447
号; noodles ¥18-22; ◎10am-10pm) You can
slurp down your moreish noodles hot or
cold, dry or in soup, with meat or without,
and with side dishes that include broccoli
or Chinese spinach at this popular 2nd-floor
eatery overlooking busy Tongzhi Jie. Picture menu.

Sānyú Zhúyuàn   SICHUAN **$**

(三俞竹苑; ☑0431 8802 8127; 2222 Tongzhi Jie,
同志街????号; mains ¥32-88; ◎10am-10pm;
❄🛜♪) The decoration starts with the
lovely faux-antique interior and continues with fistfuls of chilli adorning every
platter – meat, seafood, even frog. In true
Sìchuān style, mildly spicy can translate to
very spicy. The picture English menu also
contains lots of veg and nonspicy options.

① Information

There are 24-hour ATMs all over town and in the
north bus station.

Changchun Live (www.changchunlive.com) is
a useful site started by long-term expats.

① Getting There & Away

AIR
Chángchūn Lóngjiā International Airport
(长春龙嘉国际机场, Chángchūn Lóngjiā Guójì
Jīchǎng) has daily flights to major cities,
including Běijīng (¥900, two hours) and Shànghǎi (¥1000, 2½ hours) and also Chángbái Shān
(¥1000, one hour).

BUS
The **long-distance bus station** (长途汽车站,
chángtú qìchēzhàn; 226 Renmin Dajie, 人民大街
226号) is two blocks south of the train station.
Buses to Harbin leave from the **north bus station** (客运北站, kèyùn běi zhàn) behind the train
station. Facing the station, head left and take
the underpass just past the 24 hour KFC (not
to be confused with the non-24-hour KFC to the
right of the train station, or the two across the
street). Bus services include the following:
Harbin ¥76, 3½ hours, 8.30am, 10am and noon
Shěnyáng ¥83, 4½ hours, 10am and 2pm
Yanji ¥116, five hours, hourly, 7am to 5pm

TRAIN
Avoid getting tickets for Chángchūn's west
station (xī zhàn), 13km out of town. Instead use
Chángchūn's **main railway station** (长春火车
站, Chángchūn huǒchē zhàn), which serves the
following destinations.
Běijīng (D/G trains) Seat ¥268, seven hours,
eight daily
Běijīng Hard seat/sleeper ¥129/252, eight to
16½ hours, nine daily
Harbin (D/G trains) Seat ¥74 to ¥110, one to 1½
hours, hourly
Shěnyáng (D/G trains) Seat ¥92 to ¥145, 1½ to
two hours, 33 daily

① Getting Around

TO/FROM THE AIRPORT
The airport is 20km east of the city centre,
between Chángchūn and Jílín. Shuttle buses to
the airport (¥20, 50 minutes, every 30 minutes
from 6am to 7pm) leave from the **Civil Aviation
Administration of China** (CAAC, 中国民航,
Zhōngguó Mínháng; ☑0431 8298 8888; 480
Jiefang Dalu, 解放大路480号) on the east side
of town. Taxi fares to the airport are ¥80 to ¥100
for the 40-minute trip.

BUS
Buses heading south leave from the train station
bus stop outside the south exit. Bus 6 follows
Renmin Dajie all the way to the south part of
town. Buses 62 and 362 run to the Chongqing Lu
and Tongzhi Jie shopping districts.

LIGHT RAIL & METRO
The **Chángchūn Light Rail** (长春轻轨, Chángchūn Qīngguǐ; ◎6.30am-9pm) service is only
useful for getting to **Jìngyuètán National Forest
Park** (净月潭国家森林公园, Jìngyuètán Guójiā
Sēnlín Gōngyuán; ¥30; ◎8.30am-5.30pm).
The station is just west of the train station. The
opening of the Line 1 subway, passing through
the train station and city centre, has seen delays
but is on its way along with other lines.

TAXI
Taxi fares start at ¥5.

Hēilóngjiāng

POP 38.3 MILLION

Best Places to Eat

→ Wángmáolú Dòufu Měishí Diàn (p199)

→ Orient King of Eastern Dumplings (p192)

→ Harbin Food Market (p193)

Best Places to Sleep

→ Sunny Date International Hotel (p195)

→ Lungmen Grand Hotel (p192)

→ Jīndì Bīnguǎn (p192)

Why Go?

Hēilóngjiāng (黑龙江) means 'Black Dragon River', and this particular coiling dragon is the separating line between China and Russia. Across the province a neighbourly influence is evident in architecture, food and even souvenirs. Capital Harbin (Hā'ěrbīn), famed for its cobblestoned streets and European-style facades, is ground zero for this hybrid experience.

Of course, it gets cold – sub-Arctic cold – in China's northernmost province, but that frigid weather is put to good use in winter, the peak tourist season. Harbin hosts a world-renowned ice-sculpture festival and the region has some of China's finest ski runs. It gets busy, but it's worth swaddling yourself in layers and joining the crowds.

Outside the cities, Hēilóngjiāng is a rugged, beautiful landscape of forests, lakes, mountains and dormant volcanoes. From Mòhé, China's most northerly city, you can access the remote Běijícūn and Běihóngcūn for bragging rights to say you have stood at the very top of the Middle Kingdom.

When to Go
Harbin

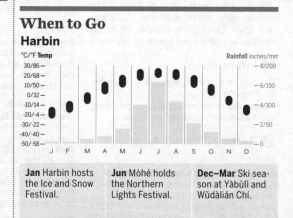

Jan Harbin hosts the Ice and Snow Festival.

Jun Mòhé holds the Northern Lights Festival.

Dec–Mar Ski season at Yàbùlì and Wǔdàlián Chí.

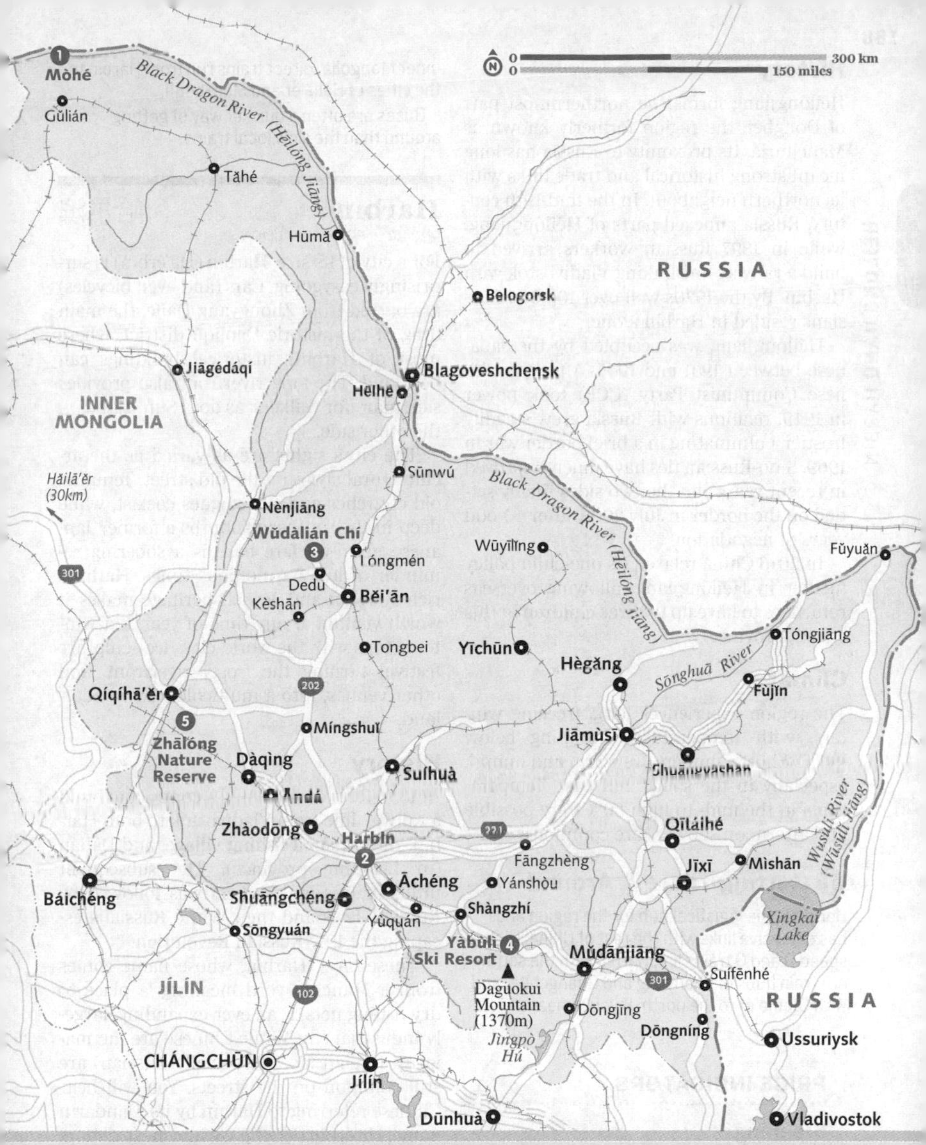

Hēilóngjiāng Highlights

1 Mòhé (p199) Exploring China's northernmost village, where every day feels like Christmas, while hoping to catch the elusive but spectacular aurora borealis.

2 Harbin (p188) Braving the cold to join the crowds who flock to Harbin's world-famous Ice & Snow Festival, and then walking the brick-lined streets of Dàolǐqū district to explore Harbin's Russian and Jewish past.

3 Wǔdàlián Chí (p197) Hiking to the top of a dormant volcano's crater mouth and through petrified lava fields, which fringe five lakes.

4 Yàbùlì Ski Resort (p196) Skiing and snowboarding at one of China's finest ski resorts.

5 Rare Cranes (p198) Searching for these beautiful, endangered birds across the north in sanctuaries, such as in Zhālóng Nature Reserve, where Siberian cranes take flight.

History

Hēilóngjiāng forms the northernmost part of Dōngběi, the region formerly known as Manchuria. Its proximity to Russia has long meant strong historical and trade links with its northern neighbour. In the mid-19th century, Russia annexed parts of Hēilóngjiāng, while in 1897 Russian workers arrived to build a railway line linking Vladivostok with Harbin. By the 1920s well over 100,000 Russians resided in Harbin alone.

Hēilóngjiāng was occupied by the Japanese between 1931 and 1945. After the Chinese Communist Party (CCP) took power in 1949, relations with Russia grew steadily frostier, culminating in a brief border war in 1969. Sino-Russian ties have much improved in recent years and the two sides finally settled on the border in July 2008, after 40-odd years of negotiation.

In 2016 China relaxed its one-child policy further in Hēilóngjiāng, allowing overseas returnees to have up to three children in this ageing province.

Climate

The region experiences long, freezing winters, with temperatures dropping below -30°C. Short summers are warm and humid, especially in the south and east. Temperatures in the mid- to high 30°Cs are possible and afternoon showers are common.

❶ Getting There & Around

Harbin is the logistical hub for the region and has extensive links with the rest of China. High-speed D and G trains link Harbin with the southern train hubs of Shěnyáng and Chángchūn, and with Qíqíhā'ěr to the north. If you're headed for

PRICE INDICATORS

Sleeping

Price ranges for a double room:

$ Less than ¥150

$$ ¥150–¥300

$$$ More than ¥300

Eating

Price ranges for meals, per person:

$ Less than ¥30

$$ ¥30–¥80

$$$ More than ¥80

Inner Mongolia, direct trains run from Harbin to the cities of Hǎilā'ěr and Mǎnzhōulǐ.

Buses are often a quicker way of getting around than the slow local trains.

Harbin 哈尔滨

📋 0451 / POP 4.59 MILLION

For a city of its size, Harbin (Hā'ěrbīn) is surprisingly easygoing. Cars (and even bicycles) are barred from Zhongyang Dajie, the main drag of the historic Dàolǐqū district, where most of Harbin's historical buildings can be found. The long riverfront also provides sanctuary for walkers, as does Sun Island on the other side.

The city's sights are as varied as the architectural styles on the old street. Temples, old churches and synagogues coexist, while deep in the southern suburbs a former Japanese germ-warfare base is a sobering reminder of less harmonious times. Harbin's rich Russian and Jewish heritage makes it worth visiting at any time of year, but winter is tops with the world-class ice-sculpture festival turning the frosty riverfront, and other venues, into a multicoloured wonderland.

History

In 1896 Russia negotiated a contract to build a railway line from Vladivostok to both Harbin, then a small fishing village, and Dàlián (in Liáoníng province). The subsequent influx of Russian workers was followed by Russian Jews and then White Russians escaping the 1917 Russian Revolution.

These days, Harbin, whose name comes from a Manchu word meaning 'a place to dry fishing nets', is an ever-expanding, largely industrial city. While Chinese are the majority, foreign faces (especially Russian) are still common on the streets. You will hear Chinese referring to Harbin by its Mandarin name, Hā'ěrbīn (哈尔滨), while most visitors use the older Harbin.

❍ Sights

The Dàolǐqū district (道里区, Old Harbin), in particular the brick-lined street of Zhongyang Dajie, is the most obvious legacy of Russia's involvement with Harbin. Now a pedestrian-only zone, the street is lined with buildings that date back to the early 20th century. Some are imposing, others distinctly dilapidated, but the mix of architectural styles is fascinating. Other nearby streets

Harbin

Harbin

⦿ **Top Sights**
1 Church of St Sophia B2

◎ **Sights**
2 Dàolǐqū district B2
3 Harbin Main Synagogue....................... A2
  Jewish Middle School.................. (see 3)
4 Stalin Park.. A1
5 Zhāolín Park B1

🛏 **Sleeping**
6 Hàolín Business Hotel A2
7 Ibis Hotel B2
8 Jìndì Bīnguǎn B1
9 Kazy International Youth Hostel B2
10 Lungmen Grand Hotel........................... C4
11 Modern Hotel B2

✕ **Eating**
12 Cafe Russia B1
13 Harbin Food Market B2
14 Láifùbiǎndàn Chóngqìng Xiǎo
   Miàn.. A1
15 Lóngjiāng Xiǎochī Jiē........................... B2

16 Old Chang's Spring Rolls B2
17 Orient King of Eastern Dumplings B2
18 Orient King of Eastern Dumplings C4
19 Sùxīn Shídù Vegetarian B2

🍷 **Drinking & Nightlife**
20 Ming Tien B1

🛍 **Shopping**
21 Hóngbó Century Square........................D4
22 Tòulóng Shopping City C2

ℹ **Information**
23 Harbin Modern Travel Company B2

ℹ **Transport**
24 Cable Car A1
25 Ferries to Sun Island Park A1
26 Harbin Airport Shuttle C4
27 Harbin Railway International Travel
   Service C4
  Harbin Train Booking Office .... (see 26)
28 Local Bus Stop C4
29 Long-Distance Bus Station C4

JEWISH HARBIN

The Jewish influence on Harbin was surprisingly long lasting; the last original Jewish resident of the city died in 1985. In the 1920s Harbin was home to some 20,000 Jews, the largest Jewish community in the Far East at the time. **Tongjiang Jie** was the centre of Jewish life in the city till the end of WWII, and many of the buildings on the street are from the early 20th century.

lined with handsome old buildings include **Shangzhi Dajie** and **Zhaolin Jie**.

Elsewhere in the city, **Hongjun Jie**, heading south from the train station, and **Dongdazhi Jie** also feature rows of stately old buildings, including a few churches. The latter street and some of its arteries also have the dubious reputation of sporting some heady postmodern Russian-style architecture of questionable taste.

In all of these areas, the city has erected plaques on the most worthy buildings giving short English and Chinese descriptions of the date of construction, the architect and the former usage.

A number of temples are within walking distance of each other in the Nángàng district. The **Temple of Bliss** (极乐寺, Jílè Sì; 9 Dongdazhi Jie, 东大直街9号; ¥10; ⊘8.30am-4pm) sits off a pedestrian-only street reachable by bus 53 (¥1) or taxi (¥12) from the Dàolǐqū district 5km away. For **Harbin Confucius Temple** (哈尔滨文庙, Hā'ěrbīn Wénmiào; 25 Wenmiao Jie, 文庙街25号; ⊘9am-3.30pm, closed Wed), look for an arch down to the right at the start of the pedestrian street. Pass through this and then a second arch on the left. The temple is a 10-minute walk along Wenmiao Jie. You can also cut through Harbin Culture Park after the Temple of Bliss en route to Harbin Confucius Temple.

★ Church of St Sophia   CHURCH
(圣索菲亚教堂, Shèng Suǒfēiyà Jiàotáng; 88 Toulong Jie, cnr Zhaolin Jie, 透笼街88号; ¥20; ⊘8.30am-5pm) The red-brick Russian Orthodox Church of St Sophia, with its distinctive green onion dome and roosting pigeons, is Harbin's most famous landmark. Built in 1907, the church has traded religion for photographs of Harbin from the early 1900s. Its unrestored interior and dusty chandeliers evoke a faded yesteryear glamour.

Harbin Culture Park   AMUSEMENT PARK
(哈尔滨文化公园, Hā'ěrbīn Wénhuà Gōngyuán; 208 Nantong Dajie, 南通大街208号; ¥5, rides from ¥30; ⊘8.30am-5pm) If culture equals amusement, then the creators of this park have certainly ticked all the right boxes. The gigantic Ferris wheel offers panoramic views of the city and it's worth strolling around the grounds to see the locals having a great time. The park is in between the Temple of Bliss and the Harbin Confucius Temple near an atmospheric old Russian church. A taxi here costs ¥12.

Jewish Middle School   HISTORIC BUILDING
(犹太中学, Yóutài Zhōngxué; Tongjiang Jie, 通江街) This was the first Jewish middle school in the Far East and most recently housed a Korean (!) school. It has since been immaculately restored as part of a shared compound with the original synagogue.

Zhāolín Park   PARK
(照林公园, Zhàolín Gōngyuán; 377 Senlin Jie, 森林街377号; Ice Lantern venue ¥200) During the Harbin Ice & Snow Festival, the Ice Lantern venue is in Zhāolín Park, though many consider it the least interesting venue. If you do visit, go at night when the lanterns are lit.

Sun Island Park   PARK
(太阳岛公园, Tàiyángdǎo Gōngyuán; cable car 1-way/return ¥50/80; ⊘cable car 8.30am-5pm) Across the river from **Stalin Park** (斯大林公园, Sīdàlín Gōngyuán) is Sun Island Park, a 38-sq-km recreational zone with landscaped gardens, a 'water world', a 'Russian-style' town, and various small galleries and museums. It's a pleasant place to have a picnic, walk or bike (¥60 per hour), though as usual you need to pay extra to get into many areas (most people find it too kitsch and not worth the money).

A ticket is required for entry during the Harbin Ice and Snow Festival.

Ferries (p194) across depart from one of many docks just north of the Flood Control Monument in warmer months. During the Ice Festival when the waters are frozen, catch the nearby cable car (p194).

Harbin Main Synagogue   SYNAGOGUE
(哈尔滨犹太会堂, Hā'ěrbīn Yóutài Huìtáng; 82 Tongjiang Jie, Yóutài Jiùhuìtáng, 通江街82号) **FREE** The beautiful old Main Synagogue, built in 1909, has been refurbished as a con-

cert venue with a small museum. Close by is the former Jewish Middle School.

Huángshān Jewish Cemetery CEMETERY
(皇山公墓, Huángshān Gōngmù) Located in the far eastern suburbs of Harbin, this is the largest Jewish cemetery in East Asia. There are more than 600 graves here, all well maintained. A taxi here takes around 45 minutes and costs about ¥100.

Japanese Germ Warfare Experimental Base MUSEUM
(侵华日军第731部队遗址, Qīnhuá Rìjūn Dì 731 Bùduì Yízhǐ; www.731yz.com; Xinjiang Dajie, 新疆大街; ⊙9-11am & 1-3.30pm Tue-Sun; FREE) This museum is set in the notorious Japanese Germ Warfare Experimental Base (Division 731). Between 1939 and 1945, prisoners of war and civilians were frozen alive, subjected to vivisection or infected with bubonic plague, syphilis and other virulent diseases. Three to four thousand people died here in the most gruesome fashion. The museum includes photos, sculptures and exhibits of the equipment used by the Japanese. There are extensive English captions and an audio guide is available for ¥15.

The base is in the south of Harbin and takes an hour to get to by bus. In the alley beside the Kunlun Hotel on Tielu Jie, catch bus 338 or 343 (¥2). Get off at the stop called Xinjiang Dajie. Walk back 500m along Xinjiang Dajie and look for the base on the left-hand side of the road. If you get lost, just ask the locals the way to Qī Sān Yī (731). Note that Chinese people can be, un-derstandably, uncomfortable talking about this museum.

★ Festivals & Events

Harbin Ice & Snow Festival ICE SCULPTURE
(冰雪节, Bīngxuě Jié, Harbin International Ice & Snow Sculpture Festival; ✆0451 8625 0068; day/evening ticket ¥150/300; ⊙11am-9.30pm) Every winter, from December to February (officially the festival opens 5 January), Zhàolín Park and Sun Island Park become home to extraordinarily detailed, imaginative and downright wacky snow and ice sculptures. They range from huge recreations of iconic buildings, such as the Forbidden City and European cathedrals, to animals and interpretations of ancient legends. At night they're lit up with coloured lights to create a magical effect.

🛏 Sleeping

The most convenient and pleasant place to stay is within a few blocks of Zhongyang Dajie in the Dàolǐqū district. If you need to catch an early train, staying in one of the many hotels surrounding the hectic station can be handy, but be aware that the broad highways are difficult to cross. During the ice and snow festival expect hotel prices to go up by at least 20%.

Hàolín Business Hotel HOTEL $
(昊琳商务连锁酒店, Hàolín Shāngwù Liánsuǒ Jiǔdiàn; ✆0451 8467 5555; 26 Tongjiang Jie, 通江街26号; d & tw ¥138-198; ❀@) In the centre of Jewish Harbin, a neighbourhood now loaded with restaurants and barbecue stalls

THE GREAT CATS

As with many of the world's powerful wild creatures, size did not give the Amur (Siberian) tiger much of an advantage during the 20th century. The largest feline in the world, topping 300kg for males and capable of taking down a brown bear in a fair fight, was no match for the poachers, wars, revolutions, railway construction and economic development in its traditional territory in Russia, China and Korea. These days it's believed that fewer than 540 of the great cats still prowl the wilds of Russia. Perhaps 60 are divided between Hēilóngjiāng and Jílín provinces in China, and none are left in South Korea.

It's a dismal figure, and in 1986 the Chinese government set about boosting numbers by establishing the world's largest tiger breeding centre in Harbin.

The majority of these are in captivity, with 28 born in the first half of 2016, but the centre's conditions are dubious. This makes any wild sighting a cause for celebration. In December 2015 the figurative champagne flowed when Amur tigers were captured on film in Jílín province (bringing the province's numbers up to 27 cats) in the Tianqiaoling area, a zone they had been absent from since the 1980s. It is evidence that the cats are expanding their range south – back into traditional Chinese territory.

at night, is this business-style express hotel with surprisingly comfortable rooms sporting high ceilings, bright interiors and good modern bathrooms. It's a two-minute walk to Zhongyang Dajie.

Kazy International Youth Hostel   HOSTEL $
(卡兹国际青年旅舍, Kǎzī Guójì Qīngnián Lǔshě; ☏0451 8469 7113; kazyzcl@126.com; 27 Tongjiang Jie, 通将街27号; dm/s/tw without bathroom ¥40/60/80, d/tw with bathroom ¥180/120; ☏; 🖥13) True, the cosy lounge area is a bit dark and grubby, but the friendly staff are a great source of travel information for the city and province. The eight-bed dorms are better value than the musty (some are windowless) private rooms. Popular with Chinese travellers, so book ahead. A taxi from Harbin station is ¥12.

Jīndì Bīnguǎn   HOTEL $$
(金地宾馆; ☏0451 8461 8013; 16 Dongfeng Jie, 东风街16号; s & d ¥218-298, tw ¥458; ✳@☏) If you're looking for a river view on the cheap, then this is the place. The owners are friendly, rooms are spacious and there are computers in the more expensive twins. To get to the hotel, turn right at the very end of Zhongyang Dajie. Discounts of up to 30% available.

Ibis Hotel   HOTEL $$
(宜必思酒店, Yíbìsī Jiǔdiàn; ☏0451 8750 9999, www.ibis.com; 92 Zhaolin Jie, 兆麟街92号; d & tw ¥210, ✳@☏) The spotless rooms and handy location, minutes up the road from the Church of St Sophia and Zhongyang Dajie, make up for the sometimes surly front-desk staff. Book online for deals.

★Lungmen Grand Hotel   HISTORIC HOTEL $$$
(龙门贵宾楼酒店, Lóngmén Guìbīn Lóu Jiǔdiàn; ☏0451 8317 7777; 85 Hongjun Jie, 红军街85号; d/tw ¥580/680; ✳@) With its turn-of-the-

century old-world styling almost entirely intact (including marble staircase, dark wood-panelled hallways and copper revolving door), the Lungmen is one of the most atmospheric top-end options in town. Beds and rooms can feel a bit worn, however. Across from the train station, the hotel lobby opens onto Hongjun Jie and its rows of heritage buildings.

A quick walk up the street's wide pavements takes you into the shopping heart of Harbin. Discounts available.

Modern Hotel   HISTORIC HOTEL $$$
(马迭尔宾馆, Mǎdié'ěr Bīnguǎn; ☏0451 8488 4000; www.madieer.cn; 89 Zhongyang Dajie, 中央大街89号; r incl breakfast from ¥980; ✳@☏✉) While hardly 'modern', this 1906 construction impressively features some of its original marble, blond-wood accents and art nouveau touches. Spend some time checking out the lobby bar's display of hotel memorabilia before retiring to (thankfully) modern rooms. Note that the entrance to the hotel is around the back. Discounts of up to 30% available.

✕ Eating

Harbin dishes tend to be thick stew-like concoctions. You'll also find delicious hotpot, barbecued meats and Russian dishes in the tourist areas. Zhongyang Dajie and its side alleys are full of small restaurants and bakeries, as well as the creamy ice-cream popsicles that Harbin is known for. Tongjiang Jie has fruit stands, sit-down restaurants and outdoor barbecue stalls set up in the evenings.

★Orient King of Eastern Dumplings   DUMPLING $
(东方饺子王, Dōngfāng Jiǎozi Wáng; 81 Zhongyang Dajie, 中央大街81号; dumpling plates ¥13-

---

HARBIN CHEAP EATS

It's hard to stop eating in Harbin. In any season, the city is abuzz with visitors snacking their way through the day and night. In summer the streets off Zhongyang Dajie come alive with open-air food stalls and beer gardens, where you can sip a Hāpí (the local beer), while munching on squid on a stick, *yángròu chuàn* (lamb kebabs) and all the usual street snacks.

The year-round indoor **food market** (p193) has stalls selling decent bread, smoked meats, sausages, wraps and fresh dishes, as well as nuts, cookies, fruits and sweets. It's a great place to grab a quick breakfast or to stock up on food for a long bus or train ride.

Just south of the market, on the opposite side of the street, look for the underground **Lóngjiāng Xiǎochī Jiē** (龙江小吃街; Zhongyang Dajie, 中央大街; dishes ¥8-18; ⏱9am-6pm; ✳), a clean, modern food court with a range of inexpensive noodle and rice dishes, as well as kebabs.

38; ⊗10.30am-9.30pm; ☎) It's not just the freshly made *jiǎozi* (饺子; stuffed dumplings) that are good at this always busy and ever-expanding chain restaurant: there are also plenty of tasty vegie dishes and draft beer on tap. There's **another location** (东方饺子王, Dōngfāng Jiǎozi Wáng; Kunlun Hotel, 8 Tielu Jie, 铁路街8号昆仑大厦; dumpling plates ¥13-38; ☑) near the train station in the Kunlun Hotel. Picture menu available.

Harbin Food Market   MARKET $
(小吃城, Xiǎochi Chéng; 96 Zhongyang Dajie, 中央大街96号; snacks ¥5-20; ⊗8.30am-7.30pm) A food market with stalls offering buns, cookies, sausages, fruits and sweets. The market extends out to the main pedestrian street Zhonyang Dajie, where busy stalls serve kebabs, dumplings and ice cream.

Sùxīn Shídù Vegetarian   VEGETARIAN $
(素心食度素食餐厅, Sùxīn Shídù Sùshí Cāntīng; ☑0451 8469 8934; 8 Qidao Jie, 七道街8号; buffet ¥18; ⊗11am-2pm & 5-9pm) A vegetarian all-you-can-eat buffet that is on the filling, stir-fried side – think yams, cauliflower, tofu, spinach and mung beans. You can self serve yourself a variety of congee and hot drinks too.

Láifùbiǎndān Chóngqìng Xiǎo Miàn   SICHUAN $
(来负扁担重庆小面; 134-1 Youyi Lu, 友谊路134-1号; noodles ¥9-18; ⊗9am-10pm) A cute hole-in-the-wall eatery serving fiery Sìchuān noodles to a steady stream of customers. Pull up a rustic wooden chair and slurp down sweat-inducing *xiǎo miàn* (小面; spicy soup noodles) plain or with *niú ròu* (牛肉; beef). If you can't take the heat, order *qīng tāng* (清汤; clear soup noodles) instead. No one will notice...they're too busy eating!

Old Chang's Spring Rolls   CHINESE $
(老昌春饼, Lǎo Chāng Chūnbǐng, 180 Zhongyang Dajie, 中央大街180号; dishes ¥12-38; ⊗10.30am-9pm) At this well known basement spring-roll shop, order a set of wheat roll skins (per roll ¥2), a few plates of meat and vegetable dishes, and then wrap your way to one enjoyable repast.

Cafe Russia   RUSSIAN $$
(露西亚咖啡西餐厅, Lùxīyà Kāfēi Xī Cāntīng; 57 Xitoujiao, 西头到街57号; dishes ¥20-78; ⊗10am-midnight) Step back in time at this ivy-covered cafe restaurant. Photos illustrating Harbin's Russian past line the walls, while the old-school furniture and fireplace evoke a different era. There are standard, passable Russian offerings such as borscht, *piroshki* (cabbage, potato and meat dumplings) and vodka.

The restaurant is off Zhongyang Dajie in a little courtyard.

🍷 Drinking & Nightlife

Ming Tien   CAFE
(名典西餐, Míngdiǎn Xīcān; ☑0451 8465 7070; 214 Shangzhi Dajie, 尚志大街214号; drinks ¥35-60; ⊗10am-10pm) For afternoon tea or coffee head to this slightly over-the-top cafe occupying two floors of a heritage building on Shangzhi Dajie. Enter via the subdued parlour, wind your way up the tree-enshrouding staircase and ease into a big brown leather booth with views of Zhāolín Park. There's an equally eclectic menu ranging from borscht to pizza if you get hungry.

🛍 Shopping

Shops along Zhongyang Dajie (and all over the city) flog 'Russian' knick-knacks, vodka and souvenirs. There are also department stores and Western clothes chains here.

Locals shop along Dongdazhi Jie and at **Hóngbó Century Square** (红博世纪广场, Hóngbó Shìjì Guǎngchǎng; Dongdazhi Jie; ⊗6.30am-5pm), a subterranean complex of men's and women's clothing.

The best bargains are at **Tòulóng Shopping City** (透笼国际商品城, Tòulóng Guójì Shāngpǐn Chéng; 58 Shitou Dajie, 石头道街58号; ⊗9am-6pm), an 11-floor indoor market. Clothes and souvenirs are on the first of couple levels, with the 4th floor dedicated to luggage and sunglasses. Haggle hard.

ⓘ VISAS

The 72-Hour Visa-Free Transit policy allows passport-holders of many countries a stopover in Harbin without arranging a visa before arrival. This includes most European countries, the USA, Canada, Brazil, Mexico, Australia and Japan. You must have an onward ticket to a third country (ie not the country you arrived from). Inform your airline at check-in and seek the '72-hour Visa-Free Transit' counter on arrival. Check the website well before flying: http://english.gov.cn/services/visitchina.

ℹ️ Information

There are ATMs all over town. Most large hotels will also change money.

Bank of China (中国银行, Zhōngguó Yínháng; Xi'er Daojie, 西二道街) has a 24-hour ATM and will cash travellers cheques. Easy to spot on a side road as you walk up Zhongyang Dajie.

Harbin Modern Travel Company (哈尔滨马迭尔旅行社, Hā'ěrbīn Mǎdié'ěr Lūxíngshè; 2nd fl Modern Hotel, 89 Zhongyang Dajie, 中央大街89号) offers one- and two-day ski trips to Yàbùlì and can handle flight tickets to Mòhé and other regions.

ℹ️ Getting There & Away

AIR

Harbin Taiping International Airport (哈尔滨太平国际机场, Hā'ěrbīn Tàipíng Guójì Jīchǎng) has flights to Russia, Japan, South Korea and Taiwan, as well as domestic routes, including the following:

Běijīng ¥810, two hours
Dàlián ¥1050, 1½ hours
Mòhé ¥2100, 1¾ hours

BUS

The main **long-distance bus station** (长途客运站, Chángtú Kèyùn Zhàn) is directly opposite the train station. Buy tickets on the 2nd floor.

Běi'ān ¥99, five hours, five daily (7.10am, 8.30am, 12.30pm, 2.20pm and 4.30pm)
Chángchūn ¥76, four hours, six daily (10am, noon, 1pm, 1.30pm, 3pm and 4pm)
Mǔdānjiāng ¥94, 4½ hours, hourly (6.30am to 6pm)

ℹ️ **BORDER CROSSING: GETTING TO RUSSIA**

Trains no longer depart from Harbin East Train Station to Vladivostok. Trains do run as far as Suífēnhé, however, from where you can make an onward connection to Vladivostok.

Travellers on the Trans-Siberian Railway to or from Moscow can start or finish in Harbin (six days). Contact the **Harbin Railway International Travel Service** (哈尔滨铁道国际旅行社, Hā'ěrbīn Tiědào Guójì Lūxíngshè; 📞 0451 5361 6718; www.ancn.net; 7th fl, Kunlun Hotel, 8 Tielu Jie, 铁路街8号昆仑大厦; ⊙9am-5pm) for information on travelling through to Russia.

Qíqíhāěr ¥78, 3½ hours, hourly (7am to 6pm)
Wǔdàlián Chí ¥95 to ¥117, five to six hours, five daily (9am, 11.30am, noon, 1.30pm and 2.45pm). The noon bus goes to the scenic area while the others stop at Wǔdàlián Chí Shì, a ¥40 taxi ride from the scenic area.

TRAIN

Harbin is a major rail transport hub with routes throughout the northeast and beyond. If you don't want to brave the lines in the **main station** (哈尔滨站, Hā'ěrbīn Zhàn; 1 Tielu Jie, 铁路街1号), buy tickets at the nearby **train booking office** (铁路售票处, Tiělù Shòupiàochù; Tielu Jie, 铁路街; ⊙7am-9pm) to the left of Dico's (fast-food restaurant). Note that some fast D and G trains leave from **Harbin West Station** (西站; Xīzhàn), 10km from town. A taxi will cost ¥30-40.

Běijīng Hard seat/sleeper ¥159/293, 10 to 16 hours, eight daily
Běijīng (D/G train) Seat ¥307/542, eight/seven hours, six daily
Chángchūn (D/G train) Seat ¥74/110, 1½/one hour, regular
Mòhé Hard/soft sleeper ¥153/296, 17–21 hours (6pm and 7pm)
Mǔdānjiāng Hard seat/sleeper ¥52/110, five to six hours, regular
Shěnyáng Hard seat/sleeper ¥75/151, six to seven hours
Shěnyáng (D/G train) Seat ¥166/247, three/two hours, five daily

ℹ️ Getting Around

A **cable car** (1-way ¥50, return ¥80) crosses Sōnghuā River from Tongjiang Jie to Sun Island.

TO/FROM THE AIRPORT

Harbin's airport is 46km from the city centre. From the airport, **shuttle buses** (¥20) will drop you at the train station. To the airport, shuttles leave every 30 minutes from a stand just beside Dico's opposite the train station from 5.30am to 7.30pm. A taxi (¥100 to ¥125) takes 45 minutes to an hour.

BOAT

Ferries (return ¥10) cross the Sōnghuā River to Sun Island Park.

BUS

Buses 101 and 103 run from the **train station** to Shangzhi Dajie, dropping you off at the north end of Zhongyang Dajie (the main pedestrianised, old street). Buses leave from a **local bus stop** across the road and to the left as you exit the train station (where Chunshen Jie and Hongjun Jie meet).

METRO

Harbin's metro has a single line that doesn't serve any of the tourist sights. Construction for further lines is underway.

TAXI

Taxis are fairly plentiful, though they fill up quickly when it's raining. Taxi flag fall is ¥8.

Mǔdānjiāng 牡丹江

✓ 0453 / POP 805,000

A pleasant and surprisingly modern small city surrounded by some lovely countryside, Mǔdānjiāng is the jumping-off point for nearby Jìngpò Lake (Mirror Lake) and the Underground Forest. Taiping Jie is the main drag in town and runs directly south of (opposite) the train station.

🛏 Sleeping

The train-station area has a number of good hotels and there is no reason to look further into town. For budget accommodation head right as you exit the station. Just past the station square on Guanghua Jie runs a row of guesthouses. There are at least half a dozen to choose from, all offering similar prices and decent digs: dorm beds go for ¥30, rooms with shared bathroom for around ¥40 and rooms with their own bathroom (and sometimes even a computer) from ¥90.

Home Inn   HOTEL $$
(如家快捷酒店, Rújiā Kuàijié Jiǔdiàn; ✓ 0453 6911 1188; 651 Guanghua Jie, 光花街651号; r ¥129-179; ⊕ ❋ @ ☎) Probably the best-value rooms around the train station are in this well managed chain just to the right as you exit. Top floors are nonsmoking and very quiet despite the location.

★ Sunny Date
International Hotel   HOTEL $$$
(禧禄达国际酒店, Xǐlùdá Guójì Jiǔdiàn; ✓ 0453 687 8888; 8 Dongyitiao Lu, 东一条路8号; d & tw ¥298-498; ❋ ☎) It's hard not to be impressed (or blinded) by the sunny opulence of the chandelier-lined lobby. Some rooms come equipped with a mah-jong table, but all rooms are top-notch with comfy beds, wi-fi and clean bathrooms. The gigantic attached bathhouse is equally opulent. Discounts bring rooms down to as low as ¥138...bargain!

The hotel is located 200m to the left opposite the road as you exit the train station. It opens up to the busy Dongyitiao Lu pedestrian street.

🍴 Eating

There are plenty of cheap restaurants in the alleys off Qixing Jie, which intersects with Taiping Jie 500m up from the train station. Dongyitiao Lu (off Qixing Jie) is a lively pedestrian-only street with a wide range of BBQ, noodle and snack venues open in the evening.

Shuānglóng Jiǎozi Wáng   DUMPLING $
(双龙饺子王; cnr Qixing Jie & Taiping Jie; dumplings ¥13 38; ⊙ 9am 9pm) There's a wide selection of jiǎozi (stuffed dumplings) here, as well as the usual Dōngběi classics. As you turn left off Taiping Jie, the restaurant is the big glass building with the red signboard on the right. It has an English sign out front and a partial picture menu inside to help you order.

ℹ Information

There's a **Bank of China** (中国银行; Zhōngguó Yínháng) with a 24-hour ATM three blocks south of the train station along Taiping Jie.

ℹ Getting There & Away

BUS

Long-distance buses sometimes drop you off near the train station and depart from a long-distance station (客车站; kè chēzhàn) a few kilometres away on Xi Ping'an Jie. A taxi to the station costs ¥7.

Dōngjīng Chéng ¥18, 1¼ hours, half-hourly

Harbin ¥100, 4½ hours, hourly (5.30am to 6pm)

Yánjí ¥72, five hours, 6.30am, 11.30am and 2pm

TRAIN

Mǔdānjiāng has rail connections:

Harbin Hard seat/sleeper ¥52/107, 4½ to 6½ hours, frequent services

Suífēnhé Seat ¥19 to ¥22, one to two hours, 12 daily

Yánjí Hard seat/sleeper ¥22/61, 6½ hours, one daily (4.24pm)

Jìngpò Lake 镜泊湖

Formed on the bend of the Mǔdān River 5000 years ago by the falling lava of five volcanic explosions, Jìngpò Lake (Jìngpò Hú, Mirror Lake), 110km south of Mǔdānjiāng, gets its name from the unusually clear reflections of the surrounding lush green forest in its pristine blue water.

Hugely popular in summer with Chinese day trippers who come to paddle or picnic by the lakeside, Jìngpò Lake (2-day admission ¥80) is a pleasant spot if you hike along the lake to escape the crowds. Shuttle buses (¥12 per trip) run to various sights, and ferries (¥100, 1½ hours) make leisurely tours of the lake.

around the thick pine forest and several of the 10 craters takes about an hour.

The forest is 50km from Jìngpò Lake. Some day tours include it in their itinerary. Otherwise, you have to take a bus from the north gate of Jìngpò (¥40 return, one hour), which is doable but very tight if you only have a day at the lake.

◉ Sights

Diàoshuǐlóu Waterfall   WATERFALL
(吊水楼瀑布, Diàoshuǐlóu Pùbù) This waterfall boasts a 12m drop and 300m span. During the rainy season (June to September), when Diàoshuǐlóu is in full throttle, it's a spectacular raging beauty, but during spring and autumn it's little more than a drizzle.

You can walk to the waterfall from the north-gate entrance in about five minutes. Just stay on the main road and follow the English signs.

Underground Forest   FOREST
(地下森林, Dìxià Sēnlín; ¥55, internal shuttle bus ¥30) Despite its name, the Underground Forest isn't below the earth; instead it has grown within volcano craters that erupted some 10,000 years ago, giving the appearance of trees sinking into the earth. Hiking

🛏 Sleeping & Eating

It's pleasant to spend the night in the park and enjoy the lake when the crowds return to their hotels in Mǔdānjiāng.

There are a few places to eat standard Chinese fare and snacks around the lake and ferry dock. For a day trip, you're better off bringing your own food for quality and cost.

Jìngpò Hú
Shānzhuāng Jiǔdiàn   HOTEL $$$
(镜泊湖山庄酒店; ☑0453 627 0039, 139 0483 9459; Jìngpò Lake; r ¥480-580; ❄@) This hotel sits just back from the water at the first lakeside drop-off point for the shuttle buses. Rooms are very modern, some with lake views, and the hotel's restaurant has decent food (if a little overpriced). Discounts can knock prices down to the ¥240 range or less if you choose a room without a view.

SKIING IN CHINA

China's ski industry has all the appearance of a success story. From 20,000 visits to the slopes in 1996, numbers grew to around 15 million by 2012. There are now over 20 large resorts across the country in areas as diverse as Jílín, Hēilóngjiāng, Yúnnán and Héběi provinces, many of them also popular with foreigners and expats. With the lead up to the Winter Olympics in China in 2022, there is a new local sense of urgency to learn how to ski or at least to be seen doing it.

Building slopes and resorts has been easy; maintaining them while a ski culture develops has not. In 2012 there was renewed hope, however, as another round of investment hit the industry. This time the focus would be on upping the luxury quotient, and also opening more runs and facilities for absolute beginners.

In China's north, the largest resorts are Jílín's **Běidàhú Ski Resort** (p183) and Hēilóngjiāng's **Yàbùlì Ski Resort** (亚布力滑雪中心, Yàbùlì Huáxuě Zhōngxīn; www.yabuliski.com) 200km southeast of Harbin. Yàbùlì was China's first destination ski resort, and remains the training centre for the Chinese Olympic ski team. Since 2009 the resort has expanded to cover two mountains and now has a good division of advanced, intermediate and beginner runs, as well as a four-star lodge that can reasonably cater to Western guests.

The latest slopes to be developed in the region are at Chángbái Shān on the China–North Korean border located about 15km from the new airport. At the **Wanda Chángbái Shān International Resort** (p177), you'll find 20 runs on two mountains as well as a luxury alpine village offering hotels, restaurants and private condos. Top-notch hotels in the area include the Sheraton and Westin chain of hotels. They offer guest pick-ups from the train station or airport.

Lift tickets in the north average around ¥500 per day on weekends, and a little less on weekdays. Clothing and equipment rental comes to another ¥140.

ⓘ Getting There & Away

The easiest way to get to Jìngpò Lake is on the one-day tours that leave from the train station in Mǔdānjiāng from 6.30am to 7.30am. Tours cost ¥235 and include transport and admission, but no guide. Transport to the Diàoshuǐlóu Waterfall and Underground Forest are an extra ¥50 and ¥80 respectively, including waiting but not admission. Call 139 4533 1797 or book at a booth in front of the train station.

If you want to come here under your own steam, you can get a direct bus from the Mǔdānjiāng bus station (¥25, 2½ hours, 1.30pm and 2.30pm) or train station (¥25, two hours, 7.30am). If you want an earlier start from Mǔdānjiāng, first go to Dōngjīng Chéng (东京城, ¥15, 1½ hours, frequent) then change to a minibus (¥10, 40 to 60 minutes) to the lake. In the late afternoon you can try to get a seat on one of the tour buses directly back to Mǔdānjiāng from the lake (¥30) or head back again via Dōngjīng Chéng.

ⓘ Getting Around

The ticket centre for the lake is at the North Gate (Běimén). From here walk about five minutes to a car park for shuttle buses to the lake and ferry dock (get a ticket to the stop 'Jìngpò Shānzhuāng'; 镜泊山庄) and other sights (¥12 per ride). Diàoshuǐlóu Waterfall is just behind this car park.

Wǔdàlián Chí 五大连池

☎ 0456

Formed by a series of volcanic eruptions, the Wǔdàlián Chí is a nature reserve boasting one of northern China's most mesmerising landscapes. It's a genuine Lost World with vast fields of hardened lava, rivers of basalt, volcanic peaks, azure lakes and the odd little reed-lined pond. Although one day is enough for most people, you could spend days exploring.

The last time the volcanoes erupted was in 1720, when the lava flow blocked the nearby North River (Běi Hé), forming the series of five interconnected lakes that give the area its name. Wǔdàlián Chí is about 250km northwest of Harbin and, in addition to the volcanic landscape, is home to mineral springs that draw busloads of Chinese and Russian tourists to slurp the allegedly curative waters. So many Russians roll up that the town's street signs are in both Chinese and Russian.

It's only really viable to visit Wǔdàlián Chí between May and October because of the cold and wind the rest of the year.

ⓞ Sights

There's no real town here, just a long, pleasant tree-lined street called Yaoquan Lu (药泉路). Everything you want is on a section that runs west of the bus station. The intersection of Yaoquan Lu and Shilong Lu (about 3km from the bus stop) is the main crossroad and is smack in the middle of the hotel area.

★ Lǎohēi Shān   VOLCANO
(老黑山; ¥80 plus compulsory shuttle fee ¥25; ⊗ 7.30am-7pm May-Oct) This huge area is a fascinating mix of hardened lava fields, a crater, a lake and austere white trees. It's mostly easy walking with the exception of the mainly uphill 1km stair climb to the summit of Lǎohēi Shān itself, one of the area's 14 volcanoes. Do a circuit of the windy crater lip for panoramic views of the lakes and other volcanoes dotting the landscape.

Taxis drop you at the ticket booth, from where park shuttle buses take you to a large car park. To the left is the trail up the mountain. Returning down the same path, this time take the right path from the drop off, along a boardwalk to the aptly named **Shí Hǎi** (石海; Stone Sea), a magnificent lava field.

Back in the car park smaller green shuttle buses take you to **Huǒshāo Shān** (火烧山) and the end of the road at another collection of weirdly shaped lava stones. This stretch is one of Wǔdàlián Chí's most enchanting, with lava-rock rivers, birch forests, grassy fields, ponds around Third Lake and more wide stretches of lava fields.

There are only two (expensive) shops, so bring water and snacks.

Lóngmén 'Stone Village'   NATURAL FEATURE
(龙门石寨, Lóngmén Shízhài; ¥50; ⊗ 7am-6pm May-Oct) At this impressive lava field reminiscent of Middle Earth's Mordor (minus the orcs), walk through a forest of white and black birch trees on a network of boardwalks, with the lava rocks stretching away in the distance on both sides.

If you're visiting Wǔdàlián Chí's other volcanic sites, especially Lǎohēi Shān, you could easily skip this more distant (but very similar) site without missing much.

Wēnbó Lake   VOLCANO
(温泊湖, Wēnbó Hú; ¥50; ⊗ 7.30am-5.30pm) A long boardwalk takes visitors through a lava field dotted with ponds and informative interpretive boards explaining lava-related phenomenon such as fissures and, of course, the field itself. The boardwalk ends at a

small dock where you transfer to a boat for a slow putter down a reed-lined river. Your taxi will arrange to pick you from where the boat docks.

Third Lake   LAKE

(三池, Sān Chí; boat tour ¥80) Welcome to Third Lake, the largest of the five interconnected lakes that give rise to the region's name. Here, you can feel the wind whip through your hair on a zippy 40-minute boat ride across the still water. Or just inspect the hardened lava edges.

🏃 Activities

For a loop taking in lakes, volcanoes and caves, most people hire a taxi (¥150). If your time is short, just visit Lǎohēi Shān and you will get most of what the area has to offer, as the other sites tend to be repeats of the hardened lava landscape on a smaller scale.

🛏 Sleeping

Yaoquan Lu, the main east–west drag in Wǔdàlián Chí, has a dozen or more hotels operating from May to October. The newest hotels are about 500m up the road from the bus station.

Some travellers base themselves in Wǔdàlián Chí Shì (五大连池市), a larger town 20km away where most buses drop you off from Harbin. Close to the bus station there are some hotels and plenty of restaurants. However, it's worth making the effort to base yourself in Wǔdàlián Chí itself.

Liu Jie   HOSTEL $

(刘姐, Liú Jiě; ☑ 158 4687 3866; dm ¥40; 🛜) This friendly teacher has converted a few new-build apartments on the outskirts of town into comfortable dorms/hostels. There are only a few shops and restaurants nearby, but it's a perfectly fine base. She will organise pick-up from/drop-off at the bus station as well as a taxi to see the local sights.

Liu Jie speaks barely any English but is willing to use translation and chat apps to communicate.

Quanshan New Holiday Inn   HOTEL $$

(新泉山假日酒店, Xīnquánshān Jiàrì Jiǔdiàn; ☑ 0456 722 6999; Yaoquan Donglu, 药泉东路; d & tw incl breakfast ¥368-698; ✳ @ 🛜) Unrelated to the Western Holiday Inn chain, this Chinese-run hotel is located 500m up the road from the bus station just off the main road. Mod-

---

CRANE COUNTRY

Northeastern China is home to several nature reserves established to protect endangered species of wild cranes. **Zhālóng Nature Reserve** (扎龙自然保护区, Zhālóng Zìrán Bǎohùqū; ¥60; ⊙ 8am-5.30pm) near Qíqíhā'ěr is the most accessible and most visited of these sanctuaries. The reserve is home to some 260 bird species, including several types of rare cranes. Four of the species that migrate here are on the endangered list: the extremely rare red-crowned crane, the white-naped crane, the Siberian crane and the hooded crane.

The reserve comprises some 2100 sq km of wetlands that are on a bird migration path extending from the Russian Arctic down into Southeast Asia. Hundreds of birds arrive in April and May, rear their young from June to August and depart in September and October. Unfortunately, a significant percentage of the birds you can see live are in captivity and are periodically released so that visitors can take photos.

The best time to visit Zhālóng is in spring. In summer the mosquitoes can be more plentiful than the birds – take repellent! To get here, head to Qíqíhā'ěr and board bus 306 (¥20, 45 minutes, half-hourly) from Dàrùnfā (大润发). Birds are released at 9.30am, 11am, 2pm and 3.30pm.

The **Xiānghǎi National Nature Reserve** (向海, Xiànghǎi Guójiā Zìrán Bǎohùqū), 310km west of Chángchūn in Jílín province, is on the migration path for Siberian cranes, and the rare red-crowned, white-naped and demoiselle cranes breed here. More than 160 bird species, including several of these cranes, have been identified at the **Horqin National Nature Reserve** (科尔沁, Kē'ěrqin Guójiā Zìrán Bǎohùqū), which borders Xianghai in Inner Mongolia. The **Mòmògé National Nature Reserve** (莫莫格, Mòmògé Guójiā Zìrán Bǎohùqū) in northern Jílín province is also an important wetlands area and bird breeding site.

For more information about China's crane population and these nature reserves, contact the International Crane Foundation (www.savingcranes.org) or see the website of the Siberian Crane Wetland Project (www.scwp.info).

ern rooms are fitted with plush carpets and large comfy beds. The cheaper rooms are windowless but just as comfortable. Discounts bring rooms down to ¥150 during the shoulder season.

✖ Eating

There are eateries on Guotu Jie, the street parallel to Yaoquan Lu near the Quanshan New Holiday Inn, or at the intersection of Yaoquan and Shilong Lu. Plenty of greasy-spoon choices (dishes ¥8 to ¥48) largely serve the same five types of local fish the area is famous for. You can also get cheap *jiǎozi*, noodles and BBQ. Several grocery stores sell fruit and imported snacks.

★ Wángmáolǘ Dòufu

Měishí Diàn   DONGBEI **$$**
(王毛驴豆腐美食店; off Guotu Jie; dishes ¥22-58; ⊙11am-9.30pm) The locally made tofu is some of the best you'll taste in China. It's soft and delicate, and served in a variety of ways: with fish, vegies and such. If you can't decide, take your pick from the picture menu on the wall. It's located off Guotu Jie, the street parallel to the main drag where the Quanshan New Holiday Inn hotel is.

If you get lost, ask locals for directions; it's a famous restaurant.

ℹ Information

There is an **ICBC** (工商银行; Gōngshāng Yínháng) ATM accepting foreign cards in Wǔdàlián Chí on Guotu Jie. Bringing a little extra cash is not a bad idea because it would be easy to get stuck nowhere near a bank.

ℹ Getting There & Away

Both Wǔdàlián Chí and Wǔdàlián Chí Shì have bus stations. Direct buses run from Harbin (¥100, six hours, four daily at 9am, 11.30am, 1.30pm and 2.45pm). The 1.30pm bus terminates at Wǔdàlián Chí (making it the best choice for most visitors) while the other two terminate at the city proper of Wǔdàlián Chí Shì, further from the sights. A taxi the rest of the way to the 'tourist zone' costs ¥40.

Buses leave for Harbin from Wǔdàlián Chí (¥100, six hours, 5.40am and 8.10am) and Wǔdàlián Chí Shì (6.50am and 9.30am). There are also buses to Hēihé and Běi'ān (1½ hours), the nearest train station, which has connections on to Harbin (seats ¥29 to ¥51, five to seven hours).

ℹ Getting Around

Taxis make the trip from the bus station to the hotel area for ¥5 to ¥10.

Mòhé   漢河
☑ 0457 / POP 83,465

China's northernmost town, Mòhé, stands amid spindly pine forests and vast bogs. In this region it's possible to see Siberian forests and dwindling settlements of northern minorities, such as the Daur, Ewenki, Hezhen and Oroqen.

It's one of China's most intriguing outliers, sharing not just a border with Russia, but architecture as well. In 1985 the town burned to the ground in a raging forest fire and when it came time to rebuild, Mòhé decided to redo the main streets in an imperial-era Russian style with spired domes, pillared entrances and facades with rows of narrow windows.

Mòhé holds the record for the lowest plunge of the thermometer: -52.3°C, recorded in 1956. That same day in China's southern extreme at Sānyà, a tropical beach paradise of azure waters and coconut palms, the temperature was likely in the high 20°Cs.

◉ Sights

Běijícūn   VILLAGE
(北极村, North Pole Village; ¥60) Further north from Mòhé is Běijícūn, a sprawling village and recreation area on the banks of the Hēilóng Jiāng, separating China and Russia. The area is fast expanding with new hotels and resorts under construction.

Běijícūn covers an area of forest, meadows and bog, with the occasional hamlet, log cabin and Russian-style structure dotting the pretty surroundings. If the mood strikes, you can stand at the top of a map of China that has been etched into a square. Step up on the podium and you are at the official 'most northerly point' (though Běihóngcūn village is actually further north) one can be within China's 9,671,018 sq km of land. One house has even been labelled **China No 1** (中国最北一家), ie China's northernmost house. You can walk east along the river to a point where you can see a Russian village across the water.

Běihóngcūn   VILLAGE
(北红村) With the northern village of Běijícūn on the tourist radar, intrepid travellers and enterprising locals have opened up a route to the even more northerly village of Běihóngcūn, 100km away. There's nowhere to go but back south here and while there's not much beyond wooden houses and swaths of farmland, it is a quiet, idyllic spot

and lays claim to being China's real northernmost village.

From Běihóngcūn, you can push across to Hēilóng Jiāng Dìyī Wān (黑龙江第一弯), the first bend in the river. The 800-plus steps to the viewing point are well worth the gorgeous panorama of the amazing horseshoe bend.

✸ Festivals & Events

Festival of Aurora Borealis   CULTURAL
(北极光节, Běijíguāng Jié; late Jun) The area around Mòhé is best known for its midnight sun, visible for as long as 22 hours during this annual festival. Oddly, this is one of the few times you can see the Northern Lights, according to locals. Later in the summer, when there are more hours of darkness, the lights don't appear. Odds of seeing the aurora are fairly slim with the last period of high activity in 2012, and the next likely in 2023.

🛏 Sleeping & Eating

The best place to base yourself is at Běijícūn for easy access to sights and getting help with getting around. In Mòhé there are a number of cheap guesthouses down the alleys off Fanrong Xiang, which is off Zhenxing Jie (the main street).

For cheap restaurants head to the alleys off Fanrong Xiang, which runs off the main street, Zhenxing Jie. Fresh produce isn't cheap in winter as everything has to be imported from warmer provinces.

Mòhé International Youth Hostel   HOSTEL $
(漠河北极村驴友之家国际青年旅舍, Mòhé Běijícūn Lǘyóu Zhījiā Guójí Qīngnián Lǚshè; ☑0457 282 6326, 138 0484 1364; Běijícūn; dm ¥30, d & tw ¥80; ❈⃝🖢) This cute farmhouse can organise onward transport to see Běihóngcūn and the other sights before looping back to Mòhé. Rooms are comfortable and you can get home-cooked meals from the attached

kitchen. If you ring ahead, a car can pick you up from the train station or airport. You can also rent bicycles here in summer for ¥25 per day.

Only Chinese is spoken, but the friendly owner encourages communicating through WeChat (conversation translation available) on the hostel's mobile number.

Mòhé Jiā Xīn Bīnguǎn   HOTEL $$
(漠河佳鑫宾馆; ☑0457 287 0666; Běijícūn; r ¥180-220) This comfortable Běijícūn hotel can organise onward transport to see Běihóngcūn and the other sights before looping back to Mòhé. The almost-modern rooms and bathrooms are compact and clean, with steady hot water. If you ring ahead, a car can pick you up from the train station or airport. You can also rent bicycles (¥5 per hour) to explore the town.

ℹ Getting There & Away

China Southern has one direct flight a day from Harbin to Mòhé (¥1510, 1¾ hours). Trains from Harbin (hard/soft sleeper ¥288/449, 5.55pm and 6.57pm) take 13 or 15 hours to reach the northern town. Heading back, trains leave at 2.30pm and 7.50pm and take 16 hours.

Buses for Běijícūn (¥30, 1½ to two hours, 8.40am, 2.20pm and 6pm) leave from Mòhé's bus station at the corner of Zhenxing Jie and Zhonghua Jie. Return buses from Běijícūn depart at 10am and 2pm.

ℹ Getting Around

To/from the airport, taxis charge ¥20. Mòhé's train station is about 2km from the centre of town and it costs ¥12 to get here by taxi.

A good way to visit the area would be to hire a private car or taxi for two days. Expect to pay around ¥300 per day; you can start your trip from Mòhé and do all the sights listed in a loop back. You can usually find fellow travellers to share the cost at the Mòhé International Youth Hostel.

Shāndōng

POP 95.8 MILLION

Best Places to Eat

➡ Cafè Yum (p226)

➡ Yù Shū Fáng (p218)

➡ Seasons Mínghú (p205)

➡ China Community Art & Culture (p226)

Best Places to Sleep

➡ Kǎiyuè Hostelling International (p225)

➡ Shangri-La Hotel (p225)

➡ Sea View Garden Hotel (p225)

➡ Hóngmén International Youth Hostel (p209)

Why Go?

Steeped in natural and supernatural allure, the Shāndōng (山东) peninsula on China's northeastern coast is the stuff of legends. Its captivating landscape – a fertile flood plain fed by rivers and underground springs, capped by granite peaks and framed in wild coastline – can't help but inspire wonder.

A lumpy-headed boy named Confucius was born here and grew up to develop a philosophy of virtue and ethics that would reach far beyond his lectures under an apricot tree. Three centuries later China's first emperor, Qín Shǐ Huáng, would climb Tài Shān, Shāndōng's highest peak, to proclaim a unified empire in 219 BC.

But Shāndōng is more than the sum of its historical parts. The energetic buzz in seaside Qīngdǎo ranks the city among the best places to live in Asia. This is Shāndōng's real draw: you can climb mountains, feast on fine seafood, quaff beer and still find time to hit the beach.

When to Go
Qīngdǎo

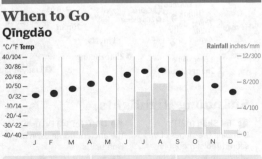

Jun–Aug Cool sea breezes and the beer festival make summer the time to explore Qīngdǎo.

Sep–Oct Sacred Tài Shān is gloriously shrouded in mist for just part (not all) of the day.

Dec & Jan Dress warmly and ascend Shāndōng's frosted peaks in the dry winter.

History

Shāndōng's tumultuous history is tied to the capricious temperament of the Yellow River, which crosses the peninsula before emptying into the Bo Sea. The 'Mother River' nurtured civilisation but when unhinged left death, disease and rebellion in its wake. After a long period of floods followed by economic depression and unrest, the river again devastated the Shāndōng plain in 1898.

Europeans had also arrived. After two German missionaries died in a peasant uprising in western Shāndōng in 1897, Germany readily seized Qīngdǎo, Britain forced a lease of Wēihǎi, and soon six other nations scrambled for concessions. These acts coupled with widespread famine emboldened a band of superstitious nationalists, and in the closing years of the 19th century, the Boxers rose out of Shāndōng, armed with magical spells and broadswords to lead a rebellion against the eight-nation alliance of Austria-Hungary, France, Germany, Italy, Japan, Russia, the UK and the USA. After foreign powers violently seized Běijīng in 1900, the Empress Cixi effectively surrendered and Boxer and other resistance leaders were executed. The Qing dynasty would soon collapse.

It was not until Japan's surrender in WWII that Shāndōng emerged from decades of war and recovered its cities. In 1955 engineers began an ambitious 50-year flood-control program, and 1959 marked Shāndōng's last catastrophic flood, though now China's economic boom threatens to suck the Yellow River dry.

Today Jǐ'nán, the provincial capital, and the prospering coastal cities of Yāntái and Wēihǎi, all play a supporting role to Qīngdǎo, the province's headliner.

🛈 Getting There & Away

With South Korea and Japan just across the water, there are direct international flights through three airports – Jǐ'nán, Qīngdǎo and Yāntái. Ferries (p234) also sail from Qīngdǎo to South Korea

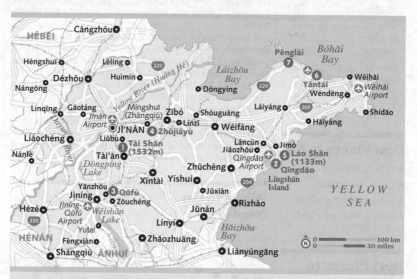

Shāndōng Highlights

1 Tài Shān (p211)
Climbing the slopes of this sacred Taoist mountain, where stones speak the wisdom of millennia.

2 Qīngdǎo (p220) Chilling by the sea with a pitcher (or bag) of China's most famous brew.

3 Qūfù (p214) Perusing the ancient home town of Confucius.

4 Zhūjiāyù (p207) Relaxing in this charming, rural village.

5 Láo Shān (p229) Hiking in search of magical springs and Taoist secrets.

6 Yāntái (p231) Savouring the ocean breeze as you explore the history of this prosperous port city.

7 Pénglái Pavilion (p235) Discovering the legends of immortals, pirates and mirages.

(Incheon) and Japan (Shimonoseki), and from Yāntái to Incheon and Pyeongtaek in South Korea.

Shāndōng is linked to neighbouring and distant provinces by both bus and rail. Jǐ'nán is the transport hub, with rail connections to all major towns and cities in Shāndōng. The high-speed rail now links Jǐ'nán, Tàishān, Qūfù and Qīngdǎo to Běijīng and Shànghǎi.

ℹ Getting Around

With rail connecting all the big towns, cities and drawcard sights, getting around Shāndōng by train is straightforward, with buses playing second fiddle, but the roads are useful for opening up the smaller corners of the province.

Jǐ'nán　济南

 0531 / POP 3.5 MILLION

Jǐ'nán is Shāndōng's busy and prosperous capital city, serving as the transit hub to other destinations around the province. On its surface the city is in a state of restless flux, but beneath the dusty construction and sprawl are 72 artesian springs, which gently roil in azure pools and flow steadily into Dàmíng Lake.

◉ Sights

Strolling among the swaying willows and quiet waterways of Jǐ'nán's particularly lovely parks is a pleasant escape from the urban din. The most central include the most famous, Bàotū Spring (p204); Huánchéng Park (p204), where Black Tiger Spring empties into the old city moat, the Húchéng River; and Five Dragon Pool (p204).

Dàmíng Lake　LAKE
(大明湖, Dàmíng Hú; ¥30) All the water from Jǐ'nán's springs eventually flows into Dàmíng Lake, set within the largest park in the city, with boat rides, paddle boats, temples, bridges, and little islands to explore. In summer lotuses bloom in pink and white. The park has been a scenic site since the Tang dynasty, inspiring everyone from Marco Polo to Deng Xiaoping to wax about its beauty.

Great Southern Mosque　MOSQUE
(清真南大寺, Qīngzhēn Nán Dà Sì; 47 Yongchang Jie; 🚌 K50, 101) FREE Jǐ'nán's oldest mosque has stood in one form or another in the centre of town since 1295. Cover arms and remove hats before entering. A lively Hui (Muslim Chinese) neighbourhood is to the north.

Xīnguóchán Temple　BUDDHIST TEMPLE
(兴国禅寺, Xīngguó Chánsì; ¥5; ⊙ 7.30am-4.30pm) The oldest Buddha statues on Thousand Buddha Mountain are contained here, in this golden-roofed temple complex.

Wángfǔ Pool　SPRING
(王府池子, Wángfǔ Chízi) FREE In a quiet alleyway off busy, walking street Furong Jie (turn right at the police stand), the neighbourhood comes to bathe and soak in this spring-fed pool. It's a brisk 18°C year-round, so indulge in frequent barbecue and beer breaks at one of the nearby stands.

Shāndōng Museum　MUSEUM
(山东博物馆, Shāndōng Bówùguǎn; 🚌 0531 8505 8201; www.sdmuseum.com; 11899 Jingshi Lu, 经十路11899号; audio tour ¥30; ⊙ 9am-4pm Tue-Sun; 🚌 115, 202, 18) FREE The enormous provincial museum – 7km east of the city centre – surveys local culture from the mesolithic age to the present. Its collection began as one of the first organised museums in China in 1904. On display are oracle bones, Qi and Lu kingdom pottery, Han tomb murals and clothing worn by the Kong clan (Confucius' descendants).

Jǐ'nán Museum　MUSEUM
(济南市博物馆, Jǐ'nán Shì Bówùguǎn; 🚌 0531 8295 9204; www.jnmuseum.com; 30 Jing Shiyilu, 经十一路30号; audio tour ¥10; ⊙ 8.30am-4pm Tue-Sun; 🚌 K51) FREE North of Thousand Buddha Mountain's main entrance, the Jǐ'nán Museum has a small, distinctive collection that includes paintings, calligraphy, ceramics, Buddhist figures from the Tang dynasty and a delightful boat carved from a walnut shell.

Thousand Buddha Mountain　MOUNTAIN
(千佛山, Qiānfó Shān; 18 Jingshi Yilu; ¥30, one-way/return cable car ¥20/30, luge ¥25/30; ⊙ 5am-9pm; 🚌 K51) Beginning in the Sui dynasty

PRICE INDICATORS

Sleeping

The following price ranges refer to a double room with private shower.

$ less than ¥200

$$ ¥200–¥500

$$$ more than ¥500

Eating

The following price ranges refer to a main course.

$ less than ¥30

$$ ¥30–¥60

$$$ more than ¥60

Jǐ'nán

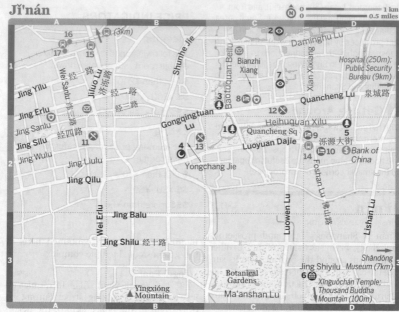

Jǐ'nán

(581–618), pious folk carved Buddhas into this mountain southeast of the city centre. The oldest are at Xīnguóchán Temple (p203), the golden-roofed complex near the **cable car** and **luge** drop-off on the mountaintop. On the rare clear day looking south, you can spot Tài Shān, the anthill in the distance.

Five Dragon Pool Park PARK
(五龙潭公园, Wǔlóngtán Gōngyuán; 18 Kuangshi Jie, 筐市街18号; ¥5; 🚌5, 101) These waters swirl up from the deepest depths of all the springs in the city to fill blue-green pools teeming with lucky carp. The park is a serene study of local life, where elders paint calligraphy on the steps and kids chase the goldfish.

Huánchéng Park PARK
(环城公园, Huánchéng Gōngyuán; 2 Nanmen Jie) FREE This park on the Húchéng River is built around Black Tiger Spring (黑虎泉, Hēihǔ Quán), which empties into the old city moat through three stone tiger heads. It gets its name from the sound of the roaring water as it rushed over a tiger-shaped stone, long gone but immortalised in Ming dynasty poetry.

Bàotū Spring PARK
(趵突泉, Bàotū Quán; 1 Baotuquan Nanlu, 趵突泉南路1号; ¥40; 🚌K51) This park's namesake 'spurting spring' once shot metres into the air, inspiring ancient poets and painters alike. Today, as more water has been chan-

neled from the city's underground limestone aquifers, it arrives with more of a gurgle. Jǐnán's local brew proudly bears its name.

🏃 Activities

Sightseeing Boats
BOATING

(☑0531 8690 5886; per stop ¥10; ☺every 20min 9am-5pm) These fun, open-air, motorised boats circle clockwise around the lovely Húchéng River and the south side of Dàmíng Lake, making 10 stops at all the major sights including Bàotū Spring, Black Tiger Spring, Five Dragon Pool, and Quancheng Sq, as well as rising and falling several stories via two fascinating locks. It takes about 1½ hours for the full circuit.

🛏 Sleeping

Jǐnán doesn't have much in the way of budget accommodation, but is reasonably well supplied in the midrange and top-end bracket. Budget hotels with rooms for around ¥160 to ¥180 are clustered around the main train station, though not all cater to foreigners and rooms vary greatly. It helps if you speak some Chinese too, but inspect the rooms first if you choose to stay here.

Chéngběi Youth Hostel
HOSTEL $

(城北国际青年旅舍, Chéngběi Guójì Qīngnián Lǚshè; ☑0531 8691 7661; w454488201@gmail. com; 111 Bianzhi Xiang, off Quancheng Lu, 鞭指巷111号; dm ¥35-55, d ¥120; 🅰🛜; 🚇3, 5, K50) This youth hostel in a small, converted courtyard residence is your best option for a cheap bed. Dorms and common bathrooms are decent, but the one available double room is just a mattress on the ground. There's a small bar, solid travel advice, train ticketing, organised biking trips to interesting sites in and around Jǐnán, and hiking gear for rent.

To get here, follow the flow of traffic, turn right off Quancheng Lu down Bianzhi Xiang, a small alley, and at the police station turn left down an even smaller alley. The hostel is through the gate with the red horse.

Silver Plaza Quancheng Hotel
HOTEL $$

(银座泉城大酒店, Yínzuò Quánchéng Dàjiǔdiàn; ☑0531 8692 1911; 2 Nanmen Dajie, 南门大街2号; d/tr ¥493/531; 🅰🛜@) You know this is a Chinese business hotel from the blinding Euro-style bling in the lobby. Professional staff and a prime spot overlooking Quancheng Sq make up for that and the compact rooms with stained tile ceilings. Shell out for an upgrade in the renovated B-wing.

Sofitel Silver Plaza
HOTEL $$$

(索菲特银座大饭店, Suǒfēitè Yínzuò Dàfàndiàn; ☑0531 8606 8888; www.sofitel.com; 66 Luoyuan Dajie, 泺源大街66号; r from ¥690, plus 10% service charge; 🅰❄@🏊) This five-star hotel in the commercial district is still an excellent option, though we wish standard rooms were as spacious as the lobby suggests.

🍴 Eating

Jǐnán is a famed centre of Lǔ (Shāndōng) cuisine, characterised by bold flavours brought out by cooking over a high heat with plenty of oil and spices. Most of the best eating is had in the city's streets and alleys.

Off Quancheng Lu's shopping strip, **Furong Jie** is a pedestrian alley crammed with restaurants and food stalls.

Dàguān Gardens
SHANDONG $

(大观园, Dàguān Yuán; Jing Silu, 经四路; dishes from ¥10)' An enclave of modern eateries. Just inside the north gate, **Lǔxī'nán Flavor Restaurant** (鲁西南老牌坊, Lǔxī'nán Lǎopáifāng; ☑0531 8605 4567; dishes ¥28-98; ☺11am-2.30pm & 5-10pm) is the place for a refined take on Lǔ (Shāndōng) cuisine. Order the home classics like sweet and spicy cabbage with glass noodles (¥22) and lamb (braised or sautéed, from ¥19), accompanied with sesame cakes (¥2) – not rice. Chinese menu with pictures.

Yǐnhǔchí Jie
STREET FOOD $

(饮虎池街; dishes from ¥10) Evenings are smoky on Yǐnhǔchí Jie in the Hui district near the Great Southern Mosque. Hawkers fan the flames of charcoal grills lining the street, roasting up all manner of *shāokǎo* (barbecue on a stick). They make crisp scallion pancakes and fresh noodles too.

Seasons Mínghú
CANTONESE $$

(四季明湖, Sìjì Mínghú; ☑0531 6666 9898; 7th fl, Parc66, 188 Quancheng Lu, 泉城路188号; dim sum from ¥18, mains from ¥38; ☺11am-10pm) It may be a chain, but this is an elegant choice on the top of the Parc66 Mall, where dandy waiters don gloves while serving southern Chinese classics, including dim sum, salt-baked chicken and durian cakes.

ℹ Information

Bank of China (中国银行, Zhōngguó Yínháng; 22 Luoyuan Dajie, 泺源大街22号; ☺9am-5pm Mon-Fri) Currency exchange/24-hour ATMs accepting foreign cards.

China Post (中国邮政, Zhōngguó Yóuzhèng; 162 Jing Erlu, 经二路162号; ☺8.30am-6pm) A red-brick building on the corner of Wei Erlu.

Public Security Bureau (PSB, 公安局, Gōng'ānjú; ☑ 0531 8508 1000, visa inquiries ext 2459; 777 Shuhuaxi Lu, 舜华西路777号; ◷ 9am-noon & 2-4.40pm Mon-Fri) About 9km (a ¥18 taxi ride) east of the city centre.

Shāndōng Provincial Qiānfó Shān Hospital International Clinic (千佛山医院国际医疗中心, Qiānfó Shān Yīyuàn Guójì Yīliáo Zhōngxīn; ☑ 0531 8926 8017, 0531 8926 8018; www. sdhospital.com.cn; 16766 Jingshi Lu, 经十路16766号; ◷ 8-11am & 2-5.30pm Mon-Fri) English and Japanese spoken. Take bus K51 or K68 to the Nánkǒu (南口) stop on Lishan Lu.

ℹ Getting There & Away

AIR

Jǐ'nán's **Yáoqiáng Airport** (☑ 0531 8208 6666) is 40km from the city and connects to most major cities, with daily flights to Běijīng (¥630, one hour 15 minutes), Dàlián (¥502, one hour), Guǎngzhōu (¥1660, 2½ hours), Hā'ěrbīn (¥1450, two hours), Seoul (¥1034, one hour 40 minutes), Shànghǎi (¥1310, 1½ hours), and Xī'ān (¥910, one hour 50 minutes).

BUS

Jǐ'nán's most convenient station is the **main long-distance bus station** (长途总汽车站, Chángtú Zǒng Qìchē Zhàn; ☑ 0531 8594 1472; 131 Jiluo Lu), about 3km north of the train station, though buses to destinations within the province also leave from the **bus station** (☑ 8830 3030; 22 Chezhan Jie, 车站街22号) directly across from the train station.

Some buses departing regularly from the main long-distance bus station:

Běijīng ¥129, 5½ hours, nine daily (8.30am to 9pm)

Qīngdǎo ¥96 to ¥109, 4½ hours, hourly (8.10am to 9.20pm)

Qūfù ¥55, two hours, every 50 minutes (7am to 6pm)

Shànghǎi ¥266, 12 hours, four daily (10.30am, 6pm, 7pm and 8.30pm)

Tài'ān ¥25, two hours, every 30 minutes (6.30am to 6pm)

Tiānjīn ¥124, 4½ hours, six daily (9am, 9.30am, 11.40am, 2pm, 2.20pm and 9pm)

Yāntái ¥150, 5½ hours, hourly (6.30am to 9.30pm)

TRAIN

Jǐ'nán is a major hub in the east China rail system and has several busy train stations. Most travellers can rely on the main train station (火车总站; huǒchē zǒng zhàn), a 4km ride on bus 3 (¥2) from the city centre, but there is also **Jǐnán West train station** (济南西站, Jǐnán Xīzhàn; Dajinzhuang Lu, 大金庄路), which largely services high-speed trains.

Lines at the station's ticket office can be very slow, and automatic ticket machines don't work for foreigners. Ticket offices only charge ¥5 commission and are all around the train-station square, including the **plane/train ticket office** (盛祥源航空铁路售票处, Shèngxiángyuán Hángkōng Tiělù Shòupiàochù; ☑ 0531 8610 9666; Quánchéng Hotel lobby, 115 Chezhan Jie; ◷ plane 7.30am-10pm, train 8am-8pm) in the Quánchéng Hotel lobby and the **Jǐ'nán Railway Hotel** (济南铁道大酒店, Jǐ'nán Tiědào Dàjiǔdiàn; 19 Chezhan Jie, Jǐ'nán Railway Hotel lobby; commission ¥5; ◷ 8am-midnight). **Chéngběi Youth Hostel** (p205) can also book tickets.

Some express trains (1st-/2nd-class seat) departing from the main train station:

Běijīng ¥330/195, two hours, frequently (7.15am to 8.02pm)

Qīngdǎo ¥145/120, two hours 40 minutes, every 10 minutes (7.20am to 8.20pm)

Qūfù ¥100/60, 30 minutes, regular

Shànghǎi ¥674/399, four hours, four daily (9.40am, 12.08pm, 4.37pm and 7.08pm)

Tài'ān ¥50/30, 24 minutes, five daily (7.26am, 9.40am, 12.08pm, 12.32pm and 5.22pm)

Wéifāng ¥80/65, one hour 20 minutes, every 20 minutes (6.09am to 8.20pm)

Some regular trains (seat/hard sleeper):

Xī'ān ¥149/264, 13 to 18 hours, six daily (11.13am to 10.36pm)

Yāntái ¥165/198, three hours 20 minutes, 12 daily (7.16am to 6.10pm)

ℹ Getting Around

TO/FROM THE AIRPORT

Airport shuttles (☑ 96888; adult ¥20; ◷ hourly 6am-6pm) connect the main train station and the Yùquán Simpson Hotel with Jǐ'nán's Yáoqiáng airport. The shuttle also runs directly to Tài'ān (¥80, two hours, eight daily from 11.30am to 8pm).

PUBLIC TRANSPORT

Bus 15 or 84 (¥1) connects the main long-distance bus station with the main train station. Bus K51 (¥2) runs from the main train station through the city centre and then south past Bàotú Spring park to Thousand Buddha Mountain.

TAXI

Taxis cost ¥8 for the first 3km then ¥1.75 (slightly more at night) per kilometre thereafter.

WATER TAXI

Open-air, motorised boats circle clockwise around the lovely Húchéng River and the south side of Dàmíng Lake, making stops at 10 major sights including Bàotú Spring, Black Tiger Spring, Five Dragon Pool and Quancheng Sq, as well as rising and falling several storeys via two fascinating locks. It takes about 1½ hours for the full circuit.

Zhūjiāyù 朱家峪

☑ 0531 / POP 1550

Eighty kilometres east of Jǐ'nán is one of Shāndōng's oldest hamlets. Zhūjiāyù's intact structures mostly date back to the Ming and Qing dynasties, and many have been recently spruced up to serve as movie and soap-opera sets, but strolling the stone-paved streets is still a journey back in time.

Zhūjiāyù and its bucolic panoramas of rolling-hills can be explored in an easy day trip from Jǐ'nán. Admission to the village is ¥10. You can wander on your own, though there are official, Chinese-speaking guides (¥60) and eager long-time residents (¥30) ready to show you around. Posted maps are in English.

In a bid to keep kids' attention, there is also a half-hour, **immersive movie experience** (incl entry ¥80; ⏱ 10am Mon-Fri, 10am & 2pm Sat & Sun) loosely based on the harrowing journeys of Shāndōng natives seeking opportunity.

Follow the Ming-dynasty, double-track **ancient road** (双轨古道; shuāngguǐ gǔdào) to the Qing-dynasty **Wénchāng Pavilion** (文昌阁; Wénchāng Gé), an arched gate topped by a single-roofed shrine where teachers would take new pupils to make offerings to Confucius before their first lesson. On your left is **Shānyīn Primary School** (山阴小学; Shānyīn Xiǎoxué), a series of halls and courtyards with exhibits on local life.

Walk on to see the many ancestral temples, including the **Zhu Family Ancestral Hall** (朱氏家祠; Zhūshì Jiācí), with packed mudbrick homesteads, and quaint, arched shíqiáo (stone bridges). The **Kāngxī Overpass** (康熙双桥; Kāngxī Shuāng Qiáo) is one of the earliest examples in the world of such a traffic structure and dates from 1671. A further 30-minute climb past the last dry-stone walls of the village will take you to the gleaming white **Kuíxīng Pavilion** (魁星楼; Kuíxīng Lóu) crowning the hill.

If you want to stay overnight, look for flags posting '农家乐' (nóngjiālè; a guesthouse or homestay) or '住宿' (zhùsù; accommodation). There are plenty of options in the village. The earthy **Gǔcūn Inn** (古村酒家; Gǔcūn Jiǔjiā; ☑ 0531 8380 8135; dm ¥30, d with bathroom ¥100; 🐾) has basic but clean rooms in a courtyard house with chickens roaming the yard. The friendly Zhang family running the place also cook up meals using ingredients they forage and grow in the garden (English menu, mains ¥15 to ¥40). Pass under the Kāngxī Overpass and take the low road at the split, following the bend to the left.

Humble restaurants in the village cook up excellent fare from local ingredients, although proprietors may steer you to the more expensive free-range chicken and pork.

Humble **Lǎo Yī Mín Restaurant** (老衣民菜馆, Lǎo Yī Mín Càiguǎn; ☑ 138 8498 9061; dishes ¥14-25) cooks up excellent fare from local ingredients, about 100m past Zhūjiāyù's large Mao portrait. The genial owners take their yellow dog hunting for wild rabbit (¥40 per jīn) and forage for fresh mushrooms and greens in the surrounding hills.

To get here from Jǐ'nán, catch bus K301 (¥14, 1½ hours, 7am to 6.30pm) to the Jìshī Xuéyuàn (技师学院) stop in front of a large technical college. From the Jìshī Xuéyuàn stop, catch bus 9 (¥1) to the large white gate marking the village drop-off. It's another 2km walk (locals offer lifts) to the tourist centre. Taxis from the college will go the whole way for ¥15. Returning to Jǐ'nán, reverse the process or flag down a bus across from the white gate on the main road. Buses back after 5pm are rare.

Tài'ān 泰安

☑ 0538 / POP 1.1 MILLION

The gateway to Tài Shān's sacred slopes is the town of Tài'ān, which has had a tourist industry in full swing since before the Ming dynasty. In the 17th century, historian Zhang Dai described package tours that included choice of lodging (enormous inns with more than 20 kitchens and hundreds of servants, opera performers and courtesans), a post summit banquet, plus an optional sedan-chair upgrade (climbing tax not included).

⊙ Sights

Dài Temple TAOIST TEMPLE
(岱庙, Dài Miào; Daimiao Beijie, 岱庙北街; adult/child ¥30/15; ⏱ 8am-6pm summer, to 5pm winter) This magnificent Taoist temple complex is where all Tài'ān roads lead, being the traditional first stop on the pilgrimage route up Tài Shān. The grounds are an impressive example of Song-dynasty (960–1127) temple construction with features of an imperial palace, though other structures stood here 1000 years before that.

Many visitors enter from the north through **Hòu Zài gate** (候载门), but entering from the south through **Zhèngyáng gate** (正阳门) allows you to follow the traditional passage through the main temple and up Hongmen Lu to the start of Tài Shān's central route ascent.

Tài'ān

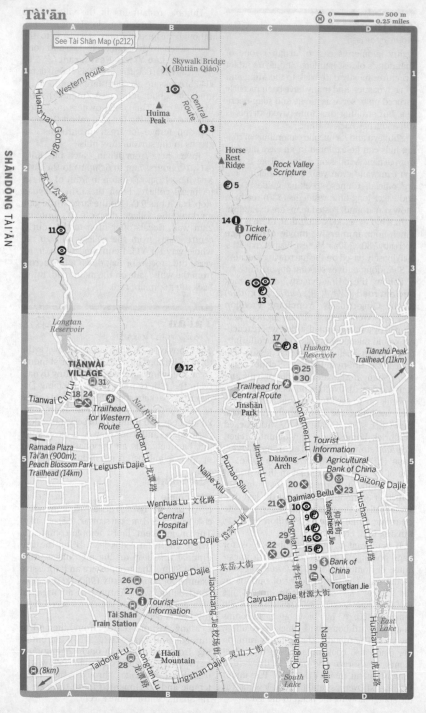

See Tài Shān Map (p212)

N
0 — 500 m
0 — 0.25 miles

SHĀNDŌNG TÀI'ĀN

Western Route

Huanshan Gonglu

汶山公路

Skywalk Bridge
(Bùtiān Qiáo)

1

Central Route

Huima Peak

3

Horse
Rest
Ridge

Rock Valley
Scripture

5

14

Ticket
Office

11

2

6 7

13

Longtan
Reservoir

17 8

Hushan
Reservoir

Tiānzhú Peak
Trailhead (11km)

12

25

30

TIĀNWÀI
VILLAGE

31

Trailhead for
Central Route

Jinshān
Park

Tianwai Cun Lu

18 24

Nai River

Trailhead
for Western
Route

Longtan Lu 龙潭路

Hongmen Lu

Tourist
Information

Ramada Plaza
Tài'ān (900m);
Peach Blossom Park
Trailhead (14km)

Leigushi Dajie

Naihe Xilu

Puzhao Silu

Jinshan Lu

Dàizōng
Arch

Agricultural
Bank of China

Daizong Dajie

Wenhua Lu 文化路

20

Daimiao Beilu

23

Yangsheng Jie 仰老街

21

10

Central
Hospital

Daizong Dajie 岱宗大街

Qingnian Lu 青年路

9

4

29

16

15

22

Hushan Lu 虎山路

Dongyue Dajie 东岳大街

19

Bank of
China

26

Jiaochang Jie 校场街

Caiyuan Dajie 财源大街

Tongtian Jie

27

Tourist
Information

Tài Shān
Train Station

Taidong Lu

28

Longtan Lu 龙潭路

Hāolǐ
Mountain

Lingshan Dajie 灵山大街

Nanguan Dajie

Qingnian Lu

South
Lake

East
Lake

Hushan Lu 虎山路

(8km)

Tài'ān

From the south end, two lions watch cars pass by on Dongyue Dajie, flanking the splendid *páifāng* (ornamental arch). Beyond this and the Zhèngyáng gate is the **Yáocān Pavilion** (遥参亭, Yáocān Tíng; ⊙6.30am-6pm).

Between the buildings, the courtyards are filled with prized examples of poetry and imperial records. Fossilised-looking *bìxì* (the mythical tortoise son of the dragon), dating from the 12th century onward, carry stelae on their backs documenting everything from the civil exam process to emperors' birthdays. The Han Emperor Wudi himself is said to have planted some of the massive, twisting trees in the **Cypress Tree Pavilion** 2100 years ago.

The main hall is the colossal **Hall of Heavenly Blessing** (天贶殿, Tiānkuàng Diàn; shoe covers ¥1).

🛏 Sleeping

Since you will need at least a full day to explore the mountain, spending the night in Tài'ān or at the summit is advised. It's cheaper and more comfortable to sleep in Tài'ān, and there's far more choice, although staying on the mountain naturally has its own appeal. There are many midrange options in town, mostly clustered around the Tàishān train station. Ask for discounts.

★Hóngmén International Youth Hostel
HOSTEL $

(红门国际青年旅舍, Hóngmén Guójì Qīngnián Lǚshě; ☑0538 808 6188; www.yhachina.com; 89 Hongmen Lu, 红门路89号; dm ¥45-65, s & d

¥188, tr ¥218; ⊛; ⬚K3, K37) In a red courtyard building, and formerly part of the Taoist Guandi Temple next door, this fresh hostel offers the best of all worlds – the mountain within a few steps, a cafe-bar and bright rooms with all necessary conveniences including wi-fi. The very knowledgeable staff organise night climbs.

Tàishān International Youth Hostel
HOSTEL ●

(泰山国际青年旅舍, Tàishān Guójì Qīngnián Lǚshè; ☑0538 628 5196; 65 Tongtian Jie, 通天街65号; dm ¥40-60, s & d ¥100-188; ⊛@⊛; ⬚1, 4, 7, 8, 17) This youth hostel is rather simple, with clean spartan rooms, pine furnishings and old propaganda posters, but staff are very helpful and the location is superb. Bike rental, free laundry and a bar on the 4th floor make this a pleasant experience. Look for the pair of arches just off Tongtian Jie. Discounts get rooms down to around ¥128.

Ramada Plaza Tài'ān
HOTEL $$$

(东尊华美达大酒店, Dōngzūn Huáměidá Dàjiǔdiàn; ☑0538 836 8666; www.ramadaplazataian. com; 16 Yingsheng Donglu, 迎胜东路16号; s & d ¥1160-1400, ste ¥1960-3360; ⊛⊛⊛; ⬚8) This decent five-star choice in the northwest has all the usual comforts plus fantastic views of the main attraction, although service can be a bit below par. Discounts of 40%.

🍴 Eating

There are three busy food streets in Tài'ān. The night market (p210) on the Nài River's east bank has many hotpot stalls. Vendors on **Beǐxīn Snack Street** (北新小吃步行街, Beǐxīn Xiǎochī Bùxíng Jiē; snacks from ¥5) set up carts for lunch (except Saturday) and dinner. Look for *mántóu* (馒头; steamed buns), various meats on skewers, fried chicken and more. Hawkers serve similar delights by the temple at Dài Beǐ Market.

Dài Beǐ Market   MARKET $
(贷北市场, Dàibeǐ Shìchǎng) Hawkers serve up snacks by the Dài Temple at this market, but expect tourist prices.

Ā Dōngde Shuǐjiǎo   CHINESE $
(阿东的水饺; ☑ 139 5489 8518; 31 Hongmen Lu, 红门路31号; mains from ¥20; ☺ 9am-10pm) This centrally located restaurant has been knocking around for years, feeding legions of travellers with Chinese staples including *shuǐjiǎo* (水饺; dumplings), with loads of fillings including lamb (羊肉; *yángròu*; ¥35 per *jīn* – enough for two) and vegetarian tofu (豆腐; *dòufu*; ¥20 per *jīn*). The English menu is challenging, so be prepared to point (or wave your arms around).

Central Night Market   MARKET $
(夜市, Yèshì; meals from ¥25; ☺ 5.30pm-late) Situated in the centre of town, this night market has hotpot stalls that start cooking from late afternoon. Pick your ingredients (thinly sliced meats, fish balls, vegetables, tofu etc) and take a seat at a low table. Meals cost about ¥25 and a large jug of beer is ¥8.

Dōngzūn Court   CHINESE $$
(东尊阁, Dōngzūn Gé; ☑ 0538 836 8888; 16 Yingsheng Donglu, 迎胜东路16号; mains from ¥30; ☺ 11.30am-2.30pm & 5.30-8.30pm) Cuisine styles at this elegant and smart tablecloth affair at the Ramada Plaza are Lǔ, Cantonese and Sìchuān, with an entire room dedicated to live freshwater fish and shrimp (priced by the *jīn*) and freshly made spring-water bean curd (¥38).

🍷 Drinking & Nightlife

Rather a sedate destination, Tài'ān doesn't have many bars, but you can get a beer at any of the restaurants or at the night market, where a jug of beer will set you back ¥8.

ℹ️ Information

Agricultural Bank of China (22 Daizong Jie, 岱宗街22号; ☺ 8.30am-4pm Mon-Fri) Currency exchange and 24-hour ATM that accepts foreign cards.

Bank of China (中国银行, Zhōngguó Yínháng; 116 Tongtian Jie, 通天街116号; ☺ 8.30am-

4.30pm) Currency exchange and 24-hour ATM that accepts foreign cards.

Central Hospital (中心医院, Zhōngxīn Yīyuàn; ☑ 822 4161; 29 Longtan Lu, 龙潭路29号) There's limited English here.

Public Security Bureau (PSB, 公安局, Gōng'ānjú; ☑ 0538 827 5264; cnr Dongyue Dajie & Qingnian Lu, 东岳大街青年路的路口; ☺ visa office 8.30am-noon & 1-5.30pm Mon-Fri, or by appointment) The **visa office** (出入境管理处) is on the east side of the shiny grey building.

Tourist Information (Taishanzhan Lu, 泰山站路) Tourist information office at the train station.

ℹ️ Getting There & Away

Whether by road or track, most routes pass through Jǐ'nán, 80km north. Buses and trains are cheapest. Another option is picking up the **airport shuttle** (☑ 0538 850 2600; 26 Hongmen Lu, 红门路26号; adult ¥80; ☺ 5.30am, 8.30am, 10am, 1.30pm, 4.40pm) in front of the Taishan Hotel; it connects to Jǐ'nán's Yáoqiáng airport, taking two hours.

Buy train and plane tickets at the Hongmen Lu **ticket office** (红门火车票代售点; ☑ 0538 218 7989; 22 Hongmen Lu, 红门路22号; commission ¥5; ☺ 8am-6pm), or at the **ticket office** (火车票代售处, 空售票处; ☑ plane 0538 218 3333, train 0538 611 1111; 111 Qingnian Lu, 青年路111号; ☺ 8.30am-5.30pm) on Qingnian Lu. Hostels can also help and you can also purchases train tickets online at http://english.ctrip.com/trains. Tickets sell out quickly so book early. Bear in mind that bus and train agents sometimes refer to Tài'ān and Tài Shān interchangeably.

BUS

The **long-distance bus station** (Old Station, 长途汽车站, Chángtú Qìchēzhàn; ☑ 0538 218 8777; cnr Tài'shān Dalu & Longtan Lu, 太山大路龙潭路的路口) – locally referred to as *lǎo zhàn* (老站) – is just south of the train station. Buses regularly depart for the following destinations:

Beǐjīng ¥164, seven hours, 11 daily

Jǐ'nán ¥27, 1½ hours, every 30 minutes (6am to 6pm)

Qīngdǎo ¥126, 5½ hours, three daily (7.40am, 9.10am and 2.30pm)

Qūfù ¥23, one hour, every 30 minutes (7.20am to 5.20pm)

Wēihǎi ¥165, seven hours, two daily (7.20am and 9am)

Yāntái ¥150, six hours, one daily (7.20am)

TRAIN

Two train stations service this region. **Tài Shān Train Station** (p214) is the most central, but express trains only pass through **Tài'ān Train Station** (泰安火车站, Tài'ān Huǒchē Zhàn; ☑ 138 0538 5950; Xingaotiezhan Lu, 新高铁站

路), sometimes referred to as the new station (新站; *xīn zhàn*), 9km west of the town centre.

Some regular trains (seat/hard sleeper) departing from Tài Shān Train Station:

Jǐ'nán ¥13/64, one hour, frequent (24 hours)

Qīngdǎo ¥69/126, five to seven hours, hourly (12.28am to 2.52pm)

Qūfù ¥19/29, 1½ hours, two daily (6.05am and 10.50am)

Express trains (1st-/2nd-class seat) departing from Tài'ān Train Station:

Běijīng ¥359/214, two hours, hourly (8.05am to 9.21pm)

Jǐ'nán ¥50/30, 20 minutes, frequent (7.48am to 10.14pm)

Nánjīng ¥429/254, 2½ hours, every 30 minutes (7.24am to 8.05pm)

Qīngdǎo ¥194/119, three hours 10 minutes, six daily (11.14am, 12.54pm, 3.10pm, 5.14pm, 5.46pm and 6.32pm)

Shànghǎi ¥634/374, 3½ hours, every 30 minutes (7.24am to 7.45pm)

Tài Shān 泰山

♪ 0538

The Shāndōng Chinese love to boast their province has '一山一水一圣人', which means 'One mountain, One river, One saint', namely Tài Shān, the Yellow River and Confucius. If you have to choose a sacred mountain to scale in China, climb Tài Shān. The mountain and Unesco World Heritage Site has been worshipped since at least the 11th century BC. To scholars and poets it is known as Dōng Yuè (东岳), the Eastern Great Mountain, one of China's five most sacred Taoist peaks.

Qin Shi Huang, the first emperor, chose its summit to proclaim the unified kingdom of China in 219 BC. From its heights Confucius uttered the dictum 'The world is small.' Pilgrims – young, old and *very* old – still make their way up the steps as a symbol of their devotion to Taoist and Buddhist teachings.

It is said that if you climb Tài Shān, you will live to see 100. Beyond Qin Shi Huang, 71 other emperors and countless figures also paid this mountain their respects. To follow in their footsteps, there are four routes up to the highest peak (1532m) that can be done on foot: **Central route**, historically the Emperor's Route, winds 8.9km from Dài Temple to the summit and gains 1400m in elevation; **Peach Blossom Park route** climbs 13km on the west side; and the least travelled 5.4km **Tiānzhú Peak route** goes up the back of the mountain from the east. **Western route** follows the 14km shuttle-bus route and converges with the Central route at the halfway point (Midway Gate to Heaven), from where it's another 3.5km up steep steps to the summit.

If this sounds like too much for your knees, there are alternatives: cover the Western route by bus to Midway Gate to Heaven and then take the cable car to South Gate to Heaven near the summit. Reverse the journey or nab a bus to get back down.

Sights on the mountain close around 5pm. Weather can change suddenly and the summit gets very bitter, windy and wet, so bring warm layers and rain gear. Wear lightweight but durable and waterproof shoes: you don't want to be dragging heavyweight boots all the way to the top. You can buy brightly coloured rain ponchos and, at the top, rent overcoats (¥30).

As with all Chinese mountain hikes, viewing the sunrise is considered an integral part of the experience. You can either do a night hike (with torches) or, easier, stay overnight at one of the (expensive) summit guesthouses to greet the first rays of dawn.

The best times to visit are in September, when humidity is low and the sting of the summer heat has ebbed away; in early October for the clearest weather on the mountain; and in spring, to see the mountain flowers and trees in bloom, and before the summer hothouse begins.

🏃 Climbing Tài Shān

🏃 Central Route (中路)

The Central Route has been the main route up the mountain since the 3rd century BC, and over the past two millennia a bewildering number of bridges, trees, rivers, gullies, inscriptions, caves, pavilions and temples have become famous sites in their own right. The central route is well paved so you won't need sherpas, climbing ropes, crampons or oxygen, but don't underestimate the challenge of its 7000 knee-wrenching steps. Figure at least six hours from Dài Temple to get to the top.

As well as being a *ne plus ultra* stepmaster, Tài Shān functions as an outdoor museum of antiquities. Two of the most prized are **Rock Valley Scripture** (经石峪; Jīngshí Yù), in the first part of the climb, a massive inscription of a Buddhist text that was once hidden behind a waterfall, and **North Prayer Rock** (拱北石; Gǒngběi Shí), a huge boulder pointing skyward and a site of imperial sacrifices to heaven, at the summit.

Purists begin with a south–north perambulation through Dài Temple, 1.7km south

Tài Shān

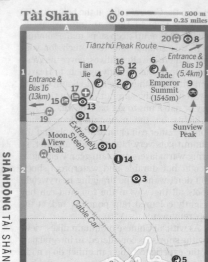

N
0 _____ 500 m
0 _____ 0.25 miles

Tiānzhù Peak Route

Entrance &
Bus 19
(5.4km)

Tian
Jie

Jade
Emperor
Summit
(1545m)

Entrance &
Bus 16
(13km)

Sunview
Peak

Moon
View
Peak

Extremely Steep

Cable Car

See Tài'ān
Map (p208)

Central
Western
Route

Route

Tiānwài Village (13km)

Dài Temple
(5.5km)

Tài Shān

◉ Sights
1 Archway to Immortality A1
2 Azure Clouds Temple B1
3 Cloud Step Bridge B2
4 Confucius Temple A1
5 God of Wealth Temple B3
6 Jade Emperor Temple B1
7 Midway Gate to Heaven B3
8 North Gate to Heaven B1
9 North Pointing Rock B1
10 Opposing Pines Pavilion A2
11 Path of 18 Bends A2
12 Qīngdì Palace B1
13 South Gate to Heaven A1
14 Ten-Thousand Zhàng Tablet B2

⊟ Sleeping
15 Nán Tiān Mén Bīnguǎn A1
16 Shénqì Hotel B1
17 Xiānjū Bīnguǎn A1

ⓘ Transport
18 Main Tài Shān Cable Car B3
19 Peach Blossom Park Cable Car A1
20 Rear Rocky Recess Cable Car B1
21 Western Route Midway Gate Bus
    Stop B3

of the actual ascent, in accordance with imperial tradition, but there is no shame in starting at the bus stop by **Guandi Temple** (关帝庙, Guāndì Miào; ¥10), the first of many dedicated to the Taoist protector of peace. Passing **First Gate of Heaven** (一天门; Yìtiān Mén) marks the start of the incline, though the **ticket office** (售票处, Shòupiào Chù; ☎ 0538 806 6077; ⊙ 24hr) is still a way further at **Wànxiān Tower** (万仙楼). The **Red Gate Palace** (红门宫, Hóng Mén Gōng; ¥5; ⊙ 8am-5pm) is the first of a series of temples dedicated to Bixia – the Heavenly Jade Maiden – daughter of the god of Tài Shān.

Take a detour into the **Geoheritage Scenic Area** (地质园区; Dìzhí Yuánqū) for a look at unusual radial rock formations that mesmerised Confucius himself. Back on the main path is the **Dǒumǔ Hall** (斗母宫; Dǒumǔ Gōng), dedicated to the Taoist Mother of the Big Dipper, first constructed in 1542 under the name 'Dragon Spring Nunnery'. Continue through the tunnel of cypresses known as **Cypress Cave** (柏洞; Bó Dòng) to **Balking Horse Ridge** (回马岭; Huímǎ Lǐng), which marks the point where Emperor Zhenzong had to dismount and continue by litter because his horse refused to go further.

The **Midway Gate to Heaven** (中天门; Zhōng Tiān Mén) marks the point where

some travellers, seeing the stairway disappearing into the clouds, head for the cable car. Don't give up! Rest your legs, visit the small and smoky **God of Wealth Temple** (财神庙; Cáishén Miào) to seek inspiration and strength and stock up on calorific snacks.

If you decide to make a float for the summit, the **main cable car** (空中索道, kōngzhōng suǒdào; one-way/return ¥100/200; ⊙ 7.30am-6.30pm 16 Apr-15 Oct, 8.30am-5pm 16 Oct-15 Apr) is a 15-minute ride to **Moon View Peak** (月观峰; Yuèguān Fēng) at the South Gate to Heaven. Be warned: peak season and weekend queues can take two hours. Also, the cable car stops when there is any risk of lightning.

If you continue on foot you'll come next to **Cloud Step Bridge** (云步桥; Yúnbù Qiáo), once a modest wooden bridge spanning a torrent of waterfalls, and the withered and wiry **Wǔdàfū Pine** (五大夫松; Wǔdàfū Sōng), under which Emperor Qin Shi Huang, overtaken by a violent storm, sought shelter. Across the valley, each character carved in the **Ten-Thousand Zhàng Tablet** (万丈碑), dated 1748, measures 1m across.

You'll pass **Opposing Pines Pavilion** (对松亭, Duìsōng Tíng) and then finally reach the arduous **Path of 18 Bends** (十八盘,

Shíbāpán), a 400m extremely steep ascent to the mountain's false summit. If you have the energy, see if you can spot the small shrine dedicated to the Lord of Tài Shān's grandmother along the way. There is an alternate route to the Azure Clouds Temple here via another steep, narrow staircase to the right. If you continue on the main route, at the top is the **Archway to Immortality** (升仙坊; Shēngxiān Fāng), once believed to bestow immortality on those dedicated enough to reach it.

The final stretch takes you to the **South Gate to Heaven** (南天门; Nán Tiān Mén), the third celestial gate, which marks the beginning of the summit area. Bear right on Tian Jie (天街), the main strip, and pass through the gate to reach the sublimely perched **Azure Clouds Temple** (碧霞祠, Bìxiá Cí; ⊙8am-5.15pm) `FREE`, dedicated to Bixia. You have to climb higher to get to the **Confucius Temple** (孔庙; Kǒng Miào), where statues of Confucius, Mencius, Zengzi and other Confucian luminaries are venerated. The Taoist **Qīngdì Palace** (青帝宫; Qīngdì Gōng) is right before the fog- and cloud-swathed **Jade Emperor Temple** (玉皇顶; Yùhuáng Dǐng), which stands at the summit, the highest point of the Tài Shān plateau.

The main sunrise vantage point is the **North Pointing Rock** (拱北石; Gǒngběi Shí); if you're lucky, visibility extends over 200km to the coast.

At the summit, you can see another side of the mountain by descending via the Tiānzhú Peak or Peach Blossom Park route.

Western Route (西路)

The most popular way to descend is by **bus** (one way ¥30; ⊙6am-6pm & midnight-2am peak, 7am-6pm off-peak) via the Western Route. These buses are also very handy for night hikes up to catch the sunrise. They zip every 20 minutes (or when full) between Tiānwài Village and Midway Gate to Heaven, not stopping in between.

Walking the route is not always pleasant as the poorly marked footpath and road often intercept or coincide, but it rewards you with a variety of scenic orchards and pools. At the mountain's base, **Pervading Light Temple** (普照寺, Pǔzhào Sì; ¥5; ⊙8am-5.30pm) is a serene Buddhist temple dating from the Southern and Northern dynasties (420–589). The main attraction is **Black Dragon Pool** (黑龙潭, Hēilóng Tán), just below **Longevity Bridge** (长寿桥, Chángshòu Qiáo).

Tiānzhú Peak Route

The less-travelled route through the **Tiānzhú Peak Scenic Area** (天烛峰景区; Tiānzhú Fēng Jǐngqū) offers a rare chance to experience Tài Shān with fewer crowds. It's largely ancient pine forest, ruins and peaks back there, so consider combining it with the Central route for an entirely different view.

If you ascend this way, get an early start to the trailhead, which is 15km by bus 19 (¥2) from Tài Shān Train Station. The challenging climb itself can take five hours.

It's 5.4km from the trailhead to the **Rear Rocky Recess Cable Car** (后石坞索道, Hòu Shíwù suǒdào; ☎0538 833 0765; one way ¥20; ⊙8.30am-4pm Apr-Oct, closed 16 Oct-15 Apr), which takes you from the back of the mountain to the **North Gate to Heaven** (北天门, Běi Tiānmén) cable-car stop (北天门索道站; Běi Tiānmén suǒdào zhàn) and views of Tiānzhú Peak – when it's running. Call in advance.

Peach Blossom Park Route

This route to the summit passes through a scenic valley of striking geological formations and trees that explode with colour in early spring and fall. It makes for an especially pleasant descent.

Near the South Gate to Heaven, take Peach Blossom Park **cable car** (桃花源索道, Táohuā Yuán suǒdào; ☎0853 833 0763; one-way/return ¥100/200; ⊙7.30am-5pm) down to Peach Blossom Valley. This cable car operates infrequently, so call ahead. From the cable car drop-off it is another 9km on foot or by bus (one way ¥30, departs when full 6am to 6pm and midnight to 2am) to reach the park exit and bus 16 back into town.

Festivals & Events

Trail runners and stair steppers converge to race up the Central route for the **International Climbing Festival** (www.zgjqdh.com/zt/tsgjdsj/index.shtml) every September.

Sleeping

Sleeping on the mountain is convenient for the sunrise, but it is much more expensive and rooms are simpler than in Tài'ān. Look for signs posting 如家 (rújiā) or 宾馆 (bīnguǎn) at the summit area along Tian Jie for inns starting from around ¥120 and going *way* up on weekends. Rates can triple during holiday periods, but during slack periods you can bargain for discounts.

Xiānjū Bīnguǎn HOTEL $$
(仙居宾馆; ☑0538 823 9984; 5 Tian Jie, 天街5
号; tw ¥120-380, d & tr ¥420-740; ❄🐾) By the
South Gate to Heaven, this two-star hotel of-
fers comfortable enough rooms, some with
large windows overlooking greenery and
views. Discounts of 30%.

Shénqì Hotel HOTEL $$$
(神憩宾馆, Shénqì Bīnguǎn; ☑0538 822 3866; 18
Tian Jie, 天街18号; s & d ¥1200-1800, ste ¥6000;
❄🐾) This old-timer is the only hotel on the
actual summit, with prices reflecting that.
The priciest mountain-view, standard rooms
are very pleasant and are pretty much the
pick of the mountain crop. The restaurant
serves Taoist banquet fare (from ¥28).

Nán Tiān Mén Bīnguǎn HOTEL $$$
(南天门宾馆; ☑0538 833 0988; 1 Tian Jie, 天
街1号; d ¥980, without bathroom ¥680-780, tr
¥880-980; ❄🐾) Located smack bang before
you turn onto Tian Jie, this is the easiest
place for weary legs to reach at the summit.
Rooms have seen quite a bit of wear and
tear but are still clean and airy; the cheapest
have common shower and toilet. There's 24-
hour hot water.

✖️ Eating

The Central Route is dotted with stalls and
restaurants, with clusters at the cable cars.
Prices rise as you do; expect to pay double
the usual. Hawkers line the path to the sum-
mit, selling fruit and snacks that similarly
increase in price with altitude. Stock up in
town before you climb. Many of the hotels
have restaurants where you can find a de-
cent (but pricey) meal.

❶ Information

Twenty-four-hour first-aid stations are at both
the Midway and South Gate.

❶ Getting There & Away

Regular buses connect **Tài Shān Train Station**
(泰山火车站, Tàishān Huǒchē Zhàn; ☑0538
688 7358; cnr Dongyue Dajie & Longtan Lu, 东
岳大街龙潭路的路口) with access points to the
mountain, mostly from 6.30am to 7.30pm dur-
ing peak season and to 5.30pm otherwise.

Bus 3 (¥2) Runs until 11pm during peak sea-
son, going in one direction to the Central route
trailhead and the other to Tiānwài Village (天外
村; Tiānwài Cūn).

Bus 4 (¥2) Also runs until 11pm during peak
season; it goes to Dài Temple and around the
town centre.

Bus 16 (¥2) Connects to Peach Blossom Valley.

Bus 19 (¥2; ⏱50 minutes) Runs from Dongyue
Dajie across from the Tài Shān Train Station to
Tiānzhú Peak trailhead.

Taxis cost ¥7 for the first 3km and ¥1.50
(slightly more at night) per kilometre thereafter.
It costs ¥12 from the Tài Shān Train Station or
¥26 from the Tài'ān Train Station to the Central
route trailhead.

❶ Getting Around

Frequent buses (¥30) run up and down the
mountain all day between Tiānwài Village and
Midway Gate to Heaven. Cable cars reach the
summit area from Midway Gate to Heaven,
Peach Blossom Park and Rear Rocky Recess.

Qūfù 曲阜
☑0537 / POP 302,805

The hometown of the great sage Confucius
and his descendants, the Kong clan, Qūfù is
a testament to the importance of Confucian
thought in imperial China to this day. The
town is one of Shāndōng's top sights, and
is a mandatory stop for anyone keen to see
how revered the social philosopher remains.

Viewing the main sights within the city
walls of ancient Qūfù, a Unesco World Her-
itage Site, will take a full day.

⊙ Sights

The principal sights – Confucius Temple,
Confucius Mansion and Confucius Forest –
are known collectively as 'Sān Kǒng (三孔;
'Three Kongs'). The main ticket office (p218)
is on Shendao Lu just outside the Confucius
Temple's main entrance. You can buy admis-
sion to the individual sights, but the **combi-
nation ticket** (per person ¥150) grants access
to all three Confucius-related sights.

From 15 November to 15 February, admis-
sion to individual sights is ¥10 cheaper (the
combined ticket stays the same) and sights
close about a half hour earlier.

Confucius Temple CONFUCIAN TEMPLE
(孔庙, Kǒng Miào; incl in combination ticket, or
¥90; ⏱8am-5.10pm) Like shrines to Confucius
throughout China and Asia, this is more mu-
seum than altar. The heart of the complex
is the huge yellow-eaved **Dàchéng Hall** (大
成殿; Dàchéng Diàn), which in its present
form dates from 1724. Craftspeople carved
the 10 dragon-coiled columns so expertly
that they were covered with red silk when
Emperor Qianlong visited, lest he feel that
the Forbidden City's Hall of Supreme Har-

Qūfù

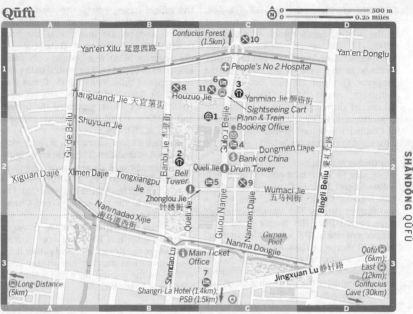

mony paled in comparison. Inside is a huge statue of Confucius resplendent on a throne.

Above him are the characters for '*wàn-shī shìbiǎo*', meaning 'model teacher for all ages'.

The temple has nine courtyards arranged on a central axis. China's largest imperial building complex after the Forbidden City began as Confucius' three-room house, but after his death in 478 BC the Duke of the Lǔ (鲁) state consecrated his simple abode as a temple. Everything in it, including his clothing, books, musical instruments and a carriage, was perfectly preserved. The house was rebuilt for the first time in AD 153, kicking off a series of expansions and renovations in subsequent centuries. By 1012 it had four courtyards and over 300 rooms. An imperial-palace-style wall was added. After a fire in 1499, it was rebuilt to its present scale.

Over 1000 stelae documenting imperial gifts and sacrifices from the Han dynasty onwards as well as treasured examples of calligraphy and stone reliefs are preserved on the grounds. Look for a *bìxì* bearing the **Chéng Huà stele** (成化碑; Chénghuà bēi), dedicated by the Ming emperor in 1468, which praises Confucius in a particularly bold, formal hand. The characters are so perfect that copies were used to teach penmanship. The **Shèngjì Hall** (圣迹殿; Shèng-

Qūfù

Sights
1 Confucius Mansion...........................C1
2 Confucius Temple B2
3 Yán Temple C1

Sleeping
4 Fúyuàn Hotel..................................C2
5 Quèlǐ Hotel.....................................C2
6 Qūfù International Youth Hostel C1
7 Shangri-La Hotel.............................C3

Eating
8 Mù'ēn Lóu Halal Food & Drink B1
9 Qūfù Night Market...........................C2
10 Street Vendors C1
11 Yù Shū Fáng C1

jī Diàn) houses 120 famed Tang-dynasty paintings depicting Confucius' life immortalised as carvings.

Halfway through the complex rises the triple-eaved **Great Pavilion of the Constellation of Scholars** (奎文阁; Kuíwén Gé), an imposing Song-dynasty wooden structure. A series of gates and colossal, twin-eaved stele pavilions lead to the **Apricot Altar** (杏坛; Xìng Tán), which marks the spot where Confucius taught his students under an apricot tree.

South of **Chóngshèng Hall** (崇圣祠; Chóngshèng Cí), which was once the site of the original family temple, the **Lǔ Wall** (鲁壁; Lǔ Bì) stands where Confucius' ninth-generation descendant hid Confucius' writings in the walls of his house during Emperor Qin Shi Huang's book-burning campaign around 213 BC. The texts were uncovered during an attempt to raze the grounds in 154 BC, spurring new schools of Confucian scholarship and long debates over what Confucius really said.

Confucius Mansion   MUSEUM

(孔府, Kǒng Fǔ; incl in combination ticket, or ¥60; ◷8am-5.15pm) Next to Confucius Temple is this maze of living quarters, halls, studies and further studies. The mansion buildings were moved from the temple grounds to the present site in 1377 and vastly expanded into 560 rooms in 1503. More remodelling followed, including reconstruction following a devastating fire in 1885. The mansion was for centuries the most sumptuous private residence in China, thanks to imperial sponsorship and the Kong clan's rule, which included powers of taxation and execution, over Qūfù as an autonomous estate.

The clan indulged in 180-course meals, and kept servants and consorts. Male heirs successively held the title of Duke Yan Sheng from the Song dynasty until 1935.

Confucius Mansion is built on an 'interrupted' north–south axis with administrative offices (taxes, edicts, rites, registration and examination halls) at the entrance (south) and private quarters at the back (north). The **Ceremonial Gate** (重光门; Chóngguāng Mén) was opened only when emperors dropped in. The central path passes a series of halls, including the **Great Hall** (大堂; Dà Táng) and **Nèizhái Gate** (内宅门; Nèizhái Mén), which separated the private and public parts of the residence and was guarded at all times.

The large *'shòu'* character (壽; longevity) presented in traditional Chinese script within the single-eaved **Upper Front Chamber** (前上房; Qián Shàng Fáng) north of Nèizhái Gate was a gift from Qing Empress Cixi. The Duke lived in the two-storey **Front Chamber** (前堂楼; Qián Táng Lóu).

Just east of Nèizhái Gate is the **Tower of Refuge** (奎楼; Kuí Lóu), not open to visitors, where the Kong clan could gather if the peasants turned nasty. It has an iron-lined ceiling on the ground floor and a staircase that could be yanked up.

Confucius Forest   CEMETERY

(孔林, Kǒng Lín; incl in combination ticket, or ¥40; ◷8am-5.20pm) About 2km north of town on Lindao Lu is the peaceful Confucius Forest, a cemetery of pine and cypress covering 200 hectares bounded by a 10km-long wall. Confucius and more than 100,000 of his descendants have been buried here for the past 2000 years, a tradition still ongoing. Today the

CONFUCIUS: THE FIRST TEACHER

An idealist born into a world of violent upheaval, Confucius (551–479 BC) spent his life trying to stabilise society according to traditional ideals. By his own measure he failed, but over time he became one of the most influential thinkers the world has known. Confucius' ideals remain at the core of values in East Asia today and still exercise massive power over Chinese thinking.

Confucius was born Kong Qiu (孔丘), earning the honorific Kongfuzi (孔夫子), literally 'Master Kong', after becoming a teacher. His family was poor but of noble rank, and eventually he became an official in his home state of Lǔ (in present-day Shāndōng). At the age of 50 he put a plan into action to reform government that included routing corruption. This resulted in his exile, and he spent 13 years travelling from state to state, hoping to find a ruler who would put his ideas into practice. Eventually he returned to his home town of Qūfù and spent the remainder of his life expounding the wisdom of the Six Classics (*The Book of Changes, Songs, Rites, History, Music* and the *Spring and Autumn Annals*). Taking on students from varied backgrounds, he believed that everyone, not just aristocracy, had a right to knowledge. This ideal became one of his greatest legacies.

Confucius' teachings were compiled by his disciples in *The Analects* (论语, Lúnyǔ), a collection of 497 aphorisms. Though he claimed to be merely transmitting the ideals of an ancient golden age, Confucius was in fact China's first humanist philosopher, upholding morality (humaneness, righteousness and virtue) and self-cultivation as the basis for social order. 'What you do not wish for yourself,' he said, 'do not do to others.'

tomb is a simple grass mound enclosed by a low wall and faced with a Ming-dynasty stele. Pairs of stone guardians stand at the ready.

The sage's son and grandson are buried nearby, and scattered through the forest are dozens of temples and pavilions.

When Confucius died in 479 BC, he was buried on the bank of the Si River beneath a simple marker. In the Western Han dynasty, Emperor Wudi deemed Confucianism the only worthy school of thought, and then the **Tomb of Confucius** (孔子墓; Kǒngzǐ Mù) became a place of pilgrimage.

A slow walk through the parklike cemetery can take a couple of hours, though Confucius' tomb is just a 15-minute walk from the entrance (turn left after the carts). Open-air **shuttles** (one-way/return ¥10/20) allow you to hop on and off in the forest.

Sightseeing carts (p219) depart for the forest from the corner of Houzuo Jie and Gulou Dajie. Otherwise, take a pedicab (¥10) or bus 1 (¥2) from Gulou Beijie. Walking takes about 30 minutes.

Confucius Cave
PARK

(夫子洞, Fūzǐ Dòng; ¥50; ☺8.10am-5pm) About 30km southeast of Qūfù, this cave on Ní Shān (尼山) is where, according to legend, a frighteningly ugly Confucius was born, abandoned and cared for by a tiger and an eagle, before his mother realised he was sent from heaven and decided to care for him. The gravitas is a bit hokey, but the sight offers a chance for some fresh air.

Buses for Ni Shān (¥8) leave regularly from the long-distance bus station. A taxi there is about ¥40.

Yán Temple
CONFUCIAN TEMPLE

(颜庙, Yán Miào; Yanmiao Jie, 颜庙街; ¥50; ☺8am-5.10pm; 🚌1, 3) This tranquil temple northeast of Confucius Mansion is dedicated to Confucius' beloved disciple Yan Hui, whose death at age 32 caused the understated Confucius 'excessive grief'. The main structure, **Fùshèng Hall** (复圣殿; Fùshèng Diàn), has a magnificent ceiling decorated with a dragon head motif. Outside a *bìxì* carries a stele that posthumously granted Yan the title of Duke of Yanguo (in both Han and Mongol script) in AD 1331.

✨ Festivals & Events

Every morning at 8am, following a recitation, a costumed procession raucously walks up Shendao Lu from Jingxian Lu to the main gate to officially open the city.

MAKING COPIES

For millennia, everything from imperial decrees to poetry, religious scriptures and maps were preserved by carving them into stone. This was done either as an inscription (yin-style) or a relief (yang-style). Copies were made by applying ink to the stone and pressing rice paper onto it, or by tamping a damp sheet of paper into the crevices and allowing it to dry, before patting ink onto the paper's surface. Over time, even stone would wear and the clearest, best-made prints became works of art themselves. Unfortunately, this prompted unscrupulous collectors to damage carvings to ensure they had the very best copy. These are some of the gouges and scratches you see in many of the most prized tablets and stelae.

Confucius Temple holds two major festivals a year: **Tomb Sweeping Day** (usually 5 April; celebrations may last all weekend) and the **Sage's Birthday** (28 September), both involving elaborate, costumed ceremonies. The city also comes alive with craftspeople, healers, acrobats and peddlers during annual fairs in the spring and autumn.

🛌 Sleeping

As a drawcard town for domestic and Asian tourists, Qūfù is loaded with hotels. This doesn't mean they are necessarily good value for money, but there is a reasonable range of choice, from hostels to smart, five-star options.

★ Qūfù International Youth Hostel
HOSTEL $

(曲阜国际青年旅舍, Qūfù Guójì Qīngnián Lǚshè; ☎0537 441 8989; Gulou Beijie, 鼓楼北街北首路西; dm/tw/tr ¥45/128/158; ❀🛜) This friendly and popular hostel at the north end of Gulou Beijie has particularly clean rooms. There's bike rental, ticket bookings and a cafe-bar serving Chinese and Western fare and cocktails. Dorms are four to eight beds and share a nice bathroom. Staff speak English and are helpful with travel tips and info.

Fúyuàn Hotel
HOTEL $$

(福苑酒店, Fúyuàn Jiǔdiàn; ☎138 6372 3660; 8 Gulou Beijie, 鼓楼北街8号; s/d incl breakfast ¥198/208; ❀🛜) Smack-bang in the middle of the old town, this hotel's courteous staff make up for a slightly worn look. Go for the 2nd-floor rooms, and avoid the stuffy, windowless economy rooms, which are dispiriting. Discounts up to 40%.

Shangri-La Hotel
HOTEL $$$

(香阁里拉大酒店; ☑0537 505 8888; www. shangri-la.com; 3 Chunqiu Lu,春秋路3号; incl breakfast r ¥805-1035, ste ¥2288; ◉❀☎) The Shangri-La is a winning brand, with slick, top-end facilities, kids' activities and impressive buffets. Rooms are stylish and comfortable and service is always polite. It's just south of the old town of Qūfù.

Quēlǐ Hotel
HOTEL $$$

(阙里宾舍, Quēlǐ Bīnshè; ☑0537 486 6400; www. quelihotel.com; 15 Zhonglu Jie, 钟楼街15号; incl breakfast s ¥280-600, d ¥350-460, ste from ¥1000; ❀☎) For many years the traditional-style four-star Quēlǐ was the fanciest hotel in Qūfù. It has been refurbed but some rooms are still nicer than others. Look at the rooms first. If you want a temple view room, it will cost sightly more.

✗ Eating

The local speciality is Kong-family cuisine (孔家菜), which, despite its name, is the furthest thing from home cooking since it developed as a result of all the imperial-style banquets the family threw.

Mù'ēn Lóu Halal Food & Drink
HUI MUSLIM $

(穆恩楼清真餐飲, Mùēn Lóu, Qīngzhēn Cānyǐn; ☑0537 448 3877; Houzuo Jie, 后作街; mains ¥15-68; ☺8.30am-1.30pm & 5-8.30pm) A friendly Hui family runs this simple, convenient place behind the Confucius Mansion, serving house specialities like beef spiced with cumin, star anise and turmeric (南前牛肉片; *nánqián niúròu piàn*; ¥68) and tongue-numbing, spicy tofu (麻辣豆腐; *málà dòufu*; ¥12).

Qūfù Night Market
MARKET $

(曲阜夜市, Qūfù Yèshì; Wumaci Jie & Gulou Nanjie, 五马祠街鼓楼南街的路口; snacks from ¥3, dishes from ¥9; ☺from 5pm) The busy, aromatic and central night market cooks up lamb kebabs, noodles, *húntún* (wontons), tofu and many other dishes and street snacks.

Yù Shū Fáng
CHINESE $$$

(御书房; ☑0537 441 9888; www.confuciusfood. com; 2nd fl, Houzuo Jie, 后作街2楼; banquet per person ¥138-500; ☺11am-2pm & 5-8.30pm) On dining, Confucius duly noted 'Food can never be too good, and cooking can never be done too carefully'. This restaurant of pri-

vate rooms behind the Confucius Mansion takes this to heart, serving fine Iron Guanyin teas (铁观音; *tiě guānyīn*) from ¥40 per pot (壶) and Kong-family banquet meals (套餐; *tào cān*), for a never-ending succession of dishes.

The most basic set involves six or so small cold dishes, followed by about 16 more hot dishes – from soup to vegetables, braised sea cucumber, spicy chicken and so on in quick succession. There's no English menu and staff do not speak much English but ordering is pretty straightforward (just pick a price). Reservations are recommended, and some dishes can be ordered à la carte (from ¥40).

🍷 Drinking & Nightlife

In accordance with its Confucian disposition, Qūfù is a rather sober place, so does not have many bars. Grabbing a beer at the restaurants, night markets or the Qūfù International Youth Hostel (p217) is an option.

ℹ Information

Buy plane and train tickets at the booking office next to China Post. **Qūfù International Youth Hostel** (p217) also books tickets (¥15 to ¥20 commission).

Bank of China (中国银行, Zhōngguó Yínháng; 96 Dongmen Dajie, 东门大街96号; ☺8.30am-4.30pm) Foreign exchange and ATM.

China Post (中国邮政, Zhōngguó Yóuzhèng; Gulou Beijie, 鼓楼门分理处; ☺8am-6pm summer, 8.30am-5.30pm winter) Near the Drum Tower.

Main Ticket Office (售票处, shòupiàochù) The main ticket office sells the combination ticket for access to all the Confucian sights, or purchase them individually here.

People's No 2 Hospital (第二人民医院, Dì'èr Rénmín Yīyuàn; ☑0537 448 8120; 7 Gulou Beijie, 鼓楼北街7号) Just north of the Qūfù International Youth Hostel.

Public Security Bureau (PSB, 公安局, Gōng'ānjú; ☑0537 443 0007; 1 Wuyutai Lu, 舞雩台路1号; ☺8.30am-noon & 2-6pm Mon-Fri) About 1.5km south of the city walls. Can help with initial paperwork for lost passports, but cannot extend visas; for more you'll have to go to Jìníng (济宁).

ℹ Getting There & Away

Plane & Train Booking Office (售票处; ☑150 5377 1869; Gulou Beijie, 鼓楼北街; commission ¥5; ☺8.30am-noon & 2-6pm) Very useful for obtaining train tickets in particular, for all of the town's stations.

AIR

Jining Qūfù Airport is 80km southwest of Qūfù's old town and connects to Běijīng (¥600, 1½ hours), Chéngdū (¥1200, two hours), Guǎngzhōu (¥900, 2½ hours), Shànghǎi (¥868, two hours), Xi'an (¥674, 55 minutes) and a handful of other cities.

BUS

Qūfù's **long-distance bus station** (长途汽车站, chángtú qìchēzhàn; ☑ 0537 441 2554; Yulong Lu & Yulan Lu, 裕隆路与玉兰路) is 3km west of the city walls. There is a left luggage office (⊙ 6am-6pm) available here; it's ¥5 per small item.

Buses regularly depart for the following destinations:

Jǐ'nán ¥55, three hours, every 30 minutes (7.30am to 6pm)

Qīngdǎo ¥135, five hours, two daily (8.30am and 1.30pm)

Tài'ān ¥23, 1½ hours, every 30 minutes

TRAIN

Trains are the best way to reach Qūfù. Leaving Qūfù, catch high-speed trains from the **East Train Station** (高铁东火车站, ☑ 0537 442 1571),12km east of the walled city. **Qūfù Train Station** (曲阜火车站, Qūfù Huǒchēzhàn; ☑ 0537 442 1571; Dianlan Lu, 电缆路) is closest to the walled city (6km east), but only regular trains stop there. If tickets are sold out, try **Yǎnzhōu Train Station** (兖州火车站; ☑ 0537 346 2965; Beiguan Lu), 16km west of Qūfù, which is on the Běijīng–Shànghǎi line and has more frequent regular trains.

Some express trains (1st-/2nd-class seat) departing from East Train Station:

Běijīng ¥409/244, 2½ hours, frequent (8.03am to 9.01pm)

Jǐ'nán ¥100/60, 30 minutes, frequent (7.20am to 10.19pm)

Nánjīng ¥379/224, two hours, frequent (7.53am to 9.15pm)

Qīngdǎo ¥244/179, 3½ hours, six daily (9.10am to 5.43pm)

Shànghǎi ¥584/344, 3½ hours, frequent (7.53am to 8.11pm)

Tiānjīn ¥320/190, one hour 50 minutes, hourly (8.03am to 8.23pm)

Some regular trains departing from Qūfù Train Station:

Jǐ'nán hard/soft seat ¥29/45, 2½ hours, three daily (8.08am, 4.24pm and 8.39pm)

Yāntái hard seat/hard sleeper ¥72/145, 9½ hours, two daily (8.57am and 11.48pm)

ⓘ Getting Around

There are no direct buses from the airport to the old town of Qūfù, so you will need to transfer to a bus or taxi at the bus station in Jīning (济宁),

---

about 50km away. Flying into the provincial capital Jǐnán is probably as convenient.

If you're arriving or departing by bus or high-speed train, bus K01 handily connects the long-distance bus station to Qūfù's main gate (¥2) and the East Train Station (¥3). A taxi from within the walls is about ¥40 to the East Train Station and ¥20 to the long-distance bus station. Minibuses (¥5 to ¥8) connect the main gate to Yǎnzhōu Train Station from 6.30am to 5.30pm; otherwise, a taxi costs about ¥50. Bus 1 (¥2) traverses the old town along Gulou Beijie to Confucius Forest.

Ubiquitous pedicabs (¥6 to ¥8 within Qūfù, ¥10 to ¥20 outside the walls) – they will find you – are the most pleasant way to get around. Take one (or a regular taxi) to the Qūfù Train Station, as there are no direct buses.

Tired ponies pull brightly decorated carts (¥50) from Queli Jie to the Confucius Forest, or you can take **sightseeing carts** (电动旅游车, diàndòng lǚyóu chē; cnr Houzuo Jie & Gulou Dajie, 后作街鼓楼大街的路口; one way/return ¥10/15; ⊙ 7.40am-6pm) to the cemetery.

Zōuchéng 邹城

☑ 0537 / POP 1.15 MILLION

Twenty-three kilometres south of Qūfù is Zōuchéng (also called Zōuxiàn 邹县), where the revered Confucian scholar Mencius (孟子; Mengzi; c 372–289 BC) was born. Like Confucius, Mencius was raised by a single mother and grew up to travel the country trying to reform government. His belief that humanity is by nature good formed the core of all his teachings, including his call to overthrow self-serving rulers. Not surprisingly, his criticism made him unpopular with those in power, but a thousand years after his death Mencius' work was elevated a step below Confucius'.

Zōuchéng today is a pretty quiet town, with fewer tourist hassles than Qūfú. Tickets (¥40) get you access to the two adjacent main attractions – Mencius Temple and Mencius Family Mansion – and are sold at both.

Mencius Family Mansion   HISTORIC SITE

(孟府, Mèng Fǔ; incl Mencius Temple ¥40; ⊙ 8am-5.50pm) Mencius Family Mansion exhibits the family's living quarters, including tea-cups and bedding left by Mencius' 74th-generation descendant, who lived there into the 1940s.

Mencius Temple   TEMPLE

(孟庙, Mèng Miào; incl Mencius Family Mansion ¥40; ⊙ 8am-5.50pm) A portrait of ancient China and tranquillity, the Mencius Temple originally dates to the Song dynasty; it bears the marks of past anti-Confucian mood swings, though restoration is always ongoing. With few visitors around, you can sit in the shade of ancient gnarled cypresses, absorbing the serene surroundings. The twin-roofed **Hall of the Second Sage** (亚圣殿; Yàshèng Diàn) looms in the centre of the grounds, a small shrine next to it dedicated to Mencius' mother, the 'model for all mothers'.

Zōuchéng Museum   MUSEUM

(邹城博物馆; ☑ 0537 525 3301; 56 Shunhe Lu, 顺和路56号; ⊙ 9am-5pm Tue-Sun) FREE This museum on Shunhe Lu displays a collection of items relating to Zōuchéng through history, from the earliest times.

Zōuchéng is a rather sleepier alternative to Qūfù, and there are places to stay, yet it does not have the same level of choice or variety. As it's a short trip from Qūfù, most visitors return there to spend the night.

Several eateries, hotpot restaurants, dumpling places, steamed bread outlets and Sìchuān restaurants can be found in the roads around the Mencius Temple.

Zōuchéng is any easy bus ride from Qūfù. Bus C609 (¥3, 35 minutes, 6.30am to 6.30pm) departs from Confucius Temple's main entrance and drops off at Zōuchéng Museum (p220), less than a kilometre from the sights (just walk, keeping the river on your left).

Qīngdǎo   青岛

☑ 0532 / POP

Combining fresh sea air and dashing good looks, Qīngdǎo – the name means 'Green Island' – is a rare modern city that has managed to preserve some of its past while angling a dazzling modern face to the future. Its blend of concession-era and modern architecture puts China's standard white-tile and blue-glass developments to shame. The winding cobbled streets, historic German architecture and red-capped hillside villas are captivating and there's so much to enjoy in the city's diverse food scene, headlined by the ubiquitous home town beer Tsingtao. Meanwhile, the seaside aspect keeps the town cooler than the inland swelter zones during summer, and slightly warmer in winter.

History

Before catching the acquisitive eye of Kaiser Wilhelm II, Qīngdǎo was a harbour and fishing village known for producing delicious sea salt. Its excellent strategic location was not lost on the Ming dynasty, which built a defensive battery – nor on the Germans who wrested it from them in 1897. China signed a 99-year concession, and it was during the next decade the future Tsingtao Brewery was opened, electric lighting installed, missions and a university established, and the railway to Jǐ'nán built.

In 1914 Japan seized control with a bombing assault on the city. When the Treaty of Versailles strengthened Japan's occupation in 1919, student demonstrations erupted in Běijīng and spread across the country in what became known as the May 4th Movement. After a period of domestic control, the Japanese took over again in 1938 and held on until the end of WWII.

In peacetime Qīngdǎo became one of China's major ports and a flourishing centre of trade and manufacturing (home to both domestic and international brands). The port town hosted the sailing events of the 2008 Olympic Games and seems to hold a permanent spot on the list of Asia's most liveable cities (despite the larger-than-life green tide of algal blooms that infest Qīngdǎo's waters in summer).

⊙ Sights

Most sights in the Shì'nán district are squeezed into Old Town (the former concession area), with the train and bus stations, historic architecture and budget accommodation, and Bādàguān, a serene residential area of parks, spas and old villas.

East of Shandong Lu rises the modern city, with the central business district (CBD) to the north and the latest in retail and dining in Dōngbù, closer to the water to the south. Further east still is the developing Láo Shān district (崂山区), anchored by the Municipal Museum, Grand Theatre and International Beer City (site of the annual International Beer Festival).

Han Dynasty Brick Museum   MUSEUM

(崇汉轩汉画像砖博物馆, Chóng Hànxuān Hàn Huàxiàng Zhuān Bówùguǎn; ☑158 6552 0097, 0532 8861 6533; http://zhangxinkuan.com; Binhai Dadao Kutao, inside 409 Hospital, 滨海大道枯桃409医院院内; adult/student ¥40/free; ⊗8-11.30am & 2-5.30pm) Thirty years ago, Zhang Xinkuan was a young army officer laying a road in Hénán province when he noticed the huge granite slabs they were smashing into gravel were covered in exquisite carvings. Thus began his life's pursuit to save more than 5000 Han dynasty relics, now housed in his truly unique, private museum at the southwestern foot of Láo Shān.

Huílán Pavilion   NOTABLE BUILDING

(回澜阁, Huílán Gé; 12 Taiping Lu, 太平路12号; ¥4; ⊗8am-5pm) Lit up at night, this graceful pavilion decorates the end of Zhàn Bridge poking into Qīngdǎo Bay.

Governor's House Museum   MUSEUM

(青岛德国总督楼旧址博物馆, Qīngdǎo Déguó Zǒngdū Lóu Jiùzhǐ Bówùguǎn; ☑0532 8286 8838; 26 Longshan Lu, 龙山路26号; summer/winter ¥20/13, multilingual audio tour ¥10; ⊗8.30am-5.30pm; ☐1, 221) East of Signal Hill Park stands one of Qīngdǎo's best examples of concession-era architecture – the former German governor's residence constructed in the style of a German palace. The building's interior is characteristic of Jugendstil, the German arm of art nouveau, with some German and Chinese furnishings of the era.

Tsingtao Beer Museum   BREWERY, MUSEUM

(青岛啤酒博物馆, Qīngdǎo Píjiǔ Bówùguǎn; ☑0532 8383 3437; www.tsingtaomuseum.com; 56-1 Dengzhou Lu, 登州路56-1号; ¥60, English guide ¥60; ⊗8.30am-6pm; ☐1, 205, 221, 307, 308) For a self-serving introduction to China's iconic beer, head to the original and still-operating brewery. On view are old photos, preserved brewery equipment and statistics, but there are also a few fascinating glimpses of the modern factory line. The aroma of hops is everywhere. Thankfully, you get to sample brews along the way.

St Michael's Cathedral   CHURCH

(天主教堂, Tiānzhǔ Jiàotáng; ☑0532 8286 5960; 15 Zhejiang Lu, 浙江路15号; ¥10; ⊗8.30am-5pm Mon-Sat, 10am-5pm Sun; ☐1, 221, 367) Up a hill off Zhongshan Lu looms this grand Gothic- and Roman-style edifice. Completed in 1934, the church spires were supposed to be clock towers, but Chancellor Hitler cut funding of overseas projects and the plans were scrapped. The church was badly damaged during the Cultural Revolution and the crosses capping its twin spires were torn off. Devout locals buried the crosses for safe keeping. In 2005 workers uncovered them while repairing pipes in the hills, and they have since been restored.

Tiānhòu Temple   TEMPLE

(天后宫, Tiānhòu Gōng, 19 Taiping Lu, 太平路19号; ⊗8am-6pm; ☐25) FREE This small restored temple dedicated to Tiānhòu (天后), the patron of seafarers, has stood by the shore since 1467. The main hall contains a colourful statue of the goddess, flanked by fearsome guardians. There is also **Dragon King Hall** (龙王殿; Lóngwáng Diàn), where a splayed pig lies before the ruler of oceans and king of the rains, and a shrine to the God of Wealth. A temple fair is held here annually during the Spring Festival.

Chinese Navy Museum   MUSEUM

(中国海军博物馆, Zhōngguó Hǎijūn Bówùguǎn; ☑0532 8286 6784; www.hjbwg.com; 8 Caiyang Lu, 菜阳路8号; ¥50; ⊗8.30am-5.30pm; ☐26, 202, 501) Adjacent to Little Qīngdǎo lighthouse, this museum's main attractions are the rusty submarine and destroyer anchored in the harbour. There are also, of course, displays on Chinese naval history.

Huāshí Lóu   NOTABLE BUILDING

(花石楼, Huāshí Lóu; ☑0532 8387 2168; 18 Huanghai Lu, 黄海路18号; ¥8.50; ⊗9am-6pm; ☐26, 231, 604) This granite and marble villa built in 1930 was first the home of a Russian aristocrat, and later the German governor's hunting lodge. It is also known as the 'Chiang Kaishek Building', as the generalissimo secretly stayed here in 1947. While most of the rooms are closed, you can clamber up two narrow stairwells to the turret for a great view. It's located on the east end of No 2 Bathing Beach at the southern tip of Zijingguan Lu in Bādàguān.

Qīngdǎo

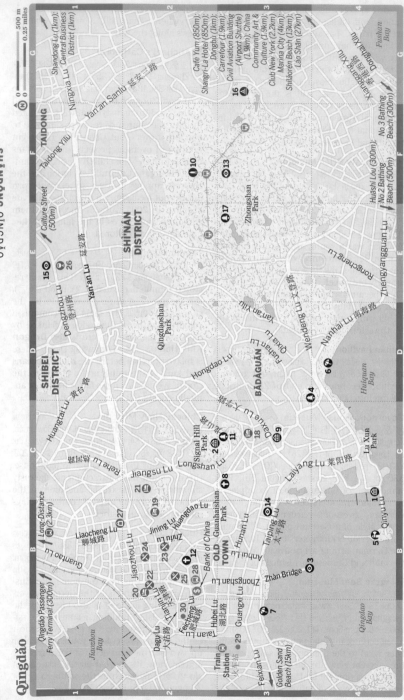

Qīngdǎo

Little Qīngdǎo
LIGHTHOUSE, ISLAND

(小青岛, Xiǎo Qīngdǎo; 26 Qinyu Lu, 琴屿路26号; summer/winter ¥15/10; ☺ 7.30am-6.30pm; ☐ 6, 26, 202, 231, 304) In the shape of a *qín* (a stringed instrument) jutting into Qīngdǎo Bay, this former island – which lends its name to the city – was connected to the mainland in the 1940s. The Germans built the white lighthouse in 1900 on the leafy promontory. It is an excellent spot for watching the city come to life in the morning, and there's free entry from 6am to official opening.

Protestant Church
CHURCH

(基督教堂, Jīdū Jiàotáng; 15 Jiangsu Lu, 江苏路15号; ¥10; ☺ 8.30am-5.30pm; ☐ 1, 221, 367) On a street of German buildings, this copper-capped beauty was designed by Curt Rothkegel and built in 1908. The interior is simple and Lutheran in its sparseness, apart from some carvings on the pillar cornices. You can climb up to inspect the clock mechanism (from Bockenem, dated 1909).

Qīngdǎo City Art Museum
MUSEUM

(青岛市美术馆, Qīngdǎo Shì Měishùguǎn; ☑ 0532 8288 8886; http://qdmsg.sdgw.com; 7 Daxue Lu, 大学路7号; ☺ 9am-5pm; ☐ 1, 25, 221, 367) FREE Contemporary works are on display in this compact museum housed in its own architectural masterpiece, a 1930s structure reflecting an eclectic mix of architectural styles from deco to Byzantine, Islamic and imperial Chinese.

Qīngdǎo Municipal Museum
MUSEUM

(青岛市博物馆, Qīngdǎo Shì Bówùguǎn; ☑ 0532 8889 6286; http://qingdaomuseum.com; 51 Meiling Lu, 梅岭路51号; ☺ 9am-5pm, closed Mon; ☐ 230, 321) FREE This massive collection of relics anchors the budding cultural zone about 13km east of Old Town in Láo Shān district. It has the usual broad span of exhibits expected in a big-city museum, ranging from the prehistoric to the industrial age. Collections of folk-art woodcuts and intriguing coins pressed with Kyrgyz script stand out.

Parks

Many parks with ticket booths, including Little Fish Hill (p224) by No 1 Bathing Beach and Signal Hill Park (p224) in Old Town, are free to wander in after 6.30pm.

Zhōngshān Park
PARK

(中山公园, Zhōngshān Gōngyuán; ☺ 24hr; ☐ 25, 26) Within central Qīngdǎo, Zhōngshān Park is a vast 69 hectares of lakes, gardens and walking paths; it's an amusement park for kids and is also the venue of lively festivals in the spring and summer. In the park's northeast rises Tàipíng Hill (p224) with a cable car to the TV Tower (p224) at the top. Also within the park is Qīngdǎo's largest temple, **Zhànshān Temple** (湛山寺, Zhànshān Sì; ¥10; ☺ 8am-4pm), an active Buddhist sanctuary.

When you get off the cable car at the temple, look for a round concrete dome on the right. This is the entrance to a bunker, which the Germans used as a wine cellar, and today houses a wine bar.

Tàipíng Hill   MOUNTAIN
(太平山, Tàipíng Shān) Rising up on the northeast side of Zhōngshān Park (p223), Tàipíng Hill hosts **Qīngdǎo TV Tower** (电视塔, Diànshì Tǎ; ✆0532 8361 2286; admission depending on view ¥50-100) at its summit, connected to the base by a scenic cable car (p229).

Little Fish Hill   PARK
(小鱼山公园, Xiǎoyúshān Gōngyuán; ✆0532 8286 5645; 24 Fushanzhi Lu, 福山支路24号; ¥10; ⊙6am-8pm) This sweet little park is located near No 1 Bathing Beach. Admission is free after 6.30pm.

Signal Hill Park   PARK
(信号山, Xìnhào Shān; 16 Longshan Lu, 龙山路16号; viewing platform ¥15; ⊙8.30am-5.30pm) This park in Qīngdǎo's Old Town is free to wander in after 6.30pm.

🏖 Beaches

Qīngdǎo has very pleasant beaches, though they are often afflicted in summer with outrageous blue-green algae blooms and litter. Chinese beach culture is low-key, with men sporting the skimpy swimwear and women covering up – even under Spandex ski-masks. Swimming season (June to September) means hordes of sun-seekers fighting for towel space on weekends. Shark nets, lifeguards, lifeboat patrols and medical stations are on hand.

There are ways to enjoy the water without jumping in. If you give in to touts, 20-minute rides around the bay are ¥10 to ¥40, depending on the boat. Or stroll the **Bīnhǎi boardwalk** (滨海步行道; *Bīnhǎi bùxíngdào*), which stretches 30km along the city's shoreline.

Shílǎorén Beach   BEACH
(石老人海水浴场, Shílǎorén Hǎishuǐ Yùchǎng; 🚌301) On the far east side of town in Láo Shān district, this 2.5km-long strip of clean sand is Qīngdǎo's largest and has the highest waves in town (decent for bodyboarding); it can be very quiet in the morning too. The 'Old Stone Man' from which the beach gets its name is the rocky outcrop to the east. Take bus 301 (¥2, 50 minutes) or a taxi (¥50) from Old Town.

No 6 Bathing Beach   BEACH
(第六海水浴场, Dì Liù Hǎishuǐ Yùchǎng; 🚌25, 202) Closest to the train station is the No 6 Bathing Beach, a short strip of sand and tide pools, next to **Zhàn Bridge** (栈桥, Zhàn Qiáo), the pier that reaches into the bay. At its tip, the eight-sided Huílán Pavilion (p221) is a graceful sight, but is often packed to the rafters. If the pavilion looks familiar, that's because it's on every Tsingtao beer label.

No 1 Bathing Beach   BEACH
(第一海水浴场, Dì Yī Hǎishuǐ Yùchǎng; 🚌304) South of tree-lined Bādàguān, No 1 Bathing Beach is a very popular spot, perhaps for its snack stalls and kiddie toy selection, but more likely for its muscle beach.

No 2 Bathing Beach   BEACH
(第二海水浴场, Dì Èr Hǎishuǐ Yùchǎng; 🚌214) Once reserved only for the likes of Mao and other state leaders, this sheltered cove just east of Bādàguān has calm waters good for a swim. Take bus 214 directly, or bus 26 to the Wǔshèngguān (武胜关) stop to first wander past the villas and sanatoriums scattered in Bādàguān's wooded headlands down to the sea.

No 3 Bathing Beach   BEACH
(第三海水浴场, Dì Sān Hǎishuǐ Yùchǎng; 🚌26, 202) On the eastern side of Tàipíng Cape in Bādàguān is this cove with dedicated swim lanes, paddle boats and gentle waves.

Golden Sand Beach   BEACH
(金沙滩, Jīnshā Tān; 🚌2) For wide open spaces of sand, sea and sky, there's Golden Sand Beach on the western peninsula of Huángdǎo district (团岛区). An undersea tunnel linking Huángdǎo and Shìnán puts it within easy reach of Old Town. Take red double-decker sightseeing bus 2 (¥15, 50 minutes) by the train station at 9am, 11am or 1.30pm, or tunnel bus 3 (隧道3; ¥2) from in front of the Municipal Hospital (市立医院) on Jiaozhou Lu in Old Town to the terminus and then transfer to bus 18 (¥1).

A taxi the whole way costs ¥70 including toll.

✨ Festivals & Events

Cherry Blossom Festival   CULTURAL
(⊙Apr) The cherry blossoms explode with colour in Zhōngshān Park around April, bring splashes of colour to Qīngdǎo's oldest and largest park.

International Beer Festival   BEER
(www.qdbeer.cn; adult 9am-3pm ¥10, 3-10.30pm ¥20; ⊙Aug) The city's premier party draws more than three million tipplers every August. It's not just Tsingtao on the menu, so expect a galaxy of international and domestic brands.

International Sailing Week SPORTS
(www.qdsailing.org; ☉ Aug/Sep) Watch (or join) the regattas and windsurfing by the Olympic Sailing Center every August/September.

🛏 Sleeping

Old Town has excellent budget and midrange options. The CBD and Dōngbù have the top-end international chains but a lot less soul. Rates increase by as much as 30% in July and August, when sun-seekers fill the beaches.

★ Kǎiyuè
Hostelling International HOSTEL $
(凯越国际青年旅馆, Kǎiyuè Guójì Qīngnián Lǚguǎn; ☑ 0532 8284 5450; kaiyuehostel@126. com; 31 Jining Lu, 济宁路31号; dm ¥55 75, r ¥100-300, without bathroom ¥70-150; ❋ 🛈) This spacious, sociable, friendly and helpful hostel in a historic church at Sifang Lu and Jining Lu has a lively congregation. They come to worship in the slick new bar and restaurant (Jinns' Café), which serves great pizza and desserts on the ground floor; there's a great movie room too. Rooms are good value for money. Live music kicks off in the bar.

Héngshān No 5 Hostel HOSTEL $
(恒山路5号国际青年旅社; ☑ 0532 8288 9888; http://hengshan5.com; 5 Hengshan Lu, 恒山路5号; dm/r ¥60/175; ❋ 🛈) On a short street south of the Governor's House Museum, this bright and cheery hostel in a white, three-storey mansion was once the servants' quarters. Beds and bunks in dorms and doubles are similar (tidy, pine frame, reasonably soft). In the garden, sunny Luka Garden Cafe & Bistro serves fantastic coffee and Kiwi fare, and feels like home on the patio.

YHA Old Observatory HOSTEL $
(奥博维特国际青年旅舍, Àobówéitè Guójì Qīngnián Lǚshè; ☑ 0532 8282 2626; www.hostelqing-dao.com; 21 Guanxiang Erlu, 观象二路21号; dm ¥80-90, r with/without bathroom from ¥428/380, discounted to ¥198/168; ❋ @ 🛈) Perched on a hill in a working observatory, this quiet hostel has unbeatable views of the city and bay. Take them in with a drink in hand in the pleasant rooftop Sunset Lounge. Staff provide all the usual hostel services, plus they organise outings around town and Láo Shān. Comfort levels vary – some doubles have nicer bathrooms. Book in advance.

Wheat Youth Hostel HOSTEL $$
(麦子青年旅社, Màizi Qīngnián Lǚshè; ☑ 0532 8285 2121; www.qdmaizi.com; 35 Hebei Lu, 河北路35号; dm ¥80-148, r with/without bathroom ¥385/355; ❋ @ 🛈) The Maizis fell in love with backpacking and each other in western China, and this fine hostel is the result of their partnership. It's in a beautiful, restored pícháiyuàn, the courtyard apartments of 1920s Qīngdǎo, within in a 10-minute walk of the train station. They designed this to provide all the services a weary traveller could possibly hope for.

Rooms are spotless with nostalgic details and creaky hardwood floors (if only there was more than one common shower room on busy mornings). There's a modern library and entertainment lounge, plus a bar where you can pick up good travel advice. Discounts of 50%.

★ Shangri-La Hotel HOTEL $$$
(香格里拉大酒店; ☑ 0532 8388 3838; www. shangri-la.com/qingdao/shangrila/; 9 Xianggang Zhonglu, 香港中路9号; d ¥1100-1500, ste ¥1800-6000; ☷❋🛈❒) The Shangri La brand is a reliable symbol of excellence throughout China, and even more so in this outstanding hotel. We could point to the stylish and comfortable rooms, the dazzling 25m swimming pool or the panoply of fine dining choices and we would be right on the money. But it's the staff that make this place a clear cut above the rest.

Sea View Garden Hotel HOTEL $$$
(海景花园大酒店, Hǎijīng Huāyuán Dàjiǔdiàn; ☑ 0532 8587 5777; http://seaviewgardenqingdao. com; 2 Zhanghua Lu, 彰化路2号; r ¥900-1700, ste from ¥1360; ☷❋@🛈❒; ☐231, 232) Numerous five-star offerings have brought intense competition to the top bracket, but this hotel on the water distinguishes itself with beyond professional service. Refreshments, hot towels and even unsolicited delivery of homemade soup to ease a cough – we could get used to this, assuming our credit cards don't max out. Fortunately, the service charge is already included and discounts up to 40% are available.

China Community Art & Culture HOTEL $$$
(老转村公社文华术酒店, Lǎozhuǎncūn Gōngshè Wénhuá Yìshù Jiǔdiàn; ☑ 0532 8576 8776; www.chinagongshe.com; 8 Minjiang Sanlu, 闽江三路8号; s/d from ¥288/328, ste ¥1088; ☐228, 402, 604) With silk lanterns illuminating the hallways, ceramic bowls serving as sinks, wood-floor showers and antique furnishings, each sumptuously decorated room in this polished hotel in the heart of Dōngbù has the feel of a courtyard residence. There's a fantastic restaurant on premises. Discounts of 10%. Some English spoken.

✖ Eating

Qīngdǎo's kitchens have no problem satisfying all tastes. The waterfront area from No 6 to No 1 Bathing Beach is brimming with restaurants – priced for tourists. The Dōngbù neighbourhood of **Hong Kong Garden** (香港花园; Xiānggǎng Huāyuán) around Xianggang Zhonglu is jam-packed with hip, international eateries: Korean, Japanese, Thai, Italian and Russian are just some of the cuisines on offer. Take bus 222 or 231.

Chūn Hé Lóu   SHANDONG $
(春和楼; ☑0532 8282 4346; 146-150 Zhongshan Lu, 中山路146-150号; mains from ¥25; ⊙11am-3.30pm & 5-9.30pm; ⊒2, 228) In the old quarter of town, this Lǔ (Shāndōng) cuisine institution was founded in 1891 and makes legendary pot stickers (锅贴; guōtiē) and crispy, fragrant chicken (香酥鸡; xiāngsū jī). The top-floor tables have the most atmosphere and get the full attention of the chefs. Downstairs is a fast-food version, with a takeaway counter for dumplings.

Wángjiě Shāokǎo   ROAST GRILL $
(王姐烧烤; 113 Zhongshan Lu, 中山路113号; skewers ¥3-12; ⊙10am-9.30pm) Qīngdǎo's kebabs are legendary and these are among the best, so give them your palate's undivided attention. Join the throng outside this streetside stand gorging on lamb (羊肉; yángròu), cuttlefish (鱿鱼; yóuyú) and chicken hearts (鸡心; jīxīn), and toss your spent skewers in the bucket. There's a sit-down restaurant around the corner.

LOCAL SEAFOOD

For the staple local seafood, stick to the streets. The **Táidōng** neighbourhood between Taidong Yilu (台东一路) and Taidong Balu (台东八路) in Shiběi district (市北区) north of Old Town is packed with restaurants, street markets and carts. Take bus 2, 222 or 217. For the quintessential Qīngdǎo meal, buy a *jīn* of clams – in local-speak *gálá* (蛤蜊; from ¥18) – and take it to a streetside stall with '加功' (*jiā gōng*) on its sign. They'll cook up your catch for ¥5, and pour you a bag of fresh Tsingtao beer for ¥8 more (decanting it into a glass is tricky). (Pints and pitchers also available if you want to be fancy.)

Huángdǎo Market   STREET FOOD $
(黄岛路市场, Huángdǎo Lù Shìchǎng; mains from ¥8; ⊙7am-late; ⊒228, 231) In the heart of Old Town, this long-standing, frenetic street market is chock-a-block with vendors selling (depending on the time of day) squirming seafood, fried chicken, pancakes, fruit, soy milk...it's all cheap, so just stop when something catches your fancy. Nearby **Zhifu Lu** has sit-down, curbside joints (look for a '加功' – *jiā gōng* – sign) that will prepare whatever seafood you bring them for ¥5.

Mǎ Jiā Lāmiàn   NOODLES $
(马家拉面; 44 Gaomi Lu, near Yizhou Lu, 高密路44号; noodles ¥8-14; ⊙9am-11pm; ⊒222, 308) This Old Town hole-in-the-wall isn't as done up as its neighbours, but the Hui family that runs it makes a variety of handmade noodles and skewers without short cuts. You can taste the effort. The beef noodle soup (牛肉面; niúròu miàn) is savoury and good, but you can't go wrong and it's all cheap.

Bottomless refills of soup and raw garlic or chilli sauce for accompaniment.

China Community Art
& Culture   SHANDONG, SICHUANESE $$
(老转村公社文华艺术酒店, Lǎozhuǎncūn Gōngshè Wénhuá Yìshù Jiǔdiàn; ☑0532 8077 6776; 8 Minjiang Sanlu, 闽江三路8号; mains from ¥48, 8-course set meal ¥68; ⊙11.30am-10pm; ⊒228, 312) This lovely restaurant next to its namesake hotel is in a stylised Hakka roundhouse (the sort once mistaken by the CIA for missile silos). The kitchen turns out sophisticated regional cuisine from Shāndōng and Sìchuān. Everything from the mushrooms to water for the tea is locally sourced from Láo Shān.

Cafè Yum   INTERNATIONAL $$$
(☑0532 8388 3838 ext 6008; 9 Xianggang Zhonglu, 香港中路9号; buffet breakfast/lunch/dinner ¥159/193/274; ⊙6-10am, 11.30am-2.30pm & 5.30-9.30pm) All-you-can-eat buffets go on all day in the swish Shangri-La Hotel, so save it for an empty tummy. They're pricey, perhaps, but the international spreads are a glutton's paradise. Did we mention the free-flow beer? Dress is smart-casual, so ditch the beachwear. Reservations recommended.

♀ Drinking & Nightlife

The first stop for any committed tipplers should probably be the many drinking holes along **Beer Street** (啤酒街, Píjiǔ Jiē; Dengzhou Lu, 登州路; ⊒221, 301) where you can sample the delicious dark, unfiltered yuánjiāng

(原浆啤酒; pint ¥15), which is hard to find elsewhere.

The youth hostel bars are pleasant, particularly **Sunset Lounge** on the top of YHA Old Observatory and **Jinns' Café** in Kǎiyuè Hostelling International.

Luka Garden Cafe & Bistro CAFF
(路过花园咖啡, Lùguò Huāyuán Kāfēi; ☑185 0024 2021; 5 Hengshan Lu, 恒山路5号; ⏰8.30am-9pm; 🛜) In a city where new coffee shops open up daily, here in the garden of Hengshan No 5 Hostel there's excellent java a-brewing (from ¥25). There's also food inspired by barista Matt's New Zealand roots, from legit meat pies (¥62) to fresh lamb chops (¥120) and fish and chips (¥52).

Club New York BAR
(纽约吧, Niǔyuē Ba; ☑0532 8573 9199; 2nd fl, 41 Xianggang Zhonglu, 香港中路41号2楼; beer from ¥28; ⏰7pm-2am; 🚌208, 216) Despite rather expensive drinks, this expat favourite overflows with revellers and sports fans when there's a match on TV. Take advantage of happy hour, which is any time before 9.30pm and after midnight. There's a live band most nights (9pm to 1am) and an incongruously classy sushi bar (11.30am to 9pm) adjoining. It's above the Overseas Chinese International Hotel lobby in Dōnghú.

☆ Entertainment

Qīngdǎo Grand Theatre THEATRE
(青岛大剧院, Qīngdǎo Dàjùyuàn; ☑0352 8066 5555; www.qingdaograndtheatre.com; 5 Yunling Lu, 云岭路5号; 🚌230, 321) North of Shílǎorén in the Láo Shān district, the city's grand performing-arts centre puts world-class theatre, music, dance, comedy and kiddie acts on its three stages.

Broadway Cinemas CINEMA
(百老汇影城, Bǎilǎohuì Yǐngchéng; www.b-cinema.cn; 88 Aomen Lu, 澳门路88号; tickets from ¥90) Domestic and Hollywood blockbusters on the 3rd floor of Marina City shopping mall in the CBD.

🔒 Shopping

Qīngdǎo's main shopping drags are in Dōngbù, around Xianggang Zhonglu, but there are plenty of other places to spend.

Jímòlù Market MALL
(即墨路小商品市场, Jímòlù Xiǎoshàngpǐn Shìchǎng; 45 Liaocheng Lu, 聊城路45号; ⏰9am-5.30pm) A four-storey bargain bonanza north of Old Town. Pearls, fake Chanel,

The beer of choice in Chinese restaurants around the world, Tsingtao is one of China's oldest and most respected brands. Established in 1903 by a joint German–British corporation, the Germania-Brauerei began as a microbrewery of sorts using spring water from nearby Láo Shān to brew a Pilsener Light and Munich Dark for homesick German troops. In 1914 the Japanese occupied Qīngdǎo and confiscated the plant, rechristening it Dai Nippon and increasing production to sell under the Tsingtao, Asahi and Kirin labels. In 1945 the Chinese took over and gave the brewery its current name. At first, only China's elite could afford to drink it, but advertisements touting Tsingtao as a health drink boosted its appeal. In 2014 the world drank more than 181 million kegs of the golden brew.

clothing, shoes, backpacks, jade, wigs – all for the haggling.

Marina City MALL
(百丽广场, Bǎilì Guǎngchǎng; ☑0532 6606 1177; 88 Aomen Lu, 澳门路88号; ⏰10am-10pm) International brands plus an ice rink.

Culture Street ANTIQUES
(文化路, Wénhuà Lù; Changle Lu btwn Lijin Lu & Huayang Lu, 长乐路 介利津路华阳路之间; ⏰8am-4pm) 'Antiques' and handicrafts sold in front of a tidy row of concession architecture north of Old Town. The most vendors come out on Saturday and Sunday.

Book City BOOKS
(书城, Shū Chéng; 67 Xianggang Zhonglu at Yan'erdao Lu, 香港中路67号; ⏰9am-7pm) Vast aisles of Chinese media and some books in English too.

Carrefour DEPARTMENT STORE
(家乐福, Jiālèfú; ☑0532 8584 5867; 21 Xianggang Zhonglu, 香港中路21号; ⏰8.30am-10pm; 🚌12, 26, 304) Massive general store at Nanjing Lu and Xianggang Zhonglu, fantastic for food too.

ℹ️ Information

Skip the travel agencies and consult with one of the city's excellent hostels for travel advice.

Useful websites include **That's Qingdao** (www.thatsqingdao.com), with listings and news clips,

---

ℹ️ BORDER CROSSINGS: QĪNGDĂO TO JAPAN & SOUTH KOREA

International boats cross the Yellow Sea from Qīngdǎo's **Passenger Ferry Terminal** (青岛港客运站, Qīngdǎogǎng Kèyùnzhàn; ☑0532 8282 5001; 6 Xinjiang Lu, 新疆路6号), a kilometre north of Old Town along Xinjiang Lu.

Orient Ferry (奥林汽船; ☑0532 8593 8919, 0532 8387 1160; www.orientferry.co.jp; Office, HiSense Plaza, 17 Donghai Xilu, 东海西路17号海信大厦1410室; tickets from ¥1350) sails twice weekly for Shimonoseki, Japan (下关; 36 hours, Monday and Thursday, check in by 3.30pm, departs 8pm), while **Weidong Ferry Company** (威东航运, Wēidōng Hángyùn; ☑0532 8280 3574; www.weidong.com; 4 Xinjiang Lu, next to Qīngdǎo Passenger Ferry Terminal, 东海西路15号; tickets ¥750-1090) operates boats from Qīngdǎo to Incheon, South Korea (仁川; 18 hours, Monday, Wednesday and Friday, check in by 2pm, departs 4pm), as well as from Yāntái and Wēihǎi. The cheapest tickets are usually for spots on the floor in large carpeted rooms, so upgrade at least one level if you want privacy.

Buy advance or same-day tickets at the passenger ferry terminal and from some ticket offices like the **Xīn Tiānqiáo Hotel** around town. The ferry terminal also exacts a ¥30 exit fee per passenger.

---

and **Red Star** (www.myredstar.com), an online entertainment guide and monthly magazine available in hostels, bars and foreign restaurants.

China Post offices are located on the west edge of **Táidōng** (23-1 Taidong Yilu, 台东一路23-1号; ⊙8.30am-6pm), north of Old Town, and by the ICBC tower in the **CBD** (119 Nanjing Lu, 南京路119号; ⊙9am-5pm Mon-Fri, 9am-4.30pm Sat & Sun).

ATMs are easy to find in Qīngdǎo.

Bank of China (中国银行, Zhōngguó Yínháng; 68 Zhongshan Lu, 中山路68号; ⊙9am-5pm Mon-Sat) On Zhongshan Lu at Feicheng Lu in Old Town. Also in the tower at the intersection of **Fuzhou Nanlu and Xianggang Zhonglu** (59 Xianggang Zhonglu, 香港中路59号; ⊙8.30am to 5pm) in the CBD. Branches have currency exchange and 24-hour ATMs.

Public Security Bureau (PSB, 公安局, Gōng'ānjú; ☑general hotline 0532 6657 0000, visa inquiries 6657 3250 ext 2860; 272 Ningxia Lu, 宁夏路272号; ⊙9am-noon & 1.30-5pm Mon-Fri) Take bus 301 from the train station to the Xiǎoyáo Lù (逍遥路) stop and cross the street to the terracotta-coloured building with the flag on top.

Qīngdǎo Municipal Hospital, International Clinic (青岛市立医院东院区国际门诊, Qīngdǎo Shìlì Yīyuàn Dōngyuàn Qū, Guójì Ménzhěn; ☑emergency 8278 9120, international clinic 0532 8593 7690 ext 2266; 5 Donghai Zhonglu, 东海西路5号; ⊙7.30am-noon & 1.30-5pm Mon-Fri, by appointment Sat; 🚍210, 317)

ℹ️ Getting There & Away

A handy ticket office sells air, train and ferry tickets on the ground floor of the **Xīn Tiānqiáo Hotel** (青岛新天桥宾馆售票处, Qīngdǎo Xīn Tiānqiáo Bīnguǎn Shòupiàochù; ☑air & boat 0532 8612 0222, train & bus 0532 8612 0111; 47 Feicheng Lu, 肥城路47号; usual commission ¥5;

⊙7.30am-9pm), near the train station. Otherwise, hostels can help.

AIR

Qīngdǎo's **Liúting International Airport** (☑booking & flight status 0532 8471 5139, hotline 96567; www.qdairport.com) is 30km north of the city. There are flights to most large cities in China, including daily services to Běijīng (¥970, 1¼ hours), Shànghǎi (¥780, one hour 40 minutes) and Hong Kong (¥2500, return, three hours). International flights include daily flights to Seoul (¥1600 return) and Tokyo (¥7000 return).

Book tickets online using www.english.ctrip.com or www.elong.net.

BUS

Among Qīngdǎo's many bus stations, the **long-distance bus station** (长途汽车站, chángtú qìchēzhàn; ☑400 691 6916; 2 Wenzhou Lu) in the Sifang district (四方区), north of most tourist sights, best serves most travellers. A limited number of buses also depart for provincial destinations, including Yāntái (¥84, four hours, hourly, 6am to 5.30pm), directly across from the train station.

Daily direct buses from the long-distance bus station:

Běijīng ¥231, 11 hours, five daily (6am to 8.10pm)

Hángzhōu ¥310, 12 hours, two daily (6pm and 6.30pm)

Héféi ¥276, 10 hours, three daily (8am, 5pm and 7.10pm)

Jǐ'nán ¥109, 4½ hours, every 30 minutes (6.50am to 6.30pm)

Qūfù ¥96, six hours, two daily (6.50am and 3.30pm)

Shànghǎi ¥258, 11 hours, hourly (5pm to 9pm)

Tài'ān ¥126, six hours, five daily (6am, 8.30am, 12.30pm, 2pm and 3.30pm)

Wēihǎi ¥104, four hours, every 40 minutes (6.30am to 6pm)

Yāntái ¥84, four hours, every 40 minutes (6am to 7pm)

TRAIN

All trains from Qīngdǎo pass through Jǐ'nán except the direct Qīngdǎo to Yāntái and Wēihǎi trains. Buy tickets at the **train station** (火车站, Huǒchē Zhàn; ☑ 0532 9510 5175; 2 Tai'an Lu, 泰安路2号), which has a 24-hour ticket office on the hectic east side (bring your passport). The west side is less crowded. Booking offices around town collect a service charge, typically ¥5. Some fast trains depart from **Qīngdǎo North Train Station** (青岛北站, Qīngdǎo Běizhàn; Cangtai Lu, 沧台路). Tickets tend to sell out early in peak season.

Express trains (1st-/2nd-class seat) depart for the following destinations:

Běijīng South ¥474/314, 4½ to five hours, 16 daily (5.32am to 5.07pm)

Jǐ'nán ¥159/117, 2½ to three hours, hourly (5.32am to 7.50pm)

Qūfù ¥244/179, three hours, three daily (6.23am, 8.31am and 4.21pm)

Shànghǎi ¥818/518, six hours 50 minutes, four daily (6.55am, 9.17am, 1.54pm and 4.23pm)

Tài'ān ¥194/149, three hours, six daily (6.55am to 2.36pm)

Wéifāng ¥70/57, one hour, frequently (5.32am to 7.50pm)

Regular trains (seat/hard sleeper) depart for the following destinations:

Jǐ'nán ¥55/100, five to six hours, every 30 minutes (6.39am to 7.32pm)

Tài Shān ¥69/126, 5½ to seven hours, eight daily (6.39am to 5.37pm)

Wéifāng ¥29/80, 2½ hours, regular (6.39am to 7.19pm)

Xī'ān ¥190/334, 19 to 24 hours, three daily (10am, 11.02am and 2.06pm)

Yāntái ¥38/57, four hours, one daily (2.46pm)

ⓘ Getting Around

TO/FROM THE AIRPORT

Bright blue airport shuttles follow three routes through town. Shuttles leave hourly from the train station's south lot and then **Airlines Hotel** (航空快线商务酒店, Hángkōng Kuàixiàn Shāngwù Jiǔdiàn; ☑ 96567; 77 Zhongshan Lu, 中山路77号; ¥20) in Old Town from 5.30am to 8.40pm; the **Civil Aviation Building** (民航大厦, Mínháng Dàshà; ☑ 0532 8286 0977; 30 Xianggang Xilu, 香港西路30号; ¥20) across from the Carrefour from 6am to 9pm; and the CBD's **Century Mandarin Hotel** (世纪文化酒店; ☑ 0532 8286 0977; 10 Haijiang Lu, 海江路10号; ¥20) from 6.45am to 4.45pm. A taxi to/from Shìnán district is ¥90 to ¥120. A metro line connecting town with the airport is under construction.

PUBLIC TRANSPORT

From the train station, buses 26 and 501 head east past Zhōngshān Park and continue north on Nanjing Lu and east along Xianggang Lu, respectively. From the long-distance bus station, buses 210 and 362 go to Old Town and Shílǎorén, respectively. Bus 5 connects the long-distance bus and train stations. Bus 2 (¥15) goes west to Huángdǎo district. Most city buses cost ¥1 to ¥2, but onboard conductors issue tickets for further destinations.

For ocean sights, bus 304 (¥7, two hours, from 6.30am) picks up at the Zhàn Qiáo stop by No 6 Bathing Beach and stops at all the biggies, ending at Dàhédòng in Láo Shān.

Outside the train station, red double-decker sightseeing buses (one stop/unlimited ¥10/30, depart 8am onwards) also pass the sights along the water, going east to Shílǎorén or Láo Shān's various gates.

The northern section of Line 3 of the highly anticipated underground metro started running in 2016, which in the long term will make travelling around town much easier. At present, Line 3 connects Qīngdǎo North Train Station with Shuangshan station, which will then connect via the southern arm of Line 3 with Qīngdǎo train station, passing by Zhōngshān Park and the centre of town. Line 2 is due to start operating by 2017 and further lines are under construction.

For those traipsing around Zhōngshān Park, a cable car (one way/return ¥60/80, ☺ 7.30am-6.30pm) runs up Tàipíng Hill.

TAXI

Flag fall is ¥9 or ¥12 for the first 6km and then ¥2.10 (slightly more at night) per kilometre thereafter, plus a ¥1 fuel surcharge. If your driver takes detours, it's because many city streets are restricted from 7am to 10pm.

Láo Shān   崂山

☑ 0532

A quick ride 28km east from Qīngdǎo, an arresting jumble of sun-bleached granite and hidden freshwater springs rises over the sea. It's easy to understand why Láo Shān has attracted spiritual pilgrims throughout the centuries. These days it's a great place to escape the city and recharge.

In his quest for immortality, Emperor Qin Shi Huang ascended these slopes (with the help of a litter party of course), and in the 5th century Buddhist pilgrim Faxian landed here returning from India with a complete set of Buddhist scriptures. Láo Shān has its share of religious sites, but it is most steeped in Taoist tradition. Adepts of the Quanzhen sect, founded near Yāntái in the 12th century, cultivated themselves in hermitages scattered all over the mountain.

Paths wind past ancient temples (and ruins), bubbling springs trickling into azure pools, and inscriptions left by Chinese poets (and German alpinists).

⊙ Sights

There are a number of ways to enter the Láo Shān park. Dàhédòng gate to the south is the main one and the start of the picturesque hike to Jùfēng. For the most part, routes are paved but there are plenty of opportunities to off-road as well (look for red flags tied to branches marking trails).

Cháoyīn Waterfall   WATERFALL
(潮音瀑, Cháoyīn Pù) This waterfall roars like an ocean tide in the wet season (in drier months the water falls in pieces, hence its ancient name, Fish Scales Waterfall).

Tàiqīng Palace   TAOIST TEMPLE
(太清宫, Tàiqīng Gōng; ¥30; ⊙ closes 5.30pm) Láo Shān's oldest and grandest temple, Tàiqīng Palace was established by the first Song emperor around AD 960 to perform Taoist rites to protect the souls of the dead. Taoist devotees in blue and white still live here, and many credit their good health to drinking from the **Spring of the Immortals** (神水泉), which feeds into the grounds. The massive ancient gingko, cedar and cypress trees also apparently benefit your health.

Yǎngkǒu Scenic Area   MOUNTAIN
(仰口景区, Yǎngkǒu Jǐngqū; Apr-Oct ¥90, Nov-Mar ¥60) You can ascend this scenic area by foot or **cable car** (仰口景区索道, Yǎngkǒu Jǐngqū Suǒdào; one-way/return ¥45/80) past wind- and water-carved granite. There's a 30m scramble in total darkness up a crevice to the top of **Looking for Heaven Cave** (觅天洞; Mìtiān Dòng) and then upward still for bright views to the sea. The hike up takes about three hours.

Jùfēng   MOUNTAIN
(巨峰; admission Apr-Oct ¥120, Nov-Mar ¥90) This peak – the name literally means 'Huge Mountain' – is Láo Shān's highest point at 1133m above sea level. If you take the **cable car** (巨峰索道, Jùfēng Suǒdào; one-way/return ¥40/80) part way up the mountain, it's another four hours up steps past temples and a spring to the stone terrace at the peak and awe-inspiring views of mountains, sky and sea. It's a tremendous walk, but load up with water on a hot day.

Běijiǔshuǐ Scenic Area   CANYON
(北九水景区, Běijiǔshuǐ Jǐngqū; admission Apr-Oct ¥130, Nov-Mar ¥100) This canyon area at the north end of the Láo Shān park is mostly flat and takes a couple of hours to traverse. The path winds alongside and across clear, blue streams before reaching Cháoyīn Waterfall.

🛏 Sleeping & Eating

There are several sleeping options if you want to spend the night in the area: although rooms are more expensive than staying in Qīngdǎo, the tranquillity can be infectious.

If you want to extend your stay, pick-your-own seafood restaurants and a range of guesthouses line the main road hugging the coast.

Abalone Island Hotel   HOTEL $$
(鲍鱼岛酒店, Bàoyú Dǎo Jiǔdiàn; ☑ 0532 8882 1678; Shazi Kou, Liuqing River Village, 沙子口镇流清河村; r ¥422; ❄ @) About 4km from the Dàhédòng gate on Láo Shān's south end, Abalone Island Hotel has a handful of frugal rooms (some with ocean views) above an excellent abalone-serving seafood restaurant. Discounts usually bring prices down to around ¥280. To get here, take local bus 104 or 113 to the Liúqínghé (流清河总站) stop, then walk another kilometre, keeping the ocean on your right.

No English spoken.

Seagrass House   BOUTIQUE HOTEL $$$
(海草房; ☑ English 186 6394 2253; Quanxin He, 泉心河; r incl meals from ¥1200; ❄ 🛜) Set in former rangers' quarters by a crystal-clear stream and surrounded by mountains and sea, this little hotel is the most sophisticated option in the park. Rooms are elegantly rustic; some have plush mattresses set on *kàng* (炕), platforms heated on chilly nights. All meals are included and highlight Láo Shān-sourced ingredients.

ℹ Getting There & Away

From Qīngdǎo, red double-decker sightseeing buses (one stop/unlimited ¥10/30) stop at sights along the water going east to Yǎngkǒu (仰口; departing 8am to 3pm, returning 2pm to 3pm), and go directly to Dàhédòng (大河东; departing 9am to 3pm, returning 1pm to 5pm) and Běijiǔshuǐ (北九水; departing 8.40am, returning 3pm). Another option is bus 304 (¥7, two hours, from 6.30am), which picks up at the Zhàn Qiáo stop by No 6 Bathing Beach and ends at Dàhédòng. Private tour buses to Láo Shān (return from ¥40) also ply Qīngdǎo's streets from

6am onwards but stop at 'sights' on the way to the mountain and back, so are the slower option.

❶ Getting Around

Private cars and taxis aren't allowed within park boundaries, but park shuttles (unlimited rides ¥40) at each gate cover the routes. There are also local buses (¥2).

Most of your travel will be on foot, although a cable car (p230) runs part way up Jùfēng, and there is another cable car (p230) that ascends the Yángkǒu Scenic Area.

Yāntái 烟台
 0535 / POP 1.8 MILLION

The sleepy portside town of Yāntái somehow has one of the fastest-developing economies in China – no small feat in a country of exponential growth. It managed to court foreign investment in its high-tech industry while building itself into a popular beach resort with a distinctive treaty port history. A tunnel connects the old district of Zhīfú with the booming Láishān district to the southeast. For now, this is still a place where you can take things easy. With Pénglái Pavilion not far away, the town makes for a relaxing two-day sojourn.

History

Starting life as a defence outpost and fishing village, Yāntái's name literally means 'Smoke Terrace': wolf-dung fires were lit on the headlands during the Ming dynasty to warn villagers of Japanese marauders. Yāntái was thrust under the international spotlight in the late 19th century when the Qing government, reeling from defeat in the Opium War, signed over the city to the British and French, who established a treaty port here, when it was known as Chefoo (Zhifu). The rest of the eight-nation alliance followed with outposts, which remained until the province was captured by the Japanese in WWII. After the war, China kept Yāntái's ports (ice-free in winter) open for foreign trade.

◉ Sights

Yāntái Folk Custom Museum   MUSEUM
(烟台民俗博物馆, Yāntái Mínsú Bówùguǎn; 257 Nan Dajie, 南大街257号; ⊙ 8.30-11.30am & 1.30-4.30pm; 🚌 43, 46) FREE It's really architecture on display at this museum, an amazing guild hall built between 1884 and 1906 by arrivals from Fújiàn. In the centre of the courtyard is a spectacularly intricate, decorated gate.

Supported by 22 pillars, it's adorned with hundreds of carved and painted figures, phoenixes and other beasties, depicting classic folk tales including The Eight Immortals Crossing the Sea.

The centerpiece is the **Hall of the Heavenly Goddess**, where the goddess Tianhou is surrounded by a set of tin instruments in the shapes of gourds and tiny mice, crawling dragons and dragon heads.

Yāntái Hill Park   PARK
(烟台山公园, Yāntáishān Gōngyuán; ¥50, lighthouse ¥10; ⊙ 7am-6pm) This quaint park of stone paths, leafy gardens and ocean vistas is also a museum of Western treaty port architecture. Wolf-dung fires burned continuously along the smoke terrace above, beginning in the 14th-century reign of Emperor Hongwu. Stroll by the former **American Consulate Building**, which retains some original interior features and contains an exhibit on Yāntái's port days. Nearby, the former **Yāntái Union Church** dates from 1875. The former **British Consulate** overlooks the bay with its annexe surrounded by an overgrown English garden.

Láishān Beach   BEACH
(莱山海水浴场, Láishān Hǎishuǐ Yùchǎng; 🚌 17) This vast expanse of golden sand in the developing district 11km east of the old town attracts clam diggers and sunbathers alike. Get off at the Huánghǎi City Flower Garden (黄海城市花园) stop.

No 1 Beach   BEACH
(第一海水浴场, Dìyī Hǎishuǐ Yùchǎng; 🚌 17) One of Yāntái's two main beaches, No 1 Beach is a long stretch of soft sand in a calm bay.

No 2 Beach   BEACH
(第二海水浴场, Dì'èr Hǎishuǐ Yùchǎng; 🚌 17) About 3km east of the old town, No 2 Beach is rocky in parts but surrounded by lively tide pools.

Yāntái Museum   MUSEUM
(烟台市博物馆, Yāntái Shì Bówùguǎn; ☎ 0535 623 2976; 61 Nan Dajie, 南大街61号; ⊙ 9am-4pm, closed Mon; 🚌 43, 46) FREE The sparkling museum traces the historical development of the Jiāodōng peninsula, where Yāntái currently stands, from the prehistoric age and successive kingdoms to the present day. There's a display on the 'Shell Mound' culture (a glimpse at a neolithic civilisation's rubbish) and a wonderful collection of rare porcelain. There are reasonable English descriptions.

Yāntái

🛏 Sleeping

Many hotels are clustered around the train and bus stations where it's noisy and dull. It's much more pleasant on the charming old streets around Chaoyang Jie's north end.

Coast International Youth Hostel HOSTEL $
(海岸国际青年旅舍, Hǎi'àn Guójì Qīngnián Lǚshě; ☑ 0535 623 0655, English 180 5358 8599; 41 Chaoyang Jie, 朝阳街41号; dm ¥50-60, s/d ¥128/198; ✳ @ 🛈 🛜) Smack in the heart of Yāntái's charming old town is this cheery hostel with a bright common room and evening movies, a coffee bar and an open kitchen. In between mixing drinks and weekend barbecues, staff lead walking tours of the neighbourhood and bike rides to Yāngmǎ Island (bike rental ¥20), plus they can help book tickets.

Shāndōng Machinery Hotel HOTEL $$
(山东机械大厦, Shāndōng Jīxiè Dàshà; ☑ 0535 622 4561; 162 Jiefang Lu, 解放路162号; s & d ¥308-480, ste ¥580; ✳ 🛜) With Korean and

Japanese restaurants, and an international ticketing office on the premises, staff here know how to cater to non-Mandarin-speaking guests. The Asian-decor rooms have nicer details (wooden soaking tubs) than the Western ones, but all are way nicer than the building's exterior suggests. Discounts of up to 30%. Look for the 'SD MACH' sign on the rooftop.

Waitinn HOTEL $$
(维特风尚酒店, Wéitè Fēngshàng Jiǔdiàn; ☑ 0535 212 0909; www.waitinn.com; 73 Beima Lu, 北马路 73号; tw & d ¥288-328, tr ¥358; ✳ @) Opposite the train station, this refurbished hotel is a decent place to, as it were, wait in. Rooms are large, comfortable and equipped with flat-screen TVs. Add breakfast for ¥15 and ask for a discount. Another branch is right by the bus station.

Golden Gulf Hotel HOTEL $$$
(金海湾酒店, Jīnhǎiwān Jiǔdiàn; ☑ 0535 663 6999; fax 0535 663 2699; 34 Hai'an Lu, 海安路34 号; s & d incl breakfast ¥986-1280; ✳ 🛜) This im-

pressive five-star hotel has a superb sea and parkside location, and bright, well maintained rooms. Expect discounts of up to 50% off room prices during the low season.

X Eating

South of Yāntái Hill, the old town pedestrian streets branching off Chaoyang Jie (朝阳街) are crammed with vendors serving some of the freshest seafood and tastiest street food in these parts. There's also international restaurants, bars, cafes and even an Irish pub or two, though some are shut outside of summer.

A good variety of restaurants can also be found in the luxury Joy City (大悦城, Dàyuè Chéng; 150 Beima Lu, 北马路150号; ⊙10am-10pm) shopping mall.

Nan Dajie Food Stalls STREET FOOD $
(Nan Dajie, 南大街; snacks from ¥2; ⊙noon-9pm) This small cluster of food stalls along the park next to the Parkson department store in the heart of the shopping district is a good place for a snack.

Xiāngfǔ Ròudīng Shuǐjiǎo DUMPLING $
(乡府肉丁水饺; ☑155 0545 3700; Fulai Lijie, 福来里街近烟台华侨小学西大门; mains from ¥20; ⊙10.30am-2pm & 4.30-9pm; 🚇6) At the south end of Fulai Lijie by the elementary school, this tiny restaurant draws foodies from afar with its speciality dumplings (水饺; shuǐjiǎo); the ones stuffed with tender bàyú (鲅鱼; ¥30 per jīn, enough for two), a locally caught mackerel, are delicious.

★ Róngxiáng Hǎixiān SEAFOOD $$
(荣祥海鲜; ☑155 0663 3177; 25-1 Fumin Jie, at Haiguan Jie, 阜民街25-1号, 海关街; mains from ¥35; ⊙11am-1pm & 5-8.40pm) At this perpetually packed local institution, the seafood is crawling/swimming/blinking in the back room where you put in your order. Quicktongued staff toss out price per jīn for creatures from the briney deep and suggested cooking methods as you point – clams, ¥38, spicy (辣炒; làchǎo); crab, ¥38, ginger scallion (姜葱; jiāngcōng); abalone, ¥75, sautéed without chilli (清炒; qīng chǎo); and so on. Everything is in Chinese, so if intimidated, tell them your overall budget, point and just go with the flow. Then grab the first table you find.

Shidé Wū JAPANESE $$
(食德屋; ☑0535 621 6676; 23 Hai'an Jie, 海岸街23号; mains from ¥25; ⊙11am-1pm & 5-9.30pm) Chef Hao lived in Japan for a decade before opening up this place with his wife. Now it's a popular spot for sashimi (from ¥38), fried pork cutlets (¥30), and udon and ramen (¥26 to ¥36). The soothing wood decor balances out the Japanese TV turned up full blast.

Crowne Plaza INTERNATIONAL $$
(☑0535 689 9999; 299 Gangcheng Dongdajie, 港城东大街299号) The Korean, Latin and Chinese restaurants in the Crowne Plaza are all excellent, but they are a 50-minute ride to Láishān district. Take bus 50 (¥2) or a taxi (¥50) from the town centre.

🍷 Drinking & Nightlife

Chaoyang Jie and the streets branching off it in the old town south of Yāntái Hill are good for Irish pubs, bars and cafes.

ℹ️ Information

Bank of China (中国银行, Zhōngguó Yínháng; 166 Jiefang Lu, 解放路166号; ⊙9am-5pm Mon-Sat) ATM accepts all cards; changes money.

China Post (28 Hai'an Jie, 海岸街28号)

China Post (中国邮政, Zhōngguó Yóuzhèng; Beima Lu & Dahaiyang Lu, across from train station, 北马路大海阳路路口; ⊙8am-noon & 1-5pm)

Public Security Bureau (公安局, Gōng'ānjú; ☑0535 629 7046; 7 Chang'an Lu, 长安路7号; ⊙8-11.30am & 1.30-5pm Mon-Fri; 🚇17) Office for entry/exit visas (出入境管理处) in Láishān district.

Yāntái Shān Hospital (烟台山医院, Yāntái Shān Yīyuàn; ☑0535 660 2001; 91 Jiefang Lu, 解放路91号) Chinese-speaking only.

ℹ️ Getting There & Away

AIR

Yāntái Pénglái International Airport (烟台蓬莱国际机场, Yāntái Pénglái Guójì Jīchǎng) serves both Yāntái and Pénglái and is around 43km northwest of Yāntái. Book tickets online at www.english.ctrip.com.

There are regular flights to Běijīng (¥690, one hour 20 minutes), Shànghǎi (¥940, one hour 50 minutes) and Guǎngzhōu (¥2050, three hours 10 minutes).

BOAT

Purchase tickets for ferries to Dàlián (seat ¥180, bed ¥210 to ¥1200, seven hours, nine daily 8am to 11.30pm) at the **Yāntái Harbour Passenger Transit Terminal** (烟台港客运站, Yāntáigǎng Kèyùnzhàn; ☑0535 650 6666; www.bohaiferry.com; 155 Beima Lu, 北马路155号) or ticket offices east of the train station or in the bus station. There are also two boats to Lǚshùn (tickets from ¥100, 6½ hours) at 2.10pm and 10pm.

ⓘ BORDER CROSSING: SOUTH KOREA

Shāndōng's coastline offers easy access to international cities across the Yellow Sea. Boats regularly depart from **Yāntái's Passenger Ferry Terminal** (烟台港客运站, Yāntái Gǎng Kèyùnzhàn; ☑ 0535 624 2715; 155 Beima Lu, 北马路155号) for Incheon (仁川) and Pyeongtaek (平泽), South Korea.

Next to Yāntái Passenger Ferry Terminal, **Wēidōng Ferry Company** (威东航运, Wēidōng Hángyùn; ☑ 0535 660 3721; www.weidong.com; 155 Beima Lu, 北马路155号; dm from ¥600, r ¥890-1370) sails three times a week from Yāntái (16 hours, Monday, Wednesday and Friday, departs 6.30pm). Tickets sell out, so book in advance by phone or at the ticket office next to the ferry terminal. Plan to check in early, generally before 3pm, as customs and other inspections are required. The cheapest tickets are usually for spots on the floor in large carpeted rooms, so upgrade at least one level if you need privacy.

There are also boats (from ¥950, 6pm, 14½ hours) every Tuesday, Thursday and Sunday to Pyeongtaek in South Korea.

Wēidōng Ferry (威东航运, Wēidōng Hángyùn; ☑ 0631 522 6173; 48 Haibin Beilu, 海滨北路48号, Wēihǎi; dm ¥750, r ¥890-1370) also sails from Wēihǎi (Tuesday, Thursday and Sunday, departs 7pm) from **Wēihǎi's passenger ferry terminal** (威海港国际客运码头, Wēihǎi Gǎng Guójì Kèyùn Mǎtóu; ☑ 0631 523 6799; www.whport.com.cn; 288 Shū Gǎng Lù, 疏港路/海埠路288号, Wēihǎi). Buses from Yāntái's long-distance main bus station (¥38) make the 70km drive to Wēihǎi's station every 10 minutes from 5.30am to 7pm, then you transfer to bus K01 for the 10km drive north to the ferry terminal.

BUS

From the **long-distance main bus station** (长途总汽车站, Chángtú Zǒng Qìchē Zhàn; ☑ 0535 666 6111; 86 Xi Dajie & Qingnian Lu, 西大街青年路的路口) there are buses to numerous destinations:

Běijīng ¥246, 10 hours, four daily (8.45am, 9.20am, 7pm and 7.10pm)

Jǐ'nán ¥147, 5½ hours, every 30 minutes (6am to 6.20pm)

Pénglái ¥23 to ¥27, 1½ hours, frequently (5.30am to 6pm)

Qīngdǎo ¥84, four hours, every 30 minutes (5am to 6.30pm)

Shànghǎi ¥310, sleeper bus, 12 hours, three daily (7pm, 8pm and 8.20pm)

Tiānjīn ¥198, 11 hours, one to two daily (10am and 7.30pm)

Wēihǎi ¥38, one hour, frequently (6am to 6pm)

TRAIN

Regular trains depart from Yāntái **train station** (火车站, Huǒchē Zhàn; ☑ 0535 9510 5175; Beima Lu, 北马路) for the following destinations:

Běijīng 1st/2nd class ¥523/357, 5½ hours, two daily (9.43am and 2.20pm)

Jǐ'nán 1st/2nd class ¥194/162, three hours, 16 daily (6.50am to 6.15pm)

Qīngdǎo seat/hard sleeper ¥38/57, 4½ hours, one daily (8.27am)

Shànghǎi 1st/2nd class ¥874/566, eight hours, two daily (9.10am & 2.21pm)

Xī'ān seat/hard sleeper ¥198/349, 24 hours, one daily (3.15pm)

ⓘ Getting Around

TO/FROM THE AIRPORT

Airport shuttle (机场巴士, Jīchǎng Bāshì; ☑ 0535 629 9146; ¥20) buses leave from the long-distance bus station for the airport between 4.45am and 8pm. Shuttle buses also leave every hour from the **Crowne Plaza** (机场巴士, Jīchǎng Bāshì; Crowne Plaza, 299 Gangcheng Dongdajie, 港城东大街99号; ¥20) between 4.30am and 7.30pm.

BUS

Bus 17 (¥2) conveniently runs along Yāntái's coastline, passing a number of sandy strips and tide pools in between the main beaches that are worth jumping off for. Bus 6 runs along Beima Lu from the old town to the **bus station** (北马路汽车站, Běimǎ Lù Qìchē Zhàn; ☑ 0535 665 8714; cnr Beima Lu & Qingnian Lu, 北马路青年路的路口). Bus 10 reaches Láishān district's main streets.

TAXI

Taxi flag fall is ¥8 for the first 6km and ¥1.80 (slightly more at night) per kilometre thereafter. It's about a ¥50 ride from the airport.

Pénglái 蓬莱

☑ 0535 / POP 450,000

The city of Pénglái has long been connected with the Taoist legend of the Eight Immortals Crossing the Sea. Though the exact location of the legendary land of Pénglái, where the Four Immortals were said to live, is disputed, Pénglái City in Shāndōng (about

75km northwest of Yāntái) enjoys an understandable connection to the legend, especially thanks to the 1000-year-old Pénglái Pavilion, which sits on a mountain overlooking the Bo Sea.

◉ Sights

Pénglái Pavilion   HISTORIC SITE
(蓬莱阁, Pénglái Gé; ¥140; ⊙6.30am-6.30pm summer, to 5pm winter) About 75km northwest of Yāntái perched on a bluff overlooking the waves, the 1000-year-old Pénglái Pavilion is closely entwined with Chinese mythology and the Taoist legend of the Eight Immortals Crossing the Sea. The route up to the pavilion passes the grounds of an ancient naval base and a series of temples. The pavilion itself is unassuming as its restored exterior is rather similar to surrounding structures.

Inside is a collection of prized inscriptions left by famous visitors since the Song dynasty, and a beautiful modern rendering of the Eight Immortals by Zhou Jinyun. There are many versions of the story, but in this one the immortals, who came from different walks of life, shared drinks at the pavilion before crossing the Bo Sea using unique superpowers.

After the pavilion, zip across the bay by cable car (one-way/return ¥30/50; ⊙8am-5.10pm) for cliffside walks overlooking the Bo and Yellow Seas. There are also **museums** (open 7.30am to 5.30pm) dedicated to ancient shipbuilding, regional relics and Qi

Jiguang, a local-born Ming-dynasty general who battled pirates.

If you arrive after a heavy rain, keep an eye out for mirages at sea that have appeared every few years. Long ago, this earned Pénglái a reputation as a gateway to immortal lands and compelled Emperor Qin Shi Huang to send ships in search of islands of immortality further east.

⊫ Sleeping & Eating

There are many hotels in Pénglái city, but most travellers visit as a day trip from Yāntái, which has better accommodation choices.

Pénglái city has loads of restaurants; the roads around Zhonglou Beilu, not far from the bus station, are a good place to start.

❶ Getting There & Away

Pénglái is an easy day trip by bus from Yāntái (¥23 to ¥27, 1½ hours, frequently, 5.30am to 6pm), with the last bus returning at 7.30pm/6pm summer/winter. The **bus station** (166 Zhonglou Beilu, 钟楼北路166号) is a 15-minute walk to the park, near the corner of Zhonglou Beilu and Beiguan Lu (北关路). Pénglái is also served by Yāntái Pénglái International Airport (p233), in between the town and Yāntái, although most people arrive by bus.

❶ Getting Around

Zip across the bay by cable car. Taxi drivers will go from the bus station to the pavilion for ¥9.

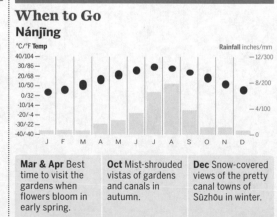

Jiāngsū

POP 78.9 MILLION

Best Places to Eat

➡ Běijīng Kǎoyādiàn (p246)

➡ Motu (p246)

➡ Wúmén Rénjiā (p256)

➡ Element Fresh (p246)

Best Places to Sleep

➡ Nánjīng Time International Youth Hostel (p245)

➡ Hilton Hotel (p246)

➡ Garden Hotel (p255)

➡ Sūzhōu Mingtown Youth Hostel (p255)

Why Go?

A zip – and an entire world – away from Shànghǎi, lush and well irrigated Jiāngsū (江苏) spills over as much charm and history as the waters that flow through its sparkling web of canals. The province, which owed its historical wealth to silk and salt production, boasts the Grand Canal as well as elaborate waterways that thread through this Yangzi River (Cháng Jiāng) region. It's known throughout China for its cute canal towns, enchanting gardens and sophisticated opera and folk arts.

Tourists descend on Sūzhōu all four seasons of the year, but kick-start your day early, go slightly off the main streets, and you'll see the old-world charm and have the place to yourself. In the lovely provincial capital and university town of Nánjīng there's a lot that remains relatively undiscovered by outsiders: Ming dynasty heritage, leafy boulevards, superb museums and some fantastic restaurants.

When to Go
Nánjīng

Mar & Apr Best time to visit the gardens when flowers bloom in early spring.

Oct Mist-shrouded vistas of gardens and canals in autumn.

Dec Snow-covered views of the pretty canal towns of Sūzhōu in winter.

Jiāngsū Highlights

1 Nánjīng (p238) Getting a grade A cultural fix at the Nánjīng Museum' climbing the City Walls and going to the scenic Míng Xiàolíng Tomb.

2 Sūzhōu (p250) Feasting your eyes on the modern Sūzhōu Museum's exhibits, exploring the charming Garden of the Master of the Nets, walking along delightful Píngjiāng Lù and getting a highbrow culture fix with a *kūnqǔ* opera performance.

3 Tónglǐ (p259) Losing yourself in the water town's alleys and canals and examining the eye-opening collection of the Chinese Sex Culture Museum.

4 Lùzhí (p260) Relaxing in the charming canalside atmosphere of this water town.

5 Mùdú (p258) Wandering this historic canal town's streets and alleys.

6 Zhōuzhuāng (p261) Ticking off the ancient bridges and residences of this good-looking canalside settlement.

History

Jiāngsū was a relative backwater until the Song dynasty (960–1279), when it emerged as an important commercial centre as trading routes were opened up by the Grand Canal. In particular, the south of the province flourished: the towns of Sūzhōu and Yángzhōu played an important role in silk production, overseen by a large mercantile class.

Prosperity continued through the Ming and Qing dynasties, and with the incursion of Westerners into China in the 1840s, southern Jiāngsū opened up to Western influence. During the catastrophic Taiping Rebellion (1851–64), the Taiping established Nánjīng as their quasi-Christian capital, naming it Tiānjīng (天京; Heavenly Capital).

Jiāngsū was also to play a strong political role in the 20th century when Nánjīng was established as the capital by the Nationalist Party until taken over by the communists in 1949, who moved the capital to Běijīng.

Today, proximity to Shànghǎi guarantees southern Jiāngsū a fast-growing economy and rapid development, although northern Jiāngsū still lags behind.

THE RAPE OF NÁNJĪNG

In 1937, with the Chinese army comparatively weak and underfunded and the Japanese army on the horizon, the invasion and occupation of Nánjīng appeared imminent. As it packed up and fled, the Chinese government encouraged the people of Nánjīng to stay and the city gates were locked, trapping more than half a million citizens inside.

What followed in Nánjīng was six weeks of brutality to an extent unwitnessed in modern warfare. According to journalists and historians such as Iris Chang and Joshua Fogel, between 200,000 and 300,000 Chinese civilians were killed, either in group massacres or individual murders, during Japan's occupation of Nánjīng. Within the first month at least 20,000 women between the ages of 11 and 76 were raped. Women who attempted to refuse or children who interfered were often bayoneted or shot.

The Japanese, however, underestimated the Chinese. Instead of breaking the people's will, the invasion fuelled a sense of identity and determination. Those who did not die survived to fight back.

ⓘ Getting There & Around

Jiāngsū is well connected to all major cities in China. There are numerous flights daily from Nánjīng to points around the country, as well as frequent bus and train connections. Getting to Jiāngsū from Shànghǎi is very easy, as high-speed rail connections head to Nánjīng and Sūzhōu.

Jiāngsū has a comprehensive bus system that allows travellers to get around within the province without difficulty – many of the small canal towns are linked to each other by bus – but travelling by train is most straightforward as high-speed trains zip between the major towns.

Nánjīng　　　南京

⌀ 025 / POP 8.2 MILLION

Many visitors only pass through handsome Nánjīng (literally 'Southern Capital') when travelling from Shànghǎi to Běijīng (or vice versa), but the capital of Jiāngsū, lying on the lower stretches of the Yangzi River, boasts a rich and impressive historical heritage. It's also one of the cleanest and best-looking cities in China.

The major attractions are the echoes of the city's brief, former glory as the nation's capital during its Ming dynasty apogee and then as the capital of the Republic of China. A magnificent city wall still encloses most of Nánjīng, and elegant republican-era buildings dot the centre.

The famous university town's atmosphere is both cultured and relaxed, with wide, tree-lined boulevards, chic cafes and excellent museums, in a fine landscape of lakes, forested parks and rivers. The countless *wutong* trees afford glorious shade on sunny days and lend the city a very leafy complexion, although summer temperatures are poleaxing.

History

During the Qin dynasty (221–207 BC), Nánjīng prospered as a major administrative centre. The city was razed during the Sui dynasty (AD 589–618) but later enjoyed some prosperity under the long-lived Tang dynasty, before slipping once more into obscurity.

In 1356 a peasant rebellion led by Zhu Yuanzhang against the Mongol Yuan dynasty was successful and in 1368 Nánjīng became capital under Zhu's Ming dynasty, but its glory was short-lived. In 1420 the third Ming emperor, Yongle, moved the capital back to Běijīng. From then on Nánjīng's fortunes variously rose and declined as a regional centre, but it wasn't until the 19th and 20th centuries that the city returned to the centre stage of Chinese history.

In the 19th century the Opium Wars brought the British to Nánjīng and it was here that the first of the 'unequal treaties' was signed, opening several Chinese ports to foreign trade, forcing China to pay a huge war indemnity, and officially ceding the island of Hong Kong to Britain. Just a few years later Nánjīng became the Taiping capital during the Taiping Rebellion, which succeeded in taking over most of southern China.

In 1864 the combined forces of the Qing army, the British army and various European and US mercenaries surrounded the city. They laid siege for seven months, before finally capturing it and killing the defenders.

The Kuomintang made Nánjīng the capital of the Republic of China from 1928 to 1937. But in the face of advancing Japanese soldiers, the capital was moved to Chóngqìng in 1937. Nánjīng was again capital between 1945 and 1949, when the communists 'liberated' the city and made China their own.

⊙ Sights

⊙ East Nánjīng

★ **Nánjīng Museum** MUSEUM
(南京博物院, Nánjīng Bówùyuàn; 321 Zhongshan Donglu, 中山东路321号; ⊙ 9am-noon Mon, 9am-4pm Tue-Sun; M Minggugong) FREE This fabulous museum had a massive and lavish expansion in 2013 with a brand new, dramatically modern exhibition block added next to its traditional, temple-style hall. All sleekly designed with lashings of marble and wood, alluring displays abound: from Jiāngsū landscape painting, ancient calligraphy (including sutra scrolls from Dūnhuáng) to sculpture (the Ming dynasty carved wood Guanyin beneath the atrium is gorgeous) and much more. Look out for two magnificent Han dynasty jade burial suits among treasures from a royal mausoleum.

On the 3rd floor there's a spectacular selection of gold and copper Tibetan Buddha statues that belonged to the Qing emperors, as well as some extravagant clocks. Ceramics and Qing dynasty furnishings round out a stunning collection. Several exhibition halls are temporary and will receive new collections down the line.

Zhōngshān Gate MONUMENT
(中山门, Zhōngshān Mén) One of the original 13 Ming city gates in town, located in the east of town. Long walks extend along the

PRICE RANGES

Eating
Price ranges for a main course for one.

$ less than ¥30

$$ ¥30–¥70

$$$ more than ¥70

Sleeping
Price ranges for a double room with private bathroom or shower room

$ less than ¥250

$$ $$¥250–¥800

$$$ more than ¥800

wall from here and it's quite common to see locals walking their dogs or taking post-dinner jaunts along the weathered path; there is no charge for climbing the wall here.

Ming Palace Ruins PARK
(明故宫, Míng Gùgōng; M Minggugong) The Ming Palace Ruins lie scattered around peaceful but maudlin Wǔcháomén Park. Built by Zhu Yuanzhang, the imperial palace was reportedly a magnificent structure and served as a template for Běijīng's Forbidden City. Clamber atop ruined Meridian Gate (Wǔ Mén), which once had huge walls jutting out at right angles from the main structure, along with watchtowers.

Wǔcháomén Park PARK
(Wǔcháomén Gōngyuán; Zhongshan Donglu, 中山东路; ⊙ 6.30am-9.30pm) FREE Peaceful but maudlin Wǔcháomén Park is home to the Ming Palace Ruins, and usually filled with locals practising ballroom dancing while saxophonists, clarinet players and other musicians gather in the resonant tunnels beneath the gate.

Presidential Palace HISTORIC BUILDING
(总统府, Zǒngtǒng Fǔ; 292 Changjiang Lu, 长江路292号; ¥40; ⊙ 7.30am-5.30pm, to 6pm in summer; M Daxinggong) After the Taiping took over Nánjīng, they built the **Mansion of the Heavenly King** (天王府; Tiānwáng Fǔ) on the foundations of a former Ming dynasty palace. This magnificent palace did not survive the fall of the Taiping, but there is a reconstruction and a classical Ming garden, now known as the Presidential Palace. Other buildings on the site were used briefly as presidential offices by Sun Yatsen's government in 1912 and by the Kuomintang from 1927 to 1949.

Nánjīng

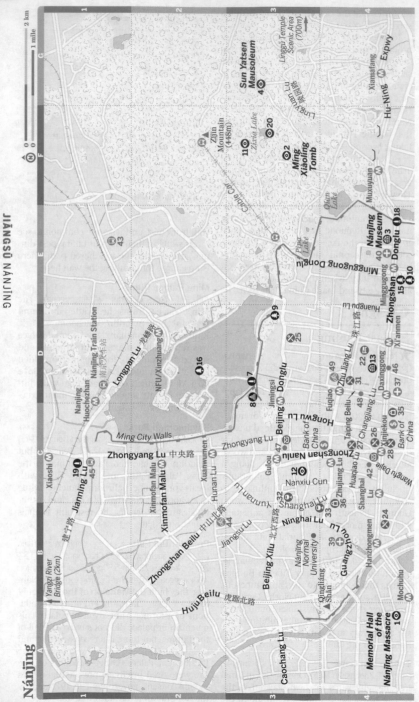

0 — 2 km
0 — 1 mile

Linggǔ Temple Scenic Area (700m)

Sun Yatsen Mausoleum 4

Linggǔ Lu 灵谷路

Xiamafang

Hu-Níng Expwy

Zǐxia Lake 20

Zǐjīn Mountain (448m) 11 2

Cable Car

Ming Xiàolíng Tomb

Muxuyuan

Qian Lake

Pípa Lake

Nánjīng Museum 40 3 Dònglù 18

Mínggùgōng Dònglù

Mínggùgōng Lu

Huángchéng Lu

珠江路

Zhongshan 15 3 10

Xī'ānmén

43

Nánjīng Train Station 南京火车站

Longpán Lu 龙蟠路

NFU/Xìnzhuāng

16

Nánjīng Huǒchēzhàn

Ming City Walls

9

25

Jīmíngsì

7

8 17

Beijing M Dōnglù

Hóngwǔ Lu

49

Zhū Jiāng Lu 22 13

Dàxīnggōng

31

Fùqiáo 48

37 46

Táipíng Běilù

27 Chángjiāng Lu

Xīnjiēkǒu

26 28 Bank of China 35

Bank of China

Zhōngshān Nánlù

Huáqiáo

42

Wángfǔ Dàjiē

Xiǎoshí M

Jiànníng M Lu

19 45

Zhōngyāng Lu 中央路

Xuānwǔmén

Hùnán Lu

Zhōngyāng Lu

Gǔlóu

Nánxiù Cūn 12

Xīnmófàn Mǎlù

Xīnmófàn Mǎlù

Zhōngshān Běilù 中山北路

44

Jiāngsū Lu

Běijīng Xīlù 北京西路

Yúnnán Lu

Shànghǎi Lu

32

Nínghǎi Lu

36

Zhūjiāng Lù

Shànghǎi M

33

Nánjīng Normal University

Qīngliáng Shān

Guǎngzhōu Lù

39

Hànzhōngmén

24

Mòchóuhú M

Memorial Hall of the Nánjīng Massacre 1

Hǔjù Běilù 虎踞北路

Cǎochǎng Lù

建宁路 Jiànníng

Yángzǐ River Bridge (2km)

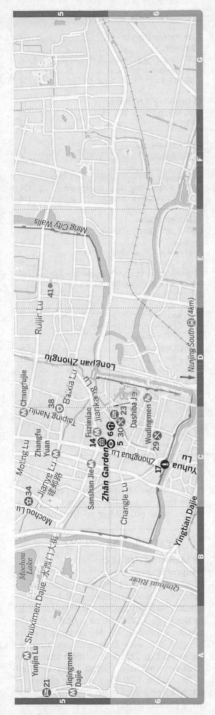

◉ South Nánjīng

★ Zhān Garden GARDENS

(詹园, Zhān Yuán; Zhonghua Lu, 中华路; ¥30; ⊘8am-6pm; MFuzimiao) If you don't have time to get to Sūzhōu, visit this delightful traditional Chinese garden at the heart of town. The Taiping History Museum belongs to the garden, but it's the garden itself that's the real draw. With willows, acers, magnolias, bamboo, potted bonsai pines and a lovely lawn, the garden is also decorated with courtyards, pools, corridors and rockeries. Admission to the garden includes entry to the museum.

Zhōnghuá Gate MONUMENT

(中华门, Zhōnghuá Mén; ¥20; ⊘7am-9pm) Zhōnghuá Gate has four rows of gates, making it almost impregnable, and could house a garrison of 3000 soldiers in vaults in the front gate building. When walking through, observe the trough in either wall of the second gate, which held a vast stone gate that could be lowered into place. Horse ramps lead up the side to the wall; also note how the roads immediately north of the gate follow the circular line of the now missing **enceinte** (瓮城; *wèngchéng*), a further fortification.

Fūzǐ Temple CONFUCIAN TEMPLE

(夫子庙, Fūzǐ Miào; Gongyuan Jie, 贡院街; ¥30; ⊘0am-10pm; MFuzimiao) The Confucian Fūzǐ Temple, in the south of the city in a smartened up pedestrian zone full of restaurants, was a centre of Confucian study for more than 1500 years. But what you see here today are newly restored, late Qing dynasty structures or wholly new buildings reconstructed in traditional style. The area surrounding Fūzǐ Temple has become Nánjīng's main shopping quarter and is particularly crowded, but is attractively lit up at night.

Tour boats (游船; *yóuchuán*) leave from the dock across from the temple itself for 30-minute day (¥60) and evening (¥80) trips along the Qínhuái River (秦淮河; Qínhuái Hé) between 9am and 10pm.

Taiping Heavenly Kingdom
History Museum MUSEUM

(太平天国历史博物馆, Tàipíng Tiānguó Lìshǐ Bówùguǎn; 128 Zhonghua Lu, 中华路128号; ¥30; ⊘8am-5pm; MSanshan Jie) Hong Xiuquan, the Hakka leader of the quasi-Christian Taiping, had a palace built in Nánjīng (then named Tiānjīng or 'Heavenly Capital'), but the building was completely destroyed when Nánjīng was bloodily retaken in 1864, after

Nánjīng

a long siege. This museum is set in a beautiful Ming dynasty garden complex that once housed Taiping officials. Displays of maps show the progress of the Taiping army, Taiping coins, weapons, uniforms and texts that describe the radical Taiping laws on agrarian reform, social law and cultural policy.

The museum was closed for refurbishment at the time of writing, although some of its contents had been moved to a nearby hall within Zhān Garden.

Imperial Examinations
History Museum   MUSEUM
(江南贡院历史陈列馆, Jiāngnán Gòngyuàn Lìshǐ Chénlièguǎn; 1 Jinling Lu, 金陵路1号; ¥20; ⊙8.30am-10pm; MFuzimiao) This museum is a reconstruction of the building where scholars once spent months – or years – in tiny cells studying Confucian classics in

preparation for the exacting civil-service examinations. The exhibition provides valuable insights into the overexacting culture of Confucian officialdom in dynastic China.

◎ West Nánjīng

★Memorial Hall of the
Nánjīng Massacre   MEMORIAL
(南京大屠杀纪念馆, Nánjīng Dàtúshā Jìniànguǎn; 418 Shuiximen Dajie, 水西门大街418号; ⊙8.30am-4.30pm Tue-Sun; MYunjin Lu) FREE
In the city's southwestern suburbs, the disturbing exhibits in the Memorial Hall of the Nánjīng Massacre document the atrocities committed by Japanese soldiers against the civilian population during the occupation of Nánjīng in 1937. They include pictures of actual executions – many taken by Japanese army photographers – and a gruesome view-

ing hall built over a mass grave of massacre victims. At times it feels overwhelming but visitors will begin to fathom the link between the massacre and the identity of the city.

North Nánjīng

Jīmíng Temple   BUDDHIST TEMPLE
(鸡鸣寺, Jīmíng Sì; Jimingsi Lu, 鸡鸣寺路; ¥5; ⊙7.30am-5pm, to 5.30pm summer; Ⓜ Jimingsi) Alongside the city's Ming walls and Xuánwǔ Lake (Xuánwǔ Hú) is Buddhist Jīmíng Temple, first built in AD 527 during the Three Kingdoms period and rebuilt many times. The seven-storey-tall Yàoshīfó Pagoda (药师佛塔) offers views over Xuánwǔ Lake. Enter the base of the pagoda to see the spectacle of hundreds of gold Buddha figures in cabinets and then head up to the rear of the temple for a lovely walk along the **city wall** (admission ¥15; 8am-4pm).

Xuánwǔ Lake Park   PARK
(玄武湖公园, Xuánwǔhú Gōngyuán; ⊙7am-9pm; Ⓜ Xuanwumen) FREE The vast lake within this lovely, verdant 530-hectare park – backing onto the towering city wall – is studded with five interconnected isles, scattered with bonsai gardens, camphor and cherry-blossom trees, temples and bamboo groves. It's a lovely escape from Nánjīng's urban expanses, while the entire lake circuit is a whopping (and enjoyable) 9.5km jaunt. There are also boat rides (¥70 per hour), pedalos (¥60 to ¥100 per hour) and buggy rides (¥12).

Zhōngyāng Gate   MONUMENT
(中央门, Zhōngyāng Mén) One of the original 13 Ming city gates, located in the north of town. The name means 'Central Gate'.

Nánjīng University   UNIVERSITY
(南京大学, Nánjīng Dàxué; Hankou Lu, 汉口路) This delightfully historic campus is worth a stroll to appreciate its traditional architecture, lovely trees and green spaces.

Nánjīng Normal University   UNIVERSITY
(南京师范大学, Nánjīng Shīfàn Dàxué; www.njnu.edu.cn; 122 Ninghai Lu, 宁海路122号; Ⓜ Zhujianglu) Established in 1902 and located in the centre of town; the lovely campus is well worth an exploration.

Yangzi River Bridge   BRIDGE
(南京长江大桥, Nánjīng Chángjiāng Dàqiáo; 🚌67, Ⓜ Shangyuanmen) Opened on 23 December 1968, the Yangzi River Bridge is one of the longest bridges in China – a double-decker with a 4.5km-long road on top and a train line below. Stirring socialist-realist sculptures can be seen on the approaches. Odds are that you'll probably cross the bridge if you take a train from the north. Probably the easiest way to get up on the bridge is to go through the **Bridge Park** (Dàqiáo Gōngyuán; Baotaqiao Dongjie, 宝塔桥东街; adult/child ¥12/10; ⊙7.30am-6.30pm; 🚌67).

Tragically, it has become the world's premier suicide site, surpassing even the Golden Gate Bridge in San Francisco.

Catch bus 67 from Jiangsu Lu, northwest of the Drum Tower (鼓楼; Gǔlóu), to its terminus opposite the park. The nearest metro station is at Shangyuanmen, but that's a few kilometres away to the northeast.

Zǐjīn Mountain

Dominating the eastern fringes of Nánjīng is Zǐjīn Mountain (紫金山; Zǐjīn Shān), or 'Purple-Gold Mountain', a heavily forested and hilly area of parks, and the site of the lion's share of Nánjīng's historical attractions. It's one of the coolest places to flee the steamy summer heat, but it can get crowded. Give yourself a day to explore it properly; discounts exist if tickets to various sights are purchased together. The area is accessible by bus, metro and taxi, and small tourist buses shuttle between some of the main sights.

★ Sun Yatsen Mausoleum   MEMORIAL
(中山陵, Zhōngshān Líng; ⊙6.30am-6.30pm; 🚌9, Y1, Y2, Y3, Ⓜ Xiamafang) An astonishing sight at the top of an enormous stone stairway (a breathless 392 steps), Sun Yatsen's tomb is a mandatory stop for Chinese visitors. Reverentially referred to as *guófù* (国父; Father of the Nation), Dr Sun is esteemed by both communists and Kuomintang. He died in Běijīng in 1925, and had wished to be buried in Nánjīng, no doubt with far less pomp than the Ming-style tomb his successors fashioned for him. Within a year of his death, however, construction of this mausoleum began.

At the start of the path stands a dignified marble gateway, capped with a roof of blue-glazed tiles. The blue and white of the mausoleum symbolise the white sun on the blue background of the Kuomintang flag.

The crypt lies at the top of the steps at the rear of the memorial chamber. A tablet hanging across the threshold is inscribed with the 'Three Principles of the People', as formulated by Dr Sun: nationalism, democracy and people's livelihood. Inside is a statue of a seated Dr Sun (who is better known to the Chinese as Sun Zhongshan, rather than Sun Yatsen). The walls are carved with the complete text of the 'Outline of Principles for the Establishment of the Nation' put forward by the Nationalist government. A prostrate marble statue of Dr Sun seals his copper coffin.

Shuttle buses (¥5) resembling red steam trains speed to and from the Línggǔ Temple Scenic Area.

★ **Línggǔ Temple**
Scenic Area   BUDDHIST TEMPLE
(灵谷寺风景区, Línggǔ Sì Fēngjǐng Qū; ¥80; ⊙7am-6.30pm; 🚌Y2, Y3, Ⓜ Zhonglingjie) This expansive temple complex contains some of the most historic buildings in Nánjīng – the **Beamless Hall** (无梁殿; Wúliáng Diàn), built in 1381 entirely out of brick and stone and containing no beam supports. Buildings during the Ming dynasty were normally constructed of wood, but timber shortages meant that builders had to rely on brick. The structure has a vaulted ceiling and a large stone platform where Buddhist statues once sat.

A road runs on both sides of the hall and up two flights of steps to the graceful **Pine Wind Pavilion** (松风阁; Sōngfēng Gé), originally dedicated to Guanyin as part of Línggǔ Temple. The ochre-walled temple is also home to the **Dàbiàn Juétáng** (大遍觉堂) memorial hall, dedicated to Xuan Zang (the Buddhist monk who travelled to India and brought back the Buddhist scriptures). Inside the memorial hall is a statue of the travelling monk, pen aloft, with a cabinet housing a golden model of a pagoda with part of Xuan Zang's skull within it. To his right is a model wooden pagoda, also within a cabinet.

Uphill to the rear of the temple is the colourful **Línggǔ Pagoda** (灵谷塔; Línggǔ Tǎ). This nine-storey, 60m-high, octagonal pagoda was finished in 1933 under the direction of a US architect, to remember those who died during the Kuomintang revolution. A vegetarian restaurant can be found nearby. Both tour buses Y2 and Y3 run to the Línggǔ Temple from Nánjīng Train Station. Alternatively, take the metro to Zhonglingjie station, then hop on tour bus Y2 from a stop

MING CITY WALLS

Běijīng will be forever haunted by the 20th-century felling of its magnificent city walls, an act of destruction that left a mere handful of isolated gates. Xī'ān's mighty Tang dynasty wall – which was far, far larger than its current (still huge) Ming wall – is a mere memory. Even Shànghǎi's modest city wall came down in 1912. Dàtóng took the dramatic step recently of entirely rebuilding its vast city walls (at enormous cost).

The same story repeats across China, where if a wall survives at all, it may just be an earthen mound. Nánjīng's fabulous surviving city wall is a constant reminder of the city's former glories and an exception to the rule. The wall may be overgrown, but this neglect – in a land where historical authenticity has too often courted destruction – has helped ensure its very survival.

The most absolute remnant of Nánjīng's Ming dynasty apogee, the imposing, five-storey Ming bastion, which measures over 35km, is the longest city wall ever built. About two-thirds of it still stands.

Built between 1366 and 1393, by more than one million labourers, the layout of the wall is irregular, an exception to the usual square format of these times; it zigzags around Nánjīng's hills and rivers, accommodating the landscape. Averaging 12m high and 7m wide at the top, the fortification was built of bricks supplied from five Chinese provinces. Each brick had stamped on it the place it came from, the overseer's name and rank, the brick-maker's name and sometimes the date. This was to ensure that the bricks were well made; if they broke, they had to be replaced. Many of these stamps remain intact.

Some of the original 13 heavily fortified Ming city gates remain, including the **Zhōngyāng Gate** (p243) in the north, **Zhōngshān Gate** (p239) in the east, and **Zhōnghuá Gate** (p241) in the south. You can climb onto the masonry for exploration at several points, for long walks and fantastic views of town.

One of the best places to access the wall is from the rear of **Jīmíng Temple** (p243). Walk to **Jiǔhuáshān Park** (Ⓜ Jimingsi) off Taiping Beilu, looking out over huge **Xuánwǔ Lake Park** (玄武湖公园) and passing crumbling hillside pagodas along the way. Another access point is at **Jiěfàng Gate** (解放门, Jiěfàng Mén; ¥15; ⊙8.30am-6pm winter, 8am-6pm summer; Ⓜ Jimingsi).

a short walk west. Bright red shuttle buses (¥5) resembling steam trains regularly connect the area to the Sun Yatsen Mausoleum, shuttling to and fro.

★ Míng Xiàolíng Tomb   TOMB
(明孝陵, Míng Xiàolíng; ¥70; ◎8am-5.30pm, to 6.30pm summer; 圓Y3, ⓂMuxuyuan) Zhu Yuanzhang (1328–1398), the founding emperor of the Ming dynasty (also known as the Hongwu Emperor), was buried in the tomb of Míng Xiàolíng; he was the only Ming emperor buried outside Běijīng. The area surrounding the tomb is the **Míng Xiàolíng Scenic Area** (明孝陵风景区; Míng Xiàolíng Fengjingqu). A tree-lined pathway winds around pavilions and picnic grounds and ends at scenic **Zǐxiá Lake** (Zǐxiá Hú, 紫霞湖; ¥10; ◎6.30am-6pm), ideal for strolling. A combo ticket for the tomb and the Línggǔ Temple Scenic Area is ¥100.

The first section of this magnificent mausoleum is a 618m 'spirit path', lined with stone statues of lions, camels, elephants and horses that drive away evil spirits and guard the tomb. Among them lurk two mythical animals: a *xiè zhì*, which has a mane and a single horn on its head, and a *qílín*, which has a scaly body, a cow's tail, a deer's hooves and one horn.

As you enter the first courtyard, a paved pathway leads to a pavilion housing several stelae. The next gate leads to a large courtyard with the **Línghún Pagoda** (Línghún Tǎ), a mammoth rectangular stone structure. Follow the crowds through a long uphill tunnel to a wall (which children and visitors clamber up!) and a huge earth tumulus (called the **Soul Tower**; 明楼; Mínglóu), beneath which is the unexcavated tomb vault of the emperor. On the wall are inscribed the characters '此山明太祖之墓' ('This hill is the tomb of the first Ming emperor'). The other Ming emperors are buried outside Běijīng at the Ming Tombs (十三陵; Shísān Líng).

Near the entrance is Plum Blossom Hill.

From Muxuyuan metro station (Line 2), it's a 1.6km walk uphill. Tour bus Y3 from the city centre also takes you here.

Plum Blossom Hill   HILL
(梅花山, Méihuā Shān) Near the entrance to the Míng Xiàolíng Tomb, this large copse of plum trees bursts into floral fragrance each spring, drawing crowds. It's the site of the Nánjīng International Plum Blossom Festival.

★ Festivals & Events

Held yearly from the last Saturday of February to early March, **Nánjīng International Plum Blossom Festival** (梅花节, Méihuā Jié; ◎Feb/Mar) takes place on Plum Blossom Hill near the Míng Xiàolíng Tomb when the mountain explodes into pink and white blossoms. It's a gorgeous sight.

🛏 Sleeping

Most of Nánjīng's accommodation is midrange to top end in price and it's very hard to score a bargain. Cheaper guesthouses will not take foreigners, but you can try your luck. All places have wi-fi (signal strength can vary from room to room) and most places can also help to book air and train tickets. There are a couple of hostels of note, however, and at least one of excellent repute.

★ Nánjīng Time
International Youth Hostel   HOSTEL $
(南京时光国际青年旅舍, Nánjīng Shíguāng Guójì Qīngnián Lǚshè; ☑025 8556 9053; www. yhachina.com; 6-5 Yongyuan, Méiyuán Xīncūn, 梅园新村雍园6-5号; dm ¥60, r ¥180-220; ✳@; ⓂXi'anmen) Time – for atmosphere alone it's the best in town – is in a republican-era mansion not far from the Presidential Palace. The area is lovely: small, leafy alleys with period properties and some serious tranquillity. Dorms are very clean and rooms offer a simplistic charm. There are a lot of common areas, including a relaxing rooftop terrace and a fine ground-floor bar.

The cheapest double rooms come without window. The salubrious – central yet very quiet – neighbourhood guarantees you a good night's sleep. The hostel is hidden away down an alley with lots of twists and turns in the Méiyuán Xīncūn district, north of Changjiang Lu. Download a map from the hostel website for directions.

Orange Hotel (Dashiba)   HOTEL $$
(桔子酒店, Júzi Jiǔdiàn; ☑025 8696 8090; www. orangehotel.com.cn; 26 Dashiba Jie, 大石坝街 26号; r ¥329-529; ✳@🗟; ⓂFuzimiao or Wudingmen) In a great riverside location within walking distance to the Fūzǐ Temple area, this branch of the very popular chain has modern rooms, with good bedding and lighting and every gizmo and gadget your computer, tablet or mobile phone might ever need. It's worth paying a few more bucks for the rooms with river-facing balconies. Other pluses include complimentary fruit and free use of the hotel's bikes.

★ **Hilton Hotel** HOTEL $$$

(南京万达希尔顿酒店, Nángjīng Wàndá Xī'ěrdùn Jiǔdiàn; 🕿 025 8665 8888; www3.hilton.com; 100 Jiangdong Zhonglu, 江东中路100号; d/ste ¥1200/2300; 🏵🛜🏊; Ⓜ Jiqingmen) This sleek five-star hotel, opening to a gargantuan marbled lobby with a huge calligraphic dedication and a vast and stylised depiction of Zǐjīn Mountain behind reception, is the town's best choice. Rooms are spacious and modern, there are three restaurants and service is tip-top. It's slightly out of the action in the southwest of town, but the metro is nearby.

✖ Eating

Nánjīng abounds with a fantastic choice of restaurants. For street food, snacking zones and loads of restaurants, the main eating quarters include the Fūzǐ Temple complex and Shīzǐqiáo (狮子桥) off Hunan Lu, where you can find snack stands and small eateries. Slick restaurants can be found towards the centre around Xinjiekou, and dotted around town.

★ **Dàpái Dàng** JIĀNGSŪ $

(大牌档, Nanjing Impressions; 7th fl, Deji Plaza, 18 Zhongshan Lu, 中山路18号德基广场7楼; mains from ¥16; ⏰ 11am-10.30pm; Ⓜ Xinjiekou) This hectic, fun and vast place, decorated like a Qing dynasty eatery, with waiters scurrying around in period garb and lanterns hanging overhead, is deservedly packed out. There's a handy photo menu for ordering fried dumplings with pork, leek and mushroom (¥12 for three), sliced fish soup with preserved vegetables (¥48), Nánjīng fried noodles (¥16) and oodles of other tasty local dishes.

With eight branches in town, it's a big name in Nánjīng, but if you arrive during a busy period (such as weekends), you'll have to grab a ticket and wait in line outside. It's on the 7th floor of Deji Plaza just north of the Xinjiekou intersection at the heart of town: take exit 7 from the Xinjiekou metro station and take the lift or escalators upstairs.

★ **Xiānmǎn Táng Shíguō Mǐxiàn** NOODLES $

(鲜满堂石锅米线; 🕿 025 853 0017; 488 Zhujiang Lu, 珠江路488号; noodles from ¥16; ⏰ 9am-9pm; Ⓜ Fuqiao) If you've only ¥16 to your name and you're half-starved, hand your cash over to the staff. For ¥16 to ¥18 you can get a vast steaming bowl of rice noodles with copious amounts of chicken, beef, pork or fish thrown in. The fish noodles (水煮鱼片米线; *shuǐzhǔ yúpiàn mǐxiàn*) in particular is superb (watch out for bones); free refills of noodles available.

There are three degrees of spiciness: slightly (微辣; *wēilà*), moderately (中辣; *zhōnglà*) and full-on (香辣; *xiānglà*). It's not a hole in the wall and is pleasantly designed with blond wood and grey brickwork. Packed at meal times.

Běijīng Kǎoyādiàn PEKING DUCK $

(北京烤鸭店, Běijīng Roast Duck Restaurant; 🕿 025 8335 9839; 40-7 Beijing Donglu, 北京东路40-7号; ⏰ 11am-2pm & 5-10pm) This place is reasonably elegant and certainly no dive, yet you can order up half a Peking duck (半只烤鸭; *bànzhī kǎoyā*) here for a paltry ¥39, including scallions, cucumbers and pancakes. That's a meal for one sorted. With a large chilled beer thrown in for another ¥8, it's a steal and only slightly more than what you'd pay for fast food.

There are loads of other dishes on the photo menu on the wall, but it's the duck that's the main draw. Appropriately enough, it's located on Beijing Donglu.

Héfēng Biàndāng JAPANESE $

(和风便当; 21-2 Zhongshan Donglu, 中山东路21-2号; mains from ¥20; ⏰ 9am-9pm; 🛜; Ⓜ Xinjiekou) This small wood-themed sushi spot with Japanese lanterns hanging outside does some excellent sets – the curry shrimps (¥38) in particular is very tasty and filling, with miso soup, a small salad and a dessert; great value. No English menu, but there's a picture menu outside.

★ **Element Fresh** CAFE $$

(新元素, Xīnyuánsù; www.elementfresh.com; 1st fl, IST Mall, 100 Zhongshan Nanlu, 中山南路100号艾尚天地1楼; mains from ¥48; ⏰ 11am-10.30pm Mon-Thu, 11am-11pm Fri, 9am-11pm Sat & Sun; 🛜; Ⓜ Xinjiekou) Ever-trendy Element Fresh gives the iffy Nánjīng cafe culture a good kick in the pants. The setting is smooth, the ambient tunes funky, the lines clean, the wholesome menu a delight and candles come on at night. Balk you may at paying ¥69 for homemade hummus, but it comes loaded with tons of pitta, tomatoes, carrots, cucumber, celery plus green and black olives.

Motu BURGERS $$

(🕿 177 0159 8220; 107 Gutong Xiang, 箍桶巷107号; mains from ¥53; ⏰ 10am-9pm; 🛜; Ⓜ Wudingmen) 🖋 Down along spruced-up Laomen Dong, New Zealander–owned Motu does a brisk trade in fine burgers. Order at the till, take a numbered flag and try and grab one of the balcony seats overlooking Gutong Alley (Gutong Xiang). Ingredients, including beef, are organic, with an emphasis on quality. Burgers are full, fat and juicy; herbivores can size up the tasty Kumara Burger.

Aladdin
XINJIANG $$

(阿拉丁, Ālādīng; 43 Luolang Xiang, 罗廊巷43号; mains from ¥35; ⊙11am-9.30pm) This smartly attired Xīnjiāng restaurant is done up in lime green and cream, with a mezzanine floor above. The sizeable menu is, of course, packed with lamb: ribs (¥10 each), kebabs (¥5 each) or the whole roasted lamb (¥168); but there's lots else besides, including beef bacon naan pizza (¥36), green cabbage tofu soup (¥28) and Aladdin milk rice (¥16) for pudding.

Accompany the meal with a Xīnjiāng black beer (¥15).

Wagas
CAFE $$

(沃歌斯, Wògēsī; www.wagas.com.cn; A108, IST Mall, 100 Zhongshan Nanlu, 中山南路100号艾尚天地A108室; mains from ¥55; ⊙10am-10pm Mon-Fri, 8am-10pm Sat & Sun; 🛜; Ⓜ Xinjiekou) Wagas is everyone's darling. The setting is all industrial chic: concrete floor, patchy and distressed white painted grey brick, staff in snappy but casual black outfits and a relaxed, casual crowd. The menu is sandwiches, wraps, pasta, modern Asian dishes, brekkies and brunches. Good deals and offers abound, chalked up on the wall: express sandwiches are 50% off before 11am Monday to Friday.

Sculpting in Time
WESTERN, CAFE $$

(雕刻时光, Diāokè Shíguāng; 32 Dashiba Jie, 大石坝街32号; mains ¥50; ⊙9am-11pm; 🛜; Ⓜ Fuzimiao) This simply adorable and very spacious riverside cafe is an appealing, relaxed spot with a delightful outdoor terrace overlooking the water. Grab a coffee and a seat outside and watch the pleasure boats drift by. The crowd is cool but unpretentious, the music soft and dreamy, while the fixtures are all birdcage lampshades, cream curtains and comfy chairs. The pastries and cakes make a good afternoon treat.

🍷 Drinking & Nightlife

Western-style drinking holes, sports bars and specialist beer bars congregate along Shanghai Lu. Nánjīng 1912, a large and attractively housed quadrant of neon-lit bars and cafes on the corner of Taiping Beilu and Changjiang Lu, is interesting for a stroll, but none of the bars are of much interest; you can find a branch of Starbucks here and other chain names.

In the summer swelter, look no further than branches of Coco for bubble tea (from ¥8).

★ Brewsell's
BAR

(www.brewsells.com; 77-1 Shanghai Lu, 上海路77-1号; beers from ¥30; ⊙5pm-2am; Ⓜ Zhujiang Lu) There's a great vibe at this enterprising bar with Vedett (¥38), La Chouffe (¥38) and Asahi (¥28) on tap, and Trappistes Rochefort, blue/red Chimay (¥40) and other Belgian brews cooling in the fridge. This small, specialist imported beer bar (named after 'Brussels') has expat ale fiends descending in droves for fine beer and a fun quiz night. It also does Belgian waffles.

Asahi is ¥10 11am to 8pm; otherwise happy hour is 5pm to 8pm for premium drafts. The bar staff are friendly and speak good English.

Behind the Wall
BAR

(答案, Dá'àn; www.behindthewall-nanjing.com; 150 Shanghai Lu, 上海路150号; pint ¥30; ⊙6pm-1am; 🛜; Ⓜ Gulou) Doubling as a Mexican restaurant, this atmospheric, recently repainted and dimly illuminated bar on the bar street of Shanghai Lu divides into many rooms and alcoves, with a terrace outside for warmer months. There's draught beer, sangria and hypnotising live Flamenco guitar performances on Friday and Saturday evenings from Louis 'wu el lobo' (who really is very good). A bottle of Tsingtao is ¥15.

☆ Entertainment

Lányuàn Theatre
CHINESE OPERA

(兰苑剧场, Lányuàn Jùchǎng; ☎025 8446 9284; 4 Chaotiangong, 朝天宫4号; Ⓜ Shanghai Lu) Kūnqǔ (昆曲), an extant form of Chinese opera originating from Jiāngsū, is staged at this small theatre every Saturday evening at 7.15pm. There are English subtitles and tickets are between ¥120 and ¥150.

🛍 Shopping

The pedestrian area around Fūzǐ Temple has souvenirs, clothing, shoes and antiques for sale, while shopping malls such as Deji Plaza are excellent for finding everything under one roof.

★ Librairie Avant-Garde
BOOKS

(先锋书店, Xiānfēng Shūdiàn; 173 Guangzhou Lu, 广州路173号; ⊙10am-9.30pm; Ⓜ Shanghai Lu) Housed in a vast and disused bomb shelter, this astonishing indie bookshop has very few foreign-language books, but the underground, left-field ambience makes it a must for bibliophiles. With miles of books and a cavernous concrete floor, it's a Nánjīng cultural landmark, loved by students and literati for its sizeable collection of social science and humanities books.

Foreign Languages Bookstore BOOKS
(外文书店, Wàiwén Shūdiàn; 218 Zhongshan Donglu, 中山东路218号; ⊙9am-7pm Mon-Thu, to 8pm Fri & Sat; Ⓜ Daxinggong) There's a big collection of hardback and paperback novels on the 2nd floor, where there's also a small and very quiet cafe.

ⓘ Information

Nanjing Expats (www.nanjingexpat.com) and *Map* (www.mapmagazine.com.cn) are handy expat listings magazines, available at restaurants and bars. *Nanjing Expats* comes in a handy pocket-size version.

MEDICAL SERVICES

Angel Flossy-Care Dental Center (天使福乐氏口腔, Tiānshǐ Fúlèshì Kǒuqiāng; ☑025 8650 2567; www.tskq025.net; 4th fl, 10 Kexiang Xiang (Kexiang Alley), 科巷10号4楼; Ⓜ Daxinggong) Courteous English-speaking staff and very professional treatment.

Jiāngsū People's Hospital (江苏省人民医院, Jiāngsū Shěng Rénmín Yīyuàn; ☑025 8371 8836; 300 Guangzhou Lu, 广州路300号; ⊙8am-noon & 2-5.30pm) Runs a clinic for expats and has English-speaking doctors available.

Nánjīng International SOS Clinic (南京国际 SOS 紧急救援诊所, Nánjīng Guójì SOS Jǐnjí Jiùyuán Zhěnsuǒ; ☑025 8480 2842; www.clinicsinchina.com; 319 Zhongshan Donglu, 中山东路319号; ⊙9am-6pm Mon-Fri, 9am-noon Sat; Ⓜ Minggugong) On the ground floor of the Grand Metropark Hotel.

MONEY

Most bank ATMs are open 24 hours and take international cards. The banks listed here change major currency and travellers cheques.

Bank of China (中国银行, Zhōngguó Yínháng; 29 Hongwu Lu, 洪武路29号; ⊙8am-5pm Mon-Fri, to 12.30pm Sat; Ⓜ Xinjiekou) Handily located branch at the centre of town.

Bank of China (中国银行, Zhōngguó Yínháng; 3 Zhongshan Donglu, 中山东路3号; ⊙8am-5pm Mon-Fri, to 12.30pm Sat; Ⓜ Xinjiekou) Centrally located.

POST

China Post (Yóujú; 19 Zhongshan Lu; ⊙8am-6pm) Set in a lovely old detached building on Zhongshan Lu just north of the Xinjiekou intersection.

China Post (中国邮政, Zhōngguó Yóuzhèng; 2 Zhongshan Nanlu, 中山南路2号; ⊙8am-6.30pm; Ⓜ Gulou) Postal services and international phone calls.

PUBLIC SECURITY BUREAU

Exit & Entry Administration Service Center (南京市公安局出入境办证服务中心, Nánjīngshì Gōng'ānjú Chūrùjìng Bānzhèng Fúwù Zhōngxīn; ☑025 8442 0018; 173 Baixia Lu, 白下路173号; ⊙8.30am-5.30pm Mon-Fri, 9am-5pm Sat, 9am-noon & 2-5pm Sun; Ⓜ Changfu Jie) For visa extensions.

ⓘ Getting There & Away

AIR

Nánjīng Lùkǒu International Airport (南京禄口国际机场, Nánjīng Lùkǒu Guójì Jīchǎng) has regular air connections to all major Chinese cities. The main office for the **Civil Aviation Administration of China** (CAAC, 中国民航, Zhōngguó Mínháng; ☑025 8449 9378; 50 Ruijin Lu, 瑞金路50号) is near the terminus of bus 37, but you can also buy tickets at most top-end hotels and also on www.english.ctrip.com. **Dragonair** (港龙航空, Gǎnglóng Hángkōng; ☑025 8471 0181; room 751-53, World Trade Centre, 2 Hanzhong Lu, 汉中路2号) has daily flights to Hong Kong.

BUS

Of Nánjīng's numerous long-distance bus stations, **Nánjīng Long-Distance Bus Station** (南京中央门长途汽车站, Nánjīng Zhōngyāng Chángtú Qìchēzhàn; ☑025 8533 1288; 1 Jianning Lu, 建宁路1号), aka Zhōngyángmén long-distance station, is the largest. It is located southwest of the wide-bridged intersection with Zhongyang Lu. Regular buses departing from here include:

Hángzhōu ¥128, four hours

Héféi ¥53 to ¥62, 2½ hours

Shànghǎi ¥88, four hours

Sūzhōu ¥65 to ¥72, 2½ hours

Túnxī (for Huángshān) ¥114, five hours

Wúxī ¥59, two hours

Buses departing the **East Bus Station** (长途汽车东站, Chángtú Qìchē Dōngzhàn):

Yángzhōu ¥37, 1½ hours

Zhènjiāng ¥18, 1½ hours

From Nánjīng Train Station, take bus 13 north to Zhōngyāngmén long-distance bus station. Bus 2 from Xīnjiēkǒu goes to the East Bus Station. A taxi from town will cost ¥20 to ¥25 to either station.

TRAIN

Nánjīng Train Station (☑025 8582 2222) is a major stop on the Běijīng–Shànghǎi train line. Heading eastward from Nánjīng, the line to Shànghǎi connects with Zhènjiāng, Wúxī and Sūzhōu. Many G and D trains depart or terminate at the Nánjīng South Train Station (南京南站; Nánjīng Nánzhàn), so check when you buy your ticket. G trains to Běijīng all depart from Nánjīng South Train Station.

QĪXIÁ TEMPLE

On **Qīxiá Mountain** (栖霞山; Qīxiá Shān), 22km northeast of Nánjīng, the sacred site of **Qīxiá Temple** (栖霞寺, Qīxiá Sì; Jan-Sep ¥25, Oct-Dec ¥40; ⊙7am-5.30pm) was founded by the Buddhist monk Ming Sengshao during the Southern Qi dynasty, and remains an active place of worship. Long one of China's most important monasteries, today it's still one of its largest Buddhist seminaries. Relics believed to be part of Gautama Buddha's skull were unveiled and interred here. The mountain's **maple trees** are a major draw in spring when the hills are splashed in crimson and bronze.

The two main halls are the **Maitreya Hall**, with a statue of the Maitreya Buddha sitting cross-legged at the entrance; and the **Vairocana Hall**, housing a 5m tall statue of the Vairocana Buddha.

Behind Qīxiá Temple is the **Thousand Buddha Cliff** (千佛岩; Qiānfó Yán). Several grottoes housing stone statues are carved into the hillside, the earliest of which dates as far back as the Qi dynasty (AD 479–502); others are from the Tang, Song, Yuan and Ming dynasties. There is also a small stone pagoda, **Shèlì Pagoda** (舍利塔; Shèlì Tǎ), which was built in AD 601 and rebuilt during the late Tang period. The upper part has engraved sutras and carvings of Buddha; around the base, each of the pagoda's eight sides depicts tales from the life of Sakyamuni.

Continue northwards to admire lovely views in the **scenic area** behind the temple. The steep path meanders via an array of pavilions and rocky outcrops: it's serene, so consider bringing lunch and spending time here.

Get to the temple from Nánjīng by public bus (南上; Nán Shàng; ¥2.50, one hour) from a stop by Nánjīng Train Station. When you get off the bus, you will be approached by motorcycle taxis that will offer to take you into the temple the 'back' way for ¥10 or more. Be warned, it's an arduous hike up and down a large hill to the temple if you do this.

Trains from Nánjīng train station in the north of town:

Huángshān (Túnxī) hard/soft sleeper ¥108/159, six to eight hours, six daily

Shànghǎi G train (main train station, Hóngqiáo and Shànghǎi), 1st/2nd class ¥220/140, 1½ to two hours, regular

Sūzhōu G train, 1st/2nd class ¥160/100, 85 minutes, regular

Yángzhōu hard/soft seat ¥17/28, 80 minutes, nine daily

Xī'ān overnight Z train hard sleeper ¥280, 12 hours, five per day

Xī'ān North D train 2nd-class seat/soft sleeper ¥279/685, eight hours, one daily (12.37am)

Trains leaving from Nánjīng South train station:

Běijīng South G train, 1st/2nd class ¥749/444, 4½ hours, regular

Hángzhōu East G train 1st/2nd class ¥198/118, 1½ to two hours, regular

Xiàmén North D train, 1st/2nd class ¥528/424, nine to 11 hours, four daily

Try to get tickets via your hotel or the **train ticket office** (火车票售票处, Huǒchēpiào Shòupiàochù; 2 Zhongshan Nanlu, 中山南路2号; ⊙8.30am-5pm) on the 3rd floor of the post office, the **train ticket office** (火车票售票处, Huǒchēpiào Shòupiàochù; 35 Taiping Beilu, 太平北路35号; ⊙8-11am & noon-5pm) on Taiping Beilu or the **train ticket office** (火车票售票处, Huǒchēpiào Shòupiàochù; 416 Zhongshan Donglu, 中山东路416号; ⊙8.30am-6pm Mon-Fri, 8.30am-5pm Sat) on Zhongshan Donglu.

ℹ️ Getting Around

TO/FROM THE AIRPORT

The S1 Airport Line express metro link (¥6 to ¥8, 35 minutes, first/last train to airport 6am/10pm, first/last train from airport 6.40am/10pm) connects directly to the airport from Nánjīng South train station, itself on Lines 1 and 3. Buses (¥20, 90 minutes) also run to Nánjīng Lùkǒu Airport every 20 minutes between 6am and 9pm from the square east of Nánjīng train station. Another airport bus runs from Nánjīng South train station (¥20, 40 minutes, 6am to 9pm). Most hotels have hourly shuttle buses to and from the airport too. A taxi to the airport will cost around ¥140 to ¥150.

BICYCLE

There is a bike-hire scheme in town, but it is not that easy for short-stay foreigners to use. You need to apply for a swipe card by taking your passport along to an office and paying ¥250 (¥200 of that is deposit) to activate the card. English skills will be limited. Then hire of the orange bikes that can be found in stations across the city centre is free for the first two hours, the third hour is ¥1 and then it's ¥3 per hour thereafter.

Offices where you can apply:

Gǔlóu District Service Centre (鼓楼区行政服务中心, Gǔlóu Qū Xíngzhèng Fúwù Zhōngxīn; 84 Shanxi Lu, 山西路84号)

Xuánwǔ District Service Centre (玄武区行政服务中心, Xuánwǔ Qū Xíngzhèng Fúwù Zhōngxīn; 455 Zhujiang Lu, 珠江路455号; Ⓜ Fuqiao)

BUS

There are tourist bus routes that visit many of the sights:

Bus Y1 Goes from Nánjīng Train Station and Nánjīng Long-Distance Bus Station through the city to the Sun Yatsen Mausoleum.

Bus Y2 Starts in the south at the Martyrs' Cemetery (烈士墓地; Lièshì Mùdì), passes Fūzǐ Temple and terminates halfway up Zǐjīn Mountain.

Bus Y3 Passes by Nánjīng Train Station en route to the Míng Xiàolíng Tomb and Línggǔ Temple.

Many local maps contain bus routes. Normal buses cost ¥1 and tourist buses cost ¥2.

A stored-value transport card (jīnlíngtōng; 金陵通) is available for a deposit of ¥25 with a minimum top-up credit of ¥50. The card can be used on buses, the metro and taxis.

METRO

Nánjīng has a very efficient, rapidly expanding metro system that cuts through the city centre and runs out to the suburbs. Line 1 runs north to south and links both train stations. Line 2 goes east from Jīngtiānlù to Yóufāngqiáo in the west. Line 10 connects Andemen to Yushan Lu, while the S1 Line runs to the airport from Nanjing South Railway Station. The S8 Line runs north of the Yangzi River (Cháng Jiāng). Other lines are under construction. Tickets are ¥2 to ¥5 and trains generally run between around 6am and 10pm or 11pm.

TAXI

Taxi flagfall is ¥11 and it's ¥2.40 for each 3km thereafter. Trips to most destinations in the city are ¥11 to ¥14. Taxis are easy to flag down anywhere in the city.

Sūzhōu 苏州

☑ 0512 / POP 1.4 MILLION

Historically, Sūzhōu was synonymous with high culture and elegance, and generations of artists, scholars, writers and high society in China were drawn by its exquisite art forms and the delicate beauty of its gardens. Like all modern Chinese towns, Sūzhōu has unfortunately endured much destruction of its heritage and its replacement with largely arbitrary chunks of modern architecture.

Having said that, the city still retains enough pockets of charm to warrant two to three days' exploration on foot or by bike. And the gardens, Sūzhōu's main attraction, are a symphonic combination of rocks, water, trees and pavilions that reflects the Chinese appreciation of balance and harmony. Adding to the charm are some excellent museums, surviving canal scenes, pagodas and humpbacked bridges. The gardens in particular can get busy, so avoid visiting at the weekend or during public holidays, if possible.

History

Dating back some 2500 years, Sūzhōu is one of the oldest towns in the Yangzi Basin. With the completion of the Grand Canal during the Sui dynasty, Sūzhōu began to flourish as a centre of shipping and grain storage, bustling with merchants and artisans.

By the 14th century Sūzhōu had become China's leading silk-producing city. Aristocrats, pleasure seekers, famous scholars, actors and painters arrived, constructing villas and garden retreats.

The town's winning image as a 'Garden City' or a 'Venice of the East' came from its medieval blend of woodblock guilds and embroidery societies, whitewashed housing, cobbled streets, tree-lined avenues and canals. The local women were considered the most beautiful in China, largely thanks to the mellifluous local accent, and the city was home to a variety of rich merchants and bookish scholars...no doubt drawn by the beautiful women.

In 1860 Taiping troops took the town without a blow and in 1896 Sūzhōu was opened to foreign trade, with Japanese and other international concessions. Since 1949 much of the historic city, including its city walls, has vanished. A conscious prettification of the city has set the tone for the last decade or so, and areas such as Pingjiang Lu and the Pán Gate Scenic Area suggest the Sūzhōu of old.

◎ Sights

High-season prices apply from March to early May and September to October. Gardens and museums stop selling tickets 30 minutes before closing, and are best visited early in the mornings before crowds arrive. The gardens were not designed for tour groups, so don't expect too much Zen-like tranquillity.

⭐**Pingjiang Lu** STREET

(平江路; Ⓜ Lindun Lu or Xiangmen) While most of the town canals have been sealed and paved into roads, the pedestrianised Pingjiang Lu offers clues to the Sūzhōu of yesteryear. On the eastern side of the city, this canalside road has whitewashed local houses, many now converted to guesthouses, teahouses or trendy cafes selling overpriced beverages, sitting comfortably side-by-side. Duck down some of the side streets that jut out from the main path for a glimpse at slow-paced local life. It's a lovely place for a stroll.

Along the main drag it's all rice wine, Tibetan trinkets, cigar sellers, fried potatoes, cake, dumplings and ice-cream vendors.

⭐**Pán Gate Scenic Area** LANDMARK

(盘门, Pán Mén; 1 Dong Dajie, 东大街1号; Pán Gate only/with Ruìguāng Pagoda ¥40/46; ⊙7.30am-6pm; 🚍Y2) This far quieter part of Sūzhōu is lovely, with a section of the city wall straddling the outer moat in the southwest corner of the city. You can find Sūzhōu's only remaining original coiled gate, Pán Gate, dating from 1355; the overgrown double-walled **water gate** was used for controlling waterways, with defensive positions at the top. From the gate you can view the exquisite arched **Wúmén Bridge** (Wúmén Qiáo) to the east, the long moat and the crumbling **Ruìguāng Pagoda** (瑞光塔, Ruìguāng Tǎ; Dong Dajie, 东大街, ¥6), constructed in 1004.

The gate is also connected to 300m of the **ancient city wall**, which visitors can walk along, past old women who come here to harvest dandelions. The gate also backs onto a delightful scenic area, dotted with old halls, bell towers, bridges, pavilions and a lake as well as the small **Wùxiàng Temple** (Wùxiàng Cí). It's far less crowded than Sūzhōu's gardens and, in many ways, more attractive. To get here, take tourist bus Y2 or a taxi.

⭐**Garden of the Master of the Nets** GARDENS

(网师园, Wǎngshī Yuán; high/low season ¥30/20; ⊙7.30am-5pm) Off Shiquan Jie, this pocket-sized garden is considered one of Sūzhōu's best preserved. Laid out in the 12th century, it went to seed and was later restored in the 18th century as part of the home of a retired official turned fisherman (hence the name). A striking feature is the use of space: the labyrinth of courtyards, with windows framing other parts of the garden, is ingeniously designed to give the illusion of a much larger area.

The central section is the main garden and the western section is an inner garden with a courtyard containing the master's study. Trivia nuts note: the Peony Study was used as the model for the Astor Court and Ming Garden in the Museum of Modern Art, New York.

In the warmer months (March to November), music performances (¥100) are held nightly here from 7.30pm.

There are two ways to the entry gate, with English signs and souvenir stalls marking the way. you can enter from the alley on Shiquan Jie; or via Kuojiatou Xiang (阔家头巷), an alley off Daichengqiao Lu.

⭐**Humble Administrator's Garden** GARDENS

(拙政园, Zhuōzhèng Yuán; 178 Dongbei Jie, 东北街178号; high/low season ¥90/70, audio guide free; ⊙7.30am-5.30pm) The largest of Suzhou's gardens, the Humble Administrator's Garden is often considered to be the most impressive, but its fame draws in constant crowds, so get here early in the morning if you can. First built in 1509, this 5.2-hectare garden is clustered with water features, a museum, a teahouse, zigzagging bridges, bamboo groves and fragrant lotus ponds, along with at least 10 pavilions with poetic names such as 'Listening to the Sound of Rain' and 'Faraway Looking' pavilions.

⭐**Sūzhōu Museum** MUSEUM

(苏州博物馆, Sūzhōu Bówùguǎn; 204 Dongbei Jie, 东北街204号; audio guide ¥30; ⊙9am-5pm; 🚍Y5) 🆓 This cubist/geometric IM Pei-designed triumph has a modern interpretation of a Sūzhōu garden, with its confluence of water, bamboo and straight lines, and mixes it with a fascinating array of jade, ceramics, wooden carvings, textiles and other displays, all labelled with good and informative English captions. Look out for the boxwood statue of Avalokiteshvara (Guanyin), dating from the republican period. No flip-flops.

Sūzhōu Art Museum MUSEUM

(苏州美术馆, Sūzhōu Měishùguǎn; 2075 Renmin Lu, 人民路2075号; ⊙9am-5pm Tue-Sun; Ⓜ Sūzhōu Train Station) 🆓 A dazzling use of daylight and design merges in this new museum, hung with contemporary landscapes, calligraphy and modern art that stands out boldly from a seemingly infinite white space. In a nod to the local vernacular, the interior composition includes a lovely courtyard, sprouting bamboo. The museum is an element of a large complex that also includes the Sūzhōu Cultural Center and a theatre.

Sūzhōu

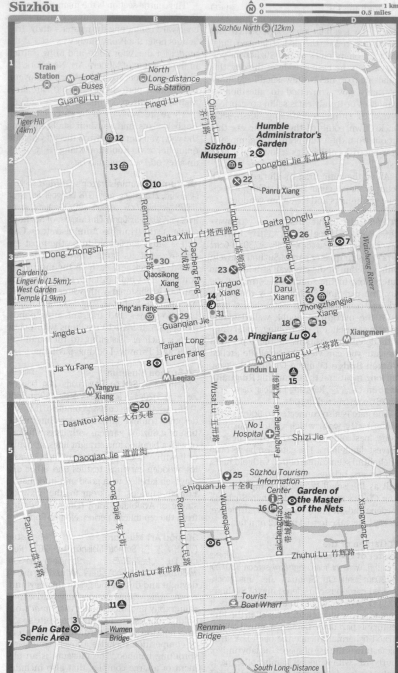

N

0 ———— 1 km
0 ———— 0.5 miles

↑ Sūzhōu North ❷ (12km)

A **B** **C** **D**

Train Station
Local Buses
Guangji Lu

North Long-distance Bus Station

Pingqi Lu

Tiger Hill (4km)

🏛 12

🏛 13

◎ 10

Qīmén Lù 齐门路

Sūzhōu Museum

🏛 5

Humble Administrator's Garden ❷ 2

Dongbei Jie 东北街

✕ 22

Panru Xiang

Lindun Lu 临顿路

Baita Donglu

Pingjiang Lu

🏛 26

◎ 7

Cang Jie

Renmin Lu 人民路

Dong Zhongshi

Baita Xilu 白塔西路

Dacheng Fang 大成坊

● 30

Qiaosikong Xiang

Garden to Linger In (1.5km); West Garden Temple (1.9km)

Yinguo Xiang

23 ✕

Daru Xiang

21 ✕

27 ⊙ 9

Zhongzhangjia Xiang

Ping'an Fang

28 ●

✉ 29

Guanqian Jie

14 ⊙

◎ 31

18 🏠 19 🏠

Jingde Lu

Taijian Long

✕ 24

Pingjiang Lu ◎ 4

Xiangmen

Jia Yu Fang

Furen Fang

8 ◎

Ⓜ Leqiao

Yangyu Xiang

Ganjiang Lu 干将路

Lindun Lu

🔺 15

Fenghuang Jie 凤凰街

20 🏠

Dashitou Xiang 大石头巷

Daoqian Jie 道前街

Wusa Lu 五卅路

No 1 Hospital ✚

Shizi Jie

Dong Daije 东大街

Shiquan Jie 十全街

🏠 25

Sūzhōu Tourism Information Center

Garden of the Master of the Nets ◎ 1

ℹ

16 🏠

Renmin Lu 人民路

Daichengqiao Lu 带城桥路

Xiangwang Lu

Zhuhui Lu 竹辉路

◎ 6

Panxu Lu 盘胥路

Xinshi Lu 新市路

17 🏠

11 🔺

Tourist Boat Wharf 🚢

Pán Gate Scenic Area ◎ 3

Wumen Bridge

Renmin Bridge

Waicheng River

Wuqueqiao Lu

South Long-Distance ❷ (0.5km)

Sūzhōu

Twin Pagodas   BUDDHIST TEMPLE, PAGODA
(双塔, Shuāng Tǎ; Dìnghuìsì Xiàng, 定慧寺巷; ¥8;
⊙8am-4.30pm; Ⓜ Lindun Lu) Beautifully enhanced with flowering magnolias in spring,
this delightful courtyard and former temple
contains a pair of sublime pagodas, which
don't often come in couples. It's one of the
more relaxing, peaceful and composed parts
of town, so come here for a break. It's also
home to the small and little-visited **Sūzhōu
Ancient Stone Carving Art Museum**.

Sūzhōu Silk Museum   MUSEUM
(苏州丝绸博物馆, Sūzhōu Sīchóu Bówùguǎn;
2001 Renmin Lu, 人民路2001号; ⊙9am-5pm;
Ⓜ Sūzhōu Train Station) FREE By the 13th
century Sūzhōu was the place for silk production and weaving, and the Sūzhōu Silk
Museum houses fascinating exhibitions detailing the history of Sūzhōu's 4000-year-old
silk industry. Exhibits include a section on
silk-weaving techniques and silk fashion
through the dynasties, while you can amble
among mulberry shrubs outdoors. You can
also see functioning looms and staff at work
on, say, a large brocade.

Precious Belt Bridge   BRIDGE
(宝带桥, Bǎodài Qiáo) Straddling the Grand
Canal southeast of Sūzhōu, and boasting 53
arches, the lovely Precious Belt Bridge was
once a Tang dynasty construction, although
the current bridge actually dates to the
Ming. It's a 40-minute bike ride. Head south
on Renmin Lu, past the south moat, then
left at the TV towers, and the bridge will be
on your right. If you're heading to Tónglǐ,
you'll see the bridge on your right.

Temple of Mystery   TAOIST TEMPLE
(玄妙观, Xuánmiào Guàn; Guanqian Jie, 观前
街; ¥10; ⊙7.30am-5pm; Ⓜ Lindun Lu or Leqiao)
Lashed by electronic music from the shops
alongside, the Taoist Temple of Mystery
stands in what was once Sūzhōu's old bazaar, a rowdy entertainment district with
travelling performers, acrobats and actors.
The temple dates from 1181 and is the sole
surviving example of Song architecture in
Sūzhōu. The complex contains several elaborately decorated halls, including the huge
Sānqīng Diàn (三清殿; Three Purities Hall),
which is supported by 60 pillars and capped
by a double roof with upturned eaves.

West Garden Temple   GARDENS
(西园寺, Xīyuán Sì; Xiyuan Lu, 西园路; ¥25;
⊙8am-5pm; ⊒Y1, Y3) This magnificent temple, with its mustard-yellow walls and gracefully curved eaves, was burnt to the ground
during the Taiping Rebellion and rebuilt in
the late 19th century. Greeting you as you

enter the stunning **Arhat Hall** (罗汉堂; Luóhàn Táng) is an amazing four-faced and thousand-armed statue of Guanyin. Beyond lie mesmerising and slightly unnerving rows of 500 glittering *luóhàn* (arhats; monks who have achieved enlightenment and passed to nirvana at death) statues, each unique and near life-size.

Luóhàn usually only appear in two rows of nine on either side of the main temple, equalling 18 in total, but on occasion – and in noteworthy temples – they can appear in a huge multitude. A vegetarian restaurant at the temple serves noodles and other simple meat-free fare. The temple is 400m west of the Garden to Linger In. Take Y1 or Y3 from the train station.

Blue Wave Pavilion
GARDENS

(沧浪亭, Cānglàng Tíng; Renmin Lu, 人民路; high/low season ¥20/15; ⊙ 7.30am-5pm) Originally the home of a prince, the oldest garden in Sūzhōu was first built in the 11th century, and has been repeatedly rebuilt since. Instead of attracting hordes of tourists, the wild, overgrown garden around the Blue Wave Pavilion is one of those where the locals actually go to chill and enjoy a leisurely stroll. Lacking a northern wall, the garden creates the illusion of space by borrowing scenes from the outside.

North Temple Pagoda
PAGODA

(北寺塔, Běisì Tǎ; 1918 Renmin Lu, 人民路1918号; ¥25; ⊙ 7.45am-5pm) The tallest pagoda south of the Yangzi is a beauty, dominating the northern end of Renmin Lu. The nine-storey pagoda is an element of Bào'ēn Temple (报恩寺; Bào'ēn Sì) and you can climb it for sweeping views of hazy modern-day Sūzhōu.

The temple complex goes back 1700 years and was originally a residence; the current reincarnation dates to the 17th century. Off to one side is **Nánmù Guānyīn Hall** (楠木观音殿; Nánmù Guānyīn Diàn), which was rebuilt in the Ming dynasty with some features imported from elsewhere.

Garden to Linger In
GARDENS

(留园, Liú Yuán; 79 Liuyuan Lu; high/low season ¥55/45; ⊙ 7.30am-5pm; 🚌 Y1) One of the largest gardens in Sūzhōu, this 3-hectare plot was originally built in the Ming dynasty by a doctor as a relaxing place for his recovering patients. It's easy to see why the patients took to it: the winding corridors are inlaid with calligraphy from celebrated masters, their windows and doorways opening onto unusually shaped rockeries, ponds

and dense clusters of bamboo. Stone tablets hang from the walls, inscribed by patients recording their impressions of the place.

The teahouse is a fantastic spot to recover from crowd overload. Order a cup of *lóngjǐng* (龙井; dragon well tea; ¥15) and relax. The garden is about 3km west of the city centre and can be reached on tourist bus Y1 from the train station or Renmin Lu.

Couple's Garden
GARDENS

(耦园, Ǒu Yuán; 6 Xiaoxinqiao Xiang, 小新桥巷6号; high/low season ¥20/15; ⊙ 8am-4.30pm; Ⓜ Xiangmen) The tranquil Couple's Garden is off the main tourist route and sees slightly fewer visitors than the other gardens, and its pond, courtyards and garden features are quite lovely.

Grand Canal
CANAL

(大运河, Dà Yùnhé) The Grand Canal – its name much grander than its modern-day appearance – passes to the west and south of Sūzhōu, within a 10km range of the town. Hop on suburban buses 13, 14, 15 or 16 to get there. In the northwest, bus 11 follows the canal for a fair distance, taking you on a pleasant tour of the surrounding countryside.

Garden of Harmony
GARDENS

(怡园, Yí Yuán; Renmin Lu, 人民路; ¥15) One of the less visited gardens around Sūzhōu is the charmingly small Qing dynasty Garden of Harmony, which has assimilated many of the features of older gardens and delicately blended them into a style of its own.

Tiger Hill
PARK

(虎丘山, Hǔqiū Shān; ☎ 0512 6723 2305; Huqiu Lu, 虎丘路; high/low season ¥80/60; ⊙ 7.30am-6pm, to 5pm winter; 🚌 Y1, Y2) In the far northwest of town, Tiger Hill is a major drawcard for Chinese tourists and the beacon that draws them is the leaning **Cloud Rock Pagoda** (云岩塔; Yúnyán Tǎ) atop the hill. The octagonal seven-storey pagoda was built in the 10th century entirely of brick, an innovation in Chinese architecture at the time. It began tilting over 400 years ago, and today the highest point is displaced more than 2m from its original position.

The hill itself is artificial and is the final resting place of He Lu, founding father of Sūzhōu. He Lu died in the 6th century BC and myths have coalesced around him – he is said to have been buried with a collection of 3000 swords and be guarded by a white tiger. Tourist buses Y1 and Y2 from the train station go here.

Kūnqǔ Opera Museum MUSEUM
(昆曲博物馆, Kūnqǔ Bówùguǎn; 14 Zhongzhang-jia Xiang, 中张家巷14号; ⏰8.30am-4pm) FREE
Down a warren of narrow lanes, the small Kūnqǔ Opera Museum is dedicated to *kūnqǔ*, the opera style of the region. The beautiful old theatre houses a stage, musical instruments, costumes and photos of famous performers and also puts on regular performances of *kūnqǔ*.

👉 Tours

Evening boat tours wind their way around the outer canal leaving nightly from 6pm to 8.30pm (¥120, 55 minutes, half-hourly). The trips, usually with *píngtán* (singing and storytelling art form sung in the Sūzhōu dialect) performance on board, are a great way to experience old Sūzhōu, passing Pán Gate and heading up to Chāng Gate (in the west of the city wall). Remember to bring bug repellent as the mosquitoes are tenacious. Tickets can be bought at the **Tourist Boat Wharf** (游船码头, Yóuchuán Mǎtóu) down the alley east of Rénmín Bridge, which shares the same quarters with the **Grand Canal Boats** (划船售票处, Huáchuán Shòupiàochù) ticket office. Buses 27 or 94 run to the wharf.

🎎 Festivals & Events

Sūzhōu Silk Festival CULTURAL
(丝绸节, Sīchóu Jié) September sees Sūzhōu hosting its silk festival, with exhibitions devoted to silk history and production, and silk merchants showing off their wares to crowds of thousands.

🛏 Sleeping

Hotels in Sūzhōu are not cheap, but there's no shortage of choice, from canalside hostels to comfortable boutique options and professional five-star hotels. Prices can rise across the board at weekends, when rooms can be harder to book, so try to visit from Sunday through to Thursday if possible.

★ Sūzhōu Mingtown Youth Hostel HOSTEL $
(苏州明堂青年旅舍, Sūzhōu Míngtáng Qīngnián Lǚshè; ☎0512 6581 6869; 28 Pingjiang Lu, 平江路28号; 6-bed dm ¥60-65, s/tw ¥200/220; ❄@☎; ⓜXiangmen or Lindun Lu) This well run youth hostel has a fantastic location on Pingjiang Lu and a charming lobby with rooms and dorms decorated with dark wooden 'antique' furniture. Rooms are not very well soundproofed but there's free laundry and bike rental. Staff speak English and can help

with travel tips around town. Rooms are around ¥20 pricier on Friday and Saturday.

Sūzhōu Watertown Youth Hostel HOSTEL $
(苏州浮生四季国际青年旅舍, Sūzhōu Fúshēngsìjì Qīngnián Lǚshè; ☎0512 6521 8885; www.watertownhostel.com; 27 Dashitou Xiang, Renmin Lu, 人民路大石头巷27号; 6-/4-bed dm ¥50/60, s ¥160, d ¥130-220; ❄@☎; ⓜLeqiao) Tucked away down Dashitou Xiang (Big Stone Alley), a lane off Renmin Lu, this 200-year-old courtyard complex houses an OK hostel. Rooms on the 2nd floor are quieter while ground-floor rooms have better wi-fi reception. Dorms are compact but clean enough. The cosy Sūzhōu-styled patio invites you to chill, and big bottles of Qīngdǎo are cheap.

The cheapest twins and the triples are with shared shower. The airport bus station is just a stone's throw away.

★ Garden Hotel HOTEL $$$
(苏州南园宾馆, Suzhou Nányuán Bīnguǎn; ☎0512 6778 6778; www.gardenhotelsuzhou.com; 99 Daichengqiao Lu, 带城桥路99号; r from ¥1558; ❄☎) Within huge, green grounds, the very popular five-star Garden Hotel has elegant, spacious and attractively decorated rooms. Washed over with Chinese instrumental *pípá* music, the lobby is a picture of Sūzhōu, with a clear pond, grey bricks and white walls. Serene stuff and an oasis of calm. It's often possible to get a room here for under ¥800.

Pan Pacific Sūzhōu HOTEL $$$
(苏州吴宫泛太平洋酒店, Sūzhōu Wúgōng Fàntàipíngyáng Jiǔdiàn; ☎0512 6510 3388; www.panpacific.com/Suzhou; 259 Xinshi Lu, 新市路259号; d ¥1880-2680, ste ¥3680; ❄☎) There's a kitschy feel to the exterior of this former Sheraton Hotel, which looks like a faux Forbidden City. But once you step into the lobby, you'll know this is five-star luxury. The 500+ rooms are spacious and stylish, fitted with all the latest gadgets to make you happy. Service is polite and impeccable. Discounts of over 50% usually available.

A bonus is guests get to enjoy free access to the adjacent Gán Gate Garden.

Píngjiāng Lodge BOUTIQUE HOTEL $$$
(苏州平江客栈, Sūzhōu Píngjiāng Kèzhàn; ☎0512 6523 2888; www.pingjianglodge.com; 33 Niujia Xiang, 钮家巷33号; d ¥988-1588, ste ¥1888-2588; ❄@; ⓜXiangmen or Lindun Lu) Capturing the canalside Sūzhōu aesthetic, this 17th-century traditional courtyard building has well kept gardens and 51 rooms bedecked in traditional furniture. Rooms

at the pointy end are very nice suites with split-level living spaces; standard rooms are bit bashed and could do with new carpets. Staff speak (faltering) English. Discounts of up to 50% are available.

✗ Eating

In reflection of its busy and year-round tourist traffic, Sūzhōu has some excellent restaurants, both Chinese and international. The area around Guanqian Jie, especially down the road from the Temple of Mystery, is stuffed with choices, but you'll find good options dotted all over the town.

Yǎba Shēngjiān   DUMPLING $

(哑巴生煎; 12 Lindun Lu, 临顿路12号; 8 dumplings ¥13; ⏱ 5.30am-6.30pm) With great clouds of steam rising from the kitchen, this 60-year-old institution mainly flogs noodles but its handmade *shēngjiān bāo* (生煎包; pan-fried dumplings), stuffed with juicy pork, are outstanding and flavour-packed. During lunch hours expect to queue for 30 minutes just to order! Protocol: get a ticket, join the line, snag a table and enjoy.

Zhūhóngxīng   NOODLES $

(朱鸿兴; Taijian Long; mains from ¥15; ⏱ 6.45am-8.45pm; Ⓜ Lindun Lu) Popular with locals, this red-wood-furniture-bedecked eatery, with several branches across town, has a long history and wholesome, filling noodles – try the scrummy *xiàrén miàn* (虾仁面; noodles with baby shrimp) or the *xuěcài ròusī miàn* (雪菜肉丝面; meat and vegetable noodles).

Pingvon   TEAHOUSE $

(品芳, Pǐnfāng; 94 Pingjiang Lu, 平江路94号; dishes from ¥6) Although often busy, this seriously cute little teahouse finds itself perched beside one of Sūzhōu's most popular canalside streets, serving up excellent dumplings and delicate little morsels on small plates. The tearooms upstairs are more atmospheric. There are all sorts of bites, from pine nuts and pumpkin soup (¥6) to crab *xiǎolóngbāo* (steamed dumplings; ¥10 a portion). Picture menu. Order by ticking what you want on a paper menu and handing it over.

Wúmén Rénjiā   JIANGSU $$

(吴门人家; ☑ 0512 6728 8041; 31 Panru Xiang, 潘儒巷31号; dishes from ¥30; ⏱ 6.30-9.30am, 11am-1.30pm & 5-8.30pm) Hidden in a quiet alley north of Lion's Grove Garden, this lovely traditional courtyard restaurant attracts a mix of locals and visitors for its subtly flavoured Sūzhōu cooking. Service can sometimes be a bit slow, but the setting (with traditional Chinese music) is superlative. Reservations essential.

Try the ever-popular squirrel fish or the kung pao chicken (宫保雞丁; *gōngbǎo jīdīng*; spicy chicken with chilli and peanuts).

☕ Drinking & Nightlife

There are stacks of trendy cafe-bars scattered along Pingjiang Lu. A gem or two survives, but the nightlife scene on Shiquan Jie has fizzled out as most of the expats' watering holes have moved to the soulless Sūzhōu Industrial Park, 9km east of the centre of town (get there on the metro).

★ Bookworm   BAR

(老书虫, Lǎo Shūchóng; ☑ 0512 6526 4720; www.suzhoubookworm.com; 77 Gunxiu Fang, 滚绣坊77号; ⏱ 11am-1am Mon-Fri, 10am-1am Sat & Sun) Běijīng's excellent Bookworm wormed its way down to Sūzhōu, serving as a kind of comfy cultural hub, library, bookshop and cafe. The food is crowd-pleasing (lots of Western options) and the cold beers include Tsingtao and Erdinger. There are readings, live music, an open mic and you can borrow or buy books. Ask about its literary festival, held in March.

★ Locke Pub   BAR

(240 Pingjiang Lu, 平江路240号; ⏱ 10am-midnight) Any place that plays Tom Waits is good in our book and we're also partial to friendly labradors. This charming spot has ample space, comfy sofas, homemade ice cream, a whole wall of English books, hot whisky, Leffe, Corona and Guinness, all set in a traditional building along Pingjiang Lu.

☆ Entertainment

Regular performances of *kūnqǔ* opera and *píngtán*, two of the exquisite performance arts sung in local dialects, are regularly scheduled at the Kūnqǔ Opera Museum and the Píngtán Museum. Music performances are also held nightly from 7.30pm to 9.30pm in the Garden of the Master of the Nets in the warmer months, from March through to November.

Garden of the Master of the Nets LIVE MUSIC

(网师园, Wǎngshī Yuán; tickets ¥100) From March to November, music performances are held nightly from 7.30pm to 9.30pm for tourist groups at this garden. Don't expect anything too authentic.

Kūnqǔ Opera Museum
CHINESE OPERA

(昆曲博物馆, Kūnqǔ Bówùguǎn; 14 Zhongzhangjia Xiang, 中张家巷14号; tickets ¥30) This place puts on performances of *kūnqǔ* at 2pm on Sundays.

Píngtán Museum
PERFORMING ARTS

(评弹博物馆, Píngtán Bówùguǎn; 3 Zhongzhangjia Xiang, 中张家巷3号; ¥4, performances ¥6; ⊗9.30am-noon & 3.30-5pm) The Píngtán Museum puts on wonderful performances of *píngtán*, a singing and storytelling art form sung in the Sūzhōu dialect. Two-hour shows are at 1.30pm daily.

🛈 Information

Major tourist hotels have foreign-exchange counters.

Bank of China (中国银行, Zhōngguó Yínháng; 1450 Renmin Lu, 人民路1450号) Changes travellers cheques and foreign cash. There are ATMs that take international cards at most larger branches of the Bank of China.

China Post (中国邮政, Zhōngguó Yóuzhèng; cnr Renmin Lu & Jingde Lu) Centrally located.

Industrial & Commercial Bank of China (工商银行, Gōngshāng Yínháng; 222 Guanqian Jie, 观前街222号) Twenty-four-hour ATM facilities.

No 1 Hospital (苏大附一院, Sūdà Fùyīyuàn; 96 Shizi Jie, 十梓街96号) At the heart of Sūzhōu.

Public Security Bureau (PSB, 公安局, Gōng'ānjú; ☑ 0512 6522 5661, ext 20593; 1109 Renmin Lu, 人民路1109号) Can help with emergencies and visa problems. The visa office is about 200m down a lane called Dashitou Xiang (大石头巷).

Sūzhōu Tourism Information Center (苏州旅游咨询中心, Sūzhōu Lǚyóu Zīxún Zhōngxīn; ☑ 0512 6530 5887; 101 Daichengqiao Lu, 带城桥路101号) This branch is just north of the Garden Hotel; there are several other branches in town including at bus stations. Can help with booking accommodation and tours; English skills vary.

🛈 Getting There & Away

AIR

Sūzhōu does not have an airport, but you can book flights out of Shànghǎi through www.english.ctrip.com. Buses leave Sūzhōu North Long-distance Bus Station frequently between 6am and 5.30pm for Hóngqiáo Airport (¥53) and Pǔdōng International Airport (¥84) in Shànghǎi.

BUS

Sūzhōu has three long-distance bus stations and the two listed here are the most useful. Tickets for all buses can also be bought at the **Liánhé ticket centre** (联合售票处, Liánhé Shòupiàochù; ☑ 0512 6520 6681; 1606 Renmin Lu, 人民路1606号; ⊗ bus tickets 8.30-11.30am & 1-5pm, train tickets 7.30-11am & noon-5pm).

The principal station is the **North Long-distance Bus Station** (汽车北站, Qìchē Běizhàn; ☑ 0512 6577 6577; 29 Xihui Lu, 西汇路29号) at the northern end of Renmin Lu, next to the train station:

Hángzhōu ¥74, two hours, regular (6.35am to 7pm)

Nánjīng ¥72, 2½ hours, regular (7.20am to 5.50pm)

Wūzhèn ¥36, 90 minutes, regular (8.15am to 5.20pm)

Zhōuzhuāng ¥16, one hour, every 40 minutes (7am to 6.20pm)

Tónglǐ ¥8, 30 minutes, every 30 minutes (6am to 7pm)

The **South Long-distance Bus Station** (汽车南站, Qìchē Nánzhàn; cnr Yingchun Lu & Nanhuan Donglu, 迎春路南环东路的路口) has buses to the following destinations:

Hángzhōu ¥74, two hours, every 20 minutes (7.35am to 7.05pm)

Nánjīng ¥72, two hours, every 40 minutes (7.20am to 5.30pm)

Shànghǎi ¥34, 1½ hours, every 30 minutes (6.50am to 7.40pm)

Yángzhōu ¥76, two hours, hourly (8am to 6pm)

Buses for Lúzhí leave from the **Local Bus Stop**, just east of the train station.

TRAIN

Sūzhōu is on the Nánjīng–Shànghǎi express G line. Trains stop at either the more centrally located Sūzhōu Train Station (苏州站; Sūzhōu Zhàn) or the Sūzhōu North Train Station (苏州北站; Sūzhōu Běizhàn), 12km north of the city centre. Book train tickets on the 2nd floor of the Liánhé ticket centre or at the **ticket office** (Guanqian Jie, 观前街) along Guanqian Jie across from the Temple of Mystery; there's another **office** (⊗8am-8pm) by the Confucian Temple. Yet another ticket office can be found on the other side of the road from the South Long-distance Bus Station. Tickets can be also be booked online at http://english.ctrip.com.

Trains departing from the Sūzhōu North Train Station:

Běijīng South 1st/2nd class ¥884/524, five hours, 17 daily

Trains departing from both stations:

Nánjīng 1st/2nd class ¥160/100, one hour, frequent

Shànghǎi 1st/2nd class ¥60/40, 26 to 46 minutes, frequent

Wúxī 1st/2nd class ¥30/20, 15 minutes, frequent

Around Sūzhōu

0 ____ 10 km
0 ____ 5 miles

ⓘ Getting Around

BICYCLE

You can rent bikes from most hostels.

PUBLIC TRANSPORT

Convenient tourist buses visit all sights and cost ¥2, passing by the train station.

Bus Y5 Goes around the western and eastern sides of the city and has a stop at Sūzhōu Museum.

Bus Y2 Travels from Tiger Hill, Pán Gate and along Shiquan Jie.

Buses Y1 & Y4 Run the length of Renmin Lu.

Bus 80 Runs between the two train stations.

Sūzhōu metro Line 1 runs along Ganjiang Lu, connecting Mùdú in the southwest with Zhongnan Jie in the east and running through the Culture & Expo Centre and Times Sq, in the Sūzhōu Industrial Park. Line 2 runs north–south from Sūzhōu North Train Station to Baodaiqiaonan in the south, via Sūzhōu Train Station. Lines 3 and 4 were under construction at the time of writing.

TAXI

Fares start at ¥12 and drivers generally use their meters. A trip from Guanqian Jie to Sūzhōu Train Station should cost around ¥15 to ¥20. From Sūzhōu North Train Station to downtown, the fare is around ¥50 to ¥60. Pedicabs hover around the tourist areas and can be persistent (¥5 to ¥10 for short rides is standard).

Mùdú   木渎

📞 0512 / POP 80,000

Dating to the Ming dynasty, the canal town of Mùdú was once the haunt of wealthy officials, intellectuals and artists, and even the Qing Emperor Qianlong visited six times. Today, the village has become part of Sūzhōu as the city develops outwards. While it's not as picturesque as Jiāngsū's canal towns, it's easy peasy to reach from Sūzhōu (the metro runs here) and Mùdú offers a glimpse of traditional Jiāngsū canal-town heritage architecture in its bridges, ancient residences and gardens.

⊙ Sights

The village is free if you merely want to soak up the atmosphere. Entrance fees are for the top sights alone; however, they contain most of Mùdú's character and history. A through ticket to all the sights is ¥78.

Yan Family Garden   HISTORIC BUILDING

(严家花园, Yánjiā Huāyuán; cnr Shantang Jie & Mingqing Jie, 山塘街明清街的路口; ¥40; ⊙8.30am-4.30pm; Ⓜ Mudu) This beautiful complex in the northwest corner of the village is the highlight of the town, dating to the Ming dynasty. It was once the home of a former magistrate. The garden, with its rockeries and a meandering lake, is divided into five sections by walls, each section designed to invoke a season. If you visit just one sight in Mùdú, come here.

Ancient Pine Garden   HISTORIC BUILDING

(古松园, Gǔsōngyuán; Shantang Jie, 山塘街; ¥20; ⊙8.30am-4.30pm; Ⓜ Mudu) In the middle of Shantang Jie, this attractive courtyard complex is known for its intricately carved beams. Look out for wooden impressions of officials, hats, phoenixes, flowers and other designs.

Hóngyǐn Mountain Villa   HISTORIC BUILDING

(虹饮山房, Hóngyǐn Shānfáng; Shantang Jie, 山塘街; ¥40; ⊙8.30am-4.30pm; Ⓜ Mudu) By far the most interesting place in Mùdú is this villa, with its elaborate opera stage, exhibits and even an imperial pier where Emperor Qianlong docked his boat. The stage in the centre hall is impressive; honoured guests were seated in front and the galleries along the sides of the hall were for women. The emperor was a frequent visitor and you can see his uncomfortable-looking imperial chair. Opera is still performed here on festival days.

Bǎngyǎn Mansion HISTORIC BUILDING

(榜眼府第, Bǎngyǎn Fǔdì; Xiatang Jie, 下塘街; ¥10; ◎8.30am-4.30pm; M Mudu) With a rich collection of antique furniture and intricate carvings of stone, wood and brick (it often serves as a movie set) this dignified complex was the home of the 19th-century writer and politician Feng Guifen. The surrounding garden is very attractive, with lotus ponds, arched bridges, bamboo and other plants.

Míngyuè Temple BUDDHIST TEMPLE

(明月古寺, Míngyuè Gǔsì, Shantang Jie, 山塘街; ◎8.30am-4.30pm, M Mudu) This large and attractive temple originally dates to the 10th century, but has been largely reconstructed (since last being mostly destroyed during the Cultural Revolution). The 1000-arm, four-faced Guanyin statue is worth hunting down – notice the ruler she holds in one of her lower hands, among other Buddhist ritual objects.

Mùdú Old Town VILLAGE

(老城区, Lǎochéngqū; ☑0512 6636 8225; ◎8.30am-4.30pm; M Mudu) The old town of Mùdú is principally hemmed in by the canal and Xiangxi Xilu. It's a small area to explore, and you only need half a day to do it justice.

👉 Tours

The most pleasurable way to experience Mùdú is along the canal by boat. You'll find a collection of traditional skiffs with boatsmen docked outside the Bǎngyǎn Mansion. A short 10- to 15-minute boat ride is ¥15 per person (¥35 per boat minimum charge).

🛏 Sleeping & Eating

Mùdú doesn't cater well to those who want to spend the night, as Sūzhōu is so near by, so most people return to spend the night there.

There's no shortage of places to eat along the canalside Shangtang Jie.

ℹ Getting There & Away

Getting to Mùdú is easy as pie. From Sūzhōu, jump aboard metro line 1 to Mùdú station then take exit 1 and hop on bus 2, 38 or 622 (all ¥1), 4km (four stops) away from the old town (木渎古镇站; Mùdú Gǔzhèn zhàn).

Tónglǐ 同里

☑0512 / POP 60,000

Once called Fùtǔ (富土) before changing its name to Tónglǐ (铜里) and then ending up with the name Tónglǐ (同里; different first character), this lovely village is only 18km southeast of Sūzhōu. A leisurely day trip from town (or for those en route to Shànghǎi), Tónglǐ boasts a rich, historical canalside atmosphere and weather-beaten charm. A restrained carnival atmosphere reigns but the languorous tempo is frequently shredded by marauding tour groups that sweep in, especially at weekends.

⊙ Sights

★ Chinese Sex Culture Museum MUSEUM

(中华性文化博物馆, Zhōnghuá Xìngwénhuà Bówùguǎn; ¥20; ◎9am-5.30pm) This private museum is quietly housed in a historic but disused girls' school campus with an attractive garden and courtyard. Despite occasionally didactic and inaccurate pronouncements, it's fascinating, and ranges from the penal (sticks used to beat prostitutes, chastity belts) and the penile (Qing dynasty dildos), to the innocent (small statues of the Goddess of Mercy) and the positively charming (porcelain figures of courting couples).

Founded by sociology professors Liu Dalin and Hu Hongxia against all odds, the museum's aim is not so much to arouse, but rather to educate and reintroduce an aspect of the country's culture that, ironically, has been forcefully repressed since China was 'liberated' in 1949. The pair have collected several thousand artefacts relating to sex, from erotic landscape paintings, fans and teacups to chastity belts and saddles with wooden dildos used to punish 'licentious' women and some bizarre objects (a pot-bellied immortal with a penis growing out of his head topped by a turtle). This is also one of the only places in the country where homosexuality is openly recognised as part of Chinese culture. Fascinating. The only drawback is that the museum is not included in the through ticket to the village.

Tónglǐ Old Town VILLAGE

(老城区, Lǎochéngqū; ☑0512 6333 1140; ¥100, after 5.30pm free) This lovely old town, only 18km southeast of Sūzhōu, boasts a rich, historical canalside atmosphere and weather-beaten charm. Many of the buildings have kept their traditional facades, with stark whitewashed walls, black-tiled roofs, cobblestone pathways and willow-shaded canal views adding to a picturesque allure. The town is best explored the traditional way: aimlessly meandering along the canals and alleys until you get lost.

A restrained carnival atmosphere reigns here but the languorous tempo is frequently upset by marauding tour groups that sweep in, especially at weekends.

The admission fee to the town includes access to the best sights, except the Chinese Sex Culture Museum.

Gēnglè Táng
HISTORIC BUILDING

(耕乐堂; ⊘9am-5.30pm) Of the three old residences in Tónglǐ that you'll pass at some point, the most pleasant is this elegant, lovely and composed Ming dynasty estate with 52 halls spread out over five courtyards in the west of town. The buildings have been elaborately restored and redecorated with paintings, calligraphy and antique furniture, while the black-brick paths, osmanthus trees and cooling corridors hung with *mǎdēng* lanterns (traditional Chinese lanterns) conjure up an alluring charm.

Pearl Pagoda
PAGODA

(珍珠塔, Zhēnzhū Tǎ; ⊘9am-5.30pm) In the north of town, this compound dates from the Qing dynasty and contains a spacious residential complex decorated with Qing-era antiques, an ancestral hall, a garden and an opera stage. It gets its name from a tiny pagoda draped in pearls.

Tuìsī Garden
GARDENS

(退思园, Tuìsī Yuán; ⊘9am-5.30pm) This beautiful 19th-century garden in the east of the old town delightfully translates as the 'Withdraw and Reflect Garden', so named because it was a Qing government official's retirement home. The 'Tower of Fanning Delight' served as the living quarters, while the garden itself is a meditative portrait of pond water churning with koi, rockeries and pavilions, caressed by traditional Chinese music.

👉 Tours

Slow-moving six-person **boats** (¥90 for 25 minutes) ply the waters of Tónglǐ's canal system. The boat trip on Tónglǐ Lake is free, though of no particular interest.

🛏 Sleeping

Most visitors come as day trippers, but guesthouses are plentiful if you'd like to spend the night, with basic rooms starting at about ¥100. The village is much quieter in the evening too, as there's an exodus in the late afternoon as travellers depart.

Tongli International Youth Hostel
HOSTEL $

(同里国际青年旅舍, Tónglǐ Guójì Qīngnián Lǚshè; ☑0512 6333 9311; 10 Zhuhang Jie, 竹行街10号; dm¥55, r from¥110; ✳@🛜) This youth hostel

has two locations. The main one is slightly off Zhongchuan Beilu and near Zhongchuan Bridge. With a charming wooden interior, rooms here have traditional furniture (some with four-poster beds) and ooze old-China charm. The lobby area is attractive, decked out with international flags and sofas draped in throws.

The alternative location (234 Yuhang Jie; 鱼行街234号) beside Taiping bridge is simpler, with doubles (¥130) with shared bathroom only.

Zhèngfú Cǎotáng
BOUTIQUE HOTEL $$

(正福草堂; ☑0512 6333 6358; 138 Mingqing Jie, 明清街138号; s/d/ste ¥480/680/1380; ✳@🛜) *The* place to stay in town. Each one unique, the 14 deluxe rooms and suites are all aesthetically set with Qing-style furniture and antiques, with four-poster beds in some. Facilities like bathrooms and floor heating are modern.

🍴 Eating

Restaurants are everywhere, but food prices here are much higher than Sūzhōu. Some local dishes to try include *méigāncài shāoròu* (梅干菜烧肉; stewed meat with dried vegetables), *yínyú chǎodàn* (银鱼炒蛋; silver fish omelette) and *zhuàngyuángtí* (状元蹄; stewed pig's leg).

ℹ Getting There & Away

You can reach Tónglǐ from either Sūzhōu or Shànghǎi, but aim for a weekday visit to escape the crowds on both the bus and in the water town.

From Sūzhōu, take a bus (¥8, 50 minutes, every 30 minutes) at the South or North Long-distance Bus Station for Tónglǐ. Electric carts (¥5) run from beside the Tónglǐ bus station to the Old Town, or you can walk it in about 15 minutes.

Regular buses leave Tónglǐ bus station for Sūzhōu (¥8), Shànghǎi (¥34) and Zhōuzhuāng (¥7, 30 minutes). There is also one bus per day to Nánjīng (¥70) and Hángzhōu (¥55). For Zhōuzhuāng, there's also the very handy public bus 263 (¥2).

Lùzhí
甪直

A lovely day trip away from Sūzhōu, the charming and petite canal town of Lùzhí is only a 25km public bus trip east of town. You can wander the streets, alleys and bridges at will, but you will need to buy a ticket (¥78) to enter the sights (8am to 5pm), such as the **Wànshèng Rice Warehouse** (万盛米行; Wànshèng Mǐháng), the **Bǎoshèng Temple**

(保圣寺; Bǎoshèng Sì) and a handful of museums, but these can be safely missed without diminishing its charm.

The **Lùzhí Cultural Park** (甪直文化园, Lùzhí Wénhuà Yuán) FREE is a huge, faux-Ming-dynasty complex is filled with tourist shops and a couple of exhibition halls. Admission is free and the landscaped gardens, ponds, pavilions and an opera stage make it a nice area to amble.

Despite its charming canalside hues, Lùzhí is not terribly well provided with decent or clean accommodation and most people return to Sūzhōu for the night. The Ramada Suzhou Luzhi is a very good choice, though not at the budget end

The restaurant trade here is built upon river clams, shrimps and crabs and boiled, soft-textured water caltrop (菱角; *língjiǎo*; like a water chestnut), which you will see served up everywhere. Finding somewhere to eat is not hard.

Getting to Lùzhí is easy: take bus 518 from Sūzhōu Train Station (¥5, one hour, first/last bus 5.30am/8pm) or from the bus stop south of the station on Pingqi Lu (平齐路) to the last stop, which is Lùzhí bus station. When you get off, take the first right along Dasheng Lu (达圣路) to the decorative arch; crossing the bridge takes you into the back of the old town in about five minutes. The bus is a local bus, so it stops at a lot of stops, but direct buses also run from the train station.

The last bus back from Lùzhí is at 7.30pm. If you want to continue to Shànghǎi from Lùzhí, buses (¥20, two hours) from the Lùzhí bus station run between 6.20am and 5pm.

Zhōuzhuāng 周庄

📋 0512 / POP 22,000

The 900-year-old water village of Zhōuzhuāng is the best-known canal town in Jiāngsū. Located some 30km southeast of Sūzhōu, it is very popular with tour groups, thanks to Chen Yifei, the late renowned Chinese painter whose works of the once-idyllic village are its claim to fame.

It does, however, have considerable old-world charm. Get up early or take an evening stroll, before the crowds arrive or when they begin to thin out, to catch some of Zhōuzhuāng's architectural highlights. The village has 14 stone bridges, dating from the Yuan dynasty through to the Qing.

HUMPBACKED BRIDGES

Lùzhí's darling humpbacked bridges are a delight. Bridges of note include the centuries-old **Jinli Bridge** (进利桥; Jìnlì Qiáo) and **Xīnglóng Bridge** (兴隆桥; Xīnglóng Qiáo). Half-hour **boat rides** (¥40) also drift up and down the canal from several points, including **Yǒng'ān Bridge** (永安桥; Yǒng'ān Qiáo).

⊙ Sights & Activities

Admission to Zhōuzhuāng is ¥100 (access is free after 8pm); make sure you get your photo digitally added to the ticket at purchase, as this entitles you to a three-day pass.

Shen's House HISTORIC BUILDING

(沈厅, Shěntīng; Nanshi Jie, 南市街; ⊙8am-7pm) Near Fú'ān Bridge, this property of the Shen clan is a lavish piece of Qing-style architecture boasting three halls and over 100 rooms. The first hall is particularly interesting, as it has a water gate and a wharf where the family moored their private boats. You can picture the compound entirely daubed in Maoist graffiti circa 1969 (note the crudely smoothed carvings above the doors).

You'll need a separate ticket for the **Zǒumǎ Lóu** (走马楼; ¥10; ⊙8am-4.30pm), where a further six courtyards and 45 rooms await (a third of the entire building).

Quánfú Temple BUDDHIST TEMPLE

(全福讲寺, Quánfú Jiǎngsì; ⊙8.30am-5.30pm) It's hard to miss this eye-catching amber-hued temple complex. The 'Full Fortune' temple was originally founded during the Song dynasty, but has been repeatedly rebuilt. The structure you see today is an incarnation from 1995, when a handful of halls and gardens were added to the mix. The grounds steal the show, with willow-lined lakes seething with plump goldfish.

Zhang's House HISTORIC BUILDING

(张厅, Zhāngtīng; ⊙8am-7pm) To the south of the Twin Bridges, this beautiful 70-room, three-hall structure was built in the Ming era and bought by the Zhang clan in early Qing times as their residence. There's an opera stage to keep the ladies entertained (they were not supposed to leave home or seek entertainment outside). Also note the chairs in the magnificently named Hall of Jade Swallows. Unmarried women could only sit on

JIĀNGSŪ ZHŌUZHUĀNG

those with a hollow seatback, symbolising that they had nobody to rely on!

Don't overlook the garden, where boats could drift straight up to the house to its own little wharf. Trek back to the road via the 'side lane', a long and narrow walkway for the servants.

Twin Bridges   BRIDGE
A total of 14 bridges grace Zhōuzhuāng, but the most beautiful and iconic are this pair of Ming dynasty bridges (双桥; Shuāngqiáo) gracing the intersection of two waterways in the heart of this canal town. Shìdé Bridge (世德桥; Shìdé Qiáo) is a humpbacked bridge while the connecting Yǒngān Bridge (永安桥; Yǒngān Qiáo) is the one with a square arch. The bridges were depicted in Chen Yifei's *Memory of Hometown*, which shot the whole town to fame from the 1980s onwards.

Boat Rides   BOATING
It's fun to go under bridge after bridge by boat. There are loads on offer, including an 80-minute boat ride (¥180 per boat; six people) from outside the international youth hostel.

🛏 Sleeping & Eating

There are a handful of guesthouses and hostels in town. Expect to pay from around ¥80 for a basic room.

With eateries at almost every corner, you won't starve, but avoid the local *āpó* tea (*āpó chá;* old woman's tea), which is extortionate.

Zhōuzhuāng
International Youth Hostel   HOSTEL $
(周庄国际青年旅舍; ☑ 0512 5720 4566; 86 Beishi Jie, 北市街86号; dm/s/d ¥45/120/140; ❋ @ ☎) Near an old opera stage, this efficient youth hostel occupies a converted

courtyard. It has tidy rooms and a clean (but dim) dorm, and offers free laundry. The hostel owner is a barista, so enjoy a perfect brew in the ground-floor cafe. When it's slow, dorms go for ¥35; singles go for ¥100 and doubles for ¥120 on weekdays.

Zhèngfú Cǎotáng   BOUTIQUE HOTEL $$
(正福草堂; ☑ 0512 5721 9333; 90 Zhongshi Jie, 中市街90号; d ¥480-880, ste ¥1080; ❋ @ ☎) This very attractive and lovingly presented seven-room boutique hotel – a converted historic residence, restored to within an inch of its life – combines antique furniture with top-notch facilities, wood flooring and a lovely courtyard.

ℹ Information

Zhōuzhuāng Visitor Centre (周庄游客中心, Zhōuzhuāng Yóukè Zhōngxīn; ☑ 0512 5721 1655; Quanfu Lu, 全福路) Near memorial archway.

ℹ Getting There & Away

From the North Long-distance Bus Station in Sūzhōu, buses (¥16, one hour) leave for Zhōuzhuāng every 40 minutes between 7am and 6.20pm. From the bus station in Zhōuzhuāng, turn left and walk till you see the bridge. Cross the bridge and you'll see the gated entrance to the village. The walk is about 20 minutes; a taxi should cost no more than ¥10.

Local bus 263 (¥2) from Tónglǐ runs to Jiāngzé (江泽) bus station, a 10-minute walk from Zhōuzhuāng. There are also buses from Jiāngzé bus station to Sūzhōu South Long-distance Bus Station (¥13, first/last 6.33am/4.10pm) and Shànghǎi Hóngqiáo bus station (¥30, first/last bus 7.30am/6.10pm). If you want to get to Hángzhōu, you will need to go back to Sūzhōu (frequent) or Tónglǐ (four a day).

It's also possible to run to Tónglǐ by fast boat (¥180, 20 minutes).

Zhèjiāng

POP 55 MILLION

Best Places to Eat

➡ Green Tea Restaurant (p271)

➡ Xiánhēng Jiǔdiàn (p289)

➡ Zǎozǐshù (p287)

➡ Gāngyágǒu (p288)

➡ Nan Fang Mi Zong (p273)

Best Places to Sleep

➡ Le Passage Mohkan Shan (p276)

➡ Four Seasons Hotel Hángzhōu (p271)

➡ Hofang International Youth Hostel (p271)

➡ Lǚxùn Native Place (p289)

Why Go?

It's Hángzhōu, the handsome capital city, that lands Zhèjiāng (浙江) on many a traveller's itinerary. Home to picture perfect landscapes of classical Chinese beauty (and just a short train ride from Shànghǎi), Hángzhōu is the obvious highlight. Yet the province offers so much more. There are water towns with spiderweb networks of canals and restored Ming and Qing dynasty merchants' homes (Wūzhèn and Nánxún), also in easy striking distance. Among the thousands of islands dotting a ragged and fragmented shoreline is the island of Pǔtuóshān, one of China's four most important Buddhist pilgrimage sites. More intrepid travellers can head west, where ancient villages retain their traditional architecture and bucolic charms. Meanwhile travellers looking for the opposite of intrepid can hole up in one of the stylish resorts nestled among the hillside bamboo groves and tea fields of naturally cool Mògànshān.

When to Go
Hángzhōu

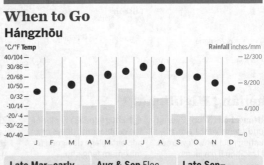

Late Mar–early May Spring sees low humidity and vegetation turning a brilliant green.

Aug & Sep Flee the simmering lowland heat to the cooler heights of Mògànshān.

Late Sep–mid-Nov Steal a march on winter and evade the sapping summer in Hángzhōu.

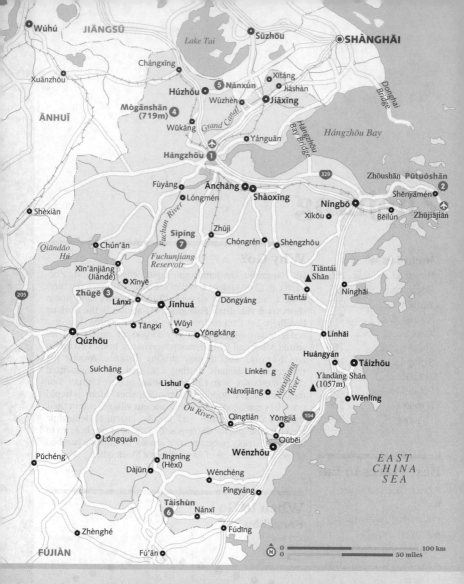

Zhèjiāng Highlights

1 Hángzhōu (p265) Cycling around scenic West Lake, a reflecting pool for willow trees and traditional pavilions.

2 Pǔtuóshān (p284) Basking in the glow of the goddess of mercy on a sacred island.

3 Zhūgě (p281) Exploring the cobblestone alleys of an ancient village designed for maximum feng shui.

4 Mògànshān (p276) Trading urban landscapes for the lush forested ones of a 19th-century hill station.

5 Nánxún (p279) Strolling alongside the waterways of

Zhèjiāng's most charming canal town.

6 Tàishùn (p280) Riding through the countryside to discover China's best collection of antique covered bridges.

7 Sìpíng (p283) Getting into the rhythms of village life with a homestay.

History

By the 7th and 8th centuries, Hángzhōu, Níngbō and Shàoxīng had emerged as three of China's most important trading centres and ports. Fertile Zhèjiāng was part of the great southern granary from which food was shipped to the depleted areas of the north via the Grand Canal (Dà Yùnhé), which commences here. Growth accelerated when the Song dynasty moved court to Hángzhōu in the 12th century after invasion from the north. Due to intense cultivation, northern Zhèjiāng has lost a lot of natural vegetation and much of it is now flat, featureless plain.

ℹ️ Getting There & Around

Zhèjiāng is well connected to the rest of the country by plane, high-speed train and bus. The provincial capital Hángzhōu is effortlessly reached by train from Shànghǎi and Sūzhōu, and serves as a useful first stop in Zhèjiāng. Hángzhōu and Pǔtuóshān are both served by nearby airports.

The province is quite small and getting around is straightforward. High-speed trains service hubs like Hángzhōu and Jīnhuá, from where you can get buses to surrounding villages, and Níngbō, the jumping-off point for sea journeys to Pǔtuóshān.

Hángzhōu 杭州

📍 0571 / POP 9 MILLION

One of China's most enduringly popular holiday spots, Hángzhōu's dreamy West Lake panoramas and fabulously green hills can easily tempt you into long sojourns. Eulogised by poets and applauded by emperors, the lake has intoxicated the Chinese imagination for aeons. Kept spotlessly clean by armies of street sweepers and litter collectors, its scenic vistas draw you into a classical Chinese watercolour of willow-lined banks, mist-covered hills and the occasional *shíkùmén* (stone-gate house) and old *lòòng* (residential lane).

Away from the tourist drawcards exists a charismatic and buzzing city in its own right, with wide pedestrian walkways to wander, an unpretentious and exciting food scene, upbeat nightlife and increasingly cosmopolitan population.

◎ Sights

★ West Lake   LAKE
(西湖, Xīhú) The very definition of classical beauty in China, West Lake is utterly mesmerising: pagoda-topped hills rise over willow-lined waters as boats drift slowly through a vignette of leisurely charm. Walk-ways, perfectly positioned benches, parks and gardens around the banks of the lake offer a thousand and one vantage points for visitors to admire the faultless scenery.

Originally a lagoon adjoining the Qiántáng River, the lake didn't come into existence until the 8th century, when the governor of Hángzhōu had the marshy expanse dredged. As time passed, the lake's splendour was gradually cultivated: gardens were planted, pagodas built, and causeways and islands were constructed from dredged silt.

Celebrated poet Su Dongpo himself had a hand in the lake's development, constructing the **Sū Causeway** (苏堤; Sūdī) during his tenure as local governor in the 11th century. It wasn't an original idea – the poet-governor Bai Juyi had already constructed the **Bái Causeway** (白堤; Báidī) some 200 years earlier. Lined by willow, plum and peach trees, today the traffic-free causeways with their half-moon bridges make for restful outings.

Lashed to the northern shores by the Bái Causeway is **Gūshān Island** (孤山岛; Gūshān Dǎo), the largest island in the lake and the location of the **Zhèjiāng Provincial Museum** (浙江省博物馆, Zhèjiāng Shěng Bówùguǎn; 25 Gushan Lu, 孤山路25号; audio guide ¥10; ⊙9am-5pm Tue-Sun) FREE and **Zhōngshān Park** (中山公园, Zhōngshān Gōngyuán). The island's buildings and gardens were once the site of Emperor Qianlong's 18th-century holiday palace and gardens. Also on the island is the intriguing **Seal Engravers Society** (西泠印社, Xīlíng Yìnshè; ⊙9am-5.30pm) FREE, though it was closed for renovations at the time of research, dedicated to the ancient art of

---

PRICE RANGES

Eating

The following price ranges refer to the cost of a main course.

$ less than ¥30

$$ ¥30–¥70

$$$ more than ¥70

Sleeping

The following price ranges refer to the cost of a double room with private bathroom or shower room.

$ less than ¥250

$$ ¥250–¥800

$$$ more than ¥800

carving the name seals (chops) that serve as personal signatures.

The northwest of the lake is fringed with the lovely **Qūyuàn Garden** (曲院风荷; Qūyuàn Fēnghé), a collection of gardens spread out over numerous islets and renowned for their fragrant spring lotus blossoms. Near Xīlíng Bridge (Xīlíng Qiáo) is **Su Xiaoxiao's Tomb** (苏小小墓; Sū Xiǎoxiǎo Mù), a 5th-century courtesan who died of grief while waiting for her lover to return. It's been said that her ghost haunts the area and the tinkle of the bells on her gown are audible at night.

The smaller island in the lake is **Xiǎoyíng Island** (小瀛洲; Xiǎoyíng Zhōu), where you can look over at **Three Pools Mirroring the Moon** (三潭印月; Sāntán Yìnyuè), three small towers in the water on the south side of the island; each has five holes that release shafts of candlelight on the night of the mid-autumn festival. From Lesser Yíngzhōu Island, you can gaze over to **Red Carp Pond** (花港观鱼; Huāgǎng Guānyú), home to a few thousand red carp.

Impromptu opera singing, ballroom dancing and other cultural activities often take place around the lake, and if the weather's fine, don't forget to earmark the east shore for sunset over West Lake photos.

It's hardly needed, but musical dancing fountains burst into action at regular intervals throughout the night and day, close to Lakeview Park.

Crowds can be a real issue here, especially on public days off when it can seem as if every holidaymaker in China is strolling around the lake. Escape the jam of people by getting out and about early in the morning – also the best time to spot the odd serene lakeside taichi session.

The best way to get around the lake is by bike or on foot.

Dragon Well Tea Village VILLAGE
(龙井问茶, Lóngjǐng Wènchá; ⊘ 8am-5.30pm) The lush, green scenery around this tea village up in the hills southwest of West Lake (p265) makes for a wonderful break from the bustle of Hangzhou. Visitors can wander through the village and up into the tea plantations themselves. During the spring, which is the best time to visit, straw-hatted workers can be seen picking the tea leaves by hand in the fields, and baskets of the fresh leaves are left out to dry in the sun back in the village.

Sunrise Terrace VIEWPOINT
(初阳台, Chūyáng Tái) Vantage point on Bǎoshí Shān.

Língyǐn Temple BUDDHIST SITE
(灵隐寺, Língyǐn Sì; Lingyin Lu, 灵隐路; grounds ¥45, temple ¥30; ⊘ 7am-5pm) Hángzhōu's most famous Buddhist temple, Língyǐn Temple was originally built in AD 326, but has been destroyed and rebuilt no fewer than 16 times. During the Five Dynasties (AD 907–960) about 3000 monks lived here. The Hall

HÁNGZHŌU IN...

One Day
Day trippers should start as early as possible to enjoy the misty air and relative solitude of the early-morning **West Lake** (p265). Stroll along the water's edge until you come to one of the **cruise boat** (p267) departure points and settle back to enjoy the ride to **Xiǎoyíng Island** (p266) and **Gushan Island.** Both deserve at least an hour to explore at a leisurely pace. Jump in a taxi to the glorious **Léifēng Pagoda** (p269), climbing to the top to see Hángzhōu's finest panorama, then cross the road to visit **Jìngcí Temple** (p267) and admire the huge seated Buddha effigy. Finish the day with a slap-up meal at **Green Tea** (p271).

Two Days
Take a morning hike into Hángzhōu's hills (p272), stopping off to see the serene **Bàopǔ Taoist Temple** (p272) along the route. Coming back into town, take some time to stroll through one of Hángzhōu's green spaces, such as **Qūyuàn Garden** (p266) or **Tàizǐwān Park** (p267) before continuing to the noisy buzz of **Qīnghéfāng Old Street** (p270) for a spot of shopping. Walk to **Zhongshan South Road Food Street** (p272) to try everything from local delicacy Beggar's Chicken or squid on sticks to fresh seafood and juice. Once full, head to **JZ Club** (p273) or **Midtown Brewery** (p273) for great drinks, music and a taste of Hángzhōu's increasingly sophisticated nightlife.

of the Four Heavenly Kings is astonishing, with its four vast guardians and an ornate cabinet housing Milefo (the future Buddha). The **Great Hall** contains a magnificent 20m-high statue of Siddhartha Gautama (Sakyamuni), sculpted from 24 blocks of camphor wood in 1956 and based on a Tang dynasty original.

Behind the giant statue is a startling montage of Guanyin surrounded by 150 small figures, including multiple *luóhàn* (arhat), in a variety of poses. The earlier hall collapsed in 1949, crushing the Buddhist statues within, so it was rebuilt and the statue conceived. The Hall of the Medicine Buddha is beyond.

The walk up to the temple skirts the flanks of **Fēilái Peak** (飞来峰, Fēilái Fēng; Peak Flying from Afar), magically transported here from India according to legend. The Buddhist carvings (all 470 of them) lining the riverbanks and hillsides and tucked away inside grottoes date from the 10th to 14th centuries. To get a close-up view of the best carvings, including the famed 'laughing' Maitreya Buddha, follow the paths along the far (east) side of the stream.

There are several other temples near Língyǐn Temple that can be explored, including Yǒngfú Temple and Tāoguāng Temple.

Behind Língyǐn Temple is the **Northern Peak** (Běi Gāofēng), which can be scaled by cable car (up/down/return ¥30/20/40). From the summit there are sweeping views across the lake and city.

Jìngcí Temple
BUDDHIST SITE

(净慈寺, Jìngcí Sì; Nanshan Lu, 南山路; ¥10; ⊙6am-5.15pm summer, 6.30am-4.45pm winter) The serene yet monastically active Chan (Zen) Jìngcí Temple was originally built in AD 954 and is now fully restored. The splendid first hall contains the massive, foreboding Heavenly Kings and an elaborate red and gold case encapsulating Milefo (the future Buddha) and Weituo (protector of the Buddhist temples and teachings). The main hall – known as the **Great Treasure Hall** – contains a vast seated effigy of Sakyamuni (Buddha).

No 1 Park
PARK

(一公园, Yī Gōngyuán; Hubin Lu, 湖滨路) Cruise boats across West Lake depart from here to Xiǎoyíng Island.

Hángzhōu Botanical Garden
GARDENS

(杭州植物园, Hángzhōu Zhíwùyuán; www.hzbg. cn; 1 Taoyuan Ling, 桃源岭1号; ¥10; ⊙7am-5pm) With huge tracts of towering bamboo,

WEST LAKE CRUISE BOATS

West Lake Cruise Boats (游船, Yóuchuán; Hubin Lu, 湖滨路; round trip adult/child ¥70/35; ⊙7am-5pm) shuttle from a number of points around West Lake (including Gushan Island, Yue Fei Temple, Red Carp Pond and No 1 Park at the south end of Hubin Lu) past the **Mid-Lake Pavilion** to **Xiǎoyíng Island**, which has a fine central pavilion and 'nine-turn' causeway. Boats depart either every 20 minutes or when full.

Your ticket allows you to take another boat on to Gushan Island or to any of the other cruise-boat docks.

If you want to contemplate the moon at a slower pace, hire one of the smaller **six or 11 person boats** (小船; *xiǎo chuán*; about one hour; small boat ¥150, large boat ¥180) rowed by a boatsperson. Look for them along the causeways. Self-rowing boats are also available, but foreign tourists are not allowed to access these without a Chinese escort.

flowering magnolias and other delightful plants and trees, these vast gardens make for lovely walks to the northwest of West Lake. Sprawling over 245 hectares, they're just as well kept as you'd expect in a city that prides itself on its beautiful environment.

Mid-Lake Pavilion
LANDMARK

(湖心亭, Húxīn Tíng) A Ming dynasty Chinese pavilion sits on this small islet in the West Lake. Many of the cruise boats pass close by it, but it's not accessible to tourists.

Bǎoshí Shān
HILL

(宝石山) Bǎoshí Hill is one of the loveliest places in Hángzhōu to take a hike (p272). Numerous well kept paths wind through the forest, taking you up steep slopes and past pagodas, West Lake viewpoints and a temple. A perfect escape from the city bustle.

Tàizǐwān Park
PARK

(太子湾公园, Tàizǐwān Gōngyuán; Nanshan Lu, 南山路) This exquisite and serene park just south of the Sū Causeway off West Lake offers quiet walks among lush woodland, ponds, lakes, rose gardens and lawns along a wooden walkway. Just take off and explore. It's heavenly in spring, with gorgeous beds of tulips and daffodils and flowering trees.

ZHĒJIĀNG HÁNGZHŌU

Hángzhōu

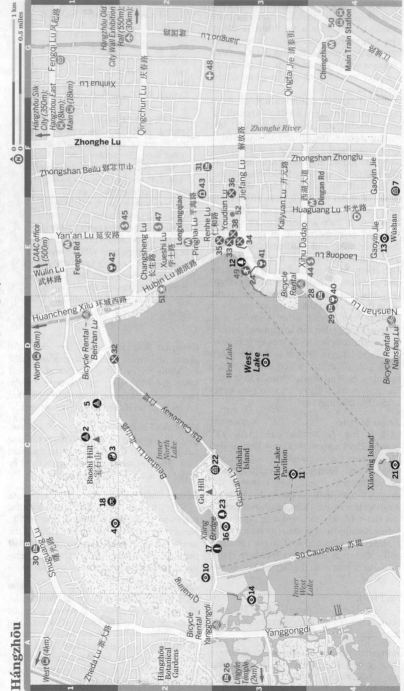

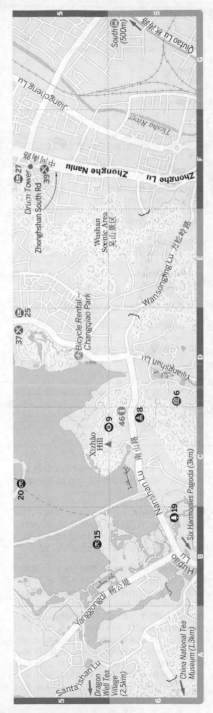

China Silk Museum
MUSEUM

(中国丝绸博物馆, Zhōngguó Sīchóu Bówùguǎn; www.chinasilkmuseum.com, 73-1 Yuhuangshan Lu, 玉皇山路73-1号; ⏱9am-5pm Tue-Sun, noon-5pm Mon) **FREE** This vast museum is devoted to all things silk, covering fashion, craftsmanship and the historic Silk Road in great depth. Extensive galleries showcase the evolution of the *qípáo* (Chinese dress) from the 1920s onward, as well as some fabulously ornate European gowns from the 1600s to the 1800s.

Húqìngyú Táng Chinese Medicine Museum
MUSEUM

(中药博物馆, Zhōngyào Bówùguǎn; 95 Dajing Xiang, 大井巷95号; ¥10; ⏱8.30am-5pm) The Huqing Yutang Chinese Medicine Museum has an actual dispensary and clinic adjoined to the museum. Originally established by the Qing dynasty merchant Hu Xueyan in 1874, the medicine shop and factory retain the typical style of the period. The museum itself is housed in a lovely, musty old building with a bright courtyard full of TCM plants.

Displays range from the fascinating, such as an ancient instruction book for medicine-making and old medical implements, to the surreal – including a giant rhino model.

Léifēng Pagoda
PAGODA

(雷峰塔, Léifēng Tǎ; Nanshan Lu, 南山路; adult/child ¥40/20; ⏱8am-8.30pm Mar-Nov, to 5.30pm Dec-Feb) Topped with a golden spire, the eye-catching Léifēng Pagoda can be climbed for fine views of the lake. The original pagoda, built in AD 977, collapsed in 1924. During renovations in 2001, Buddhist scriptures written on silk were discovered in the foundations, along with other treasures. There's now an elevator and escalator to help visitors reach the top.

Six Harmonies Pagoda
PAGODA

(六和塔, Liùhé Tǎ; 16 Zhijiang Lu, 之江路16号; grounds ¥20, grounds & pagoda ¥30; ⏱6am-6.30pm) Three kilometres southwest of West Lake, an enormous rail and road bridge spans the Qiántáng River. Close by rears up the 60m-high octagonal Six Harmonies Pagoda, first built in AD 960. The stout pagoda also served as a lighthouse, and was said to possess magical powers to halt the 6.5m-high tidal bore that thunders up Qiántáng River. You can climb the tight stairs of the pagoda, while behind stretches a charming walk through terraces dotted with sculptures, bells (¥10 buys you six chimes and a lucky bracelet), shrines and inscriptions.

ZHĒJIĀNG HÁNGZHŌU

Hángzhōu

Qīnghéfāng Old Street   STREET
(清河坊历史文化街, Qīnghéfāng Lìshǐ Wénhuà
Jiē; Hefang Jie, 河坊街) At the south end of
Zhongshan Zhonglu is this touristy, crowded
and bustling pedestrian street, with makeshift puppet theatres, teahouses and gift and
curio stalls, selling everything from stone
teapots to boxes of *lóngxūtáng* (龙须糖;
dragon whiskers sweets), ginseng and silk.
It's also home to several traditional medicine shops, including the Húqìngyú Táng
Chinese Medicine Museum (p269), which is
an actual dispensary and clinic.

Big Buddha Temple   BUDDHIST TEMPLE
(大佛寺, Dàfó Sì) The remains of this historic
temple on the western slope of Bǎoshí Shān
north of West Lake only run to a weather-
beaten and dilapidated vast stone head of a
Buddha; all the temple halls have vanished.
It's easy to miss, unless you're hunting for it,
as it lies behind a residential building and
can only be seen from the top of the steps
that lie along the hill's slope.

Bǎochù Pagoda   BUDDHIST SITE
(保俶塔, Bǎochù Tǎ) Visiting this charming
pagoda overlooking West Lake makes for a
lovely walk in the hills north of the lake.

Mausoleum of General Yue Fei   TEMPLE
(岳庙, Yuè Fēi Mù; Beishan Lu; ¥25; ⊙ 7.30am-
5.30pm) Commander of the southern Song
armies, General Yue Fei (1103–42) led successful battles against northern Jurchen
invaders in the 12th century. Despite initial
successes, he was recalled to the Song court,
where he was executed, along with his son,
after being deceived by the treacherous
prime minister Qin Hui. In 1163, Song emperor Gao Zong exonerated Yue Fei and had
his corpse reburied here.

🛏 Sleeping

Book well ahead in the summer months, at weekends and during the busy holiday periods. Room prices at hostels and some hotels get a significant weekend hike.

Hofang International Youth Hostel HOSTEL **$**
(荷方国际青年旅社, Héfāng Guójì Qīngnián Lǚshè; ☑ 0571 8706 3299; 67 Dajing Xiang, 大井巷67号; dm ¥55, d/d ¥188/288; ※ @ ☎) Pleasantly tucked away from the noise down a historic alley off Qīnghéfāng Old Street, this hostel has an excellent location and exudes a pleasant and calm ambience, with attractive rooms, the cheapest of which come with tatami. Note that prices go up by between ¥30 and ¥60 on weekends and holidays. The adjoining hostel cafe is a cosy place to check emails with a coffee.

In Lake Youth Hostel HOSTEL **$**
(柳湖小筑青年旅社, Liǔhú Xiǎozhù Qīngnián Lǚshè; ☑ 0571 8682 6700; 5 Luyang Lu, 柳杨路5号; dm ¥70, tw/d ¥378/408; ※ ☎) Well located a few steps from West Lake off Nanshan Lu, this attractive choice is all Mediterranean arches and ochre shades, with a lovely plant-filled interior courtyard. Rooms have wood flooring and tall radiators, six-person dorms (all with shower) are clean and there's a roof terrace for barbecues, a downstairs cafe and bar, and welcoming staff. Prices rise at weekends.

Mingtown Youth Hostel HOSTEL **$**
(明堂杭州国际青年旅社, Míngtáng Hángzhōu Guójì Qīngnián Lǚshè; ☑ 0571 8791 8948; 101-11 Nanshan Lu, 南山路101-11号; dm/s/d ¥65/180/210; ※ ☎) With its pleasant lakeside location, this friendly and highly popular hostel is often booked out, so reserve well ahead. It has a relaxing cafe-bar, offers ticket booking, internet access, self-service kitchen and laundry and has an attractive outdoor area.

West Lake 7
Service Apartments APARTMENT **$$**
(西湖柒号酒店公寓, Xīhú Qīhào Jiǔdiàn Gōngyù; 1 Yuewang Lu, 岳王路1号; d ¥320) These large and comfortable serviced apartments offer excellent value for money, with facilities including a washing machine, kitchen and surprisingly speedy wi-fi. The location is not bad, set right next to the Wushan Lu Night Market (p273), and just a few blocks' walk from the West Lake.

Crystal Orange Hotel HOTEL **$$**
(桔子水晶酒店, Júzi Shuǐjīng Jiǔdiàn; ☑ 0571 2887 8988; www.orangehotel.com; 122 Qingbo Jie, 清波街122号; d from ¥408; ※ @ ☎) Sleek chain hotel with a modern and stylish interior. Bold Warhol prints decorate the high lobby walls, and there's a glass lift to take you up the four floors. Sadly no views of West Lake from the neat rooms (some of which don't have windows), but this is reflected in the reasonable room rates.

Tea Boutique Hotel HOTEL **$$$**
(杭州天伦精品酒店, Hángzhōu Tiānlún Jīngpǐn Jiǔdiàn; ☑ 0571 8799 9888; www.teaboutiquehotel.com, 124 Shuguang Lu, 曙光路124号; d incl breakfast ¥898; ⊜ ※ @ ☎) The simple but effective wood-sculpted foyer area with its sinuously shaped reception is a perfect introduction to the lovely accommodation at this hotel. A Japanese-minimalist mood holds sway with celadon tea sets and tall, elegant stems of greenery artfully arranged. Muted colours and natural materials in the bedrooms create a zen atmosphere.

Four Seasons Hotel Hángzhōu HOTEL **$$$**
(杭州西子湖四季酒店, Hángzhōu Xīzihú Sìjì Jiǔdiàn; ☑ 0571 8829 8888; www.fourseasons.com/hangzhou; 5 Lingyin Lu, 灵隐路5号; d ¥3500, ste from ¥6500; ⊜ ※ @ ☎ ☎) More of a resort than a hotel, the fabulous 78-room, two-pool Four Seasons enjoys a seductive position in lush grounds next to West Lake. Low rise buildings and three private villas echo traditional China, a sensation amplified by the osmanthus trees, ornamental shrubs, ponds and general tranquillity.

🍴 Eating

Hángzhōu has endless zones dedicated to the art of feasting – try **Gaoyin Jie**, a long sprawl of neon-lit restaurants or Zhongshan South Road Food Street (p272). Many of the smarter restaurants around the West Lake itself also offer good-value and interesting meals.

★ Green Tea Restaurant HANGZHOU **$**
(绿茶, Lǜchá; 250 Jiefang Lu, 解放路250号; mains from ¥20; ⊙ 10.30am-11pm; M Longxiangqiao) Often packed, this excellent Hángzhōu restaurant has superb food. With a bare-brick finish and rows of clay teapots, the low-lit dining room is sleek and trendy. Prices are surprisingly low, with the signature fish-head dish the most expensive thing on the menu at ¥48. Eggplant claypot and a Cantonese bread and ice-cream dessert are also sensational.

Ordering can get complicated: scan the QR code on the table and select dishes direct through the menu that will load up on your phone. If you're having trouble, staff are happy to help.

★ Grandma's Home
HANGZHOU **$**

(外婆家, Wàipójiā; 3 Hubin Lu, 湖滨路3号; mains ¥15-35; ⊙lunch & dinner; Ⓜ Longxiangqiao) There's no end to the hype about this restaurant, which now has branches across the whole country, with eager diners constantly clustering outside. It almost lives up to its reputation, with low prices and generous portions but dishes do vary enormously in quality. The braised pork and tea-scented chicken are both good bets to get a taste of classic Hangzhou flavours.

Take a paper ticket when you arrive and be prepared to wait a long time for a table.

Zhongshan South Road Food Street
MARKET **$**

(中山南路美食街, Zhōngshān Nánlù Diàn; Zhongshan Nanlu, 中山南路美食街; ⊙5.30pm-late) Hángzhōu is spoilt for choice when it comes to foodie streets, and this stretch of Zhongshan Nanlu (starting at the Drum Tower) is an absolute delight. Casual sit-down restaurants line the road, and stalls that run along the middle of the road sell everything from fresh seafood and deep-fried insects to Beggar's Chicken and the absolute stinkiest of stinky tofu.

Innocent Age Book Bar
CHINESE **$**

(纯真年代书吧, Chúnzhēn Niándài Shūbā; 8 Baochuta Qian Lu, 保俶塔前山路8号; dishes from ¥22; ⊙9.30am-midnight) You couldn't ask for a prettier setting than this cafe, set just down the slope of Bǎoshí Shān from Bǎochù Pagoda. Indoors, there's a quiet reading-room atmosphere and the shelves are full of books. Outside is a glorious terrace overlooking the West Lake. Snacks, cakes, tea and coffee are available or for good-value fuel before you continue your walk, go for a huge and flavoursome bowl of Hángzhōu beef noodles.

Nan Fang Mi Zong
DUMPLINGS **$**

(Youdian Lu, 邮电路; per bun ¥2; ⊙6.30am-6.30pm) Who would have thought the humble *bāozi* could taste so good? The fluffy steamed buns served at this small stall near the Rénhé Hotel building are simply huge, and come with either pork or a sweet bean filling. The pork ones are sensational, with top-quality meat and a rich gravy. Queues stretch right down the street in the morning.

Yīhé Zàngxiāng Beef Noodles
NOODLES **$**

(伊禾藏香牛肉面, Yīhé Zàngxiāng Niúròu Miàn; 238 Yan'an Lu, 延安路238号; noodles from ¥19; ⊙6.30am-11.30pm) A superb lunch stop, where the restaurant's namesake – beef noodles – is a must-order. These are done Lanzhou-style (read: magnificently fiery) and the meat is served separately so you can drop it in yourself. Long spacious tables looking out onto bustling Yan'an Lu make this a great stop for families or solo diners, and service is efficient and friendly.

WEST LAKE HILLS WALK

For a manageable and breezy trek into the forested hills above West Lake, walk up a lane called Qixialing, immediately west of the Yuè Fēi Temple. The road initially runs past the temple's west wall to enter the shade of towering trees, with stone steps leading you up. At **Zǐyún Cave** (Purple Cloud Cave, 紫云洞) the hill levels out and the road forks; take the right-hand fork towards the Bàopǔ Taoist Temple, 1km further, and the Bǎochù Pagoda. At the top of the steps, turn left and, passing the **Sunrise Terrace** (p266), again bear left. Down the steps, look out for the tiled roofs and yellow walls of the charming **Bàopǔ Taoist Temple** (抱朴道院, Bàopǔ Dàoyuàn; ¥5; ⊙6am-5pm) to your right; head right along a path to reach it. Come out of the temple's back entrance and turn left towards the Bǎochù Pagoda and, after hitting a confluence of three paths, take the middle track towards and up **Toad Hill** (蛤蟆峰; Hámá Fēng), which affords supreme views over the lake, before squeezing through a gap between huge boulders to meet the **Bǎochù Pagoda** (p270) rising ahead. Restored many times, the seven-storey grey brick pagoda was last rebuilt in 1933, although its spire tumbled off in the 1990s. Continue on down and pass through a **páilou** (牌楼) – or decorative arch – erected during the Republic (with some of its characters scratched off) to a series of stone-carved **Ming-dynasty effigies**, all of which were vandalised in the tumultuous 1960s, save two effigies on the right. Turn left here and walk a short distance to some steps heading downhill to your right past the remarkable weathered remains of a colossal stone **Buddha** by the cliff-face (with square niches cut in him) – all that remains of the **Big Buddha Temple** (p270). Continue on down to Beishan Lu.

Northwest Family Restaurant   XINJIANG $
(西北人家, Xīběi Rénjiā; 22 Youdian Lu, 上城区
邮电路9号; mains ¥35-45; ⊙9.30am-11.30pm)
A busy neighbourhood restaurant serving
typical Uighur fare with rich, hearty gravies,
lots of lamb and bread. The range of fresh
fish and traditional soups is also excellent.
Quiet during the day, this place does a roaring trade at night, with a barbecue of meat
skewers outside, available to have at your
table or takeaway.

Xièxie Tea & Coffee   CAFE ⚲
(谢谢咖啡, Xièxie Kāfēi; 180 Nanshan Lu, 南山
路180号; mains ¥47-67; ⊙9am-midnight; 🛜)
A beautifully airy three-storey cafe, Xièxie
looks out onto the treetops of the park over
the road and is a great spot to unwind over
a cup of tea or coffee. A young crowd armed
with phones, laptops and tablets sprawl on
comfy sofas that are never more than arm's
reach from a plug socket.

Carbon   EUROPEAN
(10 Beishan Lu, 北山路10号; mains ¥130-250;
⊙11am-11pm) The crowd is super-stylish, the
lakeside location is outstanding, and the
chandeliers, gorgeous botanical arrangements and soft-wood decor make Carbon a
fine place for an evening meal. The food itself
doesn't quite live up to the lovely setting, with
a menu that's trying to please everyone and
zigzags between cuisines (think baked snails
to flammekueche via pineapple fried rice).

Follow up your meal with a drink in the
balmy night air on the outdoor terrace if the
mood takes you.

🍸 Drinking & Nightlife

⭐ **JZ Club**   CLUB
(黄楼, Huáng Lóu; ☑0571 8702 8298; www.jzclub.
cc; 6 Liuying Lu, by 266 Nanshan Lu, 柳营路6号;
⊙7pm-2.30am) The folk that brought you JZ
Club in Shànghǎi have the live jazz scene
sewn up in Hángzhōu with this neat three-
floor venue in a historic building near West
Lake. There are three live jazz sets nightly, with music kicking off at 9.15pm (until
12.30am). There's no admission charge, but
you'll need to reserve a seat on Fridays and
Saturdays. Smokers get to go upstairs.

Midtown Brewery   PUB
(1st fl, Shangri-La Hotel, 6 Changshou Lu, 长寿路6
号杭州城中香格里拉大酒店1楼) The craft-
beer craze has certainly hit Hángzhōu and
the standout place to sample some top-notch
craft beers is Midtown Brewery. Housed in
the Shangri-La hotel, the beers are brewed

on-site and are genuinely outstanding.
If you need convincing, order the tasting
paddle (¥99) of seven samplers, including
pale ale, porter and stout. Service is smooth
and the setting smart and contemporary.

Eudora Station   BAR
(亿多瑞站, Yìduōruìzhàn; 101-107 Nanshan Lu, 南
山路101-107号; ⊙9.30am-2am) A fab location
by West Lake, roof terrace, outside seating
and great happy-hour deals conspire to make
this welcoming watering hole a solid choice.
There's sports TV, live music, a good range of
imported beers, and barbecues fire up on the
roof terrace in the warmer months.

🛍 Shopping

Hángzhōu Silk City   SILK
(丝绸城, Sīchóu Shìchǎng; 253 Xinhua Lu, 新华路
253号; ⊙8am-5pm) Hángzhōu is famous for
its silks and there are certainly bargains to
be found in this seven-storey market. You'll
have to work hard to get them, though. Head
straight for the 5th and 6th floors (lower levels just sell regular clothes) to find scarves,
slinky nightwear, dresses, qípáo (traditional
Chinese sheath dresses) and other silk items.
If you haggle persistently, vendors will usually let you bargain them down by around 30%.

Wushan Lu Night Market   MARKET
(吴山路夜市, Wúshān Lù Yèshì; Huixing Lu, 惠兴
路; ⊙7-10.30pm) Wushan Lu Night Market
doesn't have too much to offer by way of
interesting souvenirs, but it's still a pleasant
place to stroll for half an hour or so. Stalls
sell knock-off cosmetics and bags, cheap
clothes, shoes, plastic jewellery and other
knick-knacks to an excited crowd of mostly teenagers. Get the gloves off and haggle
hard if something catches your eye.

Better still, spend your cash at the street-
food stalls that line Renhe Lu, where you
can pick up skewers of spicy beancurd, seasoned sweetcorn, noodles, fried dumplings
and a vast range of other snacks.

The market is located on Huixing Lu
(惠兴路), between Youdian Lu (邮电路) and
Renhe Lu (仁和路).

ℹ Information

DANGERS & ANNOYANCES
Hángzhōu is overall a safe, clean city. It's wise to
take extra care on public holidays when crowds
can be overwhelming.

GAY & LESBIAN TRAVELLERS
Check out local listings mag More Hangzhou
(http://morehangzhou.com) for more info.

QIÁNTÁNG RIVER TIDAL BORE

An often spectacular natural phenomenon occurs every month on Hángzhōu's Qiántáng River (钱塘江), when the highest tides of the lunar cycle dispatch a wall of water – sometimes almost 9m tall – thundering along the narrow mouth of the river from Hángzhōu Bay, at up to 40km per hour. Occasionally sweeping astonished sightseers away and luring bands of intrepid surfers, this awesome tidal bore (钱塘江潮; *qiántáng jiāngcháo*) is the world's largest and can be viewed from the riverbank in Hángzhōu, but one of the best places to witness the action is on the north side of the river at **Yánguān** (盐官), a delightful ancient town about 38km northeast of Hángzhōu.

The most popular viewing time is during the International Qiántáng River Tide Observing Festival, on the 18th day of the eighth month of the lunar calendar (the same day as the mid-autumn festival), which usually falls in September or October. You can, however, see it throughout the year when the highest tide occurs at the beginning and middle of each lunar month; access to the park in Yánguān for viewing the tide is ¥25. The Hángzhōu Tourist Information Centre can give you upcoming tide times. To make it a day trip, a through ticket (¥100) is available in Yánguān to explore the charming historic temples and buildings of the town.

Take a train (¥92, 35 minutes) fom Hángzhōu East to Hǎiníng (海宁) and change to bus 109 (¥10, 25 minutes) to Yánguān.

ZHÈJIĀNG HÁNGZHŌU

INTERNET ACCESS
Twenty-four-hour internet cafes are in abundance around the main train station (typically ¥8 per hour); look for the neon signs '网吧'.

MEDICAL SERVICES
Zhèjiāng University First Affiliated Hospital (浙江大学医学院附属第一医院, Zhèjiāng Dàxué Yīxuéyuàn Fùshǔ Dìyī Yīyuàn; ☑ 0571 8723 6114; 79 Qingchun Lu, 庆春路79号; ☺8am-4pm)

MONEY
Bank of China – Yanan Lu (中国银行, Zhōngguó Yínháng; 320 Yanan Lu, 延安路320号; ☺9am-5pm) A useful central branch with currency exchange.

Bank of China – Laodong Lu (中国银行, Zhōngguó Yínháng; 177 Laodong Lu, 劳动路177; ☺9am-5pm) Offers currency exchange plus 24-hour ATM.

Industrial & Commercial Bank of China (ICBC, 工商银行, Gōngshāng Yínháng; 300 Yan'an Lu, 延安路300号) Has a 24-hour ATM.

POST
China Post (中国邮政, Zhōngguó Yóuzhèng; 284 Fengqi Lu, 凤起路284號; ☺9am-5.30pm) Western Union, ATM and currency exchange service offered here.

PUBLIC SECURITY BUREAU
Public Security Bureau (PSB, 公安局, Gōng'ānjú; ☑ 0571 8728 0600; 35 Huaguang Lu; ☺8.30am-noon & 2-5pm Mon-Fri) Can extend visas.

TOURIST INFORMATION
Asking at, or phoning up, your hostel or hotel for info can be very handy.

Hángzhōu Tourist Information Centre (杭州旅游咨询服务中心, Hángzhōu Lǚyóu Zīxún Fúwù Zhōngxīn; ☑ 0571 8797 8123; Léifēng Pagoda, Nanshan Lu, 雷峰塔 南山路; ☺8am-5pm) Provides basic travel info, free maps and tours. Other branches include Hángzhōu train station and 10 Huaguang Lu, just off Qīnghéfáng Old Street.

Tourist Complaint Hotline (☑ 0571 8796 9691) Can assist visitors with problems or issues during their stay. No English is spoken.

Travellers Infoline (☑ 0571 96123; ☺6.30am to 9pm) Helpful 24-hour information, with English service from 6.30am to 9pm.

ⓘ Getting There & Away

AIR
Hángzhōu Airport has flights to all major Chinese cities (bar Shànghǎi) and international connections to Hong Kong, Macau, Tokyo, Singapore and other destinations. Several daily flights connect to Běijīng and Guǎngzhōu.

Most hotels will also book flights, generally with a ¥20 to ¥30 service charge. The **Civil Aviation Administration of China** (CAAC, 中国民航, Zhōngguó Mínháng; ☑ 0571 8666 8666; 390 Tiyuchang Lu; ☺7.30am-8pm) office is in the north of town.

BUS
All four bus stations are outside the city centre; tickets can be conveniently bought for all stations from the **bus ticket office** (长途汽车售票处, Chángtú Qìchē Shòupiàochù; Chengzhan Lu, 城站路; ☺6.30am-5pm) right off the exit from Hángzhōu's main train station.

Buses leave Shànghǎi's South Station frequently for Hángzhōu's various bus stations (¥68, 2½ hours). Buses to Hángzhōu also run every 30 minutes between 10am and 9pm from Shànghǎi's Hóngqiáo airport (¥100, two hours). Regular buses also run to Hángzhōu from Shànghǎi's Pǔdōng International Airport (¥110, three hours).

Buses from the huge **Main Bus Station** (客运中心站, Kèyùn Zhōngxīn; ☑ 0571 8765 0678; Jiubao Zhijie, 九堡直街) at Jiǔbǎo, in the far northeast of Hángzhōu (and linked to the centre of town by metro, a taxi will cost around ¥65):

Níngbō ¥62, two hours, frequent

Wūzhèn ¥27 to ¥30, one hour, 16 daily

Xīn'ānjiāng ¥35 ¥42 two hours, eight daily

Buses from the **North Bus Station** (汽车北站, Qìchē Běizhàn; 766 Moganshan Lu):

Níngbō ¥65, two hours, frequent

Shànghǎi ¥70, 2½ hours, frequent

Sūzhōu ¥73, two hours, frequent

Tónglǐ ¥64, two hours, frequent

Buses from the **West Bus Station** (汽车西站, Qìchē Xīzhàn; 357 Tianmushan Lu):

Wùyuán ¥140, 4½ hours, 9.20am and 1.40pm

Xīnyè ¥61, 2½ hours, 8.20am and 1.50pm

TRAIN

The easiest way to travel to Hángzhōu from Shànghǎi Hóngqiáo Train Station is on the high-speed G- and D-class trains to **Hángzhōu East Train Station** (杭州东站, Hángzhōu Dōngzhàn; Dongning Lu, 东宁路). For Běijīng, the overnight Z10 (soft sleeper ¥537) departs **Hángzhōu Main Train Station** (杭州火车站, Hángzhōu Huǒchēzhàn; ☑ 0571 8762 2362; Chengzhan Lu, 城站路) at 6.05pm, arriving at 7.40am, and the handy T32 (hard/soft sleeper ¥351/¥537) departs at 6.20pm, arriving at 10.21am. Most G class trains to Běijīng leave from Hángzhōu East Train Station.

G-class trains running from the huge new Hángzhōu East Train Station, linked to the centre of town by metro, include:

Běijīng South 2nd/1st class ¥538/907, six hours, frequent

Shànghǎi Hóngqiáo Train Station 2nd/1st class ¥73/117, one hour, frequent

Shàoxīng North 2nd/1st class ¥20/33, 20 minutes, frequent

Sūzhōu 2nd/1st class ¥111/178, 1½ hours, three daily

Xiàmén North Train Station 2nd/1st class ¥281/357, seven hours, one daily

Wēnzhōu South Train Station 2nd/1st class ¥153/218, three hours, frequent

Daily G-class high-speed trains from Hángzhōu Main Train Station:

Běijīng South Train Station 2nd/1st class ¥629/1056, 6½ hours, two daily

Nánjīng South Train Station 2nd/1st class ¥117/198, 2½ hours, five daily

Shànghǎi Hóngqiáo Train Station 2nd/1st class ¥78/124, 55 minutes, frequent from 6.10am until 8.26pm

Sūzhōu 2nd/1st class ¥118 to ¥184, 1½ hours, two daily

The daily Beijing sleeper trains go from **Hángzhōu Main Train Station** (杭州火车站, Hángzhōu Huǒchēzhàn; ☑ 0571 8762 2362; Chengzhan Lu, 城站路) at 5.17pm, 6.20pm and 7.24pm, soft/hard sleeper ¥583/351, 16.30 hours.

A handy **train ticket office** (火车票售票处, Huǒchēpiào Shòupiàochù; 147 Huansha Lu, 浣纱路147号; ⊙ 8am-5pm) is north of Jiefang Lu, just east of West Lake. Other offices are at 72 Baochu Lu (near turning with Shengfu Lu) and 149 Tiyuchang Lu. Train tickets are also available at certain China Post branches including 10 Desheng Lu and 60 Fengqi Lu.

ℹ Getting Around

TO/FROM THE AIRPORT

Hángzhōu's airport is 30km from the city centre; taxi drivers ask around ¥100 to ¥130 for the trip. Shuttle buses (¥20, one hour) run every 15 minutes between 5am and 9pm from the CAAC office (also stopping at the train station).

BICYCLE

The best way to rent a bike is to use the **Hángzhōu Bike Hire Scheme** (☑ 0571 8533 1122; www.hzzxc.com.cn; deposit ¥200, credit ¥100; ⊙ 6.30am-9pm Apr-Oct, 6am-9pm Nov-Mar). Stations (2700 in total) are dotted in large numbers around the city, in what is one of the world's largest networks. Apply at one of the booths at numerous bike stations near West Lake; you will need your passport as ID. Fill in a form and you will receive a swipe card, then swipe the pad at one of the docking stations till you get a steady green light, free a bike and Bob's your uncle.

Return bikes to any other station (ensure the bike is properly docked before leaving it). The first hour on each bike is free, so if you switch bikes within the hour, the rides are free. The second hour on the same bike is ¥1, the third is ¥2 and after that it's ¥3 per hour. Your deposit and unused credit are refunded to you when you return your swipe card (check when it should be returned as this can vary). Note you cannot return bikes outside booth operating hours as the swipe units deactivate (you will be charged a whole night's rental).

BUS

Hángzhōu has a clean, efficient bus system and getting around is easy (but roads are increasingly gridlocked). 'Y' buses are tourist buses; 'K' is simply an abbreviation of 'kōngtiáo' (air-con).

Tickets are ¥2 to ¥5. The following are popular bus routes:

Bus K7 Usefully connects the Main Train Station to the western side of West Lake and Língyǐn Temple.

Tourist bus Y2 Goes from the Main Train Station, along Beishan Lu and up to Língyǐn Temple.

Buses 15 and K15 Connects the North Bus Station to the northwest area of West Lake.

Bus 27 Runs from Beishan Lu to Lóngjǐng Tea Village.

Buses K4 and 334 Run from downtown to the Six Harmonies Pagoda.

METRO

Hángzhōu's metro line 1 (tickets ¥2 to ¥8; first/last train 6.06am/11.32pm) runs from the southeast of town, through the Main Train Station, along the east side of West Lake and on to the East Train Station, the Main Bus Station and the northeast of town. It's not very useful for sightseeing around town. Line 2 runs south from Chaoyang to Qianjiang Road and Line 4 runs from Pengbu to Jinjiang, with a south extension to Puyan expected to open in 2017. Other lines are planned for the future.

TAXI

Metered Hyundai taxis are ubiquitous and start at ¥11; figure on around ¥20 to ¥25 from the main train station (queues can be horrendous) to Hubin Lu.

Mògànshān 莫干山

📞 0572

Sixty kilometres northeast of Hángzhōu, refreshingly cool in summer and sometimes smothered in spectral fog, Mògànshān (¥80) is famed for its scenic vistas, forested views, towering bamboo and stone villa architecture. It was developed as a hilltop resort by 19th-century Europeans living in Shànghǎi. Largely abandoned during the second half of the last century, it is now seeing a new buzz of activity (and construction), reclaiming its reputation as a weekend bolt-hole for expat *tàitai* (wives) fleeing the simmering lowland heat.

◉ Sights

The best way to enjoy Mògànshān is just to wander the winding forest paths, taking in some of the architecture en route. There's Shànghǎi gangster **Du Yuesheng's old villa** (杜月笙别墅, Dù Yuèshēng biéshù) – now serving as a hotel; the villa where Chiang Kaishek spent his honeymoon; a couple of churches (375 Moganshan and 419 Moganshan); and many other villas linked (some-

times tenuously) with the rich and famous, including a **house** (毛主席下榻处, Máo Zhǔxí Xiàtàchù; 126 Moganshan, 莫干山126号) FREE where Chairman Mao once napped.

To preserve the mood you will have to work hard to ignore the often slapdash new constructions. Genuine, older villas are identifiable by their irregularly shaped stones.

🏃 Activities

Besides the attractions on the summit, you can strike out on longer hikes, including the five-hour loop, known colloquially as the 'temple hike', to an old, deserted temple; pick up a map at Mògànshān Lodge. Containing Tǎ Mountain (塔山; Tǎ Shān) in the northwest, the Dàkēng Scenic Area (大坑景区; Dàkēng Jǐngqū) is great for rambling.

Many accommodations also offer excursions, such as picking tea leaves in the fields nearby.

🛏 Sleeping

Mògànshān is full of hotels of varying quality, many housed in former villas; room prices nearly double at weekends and some places require a two-night-minimum booking. If you come in low season (eg early spring) you can expect good rates. Many hotels either shut up shop or close for renovation over the winter.

Mògànshān Fleecity Resort GUESTHOUSE **$$**
(莫干山离城度假别墅, Mògànshān Líchéng Dùjià Biéshù; 📞 0188 5722 9640; www.moganshan395.com; Láolǐngcūn Sānjiúwù, 劳岭村三九坞; d weekday/weekend from ¥599/799; P ⊗ ❄ 🛈) 🍃 Fleecity is located halfway up the mountain (meaning you can stay here and dodge the entry fee), surrounded by bamboo (though construction sites inch ever nearer). There are only eight rooms; some have balconies while some have Japanese-style tatami floors. The best part is the food: dinners (¥80 per person) feature local produce, like wild mushrooms and bamboo, prepared home-style.

★ Le Passage
Mohkan Shan BOUTIQUE HOTEL **$$$**
(莫干山里法国山居, Mògànshānlǐ Fǎguóshānjū; 📞 0572 805 2958; www.lepassagemoganshan.com; Xiānrénkēng Tea Plantation, Zǐlíng Village, 紫岭村仙人坑茶厂; weekday/weekend from ¥2680/3180; ⊖ 🛈 ❄) 🍃 Le Passage evokes the glamorous cosmopolitan history of Mògànshān perhaps better than the actually historic villas do. Ensconced within an organic tea plantation, the main house and five bungalows were designed by owners

Christophe Peres and Pauline Lee to look like a classic colonial-era hill station, with high ceilings, a wood-burning stove in the salon and a spring-fed swimming pool.

Mògànshān House 23   HOTEL $$$
(莫干山杭疗23号, Mògànshan Hángliáo 23 Hào; ☑ 0572 803 3822; www.moganshanhouse23. com; 23 Moganshan, 莫干山23号; d & tw weekday/weekend from ¥900/1200; ❀❉❞) This restored, 100 year-old villa on top of the mountain has heaps of period charm. It's also kid-friendly with a family room, baby chairs and swings in the garden. With only six rooms, book well in advance, especially for weekend stays (when it's a minimum two-night stay). Staff speak English.

✖ Eating

Yinshan Jie (荫山街), the main strip on the summit, has a few restaurants, but most visitors eat in their lodgings.

Mògànshān Lodge   INTERNATIONAL $$
(马克的咖啡厅, Mǎkè de Kāfēitīng; ☑ 0572 803 3011; www.moganshanlodge.com; Songliang Shanzhuang, off Yinshan Jie, 松粮山庄; ⊙ 9am-9pm; ❀❀❞) Grab a book from the shelves (there are many in English) and curl up in one of the vintage armchairs here with a pot of tea. Should you decide to stretch your legs, Mògànshān Lodge is your best source for advice and local maps. The kitchen cooks up roast dinners (by reservation only), full English breakfasts and sandwiches.

❶ Information

Be warned that the sole ATM on the mountain, on Yinshan Jie, often has no cash.
China Post (中国邮政, Zhōngguó Yóuzhèng; 40 Moganshan, 莫干山40号; ⊙ 8.30-11am & 1-4pm)

❶ Getting There & Away

The nearest train station is Déqīng (德清), a 15-minute ride (¥11 to ¥18) on one of the frequent high-speed trains from Hángzhōu East. The last return train is at 10.06pm. There are two trains daily from Shànghǎi Hóngqiáo (¥94, 1¾ hours, 7.28am and 6.05pm).

You can also go by bus from Hángzhōu's main bus station to Déqīng (¥18, one hour, six daily).

Now comes the expensive part: getting a taxi from the bus or train station to Mògànshān, which will cost ¥120 to ¥150. Most lodgings can arrange transport from Déqīng, Hángzhōu or even Shànghǎi – at a mark-up of course.

Don't take a *sānlúnchē* (three-wheel scooter) as they will drop you at the foot of the mountain.

Wūzhèn   乌镇

☑ 0573 / POP 59,000

Like many of the other famous water towns, Wūzhèn was part of the Grand Canal and prospered from trade and silk production. It's a major tourist attraction, and with its crowds and rows of souvenir shops its easy to write off Wūzhèn as inauthentic. But then you turn a corner and get a view of, say, an ancient stone bridge curving over a canal or a row of weathered Qīng dynasty wooden homes, and realise: this place really is beautiful. It's also easily explored, with good transit links and plenty of English on the ground.

◉ Sights

The old town is divided into two scenic areas: **Dōngzhà** (东栅; ¥100; ⊙ 7am-5.30pm, till 6pm in summer) and **Xīzhà** (西栅; ¥120, ¥80 after 5pm; ⊙ 9am-10pm, till 10.30pm in summer); a combined ticket to visit the two areas costs ¥150. Most of the row homes in both areas have been transformed into museums, galleries and artisan workshops (with giftshops), snack vendors and restaurants. All are free to enter, though you may be required to show your village admission ticket.

The Xīzhà scenic zone covers more ground than Dōngzhà, has the visitor centre and is where bus 305 drops passengers off first. For day trippers it makes sense to start here, take the free shuttle to Dōngzhà and then grab a *sānlúnchē* on Xinhua Lu (新华路), which runs perpendicular to Dōngzhà's main drag, Dong Dajie, back to the bus station. If you're overnighting in Xīzhà, you might want to start in Dōngzhà. Admission tickets are for one day only, but if you spend the night in Xīzhà you won't need a ticket to enter the next day.

◉ Dōngzhà Scenic Zone

The main street of the Dōngzhà scenic zone, Dongda Jie (东大街), is a narrow path paved with stone slabs and flanked by wooden buildings. There are workshops here turning out indigo-dyed cloth, bamboo weavings and the like. Most sights are open from 8am to 5pm. Dōngzhà feels more lived in than Xīzhà, though as the road is narrow it can feel a bit claustrophobic when busy.

Jiāngnán Wood Carving Museum   MUSEUM
(江南木雕陈列馆, Jiāngnán Mùdiāo Chénlièguǎn; 420 Dong Dajie, 东大街420号; ⊙ 8am-5pm) A fine collection of wood carvings from around the region, though unfortunately no

explanations as to when they were created or what symbolism is evoked.

Ancient Beds Museum MUSEUM
(百床馆, Bǎichuángguǎn; 212 Dong Dajie, 东大街212号; ⊙8am-5pm) Though very few beds here qualify as even remotely ancient, there are some beautiful examples of elaborately carved traditional beds, along with some explanations of the symbolism etched upon them (grapes, for example, signify a hope for plenty of sons and grandsons).

Huìyuán Pawn House HISTORIC BUILDING
(汇源当铺, Huìyuán Dàngpù; Changfeng Jie, 常丰街; ⊙8am-5pm) Once a famous pawnshop that eventually expanded to branches in Shànghǎi, this old shop is bare now, though the high counter – where the owner lorded over those who came to pawn their possessions – remains.

◉ Xīzhà Scenic Zone

The Xīzhà scenic zone is the more photogenic of the two zones, as its main street, Xizha Dajie (西栅大街) is criss-crossed with bridges from where you can gaze upon the canals. This is where visitors spend most of their time.

Chinese Footbinding Culture Museum MUSEUM
(三寸金莲馆, Sāncùn Jīnlián Guǎn; 349 Xizha Dajie, 西栅大街349号; ⊙8am-5pm) With plenty of English, this fascinating museum covers the thousand-year history of female footbinding in China with examples of the shoes that constituted, as captions in the museum attest to, 'The Golden Lotus complex that was the freakish mentality of the males at that time'. Periodically banned, footbinding was final abolished in the 20th century.

Yuèlǎo Temple BUDDHIST SITE
(月老庙, Yuèlǎo Miào) Singles and couples alike come here to win the favour of the god of love (who, interestingly, appears here as an old man) by lighting incense and tying red-stringed charms to trees around the temple.

White Lotus Pagoda BUDDHIST SITE
(白莲塔, Báilián Tǎ; ⊙8am-5pm) This seven-storey pagoda is a beacon at the far west end of the Xīzhà scenic zone. You can climb up to the 3rd floor for excellent views over the Grand Canal.

🛏 Sleeping & Eating

Wūzhèn is a lovely place to stay overnight, although you can easily make it a day trip from either Shànghǎi or Hángzhōu. Only the Xīzhà scenic zone is set up for overnight guests, with both budget and boutique inns. The visitor centre can make bookings, though you'll need to book ahead on weekends and holiday periods.

Restaurants and snack vendors are plentiful. Prices are fixed though not outrageous; for cheaper food look to restaurants along Xinhua Lu, which bisects the Dōngzhà scenic zone. Everything in Dōngzhà shuts up at 5pm; restaurants and stalls stay open until 9pm or 10pm in Xīzhà.

Wisteria Youth Hostel HOSTEL $
(紫藤国际青年旅社, Zǐténg Guójì Qīngnián Lǚshè; ☑0573 8873 1332; wuzhenwisteria@163.com; 43 Sizuo Jie, 丝作街43号; 4-/6-/8-bed dm ¥100/80/60, d from ¥350; 🛜) At the far west end of Xīzhà, in a creaky wooden building within stumbling distance of the bar strip, this hostel has basic but clean rooms and a pleasant common area that opens on to a large square. The dorms are the best value you'll find on a budget in Wūzhèn but the double rooms are only worthwhile with a discount.

Wūzhèn Guesthouse GUESTHOUSE $$
(乌镇民宿, Wūzhèn Mínsù; ☑0573 8873 1088; wuzhen1@wuzhen.com.cn; 137 Xizha Dajie, 西栅大街137号; r from ¥340; 🌐) Stretching the length of Xizha Dajie, in the Xīzhà scenic zone, is this loose collection of canalside, family-run B&Bs in old wooden homes with modern amenities. Prices rise for rooms with river views and verandahs, and those in the middle of town (rooms are numbered 1 to 65) are generally considered more desirable as they're away from the main gates.

Reserve in advance (through the visitor centre booking hotline) if you've got your heart set on a verandah; otherwise you can book on arrival at the visitor centre or at the reception at 137 Xizha Dajie.

★ Entertainment

Ten-minute martial-arts performances are held eight times daily on the aptly named **Kungfu Boat** (拳船; quán chuán), just inside the main entrance to the Dōngzhà scenic zone. Other performances, such as shadow puppet shows (píyǐngxì), take place irregularly in halls around both zones; look out for signs or inquire at the visitor centre for the day's schedule.

ℹ Information

There are ATMs at the main entrances to both scenic zones.

China Post (中国邮政, Zhōngguó Yóuzhèng; 500 Xizha Dajie, 西栅大街500号; ⊗ 8am-5pm) Midway down Xizha Dajie.

Wūzhèn Visitor Centre (乌镇游客服务中心, Wūzhèn Yóukè Fúwù Zhōngxīn; ☑ 0573 8873 1088; www.wuzhen.com.cn; Hongqiao Lu, 虹桥路; ⊗ 8am-5.30pm) At the entrance to the Xizhà scenic zone, with left luggage and an accommodation booking counter.

ℹ Getting There & Away

From Hángzhōu, buses (¥31, 75 minutes, hourly from 7am to 6.20pm) run regularly to Wūzhèn from the Main Bus Station. The last bus returns at 6.25pm.

From Shànghǎi, buses (¥61, two hours) run roughly every 30 minutes from Shànghǎi South Bus Station; the last return bus is at 6pm. Eight buses (¥35, 110 minutes) also run between Wūzhèn and Sūzhōu train station.

There are two daily buses to Nánxún at 8.30am and 1.30pm (60 minutes, ¥10), but no direct buses in the opposite direction.

ℹ Getting Around

Bus 350 (¥2, 7am to 5.30pm, frequent) runs in a loop from Wūzhèn bus station to Xīzhà scenic zone and Dōngzhà scenic zone and then back to the bus station. A free shuttle bus (7.40am to 5.20pm, every 20 minutes) runs between the main entrance to both scenic zones.

Sānlúnchē (pedicabs) can be picked up at Wūzhèn bus station and on Xinhua Lu (新华路), at the west end of the Dōngzhà scenic zone. Rides between the two zones or the bus station cost ¥10. It is possible to walk between the two zones in 20 minutes.

Nánxún 南浔

☑ 0572 / POP 491,000

Established during the Southern Song dynasty, Nánxún rose to prominence in the Ming and Qing dynasties, when it became a key trading point along the grand canal from Běijīng to Hángzhōu. Merchants made fortunes in silk and translated it into decadent homes. It's now a sprawling city, on the border with Jiāngsū province, but the old town within it is well preserved. Like other towns on the water, Nánxún has arched stone bridges, meandering lanes and old wooden houses. What sets it apart is its fascinating mix of Chinese and European architecture – and comparatively few visitors.

Nánxún's **scenic area** (¥100; ⊗ 7.30am-5pm Apr-Oct, 8am-4.30pm Nov-Mar) stretches a couple of kilometres along a network of canals and is easily walkable in half a day. The waterway along Nanxi Lu (南溪路) is the largest, and the most touristy; it runs perpendicular to Dongdajie (东大街), another canal-lined street. From Dongdajie, several bridges cross over to Bǎijiānlóu, the most atmospheric – and least crowded – part. If you arrive by public bus, you'll enter from Bǎijiānlóu. The main ticket office is at the opposite end of Nanxi Lu, which means you may be able to dodge the admission fee, though you'll need a ticket to enter any of the sights (the ticket covers entry to all of them). The scenic area is well signposted in English.

Oddly overlooked by most visitors, **Bǎijiānlóu** (百间楼, Hundred Room Corridor) a stretch of 100 (or so) wooden row houses flanking a narrow canal, is Nánxún's most charming spot. Most houses are still lived in, with residents running small tea shops on their waterfront patios.

The grandest of Nánxún's wealthy merchant homes, **Zhangshiming's Former Residence** (张石铭旧居, Zhāng Shí Míng Jiùjū; Nanxi Lu, 南溪路) looks like a classic Chinese manor, with ornate carvings in wood, stone and brick – until you reach deep into the interior, which hides a European-style ballroom, complete with crown moulding, crystal chandelier and brocade drapery. Other European touches draw on both Renaissance and Baroque styles. The combined effect is both fascinating and bizarre, a well preserved portrait of the cultural exchange between China and the West at the turn of the last century.

Nánxún is an easy day trip from Hángzhōu, though there are a handful of inns here nestled among the canals if you choose to stay.

The best value inn on the water in Nánxún is **Bayside Inn** (云水谣客栈, Yúnshuǐyáo Kèzhàn; ☑ 0572 301 7919; 71 Dongdajie, 东大街71号; d from ¥360; ❀ ☎). It has clean, if compact, rooms with modern amenities and friendly staff, who try their best at English. All the rooms are a little different, so have a look around. Naturally the best ones have windows opening over the canal.

Tourist restaurants line Nanxi Lu, which runs alongside the town's largest canal. For cheap eats head to Nandongjie (南东街), lined with noodle shops, just over Tōngjīn Bridge (通津桥; Tōngjīnqiáo) from Dongdajie.

One of Nánxún's local specialities is *shuāng jiāo miàn* (双浇面), a kind of long thin wheat noodle in a rich, dark soy broth.

ZHÈJIĀNG NÁNXÚN

Zhuàngyuánlóu (状元楼; Nandongjie, 南东街; noodles ¥7-12; ☺5am-10pm) is the most popular shop in which to try it, though it looks nearly identical to others just like it (to spot it, look for the coal furnace outside). Once inside, you'll be led into the tiny kitchen to choose your toppings.

❶ Getting There & Away

Buses leave every 45 minutes (¥45, 1½ hours) from Hángzhōu's north bus station (7.20am to 5.20pm); the last return bus is at 5.20pm.

Buses also depart for:

Shànghǎi ¥50, 2½ hours, frequent

Sūzhōu ¥25, one hour, every 20 to 40 minutes (7am to 5.50pm)

There is no direct bus from Nánxún to Wūzhèn; you'll need to take one of the hourly buses to Jiāxìng (嘉兴; ¥23, one hour) and transfer there for the hourly bus to Wūzhèn (¥11, one hour).

Nánxún's bus station is at the back entrance to the scenic area. Cross the overpass and in 50m you'll see a sign pointing you to the main sights.

ZHÈJIĀNG NÁNXÚN

THE BRIDGES OF TÀISHÙN COUNTY

Soggy Tàishùn (泰顺), in southeast Zhèjiāng, is China's living bridge museum: there are hundreds of covered wooden bridges – many centuries old, in varying stages of preservation and crumble – scattered around the countryside. The best of those that are easily accessible are the four clustered around the village of Sìxī (泗溪), which sits on the confluence of two streams.

From the nearby bus stop in Nánxī (南溪), it's a short 400m walk back through the village to **Nánxī Bridge** (南溪桥, Nánxī Qiáo). What this level bridge lacks in grandeur it makes up for in usefulness: built in 1842, it's more local thoroughfare than tourist attraction.

Next head back 200m to the main village junction and turn right. In 1km you can turn right again and take a 3km detour up to **Nányáng Bridge** (南阳桥, Nányáng Qiáo), a level wooden cantilever bridge, built in 1870 and situated in the grassy hills above town. Otherwise veer left for **Xīdōng Bridge** (溪东桥, Xīdōng Qiáo, Creek East Bridge), in Sìxī proper, another 500m. Easily identified by its dramatic winged roof and deep vermilion staining, this Ming dynasty arched wooden bridge was first built in 1570 and later rebuilt in 1827.

From here, the village is well signposted in English. Follow signs to gracefully arching **Běijiàn Bridge** (北涧桥, Běijiàn Qiáo, North Stream Bridge), the most picturesque of Sìxī's bridges, accessed by stone steps. It was originally built in 1674 and last rebuilt in 1803. Don't miss the 1000-year-old camphor tree just before it.

Just past Běijiàn Bridge, at the far end of the village, is the **Covered Bridge Culture Hall** (廊桥文化展厅, Lángqiáo Wénhuà Zhǎntīng) `FREE`, which has models and information (in English!) on other noteworthy bridges in the area. If you're feeling ambitious, you can hire one of the unofficial taxi drivers (¥150 to ¥400, depending on the route) who haunt the Nánxī bus stop to take you around. Make sure the driver understands where to go before setting out, as some might not know the location of all the bridges. This map (www.langqio.net/map.asp) comes in handy.

Getting There & Away

To get to Sìxī you need to first get to Wēnzhōu (温州), which is serviced by frequent high-speed trains from Shànghǎi Hóngqiáo (¥178 to ¥226, four hours) and Hángzhōu East (¥129 to ¥153, three hours). High-speed trains arrive at Wēnzhōu South (温州火车南站; Wēnzhōu Huǒchē Nánzhàn), 15km from downtown, from where you'll need to take a taxi (¥40, 25 minutes) to Niúshān Transport Centre (牛山客运中心; Niúshān Kèyùn Zhōngxīn), Wēnzhōu's central bus station. The sleeper train from Shànghǎi South (soft/hard sleeper ¥186/288, 11 hours, 11.30pm) arrives at the more convenient main train station, from where you can catch local buses 21, 23 and 107 (¥2, 20 minutes, frequent) to Niúshān.

At the bus station buy a ticket to Nánxī (南溪; ¥46, two hours, every 40 minutes 6.20am to 6.40pm) on the Tàishùn-bound bus. The last return bus leaves at 5pm; buy your ticket from the stall opposite the Nánxī bus stop, which has the timetable posted.

If you find yourself overnighting in Wēnzhōu, the **E-X Palm D'or Hotel** (意杰金棕榈酒店, Yìjié Jīnzōnglǘ Jiǔdiàn; ☎0577 8802 2222; www.expalmhotel.com; 23 Minhang Lu, 明航路23号; r from ¥600; ❷☺❋@☂), 3km from the bus station (and 15km from the high-speed-train station), is a comfortable choice.

Xīnyè 新叶

📞0571 / POP 3000

Cut with sparkling streams, centred on placid ponds and embraced by silent hills, the picturesque village of Xīnyè (¥68, ⊙8am-4pm) is populated by families sharing the surname Ye (叶) and an abundance of free-roaming chickens. The village is laid out in accordance with the traditional five element (五行; *wǔ xíng*) theory, so it's a balanced exercise in feng shui aesthetics. During spring, the village is framed by fields of bright yellow rapeseed.

The elegant white **Tuányún Pagoda** (抟云 塔, Tuányún Tǎ; ⊙8am-4pm) is the definitive image of Xīnyè and a good place to start a tour of the village. Built in 1567, the seven-storey tower symbolises hopes by its architects for a 'meteoric rise' for the village and generations to come. It's located near the tourist centre and next to **Wénchāng Hall** (文昌阁, Wénchāng Gé; ⊙8am-4pm), another noteworthy attraction. The latter contains a portrait of Confucius and an adjacent shrine (土地祠; *tǔdì cí*) to the village god (for good harvests). Smudged red Maoist slogans add their own narrative. Not far away, the **Xīshān Ancestral Temple** (西山祠堂, Xīshān Cítáng; ⊙8am-4pm) is the highest-ranking ancestral temple in the village and dates to the Yuan dynasty.

The **Hall of Good Order** (有序堂, Yǒuxù Táng; ⊙8am-4pm) is central to the village; its front door does not open so its accessible side door faces out onto pyramid-shaped **Dàofēng Mountain** (道峰山; Dàofēng Shān), across the waters of half-moon shaped **South Pond** (南塘; Nántáng), from where eight alleys radiate out through the village. Originally built in 1290 and rebuilt during the Republic, the hall contains some astonishing wood carvings of a deer, small birds and a monkey in the trees. At the end of the day, sit out next to the pond and watch old folk gathering to chat.

Shuāngměi Hall (双美堂, Shuāngměi Táng; ⊙8am-4pm) is another lovely wood-panelled structure containing intricate and exquisite carvings above pillars. At the time of research, **Chóngrén Temple** (崇仁堂, Chóngrén Táng; ⊙8am-4pm), located next to **Half Moon Pond** (半月塘; Bànyuè Táng), was undergoing reconstruction.

There are several guesthouses here and you'll see signs posted around the village. **Dàojīn Rénjiā** (道金人家; 📞159 8816 0523; r ¥100) is a reliable option with well kept but basic singles and doubles and meal service. The easiest way to get here from the bus stop is to continue down the main road and then turn right on the market lane; follow it around the bend and look for the guesthouse down an alley on the right. There are also signs in English directing you from nearby South Pond.

Xīnyè has just a couple of small eateries, though all guesthouses offer meals.

The village is signposted in Chinese; you can get a map at the tourist centre. The admission fee covers all the village sights; hold onto your ticket for entry.

The nearest international ATMs are in Xīn'ānjiāng or Jīnhuá.

ℹ️ Getting There & Away

There is a direct bus service from Hángzhōu's main bus station (¥61, two hours, 6.35am) and also from Hángzhōu's west bus station (¥61, two hours, 8.20am and 1.50pm). A return bus leaves at 12.45pm.

Xīnyè also works as a convenient day trip from Zhūgě: buses to Xīnyè (¥4, 30 minutes) depart at 7.45am, 10.20am, 1.30pm and 5.15pm and return at 6.10am, 8.30am, noon and 3.20pm.

To get to the village from the bus dropoff, turn right and follow the stone path for a few minutes. Note that to get an admission ticket covering the sights, you'll need to go to the tourist centre at the far northeast corner of the village.

Zhūgě 诸葛

📞0579 / POP 4000

Photogenic **Zhūgě** (www.zhugevillage.cn, ¥100, ⊙7.30am-5pm summer, 8am-4.30pm winter) is a fascinating composition of traditional Chinese village architecture and feng shui planning: the village was designed according to the *bāguà* (八卦; eight trigrams) of the *I Ching*. Included in Zhūgě's meticulous plans are numerous snaking cobblestone alleyways – some only wide enough for one person to pass – intentionally designed (for purposes of protection) for outsiders to get hopelessly lost. This is naturally one of the pleasures of visiting.

Though Zhūgě is one of the most commercialised of the area villages, it remains visibly lived in. Residents are largely descendants of Zhuge Liang, who was a prime minister during the Three Kingdoms period.

👁️ Sights

Entering from Gaolong Lu (高隆路), proceed downhill and around the corner to reach the lovely, huge **Upper Pond** (上塘; *Shàng Táng*). At the southern end of the pond, look for a sign leading to **Tiānyī Hall** (天一堂, Tiānyī Táng; 7.30am-5pm summer, 8am-4.30pm winter), most noteworthy for its beautiful garden with flowering trees and hundreds of potted plants – all used for Chinese medicine.

Double back and look for **Shòuchūn Hall** (寿春堂, Shòuchūn Táng; ⊙7.30am-5pm summer, 8am-4.30pm winter) – one of Zhūgě's 18 halls – itself a long sequence of chambers and courtyards. Just past it is **Lower Pond** (下塘; Xià Tǎng) and two additional halls: **Dàjīng Hall** (大经堂, Dàjīng Táng; ⊙7.30am-5pm summer, 8am-4.30pm winter) – housing a traditional Chinese medicine museum – and, up the steps, the **Yōngmù Hall** (雍睦堂, Yōngmù Táng; ⊙7.30am-5pm summer, 8am-4.30pm winter), a fine Ming dynasty hall with an eye-catching central stone door frame.

Eight (the number mirroring the eight trigrams of the *bāguà*) lanes radiate from **Zhōng Pond** (钟池, Zhōng Chí) at the heart of the village. The feng shui symbol of the village, the circular pond resembles the Chinese twin-fish, *yīn-yáng tàijí* diagram, half filled in and the other half occupied with water. You can also spot the black trigrams (八卦; *bāguà*) above some windows of the whitewashed houses.

Overlooking the water is the splendid **Dàgōng Hall** (大公堂, Dàgōng Táng; ⊙7.30am-5pm summer, 8am-4.30pm winter), a huge, airy space with a pairing of huge black Chinese characters 武 ('Wǔ' or 'Martial') and 忠 ('Zhōng' or 'Loyal') on the walls outside. The memorial hall originally dates to the Yuan dynasty; note its two large and smooth drum stones. The **Prime Minister's Temple** (丞相祠堂, Chéng Xiàng Cítáng; ⊙7.30am-5pm summer, 8am-4.30pm winter), an impressive and massive old hall with some intricately carved cross-beams in the roof, is nearby.

Admission to the village gets you into all the sights described above, so hold on to your ticket.

🛏 Sleeping & Eating

The vast majority of visitors are day trippers so there is an advantage to overnighting in one of the few guesthouses here. Also the village is beautiful at dusk.

Restaurants are dotted around the village, but most are aimed at tourists. Along the eastern edge of the Upper Pond are some more local options, where villagers gather to drink tea and play mah-jong and you can get a bowl of noodles for ¥10. Food carts and fruit sellers gather at the bottom of Gaolong Lu, just outside the village.

Huāyuán Gōngyù   HOTEL $$
(花园公寓; ☑0579 8860 0336; 48 Yitai Xiang, 义泰巷48号; r with/without bathroom ¥60/288; ❋) This quiet choice is set amid the garden at Tiānyī Hall, embellished with views over the village rooftops from the 2nd-floor corridor. The cheapest rooms come without shower and have rather flaky ceilings; of the pricier rooms, go for the less damp ones on the 2nd floor. Discounts are common.

🍷 Drinking & Nightlife

Sunshine House   TEAHOUSE
(昱栈, Yùzhàn; ⊙10am-9.30pm; ☎) Overlooking Upper Pond, Sunshine House serves big pots of tea and espresso drinks (¥25 to ¥40).

ⓘ Information

The nearest international ATMs are in Xīn'ānjiāng or Jīnhuá.

China Post (中国邮政, Zhōngguó Yóuzhèng; 330 Guodao, 国道330号; ⊙8am-4.40pm) At the bottom of Gaolong Lu, across the street.

ⓘ Getting There & Away

From Hángzhōu south bus station, direct buses to Zhūgě (¥60, two hours) leave at 8.40am and 3.50pm; there's also a bus from Hángzhōu's central bus station (¥59, two hours) at 12.30pm and west bus station (¥60, two hours) at 2.40pm. Going back to Hángzhōu there are 12 buses daily (6.15am to 6.20pm).

From Jīnhuá west bus station, buses depart nine times daily for Zhūgě (¥18 to ¥21, one hour, 6am to 3.10pm). Return buses (7.15am, 8.50am, 9am, 1.40pm, 5pm) depart from in front of the bus station, on the opposite side of the street.

Buses from Lánxī en route to Xīnyè swing by Zhūgě around 7.45am, 10.20am, 1.30pm and 5.15pm. You'll need to flag one down from the road in front of the bus station. In the return direction, buses from Xīnyè (¥4, 30 minutes) depart at 6.10am, 8.30am, noon and 3.20pm; the bus drops off at the foot of Gaolong Lu.

ⓘ Getting Around

Zhūgě bus station (诸葛汽车站, Zhūgě Qìchēzhàn; 330 Guodao, 国道330号) is on Rte 330, a 15-minute walk from the village. Walk east for 500m until you see the cluster of pedicabs and snack vendors that mark the entrance to Gaolong Lu. At the top of the road (300m) is the entrance to the village. You can also hire a pedicab from the bus station for ¥5. Some drivers will bypass the admission gate and take you straight into the village; note that without a ticket you won't be able to enter any of the ticketed structures (though you are free to walk around).

ZHĒJIĀNG ZHŪGĚ

Sìpíng 寺平

📶 0579 / POP 1600

Tiny Sìpíng, 30km west of Jīnhuá, was founded 700 years ago, and remains a remarkable repository of brick and wood carvings. Its seven original halls, built by generations of the Dai (戴) family, are arranged in the shape of the Big Dipper – to communicate harmony between the human and natural world. The village is blissfully uncommercial – though thanks to a new homestay program, it's well set up for visitors.

The main entrance to Sìpíng (¥20, 8am to 4pm) is along the handle of the dipper. On your right will be Liben Hall, an early Qing dynasty structure with some wood carvings that remain impressively vivid; keep an eye out for the bats (carvings of, that is). In the cosmology of the village, this hall represents the star Phad.

Just a few paces from Chóngdé Hall (崇德堂; Chóngdé Táng), is Wǔjiān Huāxuān (五问花轩), marked by flowery brick carvings over the door. This is the birthplace of Dai Yinniang, Sìpíng's most famous historical resident – the village girl who became an imperial concubine. According to legend, when Yinniang was ill as a child, a monk in a vision told her father to construct a well near the house. He did, and after giving his daughter water from it to drink and wash, she became well – and more beautiful. The well still exists, adjacent to the house.

At the base of the dipper, and standing in for the star Alioth, is Chónghòu Hall (崇厚堂, Chónghòu Táng). Its brick carving, 'Nine Lions Scrambling for a Ball', is noteworthy as much for its detail as for its seemingly impudent use of five-toed lions (usually an imperial symbol).

The village is well signposted in English. While the halls are the most dramatic structures, many ordinary houses have fantastic carvings as well, depicting popular Chinese symbols of luck, upward mobility and prosperity.

The only accommodations in Sìpíng are the 15 homes open to guests through Jīnhuá Homestay (www.jinhua-homestay.com; s/d incl 2 meals per person ¥128) – the small number keeps the village uncrowded. While Sìpíng has plenty of heritage structures, the homes are modern (with modern amenities); bathrooms are shared. Host families are keen to have guests at their table and to take them around the village.

While it may not have restaurants, Sìpíng does have a single cafe (irregular hours) with an espresso machine, in the centre of the village, with an outdoor terrace. The nearest reliable international ATMs are in Jīnhuá.

Bus 502 runs to/from Jīnhuá's south bus station to Tāngxī (汤溪; ¥5.50, one hour, frequent 6am to 6.30pm). In Tāngxī, pick up a pedicab (¥30) for the last 5km to Sìpíng. If you've booked a homestay, transportation from Tāngxī can be arranged.

Jīnhuá 金华

📶 0579 / POP 4.73 MILLION

As provincial Chinese cities go, Jīnhuá is an agreeable one with tree-lined streets and a central river flanked by parkland. It's a useful transport hub and a springboard for visiting the attractive villages of central Zhèjiāng.

Jīnhuá Architecture Park (金华建筑艺术公园, Jīnhuá Jiànzhù Yìshù Gōngyuán) FREE is made up of 16 pavilions, designed by international and domestic architects, strung over 2km along the Yìwū River. It was conceived and curated by the artist Ai Wei Wei, to honour his father, poet and native son Ai Qing. Though the buildings – intended to be coffee shops, libraries, wi fi enabled work spaces and the like – are shuttered, it is still a fascinating sight, a modern meditation on memorial architecture.

The park, created in 2002, could have put the city on the international map: The star power of the names attached to the project (like Herzog & de Meuron), are a testimony to Ai's global renown as an artist. Yet he is also a controversial, outspoken figure: despite having once been named artistic director for the Běijīng Oympic stadium, he was arrested in 2011 on vague charges.

The park is all but abandoned and, given southeast China's propensity for rain, the buildings are already succumbing to rust and mould – acquiring the patina of ruins, despite their contemporary nature. Local children play in the open-air structures; the rest can be appreciated only from the outside. A taxi to the park costs around ¥25.

As befitting its transit hub status, Jīnhuá has many hotels. None of them are great, but World Trade Hotel (世贸大饭店, Shìmào Dàfàndiàn; 📶 0579 8258 8888; 737 Bayi Beijie, 八一北街737号; r from ¥760; ❋ @ 🛜) is the best of the bunch: convenient, clean and well appointed. It's 2km from the train station, across from Bayi Park. Breakfast is included and discounts are common.

ZHÈJIĀNG SÌPÍNG

Cheap noodle and hotpot joints can be found on Wuyi Lu, which runs diagonally southeast from the train station. Jīnhuá is famous for its dry-cured ham – so rich and salty it's used more to flavour dishes than to eat on its own – though unfortunately it's largely considered an export and is hard to come by in restaurants in town.

ⓘ Information

Bank of China (中国银行, Zhōngguó Yínháng; cnr Bayi Beijie & Renmin Donglu, 八一北街人民东路的路口; ⊙8.30am-5pm) Money exchange and 24-hour ATM.

ⓘ Getting There & Away

Jīnhuá has excellent high-speed train connections, thanks to the new rail line between Hángzhōu and Chángshā, including:

Hángzhōu East ¥74, one hour, frequent
Huángshān North ¥157, 2½ hours, one daily
Shànghǎi Hóngqiáo ¥147, two hours, frequent
Wēnzhōu South ¥77, two hours, 10 daily

The **west bus station** (汽车西站, Qìchē Xīzhàn), where buses depart for Zhūgě, is 500m west of the high-speed train station; the walk is well signposted. The **south bus station** (汽车南站, Qìchē Nánzhàn; Bayi Nanjie, 八一南街), where buses depart for Tāngxī (for Sìpíng), is at the southern end of the city.

ⓘ Getting Around

Bus K11 (¥2) runs from the train station via the west bus station to the south bus station in 45 minutes.

Taxis start at ¥8. The 20-minute ride from the west to the south bus station costs around ¥40.

Pǔtuóshān 普陀山

🎵 0580

Pǔtuóshān – the Zhōushān Archipelago's most celebrated isle and one of China's four sacred Buddhist mountains – is the abode of Guanyin, the eternally compassionate Goddess of Mercy. With pine groves, sandy beaches, grand temples and hidden grottoes, it is immensely scenic, but also very popular (despite the fact that it is only accessible by boat). Aim for a midweek visit outside of holiday periods.

◎ Sights

Pǔtuóshān's temples are all shrines for the merciful goddess Guanyin. Besides the three main temples, you will stumble upon nunneries and monasteries everywhere

you turn, while decorative archways may suddenly emerge from the sea mist. Several sights, including Pǔjì Temple, and most amenities are clustered at the southern end of the island, which is easily walkable. If you want to stretch your legs, trails (often empty) line much of the coastline.

Pay the entrance fee (summer/winter ¥160/140) before you board the ferry and (usually ¥5).

Sights in Pǔtuóshān don't have addresses, but are well signposted in English.

Fǎyǔ Temple   BUDDHIST TEMPLE
(法雨禅寺, Fǎyǔ Chánsì; Fayu Lu, 法雨路; ¥5; ⊙5.30am-6pm) Colossal camphor trees and a huge gingko tree tower over this Chan (Zen) temple, where a vast glittering statue of Guanyin sits resplendently in the main hall, flanked by 18 *luóhàn* (arhat) effigies. Each *luóhàn* has a name – for example, the Crossing the River *luóhàn* or the Long Eyebrows *luóhàn* – and worshippers pray to each in turn. In the hall behind stands a dextrous 1000-arm Guanyin.

Pǔjì Temple   BUDDHIST TEMPLE
(普济禅寺, Pǔjì Sì; ¥5; ⊙5.30am-6pm) Fronted by large ponds and overlooked by towering camphor trees and Luóhàn pines, this recently restored Chan (Zen) temple stands by the main square and dates to at least the 17th century. Beyond chubby Milefo sitting in a red, gold and green burnished cabinet in the Hall of Heavenly Kings, throngs of worshippers stand with flaming incense in front of the colossal main hall. Note the seated 1000-arm effigy of Guanyin in the Pǔmén Hall (普门殿; Pǔmén Diàn).

South Sea Guanyin   STATUE
(南海观音, Nánhǎi Guānyīn; ⊙6am-6pm) The first thing you see as you approach Pǔtuóshān by boat is this 33m-high glittering statue of Guanyin, overlooking the waves at the southernmost tip of the island. It's the symbol of the island.

Luòjiāshān   ISLAND
(洛伽山) The very small island of Luòjiāshān, southeast of Pǔtuóshān, has its own temples and pagodas and makes for a fun expedition. The **ferry** (round trip including admission to Luòjiāshān ¥70, 25 minutes) departs at 7am, 8am, 9am and 1pm when conditions are good. You have to take a returning boat two hours later.

Guānyīn Cave
CAVE

(观音洞, Guānyīn Dòng) Crouch with an arched back into this magnificent, smoky and mysterious old grotto with a low, head-scraping ceiling to witness its assembly of Guanyins carved from the rock face along with small effigies of the goddess in porcelain and stone, draped in cloth.

Duōbǎo Pagoda
PAGODA

(多宝塔, Duōbǎo Tǎ; 9am-4pm) FREE Pǔtuóshān's oldest structure is this five-storey, 18m-high stone pagoda, with alcoves carved from the rock sheltering Buddhist statues. Built in 1335, its name literally means the 'Many Treasures Pagoda'.

One Hundred Step Beach
BEACH

(百步沙, Bǎibùshā; ☉6am-6pm) The most popular of Pǔtuóshān's beaches has a pretty pagoda perched on terraced rock that always has a crowd. Swimming is allowed between May and August, until 6pm.

One Thousand Step Beach
BEACH

(千步金沙, Qiānbù Jīnshā; ☉6am-6pm) Pǔtuóshān's largest beach stretches all along the northeast coast of the island – a long unspoilt stretch of blonde sand. Swimming is only permitted between May and August until 6pm, but any time of year it's a lovely place to plonk down on the sand.

Cháoyáng Cave
CAVE

(朝阳洞, Cháoyáng Dòng) At the jutting point that marks the boundary between One Hundred Step Beach and One Thousand Step Beach, 'Sun-facing' Cave is a small, rarely visited grotto with altars inside to Guanyin. The sound of the roaring waves here is said to imitate the chanting of the Buddha; it's also known as the island's best sunrise spot.

Shàncái Cave
CAVE

(善财洞, Shàncái Dòng) This cave is named after a boy attendant to Guanyin, often seen in Chinese Buddhist temples. He's also known as the 'child god of wealth' and you'll see visitors pulling out money for him to bless. There's a path leading here from Guānyīn Cave.

Huìjì Temple
BUDDHIST TEMPLE

(慧济禅寺, Huìjì Chánsì; ¥5; ☉5.30am-6.30pm) Less grand than the temples at sea level, hilltop Huìjì draws pilgrims who make the climb up Fódǐng Mountain. The temple has a small **vegetarian canteen** (慧济禅寺素菜馆, Huìjì Chánsì Sùcàiguǎn; breakfast ¥5, lunch & dinner ¥10; ☉4.30-6.30am, 9am-noon, 3.30-5.30pm; 🖉) for post-hike sustenance.

Buddhism Museum
MUSEUM

(佛教博物馆, Fójiào Bówùguǎn; ☉9am-4pm Tue-Sun) FREE This small museum contains some of the Ming and Qing dynasty relics from Pǔtuóshān's temples, including effigies in bronze and jade and ritual implements, with some English signage. The entrance is not well marked, but it's behind Duōbǎo Pagoda.

Fànyīn Cave
CAVE

(梵音洞, Fànyīn Dòng; ☉5.30am-6pm) FREE On the far eastern tip of the island, this cave contains a temple dedicated to Guanyin perched between two cliffs with a seagull's view of the crashing waves below.

Fódǐng Mountain
MOUNTAIN

(佛顶山, Fódǐng Shān; ¥5) A steep but beautifully shaded half-hour climb can be made up Fódǐng Mountain – Buddha's Summit Peak – the highest point on the island. This is also where you will find Huìjì Temple. Watch devout pilgrims and Buddhist nuns stop every three steps to either bow or kneel in supplication. The less motivated take the **cable car** (索道, suǒdào, one-way/return ¥40/70, ☉6.30am-5pm).

The **Xiāngyún Pavilion** (香云亭; Xiāngyún Tíng) is a pleasant spot for a breather.

🛏 Sleeping

Most hotels on Pǔtuóshān aim squarely at tour groups and holidaying Chinese, with prices to match. Room rates are generally discounted from Sunday to Thursday. Larger hotels have shuttle buses to and from the pier.

As you leave the arrivals building, local hotel touts flapping plastic photo placards will descend; these rooms are generally at the cheaper end in a nearby village. You can do your own legwork in the villages of Xīshān Xīncūn (西山新村), a short walk over the hill to the west from the ferry terminal, and Lóngwān Cūn (龙湾村), around a 15-minute walk east of the ferry terminal. Look for the characters '内有住宿', which means rooms are available. All the rooms are very similar, going for around ¥150 on a weekday, and double at weekends; bargain if you can.

Chánzōng Rúshì Sea View Hotel
HOTEL $$

(禅宗如是大酒店, Chánzōng Rúshì Dàjiǔdiàn; 🕿0580 669 6898; 1 Meicen Lu, 没岑路1号; d from ¥600) It's not the most scenic area of the island but you can't beat the location for convenience – just steps from the jetty. It's worth paying an extra 25% to upgrade to a seaview room; nonview rooms have windows but are dark. Chánzōng Rúshì is a step up

Pǔtuóshān

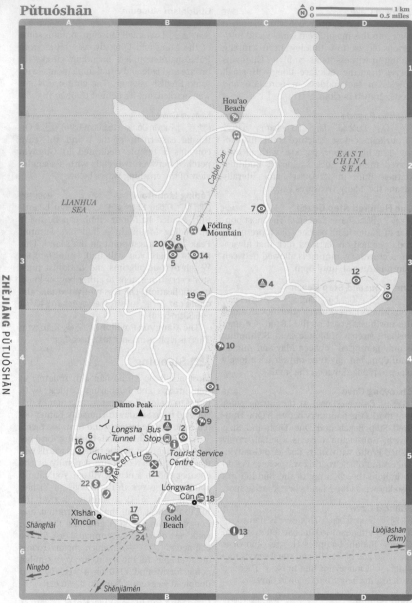

from a basic guesthouse and good value for Pǔtuóshān. Discounts likely midweek.

Hǎibiān Rénjiā
GUESTHOUSE $$

(海边人家; ☏130 5984 6649; 77, Bldg 34, Long-wan Village, 龙湾村34幢77号; r from ¥300; 🕾) This very clean budget choice up the steps in Lóngwān Village and not far from Gold Beach in the southeast of the island has 10 rooms with showers (including a sweet attic room with a skylight) and a tip-top, clean ambience. There's no English spoken but the owners are hard-working and efficient. You're likely to get a discount during the week.

Pǔtuóshān

ZHÈJIĀNG PǓTUÓSHĀN

Landison Pǔtuóshān Resort   HOTEL $$$
(雷迪森广场酒店, Léidísēn Guǎngchǎng Jiǔdiàn; ☑ 0580 669 0666; www.landisonputuoshan.com; 115 Fayu Lu, 法雨路115号; tw with/without balcony ¥1588/2588; ❄ @ 🛇) One of the island's fanciest places to stay, the Landison adds little touches of serenity like bowls of floating orchid petals and Buddhist statuary, though the whole place could use freshening up. Rooms, spacious and with plenty of natural light, surround a courtyard with an 800-year-old camphor tree; some have balconies. Weekday discounts bring rooms down to ¥1000, plus a 15% service charge.

✕ Eating

Pǔtuóshān dining is largely seafood and hotel restaurants and therefore expensive. Less expensive are the makeshift restaurants set up by villagers in hillside Lóngwān Cūn (龙湾村); when the weather's good look for plastic tables and chairs. You can also get noodles (from ¥20) on Meicen Lu, just east of the ferry port. The best places to eat are the vegetarian canteens inside the temples; both **Pǔjì** (普济寺素菜馆, Pǔjìsì Sùcàiguǎn; breakfast ¥5, lunch & dinner ¥10; ⊙ 5.30-6.30am, 10.30-11am & 4.10-5.10pm; 🍴) and **Huìjì** (p285) have them.

Zǎozǐshù   VEGETARIAN $$
(枣子树; 84-86 Meicen Lu, 梅岑路84-6号; dishes ¥28-108; ⊙ 10.30am-9.30pm; 🍴) Far more upscale (and with prices to match) than a typical temple canteen, Zǎozǐshù serves up delicacies like stir-fried tea mushrooms

(干煸茶菇; *gānbiān chágū*) and stewed papaya with snow lotus seed (瓜田雪莲; *guātián xuělián*). It's part of the Meicen Restaurants complex; look for the English sign inside that says 'vegetarian life style'.

ⓘ Information

Wi-fi is easy to come by; most accommodations have it.

Bank of China (中国银行, Zhōngguó Yínháng; 85-7 Meicen Lu, 梅岑路85-7号; ⊙ 8am-noon & 1.30-4.30pm) Currency exchange and a 24-hour ATM that accepts international cards. There are several different banks here, on what is dubbed 'Financial Street'.

China Mobile (中国移动, Zhōngguó Yídòng; 85-3 Meicen Lu, 梅岑路85-3号; ⊙ 8am-5pm) For mobile phone SIM cards.

China Post (中国邮政, Zhōngguó Yóuzhèng; 124 Meicen Lu, 梅岑路124号; ⊙ 8am-5pm summer, 8am-4.30pm winter)

Clinic (诊所, Zhěnsuǒ; ☑ 0580 609 3102; 95 Meicen Lu, 梅岑路95号; ⊙ 8am-5pm)

Industrial & Commercial Bank of China (ICBC, 工商银行, Gōngshāng Yínháng; 85-15 Meicen Lu, 梅岑路; ⊙ 8-11am & 2-5pm) Forex currency exchange.

Left Luggage Office (行李寄存, Xínglǐ Jìcúnchù; per day ¥5-10; ⊙ 6.45am-4.15pm) At the ferry terminal and also at the Zhōushān Pǔtuó Tourist Destination Service Centre, if you want to leave large luggage behind.

Tourist Service Centre (旅游咨询中心, Lǚyóu Zīxún Zhōngxīn; ☑ 0580 319 1919; ⊙ 8.30am-4.30pm)

ℹ Getting There & Away

Getting to Pǔtuóshān looks daunting as it requires multiple forms of transportation (most visitors do it on a package tour). Even coming from Níngbō, the nearest major hub, the journey takes a minimum of three hours. However, transfers are seamless and the construction of bridges lashing the principle islands of the Zhōushān archipelago to the mainland means the journey is largely made by bus (unless you choose otherwise).

First you need to get to Pǔtuó Central bus station (普陀中心站; Pǔtuó zhōngxīnzhàn), also called Shěnjiāmén (沈家门), on the island of Zhōushān. Buses depart from:

Hángzhōu south ¥65, four hours, hourly

Níngbō south ¥52, 90 minutes, frequent from 5.55am

Shànghǎi south ¥130 to ¥220, five hours, every 40 minutes

From Pǔtuó Central you'll be immediately funnelled onto a minibus (¥10) that will take you the last 10 minutes to the dockside Zhōushān Pǔtuó Tourist Destination Service Center (舟山旅游目的地服务中心; Zhōushān Lǚyóu Mùdìdì Fúwù Zhōngxīn) on Zhūjiājiān (朱家尖), where you get your ferry ticket (¥25) and admission ticket to the island. The crossing from here takes just 10 minutes. Ferries depart frequently between 6.30am and 5.30pm, after which there half-hourly departures until 8.30pm and a last boat at 9.50pm.

The other option is the slow overnight ferry direct from Shànghǎi, which takes 12 hours. From Shànghǎi, the boat leaves at 7.30pm on Monday, Wednesday and Friday, reaching Pǔtuóshān at around 8am. In the other direction, it leaves on Tuesday, Thursday and Saturday at 4pm (winter) or 5pm (summer), reaching Shànghǎi at around 6am. Tickets cost anywhere from ¥139 (4th class) to ¥499 (special class); it's easy to upgrade (bǔpiào) once you're on-board. In Pǔtuóshān boats depart from the main **ferry terminal** (普陀山客运码头, Pǔtuóshān Kèyùn Mǎtóu; ☑ 0580 609 1121); in Shànghǎi, from Wusong Passenger Transportation Centre, in the north of the city. On Pǔtuóshān, ferry tickets can be bought at the ticket office at the jetty.

The nearest airport is at Zhōushān (Pǔtuóshān) on the neighbouring island of Zhūjiājiān (朱家尖); get the ferry from the dock.

ℹ Getting Around

Minibuses zip from the passenger ferry terminal to various points around the island, including Pǔjì Temple (¥5), One Thousand Step Beach (¥8), Fǎyǔ Temple (¥10) and the cable car station (¥10), leaving every 20 minutes or when full between 7am and 4.30pm. There are more bus stations at Pǔjì Temple, Fǎyǔ Temple and other spots around the island serving the same and other destinations. If you're heading to Pǔjì Temple and the sights in the south of the island, walking is fine.

Níngbō 宁波

☑ 0574 / POP 5.77 MILLION

Níngbō, an ancient harbour city, has been an important trading port for millennia, and today is one of China's busiest. One of the five ports opened during the Treaty of Nanjing in 1842, it has a former foreign concession, Lǎo Wàitān (老外滩), now a vibrant, pedestrian-only entertainment district along the Yǒng River. For travellers, Níngbō is primarily a waypoint on the journey to Pǔtuóshān.

Should you find yourself overnighting in Níngbō, the city's main east–west thoroughfare Zhongshan Lu (中山路) is lined with midrange business hotels, including many chains, such as 7 Days Inn. There are more hotels, as well as some more upscale options (including international chains), in Lǎo Wàitān.

With it's convenient location just off Zhongshan Lu, 2km either way from the train station or Lǎo Wàitān, and just seconds from subway line 1, **Nányuàn Wénchāng Business Hotel** (南苑文昌商务酒店, Nányuàn Wénchāng Shāngwù Jiǔdiàn; ☑ 0574 5586 3999; 2 Wenchang Lu, 文昌路2号; s/d ¥298/398; ✆ ❋ ☎) is an easy choice. Rooms are spacious, clean and modern and the savvy manager speaks decent English. Wifi is fast and there's a no-smoking floor, too.

Tiānyī Guǎngchǎng (天一广场), Níngbō's spiderweb-shaped central square is full of restaurants offering an international spread of cuisines, including plenty of wallet-friendly fast-food joints and a supermarket.

Gāngyāgǒu (缸鸭狗; 68 Shuijing Jie, 水晶街68号, Tiānyī Guǎngchǎng, 天一广场; dishes ¥8-48; ◷10.30am-9.30pm) has been making Níngbō's signature dumplings (宁波汤圆; Níngbō *tāngyuán*; six for ¥10), silky boiled rice cakes stuffed with sugar-spiked ground sesame, since 1926. They come in more inventive flavours too, such as rose (玫瑰; *méiguī*) and pumpkin (南瓜; *nánguā*). You can make a meal out of it by ordering some *xiǎolóngbāo* (小笼包; soup dumplings; ¥19 to ¥36). There's a picture menu.

ℹ Information

Bank of China (中国银行, Zhōngguó Yínháng; Waima Lu, 外马路; ◷8.30am-4.30pm Mon-Fri) Currency exchange and a 24-hour ATM in Lǎo Wàitān.

ℹ Getting There & Away

Buses to Pǔtuó **central bus station** (普陀中心站; Pǔtuó zhōngxīnzhàn), also known as Shěnjiāmén (沈家门), from where you can travel onward to Pǔtuóshān, leave frequently from

Níngbō's **south bus station** (汽车南站, Qìchē Nánzhàn; 408 Jiaoshuiqiao Lu, 角水桥路408号).

Buses also run frequently between the south bus station and Hángzhōu (¥65 to ¥75, two hours).

Níngbō is well connected to China's high-speed rail network. Destinations include:

Hángzhōu East ¥71, one hour, frequent

Jīnhuá ¥145, two hours, seven daily

Shànghǎi Hóngqiáo ¥97 to ¥144, two hours, frequent

ℹ Getting Around

Níngbō has just one train station for high-speed and ordinary trains, 3km south of downtown. The south bus station is just across the plaza from the train station's south exit.

Subway line 1 runs east–west along Zhongshan Lu, stopping at Tiānyī Guǎngchǎng; rides cost ¥2 to ¥3. Taxis start at ¥11.

Shàoxīng 绍兴

☑ 0557 / POP 2.16 MILLION

Sprawling, ancient Shàoxīng, built on a network of canals, is among the oldest cities in the province. Unlike the more touristy water towns, which have concentrated historic areas, Shàoxīng is a contemporary city marbled with old, where modern housing blocks are shot through with rivulets and white-washed homes. The city is also the birthplace of many influential and colourful figures, including the writer Lu Xun.

Many of Shàoxīng's sights are related to Lu Xun (1881–1936), China's first great modern novelist, who lived here until he went abroad to study. (He later returned to China, but was forced to hide out in Shànghǎi's French Concession when the Kuomintang decided his books were too dangerous). These are clustered on the cobblestone pedestrian area known as **Lǔxùn Native Place** (鲁迅故里, Lǔxùn Gùlǐ; Luxun Zhonglu, 鲁迅中路; ☉ 8.30am-5pm). The most interesting of the bunch is the **Sānwèi Shūwū** (三味书屋), the one-room schoolhouse where the author studied as a boy. There are also two residences through which you can stroll. Entry is free, though you'll need to show your passport.

From here you can walk north along the quays, some of which are shaded with wooden overhangs, past quiet slices of residential life. The most noteworthy among the numerous stone bridges (some ancient and many still in use) you'll pass is **Bāzǐ Bridge** (八子乔, Bāzǐ Qiáo), shrouded in ivy and shaped like the character for lucky number eight (八; bā). It dates to the first years of the 13th century.

Two kilometres west of Bāzǐ Bridge is **Cāngqiáo Street** (仓桥直街; Cāngqiáo Zhíjiē), a restored stretch of old shophouses, several of which now house cafes.

Filling the meandering corridors of a centuries-old courtyard house, **Lǔxùn Native Place Youth Hostel** (老台门鲁迅故里国际青年旅舍, Lǎotáimén Lǔxùn Gùlǐ Guójì Qīngnián Lǚshè; ☑ 0575 8508 0288; www.yhachina.com/ls.php?id=260; 558 Xinjian Nanlu, 新建南路558号; dm ¥55, d ¥198-398; ❈ @ ⧉) is right in line with the city's other historic sites. The renovations are a bit patchwork but the rooms are clean and comfortable. There's also a restaurant and lounge where you can unwind with some Shàoxīng wine. Staff speak some English and are friendly. The hostel is just south of Lǔxùn Native Place, on a small road running perpendicular from the tourist strip. It's also a five-minute walk from the BRT station on Zhongxing Zhonglu (中兴中路).

Shàoxīng's custard tarts are different from the ones you find in Shànghǎi or Macau, with thin crisp shells, the lightest of custard and wispy caps of meringue. Get 'em to go from tiny **Gāo Lǎotài Nǎiyóu Xiǎopān** (高老太奶油小攀; 608 Xinjian Nanlu, 新建南路608号; tart ¥3; ☉ 8.30am-9pm).

Just west of Lǔxùn Native Place, **Xiánhēng Jiǔdiàn** (咸亨酒店; ☑ 0557 8512 7170; 179 Luxun Zhonglu, 鲁迅中路179号; dishes ¥20-55; ☉ 10.30am-2.30pm & 4.30-8.30pm) is a fantastic, if touristy, place to sample local food and drink. Dishes include dried broad beans stewed in fennel water (茴香豆; huíxiāng dòu) and 'drunk' river crab (醉蟹; zuì xiè) that has been pickled and cooked with wine vinasse, the residue from the winemaking process. Order Shàoxīng wine from the counter out front. You'll need to first purchase a prepaid card (minimum ¥100), which you'll use to purchase dishes inside. The remaining balance and deposit will be returned to you when you return the card.

ℹ Getting There & Around

Frequent high-speed trains run between Hángzhōu East and Shàoxīng North (¥20 to ¥63, 20 minutes); however, the high-speed train station is far north of the city, either 30 minutes in a taxi (¥50) or an hour on the BRT1 express bus (¥4). There are seven K trains daily between 7am and 2.12pm from either Hángzhōu or Hángzhōu East that run to Shàoxīng train station (¥11 to ¥13, one hour), which is downtown.

Frequent buses also run from Hángzhōu to Shàoxīng Passenger Transport Centre (¥24 to ¥27, one hour), although the bus station is also north of the city centre. Shàoxīng taxis start at ¥7.

ZHÈJIĀNG SHÀOXĪNG

Shànghǎi

Includes ➡

Best Places to Eat

➡ Yang's Fry Dumplings (p318)

➡ El Willy (p319)

➡ Table No 1 by Jason Atherton (p320)

➡ Din Tai Fung (p323)

➡ Lost Heaven (p320)

Best Places to Sleep

➡ Fairmont Peace Hotel (p313)

➡ Mandarin Oriental Pudong (p316)

➡ Kevin's Old House (p315)

➡ Waterhouse at South Bund (p314)

➡ Urbn (p316)

Why Go?

You can't see the Great Wall from space, but you'd have a job missing Shànghǎi (上海). One of the country's largest and most vibrant cities, Shànghǎi somehow typifies modern China while being unlike anywhere else in the land. Shànghǎi is real China, but – rather like Hong Kong or Macau – just not the China you had in mind.

This is a city of action, not ideas. You won't spot many Buddhist monks contemplating the dharma, oddball bohemians or wild-haired poets handing out flyers, but skyscrapers will form before your eyes. Shànghǎi best serves as an epilogue to your China experience: submit to its debutante charms after you've had your fill of dusty imperial palaces and bumpy 10-hour bus rides. From nonstop shopping to skyscraper-hopping to bullet-fast Maglev trains and glamorous cocktails – this is Shànghǎi.

When to Go
Shànghǎi

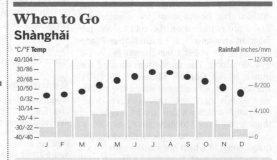

Feb or Mar Visit Yùyuán Gardens for the lantern festival, two weeks after Chinese New Year.	**Apr & May** March is chilly and 1 May is chaos, but otherwise spring is ideal.	**Late Sep–Oct** The optimal season: neither too hot nor too rainy.

History

As the gateway to the Yangzi River (Cháng Jiāng), Shànghǎi (the name means 'by the sea') has long been an ideal trading port. However, although it supported as many as 50,000 residents by the late 17th century, it wasn't until after the British opened their concession here in 1842 that modern Shànghǎi really came into being.

The British presence in Shànghǎi was soon followed by the French and Americans, and by 1853 Shànghǎi had overtaken all other Chinese ports. Built on the trade of opium, silk and tea, the city also lured the world's great houses of finance, which erected grand palaces of plenty. Shànghǎi also became a byword for exploitation and vice; its countless opium dens, gambling joints and brothels managed by gangs were at the heart of Shànghǎi life. Guarding it all were the American, French and Italian marines, British Tommies and Japanese bluejackets.

After Chiang Kaishek's coup against the communists in 1927, the Kuomintang cooperated with the foreign police and the Shànghǎi gangs, and with Chinese and foreign factory owners, to suppress labour unrest. Exploited in workhouse conditions, crippled by hunger and poverty, sold into slavery, excluded from the high life and the parks created by the foreigners, the poor of Shànghǎi had a voracious appetite for radical opinion. The Chinese Communist Party (CCP) was formed here in 1921 and, after numerous setbacks, 'liberated' the city in 1949.

The communists eradicated the slums, rehabilitated the city's hundreds of thousands of opium addicts, and eliminated child and slave labour. These were staggering achievements; but when the decadence went, so did the splendour. Shànghǎi became a colourless factory town and political hotbed, and was the power base of the infamous Gang of Four during the Cultural Revolution.

Shànghǎi's long slumber came to an abrupt end in 1990, with the announcement of plans to develop Pǔdōng, on the eastern side of the Huángpǔ River. Since then Shànghǎi's burgeoning economy, leadership and intrinsic self-confidence have put it miles ahead of other Chinese cities. Its bright lights and opportunities have branded Shànghǎi a Mecca for Chinese (and foreign) economic migrants. In 2010, 3600 people were squeezed into every square kilometre, compared with 2588 per sq km in 2000 and by 2014, the city's population had leaped to a staggering 24 million. Over nine million migrants make Shànghǎi home, colouring the local complexion with a jumble of dialects, outlooks, lifestyles and cuisines.

⊙ Sights

The majority of sightseeing in Shànghǎi centres on the Bund and People's Square with its cluster of museums and lovely park. Roaming the Bund promenade provides a non-stop show of heritage architecture with views over the river to the futuristic skyscrapers of Pǔdōng. A quick ferry ride across will have you zipping up to the observation decks of the Shànghǎi Tower and the iconic Oriental Pearl TV Tower. Back on the Pǔxī side, it's all about peeking inside historic mansions in the former French Concession and seeking out a much-needed culture hit in the sacred temples and traditional teahouses of the Old Town and Jìng'ān.

◉ The Bund & People's Square 外滩、人民广场

People's Square is ground central for Shànghǎi sightseeing with world-class museums, diverse architecture, art galleries and a beautiful park.

★ **The Bund** ARCHITECTURE
(外滩, Waitàn; Map p296; 3 East Zhongshan No 1 Rd, 3 中山东   路; M Line 2, 10 to East Nanjing Rd) Symbolic of concession-era Shànghǎi, the Bund was the city's Wall Street, a place of feverish trading and fortunes made and lost. Originally a towpath for dragging barges of rice, the Bund (an Anglo-Indian term for the embankment of a muddy waterfront) was gradually transformed into a grandiose sweep of the most powerful banks and

SHÀNGHǍI SIGHTS

PRICE RANGES

Sleeping

Price ranges per night of an en suite double room in high season:

$ Less than ¥500

$$ ¥500–¥1300

$$$ More than ¥1300

Eating

Price ranges for a main course for one:

$ less than ¥60

$$ ¥60–¥160

$$$ more than ¥160

Shànghǎi Highlights

❶ The Bund (p291) Strolling down the promenade or raising an evening glass to phosphorescent Pǔdōng.

❷ Shànghǎi Museum (p294) Loading up on Chinese culture's greatest hits.

❸ Skyline Admiring the curvature of the earth from atop the Shànghǎi Tower (p307) or the Shànghǎi World Financial Center (p307).

❹ Rockbund Art Museum (p295) Catching up with the latest trends in contemporary Chinese art.

❺ Tiánzǐfáng (p299) Weaving through a forest of shoppers' elbows in this charming *shíkùmén* warren.

❻ French Concession (p299) Putting on your best shoes and stepping out.

❼ East Nanjing Road (p295) Plunging into the neon-lit swell.

❽ Bund restaurants (p318) Dining at some of Shànghǎi's signature restaurants, all with show-stopping views.

❾ Jade Buddha Temple (p303) Fathoming the fantastic at Shànghǎi's most sacred shrine.

❿ Yùyuán Gardens (p298) Seeking out a quiet pocket and sitting down.

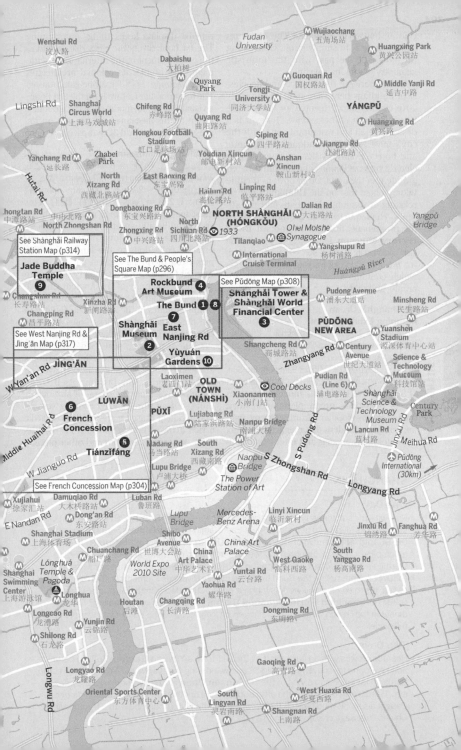

Wenshui Rd
汶水路

Fudan
University

Wujiaochang
五角场站

Huangxing Park
黄兴公园站

Dabaishu
大柏树

Guoquan Rd
国权路站

Middle Yanji Rd
延吉中路

Lingshi Rd

Shanghai
Circus World
上海马戏城站

Quyang
Park

Tongji
University
同济大学站

YÁNGPǓ

Chifeng Rd
赤峰路

Quyang Rd
曲阳路站

Siping Rd
四平路站

Huangxing Rd
黄兴路

Yanchang Rd
延长路

Zhabei
Park

Hongkou Football
Stadium
虹口足球场站

Youdian Xincun
邮电新村站

Jiangpu Rd
江浦路站

Anshan
Xincun
鞍山新村站

North
Xizang Rd
西藏北路站

East Baoxing Rd
东宝兴路

Hailun Rd
海伦路站

Linping Rd
临平路站

Dalian Rd
大连路站

Yangpǔ
Bridge

hongtan Rd
中源路站

North Zhongshan Rd
中山北路

Dongbaoxing Rd
东宝兴路站

NORTH SHÀNGHǍI
(HÓNGKǑU)

Ohel Moishe
Synagogue

Huángpǔ River

See Shànghǎi Railway
Station Map (p314)

Jade Buddha
Temple
9

Changshou Rd
长寿路站

Changping Rd
昌平路站

Xinzha Rd
新闸路站

Zhongxing Rd
中兴路站

North
Sichuan Rd
四川北路站

1933

Tilanqiao
提篮桥

International
Cruise Terminal
国际客运中心

Yangshupu Rd
杨树浦路

Pudong Avenue
浦东大道站

Minsheng Rd
民生路

See The Bund & People's
Square Map (p296)

Rockbund
Art Museum 4

The Bund 1 8

See Pǔdōng Map (p308)

Shànghǎi Tower &
Shànghǎi World
Financial Center
3

PǓDŌNG
NEW AREA

Yuanshen
Stadium
源深体育中心站

Science &
Technology
Museum

See West Nanjing Rd &
Jing'ān Map (p317)

Shànghǎi
Museum 2

East
Nanjing Rd 7

Shangcheng Rd
商城路站

Century
Avenue
世纪大道站

W Yan'an Rd JING'ĀN

Yùyuán
Gardens 10

Zhangyang Rd

Pudian Rd
(Line 6)
浦电路站

Shànghǎi
Science &
Technology
Museum
科技馆站

Century
Park

Laoximen
老西门站

OLD
TOWN
(NÁNSHÌ)

Xiaonanmen
小南门站

Cool Docks

S Pudong Rd

Lancun Rd
蓝村路

LÚWĀN

PǓXĪ

Lujiabang Rd
陆家浜路站

Nanpu Bridge
南浦大桥

Meihua Rd

6

French
Concession

Madang Rd
马当路站

South
Xizang Rd
西藏南路

S Zhongshan Rd

Pǔdōng
International
(30km)

Middle Huaihai Rd

Tiánzǐfáng 5

Lupu Bridge
卢浦大桥

Nanpu
Bridge

Linyi Xincun
临沂新村

Longyang Rd

W Jianguo Rd

See French Concession Map (p304)

The Power
Station of Art

Mercedes-
Benz Arena

Jinxiù Rd
锦绣路

Fanghua Rd
芳华路

Xujiahui
徐家汇站

Damuqiao Rd
大木桥路站

Dong'an Rd
东安路站

Lúban Rd
鲁班路

Shibo
Avenue
世博大会站

China Art
Palace

West Gaoke
高科西路

South
Yanggao Rd
杨高南路

E Nandan Rd

Shanghai Stadium
上海体育场

Chuanchang Rd
船厂路

China
Art Palace
中华艺术宫

Yuntai Rd
云台路

Dongming Rd
东明路

Shanghai
Swimming
Center
上海游泳池

Lónghuá
Temple &
Pagoda

World Expo
2010 Site

Houtan
后滩

Yaohua Rd
耀华路

Longhua

Longcao Rd
龙漕路

Yunjin Rd
云锦路

Changqing Rd
长清路

Shilong Rd
石龙路

Gaoqing Rd
高青路

Longwu Rd

Longyao Rd
龙耀路

Oriental Sports Center
东方体育中心站

South
Lingyan Rd
灵岩南路

West Huaxia Rd
华夏西路

Shangnan Rd
上南路

trading houses in Shànghǎi. The optimum activity here is to simply stroll, contrasting the bones of the past with the futuristic geometry of Pǔdōng's skyline.

The majority of the art deco and neoclassical buildings here were built in the early 20th century and presented an imposing – if strikingly un-Chinese – view. Today it is a designer retail and restaurant zone with the city's most exclusive boutiques, restaurants and hotels. Evening visits are rewarded by electric views of Pǔdōng and the illuminated grandeur of the Bund. Other options include taking a boat tour on the Huángpǔ River or relaxing at some fabulous bars and restaurants. Huángpǔ Park, at the north end of the promenade, features the modest **Bund History Museum** (外滩历史纪念馆, Wàitān Lìshǐ Jìniànguǎn; Map p296; ⊙9am-4pm Mon-Fri; Ⓜ Line 2, 10 to East Nanjing Rd, exit 7) **FREE**, which contains a collection of old photographs and maps.

★**Shànghǎi Urban Planning Exhibition Hall**   MUSEUM
(上海城市规划展示馆, Shànghǎi Chéngshì Guīhuà Zhǎnshìguǎn; Map p296; www.supec.org; 100 Renmin Ave, entrance on Middle Xizang Rd, 人民大道100号; adult/child ¥30/15; ⊙9am-5pm Tue-Sun, last entry 4pm; Ⓜ Line 1, 2, 8 to People's Square, exit 2) Set over five levels, this modern museum covers Shànghǎi's urban planning history, tracing its development from swampy fishing village to modern-day megacity. Its mix of photography, models and interactive multimedia displays keeps things entertaining. The 1st floor covers the city's rise, including the establishment of the international settlement, and profiles its colonial architecture and *shíkùmén* (石库门; stone-gate houses). The most popular feature is on the 3rd floor – a visually stunning model showing a detailed layout of this megalopolis-to-be, plus an impressive Virtual World 3D wraparound tour.

★**Shànghǎi Museum**   MUSEUM
(上海博物馆, Shànghǎi Bówùguǎn; Map p296; www.shanghaimuseum.net; 201 Renmin Ave, 人民大道201号; ⊙9am-5pm, last entry 4pm; Ⓜ; Ⓜ Line 1, 2, 8 to People's Square) **FREE** This must-see museum escorts you through the craft of millennia and the pages of Chinese history. It's home to one of the most impressive collections in the land: take your pick from the archaic green patinas of the Ancient Chinese Bronzes Gallery through to the silent solemnity of the Ancient Chinese Sculpture Gallery; from the exquisite beauty of the ceramics in the Zande Lou Gallery to the measured and timeless flourishes captured in the Chinese Calligraphy Gallery.

Chinese painting, seals, jade, Ming and Qing furniture, coins and ethnic costumes are also on offer, intelligently displayed in well lit galleries. The building itself is designed to resemble the shape of an ancient Chinese *dǐng* (three-legged cooking vessel). The excellent museum shop sells postcards, a rich array of books, and faithful replicas of the museum's ceramics and other pieces.

SHÀNGHǍI IN...

One Day

Rise with the sun for early morning riverside scenes on the **Bund** (p291) as the vast city stirs from its slumber. Then stroll down East Nanjing Rd to **People's Square** and either the **Shànghǎi Museum** or the **Shànghǎi Urban Planning Exhibition Hall**. After a dumpling lunch on Huanghe Rd food street, hop on the metro at People's Square to shuttle east to Pǔdōng. Explore the fun and interactive **Shànghǎi History Museum** (p307) or contemplate the Bund from the breezy Riverside Promenade, then take high-speed lifts to some of the world's highest observation decks, in the **Shànghǎi Tower** (p307) or **Shànghǎi World Financial Center** (p307). Stomach rumbling? Time for dinner in the French Concession, followed by a nightcap on the Bund if you want to go full circle.

Two Days

Beat the crowds with an early start at the Old Town's **Yùyuán Gardens** (p298) before poking around for souvenirs on Old St and wandering the alleyways. Make your next stop Xīntiāndì for lunch and a visit to the **Shíkùmén Open House Museum** (p302). Taxi it to **Tiánzǐfáng** (p299) for the afternoon, before another French Concession dinner. Caught a second wind? Catch the acrobats, hit the clubs or unwind with a traditional Chinese massage or some Shànghǎi jazz.

The audio guide is well worth the ¥40 (deposit ¥400 or your passport). Expect to spend half, if not most, of, a day here.

Yuanmingyuan Road   AREA
(圆明园路, Yuánmíngyuán Lù; Map p296; M Line 2, 10 to East Nanjing Rd) Like a smaller, more condensed version of the Bund, the pedestrianised, cobblestone Yuanmingyuan Rd is lined with a mishmash of colonial architecture. Running parallel with the Bund, just one block back, the road features some fine examples of renovated red-brick and stone buildings dating from the 1900s. Look for the art deco YWCA building (No 133) and Chinese Baptist Publication building (No 209), the ornate 1907 red-brick Panama Legation building (No 97) and the 1927 neoclassical Lyceum building.

Former British Consulate   HISTORIC BUILDING
(英国驻上海总领事馆, Yīngguó Zhù Shànghǎi Zǒng Lǐngshìguǎn; Map p296; 33 East Zhongshan No 1 Rd, 33 中山东路 1 号; M Line 2, 10 to East Nanjing, exit 7) The original British Consulate was one of the first foreign buildings to go up in Shànghǎi in 1852, though it was destroyed in a fire and replaced with the current structure in 1873. Now renovated, it is used as a financiers' club and restaurant, **No 1 Waitanyuan** (外滩源一号, Wàitān Yuán Yī Hào; Map p296; 021 5308 9803; www.wtysh.com; 33 East Zhongshan No 1 Rd, 中山东一路33号; platter for 2 persons ¥288; high tea 2-5pm; M Line 2, 10 to East Nanjing Rd), which serves high tea. Also within the grounds are the former Consul's Residence (1884) – now a atek Philippe store – and several century-old magnolia trees.

Hongkong & Shanghai Bank Building   HISTORIC BUILDING
(HSBC Building, 汇丰大厦; Map p296; 12 East Zhongshan No 1 Rd, 中山东一路12号; M Line 2, 10 to East Nanjing Rd) Adjacent to the Custom House (p295), the Hongkong & Shanghai Bank building was constructed in 1923. The bank was first established in Hong Kong in 1864 and in Shànghǎi in 1865 to finance trade, and soon became one of the richest in Shànghǎi, arranging the indemnity paid after the Boxer Rebellion. The magnificent mosaic ceiling inside the entrance was plastered over until its restoration in 1997 and is therefore well preserved.

Custom House   NOTABLE BUILDING
(自订的房子, Zì Dìng De Fángzi; Map p296; 13 East Zhongshan No 1 Rd, 中山东一路13号; M Line 2, 10 to East Nanjing Rd, exit 1) The neoclassical Custom House, established at this site in 1857 and rebuilt in 1927, is one of the most important buildings on the Bund. Capping it is Big Ching, a bell modelled on London's Big Ben. Clocks were by no means new to China, but Shànghǎi was the first city in which they gained widespread acceptance and the lives of many became dictated by a standardised, common schedule. During the Cultural Revolution, Big Ching was replaced with loudspeakers that blasted out revolutionary songs ('The East is Red') and slogans.

East Nanjing Road   AREA
(南京东路, Nánjīng Dōnglù; Map p296; M Line 2, 10 to East Nanjing Rd) Linking the Bund with People's Square is East Nanjing Rd, once known as Nanking Rd. The first department stores in China opened here in the 1920s, when the modern machine age – with its new products, automobiles, art deco styling and newfangled ideas – was ushered in. A glowing forest of neon at night, it's no longer the cream of Shànghǎi shopping, but its pedestrian strip remains one of the most famous and crowded streets in China.

Shànghǎi Gallery of Art   GALLERY
(外滩三号沪申画廊, Wàitān Sānhào Hùshēn Huàláng; Map p296; www.shanghaigalleryofart. com; 3rd fl, Three on the Bund, 3 East Zhongshan No1 Rd, 中山东一路三号三楼; 10am-7pm; M Line 2, 10 to East Nanjing Rd) FREE Take the lift up to the 3rd floor of **Three on the Bund** (外滩三号, Wàitān Sān Hào; Map p296) to this neat, minimalist art gallery showcasing

---

ROCKBUND ART MUSEUM

Housed in the magnificent former Royal Asiatic Society building (1932) – once Shànghǎi's first museum – world-class **Rockbund Art Museum** (RAM, 上海外滩美术馆, Shànghǎi Wàitān Měishùguǎn; Map p296; www.rockbundartmuseum. org; 20 Huqiu Rd, 虎丘路20号; adult/child ¥30/15; 10am-6pm Tue-Sun; M Line 2, 10 to East Nanjing Rd) focuses on contemporary Chinese and international art, with rotating exhibits year-round and no permanent collection. One of the city's top modern-art venues, the building's interior and exterior are both sublime. Check out the unique art deco eight-sided *bāguà* (trigram) windows at the front, a fetching synthesis of Western modernist styling and traditional Chinese design.

SHÀNGHǍI SIGHTS

The Bund & People's Square

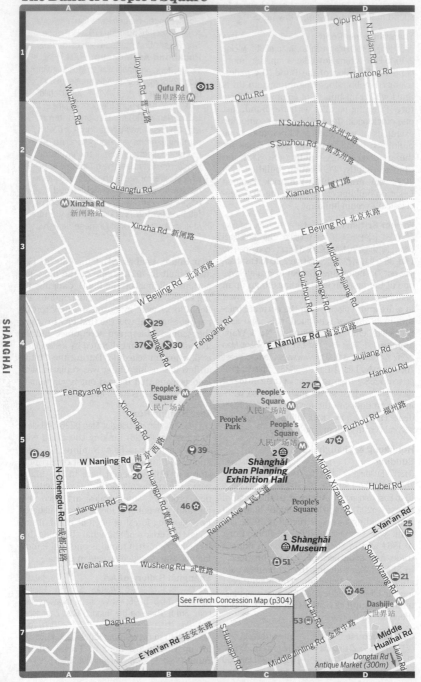

SHÀNGHĂI

Qipu Rd

N Fujian Rd

Tiantong Rd

Wuzhen Rd

Jinyuan Rd 晋元路

Qufu Rd 曲阜路站 ⊙13

Qufu Rd

N Suzhou Rd 苏州北路

S Suzhou Rd 南苏州路

Guangfu Rd

Xiamen Rd 厦门路

Xinzha Rd 新闸路站

Xinzha Rd 新闸路

E Beijing Rd 北京东路

W Beijing Rd 北京西路

Middle Zhejiang Rd

N Guangxi Rd

Guizhou Rd

Fengyang Rd

E Nanjing Rd 南京东路

Jiujiang Rd

Hankou Rd

⊗29

37⊗ ⊗30

Huangle Rd

Fengyang Rd

Fengyang Rd

27⊡

People's Square 人民广场站

People's Square

People's Square 人民广场站

Fuzhou Rd 福州路

Xinchang Rd

N Huangpi Rd 黄陂北路

People's Park

47✿

Middle Xizang Rd

⊡49

W Nanjing Rd 南京西路

⊟20

⊟39

2🏛 Shànghăi Urban Planning Exhibition Hall

Hubei Rd

N Chengdu Rd 成都北路

Jiangyin Rd

⊟22

46✿

People's Square

E Yan'an Rd

25⊟

Weihai Rd

Wusheng Rd 武胜路

1 🏛 Shànghăi Museum

⊡51

South Xizang Rd

Dashijie 大世界站 Ⓜ

⊟21

See French Concession Map (p304)

45✿

Dagu Rd

E Yan'an Rd 延安东路

S Huangpi Rd

53⊡

Puan Rd

Middle Jinling Rd 金陵中路

Middle Huaihai Rd

Lilin Rd

Dongtai Rd Antique Market (300m)

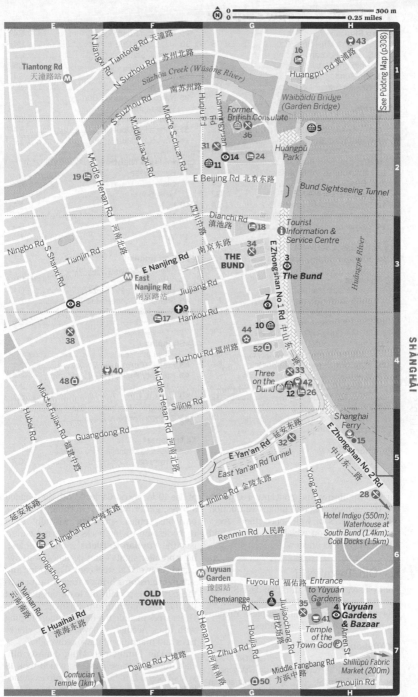

0 — 300 m
0 — 0.25 miles

N

See Pùdōng Map (p308)

43

16

Huangpu Rd 黄浦路

Tiantong Rd
天潼路站 **M**

N Jiangxi Rd

N Suzhou Rd

Tiantong Rd 天潼路

Sūzhōu Creek (Wúsōng River)

南苏州路：

Middle Sch.an Rd

S Suzhou Rd

Huqiu Rd

Yuanmingyuan Rd

Middle Jiangxi Rd

Middle Henan Rd

河南北路

19

Wàibáidù Bridge
(Garden Bridge)

Former
British Consulate

36

5

Huángpù
Park

31

14 **24**

11

E Beijing Rd 北京东路

Ningbo Rd

S Shanxi Rd

Tianjin Rd

Dianchi Rd
滇池路

18

Bund Sightseeing Tunnel

Huángpǔ River

**East
Nanjing Rd**
南京路站

E Nanjing Rd

四川中路

南京东路

34

**THE
BUND**

E Zhongshan No.1 Rd

中山东一路

i Tourist
Information &
Service Centre

3
The Bund

8

Jiujiang Rd

9

17

Hankou Rd

7

38

Fuzhou Rd 福州路

44 **10**

52

Sijing Rd

Middle Henan Rd

河南北路

48

40

*Three
on the
Bund*

33

42

12 **26**

Guangdong Rd

Hubei Rd

Middle Fujian Rd 福建中路

**Shanghai
Ferry**

15

E Yan'an Rd 延安东路

32

East Yan'an Rd Tunnel

E Jinling Rd 金陵东路

E Zhongshan No 2 Rd

中山东二路

Yong'an Rd

28

延安东路

Hotel Indigo (550m);
Waterhouse at
South Bund (1.4km);
Cool Docks (1.5km)

23

E Ninghai Rd 宁海东路

Renmin Rd 人民路

Yongshou Rd

S Yunnan Rd
云南南路

M **Yuyuan
Garden**
豫园站

Fuyou Rd 福佑路

*Entrance
to Yùyuán
Gardens*

E Huaihai Rd
淮海东路

**OLD
TOWN**

Chenxiangge
Rd

6

Jiujiaochang Rd 旧校场路

35

41

4
**Yùyuán
Gardens
& Bazaar**

Anren St

S Henan Rd 河南南路

Houjia Rd

*Temple
of the
Town God*

Confucian
Temple (1km)

Zihua Rd

Dajing Rd 大境路

Middle Fangbang Rd
方浜中路

50

*Shílìùpù Fabric
Market (200m)*

Zhoujin Rd

SHÀNGHǍI

The Bund & People's Square

⊙ Top Sights
1 Shànghǎi Museum............................C6
2 Shànghǎi Urban Planning
   Exhibition Hall..........................C5
3 The Bund..G3
4 Yùyuán Gardens & Bazaar.................H7

◎ Sights
5 Bund History Museum......................H2
6 Chénxiānggé Monastery...................G6
7 Custom House...............................G3
8 East Nanjing Road..........................E3
9 Holy Trinity Church.........................F3
10 Hongkong & Shanghai Bank
    Building.....................................G4
11 Rockbund Art Museum....................G2
12 Shànghǎi Gallery of Art.................G4
13 Sky Ring.......................................B1
14 Yuanmingyuan Rd..........................G2

⊙ Activities, Courses & Tours
15 Huángpǔ River Cruise.....................H5

🛏 Sleeping
16 Astor House Hotel...........................G1
17 Bund Garden Shanghai....................F4
18 Fairmont Peace Hotel......................G3
19 Fish Inn Bund.................................E2
20 JW Marriott Tomorrow Square...........B5
21 Metropolo Hotel – People's
    Square.......................................D6
22 Mingtown E-Tour Youth Hostel...........B6
23 Mingtown People's Square Youth
    Hostel.......................................E6
24 Peninsula Hotel..............................G2
25 Phoenix..D6
26 Waldorf Astoria..............................H4
27 Yangtze Boutique Shànghǎi..............C4

✗ Eating
28 El Willy...H5

29 Huanghe Road Food Street.................B4
30 Jiājiā Soup Dumplings......................B4
31 Light & Salt...................................G2
32 Lost Heaven..................................G5
33 M on the Bund................................G4
34 Mr & Mrs Bund...............................G3
35 Nánxiáng Steamed Bun
    Restaurant..................................H7
36 No 1 Waitanyuan............................G2
37 Yang's Fry Dumplings.......................B4
38 Yúxìn Chuāncài..............................E4

🍷 Drinking & Nightlife
39 Barbarossa....................................B5
   Glam......................................(see 33)
   Long Bar.................................(see 26)
40 M1NT...F4
41 Mid-Lake Pavilion Teahouse.............H7
42 Pop...G4
43 Vue...H1

✪ Entertainment
   Fairmont Peace Hotel Jazz
    Bar..(see 18)
44 House of Blues & Jazz......................G4
45 Shànghǎi Concert Hall.....................D7
46 Shànghǎi Grand Theatre..................B6
47 Yifū Theatre...................................D5

🛍 Shopping
   Amy Lin's Pearls........................(see 49)
48 Foreign Languages Bookstore............E4
49 Han City Fashion & Accessories
    Plaza..A5
50 Old Street.....................................G7
51 Shànghǎi Museum Art Store..............C6
52 Sūzhōu Cobblers............................G4

🚍 Transport
53 Buses to Zhūjiājiǎo (Pu'an Rd
    terminal)....................................C7

current highbrow and conceptual Chinese art. It's all bare concrete pillars, ventilation ducts and acres of wall space; there are a couple of divans on which you can sit and admire the works on view.

⊙ Old Town 南市

That elusive sense of an olden-days Shànghǎi can be glimpsed through the sights of this neighbourhood: the temples, Yùyuán Gardens and old *shíkùmén* lanes.

★**Yùyuán Gardens &
Bazaar**   GARDENS, BAZAAR
(豫园、豫园商城, Yùyuán & Yùyuán Shāngchéng; Map p296; Anren St, 安仁街; high/low season ¥40/30; ⊙8.30am-5.15pm, last entry at 4.45pm;

Ⓜ Line 10 to Yuyuan Garden) With its shaded alcoves, glittering pools churning with fish, pavilions, pines sprouting wistfully from rockeries and roving packs of Japanese tourists, the **Yùyuán Gardens** is one of Shànghǎi's premier sights – but becomes overpoweringly crowded at weekends. The spring and summer blossoms bring a fragrant aspect to the gardens, especially the luxurious petals of its *Magnolia grandiflora,* Shànghǎi's flower. Other trees include the luohan pine, bristling with thick needles, willows, gingkos, cherry trees and magnificent dawn redwoods.

The Pan family, rich Ming dynasty officials, founded these gardens, which took 18 years (1559–77) to be nurtured into existence before bombardment during the Opium War in 1842. The gardens took another trashing during French reprisals for attacks on their nearby concession during the Taiping Rebellion. Restored, they are a fine example of Ming garden design.

Next to the **garden entrance** (Map p296) is the Mid-Lake Pavilion Teahouse (p324), once part of the gardens and now one of the most famous teahouses in China.

The adjacent bazaar may be tacky, but it's good for a browse if you can handle the push and pull of the crowds. The nearby Taoist Temple of the Town God (p299) is also worth visiting. Just outside the bazaar is Old Street (p328), known more prosaically as Middle Fangbang Rd, a busy street lined with curio shops and teahouses.

Temple of the Town God   TAOIST TEMPLE
(城隍庙, Chénghuáng Miào; Map p296; Yùyuán Bazaar, off Middle Fangbang Rd, 豫园商城方浜中路; ¥10; ☉8.30am-4.30pm; Ⓜ Line 10 to Yuyuan Garden) Chinese towns traditionally had a Taoist temple of the town god, but many fell victim to periodic upheaval. Originally dating to the early 15th century, this particular temple was badly damaged during the Cultural Revolution and later restored. Note the fine carvings on the roof as you enter the main hall, which is dedicated to Huo Guang, a Han dynasty general, flanked by rows of effigies representing both martial and civil virtues.

Chénxiāngge Monastery   BUDDHIST TEMPLE
(沉香阁, Chénxiāng Gé; Map p296; 29 Chenxiangge Rd, 沉香阁路29号; ¥10; ☉7am-5pm; Ⓜ Line 10 to Yuyuan Garden) Sheltering a community of dark-brown-clothed monks from the Chénhǎi (Sea of Dust) – what Buddhists call the mortal world, but which could equally refer to Shànghǎi's murky atmosphere – this lovely yellow-walled temple is a tranquil refuge. At the temple rear, the **Guanyin Tower** guides you upstairs to a glittering effigy of the male-looking goddess, Guanyin herself (p960), within a resplendent gilded cabinet.

Cool Docks   ARCHITECTURE
(老码头, Lǎomǎtóu; www.thecooldocks.com; 479 South Zhongshan Rd, 中山南路479号; Ⓜ Line 9 to Xiaonanmen) The riverside Cool Docks consist of several shíkùmén surrounded by red-brick warehouses, near (but not quite on) the waterfront. Now full of restaurants and bars and all lit up at night, the Cool Docks' isolated positioning (it lacks the central location and transport connections of Xīntiāndì in the French Concession) has hobbled ambitions. Although high-profile and trendy restaurant,

bar and hotel openings have helped give it a much-needed lift, it remains an entertainment backwater.

Power Station of Art   GALLERY
(上海当代艺术博物馆, Shànghǎi Dāngdài Yìshù Bówùguǎn; Lane 20 Huayuangang Rd, 花园港路200号; ☉11am-7pm Tue-Sun, last entry 6pm; Ⓜ Line 4, 8 to South Xizang Rd) FREE The vast Power Station of Art in the disused Nánshì Power Plant holds modern large scale installations, design shows and other temporary exhibitions, some quite provocative. It also hosts the Shànghǎi Biennale.

◉ French Concession 法租界

The former French Concession is where the bulk of Shànghǎi's disposable cash is splashed. The low-rise, villa-lined leafy backstreets are perfectly geared to shopping, dining and entertainment, but a brood of museums makes the area a cultural experience as well.

★ **Tiánzǐfáng**   AREA
(田子坊; Map p304; www.tianzifang.cn; Taikang Rd, 泰康路; Ⓜ Dapuqiao) Tiánzǐfáng and Xīntiāndì (p302) are based on a similar idea – an entertainment complex housed within a warren of traditional *lòngtáng* (弄堂; alleyways) – but when it comes to genuine charm and vibrancy, Tiánzǐfáng is the one that delivers. You do need to wade through the souvenir stalls to get to the good stuff, but this network of design studios, cafes, bars and boutiques is the perfect antidote to Shànghǎi's oversized malls and intimidating skyscrapers. With some families still residing in neighbouring buildings, a community mood survives.

There are three main north–south lanes (Nos 210, 248 and 274) criss-crossed by irregular east–west alleyways, which makes exploration slightly disorienting and fun. Among the art galleries is **Beaugeste** (Bǐjí Yìngxiàng; www.beaugeste-gallery.com; 5th fl, No 5, Lane 210; ☉10am-6pm Sat & Sun), a forward-thinking photography gallery (only open at the weekends, by appointment at other times). The real activity is shopping, and the recent explosion of creative start-ups makes for some interesting finds, from vintage spectacle frames at **Shanghai Code** (Shànghǎi Mìmǎ; No 9, Lane 274; ☉1-9pm) and cool homewares at concept store **Taste** (www.taste-shop. com; Room 105, Bldg 3, Lane 210; ☉12.30-8.30pm Tue-Sun), to hand-wrapped *pǔ'ěr* teas from Zhēnchálín (p330). Elsewhere, a growing band of cool cafes, restaurants and bars, such

SHÀNGHǍI SIGHTS

The Bund

ARCHITECTURAL HIGHLIGHTS

The best way to get acquainted with Shànghǎi is to take a stroll along the Bund.

This illustration shows the main sights along the Bund's central stretch, beginning near the intersection with East Nanjing Rd. The Bund is 1km long and walking it should take around an hour.

Head to the area south of the Hongkong & Shanghai Bank Building to find the biggest selection of drinking and dining destinations.

Hongkong & Shanghai Bank Building (1923)

Head into this massive bank to marvel at the beautiful mosaic ceiling, featuring the 12 zodiac signs and the world's (former) eight centres of finance.

Custom House (1927)

One of the most important buildings on the Bund, Custom House was capped by the largest clock face in Asia and 'Big Ching', a bell modelled on London's Big Ben.

OSTILL / SHUTTERSTOCK ©

Former Bank of Communications (1947)

Bund Public Service Centre (2010)

SEAN PAVONE / SHUTTERSTOCK ©

TOP TIP

The promenade is open around the clock, but it's at its best in the early morning, when locals are out practising taichi, or in the early evening, when both sides of the river are lit up and the majesty of the waterfront is at its grandest.

North China Daily News Building (1924)

Known as the 'Old Lady of the Bund'. The *News* ran from 1864 to 1951 as the main English-language newspaper in China. Look for the paper's motto above the central windows.

Fairmont Peace Hotel (1929)

Originally built as the Cathay Hotel, this art deco masterpiece was *the* place to stay in Shànghǎi and the crown jewel in Victor Sassoon's real-estate empire.

Former Chartered Bank Building (1923)

Reopened in 2004 as the upscale entertainment complex Bund 18; the building's top-floor Bar Rouge is one of the Bund's premier late-night destinations.

Russo-Chinese Bank Building (1902)

Former Bank of Taiwan (1927)

Former Palace Hotel (1906)

Now known as the Swatch Art Peace Hotel (an artists' residence and gallery, with a top-floor restaurant and bar), this building was completed in 1908 and hosted Sun Yatsen's victory celebration in 1911 following his election as the first president of the Republic of China.

Bank of China (1942)

This unusual building was originally commissioned to be the tallest building in Shànghǎi but, probably because of Victor Sassoon's influence, wound up being 1m shorter than its neighbour.

as **Kommune** (Gōngshè; www.kommune.me, The Yard, No 7, Lane 210; meals from ¥77; ⊘9am-midnight; 🛜), **East** (www.east-eatery.com; No 39, Lane 155, Middle Jianguo Rd, 建国中路155弄39号; bǎo 1/3 pieces ¥12/30, dishes from ¥50; ⊘11am-11pm; 🛜; Ⓜ Dapuqiao), Bell Bar (p325) and **I Love Shanghai** (Wǒ Ài Shànghǎi; Lane 1, 248 Taikang Rd, 泰康路248弄内1号后门; ⊘6pm-late), can sort out meals and drinks and help take the weight off your feet.

★ **Xīntiāndì**　　　　　　　　　　　　　AREA
(新天地; Map p304; www.xintiandi.com; 2 blocks btwn Taicang, Zizhong, Madang & South Huangpi Rds, 太仓路与马当路路口; Ⓜ South Huangpi Rd, Xintiandi) With its own namesake metro station, Xīntiāndì has been a Shànghǎi icon for a decade or more. An upscale entertainment and shopping complex modelled on traditional alleyway homes, this was the first development in the city to prove that historical architecture makes big commercial sense.

Well heeled shoppers and alfresco diners keep things lively until late, and if you're looking for a memorable meal or to browse through some of Shànghǎi's more fashionable boutiques, you're in the right spot. The heart of the complex, divided into a pedestrianised north and south block, consists of largely rebuilt traditional *shíkùmén* houses, brought bang up-to-date with a stylish modern spin. But while the layout suggests a flavour of yesteryear, you should not expect much in the cultural realm. Xīntiāndì doesn't deliver any of the lived-in charm of

---

MAOIST PROPAGANDA IN SHÀNGHǍI

If phalanxes of red tractors, bumper harvests, muscled peasants and lantern-jawed proletariats fire you up, **Propaganda Poster Art Centre** (宣传画年画艺术中心, Xuānchuánhuà Niánhuà Yìshù Zhōngxīn; Map p304; 📋 021 6211 1845; www.shanghaipropagandaart.com; Room B-OC, President Mansion, 868 Huashan Rd, 华山路868号B-OC室; ¥20; ⊘10am-5pm; Ⓜ Shanghai Library), a small gallery in the bowels of a residential block should intoxicate. The collection of original posters from the 1950s, '60s and '70s – the golden age of Maoist poster production – will have you weak-kneed at the cartoon world of anti-US defiance. The centre divides into a showroom and a shop selling posters and postcards.

Tiánzǐfáng (p299) or the rickety simplicity of the Old Town. Beyond two worthwhile sights – the **Shíkùmén Open House Museum** (石库门屋里厢, Shíkùmén Wūlǐxiāng; Map p304; Xīntiāndì North Block, Bldg 25, 太仓路181弄新天地北里25号楼; adult/child ¥20/10; ⊘10.30am-10.30pm; Ⓜ South Huangpi Rd, Xintiandi) and the **Site of the 1st National Congress of the CCP** (中共一大会址纪念馆, Zhōnggòng Yīdàhuìzhǐ Jìniànguǎn; Map p304; Xīntiāndì North Block, 76 Xingye Rd, 兴业路76号; ⊘9am-5pm; Ⓜ South Huangpi Rd, Xintiandi) FREE – it's best for strolling the alleyways and enjoying a summer evening over drinks or a meal.

Ren Weiyin Art Gallery　　　　　　GALLERY
(Map p304; www.renweiyinart.com; Bldg 3, Lane 210, Tiánzǐfáng, 泰康路210弄; ⊘10am-6pm; Ⓜ Dapuqiao) FREE This gallery exhibits around 150 paintings by one of China's most well known post-impressionists, Ren Weiyin. In 1961 his studio was forcibly closed and he was sent to a forced labour camp. He spent most of his life as a shoe repairman. His daughter opened this gallery to showcase her father's work and life.

Liúli China Museum　　　　　　　　MUSEUM
(琉璃艺术博物馆, Liúli Yìshù Bówùguǎn; Map p304; 📋 021 6461 3189; www.liulichinamuseum.com; 25 Taikang Rd, 泰康路25号; adult/child under 18yr ¥20/free; ⊘10am-5pm Tue-Sun; Ⓜ Dapuqiao) Founded by Taiwanese artists Loretta Yang and Chang Yi, this museum is dedicated to the art of glass sculpture (*pâte de verre* or lost-wax casting). Peruse the collection of ancient artefacts – some of which date back more than 2000 years – to admire the pieces such as earrings, belt buckles and even a Tang dynasty crystal *wéiqí* (go) set.

Shànghǎi Arts & Crafts Museum　　MUSEUM
(上海工艺美术博物馆, Shànghǎi Gōngyì Měishù Bówùguǎn; Map p304; 📋 021 6431 4074; www.shgmb.com; 79 Fenyang Rd, 汾阳路79路; ¥8; ⊘9am-5pm, last entry 4pm; Ⓜ Changshu Rd) Repositioned as a museum, this arts and crafts institute displays traditional crafts such as needlepoint embroidery, paper cutting, lacquer work, jade cutting and lantern making. Watch traditional crafts being performed live by craftspeople and admire the wonderful exhibits, from jade, to ivory to ink stones and beyond. The 1905 building itself is a highlight, once serving as the residence for Chen Yi, Shànghǎi's first mayor after the founding of the Chinese Communist Party.

⊙ Jìng'ān 静安

From its sacred Buddhist temples and heritage architecture to its edgy arts scene and modern museums, Jìng'ān has a strong case for being Shànghǎi's most interesting neighbourhood for sightseeing.

★ M50   GALLERY

(M50创意产业集聚区, M50 Chuàngyì Chǎnyè Jíjùqū; Map p314; www.m50.com.cn/en; 50 Moganshan Rd, 莫干山路50号, Ⓜ Line 3, 4 to Zhongtan Rd, exit 5, Line 1, 3, 4 to Shànghǎi Railway Station, exit 3) FREE Shànghǎi may be known for its glitz and glamour, but it's got an edgy subculture, too. The industrial M50 art complex is one prime example, where galleries have set up in disused factories and cotton mills, utilising the vast space to showcase contemporary Chinese emerging and established artists. There's a lot to see, so plan to spend half a day poking around the site.

It's not just galleries either – there's some great street art en route as you pass the graffiti-splashed, mural-decorated walls along gritty Moganshan Rd.

The most established galleries here include **ShanghART** (Xiānggénà Huàláng, www.shanghartgallery.com; Bldg 16 & 18, M50) with a big, dramatic space showcasing the work of some of the 40 artists it represents. The forward-thinking, provocative and downright entertaining **island6** (Liù Dǎo; www.island6.org; Bldg 6, M50) focuses on collaborative works created in a studio behind the gallery; it has a smaller gallery on the 1st floor of Building Seven. Other notable galleries include **Sanzi Art** (Sānzǐ Yìshù; www.sanziart.com; Room 4a-107, M50), featuring the work of notable Shànghǎi artist Sanzi, and Yu Nancheng's **Fish Studio** (Yú Gōngzuò Shì; www.yunancheng.com; Bldg 4, Room B-101, M50) – both local artists of international repute. For new media by avant-garde local and foreign artists try **Antenna Space** (Tiānxiàn Kōngjiān; www.antenna-space.com/en; Bldg 17, M50) or **Chronus Art Center** (CAC, Xīn Shíjiān Méitǐ Yìshù Zhōngxīn; www.chronusartcenter.org; Bldg 18, M50). Across the road is the **Gallery** (Huàláng; www.thegallery.com.cn; 87 Moganshan Rd, 莫干山路87号), another innovative art collective featuring Chinese contemporary art and photography. Budding photographers should absolutely pop into **DN Club** (Dāngnián; Room 107, Bldg 17, M50, course ¥380), with its classes using vintage SLRs and a dark room for developing prints.

Most galleries are open from 10am to 6pm, with the majority closed Mondays.

★ Shànghǎi Natural History Museum   MUSEUM

(上海自然博物馆, Shànghǎi Zìrán Bówùguǎn; ☎021 6862 2000; www.snhm.org.cn; 510 West Beijing Rd, 北京西路510号; adult/teen/under 13yr ¥30/12/free; ⊙9am-5.15pm Tue-Sun; Ⓜ Line 2, 12, 13 to West Nanjing Rd) Perhaps not quite on the same scale as the Smithsonian, Shànghǎi's new sleek space would nevertheless be a fitting choice for a *Night at the Museum* movie. As comprehensive as it is entertaining and informative, the museum is packed with displays of taxidermied animals, dinosaurs and cool interactive features. Its architecture is also a highlight, with a striking design that is beautifully integrated in its art-filled **Jìng'an Sculpture Park** (静安雕塑公园, Jìng'an Diāosù Gōngyuán; 128 Shimen 2nd Rd, 石门二路128号; ⊙6am-8.30pm; Ⓜ Lines 2, 12, 13 to West Nanjing Rd) FREE setting.

★ Jìng'ān Temple   BUDDHIST TEMPLE

(静安寺, Jìng'ān Sì; Map p317; 1686-1688 West Nanjing Rd, 南京西路1686-1688号; ¥50; ⊙7.30am-5pm; Ⓜ Line 2, 7 to Jing'an Temple, exit 1) With the original temple dating back to AD 1216, the much-restored Jìng'ān Temple was here well before all the audacious skyscrapers and glitzy shopping malls. Today it stands like a shimmering mirage in defiance of West Nanjing Rd's soaring modern architecture; a sacred portal to the Buddhist world that partially, at least, underpins this metropolis of 24 million souls.

★ Jade Buddha Temple   BUDDHIST TEMPLE

(玉佛寺, Yùfó Sì; Map p314; cnr Anyuan & Jiangning Rds, 安远路和江宁路街口; high/low season ¥20/10; ⊙8am-4.30pm; Ⓜ Line 7, 13 to Changshou Rd, exit 5) One of Shànghǎi's few active Buddhist monasteries, this temple was built between 1918 and 1928. The highlight is a transcendent Buddha crafted from pure jade, one of five shipped back to China by the monk Hui Gen at the turn of the 20th century. It's a popular stopover for tour buses, so be prepared for crowds. In February, during the Lunar New Year, the temple is very busy, as some 20,000 Chinese Buddhists throng to pray for prosperity.

The first temple on your immediate left upon entering is the **Hall of Heavenly Kings**, holding the statues of the Four Heavenly Kings who each look upon the four cardinal points. Directly opposite is the twin-eaved **Grand Hall**, the temple's most significant building, where worshippers pray to the past, present and future Buddhas.

French Concession

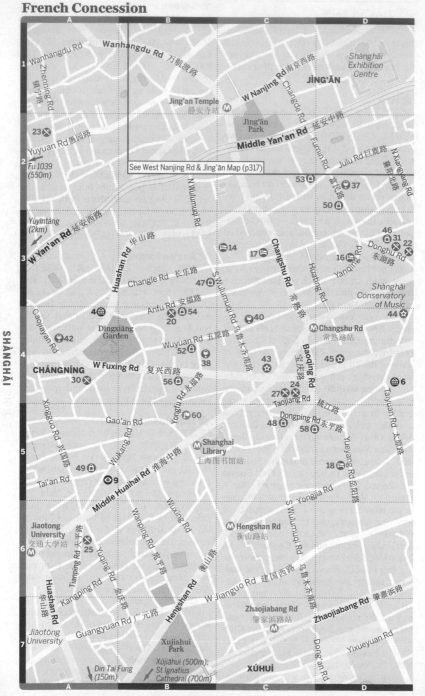

See West Nanjing Rd & Jing'ān Map (p317)

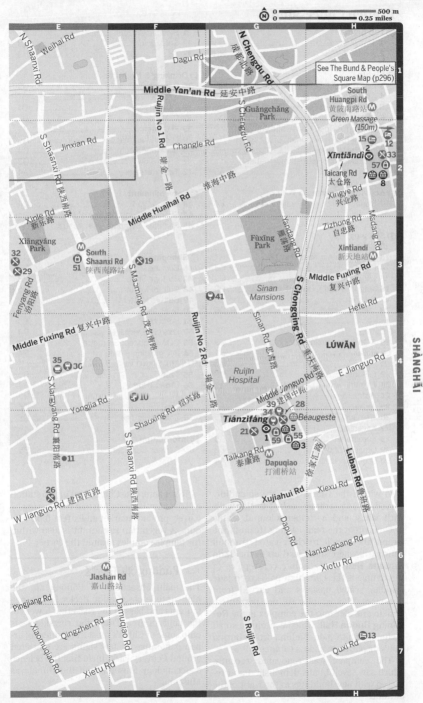

N

0 ——————— 500 m
0 ——————— 0.25 miles

See The Bund & People's Square Map (p296)

Weihai Rd

N Shaanxi Rd

Dagu Rd

N Chengdu Rd 成都北路

Middle Yan'an Rd 延安中路

Guǎngchǎng Park 广场公园

South Huangpi Rd 黄陂南路站

Green Massage (150m)

Changle Rd

S Shaanxi Rd

Jinxian Rd

Ruìjīn No 1 Rd 瑞金一路

S Chengdu Rd 成都南路

15 🛏 2
🏪 12

Xīntiāndì ⊙ ✕33
57 🛏
Taicang Rd 太仓路 7 🛏
🛏 8

Xinye Rd 兴业路

S Shaanxi Rd 陕西南路

Xinle Rd 新乐路

Middle Huaihai Rd 淮海中路

Yandang Rd 雁荡路

Zizhong Rd 自忠路

Madang Rd 马当路

Xintiandi 新天地站 Ⓜ

Xiāngyáng Park

Ⓜ South Shaanxi Rd
51 陕西南路站

Fùxīng Park 复兴公园

32 🛏
✕29

Fenyang Rd 汾阳路

✕19

S Mǎomíng Rd 茂名南路

Sinan Mansions

Middle Fuxing Rd 复兴中路

Hefei Rd

Middle Fuxing Rd 复兴中路

🍴41

S Chongqing Rd 重庆南路

LÚWĀN

35 🛏
🛏36

Ruìjīn No 2 Rd 瑞金二路

Ruìjīn Hospital

Sinan Rd 思南路

E Jianguo Rd

S Xiangyang Rd 襄阳南路

Yongjia Rd

🍴10

Shaoxing Rd 绍兴路

Middle Jianguo Rd 建国中路

39 🏛
🛏 28

Luban Rd 鲁班路

34 🛏
Tiánzǐfáng 59 🛏 🏛 Beaugeste

21 ✕
🛏 5
1 🛏 🛏55

●11

Taikang Rd 泰康路

🛏 3

26 ✕

W Jianguo Rd

S Shaanxi Rd 陕西南路

Ⓜ Dapuqiao 打浦桥站

Xujiahui Rd

Xiexu Rd

Ⓜ Jiashan Rd 嘉山路站

Dapu Rd

Nantangbang Rd

Pingjiang Rd

Damuqiao Rd

Xietu Rd

Qingzhen Rd

Xiaomuqiao Rd

S Ruijin Rd

Xietu Rd

Quxi Rd 🛏13

SHÀNGHǍI

French Concession

Also within the Grand Hall are splendidly carved *luóhàn* (arhats), lashed to the walls with wires, and a copper-coloured statue of Guanyin at the rear. Passing through the Grand Hall you'll reach a gated tranquil courtyard, where stairs lead up to the **Jade Buddha Hall**. The absolute centrepiece of the temple is the 1.9m-high pale-green jade Buddha, seated upstairs and carved from one piece. Photographs are not permitted. Walking further into the complex is the **Reclining Budda Hall**, which contains a small reclining white jade Buddha from Burma that's displayed in a glass cabinet.

The complex was renovated recently, which saw several halls demolished and replaced with new buildings to the right of the entrance.

To get here, take Changshou metro station exit 5 and walk along Anyuan Rd, passing by a lively produce market and street-food vendors. A vegetarian restaurant is also within the temple complex around the corner.

⦿ Pǔdōng 浦东新区

The main attractions of Pǔdōng are the high-altitude observation decks, hotels, restaurants and bars in the rocketing towers of the Lùjiāzuǐ area. They offer ringside seats onto some of China's most mind-altering urban panoramas. A few sights are scattered around Century Park, including the Science & Technology Museum and the Himalayas Museum.

SHÀNGHǍI SIGHTS

★ **Shànghǎi Tower** NOTABLE BUILDING
(上海中心大厦, Shànghǎi Zhōngxīn Dàshà; Map p308; www.shanghaitower.com.cn; cnr Middle Yincheng & Huayuanshiqiao Rds; ¥160; ⊙9am-9pm; MⓁLujiazui) China's tallest building dramatically twists skywards from its footing in Lùjiāzuǐ. The 121-storey 632m-tall Gensler-designed Shànghǎi Tower topped out in August 2013 and opened in mid-2016. The spiral-shaped tower houses office space, entertainment venues, shops, a conference centre, a luxury hotel and 'sky lobbies'. The gently corkscrewing form – its nine interior cylindrical units wrapped in two glass skins – is the world's second-tallest building at the time of writing. The observation deck on the 118th floor is the world's highest.

The twist is introduced by the outer skin of glass which swivels through 120 degrees as it rises, while atrium 'sky gardens' in the vertical spaces sandwiched between the two layers of glass open up a large volume of the tower to public use. The tower is sustainably designed: as well as providing insulation, the huge area of glass will vastly reduce electrical consumption through the use of sunlight. The tower's shape furthermore reduces wind loads by 24%, which generated a saving of US$58m in construction costs. Before the tower even went up, engineers were faced with building the 61,000m³ concrete mat that would support its colossal mass in the boggy land of Pǔdōng.

Uppermost floors of the tower are reserved for that obligatory Shànghǎi attraction – the world's highest skydeck above ground level – with passengers ferried skywards in the world's fastest lifts (64km/h), and the world's tallest single-lift elevator. Visitors can gaze down on both the Jīnmào Tower (p308) and Shànghǎi World Financial Center. A six-level luxury retail podium fills the base of the tower.

★ **Oriental Pearl TV Tower** NOTABLE BUILDING
(东方明珠广播电视塔, Dōngfāng Míngzhū Guǎngbō Diànshì Tǎ; Map p308; ☑021 5879 1888; 1 Century Ave, 世纪大道1号; ¥160-220; ⊙8am-10pm, revolving restaurant 11am-2pm & 5-9pm; MⓁLujiazui) This 468m-tall poured-concrete tripod tower is the most iconic contemporary building in the city, and its image is flashed around town on everything from postcards to T-shirts. Love it or hate it, the Deng Xiaoping–era design is inadvertently retro; a certain mix of sci-fi meets Soviet brutalist architecture. Inside, the highlight is the Transparent Observatory (259m), where you can peer way down through the glass-bottomed walkway. Also don't miss the excellent Shànghǎi History Museum in the basement.

★ **Aurora Museum** MUSEUM
(震旦博物馆, Zhèn Dàn Bówùguǎn; Map p308; ☑021 5840 8899; www.auroramuseum.cn; Aurora Bldg, 99 Fucheng Rd, 富城路99号震旦大厦; ¥60; ⊙10am-5pm Tue-Sun, to 9pm Fri, last entry 1hr before closing; MⓁLujiazui) Designed by renowned Japanese architect, Andō Tadao, the Aurora Museum is set over six floors of the Aurora building and houses a stunning collection of Chinese treasures. Artefacts and antiquities on display include pottery from the Han dynasty; jade dating back from the Neolithic to the Qing dynasty; blue-and-white porcelain spanning the Yuan, Ming and Qing dynasties; as well as Buddhist sculptures from the Gandharan and Northern Wei period. Don't miss the jade burial suit of 2903 tiles sewn with gold wire.

★ **Shànghǎi World Financial Center** NOTABLE BUILDING
(上海环球金融中心, Shànghǎi Huánqiú Jīnróng Zhōngxīn; Map p308; ☑021 5878 0101; www.swfc-observatory.com; 100 Century Ave, 世纪大道100号; observation decks 94th fl adult/child ¥120/60, 94th, 97th & 100th fl ¥180/90; ⊙8am-11pm, last entry 10.30pm, MⓁLujiazui) Although trumped by the adjacent Shànghǎi Tower as the city's most stratospheric building, the awe-inspiring 492m high Shànghǎi World Financial Center is an astonishing sight, even more so come nightfall when its 'bottle opener' top dances with lights. There are three observation decks – on levels 94, 97 and 100 – with head-spinningly altitude-adjusted ticket prices and wow-factor elevators thrown in.

★ **Shànghǎi History Museum** MUSEUM
(上海城市历史发展陈列馆, Shànghǎi Chéngshì Lìshǐ Fāzhǎn Chénlièguǎn; Map p308; ☑021 5879 8888; 1 Century Ave, 世纪大道1号, Oriental Pearl TV Tower basement; ¥35, English audio tour ¥30; ⊙8am-9.30pm; MⓁLujiazui) The entire family will enjoy this informative museum with a fun presentation on old Shànghǎi. Learn how the city prospered on the back of the cotton trade and junk transportation, when it was known as 'Little Sūzhōu'. Life-sized models of traditional shops are staffed by realistic waxworks, amid a wealth of historical detail, including a boundary stone from the International Settlement and one of the bronze lions that originally guarded the entrance to the HSBC bank on the Bund.

Some exhibits are hands-on or accompanied by creative video presentations. The

Pǔdōng

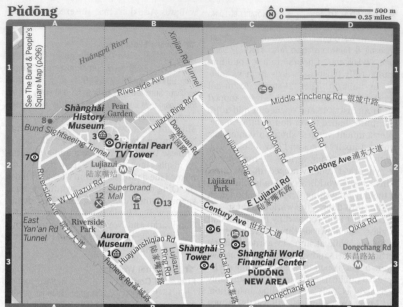

Pǔdōng

city's transport history gets a look-in; you can size up an antique bus, an old wheelbarrow taxi and an ornate sedan chair.

★ **Shànghǎi Disneyland** AMUSEMENT PARK
(上海迪士尼乐园, Shànghǎi Díshìní Lèyuán; ☑ 021 3158 0000; www.shanghaidisneyresort.com; Shànghǎi Disney Resort, Pǔdōng; adult/child 1.0-1.4m & senior ¥499/375; ⊗9am-9pm; M Disney Resort) Disney has magicked-up a spectacular theme park in Shànghǎi, offering a subtly Chinese take on Mickey and co. Six themed areas encircle Disney's biggest-ever Enchant-

ed Storybook Castle, with attractions including a TRON roller coaster joining high-tech reboots of old favourites like Pirates of the Caribbean. With an estimated 350 million people living less than three hours away, expect long queues for rides – arrive before 9am if you plan to do it all in a day.

Jīnmào Tower NOTABLE BUILDING
(金茂大厦, Jīnmào Dàshà; Map p308; ☑021 5047 5101; 88 Century Ave, 世纪大道88号; adult/student/child ¥120/90/60; ⊗8.30am-10pm; M Lujiazui) Resembling an art deco take on a

pagoda, this crystalline edifice is a beauty. It's essentially an office block with the high-altitude **Grand Hyatt** (金茂君悦大酒店, Jīnmào Jūnyuè Dàjiǔdiàn; Map p308; ☑ 021 5049 1234; www.shanghai.grand.hyatt.com; d ¥1500 2000; ❄@🏊🛗; Ⓜ Lujiazui) renting space from the 53rd to 87th floors. You can zip up in the elevators to the 88th-floor **observation deck**, accessed from the separate podium building to the side of the main tower (aim for clear days at dusk for both day and night views).

Alternatively, sample the same view through the carbonated fizz of a gin and tonic at **Cloud 9** (九重天酒廊, Jiǔchóngtiān Jiǔláng; Map p308; ☑ 021 504/ 8838; http://shanghai.grand. hyatt.com; 87th fl, 金茂大厦87楼; ⊗ 5pm-1am Mon-Fri, 2pm-2am Sat & Sun; Ⓜ Lujiazui) on the 87th floor of the Grand Hyatt (accessed on the south side of the building), and photograph the hotel's astonishing barrel-vaulted atrium.

Riverside Promenade
WATERFRONT
(滨江大道, Bīnjiāng Dàdào; Map p308; Ⓜ Lujiazui) Hands down the best stroll in Pǔdōng. The sections of promenade alongside Riverside Ave on the eastern bank of the Huángpǔ River offer splendid views to the Bund across the way. Choicely positioned cafes look out over the water.

⊙ Hóngkǒu & North Shànghǎi 虹口

The highlight of Hóngkǒu and North Shànghǎi is just wandering the streets, soaking up the Jewish history and admiring the art deco and heritage architecture. The Ohel Moishe Synagogue makes for a good starting point before a stroll around the North Bund area to check out the Astor House Hotel, Broadway Mansions, Main Post Office and Embankment Building. You can easily combine a day out strolling historic Duolun Rd and the Lu Xun Park area.

★ Ohel Moishe Synagogue & Jewish Refugees Museum
MUSEUM
(摩西会堂, Móxī Huìtáng; ☑ 021 6512 6669; 62 Changyang Rd, 长阳路62号; ¥50; ⊗ 9am-5pm, last entry 4.30pm; Ⓜ Tilanqiao) Built by the Russian Ashkenazi Jewish community in 1927, this synagogue lies in the heart of the 1940s Jewish ghetto. Today it houses the synagogue and the Shànghǎi Jewish Refugees Museum, with exhibitions on the lives of the approximately 20,000 Central European refugees who fled to Shànghǎi to escape the Nazis. There are English-language tours every hour, from 9.30am to 11.30am and 1pm to 4pm.

1933
ARCHITECTURE
(上海1933老场坊, Shànghǎi 1933 Lǎochǎngfáng; 10 Shajing Rd, 沙泾路10号; Ⓜ Hailun Rd) This vast concrete former abattoir is one of Shànghǎi's unique buildings, today converted to house a number of boutiques, galleries and restaurants (though, sadly, none are of much interest). An extraordinary place built around a central core, its structure is a maze of flared columns, sky-bridges (across which cattle would be led to slaughter), ramps, curved stairwells – and jostling photo opportunities.

Sky Ring
FERRIS WHEEL
(天空指环, Tiānkōng Zhǐhuán; Map p296; ☑ 021 3633 8833; www.shjoycity.com; 8F, North Bldg, Shànghǎi Joy City, 198 Xizang North Rd, 上海大悦城座8楼, 西藏北路198号; ¥60; ⊗ 10am-9.30pm; 🚇; Ⓜ Qufu Rd) Sky Wheel's rooftop location in a rapidly developing neighbourhood is perfect for sweeping views contrasting old Shànghǎi with new. The 12 minute ride above a neighbourhood of historic *lǐlòng* (里弄) houses offers glimpses of the Huángpǔ River and, at the very top, Shànghǎi's newest skyscrapers peeking over even newer riverside construction. When the ride is finished, head to the roof for boutique shopping and a closer look at the wheel itself. Book via smartphone to save time (but not money). Kids under 1.2m tall ride free

⊙ Xújiāhuì & South Shànghǎi 徐家汇

Originally a Jesuit settlement dating back to the 17th century, Xújiāhuì today is more characterised by shopping malls, while south Shànghǎi sprawls to the Lónghuá Temple and Pagoda and beyond.

Yuz Museum
GALLERY
(余德耀美术馆, Yúdéyào Měishùguǎn; www.yuzmshanghai.org; 35 Fenggu Rd, 丰谷路35号近龙腾大道; Tue-Fri ¥120, Sat & Sun ¥150; ⊗ 10am-9pm Sun-Thu, to midnight Fri & Sat; Ⓜ Line 11 to Yun Jin Rd) A huge development for Shànghǎi's contemporary art scene, this enormous gallery is housed in the former hangar of Lónghuá Airport and sprawls over 9000 sq metres. The temporary exhibitions have been world-class and beautifully curated so far, making an important contribution to the fast-developing West Bund cultural hub. The airy atrium contains a cafe and gift shop. Check in advance what exhibitions and workshops (some held in English) are running.

Lónghuá Temple & Pagoda   BUDDHIST TEMPLE
(龙华寺、龙华塔, Lónghuá Sì & Lónghuá Tǎ; ☑ 021 6457 6327; 2853 Longhua Rd, 龙华路2853号; ¥10, incl incense ¥50; ⊗ 7am-4.30pm; Ⓜ Line 11 Longhua) Shànghǎi's oldest and largest monastery is named after the pipal tree (*lónghuá*) under which Buddha achieved enlightenment. Trees are decorated with red lanterns, incense smoke fills the front of the grounds and monks can regularly be heard chanting, making this one of the city's most atmospheric sites. The much-renovated temple is said to date from the 10th century.

St Ignatius Cathedral   CATHEDRAL
(徐家汇天主教堂, Xújiāhuì Tiānzhǔjiàotáng; ☑ 021 6438 4632; 158 Puxi Rd, 蒲西路158号; Ⓜ Line 1, 9, 11 to Xujiahui) The dignified twin-spired St Ignatius Cathedral (1904) is a major Xújiāhuì landmark, closed while undergoing restoration at the time of writing. Its nave is a long span of Gothic arches, while the exterior is ornamented with rows of menacing gargoyles. Note how the church spires find reflection in much of the more recently built local architecture. The original stained glass was destroyed in the Cultural Revolution, but the vivid colours of the recent red, azure and purple replacements (with archaic Chinese inscriptions from the Bible) are outstanding.

⊙ West Shànghǎi

West Shànghǎi is mainly of interest for long-term expats and those on business, although the village of Qībǎo is worth a visit.

★ **Qībǎo**   VILLAGE
(七宝; www.goqibao.com; 2 Minzhu Rd, Mínháng district, 闵行区民主路2号; high/low season ¥45/30; ⊗ sights 8.30am-4.30pm; Ⓜ Qibao) If you tire of Shànghǎi's incessant quest for modernity, this tiny town is only a hop, skip and metro ride away. An ancient settlement that prospered during the Ming and Qing dynasties, it is littered with traditional historic architecture, threaded by small, busy alleyways and cut by a picturesque canal. If you can somehow blot out the crowds, Qībǎo brings you the flavours of old China. When you exit the station, head down Minzhu Rd and follow the signs to the Old Street.

🏃 Activities

There are plenty of activities on offer in Shànghǎi, whether you're in the mood for a workout with some martial arts, cooking up a storm, learning a craft or loosening up the muscles with a traditional Chinese massage.

★ **Double Rainbow Massage House**   MASSAGE
(双彩虹保健按摩厅, Shuāng Cǎihóng Bǎojiàn Ànmó Tīng; Map p304; ☑ 021 6473 4000; 45 Yongjia Rd, 永嘉路45号; 45/68/90 minutes ¥60/90/120; ⊗ noon-midnight; Ⓜ South Shaanxi Rd) Perhaps Shànghǎi's best neighbourhood massage parlour, where the shared rooms have little ambience but the facilities are spotless and the prices are unbeatable. Choose your preference of soft, medium or hard, and the visually impaired masseuses here will have you groaning in agony in no time as they seek out those little-visited pressure points. Choose between traditional massage or a herbal foot bath, or try both.

Kitchen At...   COOKING
(Map p304; ☑ 021 6433 2700; www.thekitchenat.com; 3rd fl, Bldg 20, Lane 383, South Xiangyang Rd, 襄阳南路383弄20号3楼; Ⓜ Jiashan Rd) Great culinary school offering courses in regional Chinese and Western cuisines; good for both long-term residents and short-term visitors.

Lóngwǔ Kung Fu Center   MARTIAL ARTS
(龙武功夫馆, Lóngwǔ Gōngfu Guǎn; Map p317; ☑ 021 6287 1528; 3rd fl,1 South Maoming Rd, 茂名南路1号; 1/20 lessons ¥150/2400, 6 months ¥3600; Ⓜ South Shaanxi Rd) Brush up on your taekwondo *poomsae,* hone your Chinese kung fu skills or simply learn a few taichi moves to help slip aboard the bus at rush hour. The largest centre in the city, Lóngwǔ also offers children's classes on weekend mornings and lessons in English.

Hóngkǒu's Jewish Heritage Tours   WALKING
(☑ 130 0214 6702; www.shanghaijews.com; half-day tour ¥450) These informative and interesting half-day walking tours run by passionate Israeli expat Dvir Bar-Gal will take you to the landmarks of the Hóngkǒu district, once known as the Jewish ghetto, and give you a lesson on this part of Shanghai's Jewish history. Tours run every day and usually start at 9.30am.

Huángpǔ River Cruise   CRUISE
(黄浦江游览, Huángpǔ Jiāng Yóulǎn; Map p296; 219-239 East Zhongshan No 2 Rd, 中山东二路219-239号; tickets ¥120; ⊗ 11am-9.30pm; Ⓜ Line 2, 10 to East Nanjing Rd) The Huángpǔ River offers intriguing views of the Bund, Pǔdōng and riverfront activity. The night cruises are arguably more scenic, though boat traffic during the day is more interesting. Most cruises last 50 minutes.

Departures are from the docks on the south end of the Bund (near East Jinling Rd) or, less conveniently, from the Shíliùpù Docks (十六铺; Shíliùpù), a 20-minute walk south of the Bund. Buy tickets at the departure points or from the Bund tourist information and service centre (p332), beneath the Bund Promenade and opposite the intersection with East Nanjing Rd. Departure times vary.

Shànghǎi Tour Bus Centre BUS
(上海旅游集散中心, Shànghǎi Lǚyóu Jísàn Zhōngxīn; ☑021 2409 5555; www.chinassbc.com; 2409 South Zhongshan No 2 Rd, 中山南二路2409号; ⊙6.30am-7pm; Ⓜ Line 3 to Caoxi Rd) Daily tours to canal towns including Tónglǐ, Nánxún and other nearby tourist destinations.

👉 Tours

Shopping Tours Shanghai TOURS
(www.shoppingtoursshanghai.com; half-day tours from ¥800; ⊙ group tours run Mon, Wed & Fri) This highly regarded group takes the stress out of shopping in Shànghǎi with its tours of markets and specialist stores around the city. The guides are seriously experienced shoppers who have a great understanding of the city's best buys (bespoke tailoring, jewellery, porcelain, handicrafts and more) and the contacts to source any particular items you might have your heart set on.

Newman Tours TOURS
(新漫; Xīnmàn; ☑138 1777 0229; www.newmantours.com; from ¥190) A Bund tour, gangster tour, ancient Shànghǎi tour, ghost tour and a host of other informative and fun walking jaunts around the city. Also covers Hángzhōu and Sūzhōu.

Insiders Experience DRIVING
(☑138 1761 6975; www.insidersexperience.com; from ¥800) Fun motorcycle-sidecar tours of the city for up to two passengers, setting off from the Andaz in Xīntiāndì (but can pick up from anywhere, at extra cost).

City Sightseeing Buses TOURS
(都市观光, Dūshì Guānguāng; ☑021 4008206222; www.springtour.com; tickets ¥30; ⊙9am-8.30pm summer, to 6pm winter) Tickets for the hop-on, hop-off, open-top buses last 24 hours. Besides enabling you to tour Shànghǎi's highlights, they're a great way to get around the centre of town and Pǔdōng. A recorded commentary runs in eight languages; just plug in your earphones (supplied). Buses have stops across central Shànghǎi, including the Bund, the Old Town and People's Square.

Big Bus Tours BUS
(上海观光车, Shànghǎi Guānguāngchē; ☑021 6351 5988; www.bigbustours.com; adult/child ¥300/200) Operates hop-on, hop-off services, lassoing the sights along 22 stops across two routes. Tickets are valid for 48 hours and include a 90-minute boat tour of the Huángpǔ River, entry to the Jade Buddha Temple and admission to the 88th-floor observation deck of Jīnmào Tower.

UnTour Shanghai FOOD & DRINK
(https://untourfoodtours.com; per person ¥450) See a whole new side to the Old Town on an evening Night Markets Food Tour. Gregarious and knowledgeable guides introduce you to the city's vibrant scene through a walk around neighbourhood alleys famous for their street food.

Huángpǔ River Cruise (Pǔdōng) BOATING
(黄浦江游览船, Huángpǔjiāng Yóulǎnchuán; Map p308; Pearl Dock, 明珠码头; per person ¥100; ⊙9am-10pm; Ⓜ Lujiazui) Forty-minute cruises departing hourly in Pǔdōng. You can buy tickets at the tourist information office (p332).

✨ Festivals & Events

China Shanghai International Arts Festival ART
(中国上海国际艺术节, Zhōngguó Shànghǎi Guójì Yìshù Jié; www.artsbird.com) A month-long program of cultural events held in October and November, including the Shanghai Art Fair, international music, dance, opera, acrobatics and the Shanghai Biennale.

Lantern Festival CULTURAL
The Lantern Festival falls on the 15th day of the first lunar month (2 March 2018, 19 February 2019). Families make yuán xiāo (also called tāng yuán; delicious dumplings of glutinous rice with a variety of sweet fillings) and sometimes hang paper lanterns. It's a colourful time to visit Yùyuán Gardens.

Formula 1 Chinese Grand Prix SPORTS
(www.formula1.com; 2000 Yining Rd, Jiādìng; Ⓜ Line 11 to Shanghai Circuit) The slick Shànghǎi International Circuit has hosted F1's Chinese Grand Prix every year since 2004. The race usually comes to town for three days in mid-April.

🛏 Sleeping

There's never been a better time to find a bed in Shànghǎi. From ultrachic, carbon-neutral boutique rooms to sumptuous five-star hotels housed in glimmering towers, grand heritage affairs and snappy, down-to-earth backpacker haunts, the range of accommodation in town is just what you would expect from a city of this stature.

🛏 The Bund & People's Square

With many luxury hotels setting up in the heritage buildings along the Bund and People's Square, this area has some stunning accommodation options. However, it's not all five-star choices, with many hostels in the backstreets offering a fantastic local flavour. There's also no shortage of reliable, inexpensive local chain hotels that offer good value.

★ **Mingtown E-Tour Youth Hostel**   HOSTEL $
(明堂上海青年旅舍, Míngtáng Shànghǎi Qīngnián Lǚshè; Map p296; ☑ 021 6327 7766; www.yhachina. com; 55 Jiangyin Rd, 江阴路55号; dm ¥90, d with/ without bathroom ¥300/220; ❄ @ 🛜; Ⓜ Line 1, 2, 8 to People's Square, exit 2) One of Shànghǎi's best youth hostels, E-Tour has fine feng shui, a historic alleyway setting and pleasant rooms. But it's the tranquil courtyard with fish pond and the superb split-level bar-restaurant with cheap cocktails, pool table and comfy sofas that really sell it; plus there's plenty of outdoor seating on wooden decking. Private rooms come with small desks, TV and kettle.

There are both women-only and mixed dorms. YHA members get a small discount, and prices fluctuate slightly between high and low seasons. Reception is only open from 7am to 11pm, so notify the hostel if you're checking in outside these hours.

Mingtown People's Square Youth Hostel   HOSTEL $
(明堂青年旅舍人民广场店, Míngtáng Qīngnián Lǚshě Rénmín Guǎngchǎng Diàn; Map p296; ☑ 021 3330 1556; www.yhachina.com; 35 Yongshou Rd, 永 寿路35号; dm/r from ¥70/220; ❄ @ 🛜; Ⓜ Line 1, 2, 8 to People's Square, Line 8 to Dashijie) Centrally located between People's Square and the Bund, private rooms here have homely touches and Chinese porcelain wash basins, while single-sex dorms have pine-frame bunks with bed lamps, power sockets and large storage lockers. There's a cool bar with pool table and plenty of seating. Its proximity to Yunnan Rd's food street is handy.

Fish Inn Bund   HOTEL $
(子鱼居, Zǐyújū; Map p296; ☑ 021 3330 1399; www.fishinn.com.cn; 639 Middle Henan Rd, 河南中 路639号; r ¥348-450; ❄ 🛜; Ⓜ Line 2, 10 to East Nanjing Rd, Lines 10, 12 to Tianlong Rd) With a handy location about a 10-minute walk from the Bund and East Nanjing Rd, this friendly little place is like a hotel with a vibrant youth hostel energy. Rooms are decent although they are a bit small and dark. Deluxe rooms come with balcony/patio. Staff are eager to please and the tariff is excellent value for the hotel's position. There are suites for more room and comfort.

Phoenix   HOSTEL $
(老陕客栈, Lǎoshǎn Kèzhàn, Lǎoshǎn Hostel; Map p296; ☑ 021 6328 8680; www.phoenixhostelshanghai.com; 17 South Yunnan Rd, 云南南路17号; dm ¥80-90, s ¥158-248, d ¥298; ❄ @ 🛜; Ⓜ Line 1, 2, 8 to People's Square, Line 8 to Dashijie) For those looking for a more authentic, local experience, the Phoenix is a good choice right among great street food. Appealingly grungy, rooms are clean and bright; dorms sleep from four to eight people. A rooftop bar, ground-floor Shaanxi restaurant, dumpling cooking classes and Chinese language lessons add to the appeal. Good location close to People's Square.

Metropolo Hotel – People's Square   HOTEL $$
(锦江都城上海青年会经典酒店, Jǐnjiāng Dūchéng Shànghǎi Qīngnián Huì Jīngdiǎn Jiǔdiàn; Map p296; ☑ 021 3305 9999; www.metropolohotels. com; 123 South Xizang Rd, 西藏南路123号; r ¥939-2039; Ⓜ Line 8 to Dashijie) Occupying the former Chinese YMCA building (1931) just south of People's Square, this member of the Metropolo chain is one of the city's better midrange hotels. The brown-and-cream rooms offer a reassuring degree of style, and are large and comparable in standard to pricier business hotels. Staff are professional and online discounts can slash room rates by 20%.

The building resembles Běijīng's Southeast Corner Watchtower, with a traditional hammerbeam ceiling. Its lobby has lavish art deco features.

JW Marriott Tomorrow Square   HOTEL $$
(明天广场JW万豪酒店, Míngtiān Guǎngchǎng JW Wànháo Jiǔdiàn; Map p296; ☑ 021 5359 4969; www.jwmarriottshanghai.com; 399 West Nanjing Rd, 南京 西路399号; d from ¥1500; ❄ 🛜 🏊; Ⓜ Line 1, 2, 8 to People's Square, exit 11) Victor Sassoon probably would have traded in his old digs in a heartbeat if he could have stayed in the chairman's suite here. Housed across the upper 24 floors of one of Shànghǎi's most dramatic towers, the JW Marriott boasts marvellously appointed rooms with spectacular vistas, coffeemaker, and showers with hydraulic massage functions to soak away the stress.

Service and facilities are top class, with two pools (indoor and outdoor) and an excellent spa. Internet costs ¥120 a day for nonmembers (¥600 per week). Its library is in the *Guinness Book of Records* for the world's highest at 230.9m, but it's only accessible to executive-lounge members.

Bund Garden Shanghai   HERITAGE HOTEL $$
(外滩花园酒店, Wàitān Huāyuán Jiǔdiàn; Map p296; ☑021 6329 8800; 200 Hankou Rd, 汉口路200号; r ¥980; ❈ 🛜; Ⓜ Line 2, 10 to East Nanjing Rd) Set in a beautiful colonial villa dating from the 1930s, the Bund Garden retains its distinct classic British feel with red-brick Gothic features, chimneys and a beautiful wooden staircase. With only nine rooms, the standard here is more dated B&B than luxury hotel, but all rooms are large, with fireplaces, and are decorated in period style.

Leading off the lobby is a suitably posh dining room, and a large garden enclosed by heritage buildings, including the charming **Holy Trinity Church** (圣三一教堂, Shèng Sānyī Jiàotáng; Map p296; 219 Jiujiang Rd, 九江路219号; Ⓜ Line 2, 10 to East Nanjing Rd, exit 1). Rates include breakfast.

★**Waldorf Astoria**   HOTEL $$$
(华尔道夫酒店, Huá'ěr Dàofū Jiǔdiàn; Map p296; ☑021 6322 9988; www.waldorfastoriashanghai.com; 2 East Zhongshan No 1 Rd, 中山东一路2号; r new/old wing from ¥2500/6000; ❈@🛜; Ⓜ Line 2, 10 to East Nanjing Rd) Grandly marking the southern end of the Bund is the former Shànghǎi Club (1910), once the Bund's most exclusive gentlemen's hang-out. The 20 original rooms have been converted to house the Waldorf Astoria's premium suites, six of which look out onto the Huángpǔ River. Behind this heritage building is a new hotel tower with 252 state-of-the-art rooms.

Each room features touch digital controls, espresso machine, walk-in closet and a TV in the mirror. There's a pronounced New York–meets-Shànghǎi theme, from the Peacock Lounge to the cocktail list at the Long Bar.

★**Fairmont Peace Hotel**   HISTORIC HOTEL $$$
(费尔蒙和平饭店, Fèi'ěrméng Hépíng Fàndiàn; Map p296; ☑021 6321 6888; www.fairmont.com; 20 East Nanjing Rd, 南京东路20号; d ¥2500-4000; ♨❈🛜☒; Ⓜ Line 2,10 to East Nanjing Rd) If anywhere in town fully conveys swish 1930s Shànghǎi, it's the old Cathay, rising imperiously from the Bund. One of the city's most iconic hotels, the Fairmont Peace is cast in the warm, subdued tints of a bygone era. Expect all the luxuries of a top-class establishment,

with rooms decked out in art deco elegance, from light fixtures down to coffee tables.

Standard rooms come without a view, deluxe rooms with a street view and suites with the coveted river view. Note that wifi and broadband access cost an extra ¥99 per day for guests. The hotel is also home to a luxury spa, two upmarket restaurants and several bars and cafes. Even if you're not staying here, it's worth popping in to admire the magnificent lobby (1929), or taking in an evening show at the jazz bar.

★**Yangtze Boutique Shànghǎi**   BOUTIQUE HOTEL $$$
(朗廷扬子精品宾馆, Lǎngtíng Yángzǐ Jīngpǐn Bīnguǎn; Map p296; ☑021 6080 0800; www.theyangtzehotel.com; 740 Hankou Rd, 汉口路740号; d ¥1200-2000; ❈🛜; Ⓜ Line 1, 2, 8 to People's Square, exit 14) Dating from the 1930s, this art deco beauty was a famous hang-out for the glitterati in the swinging 1930s. Splendidly refurbished, it features a sumptuous stained-glass skylight in the lobby, above a deco-style curved staircase. In addition to period decor, rooms feature deep baths, picture-frame TVs, glass-walled bathrooms with Venetian blinds and tiny balconies.

Peninsula Hotel   LUXURY HOTEL $$$
(半岛酒店, Dàndǎo Jiǔdiàn; Map p296; ☑021 2327 2888; http://shanghai.peninsula.com; 32 East Zhongshan No 1 Rd, 中山东一路32号; d incl breakfast from ¥2700; ❈@🛜☒; Ⓜ Line 2, 10 to

MORNING EXERCISES ALONG THE BUND

Early risers wandering along the Bund are rewarded with the fascinating sight of locals doing their morning exercises, posed against the backdrop of Pǔdōng's skyline – there are brilliant photo opportunities to be had in the morning light.

You'll see myriad offbeat ways to get the circulation flowing, with everything from groups of taichi practitioners with synchronised hand fans, to those honing their sword-wielding techniques, to bunny hopping down stairs or walking backwards along the promenade.

Kite flying is also a popular pastime. It's an impressive sight as middle-aged men take control of these magnificent crafts as they soar to stunning heights.

Aim to get here around 7.30am (or earlier) as things wind up around 9am.

Shànghǎi Railway Station

N 0 _____ 500 m
0 _____ 0.25 miles

Shànghǎi Railway Station

⊙ Top Sights

⊙ Sights

⊙ Activities, Courses & Tours

⊙ Transport

East Nanjing Rd) Though built in 2009, this spiffy hotel at the Bund's northern end has a heritage look achieved by combining art deco motifs with Shànghǎi modernity. It's a grade above many other market rivals, with TVs in the tub, well equipped dressing rooms (with fingernail driers), valet boxes for dirty clothes, Nespresso machines and fabulous views across the river or out onto the gardens of the former British consulate.

Part of the Rockbund development project, it includes an enormous luxury shopping arcade on the ground floor, and a back entrance that leads to the beautifully renovated Yuanmingyuan Rd.

🛏 Old Town

★Waterhouse at South Bund
BOUTIQUE HOTEL $$

(水舍时尚设计酒店, Shuǐshè Shíshàng Shèjì Jiǔdiàn; ☎021 6080 2988; www.waterhouse shanghai.com; 1-3 Maojiayuan Rd, Lane 479, South Zhongshan Rd, 中山南路479弄毛家园路1-3号; d ¥1100-2800; ❀🛜; Ⓜ Line 9 to Xiaonanmen) There are few cooler places to base yourself in Shànghǎi than this awfully trendy 19-room, four-storey South Bund converted 1930s warehouse right by the Cool Docks. Gazing out onto supreme views of Pǔdōng (or into the crisp courtyard), the Waterhouse's natty rooms (some with terrace) are swishly dressed. Service can be wanting, though, and it's isolated from the action.

A lovely rooftop bar caps it all and trim ground-floor Table No 1 (p320) throws in culinary excellence.

French Concession

Blue Mountain Youth Hostel HOSTEL $
(蓝山国际青年旅舍, Lánshān Guójì Qīngnián Lûshè; Map p304; ☎021 6304 3938; www.bmhostel.com; 2nd fl, Bldg 1, 1072 Quxi Rd, 瞿溪路1072号1号甲2楼; dm ¥85-90, d ¥260-280, tr ¥330; ❄@📶; [M] Luban Rd) Although slightly out of the action, this hostel is almost next door to Luban Rd metro station, so transport is sorted. Rooms are clean and simple with pine furniture and flooring, TV and kettle. There are women-only, men-only and mixed four-to eight-bed dorms, and there's a bar-restaurant area with free pool table and free movie screenings. Wi-fi is in the public areas only.

Staff members speak English and are very friendly.

Yuèyáng Hotel HOTEL $
(悦阳商务酒店, Yuèyáng Shāngwù Jiǔdiàn; Map p304; ☎021 6466 6767; 58 Yueyang Rd, 岳阳路58号; s ¥198, d ¥338-368; ❄; [M] Hengshan Rd) One of the best budget options in the French Concession that's within easy walking distance of a metro station, Yuèyáng has well kept spacious rooms with big double beds and laminated flooring. Shower rooms are clean and modern, although, annoyingly, the hot water isn't always piping hot. Expect only small discounts, if any.

★**Quintet** B&B $$
(Map p304; ☎021 6249 9088; www.quintet-shanghai.com; 808 Changle Rd, 长乐路808号; d incl breakfast ¥850-1100; 🚭❄📶; [M] Changshu Rd) This chic B&B has five homely double rooms in a 1930s townhouse full of character. Some of the rooms are small, but each is decorated with style, incorporating modern luxuries such as large-screen TVs and laptop-sized safes, with more classic touches such as wood-stripped floorboards and deep porcelain bathtubs. The loft room comes with a private rooftop terrace.

Staff members sometimes get a BBQ going in the downstairs restaurant terrace in summer. No sign – just buzz on the gate marked 808 and wait to be let in. Be aware there is no elevator.

★**Kevin's Old House** B&B $$
(老时光酒店, Lǎoshíguāng Jiǔdiàn; Map p304; ☎021 6248 6800; www.kevinsoldhouse.com; No 4, Lane 946, Changle Rd, 长乐路946弄4号; ste incl breakfast from ¥900; ❄📶; [M] Changshu Rd) Housed in a secluded 1927 four-storey French Concession villa, this lovely, quiet place is run by a friendly, English-speaking owner. Six spacious suites are spread throughout the house, featuring wooden floorboards, traditional Chinese furniture and a few antiques, as well as fridges, flat-screen TVs and washing machines. Suite 328 is the pick of the bunch. There's an attached Italian restaurant with a long menu of pizza and pasta dishes.

★**Magnolia Bed & Breakfast** B&B $$
(Map p304; ☎021 5403 5306; www.magnoliabnbshanghai.com; 36 Yanqing Rd, 延庆路36号; r ¥702-1296; ❄@📶; [M] Changshu Rd) Opened by Miranda Yao of the cooking school Kitchen at... (p310), this cosy five-room B&B is located in a 1927 French Concession home. It's Shànghǎi all the way, with original art deco features combined with comfort and design; a true labour of love. There are discounts for stays of seven nights or more. There's no front desk, so phone ahead before visiting.

★**Andaz** LUXURY HOTEL $$$
(安达仕酒店, Āndáshì Jiǔdiàn; Map p304; ☎021 2310 1234; http://shanghai.andaz.hyatt.com; 88 Songshan Rd, 嵩山路88号; r ¥1800-3300; ❄📶≋; [M] South Huangpi Rd) Housed in a tower with retro '70s style windows, this fab hotel's design-led lobby – a pronouncement of metal latticework – suggests an art space, a sensation that persists when you hunt for the open-plan reception (it's on the right). Along curving corridors, guest rooms are cool and modern, with basins and bathtubs that glow in different colours, coffee machines and monumental flat-screen TVs.

With room design courtesy of Japanese interior designer Super Potato, all mod cons are operated by iPad, while views of Pǔxī or Pǔdōng – depending on your choice – range out beyond curved and chunky windows. Extra bonus: free drinks for guests in the bar during happy hour 6pm to 8pm daily. Discounts of up to 35% online.

★**Langham Xīntiāndì** LUXURY HOTEL $$$
(新天地朗廷酒店, Xīntiāndì Lǎngtíng Jiǔdiàn; Map p304; ☎021 2330 2288; xintiandi.langhamhotels.com; 99 Madang Rd, 马当路99号; r/ste ¥1800/2400; ❄📶≋; [M] South Huangpi Rd) Xīntiāndì has become a magnet for luxury hotels, and they don't come much nicer than this one. Its 357 smart, stylish rooms all feature huge floor-to-ceiling windows, plenty of space to spread out in, and an attention to the minute details that make all the difference: Japanese-style wooden tubs in some suites, heated bathroom floors, Nespresso machines, VPN wi-fi and fresh flowers.

Amenities include the much-lauded Cantonese restaurant **T'ang Court**, an indoor pool and the award-winning, stunning **Chuan** spa.

Jìng'ān

★Le Tour Traveler's Rest HOSTEL $
(乐途静安国际青年旅舍, Lètú Jìng'ān Guójì Qīngnián Lǘshè; Map p317; ☑ 021 6267 1912; www.letourshanghai.com; 319 Jiaozhou Rd, 胶州路319号; dm ¥100-150, r ¥340-400; ❈@🛜; ⓜ Line 2, 7 to Jing'an Temple, exit 2) Housed in a former towel factory, this fabulous youth hostel leaves most others hanging out to dry. You'll pass a row of splendid *shíkùmén* on your way down the alley to get here. The old-Shànghǎi textures continue once inside, with red-brick walls decorated in graffiti, polished concrete floors and reproduced stone gateways above doorways leading to simple but smart rooms and six-person dorms (with shared bathrooms).

Double rooms are not very spacious, but they have flat-screen TVs and they're clean. Rooms are ¥10 to ¥30 pricier on Fridays and Saturdays. The hostel also has small apartments next door for short- and long-term rental. The ground floor has a ping-pong table, a pool table and wi-fi, all of which are free to use, and there's a fine rooftop bar-restaurant with outdoor seating. Bicycles can also be rented for ¥30 per day.

It's down an alley off Jiaozhou Rd.

★Urbn BOUTIQUE HOTEL $$$
(雅悦酒店, Yǎ Yuè Jiǔdiàn; Map p317; ☑ 021 5153 4600; www.urbnhotels.com; 183 Jiaozhou Rd, 胶州路183号; r incl breakfast ¥1400-1700; ❈; ⓜ Line 2, 7 to Jing'an Temple, exit 1) 🌿 Within a former post office, China's first carbon-neutral hotel not only incorporates recyclable materials and low-energy products where possible, it also calculates its complete carbon footprint – including staff commutes and delivery journeys – and offsets it by donating money to environmentally friendly projects. The 26 open-plan rooms are beautifully designed using recycled brick and timber from a French Concession *shíkùmén*, with low furniture and sunken living areas that exude space.

Púlì LUXURY HOTEL $$$
(璞丽酒店, Púlì Jiǔdiàn; Map p317; ☑ 021 3203 9999; www.thepuli.com; 1 Changde Rd, 常德路1号; d from ¥2300; ❈🛜; ⓜ Line 2, 7 to Jing'an Temple, exit 9) With open-space rooms divided by hanging silk screens and an understated beige-and-mahogany colour scheme accentuated by the beauty of a few well placed orchids, the Púlì is an exquisite choice. The Zen calm and gorgeous design of this 26-storey hotel make a strong case for stylish skyscrapers. Other perks are the free minibar and coffee pod machine. Book ahead for discounts of up to 60%.

Pǔdōng

★Mandarin Oriental Pudong HOTEL $$$
(上海浦东文华东方酒店, Shànghǎi Pǔdōng Wénhuá Dōngfāng Jiǔdiàn; Map p308; ☑ 021 2082 9888; www.mandarinoriental.com; 111 South Pudong Rd, 浦东南路111号; d ¥1800-2800, ste from ¥3600; ❈@🛜🏊; ⓜ Lujiazui) Slightly tucked away from the Lùjiāzuǐ five-star hotel melee in a sheltered riverside spot, the 362-room Mandarin Oriental is a visual feast, from the beautiful oval chandeliers and multi-coloured glass murals (depicting forests) in the lobby to the excellent dining choices, such as Fifty 8° Grill. All five-star expectations are naturally met, but it's the meticulous service that ices this cake.

Sumptuous rooms aside, there's a 24-hour pool and gym, spa and fantastic views. The address may seem a bit stranded, but it's a short walk to the heart of Lùjiāzuǐ and there's a complimentary shuttle bus within the area.

★Ritz-Carlton Shanghai Pudong HOTEL $$$
(上海浦东丽思卡尔顿酒店, Shànghǎi Pǔdōng Lìsī Kǎ'ěrdùn Jiǔdiàn; Map p308; ☑ 021 2020 1888; www.ritzcarlton.com; Shànghǎi IFC, 8 Century Ave, 世纪大道8号; d from ¥2800; ❈@🛜🏊; ⓜ Lujiazui) From the stingray-skin-effect wallpaper in the lift to its stunning alfresco Flair (p326) bar and exceptional service, the exquisitely styled 285-room Ritz-Carlton in the Shànghǎi IFC is a peach. The beautifully designed rooms – a blend of feminine colours, eye-catching art deco motifs, chic elegance and dramatic Bund-side views – are a stylistic triumph. Open-plan bathrooms (divided by a screen) feature deep and inviting free-standing bathtubs.

★Park Hyatt HOTEL $$$
(柏悦酒店, Bóyuè Jiǔdiàn; Map p308; ☑ 021 6888 1234; www.parkhyattshanghai.com; Shànghǎi World Financial Center, 100 Century Ave, 世纪大道100号 世界金融中心; d from ¥2200; ❈@🛜🏊; ⓜ Lujiazui) Spanning the 79th to 93rd floors of the towering Shànghǎi World Financial Center, this soaring hotel sees Pǔdōng's huge buildings (bar the Shànghǎi Tower) dwarfing into Lego blocks as lobby views graze the tip of

West Nanjing Rd & Jìng'ān

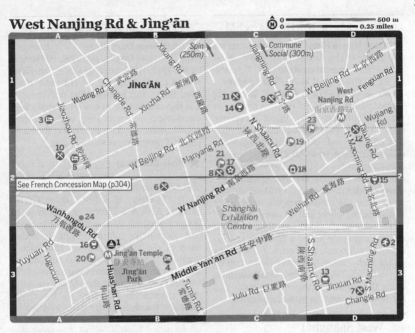

West Nanjing Rd & Jìng'ān

the Jīnmào Tower. Smaller than the Grand Hyatt, it's a subdued but stylish 174-room affair with a deco slant, high-walled corridors of brown fabric and grey stone textures.

Rooms are luxurious, with nifty features (mist-free bathroom mirror containing a small TV screen, automatically opening toilet seats). All come with huge TVs, deep bathtubs, leather chaise longues, sumptuous beds and outrageously good views. There are a few dining options including **100 Century Avenue** with its exceptional views. Access is from the south side of the tower.

Hóngkǒu & North Shànghǎi

★ Astor House Hotel
HISTORIC HOTEL $$$

(浦江饭店, Pǔjiāng Fàndiàn; Map p296; ☑021 6324 6388; www.astorhousehotel.com; 15 Huangpu Rd, 黄浦路15号; d ¥1880-2580, 'celebrity' r ¥3080, ste from ¥4800; ✲@🎧; MTiantong Rd) Stuffed with history (and perhaps a ghost or two), this old-timer shakes up an impressive cocktail from select ingredients: a location just off the Bund; old-world, Shànghǎi-era charm; great discounts; and colossal rooms. It's played host to the likes of Albert Einstein and Charlie Chaplin, and the original polished wooden floorboards, corridors and galleries pitch the mood somewhere between British public school and Victorian asylum.

There's enough wood panelling to build an ark; you could shunt a bed into the capacious bathrooms; and some of the rooms on the higher floors have river views. Pop up the stairs and hang a left to a small museum along the corridor to explore the history of the hotel. Discounts of 40% are common.

West Shànghǎi

Rock & Wood International Youth Hostel
HOSTEL $

(老木国际青年旅舍, Lǎomù Guójì Qīngnián Lǚshè; ☑021 3360 2361; No 278, Lane 615, Zhaohua Rd, 昭化路615弄278号; dm ¥75-80, s ¥110-120, d ¥180-190; ✲@🎧; MWest Yan'an Rd) With a serene bamboo-edged pond in its courtyard, and a bright and inviting lounge and bar area, this is an affordable and tranquil choice that sees a steady stream of travellers. Rooms and mixed dorms are clean and quiet, and the deluxe double (¥270 to ¥280) is the nicest of the bunch – basic but clean and comfy with a four-poster pine bed. The staff is very welcoming.

The cheapest single has a shared shower room. There's no kitchen but guests can use the fridge, and the hostel restaurant serves well priced Western and Chinese cuisine, as well as great coffee.

✕ Eating

Brash, stylish and forward-thinking, Shànghǎi's culinary scene typifies the city's craving for foreign trends and tastes. As much an introduction to regional Chinese cuisine as a magnet for talented chefs from around the globe, Shànghǎi has staked a formidable claim as the Middle Kingdom's hottest dining destination.

✕ The Bund & People's Square

★ Jiājiā Soup Dumplings
DUMPLING $

(佳家汤包, Jiājiā Tāngbāo; Map p296; 90 Huanghe Rd, 黄河路90号; 12 dumplings ¥25; ☉7am-10pm; MLines 1, 2, 8) A fixture on Huanghe Road Food Street, this humble tiled restaurant is a real contender for one of Shànghǎi's best dumpling places, with juicy pork and crab *xiǎolóngbāo* served up in bamboo steamers. Expect a queue and to share a table.

★ Yúxìn Chuāncài
SICHUAN $

(渝信川菜, Yú Xìn Chuāncài; Map p296; ☑021 6361 1777; 5th fl, Huasheng Tower, 399 Jiujiang Rd, 九江路399号华盛大厦5楼; dishes ¥20-98; ☉11am-2.30pm & 5-9.30pm; 🎧; MLine 2, 10 to East Nanjing Rd) At the top of Shànghǎi's best Sìchuān restaurants, Yúxìn is a dab hand in the art of blistering chillies and numbing peppercorns. All-stars include the 'mouth-watering chicken' starter (口水鸡; *kǒushuǐ jī*), or opt for the simply smoking spicy chicken (辣子鸡; *làzǐ jī*), the crispy camphor tea duck (half/whole ¥38/68) or catfish in chilli oil. There's an occasionally misfiring English menu ('Impregnable Sibao' anyone?). Take the lift.

★ Yang's Fry Dumplings
DUMPLING $

(小杨生煎馆, Xiǎoyáng Shēngjiān Guǎn; Map p296; 97 Huanghe Rd, 黄河路97号; dumplings from ¥8; ☉6.30am-8.30pm; MLine 1, 2, 8 to People's Square) The city's most famous place for sesame-seed-and-scallion-coated *shēngjiān* (生煎; fried dumplings) gets nil points for decor or service, but queues can stretch to the horizon as eager diners wait for *shēngjiān* to be dished into mustard-coloured bowls. Watch out for boiling meat juices that unexpectedly jet down your shirt (and your neighbour's). Per *liǎng* (两; four dumplings) ¥8.

Huanghe Road Food Street
CHINESE $

(黄河路美食街, Huánghé Lù Měishí Jiē; Map p296; MLine 1, 2, 8 to People's Square) With a prime central location near People's Park, Huanghe Rd covers all the bases from cheap lunches to late-night post-theatre snacks. You'll find large restaurants, but Huanghe Rd is best for dumplings – get 'em fried at Yang's or served up in bamboo steamers across the road at Jiājiā Soup Dumplings.

★ Light & Salt
INTERNATIONAL $$$

(光与盐, Guāng Yǔ Yán; Map p296; ☑021 6361 1086; www.light-n-salt.com; 6th fl, YMCA Bldg, 133 Yuanmingyuan Rd, 圆明园路133号6楼; mains

¥167-330, set lunch 2-/3-course ¥158/188; ☻ noon-2.30pm & 6-10.30pm Mon-Fri, 11.30am-4pm & 6-10.30pm Sat & Sun; Ⓜ Line 2, 10 to East Nanjing Rd) In the elegant art deco former YMCA building, this classy yet casual restaurant is divided into different sections to suit many moods. Diners will appreciate smart leather booths, dining tables and an outdoor terrace with brilliant Bund views from which you can enjoy contemporary European-influenced mains. If you're needing a drink, check out quality cocktails at its speakeasy-style Library Distillery, or enjoy a coffee in the plant-filled cafe stocked with art and design books.

★ Ultraviolet   GASTRONOMY $$$

(紫外线, Zǐwàixiàn; www.uvbypp.cc; dinner from ¥5000; ☻ dinner Tue-Sat; Ⓜ Line 2, 10 to East Nanjing Rd) You've probably paired food and wine before, but what about coupling an illuminated apple-wasabi communion wafer with purple candles and a specially designed cathedral scent? Welcome to China's most conceptual dining experience. The evening's diners gather first at Mr & Mrs Bund for an aperitif before they're whisked away to a secret location.

The meal consists of 20 courses – each accompanied by a different sensory mood (sounds, scents and images) This is Paul Pairet's masterpiece, years in the making. Revolving around his signature mischievous creations, a dinner here is bound to be unlike anything you've ever experienced before.

Reservations must be made online; book months in advance.

★ M on the Bund   EUROPEAN $$$

(米氏西餐厅, Mǐshì Xīcāntīng; Map p296; ☑ 021 6350 9988; www.m-restaurantgroup.com/mbund/home.html; 7th fl, 20 Guangdong Rd, 广东路20号7楼; mains ¥200-400, 2-course set lunch ¥188, weekend brunch 2-/3-courses ¥268/298; ☻ 11.30am-2.30pm & 6-10.30pm; Ⓜ Line 2, 10 to East Nanjing Rd) M exudes a timelessness and level of sophistication that eclipses the razzle-dazzle of many other upscale Shànghǎi restaurants. The menu ain't radical, but that's the question it seems to ask you – is breaking new culinary ground really so crucial? Crispy suckling pig and tagine with saffron are, after all, simply delicious just the way they are.

The art deco dining room and 7th-floor terrace overlooking the Bund are equally gorgeous. It's also a heavenly spot for afternoon tea (¥88 to ¥138). Make reservations well in advance.

★ Mr & Mrs Bund   FRENCH $$$

(先生及夫人外滩, Xiānshēng Jí Fūrén Wàitān; Map p296; ☑ 021 6323 9898; www.mmbund.com; 6th fl, Bund 18, 18 East Zhongshan No 1 Rd, 中山东一路18号6楼; mains ¥160-800, 2-/3-course set lunch ¥200/250; ☻ 5.30-10.30pm Mon-Wed, 5.30pm-2am Thu &Fri, 11.30am-2.30pm & 5.30pm-2am Sat, 11.30am-2.30pm & 5.30-10.30pm Sun; Ⓜ Line 2, 10 to East Nanjing Rd) French chef Paul Pairet's casual eatery aims for a space that's considerably more playful than your average fine-dining Bund restaurant. The mix-and-match menu has a heavy French bistro influence, reimagined and served up with Pairet's ingenious presentation. But it's not just the food you're here for: it's the post-midnight menu deal (two-/three-course meals ¥250/300), the bingo nights and the wonderfully wonky atmosphere. Ring the doorbell for entry.

✖ Old Town

Element Fresh   SANDWICHES $

(新元素, Xīnyuánsù; www.elementfresh.com; 6th fl, Fraser Residence, 228 South Xizang Rd, 西藏南路228号6楼; breakfast from ¥38, meals ¥60-100; 🛜; Ⓜ Line 8 to Dashijie) Handy Old Town outpost of the health-conscious chain dedicated to pick-me-up breakfasts, crisp salads, sandwiches, and feel-good juices and smoothies.

Nánxiáng Steamed Bun Restaurant   DUMPLING $

(南翔馒头店, Nánxiáng Mántou Diàn; Map p296; 85 Yuyuan Rd, Yùyuán Bazaar, 豫园商城豫园路85号; 12 dumplings on 1st fl ¥22; ☻ 1st fl 10am-9pm, 2nd fl 7am-8pm, 3rd fl 9.30am-7pm; Ⓜ Line 10 to Yuyuan Garden) Shànghǎi's most famous dumpling restaurant divides the purists, who love the place, from the younger crowd, who see an overrated tourist trap. Decide for yourself how the *xiǎolóngbāo* rate, but lines are long and you won't even get near it on weekends. There are three dining halls upstairs, with the prices escalating (and crowds diminishing) in each room.

The takeaway deal (including crab meat) is comparable to what you pay elsewhere for *xiǎolóngbāo*, but the queue snakes halfway around the Yùyuán Bazaar.

★ El Willy   SPANISH $$

(Map p296; ☑ 021 5404 5757; www.elwillygroup.com; 5th fl, South Bund 22, 22 East Zhongshan No 2 Rd, 中山东二路22号5楼; mains from ¥65, 3-course set menus ¥168; ☻ 11am-2.30pm & 6-10.30pm Mon-Sat; Ⓜ Line 10 to Yuyuan Garden) Ensconced in the stunningly converted South Bund 22, bright, vivacious and relocated from the French

Concession, Willy Trullas Moreno's fetching and fun restaurant is a more relaxed counterpoint to many other overdressed Bund operations. Seasonally adjusted scrumptious tapas and paellas are Willy's forte, paired with some serene Bund views beyond the windows. Chopsticks encourage the communal Chinese dining approach.

★ Table No 1
by Jason Atherton　　EUROPEAN $$$

(☎ 021 6080 2918; www.tableno-1.com; The Waterhouse at South Bund, 1-3 Maojiayuan Rd, 毛家园路 1-3号; mains ¥148-268; ⊙ lunch & dinner; 🐾; Ⓜ Line 9 to Xiaonanmen) On the ground floor of the Waterhouse (p314) by the Cool Docks, British chef Jason Atherton's Table No 1 fits in perfectly with the distressed industrial-chic theme. A low-key cocktail bar gives way to a deceptively casual dining room where candlelit wooden tables are arranged in communal dining style. A short selection of modern European dishes make up a beautifully considered menu. Sharing options are also available.

✖ French Concession

★ Ā Dà Cōngyóubǐng　　SHANGHAI $

(阿大葱油饼; Map p304; 2, Lane 159, South Maoming Rd, 茂名南路159弄2号; cōngyóubǐng ¥5; ⊙ 6am-3pm Thu-Tue; Ⓜ South Shaanxi Rd) *The* very definition of a hole-in-the-wall, Ā Dà Cōngyóubǐng is a takeaway spot with a long queue of hungry locals (a one-hour wait is not unheard of), serving the tastiest of that crispy Shànghǎi snacking stalwart: *cōngyóubǐng* (spring-onion pancake). You can get them all over town, but this simple place frequently edges into Top 10 lists (as voted by local diners).

Follow the aroma down the small alley, which actually leads off Nanchang Rd near the intersection of South Maoming Rd.

★ Spicy Joint　　SICHUAN $

(辛香汇; Xīnxiānghuì; Map p304; ☎ 021 6470 2777; 3rd fl, K Wah Center, 1028 Middle Huaihai Rd, 淮海中路1028号嘉华中心3楼; dishes ¥12-60; ⊙ 11am-10pm; 🐾; Ⓜ South Shaanxi Rd) If you only go to one Sìchuān joint in town, make it this one, where the blistering heat is matched only by its scorching popularity. Dishes are inexpensive by the city's standards; favourites include massive bowls of spicy catfish in hot chilli oil, an addictive garlic-cucumber salad, smoked-tea duck and chilli-coated lamb chops. Be forewarned that the wait can be excruciatingly long at peak times; you'll need a mobile number to secure a place in the queue.

★ Jian Guo 328　　SHANGHAI $

(建国, Jiànguó; Map p304; ☎ 021 6471 3819; 328 West Jianguo Rd, 建国西路328号; mains ¥22-58; ⊙ 11am-2pm & 5-9.30pm; Ⓜ Jiashan Rd) Frequently crammed, this boisterous narrow two-floor MSG-free spot tucked away on Jianguo Rd does a roaring trade on the back of excellent well priced Shanghainese cuisine. You can't go wrong with the menu; highlights include the deep-fried duck legs, aubergine casserole, scallion-oil noodles and yellow croaker fish spring rolls. Reserve.

Baker & Spice　　CAFE $

(Map p304; www.bakerandspice.com.cn; 195 Anfu Rd, 安福路195号; sandwiches & salads from ¥50; ⊙ 6am-10.30pm; 🐾; Ⓜ Changshu Rd) Whether you're craving a healthy sit-down lunch or a takeaway treat, Baker & Spice has you covered. The long wooden communal table suits solo diners, while couples and groups natter away at tables spread out in this bright and airy bakery-cafe. Everything comes lovingly presented: sandwiches on dense, fibre-rich bread; quinoa and kale salads; muffins; pains-au-chocolate; tartines; cakes; and sizeable vanilla custard Berliners.

★ Lost Heaven　　YUNNAN $$

(花马天堂, Huāmǎ Tiāntáng; Map p304; ☎ 021 6433 5126; www.lostheaven.com.cn; 38 Gaoyou Rd, 高邮路38号; dishes ¥48-96; ⊙ 11.30am-1.30pm & 5.30-10.30pm; Ⓜ Shanghai Library) Located on a quiet street in Shànghǎi's most desirable neighbourhood, Lost Heaven is stylish and atmospheric with subdued red lighting and a giant Buddha dominating the main dining area. The Yúnnán food is delicately flavoured and nicely presented, although purists may bemoan the way some dishes, such as the Dali chicken, aren't as spicy as they should be.

The Yúnnán vegetable cakes come with a salsa-like garnish and make a fantastic starter. There are a few branches around town, including **one on the Bund** (Map p296; ☎ 021 6330 0967; 17 East Yan'an Rd, 延安东路17号; dishes ¥50-160; ⊙ 11.30am-3pm & 5.30-10.30pm; Ⓜ Line 2, 10 to East Nanjing Rd). Reserve.

★ Jesse　　SHANGHAI $$

(吉士酒楼, Jíshì Jiǔlóu; Map p304; ☎ 021 6282 9260; www.xinjishi.com; 41 Tianping Rd, 天平路 41号; dishes ¥28-188; ⊙ 11am-4pm & 5.30pm-midnight; Ⓜ Jiaotong University) Jesse specialises in packing lots of people into tight spaces, so if you tend to gesture wildly when you talk, watch out with those chopsticks. This is Shanghainese home cooking at its best: crab dumplings, jujubes (red dates) stuffed with glutinous rice, Grandma's braised pork and plenty of fish, drunken shrimp and eel.

★ Dĭ Shuĭ Dòng
HUNANESE $$

(滴水洞; Map p317; ☑ 021 6253 2689; 2nd fl, 56 South Maoming Rd, 茂名南路56号2楼; dishes ¥25-128; ⊙ 11am-1am; M South Shaanxi Rd) Until the chilled lagers arrive, the faint breeze from the spreading of the blue-and-white tablecloth by your waiter may be the last cooling sensation at Dĭ Shuĭ Dòng, a rustic upstairs shrine to the volcanic cuisine of Húnán. Loved by Shanghainese and expats in equal measure, dishes are ferried in by sprightly peasant-attired staff to tables stuffed with enthusiastic, red-faced diners.

The claim to fame is the Húnán-style cumin-crusted ribs, but there's no excuse not to sample the *làzi jīdīng* (fried chicken with chillies), the excellent Húnán-style fried crab in claypot or even the classic boiled frog. Cool down with plenty of beers and caramelised bananas for dessert.

Liquid Laundry
AMERICAN $$

(Map p304; ☑ 021 6445 9589; www.theliquidlaundry.com; 2nd fl, Kwah Centre, 1028 Middle Huaihai Rd, 淮海中路1028号2楼; mains ¥48-128; ⊙ 11am-midnight Sun-Wed, to 2am Thu-Sat; ☎; M South Shaanxi Rd) With bow-tied 'mixologists', subway-tiled walls and exposed warehouse piping, Liquid Laundry will have you thinking you've just walked off the elevator into NYC. This vast gastropub/cocktail bar offers several options – wood-fired pizza at the counter, American bourbon whiskies in the lounge area, rotisserie chicken with homemade hot sauce to a backdrop of shiny brewery vats, and 15 craft beer taps.

★ ElEfante
MEDITERRANEAN $$$

(Map p304; ☑ 021 5404 8085; www.el-efante.com; 20 Donghu Rd, 东湖路20号; lunch set ¥128, weekend brunch from ¥198; ⊙ 11.30am-3pm & 6-10.30pm Mon-Fri, 11am-3pm Sat & Sun; M South Shaanxi Rd) Willy Trullas Moreno's ElEfante sits squarely at the heart of the French Concession – in the same spot as his first venture – with a choice patio and romantic 1920s villa setting. Its tantalising Mediterranean menu, with tapas-style dishes, has pronounced Spanish and Italian inflections, and has local gastronomes buzzing.

★ T8
FUSION $$$

(Map p304; ☑ 021 6355 8999; http://t8-shanghai.com; Xīntiāndì North Block, Bldg 8, 太仓路181弄新天地北里8号楼; mains ¥238-598, set lunch weekdays ¥158; ⊙ 11am-2.30pm & 6.30-10.30pm;

M South Huangpi Rd, Xintiandi) T8 aims to seduce, which it does exceptionally well. Catalan chef Jordi Servalls Bonilla is at the helm, bringing a preference for molecular cuisine with dishes such as *tataki* of sesame-crusted tuna and foie gras millefeuille (a layered pastry cake). The renovated grey-brick *shíkùmén* with striking feng shui–driven entrance is the perfect setting. Reserve ahead.

Kagen
JAPANESE $$$

(隐泉源铁板烧. Yīnquán Yuán Tiĕbǎnshāo; Map p304; ☑ 021 6433 3232; 28d Taojiang Rd, 桃江路28号丁; all-you-can-eat-&-drink teppanyaki ¥328; ⊙ 5.30-11pm Mon-Thu & Sun, 11.30am-midnight Fri & Sat; M Changshu Rd) Opened by the folks at **Haiku** (隐泉之语, Yīnquán Zhī Yǔ; Map p304; ☑ 021 6445 0021; 28b Taojiang Rd, 桃江路28号乙; maki rolls ¥70-140; ⊙ 11am-2pm & 5.30-10pm; M Changshu Rd) next door, supersleek Kagen offers excellent value all-you-can-eat-and-drink teppanyaki. Wagyu beef, tiger prawns and foie gras are some of the finer ingredients on the menu, and quality sushi, sashimi, sake and wine are all part of the buffet deal. It also offers an à la carte menu. Reserve.

🍴 Jìng'ān

★ Yang's Fry Dumplings
DUMPLING $

(小杨生煎馆, Xiǎoyáng Shēngjiān Guǎn; Map p317; 2nd fl, 269 Wujiang Rd, 吴江路269号2楼; 4 fried dumplings from ¥8; ⊙ 10am-10pm; M Line 2, 12, 13 to West Nanjing Rd, exit 4) A much-too-small outlet of this famous dumpling-house chain, specialising in delicious pork and prawn *shēngjiān*. Pass your receipt to the kitchen to collect your dumplings.

★ Sumerian
CAFE $

(苏美尔人, Sū Měi Ěr Rén; Map p317; www.sumeriancoffee.com; 415 North Shaanxi Rd, 陕西北路415号; mains from ¥20; ⊙ 7am-8pm; ☎; M Line 2, 13 to West Nanjing Rd, exit 1) Run by a bright and sunny team of staff, good-looking Sumerian packs a lot into a small space. The real drawcard here is the coffee – the cafe roasts its own single-origin beans sourced seasonally from Ethiopia, El Salvador and China. It does good pour-overs and lattes, as well as a nitro and eight-hour cold drip. The homemade bagels are also a standout, with a delicious selection of toppings and spreads.

Co. Cheese Melt Bar
SANDWICHES $

(Map p317; 32 Yuyuan East Rd, 愚园东路32号; sandwiches from ¥25; ⊙ 11.30am-10pm Tue-Thu & Sun, to 1am Sat; ☎; M Line 2, 7 to Jing'an Temple) A godsend for those with a hankering for the ultimate in Western comfort food, this joint is dedicated entirely to the humble grilled-cheese sandwich. Run by a Canadian expat, this intimate bar offers a selection of 20 gourmet cheese melts on sourdough, or build your own classic grilled cheese on white bread with a side of pickles and hot sauces.

There's an IPA and cider on tap, bottled craft beers and a good bar selection. Jars of homemade Polish pickles line the walls. Don't miss the signature pickleback – a shot of whisky with briny pickle-juice chaser. If you want something different for a boozy brunch, try the alcoholic cereal served with Baileys milk.

Pure and Whole　　　　VEGETARIAN $
(純和整個, Chún Hé Zhěnggè; Map p317; ☑ 021 5175 9822; www.pureandwhole.com; 98 Yanping Rd, 延平路98号; ☉ 11.30am-10pm; ❀🔊⏼; Ⓜ Line 2, 7 to Jing'an Temple, exit 2) When you've overdosed on dumplings, this popular vegetarian restaurant offers much-needed respite with detox salads, wholewheat wraps stuffed with tofu 'chorizo', chickpeas and avocado, or white-bean stews. It does cleansing juices and creative blended drinks. Grab a seat upstairs overlooking the main road.

★**Commune Social**　　　　TAPAS $$
(食社, Shìshè; www.communesocial.com; 511 Jiangning Rd, 江宁路511号; tapas ¥38-198, set-lunch menu 3/5 course ¥178/218; ☉ noon-2.30pm & 6-10.30pm Tue-Fri, noon-3pm & 6-10.30pm Sat, to 3pm Sun; Ⓜ Line 7 to Changping Rd) A venture by UK celebrity chef Jason Atherton, this natty Neri & Hu–designed restaurant blends a stylish, yet relaxed, vibe with sensational tasting dishes, exquisitely presented by chef Scott Melvin. It's divided neatly into upstairs cocktail bar with terrace, downstairs open-kitchen tapas bar and dessert bar. It's the talk of the town, but has a no-reservations policy, so prepare to queue.

There's a range of tapas menus, including a vegetarian option, and set-lunch menus all featuring modern European creations.

★**Hǎi Dǐ Lāo**　　　　HOTPOT $$
(海底捞; Map p317; ☑ 021 6258 9758; 3rd fl, 1068 West Beijing Rd, 北京西路1068号3楼; hotpot per person ¥100-120; ☉ 10.30am-late; 🔊; Ⓜ Line 2, 12, 13 to West Nanjing Rd) This Sichuanese hotpot restaurant is all about service, and the assault begins the minute you walk in the door. Pre-dining options include complimentary shoeshines, manicures and

trays of fresh fruit; once you've actually sat down, the buzz of activity continues with the donning of matching red aprons and a YouTube-worthy noodle-stretching dance performance (order *lāo miàn;* 捞面).

Din Tai Fung　　　　DUMPLING $$
(鼎泰丰, Dǐng Tài Fēng; Map p317; ☑ 021 6289 9182; www.dintaifung.com.tw/en; Shànghǎi Centre, 1376 West Nanjing Rd, 南京西路1376号; 10 dumplings ¥58-88; ☉ 10am-10pm; 📷; Ⓜ Line 2, 7 to Jing'an Temple, exit 1) Critically acclaimed dumplings and flawless service from Taiwan's most famous dumpling chain. Reserve ahead.

★**Fu 1088**　　　　SHANGHAI $$$
(福1088; Map p304; ☑ 021 5239 7878; 375 Zhenning Rd, 镇宁路375号; ☉ 11am-2pm & 5.30-11pm; Ⓜ Line 2, 11 to Jiangsu Rd) In a 1930s villa, exclusive Fu 1088 has 17 rooms filled with Chinese antiques. Rooms are rented out privately, with white-gloved service and an emphasis on elegant Shanghainese fare with a modern twist such as shredded crab and drunken chicken. There's a minimum charge of ¥300 per person for lunch, and ¥400 for dinner, excluding drinks.

🍴 Pǔdōng

Baker & Spice　　　　CAFE $
(Map p308; IFC Mall, 8 Century Ave, 世纪大道8号; sandwiches & salads from ¥50; ☉ 10am-10pm; Ⓜ Lujiazui) Small branch in the IFC Mall (p330) with baked pastries, bagels, salad bowls and weekend brunch.

Food Opera　　　　ASIAN $
(食代馆, Shídàiguǎn; Map p308; B2, Superbrand Mall, 168 West Lujiazui Rd, 陆家嘴西路168号B2楼; dishes from ¥15; ☉ 10am-10pm; Ⓜ Lujiazui) Grab a card from the booth (¥10 deposit), load up with credits and then spend, spend, spend on a whole host of open kitchens in this hopping food court. There's Korean, teppanyaki, Japanese noodles, pasta and much more. The spicy *shoyu ramen* at **Ramen Play** is a good place to start. Just point at what you want and hand over your card.

★**Sichuan Folk**　　　　SICHUAN $$
(☑ 021 3111 8055; Room 110, 1368 Shibo Ave, 世博大道1368号110室; mains from ¥22; ☉ 11am-2pm & 5-9pm; Ⓜ China Art Museum) Formerly known as Bāguó Bùyī, Sichuan Folk is pretty much the most authentic Sìchuān food in town, cooked up by the diligent chefs at this famous restaurant at the World Expo site, originally founded in Chéngdū. With no

concessions to the dainty Shànghǎi palate, prepare for a spicy firecracker of a meal. It's located in a complex opposite the Mercedes-Benz Arena.

★ **Grand Café** BISTRO $$$
(Map p308; ☑ 021 5047 8838; http://shanghai. grand.hyatt.com; Grand Hyatt, Jīnmào Tower, 88 Century Ave, 世纪大道88号君悦大酒店; buffet lunch/dinner from ¥288/388; ⊙ buffet lunch 11.30am-2.30pm, à la carte 24hr; M Lujiazui) On the 54th floor of Jīnmào Tower (in the Grand Hyatt lobby), the Grand Café offers stunning panoramas through its glass walls and an excellent-value lunch buffet; pile your plate with endless crab legs, Peking duck, fresh prawns, mini burgers, dumplings, made-to-order noodles: you name it. Finish it off with gelato, delectable cakes, fruit and French cheeses. Book well in advance for a window table. Service charge 10%.

✕ Hóngkǒu & North Shànghǎi

★ **Guǒyuán** HUNANESE $
(果园; 524 Dongjiangwan Rd, 东江湾路524号; mains from ¥18; ⊙ 11am-2pm & 5-10pm Mon-Fri, 11am-3pm & 5-10pm Sat & Sun; M Hongkou Football Stadium) The cool lime-green tablecloths do little to tame the tempestuous flavours of this fantastic Húnán restaurant. The *tiěbǎn dòufu* (铁板豆腐; sizzling tofu platter) here is a magnificent dish, but its fiery flavours are almost eclipsed by the enticing *xiāngwèi qiézibāo* (湘味茄子煲; Húnán aubergine hotpot) and the lovely *zīrán yángròu* (孜然羊肉; lamb with cumin; ¥32).

✕ Xújiāhuì & South Shànghǎi

★ **Hóng Làjiāo Xiāngcàiguǎn** HUNANESE $
(红辣椒湘菜馆; ☑ 021 6283 2970; 754 Panyu Rd, 番禺路754号; mains ¥28-58; ⊙ 11am-midnight; M Line 11 to Jiaotong University) There's no shortage of decent Húnán restaurants in Shànghǎi but you won't find much better than this one. Wooden benches and an exposed-brick effect make for a rough-and-ready atmosphere, but there's nothing casual about the food: a feast of unforgettably smoky, spicy flavours. Many of the dishes are prepared in the typical 'dry pot' (干锅; *gān guō*) style, and are served up in an iron pot placed over a burner at the table.

★ **Din Tai Fung** SHANGHAI $
(鼎泰丰, Dǐng Tài Fēng; ☑ 021 3469 1383; 5th fl, Grand Gateway 66, 1 Hongqiao Rd, 虹桥路1号 港汇广场5楼; mains ¥38-58; ⊙ 10am-10pm;

M Line 1, 9, 11 to Xujiahui) This brightly lit and busy Taiwan-owned restaurant chain may still be peddling its 'Top 10 restaurants of the world' mantra after a two-decades-old review in the *New York Times,* but it does deliver some absolutely scrummy Shànghǎi *xiǎolóngbāo* dumplings. Not cheap perhaps (the pork variety are five for ¥30, or 10 for ¥60), but they're delicate, flavoursome and worth every *jiǎo*.

Service is top notch and you can watch masked chefs prepare your dumplings through sheet glass on arrival, where you can also peruse pictures of Tom Cruise giving his thumbs up. Vegetable or pricey black truffle *xiǎolóngbāo* options are also on offer.

✕ West Shànghǎi

★ **1221** SHANGHAI $$
(Yī Èr Èr Yī; ☑ 021 6213 6585; 1221 West Yan'an Rd, 延安西路1221号; dishes ¥28-128; ⊙ 5-11pm; M West Yan'an Rd) No one has a bad thing to say about this dapper expat favourite, and rightly so: it has never let its standards dip over the years. Meat dishes start at ¥58 for the beef and *yóutiáo* (dough strips), and the plentiful eel, shrimp and squid dishes cost around twice that. Other tempting fare includes the roast duck and braised pork.

★ **Fú Hé Huì** VEGETARIAN $$$
(福和慧; ☑ 021 3980 9188; 1037 Yuyuan Rd, 愚园路1037号; set menus ¥380, ¥680 & ¥880; ⊙ 11am-2pm & 5-10.30pm; ☑; M Jiangsu Rd) The most recent venture from owner Fang Yuan and chef Tony Lu, the Shànghǎi team behind Fu 1015, Fu 1088 (p322) and **Fu 1039** (福一零三九, Fú Yào Líng Sān Jiǔ; ☑ 021 5237 1878; 1039 Yuyuan Rd, 愚园路1039号; dishes ¥60-108; M Jiangsu Rd), this is the standout in an amazing bunch. Set in an elegant private room, the strictly vegetarian menu draws on Yuan's Buddhist faith. Choose from three set menus featuring creative and delicate flavours that won it a place in Asia's 50 Best Restaurants 2016.

🍷 Drinking & Nightlife

Shànghǎi adores its lychee martinis and cappuccinos to go and, with dazzling salaries and soaring property prices leaving the streets sloshing with cash, there are more than enough bars and cafes to wet the lips of the thirsty white-collar set. There's a happening nightlife scene that keeps everyone – VIP or not – well entertained.

The Bund & People's Square

★ Glam
LOUNGE

(魅力, Mèilì; Map p296; 7th fl, 20 Guangdong Rd, 广东路20号7楼; cocktails ¥80-100; ⏰5pm-late; Ⓜ Line 2, 10 to East Nanjing Rd) The decor here is decidedly bohemian – full of art and curiosities – and its cool retro feel makes it one of the Bund's most atmospheric spots for a drink. Cocktail prices are accessible, as is the bar menu, ranging from truffle cheese toasties to soft-serve ice cream.

★ Long Bar
BAR

(廊吧, Láng Bā; Map p296; ☎021 6322 9988; 2 East Zhongshan No 1 Rd, 中山东一路2号; drinks from ¥70; ⏰4pm-1am Mon-Sat, 2pm-1am Sun; ☎; Ⓜ Line 2, 10 to East Nanjing Rd) For a taste of colonial-era Shànghǎi's elitist trappings, you'll do no better than the Long Bar. This was once the members-only Shànghǎi Club, whose most spectacular accoutrement was a 34m-long wooden bar. Foreign businessmen would sit here according to rank, comparing fortunes, with the taipans (foreign heads of business) closest to the view of the Bund.

Now part of the Waldorf Astoria, the bar's original wood-panelled decor has been painstakingly re-created from old photographs. There's a good selection of old-fashioned cocktails as well as an oyster bar (and jazz, naturally).

★ Barbarossa
BAR

(芭芭露莎会所, Bābālùshā Huìsuǒ; Map p296; www.barbarossa.com.cn; People's Park, 231 West Nanjing Rd, 南京西路231号人民公园内; ⏰11am-2am; ☎; Ⓜ Line 1, 2, 8 to People's Square, exit 11) Set back in People's Park alongside a pond, Barbarossa is all about escapism. Forget Shànghǎi, this is Morocco channelled by Hollywood set designers. The action gets steadily more intense as you ascend to the roof terrace, via the cushion-strewn 2nd floor, where the hordes puff on fruit-flavoured hookahs. At night, use the park entrance just east of the former Shànghǎi Race Club building (上海跑马总会; Shànghǎi Pǎomǎ Zǒnghuì).

Happy hour (from 2pm to 8pm) is a good time to visit for two-for-one cocktails.

M1NT
CLUB

(Map p296; ☎021 6391 2811; www.m1ntglobal.com; 24th fl, Cross Tower, 318 Fuzhou Rd, 福州路318号24楼; ⏰9.30pm-late Wed-Sat; Ⓜ Line 2, 10 to East Nanjing Rd) Exclusive penthouse-style club with knockout city views and snazzy fusion food but not a lot of dance space. Dress to impress or you'll get thrown into the shark tank. No sports shoes etc.

Pop
BAR

(流行音乐, Liúxíng Yīnyuè; Map p296; ☎021 6321 0909; www.threeonthebund.com; 7th fl, Three on the Bund, 3 East Zhongshan No 1 Rd, 中山东一路3号7楼; ⏰11am-late; Ⓜ Line 2, 10 to East Nanjing Rd) On the top floor of Three on the Bund, Pop's splendid roof terrace is divided into multiple entities, all with choice views of Pǔdōng's hypnotising neon performance. There's always a crowd, whether they're here for the Miami art deco–themed cocktail bar or the Louisiana-style Whisper bar, specialising in American rye whiskies and bourbon. There's also a stylish restaurant that channels a retro New York brasserie.

The menu is mainly Western comfort food, with mains from ¥120.

Old Town

Mid-Lake Pavilion Teahouse
TEAHOUSE

(湖心亭, Húxīntíng; Map p296; Yùyuán Bazaar, 豫园商城; tea ¥50; ⏰8am-9pm; Ⓜ Line 10 to Yuyuan Garden) Next to the entrance to the Yùyuán Gardens is the Mid-Lake Pavilion Teahouse, once part of the gardens and now one of the most famous teahouses in China, visited by Queen Elizabeth II and Bill Clinton, among others. The zigzag causeway is designed to thwart spirits (and trap tourists), who can only travel in straight lines.

The wonderfully lengthy menu recommends suitable brews to drink in each season and the tea is served elegantly with tiny nibbles.

French Concession

★ Senator Saloon
COCKTAIL BAR

(Map p304; ☎021 5423 1330; www.senatorsaloon.com; 98 Wuyuan Rd, 五原路98号; ⏰5pm-1am Mon-Fri, to late Sat & Sun; Ⓜ Changshu Rd) From the team behind Sìchuān Citizen (龙门阵茶屋, Lóngménzhèn Cháwū; Map p304; ☎021 5404 1235; 30 Donghu Rd, 东湖路30号; dishes ¥26-98, set lunch ¥38-68; ⏰11am-10.30pm; ☎; Ⓜ South Shaanxi Rd) and Citizen Café (p325) comes this classy 1920s Prohibition Era–style cocktail bar in a quiet spot on Wuyuan Rd. Slink into a dark-wood booth under pressed metal ceilings and dim art deco lights to order a barrel-aged Negroni from waitstaff decked out in braces and bow ties. There's a long menu of American bourbon and whisky rye-based cocktails, and excellent table service.

★ Speak Low COCKTAIL BAR
(Map p304; ☎021 6416 0133; 579 Middle Fuxing Rd, 复兴中路579号; ⏲6pm-1.30am Sun-Thu, to 2.30am Fri & Sat; Ⓜ South Shaanxi Rd) Speak Low is a standout in a city overrun with speak-easy-style bars. Once you find your way in through Ocho bar equipment shop, start with a drink on the 2nd floor; cocktails run ¥75 to ¥85. Then head upstairs (hint: find China and you'll find the entrance) to the intimate, seating-only bar for expertly crafted Japanese-influenced cocktails from ¥100.

★ Café del Volcán CAFE
(Map p304; www.cafevolcan.com; 80 Yongkang Rd, 永康路80号; espressos ¥26, flat whites ¥36; ⏲8am-8pm Mon-Fri, 10am-8pm Sat & Sun; 📶; Ⓜ South Shaanxi Rd) Tiny Café del Volcán offers a pit stop from the bustle of bar-heavy Yongkang Rd. The minimalist cafe has just a few wooden box tables sharing the space with the roasting machine. The coffee here is excellent and its signature beans come from the owner's coffee plantation in Guatemala – in the family for 120 years – while other single-origin beans are from Ethiopia, Kenya, Panama and Yúnnán.

★ Dr Wine WINE BAR
(葡萄酒博士, Pútáojiǔ Bóshì; Map p304; 177 Fumin Rd, 富民路177号; ⏲11am-2am; 📶; Ⓜ Jing'an Temple) Black-leather armchairs, salvaged *shíkùmén* brick walls and worn-in tables set the mood at this casual, two-storey wine bar on Fumin Rd. Wines are sold by both the glass (from ¥48) and bottle. Pair it with the usual French accompaniments – a cheeseboard (from ¥88) or charcuterie plate (saucisson, pâté etc from ¥120) – and settle in for the night.

★ El Cóctel BAR
(Map p304; ☎021 6433 6511; 2nd fl, 47 Yongfu Rd, 永福路47号; ⏲5.30pm-late; Ⓜ Shanghai Library) What do you get when you cross an ever-inventive Spanish chef with a perfectionist bartender from Japan? El Cóctel, of course – a retro cocktail lounge that mixes up some damn fine drinks, but make sure you come with cash to spare. Like a lot of bars in the city, it can get very smoky, and if you don't reserve you might find it hard to get in.

★ Citizen Café CAFE
(天台餐厅, Tiāntái Cāntīng; Map p317; 222 Jinxian Rd, 进贤路222号; ⏲11am-12.30am; 📶; Ⓜ South Shaanxi Rd) Decked out with Chesterfield seating, dark-wood-panelled walls, whirring ceiling fans and small lamps, this feels like a snug private gentleman's club by day and romantic candlelit hideaway come sundown. Weekday lunch sets (11am to 2pm) are great value where you can recharge with a club sandwich, fries and a latte for ¥45. The small 2nd-floor terrace is a great spot for sipping cocktails while watching street scenes unfold.

SHÀNGHǍI PUB CRAWL

Every Saturday at 9.30pm, an organised **pub crawl** (http://pubcrawlshanghai.com; ¥150) starts with an hour-long open bar (with free snacks), followed by a series of bars around town, with free shots and cut-price booze to follow. It's a great way to size up the Shànghǎi bar scene and make new friends. Sign up online; cost ¥150.

★ Café des Stagiaires BAR
(Map p304; www.cafestagiaires.com; 54-56 Yongkang Rd, 永康路54-56号; mains from ¥45; ⏲10am-midnight; 📶; Ⓜ South Shaanxi Rd) One of the original bars on buzzing Yongkang Rd, this hip oasis of Francophilia spills over with slightly zany Gallic charm. There's a coke bottle chandelier and a (French) geography lesson via the wine list. Languedoc, Provence, Côte du Rhône, Loire, Alsace, Bourgogne, Bordeaux and, *bien sûr,* Rest of the World. Each table is regularly stocked with addictive chilli peanuts.

If that's insufficient, sample the quality charcuterie, cheese and pizzas. Happy hour is 5pm to 8pm weekdays and 2pm to 6pm weekends, with great-value wine at ¥20 per glass.

★ Bell Bar BAR
(Map p304; http://bellbar.cn; Tiánzǐfáng, back door No 11, Lane 248, Taikang Rd, 泰康路248弄11号后门田子坊; ⏲11am-2am Wed-Mon, 2pm-2am Tue; 📶; Ⓜ Dapuqiao) This eccentric, unconventional boho haven is a delightful Tiánzǐfáng hideaway, with creaking, narrow wooden stairs leading to a higgledy-piggledy array of rooms and the tucked-away attic slung out above. Expect hookah pipes, mismatched furniture and a small, secluded mezzanine for stowaways from the bedlam outside. It's in the second alley (Lane 248) on the right.

Time Passage BAR
(昨天今天明天, Zuótiān Jīntiān Míngtiān; Map p304; ☎021 6240 2588; No 183, Lane 1038, Caojiayan Rd, 曹家堰路1038弄183号; ⏲5pm-late; 📶; Ⓜ Jiangsu Rd) Time Passage has real staying power, clocking up around 20 years in the

business of cheap beer and good music. Beyond its no-nonsense Gucci-free vibe – not a suit in sight – it's a relaxing, down-to-earth spot for an evening beer or a daytime coffee.

There's live music on Friday and Saturday nights, and a daily happy hour from 5.30pm to 7.30pm.

🍷 Jìng'ān

★Dogtown
BAR

(狗镇, Gǒu Zhèn; Map p317; 409 N Shaanxi Rd, 陕西北路409号; ⊙4-10pm Mon-Fri, noon-11pm Sat & Sun; Ⓜ Line 2, 7 to Jing'an Temple, Line 2, 12, 13 to West Nanjing Rd) Run by the team from Sumerian (p321) next door, this pocket-sized bar is literally a streetside shack with a few stools at its bar, though most revellers stand on the pavement with beer in hand. It's a great place to get chatting to random strangers. For early starters, there's a free keg of Asahi going on weekends from noon until it runs out.

If that wasn't a sweet enough deal, Dogtown also serves homemade soft-corn tortilla tacos (from ¥15) and bagels. Note it's closed during the winter months.

Tailor Bar
COCKTAIL BAR

(裁缝栏, Cáiféng Lán; Map p317; ☑183 0197 7360; 4th fl, 2 Huashan Rd, 华山路2号4楼; cocktails ¥90-150; ⊙6.30pm-late; Ⓜ Line 2, 7 to Jing'an Temple) Set up by London-trained mixologist Eddie Yang, this swanky speakeasy is accessed via a nondescript lift next to a Chinese medicine shop. It lives up to its name with cocktails tailormade to suit your tastes; there's no menu, so pick a few items and let the staff do their thing. During the day they serve coffee and there are good views of Jìng'ān Temple.

Mokkos Lamu
BAR

(1245 Wuding W Rd, 武定西路1245号; ⊙7pm-2am; Ⓜ Line 2, 11 to Jiangsu Rd, exit 5) Hidden away on a residential side street, Mokkos is a long-running local fave that specialises in nothing but *shōchū* (Japanese spirit made from grains). It's an intimate, jovial and welcoming bar where drinkers sit on stools around the curved bar lined with large, aesthetically pleasing *shōchū* bottles. There's a choice of wheat, rice or potato varieties, and it also does *shōchū* cocktails for ¥40.

There's a guitar on the wall for regular impromptu jams.

Helen's
BAR

(海倫的, Hǎilún De; Map p317; 148 N Maoming Rd, 茂名北路148号; ⊙5pm-2am; Ⓜ Line 2, 12, 13 West Nanjing Rd, exit 12) Had enough of wall-to-wall suits and sky-high prices? Helen's speciality is the bargain-basement, no-frills, student-set dive-end of the bar market. Enjoy.

🍷 Pǔdōng

★Flair
BAR

(Map p308; 58th fl, Ritz-Carlton Shanghai Pudong, 8 Century Ave, 世纪大道8号58楼; cocktails from ¥95; ⊙5.30pm-late; ☎; Ⓜ Lujiazui) Wow your date with Shànghǎi's most intoxicating nocturnal visuals from the outdoor terrace on the 58th floor of the Ritz-Carlton, where Flair nudges you that bit closer to the baubles of the Oriental Pearl TV Tower. If it's raining, you'll end up inside, but that's OK as the chilled-out interior, designed by the firm Super Potato, is very cool. Book well in advance for the terrace.

🍷 Hóngkǒu & North Shànghǎi

★Vue
BAR

(非常时髦, Fēicháng Shímáo; Map p296; www. hyattonthebundsh.com; 32nd & 33rd fl, Hyatt on the Bund, 199 Huangpu Rd, 黄浦路199号外滩茂悦大酒店32-33楼; ⊙5.30pm-late; Ⓜ Tiantong Rd) Take in the extrasensory nocturnal views of the Bund and Pǔdōng from Vue bar at the Hyatt on the Bund, complete with outdoor jacuzzi to dip your toes in while you raise your glass of bubbly. There's a cover charge of ¥100 for those not staying at the hotel, which includes a free drink.

☆ Entertainment

Shànghǎi is no longer the decadent city that slipped on its dancing shoes as the revolution shot its way into town, but entertainment options have blossomed again over the past decade. Plug into the local cultural scene for a stimulating shot of gallery openings, music concerts and laid-back movie nights at the local bar.

★Shànghǎi Grand Theatre
CLASSICAL MUSIC

(上海大剧院, Shànghǎi Dàjùyuàn; Map p296; ☑021 6386 8686; www.shgtheatre.com; 300 Renmin Ave, 人民广场人民大道300号; ⊙box office 9am-8pm; Ⓜ Line 1, 2, 8 to People's Square) Shànghǎi's state-of-the-art concert venue hosts everything from Broadway musicals to symphonies, ballets, operas, and performances by internationally acclaimed classical soloists. There are also traditional Chinese-music performances. Pick up a schedule at the ticket office.

★ **Yùyīntáng** LIVE MUSIC
(育音堂; ☎021 5237 8662; www.yytlive.com; 851 Kaixuan Rd, 凯旋路851号; Ⓜ West Yan'an Rd) Small enough to feel intimate, but big enough for a sometimes pulsating atmosphere, Yùyīntáng has long been one of the top places in the city to see live music. Any Shànghǎi rock band worth its amps plays here, but you can also catch groups on tour from other cities in China, as well as international acts. Rock is the staple diet, but anything goes, from hard punk to jazz.

★ **Shànghǎi Centre Theatre** ACROBATICS
(上海商城剧院, Shànghǎi Shāngchéng Jùyuàn; Map p317; ☎021 6279 8948; Shànghǎi Centre, 1376 West Nanjing Rd, 南京西路1376号; tickets ¥120-300; Ⓜ Line 2, 7 to Jing'an Temple) The Shànghǎi Acrobatics Troupe has popular performances here at 7.30pm most nights. It's a short but fun show and is high on the to-do list of most first-time visitors. Buy tickets a couple of days in advance from the ticket office on the right-hand side at the entrance to the Shànghǎi Centre.

Fairmont Peace Hotel Jazz Bar JAZZ
(爵士吧, Juéshì Bā; Map p296; ☎021 6138 6883; 20 East Nanjing Rd, 南京东路20号费尔蒙和平饭店; ◷5.30pm-2am, live music from 7pm; Ⓜ Line 2, 10 to East Nanjing Rd) Shànghǎi's most famous hotel features Shànghǎi's most famous jazz band (starts at 7pm), a septuagenarian sextet that's been churning out nostalgic covers such as 'Moon River' and 'Summertime' since the dawn of time. There's no admission fee, but you'll need to sink a drink from the bar (draught beer starts at ¥70, a White Lady is ¥98). The original band takes the stage from 7pm to 9.45pm; to get the pulse moving, a 'sultry female vocalist' does her bit from 9.45pm.

House of Blues & Jazz LIVE MUSIC
(布鲁斯乐爵士之屋, Bùlǔsī Yuè Juéshì Zhīwū; Map p296; ☎021 6323 2779; 60 Fuzhou Rd, 福州路60号; beer from ¥70; ◷5pm-1am Tue-Sun; Ⓜ Line 2, 10 to East Nanjing Rd) Fittingly dark and divey, this vintage jazz and blues bar exudes plenty of class with its polished heavy wood decor. The house band delivers live jazz or blues from 9.30pm (10pm on Friday and Saturday) to 1am. Sunday night is a free-for-all jam. Entry is free if you're here to eat or drink; happy hour offers half-priced beers to 8pm.

Shànghǎi Concert Hall CLASSICAL MUSIC
(上海音乐厅, Shànghǎi Yīnyuè Tīng; Map p296; ☎021 6386 2836; www.shanghaiconcerthall.org;

523 East Yan'an Rd, 人民广场延安东路523号; tickets ¥80-480; Ⓜ Line 1, 2, 8 to People's Square, Line 8 to Dashijie) A decade or so ago, the government shunted all 5650 tonnes of this classic 1930s building 66m away from busy East Yan'an Rd to a quieter parkside setting. It features smaller-scale concerts plus local and international soloists.

The website is in Chinese, but you can pick up the program from the box office.

Yifū Theatre CHINESE OPERA
(逸夫舞台, Yifū Wǔtái; Map p296; ☎021 6322 5294; www.lianchan.com; 701 Fuzhou Rd, 人民广场福州路701号; tickets ¥30-280; Ⓜ Line 1, 2, 8 to People's Square) One block east of People's Square, this is the main opera theatre in town. The theatre presents a popular program of Běijīng, Kun and Yue (Shàoxīng) opera. A Běijīng opera highlights show is performed several times a week at 1.30pm and 7.15pm; pick up a brochure at the ticket office.

Shanghai Symphony Orchestra Hall CLASSICAL MUSIC
(上海交响乐团, Shànghǎi Jiāoxiǎngyuè Tuán; Map p304; www.shsymphony.com; 1380 Middle Fuxing Rd, 复兴中路1380号; Ⓜ Changshu Rd) Designed by architects Isozaki Arata and Yasushisa Toyota, and opening in 2014, this concert venue is now the home of the Shanghai Symphony Orchestra, which has been going strong since 1949. Small chamber music concerts are held most Friday evenings at affordable prices, but they sell out, so book in advance. Tickets can be bought at the venue box office or on the website.

Cotton Club LIVE MUSIC
(棉花俱乐部, Miánhuā Jùlèbù; Map p304; ☎021 6437 7110; www.thecottonclub.cn; 1416 Middle Huaihai Rd, 淮海中路1416号; ◷7.30pm-2am Tue-Sun; Ⓜ Changshu Rd) Harlem it ain't, but this is still the best and longest-running bar for live jazz in Shànghǎi. It features blues and jazz groups throughout the week. Wynton Marsalis once stepped in to jam, forever sealing the Cotton Club's reputation as the top live-music haunt in town. The music gets going around 9pm or 10pm.

Shànghǎi Conservatory of Music CLASSICAL MUSIC
(上海音乐学院, Shànghǎi Yīnyuè Xuéyuàn; Map p304; ☎021 6431 1792; 20 Fenyang Rd, 汾阳路20号; ◷ticket office 9am-8.30pm; Ⓜ South Shaanxi Rd) The auditorium here holds classical-music performances (Chinese and Western), usually on weekends at 7.30pm, and the

musicians are often the stars of the future. You can buy tickets next door to the campus at Music Ticket; it also sells tickets to performances at other venues in the city.

Oriental Art Center
CLASSICAL MUSIC
(上海东方艺术中心, Shànghǎi Dōngfāng Yìshù Zhōngxīn; ☑ 021 6854 1234; www.shoac.com.cn; 425 Dingxiang Rd, 浦东丁香路425号; M Science & Technology Museum) Home of the Shànghǎi Symphony Orchestra, the Oriental Art Center was designed to resemble five petals of a butterfly orchid. There are three main halls that host classical, jazz, dance and Chinese and Western opera performances. Saturday brunch concerts (10am, held on the first and third Saturday of the month) cost from ¥30 to ¥80. Free tours of the centre are conducted on the first Saturday of the month (from 1.30pm to 4.30pm).

Shànghǎi Circus World
ACROBATICS
(上海马戏城, Shànghǎi Mǎxìchéng; ☑ 021 6652 7501; www.era-shanghai.com/era/en/; 2266 Gonghexin Rd, 共和新路2266号; tickets ¥120-600; M Shanghai Circus World) Out on the far northern outskirts of town, you'll find this impressive complex. The show – *Era: Intersection of Time* – combines awesome acrobatics with new-fangled multimedia elements. Shows start at 7.30pm. Tickets are available at the door, but booking ahead is advised.

🛍 Shopping

Shànghǎi's runaway property market and thrusting economy have filled pockets citywide: Shànghǎi shoppers buy up big-time. While locals have a passion for luxury goods and designer labels, it's not all about Gucci, Prada and Louis Vuitton. Whether you're after boutique threads, a set of snappy heels, Chinese antiques, handmade ceramics or a period poster from the Mao era, Shànghǎi is an A to Z of shopping.

🛍 The Bund & People's Square

★ Shànghǎi Museum Art Store
GIFTS & SOUVENIRS
(上海博物馆艺术品商店, Shànghǎi Bówùguǎn Yìshùpǐn Shāngdiàn; Map p296; 201 Renmin Ave, 人民大道201号; ⊙9.30am-5pm; M Line 1, 2, 8 to People's Square) Attached to the Shànghǎi Museum and entered from East Yan'an Rd, this shop offers a refreshing change from the usual tourist tat. Apart from the excellent range of books on Chinese art and architecture (including many Shànghǎi-centric titles), there's a good selection of quality

cards, prints and slides. The annex shop sells fine imitations of some of the museum's ceramic pieces, as well as scarves and bags.

★ Sūzhōu Cobblers
FASHION & ACCESSORIES
(上海起想艺术品, Shànghǎi Qǐxiǎng Yìshùpǐn; Map p296; www.suzhou-cobblers.com; Unit 101, 17 Fuzhou Rd, 福州路17号101室; ⊙10am-6.30pm; M Line 2, 10 to East Nanjing Rd) Right off the Bund, this cute boutique sells exquisite hand-embroidered silk slippers, bags, hats and clothing. Patterns and colours are based on the fashions of the 1930s, and as far as the owner, Huang 'Denise' Mengqi, is concerned, the products are one of a kind. Slippers start at ¥650 and can be made to order.

★ Foreign Languages Bookstore
BOOKS
(外文书店, Wàiwén Shūdiàn; Map p296; www.sbt.com.cn; 390 Fuzhou Rd, 福州路390号; ⊙10am-6.30pm; M Line 2, 10 to East Nanjing Rd) Open since the 1950s, this monumental red-brick bookshop is Shànghǎi's best for English-language fiction, nonfiction and travel guides. There's also a stellar selection of Chinese cultural, cooking and language books. Kids' literature is on the 4th floor.

🛍 Old Town

★ Old Street
GIFTS & SOUVENIRS
(老街, Lǎo Jiē; Map p296; Middle Fangbang Rd, 方浜中路; M Line 10 to Yuyuan Garden) This renovated Qing dynasty stretch of Middle Fangbang Rd is lined with specialist tourist shops, spilling forth with shadow puppets, jade jewellery, embroidered fabrics, kites, horn combs, chopsticks, *zǐshā* teapots, old advertising posters, banknotes, Tibetan jewellery, the usual knock-off Mao memorabilia, reproduction 1930s posters, old illustrated books and calligraphy manuals, and surreal 3D-dazzle kitten photos.

★ South Bund Fabric Market
CLOTHING
(南外滩轻纺面料市场, Nán Wàitān Qīngfǎng Miànliào Shìchǎng; 399 Lujiabang Rd, 陆家浜路399号; ⊙8.30am-6pm; M Line 4 to Nanpu Bridge) This old building with more than 100 stalls is one of the best and easiest fabric markets for tourists as many of the stallholders speak a little English. Dresses and suits can be chosen from pattern books or copied from pictures and made up in a dizzying range of fabrics.

Shíliùpù Fabric Market
CLOTHING
(十六铺面料城, Shíliùpù Miànliào Chéng; ☑ 021 6330 1043; 2 Zhonghua Rd, 中华路2号; ⊙8.30am-6pm; M Line 9 to Xiaonanmen) Hav-

ing silk shirts, dresses and cashmere coats tailor-made for a song is one of Shànghǎi's great indulgences. This three-storey building, one of several fabric markets in the city, is conveniently located near the Yùyuán Bazaar. It's a cheaper source of silk than many shops, with prices around ¥200 per metre.

🏛 French Concession

★ Dòng Liáng
FASHION & ACCESSORIES

(棟梁; Map p304; ☑ 021 3469 6926; www.dong liangchina.com; 184 Fumin Rd, 富民路184号; ☺ noon-9pm; 🅼 Changshu Rd, Jing'an Temple) For an up-to-the-minute look at what's hot in local fashion, head to this beautiful boutique housed in a converted villa. Showcasing new Chinese design talent, pieces don't come cheap. The offerings are some of the coolest fashion and accessory collections from designers such as Ms Min, Yifang Wan, Hefang and Comme Moi together in one studio. There is another shop nearby on Changle Rd.

★ Culture Matters
SHOES

(Map p304; 15 Dongping Rd, 东平路15号; ☺ 11am-9.30pm; 🅼 Hengshan Rd, Changshu Rd) Sneaker freaks should stop by this small Dongping Rd shop to ogle its fine selection of cool Feiyue and Warrior trainers (originating in Shànghǎi in the 1920s as martial arts shoes). There are a few branches around town including one at Tai'an Rd (Map p304; 20 Tai'an Rd, 泰安路20号; ☺ 11am-9.30pm; 🅼 Jiatong University) and prices start at an incredible ¥60.

★ OOAK Concept Boutique
JEWELLERY

(OOAK设计师品牌概念店, OOAK Shèjìshī Pǐnpái Gàiniàndiàn; Map p304; www.theooak.com; 30, Lane 820, Julu Rd, 巨鹿路820弄30号; ☺ 11am-8pm; 🅼 Jiashan Rd, Hengshan Rd) Tall and skinny OOAK ('One of a Kind') has three floors of inspiring jewellery; catchy and attractive modern clothing for women; and bags and shoes from a host of talented big-name and aspiring independent designers from Europe and far-flung parts of the globe.

★ Lolo Love Vintage
VINTAGE

(Map p304; 2 Yongfu Rd, 永福路2号; ☺ noon-9pm; 🅼 Shanghai Library, Changshu Rd) There's rock and roll on the stereo and a huge white rabbit, stuffed peacock and plastic cactus outside this wacky shrine to vintage 1940s and 1950s glad rags, behind the blue steel door on Yongfu Rd. It's stuffed with frocks, blouses, tops, shoes, brooches and sundry togs spilling from hangers, shelves and battered suitcases. There's a lovely garden out the front.

★ Pílíngpālāng – Anfu Lu
CERAMICS

(噼吟啪啷; Map p304; www.pilingpalang.com; 183 Anfu Rd, 安福路183号; ☺ 10am-9.30pm; 🅼 Changshu Rd) You'll find gorgeous vibrant-coloured ceramics, cloisonné and lacquer, in pieces that celebrate traditional Chinese forms while adding a modern and deco-inspired slant here at Pílíngpālāng. Tea caddies and decorative trays make for great gifts or souvenirs.

Comme Moi
FASHION & ACCESSORIES

(Map p304; ☑ 021 5466 4689; www.commemoi. com.cn; 169 Xinle Rd, 新乐路169号; 🅼 South Shaanxi Rd) Fitted out by Shànghǎi-based designers Neri & Hu, and located in the art deco Donghu Hotel building, this is the flagship store of Comme Moi. Created by one of China's most successful supermodels, Lu Yan, the Comme Moi label features relaxed chic styles in classic muted tones.

Cottage Shop
ACCESSORIES, VINTAGE

(Map p304; ☑ 021 3416 0523; 170 Wulumqi Middle Rd, 乌鲁木齐中路170号; ☺ 11am-8pm; 🅼 Changshu Rd) If you're in the market for an antique camera, bowler hat, vintage checked shirt, kerosene lamp or designer leather wallet, duck into the Cottage Shop and you won't be disappointed.

Yizidi
GIFTS & SOUVENIRS

(蚁总店, Yàn Zhǐ Diàn; Map p304; Xintiandi North Block, Bldg 25, 太仓路181弄新天地北里25号楼; ☺ 10am-10pm Mon-Thu & Sun, 10.30am-10.30pm Fri & Sat; 🅼 South Huangpi Rd) It might be the tiniest shop imaginable but Yizidi – part of the **Zen Lifestore** (钲艺廊, Zhēng Yìláng; Map p304; 7 Dongping Rd; 东平路7号; ☺ 10am-10pm Sun-Thu, 10.30am-10.30pm Fri & Sat; 🅼 Changshu Rd) group – manages to pack in a number of great gifts and souvenirs, from hand-sewn brightly coloured slippers made in Shànghǎi to Saint John wind-up toys (robots, planes, cars).

IAPM Mall
MALL

(Map p304; www.iapm.com.cn/; 999 Middle Huaihai Rd, 淮海中路999号; ☺ 10am-11pm; ☎; 🅼 South Shaanxi Rd) There is a mix of high-end designers (Stella McCartney, Alexander McQueen, Miu Miu, Prada) and younger casual brands such as Mango, Camper and Muji at this upscale mall, worth a look for the spectacular and well considered interior design alone. You'll also find a branch of the supermarket city'super here, packed with imported goods.

SHÀNGHǍI SHOPPING

Zhēnchálín Tea
DRINKS

(臻茶林, Zhēnchálín; Map p304; No 13, Lane 210, Taikang Rd, Tiánzǐfáng, 泰康路210弄13号田子坊; ⊙10am-8.30pm; Ⓜ Dapuqiao) From the entrance this looks like just another tea shop, but poke around inside and you'll find specially blended herbal teas from Ayako, a traditional Chinese medicine-certified nutritionist. Peruse the hand-wrapped *pǔ'ěr* teas and ceramic and crystal teaware while staff ply you with tiny cups of ginseng oolong and offer tasters of whatever takes your fancy to keep you lingering. Bags of tea start at around ¥45.

Urban Tribe
CLOTHING

(城市山民, Chéngshì Shānmín; Map p304; www.urbantribe.cn; 133 West Fuxing Rd, 复兴西路133号; 10am-10pm; Ⓜ Shanghai Library) Urban Tribe draws inspiration from the ethnic groups of China and Southeast Asia. The collection of loose-fitting blouses, pants and jackets made of natural fabrics are a refreshing departure from the city's on-the-go attitude and usual taste for flamboyance. Don't miss the collection of silver jewellery, nor the lovely tea garden behind the store.

⌂ Jìng'ān

★ Spin
CERAMICS

(旋, Xuán; www.spinceramics.com; 360 Kangding Rd, 康定路360号; ⊙11am-8pm; Ⓜ Line 7 to Changping Rd, exit 2) High on creative flair, Spin brings Chinese ceramics up to speed with oblong teacups, twisted sake sets and all manner of cool plates, chopstick holders and 'kung fu' vases. Pieces are never overbearing, but trendily lean towards the whimsical, geometric, thoughtful and elegant. All are made by Shànghǎi designers in the famous pottery town of Jǐngdézhèn. Prices are reasonable – pick up contemporary (beautiful) spiral teacups for ¥70.

★ Design Commune
HOMEWARES

(設計公社, Shèjì Gōngshè; www.thedesignrepublic .com; 511 Jiangning Rd, 江宁路511号; ⊙10am-7pm; Ⓜ Line 7 to Changping Rd) Run by esteemed interior-design duo Neri & Hu – the last word on everything tasteful in Shanghai – Design Republic has set up this multilevel showroom displaying products from acclaimed local and international designers. Within a beautiful red-brick building that was a former police headquarters (c 1909), here you'll encounter anything from Scandinavian furniture to designer glassware, ceramics and accessories.

Jǐngdézhèn Porcelain Artware
CERAMICS

(景德镇艺术瓷器, Jǐngdézhèn Yìshù Cíqì; Map p317; ☑ 021 6253 8865; 212 North Shaanxi Rd, 陕西北路212号; ⊙10am-9pm; Ⓜ Line 2, 12, 13 to West Nanjing Rd, exit 1) This is one of the best places for high-quality traditional Chinese porcelain. Blue-and-white vases, plates, teapots and cups are some of the many choices available. Credit cards are accepted, and overseas shipping can be arranged.

Amy Lin's Pearls
JEWELLERY

(艾敏林氏珍珠, Àimǐn Línshì Zhēnzhū; Map p296; ☑ 139 1631 3466; www.amylinspearls.com; Room 30, 3rd fl, 580 West Nanjing Rd, 南京西路580号3楼30号; ⊙10am-8pm; Ⓜ Line 2, 12, 13 to West Nanjing Rd, exit 1) It may be in a market known for fake goods, but Amy Lin's is the most reliable retailer of pearls of all colours and sizes. Freshwater pearls (from ¥80), including prized black Zhèjiāng pearls (from ¥1500) and saltwater pearls (from ¥200), are available here. The staff speak English and will string your selection for you. This place sells jade and jewellery, too.

Han City Fashion & Accessories Plaza
CLOTHING

(韩城服饰礼品广场, Hánchéng Fúshì Lǐpǐn Guǎngchǎng; Map p296; 580 West Nanjing Rd, 南京西路580号; ⊙10am-10pm; Ⓜ Line 2, 12, 13 to West Nanjing Rd, exit 1) This unassuming building is a popular location to pick up knockoffs, with hundreds of stalls spread across four floors. Scavenge for bags, belts, jackets, shoes, suitcases, sunglasses, ties, T-shirts, DVDs and electronics. Prices are all inflated, so bargain hard.

⌂ Pǔdōng

IFC Mall
MALL

(上海IFC商场, Shànghǎi IFC Shāngchǎng; Map p308; www.shanghaiifcmall.com.cn; 8 Century Ave, 世纪大道8号; ⊙10am-10pm; Ⓜ Lujiazui) This incredibly glam and glitzy six-storey mall beneath the Cesar Pelli–designed twin towers of the Shànghǎi International Finance Center hosts a swish coterie of top-name brands, from Armani via Prada to Miu Miu and Vuitton, a host of great dining options including Lei Garden, and branches of Baker & Spice, Simply Thai and Haiku by Hatsune.

AP Xīnyáng Fashion & Gifts Market
GIFTS & SOUVENIRS

(亚太新阳服饰礼品市场, Yàtài Xīnyáng Fúshì Lǐpǐn Shìchǎng; ⊙10am-8pm; Ⓜ Science & Technology Museum) This mammoth underground market by the Science & Technology Museum metro station is Shànghǎi's largest collection of shopping stalls. There's tonnes of merchandise and fakes, from suits to moccasins, glinting copy watches, Darth Vader toys, jackets, Lionel Messi football strips, T-shirts, Indian saris, Angry Birds bags, Bob Marley Bermuda shorts, Great Wall snow globes: everything under the sun.

It includes a branch of the **Shíliùpù Fabric Market** and a separate market devoted to pearls, the **Yada Pearl Market** (Yádà Zhēnzhū Shìchǎng). Shop vendors are highly persistent and almost clawing, sending out scouts to wait at the metro exit turnstiles to ensnare shoppers. Haggling is a common language – mixed with much huffing and puffing – so start with a very low offer and take it from there.

🏠 Xújiāhuì & South Shànghǎi

Grand Gateway 66　　　　　　　　　MALL
(港汇恒隆广场, Gǎnghuì Hénglóng Guǎngchǎng; ☑021 6407 0111; 1 Hongqiao Rd, 虹桥路1号; ◎10am-10pm; Ⓜ Line 1, 9, 11 to Xujiahui) Fed by the metro station below ground, Grand Gateway 66 is a vast, airy space and one of Shànghǎi's most high-end malls. It has a wide range of designer and international fashion brands, including the likes of Gucci, Calvin Klein and Lacoste, as well as a constellation of cosmetics and sports-gear outlets.

The complex also has a decent range of restaurants on the 5th and 6th floors, an outside food strip, a cinema, and seating for resting weary shopping legs.

ℹ️ Information

DANGERS & ANNOYANCES
Shànghǎi feels very safe, and crimes against foreigners are rare. If you have something stolen, you need to report the crime at the district Public Security Bureau (PSB; 公安局; Gōng'ānjú) office and obtain a police report.

INTERNET ACCESS
The majority of hostels and hotels have broadband internet access, and many hotels, cafes, restaurants and bars are wi-fi enabled.

MEDICAL SERVICES
Huàshān Hospital (华山医院国际医疗中心, Huàshān Yīyuàn Guójì Yīliáo Zhōngxīn; ☑021 5288 9998; www.sh-hwmc.com.cn; 12 Middle Wulumuqi Rd, 乌鲁木齐中路12号; Ⓜ Changshu Rd) Hospital treatment and outpatient consultations are available at the 8th-floor foreigners' clinic (☑021 6248 3986), and there's 24-hour

emergency treatment on the 15th floor in building 6.

Parkway Health (以极佳医疗保健服务, Yǐjíjiā Yīliáo Bǎojiàn Fúwù; ☑24hr 021 6445 5999; Suite 203, Shànghǎi Centre, 1376 W Nanjing Rd, 南京西路1376号203室; Ⓜ Line 2, 7 to Jing'an Temple) Offers comprehensive private medical care from internationally trained physicians and dentists. Members can access after-hours services and an emergency hotline. Has numerous locations around town.

Watson's (屈臣氏, Qūchénshì; ☑021 6474 4775; 787 Middle Huaihai Rd, 淮海中路787号; ◎24hr) The Hong Kong pharmacy Watson's can be found in the basements of malls all over town, mainly selling imported toiletries and a limited range of simple over-the-counter pharmaceuticals.

MONEY
Most tourist hotels, upmarket restaurants and banks accept major credit cards. ATMs are widespread and generally accept Visa, MasterCard, Cirrus and Maestro cards. Most operate 24 hours.

You can change foreign currency at money-changing counters at almost every hotel and at many shops, department stores and large banks such as the Bank of China and HSBC, as long as you have your passport; you can also change money at both Pǔdōng International Airport and Hóngqiáo International Airport. Some top-end hotels will change money only for their guests. Exchange rates in China are uniform wherever you change money, so there's little need to shop around.

Bank of China (中国银行, Zhōngguó Yínháng; East Zhongshan No 1 Rd, 中山东一路; ◎9am-noon & 1.30-4.30pm Mon-Fri, 9am-noon Sat; Ⓜ Line 2, 10 to East Nanjing Rd) Right next to the Peace Hotel. Tends to get crowded, but is better organised than many banks in China (it's worth a peek for its grand interior). Take a ticket and wait for your number. For credit-card advances, head to the furthest hall (counter No 2).

Citibank (花旗银行, Huāqí Yínháng; East Zhongshan No 1 Rd, E 中山东一路; ◎24hr; Ⓜ East Nanjing Rd) Useful ATM open 24 hours.

POST
The larger tourist hotels and business towers have convenient post offices from where you can mail letters and small packages. China Post (中国邮政; Zhōngguó Yóuzhèng) offices and post boxes are green. The **Main China Post Office** (中国邮政, Zhōngguó Yóuzhèng; ☑021 6393 6666; 276 North Suzhou Rd, 苏州北路276号; ◎7am-10pm) is just north of Sūzhōu Creek in Hóngkǒu.

PUBLIC SECURITY BUREAU
Public Security Bureau (PSB, 公安局, Gōng'ānjú; ☑021 2895 1900; 1500 Minsheng Rd, 民生路1500号; ◎9am-5pm Mon-Sat) Visa extensions in Shànghǎi are available here.

TELEPHONE

Mobile-phone shops (手机店; *shǒujīdiàn*) can sell you a SIM card, which will cost from ¥60 to ¥100 and will include ¥50 of credit. SIM cards are also available from newspaper kiosks (报刊亭; *bàokāntíng*). When credit runs out, you can top up the number by buying a credit-charging card (充值卡; *chōngzhí kǎ*) for ¥50 or ¥100 worth of credits. The main networks are China Mobile, China Unicom and China Telecom, with branches throughout the city.

Buying a mobile phone in Shànghǎi is also an option as they are generally inexpensive. Cafes, restaurants and bars in larger towns and cities usually have wi-fi.

TOURIST INFORMATION

For competent English-language help, call the **Shànghǎi Call Centre** (☑ 021 962 288), a free 24-hour English-language hotline that can respond to cultural, entertainment or transport enquiries (and even provide directions for your cab driver).

Other branches of tourist information offices:

The Bund (旅游咨询服务中心, Lǚyóu Zīxún Fúwù Zhōngxīn; Map p296; ☑ 021 6357 3718; 518 Jiujiang Rd, 九江路518号; ⊙ 9.30am-8pm; Ⓜ East Nanjing Rd) Beneath the promenade, opposite the intersection with East Nanjing Rd.

French Concession (旅游咨询服务中心, Lǚyóu Zīxún Fúwù Zhōngxīn; ☑ 021 5386 1882; 138 S Chengdu Rd, 成都南路138号; ⊙ 9am-9pm; Ⓜ South Huangpi Rd)

Jing'ān (旅游咨询服务中心, Lǚyóu Zīxún Fúwù Zhōngxīn; ☑ 021 6248 3259; Lane 1678, 18 West Nanjing Rd, 南京西路1678弄18号; ⊙ 9.30am-5.30pm Mon-Fri; Ⓜ Line 2, 7 to Jing'an Temple)

Old Town (旅游咨询服务中心, Lǚyóu Zīxún Fúwù Zhōngxīn; ☑ 021 6355 5032; 149 Jiujiaochang Rd, 旧校场路149号; ⊙ 9am-7pm; Ⓜ Line

10 to Yuyuan Garden) Southwest of Yùyuán Gardens.

Pǔdōng (旅游咨询服务中心, Lǚyóu Zīxún Fúwù Zhōngxīn; Map p308; Base of Oriental Pearl TV Tower, 东方明珠广播电视塔1楼; ⊙ 9am-5pm; Ⓜ Lujiazui)

The **Tourist Hotline** (☑ 021 962 020) offers a limited English-language service.

TRAVEL AGENCIES

The following agencies can help with travel bookings.

CTrip (http://english.ctrip.com) Excellent online agency, good for hotel and flight bookings.

eLong (www.elong.net) Hotel and flight bookings.

STA Travel (☑ 021 2281 7723; www.statravel.com.cn; Room 1609, Shànghǎi Trade Tower, 188 Siping Rd; ⊙ 9.30am-6pm Mon-Fri; Ⓜ Hailun Rd)

WEBSITES

For a plug into what's on in town:

City Weekend (www.cityweekend.com.cn/shanghai)

That's Shanghai (http://online.thatsmags.com/city/shanghai)

Time Out Shanghai (www.timeoutshanghai.com).

ⓘ Getting There & Away

With two airports, rail and air connections to places all over China, and buses to destinations in adjoining provinces and beyond, Shànghǎi's a handy springboard to the rest of the land.

AIR

Pǔdōng International Airport (PVG, 浦东国际机场, Pǔdōng Guójì Jīchǎng, ☑ 021 6834 7575, flight information 96990, www.shairport.com) is located 30km southeast of Shànghǎi, near the East China Sea. Most international flights

---

BORDER CROSSING: GETTING TO JAPAN

Shànghǎi Port International Cruise Terminal (上海港国际客运中心, Shànghǎi Gǎng Guójì Kèyùn Zhōngxīn; Gaoyang Rd, 高阳路) Located north of the Bund and mostly serving cruise ships. A few international passenger routes serve Shànghǎi, with reservations recommended in July and August. Passengers must be at the harbour three hours before departure to get through immigration.

China-Japan International Ferry Company (中日国际轮渡有限公司, Zhōngrì Guójì Lúndù Yǒuxiàn Gōngsī; ☑ 021 6325 7642; www.shinganjin.com/index_e.php; 18th fl, Jin'an Bldg, 908 Dongdaming Rd, 东大明路908号金岸大厦; tickets from ¥1300, plus ¥150 fuel surcharge) Has staggered departures every week to either Osaka or Kobe (46 hours) in Japan on Saturdays at 12.30pm. Fares range from ¥1300 in an eight-bed dorm to ¥6500 in a deluxe twin cabin.

Shànghǎi International Ferry Company (上海国际轮渡, Shànghǎi Guójì Lúndù; ☑ 021 6537 5111; www.shanghai-ferry.co.jp/english/; 15th fl, Jin'an Bldg, 908 Dongdaming Rd, 东大明路908号金岸大厦; tickets from ¥1300, plus ¥150 fuel surcharge; ⊙ 8.30am-5pm Mon-Fri) Has departures to Osaka (46 hours) on Tuesdays at 11am. Fares range from ¥1300 in an eight-bed dorm to ¥6500 in a deluxe twin cabin.

(and some domestic flights) operate from here. If you're making an onward domestic connection from Pǔdōng International Airport, it's crucial that you find out whether the domestic flight leaves from Pǔdōng or Hóngqiáo, as it will take at least an hour to cross the city.

There are two main passenger terminals (with a new satellite terminal under construction), which are easy to navigate. Departures are on the upper level and arrivals on the lower level, where there is a tourist information counter.

Hóngqiáo International Airport (SHA; 虹桥国际机场; Hóngqiáo Guójì Jīchǎng; ☏ 021 5260 4620, flight information 021 6268 8899; www.shairport.com, mHongqiao Airport Terminal 1, M Hongqiao Airport Terminal 2), 18km west of the Bund, has two terminals: the older and less-used **Terminal 1** (east terminal; halls A and B), and the new and sophisticated **Terminal 2** (west terminal; attached to Shànghǎi Hóngqiáo Railway Station), where most flights arrive. If flying domestically within China from Shànghǎi, consider flying from here; it is closer to central Shànghǎi than Pǔdōng International Airport. If transferring between Hóngqiáo and Pǔdōng International Airports, note they are a long way apart and it will take at least an hour.

BUS

As trains are fast, regular and efficient, and traffic on roads unpredictable, travelling by bus is not a very useful way to leave or enter Shànghǎi, unless you are visiting local water towns. Buses to Běijīng take between 14 and 16 hours: it is far faster and more comfortable (but more expensive) to take the 5½-hour high-speed G-class trains to the capital, or even the eight-hour D-class trains.

The huge **Shànghǎi South Long-Distance Bus Station** (上海长途客运南站; Shànghǎi Chángtú Kèyùn Nánzhàn; ☏ 021 5436 2835; www.ctnz.net; 666 Shilong Rd; M Shanghai South Railway Station) has buses largely to destinations in south China. Destinations include Sūzhōu (苏州; ¥38, very frequent), Nánjīng (南京; ¥96, four per day), Hángzhōu (杭州; ¥68, very frequent) and Níngbō (宁波; ¥127, very frequent).

Although it appears close to Shànghǎi Railway Station, the vast **Shànghǎi Long-Distance Bus Station** (上海长途汽车客运总站; Shànghǎi Chángtú Qìchē Kèyùn Zǒngzhàn; Map p314; ☏ 021 6605 0000; www.kyzz.com.cn; 1666 Zhongxing Rd, 中兴路1666号; M Shanghai Railway Station) is a pain to get to (taxi is easiest), but has buses to everywhere, including regular buses to Sūzhōu (¥38, two hours) and Hángzhōu (¥68, 2½ hours), as well as two buses to Nánjīng (¥105, 4½ hours, 9.30am and 2.50pm), Zhōuzhuāng (¥29, six daily, two hours) and Běijīng (¥354, 4pm, 18 hours).

Regular buses also depart for Hángzhōu (¥100, two hours) and Sūzhōu (¥84, two hours) from Pǔdōng International Airport. Buses for Háng-zhōu, Sūzhōu and a host of destinations also leave from the **Hóngqiáo Long-Distance Bus Station** (虹桥长途客运站; Hóngqiáo Chángtú Kèyùn Zhàn) at Hóngqiáo Airport Terminal 2.

From the **Shànghǎi Sightseeing Bus Centre** (上海旅游集散中心; Shànghǎi Lǚyóu Jísàn Zhōngxīn) at Shànghǎi Stadium, you can join tours to Sūzhōu, Hángzhōu, Tónglǐ, Zhōuzhuāng, Zhūjiā-jiāo and other destinations around Shànghǎi.

TRAIN

The new and sophisticated **Shànghǎi Hóngqiáo Railway Station** (上海虹桥站; Shànghǎi Hóng-qiáo Zhàn; M Hongqiao Railway Station) is Asia's largest train station. It is located at the western end of metro line 10 and on line 2, near Hóngqiáo International Airport. It's the terminus for the high-speed G-class trains and other trains, and includes services to Běijīng (from ¥555, very regular), Hángzhōu (from ¥73, very regular), Nánjīng South (from ¥95, frequent) and Sūzhōu (from ¥25, regular).

The vast, hectic and sprawling **Shànghǎi Railway Station** (上海火车站; Shànghǎi Huǒchē Zhàn; Map p314; ☏ In Chinese 12306; 385 Meiyuan Rd, 梅园路385号; M Shanghai Railway Station), located in the north of town, is easily reached by metro lines 1, 4 and 3 and has G-class, D-class and express trains to Běijīng (¥309, three daily), Hángzhōu (¥95, four daily), Hong Kong (¥226, 6.20pm), Huángshān (¥93, two daily), Nánjīng (¥144, frequent), Sūzhōu (¥40, frequent) and Xī'ān (¥180, frequent).

Modern **Shànghǎi South Railway Station** (上海南站; Shànghǎi Nánzhàn; ☏ 021 9510 5123; 200 Zhaofeng Rd) is easily accessed on metro lines 1 and 3. It has trains largely to southern and southwestern destinations including Guìlín (¥190, four daily) and Hángzhōu (¥29, frequent).

A few trains also leave from the renovated West Station (上海西站; Shànghǎi Xīzhàn), including trains to Nánjīng; however, it's less convenient.

Ticket Offices

There are several options for getting hold of train tickets in Shànghǎi. You can queue at the ticket offices (售票厅; shòupiàotīng) at train stations, but brace for a long wait. There are two ticket halls at the Shànghǎi Railway Station, one in the main building (same-day tickets) and another on the east side of the square (advance tickets). One counter should have English-speakers.

Your hotel will be able to obtain a ticket for you; however, a surcharge may be levied.

Tickets can be purchased for a small surcharge from travel agencies. You can also book tickets online using **CTrip** (http://english.ctrip.com), which will then be delivered to your address in China, but you cannot buy e-tickets, print them out or collect them. **China Highlights** (www.chinahighlights.com) offers a similar service, but can also deliver e-tickets by email.

Train information is available over the phone in Chinese only (📞 800 820 7890).

Advance Train Ticket Office (Map p314; 824 Hengfeng Rd, 恒丰路; ◷ 8am-7pm) If you can't handle the queues at Shànghǎi Railway Station, this small office under the bridge a short walk west is very useful.

Jing'ān Train Ticket Office (静安火车售票处, Jìng'ān Huǒchē Shòupiào Chù; Map p317; 77 Wanhangdu Rd, 万航渡路77号; ◷ 8am-6pm) Useful train ticket office, located to the west of Jìng'ān Temple.

🛈 Getting Around

The best way to get around Shànghǎi is the metro, which now reaches most places in the city, followed by cabs. Buses (¥2 to ¥3) are tricky to use unless you are a proficient Mandarin speaker. Whatever mode of transport you use, try to avoid rush hours between 8am and 9am, and 4.30pm and 6pm.

Walking from A to B, unless it's a short journey, is generally an exhausting and sometimes stressful experience.

TO/FROM PǓDŌNG AIRPORT

The warp-speed **Maglev** (磁浮列车, Cífú Lièchē; www.smtdc.com; economy one-way/return ¥50/80, with same-day air ticket ¥40, children under/over 1.2m free/half price) runs from Pǔdōng International Airport to Longyang Rd metro stop (just south of Century Park) on metro line 2 in eight minutes, running every 20 minutes in both directions. Trains from Pǔdōng International Airport run from 6.45am to 9.40pm. Trains to the airport run from 7.02am to 10.40pm.

Metro line 2 zips from Pǔdōng International Airport to Hóngqiáo International Airport, passing through central Shànghǎi. You will, however, need to disembark at Guanglan Rd station and transfer to another train on the same platform

to continue your journey. Pǔdōng International Airport is a long way out: it takes about 45 minutes to People's Square (¥7).

Airport buses take between 60 and 90 minutes to reach destinations in Pǔxī, west of the Huángpǔ River. Buses drop off at all departures halls and pick up outside arrivals, at both Terminals 1 and 2, leaving the airport roughly every 15 to 30 minutes from 7am to 11pm and heading to the airport from roughly 5.30am to 9.30pm (bus 1 runs till 11pm). The most useful buses are **airport bus 1** (¥30), linking Pǔdōng International Airport with Hóngqiáo International Airport (Terminals 1 and 2), and **airport bus 5** (Map p314, ¥16 to ¥22) linking Pǔdōng Airport with Shànghǎi Railway Station via People's Square. **Airport bus 7** (¥20) runs to Shànghǎi South Railway Station; and a **midnight line** (¥16 to ¥30) operates from 11pm to the last arrival, running to Hóngqiáo Airport Terminal 1 via Longyang Rd metro station to Shimen No 1 Rd and Huashan Rd.

Taxis into central Shànghǎi cost around ¥160 and take about an hour; to Hóngqiáo airport it costs around ¥200. Most Shànghǎi taxi drivers are honest, but ensure they use the meter. Avoid monstrous overcharging by using the regular taxi rank outside the arrivals hall.

TO/FROM HÓNGQIÁO AIRPORT

Bus From Terminals 1 and 2, airport bus 1 (¥30, 6am to 9.30pm) runs to Pǔdōng International Airport; and bus 941 (Map p314; ¥6; ◷ 5.30am to 11pm) runs to the main Shànghǎi Railway Station.

Night buses 316 (11am to 5pm) and 320 (11am to 5pm) run from Terminal 2 to East Yan'an Rd near the Bund.

From Terminal 1, the **airport shuttle bus** (¥4, 7.50am to 11pm) runs to the largely defunct Airport City Terminal in Jìng'ān; it's useful for accessing the Jìng'ān area. **bus 925** (¥4, 5.30am to 10.30pm) runs to People's Square via Hongmei Rd and Shimen No 1 Rd; **bus 938** (¥7, 6am to midnight) runs to Yángjiādù in Pǔdōng via Hongxu Rd, North Caoxi Rd and South Xizang Rd; and **bus 806** (¥5, 6am to 11pm) runs to Lùpǔ Bridge in the south of Pǔxī.

Metro Terminal 2 is connected to downtown Shànghǎi by lines 2 and 10 (30 minutes to People's Square) from Hóngqiáo International Airport Terminal 2 metro station; both lines run through East Nanjing Rd station (for the Bund). Line 2 runs to Pǔdōng and connects with Pǔdōng International Airport (¥8, 1¾ hours) and Longyang Rd metro station, south of Century Park, from where you can hop aboard the Maglev. The next stop west from Hóngqiáo Airport Terminal 2 is Hóngqiáo Railway Station (connected to the airport and accessible on foot).

Hóngqiáo Airport Terminal 1 is the next stop east on line 10 from Hóngqiáo Airport Terminal 2 metro station.

TRANSPORT CARDS & TOURIST PASSES

If you are making more than a fleeting trip to Shànghǎi, it's worth getting a Transport Card (交通卡, Jiāotōng Kǎ). Available at metro stations and some convenience stores, cards can be topped up with credit and used on the metro, some buses and ferries, and all taxis. Credit is electronically deducted from the card as you swipe it over the sensor, at metro turnstiles and near the door on buses; when paying your taxi fare, hand it to the taxi driver, who will swipe it. Cards don't save you money, but will save you from queuing for tickets or hunting for change. A refundable deposit of ¥20 is required.

Taxi A taxi from Terminal 2 to the Bund will cost around ¥100; to Pǔdōng International Airport, around ¥200.

Taxi queues at Terminal 1 can be long; it can be quicker to take the metro or the bus.

BICYCLE

If you can handle the fumes and menace of Shànghǎi's intimidating traffic, cycling can be a good way to get around town, but you will need to link it in with public transport.

➼ Make sure that you have your own bicycle cable lock and try to leave your bike at bike parks.

➼ Cyclists never use lights at night and Chinese pedestrians favour dark clothing, so ride carefully.

Several hostels around town, including Le Tour Traveler's Rest (p316), can rent you a bike.
BOHDI (☑ 021 5266 9013; www.bohdi.com.cn; Bldg 15, 271 Qianyang Rd, 千阳路271号; ☺ 8am-5pm Mon-Fri; Ⓜ Zhenbei Rd) also sells and rents quality bikes.

BOAT

Ferries cross the Huángpǔ River between Pǔxī on the west bank and Pǔdōng on the east. Most useful is the **Shanghai Ferry** (Map p296; 127 East Zhongshan No 2 Rd, 中山东二路127号; one way ¥2; Ⓜ Line 2, 10 to East Nanjing Rd, exit 1), which operates between the southern end of the Bund and Dongchang Rd in Pǔdōng, running every 15 minutes from 7am to 10pm. Tickets are sold at the kiosks out the front. The **Fuxing Road Ferry** (复兴路轮渡站, Fùxīng Lù Lúnduzhàn; one way ¥?) runs from Fuxing Rd north of the Cool Docks in the South Bund to Dongchang Rd. Ferries run every 10 to 20 minutes from 5am to 11pm.

BUS

Although sightseeing buses can be extremely handy, the huge Shànghǎi public bus system is unfortunately very hard for foreigners who don't speak or read Chinese to use. Bus-stop signs and routes are in Chinese only. Drivers and conductors speak little, if any, English, although onboard announcements in English will alert you to when to get off. The conductor will tell you when your stop is arriving, if you ask. Bus stops are widely spaced and your bus can race past your destination and on to the next stop up to a kilometre away. Suburban and long-distance buses don't carry numbers – the destination is in characters.

➼ Air-con buses (with a snowflake motif and the characters 空调 alongside the bus number) cost ¥2 to ¥3. The far rarer buses without air-con cost ¥1.5.

➼ On buses without conductors, drop your cash into the slot by the driver. Always carry exact money; no change is given.

➼ The swipe-able Transport Card works on many but not all bus routes.

➼ Buses generally operate from 5am to 11pm, except for 300-series buses, which run all night.

➼ For English-language bus routes in town, go to http://msittig.wubi.org/bus.

CAR & MOTORCYLE

It is possible to hire a car in Shànghǎi, but you will need a temporary or long-term Chinese driving licence.

For most visitors, it is more advisable to hire a car and a driver. A Volkswagen Santana with driver and petrol starts at around ¥600 per day; it is likely to be cheaper to hire a taxi for the day. Ask for more information at your hotel.

METRO

The Shànghǎi metro (www.shmetro.com) is fast, cheap, clean and easy, though hard to get a seat on at the best of times (unless you get on at a terminus). The rush hour sees carriages filled beyond capacity, but trains are frequent and the system has been rapidly expanded to envelop more and more of the city.

➼ There are 14 lines serving more than 366 stations over 617km.

➼ There are plans to extend the network with nine new lines and 250km of track, starting in 2017, with a 2025 completion date.

➼ Metro maps are available at most stations. The free tourist maps also have a small metro map printed on them, and there's an English section on the metro website.

➼ Metro station exits can be confusing, so look for a street map (usually easy to find) in the ticket hall before exiting to get your bearings.

➼ To find a metro station look for the red M.

➼ The *Explore Shanghai* app helps you calculate how long your journey will take, how much it will cost and where the nearest metro station is.

➼ In 2016 wi-fi was rolled out to most metro lines and platforms. To access the internet, users need to download an application on their phones and register.

Fares & Tickets

➼ Tickets range from ¥3 to ¥15, depending on the distance.

➼ One-day (¥18) and three-day travel passes (¥45) for use on the metro are available from service counters in stations.

➼ There can be huge distances between different lines at interchange stations, such as between line 9 and 1 at Xújiāhuì station, so factor this into your journey time.

TAXI

Shànghǎi's taxis are reasonably cheap, hassle-free and generally easy to flag down except during rush hour and in summer storms.

Shànghǎi's main taxi companies include turquoise-coloured **Dàzhòng** (大众; ☑ 021 96822), gold **Qiángshēng** (强生; ☑ 021 6258 0000) and green **Bāshì** (巴士; ☑ 021 96840).

AROUND SHÀNGHĂI

The most popular day trips from Shànghǎi are to Hángzhōu (p265; a quick zip away on the train) and Sūzhōu (p250).

Zhūjiājiǎo 朱家角

Thirty kilometres west of Shànghǎi, Zhūjiājiǎo is easy to reach and charming – as long as your visit does not coincide with the arrival of phalanxes of tour buses.

What survives of this historic canal town today is a charming tableau of Ming and Qing dynasty alleys, bridges and *gǔzhèn* (古镇; old town) architecture, its alleyways steeped in the aroma of *chòu dòufu* (stinky tofu).

While first impressions aren't fabulous when you step off the bus as soon as you hit the old town and its canals (a 10-minute walk from the bus station), you'll be glad you came. The riverside settlement is small enough to wander completely in three hours. Souvenir shops and restaurants line the scenic canal, connected by quaint bridges and narrow laneways that make it genuinely reminiscent of Venice – albeit a very Chinese version.

Sights & Activities

If you plan on doing a full day's sightseeing, you can buy a variety of packages from Zhūjiājiǎo's **tourist information office** (旅游办事处, Lǚyóu Bànshì Chù; ☑021 5924 0077; www.zhujiajiao.com/en; Xinfeng Lu, 新丰路; English guide half-/whole day ¥120/200; ◷8.30am-4.30pm). They also have a useful map here.

You can tour the canals in one of the Chinese gondola-style row boats (short/long tour ¥80/150 per boat), which seat six people. They depart from the dock out the front of City God Temple.

Kèzhí Garden   GARDENS
(课植园, Kèzhí Yuán; 109 Xijing St, 朱家角镇西井街109号; ¥20) It's a little pricey, but this Chinese garden established in 1912 is a nice spot for a stroll with pavilions, ponds, quaint bridges and rocky outcrops.

Qing Dynasty Post Office   HISTORIC BUILDING
(清王朝邮局, Qīng Wángcháo Yóujú; 35 Xihu Rd, 西湖路35号; ¥5; ◷8.30am-4.30pm) A historic 1903 outpost of the Qing dynasty postal service, this is not a huge place but it's nice to walk through the old wooden building's interior, with mildly interesting exhibits such as vintage postcards and a postie's uniform dating from the Qing dynasty.

Yuánjīn Buddhist Temple   BUDDHIST TEMPLE
(圆津禅院, Yuánjīn Chányuàn; 193 Caohe Jie, 漕河街; ¥10; ◷8am-4pm) This temple is famed for its **Qīnghuá Pavilion** (Qīnghuá Gé) at the rear, a towering hall visible from many parts of town. It's located on Caohe St near the distinctive Tài'ān Bridge (泰安桥; Tài'ān Qiáo).

City God Temple   TAOIST TEMPLE
(城隍庙, Chénghuáng Miào; 69 Caohe Jie, 漕河街; ¥10; ◷7.30am-4pm) Moved here in 1769 from its original location in Xuějiābāng, this temple stands on the west side of the Chénghuáng Bridge.

Zhūjiājiǎo Catholic Church of Ascension   CHURCH
(朱家角耶稣升天堂, Zhūjiājiǎo Yēsū Shēngtiāntáng; 27 Caohe Jie, No 317 Alley, 漕河街27号317弄) A gorgeous church dating from 1863 with its belfry rising in a detached tower by the rear gate.

Fàngshēng Bridge   BRIDGE
(放生桥, Fàngshēng Qiáo) Of Zhūjiājiǎo's quaint band of ancient bridges, the standout must be the graceful, 72m-long, five-arched Fàngshēng Bridge, first built in 1571 with proceeds from a monk's 15 years of alms-gathering. It passes over a wide expanse of water, reminiscent of sections of Venice's famous waterways.

🛏 Sleeping

Given its proximity to Shànghǎi, there's no real reason to stay in Zhūjiājiǎo; though if you do, you'll get to enjoy it crowd-free once the tourists have gone home. A charming choice is **Cǎo Táng Inn** (草堂客栈, Cǎotáng Kèzhàn; ☑021 5978 6442; 31 Dongjing Jie, 东井街31号; dm ¥80-100, d ¥300-320; ※@奈) a friendly and atmospheric hostel set within a century-old house. Its common area has a well stocked bar and a fire pit to hang out by. There's a lovely courtyard garden too. The rooms are clean and well kept, including dorms and traditionally dressed doubles and twins.

ⓘ Getting There & Away

To reach Zhūjiājiǎo, hop on the direct pink and white Hùzhū Gāosù Kuàixiàn bus (沪朱高速快线; ¥12, one hour, every 20 minutes from 6am to 10pm, less frequently in low season) from the **Pu'an Rd Bus Station** (普安路汽车站, Pǔ'ān Lù Qìchē Zhàn; Map p296; Pu'an Lu, 普安路; Ⓜ Dashijie) just south of People's Square. Note local buses also ply this route – these are best avoided and take double the time.

Zhūjiājiǎo can also be reached from the bus station in Tónglǐ (¥15, 1½ hours).

Fújiàn

POP 37.2 MILLION

Best Places to Eat

➡ Lucky Full City Seafood (p342)

➡ Lǎohǎi Wù (p346)

➡ Gǔcuò Cháfáng (p353)

Best Places to Sleep

➡ Xiàmén International Youth Hostel (p340)

➡ Miryam Boutique Hotel (p346)

➡ 54 Coffee Inn (p352)

➡ Fúyù Lóu Chángdì Inn (p349)

Why Go?

Fújiàn (福建) is an attractive coastal province with a long seafaring history. As a significant stop on the maritime Silk Road, its cities developed an easy cosmopolitan outlook and visitors are surprised by the traces of elsewhere in its architecture, food, language and people.

Xiàmén is the star attraction to visitors, with its long seaside promenade and easy access to little Gǔlàng Yǔ, a hip island enclave just offshore. Many travellers also pass through the area en route to the Taiwanese island of Kinmen.

Away from the coast, the Unesco World Heritage-listed *tǔlóu* (roundhouses) rise out of the countryside and for generations have housed traditional Hakka and Fujianese communities. Further north, the hill station of Wǔyí Shān offers year-round hiking opportunities and a memorable river cruise on bamboo rafts.

When to Go
Xiàmén

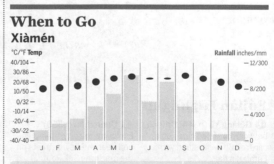

Mar & Apr Sleeping in a traditional *tǔlóu* in spring is an inspiring way to experience rural life.

Jun & Sep Relax in one of Gǔlàng Yǔ's countless cafes and cool off in the sea.

Oct Hike away from the crowds around the lush Wǔyí Shān in the northwest of the province.

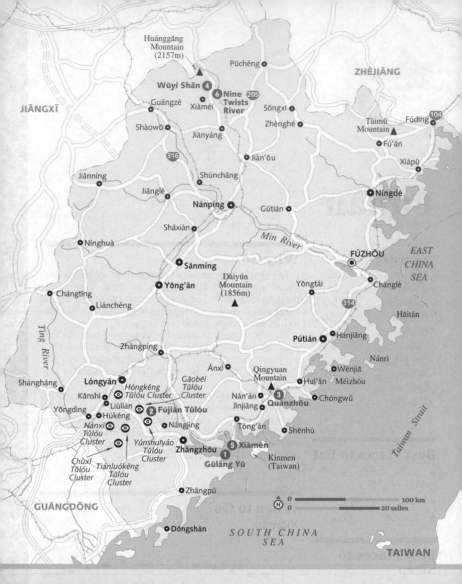

Fújiàn Highlights

1 **Gǔlàng Yǔ** (p344) Drifting between cat-filled cafes on a car-free Chinese island with European flair.

2 **Fújiàn Tǔlóu** (p347) Sleeping in packed-earth fortresses like a character from *Game of Thrones*.

3 **Quánzhōu** (p350) Exploring the city's temples and near-medieval streets on the maritime Silk Route.

4 **Wǔyí Shān** (p356) Hiking and cleansing your lungs at a quaint hill station in the province's northwest.

5 **Xiàmén** (p339) Strolling the seaside promenade of one of China's most attractive cities.

6 **Nine Twists River** (p357) Reclining in a rattan chair on a *zhúpái* (bamboo raft) cruise.

History

The coastal region of Fújiàn, known in English as Fukien or Hokkien, has been part of the Chinese empire since the Qin dynasty (221–207 BC), when it was known as Min. Sea trade transformed the region from a frontier into one of the centres of the Chinese world. During the Song and Yuan dynasties the coastal city of Quánzhōu was one of the main ports on the maritime Silk Road, which transported not only silk but other textiles, precious stones, porcelain and a host of other valuables. The city was home to more than 100,000 Arab merchants, missionaries and travellers.

Despite a decline in the province's fortunes after the Ming dynasty restricted maritime commerce in the 15th century, the resourcefulness of the Fújiàn people proved itself in the numbers heading for Taiwan, Singapore, the Philippines, Malaysia and Indonesia. Overseas links that were forged continue today, contributing much to the modern character of the province.

ℹ Getting there & Around

Fújiàn is well connected to the neighbouring provinces of Guǎngdōng and Jiāngxī by train and coastal highway. Xiàmén and Fúzhōu have airline connections to most of the country, including Hong Kong, and Taipei and Kaohsiung in Taiwan. Wǔyí Shān has flight connections to China's larger cities, including Běijīng, Shànghǎi and Hong Kong. The coastal freeway also goes all the way to Hong Kong from Xiàmén. The D class train links Xiàmén to Shànghǎi in eight hours.

For exploring the interior, high-speed D trains are more comfortable than travelling by bus, but not always more convenient. Wǔyí Shān is linked to Fúzhōu, Quánzhōu and Xiàmén by train. There are also daily flights between Xiàmén and Wǔyí Shān.

Xiàmén 厦门

♫ 0592 / POP 2.1 MILLION

Xiàmén, the island city formerly known in Western circles as Amoy, is emerging as southern China's most sophisticated city. Chinese travellers have long understood the lure of its long seaside promenade and European city architecture, but international 'jetizens' are now descending on the fun.

Many use Xiàmén as a stepping-off point for the much smaller island of Gǔlàng Yǔ (p344), perhaps the highlight of the entire province. Strewn with crumbling embassies, lush gardens and beaches, and hip boutique

cafes and hotels, this island feels like a kind of Chinese Mediterranean, in all its wonderful oddity.

History

Xiàmén was founded around the mid-14th century in the early years of the Ming dynasty, when the city walls were built and the town was established as a major seaport and commercial centre. In the 17th century it became a place of refuge for the Ming rulers fleeing the Manchu invaders. Xiàmén and nearby Kinmen (金门; Jīnmén) were bases for the Ming armies who, under the command of the general Koxinga, raised their anti-Manchu battle cry, 'resist the Qing and restore the Ming'.

The Portuguese arrived in the 16th century, followed by the British in the 17th century, and later by the French and the Dutch, all attempting, rather unsuccessfully, to establish Xiàmén as a trade port. The port was closed to foreigners in the 1750s and it was not until the Opium Wars that things began to change. In August 1841 a British naval force of 38 ships carrying artillery and soldiers sailed into Xiàmén harbour, forcing the port to open. Xiàmén then became one of the first treaty ports.

Japanese and Western powers followed soon after, establishing consulates and making Gǔlàng Yǔ a foreign enclave. Xiàmén turned Japanese in 1938 and remained that way until 1945.

◉ Sights

The town of Xiàmén is on the island of the same name. It's connected to the mainland by a 5km-long causeway bearing a railway, a Bus Rapid Transit (BRT) line, road and footpath. The most absorbing part of Xiàmén is near the western (waterfront) district, directly opposite the small island of Gǔlàng Yǔ. This is the old area of town, known for its colonial-era architecture, parks and winding streets.

Báilùzhōu Park   PARK

(白鹭洲公, Báilùzhōu Gōngyuán; Bailuzhou Lu, 思明区白鹭洲路) Xiàmén positions itself as China's most liveable city and this huge green expanse on an islet north of town is a quiet exclamation mark on that claim. Perfect for families or broken souls who need to touch grass for a while.

Kāihé Lù Fish Market   MARKET

(开禾路菜市场, Kāihélù Càishìchǎng; Kaihe Lu) In the old district of Xiàmén, this tiny but lively market sells various (weird) sea creatures to a backdrop of *qílóu* (骑楼; shophouses) and a church. Access is from Xiahe Lu, where you can also find lots of Taiwanese food.

Nánpǔtuó Temple   BUDDHIST SITE

(南普陀寺, Nánpǔtuó Sì; Siming Nanlu; ⊙8am-6pm) **FREE** This Buddhist temple complex on the southern side of Xiàmén is one of the most famous temples among the Fujianese, and is also considered a pilgrimage site by dedicated followers from Southeast Asia. The temple has been repeatedly destroyed and rebuilt. Its latest incarnation dates to the early 20th century, and today it's an active and busy temple with chanting monks and worshippers lighting incense.

THE HEYDAY OF AMOY

When you are in Xiàmén, get a copy of *Old Xiamen, Cradle of Modern Chinese Business & Chinese Business Education*, edited by Dr Bill Brown, a long-time local resident from the US. The book explains in a most readable way how Xiàmén has historically played a vital role in fostering cultural interactions between the East and the West, and it also has a wonderful collection of old prints, news clips and literary extracts about the city dating back to as early as Marco Polo's time. The affordable paperback (¥30) is available in **Xinhua Bookshop** (新华书店, Xīnhuá Shūdiàn; 155 Zhongshan Lu; ⊙9am-5pm).

Báichéng Beach   BEACH

(Báichéng Shātān, 白城沙滩) You can rarely swim here due to council restrictions, but there are few more convenient places in the city to enjoy a beautiful natural environment, especially at sunset. Except on weekends, when every man and his mobile turn up.

Railroad Culture Park   PARK

(铁路文化公园, Tiělù Wénhuà Gōngyuán; Huyuan Lu, 虎园路) The charming 3km walking trail on an abandoned railway track in this park makes a welcome change from the crowds of the city. It is reached by bus number 1, 15, 20, 122, 135. Get off at Dashengli (大生里站).

Húlǐ Shān Fortress   NOTABLE BUILDING

(胡里山炮台, Húlǐ Shān Pàotái; ¥25; ⊙7.30am-5.30pm) Across Daxue Lu, south of Xiàmén University, is this gigantic German gun artillery built in 1894. You can rent binoculars to peer over the water to the Taiwanese-occupied island of Kinmen (金门; Jīnmén), formerly known as Quemoy and claimed by both mainland China and Taiwan. To get here, walk for 2km south along the coastal path.

🎊 Festivals & Events

Dragon Boat Races   SPORTS

(龙舟竞渡, Lóngzhōu Jìngdù) Held in Xiàmén at the Dragon Pool (龙舟池; Lóngzhōu Chí) in Jíměi every June. They are quite a sight.

🛏 Sleeping

Xiàmén International Youth Hostel   HOSTEL $

(厦门国际青年旅舍, Xiàmén Guójì Qīngnián Lǚshè; ☑0592-208 2345; www.yhaxm.com; 41 Nanhua Lu, 南华路41号; dm from ¥60, d ¥218-298, f ¥318-348; ❄@🛜) This is the best hostel in Fújiàn. Spacious mixed dorms share a clean bathroom between up to six guests; stylish double rooms – some with balcony – would suit a boutique hotel; and the excellent family rooms make it a popular base for the entourage. Reception can be a little regimented, but sunlight pours through the splendid backyard and into the communal lounge room.

Xiàmén Locanda International Youth Hostel   HOSTEL $

(厦门卢卡国际青年旅舍, Xiàmén Lúkǎ Guójì Qīngnián Lǚshè; ☑0592-208 2918; www.locanda hostel.com; 35 Minzu Lu, 民族路35号; 4-/6-bed dm ¥60/55, s/d & tw ¥208/258; ❄@🛜) Xiàmén's 'other' hostel feels like a family guesthouse set over two levels and has a large, pleasant garden, though the dorm

Xiàmén & Gǔlàng Yǔ

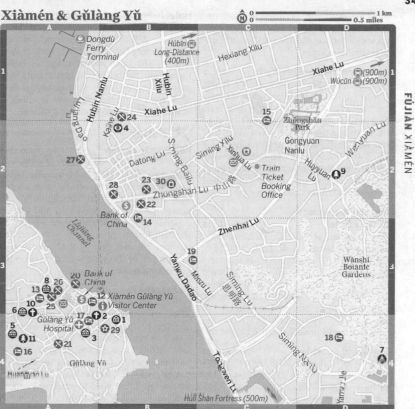

Xiàmén & Gǔlàng Yǔ

◎ Sights
1 Bo'ai Hospital	B4
Consulate Inn	(see 1)
2 Ecclesia Catholica	A4
3 Former Japanese Consulate	A4
Former Spanish Consulate	(see 3)
Guāncǎi Lóu	(see 6)
4 Kāihé Lù Fish Market	B2
5 Koxinga Memorial Hall	A4
6 Law Court	A3
7 Nánpǔtuó Temple	D4
8 Organ Museum	A3
9 Railroad Culture Park	D2
10 Sānyī Church	A3
11 Sunlight Rock Park	A4
Yìzú Shānzhuāng	(see 6)

🛏 Sleeping
12 Gǔlàng Yǔ International Youth Hostel	A3
13 Gǔlàng Yǔ Lù Fēi International Youth Hostel	A3
14 Hotel Indigo Xiàmén Harbour	B3
15 Liángzhù Boutique Lifestyle Hotel	C1
16 Miryam Boutique Hotel	A4
17 Mogo Cafe Hotel	A4
18 Xiàmén International Youth Hostel	D4
19 Xiàmén Locanda International Youth Hostel	B3

🍴 Eating
32/HOW cafe	(see 15)
20 Babycat Café	A3
21 Chu Family Coffee	A4
22 Huángzéhé Peanut Soup Shop	B2
23 Huìyí Mǐntái Tèchǎn	B2
24 Kāihé Shāchámiàn	B1
25 Líjì Mǔdān Fishball	A3
26 Lóngtóu Fishball	A3
27 Lucky Full City Seafood Dim Sum	A2
28 Seaview Restaurant	B2

✪ Entertainment
29 Huáng Róngyuǎn Villa	B4

🛍 Shopping
30 Xinhua Bookshop	B2

FÚJIÀN XIÀMÉN

rooms are much smaller than at the more famous rival. Staff compensate though with gregarious service and the location in Siming is very relaxing.

Jinjiang Inn Xiamen University HOSTEL $

(厦门锦江之星大学店, Xiàmén Jǐnjiāng Zhīxīng Dàxuédiàn; ☎ 0592 252 2666; www.jinjiang.com; 5 Fengchaoshan Lu, Siming District, 思明区蜂巢山路5号; r ¥200-300; 率率) You won't need to re-visit your university days just yet – this branch of the J1 budget hotel franchise is far from a frat house – but you will have easy access to the beautiful grounds of Xiàmén University. Rooms are blissfully quiet and self-contained. Top value.

Liángzhù Boutique
Lifestyle Hotel BOUTIQUE HOTEL $$

(良筑, Liángzhù; ☎ 0592 207 1322; www.liangzhu22.com; 22 Huaxin Lu, 华新路22号; r ¥410-618; 率率) Old-world hospitality makes a guest appearance at this 1950s chocolate-coloured villa discreetly located in central Xiàmén. The eight rooms are designed in competing aesthetics – some busier than others – so look at a few before settling. The garden provides a lovely breakfast setting.

Ring Island Coast Inn GUESTHOUSE $$

(环岛海岸客栈, Huándǎo Hǎiàn Kèzhàn; ☎ 0592-219 6677; www.xm-inn.com; 20 Zeng Cuo An, Huandao Nanlu, 环岛南路曾厝安20号; r ¥150-350; 率@) Further southeast of Xiàmén University is the fishing village of Zēng Cuò Ān where locals tourists descend on weekends for street food and coastal breezes. Of the numerous guesthouses, Ring Island has the most experience with foreigners and perhaps the best views from its two elevated rooms. The cheaper rooms, all decorated like vibrant student digs, have neither the view nor an attached bathroom. To get there, catch bus 29 from Siming Nanlu.

Kempinski Hotel Xiamen LUXURY HOTEL $$$

(厦门源昌凯宾斯基大酒店, Xiàmén Yuánchāng Kǎibīnsījī Dàjiǔdiàn; ☎ 0592 258 8888; www.kempinskihotel.com/en/xiamen; 98 Hubin Zhonglu, 湖滨中路98号; d ¥920-1220; P率率率) The Kempinski label is growing in stature and the futuristic design of the Xiàmén branch, located splendidly on Bailuzhou Lake, will do its reputation no harm. Inside the lobby glitters, and the ceilings are high enough for an abseiling wall. When you reach the rooms, enjoy the beauty products and fluffy pillows. There's a top gym to work off your meal at the German restaurant.

Hotel Indigo Xiàmén Harbour HOTEL $$$

(厦门海港英迪格酒店, Xiàmén Hǎigǎng Yīndígé Jiǔdiàn; ☎ 0592-226 1666; www.hotelindigo.com; 16 Lujiang Dao, 鹭江道16号; d ¥1200-1400; 率率@) The small rooms at the sea-facing Indigo are daubed in bright colours and have Gulang Yu firmly in their sights. Staff work hard to please, especially at check-in where generous discounts are common.

✕ Eating

Kāihé Shāchámiàn NOODLES $

(开禾沙茶面; 126 Xiahe Lu, 厦禾路126号; noodles from ¥12; ⊘24hr) Shāchámiàn is Fújiàn's favourite street noodle dish sauced with dried fish, onion and chilli. Which animal protein you choose to add on top depends on personal preference – pork and shellfish feature prominently – or you can opt for tofu and egg. This simple shop is identifiable by the yellow characters on the green front panel.

Huángzéhé Peanut Soup Shop SOUP $

(黄则和花生汤店, Huángzéhé Huāshēng Tāngdiàn; 22-24 Zhongshan Lu, 中山路20号; snacks ¥4-10; ⊘6.30am-10.30pm) For 60 years this humble counter-service restaurant has filled an unusual craving for sweet huāshēng tāng (花生汤; peanut soup). Other snacks include fried zǎo (枣; red dates) and hǎlìjiān (海蛎煎; oyster omelette). You need to purchase coupons that you hand over when you order food.

Huìyí Mǐntái Tèchǎn SWEETS $

(汇怡闽台特产; 75 Zhongshan Lu, 中山路75号; ⊘9am-9pm) Fújiàn sweets include zǐcài huāshēng (紫菜花生, sweet seaweed peanuts; ¥20 per bag), liúlián táng (榴莲糖, durian candy) and li hing mui (旅行梅, sugared plum kernels). Box them up to go.

★ Lucky Full City Seafood DIM SUM $$

(潮福城, Cháofú Chéng; 28 Hubin Beilu, 湖滨北路28号; dim sum from ¥14, meals from ¥70; ⊘10am-1am) If you eat out once in Xiàmén, join the queues for this Cantonese culinary masterclass. Stack up the exquisite dim sum dishes like egg buns, roasted pigeon and pork dumplings. Try to visit outside peak times. Catch a taxi here: the driver will know where it is. It also has a branch 200m north of Lúndù ferry terminal.

Lucky Full City
Seafood Dim Sum DIM SUM $$

(幸运的全城海鲜点心, Xìngyùn de Quánchéng Hǎixiān Diǎnxīn; 33 Lujiang Dao, 鹭江道33号; meals from ¥60; ⊘8am-2.30am) Authentic and

MSG-free dim sum is served in this ever-popular restaurant. Expect to wait at least 30 minutes to get a table.

32/HOW cafe
CAFE $$

(Cherry 32 Cafe; 32 Huaxin Lu, 华新路32号; coffee from ¥45; ⊙11am-11pm) If Xiàmén starts to wear you down, hide out in this atmospheric Taiwanese coffee shop located in an old house. The coffee is brewed with aplomb and the decor is mid-century Europe: velvety reds and browns, towering wine racks, abstract artwork and hard leather lounges. Lean back and percolate.

Seaview Restaurant
DIM SUM $$$

(鹭江宾馆观海厅, Lùjiāng Bīnguǎn Guānhǎitīng; 7th fl, 54 Lujiang Dao, 鹭江道54号7楼; meals from ¥80; ⊙10am-10pm) The prime viewing deck in the city also serves Fujianese snacks. It's ideal for a predinner drink and the sunset may make you linger longer than expected.

🛍 Shopping

Zhongshan Lu is essentially a long shopping strip filled with souvenir shops and the latest fashion brands.

ℹ Information

Bank of China (中国银行, Zhōngguó Yínháng; 6 Zhongshan Lu) The 24-hour ATM accepts international cards.

China Post (中国邮政, Zhōngguó Yóuzhèng; cnr Xinhua Lu & Zhongshan Lu; ⊙7.30am-7.30pm) Telephone services available.

City Medical Consultancy (来福诊所, Láifú Zhěnsuǒ; ☑0532 3168; 123 Xidi Villa Hubin Beilu; ⊙8am-5pm Mon-Fri, to noon Sat) English-speaking doctors; expat frequented. Telephone operated 24 hours. It's near the western shore of Yuandang Lake.

Discover Fujian (☑0592-398 9966; www.discoverfujian.com; 10th fl, Jiari Shangcheng, 1118 Xiahe Lu, 厦禾路1118) This travel agent can arrange English-speaking tours and accommodation in the *tǔlóu* areas of Fújiàn, as well as other parts of the province. One-day tours start at around Y500 per person.

Public Security Bureau (PSB, 公安局, Gōng'ānjú; ☑0592-226 2203; 45-47 Xinhua Lu; visa section 8.10-11.45am & 2.40-5.15pm Mon-Sat) Opposite the main post and telephone office. The visa section (出入证管理处, *chūrùjìng guǎnlǐchù*) is in the northeastern part of the building, on Gongyuan Nanlu.

ℹ Getting There & Away

AIR

Air China, China Southern, Xiàmén Airlines and several other domestic airlines operate flights between Xiàmén and all major domestic airports in China. There are innumerable ticket offices around town, many of which are in the larger hotels.

There are direct international flights to/from Bangkok, Hong Kong, Jakarta, Kuala Lumpur, Los Angeles, Manila, Osaka, Penang, Singapore and Tokyo.

BOAT

Fast boats (¥14, 20 minutes) leave for the nearby coastal Fújiàn town of Zhāngzhōu (漳州) from the passenger ferry terminal (客运码头; *kèyùn mǎtóu*). Boats run every 15 minutes between 6.30am and 9.30pm. Boats to Kinmen (金门; Jīnmén), Taiwan (¥160, 30 minutes, hourly) leave from Wǔtōng ferry terminal (五通码头; Wǔtōng Mǎtóu) between 8am and 6.30pm.

BUS

There are three major bus stations in Xiàmén. **Húbīn long-distance bus station** (湖滨长途汽车站, Húbīn Chángtú Qìchēzhàn; 58 Hubin Nanlu) serves destinations south of Xiàmén; tickets can be bought two days in advance at the

---

ℹ BORDER CROSSINGS: GETTING TO TAIWAN

Ferries ply between Xiàmén and Kinmen (金门; Jīnmén) Island in Taiwan half-hourly between 8am and 6.30pm. You can catch the boat from Wǔtōng ferry terminal (五通码头; Wǔtōng Mǎtóu; ¥160, 30 minutes), 8km east of Xiàmén's airport.

Tickets can only be bought an hour before the departure time. In Kinmen, visas are issued on the spot for most nationalities. But you need a multiple-entry China visa if you want to return to Fújiàn.

Wǔtōng ferry terminal can only be reached by taxi. Expect to pay ¥20 from the airport to the terminal.

Rénmínbì is the only currency accepted in the money-exchange counters at Kinmen's ferry terminal. From Kinmen, there are flights to other major cities in Taiwan.

Alternatively, you can catch a ferry (¥300, 1½ hours, 9.15am) from Fúzhōu's Máwěi ferry terminal (马尾码头; Máwěi Mǎtóu) to Taiwan's archipelago of Matzu (马祖; Mázǔ). From there, you'll find boats to Keelung and flights to other cities in Taiwan.

ticket booth in the local bus terminal adjacent to Xiàmén University at the end of Siming Nanlu.

Guǎngzhōu ¥250, nine hours, two daily
Lóngyán (Tǔlóu) ¥75, three hours, eight daily
Nánjìng (in Fújiàn) ¥28, two hours, 11 daily
Yǒngdìng (Tǔlóu) ¥75, four hours, nine daily

Wúcūn bus station (梧村汽车站, Wúcūn Qìchēzhàn; 925 Xiahe Lu), directly opposite Xiàmén's main train station, serves destinations north of the city, including Jìnjiāng (¥33, 1½ hours, every 20 minutes) and Quánzhōu (¥45, two hours, every 20 minutes).

Note that buses to Fúzhōu (¥115, four hours, every 20 minutes) and Wǔyí Shān (¥191, nine hours, one daily, 9.30am) leave from the far-flung Fānghú bus station (枋湖客运中心; Fānghú Kèyùn Zhōngxīn).

TRAIN

Xiàmén's main train station is on Xiahe Lu. All trains stop at Xiàmén north station 25km north of the city centre. Tickets can be booked through the **train ticketing booth** (☎0592-203 8565; cnr Xinhua Lu & Zhongshan Lu; 9am-6pm) behind the Gem Hotel (金后酒店; Jīnhòu Jiǔdiàn).

Fúzhōu ¥66 to ¥85, two hours
Hángzhōu ¥282 to ¥357, seven hours
Quánzhōu ¥21 to ¥25, 30 minutes
Shànghǎi ¥328 to ¥413, 7½ hours
Wǔyí Shān ¥144 to ¥223, 13½ hours

❶ Getting Around

Xiàmén airport is 15km from the waterfront district. Taxis cost about ¥55. Bus 27 travels from the airport to Dìyī ferry terminal (but not vice versa). From the city centre, airport shuttle buses (¥10) leave from Chūnguāng Hotel, opposite the Lúndù ferry terminal.

BRT line 1 links the waterfront to both train stations via Xiahe Lu (¥1). Bus 19 runs to the train station from the ferry terminal (¥1). Buses to Xiàmén University leave from the train station (bus 1) and from the ferry terminal (bus 2). Taxis start at ¥8, plus a ¥3 fuel surcharge.

Gǔlàng Yǔ 鼓浪屿
☎ 0592 / POP 15,000

China is not known for its island escapes but a visit to Gǔlàng Yǔ, which is seeking Unesco World Heritage status, is more than a novel experience. A short hop from the large island city of Xiàmén, this car-free gem was a turn-of-the-20th-century international enclave where consulates from Europe, America and Japan managed their affairs among banyan trees and vine-strewn villas.

A day or two spent wandering its museums, tunnels, trails and beaches is a highlight of a visit to Southern China, but for now it's still mostly locals who hang out in the increasingly slick cafe scene. Breathe deeply if the weekend crowds get too heavy; there is sanctuary to be found if you seek it.

History

The foreign community was well established on Gǔlàng Yǔ by the 1880s, with a daily English newspaper, churches, hospitals, post and telegraph offices, libraries, hotels and consulates. In 1903 the island was officially designated an International Foreign Settlement, and a municipal council with a police force of Sikhs was established to govern it. Today memories of the settlement linger in the many charming colonial-era buildings and the sound of classical piano wafting from speakers (the island is nicknamed 'piano island' by the Chinese). Many of China's most celebrated musicians have come from Gǔlàng Yǔ, including the pianists Yu Feixing, Lin Junqing and Yin Chengzong.

◉ Sights

Aside from the hawkers on Longtou Lu and Quanzhou Lu, Gǔlàng Yǔ is an open-air museum perfect for wandering on foot. You can circumnavigate the island's rocky beaches, short cut through man-made tunnels, or make the skip over Sunlight Rock in the middle. The colonial-era architecture is distinctly European, but life spills out into the narrow alleys where hip Chinese snap their way around this incongruously cool cafe scene.

An inclusive ticket (¥100) covers your entrance to the Koxinga Memorial Hall, Sunlight Rock (and cable-car ride), the Organ Museum and the International Calligraphic Carving Art Gallery.

Organ Museum MUSEUM
(风琴博物馆, Fēngqín Bówùguǎn; 43 Guxin Lu, 鼓新路43号; ¥20; ⊙8.40am-5.30pm) Housed in the highly distinctive Bāguà Lóu (八卦楼) building is the Organ Museum, with a fantastic collection including a Norman & Beard organ from 1909.

Sunlight Rock Park PARK
(日光岩公园, Rìguāng Yán Gōngyuán; ¥60; ⊙8am-7pm) Sunlight Rock (Rìguāng Yán), in Sunlight Rock Park, is the island's highest point at 93m. At the foot of Sunlight Rock is a large colonial-era building known as the Koxinga Memorial Hall. Also in the park is **Yīngxióng Hill** (Yīngxióng Shān), near the memorial hall and connected via a cable-car

ride. It has an open-air aviary (admission free) with chattering egrets and parrots.

Octagonal Villa   ARCHITECTURE
(八角楼, Ba Jiao Lou; 15 Lujiao Lu, 鹿角路15号) This is the former family residence of Mr Lin, a prominent Taiwanese tycoon who lived here in the late 19th century. It's near Ecclesia Catholica.

Koxinga Memorial Hall   MUSEUM
(郑成功纪念馆, Zhèngchénggōng Jìnlànguǎn; Quanzhou Lu, 泉州路; ☺8-11am & 2-5pm) Commemorates the life of the charismatic military man who defeated the Dutch East Indies Company in the 17th century.

🛏 Sleeping

Gǔlàng Yǔ has a variety of excellent boutique guesthouses, hotels and hostels. It's a little more expensive than Xiàmén, but a very different experience altogether. Note that whatever luggage you bring you will have to carry or wheel from the ferry terminal as there are no cars on the island.

Gǔlàng Yǔ Lù Fēi
International Youth Hostel   HOSTEL $
(鼓浪屿鹭飞国际青年旅舍, Gǔlàng Yǔ Lù Fēi Guójì Qīngnián Lǚshè; ☎0592-208 2678; www.yhalt.cn; 20 Guxin Lu, 鼓新路20号; dm ¥70, s &

d ¥270-390; ✴@🛜) In a surprisingly quiet location near the Piano Museum, this is the pick of the two hostels on the island, thanks to the fine staff and pleasant communal areas. The dorm rooms are tight, though, and the mattresses not particularly comfortable.

Gǔlàng Yǔ
International Youth Hostel   HOSTEL $
(鼓浪屿国际青年旅馆, Gǔlàng Yǔ Guójì Qīngnián lǚguǎn; ☎0592 206 6066, yha@yhagly.com; 8 Lujiao Lu, 鹿礁路18号; dm ¥70, s/d ¥270/390; ✴@🛜) A wooden boat greets guests at the reception of this popular hostel 400m west of the ferry terminal. It's enthusiastically managed but tiring with the tide. The double rooms are huge for the price and the communal areas are abundant with natural light. Look for a small red sign.

Penero Hotel   BOUTIQUE HOTEL $$
(磐诺假日酒店, Pánnuò Jiàrì Jiǔdiàn; ☎592 256 1152; 111-1 Kangtai Lu, 康泰路111-1号; d ¥450-550; ✴🛜) The Penero has undergone extensive renovations to be among the top bracket of hotels here. Located on the quieter western side of the island, the place has a marina feel in its airy rooms and wooden decking throughout. The upstairs rooms have nice views and are dead quiet. There's a terrific European restaurant downstairs.

HISTORIC BUILDINGS

Old colonial-era residences and consulates are tucked away in the maze of streets leading from the pier, particularly along Longtou Lu and the back lanes of Huayan Lu. Some of Gǔlàng Yǔ's buildings are deserted and tumbledown, with trees growing out of their sides, as residents cannot afford their upkeep.

Southeast of the pier you will see the two buildings of the **former British Consulate** (永顺卡斯特宾馆, Yǒngshùn Kǎsìtè Bīnguǎn), currently running as a hotel, above you, while further along is the cream-coloured former Japanese **Bo'ai Hospital** (1 Lujiao Lu, 鹿角路1号), built in 1936. Up the hill on a different part of Lujiao Lu stands the red-brick **former Japanese Consulate** (日本领事馆, Rìběn Lǐngshìguǎn; 26 Lujiao Lu, 鹿角路26号), just before you reach the magnificent snow-white **Ecclesia Catholica** (鼓浪屿天主堂, Gǔlàngyǔ Tiānzhǔtáng; 34 Lujiao Lu, 鹿角路34号), dating from 1917. The white building next to the church is the **former Spanish Consulate** (西班牙领事馆, Xībānyá Lǐngshìguǎn). Just past the church on the left is the **Huáng Róngyuǎn Villa** (黄荣远堂, Huángróngyuǎn Táng; ☎0592-257 0510; 32 Fujian Lu, 福建路32号; show ¥118; ☺8.30am-5pm), a marvellous pillared building, now the Puppet Art Centre. Other buildings worth looking at include the Protestant **Sānyī Church** (三一堂, Sānyī Táng), a red-brick building with a classical portico and cruciform-shaped interior on the corner of Anhai Lu (安海路) and Yongchun Lu (永春路). Where Anhai Lu meets Bishan Lu is the former **Law Court**, now inhabited by local residents.

Doing a circuit of Bishan Lu will take you past a rarely visited part of the island. **Guāncǎi Lóu** (观彩楼, 6 Bishan Lu), a residence built in 1931, has a magnificently dilapidated interior with a wealth of original features. The building stands in stark contrast next to the immaculate **Yìzú Shānzhuāng** (亦足山庄, 9 Bishan Lu, 壁山路9号), a structure dating from the 1920s.

Mogo Cafe Hotel
HOTEL $$

(蘑菇旅馆, Mógū Lǚguǎn; ☑0592-208 5980; www.mogo-hotel.com; 3-9 Longtou Lu, 龙头路 3-9号; r ¥280-650; ❄@) The Mogo is a well known hotel and its small, atmospheric rooms are still in reasonable nick. There are conscious style choices like rain showers and down lighting, which lift it above the many similar hotels around Longtou Lu. Staff do not speak English.

★Miryam Boutique Hotel
BOUTIQUE HOTEL $$$

(老别墅旅馆, Miryam Lǎo Biéshù Lǚguǎn; ☑0592-206 2505; www.miryamhotel.com; 70 Huangyan Lu, 晃岩路70号; r ¥688-1688; ❄@🛜) Our favourite hotel on the island is located right below Sunlight Rock and affords views across villa roofs and out to sea. Busy staff will meet you at the ferry and show you to the Victorian mansion where rooms have period furniture and decadent beds. The restaurant is superb.

✕ Eating

The cafe scene is a feature for many visitors. The lanes off Longtou Lu hide many terrific little eateries, but anything on the street here will be decent. Let the crowds decide. Local specialities include shark fishballs and Amoy pie (a sweet filled pastry).

Lóngtóu Fishball
SEAFOOD $

(龙头鱼丸店, Lóngtóu Yúwán Diàn; 183 Longtou Lu, 龙头路183号; meals from ¥10; ⏰8.30am-8pm) You won't go far wrong at any of the nondescript restaurants on Longtou Lu, but the eponymous one is the most popular for a bowl of *shāyú wán fěnsī* (鲨鱼丸粉丝; shark fishball noodles) or the *hǎilìjiān* (海蛎煎; oyster omelette).

Líjì Mùdān Fishball
SEAFOOD $

(林记木担鱼丸, Línjì Mùdān Yúwán; 56 Longtou Lu, 龙头路56号; meals from ¥15; ⏰10am-9pm) The stakes are high on Longtou Lu, and the staff at Líjì Mùdān will shout you into a plastic seat for some of that fishball goodness.

Slowly Cafe
CAFE $

(花时间, 2nd fl, 36 Anhai Lu, 安海路36号2楼; meals from ¥10, coffee from ¥30; ❄🛜) In a regal old European villa is one of the old breed of cafes on the island, specialising in flavoured coffee varieties like honey and orange. Service is faster than the name suggests.

★Lǎohǎi Wù
CHINESE $$

(捞海坞, ☑0592 206 7918; 35 Wudai Lu, 乌埭路 35号; meals ¥30-60) It feels like you're cutting through on the way to somewhere else, but stop at the wooden benches for incredible noodle and fish dishes at this friendly outdoor restaurant loved by Fujianese food fanatics. There's an attached ceramics gallery and cold beer (¥30) available.

Chu Family Coffee
CAFE $$

(褚家园咖啡馆, Chǔjiāyuán Kāfēiguǎn; ☑0592-206 3651; 15 Zhonghua Lu, 中华路54号; meals from ¥60; ⏰11am-9pm) A little afternoon delight is found in this garden cafe where cats roam and an award-winning barista brews his magic. The Western desserts don't scrounge on the cream.

Babycat Café
CAFE $$

(☑0592-206 3651; 143 Longtou Lu, 龙头路143号; ⏰10.30am-11pm; 🛜) The sweet Amoy pies are the attraction at Babycat, a dimly lit haunt with a graffiti wall and feline and nautical touches. Go for the red bean or pistachio flavour. There's another fancier branch nearby.

ℹ Information

There are various maps for sale (¥5 to ¥10) in cafes and souvenir shops, some in English.

Bank of China (中国银行, Zhōngguó Yínháng; 2 Longtou Lu, 龙头路2号; ⏰9am-7pm) Forex and 24-hour ATM.

China Post (中国邮政, Zhōngguó Yóuzhèng; 102 Longtou Lu, 龙头路102号; ⏰8.30am-5.30pm) Sells stamps and postcards.

Gǔlàng Yǔ Hospital (鼓浪屿医院, Gǔlàng Yǔ Yīyuàn; 60 Fujian Lu, 福建路60号) A significant upgrade includes 24-hour service. Has its own miniature ambulance for the small roads.

Xiàmén Gǔlàng Yǔ Visitor Center (厦门鼓浪屿游客中心, Xiàmén Gǔlàng Yǔ Yóukè Zhōngxīn; Longtou Lu, 龙头路) Left luggage costs ¥3 to ¥5.

ℹ Getting There & Away

Ferries for the 10-minute trip to Gǔlàng Yǔ now leave the **Dōngdù ferry terminal** (东渡码头, Dōngdù Mǎtóu) just north of the city, but return to the old terminal at the main **Huangu ferry terminal** off Lujiang Lu. The round-trip fare is ¥35. Boats run from 5.45am to midnight.

ℹ Getting Around

Circuits of the island can be done by boat (¥20), with half-hourly departures from the passenger ferry terminal off Lujiang Lu between 7.40am and 5pm.

Fújiàn Tǔlóu 福建土楼

0597 / POP 43,000

The Hakka and the Mǐnnán (Fujianese) people have lived in the fabled earthen structures known as *tǔlóu* (土楼) for centuries. Spread across a southwestern section of the province, many are still inhabited and welcome visitors for the day or night. The circular edifices are remarkable for their ingenuity, but the idyllic rural setting lends an ethereal quality hard to find in modern China. Sleeping here and sharing a meal with local families can be life-affirming.

Take note: since Unesco rubber-stamped the region in 2008, tour buses have rumbled in on freshly paved highways. But it's hardly reason to stay away. With more than 30,000 *tǔlóu* still intact, you can find one to take your fancy.

◉ Sights

The most notable of the *tǔlóu* are lumped into various clusters, in the vicinity of Nánjìng (南靖) and Yǒngdìng (永定). Only the three most developed clusters: Hóngkēng, Tiánluókēng and Yúnshuǐyáo are accessible by public transport. However, bus services are neither frequent nor punctual. Booking a tour or hiring a vehicle is recommended if you want to venture off the beaten path and see more.

◉ Hóngkēng

This cluster is 50km east of Yǒngdìng. From Xiàmén, three buses (¥63, 3½ hours, 6.50am, 9.10am and 1pm) go directly to the cluster, which is also known as Tǔlóu Mínsú Wénhuàcūn (土楼民俗文化村). Admission is ¥90.

Zhènchéng Lóu NOTABLE BUILDING
(振成楼) This most visited *tǔlóu* is a grandiose structure built in 1912, with two concentric circles and 222 rooms. The ancestral hall in the centre of the *tǔlóu* is complete with Western-style pillars. The locals dub this *tǔlóu wángzǐ* (土楼王子), the prince *tǔlóu*.

Fúyù Lóu NOTABLE BUILDING
(福裕楼) Along the river, this five-storey square *tǔlóu* boasts some wonderfully carved wooden beams and pillars. Rooms (from ¥100) are available here.

Kuíjù Lóu NOTABLE BUILDING
(奎聚楼) Near Zhènchéng Lóu, this much older, square *tǔlóu* dates back to 1834.

◉ Tiánluókēng

A pilgrimage to the earthen castles is not complete if you miss Tiánluókēng (田螺坑), which is 37km northeast of Nánjìng and home to arguably the most picturesque cluster of *tǔlóu* in the region. The locals affectionately call the five noble buildings 'four dishes with one soup' because of their shapes: circular, square and oval.

There's one direct bus (¥47, 3½ hours) to the cluster from Xiàmén, leaving at 8.30am.

Make sure your driver, if you've hired one, takes you up the hill for a postcard-perfect view of Tiánluókēng.

Cluster admission, which includes entry to Yùchāng Lóu and Tǎxià village, is ¥100. A shuttle bus (¥15) from the cluster's ticket office goes to the above two places, but the vehicle won't leave until it gets 10 passengers.

Yùchāng Lóu NOTABLE BUILDING
(裕昌楼) The tallest roundhouse in Fújiàn, this vast five-floor structure has 270 rooms and an observation tower to check for marauding bandits. Interestingly, this 300-year-old property's pillars bend at an angle on the 3rd floor and at the opposite angle on the 5th floor. Each room and kitchen on the ground floor has its own well.

Tǎxià VILLAGE
(塔下村) This delightful river settlement boasts several *tǔlóu*-converted guesthouses and it is a great base from which to explore the *tǔlóu* areas. The highlight of the village is the **Zhang Ancestral Hall** (张氏家庙, Zhāngshì Jiāmiào; Tǎxià Village, 塔下村; ◉9am-5pm). It is surrounded by 23 elaborately carved spear-like stones, which celebrate the achievements of prominent villagers. The bus station in Nánjìng runs six buses (¥17, 1½ hours) to the village between 8am and 5.30pm.

Wénchāng Lóu NOTABLE BUILDING
(文昌楼) The Tiánluókēng cluster's oval-shaped building.

Bùyún Lóu NOTABLE BUILDING
(步云楼) At the heart of the Tiánluókēng Tǔlóu cluster is this square building. First built in the 17th century, it burnt down in 1936 and was rebuilt in the 1950s.

◉ Gāoběi

Home to the 'King of Tǔlóu', Chéngqǐ Lóu (承启楼), this cluster is on the road from Xiàmén, roughly 45km east of Yǒngdìng. Admission is ¥50.

JUST WHAT IS A TǓLÓU?

Tǔlóu (literally mud houses) are outlandish, multistorey, fortified mud structures built by the inhabitants of southwest Fújiàn to protect themselves from bandits and wild animals.

Tǔlóu were built along either a circular or square floor plan. The walls are made of rammed earth and glutinous rice, reinforced with strips of bamboo and wood chips. These structures are large enough to house entire clans, and they did, and still do! They are a grand exercise in communal living. The interior sections are enclosed by enormous peripheral structures that could accommodate hundreds of people. Nestled in the mud walls were bedrooms, wells, cooking areas and storehouses, circling a central courtyard. The later *tǔlóu* had stone firewalls and metal-covered doors to protect against blazes.

The compartmentalised nature of the building meant that these structures were the ancient equivalent of modern apartments. A typical layout would be the kitchens on the ground floor, storage on the next level and accommodation on the floors above this. Some *tǔlóu* have multiple buildings built in concentric rings within the main enclosure. These could be guest rooms and home schools. The centre is often an ancestral hall or a meeting hall used for events such as birthdays and weddings. For defence purposes, usually there is only one entrance for the entire *tǔlóu* and there are no windows on the first three storeys.

No matter what type or shape of *tǔlóu* you're looking at, many of them are still inhabited by a single clan, and residents depend on a combination of tourism and farming for a living. The *tǔlóu* are surprisingly comfortable to live in, being '*dōng nuǎn, xià liáng*' (冬暖夏凉), or 'warm in winter and cool in summer'. These structures were built to last.

Chéngqǐ Lóu
NOTABLE BUILDING

(承启楼) In the village of Gāoběi (高北), this 300-year-old *tǔlóu* has 400 rooms and once housed 1000 inhabitants. It's built with elaborate concentric rings, with circular passageways between them and a central shrine. It's one of the most iconic and photographed *tǔlóu* and it's no surprise that it has been dubbed the king *tǔlóu*.

Yìjīng Lóu
NOTABLE BUILDING

(遗经楼) The largest rectangular *tǔlóu* in Fújiàn. The crumbling structure, built in 1851, has 281 rooms, two schools and 51 halls.

Wǔyún Lóu
NOTABLE BUILDING

(五云楼) Deserted and rickety, this square building took on a slant after an earthquake in 1918.

◉ Yúnshuǐyáo

This cluster, 48km northeast of Nánjìng, is set in idyllic surrounds with rolling hills, verdant farms and babbling streams. Six buses run from Nánjìng bus station (¥20, one hour) to Yúnshuǐyáo (云水谣) and seven go from Nánjìng train station (¥25, one hour) between 8.30am and 5.25pm. Cluster admission is ¥90.

Yúnshuǐyáo Village
VILLAGE

(长教村) Between the Héguì and Huáiyuǎn *tǔlóu* in the Yúnshuǐyáo Tǔlóu Cluster is this beautiful village (formerly known as ancient Chángjiào) where you can sip tea under the big banyan trees and watch water buffalo in the river. The village has a few guesthouses that offer rooms (from ¥100).

Héguì Lóu
NOTABLE BUILDING

(和贵楼) This tallest rectangular *tǔlóu* in Fújiàn has five storeys and was built on a swamp. It boasts 120 rooms, a school, two wells, and a fortified courtyard in front of the entrance. The mammoth structure was built in 1732.

Huáiyuǎn Lóu
NOTABLE BUILDING

(怀远楼) This relatively young *tǔlóu* (built in 1909) has 136 equally sized rooms and a concentric ring that houses an ancestral hall and a school.

◉ Chūxī

This lesser-visited yet picturesque cluster is located 48km southeast of Yǒngdìng. Admission is ¥70.

Jíqìng Lóu
NOTABLE BUILDING

(集庆楼) This 600-year-old *tǔlóu* was built without using a single nail and is still pretty intact. It now houses an exhibition hall.

Zhōngchuān Village
VILLAGE

(中川村, Zhōngchuān Cūn) This village, 17km northwest of the Chūxī Tǔlóu Cluster, is the ancestral home of the Burmese-Chinese businessman Aw Boon Haw, the inventor of the medicinal salve Tiger Balm and owner of the (in)famously quirky Haw Par Villa theme park in Singapore. Here you'll find another **villa** (虎豹别墅, Hǔbào Biéshù; ¥30; ⊙8am-5pm), but its scale and decor can't compete with its Singaporean (big) sister. More interesting is his family's **ancestral hall** (胡氏家庙; Húshì Jiāmiào), 100m behind the villa. The shrine, the spear-like pillars that celebrate the achievements of their family members, and the setting itself are spectacular.

⊙ Nánxī

The Nánxī Tǔlóu Cluster, 35km east of Yǒngdìng, is a densely packed cluster known for its large rectangular structures. Admission is ¥70.

Yǎnxiāng Lóu
NOTABLE BUILDING

(衍香楼) This four-storey *tǔlóu* rises up beautifully next to a river, and is in the same direction as Huánjí Lóu *tǔlóu*.

Huánjí Lóu
NOTABLE BUILDING

(环极楼) Sitting midway between Yǒngdìng and Nánjìng, this four-storey building is a huge roundhouse with inner concentric passages, tiled interior passages and a courtyard. It also sports a *huíyīnbì* (回音壁) – a wall that echoes and resonates to sharp sounds.

Qìngyáng Lóu
NOTABLE BUILDING

(庆洋楼) Not far from Yǎnxiāng Lóu *tǔlóu*, this huge, rectangular, semidecrepit structure was built between 1796 and 1820.

Lìběn Lóu
NOTABLE BUILDING

(立本楼) To the rear of Yǎnxiāng Lóu is this derelict *tǔlóu* with crumbling walls. It was burnt down during the civil war and stands without its roof.

⊂₣ Tours

Amazing Fujian Tulou (p350) and Discover Fujian (p343) can organise English-speaking guided tours.

🛏 Sleeping & Eating

In short, unless you came on a day trip, we strongly recommend spending a night (or two) in a *tǔlóu*, which must rank among the most novel sleeping experiences in the world.

It's not quite roughing it, but it isn't hotel quality either. Some *tǔlóu* have modern facilities, but most are still very basic – a bed, a thermos of hot water and a fan. You might also find that the toilets are outside. Bring a flashlight and bug repellent.

Most *tǔlóu* owners can also organise a pick-up from Yǒngdìng or Nánjìng and transport for touring the area. There are many hotels in Yǒngdìng and Nánjìng, but neither town is attractive. Still, it can be convenient to stay if you arrive late, and to find a local taxi driver to scoot you around the following day.

Yúnshuǐyáo (ancient Chángjiàn) and Tǎxià villages are other convenient options, with some basic *tǔlóu* guesthouses available.

If you stay in a *tǔlóu*, most families can cook up meals for you (¥150 to ¥200 for two people; confirm before ordering). Tasty food stalls will do the trick near the Yǒngdìng and Nánjìng bus stations if you are travelling by public transport. Hakka dishes are often braised. Expect a set menu, but look out for the *niúròuwán tāng* (牛肉丸汤; beef soup with meatballs) or *niàng dòufù* (酿豆腐; braised tofu with pork).

Fúyù Lóu Chángdì Inn
INN $

(福裕楼常棣客栈, Fúyù Lóu Chángdì Kèzhàn; ☑1379 9097 962, 0597-553 2800; www.fuyulou.com; Hóngkēng Tǔlóu Cluster; d incl breakfast ¥100-150; 🛜) The English-speaking owners are very welcoming at the Chángdì Inn. Fans and TVs in the basic rooms don't hurt either. Other bonuses include cold beer, a lending library and bike rental.

Tǔlóu Sunshine International Youth Hostel
HOSTEL $

(土楼沐浴阳光国际青年旅舍, Tǔlóu Mùyù Yángguāng Guójì Qīngnián Lǚshè; ☑777 1348; Tǎxià village; dm/d¥45/140; @🛜) Part converted *tǔlóu*, part newly built premises, this HI-affiliated hostel is very friendly and far simpler to negotiate than Tǎxià family life. Dorms are clean and very presentable. Carpooling and bike rental can be arranged. Follow the HI signs after you get off the bus at Xueying bridge (雪英桥; Xuěyīng Qiáo) in Tǎxià.

Qìngdé Lóu
INN $

(庆德楼; ☑1890 6951 868, ext 777; Tǎxià Village; d¥138-168; ❀🛜) Beautiful lantern-lit nights await in this modern rectangular compound. The 30 modern rooms have air-con and wi-fi. Upstairs rooms are cheaper, but you share a bathroom.

Yúqìng Lóu
INN $

(余庆楼; Chūxī, 永定县下洋镇初溪村; d ¥110-150, f ¥220) Built in 1729, this *tǔlóu* with two concentric wings is now a guesthouse. The family room is handy for some.

Qiáofú Lóu
INN $

(侨福楼; Gāobĕi Tŭlóu Cluster; r from ¥100) This modern *tŭlóu* in the Gāobĕi Tŭlóu Cluster was constructed in 1962 and houses 90 rooms across three levels. Decent sleeping arrangements are available.

Dōngfú Hotel
BUSINESS HOTEL $

(东福酒店, Dōngfú Jiŭdiàn; ☑ 0597 583 0668; 1-2 Wenquan Lu, Yŏngdìng; d ¥150) On a roundabout close to the Yŏngdìng bus station, this helpful business hotel offers a pleasant alternative to the earthy roundhouses. Rooms are neat and tidy and very comfortable.

Défēng Lóu
INN $$

(德风楼; ☑ 0597 775 6669; d ¥130-162; ❄ 🛜) The *tŭlóu* with the big red star above the entrance is a reliable place to stay. As the villagers move out, the tourists move in, partly for the en suite bathrooms. It's conveniently located near the bridge to the Yúnshuĭyáo Tŭlóu Cluster and all buses stop in front of it.

❶ Information

Amazing Fujian Tulou (www.amazingfujian tulou.com) is a Bĕijīng-based company that organises English-speaking tours to the *tŭlóu* areas in Fújiàn. Bookings can be made online. Group tours start at US$140 per person per day.

❶ Getting There & Away

From Xiàmén's **Húbīn long-distance bus station** (p343), take a bus headed to Nánjìng (¥32, two hours, 12 daily from 7am to 5.30pm). Upon arrival, you can either take the respective buses to some of the clusters, or hire a private vehicle to take you there.

Xiàmén has buses to Yŏngdìng (永定县; ¥75, four hours, seven daily) between 7.10am and 4pm, from where there are infrequent buses to Gāobĕi Tŭlóu Cluster. Yŏngdìng can also be accessed by bus from Guăngdōng and Lóngyán (¥20, one hour, regular).

Ten high-speed D trains link Xiàmén and Lóngyán via Nánjìng (¥27, 35 minutes) daily. Local buses 1 and 2 link the train and bus stations in Nánjìng.

❶ Getting Around

The easiest way to see the *tŭlóu* is to book a tour, or hire a vehicle either from Xiàmén, Nánjìng or Yŏngdìng. You'll find taxi drivers in Yŏngdìng and Nánjìng offering their services for around ¥500 a day (¥800 if you hire for two days), setting off early morning and returning late afternoon. Expect to see two clusters per day.

If you book a place to stay in one of the *tŭlóu*, most owners can help with transport and they usually arrange pick-up from Nánjìng or Yŏngdìng.

Quánzhōu
泉州

📞 0595 / POP 1.2 MILLION

The role of Quánzhōu as an integral part of the maritime Silk Road during Song and Yuan rule is still felt in the city's architecture, cuisine and ethnic diversity. Today it's a handsome, if grossly undervisited place – due partly to the lure of nearby Xiàmén – but what Marco Polo described in the 13th century as 'one of the two ports in the world with the biggest flow of merchandise' does not easily fade away.

Wandering Quánzhōu's ancient stone streets and temples of many faiths creates a rare sense of timelessness in urban China. Hints of a rich Islamic and maritime past are readily visible, and the atmosphere at times feels like a city further west. There are also easy day trips from here to the fascinating historic villages of Chongwu and Xunpu which have long faced out towards the sea.

◉ Sights

Guāndì Temple
TAOIST TEMPLE

(关帝庙, Guāndì Miào; Tumen Jie, 涂门街) FREE This smoky and magnificently carved temple is southeast of Qīngjìng Mosque. A furnace burns prayer books stuffed in by devotees. It's dedicated to Guan Yu, a Three Kingdoms general who was deified as the God of War. Inside the temple are statues of the god and wall panels that detail his life. Busy merchants gather outside.

Língshān Islamic Cemetery
CEMETERY

(灵山伊斯兰教圣墓, Língshān Yīsīlán Shèngmù; cnr Donghu Lu & Lingshan Lu, 在东湖路与灵山路的路口) Set at the foot of the mountain of Língshān, this leafy cemetery is one of the most intact historic cemeteries in China. Two of Mohammed's disciples are said to be buried here, and you'll also find some granite steles dating from the Míng dynasty. Take bus 7 or 203 and hop off at Shèngmùzhàn (圣墓站).

Maritime Museum
MUSEUM

(泉州海外交通史博物馆, Quánzhōu Hăiwài Jiāotōngshĭ Bówùguăn; Donghu Lu, 东湖路; ⊙ 8.30am-5.30pm Tue-Sun) FREE On the northeast side of town, this fabulous museum explains Quánzhōu's trading history, the development of Chinese shipbuilding and the kaleidoscope of religions in the port's heyday. The Religious Stone Hall and Islamic Culture Hall are highlights, boasting a beautiful collection of gravestones and reliefs of different religions dating from the Yuan dynasty. Take bus 7 or 203 and alight at Qiáoxiāng Tǐyùguǎn (侨乡体育馆).

Kāiyuán Temple
BUDDHIST SITE

(开元寺, Kāiyuán Sì; 176 Xi Jie, 西街176号; ¥10; ⏱7.30am-7pm) In the northwest of the city, one of the oldest temples in Quánzhōu dates back to AD 686. Surrounded by trees, Kāiyuán Temple is famed for its pair of rust-coloured five-storey stone pagodas, stained with age and carved with figures, which date from the 13th century. Behind the eastern pagoda is a **museum** containing the enormous hull of a Song dynasty seagoing junk, which was excavated near Quánzhōu in 1974.

Confucius Temple
CONFUCIAN TEMPLE

(府文庙, Fǔwén Miào; Zhongshan Zhonglu, 鲤城区中山中路) [FREE] A living relic of the Song dynasty built in 976 and the largest Confucian Temple in southern China.

Jǐnxiùzhuāng Puppet Museum
MUSEUM

(锦绣庄木偶艺术馆, Jǐnxiùzhuāng Mù'ǒu Yìshùguǎn; 10-12 Houcheng Jie, 后城街10-12号; ⏱9am-9pm) [FREE] A very simple museum behind Tumen Jie displaying puppet heads, intricate 30-string marionettes and comical hand puppets. Shows run intermittently.

Qīngjìng Mosque
MOSQUE

(清净寺, Qīngjìng Sì; 108 Tumen Jie, 涂门街108号; ¥3; ⏱8am-5.30pm) Built by the Arabs in 1009 and restored in 1309, this stone edifice is one of China's only surviving mosques from the Song dynasty. Only a few sections (mainly walls) of the original building survive, largely in ruins. The adjacent mosque is a donation from the government of Saudi Arabia.

✦ Festivals & Events

Lantern Festival
CULTURAL

The Lantern Festival is celebrated on the 15th day of the first lunar month. Streets in downtown Quánzhōu swell with people after dark, flashing their glow sticks or lanterns and marching to **Tiānhòu Temple** (天后宫, Tiānhòu Gōng; 1 Nanmen Tianhou Lu, 南门天后路1号; ⏱9am-5pm) [FREE] to pray for prosperity.

🛏 Sleeping

There are plenty of nondescript midrange hotels along Wenling Nanlu heading north, as well as some decent accommodation near

Quánzhōu

the old town. The high-end options are also excellent value; enquire about discounts.

54 Coffee Inn
GUESTHOUSE $

(泉州新街54咖啡客栈, Quánzhōu Xīnjiē Wǔshísì Kāfēi Kèzhàn; ☑0595-2287 5167; 54 Xin Jie, 新街 54号; dm ¥85, s & d ¥158-178; ❀🛜) It's worth the effort to seek out this welcoming red-brick building managed by two friendly women. The four-bed dormitory is excellent value, while the courtyard is a great place to meet other China travellers. The entrance to the unmarked Xin Jie is on Xi Jie, about 150m west of the intersection at Zhongshan Zhonglu. From there, walk north for another 150m and the guesthouse is to your right.

Tíhò Cafe & Hostel
HOSTEL $

(堤后咖啡客栈, Tíhòu Kāfēi Kèzhàn; ☑1865 9009 055, 0595-2239 0800; caimj@126.com; 114 Tihou Lu, 堤后路114号; dm ¥50, s & d ¥108-158; ❀@🛜) A little quirk goes a long way in Quánzhōu's fairly routine hotel scene, so this place is a welcome sight for independent travellers. Located at the western edge of the old town, the six-bed mixed dorm here is small but clean. Private rooms sport unusual furniture choices, but most of your time will

---

NÁNYĪN: THE SOUL MUSIC OF QUÁNZHŌU

The square in front of Confucius Temple (p351) on Tumen Jie is one of the busiest spots in Quánzhōu during daytime, but once the sun sets, amateur and professional musicians start to gather to practise Nányīn (南音), one of the oldest music genres in China.

The music of Nányīn can be traced as early as Han dynasty, and it was inscribed onto the Unesco Representative List of Intangible Cultural Heritage in 2009. These slow, haunting melodies are performed with Chinese musical instruments like the bamboo flute, the Chinese lute (pipa) as well as other percussive instruments like clappers. Sometimes the music is purely instrumental, sometimes with ballad singing in the local dialect by a solo singer or by a quartet. The lyrics sung revolve around classical Chinese poems and Buddhist sutras.

The performance in front of Confucius Temple usually starts at 7pm every night. The shows are free.

---

be spent in the cool communal areas, sipping cappuccino and comparing purchases from the market.

Catch bus 40 (westbound) from the long-distance bus station and alight at Línzhāngmén (临漳门). A taxi from the train station and the centre of town is around ¥20.

Super 8 Hotel Creative Park
BUSINESS HOTEL $$

(泉州速8创意园店; ☑0595 2866 5100; service @bestchinahotel.com; Quanxiu Lu Lingtian 1, 丰泽区秀路领SHOW天地1号楼; r ¥250-300; P❀🛜) The Super 8 brand rarely disappoints and this new branch located in 'Live Show Wonderland' gives you a clean, warm, relatively quiet bed in the middle of a designated party zone about 2km southeast of the city centre. Check in and sleep it off.

Quánzhōu Humei Holiday Hotel
BUSINESS HOTEL $$

(泉州湖美假日酒店, Quánzhōu Húměi Jiàrì Jiǔdiàn; ☑0595 6531-8858; Wenling Nanlu, 温陵南路; d ¥215-225; P❀🛜) The former Lake Hotel retains its great location, while a recent makeover has given the small rooms a sense of colour and style beyond the business basics, especially in the bathrooms. Service is commendably earnest.

Jīnjiāng Hotel
HOTEL $$

(锦江之星旅馆, Jīnjiāng Zhīxīng Lǚguǎn; ☑2815 6355; 359 Wenling Beilu, 温陵北路359号; tw/d ¥176/189; ❀@🛜) Not many midrange chain hotels are as good value as this one. It's opposite a fine park and there are good restaurants in the neighbourhood. All rooms are large and the bathrooms sparkle.

Wàndá Vista Quánzhōu
HOTEL $$$

(泉州万达文华酒店, Quánzhōu Wàndá Wénhuá Jiǔdiàn; ☑0595-6829 8888; www.wandahotels. com; 719 Baozhou Lu, 宝洲路719号; d ¥1288-1588; ❀@🛜) Located at the southern edge of Quánzhōu's city centre, the Wàndá Vista looks like a Las Vegas mall from the outside, but inside it's more like a shiny craps table. Rooms on the upper floors have good views of Jīnjiāng River, though, and all are huge. The buffet comes highly recommended.

C & D Quanzhou Hotel
HOTEL $$$

(泉州悦华酒店, ☑0595-2801 9999; www.yeohwa hotels.com; 129 Citong Xilu, 刺桐西路129号; d ¥1650-2200; ❀@🛜) The name has changed but the C & D is still the best hotel in the city, with four restaurants, a complete spa and friendly English-speaking staff. Generous rack-rate discounts will please tired travellers. It's about 2km southeast of the centre.

🍴 Eating

You can find the usual noodle and rice dishes served in the back lanes around Kāiyuán Temple (p351) and also along the food street close to Wenling Nanlu.

Ānjì Kèjiāwáng HAKKA $$
(安记客家王; 461 Tumen Jie; meals from ¥50; ⊙11am-9pm) The Ān family are well known across town for their Cantonese-style dim sum, which sneaks a few Hakka delights onto the trolley. The *xiāmǐ chángfěn* (虾米肠粉; shrimp in rice paper) and *xián dànjuǎn* (咸蛋卷; salty egg rolls) will do just nicely thanks.

Lánshì Zhōnglóu HAKKA $$
(蓝氏钟楼肉粽; 9-21 Dong Jie; meals from ¥25; ⊙11am-9.30pm) In an area flush with eateries, this Hakka favourite draws a return crowd for its honest, affordable fare. The signature *hēimǐzòng* (黑米粽; black rice dumplings) and *dànhuángzòng* (蛋黄粽; rice dumpling with yolk) are recommended by staff for a reason. There's another branch in Xiàmén.

🍷 Drinking & Nightlife

New Overseas Chinese Village west of Zhōngshān Park and **Yuanhe 1916 Idea Land** on Xinmen Jie are like the many designated 'party' areas in Fújiàn, full of old houses turned into cafes, bars and restaurants. Young people are often out in abundance here.

Gǔcuò Cháfáng TEAHOUSE
(古厝茶坊; 44 Houcheng Xiang; tea ¥50-480, snacks from ¥20; ⊙9am-1am) Curious travellers will find many answers in the alley behind Guāndì Temple, often provided by smiling old men reading poems and playing games in this classic Chinese teahouse. Pull up a bamboo chair on the flagstone floor and slow right down for the afternoon.

The Brickyard BEER GARDEN
(📱0595 6043 1105; Quanxiu Lu, 丰泽区乐其道 6号101; 🛜📶) Every midsized Chinese city has a place where expats go to meet up and whinge about living in a midsized Chinese city. Quánzhōu has the Brickyard, and it's absolutely fantastic. Heaps of beers on tap, reliable pub food and an atmosphere convivial enough to make you want to pack it in and make the nearby-sea change.

ⓘ Information

Bank of China (中国银行, Zhōngguó Yínháng; 9 Jiuyi Jie, 九一街9号; ⊙9am-5pm) Has a 24-hour ATM.

China Post (中国邮政, Zhōngguó Yóuzhèng; cnr Dong Jie & Nanjun Lu, 在东街与南骏路的路口; ⊙8.30am-6pm) Sells stamps and postcards.

Public Security Bureau (PSB, 公安局, Gōng'ānjú; 📱2218 0323; 62 Dong Jie, 东街62号; ⊙ visa section 8-11.30am & 2.30-5.30pm) You can extend your visa here.

Quánzhōu Xiéhé Hospital (泉州协和医院; Quánzhōu Xiéhé Yīyuàn, Tian'an Nanlu, 天安南路) In the southern part of town.

ⓘ Getting There & Away

BUS
Both **Quánzhōu bus station** (泉州汽车站, Quánzhōu Qìchēzhàn; cnr Wenling Nanlu & Quanxiu Jie) and the **long-distance bus station** (泉州客运中心站, Quánzhōu Kèyùn Zhōngxīnzhàn; cnr Quanxiu Jie & Pingshan Lu) further east along Quanxiu Jie have buses to the following destinations:

Guǎngzhōu ¥250, seven hours, four daily

Shēnzhèn ¥280, eight hours, four daily

Regular deluxe buses:
Fúzhōu ¥70, 2½ hours

Xiàmén ¥37, 1½ hours

TRAIN
D trains depart from the high-speed train station (高铁泉州站; Gāotiě Quánzhōu Zhàn), 15km from the town centre:

Fúzhōu ¥55, one hour, half-hourly

Shànghǎi ¥307, 8½ hours, 12 daily

Xiàmén ¥21, 45 minutes, half-hourly

In town, train tickets can be bought at the **Wenling Nanlu ticket office** (铁路火车票代售点, Tiělù Huǒchēpiào Dàishòudiǎn; 166 Wenling Nanlu, 温岭南路166号; ⊙9am-6pm) or from the **ticket office** (火车售票亭, Huǒchē Shòupiàotíng; 675 Quanxiu Jie, 泉秀街675号; ⊙7am-6pm) just east of the long-distance bus station. There's a ¥5 booking fee.

ⓘ Getting Around
Buses 17 and K1 run from the high-speed train station to Quánzhōu bus station and the long-distance bus station respectively, via Zhōnglóu (钟楼), the intersection of Zhongshan Zhonglu and Xijie. Bus 203 links the train station to Maritime Museum and Islamic Cemetery. A taxi from the centre of town to the train station costs ¥50. Local bus 15 links both bus stations. Bus 2 goes from the bus station to Kāiyuán Temple. Taxi flag fall is ¥7, then ¥1.80 per kilometre.

FÚJIÀN AROUND QUÁNZHŌU

Around Quánzhōu

Chóngwǔ 崇武

☎ 0595 / POP 50,000

One of the best-preserved city walls in China can be found in the ancient 'stone city' of Chóngwǔ. The granite walls date back to 1387, stretch over 2.5km and average 7m in height. Scattered around the walls are 1304 battlements and four gates into the city.

The town wall was built by the Ming government as a frontline defence against marauding Japanese pirates, and it has survived the past 600 years remarkably well. You can also walk along the top of the wall at some points.

If your interest here is solely architectural, enter the old town through a narrow gate roughly 200m before the ticketed entrance. From there you can weave your way past intact 14th-century houses and up towards the wall. Adjacent to the old town is **Chóngwǔ Stone Arts Expo Park** (崇武石雕工艺博览园, Chóngwǔ Shídiāo Gōngyì Bólǎnyuán; ¥45). It is filled with 500 stone sculptures made by local craftspeople, a small beach, a lighthouse and some basic seafood restaurants. The open spaces and clean ocean air make it worth the effort, especially if you have kids.

There are a handful of decent hotels within walking distance or a short taxi ride of the old city, but most travellers make day trips from Quánzhōu. It was a bit of a building site when we visited **West Gulf Holiday Hotel** (湾假日酒店, Wān Jiàrì Jiǔdiàn; ☎ 0595 2787 7777; www.xswhotel.com; r ¥440-680; P ❄ ☎ ☲) – Holiday Inn has moved in and renovated – but the beautiful ocean views, three-star hotel rooms, friendly service and convenient access to the old town lift the hotel into its own, somewhat uncompetitive, category.

The strip of cafes adjacent to the old city serve congee with crab meat (¥20), while many vendors inside the park sell barbecued squid on sticks (¥10). There are comfortable, modern eateries frequented by a younger crowd on the pedestrian-only Xinhua Jie, which is about 2km west of the old town.

Frequent buses depart Quánzhōu's long-distance bus station (¥13, 1½ hours), taking you past arrays of stone statues (the area is famed for its stone-carving workshop) before ending up in Chóngwǔ. Motorbikes (¥5) will take you from the bus drop-off to the stone city. From Chóngwǔ,

it's best to take the a return bus Quánzhōu where numerous connections are available.

Xúnpǔ Village 蟳埔村

The fishing village of Xúnpǔ, some 10km southeast of the city centre of Quánzhōu, was on the old trade route of the maritime Silk Road and was perhaps the Arabs' first port of call when they set foot in Quánzhōu during the Song dynasty. The village, now under encroaching urbanisation, is still fascinating and you'll find some old houses built with oyster shells behind the main road in the village and older women still wearing flamboyant traditional head ornaments.

The **Māzǔ Temple** (妈祖庙; Māzǔ Miào) on the knoll in the village is the local centre of worship. It's dedicated to the goddess of seafarers and turns very lively on the 29th day of the first lunar calendar month, the birthday of the protector. All the women in the village turn out in traditional costumes to join in the annual Māzǔ procession. A taxi from Quánzhōu bus station is about ¥25.

Cǎo'ān Manichaean Temple 草庵摩尼教寺

This **temple** (Cǎo'ān Móníjiào Sì; Huábiǎo Hill, 华表山; ¥20; ⊙8am-6pm) is dedicated to Manichaeism, a religion originating in Persia in the 3rd century, combining elements of Zoroastrian, Christian and Gnostic thought, which reached China in the 7th century.

The well restored stone complex you see today is a rebuild dating to the Yuan dynasty (14th century). The most remarkable relic in the temple is the 'Buddha of Light', a sitting stone statue in the main hall, which is actually the prophet Mani, founder of Manichaeism, in a Buddhist disguise.

Manichaeism was considered an illegal religion during the Song period and the religion had to operate in the guise of an esoteric Buddhist group. Take a closer look at the statue, and you'll find its hairstyle (straight instead of curly), hand gestures and colour combinations are distinctly different from most representations of the Buddha.

The temple is 19km south of Quánzhōu. From the long-distance bus station in Quánzhōu, board a bus to Ānhǎi (安海; ¥12) and tell the driver to drop you off at Cǎo'ān Lùkǒu (草庵路口). Then look for the English signage saying Grass Temple and it's a 2km walk uphill. The road is not well marked so taking a taxi is a recommended alternative; a taxi from Quánzhōu is around ¥65.

Fúzhōu 福州

☎ 0591 / POP 2.1 MILLION

Fúzhōu is a handsome provincial capital most often passed through en route to other destinations in southern China. Its tea culture is renowned, though, and you'll find plenty of purveyors along the banks of the Minjiang River. A short trip to the west lies Gu Mountain and its delightful, accessible hiking paths.

Sights

★ Sānfāng Qīxian ARCHITECTURE

(三坊七巷; Yangqiao Donglu & Nánhou Jie, 杨桥东路) The 'downtown' area of the city is actually a series of ancient residential buildings known as 'Three Lanes and Seven Paths'. Constructed in the late Jin dynasty around the 12th century, the residences prospered 400 years later during Ming and then Qing rule. Today thousands of visitors wander through the white-walled streets every day, from the traditional architecture to the hectic shopping strip on Nanhou Jie, and take a break at a cafe on the canal. A taxi here from the south long-distance bus station costs around ¥25.

Linzexu Memorial Hall MUSEUM

(福州林则徐纪念馆, Fúzhōu Línzéxú Jìniàn Guǎn; ☎0591 8762 2782; www.linzexu.cn; 16 Aomen Lu, 澳门路16号; ¥30; ⊙8.30am-5.30pm Mon-Sun) The former residence of the anti-opium trade reformer is a surprisingly well presented museum. It offers an overview of Fuzhou's seafaring history, attractive gardens and courtyards to escape the busy weekend foot traffic.

Jade Hill Scenic Area PARK

(于山风景区, Yú Shān Fēngjǐngqū) This rocky hill park in the centre of Fúzhōu rises above a snow-white **statue of Mao Zedong** playing 'traffic cop'. Check out the seven-storey **White Pagoda**, built in AD 904. At the foot of Jade Hill are the remains of Fúzhōu's **Ming dynasty city wall**; originally boasting seven gates, the wall was pulled down for road widening.

Sleeping

Hǎixī Hostel HOSTEL $

(海西青年旅舍, Hǎixī Qīngnián Lǚshè; ☎0591 8364 4944; 39 Meixian Jie, Tatou Lu, 塔头路梅仙街39号; s from ¥65) This friendly hostel in the eastern part of the city is terrific value. Beds are new and firm, while each dormitory has writing desks and small bedside tables. Bike rental is available. The vine-covered entrance is tucked away next to a busy market.

7 Days Inn HOTEL $

(7天, Qītiān; ☎0591-8803 8377; www.7daysinn.cn; 98 Wuyi Nanlu, 五一南路98号; r ¥150-190; ❄@) This hugely popular chain has a decent branch 500m south of the south long-distance bus station. Reception is friendly and staff speak some English. The university hall–style rooms are all spotless.

Jùchūnyuán Inn Fuzhou HOTEL $$

(福州聚春园驿馆, Fúzhōu Jùchūnyuán Yìguǎn; ☎0591-6303 3888; 22 Gong Xiang, Sānfáng Qīxiàn, 三坊七巷宫巷22号; d ¥435-515; ⊖❄@📶) A beautiful inn housed in a historic mansion in the pedestrianised Sānfáng Qīxiàn area. All 56 rooms are tastefully and modernly appointed.

Intercontinental Fúzhōu LUXURY HOTEL $$$

(福州世茂洲际酒店, Fúzhōu Shìmào Zhōujì Jiǔdiàn; ☎0591-8612 8888; www.ihg.com; 108 Guangda Lu, 广达路108号; r from ¥1000, f ¥1300; P❄📶🏊) The tallest building in town is a classic five-star number with a stunning breakfast buffet and gym. The family suites are excellent value.

Shangri-La Hotel HOTEL $$$

(香格里拉大酒店, Xiānggélǐlā Dàjiǔdiàn; ☎0591-8798 8888; www.shangri-la.com; 9 Xinquan Nanlu, 新权南路9号; d ¥1450; ❄@📶🏊) Overlooking Wuyi Square, this hotel is the finest in Fúzhōu. The swimming pool, lobby and breakfast spread live up to the brand's reputation. The suites are good value when discounts apply. A cab from the south long-distance bus station is around ¥25.

Eating

Sānfáng Qīxiàn is by far the most atmospheric area to eat out in Fúzhōu. Its narrow laneways and Ming-style houses have been impeccably maintained, while stylish cafes line small canals. You'll find small eateries on both sides of Nanhou Jie (南后街), which also fills with shoppers on weekends.

Shíjǐnzhāi VEGETARIAN $

(食锦斋; ☎0591-8751 5500; 332 Tatou Lu, 福清市石竹山道院内332; mains ¥20-30; ⊙9.30am-9pm Mon-Sun; 🌱) This reputable, 20-year old vegetarian restaurant has a welcoming outdoor area and a variety of mock-meat dishes. It gets busy with workers at lunchtime. It's about 2km east of Sānfāng Qīxian.

30ml Coffee Studio CAFE $$

(☎0591 8789 1230; Yushuanjian Xiang, 号闽发西湖广场楼号店; snacks ¥35-45; ⊙9am-9pm; 📶) Near the corner of 'Seven Alleys', on the edge of the canal, 30ml is almost too cool for Fúzhōu. Here you'll find delicious coffee (¥28-32), cake, chicken wings, imported fruit beer and the diverse sounds of Cash, Cook, Dylan et al. Reasonable English spoken, with a Chinese sensibility.

ⓘ Getting There & Away

AIR

Fúzhōu airport is 45km southeast of the city centre and has daily flights to Běijīng (¥1700, 2½ hours), Guǎngzhōu (¥900, one hour), Shànghǎi (¥800, 70 mins) and Hong Kong (¥1400, 80 mins).

Airport buses leave from at least three locations in town: the Apollo Hotel (阿波罗大酒店; Ābōluó Dàjiǔdiàn; ¥25) on Wuyi Zhonglu, 400m north of the south long-distance bus station, has departures every 20 minutes between 5.30am and 10pm; the north long-distance bus station (¥25) near the North Rail Station has departures every hour between 6am and 8pm; the South Rail Station has departures every hour between 12pm and 5pm. The trip takes about an hour.

BUS

The **north long-distance bus station** (长途汽车北站; Chángtú Qìchē Běizhàn; 317 Hualin Lu, 华林路317号) is 400m south of the North Rail Station. Services include the following:

Guǎngzhōu ¥320, 12 hours, seven daily
Quánzhōu ¥70, two hours, regular
Shànghǎi ¥310, 10 hours, two daily
Wǔyí Shān ¥100, eight hours, 5.30pm
Xiàmén ¥105, 3½ hours, every 20 minutes

The **south long-distance bus station** (长途汽车南站; Chángtú Qìchē Nánzhàn; cnr Guohuo Xilu & Wuyi Zhonglu, 在国货西路与五一中路的路口) services the following destinations:

Guǎngzhōu ¥270, 13 hours, eight daily
Hong Kong ¥404, 15 hours, four daily
Shēnzhèn ¥340, 12 hours, five daily
Xiàmén ¥115, 3½ hours, every 15 minutes

TRAIN

Fúzhōu has a good network of trains to many major cities. D trains sometimes leave from the more centrally located **North Rail Station** (福州北站, Fúzhōu Běizhàn; 502 Hualin Lu, 华林路502号), but more often from the **South Rail Station** (福州南站; Fúzhōu Nánzhàn; East of

---

ⓘ GETTING TO TAIWAN

A ferry departs from Fúzhōu's Máwěi ferry terminal (马尾码头; Máwěi Mǎtóu) to Taiwan's archipelago of Matzu (马祖; Mázǔ). The boat leaves at 11am, takes about 1½ hours and costs ¥150.

Lulei Village, Canshan District), 17km southeast of the town centre:

Běijīng ¥719 to ¥765, 7½ to 10½ hours, six daily
Quánzhōu ¥55, one hour, half-hourly
Shànghǎi ¥333, 6½ hours, 16 daily
Wǔyí Shān ¥174, five to 6½ hours, seven daily
Xiàmén ¥80, 1½ hours, every 15 minutes

Wǔyí Shān 武夷山

☏ 0599 / POP 230,000

Despite a long association with domestic travellers, Wǔyí Shān is a mountain retreat which retains a sense of untouched natural splendour. Set high up in the northwest of Fújiàn, its hiking trails through protected forests and the famed bamboo rafting trip are well worth the effort to come here. Try to visit midweek or in low season (November, March and April) and you might have the area to yourself. Avoid the area during heavy rain (especially during summer months) even if the hotels and tour organisers advise otherwise.

The scenic part lies on the west bank of Chóngyáng Stream (Chóngyáng Xī). The main settlement is Wǔyí Shān city, about 10km to the northeast, with the train station and airport roughly halfway in between.

⊙ Sights

Wǔyí Shān Scenic Area PARK
(武夷宫; 1-/2-/3-day access ¥140/150/160; ⊙7am-5pm) The entrance to the Wǔyí Shān Scenic Area is at Wǔyí Gōng, about 200m south of the Wǔyí Mountain Villa. Trails within the scenic area connect all the major sites. Good walks include the 530m **Great King Peak** (大王峰; Dàwáng Fēng), accessed through the main entrance, and the 410m **Heavenly Tour Peak** (天游峰; Tiānyóu Fēng), where an entrance is reached by road up the Nine Twists River.

It's a moderate two-hour walk to Great King Peak among bamboo groves and steep-cut rock walls. The trail can be slippery and wet, so bring suitable shoes.

The walk to Heavenly Tour Peak is more scenic, with better views of the river and mountain peaks. But the path is also the most popular with tour groups. At the northern end of the scenic area, the **Water Curtain Cave** (水帘洞; Shuǐlián Dòng) is a cleft in the rock about one-third of the way up a 100m cliff face. In winter and autumn, water plunges over the top of the cliff, creating a curtain of spray.

Xiàméi

VILLAGE

(下梅; ¥60) This village dates to the Northern Song dynasty and boasts some spectacular Qing dynasty architecture from its heyday as a wealthy tea-trading centre. Motorbikes in Wǔyí Shān city can take you to Xiàméi (¥50 round trip) for this 12km journey.

🏃 Activities

Nine Twists River

RAFTING

(九曲溪, Jiǔqū Xī; boat rides ¥120; ⊙7am-5pm) One of the highlights for visitors to Wǔyí Shān is floating down the river on *zhúpái* (bamboo rafts) fitted with rattan chairs. Departing from Xīngcūn (星村), a short bus ride west of the resort area, the trip down the river takes over an hour and brings you through some magnificent gorge scenery, with sheer rock cliffs and lush green vegetation.

🛏 Sleeping

Most of the accommodation in Wǔyí Shān is in the midrange category and most is overpriced unless you come here during low season. Hotels are mostly on the eastern side of the river, while family-run guesthouses and hostels are in the village of Lántáng on the relatively quieter western side. The village is 700m north of Wǔyí Mountain Villa.

Wǔyíshān Shāncháhuā Youth Hostel

HOSTEL $

(武夷山山茶花青年旅舍, Wǔyíshān Shāncháhuā Qīngnián Lǚshè; ☑1890 5093 345, 0599 523 2345; wulifang21@yahoo.com.cn; 27 Sangu Lantangcun, 三菇兰汤村27号; 8-/4-bed dm ¥35/50, d ¥118-190; @) Situated on the west bank in the village of Sángū Lántáng, away from anything like action, our favourite hostel in the area is by no means impressive on arrival. But the 'Camellia' offers bucolic seclusion and good double rooms for the price. To get there, take bus 5, or take a taxi (about ¥30 to ¥40) from the train station.

Wǔyí Mountain Dàwáng Peak Youth Hostel

HOSTEL $

(武夷山大王峰青年旅舍, Wǔyíshān Dàwángfēng Qīngnián Lǚshè; ☑0599 520 9518; 46 Lantang Village, 兰汤村46号; dm ¥50, d ¥148-178; @ 🛜) Walking paths lead to the back door of this attractive hostel where independent travellers hang out below the gaze of a giant Che Guevara image. No revolution in the cramped dorms, but the mood is bright and the non-English-speaking staff are very accommodating. To get there, take bus 5, or pay about ¥30 to ¥40 for a taxi ride from the train station.

Elite Boutique Hotel

BOUTIQUE HOTEL $$

(逸精品酒店, Yìjīngpǐn Jiǔdiàn; ☑0599 520 6088; 1 Qingliang Xia, 武夷山三菇度假区清凉峡1号; r ¥310-510; 🌀 🛜) Excellent price for a clean, well appointed room and a perfectly adequate breakfast. It's ideally located at the southern gate to the park proper.

C & D Resort Wǔyí Mountain

HOTEL $$$

(武夷山悦华酒店; ☑0599 523 8999; www. yeohwahotels.com; Dawangfeng Lu, 大王峰路; s/d ¥748/848; 🌀 @ 🛜) New management have taken over at the flashest resort on the mountain. Expect the same couple of hundred five-star rooms, loads of tourists in high season, impeccable service and tremendous views of Great King Peak. You can take comfort in the on-site restaurants and rooms that are not expensive for the size.

ℹ Information

There are some grubby internet cafes in the back alleys south of Wangfeng Lu (望峰路), charging ¥3 to ¥4 an hour.

Chinese maps of the Scenic Area are available in bookshops and hotels in the resort district.

Bank of China (中国银行, Zhōngguó Yínháng; Wujiu Lu, 无爸路; ⊙9am-5pm) Has an ATM.

China International Travel Service (CITS, 中国国际旅行社, Zhōngguó Guójì Lǚxíngshè; ☑0599 5134 666, www.cits.net, Guolu Dalou, Sangu Jie; ⊙9am-4pm Mon-Sat) The staff can arrange train tickets and tours.

ℹ Getting There & Away

Wǔyí Shān's airport, about 15km south of the town and east of the mountain, has air links to several cities. A taxi should cost about ¥40 to either.

Běijīng ¥1350, two hours, two daily
Guǎngzhōu ¥890, 2½ hours, one daily
Shànghǎi ¥660, one hour, one daily
Xiàmén ¥720, 50 minutes, two daily

Buses run from the long-distance bus station in Wǔyí Shān city, about 1km west of the town.

Fúzhōu ¥174, five to six hours, two daily
Xiàmén ¥144 to ¥223, nine hours, four daily

Trains go to Wǔyí Shān from Quánzhōu (¥148, one to two hours, hourly) and Xiàmén (¥149 to ¥232, 12 hours, hourly).

ℹ Getting Around

Bus 6 links the long-distance bus station, train station, airport, resort area and Wǔyí Mountain Villa.

The resort area is small enough for you to walk everywhere. Expect to pay about ¥15 for a motorised trishaw from the resort district to most of the scenic area entrances. A ride from the train station or airport to the resort district will cost ¥30.

Shānxī

POP 35.7 MILLION

Best Places to Eat

➡ Fènglín Gé (p362)

➡ Dōngfāng Xiǎo Miàn (p362)

➡ Tónghé Dàfàndiàn (p363)

➡ Déjūyuán (p374)

Best Places to Sleep

➡ Jing's Residence (p374)

➡ Harmony Guesthouse (p374)

➡ Garden Hotel (p362)

➡ Déjūyuán Guesthouse (p374)

➡ Hongqi Hotel (p362)

Why Go?

Waist-deep in handsome history, Shānxī (山西) is home to an impressive roll-call of must-see, ancient sights. Most travellers start with the walled city of Píngyáo. Basing yourself here and jumping to the town's surrounding sights is practically all you need: you'll encounter time-worn temples, traditional Qing dynasty courtyard architecture, some of the warmest people in the Middle Kingdom and the opportunity for a day trip to the dizzying mountain cliffs and gorges of Mián Shān.

Travellers shouldn't overlook Dàtóng, a forward-thinking city with a brand-new city wall and a great-looking old town, but it's the astonishing cave sculptures at Yúngāng outside town that give expression to the province's other great source of magic: a rich vein of Buddhist heritage, which splendidly litters the rolling mountain vastness of Wǔtái Shān with temples. Add the still-inhabited cave dwellings of Lǐjiā Shān and vestiges of the Great Wall, and you could find yourself staying longer than planned.

When to Go
Dàtóng

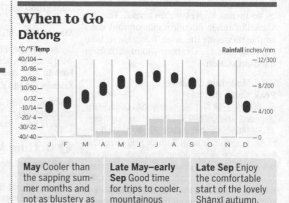

May Cooler than the sapping summer months and not as blustery as early spring.	**Late May–early Sep** Good time for trips to cooler, mountainous Wǔtái Shān.	**Late Sep** Enjoy the comfortable start of the lovely Shānxī autumn.

Shānxī Highlights

1 Píngyáo (p371)
Wandering the cobblestone ancient streets of this time-warped, walled town.

2 Yúngāng Caves (p363) Discovering the grandeur of these magnificent Buddhist statues.

3 Dàtóng (p360)
Checking out the lavish restoration of the city wall and the old town.

4 Wǔtái Shān (p365) Hanging up your traveller's hat in this scenic and mountainous monastic enclave.

5 Guōyù (p378)
Journeying to this still-inhabited historical walled village in Shānxī's remote southeast.

6 Lǐjiā Shān (p377) Experiencing 'old' China with an overnight stay at the Ming-dynasty cave village.

7 Mián Shān (p375) Hiking among the sublime and vertigo-inducing scenery on this magnificent mountain.

8 Shuānglín Temple (p376)
Admiring some of China's most ancient in situ temple statuary.

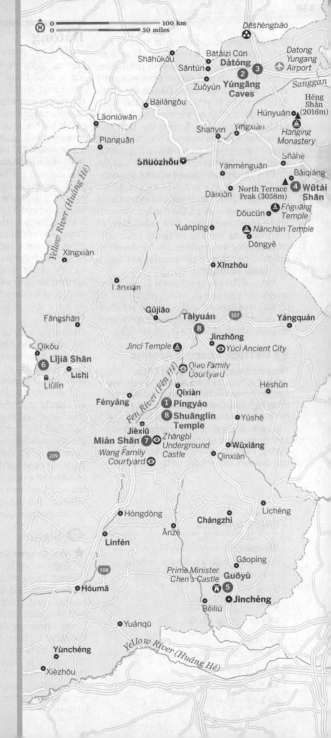

History

Though home to the powerful state of Jin, which split into three in 403 BC, Shānxī really only rose to greatness with the Tuoba, a clan of the Xianbei people from Mongolia and Manchuria who made Dàtóng their capital during the Northern Wei (AD 386–534). Eventually the Tuoba were assimilated, but as China weakened following the Tang collapse, the northern invaders returned; most notable were the Khitan (907–1125), whose western capital was also in Dàtóng.

After the Ming regained control of northern China, Shānxī was developed as a defensive outpost, with an inner and outer Great Wall constructed along the northern boundaries. Local merchants took advantage of the increased stability to trade, eventually transforming the province into the country's financial centre with the creation of China's first banks in Píngyáo.

Today Shānxī is best known for its many mines; the province contains one-third of all China's coal deposits and parts of it are heavily polluted, while Dàtóng has experienced an astonishing, if controversial, facelift.

ℹ️ Getting There & Around

There are airports at Dàtóng and Tàiyuán, with flights to cities across China. Tàiyuán and Píngyáo are connected to Běijīng and other cities by high-speed rail, while long-distance buses run to neighbouring provinces and further afield.

Modern railway lines and roads split Shānxī on a northeast–southwest axis, so getting between Dàtóng, Tàiyuán and Píngyáo is no problem, with long-distance buses taking up the slack.

PRICE RANGES

Sleeping
Prices for a double room with private bathroom or shower room:

$ less than ¥200

$$ ¥200–¥500

$$$ more than ¥500

Eating
Prices for a main dish at a restaurant:

$ less than ¥30

$$ ¥30–¥60

$$$ more than ¥60

Dàtóng 大同

📞 0352 / POP 3.3 MILLION

Dàtóng today is fascinating, and charming to boot. Come night-time, the old-town sensations – with red lanterns swinging in the breeze and wind chimes tinkling on the illuminated city walls – are hard to beat. Most of this has been re-created from scratch by an overambitious mayor: a mountain of cash – an estimated ¥50 billion – has been ploughed into a colossal renovation of the old quarter. The city wall has been rebuilt in its entirety (well, almost) and the city has shown how it can cut it with other drawcard cities such as Hángzhōu and Xī'ān. What's more, the town is the gateway to the awe-inspiring Yúngāng Caves, one of China's most outstanding Buddhist treasures. Dàtóng is also a launchpad to the photogenic Hanging Monastery, the world's oldest wooden pagoda, crumbling earthen sections of the Great Wall and onward trips to sacred Wǔtái Shān.

History

Dàtóng has long held a strategic position on the edge of the Mongolian grasslands, first rising to greatness as the capital of the Tuoba. A federation of Turkic-speaking nomads who united northern China (AD 386–534) and converted to Buddhism, the Tuoba were eventually assimilated into Chinese culture (like most other invaders). The Tuoba established the Northern Wei dynasty, whose greatest achievement here was the Yúngāng Caves, a collection of sublime 5th-century Buddhist carvings that capture a quiet, timeless and evocative beauty. The dynastic capital was later moved to Luòyáng in Hénán province and the rock carving continued at the astonishing Lóngmén Grottoes.

◉ Sights

★ **Nine Dragon Screen** WALLS
(九龙壁, Jiǔlóng Bì; Da Dongjie, 大东街; ¥10; ⊙8am-6.30pm) With its nine beautiful multicoloured coiling dragons, this 45.5m-long, 8m-high and 2m-thick Ming dynasty spirit wall was built in 1392. One of the finest in China (there are two more in Běijīng), it's the largest glazed-tile *yǐngbì* (影壁) spirit wall in China and is a truly amazing sight; the palace it once protected belonged to the 13th son of a Ming emperor and burnt down in 1644. Amazingly, the palace is being rebuilt in its entirety, covering a vast area of town.

Dàtóng

SHĀNXĪ DÀTÓNG

the west is still under construction. The wall is not the original, but looks sublime.

★ **Dài Wángfǔ** PALACE
(代王府) Originally built in 1392 but burned to the ground in a huge conflagration in 1644 during the last gasps of the Ming dynasty, this vast palace (191,000 sq metres) complex reaches all the way north from Da Dongjie to a street shy of the city walls. Under construction since 2011, all that survives of the original palace is the Nine Dragon Screen. The palace was still undergoing construction at the time of writing.

★ **China Sculpture Museum** GALLERY
(中国雕塑博物馆, Zhōngguó Diāosù Bówùguǎn; Da Beijie, 大北街; ◎8.30am-11.30am & 2.30-5.30pm Tue-Sun) FREE This cavernous museum is built within the north Wǔdìng Mén gate section of the restored city walls, with seemingly endless corridors of excellent contemporary sculpture by Chinese and foreign artists. When you get bored of looking at statues and photography, look out for uncovered sections of the original city walls at the very rear, dating from the Ming, Jin, Liao and Northern Wei dynasties. You will need your passport for admission.

Dàtóng Cathedral CHURCH
(大同天主堂, Dàtóng Tiānzhǔtáng; Lǐhuáijiǎo, 李怀角) This cathedral – also called the

Old Town
HISTORIC SITE
(老城区, Lǎochéngqū) Dàtóng's old town has been massively resurrected at colossal expense to put Dàtóng back on the map. The former mayor – now Tàiyuán's mayor – ploughed a fortune into trying to turn Dàtóng back into an old town (by rebuilding it). Sadly, and typical in China, a considerable amount of the original old town was levelled before being rebuilt. Nonetheless, what is on show is alluring, especially at night when lanterns delightfully illuminate the old town.

★ **Dàtóng City Wall** FORTRESS
(大同城墙, Dàtóng Chéngqiáng; ¥30; ◎8am-9.30pm) This incredible city wall has been rebuilt from the soles up in what must be one of the greatest feats of engineering to hit Dàtóng since, well, since the last time it was built. Prior to the rebuild, the wall had been denuded of bricks and reduced to earthen stumps. At present, you can only walk around three sides of the wall – the gate in

Cathedral of the Immaculate Heart of Mary – is an astonishing sight once you find it and stand before its twin bell towers. Built in 1891, the church was burned down on 13 July 1900 during the xenophobic and anti-Christian Boxer Rebellion, taking a few Catholics with it; it was rebuilt in 1906. Both bell towers were destroyed in 1966 during the Cultural Revolution, but the house of worship was repaired in 1982 and 2006.

Shànhuà Temple
BUDDHIST SITE

(善化寺, Shànhuà Sì; Nansi Jie, 南寺街; ¥40; ☺8am-6pm) Originally constructed in AD 713 and today standing just inside the magnificent and rebuilt city walls, Shànhuà Temple was rebuilt during the Jin dynasty. The grand wooden-bracketed hall at the rear contains five beautiful central Buddhas and expressive statues of celestial generals in the wings. Look out for the impressive and quite colossal turquoise, yellow and ochre five-dragon screen (五龙壁; wǔlóngbì). It stands outside the current temple perimeter, so is free to admire.

Huáyán Temple
BUDDHIST SITE

(华严寺, Huáyán Sì; Huayan Jie, 华严街; ¥80; ☺8am-6.30pm; ☒38) Built by the Khitan during the Liao dynasty (AD 907–1125), this temple faces east, not south (it's said the Khitan were sun worshippers) and is divided into two separate complexes. One of these is an active monastery (upper temple), while the other is a museum (lower temple). Dating to 1140, the impressive main hall of the **Upper Temple** (上华严寺; Shàng Huáyán Sì) is one of the largest Buddhist halls in China, with Ming murals and Qing statues within.

🛏 Sleeping

★ Green Island Youth Hostel
HOSTEL $

(绿岛青年旅舍, Lǜdǎo Qīngnián Lǚshě; ☒158 3524 4211; www.facebook.com/datongyouthhostel; 5th fl, block A, Jinhu Guoji building, 1029 Weidu Dadao, 魏都大道1029号金湖国际A座5层; dm ¥50-55, d ¥160-210; ❇☎) This new hostel in a huge tower block puts dorm beds and comfortable double rooms within an easy stroll of the train station; numerous buses trundle into the walled city not far away. The main common area is a bit small, but everything is neat and Simon the owner is helpful and friendly. It has excellent coffee too.

The entrance is at the rear of the building; go in and you will find a lift. The hostel can sort out ticketing and offers very handy travel tips. It's also very convenient for the

bus to the Yúngāng Caves (p363), which leaves from just outside.

★ Hongqi Hotel
HOTEL $$

(红旗饭店, Hóngqí Fàndiàn; ☒0352 536 6666, 0352 536 6111; www.hongqihotel.com; 11 Zhanqian Jie, 站前街11号; s & tw ¥380, ste ¥680-1288, all incl breakfast; ❇☎) This classic place opposite the train station has excellent rooms, drinkable tap water, fully equipped shower rooms with regularly restocked toiletries, very friendly staff and prices that regularly dip to a very attractive ¥218. The included buffet-style breakfast is also excellent, with a Western option provided.

★ Garden Hotel
HOTEL $$$

(花园大饭店, Huāyuán Dàfàndiàn; ☒0352 586 5888; www.gardenhoteldatong.com; 59 Da Nanjie, 大南街59号; d & tw incl breakfast ¥1080-1780, tw ¥1380-1580, ste ¥2880-3880; ❇❇@☎) The large impeccable rooms at this hotel feature goose-down quilts, carved rosewood bed frames, reproduction antique furnishings and superb bathrooms. There's an attractive atrium with a cafe lounge and fake palms, Latin American and Chinese restaurants, plus excellent staff. The impressive breakfast spread includes decent espresso coffee. Significant discounts (even in high season) knock prices as low as ¥320: excellent value.

🍴 Eating

Fènglín Gé
CHINESE $

(凤临阁; ☒0352 205 9799; near cnr Gulou Xijie & Huayan Jie, 鼓楼西街华严街路口; mains from ¥25; ☺6.30-9.30am, 11.30am-2pm & 5.30-9pm; ❇☎) Exquisite and delectable *shāomai* (steamed dim-sum dumpling) is the star of the show at this traditionally styled restaurant at the heart of the old town. Order by the steamer (笼; *lóng*) or half steamer. The crab *shāomai* are succulent and gorgeous, but not cheap (¥15 each, half steamer ¥45); there's lamb too (¥7 each, half steamer ¥26) and other tempting fillings.

Dōngfāng Xiǎo Miàn
NOODLES $

(East Wheat, 东方削面; Yingze Jie, 迎泽街; noodles from ¥6; ☺7am-10pm) Forgive the chain-store decor and bear the long queues (always a good sign) and you'll soon be in noodle heaven. Steaming bowls of the humble Shānxī speciality (削面; *xiāo miàn*) is the star here; have it with pork, beef or lamb and pair it with a variety of side dishes such as sliced cucumbers. A beer will help top it all off. A large bowl of noodles with pork will only set you back ¥7.50, for lamb it's ¥10.

Tónghé Dàfàndiàn   CHINESE $

(同和大饭店; Zhanqian Jie; dishes ¥16-40; ⊙ 11am-2pm & 6-9pm) This fantastic, bright and cheery spot alongside the Hongqi Hotel can look a little intimidating with its big round tables better suited to functions, but solo diners can pull up a chair no problem. There's a huge range of tasty, well presented dishes on the picture menu, suiting all budgets.

ℹ Information

Agricultural Bank of China (ABC, 中国农业银行, Zhōngguó Nóngyè Yínháng; Da Nanjie, 大南街) ATM and money exchange.

China Post (Da Nanjie, 大南街) A short walk south from the Garden Hotel.

China Post (cnr Weidu Dadao & Zhanbei Jie, 魏都大道站北街路口)

Industrial & Commercial Bank of China (ICBC, 工商银行, Gōngshāng Yínháng; Weidu Dadao, 魏都大道)

Public Security Bureau (PSB, 公安局出入境接待处, Gōng'ānjú Chūrùjìng Jiēdàichù; ☑ 0352 206 1833; junction Heng'an Jie & Wenxing Lu, 恒安街与文兴路交汇处; ⊙ 9am-noon & 3-5.30pm Mon-Fri) In the east of town, beyond the city walls.

ℹ Getting There & Away

AIR

Located 20km east of the city, small Dàtóng Yúngāng Airport has flights to Běijīng (¥450, one hour), Shànghǎi (¥1450, 2½ hours) and Guǎngzhōu (¥1650, 4½ hours). Buy tickets at www.ctrip.com or www.elong.net.

BUS

Buses from the **south bus station** (新南站; xīnnán zhàn), located 9km from the train station:

Běijīng ¥120, four hours, hourly, 8am to 5.30pm

Mùtǎ ¥26, 1½ hours, hourly, 7.30am to 7pm

Tàiyuán ¥100, 3½ hours, 8.50am, 10am, 11am and 1.30pm

Wǔtái Shān ¥75, 3½ hours, two daily, 8.30am, 9am and 2pm; summer only

You can also catch minibuses to some of these destinations from outside the train station.

Buses from the **main bus station** (大同汽车站, Dàtóng Qìchēzhàn; ☑ 0352 246 4464; Weidu Dadao, 魏都大道)

Hanging Monastery ¥30, two hours, hourly, 7am to 11am

Hohhot ¥65, 3½ hours, hourly, 7.20am to 4.20pm

Regular buses (¥80) to Hohhot depart hourly from next to the Tónghé Dàfàndiàn by the train station.

TRAIN

Train departures from Dàtóng include the following:

Běijīng Hard seat/sleeper ¥48/108, six hours, 11 daily

Hohhot Hard seat ¥42, four hours, 16 daily

Píngyáo Hard seat/sleeper ¥63/122, seven to eight hours, four daily

Tàiyuán Hard seat/sleeper ¥44/98, four hours, seven daily

Xī'ān Hard seat/sleeper ¥114/223, 16½ hours, one daily (4 40pm)

ℹ Getting Around

No public transport goes to the airport. A taxi costs around ¥50. Taxi flagfall is ¥7.

Bus routes are being readjusted owing to the massive construction all around town, so expect changes. Buses 4 and 15 run from the train station to the main bus station. Bus 30 takes 30 minutes to run from the train station to the new south bus station. Buses 27 and 35 go to the old town from Weidu Dadao. Bus 603 runs to the Yúngāng Caves.

Around Dàtóng

Yúngāng Caves   云冈石窟

One of China's most supreme examples of Buddhist cave art, the **Yúngāng Caves** (Yúngāng Shíku; ☑ 0352 302 6230; Dec-Feb ¥80, Mar-Nov ¥125; ⊙ 8.30am-5.30pm 1 Apr-15 Oct, to 4.50pm 16 Oct-31 Mar) are simply magnificent. With 51,000 ancient statues and celestial beings, they put virtually everything else in the Shānxī shade. Carved by the Turkic-speaking Tuoba, these 5th-century caves drew their designs from Indian, Persian and even Greek influences that swept along the Silk Road. Work began in AD 460, continuing for 60 years before all 252 caves, the oldest collection of Buddhist carvings in China, had been completed.

Pass through the slick visitors centre and a re-created temple on a lake before arriving at the caves. You may find some caves shut for restoration and this is done on a rotational basis; at the time of writing Caves 11 to 13 were closed to visitors. That still leaves around 40 showcasing some of the most precious and elegant Buddhist artwork in China. Despite weathering, many of the statues at Yúngāng still retain their gorgeous pigment, unlike the slightly more recent statues at Lóngmén in Hénán. The caves that are deeply recessed, in particular, have been well protected from the outside weather, although the penetration of water from above is a constant hazard.

A number of caves were once covered by wooden structures. Many of these are long gone, although the very impressive Caves 5 to 13 are still fronted by recently constructed wooden temples.

Some caves contain intricately carved square-shaped pagodas or central columns which you can circumambulate, while others depict the inside of temples, carved and painted to look as though they're made of wood. Frescoes are in abundance and there are graceful depictions of animals, birds and angels, some still brightly painted, and almost every cave contains the 1000-Buddha motif (tiny Buddhas seated in niches).

Eight of the caves contain enormous Buddha statues; the largest can be found in Cave 5, an outstanding 17m-high, seated effigy of Sakyamuni with a gilded face. As with many here, the frescoes in this cave are badly scratched and vandalised, but note the painted vaulted ceiling. Bursting with colour, Cave 6, the Cave of Sakyamuni, is also stunning, resembling an overblown set from an *Indiana Jones* epic with legions of Buddhist angels, Bodhisattvas and other celestial figures. In the middle of the cave, a square block pagoda or column fuses with the ceiling, with Buddhas on each side across two levels. Most foreign visitors are oblivious to the graffiti in bright red oil paint on the right-hand side of the main door frame within the cave, which reads 大同八中 (Dàtóng Bāzhōng; Datong No 8 Middle School), probably courtesy of pupils during the Cultural Revolution. The frescoes here are also badly scratched by recent visitors from the years of turmoil – the 40-year-old date '76.12.8' is etched crudely.

The dual chamber Cave 9, the Aksokhya Buddha Cave, is an astonishing spectacle too, with its vast seated and gold-faced Buddha.

Caves 16 to 20 are the earliest caves at Yúngāng, carved under the supervision of monk Tanyao. Cave 16, the Standing Buddha Cave, contains a huge standing Buddha whose middle section is badly eroded. The walls of the cave are perforated with small niches containing Buddhas. Cave 17 houses a colossal 15.6m seated Maitreya Buddha. Examine the exceptional quality of the carvings in Cave 18; some of the faces are perfectly presented. Cave 19 contains a vast 16.8m-high effigy of Sakyamuni.

Entirely exposed to the elements, Cave 20 (AD460–470) is similar to the Losana Buddha Statue Cave at Lóngmén (p432), originally depicting a trinity of Buddhas (the past, present and future Buddhas). The huge seated Buddha in the middle is the representative icon at Yúngāng, while the Buddha on the left has somehow vanished. Prayer mats are arrayed out front so that pilgrims can worship.

Some effigies, such as in Cave 39, have had their heads crudely bludgeoned off. Past the last set of caves, you can turn off the path down to the slick and highly informative **museum** (◷9.30am-5pm) detailing the Wei Kingdom and the artwork at the caves. Sadly, English captions are very limited.

Most of the caves, however, come with good dual Chinese/English captions. English-speaking tour guides can be hired for ¥150; their services include a trip to the museum. Note that photography is permitted in some caves but not in others.

To get to the caves, take bus 603 (¥3, 45 minutes) from Dàtóng train station to the terminus. Buses run every 10 to 15 minutes. A taxi from Dàtóng is around ¥40 each way. You will pass the rather less appealing Dàtóng Coal Mine en route.

Bā Táizi 八台子

Alongside magnificently dilapidated earthen sections of the Great Wall that disappear over the top of Horsehead Hill (马头山; Mǎtóu Shān), a fabulous Gothic church ruin is quite a sight. All that remains of the **Holy Mother Church** (圣母堂; Shèngmǔ Táng), built in 1876, is its front gate and bell tower and lopped-off spire above it. No explanation for the church's demise is given in the blurb on the board alongside, nor how the church arrived in such a remote spot.

Fourteen recently built stations of the cross lead the way to the church ruin. You can hike along the wall for some thrilling views, but pack water.

This entire area is very near the border with Inner Mongolia. To reach Bā Táizi, hop on a bus (¥18, regularly 6.15am to 6.20pm, 80 minutes) from Dàtóng's main bus station to Zuǒyún (左云), then negotiate with a taxi driver to take you to Bā Táizicūn (八台子村), around 20km away. Expect to pay between ¥80 and ¥100 return; the driver will wait for you for around 30 minutes. If you want to spend longer hiking along the wall, you will need to pay the driver more to wait for you.

If you ask nicely (or cross the driver's palm with a bit more silver), the driver may take you up winding mountain roads to a **scenic lookout** on top of Mótiān Lǐng (摩天岭), on the road to Liángchéng (凉城),

where you can get an elevated perspective down onto the earthen Great Wall trailing off into the distance.

The last bus to Dàtóng leaves Zuǒyún at 6.30pm.

Hanging Monastery 悬空寺

Built precariously into the side of a cliff, the Buddhist **Hanging Monastery** (Xuánkōng Sì; ¥130; ⊙8am-7pm summer, 8.30am-5.30pm winter) is made all the more stunning by its long support stilts. The halls have been built along the contours of the cliff face, connected by rickety catwalks and narrow corridors, which can get very crowded in summer. It's a sight to behold, but we hear that the access up into the monastery itself might (understandably) eventually be closed owing to the large number of visitors. Get here soon.

Buses travel here from Dàtóng's main bus station (¥31, two hours). Most will transfer passengers to the monastery into a free taxi for the last 5km from Húnyuán (浑源). Heading back, you'll be stung for ¥20 for a taxi (per person) to Húnyuán. If you want to go on to Mùtǎ, there are frequent buses from Húnyuán (¥14, one hour), or shared taxis make the run from the monastery car park for ¥50 per person (when full).

Mùtǎ 木塔

Built in 1056, impressive **Mùtǎ Tower** (¥60; ⊙7.30am-7pm summer, 8am-5.30pm winter) is the world's oldest and tallest (67m) wooden pagoda. The clay Buddhist carvings it houses, including an 11m-high Sakyamuni on the 1st floor, are as old as the pagoda itself. Due to its fragile state, visitors can no longer climb the pagoda, but there are photos of the higher floors to the side of the pagoda.

Mùtǎ is located in unlovely Yìngxiàn (应县). Buses from Dàtóng's south bus station (¥32, two hours) run to its west bus station (西站; xīzhàn). From there, get public bus 1 (¥1) to Mùtǎ, 2km up the road. Hourly buses return to Dàtóng until 6pm, or you can travel onto Tàiyuán (¥90, 3½ hours, last bus 2.30pm).

Déshèngbǎo 得胜堡

A good place to see some raw sections of the Great Wall is little-visited Déshèngbǎo, a 16th-century walled fort almost on the border with Inner Mongolia that is now a small farming village. The fort's north and south gates are still standing, as are parts of its walls. Walk through the village (many of its houses are built out of Great Wall bricks) to the north gate and beyond it you'll see wild wall – 10m-high sections of it.

To get here, take a minibus to Fēngzhèn (丰镇; ¥19, one hour) from opposite Tónghé Dàfàndiàn, next to Dàtóng train station. The bus will drop you at the turn-off for Déshèngbǎo, from where it's a 1km walk to the south gate. Heading back, return to the highway and flag down any Dàtóng-bound bus.

Wǔtái Shān 五台山

📱 0350 / POP 10,600

The mountainous, monastic enclave of Wǔtái Shān (Five Terrace Mountains) is Buddhism's sacred northern range and the earthly abode of Manjusri (文殊; Wénshū), the Bodhisattva of Wisdom. Chinese students sitting the ferociously competitive *gāokǎo* (university entrance) exams troop here for a nod from the learned Bodhisattva, proffering incense alongside saffron-robed monks and octogenarian pilgrims.

A powerful sense of the divine holds sway in Wǔtái Shān and the port-walled monasteries – the principal sources of spiritual power – find further amplification in the sublime mountain scenery.

The forested slopes overlooking the town eventually give way to alpine meadows where you'll find more temples and great hiking possibilities. Wǔtái Shān is also famed for its mysterious rainbows, which can appear without rain and are said to contain shimmering mirages of Buddhist beings, creatures and temple halls.

Avoid Wǔtái Shān during the holiday periods (first week of May in particular) and high-season weekends.

Climate

Wǔtái Shān is at high altitude and powerful blizzards can sweep in as late as May and as early as September; check ahead to ensure the roads are passable. Winters are freezing with snow; summer months are the most pleasant, but always pack a jacket, as well as suitable shoes or boots for rain, as temperatures fall at night. If you are climbing up the peaks to see the sunrise, warm coats can be hired.

History

It's believed that by the 6th century there were already 200 temples in the area, although all but two were destroyed during the official persecution of Buddhism in the

9th century. During the Ming dynasty, Wŭtái Shān began attracting large numbers of Tibetan Buddhists (principally from Mongolia), for whom Manjusri holds special significance.

◉ Sights

Enclosed within a lush valley between the five main peaks is an elongated, unashamedly touristy town, called **Táihuái** (台怀) but everyone simply calls it Wŭtái Shān. It's here that you'll find the largest concentration of temples, as well as all the area's hotels and tourist facilities. The five main peaks are north (北台顶; *běitái dǐng*), east (东台顶; *dōngtái dǐng*), south (南台顶; *nántái dǐng*), west (西台顶; *xītái dǐng*) and central (中台顶; *zhōngtái dǐng*).

There's a steep ¥218 entrance fee for the area – including a mandatory ¥50 'sightseeing-bus' ticket (旅游观光车票; *lǚyóu guānguāng chēpiào*) for transport within the area, valid for three days. Some of the more popular temples charge an additional small entrance fee. On the way in, the bus will stop at a large visitors centre where you buy tickets and reboard after your tickets are checked. Note that your bus might drop you behind the main town area from where you'll need to walk to the main drag. From the main bus station in Wŭtái Shān, you can jump on a free shuttle bus along the main road to get to different points.

Táihuái Temple Cluster

More than 50 temples lie scattered in town and across the surrounding countryside, so knowing where to start can be a daunting prospect. Most travellers limit themselves to what is called the Táihuái Temple Cluster (台怀寺庙群; *Táihuái Sìmiàoqún*), about 20 temples around Táihuái itself, among which Tǎyuàn Temple and Xiǎntōng Temple are considered the best. Many temples in Táihuái contain a statue of Manjusri, often depicted riding a lion and holding a sword used to cleave ignorance and illusion.

Wŭtái Shān

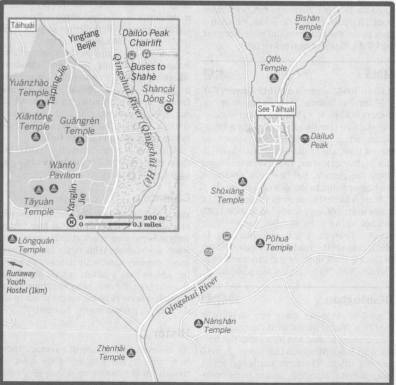

★**Tǎyuàn Temple** BUDDHIST SITE
(塔院寺, Tǎyuàn Sì; ¥10; ⏱6am-6pm) At the
base of **Spirit Vulture Peak** (灵鹫峰; Língjiù Fēng), the distinctive white stupa rising
above, Tǎyuàn Temple is the most prominent landmark in Wǔtái Shān and virtually all pilgrims pass through here to spin
the prayer wheels at its base or to prostrate
themselves, even in the snow. Even Chairman Mao did his tour of duty, staying in the
Abbot Courtyard in 1948.

Beyond the **Devaraja Hall** (Hall of Heavenly Kings), with its candlelit gilded statue
of Avalokitesvara (instead of Milefo, who
you usually find in this position), at the
rear of the **Dàcí Yánshòu Hall** is an altar
where worshippers leave canned drinks as
offerings to Guanyin. Hung with small yellow bells chiming in the Wǔtái Shān winds,
the **Great White Stupa** (大白塔; Dàbái
Tǎ) dates originally from 1301 and is one
of 84,000 stupas built by King Asoka, 19
of which are in China. The **Great Sutra-Keeping Hall** is a magnificent sight; its
towering 9th-century revolving Sutra case
originally held scriptures in Chinese, Mongolian and Tibetan.

★**Xiàntōng Temple** BUDDHIST SITE
(显通寺, Xiàntōng Sì; ⏱6am-6pm) FREE
Xiàntōng Temple – the largest temple in
town – was erected in AD 68 and was the
first Buddhist temple in the area. It comprises more than 100 halls and rooms. The **Qiānbō Wénshū Hall** contains a 1000-armed,
multifaced Wenshu, whose every palm supports a miniature Buddha. The squat brick
Beamless Hall (无梁殿; Wúliáng Diàn)
holds a miniature Yuan dynasty pagoda, remarkable statues of contemplative monks
meditating in the alcoves and a vast seated
effigy of Wenshu.

Further on, up some steps is the blindingly beautiful **Golden Hall**, enveloped in
a constellation of small Buddhas covering
the walls. Five metres high and weighing
50 tonnes, the metal hall was cast in 1606
before being gilded; it houses an effigy of
Wenshu seated atop a lion.

Further Temples
North beyond Xiàntōng Temple, is a cluster
of temples that you can explore. **Yuánzhào
Temple** (圆照寺, Yuánzhào Sì; ¥6) contains a
smaller stupa than the one at Tǎyuàn Temple. A 10-minute walk south down the road,
Shūxiàng Temple (殊像寺, Shūxiàng Sì) FREE
can be reached up a steep slope beyond its

ANCIENT WOODEN TEMPLES

Two of the oldest wooden buildings in
China, dating from the Tang dynasty,
can be found at **Fóguāng Temple**
(佛光寺; Fóguāng Sì; ¥15; ⏱8am-6.30pm) and **Nánchán Temple** (南禅
寺; Nánchán Sì; ¥15) Not many visitors
make it out here, but it's worth the
journey for the sheer rarity and the
tranquillity Many of the buses between
Wǔtái Shān and Taiyuán pass through
the countryside where they are located,
so both can be seen as a day trip.

spirit wall by the side of the road; the temple
contains Wǔtái Shān's largest statue of Wenshu riding a lion.

For great views of the town, you can trek,
take a **chairlift** (one way/return ¥50/85; ⏱7am
to 5pm) or ride a horse (¥50 one way) up to
the temple on **Dàiluó Peak** (黛螺顶, Dàiluó
Dǐng; ¥10), on the eastern side of Qīngshuǐ
River (清水河; Qīngshuǐ Hé). For even better
views of the surrounding hills, walk 2.5km
south to the isolated, fortresslike **Nánshān
Temple** (南山寺, Nánshān Sì; ¥4), which sees
far fewer tour groups than the other temples
and has beautiful stone carvings.

🏃 Activities

Opportunities for hiking are immense, but
there are no good maps, and no marked
trails. Contact the Runaway Youth Hostel (p367) for organised hikes and mountain-bike rides. Roads lead to the summits
of the five main peaks, so you can take a taxi
up to one of them before hiking back into
town using the road as a bearing. Minibuses
run to all five peaks for ¥350 (7.30am departure, return 5pm). They can be found at the
big car park by the chairlift to Dàiluó Peak.

🛏 Sleeping

While Wǔtái Shān attracts tens of thousands
of tourists, accommodation is fairly basic and
most hostels are identical in terms of pricing
and standard. Touts are happy to lead you to
family-run hotels with decent rooms from
¥100. Find one that's close to the main road
so you can easily get to the temples.

★**Runaway Youth Hostel** HOSTEL $
(Runaway国际青年旅舍, Runaway Guójì Qīngnián Lǚshě; ☎186 3604 2689, 0350 654 9505;
648984355@qq.com; Xiazhuang Village, 下庄村;

dm ¥50, d & tw ¥128-148; ☺ closed Oct-Apr; @🛜)
Húběi owner Zhou Jin is a passionate traveller who set up this 15-room hostel with his
local wife in a quiet southwestern section
of the mountain. Enter via a cosy lounge
area that leads up to clean, hotel-standard,
private rooms and rooftop bunk rooms, all
with en suite. Ask about organised hikes and
mountain-bike rides to the peaks.

Take internal shuttle bus 4 from Zhēnhǎi
Temple (镇海寺, Zhènhǎi Sì) to the terminal
station (西线换乘区, Xīxiàn Huànchéng Qū),
then walk up the hill 100m and look for a YHA
sign; the hostel is on the left. Phone ahead to
check that the shuttle bus is running.

🍷 Drinking & Nightlife

As a sacred Buddhist mountain, Wǔtái Shān
does not have much in the way of bars; continue on to Píngyáo for a drink.

ℹ️ Information

ATMs are found in the visitors centre and along
the town's main road.

There is a **China Post** (中国邮政, Zhōngguó
Yóuzhèng; ☺ 8am-7pm) south of the bus station.

ℹ️ Getting There & Away

BUS

Buses from **Wǔtái Shān bus station** (五台山汽
车站, Wǔtái Shān Qìchēzhàn; ☑ 0350 654 3101):
Běijīng ¥145, five hours, 9am and 2pm
Dàtóng ¥75, four hours, three daily, 7.30am,
1pm and 2pm, summer only
Hanging Monastery ¥65, three hours, one
daily, 8.30am
Tàiyuán ¥75, five hours, hourly, 6.30am to 4.30pm
Buses to Shāhé (¥25, 1½ hours, hourly, 8am
to 5pm) leave from the car park by the **chairlift**
(p367) to Dàiluó Peak.

TRAIN

The station known as Wǔtái Shān is actually
50km away in the town of Shāhé (砂河) from
where you can get a minibus taxi the rest of the
way from around ¥70, or a bus (¥25). Destinations include Píngyáo (hard seat ¥51, five hours,
one daily), Tàiyuán (hard seat ¥19, four to five
hours, three daily) and Běijīng (hard seat ¥50,
six to seven hours, two daily).

Tàiyuán 太原

☑ 0351 / POP 4.2 MILLION

Most travellers pass through Shānxī's capital en route to Píngyáo or heading north
to Dàtóng or Wǔtái Shān, but Tàiyuán is
well worth a day or two of your time. It's a
huge, modern and cosmopolitan city, but
it's certainly not short on history or culture;
there's a first-rate museum, several notable
temples – including a beautiful and rare set
of twin pagodas – and a stunning Catholic cathedral that wouldn't look out of place in Italy.

⊙ Sights

★ Cathedral of the Immaculate Conception
CHURCH

(圣母无染原罪主教座堂, Tàiyuán Shèngmǔ
Wúrǎn Yuánzuì Zhǔjiào Zuòtáng; 178 Jiefang Lu,
解放路178号) This quite astonishing sight
along Jiefang Lu is worth going out of your
way to explore. Built in 1870, the neoclassical house of worship was badly damaged
during the Boxer Rebellion but today stands
magnificently amid the modern buildings of
the Shānxī capital. The church is often open,
and hopefully will be when you visit, so you
can look at the amazing interior – a blaze
of white, blue, red and gold. The ceiling in
particular is amazing.

★ Twin Pagoda Temple/ Yǒngzuò Temple
BUDDHIST SITE

(双塔寺/永祚寺, Shuāngtǎ Sì/Yǒngzuò Sì; ¥30;
☺ 8.30am-5.30pm) These gorgeous twin brick
pagodas rise photogenically south of the
Nansha River in Tàiyuán's southeast; they're
lovely with the wind in their tinkling bells.
Not much of the original Yǒngzuò Temple,
which the pagodas belong to, is left, but the
area is well tended with shrubs and greenery. Of the two pagodas, 13-storey **Xuānwén
Pagoda** (宣文塔; Xuānwén Tǎ), dating from
the reign of Ming emperor Wanli, can be
climbed. The adjacent pagoda dates from the
same period but sadly cannot be climbed.

Pagodas in pairs are very rare in China,
but there are others (there is a set of smaller
twin pagodas in Sūzhōu). Take bus 820 or
812 from the train station.

Chóngshàn Temple
BUDDHIST SITE

(崇善寺, Chóngshàn Sì; Dilianggong Jie, 狄梁
公街; ¥2; ☺ 8am-4.30pm) The double-eaved
wooden hall in this Ming temple contains
three magnificent statues: Samantabhadra
(the Bodhisattva of Truth), Guanyin (the
Goddess of Mercy with 1000 arms) and
Manjusri (the Bodhisattva of Wisdom with
1000 alms bowls). The entrance is down an
alley off Dilianggong Jie behind the **Confucius Temple** (文庙, Wén Miào; 40 Wenmiao
Xiang, 文庙巷40号; ¥30; ☺ 9am-5pm Tue-Sun),
which still has its spirit wall standing guard,
as well as a folk-art museum.

Tàiyuán

Shānxī Museum MUSEUM

(山西博物馆, Shānxī Bówùguǎn; ☑ 0351 878 9015; http://shanximuseum.com; 13 Binhe Xilu Belduan, 滨河西路北段13号; ⊙ 9am-5pm Tue-Sun, last entry 4pm) FREE This top-class museum has three floors that walk you through all aspects of Shānxī culture, from prehistoric fossils to detailed local opera and architecture exhibits. All galleries are imaginatively displayed and some contain good English captions. Take bus 6 (¥1) from the train station, get off at Yifen Qiaoxi (漪汾桥西) bus stop across the river and look for the inverted pyramid.

🛏 Sleeping

Guesthouses offering rooms from ¥50 can be found on Yingze Nanjie, but not all places will take foreigners. Touts will find you near the train station with offers of cheapies. The city is well supplied with a decent selection of upper-midrange hotels and chain-express hotels.

Jīnjiāng Zhī Xīng HOTEL $$

(锦江之星; 7 Bingzhou Beilu, 并州北路7号; d ¥219-309) This central branch of this efficient chain hotel has lovely rooms: clean, bright and spacious enough, with telephone, flatscreen TV, ample work desk, lamp, kettle and very clean shower, the latter fully stocked with all you might need. Service is professional and there's a very good **restaurant** attached for breakfast (¥18 for guests) and dinner.

Try the restaurant's tasty spicy pork-rib noodles (麻辣排骨面; *málà páigǔmiàn*; ¥18).

Jīnlín Oriental Hotel HOTEL $$

(锦麟东方酒店, Jīnlín Dōngfāng Jiǔdiàn; ☑ 0351 839 0666; Yingze Nanjie, 迎泽南街; d/ste incl breakfast ¥418/588; ✳ @ 🗢) Conveniently located

across the road from the main entrance of the train station (on the left as you exit), the Jinlin has clean, quiet and comfortable rooms with discounts of up to 40%. Staff are helpful.

✖ Eating

Shānxī is famed for its noodles – including *dāoxiāo miàn* (刀削面; knife-pared noodles) and *lāmiàn* (拉面; hand-pulled noodles) – and vinegar, both in abundance in Tàiyuán. *Yángròu tāng* (羊肉汤; mutton soup) is lapped up by locals for breakfast.

Tàiyuán Noodle House NOODLES $

(太原面食店, Tàiyuán Miànshí Diàn; 5 Jiefang Lu, 解放路5号; noodles ¥6-16; ⊙ 11am-9.30pm) With a cake shop on the ground floor, head up to the bustling 2nd floor of this restaurant for Shānxī's famous vinegar/noodle combo. If you're bewildered by the choices, go for the six-type taster (六中面套餐;

liùzhōng miàntào cān; ¥35), otherwise choose pork noodles (排骨烩锅面；*páigǔ qiàngguōmiàn;* ¥16). It also does *shāomài* (烧麦; ¥12). No English menu, but there are pictures. Aim for a window seat.

★ **Shānxī Huìguǎn** — DONGBEI $$$

(山西会馆; ☑ 0351 718 9999; 7 Tiyu Lu, 体育路 7号; dishes ¥20-370; ⊙ 11am-9.30pm) Behind the imposing grey exterior is a refined restaurant serving quality northern-Chinese cuisine. There's everything from hotpot to homemade tofu and, of course, noodles, served by eager staff. If you're lucky, you might catch a noodle-making demonstration at dinner time. The picture menu has fairly accurate English translations. A taxi from the train station costs around ¥12.

There are several other branches in town.

ⓘ Information

Agricultural Bank of China (ABC, 中国农业银行, Zhōngguó Nóngyè Yínháng; Yingze Nanjie, 迎泽南街) ATM next to the Jīnlín Oriental Hotel (p369).

Bank of China (中国银行, Zhōngguó Yínháng; 47 Wuyi Lu, 五一路47号; ⊙ 9am-5pm) For foreign exchange and ATM.

China Post (中国邮政, Zhōngguó Yóuzhèng; Yingze Dajie, 迎泽大街; ⊙ 8am-7pm) Opposite the train station.

Industrial & Commercial Bank of China (ICBC, 工商银行, Gōngshāng Yínháng; Yingze Dajie, 迎泽大街) ATM.

Public Security Bureau (PSB, 公安局, Gōng'ānjú; ☑ 0351 895 5355; Wuyi Dongjie, 五一东街; ⊙ 8.30am-5.30pm Mon-Fri) Can extend visas, but be warned they need seven working days to do so.

ⓘ Getting There & Away

AIR

Destinations from Tàiyuán Wǔsù International Airport include Běijīng (¥550), Hángzhōu (¥650), Hong Kong (¥1150), Kūnmíng (¥1440), Nánjīng (¥650), Shànghǎi (¥850) and Shēnzhèn (¥1100).

BUS

Tàiyuán's seriously old-school long-distance **bus station** (长途汽车站, Chángtú Qìchēzhàn; Yingze Dajie, 迎泽大街) is 500m west of the train station on Yingze Dajie. Buses travel to the following destinations:

Běijīng ¥190, seven hours, three daily (8.30am, 10.30am and 2.30pm)

Dàtóng ¥117, 3½ hours, every hour (7am to 7pm)

Shànghǎi ¥409, 17 hours, one daily (1pm)

Shíjiāzhuāng ¥65, 3½ hours, one daily (12.40pm)

Xī'ān ¥180, eight hours, five daily (noon)

Zhèngzhōu ¥152, seven hours, five daily (7am to 5pm)

Buses from the Jiànnán bus station (建南站; Jiànnán zhàn), 3km south of the train station:

Jièxiū ¥63, two hours, half-hourly (7.40am to 6.40pm)

Jìnchéng ¥115, five hours, every 40 minutes (7am to 7pm)

Píngyáo ¥26, two hours, half-hourly (7.30am to 7.30pm)

Qíxiàn ¥23, two hours, half-hourly (7.30am to 7.30pm)

The east bus station (东客站; *dōng kèzhàn*) has buses to Wǔtái Shān (¥75, four to five hours, hourly, 6.40am to 6pm).

The west bus station (客运西站; *kèyùn xīzhàn*) has the following services:

Líshí ¥70, two hours, frequent (7am to 7.30pm)

Qìkǒu ¥80, four hours, one daily (10.30am)

TRAIN

Sample routes from Tàiyuán train station (火车站; *huǒchē zhàn*):

Běijīng normal train seat/sleeper ¥72/136, eight to 12 hours, six daily

Běijīng West G-class train 1st/2nd class ¥197/288, three hours, regular

Dàtóng hard seat/sleeper ¥44/98, five to seven hours, eight daily

Jìnchéng hard seat/sleeper ¥54/108, seven hours, four daily

Píngyáo ¥17, 1½ hours, frequent

Wǔtái Shān ¥38, 3½ hours to five hours, three daily

High-speed trains depart from the new Tàiyuán South train station (火车南站; Huǒchē Nánzhàn), 8km south of the old train station in the Běiyíng (北营) district. The best way to get here is via taxi (¥20, 25 minutes) or bus 861 from the old station.

Běijīng West D/G-class train ¥197/288, 3½/three hours, regular

Xī'ān 1st/2nd class ¥222/179, four hours, regular

Zhèngzhōu East G-class train 1st/2nd class ¥384/257, four hours, 10.35am

ⓘ Getting Around

Shuttle buses (机场大巴, Jīchǎng Dàbā; Yingze Dajie, 迎泽大街) to the airport (¥16, 40 minutes, hourly from 6am to 8pm) run from the side of the Sanjin International Hotel on Wuyi Guangchang. The airport is 15km southeast of downtown Tàiyuán; a taxi costs around ¥50.

The Tàiyuán metro is currently undergoing construction, with the north–south Line 2 due to open in 2018. Bus 1 (¥1) runs the length of Yingze Dajie. For the Jiànnán bus station and the west bus

QIAO FAMILY COURTYARD

An 18th-century complex of courtyards, **Qiao Family Courtyard** (乔家大院, Qiáojiā Dàyuàn; ¥72; ☺8am-7pm) is one of the finest remaining examples of a traditional private residence in all of China. Once home to a celebrated merchant, it's an austere (yet compelling) maze of doorways and courtyards that lead onto a seemingly infinite number of rooms (more than 300). The complex is famous in China as the set of Zhang Yimou's beautiful, required-viewing Fifth Generation tragedy *Raise the Red Lantern* (大红灯笼高高挂; *Dàhóng Dēnglóng Gāogāo Guà*).

If you have seen the film and enjoyed it, a visit is a must. Sure enough, the place is festooned with red lanterns; but many fascinating exhibits of Qing-era furniture and clothes are also displayed, as well as Shānxī opera costumes and props. English signage helps convey northern Chinese traditions and rites to foreign visitors.

The site is massively popular with domestic tour groups so get here as early as you can to steal a lead on the colour-coordinated baseball-hatted tour groups from across China. While the entrance is glossed up, and souvenir and food stalls besiege the courtyard, the residence is still big enough to flee the crowds: step through one of the many doorways and they magically vanish.

To get here, catch any bus going to Qíxiàn (祁县; ¥23, 1½ hours) from Tàiyuán's Jiànnán bus station. Tell the driver where you're headed and they'll drop you at the main gate. You can also visit from Píngyáo (¥13, 45 minutes, every 30 minutes to 6.40pm).

station, take bus 23 or 611 (¥1.50) from Yingze Dajie. For the east bus station take any bus (¥1.50) heading east from Wulongkou Jie. A taxi to Jiànnán bus station costs ¥13. Taxi flagfall is ¥8.

Around Tàiyuán

Jìncí Temple   晋祠

The highlight of this sprawling Buddhist **temple complex** (¥70; ☺8am-6pm) is the **Hall of the Sacred Mother** (圣母殿; Shèngmǔ Diàn), a magnificent wooden structure first built (without using a single nail) in AD 984, then renovated in 1102. Eight dragons twine their way up the first row of pillars. Inside are 42 Song dynasty clay maidservants of the sacred lady, the mother of Prince Shuyu, who founded the state of Jin (772–403 BC).

Adjacent is the **Zhou Cypress**, an unusual tree that has been growing at an angle of about 30 degrees for the last 900 years. Take bus 804 or 308 from the train station (¥3, 45 minutes).

Yùcì Ancient City   榆次老城

A favourite location for Chinese film producers, **Yùcì Ancient City** (Yùcì Lǎochéng; ¥60) has more than 400 rooms and halls to explore in the preserved section of this **Ming town**. You can walk the streets and some of the gardens for free, but you'll need a ticket

to enter the temples or the numerous former government offices. The oldest building is the impressive **God Temple** (隍庙; Huáng Miào), built in 1362. Take bus 901 (¥3, 80 minutes, first/last bus 6am/8pm) from near Tàiyuán train station.

Píngyáo   平遥

☎0354 / POP 502,000

Píngyáo is China's best-preserved ancient walled town. If you have any China mileage under your belt you'll appreciate the town's age-old charms; charms squandered away – or forever lost – elsewhere across the Middle Kingdom. While other 'ancient' cities in China will rustle together an unconvincing display of old city walls, sporadic temples or the occasional ragged alley thrust beneath an unsightly melange of white-tile architecture and greying apartment blocks, Píngyáo has managed to keep its beguiling narrative largely intact: red-lantern-hung lanes set against night-time silhouettes of imposing town walls, elegant courtyard architecture, ancient towers poking into the north China sky, and an entire brood of creaking temples and old buildings.

Píngyáo is also a living and breathing community where the 30,000-odd locals who reside in the old town hang laundry in courtyards, career down alleyways on bicycles, sun themselves in doorways or chew the fat with neighbours.

Píngyáo

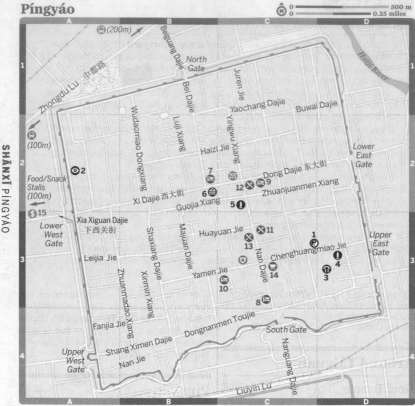

History

Already a thriving merchant town during the Ming dynasty, Píngyáo's ascendancy arrived in the Qing era when merchants created the country's first banks along with cheques to facilitate the transfer of silver from one place to another. The city escaped the shocking reshaping much loved by communist town planners, and almost 4000 Ming- and Qing-dynasty residences remain within the city walls.

Even as late as the early 1990s, foreign visitors would come to Píngyáo, but they'd stay in a hotel outside the walls and only visit the more famous Shuānglín Temple, 7km away. Then they would return to Běijīng or proceed to Xī'ān. Gradually the occasional *lǎowài* (foreigner) crept through the gates and discovered the amazingly well preserved town hiding behind it. The rest is history.

◉ Sights

If you have even the remotest interest in Chinese history, culture or architecture, you could easily spend a couple of days wandering across the pinched lanes of Píngyáo, stumbling across hidden gems while ticking off all the well known sights. You will always find something new, whether it's an ancient temple or alleyway, or an old courtyard house. It's free to walk the streets, but you must pay ¥150 to climb the city walls or enter any of the 18 buildings deemed historically significant. Tickets are valid for three days and can be purchased from near the gate openings and at other ticket offices near the big sights. Opening hours for sights are 8am to 7pm in summer and 8am to 6pm in winter.

City Walls

HISTORIC SITE

(城墙, Chéng Qiáng) A good place to start your Píngyáo experience is the magnificent city walls; they date from 1370 and are among

Píngyáo

the most complete in the nation. At 10m high and more than 6km in circumference, they are punctuated by 72 watchtowers, each containing a paragraph from Sunzi's *The Art of War*. You can wander around the walls gazing down into the old town.

Píngyáo City Tower TOWER
(市楼, Shì Lóu; Nan Dajie, 南大街) This is the signature structure standing proud above Píngyáo, the tallest building in the old town – snap a photo before passing under it en route to other sites. Sadly, you can no longer climb it for city views and a gate bars its stone steps. An antiques vendor works in the shop next to the tower.

Rìshēngchāng Financial House Museum MUSEUM
(日升昌, Rìshēngchāng; 38 Xi Dajie, 西大街38号; ⊙8am-7pm) Not to be missed, this museum began life as a humble dye shop in the late 18th century before its tremendous success as a business saw it transform into China's first draft bank (1823), eventually expanding to 57 branches nationwide. The museum has nearly 100 rooms, including offices, living quarters and a kitchen, as well as several cheques from the days of yore.

Entry included with ticket to the town.

City God Temple TAOIST SITE
(城隍庙, Chénghuáng Miào; Chenghuangmiao Jie, 城隍庙街) Within the venerable halls of this astonishing temple are some intriguing frescoes, including the hall at the very rear of the temple, the Qǐn Gōng (寝宫). Also look out for the two-faced fertility goddess in the Songsheng Dian (送生殿) – she is the *zhuǎnshēng pópo* (转生婆婆; reincarnation mother), responsible for sending out babies to the world. Her face at the back is, however, ferocious. She is helped in her work by assistants standing next to her who deliver babies from baskets. Admission is included with entrance ticket to the town.

Nine Dragon Screen MONUMENT
(九龙壁, Jiǔlóng Bì; Chenghuangmiao Jie, 城隍庙街) The old Píngyáo Theatre (大戏堂; Dàxì Táng) has been converted into a hotel's banquet hall, but it is fronted by this magnificent stone wall.

Confucius Temple CONFUCIAN SITE
(文庙, Wén Miào; Wenmiao Jie, 文庙街; ⊙8am-7pm) Píngyáo's oldest surviving building is **Dàchéng Hall** (大成殿; Dàchéng Diàn), dating from 1163. It can be found in the Confucius Temple, a huge complex where bureaucrats-to-be came to take the Imperial exams. Within the hall, beneath the roosting and cooing pigeons, is the seated sage with his fellow disciples. Admission is included with entrance ticket to the town.

🛏 Sleeping

Most old-town hotels are conversions of old courtyard homes, and finding a bed isn't hard. Hoteliers are increasingly aware of the needs of Western travellers, some English is spoken and they can make a passable Western breakfast. Most places offer train- or bus-station pick-ups.

Upon arrival, touts will direct you to rooms with air-con, private bathrooms and wi-fi from ¥80. Make sure it's not too far from the centre and don't be afraid to say no.

Zhèngjiā Kèzhàn COURTYARD HOTEL $
(郑家客栈; ☎0354 568 4466; 68 Yamen Jie, 衙门街68号; dm ¥50, d from ¥140; ❀@🛜) With two locations virtually next door to each other, head to the one closest to the Listen to the Rain Pavilion for decent doubles with *kàng* (raised sleeping platform) beds set around a very pleasant courtyard. The cramped but fresh, sweet and clean dorms are under the eaves at the neighbouring courtyard (which also has doubles), but the tiny bathrooms

are dark. The lobby and communal area at the front has been half-converted to a bookshop (with many travel books). It sees more Chinese travellers than the other guesthouses, making it a good place to meet the locals.

⭐ **Harmony Guesthouse**   COURTYARD HOTEL **$$**
(和义昌客栈, Héyìchāng Kèzhàn; ☑134 5327 0465, 0354 568 4963; www.py-harmony.com; 1 Duan Xiang, 段巷1号; r ¥180-480; ✳ @ 🛜) The rooms in these three lovingly preserved 300-year-old Qing courtyards are superb and the tranquil atmosphere is sublime. The English-speaking husband-and-wife team also offer good local information and breakfasts. The location is excellent, tucked away quietly down a charming alleyway. The hotel also offers tours, ticketing, bike rental, laundry and pick-up.

Private rooms have traditional stone *kàng* beds, wooden bed-top tea tables and wooden inlaid windows. At night, when red lanterns light up the courtyards, it's even more picturesque.

Déjūyuán Guesthouse   COURTYARD HOTEL **$$**
(德居源客栈, Déjūyuán Kèzhàn; ☑0354 568 5266; www.pydjy.net; 43 Xi Dajie, 西大街43号; s ¥150, d & tw ¥280-488, ste ¥1480; ✳ @ 🛜) If it's good enough for former French president Giscard D'Estaing who spent two nights here, it's good enough for you. The lovely rooms at this efficient and friendly place are set around two of the oldest courtyards in Píngyáo. The cheapest rooms are excellent value, while the suites are exquisite, with walnut-wood 'phoenix' beds (rather like four-posters).

⭐ **Jing's Residence**   COURTYARD HOTEL **$$$**
(锦宅, Jǐn Zhái; ☑0354 584 1000; www.jingsresidence.com; 16 Dong Dajie, 东大街16号; r ¥1500, ste ¥2000-3200; ✳ @ 🛜) With the super-hushed atmosphere that's unique to the most exclusive (and expensive) hotels, Jing's is a soothing blend of old Píngyáo and modern flair that's squarely aimed at upmarket Western travellers. At 260 years old, the former home of a Qing dynasty silk merchant is sleek and well finished with polished service from the English-speaking staff.

🍴 Eating

Most guesthouses can rustle up (Western or Chinese) meals. Píngyáo's lanes are stuffed with *xiǎochī guǎn* (小吃馆; hole-in-the-wall restaurants), most offering the same dishes at similar prices. For something cheaper and less touristy, head to Xia Xiguan Jie (下西关街) just outside Lower West Gate, where food stalls sell noodles for ¥5 and up, plus *ròujiāmó*

(肉夹馍; fried pork or beef with green peppers in bread), and meat and veggie skewers.

⭐ **Déjūyuán**   SHĀNXĪ **$**
(德居源, Petit Resto; 82 Nan Dajie, 南大街82号; mains from ¥25; ⏲8.30am-10pm; 🛜) Traveller-friendly, but no worse for that, this welcoming and popular little restaurant has a simple and tasty menu (in English) of northern Chinese dishes such as dumplings (¥25), plus all the local faves. Try the famed Píngyáo beef (¥45), the mountain noodles (¥15) or the fried shrimps with green pepper (¥48). It's often packed, so you may have to share a table.

⭐ **Tiānyuánkuí Guesthouse**   SHĀNXĪ **$$**
(天元奎客栈, Tiānyuánkuí Kèzhàn; ☑0354 568 0069; 73 Nan Dajie, 南大街73号; dishes ¥10-68; ⏲7.30am-10pm; 🛜) With warm wooden furnishings and floral cushions, friendly staff, free wi-fi and soft music, this restaurant has an easygoing vibe that invites travellers to linger over their meals. The English iPad menu has photos of the dishes (a range of traditional favourites such as Píngyáo beef sit next to the usual meat, veg and tofu offerings) making ordering a snap.

It's a good place for an early-morning breakfast before other places open. There are also comfortable rooms (from ¥400) in the rear courtyard compound.

Sakura Cafe   CAFE **$$**
(樱花屋西餐酒吧, Yīnghuāwū Xīcān Jiǔbā; 6 Dong Dajie, 东大街6号; mains from ¥30; ⏲8am-11pm; 🛜🍴) This eclectic and fun cafe-bar attracts both locals and foreigners with its daily food and drink specials. It does decent, if pricey, pizzas (from ¥65), burgers, sandwiches and omelettes, plus breakfasts, coffee, beer (from ¥15) and cocktails. Staff are welcoming. There's another equally popular branch at 86 Nan Dajie, which is more aimed at Chinese (this branch is aimed at Westerners).

🍷 Drinking & Nightlife

Coffee by Shrew   CAFE
(池池咖啡馆, Chíchí Kāfēiguǎn; 9 Chenghuang-miao Jie, 城隍庙街9号; coffee from ¥25, cakes ¥28, alcohol from ¥35; ⏲11am-9pm; 🛜) Behind its green doors is a cute-as-pie, blink-and-you'll-miss-it cafe serving some of Píngyáo's best espresso, lattes and single-origin brews in a warm setting lined with bookshelves and cosy seats. Come night-time, swap caffeine for simple cocktails and start a conversation with the Fujianese owner Shrew. Shrew has rooms too – they're not at this address, but she can take you there.

Shopping

Nan Dajie (南大街) is stuffed with wood-panelled shops selling Píngyáo snacks, knick-knacks, faux Cultural Revolution memorabilia, 'antiques', jade, shoes and slippers, and loads more. Look out for red and black Shānxī paper cuts, which make excellent presents.

Information

China Post (中国邮政, Zhōngguó Yóuzhèng; Xi Dajie, 西大街; ⊗8am-6pm) Handily located at the centre of the old town.

Industrial & Commercial Bank of China (ICBC, 工商银行, Gōngshāng Yínháng; Xia Xiguan Dajie, 下西关大街) ATM just west of the old city wall.

Public Security Bureau (PSB, 公安局, Gōng'ānjú; ☑0354 563 5010; off Yamen Jie, 衙门街; ⊗8am-noon & 3-6pm Mon-Fri) Next to the Píngyáo fire station on Yamen Jie, also known as Zhengfu Jie. You cannot extend visas here, but you can in Tàiyuán (although it takes seven working days).

Getting There & Away

BUS

Píngyáo's **bus station** (汽车新站, Qìchēxīnzhàn; ☑0354 569 0011; Zhongdu Dongjie, 中都东街) has buses to the following locations:

Tàiyuán (¥26, two hours, frequent, 6.30am to 7.40pm)

Líshí (¥44, two hours, 8.30am and 12.30pm)

Chángzhì (¥79, three hours, 7.50am and 1.40pm)

Qiao Family Courtyard (¥13, 45 minutes, half-hourly)

TRAIN

Píngyáo has two train stations: the older **Píngyáo Train Station** (平遥站; Píngyáo Zhàn) just north of the city walls and the new **Píngyáo Gǔchéng Train Station** (平遥古城站; Píngyáo Gǔchéng Zhàn) further away to the south; the latter mainly services high-speed trains. Check to see which station your train is pulling in at.

Tickets for trains (especially to Xī'ān) are tough to get in summer, so book ahead. Your hotel/hostel should be able to help. Trains depart for the following destinations:

Běijīng D-class train 1st/2nd class ¥255/183, 4½ hours, two daily

Běijīng G-class train 1st/2nd class ¥323/226, four hours, one daily

Dàtóng hard seat/sleeper ¥61/122, six to eight hours, four daily

Tàiyuán ¥18, 1½ hours, frequent

Tàiyuán South D-class train 1st/2nd class ¥35/29, 40 minutes, 15 per day

Tàiyuán South G-class train 1st/2nd class ¥35/29, 40 minutes, one daily 1.40pm

Xī'ān D-class train 1st/2nd class ¥188/150, three hours, six daily

Getting Around

Many hotels and hostels arrange pick-up from the train station, so check up front.

A rickshaw will run from Píngyáo train station and the bus station to the old town for ¥10. A taxi from Píngyáo Gǔchéng train station to the old town costs ¥30. Note that taxis are not allowed to enter the old town (to keep traffic under control), so you will be dropped outside the gates of the city wall.

From Píngyáo Gǔchéng train station, take bus 108 (¥1) to the old town.

Píngyáo can be easily navigated on foot or bicycle (¥10 per day). Bike rental is available all over; most guesthouses offer it and there are many spots along Nan Dajie and Xi Dajie.

Around Píngyáo

Most hostels and guesthouses will arrange transport to the surrounding sights. Day tours to the Wang Family Courtyard (p376) and Zhangbì Underground Castle (p376) are ¥80 per person (excluding the admission price or food) and depart at 8.30am, returning late afternoon. You can also hire a private car for ¥350 per day.

Sights

★**Mián Shān** MOUNTAIN
(绵山; incl bus ¥160) With vertiginous and dizzying cliffs alongside a deep gorge, this astonishing mountain area is a splendid day trip from Píngyáo. Lined with precariously perched temple architecture, scenic gully walks and breathtaking views, the road snaking around the mountain is an undemanding hike, with buses linking the main sights. From the bus drop-off, it's a short walk to **Dragon Head Temple** (龙头寺; Lóngtóu Sì), from where a long, flat road links to the **Shuǐtāogōu Scenic Area** (水涛沟景区; Shuǐtāogōu Jǐngqū), a few hours' walk.

From Dragon Head Temple, the wide road (which accommodates the hop-on, hop-off buses that rattle along the route) hugs the side of the mountain, overlooking a deep and perilous drop into the gorge below. The distant sound of the river at the bottom accompanies you as you hike, with vertical cliffs on either side. You will pass a spring and then the **Dàluó Temple** (大罗宫; Dàluó Gōng), built up the side of the cliff. Winding around the mountain with a stomach-wrenching view below your feet is

Rabbit Bridge (兔桥; Tùqiáo). It was out of bounds at the time of writing, so you needed to walk through the tunnel. Ahead is **Yúnfēng Temple** (云峰寺; Yúnfēng Sì) and the **Sky Ladder** (天桥; Tiānqiáo), a scary-looking walkway climbing up the side of the mountain. Past **Five Dragon Peak** (无龙峰; Wǔlóng Fēng) is the exhilarating **Qīxián Gǔ** (栖贤谷), a lovely river-gorge walk. Beyond lie the waterfalls, bridges and water-curtain caves of the Shuǐtāogōu Scenic Area.

Buses run regularly between the sights, so just hop-on and hop-off, although walking between the different areas is not difficult. The first/last bus up the mountain from the ticket office is at 7am/7pm. You must buy the bus ticket (¥50) as you cannot walk up from the main ticket office and the ticket entitles you to free transport between the sights. Pick up a map at the ticket office for ¥5. Take water, sunscreen and, if travelling in the colder months, some warm clothes.

Take a train (¥7 to ¥9, 25 minutes, regular) to Jièxiū (介休) from Píngyáo train station or take a bus (¥11, one hour) from Píngyáo bus station to Jièxiū bus station. Buses (¥10) to Mián Shān leave from in front of the train station, around 300m east along Xinjian Xilu (新建西路) from the long-distance bus station in Jièxiū. Booking a car from Píngyáo would cost around ¥300 for the return trip; this can be arranged at hotels such as the Harmony Guesthouse (p374).

★ **Shuānglín Temple**   BUDDHIST SITE
(双林寺, Shuānglín Sì; ¥40; ◎8.30am-6.30pm) Within easy reach of Píngyáo, this astonishing Buddhist temple houses many incredibly rare, intricately carved Tang, Song and Yuan painted statues. Rebuilt in 1571, it's an impressive complex of ancient halls: the interiors of the Sakyamuni Hall and flanking buildings are exquisite. The Four Heavenly Kings date to the Tang dynasty and the Thousand Buddha Hall contains an astonishing 1000-arm Guanyin. Dark-faced Buddha statues hide within the Great Treasure Hall, while young sculptors come here to cast their likeness from clay.

Guanyin is portrayed sitting *lalitasana* (a very lithe and relaxed regal posture) in another hall, while in the Luohan Hall, one of the ancient *luóhàn* (arhat) is depicted boozing. Note how some of the statues have a wooden skeleton, covered in clay. You can also go up and walk along the wall around the temple. A rickshaw or taxi from town will cost ¥50 return, or you could cycle the 7km here.

★ **Zhènguó Temple**   BUDDHIST SITE
(镇国寺, Zhènguó Sì; ¥25; ◎8am-6pm) While not as famous as Shuānglín Temple, Zhènguó Temple also houses a magnificent collection of old halls and ancient statues. Don't miss the still-living 1000-year-old Dragon Scholar Tree. The incredible Hall of the Ten Thousand Buddhas, built in 963 AD (Northern Han dynasty), is one of the oldest wooden halls in the land. Housed within its time-worn timbers is a collection of 11 10th-century painted sculptures and frescoes.

The temple lies around 12km northeast of Píngyáo. Take bus 9 (¥4, 30 minutes) from Guāngdà Shāngchéng (光大商城) on Shuncheng Beilu (顺城北路) to the west of the city wall.

Wang Family Courtyard   HISTORIC BUILDING
(王家大院, Wángjiā Dàyuàn; ¥55; ◎8am-7pm) More castle than cosy home, this grand Qing-dynasty **former residence** has been very well maintained (note the wooden galleries fronting many of the courtyard buildings). Due to the sheer size, the seemingly endless procession of courtyards (123 in all) become a little repetitive, but it's still beautiful and the complex is interspersed with gardens. Four direct buses (¥17, one hour, 7.10am, 8.40am, 12.40pm and 2.20pm) leave from Píngyáo's bus station, returning at 10.50am, 12.30pm, 3.30pm and 5.20pm.

You can join a tour or hire a car to get here. Climb up onto the walls around the vast courtyard for excellent views. Behind the castle walls are interesting and still-occupied **cave dwellings** (窑洞; *yáodòng*), while in front of the complex is a Yuan dynasty Confucius Temple (p373), with a beautiful three-tiered wooden pagoda. An audio guide to the courtyard complex is ¥20 (¥50 deposit).

Zhāngbi Underground Castle   CAVE
(张壁古堡, Zhāngbì Gǔbǎo; ¥60; ◎8am-6.30pm) This 1400-year-old network of **defence tunnels**, stretching underground for 10km, are the oldest and longest series of such tunnels in China. Built at the end of the Sui dynasty in case of attack by Tang dynasty invaders, they were never used and subsequently fell into disrepair. Today, 1500m of tunnels on three levels have been restored. You descend as low as 26m in places and tour narrow and low subterranean passages, which were once storage rooms, guardhouses and bedrooms.

Holes cut into the side of shafts leading to the surface indicate escape routes and places where soldiers stood sentry to spy on would-be attackers. Chinese-speaking guides (included in the ticket price) are compulsory; you don't want to get lost here.

The tour includes a visit to fascinating Zhāngbì Cūn (张壁村), a still-occupied Yuan-dynasty farming village above the tunnels. You can wander its cobblestone streets and temples for free if you don't mind skipping the underground castle.

You can only get here on tour or by private car (per day ¥350). Check with your accommodation in Píngyáo.

Qìkǒu 碛口

☑ 0358 / POP 32,000

Separated from neighbouring Shaanxi (Shǎnxī) province by the fast-flowing Yellow River (黄河; Huáng Hé), this tiny Ming River port found prosperity during its Qing heyday when hundreds of merchants lived here, only to lose it when the Japanese army arrived in 1938. Qìkǒu is well worth visiting for its evocative stone courtyards and cobbled pathways. All wind their way, eventually, up to the Black Dragon Temple, which overlooks the town.

While it's lost a bit of charm due to recent construction of tourist amenities in the main town, considerable appeal survives, for now. The weekly market on Saturday is a good time to visit.

◉ Sights

Qìkǒu's main draw is the nearby ancient village of Lǐjiā Shān, a settlement of hundreds of cave dwellings (窑洞; yáodòng), some of which remain inhabited today.

Lǐjiā Shān   CAVE

(李家山) For anyone wanting to experience Shǎnxī's **cave houses**, this remote, supremely peaceful 550-year-old village, hugging a hillside with terraces of crops running up it, has hundreds of cave dwellings scaling nine storeys. Once home to more than 600 families, most with the family name Li, today's population is much depleted at around 45. Some stone paths and stairways that twist up the hill date from Ming times; note the rings on some walls that horses were tied to.

As with many semiabandoned villages in China, almost all inhabitants today are elderly: the local school, with caves for classrooms, no longer operates. The village is however very popular with artists who have come to walk in the footsteps of the late Chinese painter Wu Guanzhong, a pioneer in modern Chinese painting who

found inspiration here. The surrounding countryside offers ample opportunities for hikes and there are now **homestays** (农家乐; nóngjiālè; ¥60 including meals) offering basic accommodation for those who wish to get away from it all. People here speak Jin, although most understand Mandarin.

To get here, cross the bridge by Qìkǒu's bus stop and follow the river for about 30 minutes until you see a blue sign indicating Lǐjiā Shān. Walk on for about 100m and then take the road up the hill for another 30 minutes and you'll reach the old village. Local cars do a return run for around ¥50 to ¥60. If you're planning on staying, you'll need to negotiate a rate or walk out.

Black Dragon Temple   TAOIST SITE

(黑龙庙, Hēilóng Miào) **FREE** They say the acoustics of this Ming Taoist temple, with wonderful views of the Yellow River, were so excellent that performances held on its stage were audible on the other side of the river in Shaanxi (Shǎnxī) province. Sadly, the stage is unused today. You can't miss the temple: from Qìkǒu's main road, head up any number of old cobbled pathways up the hill, via the odd courtyard or two.

🛏 Sleeping

Some locals offer clean beds (with an outhouse) for around ¥60; look for the characters 住宿 (zhùsù), which means 'accommodation', or 有房 (yǒufáng), which means 'rooms available'. For something more comfortable, with views onto the Yellow River, the Qìkǒu Kèzhàn (p377) is a good choice.

Qìkǒu Kèzhàn   GUESTHOUSE $

(碛口客栈; ☑ 0358 446 6188; d/tw/tr ¥188/218/388; @ ⟨) Overlooking the Yellow River in Qìkǒu, this distinctive, friendly, 180-year-old (the Red Army used it as a base in WWII) place has comfortable and very large, yáodòng style rooms with kàng beds set off by two 300-year-old courtyards. Up the stone stairs is a wonderful terrace with great views over the river.

❶ Getting There & Away

One bus runs from the west bus station in Tàiyuán to Qìkǒu (¥70, four hours, 10.30am). If you miss it, or are coming from Píngyáo, you will have to go through nearby Líshí (离石).

Regular buses go from Tàiyuán to Líshí (¥75, three hours, half-hourly from 7am to 7pm). There are two daily buses from Píngyáo (¥45, two hours, 8.30am and 12.30pm). From Líshí's long-distance bus station (长途汽车站; chángtú qìchēzhàn), take bus 5 (¥1, 25 minutes) to the Jìnián Běi (纪念北) crossroads where buses to Qìkǒu (¥20, 1½ hours, 7am to 7pm) depart.

There's one daily bus from Qìkǒu to Tàiyuán (¥80), but it leaves very early at 5.30am. There are hourly buses to Líshí from Qìkǒu until around 4pm. From Líshí, there are many buses back to Tàiyuán (¥70, from 7am to 8pm), two to Píngyáo (¥45, 8am and 1.40pm) and one to Xī'ān (¥183, eight hours, 11.30am).

Jìnchéng 晋城

Jìnchéng has few sights in itself, but this small, little-visited city is the launch pad for a historical adventure into Shānxī's southeast. The surrounding countryside conceals a rich vein of impressive ancient architecture, making this a rewarding stop, particularly if you are continuing south into Hénán.

The only sight of note in Jìnchéng is **Bǐfēng Temple** (笔峰寺, Bǐfēng Sì; ⊙6am-6pm), which sits atop a hill close to the train station. The temple itself is newly built but the nine-storey pagoda dates to the Ming dynasty.

Most hotels in town are either overpriced or won't accept foreigners, but a small number do, including the **Sunshine Hotel** (阳光大酒店, Yángguāng Dàjiǔdiàn; ☑0356 222 9001; 568 Zezhou Lu, 泽州路568号; d ¥400, tw ¥500 incl breakfast; ✳🛜), a smart business hotel. Discounts of 50% are usually available.

ⓘ Getting There & Around

Buses depart from the east bus station (客运东站; kèyùn dōngzhàn). Destinations include Tàiyuán (¥115, four hours, every 1½ hours, 6.30am to 6.30pm), Píngyáo (¥110, five hours, 7am, 8am, 9.30am), Zhèngzhōu (¥65, 1½ hours, half-hourly, 5.40am to 6pm), Luòyáng (¥55, hourly, 7.20am to 6.30pm) and Xī'ān (¥180, seven hours, 8.30am and 10am).

The few trains that pass Jìnchéng shuttle between Tàiyuán (hard seat/sleeper ¥54/108, seven hours, eight daily), Zhèngzhōu (¥30 to ¥33, 3½ hours, three daily) and the handy overnighter to Dàtóng (hard sleeper ¥174, 12 hours, 9.18pm).

Bus 2, 3 and 19 (¥1) connect the train station with the east bus station. Bus 5 from the train station travels along the main road, Wenchang Dongjie (文昌东街). Taxi flagfall is ¥5.

Around Jìnchéng

Guōyù 郭峪古城

This atmospheric **walled village** (Guōyù Gǔchéng) is the highlight of a trip to this part of Shānxī. Although there's now an entrance fee (¥50), there's little tourist paraphernalia or nonsense; just the genuine charm of a historic and still-inhabited Ming-dynasty settlement.

The crumbling remains of this one-time fort's south gate and some of its old walls still stand sentry at the entrance to the village close to the road. Walk 200m and it's as if you've stepped back in time. Narrow alleys and stone streets run past courtyard houses, where the locals sit and chatter in their native dialect.

Guōyù's oldest building is **Tāngdì Miào** (汤帝庙), a 600-year-old Taoist temple. Make sure you climb up to the stage where there are two very rare Cultural Revolution–era paintings adorned with slogans exhorting the locals to work harder (the temple was a government building during that time). It's also worth looking inside the former courtyard residence of Minister Chen's grandfather at **1 Jingyang Beilu** (景阳北路1号). Admission is included with the entrance to the walled village (郭峪古城; Guōyù Gǔchéng; ¥50).

To get here, catch one of the frequent buses headed to Prime Minister Chen's Castle (¥15, 1½ hours, 6am to 6.30pm) from Jìnchéng's east station. Guōyù is a 10-minute walk south of the castle. Return transport is scarce, so it's best to take a minibus to the small town of Běiliú (北留; ¥5, 15 minutes), then catch an ordinary bus back to Jìnchéng (¥12).

Prime Minister Chen's Castle 皇成相府

This beautifully preserved Ming-dynasty **castle** (Huángchéng Xiàngfǔ; ¥100; ⊙8am-6.30pm) is the former residence of Chen Tingjing, prime minister under Emperor Kangxi in the late 17th century, and coauthor of China's most famous dictionary. The Chen family rose to prominence as senior officials in the 16th century and the castle walls were originally constructed to keep revolting peasants out. While it may have tourist trappings today, it remains an attractive and impressive maze of battlements, courtyards, gardens and stone archways.

Don't bother buying the pricier ¥120 ticket, which includes entry to a nearby garden. Regular buses (¥15) run to the ticket office from Jìnchéng's east bus station. If there isn't a minibus back to Jìnchéng, minibuses zip to the small town of Běiliú (北留; ¥3, 15 minutes), where you can catch an ordinary bus back to Jìnchéng (¥10).

Shaanxi

POP 37.4 MILLION

Best Places to Eat

➡ Sānjiǎoméi Jiǎozi (p387)

➡ Hǎiróng Guōtiēdiàn (p387)

➡ Muslim Family Restaurant (p387)

Best Places to Sleep

➡ Hàn Táng House (p386)

➡ Hàn Táng Inn (p385)

➡ Huá Shān Guesthouse (p396)

Why Go?

Shaanxi (陕西; Shǎnxī) is where it began for China. As the heartland of the Qin dynasty (秦朝), whose warrior emperor united much of China for the first time, Shaanxi was the cradle of Chinese civilisation and the fountainhead of Han culture. Xī'ān marked the beginning and end of the Silk Road and was a buzzing capital long before anyone knew of Běijīng and its Forbidden City.

Shaanxi's archaeological sites make it an essential destination. Around Xī'ān there's an excavated Neolithic village and royal graves, including the tomb of Qin Shi Huang and his Army of Terracotta Warriors, one of the world's foremost heritage sites. Shaanxi also serves up some of the most wholesome and appetising food in the land, especially in Xī'ān's Muslim Quarter.

Xī'ān is an emergent travellers' hub, with hotels, restaurants, museums, ancient pagodas, and a marvellous city wall and Muslim Quarter. Rural areas have fascinating villages barely touched by modernity and mountains that were once home to hermits and sages.

When to Go

Xī'ān

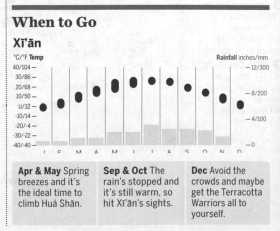

Apr & May Spring breezes and it's the ideal time to climb Huá Shān.

Sep & Oct The rain's stopped and it's still warm, so hit Xī'ān's sights.

Dec Avoid the crowds and maybe get the Terracotta Warriors all to yourself.

Shaanxi Highlights

1 **Army of Terracotta Warriors** (p391) Seeing what guardians an emperor enlists to protect him in the afterlife.

2 **Big Goose Pagoda** (p383) Admiring Xī'ān's classically styled Tang dynasty Buddhist pagoda, the centrepiece for a stunning sound and light show.

3 **Huá Shān** (p394) Watching the sun rise over the Qínlíng Mountains from atop Taoism's sacred and dramatic western peak.

4 **Hánchéng** (p397) Exploring this old town with its quaint quarter of buildings dating from the Yuan, Ming and Qing eras.

5 **Tomb of Emperor Jingdi** (p394) Taking a different look at China's past by gazing down at enthralling excavations.

6 **Muslim Quarter** (p382) Getting lost wandering the backstreets of this ancient Xī'ān quarter.

7 **Xī'ān City Walls** (p381) Hopping on a bike and riding atop these glorious walls that form a 14km loop of the old city.

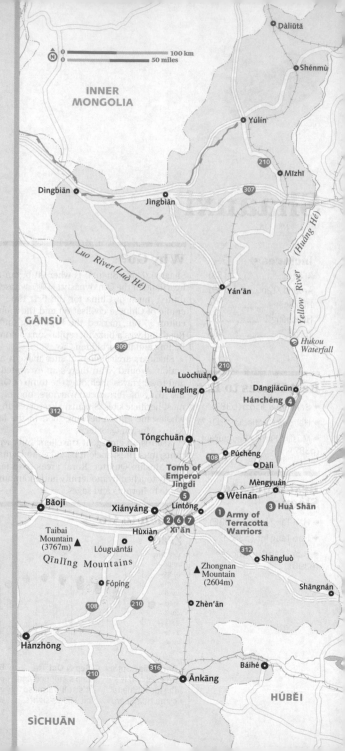

History

Around 3000 years ago, the Zhou people of the Bronze Age moved out of their Shaanxi homeland, conquered the Shang and became dominant in much of northern China. Later the state of Qin, ruling from its capital Xiányáng (near modern-day Xī'ān), became the first dynasty to unify much of China. Subsequent dynasties, including the Han, Sui and Tang, were based in Xī'ān, then known as Cháng'ān, which was abandoned for the eastern capital of Luòyáng (in Hénán) whenever invaders threatened.

Shaanxi remained the political heart of China until the 10th century. However, when the imperial court shifted eastward, the province's fortunes began to decline. Rebellions and famine were followed in 1556 by the deadliest earthquake in history, when an estimated 830,000 people died (the unusually high death toll was attributed to the fact that millions were living in cave homes, which easily collapsed in the quake). The extreme poverty of the region ensured that it was an early stronghold of the CCP (Chinese Communist Party).

❶ Getting There & Around

Xī'ān has one of China's best connected airports. Xī'ān is also a hub for road transport and megahighways spread out in all directions. High-speed trains connect Xī'ān to Běijīng, Shànghǎi and other destinations while long-distance buses link to neighbouring provinces and further afield.

Regular trains run between Xī'ān and the other main towns in the region. These trips can also be taken by bus.

Xī'ān　　　　西安

🎯 029 / POP 8.5 MILLION

Once the terminus of the Silk Road and a melting pot of cultures and religions, as well as home to emperors, courtesans, poets, monks, merchants and warriors, the glory days of Xī'ān (西安; pronounced 'see-an') may have ended in the early 10th century, but a considerable amount of ancient Cháng'ān, the former city, survives behind the often roaring, modern city.

Xī'ān's Ming-era city walls remain intact, vendors of all descriptions still crowd the narrow lanes of the warren-like Muslim Quarter, and there are enough places of interest to keep even the most amateur historian riveted.

Most people only spend two or three days in Xī'ān; dynastic enthusiasts could easily stay busy for a week. Must-sees include the Terracotta Warriors, the Tomb of Emperor Jingdi, the City Walls and the Muslim Quarter, but try to set aside time for its pagodas and museums, plus a side trip to nearby Huá Shān.

⊙ Sights

⊙ Inside the City Walls

Xī'ān City Walls　　　　HISTORIC SITE
(西安城墙, Xī'ān Chéngqiáng; ¥54; ⊙8am-8.30pm Apr-Oct, to 7pm Nov-Mar) Xī'ān is one of the few cities in China where the imposing old city walls still stand. Built in 1370 during the Ming dynasty, the magnificent 12m-high walls are surrounded by a dry moat and form a rectangle with a perimeter of 14km. Most sections have been restored or rebuilt, and it is possible to walk the walls in their entirety in a leisurely four hours (or around two hours by bike, or at a slow jog).

Cycling from the South Gate costs ¥40 for 100 minutes (¥200 deposit), while the truly lazy can be whisked around in a golf cart for ¥200. Access ramps are located inside the major gates, with the exception of the South Gate, where the entrance is outside the walls; there's another entrance inside the walls beside the Forest of Stelae Museum (p382). En route, you get to look out over modern-day Xī'ān. From this vantage point it's clear that the city is a hodgepodge of old and new, with the new vastly in the ascendancy. Every now and then a slice of old Xī'ān, such as Guǎngrén Temple (p382),

---

PRICE RANGES

Sleeping

The following prices are for a double room with private bath or shower room.

$ less than ¥190

$$ ¥190–¥400

$$$ more than ¥400

Eating

The following prices are for the cost of a main dish.

$ less than ¥30

$$ ¥30–¥60

$$$ more than ¥60

XĪ'ĀN IN TWO DAYS

Steal a lead on the crowds and catch an early bus to the **Army of Terracotta Warriors** (p391) before returning to Xī'ān for lunch and snacking your way through the **Muslim Quarter**. Explore the **Great Mosque** but give yourself enough time to walk or cycle around the **Xī'ān City Walls** (p381) before sundown.

On day two, start your day with a history lesson at the **Shaanxi History Museum** (p383) before visiting the nearby **Big Goose Pagoda** (p383). Have lunch at **Hǎiróng Guōtiēdiàn** (p387), followed by fathoming the mysteries of the Tibetan Buddhist **Guǎngrén Temple**. Round off the day with drinks at **King Garden Bar** (p388).

appears and you are rewarded with a bird's-eye view.

To get an idea of Xī'ān's former grandeur, consider this: the Tang city walls originally enclosed 83 sq km, an area seven times larger than today's city centre.

Muslim Quarter   HISTORIC SITE

(回族区; Ⓜ Zhonglou (Bell Tower)) The backstreets leading north from the Drum Tower (p383) have been home to the city's Hui (p399) community (non-Uighur Chinese Muslims) for centuries, perhaps as far back as the Ming dynasty or further still. The narrow lanes are full of butcher shops, sesame-oil factories, smaller mosques hidden behind enormous wooden doors, men in white skullcaps and women with their heads covered in coloured scarves. It's a great place to wander and especially atmospheric at night.

Great Mosque   MOSQUE

(清真大寺, Qīngzhēn Dàsì; Huajue Xiang, 化觉巷; Mar-Nov ¥25, Dec-Feb ¥15, Muslims free; ◷ 8am-7.30pm Mar-Nov, to 5.30pm Dec-Feb; Ⓜ Zhonglou (Bell Tower)) Bigger than many temples in China, the Great Mosque is a gorgeous blend of Chinese and Islamic architecture and one of the most fascinating sacred sites in the land. The present buildings are mostly Ming and Qing, though the mosque was founded in the 8th century. Arab influences extend from the central minaret (cleverly disguised as a stumpy pagoda) to the enormous turquoise-roofed Prayer Hall (not open to vis-

itors) at the back of the complex, dating to the Ming dynasty.

Guǎngrén Temple   BUDDHIST TEMPLE

(广仁寺, Guǎngrén Sì; Guangren Si Lu, 广仁寺路; ¥20; ◷ 8am-5.30pm; Ⓜ Sajinqiao or Yuxiangmen) The sole Tibetan Buddhist temple in the entire province, Guǎngrén Temple originally dates to the early 18th century, but was largely rebuilt in the 20th century. As a sacred Tibetan Buddhist place of worship, the temple hums with mystery and spiritual energy. Perhaps the most valuable object in the temple resides in the final hall, a golden representation of Sakyamuni that rests upon a Tang dynasty pedestal. There is only one other like it, housed at the Jokhang Temple in Lhasa.

Forest of Stelae Museum   MUSEUM

(碑林博物馆, Bēilín Bówùguǎn; www.beilin-museum.com; 15 Sanxue Jie, 三学街15号; Mar-Nov ¥75, Dec-Feb ¥50; ◷ 8am-6.45pm Mar-Nov, to 5.45pm Dec-Feb, last admission 45min before closing) Housed in Xī'ān's Confucius Temple, this museum holds more than 1000 stone stelae (inscribed tablets), including the nine Confucian classics and some exemplary calligraphy. The highlight is the fantastic sculpture gallery (across from the gift shop), where animal guardians from the Tang dynasty, pictorial tomb stones and Buddhist statuary muster together. To reach the museum, follow Shuyuan Xiang east from the South Gate.

The second gallery holds a Nestorian tablet (AD 781), the earliest recorded account of Christianity in China. (The Nestorians professed that Christ was both human and divine, for which they were booted out of the Church in 431.) The fourth gallery displays a collection of ancient maps and portraits, and rubbings (copies) are made here, an absorbing process to observe.

Bell Tower   HISTORIC SITE

(钟楼, Zhōng Lóu; ¥35, combined Drum Tower ticket ¥50; ◷ 8.30am-9.30pm Mar-Oct, to 5.30pm Nov-Feb, last admission 30min before closing) Occupying a central place at the frantic intersection of Xi Dajie, Dong Dajie, Bei Dajie and Nan Dajie, the domineering form of the Bell Tower originally housed a huge bell that was rung sonorously at dawn. Initially standing two blocks to the west, it dates from the 14th century and was later rebuilt in the 1700s. Musical performances are held inside from 9am to 11.30am and 2.30pm to 5.30pm. It is entered through the underpass on the north side.

Drum Tower   HISTORIC SITE

(鼓楼, Gǔ Lóu; Beiyuanmen; ¥35, combined Bell Tower ticket ¥50; ⏱8.30am-9.30pm Mar-Oct, to 6.30pm Nov-Feb, last admission 30min before closing; Ⓜ Zhonglou (Bell Tower)) While the Bell Tower (p382) originally held a bell that was rung at dawn, the Drum Tower, standing at the foot of the smoky and uproarious street of Beiyuanmen, marked nightfall. It similarly dates from the 14th century and was later rebuilt in the 1700s. Musical performances are held inside from 9am to 11.30am and 2.30pm to 5.30pm. Close by, a covered market sells all manner of haggle-worthy goods for souvenirs and gift-giving, leading to the magnificent Great Mosque.

◎ Outside the City Walls

Big Goose Pagoda   BUDDHIST PAGODA

(大雁塔, Dàyàn Tǎ; Yanta Nanlu, 雁塔南路; grounds ¥50, pagoda ¥40; ⏱8am-7pm Apr-Oct, to 6pm Nov-Mar) This pagoda, Xi'an's most famous landmark, 4km southeast of the South Gate and formerly within the old (and huge) Tang dynasty city wall, dominates the surrounding modern buildings. One of China's best examples of a Tang-style pagoda (squarish rather than round), it was completed in AD 652 to house Buddhist sutras brought back from India by the monk Xuan Zang. His travels inspired one of the best-known works of Chinese literature, *Journey to the West.*

Xuan spent the last 19 years of his life translating scriptures with a crack team of linguist monks; many of these translations are still used today.

The brick Tang pagoda style is not seen in many parts of China, although other examples do exist, in Héběi province's Zhèngdìng, for example. Surrounding the Big Goose Pagoda is **Dà Cí'ēn Temple** (大慈恩寺, Dàcí'ēn Sì), one of the largest temples in Tang dynasty Cháng'ān. The buildings today date from the Qing dynasty. To the south of the pagoda is an open-air mall of shops, galleries, restaurants and public art; well worth a wander.

Bus 610 from the Bell Tower and bus 609 from the South Gate drop you at the pagoda square; the entrance is on the south side. An evening fountain show is held on the square.

Little Goose Pagoda   BUDDHIST PAGODA

(小雁塔, Xiǎoyàn Tǎ; grounds free, pagoda ¥30; ⏱8.30am-7pm Wed-Mon; Ⓜ Nanshaomen) Little Goose Pagoda is in the pleasant grounds of

Jiànfú Temple. Its top was shaken off by an earthquake in the middle of the 16th century, but the rest of the 43m-high structure is intact.

Jiànfú Temple was built in AD 684 to bless the afterlife of the late Emperor Gaozong. The pagoda, a rather delicate building of 15 progressively smaller tiers, was built from AD 707–709 and housed Buddhist scriptures brought back from India by the pilgrim Yi Jing.

Admission to the grounds is free but climbing up the pagoda requires a ¥30 ticket.

Shaanxi History Museum   MUSEUM

(陕西历史博物馆, Shǎnxī Lìshǐ Bówùguǎn; 91 Xiaozhai Donglu, 小寨东路91号; ⏱8.30am-6pm Tue-Sun Apr-Oct, last admission 4.30pm, 9.30am-5pm Tue-Sun Nov-Mar, last admission 4pm) FREE This museum naturally overlaps with Xi'an's surrounding sights but makes for a comprehensive stroll through ancient Cháng'ān. Most exhibits offer illuminating explanations in English. Don't miss the four original terracotta warrior statues on the ground floor. Go early and expect to queue for at least 30 minutes. In the Sui and Tang section, unique murals depict a polo match, and you'll find a series of painted pottery figurines with elaborate hairstyles and dress, including several bearded foreigners, musicians and braying camels.

The number of visitors is limited to 4000 per day (2500 tickets are distributed in the morning starting at 8.30am and another 1500 in the afternoon starting at 1.30pm). Bring your passport to claim your free ticket. Take bus 610 from the Bell Tower or bus 701 from the South Gate.

Xi'ān Museum   MUSEUM

(西安博物馆, Xī'ān Bówùguǎn; ☎029 8780 3591; www.xabwy.com; 72 Youyi Xilu, 友谊西路72号; ⏱9am-5pm Wed-Mon; Ⓜ Nanshaomen) FREE Housed in the pleasant grounds of the Jiànfú Temple is this museum featuring relics unearthed in Xi'an over the years. There are some exquisite ceramics from the Han dynasty, as well as figurines, an exhibition of Ming-dynasty seals and jade artefacts. Don't miss the basement, where a large-scale model of ancient Xi'an gives a good sense of the place in its former pomp and glory.

Temple of the Eight Immortals   TAOIST SITE

(八仙庵, Bāxiān Ān; Yongle Lu, 永乐路; ¥3; ⏱7.30am-5.30pm Mar-Nov, 8am-5pm Dec-Feb; Ⓜ Chaoyangmen) Xi'an's largest Taoist temple dates to the Song dynasty and is still an

Xi'ān

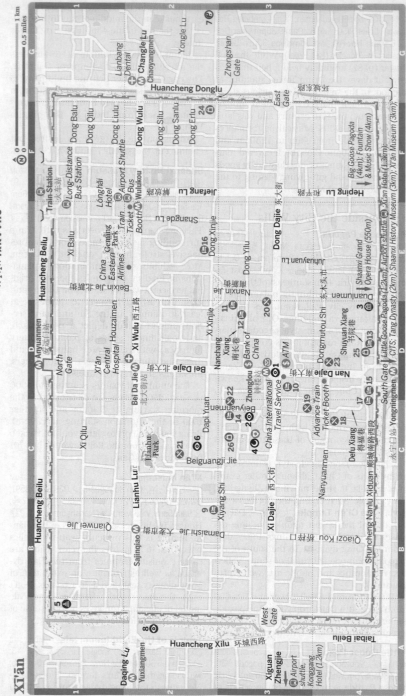

0   1 km
0   0.5 miles

Daqing Lu
Yuxiangmen

Huancheng Beilu

Xi Qilu

Qianwei Jie

Lianhu Lu
Sajinqiao

Lianhu Park

Dapi Yuan

Xiyang Shi

Damshishi Jie

Qiaozi Kou 桥梓口

Huancheng Xilu 环城西路
Taibai Beilu

Xiguan
Zhengjie

Airport
shuttle,
Konggang Hotel (1.2km);

West
Gate

Shuncheng Nanlu Xiduan 顺城南路西段

Nanyuanmen

Defu Xiang
得福巷

Xi Dajie 西大街

Beiguangji Jie

Advance Train
Ticket Booth

China International
Travel Service

Nan Dajie 南大街

Yongningmen
South Gate

Shuyuan Xiang
书院巷

Dongmutou Shi

Duanlumen
东木头市

Juhuayuan Lu

Shaanxi Grand
Opera House (550m);

Little Goose Pagoda; CITS; Tang Dynasty (2km); Shaanxi History Museum (3km); Xi'an Museum (3km);
Little Goose Pagoda (12km); Airport Shuttle; Xi'an Hotel (13km);

Big Goose Pagoda
(4km); Fountain
& Music Show (4km)

Heping Lu 和平路

East
Gate

Zhongshan
Gate

Changle Lu 长乐路
Chaoyangmen

Huancheng Donglu

Lianbang
Dental

Yongle Lu

Dong Balu
Dong Qilu
Dong Liulu

Dong Wulu

Dong Silu
Dong Sanlu
Dong Erlu

Jiefang Lu 解放路

Shangde Lu

Dong Xinjie

Dong Yilu

Dong Dajie 东大街

Nanxin Jie
南新街

Naxin Jie

Bei Dajie 北大街

Xi Xinjie

Nanchang
Xiang
南长巷

Bank of
China

Zhonglou
钟楼站

ATM

ATM

Beixin Jie 北新街

Houzaimen

Xi Wulu 西五路

Xi'an
Central
Hospital

North
Gate
Anyuanmen
安远门

Huancheng Beilu

Train Station
火车站

Long-Distance
Bus Station

Lónghǎi
Hotel

Airport Shuttle
Train
Bus

Train
Ticket
Booth

China
Eastern
Airlines

Gèming
Park

Wulukou

Huancheng Donglu

5
8
21
6
9
22
14
2
26
4
19
18
17
15
10
1
20
11
12
13
25
23
3
16
24
7

Xī'ān

SHAANXI XĪ'ĀN

active place of worship. Supposedly built on the site of an ancient wine shop, it was constructed to protect against subterranean divine thunder. Scenes from Taoist mythology are painted around the courtyard. Empress Cixi, the mother of the last emperor, stayed here in 1901 after fleeing Běijīng during the Boxer Rebellion. Bus 502 runs close by the temple (eastbound from Xi Xinjie).

The small antique market (p389) opposite is busiest on Sunday and Wednesday.

🛌 Sleeping

If you're arriving by air and have not yet booked accommodation, keep in mind that touts at the shuttle-bus drop-off points may get you discounted rooms at a wide selection of hotels.

All hostels in the city offer similar services, including bike hire, wi-fi, laundry, restaurant and travel services. Ask about free pick-up from the train station and book ahead at popular places. In low season (January to March) you can usually get 20% off at hostels.

★ Hàn Táng Inn   HOSTEL $
(汉唐驿, Hàntáng Yì; ☑ 029 8728 7772, 029 8726 6762; www.itisxian.com; 7 Nanchang Xiang, 南长巷7号; dm ¥40-50, s & d ¥160-200; ❄❋@❀; M Zhonglou (Bell Tower)) This very popular hostel has friendly and helpful staff – some of the best in China – and loads of information and tours of Xī'ān. The dorms are compact but clean and have en suite bathrooms. There's a pleasant rooftop terrace with loads

of potted plants and trees, ping-pong table (with lessons from a top coach) and even a sauna!

It's tucked down a small and quiet alley off Nanxin Jie; look for the two terracotta warriors standing guard outside. Activities are organised too, including free dumplings every Friday night. There's a pool-table room and breakfasts are a knockout. Take bus 603 from the train station and get off at Xincheng Guangchang (新城广场), from where it's a short five-minute walk.

Sahara Youth Inn   HOSTEL $
(撒哈拉青年客栈, Sāhālā Qīngnián Kèzhàn; ☑ 029 8728 7631; http://site.douban.com/219529; 180 Beiyuanmen, 北院门180号; dm ¥30-60, tw ¥158; ❀; M Zhonglou (Bell Tower)) You'd think staying smack bang in the Muslim Quarter would be noisy, but Sahara is set well back around a quiet Chinese courtyard in a lovely Qing-dynasty building replete with traditional accents. The beds are firm but rooms are clean and peaceful. You can even see the action outside from the rooftop. You'll be tripping over cats, too.

Shūyuàn Youth Hostel   HOSTEL $
(书院青年旅舍, Shūyuàn Qīngnián Lǚshè; ☑ 029 8728 0092; 2 Shuncheng Nanlu Xiduan, 南门里顺城南路西段2号; dm ¥40-60, s/d ¥160/180; ❋@❀; M Yongningmen) The longest-running hostel in Xī'ān, this converted residence has three lovely courtyards, and a welcoming and enjoyable atmosphere. The cafe has a pizza oven and serves excellent food, and the lively basement bar (guests get a free beer

voucher) is a riot in the evenings. Rooms are simple but clean, the staff is excellent and the location a winner.

Xiāngzǐmén Youth Hostel
HOSTEL $

(湘子门国际青年旅舍, Xiāngzǐmén Guójì Qīngnián Lǚshè; ☏ 029 6286 7888; www.yhaxian.com; 16 Xiangzimiao Jie, 南门里湘子庙街16号; dm/s/tr ¥50/220/240, d ¥150-220; ❄@🛜; Ⓜ Yongningmen) Set around a series of interconnected courtyards, this hostel is a big, sprawling place with an ever-busy pub known for its smoky and noisy atmosphere. Rooms are clean, modern and warm in winter, but make sure to avoid the stuffy windowless basement rooms. There's a lovely courtyard for a coffee where a caged yellow bird sings.

Alley Youth Hostel
HOSTEL $

(秦城小巷客站, Qínchéng Xiǎoxiàng Kèzhàn; ☏ 029 8732 4011; 33 Xicang Nanxiang, Miaohou Jie, 庙后街西仓南巷33号; dm ¥35-40, s ¥120, d ¥140-240; ❄🛜) A reasonable alternative if the other hostels are full, this place is buried away down an alley in the Muslim Quarter. Dorms and doubles are fine and staff are helpful, but the design is a bit sterile, despite the location. It can get busy and noisy outside on market days (Thursday and Sunday).

★ Hàn Táng House
HOSTEL $$

(汉唐驿青年旅舍, Hàntáng Yì Qīngnián Lǚshè; ☏ 029 8738 9765; www.hantanghouse.com; 32 Nanchang Xiang, 南长巷32号; ⏱ dm/s/d/tr ¥60/168/268/338; ❄❄@🛜; Ⓜ Zhonglou (Bell Tower)) A hybrid of sorts, this place has dorms and the vibe of a youth hostel but the look and feel of a three-star hotel. The smart rooms are decked out with high-quality dark-wood furnishings, slab floors and comfortable beds, but lighting is a bit gloomy. The downstairs lobby area is fun and staff are friendly and helpful. Washing is ¥12 per kilo.

There's also a great cafe with good Western food, which converts to a fun bar with live music at night (the singing finishes early). Take bus 603 from the train station and get off at Xincheng Guangchang (新城广场), from where it's a short five-minute walk.

Jano's Backpackers
HOSTEL $$

(杰诺庭院背包旅舍, Jíenuò Tíngyuàn Bēibāo Lǚshè; ☏ 029 8725 6656; www.xian-backpackers.com; 69 Shuncheng Nanlu Zhongduan, South Gate, 南门顺城南路中段69号; dm ¥50-60, d ¥150-300, f ¥320-420; ❄@🛜; Ⓜ Yongningmen) Set in a little faux *hútòng* (narrow alleyway) with artist galleries and cafes nearby, Jano's

is a pleasant place to escape bustling Xī'ān (though street-facing rooms get pub noise). Rooms are well maintained and decorated in traditional style, including some with *kang* (heated beds). There's a lovely courtyard and the family rooms with mezzanine are excellent. Staff speak English. There's a spacious cellar too, with table football.

★ Bell Tower Hotel
HOTEL $$$

(西安钟楼饭店, Xī'ān Zhōnglóu Fàndiàn; ☏ 029 8760 0000; www.belltowerhtl.com; 110 Nan Dajie, 南大街110号; d ¥900-1200, ste ¥1800-2800, incl breakfast; ❄@; Ⓜ Zhonglou (Bell Tower)) Right by the Bell Tower in the centre of downtown, this decent 300-plus-room, four-star hotel has been in business for more than three decades. The expansive foyer is all marble, gloss and the occasional dash of kitsch, while rooms are comfortable and good-looking, and staff are pleasant and welcoming. The pricier ¥1200 rooms look directly onto the Bell Tower. It has low-season discounts of up to 30%.

Sofitel
HOTEL $$$

(索菲特人民大厦, Suǒfēitè Rénmín Dàshà; ☏ 029 8792 8888; www.sofitel.com; 319 Dong Xinjie, 东新街319号; d/ste ¥1760/3150; ♿❄🛜❄; Ⓜ Zhonglou – Bell Tower) Grandly housed, the Sofitel is a fine choice, with a soothing, hushed atmosphere and that crucial central location. Rooms are elegant and comfortable, with top-notch bathrooms, while restaurants are excellent and service is professional and courteous. Reception is in the east wing. Room rates change daily, so you can score a deal when business is slow.

🍴 Eating

Xī'ān has a wide range of restaurants serving cuisine from across China and the world. The Muslim Quarter is an excellent place for snacking, while a good street to wander for a selection of more typically Chinese restaurants is Dongmutou Shi, east of Nan Dajie. All the hostels serve Western breakfasts and meals with varying degrees of success.

Mǎ Hóng Xiǎochǎo Pàomóguǎn
HUI MUSLIM $

(马洪小炒泡馍馆, ☏ 133 5918 5583; 46 Hongbu Jie, 红埠街46号; ¥17; Ⓜ Bei Da Jie) A superb choice for lamb or beef *pàomó;* you need to grab a seat before 11am, otherwise it's all elbows. Pay for your dish, take your seat and then break the round bread into a myriad tiny pieces (they *must* be small) to drop into the bowl, and wait for your meat broth to arrive, splashed over the crumbs for a filling

MUSLIM QUARTER EATS

Hit the Muslim Quarter for tasty eating in Xī'ān. Common dishes here are *májiàng liángpí* (麻酱凉皮; cold noodles in sesame sauce), *fěnzhēngròu* (粉蒸肉; chopped mutton fried in a wok with ground wheat), the 'Chinese hamburger' *ròujiāmó* (肉夹馍; fried pork or beef in pitta bread, sometimes with green peppers and cumin), *càijiāmó* (菜夹馍; the vegetarian version of *ròujiāmó*) and the ubiquitous *ròuchuàn* (肉串; kebabs).

Best of all is the delicious *yángròu pàomó* (羊肉泡馍), a soup dish that involves crumbling a flat loaf of bread into a bowl and adding noodles, mutton and broth. You can also pick up mouth-watering desserts such as *huāshēnggāo* (花生糕; peanut cakes) and *shìbǐng* (柿饼; dried persimmons), which can be found at the market or in Muslim Quarter shops.

The food market around Xīyángshì Jiē (西羊市街) is excellent for everything from lamb skewers to walnuts, cakes, pomegranate juice, flatbreads of all sorts, fried potatoes, fragrant tofu and much more.

and fine meal. Ask either for (清淡; *qīngdàn*) or spicy (辣; *là*).

Hǎiróng Guōtiēdiàn
DUMPLING $

(海荣锅贴店; 67 Zhubashi, 竹笆市67号; mains from ¥12, ⊗ 10.30am-10pm) A civilised and restful choice, this place specialises in *guōtiē* (锅贴) 'pot-sticker' fried dumplings and they are simply delicious. There's six different types to choose from, including a vegetarian choice. There are other dishes on the menu too, including the lovely *tiáozi ròu* (条子肉; ¥32), soft chunks of pork that you squeeze into white buns to consume together.

Dumpling fillings include pork and shrimp (大肉鲜虾馅; *dàròu xiānxiāxiàn*) and vegetable and egg (野菜鸡蛋馅; *yěcàijīdànxiàn*). There are 10 branches in town.

Sānjiěmèi Jiǎozi
DUMPLING $

(三姐妹饺子, Three Sisters Dumplings; ☑ 029 8725 2129; 140 Dongmutou Shi, 东木头市140号; dumplings from ¥14; ⊗ 10.30am-2.30pm & 5-9.30pm) Weary diners with dumpling fatigue will be inspired by the rustic two-room Three Sisters, with its well done twist on classics. Try succulent carrot and lamb dumplings blanketed in crisp peanuts and fried chives. Or for vegetarians, the winning texture of dry and marinated tofu (yes, two types) with the zing of crunchy cilantro and a lashing of chilli.

There's a whole range of other dishes too, including the tangy, sour, cabbage fish soup (酸菜鱼; *sāncàiyú*) and the extremely spicy black-pepper beef (黑胡椒牛柳; *hēihújiāo niúliu*), which will put hairs on your chest. Look for the words 'Restaurant of China' on the outside.

Dǐng Dǐng Xiāng
CHINESE $

(顶顶香; 130 Nanyuanmen, 南院门130号; dishes ¥18-58; ⊗ 10am-10pm; ☑) A clean cafe atmosphere spread over four floors with aspirational snaps of Europe in scattered picture frames on the walls. A lively well dressed crowd peers down onto the street, drinking beer and eating Chinese classics such as hotpots with generous servings. The extensive English picture menu includes excellent veg options.

Muslim Family Restaurant
CHINESE, MUSLIM $

(回文人家, Huiwen Renjia; Beiyuanmen, 北院门; dishes ¥10-98; ⊗ 9am-10.30pm; Ⓜ Zhonglou (Bell Tower)) Right on Beiyuanmen in the heart of the Muslim Quarter, this smart establishment serves classic Muslim dishes such as *ròujiāmó* (beef in flat bread; ¥15), lamb kebabs (¥10 each), beef- or lamb-filled *xiàbǐng* (fried, crispy bread; ¥18 to ¥20), dumplings (¥15 to ¥18) and lovely grilled golden needle mushrooms (¥18).

There's no English sign so look for the veil-adorned female waiting staff in the doorway.

Lǎo Sūn Jiā
SHAANXI $$

(老孙家; ☑ 029 8240 3205; 5th fl, 364 Dong Dajie, 东大街364号5层; dishes ¥12-49; ⊗ 8am-9.30pm; Ⓜ Zhonglou (Bell Tower)) The speciality dish at one of Xī'ān's most famous restaurants (with a 100-year-plus history) is steaming bowls of *yángròu pàomó*. The catch is that the diner is responsible for ripping up the bread before the chefs add the soup. Many other cold and hot dishes are on display, so just point if you don't speak Chinese.

It's located on the 5th floor of a large black glass building.

🍷 Drinking & Nightlife

Xī'ān's nightlife options range from bars and clubs to cheesy but popular tourist shows.

A main bar strip is near the South Gate on leafy Defu Xiang – one of the most pleasant parts of Xī'ān to stroll through by day.

Clubs get going early in Xī'ān. They are free to get into, but expect to pay at least ¥30 for a beer. Most are located along or off Nan Dajie.

ParkQin   BAR
(秦吧, Qínbā; 2 Shuncheng Nanlu Xiduan; Ⓜ Yongningmen) In the basement bowels of the Shūyuàn Youth Hostel (p385), this music bar is a tip-top riot and a fun night out. Staff are excellent and very mindful: look for lovely Kathy with her perfect English. It has lots of coloured terracotta warrior statues, blues music, balloons and delicious savoury snacks delivered to your table.

Jamaica Blue   BAR
(蓝色牙买加, Lánsè Yámǎijiā; Nanchang Xiang; Ⓜ Zhonglou (Bell Tower)) Doubling as a good restaurant, enterprising Jamaica Blue gets a daily workout come sundown as a fine and sociable bar, with live crooning nightly at around 9pm. Moreish, finger-lickin' savoury snacks are delivered free to tables. The layout is a squarish mezzanine, looking down into the lobby of a youth hostel below. Staff are polite and efficient.

The singing finishes at around 11pm to allow guests in the attached hostel to get some kip.

King Garden Bar   BAR
(老城根; Lǎo Chénggēn; ☏029 8797 3366; ⊗7pm-2am; 🛜; Ⓜ Yuxiangmen) Picturesquely located just outside the gate of Yuxiang Men, this slick bar is a cool spot to hang out with Xī'ān's high rollers. With illuminated bar top, snappily attired bar staff, subdued lights and chill-out sounds, the setting is sharp. A lovely outside garden area awaits for the warmer months. A small Tsingtao beer is ¥55, so it's not cheap.

☆ Entertainment

Xī'ān has a number of dinner-dance shows, which are normally packed with tour groups; reservations are recommended. They can be fun if you're in the mood for a bit of kitsch.

Tang Dynasty   LIVE PERFORMANCE
(唐乐宫, Tángyuè Gōng; ☏029 8782 2222; www.xiantangdynasty.com; 75 Chang'an Beilu, 长安北路75号; performance with/without dinner ¥500/220)

The most famous dinner theatre in the city stages an over-the-top spectacle with Vegas-style costumes, traditional dance, live music and singing. It's dubbed into English. Book online for discounts.

Buses can take you to the theatre 1.5km directly south of the South Gate, or walk five minutes south of South Shaomen metro.

Shaanxi Grand Opera House   LIVE PERFORMANCE
(陕歌大剧院, Shǎngē Dàjùyuàn; ☏029 8785 3295; 165 Wenyi Beilu, 文艺北路165号; performance with/without dinner ¥298/198) Also known as the Tang Palace Dance Show, this is cheaper and less flashy than other dinner-dance shows in town. Wenyi Lu starts south of the city walls. You can get a better price by buying your ticket through a reputable hostel or hotel.

Fountain & Music Show   LIVE MUSIC
(Dayan Ta Bei Guangchang, 大雁塔北广场; ⊗9pm Mar-Nov, 8pm Dec-Feb) Some travellers enjoy spending the evening at the free fountain and music show on Big Goose Pagoda Sq; it's the largest such 'musical fountain' in Asia. Try to get here around 20 minutes early for a good spot.

🔒 Shopping

Stay in Xī'ān for a couple of days and you'll be offered enough sets of miniature Terracotta Warriors to form your own army. A good place to search for gifts is the Muslim Quarter, where prices are generally cheaper than elsewhere.

Xīyáng Market   MARKET
(西羊市, Xīyáng Shì) This narrow alley running north of the Great Mosque is a great central stop for souvenirs. With vocal vendors, bargaining is a way of life here. You'll get everything from Terracotta Warriors to shadow puppets, lanterns, tea ware, 'antiques', jade, T-shirts, paintings, Cultural Revolution memorabilia and whatnot. Quality varies a lot, so look for defects, but bargains can be had.

Shuyuan Xiang   FASHION & ACCESSORIES
(书院巷, Shūyuàn Xiàng; Ⓜ Yongningmen) Near the South Gate is the Qing-style Shuyuan Xiang, the main tree-lined strip for art supplies, paintings, calligraphy, paper cuts, brushes and fake rubbings from the Forest of Stelae Museum (p382).

Temple of the Eight Immortals Antique Market
MARKET

(Ⓜ Chaoyangmen) A small antique market sells its wares by the Temple of the Eight Immortals (p383) on Sunday and Wednesday mornings.

Northwest Antique Market
MARKET

(西北古玩城, Xīběi Gǔwán Chéng; Dong Xinjie (Shuncheng Donglu), 东新街 (顺城东路北段); ⊙10am-5.30pm; Ⓜ Chaoyangmen) Serious shoppers can visit the Northwest Antique Market, by Zhongshan Gate. This three-storey warren of shops selling jade, seals, antiques and Mao memorabilia sees far fewer foreign faces than the Muslim Quarter. Dozing street sellers also display their wares south along Shuncheng Donglu (顺城东路北段). As with everywhere, however, examine everything with a critical eye.

ℹ Information

Pick up a copy of the widely available *Xi'an Traffic & Tourist Map* (¥12), a bilingual publication with listings and bus routes. It's available at the airport and some bookshops. Chinese-language maps with the bus routes are sold on the street for ¥5 to ¥6. Shūyuàn Youth Hostel has useful free maps with key bus routes. The English-language magazine *Xianese* (www.xianease.com) is available at some hotels and restaurants that cater to tourists.

China Post (中国邮政, Zhōngguó Yóuzhèng; Bei Dajie; ⊙8am-8pm) Right across from the Bell Tower; Western Union is here too.

Public Security Bureau Exit-Entry Administration Bureau (公安局出入境管理处, Gōng'ānjú Chūrùjìng Guǎnlǐchù; 2 Keji Lu; ⊙8.30am-noon & 2-6pm Mon-Fri) This is on the southeast corner of Xixie 7 Lu. Visa extensions take five working days. To get here from the Bell Tower, take bus K205 and get off at Xixie 7 Lu.

DANGERS & ANNOYANCES

The air in Xī'ān can be highly polluted, so bear this in mind if you suffer from breathing problems or allergies.

If choosing a tour to the surrounding sights, ensure there aren't any shops, commercial outlets or workshops included on the route; you may feel pressured into buying souvenirs or handicrafts.

EMERGENCY

In an emergency call ☑120.

GAY & LESBIAN TRAVELLERS

Like everywhere in China, but especially more in the conservative north, the gay and lesbian scene in town is low-key, low-profile and subtle.

For a list of gay and lesbian spots in town, see www.utopia-asia.com/xianbars.htm.

INTERNET ACCESS

All hostels and hotels offer wi-fi access, as do many restaurants, bars and cafes. Note that wi-fi signals in hostels can vary from room to room, so it can be a good idea to test out the room first.

MEDICAL SERVICES

Lianbang Dental (联邦口腔, Liánbāng Kǒuqiāng; ☑029 8360 0666; 9th fl, Chaoyang Xinshijie, Changle Xilu 长乐西路朝阳新世界9层; Ⓜ Chaoyangmen) This very friendly and professional dental practice is hard-working and has English-speaking staff. Take exit A from the metro station.

Xī'ān Central Hospital (西安市中心医院, Xī'an Shì Zhōngxīn Yīyuàn; www.xaszxyy.com; 161 Xi Wulu, 西五路161号; Ⓜ Bei Da Jie) Centrally located and a short walk from Bei Da Jie metro station.

MONEY

ATM (自动柜员机, Zìdòng Guìyuánjī; ⊙24hr) You won't find it hard to locate usable ATMs. When in doubt, try the southeast corner of the Bell Tower intersection.

Bank of China (中国银行, Zhōngguó Yínháng; 29 Nan Dajie, 南大街29号; ⊙8am-6pm) For ATMs and changing cash.

OPENING HOURS

Opening hours may vary slightly through the year. We've provided high-season opening hours; hours will generally decrease in the low and shoulder seasons. Some museums and sights may be shut either on a Monday or a Tuesday.

Banks 9am–5pm Monday to Friday, and sometimes Saturday and Sunday

Bars 7pm to late

Restaurants 9am–10pm, sometimes closed 2pm–5pm

Shops 10am–10pm

Temples Open early, from 7am or 8am to around 6pm or 7pm

TOURIST INFORMATION

Staffed by English speakers, **Hàn Táng House** (p386), **Hàn Táng Inn** (p385) and the **Shūyuàn Youth Hostel** (p385) are excellent and resourceful sources of impartial travel information for visitors.

The China International Travel Service (CITS) is really only useful for getting people on tours. You're unlikely to be offered independent advice here as it is purely a commercially driven operation. It has two branches.

CITS (CITS, 中国国际旅行社, Zhōngguó Guójì Lǚxíngshè; www.cits.net; 2nd fl, Bell Tower Hotel, 110 Nan Dajie, 南大街二楼110号; ⊙8am-8pm)

CITS (CITS, 中国国际旅行社, Zhōngguó Guójì Lǚxíngshè; www.chinabravo.com; 48 Chang'an Beilu, 长安北路48号; ⏱8am-9pm)

TRAVEL WITH CHILDREN

As an historic city with few attractions for children, Xī'ān can be a challenge for parents. The metro has made getting around town less of a challenge for parents with kids in tow, so use it as much as you can. Prams can be navigated down the road with relative ease. More and more restaurants come with baby chairs, but these can still be hard to find. Baby change facilities will be hard to find in restaurants but easier to find in department stores.

Children may find the full-on Terracotta Warrior history tour rather dull, but may enjoy walking around the Xī'ān City Walls or exploring the sights, sounds and aromas of the Muslim Quarter. Consider a side trip to Huá Shān for athletic teenagers keen to burn off calories and tick off some spectacular views.

TRAVELLERS WITH DISABILITIES

As with most cities in China, Xī'ān is not a very easy city to navigate for those with mobility problems. Pavements frequently have high kerbs and may be littered with obstacles, especially along the smaller back alleys and side streets. Some metro stations have lifts, but not all, and braille is widely used.

The Army of the Terracotta Warriors is generally quite accessible, although not everywhere at the site. The Xī'ān City Walls are usually not accessible to those in wheelchairs. Four- and five-star hotels are far better equipped to deal with travellers with disabilities than three-star hotels or hostels.

ⓘ Getting There & Away

AIR

Xī'ān's **Xiányáng Airport** (西安咸阳国际机场, Xī'ān Xiányáng Guójì Jīchǎng; 📞029 96788; www.xxia.com/en) is one of China's best connected – you can fly to almost any major Chinese destination from here, as well as several international ones. Most hostels and hotels and all travel agencies sell airline tickets.

Daily flights include Běijīng (¥790), Chéngdū (¥750), Guǎngzhōu (¥590), Shànghǎi (¥970) and Ürümqi (¥1040). **China Eastern** (中国东方航空公司, Zhōngguó Dōngfāng Hángkōng; 📞029 8208 8707; 64 Xi Wulu; ⏱8am-9pm) has international flights from Xī'ān to Hong Kong (¥1750), Seoul, Bangkok, Tokyo and Nagoya.

BUS

The **long-distance bus station** (长途汽车站, Chángtú Qìchēzhàn) is opposite Xī'ān's train station. It's a chaotic place. Note that buses to Huá Shān (6am to 8pm) depart from in front of the train station.

Other bus stations around town include the **east bus station** (城东客运站, Chéngdōng Kèyùnzhàn; Changle Lu, 长乐路) and the **west bus station** (城西客运站, Chéngxī Kèyùnzhàn; Zaoyuan Donglu, 枣园东路). Both are located outside the Second Ring Rd. Bus K43 travels between the Bell Tower and the east bus station, and bus 103 travels between the train station and the west bus station. A taxi into the city from either bus station costs between ¥15 and ¥20.

Buses from Xī'ān's long-distance bus station:

Luòyáng ¥105, five hours (10am, noon, 1pm, 3pm)

Zhèngzhōu ¥135, six hours, one daily (10am)

Buses from Xī'ān's east bus station:

Hánchéng ¥75, four hours, half-hourly (8am to 6.30pm)

Huá Shān One way ¥36, two hours, hourly (7.30am to 7pm)

Píngyáo ¥160, six hours (8am, 9.30am, 10.30am, 12.30pm, 4.30pm)

Yán'ān ¥93, five hours, every 40 minutes (8.30am to 5.35pm)

TRAIN

Xī'ān's **main train station** (huǒchē zhàn) is just outside the northern city walls. It's always busy so arrive early for your departure to account for queues and poor signage. Try to buy your onward tickets as soon as you arrive.

Most hotels and hostels can get you tickets (¥40 commission); there's also an **advance train ticket booking booth** (代售火车票, Dàishòu Huǒchēpiào; Nan Dajie, 南大街; ⏱8.50am-noon & 1.30-4.30pm) in the ICBC Bank's south entrance and another **train ticket booth** (代售火车票, Dàishòu Huǒchēpiào; Xiwu Lu, 西五路; ⏱8am-5pm & 5.30pm-midnight) just west of Wulukou metro station on Xiwu Lu. This is much easier than the hectic crowds at the main ticket hall and commission is only ¥5.

Xī'ān is well connected to the rest of the country. For an overnight journey, deluxe Z trains run to/from Běijīng west (hard/soft sleeper ¥273/416, 11½ hours), the later departures leaving Xī'ān at 7.21pm and 7.27pm and Běijīng at 8.12pm and 8.40pm. The Z94 to Shànghǎi departs 4.46pm and arrives 7.53am (hard/soft sleeper ¥332/510, 15 hours).

From Xī'ān's **north train station** (běi huǒchē zhàn) high-speed 'bullet' G trains zip to Běijīng west (2nd/1st class ¥825/516, 5½ hours, 10 daily), Luòyáng (2nd/1st class ¥280/175, 1½ hours), and Wǔhàn (2nd/1st class ¥455/728, four hours, nine daily), with other destinations starting in the next several years.

All prices listed here are for hard/soft sleeper tickets (except where indicated).

Chéngdū Hard/soft sleeper ¥194/301, 11 hours

Chóngqìng Hard/soft sleeper ¥190/285, 11 hours

Guìlín Hard/soft sleeper ¥377/582, 28 hours

Lánzhōu Hard/soft sleeper ¥174/263, seven to nine hours

Luòyáng 2nd/1st class ¥175/280, 90 minutes, 15 daily

Píngyáo 2nd/1st class ¥150/188, 2½ hours, seven daily

Shànghǎi 2nd class seat/soft sleeper ¥338/834, 11 hours, one daily, 8.35pm

Tàiyuán 2nd/1st class ¥179/222, 3½ hours, regular

Ürümqi Hard/soft sleeper ¥497/768, 25 to 35 hours

Zhèngzhōu 2nd/1st class ¥154/249, three hours, twice daily

Within Shaanxi, there are regular trains (including several night trains) to Yúlín (hard seat/sleeper ¥81/154, six to seven hours, regular) via Yán'ān (2nd/1st class ¥96/115, two hours). Buy tickets in advance. There is also an early morning train to Hánchéng (¥17 to ¥42, three to seven hours).

🛈 Getting Around

TO/FROM THE AIRPORT

Xiányáng Airport is about 40km northwest of Xī'ān. Shuttle buses (¥26, one hour) run every 20 to 30 minutes from 5.40am to 8pm between the airport and several points in the city, including the **Lónghǎi Hotel** (龙海大酒店, Lónghǎi Dàjiǔdiàn; 306 Jiefang Lu, 解放路306号). Metered taxis into the city charge more than ¥100.

Airport Bus (机场大巴, Jīchǎng Dàbā; 118 Taoyuan Nanlu, 桃园南路118号; ¥28; M Nanshao Men) Leaves regularly from the Xī'ān Hotel.

Airport Shuttle Bus (机场大巴, Jīchǎng Dàbā; 306 Jiefang Lu, 解放路306号; ¥25) Runs every 20 minutes from an alley by the Lónghǎi Hotel.

Airport Shuttle Bus (机场大巴, Jīchǎng Dàbā; 207 Laodong Nanlu, 劳动南路207号; ¥28) Leaves regularly for the airport from the Konggang Hotel.

BICYCLE

If you can cope with the congested roads, bikes are a good alternative to taxis and can be hired at the youth hostels.

BUS

If you're itching to try out the public buses, they go to all the major sights in and around the city. Bus 610 is a useful one: it passes the train station, then onto the Bell Tower, Little Goose Pagoda, Shaanxi History Museum and Big Goose Pagoda. Remember that packed buses are a pickpocket's paradise, so watch your wallet.

TAXI

Taxi flagfall is ¥9. It can be very difficult to get a taxi in the late afternoon, when the drivers change shifts. Bicycles are a good alternative.

TRAIN

The Xī'ān metro system (西安地铁, Xī'ān dìtiě) started in 2011 with Line 2, followed by Line 1 in 2013 – Line 3 was due to open in 2016, with more lines under construction or in the planning stages. Rides cost ¥2 to ¥5 depending on distance. Useful stations on Line 2 include Běihuǒchē Zhàn (north train station) and Xiǎozhài (near the Shaanxi History Museum). Line 1 has a stop at the Bànpō Neolithic Village. Trains run between around 6.10am and 11.15pm

Around Xī'ān

The ranging plains and flat ochre farmland around Xi'an are strewn with early imperial tombs, many of which have yet to be excavated. Unless you have a particular fascination for imperial burial sites, you can probably come away satisfied after visiting a couple of them. The Army of Terracotta Warriors is obviously the most famous site, but it's really worth the effort to get to the Tomb of Emperor Jingdi as well.

Tourist buses run to almost all the sites from in front of Xī'ān's main train station, with the notable exception of the Tomb of Emperor Jingdi.

👁 Sights

👁 East of Xī'ān

⭐ **Army of Terracotta Warriors** HISTORIC SITE (兵马俑, Bīngmǎyǒng; www.bmy.com.cn; adult/student Mar-Nov ¥150/75, Dec-Feb ¥120/60; ⊙8.30am-5.30pm Mar-Nov, to 5pm Dec-Feb) The Terracotta Army isn't just Xī'ān's premier sight, it's one of the most famous archaeological finds in the world. This subterranean life-size army of thousands has silently stood guard over the soul of China's first unifier for more than two millennia. Either Qin Shi Huang was terrified of the vanquished spirits awaiting him in the afterlife, or as most archaeologists believe, he expected his rule to continue in death as it had in life.

Whatever the case, the guardians of his tomb today offer some of the greatest insights we have into the world of ancient China.

The discovery of the army of warriors was entirely fortuitous. In 1974, peasants drilling a well uncovered an underground vault that eventually yielded thousands of terracotta soldiers and horses in battle formation. Throughout the years the site became so famous that many of its unusual attributes are now well known, in particular the fact that no two soldier's faces are alike.

SHAANXI AROUND XĪ'ĀN

Around Xī'ān

The on-site wrap-around theatre gives a useful primer on how the figures were sculpted. You can also employ a guide (low/high season ¥150/200) or try the audio guide (¥40, plus ¥200 deposit), although the latter is somewhat useless, being difficult to understand and not very compelling.

Then visit the site in reverse, which enables you to build up to the most impressive pit for a fitting finale.

Start with the smallest pit, **Pit 3**, containing 72 warriors and horses; it's believed to be the army headquarters due to the number of high-ranking officers unearthed here. It's interesting to note that the northern room would have been used to make sacrificial offerings before battle. In the next pit, **Pit 2**, containing around 1300 warriors and horses, you can examine five of the soldiers up close: a kneeling archer, a standing archer, a cavalryman and his horse, a mid-ranking officer and a general. The level of detail is extraordinary: the expressions, hairstyles, armour and even the tread on the footwear are all unique.

The largest pit, **Pit 1**, is the most imposing. Housed in a building the size of an aircraft hangar, it is believed to contain 6000 warriors (only 2000 are on display) and horses, all facing east and ready for battle. The vanguard of three rows of archers (both crossbow and longbow) is followed by the main force of soldiers, who originally held spears, swords, dagger-axes and other long-shaft weapons. The infantry were accompanied by 35 chariots, though these, made of wood, have long since disintegrated.

Almost as extraordinary as the soldiers is a pair of bronze chariots and horses un-

earthed just 20m west of the Tomb of Qin Shi Huang. These are now on display, together with some of the original weaponry and a mid-ranking officer you can see up close in a huge modern museum called the **Qin Shi Huang Emperor Tomb Artefact Exhibition Hall** (秦始皇帝陵文物陈列厅; Qínshǐhuángdìlíng Chénlièting).

You can take photographs, although signs forbid using flash photography (widely ignored) or tripods (also ignored by some).

Among rather tacky souvenir offerings, you can get your own warrior statue personalised with your own face (¥100) or have a photo taken next to a fake warrior (¥10). You can also pick up all manner of terracotta ornamentation – from warrior paperweights to life-size statues – from the souvenir shop in the theatre building. There's also a **Friendship Store** for jade, jewellery and so forth.

The Army of the Terracotta Warriors is easily reached by public bus. From Xī'ān train station take one of the air-conditioned buses, either 914 or 915 (¥8, one hour), which depart every four minutes from 6am to 7pm. Take the bus to the last stop; the buses also travel via the Huáqīng Hot Springs and the Tomb of Qin Shi Huang. The car park for the vehicles is a 15-minute walk from the site, but you can take an electric buggy (¥5) instead if you want. If you want to eat here, there's a good cafe in the theatre building and after you exit to walk back to the car and bus park, you will take another route past a whole assortment of restaurants and fast food, including a McDonald's. Buses head back to town from the parking lot.

Tomb of Qin Shi Huang　　HISTORIC SITE
(秦始皇陵, Qín Shǐhuáng Líng; adult/student Mar-Nov ¥150/75, Dec-Feb ¥120/60 incl with Terracotta Warrior ticket; ⊙8am 6pm Mar-Nov, to 5pm Dec-Feb) In its time this tomb must have been one of the grandest mausoleums the world had ever seen. Historical accounts describe it as containing palaces filled with precious stones, underground rivers of mercury and ingenious defences against intruders. The tomb reputedly took 38 years to complete, and required a workforce of 700,000 people. It is said that the artisans who built it were buried alive within, taking its secrets with them.

Archaeologists have yet to enter the tomb but probes and sensors have been sent inside. Levels of mercury inside exceed 100 times normal concentrations, temptingly adding credence to some of the legends. Since little has been excavated there isn't much to see but you can climb the steps to the top of the 76m-high mound for a fine view of the surrounding countryside.

The Terracotta Warriors bus from Xī'ān train station stops at the tomb, which is 2km west of the warriors.

Bànpō Neolithic Village　　VILLAGE
(半坡博物馆, Bànpō Bówùguǎn; Mar-Nov ¥65, Dec-Feb ¥45; ⊙8am-6pm) Bànpō is the earliest example of the Neolithic Yangshao culture, which is believed to have been matriarchal. It appears to have been occupied from 4500 BC until around 3750 BC. The excavated area is divided into three parts: a pottery manufacturing area, a residential area complete with moat, and a cemetery.

This village is of enormous importance for Chinese archaeological studies, but unless you're desperately interested in the subject it can be an underwhelming visitor experience.

◉ North & West of Xī'ān

Fǎmén Temple　　BUDDHIST SITE
(法门寺, Fǎmén Sì; Mar-Nov ¥120, Dec-Feb ¥90; ⊙8am-6pm) Dating way back to the 2nd century AD, this temple was built to house parts of a sacred finger bone of the Buddha, presented to China by India's King Asoka who undertook the distribution of Sakyamuni's relics. The older section is worth a visit and you can join the queue of pilgrims who shuffle past the finger bone. The real reason to make the trip out here is the superb **museum** and its collection of Tang-dynasty treasures.

There are elaborate gold and silver boxes (stacked on top of one another to form pagodas) and tiny crystal and jade coffins that originally contained the four separated sections of the holy finger.

In 1981, after torrential rains had weakened the temple's ancient brick structure, the entire western side of its 12-storey pagoda collapsed. The subsequent restoration of the temple produced a sensational discovery. Below the pagoda in a sealed crypt were more than 1000 sacrificial objects and royal offerings – all forgotten for over a millennium.

Sensing a cash cow, local authorities began enlarging the temple complex and it now includes a sprawling modern section featuring a 1.6km-long walkway lined with 10 golden Buddhas, eccentric modern sculptures and outsized gates. Shuttle buses (¥20) whisk the pious to the main temple, topped with an enormous replica of the box in which the finger bone was kept. Despite the overblown enlargements, for Buddhists this is a very sacred place.

Other notable exhibits are ornate incense burners, glass cups and vases from the Roman Empire, statues, gold and silver offerings, and an excellent reproduced cross-section of the four-chamber crypt, which symbolised a tantric mandala (a geometric representation of the universe).

Reaching Fǎmén Temple is quite an expedition, but direct buses head to the sacred site 115km northwest of town. Tour bus 2 (¥25, 8am) from Xī'ān train station runs to the temple and returns to Xī'ān at 5pm. The temple is also generally included on Western Tours.

Imperial Tombs　　HISTORIC SITE
A large number of imperial tombs (皇陵, huáng líng) dot the Guānzhōng plain around Xī'ān. They are sometimes included on tours from Xī'ān, but most aren't so remarkable as to be destinations in themselves. By far the most impressive is the **Qián Tomb** (乾陵, Qián Líng; Mar-Nov ¥122, Dec-Feb ¥82, incl Tomb of Princess Yong Tai & Tomb of Prince Zhang Huai; ⊙8am-6pm), where China's only female emperor, Wu Zetian (AD 625–705) – from when Tang dynasty Cháng'ān was at its cultural zenith – is buried with her husband Emperor Gaozong, whom she succeeded.

The long **Spirit Way** (神道, Shéndào) – an outdoor, paved path leading to the imperial tomb – is lined with enormous, lichen-encrusted sculptures of animals and officers of the imperial guard, culminating with 61 (now headless) statues of Chinese ethnic group leaders who attended the emperor's funeral. The mausoleum is 85km northwest of Xī'ān. Tour bus 2 (¥25, 8am) runs close to here from Xī'ān train station and returns in the late afternoon.

Nearby are the **tombs** (永泰公主墓、章怀太子墓, Yǒngtài Gōngzhǔ Mù, Zhāng Huái Tàizǐ Mù; Mar-Nov ¥122, Dec-Feb ¥82 incl admission to Qián Tomb) of Princess Yong Tai (永泰幕, Yǒng Tài Mù) and Prince Zhang Huai (章怀幕, Zhāng Huái Mù), both of whom fell foul of Empress Wu, before being posthumously rehabilitated. Other notable tombs are the **Zhao Tomb** (昭陵, Zhāo Líng; ¥40), where the second Tang emperor Taizong is buried, and the **Mao Tomb** (茂陵, Mào Líng; low/high season ¥60/80), the resting place of Wudi (156–87 BC), the most powerful of the Han emperors.

★ **Tomb of Emperor Jingdi**　　TOMB
(汉阳陵, Hàn Yánglíng; Mar-Nov ¥90, Dec-Feb ¥65; ⏰ 8.30am-7pm Mar-Nov, to 6pm Dec-Feb) This tomb, also referred to as the Han Jing Mausoleum, Liu Qi Mausoleum and Yangling Mausoleum, is the burial place of the Han-dynasty emperor Jingdi (188–141 BC) and is quite possibly Xī'ān's most underrated highlight. If you only have time for two sights outside Xī'ān, make it the Army of Terracotta Warriors and this impressive museum and tomb. Unlike the warriors, though, it's not inundated with visitors so you'll have elbow room to fully appreciate what you're seeing.

Much influenced by Taoist precepts, Emperor Jingdi based his rule upon the concept of *wúwéi* (无为; nonaction or noninterference) and did much to improve the life of his subjects: he lowered taxes greatly, used diplomacy to cut back on unnecessary military expeditions and even ameliorated punishments meted out to criminals. The contents of his tomb are particularly interesting, as they reveal more about daily life than martial preoccupations – a total contrast with the Terracotta Army.

The site has been divided into two sections: the museum and the excavation area. The **museum** holds a large display of expressive terracotta figurines (more than 50,000 were buried here), including eunuchs, servants, domesticated animals and even female cavalry on horseback. The figurines originally had movable wooden arms (now gone) and were dressed in colourful silk robes.

Inside the **tomb** are 21 narrow pits, some of which have been covered by a glass floor, allowing you to walk over the top of ongoing excavations and get a great view of the relics. In all, 81 burial pits are believed to be here.

To get here, take Xī'ān metro Line 2 to the station Shitushuguan. Outside exit D take bus 4 (¥1) to the tomb, which leaves at 8.30am, 9.30am, 10.30am, noon, 1.30pm, 3pm, 4pm and 5pm, returning to the Xī'ān metro station at 9am, noon, 4pm and 5pm.

Alternatively, tours (around ¥160 per person) are usually arranged by guesthouses. The tomb is 20 minutes from the airport, so makes an easy stop-off by taxi.

Huá Shān　　华山

📷 0913

One of Taoism's five sacred mountains, the granite domes of Huá Shān used to be home to hermits, sages and Taoist mystics (some of whom could fly, they say). These days, though, the trails that wind their way up to the five peaks are populated by droves of day-trippers drawn by the dreamy scenery. And it is spectacular. There are knife-blade ridges and twisted pine trees poking from crevices and clinging to ledges, while the summits offer transcendent panoramas of green mountains and countryside stretching away to the horizon. Taoists hoping to find a quiet spot to contemplate the *dào* (道) may be disappointed, but everyone else seems to revel in the tough climb and those who overnight can bask in the first glow of sunrise.

◉ Sights & Activities

There are three ways up the mountain to the **North Peak** (北峰, Běi Fēng, adults ¥180, students ¥90), the first of five summit peaks. Two of these options start from the eastern base of the mountain, at the North Peak cable-car terminus. The first option is handy if you don't fancy the climb: an Austrian-built **cable car** (北峰索道, Běifēng Suǒdào; one-way/return ¥80/150; ⏰ 7am-7pm) will lift you silently (bar the on-board announcements) to the North Peak in eight scenic minutes, though you may have to queue for over an hour at busy times.

The second option is to work your way to the North Peak under the cable-car route. This takes two sweaty hours, and two sections of 50m or so are literally vertical, with nothing but a steel chain to grab onto and tiny chinks cut into the rock for footing. It's why this route is called the 'Soldiers Path'.

The third option is the most popular, but it's still hard work, taking between three and five hours. A 6km path leads to the North Peak from the village of Huá Shān, at the base of the mountain (the other side of the moun-

Huà Shān

tain from the cable car). It's pretty easy for the first 4km, but after that it's all steep stairs.

The village at the trailhead is a good place to stock up on water and snacks; these are also available at shops on the trail but prices double and triple the further you head up the mountain. No need to fork out for the white cotton gloves purveyed by loud old ladies; they insist the rust on the chains at the steepest sections will come off on your hands, but in our experience this was not the case.

If you want to carry on to the other peaks, then count on a minimum of eight hours in total from the base of Huá Shān. If you want to spare your knees, you can take the cable car to the North Peak and then climb to the other peaks, before ending up back where you started. It takes about four to five hours to complete the circuit in this fashion, and it's still fairly strenuous and some sections are exhausting. In places, it can be a little nerve-racking, too. Huá Shān has a reputation for being dangerous, especially when the trails are crowded, or if it's wet or icy, so exercise caution.

The scenery is sublime. Along **Blue Dragon Ridge** (苍龙岭; Cānglóng Lǐng), which connects the North Peak with the **East Peak** (东峰; Dōng Fēng), **South Peak** (南峰; Nán Fēng) and **West Peak** (西峰; Xī Fēng), the way has been cut along a narrow rock ridge with impressive sheer cliffs on either side.

The West Peak **cable car** (西峰索道, Xīfēng Suǒdào; one way/return ¥140/280; ⊙7am-7pm) is less crowded than the North Peak cable car and the 20-minute ride offers clear views of all the other peaks at the top, but it is also more expensive.

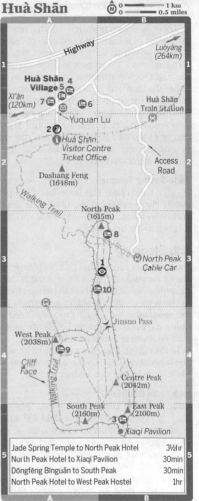

SHAANXI HUÁ SHĀN

Jade Spring Temple to North Peak Hotel	3½hr
North Peak Hotel to Xiaqi Pavilion	30min
Dōngfēng Bīnguǎn to South Peak	30min
North Peak Hotel to West Peak Hostel	1hr

The South Peak is the highest at 2160m and the most crowded. The East Peak isn't as busy, but all three rear peaks afford great views when the weather cooperates. If possible, avoid weekends when foot traffic is heaviest.

At the South Peak thrill-seekers can try the **Plank Walk** (长空栈道, Chángkōng Zhàndào; adult ¥30); a metal ladder leads down to a path made from wooden boards that hover above a 2000m vertical drop. Thankfully, the admission fee includes a harness and karabiners that you lock onto cables, but even with these safety features it's scary as hell.

At peak times, and even in the slow season, queues can get seriously long here.

There is accommodation on the mountain, most of it basic and overpriced, but it does allow you to start climbing in the afternoon, watch the sunset and then spend the night, before catching the sunrise from either the East Peak or South Peak. Some locals make the climb at night, using torches (flashlights) and some of the paths are illuminated. The idea is to start around 11pm and be at the East Peak for sunrise; you get to see the scenery on the way down.

Don't forget warm clothes.

Jade Spring Temple   TAOIST SITE
(玉泉院, Yùquán Yuàn) This large Taoist temple awaits climbers taking the 6km walk from Huá Shān village to the North Peak and lies just before the ticket office.

🛏 Sleeping

You can either stay in Huá Shān village or on one of the peaks. Prices for a bed triple during public holidays. It's best to phone ahead to check on room availability and prices on the mountain, but you'll probably need a Chinese speaker. Mountain hotels are basic, with no showers and shared bathrooms.

In the village, there are a couple of hostels and other cheapies, plus some decent hotels. Most shops have basic, budget rooms.

Huá Shān Bǎoliánjū
Guójì Qīngnián Lǚshě   HOSTEL $
(华山宝莲居国际青年旅舍; ☑ 0913 436 8010; Huashan Lu, 华山路; dm ¥60, s & d ¥198; ✳🖢) This particularly clean, smart but soulless hostel has a lot of exposed brickwork, especially in the lobby and the shower rooms. Rooms are comfortable, if characterless. It's on the main road, so there's a lot of traffic outside.

Huáyuè Quick Hotel   HOTEL $
(华岳快捷酒店; ☑ 0913 436 8555; Yuquan Donglu, 玉泉路, Huà Shān village; s/d/tr/ste ¥228/188/288/388; 🖢) This place right at the intersection has clean and simple rooms with OK bathrooms, but the location is rather noisy with traffic, albeit handy. Rooms are normally discounted to between ¥128 (single and double) and ¥180 (suite).

West Peak Hostel   HOSTEL $
(西峰旅社, Xīfēng Lǚshè; dm ¥100) Rustic and basic, but also the friendliest place on the mountain. It shares its premises with an old Taoist temple.

Huá Shān Huáyì Youth Hostel   HOSTEL $
(华山华驿青年旅舍, Huá Shān Huáyì Qīngnián Lǚshě; ☑ 0913 436 0385; Dongmian Xiang, Lianhua Shanzhuang, 莲花山庄东面巷; dm ¥45-55, r ¥128; ✳🖢) This white-tile hostel in the east of Huá Shān village is a reasonable and friendly choice, with a very quiet setting, way back from the main road. There's a pleasant courtyard, with sunloungers upstairs and excellent views of the mountain, but English is poor. Doubles are good value, although the beds are a bit hard.

The hostel is around 1km to the east of Yuquan Lu along Huashan Lu and south down a side road.

North Peak Hotel   HOTEL $$
(Yúntái Hotel, 北峰饭店, Běifēng Fàndiàn, 云台山庄, Yúntái Shānzhuāng; ☑ 157 1913 6466; dm ¥150-200, d/tr/q ¥720/900/1040) This is the busiest of the peak hotels, but a friendly enough place. Rooms are clean and pretty nice, and they have views; the 'eight-human' dorm is the cheapest. It's also home to Huá Shān Coffee (p397), with its fantastic views.

Wǔyúnfēng Fàndiàn   HOTEL $$
(五云峰饭店; ☑ 138 9135 4822; dm ¥100-180, s & d ¥780, tr ¥900, tr per bed ¥300) This basic place is along the Black Dragon Ridge and on a hillside, not a peak. An OK choice if you're planning on doing a circuit of the rear peaks the next day, or want to catch the sunrise at the East or South Peak. Rooms have views but you'll have to share the loo. There's a restaurant, but no English sign.

★ Huá Shān Guesthouse   HOTEL $$$
(华山客栈, Huàshān Kèzhàn; ☑ 0913 465 8111; www.517huashan.com; 2 Yuquan Lu, 玉泉路2号; s ¥668, d ¥418-628, ste ¥1360-2288; @🖢) This excellent and very friendly place appears less like a hotel and more like a guesthouse, but it's huge and the best hotel in the area. You can usually nab one of the rooms for around ¥280.

Dōngfēng Bīnguǎn   HOTEL $$$
(东峰宾馆; ☑ 0913 430 1312; dm/tr/q ¥150/1149/1280, d ¥960-1040) The top location on the East Peak for watching the sun come up also has the best restaurant. Triples and quads have views from upstairs.

🍴 Eating

Take your own food or eat well before ascending, unless you like to feast on instant noodles and processed meat – proper meals are very pricey on the mountain. Along

Yuquan Lu, every other outlet sells *ròujiāmó* (shredded pork or beef in a bun) for around ¥6 – perfect for stocking up on calories if you're climbing up the mountain.

🍷 Drinking & Nightlife

At the North Peak Hotel, **Huá Shān Coffee** (华山咖啡, Huàshān Kāfēi; North Peak Hotel; coffee from ¥38; ⏱8.30am-5pm, 24hr in summer) is a great place for a coffee, with ranging views through glass windows, and it's open all hours in summer. Otherwise you will be limited to drinking beer in the hotel restaurants.

ℹ️ Getting There & Away

BUS

From Xī'an to Huá Shān, catch one of the private buses (¥36, two hours, 6am to 8pm) that depart when full from in front of Xī'an train station. You'll be dropped off on Yuquan Lu, which is also where buses back to Xī'an leave from 7.30am to 7pm; they depart from the lot opposite the **post office** (Yuquan Lu). Coming from the east, try to talk your driver into dropping you at the Huá Shān highway exit if you can't find a direct bus. Don't pay more than ¥10 for a taxi into Huá Shān village. There are few buses (if any) going east from Huá Shān; pretty much everyone catches a taxi to the highway and then flags down buses headed for Yùnchéng, Tàiyuán or Luòyáng.

TRAIN

Eight high-speed G-class trains (2nd/1st class ¥55/90, 32 minutes) run daily from Xī'an North train station to the recently opened Huá Shān North train station between 9.19am and 9.06pm. In the other direction, the first/last train back to Xī'an leaves at 7.53am/8.50pm. Slower trains (¥20, 90 minutes) also link Xī'an with Huá Shān train station, a different station that services slower trains.

ℹ️ Getting Around

Regular buses (¥5) connect Huá Shān North train station with the **Huá Shān Visitor Centre Ticket Office** (华山游客中心售票处, Huá Shān Lǚyóu Zhōngxīn Shòupiàochù). A taxi will cost you around ¥20. Regular buses (¥3.50) also connect Huá Shān train station with Huá Shān Visitor Centre Ticket Office.

Shuttle buses (one-way/return ¥20/40) to the **North Peak cable car** (p394) run from the Huá Shān Visitor Centre Ticket Office; shuttle buses (one-way/return ¥40/80) also run to the **West Peak cable car** (p395) from here. A free bus runs to the Huá Shān Visitor Centre Ticket Office from the bus station near the foot of the main steps that lead to the Jade Spring Temple on Yuquan Lu. It can be a long wait, though, so you can take a taxi from the village for ¥10, or walk (20 minutes).

Hánchéng 韩城

📞 0913 / POP 59,000

Hánchéng is best known for being the hometown of Sima Qian (145–90 BC), China's legendary historian and author of the *Shiji* (Records of the Grand Historian). Sima Qian chronicled different aspects of life in the Han dynasty and set about arranging the country's already distant past in its proper (Confucian) order. He was eventually castrated and imprisoned by Emperor Wudi, after having defended an unsuccessful general.

For its historical textures and ambience, Hánchéng is a great side trip from Xī'an. Built upon a hill, the new town (新城; *xīnchéng*) located at the top is dusty and unremarkable and is where you'll find hotels, banks and transport. But the more atmospheric old town (古城; *gǔchéng*) at the bottom of the hill boasts a handful of historic sights. The unique Ming-dynasty village of Dǎngjiācūn is 9km further east.

👁️ Sights

Dǎngjiācūn   HISTORIC SITE
(党家村; ¥40; ⏱7.30am-6.30pm) This lovely and perfectly preserved, 14th-century village nestles in a sheltered location in a loess valley. Once the home of the Dang clan (党家), successful merchants who ferried timber and other goods across the Yellow River, it has since evolved into a quintessential farming community. The village is home to 125 grey-brick courtyard houses, which are notable for their carvings and mix of different architectural styles. The elegant six-storey tower is a Confucian Hall.

As with so many small villages, many of the families have moved out and their homes are now exhibition showrooms, so the village feels rather lifeless. However, it's well worth a wander to explore the old alleys and admire the historic architecture.

Dǎngjiācūn is 9km northeast of Hánchéng. To get here, take a minibus (¥4, 20 minutes) from the bus station to the entrance road, from where it's a pleasant 2km walk through fields to the village. A taxi from Hánchéng is another option (¥35 to ¥40).

Confucius Temple   CONFUCIAN SITE
(文庙, Wénmiào; ¥15; ⏱8am-5.30pm) In the heart of the old town, the tranquil Confucius Temple is the pick of the sights in Hánchéng. The weathered Yuan, Ming and Qing buildings give an understated sense of how long they have stood the test of time, along with the

dramatic towering cypress trees (often associated with Confucian sites), half-moon pool and glazed dragon screens. The city museum holds peripheral exhibits in the wings.

Buying a ticket for the Confucius Temple (p397) gets you admission to the City God Temple too. Bus 102 (¥1) runs here from the southwest corner of Huanghe Dajie, close to the bus station. A taxi is ¥10.

City God Temple   CONFUCIAN SITE
(城隍庙, Chénghuáng Miào; Huangmiao Xiang, 隍庙巷; ¥15; ⊘8am-5.30pm) At the back of the Confucius Temple (p397) is the City God Temple (Chénghuáng Temple), in a lane lined with Ming-dynasty courtyard houses. An antediluvian temple has apparently been here since the Zhou dynasty, but this whole site has undergone renovation through the dynasties and in recent years. The main attraction is the Sacrificing Hall, with its intricate roof detail, where gifts were offered to the divine protector of the city.

🛏 Sleeping

For something completely different, spend the night in Dǎngjiācūn, where basic dorm beds in some of the courtyard houses are available for around ¥30. If a local doesn't approach you, just ask and you'll be pointed in the right direction. Places are pretty relaxed about taking foreigners.

Tiānyuán Bīnguǎn   HOTEL $
(天园宾馆, ☎0913 529 9388; Longmen Dajie Beiduan, 龙门大街北段; s & d ¥120-140; ❄@) A few doors down from the main bus station, this place has simple but serviceable rooms.

Yínhé Dàjiǔdiàn   HOTEL $$
(银河大酒店, ☎0913 529 2555; Longmen Dajie Nanduan, 龙门大街南段; r from ¥398; ❄@🖥) This upmarket option offers comfortable accommodation and discounts of around 30%. From the bus station turn left and walk on the main road for about 10 minutes. The name means the 'Milky Way Hotel'.

ℹ Information

Bank of China (中国银行, Zhōngguó Yínháng; cnr Huanghe Dajie & Jinta Zhonglu; ⊘8am-6pm) This branch of Bank of China, close to the bus station, has a 24-hour ATM and will change cash.

ℹ Getting There & Away

Buses (¥75, three hours, seven daily) leave from Xī'ān's long-distance bus station near Xī'ān train station for Hánchéng from 8am onward; the last bus leaves Xī'ān at 7pm. Buses back to Xī'ān run until 6.30pm. There are two buses per day from to Hánchéng to Huá Shān (¥45, two hours) at 7am and noon. There are also two daily buses to Yán'ān (¥80, eight hours) at 6.50am and 8am.

Six trains (¥17 to ¥42, three hours to seven hours) run between Xī'ān and Hánchéng, from 8am to 6.10pm. There's also a less useful slow train at 2.20am. From Hánchéng, the daily K610 train rumbles towards Běijīng (hard sleeper ¥256, 15 hours) via Píngyáo (¥105, six hours) and Tàiyuán (¥123, eight hours), departing at 2.13pm.

Yúlín   榆林

☑ 0912 / POP 92,000

Thanks to extensive coal mining and the discovery of natural gas fields nearby (but you'll see wind farms as well as oil wells on the way up from Yán'ān), Yúlín, a one-time garrison town on the fringes of Inner Mongolia's Mu Us Desert, is booming. Despite all the construction, there's enough interesting stuff to make this a good place to break a trip if you're following the Great Wall, heading north on the trail of Genghis Khan or wandering west to the Hui culture of Yínchuān. If you're on the road from Yán'ān, look out for *yáodòng* (cave dwellings) perforating the hillsides until the land becomes desert.

Parts of Yúlín's earthen **city walls** are still intact, especially running along Changcheng Nanlu, while the main north–south pedestrian street in the elongated old town (divided into Beidajie and Nandajie) has several restored buildings. The lovely **Lingxiao Pagoda** looks down on the town from near the centre of Yúlín and is gorgeously illuminated at night. The Drum Tower is in the same area, overlooking a pleasant and *rènào* (bustling) neighbourhood come evening.

⊙ Sights

Drum Tower   TOWER
(鼓楼, Gǔ Lóu; Bei Dajie, 北大街) Yúlín's drum tower was first erected in 1380 and destroyed several times (the current tower dates to the early 20th century). With several restaurants and antique shops, the whole street is a nice place to wander, especially at night, when it's lit by lanterns and the South Gate (南门; Nánmén) is illuminated.

★**Beacon Tower**   TOWER
(镇北台, Zhènběitái; ¥30; ⊘8am-5pm, later in summer) Seven kilometres north of the Yúlín bus station, on the outskirts of town, are some badly eroded sections of the Great Wall

THE HUI

The Hui (回族) are perhaps China's most unusual ethnic minority; they are the only people to be designated as one solely because of their religious beliefs. The Hui don't have their own language, speaking only Mandarin, and are scattered throughout every province of the country with nearly 80% of the 10-million-odd Hui living outside their official homeland.

Their origins date back more than 1000 years to the time of the Silk Road, when trade thrived between China and the Middle East and Central Asia. Arab traders intermarried with the local women and now most Hui are ethnically indistinguishable from the Han Chinese. What marks them out is their adherence to Islam.

Most Hui men wear white skullcaps, while many women don headscarves. The more educated can read and speak Arabic, a result of studying the Koran in its original language. For many young Hui, learning Arabic is the path to a coveted job as a translator for the Chinese companies on the east coast doing business in the Middle East.

Although the Hui can be found all over China, they are most numerous in the northwest provinces of Gānsù, Níngxià and Shaanxi. True to their origins as traders and caravanserai operators, many Hui are still engaged in small businesses, especially the running of restaurants.

SHAANXI YÚLÍN

and this imposing Ming-era four-storey beacon tower that dates to 1607 (and has been much restored recently). You can climb to the top for long views and also walk past old eroded and wind blasted sections of wall and the stump of a disintegrated watchtower.

There are also two old surviving Siberian elm trees that Yúlín (literally Siberian Elm Forest) is named after; the tree species, now virtually wiped out here, once grew in abundance along the river. Bus 5 (¥1) runs here from Changcheng Nanlu (长城南路), about 200m west of the main bus station. Take the bus to Zhènběitái, which is the last stop, walk in the same direction a further 30m and then turn right; you will see the beacon tower on the hilltop.

Sleeping & Eating

A selection of street stalls can be found in the evenings around the Drum Tower area.

Jingdu Holiday Hotel   HOTEL $$
(晶都假日酒店, Jīngdū Jiàrì Jiǔdiàn; ☑ 0912 354 9966; 3 Yuyang Zhonglu, 榆阳中路3号; r ¥138-158, ste or tr ¥188) This cheapie is actually rather smart, with comfortable and very presentable rooms. It has a fine location near the South Gate and the Drum Tower; it's also a short walk from the main bus station. English skills are very limited, however.

Jīnyù Hotel   HOTEL $$
(金域大酒店, Jīnyù Dàjiǔdiàn; ☑ 0912 233 3333; 6 Xinjian Nanlu, 新建南路6号; s ¥218, tw ¥238-268, ste ¥598, incl breakfast; ❈ @ ☎) This midrange place has well turned-out and smart rooms, with flat-screen TV and oodles of space. It's

near the main bus station, not far from the South Gate; exit the bus station, turn left and it's facing you at the first turn.

There's a branch of Home Inn sharing the same lobby, but it does not take foreigners.

ⓘ Getting There & Around

Taxis around town and to the train station will cost you ¥6. Bus 1 (¥1) runs between the two bus stations. Bus 7 (¥1) runs between the main bus station and the train station.

There are several daily flights from Yúlín to Xī'ān (¥350).

Yúlín has two bus stations. If you get off the bus inside the town walls (near the South Gate), you are at the **main (south) bus station** (汽车站; qìchē zhàn); the **regional (north) bus station** (客运站; kèyùn zhàn) is located 3.5km northwest on Yingbin Dadao, near the intersection with Changcheng Beilu.

The main bus station has regular buses to Xī'ān (¥166 to ¥181, eight hours) from 7.25am to 7.30pm. You can also get frequent buses to Yán'ān (¥87, five hours, half-hourly) from 7.25am to 5pm, to Yínchuān (¥142, five to six hours, eight daily), and two daily buses to Tàiyuán (¥135, eight hours, 6.50am and 12.50pm).

The regional bus station has buses to Bāotóu (¥88, four hours, hourly from 7am to 5.30pm) in Inner Mongolia and to Dōngshèng (¥66, regular from 7.10am to 6.40pm). The buses to Dōngshèng pass by Genghis Khan's Mausoleum. Five buses a day also leave from here to Xī'ān (¥170, eight hours).

The train station is 4km west of the main bus station. There are trains to Xī'ān (hard seat/hard sleeper ¥81/154, six to seven hours, regular) via Yán'ān. There are also regular trains north to Bāotóu (hard seat ¥47, four to five hours).

Ānhuī

POP 66 MILLION

Best Places to Eat

➜ Lao Jie Yīlóu Shíyè (p404)
➜ Pig's Heaven Inn (p406)
➜ Qíyuán Vegetarian (p417)
➜ Gāotáng Húndūn (p403)

Best Places to Sleep

➜ Pig's Inn Bìshān (p407)
➜ Long Lane Inn (p408)
➜ Ancient Town Youth Hostel (p403)
➜ Imperial Guard Boutique Hotel (p409)

Why Go?

Fantastical mountainscapes and well preserved villages make Ānhuī (安徽) the perfect antidote to the brashness of China's larger cities. The main attraction is unquestionably Huáng-shān, a jumble of sheer granite cliffs wrapped in cottony clouds that inspired an entire school of ink painting during the 17th and 18th centuries. But the often overlooked peaks of nearby Jiǔhuá Shān, where Buddhists bless the souls of the recently departed, have a hallowed aura that offers a strong contrast to Huángshān's stunning natural scenery.

At the foot of these ranges are strewn the ancient villages of the province formerly known as Huīzhōu. With distinctive whitewashed walls and black-tiled roofs augmented by lush surroundings of buckling earth, bamboo and pine forest, they are among the most picturesque in the country.

Ānhuī's top sights are clustered in its southeast corner. Easy to navigate and within striking distance of Shànghǎi, this is rural China at its accessible best.

When to Go

Túnxī

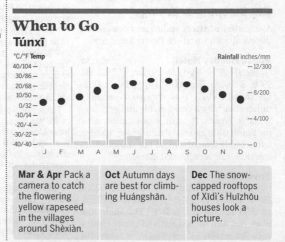

Mar & Apr Pack a camera to catch the flowering yellow rapeseed in the villages around Shèxiàn.

Oct Autumn days are best for climbing Huángshān.

Dec The snow-capped rooftops of Xīdì's Huīzhōu houses look a picture.

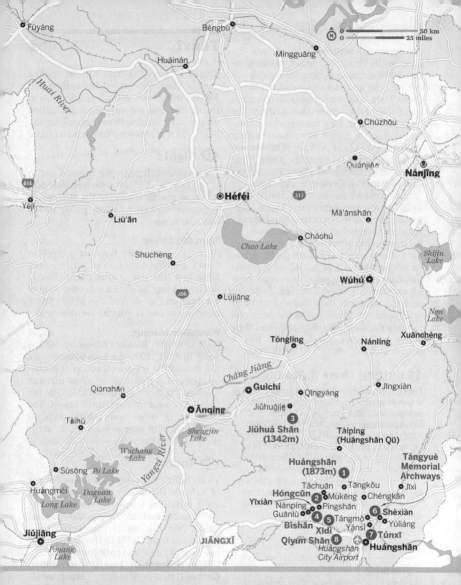

Ānhuī Highlights

1 **Huángshān** (p412)
Catching the sunrise from China's iconic mountain.

2 **Hóngcūn** (p407)
Marvelling at the sophisticated and oh-so-photogenic waterways of an ancient village.

3 **Jiǔhuá Shān** (p415)
Joining the Buddhist pilgrims in scaling the fog-shrouded peak.

4 **Bìshān** Living the grand life of a Qing dynasty merchant at the Pig's Inn Bìshān (p407).

5 **Xīdì** (p406) Wandering the lanes of a white-walled village, a living museum of traditional architecture.

6 **Tángyuè Memorial Archways** (p410) Standing in awe of this procession of stone archways.

7 **Túnxī Old Street** (p402) Sampling Huángshān's famous tea along a lane of restored Qing shopfronts.

8 **Qíyún Shān** (p405) Exploring the grottoes and dilapidated temples of this lofty Taoist haven.

History

The provincial borders of Ānhuī were defined by the Qing government, bringing together two disparate geographic regions and cultures: the arid, densely populated North China Plain and the mountainous terrain south of the Yangzi River (Cháng Jiāng). The region has a long, long history, with excavation sites in the Yangzi River basin turning up some of the oldest evidence of human settlement in Eurasia. During the Three Kingdoms Period many battles were fought here (and warlord Cao Cao was a native son).

Impoverished for much of history and today a primary source of China's hardworking army of *āyí* (nannies), rural Ānhuī's fortunes have begun to reverse. Some say the massive infrastructure improvements in the hitherto remote areas are partly due to former president Hu Jintao, whose ancestral clan hails from Jìxī County. Hu comes from a long line of Huīzhōu merchants, who for centuries left home to do business or fill official posts elsewhere, but would never fail to complete their filial duty and send their profits back home (much of it by way of large homes and ceremonial structures).

ℹ️ Getting There & Around

The historic and tourist sights of Ānhuī gather in the south around the town of Túnxī (also known as Huángshān Shì), which has an airport and high-speed train station. When the rail line to Hángzhōu is completed (in 2017 or 2018), the region will be more accessible from Shànghǎi and Nánjīng, or any other part of China. In the meantime, there are buses to major cities.

Within mountainous Ānhuī, buses are the way to get around. However, as the main sights are clustered in one region, hired taxis are also an option for groups.

PRICE RANGES

Sleeping

Prices for a double room with bathroom.

$ less than ¥250

$$ ¥250–¥750

$$$ more than ¥750

Eating

Price ranges for a main course:

$ less than ¥25

$$ ¥25–¥70

$$$ more than ¥70

Túnxī 屯溪

☑ 0559 / POP 156,000

Ringed by low-lying hills, the old trading town of Túnxī (also called Huángshān Shì; 黄山市) is the main springboard for trips to Huángshān and the surrounding Huīzhōu villages. Compared with the region's capital, Héféi, Túnxī makes for a far, far better base.

◉ Sights

Túnxī's historic heart is the restored Old St (老街; Lao Jie). Unless you're travelling outwards, to nearby villages or the atmospheric Taoist centre Qíyún Shān (p405), there's little else to see.

Túnxī Old Street   STREET

(屯溪老街, Túnxī Lǎojiē) Running a block in from the river, Old St is lined with restored Ming-style Huīzhōu buildings. It's definitely touristy – every block is a repetitive loop of tea shops and snack vendors – but it's pretty nonetheless, and nice for an evening stroll.

Wàncuìlóu Museum   MUSEUM

(万粹楼博物馆, Wàncuìlóu Bówùguǎn; 143 Lao Jie, 老街143号; ¥50; ☉8.30am-9.30pm) This is a fascinating private collection of ceramics, painted scrolls and religious carvings displayed as they were meant to be – in the halls of a wealthy merchant's house. The house itself, three storeys high, with an open-air atrium over a fishpond, is something to behold as well.

☞ Tours

Youth hostels offer day trips to the villages of Xīdì and Hóngcūn (expect to pay around ¥250 including transport, admission fees and lunch) and to Huángshān (around ¥350). They can also arrange tickets for a shuttle bus from Old St to Huángshān (¥22, one hour, 6.15am) and pack you a lunch.

The **Huángshān Tourist Distribution Center** (黄山市旅游集散中心, Huángshān Lǚyóu Jísàn Zhōngxīn; ☑0559 255 8358; 31 Qiyun Lu, 齐云路31号; ☉8.30am-5.30pm), located inside the long-distance bus station, runs day trips and tourist shuttles to surrounding villages, and sells discounted tickets.

🛏️ Sleeping

Túnxī's Old St is an established traveller base, with excellent hostels and boutique hotels in restored wooden homes.

Túnxī

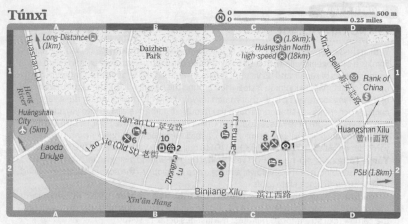

★ Ancient Town Youth Hostel HOSTEL **$**
(小镇国际青年旅舍, Xiǎozhèn Guójì Qīngnián
Lǚshè; ☎ 0559 252 2088; www.yhahs.com; 11
Sanma Lu, 三马路11号; dm ¥40 50, d & tw ¥148-
198; ✳ @ 🛜) Started by some former tour
guides, this hostel ticks all the right boxes,
with a well stocked bar, movie room, friendly and informative English-speaking staff,
bike rental and organised tours. Dorms are
spacious and comfy, but the cheapest of the
(clean) twin rooms lack natural light and
quality varies, so check them out first

Old Street Hostel HOSTEL **$**
(老街国际青年旅舍, Lǎojiē Guójì Qīngnián Lǚshè;
☎ 0559 254 0386; www.hiourhostel.com; 266 Lao
Jie, 老街266号; dm/d/f ¥50/159/220; ✳ @ 🛜)
With a convenient location and decent
rooms, this place clearly has an appeal that
extends beyond the backpacking crowd.
The four-person dorms come with proper
mattresses and private bathrooms; private
rooms are spartan but spacious and comfortable. There's a cafe/bar on the 2nd floor,
overlooking Lao Jie. Helpful staff speak
English and are happy to help make travel
arrangements.

Hui Boutique Hotel BOUTIQUE HOTEL **$$**
(黄山徽舍品酒店, Huángshān Huīshèpǐn Jiǔdiàn;
☎ 0559 235 2003; 3 Lihong Xiang, 老街李洪巷
3号; d ¥580-880; ✳ 🛜) In a Qing dynasty
building with a landscaped courtyard, down
a quiet lane off Old St, this is a cloistered
and atmospheric place to stay. The 1st-floor
rooms (the cheaper ones) have been shoddily
modernised, but the 2nd-floor ones have an-
tique rosewood beds and more natural light.
Look for online discounts to soften the tariff.

🍴 Eating & Drinking

Old St is full of restaurants and stalls sell-
ing classic local snacks like *xièké huáng*
(蟹壳黄), 'yellow crab shells' – actually
baked buns stuffed with meat or vegetables
that just look like crab shells.

There are cheaper street eats and fast-
food restaurants just east of the eastern en-
trance and also along the river on Binjiang
Xinlu.

Zhongma Lu off Old St has a string of cute
coffee shops and bars, all with free wi-fi; cof-
fee and beer starts at about ¥20. Most open
around 10am and close up around 10pm.

★ Gāotāng Húndūn DUMPLING **$**
(高汤馄饨; 1 Haidi Xiang, 海底巷1号; wontons
¥10; ⏰ 7am-10pm; 🥢) Duck down a little al-
ley opposite 120 Lao Jie for what is essen-

WORTH A TRIP

CHÉNGKǍN VILLAGE

With arched bridges over waterways cloaked with lilies, **Chéngkǎn** (呈坎; ¥107; ⊙8am-5pm) is a photogenic village that hasn't yet been completely restored: buildings are in various states of repair and its visitors are far fewer than those at villages more firmly on the tourist map. Chéngkǎn is designed around the *bāguà* (八卦), the eight trigrams of the *I-Ching*, compass points that match up with eight hills surrounding the village. A central river snakes S-shaped through the middle, dividing the village into yin and yang.

Most visitors are here to see southern China's largest ancestral temple, **Luó Dōngshū Temple** (罗东舒祠; Luó Dōngshū Cí), a massive wooden complex several courtyards deep that took 71 years (1539–1610) to build. Also worth a peek is the three-storey **Yànyì Táng** (燕翼堂), nearly 600 years old. The best time to visit is in late April when yellow irises bloom in the shallows, adding a pop of colour to the scenes of whitewashed residences with black slate roofs.

Tourist bus 3 runs from Túnxī's **Tourist Distribution Center** (p402; ¥10, 40 minutes, hourly 8am to 11am and 1pm to 4pm). To get the return bus from the exit, walk up the commercial street for 10 minutes; the last bus departs at 4pm.

Admission to Chéngkǎn is included in the combined ticket for Shèxiàn (p410).

tially an ancient food cart inside an even more ancient Qing dynasty home – run by a 12th-generation *húndūn* (wonton) seller and his family. The speciality is obviously the wontons, made to order and with super-thin skin, though there are other dishes, like fried *jiǎozi* (stuffed dumplings), on the menu too.

Měishí Rénjiā　　　　　　　　HUIZHOU $
(美食人家; 245 Lao Jie, 老街245号; dishes ¥5-108; ⊙10.30am-2pm & 5-10.30pm) Měishí Rénjiā is designed to please everyone: if you want to dig in deep on local specialities, you can find *chòu guìyú* (臭鳜鱼; fermented mandarin fish; ¥108) here. If you just want something light and cheap, you can snack on various *bāozi* (steamed buns stuffed with meat or vegetables; from ¥5). Belly-warming claypots cost ¥25 to ¥40.

Tóngjùlóu Huīcài　　　　　　　HUIZHOU $$
(同聚楼徽菜; ☑0559 257 2777; 216 Lao Jie, 老街216号; mains ¥22-68; ⊙11am-9pm) With a corner positioning at the heart of Lao Jie, this 90-year-old restaurant is a fun place to sample Huīzhōu cuisine. Various stews and dishes of braised meat are arranged in claypots, so take a look and see what you fancy, order up, grab some beers and claim an outside table.

★Lao Jie Yīlóu Shíyè　　　　HUIZHOU $$$
(老街一楼食业; ☑0559 235 9999; 247 Lao Jie, 老街247号; mains ¥28-88; ⊙11am-1.30pm & 5-8.30pm) Considered the best restaurant on Old St, this is the place to splash out on

Huīzhōu delicacies, like *tiánluó* (田螺; pond snails), here braised in a plate-licking concoction of soy sauce and spices. Also excellent is the Huīzhōu *wēisānbǎo* (徽州煨三宝), a stew of 'three treasures' – salt-cured pork, thin skins of tofu tied in decorative knots, and puffs of fried tofu stuffed with meat. There's a picture menu.

🛍 Shopping

★Xiè Yù Dà Tea　　　　　FOOD & DRINKS
(谢裕大茶行, Xiè Yù Dàchāháng; 149 Lao Jie, 老街149号) Old St is lined with tea shops but Xiè Yù Dà Tea is the real deal, founded by Xie Zhengan (1838–1910) – the man who first marketed Huángshān's now famous *máofēng* (毛峰) tea. Literally 'fur peak', the subtle, slightly floral green tea gets its name from an almost indiscernible peach fuzz.

ℹ Information

Hostels have wi-fi and computers for internet access (usually ¥4 per hour).

Bank of China (中国银行, Zhōngguó Yínháng; cnr Xin'an Beilu & Huangshan Xilu, 新安北路黄山西路的路口; ⊙8am-5.30pm) Changes travellers cheques and major currencies; 24-hour ATM.

China Post (中国邮局, Zhōngguó Yóuqú; cnr Xin'an Beilu & Yan'an Lu, 新安北路延安路的路口; ⊙8am-5pm)

Public Security Bureau (PSB, 公安局, Gōng'ānjú; ☑0559 251 2929; 108 Changgan Donglu, 长干东路108号; ⊙8am-noon & 2.30-5pm) For visa extensions and police assistance.

ℹ️ Getting There & Away

AIR

Daily flights from Huángshān City Airport (黄山市飞机场; Huángshānshì Fēijīchǎng), located 5km west of town:

Běijīng ¥1140, 2½ hours, one daily
Guǎngzhōu ¥1010, 1½ hours, one daily
Shànghǎi ¥630, one hour, one daily

Flights usually depart late in the evening.

BUS

The **long-distance bus station** (客运总站, Kèyùn Zǒngzhàn; ☏ 0559 256 6666; 31 Qiyun Dadao, 齐云大道31号; ⏱ 5.45am-5.50pm) is roughly 2km west of the train station on the outskirts of town. Destinations include the following:

Hángzhōu ¥85, three hours, hourly (7.10am to 5.50pm)
Jǐngdézhèn ¥61, 3½ hours, three daily (9.15am, noon and 2.10pm)
Nánjīng ¥122, 5½ hours, four daily (7.40am, 9.30am, 12.10pm and 4.20pm)
Shànghǎi ¥135, five hours, 10 daily (last bus 4.20pm)
Sūzhōu ¥132, six hours, three daily (6.50am, 11am and 1.30pm)
Wùyuán ¥45, two hours, one daily (8.30am)

Within Ānhuī, buses go to these destinations:
Héféi ¥114, four hours, hourly (7.30am to 4pm)

Jiǔhuá Shān ¥63, 3½ hours, one daily (1.30pm)
Shèxiàn ¥7, 45 minutes, frequent services (6am to 5pm)
Yīxiàn ¥13, one hour, frequent services (6am to 5pm)

Buses to Huángshān go to the main base at Tāngkǒu (¥20, one hour, every 20 minutes, 6am to 5pm) and on to the north entrance, Tàipíng (¥20, two hours). There are also minibuses to Tāngkǒu (¥20) from in front of the train station (6.30am to 5pm) that leave when full.

Inside the bus station (to the right as you enter) is the separate **Huángshān Tourist Distribution Center** (p402) with tourist buses following three routes to popular destinations.
Bus 1 Qíyún Shān (¥10, 45 minutes), Xīdì (¥14, one hour) and Hóngcūn (¥18, 1½ hours); hourly 8am to 4pm, last return bus 5pm
Bus 2 Tángmó (¥5.50, 45 minutes), Tángyuè (¥6, one hour), Huīzhōu Old Town (¥8, 75 minutes) and Yúliáng (¥9, 90 minutes); 8am, 10am, 2pm and 4pm, last return bus 4pm
Bus 3 Chéngkǎn (¥10, 40 minutes); hourly 8am to 11am and 1pm to 4pm, last return bus 4pm

TRAIN

At the time of research, there was one direct high-speed train departing at 2.33pm from Huángshān North station (黄山北站; Huángshān Běizhàn) for Hángzhōu East (¥304, 3½ hours) and Shànghǎi (¥549, 6½ hours). Otherwise, it's necessary to first take one of

ĀNHUĪ TÚNXĪ

WORTH A TRIP

QÍYÚN SHĀN

Qíyún Shān means 'mountain as high as the clouds' and it's an apt description for this **mountain** (齐云山; Mar-Nov ¥75, Dec-Feb ¥55; ⏱ 8am-5pm Mon-Fri, 7.30am-5.30pm Sat & Sun): though not actually that high (just 585m) its peaks do pierce the low-lying, ghostly puffs of mist that regularly envelop the region. Long venerated by Taoists, the reddish sandstone rock provides a mountain home to temples, many built into the mountain itself, and the monks who tend to them. Qíyún Shān is a 45-minute bus trip west of Túnxī.

Most tour groups get dropped off at a back entrance, so if you arrive by public bus you'll likely be on your own for the 75-minute climb up stone steps to the ticket office. Just beyond, **Zhēnxiān Cave** (真仙洞府; Zhēnxiān Dòngfǔ) houses a complex of Taoist shrines in grottoes and niches gouged from the sandstone cliffs. Further on, seated within in the smoky interior of the vast and dilapidated **Xuán Tiān Tàisù Gōng** (玄天太素宫) is an effigy of Zhengwu Dadi, a Taoist deity. A further temple hall, the **Yùxū Gōng** (玉虚宫), is erected beneath the huge brow of a 200m-long sandstone cliff, enclosed around effigies of Zhengwu Dadi and Laotzu.

A village – seemingly plonked in the middle of the mountain range – stretches along the poetically named **Moonlight Street** (月华天街; Yuehua Tian Jie). Most residents operate restaurants and snack stands from their homes.

The bus from Túnxī will likely drop you off on the side of the road, from where you'll walk through a village to **Dēngfēng Bridge** (登封桥; Dēngfēng Qiáo). Return buses sometimes hang around the bridge; otherwise wait at the side of the road for buses coming from Yīxiàn. The last bus from Yīxiàn to Túnxī departs at 5pm; the last tourist bus departs at 4pm.

the frequent trains to Shàngráo (上饶; ¥74, one hour) and transfer. When the Huángshān–Hángzhōu rail line is completed, the trip between the two will take just 1½ hours.

Regular-service trains depart from the older Huángshān station in central Túnxī:

Běijīng Hard/soft sleeper from ¥262/489, 20 hours, 9am and 4.30pm

Nánjīng Hard/soft sleeper ¥100/153, six to seven hours, six daily

Shànghǎi Hard/soft sleeper ¥163/251, 12 hours, 8.45pm and 10.17pm

🛈 Getting Around

The 5km taxi from the airport to Old St should cost ¥30.

Bus 2 (¥2) runs between the bus station and Old St; bus 12 (¥2) runs between Huángshān train station and Old St.

Taxi flag fall is ¥7, but most drivers who hang out around Old St refuse to use the meter. Grab one from Binjiang Xilu instead, or pay the accepted fares from Old St: long-distance bus station or main train station ¥10; high-speed train station (Huángshān Běizhàn) ¥50.

Xīdì   西递

☎ 0559 / POP 1000

Typical of the elegant Huīzhōu style, Xīdì's 124 surviving buildings reflect the wealth and prestige of the prosperous merchants who settled here. Its Unesco World Heritage Site status means Xīdì (¥104; 7am to 5pm) enjoys a lucrative tourist economy, yet it remains a picturesque tableau of slender lanes, cream-coloured walls topped with horse-head gables, roofs capped with dark tiles, and doorways ornately decorated with carved lintels. From here you can head out further into the countryside, to explore less-visited villages such as Nánpíng, **Guānlù** (关麓; ¥35; ⊗7.30am-5pm) and Bìshān.

◉ Sights

Dating to AD 1047, the village has for centuries been a stronghold of the Hu (胡) clan, descended from the eldest son of the last Tang emperor who fled here in the twilight years of the Tang dynasty. The magnificent three-tiered Ming dynasty decorative arch, the **Húwénguāng Páifāng** (胡文光牌坊), at the entrance to the village, is an ostentatious symbol of Xīdì's former standing.

Numerous other notable structures are open for inspection, including **Díjí Hall** (迪吉堂; Díjí Táng) and **Zhuīmù Hall** (追慕堂; Zhuīmù Táng), both on Dalu Jie (大路

街). **Jìng'ài Hall** (敬爱堂; Jìng'ài Táng) is the town's largest building, a multipurpose hall where wedding ceremonies and clan meetings were held and punishments meted out. Back in the day, women weren't allowed inside. **Xīyuán** (西园) is a small house known for its exquisite stone carvings on the windows. Unlike regular carvings, these are carved on both sides.

Paths lead out from the village to nearby hills where there are suitable spots for picture-postcard panoramas of the village (though a mobile-phone tower blights the landscape). If you want to avoid the crowds, you'll have to start early or hang out late: tour groups start roaming around at 7am and only trickle out at 5pm or so.

Nánpíng   VILLAGE

(南屏; ¥43; ⊗8am-5pm) Labyrinthine Nánpíng has a history of more than 1100 years. However, it's relatively recent history that draws most visitors, particularly film fans: much of Zhang Yimou's 1989 tragedy *Judou* was filmed inside the village's **Xùzhì Hall** (叙秩堂; Xùzhì Táng). Props from the film and behind-the-scenes photographs from the filming are on display inside the dramatic 530-year-old hall. Parts of Ang Lee's 1999 *Crouching Tiger, Hidden Dragon* were filmed next door in the Ming dynasty **Kuíguāng Hall** (奎光堂; Kuíguāng Táng).

Nánpíng is 5km west of Yīxiàn. Minibuses (¥3) depart for Nánpíng every 30 minutes (7am to 4pm) from Yīxiàn; a taxi from Xīdì costs ¥40.

🛏 Sleeping & Eating

Xīdì and nearby Bìshān have two of the most attractive boutique hotels in the region.

There are plenty of indistinguishable restaurants and snack vendors here. The best meals in town are served at the Pig's Heaven Inn, at the back of the village – it's well worth the trouble of finding it.

⭐ **Pig's Heaven Inn**   BOUTIQUE HOTEL $$
(猪栏酒吧, Zhūlán Jiǔbā; ☎0559 515 4555; http://blog.sina.com.cn/zhulanjiuba; Renrang Li, Xidi, 西递镇仁让里; s/d incl breakfast ¥390/610; ❈@◈) When Shànghǎi artist Li Guoyu discovered this Ming dynasty home it was being used as a pig's pen (hence the name). She painstakingly restored it, adding an eclectic blend of vintage furniture and mid-20th-century memorabilia. Cheaper rooms are a little pokey but all guests can make use of the common areas, including a

RETURN TO THE VILLAGES

In 2012 China's urban population exceeded its rural one. Yet while waves of farmers are moving to the cities, a small trickle of urban artists are heading back to the villages.

In the early 2000s Shànghǎi artist Li Guoyu moved to Xīdì, restoring the dilapidated Ming structure that would become the **Pig's Heaven Inn**. Two more properties, this time in Bìshān (璧山), a tiny village 10km to the west, followed. Her clientele are mostly urbanites themselves, seeking a quiet interlude and fresh air.

Li is not the only one to zero in on Bìshān: Běijīng artists Ou Ning and Zuo Jing started the Bishan Project in 2011. It began as an attempt to create a model for village revival that would see artists and villagers working together and that would favour community over commercialism. It's a work in progress, fraught with questions of authenticity, upward mobility and gentrification, discussed in their magazine, *Bishan*. Though one undeniably attractive addition they've made to the village is the temple of books that is the **Librarie Avant-Garde**, even if few villagers could afford to shop there.

3rd-floor verandah overlooking the village rooftops.

★ **Pig's Inn Bìshān**　　BOUTIQUE HOTEL $$$
(猪栏酒吧璧山, Zhūlán Jiǔbā Bìshān; ☑ 0559 517 5555; http://blog.sina.com.cn/zhulanjiuba; Bìshān, 璧山村; tw/d incl breakfast ¥790/910; 闇 ⍚) ⍝
There is no better way to experience the extravagant villas of the Huīzhōu merchants than to spend a few days living in one, waking for breakfast overlooking the courtyard, and spending a rainy afternoon in the wood-panelled study. At this boutique hotel, inside a Qing dynasty home masterfully restored by Li Guoyu, you can do exactly that.

🛍 Shopping

Librarie Avant-Garde　　BOOKS
(先锋书店, Xiānfēng Shūdiàn; Bìshān, 璧山; ⊙10am-noon & 1-6pm) An unlikely bookstore in an unlikely place, this is the Bìshān branch of storied Nánjīng bookstore, Librarie Avant-Garde, coaxed into existence by a pair of Běijīng artists who relocated to the village. While the open-air courtyard of a restored ancestral hall may not be the best environment for books (it's awfully damp), it certainly is stunning.

❶ Getting There & Around

Tourist bus 1 runs to Xīdì (¥14, one hour) from Túnxī's Huángshān Tourist Distribution Center (p402), leaving hourly from 8am to 4pm. From Xīdì buses leave hourly for Hóngcūn (¥6, 30 minutes), stopping at Píngshān (¥6, 15 minutes).

For Tāngkǒu you'll need to first get a bus to Hóngcūn.

For all other onward travel, you'll need to first get to Yìxiàn (¥3, 20 minutes, every 30 minutes, 7.30am to 3.30pm), the nearest transit hub.

From Yìxiàn, it's possible to travel on to Jiǔhuá Shān (¥50, 3½ hours, two daily, 6.50am and 1.15pm), Hángzhōu (¥91, two daily, 8.15am and 1.35pm) and Shànghǎi (¥151, two daily, 7.20am and 2.20pm). There are also frequent buses between Yìxiàn and Túnxī's long-distance bus station (¥13, one hour).

To get to Guānlù and Nánpíng, you'll need to first travel to Yìxiàn, where you can get a minibus (¥3, every 30 minutes, 7am to 4pm) that stops at both villages. Minibuses also travel to Bìshān (¥2, 15 minutes, hourly 7.30am to 3.30pm).

It's easier to pick up a taxi in Xīdì than a pedicab. A taxi ride to Nánpíng or Guānlù costs around ¥40; to Bìshān, ¥20.

Hóngcūn　　宏村
☑ 0559 / POP 4000

Hóngcūn (¥104; 7am to 5.30pm), a Unesco World Heritage Site, is the most-visited of the Huīzhōu villages. It is a standout example of ancient feng shui planning, a perfect marriage of symbolism and function, predicated on a sophisticated network of waterways. Founded in the Song dynasty, the village was remodelled in the Ming dynasty by village elders, under the direction of a geomancer, to suggest an ox; its still-functioning waterway system represents the animal's entrails.

◉ Sights

Hóngcūn has crescent-shaped **Moon Pond** (月沼; Yuè Zhǎo) at its heart, or rather at its stomach – as that's what the pond represents in the village's ox-shaped layout. Larger **South Lake** (南湖; Nán Hú), built later, is another stomach; **Léigǎng Mountain** (雷岗山; Léigǎng Shān), to the north, is the head. The busy square by **Hóngjì Bridge** (宏济桥;

Hóngjì Qiáo) on the West Stream is shaded by two ancient trees (the 'horns' of the ox), a red poplar and a gingko.

Traditionally, villagers followed a strict time regimen: collecting water before 6am, washing vegetables from 6am to 7am and doing laundry afterwards. Alleyway channels flush water through the village from West Stream to Moon Pond and from there on to South Lake. Lost? Just follow the water flow.

If the bridge at the entrance to the village looks familiar, it's because it featured in the opening scene of Ang Lee's *Crouching Tiger, Hidden Dragon*. The picturesque Moon Lake also features in the film. Built by a salt merchant, the **Chéngzhì Hall** (承志堂, Chéngzhì Táng; Shangshuizhen Lu, 上水圳路) dates from 1855 and has 28 rooms, adorned with fabulous woodcarvings, 2nd-floor balconies and lightwells. Peepholes on top-floor railings are for girls to peek at boy visitors and the little alcove in the mah-jong room was used to hide the concubine. The now-faded gold-brushed carvings are said to have required 100 taels of the expensive stuff and took over four years to complete.

Other notable buildings include the **Utopian Residency** (桃源居; Táoyuán Jū), with its elaborate carved wood panels, and the **South Lake Academy** (南湖书院; Nánhú Shūyuàn), which enjoys an enviable setting beside tranquil South Lake. Overlooking Moon Pond is a gathering of further halls, chief among which is the dignified **Lèxù Hall** (乐叙堂; Lèxù Táng), a hoary Ming antique from the first years of the 15th century.

Mùkēng Zhúhǎi FOREST
(木坑竹海; ¥30; ⊙7.30am-5pm) A forest of feathery bamboo, Mùkēng is most famous as the setting for the breathtaking bamboo-top fight scenes in *Crouching Tiger, Hidden Dragon*. You can't quite get to the exact spot, but you can hike 1km up the ridge for views over the grove of golden plumes.

Mùkēng is 5km northwest of Hóngcūn, on the route to Huángshān.

🛏 Sleeping

Hóngcūn makes for a convenient base to explore the Huīzhōu villages. It has the best budget options in the area.

Qíng Hé Yuè HOSTEL $
(清和月; ☑139 5596 8814, 0559 217 1713; 28-29 Hou Jie, 后街28-29号; dm/d ¥60/380; ❀ ⊗) Tidy, though small, dorm rooms with showers sleep six. Across the alleyway a 200-year-old villa houses the double rooms. All guests are free to use the common areas in the old house, the highlight of which is the 3rd-floor verandah, from where you can look out over the village rooftops. Friendly staff speak good English.

Hóngdá Tíngyuàn HOMESTAY $
(宏达庭院; ☑0559 554 1262; 5 Shangshui Zhen, 上水圳5号; d/tr ¥160/200; ⊗ ❀) The draw of this Hóngcūn home is the verdant courtyard filled with potted daphne, heavenly bamboo and other flowering shrubs, all set around a small pond and pavilion. Its rooms are unadorned, but the peaceful location in the upper part of the village is ideal. You can stop by for lunch (dishes from ¥20), space permitting. No English spoken.

★**Long Lane Inn** BOUTIQUE HOTEL $$
(宏村一品更楼, Hóngcūn Yìpǐn Gēng Lóu; ☑0559 554 2001; 1 Shangshui Zhen, 上水圳1号; r incl breakfast ¥380-1280; ❀ ⊛) Housed in a gorgeous Ming dynasty villa, Long Lane Inn is a tourist attraction in its own right. There are nine different rooms, some with traditional rosewood Chinese four-poster beds, arranged around a courtyard. It's in a quiet corner of the village, away from the tourist scrum. Mornings start with birdsong and a good Chinese breakfast.

❶ Getting There & Away

Tourist bus 1 runs to Hóngcūn (¥20, 1½ hours) via Xīdì from Túnxī's Huángshān Tourist Distribution Centre, leaving hourly from 8am to 4pm. Return buses run hourly from 8am to 5pm. The fare from Hóngcūn to Xīdì (30 minutes) and Píngshān (15 minutes) is ¥6.

From Hóngcūn you can travel onward to Tāngkǒu, for Huángshān (¥15, one hour, hourly 6.50am to 2.50pm).

❶ Getting Around

There are bicycle rental shops (出租自行车; chūzū zìxíngchē; per day ¥40) outside the village, on the modern street opposite Hóngjì Bridge.

Taxis and pedicabs can be picked up in front of the village. A pedicab ride to **Tǎchuān** (塔川; ¥20; ⊙7.30am-5pm) and **Mùkēng Zhúhǎi** (p408) costs ¥30. You'll need to negotiate for the driver to wait for you as returning pedicabs are rare.

Píngshān 屏山

☑0559 / POP 3050

Píngshān (¥50; 7.30am to 5pm), first settled in the Tang dynasty, was once the largest village in the county, with 38 ancestral halls and 13 archways. Its stature made it a target during the Cultural Revolution; only a handful of these structures remain. The lack of grand halls means that Píngshān sees few visitors; most who do come are art students sitting with easels in shady corners. With its canal lined with rose bushes, meandering cobblestone lanes and whitewashed homes, the village does make a pretty picture. Just a few kilometres away is Xiùlǐ, a repository of restored old buildings.

◉ Sights

Píngshān village was designed as a boat riding through the waves of hills (and historical forces), its residential houses likened to cabins. Some noteworthy structures include **Píngshān Gōngzhì** (屏山拱峙), the only gate still standing, and **Shūguāngyù Hall** (舒光裕堂; Shūguāngyù Táng), the only painted *ménlóu* (门楼; gate house) in Huīzhōu. The nearly 300-year-old **Imperial Guard Temple** (御前侍卫寺; Yùqián Shìwèi Sì), with its glorious entranceway of elaborately carved stone, has been artfully refashioned into a cafe and boutique hotel.

At the northern tip of the villages is the rouge-coloured, 900-year-old **Sāngū Miào** (三姑庙; Three Goddess Temple). In the temple's main hall are the Sānshèng Lóngnǚ (Three Sacred Dragon Girls) with 18 *luóhàn* (arhat; 罗汉) in attendance.

Yīxiàn Xiùlǐ Cinema Village HISTORIC BUILDING
(黟县秀里影视村, Yīxiàn Xiùlǐ Yǐngshìcūn; Xiùlǐ, 秀里; ¥50) Xiùlǐ, which opened in 2007, is a collection of 100-plus historic structures from around Yīxiàn County, left in ruins because their owners couldn't afford to maintain them. Here they've been restored and given new life, with art deco touches adding extra cachet. What could be a tourist trap is actually an arrestingly beautiful, if artificial, village, curated with a film-maker's eye (it's the pet project of film producer and frequent Yimou Zhang collaborator Zhenyan Zhang).

If it looks like a film set that's because some of the buildings have appeared in films. Classic Chinese films screen daily in one of the old halls, repurposed into a cinema. Xiùlǐ also runs artist-in-residence programs and holds exhibitions in some of the halls. The village is 3.5km from Píngshān, just off Rte 218.

⌂ Sleeping

Píngshān and Xiùlǐ both have splurge-worthy boutique hotels, though unless you're also planning to splurge on a driver, neither make for a convenient base. Budget accommodation in Píngshān caters exclusively to classes of art students who book en masse. Xiùlǐ has only one hotel and is very quiet.

Xiùlǐ Huīzhōu Culture Hotel BOUTIQUE HOTEL $$
(秀里惠州文化酒店, Xiùlǐ Huīzhōu Wénhuà Jiǔdiàn; ☏ 0559 518 2979; Xiùlǐ, 秀里; r ¥600-6000; ❈ ❋ ⊛) Filling several restored buildings inside the Yīxiàn Xiùlǐ Cinema Village, this new boutique hotel has 31 rooms of various configurations, from humble doubles to sprawling family suites, decorated with a careful selection of antiques. Guests can take advantage of the pool, inside another refitted historic hall, with colourful, Mondrian-esque window panes.

★ **Imperial Guard**
Boutique Hotel BOUTIQUE HOTEL $$$
(御前侍卫艺术精品酒店, Yùqián Shìwèi Yìshù Jīngpǐn Jiǔdiàn; ☏ 0599 555 2777, 133 5909 1777; imperial_guard@163.com; Píngshān, 屏山村; d & tr incl breakfast ¥900-2300; ❈ ❋) All that was left of the nearly 300-year-old Imperial Guard Temple was the facade. Film producer Zhenyan Zhang reinvented the rest using beams salvaged from other structures and concession-era antiques. The result is this new, swoon-worthy 10-room boutique hotel, favoured by movers and shakers of the Chinese film world. Zhang's son, who speaks fluent English, and his wife manage the place.

ⓘ Getting There & Away

Píngshan and Xiùlǐ are inbetween Hóngcūn and Xīdì. Hourly buses running to and from the two villages can drop you off in Píngshān or Xiùlǐ (¥6, 15 minutes); tell the driver when you get on the bus where you want to get off. You can try to hail the same bus from the side of the road going back, though this isn't always possible and it's nearly impossible to pick up a cab at either village. As such, it's best to visit these two areas with a hired taxi or pedicab from Xīdì.

Shèxiàn 歙县

☏ 0559 / POP 490,000

Shèxiàn is 25km east of Túnxī and can be visited as a day trip. The town was formerly the grand centre of the Huīzhōu culture, serving as its capital. Today, the city's classic Old Town is the main sight. The nearby port of Yúliáng harbours an architectural heritage entirely different from the other Huīzhōu villages. Shèxiàn is also the jumping-off point for visiting the memorial archways of Tángyuè, the best collection of their kind in the region.

⊙ Sights

A combined ticket for Huīzhōu Old Town, **Tángmó** (唐模; adult/student ¥80/50, child & senior free; ⊘ 8am-5pm) and Tǎngyuè Memorial Archways (¥220) is a good deal if you plan to visit everything; it also includes entry to the village of Chéngkǎn.

Tángyuè
Memorial Archways   MONUMENT
(棠樾牌坊群, Tángyuè Páifāng Qún; www.paifangqun.com; adult/student ¥100/50, child & senior free; ⊘ 7.30am-5.30pm) Over generations, the Bao (鲍) family constructed these seven carved stone *páifāng* (牌坊; memorial arches), stretching east to west in the fields outside their village, to consecrate their ancestors for feats of service and piety. Three are from the Ming dynasty, four from the Qing. Placards (in English) describe the acts – some touching, some gruesome – that earned such high esteem.

Yúliáng   VILLAGE
(渔梁; ¥30, child & senior free; ⊘ 9am-5pm) Little-visited Yúliáng is a historic riverine port village on the Liàn River (练江; Liàn Jiāng). The cobbled and picturesque alley of **Yuliang Jie** (渔梁街) houses former transfer stations for the wood, salt and tea that plied the river; the tea shop at No 87 is an example. Note the firewalls separating the houses along the road. The attraction with most historical significance is the 138m-long granite **Yúliáng Dam** (渔梁坝; Yúliáng Bà) across the river; it's believed to be 1400 years old.

Boat operators can take you on excellent 20-minute return river trips (¥20).

A pedicab from Shèxiàn's bus station or Huīzhōu Old Town to Yúliáng costs ¥10.

Huīzhōu Old Town   VILLAGE
(徽州古城, Huīzhōu Gǔchéng; adult/child & senior ¥80/50; ⊘ 8am-5pm) The entrance to the old town is marked by **Yánghé Mén** (阳和门), a double-eaved, wooden gate tower that dates to the Song dynasty. To the left are two stone *xièzhì* (獬豸; a legendary beast) and straight ahead, the main attraction: the magnificent **Xǔguó Archway** (许国石坊; Xǔguó Shífāng). This is China's sole surviving four-sided decorative archway, with 12 lions (18 in total if you count the cubs) seated on pedestals around it and a profusion of bas-relief carvings of other mythical creatures.

⊨ Sleeping

Túnxī has more accommodation options and makes for a better base; however, you could go for a quiet night in atmospheric **Yúliáng Farm Hotel** (渔梁农家饭店, Yúliáng Nóngjiā Fàndiàn; ☑ 0559 653 9731; 147 Yuliang Jie, 渔梁街147号; d ¥60-80), which has small, clean, modern rooms above a restaurant (which will naturally cook up your dinner). There's an English sign out front.

ⓘ Information

Bank of China (中国银行, Zhōngguó Yínháng; Huizhou Lu, 徽州路; ⊘ 8am-5.30pm) ATM and currency exchange; across from the entrance to Old Town.

ⓘ Getting There & Around

There are five trains daily from Huángshān station in Túnxī to Shèxiàn (¥2 to ¥9, 20 to 40 minutes), departing at 6.30am, 8.05am, 10.57am, 7.50pm and 8.45pm; the last train returns at 6.36pm. Buses from Túnxī's long-distance bus station run regularly to Shèxiàn (¥7, 45 minutes, frequent 6am to 5pm).

Tourist shuttle 2 runs from Túnxī's Tourist Distribution Center (p402) at 8am, 10am, 2pm and 4pm, to Tángmó (¥5.50, 45 minutes), stopping at Tángyuè (¥6, one hour) and Huīzhōu Old Town (¥8, 75 minutes) before terminating in Yúliáng (¥9, 90 minutes). The last bus returns to Túnxī at 4pm.

You can try to use tourist shuttle 2 to get around, but hiring a pedicab to take you to the sights (¥40/80 for a half-/full day) is more convenient. Getting return cabs in Yúliáng and Tángmó is difficult.

Huángshān   黄山
☑ 0559

When its granite peaks and twisted pines are wreathed in spectral folds of mist, Huángshān's idyllic views easily nudge it into the select company of China's top 10, nay, top five, sights. Legions of poets and painters have drawn inspiration from Huángshān's iconic beauty. Yesterday's artists seeking an escape from the hustle and bustle of the temporal world have been replaced by crowds of tourists: who bring the hustle and bustle with them: the mountain is inundated with tourist traffic at points, so the magic can rapidly evaporate, especially during holiday periods and weekends. But Huángshān still rewards visitors with moments of tranquillity, and the unearthly views are simply breathtaking.

Huángshān

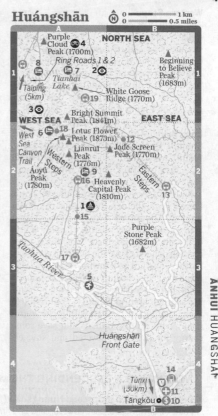

Climate

Locals claim that it rains more than 200 days a year up on the mountain. Allow yourself several days and climb when the forecast is best. Spring (April to June) generally tends to be misty, which means you may be treated to some sublime scenery, but you're just as likely to encounter a dense fog that obscures everything except for a line of yellow ponchos extending up the trail. Summer (July to August) is the rainy season, though storms can blow through fairly quickly. Autumn (September to October) is generally considered to be the best travel period. Even at the height of summer, average temperatures rarely rise above 20°C at the summit, so come prepared. Summit hotels usually offer warm jackets for sunrise watchers.

◉ Sights & Activities

Buses from Túnxī drop you off at the Tourist Distribution Center (p415) in the tourist village 2km south of Tāngkǒu, the town at the southern foot of Huángshān. The area around the bus station is a base for climbers; you can stock up on supplies (maps, rain gear and food), store luggage (¥10 per bag per day) and arrange onward transport here. Tangchuan Lu runs north to the town itself, where you can find amenities such as the post office and banks with international ATMs.

Tāngkǒu Town is small, basically two streets, Yanxi Zonglu and Yanxi Xilu, on either side of a river; look for the stairs leading down from the bridge on Tangchuan Lu.

Eastern Steps   HIKING

A medium-fast climb of the 7.5km eastern steps from Cloud Valley Station (p415), at 890m, to **White Goose Ridge** (白鹅峰; Bái'é Fēng; 1770m) can be done in 2½ hours. The route is pleasant, but lacks the awesome geological scenery of the western steps. In spring wild azalea and weigela add gorgeous splashes of colour to the wooded slopes. Much of the climb is comfortably shaded and although it can be tiring, it's a doddle compared with the western steps.

Western Steps HIKING

The 15km western steps route has some stellar scenery, but it's twice as long and strenuous as the eastern steps, and much easier to enjoy if you're clambering down rather than gasping your way up. If you take the cable car up the mountain, just do this in reverse. The western steps descent begins at the **Flying Rock** (飞来石, Fēilái Shí), a boulder perched on an outcrop 30 minutes from Běihǎi Hotel, and goes over **Bright Summit Peak** (光明顶; Guāngmíng Dǐng; 1841m), from where you can see **Áoyú Peak** (鳌鱼峰; Áoyú Fēng; 1780m), which resembles two turtles!

South of Áoyú Peak en route to Lotus Flower Peak, the descent funnels you down through **Gleam of Sky** (一线天; Yīxiàn Tiān), a remarkably narrow chasm – a vertical split in the granite – pinching a huge rock suspended above the heads of climbers. Further on, **Lotus Flower Peak** (莲花峰; Liánhuā Fēng; 1873m) marks the highest point, but is occasionally sealed off, preventing ascents. **Liánruǐ Peak** (莲蕊峰; Liánruǐ Fēng; 1776m) is decorated with rocks whimsically named after animals, but save some energy for the much-coveted and staggering climb – 1321 steps in all – up **Heavenly Capital Peak** (天都峰; Tiāndū Fēng; 1810m) and the stunning views that unfold below. As elsewhere on the mountain, young lovers have padlocks engraved with their names up here and lash them for eternity to the chain railings. Access to Heavenly Capital Peak (and other peaks) is sometimes restricted for maintenance and repair, so keep those fingers crossed when you go!

At the halfway point is **Bànshān Temple** (半山寺; Bànshān Sì), which literally means halfway temple. At the bottom of the steps is **Mercy Light Pavilion** (慈光阁; Cíguāng Gé), which has been repurposed as the cable car station. From here, you can pick up a minibus back to Tāngkǒu (¥19) or continue walking 1.5km to the hot springs area.

Huángshān Hot Springs HOT SPRINGS

(黄山温泉, Huángshān Wēnquán; ¥298; ⊙10.30am-11pm) Costing more than admission to the mountain itself, a stop here is definitely an indulgence. Still, after a long day (or several) of hiking, the tubs, filled with natural spring water, are heavenly. There are many to choose from, including ones seeped in Chinese medicinal herbs.

ASCENDING & DESCENDING THE MOUNTAIN

Regardless of how you ascend **Huángshān** (黄山, Yellow Mountain; www.chinahuangshan. gov.cn; Mar-Nov ¥230, Dec-Feb ¥150, child 1.2-1.4m ¥115, under 1.2m free), you will be stung by a dizzying entrance fee. You can pay at the eastern steps near the Cloud Valley Station (p415) or at the Mercy Light Pavilion Station (p415), where the western steps begin. Shuttle buses (¥19) run to both places from Tāngkǒu.

Three basic routes will get you up to the summit: the short, hard way (eastern steps); the longer, harder way (western steps); and the very short, easy way (cable car). It's possible to do a 10-hour circuit going up the eastern steps and then down the western steps in one day, but you'll have to be slightly insane, in good shape and you'll definitely miss out on some of the more spectacular, hard-to-get-to areas.

A basic itinerary would be to take an early morning bus from Túnxī, climb the eastern steps, hike around the summit area, spend the night at the top, catch the sunrise and then hike back down the western steps the next day, giving you time to catch an afternoon bus back to Túnxī. Most travellers do opt to spend more than one night on the summit to explore all the various trails. Don't underestimate the hardship involved; the steep gradients and granite steps can wreak havoc on your knees, both going up and down.

Most sightseers are packed (and we mean *packed*) into the summit area above the upper cable car stations, consisting of a network of trails running between various peaks, so don't go expecting peace and quiet. The volume of visitors is mounting every year and paths are being widened at bottleneck points where scrums develop. The highlight of the climb for many independent travellers is the lesser-known **West Sea Canyon** (see far right) hike, a more rugged, exposed section where most tour groups do not venture.

Make sure to bring enough water, food, warm clothing and rain gear before climbing. Bottled water and food prices increase the higher you go as porters carry everything up. As mountain paths are easy to follow and English signs plentiful, guides are unnecessary.

Shuttle buses (¥11) run from Tāngkǒu to the hot springs or from the lower stations of both cable cars (¥8). But if you're coming from the western steps, the 1.5km walk down here from the cable car station passes several waterfalls. Don't walk on the road: look for the sign to the pedestrian path at the bottom of the parking lot.

Huángshān Summit   HIKING

The summit's huge network of connecting trails and walks meander up, down and across several different peaks. More than a few visitors spend several nights on the peak, and the North Sea (北海; Běihǎi) sunrise is a highlight for those staying overnight. **Refreshing Terrace** (清凉台; Qīngliáng Tái) is five minutes' walk from Běihǎi Hotel (p414) and attracts sunrise crowds. Lucky visitors are rewarded with the luminous spectacle of *yúnhǎi* (literally 'sea of clouds'): idyllic pools of mist that settle over the mountain, filling its chasms and valleys with fog.

The staggering and other-worldly views from the summit reach out over huge valleys of granite and enormous formations of rock, topped by gravity-defying slivers of stone and the gnarled forms of ubiquitous Huángshān pine trees (*Pinus taiwanensis*). Many rocks have been christened with fanciful names by the Chinese, alluding to figures from religion and myth. **Beginning to Believe Peak** (始信峰; Shǐxìn Fēng; 1683m), with its jaw-dropping views, is a major bottleneck for photographers. En route to the North Sea, pause at the **Flower Blooming on a Brush Tip** (梦笔生花; Mèngbǐ Shēnghuā), a 1640m-high granite formation topped by a pine tree. Clamber up to **Purple Cloud Peak** (丹霞峰; Dānxiá Fēng; 1700m) for a long survey over the landscape and try to catch the sun as it descends in the west. Aficionados of rock formations should keep an eye out for the poetically named **Mobile Phone Rock** (手机石; Shǒujī Shí), located near the top of the western steps.

If you're coming via cable car, the hike between **White Goose Ridge station** (白鹅岭站; Bái'élǐng Zhàn) and **Jade Screen Tower station** (玉屏楼站; Yùpínglóu Zhàn) takes 3½ hours – though you'd be missing out if you didn't explore the summit further.

West Sea Canyon   HIKING

(西海大峡谷, Xīhǎi Dàxiágǔ) A strenuous and awe-inspiring 8.5km hike, the West Sea Canyon route descends into a gorge (Xīhǎi Dàxiágǔ) and has some impressively exposed stretches (it's not for those with vertigo), taking a minimum four hours to complete. You can access the canyon at either the northern entrance (near the Páiyúnlóu Hotel; p414) or the southern entrance near the **Báiyún Hotel** (White Clouds Hotel, 白云宾馆, Báiyún Bīnguǎn; ☑0559 558 2708; dm/d ¥388/1880; ☀ ☎). Avoid this region in bad weather.

A good option to start would be at the northern entrance. From there, you'll pass through some rock tunnels and exit onto the best bits of the gorge. Here, stone steps have been attached to the sheer side of the mountain – peer over the side for some serious butt-clenching views down. Don't worry, there are handrails. If you're pressed for time or don't have the energy to stomach a long hike, do a figure-eight loop of **Ring Road 1** (一环上路口; Yīhuán Shàng Lùkǒu) and **Ring Road 2** (二环上路口; Èrhuán Shàng Lùkǒu), and head back to the northern entrance. Sure, you'll miss some stunning views across lonely, mist-encased peaks, but you'll also miss the knee-killing dip into the valley and the subsequent thigh-shuddering climb out to the southern entrance.

The **West Sea Canyon Funicular** (西海大峡谷索道, Xīhǎi Daxiá Suǒdào; one way ¥80; ☺6am-4.30pm Mar-Nov) runs between **Tiān hǎi Station** (天海站; Tiānhǎi Zhàn), at the southern entrance, and the bottom of the valley in a startling three minutes.

🛏 Sleeping

In the tourist village around the bus station chain hotels, like 7 Days Inn and Green Tree Inn, there are rooms for around ¥200. Mediocre midrange hotels geared for tour groups line Tangchuan Lu all the way to Tāngkǒu Town, where rooms are a little cheaper; remember to look at rooms first and ask for discounts before committing. Many hotels in town offer transport to and from the Tourist Distribution Center (p415).

Huángshān visits should ideally include nights on the summit. Room prices rise on Saturday and Sunday, and are astronomical during major holiday periods.

It's possible to camp at select, though not scenic, points on the mountain, such as the plaza in front of the Běihǎi Hotel (p414). You'll need to ask for permission and pay a fee of ¥180.

ĀNHUĪ HUÁNGSHĀN

ÀNHUĪ HUÁNGSHĀN

🛏 Tāngkǒu Town

Grapevine Hotel
HOTEL $

(黄山葡萄藤酒店, Huángshān Pútaoténg Jiǔdiàn; ☎ 0559 556 7377; 92 Tangchuan Lu, 汤川路92号; r from ¥80; ✳ 🛜) With sketches on the wall, this hotel has a youthful feel lacking at most hotels around the mountain. Rooms are basic but clean. It's just past the post office, before the bridge on the way to Tāngkǒu Town (a 30-minute walk from the bus station).

Zhōngruìhuáyì Hotel
HOTEL $$

(中瑞华艺大酒店, Zhōngruìhuáyì Dàjiǔdiàn; ☎ 0559 556 6888; www.huayihotel.cn; 119 Tangchuan Lu, 汤川路119号; r from ¥580; ✳) Though this white four-star hotel doesn't look like much from the outside, it has the nicest rooms in Tāngkǒu. Staff can help with bus and flight bookings and there's a free shuttle bus to the bus station.

🛏 On the Mountain

Páiyúnlóu Hotel
HOTEL $$

(排云楼宾馆, Páiyúnlóu Bīnguǎn; ☎ 0559 558 1558; dm/d/tr ¥280/1280/1480; ✳ 🛜) With an excellent location near Tiānhǎi Lake (Tiānhǎi Hú) and the entrance to the West Sea Canyon (p413), plus three-star comfort, this place is recommended for those who prefer a slightly more tranquil setting. None of the regular rooms have views, but the newer dorms have unobstructed vistas and come with TVs and attached showers. Discounted dorms are ¥210 and doubles cost from ¥680.

PORTERS ON THE MOUNTAIN

When climbing Huángshān, spare a thought for the long-suffering, muscular and sun-tanned porters (挑山工; *tiāoshāngōng*) who totter slowly uphill with all manner of goods from rice to water and building materials for the hotels and hawkers that populate the higher levels. They then descend with rubbish. Going up, they earn ¥1.80 per kilogram hauled aloft, downhill it's ¥1.50 per kilogram. They ferry around 100kg each trip (and only ascend once per day), balanced on two ends of a stout pole across their shoulder. Remember to give way to them on your way up (and down).

Yùpínglóu Hotel
HOTEL $$$

(玉屏楼宾馆, Yùpínglóu Bīnguǎn; ☎ 0559 558 2288; www.hsyplhotel.com; dm/d ¥400/1480; ✳ 🛜) A 10-minute walk to the right from the top of the Jade Screen cable car, this four-star hotel is perched on a spectacular 1660m-high lookout just above the Welcoming Guest Pine Tree (迎客松; *Yíngkèsōng*). Aim for the doubles at the back, as some rooms have small windows with no views. Discounts bring doubles down to ¥780 and dorm beds to ¥150.

Běihǎi Hotel
HOTEL $$$

(北海宾馆, Běihǎi Bīnguǎn; ☎ 0559 558 2555; www.hsbeihaihotel.com; dm/d ¥300/1480; ✳ @ 🛜) Located a 1.2km walk from the top of the Cloud Valley cable car, the four-star Běihǎi has professional service, money exchange, cafe and 30% discounts during the week. Larger doubles have older fittings than the smaller, better-fitted-out doubles (same price). There are ¥1280 doubles in the three-star compound across the square. It's the best-located hotel, but also the busiest, and it lacks charm. Dorms can dip to ¥150 when it's quiet, but otherwise book out fast.

🍴 Eating

The tourist village next to the Tourist Distribution Center (p415) has numerous, nearly identical restaurants (dishes ¥10 to ¥100). There are supermarkets here, too.

For street food head into Tāngkǒu, where there are a few vendors on Yanxi Jie, near the bridge.

Most hotel restaurants on the mountain offer buffets (breakfast ¥60, lunch and dinner ¥100 to ¥140) plus a selection of standard dishes (fried rice ¥48), though getting service outside meal times can be tricky. It's usually a better deal to sign up for a meal plan at your hotel.

ℹ Information

Most hotels, even on the summit, have reliable wi-fi.

MEDICAL SERVICES

Běihǎi Clinic (北海医务室, Běihǎi Yīwùshì; ☎ 0559 558 1595; ⊗ 8am-10pm) On the mountain, opposite Běihǎi Hotel.

Huángshān Scenic Area Emergency Medical Center (黄山风景区卫生防疫中心, Huángshān Fēngjǐngqū Wèishēng Fángyì Zhōngxīn; ☎ 0559 562 436) On the east side of the river in Tāngkǒu Town.

MONEY

The **Bank of China** (中国银行, Zhōngguó Yínháng; ⊘ 8-11am & 2.30-5pm) opposite Běihǎi Hotel changes money and has an ATM that accepts international cards. There is another branch (Yanxi Jie, Tāngkǒu, 沿溪街; ⊘ 8am-5pm) at the southern end of Yanxi Jie.

POLICE

Police Station (派出所, pàichūsuǒ; ☑ 0559 558 1388) Opposite Běihǎi Hotel.

Public Security Bureau (PSB, 公安局, Gōng'ānjú; ☑ 0559 556 2233) At the northern end of Tāngkǒu Town.

ⓘ Getting There & Away

BUS

Buses from Túnxī (aka Huángshan Shì) take around one hour to reach Tāngkǒu from either the long-distance bus station (¥20, frequent, 6am to 5pm) or the train station (¥20, departures when full, 6.30am to 5.30pm, may leave as late as 8pm in summer).

Buses back to Túnxī (¥20) from Tāngkǒu depart on roughly the same schedule, and can be flagged down on the road to Túnxī. The last bus back leaves at 5.30pm.

The main bus depot for both long-distance buses to and from Tāngkǒu and tourist buses around Huángshan is the **Tourist Distribution Center** (新国线客车站, Xīnguóxiàn Kèchēzhàn; Tangchuan Lu, 汤川路).

Hángzhōu ¥110, 3½ hours, seven daily

Héféi ¥91, four hours, six daily

Jiǔhuá Shān ¥54, 2½ hours, two daily (6.30am and 2.20pm)

Nánjīng ¥110, five hours, three daily (8am, 1.50pm and 5pm)

Shànghǎi ¥148, 6½ hours, five daily

Wǔhàn ¥235, nine hours, two daily (8.40am and 5.30pm)

Yìxiàn ¥17, one hour, four daily (8am, 9.30am, 1.40pm and 3.30pm; stops at Hóngcūn and Xīdì)

TAXI

A taxi between Túnxī and the Huángshan Scenic Area should cost around ¥200; to the villages of Yìxiàn ¥110 to ¥140.

ⓘ Getting Around

CABLE CAR

Cloud Valley Cable Car (云谷索道, Yúngǔ Suǒdào; one way Mar-Nov ¥80, Dec-Feb ¥65; ⊘ 7.30am-4.30pm) runs from Cloud Valley Temple (云谷寺; Yúngǔ Sì) to White Goose Ridge (Báiyànlǐng; 白鹅岭), bypassing the eastern steps. Beware the long queues: it's best to arrive very early or late (if you're staying on the summit).

Jade Screen Cable Car (玉屏索道, Yùpíng Suǒdào; one way Mar-Nov ¥90, Dec-Feb ¥75; ⊘ 7am-4.30pm) runs from Merciful Light Pavilion to Jade Screen Tower (Yùpínglóu; 玉屏楼), just below the **Yùpínglóu Hotel**, bypassing the western steps.

SHUTTLE BUS

Official tourist shuttles run from the Tourist Distribution Center to Hot Springs (¥11), **Cloud Valley cable car station** (云谷站, Yúngǔ Zhàn; ¥19) and **Mercy Light Pavilion cable car station** (慈光阁站, Cíguānggé zhàn; ¥19), departing every 20 minutes from 6am to 6.30pm, though they usually wait until enough people are on board. If you're staying in Tāngkǒu Town, you can get the buses at the **east bus station** (东岭换乘分中心, Dōnglǐng Huànchéng Fēnhōngxīn; Tangchuan Lu, 汤川路) on Tangchuan Lu.

Jiǔhuá Shān　九华山

☑ 0566

The Tang dynasty Buddhists who determined Jiǔhuá Shān (Jiǔhuá Mountain; Nine Lotus Mountain) to be the earthly abode of the Bodhisattva Dizang (Ksitigarbha), Lord of the Underworld, chose well. Often shrouded in a fog that pours in through the windows of its cliff-side temples, Jiǔhuá Mountain has a powerful gravitas, heightened by the devotion of those who come here to pray for the souls of the departed. It is among the four most sacred peaks in China and there are dozens of active temples here, housing a population of some 500-plus monks and nuns.

The mountain is not untouched by commercialism; however, the hawkers of overpriced joss sticks and jade carvings come together with the ochre-coloured monasteries, flickering candles and low, steady drone of Buddhist chanting emanating from pilgrims' MP3 players to create an atmosphere that is both of this world and of another one entirely.

History

Jiǔhuá Mountain was made famous by the 8th-century Korean monk Kim Kiao Kak (Jin Qiaojue), who meditated here for 75 years and was posthumously proclaimed to be the reincarnation of Dizang. In temples, Dizang is generally depicted carrying a staff and a luminous jewel, used to guide souls through the darkness of hell.

⊙ Sights & Activities

Buses will let you off at Jiǔhuáshān bus station (九华山气车站; Jiǔhuàshān qìchēzhàn), the local bus terminus and main ticket office where you purchase your ticket for the **mountain** (九华山; Mar-Nov ¥190, Dec-Feb ¥140). You'll also then need to buy a return shuttle bus ticket (¥50, 20 minutes, half-hourly) from the counters on the left of the admission-ticket windows. The shuttle bus goes to Jiǔhuá village (九华镇), halfway up the mountain (or, as locals say, at roughly navel height in a giant Buddha's potbelly). The shuttle terminates at the bus station just before the gate (大门; *dàmén*) leading to the village, from where the main street (芙蓉路; Furong Lu; also called Jiuhua Jie, 九华街) heads south past hotels and restaurants.

Zhīyuán Temple   BUDDHIST TEMPLE
(祇园寺, Zhīyuán Sì; ⊘6.30am-8.30pm) `FREE`
Just past the village's main entrance on your left, worshippers hold sticks of incense to their foreheads and face the four directions at this enticingly esoteric yellow temple. Pilgrims can join chanting sessions in the evening, starting around 5pm.

Huàchéng Sì   BUDDHIST TEMPLE
(化成寺; ⊘6.30am-8.30pm) `FREE` Set back off the road, behind a pond, Huàchéng Sì was founded in the Tang dynasty (though the current building itself is not that old). It has ornately carved lions guarding the main steps (one male and one female), colourful eaves and beams, and three huge golden Bodhisattvas.

Bǎisuì Gōng   BUDDHIST TEMPLE
(百岁宫) ⊘6am-5.30pm) `FREE` A 30-minute hike up the ridge behind Zhīyuán Temple (p416) leads you to Bǎisuì Gōng, an active temple built into the cliff in 1630 to consecrate the Buddhist monk Wu Xia, whose shrunken, embalmed body is coated in gold and sits shrivelled within an ornate glass cabinet in front of a row of pink lotus candles. A **funicular** (百岁宫缆车, Bǎisuì Gōng Lǎnchē; one-way/return ¥55/100; ⊘7am-5.30pm) also makes the journey, departing from just off Furong Lu.

Jiǔhuá Shān Summit   HIKING
(九华山巅, Jiǔhuá Shān Diān) Hiking the summit of Jiǔhuá Mountain alongside pilgrims following a stone trail (天台正顶) shaded by pines and bamboo is a real highlight. To begin the hike from the village, walk up Furong Lu for 450m and look for a sign on your left

pointing up to **Huíxiāng Pavilion** (回香阁; Huíxiāng Gé). From here to the summit takes four to five hours; count on about two to three hours to get back down to the village.

Follow the path along the front of **Tōnghuì Nunnery** (通慧俺; Tōnghuì Ǎn) as the gentle incline transitions to steep stone steps. The 750m trek up to Huíxiāng Pavilion takes around 20 minutes. Above it is the towering seven-storey **10,000 Buddha Pagoda** (万佛塔; Wàn Fó Tǎ), fashioned entirely from bronze and prettily lit at night. Continuing along, the path dips into a pleasant valley, passing **Ròushēn Temple** (肉身寺; Ròushēn Sì) and **Welcoming Guest Pine** (迎客松; Yíngkè Sōng) en route to **Phoenix Pine** (凤凰松; Fènghuáng Sōng). From here, the two-hour, 4km walk to the summit, **Tiāntái Peak** (天台正顶; Tiāntái Zhèng Dǐng; 1304m) is tough going, passing small temples and nunneries.

The summit is slightly damp, with mist shrouding the area. Within the faded **Tiāntái Temple** (天台寺; Tiāntái Sì) on Tiāntái Peak, a statue of the Dizang Buddha is seated within the **Dizàng Hall** (地藏殿; Dìzàng Diàn), while from the magnificent **10,000 Buddha Hall** (万佛楼; Wàn Fó Lóu) above, a huge enthroned statue of the Dizang Buddha gazes at the breathless pilgrims mustering at his feet. The beams above your head glitter with rows of thousands of Buddhas.

There's another trail to your right before the main stairs to the Tiāntái Temple. This one leads you to one of the highest and quietest points of the mountain, **Shíwáng Peak** (十王峰; Shíwáng Fēng; 1344m), where you can stop and let the rolling fog sweep past you. This trail will also take you to Tiāntái Temple, with far fewer crowds.

An easier route is to take a bus (return trip included with the ¥50 shuttle bus ticket) from Jiǔhuá village up to Phoenix Pine, from where a **cable car** (天台索道, Tiāntái Suǒdào; one-way/return ¥85/160; ⊘6.50am-5pm) runs to the summit in five minutes. Note that from the terminus of the cable car, it's still a 1km climb up steps to Tiāntái Temple.

🛏 Sleeping

Jiǔhuá village has plenty of accommodation options. None are particularly good value, but you can usually bargain for something in the range of ¥150 to ¥200 for a double room outside holiday periods. The further you head from the bus stop the better deals you're likely to find.

Bǎisuìgōng Xiàyuàn Hotel   HOTEL $$
(百岁宫下院, Bǎisuìgōng Xiàyuàn; ☑ 139 0566 7465, 0566 283 3122; Furong Lu, 芙蓉路; r ¥360-1380; ❊ 🛜) Pleasantly arranged around an old temple, this hotel has the right atmosphere and a good location. Standard rooms are just that – lino floors, small showers, but comfortable enough. It's right beside Jùlóng Hotel, opposite Zhǐyuán Temple.

Jùlóng Hotel   HOTEL $$$
(聚龙大酒店, Jùlóng Dàjiǔdiàn; ☑ 0566 283 1368; Furong Lu, 芙蓉路; d & tw ¥1280-1480; ❊ 🛜) The long-standing Jùlóng's recent facelift has resulted in quality rooms decked out with easy-on-the-eye hues of brown and gold. Flat-screen TVs, good bathrooms and friendly staff round out the experience. Discounts knock rooms down to ¥690 on weekdays, ¥890 on weekends. It's opposite Zhǐyuán Temple (p416), off Furong Lu after you enter the main gate.

Shàngkètáng Hotel   HOTEL $$$
(上客堂宾馆, Shàngkètáng Bīnguǎn; ☑ 0566 283 3888; Furong Lu, 芙蓉路; d & tw ¥1280; ❊ @) With an upscale vibe that skews more towards a wellness retreat than a spiritual one, Shàngkètáng Hotel has rooms with rosewood furniture, flat-screen TVs and plush carpets (some rooms have a wet carpet smell though). Weekday discounts can knock rooms down to ¥480, ¥720 on weekends. The in-house vegetarian restaurant is the best in town.

✖ Eating

Restaurants, which are numerous in Jiǔhuá village, historically served only vegetarian food, though now some do offer meat. Look for dishes (¥10 to ¥100) featuring bamboo and mushrooms of all colours and shapes harvested from the mountain.

Zhǐyuán Temple serves vegetarian meals (5.30am, 10.40am and 4.40pm; ¥10) to the public after the monks have eaten, though often runs out of food.

★ Qíyuán Vegetarian   VEGETARIAN $$
(祇园素斋, Qíyuán Sùzhāi; Shàngkètáng Bīnguǎn; 上客堂宾馆; dishes ¥28-188, buffet ¥78; ⊙ 11am-2pm & 5-8pm; 🖉) Come here to sample (and study: the picture menu is well translated) the exotic edible fungi, shoots and roots of the mountain. Dishes range from humble Chinese chestnuts flavoured with *osmanthus* (a flowering shrub; 桂花板栗; *guìhuā bǎnlì*; ¥28) to prized 'stone ear' mushrooms

(石耳, *shí'ěr*; ¥188), a kind of lichen that grows on rock and is believed to have medicinal properties.

ℹ Information

Bank of China (中国银行, Zhōngguó Yínháng; 65 Huacheng Lu, 化城路65号; ⊙ 9am-4.30pm) Foreign exchange and 24-hour international ATM. West of the main square, halfway up Huacheng Lu.

China Post (中国邮政, Zhōngguó Yóuzhèng; 58 Huacheng Lu, 化城路58号; ⊙ 8am-5.30pm) Off the main square.

Jiǔhuáshān Red Cross Hospital (九华山红十字医院, Jiǔhuáshān Hóngshízì Yīyuàn; ☑ 0566 283 1330) Seven hundred metres up Furong Lu from the town entrance.

ℹ Getting There & Away

Buses from Jiǔhuáshān bus station (九华山汽车站; Jiǔhuàshān qìchēzhàn; the bus terminus and main Jiǔhuá Mountain ticket office) run to the following destinations:

Hángzhōu ¥125, five hours, 6.50am and 2.50pm

Héféi ¥88, 3½ hours, hourly (last bus at 4.50pm)

Huángshān ¥54, three hours, 7.20am and 2.30pm

Nánjīng ¥85, three hours, four daily (6.40am, 7.20am, 8.40am and 1pm)

Shànghǎi ¥140, six hours, two daily (7am and 2pm)

Túnxī ¥70, 3½ hours, 7.20am and 1.30pm

Wǔhàn ¥155, six hours, 7am

Yīxiàn ¥60, 2½ hours, 7.30am and 12.30pm

The nearest high-speed train station is Chízhōu (池州). Buses depart hourly (¥12, one hour, 7am to 4.50pm) for Jiǔhuáshān bus station from the bus station next to the train station. Chízhōu can be reached from Shànghǎi (¥221, four hours, four daily) and Héféi (¥69 to ¥91, 90 minutes, nine daily).

ℹ Getting Around

The ¥50 shuttle ticket includes four bus rides: from the main ticket office to Jiǔhuá village (the base for the mountain ascent), from the village to **Phoenix Pine cable car station** (凤凰松站, Fènghuáng Sōng Zhàn) and back to the village, and from the village back to the main ticket office (first bus 7am, last bus 5pm).

To get to Phoenix Pine, catch the bus (every 30 minutes or when full) from the bus station north of the main gate (cross the bridge on the right after the Jùlóng Hotel). On busy days you may need to queue for more than two hours for the cable car to/from the peak.

Héféi 合肥

♫ 0551 / POP 7.79 MILLION

Héféi is the capital of Ānhuī. Besides the excellent provincial museum, the city has little to offer tourists and works best as a transit hub.

◉ Sights

Central Héféi, a few kilometres southwest of the train station (and 6km north of the south train station) is ringed with parks and ponds. Changjiang Zhonglu, the main commercial street, cuts east–west through here. Huaihe Lu Buxing Jie, a busy pedestrian shopping street, runs parallel just to the north. The city's main historical sights are clustered around here.

Ānhuī New Provincial Museum   MUSEUM
(安徽省博物馆新馆, Ānhuīshěng Bówùguǎn Xīnguǎn; www.ahm.cn; 268 Huaining Lu, 怀宁路268号; ⊙9am-5pm Tue-Sun) FREE If you really want to get to know Ānhuī, it's worth taking a half-day to explore the four floors of this museum, which opened in 2011. It begins with Palaeolithic artefacts (some are replicas) mined from the earliest known settlements in Eurasia, which happen to be in Ānhuī. Other exhibitions cover the region's Three Kingdoms Period history (including a replica of Cao Cao's fabulous jade burial suit) and the symbolism evoked by Huīzhōu architecture and artworks.

You'll need to show your passport to enter. The museum is 10km southwest of downtown, about a ¥30 taxi ride. The building itself is a sight to behold.

🛏 Sleeping

Budget chain hotels can be found around the train station and on Huaihe Lu Buxing Jie. Midrange ones are located on the main commercial street of Changjiang Zhonglu.

Green Tree Inn   HOTEL $
(格林豪泰, Gélín Háotài; ♫0551 6265 0988; www.998.com; 24 Hongxing Lu, 红星路24号; d ¥209; 🅿️@🛜) This reliable, modern midrange chain hotel offers compact, cheap and clean accommodation in a 24-room branch along a quiet residential street. There's food and shopping within walking distance.

Holiday Inn Express Downtown   HOTEL $$$
(Héféi Zhōngxīn Zhìxuǎn Jiàrì Jiǔdiàn, 合肥中心智选假日酒店; ♫0551 6570 6888; 279 Changjiang Zhonglu, 长江中路279号; r from ¥780; 🅿️🗺@🛜) Héféi's best midrange deal is this branch of the Holiday Inn (not to be confused with all the other branches in town). It's centrally located in a building shared by a bookstore and cafe (enter the hotel around the back). Rooms are modern, clean and comfortable. Look for 50% discounts online.

Westin   HOTEL $$$
(合肥万达威斯汀酒店, Héféi Wàndá Wēisītīng Jiǔdiàn; ♫0551 6298 9888; www.starwoodhotels.com/westin; 150 Ma'anshan Lu, 马鞍山路150号; d ¥2800; 🗺@🛜) If you're counting on a good night's sleep, the Westin, Héféi's top hotel, is a safe bet. Facilities include a fitness centre, swimming pool, spa, good restaurants, and elegant and modern rooms, equipped with Westin's trademark Heavenly Beds. Look online for discounts of up to 60%.

🍴 Eating

For food, head to the pedestrianised Huaihe Lu Buxing Jie. The side streets have cheap eats and there's everything from fast-food chains to noodle shops. A night market sets up in the area too.

🍷 Drinking & Nightlife

The little alley Dongxi Xiang (东西巷), off Shuguang Lu (曙光路), is a colourful strip of tiny bars and cafes with a DIY vibe – a refreshing change from the usual KTV. It's a 15-minute taxi ride from downtown, just south of Tunxi Lu (屯溪路).

Shipyard   BAR, CAFE
(造船厂咖啡店, Zàochuánchǎng Kāfēidiàn; 50 Shuguang Lu, 曙光路50号; ⊙2pm-2am) Popular expat hang-out Shipyard has decent burgers (¥55), Guinness on tap (¥60) and live music on weekends. If it gets too loud, retreat to the small courtyard out back. In the afternoon it serves coffee.

ℹ Information

Internet cafes (网吧; wǎngbā) are clustered about 80m west of Motel 168, off Huaihe Lu Buxing Jie. You'll need to show a passport. They're generally open from 8am to midnight and cost ¥2 per hour.

Bank of China (中国银行, Zhōngguó Yínháng; ⊙8.15am-5pm) Branches on Wuwei Lu and Shouchun Lu, with currency exchange and international ATMs.

China Post (中国邮政, Zhōngguó Yóuzhèng; cnr Changjiang Zhonglu & Suzhou Lu, 长江中

路宿州路的路口; ⊙8am-5pm) There's also a branch beside the train station.

Civil Aviation Ticket Center (民航合肥售票中心, Mínháng Héféi Shòupiào Zhōngxīn; ☑0551 637 7777; 212 Shouchun Lu, 寿春路212号; ⊙8am-6pm) Air and train tickets.

First People's Hospital (第一人民医院, Dìyī Rénmín Yīyuàn; ☑front desk 0551 218 3401; 390 Huaihe Lu, 淮河路390号)

Public Security Bureau (PSB, 公安局, Gōng'ānjú; cnr Shouchun Lu & Liu'an Lu, 寿春路六安路的路口)

❶ Getting There & Away

AIR

Héféi Xīnqiáo International Airport is 32km northwest of Héféi.

Daily flights include the following:

Běijīng ¥1760, two hours, five daily

Guǎngzhōu ¥1080, two hours, seven daily

Shànghǎi ¥1130, one hour, two daily

Xiàmén ¥910, 1½ hours, four daily

Airport shuttles (¥25, one hour) depart hourly (5.40am to 7.30pm) from the main bus station and the long-distance bus station. A taxi (45 minutes) costs around ¥100, including the ¥10 toll for the highway.

BUS

Centrally located **Héféi long-distance bus station** (合肥长途汽车站, Héféi Chángtú Qìchēzhàn; 168 Mingguang Lu, 明光路168号; ⊙5.30am-9pm), near Xiāoyáojīn Park, has buses to destinations in the surrounding provinces, including:

Hángzhōu ¥138, six hours, 10 daily

Nánjīng ¥63, 2½ hours, hourly 6.55am to 5.30pm

Shànghǎi ¥160, six hours, 10am

Wǔhàn ¥148, six hours, 9am

Buses to Jiǔhuá Shān (¥88, 3½ hours, every 40 minutes, 6.40am to 5pm) leave from the **tourist bus station** (旅游汽车站, Lǚyóu Zìchēzhàn; Zhanqian Jie, 站前街), 500m west of the train station.

Buses to Túnxī (¥98, four hours, 7.50am, 10.10am, 1pm and 3.20pm) via Huángshān (¥98, 3½ hours) depart from the **east bus station** (汽车东站, qìchē dōngzhàn; 517 Changjiang Donglu, 长江东路517号), 5km east of the city centre.

The so-called **main bus station** (客运总站, Kèyùn Zǒngzhàn; Zhanqian Jie, 站前街), just outside the train station, is for local buses only.

TRAIN

Most (but double-check your ticket) high-speed trains depart from the new **Héféi South station** (合肥火车南站, Héféi Huǒchē Nánzhàn), 6km southeast of the city centre. Express D and G trains:

Běijīng ¥436, 4½ hours, hourly

Huángshān North ¥141, 75 minutes, frequent

Nánjīng South ¥61, one hour, frequent

Shànghǎi Hóngqiáo ¥156 to ¥205, 3½ hours, frequent

Wǔhàn & Wǔhàn Hànkǒu ¥105 to ¥127, 2½ hours, frequent

Regular-service trains depart from **Héféi train station** (合肥火车站, Héféi Huǒchēzhàn), 4km northeast of the city centre:

Běijīng hard/soft sleeper from ¥270/420, 10 to 14 hours, six daily

Shànghǎi hard/soft sleeper from ¥173/268, 6½ to 8½ hours, seven daily

Túnxī hard/soft sleeper from ¥114/176, six to seven hours, four daily

❶ Getting Around

Héféi has an extensive local bus system (rides ¥1) though it isn't helpful for visitors. Metered taxis start at ¥8. The 25-minute ride from Héféi South station to the city centre should cost ¥25; from Héféi train station expect to pay ¥20.

ĀNHUĪ HÉFÉI

Hénán

POP 94 MILLION

Best Places to Eat

➡ Luòyáng's Old Town Night Market (p430)

➡ Xīsī Square Night Market (p438)

➡ Hé Jì (p423)

Best Places to Sleep

➡ Courtyard & Sunlight Inn (p437)

➡ Luòyáng Yìjiā International Youth Hostel (p430)

➡ Kungfu Hostel (p428)

➡ Sofitel (p423)

Why Go?

Affluent Chinese may roll their eyes at the mention of impoverished and land-locked Hénán (河南), but the province's heritage takes us back to the earliest days of Chinese antiquity. Ancient capitals rose and fell in Hénán's north, where the capricious Yellow River (Huáng Hé) nourished the flowering of a great civilisation.

Hénán is home to China's oldest surviving Buddhist temple and one of the country's most astonishing collections of Buddhist carvings, the Lóngmén Grottoes. There is also the Shàolín Temple, that legendary institution where the martial way and Buddhism found an unlikely but powerful alliance. Hénán's inability to catch up with the rest of the land perhaps helps to explain why the unusual village of Nánjiēcūn still sees a future in Maoist collectivism. Hénán is also home to the excellent walled town of Kāifēng and the 1000-year-old craft of woodblock printing in Zhūxiān.

When to Go
Zhèngzhōu

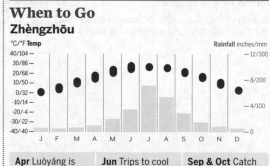

Apr Luòyáng is a blaze of floral colour during the peony festival.

Jun Trips to cool Guōliàngcūn up in the Mountains of the Ten Thousand Immortals.

Sep & Oct Catch the lovely and fleeting north China autumn.

Hénán Highlights

1 Shàolín Temple (p425) Fathoming the mysteries of Shàolín boxing and hiking the surrounding peaks.

2 Lóngmén Grottoes (p431) Admiring the artistry of 1500-year-old carved Bodhisattvas.

3 Guōliàngcūn (p433) Discovering the unreal scenery of the Mountains of the Ten Thousand Immortals from the perch of a cliff-top village.

4 Kāifēng (p434) Taking a trip back in time to the former capital of the Northern Song dynasty.

5 White Horse Temple (p432) Exploring the vast complex of China's oldest Buddhist shrine, found outside Luòyáng.

6 Zhūxiān (p439) Getting acquainted with the ancient craft of Chinese woodblock printing.

7 Nánjiēcūn (p425) Rediscovering communism with Chinese characteristics.

PRICE RANGES

Sleeping

Prices given are for a double room.

$ less than ¥200

$$ ¥200–¥500

$$$ more than ¥500

Eating

Prices given are for a meal for one.

$ less than ¥35

$$ ¥35–¥100

$$$ more than ¥100

History

It is believed that the first Shang capital, perhaps dating back 3800 years, was at Yǎnshī, west of modern-day Zhèngzhōu. Around the mid-14th century BC, the capital is thought to have moved to Zhèngzhōu, where its ancient city walls remain visible.

Hénán again occupied centre stage during the Song dynasty (AD 960–1279), but political power deserted it when the government fled south from its capital at Kāifēng following the 12th-century Jurchen invasion.

Modern Hénán has been poor and strife-prone. In 1975 Bǎnqiáo Dam collapsed after massive rainfall, leading to a string of other dam failures that caused the deaths of 230,000 people. In the 1990s a scandal involving the sale of HIV-tainted blood led to a high incidence of AIDS in several Hénán villages.

🛈 Getting There & Around

Hénán is that rarity in China: a province in which travellers can get in, out and around with ease. Zhèngzhōu is the main regional rail hub; high-speed trains zip between Zhèngzhōu, Luòyáng and, to a lesser extent, Kāifēng.

Luòyáng has a small airport, but Zhèngzhōu is the main hub for flying to/from Hénán.

Zhèngzhōu 郑州

📞 0371 / POP 6.4 MILLION

The provincial Hénán capital of Zhèngzhōu is a rapidly modernising, smog-filled metropolis with few relics from its ancient past (due to Japanese bombing in WWII). Zhèngzhōu can be largely zipped through, serving as a major transport hub and access point for the Shàolín Temple and the left-field Maoist collective of Nánjiēcūn.

👁 Sights

Despite a history reaching back to the earliest chapters of Chinese history, the city now has few sights of interest to travellers.

Chénghuáng Temple TAOIST TEMPLE
(城隍庙, Chénghuáng Miào; Shangcheng Lu, 商城路; ⏰9am-6pm) **FREE** The 600-year-old City God temple bustles with worshippers who leave its trees festooned with red ribbons and its entrances swirling with incense smoke. Take bus 2 from the train station.

Hénán Museum MUSEUM
(河南博物院, Hénán Bówùyuàn; http://english.chnmus.net; 8 Nongye Lu, 农业路8号; ⏰9am-5.30pm Tue-Sun, shorter hours rest of year) **FREE** Closed for renovations (estimated to last until 2018), only temporary exhibits in a side building are currently on display. An **audio guide** (¥20, deposit ¥200) in English is available. Take your passport as ID for admission. The museum is around 2km north of Jinshui Lu; a taxi there will cost about ¥20. (A huge swath of Nongye Lu was also closed for total renovation during research; as a result no buses were running here.)

Shang City Walls RUINS
(商代城墙遗址, Shāngdài Chéngqiáng Yízhǐ) **FREE** Zhèngzhōu's eastern outskirts are marked by long, high mounds of earth, the remains of the old city walls. You can climb up to explore.

🛏 Sleeping

At the time of research, only international chains and a select few domestic hotels were accepting foreigners.

Jǐnjiāng Inn MOTEL **$$**
(锦江之星, Jǐnjiāng Zhīxīng; 📞0371 6693 2000; 77 Erma Lu, 二马路77号; d from ¥200; ❋🛜) This modern chain has crisp, well looked-after rooms (work desks, flat-screen TVs) in a convenient location near the train station. The cheapest rooms have no windows; staff will likely upgrade you to the mid-level rooms. It is currently the city's only midrange hotel accepting foreigners.

Hilton Zhèngzhōu HOTEL **$$$**
(希尔顿酒店, Xīěrdùn Jiǔdiàn; 📞0371 8996 0888; www3.hilton.com; 288 Jinshui Lu, 金水路288号; d from ¥688; ❋@🛜🏊; Ⓜ Minhang Rd) The Hilton combines stylish elegance with a highly exacting level of service and a tempting range of five-star amenities and dining choices in a tower on Jinshui Lu. Rooms are contempo-

Zhèngzhōu

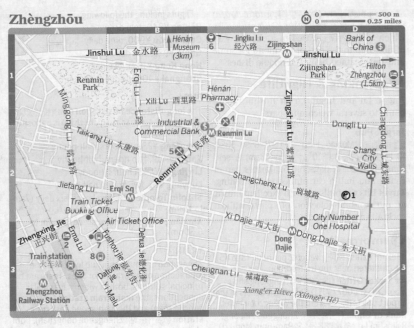

rary, invitingly spacious and fully equipped. It's close to the city's Central Business District.

Sofitel
HOTEL $$$

(索菲特国际饭店, Suǒfēitè Guójì Fàndiàn; ☑ 0371 6595 0088; www.sofitel.com; 289 Chengdong Lu, 城东路289号; d from ¥600; ❀❄@🛜🏊; Ⓜ Yanzhuang) Fresh off a multi-year renovation in 2016, rooms at the five-star Sofitel are excellent. Muted gold and brown tones provide a soothing counterpoint to Zhèngzhōu's chaotic streets, and plusher rooms are equipped with plenty of modern conveniences, including Nespresso machines and swivel TVs. Note that the entrance is off Jinshui Lu.

🍴 Eating

A short walk north of the train station is the busy **February 7 Sq** (二七广场; Èrqī Guángchǎng), also called Èfqī Sq, with nearby shops, restaurants and a **night market**. Look out for the large white pagoda.

Hé Jì
HENAN $

(合记; 3 Renmin Lu, 人民路3号; noodles ¥14-25; ⊙10.30am-10pm; Ⓜ Renmin Rd) This Zhèngzhōu stalwart has racked up numerous awards over the years, and judging by the raucous crowds inside, it hasn't lost its touch. There's only one thing on the menu – noodle soup in a nourishing mutton broth (烩面;

Zhèngzhōu

huìmiàn). Order at the window: basic (普通; pǔtōng) or deluxe (特优; tèyōu), with a bit more meat. Add coriander and chilli to taste, but eat the pickled garlic on the side.

Hénán Shífǔ
HENAN $$

(河南食府; ☑ 0371 6622 2108; 25 Renmin Lu, 人民路25号; dishes ¥22-98; ⊙10am-2pm & 5-9.30pm; Ⓜ Renmin Rd) Tucked away in a courtyard off Renmin Lu, this well known restaurant's photo menu is full of local specialities, such as tofu potstickers (锅贴豆腐; *guōtiē dòufu*) or Hakka beef (客家牛肉粒; *Kèjiā niúròu lì*), which is cleverly encased in a circular wall of rice. Flip to the end of the menu for some unusual steamed buns and noodle dishes.

🍸 Drinking & Nightlife

Jingliu Lu and Jingqi Lu off Jinshui Rd are home to several welcoming bars.

Target Pub   PUB
(目标酒吧, Mùbiāo Jiǔbā; ☑0371 6590 5384; 10 Jingliu Lu, 经六路10号; ⊗5pm-3am) A seasoned portrait of flags, old banknotes, rattan chairs and half a car pinned to the ceiling, Target hits the bullseye with excellent music, an outstanding selection of spirits, offbeat cocktails and a laid-back vibe.

ℹ️ Information

Internet cafes (网吧; *wǎngbā*; per hour ¥3 to ¥5) are clustered near the train station.
Air Ticket Office (航空售票, hángkōng shòupiào; ☑0371 6677 7111) Sells flight tickets in the airport bus office, next to the Zhèngzhōu Hotel.
Bank of China (中国银行, Zhōngguó Yínháng; 8 Jinshui Lu, 金水路8号; ⊗9am-5pm Mon-Fri) North of the Sofitel, on Jinshui Lu.
China Post (中国邮政, Zhōngguó Yóuzhèng; ⊗8am-8pm) South end of train station concourse.
City Number One Hospital (市一院, Shì Yīyuàn; Dong Dajie, 东大街) West of the Confucius Temple.
Civil Aviation Administration of China (CAAC, 中国民航, Zhōngguó Mínháng; ☑0371 6599 1111; 3 Jinshui Lu, at Dongmin Lu, 金水路3号) East of the city centre, the CAAC sells flight tickets.
Hénán Pharmacy (河南大药房, Hénán Dàyàofáng; ☑0371 6623 4256; 19 Renmin Lu, 人民路19号; ⊗24hr)
Industrial & Commercial Bank (ICBC, 工商银行, Gōngshāng Yínháng; Renmin Lu, 人民路; Ⓜ Renmin Rd) Has a 24-hour ATM.
Public Security Bureau (PSB, 公安局出入境管理处, Gōng'ānjú Chūrùjìng Guǎnlǐchù; ☑0371 6962 5990; 66 Huanghe Nanlu, 黄河南路66号; ⊗9am-noon & 2-5pm Mon-Fri) For visa extensions; in the north of town.
Train Ticket Booking Office (火车预售票处, huǒchē yùshòupiàochù; ☑0371 6835 6666; cnr Zhengxing Jie & Fushou Jie, 正兴街与福寿街路口; ⊗8am-8pm)

ℹ️ Getting There & Away

AIR
Zhèngzhōu Airport is located 37km southeast of town. The **ticket office** is in the airport bus office, next to the Zhèngzhōu Hotel.

Flights include the following:
Běijīng ¥840, two daily
Guǎngzhōu ¥900, nine daily
Guìlín ¥925, two daily
Hong Kong ¥1021, two daily
Shànghǎi ¥400, frequent service

BUS
The **long-distance bus station** (郑州长途汽车站, Zhèngzhōu chángtú qìchēzhàn) is opposite the train station.
Dēngfēng ¥28, 1¾ hours, half-hourly
Kāifēng ¥19, two hours, half-hourly
Línyǐng ¥40, 2¼ hours, hourly
Luòyáng ¥57, two hours, half-hourly
Shàolín Temple ¥29, two hours, six daily (7am to 11am)
Xīnxiāng ¥25, two hours, six daily (6am to 6.30pm)

TRAIN
Zhèngzhōu is a major rail hub located at the intersection of several major lines. There are two principal stations, both of which have similar connections: the **main train station** (火车站; huǒchē zhàn) and the high-speed **east train station** (郑州东站; Zhèngzhōu dōngzhàn). Both stations are on metro line 1.

For a ¥5 commission, skip waiting in line and get tickets at the **advance booking office**.
Běijīng West G train ¥315, 2½ to four hours, frequent service
Guǎngzhōu South G train ¥653, six hours, frequent service
Kāifēng C/D train ¥19, 30 minutes, frequent service
Luòyáng Lóngmén G train ¥60, 40 minutes, frequent service
Nánjīng South D train ¥204, 5½ hours, five daily
Shànghǎi D train ¥237, seven hours, four daily
Xī'ān North G train ¥229, 2½ hours, frequent service

ℹ️ Getting Around

The **airport bus** (飞机巴士, fēijī bāshì; ¥20, 90 minutes, half-hourly from 6.30am to 8.30pm) leaves from the sidewalk next to the Zhèngzhōu Hotel (郑州大酒店; Zhèngzhōu Dàjiǔdiàn). A taxi costs around ¥100 and takes 50 minutes.

Bus 26 travels from the train station past 7 February Sq, along Renmin Lu and Jinshui Lu to the CAAC office. Local buses cost ¥1 to ¥2.

The east–west Line 1 of the metro (tickets from ¥2) runs through the train station, up Renmin Lu and Jinshui Lu to the Central Business District (CBD), eventually passing the east train station. Note that the main train station metro stop only exits on the west side and is not conveniently accessed from the front of the train station.

The north–south Line 2 following Zijingshan Lu is under construction but should be completed by 2017, while Lines 3 and 5 will only open in 2018 at the very earliest.

Taxi fares start at ¥8 (¥10 at night).

Nánjiēcūn 南街村

📞 0395 / POP 3180

Nánjiēcūn is China's very last Maoist collective (*gōngshè*), and a visit here is a surreal trip back in time – a journey to the puritanical and revolutionary China of the 1950s, when Chairman Mao was becoming a supreme being, money was yesterday's scene and the menace of karaoke had yet to be prophesied by even the most paranoid party faithful.

The first inkling you have arrived in an entirely different world comes from the roads: relatively clean, tree-lined streets run in straight lines with a kind of austere socialist beauty (or, perhaps, the quiet menace of an autocratic sci-fi dystopia), past noodle factories, schools, and rows of identikit blocks of workers' flats emblazoned with vermilion communist slogans. There are no advertising billboards, but beatific portraits of Chairman Mao gaze down on all.

👁 Sights

To find your way from the town of Línyǐng into the collective, head down the main drag, Yingsong Dadao (颍松大道), to the rainbow-arch-adorned East Is Red Square. A short stroll to the left brings you to Cháoyáng Gate Square.

East Is Red Square SQUARE
(东方红广场, Dōngfānghóng Guǎngchǎng) In this square, guards maintain a 24-hour vigil at the foot of a statue of Chairman Mao, and portraits of Marx, Engels, Stalin and Lenin (the original 'Gang of Four') rise up on all four sides. Behind the ensemble, a tri-coloured rainbow proclaims 'Mao Zedong thought will shine forever'. The square is deluged in shrill propaganda broadcast from speakers in true 1950s style, kicking off at 6.15am daily.

Cháoyáng Gate Square SQUARE
(朝阳门广场, Cháoyángmén Guǎngchǎng) Not far from East is Red Square, this square is known primarily for the rebuilt, traditional architecture of **Cháoyáng Gate** (朝阳门; Cháoyáng Mén).

ℹ️ Information

You can safely avoid the **Tourist Service Centre** near the entrance (off the west end of Yingsong Dadao), as they'll ask you to buy an admission ticket (¥80) that you don't actually need to visit Nánjiēcūn. But if you do take up their offer, it comes with a Chinese-speaking guide and a jaunt around town on an electric cart.

ℹ️ Getting There & Away

From Zhèngzhōu bus station, buses (¥40, 2¼ hours) run south every hour between 6.20am and 6.20pm to the bus station at Línyǐng (临颍), from where it's a ¥5 *sānlúnchē* (pedicab) journey south to Nánjiēcūn.

Sōng Shān & Dēngfēng 嵩山、登封

📞 0371 / POP 650,000

In Taoism, **Sōng Shān** (嵩山) is considered the central mountain (中岳; *zhōngyuè*) of the five sacred peaks, symbolising earth (土; *tǔ*) among the five elements and occupying the axis directly beneath heaven. Despite this Taoist persuasion, the mountains are also home to one of China's most famous and legendary Zen (禅; Chán) Buddhist temples: the inimitable Shàolín Temple. Two main mountains crumple the area, the 1494m-high **Tàishì Shān** (太室山) and the 1512m-high **Shàoshì Shān** (少室山) whose peaks compose Sōng Shān about 80km west of Zhèngzhōu.

At the foot of Tàishì Shān, 12km southeast of the Shàolín Temple and 74km from Zhèngzhōu, sits the squat little town of **Dēngfēng** (登封). Tatty in parts, travellers use it as a base for trips to surrounding sights or exploratory treks into the hills.

👁 Sights

In Dēngfēng, Zhongyue Dajie (中岳大街) is the main east–west street; Shaolin Dadao (少林大道) runs parallel to the south.

Shàolín Temple BUDDHIST TEMPLE
(少林寺, Shàolín Sì; 📞 0371 6370 2503; ¥100; ⏰ 6.30am-5.30pm Mar-Sep, shorter hours rest of year) The largely rebuilt Shàolín Temple is a commercialised victim of its own incredible success. A frequent target of war, the ancestral home of *wǔshù* was last torched in 1928, and the surviving halls – many of recent construction – are today assailed by relentless waves of selfie-shooting tour groups. The temple's claim to fame, its dazzling *gōngfū* (kung fu) based on the movements of animals,

insects and sometimes mythological figures, guarantees that martial arts clubs around the world make incessant pilgrimages.

A satisfying visit to the Shàolín Temple requires, rather than bestows, a Zen mentality (to handle the visiting hordes and looped recordings broadcast from competing loudspeakers). But if you explore away from the main areas, you could spend an entire day or two visiting smaller temples, climbing the surrounding peaks and eking out crumbs of solitude.

Coming through the main entrance, you'll pass several *wǔshù* schools. On the right, about 500m in, is the Wǔshù Training Centre (p428), with entertaining shows featuring novices tumbling around and breaking sticks and metal bars over their heads – an integral part of the Shàolín experience.

The main temple itself is another 600m along. Many buildings, such as the main **Dàxióng Hall** (大雄宝殿; Dàxióng Bǎodiàn; reconstructed in 1985) burned to the ground in 1928. Although the temple seems to have been founded in approximately the year 500 (accounts vary), some halls only date back as far as 2004. Among the oldest structures at the temple are the decorative arches and stone lions, both outside the main gate.

BODHIDHARMA AND HIS SOLE SHOE

Called Damo (达摩) by the Chinese, Bodhidharma was a 5th-century Indian monk who travelled to the Shàolín Temple, bringing Chán (禅; Zen) Buddhism to China in the process. The monk is also traditionally revered for establishing the breathing and meditation exercises that lay the foundations of Shàolín Boxing. Bodhidharma's bearded, heavy-browed and serious expression can be seen in temples across China, especially Chán temples. Accomplishments and legends swarm around his name: he is said to have sat in a cave silently staring at a wall for nine years.

Damo is also often depicted carrying a shoe on a stick. Folklore attests that he was spotted wandering in the Pamir Mountains holding a single shoe. When the news reached the Shàolín Temple, it caused consternation as Bodhidharma had passed away and was buried nearby. His grave was exhumed and discovered to contain nothing but a solitary shoe.

At the rear, the **West Facing Hall** (西方圣人殿; Xīfāng Shēngrén Diàn) has depressions in the floor, famously (and apocryphally) the result of generations of monks practising their stance work, and huge colour frescoes. Always be on the lookout for the ubiquitous Damo (Bodhidharma), whose bearded Indian visage gazes sagaciously from stelae or peeks out from temple halls.

Across from the temple entrance, the **Arhat Hall** within the **Shífāng Chányuàn** (十方禅院) contains legions of crudely fashioned *luóhàn* (monks who have achieved enlightenment and passed to nirvana at death). Past the main temple on the right, the **Pagoda Forest** (少林塔林; Shàolín Tǎlín), a cemetery of 248 brick pagodas, which includes the ashes of eminent monks, is well worth visiting.

Further along, past the Pagoda Forest, paths lead up **Wǔrǔ Peak** (五乳峰; Wǔrǔ Fēng). Flee the tourist din by heading towards the peak to see the **cave** (达摩洞, Dámó Dòng) where Damo meditated for nine years; it's 4km uphill. From the base, you may spot the peak and the cave, marked by a large Bodhisattva figure. En route to the cave, detour to the **Chūzǔ Temple** (初祖庵; Chūzǔ Ān), a quiet and battered counterpoint to the main temple. Its main structure is the oldest wooden one in the province (c 1125).

At 1512m above sea level and reachable on the **Sōngyáng Cableway** (嵩阳索道; Sōngyáng Suǒdào; return ticket ¥50), **Shàoshì Shān** (少室山) is the area's tallest summit. The area beyond the cable car is home to the peak, and to **Èrzǔ Nunnery** (二祖庵; Èrzǔ Ān; ¥2) with four wells where you can sample its various tasting waters (sour, sweet, peppery and bitter).

Perhaps the most famous hike, however, is to neighbouring **Sānhuángzhài** (三皇寨), which takes about six hours return and covers 9km one-way (and 7398 steps!). The path goes past precipitous cliffs along a roller coaster of a route that often hugs the striated rock face to the 782-step **Rope Bridge** (连天吊桥; Lián Tiān Diào Qiáo). The scenery is superb.

Consider bypassing the initial 3km with the **Shàolín Cableway** (少林索道; Shàolín Suǒdào; one-way/return ¥50/80), which conveys you effortlessly to the start of the most dramatic section. No matter how you do this hike, start early and be prepared for some noise – it's very popular and the echoes are a big draw. Once you get to the first suspension bridge (one hour), most people turn around and the crowds thin out considerably.

To do this hike one-way – probably the most satisfying option – you can start from the end (catch a cab to Sānhuángzhài from Dēngfēng; aim for ¥30) and walk towards Shàolín. You can do it the other way too, but you're at the mercy of the drivers (assuming there are any) when you finish. Note that the bridge may be closed at times for repair or during inclement weather. Food is plentiful along the part closest to Shàolín.

To reach the Shàolín Temple, take a bus (15 minutes) from Dēngfēng's west bus station (¥3.50) or main station (¥5). A taxi to the temple from Dēngfēng will cost ¥30 (unofficial fare, no meter). Alternatively, take a minibus from either Luòyáng (¥19, 1½ hours) or Zhèngzhōu (¥29, two hours).

From the ticket office, it's then a 20-minute walk to the actual temple (passing the Wǔshù Training Centre on the way); electric carts (one-way/return ¥15/25, 7.30am to 6pm) run from the ticket office to the main temple entrance and beyond.

Note that tickets to the scenic area (including all hikes) are valid for 10 days, *except* for the temple itself, which can only be visited once on the date of purchase.

Mt Tàishì   MOUNTAIN
(太室山, Tàishì Shān; ¥50; ⊙6.30am-5.30pm) Arguably the best hike in the area, Mt Tàishì serves as a much quieter counterpoint to Shàolín Temple. It's not for slackers, however; like all Chinese mountains, the steps go straight up, and these ascend a leg-busting 1000m in altitude before reaching **Jùnjí Peak** (1492m). Along the way you'll pass some fantastical landscapes and a host of ravaged temples, the most interesting being **Lǎojūn Cave**, where according to one legend Laotzu lived for six years while writing the *Tao Te Ching*.

If you want to make a day of it, it's possible to do a loop, descending past **Fǎwáng Temple** (法王寺; Fǎwáng Sì) and then **Sōngyuè Pagoda** (嵩岳塔; Sōngyuè Tǎ), built in the year 509, on the return trip. Ask for directions at Tiānyé Temple. If you don't do the loop, figure on spending four to six hours hiking (return).

The entrance is located at Sōngyáng Academy; take bus 6 or 2 to get here. Don't forget to pick up a map (地图; dìtú) with your ticket.

Zhōngyuè Temple   TAOIST TEMPLE
(中岳庙, Zhōngyuè Miào; Shaolin Dadao, 少林大道; ¥30; ⊙8am-5pm) A few kilometres east of Dēngfēng, the ancient and hoary Zhōngyuè Miào is a colossal active Taoist monastery

complex that originally dates back to the 2nd century BC. The complex – embedded in a mountainous background, its monks garbed in traditional dress and sporting topknots – is less visited and exudes a more palpable air of reverence than its Buddhist sibling, the Shàolín Temple (p425).

Sōngyáng Academy   HISTORIC BUILDING
(嵩阳书院, Sōngyáng Shūyuàn; ¥30; ⊙7.30am-5.30pm) At the foot of Tàishì Shān sits one of China's oldest academies, the lush and well tended Sōngyáng Academy, a building complex which dates to 484 and rises up the hill on a series of terraces. In the courtyard are two cypress trees believed to be around 4500 years old – and they're still alive.

Both bus 2 and bus 6 (¥1) run to the Sōngyáng Academy.

🛏 Sleeping & Eating

Luxury sleeping options are nonexistent – if you'd prefer an international hotel with English-speaking staff and nonsmoking rooms, stay in Zhèngzhōu and visit Shàolín as a day trip.

Shàolín Temple has scores of stands in every conceivable location selling instant noodles, snacks and water. Hikers can also grab bags of peanuts.

In Dēngfēng, the local speciality is thickly cut handmade soup noodles (烩面; huì miàn). Head to the intersection of Aimin Lu (爱民路) and Songshan Lu (嵩山路) for a good choice of restaurants.

WǓSHÙ OR GŌNGFÙ?

When planning to study Chinese martial arts, the first question you should ask is: shall I learn *wǔshù* (武术) or *gōngfù* (功夫)? There may be considerable overlap, but there are crucial differences.

Wǔshù is a more recently coined term that's strongly associated with athletic martial arts displays and competition-based martial arts patterns or forms. *Gōngfù* (kung fu), however, is more about the development of internal and more esoteric skills, rather than physical prowess or mainstream athleticism.

If you're lucky enough to see a martial arts master break a piece of ceramic from a bowl and grind it to dust with his bare fingers, this is *gōngfù*, not *wǔshù*.

Kungfu Hostel
HOSTEL **$**

(功夫客栈, Gōngfù Kèzhàn; ☑ 0371 6274 8889; 20 Dujia Village, Shàolín Temple Grounds, 少林景区内度假村20号院; dm/d ¥80/198; ❋ 🛜) If waking up to the sounds of crowing roosters and future Jet Lis jogging laps past the door sounds like your cup of *chá*, don't miss this opportunity to stay at Shàolín Temple. Set in a residential compound on a hillside opposite the main temple, this is without a doubt the best place to soak up the full Shàolín experience.

Make sure to reserve in advance – it's hard to find (about a 20- to 30-minute walk from the ticket office), and you need to purchase a ticket before you check in (unless it's after 6pm). They can help arrange private martial arts classes, too.

Dēngfēng Climb Hostel
HOSTEL **$**

(登封攀登国际青年旅舍, Dēngfēng Pāndēng Guójì Qīngnián Lúshě; ☑ 138 3853 6111; Songyang Lu, 嵩阳路; dm/d ¥30/120; ❋ 🛜) The simple and friendly Climb Hostel has an enviable location set against the mountains, just steps from the entrance to Mt Tàishì (p427). Located all the way in the north of town, it can be a bit tricky to reach on your first try, though. Bus 6 runs almost here from the bus station (last stop, then ask directions).

Shàolín Hotel
HOTEL **$$**

(少林宾馆, Shàolín Bīnguǎn; ☑ 0371 6016 1616; 66 Zhongyue Dajie, 中岳大街66号; d from ¥238; ❋ 🛜) Bright and cheery staff, good discounts and clean rooms make this neat and trim midrange hotel a good choice. Look for the four-storey white building east of Dicos (a fast-food restaurant) with the yellow-and-red sign. It's a ¥7 taxi ride from the bus station. Discounts of ¥100 available.

☆ Entertainment

Wǔshù Training Centre
MARTIAL ARTS

(武术馆, Wǔshù Guǎn; ⊘ 9.30am, 10.30am, 11.30am, 2pm, 3pm, 4pm) Coming through Shàolín Temple's main entrance, you'll pass several *wǔshù* schools. On the right, about 500m in, is the Wǔshù Training Centre, with free entertaining performances by the novices – a quintessential part of the Shàolín experience. (There is no 9.30am show in the off-season.)

ⓘ Information

Bank of China (中国银行, Zhōngguó Yínháng; 52 Zhongyue Dajie, 中岳大街52号; ⊘ 9am-5pm Mon-Fri) Has a 24-hour ATM and foreign exchange.

Bank of China (186 Shaolin Dadao, 少林大道186号; ⊘ 9am-noon & 2-5pm Mon-Fri)

China International Travel Service (CITS, 中国国际旅行社, Zhōngguó Guójì Lǚxíngshè; ☑ 0371 6287 3387; www.cits.net; Dayu Lu, 大禹路)

China Post (中国邮政, Zhōngguó Yóuzhèng; cnr Zhongyue & Wangji Rd, 中岳路与望箕路) Centrally located post office.

Number Two People's Hospital (第二人民医院, Dì'èr Rénmín Yīyuàn; ☑ 0371 6289 9999; 189 Shaolin Dadao, 少林大道189号) On the main road.

Train Ticket Office (火车预售票处, huǒchē yùshòupiàochù; 72 Shaolin Dadao, 少林大道72号; ⊘ 8am-6pm)

ⓘ Getting There & Away

The **main bus station** (总站; *zǒng zhàn*) is in the east of town; jump on bus 1 (¥1) to reach Zhongyue Dajie and the town centre. There's also a **west bus station** (西站; *xī zhàn*), which some buses head to after dropping people off at the main station. Buses run to the following:

Kāifēng ¥40, three hours, four daily

Luòyáng ¥25, two hours, half-hourly

Zhèngzhōu ¥27, two hours, half-hourly

Don't buy the cheaper Zhèngzhōu bus ticket (¥22) – it won't take you to the central bus station.

To purchase tickets in advance for trains departing from Zhèngzhōu, go to the train ticket office (p428).

Taxis are a cheap and easy way to get around. Fares start at ¥5, though many drivers insist on a ¥10 flat fee (accept or switch taxis).

Luòyáng
洛阳

☑ 0379 / POP 1.8 MILLION

Access point for the incredible Lóngmén Grottoes outside town, Luòyáng was one of China's true dynastic citadels. The city was the prosperous capital of 13 dynasties, until the Northern Song dynasty shifted its capital east along the Yellow River to Kāifēng in the 10th century. The mighty Sui- and Tang-dynasty walls formed an imposing rectangle north and south of the Luò River, while worshippers flocked to 1300 Buddhist temples through the city.

Luòyáng was once the very centre of the Chinese universe and the eastern capital of the resplendent Tang dynasty. Tragically, little remains of this glorious past: the heart of the magnificent Sui dynasty palace complex was centred on the point where today's Zhongzhou Zhonglu and Dingding Lu intersect in a frenzy of traffic.

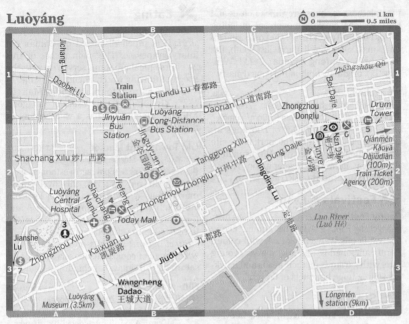

Luòyáng

⊙ Sights

★ Luòyáng Museum
MUSEUM

(洛阳市博物馆, Luòyáng Shì Bówùguǎn; www.ly museum.com; Nietai Lu, 聂泰路; ⊙9am-4.30pm Tue-Sun) FREE This huge museum, situated out of the action south of the river, has ex-hilarating displays across two huge floors and is one of the few places to get ancient Luòyáng in any kind of perspective. There's an absorbing collection of three-colour Tang dynasty *sāncǎi* porcelain; the city's rise is traced through dynastic pottery, bronzeware and other magnificent objects. An **audio guide** (¥40) is also available.

Ancient Tombs Museum
MUSEUM

(古墓博物馆, Gǔmù Bówùguǎn; Airport Rd, 机场路; ⊙9am-4.30pm Tue-Sun) FREE This superb but little-visited museum has three main exhibits: 20 reconstructed tombs (spanning five main dynasties, or over 1000 years), re-created using original building materials; original tomb murals; and a Northern Wei royal burial mound (closed at the time of research). Grab an **audio guide** (¥20) on the way in and let loose your inner Indiana Jones: crawl on hands and knees into a 2000-year-old tomb to admire delicately carved peony panels and the faded frescoes on a domed ceiling.

The museum is 7km north of town. To get here, take bus 83 north from the train station (¥1, 20 minutes). A taxi will run about ¥30.

Luòyáng Old Town
AREA

(老城区, lǎochéngqū) Any Chinese city worth its rice has an Old Town. Luòyáng's is east of the rebuilt **Lǐjīng Gate** (丽景门, Lǐjīng Mén; Xi Dajie, 西大街; ¥30; ⊙8am-8pm summer, shorter hours rest of year), where the narrow Xi Dajie yields up a plethora of shops, grey-brick houses and the occasional creaking monument, including the old **Drum Tower** (鼓楼; Gǔ Lóu) rising up on Dong Dajie (东大街) and, just south, the lovely brick **Wénfēng Pagoda** (文峰塔; Wénfēng Tǎ), originally built in the Song dynasty.

Wángchéng Park   PARK
(王城公园, Wángchéng Gōngyuán; Zhongzhou Zhonglu, 中州中路; ☺6am-9.30pm summer, shorter hours rest of year) One of Luòyáng's indispensable green lungs, this park is the site of the annual Peony Festival. Unfortunately, the park is home to a decrepit zoo. There's also an **amusement park** (rides ¥15 to ¥20).

✨ Festivals & Events

Peony Festival   CULTURAL
(Wángchéng Park; ☺Apr) The annual peony festival floods Wángchéng Park with colour, floral aficionados, photographers, young girls with garlands on their heads and hawkers selling huge bouquets of flowers.

🛏 Sleeping

Luòyáng has a large range of hotels in every budget bracket dotted all over the city.

Luòyáng Yijiā
International Youth Hostel   HOSTEL $
(洛阳易家国际青年旅舍, Luòyáng Yìjiā Guójì Qīngnián Lǚshè; ☎0379 6351 2311; 329 Zhongzhou Donglu, 中洲东路329号; dm ¥30-50, d & tw ¥158; ❋@☎) Located in the busy Old Town, this hostel hits its stride with a lively communal area and bar. Six-bed dorms are a little tight; private rooms are the equivalent of a two-star Chinese room. Rooms facing the main road are noisy (and bright), so check first. Transport to town and all the major sights is within walking distance.

Buses 5 and 41 from the train and bus stations come past. From the Lóngmén train station, take bus 49, then switch to bus 9 at Xiguan.

Christian's Hotel   BOUTIQUE HOTEL $$$
(克丽司汀酒店, Kèlìsītīng Jiǔdiàn; ☎0379 6326 6666; www.5xjd.com; 56 Jiefang Lu, 解放路56号, entrance on Tanggong Xilu; d from ¥1499; ❋@☎) This boutique hotel scores points for its variety of rooms, each with a kitchen and dining area, large plush beds, flat-screen TVs, and mini-bar. Do you go for Tang dynasty style or white walls and a circular bed? Regardless, you'll be thanking the eponymous Christian each time you step into the room. Outside of April, discounts usually slash rates in half.

🍴 Eating

Luòyáng's famous 'water banquet' (水席; shuǐxí) is much discussed on China's culinary grapevine. The main dishes of this 24-course meal are soups served up with the speed of flowing water – hence the name.

In the centre of town, the **Today Mall** (新都汇; Xīndùhuì), at the corner of Tanggong Xilu and Jiefang Lu, has a wide variety of things to eat.

Old Town Night Market   STREET FOOD $
(十字街夜市, Shízìjiē Yèshì; Xinghua Jie, 兴华街; meals ¥10-50; ☺6pm-1am) Festooned with brightly lit red lanterns, this lively night market has a cornucopia of snacks from lamb kebabs (羊肉串; yángròu chuàn) and fermented soup noodles (浆面; jiāng miàn) to roasted garlic-stuffed eggplant (蒜香茄子; suànxiāng qiézi). Stalls on the left offer a wide range of cooked dishes served at tables set up on the sidewalk behind.

Niūniū Dàpánjī   XINJIANG $
(妞妞大盘鸡; 329 Zhongzhou Donglu, 中州东路329号; big-plate chicken ¥32; ☺11.30am-2pm & 5.30-10pm) A Xīnjiāng speciality, dàpánjī (大盘鸡; big-plate chicken) is a spicy chicken, potato and pepper stew; halfway through the meal, handmade noodles and greens are added to the mix – the ensemble is absolutely delicious. A small portion feeds two people, and this is the only dish they serve, so you can be assured they do it well!

Qiánmén Kǎoyā Dàjiǔdiàn   PEKING DUCK $$
(前门烤鸭大酒店; ☎0379 6395 3333; cnr Zhongzhou Donglu & Minzu Jie; half/whole duck ¥70/138, other dishes from ¥22; ☺10am-2pm & 5-9pm) This efficient and smart choice serves up rich and tasty roast duck, cooked by an army of white-clad chefs. There are other vegetable and meat dishes on the menu, but why bother?

ℹ Information

Internet cafes (¥3 per hour) are scattered around the train station and sprinkled along nearby Jinguyuan Lu.

Bank of China (中国银行, Zhōngguó Yínháng; Daonan Lu, 道南路) Handy branch just west of the train station.

Bank of China (Zhongzhou Xilu, 中州西路) For foreign exchange and cashing travellers cheques.

Bank of China (中国银行, Zhōngguó Yínháng; Zhongzhou Zhonglu, 中州中路; ☺8am-4.30pm)

China Post (中国邮政, Zhōngguó Yóuzhèng; Zhongzhou Zhonglu, 中州中路)

Industrial & Commercial Bank (ICBC, 工商银行, Gōngshāng yínháng; Zhongzhou Zhonglu, 中州中路) Huge branch; foreign exchange and 24-hour ATM.

Luòyáng Central Hospital (洛阳市中心医院, Luòyáng Shì Zhōngxīn Yīyuàn; ☑ 0379 6389 2222; 288 Zhongzhou Zhonglu, 中州中路288号) Works in cooperation with SOS International; also has a 24-hour pharmacy.

Public Security Bureau (PSB, 公安局, Gōng'ānjú; ☑ 0379 6313 3313; cnr Taitang Lu & Guanxi Lu, 太康路与馆西路交义口; ☑8am-noon & 2-5.30pm Mon-Fri) The exit-entry department (出入境大厅; chūrùjìng dàtīng) is across the river to the southwest.

Train Ticket Agency (火车票代售处, Huǒchēpiào Dàishòuchù; 249 Zhongzhou Dongu, 中州东路249号; ☑9am-5pm) Sells train tickets for a ¥5 commission.

❶ Getting There & Away

AIR

You would do better to fly into or out of Zhèngzhōu. One or two daily flights operate to Běijīng (¥275, 1½ hours), Shànghǎi (¥710, 1½ hours), Guǎngzhōu (¥900, two hours) and other cities. Obtain tickets through hotels or Ctrip.

BUS

Regular departures from the **long-distance bus station** (洛阳一运汽车站, Luòyáng yīyùn qìchēzhàn; 51 Jinguyuan Lu, 金谷园路), located diagonally across from the train station, include the following:

Dēngfēng ¥24, two hours, every 40 minutes (5.30am to 6.50pm)

Kāifēng ¥60, four hours, half-hourly

Shàolín Temple ¥19, 1½ hours, every 40 minutes (5.30am to 6.50pm)

Zhèngzhōu ¥50, two hours, half-hourly

Buses to similar destinations also depart from the friendly and less frantic **Jǐnyuǎn bus station** (锦远汽车站, Jǐnyuǎn qìchēzhàn), just west of the train station.

TRAIN

Luòyáng's **Lóngmén Station** (洛阳龙门站, Lùoyáng Lóngmén Zhàn), over the river in the south of town, is the high-speed station. The **main train station** (洛阳火车站, Luòyáng huǒchē zhàn) has slower trains.

You can get tickets for a ¥5 commission from a **train ticket agency**.

Destinations departing the main train station:

Běijīng West Seat/sleeper ¥105/208, 7½ to 11 hours, seven daily

Kāifēng Hard seat ¥30, three hours, nine daily (afternoon only)

Nánjīng Seat/sleeper ¥112/219, eight to 12 hours, seven daily

Shànghǎi Seat/sleeper ¥142/276, nine to 17 hours, six daily

From Luòyáng Lóngmén Station:

Běijīng West G train 2nd/1st class ¥367/587, four hours, seven daily

Shànghǎi D train sleeper ¥765, nine hours, 22.52pm

Wǔhàn 2nd/1st class ¥302/483, three hours, regular

Xī'ān North G train 2nd/1st class ¥175/280, 1¾ hours, frequent

Zhèngzhōu G train 2nd/1st class ¥60/90, 40 minutes, frequent

❶ Getting Around

The airport is 12km north of the city. Bus 83 (¥1, 30 minutes) runs to/from the parking lot to the left of the train station. A taxi to/from the train station costs about ¥35.

Buses 5 and 41 go to the Old Town from the train station, running via Wángchéng Sq. Bus 49 (among others) runs from Lóngmén station to the centre of town.

Taxis are ¥5 at flag fall, making them good value. Expect to pay about ¥30 to Lóngmén station and ¥10 to the main train and bus station area.

Around Luòyáng

Lóngmén Grottoes　　龙门石窟

The ravaged **Lóngmén Grottoes** (Lóngmén Shíkū; ¥100, English-speaking guide ¥100; ☑8am-5.30pm Apr-Oct, shorter hours rest of year) constitute one of China's handful of surviving masterpieces of Buddhist rock carving. A sutra in stone, the epic achievement of the grottoes was commenced by chisellers from the Northern Wei dynasty after the capital relocated here from Dàtóng in the year 494. Over the next two centuries, more than 100,000 images and statues of Buddha and his disciples emerged from over a kilometre of limestone cliff wall along the Yī River (伊河; Yī Hé).

A disheartening amount of decapitation disfigures the statuary at this Unesco World Heritage Site. In the early 20th century, many effigies were beheaded by unscrupulous collectors or simply extracted whole, many ending up abroad in such institutions as the Metropolitan Museum of Art in New York, the Atkinson Museum in Kansas City and the Tokyo National Museum. Many statues have clearly just had their faces crudely bludgeoned off, vandalism that probably dates to the Cultural Revolution and earlier episodes of anti-Buddhist fervour. The elements have also intervened, wearing smooth the faces of many other statues.

The grottoes are scattered in a line on the west and east sides of the river. Most of the significant Buddhist carvings are on the west side, but a small crop can also be admired after traversing the bridge to the east side. Admission also includes entry to a temple and garden on the east side. English captions are rudimentary.

The grottoes are 13km south of Luòyáng and can be reached by taxi (¥30); bus 81 (¥1, 40 minutes) from the east side of Luòyáng's train station; or bus 53 from Zhongzhou Donglu.

From the west side, you can take a boat (¥25) back to the main entrance to get a riverside view of the grottoes (note that you can't re-enter the west side once you leave). On the east side, electric carts (¥10) can take you to a variety of locations. All in all, it's a 3km walk; expect to spend at least 2½ hours here.

WEST SIDE

Work began on the **Three Bīnyáng Grottoes** (宾阳三洞; Bīnyáng Sān Dòng) during the Northern Wei dynasty. Despite the completion of two of the grottoes during the Sui and Tang dynasties, statues here all display the benevolent expressions that characterised Northern Wei style. Traces of pigment remain within the three large grottoes and other small niches honeycomb the cliff walls. Nearby is the **Móyá Three Buddha Niche** (摩崖三佛龛, Móyá Sānfó Kān), with seven figures that date to the Tang dynasty.

The Tang dynasty **Ten Thousand Buddha Grotto** (万佛洞; Wànfó Dòng) dates from 680. In addition to its namesake galaxy of tiny bas-relief Buddhas, there is a fine effigy of the Amitabha Buddha. Note the red pigment on the ceiling.

The most physically imposing and magnificent of all the Lóngmén carvings, the vast **Losana Buddha Statue Grotto** (奉先寺; Fèngxiān Sì) was created during the Tang dynasty between 672 and 675; it contains the best examples of sculpture, despite evident weathering and vandalism. Nine principal figures dominate: the Buddha, two disciples, two Bodhisattvas, two heavenly kings and two guardians. The 17m-high central Buddha is said to be Losana, whose face is allegedly modelled on Tang empress and Buddhist patron Wu Zetian, who funded its carving.

The Tang figures tend to be more three-dimensional than the Northern Wei figures, while their expressions and poses also seem more natural. In contrast to the otherworldly effigies of the Northern Wei, many Tang figures possess a more fearsome ferocity and muscularity, most noticeable in the huge guardian figure in the north wall.

EAST SIDE

Although the **east side grottoes** (东山石窟; Dōngshān Shíkū) lack comparable grandeur – many are even gated shut – there are still some gems to seek out here. The first stop you'll come across after crossing the bridge is the **Léigǔtái Architectural Site** (擂鼓台建筑遗址; Léigǔtái Jiànzhù Yízhǐ), which takes visitors through an earlier excavation, with various Tang and Song relics on display. It's through a pair of doors at the top of the steps.

Although badly faded, the delicate **Thousand Arm and Thousand Eye Guanyin** (千手千眼观音龛; Qiānshǒu Qiānyǎn Guānyīn Kān) in Grotto 2132 is a splendid bas-relief dating to the Tang dynasty, revealing the Goddess of Mercy framed in a huge fan of carved hands, each sporting an eye.

Further is the eastern side's largest site, the **Reading Sutra Grotto** (看经寺洞; Kàn Jīng Sìdòng), with a carved lotus on its ceiling and 29 expressive *luóhàn* (Buddhists who have achieved nirvana) around the base of the walls.

At the top of a steep flight of steps, the **Xiāngshān Temple** (香山寺; Xiāngshān Sì) nestles against a hill. It was first built in 516 and has been repeatedly restored. Look for a stele with a poem written by Emperor Qianlong, who visited and was moved to honour the temple's beauty. There's also a villa which once belonged to Chiang Kaishek, built in 1936 to celebrate his 50th birthday.

The final stop is a lovely garden built around the **tomb of Bai Juyi** (白居易墓地; Bái Jūyì Mùdì), a poet from the Tang dynasty. It's a peaceful, leafy place where you can rest your tired feet. There's an alfresco **teahouse** here where you can get tea (from ¥98), snacks and instant noodles.

White Horse Temple 白马寺

Although its original structures have all been replaced and older Buddhist shrines may have vanished, this vast, active **monastery** (Báimǎ Sì; ¥35; ⊙ 7.40am-6pm) outside Luòyáng is regarded as China's first surviving Buddhist temple, originally dating from the 1st century

AD. When two Han dynasty court emissaries went in search of Buddhist scriptures, they met two Indian monks in Afghanistan; the monks returned to Luòyáng on white horses carrying Buddhist sutras and statues. The impressed emperor built the temple for the monks; it's also their resting place.

Tucked amid the smoky incense burners and usual Buddhist halls are some unusual sights; plan on spending at least two hours here. In the back of the complex, beneath a raised hall, is the **Shìyuán Art Gallery** (释源美术馆; Shìyuán Měishùguǎn), displaying temporary exhibitions. Also in the back of the complex is a surprisingly chic **teahouse** (止语茶舍; zhǐyǔ cháshě), an excellent place to take refuge and relax with a pot of weak tea (free).

West of the historic grounds is the new **International Zone**, featuring a large collection of temples built by Thailand, Myanmar and India. It's certainly worth strolling around.

Way at the opposite end of the grounds are **gardens** and the ancient 12-tiered **Qíyún Pagoda** (齐云塔; Qíyún Tǎ), encircled by worshippers.

The temple is 13km east of Luòyáng, around 40 minutes away on bus 56 from the Xīguān (西关) stop. Bus 58 from Zhongzhou Donglu in the Old Town also runs here.

Guōliàngcūn　郭亮村

⌖ 0373 / POP 500

On its cliff-top perch high up in the Mountains of the Ten Thousand Immortals (万仙山; Wànxiān Shān) in north Hénán, this delightful high-altitude stone hamlet was for centuries sheltered from the outside world by a combination of inaccessibility and anonymity. Guōliàngcūn shot to fame as the bucolic backdrop to a clutch of Chinese films, which firmly embedded the village in contemporary Chinese mythology.

Today, the village attracts legions of artists, who journey here to capture the unreal mountain scenery on paper and canvas. Joining them are Chinese tourists who get disgorged by the busloads. For a true rustic mountaintop experience, come on an out-of-season weekday when it's more tranquil. New buildings have sprung up at the village's base, but the original dwellings – climbing the mountain slope – retain their simple, rustic charms. Long treks beneath the marvellous limestone peaks more than compensate for the hard slog of journeying here.

⊙ Sights & Activities

All of the **village dwellings**, many hung with butter-yellow bàngzi (sweetcorn cobs), are hewn from the same local stone that paves the slender alleyways, sculpts the bridges and fashions the picturesque gates of Guōliàngcūn. Swallowed up by new construction, the original village can be easy to miss – it's on the right and up the hill from the rest of town.

You will have passed by the **Precipice Gallery** (绝壁长廊, Juébì Chángláng), also referred to on some signs as 'Long Corridor in the Cliffs', en route to Guōliàngcūn, but backtrack down for a closer perspective on these plunging cliffs, with dramatic views from the tunnel carved through the rock. Before this tunnel was built (between 1972 and 1978) by a local man called Shen Mingxin and some others, the only way into the village was via the **Sky Ladder** (天梯, Tiān Tī) – Ming dynasty steps hewn from the local stone, with no guard rails but amazing views.

The walk to the Sky Ladder is among the area's most scenic (and tranquil). To get here, take the left fork of the road heading towards the tunnel and walk for 2km.

Over the bridge on the other side of the precipice from the village, walk past the small row of cottages, set almost on the edge of the cliff, called **Yáshàng Rénjiā** (崖上人家); you can step onto a platform atop a pillar of rock for astonishing views into the canyon.

Otherwise, head up valley through the strip of street stalls and hotels to get to the start of a 5km circuit. From the end of the street, it's an additional 1.3km to the starting point of the loop. (Sadly, the mood of the area has been spoilt in parts by the addition of several constructed oddities, including a mini zip-line and a drain-like slide ride

HÉNÁN GUŌLIÀNGCŪN

from the top of the mountain.) If you start on the left-hand set of steps, you'll first go past the awe-inspiring curtain of rock above the **Shouting Spring** (喊泉, Hǎn Quán). According to local lore, its flow responds to the loudness of your whoops (it doesn't, but the site is predictably a riot of noise). You'll also pass the peaceful **Old Pool** (老潭, Lǎo Tǎn), which is thankfully out of earshot of the spring. Further along is the **Red Dragon Cave** (红龙洞, Hónglóng Dòng), now closed, and after a few steep flights of stairs, the slide ride (¥30) and then the small **White Dragon Cave** (白龙洞, Báilóng Dòng; ¥20), which you can skip with no regrets. The last sight is a set of steps that lead up to **Pearl Spring** (珍珠泉, Zhēnzhū Quán), a fissure in the mountain from which pours out cool, clear, spring water. You can, of course, do the loop in the opposite direction.

Once you've seen the big sights, get off the beaten trail and onto one of the small paths heading into the hills (such as the boulder-strewn, brook-side trail along the flank of Guōliàngcūn that leads further up into the mountain). Take your own water with you.

Several kilometres before the village, you'll need to purchase an admission ticket to the **Wànxiān Shān Scenic Area** (¥125); the required ticket includes free transport on the park's green shuttle buses.

🍽 Sleeping & Eating

There are hotels galore in Guōliàngcūn, most heading up the valley, though the village and road opposite also have rooms. All offer identical two-star quality, with hot showers, wi-fi and TVs (no toiletries or towels though). Rooms cost ¥40 to ¥100 depending on size and orientation. Prices are a bit higher during the summer but negotiable in the low season and on weekdays.

Small restaurants and eateries are everywhere you turn, with most attached to one of the innumerable village guesthouses. Expect a sampling of classic Chinese dishes and noodles, costing in the range of ¥15 to ¥40.

ℹ Information

There are no ATMs and there is nowhere to change money in Guōliàngcūn.

ℹ Getting There & Away

You can reach Guōliàngcūn from Xīnxiāng (新乡), between Ānyáng and Zhèngzhōu. Fast trains run from Zhèngzhōu east train station to Xīnxiāng east train station (¥24, 45 minutes), as do regular buses (¥25, two hours). From here, you'll need to take a cab to Xīnxiāng's **main bus station** (客运总站; kèyùn zǒngzhàn; about ¥12) to catch the bus to Huīxiàn (辉县; ¥7, 45 minutes), which runs regularly. Bus 66 (¥1) also runs to the main bus station.

Seven buses (¥15, 1¾ hours, first/last bus 7.20am/5.25pm) from Huīxiàn's **bus station** (辉县站; Huīxiàn zhàn) run to the Wànxiān Shān ticket office. Here, you will need to switch to the green shuttle, which will take you the rest of the way to the village.

To return, take the green shuttle down to Nánpíng (南坪; 25 minutes), a village below Guōliàngcūn, from where minibuses depart for Huīxiàn (¥20) at 6.20am, 9am, noon, 1pm, 1.30pm, 3pm and 5pm. Most say they go directly to Xīnxiāng, but unless it's standing room only, they only go as far as Huīxiàn.

ℹ Getting Around

Electric carts (¥20 return) run to the Sky Ladder (2km) and the trail for the Shouting Spring loop (1.3km). Follow the signs to each and you'll find the carts waiting along the way.

Kāifēng   开封

♪ 0371 / POP 1.25 MILLION

More than any other of Hénán's ancient capitals, Kāifēng has made an effort to recall its former grandeur. The walled town has character: you may have to squint a bit and sift the reproductions from its genuine historical narrative, but the city still offers up an intriguing display of age-old charm, magnificent market food, relics from its long-vanished apogee and colourful chrysanthemums, the city flower (Kāifēng is also known as Júchéng, or 'Chrysanthemum Town').

You won't see soaring skyscrapers, though – one reason being that buildings requiring deep foundations are prohibited, for fear of destroying the ancient northern Song dynasty city below.

History

Once the prosperous capital of the Northern Song dynasty (960–1126), Kāifēng was established south of the Yellow River, but not far enough to escape the river's capricious wrath. After centuries of flooding, the city of the Northern Song largely lies buried 8m to 9m deep in hardened silt. Between 1194 and 1938 the city flooded 368 times, an average of once every two years.

Kāifēng was also the first city in China where Jewish merchants, travelling along the Silk Road during the Song dynasty, settled when they arrived. A small Christian and Catholic community also lives in Kāifēng alongside a much larger local Muslim Hui community.

◉ Sights

★ Temple of the Chief Minister
BUDDHIST TEMPLE

(大相国寺, Dà Xiàngguó Sì; Ziyou Lu, 自有路; ¥40; ⊙ 8am 6.30pm summer, shorter hours rest of year) First founded in AD 555, this frequently rebuilt temple vanished along with Kāifēng in the early 1640s, when rebels breached the Yellow River's dykes. During the Northern Song, the temple covered a massive 34 hectares and housed over 10,000 monks. The show-stopper today is the mesmerising **Four-Faced Thousand Hand Thousand Eye Guanyin** (四面千手千眼观世音), towering within the octagonal **Arhat Hall** (罗汉殿, Luóhàn Diàn), beyond the **Hall of Tathagata** (大雄宝殿, Dàxióng Bǎodiàn).

Kāifēng Fǔ
HISTORIC SITE

(开封府; north side, Baogong East Lake, 包公湖北岸; ¥60; ⊙ 7am-7pm summer, shorter hours rest of year) This reconstructed site of the government offices of the Northern Song has daily theatricals commencing daily outside the gates – as the doors are thrown open costumed actors play period scenes, complete with cracking whips and the sound of gongs. They then retreat inside to continue the play (in Chinese). Drama aside, the site is one of Kāifēng's better re-creations of Song imperial life, with English explanations, martial parade grounds, a prison and several appearances by the famed Judge Bao.

Kāifēng City Walls
WALLS

(城墙, Chéng Qiáng) FREE Kāifēng is ringed by a relatively intact, much-restored Qing dynasty wall, which you can climb up at various points. Today's bastion was built on the foundations of the Song dynasty **Inner Wall** (内城; Nèichéng). Encased with grey bricks, rear sections of the ramparts have been recently buttressed unattractively with concrete. Rising up outside was the mighty, now buried **Outer Wall** (外城; Wàichéng), a colossal construction containing 18 gates, which looped south of Pó Pagoda.

Former Site of Kāifēng Synagogue
RUINS

(开封犹太教堂遗址, Kāifēng Yóutài Jiàotáng Yízhǐ; Jiefang Rd Tujie Section, 解放路土街段) Sadly, nothing remains of the synagogue – finally swept away in mid-19th-century floodwaters – except a well with an iron lid in the boiler room of the Kāifēng Traditional Chinese Medicine Hospital (开封中医院, Kāifēng Zhōngyīyuàn), which may allow you to examine it. The spirit of the synagogue lingers, however, in the name of the brick alley immediately south of the hospital – **Jiaojing Hutong** (教经胡同, Teaching the Torah Alley).

A local English-speaking **guide** (☑ 137 8172 2704; yisrael-kaifeng@hotmail.com) familiar with local Jewish history lives in the house with the blue sign. Send an email prior to visiting if you intend to engage her guide services or want an extended chat.

Shānshǎngān Guild Hall
HISTORIC BUILDING

(山陕甘会馆, Shānshǎn'gān Huìguǎn; 85 Xufu Jie, 徐府街85号; ¥25; ⊙ 8am-6.30pm summer, shorter hours rest of year) This tiny, elaborately

---

ALONG THE RIVER DURING THE QINGMING FESTIVAL

Now held in the Forbidden City and widely acknowledged as China's first *shén* (godly) painting, *Along the River During the Qingming Festival* was completed by Zhang Zeduan (张择端) in the early 12th century. These days, you'll see it everywhere in Kāifēng. Museums and parks have it in carved wood and stone bas-relief, it's found in scale dioramas, souvenir posters and advertising (it's on the Kāifēng Hostel's poster), and there's even a historical theme park modelled on it.

The long (about 25cm x 529cm) painting depicts life in a city that experts have attributed as Kāifēng. It's packed to the gills with details of the period: boats unloading goods at a harbour, an inn crowded with customers and children playing on the streets. As you would imagine, it offers valuable insight into the life and times of a large Song dynasty town. When the original is displayed in Beijing, queues to see it last hours. Art enthusiasts will no doubt recognise later copies of the work, some of which are equally famous – the 1737 version, presented to Emperor Qianlong, is now held in Taipei's national Palace Museum.

You can see versions at several places in Kāifēng, including the Riverside Scenic Park, the scale diorama in the **Shānshǎngān Guild Hall** and the replica version in the **Kāifēng Museum** (p437).

Kāifēng

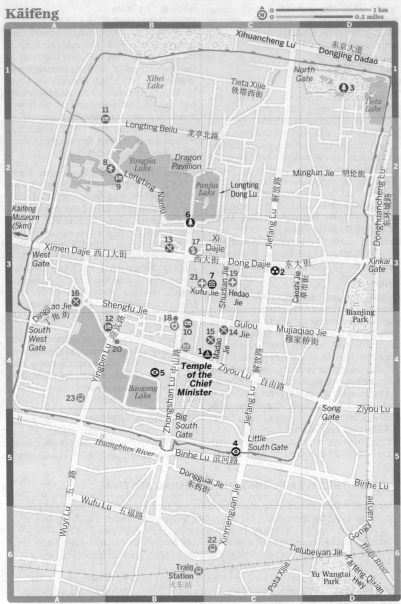

Xihuancheng Lu

东京大道
Dongjing Dadao

Xibei Lake

Tieta Xijie 铁塔西街

North Gate

Tieta Lake

Longting Beilu 龙亭北路

Dragon Pavillion

Minglun Jie 明伦街

Yangjia Lake

Longting Nanlu

Panjia Lake

Longting Dong Lu

Kāifēng Museum (5km)

West Gate

Ximen Dajie 西门大街

Xi Dajie 西大街

Dong Dajie 东大街

Jiefang Lu 解放路

Xinkai Gate

Xufu Jie

Shudian Jie

Hedao Jie

Caoshi Jie 草市街

Bianjing Park

Dingjiao Jie 丁角街

Shengfu Jie

Gulou Jie

Mujiaqiao Jie 穆家桥街

South West Gate

Yingbin Lu 迎宾路

Zhongshan Lu 中山路

Madao Jie

Ziyou Lu 自由路

Jiefang Lu

Temple of the Chief Minister

Baogong Lake

Big South Gate

Song Gate

Ziyou Lu

Little South Gate

Huangbian River

Binhe Lu 滨河路

Binhe Lu

Dongguai Jie 东拐街

Wufu Lu 五福路

Xinmenguan Jie

Gongyuanjie

Tielubeiyan Jie

Kaifeng-Qixian Hwy

Yu Wangtai Park

Train Station 火车站

Pota Xijie

HÉNÁN KĀIFĒNG

styled guild hall was built as a lodging and meeting place during the Qing dynasty by an association of merchants from Shānxi (山西), Shaanxi (陕西) and Gānsù (甘肃) provinces. Note the ornate carvings on the roof beams. You can delve into the exhibition on historic Kāifēng and see a fascinating diorama of the old Song city – with its palace in the centre of town – and compare it with a model of modern Kāifēng.

Kāifēng

Kāifēng Museum   MUSEUM
(开封博物馆, Kāifēng Bówùguǎn; ☑ 0371 393 2178, ext 8010; Zhengkai Dadao, near Wu Dajie, 郑开大道与五大街交叉口; ⏱ 9am-5pm Tue-Sun) FREE Containing a modest collection of archaeological finds, woodblock prints and historical objects, the Kāifēng Museum was slated to move into a new home 5km west of the city in 2017. The draw for most is two notable Jewish stelae, managed by the Kāifēng Institute for Research on the History of Chinese Jews. A ticket to see the stelae was ¥50 at the old museum (at time of research the future price was unknown).

Iron Pagoda Park   PARK
(铁塔公园, Tiě Tǎ Gōngyuán; 210 Beimen Dajie, 北门大街210号; day/night ¥40/80; ⏱ 8am-6.30pm) Rising up within Iron Pagoda Park is a magnificent 11th-century **pagoda** (55m tall), a gorgeous, slender brick edifice wrapped in glazed rust-coloured tiles (hence the name); its narrow stairs are climbable for ¥35. A 30-minute evening **light show** is held at 7.30pm, 8pm, 9pm and 9.30pm. Take bus 1 from Zhongshan Lu; alternatively, a taxi will cost ¥10.

🎉 Festivals & Events

Chrysanthemum Festival   CULTURAL
(⏱ Oct) Millions of chrysanthemums are on full display at **Lóngtíng Park** (龙亭公园, Lóngtíng Gōngyuán; ☑ 0371 566 0316; Zhongshan Lu, 中山路; ¥80; ⏱ 8am-6pm) and elsewhere around the city during this autumn festival. In 2015, botanists grafted 641 flowers together, earning a spot in the Guinness World Records.

🛏 Sleeping

At the time of research, Kāifēng had closed all hotels to foreigners except for a few four- and five-star options. However, both the **Jǐnjiāng Inn** (锦江之星, Jǐnjiāng Zhīxīng; ☑ 0371 2399 6666; 88 Zhongshan Lu, 中山路88号; d ¥208-246; ❋ @ ⏱) and the Tiānfú Hostel have accepted foreigners in the past; check with them if you're looking for budget accommodation. If nothing is available, you can always visit as a day trip from Zhèngzhōu.

Tiānfú International Youth Hostel HOSTEL $
(天福国际青年旅舍, Kāifēng Guójì Qīngnián Lǚshè; ☑ 0371 2315 3789; 30 Yingbin Lu, 迎宾路30号; dm ¥80, d from ¥298; ❋ @ ⏱) On our last visit, this so-so hostel was being managed by three middle-aged women who seemed unlikely candidates for conveying that fun youth hostel experience. Shooing us out the door with claims that the hostel was closed for renovations (it wasn't), they were neither helpful nor particularly friendly. Definitely confirm before you book here. No English.

Courtyard & Sunlight Inn BOUTIQUE HOTEL $$
(阳光纳里酒店, Yángguāng Nàlǐ Jiǔdiàn; ☑ 0371 2238 2222; 5 Qishengjiao Commercial Area, Longting Xilu, 龙亭西路七盛角商业街5号楼; d from ¥468; ❋ ⏱) Part of a re-created Song dynasty tourist street, this boutique hotel offers a peaceful setting where you can unwind at the end of the day. Expect some semblance of style with a faux interior courtyard, decorated with upside-down parasols, and traditional-style furnishings in the rooms. Bike

HÉNÁN KĀIFĒNG

rental is also available. It's just east of the **Millennium City Park** (清明上河园, Qīng-míng Shànghéyuán; Longting Nanlu, 龙亭南路; day ¥100, night ¥219-299; ⏰8am-6pm).

Pullman Hotel HOTEL $$$
(铂尔曼酒店, Bó'ěrmàn Jiǔdiàn; ☎0371 2358 9999; www.pullmanhotels.com; 16 Longting Beilu, 龙亭北路16号; d from ¥2062; ❷❄☎️❄️) Set in expansive, park-like grounds, Kāifēng's top hotel choice opened in 2015. Rooms are stylish, with woven tapestries featuring the city's famous sights, though it must be said the bathrooms are a bit jarring, featuring an unusually garish marble. Discounts of 66% make this an excellent, affordable luxury choice.

🍴 Eating

Kāifēng is particularly famous for its snacks and night markets, and you'll find several food streets scattered around town. Xīsī Square is the best of the night markets; the Drum Tower night market is more central but with less variety.

Xīsī Square Night Market STREET FOOD $
(西司广场夜市, Xīsī Guǎngchǎng Yèshì; Dingjiao Jie, 丁角街; meals from ¥20; ⏰6.30pm-late) Join the scrum weaving between stalls busy with red-faced popcorn sellers and hollering Hui Muslim chefs cooking up kebabs and *náng* bread. There are loads of vendors, selling cured meats, hearty *jiānbǐng guǒzi* (煎饼裹子; pancake with chopped onions), sweet potatoes, roast rabbit, *xiǎolóngbāo* (Shànghǎi-style dumplings), peanut cake (花生糕, *huāshēng gāo*) and cups of sugarcane juice.

Look for *yángròu kàngmó* (羊肉炕馍; lamb in a parcel of bread), a local Kāifēng Muslim speciality, and for noodle vendors who pull and twist fresh *niúròu lāmiàn* (牛肉拉面; noodles in beef broth). Take bus 24 to get here.

Bǎiqíyuán Food Court FOOD HALL $
(百奇源美食, Bǎiqíyán Měishí; 4th fl, New Mart Mall, Ximen Dajie, 西门大街新玛特4楼; meals from ¥20; ⏰9.30am-8pm) This tempting food court offers plenty of easy-to-order meals, with noodles, dumplings, fried rice, soups and personal stir-fries to choose from. Prepay at the entrance (¥10 deposit), take your card and enjoy!

Gǔlóu Night Market STREET FOOD $
(鼓楼夜市, Gǔlóu Yèshì; Sihou Jie, 寺后街; meals from ¥15; ⏰6.30pm-late) Kāifēng's bustling night market wraps around the Drum Tower, sprawling in various directions, and serves

the usual run of point-and-grill kebabs and steamers of soup dumplings. It's always crowded with locals out enjoying themselves.

Vegetarian Restaurant VEGETARIAN $$
(素斋部, Sùzhāibù; Temple of the Chief Minister, 大相国寺, Dà Xiàngguó Sì; ¥32-88; ⏰11.30am-2pm; 🚫) Looking out onto the grounds of the Temple of the Chief Minister (p435), the outdoor tables at this small Buddhist dining hall offer the city's most atmospheric setting. Sample braised spare ribs or stewed fish – all made of tofu and vegetables, of course – or simply relax with a pot of tea.

ℹ️ Information

The area around Zhongshan Lu has internet cafes, but at the time of research, you needed local ID to use the computers. Some places may let you go online for an hour or so.

Bank of China (中国银行, Zhōngguó Yínháng; cnr Xi Dajie & Zhongshan Lu, 西大街与中山路交叉口) Has a 24-hour ATM.

China Post (中国邮政, Zhōngguó Yóuzhèng; Ziyou Lu, 自由路; ⏰8am-5.30pm) West of the Temple of the Chief Minister.

IATA Air Ticket Office (☎0371 2595 5555; cnr Zhongshan Lu & Shengfu Jie, 中山路与省府街交叉口; ⏰9am-5pm)

Kāifēng Number One People's Hospital (开封第一人民医院, Kāifēng Dìyī Rénmín Yīyuàn; ☎0371 2567 1288; 85 Hedao Jie, 河道街85号) Located right in the heart of town.

Public Security Bureau (PSB, 公安局, Gōng'ānjú; ☎0371 2595 8899; 86 Zhongshan Lu, 中山路86号; ⏰8.30am-noon & 2.30-6pm Mon-Fri) Visa renewals.

Railway Ticket Office (火车票代售, Huǒchēpiào Dàishòu; Yingbin Lu, 迎宾路; ⏰8am-noon & 1.30-5.30pm)

Zhāngzhòngjǐng Pharmacy (张仲景大药房, Zhāngzhòngjǐng Dàyàofáng; Xufu Jie, 徐府街; ⏰7.30am-10pm summer, 8am-9pm winter) Next to Shānshǎngān Guild Hall.

ℹ️ Getting There & Away

AIR

The nearest airport is at Zhèngzhōu. Tickets can be bought at the IATA Air Ticket Office, next to the Public Security Bureau. The **airport shuttle** (机场巴士, Jīchǎng Bāshì) runs from the corner of Gulou Jie and Jiefang Lu (¥40, two hours, half-hourly, 5.10am to 6.40pm).

BUS

Buses leave from the main **long-distance bus station** (开封长途汽车中心站, Kāifēng chángtú qìchē zhōngxīnzhàn), opposite the train station:
Ānyáng ¥63, four hours, half-hourly
Luòyáng ¥60, three hours, hourly

Xīnxiāng ¥29.50, three hours, hourly
Zhèngzhōu ¥7, 1¾ hours, every 15 minutes

Buses also run from the **west long-distance bus station** (开封长途汽车西站, Kāifēng chángtú qìchē xīzhàn):

Dēngfēng ¥42, 3¼ hours, one daily (9.30am)

Luòyáng ¥63, three hours, two daily (8.50am and 2pm)

Xīnxiāng ¥29.50, three hours, six daily

Zhèngzhōu ¥7, 1¾ hours, every 15 minutes

Zhūxiān Zhèn ¥6, 45 minutes, every 15 minutes

Note that almost all buses to Zhèngzhōu terminate at its east train station; to get into town either take the metro or the transfer bus running between the two train stations.

TRAIN

Kāifēng's train station is located in the south of town, around 1km beyond the city walls. You can buy tickets at the **railway ticket office**. Rail options – and tickets – from Kāifēng are limited; your options are much better leaving from Zhèngzhōu.

A new Zhèngzhōu–Kāifēng intercity train was nearing completion at the time of research. Most trains leave from the Zhèngzhōu east train station and will eventually terminate at the Kāifēng station, but so far only go to the Songcheng Lu station, a ¥20 cab ride from Kāifēng.

Běijīng West Hard sleeper ¥195, 12 hours, two daily

Luòyáng Hard seat ¥30, 2½ hours, eight daily (few tickets available)

Shànghǎi Hóngqiáo D train 2nd/1st class ¥232/371, six to seven hours, three daily

Xī'ān Seat/sleeper ¥81/163, eight hours, three morning trains (few tickets available)

Zhèngzhōu East ¥18 to ¥22, 30 minutes, frequent service

ⓘ Getting Around

Zhongshan Lu is a good place to catch buses (¥1) to most sights. Taxis (flag fall ¥5, pollution tax ¥1) are the best way to get about; a journey from the train station to Zhongshan Lu should cost around ¥7. Avoid pedicabs as they frequently rip off tourists.

Zhūxiān Zhèn   朱仙镇

☏ 0371 / POP 210,000

Zhūxiān Zhèn, where the 1000-year-old craft of woodblock printing (木板年画; *mùbǎn niánhuà*) is still practised, is known as one of China's four 'ancient' towns: the other three are Hànkǒu (trade), Jǐngdézhèn (porcelain) and Fóshān (silk). An easy day trip from Kāifēng, the woodblock prints here are

a sure highlight for anyone interested in traditional Chinese arts and crafts.

⊙ Sights

Zhūxiān Mosque   MOSQUE

(朱仙清真寺, Zhūxiān Qīngzhēn Sì) FREE Originally founded in the Northern Song dynasty, this mosque is housed in a traditional Chinese temple compound with a pretty rose garden. Examine the elaborately carved lintels and the examples of Chinese/Arabic calligraphy. It's a pleasant walk, 700m south of Zhūxiān's main road along a wide stone path.

Guānyǔ Temple   TEMPLE

(关羽庙, Guānyǔ Miào; ¥10; ⊙8am-5pm) Dedicated to Guandì, the god of war and protection (among other things), this temple was originally built during the Ming dynasty (then dedicated to the god of wealth); the present structure dates back to 1708. Consisting of a single hall, there is not much to see here besides the building.

Yuè Fēi Temple   TEMPLE

(岳飞庙, Yuè Fēi Miào; ¥30; ⊙8.30am-6.30pm) Dedicated to the Southern Song military hero Yuè Fēi, this temple was first founded in 1478. Although the hall interiors are largely without interest, there are some old stelae in the courtyard, carried by weathered stone *bìxì* (碧玺; mythical tortoise like dragons).

🛏 Sleeping & Eating

As it's an easy day trip from Kāifēng, there is no need to spend the night in Zhūxiān.

Look for freshly baked naan (flat bread; ¥1.50), sold by Muslim vendors in the street.

🛍 Shopping

Yīnshì Lǎo Tiānchéng   ARTS & CRAFTS

(尹氏老天成; ☏0371 2671 2924) The artist/owner of this woodblock printing workshop, Mr Yin (尹), is a fifth-generation artisan whose family has been in business for more than 200 years. A beautifully bound book of prints, with English explanations, housed in a wooden presentation box costs ¥200 (but if you're nice, he might knock ¥20 off the price). Located 100m east of the Yuè Fēi Temple.

ⓘ Getting There & Away

Head to Kāifēng's **west bus station**, from where buses (¥6, 45 minutes, every 15 minutes) run all the way to Zhūxiān. The last bus from Zhūxiān leaves at 5.50pm. The driver can let you off at the mosque, or you can get off at a busy thoroughfare closer to the centre of town.

Húběi

POP 57.9 MILLION

Best Places to Eat

➡ Xiǎo Bèiké (p445)

➡ Bàyú Rénjiā (p448)

➡ Piān Qiáo Wān (p452)

Best Places to Sleep

➡ Wǔhàn Bingo International Youth Hostel (p443)

➡ Tomolo (p445)

➡ Taichi Hotel (p450)

Why Go?

Like much of central China, Húběi (湖北) is better known for its industrial belt rather than the searing beauty of its lush and fertile landscape of mountain parks and plains sluiced by rivers, lakes and sacred Taoist sites.

The Three Gorges snakes across the border, carrying gobsmacked visitors into its belly, while the mountainous west rises to the sacred peaks of Wǔdāng Shān, the kind of kung-fu film setting where courtyards of taichi masters cling to mountaintops and adhere to Taoist virtues. And hikers will find Shénnóngjià National Park in its sparse, water-coloured natural state.

Húběi's central location ensured it played a key role in Chinese history – there's evidence around Jīngzhōu of the great Chu kingdom that ruled here more than 2000 years ago. China's modern history echoes through the cultural sites of Wǔhàn, one of China's most dynamic cities, where the hum of commerce spills over into jumping nightlife.

When to Go
Wǔhàn

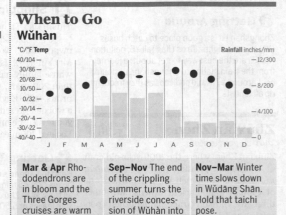

Mar & Apr Rhododendrons are in bloom and the Three Gorges cruises are warm and breezy.

Sep–Nov The end of the crippling summer turns the riverside concession of Wǔhàn into an outdoor party.

Nov–Mar Winter time slows down in Wǔdāng Shān. Hold that taichi pose.

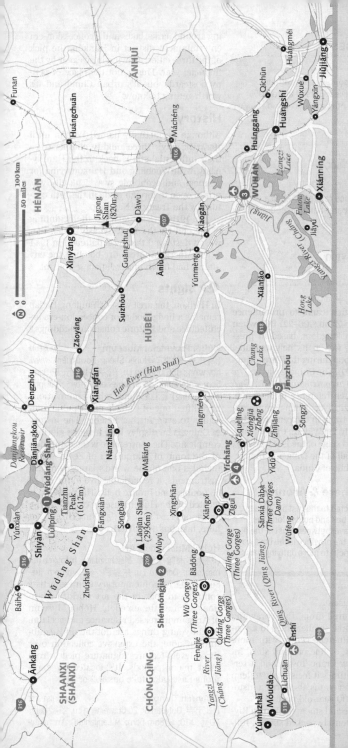

Húběi Highlights

1 Wǔdāng Shān (p449)
Learning taichi on the majestic cloud-covered mountain where it was invented, then wandering off-path to quiet temples hanging over yonder.

2 Shénnóngjià (p451)
Spotting the famed 'wild man' as you hike in the wilds of northeast Húběi and camping under the stars on elevated grassy knolls.

3 Wǔhàn (p442) Doing the cultural dance around Wǔhàn's fine museums and temples before snuffling to the dance floors of the riverfront concession.

4 Yíchāng (p452) Tackling the Three Gorges the Húběi way from this humble river city, rather than the better known Chóngqìng.

5 Jīngzhōu (p447) Cycling around the historic gates, city walls and ruined temples of ancient Jīngzhōu.

PRICE RANGES

Sleeping
Prices are for a double room with private bathroom. Discounts of up to 40% are available at most midrange and high-end hotels.

$ less than ¥150

$$ ¥150–¥500

$$$ more than ¥500

Eating
The following price ranges refer to a standard but substantial main course.

$ less than ¥40

$$ ¥40–¥100

$$$ more than ¥100

History

The Húběi area first came to prominence during the Eastern Zhou (700–221 BC), when the powerful Chu kingdom, based in present-day Jīngzhōu, was at its height. Húběi again became pivotal during the Three Kingdoms (AD 220–280). The Chinese classic *The Romance of the Three Kingdoms (Sān Guó Yǎnyì)* makes much reference to Jīngzhōu. The mighty Yangzi River (Cháng Jiāng) ensured prosperous trade in the centuries that followed, especially for Wǔhàn, China's largest inland port and stage of the 1911 uprising, which led to the fall of the Qing and the creation of the Republic of China.

🛈 Getting There & Around

Húběi is well connected to the rest of China by high-speed rail, air, bus and boats along the Yangzi River. Rail travel between most of the big destinations within the province is the best way to go, with bus journeys to more outlying parts.

Wǔhàn 武汉

🎵 027 / POP 10.6 MILLION

Wǔhàn has matured from the sprawling convergence of three smaller cities to an industrial and commercial centre with more than a smattering of fine cultural sites, including the Yellow Crane Tower and a terrific museum. At times it feels ready to leap from its second-tier status, its warring history a thing of a 2000-year-old past.

Amid the traffic and smog, the Yangzi River opens up the densely packed streets, rolling around parks, lakes and a concession-era entertainment district in Hànkǒu, the pick of the three cities, growing in swagger by the financial year. This is not the place of penny postcards, but it's urban China and it's worth getting to know.

History

Although not actually named Wǔhàn until 1927, the city's three mighty chunks trace their influential status back to the Han dynasty, with Wǔchāng and Hànkǒu vying for political and economic sway. The city was prised open to foreign trade in the 19th century by the Treaty of Nanking.

The 1911 uprising sparked the beginning of the end for the Qing dynasty. Much that wasn't destroyed then was flattened in 1944 when American forces fire-bombed the city after it had fallen under Japanese control.

👁 Sights

In Hànkǒu, the area west of Yanjiang Dadao remains a hodgepodge of concession-era architecture and historic consulate buildings.

Húběi Provincial Museum   MUSEUM
(湖北省博物馆, Húběi Shěng Bówùguǎn; www.hbww.org; 156 Donghu Lu, 东湖路156号; ⊙9am-5pm Tue-Sun, no admission after 3.30pm; Ⓜ Dongting) FREE Some minor renovations have lifted one of China's finest public museums to even further heights. The history of China is on display here in all its glorious complexity. The centrepiece is the exhibition of the tomb of Marquis Yi of Zeng, which includes one of the world's largest musical instruments, a remarkable five-tonne set of 65 double-tone bronze bells. The museum is located by the Húběi Museum of Art and the enormous East Lake (东湖; Dōng Hú). To get here, take bus 402 or 411.

Húběi Museum of Art   MUSEUM
(湖北美术馆, Húběi Měishùguǎn; http://en.hbmoa.com; Donghu Lu, 东湖路; ⊙9am-5pm Tue-Sun) FREE As contemporary Chinese artists continue to soar in the art world, institutions such as the excellent Húběi Museum of Art gain increased relevance and acclaim. Bright young things are not the only exhibitors of note; the extensive collection over three levels features signature pieces from most major periods. It's located by enormous East Lake; take bus 402 or 411.

Guīyuán Temple   BUDDHIST SITE
(归元寺, Guīyuán Sì; 20 Cuiweiheng Lu, 翠微横路20号; ¥10; ⊙8am-5pm; Ⓜ Lanjianglu) An after-

noon at this revered 350-year-old Buddhist temple can fluctuate between serenity and chaos, depending on the tour buses. Pass a large rectangular pond where turtles cling like shipwrecked sailors to two metal lotus flowers and examine the magnificently burnished cabinet housing Milefo in the first hall. Also seek out the more than 500 statues of enlightened disciples in the **Hall of Arhats** (罗汉堂; Luóhàn Táng). Completed in 1890, after nine years in the making, they remain in pristine condition.

Yellow Crane Tower HISTORIC SITE
(黄鹤楼, Huánghè Lóu; Wuluo Lu, 武珞路; ¥80; ⏰ 7.30am-5.30pm, to 6.30pm in summer) Wǔhàn's magical dancing crane, immortalised in the 8th-century poetry of Cui Hao, has long flown, but the city's pride and joy remains perched atop Snake Hill. The tower has had its history rebuilt out of it since the original was constructed in AD 223, and today's beautiful five-storey, yellow-tiled version is a 1980s remake of the Qing tower that combusted in 1884. Buses 401, 402 and 411, and trolley buses 1 and 10, all go here.

Hànkǒu Bund PARK
(汉口江滩, Hànkǒu Jiāngtān) FREE The Hànkǒu Bund is a roughly 4km stretch of curated park running parallel to the Yangzi where locals gather to amble or gossip at varying levels of intensity. There are some teahouses and bars, a swimming-pool complex, mahjong and chess boards, and some green areas. Mostly, though, it's locals escaping the concrete and shooting the breeze, especially around sunrise and sunset.

🛏 Sleeping

Wǔhàn has excellent high-end hotels, solid midranges and a handful of very pleasant budget options to meet fellow Sinophiles.

★ Wǔhàn Bingo International Youth Hostel HOSTEL $
(汉阳造青年公寓, Hànyáng Zàoqīngnián Gōngyù; ☑ 027 8477 0648; hymhostel@126.com; 9-10 Hànyáng Creative Garden, 1 Guibei Lu, Hànyáng, 龟北路1号汉阳造创意园9-10号; dm ¥50-70, s/d ¥138/148; ❄ @ 🛜) Wǔhàn welcomes a fab new hostel into a Cultural District that signals the city's expanding civic pride. Private rooms are smartly presented, with quality beds, bedside tables, kettles and bathrooms (strong, hot water!) of sound proportions; dorms are orderly and very clean. There's a friendly on-site cafe and some cute shared spaces.

Pathfinder Youth Hostel HOSTEL $
(探路者国际青年旅社, Tànlùzhě Guójì Qīngnián Lǚshè; ☑ 091 8884 4092; yhawuhan@hotmail.com; 368 Zhongshan Lu, 中山路368号; dm ¥45-60, d/tr ¥160/210; ❄ @ 🛜; M Pangxiejia) Wǔhàn's longest-running youth hostel is a communal place full of artistic temperament, but the cool graffiti also hides some fairly scrubby walls. Dorm rooms are quite spacious and the doubles are bright, but the bathrooms need attention. The real upsides though are the popular bar hang-out and on-the-ball English-speaking staff.

Walk south from exit A2 of Pangxiejia (螃蟹岬) metro station along Zhongshan Lu, and it's on your right.

Dorsett Wǔhàn HOTEL $$
(武汉帝盛酒店, Wǔhàn Dìshèng Jiǔdiàn; ☑ 027 6882 2899; www.dorsetthotels.com/wuhan; 118 Jianghan Lu, Hankou, Hong Kong & Macau Centre, 汉口江汉路步行街118号; r ¥480-600; P ❄ 🛜) With a handy location on the doorstop of Wǔhàn's best shopping district, the Dorsett is a very attentive and efficient four-star

---

YELLOW CRANE TOWER BY CUI HAO

Penned in the 8th century by Tang dynasty luminary Cui Hao (崔颢), this poem recalls the departure of someone on the back of a yellow crane, possibly to become an immortal. The spot he left from is now occupied by a tower named after the bird.

黄鹤楼

昔人已乘黄鹤去，此地空余黄鹤楼。
黄鹤一去不复返，白云千载空悠悠。
晴川历历汉阳树，芳草萋萋鹦鹉洲。
日暮乡关何处是，烟波江上使人愁。

Yellow Crane Tower

A man of old left a long time ago on the Yellow Crane; this place is empty save for the Yellow Crane Tower.

Once the Yellow Crane left, it would never return; for a thousand years, the white clouds leisurely drifted.

The trees in Hànyáng are all arrayed by the clear river and the fragrant grasses grow luxuriously on Parrot Isle.

Where are the gates of my home at dusk? The mist and ripples on the river waters make me sad.

Wǔhàn

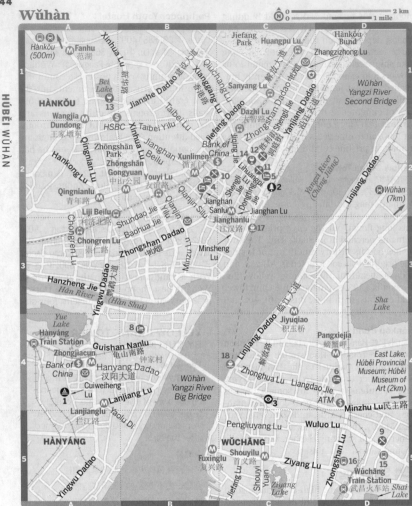

Wǔhàn

hotel. It's set inside a relaxed mall which has a cinema and nightclubs. Rooms are large, with leather furniture, exquisite bedding and rainforest showers. There's a Hong Kong–style cafe, small gym and well-informed English-speaking staff.

Tomolo
BOUTIQUE HOTEL $$$

(天美乐饭店, Tiānměilè Fàndiàn; ☑ 027 8275 7288; 56 Jianghan Sanlu, 江汉三路56号; r ¥698; ❄ @ 🛜; M Xunlimen) Tomolo is a Wǔhàn brand known for style and panache. You'll enjoy the oversized rooms with sofas, wide-screen TVs and lush carpets, while the bathrooms are some of the brightest we encountered in the city, with artisan tiling and power showers. Try to angle for a discount at this central branch. The entrance is tucked down a laneway.

Marco Polo
HOTEL $$$

(马哥孛罗酒店, Mǎgē Bóluó Jiǔdiàn; ☑ 027 8277 8888; www.marcopolohotels.com; 159 Yanjiang Dadao, 沿江大道159号; r from ¥897; ❄ @ 🛜 🏊; M Jianghanlu) Wǔhàn's growing luxury-hotel scene is still led by Marco Polo, which enjoys sweeping river views and an easy stumbling distance from the tree-lined former concession area, which fills with bar-hoppers on weekends.

🍴 Eating

In Hànkǒu, the alleyways north of Zhongshan Dadao, between Qianjin Yilu (前进一路) and Qianjin Silu (前进四路), are particularly lively. **Jiqing Jie** (吉庆街) has *dàpáidàng* (open-air food stalls) selling seafood and duck, especially the Dazhi Lu end. **Cai'e Lu** (蔡锷路) has smoky *shāokǎo* (烧烤, barbecue). Breakfast – called *guōzǎo* (过早) in Wǔhàn – is all about *règānmiàn* (热干面; 'hot-dry noodles'; from ¥4). Don't miss **Hùbù Xiàng Snack Street** (户部巷小吃; Hùbù Xiàng Xiǎochī).

Lǎojiē Shāokǎo
BARBECUE $

(老街烧烤, Lǎojiē Shāokǎo; Jianghan Lu, 武汉路; skewered meat/vegetable ¥14/10; ⏱ 11am-10pm) 'Old Street Barbecue' takes the popular hawker-style meat-on-stick philosophy espoused on corners nightly around the city, and poshes it up just a little. Large bottles of cheap beer are served by young, well trained staff who try hard to accommodate despite limited English. You can sit on a swing seat and rock yourself to sleep after eating.

⭐ Xiǎo Bèiké
CHINESE $$

(小贝壳; 129 Dongting Jie, 洞庭街129号; mains ¥20-50; ⏱ 9.30am-10.30pm) This stylish restaurant, with lovely tree-shaded terrace seating,

offers an excellent range of pan-Chinese cuisine, with dishes from Húběi, Sìchuān and Chóngqìng featuring highly. It also does a number of fish dishes, including braised catfish and delicious scallops. There's no English sign; it's in the yellow building on the corner of Dongting Jie and Cai'e Lu (蔡锷路). It has an English menu with photos.

MADE Cafe
CAFE $$

(☑ 027 8558 1506; 4 Lihuangbei Lu, 黎黄陂路4号; coffee ¥25-35, cakes from ¥15; ⏱ 8am-6pm) This stylish coffee house and cake store serves delicious brews over two levels. The young, funky crowd on laptops also sip fruit beer, wine and tea while planning the night ahead, the looming essay or their next meeting.

Chángchūn Temple Vegetarian Restaurant
VEGETARIAN $$

(长春观素菜餐厅, Chángchūnguān Sùcài Cāntīng; 269 Wuluo Lu, 武珞路269号; mains ¥20-50; ⏱ 9am-8.30pm; 🌱) Housed next door to the Chángchūn Temple, this place serves mock-meat creations but also cooks up fish dishes. It has a photo menu.

🍷 Drinking & Nightlife

Hànkǒu is the place to go for a night out; Yanjiang Dadao (沿江大道) and its surrounding lanes are the best places to start. There are neon-tastic nightclubs towards the ferry port, while Lihuangpi Lu (黎黄陂路) is one of a number of lanes with cutesy Western-style cafes.

⭐ Vox Livehouse
CLUB

(VOX音乐教室; ☑ 027 8759 6030; 163 Shengli Jie, 胜利街163电; tickets usually ¥50-250; ⏱ 8pm-1am Thu-Sat, other times vary) Wǔhàn has a surprisingly good indie and heavy-rock scene, and Vox Livehouse is an institution for late-night revelling. Some interesting mainland acts often share the stage with international underground bands.

Brussels Beer Garden
BEER GARDEN

(☑ 150 3351 5822; www.brusselsbg.com; 8-8 Xibcihu Lu, 西北湖路8附8号; beer ¥25-45) The expatriate bar of choice is a Belgian affair by Běi Lake which serves yummy mini pizzas and burgers to accompany tall, creamy glasses of beer from across the world. Great place to get the scoop on the city from seasoned travellers.

ℹ️ Information

ATM (Wǔchāng) Located in Wǔchāng.

Bank of China (中国银行, Zhōngguó Yínháng; 65 Huangshi Lu, 黄石路65号; ⏱ 8.30am-5.30pm

Mon-Fri, 9am-5pm Sat) Centrally located in Hànkǒu.

Bank of China (中国银行, Zhōngguó Yínháng; 677 Jianshe Dadao, 建设大道677号; ⊙8.30am-5.30pm Mon-Fri, 9am-5pm Sat) Located in Hànyáng.

China Post (中国邮政, Zhōngguó Yóuzhèn; 2 Zizhi Jie, 自治街2号; ⊙9am-5pm Mon-Fri) Centrally located post office in Hànkǒu.

China Post (中国邮政, Zhōngguó Yóuzhèn; Hanyang Dadao, ⊙9am-5pm Mon-Fri) Handy post office situated in Hànyáng.

China Post (中国邮政, Zhōngguó Yóuzhèng; 10 Jianghan Lu, 江汉路10号; ⊙9am-5pm Mon-Fri) Not far from the river in Hànkǒu.

HSBC (汇丰银行, Huìfēng Yínháng; 632 Jianshe Dadao, 建设大道632号) Has an ATM.

Public Security Bureau (PSB, 公安局, Gōng'ānjú; ☑027 8539 5351; 7 Zhangzizhong Lu, 张自忠路7号; ⊙8.30am-noon & 2.30-5.30pm) Can extend visas.

🛈 Getting There & Away

AIR

Tiānhé International Airport (天河飞机场, Tiānhé Fēijīchǎng; ☑027 8581 8888) is 30km northwest of town, with daily direct flights to:

Běijīng ¥1440

Chéngdù ¥910

Guǎngzhōu ¥1230

Hong Kong ¥1480

Shànghǎi ¥1080

Xī'ān ¥920

Use www.elong.net or www.ctrip.com to book flights.

BUS

There are several long-distance bus stations, all of which run very similar services. In Hànkǒu, the main one is beside Hànkǒu train station. In Wǔchāng, the main two are **Fùjiāpō long-distance bus station** (傅家坡汽车客运站, Fùjiāpō Qìchē Kèyùnzhàn; 358 Wulou Lu, 五楼路358号) and **Hóngjī long-distance bus station** (宏基长途汽车站, Hóngjī Chángtú Qìchēzhàn; 519 Zhongshan Lu, 中山路519号).

You can get buses to most major cities, even as far away as Shànghǎi and Běijīng. The following are sample services from Hóngjī long-distance bus station:

Jīngzhōu ¥75, three hours, every 45 minutes (7am to 8pm)

Mùyú (for Shénnóngjià) ¥150, eight hours, one daily (8.50am)

Shíyàn (for Wǔdāng Shān) ¥145, six hours, three daily (8.40am, 11.40am and 1.30pm)

Yíchāng ¥85 to ¥120, four hours, half-hourly (6.50am to 6pm)

TRAIN

Wǔhàn has three major train stations: **Hànkǒu train station** (汉口火车站; Hànkǒu huǒchēzhàn), **Wǔchāng train station** (武昌火车站; Wǔchāng huǒchēzhàn) and **Wǔhàn train station** (武汉火车站; Wǔhàn huǒchēzhàn), all of which should be linked up to the metro system by the time you read this.

Services from Hànkǒu station:

Běijīng D train 2nd-/1st-class seat ¥267/333, 10 hours, two daily (8.06am and 9.05am)

Běijīng Z train hard/soft sleeper ¥263/411, 10 hours, two daily (8.24pm and 9.12pm)

Shànghǎi Hóngqiáo D train 2nd-/1st-class seat ¥264/316, six hours, 11 daily (7.05am to 5.23pm)

Wǔdāng Shān Hard seat ¥70, six to seven hours, two daily (10.35am and 4pm)

Xī'ān D train 2nd-/1st-class seat ¥307/432, 7½ hours, one daily (9.15am)

Services from Wǔchāng station:

Běijīng Z train hard/soft sleeper ¥263/411, 10 hours, two daily (9.03pm and 9.09pm)

Kūnmíng Hard/soft sleeper ¥380/600, 23 to 25 hours, five daily

Yíchāng Hard seat ¥54, five hours, four daily (7.36am, 11.26am, 12.10pm and 5.35pm)

Services from Wǔhàn station:

Běijīng D train 2nd/1st class ¥267/333, 10 hours, one daily (11.57am)

Chángshā G train 2nd/1st class ¥165/265, 1½ hours, more than 40 daily (7am to 7.55pm)

Guǎngzhōu G train 2nd/1st class ¥464/739, four hours, more than 40 daily (7am to 7.55pm)

Shànghǎi Hóngqiáo G train, 2nd/1st class ¥303/428, five hours, two daily (1.35pm and 3.10pm)

Xī'ān North G train 2nd/1st class ¥458/733, 4½ hours, seven daily

🛈 Getting Around

TO/FROM THE AIRPORT

Regular airport shuttle buses reach Hànkǒu train station (¥15, 45 minutes) and Fùjiāpō long-distance bus station (¥30, one hour). A taxi is about ¥100.

BUS

Bus 10 (¥1.50) Connects Hànkǒu and Wǔchāng train stations.

Bus 401 (¥2) From Hànyáng past Guīyuán Temple, Yellow Crane Tower and Chángchūn Temple to East Lake.

Bus 402 (¥2) From Wǔchāng train station to Chángchūn Temple and Yellow Crane Tower, then via Hànyáng to Yanjiang Dadao in Hànkǒu before returning over the river for the provincial museum and half a circuit of East Lake.

Bus 411 (¥1.50) Travels a more direct route from the museum to Yellow Crane Tower and Chángchūn Temple before carrying on to Hànkǒu train station.

FERRY

Ferries (¥1.50, 6.30am to 8pm) make swift daily crossings of the Yangzi between **Zhonghua Lu Dock** (中华路码头, Zhōnghuá Lù Mǎtóu) and **Wǔhàn Guān Dock** (武汉关码头, Wǔhàn Guān Mǎtóu).

METRO

Wǔhàn's fledgling metro system (地铁; *dìtiě*) includes Line 1, an overground light rail line in Hànkǒu, and Lines 2 and 4, which tunnel under the river, linking the main train stations. Four more lines are under construction.

Jīngzhōu 荆州

☑ 0716 / POP 1.5 MILLION

Easily reached by fast train from Wǔhàn, Jīngzhōu is the charming former capital of the Chu kingdom during the Eastern Zhou. Its ancient origins are found within the city wall, one of China's finest. There are a number of period temples still standing plus a tremendous museum which holds a 2000-year-old Han body. The largest collection of Chu kingdom tombs ever discovered lies underground at Xióngjiā Zhǒng, the best known of several ancient burial sites scattered across the fertile neighbouring countryside.

◉ Sights

The walled section of Jīngzhōu is approximately 3.5km from east to west and 2.5km from north to south, with impressive city gates at each cardinal point, as well as several lesser gates. Passing through the wall at **New East Gate** (新东门; Xīn Dōngmén), which you will do if you're on the bus from the main stations, you'll have Jingzhou Nanlu (荆州南路) stretching out in front of you, and you'll see the older **East Gate** (老东门; Lǎo Dōngmén) off to your right. Zhangjuzheng Jie (张居正街) leads away from East Gate and runs parallel to Jingzhou Nanlu.

City Wall HISTORIC SITE

(城墙, Chéngqiáng) Jīngzhōu's original city wall was a tamped mud wall dating from the Eastern Han dynasty, later clad in stone during the Five Dynasties and Ten Kingdoms. The oldest surviving sections today, around **South Gate** (南门; Nánmén), are Song, but most date to the Ming and Qing. The South Gate, with its enceinte (瓮城; *wèngchéng*) still attached, concocts flavours of medieval

Jīngzhōu, swarming with Taoist soothsayers, craftsfolk and vegetable sellers.

Jīngzhōu Museum MUSEUM

(荆州博物馆, Jīngzhōu Bówùguǎn; Jingzhou Zhonglu, 荆州中路; audio tour ¥20, English tour guide ¥200; ⊙9am-5pm Tue-Sun) **FREE** Next to Kāiyuán Temple is a small, yet architecturally superb museum surrounded by water. Here you'll find wonderful artefacts unearthed from Chu tombs around the area. The jade and porcelain halls are marvellous, and there is a collection of old silks which appear to float in their cabinets. The highlight is the incredibly well preserved 2000-year-old body of a man found in his tomb with ancient tools, clothing and even food; the airtight mud seal around his crypt helped preserve him.

Tiěnǚ Temple BUDDHIST SITE

(铁女寺, Tiěnǚ Sì; off Jingbei Lu, 荆北路) **FREE** Located in the north of town, off Jingbei Lu, the name of this intriguing temple translates as the Iron Girl Temple.

Kāiyuán Temple TAOIST SITE

(开元观, Kāiyuán Guàn; Jingzhou Zhonglu, 荆州中路) **FREE** Explore the fascinating empty Taoist remains attached to the Jīngzhōu Museum.

Xuánmiào Temple TAOIST SITE

(玄妙观, Xuánmiào Guàn; north of Jingbei Lu, 荆北路的北侧面) **FREE** This Taoist temple, just north of New North Gate (新北门; Xīnběimén), literally translates as the 'Temple of Mystery'.

🛏 Sleeping

Sānguó Kèzhàn HOTEL $

(三国客栈; ☑0716 418 2080; 12 Jingtan Lu, 景昌路12号; r ¥90-150; ✽🛜) This modest hotel within the city walls is fairly new and very well maintained.

King Kowloon Hotel HOTEL $$

(金九龙大酒店, Jīnjiǔlóng Dàjiǔdiàn; ☑0716 847 8888; 18 Nanhuan Lu, 南环路18号; d ¥250; 🅿✽🛜) Located just outside the East Gate is a smart business hotel at an impressive price. The rooms are open and bright and the staff speak some English.

🍴 Eating

Liánxīn Sùcàiguǎn VEGAN $

(莲心素菜馆; Shiyuan Lu, beside Zhanghua Temple, 渊路章华寺内; ¥30 buffet; ⊙10am-9pm) Wholesome vegan food is served, buffet-style, at this friendly Buddhist restaurant next to Zhanghua Temple. Mock-meat dishes are overshadowed by the many bright, green vegetable dishes infused with chilli, garlic and mushroom.

Grandma's Home   CHINESE $$
(外婆家, Wàipójiā; ☑ 0151 3407 7507; www.waipojia.com; Minzhu Lu, 民主路; mains ¥15-30) This new restaurant chain has taken off in China, and while we don't necessarily advocate seeking out the easy-to-find, Jīngzhōu's modest dining scene means delicious, freshly prepared hotpots and stir-fries warrant our thumbs creaking up.

Bàyú Rénjiā   HUBEI $$
(巴渝人家; New East Gate, Donghuan Lu, 东环路新东门外; mains ¥20-50; ⊙ 11am-9pm) Great location by the moat, outside New East Gate. Grab a table overlooking the city wall and moat and tuck into the restaurant speciality, gānguō (干锅), an iron pot of spicy delights, kept bubbling hot with a small candle burner. Varieties include chicken (干锅仔鸡; gānguō zǐjī; ¥38), bullfrog (干锅牛蛙; gānguō niúwā; ¥48) and tofu (干锅千叶豆腐; gānguō qiānyè dòufu; ¥32).

One pot is enough for two or three people with rice (米饭; mǐfàn), which is free. Exit New East Gate, cross the moat and the restaurant is on your right.

❶ Information

There are 24-hour internet cafes (网吧; wǎngba) dotted around town.

China Construction Bank (中国建设银行, Zhōngguó Jiànshè Yínháng) has a foreign-friendly ATM. Located between New East Gate and Jiǔgē Holiday Hotel (九歌假日酒店, Jiǔgē Jiàrì Jiǔdiàn; 13 Jingzhou Nanlu, 荆州南路13号).

❶ Getting There & Away

BUS
Buses from Shāshì long-distance bus station:
Wǔdāng Shān ¥120, five hours, two daily (7.45am and 1pm)
Wǔhàn ¥80, four hours, frequent (6.30am to 8pm)
Yíchāng ¥44, two hours, frequent (7am to 6pm)

TRAIN
D- and G-class trains (and slower trains) link Jīngzhōu with:
Shànghǎi Hóngqiáo 2nd/1st class ¥322/385, eight hours, six daily
Wǔhàn 2nd/1st class ¥70/85, 1½ hours, regular
Yíchāng East 2nd/1st class ¥26/31, 40 minutes, regular

❶ Getting Around

You'll probably arrive at either **Shāshì long-distance bus station** (沙市长途汽车站; Shāshì chángtú qìchēzhàn) or **Shāshì central bus station** (沙市中心客运站; Shāshì zhōngxīn kèyùnzhàn). Turn right out of either, walk to the first bus stop and take bus 101 (¥2) to East Gate (老东门, Lǎo Dōngmén).

Bus 49 (¥2) connects the train station (火车站; huǒchē zhàn) with the East Gate.

The **bicycle rental place** (Lao Dongmen, 老东门; per hr/day ¥7/50) by East Gate is one of many around the walled section of the city.

Around Jīngzhōu

Forty kilometres north of Jīngzhōu, the 2300-year-old tombs of **Xióngjiā Zhǒng** (熊家冢; ¥30; ⊙ 9.30am-4.30pm) are the source of a large collection of jade – on display at the Jīngzhōu Museum (p447) – while there is a fascinating and huge collection of skeletal horses and chariots in a section of the tomb in a hangar-like museum that is open to visitors.

Buses (¥10, 70 minutes) leave hourly from the back of the bus station called Chǔdū Kèyùn Zhàn (楚都客运站) in Jīngzhōu. Bus 24 links this station with Jīnfèng Guǎngchǎng (金凤广场) bus stop, just outside East Gate (over the moat and turn left). A taxi will be at least ¥100 return.

Wǔdāng Shān   武当山
☑ 0719

There are not many places in the world quite like Wǔdāng Shān, a Unesco World Heritage Site and wellspring of the gentle art of taichi. Misty clouds cover haunting Taoist courtyards where masters and disciples make bird-like moves in unison and travellers make the three-hour ascent up ancient stone steps in giddy reverence. The 'No 1 Taoist Mountain in the Middle Kingdom' is more than a place of pilgrimage though; its flora contains elixirs for natural health remedies sold on every second precipice and its mountain views rival any in China. Press away from the building and the selling and you'll find unmarked paths to moss-strewn temples and ethereal splendour. Just take your time, breathe, repeat.

◉ Sights & Activities

The town's main road, Taihe Lu (太和路) – which at various sections is also labelled Taihe Donglu (太和东路; Taihe East) and Taihe

Zhonglu (太和中路; Taihe Central) – runs east–west on its way up towards the main gate of the mountain. Everything of interest in town is either on or near this road and road numbers are clearly labelled. Buses often drop you at the junction by the main expressway, a 1km walk east of the town centre. From here, turn left to the mountain entrance (100m) or right into town.

You can buy Chinese (¥3) or English (¥8) maps at the main gate of the mountain.

Wǔdāng Shān   MOUNTAIN

(武当山; ¥140, bus ¥100, audio guide ¥30) Wǔdāng Shān attracts a diverse array of climbers, from Taoist nuns with knapsacks, porters shouldering paving slabs and sacks of rice, business people with laptops and bright-eyed octogenarians hopping along. It's a gruelling climb but the scenery is worth every step; plenty of Taoist temples line the route (where you can take contemplative breathers) and you'll see the occasional Taoist cairn or trees garlanded with scarlet ribbons weighed with small stones. On the way down, note how some pilgrims descend backwards!

To start your ascent, take bus 1 (¥1) or walk from Taihe Lu to the Main Gate (山门口; Shān Ménkǒu) and ticket office. The bus ticket (compulsory with your admission) gives you unlimited use of shuttle buses (from 6am to 6.30pm).

One bus – often only leaving when full – runs to the start of the cable car (索道, Suǒdào; up/down ¥50/45). For those who don't mind steps, take the bus to South Cliff (南岩; Nányán), where the trail to 1612m Heavenly Pillar Peak (天柱峰; Tiānzhù Fēng), the highest peak, begins. Consider disembarking early at the beautiful, turquoise-tiled Purple Cloud Temple (紫霄宫, Zǐxiāo Gōng; ¥20), from where a small stone path leads up to South Cliff (45 minutes). From South Cliff it's an energy-sapping, two-hour, 4km climb to the top.

The enchanting red-walled Cháotiān Temple (朝天宫; Cháotiān Gōng) is about halfway up, housing a statue of the Jade Emperor and standing on an old, moss-hewn stone base with 4m-high tombstones guarding its entrance. From here you have a choice of two ascent routes, via the 1.4km Ming dynasty route (the older, Back Way) or the 1.8km Qing dynasty path (the 'Hundred Stairs'). The shorter but more gruelling Ming route ascends via the Three Heaven's Gates, including the stupefying climb to the Second Gate of Heaven (二天门; Èrtiān Mén). You can climb by one route and de-

THE BIRTH OF TAICHI

Zhang San Feng (张三丰), a semi-legendary Wǔdāng Shān monk from the 10th or 13th century (depending on what source you read). is reputed to be the founder of the martial art tàijíquán (literally 'Supreme Ultimate Boxing') or taichi. Zhang had grown dissatisfied with the 'hard' techniques of Shàolín Boxing and searched for something 'softer' and more elusive. Sitting on his porch one day, he became inspired by a battle between a huge bird and a snake. The sinuous snake used flowing movements to evade the bird's attacks. The bird, exhausted, eventually gave up and flew away. Taichi is closely linked to Taoism, and many priests on Wǔdāng Shān practise some form of the art.

scend by the other. Temple ruins, fallen trees, shocking inclines and steep steps misshapen by centuries of footslogging await you.

Near the top, beyond the cable-car exit, is the magnificent Forbidden City (紫金城, Zǐjīn Chéng; ¥20) with its 2.5m-thick stone walls hugging the mountainside and balustrades festooned with lovers' locks. From here you can stagger to magnificent views from the Golden Hall (金殿, Jīn Diàn; ¥20), constructed entirely from bronze, dating from 1416 and in dire need of some buffing up. A small statue of Zhenwu – Ming emperor and Wǔdāng Shān's presiding Taoist deity – peeks out from within.

Wǔdāng Museum of China   MUSEUM

(武当博物馆, Wǔdāng Bówùguǎn; Culture Sq, 文化广场; audio tour ¥20, deposit ¥200; ⊙ 9-11.30am & 2.30-5pm) FREE This is a great opportunity to get a grip on Wǔdāng Shān history, lore and architecture. There's a whole pantheon of gods, including the eminent Zhenwu (patriarch of the mountain) and a section on Taoist medicine including the fundamentals of nèidān xué (内丹学; internal alchemy). There are also some stunning bronze pieces.

The museum is down Bowuguan Lu (博物馆路), which leads to Culture Sq (Wenhua Guangchang).

Courses

⭐ Wǔdāng Taoist Kungfu Academy SPORTS
(武当道教功夫学院, Wǔdāng Dàojiào Gōngfu Xuéyuàn; ☑ 0719 568 9185; www.wudang.org; Purple Cloud Temple; fees per day classes ¥300,

accommodation ¥200-300, meals ¥80) Dozens of taichi schools pepper these parts, but this one has the edge for location, its qualities as a school and accessibility to foreigners. The setting is magical; in a large, secluded courtyard surrounded by pine trees halfway up the mountain. Classes follow a strict regime; they're held either at the school or at various scenic spots on the mountain. You can sign up for anything from a few days to one year; the longer you study, the cheaper the rates.

It's down the steps to your left, just past Purple Cloud Temple; no English sign.

🛏 Sleeping

There are a few reasonable hotels in town, but most travellers prefer to stay on the mountain. Despite the price hikes, it's by far the best way to enjoy the experience of Wŭdāng. There are about a dozen hotels and guesthouses by South Cliff. The cheapest rooms go for around ¥90, but you can bargain, especially during low season.

Yínjiē Holiday Inn   HOTEL $$
(银街假日酒店, Yínjiē Jiàrì Jiŭdiàn; 1 Jin Jie, 金街1号; r from ¥200; ❄ 🔊) Attractive rooms with fresh flowers and new carpets await guests at this great-value hotel by the national-park entrance. The lobby feels like a shady office block but the welcome is honest and there's a spacious breakfast hall.

Jiànguó Hotel   HOTEL $$
(建国饭店, Jiànguó Fàndiàn; ☑ 0719 590 8888; www.hotelsjiangou.com; Wŭdāngshān Scenic Area, Shíyàn, 武当山风景区; d from ¥500; ❄ 🔊) The Jiànguó is a large, spacious, luxury hotel at the foot of Wŭdāng. English-speaking management, top-shelf room service and a bucolic outlook make this the pick of the hotels in town.

Nányán Hotel   HOTEL $$
(南岩大岳宾馆, Nányán Dàyuè Bīnguǎn; ☑ 0719 568 9182; beside the Nányán car park, 南岩的停车场; r ¥300-400; ❄ @) Near the bus stop at South Cliff is this welcoming hotel, popular with large groups. Rooms are clean and comfortable and the breakfast is decent. It's beside the Nányán parking lot.

Xuán Yuè Hotel   HOTEL $$
(玄岳饭店, Xuányuè Fàndiàn; ☑ 0719 566 3222; 27 Yuxu Lu, 玉虚路27号; r from ¥380; ❄ @ 🔊) This smart, midrange hotel has comfortable rooms with clean bathrooms. It's on the corner of Yuxu Lu and Taihe Zhonglu and is accessed through an entranceway to the right of the one with the English sign for the hotel (the one with the English sign leads to the restaurant).

Shèngjǐngyuàn Bīnguǎn   HOTEL $$
(圣景苑宾馆; ☑ 0719 566 2118; 7 Taihe Zhonglu, 太和中路7号; r ¥278-318; ❄ @ 🔊) Simple, bright, pleasant rooms come with firm mattresses and spacious bathrooms. It's a couple of doors down from the Bank of China.

Taichi Hotel   HOTEL $$$
(太极会馆, Tàijí Huìguǎn; ☑ 0719 568 9888; r ¥568; ❄ @ 🔊) This quality hotel on the mountain may not have discounts as good as elsewhere, but rooms with windows go for ¥348, and have fabulous mountain views. Rooms without windows are identical (apart from the views) but are generally not discounted. It's 200m downhill from the bus stop at South Cliff.

🍴 Eating

In town a few *shāokǎo* stalls set up every evening in an alley off Taihe Lu. Look for the neon-lit archway with the characters 鱼羊鲜, beside No 14.

On the mountain there are plenty of food options by South Cliff, although not many English menus.

Taste of Wŭdāng   CHINESE $
(味道武当, Wèidào Wŭdāng; mains ¥15-32) This fast-food-style restaurant, right by the bus station, does basic noodle dishes and has an English menu.

Taìhé Xuánwǔ Dàjiǔdiàn   CHINESE $$
(太和玄武大酒店; 8 Taihe Zhonglu, 太和路8号; mains ¥20-50; ⊙ 6.30am-11.30pm) Large bustling restaurant with half its menu helpfully translated into English. Various regional cuisines are represented, from Sichuanese to Cantonese; even Běijīng roast duck! No English sign.

☆ Entertainment

Wŭdāng Grand Theatre   THEATRE
(武当大剧院, Wŭdāng Dàjùyuàn; ☑ 0719 506 2366; Culture Sq, 文化广场; Wŭdāng Taichi Show tickets ¥200-280; ⊙ Wŭdāng Taichi Show 8-9pm) Modern theatre opposite the Wŭdāng Museum of China. It hosts the **Wŭdāng Taichi Show** every Thursday, Friday and Saturday.

ⓘ Information

Bank of China (中国银行, Zhōngguó Yínháng; 1 Taihe Zhonglu, 太和中路1号; ⊙ 8.30am-5.30pm) Foreign-friendly ATM and money-exchange facility.

ⓘ Getting There & Away

BUS

The bus station (客运汽车站; kèyùn qìchēzhàn), 200m downhill from the expressway, is on the right of the road leading into town.

Jīngzhōu ¥125, five hours, one daily (9am)

Wǔhàn ¥150, five hours, two daily (8.30am and 11am)

Xī'ān ¥159, eight hours, one daily (8.30am)

Yíchāng ¥120, five hours, one daily (9.30am)

A fleet of small green buses shuttles between the two nearest train stations – Wǔdāngshān and Shíyàn (十堰; ¥15, one hour, 5.10am to 8pm) – via Liùlǐpíng (六里坪; ¥4, 20 minutes). They leave from outside Taìhé Xuánwǔ Dàjiǔdiàn restaurant.

TRAIN

Wǔdāng Shān no longer has a train station, although the train station at Liùlǐpíng is often referred to as Wǔdāng Shān. You can buy train tickets from the **train ticket office** (铁路客票代售, Tiělù Piàodàishòu; ⏰8.30am-6pm), beside Wǔdāng Shān's old train station on Chezhan Lu (车站路), the road opposite Taìhé Xuánwǔ Dàjiǔdiàn restaurant.

Liùlǐpíng (Wǔdāng Shān) trains:

Běijīng West Hard seat/hard sleeper ¥164/300, 19 to 22 hours, two daily

Chángshā Hard seat/hard sleeper ¥112/208, 10½ hours, three daily

Chéngdū Hard seat/hard sleeper ¥128/230, 11 to 14 hours, four daily

Shànghǎi South Hard seat/hard sleeper ¥192/328, 24 to 26 hours, two daily

Wǔhàn (Wǔchāng) Hard seat/hard sleeper ¥69/130, 6½ to 8½ hours, seven daily

Xī'ān Hard seat/hard sleeper ¥69/130, five to six hours, three daily

Xī'ān North Hard seat/hard sleeper ¥69/130, five to six hours, three daily

Xiāngyáng Hard seat/hard sleeper ¥24/78, two hours, regular (6am to 11.30pm)

Yíchāng East Hard seat/hard sleeper ¥55/109, three hours, one daily (4.23pm)

Shénnóngjià 神农架

☑ 0719 / POP 80,000

Húběi's natural beauty is on show in the northeast of the province, especially around the Yāzikǒu National Park in the region known as Shénnóngjià. Reached via a dramatic climbing road best left to the bus driver, here the ape-like yěrén (wild-man; 野人) roams wild among the hikers, in between a 3000-step trail, brooks, ravines and thickly forested peaks. Below winds the Yangzi River, wearing away the sheer rock faces and rejuvenating the snub-nosed monkeys and salamanders which scamper about the forest floor.

The small but well developed tourist village of **Mùyú** (木鱼) is the main jumping-off point, where you can find a few hotels, restaurants and basic provisions.

⊙ Sights

Yāzikǒu NATIONAL PARK

(鸭子口; ¥140) Foreigners are only allowed into one of the four sections of this national park, at Yāzikǒu, but the area is big enough for good walking and you can also camp here. **Xiǎolóngtán** (小龙潭), about 10km from the entrance, is a good place to spot monkeys (Shénnóngjià is home to the rare golden snub-nosed monkey; 川金丝猴; chuān jīnsīhóu), while **Shénnóngdǐng** (神农顶), 20km from the entrance, is the highest peak in the park (3105m).

Once inside the park, you can board shuttle buses (¥90) to various points of interest. There's a camping area (¥30) at the base of Shénnóngdǐng, called **Shénnóngyíng** (神农营).

Winter is bitterly cold and snow often blocks roads.

Yāzikǒu is accessed from Mùyú, a about 14km down the mountain. All buses drop you in Mùyú.

🛏 Sleeping

There are some basic hotels and a few flashier numbers spread out in the surrounding area, with the highest concentration around Mùyú. You can normally rent tents (帐篷; zhàngpéng; ¥100 to ¥200) once inside the park, or buy them (¥700 to ¥800) from a couple of camping shops in Mùyú.

Wǔyuè Scenic Area Hotel HOTEL $

(五悦景区连锁酒店, Wǔyuè Jǐngqū Liánsuǒ Jiǔdiàn; ☑ 400 650 5151; www.5yue.com; Yuányì Chǎngshí Shìdàn Cáohé Xiǎoqū, 木鱼园艺场石槽河小区; d ¥135) Just outside Mùyú Village (木鱼镇; Mùyú Zhèn) is this well maintained hotel with tasteful rooms and a lovely location. It's a good base for exploring the region, and staff are friendly and will throw in a solid breakfast for your troubles.

Shuānglín Hotel HOTEL $

(双林酒店, Shuānglín Jiǔdiàn; ☑ 0719 345 2803; 25 Muyu Lu, 木鱼路25号; r from ¥88, with computer ¥128; ❄ @) The modest Shuānglín Hotel, where buses drop you off, has tidy rooms and welcoming management.

✖ Eating

Mùyú has some basic restaurants; otherwise, the hotels will feed you.

Piān Qiáo Wān
CHINESE $

(偏桥湾; 53 Muyu Lu, 木鱼路53号; mains ¥20-40; ⏰10am-9pm) This is the coolest place to eat in Mùyú. It's accessed via a wobbly bridge and backs onto a small tea plantation (you can buy tea here). The menu is in Chinese only. Try the *huíguō niúròu* (回锅牛肉; spicy fried beef), the *cháshùgū chǎolàròu* (茶树菇炒腊肉; wild mushrooms and cured pork) or the *xiānggū ròusī* (香菇肉丝; shiitake mushrooms with pork shreds).

ℹ Information

The ICBC Bank at the top of Mùyú village has an ATM that accepts foreign cards.

ℹ Getting There & Away

Buses leave from outside Shuānglín Hotel, where you can also buy tickets. Foreigners aren't allowed to continue north to Wǔdāng Shān from Mùyú.

Bādōng ¥55, three hours, one daily (9.30am)

Yíchāng ¥60, 2½ hours, five daily (7am to 3.30pm)

Shared minibuses to Yāzikǒu (per person ¥10) leave from the top end of Mùyú.

Yíchāng 宜昌

☑ 0717 / POP 1.5 MILLION

Yíchāng is a small, compact city known as the culmination point for many a Three Gorges cruise. It's a remarkable feeling to glide through this iconic geological formation and quickly becomes the highlight for many travellers to China. There is not a lot to see for the waylaid traveller in Yíchāng – other than get psyched for, or decompress from, the boat trip – but the Yangzi offers an attractive backdrop to the unpretentious urban hum and a vibrant street-food scene.

◉ Sights

Three Gorges Dam
ARCHITECTURE

(三峡大坝, Sānxiá Dàbà; ¥105) The huge, hulking Three Gorges Dam is the world's largest dam due to its length (2.3km) rather than its height (101m), and while it isn't the most spectacular dam, it is worth a peek. You can't walk on it, but there's a tourist viewing area to the north. The view from the south is much the same, and free.

Take a bus from the long-distance station to Máopíng (茅坪; ¥15, 8.30am to 3pm), but get off at Bālù Chēzhàn (八路车战). Alternatively, bus 8 (¥20, one hour, 8am to 4pm) leaves from Yíchāng's east train station.

Day trips can also be taken by boat (¥280 including entrance fee and lunch) from the old ferry port (老码头; *lǎo mǎtóu*). Boats leave at 7.30am and return around 5pm. Buy tickets from Yangtze River International Travel at the port.

Three Gorges Village
VILLAGE

(三峡村, Sānxiácūn; ¥120) It's a little tacky and overrun on weekends, but nonetheless a neat, convenient way to take in the stunning views over Xīlíng Gorge (西陵峡; Xīlíngxiá) and an interesting guided cave ramble. Catch bus 10 (¥2, 30 minutes) from the city centre.

🛏 Sleeping

Yíchāng has a few good business hotels, especially near the river.

Xīndǎo International Hotel
HOTEL $$

(馨岛国际酒店, Xīndǎo Guójì Jiǔdiàn; ☑0717 609 9999; www.xindaohotel.com; 51 Dongshan Dajie, 东山大道51号; d ¥390; P ❈ @ ☎) 'Hope Island' Hotel offers excellent value for travellers who want to put their feet up before or after the Three Gorges cruise, or are in town on business and need some leisure. It's four-star on the old scale, with friendly service and huge, plush-carpeted rooms.

Yíchāng Hotel
HOTEL $$

(宜昌饭店, Yíchāng Fàndiàn; ☑0717 644 1616; 113 Dongshan Dadao, 东山大道113号; r from ¥288; ❈ @ ☎) This jolly place has an elegant foyer plus large and pleasant rooms. English is limited but it's all smiles. It's diagonally opposite the long-distance bus station. Discounts may apply.

✖ Eating

There's a modest restaurant scene, or get bus 2 or 6 (¥1) or a taxi (¥7) to **Běimén** (北门), for *xiǎoyè* (宵夜; 'midnight snacks') at stalls which spill onto the streets nightly (5pm to 2am). Try skewers (串; *chuàn*), dumplings (饺子; *jiǎozi*), noodles (面; *miàn*) and barbecued fish (烤鱼; *kǎoyú*). A **pancake stall** makes *fēi bǐng* (飞饼; 'flying pancakes'; ¥12 to ¥15); the banana ones (香蕉; *xiāngjiāo*) are delicious.

Xiǎo Hú Niú
HUBEI $

(小胡牛; 73 Shangshu Xiang, Běimén, 北门尚书巷73号; ingredients ¥8-26; ⏰4pm-2am) Our favourite restaurant in Běimén specialises in a local beef hotplate called *xiǎo hú niú*. Order that first, stipulating how spicy you want your beef (¥25 for 250g) or lamb (¥26 for 250g) – mild (微辣; *wēi là*), medium (中辣; *zhōng là*) or hot (麻辣; *má là*) – before ordering other raw ingredients to fry with it on your hotplate.

Choices include *qīngjiāo* (青椒; green peppers), *xiānggū* (香菇; shiitake mushrooms), *tǔdòu piàn* (土豆片; potato slices) and *ǒu piàn* (藕片; lotus root slices).

Hánlìgōng Liàolǐ KOREAN $
(韩丽宫料理; ⊙11am-9pm; ☒) Opposite **Yílíng Hotel** (夷陵饭店, Yílíng Fàndiàn, 41 Yunji Lu, 云集路41号), and next door to a Western-style cafe, is this smart Korean restaurant with good-value dishes, claypots and barbecues.

★ **Fàngwēng Restaurant** HUBEI $$
(放翁酒家, Fàngwēng Jiǔjiā; ☑0717 886 2179; Nanjin Guan Sanyoudong Bridge, 南津关二游洞桥头; dishes ¥60-160; ⊙9am-9.30pm) At Xīlíng Gorge (西陵峡; Xīlíngxiá), 12km north of Yíchāng, is a peculiar restaurant perched precariously against a cliff. Claimed to be the ninth 'cave restaurant' in the world, the cuisine is distinctly Húběi, the service brisk and the view quite amazing. Taxis know it well (for about ¥80 one way).

ℹ Information

There are plentiful 24-hour internet cafes (网吧; *wǎngbā*; per hour ¥3).

China International Travel Service (CITS, 中国国际旅行社, Zhōngguó Guójì Lǚxíngshè; ☑0717 625 3088; www.cits.net; Yunji Lu, 云集路; ⊙8am-6pm) Sells luxury cruises (from ¥2800) and tourist boat tickets (¥880 to ¥900) to Chóngqìng, but not hydrofoil tickets. Some English is spoken.

Three Gorges Tourist Centre (三峡游客中心, Sānxiá Yóukè Zhōngxīn; ☑0717 696 6116; Yanjiang Dadao, 沿江大道; ⊙7am-8pm) Commission-free, so cheaper than CITS. Sells hydrofoil tickets to Fèngjié (¥245) plus passenger ferry tickets to various destinations between Yíchāng and Chóngqìng. Minimal English is spoken, but staff members are helpful. Enter the modern tourist centre (no English sign) and head to the ticket counters at the far right of the building.

Yangtze River International Travel (宜昌长江国际旅行社, Yíchāng Chángjiāng Guójì Lǚxíngshè; ☑0717 692 1808; Yanjiang Dadao, 沿江大道; ⊙7am-8pm) Marginally cheaper than CITS for ordinary tourist-boat tickets to Chóngqìng (from ¥890). Also sells luxury cruises. Housed inside the Three Gorges Tourist Centre, but has a separate desk beside the passenger-boat ticket counters.

ℹ Getting There & Away

AIR
Daily flights from **Three Gorges Airport** (三峡机场; Sānxiá Jīchǎng) include Běijīng (¥1100), Guǎngzhōu (¥860), Shànghǎi (¥1080) and Xī'ān (¥640).

BUS
There are three main long distance bus stations: Yíchāng **long-distance bus station** (长途汽车站; *chángtú qìchēzhàn*), plus one at the east train station and at the old ferry port. All are modern and well run, and offer very similar bus services. Services from the Yíchāng long-distance bus station include:

Jīngzhōu ¥40 to ¥65, two hours and 10 minutes, half-hourly (6.40am to 6.30pm)

Lǎoyíng (for Wǔdāng Shān) ¥130, six hours, regular (8am to 1pm)

Mùyú (for Shénnóngjià) ¥70, five hours, seven daily (7.45am to 3.30pm)

Wǔdāng Shān ¥120, six hours, two daily (8am and 12.20pm)

Wǔhàn (Wǔchāng) ¥78 to ¥110, 4½ hours, every hour (7am to 8pm)

TRAIN
Yíchāng's **east train station** (火车东站; *huǒchē dōngzhàn*) is the station that almost all trains use. Train tickets (¥5 service charge) can also be bought at window 1 of Yíchāng long-distance bus station. Trains include:

Běijīng West G train 2nd/1st class ¥606/931, eight hours, four daily (8.35am, 10.41am, 12.40pm, 1.52pm)

Chéngdū D train 2nd/1st class ¥259/311, seven hours, 11 per day (some to Chéngdū East)

Chóngqìng North D train 2nd/1st class ¥162/195, four hours, regular

Shànghǎi Hóngqiáo D train 2nd/1st class ¥348/416, eight hours, six daily

Wǔdāng Shān Hard seat/hard sleeper ¥5 to ¥109, five hours, one daily (7.30pm)

Wǔhàn D train 2nd/1st class ¥96/116, 2½ hours, regular

Xī'ān Hard sleeper ¥200, 11 hours, 7.45pm

ℹ Getting Around

Airport shuttle buses (¥20, 50 minutes) run to and from the Qīngjiāng building (清江大厦; Qīngjiāng dàshà), leaving two hours before outgoing flights and meeting all incoming flights.

Local buses cost ¥1. Useful routes for frequently running buses include:

Bus 4 Old ferry port (老码头; lǎo mǎtóu) via Yíling Hotel (夷陵饭店, Yíling Fàndiàn) and the old train station (火车站, huǒchē zhàn) or long-distance bus station.

Bus 6 Long-distance bus station to Běimén (北门).

Bus 9 East train station to the long-distance bus station.

Jiāngxī

POP 45.2 MILLION

Best Places to Eat

➡ Kǎlúnbì Kāfēi (p458)

➡ Sānbǎo Shíguāng Jiǔbā (p461)

➡ Helen's (p458)

Best Places to Sleep

➡ Go Home Hotel (p467)

➡ Jǐngdézhèn International Youth Hostel (p461)

➡ Sānqīngshān International Resort (p468)

Why Go?

The underrated province of Jiāngxī (江西) offers a bucolic entrée into semirural Chinese life. It's a succulent, green place, connected by waterways of natural and human design, rice paddies teeming with bird life and fields draped in wildflowers. Tea seemingly grows out of every patch of land until dramatic mountain ranges, swirling with mist, rise up at its edges.

Jiāngxī has joined the high-speed rail circuit and now there's a new breed of local, prosperous traveller. They come here for the story-book villages around Wùyuán, the remote mountain parks of great spiritual significance and matching hiking trails in the northeast, and the surprisingly pleasant provincial capital, Nánchāng.

The altogether slower pace of life is the real highlight of a visit to this charming pocket of southeast China.

When to Go
Nánchāng

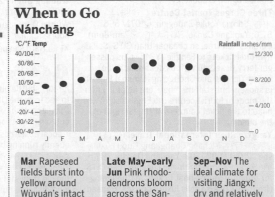

| Mar Rapeseed fields burst into yellow around Wùyuán's intact Song and Qing villages. | Late May–early Jun Pink rhododendrons bloom across the Sānqīng Shān and Lúshān canopies. | Sep–Nov The ideal climate for visiting Jiāngxī; dry and relatively mild. |

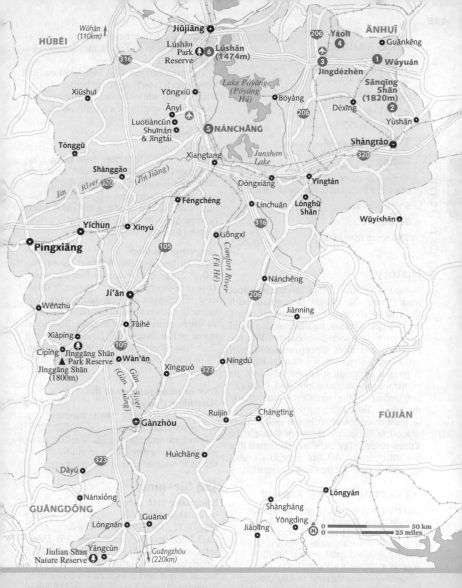

Jiāngxī Highlights

1 **Wùyuán & Around**
(p464) Hiking the ancient postal trail between villages before sipping rice wine and chrysanthemum tea.

2 **Sānqīng Shān** (p467)
Looking out over a forest of granite spires in one of eastern China's most underrated national parks.

3 **Jǐngdézhèn** (p460)
Shopping for porcelain pieces in this world-renowned and revitalised arts district.

4 **Yáolǐ** (p462) Visiting this ancient riverside village with its moss-hewn residences and traditional pottery kilns.

5 **Bāyī Square** (p456)
Starting your long morning walk where the Long March was inspired, in Nánchāng, the energetic, riverside capital with surprisingly decent nightlife.

6 **Lúshān** (p459) Seeking respite from the heat in this former Communist Party summer playground atop a misty national park dotted with European-style villas.

JIĀNGXĪ NÁNCHĀNG

History

Jiāngxī's Gán River Valley was the principal trade route that linked Guǎngdōng with the rest of the country in imperial times. Its strategic location, natural resources and long growing season have ensured that the province has always been relatively well off. Jiāngxī is most famous for its imperial porcelain (from Jǐngdézhèn), although its contributions to philosophy and literature are perhaps more significant, particularly during the Tang and Song dynasties.

Peasant unrest arose in the 19th century when the Taiping rebels swept through the Yangzi River Valley. Rebellion continued into the 20th century, and Jiāngxī became one of the earliest bases for the Chinese communists.

ℹ️ Getting There & Around

Nánchāng is connected by air to most major cities in China. There's also a small airport at Jǐngdézhèn. Bullet trains link Nánchāng with an ever-growing number of cities, including Wǔhàn and Shànghǎi and, most recently, beautiful Wùyuán in the north of the province.

Travelling around the province, long-distance buses are usually quicker and more frequent than trains. Within towns and cities, local buses cost ¥1 (carry exact change). Around the villages, you may sometimes have to resort to motorbike taxis.

Nánchāng 南昌

🚉 0791 / POP 2.5 MILLION

Known reverently in textbooks for fomenting Chinese Communist Party (CCP) rule, Nánchāng now galvanises support for its attractive, tree-lined streets and easy urban charm. It's a handy base for Jiāngxī's immediate country to the north and is now on a number of bullet-train lines.

The area around Bāyī Park – where the Long March (p947) arguably began – buzzes after sunset, while the old quarter near the Gán River is worthy of a lengthy stroll.

👁 Sights

Bāyī Square   PARK

(南昌八一广场, Nánchāng Bāyī Guǎngchǎng; Zhongshan Lu, 中山路) Where the Communist Party first insurged, you'll now find groups of Chinese, young and old, walking, dancing, hawking and laughing throughout this popular park in the heart of the city. Best enjoyed just after dusk or dawn.

Téngwáng Pavilion   MONUMENT

(腾王阁, Téngwáng Gé; Rongmen Lu, 榕门路; ¥50; ⊙7.30am-6.30pm summer, 8am-5pm winter) This nine-storey pagoda is the city's drawcard monument, first erected during Tang times, but destroyed and rebuilt no less than 29 times, most recently in 1989. Traditional music performances are played on the 6th floor. Take Bus 2内 from the train station. Visitors can climb to the top for views of the modern city.

Former Headquarters of the
Nánchāng Uprising   MUSEUM

(八一南昌起义纪念馆, Bāyī Nánchāng Qǐyì Jìniànguǎn; 380 Zhongshan Lu, 中山路380号; ⊙9am-5pm, closed Mon) FREE Wartime paraphernalia for rainy days and enthusiasts of the CCP. Admission free with passport.

🛏 Sleeping

Nánchāng YHA Letu
International Hostel   HOSTEL $

(国际旅馆, Nánchāng Guójì Lǚguǎn; 🚉0791 8523 9191; service@yhachina.com; 253 Shengjinta Jie, 绳金塔街253号; dm/s/d ¥25/50/80) Nánchāng's best hostel is on the historic 'snack' street and does a steady business in itinerant Chinese backpackers and Chinese-language-student drifters from afar. Dorms are perfectly kept, while the private rooms are compact but bright and airy.

7 Days Inn   HOTEL $$

(七天连锁酒店, Qītiān Liánsuǒ Jiǔdiàn; 🚉0791 8610 5088; www.7daysinn.cn; 19 Zhanqian Lu, 站前路19号; r from ¥165; ❀@🛜) The Bāyī Square branch of this 24/7 chain has clean rooms with wooden floors, and service is always earnest. The breakfast will fill a hole too.

Nánchāng

Nánchāng

Swiss International Hotel LUXURY HOTEL **$$$**
(南昌瑞颐大酒店, Nánchāng Ruìyí Dàjiǔdiàn; ☎0791 8777 7777; www.swissinternationalhotels.com/nanchang; 69 Yanjiang Bei Lu, 沿江北路69号; r from ¥900; ㊾❀❄✉) On the mighty Gàn River is Nánchāng's finest high-end hotel. Rooms are understated and spacious with big-window views of barges and bridges. Staff provide real expertise on the area and can arrange trips around the province. The day spa and swimming-pool area were under renovation when we visited.

Galactic Classic International Hotel HOTEL **$$$**
(嘉莱特精典国际酒店, Jiāláitè Jīngdiǎn Guójì Jiǔdiàn; ☎0791 8828 1888; www.glthp.com; 2 Bayi Dadao, 八一大道2号; r from ¥1288; ❀❄) Not exactly out of this world, but this classy Chinese luxury hotel near the train station has quite the futuristic exterior. Rooms are a little dated, but very big and the soft colours ease the jet lag. Over the road, its older sister, **Galactic Peace Hotel** (嘉莱特和平国际酒店, Jiāláitè Hépíng Guójì Jiǔdiàn; ☎0791 8611

1118; 10 Guangchang Nanlu, 广场南路10号; r from ¥1080; ⊞@🛜), is a slightly cheaper option. Discounted to ¥699 when not busy.

✕ Eating

★ Kǎlúnbǐ Kāfēi   ASIAN $$
(卡伦比咖啡; Bāyī Park, 八一公园西门; mains ¥40-100; ⊙9am-1.30am; 🛜) This modern cafe-restaurant, with a charming lakeside location inside Bāyī Park, does fresh coffee (¥40), Chinese tea (¥90) and imported beer (¥30) as well as good quality food. The steaks (¥100 to ¥200) are expensive. Instead, go for noodles (¥45) or one of the tasty casserole pots (¥50 to ¥60).

Pay a few extra kuài to upgrade your dish to a *tàocān*, a set meal with rice, soup and other small accompaniments. No English sign, but it does have an English menu.

Le Bistro 100   FRENCH $$$
(法国小厨100, Fǎguó Xiǎochú 100; ☑0791 610 0100; 100 Rongmen Lu, 榕门路100号; mains ¥60-100; ⊙noon-10pm) It's not *totally* French, but you're in the middle of China, so be grateful that you can vary your cuisine. Pull up a seat at this small restaurant and order beef, fish and chicken dishes of the utmost quality. The wine list (bottles only) is good too.

🍷 Drinking & Nightlife

★ Helen's   BAR
(☑0791 8671 9023; 536 Dieshan Lu, 叠山路536号; beer from ¥30, snacks from ¥20) Helen's large tables and booths fill with groups of young and well heeled Chinese playing drinking games, smoking hookah pipes, dancing to hip hop and house, and eating delicious miniburgers. It's dimly lit, very friendly and a lot of fun.

1923 Zuǒàn Cafe   CAFE
(1923-左岸艺文咖啡馆, 1923 Zuǒ'àn Yìwén Kāfēi Guǎn; Minde Lu, 民德路; drinks ¥30-60) This

---

Parisian-themed bar-cafe on the shopping street of Minde Lu is remarkably cool for a second-tier Chinese city. The owner has sourced antiques and bric-a-brac from across Europe to create an intimate, kooky venture where you can sip martinis or hot espressos in period splendour.

Caffé Bene   CAFE
(1 Minde Lu, 民的路1号佑民寺旁; coffee ¥25; ⊙10.30am-11pm; 🛜) Spacious branch of the stylish Korean coffee chain. Does good coffee plus a small selection of Western food, including Belgian waffles and ice cream. Free wi-fi.

ℹ Information

There are 24-hour internet cafes by the train station.

Bank of China (中国银行, Zhōngguó Yínháng; 161 Minde Lu, 民的路161号) Bank of China ATM.

Bank of China (中国银行, Zhōngguó Yínháng; Zhanqian Xilu, 站前西路) Includes foreign exchange.

China Post (中国邮政, Zhōngguó Yóuzhèng; Youzheng Rd, 邮政路)

Public Security Bureau (PSB, 公安局, Gōng'ānjú; ☑0791 8728 8493; 131 Yangming Lu, 阳明路131号; ⊙8am-noon & 2.30-6pm)

The 1st Hospital of Nánchāng City (南昌市第一医院, Nánchāng Shì Dìyī Yīyuàn; ☑0791 870 0989, 0791 886 2288; 128 Xiangshan Beilu, 象山北路128号)

ℹ Getting There & Away

AIR
Chāngběi airport, 28km north of Nánchāng, has flights to all major Chinese cities as well as Bangkok and Singapore. Book tickets through www.ctrip.com.

BUS
Bus 89 links the train station with **Xúfāng bus station** (徐坊客运站, Xúfāng Kèyùnzhàn; 850 Jinggangshan Dadao, 井冈山大道850号). Bus 18 links the train station with **Qīngshān bus station** (青山客运站, Qīngshān Kèyùnzhàn; 19 Qingshan Nanlu, 青山南路19号), which will eventually be connected to the metro.

Services from Qīngshān bus station:
Lúshān ¥59, 2½ hours, 8am, 9.30am and 10.40am
Wùyuán ¥106, 3½ hours, 8am, 10.25am, 12.40pm, 2.15pm and 4.25pm

Services from Xúfāng bus station:
Gànzhōu ¥120, 5½ hours, hourly, 7.20am to 6.50pm
Jǐngdézhèn ¥85, three hours, hourly, 7am to 7.30pm

THE NÁNCHĀNG UPRISING

The Nánchāng Uprising is known as the first appearance of the People's Liberation Army. On 1 August 1927, Zhou Enlai and Zhu De broke ranks with the Nationalist-controlled military and, together with 30,000 communist troops, held the city for four days. The communists were eventually forced to retreat to the nearby mountains where they continued their gruelling campaign, and eventually the fabled Long March in 1934.

Jiǔjiāng ¥41, two hours, every 40 minutes, 8am to 7pm

Yīngtán ¥43, two hours, every 90 minutes, 7.45am to 6.15pm

Yùshān ¥84, four hours, 2.40pm

TRAIN

An increasing number of bullet trains leave from Nánchāng's colossal west train station, which will be connected to the metro. Shuttle bus 1 (高铁巴士1号线; *gāotiě bāshi yīhàoxiàn*; ¥5, 45 minutes, half hourly 6am to 11pm) links the two train stations.

Services from **Nánchāng train station** (南昌 火车站, Nánchāng Huǒchēzhàn; Erqi Nanlu, 二 七南路):

Běijīng West Z-class hard sleeper ¥317, 11½ hours, two daily (7.55pm, 8.02pm)

Běijīng West K/T-class hard sleeper ¥317, 16 to 22 hours, six daily

Gànzhōu K/T-class hard seat ¥63, four to five hours, 14 daily

Guǎngzhōu T/K-class hard sleeper ¥230 to ¥250, 11 to 13 hours, six daily

Hángzhōu East G-class bullet ¥264, two to three hours, 30 daily, 7.32am to 9pm.

Jǐngdézhèn K-class hard seat ¥41 to ¥47, five hours, two daily (7.08am, 4.34pm)

Xī'ān G-class hard sleeper ¥748, 7½ hours, 7.05am

Yùshān K-class hard seat ¥44, 4½ hours, seven daily

Services from **Nánchāng West train station** (南 昌西站, Nánchāng Xīzhàn; Xizhan Jie, 西站街):

Běijīng West G-class hard seat ¥806, eight to nine hours, two daily (8.48am and 1.12pm)

Shànghǎi (Hóngqiáo) G-class bullet ¥337, 3½ hours, 30 daily

Wǔhàn D-class bullet ¥100 to ¥110 , 2½ hours, 13 daily (8.02am to 7.39pm)

Wùyuán D-class bullet ¥150 to 250, 2½ hours

You can pick up tickets at either the **Nánchāng Railway International Ticket Office** (南铁国 旅, Nántiě Guólǚ; 393 Bayi Dadao, 八一 大道393 号; ⊘ 8.30am-6pm) on the day of travel or the **Advance Rail Ticket Office** (火车铁路售票处, Huǒchē Tiělù Shòupiàochù; 393 Bayi Dadao, 八一 大道393号; ⊘ 8am-noon & 12.30-5pm) if you're a little more organised. They're in the same building.

ⓘ Getting Around

Airport buses (¥15) leave every 20 minutes from 5.30am to 9pm from the north side of the train-station square and take 50 minutes. A taxi to the airport (机场; *jīchǎng*) costs around ¥120.

Line 1 of Nánchāng's flash metro (地铁; *dìtiě*) is up and running. Line 2 (connecting both train stations with Bāyī Sq) should also be open. Tickets starts at ¥1.50 for single trips.

Around Nánchāng

The rarely visited, 1100-year-old village of **Luótiáncūn** (罗田村; ¥40, incl admission to Shuǐnán & Jǐngtái villages), its uneven stone-flagged alleys etched with centuries of wear, provides a history-laden rural escape from urban Nánchāng.

A lazy amble around the village will take you through a tight maze of lanes, past hand-worked pumps, ancient wells, stone steps, scattering chickens, lazy water buffalo and conical haystacks. Rudimentary walking-tour signs – 'visit and go ahead' – will point you towards the most notable old buildings.

A 1km-long flagstone path links Luótiáncūn with its sibling village, Shuǐnán (水南). A further 500m down the stone path (and across the road) is the forlorn village of Jǐngtái (京台). Both also contain some wonderful old buildings.

Simple guesthouses (around ¥30 per person) are available in Luótiáncūn – ask for *zhùsù* (住宿; accommodation) – and there are a few restaurants by the main square.

To get here, take Bus 22 (¥1) from Nánchāng train station to a bus stop called Bayi Qiao (八一桥; 30 minutes), then walk 400m straight ahead to catch bus 136, from a bus stop underneath the flyover, to the small town of Ānyì (安义; ¥10, 90 minutes, frequent from 6am to 6pm). From Ānyì bus station, where the 136 terminates, take a bus to nearby Shíbí (石鼻; ¥5, 30 minutes, half-hourly, 7am to 5.30pm), but tell the ticket seller on the bus that you want to go to Luótiáncūn. They will then sell you a bus ticket which is also valid for the final 5km minibus ride to the village entrance. The last bus back to Nánchāng leaves Ānyì at 6.30pm.

Lúshān　　　　庐山

☑ 0792 / POP 111,000

The drive up to Lúshān weaves through thick forest and low-hanging clouds until you reach a town indelibly inked in the Chinese consciousness. Long revered as a Buddhist centre and as a spiritual retreat for European missionaries, Lúshān infiltrated the public imagination as the official summer residence of the Chinese Community Party.

The Taiping Rebellion in the mid-19th century destroyed most of the spiritual sites, though some 20th-century European-style villas still dot the hillsides. These days, however, most people come simply to escape the scorching summer heat of Nánchāng (it's particularly popular at weekends).

When it's not covered in mist, walking around here is pleasant: there are plenty of viewpoints, some waterfalls and a few notable villas to head for. Buy a bilingual map (地图 dìtú; ¥6) in **Xīnhuá Bookstore** (新华书店, Xīnhuá Shūdiàn; 11 Guling Zhengjie, 牯岭政街11 号), opposite the main square – called Jiēxīn Park (街心公园; Jiēxīn Gōngyuán) – and head off in whatever direction takes your fancy.

Venturing in any direction will take you into the wilds of one of the most ethereal environments in this province. The 300-sq-km **Lúshān National Park** (庐山国家公园, Lúshān Guójiā Gōngyuán; adult/student ¥180/135) is best known for its strange rock formations that seem almost perennially covered in cloud. Loads of hiking trails are clearly marked and often paved. You pay to enter upon arrival at the foot of the mountain; all accommodation, restaurants and hiking trails are at the top.

Sāndiéquán Waterfall (三叠泉瀑布, Sāndiéquán Pùbù), the three-tiered waterfall inside Lúshān National Park is a highlight and just reward for hikers. The ascent of 1600m will test your knees, but press on to the top (or take the **cable car**) for tremendous, misty vistas.

There are dozens of hotels lining the main road. You can negotiate during the week and in low season. **Lúshān Hotel** (庐山饭店, Lúshān Fàndiàn; ☑ 0792 828 5430; www.lsfd.lsw. cn; 4 Guling Jie, 牯岭街4号; r ¥80-130) is cheap and close to the bus station.

About 1km from the bus station (turn left from Guling Zhengjie onto Henan Lu and continue for about 600m), **Dàzìrán Youth Hostel** (大自然青年旅社, Dàzìrán Qíngnián Lǚshè; ☑ 0792 829 6327; www.yhalushan.com; 1 Hubei Lu, 湖北路1号; dm/d ¥50/180, weekends dm/d ¥70/260; ❀@☎) is well maintained with a school-camp vibe. Book ahead in summer, especially for the dorm beds.

ℹ️ Getting There & Away

In summer there are three direct buses to Lúshān from Nánchāng's Qīngshān bus station. Otherwise, you'll have to first go to the small city of Jiǔjiāng (九江) at the foot of the mountain, then catch a bus up to Lúshān (¥15.5, one hour, hourly 6.50am to 4.30pm) from there. The last bus back down to Jiǔjiāng from Lúshān is at 5pm.

Buses from Jiǔjiāng long-distance bus station (九江长途汽车站, Jiǔjiāng chángtú qìchēzhàn):

Nánchāng ¥37, two hours, hourly until 7pm
Wǔhàn ¥100, 3½ hours, hourly until 5.30pm
Wùyuán ¥100, three hours, 8.30am, 11.50am and 2.30pm

Jǐngdézhèn　景德镇

☑ 0798 / POP 1.6 MILLION

Jǐngdézhèn is a bustling, regional city synonymous with a thriving porcelain industry. For more than 1700 years, the kilns have fired some of the world's most recognisable and highly sought-after ceramic creations. Even those unaccustomed to the ways of the wheel will be stoked by the range of glazed wares on offer at the many small galleries around town.

Little of the city's architectural heritage remains – and the city's rich cultural history does not leap out at the unsuspecting visitor – but the city boasts a rejuvenated arts district known as the Sculpture Factory and it is well worth a day or two getting to know more about the precious 'white gold'.

◉ Sights

★ Sculpture Factory　ARTS CENTRE
(雕塑瓷厂, Diāosù Cíchǎng; 139 Xinchang Donglu, 新厂东路139号) FREE This tree-lined street, and the pathways that branch off it, form a kind of porcelain-production arts district, which is a centre for contemporary ceramics in China. Some of the world's leading porcelain artists work and teach here and visitors can wander freely around the kilns, workshops and small factories as the latest masterpieces are being sculpted. This is also the most pleasant place in town to shop for ceramics, including tea sets.

Ceramics enthusiasts should pay a visit to the Pottery Workshop. Casual visitors can ask to look around. Staff speak English, and there's a pleasant cafe on-site.

Bus 1, which runs along Zhushan Zhonglu in the centre of town, stops outside the south gate of the complex. Get off at Caojialing (曹家岭) bus stop, then walk through the archway opposite.

Sānbǎo　GALLERY
(三宝; ☑ 798 849 7505; www.chinaclayart.com; 588-680 Sanbao Lu, 三宝路588-680号) FREE About 12km southeast of the city is this wonderful ceramics 'institute' spread across four converted houses. The passion project of Jackson Li, a prominent Chinese artist, the set-up includes a high-end gallery featuring overseas exhibitions, workshops, and a very hip bar-restaurant.

Jǐngdézhèn Ancient Kiln　MUSEUM
(古窑, Gǔyáo; Cidu Dadao, 瓷都大道; ¥95; ☺8am-5pm) A bit like a living museum, this large, nicely landscaped site contains tradi-

Jǐngdézhèn

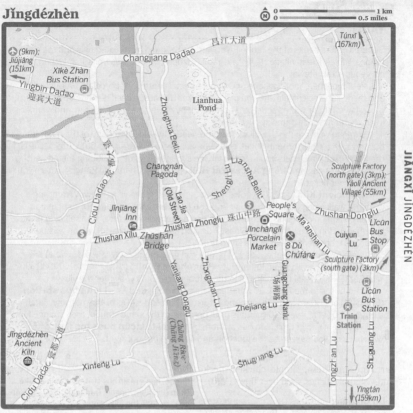

(9km);
Jiǔjiāng
(151km)
Xīkè Zhàn
Bus Station
Yíngbīn Dàdào
迎宾大道

Changjiang Dadao
昌江大道

Túnxī
(167km)

Zhonghua Beilu

Lianhua
Pond

Cídū Dàdào 瓷都大道

Chāngnán
Pagoda

Lianshe Beilu

Shengli

Jǐnjiāng
Inn

Lao Jie
(Old Street)

Zhushan Zhonglu 珠山中路

People's
Square

Sculpture Factory
(north gate) (3km);
Yáolǐ Ancient
Village (55km)

Zhushan Donglu

Zhushan Xilu

Zhūshān
Bridge

Jǐnchānglì
Porcelain
Market

8 Dù
Chúfáng

Ma'anshan Lu

Cuiyun
Lu

Lǐcūn
Bus
Stop

Sculpture Factory
(south gate) (3km)

Yanjiang Donglu

Zhongshan Lu

Guangchang Nanlu

海南路

Lǐcūn
Bus
Station

Zhejiang Lu

Train
Station

Shiguang Lu

Jǐngdézhèn
Ancient
Kiln

Cídū Dàdào 瓷都大道

Xinfeng Lu

Chāng Rivér
(Chāng Jiāng)

Shuguang Lu

Tongzi Lu

Yīngtán
(159km)

tional porcelain-making equipment, including revived ancient kilns, and has teams of staff demonstrating how they were once used. Some of the buildings here date from Qing and Ming times, although have been largely rebuilt. Bus 5 runs here from the train station, via Zhushan Xilu.

🎒 Courses

Pottery Workshop ARTS CENTRE
(乐天陶社, Lètiān Táoshè; ☑ 0798 844 0582; www.potteryworkshop.com.cn; inside Sculpture Factory arts district, 雕塑瓷厂内; residencies incl accommodation & meals per week ¥2600) Runs highly regarded, month-long residency programs for artists.

🛏 Sleeping

Jǐngdézhèn has a decent smattering of business hotels, and one excellent hostel – **Jǐngdézhèn International Youth Hostel** (景德镇国际青年旅舍, Jǐngdézhèn Guójì Qīng-

niánlǚshè; ☑ 0798 844 9998, 0798 844 8886; jdzhostel@hotmail.com; south end of Sculpture Factory, 139 Xinchangdong Lu, 新厂东路139号, 雕塑瓷厂前门口内; dm ¥45-50, r ¥128-148). Located inside the Sculpture Factory arts district, about 3km east of the town centre, this is the only hostel in Jǐngdézhèn but is smart, clean and has English-speaking staff and a cafe. No website, but you can book through www.yhachina.com.

🍴 Eating

Jǐngdézhèn's restaurants are the typical second-tier city range of delicious street fare, working-class restaurants and pan-Chinese banquet halls. Dig in.

⭐ Sānbǎo Shíguāng Jiǔbā CHINESE $$
(三宝时光酒吧; ☑ 0798 848 3665; 588-680 Sanbao Lu, 三宝路588-680号; mains ¥20-50) The Sānbǎo gallery's signature restaurant is perhaps the best in the city. A homely, artsy mood permeates the two floors of wooden

WORTH A TRIP

YÁOLǏ

Situated on the banks of the Yáohé River, and surrounded by forested hills and tea plantations, Yáolǐ Ancient Village (瑶里古镇; Yáolǐ Gǔzhèn), 90 minutes from Jǐngdézhèn, is a gorgeous rural getaway.

Like Jǐngdézhèn, Yáolǐ was one of China's original centres for porcelain production, and there's an ancient kiln site you can visit here. The village itself is made up of elegant, moss-hewn, stone-walled courtyard homes, many of which are still lived in, and wandering its tight, riverside pathways is a treat.

It's free to walk around the village but you need a ticket to enter any of the notable buildings. The ¥150 'through ticket' gives you access to all the sights, but better value is the ¥60 ticket, which gets you in to the village's four best sights, including the Ancient Kiln and the engaging **Chéng Ancestral Hall** (程民宗祠; Chéngmín Zōngcí), where you can buy your ticket.

The **Ancient Kiln** (古窑; Gǔyáo) is about 3km beyond the village (away from Jǐngdézhèn); walk along the country road and you'll see the entrance on your right. It contains a collection of sights, all strung out along a riverside walk (give yourself at least an hour here). Don't miss the Song dynasty 'dragon kiln' (龙窑; lóngyáo), which was built up a slope to increase the heat of the kiln's fire.

Simple restaurants, teahouses and family-run guesthouses (农家乐; nóngjiālè) are dotted around the village, including cute **Píngcháng Rénjiā** (平常人家; ☎ 150 7980 8902; Yáolǐ Gǔzhèn, 瑶里古镇; r ¥80; 閣 ☎), to the left of the river as you enter the village.

Direct buses to Yáolǐ (¥14, 90 minutes) leave from Jǐngdézhèn's **Lìcūn bus station** (Map p461) at 7.30am and 2.30pm, and return at 9am and 3.40pm. Alternatively, catch a bus to Éhú (鹅湖; every 20 minutes until 5pm) from the same station, then change for Yáolǐ (frequent). To get to Lìcūn bus station, take Bus 1 to **Lìcūn bus stop** (Map p461), walk back on yourself, cross the junction and it will be on your right.

furniture and fresh, simple chicken, pork and vegetable dishes. Cold beer flows (¥20).

8 Dù Chúfáng
JIANGXI $$

(八渡厨房, Bādù Chúfáng; 57 Guangchang Nanlu, 广场南路57号; mains ¥20-50; ⏰11am-9.30pm) Popular modern restaurant serving Jiāngxī specialities such as *niúqì chōngtiān* (牛气冲天; spicy beef claypot), *xiāngcūn lǎodòufu* (乡村老豆腐; village-style tofu) and *hóngshāo huángyātou* (红烧黄丫头; braised river fish).

🔒 Shopping

Jīnchānglì Porcelain Market
MALL

(金昌利陶瓷大厦, Jīnchānglì Táocí Dàshà; 2 Zhushan Zhonglu, 珠山中路2号; ⏰9am-6pm) This multistorey shopping centre, specialising entirely in porcelain, isn't as pleasant a place to shop for ceramics as the Sculpture Factory, but it sure does stock a lot of tea sets!

ⓘ Getting There & Away

AIR

From Jǐngdézhèn Luójiā Airport (景德镇罗家机场), Air China flies daily to Běijīng and Shenzhen Airlines makes the daily Shànghǎi trip.

BUS

Jǐngdézhèn's main bus station is called **Xīkè Zhàn** (西客站; Yingbin Dadao, 迎宾大道). Services include the following:

Jiǔjiāng ¥56, 90 minutes, hourly 7.30am to 6.30pm

Nánchāng ¥85, three hours, hourly 6.50am to 7.30pm

Nánchāng Airport ¥60, three hours, every two hours, 6.50am to 5.50pm

Wùyuán ¥30, one hour, 7.40am and 1.40pm

Yīngtán ¥61, 2½ hours, 7.40am, 9.15am, 1.20pm and 5pm

Yùshān ¥91, four hours, 8.20am

TRAIN

There's a train-ticket booking office beside **Jǐnjiāng Inn** (锦江之星, Jǐnjiāng Zhīxīng; 1 Zhushan Xilu, 珠山西路1号). Services include the following:

Běijīng K-class hard sleeper ¥337, 23 hours, 5.31am

Huáng Shān K-class hard seat ¥25, three to four hours, two daytime trains (5.21am and 6.43pm)

Nánchāng K-class hard seat ¥41 to ¥47, five hours, two daily (7.05am and 1.49pm)

Shànghǎi K-class hard sleeper ¥194, 16 hours, 6.43pm

ℹ️ Getting Around

The airport shuttle bus (机场巴士; *jīchǎng bāshì*; ¥10) meets arriving flights and goes to the train station, via the bus station and People's Sq (人民广场; Rénmín Guǎngchǎng). A taxi costs at least ¥70.

Wùyuán
婺源

 0793 / POP 134,100

Wùyuán is home to some of southeastern China's most immaculate views. Parcelled away in this hilly pocket is a scattered cluster of picturesque Huīzhōu villages, where old China remains preserved in enticing panoramas of ancient bridges, trickling streams and stone-flagged alleyways.

Despite lending its name to the entire area, the main town of Wùyuán itself is a fairly bog-standard town, but it has some comfortable hotels, and you can arrange bicycle hire here for cycling trips into the far more arresting countryside.

🏃 Activities

Wùyuán county has a number of villages spread out of a roughly 30km radius. Wengong Beilu (文公北路), and its southern extension Wengong Nanlu (文公南路), is the main north–south drag in the more modern town centre, also known as Wùyuán.

Merida Bike Shop   CYCLING
(美利达自行车, Měilìdá Zìxíngchē; ☑ 0793 734 1818, 135 1703 3662; Liangli Shanlu, 凉笠山路二环路南段; ⊙ 8.30am-9pm) Rents good-quality second-hand mountain bikes for ¥30 per day (deposit ¥500). It has helpful staff. It's located a short walk downhill from Tiānmǎ Hotel. Turn left at the crossroads, then second left.

Héngyuán Chēháng   CYCLING
(恒元车行; ☑ 0793 734 6328; Wengong Beilu, 文公北路; ⊙ 7am-7pm) Rents cheap, but brandnew mountain bikes for ¥50 per day (deposit ¥600). Just up from the crossroads with Chaxiang Xilu (茶乡西路), next to 'Heaven and the World' KTV club.

🛏️ Sleeping

Yíngdū Bīnguǎn   HOTEL $
(迎都宾馆; ☑ 0793 734 8620; 13 Wengong Nanlu, 文公南路13号; r ¥100; ❋@🛜) Centrally located hotel in reasonable condition. Get Bus 1 to People's Hospital (Rénmín Yīyuàn); it's on the right.

Tiānmǎ Hotel   HOTEL $$
(天马大酒店, Tiānmǎ Dàjiǔdiàn; ☑ 0793 736 7123; www.wytm.cn; 119 Wengong Beilu, 文公北路119号; r incl breakfast from ¥628; ❋@🛜) This smart hotel, opposite Běizhàn (north bus station), is comfortable. Can be discounted to ¥158 when quiet.

ℹ️ Information

ATMs are plentiful in Wùyuán, but not in the villages, so load up with cash here.

People's Hospital (人民医院, Rénmín Yīyuàn; Wengong Nanlu, 文公南路) Bus 1 goes here.

Public Security Bureau (PSB, 公安局, Gōng'ānjú; 2 Huancheng Beilu; ⊙ 8-11.30am & 2.30-5.30pm) Bus 1 goes here.

Qǐháng Wǎngbā (启航网吧; Wengong Nanlu, 文公南路; per hour ¥3; ⊙ 24hr) Internet cafe; next to People's Hospital.

Xīnhuá Bookstore (新华书店, Xīnhuá Shūdiàn; Tianyou Xilu, 天佑西路; ⊙ 8am-8pm) The Wùyuán Tourist Map (旅游交通图; *lǚyóu jiāotōng tú*; ¥6) sold here is in Chinese only, but includes a street map of Wùyuán town and a road map of the surrounding countryside. Very useful if you intend to cycle out to the villages. Bus 1 goes here, or walk downhill along Wengong Nanlu, bear left and it's on your left.

ℹ️ Getting There & Around

Local Bus 1 (¥1; 6am to 6pm), from Wùyuán bus station forecourt, goes to north bus station and People's Hospital before terminating at the new train station.

Wùyuán bus station (婺源汽车站; *Wùyuán qìchēzhàn*) is about 2km west of town. Bus services include the following:

Hángzhōu ¥140, 3½ hours, 9.10am, 1.30pm and 4.30pm

Jiǔjiāng ¥100, 2½ hours, 8.20am, 11.50am and 2.30pm

Nánchāng ¥111, 3½ hours, 8am, 10am, 12.10pm, 2pm and 5pm

Sānqīng Shān (east section) ¥32, 1½ hours, 11am

Shànghǎi South ¥210, six hours, 9.50am and 10.30am

Túnxī ¥46, 2½ hours, 8.20am and 1.20pm

Yùshān ¥46, 2½ hours, 8.10am, 11am and 1.20pm

Services from the smaller north bus station (北站; *Běizhàn*) include the following:

Guānkēng ¥23, 2½ hours, 7am, 8.30am, 11am and 2.30pm

Lǐkēng ¥6, 20 minutes, half-hourly (6.30am to 5.20pm)

Língjiǎo ¥20, 90 minutes, 8am, 9.20am, 10.30am, 1.30pm and 3.10pm

Qīnghuá (via Sīkǒu) ¥10, 30 minutes, half-hourly (7am to 5pm)

Xiǎoqǐ ¥15, one hour, hourly (6.30am to 3.30pm)

Wùyuán's **train station** (火车站; *huǒchēzhàn*) is an impressive structure on the outskirts of the city centre. Moto-taxis line the exit to take you to the various villages. The high-speed rail line connects Fúzhōu to Héféi, where it connects with another high-speed line to Běijīng.

Destinations include:

Běijīng South, G-class, hard seat, ¥577, seven hours, 9.13am, 11.25am and 1.02pm

Fúzhōu, G-class, hard seat, ¥196, two to 2½ hours, 10 daily

Guǎngzhōu South G-class, hard seat, seven hours, 4.33pm

Nánchāng West K-class, hard seat ¥150, two to 2½ hours, 11.10am, 11.58am and 4.33pm

Shànghǎi Hongqiao G-class, hard seat, ¥269, four hours, 2.57pm

Around Wùyuán

The main reason to come to this region is to explore the numerous villages which retain their architectural integrity amid splendid pastoral settings.

It is enjoying a renaissance among domestic tourists; hence the weekend crowds.

Wāngkǒu   汪口

Less popular than some of the other ticketed villages, Wāngkǒu (¥60), 9km northeast of Lǐkēng, enjoys a fine location beside a rushing weir at the confluence of two large rivers.

Xiǎoqǐ   晓起

About 35km from Wùyuán, Xiǎoqǐ (¥60) dates to AD 787. There are actually two villages here: the larger, more touristy lower Xiǎoqǐ (下晓起; Xià Xiǎoqǐ) and the much quieter upper Xiǎoqǐ (上晓起; Shàng Xiǎoqǐ), where you'll find a fascinating old **tea factory** (传统生态茶作坊; *chuántǒng shēngtài chá zuòfang*). The two are linked by a time-worn, 500m-long stone pathway. Both parts of the village have accommodation.

Lǐngjiǎo   岭脚

Lǐngjiǎo is best known as one end of the old Qing postal route which now serves as one of Wùyuán's most spectacular and manageable hikes. The village itself is magical and pristine. There is not much to do, but it has a couple of basic restaurants for pre- or post-hike sustenance. A new guesthouse has just opened up, run by an ex-Shanghai travel writer.

CYCLING AROUND WÙYUÁN

Though you can reach most of Wùyuán's villages by bus, cycling gives you more freedom to village-hop around the surrounding countryside. Roads are in good nick and well signposted in pinyin as well as Chinese characters. You can pick up a Chinese map of the area from Xīnhuá Bookstore (p463).

One possible two- to three-day trip is the 130-km circuit from Wùyuán, passing Lǐkēng, Xiǎoqǐ and the Duànxīn Reservoir, before looping back to Wùyuán via Qīnghuá and Sīkǒu. Follow Wengong Beilu north out of Wùyuán to pick up signs to Lǐkēng.

How long the circuit takes you depends on how much time you spend in each village, but the total cycling time (not including side trips to villages such as Guānkēng and Lǐngjiǎo, both 30 minutes from the main road) is about seven or eight hours. You could do it in two days, but taking three days makes more sense.

Some roads are hilly, but the only really tough climb is the one-hour slog from Jiānglǐng up to the Duànxīn Reservoir.

Individual cycling times from Wùyuán to various villages:

➡ **Lǐkēng** one hour

➡ **Wāngkǒu** 90 minutes

➡ **Xiǎoqǐ** 2½ hours

➡ **Guānkēng** 4½ hours

➡ **Sīkǒu** one hour

➡ **Qīnghuá** 90 minutes

In Wùyuán, numerous places rent bikes; don't forget to ask for a bike lock (车锁; *chēsuǒ*).

Around Wùyuán

Little Lǐkēng 小李坑

📶 0793 / POP 15,000

Little Lǐkēng (Xiǎo Lǐkēng) is the most popular village in the area due to its Song dynasty houses and buzzing laneways. The walk in from the car park is beautiful, despite the train line running overhead: winding, lantern-strewn river with punters offering lifts on bamboo barges, narrow footbridges dissecting the valley floor. After sunset, visitors fill the riverside lanes for chrysanthemum tea, rice wine and trinkets, snapping photos of rooftops glowing under red lanterns and old-fashioned street lamps.

Note, there is another, plain-old Lǐkēng (李坑) village in the north of the county.

◎ Sights & Activities

Walk in any direction and you will hit the countryside.

Lǐkēng's highly photogenic focal point hinges on the confluence of its two streams, traversed by the bump of the 300-year-old **Tōngjì Bridge** (通济桥; Tōngjì Qiáo) and signposted by the **Shēnmíng Pavilion** (申明亭; Shēnmíng Tíng), one of the village's signature sights, its wooden benches polished smooth with age.

Among the *báicài* (Chinese cabbage) draped from bamboo poles and chunks of cured meat hanging out in the air from crumbling, mildewed buildings, notable structures include the **Patina House** (铜录坊; Tónglù Fáng), erected during Qing times by a copper merchant, the rebuilt **old stage** (古戏台; gǔxìtái), where Chinese opera and performances are still held during festivals, and spirit walls erected on the riverbank to shield residents from the sound of cascading water. Admission to the village costs ¥60.

Dáfū Mansion HISTORIC BUILDING
(达夫大厦, Dáfū Dàshà) This former Qing governor residence is a fine example of the period. Pay special attention to the doorway and entrance gate.

🛏 Sleeping & Eating

Lǐsi Cháhàn Guesthouse GUESTHOUSE $$
(李斯察汗, Lǐsi Cháhàn; 📶 0793 737 0149; Little Lǐkēng, 小李坑; d ¥150-200; ❄ 🛜) Above the Lǐsi family tea shop is a new guesthouse featuring large, clean rooms, with TV, hot running water and village views from some of the rooms. The old couple in charge will do everything they can to make you feel comfortable.

Brook Hotel GUESTHOUSE $$
(傍溪居, Bàng Xī Jū; 📶 138 7032 7901, 138 7934 9519; limin608058@126.com; d ¥120; ❄ 🛜) The most established guesthouse in the village is on the right-hand side of Tōngjì Bridge as you walk into the village. Rooms are clean and spacious, and there are also some slightly cheaper ones in a newer build just off the river. The owner 'Linda' speaks some English and yummy meals are available on-site.

Guāngmíng Teahouse CHINESE $$
(光明茶楼, Guāngmíng Chálóu; 📶 0793 737 0999; mains ¥15-50; ❄ 🛜) The best restaurant in Little Lǐkēng is the charming Guāngmíng Teahouse. It acts as an informal thoroughfare to the best photo spot in the village, perched above the village stream. It's a lovely spot to try the local *hóng lǐyú* (red carp; 红鲤鱼). There's an English menu.

OFF THE BEATEN TRACK

WALKING WÙYUÁN'S TRAILS

Many of Wùyuán's villages are linked by time-worn **postal roads** (驿道; yìdào) that today provide hikers with the perfect excuse to explore the area's gorgeous backcountry: imagine wild azalea, wisteria and iris blooms dotting steep hills cut by cascading streams and you're off to the right start.

Most trails are difficult to navigate without help from a local, but one fabulous 8km-long, three-hour trail linking the villages of **Guānkēng** (官坑) and **Lǐngjiǎo** (岭脚) has bilingual signposts along its route, so can be done independently.

The path takes you up and over a pass, and has numerous steps, so it's not feasible if you've cycled out here.

Follow the hiking sign beside Guānkēng Fàndiàn, in Guānkēng village, and head straight upstream. After the second pavilion (near the top of the pass) turn left, then right immediately afterwards, to continue on the path to Lǐngjiǎo, from where you can catch a bus back to Wùyuán (¥20, 90 minutes, 7am, 11.30am and 1pm).

ⓘ Getting There & Around

Irregular buses travel the road past the village turn-off, from where it's a five-minute walk to the ticket office. It's easier and more reliable to catch a moto-taxi (¥40 from Wùyuán, 20 minutes) or a regular taxi.

Qīnghuá 清华
✔ 0793 / POP 40,000

Qīnghuá is the main village in Wùyuán. While there is not a lot to endear it to travellers, it's conveniently located for access to a number of the tourist villages, plus it's a handy place to stock up on supplies, including cash at the one ATM.

Laojie (老街; Old Street), which leads down to the 800-year-old **Rainbow Bridge** (彩虹桥; Cǎihóng Qiáo), is the town's most interesting street. It's also where the best restaurants are to be found.

There are a few simple guesthouses (客栈; kèzhàn) on Laojie and one or two decent business hotels, including the welcoming **Lǎojiē Kèzhàn** (老街客栈; ✔ 0793 724 2359; 355 Qinghua Laojie, 清华老街355号; s/d ¥50/60; ❊ 🛜). It has simple, spotless rooms and the manager has good local knowledge.

Qinghua Hostel (清华宾馆, Qīnghuá Bīnguǎn; ✔ 0793 724 2789; Zhengfu Lu, 镇政府路; r ¥138; ❊ 🛜) is more hotel than hostel, but nonetheless friendly and fairly new. It's next door to a supermarket and close to the famed Rainbow Bridge.

Buses leave from the turn-off into the town **to** Jǐngdézhèn(¥25, two hours, 7.20am, 8.30am and 2pm) and Wùyuán (via Sīkǒu; ¥10, 30 minutes, half-hourly 6am to 5pm).

Buses between Wùyuán and Lǐngjiǎo also stop here.

Guānkēng 官坑
✔ 0793 / POP 3500

Guānkēng is a low-key Wùyuán village set between two valleys in the north of the county. It may lack the architectural heritage of its neighbours, but the absence of tour buses more than compensates. It is best known in travel circles as the start or end point of a wonderful three-hour hike to the equally quiet village of Lǐngjiǎo.

A handful of guesthouses cater to independent travellers, and can provide information on hiking. **Guānkēng Fàndiàn** (官坑饭店; ✔ 0793 725 9588; per person ¥40; ❊ 🛜) is a friendly and welcoming guesthouse beside the arched bridge. It serves hearty hiking fare and the man of the house speaks some English.

By far the easiest and fastest way to get here is via taxi (¥100, 30 minutes) or moto-taxi (¥80 per person), which are usually waiting in the car park or on the main road. Buses from here to Wùyuán (¥22, two hours) leave at 6am, 6.40am, 7.30am and 11am.

Sīxī & Yáncūn 思溪·延村
✔ 0793 / POP 30,000

Less hectic than other parts of Wùyuán, but with a small independent travel scene and stunning natural surrounds, these charming twin villages are among the most favoured by return visitors to the county.

Sīxī and Yáncūn are quintessential Qing chic, with the prow-shaped, covered wooden **Tōngjì Bridge** (通济桥; Tōngjì Qiáo) at Sīxī's entrance, dating to the 15th century. Follow the signs to the numerous Qing dynasty residences, making sure not to miss the large **Jìngxù Hall** (敬序堂; Jìngxù Táng). A 15-minute walk back along the road, towards Sīkǒu, brings you to Yáncūn, Sīxī's more homely sibling, where you'll find yet more Qing architecture. Admission to the villages costs ¥60.

The most appealing place to stay in any of the villages around Wùyuán is **Go Home Hotel** (归去来兮, Guīqù Láixī; ☑ 0793 733 5118; Yáncūn Village, 延村; r incl breakfast ¥328-1180; ✳ ❄ 🛜). Housed in a 270-year-old former residence, this immaculately renovated boutique hotel is beautifully decorated with period wooden furniture. Lunch and dinner cost ¥50 each. No website, but you can book a room through www.ctrip.com (search for Guiqulaixi Hotel).

There are a few more typical guesthouses in Sīxī. You can also stay outside the paid area in Sīkǒu town at splendid **Wángjiā Huīyuàn Inn** (王家徽院, Wángjiā Huīyuàn; Sīkǒu town, 思口镇政府侧; d from ¥250; ✳ 🛜), a deftly re-created period mansion.

Sīkǒu is a much larger town than the more popular Sīxī and Yáncūn and buses run more regularly around the region.

To get to the villages take any Wùyuán–Qīnghuá bus (¥3, 20 minutes) and get off at Sīkǒu (思口). Motorbikes will take you the rest of the way (¥5), or just walk (3km).

Sānqīng Shān 三清山

☑ 0793

Sānqīng (三清) means 'The Three Pure Ones', and you won't find a mountain park in China more serendipitous than this triumvirate of natural majesty, believed to resemble Taoism's three most important deities. Concrete may encroach underfoot, and a cable car whir overhead, but consider the architectural feat as you hike around sheer rock face, looking out onto a forest of fantastical granite spires and a gorgeous canopy sprinkled with white rhododendron blooms.

Unlike Huáng Shān, its more famous neighbour to the north, Sānqīng Shān has a spiritual legacy and has been a place of retreat for Taoist adepts for centuries. Views are spectacular in any season, reaching a climax amid the flowering buds of late May.

The main town near the mountain park is Yùshān; this is where you'll find the train and bus station.

👁 Sights & Activities

Hiking is the activity you come for, or at least some kind of gazing into the great abyss. There are two main access points: the southern section (南部; *nán bù*) and the eastern section (东部; *dōng bù*). You can buy maps (¥5), or photograph the ones

on the signboards. Estimated hiking times from the southern-section trailhead are as follows:

➡ top of southern-section cable car: 1½ hrs

➡ top of eastern-section cable car: 3 hrs

➡ bottom of eastern-section cable car: 5 hrs

➡ Nánqīng Garden loop and back: 4 hrs.

Nánqīng Garden   MOUNTAIN

(南清苑, Nánqīng Yuàn) Sānqīng Shān's main summit area is known as the Nánqīng Garden, a looping trail that wends beneath strange pinnacles and connects the southern and eastern sections.

West Coast Trail   HIKING

(西海岸, Xī Hǎi'àn) The spectacularly exposed West Coast Trail was built into the cliff face at an average altitude of 1600m. This trail eventually leads to the secluded **Taoist Sānqīng Temple** (三清宫, Sānqīng Gōng), established during the Ming dynasty. It's one of the few Taoist temples in Jiāngxī to have survived the Cultural Revolution.

Sunshine Coast Trail   HIKING

(阳光岸, Yángguāng Àn) The Sunshine Coast Trail winds through a forest of ancient rhododendrons, sweet chestnut, bamboo, magnolia and pine, and even features a glass-floored observation platform. There are lots of steps here; take it on the way back from the temple.

🛏 Sleeping

You can sleep in three areas: on the summit, at the trailheads or in the town of Yùshān. Prices rise on weekends, when it's a good idea to reserve if you want to sleep at the trailheads or on the summit.

Fāngfāng Bīnguǎn   GUESTHOUSE $

(芳芳宾馆, ☑ 0793 220 5890, 187 7931 6629; off Renmin Dadao, 人民大道日景现代城; s/d ¥60/100; ✳ @) In the collection of simple family-run guesthouses near the Yùshān bus station, Fāngfāng is our pick thanks to that age-old combination of cleanliness, friendliness and value. Left, then second left.

International Trade Hotel   HOTEL $$

(国贸大酒店, Guómào Dàjiǔdiàn; ☑ 0793 235 3922; Renmin Beilu, 人民北路汽车站对面; r ¥218; P ✳ @) If you need to iron your fanny pack or test your new hiking shoes on faux-marble lobby floors, this smart business hotel with good-value, spacious rooms will prepare you for the challenge ahead. It's opposite the bus station.

Sānqīngshān International Resort HOTEL $$$
(三清山国际度假酒店, Sānqīngshān Guójì Dùjià
Jiǔdiàn; ☑0793 223 3333; 三清山风景名胜区
南部外双溪; tw from ¥1788; ❇🛜) Surprising-
ly luxurious hotel located at the southern
trailhead outdoes Sānqīng Shān's oft-greedy
hoteliers at every level. Wrangle the price
down and you have yourself an excellent-
value, customer-focused, amenity-stacked,
buffet-breakfast-serving oasis on the edge of
the great outdoors. Rates may be discounted
to ¥888 during off-peak periods.

Rìshàng Bīnguǎn HOTEL $$$
(日上宾馆; ☑0793 218 9377; r from ¥480) About
a 10-minute climb from Sānqīng's southern
chairlift is the welcoming, pale blue-Rìshàng,
which has a stupendous viewing deck and
neat, renovated rooms. If it's full, you won't
go wrong with the options either side.

🍴 Eating

Yùshān has the greatest variety of restaurants at competitive prices. As you ascend
the mountain, the food gets a little greasy
and overpriced.

Xīntíngjì Tǔcàiguǎn JIANGXI $$
(新廷记土菜馆; Renmin Dadao, 日景现代城
国际公寓号; mains ¥20-50; ⏱9am-9pm) The
shiny photos match the delicious offerings
at this quiet eatery near the Yùshān bus sta-
tion. Specialities include *jīnpái guōmèn tǔjī*
(金牌锅焖土鸡); free-range chicken casse-
role), *xiǎochǎo huángniúròu* (小炒黄牛肉;
spicy beef stir-fry) and *suìjiāo báiyù dòu*
(碎椒白玉豆; a simple but tasty broad-bean
dish). Turn left out of the bus station and it's
on your left, just before the crossroads.

ℹ Getting There & Away

Sānqīng Shān is accessed via the town of Yùshān
(玉山). The 11am bus from Wùyuán to Yùshān
stops at Sānqīng Shān (eastern section). The
return to Wùyuán leaves at around 7pm.

BUS
Yùshān bus station (玉山汽车站; *Yùshān
qìchēzhàn*) services:
Hángzhōu ¥105, four hours, 7.30am, 9am,
11.20am and 3.30pm
Nánchāng ¥80, four to five hours, 7.10am
and 3pm
Shànghǎi ¥145, 5½ hours, 10am
Wùyuán ¥45, 2½ hours, 7.55am and 1.20pm

TRAIN
Local bus 8 (¥1) links the train and bus stations,
but is only hourly. A motor-rickshaw costs

around ¥8. Destinations from **Yùshān train sta-
tion** (玉山火车站; Yùshān huǒchēzhàn) include
the following:
Hángzhōu K-class hard seat ¥52, four to five
hours, four morning trains (6.47am, 6.54am,
7.05m and 8.38am)
Shànghǎi South K-class hard seat/sleeper
¥75/138, seven hours, seven daily
Yīngtán K-class hard seat ¥24, two hours, six
daytime trains (8.39am to 5.10pm)

The bullet train from Chángshā to Hángzhōu
passes through the **Yùshān South train station**
(玉山火车南站; Yùshan Huǒchē Nánzhàn).
 Services include the following:
Nánchāng G-class hard seat ¥44, one hour,
13 daily
Shànghǎi Hongqiao G-class hard seat, ¥214,
2½ hours, nine daily

ℹ Getting Around

Buses (¥17, 80 minutes, 6.30am to 5.20pm) run
from Yùshān bus station to the start of both the
eastern section (东部) and southern section (
南部) – make sure you specify your destination,
as no buses link the two sections and they are at
least 20km apart. The last buses back to Yùshān
leave just after 4.30pm.
 A **cable car** (三清山索道, Sānqīng Shān
Suǒdào; one-way/return ¥70/125) leaves from
both sections. The eastern-section cable-car ride
is more spectacular, but leaves you further from
the West Coast Trail; if you're walking, the south-
ern section is a much shorter hike. Note, you can
use your return ticket on either cable car.

Lónghǔ Shān 龙虎山
☑0701

Lónghǔ Shān is billed as a natural Tao-
ist wonderland, welcoming visitors of all
ages to find 'The Way'. While the family-
centred entertainment – gentle raft rides,
climbing shows, miniature train and 4D
cinema – make passable fun, the real draw
is the park's location by a winding river,
where clusters of red sandstone peaks over-
look grazing water buffalo and solitary her-
ons. It's an easily packaged taste of the lush
Jiāngxī countryside.
 During the Song dynasty (960–1279)
Lónghǔ Shān became the centre of the
emergent Zhèngyī sect, which claimed to
represent the teachings of religious Taoism's
founder, Zhang Daoling (34–156). Together
with the Quánzhēn sect, Zhèngyī Taoism
was one of the most prominent schools of
Taoism in late imperial China, and there
were more than 100 temples and monas-

teries here before the Cultural Revolution swept into town.

Sights

The Lónghǔ Shān scenic area encompasses 200 sq km, most of which is located along the eastern bank of the Lúxī River. Entrance costs ¥150, but most people buy the **combined ticket** (¥260), which includes admission to seven sites and a raft ride, as well as transport on miniature trains (at the main entrance to Zhèngyī Temple) and shuttle buses (from Zhèngyī Temple to the Residence of the Celestial Masters). To get the most out of your visit, narrow your sightseeing to two main areas: the Residence of the Celestial Masters and Elephant's Trunk Hill.

At the main entrance are two small museums, the **Taoist Museum** (龙虎山道教博物馆, Lónghǔ Shān Dàojiào Bówùguǎn; ⊙8am-5pm) FREE, with information in Chinese only, and the **Geology Museum** (龙虎山地质博物馆, Lónghǔ Shān Dìzhí Bówùguǎn; ⊙8am-5pm) FREE, with detailed explanations of Lónghǔ Shān's formation. The dinosaur-themed **4D-cinema** (电影院, Diànyǐngyuàn; ¥25) is above the ticket office.

Residence of the Celestial Masters   TAOIST SITE
(天师府, Tiānshī Fǔ) This is the largest and best-preserved temple in the area. It was originally built in the Song dynasty, thoroughly renovated in the Qing dynasty and then again in the 1990s. The oldest building still standing is the **Sanctuary of Triple Introspection** (三省堂; Sān Xǐng Táng), which dates to 1865. To get here, walk for 15 minutes through old Shàngqīng village from the shuttle drop-off. Another 500m along Fuqian Jie (府前街) is an abandoned **Catholic church** (天主教堂; Tiānzhǔjiào Táng).

It's located about 28km from Lónghǔ Shān's main entrance. Entrance is via the ¥150 scenic area ticket, or the combined ticket (¥260).

Elephant's Trunk Hill   HILL
(象鼻山, Xiàngbí Shān) Close to Lónghǔ Shān's main entrance, this is the first stop you'll reach if you catch the **miniature train**. Here you can hike a loop past rock formations and rebuilt temples, then descend to the river from where you'll be able to spy the mountain's 2500-year-old **hanging coffins** (悬棺; *xuán guān*) on the opposite side of the bank.

Sleeping

A number of decent guesthouses at very reasonable prices are located just outside the main entrance to the ticketed scenic area.

Lónghǔ Shān Kèzhàn   GUESTHOUSE $
(龙虎山客栈; ☑0701 665 9506; 39 Xianrencheng Lu, 仙人城路39号; r with/without air-con ¥80/60; ❈ 🛜) One block back from the main entrance to the Lónghǔ Shān scenic area, this little guesthouse is clean and friendly.

Róngshèng Bīnguǎn   HOTEL $$
(荣盛宾馆, Róngshèng Bīnguǎn; ☑0701 665 7666; Xin Damen Daimian, 龙虎山新大门对面; tw from ¥168; ❈ @ 🛜) Tasteful and surprisingly sophisticated, Róngshèng is opposite the Lónghǔ Shān park entrance, on the corner.

Ask for a discount. Outside peak periods it can be discounted to ¥150.

Eating

Hotels and restaurants are conveniently based near the main entrance. There are also small restaurants inside the park, at Shàngqīng village.

Information

There are **internet cafes** (网吧; *wǎngba*) by the train station in Yīngtán.

Getting There & Away

Lónghǔ Shān is near the small city of Yīngtán (鹰潭). To get to Lónghǔ Shān from Yīngtán, take bus K2, which runs from the train station, past the **bus station** (鹰潭客运站, Yīngtán Kèyùnzhàn; Jiaotong Lu, Guìxī, 交通路贵溪) and on to the main entrance (¥3, 25 minutes, 6.15am to 7pm, every 15 minutes).

Services from Yīngtán bus station (鹰潭客运站; Yīngtán kèyùnzhàn):

Jǐngdézhèn ¥55, three hours (7.40am, 8.40am, 12.40pm and 1.50pm)

Nánchāng ¥42, two hours, hourly (7.30am to 6.15pm)

Wùyuán ¥76, 3½ hours (8.30am, 11.50am and 1.20pm)

The Hángzhōu-Changsha bullet-train line passes through the **Yīngtán north train station** (鹰潭北火车站, Yīngtán Běihuǒchēzhàn; Yingdong Dadao, Guìxī, 鷹東大道贵溪). Services include:

Chángshā G-class bullet, hard seat, ¥222, two hours, 30 daily

Nánchāng West G-class bullet ¥65, 30 minutes, 40 daily

Shànghǎi Hóngqiáo G-class bullet, hard seat, ¥276, three to 3½ hours, 22 daily

Services from Yīngtán train station (鹰潭北火车站; Yīngtán huǒchēzhàn):

Hángzhōu D-class bullet ¥148, four hours, five daily (9.17am to 3.42pm)

Hángzhōu T/K-class hard seat/sleeper ¥72/132, six to seven hours, 20 daily

Jǐngdézhèn K-class hard seat, ¥24, three hours, four daytime trains (8.32am, 10.23am, 1.17pm and 2.52pm)

Nánchāng K-class hard seat ¥24, two hours, 20 daily

Yùshān K-class hard seat ¥24, two hours, six daytime trains (6.27am to 5.56pm)

Lóngnán 龙南

📞 0797 / POP 152,000

If you have never encountered Fújiàn's famous circular *tǔlóu* (土楼; roundhouses), try Jiāngxī's equally marvellous rectangular versions. In the verdant Hakka countryside in the south of the province, there are estimates of some 370 such dwellings in Lóngnán County. These unusual structures have housed neighbouring families for generations in earthen compounds; the villages of Guānxī (关西) and Yángcūn (杨村) are the most interesting and accessible.

◉ Sights

Yànyì Wéi HISTORIC BUILDING
(燕翼围; ¥10) The fascinating, 350-year-old, four-storey-tall Yànyì Wéi is the tallest of a number of crumbling old fortified villages in the vicinity of Yángcūn. It's still lived in by villagers and you can climb all four storeys.

Wǔdāng Shān MOUNTAIN
(武当山; ¥15; ⊙8am-5.30pm) Also known as Xiǎo (little) Wǔdāng Shān, this group of weathered sandstone peaks reward an easy one-hour climb with stunning views of the surrounding subtropical forest. Not to be confused with Húběi's more famous Wǔdāng Shān.

To get to Yángcūn, take a bus (¥12.50, 1¼ hours, frequent) from the small bus station at 99 Longding Dadao (龙鼎大道99号) in Lóngnán. The bus passes Wǔdāng Shān (one hour).

Guānxī New Fort FORT
(关西新围, Guānxī Xīn Wéi; ¥10) Built in 1827 by Xu Mingjun, a wealthy lumber merchant, Guānxī New Fort is the largest and most ornate fortified village in the county. The smaller, more rundown fort just behind it is known as *lǎo wéi* (old fort) and was built by Xu's father.

COILED-DRAGON HOUSES

If you're interested in further exploring traditional Hakka dwellings – or just fancy taking the back route into Guǎngdōng province – you can catch a bus from Lóngnán's long-distance bus station to Méizhōu (梅州; ¥80, four hours, 7.20am), where you'll find China's largest cluster of *wéilóngwū* (coiled-dragon houses). From there you can catch a bus on to Yǒngdìng, to see Fújiàn's famed *tǔlóu* (土楼).

🛏 Sleeping & Eating

In Lóngnán, there are a few passable guesthouses and business hotels, especially around Binjiang Sq.

Lóngnán has a modest selection of places to eat. For cheap fare, stick to the bus-station area or near Binjiang Sq.

Fùyě Hotel BUSINESS HOTEL $
(富野酒店, Fùyě Jiǔdiàn; 500 Jinshui Dajie, 金水大道500号; r from ¥290; ▣❈🛜) This gaudy old darling of a hotel on the river is actually quite fun. As long as there isn't a conference in town you can slide across the empty banquet room in your socks. The nonsmoking rooms are pleasant enough, with some thread still left in the carpet, the beds are well presented and the bathrooms have been jazzed up. Staff don't speak English, but are enthusiastic in their efforts.

❶ Getting There & Away

Two direct trains to Lóngnán run from Nánchāng (hard seat ¥75, 7½ hours, 3.33pm and 3.47pm) while one runs from Guǎngzhōu East (hard seat ¥87, 5½ hours, 11.25am). Otherwise take a bus from Nánchāng to Gànzhōu (赣州; ¥120, 5½ hours, hourly, 7.20am to 6.50pm), where you can transfer to a Lóngnán bus (¥58, two hours, hourly until 6pm). The bus from Gànzhōu will stop at Lóngnán's long-distance bus station (长途汽车站; chángtú qìchēzhàn) before terminating at the small bus station at 99 Longding Dadao, which is 200m from Binjiang Sq (turn left).

❶ Getting Around

Local bus 1 (¥1) goes from the train station in Lóngnán, past the long-distance bus station and onto Binjiang Sq (滨江广场; Bīnjiāng Guǎngchǎng).

Húnán

POP 66 MILLION

Best Places to Eat

➡ Huǒgōngdiàn (p474)

➡ Sōnghuājiāng Jiǎoziguǎn (p474)

➡ Miss Yang Restaurant (p488)

➡ Máo Jiā Fàndiàn (p478)

Best Places to Sleep

➡ A Good Year (p488)

➡ Bājiè Youth Hostel (p482)

➡ Guìguān International Hotel (p482)

➡ Sheraton Chángshā Hotel (p474)

Why Go?

As the birthplace of Mao Zedong, Communist Party cadres might wax lyrical about the sacred standing of Húnán (湖南) in the annals of Chinese history, but it's Húnán's dramatic scenery that is the real draw.

A magnificent landscape of isolated mountain ranges and jagged, karst peaks envelops more than 80% of the province. The most astonishing example is found at the phantasmagorical Zhāngjiājiè, one of China's most surreal national parks. Here, as in other parts of the province, geological marvels thrust up majestically from green vales fed by tributaries in the fertile Yangzi River basin.

People have long made a home amid Húnán's natural wonders, taming the rocky slopes into terraces of lush fields, and their distinctive cultures live on in charming villages and towns, the most alluring being the historic riverside settlement of Fènghuáng.

When to Go
Chángshā

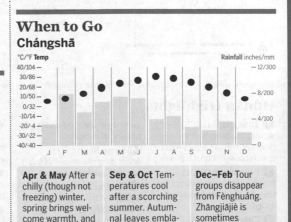

Apr & May After a chilly (though not freezing) winter, spring brings welcome warmth, and mountain flowers.

Sep & Oct Temperatures cool after a scorching summer. Autumnal leaves emblazon Zhāngjiājiè.

Dec–Feb Tour groups disappear from Fènghuáng. Zhāngjiājiè is sometimes brushed with snow.

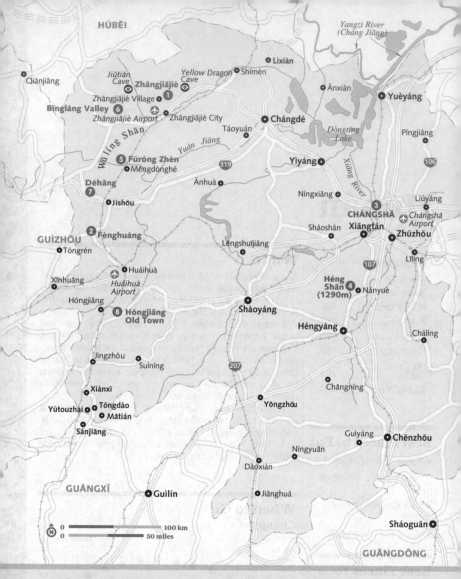

Húnán Highlights

1 Zhāngjiājiè (p480) Hiking among the otherworldly peaks of one of China's most spectacular national parks.

2 Fènghuáng (p486) Wandering this gorgeous river town at night, marvelling at its lights.

3 Chángshā (p473) Sampling authentic, chilli-laden *xiāng cài* (Húnán cuisine) in the food-loving provincial capital.

4 Héng Shān (p478) Ascending the slopes of the sacred Taoist mountain.

5 Fúróng Zhèn (p490) Sizing up the magnificent waterfall alongside this quaint old town.

6 Bīngláng Valley (p484) Exploring its magnificent 1km-long pitch-black cave before emerging into the sun.

7 Déhāng (p485) Hiking off in search of waterfalls amid the greenery of west Húnán.

8 Hóngjiāng Old Town (p489) Meandering around the old town, checking out its ancient buildings.

History

During the Ming and Qing dynasties, Húnán was one of the empire's granaries, transporting vast quantities of rice to the embattled north. By the 19th century, land shortages and feudalism caused widespread unrest among farmers and hill-dwelling minorities. These economic disparities galvanised the Taiping Rebellion in the 1850s, ensuring widespread support by the 1920s for the Chinese Communist Party (CCP) and Húnán's Mao Zedong.

ℹ Getting There & Around

Chángshā is loaded with bullet trains, heading south to Guǎngzhōu (2½ hours), north to Běijīng (six hours), east to Shànghǎi (seven hours), west to Sháoshān (25 minutes) and northwest to Xī'ān (six hours). It also has flights to every major city.

Local trains can get you around the province, although long-distance buses are more frequent and often faster. Within towns and cities, local buses cost ¥1 or ¥2. Carry exact change.

Chángshā 长沙

☑ 0731 / POP 2.5 MILLION

For three millennia, this city on the Xiāng River (湘江; Xiāng Jiāng) flourished steadily as a centre of agriculture and intellect. In the 1920s it was still so well preserved that British philosopher Bertrand Russell is said to have compared it to a medieval town, but not long after, the Sino-Japanese War and a massive fire in 1938 gave Chángshā an irreversible facelift, leaving little of its early history. These days it's a modern, energetic city, known mainly for sights relating to Mao Zedong, but with its magnolia-lined streets and riverine aspect, it's a pleasant enough stopover and provincial capital.

◉ Sights

Old City Walls &
Tiānxīn Pavilion   HISTORIC SITE
(古城墙、天心阁, Gǔchéngqiáng、Tiānxīn Gé; 3 Tianxin Lu, 天心路3号; park free, pavilion ¥32; ☺7.30am-6pm; ☐202) The old city walls, which once stretched for 9km around ancient Chángshā, were built of rammed earth in 202 BC, reinforced with stone in AD 1372 (during the Ming dynasty), damaged by the Taiping in 1852 and finally demolished in 1928, save for this imposing 251m-long section. You can enter Tiānxīn Park for free and wander around the old wall, but you have to pay to climb up on top of it, and to

PRICE RANGES

Sleeping

The following price ranges refer to a double room with bathroom.

$ less than ¥150

$$ ¥150–400

$$$ more than ¥400

Eating

The following price ranges refer to a meal for one.

$ less than ¥40

$$ ¥40–80

$$$ more than ¥80

---

visit the attractive Tiānxīn Pavilion atop it. The extant section was restored in 1983.

Tangerine Isle   PARK
(橘子洲, Júzi Zhōu; ☺24hr; ⓜ Juzizhou; FREE) The most famous of the city's parks is a 5km-long sliver of an island smack bang in the middle of the Xiāng River. A reflective 32-year-old Mao immortalised it in 'Changsha', probably his best regarded poem, after standing at its southern tip and looking west towards Yuèlù Mountain one autumn day. A towering granite bust of a youthful Chairman with flowing locks now stands at the spot – but faces in a new direction.

You can walk a circuit of the island on the pleasant riverside promenade, or catch a hop-on, hop-off sightseeing electric trolley (¥20) for the 9km round trip by the metro entrance, or rent tandem bicycles (¥30 per hour).

Húnán Provincial Museum   MUSEUM
(湖南省博物馆, Húnán Shěng Bówùguǎn; ☑0731 8451 4630; 50 Dongfeng Lu, 东风路50号; ☐136 from train station) FREE This formerly first-rate museum was undergoing a complete rebuild at the time of research and was far from completion at that time.

🛏 Sleeping

You can find basic rooms clustered around the train station, but you get what you pay for and there are better pickings further afield.

Chángshā
International Youth Hostel   HOSTEL $
(长沙国际青年旅舍, Chángshā Guójì Qīngnián Lǚshè; ☑0731 8299 0202; www.hnhostel.com; 61 Gongshang Xiang, 东风路下大垅工商巷61号;

dm ¥35-40, s/d/tw/tr ¥88/108/118/138; ❀ @ 🛜; 🖥 136 from train station) Chángshā's first youth hostel, and still its best, although rooms – simple, bright and clean – could do with freshening up. The lovely lobby is great for sitting down with a coffee or beer, and there's a backyard with table tennis and a pool table. Travel notices pinned up around the place are in Chinese only, but some staff speak a little English and are happy to help out.

The location is pleasant – tucked away on a quiet, tree-lined residential street – but out of the way. Take bus 136 from the train station and get off at Xiàdàlóng (下大垅) bus stop. Cross the road, walk along the alley called Dongfeng Ercun Xiang (东风二村巷), which is opposite the bus stop, and you'll find Gongshang Xiang behind the shops, running parallel to the main road. From Xiàdàlóng bus stop, buses 112 and 901 go to Jiefang Xilu.

Its sister hostel – **Yuèlù Mountain International Youth Hostel** (岳麓山国际青年旅舍, Yuèlù Shān Guójì Qīngnián Lǚshè; ☎ 0731 8536 8418; 50 Xinmin Lu, 新民路50号; dm/s/d ¥40/98/128; 🖥 旅1, Ⓜ Yingwanzhen) – isn't as nice, but is OK if this place is full. It's on Xinmin Lu, which is opposite the entrance to Yuèlù Mountain.

Old Street
International Youth Hostel   HOSTEL $
(古巷国际青年旅舍, Gǔxiàng Guójì Qīngnián Lǚshè; ☎ 0731 8225 3500; gxhostel@126.com; 56 Duzheng Jie, 都正街56号; dm/s/tw/d ¥45/98/108/138; ❀ @ 🛜) This small hostel, parcelled away along the restored old street of Duzheng Jie, has a fabulous location in a charming area not far from Chángshā's pulsing nightlife. The staff are friendly and speak English. From the train station, take bus 139 to the Tianxinge (天心阁) stop, which takes you close to Duzheng Jie.

★ **Sheraton Chángshā Hotel**   HOTEL $$$
(喜来登酒店, Xǐláidēng Jiǔdiàn; ☎ 0731 8488 8888; www.starwoodhotels.com; 478 Furong Zhonglu, 芙蓉中路一段478号; r from ¥750, plus 15% service charge; 🏊 ❀ @ 🛜 ❄) The 380-room Sheraton is a benchmark of luxury in Chángshā, with contemporary, fully equipped rooms and a glass-window enclosed swimming pool, among other tempting amenities and restaurants.

✕ Eating

The lanes off the major shopping street, Huangxing Lu, and on and around the nightlife hub Taiping Jie, are good for street food. Follow your nose to the stalls selling *chòu dòufu* (臭豆腐; stinky tofu), a popular local delicacy.

Breakfast here is all about *mǐfěn* (米粉; rice noodles). Almost anywhere open early will serve them, usually in a number of varieties; beef (牛肉粉; *niúròu fěn*) is popular.

★ **Sōnghuājiāng Jiǎoziguǎn**   DUMPLING $
(松花江饺子馆; 102 Wuyi Dadao, 五一大道102号; dumplings from ¥6, mains ¥30-60; ⏰ 10.30am-10pm) Not a romantic choice, this bustling eatery specialises in the mellow cuisine of northern China. Dumplings (饺子; *jiǎozi*) are the speciality and come in many varieties, including pork and chives (¥6), lamb and onion (¥8) and just pork (¥6). There are also tasty lamb kebabs (¥6) and fine beef-filled fried bread (¥8). There's a picture menu.

The dumplings are priced by the *liǎng* (两; 50g), which gets you six dumplings. You must order at least two *liǎng (èr liǎng)* of each type of dumpling and one portion is generally sufficient.

★ **Huǒgōngdiàn**   HUNAN $$
(火宫殿; ☎ 0731 8581 4228; 127 Pozi Jie, 坡子街127号; dishes ¥5-88; ⏰ 6am-2am) There's a great buzz at this landmark eatery, established in 1747 and set in and around a small templelike courtyard. Even Mao has eaten here, in 1958, and he praised the homemade *chòu dòufu* (臭豆腐; stinky tofu; ¥18). The *xiǎo chī* (小吃; snacks) menu is for those eating in the courtyard and off to one side. The *xiāngcài* (湘菜; Húnán cuisine) menu is for those seated in the back room.

ⓘ Information

Bank of China (中国银行, Zhōngguó Yínháng; 43 Wuyi Dadao, 五一大道43号) By the Civil Aviation Hotel. Has an exchange.

China Post (中国邮政, Zhōngguó Yóuzhèng; 480 Chezhan Lu, 车站路480号; ⏰ 9am-5pm) By the train station.

HSBC ATM (汇丰银行, Huìfēng Yínháng; 159 Shaoshan Lu, 韶山路159号) Twenty-four-hour ATM in Dolton Hotel lobby.

Provincial People's Hospital (省人民医院, Shěng Rénmín Yīyuàn; ☎ 0731 8227 8120; 61 Jiefang Xilu, 解放西路61号) One of the largest hospitals in the city, centrally located on Jiefang Xilu.

Public Security Bureau (PSB, 公安局, Gōng'ānjú; ☎ 0731 8887 8741; 2 Fenglin Yilu, 枫林一路2号) For visa extensions, go to this PSB about 2km west of the river. Yingwanzhen metro station is closest.

Chángshā

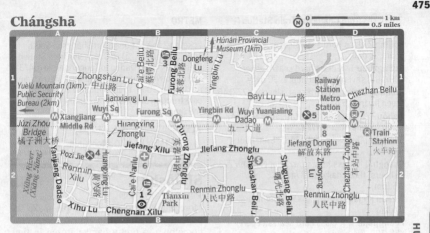

Chángshā

◎ Sights
1 Old City Walls & Tiānxīn Pavilion B2

🛏 Sleeping
2 Old Street International Youth Hostel . B2
3 Sheraton Chángshā Hotel B1

✕ Eating
4 Huǒgōngdiàn A2
5 Sōnghuājiāng Jiǎoziguǎn D1

ℹ Information
Bank of China .... (see 8)
6 Provincial People's Hospital B2

ℹ Transport
Airport Shuttle Bus .... (see 8)
7 Bus Ticket Office D1
8 Civil Aviation Administration of
China D2

ℹ Getting There & Away

AIR

Chángshā's **Huánghuā International Airport** (黄花国际机场, Huánghuā Guójì Jīchǎng; ☎0731 8479 8777) has flights to pretty much every city in China plus services to Bangkok, Seoul, Phnom Penh and Singapore. Also has daily local flights to Huáihuà (¥820, one hour) and Zhāngjiājiè (¥500, one hour).

Book tickets through www.elong.net or www.ctrip.com, or at the **Civil Aviation Administration of China** (CAAC, 中国民航售票处, Zhōngguó Mínháng Shòupiàochù; ☎0731 8411 2222; 49 Wuyi Dadao, 五一大道49号; ⊗8.30am-5.30pm) near the train station.

BUS

Chángshā has multiple bus stations, but most travellers use **South Bus Station** (汽车南站, qìchē nánzhàn) (take bus 107 or 7 from Chángshā Train Station, or bus 16 from Chángshā South Train Station) or **West Bus Station** (汽车西站, qìchē xīzhàn) (at Wangchengpo metro station). Long-distance buses also leave from both train stations.

Buy bus tickets at the bus stations, or at the **bus ticket office** (长途汽车售票处, Chángtú Qìchē Shòupiào Chù; north side, train station square) in the train station square.

Services from South Bus Station):

Fènghuáng ¥134, five hours, four daily (9am to 3.40pm)

Guìlín ¥144, seven hours, 3.40pm

Héng Shān ¥46, three hours, hourly 8am to 5.20pm

Héngyáng ¥60, two hours, hourly 7.50am to 6.20pm

Huáihuà ¥105, six hours, hourly 10.30am to 3pm

Nánchāng ¥118, five hours, one daily (8.30am)

Shànghǎi sleeper ¥326, 16 hours, 5pm

Sháoshān ¥32, 1½ hours, half-hourly 8am to 5.30pm

Services from West Bus Station:

Fènghuáng ¥145, five hours, eight daily (9am to 5.20pm)

Jíshǒu ¥136, 4½ hours, regular from 8.30am to 7.10pm

Zhāngjiājiè ¥119, four hours, hourly 8.20am to 6.30pm

TRAIN

Both train stations are connected to the metro. Bullet trains leave from **Chángshā South Train Station** (长沙南站, Chángshā Nánzhàn; Huahou Lu, 花候路).

Services from **Chángshā Train Station** (长沙
火车站, Chángshā huǒchēzhàn):

Běijīng Z-class hard seat/sleeper ¥190/334, 14
hours, 11 daily

Guǎngzhōu T/K-class hard seat/sleeper
¥99/193, seven to eight hours, 30 daily

Huáihuà T/K-class hard seat/sleeper ¥72/146,
seven hours, 15 daily

Jíshǒu T/K-class hard seat/sleeper ¥75/142,
seven to nine hours, five daily

Shànghǎi D-class bullet ¥258, seven hours,
10.35am

Shànghǎi K-class hard seat/sleeper ¥149/273,
15 hours, three daily (12.37am, 6.36pm,
9.53pm)

Wǔhàn K-class hard seat ¥54, four hours,
10 daily

Zhāngjiājiè T/K-class hard seat/sleeper
¥55/109, 5½ hours, six daily

Services from Chángshā South Train Station:

Běijīng West G-class bullet ¥649, 5¾ to seven
hours, 16 daily (7.30am to 4pm)

Guǎngzhōu South G-class bullet ¥314, 2½
hours, every 10 minutes (7am to 9.15pm)

Huáihuà South G-class bullet ¥153, 100
minutes, regular

Shànghǎi Hóngqiáo G-class bullet ¥478, five
hours, regular

Sháoshān South G-class bullet 2nd/1st class
¥31/51, 25 minutes, regular from 8.10am to
6.45pm

Shēnzhèn North G-class bullet ¥389, 2½
hours, half-hourly 7am to 8.30pm

Wǔhàn G-class bullet ¥165, 1½ hours, half-
hourly 7.30am to 9.58pm

Xī'ān G-class bullet ¥590, six hours, nine daily
(8.20am to 4.32pm)

ⓘ Getting Around

TO/FROM THE AIRPORT

Huánghuā International Airport is 26km from the
city centre. **Airport shuttle buses** (机场巴士,
jīchǎng bāshì; Wuyi Dadao, 五一大道; ¥15.50)
depart from the CAAC office on Wuyi Dadao
near the train station, every 15 minutes between
5.20am and 10.30pm, and take 40 minutes.

Local bus 114 (¥3, 70 minutes, 6.30am to
6.30pm) also links the train station to the airport.

A taxi from the city centre is about ¥90.

The eagerly anticipated Maglev (磁浮; cífú;
magnetic levitation train) was due to start operating by the time you read this, whooshing passengers from the airport to South Train Station
in a mere 10 minutes.

BUS

Local buses cost ¥1 or ¥2 per trip. Carry exact
change.

METRO

Handy Line 2 of Chángshā's metro (地铁; dìtiě;
tickets ¥2 to ¥5) goes from Chángshā South
Train Station (p475) to Chángshā Train Station
then along Wuyi Dadao to Tangerine Isle (p473)
and on to West Bus Station (p475). Metro trains
run from 6.30am to 10.30pm. Line 1 is under
construction and may be operating by the time
you read this.

TAXI

Taxi flag fall is ¥8; ¥10 after 10pm.

Sháoshān 韶山

☑ 0732 / POP 120,000

More than three million people make the
pilgrimage each year to Mao Zedong's rural
hometown, a pretty hamlet frozen in time
130km southwest of Chángshā. The swarms
of young and old drop something to the tune
of ¥1.8 billion annually in Sháoshān. Mao
statues alone are such big business that each
must pass inspection by no fewer than five
experts checking for features, expression,
hairstyle, costume and posture. The 6m-high
bronze statue of Mao erected in 1993 in Mao
Zedong Sq is considered a model example.

Sháoshān can be easily done as a day trip,
especially with the advent of the high-speed
train from Chángshā, so there's little reason
to spend the night here.

⊙ Sights

Sháoshān is in two parts: the modern town
with the train and bus stations, and the original village about 5km away, where all the
sights cluster. Only a handful of the popular
sights have a genuine connection to Mao.

The minibus from town will drop you on
the main road by the village, a few hundred
metres from Mao's former residence; cross
the small river to the left of the road. You'll
then see **Mao Zedong Square** (with its Mao
statue) to your right, but turn left to reach
Mao's former residence.

Relic Hall of Mao Zedong MUSEUM
(毛泽东遗物馆, Máo Zédōng Yíwùguǎn; ⊙9am-
4.30pm) FREE This museum includes everyday artefacts used by the Great Helmsman,
clothing he wore and photos from his life; it
benefits from good English captions.

Sháo Peak MOUNTAIN
(韶峰, Sháo Fēng; incl cable car ¥80; ⊙8.30am-
5pm) This cone-shaped mountain is visible
from the village. On the lower slopes is the
forest of stelae, stone tablets engraved

with Mao's poems. You can hike to the summit, where there's a **lookout pavilion**; this takes about an hour.

Dripping Water Cave   PARK
(滴水洞, Dī Shuǐ Dòng; ¥50; ⊙8am-5.30pm) Mao secluded himself here for 11 days in June 1966, 3km outside of Sháoshān village, to contemplate the start of the Cultural Revolution. His retreat was actually a low-slung, cement and steel bunker (not the cave, which was a few kilometres away). Members of the Mao clan are entombed nearby.

Mao Zedong Memorial Museum   MUSEUM
(毛泽东同志纪念馆, Máo Zédōng Tóngzhì Jiniànguǎn; ⊙9am-4.30pm) FREE Exiting Mao's home, turn left and walk straight on to Mao Zedong Sq where, on your left, you'll see the entrance to this museum, which celebrates Mao's life through paintings and old photos, assisted with decent English captions.

Former Residence of
Mao Zedong   HISTORIC SITE
(毛泽东故居, Máo Zédōng Gùjū; ⊙8.30am-5pm) FREE Surrounded by lotus ponds and rice paddies, this modest mud-brick house is like millions of other country homes except that Mao was born here in 1893. By most accounts, his childhood was relatively normal, though he tried to run away at age 10. He returned briefly in 1921 as a young revolutionary and firebrand. On view are some original furnishings, photos of Mao's parents and a small barn. No photography allowed inside.

HÚNÁN SHÁOSHĀN

MAO: THE GREAT HELMSMAN

Mao Zedong was born in the village of Sháoshān in 1893, the son of 'wealthy' peasants. Mao worked beside his father on the 8-hectare family farm from age six and was married by 14.

At 16, he convinced his father to let him attend middle school in Chángshā. In the city, Mao discovered Sun Yatsen's revolutionary secret society. When the Qing dynasty collapsed that year, Mao joined the republican army but soon quit, thinking the revolution was over.

At the Húnán County No 1 Teachers' Training School, Mao began following the Soviet socialism movement. He put an ad in a Chángshā newspaper 'inviting young men interested in patriotic work to contact me', and among those who responded were Liu Shaoqi, who would become president of the People's Republic of China (PRC), and Xiao Chen, who would be a founding member of the Chinese Communist Party (CCP).

Mao graduated in 1918 and went to work as an assistant librarian at Peking University, where he befriended more future major CCP figures. By the time he returned to teach in Chángshā, Mao was active in communist politics. Unlike orthodox Marxists, Mao saw peasants as the lifeblood of the revolution. The CCP was formed in today's Xīntiāndì area in Shànghǎi in 1921, and soon included unions of peasants, workers and students.

In April 1927, following Kuomintang leader Chiang Kaishek's attack on communists, Mao was tasked with organising what became the 'Autumn Harvest Uprising'. Mao's army scaled Jǐnggāng Shān, on the border with Jiāngxī province, to embark on a guerrilla war. The campaign continued until the Long March in October 1934, a 9600km retreat that ended up in Yán'ān in north Shǎnxī province. Mao emerged from the Long March as the CCP leader.

Mao forged a fragile alliance with the Kuomintang to expel the Japanese, and from 1936 to 1948 the two sides engaged in betrayals, conducting a civil war simultaneously with WWII. Mao's troops eventually won, and the PRC was established on 1 October 1949.

As chairman of the PRC, Mao embarked on radical campaigns to repair his war-ravaged country. In the mid-1950s he began to implement peasant-based and decentralised socialist developments. The outcome was the ill-fated Great Leap Forward in the late 1950s and the chaos of the Cultural Revolution (1966–76).

China saw significant gains in education, women's rights and average life expectancy under Mao's rule; however, by most estimates, between 40 and 70 million people died during that era of change, mainly from famine. Five years after Mao's death, Deng Xiaoping famously announced Mao had been 70% right and 30% wrong in an effort, some say, to tear down Mao's cult of personality. Yet today, Mao remains revered as the man who united the country, and he is still commonly referred to as the 'Great Leader', 'Great Teacher' and 'supremely beloved Chairman'. His image hangs everywhere – in public places, schools, taxis, restaurants and living rooms – but exactly what he symbolises now is the question that China grapples with today.

🛏 Sleeping

With the advent of the high-speed train connection from Chángshā, there is even less need to overnight here. Nondescript hotels with rooms for around ¥140 after discounts are close to the bus station in the new town. In the village itself, touts are happy to lead you to a *nóngjiālè* (农家乐), a local family's guesthouse.

Máo Jiā Fàndiàn   HOTEL $
(毛家饭店; ☑ 0731 5568 5132; r from ¥160) Has huge rooms facing onto an overgrown courtyard.

Sháoshān Bīnguǎn   HOTEL $$
(韶山宾馆; ☑ 0731 5568 5262; 16 Guyuan Lu, 故园路16号; s & d ¥468, plus 10% service charge; ❋ @) The rooms here are clean and bright – four-star standard issue. You're paying for location and the fact that Mao and various CCP bigwigs slept in the building next door in June 1959.

🍴 Eating

Restaurants are all over the village, each and every one serving Mao's favourite dish, *Máo jiā hóngshāoròu* (毛家红烧肉; Mao family red-braised pork) from around ¥45 and up. It's almost mandatory to partake.

★ Máo Jiā Fàndiàn   HUNAN $$
(毛家饭店; Sháoshān Village, 韶山; mains ¥25-65; ⏱ 6am-9pm) The best-known restaurant in the village was opened in 1987 by business-savvy octogenarian Madam Tang, who used to live in the house opposite Mao, but who now owns a restaurant empire with more than 300 outlets worldwide. *Máo Zédōng hóngshāoròu* (毛泽东红烧肉; Mao's favourite braised pork belly; ¥58) takes pride of place as first dish on the menu.

ℹ Getting There & Away

BUS
Buses (¥32, 1½ hours) from Chángshā South Bus Station terminate at **Sháoshān Bus Station** (韶山汽车站, Sháoshān Qìchēzhàn; Yingbin Lu, 迎宾路), where you need to transfer to a minibus (¥2.50 one way, ¥10 hop-on, hop-off) for the village, 5km away. Minibuses also shuttle between the sights, but it's nicer just to walk around once you're there.

The last bus back to Chángshā from the bus station leaves at 5.30pm.

TRAIN
The new fast-train service (2nd/1st class ¥31/51) zips regularly to Sháoshān South Train Station (韶山南站; Sháoshān Nánzhàn) from Chángshā South Train Station between 8.10am and 6.45pm, making it the fastest way to reach Sháoshān. The journey takes a mere 25 minutes. The last train back to Chángshā departs at 9.26pm.

ℹ Getting Around

A tourist minibus (中巴; ¥10) lets you hop on and off at the key sights with one ticket from 7am to 6pm. Pick it up in front of sights and the Sháoshān Bīnguǎn. Expect to pay ¥100 for a taxi to take you around. Local minibuses (¥2.50) also take you to the sights from Sháoshān South Train Station; a taxi will cost you around ¥20.

Héng Shān   衡山
☑ 0734

About 130km south of Chángshā rises the southernmost of China's five sacred Taoist mountains – Héng Shān – to which emperors came to make sacrifices to heaven and earth. The ancients called it Nányuè (南岳; Southern Mountain), a name it now shares with the town at its base. The imperial visits left a legacy of Taoist temples and ancient inscriptions scattered amid gushing waterfalls, dense pine forests and terraced fields cut from lush canyons. Bring extra layers, as the weather can turn quickly and the summit is often cold and wet.

◉ Sights & Activities

Turn right out of the main bus station to reach the *páifāng* (牌坊), a decorative stone archway, and a focal point in town.

Walk through the *páifāng* to reach the tourist centre (1km; follow signs for Zhùróng Peak) and the town's temples, all of which are also signposted.

Héng Shān   MOUNTAIN
(衡山) Seventy-two peaks spanning 400km comprise Héng Shān, but most visitors focus on **Zhùróng Peak** (祝融峰, Zhùróng Fēng; ¥120), rising 1290m above sea level.

The lung- and knee-busting, 13km ascent up winding paths, steep staircases and, in places, a road busy with tourist shuttle buses, takes around four hours one way, although it can fill the best part of a day if you take in the many temples en route. Alternatively, tourist buses, or a combination of bus and cable-car, can ferry you almost the whole way up in a sedentary posture.

If you want to take the bus, buy the bus ticket (车票; chē piào; ¥80 return, including cable car), along with your entrance ticket (门票; mén piào; ¥120) on the 2nd floor of the modern tourist centre, where you can also store luggage (¥10 per bag) and pick up a free leaflet with a map (地图; *dìtú*) on it. Buses depart directly from here to the mountain's **halfway point** (半山亭; Bànshān Tíng; 15 minutes). From there, you can either take the **cable car** (横山索道, suǒdào; return trip included with bus ticket) to **Nántiānmén** (南天门; five minutes), or change to another bus. From Nántiānmén, it's a 30-minute hike to Zhùróng Peak.

Note, the mountain is open 24 hours, but the buses and cable car only run until around 6pm. It's worth packing a waterproof jacket, although you can buy plastic ponchos (¥10) from hawkers.

If you decide to hike up the mountain (a wise choice, as you'll miss most of the temples if you take the bus), it's nicer to start up the tree-lined road 300m east of the tourist centre marked by the stone **Shènglì Archway** (胜利坊; Shènglì Fāng). This road leads to another entrance, where you can pay admission, and then to a tranquil path that winds 5km past lakes, waterfalls and streams in **Fànyīn Valley** (梵音谷; Fànyīn Gǔ), almost to the cable car departure point at Bànshān Tíng. Along the way, you can stop to see the colourful figures of Taoist and Buddhist scripture on display in **Shénzhōu Temple** (神州祖庙; Shénzhōu Zǔmiào), the grand and dignified **Nanyue Martyrs Memorial Hall** (南岳忠烈祠; Nányuè Zhonglièci), dedicated to the anti-Japanese resistance, and a **stele** inscribed with a dedication from Kuomintang leader Chiang Kaishek celebrating the pine forest. Before you jump on the cable car, take a break at **Xuándōu Guàn** (玄都观), an active Taoist temple. The couplet carved at the entry reminds weary climbers that the path of righteousness is long, so don't give up halfway through!

The next 4.5km up to Nántiānmén frequently takes the busy road and scattered staircases, but there are plenty more inspiring temples along the way. Once you reach Nántiānmén, it's a chilly (outside of July and August) 30-minute ascent to the peak – you can rent coats (¥20) by the cable car station.

At the top is **Zhù Róng Palace** (祝融殿; Zhù Róng Diàn), an iron-tiled, stone structure built for Zhu Rong, an ancient official who devised a method of striking stones to create sparks. After his death, he became revered as the god of fire.

Nányuè Temple
TAOIST, BUDDHIST

(南岳大庙, Nányuè Dàmiào; ¥60; ⏰7.30am-5.30pm) This huge Taoist and Buddhist temple originally dates to the Tang dynasty and was moved from Héng Shān summit to its foot in the Sui dynasty and then rebuilt many times, most recently in the Qing dynasty. Each carved panel in the main pavilion's balustrade tells a legend of one of Héng Shān's peaks. Its north gate is opposite the tourist centre.

Zhùshèng Temple
BUDDHIST TEMPLE

(祝圣寺, Zhùshèng Sì; 67 Dong Jie, 东街67号; ⏰5am-6pm) **FREE** A 10-minute walk east of Nányuè Temple, this Zen (Chan; 禅) Buddhist temple, with an attractive stone carved entranceway, dates as far back as the Tang dynasty. Outside, on Dong Jie, you can watch carpenters making wooden Buddha statues for the various temples in town.

🛏 Sleeping & Eating

The cheapest hotels can be found near Nányuè Bus Station. On the lower slopes of the mountain, basic hotels line the road at various places, while some places exist higher up on the mountain, for those who want to catch the sunrise.

Nányuè has more than its share of restaurants. Zhurong Lu, the road that Nányuè Telecom Hotel is on, is a good choice for a variety of eateries. Accommodation places cook up meals on the mountain, although they can be pricey (but the vegetarian meals at Zǔshī Temple (p480) are decent value).

🛏 In Town

Auspicious Margin Hotel
HOTEL $

(吉缘宾馆, Jíyuán Bīnguǎn; ☎187 1149 7187; 338 Hengshan Lu, 衡山路338号; r ¥70-100; ✴@🛜) Opposite the bus station, this simple place has a slightly bizarre name and a variety of room choices, all with air-con, TV, bathroom and wi-fi.

Nányuè Telecom Hotel
HOTEL $$

(南岳电信宾馆, Nányuè Diànxin Bīnguǎn; ☎153 0734 2269; www.nydxhotel.com; 173 Zhurong Lu, 祝融路173号; s/tr/ste ¥228/248/578, d ¥198-268; ✴@🛜) This large hotel has comfortable, smart twins and doubles and a good restaurant, serving up some tasty dishes. Turn right out of the bus station, left through the *páifāng* (decorative stone archway) and it's on your left.

Cohere Hotel
HOTEL $$$

(枕岳楼大酒店, Zhěnyuèlóu Dàjiǔdiàn; ☎0734
539 8888; 8 Jinsha Lu, 金沙路8号; s/d/ste
¥688/888/1088; P👤❄@📶🏊) The nicest ho-
tel in Nányuè is this attractive health resort
that doesn't serve soda in the lobby bar. It has
everything else you might need though – foot
massages, gym, pool, roof garden, ping-pong
room, three restaurants and an ATM. Rooms
discounted by 40% in slow periods; another
reason to avoid the peak holiday crush.

🏕 On the Mountain

Zǔshī Temple
GUESTHOUSE $$

(祖师殿, Zǔshī Diàn; near Nántiānmén, 南天门附
近; d ¥348; @) The rooms in this Taoist temple are spartan for sure, but the views are
magic and vegetarian rice meals are served
up throughout the day. It's a five-minute
walk from the cable-car station by Nántiānmén – turn left as you exit the cable car.

Wàngrì Tái Jiēdàizhàn
HOTEL $$

(望日台接待站, Wàngrì Tái Jiēdàizhàn; ☎0734
566 3188; Wàngrì Tái; r from ¥360; 📶) The moun-
tain's highest accommodation, this place is
just a 10-minute walk below Zhùróng Peak
(up to your right as you are climbing), and
has small but modern twins with air-con-
heaters, TV, bathroom and wi-fi. Cooked
meals also available (mains ¥30 to ¥60).

ℹ Information

Bank of China (中国银行, Zhōngguó Yínháng;
270 Hengshan Lu, 衡山路270号; ⏰9am-5pm)
Just past the *páifāng* (decorative arch), this
branch changes money and has a 24-hour ATM.
Tourist Centre (旅客服务中心, Lǚkè Fùwù
Zhōngxīn; Yanshou Lu, 延寿路; ⏰7am-5.30pm)
Tourist leaflets and maps are available at this
modern tourist centre, where you can also
store luggage.

ℹ Getting There & Away

Very regular bullet trains from Chángshā South
Station (2nd/1st class ¥65/100, 29 minutes,
7.11am to 9pm) stop at Héng Shān West Station
(衡山西站; Héng Shān Xīzhàn), 10km from
Nányuè town centre.

Returning to Chángshā, bullet trains leave
Héng Shān West Station roughly half-hourly
from 9.09am to 9.09pm; trains take 34 minutes
in this direction. You can buy tickets at a **train
ticket office** (火车票代售, huǒchē piàodàishòu;
☎0734 568 2222; 167 Zhurong Lu, 祝融路167
号; commission per ticket ¥5; ⏰7.40am-9pm)
near the *páifāng* – walk through the *páifāng*, and
it's on your left (on the way into town).

Buses from Chángshā arrive at Nányuè Bus
Station, which has 12 buses a day back to Cháng-
shā (¥42, three hours, 7.50am to 4.30pm).

ℹ Getting Around

Local buses wait at the train-station car park to
take passengers to Nányuè (¥6). They will drop
you at a small local bus station, called **Zhōngxīn
Zhàn** (中心站), which is diagonally opposite
the main **Nányuè Bus Station** (南岳汽车站;
Nányuè Qìchēzhàn).

Zhāngjiājiè
张家界

☑0744 / POP 1.7 MILLION

Rising from the subtropical and temperate
forests of northwest Húnán, Zhāngjiājiè has
a concentration of quartzite-sandstone for-
mations found nowhere else in the world.
Some 243 peaks and more than 3000 karst
pinnacles and spires dominate the scenery
in this Unesco-protected park. If caught in
the right light or when the early-morning
mountain mist rolls in around them, the ef-
fect is otherworldly.

For thousands of years, this was a re-
mote land known mainly to three minority
peoples: Tujia, Miao and Bai. Today more
than 20 million visitors come here every year.
It is also home to more than 3000 distinct
plant species as well as diverse fauna. You'll
see lots of macaques on the main trails (re-
member, they are wild so don't feed them),
while endangered species such as the Chi-
nese giant salamander, Chinese water deer
and the elusive clouded leopard (only their
tracks have been seen) lurk deep in the park.

⊙ Sights

⊙ The National Park

Wǔlíngyuán Scenic &
Historic Interest Area
NATIONAL PARK

(武陵源风景区, Wǔlíngyuán Fēngjǐngqū; adult/
student ¥248/160) The national park's official
name is the Wǔlíngyuán Scenic & Historic
Interest Area, but almost everyone refers
to it simply as Zhāngjiājiè, the name of one
section of the park.

The park, covering a vast 264 sq km, is di-
vided into three main areas: the **Zhāngjiājiè**,
Tiānzǐ Shān and **Suǒxī Valley** scenic areas.

Zhāngjiājiè is also the name of the city (张
家界市; Zhāngjiājiè Shì) 30km south of the
park, and the village (张家界村; Zhāngjiājiè
Cūn) by the 'Forest Park' entrance.

There are access points on all sides of the
park, but most enter from the south, passing

Zhāngjiājiè

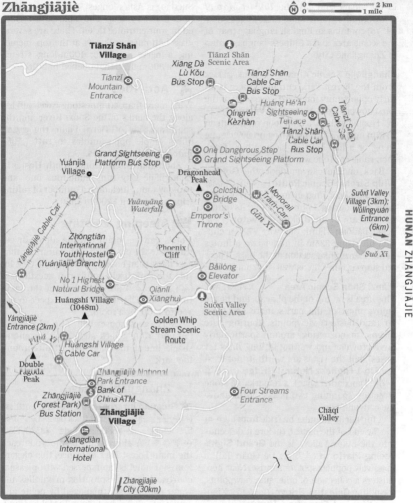

through Zhāngjiājiè village to the Zhāngjiā-jiè National Park entrance (张家界公园门票站; Zhāngjiājiè Gōngyuán *ménpiàozhàn*), more commonly called Forest Park (森林公园; Sēnlín Gōngyuán). Otherwise, many enter from the east through the less spectacular Wǔlíngyuán entrance (武陵源门票站; Wǔlíngyuán *ménpiàozhàn*).

Organised tours to the park and **Jiǔtiān Cave** (九天洞, Jiǔtiān Dòng; ¥76; ☺8am-6pm) often include a rafting trip (漂流; *piāoliú*), or you can join a tour and just do the rafting trip. While good white-water rafting is possible northwest of Zhāngjiājiè near the Húběi border, you'll have to make spe-

cial arrangements for the equipment and transport.

Most rivers are pretty tame, so don't expect great thrills, but the scenery is fantastic. The actual rafting usually lasts about four hours, with about the same amount of time taken up in travel to and from the launch area.

A simply staggering admission fee includes ¥3 compulsory insurance and buys a ticket that is valid for two days. It must be used on consecutive days, and thumb prints are taken at the entrance, so tickets can't be resold or passed on. There are admission fees to some other sights within the park as well. Available from the ticket office, and hotels in the village and city, the *Tourist Map of Wulingyuan Scenic Zone* (武陵源景区导游图; ¥5) contains an English-language map of the scenic area and a Chinese-language map of Zhāngjiājiè City.

Zhāngjiājiè Scenic Area   NATIONAL PARK

From the 'Forest Park' entrance, there is an early opportunity for a bird's-eye view of the karst towers from **Huángshí Village** (黄石寨; Huángshízhài), a 3km loop on a plateau 1048m up. It's a two-hour slog up 3878 stone steps, or a half-hour by electric bus (free), then cable car (one way ¥67).

Back on the canyon floor, the **Golden Whip Stream Scenic Route** (金鞭溪精品游览线; Jīnbiānxī Jīngpǐn Yóulǎnxiàn) is a flat path meandering 5.7km east along its namesake stream to the **Báilóng Elevator** (白龙天梯; Báilóng Tiāntī; one way ¥72), a cliffside lift rising 335m in under two minutes to the Tiānzǐ Shān section of the park. There are steps up the cliff as well (one hour).

Tiānzǐ Shān Scenic Area   NATIONAL PARK

This area is on top of the plateau, and hence enjoys most of the park's more spectacular (and busiest) viewpoints. Touring here means manoeuvring around particularly large crowds (and waiting in long lines for buses), but the vistas are worth it; not least the **No 1 Highest Natural Bridge** (天下第一桥; Tiānxiàdìyī Qiáo), a remarkable stone structure spanning two peaks, 357m above the canyon floor.

A further 30-minutes bus ride from here, at the far end of the plateau (before it descends into the Suǒxī Valley), is the **Grand Sightseeing Platform** (大观台; Dà Guān Tái), a massively popular spot for sunrise. Near here clusters a collection of other fine viewpoints, including **Celestial Bridge** (仙人桥; Xiānrén Qiáo) and **Emperor's Throne** (天子座; Tiānzǐ Zuò). A cable car (索道; *suǒdào*; one way ¥67) can whisk you down into the Suǒxī Valley, or you can hike down then take a cute **monorail tram-car** (电车; *diànchē*; one way ¥52) along a short stretch of the valley.

Zhāngjiājiè City

Tiānmén Mountain   MOUNTAIN

(天门山, Tiānmén Shān; ¥258; 8am-4.30pm) Visible from anywhere in Zhāngjiājiè City, this distinctive mountain range features **Tiānmén Dòng** (天门洞), a prominent keyhole cut through the mountainside. The seriously lengthy 7km-long **Tiānmén Mountain Cable Car** (天门山索道; Tiānmén Shān

Suǒdào) is Asia's longest, and takes half an hour to hoist you up. The cable car is included in your entrance ticket. There are several glass-bottomed walkways at the top, including a nerve-shredding 100m-long stretch over a 300m drop that opened in 2016.

Activities

With more than 40 limestone caves hidden along the banks of the Suǒxī River and the southeast side of Tiānzǐ Shān, the region offers ample opportunities to **raft** (漂流; *piāoliú*) and tour **caves**.

Zhōngtiān International Youth Hostel in Zhāngjiājiè City runs numerous one- and two-day tours, including a number of rafting trips (per person ¥200 to ¥500).

Sleeping & Eating

Hotels can be found outside all main entrances to the park, although, naturally, they cost more than hotels in Zhāngjiājiè City. Inside the park itself, family-run guesthouses (客栈; *kèzhàn*) are dotted along the main road in the Tiānzǐ Shān area. Expect to pay ¥50 to ¥100 for a room.

Every guesthouse will also do meals (around ¥30). Snack stalls and restaurant shacks line all the main hiking trails around the park.

Zhāngjiājiè Village

★ Guìguān International Hotel   HOTEL $$$

(桂冠国际酒店, Guìguān Guójì Jiǔdiàn; 0744 571 2999; d ¥680-1280, ste ¥3380-3980;) A short walk before you reach the main Forest Park entrance, this elegant four-star hotel is interspersed with pleasant courtyard gardens sprouting magnolias and water features, and managed by polite and courteous staff. The most affordable standard rooms can come down to ¥380, which is a steal, although rooms with mountain view will set you back more.

Zhāngjiājiè City

★ Bājiè Youth Hostel   HOSTEL $

(八戒青年旅舍, Bājiè Qīngnián Lǚshě; 0744 829 9577; Dayong Fucheng, Jiefang Lu, 大庸府城解放路; dm ¥40, s & d ¥98-128, tr/q ¥168/198;) The nearby bars can get noisy at night, but this hostel in Zhāngjiājiè City has a lovely atmosphere, with well kept rooms, pool table, ping pong and a quiet library. Rooms are smart and comfortable and staff are helpful, although they're more used to

ZHĀNGJIĀJIÈ IN TWO DAYS

If you're stuck for ideas, the following mini-itinerary takes in all three of the park's main zones, and can be done leisurely in two days, or in one day at a push.

Enter the park at the **Zhāngjiājiè National Park entrance**, more commonly known as **Forest Park**. Follow the **Golden Whip Stream Scenic Route**, an easy 5.7km path along the canyon floor, which leads to the **Bǎilóng Elevator**. Before you reach the elevator, though, take the steps up to your left at a point called **Qiānlǐ Xiāng-huì** (千里相会), about one hour from where you started.

It's a tough one-hour climb to the top (you're now in the Tiānzǐ Shān Nature Reserve), from where you can follow a short path to various viewpoints, including the famous **No 1 Highest Natural Bridge**. From here you can either hop on one of the free tourist buses, or walk along the main road (20 minutes) to Zhōngtiān International Youth Hostel, where you can either stop for the night, or just for lunch or a drink. Either way, don't forget to check out the path behind the hostel, which accesses two stunning viewpoints.

The hostel is right beside **Wàng Qiáo Tái** (望桥台) bus stop. From here, take a free bus about 30 minutes further up the mountain to the bus stop for the **Grand Sight-seeing Platform**, and find a rarely taken trail, which starts near a place called **One Dangerous Step** (一步难行; *Yī Bù Nán Xíng*). Follow this cliff-hugging trail through dripping-wet forest and past numerous small waterfalls, until, after about an hour, you reach a small rural hamlet where, if it's getting late, you can stay the night in the rustic family guesthouse **Qíngrén Kèzhàn** (p484). Or turn left to follow the lane back up to the main road where you can pick up another free bus, at **Xiāng Dà Lù Kǒu** (湘大路口) bus stop, to the terminus at the **Tiānzǐ Shān cable car station** (天子山索道站; Tiānzǐ Shān suǒdàozhàn).

It's ¥67 to descend in the cable car. Alternatively, follow the stepped path down (about one hour – the views are fabulous in places). At the bottom (you're now in the Suǒxī Valley area) you can take the **monorail tram-car** (¥52 one way, 10 minutes) or walk another 20 minutes to a bus depot. From the depot you can either take a free bus 10km to the Wǔlíngyuán park entrance (武陵源门口; Wǔlíngyuán *ménkǒu*), from where buses head back to Zhāngjiājiè City (¥12, 45 minutes), or turn right to get back to the path where you began your hike. After a few hundred metres you'll reach the bottom of the Bǎilóng Elevator before continuing for about 90 minutes along the Golden Whip Stream Scenic Route again, back to the Zhāngjiājiè entrance.

dealing with Chinese guests. From the airport, take bus 4 to the Dayong Fucheng stop (大庸府城) and climb the steps to the hostel.

From the train station, hop on bus 6 to the Dayong Fucheng stop. There's another branch (p484) within the National Forest Park itself, located in Dīngxiángróng village (丁香榕村).

Zhōngtiān International Youth Hostel
HOSTEL **$**

(中天国际青年旅舍, Zhōngtiān Guójì Qīngnián Lǚshè; ☑ 0744 832 1678; 4th fl, Zhōngtiān Bldg, cnr Ziwu Lu & Beizheng Lu, 子午路和北正路街角, 中天大厦4楼; dm from ¥40, tw & d from ¥138; ❄@🛜) In an anonymous office block, this OK hostel has a rooftop garden, a small bar and sofa-strewn area for sitting in. Rooms are only passable though and seriously need a refurb. Helpful staff speak some English, which is a plus, and the claypot rice meals (¥15 to ¥20), delivered from outside, are not bad.

You can have luggage delivered to its branch inside the park for ¥20. It also runs day trips, including rafting. To get here, take bus 6 (¥2) from outside Zhāngjiājiè Central Bus Station to Lieshi Gongyuan (烈士公园) bus stop, then take bus 3 (¥2) to Beizheng Lu (北正路) and the Zhōngtiān Building will be up on your left. Go down the side of the building and take the crummy lift to the 4th floor.

🛏 The National Park

Zhōngtiān International Youth Hostel (Yuánjiājiè branch)
HOSTEL **$**

(中天国际青年旅舍, 袁家界店, Zhōngtiān Guójì Qīngniánlǚshè, Yuánjiājièdiàn; ☑ 0744 571 3568; Wang Qiao Tai bus stop, Yuánjiājiè, 望桥台 袁家界; dm ¥50, d from ¥150, q ¥260; ❄) This quiet hostel is a good choice within the park. Rooms are rather musty (everywhere's musty up here), but are clean and tidy. There's not much English spoken, but the food menu (mains ¥15 to ¥35), and notices around the hostel, are all in English. Air-con is an extra ¥20.

A path behind the hostel leads to two stunning viewpoints, while about 50m beyond the hostel are steps leading down into the canyon below.

The easiest and quickest way to get here is to enter the park through the Tiānzǐ Shān entrance (天子山门票站; Tiānzǐshān *mén-piàozhàn*) then take the free bus to Wang Qiao Tai (望桥台) bus stop (about 40 minutes). You can also get here from the Zhāngjiājiè entrance.

Bājiè Youth Hostel　　　　HOSTEL **$**
(☑150 7446 9955; Dīngxiāngróng village, 丁香榕村; dm ¥50, s & d ¥138; 🛜) This rather simple hostel is clean, well located within the park

for sunrise viewings from the Grand Sightseeing Platform and well staffed by English-speakers.

Qíngrén Kèzhàn　　　　GUESTHOUSE **$**
(情人客栈; ☑189 0744 1378; Xiangda Lukou bus stop, Tianzi Shan area, 天子山, 湘大路口; r ¥80; 🛜) This remote, rustic, family-run guesthouse, has simple rooms, home-cooked meals and farmyard animals running around the courtyard. There's no English spoken, but the owners are friendly and there's wi-fi (no air-con, though). The simplest way to get here is via the free bus from the Tiānzǐ Shān park entrance to Xiangda Lukou (湘大路口) bus stop, not far before the Tiānzǐ Shān cable-car station.

BĪNGLÁNG VALLEY 槟榔谷

A free alternative to Zhāngjiājiè national park, **Bīnglláng Valley** (Bīnglláng Gǔ) is a staggeringly beautiful mountain valley and its caves, natural arches and vertiginous cliffs, 90 minutes by bus from town, make for a sublime day trip or overnight expedition. And it's free to enter. You begin by descending through a beautiful flat valley called **Moon Valley** (月之谷; Yuè Zhī Gǔ) surrounded by limestone cliffs before climbing to a vast cave called **Cathedral Gate** (教堂们; Jiàotáng Mén), after which you thread through a bamboo forest to make your way towards a 1km-long **subterranean cave**.

On the way you will pass the **Two Layer Cave** (双层洞; Shuāngcéng Dòng) before reaching the astonishing **Angel Castle** (天使城; Tiānshǐ Chéng) – a formation of vast limestone cliffs that encircles you – with the **Angel Gate** (天使门; Tiānshǐ Mén) at the far end, a further cave that drills through the entire cliff to the far side.

A low-hanging cave entrance on the far side of the valley leads to the **Mí Cave** (迷洞; Mí Dòng), but whatever you do, don't enter without a **guide** and a **head lamp**. It's 1km long, pitch black, devoid of mobile signals and if you take a wrong turn, you could easily get lost. But it's an astonishing experience. One section is full of litter, not dropped by visitors, but swept in by river waters that flow in here during the rainy season (though usually only to a shallow depth). Eventually – after about half an hour of walking in the dark – you will see the faint glow of the exit, a cavernous opening leading to a breathtaking valley called **Star Valley** (星之谷; Xīng Zhī Gǔ) surrounded by colossal limestone cliffs. Give a good shout: the echo acoustics are phenomenal.

Not far away is **Bīngláng Hole** (槟榔孔; Bīnláng Kǒng), another natural cave leading through to the other side, from where you can make your way back to the bus drop-off point. Locals still use the naturally formed cave to reach villages on the far side, thus avoiding a circuitous detour.

To reach Bīngláng Valley, take a bus (¥17, 90 minutes) towards Qīng'ān Píng (青安坪) from the west bus station (汽车西站; qìchē xīzhàn) on Ziwu Lu (子午路) in Zhāngjiājiè City and disembark at Bīnglángǔ Nóngjiā Lè (槟榔谷农家乐), simply the name of a family homestead by the valley access point. Buses leave at 8.20am and 1.30pm; the last bus back is at 3.30pm. It is, however, best to take a guide; arrange one through the **Bājiè Youth Hostel** (p482). Cheng Lifeng is an expert guide who takes visitors for around ¥100 per person; he does not speak much English, however, but should be able to arrange an English-speaking guide for you.

If you want to spend the night here, **Bīnglángǔ Nóngjiā Lè** (槟榔谷农家乐; ☑153 8744 3709, 153 8744 3719; r ¥40) at the drop-off point has simple and cheap rooms for around ¥40 and can cook meals, but the hosts don't speak any English.

🍷 Drinking & Nightlife

Bars are largely limited to Zhāngjiājiè City. The Dàyōng Fǔchéng (大庸府城) complex north of Jiefang Lu (解放路) and just west of Beizheng Jie (北正街) has loads of bars and karaoke spots.

ℹ️ Information

In Zhāngjiājiè City, tree-lined Beizheng Jie has everything you need: accommodation, restaurants, snack stalls, pharmacies, ATMs, Internet cafes and bars tucked away down alleys, as well as a street-food market and a street-food **night market** (南门夜市; Nánmén Yèshì; Nanzheng Jie, 南正街; ☺ 5am-2am) at its southern extension.

ℹ️ Getting There & Away

AIR

Zhangjiajie Héhuā Airport (张家界荷花机场, Zhāngjiājiè Héhuā Jīchǎng; ☑ 0744 823 8417) is 6km southwest of Zhāngjiājiè City and about 40km from the Zhāngjiājiè National Park entrance.

There are flights to Běijīng, Chángshā, Chóngqìng, Guǎngzhōu, Hángzhōu, Shànghǎi, Xī'ān and other domestic destinations. Use www.english.ctrip.com for bookings.

BUS

Buses leave from **Central Bus Station** (中心汽车站, Zhōngxīn Qìchēzhàn; ☑ 0744 822 2417), right beside Zhāngjiājiè train station. As well as those listed here, there are daily sleeper buses to cities such as Běijīng, Shànghǎi, Wǔhàn and Xī'ān.

Chángshā ¥110, four hours, at least hourly 7am to 7pm

Fènghuáng ¥80, four hours, 8.30am, 9.30am, 12.30pm, 2.30pm, 3.30pm and 5.20pm

Jíshǒu ¥50, two hours, hourly 7am to 5pm

TRAIN

The **train station** (火车站, huǒchēzhàn; ☑ 0744 214 5182) is right beside Central Bus Station. Note, Huáihuà trains also stop at Jíshǒu (¥20, two hours).

Běijīng hard/soft sleeper ¥361/552, 24 to 26 hours, three daily (12.36pm, 2.40pm and 6.16pm)

Chángshā hard seat ¥55 to ¥84, six hours, six daily between 3.36pm and 7pm

Huáihuà hard seat ¥38, three to four hours, 12 daily

Yíchāng hard seat ¥44, five hours, three daily (5.58am, 9.15am and 4.10pm)

ℹ️ Getting Around

A taxi from the airport costs about ¥100 to the park and ¥20 to town. To reach the airport from the city, take local bus 4 (¥2, 5.30am to 8.30pm) from outside the Tiānmén Mountain Cable Car; the journey takes around 30 minutes.

Shuttle buses travel every 10 minutes from Zhāngjiājiè Central Bus Station to the three main park entrances: Zhāngjiājiè (better known as Forest Park; 森林公园; Sēnlín Gōngyuán; ¥10, 45 minutes), Wǔlíngyuán (武陵源) ¥12, one hour) and Tiānzi Shān (¥13, one hour, less frequent). To find the various buses, go to the far left-hand door of the bus-station waiting room, turn left and follow the route to the buses. Buy tickets on-board the bus. Once inside the park, all buses are free with your park ticket, but other transport (cable car, elevator, monorail tramcar) costs extra, typically around ¥70 per ride.

A taxi from the city to the Forest Park entrance costs around ¥120.

Déhāng 德夯

☑ 0743 / POP 500

Set against a backdrop of forested peaks, the Miao village of Déhāng (admission ¥100) has been tarted up for tourism these days and lacks authenticity, but it's merely a base for exploring the stunning scenery with short and easy-to-follow hikes.

Bilingual signs and map-boards around the main square (where the bus terminates) show you the way to the various trailheads, including the Nine Dragon Stream Scenic Area, which energetically leads to the 216m-tall Liúshā Waterfall, one of China's tallest (although very skinny) waterfalls and the lovely Yùquánxī Scenic Area.

Liúshā Waterfall (流沙瀑布, Liúshā Pùbù) – very thin, but very tall indeed – concludes a pleasant walk through a scenic area beyond the village. You can climb up behind the curtain of water, which is fun after the rains. It takes about two hours to walk to the waterfall and back, walking alongside a stream and across a bridge and past lush, green fields. The best time to walk to the waterfall is either early in the morning or late in the afternoon, when visitor numbers are down.

Winding along a stream beyond the village and going past lush gren fields, beautiful **Nine Dragon Stream Scenic Area** (九龙溪景区, Jiǔlóngxī Jǐngqū) takes around an hour to walk along its length, reaching the Liúshā Waterfall at its conclusion.

Yùquánxī Scenic Area (玉泉溪景区, Yùquánxī Jǐngqū) is a 2.6km-long hike that follows a path along the Yùquán Stream, past terraced fields and delightful views. Cross the **Jade Fountain Gate** (玉泉门; Yùquán Mén) to make your way to a waterfall and if you've the energy, climb the steps up to the

Tiānwèn Platform (天问台; Tiānwèn Tái) for glorious views.

Simple inns (客栈; *kèzhàn*) are around the square and suspended over the river. The most attractive is the simple **Jiēlóngqiáo Inn** (接龙桥客店, Jiēlóngqiáo Kèdiàn; 🎵135 1743 0915; r ¥80-150; 🛰), overlooking the arched Jiēlóng Bridge (接龙桥; Jiēlóng Qiáo). Rooms are well kept but the shared bathroom is in the basement. Travellers wanting midrange comfort can find it in nearby (but soulless) Jíshǒu.

Restaurants are clustered around the square and main road. The inns also have restaurants, though their meals are more expensive than their rooms. Hawkers in the alleys proffer small bites, including skewers of grilled fish (*táohuāyú*; ¥3) and tiny crabs (*xiǎo pángxiè*; ¥5).

ⓘ Getting There & Around

Déhāng is accessed from the town of Jíshǒu (吉首). Buses to Déhāng (¥8, 45 minutes) leave frequently from outside Jíshǒu train station.

You can catch frequent buses to Fènghuáng (¥24, one hour, 7.30am to 7pm), Zhāngjiājiè (¥50, three hours, 8am to 5pm), Huáihuà (¥50, regular) and Chángshā (¥140, regular, 7.30am to 6.30pm) from Jíshǒu bus station.

Local bus 3 (¥2) links Jíshǒu's train and bus stations.

Fènghuáng 凤凰

☑0743 / POP 421,000

Once a frontier town, Fènghuáng marked the boundary between the Han civilisations of the central plains and the Miao (苗), Tujia (土家) and Dong (侗) minorities of the southwest mountains. Protective walls went up in the Ming dynasty, but despite the implications Fènghuáng prospered as a centre of trade and cultural exchange. Its diverse residents built a breathtaking riverside settlement of winding alleys, temples and rickety stilt houses, which these days attract tourists by the bucketload. Do try to stay overnight – the town is bursting with accommodation options, and the sight of an illuminated Fènghuáng at night is quite awesome.

◉ Sights

Wandering aimlessly is the best way to experience the charms of the **old town** (古城; *gǔchéng*). The back alleys are a trove of shops, temples, ancestral halls and courtyard homes.

The through ticket (通票; *tōngpiào*; ¥148) gains you three-day access to the old town, plus entrance to all the major sights and a half-hour boat trip on the river. Ticket checks with almost military efficiency have plugged most of the gaps, so it's hard to avoid buying the ticket, which you will certainly need to enter the ticketed sights. Hang on to your hotel deposit receipt as this can be used at some of the entry points.

At the time of writing, there was word that the through ticket may be scrapped for entry to the town, but admission charges would apply to individual sights, so a new ruling may be in effect by the time you read this. Ticket offices are scattered around town. Sights are generally open 8am to 6pm. Come nightfall, much of the old town is dazzlingly illuminated, making it one of the most photogenic sights in China.

◉ Inside the City Wall

Hóng Bridge   BRIDGE
(虹桥, Hóng Qiáo; through ticket for upstairs galleries) In the style of the Dong minority's wind and rain bridges, this attractive bridge vaults the waters of the Tuó River and is illuminated at night. Like some other sights in Fènghuáng, it's best viewed from a distance.

Stepping Stones   BRIDGE
Stones laid out for crossing the river. Not a great idea to cross them after too many glasses of the local strong stuff.

Fènghuáng City Wall   HISTORIC SITE
(城墙, Chéngqiáng) Restored fragments of the city wall lie along the south bank of the Tuó River. Carvings of fish and mythical beasts adorn the eaves of the North Gate Tower, one of four original main gates. Another, the **East Gate Tower** (东门城楼, Dōngmén Chénglóu; with through ticket), is a twin-eaved tower of sandstone and fired brick, dating from 1715.

Yáng Family Ancestral Hall   HISTORIC SITE
(杨家祠堂, Yángjiā Cítáng; with through ticket) West of East Gate Tower. Built in 1836, its exterior is covered with slogans from the Cultural Revolution. There are two lovely black-and-white frescoes of mythical animals on the rear walls of the main hall.

North Gate Tower   GATE
(北门城楼, Běimén Chénglóu) Carvings of fish and mythical beasts adorn the eaves of this tower, one of four original main gates.

Jiāngxīn Buddhist Temple   BUDDHIST TEMPLE
(江心禅寺, Jiāngxīn Chánsì; Huilong Ge, 回龙阁) Secreted away on Huilong Ge, a narrow al-

Fènghuáng

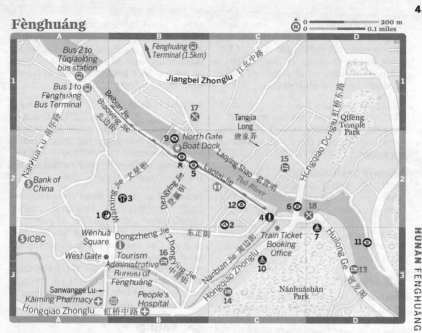

Fènghuáng

◎ Sights

1 Cháoyáng Temple	A2
2 Chóngdé Hall	C2
3 Confucian Temple	B2
4 East Gate Tower	C2
5 Fènghuáng City Wall	B2
6 Hóng Bridge	C2
7 Jiāngxīn Buddhist Temple	D3
8 North Gate Tower	B2
9 Stepping Stones	B2
10 Three Kings Temple	C3
11 Wànmíng Pagoda	D3
12 Yáng Family Ancestral Hall	C2

⊨ Sleeping

13 A Good Year	D3
14 Border Town International Youth Hostel	C3
15 Phoenix Jiāngtiān Holiday Village	C2
16 Shí'èr Hào Shíguāng	B3

⊗ Eating

17 Miss Yang Restaurant	B1
18 Soul Cafe	D2

ley. The temple is inscribed with the characters 準提庵 above the door, identifying it as a former nunnery.

Chóngdé Hall · HISTORIC SITE
(崇德堂, Chóngdé Táng; Shijia Long, 史家弄; with through ticket) The town's wealthiest resident, Pei Shoulu has his personal collection of antiques on display in his former residence on Shijia Long. The collection of carved wood lintels, decorative woodwork and inscribed wooden wall plaques is simply gorgeous.

Cháoyáng Temple · TAOIST TEMPLE
(朝阳宫, Cháoyáng Gōng; 41 Wenxing Jie, 文兴街) Features an ancient theatrical stage and hall, and is now home to a silver-forging training centre.

Confucian Temple · CONFUCIAN TEMPLE
(文庙, Wén Miào; Wenxing Jie, 文星街) This 18th-century walled temple and shrine to the celebrated sage is now a middle school.

Three Kings Temple · BUDDHIST TEMPLE
(三皇庙, Sānhuáng Miào) Great views of town, colourfully carved dragons, and thousands of lucky charms await up stone steps.

◎ Outside the City Wall

The north bank of the river offers lovely views of Fènghuáng's *diàojiǎolóu* (吊脚楼; stilt houses). Cross by stepping stones (跳岩; *tiàoyán*) – best navigated when sober – or the wooden footbridge (木头桥; *mùtóu qiáo*).

Wànmíng Pagoda PAGODA
(万名塔, Wànmíng Tǎ) This elegant and slim pagoda was built during the reign of Emperor Jiaqing. It cannot be climbed, but is gloriously illuminated at night and makes for simply beautiful photographs.

Huángsī Bridge Old Town VILLAGE
(黄丝桥古城, Huángsī Qiáo Gǔchéng; ¥20) A Tang dynasty military outpost 25km from town. The Southern Great Wall bus continues to here.

Southern Great Wall ARCHITECTURE
(南方长城, Nánfāng Chángchéng; ¥45) The Ming dynasty defensive wall, 13km from town, once stretched to Guìzhōu province. Take bus 2 from Nánhuá Gate to its terminus at Tǔqiáolǒng bus station (土桥垅车站; Tǔqiáolǒng *chēzhàn*), from where you can catch a bus here.

🛏 Sleeping

Fènghuáng is stuffed with guesthouses (客栈; *kèzhàn*). River-view rooms come at a premium, but may also be a bit damp. All places have wi-fi, but reception can be bad in many rooms, so check first. Look for the sign 今日有房, which means 'rooms available'; book ahead for weekends and holidays. Many guesthouses only come with squat toilets. Using air-con costs an extra ¥20 at a lot of guesthouses.

★**A Good Year** GUESTHOUSE $
(一年好时光, Yī Nián Hǎo Shíguāng; ☎ 0743 322 2026; 91 Huilong Ge, 迴龙阁91号; r ¥100-130; ❀🛜) There are just 10 rooms in this sweet, wood-framed inn on the river; all have balconies, showers and TVs but six have fantastic river views (¥130), with swings on their balconies. Staff are friendly and the location is quiet and secluded, tucked away a fair distance along Huilong Ge.

Shí'èr Hào Shíguāng Hostel HOSTEL $
(十二号时光国际青年旅舍, Shí'èr Hào Shíguāng Guójì Qīngnián Lǚshě; ☎ 0743 350 0302, 137 6210 6759; 12 Zhongying Jie, 中营街12号; dm ¥47, r ¥118, with private bathroom ¥158; ❀@🛜) Friendly, laid-back hostel with a quiet, back-alley location on historic Zhongying Jie. All rooms come with squat loo.

**Border Town
International Youth Hostel** HOSTEL $
(边城国际青年旅舍, Biānchéng Guójì Qīngnián Lǚshè; ☎ 0743 322 8698; 45 Hongqiao Zhonglu, 虹桥中路45号; dm ¥35, d ¥70-90; ❀@) Named

after a novel by Fènghuáng's famous son Shen Congwen, this hostel is a five-minute walk south of the Hóng Bridge. The pricier doubles are especially spacious, and those on the top floor have great views of the old town. Squat toilets.

Běiyīmén Lǚshè GUESTHOUSE $$
(北一门旅舍; ☎ 153 0743 8250, 0743 366 6508; 32 Laoying Shao, 老营哨32号; d ¥288-388; ❀@🛜) This modern guesthouse has seven comfortable and tastefully decorated rooms with balconies overlooking the river. Bathrooms are small and there's a bar down below.

Phoenix Jiāngtiān Holiday Village HOTEL $$$
(凤凰江天旅游度假村, Fènghuáng Jiāngtiān Lǚyóu Dùjiàcūn; ☎ 0743 326 1998; Jiangtian Sq, 虹桥路江天广场; s/d/tr/ste ¥658/688/858/1098; ❀@🛜) The only proper hotel by the old town, Phoenix has decent, good-sized rooms, but bathrooms are small and there are no river views. Discounts are the rule, with singles and doubles being reduced to ¥298, except at the busiest times.

🍴 Eating

Fènghuáng has plenty of cheap, tasty street food – everything from kebabs to spicy *dòufu* (tofu), homemade ginger sweets (姜糖; *jiāngtáng*) and duck-blood sausages. Look out for evening *shāokǎo* (street barbecues) on the north side of Hóng Bridge. If you crave fast food or an easy coffee, KFC is on Hongqiao Donglu.

★**Miss Yang Restaurant** HUNAN $$
(杨小姐的餐厅, Yángxiǎojiě de Cāntīng; 45 Laoying Shao, 老营哨45号; mains ¥30-80; ⊙10am-midnight) Specialising in local cuisine, particularly that of the Miao and Tujia people, such as Tuó River fish (沱江小鱼; *Tuó Jiāng xiǎoyú*), this intimate restaurant serves tasty delights in an atmospheric upstairs setting of varnished-wood furniture and colourful cushions. It also does a classic Jiāngxī chicken stew called *sān bēi jī* (三杯鸡), and its cured pork (腊肉; *là ròu*) dishes are superb.

There's also *tǔdòu fěn* (土豆粉), a rice-noodle dish from Guìzhōu province. You'll also find classic home-style dishes on the menu: the fried aubergine (家常茄子; *jiācháng qiézi*) is lovely. Downsides: the beer is expensive and there's no wi-fi. Photo menu.

Soul Cafe ITALIAN $$
(亦素咖啡, Yìsù Kāfēi; 17 Huilong Ge, 回龙阁17号; mains ¥35-65; ⊙8.30am-11.30pm; 🛜) This upmarket cafe serves proper coffee (from ¥25)

and the setting is lovely, with sofas, comfy chairs, lampshades everywhere and river views, but the food is overpriced (and toast in the breakfast sets comes without butter, which costs a further ¥20). If you want to push the boat out, there are imported wines, Cuban cigars and hookah pipes (¥90).

ℹ Information

Bank of China (中国银行, Zhōngguó Yínháng; Nanhua Lu, 南华路) You can change money at this branch on Nanhua Lu, a short walk from the Nánhuá Gate Tower.

Kāimíng Pharmacy (开明大药房, Kāimíng Dàyàofáng; 132-1 Hongqiao Zhonglu, 虹桥中路132-1号; ⊗7.30am-10pm) Round the corner from China Post.

People's Hospital (人民医院, Xīn Rénmín Yīyuàn; ☑0743 322 1199; Hongqiao Zhonglu, 虹桥西路) Southwest of the old town.

Tourism Administrative Bureau of Fènghuáng (凤凰旅游中心, Fènghuáng Lǚyóu Zhōngxīn; ☑0743 322 8365; ⊗6.30am-6pm) Off Wenhua Sq.

ℹ Getting There & Away

Buses from Fènghuáng Bus Terminal (凤凰汽车客运总站; Fènghuáng Qìchē Kèyùn Zǒngzhàn) include the following:

Chángshā ¥140, five hours, hourly 7.30am to 5.30pm

Guìyáng ¥160, seven hours, one daily, 3pm

Huáihuà ¥40, three hours, hourly 8am to 6pm

Jíshǒu ¥22, one hour, frequent 6.30am to 7.30pm

Zhāngjiājiè ¥80, 4½ hours, hourly 8am to 5pm

There are also frequent buses to Tóngrén (铜仁; ¥25, 1½ hours, 8am to 4pm), from where you can change for Zhènyuǎn in Guìzhōu province.

There's no train station in Fènghuáng, but you can book tickets at the **train ticket booking office** (火车代票处, Huǒchē Dàipiàochù; ☑0743 322 2410; 12 Hongqiao Zhonglu, 虹桥中路12号; ⊗7.55am-10pm) south of Hóng Bridge.

ℹ Getting Around

Local bus 1 goes from Fènghuáng Bus Terminal to Nánhuá Gate Tower.

Hóngjiāng Old Town 洪江古商城

☑0745 / POP 60,783

This little-known town (Hóngjiāng Gǔ Shāngchéng) boasts an extraordinary history as a Qing dynasty financial and trading centre, due to its fortuitous location at the confluence of the Yuán (沅江; Yuán Jiāng) and Wū (巫水; Wū Shuǐ) Rivers. At one time it was the main opium-distribution hub in southwest China. Dating as far back as the Northern Song dynasty, the surrounding city is mostly modern now, but the past lives on in the remarkable **old town**, which is still home to a few thousand people. When arriving or departing by bus, look out for the delightful old white pagoda on the south side of the river to the west of town.

◉ Sights

The old town can be visited in half a day. It spreads in a maze of alleys running uphill from Yuanjiang Lu (沅江路) – a road running close to the riverbank – but can be accessed from all sides.

Admission to the old town includes guided two-hour tours in Chinese. If you enter via any of the alleys connecting to the main roads, you may get in for free, but you won't be allowed into the notable buildings without a ticket and you may also be stopped by a random ticket-checker and directed to the ticket office.

The old town undulates in a delightful, higgledy-piggledy, often steep, maze of narrow stone-flagged alleys and lanes. Many of the less important buildings remain in a charming state of dilapidation, but a consistent program of restoration is underway. English and Chinese signposts point the way to the more notable buildings, most of which have been fully restored, and there's a metal map on a board at the heart of town for you to consult. Notable buildings include the **tax office**, an **opium shop**, a **brothel**, a **pharmacy**, a **newspaper office**, ancestral halls, **courtyard homes** of prominent merchants as well as several **guildhalls** (会馆; huìguǎn), including the superb facade of the **Tàipíng Palace** (太平宫; Tàipíng Gōng).

Liú Yuán　　　　　　　　　　　HOUSE
(留园) The Liú Yuán is a magnificent old house – it's now lived in by several families, but it used to belong to a wealthy merchant and is named after the garden in Sūzhōu; it stands in front of a colossal courtyard. Most buildings are of the yìnzìwū (窨子屋) style, characterised by a series of adjoining courtyards, high exterior walls and concave roofs. You can enter many to admire their interiors; look out for the numerous **Tàipíng Gāng** (太平缸), huge water vats for putting out fires.

🛏 Sleeping

Wǔlíngchéng Hotel HOTEL $$
(武陵城酒店; Wǔlíngchéng Jiǔdiàn; ☎0745 766 6717; 40 Xinmin Lu, 新民路40号; d ¥298-588, ste ¥1288; ❀@🛜) Uphill along Xinmin Lu and set back from the road up some steps, this place is quite a smart choice, with well turned-out staff, a restaurant, and rooms that are clean, tidy and well presented. The hotel is almost at the junction with Xingfu Xilu, towards the post office. Rooms are regularly largely discounted.

ℹ Information

The official entry point to the old town is at **Hóngjiāng Old Town Ticket Office** (off Yuanjiang Lu, 沅江路; ¥140; ⏱8am-6.30pm). You can try to enter by any of the other side alleys off Yuanjiang Lu, but you may be stopped by one of the wandering ticket collectors who will direct you to the main ticket office.

Bank of China (中国银行, Zhōngguó Yínháng; 318 Xinmin Lu, 新民路318号) changes foreign currency, if you ask politely. It's around 400m downhill from the Wǔlíngchéng Hotel.

ℹ Getting There & Away

Don't confuse Hóngjiāng Old Town with Hóngjiāng City (洪江市; Hóngjiāng Shì), the town on the railway 30km west. The old town is most easily reached via the town of Huáihuà (怀化).

Buses from Huáihuà:

Chángshā ¥150, four hours, frequent 7.30am to 6.20pm

Fènghuáng ¥39, one hour, frequent 7am to 6pm

Hóngjiāng Old Town ¥18, 90 minutes, half-hourly 6.30am to 6pm

Jíshǒu ¥52, two hours, eight daily

Buses to and from Fènghuáng use Huáihuà West Bus Station (汽车西站; Qìchē Xīzhàn) at 80 Huaixi Lu, which is walking distance from Huáihuà train station – turn right out of the train station, walk down Yingfeng Dajie (迎丰大街) and then turn right at the roundabout along Huaixi Lu (怀西路).

Buses to and from Chángshā and Hóngjiāng old town use Huáihuà South Bus Station (汽车南站; Qìchē Nánzhàn).

Local bus 12 links Huáihuà's train station and South Bus Station.

Buses back to Huáihuà (6.30am to 6pm) from Hóngjiāng old town leave from the **bus station** (416 Nanyue Lu, 南岳路416号). It's a 15-minute walk to the old town across the bridge from the bus station, or a ¥5 taxi ride.

Fúróng Zhèn   芙蓉镇

The road between Jíshǒu and Zhāngjiājiè runs through hills, terraced fields and minority villages, and past rivers and lush, verdant scenery via the Tujia settlement of Fúróng Zhèn, an old town (古镇; gǔzhèn) elevated to fame in the 1986 film *Hibiscus Town*. Until around 10 years ago, the town was simply called Wáng Cūn (王村; Wang Village), before being renamed in honour of the movie. Wandering down the steps of the old riverside town is charming, but the main draw is the gushing waterfall alongside the hamlet, splendidly illuminated come nightfall.

Wandering down the main old village street (admission ¥110), which descends in steps to the wharf and the Yōu River (酉水) at its foot, is a charming excursion. Historic buildings on the way down include the **Guanyin Hall** (观音阁, Guānyīn Gé; No 105) at No 105 and the **Tóngzhù Guǎn** (铜柱馆; No 15). The highlight, however, is the **Fúróng Zhèn Waterfall** (芙蓉镇瀑布, Fúróng Zhèn Pùbù; included in old town ticket), which divides the village and can be crossed via stepping stones to the far side, affording the most amazing views of the town, especially at sundown as the lights begin twinkling. Have a camera ready. Note: it's possible to slip into the old town without paying, but you won't be able to enter any of the ticketed sights.

There are numerous hotels and guesthouses where you can find a double room with shower for the night for around ¥100. If you want a room overlooking the falls, you can find rooms for around ¥150.

There are a few **restaurants** (mains ¥20-40) on your left as you walk down the main steps to the river, with tables overlooking the waterfall, serving up a variety of local and regional dishes. One such cafe and bar is **Silencio Cafe** (默啡, Mòfēi; cappuccino ¥25, ⏱9am-6.30pm winter, 8am-11.30pm summer), which has a superb position overlooking the falls, with later hours during the busy months.

Most of the restaurants overlooking the falls also double as spots where you can sit back with a beer; they stay open till late, especially during the summer months. Regular buses (¥25, one hour) run between Jíshǒu north bus station and Fúróng Zhèn from 7.30am to 5pm. Take the bus for Wáng Cūn (王村), the old name for Fúróng Zhèn. Buses (¥30, 90 minutes) run every hour from the bus station in Fúróng Zhèn to Zhāngjiājiè between 7.30am and 5pm.

Essential China

Cuisine »

Hiking »

Temples »

Festivals »

Above Píngyáo City Tower (p373)

Cuisine

To the Chinese, food is life. Dining is the cherished high point of the daily social calendar and often the one occasion to stop work and fully relax. The only problem is knowing where to begin: the sheer variety on offer can have your head spinning and your tummy quivering.

Peking Duck

Purists insist you must be in Běijīng for true Peking duck roasted to an amber hue over fruit-tree wood. You might as well take their advice as that's where you'll find the best Peking duck restaurants.

Dumplings

Set your compass north and northeast for the best *jiǎozi* (dumplings) – leek, pork, lamb, crabmeat wrapped in an envelope of dough. If you like them crispy, get them *guōtiē* (fried). Shànghǎi's interpretation is *xiǎolóngbāo* – scrummy and steamed.

Noodles

Marco Polo may have nicked the recipe to make spaghetti (so they say), but he didn't quite get the flavouring right. Noodles range across an exciting spectrum of taste, from the wincingly spicy *dàndan miàn* (spicy noodles) through to the supersalty *zhájiàng miàn* (fried sauce noodles).

Dim Sum

Dim sum is steamed up across China, but like the Cantonese dialect, it's best left to the masters of the south to get it right. Hong Kong, Macau and Guǎngzhōu should be your first stops – they set the dim-sum benchmark.

Hotpot

An all-weather meal, hotpot is ideal for banishing the bitter cold of a northern winter, while in steaming Chóngqìng, old folk devour the spiciest variety in the height of summer.

1. Peking duck 2. *Xiǎolóngbāo*
3. Rice noodles with peanuts 4. Dim sum

494

KAY DULAY/GETTY IMAGES ©

1. Hong Kong's New Territories 2. Huángshān
3. Jīnshā River, Tiger Leaping Gorge 4. Rock climbing, Yángshuò

APHOTOSTORY/SHUTTERSTOCK ©

Hiking

If you're keen to escape the cities into the great outdoors, China's dramatic variety of landscapes is the perfect backdrop for bracing walks – whether island-hopping in Hong Kong, exploring the foothills of the Himalayas or trekking through gorges in Yúnnán province.

Hong Kong's Outlying Islands & New Territories

A whopping 70% of Hong Kong is hiking territory, so fling off your Gucci loafers, lace up your hiking boots and go from island to island or make a break for the New Territories, where fantastic hiking trails await.

Huángshān, Ānhuī

Sooner or later you'll have to hike uphill, and where better than up China's most beautiful mountain. The steps may be punishing, but just focus on the scenery: even if the fabled mists are nowhere to be seen, the views are incredible.

Yángshuò, Guǎngxī

Yángshuò's karst topography is truly astonishing. Base yourself in town, give yourself three or four days, and walk your socks off (or hire a bike). Adventurous types can even try rock climbing.

Tiger Leaping Gorge, Yúnnán

The mother of all southwest China's treks, this magnificently named Yúnnán hike is at its most picturesque in early summer. It's not a walk in the park, so plan ahead and give yourself enough time.

Ganden to Samye, Tibet

You'll need four to five days for this glorious high-altitude hike connecting two of Tibet's most splendid monasteries. The landscape is beautiful, but the trek requires preparation both physically and mentally, plus a Tibet travel permit.

ZHAO JIAN KANG/SHUTTERSTOCK ©

Temples

Divided between Buddhist, Taoist and Confucian faiths, China's temples are places of introspection, peace and absolution. Find them on mountain peaks, in caves, on side streets, hanging from cliffsides or occupying the epicentre of town, from Tibet to Běijīng and beyond.

Pǔníng Temple, Chéngdé

On a clear day this temple stands out against the hills around Chéngdé, while in the Mahayana Hall is the Guanyin statue, a 22m-high, multiarmed embodiment of Buddhist benevolence – this is perhaps China's most astonishing statue.

Confucius Temple, Qūfù

This is China's largest and most important Confucius Temple. The Shāndōng sage has had an immeasurable influence on the Chinese persona through the millennia – visit the town where it began and try to put his teachings in perspective.

1. Temple of Heaven, Běijīng 2. Mandala, Jokhang Temple
3. Labrang Monastery, Xiàhé

Temple of Heaven, Běijīng

Not really a temple, but let's not quibble. Běijīng's Temple of Heaven was China's graceful place of worship for the Ming and Qing emperors, encapsulating the Confucian desire for symmetry and order, and harmony between heaven and earth.

Labrang Monastery, Xiàhé

If it's a hassle to rustle up a Tibet travel permit, pop down to this gargantuan Tibetan monastery in the scenic southwest corner of Gānsù. Its aura of devotion is amplified by the nonstop influx of Tibetan pilgrims and worshippers.

Jokhang Temple, Lhasa

Tibet's holiest place of worship, the Jokhang Temple in Lhasa is a place of pilgrimage for every Tibetan Buddhist at least once in their lifetime.

Ice & Snow Festival, Harbin

Festivals

China is a nation of hard workers and entrepreneurs, but considerable energy is reserved for its festivals and celebrations. Festivals can be religious, fun-filled, commemorative or seasonal. Locals don their best clothes and get seriously sociable. Join in and be part of the party.

Dragon Boat Festival

Commemorating the death of Qu Yuan, the celebrated 3rd-century-BC poet and statesman, dramatic dragon boat races can be seen in May or June churning up the waterways across China, including in Shànghǎi, Hong Kong and Tiānjīn.

Ice & Snow Festival, Harbin

The arctic temperatures may knock the wind from your lungs, but in January the frost-bitten capital of Hēilóngjiāng province twinkles with an iridescent collection of carved ice sculptures.

Third Moon Fair, Dàlǐ

One of China's many ethnic minority festivals, and usually held in April, this Bai festival commemorates the appearance of Guanyin, the Bodhisattva of Mercy, to the people of the Nanzhao kingdom.

Spring Festival

China's most commercially driven and full-on celebration takes the entire nation by storm at midnight on the first day of the first lunar month. The fuse is lit on a nationwide arsenal of fireworks.

Monlam (Great Prayer) Festival, Xiàhé

Celebrated across Tibet, the highlight of this Buddhist festival (in February or March) is easiest to witness in the monastic town of Xiàhé, where a host of celebrations include the unfurling of a huge *thangka* (sacred painting) on the hillside.

Hong Kong

📞852 / POP 7.18 MILLION

Best Places to Eat

➡ Choi's Kitchen (p525)

➡ Kam's Roast Goose (p525)

➡ Fortune Kitchen (p525)

➡ Aberdeen Fish Market Yee Hope Seafood Restaurant (p525)

➡ Atum Desserant (p525)

➡ Lung King Heen (p524)

Best Places to Sleep

➡ Peninsula Hong Kong (p522)

➡ TUVE (p521)

➡ Hotel Indigo (p522)

➡ Campus Hong Kong (p523)

➡ Upper House (p521)

Why Go?

Like a shot of adrenalin, Hong Kong quickens the pulse. Skyscrapers march up jungle-clad slopes by day and blaze neon by night across a harbour criss-crossed by freighters and motor junks. Above streets teeming with traffic, five-star hotels stand next to ageing tenement blocks.

The very acme of luxury can be yours, though enjoying the city need not cost the earth. The HK$2.50 ride across the harbour must be one of the world's best-value cruises. A meander through a market offers similarly cheap thrills. You can also escape the crowds – just head for one of the city's many country parks.

It's also a city that lives to eat, offering diners the very best of China and beyond. Hong Kong, above all, rewards those who grab experience by the scruff of the neck, who'll try that jellyfish, explore half-deserted villages or stroll beaches far from neon and steel.

When to Go
Hong Kong

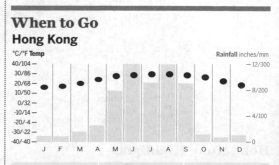

| Mar–May Asia's top film festival and deities' birthdays beckon beyond a sea of umbrellas | Jun–Sep Get hot (beach, new wardrobe), get wet (rain, beer): antidotes to sultry summers | Nov–Feb Hills by day, arts festival by night, celebrate Chinese New Year under Christmas lights. |

Hong Kong Highlights

1 **Ferries** Crossing Victoria Harbour on the legendary Star Ferry (p515).

2 **Victoria Peak** Taking the steep ascent on the Peak Tram (p507).

3 **Yum Cha** Eating under whirling fans at Luk Yu Tea House (p524).

4 **Man Mo Temple** (p507) Soaking up the incensed air.

5 **Trams** Feeling the chug of the world's last double-decker trams.

Sha Tau Kok ⊗
Crooked Island
Kat O Hoi
Tung Ping Chau
Lung Yeuk Tau Heritage Trail
Starling Inlet
Yan Chau Tong
Crescent Island
heung hui
Pat Sin Leng Nature Trail
Pat Sin Leng Country Park
Luk Keng
Double Island
Port Island
Tai Pang Wan (Mirs Bay)
Fanling ⓜ Hok Tau Wai
Fanling
ng ⓜ
Wong Leng Shan (639m)
Plover Cove Country Park
Plover Cove Reservoir
Hoi Ha Wan Marine Park
Tap Mun Chau
Tai Mei Tuk
Hoi Ha
Tai Po
Tap Mun
Tai Po Market
San Mun
Tsai
Tolo Channel
Lai Chi Chong
Ku Lau Wan
lung hai
Tung
Tsung Tsai
Tai Po Kau
Wu Kai Sha
Nai Chung
Sham Chung
Sai Kung Peninsula
Wong Shek
Tolo Harbour
Ma Liu Shui
Lead Mine Pass
Yuen Tai Po Kau Nature Reserve
University
Ma On Shan
Heng On
Wong Shek
Tai Long
Tai Mo Shan (957m)
Shing Mun Country Park
Racecourse ⓜ
Tai Shui Hang
Ma On Shan (702m)
Sai Kung West Country Park
Pak Tam Au
Chek Keng
Ham Tin
Tai Long Wan
Fo Tan
Pak Tam Chung
Sai Wan
Sha Tin ⑧ Hong Kong Heritage Museum
Sai Kung
Cham Tau Chau
Sai Kung East Country Park
Sai Wan
Sha Tin ⓜ
Sha Tin
Tai Wei ⓜ
Kam Shan Country Park
①
Buffalo Hill
Marina Cove
Habe Haven
Vim Tin Tsai
Tai Tau Chau
High Island Reservoir
South China Sea
Kiu Tsui Chau
Lion Rock Country Park
Chi Lin Nunnery
Trio Beach
Kau Sai Chau
Leung Sheun Wan
emple Street Night Market ⑨
Kowloon Tong ⓡ
Kowloon Peak (602m)
Port Shelter
Tiu Chung Chau
See Chau
Wong Nai Chau
KWUN TONG
Po Lam
Shelter Island
Kong Tau Pai
KOWLOON
Tsim Sha
Hang Hau
Lang Ha Wan
Bluff Island
Basalt Island
Man Mo emple
Star Ferry ①
Tsui East Promenade ⑥
Yau Tong
High Junk Peak (344m)
Tseung Kwan O
Lei Yue Mun
Tai Au Mun
④ Luk Yu Teahouse
②
Victoria Peak (552m)
Peak Tram
Hong Kong Island
Junk Bay
Tin Ha Shan (273m)
Clearwater Bay
Clearwater Bay Country Park
Aberdeen
Ocean Park
Chai Wan
Joss House Bay
Tung Lung Chau
Ap Lei Chau
Repulse Bay
Stanley Main Beach
Big Wave Bay
ok
Mo Tat Wan
⑦
Stanley
St Stephens Beach ⑦
Shek O
Shek O Beach ⑦
vu
Van
Tung O Wan
Tai Tam Bay
Sung Kong
East Lamma Channel
Stanley Peninsula
Sham Wan
Lo Chau
Po Toi

Ⓝ ▲ 0 ————————— 10 km
0 ————————— 5 miles

---

⑥ Tsim Sha Tsui East Promenade (p511) Indulging in the visual feast.

⑦ Ping Shan Heritage Trail (p514) Losing yourself in a walled village.

⑧ History Getting some context for it all at **Hong Kong Heritage Museum** (p514).

⑨ Temple Street Night Market (p512) Taking in the sights, sounds and smells.

⑩ Po Lin Monastery (p516) Paying your respects to the magnificent Big Buddha.

History

Until European traders started importing opium into the country, Hong Kong was an obscure backwater in the Chinese empire. The British developed the trade aggressively and by the start of the 19th century traded this 'foreign mud' for Chinese tea, silk and porcelain.

China's attempts to stamp out the opium trade gave the British the pretext they needed for military action. Gunboats were sent in. In 1841 the Union flag was hoisted on Hong Kong Island and the Treaty of Nanking, which brought an end to the so-called First Opium War, ceded the island to the British crown 'in perpetuity'.

At the end of the Second Opium War in 1860, Britain took possession of Kowloon Peninsula, and in 1898 a 99-year lease was granted for the New Territories.

Through the 20th century Hong Kong grew in fits and starts. Waves of refugees fled China for Hong Kong during times of turmoil. Trade flourished, as did British expat social life, until the Japanese army crashed the party in 1941.

By the end of WWII Hong Kong's population had fallen from 1.6 million to 610,000. But trouble in China soon swelled the numbers again as refugees (including industrialists) from the communist victory in 1949 increased the population beyond two million. This, together with a UN trade embargo on China during the Korean War and China's isolation in the next three decades, enabled Hong Kong to reinvent itself as one of the world's most dynamic ports and manufacturing and financial-service centres.

In 1984 Britain agreed to return what would become the Special Administrative Region (SAR) of Hong Kong to China in 1997, on condition it would retain its free-market economy and its social and legal systems for 50 years. China called it 'One country, two systems'. On 1 July 1997, in pouring rain, outside the Hong Kong Convention & Exhibition Centre, the British era ended.

In the years that followed, Hong Kong weathered major storms – an economic downturn, the outbreak of the SARS virus and a nagging mistrust of the government.

In March 2012, Leung Chun-ying, a former property surveyor, became Hong Kong's fourth chief executive. Though a seemingly more decisive man than his predecessors, Leung's unsubstantiated 'red' connections have many Hong Kongers worried, something not helped by spiralling living costs and China's treatment of its dissidents.

Pro-democracy protesters took over the streets of downtown Hong Kong in September 2014, demanding free elections. Demonstrations continued until mid-December, with Běijīng refusing to budge.

What is certain is that, two decades on from the handover, Hong Kong people are asking questions about their identity more intensely than ever as Hong Kong and mainland China, for better or worse, increasingly intertwine.

⊙ Sights

Hong Kong is quite an eyeful offering architecture, museums and some of the world's most iconic sights. And if you head out to the countryside, green and blue imprint themselves on your retina.

⊙ Central District

Whatever time of the day you plan on visiting Hong Kong's CBD, it's worth remembering that shops here close relatively early (6pm or 7pm), and that by mid-evening the dust has settled. It's also advisable to have

---

PRICE RANGES

Sleeping
Nightly rates for a double room:

$ less than HK$900

$$ HK$900–1900

$$$ more than HK$1900

Eating
A two-course meal with a drink.

$ less than HK$200

$$ HK$200–500

$$$ more than HK$500

EXCHANGE RATES

Australia	A$1	HK$5.99
Canada	C$1	HK$5.92
China	¥1	HK$1.13
Euro	€1	HK$8.21
Japan	¥100	HK$6.88
Macau	MOP$1	HK$0.97
New Zealand	NZ$1	HK$5.78
UK	UK£1	HK$9.74
USA	US$1	HK$7.76

Central Hong Kong & Kowloon

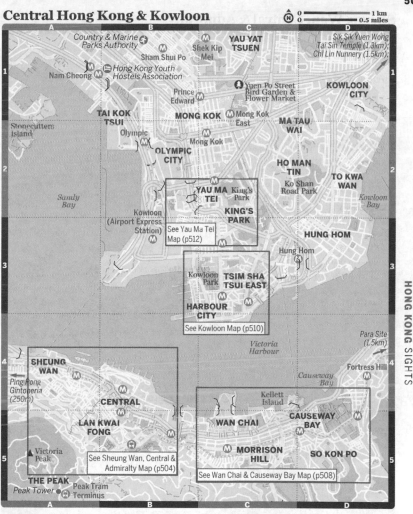

lunch outside the noon-to-2pm insanity when hordes of hungry suits descend on every table in sight.

Travelling on the MTR, take the Statue Sq exit and spend an hour looking around the Former Legislative Council Building and other memorials to Hong Kong's past. In the next couple of hours, check out the architecture in the vicinity – glass-and-steel modernity like the HSBC Building and colonial-era survivors like the Gothic St John's Cathedral.

Head over to the Zoological and Botanical Gardens for some hobnobbing with the rhesus monkeys. Recharged after an hour, make

a beeline for the harbour for some retail therapy at the IFC Mall. Take as long as you like, then hop on the Star Ferry to Kowloon.

★ **Peak Tram**   FUNICULAR
(Map p504; ☑ 852 2522 0922; www.thepeak.com. hk; Lower Terminus, 33 Garden Rd, Central; one-way/return adult HK$28/40, child 3-11yr & seniors over 65yr HK$11/18; ☺ 7am-midnight; Ⓜ Central, exit J2) The Peak Tram is not really a tram but a cable-hauled funicular railway that has been scaling the 396m ascent to the highest point on Hong Kong Island since 1888. A ride on the tram is a classic Hong Kong experience, with vertiginous views

Sheung Wan, Central & Admiralty

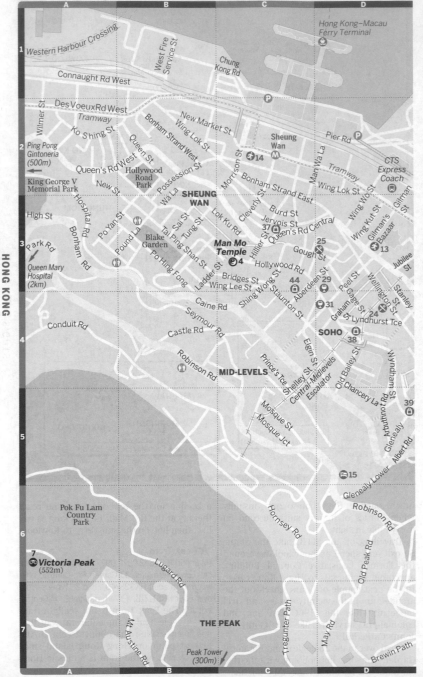

Western Harbour Crossing

Hong Kong–Macau
Ferry Terminal

Connaught Rd West

West Fire
Service St

Chung
Kong Rd

Des Voeux Rd West
Tramway

Pier Rd

Wilmer St

Ko Shing St

New Market St

Wing Lok St

Bonham Strand West

Queen St

Ping Pong
Gintoneria
(500m)

Queen's Rd West

Hollywood
Road
Park

Possession St

Morrison St

Sheung
Wan

Man Wa La

Tramway

CTS
Express
Coach

King George V
Memorial Park

New St

Wa La

SHEUNG
WAN

Bonham Strand East

Wing Lok St

Wing Wo St

Gilman St

14

M

High St

Hospital Rd

Bonham Rd

Po Yan St

Pound La

Tai Ping Shan St

Tung St

Sai St

Lok Ku Rd

Cleverly St

Burd St

Jervois St

37

Queen's Rd Central

Wing Kut St

Gilman's
Bazaar

Park Rd

Blake
Garden

Po Hing Fong

Ladder St

Man Mo
Temple

Hollywood Rd

Gough St

25

13

Queen Mary
Hospital
(2km)

4

Bridges St

Wing Lee St

Shing Wong St

Staunton St

Aberdeen St

44

29

Peel St

Gage St

Graham St

Wellington St

Stanley St

Jubilee St

Conduit Rd

Castle Rd

Seymour Rd

Caine Rd

31

SOHO

Lyndhurst Tce

24

Robinson Rd

MID-LEVELS

Prince's Tce

Shelley St

Elgin St

38

Old Bailey St

Wyndham St

Chancery La

Arbuthnot Rd

Glenealy

39

Central-Midlevels
Escalator

Mosque St

Mosque Jct

15

Pok Fu Lam
Country
Park

Hornsey Rd

Glenealy Lower

Albert Rd

Robinson Rd

Old Peak Rd

7

Victoria Peak
(552m)

Lugard Rd

Mt Austine Rd

THE PEAK

Treganter Path

May Rd

Brewin Path

Peak Tower
(300m)

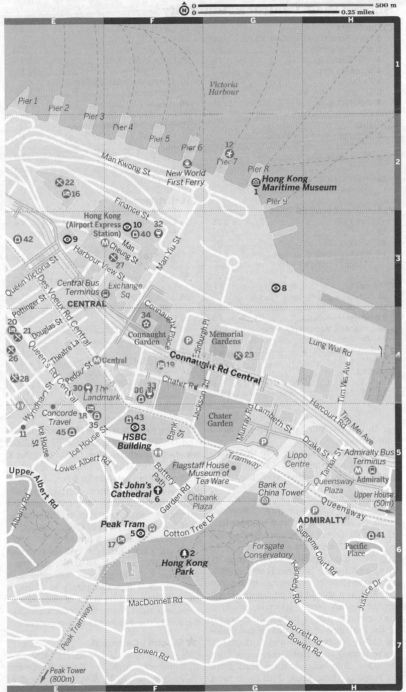

N

0 —————— 500 m
0 —————— 0.25 miles

Victoria
Harbour

Pier 1
Pier 2
Pier 3
Pier 4
Pier 5
Pier 6
12
Pier 7
Pier 8
Pier 9

Man Kwong St

New World
First Ferry

Hong Kong
Maritime Museum
1

22
16

Finance St

Hong Kong
(Airport Express
Station)
10
32
40

Man
Cheung St
27

Man Yiu St

42

9

Harbour View St

Queen Victoria St

Des Voeux Rd Central

Central Bus
Terminus

CENTRAL

Exchange
Sq

8

Pottinger St

Douglas St

34

Connaught Place

Connaught
Garden

Edinburgh Pl

Memorial
Gardens

Lung Wui Rd

20
21

Theatre La

Central

Peddar St

19

Connaught Rd Central

23

Tim Wa Ave

26

Queen's Rd Central

Chater Rd

Jackson Rd

28

Wyndham St

30
The
Landmark

33

Concorde
Travel
18

35

45

43
3

HSBC
Building

Bank St

Chater
Garden

Lambeth St

Murray Rd

Harcourt Rd

Tim Mei Ave

Admiralty Bus
Terminus

11

Ice House
St

Ice House St

Lower Albert Rd

Flagstaff House
Museum of
Tea Ware

Tramway

Lippo
Centre

Drake St

Tamar St

Admiralty

Upper House
(50m)

Upper Albert Rd

St John's
Cathedral
6

Battery
Path

Garden Rd

Citibank
Plaza

Bank of
China Tower

Queensway
Plaza

Queensway

ADMIRALTY

Peak Tram
5

17

Cotton Tree Dr

Forsgate
Conservatory

Supreme Court Rd

41

Pacific
Place

Albany Rd

2
Hong Kong
Park

MacDonnell Rd

Kennedy Rd

Justice Dr

Peak Tramway

Bowen Rd

Borrett Rd

Bowen Rd

Peak Tower
(800m)

Sheung Wan, Central & Admiralty

⊙ Top Sights
1 Hong Kong Maritime Museum..............G2
2 Hong Kong Park F6
3 HSBC Building.......................................F5
4 Man Mo Temple C3
5 Peak Tram F6
6 St John's Cathedral F5
7 Victoria Peak A6

⊙ Sights
8 Clockenflap Outdoor Music
   Festival...G3
9 One International Finance
   Centre..E3
10 Two International Finance
   Centre...F3

⊙ Activities, Courses & Tours
11 Fringe Club...E5
12 Star Ferry..G2
13 Ten Feet Tall D3
14 Wan Kei Ho International
   Martial Arts Association C2

⊙ Sleeping
15 Bishop Lei International House.............D5
16 Four Seasons E2
17 Helena May F6
18 Landmark Mandarin Oriental.................E5
19 Mandarin Oriental................................F4
20 Pottinger E4

⊗ Eating
21 Boss...E4
22 Caprice...E2

23 City Hall Maxim's Palace.......................G4
24 Dumpling Yuan D4
25 Kau Kee Restaurant..............................D3
26 Luk Yu Tea House..................................E4
   Lung King Heen ....(see 16)
27 Tim Ho Wan, the Dim Sum
   Specialists.......................................F3
28 Yung Kee Restaurant...........................E4

⊙ Drinking & Nightlife
29 Club 71..D3
30 MO Bar E4
31 Quinary D4
32 Red Bar F3
33 Sevva...F4

⊙ Entertainment
   Fringe Club ....(see 11)
34 Grappa's Cellar F4
   Peel Fresco..................................(see 31)

⊙ Shopping
35 Armoury..E5
36 Blanc de Chine......................................F4
37 Chan Shing Kee C3
38 Gallery of the Pottery
   Workshop D4
39 Grotto Fine Art D5
40 IFC Mall F3
41 Joyce...H6
42 PCCW...E3
43 Picture This F5
44 PMQ..C3
45 Shanghai Tang.......................................E5

HONG KONG SIGHTS

over the city as you ascend up the steep mountainside.

The Peak Tram runs every 10 to 15 minutes from 7am to midnight. Octopus cards can be used. On clear days, expect long lines.

★ HSBC Building   NOTABLE BUILDING
(滙豐銀行總行大廈; Map p504; www.hsbc. com.hk/1/2/about/home/unique-headquarters; 1 Queen's Rd, Central; ⊙escalator 9am-4.30pm Mon-Fri, 9am-12.30pm Sat; Ⓜ Central, exit K) FREE This stunning building, designed by British architect Sir Norman Foster in 1985, is a masterpiece of precision and innovation. And so it should be; on completion it was the world's most expensive building. Don't miss the pair of bronze lions guarding the harbour-side entrance of the building. Called Stephen (left) and Stitt (right), they're named after HSBC managers from the 1920s. Both bear shrapnel scars from the Battle of Hong Kong. Rub their paws for luck.

★ Hong Kong Maritime Museum   MUSEUM
(香港海事博物館; Map p504; ☎852 3713 2500; www.hkmaritimemuseum.org; Central Ferry Pier 8, Central; adult/child & senior HK$30/15; ⊙9.30am-5.30pm Mon-Fri, 10am-7pm Sat & Sun; ♿; Ⓜ Hong Kong, exit A2) Relocation and expansion have turned this into one of the city's strongest museums, with 15 well curated galleries detailing over 2000 years of Chinese maritime history and the development of the Port of Hong Kong. Exhibits include ceramics from China's ancient sea trade, shipwreck treasures and old nautical instruments. A painted scroll depicting piracy in China in the early 19th century is one of Hong Kong's most important historical artefacts, and, like the rest of the museum, a real eye-opener.

★ St John's Cathedral   CHURCH
(聖約翰座堂; Map p504; ☎ 852 2523 4157; www. stjohnscathedral.org.hk; 4-8 Garden Rd, Central; ⊙7am-6pm; 🚌12A, 40, 40M, Ⓜ Central, exit K) FREE Services have been held at this Angli-

can cathedral since it opened in 1849, with the exception of 1944, when the Japanese army used it as a social club. It suffered heavy damage during WWII, and the front doors were subsequently remade using timber salvaged from HMS *Tamar,* a British warship that guarded Victoria Harbour. You walk on sacred ground in more ways than one here: it is the only piece of freehold land in Hong Kong. Enter from Battery Path.

**Two International
Finance Centre**   NOTABLE BUILDING
(國際金融中心, Two IFC; Map p504; 8 Finance St, Central; Ⓜ Hong Kong, exit A2 or F) A pearl-coloured colossus resembling an electric shaver, this is the tallest building on Hong Kong Island. You can't get to the top, but you can get pretty high by visiting the Hong Kong Monetary Authority Information Centre. The building sits atop IFC Mall (p530), which stretches to the lower levels of its sister building, the much-shorter **One IFC** (國際金融中心, One IFC; Map p504; 1 Harbour View St, Central; Ⓜ Hong Kong, exit A2 or F).

Bank of China Tower   NOTABLE BUILDING
(中銀大廈, BOC Tower; Map p504; 1 Garden Rd, Central; ⓂCentral, exit K) The awesome 70-storey Bank of China Tower, designed by IM Pei, rises from the ground like a cube, and is then successively reduced, quarter by quarter, until the south-facing side is left to rise on its own. Some geomancers believe the four prisms are negative symbols; being the opposite of circles, these triangles contradict what circles suggest – money, union and perfection.

The lobby of the BOC Tower features the **Prehistoric Story Room** (open 9am to 6pm, closed Tuesday), a small exhibition depicting Earth's life history through fossil displays.

◉ The Peak & Northwest Hong Kong Island

You'll find many of Hong Kong's most intriguing sights around the Peak and in the neighbourhoods below it, from quirky museums and historic buildings to fragrant temples.

★Victoria Peak   VIEWPOINT
(維多利亞山頂; Map p504; ☑852 2522 0922; www.thepeak.com.hk; ⊗24hr; 🚌Bus 15 from Central, below Exchange Sq, 🚃Peak Tram Lower Terminus) FREE Standing at 552m, Victoria Peak is the highest point on Hong Kong Island. The Peak is also one of the most visited spots

by tourists in Hong Kong, and it's not hard to see why. Sweeping views of the vibrant metropolis, verdant woods, easy but spectacular walks – all reachable in just eight minutes from Central by Hong Kong's earliest form of transport.

The best way to reach the Peak is by the 125-year-old gravity-defying **Peak Tram** (p503). Some 500m to the northwest of the upper terminus, up steep Mt Austin Rd, is the site of the old governor's summer lodge, which was burned to the ground by Japanese soldiers during WWII. The beautiful gardens still remain, however, and have been refurbished with faux-Victorian gazebos, sundials, benches and stone pillars. They are open to the public.

The dappled 3.5km circuit formed by Harlech Rd on the south, just outside the Peak Lookout, and Lugard Rd on the northern slope, which it runs into, takes about 45 minutes to cover. A further 2km along Peak Rd will lead you to Pok Fu Lam Reservoir Rd. Hatton Rd, reachable by Lugard or Harlech Rds, on the western slope goes all the way down to the University of Hong Kong. The 50km Hong Kong Trail also starts on the Peak.

★Man Mo Temple   TAOIST TEMPLE
(文武廟; Map p504; ☑852 2540 0350; 124-126 Hollywood Rd, Sheung Wan; ⊗8am-6pm; 🚌26) FREE One of Hong Kong's oldest temples and a declared monument, atmospheric Man Mo Temple is dedicated to the gods of

HONG KONG IN...

One Day
Catch a tram up to **Victoria Peak** for great views of the city, stopping for lunch in Central on the way down. Head to **Man Mo Temple** for a taste of history before boarding the **Star Ferry** (p515) to Kowloon. Enjoy the views along Tsim Sha Tsui East Promenade as you stroll over to the Hong Kong Museum of History. Dine on ultraluxe Cantonese cuisine (think seafood) at **Boss** (p524) in Central. After dinner, take the MTR to Soho for drinks at **Club 71** (p527).

Two Days
On the second day, you could go to **Aberdeen** (p510) for a boat ride, then seafood and shopping. After dark, head to the **Temple Street Night Market** (p512) for sightseeing, shopping and street food.

HONG KONG SIGHTS

Wan Chai & Causeway Bay

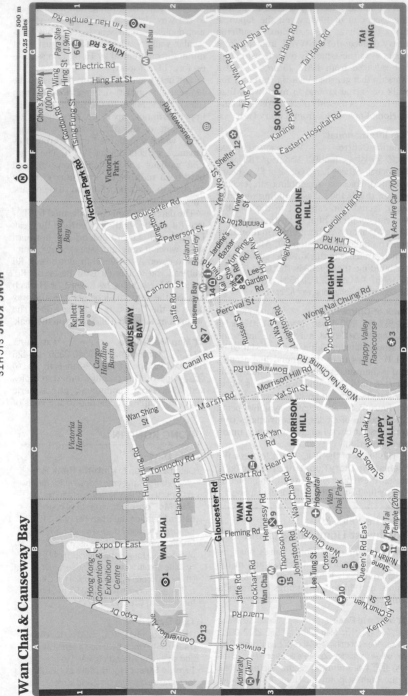

Tin Hau Temple Rd

Para Site (1.9km)
Choi's Kitchen (100m)
Wing Hing St
Para Site 6
King's Rd
Tin Hau
Electric Rd
Hing Fat St
Gordon Rd
Tsing Fung St

Tin Hau Temple Rd 2

Wun Sha St
Tung Lo Wan Rd
Tai Hang Rd
Tai Hang Rd

TAI HANG

500 m
0.25 miles

Victoria Park Rd

SO KON PO
Kaning Path
Eastern Hospital Rd

Causeway Bay
Gloucester Rd
Kingston St
Paterson St
Island Beverley St
Jardine's Bazaar
Irving St
Pennington St
Shelter St
Yee Wo St
12

Caroline Hill Rd
Broadwood Link Rd
Leighton Rd

CAROLINE HILL

Ace Hire Car (700m)

Victoria Park

Kellett Island

Cargo Handling Basin

CAUSEWAY BAY
Jaffe Rd
Cannon St
Cannon St
Causeway Bay
14
Kai Chiu Rd
Pak Sha Rd
Lee Garden Rd
Lan Fong Rd
Yun Ping Rd
Hysan Ave
8
Lee Garden Rd
Leighton Rd

LEIGHTON HILL

Percival St
Russell St
Wong Nai Chung Rd

Victoria Harbour

Canal Rd
Bowrington Rd
Yiu Wa St
Leighton Rd
Sports Rd
Wong Nai Chung Rd

Happy Valley Racecourse
3

Wan Shing St
Marsh Rd
Morrison Hill Rd
Yat Sin St
MORRISON HILL

Hung Hing Rd
Tonnochy Rd
Tak Yan Rd
Heard St

HAPPY VALLEY
Hau Tak La
S'tubbs Rd

Expo Dr East
Stewart Rd
4
Wan Chai Rd
Ruttonjee Hospital
Wan Chai Park

WAN CHAI
Gloucester Rd
Hennessy Rd
9
Fleming Rd
Thomson Rd
Johnston Rd
Wan Chai Rd
Cross St
Queen's Rd East
5
11
Pak Tai Temple (20m)
Stone La
Nullah La
B

Hong Kong Convention & Exhibition Centre
Expo Dr East
1

Expo Dr
Convention Ave
13
Fenwick St
Jaffe Rd
Lockhart Rd
Luard Rd
Wan Chai
15
Lee Tung St
10
Queen's Rd East
Kennedy Rd
Chun Yuen St

Admiralty (1km)

Wan Chai & Causeway Bay

literature ('Man'), holding a writing brush, and of war ('Mo'), wielding a sword. Built in 1847 during the Qing dynasty by wealthy Chinese merchants, it was, besides a place of worship, a court of arbitration for local disputes when trust was thin between the Chinese and the colonialists.

◉ Wan Chai & Northeast Hong Kong Island

Admiralty's location between water and hills means sights are clustered on slopes or by the sea. Scenic stretches of manicured green are dotted with low-rises with a military past or skyscrapers housing government offices. The section of Wan Chai between Queen's Rd East and Johnston Rd, where the old coastline used to be, is rich with ancient and modern heritage, while the new harbourfront, to the north on reclaimed land, has monuments to culture, commerce and sovereignty. A park lies between Causeway Bay and the area served by Tin Hau MTR station. The latter also features a temple and the leisurely neighbourhood of Tai Hang.

★**Happy Valley Racecourse** HORSE RACING
(跑馬地馬場; Map p508; ☑852 2895 1523; www.hkjc.com/home/english/index.asp; 2 Sports Rd, Happy Valley; HK$10; ⊗7-10.30pm Wed Sep-Jun; 🚃Happy Valley) An outing at the races is one of the quintessential Hong Kong things to do, especially if you happen to be around during one of the weekly Wednesday evening races here. The punters pack into the stands and trackside, cheering, drinking and eating, and the atmosphere is electric.

The first horse races were held here in 1846. Now meetings are held both here and at the newer and larger (but less atmospher-

ic) **Sha Tin Racecourse** (沙田賽馬場; Penfold Park; race-day public stands HK$10, members' enclosures HK$100-150; 🚇Racecourse) in the New Territories. Check the website for details on betting and tourist packages. Take the eastbound Happy Valley tram to the final stop and cross the road to the racecourse.

★**Hong Kong Park** PARK
(香港公園; Map p504; ☑852 2521 5041; www.lcsd.gov.hk/parks/hkp/en/index.php; 19 Cotton Tree Dr, Admiralty; ⊗park 6am-11pm; ♿; 🚇Admiralty, exit C1) FREE Designed to look anything but natural, Hong Kong Park is one of the most unusual parks in the world, emphasising artificial creations such as its fountain plaza, conservatory, waterfall, indoor games hall, playground, taichi garden, viewing tower, museum and arts centre. For all its artifice, the 8-hectare park is beautiful in its own weird way and, with a wall of skyscrapers on one side and mountains on the other, makes for some dramatic photographs.

Hong Kong Park is an easy walk from either Central or the Admiralty MTR station.

Para Site GALLERY
(☑852 2517 4620; www.para-site.org.hk; 22/F, Wing Wah Industrial Bldg, 677 King's Rd, Quarry Bay; ⊗noon-7pm Wed-Sun; 🚇Quarry Bay, exit C) From this new address in Quarry Bay, the respected independent art space Para Site continues to mount exhibitions of contemporary art that question the very values of society and contemporary existence. The exhibitions usually have a Hong Kong or Asian focus but universal relevance.

Tin Hau Temple TEMPLE
(天后廟; Map p508; 10 Tin Hau Temple Rd, Causeway Bay; ⊗7am-5pm; 🚇Tin Hau, exit B) Hong Kong Island's most famous Tin Hau

Kowloon

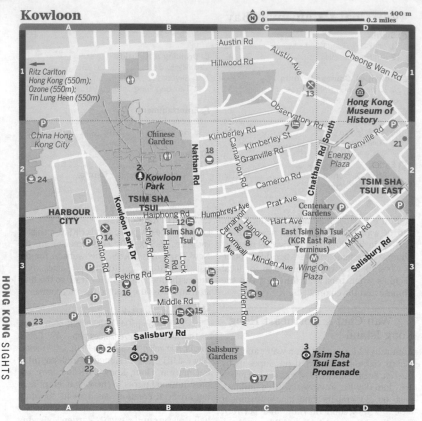

(Goddess of the Sea) temple has lent its name to an entire neighbourhood, a metro station and a street. It has been a place of worship for 370 years and, despite renovations, imparts an air of antiquity, particularly in the intricate stone carvings near the entrance and the ceramic figurines from Shiwan decorating the roof. The main altar contains an effigy of the goddess with a blackened face.

Flagstaff House
Museum of Tea Ware   MUSEUM
(旗桿屋茶具文物館; Map p504; ☎852 2869 0690; www.lcsd.gov.hk/CE/Museum/Arts/en_US/web/ma/tea-ware.html; 10 Cotton Tree Dr, Admiralty; ⊗10am-6pm Wed-Mon; Ⓜ Admiralty, exit C1) FREE
Built in 1846 as the home of the commander of the British forces, Flagstaff House is the oldest colonial building in Hong Kong still standing in its original spot. Its colonnaded verandahs exude a Greek Revival elegance that is complemented by the grace of the

tea ware from the 11th to the 20th century – bowls, brewing trays, sniffing cups (used particularly for enjoying the fragrance of the finest oolong from Taiwan) and teapots made of porcelain or purple clay from Yíxìng.

The ground-floor cafe is a great place to recharge over a pot of fine tea. The museum also runs tea-appreciation classes. Call for details. Flagstaff House sits on Hong Kong Park's northernmost tip.

⊙ Aberdeen & South Hong Kong Island

The southern part of Hong Kong Island lays claim to Hong Kong's richest fishing culture. You'll see the homes, markets and temples, both traditional and modern, of Hong Kong's 'people of the water'. The island's south is also home to its last surviving urban village and remnants of a dairy, as well as some of the territory's most popular sunbathing spots.

Kowloon

HONG KONG SIGHTS

★**Aberdeen Promenade** WATERFRONT
(香港仔海濱公園; Aberdeen Praya Rd, Aberdeen)
FREE Tree-lined Aberdeen Promenade runs
from west to east on Aberdeen Praya Rd
across the water from Ap Lei Chau. On its
western end is sprawling **Aberdeen Wholesale Fish Market** (香港仔魚市場) with its
industrial-strength water tanks teeming
with marine life. It's pungent and grimy,
but 100% Hong Kong. Before reaching the
market, you'll pass berthed house boats and
seafood-processing vessels.

Stanley VILLAGE
(赤柱) This crowd pleaser is best visited on
weekdays. **Stanley Market** (赤柱市集; Stanley Village Rd, Stanley; ◎9am-6pm; ☐6, 6A, 6X or
260) is a maze of alleyways that has bargain
clothing (haggling is a must!), while **Stanley Main Beach** (赤柱正灘; ☐6A, 14) is for
beach-bumming and windsurfing. With
graves dating back to 1841, **Stanley Military
Cemetery** (赤柱軍人墳場; ☑852 2557 3498;
Wong Ma Kok Rd, Stanley; ◎8am-5pm; ☐14, 6A),
500m south of the market, is worth a visit.

◎ Kowloon

Kowloon has most of Hong Kong's major
museums, as well as some of its most fascinating street markets. Many of its attractions revolve around views of the Hong

Kong Island skyline, which can be best seen
from the Kowloon waterfront and various
high-rise bars and restaurants.

★**Tsim Sha Tsui East Promenade** HARBOUR
(尖沙嘴東部海濱花園; Map p510; Salisbury
Rd, Tsim Sha Tsui; ⓜTsim Sha Tsui, exit E) One
of the finest city skylines in the world has
to be that of Hong Kong Island, and the
promenade here is one of the best ways to
get an uninterrupted view. It's a lovely place
to stroll around during the day, but it really
comes into its own in the evening, during
the nightly **Symphony of Lights** (◎8-
8.20pm), a spectacular sound-and-light show
involving 44 buildings on the Hong Kong
Island skyline.

★**Shanghai Street** STREET
(上海街; Map p512; Yau Ma Tei; ⓜYau Ma Tei, exit
C) Strolling down Shanghai St will take you
back to a time long past. Once Kowloon's
main drag, it's flanked by stores selling Chinese wedding gowns, sandalwood incense
and Buddha statues, as well as mah-jong
parlours and an old pawn shop (at the junction with Saigon St). This is a terrific place
for souvenirs – fun picks include wooden
mooncake moulds stamped with images
of fish or pigs or lucky sayings, bamboo
steamer baskets, long chopsticks meant for
stirring pots and pretty ceramic bowls.

Yau Ma Tei

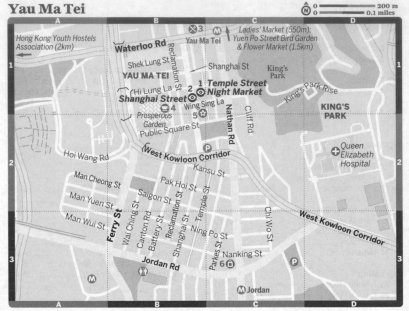

Yau Ma Tei

★ **Temple Street Night Market**   MARKET
(廟街夜市; Map p512; Temple St, Yau Ma Tei; ⊙6-
11pm; Ⓜ Yau Ma Tei, exit C) The liveliest night
market in Hong Kong, Temple St extends
from Man Ming Lane in the north to Nanking St in the south and is cut in two by the
Tin Hau Temple complex. While you may
find better bargains further north in New
Kowloon, and certainly over the border in
Shēnzhèn, it is still a good place to go for

the bustling atmosphere and the smells and
tastes on offer from the *dai pai dong* (open-
air street stall) food.

★ **Yuen Po Street Bird Garden &
Flower Market**   PARK
(園圃街雀鳥花園, 花墟; Map p503; Yuen Po &
Boundary Sts, Mong Kok; ⊙7am-8pm; Ⓜ Prince
Edward, exit B1) In this enchanting corner of
Mong Kok, you will find a handful of old
men out 'walking' their caged songbirds.
Stick around long enough and you should
see birds being fed squirming caterpillars
with chopsticks. There are also feathered
creatures for sale, along with elaborate cages
carved from teak (an excellent souvenir, in
our opinion). Adjacent to the garden is the
flower market, which theoretically keeps the
same hours, but only gets busy after 10am.

Don't miss shops choked with thousands
of multihued orchids, all cheap as chips.

★ **Sik Sik Yuen
Wong Tai Sin Temple**   TAOIST TEMPLE
(嗇色園黃大仙祠; ☎852 2327 8141, 852 2351
5640; www.siksikyuen.org.hk; 2 Chuk Yuen Village,
Wong Tai Sin; donation HK$2; ⊙7am-5.30pm;
Ⓜ Wong Tai Sin, exit B2) An explosion of colourful pillars, roofs, lattice work, flowers and
incense, this busy temple is a destination for
all walks of Hong Kong society, from pen-

sioners and business people to parents and young professionals.

Some come simply to pray, others to divine the future with *chīm* – bamboo 'fortune sticks' that are shaken out of a box on to the ground and then read by a fortune-teller (they're available free from the left of the main temple).

⭐ **Chi Lin Nunnery**   BUDDHIST NUNNERY
(志蓮淨苑; ☑852 2354 1888; www.chilin.org; 5 Chi Lin Dr, Diamond Hill; ⊙nunnery 9am 4.30pm, garden 6.30am 7pm; Ⓜ Diamond Hill, exit C2) FREE One of the most beautiful and arrestingly built environments in Hong Kong, this large Buddhist complex, originally dating from the 1930s, was rebuilt completely of wood (and not a single nail) in the style of the Tang dynasty in 1998. It is a serene place, with lotus ponds, immaculate bonsai tea plants and bougainvillea, and silent nuns delivering offerings of fruit and rice to Buddha and arhats (Buddhist disciples freed from the cycle of birth and death) or chanting behind intricately carved screens.

⭐ **Hong Kong Museum of History**   MUSEUM
(香港歷史博物館; Map p510; ☑852 2724 9042; http://hk.history.museum; 100 Chatham Rd South, Tsim Sha Tsui; adult/concession HK$10/5, Wed free; ⊙10am 6pm Mon & Wed-Sat, to 7pm Sun; 🚌; Ⓜ Tsim Sha Tsui, exit B2) For a whistle-stop overview of the territory's archaeology, ethnography, and natural and local history, this museum is well worth a visit, not just to learn more about the subject but also to understand how Hong Kong presents its stories to the world. 'The Hong Kong Story' takes visitors through the territory's past via eight galleries, starting with the natural environment and prehistoric Hong Kong – about 6000 years ago, give or take a lunar year – and ending with the territory's return to China in 1997.

⭐ **Kowloon Park**   PARK
(九龍公園; Map p510; www.lcsd.gov.hk; Nathan & Austin Rds, Tsim Sha Tsui; ⊙6am-midnight; 🚌; Ⓜ Tsim Sha Tsui, exit C2) Built on the site of a barracks for Indian soldiers in the colonial army, Kowloon Park is an oasis of greenery and a refreshing escape from the hustle and bustle of Tsim Sha Tsui. Pathways and walls criss-cross the grass, birds hop around in cages, and ancient banyan trees dot the landscape. In the morning the older set practise taichi amid the serene surrounds, and on Sunday afternoon Kung Fu Corner stages martial-arts displays.

Hong Kong Cultural Centre   NOTABLE BUILDING
(香港文化中心; Map p510; www.lcsd.gov.hk; 10 Salisbury Rd, Tsim Sha Tsui; ⊙9am-11pm; 🚢Star Ferry, Ⓜ East Tsim Sha Tsui, exit J) Overlooking the most beautiful part of the harbour, the aesthetically challenged and windowless Cultural Centre is a world-class venue (p529) containing a 2085-seat concert hall, a Grand Theatre that seats 1750, a studio theatre, and rehearsal studios. On the building's south side is the beginning of a viewing platform from where you can gain access to the Tsim Sha Tsui East Promenade (p511).

◉ New Territories

The New Territories offers much cultural and natural interest. Ancient walled villages (Sheung Shui, Fan Ling, Yuen Long), wetlands teeming with birds and aquatic life (Yuen Long), temples (Tsuen Wan, Sha Tin, Fan Ling), a solid museum in Sha Tin, and generous expanses of unspoiled country are just some of its attractions. Notably, Sai Kung Peninsula has fabulous hiking trails, delicious seafood and attractive beaches. And, of course, there's the awe-inspiring Hong Kong Unesco Global Geopark.

⭐ **Hong Kong Global Geopark**   PARK
(香港地質公園; www.geopark.gov.hk) Part of the Unesco Global Geopark Network, the spectacular Hong Kong Global Geopark consists of two regions of rock formations – volcanic rock formations from 140 million years ago and sedimentary rock formations from 400 million years ago – and a total of eight major groups of sites dispersed over 50 sq km in the eastern and northeastern New Territories. The best way to experience either region is by joining a guided boat tour. The Recommended Geopark Guide System (hkr2g.net) has recommendations.

⭐ **Lai Chi Wo**   VILLAGE
(荔枝窩; hakkahomelcw@gmail.com) This 400-year-old village inside Plover Cove Country Park is arguably Hong Kong's best-preserved Hakka walled village and has an intact feng shui woodland. Featuring 200 houses, three ancestral halls, two temples, and a breezy square fringed by banyans and opening onto recently revived rice paddies, Lai Chi Wo is not only a sight to behold, but also one of Hong Kong's most biologically diverse freshwater wetlands.

Along a stream leading to the village is the looking-glass **mangrove** with buttress roots forming a lace-like pattern. Also here is the white-flower Derris, a climbing vine with long, supple branches like elongated arms that form a natural swing. The Derris plant is poisonous and can be used as a fish stunner or insecticide, but only the root is harmful and only when crushed – there are butterflies and dragonflies aplenty here, hovering over scuttling mangrove crabs.

A 5- to 7-hectare crescent-shaped **wood** embraces the village from behind – this is ideal for the feng shui of a Hakka village. Not only does having the backing of wood bring good luck, it fosters a good life. Thickly grown trees and shrubs serve as a natural barrier against enemies and the elements, and are a source of food, fuel and construction materials. Lai Chi Wo was once the most affluent Hakka walled village in the northeastern New Territories.

Though almost completely abandoned in the 1960s, Lai Chi Wo has been undergoing a revival thanks to the efforts of villagers, academics and conservationists. The growing of rice and vegetables has resumed on a cautious scale, pig and cow sheds have been restored, and shuttered village houses now function as education and research facilities.

The village runs 90-minute **guided tours** every Sunday and public holiday – the ecological tour at 11am, and the cultural tour at 11am and 1.30pm. There's also a fabulous Hakka sticky-rice dumpling making workshop from 1.30pm to 3pm. Register at the village square or inform them before you go to ensure a place.

Bespoke tours can be arranged on weekdays, but make contact at least two weeks in advance. Currently the 9am Sunday ferry from the Ma Liu Shui Pier is the only direct public transport to the village, but sailings are expected to increase in the near future. The return sailing is at 3.30pm. Lai Chi Wo is only a 10-minute boat ride from the frontier town of Sha Tau Kok, but you'll need the Lai Chi Wo volunteers to get you a permit as the pier is in a closed area.

Most Hong Kong Global Geopark (p513) Sedimentary Rock tours make a stop at Lai Chi Wo, or just hike there from Wu Kau Tang or Luk Keng, and lunch at **Yau Kee** (有記; ☑ 852 9558 7787, 852 2674 0172; Lai Chi Wo; HK\$60-160; ⊙10.30am-2pm Sun & public holidays, closed on rainy days).

All tour, workshop and sailing times given were valid at the time of research, but may be subject to change in the coming months.

Green minibus 20C, operating between Tai Po Market MTR station and Tai Mei Tuk, goes beyond Tai Mei Tuk to Wu Kau Tang once every one to two hours between 5.45am to 7.45pm daily, with the last minibus returning from Wu Kau Tang at around 8.15pm. From Wu Kau Tang, it's a 90-minute walk to Lai Chi Wo.

On Sundays and public holidays, bus route 275R goes from Tai Po Market MTR station to Bride's Pool, which is only a 15-minute walk from Wu Kau Tang.

Green minibus 56K leaves Fanling MTR station for Luk Keng at 30-minute intervals on weekdays, and 10-minute intervals on Saturdays, Sundays and public holidays. From Luk Keng, it's a two-hour walk to Lai Chi Wo.

★**Hong Kong Heritage Museum** MUSEUM
(香港文化博物館; ☑852 2180 8188; www.heritagemuseum.gov.hk; 1 Man Lam Rd; adult/concession HK\$10/5, Wed free; ⊙10am-6pm Mon & Wed-Sat, to 7pm Sun; 🚻; ⓂChe Kung Temple, exit A) Southwest of Sha Tin town centre, this spacious, high-quality museum inside an ugly building gives a peek into local history and culture. Highlights include a **children's area** with interactive play zones, the **New Territories Heritage Hall** with mock-ups of traditional minority villages, the **Cantonese Opera Heritage Hall**, where you can watch old operas with English subtitles, and an elegant gallery of Chinese art. There's also a **Bruce Lee exhibit**, with some 600 items of the kung fu star's memorabilia on display until July 2018.

To reach the Hong Kong Heritage Museum from Che Kung Temple MTR station, walk east along Che Kung Miu Rd, go through the subway and cross the footbridge over the channel. The museum is 200m to the east.

Tai Po Market MARKET
(大埔街市; Fu Shin St, Tai Po; ⊙6am-8pm; ⓂTai Wo) Not to be confused with the MTR station of the same name, this street-long outdoor wet market is one of the most winning in the New Territories. Feast your eyes on a rainbow of fruit and vegetables, tables lined with dried seafood, old ladies hawking glutinous Hakka rice cakes, and stalls selling fresh aloe and sugar cane juices.

★**Ping Shan Heritage Trail** VILLAGE
(屏山文物徑; ☑852 2617 1959; Hang Tau Tsuen, Ping Shan, Yuen Long; ⊙ancestral halls & Tsui Sing Lau Pagoda 9am-1pm & 2-5pm Wed-Mon; ⓂTin Shui Wai, exit E) Hong Kong's first-ever heritage trail features historic buildings belonging to the Tangs, the first and the most powerful of the 'Five Clans'. Highlights of the 1km trail include Hong Kong's oldest pagoda

Tsui Sing Lau Pagoda (聚星樓; Ping Ha Rd; ⊙9am-1pm & 2-5pm Wed-Sun; ⒭Tin Shui Wai) FREE, the magnificent **Tang Clan Ancestral Hall** (鄧氏宗祠; Hang Tau Tsuen; ⊙9am-1pm & 2-5pm Wed-Sun; ⓜTin Shui Wai, exit E) FREE, a temple, a study hall, a well and **Ping Shan Tang Clan Gallery** (屏山鄧族文物館; ☑852 2617 1959; Hang Tau Tsuen; ⊙10am-5pm Tue-Sun; ⒭Ping Shan) FREE inside an old police station built by the British as much to monitor the coastline as to keep an eye on the clan.

Cross Tsui Sing Rd from the ground floor of the MTR station and you'll see the pagoda. Set aside two hours for the trail.

★**Hong Kong Wetland Park**　　PARK
(香港濕地公園; ☑852 3152 2666; www.wetlandpark.gov.hk; Wetland Park Rd, Tin Shui Wai; adult/concession HK$30/15; ⊙10am-5pm Wed-Mon; ⒨; ⒟967, ⒭705, 706) This 60-hectare ecological park is a window on the wetland ecosystems of northwest New Territories. The natural trails, bird hides and viewing platforms make it a handy and excellent spot for birdwatching. The futuristic grass-covered headquarters houses interesting galleries (including one on tropical swamps), a film theatre, a cafe and a viewing gallery. If you have binoculars, bring them; otherwise be prepared to wait to use the fixed points in the viewing galleries and hides (towers or huts from where you can watch birds up close without disturbing them).

To reach Hong Kong Wetland Park, take the MTR West Rail to Tin Shui Wai and board light-rail line 705 or 706, alighting at the Wetland Park stop. It can also be reached directly from Hong Kong Island: jump on a 967 bus at Admiralty MTR bus station.

Mai Po Nature Reserve　　NATURE RESERVE
(米埔自然護區; ☑852 2526 1011; www.wwf.org.hk; Mai Po, Sin Tin, Yuen Long; ⊙9am-5pm; ⒟76K from Sheung Shui East Rail or Yuen Long West Rail stations) The 270-hectare nature reserve includes the Mai Po Visitor Centre at the northeastern end, where you must register; the Mai Po Education Centre to the south, with displays on the history and ecology of the wetland and Deep Bay; floating boardwalks and trails through the mangroves and mudflats; and a dozen hides. Disconcertingly, the cityscape of Shēnzhèn looms to the north.

◉ **Outlying Islands**

From the old-world streetscapes of Cheung Chau and Peng Chau, to the monasteries and hiking trails of Lantau, and the waterfront seafood restaurants of Lamma, Hong Kong's 'Outlying Islands' offer a host of sights and activities.

The sheer size of **Lantau**, Hong Kong's largest island, makes for days of exploration. The north tip of the island, home to the airport, Disneyland and the high-rise Tung Chung residential and shopping complex, is highly developed. But much of the rest of Lantau is still entirely rural. Here you'll find

HONG KONG SIGHTS

STAR FERRY

You can't say you've 'done' Hong Kong until you've taken a ride on a **Star Ferry** (天星小輪; Map p504; ☑852 2367 7065; www.starferry.com.hk; adult HK$2.50-3.40, child HK$1.50-2.10; ⊙every 6-12min, 6.30am-11.30pm; ⓜHong Kong, exit A2), that wonderful fleet of electric-diesel vessels with names like *Morning Star, Celestial Star* and *Twinkling Star*. Try to take your first trip on a clear night from Kowloon to Central. It's not half as dramatic in the opposite direction.

At any time of the day, the journey, with its riveting views of skyscrapers and jungle-clad hills, must be one of the world's best-value cruises. At the end of the 10-minute journey, a hemp rope is cast and caught with a billhook, the way it was in 1888 when the first boat docked.

Star Ferry also runs a 60-minute **Harbour Tour** (HK$80 to HK$200) covering calling points at Tsim Sha Tsui, Central and Wan Chai. Get tickets at the piers.

The Star Ferry was founded by Dorabjee Nowrojee, a Parsee from Bombay. Parsees believe in Zoroastrianism, and the five-pointed star on the Star Ferry logo is an ancient Zoroastrian symbol – in fact the same as the one followed by the Three Magi (who may have been Zoroastrian pilgrims) to Bethlehem in the Christmas tale.

Zoroastrians consider fire a medium through which spiritual wisdom is gained, and water is considered the source of that wisdom. No wonder that on an overcast day, the only stars you'll see over Victoria Harbour are those of the Star Ferry.

traditional fishing villages, empty beaches and a mountainous interior criss-crossed with quad-burning hiking trails.

Most visitors come to Lantau to visit Mickey or see the justly famous 'Big Buddha' statue, but be sure you get beyond the north side for a taste of a laid-back island where cows graze in the middle of the road, school kids gather seaweed with their grandparents in the shallow bays, and the odd pangolin is said to still roam the forested hillsides.

Lamma, Hong Kong's laid-back 'hippie island', is easily recognisable at a distance by the three coal chimneys crowning its hilly skyline. The chimneys stand out so much because Lamma, home to 6000 or so, is otherwise devoid of high-rise development. Here it's all about lush forests, hidden beaches and chilled-out villages connected by pedestrian paths. You won't see any cars here, but be prepared for spotting the odd snake.

Most visitors arrive in the main town of Yung Shue Wan, a counterculture haven popular with expats.

Small, dumb-bell–shaped **Cheung Chau** island is a popular getaway thanks to its beaches and its cute downtown lined with snack shops and incense-filled temples. Come here for an afternoon of temple touring, noshing on fish balls and exploring the rocky coastline. Or stay for a weekend at one of the many holiday rentals and treat yourself to a day of windsurfing lessons followed by an alfresco seafood dinner at one of several harbourside restaurants.

Hong Kong Disneyland   AMUSEMENT PARK
(香港迪士尼樂園; ☑ 852 183 0830; http://park. hongkongdisneyland.com; adult/child one-day ticket HK$539/385; ⊙10am-8pm Mon-Fri, to 9pm Sat & Sun; 👶; Ⓜ Disney Resort Station) Ever since it claimed Hong Kong in 2005, Disneyland has served as a rite of passage for the flocks of Asian tourists who come daily to steal a glimpse of one of America's most famous cultural exports. It's divided into seven areas – Main Street USA, Tomorrowland, Fantasyland, Adventureland, Toy Story Land, Mystic Point and Grizzly Gulch – but it's still quite tiny compared to the US version, and most of the attractions are geared towards families with small children.

🏃 Activities

Hong Kong offers countless ways to have fun and keep fit. From golf and soccer to cycling and windsurfing, you won't be stumped for something active to do or somewhere to do it – for lists of fields, stadiums, beaches, water-sports centres etc, including equipment for hire, check the website of the Leisure and Cultural Services Department (www.lcsd.gov.hk). There are also gyms, yoga studios and spas offering everything from aromatherapy to foot massage. If you prefer watching people play, the world's most exciting dragon boat racing takes place right here!

★ **High Island Reservoir East Dam**   HIKING
(萬宜水庫東霸) A reservoir built in the 1970s, the South China Sea, and 14-million-year-old volcanic rocks make this one of Hong Kong's most breathtaking places. High Island Reservoir East Dam is in the only part of Hong Kong Global Geopark that's reachable on foot, and the only place where you can touch the hexagonal rock columns. The scenery is surreal and made even more so by the presence of thousands of dolosse (huge cement barriers shaped like jacks) placed along the coast to break sea waves.

Hong Kong's second reservoir built by sealing off the coast with dams – Plover Cove was the first – High Island was constructed to provide fresh water to the territory when mainland China shut down supply during the 1967 riots. It was designed by Binnie & Partners of London and constructed by an Italian company, Vianini Lavori. At the southern end of East Dam, you'll see a giant

PO LIN MONASTERY & BIG BUDDHA

Built in 1924, **Po Lin Monastery & Big Buddha** (寶蓮禪寺; ☑ 852 2985 5248; Lantau Island; ⊙ 9am-6pm) is a huge Buddhist monastery and temple complex. Today it seems more of a tourist honeypot than a religious retreat, attracting hundreds of thousands of visitors a year and still being expanded. Most of the buildings you'll see on arrival are new, with the older, simpler ones tucked away behind them. The big draw is the enormous seated bronze Buddha, a must-see on any Hong Kong trip.

Commonly known as the 'Big Buddha', the Tian Tan Buddha is a representation of Lord Gautama some 23m high (or 26.4m with the lotus), or just under 34m if you include the podium. It was unveiled in 1993, and today it still holds the honour of being the tallest seated bronze Buddha statue in the world.

dolos block in sky blue. It's a memorial erected by Vianini Lavori to those who died on the project. Nearby there's a slab of concrete that commemorates, in Chinese and English, the inauguration of the reservoir in 1978. The construction of the reservoir had one unintentional effect – it made a part of what 30 years later became Hong Kong Global Geopark accessible on foot. Off the coast of the southern end of the dam is Po Pin Chau (literally, Broken-Sided Island), a massive sea stack with rock columns all over its face like a giant pipe organ.

Country & Marine Parks Authority   PARK
(Map p503; ☑ 852 2150 6868; www.afcd.gov.hk/english/country/cou_vis/cou_vis.html) Has information about visiting Hong Kong's various country and marine parks.

Lantau Peak   HIKING
(Fung Wong Shan) Known as Fung Wong Shan (Phoenix Mountain) in Cantonese, this 934m-high peak is the second-highest in Hong Kong after Tai Mo Shan (957m) in the New Territories. The view from the summit is absolutely stunning, and on a clear day it's possible to see Macau 65km to the west. Watching the sun rise from the peak is a popular choice among hardy hikers. Some choose to stay at the **Ngong Ping SG Davis Hostel** (☑ 852 2985 5610; www.yha.org.hk; Ngong Ping; dm from HK$110, r from HK$400; ☐☑ from Mui Wo, or 21, 23 from Tung Chung) and leave around 4am for the two-hour summit push.

If you're hiking Lantau Peak as a day trip, take the MTR to Tung Chung, then take bus 3M to Pak Kung Au (tell the driver where you're getting off beforehand). From here, you'll follow the markers for section 3 of the **Lantau Trail**, ascending the peak and then descending the steps into Ngong Ping. This 4.5km route takes about three hours.

Tai Tam Waterworks Heritage Trail   HIKING
(大潭水務文物徑) This scenic 5km trail runs past reservoirs and a handsome collection of 20 historic waterworks structures – feats of Victorian utilitarian engineering that include bridges, aqueducts, valve houses, pumping stations and dams, many still working.

The trail, which ends at Tai Tam Tuk Raw Water Pumping Station, takes about two hours. Enter at Wong Nai Chung Gap near the luxury flats of Hong Kong Parkview, or at the junction of Tai Tam Rd and Tai Tam Reservoir Rd. On weekends you'll see residents taking a walk with their dogs, kids, maids, chauffeurs and nannies.

From Admiralty MTR station, bus 6 takes you to Wong Nai Chung Reservoir. Walk east along Tai Tam Reservoir Rd.

Hong Kong Golf Association   GOLF
(☑ 852 2504 8659; www.hkga.com) The HKGA is the authority that governs and promotes golfing events in Hong Kong, including the Hong Kong Open.

HKTB Island Tour   BUS
(☑ 852 2368 7111; www.discoverhongkong.com; half-/full-day adult HK$530/740, child HK$400/620) Includes Man Mo Temple, the Peak, Aberdeen, Repulse Bay and Stanley Market.

Big Foot Tours   WALKING
(☑ 852 6075 2727; www.bigfoottour.com) Small group tours tailored to your interests really get behind the scenes of daily Hong Kong life. Itineraries can focus on food (wanna try snake soup?), architecture, nature or whatever strikes your fancy, and guides are full of interesting facts. Four-hour tours are about HK$700 per person, depending on group size. Private tours start from HK$2200 for two people.

Walk Hong Kong   WALKING
(☑ 852 9187 8641; www.walkhongkong.com) Offers a range of hiking tours to some of most beautiful places in Hong Kong, including deserted beaches (HK$800 per person, 8½ hours), Dragon's Back in Shek O (HK$500 per person, four hours), WWII battlefields (HK$500, half-day), as well as half-day local market tours (HK$450).

Ten Feet Tall   MASSAGE
(Map p504; ☑ 852 2971 1010; www.tenfeettall.com.hk; 20th & 21st fl, L Place, 139 Queen's Rd, Central; ☉ 11am-midnight Mon-Thu, 10.30am-1.30am Fri & Sat, 10.30am-12.30am Sun; Ⓜ Central, exit D2) This sprawling comfort den (745 sq metres) offers a range of treatments from foot reflexology and shoulder massage to hardcore pressure-point massage and aromatic oil treatments. The interiors were created by French restaurant designers.

Hong Kong Dolphinwatch   WILDLIFE WATCHING
(香港海豚觀察; Map p510; ☑ 852 2984 1414; www.hkdolphinwatch.com; 15th fl, Middle Block, 1528A Star House, 3 Salisbury Rd, Tsim Sha Tsui; adult/child HK$420/210; ☉ cruises Wed, Fri & Sun) ⬐ Hong Kong Dolphinwatch was founded in 1995 to raise awareness of Hong Kong's wonderful pink dolphins and promote responsible ecotourism. It offers 2½-hour cruises to see them in their natural habitat.

Walking Tour
Hong Kong's Wholesale District

START SUTHERLAND ST STOP, KENNEDY TOWN TRAM
END SHEUNG WAN MTR STATION, EXIT B
LENGTH 1.9KM; ONE HOUR

Set off from the Sutherland St stop of the Kennedy Town tram. Have a look at (and a sniff of) Des Voeux Rd West's many ❶ **dried seafood shops** piled with all manner of desiccated sea life. Walk south on Sutherland St to Ko Shing St to browse the medieval-sounding goods on offer from the ❷ **herbal-medicine traders**.

At the end of Ko Shing St, re-enter Des Voeux Rd West and head northeast. Continue along Connaught Rd West, where you'll find the attractive colonial building that houses the ❸ **Western Market** (⏱9am-7pm).

At the corner of Morrison St, walk south past Wing Lok St and Bonham Strand, which are both lined with ❹ **shops selling ginseng root and edible birds' nests**. Then turn right onto Queen's Rd Central to the ❺ **incense shops** selling paper funeral offerings for the dead.

If you're hungry, progress to Queen's Rd West for a quick Chiu Chow meal at ❻ **Chan Kan Kee**. Retrace your steps, and climb up Possession St, then take a left into Hollywood Rd, before turning right to ascend Pound Lane to where it meets Tai Ping Shan St. Here you'll see four charming ❼ **temples**.

Head southeast down Tai Ping Shan St, then left to descend Upper Station St to the start of Hollywood Rd's ❽ **antique shops**. There's a vast choice of curios and rare, mostly Chinese, treasures.

Continuing east on Hollywood Rd brings you to ❾ **Man Mo Temple** (p507), one of the oldest and most significant temples in the territory.

Take a short hop to the left down Ladder St to Upper Lascar Row, home of the ❿ **Cat Street Market** (⏱10am-6pm), which is well stocked with inexpensive Chinese memorabilia. Ladder St brings you back to Queen's Rd Central. Cross the road and follow Hillier St to Bonham Strand. Sheung Wan MTR station is due north.

About 97% of the cruises result in the sighting of at least one dolphin; if none are spotted, passengers are offered a free trip.

Wan Kei Ho International Martial Arts Association MARTIAL ARTS
(尹圻灝國際武術總會; Map p504; ☑ 852 9506 0075, 852 2544 1368; www.kungfuwan.com; 3rd fl, Yue's House, 304 Des Voeux Rd Central, Sheung Wan; ⊙10am-8pm Mon-Fri, 9am-1pm Sat & Sun; Ⓜ Sheung Wan, exit A) English-speaking Master Wan teaches northern Shàolín kung fu to a wide following of locals and foreigners. Classes are offered in the evenings from Monday to Thursday. Depending on how many classes you take, the monthly fees may range from HK$350 to HK$1600.

Fringe Club COURSE
(Map p504; ☑ 852 2521 7251; www.hkfringe.com.hk; 2 Lower Albert Rd, Lan Kwai Fong) The Fringe Club offers any number of courses and workshops centred on visual arts.

Tours

Mai Po Nature Reserve Tours NATURE TOURS
(米埔自然保護區導賞團; ☑ 852 2526 1011; www.wwf.org.hk; Mai Po, Sin Tin, Yuen Long; tours HK$120-220; ⊙weekends & public holidays; 🚌 76K from Sheung Shui East Rail or Yuen Long West Rail stations) World Wide Fund for Nature Hong Kong (WWF) runs year-round and seasonal tours of Mai Po Nature Reserve (p515). The three- or four-hour tours are led by bilingual guides when there are English speakers present. Note that different age requirements for child participants apply. Details and booking online.

Festivals & Events

Hong Kong Arts Festival ART
(香港藝術節; www.hk.artsfestival.org; from HK$150; ⊙Feb-Mar) A feast of music and performance arts, ranging from classical to contemporary, by hundreds of local and international talents.

Art Basel Hong Kong ART
(香港巴塞爾藝術展; Map p508; www.artbasel.com/hong-kong; HK$180-850; ⊙Mar) The Hong Kong edition of the world's premier art fair is a mega event where hundreds of galleries, thousands of artists, as well as art collectors from all over the world flock to Hong Kong for five days of buying, selling, mingling and viewing. Satellite happenings are hosted by galleries all over town but the big shows are at the Hong Kong Convention & Exhibition Centre in Wan Chai.

Hong Kong International Film Festival FILM
(香港國際電影節; www.hkiff.org.hk; from HK$45; ⊙Mar & Apr) One of Asia's top film festivals, the 40-year-old HKIFF screens the latest art-house and award-winning movies from around the world for two to three weeks straddling the Easter holidays. Those who missed the festival can catch screenings all year round at regular cinemas through the festival's Cine Fan program (http://cinefan.com.hk).

Cheung Chau Bun Festival FOOD & DRINK
(www.cheungchau.org; Apr or May) Taking place over four days in late April or early May, Cheung Chau's annual Bun Festival is one of Hong Kong's most unique cultural experiences. Honouring the Taoist god Pak Tai, the festival involves days of parades, music and sweet buns galore. The main event is the scramble up the 'bun tower' – whoever grabs the top bun first wins.

Hong Kong International Dragon Boat Races SPORTS
(香港國際龍舟邀請賽; www.hkdba.com.hk; ⊙May or Jun) For several days round the fifth day of the fifth lunar month, as has been the custom for hundreds of years, dragon-boaters race in waterways all over Hong Kong. It's also around this time that the government-hosted Hong Kong International Dragon Boat Races take place at Victoria Harbour. The event features thousands of the world's top dragon-boaters over three exciting days of racing and partying.

Clockenflap Outdoor Music Festival MUSIC
(香港音樂及藝術節; Map p504; www.clockenflap.com; tickets HK$600-1800; ⊙Nov or Dec) Hong Kong's largest outdoor music festival incorporates international, regional and local live music of a mostly indie variety, as well as art installations and pop-ups. Acts that have played the festival include New Order, The Libertines, A$AP and Primal Scream.

Sleeping

Hong Kong offers a full range of accommodation, from closet-sized rooms to palatial suites. Most hotels on Hong Kong Island are between Central and Causeway Bay; in Kowloon, they fall around Nathan Rd, where you'll also find budget places. During low seasons prices fall sharply, particularly the midrange and top-end options, when booking online can get you discounts of up to 60%.

Central District

The lion's share of Hong Kong Island's luxury hotels is in Central, catering predominantly to moneyed leisure travellers and busy, corporate types. The service and facilities you'll find here are the best in town. Whether it's child-minding service, dinner reservations or combating jetlag you need, it will be done with efficiency, and possibly a smile.

★**Helena May** HOTEL **$**
(梅夫人婦女會主樓; Map p504; ☑852 2522 6766; www.helenamay.com; 35 Garden Rd, Central; s/d HK$580/760, studio per month HK$16,300-21,240; ☐23) If you like the peninsula's colonial setting but not its price tag, this grand dame could be your cup of tea. Founded in 1916 as a social club for single European women, it is now a private club for women of all nationalities and a hotel with 43 creaky but charming rooms. Rooms are women-only; studios are open to men.

Rooms are in the main building and have shared bathrooms, while the rent-by-the-month studios are in an adjacent building. You must be 18 or above to stay at the Helena May. The building is a stone's throw from the Peak Tram Terminus and the Zoological & Botanical Gardens.

All guests must pay a HK$180 membership fee, plus a HK$120 monthly subscription.

★**Mandarin Oriental** LUXURY HOTEL **$$$**
(文華東方酒店; Map p504; ☑852 2522 0111; www.mandarinoriental.com/hongkong; 5 Connaught Rd, Central; r HK$3655-7400, ste HK$6120-65,000; @☎☒; ⓂCentral, exit J3) The venerable Mandarin has historically set the standard in Asia and continues to be a contender for the top spot, despite competition from the likes of the Four Seasons. The styling, service, food and atmosphere are stellar throughout and there's a sense of gracious, old-world charm. The sleek **Landmark Oriental** (Map p504; ☑852 2132 0088; www.mandarin oriental.com/landmark; 15 Queen's Rd, Central; r HK$5470-9000, ste HK$9300-45,000; @☎☒; ⓂCentral, exit D1), just across the way, offers modern luxury, but with a business vibe.

Four Seasons LUXURY HOTEL **$$$**
(四季酒店; Map p504; ☑852 3196 8888; www.fourseasons.com/hongkong; 8 Finance St, Central; r HK$4800-8100, ste HK$9800-65,000; @☎☒; ⓂHong Kong, exit F) The Four Seasons arguably edges into top place on the island for its amazing views, pristine service, and its location close to the Star Ferry Pier, Hong Kong

station and Sheung Wan. Also on offer are palatial rooms, a glorious pool and spa complex, and award-winning restaurants **Caprice** (Map p504; set lunch/dinner from HK$540/1740; ⏰noon-2.30pm & 6-10.30pm; ☎; ⓂHong Kong, exit E1) and Lung King Heen (p524).

The Peak & Northwest Hong Kong Island

Some of the city's better midrange hotels can be found in the Sheung Wan area, which is close enough to the action, but too far for the well heeled business crowds.

★**Bishop Lei International House** HOTEL **$**
(宏基國際賓館; Map p504; ☑852 2868 0828; www.bishopleihtl.com.hk; 4 Robinson Rd, Mid-Levels; s/d/ste from $550/700/1250; @☒; ☐23 or 40) This hotel in residential Mid-Levels, though out of the way, provides a lot of bang for your buck. It boasts good service, a swimming pool, a gym and proximity to the Zoological & Botanical Gardens. The standard single and double rooms are small. It's worth paying a little more for the larger, harbour-facing rooms, which offer good views of the skyline and the cathedral from high up. Buses to Central and Wan Chai stop in front of the hotel.

Jockey Club Mt Davis Youth Hostel HOSTEL **$**
(☑852 2817 5715; www.yha.org.hk; 123 Mount Davis Path, Pok Fu Lam; dm high season/low season HK$250/180, r from HK$500; ☎) If you're not afraid of ghosts (Mt Davis, an isolated Pok Fu Lam peak, is said to be haunted) then this newly refurbished hostel may be for you. Though it's not walking distance from anything, it makes up for it with a free shuttle bus and killer views of Victoria Harbour. Guests must be a **Hong Kong Youth Hostels Association** (香港青年旅舍協會, HKYHA; ☑852 2788 1638; www.yha.org.hk; HI card under/over 18yr $70/150) member, or arrive with one.

★**Pottinger** BOUTIQUE HOTEL **$$$**
(Map p504; ☑852 2308 3188; www.thepottinger.com; 74 Queen's Rd Central, enter from Stanley St, Central; r from HK$2700, ste from HK$4200; ⓂCentral D2) Smack in the heart of Central, this unobtrusive new boutique hotel has 86 airy, white-and-cream rooms with subtle Asian touches – carved wooden screens, calligraphy work, black-and-white photos of old Hong Kong. The Envoy, the Pottinger's excellent hotel bar, has a colonial theme, with dark panelling and afternoon high tea, a tribute to Sir Henry Pottinger, Hong Kong's first governor and the hotel's namesake.

Wan Chai & Northeast Hong Kong Island

Admiralty, with easy access to Hong Kong Park, the Pacific Place mall and the Asia Society Hong Kong Centre, has a handful of high-end hotels. Wan Chai, favoured by trade-fair regulars and mainland tourists, has midrange lodging, with a sprinkling of cheaper options in old residential buildings and some luxury addresses near the harbour. In addition to good-value midrange options, Causeway Bay is served by some inexpensive hostels. During the low season, guesthouses often struggle to fill beds and rooms; most will offer discounts to anyone staying longer than a few nights.

Check Inn   HOSTEL **$**
(卓軒旅舍; Map p508; ☑852 2955 0175; www.checkinnhk.com; Room A, 3rd fl, Kwong Wah Mansion, 269-273 Hennessy Rd, Wan Chai; dm HK$160-200, r HK$450-600; ি; Ⓜ Wan Chai, exit A2) Twelve basic dorms (female and mixed) and four simple en suite rooms in an old, centrally located building. The reception and hangout area (2nd floor) is cosy and spacious, featuring books and coffee next to a wall of windows. The knowledgeable staff hosts two or three free tours a week for guests, who just need to pay for food and transport.

★ **Tuve**   BOUTIQUE HOTEL **$$**
(Map p508; ☑852 3995 8800; www.tuve.hk; 16 Tsing Fung St, Tin Hau; from HK$980; @ি; Ⓜ Tin Hau, exit A1) From the dungeon-like entrance to the noir-ish reception area with black iron grille and the brass and concrete slab that is the front desk, everything here spells design. Industrial glam continues in the rooms where concrete walls are discreetly highlighted with gold foil, and grey-and-white marble plays off against oak and wired glass, and all are grounded by immaculate white linen and excellent service.

★ **Upper House**   BOUTIQUE HOTEL **$$$**
(☑852 2918 1838; www.upperhouse.com; 88 Queensway, Pacific Pl, Admiralty; r/ste from HK$5000/17,000; @ি; Ⓜ Admiralty, exit F) Every corner here spells Zen-like serenity: the understated lobby, the sleek ecominded rooms, the elegant sculptures, the warm and discreet service, and the manicured lawn

---

CHUNGKING MANSIONS

Say 'budget accommodation' and 'Hong Kong' in one breath and everyone thinks of Chungking Mansions. Built in 1961, CKM is a labyrinth of homes, guesthouses, Indian restaurants, souvenir stalls and foreign-exchange shops spread over five 17-storey blocks in the heart of Tsim Sha Tsui. According to anthropologist Gordon Mathews, it has a resident population of about 4000 and an estimated 10,000 daily visitors. More than 120 different nationalities – predominantly South Asian and African – pass through its doors in a single year.

Though standards vary significantly, most of the guesthouses at CKM are clean and quite comfortable. It's worth bearing in mind, however, that rooms are usually the size of cupboards and you have to shower right next to the toilet. The rooms typically come with air-con and TV and, sometimes, a phone. Many guesthouses can get you a Chinese visa quickly, most have internet access and some have wi-fi and laundry service.

Bargaining for a bed or room is always possible, though you won't get very far in the high season. You can often negotiate a cheaper price if you stay more than, say, a week, but never try that on the first night – stay one night and find out how you like it before handing over more rent. Once you pay, there are usually no refunds.

Though there are dozens of ever-changing hostels in Chungking Mansions, some reliable ones include **New China Guesthouse** (新欣欣賓館; Map p510; ☑852 9489 3891; http://newchinaguesthouse.com; Flat D7, 9th fl, D Block; r from HK$230; ি; Ⓜ Tsim Sha Tsui, exit D1), **Park Guesthouse** (百樂賓館; Map p510; ☑852 2368 1689; fax 852 2367 7889; Flat A1, 15th fl, A Block; s from HK$250, d from HK$450, without bathroom HK$200; ি; Ⓜ Tsim Sha Tsui, exit D1), **Holiday Guesthouse** (Map p510; ☑852 2316 7152, 852 9121 8072; fax 852 2316 7181; Flat E1, 6th fl, E Block; s HK$250-600, d HK$350-700; @ি; Ⓜ Tsim Sha Tsui, exit D1) and **Dragon Inn** (龍滙賓館; Map p510; ☑852 2368 2007; www.dragoninn.info; Flat B5, 3rd fl, B Block; s HK$180-400, d HK$360-680, honeymoon rooms HK$660, tr HK$480, q HK$520; ি; Ⓜ Tsim Sha Tsui, exit D1).

Movie buffs note: it was at nearby Mirador Mansion – and not Chungking Mansions – where Wong Kar-wai filmed most of *Chungking Express* (1994).

where guests can join free yoga classes. Other pluses include a free and 'bottomless' minibar, a 24-hour gym, and easy access to Admiralty MTR station. The cafe is famous for its afternoon tea.

★ **Hotel Indigo**   BUSINESS HOTEL $$$
(Map p508; ☑ 852 3926 3888; www.ihg.com; 246 Queen's Rd E, Wan Chai; dm HK$2000-3800, ste HK$4500-6000; @奈窶; Ⓜ Wan Chai, exit A3) Excitingly located near markets and hipster hang-outs, Indigo has slightly over-the-top modern Chinese decor and 138 large-ish, tech-forward, and very comfortable rooms. A dragon-shaped heat-absorbing grid covers its exterior, giving texture to scenery framed by the rooms' floor-to-ceiling windows. The rooftop pool has views of the hills and, dizzyingly – the courteous staff will remind you – the street below.

Choose an upper-floor 'deluxe' room for the best views and more natural light. Indigo also has a small 24-hour gym, a meeting room seating eight, a quaint cafe that makes attractive use of the eponymous colour, and **Skybar** (Map p508; ☑ 852 3926 3888; www.ihg. com; 29th fl, Hotel Indigo; ⊙ 4pm-1am, happy hour 5-8pm), which has killer views.

🛏 Kowloon

Splendour rubs shoulders with squalor in Kowloon. There is a huge range of hotels and guesthouses, catering to all budgets, between the two extremes. Tsim Sha Tsui has a number of top-end hotels, some glamorous, some anonymous. Things start getting cheaper as you go north. Yau Ma Tei has several midrange options, plus cheap, basic hotels and a good assortment of guesthouses.

★ **Urban Pack**   HOSTEL $
(休閒小窩; Map p510; ☑ 852 2732 2271; www.urban -pack.com; Unit 1410, 14th fl, Haiphong Mansion, 99-101 Nathan Rd, Tsim Sha Tsui; dm HK$200-500, r from HK$500, apt from HK$700; 奈; Ⓜ Tsim Sha Tsui, exit A1) If your idea of a great hostel involves a chilled vibe, lots of interaction with fellow travellers, and bar-hopping with the owners, Urban Pack is *the* place for you. Run by two friendly Canadian-Chinese, Albert and Jensen, Urban Pack also offers solid dorms (mixed and women's), as well as new private rooms and suites.

★ **Mariner's Club**   HOTEL $
(海員之家; Map p510; ☑ 852 2368 8261; www. themarinersclubhk.org; 11 Middle Rd, Tsim Sha Tsui;

s/d without bathroom from HK$370/520, with bathroom from HK$550/750, ste from HK$1140; @奈窶; Ⓜ East Tsim Sha Tsui, exit K) The Mariner's Club, overlooking the Middle Road Children's Playground, offers a lazy, old-world charm, as well as a first-rate swimming pool. The hotel has 100 rooms – 30 new (with wi-fi, on the 4th and 5th floors), and 70 old (austere-looking with retro furniture). Anyone can book this great budget option but there may be discounts if you have a mariner's ID or proof of shipping-company employment at check-in.

★ **Salisbury**   HOTEL $
(香港基督教青年會; Map p510; ☑ 852 2268 7888; www.ymcahk.org.hk; 41 Salisbury Rd, Tsim Sha Tsui; dm HK$360, s/d/ste from HK$1200/1360/2200; ⊜@奈窶; Ⓜ Tsim Sha Tsui, exit E) If you can manage to book a room at this fabulously located YMCA hotel, you'll be rewarded with professional service and excellent exercise facilities. Newly renovated rooms and suites are comfortable but simple, so keep your eyes on the harbour: that view would cost you five times as much at the Peninsula next door. The dormitory rooms are a bonus, but restrictions apply.

The four-bed dorm rooms are meant for short-stay travellers, hence no one can stay there more than 10 nights in a 30-day period, and walk-in guests aren't accepted if they've been in Hong Kong for more than seven days; check-in is at 2pm. The same restrictions do not apply to the other rooms at the Salisbury. Sports enthusiasts will love it here – the hotel has a 25m swimming pool, a fitness centre and a climbing wall.

Empire Kowloon   HOTEL $$
(尖沙咀皇悅酒店; Map p510; ☑ 852 3692 2222; www.empirehotel.com.hk; 62 Kimberley Rd, Tsim Sha Tsui; r/ste from HK$1045/2000; @奈窶; Ⓜ Tsim Sha Tsui, exit B2) This hotel offers decent rooms and an excellent indoor atrium swimming pool and spa. It's in the old residential quarter of Tsim Sha Tsui. Weekday rates can be 30% lower or more. Guests get use of a free mobile phone with data for use around the city.

★ **Peninsula Hong Kong**   HOTEL $$$
(香港半島酒店; Map p510; ☑ 852 2920 2888; www.peninsula.com; Salisbury Rd, Tsim Sha Tsui; r/ste from HK$4000/6000; @奈窶; Ⓜ Tsim Sha Tsui, exit E) Lording it over the southern tip of Kowloon, Hong Kong's finest hotel exudes colonial elegance. Your dilemma will be how to get here: landing on the rooftop helipad or arriving in one of the hotel's 14-strong fleet

of Rolls-Royce Phantoms. Some 300 classic European-style rooms sport wi-fi, CD and DVD players, as well as marble bathrooms.

★**Hyatt Regency Tsim Sha Tsui** HOTEL $$$
(尖沙咀凱悅酒店; Map p510; ☑852 2311 1234; http://hongkong.tsimshatsui.hyatt.com; 18 Hanoi Rd, Tsim Sha Tsui; r/ste from HK$2150/3600; @🛇🕿; MTsim Sha Tsui, exit D2) Top marks to this classic that exudes understated elegance and composure. Rooms are plush and relatively spacious, with those on the upper floors commanding views over the city. Black-and-white photos of Tsim Sha Tsui add a thoughtful touch to the decor. The lobby gets crowded at times, but the helpful and resourceful staff will put you at ease.

Ritz-Carlton Hong Kong HOTEL $$$
(麗思卡爾頓酒店; ☑852 2263 2263; www.ritzcarlton.com/hongkong; 1 Austin Rd W, Tsim Sha Tsui; r HK$5000-9900, ste from HK$9000; 🛇🕿; MKowloon, exit C1 or D1) Sitting on Kowloon Station, this out-of-the-way luxury hotel is the tallest hotel on earth (the lobby's on the 103rd floor). To echo the theme of excess, the decor is over the top with imposing furniture and a superfluity of shiny surfaces, the service is stellar, **Tin Lung Heen** (天龍軒; ☑852 2263 2270; 102nd fl, Ritz-Carlton Hong Kong; meals HK$400-1700; ⊙noon-2.30pm & 6-10.30pm, MKowloon, exit U3) serves top-notch Chinese food, and the views on a clear day are mind-blowing

⌂ New Territories

Tao Fong Shan Ascension House HOSTEL $
(道風山昇天屋; www.ascensionhousehk.com; 33 Tao Fong Shan Rd, Sha Tin; dm HK$180-300; MSha Tin, exit B) Located at the edge of the Tao Fong Shan compound is Ascension House with four basic air-conditioned dorms accommodating two or three people. Bathrooms are shared and guests have use of a kitchen. It's managed by volunteers from Scandinavia, who also lead daily prayers, host cookouts and arrange weekend outings. Participation is optional.

Ascension House is only open to overseas backpackers. At exit B of Sha Tin MTR station, walk down the ramp, passing a series of old village houses on the left. To the left of these houses is a set of steps signposted 'To Fung Shan'. Follow the path all the way to the top. The walk should take around 20 minutes. A taxi from the nearest MTR station in Sha Tin will cost about HK$38, under HK$30 from Tai Wai MTR station.

★**Campus Hong Kong** HOSTEL $
(☑852 2945 1111; www.campushk.com; 123 Castle Peak Rd, Yau Kom Tau, Tsuen Wan; dm HK$190-260, r HK$700-1000; 🛇; MTsuen Wan) Fabulous hostel for university students that also entertains backpackers whenever rooms are available, but especially during the summer months. The 48 rooms with four beds each feature nifty communal and study spaces, kitchenette and shower. It's part of a serviced apartment complex (Bay Bridge Hong Kong) and hostel guests also get to enjoy the sea views, the fitness room and the swimming pool.

Weekly rates are HK$1200 to HK$1500 per room, and monthly HK$5000 (over six months) or HK$5500 (under six months). There's free shuttle bus service to Tsuen Wan MTR station. At exit B of Tsuen Wan MTR station, turn right and ascend some stairs to Tai Ho Rd North and you'll see the shuttle bus station for Bay Bridge Hong Kong.

⌂ Outlying Islands

With the exception of Lantau, there are no international-style hotels on any of the Outlying Islands. Instead, you'll find local guesthouses and beach inns, as well as some camping opportunities.

✖ Eating

One of the world's top culinary capitals, the city that worships the God of Cookery has many a demon in the kitchen, whether the deliciousness in the pot is Cantonese, Sichuanese, Japanese or French. So deep is the city's love of food and so broad its culinary repertoire that whatever your gastronomic desires, Hong Kong will find a way to sate them. The answer could be a bowl of wonton noodles, freshly steamed dim sum, a warm pineapple bun wedged with butter, a pair of the sweetest prawns, your first-ever stinky tofu, or the creations of the latest celebrity chef.

✖ Central District

Many of the city's poshest, most multistarred restaurants are in Central, though there's also no shortage of affordable lunch spots popular with local workers.

★**Tim Ho Wan,**
the Dim Sum Specialists DIM SUM $
(添好運點心專門店; Map p504; ☑852 2332 3078; www.timhowan.com; Shop 12a, Podium Level 1, 8 Finance St, IFC Mall, Central; dishes HK$50;

⊙9am-8.30pm; Ⓜ Hong Kong, exit E1) Opened by a former Four Seasons chef, Tim Ho Wan was the first-ever budget dim sum place to receive a Michelin star. Many relocations and branches later, the star is still tucked snugly inside its tasty titbits, including the top-selling baked barbecue pork bun. Expect to wait 15 to 40 minutes for a table.

City Hall Maxim's Palace DIM SUM $

(美心皇宮; Map p504; ✆852 2521 1303; 3rd fl, Lower Block, Hong Kong City Hall, 1 Edinburgh Pl, Central; meals from HK$150; ⊙11am-3pm Mon-Sat, 9am-3pm Sun; 🛜🚻; Ⓜ Central, exit K) This 'palace' offers the quintessential Hong Kong dim sum experience. It's cheerful, it's noisy and it takes place in a huge kitschy hall with dragon decorations and hundreds of locals. A dizzying assortment of dim sum is paraded on trolleys the old-fashioned way. There's breakfast on Sunday from 9am, but people start queuing for a table at 8.30am.

A seat by the window will let you see the harbour or, a more common sight, land reclamation in progress.

★ Lung King Heen CANTONESE, DIM SUM $$$

(龍景軒; Map p504; ✆852 3196 8888; www.fourseasons.com/hongkong; Four Seasons Hotel, 8 Finance St, Central; lunch HK$200-500, dinner HK$500-2000; ⊙noon-2.30pm & 6-10.30pm; 🛜; Ⓜ Hong Kong, exit E1) The world's first Chinese restaurant to receive three Michelin stars still retains them. The Cantonese food, though by no means peerless in Hong Kong, is excellent in both taste and presentation, and when combined with the harbour views and the impeccable service, provides a truly stellar dining experience. The signature steamed lobster and scallop dumplings sell out early.

The Peak & Northwest Hong Kong Island

Restaurants in Soho have a pre-clubbing vibe; the majority are midrange or above. Sheung Wan has more local flavour, and is known for Chinese places that keep their quality high but profiles low. Further west, a hip new dining scene is taking shape. Quality choices on the Peak are sparse, though eateries make smart use of the gorgeous views.

★ Dumpling Yuan DUMPLING $

(餃子園; Map p504; ✆852 2541 9737; 98 Wellington St, Soho; meals from HK$40; ⊙11am-10.30pm Mon-Sat; ✐; ☐40M) Locals and visitors from the north flock to this little shop for its nine varieties of juicy bundles of heaven, more

commonly known as lamb and cumin, pork and chives, egg and tomato or vegetarian dumplings.

★ Kau Kee Restaurant NOODLES $

(九記牛腩; Map p504; ✆852 2850 5967; 21 Gough St, Sheung Wan; meals from HK$40; ⊙12.30-7.15pm & 8.30-11.30pm Mon-Sat; Ⓜ Sheung Wan, exit E2) You can argue till the noodles go soggy about whether Kau Kee has the best beef brisket in town. Whatever the verdict, the meat – served with toothsome noodles in a fragrant beefy broth – is hard to beat. During the 90 years of the shop's existence, film stars and politicians have joined the queue for a table.

★ Luk Yu Tea House CANTONESE $$

(陸羽茶室; Map p504; ✆852 2523 5464; 24-26 Stanley St, Lan Kwai Fong; meals HK$300; ⊙7am-10pm, dim sum to 5.30pm; 🚻; Ⓜ Central, exit D2) This gorgeous teahouse (c 1933), known for its masterful cooking and Eastern art deco decor, was the haunt of opera artists, writers and painters (including the creator of one exorbitant ink-and-brush gracing a wall) who came to give recitals and discuss the national fate. The food is old-school Cantonese fare such as sweet-and-sour pork, prawn toast and a variety of dim-sum dumplings and pastries.

★ The Boss CANTONESE $$$

(波士廳; Map p504; ✆852 2155 0552; www.theboss1.com; Basement, 58-62 Queen's Rd Central, Central; lunch/dinner sets from HK$230/680; ⊙11.30am-midnight Mon-Sat, from 11am Sun; 🛜; Ⓜ Central, exit D2) Awarded one Michelin star, the Boss is a perfectionist. The flawless service, austere modern decor, and meticulous kitchen point to high expectations being imposed. The old-school Cantonese dishes are impressive, notably the deep-fried chicken pieces with home-fermented shrimp paste, and the baked-crab casserole. Dim sum, made with first-rate ingredients, is available at lunch.

Aberdeen & South Hong Kong Island

Choices in Shek O and Repulse Bay are sparse, but you'll still manage to eat decently and enjoy the views on the coast. Aberdeen and Ap Lei Chau are home to quite a few excellent seafood places that offer a unique cultural experience. These warehouse districts also have a growing number of restaurants that cater to more Westernised palates.

★**Aberdeen Fish Market Yee Hope Seafood Restaurant** CANTONESE, SEAFOOD $$
(香港仔魚市場二合海鮮餐廳; ☑852 2177 7872, 852 5167 1819; 102 Shek Pai Wan Rd, Aberdeen; meals from $350; ⊘4am-4pm; ☐107) Hidden in Hong Kong's only wholesale fish market, this understated eatery run by fishers is truly an in-the-know place for ultrafresh seafood. There's no menu, but tell them your budget and they'll source the best sea creatures available, including ones you don't normally see in restaurants, and apply their Midas touch to them.

The restaurant serves as a canteen for the fishers in the market and you'll see men in gumboots dropping in for beer, Hong Kong–style French toast and other *cha chaan tang* (teahouse) staples throughout the day. Walk-in customers can do the same. There's no English sign; look for the nondescript one-storey yellow building with a green roof at the end of the fish market.

You'll need a Cantonese-speaking friend to help you if you'd like to book a table; organise at least two days in advance (two weeks for weekends).

✕ Wan Chai & Northeast Hong Kong Island

Admiralty has a few exceptional restaurants. Wan Chai, with a wealth of cuisines in all price ranges, is Hong Kong's food capital, while Causeway Bay is an eclectic amalgam of eateries, many upscale, many Japanese. Down-at-heel North Point is home to a wonderful *dai pai dong* (大牌檔; food stall). Further afield, Shau Kei Wan and Sai Wan Ho offer good-value Canto staples and street eats.

★**Atum Desserant** SWEETS $
(Map p508; ☑852 2377 2400, 852 2956 1411; www.atumhk.com; 16th fl, The L Square, 459-461 Lockhart Rd, Causeway Bay; desserts from HK$138; ⊘2.45pm-midnight Mon-Thu, from 1pm Fri-Sun; Ⓜ Causeway Bay, exit C) Hop onto a stool, hook your bag under the counter and watch museum-worthy desserts materialise with some help from liquid nitrogen and the owner's years as a pastry chef at the Mandarin Oriental. Improvisation (HK$348 for two) is confectionery, fruits and ice cream arranged like a Jackson Pollock crossbred with a Monet. And it's not just for show – flavours are surprisingly well balanced. Booking advised.

Kam's Roast Goose CANTONESE $
(甘牌燒鵝; Map p508; ☑852 2520 1110; www.krg.com.hk; 226 Hennessy Rd, Wan Chai; meals HK$70-

200; ⊘11.30am-9pm; Ⓜ Wan Chai, exit A2) One of two spin-offs from Central's famed **Yung Kee Restaurant** (鏞記; Map p504; ☑852 2522 1624; www.yungkee.com.hk; 32-40 Wellington St, Lan Kwai Fong; lunch HK$150-400, dinner from HK$450; ⊘11am-10.30pm; [✚]; Ⓜ Central, exit D2), Kam's clearly still upholds the same strict standards in the sourcing and roasting of the city's most glorified roast goose. Besides the juicy crisp-skinned fowl (of which the best cut is the leg), other barbecued meats such as roast suckling pig are well worth sinking your teeth into.

★**Choi's Kitchen** CANTONESE $$
(私房蔡; ☑852 3485 0501; Shop C, ground fl, Hoi Kok Mansion, 9 Whitfield Rd, Tin Hau; mains from HK$128; ⊘11am-3pm & 6-10pm; Ⓜ Tin Hau, exit A) This charming shop refines common Cantonese dishes by using only fresh, high-quality ingredients and restraint in seasoning. The signature claypot rice is made to order and is only available at dinner. Decor is understated faux-retro to reflect the restaurant's origin as a *dai pai dong* (大牌檔; food stall). Prices are a far cry from those days, but the (well heeled) customers keep coming. Booking advised or go early.

★**Fortune Kitchen** CANTONESE $$
(盆福小廚; Map p508; ☑852 2697 7317; 5 Lan Fong Rd, Causeway Bay; mains HK$100-500; ⊘11.30am-5pm & 6-10.30pm; Ⓜ Causeway Bay, exit A) Despite the old-fashioned Chinatown name, Fortune Kitchen is decorated like an old teahouse and serves homey but sophisticated Cantonese at wallet-friendly prices. The owner was a sous-chef at a Michelin-star restaurant and his culinary skills are evident in dishes such as the signature steamed chicken with dried scallops and the eponymous fried rice. Booking advised.

✕ Kowloon

Kowloon doesn't have quite as many upmarket restaurants as Hong Kong Island but there's a riveting assortment of Chinese and Asian eateries to fit all budgets in Tsim Sha Tsui. For hearty local fare, head for Yau Ma Tei or Mong Kok. Kowloon City is renowned for its many Thai eateries.

★**Sun Sin** NOODLES $
(新仙清湯腩; Map p512; ☑852 2332 6872; 37 Portland St, Yau Ma Tei; meals HK$40-65; ⊘11am-midnight; Ⓜ Yau Ma Tei, exit B2) A Michelin-praised brisket shop in a 'hood known for brothels, Sun Sin has kept quality up and

prices down despite its laurels. The succulent cuts of meat are served in a broth with radish, in a chunky tomato soup, or as a curry. At peak times, makeshift tables are available upstairs for those who prize food over comfort.

★ **Chicken HOF & Soju Korean** KOREAN $
(李家, Chicken; Map p510; ☑852 2375 8080; ground fl, 84 Kam Kok Mansion, Kimberley Rd, Tsim Sha Tsui; meals from HK$150; ☺5pm-4am; Ⓜ Jordan, exit D) This place with darkened windows may look dodgy from the outside, but in fact it's a Korean gastropub with a friendly owner who'll holler a greeting when customers enter. The excellent fried chicken, made with a light and crispy batter, comes in five versions. Traditional fare such as Korean barbecue is also available. If you need to ask directions, locals often refer to this place as 'Lee Family Chicken'. A long queue is the norm.

★ **Din Tai Fung** TAIWANESE, NOODLES $$
(鼎泰豐; Map p510; ☑852 2730 6928; www.dintaifung.com.hk; Shop 130, 3rd fl, Silvercord, 30 Canton Rd, Tsim Sha Tsui; meals HK$120-300; ☺11.30am-10.30pm; ⓐ; Ⓜ Tsim Sha Tsui, exit C1) Whether it's comfort food or a carb fix you're craving, the juicy Shànghǎi dumplings and hearty northern-style noodles at this beloved Taiwanese chain will do the trick. Queues are the norm and there are no reservations, but service is excellent. Must-eats include the famous *xiǎolóngbāo* (soup dumplings), fluffy steamed pork buns and the greasy-but-oh-so-good fried pork chop.

Gaddi's FRENCH $$$
(Map p510; ☑852 2696 6763; www.peninsula.com; 1st fl, The Peninsula, 19-21 Salisbury Rd, Tsim Sha Tsui; set lunch/dinner HK$500/2000; ☺noon-2.30pm & 7-10.30pm; Ⓜ Tsim Sha Tsui, exit E) Gaddi's, which opened just after WWII, was the kind of place where wealthy families went to celebrate special occasions. Today the classical decor may be a tad stuffy and the live Filipino band gratuitous, but the food – traditional French with contemporary touches – is without a doubt still some of the best in town.

✕ New Territories

The New Territories whips up Hong Kong's best Hakka and walled village cuisines (Yuen Long, Fan Ling) and makes a solid bowl of noodles (Tai Po, Yuen Long, Fan Ling). Waterfront areas in Sai Kung, Tuen Mun (Sam Shing Hui) and Po Toi O fishing village feature exciting seafood places. Village teahouses can be found in Tai Mo Shan and world-famous roast goose in Tsuen Wan and Tai Po.

★ **Yat Lok Barbecue Restaurant** CANTONESE $
(一樂燒臘飯店; ☑852 2656 4732; 5 Tai Ming Lane; meals HK$50-180; ☺11am-11pm; Ⓜ Tai Po Market, exit A2) Glossy roast goose with shatteringly crisp skin and a pillow of succulent fat is the order of the day at this one-Michelin-star, family-run eatery, which counts celebrity chef Anthony Bourdain among its many fans. *Char siu* (roast pork) is a bit dry, so focus on the bird. Chinese menu only, but friendly servers will help you order.

★ **Loaf On** CANTONESE, SEAFOOD $$
(六福菜館; ☑852 2792 9966; 49 See Cheung St, Sai Kung; dishes from HK$100; ☺11am-11pm; ☐1) The motto here is: eat what they hunt. This three-storey Michelin-star restaurant is where fish freshly caught from Sai Kung waters in the morning lands on customers' plates by midday. The signature fish soup and steamed fish sell out fast. There is no English signage, but it's identifiable by a lone dining table set outside and the shiny brass sign. Reservations recommended.

★ **Sha Tin 18** CANTONESE, CHINESE $$
(沙田18; ☑852 3723 7932; www.hongkong.shatin.hyatt.com; 18 Chak Cheung St, Hyatt Regency Hong Kong; meals HK$300-700; ☺11.30am-3pm & 5.30-10.30pm; ⓂUniversity) The Peking duck (whole HK$785, half HK$500) here has put this hotel restaurant, adjacent to the Chinese University, in the gastronomic spotlight. Book your prized fowl 24 hours in advance, and tantalise your taste buds in three ways – pancakes with the crispy skin, meat and leeks, duck soup and wok-fried minced duck. The Asian fusion desserts here are also famous.

★ **Yue Kee Roasted Goose Restaurant** CANTONESE $$
(裕記大飯店; ☑852 2491 0105; www.yuekee.com.hk/en; 9 Sham Hong Rd, Sham Tseng; meals HK$150-500; ☺11am-11pm; ☐minibus 302 from Tai Wo Hau MTR) In an alley lined with roast-goose restaurants, 54-year-old Yue Kee is king. Order gorgeous plates of coppery-skinned charcoal-roasted goose (half is plenty for four people) and sample house specialities including soy-braised goose web (feet), wine-infused goose liver, and stir-fried goose intestines. If that's not your speed, there are plenty of standard Cantonese dishes on offer. Book ahead.

✕ Outlying Islands

Eating on the Outlying Islands is all about seafood. Many local villages have rows of eateries dedicated to frying, poaching and sautéing everything that swims or wriggles in the ocean. Lamma's large foreign population ensures there's lots of funky international eateries as well.

★**Mavericks**   BURGERS, INTERNATIONAL $
(☑ 852 5402 4154; Pui O beach; meals from HK$100; ⊙ 5.30-11.30pm Fri, 11.30am-11.30pm Sat & Sun; 🔲1 from Mui Wo) 🍴 Sunburned beach-goers gather for house-made sausages and burgers on artisan buns at this hip surf-themed weekend spot, right on the water in Pui O. Many of the veggies are grown on the restaurant's own farm, the meat and dairy used are hormone-free, and menus are printed on recycled bamboo paper. Wash your meal down with a locally brewed Young Master Ale.

★**Rainbow**
Seafood Restaurant   CHINESE, SEAFOOD $$
(天虹海鮮酒家; ☑ 852 2982 8100; www.rainbow rest.com.hk; Shops 1A-1B, ground fl, 23-25 First St, Sok Kwu Wan; meals from HK$180; ⊙ 10am-10.30pm; 🚢 Sok Kwu Wan) Gigantic Rainbow may boast 800 seats but you still need to book ahead for prime hours. Steamed grouper, lobster and abalone are the specialities at this waterfront restaurant. You have the option of being transported by its own ferries from Central pier 9 or Tsim Sha Tsui Public Pier; call or check its website for sailings.

🍸 Drinking & Nightlife

Energetic Hong Kong knows how to party and does so visibly and noisily. Drinking venues run the gamut from British-style pubs through hotel bars and hipster hang-outs, to karaoke bolt-holes aimed at a young Chinese clientele. The last few years have seen a heartening surge in the number of wine bars and live-music venues, catering to a diverse, discerning and fun-loving population.

🍷 Central District

MO Bar   BAR
(Map p504; ☑ 852 2132 0077; 15 Queen's Rd Central, Landmark, Central; ⊙ 7am-1.30am; 🍴; Ⓜ Central, exit D1) If you want to imbibe in the quiet or catch up with a chat, the swish MO Bar, attached to the Mandarin's swanky outpost at the Landmark (p520), offers peace, soft lighting and a first-rate drinks list of wines and cocktails.

Sevva   COCKTAIL BAR
(Map p504; ☑ 852 2537 1388; www.sevva.hk; 25th fl, Prince's Bldg, 10 Chater Rd, Central; ⊙ noon-midnight Mon-Thu, to 2am Fri & Sat; 🍴; Ⓜ Central, exit H) If there was a million-dollar view in Hong Kong, it'd be the one from the balcony of ultra-stylish Sevva – skyscrapers so close you can see their arteries of steel, with the harbour and Kowloon in the distance. At night it takes your breath away. To get there, though, you have to overcome expensive drinks and patchy service.

Book ahead if you want a table on the balcony, but even if you don't, you can go out to take pictures.

Red Bar   BAR
(Map p504; ☑ 852 8129 8882; www.pure-red.com; Level 4, 8 Finance St, Two IFC, Central; ⊙ noon-midnight Mon-Wed, to 1am Thu, to 3am Fri & Sat, to 10pm Sun, happy hour 6-9pm; 🍴; Ⓜ Hong Kong, exit E1) Red Bar's combination of alfresco drinking and harbour views is hard to beat. Expect to meet lots of smartly dressed finance types from the corporate offices nearby. DJs playing funk and jazz turn up the volume as the weekend approaches.

Hint: if you're on a budget, grab some beers at a 7-Eleven and take one of the rooftop tables adjacent to Red; it's public space.

⊟ The Peak & Northwest Hong Kong Island

★**Quinary**   COCKTAIL BAR
(Map p504; ☑ 852 2851 3223; www.quinary.hk; 56-58 Hollywood Rd, Soho; ⊙ 5pm-2am Mon-Sat; Ⓜ Central, exit D2) A sleek, moodily lit cocktail bar, Quinary attracts a well dressed crowd to sip Asian-inspired cocktail creations such as the Quinary Sour (whisky, licorice root, Chinese black sugar), the Oolong Tea Collins (vodka, oolong tea cordial) or the Checkers (vodka, black sesame syrup, vanilla ice cream). Prices are high, making this a good place to start the evening before moving on to cheaper and less elegant environs.

★**Club 71**   BAR
(Map p504; Basement, 67 Hollywood Rd, Soho; ⊙ 3pm-2am Mon-Sat, 6pm-1am Sun, happy hour 3-9pm; 🔲26, Ⓜ Central, exit D1) This friendly bar with a bohemian vibe is named after a protest march on 1 July 2003. It's a favourite haunt of local artists and activists who come for the beer and jamming sessions. In the garden out the front, revolutionaries plotted to overthrow the Qing dynasty a hundred years ago. Enter from the alley next to 69 Hollywood.

★ **Ping Pong Gintoneria** BAR

(☑852 9835 5061; www.pingpong129.com; 135 Second St, Sai Ying Pun; ⊙6-11.30pm; Ⓜ Sai Ying Pun, exit B2) An unmarked red door leads you downstairs into a cavernous former ping-pong hall, now one of Hong Kong's coolest bars. The drink here is gin – the bar stocks more than 50 types from across the globe, served in a variety of cocktails both classic and creative. Crowds here are artsy, and the decor is even artsier – look out for original work by infamous Hong Kong graffiti artist the King of Kowloon.

🍷 Wan Chai & Northeast Hong Kong Island

★ **MyHouse** WINE BAR

(Map p508; ☑852 2323 1715; www.myhousehk. com; 26th fl, QRE Plaza, 202 Queen's Rd E, Wan Chai; ⊙6pm-2am Tue & Wed, to 3am Thu-Sat, closed Sun; Ⓜ Wan Chai, exit A3) 🎶 MyHouse brings together vinyls and natural wine in a spacious Euro-chic setting. Furniture is made from natural wood, illuminated wine bottles hang alongside cured meats, and guests can take their pick from a vinyl library, slip it on individual turntables, and kick back with an organic, chemical-free Beaujolais, or surrender to the whims of a resident DJ (analogue, of course).

★ **Tai Lung Fung** BAR

(大龍鳳; Map p508; ☑852 2572 0055; 5-9 Hing Wan St, Wan Chai; ⊙noon-1am Mon-Thu, to 1.30am Fri & Sat, happy hour noon-9pm; Ⓜ Wan Chai, exit A3) This capriciously retro bar takes its name from a 1960s Cantonese opera troupe. In common parlance, Tai Lung Fung (Big Dragon Phoenix) means 'much ado'. Appropriately, the decor is fabulously over-the-top. Tai Lung Fung attracts artsy types who prefer its funky aesthetics and quiet environment to a more conventional partying vibe. Cocktails, less adventurous than the decor, are the speciality.

🍷 Kowloon

★ **Kubrick Bookshop Café** CAFE

(Map p512; ☑852 2384 8929; www.kubrick. hk; Shop H2, Prosperous Garden, 3 Public Square St, Yau Ma Tei; ⊙11.30am-9.30pm; Ⓜ Yau Ma Tei, exit C) The airy bookshop-cafe attached to the **Broadway Cinematheque** (百老匯電影中心; Map p512; ☑852 2388 3188; Ground fl, Prosperous Gardens, 3 Public Square St, Yau Ma Tei; Ⓜ Yau Ma Tei, exit C) serves decent coffee and simple eats, attracting an eclectic, arty crowd. While waiting for your cuppa, you can browse the shop's strong collection of art, film and cultural studies titles.

★ **InterContinental Lobby Lounge** BAR

(Map p510; ☑852 2721 1211; www.hongkong-ic. intercontinental.com; Hotel InterContinental Hong Kong, 18 Salisbury Rd, Tsim Sha Tsui; ⊙7am-12.30am; 🛜; Ⓜ East Tsim Sha Tsui, exit J) Soaring plate glass and an unbeatable waterfront location make this one of the best spots to soak up the Hong Kong Island skyline and take in the busy harbour, although you pay for the privilege. It's also an ideal venue from which to watch the evening light show at 8pm.

★ **Aqua** BAR

(Map p510; ☑852 3427 2288; www.aqua.com. hk; 29 & 30th fl, 1 Peking Rd, Tsim Sha Tsui; ⊙4pm-2am, happy hour 4-6pm; 🛜; Ⓜ Tsim Sha Tsui, exit L5) When night falls, you'll know why this uberfashionable bar has dim illumination and black furniture – the two-storey, floor-to-ceiling windows command sweeping views of the Hong Kong Island skyline that come to life after sundown. The tables by the windows are awesome for bringing a date. On the weekends, a DJ spins hip hop and lounge jazz.

Ozone BAR

(☑852 2263 2263; www.ritzcarlton.com; 118th fl, ICC, 1 Austin Rd, Tsim Sha Tsui; ⊙5pm-1am Mon-Wed, to 2am Thu, to 3am Fri, 3pm-3am Sat, noon-midnight Sun; 🛜; Ⓜ Kowloon, exit U3) Ozone is the highest bar in Asia. The imaginative interiors, created to evoke a cyber-esque Garden of Eden, have pillars resembling chocolate fountains in a hurricane and a myriad of refracted glass and colour-changing illumination. Equally dizzying is the wine list, with the most expensive bottle selling for over HK$150,000. Ozone offers potential for a once-in-a-lifetime experience, in more ways than one. Oh, that temptingly empty corner table? That's HK$10k just to sit there.

🍷 Outlying Islands

On Lamma, **Island Bar** (⊙5pm-late Mon-Fri, noon-late Sat & Sun, happy hour 5-8pm; 🛜 Yung Shue Wan) is the closest bar to Yung Shue Wan's ferry pier. It's a favourite with older expats and hosts the best jam sessions on the island.

☆ Entertainment

Hong Kong's arts and entertainment scene is healthier than ever. The increasingly busy cultural calendar includes music, drama and dance hailing from a plethora of traditions.

The schedule of imported performances is nothing short of stellar. And every week, local arts companies and artists perform anything from Bach to stand-up to Cantonese opera and English versions of Chekhov plays.

Hong Kong Ticketing BOOKING SERVICE
(852 3128 8288; www.hkticketing.com; ⊘10am-8pm) You can book tickets to plays, concerts and other cultural events here.

Urbtix BOOKING SERVICE
(852 2734 9009; www.urbtix.hk; ⊘10am-8pm) Books tickets to shows at venues operated by the government's Leisure and Cultural Services Department.

Grappa's Cellar LIVE MUSIC
(Map p504; 852 2521 2322; http://elgrande. com.hk/restaurant/grappas-cellar/; 1 Connaught Pl, Central; ⊘9pm-late; Hong Kong, exit B2) For at least two weekends a month, this subterranean Italian restaurant morphs into a jazz or rock music venue – chequered tablecloths and all. Call or visit the website for event and ticketing details.

★Peel Fresco JAZZ
(Map p504; 852 2540 2046; www.peelfresco. com; 49 Peel St, Soho; ⊘5pm-late Mon-Sat; 13, 26, 40M) Charming Peel Fresco has live jazz six nights a week, with local and overseas acts performing on a small but spectacular stage next to teetering faux-Renaissance paintings. The action starts around 9.30pm, but get there at 9pm to secure a seat.

Fringe Club LIVE MUSIC, THEATRE
(藝穗會; Map p504; theatre bookings 852 2521 9126, 852 2521 7251; www.hkfringe.com.hk; 2 Lower Albert Rd, Lan Kwai Fong; ⊘noon-midnight Mon-Thu, to 3am Fri & Sat; Central, exits D1, D2 & G) The Fringe, housed in a Victorian building (c 1892) that was part of a dairy farm, offers original music in the Dairy several nights a week, with jazz, rock and world music getting the most airplay. The intimate theatres host eclectic local and international performances. The Fringe sits on the border of Lan Kwai Fong.

Focal Fair LIVE MUSIC
(Map p508; www.facebook.com/focalfair; 28th fl, Park Avenue Tower, 5 Moreton Tce, Causeway Bay; Tin Hau, exit A1) Finally, a conveniently located indie music venue – Focal Fair is right by the Hong Kong Central Library! It hosts several gigs a month, and everyone from Canadian hardcore punks Career Suicide to local noise artists Dennis Wong and Eric Chan

have played here. See the Facebook page for the latest.

Hong Kong Arts Centre DANCE, THEATRE
(香港藝術中心; Map p508; 852 2582 0200; www.hkac.org.hk; 2 Harbour Rd, Wan Chai; Wan Chai, exit C) A popular venue for dance, theatre and music performances, the Arts Centre has theatres, a cinema and a gallery.

★Canton Singing House LIVE MUSIC
(艷陽天; Map p512; 49-51 Temple St, Yau Ma Tei; HK$20, ⊘3-7pm & 8pm-5am; Yau Ma Tei, exit C) The oldest and most atmospheric of the singalong parlours, Canton resembles a film set with its mirror balls and glowing shrines. Each session features 20 singers, all with fan following. Patrons tip a minimum of HK$20 (per patron) if they like a song.

Even if you don't, it's nice to tip every now and then for the experience – just slip your money into a box on stage. For HK$100, you can sing a song.

★Hidden Agenda LIVE MUSIC
(852 9170 6073; www.hiddenagenda.hk; 2A, Wing Fu Industrial Bldg, 15-17 Tai Yip St, Kwun Tong; Ngau Tau Kok, exit B6) Hong Kong's best-known music dive has the setting (former warehouse), line-up (solid indie acts) and elusiveness (it's out of the way) all other dives wish they had. Located in the gritty industrial hub of Kwun Tong (about a five-block walk from the MTR), Hidden Agenda is synonymous with underground music. The entrance has a small metal gate that's open after-hours.

Hong Kong Cultural Centre THEATRE, MUSIC
(香港文化中心; Map p510; www.lcsd.gov.hk; 10 Salisbury Rd, Tsim Sha Tsui; ⊘9am-11pm; ☎; East Tsim Sha Tsui, exit L6) Hong Kong's premier arts performance venue, this world-class cultural centre contains a 2085-seat concert hall with an impressive Rieger pipe organ, plus two theatres and rehearsal studios.

🔒 Shopping

Everyone knows Hong Kong as a place of neon-lit retail pilgrimage. This city is positively stuffed with swanky shopping malls and brand-name boutiques. All international brands worth their logo have outlets here. These are supplemented by the city's own retail trailblazers and a few creative local designers. Together they are Hong Kong's shrines and temples to style and consumption.

Central District

★ Shanghai Tang
CLOTHING, HOMEWARE
(上海灘; Map p504; ☑852 2525 7333; www.
shanghaitang.com; 1 Duddell St, Shanghai Tang
Mansion, Central; ⊙10.30am-8pm; Ⓜ Central,
exit D1) This elegant four-level store is the
place to go if you fancy a body-hugging
qípáo (cheongsam) with a modern twist, a
Chinese-style clutch or a lime-green mandarin jacket. Custom tailoring is available; it
takes two weeks to a month and requires a
fitting. Shanghai Tang also stocks cushions,
picture frames, teapots, even mah-jong tile
sets, designed in a modern chinoiserie style.

★ Armoury
CLOTHING
(Map p504; ☑852 2804 6991; www.thearmoury.
com; 307 Pedder Bldg, 12 Pedder St, Central; ⊙11am-
8pm Mon-Sat; Ⓜ Central, exit D1) The Armoury
can help any man look like a dapper gentleman, whatever his build – the elegant shop
is a specialist in refined menswear sourced
from around the world. You can choose from
British-, Italian- and Asian-tailored suits, and
a high-quality selection of shoes and ties to
match. Still not good enough? Ask about their
bespoke suits and custom footwear.

★ Picture This
GIFTS & SOUVENIRS
(Map p504; ☑852 2525 2803; www.picturethiscol
lection.com; 13th fl, 9 Queen's Rd, Central; ⊙10am-
7pm Mon-Sat, noon-5pm Sun; Ⓜ Central, exit H)
The vintage posters, photographs, prints and
antique maps of Hong Kong and Asia on sale
here will appeal to collectors or anyone seeking an unusual gift. There's also an assortment of antiquarian books related to Hong
Kong. Prices are not cheap but they guarantee all maps and prints to be originals.

★ Blanc de Chine
FASHION & ACCESSORIES
(源; Map p504; ☑852 2104 7934; www.blanc
dechine.com; Shop 123, Prince's Bldg, 10 Chater Rd,
Central; ⊙10.30am-7.30pm Mon-Sat, noon-6pm Sun;
Ⓜ Central, exit H) This sumptuous store specialises in Chinese men's jackets and silk dresses
for women, both off-the-rack and made-to-
measure. A gorgeous sequinned gown takes
about four weeks to make, including one
fitting. If you're not in Hong Kong after a
month, the shop will ship it to you. The satin
bed linens are also exquisite (as are the old
ship's cabinets in which they are displayed).

IFC Mall
MALL
(Map p504; ☑852 2295 3308; www.ifc.com.hk;
8 Finance St, Central; Ⓜ Hong Kong, exit F) Hong
Kong's most luxurious shopping mall boasts
200 high-fashion boutiques linking the One
(p507) and Two (p507) IFC towers and the
Four Seasons Hotel (p520). Outlets include
Prada, Gucci, Céline, Jimmy Choo, Vivienne
Tam, Zegna...we could go on. The Hong Kong
Airport Express Station is downstairs.

The Peak &
Northwest Hong Kong Island

★ PMQ
HANDICRAFTS, JEWELLERY
(Map p504; ☑852 2870 2335; www.pmq.org.hk; 35
Aberdeen St, Central; ⊙most shops 11am-7pm) The
modernist building that was once the police
married quarters is now one of the best places in Hong Kong to shop for pieces by local
designers, jewellery makers and artisans,
with dozens of shops and boutiques occupying the old apartments. Top picks include the
hip streetwear of Kapok, Hong Kong–themed
gifts at HKTDC Design Gallery, industrially
inspired jewellery at The Little Finger, and
bamboo kitchenware at Bamboa Home.

★ Chan Shing Kee
ANTIQUES
(陳勝記; Map p504; ☑852 2543 1245; www.chan
shingkee.com; 228-230 Queen's Rd Central, Sheung
Wan; ⊙9am-6pm Mon-Sat; ☐101, 104) This shop
with a three-storey showroom is run by Daniel Chan, the third generation of a family
that's been in the business for 70 years. Chan
Shing Kee is known to collectors and museums worldwide for its fine classical Chinese
furniture (16th to 18th century). Scholars'
objects, such as ancient screens and wooden
boxes, are also available.

★ Gallery of the
Pottery Workshop
ART, HOMEWARES
(樂天陶社; Map p504; ☑852 2525 7949, 852
9842 5889; www.potteryworkshop.com.cn; 3rd fl,
Hollywood House, 27-29 Hollywood Rd, Soho; ⊙1-
6pm Tue-Sun; ☐26) This gallery showcases
playful ceramic objects made by local ceramic artists and artisans from the mainland and overseas. The lovely pieces range
from crockery to sculptures.

★ Grotto Fine Art
ART
(嘉圖; Map p504; ☑852 2121 2270; www.grottofine
art.com; 2nd fl, 31C-D Wyndham St, Lan Kwai Fong;
⊙11am-7pm Mon-Sat; Ⓜ Central, exit D2) This exquisite gallery, founded by a scholar in Hong
Kong art, is one of very few that represents
predominantly local artists. The small but
excellent selection of works shown ranges
from painting and sculpture to ceramics and
mixed media. Prices are reasonable too.

☐ Aberdeen & South Hong Kong Island

★ G.O.D.   CLOTHING, HOUSEWARES
(Goods of Desire; ☑ 852 2673 0071; www.god.
com.hk; Shop 105, Stanley Plaza, 22-23 Carmel Rd,
Stanley; ⊙ 10.30am-8pm Mon-Fri, to 9pm Sat; ☐ 6,
6A, 6X, 260) One of the coolest born-in-Hong
Kong shops around, G.O.D. does irreverent
takes on classic Hong Kong iconography.
Think cell phone covers printed with pictures of Hong Kong housing blocks, light fixtures resembling the ones in old-fashioned
wet markets, and pillows covered in lucky
koi print. There are a handful of G.O.D.
shops in town, but this is one of the biggest.

☐ Wan Chai & Northeast Hong Kong Island

★ Eslite   BOOKS
(誠品; Map p508; ☑ 852 3419 6789; 8th-10th
fl, Hysan Place, 500 Hennessy Rd, Causeway Bay;
⊙ 10am-10pm Sun-Thu, to 11pm Fri & Sat; ☑;
Ⓜ Causeway Bay, exit F2) You could spend an
entire evening inside this swanky three-floor
Taiwanese bookstore, which features a massive collection of English and Chinese books
and magazines, a shop selling gorgeous sta-
tionery and leather-bound journals, a cafe, a
bubble-tea counter, and a huge kids' toy and
book section.

★ Wan Chai Computer Centre   ELECTRONICS
(灣仔電腦城, Map p508; 1st fl, Southorn Centre,
130-138 Hennessy Rd, Wan Chai; ⊙ 10am-9pm
Mon-Sat, noon-8pm Sun; Ⓜ Wan Chai, exit B2) This
gleaming, beeping warren of tiny shops is a
safe bet for anything digital and electronic.

Joyce   FASHION & ACCESSORIES
(Map p504; ☑ 852 2523 5944; www.joyce.com;
Shop 232, Pacific Place, 88 Queensway, Admiralty;
⊙ 10.30am-8pm Sun-Thu, to 8.30pm Fri & Sat; Ⓜ Admiralty, exit F) This Pacific Place outlet of one of
Hong Kong's most famous luxury fashion retailers features a shrewdly curated collection
of international brands that strikes a balance
between the popular and the edgy.

☐ Kowloon

★ Shanghai Street   MARKET
(上海街; Map p512; Yau Ma Tei; Ⓜ Yau Ma Tei,
exit C) Wander Kowloon's kitchen district
for food-related souvenirs such as wooden
mooncake moulds, chopsticks, woks and ceramic teapots.

★ Yue Hwa Chinese Products Emporium   DEPARTMENT STORE
(裕華國貨; Map p512; ☑ 852 3511 2222; www.
yuehwa.com; 301-309 Nathan Rd, Jordan; ⊙ 10am-
10pm; Ⓜ Jordan, exit A) This five-storey behe-
moth is one of the few old-school Chinese
department stores left in the city. Gets here
include silk scarves, traditional Chinese
baby clothes and embroidered slippers,
jewellery both cheap and expensive, pretty
patterned chopsticks and ceramics, plastic
acupuncture models and calligraphy equipment (to name a few). The top floor is all
about tea, with various vendors offering free
sips. Food is in the basement.

★ Ladies' Market   MARKET
(通菜街, 女人街, Tung Choi Street Market; Tung
Choi St; ⊙ noon-11.30pm; Ⓜ Mong Kok, exit D3)
The Tung Choi Street market is a cheek-by-
jowl affair offering cheap clothes and trinkets. Vendors start setting up their stalls
as early as noon, but it's best to get here
between 1pm and 6pm when there's much
more on offer. Beware, the sizes stocked here
tend to suit the lissom Asian frame. A terrific place to soak up local atmosphere.

★ K11 Select   ACCESSORIES, CLOTHING
(Map p510; Shop 101, K11 Mall, 18 Hanoi Rd, Tsim
Sha Tsui; ⊙ 10am-10pm) In the K11 (Map p510;
18 Hanoi Rd, Tsim Sha Tsui; Ⓜ East Tsim Sha Tsui,
exit D2) mall, this shop gathers the best of
Hong Kong designers in one spot. Look for
theatrical clothing from Daydream Nation,
founded by a pair of Hong Kong siblings,
and unisex accessories from Kapok.

ℹ Information

EMERGENCY
Dial ☑ 999 for emergency services.
For non-emergency police services, call ☑ 852
2527 7177.

INTERNET ACCESS
Free wi-fi is increasingly available in hotels and
public areas, including the airport, public libraries, key cultural and recreational centres, large
parks, major MTR stations, shopping malls and
almost all urban cafes and bars.

You can also purchase a **PCCW account** online
or at convenience stores and PCCW stores, and
access the internet via any of PCCW's 7000-plus
wi-fi hot spots in Hong Kong.

Hong Kong's home-grown version of Starbucks, **Pacific Coffee Company** (Map p510;
www.pacificcoffee.com) has free internet for
customers. There are more than 100 branches
through the city.

LGBTIQ TRAVELLERS

Hong Kong has a small but vibrant and growing gay-and-lesbian scene and the annual Pride Parade in November now attracts rainbow flag-wavers by the thousands.

Contact **Pink Alliance** (http://tcjm.org) for information about LGBTIQ culture and events in Hong Kong. Or check out the latest events in Hong Kong's first free gay lifestyle magazine, *Dim Sum Magazine* (http://dimsum-hk.com).

Les Peches (☑ 852 9101 8001; lespechesinfo@ yahoo.com) is Hong Kong's premier lesbian organisation and has monthly events for lesbians, bisexual women and their friends.

MEDICAL SERVICES

Hong Kong Island

Queen Mary Hospital (瑪麗醫院; ☑ 852 2255 3838; www3.ha.org.hk/qmh; 102 Pok Fu Lam Rd, Pok Fu Lam; ☐ 30x, 55, 90B, 91) Public.

Ruttonjee Hospital (律敦治醫院; Map p508; ☑ 852 2291 2000; www.ha.org.hk; 266 Queen's Rd E, Wan Chai; Ⓜ Wan Chai, exit A3) Public.

Kowloon

Hong Kong Baptist Hospital (瑪嘉烈醫院; ☑ 852 2339 8888; 222 Waterloo Rd, Kowloon Tong) Private.

Princess Margaret Hospital (瑪嘉烈醫院; ☑ 852 2990 1111; www.ha.org.hk; 2-10 Princess Margaret Hospital Rd, Lai Chi Kok) Public.

Queen Elizabeth Hospital (伊利沙伯醫院; Map p512; ☑ 852 2958 8888; 30 Gascoigne Rd, Yau Ma Tei; ☐ 112, Ⓜ Jordan, exit C1) Public.

MONEY

ATMs are widely available. Credit cards are accepted in most hotels and restaurants; some budget places only take cash.

➡ Most ATMs are linked up to international money systems such as Cirrus, Maestro, Plus and Visa Electron.

➡ Some of HSBC's so-called Electronic Money machines offer cash withdrawal facilities for Visa and MasterCard holders.

➡ American Express (Amex) cardholders have access to Jetco ATMs and can withdraw local currency and travellers cheques at Express Cash ATMs in town.

NEWSPAPERS & MAGAZINES

The main English-language newspaper in the city is the *South China Morning Post* (www.scmp. com), a daily broadsheet that has always toed the government line. It has the largest circulation and is read by more Hong Kong Chinese than expatriates.

Other publications include *Hong Kong Standard* (www.thestandard.com.hk), *Hong Kong Economic Journal* (www.ejinsight.com), *Time, Newsweek, the Economist,* and the Běijīng mouthpiece *China Daily* (www.chinadaily.com.cn).

POST

Hong Kong Post (www.hongkongpost.com) is generally excellent; local letters are often delivered the same day they are sent and there is Saturday delivery. The staff at most post offices speak English, and the green mail boxes are clearly marked in English.

TELEPHONE

To make a phone call to Hong Kong, dial your international access code, Hong Kong's country code (☑ 852), then the eight-digit number.

To call someone outside Hong Kong, dial 001, then the country code, the local area code and the number.

Mobile service providers, including **PCCW** (Map p504; Ground fl, 113 Des Voeux Rd, Central; ☺10am-8.30pm Mon-Sat, 11am-8pm Sun; Ⓜ Hong Kong Station, exit A1 or A2), have mobile phones and accessories along with rechargeable SIM cards for sale from HK$98. Local calls cost between 6¢ and 12¢ a minute (calls to the mainland are about HK$1.80/minute).

TOURIST INFORMATION

Hong Kong Tourism Board (香港旅遊發展局; Map p510; Star Ferry Concourse, Tsim Sha Tsui; ☺8am-8pm; 🛳 Star Ferry) has helpful and welcoming staff, and reams of information – most of it free. Also sells a few useful publications.

In addition to the office at the Star Ferry Visitor Concourse, HKTB has visitor centres at the **airport** (Chek Lap Kok; ☺7am-11pm), in Halls A and B on the arrivals level in Terminal 1 and the E2 transfer area; at **The Peak** (Map p508; www. discoverhongkong.com; Peak Piazza, The Peak; ☺11am-8pm; Peak Tram), between the Peak Tower and the Peak Galleria; and at the border to **mainland China** (2nd fl, Arrival Hall, Lo Wu Terminal Bldg; ☺8am-6pm).

China Travel Service has four counters at the **airport** (中國旅行社, CTS; ☑ customer service 852 2998 7333, tour hotline 852 2998 7888; www.ctshk.com; ☺7am-10pm).

Outside these centres, and at several other places in the territory, you'll be able to find iCyberlink screens, from which you can conveniently access the HKTB website and database 24 hours a day.

TRAVEL AGENCIES

The following are among the most reliable agencies and offer the best deals on air tickets:

Concorde Travel (Map p504; ☑ 852 2526 3391; www.concorde-travel.com; 7th fl, Galuxe Bldg, 8-10 On Lan St, Central; ☺9am-5.30pm Mon-Fri, to 1pm Sat)

Forever Bright Trading Limited (Map p510; ☑ 852-2369 3188; www.fbt-chinavisa.com. hk; Room 916-917, Tower B, New Mandarin Plaza, 14 Science Museum Rd, Tsim Sha Tsui East, Kowloon; ☺8.30am-6.30pm Mon-Fri, to 1.30pm Sat; Ⓜ East Tsim Sha Tsui, exit P2)

Traveller Services (☑852 2375 2222; www.
traveller.com.hk; 18E, Tower B, Billion Centre,
1 Wang Kwong Rd, Kowloon Bay; ◷9am-6pm
Mon-Fri, to 1pm Sat)

WEBSITES

Lonely Planet (lonelyplanet.com/china/
hong-kong/hotels) Book LP's top picks online.

Hotel.com (www.hotels.com/Hong-Kong)
Specialises in cheap lodging.

Discover Hong Kong (www.discoverhongkong.
com) Provides a hotel search based on location
and facilities.

Asia Travel (www.hongkonghotels.com) Has
better deals than others.

ℹ Getting There & Away

Most international travellers arrive and depart
via Hong Kong International Airport. Travellers
to and from mainland China can use ferry, road
or rail links to Guǎngdōng and points beyond.
Hong Kong is also accessible from Macau via
ferry or helicopter.

AIR

More than 100 airlines operate between **Hong
Kong International Airport** (HKG; www.hkair
port.com; ☑852 2181 8888) and some 190
destinations around the world. There are flights
between Hong Kong and around 50 cities in
mainland China, including Běijīng, Chéngdū,
Kūnmíng and Shànghǎi. One-way fares are a bit
more than half the return price. The national
carrier is **Air China** (☑852 3970 9000; www.
airchina.hk). Other carriers include:

Cathay Pacific (Map p510; www.cathay
pacific.com; 7th fl, The Cameron, 33 Cameron
Rd, Tsim Sha Tsui; Ⓜ Tsim Sha Tsui, exit A2)
From Hong Kong, with connections to Cape
Town, Port Elizabeth and Durban.

Dragonair (www.dragonair.com) Owned by Cathay Pacific, Dragonair specialises in regional
flights and flies to 20 cities in mainland China.

Hong Kong Airlines (HX; ☑852 3151 1888;
www.hongkongairlines.com) Cheaper airline
that specialises in regional routes, including 22
cities in mainland China.

BOAT

Regularly scheduled ferries link the **China Ferry
Terminal** (Map p510) in Kowloon and/or the
Hong Kong–Macau Ferry Terminal (Map p504)
on Hong Kong Island with a string of towns and
cities on the Pearl River Delta, including Macau.
Trips take two to three hours.

Mainland destinations from Hong Kong include:
Shékǒu One hour
Shùndé Two hours
Zhàoqìng Four hours
Zhōngshān 1½ hours
Zhūhǎi 70 minutes

A fast ferry service called the **SkyPier** (☑852
2215 3232) links Hong Kong airport with nine
Pearl River Delta destinations: Shēnzhèn
Shékǒu, Shēnzhèn Fúyǒng, Dōngguǎn, Zhōngshān, Zhūhǎi, Guǎngzhōu Nánshā, Guǎngzhōu
Lianhuashan, Macau (Maritime Ferry Terminal)
and Macau (Taipa). The service enables travellers to board ferries directly without clearing
Hong Kong customs and immigration. Book
a ticket prior to boarding from the ticketing
counter located at Transfer Area E2 at least
60 minutes before ferry departure time.
Take the Automated People Move to the ferry
terminal.

BUS

There are regular buses connecting Hong Kong
with major destinations in neighbouring Guǎng
dōng province.

CTS Express Coach (Map p504; ☑852 2764
9803; http://ctsbus.hkcts.com) Buses to
mainland China.

Eternal East Cross-Border Coach (Map p510;
☑852 3760 0888, 852 3412 6677; www.eebus.
com; 13th fl, Kai Seng Commercial Centre,
4-6 Hankow Rd, Tsim Sha Tsui; ◷7am-8pm)
Mainland destinations from Hong Kong include
Dōngguǎn, Fóshān, Guǎngzhōu, Huìzhōu,
Kāipíng, Shēnzhèn's Bǎoān airport and Zhōngshān.

TRAIN

One-way and return tickets for Guǎngzhōu,
Běijīng and Shànghǎi can be booked 30 to 60
days in advance at MTR stations in Hung Hom,
Mong Kok East, Kowloon Tong and Sha Tin, and
at Tourist Services at Admiralty station. Tickets
to Guǎngzhōu can also be booked with a credit
card on the **MTR website** (www.it3.mtr.com.hk)
or via the **Tele-Ticketing Hotline** (☑ bookings
852 2947 7888, enquiries 852 2314 7702; www.
lcsd.gov.hk/en/leisurelink/ls_booking_5.html).

Visas are required to cross the border to the
mainland.

Destinations include:

Guǎngzhōu East train station 12 trains
daily from Hung Hom station (1st/2nd-class
HK$250/210, two hours)

Shànghǎi Trains depart alternate days at
3.15pm, arriving at 10.22am the following day (hard/soft/deluxe sleeper from
HK$530/825/1039)

Běijīng West train station Trains depart alternate days at 3.15pm, arriving at 3.13pm the
following day (hard/soft/deluxe sleeper from
HK$601/934/1191).

Shēnzhèn Board the MTR East Rail and ride it
to Lo Wu or Lok Ma Chau; the mainland is 200m
away. The border crossing at Lo Wu opens at
6.30am and closes at midnight. The crossing at
Lok Ma Chau is open around the clock.

ℹ Getting Around

Hong Kong is small and crowded, and public transport is the only practical way to move people. The ultramodern Mass Transit Railway (MTR) is the quickest way to get to most urban destinations. The bus system is extensive and as efficient as the traffic allows, but it can be bewildering for short-term travellers. Ferries are fast and economical and throw in spectacular harbour views at no extra cost. Trams serve the purpose if you're not in a hurry.

TO/FROM THE AIRPORT

The **Airport Express line** (🖉 2852 881 8888; www.mtr.com.hk; one way Central/Kowloon/Tsing Yi HK\$100/90/60; ⊙ every 10min) is the fastest (and most expensive, other than a taxi) way to get to and from the airport.

Shuttles run from 5.54am to 12.48am for Central, calling at Kowloon station in Jordan, Tsing Yi island en route; the full trip takes 24 minutes. Tickets are available from vending machines at the airport and train stations.

Return fares for Central/Kowloon/Tsing Yi, valid for a month, cost HK\$180/160/110. Children three to 11 years pay half-price. An Airport Express Travel Pass allows three days of unlimited travel on the MTR and Light Rail and one-way/return trips on the Airport Express (HK\$250/350).

Airport Express also has two shuttle buses on Hong Kong Island (H1 and H2) and five in Kowloon (K1 to K5), with free transfers for passengers between Central and Kowloon stations and major hotels. The buses run every 12 to 20 minutes between 6.12am and 11.12pm. Schedules and routes are available at Airport Express and MTR stations and on the Airport Express website.

A taxi to Central is about HK\$300 plus luggage charge of HK\$5 per item.

Bus

There are good bus links to/from the airport. These buses have plenty of room for luggage, and announcements are usually made in English, Cantonese and Mandarin notifying passengers of hotels at each stop. For more details on the routes, check the Transport section at www.hkairport.com.

Buses run every 10 to 30 minutes from about 6am to between midnight and 1am. There are also quite a few night buses (designated 'N').

Major hotel and guesthouse areas on Hong Kong Island are served by the A11 (HK\$40) and A12 (HK\$45) buses; the A21 (HK\$33) covers similar areas in Kowloon. Bus drivers in Hong Kong do not give change, but it is available at the ground transportation centre at the airport, as are Octopus cards. Normal returns are double the one-way fare. Unless otherwise stated, children aged between three and 11 years and seniors over 65 pay half-fare.

Buy your ticket at the booth near the airport bus stand.

BICYCLE

Cycling in urbanised Kowloon or Hong Kong Island would be suicide, but in the quiet areas of the islands (including southern Hong Kong Island) and the New Territories, a bike can be a lovely way to get around. It's more recreational than a form of transport, though – the hilly terrain will slow you down (unless you're mountain biking). Be advised that shops and kiosks renting out bicycles tend to run out early on weekends if the weather is good.

Wong Kei (旺記單車; 🖉 852 2662 5200; Ting Kok Rd, Tai Mei Tuk) offers bicycle hire.

BOAT

The cross-harbour **Star Ferry** (p515), operates on two routes: Central–Tsim Sha Tsui and Wan Chai–Tsim Sha Tsui.

The coin-operated turnstiles do not give change, but you can get change from the ticket window or use an Octopus card.

Three separate ferry companies operate services to the Outlying Islands from the ferry terminal in Central. Another, **Tsui Wah Ferry Service** (翠華旅遊有限公司; 🖉 852 2527 2513, 852 2272 2022; www.traway.com.hk), offers services to less-visited but scenic spots.

Discovery Bay Transportation Services (www.dbcommunity.hk) Between Central (Pier 3) and Discovery Bay on Lantau Island.

Hong Kong & Kowloon Ferry (HKKF; 🖉 852 2815 6063; www.hkkf.com.hk) Serves destinations on Lamma Island and Peng Chau only.

New World First Ferry (NWFF; Map p504; 🖉 852 2131 8181; www.nwff.com.hk; Ⓜ Hong Kong, exit A1 or A2) Boats sail to/from Cheung Chau, Peng Chau and Lantau Island, and connect all three via an interisland service (regular/deluxe class/fast ferry HK\$13.20/20.70/25.80), every 1¾ hours from 6am to 10.50pm.

BUS

On Hong Kong Island the most important bus stations are the bus terminus in **Central** (Map p504) and the one at **Admiralty** (Map p504). From these stations you can catch buses to Aberdeen, Repulse Bay, Stanley and other destinations on the southern side of Hong Kong Island. In Kowloon the **Star Ferry bus terminal** (Map p510) has buses heading up Nathan Rd and to the Hung Hom train station.

Most buses run from 5.30am or 6am until midnight or 12.30am, though there are some night buses that run from 12.45am to 5am or later.

Fares cost HK\$4 to HK\$46, depending on the destination. Night buses cost from HK\$7 to HK\$32. You will need exact change or an Octopus card.

Figuring out which bus you want can be difficult, but **City Bus** (🖉 852 2873 0818; www.nwstbus.com.hk) and **New World First Bus** (🖉 852 2136 8888; www.nwstbus.com.hk), owned by the same company, plus **Kowloon Motor Bus** (KMB; ☑ 852 2745 4466; www.kmb.hk) provide user-friendly route searches on their websites. KMB also has a route app for smartphones.

Most parts of Lantau Island are served by the **New Lantau Bus** (☑ 852 2984 9848; www.newlantaobus.com). Major bus stations are located in Mui Wo ferry terminal and Tung Chung MTR station.

Public Light Bus

Better known as 'minibuses', these 16 seaters come in two varieties: red and green.

↦ **with red roof/stripe** (HK$7 to HK$40) pick up and discharge passengers wherever they are hailed or asked to stop along fixed routes. The destination and price are displayed on a card propped up on the windscreen, but these are often only written in Chinese. You usually hand the driver the fare when you get off, and change is given. You can use your Octopus card on certain routes.

↦ **with green roof/stripe** (HK$3 to HK$24) make designated stops. You must put the exact fare in the cash box when you get in or you can use your Octopus card. Two popular routes are the 6 (HK$6.40) from Hankow Rd in Tsim Sha Tsui to Tsim Sha Tsui East and Hung Hom station in Kowloon, and the 1 (HK$10) to Victoria Peak from next to Hong Kong station.

CAR & MOTORCYCLE

Hong Kong's maze of one-way streets and dizzying expressways isn't for the faint-hearted. Traffic is heavy and finding a parking space is difficult and very expensive. If you are determined to see Hong Kong under your own steam, do yourself a favour and rent a car with a driver.

Ace Hire Car (☑ 852 2572 7663, 24hr 852 6108 7399; www.acehirecar.com.hk; Flat F, 1st fl, Nam Wing Bldg, 49-51A Sing Woo Rd, Happy Valley; ☐ 1 from Des Voeux Rd Central) hires out chauffeur-driven Mercedes-Benz for HK$250 per hour (minimum two to five hours, depending on location).

TRAIN

The **Mass Transit Railway** (MTR; ☑ 852 2881 8888; www.mtr.com.hk; fares HK$4-25) is the name for Hong Kong's rail system comprising underground, overland and Light Rail (slower tram-style) services. Universally known as the 'MTR', it is clean, fast and safe, and transports around four million people daily.

There are around 90 stations on nine underground and overland lines, and a Light Rail network that covers the northwest New Territories. Smoking, eating and drinking are not permitted in MTR stations or on the trains, and violators are subject to a fine of HK$5000.

Trains run every two to 14 minutes from around 6am to sometime between midnight and 1am.

TICKETS & PASSES

Octopus Card (www.octopuscards.com) A rechargeable smartcard valid on the MTR and most forms of public transport. It also allows you to make purchases at retail outlets across the territory (such as convenience stores and supermarkets). The card costs HK$150 (HK$70 for children and seniors), which includes a HK$50 refundable deposit and HK$100 worth of travel. Octopus fares are about 5% cheaper than ordinary fares on the MTR. You can buy one and recharge at any MTR station.

Airport Express Travel Pass (one-way/return HK$250/350) As well as travel to/from the airport, it allows three consecutive days of unlimited travel on the MTR.

MTR Tourist Day Pass (adult/child 3-11yr HK$65/35) Valid on the MTR for 24 hours after the first use.

Tourist Cross-Boundary Travel Pass (1/2 consecutive days HK$85/120) Allows unlimited travel on the MTR and two single journeys to/from Lo Wu or Lok Ma Chau stations.

Tickets cost HK$8 to HK$35, but trips to stations bordering mainland China (Lo Wu and Lok Ma Chau) can cost up to HK$60. Children aged between three and 11 years and seniors over 65 pay half-fare. Ticket machines accept notes and coins and dispense change. Once you've passed through the turnstile to begin a journey you have 90 minutes to complete it before the ticket becomes invalid. If you have underpaid (by mistake or otherwise), you can make up the difference at an MTR service counter next to the turnstile.

If possible, it's best to avoid the rush hours: 7.30am to 9.30am and 5pm to 7pm weekdays.

TAXI

Cheap compared to Europe and North America. Most taxis are red; green ones operate in certain parts of the New Territories; blue ones on Lantau Island. All run on meter.

TRAM

Hong Kong's venerable old trams, operated by **Hong Kong Tramways** (☑ 852 2548 7102; www.hktramways.com; fares HK$2.30; ☉ 6am–midnight), are tall, narrow double-deckers. They are slow, but they're cheap and a great way to explore the city. Try to get a seat at the front window on the upper deck for a first-class view while rattling through the crowded streets.

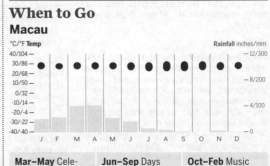

Macau

📞 853 / POP 566,375

Best Places to Eat

➡ António (p551)

➡ Restaurante Fernando (p551)

➡ Clube Militar de Macau (p550)

➡ Robuchon au Dôme (p550)

➡ Lord Stow's Bakery (p551)

Best Places to Sleep

➡ Pousada de São Tiago (p549)

➡ Banyan Tree (p550)

➡ Mandarin Oriental (p549)

➡ Pousada de Mong Há (p549)

➡ 5Footway Inn (p549)

Why Go?

Best known globally as the 'Vegas of China', the Macau Special Administrative Region is indeed a mecca of gambling and glitz. But the city is so much more than that. A Portuguese colony for more than 300 years, it is a city of blended cultures. Ancient Chinese temples sit on streets paved with traditional Portuguese tiles. The sound of Cantonese fills the air on streets with Portuguese names. You can eat Chinese *congee* for breakfast, enjoy a Portuguese lunch of *caldo verde* soup and *bacalhau* (cod) fritters, and dine on hybrid Macanese fare such as *minchi* (ground beef or pork, often served over rice).

The Macau Peninsula holds the old city centre, where colonial ruins sit next to arty new boutiques. Further south are the conjoined islands of Taipa, Cotai and Coloane. Taipa has gloriously preserved Macanese architecture, Cotai is home to the new megacasinos and Coloane is lined with colonial villages and pretty beaches.

When to Go
Macau

Mar–May Celebrate the arts, a sea goddess and a dragon as mist hangs over the harbour.

Jun–Sep Days in the shade of temples and dragon boats; nights aglow with fireworks.

Oct–Feb Music and grand prix in a high-octane run-up to Christmas and New Year.

History

Portuguese galleons first visited southern China to trade in the early 16th century, and in 1557, as a reward for clearing out pirates, they obtained a leasehold for Macau. The first Portuguese governor of Macau was appointed in 1680, and as trade with China grew, so did Macau. However, after the Opium Wars between the Chinese and the British, and the subsequent establishment of Hong Kong, Macau went into a long decline.

In 1999, under the Sino-Portuguese Joint Declaration, Macau was returned to China and designated as a Special Administrative Region (SAR). Like Hong Kong, the pact ensures Macau a 'high degree of autonomy' in all matters (except defence and foreign affairs) for 50 years. The handover, however, did not change Macau socially and economically as much as the termination of the gambling monopoly in 2001. Casinos mushroomed, redefining the city's skyline, and tourists from mainland China surged, fattening up the city's coffers.

Yet the revenue boost, coupled with government policies (or the lack thereof), also led to income inequality and a labour shortage. Macau residents are also increasingly critical of their chief executive's pro Beijing stance In May 2014 thousands in the formerly placid city took to the streets to protest Chief Executive Fernando Chui, who was re-elected three months later.

Language

Cantonese and Portuguese are the official languages of Macau, though few people actually speak Portuguese. English and Mandarin are reasonably well understood, though the former is harder to find here than in Hong Kong.

◉ Sights

◉ Central Macau Peninsula

★**Ruins of the Church of St Paul**   RUINS
(大三巴牌坊, Ruinas de Igreja de São Paulo; Map p540; Travessa de São Paulo; 🚍8A, 17, 26, disembark at Luís de Camões Garden) **FREE** The most treasured icon in Macau, the towering facade and stairway are all that remain of this early-17th-century Jesuit church. With its statues, portals and engravings that effectively make up a 'sermon in stone' and a *Biblia pauperum* (Bible of the poor), the church was one of the greatest monuments to Christianity in Asia, intended to help the illiterate understand the Passion of Christ and the lives of the saints.

The church was designed by an Italian Jesuit and completed by early Japanese Christian exiles and Chinese craftsmen in 1602. It was abandoned after the expulsion of the Jesuits

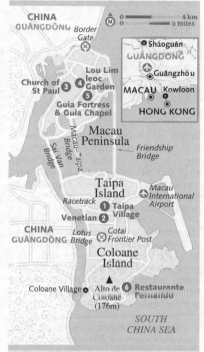

MACAU SIGHTS

Macau Highlights

❶ **Taipa Village** (p546) Dining on Portuguese fare and wandering the narrow lanes of this charming colonial village.

❷ **Venetian** (p553) Wandering the baroque indoor canals of this mind-blowingly huge casino complex.

❸ **Ruins of the Church of St Paul** (p537) Exploring the ethereal ruins of the very symbol of Macau.

❹ **Lou Lim Ieoc Garden** (p545) Losing yourself in maze-like spaces at Lou Lim Ieoc Garden.

❺ **Guia Fortress & Guia Chapel** (p543) Taking the cable car to handsome Guia Fort and its gorgeous chapel.

❻ **Restaurante Fernando** (p551) Indulging in a long lunch of garlicky clams and crisp suckling pig at this beloved beachside institution in Coloane.

PRICE RANGES

Sleeping
Breakfast is usually included in the rates for hotels marked $$ and $$$.

$ under MOP$700

$$ MOP$700-2000

$$$ over MOP$2000

Eating

$ less than MOP$200

$$ MOP$200-400

$$$ more than MOP$400

in 1762 and a military battalion was stationed here. In 1835 a fire erupted in the kitchen of the barracks, destroying everything, except what you see today. At the top is a dove, representing the Holy Spirit, surrounded by stone carvings of the sun, moon and stars. Beneath the Holy Spirit is a statue of the infant Jesus, and around it, stone carvings of the implements of the Crucifixion (the whip, crown of thorns, nails, ladder and spear). In the centre of the third tier stands the Virgin Mary being assumed bodily into heaven along with angels and two flowers: the peony, representing China, and the chrysanthemum, representing Japan. To the right of the Virgin is a carving of the tree of life and the apocalyptic woman (Mary) slaying a seven-headed hydra; the Japanese *kanji* next to her read: 'The holy mother tramples the heads of the dragon'. To the left of the central statue of Mary, a 'star' guides a ship (the Church) through a storm (sin); a carving of the devil is to the left. The fourth tier has statues of four Jesuit doctors of the church: (from left) Blessed Francisco de Borja; St Ignatius Loyola, the founder of the order; St Francis Xavier, the apostle of the Far East; and Blessed Luís Gonzaga.

★ **St Lazarus Church District**   AREA
(瘋堂斜巷, Calcada da Igreja de São Lazaro; Map p544; www.cipa.org.mo; 🚍7, 8) A lovely neighbourhood with colonial-style houses and cobbled streets makes for some of Macau's best photo-ops. Designers and other creative types like to gather here, setting up shop and organising artsy events.

★ **AFA (Art for All Society)**   GALLERY
(全藝社; Map p540; ☎853 2836 6064; www.afamacau.com; 1st fl, Art Garden, Avenida Dr Rodrigo Rodrigues N 265, Macau; ⏰11am-7pm Tue-Sun; 🚍8, 8A,

18A, 7) Macau's best contemporary art can be seen at this nonprofit gallery, which has taken Macau's art worldwide and holds monthly solo exhibitions by Macau's top artists. AFA is near the Mong Há Multi-Sport Pavilion. Disembark from the bus at Rua da Barca or Rua de Francisco Xavier Pereira. Alternatively, it's a 20-minute walk from Largo do Senado.

★ **Mandarin's House**   HISTORIC BUILDING
(鄭家大屋, Caso do Mandarim; Map p540; ☎853 2896 8820; www.wh.mo/mandarinhouse; 10 Travessa de António da Silva; ⏰10am-5.30pm Thu-Tue; 🚍28B, 18) FREE Built around 1869, the Mandarin's House, with over 60 rooms, was the ancestral home of Zheng Guanying, an influential author-merchant whose readers included emperors, Dr Sun Yatsen and Chairman Mao. The compound features a moon gate, tranquil courtyards, exquisite rooms and a main hall with French windows, all arranged in that labyrinthine style typical of certain Chinese period buildings. There are guided tours in Cantonese on weekend afternoons.

★ **St Joseph's Seminary & Church** CHURCH
(聖若瑟修院及聖堂, Capela do Seminario São José; Map p544; Rua do Seminario; ⏰church 10am-5pm; 🚍9, 16, 18, 28B) St Joseph's, which falls outside the tourist circuit, is one of Macau's most beautiful models of tropicalised baroque architecture. Consecrated in 1758 as part of the Jesuit seminary (not open to the public), it features a white-and-yellow facade, a scalloped entrance canopy (European) and the oldest dome, albeit a shallow one, ever built in China. The most interesting feature, however, is the roof, which features Chinese materials and building styles.

★ **Sir Robert Ho Tung Library**   LIBRARY
(何東圖書館; Map p544; 3 Largo de St Agostinho; ⏰10am-7pm Mon-Sat, 11am-7pm Sun; 🚍9, 16, 18) This charming building founded in the

EXCHANGE RATES

Australia	A$1	MOP$6.17
Canada	C$1	MOP$6.10
China	¥1	MOP$1.16
Euro	€1	MOP$8.46
Hong Kong	HK$1	MOP$1.03
Japan	¥100	MOP$7.09
New Zealand	NZ$1	MOP$5.78
UK	UK£1	MOP$10.04
USA	US$1	MOP$7.99

MACAU SIGHTS

19th century was the country retreat of the late tycoon Robert Ho Tung, who purchased it in 1918. The colonial edifice, featuring a dome, an arcaded facade, Ionic columns and Chinese-style gardens, was given a modern extension by architect Joy Choi Tin Tin not too long ago. The new four-storey structure in glass and steel has Piranesi-inspired bridges connecting to the old house and a glass roof straddling the transitional space.

Bishop's Palace   HISTORIC BUILDING
(土教府; Map p540; Penha Hill) This butter-yellow colonial palace is the office of the Bishop of Macau, the highest Catholic authority in the city.

Street of Happiness   STREET
(福隆新街; Map p544; Rua da Felicidade; ☒ 3, 6, 26A) Not far west of Largo do Senado is Rua da Felicidade (Street of Happiness). Its shuttered terraces were once Macau's main red-light district. Several scenes from *Indiana Jones and the Temple of Doom* were shot here. The government has plans to repaint the famous red shutters in the original colour – green. But whether it's wise to change the distinguishing feature of so iconic a landmark remains to be seen.

Leal Senado   HISTORIC BUILDING
(民政總署大樓; Map p544; ☑ 853 2857 2233; 163 Avenida de Almeida Ribeiro; ☉ 9am-9pm Tue-Sun; ☒ 3, 6, 26A, 18A, 33, disembark at Almeida Ribeiro) Facing Largo do Senado is Macau's most important historical building, the 18th-century 'Loyal Senate', which houses the Instituto para os Assuntos Cívicos e Municipais (IACM; Civic and Municipal Affairs Bureau). It is so-named because the body sitting here refused to recognise Spain's sovereignty during the 60 years that it occupied Portugal. In 1654, a dozen years after Portuguese sovereignty was re-established, King João IV ordered a heraldic inscription to be placed inside the entrance hall, which can still be seen today.

Inside the entrance hall is the **IACM Temporary Exhibition Gallery** (民政總署臨時展覽廳; ☑ 853 8988 4100; ☉ 9am-9pm Tue-Sun) **FREE**. On the 1st floor is the **Senate Library** (民政總署圖書館; ☑ 853 2857 2233; ☉ 1-7pm Tue-Sat) **FREE**, which has a collection of some 18,500 books, and wonderful carved wooden furnishings and panelled walls.

Monte Fort   FORT
(大炮台; Fortaleza do Monte; Map p544; ☉ 7am-7pm; ☒ 7, 8, disembark at Social Welfare Bureau) Just east of the Ruins of the Church of St Paul, Monte Fort was built by the Jesuits between 1617 and 1626 as part of the College of the Mother of God. Barracks and storehouses were designed to allow the fort to survive a two-year siege, but the cannons were fired only once, during the aborted attempt by the Dutch to invade Macau in 1622. Now the cannons on the south side are trained at the gaudy Grand Lisboa Casino like an accusing finger.

Lou Kau Mansion   HISTORIC BUILDING
(盧家大屋, Casa de Lou Kau; Map p544; ☑ 853 8399 6699; 7 Travessa da Sé; ☉ 9am-7pm Tue-Sun; ☒ 3, 4, 6A, 8A, 19, 33) **FREE** Built around 1889, this Cantonese-style mansion with southern European elements belonged to merchant Lou Wa Sio (aka Lou Kau), who also commissioned the Lou Lim Ieoc Garden (p545). Behind the grey facade, an intriguing maze of open and semi-enclosed spaces blurs the line between inside and outside. The flower-and-bird motif on the roof can also be found in the Mandarin's House and A-Ma Temple. Traditional craft workers often practise their art here during weekdays. Free guided tours in Chinese on weekends (10am to 7pm).

Church of St Dominic   CHURCH
(玫瑰堂, Igreja de São Domingos; Map p544; Largo de São Domingos; ☉ 10am-6pm; ☒ 3, 6, 26A) Smack in the heart of Macau's historic centre, this sunny yellow baroque church with a beautiful altar and a timber roof was founded by three Spanish Dominican priests from Acapulco, Mexico, in the 16th century, though the current structure dates from the 17th century. It was here, in 1822, that the first Portuguese newspaper was published on Chinese soil. The former bell tower now houses the **Treasure of Sacred Art** (聖物寶庫, Tesouro de Arte Sacra; Map p544; ☉ 10am-6pm) **FREE**, an Aladdin's cave of ecclesiastical art and liturgical objects exhibited on three floors.

Macau Museum   MUSEUM
(澳門博物館, Museu de Macau; Map p544; ☑ 853 2835 7911; www.macaumuseum.gov.mo; 112 Praceta do Museu de Macau; MOP$15, 15th of month free; ☉ 10am-5.30pm Tue-Sun; ☒ 7, 8, disembark at Social Welfare Bureau) This interesting museum inside Monte Fort will give you a taste of Macau's history. The 1st floor introduces the territory's early history and includes an elaborate section on Macau's religions. Highlights of the 2nd floor include a re-created firecracker factory and a recorded reading in the local dialect by Macanese

Macau Peninsula

MACAU

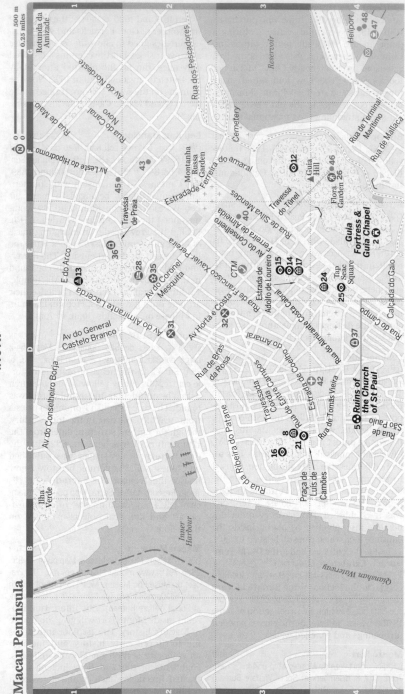

500 m
0.25 miles

Rotunda da Amizade

Av do Nordeste

Rua do Canal Novo

Rua de Maio

Av Leste do Hipódromo

Rua dos Pescadores

Reservoir

Heliport

48
47

Montanha Russa Garden

Cemetery

Rua de Terminal Marítimo

Rua de Mallaca

Estrada de Ferreira do amaral

43

45

Travessa de Praia

12

Guia Hill

46

Flora Garden

26

Guia Fortress & Guia Chapel
2

E do Arco

13

36

28

35

Av do Coronel Mesquita

Ferreira de Almeida

Av do Conselheiro

Travessa do Túnel

Rua de Silva Mendes

CTM

15
14
17

24

25

Tap Seac Square

Calçada do Galo

Av do Conselheiro Borja

Av do General Castelo Branco

Av do Almirante Lacerda

31

Av Horta e Costa

32

Rua de Francisco Xavier Pereira

Estrada de Adolfo de Loureiro

Rua de Almirante Costa Cabral

37

Rua do Campo

Ilha Verde

Inner Harbour

Rua da Ribeira do Patane

Rua de Brás da Rosa

Rua de Coelho do Amaral

Travessada Corda

Rua de Entre Campos

Estrada

42

Rua de Tomás Vieira

Ruins of the Church of St Paul
5

Rua de São Paulo

Praça de Luís de Camões

16

8

21

Quanshan Waterway

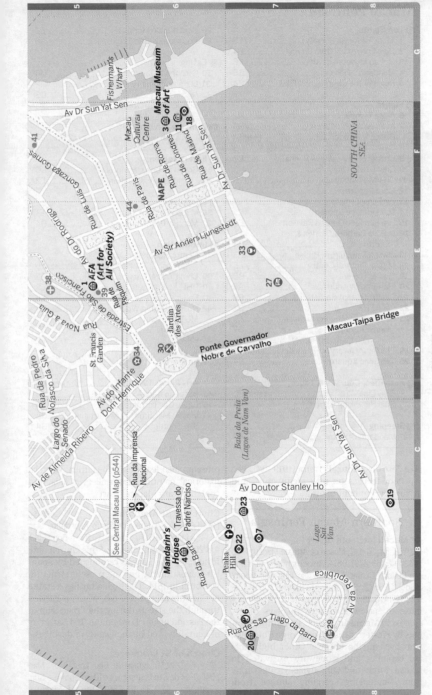

MACAU

South China Sea

Fisherman's Wharf

Av Dr Sun Yat Sen

Macau Museum

Macau Cultural Centre

Macau Museum of Art 3

11 18

NAPE

Rua de Roma

Rua de Londres

Rua de Madrid

Av Dr Sun Yat Sen

Rua de Paris

41

Rua de Luís Gonzaga Gomes

Rua de Dr Rodrigo

44

Av Sir Anders Ljungstedt

33

AFA (Art for All Society) 1

Av do Dr Rodrigo

38

39

Rua de São Francisco

Rua de Pequim

27

Rua Nova à Guia

Estrada de São Francisco

Jardim des Artes

Macau-Taipa Bridge

Rua de Pedro Nolasco da Silva

St Francis Garden

34

Av do Infante Dom Henrique

30

Ponte Governador Nobre de Carvalho

Largo do Senado

Av de Almeida Ribeiro

Rua da Imprensa Nacional

See Central Macau Map (p544)

Baía da Praia (Lagos de Nam Van)

10

Travessa do Padré Narciso

23

Mandarin's House 4

9

22

7

Av Doutor Stanley Ho

19

Rua da Barra

Penha Hill

Lago Sai Van

Av da República

6

20

Rua de São Tiago da Barra

29

Macau Peninsula

poet José dos Santos Ferreira (1919–93). The top floor focuses on new architecture and urban-development plans.

◉ Southern Macau Peninsula

★ **Macau Museum of Art**   MUSEUM
(澳門藝術博物館, Museu de Arte de Macau; Map p540; ☏853 8791 9814; www.mam.gov.mo; Macau Cultural Centre, Avenida Xian Xing Hai; adult/child MOP$5/2, Sun free; ◷10am-6.30pm Tue-Sun; ☐1A, 8, 12, 23) This excellent five-storey museum has well curated displays of art created in Macau and China, including paintings by Western artists like George Chinnery, who lived in the enclave. Other highlights are ceramics and stoneware excavated in Macau, Ming- and Qing-dynasty calligraphy from Guǎngdōng, ceramic statues from Shíwān (Guǎngdōng) and seal carvings. The

museum also features 19th-century Western historical paintings from all over Asia, and contemporary Macanese art.

Church of St Augustine   CHURCH
(聖奧斯定教堂, Igreja de Santo Agostinho; Map p544; 2 Largo de St Agostinho; ◷10am-6pm; ☐3, 4, 6, 26A) The foundations of this church date from 1586 when it was established by Spanish Augustinians, but the present structure was built in 1814. The high altar has a statue of Christ bearing the cross, which is carried through the streets during the Procession of the Passion of Our Lord on the first Saturday of Lent, followed by thousands of devotees.

Church of St Lawrence   CHURCH
(聖老楞佐教堂, Igreja de São Lourenço; Map p540; Rua de São Lourenço; ◷10am-5pm Tue-Sun, 1-2pm Mon; ☐9, 16, 18, 28B) One of Macau's

three oldest churches, St Lawrence was originally constructed of wood in the 1560s, then rebuilt in stone in the early 19th century. The neoclassical church has a magnificent painted ceiling and one of its towers once served as an ecclesiastical prison. Enter from Rua da Imprensa Nacional.

Avenida da República   AREA

(Map p540, ☐6, 9, 16) Avenida da República, along the northwest shore of Sai Van Lake, is Macau's oldest Portuguese quarter. There are several grand colonial villas not open to the public here. The former Bela Vista Hotel, one of the most-fabled hotels in Asia, is now the **Residence of the Portuguese Consul-General** (葡國駐澳門領事官邸, Consulado-Geral de Portugal em Macau; Map p540; Rua do Boa Vista). Nearby is the ornate **Santa Sancha Palace**, once the residence of Macau's Portuguese governors, and now used to accommodate state guests. Not too far away are beautiful, abandoned art deco–inspired buildings.

A-Ma Temple   TAOIST TEMPLE

(媽閣廟, Templo de A-Ma; Map p540; Rua de São Tiago da Barra; ⊙7am-6pm; ☐1, 2, 5, 6B, 7) A-Ma Temple was probably already standing when the Portuguese arrived, although the present structure may date from the 16th century. It was here that fisherfolk once came to replenish supplies and pray for fair weather. A-Ma, aka Tin Hau, is the goddess of the sea, from which the name Macau is derived. It's believed that when the Portuguese asked the name of the place, they were told 'A-Ma Gau' (A-Ma Bay). In modern Cantonese, 'Macau' (Ou Mun) means 'gateway of the bay'.

Penha Hill   AREA

(西望洋山, Colina da Penha; Map p540; ☐6, 9, 16) Towering above the colonial villas along Avenida da República is Penha Hill, the most tranquil and least-visited area of the peninsula. From here you'll get excellent views of the central area of Macau. Atop the hill is the Bishop's Palace (p539), built in 1837 and a residence for bishops (not open to the public), and the **Chapel of Our Lady of Penha** (主教山小堂, Ermida de Nossa Senhora da Penha; ⊙9am-5.30pm; ☐6B, 9, 16, 28B), once a place of pilgrimage for sailors.

Maritime Museum   MUSEUM

(海事博物館, Museu Marítimo; Map p540; ☑853 2859 5481; www.museumaritimo.gov.mo; 1 Largo do Pagode da Barra; adult MOP$3-10, child free; ⊙10am-5.30pm Wed-Mon; ☐1, 2, 5, 6B, 7, 10) The highlights here are the interactive displays detailing the maritime histories of

Portugal and China, the artefacts from Macau's seafaring past, and the mock-ups of boats – including the long, narrow dragon boats used during the Dragon Boat Festival – and a Hakka fishing village.

Macau Cultural Centre   NOTABLE BUILDING

(澳門文化中心, Centro Cultural de Macau; Map p540; ☑853 2870 0699; www.ccm.gov.mo; Avenida Xian Xing Hai; ⊙9am-7pm Tue-Sun; ☐1A, 8, 12, 23) This US$100-million, 45,000-sq-metre contemporary concrete structure is the territory's prime venue for cultural performances, from dance to theatre to multimedia shows. **Creative Macau** (創意空間; Map p540; ☑853 2875 3282; www.creativemacau. org.mo; Ground fl, ⊙2-7pm Mon-Sat), an art space that runs exhibitions and poetry readings, is on the ground floor.

⊙ Northern Macau Peninsula

★ Guia Fortress & Guia Chapel   FORT

(東望洋炮台及聖母雪地殿聖堂, Fortaleza da Guia e Capela de Guia; Map p540; ⊙fortress 6am-6pm, chapel 10am-5.30pm; ☐2, 2A, 6A, 12, 17, 18, Flora Garden stop) FREE As the highest point on the peninsula, Guia Fort affords panoramic views of the city and, when the air is clear, across to the islands and China. At the top is the stunning Chapel of Our Lady of Guia, built in 1622 and retaining almost 100% of its original features, including some of Asia's most important frescoes. Next to it stands the oldest modern lighthouse on the

MACAU SIGHTS

MACAU IN ONE DAY

Start in the **Largo do Senado** and wander up to the **Ruins of the Church of St Paul** (p537). Spend an hour or so in the **Macau Museum** (p539) to give it all some context. Have lunch at **Clube Militar de Macau** (p550), before getting a feel for Macau's living history as you wander back through the tiny streets towards the Inner Harbour port and **A-Ma Temple**. Jump on a bus to sleepy **Coloane Village**. Take an easy stroll around here and bus it back to Taipa for some sightseeing and dinner at the lovely **António** (p551). Then head for the gaudy magnificence of the **Grand Lisboa Casino** (新葡京; Map p540; ☑853 2838 2828; www.grandlisboa. com; Avenida de Lisboa, Macau Peninsula; ☐3, 10), before sauntering over to **Macau Soul** (p552) for wine and jazz.

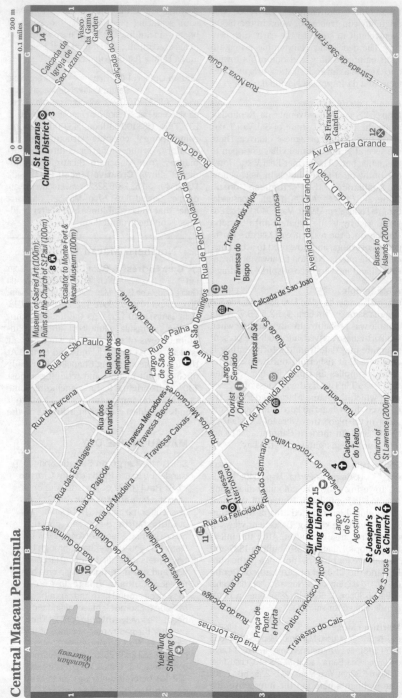

Central Macau Peninsula

MACAU SIGHTS

200 m
0.1 miles

Qianshan Waterway

Yuet Tung Shipping Co

St Lazarus Church District 3

Calçada da Igreja de São Lázaro

14

Vasco da Gama Garden

Calçada do Gaio

Rua Nova a Guia

Estrada de São Francisco

St Francis Garden

12

Av da Praia Grande

Av de D. João IV

Buses to Islands (200m)

Avenida da Praia Grande

Rua Formosa

Rua do Campo

Rua de Pedro Nolasco da Silva

Travessa dos Anjos

Travessa do Bispo

Calçada de São João

Museum of Sacred Art (100m); Ruins of the Church of St Paul (100m)

Escalator to Monte Fort & Macau Museum (100m)

8

13

Rua de São Paulo

Rua de Nossa Senhora do Amparo

Rua da Palha

Rua da Sé

Rua de São Domingos

16

7

Calçada de São João

Rua da Tercena

Rua dos Ervanários

Largo de São Domingos

Rua da Madeira

Rua das Estalagens

Rua do Pagode

Travessa Mercadores

Travessa Becos

Travessa Caixas

Rua dos Mercadores

5

Largo do Senado

Tourist Office

Travessa da Sé

Av de Almeida Ribeiro

6

Rua Central

Church of St Lawrence (200m)

Rua do Cinco de Outubro

Rua de Guimarães

10

Travessa da Caldeira

Rua da Caldeira

Travessa AterroNovo

Rua de Seminario

Calçada do Tronco Velho

Calçada do Teatro

4

9

Rua da Felicidade

11

Rua do Gamboa

Rua do Bocage

Praça de Ponte e Horta

Rua das Lorchas

Largo de St Agostinho

Sir Robert Ho Tung Library 1

15

St Joseph's Seminary & Church 2

Rua de S José

Patio Francisco António

Travessa do Cais

Central Macau Peninsula

◎ Top Sights
1 Sir Robert Ho Tung Library B4
2 St Joseph's Seminary & Church B4
3 St Lazarus Church District F1

◎ Sights
4 Church of St Augustine C4
5 Church of St Dominic D2
   IACM Temporary Exhibition
   Gallery .... (see 6)
6 Leal Senado C3
7 Lou Kau Mansion D3
   Macau Museum .... (see 8)
8 Monte Fort E1
   Senate Library .... (see 6)
9 Street of Happiness B3
   Treasure of Sacred Art .... (see 5)

🛏 Sleeping
10 5Footway Inn B1
11 San Va Hospedaria B2

✕ Eating
12 Clube Militar de Macau F4

◎ Drinking & Nightlife
13 Macau Soul D1
14 Single Origin G1
15 Terra Coffee House C4

🛍 Shopping
16 Livraria Portuguesa E3

China coast (1865) – an attractive 15m-tall structure that is closed to the public.

You could walk up, but it's easier to take the Guia cable car that runs from the entrance of Flora Gardens, Macau's largest public park.

Casa Garden　　　　HISTORIC BUILDING
(東方基金會會址; Map p540; 13 Praça de Luís de Camões; ⊙ garden 9.30am-6pm daily, gallery open only during exhibitions 9.30am-6pm Mon-Fri; 🚍 8A, 17, 26) One of the oldest buildings in the city, this beautiful colonial villa was built in 1770. It was the headquarters of the British East India Company when it was based in Macau in the early 19th century. Today it's home to a small gallery that mounts interesting art exhibitions. Visitors can wander the slightly forlorn gardens.

Flora Gardens　　　　GARDENS
(Jardim da Flora; Map p540; Travessa do Túnel; ⊙ 8am-6pm, cable car closed Mon) The former grounds of a Portuguese mansion, this European-style garden is known for its cable car, which travels the short distance up Guia Hill, the highest point in the city and home to Guia Fortress & Guia Chapel (p543). The park's tiny zoo is quite sad by global standards.

Lou Lim Ieoc Garden　　　　GARDENS
(盧廉若公園, Jardim Lou Lim Ieoc; Map p540; 10 Estrada de Adolfo de Loureiro; ⊙ 6am-9pm; 🚍 2, 2A, 5, 9, 9A, 12, 16) Locals come to this lovely Sūzhōu-style garden to practise taichi, play Chinese music or simply relax among its lotus ponds and bamboo groves. The Victorian-style **Lou Lim Ieoc Garden Pavilion** (盧廉若公園, Pavilhão do Jardim de Lou Lim Ieoc; Map p540; ☑ 853 8988 4100; ⊙ 9am-7pm Tue-Sun) was where the Lou family received guests, including Dr Sun

Yatsen, and is now used for exhibitions. Adjacent to the garden is the **Macao Tea Culture House** (澳門茶文化館, Caultura do Chá em Macau; Map p540; ☑ 853 2882 7103; ⊙ 9am-7pm Tue-Sun) FREE, displaying Chinese tea-drinking culture with exhibits of teapots and paintings related to the coveted drink.

Luís de Camões Garden & Grotto　　GARDENS
(白鴿巢公園, Jardim e Gruta de Luís de Camões; Map p540; Praça de Luís de Camões; ⊙ 6am-10pm; 🚍 8A, 17, 26) This relaxing garden with dappled meandering paths is dedicated to the one-eyed poet Luís de Camões (1524–80), who is said to have written part of his epic *Os Lusíadas* in Macau, though there is little evidence that he ever reached the city. You'll see a bronze bust (c 1886) of the man here. The wooded garden attracts a fair number of chess players, bird owners and Chinese shuttlecock kickers. The **Sr Wong Ieng Kuan Library** (白鴿巢公園黃營均圖書館; Map p540; ☑ 853 2895 3075; ⊙ 8am-8pm Tue-Sun) is also here.

Lin Fung Temple　　　　BUDDHIST TEMPLE
(蓮峰廟, Lin Fung Miu; Map p540; Avenida do Almirante Lacerda; ⊙ 7am-5pm; 🚍 1A, 8, 8A, 10, 28B) Dedicated to Kun Iam, the Goddess of Mercy, this Temple of the Lotus was built in 1592, but underwent several reconstructions from the 17th century. It used to host mandarins from Guǎngdōng province when they visited Macau. The most famous of these imperial visitors was Commissioner Lin Zexu, who was charged with stamping out the opium trade.

Macau Tower　　　　LANDMARK
(澳門旅遊塔, Torre de Macau; Map p540; ☑ 853 2893 3339; www.macautower.com.mo; Largo da Torre de Macau; observation deck adult/child

MACAU SIGHTS

MOP$135/70; ⊙10am-9pm Mon-Fri, 9am-9pm Sat & Sun; 🚌9A, 18, 23, 26, 32) At 338m, Macau Tower looms above the narrow isthmus of land southeast of Avenida da República. You can stay put on the observation decks on the 58th and 61st floors, or challenge yourself to some gravity-defying sport: the tower hosts a climbing wall, a bungee platform (said to be the highest commercial bungee jump in the world), a sky walk around the rim of the tower and more.

Tap Seac Square   SQUARE
(塔石廣場, Praca do Tap Seac; Map p540; 🚌7, 8) This beautiful square surrounded by important historic buildings from the 1920s, such as the Cultural Affairs Bureau, Tap Seac Health Centre, Central Library, Library for Macau's Historical Archives and **Tap Seac Gallery** (塔石藝文館, Galeria Tap Seac; Map p540; www.macauart.net/ts; 95 Avenida Conselheiro Ferreira de Almeida; ⊙10am-9pm; 🚌). It was designed by Macanese architect Carlos Marreiros. Marreiros also created the Tap Seac Health Centre, a contemporary interpretation of Macau's neoclassical buildings.

Old Protestant Cemetery   CEMETERY
(基督教墳場, Antigo Cemitério Protestante; Map p540; 15 Praça de Luís de Camões; ⊙8.30am-5.30pm; 🚌8A, 17, 26) As church law forbade the burial of non-Catholics on hallowed ground, this cemetery was established in 1821 as the last resting place of (mostly Anglophone) Protestants. Among those interred here are Irish-born artist George Chinnery (1774–1852), and Robert Morrison (1782–1834), the first Protestant missionary to China and author of the first Chinese-English dictionary.

⊙ The Islands
♪ 853

The islands of Taipa, Cotai and Coloane are more like one big island these days, thanks to land reclamation. Head to Taipa for dining and shopping in the narrow streets of old Taipa Village. Visit the new area of Cotai (created by infilling marsh between Taipa and Coloane, hence the name) to gamble and gawk at the biggest casinos on earth. Go south to Coloane for beachy getaways and long Portuguese lunches.

Taipa (氹仔) was once two islands that were slowly joined together by silt from the Pearl River. A similar physical joining has happened to Taipa and Coloane because of land reclamation from the sea. The new strip of land joining the two islands is known as Cotai (from Co-loane and Tai-pa). Taipa has rapidly urbanised and it's hard to imagine that just a few decades ago it was an island of duck farms and boat yards. Today the most interesting part of the area for visitors is the well preserved streets around Taipa Village.

A haven for pirates until the start of the 20th century, **Coloane** (路環), considerably larger than Taipa or Cotai, is the only part of Macau that doesn't seem to be changing at a head-spinning rate. Today it retains Macau's old way of life, though luxurious villas are finding their way onto the island. All buses stop at the roundabout in Coloane Village.

The newest part of Macau has risen out of the marshland that once divided Taipa and Coloane, with a name (from Co-loane and Tai-pa) to reflect this joining. Today, **Cotai** is Macau's answer to the Vegas Strip, an ever-growing collection of megacasinos and entertainment complexes drawing tens of millions of tourists every year. Even if you hate gambling, the casinos are marvels of giant-scale planning and detail – a faux Venice! A one-third-scale Eiffel Tower! An indoor model of Lisbon's train station!

★ Taipa Village   VILLAGE
(Map p547; 🚌22, 26, 33) The historical part of Taipa is best preserved in this village in the south of the district. An intricate warren of alleys hold traditional Chinese shops and some excellent restaurants, while the broader main roads are punctuated by colonial villas, churches and temples. Rua do Cunha, the

---

COLOANE'S STILT HOUSES

Macau was a fishing village before gambling was legalised in the mid-19th century. Now the only vestiges of that idyllic past are found in Coloane.

Along the coastline, on Rua dos Navegantes in Coloane's old fishing village, there are a few stilt houses and shipyards. These huts of colourful corrugated metal, extending like chunky chopsticks out into the harbour, were once landing spots for houseboats. A couple have been turned into dried seafood shops, such as Loja de Peixe Tong Kei (棠記魚舖) at Largo do Cais, the square just off the charming old pier of Coloane.

From the square, take the slope to the right of the Servicos de Alfangega building. After two minutes, you'll see the cavernous cadaver of a shipyard, also on stilts.

The Islands – Taipa

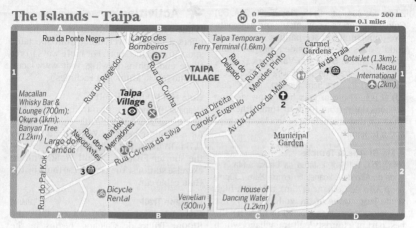

main pedestrian drag, is lined with vendors hawking free samples of Macanese almond cookies and beef jerky, and tiny cafes selling egg tarts and serradura pudding. Avenida da Praia, a tree-lined esplanade with wrought-iron benches, is perfect for a leisurely stroll.

Taipa Houses-Museum MUSEUM
(龍環葡韻住宅式博物館, Casa Museum da Taipa; Map p547; ☑853 2882 7103; Avenida da Praia, Carmo Zone, Taipa Village; adult/student MOP$5/2, child & senior free, Sun free; ☉10am-5.30pm Tue-Sun; ☐11, 15, 22, 28A, 30, 33, 34) The pastel-coloured villas (c 1921) here were the summer residences of wealthy Macanese. House of the Regions of Portugal showcases Portuguese costumes. House of the Islands looks at the history of Taipa and Coloane, with displays on traditional industries, such as fishing and the manufacture of fireworks. Macanese House offers a snapshot of life in the early 20th century.

Museum of Taipa & Coloane History MUSEUM
(路氹歷史館, Museu da História da Taipa e Coloane; Map p547; ☑853 2882 5361; Rua Correia da Silva, Taipa; adult/student MOP$5/2, child & senior free, Tue free; ☉10am-5.30pm Tue-Sun; ☐11, 15, 22, 28A, 30, 33, 34) This museum has a display of excavated relics and other artefacts on the 1st floor, while the 2nd floor contains religious objects, handicrafts and architectural models.

Church of Our Lady of Carmel CHURCH
(Igreja de Nossa Senhora de Carmo; Map p547; Rue da Restauração, Taipa Village; ☐22, 28A, 26) Built in 1885, this lovely yellow neoclassical church stands on a hill overlooking the

harbour, scenic Taipa Village and the pastel-coloured Taipa Houses-Museum. On weekends, expect to see dozens of couples taking wedding photos here.

Chapel of St Francis Xavier CHURCH
(聖方濟各教堂, Capela de São Francisco Xavier, Coloane; Map p551; Rua do Caetano, Largo Eduardo Marques; ☉10am-8pm; ☐15, 21A, 25, 26A) This chapel built in 1928 contains paintings of the infant Christ with a Chinese Madonna, and other reminders of Christianity and colonialism in Asia. It's a quirky place painted in yellow and embellished with red lanterns. In front of the chapel are a monument and fountain surrounded by four cannonballs that commemorate the successful – and final – routing of pirates in 1910.

Macau Giant Panda Pavilion ZOO
(大熊貓館, Pavihao do Panda Gigante de Macau; ☑853 2833 7676; www.macaupanda.org.mo; Seac Pai Van Park, Coloane; MOP$10; ☉10am-1pm &

MACAU SIGHTS

2-5pm Tue-Sun; [icon]; [bus]15, 21A, 25, 26, 26A, 50) Coloane offers a convenient and inexpensive opportunity to see pandas. The pair of cuddly ones are kept inside a purpose-built pavilion inside **Seac Pai Van Park** (石排灣郊野公園; Estrada de Seac Pai Van; ⊙8am-6pm Tue-Sun, aviary 9am-5pm Tue-Sun; [bus]21A, 26A, 50) **FREE**. There are six hour-long viewing sessions daily, from 10am to 4pm. Other animals on display include peacocks, monkeys and a toucan.

A-Ma Statue & Temple
MEMORIAL

(媽祖像及媽閣廟, Estátua da Deusa A-Ma; Estrada do Alto de Coloane; ⊙temple 8am-7.30pm) Atop Alto de Coloane (176m), this 20m-high white jade statue of the goddess who gave Macau its name was erected in 1998. It's the best part of a touristy 'cultural village', which also features **Tian Hou Temple**. A free bus runs from the A-Ma ornamental entrance gate (媽祖文化村石牌坊) on Estrada de Seac Pai Van (bus 21A, 25, 50) half-hourly from 8am to 6pm. You can also reach both by following the Coloane Trail (Trilho de Coloane) from Seac Pai Van Park.

Cheoc Van Beach
BEACH

(竹灣海灘; Map p551; Estrada de Cheoc Van; [bus]21A, 25, 26A) About 1.5km down Estrada de Cheoc Van, which runs east and then southeast from Coloane village, is the beach at Cheoc Van (Bamboo Bay). It's smaller but somewhat cleaner than Hác Sá beach. There are changing rooms and toilets and, in season, lifeguards on duty (from 10am to 6pm Monday to Saturday, from 9am to 6pm Sunday, May to October). There's also a large public outdoor pool.

CONFUCIANISM VERSUS CATHOLICISM

As the Portuguese lost ground to the Dutch and English in trade, religious infighting weakened the status of Macau as a Christian centre. In what came to be known as the Rites Controversy, the Jesuits maintained that central aspects of Chinese belief – such as ancestor worship and Confucianism – were not incompatible with the Christian faith. The Dominicans and Franciscans, equally well represented in Macau, disagreed. It took an edict by Pope Clement XI in 1715 condemning the rites as idolatrous to settle the matter and this stopped further missionary expansion into China.

🏃 Activities

While Macau is no adventure paradise, it offers a taste of everything from spectator sport to extreme sport. For more ways to get those endorphins flowing, visit www.iacm.gov.mo (click 'Municipal Facilities').

Guia Hill Hiking Circuit
HIKING

(Map p540) There are two trails on Guia Hill in central Macau Peninsula that are good for a stroll or jog. The **Walk of 33 Curves** (1.7km) circles the hill; inside this loop is the shorter **Fitness Circuit Walk**, with 20 exercise stations. You can access these by the Guia cable car.

Coloane Trail
HIKING

Coloane's (and Macau's) longest trail, the 8100m Trilho de Coloane, begins in the mid-section of Estrada do Alto de Coloane and winds around the island. (To get there, take bus 21A and get off at stop Estrada do Campo, then enter Estrata Militar across the road; after 600m, turn right.) You can make a detour to Alto de Coloane (170m) to see the A-Ma Statue.

The shorter **Coloane Northeast Trail** (Trilho Nordeste de Coloane), near Ká Hó, runs for 3km. Other trails that offer good hiking include the 1.5km-long **Altinho de Ká Hó Trail** and the 1.5km-long **Circuito da Barragem de Hác Sá**, which both loop around the reservoir to the northwest of Hác Sá beach.

👉 Tours

Gray Line
TOURS

(Map p540; ☏ 853 2833 6611; www.grayline.com.hk; Room 1015, ground fl, Macau Ferry Terminal; 10hr tour adult/child 3-11yr MOP$1275/1200 incl ferry ticket to Hong Kong) Quality tours organised by the Macau Government Tourist Office and tendered to agents take around 10 hours.

🎊 Festivals & Events

The blend of Cantonese and Portuguese culture and religious occasions creates an unusual and intriguing succession of holidays and festivals in Macau; Chinese festivals usually fall on dates in the lunar calendar. See the directory for the full list of other festivals and events in China, many of which are also celebrated in Macau.

Feast of the Drunken Dragon
CULTURAL

(⊙May or Jun) One of Macau's most unique festivals, on the evening of the eighth day of the fourth month of the lunar calendar (in

May or June), local fishmongers and fishers perform drunken dances with a wooden dragon and parade through the streets distributing free 'longevity rice'.

Procession of Our Lady of Fatima RELIGIOUS (⊘May) A celebration of Macau's Portuguese heritage, this event draws thousands of Catholics into the streets, where they parade from St Domingo's to Penha Chapel in honour of a 1917 sighting of the Virgin Mary in Portugal.

Macau Formula 3 Grand Prix SPORTS (☑853 2855 5555; www.macau.grandprix.gov.mo; ⊘Nov) Macau's biggest sporting event of the year is held in the third week of November.

🛏 Sleeping

The Macau Peninsula has a range of accommodation, from dated-but-serviceable business hotels at low price points to international luxury brands. Cotai has scads of brand-new casino hotels, many offering excellent weekday deals. Coloane is home to a handful of beachy inns and the city's two hostels.

All rooms listed here have air-conditioning and bathroom unless otherwise stated. Most midrange and top-end hotels have shuttle buses from the ferry terminal.

🛏 Macau Peninsula

Cheap guesthouses occupy central Macau, on and around Rua das Lorchas and Avenida de Almeida Ribeiro, with options aplenty on Rua da Felicidade (Street of Happiness), whose shuttered terraces were once Macau's main red-light district (scenes from *Indiana Jones and the Temple of Doom* were shot here). The high-end casino hotels generally occupy the southeast and the centre of town.

San Va Hospedaria GUESTHOUSE $ (新華大旅店; Map p544; ☑853 2857 3701, reservations 853 8210 0193; www.sanvahotel.com; 65-67 Rua da Felicidade; d MOP$220-620, tw MOP$360-620, tr MOP$450-650; ☑3, 6, 26A) Built in 1873, San Va, with its green partitions and retro tiles, is about the cheapest and most atmospheric lodging in town – Wong Kar-wai filmed parts of *2046* here. However, it's also very basic, with shared bathrooms and no air-conditioning (just fans).

★5Footway Inn INN $$ (五步廊旅舍; Map p544; ☑853 2892 3118; www.5footwayinn.com; 8 Rua de Constantino Brito; d/tr from MOP$1400/2200; ☀❄🛜; ☑1, 2, 10, 5, 7) This Singapore-owned accommodation con-

verted from a love motel has 23 small clean rooms, vibrant paintings in communal areas and excellent English-speaking staff. Rates include a self-service breakfast. It's opposite the Sofitel Macau at Ponte 16, which means you can take the latter's free shuttle buses to and from the ferry terminal.

★Pousada de Mong Há INN $$ (澳門望廈迎賓館; Map p540; ☑853 2851 5222; www.ift.edu.mo; Colina de Mong Há, r MOP$700-1300, ste MOP$1300-1800; ☀❄@🛜; ☑5, 22, 25) Sitting atop Mong Há Hill near the ruins of a fort built in 1849 is this Portuguese-style inn run by students at the Institute for Tourism Studies. Rooms are well appointed, with some having computers, and the service is attentive. Rates include breakfast. Discounts of 25% to 40% midweek and in low season.

Pousada de São Tiago HISTORIC HOTEL $$$ (聖地牙哥古堡; Map p540; ☑853 2837 8111; www.saotiago.com.mo; Fortaleza de São Tiago da Barra, Avenida da República; ste MOP$2800-5400; ☀❄@🛜🛆; ☑6, 9, 28B) Built into the ruins of the 17th-century Barra Fort, the landmark São Tiago is the most romantic place to stay in Macau. No other hotel has such a rich history. All 12 rooms are elegantly furnished suites. Discounts of up to 35% in low season. The restaurant serves elegant modern Spanish food.

Mandarin Oriental LUXURY HOTEL $$$ (文華東方; Map p540; ☑853 8805 8888; www.mandarinoriental.com/macau; Avenida Dr Sun Yat Sen, Novos Aterros do Porto Exterior; r from MOP$3000, ste from MOP$4800; ☀❄@🛜🛆) A great high-end option, the Mandarin has everything associated with the brand: elegance, superlative service, comfortable rooms and excellent facilities. Though relatively small, it's a refreshing contrast to the glitzy casino hotels.

🛏 The Islands

Almost all the hotels in Cotai are part of casino complexes. Some are tacky and flashy, while others are as elegant as you'll find anywhere. Prices vary vastly; you can often find incredible midweek deals, while prices during Lunar New Year and other high-season times can quadruple.

Coloane offers some solid budget options, including two HI-affiliated hostels.

Pousada de Juventude de Cheoc Van HOSTEL $ (Map p551; ☑853 2888 2024; Rua de António Francisco, Coloane; dm/tw from MOP$100/160;

❀☎; 🔲21A, 25, 26A) This government-run, beachside hostel is excellent value, but conditions apply. You'll need to book at least a week in advance and own an International Youth Card, International Youth Hostel Card or similar. It's closed to tourists in July and August. Don't expect much of a social vibe – most of the guests here are local or Chinese school groups.

Okura HOTEL $$
(🖉853 8883 8883; www.hotelokuramacau.com; Galaxy, Avenida Marginal Flor de Lotus, Cotai; r MOP$1000-5600, ste MOP$3000-20,000; 🔲25, 26A) In the Galaxy Macau, this Japanese hotel offers attentive service and subdued luxury for a price that tends to be among the area's most reasonable. Rooms are large and bathrooms are even larger, complete with heated Japanese toilet seats and freestanding tubs with televisions.

Banyan Tree LUXURY HOTEL $$$
(🖉853 8883 8833; www.banyantree.com/en/macau; Galaxy, Avenida Marginal Flor de Lotus, Cotai; ste MOP$2880-63,800, villas MOP$23,600-35,100; 🔲25, 25X) One of three hotels at the Galaxy Macau, this extravagant resort recreates tropical-style luxury in Macau. All 10 villas come with private gardens and swimming pools, while the suites have huge baths set by the window. If you need more pampering, there's a spa with state-of-the-art facilities.

🍴 Eating

Browse a typically Macanese menu and you'll find an enticing stew of influences from Chinese and Asian cuisines, as well as from those of former Portuguese colonies in Africa, India and Latin America, and from Portugal itself. Coconut, tamarind, chilli, jaggery (palm sugar) and shrimp paste can all feature. While Macau's Chinese cuisine is excellent, most people come here to sample Macanese or Portuguese food.

🍴 Macau Peninsula

★Lung Wah Tea House CANTONESE $
(龍華茶樓; Map p540; 🖉853 2857 4456; 3 Rua Norte do Mercado Aim-Lacerda; dim sum from MOP$14, tea MOP$10, meals MOP$50-180; ☺7am-2pm; 📶; 🔲23, 32) There's grace in the retro furniture and the casual way it's thrown together in this airy Cantonese teahouse (c 1963). Take a booth by the windows overlooking the Red Market, where the teahouse buys its produce every day. There's no English menu; just point and take.

Nga Heong BURMESE $
(雅馨緬甸餐廳; Map p540; 🖉853 2855 2711; 27 Rua de Fernao Mendes Pinto; mains MOP$25-45; ☺7.30am-6.30pm; 🔲23, 32) In Macau's Three Lamps district, an area known for its Burmese immigrants, this popular two-floor greasy spoon dishes out home-style Burmese classics like coconut chicken noodles, braised pig ear salad and shrimp-paste–fragrant greens. There's an English menu with pictures.

★Clube Militar de Macau PORTUGUESE $$
(陸軍俱樂部; Map p544; 🖉853 2871 4000; 975 Avenida da Praia Grande; meals MOP$150-400; ☺1.45-2.30pm & 7-10.30pm Mon-Fri, noon-2.30pm & 7-10pm Sat & Sun; 🔲6, 28C) Housed in a distinguished colonial building, with fans spinning lazily above, the Military Club takes you back in time to a slower and quieter Macau. The simple and delicious Portuguese fare is complemented by an excellent selection of wine and cheese from Portugal. The MOP$153 buffet is excellent value. Reservations are required for dinner and weekend lunches.

★Guincho a Galera PORTUGUESE $$$
(葡国餐廳; Map p540; 🖉853 8803 7676; www.hotelisboa.com; 3rd fl, Hotel Lisboa, 2-4 Avenida de Lisboa; meals MOP$550-1800; ☺noon-2.30pm & 6.30-10.30pm; 🔲3, 10) The international branch of Portugal's famous Fortaleza do Guincho, this luxuriously decorated restaurant brings Portuguese haute cuisine to Macau. The menu features well executed classical dishes, with a couple of Macanese additions. Set meals are available at lunch (from MOP$310) and dinner (from MOP$630).

Robuchon au Dôme FRENCH $$$
(Map p540; 🖉853 8803 7878; www.grandlisboahotel.com; 43rd fl, Grand Lisboa Hotel, Avenida de Lisboa; lunch/dinner set menu from MOP$598/1688; ☺noon-2.30pm & 6.30-10.30pm; 🔲3, 10) Encased in a glass dome, this is arguably the most tastefully decorated of the casino restaurants. And as one of two Macau restaurants with three Michelin stars, it has everything you'd associate with the celebrated Robuchon name: fine decor, exquisite Gallic creations and impeccable service. The wine cellar with 8000 bottles is one of the best in Asia.

🍴 The Islands

★Tai Lei Loi CHINESE $
(大利来; Map p547; 🖉853 2882 7150; www.taileiloi.com.mo; 42 Rua dos Clérigos, Taipa Village; buns MOP$40; ☺8am-6pm; 📶; 🔲22, 26) South China's most famous pork-chop bun is made

The Islands – Coloane

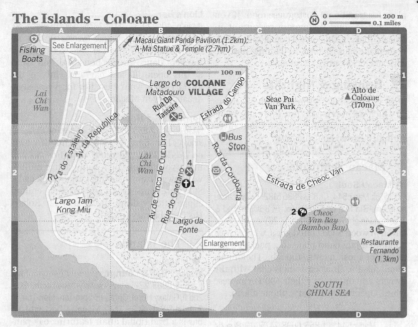

here – a shop founded in 1960 as a street stall by the mother of the current owner. Succulent slices of pork (or slivers of fish) are coupled with warm, chewy buns that emerge from the oven daily at 2pm sharp.

★**Café Nga Tim** MACANESE $
(雅憩花園餐廳; Map p551; Rua do Caetano, Coloane Village; mains MOP$70-200; ⊙noon-1am; ⊕; ⊒21A, 25, 26A) We love the Chinese-Portuguese food, the small-town atmosphere, the view of the Chapel of St Francis Xavier, the prices and the owner – a guitar- and *erhu*-strumming ex-policeman named Feeling Wong.

Lord Stow's Bakery BAKERY $
(澳門安德魯餅店; Map p551; 1 Rua da Tassara, Coloane; egg tarts MOP$9; ⊙7am-10pm Thu-Tue, to 7pm Wed) Though the celebrated English baker Andrew Stow has passed away, his cafe (9 Largo do Matadouro) and Lord Stow's Bakery keep his memory alive by serving his renowned *pastéis de nata* – a warm egg-custard tart (MOP$9) and cheesecake (MOP$14) in unusual flavours, including black sesame and green tea.

★**Restaurante Fernando** PORTUGUESE $$
(法蘭度餐廳; ☑853 2888 2264; 9 Hác Sá beach, Coloane; meals MOP$150-270; ⊙noon-9.30pm;

⊕; ⊒21A, 25, 26A) Possibly Coloane's most famous restaurant, sprawling Fernando's contains two separate dining rooms and a large courtyard bar area. Devoted customers and travellers pack the chequered-tablecloth tables to chow on plates of garlicky clams, golden roast suckling pig, and piles of codfish rice. Expect lines during peak lunch and dinner times, especially on weekends. Cash only.

★**António** PORTUGUESE $$$
(安東尼奧; Map p547; ☑853 2888 8668; www.antoniomacau.com; 7 Rua dos Clérigos, Taipa Village; meals MOP$350-1200; ⊙noon-midnight; ⊒22, 26) The cosy mahogany-framed dining room, the well thought-out menu and the entertaining chef, António Coelho, all make this the go-to

place for traditional Portuguese food. If you can only try one Portuguese restaurant in Macau, make it this one. The octopus salad, homemade sausage (served flaming) and the African chicken are exceptional.

Drinking & Nightlife

Most visitors stick to the casino bars, many of which are top-notch, but there are plenty of interesting wine bars, cafes and dives sprinkled throughout the city.

Macau Peninsula

★**Macau Soul** BAR
(澳感廊; Map p544; ☑853 2836 5182; www.macau soul.com; 31a Rua de São Paulo; ☉3-10pm Wed & Thu, to midnight Fri-Sun; ☑8A, 17, 26) An elegant haven in wood and stained glass, where twice a month a jazz band plays to a packed audience. On most nights, though, Thelonious Monk fills the air as customers chat with the owners and dither over their 430 Portuguese wines. Opening hours vary; phone ahead.

★**Single Origin** COFFEE
(單品; Map p544; ☑853 6698 7475; 19 Rua de Abreu Nunes; coffee MOP$35; ☉11.30am-8pm Mon-Sat, 2-7pm Sun; ☎; ☑2, 4, 7, 7A, 8) This airy corner cafe opened by coffee professional Keith Fong makes a mean shot of espresso. You can choose your poison from a daily selection of 10 beans from various regions. If you can't decide, the well trained barristas are more than happy to help.

Lion's Bar CLUB
(Map p540; ☑853 8802 2375; www.mgmmacau. com/lion-bar; MGM Grand, Avenida Dr Sun Yat Sen; ☉7pm-5am Thu-Tue) Sleekly dressed revellers dance to the house DJ and band at this open-till-5am bar and club in the MGM Grand, your best bet for Vegas-style debauchery in Macau.

Terra Coffee House CAFE
(Map p544; ☑853 2893 7943; 1 Largo de St Agostinho; ☉11am-8pm; ☎; ☑9, 16) This tiny haven overlooking pretty St Augustine Sq will make you forget you're only a five-minute walk away from heaving Largo do Senado. Stop here for a strong and carefully crafted cuppa after visiting the nearby Sir Robert Ho Tung Library (p538).

The Islands

★**Macallan
Whisky Bar & Lounge** BAR
(☑853 8883 2221; www.galaxymacau.com; 203, 2nd fl, Galaxy Hotel, Cotai; ☉5pm-1am Mon-Thu, to 2am Fri & Sat; ☑25, 25X) Macau's best whisky bar is a traditional affair featuring oak panels, Jacobean rugs and a real fireplace. The 400-plus whisky labels include representatives from Ireland, France, Sweden and India, and a 1963 Glenmorangie. The pre-9pm happy hour means you get your age in years discounted as a percentage from your drink (30 years old = 30% off).

BRIGHT LIGHTS, SIN CITY

A gambling mecca since the 19th century, Macau has lately been sprouting glitzy mega-casinos like mushrooms after a rain. The change began when casino mogul Stanley Ho's monopoly ended in 2001 and Las Vegas operators set up shop in competition. There are now more than 30 casinos in Macau, their total gaming revenue surpassing all of the world's major gambling jurisdictions combined. Macau Peninsula has most of the older, smaller casinos, while the newly infilled Cotai area is home to the new breed of casino-hotel-shopping-entertainment behemoths.

Table games are the staple at casinos here – mostly baccarat, then roulette and a dice game called dai sai (big small). You'll hardly hear any whooping and clunking – slot machines make up only 5% of total casino winnings (versus Vegas' 60%). Drunks are also hard to come by, as Chinese players believe that booze dulls their skill. Over 80% of gamblers and 95% of high rollers come from mainland China. The latter play inside members-only rooms where the total amount wagered on any given day can exceed a small country's GDP.

For recreational players, the only thing to watch out for is harassment by tip hustlers – scam artists who hang around tables acting like your new best friend. They may steal your chips, nag you for a cut or try to take you to a casino that will tip them for bringing clients.

Casinos are open 24 hours. To enter, you must be 21 years or older and neatly dressed.

☆ Entertainment

Macau's nightlife may be dominated by the ever-expanding casino scene, but a number of interesting live-music venues have also sprung up about town. For entertainment and cultural events listings, check out the bimonthly *CCM+* and monthly *Destination Macau* available for free at MGTO outlets and larger hotels.

★ Venetian   CASINO
(澳門威尼斯人度假村酒店; ☑853 2882 8877; www.venetianmacao.com; ☑25, 26A) Said to be one of the 10 largest buildings in the world, the Venetian is 980,000 sq metres of what might be described as Casino Gothic architecture, packed to the gills with busloads of goggle-eyed tourists. Features include some 3000 hotel suites, a full-sized arena, an onsite medical and plastic surgery clinic and more than 500,000 sq ft of gaming floor. Its centrepiece is the Grand Canal Shoppes, an indoor mall surrounding three enormous curved canals, where gondoliers push boats of tourists through pool-blue waters while singing opera. The ceiling is painted and lit to resemble the sky at dusk, the shops are housed behind Venetian-style facades, and wandering magicians dressed like carnival revellers entertain the crowds. Surreal.

★ House of Dancing Water   THEATRE
(水舞間; ☑853 8868 6688; http://thehouseof dancingwater.com; City of Dreams, Estrada do Istmo, Cotai; tickets MOP$580-1480; ☑50, 35) 'The House of Dancing Water', Macau's most expensively made show, is a breathtaking melange of stunts, acrobatics and theatre designed by Franco Dragone, the former director of Cirque du Soleil. The magic revolves around a cobalt pool the size of several Olympic-sized swimming pools. Over, around, into and under this pool a cast of 80, dressed in glorious costumes, perform hair-raising stunts.

★ Live Music Association   LIVE MUSIC
(LMA, 現場音樂協會; Map p540; www.facebook. com/LMA.Macau; 11b San Mei Industrial Bldg, 50 Avenida do Coronel Mesquita; ☑3, 9, 32, 12, 25) The go-to place for indie music in Macau, this excellent dive inside an industrial building has hosted local and overseas acts, including Cold Cave, Buddhistson, Mio Myo and Pet Conspiracy. See the website for what's on. Macau indie bands to watch out for include WhyOceans (www.whyoceans.com) and Turtle Giant (www.turtlegiant.com).

🛍 Shopping

Browsing through the shops in the old city, specifically on crumbly Rua dos Ervanários and Rua de Nossa Senhora do Amparo near the Ruins of St Paul, can be a great experience. You can also look for antiques or replicas at shops on or near Rua de São Paulo, Rua das Estalagens and Rua de São António. Rua de Madeira and Rua dos Mercadores, which lead up to Rua da Tercena and its flea market, have shops selling mah-jong tiles and bird cages.

🛍 Macau Peninsula

Livraria Portuguesa   BOOKS, GIFTS
(Portuguese Bookstore; Map p544; ☑853 2851 5915; Rua de São Domingos 18; ☺11am-7pm; ☑3, 4, 6A, 8A, 19, 33) Right in the heart of Macau's historic district, this two-storey bookshop carries both English and Portuguese titles, including some hard-to-find Macanese cookbooks. It also stocks gift items, like imported Portuguese soaps and perfumes. Founded more than 30 years ago, it's one of the few places in Macau where you can reliably hear Portuguese spoken.

Macau Design Centre   GIFTS & SOUVENIRS
(Map p540; ☑853 2852 0335; www.dcmacau.com/ en; Travessa da Fabrica 5; ☺11am-7pm; ☑1A, 2, 6A, 8, 8A, 10, 12, 19, 22, 28B, 28BX, 28C, 34) In a gritty working-class neighbourhood, this shop-gallery-exhibition space showcases Macau designers. Look out for handmade ceramics, high-quality leather bags, trendy clothes, framed graphics and more.

Mercearia Portuguesa   FOOD
(Map p540; ☑853 2856 2708; www.mercearia portuguesa.com; 8 Calçada da Igreja de São Lazaro; ☺1-9pm Mon-Fri, noon-9pm Sat & Sun; ☑7, 8) The charming Portuguese corner shop opened by a film director and actress has a small but well curated selection of provisions, which includes honey, chinaware, wooden toys and jewellery from Portugal – gorgeously packaged and reasonably priced.

🛍 The Islands

★ Cunha Bazaar   GIFTS & SOUVENIRS
(Map p547; www.cunhabazaar.com; Rua do Cunha 33-35, Taipa Village; ☺9.30am-10pm) This four-storey shop on the corner of Taipa Village's Rua do Cunha pedestrian street has the motherlode of made-in-Macau gifts, T-shirts, candies and more. You'll find traditional foods like almond cookies and jerky

on the ground floor, while the 1st floor is dedicated to goods bearing the image of Macau's own Soda Panda, a perpetually grumpy cartoon panda who likes to do Macanese things like eat egg tarts and play roulette. The remaining two floors are dedicated to leather goods, ceramics, notebooks, sketches and so on by local designers.

❶ Information

DANGERS & ANNOYANCES

Violent crime against visitors in Macau is rare, but pickpocketing and other street crime can occur in busy areas.

Take extra caution with passports and valuables in crowded areas and when visiting casinos late at night.

EMERGENCY

Visitors can utilise a dedicated 24-hour emergency hotline (⏺112) for tourists. Police, fire and ambulance can be reached by dialling ⏺999.

INTERNET ACCESS

Most cafes and hotels in Macau have free wi-fi. You can also access free public wi-fi in select government premises, tourist hot spots and public areas daily from 8am to 1am the following day. See www.wifi.gov.mo for details.

You can buy prepaid phonecards from CTM, ranging from MOP$50 to MOP$130, to enjoy mobile broadband; or buy a mobile broadband pass for unlimited internet access for one day (MOP$120) or five days (MOP$220).

MEDICAL SERVICES

Two of Macau's hospitals have 24-hour emergency services.

Centro Hospitalar Conde São Januário (山頂醫院; Map p540; ⏺853 2831 3731; Estrada do Visconde de São Januário) Southwest of Guia Fort.

Hospital Kiang Wu (鏡湖醫院; Map p540; ⏺853 2837 1333; Rua de Coelho do Amaral) Northeast of the ruins of the Church of St Paul.

MONEY

Macau's currency is the pataca (MOP$). Most ATMs allow you to choose between patacas and Hong Kong dollars. Credit cards are readily accepted at Macau's hotels, larger restaurants and casinos. You can also change cash and travellers cheques at the banks lining Avenida da Praia Grande and Avenida de Almeida Ribeiro, as well as at major hotels.

POST

Correios de Macau, Macau's postal system, is efficient and inexpensive.

The **Main Post Office** (郵政總局; Map p544; ⏺853 2832 3666; www.macaupost.gov.mo; 126 Avenida de Almeida Ribeiro; ◷9am-6pm Mon-Fri, to 1pm Sat) faces Largo do Senado; pick up poste restante from counter 1 or 2.

EMS Speedpost is available at the main post office. Other companies, such as Federal Express and DHL, can also arrange express forwarding.

TELEPHONE

Local calls are free from private telephones; at a public payphone they cost MOP$1 for five minutes. Most hotels will charge you MOP$3.

Prepaid SIM cards are available from **CTM** (澳門電訊總店; Companhia de Telecomunicações de Macau) stores or the ferry terminal for MOP$50 (for local calls) and MOP$50/100/130 (with IDD and international roaming), which allow internet access through mobile broadband.

TOURIST INFORMATION

The **Macau Government Tourist Office** (MGTO, Map p544; ⏺853 8397 1120, tourism hotline 853 2833 3000; www.macautourism.gov.mo; Edifício Ritz, Largo do Senado; ◷9am-1pm & 2.30-5.35pm Mon-Fri) is a well organised and helpful source of information. It dispenses a large selection of free literature, including pamphlets on everything from Chinese temples and Catholic churches to fortresses, gardens and walks. The MGTO also runs a 24-hour **tourist hotline** (⏺853 2833 3000) and a 24-hour **tourists' emergency hotline** (⏺110 or 112).

MGTO has a Hong Kong branch and half a dozen outlets scattered all over Macau.

The Macau Cultural Affairs Bureau (www.icm.gov.mo) lists Macau's monthly cultural offerings.

TRAVEL AGENCIES

China Travel Service (中國旅行社, Zhōngguó Lǚxíngshè, CTS; Map p540; ⏺853 2870 0888; www.cts.com.mo; Nam Kwong Bldg, 207 Avenida do Dr Rodrigo Rodrigues; ◷9am-6pm) Express China visas (MOP$1250 plus photos) are available to most passport holders in two days.

TRAVELLERS WITH DISABILITIES

Macau is not exactly friendly to travellers with disabilities. The historical part of Macau sits on a hilly landscape and pavement is often uneven, though some major sights do have provisions for disability access. The newer parts, eg around the Cotai Strip, are flat and have wider streets.

Traffic lights generally have audible signals to help the sight-impaired cross the street.

Public transport, including taxis, is not equipped to accommodate people with physical disabilities. The airport is quite accessible, but accessing the ferries from Hong Kong to Macau would require assistance from the staff.

VISAS

Most travellers can enter Macau with just their passports for between 30 and 90 days, including citizens of Australia, Canada, the EU, New Zealand, South Africa and the USA.

Travellers who do require visas can get them, valid for 30 days, on arrival in Macau. They cost MOP$100/50/200 per adult/child under 12 years/family.

❶ Getting There & Away

Macau International Airport is connected to a limited number of destinations in Asia. If you are coming from outside Asia and destined for Macau, your best option is to fly to Hong Kong International Airport and take a ferry to Macau without going through Hong Kong customs.

Nationals of Australia, Canada, the EU, New Zealand and most other countries (but not US citizens) can purchase their China visas at Zhūhǎi on the border, but it will ultimately save you time if you get one in advance. These are available in Hong Kong or in Macau from China Travel Service (see left), usually in one day.

AIR

Located on Taipa Island, **Macau International Airport** (☑ 853 2886 1111; www.macau-airport. com) is only 20 minutes from the city centre. It has frequent services to destinations including Bangkok, Chiang Mai, Kaohsiung, Kuala Lumpur, Manila, Osaka, Seoul, Singapore, Taipei and Tokyo.

Air Macau (澳門航空, NX; Map p540; ☑ 853 8396 5555; www.airmacau.com.mo; ground fl, 398 Alameda Doutor Carlos d'Assumpção; ☉ 9am-6pm) flies to more than a dozen destinations in mainland China and has codeshare flights to South Korea, Taiwan, Vietnam, Thailand and Japan. The departure tax is MOP$110, and is added to the ticket fee.

Travel to Macau by helicopter is a viable option and is becoming increasingly popular for residents and visitors alike. **Sky Shuttle** (Map p540; ☑ in Hong Kong 852 2108 9898; www.skyshuttlehk. com) runs a 15-minute helicopter shuttle service between Macau and Hong Kong (HK$4300, tax included) with daily flights leaving every half-hour between 9am and 11pm. Flights arrive and depart in Macau from the roof of the Macau Maritime Ferry Terminal. In Hong Kong, departures are from the helipad atop the ferry pier that is linked to **Shun Tak Centre** (信德中心; 200 Connaught Rd Central, Hong Kong) in Sheung Wan.

Sky Shuttle also has a helicopter shuttle linking Macau with Shēnzhèn six times a day from 10.15am to 7.45pm (11.45am to 8.30pm from Shēnzhèn) for HK$5900. The trip takes about 15 minutes.

BOAT

Ferry and catamaran tickets can be booked in advance at the ferry terminals, through travel agencies or online. You can also buy tickets on the spot, though advance booking is recommended if you travel on weekends or public holidays, as tickets are often in high demand. There is a standby queue at the pier for passengers wanting to travel before their ticketed sailing. You need to arrive at the pier at least 15 minutes before departure, but you should allow 30 minutes because of occasional long queues at immigration.

You are limited to 10kg of carry-on luggage in economy class, but oversized or overweight bags can be checked in.

To & From Hong Kong

The vast majority of travellers make their way from Hong Kong to Macau by ferry. The journey takes just an hour and there are frequent departures throughout the day, with reduced service between midnight and 7am.

Most ferries depart from the Hong Kong–Macau Ferry Terminal (Map p504) on Hong Kong Island or the China Ferry Terminal (Map p510) in Kowloon, and arrive at the **Macau Maritime Ferry Terminal** (外港客運碼頭, Terminal Maritimo de Passageiros do Porto Exterior; Map p540; Outer Harbour, Macau) in the outer harbour or the **Taipa Temporary Ferry Terminal** (☑ 853 2885 0595).

TurboJet (☑ 852 2859 3333; www.turbojet. com.hk; Shun Tak Centre, 200 Connaught Rd, Sheung Wan) has regular departures from the Hong Kong–Macau Ferry Terminal (every 15 minutes) and the China Ferry Terminal (every 30 minutes) to Macau from 7am to midnight, and less frequent service after midnight. Fares are HK$164/326 (economy/superclass), and it costs about 10% more on weekends and 20% more for night service (6.15pm to 6.30am).

CotaiJet (☑ 853 2885 0595; www.cotaijet. com.mo; weekdays to Hong Kong regular/1st class MOP$154/267) has high-speed catamarans connecting the Hong Kong–Macau Ferry Terminal and the Taipa Temporary Ferry Terminal every half-hour between 7.30am and midnight. Fares are HK$165/270 (Cotai class/Cotai first) and it costs about 10% more on weekends and 20% more for night service (after 6pm). Free shuttles at the ferry terminal in Taipa will take you to destinations along the Cotai Strip.

To & From Mainland China

TurboJet has 11 departures from the Macau Maritime Ferry Terminal daily to the port of Shékǒu in Shēnzhèn between 9.45am and 8.45pm. The journey takes 60 minutes and costs MOP$238/376 (economy/super class). Eleven ferries return from Shékǒu between 8.15am and 7.30pm. TurboJet also has nine departures to Shēnzhèn airport (MOP$235/399, one hour) from 9.40am to 7.30pm and two departures to Nánshā in Guǎngzhōu (MOP$180/280) at 10.45am and 4.15pm.

Yuet Tung Shipping Co (粵通船務有限公司; Map p544; ☑ 853 2893 9944, 853 2877 4478; www.ytmacau.com; Point 11A Inner Harbour, Inner Harbour Ferry Terminal) has ferries connecting Macau (Taipa Temporary Ferry Terminal) with Shékǒu (MOP$238, 1½ hours, 11am, 2pm, 5.30pm, 6.30pm, 8.30pm). Ferries also leave from the Macau Maritime Ferry Terminal for Wānzǎi in Zhūhǎi (MOP$90, every half-hour between 8am and 4.15pm).

BUS

Macau is an easy gateway by land into mainland China. Simply take bus 3, 5 or 9 to the **border gate** (關閘; Portas do Cerco; open 7am to midnight) and walk across. A second – and much less busy crossing – is the **Cotai Frontier Post** (open 9am to 8pm) on the causeway linking Taipa and Coloane, which allows visitors to cross the Lotus Flower Bridge by shuttle bus (MOP$4) to Héngqín in Zhūhǎi. Buses 15, 21 and 26 will drop you off at the crossing.

If you want to travel further afield in China, buses run by **Kee Kwan Motor Road Co** (歧關車路有限公司; ☑ 853 2893 3888; underground bus terminal near Border Gate; ☺ 7.15am-9pm) leave the bus station at the border gate. Buses for Guǎngzhōu (MOP$77, 2½ hours) depart every 15 minutes or so, and for Zhōngshān (MOP$40, one hour) every 20 minutes between 8am and 6.30pm. There are many buses to Guǎngzhōu (MOP$155) and Dōngguǎn (MOP$155) from **Macau International Airport Bus Terminal** (☑ 853 2888 1228).

❶ Getting Around

TO/FROM THE AIRPORT

Take buses 21 and 26 from the airport to Coloane. Bus 21 goes from the airport to A-Ma Temple.

The airport bus AP1 (MOP$4.20) leaves the airport and zips around Taipa before heading to the Macau Maritime Ferry Terminal and the border gate. The bus stops at a number of major hotels en route and departs every five to 12 minutes from 6.30am to midnight.

Other services run to Praça de Ferreira do Amaral (MT1 and MT2).

Macau is linked directly to Hong Kong International Airport by TurboJet, which has eight ferries operating between 10am and 10pm. It costs MOP$254/196/140 per adult/child/infant and takes 70 minutes. However, please note that this ferry service is for transit passengers only. It is not applicable to passengers originating in Hong Kong.

A taxi from the airport to the town centre should cost about MOP$60, plus a surcharge of MOP$5. Large bags cost an extra MOP$3.

BICYCLE

Bikes can be **rented** (Map p547; 11 Rua dos Negotiantes, Taipa Village; per hr MOP$20; ☺ 2-7pm Mon-Fri, 9am-7pm Sat & Sun) in Taipa Village. You are not allowed to cross the Macau–Taipa bridges on a bicycle.

CAR

The streets of Macau Peninsula are a gridlock of cars and mopeds that will cut you off at every turn.

Avis Rent A Car (Map p540; ☑ 853 2872 6571; www.avis.com.mo; Room 1022, ground fl, Macau Maritime Ferry Terminal; ☺ 9am-6pm) hires out cars from MOP$800 to MOP$1600 per day (10% to 20% more expensive on weekends). Chauffeur-driven services start from MOP$380 per hour. Also has an office at the Grand Lapa Hotel car park (open 8am to 10pm).

Burgeon Rent A Car (Map p540; ☑ 853 2828 3399; www.burgeonrentacar.com; Avenida do Almirante Magalhaes Correia, 61) hires out Kia cars, with the cheapest model starting at MOP$450 for the first nine hours. The cheapest car with chauffeur costs MOP$1280 for eight hours.

PUBLIC TRANSPORT

Public buses and minibuses run by TCM (www.tcm.com.mo) and **Transmac** (☑ 853 2827 1122; www.transmac.com.mo) operate from 6am until shortly after midnight. Fares – MOP$3.20 on the peninsula, MOP$4.20 to Taipa Village, MOP$5 to Coloane Village and MOP$6.40 to Hác Sá beach – are dropped into a box upon entry (exact change needed), or you can pay with a Macau Pass, which can be purchased from various supermarkets and convenience stores. The card costs MOP$130 at first purchase, which includes a refundable deposit of MOP$30. A minimum of MOP$50 is required to add money to the card each time. Expect buses to be very crowded.

The two most useful buses on the peninsula are buses 3 and 3A, which run between the ferry terminal and the city centre, near the post office. Both continue up to the border crossing with the mainland, as does bus 5, which can be boarded along Avenida Almeida Ribeiro. Bus 12 runs from the ferry terminal, past the Lisboa Hotel and then up to Lou Lim Ieoc Garden. The best services to Taipa and Coloane are buses 21A, 25 and 26A. Buses to the airport are AP1, 26, MT1 and MT2.

Free shuttle buses run from the ferry terminals and the border gates to the casinos of Cotai; anyone can ride, not just hotel guests. Public bus 25 goes all the way from the peninsula's northern border gate, through Taipa and Cotai and all the way to Coloane; 26A covers a similar route. There are plenty of taxi queues around the casinos in Cotai, but expect long lines and refusals to take you to far-flung locations (ie Coloane).

TAXI

Flag fall is MOP$17 for the first 1.6km and MOP$2 for each additional 230m. There is a MOP$5 surcharge to go to Coloane, although many taxis will refuse to take you because they're not assured a return fare. Travelling between Taipa and Coloane is MOP$2 extra. For yellow radio taxis, call ☑ 853 2851 9519 or 853 2893 9939.

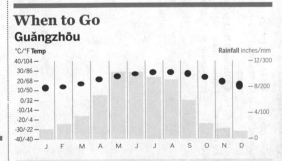

Guǎngdōng

POP 93 MILLION

Best Places to Eat

➡ Guǎngzhōu Restaurant (p566)

➡ Zhèng's Private Kitchen (p588)

➡ Qīngyún Vegetarian Restaurant (p579)

➡ Dàbù Handmade Noodles (p591)

➡ Pànxī Restaurant (p567)

Best Places to Sleep

➡ Garden Hotel (p566)

➡ Shēnzhèn Loft Youth Hostel (p582)

➡ Zàiyáng Inn (p588)

Why Go?

Guǎngdōng's unique culture and natural beauty fly under the radar and have yet to be discovered by many travellers, so you may have a plethora of sublime sights (not to mention great dim sum) all to yourself.

Northern Guǎngdōng (广东) is home to some wild and wondrous landscapes. In the blue pine forests of Nánlǐng, the music of waterfalls and windswept trees boomerangs in your direction. If it's Unesco-crowned heritage you're after, Kāipíng's flamboyant watchtowers and the stylised poses of Cantonese opera will leave you riveted. What's all the fuss about Hakka and Chiuchow cultures? Well, find out in Méizhōu and Cháozhōu.

Historically Guǎngdōng was the starting point of the Maritime Silk Road and the birthplace of revolution. On the scenic byways of the Pearl River delta, you'll uncover the glory of China's revolutionary past. While on the surf-beaten beaches of Hǎilíng Island, an ancient shipwreck and its treasures await.

When to Go
Guǎngzhōu

Apr–Jun Verdant paddy fields against the built wonders of Kāipíng and Méizhōu.

Jul–Sep Blue pines and stained-glass windows offer respite from summer.

Oct–Dec The typhoons and heat are gone; this is the best time to visit.

Guǎngdōng Highlights

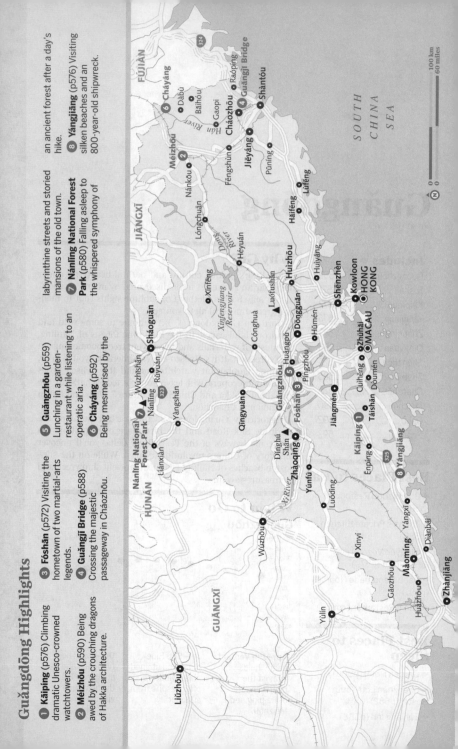

❶ **Kāipíng** (p576) Climbing dramatic Unesco-crowned watchtowers.

❷ **Méizhōu** (p590) Being awed by the crouching dragons of Hakka architecture.

❸ **Fóshān** (p572) Visiting the hometown of two martial-arts legends.

❹ **Guǎngjì Bridge** (p588) Crossing the majestic passageway in Cháozhōu.

❺ **Guǎngzhōu** (p559) Lunching in a garden-restaurant while listening to an operatic aria.

❻ **Cháyáng** (p592) Being mesmerised by the

an ancient forest after a day's hike.

❼ **Nánlíng National Forest Park** (p580) Falling asleep to the whispered symphony of

labyrinthine streets and storied mansions of the old town.

❽ **Yángjiāng** (p576) Visiting silken beaches and an 800-year-old shipwreck.

History

Guǎngdōng has had contact with the outside world for nearly two millennia. Among the first outsiders to arrive were the Romans, who appeared in the 2nd century AD. By the Tang dynasty (AD 618–907), a sizeable trade with the Middle East and Southeast Asia had developed.

The first Europeans to settle here were the Portuguese in 1557, followed by the Jesuits who established themselves in Zhàoqìng. The British came along in the 17th century and by 1685 merchant ships from the East India Company were calling at Guǎngzhōu. In 1757 an imperial edict gave the *cohong*, a local merchants' guild, a monopoly on China's trade with foreigners, who were restricted to Shāmiàn Island. Trade remained in China's favour until 1773, when the British shifted the balance by unloading 1000 chests of Bengal opium in Guǎngzhōu. Addiction spread in China like wildfire, eventually leading to the Opium Wars.

In the 19th century Guǎngdōng was a hotbed of reform and revolt. Among the political elites who sowed revolutionary ideas here was Sun Yatsen, who later became the first president of the Republic of China.

The 20th century saw Guǎngdōng serve as the headquarters of both the Nationalist and Communist Parties, and endure great suffering during the Cultural Revolution. After the implementation of the 'open door' policy in 1978, it became the first province to embrace capitalism. The province's continued economic success has made it a leading export centre for consumer goods.

Language

The vast majority of the people of Guǎngdōng speak Cantonese, a dialect distinct from Mandarin. Though it enjoys a less exalted status than the national dialect, Cantonese is older and better suited than Mandarin for the reading of classical poetry, according to many scholars.

❶ Getting There & Away

Airports at Guǎngzhōu and Shēnzhèn run domestic and international flights, while those at Zhūhǎi, Méizhōu and Cháozhōu bring every major city within a three-hour flight of the sights.

Long-distance buses are the transportation with the most frequent departures between major areas in Guǎngdōng.

High-speed rail connects Guǎngdōng to its provincial neighbours Guǎngxī, Húnán, Jiāngxī and Fújiàn.

The fastest trains on the northeast–southwest axis head for Nánchāng (four hours), Wǔhàn (four hours), Xī'ān (nine hours) and Běijīng (10 hours). A well developed network of convenient, older rail lines and expressways span the entire province. Metro and light rail in Guǎngzhōu, Shēnzhèn, Zhūhǎi and Fóshān are connected to major and high-speed train stations.

Guǎngzhōu 广州

📶 020 / POP 12 MILLION

Guǎngzhōu, once better known to Westerners as Canton, is China's busiest transport and trade hub and the third-largest city in the country. A giant metropolis, Guǎngzhōu is home to both gleaming towers and leafy alleys, and its history as a strategic trade port to the South China Sea has afforded it a colonial background and culturally diverse population that combine to give Guǎngzhōu a cosmopolitan flair. Additionally, the China Import and Export Fair (more commonly known as the Canton Fair) – China's largest trade fair – sees thousands of international visitors flocking to Guǎngzhōu twice a year. And its proximity to Hong Kong means it is one of the most well connected cities in China.

History

Guǎngzhōu's history is one dominated by trade and revolution. Since the Tang dynasty, it had been China's most important southern port and the starting point for the Maritime Silk Road, a trade route to the West. It became a trading post for the Portuguese in the 16th century, and later for the British.

After the fall of the Qing dynasty in 1911, the city was a stronghold of the republican forces led by Sun Yatsen and, subsequently,

PRICE RANGES

Price ranges for a double room with bathroom:

$ less than ¥250

$$ ¥250–¥600

$$$ more than ¥600

Price ranges for a main course:

$ less than ¥70

$$ ¥70–¥150

$$$ more than ¥150

a centre of activity also of the Chinese Communist Party (CCP) led by Mao Zedong.

During the post-1949 years of China's self-imposed isolation, the Canton Trade Fair was the only platform on which China did business with the West.

In 2010 Guǎngzhōu held the Asian Games, resulting in major expansion of the city's transport network.

◉ Sights

◉ Zhūjiāng Xīnchéng (Zhūjiāng New Town)

New Guǎngdōng Museum   MUSEUM
(广东省博物馆新馆, Guǎngdōngshěng Bówùguǎn Xīnguǎn; Map p567; ☑020 3804 6886; www.gdmuseum.com; 2 Zhujiang Donglu, Zhūjiāng New Town; ☉9am-4pm Tue-Sun; 💼; Ⓜ Line 3, Zhūjiāng Xīnchéng, exit B1) FREE This ultramodern museum has an extensive collection illuminating the human and natural history of Guǎngdōng, as well as Cantonese art, literature and architecture. English explanations are unfortunately limited to brief leaflets, but there are plenty of self-evident visual treats for kids, including dinosaur fossils and model whales. Inspired by the Chinese lacquer box, the museum's appearance is a striking contrast against the curvilinear design of the Guǎngzhōu Opera House further to the west. ID required for entry.

Guǎngzhōu Opera House   NOTABLE BUILDING
(广州大剧院, Guǎngzhōu Dàjùyuàn; Map p567; ☑020 3839 2666, tour bookings 020 3839 9847; http://guangzhouoperahouse.org; 1 Zhujiang Xilu; ¥30, tours in English per person ¥200; ☉9am-4.30pm Tue-Sun, tours 10am, 11am, 2pm, 3pm & 4pm; Ⓜ Line 3, Zhūjiāng Xīnchéng, exit B1) Authored by architect Zaha Hadid, southern China's biggest performance venue has transformed the area with its other-worldly appearance. With futuristic glass panels knitted together to form subtle curves, it's been described as pebbles on the bed of the Pearl River. To enter, you have to join one of five 45-minute daily tours. Tours in English require booking a day in advance.

◉ Hǎizhū District

Memorial Hall of the
Lǐngnán School of Painting   MUSEUM
(岭南画派纪念馆, Lǐngnán Huàpài Jìniànguǎn; ☑020 8401 7167; www.lingnans.org; 257 Changgang Donglu; ☉9am-5pm Tue-Sun; Ⓜ Xiǎogǎng, exit A) FREE This small but excellent museum

on the leafy campus of the Guǎngzhōu Academy of Fine Arts (广州美术学院; Guǎngzhōu Měishù Xuéyuàn) pays tribute to the founders of the Lǐngnán school of painting, such as Gao Jianfu, and shows the colourful ink and brush works of contemporary artists versed in the Lǐngnán style.

◉ Lìwān District

★Chen Clan Ancestral Hall   HISTORIC SITE
(陈家祠, Chénjiā Cí; Map p562; ☑020 8181 4559; 34 Enlong Li, Zhongshan Qilu; ¥10; ☉8.30am-5pm; Ⓜ Line 1, Chénjiācí, exit D) An all-in-one ancestral shrine, Confucian school and 'chamber of commerce' for the Chen clan, this compound was built in 1894 by the residents of 72 villages in Guǎngdōng, where the Chen lineage is predominant. There are 19 buildings in the traditional Lǐngnán style, all featuring exquisite carvings, statues and paintings, and decorated with ornate scrollwork throughout.

◉ Islands

★Shāmiàn Island   HISTORIC SITE
(沙面岛, Shāmiàn Dǎo; Map p562; Ⓜ Lines 1 & 6, Huángshā) To the southwest of Guǎngzhōu is the dappled oasis of Shāmiàn Island. It was acquired as a foreign concession in 1859 after the two Opium Wars. Shamian Dajie, the main boulevard, is a gentle stretch of gardens dotted by old houses, cafes and galleries. The **Church of Our Lady of Lourdes** (天主教露德圣母堂, Tiānzhǔjiào Lùdé Shèngmǔ Táng; Map p562; 14 Shamian Dajie; ☉8am-6pm; Ⓜ Line 1, Huangsha), built by the French in 1892, is on the eastern end. Shāmiàn is so picturesque that you're sure to spot photo shoots for online clothing stores on the streets.

Guǎngdōng Museum of Art   MUSEUM
(广东美术馆, Guǎngdōng Měishùguǎn; ☑020 8735 1468; www.gdmoa.org; 38 Yanyu Lu; ☉9am-5pm Tue-Sun; 🚌89, 194, 131A) FREE At the southern end of Èrshā Island (Èrshā Dǎo), this worthy enormous museum showcases the works of important Cantonese artists and has been the site of the Guǎngzhōu Triennale.

◉ Yuèxiù District

★Mausoleum of the
Nányuè King   MAUSOLEUM
(南越王墓, Nányuèwáng Mù; Map p562; ☑020 3618 2920; www.gznywmuseum.org/nanyuewang/index.html; 867 Jiefang Beilu; ¥12; ☉9am-4.45pm;

M Line 2, Yuèxiù Park, exit E) This superb mauso-leum from the 2000-year-old Nányuè king-dom is one of China's best museums. It houses the tomb of Zhao Mo, second king of Nányuè, who was sent south by the em-peror in 214 BC to quell unrest and estab-lished a sovereign state with Guǎngzhōu as its capital.

Don't miss Zhao Mo's jade burial suit – the precious stone was thought to preserve the body.

Dōngshān
HISTORIC SITE

(东山区, Dongshan Qu; Map p562; M Line 1, Dōngshān Kǒu, exit E) Tree-lined Xīnhepu Lu (新河浦路), Xuguyuan Lu (恤孤院路) and Peizheng Lu (培正路) in the historic Dōng-shān area offer a welcome respite from the city. There are schools and churches raised by American missionaries in the 1900s, and exquisite villas commissioned by overseas Chinese and military bigwigs of the Kuo-mintang.

Take the metro to Dōngshān Kǒu station: from exit E, walk left along Shuqian Lu until Miaoqianzhi Jie, then left again till Xuguyu-an Lu.

Yuèxiù Park
PARK

(越秀公园, Yuèxiù Gōngyuán; Map p562; ☑ 020 8666 1950; 988 Jiefang Beilu; ⊙ 6am-9pm; M Line 2, Yuèxiù Park) A statue of the symbol of Guǎngzhōu – the Five Rams (五羊石像, Wǔ Yáng Shíxiàng; Map p562; ⊙ 6am-9pm; M Line 2, Yuexiu Park) (五羊) that supposedly carried the five immortals who founded the city – stands guard at this park. On a hilltop is red-walled Zhènhǎi Tower (镇海楼; Zhènhǎi Lóu), built in 1380 as a watchtower to keep out pirates. The tower is home to the excel-lent Guǎngzhōu City Museum (广州市博物馆, Guǎngzhōushì Bówùguǎn; Map p562; ☑ 020 8355 0627; www.guangzhoumuseum.cn/en/main. asp; 2 Zhujiang Donglu; ¥10; ⊙ 9am-5pm; M Line 2, Yuèxiù Park), which traces the city's his-tory from the Neolithic period. To the east is Guǎngzhōu Art Gallery (广州美术馆, Guǎngzhōu Měishùguǎn; Map p562; ⊙ 9am-5pm; M Line 2, Yuexiu Park) FREE, which has displays on the city's trading history with the West.

Temple of the Six Banyan Trees
BUDDHIST SITE

(六榕寺, Liùróng Sì; Map p562; ☑ 020 8339 2843; 87 Liurong Lu; ¥5, pagoda ¥10; ⊙ 8am-5pm; 🚌 56) This Buddhist temple was built in AD 537 to

---

ENNING ROAD

If you like history, a stroll down century-old Enning Road (恩宁路; Ēnníng Lù) can be rewarding. Located in the area known traditionally as Xīguān (西关), the western gate and commercial hub of old Canton, it retains a few cultural relics such as teahouses and antique trinket stores, despite earnest urban renewal efforts.

The highlight is **Bāhé Academy** (八和会馆, Bāhé Huìguǎn; Map p562; 117 Enning Lu; M Line 1, Changshou Lu, exit D2), a guild hall for Cantonese opera practitioners. The original academy opened in 1889 to provide lodging, schooling, medical and funeral services to Cantonese opera troupes. It's now a gathering place for retired artists. It is not open to the public, but you can see the original 3m-tall wooden door from 1889. The only item that survived a bombing by the Japanese in 1937, it was used during the Great Leap For-ward as a parking plank for 4-tonne vehicles, and clearly survived that as well.

Turn right as you leave the academy and walk for about a block before making another right into a lane called Yongqing Daxiang (永庆大巷). Turn left into the second smaller lane. The second-last unit here is **Luányú Táng** (銮舆堂; Map p562; Yongqing Daxiang, 永庆 大巷; ⊙ 10am-3pm; M Line 1, Changshou Lu, exit D2), a 200-year-old union for actors playing martial and acrobatic roles in Cantonese opera. The union still gives martial-arts training for the stage to children, and its members come for operatic 'jamming' sessions on the 2nd floor. Visitors may be let in at their discretion. Otherwise there is little to see.

Interestingly, the last unit in this lane used to be the **ancestral home of Bruce Lee** (Map p562; Yongqing Daxiang, 永庆大巷; M Line 1, Changshou Lu, exit D2), the kung fu (gōng-fū) icon, whose father Lǐ Hǎiquán (李海泉) was – you guessed it – a Cantonese opera actor and a member of that union. There's now a wall in its place, but if you retrace your steps out of the alleys, turn right and head up Ēnníng Lù, you'll pass the gates of a school. In the right corner, just past the entrance, you can barely see the shuttered house.

Enning Road is easily walkable from metro station Chángshòu Lù or from Shāmiàn Island.

Guǎngzhōu

Xiwan Lu

Guangyuan Lu

Báiyún International
(30km)

SĀNYUÁNLĬ

Guǎngzhōu
Huǒchēzhàn

42 Main Train
Station

41

44 40 Guǎngzhōu
Railway Station

Huanshi Xilu

Huanshi Xilu

Zhanqian Lu

Renmin Beilu

Yuèxiù
Park

15

34

Dongfeng Xilu

XĪCŪN

Xīcháng

Liuhua Lu

Liúhuā
Lake

Liúhuāhú
Park

**Mausoleum of
the Nányuè King** 2

7

11

Bank of
China

Panfu Lu

37

Jiniàn
Táng

Zhongshan
Liulu 8

Haizhu Beilu

14

Liurong Lu

Rénmín
Park

**Chen Clan 1
Ancestral Hall**

Zhōngshān Bā

Zhongshan Balu

Chénjiācí

38 Xīmén
Kǒu

Guangta Lu

22

Renmin Zhonglu

Haizhu Zhonglu

Zhongshan Wulu

Gōngyuán
Qián

Longjin Xilu

Longjin Donglu

27

Lìwān
Lake
Park 33

Xiguan Antique
Street (Lizhwan Lu)

Wenchang Beilu

XĪGUĀN

Huifu Xilu

Jiefang Zhonglu

26

Huifu
Donglu

Chángshòu Lù

Changshou Lu

Dade Lu

Hǎizhū
Square

Táng Lì
Yuán
(500m)

12

Duobao Lu

24

25

Bohua Lu

Wenchang Nanlu

Changshou Lu

Xia Jiulu

Shang Jiu lu

Daxin Lu

32

Yide Xilu

4

Enning Lu

Dishifu Lu

Datong Lu

Qingping Lu

Yide Lu

Yide Xilu

Renmin Nanlu

Changdi Dama Lu

Yanjiang Xilu

Hǎizhū
Guǎngchǎng

Pengai Lu

Culture
Park

Huángshā

**Wénhuà
Park**

Guǎngzhōu
Riverside
International
Youth Hostel
(600m)

Shamian Dajie

Xīdī Pier

Binjiang Xilu

Tongfu Donglu

See Enlargement

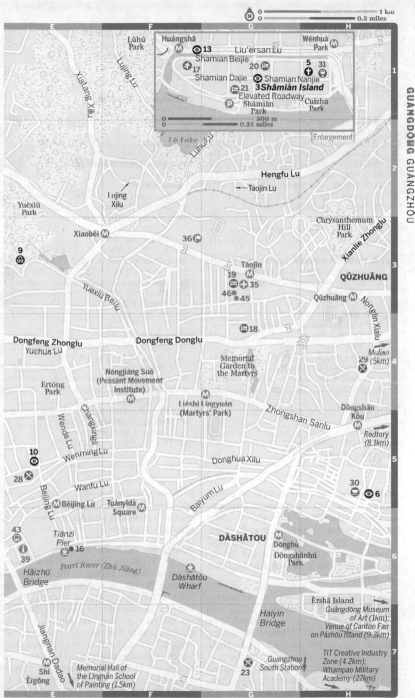

N
0 ——————— 1 km
0 ——————— 0.5 miles

Enlargement

Huángshā
Liu'érsan Lu
Wénhuà Park
Shamian Beijie
20
5 31
17
Shamian Dajie
Shamian Nanjie
3 Shāmiàn Island
21
Elevated Roadway
Shāmiàn Park
Cuìzhú Park
0 ——————— 500 m
0 ——————— 0.25 miles

Lùhú Park
Xiàtang Xilu
Lùjìng Lu

Lùjìng Lu

Lùhú Lu

Lù Lake

Hengfu Lu
Taojin Lu

Yuèxiù Park

Lùjing Xilu

9

Xiǎobĕi
36

Chrysanthemum Hill Park
Xiànliè Zhonglu

Táojīn
19
35
46 45

QŪZHUĀNG

Qūzhuāng
Nónglín Xialu

18

Dongfeng Zhonglu
Yuchua Lu
Dongfeng Donglu

Mùlian (5km)
29

Nóngjiăng Suŏ (Peasant Movement Institute)

Memorial Garden to the Martyrs

Ertóng Park

Lièshì Língyuán (Martyrs' Park)

Zhongshan Sanlu

Dōngshān Kŏu

Redtory (8.1km)

10
Wende Lu
Changxīnglì
Wenming Lu

Donghua Xilu

28
Wanfu Lu

Beijing Lu

Bĕijīng Lù
Tuányīdà Square

Báiyum Lu

30
6

43
39
Tiānzi Pier
16

DÀSHĀTOU
Dōnghú
Dōngshānhú Park

Hăizhū Bridge

Pearl River (Zhū Jiāng)

Dàshātóu Wharf

Èrshā Island
Guăngdōng Museum of Art (1km); Venue of Canton Fair on Pázhōu Island (9.3km)

Haiyin Bridge

Jiāngnán Dàdào
Shí Èrgōng
Memorial Hall of the Língnán School of Painting (1.5km)

23
Guangzhou South Station

TIT Creative Industry Zone (4.2km); Whampoa Military Academy (27km)

E   F   G   H

Guǎngzhōu

enshrine Buddhist relics brought over from India and placed in the octagonal **Decorated Pagoda** (Huā Tǎ). The temple was given its current name by the exiled poet Su Dongbo in 1099, who waxed lyrical over the (now gone) banyans in the courtyard. You can see the characters 'six banyans' *(liùróng)* that he wrote above the gates.

Guāngxiào Temple   BUDDHIST SITE
(光孝寺, Guāngxiào Sì; Map p562; ✆020 8108 7421; 109 Guangxiao Lu; ¥5; ◷6am-5.30pm; Ⓜ Line 1, Xīmén Kǒu, exit C) 'Bright Filial Piety Temple' is the oldest temple in Guǎngzhōu, dating back to the 4th century. By the time of the Tang dynasty it was well established as a centre of Buddhist learning in southern China. Bodhidharma, the founder of Zen

Buddhism, taught here. Most of the current buildings date from the 19th century, including a main hall with double eaves and a 10m-tall Buddha statue.

Guǎngzhōu Big Buddha Temple   TEMPLE
(大佛古寺, Dàfógǔsì; Map p562; 21 Huifu Lu, cnr Beijing Lu; Ⓜ Line 6, Běijīng Lù) Hidden behind bustling Beijing Lu and spanning a whole block is this calm complex featuring three 10-tonne bronze Buddha statues (representing the past, present and future). Equally gigantic are the 350-year-old cinnamon and avocado trees donated by (modern-day) Vietnam and decorated in red lanterns. The temple was built in the Nanhan period (907–971), with the latest iteration from 1649, and renovations in 2016. By night, you might

hear monks chanting, and the complex is lit up spectacularly neon-like.

Qīngpíng Chinese Medicine Market MARKET

(清平市场, Qīngpíng Shìchǎng; Map p562; Liu'ersan Lu; ⊙9am-9pm; M Line 1, Huángshā, exit E) In this busy market you'll see and definitely smell barrels of dried seahorses, ginseng, goji berries, enamel-like black mushrooms, antler horns and ingredients you can't identify at all. A sensory experience even if you don't buy a thing from the small stores. A short walk from Shāmiàn Island.

🏃 Activities

Shāmiàn Traditional Chinese Medical Centre MASSAGE

(沙面国医馆, Shāmiàn Guóyīguǎn; Map p562; ☑020 8121 8383; 85-87 Shamian Beijie, 沙面北街85-87号; ⊙11am-1.30am; M Lines 1 & 6, Huángshā) Shāmiàn Traditional Chinese Medical Centre, at the western end of Shāmiàn Island, offers body massages for ¥238 per hour. English is spoken for consultations by a Chinese doctor, though not for complicated issues. Appointments accepted.

Guǎngzhōu Star Cruises Company BOATING

(广州之星游轮有限公司, Guǎngzhōu Zhīxīng Yóulún Yǒuxiàn Gōngsī; Map p562; ☑020 8333 2222; cruises ¥48-88; ⊙6-11pm; M Line 6, Hǎizhū Square) The Guǎngzhōu Star Cruises Company has eight two-hour evening cruises on the Pearl River. Boats leave from the **Tiānzì Pier** (Tiānzì Mǎtou; Beijing Lu), just east of Hǎizhū Bridge (Hǎizhū Qiáo; catch metro line 6 to Hǎizhū Square station), and head down the river as far as Èrshā Island (Èrshā Dǎo) before turning back.

🎊 Festivals & Events

Birthday of the Fire God CULTURAL

(⊙28th day of the 9th lunar month) Every year on the birthday of the Fire God, usually around November, Bāhé Academy guild hall throws a banquet for the opera industry. From early morning, you'll hear gongs and drums, and ceremonies are performed at Luányú Táng. Hundreds show up for the day-long feasting that takes place both indoors and on the pavement.

Canton Trade Fair TRADE FAIR

(中国出口商品交易会, Zhōngguó Chūkǒu Shāngpǐn Jiāoyì Huì; ☑020 2608 8888; www.cantonfair.org.cn) The 15-day Canton Trade Fair is held twice yearly, usually in April and October, on Pázhōu Island south of the Pearl River in Guǎngzhōu.

🛏 Sleeping

Guǎngzhōu has few good budget and lower-midrange choices, but there are plenty of excellent top-end and upper-midrange hotels. During the Canton Trade Fair (usually in April and October), prices go up. All hotels offer wi-fi and air-conditioning.

In Guǎngzhōu, Shāmiàn Island is by far the quietest and most attractive area to stay in.

Koala's Home HOSTEL $

(广州考拉青年旅舍, Kǎola Qīngnián Lǚshè; Map p562; ☑020 8319 0988; 505 Huifu Donglu, 3rd fl, 惠福东路505号三楼; d & tw ¥188-268; M Lines 1 & 2, Gōngyuán Qián, exit D) An excellent, clean hostel with cheery furnishings, movies on demand and spotless modern bathrooms. From the inward-facing rooms, there isn't a peep from nearby bustling Beijing Lu. There's little social interaction, though some staff speak English and there are plans to build a rooftop bar. Access by lift inside an egg-tart shop in an alley opposite Tiger Prawn restaurant.

Lazy Gaga HOSTEL $

(春田家家, Chūntián Jiājiā; Map p562; ☑020 8192 3232; www.gagahostel.com; 215 Haizhu Zhonglu, 海珠中路215号; dm ¥55-65, d & tw ¥178, tr ¥240; ❋@🛜; M Line 1, Xīmén Kǒu, exit B) Only five minutes' walk from the metro, Lazy Gaga has 45 cheerful rooms and homey communal areas enlivened by colourful walls and furniture. Guests can have free use of the spotless kitchen and a cheap laundry service; and the pleasant English-speaking staff are up for a chat when they're not busy. In-room lockers come thoughtfully embedded with chargers for mobile devices.

Guǎngzhōu Riverside International Youth Hostel HOSTEL $

(广州江畔国际青年旅舍, Guǎngzhōu Jiāngpàn Guójì Qīngnián Lǚshè; ☑020 2239 2500; www.yhachina.com; 15 Changdi Jie, 长堤街15号; dm ¥65, s ¥140, d ¥185-288, tr ¥268; @🛜; M Line 1, Fāngcūn, exit B1) Located in Fāngcūn next to a bar street, this YHA-affiliated hostel can feel chilly on cold nights but has spotless rooms and a welcoming vibe. Turn right from the metro exit and go through the back lane next to the hospital to reach tree-lined Luju Lu (陆居路). Turn left and walk towards the river, turn right and you'll see the hostel after five minutes.

Ferries depart frequently from Huángshā pier on Shāmiàn Island to Fāngcūn pier right in front of the hostel.

Guăngzhōu Youth Hostel
HOTEL $$

(广东鹅潭宾馆, Guăngdōng Étán Bīnguăn; Map p562; ✆020 8121 8298; 2 Shamian Sijie, 沙面四街2号; d ¥200-290, tr ¥300; ➌; Ⓜ Lines 1 & 6, Huángshā) The English name remains, but the youth hostel has long gone. Dorms have been converted into huge, spotless rooms, making for great value if you want loads of space. The cheapest decent beds on Shāmiàn Island.

7 Days Inn Guăngzhōu Shimao Center
HOTEL $$

(7天连锁酒店, Qītiān Liánsuǒ Jiŭdiàn; Map p562; ✆/fax 0208364 4488; 32 Huale Lu, 华乐路32号; r ¥219-355; ✳➌➐; Ⓜ Line 5, Táojīn) This chain hotel is the cheapest decent option amid the five-star enclave in Yuèxiù (越秀) District. It's just south of the Garden Hotel.

★ Garden Hotel
HOTEL $$$

(花园酒店, Huāyuán Jiŭdiàn; Map p562; ✆020 8333 8989; www.gardenhotel.com; 368 Huanshi Donglu, 环市东路368号; r/ste from ¥1128/2628; ✳➌➐✲; Ⓜ Line 5, Táojīn) One of the most popular luxury hotels in Guăngzhōu, with waterfalls and lovely gardens in the lobby and on the 4th floor. The modern rooms are just as classy, with Chinese design accents. Bookings are essential.

Westin Guăngzhōu
HOTEL $$$

(广州天誉威斯汀酒店, Guăngzhōu Tiānyú Wēisītīng Jiŭdiàn; Map p567; ✆020 2886 6868; www.starwoodhotels.com; 6 Linhe Zhonglu, 林和中路6号; d/ste from ¥1279/2155; Ⓜ Line 3, Línhé Xī) The luxurious Westin is the best place to stay in Tiānhé, if not in Guăngzhōu. Staff are very welcoming and efficient, rooms are spacious and sparkling, and the location, near the eastern train station, is terrific.

Mulian
BOUTIQUE HOTEL $$$

(广州木莲庄酒店, Guăngzhōu Mùliánzhuāng Jiŭdiàn; ✆020 8353 8888; www.themulian.com; 715 Jinsui Lu, 金穗路715号; s/d/ste ¥448/688/1088; ✳➐; Ⓜ Line 5, Táncūn, exit D) If you don't mind windowless rooms (which is 90% of the rooms here), the Mulian is perfect for a getaway – the soundproofing is seamless; the decor is exotically Thai; there are a host of gadgets to keep you entertained indoors; and there's free afternoon tea when you get hungry.

Guăngdōng Victory Hotel
HOTEL $$$

(胜利宾馆, Shènglì Bīnguăn; Map p562; ✆020 8121 6688; www.vhotel.com; 53 & 54 Shamian Beijie, 沙面北街53、54号; r from ¥928, tr ¥1280, ste ¥1380-3880; ✳➌➐; Ⓜ Lines 1 & 6, Huángshā) There are two branches of the Victory Hotel on Shāmiàn Island: an older one at 54 Shamian Beijie (enter from 10 Shamian Sijie) and a newer wing – 胜利宾馆 (新楼) – at 53 Shamian Nanjie. Both offer decent value for money, especially as discounts of up to a third are available.

✕ Eating

Guăngzhōu is home to some excellent Cantonese restaurants. Dim sum (点心; *diănxīn*), or yum cha (饮茶; *yĭnchá*; tea drinking), may be the best-known form of Cantonese cuisine to foreigners, but in fact noodles, congee and desserts are equally popular locally.

★ Guăngzhōu Restaurant
DIM SUM $

(广州酒家, Guăngzhōu Jiŭjiā; Map p562; 2 Wenchang Nanlu, 文昌南路2号; dim dum per dish ¥9-25; ⏱7am-11pm; Ⓜ Line 1, Chángshòu Lù) Guăngzhōu's oldest restaurant is dedicated to serving well made dim sum with an exquisite selection of teas (¥8 to ¥50 per person). Times may have moved on but this is the traditonal dim sum model. Tables and dining spaces are set around a beautiful interior garden in the atrium. Go early: by 8.30am all the tables with views are taken.

Huìfú Vegetarian
VEGETARIAN $

(惠福慈心素食, Huìfú Cíxīn Sùshí; Map p562; ✆020 8323 4326; 449 Huifu Donglu, 惠福东路449号; buffet ¥25; ⏱11am-2pm & 5-8.30pm; ➐➋; Ⓜ Lines 1 & 2, Gōngyuán Qián, exit D) Serve yourself a selection of extremely fresh vegetarian Cantonese dishes such as sweet-and-sour tofu, and red bean with lotus root. Sweet ginger and rice cake soups, and dumplings are also available. No menu or Chinese needed.

Tiger Prawn
VIETNAMESE $

(Map p562; ✆020 8319 1277; www.tigerprawngz.com; 548 Huifu Donglu, 惠福东路548号; mains ¥21-108; ⏱11am-10pm; Ⓜ Line 6, Běijīng Lù) The large queue (plan on 15 to 60 minutes) between 7pm and 9pm reflects how popular Vietnamese food has become in Guăngzhōu. Tiger Prawn is the long-standing star for Southeast Asian food in the city, using the right herbs and spices in the *pho* (rice noodles in beef broth) and the lemongrass chicken. The Chinese and Thai dishes are also excellent. English and photo menu.

Chén Tiānjì
CANTONESE $

(陈添记; Map p562; ✆020 8182 8774; 59 Baohua Lu, 宝华路59号; dishes ¥9-35; ⏱9.30am-10.30pm; Ⓜ Line 1, Chángshòu Lù, exit D2) This old hole-in-the-wall serves three things – crunchy blanched fish skin (鱼皮; *yúpí*) tossed with peanuts and parsley; sampan congee (艇仔

East Guǎngzhōu

粥; *tǐngzǎi zhōu*); and rice-flour rolls (肠粉; *chángfěn*). Turn right from the metro exit, then turn into an alley; it's the second eatery.

Big Buddha Temple Vegetarian VEGETARIAN $
(大佛寺素食阁, Dàfógǔsì Sùshí Gé; Map p562; Huifu Lu, main hall, 2nd fl, cnr Beijing Lu; mains ¥15-148; ⊙11am-8.30pm; 🌐📶; Ⓜ Line 6, Běijīng Lù) On the 2nd floor of the main hall of the calm Big Buddha Temple, choose from an extensive menu of banquet-worthy vegetarian dishes in an elevated ancient-China-style restaurant. The focus is on mock meats to mimic traditional Cantonese dishes for catering to omnivore temple visitors. Photo and English menu.

★ **Pànxī Restaurant** DIM SUM $$
(泮溪酒家, Pànxī Jiǔjia; Map p562; ☎020 8172 1328; 151 Longjin Xilu, 龙津西路151号; dishes from ¥40; ⊙7.30am-midnight; Ⓜ Line 1, Chángshòu Lù) Set in a majestic garden and embracing another one within its walls, Pànxī is the most representative of Guǎngzhōu's garden-restaurants. Corridors and courtyards are brought together to give the effect of 'every step, a vista' (一步一景). Elderly diners are known to get up and sing an operatic aria or two when the mood is right. You'll need to queue for a table after 8.30am.

Social&Co INTERNATIONAL $$
(Map p567; ☎020 3804 9243; www.socialandco. com; 7 Huacheng Lu, 华成路7号; mains ¥60-140; ⊙11.30am-2am; 📶; Ⓜ Line 5, Zhūjiāng New Town) The Australian owners of this casually cool cafe command some of the best international dishes in Guǎngzhōu. Highlights are banoffee pie, Portuguese-style chicken, pork belly with plum sauce and a drinks list that includes tea-infused cocktails (¥60). Lunch packages (salad, sandwich, soup; ¥50) are good value.

East Guǎngzhōu

Wilber's EUROPEAN $$
(Map p562; ☎020 3761 1101; www.wilber.com.cn; 62 Zhusigang Ermalu, 竹丝岗二马路62号; mains ¥68-280; ⊙11am-4pm & 5-9pm; 🌐; Ⓜ Line 1, Dōngshān Kǒu) Hidden on the edge of Yuèxiù District, gay-friendly Wilber's gets top marks

for cocktails and atmosphere, and the food isn't far behind. You can munch on cold cuts and mini burgers at the sleek bar, or opt for seafood risotto and pan-fried scallops in a set menu (¥350) in the ultramodern restaurant. Look for the restored colonial villa with whitewashed walls and patio.

Táng Lì Yuán
CANTONESE $$

(唐荔园; ✓020 8181 8002; Lìwān Lake Park, ☐ 荔湾湖公园内5号; mains ¥22-200; ⊗7.30am-3pm & 5pm-3am; Ⓜ Line 1, Huángshā) This garden-restaurant, known for its roasted pigeon (金牌乳鸽; jīnpái rǔgē), is located inside Lìwān Lake Park (荔湾湖公园; Lìwān Hú Gōngyuán). A highlight are the tables on six-seater boats that you can reserve for dinner. They're inspired by Zǐdòng Chuán (紫洞船), aka 'drinking boats' or 'whore boats', used in the Qing dynasty by Xīguān merchants to entertain with banquets, opera and women. There's a cover charge and a 'seat fee' of ¥150 and ¥20, respectively, per person. The restaurant sits at the junction of Huangsha Dadao (黄沙大道) and Ruyi Fang (如意坊).

Bīngshèng Restaurant
CANTONESE $$

(炳胜海鲜酒家, Bīngshèng Hǎixiān Jiǔjiā; Map p562; ✓020 3428 6910; 33 Dongxiao Lu, 东晓路 33号; dishes from ¥48; ⊗11am-midnight; 🚌293, 886) This exquisite restaurant surprises with every visit. Shùndé (a town south of Guǎngzhōu) cuisine's freshwater fish is the speciality here. The dòufuhuā zhēngxiègāo (豆腐花蒸蟹羔; bean curd with crab roe) and hǎilú cìshēn (海鲈刺身; sea bass sashimi) are very tasty. No English menu.

🍷 Drinking & Nightlife

Guǎngzhōu's party hub is Zhūjiāng Pátí (珠江琶醍), a strip of land by the river that is the former site of the massive Zhūjiāng Brewery. Converted facilities now throb with trendy bars and clubs. With traces of the brewery still visible, it's the city's most surreal (and boozy) party place. Upmarket Yánjiāng Lù Bar Street is also worth a visit.

★ Kuí Yuán
CAFE

(逵园; Map p562; ✓020 8765 9746; 9 Xuguyuan Lu, 恤孤院路9号; ⊗10am-midnight; 🛜; Ⓜ Line 1, Dōngshān Kǒu, exit F) From its location inside the gorgeous Kuí Yuán building in the historic Dōngshān area, this cafe serves decent coffee and canapés during the day and morphs into a bar at night. Stylish, warm-toned seating areas occupy the rooms of the original residence. Built in 1922, the house is famous for its Western architectural features.

Sun's
LOUNGE

(✓020 8977 9056; www.sunsgz.com; B25-26 Yuejiang Xilu, 阅江西路25-26B号; cover from ¥50; ⊗7am-2am Sun-Thu, to 5am Fri & Sat; 🚌779, 765 (final stop)) The best of the lot in Zhūjiāng 'Party Pier' (珠江琶醍), Sun's lets you sip cocktails on couches by the river or dance to electronic music.

Shāmiàn Clubhouse
BAR

(沙面会馆, Shāmiàn Huìguǎn; Map p562; Shamian Dajie, 沙面大街; ⊗11am-11pm; 🛜; Ⓜ Lines 1 & 6, Huángshā) The 'Red Mansion' (c 1907), once known as 'Shāmiàn's grandest mansion', fuses features of British colonial architecture such as colonnades and louvre windows with the Lǐngnán fondness for skylights. It has a small, clubby bar with long teak flooring.

☆ Entertainment

★ 191 Space
LIVE MUSIC

(191Space 音乐主题酒吧, 191 Space Yīnlè Zhǔtí Jiǔbā; Map p567; ✓020 8737 9375; www.191space.com; 191 Guangzhou Dadao Zhonglu, 广州大道中路191号; ⊗8pm-2am; Ⓜ Line 5, Wǔyángcūn, exit A) Two steps from the metro exit, this is a throbbing dive that features live indie gigs from China and overseas every weekend.

Fei Live House
LIVE MUSIC

(飞, Fēi; Unit B4, 128 Yuancun Sihenglu, 员村四横路128号, Redtory; Ⓜ Line 3, Yúncūn, exit B) A live-music space with an awesome sound system and a focus on indie music, inside Redtory art village (红砖厂, Hóngzhuān Chǎng; ✓020 8557 8470; www.redtory.com.cn; ⊗6am-midnight).

Guǎngzhōu Opera House
THEATRE

(广州大剧院, Guǎngzhōu Dàjùyuàn; Map p567; ✓020 3839 2888, 020 3839 2666; http://gzdjy.org; 1 Zhujiang Xilu, 珠江西路1号; ⊗9am-4.30pm Tue-Sun; Ⓜ Line 3, Zhūjiāng Xīnchéng, exit B1) Guǎngdōng's premier performance venue. Local versions of international theatre productions, such as War Horse, are staged here.

🛍 Shopping

Xīguān Antique Street
ANTIQUES

(西关古玩城, Xīguān Gǔwánchéng; Map p562; Lizhiwan Lu, 荔枝湾路; ⊗9am-8pm; Ⓜ Line 5, Zhōngshān Bā) This street sells everything from ceramic teapots to Tibetan rugs. Even if you're not in the mood to load up your pack with ceramic vases, it's a wonderful place in which to browse. Note that most artefacts here are known to be fakes.

Shàngxiàjiǔ Pedestrian Street CLOTHING
(上下九步行街, Shàngxiàjiǔ Bùxíng Jiē; Map p562; ☉9am-late; MLine 1, Chángshòu Lù or Huángshā) Literally 'Up Down Nine Street', this pedestrianised shopping area in one of the oldest parts of the city, where the buildings retain elements of both Western and Chinese architecture, is a good place to look for discounted clothing (and street food).

Information

EMERGENCY
Ambulance ☑120
Fire ☑119
Police ☑110

INTERNET ACCESS
Most hotels provide free broadband internet access. Free wi-fi is available at all Guǎngdōng branches of Starbucks, Fairwood (大快活; Dàkuàihuó) and Cafe de Coral (大家乐; Dàjiālè), but some require a local phone number for access.

MEDICAL SERVICES
CanAm International Medical Centre (加美国际医疗中心, Jiāměi Guójì Yīliáo Zhōngxīn; Map p562; ☑020 8386 6988; www.canamhealthcare.com; 5th fl, Garden Tower, Garden Hotel, 368 Huanshi Donglu; ☉24hr) Has English-speaking doctors but you'll need to call ahead.
Guǎngzhōu First Municipal People's Hospital (广州第一人民医院, Guǎngzhōu Dìyī Rénmín Yīyuàn; Map p562; ☑020 8104 8888; www.gzhosp.cn; 1 Panfu Lu) Medical clinic for foreigners on the 1st floor.

MONEY
American Express Guǎngzhōu (美国运通广州, Měiguó Yùntōng Guǎngzhōu; Map p562; ☑020 8331 1611; fax 020 8331 1616; Room 1004, Main Tower, Guǎngdōng International Hotel, 339 Huanshi Donglu; ☉9am-5.30pm Mon-Fri) Cashes and sells Amex travellers cheques.
Bank of China (中国银行, Zhōngguó Yínháng; Map p562; ☑020 8334 0998; 686 Renmin Beilu; ☉9am-5.30pm Mon-Fri, to 4pm Sat & Sun) Most branches change travellers cheques.

POST
China Post (中国邮政, Zhōngguó Yóuzhèng; Map p562; 151 Huanshi Xilu; ☉8am-8pm) Located next to the train station.

PUBLIC SECURITY BUREAU
PSB (公安局, Gōng'ānjú; Map p562; ☑020 8311 5808, 020 8311 5800; 155 Jiefang Nanlu; ☉8-11.30am & 2.30-5pm) Helps with all 'aliens' needs. Between Dade Lu and Darin Lu.

TELEPHONE
China Telecom (中国电信, Zhōngguó Diànxìn; Map p562; ☑10000; 196 Huanshi Xilu; ☉9am-6pm) Its main branch is opposite the train station (eastern side of Renmin Beilu).

TOURIST INFORMATION
Tourist Information Centre (Map p562; www.visitgz.com; 325 Zhongshan Liulu; ☉9am-6pm) There are 19 tourist information centres, including at 325 Zhongshan Liulu, the airport and the train station.

TRAVEL AGENCIES
Most hotels offer travel services that, for a small charge, can help you book tickets and tours.
China Travel Service (Map p562; ☑020 8333 6888; 8 Qiaoguang Lu, CTS, 广州中国旅行社, Zhōngguó Lǚxíngshè; ☉8.30am-6pm Mon-Fri, 9am-5pm Sat & Sun; M Hǎizhū Guǎngchǎng, exit A) is located next to Hotel Landmark Canton, it offers various tours and books tickets.

USEFUL WEBSITES
Delta Bridges Guǎngzhōu (www.deltabridges.com/users/guangzhou) Events listings.
Guǎngzhōu Stuff (www.gzstuff.com) Entertainment listings, forums and classifieds.
Life of Guǎngzhōu (www.lifeofguangzhou.com) Yellow Pages for visitors and expats.

VISAS
The 72-Hour Visa-Free Transit policy allows passport holders of many countries a stopover in Guǎngzhōu without arranging a visa before arrival. See p1007 for more information.

Getting There & Away

AIR
Báiyún International Airport (白云国际机场, CAN, Báiyún Guójì Jīchǎng, ☑020 3606 6999, www.gbiac.net) is about 28km north of the city.

The major airline serving Guǎngzhōu, **China Southern Airlines** (中国南方航空, Zhōngguó Nánfāng Hángkōng; Map p562; ☑95539; www.csair.com; 181 Huanshi Xilu; ☉24hr), runs frequent flights to major cities in China including Guilín, Shànghǎi and Běijīng, as well as numerous international destinations.

BUS
Guǎngzhōu has many long-distance bus stations with services to destinations in Guǎngdōng, southern Fújiàn, eastern Guǎngxī and further afield. There are frequent buses to Fóshān (¥21, 45 minutes), Kāipíng (¥58, two hours), Shēnzhèn (¥65, two hours) and Zhūhǎi (¥60, two hours) from Tiānhé bus station, Fāngcūn bus station (from metro Kēngkǒu), Guǎngzhōu East coach terminal and Guǎngdōng long-distance bus station.

Other destinations:
Cháozhōu ¥170 to ¥180, six hours, hourly from Tiānhé station
Guilín ¥170, 10 hours, eight daily from Guǎngdōng long-distance bus station (8.30am to 11.30pm)

Hăikŏu ¥260 to ¥285, 12 hours, seven daily from Guăngdōng long-distance bus station

Nánníng ¥185, 10 hours, five daily from Guăngdōng long-distance bus station

Qīngyuăn ¥30 to ¥40, 1½ hours, every half-hour from Tiānhé station

Shàntóu ¥180 to ¥200, five hours, every 30 minutes from Tiānhé station

Sháoguān ¥75 to ¥85, four hours, every 45 minutes from Guăngdōng long-distance bus station

Xiàmén ¥230, nine hours, every 45 minutes from Tiānhé station

Zhàoqìng ¥35 to ¥50, 1½ hours, every 15 minutes from Tiānhé station

Deluxe buses ply the Guăngzhōu–Shēnzhèn freeway to Hong Kong, which is the easiest route to travel. **Buses** (Map p562) (from ¥110, 3½ hours) to Hong Kong and its airport leave from Hotel Landmark Canton near Hăizhū Square station or China Hotel near Yuèxiù Park station every 30 minutes.

Buses through Zhūhăi to Macau (¥80, every hour, 2½ hours) leave frequently from Tiānhé station (7.40am to 8pm).

Fāngcūn Bus Station (芳村客运站, Fāngcūn Kèyùnzhàn; ☑ 020 3708 5070; www.fangcunbus. com; Huadi Dadao, 华地大道; Ⓜ Line 1, Keng-kou) Accessible by metro (Kēngkŏu station).

Guăngzhōu East Coach Terminal (广州东站汽车客运站, Guăngzhōu Dōngzhàn Kèyùnzhàn; Map p567; Linhe Xilu; Ⓜ Lines 1 & 3, Guăngzhōu East Railway Station) Behind Guăngzhōu East Railway Station. Good for destinations within Guăngdōng; departures aren't as frequent as from other stations.

Guăngdōng Long-Distance Bus Station (广东省汽车客运站, Guăngdōng Shĕng Qìchē Kèyùnzhàn; Map p562; Huanshi Xilu; Ⓜ Lines 2 & 5, Guăngzhōu Railway Station) West of the Guăngzhōu Railway Station. There's a smaller long-distance bus station (广州市气车客运站; *Guăngzhōu Shì Qìchēzhàn*) over the footbridge.

Liúhuā Bus Station (流花车站, Liúhuā Chēzhàn; Map p562; 188 Huanshi Xilu, 环市西路188号) Opposite Guăngzhōu Main Train Station. Destinations include Cháozhōu and Shàntóu.

Tiānhé Bus Station (天河客运站, Tiānhé Kèyùnzhàn; ☑ 020 3709 0062; www.tianhebus. com; Yanling Lu, 燕玲路; Ⓜ Lines 3 & 6, Tiānhé Coach Terminal) Most frequent departures to destinations in Guăngdōng; accessible by metro.

TRAIN

Guăngzhōu's three major train stations serve destinations all over China. China Travel Service (p569), books train tickets up to five days in advance for ¥10 to ¥20. There are similar fees for booking from the Ctrip app, with tickets paid for by card and picked up from a station.

From **Guăngzhōu Main Train Station** (广州火车总站, Guăngzhōu Zhàn; Map p562; Huanshi Xilu; Ⓜ Lines 2 & 5, Guăngzhōu Railway Station):

Lhasa ¥919, 53 hours, one every two days (11.42pm)

Sháoguān ¥38, 2½ hours, frequent services

Zhàoqìng ¥17 to ¥71, two hours, 14 daily

High-speed trains leave from **Guăngzhōu South Railway Station** (广州火车南站, Guăngzhōu Nánzhàn; Shibi, Pānyú) in Pānyú:

Bĕijīng ¥709 to ¥862, eight to 11 hours, 10 daily

Chángshā ¥314, 2½ hours, frequent

Qīngyuăn ¥40, 25 minutes, frequent

Shànghăi ¥479 to ¥793, seven to 11½ hours, 10 daily

Sháoguān ¥105, 50 minutes, frequent

Shēnzhèn North Station ¥75, 45 minutes

Wŭhàn ¥464, 4½ hours, frequent

Light rail goes to Zhūhăi (¥34, one hour).

To get to Guăngzhōu South Railway Station, take metro line 2 from the main train station (¥6, 34 minutes) or one of the South Station Express buses (南站快线; Nánzhàn Kuàixiàn) that leave from Tianhe Sports Centre metro station, Garden Hotel and Hotel Landmark Canton (¥14, 45 minutes).

There is one daily service from **Guăngzhōu East Railway Station** (广州车站, Guăngzhōu Dōngzhàn; Ⓜ Lines 1 & 3, Guăngzhōu East Railway Station) to Shànghăi (¥206 to ¥377, 16 hours, 6.12pm)

The station is used mainly for bullet trains to Shēnzhèn (¥80, 1½ hours, every 15 minutes, 6.15am to 10.32pm) and a dozen direct trains to Hong Kong (¥184, HK$222, two hours, 8.19am to 9.32pm).

ⓘ Getting Around

TO/FROM THE AIRPORT

Airport shuttle buses (¥17 to ¥32, 35 to 70 minutes, every 20 to 30 minutes, 5am to 11pm) leave from half a dozen locations, including the Garden Hotel and Tiānhé bus station. A taxi to/from the airport will cost about ¥150.

Metro line 2 links the airport's south terminal (Airport South station; Jīchăng Nán) and Guăngzhōu East station. The ride takes 40 minutes (¥8, 6.10am to 11pm), or 70 minutes to Bĕijīng Lù station.

BUS

Guăngzhōu has a large network of motor buses (¥1) and bus rapid transport (BRT; ¥2).

FERRY

Riding the Pearl River is a useful and overlooked way of getting around. It can sometimes avoid multiple metro line changes and costs only ¥2 for a DIY river tour. Ferry piers near sights include:

Dàshātóu Wharf (大沙头游船码头, Dàshātóu Yóuchuán Mătóu; Map p562) Used by main river tour boats and next to Hăizhū Square station.

Tiānzì Pier (天字码头, Tiānzì Mǎtou; Map p562; Beijing Lu, 北京路; ferry one way ¥2; M Line 6, Beijing Lu) At the south end of the Beijing Lu shopping street, with ferries to Canton Tower

Xīdī Pier (西堤码头, Xīdī Mǎtou; Map p562) Just east of Shāmiàn Island.

METRO

Guǎngzhōu has nine metro lines in full service, all with free maps available in English (beware of old maps still in circulation that omit Line 6). New lines are to be added and extended from 2017 onwards. Operating hours are approximately from 6.20am to 11.30pm and fares cost from ¥2 to ¥14.

Transit passes (羊城通; yáng chéng tōng) are available at metro stations from ¥70 (deposit ¥20 included). The deposit is refundable at designated stations, including Tiyu Xilu and Gōngyuán Qián. This pass can be used on all public transport, including in yellow taxis. There are also one-day (¥20) and three-day (¥50) metro passes. Both allow unlimited use within the specified period and do not require a deposit.

TAXI

Taxis are abundant but demand is high. Peak hours are from 8am to 9am, and around lunch and dinner. Yellow or red cabs are driven by local drivers; others by migrant drivers who may not know the city well. Flag fall is ¥10 for the first 2.5km; ¥2.6 for every additional kilometre, with a ¥1 fuel surcharge. App taxi services such as Uber (www.uber.com) have gained popularity and can offer a safe, convenient service, if your Chinese is up to it.

Around Guǎngzhōu

One of Guǎngdōng's four famous classical gardens, **Yúyìn Mountain Villa** (余荫山房, Yúyìn Shānfáng; ☑020 3482 2187; Náncūn, Pānyú; adult/child ¥18/9; ☺8am-6pm; M Line 3, Dàshi, exit A) is a graceful property was built in 1871 by an official of the Qing court. It incorporates the landscaping styles of Sūzhōu and Hángzhōu, and the features of Lǐngnán architecture. The result is a photogenic collection of pavilions, terraces, halls, bridges and lakes. It also has a dessert shop selling ginger milk curd (姜汁撞奶; jiāngzhī zhuàngnǎi).

The Waterside Pavilion commands a different vista on each of its eight sides; the Deep Willow Room features ancient art and coloured 'Manchu' windows (满洲窗; mǎnzhōu chuāng) aka 'four-season windows' (四季窗; sìjì chuāng), which create an illusion of changing seasons by altering the hue of the outside scenery.

Turn left when you leave the metro. There's a stop for the Route 8 feeder bus to Qīxīnggǎng Gōngyuán (七星岗公园; ¥2). Disembark at Nánshān Gōngyuán (南山公园), the 20th stop, after 30 minutes. Cross to the opposite and leafy side of the road. Bus 30 (¥2) from the stop there takes you to the entrance of Yúyìn Mountain Villa just one stop away.

Fóshān 佛山

☑0757 / POP 6 MILLION

An easy half-hour metro ride will take day-trippers from Guǎngzhōu to this city. Fóshān (literally 'Buddha Hill') was famous for its ceramics in the Ming dynasty. Today, it's better known as the birthplace of two kung fu icons, Wong Fei Hung and Ip Man (Bruce Lee's master), and the Wing Chun style of kung fu developed here.

◉ Sights

Nánfēng Ancient Kiln Artists' Village ARTS CENTRE

(南风古灶, Nánfēng Gǔzào; ☑0757 8278 0606; 6 Gaomiao Lu, Shíwān, 高庙路6号; ¥25; ☺9am-5.30pm; ☐137) This lovely ceramics town of stone-paved paths is worth snooping around in for its artisans' ceramics workshops and the two ancient 'dragon kilns' of more than 30m in length. The modern Bruce Lee statues celebrating the local Wing Chun school of kung fu are also photogenic. Shíwān (石湾), 2km from downtown Fóshān, was once China's most important ceramics production centre. Much of the Ming dynasty pottery you see at museums comes from here (those in most shops here, however, are mass-produced copies).

Zǔmiào TAOIST SITE

(祖庙; ☑0757 8229 3723; www.fszumiao.com; 21 Zumiao Lu, 祖庙路21号; ¥20, combined with Ancient Nánfēng Kiln ¥35; ☺8.30am-5.30pm; M Zǔmiào, exit A) The 11th-century Zǔmiào temple is believed to be the site where Cantonese opera flourished. The art is still performed today during festivals to entertain the gods, and the tourists. Sharing the complex are a Confucius temple (c 1911) and memorial halls dedicated to two martial artists born in Fóshān – Wong Fei Hung (aka Huang Fei Hong) and Ip Man – and kung fu cinema in general.

There are daily performances of kung fu (10am, 2pm and 3pm) and lion dance (10.30am, 2.15pm and 3.30pm). The temple runs martial-arts classes for children every summer. Call ☑0757 8222 1680 for details.

THE MAKING OF A NATIONAL LEGEND

Fóshān-born Wong Fei Hung (1847–1924) is one of China's best-known folk heroes. Although a consummate *gōngfū* (kung fu) master in his lifetime, he didn't become widely known until his story was merged with fiction in countless movies made after 1949, most by Hong Kong directors, such as Hark Tsui's *Once Upon a Time in China*, starring Jet Li. Sadly, Wong spent his later years in desolation, after his son was murdered and his martial-arts school was destroyed by fire. Regardless, an astonishing 106 movies (and counting!) have celebrated this son of Fóshān, resulting in the world's longest movie series and the creation of a national legend.

Another Fóshān hero, Ip Man (1893–1972) rose to fame as a Wing Chun master at the outset of WWII. He fled to Hong Kong in 1949 where he founded the first Wing Chun school. His most famous student was Bruce Lee. Ip Man was immortalised by Wong Kar-wai's award-winning *The Grandmaster* and a series of semibiographical movies starring Donnie Yen.

Liáng Garden GARDENS
(梁园, Liáng Yuán; ☑0757 8224 1279; Songfeng Lu, 松风路; ¥10; ☺8.30am-5.30pm; ☐205, 212) This tranquil residence of a family that produced painters and calligraphers was built during the Qing dynasty. Designed in a Lǐngnán style, it delights with ponds, willow-lined pathways and, in summer, trees heavy with wax apple and jackfruit. Like Yúyìn Mountain Villa near Guǎngzhōu, it's one of the four great classical gardens. Liáng Garden is north of Rénshòu Temple and 300m north of the Bank of China.

🛌 Sleeping

Fóshān Marco Polo HOTEL $$$
(马哥孛罗酒店, Mǎgē Bóluó Jiǔdiàn; ☑0757 8250 1888; www.marcopolohotels.com; 97 Renmin Lu, Chánchéng Qū, 人民路97号; r/ste from ¥2380/3080; @🅿🛜🏊; Ⓜ Zūmiào, exit C) Arguably the best place to stay in town. Rates are usually in the region of ¥800.

🍴 Eating

In this temple town, vegetarian restaurants are dotted on-site or nearby. A local speciality is the shrimp wonton noodle soup.

Rénshēngyuán Vegetarian VEGETARIAN $
(仁生缘素食, Rénshēngyuán Sùshí; ☑0757 8225 2171; 22 Zumiao Lu, 祖庙路22号; mains ¥23-38; ☺11am-2.30pm & 5-8.30pm; 🍴; Ⓜ Zūmiào, exit A) Very good vegetarian dishes that include plenty of fresh greens and mock meats, made to be shared. Enter the large, neat restaurant from the laneway opposite Rénshòu Temple.

Yīngjì Noodle Shop NOODLES $
(应记面家, Yīngjì Miànjiā; ☑0757 3171 2533; 112 Lianhua Lu, 莲花路112号; noodles ¥7-12; ☺7am-11pm; ☐105, 106, 109, 114, 118, 128, 137) This excellent noodle shop opposite Liánhuā Supermarket (莲花超市; Liánhuā Chāoshì) is the go-to place in Fóshān for noodles with shrimp wonton (鲜虾云吞面; *xiānxiā yúntūnmiàn*).

ℹ Getting There & Away

Buses leaving from **Fóshān bus station** (佛山汽车站, Fóshān Shěng Qìchēzhàn; Fenjiang Zhonglu), 400m south of the train station:
Shēnzhèn ¥75 to ¥90, 2½ hours, every 30 minutes
Zhūhǎi ¥70, three hours, every 30 to 60 minutes

Buses (¥13) run hourly between Guǎngzhōu's Guǎngdōng long-distance bus station and **Zūmiào bus station** (祖庙车站, Zūmiào Chēzhàn; 104 Jianxin Lu, 建新路104号), a block east of Zūmiào metro station.

Trains go to Guǎngzhōu (¥9 to ¥24, 30 minutes, 21 daily).

The metro is the easiest way to get between Guǎngzhōu and Fóshān, via the Guǎngfó line (¥7, 30 to 60 minutes), with regular Guǎngzhōu tickets.

There's a direct express train to Hong Kong (¥210, 2½ hours, 4.13pm), and at 10.42pm from Kowloon.

ℹ Getting Around

Buses 101 and 134 (¥2) link the train station to Zūmiào and Shíwān.

Taxis start at ¥8 for the first 2km, costing ¥2.60 for every additional 1km.

Kāipíng 开平
☑0750 / POP 680,000

Kāipíng, 140km southwest of Guǎngzhōu, is home to one of the most arresting human-constructed attractions in Guǎngdōng – the Unesco-crowned *diāolóu* (碉楼), eccentric watchtowers featuring a fusion of Eastern and Western architectural styles. Out of the approximately 3000 original *diāolóu*, only 1833 remain.

Downtown Kāipíng is pleasant, especially the section near the Tánjiāng River (谭江), where you'll see people fishing next to mango and wampee trees.

Kāipíng is also the home of many overseas Chinese. Currently, 720,000 people from the county are living overseas – 40,000 more than its local population. Chinese tourists abound and it's worth dedicating at least one whole day to *diāolóu* hunting as most require renting a bike or taxi.

◉ Sights

A combo ticket for seven sights, including Lì Garden and the villages of Zìlì, Jīnjiānglǐ and Mǎjiànglóng, costs ¥180. It's only available at Lì Garden and Zìlì village. The price for just Lì Garden and one village is ¥150. A village alone costs from ¥50 to ¥80. Some towers charge an extra ¥5 to ¥10 to let you in.

★ Zìlì
VILLAGE

(自力村, Zìlì Cūn; ◷ 8.30am-5.30pm) Zìlì, 11km west of Kāipíng, has the largest collection of *diāolóu* historic watchtowers in the area, though only a few of the 15 are open to the public. The most stunning is **Míngshí Lóu** (铭石楼), which has a verandah with Ionic columns and a hexagonal pavilion on its roof. It appeared in the film *Let the Bullets Fly*. **Yúnhuàn Lóu** (云幻楼) has four towers known as 'swallow nests', each with embrasures, cobblestones and a water cannon.

Jīnjiānglǐ Historic Village
VILLAGE

(锦江里, Jīnjiānglǐ Cūn; ◷ 9am-5pm) The highlights in this village, 20km south of Kāipíng, are the privately run Ruìshí Lóu and **Shēngfēng Lóu** (升峰楼). The former (c 1923) is Kāipíng's tallest *diāolóu* and comprises nine storeys, topped off with a Byzantine-style roof and a Roman dome. The latter is one of very few *diāolóu* that had a European architect.

Ruìshí Lóu
TOWER

(瑞石楼; ¥20) One of the most marvellous of the towers around Kāipíng is located behind Jīnjiānglǐ village (锦江里), 20km south of Kāipíng. Built in 1923, the privately owned tower has nine storeys with a Byzantine-style roof and Roman dome supported by elaborately decorated walls and pillars.

Lì Garden
HISTORIC SITE

(立园, Lì Yuán; ◷ 8.30am-5.30pm) About 15 minutes by taxi from Kāipíng, Lì Garden has a fortified mansion built in 1936 by a wealthy Chinese American. The interiors featuring Italianate motifs and the gardens, with their artificial canals, footbridges and dappled pathways, are delightful.

Diāolóu here include the oldest of the historic towers, **Yínglóng Lóu** (迎龙楼), found in Sānménlǐ village (三门里), and the fortified villas of **Mǎjiànglóng** (马降龙) village.

Nánxìng Xié Lóu
HISTORIC BUILDING

(南兴斜楼, Leaning Tower) **FREE** In Nánxìng village, Nánxìng Xié Lóu was built in 1903 and tilts severely to one side, with its central axis over 2m off-centre.

Chìkǎn
VILLAGE

(赤坎) The charming old town of Chìkǎn, 10km southwest of Kāipíng, has streets of shophouses with arcades on the ground floor flanking the Tánjiāng River (谭江). These distinctive *qílóu* (骑楼) buildings were built by overseas Cantonese merchants in the 1920s. Bus 6 from Yìcí bus station terminates at Chìkǎn.

🛏 Sleeping

Tribe of Diāomín
HOTEL $

(碉民部落, Diāomín Bùluò; ☎ 0750 261 6222; 126 Henan Lu, Chìkǎn, 赤坎镇河南路126号; dm per person ¥40-50, r ¥140-230; ❉ 🍽 🛜) An old building right by Tánjiāng River in Chìkǎn has been turned into a pleasant backpacker hostel by a bicycle club. The dearest private rooms are given a rustic-China styling in another building. You can rent one of the 100-plus bikes for a full day of sightseeing with provided maps for ¥50 to ¥80. Free laundry use. Bus 6 terminates nearby.

Pan Tower Hotel
HOTEL $$

(潭江半岛酒店, Tánjiāng Bàndǎo Jiǔdiàn; ☎ 0750 233 3333; www.pantower.com; 2 Zhongyin Lu, 中银路2号; r ¥700-1700; ❉ @) *The* place to stay in Kāipíng. It's on an islet on the Tánjiāng River and only accessible by taxi (¥15 from Chángshā bus station, five minutes away). Offers discounts of 40% to 60%.

🍴 Eating

Zhōnghuá Dōnglù
CHINESE $

(中华东路; claypots ¥11-15; ◷ 11am-8pm) A short walk east of central Chìkǎn are over half a dozen stalls serving Kāipíng's speciality *bāozǎifàn* (包仔饭): rice and meat or eel cooked directly in individual claypots, making for a distinctive crispy rice skin inside – and good street theatre. Ingredients are on display too so point at what you fancy. From Chìkǎn bus terminus it's two stops on bus 6.

LĬNGNÁN CULTURE

Lǐngnán (岭南) culture is an important part of Cantonese culture and it manifests itself most notably in food, art and architecture, and Cantonese opera. Culturally Lǐngnán was a hybrid and a late bloomer that often went on to reverse-influence the rest of the country. Its development was also fuelled by the ideas of the revolution to end feudalism. Boundaries between refined and pedestrian are relaxed and there's an open-mindedness towards modernity.

Place

Lǐngnán, literally South of the Ranges, refers to the region to the south of the five mountain ranges that separate the Yangzi River (central China) from the Pearl River (southern China). Traditionally, Lǐngnán encompassed several provinces, but today it's become almost synonymous with Guǎngdōng.

People

The term Lǐngnán was traditionally used by men of letters on the Yangzi side as a polite reference to the boonies, where 'mountains were tall and emperors out of sight', as a Chinese saying goes. These northerners regarded their southern cousins as less robust (physically and morally), more romantic and less civilised. But being far-flung had its benefits. Lǐngnán offered refuge to people not tolerated by the Middle Kingdom; and played host in various diasporas in Chinese history to migrants from the north, such as the Hakkas in Méizhōu. This also explains why some Cantonese words are closer in pronunciation to the ancient speech of the Chinese.

Lǐngnán School of Painting (1900–50)

The Lǐngnán painters were an influential lot who ushered in a national movement in art in the first half of the 20th century.

Traditionally, Chinese painters were literati well versed in calligraphy, poetry and Confucian classics. These scholar-artists would later become imperial bureaucrats, and as they were often stationed somewhere far away from home, they expressed their nostalgia by recreating the landscapes of their childhood villages from memory.

The founding masters of the Lǐngnán School of Painting, however, studied abroad, where they were exposed to Japanese and European art. China, during the Qing dynasty, was being carved up by Western powers. Sharing the ideals of the revolutionaries, these artists devoted themselves to a revolution in art by combining traditional techniques with elements of Western and Japanese realist painting.

The New National Painting, as it came to be called, featured a bolder use of colours, more realism and a stronger sense of perspective – a style that was more accessible to the citizenry of China's new republic than the literati painting of the past.

You can see Lǐngnán paintings at the Guǎngdōng Museum of Art (p560) and Memorial Hall of the Lǐngnán School of Painting (p560).

Lǐngnán Architecture

The Lǐngnán school of architecture is one of three major schools of modern Chinese architecture, alongside the Běijīng and Shànghǎi schools. It was founded in the 1950s, though earlier structures exhibiting a distinctive local style had existed since the late Ming dynasty (1600s). The features of the Lǐngnán school are lucidity, openness and an organic incorporation of nature into built environments.

ANCIENT

Examples of this style of architecture include schools, ancestral halls and temples of the Ming and Qing dynasties. The Chen Clan Ancestral Hall (p560) in Guǎngzhōu and Zǔmiào in Fóshān are prime illustrations of this style.

Vernacular Lǐngnán-style houses are more decorative than their austere northern cousins. The 'wok-handle' houses (锅耳屋; guō'ěr wū) in Líchá village near Zhàoqìng have distinctive wok-handle-shaped roofs that also serve to prevent the spread of fire. You'll also see in Líchá village bas-relief sculpting and paintings (浮雕彩画; fúdiāo cǎihuà), intricate and colourful, above windows or doors, portraying classical tales, birds, flowers and landscapes.

MODERN

Excellent examples of this style of architecture, appearing in the late Qing dynasty, are the Xīguān houses on Ēnning Road (p561) in Guǎngzhōu, with their grey bricks and stained-glass windows. These windows were products of the marriage between Manchurian windows (满洲窗; *mǎnzhōu chuāng*), simple contraptions consisting of paper overlaid with wood, and coloured glass introduced to Guǎngzhōu by Westerners. It's said that when a foreign merchant presented the empress dowager with a bead of coloured glass, she was so dazzled by its beauty that she reciprocated with a pearl. Pànxī Restaurant in Guǎngzhōu and Yúyìn Mountain Villa have Manchurian windows embedded with coloured glass.

Another example of modern Lǐngnán architecture is shophouses with arcades or *qílóu* (骑楼) on the ground floor, a style that evolved from the arcades of southern Europe. You'll see them in Cháyáng Old Town in Méizhōu and Chìkǎn in Kāipíng.

CONTEMPORARY

The garden-restaurants and garden-hotels that proliferated between the 1950s and 1990s are examples of contemporary architecture. Guǎngzhōu's Garden Hotel, Guǎngzhōu Restaurant and Pànxī Restaurant all contain elaborate indoor gardens complete with trees and waterfalls, and make use of glass to blur the boundary between built and natural environments.

These indoor Edens were fashioned after the private Lǐngnán-style gardens of wealthy families, such as Liáng Garden in Fóshān, which together with the imperial gardens of Peking and the scholars' gardens of Jiāngnán, constituted the three main types of Chinese gardens. Thanks to these architects, the privilege of having gardens in the interior was now available to all.

Cantonese Opera

Cantonese opera is a regional form of Chinese opera that evolved from theatrical forms of the north and neighbouring regions. Like Peking opera, it involves music, singing, martial arts, acrobatics and acting. There's elaborate face painting, glamorous period costumes and, for some of the roles, high-pitched falsetto singing. But compared to its northern cousin, it tends to feature more scholars than warriors in its tales of courtship and romance.

You don't have to understand or even like Cantonese opera to appreciate it as an important aspect of Cantonese culture – there's no shortage of related attractions, such as Bāhé Academy and Luányú Táng in Guǎngzhōu, a festival, and a props speciality shop in Cháozhōu.

If you do decide to catch a show at Culture Park in Guǎngzhōu, those exotic strains could years later become the key that unlocks your memory of your travels in China.

Cantonese Cuisine

There's a saying 'Good food is in Guǎngzhōu' (食在广州; *shí zài Guǎngzhōu*). Regional bias aside, Cantonese food is very good. The most influential of the eight major regional cuisines of China, it's known for complex cooking methods, an obsession with freshness and the use of a wide range of ingredients.

Many Cantonese dishes depend on quick cooking over high heat – these require skills (versus patience over a stew) that are less common in other regional cuisines. Cantonese chefs are also masters at making new techniques sizzle in their language. Dishes such as sweet-and-sour pork, crab shell au gratin and tempura-style prawns show an open-mindedness to foreign ideas.

When it comes to haute cuisine, even northern cooks would acknowledge the superiority of their Cantonese colleagues in making the best of expensive items such as abalone. Also, much of the costliest marine life to grace the Cantonese table, such as deep-sea fish and large prawns, simply doesn't grow in inland rivers.

Cháojiāngchūn Restaurant CHINESE $$
(潮江春酒楼, Cháojiāngchūn Jiǔlóu; ☑ 0750 221 9963; 114 Guangming Lu; mains ¥28-98; ☑ 11am-10.30pm) This excellent restaurant serves the local speciality – braised wild-grown goose (狗仔鹅; gǒuzǎi é). The steamed tofu with shredded taro and ground pork (肉碎芋丝蒸豆腐; ròusù yùsī zhēng dòufu) and salt-baked chicken (手撕鸡; shǒusījī) are also delicious.

ℹ Getting There & Away

Kāipíng has two bus stations (www.bus.ko.com. cn) that are linked by local buses 7 and 13: **Yìcí bus station** (义祠汽车总站, Yìcí Zǒngzhàn; ☑ 0750 221 3126; Mucun Lu) and **Chángshā bus station** (长沙汽车站, Chángshā Qìchēzhàn; ☑ 0750 233 3442; Xijao Lu). Both run frequent services:

Guǎngzhōu (Fāngcūn bus station) ¥58, 2½ hours, every 40 minutes (6.30am to 7pm)

Hong Kong HK$160, four hours, three to four times daily

Shēnzhèn ¥92, three to 3½ hours, every 45 minutes (7.30am to 7.30pm)

Zhūhǎi ¥50 to ¥70, 2½ to three hours, every 40 minutes (7am to 7.43pm)

ℹ Getting Around

From both Yìcí and Chángshā bus stations, local buses (from ¥4) go to Chìkǎn and some of the diāolóu. But as the diāolóu are scattered over several counties, your best bet is to hire a taxi for the day. A full day costs around ¥600, but you can negotiate. Otherwise hiring a bike is possible to see a handful of diāolóu.

Yángjiāng 阳江

☑ 0662 / POP 2.4 MILLION

Yángjiāng is a city on the southwestern coast of Guǎngdōng. While downtown Yángjiāng is unexciting, picturesque Hǎilíng Island (海陵岛; Hǎilíng Dǎo), located 50km or an hour's drive away, is home to the Maritime Silk Road Museum and some of the finest beaches in the province.

◉ Sights

Shílǐ Yíntān BEACH
(十里银滩; Hǎilíng Island, Jiāngchéng District, 江城区海陵岛南面; ☑ 6.30am-6pm summer, 8am-7pm rest of year) Literally '10 miles of silver beach', this is the most beautiful and the longest stretch of coastline in the area. On the southern shore of Hǎilíng Island, it's where you'll find the Maritime Silk Road Museum of Guǎngdōng.

Maritime Silk Road Museum of Guǎngdōng MUSEUM
(广东海上丝绸之路博物馆, Guǎngdōng Hǎishàng Sīchóu Zhīlù Bówùguǎn; ☑ 0662 368 1111; www.msrmuseum.com; ¥80, English audio guide free; ☑ 9am-5pm, closed 1st & 2nd Mar & Nov) Sitting right on Shílǐ Yíntān (十里银滩) beach, this museum was purpose-built to house an 800-year-old Song dynasty shipwreck that was wholly salvaged near the island. The remains of the 30m-long merchant vessel (Nanhai No 1; 南海一号), and much of the

---

KĀIPÍNG'S BIZARRE TOWERS

Scattered across Kāipíng's 20km periphery are diāolóu – multistorey watchtowers and fortified residences displaying a flamboyant mix of European, Chinese and Moorish architectural styles. The majority were built in the early 20th century by some of the villagers who made a fortune working as coolies overseas. They brought home fanciful architectural ideas they'd seen in real life and on postcards, and built the towers as fortresses to protect their families from bandits, flooding and Japanese troops.

The oldest diāolóu were communal watchtowers built by several families in a village. Each family was allocated a room within the citadel, where all its male members would go to spend the night to avoid being kidnapped by bandits. These narrow towers had sturdy walls, iron gates and ports for defence and observation. The youngest diāolóu were also watchtowers, but ones equipped with searchlight and alarm. They are located at the entrances to villages.

More than 60% of diāolóu, however, combined residential functions with defence. Constructed by a single family, they were spacious and featured a mix of decorative motifs. As the builders had no exposure to European architectural traditions, they took liberties with proportions, resulting in outlandish buildings that seem to have leapt out of an American folk-art painting or a Miyazaki animation.

These structures sustain a towerlike form for the first few floors, then, like stoic folk who have not forgotten to dream, let loose a riot of arches and balustrades, Egyptian columns, domes, cupolas, corner turrets, Chinese gables and Grecian urns.

70,000 pieces of merchandise on board, now rest in a sealed glass tank. The displays are supplemented by temporary exhibitions of treasures from dynastic China.

🛏 Sleeping & Eating

If money is not an issue, stay on Hǎilíng Island – in the up-and-coming resort area near the museum or in lively Zhápō (闸坡) resort town. Downtown Yángjiāng, though, has the cheapest sleeping options.

Zhápō on Hǎilíng Island has plenty of seafood restaurants that are all quite similar. Pick what you want from the tanks, agree on prices, and it'll be cooked for you. Generally, seafood items cost ¥30 to ¥230 per 500g/1 catty (斤; jīn); nonseafood dishes are between ¥20 and ¥90. Most eateries pay drivers commission for bringing customers – it's better to choose a restaurant yourself.

7 Days Inn   HOTEL $
(7天连锁酒店, Qītiān Liánsuǒ Jiǔdiàn; ☑ 0662 321 7888; www.7daysinn.cn; 37 Dongfeng Erlu, 东风二路37号; r ¥127-187; ❄🛜) Located in Yángjiāng, this place has cheerful rooms.

Jīnhǎilì Hotel   HOTEL $$
(金海利大酒店, Jīnhǎilì Dàjiǔdiàn; ☑ 0662 389 6688; fax 0662 389 5599; 23 Haibin Lu, Zhápō Town, 闸坡市海滨路23号; r ¥265-320) This affordable option in the upmarket Zhápō area has a gloomy lobby but big, decent rooms (it's a designated host for government officials). In July and August, prices go up by 30% on Fridays and double on Saturdays.

Hǎilíng Crowne Plaza   HOTEL $$$
(海陵岛皇冠假日酒店, Hǎilíngdǎo Huángguān Jiàrì Jiǔdiàn; ☑ 0662 386 8888; www.ihg.com/crowneplaza; Shílǐ Silver Beach, 十里银滩; ¥2628-3800; 🅿❄@🛜🏊) The most luxurious place to stay in Yángjiāng offers 313 top-notch rooms, its own stretch of beach, a spa, swimming pools, barbecues and child-minding services. In July and August, expect to share all of the above with hordes of moneyed local tourists who follow rules of etiquette that may be different from yours. Packages and off-season discounts are often available.

❶ Getting There & Away

Yángjiāng's **main bus station** (阳江汽车客运总站, Yángjiāng Qìchē Kèyùn Zǒngzhàn; ☑ 0662 316 9999; Xiping Beilu) has direct services to the following:

Fóshān ¥98, three hours, six daily (8.30am to 4.50pm)

Guǎngzhōu ¥70 to ¥95, 3½ hours, frequent (6.05am to 7.20pm)

Hong Kong ¥170 to ¥260, six hours, four daily (8am to 5pm)

Shēnzhèn ¥120, four to five hours, 14 daily (8am to 8.30pm)

Zhūhǎi ¥90, 3½ to four hours, frequent (8am to 7.30pm)

Yángjiāng's **No 2 bus station** (阳江二运汽车站, Yángjiāng Èryùn Qìchēzhàn; ☑ 0662 342 9168, 666 Shiwan Beilu) has direct services to the following:

Guǎngzhōu ¥85, three hours, frequent (6.10am to 7pm)

Kāipíng ¥40, two hours, five daily (8.20am to 4.40pm)

Shēnzhèn ¥135, four hours, 11 daily (7.40am to 8.30pm)

Kāipíng's Yìcí bus station has two buses daily (12.55pm and 5.15pm) to Yángjiāng's main bus station and six (from 8.45am to 4.10pm) to its No 2 station (¥40).

❶ Getting Around

Local buses run every 20 minutes to Zhápō from No 2 station (¥13, one hour, 6.30am to 9pm) and the main station (¥13 to ¥20, one hour, 6am to 9.30pm).

Zhápō and the museum area on Hǎilíng Island are connected by pedicabs (¥10 to ¥15, 10 minutes). A taxi from downtown Yángjiāng to the Maritime Silk Road Museum of Guǎngdong costs ¥100 (one hour).

Zhàoqìng   肇庆

☑ 0758 / POP 3.9 MILLION

Bordered by lakes and limestone formations, the leisurely town of Zhàoqìng in western Guǎngdōng province was where Jesuit Mateo Ricci first set foot in China in 1583.

◉ Sights

Seven Star Crags Park   PARK
(七星岩公园, Qīxīng Yán Gōngyuán; ☑ 0758 230 2838; ¥78; ⊙8am-5.30pm) The landscape of limestone hills, grottoes and willow-graced lakes in this massive, busy park is beautiful, so it's a pity the authorities try so hard – the caves are illuminated like nightclubs and boat rides cost extra (¥15 to ¥60). The easiest way to navigate between sights is to use the battery-operated carts (¥15 to ¥30 per person). If you just want a quick jaunt, it's possible to walk around the lake without entering (or paying).

Zhàoqìng

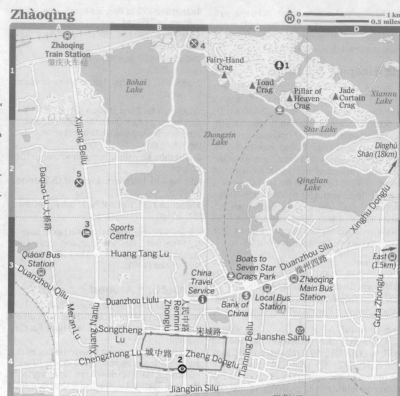

Zhàoqìng

◎ Sights
1 Seven Star Crags Park........................C1
2 Zhàoqìng City Walls............................B4

🛌 Sleeping
3 Shānshuǐ Trends Hotel A3

✕ Eating
4 Bōhǎilóu B1
5 Kuàihuólín Restaurant A2

Zhàoqìng City Walls　　　HISTORIC SITE
(古城, Gǔ Chéng) Zhàoqìng's city walls were
built during several periods – the lowest part with large mud bricks are Song
dynasty; above that is Ming; then a Qing
extension featuring smaller bricks. Anything
above that was built yesterday. Interestingly,
there are alleyways and dwellings at the top.
The **River View Tower** and **Cloud-Draped
Tower** here are only open for dignitaries.

🛌 Sleeping & Eating

For around ¥180, you can bed down at one
of the lower-midrange hotels near the **boats
to Seven Star Crags Park**, which is also
near the main bus station.

If you're hankering for local delicacies
such as sticky rice dumplings (裹蒸粽;
guǒzhēngzòng) filled with chestnuts and
egg yolk, head to **Bōhǎilóu** (波海楼; 📞 0758
230 2708; Xinghu Xilu, 星湖西路; dim sum ¥6-32;
🕙 11.30am-1.30pm & 5.30-7.30pm).

Shānshuǐ Trends Hotel　　BUSINESS HOTEL $$
(山水时尚酒店, Shānshuǐ Shíshàng Jiǔdiàn;
📞 0758 285 9999; 36 Xijiang Beilu, 西江北路36
号; d & tw ¥178-318, tr from ¥338, ste from ¥438;
🌐✳@🖐) A decent option for the price and
location, if you don't mind slightly thin walls
(pray for a quiet neighbour) and small TV
screens. There are more than 200 rooms
in this hotel that's adjacent to a shopping
centre.

Kuàihuolín Restaurant   CANTONESE $

(快活林食家, Kuàihuolín Shíjiā; ☑ 0758 285 1332; Xijiang Beilu, next to fruit market, 西江北路, 水果市场侧; mains ¥20-40; ☻ 11am-2.30pm & 5pm-2am) If you're hankering for seafood, this restaurant near a fruit market will overwhelm with its options. It's wildly popular and, at peak times, can get slightly chaotic. But the food is great. Try the broiled shrimp (白灼沙虾; *báizhuó shāxiā*; ¥24) and the fish soup with tofu and parsley (芫荽豆腐黄骨鱼汤; *yánqian dòufu huánggǔyú tāng*; ¥37). Chinese picture menu.

ℹ Information

Bank of China (中国银行, Zhōngguó Yínháng; Duanzhou Wulu; ☻ 9am-5pm Mon-Sat)

China Post (中国邮政, Zhōngguó Yóuzhèng; Jianshe Sanlu; ☻ 9am-8pm)

China Travel Service (CTS, 中国旅行社, Zhōngguó Lǚxíngshè; ☑ 0758 226 8090; Duanzhou Wulu; ☻ 8am-9pm)

ℹ Getting There & Away

The **main bus station** (肇庆汽车客运总站, Zhàoqìng Qìchē Kèyùn Zǒngzhàn; ☑ 0758 223 5173; Duanzhou Silu) has frequent services to the following:

Guǎngzhōu ¥55, 1½ hours, frequent (6.30am to 9.30pm)

Shēnzhèn ¥100, three hours, frequent (7.30am to 7.30pm)

Zhūhǎi ¥100, four hours, 13 daily (7.40am to 6.30pm)

The **east bus station** (肇庆城东客运站, Zhàoqìng Chèngdōng Kèyùnzhàn; ☑ 0758 271 8474; Duanzhou Sanlu), around 1.5km east of the main bus station, has services to Kāipíng (¥55, 2½ hours).

The fastest train to Guǎngzhōu (¥17 to ¥28, every 30 minutes) takes two hours.

ℹ Getting Around

Bus 12 links the train station (¥2, every 10 minutes) and main bus station with the ferry pier. A taxi to the train station from the centre costs about ¥15.

Around Zhàoqìng

Dǐnghú Shān   鼎湖山

Northeast of Zhàoqìng, the 11.3-sq-km **Dǐnghú Shān Reserve** (鼎湖山自然保护区, Dǐnghúshān Zìrán Bǎohù Qū; ☑ 0758 262 2510; 21 Paifang Lu; ¥78; ☻ 8am-6pm) makes for a relaxing day trip, with great walks among lush vegetation, rare trees and roaring waterfalls.

A boat (¥35) will ferry you to a butterfly reserve on a tiny wooded island on Dǐng Lake (Dǐnghú). From there, a guide will take you on an hour long hike through a scenic forest with ponds and waterfalls, to emerge near Bǎodǐng Garden (宝鼎园; Bǎodǐng Yuán), which has the world's largest *dǐng*, a three-legged ceremonial cauldron. Battery-operated carts (¥20) are useful for navigating the reserve.

Qìngyún Vegetarian Restaurant (庆云寺斋堂, Qìngyúnsì Zhāitáng; ☑ 0758 262 1585; mains ¥38-135; ☻ 8am-2pm & 5-7pm; ✐) is an excellent but pricey eatery in the reserve that serves the famous Dǐnghú Vegetarian Dish (鼎湖上素; Dǐnghú Shàngsù; ¥68), supposedly an invention by monks around here. It also does an exceptional sweet-and-sour pork (糖醋咕噜肉; *tángcù gūlùròu*; ¥50) with fried winter melon, no less. Things to note: when servers give you tea, make sure it's regular tea (普通茶; *pǔtōngchá*; ¥3 per person) and not an exotic variety that will inflate your bill by ¥30 to ¥100; snacks left at your table also cost money.

Most people visit Dǐnghú Shān as a day trip and stay in Zhàoqìng. Bus 21 (¥2) goes to Dǐnghú Shān from the local bus station in Zhàoqìng (Map p578) on Duanzhou Silu.

Bāguà Villages   八卦村

Two villages, exceptional for their shape and feng shui, make great excursions from Zhàoqìng. These '*bāguà* villages' (*bāguà cūn*) are designed according to *bāguà*, an octagon-shaped Taoist symbol with eight trigrams representing different phases in life.

Around 15km southeast of downtown Zhàoqìng, **Xiǎngǎng village** (蚬岗村, Xiǎngǎng Cūn), founded in the Ming dynasty, is a large and lively *bāguà* village, and has a market at its entrance. Its 16 ancestral halls, some opulent, only open on the first and 15th days of the lunar month. Board bus 308 (¥11, one hour) at Qiáoxī bus station (Map p578) in Zhàoqìng to get here.

At 700-year-old **Lìchá village** (黎槎村, Lìchá Cūn; ¥25; ☻ 8.15am-5.30pm), 21km east of Zhàoqìng, houses, many with wok-handle roofs and bas-relief sculptures, radiate from a taichi (a symbol of yin and yang) on a central terrace, turning the village into a maze. Most residents have emigrated to Australia; only the elders remain. Bus 315 (¥11, 40 minutes) leaves for Lìchá behind Qiáoxī bus station (Map p578) in Zhàoqìng every 15 minutes.

Qīngyuǎn 清远

☑ 0763 / POP 3.7 MILLION

The industrial town of Qīngyuǎn is where to set off for a scenic jaunt down the Běijiāng River (北江). The secluded temple in Fēilái and the monastery in Fēixiá are the main attractions. Four-hour cruises (¥380 to ¥600 for the whole boat, depending on size) leave from Qīngyuǎn's Wǔyī dock (五一码头; Wǔyī Mǎtóu).

The admission fee to the monastery at Fēixiá (飞霞; ¥50; ⊙ 7.30am-5.30pm), 4km upstream from Fēilái, includes an eight-minute ride (every 15 minutes) to the Taoist relics uphill. Cángxiá Ancient Cave (藏霞古洞; c 1863) is a maze of whispering shadows, abandoned courtyards and crumbling alleys connected by arboured paths. Further up, there is a pagoda; further down, a nunnery.

Cruise along the Běijiāng River (北江) from Qīngyuǎn's Wǔyī dock (五一码头; Wǔyī Mǎtóu), heading past ancient pagodas to the Buddhist Fēilái Temple (飞来寺, Fēilái Sì; ¥15; ⊙ 7.30am-5pm). Though it has been around for more than 1400 years, the complex was destroyed by a landslide in 1997 and subsequently rebuilt. The mountain-top pavilion offers terrific views of the river gorge below.

Most people do Qīngyuǎn boat tours as a day trip from Guǎngzhōu but if you get stuck, there are budget hotels (from ¥120) a block or two back from the docks.

ℹ Getting There & Around

To visit Fēilái and Fēixiá on a day trip from Guǎngzhōu, catch one of the 10 high-speed trains from Guǎngzhōu South railway station that stop in Qīngyuǎn (¥25 to ¥40, 30 minutes).

Buses run every 25 minutes from Guǎngzhōu's long-distance bus stations (¥37 to ¥42, 70 to 80 minutes, 6.30am to 9pm).

It's a 15-minute walk from Qīngyuǎn station to Qīngyuǎn's Wǔyī dock. Turn right as you leave the station.

Nánlǐng National Forest Park 南岭国家森林公园

☑ 0751 / POP 2000

Lying 285km north of Guǎngzhōu, the Nánlǐng (南岭; Southern Mountains) ranges stretch from Guǎngxī to Jiāngxī provinces, separating the Pearl River from the Yangzi River. Home to the only ancient forests in the province, the range is a reserve for old-growth blue pines, a species unique to this part of Guǎngdōng.

◉ Sights & Activities

Come here with water and your walking boots. There are four trails, most of which can be completed in under three hours.

The entrance to Nánlǐng National Forest Park (南岭国家森林公园, Nánlǐng Guójiā Sēnlín Gōngyuán; 327 Xian Dao, Rǔyuán Yao Autonomous Region, 乳源瑶族自治区县道327号; ¥80; ⊙ 6am-6pm) is at the southern end of the village of Wǔzhǐshān (五指山), which is small enough to cover on foot. Farmers nearby do their weekly shopping and stock clearance at Wǔzhǐshān's lively Sunday market. Staying in Orange House here will give you access to the park the next day. Just get your ticket and receipt stamped at the hotel.

From Wǔzhǐshān it's 6km to the start of the trails to Pùbù Chángláng waterfalls and Water Valley, and another 6km to Little Yellow Mountain. The best way of getting around is to hire a car from Wǔzhǐshān. For between ¥350 and ¥500 you can hire one for the whole day. The driver can drop you at one end of the trail and wait for you at the other. A one-way trip to the lower entrance of the trail to Little Yellow Mountain costs ¥120.

Water Valley HIKING
(亲水谷, Qīnshuǐgǔ) The easiest of the four walks through Nánlǐng National Forest Park, this 6km trail follows a stream and leads you through the steep-sided gorges and crystalline pools of Water Valley.

Pùbù Chángláng HIKING
(瀑布长廊) This short but interesting 3.5km trail through Nánlǐng National Forest Park takes you past roaring waterfalls.

🛏 Sleeping & Eating

As camping inside Nánlǐng National Forest Park is prohibited, the only option is to stay in Wǔzhǐshān. There are a couple of *zhāodàisuǒ* (招待所; basic lodgings), where you can get a room from ¥90.

Brings snacks and water as the only reliable places to get food are in Wǔzhǐshān.

Orange House BOUTIQUE HOTEL $$
(橙屋, Chéngwū; ☑ 0751 523 2929; www.ctrip. com; d ¥398-498, Ranger House tr ¥198; ✳ @) A cheery boutique hotel with 32 comfortable but slightly musty rooms. The hotel also manages the air-con-free Ranger House (林舍, Línshè) behind Orange House. Discounts

of 30% to 40% online. They can arrange transport to and from the park.

Feng's Kitchen
CANTONESE $

(冯家菜, Féngjiācài; ☑138 2799 2107; mains ¥10-40; ☻7am-8.30pm) A farmer restaurant that cures its own meat and grows its own vegetables (¥10 per plate). Reservations necessary. Mr Feng can arrange for car hire of any duration.

ⓘ Getting There & Away

BUS
Sháoguān (韶关) is your gateway to Nánlǐng. Buses (¥75 to ¥95, 3½ hours) leave Guǎngzhōu's long-distance bus stations for Sháoguān's Xīhé bus station every hour (6.50am to 8.30pm).

If you miss the bus to Wúzhǐshān, catch a bus to Rǔyuán (乳源; ¥10, one hour, every 15 minutes). From Rǔyuán, three buses to Wúzhǐshān (¥10) leave at 9am, 12.45pm and 4.30pm, or you can hire a taxi (¥90).

In Wúzhǐshān, buses to Sháoguān leave at 7.30am, 12.30pm and 3.30pm.

TRAIN
High-speed trains (¥105, one hour) leave from Guǎngzhōu South railway station for Sháoguān train station (韶关高铁站, Sháoguān Gāotiězhàn). From there, board bus 22 and get off at **Xīhé bus station** (西河汽车站, Xīhé Qìchēzhàn; ☑0751 875 4176; Gongye Donglu). Buses to Wúzhǐshān (¥22, two hours) depart at 8am, 11.45am and 3.30pm.

Guǎngzhōu's main train station has trains that stop over at **Sháoguān East train station** (韶关东站, Sháoguān Dōngzhàn) (¥38, 2½ hours). Buses to Wúzhǐshān leave at 7.45am, 11.15am and 3.15pm.

Shēnzhèn
深圳

☑0755 / POP 10.6 MILLION

One of China's wealthiest cities and a Special Economic Zone (SEZ), Shēnzhèn draws a mix of business people, investors and migrant workers to its golden gates. It's a popular, easy day trip from Hong Kong, surprising most visitors who just expect a peek at a very serious mainland China, but find a thriving club and indie-music nightlife, or squads of housewives breaking out dance moves in public squares into the evening. The myriad theme parks, which include fun miniature landmarks, also amuse, as do the quirky speciality markets where you can grab a bargain house decoration or dozen. Shēnzhèn is also a useful transport hub for other parts of China.

⊙ Sights

★OCT-LOFT
ARTS CENTRE

(华侨城创意文化园, Huáqiáochéng Chuàngyì Wénhuàyuán; ☑0755 2691 1976; Enping Jie, Huáqiáochéng, 南山区华侨城恩平街; ☻10am-5.30pm; ⓂQiáochéngdōng, exit A) The sprawling OCT-LOFT complex, converted from fashionably austere communist-era factories, is one of the best places to see contemporary art in Shēnzhèn, and makes for a wonderful (if ever-more commercial) browse-as-you-stroll experience. Large exhibition spaces and private galleries – many closed on Mondays – are complemented by chilled cafes (not to mention the ubiquitous Starbucks), restaurants with exposed ventilation ducts, quirky fashion boutiques, a gem of a bookstore, and the obligatory 'lifestyle' outlets.

Shēnzhèn Museum
MUSEUM

(深圳博物馆新馆, Shēnzhèn Bówùguǎn Xīnguǎn; ☑0755 8812 5800; www.shenzhenmuseum.com.cn; East Gate, Block A, Citizens' Centre, Fuzhong Sanlu, Fútián District; ☻10am-6pm Tue-Sun; ⓂLine 4, Shìmín Zhōngxīn, exit B) FREE This hulking museum provides a solid introduction to Shēnzhèn's short yet dynamic history of social transformation, both before and after the implementation of Deng Xiaoping's policies of reform. Highlights include propaganda art popular in the 1940s and the colourful scale models in the folk culture hall.

OCT Art & Design Gallery
GALLERY

(华美术馆, Huá Měishùguǎn; ☑0755 3399 3111; www.oct-and.com; 9009 Shennan Dadao, 深南大道9009号; adult/child ¥15/8; ☻10am-5.30pm Tue-Sun; ⓂHuáqiáochéng, exit C) The bare interiors of this former warehouse are filled with the works of excellent mainland and international graphic designers. Exhibits change frequently. It's a glass-encased steel structure adjacent to Hé Xiāngníng Art Gallery.

Window of the World
AMUSEMENT PARK

(世界之窗, Shìjiè Zhīchuāng; ☑0755 2660 8000; www.szwwco.com; 9037 Shennan Dadao, 深南大道9037号; adult/child under 12yr ¥180/90; ☻9am-10.30pm; 🚇; ⓡ90 or 245 from Shēnzhèn Bay Port, ⓂShìjiè Zhīchuāng, exit J) Just a few minutes' walk from the OCT Art & Design Gallery is a series of dated-but-fun theme parks that is always packed with snap-happy Chinese tourists. Window of the World sports a collection of scale replicas of famous world monuments. Foreigners being misidentified as part of the exhibits is not unheard of. Not all replicas are lit up at night, so come before sunset if you must see everything.

🛏 Sleeping

★ Shēnzhèn Loft Youth Hostel   HOSTEL $

(深圳侨城旅友国际青年旅舍, Shēnzhèn Qiáo-chéng Lǚyǒu Guójì Qīngnián Lǚshè; ☑0755 8609 5773; www.yhachina.com; 7 Xiangshan Dongjie, OCT-LOFT, Huáqiáochéng, Nánshān District, 南山区，华侨城香山东街7号; dm/d/ste from ¥70/220/410; ⊜✳@🛜; M Qiáochéngdōng, exit A) Located in a tranquil part of OCT-LOFT, near the junction of Enping Jie and Xiangshan Dongjie, this immaculate YHA hostel has over 50 private rooms, all with showers, and dormitory-type accommodation with shared bathrooms. The staff are well trained and helpful.

Shēnzhèn Vision
Fashion Hotel   BOUTIQUE HOTEL $$

(深圳视界风尚酒店, Shēnzhèn Shìjiè Fēngshàng Jiǔdiàn; ☑0755 2558 2888; www.visionfashionhotel. com; 5018 Shennan Donglu, 深南东路5018号; d ¥488-1888; ✳@🛜; M Grand Theatre, exit B) In-side a theatre complex is this boutique hotel featuring eclectic designs in its rooms. Some are chic, some bizarre. Its prime location and quiet environment make it a very good choice. Discounts of 50% to 70% are available.

Shangri-La   HOTEL $$$

(香格里拉大酒店, Xiānggélǐlā Dàjiǔdiàn; ☑0755 8233 0888; www.shangri-la.com/shenzhen; 1002 Jianshe Lu, 建设路1002号; d ¥1700-2010, ste ¥3500; P🛜✲) This classic, luxury hotel, on a corner next to Luóhú train station, is one of the best places to stay in Luóhú District. Rooms are spacious and sparkling, and there is a full-sized outdoor pool. Rates are nearly half-price on its website.

🍴 Eating

★ Bollywood Cafe   SOUTH INDIAN $

(宝莱坞印度餐厅, Bǎoláiwù Yìndù Cāntīng; ☑0755 8222 0370; 3rd fl, 2055 Renmin Nanlu, 人民南路2055-3号; mains ¥45-58; ⊙10.30am-3pm & 5.30-11.30pm; ✳🛜✎; M Guómào) One of the top restaurants for international food in Guǎngdōng – definitely the best Indian. The South Indian flavours have kick in the Kedai chicken or flaky naan. A steady flow of In-dian families and businessmen to the white-tableclothed tables gives a nod to the authen-ticity. English spoken by the Indian owners and staff. Look for yellow steps at street level.

Mǐ Mǐ Jiā   CHINESE $

(米米嘉, ☑0755 8222 9839; 3015 Dongmen Nanlu, 东门南路3015号; dishes ¥4-13; ⊙10am-9pm; M Guómào) You might get flashbacks to school dinners, but this casual restaurant is great for trying out dishes. Small plates such as whole baked fish with ginger slivers, stewed pork or chilli tofu are hot, fresh and on display, making for easy selection – no menu needed. It's opposite a 7 Days Inn on a small street off the larger Dongmen Nanlu of the same name..

Yúnláijū Vegetarian   VEGETARIAN $

(云来居素食馆(东门店), Yúnláijū Sùshíguǎn; ☑0755 8238 3253; 4th fl, Rénmín Běilù Dōngmén Xīngànxiàn, 人民北路东门新干线4层; dishes ¥13-48; ⊙10am-10pm; ✎; M Lǎojiē) Vegetarian or not, the interesting dishes in this calm, large restaurant will please many. Try skewers of mock meat, hand-pulled noodles in a rich tomato and mushroom broth, or corn tea. The iPad menus have scant English but detailed photos. It's on the 4th floor above the Dong-men food court and, ironically, McDonald's.

Laurel   DIM SUM, CANTONESE $

(丹桂轩, Dānguìxuān; ☑0755 8232 3668; Renmin Nanlu, 人民南路; dim sum ¥9-28, dishes ¥40-180; ⊙7am-11pm; M Guómào) An excellent, mod-ern, dim-sum restaurant on the 5th floor of Luóhú Commercial City. Tables are a little close together, but the environment is pleas-ant and service is warm.

Dōngméndīng   MARKET $

(东门町美食街, Dōngméndīng Měishíjiè; ☑0755 8884 6001; Renmin Beilu, 人民北路; ⊙9am-9pm; M Lǎojiē) If you want to try street food that's cleaned up and smartened up, this is the place. Three undercover strips have elabo-rate snacks such as crab claws, spicy cori-ander and yellow bean crêpes, hand-pulled noodles, squid skewers and everything else you might have seen on the street, but with seating. Look for the faux-ancient gates.

West Lake Spring   ZHEJIANG $$

(西湖春天, Xīhú Chūntiān; ☑0755 8211 6988; 3019 Sungang Donglu, 2nd-3rd fl, Parkway Tower; dishes ¥21-260; ⊙10am-11pm; 🚌18, get off at Xīhú Bīnguǎn) This Hángzhōu restaurant gets the thumbs-up from locals. Signature dishes such as Lóngjǐng Xiārén (龙井虾仁; stir-fried freshwater shrimp with Longjing tea leaves; ¥88) and Sòngsǎo Yúgēng (宋嫂鱼羹; yellow croaker soup; small/large ¥48/58) are delicately flavoured like they should be. There's no English menu but the Chinese menu has pictures.

Phoenix House   DIM SUM, CANTONESE $$

(凤凰楼, Fènghuánglóu; ☑0755 8207 6338, 0755 8207 6688; 4002 Huaqiang Beilu, East Wing, Pavil-ion Hotel, 华强北路4002号; lunch ¥60-80, dinner

Shēnzhèn

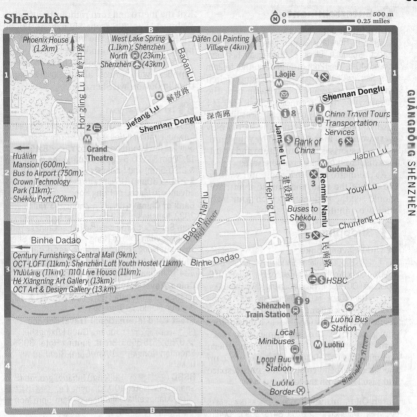

GUĂNGDŌNG SHĒNZHÈN

Map labels:

Phoenix House (1.2km)
West Lake Spring (1.1km); Shēnzhèn North (23km); Shēnzhèn (43km)
Dàfēn Oil Painting Village (4km)
Hóngling Lu 红岭中路
Bāoān Lu
Jiefang Lu 解放路
Lǎojiē
Shennan Donglu
Shennan Donglu 深南东路
China Travel Tours Transportation Services
2
Grand Theatre
Jiànshè Lu
Bank of China
Jiabin Lu
Huálián Mansion (600m); Bus to Airport (750m); Crown Technology Park (11km); Shékǒu Port (20km)
Guómào
Renmin Nanlu
Youyi Lu
Héping Lu
Bàoàn Nanlu
Bus River
Buses to Shékǒu
Chunfeng Lu
人民南路
Binhe Dadao
5
Century Furnishings Central Mall (9km); OCT-LOFT (11km); Shēnzhèn Loft Youth Hostel (11km); Yídùtáng (11km); 0110 Live House (11km); Hé Xiāngníng Art Gallery (13km); OCT Art & Design Gallery (13km)
Binhe Dadao
HSBC
Shēnzhèn Train Station
Luóhú Bus Station
Local Minibuses
Luóhú
Local Bus Station
Luóhú Border
Shēnzhèn River

¥100-350; ⊙7.30am-11pm; Ⓜ Huáqiánglù, exit A) One of the best Cantonese restaurants in town, but expect noisy waits for 30 minutes or more after 11.30am. Some of the dim sum can be ordered by the piece – good when you're dining alone.

🍷 Drinking & Nightlife

There is plenty of glitz in town but most clubs in tall buildings are just flashes in the pan and it can be difficult to find a place to drink that isn't just a show of wealth. The OCT-LOFT arts complex is the best bet for small places with personality.

Yídùtáng   BAR
(一渡堂; ☑0755 8610 6046; Enping Lu, Block F3, OCT-LOFT, Huáqiáochéng, Nánshān District; ⊙11.30am-2am; Ⓜ Qiáochéngdōng, exit A) International and local indie bands play almost every night after 10pm at this warehouse-turned-bohemian-haunt in OCT-LOFT. It's a pleasant place with large glass panes, a

Shēnzhèn

🛏 **Sleeping**
1 Shangri-La D3
2 Shēnzhèn Vision Fashion Hotel A2

🍽 **Eating**
3 Bollywood Cafe D2
4 Dōngméndīng..D1
5 Laurel D3
6 Mǐ Mǐ Jiā D2
Yúnláijū Vegetarian.....................(see 4)

ℹ **Information**
7 China Travel Service D1
8 Great Land International Travel
    Service..C1
Internet Cafe................................(see 7)
9 Tourist Office..C3

soaring ceiling (from which chandeliers hang) and velvet armchairs placed next to brick walls. During the day it's an up-market cafe.

☆ Entertainment

Brown Sugar Jar   LIVE MUSIC
(红糖罐子, Hóngtáng Guànzi; Tairan Jiulu, Fútián District, ground fl, Block 2, Huángguān Kējìyuán; tickets ¥40-120; ☺2pm-midnight Sun-Thu, to 2am Fri & Sat; M Chēgōngmiào, exit C) Sandwiched between a garage and a hair salon near the entrance of Crown Technology Park (皇冠科技園; Huángguān Kējìyuán), this loft-like bar is where local and foreign indie bands play every weekend from 9pm. Run by young musicians, it sports eclectic furniture and paintings displayed on bare concrete walls.

At the metro exit, turn right and walk to the end of the road, then make a left. You should see the park entrance on your right after two minutes.

🛍 Shopping

★ Old Heaven Books   BOOKS
(旧天堂书店, Jiùtiāntáng Shūdiàn; ☏0755 8614 8090; oldheavenbooks@gmail.com; Room 120, Block A5, OCT-LOFT, Huáqiáochéng, Nánshān District; ☺11am-10pm; M Qiáochéngdōng, exit A) This bookstore specialising in cultural and academic titles, that also doubles as a music store (vinyls anyone?). Gigs sometimes take place in the adjoining cafe. Located in the northern section of the OCT-LOFT arts complex, it's up the street perpendicular to the music space B10 Live House, on the left-hand side.

Dàfēn Oil Painting Village   ARTS & CRAFTS
(大芬村, Dàfēncūn; ☏0755 8473 2633; Dàfēn, Buji, Lónggǎng District; ☺9am-6pm; M Dàfēncūn, exit A1) A real eye-opener: 600 studios-cum-stores, churning out thousands of copies of Rembrandt, Renoir and Picasso paintings every week, and some original work, in laneways for all to see. Prices start from ¥200.

INDIE MUSIC FESTIVALS

Shēnzhèn's indie music scene is rocking, and there's irrefutable proof – China's largest indie music events, **Strawberry Music Festival** (草莓音乐节, Cǎoméi Yīnyuè Jié; www.modernsky.com) and **Midi Music Festival** (谜笛音乐节, Mídí Yīnyuè Jié; www.midifestival.com), have had Shēnzhèn editions since 2013–14. Both events feature the strongest bands from China, Taiwan and Hong Kong performing for three days. Midi takes place on New Year's Eve/New Year's Day and Strawberry is usually in May. Check their websites for details.

Exit the metro and turn right until just after Walmart. Bus 306 from Shēnzhèn's Luóhú station takes you to the village in about an hour. A taxi costs around ¥80.

It's also a good place to stock up on art supplies, with prices about 50% cheaper than in downtown Shēnzhèn.

ℹ Information

You can buy a five-day Shēnzhèn-only visa (¥168 for most nationalities, ¥469 for Brits; cash only) at the **Luóhú border** (Lo Wu; ☺8.45am-12.30pm & 2.30-5.30pm), **Huánggǎng** (9am-1pm & 2.30-5pm) and **Shékǒu** (☺8.45am-12.30pm & 2.30-5.30pm). US citizens must buy a visa in advance in Macau or Hong Kong.

Bank of China (中国银行, Zhōngguó Yínháng; 2022 Jianshe Lu; ☺9am-5.30pm Mon-Fri, to 4pm Sat & Sun) You can use either Chinese rénmínbì or yuán ('¥') or Hong Kong dollars in Shēnzhèn but Hong Kong dollars are less desired.

China Post (中国邮政, Zhōngguó Yóuzhèng; 3040 Shennan Donglu; ☺8am-8pm)

China Travel Service (CTS, 中国旅行社, Zhōngguó Lǚxíngshè; ☏0755 8228 7644; 3023 Renmin Nanlu; ☺9am-6pm)

Great Land International Travel Service (巨邦国际旅行社, Jùbāng Guójì Lǚxíngshè; ☏0755 2515 5555; 3rd fl, Jùntíng Hotel, 3085 Shennan Donglu; ☺10am-6pm) Good for air tickets.

HSBC (汇丰银行, Huìfēng Yínháng; ground fl, Shangri-La Hotel, 1002 Jianshe Lu; 香格里拉大酒店, Xiānggélǐlā Dàjiǔdiàn; ☺9am-5pm Mon-Fri, 10am-6pm Sat)

Internet Cafe (网吧; 3023 Renmin Nanlu; per hr ¥5; ☺10am-10pm) Adjacent to the CTS.

Public Security Bureau (PSB, 公安局, Gōng'ānjú; ☏0755 2446 3999; 4018 Jiefang Lu; ☺24hr)

Tourist Office (深圳旅遊咨詢中心; ☏0755 8232 3045; ground fl, Shēnzhèn train station, east exit; ☺9am-6pm) Free and reasonably detailed maps available on request. There's another branch at Fútián Port.

ℹ Getting There & Away

Shēnzhèn Airport (深圳宝安国际机场, Shēnzhèn Bǎoān Guójì Jīchǎng; ☏0755 2345 6789; http://eng.szairport.com) Has flights to most major destinations around China.

BOAT

Shékǒu Port (☏0755 2669 1213) has services to Hong Kong (take the **bus** to the port):

Hong Kong International Airport ¥260, 30 minutes, 14 daily (7.45am to 9pm)

Hong Kong–Macau Ferry Terminal, Central ¥120, one hour, six daily (7.45am, 10.15am, 11.45am, 2.15pm, 4.45pm and 7.15pm)

To Macau:

Macau Maritime Ferry Terminal ¥190, one hour, 11 daily (8.15am to 7.30pm)

Taipa Temporary Ferry Terminal ¥190, one hour, seven daily (9.30am to 7pm)

To Zhūhǎi:

Fúyǒng ferry terminal (福永码头, Fúyǒng Mǎtóu; ☑ 0755 2345 5388) at Shēnzhèn Airport runs ferries to Hong Kong and Macau:

Jiǔzhōu Port ¥150, one hour, every 30 minutes (7.30am to 8.30pm)

Macau Maritime Ferry Terminal ¥222, 80 minutes, seven daily (8.15am to 6pm)

Sky Pier, Hong Kong International Airport ¥295, 40 minutes, four daily (8.35am, 11.30am, 3.30pm and 6.30pm)

BUS

Regular intercity buses leave from **Luóhú bus station** (罗湖汽车站, Luóhú Qìchēzhàn; ☑ 0755 8232 1670).

Cháozhōu ¥150, 5½ hours, three daily (8.30am, 1.40pm and 8pm)

Guǎngzhōu ¥50 to ¥70, two hours, every 20 minutes (7am to 10pm)

Shàntóu ¥130 to ¥170, four to five hours, every 30 minutes (7.20am to 9.40pm)

Xiàmén ¥220 to ¥240, eight hours, six daily (9.30am, 11am, 7.30pm, 8.30pm, 9.30pm and 9.50pm)

For Hong Kong, book a long-distance bus with **China Travel Tours Transportation Services** (CTS; ☑ 0755 2764 9803; www.hkctsbus.com).

TRAIN

Services to Guǎngzhōu and Hong Kong leave from Luóhú train station to Guǎngzhōu East station (¥80, 1½ hours); and from Shēnzhèn North station (深圳北站; Shēnzhèn Běizhàn) in Lónghuá to Guǎngzhōu South station (¥80, 40 minutes).

The Mass Transit Railway (MTR) links Shēnzhèn with Hong Kong.

❶ Getting Around

Shēnzhèn has a good public transport network, with five metro lines (¥2 to ¥11), plus the Airport Express (Line 11). Transit passes (深圳通; Shēnzhèn Tōng) can be bought in metro stations and are good for all services except taxis. Bus and minibus fares cost ¥2 to ¥10.

Shēnzhèn's airport, 36km west of the city, is connected to Luóhú by metro line 1 (¥9, 70 minutes). Metro line 11 is due to open in June 2016, connecting the airport with the city centre.

Airport bus departures are from **Huálián Mansion** (华联大厦, Huálián Dàshà; Shennan Zhonglu; 🚌 101, Ⓜ Kexue Guan, exit B2) and cost ¥20 (40 minutes, every 15 minutes, 5am to 9pm), and Luóhú train station in Luóhú (¥20, one hour, every 15 minutes, 7am to 10pm).

Buses leave from the **local bus station** (Map p583) west of the train station.

Flag fall for **taxis** (☑ 0755 8322 8000) costs ¥12.50 (¥16 from 11pm to 6am), with a ¥4 fuel surcharge and ¥2.40 for every additional kilometre. A taxi from the airport costs ¥180 to ¥200.

Around Shēnzhèn

★ Guǎnlán Original Printmaking Base   VILLAGE

(观澜版画原创产业基地, Guǎnlán Bǎnhuà Yuánchuàng Chǎnyè Jīde; ☑ 0755 2978 2510; www.guanlanprints.com/en; Dàshuǐtián, Niúhú, Bǎo'ān District; 🚌 312, M258, M285, M288, M338, M339 to Guǎnlán Printmaking Base stop, Ⓜ Qīnghú, then bus M338, 🚌 DG50, D768, D769, L4 to Guǎnlán Jiēdàobàn Zhàn, 观澜街道办站) FREE At this 300-year-old village, rows of quaint black-and-white houses exuding a functional elegance unique to Hakka architecture are occupied by the workshops and galleries of printmaking artists from China and overseas. The village, with its tree-lined paths and lotus ponds, is open all day, but the galleries keep different hours. The journey from downtown Shēnzhèn takes about 1½ hours. Check the website for exhibitions, events and detailed directions.

Dàpéng Fortress   VILLAGE

(大鹏所城, Dàpéng Suǒchéng; ☑ 0755 8431 5618; Dàpéng Town, Lónggǎng District, 龙岗区大鹏市; adult/student & senior ¥20/10; ⊙ 10am-6pm) This walled town and lively village built 600 years ago lies on Shēnzhèn's eastern edge and was a key battle site in the Opium Wars of the 19th century. Stately mansions, fortress gates and ornate temples from the Ming and Qing dynasties are the main attractions. Having the place to yourself with very few visitors is another.

Board bus 360 at Yínhú bus station or near China Regency Hotel on Sungang Lu. The trip takes about 90 minutes. At Dàpéng bus station (大鹏总站; Dàpéng Zǒngzhàn) change to bus 966. A taxi from Luóhú costs ¥190.

Zhūhǎi   珠海

☑ 0756 / POP 1.6 MILLION

Zhūhǎi is close enough to Macau for a day trip without any maniacal driving. Never too hot or too frosty, Zhūhǎi is the just-right popular Chinese getaway – especially in summer – with plenty of seaside glitz. Yet it remains laid-back, and what helps it really shine is the natural beauty of its gardens and an attractive, relatively clean port.

⊙ Sights

Lover's Road STREET
(情侣路, Qínglǚ Lù) This balmy promenade starts at Gǒngběi (拱北), at the border with Macau, and sweeps north for 28km along the coast, passing some of Zhūhǎi's most coveted real estate. The section near Tángjiā Public Garden is the most beautiful. There are kite and bicycle rentals along the way, and snack booths at night.

🛏 Sleeping & Eating

Zhūhǎi Holiday Resort
Youth Hostel HOSTEL $
(国际青年学生旅馆, Guójì Qīngnián Xuéshēng Lǚguǎn; ☑ 0756 333 3838; www.zhuhai-holitel.com; 9 Shihua Donglu, 石花东路9号; dm ¥65) Hidden away inside the Zhūhǎi Holiday Resort in Jídà, this hostel has two eight-bed dorms. Take bus 99 to get there.

Jǐnjiāng Inn INN $$
(锦江之星, Jǐnjiāng Zhīxīng; ☑ 0756 221 9899; 1058 Fenghuang Nanlu, 凤凰南路1058号; r ¥245-450; ❋ 🛜) The best of several branches in Zhūhǎi, this one is 50m from Lover's Road, and 300m from Wānzǎishā Sq (湾仔沙广场; Wānzǐshā Guǎngchǎng). Rooms are bright and clean though those facing the street can be a tad noisy. Not all staff members speak English, but they're helpful and courteous.

The Garden INTERNATIONAL $
(健康园餐饮, Jiànkāngyuán Cānyǐn; ☑ 0756 830 5190; www.thegarden.com.cn; Unit 3115, New Century Plaza, 376 Changsheng Lu, 昌盛路376号新世纪广场3115号; mains ¥38-60; ⊙ 10.30am-11pm; ❋ 🛜) If you're craving a break from Chinese food, the Garden might please you with some international bistro favourites, such as Greek salad, good steaks and salmon, couscous and a nice selection of wines.

May Flower Restaurant CANTONESE $$
(皇朝五月花大酒楼, Huángcháo Wǔyuèhuā Jiǔjiā; ☑ 0756 818 1111; 3 Rìdōng Guǎngchǎng, 日东广场3号), 49 Qinglu Zhonglu; mains ¥32-400; ⊙ 7.30am-11pm) Where the middle classes go when they have important guests, this veteran of Zhūhǎi's fine-dining scene serves up elaborately prepared seafood dishes, claypot goodies, and other Cantonese deliciousness, including, of course, dim sum.

☆ Entertainment

Zhūhǎi Live Bar LIVE MUSIC
(珠海现场酒吧, Zhūhǎi Xiànchǎng Jiǔbà; ☑ 137 0232 9064, 0756 3352 580; 45 Jidayuan Linlu, 吉大园林路45号; ⊙ 7pm-late) A dive bar that hosts local and overseas gigs nightly from 9pm within its graffitied walls. The music can be pop, rock and everything in between. It's across the road from Xìnhǎi Building (信海大厦; Xìnhǎi Dàxià), between Píngān Insurance Building (平安保险; Píngān Bǎoxiǎn) and Chūnxīng Restaurant (春兴酒家; Chūnxīng Jiǔjiā). Get here by bus 23 or 43.

ⓘ Information

Visas (¥168 for most nationalities, ¥469 for Brits) valid for three days are available at the border (8.30am to 12.15pm, 1pm to 6.15pm, and 7pm to 10.30pm). US citizens must buy a visa in advance in Macau or Hong Kong.

Bank of China (中国银行, Zhōngguó Yínháng; cnr Yingbin Nanlu & Yuehai Donglu; ⊙ 9am-5.30pm Mon-Fri, to 4pm Sat & Sun)
Bank of China (中国银行, Zhōngguó Yínháng; Lianhua Lu; ⊙ 9am-5.30pm Mon-Fri, to 4pm Sat & Sun)
China Travel Service (CTS, 中国旅行社, Zhōngguó Lǚxíngshè; ☑ 0756 889 9228; 2nd fl, Overseas Chinese Hotel, 2016 Yingbin Nanlu; ⊙ 8am-8pm)
Public Security Bureau (PSB, 公安局, Gōng'ānjú; ☑ 0756 888 5277; 1038 Yingbin Nanlu)

ⓘ Getting There & Away

AIR
Zhūhǎi Airport (☑ 0756 777 8888; www.zhairport.com) Serves various destinations in China, including Běijīng (¥1380), Shànghǎi (¥860) and Chéngdū (¥890).

BOAT
Hong Kong–bound jetcats leave from **Jiǔzhōu Port** (九州港, Jiǔzhōu Gǎng; ☑ 0756 333 3359):
China Ferry Terminal, Kowloon ¥175, 70 minutes, six daily (8am to 5pm)
Hong Kong International Airport ¥290, one hour, four daily (9.30am, 12.40pm, 3.30pm and 6.30pm)
Hong Kong–Macau Ferry Terminal, Central ¥175, 70 minutes, nine daily (9am to 9.30pm)

Ferries leave Jiǔzhōu Port for Shēnzhèn's port of Shékǒu (¥150, one hour, every 30 minutes, 8am to 9.30pm); ferries leave Shékǒu for Jiǔzhōu every 30 minutes (7.30am to 9.30pm).

Local buses 3, 4, 12, 23, 25 and 26 go to Jiǔzhōu Port.

BUS
Gǒngběi long-distance bus station (拱北长途汽车站, Gǒngběi Chángtú Qìchēzhàn; ☑ 0756 888 5218; Lianhua Lu) at **Gǒngběi Port** runs regular buses between 6am and 9.30pm:
Fóshān ¥60 to ¥75, three hours, 10 daily
Guǎngzhōu ¥60 to ¥75, 2½ hours, frequent

Zhūhǎi

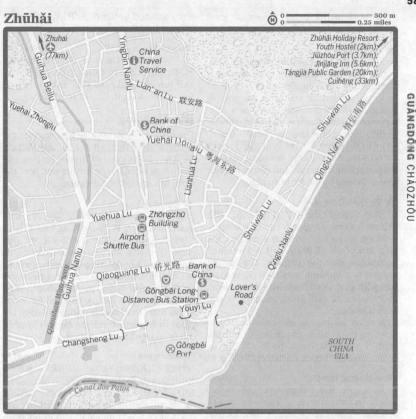

Kāipíng ¥40 to ¥75, three hours, four daily

Shàntóu ¥180, 6½ hours, two daily

Shēnzhèn ¥80, three hours, every 30 minutes

Zhàoqìng ¥100, 4½ hours, 10 daily

LIGHT RAIL

Guǎngzhōu–Zhūhǎi Light Rail (广珠城轨; ☑ 0756 9510 5105) Serves Zhūhǎi North station (珠海北站) and Guǎngzhōu South station (¥36, 70 minutes). Zhūhǎi North station can be reached by buses K1, 3A and 65.

ⓘ Getting Around

Zhūhǎi's airport, 43km southwest of the centre, runs an airport shuttle bus (¥25, 50 to 70 minutes) to the city centre (every 30 minutes, 6am to 9.30pm) from Jiǔzhōu Port and the **Zhōngzhū Building** (中珠大厦, Zhōngzhū Dàshà; cnr Yuehua Lu & Yingbin Nanlu). A taxi to the centre costs about ¥150.

Flag fall for taxis is ¥10 for the first 3km, then ¥0.60 for each additional 250m.

Cháozhōu 潮州

☑ 0768 / POP 2.7 MILLION

Charming Cháozhōu was once a thriving trading and cultural hub in southern China, rivalling Guǎngzhōu. Today, it still preserves its distinct dialect, cuisine and opera. Cháozhōu is best appreciated at a leisurely pace, so do consider spending a night here.

Paifang Jie (牌坊街; Street of Memorial Arches), running 1948m from north to south in the old quarter, has signage to the main sights and is a good place to orient yourself. It's made up of Taiping Lu (太平路; 1742m) and Dongmen Jie (东门街; 206m).

ⓞ Sights

Sights abound in Cháozhōu but admission charges can add up. Before you go sightseeing, buy a combo ticket (¥80) from Jīnlóng Travel Service (p590), located across Huangcheng Nanlu from the southern entrance of

Street of Memorial Arches. Tickets are good for two days and cover six or seven sights.

★ **West Lake** PARK
(西湖, Xīhú; ☎ 0768 222 0731; Huancheng Xilu, 环城西路; ⏰ 8am-11pm) FREE The moat of ancient Cháozhōu is a lake inside a park well loved by locals. Around the lake are a few notable buildings. **Hánbì Building** served as a military office during anti-warlord expeditions in 1925. Sitting on a knoll is **Phoenix Building** (凤楼, Fènglóu; ⏰ 6am-6pm) FREE, with its bird-like shape, iron moongate, gourd-shaped ceiling openings, and quirky interior spaces formed by the fowl's anatomy.

★ **Guǎngjǐ Bridge** BRIDGE
(广济桥, Guǎngjǐ Qiáo; ☎ 0768 222 2683; ¥50; ⏰ 10am-5.30pm) Originally a 12th-century pontoon bridge with 86 boats straddling the Hán River, Guǎngjǐ Bridge suffered repeated destruction over the centuries. The current version is a brilliant, faux-ancient passage-way with 18 wooden boats hooked up afresh every morning and 24 stone piers topped with pagodas.

A ticket allows you one crossing. If you want to come back, remember to tell the staff 'I want to come back' (我要回来; 'wǒyào huílai') before leaving the bridge.

Jǐluè Huáng Temple TEMPLE
(己略黄公祠, Jǐluè Huánggōngcí; ☎ 0768 225 1318; 2 Tie Xiang, Yi'an Lu, 义安路铁巷2号; ¥10; ⏰ 8.30am-5pm) The highlights here are the ancient Cháozhōu woodcarvings decorating the walls and thresholds – most single pieces took a decade to complete. The art form is famous for its rich and subtle details and exquisite craftsmanship. Emerging 1000 years ago, it flourished during the Qing dynasty, which was also when this small temple (1887) was built. It's a short walk from Paifang Jie. No English explanations.

Kāiyuán Temple BUDDHIST SITE
(开元寺, Kāiyuán Sì; Kaiyuan Lu, 开元路; ⏰ 6am-5.30pm) FREE Built in AD 738, Cháozhōu's most famous temple has old bodhi trees and an embarrassment of statues, including one of a 1000-arm Guanyin. Roof tiles can be daubed by a calligraphist (by donation) with your wishes, to be later installed in the complex ceiling (at least for a while).

Hánwén Temple TEMPLE
(韩文公祠, Hánwéngōng Cí; ¥20; ⏰ 8am-5.30pm) On the east bank of the Hán, this is the oldest and best-preserved temple dedicated to the Tang dynasty philosopher Han Yu, who

was banished to 'far-flung' Guǎngdōng for his anti-Buddhist views.

Cháozhōu City Wall HISTORIC SITE
(潮州古府城墙, Cháozhōu Gǔfǔ Chéngqiáng; ⏰ 24hr) FREE The remains of the ancient city wall run alongside and back from the river. You can walk on the top of most sections.

🛏 Sleeping

The most convenient place to stay to see the sights is near Guǎngjǐ Bridge and Paifang Jie. The glut of lower-midrange options and chain hotels tend to be further out, near the main bus station or city centre.

★ **Zàiyáng Inn** HOTEL $
(载阳客栈, Zàiyáng Kèzhàn; ☎ 0768 223 1272; www.czdafudi.com; 15 Zaiyang Xiang, Taiping Lu, 太平路, 载阳巷15号; s ¥128, d ¥168-368; ☎) This classy Qing-style inn with graceful courtyards and antique woodcarvings is *the* place to stay in Cháozhōu. Rooms are small, but clean and far from street noise, though wooden-gate-style doors might feel too exposed for some. Prices more than double during holidays. Located in an alley off Paifang Jie; ¥10 by pedicab from the main bus station.

Fǔchéng Inn HOTEL $
(府城客栈, Fǔchéng Kèzhàn; ☎ 0768 222 8585; 9 Fensi Houxiang, Taiping Lu, 太平路, 分司后巷9号; s/d ¥128/208; ❀ ☎) Located in an old building inside an alley off Paifang Jie, Fǔchéng Inn offers decent accommodation and opportunities to meet fellow travellers. Rooms on the ground floor can be noisy. It's ¥10 by pedicab from the main bus station (汽车总站).

🍴 Eating

Food is generally good in Cháozhōu. On Paifang Jie you'll find China's best beef balls with noodles (牛丸粉; *niúwán fěn*) and oyster omelette (蚝烙; *háolào*), though prices can be a little more local just a block away. There are also a number of trendy cafes, all offering free wi-fi.

★ **Liánhuā Vegetarian** CHINESE $
(莲华素食府, Liánhuā Sùshífǔ; ☎ 0768 223 8033; 9 Kaiyuan Sq, 2nd fl, 开元广场9号2楼; mains ¥18-48; ⏰ 11am-2pm & 5-8pm; ✍) An excellent vegetarian restaurant opposite Kāiyuán Temple. The menu also features Cháozhōu specialities, including some delightful desserts.

★ **Zhèng's Private Kitchen** CHINESE $$
(郑厨私房菜, Zhèngchú Sīfángcài; ☎ 0768 399 1310; 1 Shangdong Pinglu, 上东平路1号; per

Cháozhōu

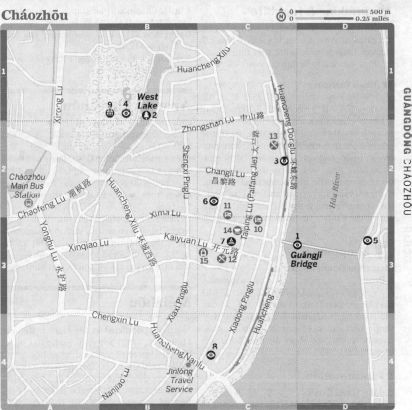

Cháozhōu

⊙ Top Sights
1 Guǎngjǐ Bridge	D3
2 West Lake	B1

⊙ Sights
3 Cháozhōu City Wall	C2
4 Hánbì Building	B1
5 Hánwén Temple	D3
6 Jīluè Huáng Temple	C2
7 Kāiyuán Temple	C3
8 Paifang Jie	C4
9 Phoenix Building	B1

🛏 Sleeping
10 Fúchéng Inn	C3
11 Zàiyáng Inn	C2

✕ Eating
12 Liánhuā Vegetarian	C3
13 Zhèng's Private Kitchen	C2

🍸 Drinking & Nightlife
14 Pǐnyǔ Teahouse	C3

🛍 Shopping
15 Cháozhōu Opera Costumes & Props	C3

person ¥50-100; ⊙ lunch & dinner) A private kitchen that whips up impressive Cháozhōu-style seafood dishes. Ask a Mandarin- or Cantonese-speaking friend to call and book at least a day in advance. Also tell them your budget per person; and if you don't want shark's fin, a speciality here, say so too. It's in the first lane opposite Shàngshuǐmén Gate Tower (上水门城楼; Shàngshuǐmén Chénglóu). Walk down the lane until you see the stairs.

♀ Drinking & Nightlife

By night you can try your luck with a few of the cafes catering to tourists on or just off Paifang Jie, but options are very limited after 9pm, especially during the week.

★ **Pínyǔ Teahouse**   TEAHOUSE
(品羽茶居, Pínyǔ Chájū; ☑133 7673 9198; 15 Xima Lu, 西马路15号; per hr ¥30; ⊙10am-10pm) A lovely place for a tea experience with an English speaker in a minimalist, modern-meets-ancient Chinese teahouse. You pay for a taste test of bottomless different Cháozhōu teas and learn the difference between exquisite brews, such as Oolong winter versus spring tea, and how to pour tea. If you're lucky, the owner might play one of the Chinese musical instruments on display.

🛍 Shopping

Cháozhōu Opera Costumes
& Props   GIFTS & SOUVENIRS
(吉元戏剧歌舞用品; ☑0768 222 6041; 12 Kaiyuan Lu; ⊙9am-10.30pm) Diagonally across the road from Kāiyuán Temple is this tiny shop that makes gowns, headdresses, swords, sedans and shoes for the Cháozhōu opera stage.

ℹ Information

Jīnlóng Travel Service (金龙旅行社, Jīnlóng Lǚxíngshè; ☑0768 222 1437; 39 Huangcheng Nanlu; ⊙9am-5.30pm) Before you go sightseeing in Cháozhōu, buy a combo ticket (¥80) from Jīnlóng Travel Service, located across Huangcheng Nanlu from the southern entrance of Paifang Jie.

ℹ Getting There & Away

Services from Cháozhōu's **main bus station** (潮州汽车总站, Cháozhōu qìchē zǒngzhàn; ☑0768 220 2552; 2 Chaofeng Lu):

Guǎngzhōu ¥110 to ¥170, 5½ hours, eight daily (8am to 11.55pm)

Méizhōu ¥58, two hours, two daily (8.30am and 3pm)

Raópíng ¥19, one hour, 13 daily (6.30am to 6.30pm)

Shànghǎi ¥389, 20 hours, one daily (2.45pm)

Shàntóu ¥14, one hour, 13 daily (7am to 6.40pm)

Shēnzhèn ¥120 to ¥140, five hours, five daily (8am to 11pm)

Xiàmén ¥100, 3½ hours, four daily (7am to 2.20pm)

Zhūhǎi ¥140, 9½ hours, two daily (8.30am and 9.10pm)

A taxi to Cháozhōu's train station, 8km west of the centre, costs about ¥35. Services:

Guǎngzhōu ¥91 to ¥167, seven hours, two daily (8.41am and 12.45pm)

Shàntóu ¥9, 35 minutes, three daily (7.45am, 3.30pm and 6.53pm)

Around Cháozhōu

China's largest octagonal Hakka earthen house, **Dàoyùnlóu** (道韵楼; ¥20; ⊙8.30am-5.30pm) is located in Raópíng (饶平), 53km from Cháozhōu. Some 600 villagers once resided in this stunning complex built in 1587; now only 100 remain. Ascend to the upper floors from unit 18 to admire the views and frescoes.

Buses to Raópíng (¥20, one hour) leave from Cháozhōu main bus station. Change to a bus to the village of Sānráo (三饶; ¥13), another 50km away. From there, motor-rickshaws will take you to Dàoyùnlóu (¥5, 10 minutes).

Méizhōu   梅州

☑0753 / POP 5 MILLION

Méizhōu, populated by the Hakka (Kèjiā in Mandarin; 客家) people, is home to China's largest cluster of 'coiled dragon houses' or *wéilóngwū* (围龙屋). Specific to the Hakka, these are dwellings arranged in a horseshoe shape evocative of a dragon napping at the foot of a mountain. You'll also see *tǔlóu* (roundhouses) dotting the fields like mysterious flying saucers, and a jumble of other architectural treasures.

👁 Sights

★ **Xuán Villa**   HISTORIC BUILDING
(旋庐, Xuánlú; 115 Dahua Lu, 大华路115号) Foreboding and beautiful Xuán Villa was built in 1936 by a wealthy Malaysian Chinese who was a member of a secret society tied to Sun Yatsen. Parts of the building doubled up as an air-raid shelter. If the owners let you in, you'll see crumbling but elegant staircases and sweeping balconies with views of tea fields.

Méizhōu Thousand Buddha Pagoda TEMPLE
(梅州千佛塔寺, Méizhōu Qiān Fó Tǎsì; ☑0753 229 0362; www.qianfotasi.com; Jinshao Jie, 梅江区金山街道东岩莲花山顶; ¥8; ⊙8am-5pm; 🚌20 to terminus, or 6 to Gangbei) Cast in AD 965, there are indeed 1000 buddha statues (250 on each side) of varying sizes on the iron pagoda that sits on a 36m-high tower. The complex itself surprises with each turn as it

takes you through an ascending journey of white, columned temples, statues built into a faux cliff, long, open corridors, bridges and finally the towering pagoda and (hazy) views across Méizhōu. A taxi here costs about ¥35.

Hakka Park   PARK, MUSEUM
(客家公园, Kèjiā Gōngyuán; Dongshan Dadao, 东山大道; ⊙Xiānqín Bldg 8.30am-5.10pm, Dáfū Bldg 8.30-11.30am & 2-5.30pm; 📷1, 6) Pebbled paths and a willow-fringed pond make this small park on the north bank of the Méijiāng River a delight to stroll around in. There are a couple of interesting 1930s buildings – Xiānqín Building (先勤楼; Xiānqínlóu), a courtyard-style Hakka house; and the East–West hybrid Dáfū Building (達大楼; Dáfūlóu), which evokes a pseudo-Western train terminal drawn by Japanese animator Miyazaki.

The **Hakka Museum** (客家博物馆, Kèjiā Bówùguǎn; 📞0753 2258 830; ⊙9am-5pm Tue-Sun; 📷1, 6) FREE here offers a good warm-up to the culture of Hakkaland with model 'coiled dragon houses'.

If you're interested, there's a part two of the museum outside the park. From the back entrance/exit near the stream, go straight ahead for 50m, turn right and you'll see the small, old houses of the **Huang Zunxian Memorial** (赏遵宪纪念馆, Huáng Zūnxiàn Jìniànguǎn, 客家公园, Kèjiā Gōngyuán; ⊙9am-5pm) FREE, the former home of famous Qing dynasty era Méizhōu writer-philosopher Huang Zunxian (1848–1905). The house is hands on, allowing you to sit in the Lingnán-style courtyard table under a small painted pagoda and ponder civilisation (文明; wénmíng), a word that Huang was the first to use in Chinese. There are no English explanations but personal items, such as the lovely gold and red bed, speak for themselves. He is credited with convincing the emperor to allow overseas Chinese to return to China, previously punishable by torture!

Nánkǒu Village   VILLAGE
(南口, Nánkǒu) This quiet village about 16km west of Méizhōu is where you'll see fine examples of wéilóngwū (围龙屋) dwellings nestled between paddy fields and the hills, like dragons in repose. If you make your way to the back of Dōnghuā Lú (東華盧) and Déxīn Táng (德馨堂), you'll see rooms arranged in a semi-circle on an undulating slope, like the coiled body of a dragon. Another of the old houses, Nánhuá Yòulú (南华又庐) charges an admission of ¥11.

Bus 9 from Méizhōu's local bus terminal and buses to Xīngníng (兴宁; ¥12, every 20 minutes) from Méizhōu's main bus station go to Nánkǒu. Once you get off, walk 1km to the village entrance. The last bus back leaves at 4.30pm. A one-way taxi ride costs around ¥35.

Méizhōu Old Street   STREET
(梅州老街, Méizhōu Lǎojiē; Lingfeng Lu, 凌风路) Méizhōu's sleepy Old Street covers four blocks on Lingfeng Lu. There's not much to see by way of building design, but there are traditional industries that cannot be found elsewhere producing fishing implements, funereal and wedding accessories, and more. Walk through the vehicular passage in the brown building opposite Huáqiáo Dàxià (華僑大廈) at 12 Jiangbian Lu (江边路) and you'll see it.

🛏 Sleeping

Jīnjiāng Inn   HOTEL $
(锦江之星旅馆, Jīnjiāng Zhīxīng Lǚguǎn; 📞0753 218 9999; www.jinjiang inns.com; 88 Binfang Dadao, 彬芳大道88号; d ¥161-218; ❄ 🛜) Near the city centre and a short walk from the Jiāngnán bus station south of the river. Modern rooms are warm in mood and tone and come with movies on demand, strong wi-fi, large comfy beds and small but spotless bathrooms. A taxi from the train station costs ¥20.

Royal Classic Hotel   HOTEL $$
(皇家名典酒店, Huángjiā Míngdiàn Jiǔdiàn; 📞0753 867 7777; www.hjmd-hotel.com; 35 Dongmen Lu, 東門路35号; r ¥128-1278, ste ¥1888-2888) This glitzy Hong Kong–owned hotel has clean, quiet rooms, with wide, comfortable beds. Lifts can only be activated with guestroom card-keys, which makes it feel safe. The extravagant breakfast buffet (¥50 per person) in the revolving restaurant offers a good selection of local delicacies. Rates are often 30% to 50% of those posted.

🍴 Eating

The local speciality is wok-tossed Hakka noodles (腌面; yānmiàn) smothered in minced pork, resembling spaghetti bolognaise. You'll find stalls all over town dishing up the noodles from 9pm and long into the night.

★ Dàbù Handmade Noodles   NOODLES $
(大埔手工面馆, Dàbù Shǒugōng Miànguǎn; 15 Bingfang Dadao; noodles ¥5-15, soup ¥5; ⊙6.30am-2pm & 5pm-2am) This neighbourhood shop whips up al dente Hakka tossed noodles (腌面; yānmiàn) and pig-innards soup (三及第湯; sānjídì tāng). The strands also come stir-fried (炒面; chǎomiàn). Bus 4, which runs from Méizhōu train station, a 15-minute walk away, stops here. Disembark at Méiyuán Xīncūn (梅園新村). It's on your left.

Chéngdé Lóu Coiled
Dragon House Restaurant CHINESE, HAKKA $
(承德楼围龙屋酒家, Chéngdélóu Wéilóngwū Jiǔjiā; ☑ 0753 233 1315; 41 Fuqi Lu, 富奇路41号; mains ¥33-120; ⊙ 8am-8pm) From inside a maze-like 19th-century Hakka house, this atmospheric eatery serves local dishes such as salt-baked chicken (盐局鸡; *yánjú jī*; ¥58) and pork braised with preserved vegetables (梅菜扣肉; *méicài kòuròu*; ¥48). The manager speaks English. A taxi here from Méizhōu centre costs ¥18.

❶ Getting There & Away

Méizhōu's airport (梅县机场; Méixiàn Jīchǎng), 4km south of town, has flights to Guǎngzhōu (¥700, daily) and Hong Kong (¥1000, Mondays and Fridays).

Méizhōu has two bus stations and a **local bus terminal** (市公共汽车总站, Shì Gōnggòng Qìchēzhàn; cnr Meijiang Dadao & Xinzhong Lu): the **main bus station** (粤运汽车总站, Yuèyùn Qìchē Zǒngzhàn; ☑ 0753 222 2427; Meizhou Dadao), north of the river, and **Jiāngnán bus station** (江南汽车站, Jiāngnán Qìchēzhàn; ☑ 0753 226 9568; Binfang Dadao) to the south. Most buses to Méizhōu drop you off at the former.

Cháozhōu ¥78, 2½ hours, two daily (10.20am and 3pm)

Cháyáng ¥29, three daily (5.45am, 7am and 11.10am)

Guǎngzhōu ¥175 to ¥193, five hours, 15 daily (7am to 10.30pm)

Hong Kong ¥280, eight hours, two daily (7.40am and 2.40pm)

Shàntóu ¥69, 2½ hours, 13 daily (8am to 5.20pm)

Shēnzhèn ¥178 to ¥187, six hours, 10 daily (6.45am to 5pm)

Yǒngdìng ¥49, three hours, two daily (6am and 12.45pm)

The train station, south of town, has four daily trains to Guǎngzhōu (¥65 to ¥142, 5½ to seven hours, 12.12am, 8.36am, 3.25pm and 10.53pm) and two early trains to Yǒngdìng (¥19 to ¥72, two hours, 2.41am and 3.14am).

❶ Getting Around

A taxi ride into Méizhōu town centre from the airport, 4km south, costs about ¥20. Buses 3 and 11 also go into town.

Bus 6 links the airport and train station to both bus stations. Anywhere within the city by taxi should cost no more than ¥25.

Most sights are scattered in different villages, and almost inaccessible by public transport, so it makes more sense to hire a taxi for a day. Expect to pay about ¥450.

Dàbù 大埔

☑ 0753 / POP 540,000

Dàbù sits on the border with Fújiàn, in the easternmost part of Guǎngdōng, about 89km from downtown Méizhōu. It's encircled by mountains and rivers, which means beautiful natural scenery and nicely preserved old towns.

There are rooms for ¥80 and upwards with air-con on Wanxiang Dadao (畹香大道), about 240m from the bus station.

Your best bet for food are the tiny eateries on Dàbù Gourmet Street (大埔美食街, Dàbù Měishí Jiē; Huliao Tongyen Lu; ⊙ 8am-5pm). Comb it (it's only 330m) for Dàbù and Hakka snacks such as pancakes (薄饼; *báobǐng*) and bamboo-shoot dumplings (笋粄; *sǔnbǎn*).

Ruìjīn Hotel (瑞锦酒店, Ruìjīn Jiǔdiàn; ☑ 0753 518 5688; www.ruijin-hotel.com; 2nd St, Long Shan, Neihuan Xilu, 内环西路龙山二街; r ¥888-988, ste ¥1688-1988; ❉ @ 🛜 🌊) is a great place to stay, with large, plush rooms and an attractive swimming pool. The hotel is a 20-minute walk from Dàbù bus station (大埔汽車客運站; Dàbù Qìchē Kèyùn Zhàn). Turn left at the hotel entrance and walk several blocks up until you reach a T-junction, then head left and you'll see the station.

❶ Getting There & Away

Méizhōu has buses to Dàbù from **Jiāngnán bus station** every 30 minutes (¥24, one hour).

Buses head daily from Dàbù to the following:

Cháozhōu ¥67, three hours, one daily (8.10am)

Cháyáng ¥5, 30 minutes, two daily (5pm, 5.30pm)

Guǎngzhōu ¥238, 6½ hours, eight daily (7.30am, 8am, 8.40am, 9am, 1.10pm, 6.30pm, 7pm, 7.30pm)

Méizhōu ¥24, one hour, frequent

Shàntóu ¥78, three hours, one daily (7.40am)

Shēnzhèn ¥226, six hours, five daily (8.20am, 9am, 1.30pm, 2.50pm, 3.30pm)

Xiàmén ¥105, 4½ hours, one daily (6.40am)

Cháyáng Old Town 茶阳古镇

☑ 0753 / POP 55,000

People still take long siestas in lazy Cháyáng (Cháyáng Gǔzhèn), 27km from downtown Dàbù County. Its old streets (老街; *lǎojiē*) with pillared arcades are nice to lose yourself in for a couple of hours.

The weather-beaten, three-storey **Soviet Department Store Building** (百货大楼, Bǎihuò Dàlóu; Shengli Lu, 胜利路) just opposite Cháyáng Guesthouse (茶陽賓館; Cháyáng

Bīnguǎn) was built in the 1950s with Soviet funds. Patches of yellow paint still cling onto its facade, and you can make out Mao-era slogans on its red pillars. If you walk along the river, cross the bridge, go straight, turn left and walk to the end of the road, you'll see the stunning Xuán Lú (旋盧) villa.

Most just pass through Cháyáng and stay in Méizhōu, but if you get stuck, there are a few simple budget options in the south of town, and a clean business hotel at the roundabout (there's only one) on the north side with rooms for around ¥100.

There are noodle joints, snacks and even a more upmarket seafood option, but for more variety, head to Méizhōu or Cháozhōu.

Buses run from Cháyáng to Méizhōu (90 minutes) every half hour from 7.10am to 6pm.

Băihóu Old Town   百侯镇
📞 0753 / POP 30,290

Scenic Băihóu (Băihóu Zhèn) is known for its Qing dynasty buildings. These were the stately residences and public spaces of the Yang (楊) family, a family known for the number of scholars and government officials it nurtured. Băihóu literally means 'a hundred noblemen'.

Buildings with a flamboyant hybrid style tend to cluster around the southern end, while ancestral halls and village houses are in the north. Between them are winding paths, peanut vines, longan and wampi trees, and a huge lily pond.

Lack of upkeep and old age (early 18th century) means **Qínán Villa** (企南軒, Qínán Xuān) looks a bit like a princeling-turned-pauper. The stone carvings around its elegant arches and the terraces fringed with urn-shaped balusters are now overgrown with black moss and weed. The villa was built as a study with 27 rooms in the early decades of the Qing dynasty.

Inhabited by the third and fourth generations of the founder, a pharmaceutical merchant, **Zhàoqìng Hall** (肇庆堂, Zhàoqìng Táng; ¥15; ⏱ 8.30am-noon & 2-5pm) is a balmy courtyard residence (c 1914) featuring stone, wood and ceramic carvings, and stained-glass windows from Italy. The stately two-storey structure in front of it was the study quarters of the younger members of the family.

Hǎiyuán Inn is an eye-catching early-20th-century mansion combining Southeast Asian features, Western details and the attributes of a *hakka* (走马楼; zǒumǎ lóu), a two-storey residence with a wide wooden corridor that keeps the rooms safe and dry.

Although there is loads of potential for a tourist town, accommodation options here are virtually nil as most people still move on and stay in nearby Méizhōu.

There are a handful of simple places to eat in the Băihóu Tourist Area (百侯旅游区; Băihóu Lǚyóu Qū) and around the bus station (百侯客运站; Băihóu Kèyùn Zhàn), 1km north.

All southbound buses from Dàbù pass through Băihóu (¥6). Tell the driver you want to get off at Băihóu Tourist Area (百侯旅游区; Băihóu Lǚyóu Qū). From Dàbù, it's 20 minutes (11km).

Shàntóu   汕头
📞 0754 / POP 4.9 MILLION

If you like history, the industrial town of Shàntóu has a couple of interesting sights on its outskirts that can be covered on a day trip from Cháozhōu.

It is more pleasant to stay in the old town of Cháozhōu, but if you do want more than a day trip in Shàntóu, there are perfectly fine accommodation options, with chain hotels near the bus stations, starting from ¥100.

Chen Cihong Memorial Home (陈慈黉故居, Chén Cíhóng Gùjū; ¥12; ⏱ 8.30am-5.30pm) is an attractive complex built by a businessman who made his fortune in Thailand in the 19th century. He had the region's best raw materials shipped here and assembled in imaginative ways that incorporated Asian, Western and Moorish motifs. Board the northbound bus 103 from People's Square (eastern edge) in Shàntóu. The hour-long ride will cost you ¥7.

Sitting atop Tǎshān Park (塔山风景区; Tǎshānfēngjǐngqū), 25km north of Shàntóu's city centre, the **Cultural Revolution Museum** (文革博物馆, Wéngé Bówùguǎn; ¥10; ⏱ 9.30am-5.30pm) is the only museum in China that honours the victims of the Cultural Revolution. Names and inscriptions are engraved on the walls. Take eastbound bus 102 from the long-distance bus station to Tǎshān Lùkǒu (塔山路口). After the 45-minute ride, cross the road and walk 800m to the entrance, then another 3.5km uphill (take the path on the left).

Buses run from Cháozhōu to Shàntóu (¥14, one hour, 13 daily, 7am to 6.40pm). Shàntóu's main bus station and CTS bus station run buses every 30 minutes to an hour to Cháozhōu (¥17, one hour, 8.20am to 4.10pm); Guǎngzhōu (¥90 to ¥150, 5½ hours, 7am to 11pm); and Méizhōu (¥60, 2½ hours, 6am and 5pm).

Hǎinán

POP 9 MILLION

Best Places to Eat

➜ Ā Bo Pó (p598)

➜ Hǎikǒu Qílóu Snack Street (p598)

➜ Sānyà Market #1 (p607)

➜ Sea Story (p604)

➜ Bǎnqiáo Road Seafood Market (p598)

Best Places to Sleep

➜ Hǎikǒu Banana Youth Hostel (p597)

➜ Narada Resort (p602)

➜ Resort Intime (p607)

Why Go?

China's largest tropical island boasts all the balmy weather, coconut palms and gold-sand beaches you could ask for. Down at Sānyà it's see-and-be-seen on the boardwalks or escape altogether at some of Asia's top luxury resorts. Thatched huts and banana pancakes haven't popped up anywhere yet, but there's a hint of hipness coming from the east coast beachside towns, and the budding surf scene is helping to spread the gospel of chill out.

Money is pouring into Hǎinán (海南) these days to ramp up the luxury quotient. You can cruise on the high-speed rail, but cycling is still the better way to get around. When you've had enough of a lathering on the coast, the cool central highlands are an ideal place to be on two wheels. The good roads, knockout mountain views, and concentration of Li and Miao, the island's first settlers, give the region an appealing distinction from the lowlands.

When to Go
Sānyà (Dàdōnghǎi)

Apr–Oct Low season is hot, hot, hot, but ideal for hotel bargains.

Nov–Mar Cool dry months are perfect for cycling under the blue South China sky.

Nov–Jan Winter winds blow in the island's best surfing season.

History

Until the economic boom of the last 30 years, Hǎinán had been a backwater of the Chinese empire since the first Han settlements appeared on the coast almost 2000 years ago. Largely ignored by a series of dynasties, Hǎinán was known as the 'tail of the dragon,' 'the gate of hell', and a place best used as a repository for high-profile exiles such as the poet Su Dongpo and the official Hai Rui.

More recently, China's first communist cell was formed here in the 1920s, and the island was heavily bombarded and then occupied by the Japanese during WWII. Li and Han Chinese guerrillas waged an effective campaign to harass the Japanese forces but the retaliation was brutal – the Japanese executed a third of the island's male population. Even today resentment over Japanese atrocities lingers among the younger generation.

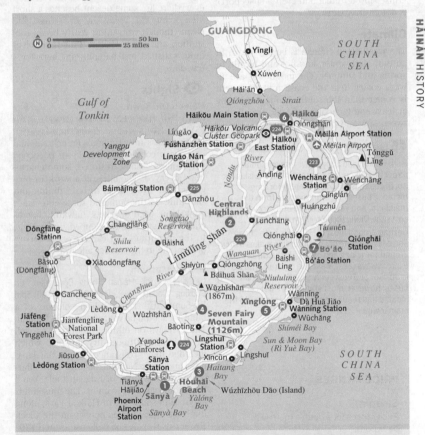

Hǎinán Highlights

❶ Sānyà (p605) Soaking up the sun, sand and cocktails at China's top beach resort.

❷ Central Highlands (p601) Cycling through the island's mountainous spine, home of the Li and Miao.

❸ Hòuhǎi Beach (p605) Surfing and chilling out at a beachside guesthouse.

❹ Seven Fairy Mountain (p601) Hiking and hot-spring soaking in the rainforest.

❺ Xīnglóng (p609) Getting a whiff of Hǎinán's unexpected coffee scene.

❻ Bǎnqiáo Road Seafood Market (p598) Bargaining for fresh local seafood in Hǎikǒu.

❼ Bó'áo (p602) Taking in traditional villages and empty beaches.

In 1988 Hăinán was taken away from Guăngdōng and established as its own province and Special Economic Zone (SEZ). After years of fits and starts, development is now focused on turning tropical Hăinán into an 'international tourism island' by 2020. What this really means, besides developing every beach, and building more golf courses and mega-transport projects (such as a high-speed rail service around the island, a cruise-ship terminal and even a spaceport), is not entirely clear.

Climate

The weather on Hăinán is largely warm in autumn and winter, and hot and humid in spring and summer. The mountains are always cooler than the coast, and the north is cooler than the south. Hăinán is hit by at least one typhoon each year, usually between May and October.

ℹ Getting There & Around

Both Hăikŏu and Sānyà have international airports. Hăikŏu, the capital city on the island's north coast, is the point of entry for long-distance buses and trains coming from the mainland. And yes, there's no bridge: even trains cross the Qióngzhōu Strait on the ferry.

Getting around most of Hăinán is both cheap and easy. A high-speed rail service makes a loop around the island and buses ply the three main expressways (east, west and central). The train is quicker and costs only slightly more than buses; however, most stations are not centrally located and require a bus or taxi transfer to the main town.

PRICE RANGES

Sleeping

Price ranges for a double room with bathroom:

$ less than ¥200

$$ ¥200–¥600

$$$ more than ¥600

Eating

Price ranges for a main course or meal:

$ less than ¥30

$$ ¥30–¥100

$$$ more than ¥100

HĂIKŎU 海口

☏ 0898 / POP 2.2 MILLION

Hăikŏu means 'Mouth of the Sea', and while sea trade remains relatively important, the buzzing provincial capital at the northern tip of Hăikŏu is most notable for its booming construction. New and restarted projects are everywhere.

Hăikŏu doesn't have much in the way of sights, save for its restored downtown; however, there are some decent beaches a short bike or bus ride away, the air is fresh and clean (though worsening yearly because of traffic), and some visitors find themselves quite satisfied just hanging out here for a few days.

⊙ Sights

Hăikŏu Old Town   AREA

(海口老街, Hăikŏu Lǎo Jiē; Zhongshan Lu, 中山路) The streets around Zhongshan Lu are a looking glass into Hăikŏu's French colonial past, with cobblestone blocks of porticoed row houses – some restored, some charmingly decayed. Though still a work in progress, 'Old Town' aims to be a dining and shopping destination, and some cute cafes, bookshops, and markets hawking handicrafts and spices have popped up recently. In the meantime, you can see active scenes of local life in the smaller alleyways.

Hăinán Museum   MUSEUM

(海南省博物馆, Hăinán Shěng Bówùguǎn; 68 Guoxing Dadao, 国兴大道68号; ⊙9am-5pm Tue-Sun) FREE This modern colossus of a building should be your first stop in Hăinán. The displays on ethnic minorities, as well as Hăinán's 20th-century history, which included fierce resistance against the Japanese and later Nationalists, are particularly informative (and in English too!). You'll need your passport to enter. The museum is about 2km southeast of Hăikŏu Park, along the river. Bus 43 runs here from the Clock Tower bus stop. A taxi will cost around ¥30.

🏃 Activities

A few kilometres west of the city centre is a long stretch of sandy beaches, of which Holiday Beach is the nicest. Take bus 37 (¥2) and get off anywhere; alternatively, rent a bike in town.

Mission Hills Resort   HOT SPRINGS

(观澜湖, Guàn Lán Hú; 1 Mission Hills Lu, 澜湖大道1号; ¥198; ⊙1pm-midnight; 🚐) With 168 different pools, Mission Hills has – officially –

more bathing options than anywhere in the world. Making use of Hǎikǒu's natural mineral springs and perfumed with different herbs and spices, the baths are arranged 'It's a Small World' style into themes by continent. This is the place to spend one of Hǎikǒu's frequently overcast days; for hot sunny days there's a wave pool with a man-made beach. You'll need a swimsuit; towels and slippers are provided.

Tourist bus 3 leaves from Báishāmén Park for Mission Hills (¥20, 45 minutes) several times a day.

Velo China CYCLING, BICYCLE RENTAL
(☑ 189 7617 5016; www.velochina.com; Mission Hills Resort) English-speaking Frank Li arranges well researched, professional cycling tours all over Hǎinán from his bases in Hǎikǒu and Wǔzhǐshān. If you just want to cycle on your own, he can arrange that too: bicycle rentals start from ¥500 per week or ¥80 per day (depending on the type of bicycle).

🛏 Sleeping

Travellers tend to stay around Hǎikǒu Park or north of the river on Hǎidiàn Island (海甸岛; Hǎidiàn Dǎo). These are both older, less flashy neighbourhoods (especially compared with the western sections of the city), but all your life-support systems, including banks, food and travel agents, can be found here.

Unlike in the more seasonal Sānyà, prices in Hǎikǒu tend to be greatly discounted from the published rates pretty much year-round.

★ Hǎikǒu Banana Youth Hostel HOSTEL $
(海口巴纳纳国际青年旅舍, Hǎikǒu Bānànà Qīngnián Lǚshè; ☑ 0898 6628 6780; www.haikou hostel.com; 3 Dong, 6 Bieshu Liyuan Xiaoqu, 21 Renmin Dadao, 人民大道21号梨园小区6号别墅3栋; dm/s/tw/tr ¥50/98/138/168; ❉@🖼) The digs of choice for international budget travellers, the simple, friendly Banana Youth Hostel is tucked away down a quiet residential alley. Staff speak English, and amenities include laundry, internet and common areas, as well as a super-informative bulletin board and website. The on-site restaurant is a popular expat hang-out, thanks to the superb pizzas (from ¥45).

Mountain bikes for multiday trips (per day ¥30; book in advance) are available for rent. This is also a good place to meet up with fellow cyclists and get current route information.

Hǎikǒu

Hǎinán Mínháng Bīnguǎn HOTEL $$
(海南民航宾馆, Hǎinán Civil Aviation Hotel; ☑ 0898 6650 6888; www.mhbgotel.com; 9 Haixiu Donglu, 海秀东路9号; r from ¥268; ❉🖼) This hotel isn't going to win any design awards, but it's solid all around: a convenient central location with clean and comfortable rooms. Bonus: the airport shuttle starts and stops here. Also known as the 'Green Hotel'.

Golden Sea View Hotel   HOTEL $$$

(黄金海景大酒店, Huángjīn Hǎijǐng Dà Jiǔdiàn;
☑ 0898 6851 9988; www.goldenhotel.com.cn; 67
Binhai Dadao, 滨海大道67号; r incl breakfast from
¥825; P ✳ 🛜) With discounts of 40% to 50%,
rooms in this well run, three-star hotel are
priced similarly to those stuck deep in the
city. The Sea View, however, sits across from
Evergreen Park (a useful bus hub), at the
start of the beaches just to the west of town.
Rates include a breakfast buffet.

✕ Eating

Hǎikǒu is a great place to sample Hainanese
cooking. Though much of the city's street-
food scene has been, unfortunately, swept
into hawker markets following a city-wide
'clean-up' campaign, you can still find barbecue stalls lining up from around 9pm on
Haidian 2 Donglu, between Renmin Dadao
and Heping Beilu. There are several branches
of the supermarket **Carrefour** (家乐福; 18 Haifu Lu, 海府路18号; ⊘ 8am-10pm) around town.

Hǎikǒu Qílóu Snack Street   HAINAN $

(海口骑楼小街, Hǎikǒu Qílóu Xiǎo Jiē; cnr Datong
Lu & Jiefang Lu, 大同路解放路的路口; dishes
¥6-30; ⊘ 7am-11.30pm) This marvellous colonial arcade is the repository of many of the
street vendors swept off the street in the
clean-up campaign and is easily the best
place to sample local Hainanese dishes. Buy
a prepaid plastic card at the window on the
right of the entrance, then use that to pay
for your snacks (you can refund the unused
amount).

★ Ā Bo Pó   HAINAN $$

(阿卜婆; stall 5, 2nd fl, Tailong Cheng, Datong Lu, 大
同路泰龙城二楼5号铺; chicken ¥138; ⊘ 11am-
8pm) Ā Bo Pó means 'grandma' in Hainanese,
though we'd also translate it as 'best chicken
ever'. Indeed made by a 70-something grandma, the chicken here is buried in sea salt and
baked for four hours, then sealed in plastic
to pull in all the juices. Just tear into it with
your hands (plastic gloves are provided). One
bird feeds two to three people.

It's on the 2nd floor of the shopping arcade next to Hǎikǒu Qílóu Snack Street. Best
to come early before they sell out for the day.

Bǎnqiáo Road
Seafood Market   SEAFOOD, MARKET $$

(板桥路海鲜市场, Bǎnqiáo Lù Hǎixiān Shìchǎng;
Banqiao Lu, 板桥路; meals per person from ¥50;
⊘ 11am-4am) For a fresh seafood dinner with
lots of noise, smoke and toasting, head to
the hectare of tables at the Bǎnqiáo Road

Seafood Market, known island-wide. First
bargain for the raw ingredients from the
market – local oysters for ¥5 or enormous tiger prawns for ¥20 per 100g – and then have
one of the restaurants cook it up for you.

It's best to go with a group; prices average
¥50 per person (not including beer).

Banqiao Lu is about 3km south of the
city centre. A taxi to the market from downtown costs ¥15.

Red Bar   SICHUAN $$

(红吧, Hóng Bā; ☑ 0898 6856 1314; Jiǔdū Villas, 38
Guomao Lu, 九都别墅国贸路38号; dishes ¥15-
128; ⊘ 11am-midnight) This moody, lantern-lit
villa down an alley in Guómào is where
you'll find Hǎikǒu's cool kids sampling fiery
Chóngqìng-style street food (refined to yup-
pie standards). On the northwestern corner
of Guomao Lu and Yusha Lu, head down the
lane in between the Soho club and an apartment tower and look for the crowd. There's
a picture menu.

🍷 Drinking & Nightlife

Guómào is the newest downtown area, with
the flashiest nightlife. Along Hadian 5 Xilu,
in front of the south gate of Hǎinán University, you'll find bars popular with students.

Small stands selling lemon drinks and
teas are plentiful. *Liángchá* (cool tea) is a
little medicinal in taste but locals swear it
helps cool the body's fires on a hot day.

Small Cafe   CAFE

(蓝庭咖啡小馆, Lántíng Kāfēi Xiǎoguǎn;
62 Zhongshan Lu, 中山路62号; coffee ¥18;
⊘ 10am-midnight; 🛜) You have your pick of
charming cafes along Old Town's pedestrian
street, but this one gets our vote thanks to
the garden patio out back.

Drunk Bear   BAR

(百熊酒馆, Báixióng Jiǔguǎn; 11 Tea Plaza, Guomao
Beilu, 国贸北路大坤茶叶园11号; ⊘ 8pm-late)
With half a dozen local craft brews on tap,
this Guómào watering hole is naturally a favourite expat hang-out.

ℹ Information

Cafes and fast-food restaurants around town
have free wi-fi.

Bank of China (中国银行, Zhōngguó Yínháng;
29-31 Datong Lu, 大同路29-31号; ⊘ 9am-5pm,
ATM 24hr) Changes money and travellers
cheques. ATMs are plentiful around town.

China Post (中国邮政, Zhōngguó Yóuzhèng; 16
Jiefang Xilu, 解放西路16号; ⊘ 8am-6pm)

ⓘ Getting There & Away

AIR

Hăikŏu's **Mĕilán Airport** (美兰国际机场, Mĕilán Guójì Jīchăng; www.mlairport.com), 25km to the east of town, is well connected to most of China's major cities, including Hong Kong and Macau, with international flights to Bangkok, Singapore, Kuala Lumpur and Taipei. Low-season one way domestic fares are cheap. Destinations include Bĕijīng, Guăngzhōu and Shànghăi.

BUS

Long-distance buses to the mainland depart from **Xiùyīng Harbour Station** (海口秀英港客运站, Hăikŏu Xiùyīnggăng Kèyùn Zhàn; 102 Binhai Dadao, 滨海大道102号), far to the west of town. To get here, take bus 37 (30 minutes) to the Marine Bureau (海事局站; Hăi Shìjú Zhàn; ¥2) stop. A taxi costs about ¥30 from downtown.

Destinations from Xiùyīng Harbour Station include:

Guăngzhōu ¥352, 12 hours, hourly
Guìlín ¥411, 13 hours, 3.30pm
Nànníng ¥280, 10 hours, hourly (11am to 9pm)

Buses from the **south bus station** (汽车南站; 32 Nanhai Dadao, 南海大道32号), 3km south of downtown, go to Qióngzhōng (¥35, 2½ hours via the central highway, half-hourly).

Buses from the **east bus station** (汽车东站; 148 Haifu Lu, 海府路148号), 1.5km south of downtown, go to:

Qiónghăi ¥30, 1½ hours, every 20 minutes
Wénchāng ¥20, 1½ hours, every 15 minutes
Sānyà ¥80, 3½ hours, 10 daily

TRAIN

Hăikŏu Railway Station (海口火车站, Hăikŏu Huŏchēzhàn), the main train station, is in the northwest corner of the city. Bus 37 (¥2) connects the train station and the Clock Tower bus stop; for destinations in the southern part of the city, take bus 40 (¥2).

There are five trains daily to/from Guăngzhōu (hard/soft sleeper ¥267/418, 12 hours). Buy tickets (¥5 service fee) at the train station or from the dedicated counter at **China Southern Airlines** (中国南方航空, Zhōngguó Nánfāng Hángkōng; 9 Haixiu Donglu; 海秀东路9号).

HIGH-SPEED TRAIN

High-speed trains running down the east coast to Sānyà mostly start from **Hăikŏu East Railway Station** (海口东站, Hăikŏu Dōngzhàn), in the southeast corner of the city. Trains down the west coast depart from Hăikŏu Railway Station, on the western side.

Qiónghăi ¥34, 50 minutes, hourly
Sānyà ¥84, two hours, hourly
Wànníng ¥49, 1½ hours, hourly

ⓘ Getting Around

TO/FROM THE AIRPORT

An airport shuttle bus (¥20, half-hourly) runs to/from Hăinán Mínháng Bīnguăn in downtown. A taxi costs around ¥80 to downtown; negotiate the price. The high-speed rail also has a stop at the airport; this train will take you to the Hăikŏu East Railway Station.

BUS

Both Hăikŏu's city centre and Hăidiàn Island are easy to get around on foot. The bus system (¥1 to ¥2) is decent, though it often takes transfers to get around. Key bus hubs include **Clock Tower** (钟楼, Zhōng Lóu) and Evergreen Park (万绿园; Wànlùyuán), both serviced by the handy bus 37. Tourist buses depart from near the entrance to Báishāmén Park (白沙门) on the northern end of Hăidiàn Island.

TAXI

Taxis charge ¥10 for the first 3km. They're easy to spot, but difficult to catch on large roads because of roadside barriers.

AROUND HĂIKŎU

Hăikŏu Volcanic Cluster Geopark   VOLCANO
(雷琼世界地质公园, Léiqióng Shìjiè Dìzhì Gōngyuán; Shíshān Town, 石山镇; ¥60; ◷8.30am-6pm) While this geopark encompasses about 108 sq km of rural countryside, the main attraction here is a corny tourist park surrounding a (genuinely cool) extinct volcano cone. Make haste past the snack stands and gift kiosks to descend the stairs winding down into the lushly vegetated crater, which feels more like a cave. Then climb back up for luscious views of the countryside all the way to the sea.

WŬZHĬSHĀN 五指山

Wŭzhĭshān (Five Finger Mountain), the highest peak in the land, rises 1867m out of the centre of Hăinán. It is the symbol of the island and is naturally steeped in local lore: the five peaks, for example, are said to represent the Li people's five most powerful gods. It is also the source of the Wànquán (万泉河) and Chānghuà (昌化江) rivers and part of the Wŭzhĭshān National Nature Reserve, a rich, threatened ecosystem containing 6.5% of all vascular plant species in China.

At the time of research, local authorities were making it very hard for foreign travellers to visit Wŭzhĭshān. You must apply for a permit through a licensed travel agency at least a week in advance – though your permit may be rejected or remain pending for no reason (as ours was) – and be accompanied by a guide. Should you receive permission and decide to climb, know that it is pretty much an all-day event to reach the summit and back. Most people can reach the top of the first finger (the second is highest) in three hours. The path is clear but very steep and includes a number of ladder climbs further up. Coming down is not much faster than going up, so give yourself six to eight hours. Be sure to bring plenty of water, as there are no amenities on the mountain.

Wŭzhĭshān sits about 4km from the village of Shuĭmăn (水满), 30km northeast of Wŭzhĭshān City. You'll need to first take a bus to Wŭzhĭshān City from Băotíng (¥10, 40 minutes, hourly), Hăikŏu (¥80, four hours, seven daily) or Sānyà (¥28, 1½ hours, frequent) and then transfer to a local bus to Shuĭmăn (¥10, one hour, hourly 7.30am to 5.30pm). Buy your ticket on the bus, which leaves across the street from the Wŭzhĭshān City bus station, 50m to the right. Make sure to get a bus going to Shuĭmăn via Nánshèng. In Shuĭmăn, motorcycle taxis will take you the remaining 4km for ¥15. The last bus back to Wŭzhĭshān leaves Shuĭmăn around 5.30pm.

If you're in Wŭzhĭshān City for a meal, **Zhèngzōng Lánzhōu Lāmiàn** (正宗兰州拉面, Authentic Lanzhou Noodles; 25 Sanyuesan Dadao, 三月三大道25号, Wŭzhĭshān City; dishes from ¥15; ⊘ 6.30am-10pm), a Hui Muslim restaurant, sells a wide range of cheap but excellent noodle and lamb dishes. Try the *gānbànmiàn* (干伴面; ¥15), a kind of stir-fried spaghetti bolognese with hand-pulled noodles.

If you need to overnight in Shuĭmăn, **Shuĭmăn Hotel** (水满园酒店, Shuĭmăn Yuán Jiŭdiàn; ☑ 0898 8655 0333; Shuĭmăn Town, 水满乡; tw ¥688; ❋ ☎), near to the bus stop and overlooking rice paddies and the Li temple, is a good bet. Steps from where the bus will let you off, **Shuĭmăn Yìjiā** (look for the yellow sign), is the best place in town for local food. Dishes to try include *Shuĭmăn* yā (水满鸭; local Shuĭmăn duck) and *wŭjiăo zhū* (五脚猪; 'five-foot pig' – local slang for the pigs that root around the villages).

The geopark entrance is about 18km west of Hăikŏu. The easiest way to get here is to take tourist bus 1 (¥30, 45 minutes, 8.30am and 12.30pm) from Báishāmén Park. The return bus leaves three hours later. A taxi to the park costs ¥60.

Tónggŭ Lĭng
MOUNTAIN
(铜鼓岭, Bronze Drum Ridge) Tónggŭ Lĭng is famous locally for its great views up and down the coast from the top, especially of the moon-shaped beach at Yuè Liàng Wān's beach. It's 3km to the top; there's a shuttle bus (¥20 round trip, 9am to 6pm) or you can hike along the road (though this is not so pleasant with the buses going up and down).

To get to Tónggŭ Lĭng, take a bus from Hăikŏu's east bus station to Dōngjiāo (¥23, 1½ hours, five daily), and then transfer to a minibus bound for Lónglóu (龙楼镇; ¥6, 30 minutes, hourly). At the Lónglóu bus stop, *sānlúnchē* (pedicab) drivers wait to take tourists the last 8km to the ridge; expect to pay about ¥20. Alternatively, you can cycle here from Dōngjiāo Yēlín in about two hours.

Měi Shè Village
HISTORIC SITE
(美社村, Měi Shè Cūn) Photogenic Měi Shè was built out of the rough grey volcanic stone so prevalent in this part of Hăinán. Wander the quiet back alleys and gawp at the castle-like five-storey gun tower in the town centre. It was built in the early 20th century to protect the village from bandits. The village is a 20-minute walk from the Hăikŏu Volcanic Cluster Geopark entrance (or a ¥60 taxi ride from Hăikŏu).

There is a network of small roads that run from Měi Shè to other villages, making this an ideal area for cycling.

CENTRAL HIGHLANDS

⏱ 0898

Hǎinán's reputation rests on its tropical beaches, but for many travellers it's in this region of dark-green mountains and terraced rice-growing valleys that they make genuine contact with the island's culture. Bǎotíng, with its rainforest and hot springs, is the most accessible destination. With more time, and especially if you're on two wheels, you can head to Wǔzhǐshān, Qióngzhōng and their surrounding villages.

Until recently, Han Chinese had left almost no footprint here, and even today visible signs of Chinese culture, such as temples or shrines, are very rarely seen. Instead, the region is predominantly Li and Miao – minority ethnic groups who have lived a relatively primitive subsistence existence for most of their time on the island. Indeed, groups of Li living as hunter-gatherers were found in the mountainous interior of Hǎinán as recently as the 1930s. Today they are by far the poorest people on Hǎinán.

The central highlands have a good range of accommodation, from luxurious rainforest resorts to village guesthouses. Transport hubs like Wǔzhǐshān City have business hotels around the bus station if you find yourself stuck.

One of the joys of visiting the highlands is getting to feast on wild mountain vegetables (野菜; yěcài) and free-range duck and pork.

On the sidewalks, Li women sell zhú tǒng fàn (rice baked in fragrant bamboo stalks; ¥10).

Travelling in the region is easy, as a decent bus system links major and minor towns. Key transit hubs include Wǔzhǐshān and Qióngzhōng.

Bǎotíng 保亭

⏱ 0898 / POP 170,000

Bǎotíng is the gateway to the **Qī Xiān Líng Hot Spring Forest Park** (七仙岭温泉国家森林公园; Qī Xiān Líng Wēnquán Guójiā Sēnlín Gōngyuán), where the main attraction is the ridge of jagged, spear-like crags that make up Seven Fairy Mountain. It's a well developed town with a large population of Li and Miao. The mountain entrance and hot-springs area are 8km out of town. The area around the bus station has some amenities, including restaurants and an ATM.

Seven Fairy Mountain (七仙岭, Qī Xiān Líng; ¥48; ⊘ ticket office 7.30am-5.30pm), named for its dramatic seven pinnacles, is found inside the Hot Spring Forest Park. It's a three-hour return trip to the top of the first point along a stepped path through a dense, healthy rainforest buzzing with bird and insect life. The final 100m climb to the peak runs up a pitted slope with chains and railings in place to aid your near-vertical climb. The views from the top are worth the effort. Purchase tickets at the excessively large park administration building at the entrance.

To get to Seven Fairy Mountain from Bǎotíng's bus station, you can take bus 1 (¥1, 10 minutes) to Xiàn Zhèng Fǔ (县政府) and then transfer to bus 2 (¥3, 15 minutes) to the entrance of the park, though it's easier to

---

THE LI & THE MIAO

The Li, who today number over one million and can only be found on Hǎinán, were the island's first-known settlers, likely immigrating from southern China several thousand years ago. The Li were followed by the Miao (H'mong), who can also be found across stretches of northern Vietnam, Laos and Thailand; their arrival pushed the Li into the central highlands. When Han settlers arrived in big numbers during the Qing dynasty, they pushed the Miao, who in turn pushed the Li even further into the mountains.

Today both populations occupy some of the most rugged terrain on the island, in the forested areas covering the Límǔlǐng Shān (Mother of the Li Mountain) range that stretches down the centre of the island. Since 1987, several counties in the central highlands have been designated as Li and Miao autonomous regions, which afford the minority groups a degree of independent governance.

Visitors to the central highlands will see visual markers of Li culture, including architecture adorned with traditional geometric symbols and children in school uniforms hemmed with colourful embroidery.

catch a motorcycle taxi (¥30). Make sure not to catch a motorcycle with a side car as they lack the power to make it the last 4km from the hot springs area up to the trailhead.

There's an ever-growing number of hot-spring resorts in the forest, which have a certain appeal after hiking. Otherwise, it's best to visit as a day trip from Sānyà as accommodation is hard to find in town. At the foot of Seven Fairy Mountain, **Narada Resort** (君澜度假酒店, Jūnlán Dùjià Jiŭdiàn; ☑0898 8388 8888; www.naradahotels.com; Qī Xiān Lǐng Hot Spring Forest Park; r from ¥2488; P❄⚛☀≋) is an elegant surprise in the middle of the peaceful (though increasingly developed) rainforest. The 222 bright, airy rooms are done up in wood with ethnic minority art; the manicured grounds are spotted with fruit trees; and the bathtubs, behind bamboo screens on the verandah, are filled with natural hot-spring water.

There are frequent buses to Băotíng's main bus station from Sānyà (¥20, 1½ hours).

THE EAST COAST

☑0898

Hăinán's east coast is a series of spectacular palm-lined beaches, long bays and headlands, most of which are, unfortunately, not usually visible from the main roads, not even at bicycle level. With the best beaches developed or being developed, there is little reason to make a special trip out here (Bó'áo being the exception) unless you are surfing or wish to stay at a resort. Biking or motorcycling is another story, however, as there are endless small villages and rural roads to explore and even a few near-deserted bays.

In the past, the east coast was the centre of Han settlement. If you are coming from the highlands you will start to notice temples, grave sites, shrines and other signs of Chinese culture dotting the landscape.

We've heard reports of travellers camping on the undeveloped beaches with no trouble. There are camping facilities at **Dà Huā Jiăo** (大花角), a pretty beach with bobbing fishing boats at the end of the outstretched finger of land due east of Wànníng.

Frequent high-speed trains and buses run down the eastern side of the island, stopping at Qiónghăi (for Bó'áo), Wànníng (for Rì Yuè Bay) and Língshuĭ.

Note that the eastern highway runs quite a bit inland; if you're keen to cycle along the coast, you'll need a good map to navigate the tiny roads that flit in and out of the waterfront towns.

Bó'áo 博鳌

☑0898 / POP 29.000

For cyclists, Bó'áo is a natural stop along the coast. For all travellers, it's an unpretentious (though rapidly developing) beach town surrounded by pretty countryside. Just to the west are small villages of stone and brick buildings where locals dry rice in the middle of the lanes, and burn incense for their local folk deities in small shrines.

Officially Bó'áo is starting to cover a large area, but the 'downtown' blocks, where most travellers both stay and eat, are tiny. The beach is a five-minute walk away.

Avoid visiting during, or the week before, the Bó'áo Forum for Asia (BFA), an annual April meet-up of top-level officials, academics and economists exclusively from the Asia region. The town is pretty much closed off under the scrutiny of high-level security (there are even warships in the harbour).

⊙ Sights & Activities

A network of small lanes and boardwalks makes the surrounding villages easily accessible to cyclists and strollers. Some places to aim for are **Dà Lù Pō Village** (大路坡村; Dà Lù Pō Cūn) and **Nánqiáng Village** (南强村; Nánqiáng Cūn) off the main road about 2km west of the downtown junction.

Cai Family Former Residence HISTORIC SITE (蔡家宅, Càijiā Zhái; Liú Kè Cùn, 留客村; ⊙9am-5pm) FREE This sprawling, and pleasantly decaying, mansion was built in 1934 by several brothers who made their fortune in the Indonesian rubber industry. The building was abandoned in 1937 after the Japanese invaded Hăinán, and later became a guerrilla outpost for resistance fighters. In 2006 it was declared a heritage site and these days you can wander around inside for a look if the caretaker is about.

It's about 5km from town. Take a *sānlúnchē* (三路车; pedicab; ¥60 round trip) or make an afternoon bike ride out of it: head west out of town and when the road ends at a junction turn left (south) and cross two long bridges. After crossing the second bridge, head right at the English sign. In a couple of blocks stay left and enjoy a sumptuous ride through green fields and collections of handsome old and new houses alongside the road.

Bó'áo Bay

(博鳌湾, Bó'áo Wān) Bó'áo's beach is a long, narrow strip of golden sand, just a few hundred metres east of the town's main road. If you plan to swim, head at least 500m north to avoid dangerous currents. The best stretches are even further north, particularly around the Asia Bay resort hotel.

🛏 Sleeping

Bó'áo has resorts that looked like they beamed in from Dubai and a growing number of hostels, but nothing in between. Note that hostels often book out completely with cycling tours; you'll want to book in advance.

CYCLING HĂINÁN

Hăinán is a great destination for recreational touring. You're rarely more than an hour from a village with food and water, and never more than a few hours from a town with a decent hotel. At the same time, you'll find most of your riding is out in nature or through pretty farming valleys, not urban sprawl. Roads, even to minor villages, are generally in excellent condition (and new ones are being created regularly). Preparation time for a tour can be minimal.

Around Hăikŏu

A network of narrow, paved lanes connect the picturesque villages around the Hăikŏu Volcanic Cluster Geopark, which are perfect for a day or afternoon trip. **Velo China** (p597) runs short, one- to three-hour cycling tours (free with the cost of bicycle rental, which starts at ¥80) that leave daily at 9am and 3pm from in front of the Mission Hills Resort; for reservations call ☎ 0898 6868 3888.

East Coast

The most popular of the multiday routes, because it is largely flat, runs from Hăikŏu to Sānyà along the eastern highway, covering about 300km. The main road runs somewhat inland, though, so if you want to strike out along the coast, you'll need a good map to follow the small roads that run to the seaside villages.

Central Highlands

This is the most spectacular ride, if you have the stamina for it. The central highway, which runs 300km from Hăikŏu to Sānyà via Wŭzhĭshān, has a good shoulder most of the way, and allows for endless side trips up small country roads and stops in tiny villages.

After a day riding through the lush Túnchāng County valley, the route climbs into some fine hill country around Shíyùn (什运). The village, 32km southwest of Qióngzhōng, sits on a grassy shelf above a river and is worth a look around. Local cyclists recommend the 42km side trip from here up a wooded canyon to Báishā (白沙). The major towns in this area are Túnchāng (屯昌) and Qióngzhōng (琼中), the latter a major settlement for the Miao.

After Shíyùn you can look forward to a long climb (at least 10km), followed by a long fast descent into Wŭzhĭshān. If you are continuing on to Sānyà, the road is one long, steep downhill after the turn-off to Băotíng.

Bicycle Rental

If you're not bringing your own wheels, you can rent decent-quality mountain bikes at **Hăikŏu Banana Youth Hostel** (p597) from ¥30 a day. The hostel's website has detailed information on cycling Hăinán. **Velo China** (p597) also rents mountain and touring bicycles (from ¥80/500 per day/week) and can arrange custom tours with English-speaking guides. Six-day tours, which include hotel accommodation, bicycle rental and maintenance, picnic lunch and insurance, start at ¥2860 per person person.

Maps

Road maps are available at **Xīnhuá Bookstore** (新华书店, Xīnhuá Shūdiàn; 10 Jiefang Xilu, 解放西路10号; ⏰ 9am-10pm) in Hăikŏu. It's worth noting that people in Hăinán call bikes *dānchē*. Buses will accept bicycles in the hold but trains require you to box them up.

Bó'áo 517 Yìzhàn
GUESTHOUSE $

(博鳌517驿站; ☑133 7991 7175; www.hn517.cn; 22 Dongning Lu, 东宁路22号; d ¥90; 🖳) Some travellers will find the rooms at tiny Bó'áo 517 Yìzhàn, occupying a traditional stone house just minutes from the main town junction and the beach, charming. (Those who find them dark and cramped can bunk at the modern, utilitarian sister hostel down the road.) There are just three rooms set in a courtyard with a shared bathroom and laundry room. Call ahead as there's no reception.

Bó'áo Golden Coast Hot Spring Hotel
RESORT $$$

(琼海博鳌金海岸温泉大酒店, Qiónghǎi Bó'áo Jīnhǎi'àn Wēnquán Dàjiǔdiàn; ☑0898 6277 8888; www.boao-golden.com.cn; 8 Jinhai'an Dadao, 金海岸大道8号; r from ¥1380; 🅿❄🖳🏊) One of the more classically resort-like options in town, this sprawling complex has more than 300 rooms, an enormous pool, manicured lawns, and several restaurants and bars. In the off-season (most of the year), when discounts upwards of 50% are available, it's great value.

🍴 Eating

Bó'áo has a good spread of eating options. Around 4pm each day look for stalls on either side of Haibin Lu near the Hainan Bank selling succulent Jiājī duck (加积鸭; *Jiājī yā*; ¥10 for a leg), a Hǎinán speciality. Don't be tardy as it sells out quickly. On the main streets there are grocery stores and fruit stands.

⭐ Sea Story
SEAFOOD, CAFE $$

(海的故事, Hǎide Gùshì; dishes ¥28-138; ⏱8am-late; 🖳) Bó'áo's most famous restaurant is surprisingly un-flashy, cobbled together from driftwood and with a courtyard full of weathered old fishing junks. The kitchen turns out excellent local and Southeast Asian dishes (think barbecued spare ribs and curried prawns). Outside, the breezy, seaside deck is an ideal spot for cocktails. Sea Story is a 15-minute walk north along the beach path.

SĀNYUÈSĀN FESTIVAL

Held on the third day of the third (lunar) month, **Sānyuèsān** (三月三, March 3rd Festival) is the biggest festival for Hǎinán's native Li people. Traditional dancing and singing contests take place in town and villages across the central highlands.

Áogōng Hǎixiān Chéng
SEAFOOD $$

(鳌宫海鲜城; ☑0898 6277 9699; meals around ¥100; ⏱11am-9pm) Come see what the local fishing boats haul in, and then splash out on a spread of fresh seafood. Pick and choose from among the tanks, which helpfully have prices listed – so you know how much that giant lobster will cost you. The 'Legendary Turtle' (as the name translates) is a 30-minute walk north along the beach road, from the town junction.

🍷 Drinking & Nightlife

The beach road leading north from downtown has been redeveloped into a 'Seaside Bar Street' lined with open-air bars and cafes, which are lit up in the evenings.

Lǎo Wood Coffee Rest Area
CAFE

(老房子, Lǎo Fángzi; drinks from ¥20; ⏱10am-10pm; 🖳) The owner of this cafe, a local dancer and art administrator, literally had a traditional old stone house taken apart and reassembled on Bó'áo's coastal path to make his dream of opening a stylish cafe come true. Inside is chock-full of antiques and objets d'art, while in front is a sculpture-filled garden dotted with cafe tables.

ℹ Information

Bank of China (中国银行, Zhōngguó Yínháng; 99 Haibin Lu, 海滨路99号) Has an ATM. It's about 200m north of the main intersection near ABC Bank.

Wàn Yuè Travel Agency (万悦旅行社, Wàn Yuè Lǚxíngshè; 60-3 Haibin Lu, 海滨路60-3号; ⏱7.30am-10pm) Sells high-speed train tickets. It's about 200m north of the main intersection, across from an ABC Bank.

ℹ Getting There & Away

From Hǎikǒu's east bus station, catch a bus to the main station in Qiónghǎi (琼海; ¥30, 1½ hours, every 20 minutes) then cross the street to the Kentucky Fried Chicken side, and look for the bus stop just down the road to the left. Catch bus 2 to Bó'áo (¥6, 30 minutes, frequent). Passengers get dropped off at the main junction in Bó'áo. All transport from Bó'áo passes through Qiónghǎi.

The nearest train station to Bó'áo is actually Qiónghǎi (not Bó'áo Station); from there you'll need to catch a taxi (¥40) the rest of the way to town. Alternatively, catch bus 6 or 7 (¥2) outside the train station to Qiónghǎi East Bus Station (琼海东站) and then take bus 2 the rest of the way.

Hǎikǒu ¥34, 50 minutes, hourly

Sānyà ¥48.50, 70 minutes, hourly

ⓘ Getting Around

There are a handful of shops around town renting bicycles (¥50 per day), though it's common for tour groups to have reserved all the stock in advance.

Shímĕi Bay & Rì Yuè Bay 石梅湾、日月湾

This is a wild, rocky stretch of coastline. Shímĕi Bay (石梅湾, Shímĕi Wān) is now lined with resorts, but Rì Yuè Bay (日月湾; Rì Yuè Wān; Sun & Moon Bay), further south, is still largely undeveloped and is popular with local surfers. Both bays have strong currents and aren't considered safe for casual swimmers.

If you like your ocean slate-blue and reckless (and largely resort free), **Rì Yuè Bay** (日月湾, Rì Yuè Wān, Sun & Moon Bay) is for you. Colour is provided by local surfers rather than the usual flotilla of inflatable children's toys. The beachside restaurant (8am to 10pm) run by the friendly people at **Surfing Hǎinán** (冲浪海南, Chōnglàng Hǎinán; ☑0898 6225 4626; www.surfinghainan. com; Rì Yuè Bay, 日月湾; board/wetsuit rental per day ¥100/50; ☺8am-7.30pm) is a good place to hangout.

Rì Yuè Bay has just one combined hotel and hostel, which is unappealing. Camping is an option: Surfing Hǎinán rents tents and sleeping bags.

There are few amenities on the beaches along this stretch of coast that aren't attached to resorts.

The most direct way to get here is on the bus that runs down the eastern expressway between Hǎikǒu and Sānyà: ask the driver to drop you off at the exit for Rì Yuè, from where it's a 500m walk down the ramp to the shore. Only the lower-class green buses will stop, so check when you buy a ticket. From Sānyà you'll have to buy a ticket to Wànníng (万宁; ¥34, 1½ hours, every 40 minutes); from Hǎikǒu, buy one to Língshuǐ (陵水; ¥43, three hours, 7.15am, 11am, 3pm). You can also take a taxi from Xīnglóng for around ¥50.

If you're cycling down the eastern highway, note that the expressway (which runs closer to the coast here) blocks your access to the beach. A county road down the coast, which would be an attractive alternative, was still under construction in parts at the time of research.

Sānyà (Dàdōnghǎi) 三亚

☑0898 / POP 580,500

China's premier beach community claims to be the 'Hawaii of China', but 'Moscow on the South China Sea' is more like it. The modern, hyper-developed resort city has such a steady influx of Russian vacationers these days that almost all signs are in Cyrillic as well as Chinese. Middle-class Chinese families are increasingly drawn to the golden shores of Sānyà as well.

While the full 40km or so of coastline dedicated to tourism is usually referred to as Sānyà, the region is actually made up of three distinct zones. Sānyà Bay is home to the bustling city centre and a long stretch of beach and hotels aimed at locals and mainland holidaymakers. Busy, cheerfully tacky Dàdōnghǎi Bay, about 3km southeast, beyond the Lùhuítóu Peninsula, is where most Western travellers stay. A further 15km east, at exclusive Yàlóng Bay, the beach is first-rate, as is the line of plush international resorts.

◉ Sights & Activities

Unsurprisingly for a beach resort, the vast majority of things to see and do revolve around sand, sea, shopping and after-hours entertainment. If you want to scuba dive or snorkel, May to August, before typhoon season, is the best time, though locals will tell you honestly that there is not that much to see in the water. Be aware that although beaches often have lifeguards they may not be properly trained.

Hòuhǎi Beach　　　BEACH

(后海) A crescent-shaped sandy beach about 30km northeast of Dàdōnghǎi, Hòuhǎi is the place for those looking to get away from the crowds (though ironically it lies in the southern reach of Hǎitáng Bay where the scale of development must be seen to be believed). It's the most low-key of the Sānyà area beaches and is a popular place for beginner surfers.

Bus 28 from the main road in Dàdōnghǎi (¥10, one hour) takes you to the beach. There's a small village here, where every house doubles as a guesthouse, and plenty of small restaurants and fruit stands.

Sānyà Bay　　　BEACH

(三亚湾, Sānyà Wān) The long sandy strip off the city centre at Sānyà Bay is where you'll find crowds of mostly mainland Chinese tourists kicking back. In little covered areas

Sānyà (Dàdōnghǎi)

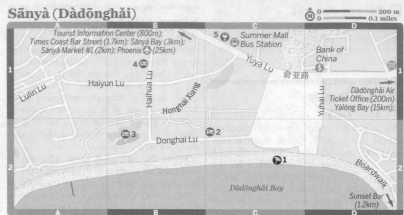

locals play music, sing, write characters in the sand and so on. There's a long pathway for strolling in the cool evenings, and if the tide is out a little, you can walk on the sand for many kilometres. In the evenings it's fun to watch the lights on Phoenix Island (the awesome cruise-ship terminal).

Dàdōnghǎi Bay   BEACH
(大东海湾, Dàdōnghǎi Wān) Dàdōnghǎi Bay sports a wider beach than Sānyà and has a shaded boardwalk running along most of its length. The setting, in a deep blue bay with rocky headlands, is simply gorgeous, but it does get busy here. At night, half the crowd is knocking back beers and eating crabs at the boardwalk restaurants, while the other half is still bobbing in the sea under the light of the moon.

Yàlóng Bay   BEACH
(亚龙湾, Yàlóng Wān, Asian Dragon Bay) Yàlóng Bay is the most picture-perfect of Sānyà's beaches, though jet skis and banana boats do buzz through (there are roped-off swimming areas in the shallows). This is resort central, with all the attendant luxuries. Budget travellers will want to head to the main plaza for fast-food and coconut stands.

China's beaches are theoretically open to everyone, but at Yàlóng Bay there can be a quasi-official entry fee if you're not staying at one of the beachfront resorts. To avoid any sporadically enforced fees, walk through one of the hotels rather than entering the beach from the main square. No one will bother you.

🛏 Sleeping

A glut of hotel rooms makes even luxury resorts affordable in Sānyà. Dàdōnghǎi Bay is the place to head for midrange and budget lodgings catering to the international set. Hòuhǎi Beach has a row of beachside guesthouses and a backpacker vibe. The top-end resorts are at Yàlóng Bay, in a private area of palm-lined roads and landscaped grounds. Outside peak periods 30% to 60% discounts are common everywhere.

White Castle Club   GUESTHOUSE $
(百城堡冲浪俱乐部, Báichéng Bǎochōnglàng Jùlèbù; ☑ 0898 8882 7103, 133 7994 6916; Hǎitáng Bay, 海棠湾; r from ¥190; 🌐 🛜) This is the hub of Hòuhǎi's nascent surf scene and a great place to base yourself if you're keen to learn and make friends. The guesthouse backs on to the sand, with a hang-out spot that serves traveller staples like yoghurt, granola and pizzas. The rooms without sea views are a little damp.

In-house licensed instructors run intro courses of three daily, 1½-hour lessons (¥900 including board rental). Just board rental costs ¥150 per day. If you're ready to splurge on your own, White Castle sells hand-shaped boards (from ¥8800). English spoken.

Sānyà Backpackers HOSTEL $
(二亚背包度假屋, Sānyà Bēibāo Dùjià Wū; ☑ 0898 8821 3963; www.sanyabackpackers.com; No 1 Type 1 Villa, Lu Ming Community, Haihua Lu, 海花路鹿鸣小区一型一一号别墅, Dàdōnghǎi; dm ¥75, s/d ¥200/240; ❄ ☎) This spick-and-span hostel is a more intimate and friendly place than others in town. Set in a whitewashed building in a residential compound it's also an oasis. Simple backpacker dishes are available, and there's a bar (which can get noisy) for hanging out in the evenings. Surf lessons and board rentals (¥150 per day) are available during the summer.

Golden Beach Villa HOTEL $$
(金沙滩海景度假别墅, Jīn Shātān Hǎijǐng Dùjià Biéshù; ☑ 0898 8821 2760; 11 Donghai Lu, 东海路11号, Dàdōnghǎi; r from ¥268; ❄ ☎) Golden Beach Villa is not as fancy as the name suggests but it's right on the beach. Rooms, which are enclosed in a walled-off garden, face the sea, and the upper floors have excellent views. Outside the busy season, you can roll up and bargain for a great rate.

Ritz-Carlton RESORT $$$
(丽思卡尔顿酒店, Lìsī Kǎěrdùn Jiǔdiàn; ☑ 0898 8898 8888; www.ritzcarlton.com; Yàlóng Bay; r from ¥4000; ❰P❱ ❄ ☎) While some of Yàlóng Bay's palatial resorts can feel a bit like a ghost town due to Sānyà's overbuilding, the Ritz is always abuzz. Well heeled matrons sip tea on the grand patio, princelings splash down water slides in the kids' pool, and young couples lie on the wide, sugar-white beach. Rooms are large and airy, all white linen and elegant mahogany.

Resort Intime RESORT $$$
(湘投银泰度假酒店, Xiāngtóu Yíntài Dùjià Jiǔdiàn; ☑ 0898 8821 0888; www.resortintime.com; 88 Haihua, 海花路88号, Dàdōnghǎi; r from ¥1989; ❒❄☎☐) This great little resort right by the beach has surprisingly large and leafy grounds with a barbecue area near the pool. The rooms aren't the most spacious, but those with sea views are set at a perfect angle to take in the bay. Nonsmoking floors are available. Discounts of over 50% are common.

Hotel Pullman HOTEL $$$
(三亚湾海居铂尔曼度假酒店, Sānyà Wānhǎi Jūbó'ěr Màndùjià Jiǔdiàn; ☑ 0898 8855 5588; www.pullmanhotels.com; Yàlóng Bay; r from ¥2000; ❰P❱❄☎☐) Directly across the street from the ocean, what you give up in oceanfront views, you make up in savings at the Pullman. Ground-floor rooms have 'swim up' entrances to the pool, which surrounds an emerald interior courtyard. Kids will dig the water-slide area. Don't expect five-star luxury, just solid midrange value and comfort.

✖ Eating

The entire beachfront at Dàdōnghǎi is one long strip of restaurants, bars and cafes, most of which are overpriced and not terribly good, even if the overall atmosphere is cool, shady and scenic. When ordering seafood, be sure to settle on price beforehand – Sānyà has had some fairly infamous restaurant scams. The narrow alley Honghai Xiang has good street food.

★ Sānyà Market #1 MARKET $
(第一市场, Dì Yī Shìchǎng; cnr Jiefang Lu & Xinjian Lu, 解放路新建路路口, Sānyà; ⏰ 11am-2am) Sānyà's most popular market is ostensibly a place to bargain for cheap and colourful clothes and accessories, but its real appeal

---

SURFING ON HǍINÁN

Surfing is slowly gaining a following in China, and Hǎinán is without question the centre of that budding scene. Conditions are never going to make this the next Indonesia, but every level, from beginner to advanced, can find suitable waves.

If you want to try your hand at the sport, Dàdōnghǎi and Hòuhǎi get decent waves from May to September and are suitable for absolute novices (especially quiet Hòuhǎi). Rì Yuè Bay (Sun & Moon Bay) is prime from November to January, but it's possible to surf all year. With up to five breaks, the area is suitable for all levels; advanced surfers can try their luck on the Ghost Hotel waves. Unlike further south, Sun & Moon Bay gets a bit chilly and overcast in the winter months, so light wetsuits are recommended.

Rentals and lessons are available year-round through **Surfing Hǎinán** (p605) in Rì Yuè Bay and **White Castle Club** (p606) in Hòuhǎi. During summer you can find rentals and basic lessons in Sānyà at Sānyà Backpackers.

LǍOBÀ CHÁ

On Hǎinán, in nearly every city, town and hovel, you can find open-air cafes filled with middle-aged men whittling away the day drinking tea, smoking and playing cards. (Many work through the night tapping rubber trees.) These local institutions are called *lǎobà chá* (老爸茶), literally 'daddy's tea.' Many open early and are a great place to start the day: you can get fresh coffee (¥4 a pot) and steaming baskets of meat-filled buns (包子; *bāozi*; around ¥6 for three). *Lǎobà chá* are easily recognised by their large bare interiors and plastic chairs that, for some reason, are often shocking pink.

lies on the fringes, where food vendors set up shop. Stop for barbecued seafood, grilled corn and local sweets like *qīngbǔliáng* (清补凉; a cold sweet soup; ¥10) and *chǎobīng* (炒冰; fried ice, like sorbet; ¥25). Things really heat up after dark.

Casa Mia Italian Restaurant ITALIAN $$
(卡萨米亚意大利餐厅, Kǎsà Mǐyà Yìdàlì Cāntīng; ☑0898 8888 9828; 88 Sanya Wan Lu, 三亚湾路88号, Sānyà; mains ¥58-98; ⊗11.30am-10pm; 🛜) A jaded traveller might pooh-pooh the thought of finding top-notch Italian in a Chinese resort town. But they'd be wrong. Casa Mia has truly divine pizzas, pastas (try the special seafood linguine) and classics like veal scallopini. The wine list is nothing to sneeze at either. The terrace gets a nice breeze from Sānyà Bay across the street.

Bus 8 (¥2) from Dàdōnghǎi will take you here in 45 minutes; otherwise it's about ¥50 in a taxi.

Baan Rim Nam THAI $$$
(水岸阁餐厅, Shuǐ Àn Gé Cāntīng; ☑0898 8888 5088; http://sanya.anantara.com; 6 Donghai Lu, 小东海路6号, Anantara Resort, 安纳塔拉度假会; dishes from ¥108-268; ⊗noon-10pm; 🛜🅿) Dine on Thai classics like curried crab, green papaya salad, and basil pork at this hushed and elegant restaurant in the Anantara Resort, a spa-like resort all done up in mirrors and dark wood. Service is extremely friendly. If it's not too hot, opt to sit on the patio.

🍷 Drinking & Nightlife

Most of the after-hours fun is in Sānyà and Dàdōnghǎi Bay. **Times Coast Bar Street** (时代海岸酒吧街, Shídài Hǎiàn Jiǔ Bā Jiē; Yuya

Lu, 榆亚路), on Yuya Lu, where it crosses the river, is the nexus of Sānyà's club scene.

Sunset Bar COCKTAIL BAR
(日落吧, Rì Luò Bā; 12 Yuhai Lu, 榆海路12号, Mandarin Oriental Hotel, 文华东方酒店; ⊗11am-1am) A two-for-one happy hour (5pm to 7pm) makes this terrace bar at the cool and collected Mandarin Oriental almost a good deal. Watch the sun drop behind the headland while sipping a signature ginger lycheetini (¥90). Smoothies from ¥60. A taxi from Dàdōnghǎi costs ¥10.

Dolphin Sports Bar & Grill PUB
(☑0898 8821 5700; www.sanyadolphin.com; 99 Yuya Lu, 榆亚路99号, Dàdōnghǎi; beer from ¥25; ⊗11am-2am) International tourists and expats mingle with locals at this always-packed Western-style pub. Wash down a (very good) cheeseburger with a pint while watching football on the multiple TVs, or wait until after 10pm, when the live music starts up and the crowd really gets rolling. Friendly servers speak impeccable English.

ℹ Information

Wi-fi is widely available in restaurants and cafes.

Bank of China (中国银行, Zhōngguó Yínháng; 119 Yuya Lu, 榆海路119号, Dàdōnghǎi; ⊗9am-5pm) Changes travellers cheques and has a 24-hour ATM.

China Post (中国邮政, Zhōngguó Yóuzhèng; 147 Yuya Lu, 榆海路147号, Dàdōnghǎi; ⊗9am-5pm)

Dàdōnghǎi Air Ticket Office (蓝色海航空售票中心, Lánsèhǎi Hángkōng Shòupiào Zhōngxīn; ☑0898 8821 5557; 172 Yuya Lu, 榆海路172号, Dàdōnghǎi; ⊗8am-9.30pm) Air and rail tickets can be purchased from the air ticket office two bus stops east of Summer Mall (the stop is called Bayi Zhongxue).

Tourist Information Center (☑0898 8836 8826; 19 Yuya Lu, 榆海路19号, Dàdōnghǎi; ⊗9am-9pm; 🛜) Has bilingual city maps of Sānyà. There's usually someone at the counter who speaks English.

ℹ Getting There & Away

AIR

Sānyà's **Phoenix Airport** (三亚凤凰国际机场, Sānyà Fèng Huáng Guójì Jīchǎng; www.sanyaairport.com) has international flights to Singapore, Hong Kong, Malaysia, Thailand, Taiwan and Japan, as well as to Běijīng, Guǎngzhōu and Shànghǎi.

BUS

Frequent buses and minibuses to most parts of Hǎinán depart from the **long-distance bus**

station (三亚汽车站, Sānyà Qìchēzhàn; Jiefang Lu, 解放路), in busy central Sānyà.

Bǎotíng ¥20, 1½ hours, half-hourly

Hǎikǒu ¥80, 3½ hours, hourly

Qióngzhōng ¥48, four hours, 8.10am, 11am, 1.35pm, 3.30pm

Wànníng ¥30, two hours, hourly

HIGH-SPEED TRAIN

The high-speed train station is far out of town. Bus 4 (¥2) runs there from Dàdōnghǎi, but takes over an hour. A taxi will cost ¥50 for a 20-minute ride.

Hǎikǒu ¥99, two hours, hourly

Qiónghǎi ¥49, one hour, hourly

🛈 Getting Around

TO/FROM THE AIRPORT

Phoenix Airport is 25km from Dàdōnghǎi Bay. The airport is a stop on the new western high-speed rail line (¥8, 10 minutes to Sānyà), though trains are infrequent and the Sānyà train station is inconveniently located. Bus 8 (¥5, one hour) leaves for the airport from Yuya Lu. A taxi costs ¥70 to ¥80.

BUS

Buses 2 and 8 (¥2, frequent) travel from Sānyà bus station to Dàdōnghǎi Bay. From Dàdōnghǎi Bay to Yàlóng Bay, catch bus 15 (¥5, 45 minutes).

TAXI

Taxis charge ¥10 for the first 2km. A taxi from Sānyà to Dàdōnghǎi Bay costs ¥15 to ¥20, and from Dàdōnghǎi Bay to Yàlóng Bay it's ¥70.

Xīnglóng　　兴隆

☑ 0898 / POP 25,800

Xīnglóng is a hot-spring town that is home to communities of overseas Chinese who returned from Southeast Asia in the 1950s.

👁 Sights

Xīnglóng Tropical Botanical Gardens　　GARDENS

(兴隆热带植物园, Xīnglóng Rèdài Zhíwùyuán; ⊙24hr) What sounds like another of Hǎinán's many tourist traps is actually a worthy retreat: a network of largely traffic-free lanes – where you're more likely to run into a butterfly than a motorbike – snaking through hills and between villages. Walk or cycle past clear springs, groves of mango trees and coffee plantations. Rental cycles (¥80 per day) are available at the **Qiáo Xiāng Yìzhàn** (桥乡驿站) cafe, which also serves excellent local coffee (¥5).

From Xīnglóng bus station, bus 4 (¥2, 20 minutes) runs to the garden entrance, or get a taxi to the cafe – all drivers should know it.

🛏 Sleeping

There are several high-end hot-spring resorts in the vicinity, but otherwise Xīnglóng is best visited as a day trip from Sānyà.

🍴 Eating

Tucking into authentic Southeast Asian food and sweets is the number one reason to visit Xīnglóng.

Xīng Xīn Gé　　INDONESIAN $$

(兴欣阁; Xingmei Dadao, 兴梅大道; dishes ¥45-75; ⊙11am-9pm) There's no menu here: just pop into the kitchen and point to whichever of the Indonesian-style stews and curries looks (or smells!) the best. In the afternoon, stop by for coffee and *qī céng gāo* (七层糕) 'seven layer' steamed cakes flavored with coffee and isatis leaf. The restaurant is on the right of the entrance to the Xīnglóng Tropical Botanical Gardens.

🍷 Drinking & Nightlife

Xīnglóng is the locus of Hǎinán's unexpected – and unexpectedly good – cafe scene. When the coffee shops close up around dusk, though, it's a quiet place.

Lín Qīng Gé　　COFFEE

(林清阁; 1 Gonghui Lu, 工会路1号; ⊙6am-4pm) In the 1950s a number of overseas Chinese returned from Southeast Asia and settled in Xīnglóng – bringing coffee back with them. Downtown Xīnglóng, around the Xīnglóng Trade Union (兴隆工会; Xīnglóng Gōnghuì) bus stop, is full of cafes selling local coffee (¥5) and Indonesian-style sweets. Lín Qīng Gé has won the local coffee competition several years running. The bus from Wànníng train station to Xīnglóng will let you off just before a bridge; follow the road another 300m and the cafe will be on your right.

🛈 Getting There & Away

Hourly buses run from Sānyà to Xīnglóng (¥28, two hours).

The nearest train station is in Wànníng (万宁), where hourly trains arrive from Hǎikǒu (¥49, 75 minutes), Qiónghǎi (¥19, 20 minutes) and Sānyà (¥41, 45 minutes). Direct buses (¥5, 40 minutes) to Xīnglóng Town meet the trains at the station.

Guǎngxī

POP 51 MILLION

Best Places to Eat

➡ Dàilóng Farmer Restaurant (p628)

➡ Luna (p626)

➡ Gānjiājiè Lemon Duck (p629)

➡ Āmóu Delicious Eats (p629)

➡ Kali Mirch (p614)

Best Places to Sleep

➡ Giggling Tree (p625)

➡ Secret Garden (p626)

➡ Backpacker Inn (p632)

➡ This Old Place Youth Hostel (p627)

Why Go?

Guǎngxī (广西) conjures up visions of cycling and bamboo-rafting upon shimmering river waters beneath the sublime karst peaks of Yángshuò and hiking between ethnic villages in the lofty Lóngjǐ Rice Terraces. That's not all though: you can take selfies in front of the dramatic Dānxiá landscape (a type of landform) at Tiānmén Mountain and Bājiǎozhài National Geopark, and get sprayed by the mighty waterfall of Détiān or splashed by live seafood in Běihǎi's Vietnamese quarter.

What's more, you'll be contemplating the 2000-year-old Huāshān cliff murals from a boat and comparing the poetry of the Dòng villages at Chéngyáng to the beauty of Japan's Kyoto.

After you've had your fill of wonders above ground, you'll be plunging into the subterranean forests of Lèyè and soaking your feet in the underground streams of Tónglíng Grand Canyon. Doing it all in reverse also makes sense, for Yángshuò is the perfect conclusion to any expedition.

When to Go
Guìlín

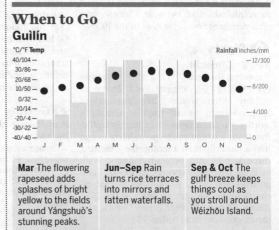

°C/°F Temp   Rainfall inches/mm

Mar The flowering rapeseed adds splashes of bright yellow to the fields around Yángshuò's stunning peaks.	**Jun–Sep** Rain turns rice terraces into mirrors and fatten waterfalls.	**Sep & Oct** The gulf breeze keeps things cool as you stroll around Wéizhōu Island.	

Guǎngxī Highlights

1. **Yángshuò** (p621) Cycling past scenery straight out of a painting alongside the Yùlóng River.

2. **Lóngjǐ Rice Terraces** (p617) Trekking among stilt houses and fields that cascade down the slopes like stairs.

3. **Sānjiāng** (p619) Stopping by the Chéngyáng Wind and Rain Bridge, drum towers and cedar-wood homes of the artistic Dòng people.

4. **Tōnglíng Grand Canyon** (p636) Letting underground rivers, ancient caves and primeval forests whisper you their secrets.

5. **Bājiǎozhài National Geopark** (p617) Watching the Dānxiá geology unfold.

6. **Lèyè Geopark** (p637) Being awestruck by massive sinkholes and their caverns.

7. **Běihǎi** (p631) Exploring the delightful old seaside quarter and taking a trip to the volcanic island of Wéizhōu.

History

In 214 BC a Qin dynasty army attempted to assimilate the Zhuang people, living in what is now called Guǎngxī, into their newly formed Chinese empire. But while the eastern and southern parts submitted, the western extremes remained largely controlled by hill-tribe chieftains.

Major tribal uprisings occurred in the 19th century, the most significant being the Taiping Rebellion (1850–64), which became one of the bloodiest civil wars in human history, resulting in 20 million deaths.

Communist bases were set up in Guǎngxī following the 1929 Bǎisè Uprising led by Deng Xiaoping, although they were eventually destroyed by Kuomintang forces. Much of Guǎngxī fell briefly under Japanese rule following highly destructive WWII invasions.

Today the Zhuang, China's largest minority group, makes up 32% of Guǎngxī's population, which led to the province being reconstituted in 1955 as the Guǎngxī Zhuang Autonomous Region. As well as Zhuang, Miao and Yao, Guǎngxī is home to significant numbers of Dong people.

Language

Travellers with a grasp of Mandarin (Pǔtōnghuà) will have few problems navigating Guǎngxī's vast sea of languages. Cantonese (Guǎngdōnghuà), known as Báihuà in these parts, is the language of choice in Nánníng, Píngxiáng and Dàxīn, but most people also understand Mandarin. Visitors will also hear a number of minority languages being spoken, such as Zhuang, Dong and Yao.

PRICE RANGES

Sleeping
The following price ranges refer to a double room with bathroom.

$ less than ¥150

$$ ¥150–¥400

$$$ more than ¥400

Eating
The following price ranges refer to a main course.

$ less than ¥40

$$ ¥40–¥100

$$$ more than ¥100

---

❶ Getting There & Around

Airports at Guìlín and Nánníng run domestic flights of three hours or less to every major city, as well as international flights mainly to destinations in Southeast Asia, such as Thailand, Vietnam, Malaysia and Singapore.

Long-distance buses are less convenient than high-speed rail for covering great distances to neighbouring and more distant provinces, but are very handy for accessing nearby towns in closer provinces.

A well developed network of rail lines links together most of the province, making train the transport option of choice for most travellers.

High-speed rail, centred in Nánníng, connects Guǎngxī to provincial neighbours including Guǎngdōng, Guìzhōu, Húnán and Yúnnán and to the far-off metropolises of Běijīng and Shànghǎi, shrinking colossal distances and journey times.

Guìlín 桂林

☑ 0773 / POP 5,189,562

Guìlín was China's first city to develop tourism after 1949. For decades, children's textbooks proclaimed 'Guìlín's landscape is the best under heaven' (桂林山水甲天下). It was the darling of Chinese politicians, the star city proudly presented to visiting dignitaries. Today Guìlín's natural endowments still amaze, yet, thanks to imperfect urban planning, there is a pervasive feeling that the city is past its prime.

No matter where you're going in Guǎngxī, you're likely to spend a night or two here – Guìlín is a convenient base to plan trips to the rest of the province. It's clean and modern, with a high percentage of English-speaking locals, but you'll have to put up with touts and high admission fees to sights.

◎ Sights & Activities

Guìlín's sights are built around scraggly karst peaks that dot the bustling city. Some, owing to exorbitant admission prices, can be skipped, especially if you are heading to Yángshuò. A ride down the magical Lí River (漓江; Lí Jiāng) and a stroll around tranquil Róng and Shān lakes offer pleasing, wallet-friendly alternatives.

South Gate   GATE, LAKE

(南门, Nán Mén) On the northern shore of **Róng Lake** (榕湖, Róng Hú), and strikingly illuminated at night, the South Gate (南门; Nán Mén) is the only surviving section of the original Song-dynasty city wall (城墙; chéng qiáng). The area is abuzz with activity and

Guìlín

is a good place to watch locals practising ta-ichi, calligraphy and dancing.

East Gate HISTORIC SITE
(东镇门, Dōngzhèn Mén) About 1km north of **Folded Brocade Hill** (叠彩山, Diécǎi Shān; ¥35; ⏰7am-6pm) is the partly reconstructed East Gate, flanked by crumbling sections of the original wall. To reach the East Gate, take bus 1 or 2 and get off at the Dōngzhèn Lù stop, then turn right down the road of the same name. Alternatively, it's a short walk or cycle north along the riverbank, just east of the entrance to Folded Brocade Hill.

Shān Lake LAKE
(杉湖, Shān Hú) Literally 'Fir Lake', Shān Lake, together with its neighbour Róng Lake, was once part of a city moat.

Sun & Moon Twin Pagodas PAGODA
(日月双塔, Rìyuè Shuāng Tǎ; ¥45; ⏰8am-10.30pm) Elegantly embellishing the scenery of Shān Lake, the Sun and Moon Twin Pa-

Guìlín

◎ Sights
1	Róng Lake	B1
2	Shān Lake	C2
3	South Gate	B1
4	Sun & Moon Twin Pagodas	C2

🛏 Sleeping
5	Ming Palace International Youth	D1
6	Sheraton	D2
7	This Old Place Hostel	B1
8	White House	B1

✕ Eating
9	Kali Mirch	D2

🍷 Drinking & Nightlife
10	Róng Coffee	B2

godas, beautifully illuminated at night, are the highlight of a stroll around Guìlín's two central lakes. The octagonal, seven-storey Moon Pagoda (月塔; Yuè Tǎ) is connected by an underwater tunnel to the 41m-high Sun Pagoda (日塔; Rì Tǎ), one of the few pagodas with a lift.

Solitary Beauty Peak   PARK
(独秀峰, Dúxiù Fēng; 1 Wangcheng, 王城1号; ¥130; ⏱7.30am-6pm; 🚌1, 2) This park is a peaceful, leafy retreat from the city centre. The entrance fee for the famous lone pinnacle includes admission to an underwhelming 14th-century Ming prince's mansion (oversold as a 'palace'). The 152m peak affords fine views of Guìlín.

🛏 Sleeping

Ming Palace International Youth   HOSTEL $
(桂林王城青年旅舍, Guìlín Wángchéng Qīngnián Lûshè; 🕿0773 283 6888; mingpalace123@hotmail.com; 10 Donghua Lu, 东华路10号, 中华小学旁; dm ¥40-45, s ¥120, d ¥160-220, tr ¥210-240; ⊛🌐@🛜; 🚌99, 100 from South Guìlín Bus Station) Well located a very short walk from the east gate of the Ming palace and next to Zhōnghuá Primary School (Zhōnghuá Xiǎoxué), this affordable option has spacious, clean and bright doubles and twins, many with wood trim; single rooms are small, but value for money, and mixed and female dorms are clean (but there's no lift). The lobby is a bit gloomy, but staff are sunny and helpful.

Disembark the bus at Lèqún Lùkǒu (乐群路口), turn right at the first crossing, walk on, passing two arches, and then you'll see the hostel. A taxi from the airport costs ¥130.

This Old Place Hostel   HOSTEL $
(老地方国际青年旅舍, Lǎodìfāng Guójì Qīngnián Lûshè; 🕿0773 281 3598; www.topxingping.com; 2 Yiwu Lu, 翊武路2号; dm ¥35-40, d ¥100-120, tr ¥200-280; ⊛@🛜) This hostel doesn't have a huge amount of character but enjoys an enviable position facing Róng Lake and it's a 10-minute walk to the main eating and shopping areas. Three-bed dorms have single beds with en suite; regular rooms have a similar, though more spacious, arrangement. Pricier rooms face the lake.

White House   BOUTIQUE HOTEL $$$
(白公馆, Bái Gōngguǎn; 🕿0773 899 9888; www.glbgg.com; Bldg 4, 16 Ronghu Beilu, 榕湖北路16号4栋; d ¥980-1380, ste ¥1980-3780; ⊝⊛@🛜) The White House is decked out in all manner of period (some genuine, some perhaps not) trappings reflecting the building it's in – part of the former residence of General Bai Chongxi (白崇禧), a powerful regional

Guǎngxī warlord and father of the Taiwanese writer Kenneth Pai Hsien-yung (白先勇). Spacious guestrooms are lavishly appointed, featuring, among other luxuries, a mini-spa and high-thread-count bedding.

Sheraton   HOTEL $$$
(喜来登酒店, Xǐláidēng Jiǔdiàn; 🕿0773 282 5588; 15 Binjiang Lu, 滨江路15号; d ¥528-640; 🛝) Guǎngxī's first five-star hotel, the Sheraton is a bit long in the tooth, but its central positioning right by the Lí River is excellent. It's now more of a four-star hotel in its decor, standards and room appearance, and the swimming pool is external, but service is efficient, you're at the heart of the Guìlín action and you get value for money.

🍴 Eating

Chóngshàn Rice Noodle Shop   NOODLES $
(崇善米粉店, Chóngshàn Mǐfěn Diàn; 🕿0773 282 6036; 5 Yiren Lu, 依仁路5号; noodles ¥3-5; ⏱6.30am-midnight) This very popular Guìlín noodle shop near junction with Zhengyang Lu has branches all over town. Order at the front, take your docket to the cook and retrieve your food from a window. The slippery rice noodles come with a variety of ingredients, but the Guìlín speciality (also the tastiest) is with stewed vegetables (卤菜粉; lǔcài fěn).

★ Kali Mirch   INDIAN $$
(黑胡椒印度餐厅, Hēi Hújiāo Yìndù Cāntīng; 15 Binjiang Lu, Zhengyang Jie, 正阳步行街滨江路15号; mains from ¥30; 🛜) Tucked away behind the Sheraton, this fantastic restaurant is run by an affable and well travelled man from Darjeeling, who speaks perfect English and ensures that every dish is true to form. The vegetable samosas, onion pakoras, butter chicken and lamb biryani are just a few excellent dishes from a tried-and-tested menu, with all spices imported from India.

Céngsān Jiāwèiguǎn   GUANGXI $$
(曾三家味馆; 🕿0773 286 3781; 10 Xinyi Lu, 信义路10号; dishes ¥20-158; ⏱11am-2pm & 5-9pm) A modern restaurant jam-packed with middle-class locals who come for the generously plated wild boar, rabbit and cured meat dishes. If you prefer tamer flavours, there are other great options in the phone book of a menu. For weekend dinner, go before 6.15pm to snag a table. There's a Chinese picture menu. It's near junction with Xicheng Lu.

♟ Drinking & Nightlife

Guìlín's streets are dotted with trendy cafes; Zhengyang Lu has a short stretch of bars with outdoor seating, while Binjiang Lu alongside the river has a slew of cute drinking spots, most with free wi-fi.

Róng Coffee   CAFE
(榕咖啡, Róng Kāfēi; Bldg 5, Rónghú Hotel, 16 Ronghu Beilu, 榕湖北路16号; coffee & tea from ¥15, cake ¥24-30; ⊙1-11pm; 🛜) Looking like a greenhouse with colourful armchairs, this peaceful cafe by the picturesque Róng Lake offers a lovely getaway from the busy streets. It's even got a tiny garden with a couple of tables and a garden swing.

🛍 Shopping

Guìlín Night Market   MARKET
(夜市, Yèshì; Zhongshan Zhonglu, 中山中路; ⊙from 7pm) For souvenirs, check out Guìlín's night market, which runs along Zhongshan Zhonglu from Ronghu Beilu to Sanduo Lu.

Bird Flower Market   MARKET
(花鸟市场, Huāniǎo Shìchǎng; ⊙8am-5pm Sat & Sun; 🚌51) This local flea market has everything from electronics to vintage magazines, calligraphy brushes, dogs and, of course, birds and flowers.

ℹ Information

Buy a map of Guìlín (桂林地图; Guìlín dìtú) from bookshops or kiosks (¥7).

Bank of China (中国银行, Zhōngguó Yínháng) Branches on Zhongshan Nanlu (near the main bus station) and Jiefang Donglu change money, give credit-card advances and have 24-hour ATMs.

Guìlín Tourist Information Service Centre (桂林旅游咨询服务中心, Guìlín Lǚyóu Zīxún Fúwù Zhōngxīn; 📞0773 280 0318; South Gate, Ronghu Beilu, 榕湖北路; ⊙8am-10pm) These helpful centres dot the city. There's a good one just west of the South Gate on Róng Lake.

People's Hospital (人民医院, Rénmín Yīyuàn; 70 Wenming Lu, 文明路70号) This large, well equipped hospital is a designated International SOS service provider, and the teaching hospital of several universities in Guǎngxī.

Public Security Bureau (PSB, 公安局, Gōng'ānjú; 📞0773 582 3492; 16 Shijiayan Lu; ⊙8.30am-noon & 3-6pm Mon-Fri) Visa extensions. Located by Xiǎodōng River and 500m south of the Seven Stars Park. A taxi from downtown will cost around ¥20.

ℹ Getting There & Away

AIR

Buy air tickets from www.english.ctrip.com or www.elong.net; tickets can also be purchased from the **Civil Aviation Administration of China** (CAAC, 中国民航, Zhōngguó Mínháng; 📞0773 384 7252; cnr Shanghai Lu & Anxin Beilu; ⊙7.30am-8.30pm). Direct flights from Guìlín Liǎngjiāng International Airport (两江国际机场; Liǎngjiāng Guójì Jīchǎng) include Běijīng (¥1700), Chéngdū (¥900), Chóngqìng (¥600), Hǎikǒu (¥1040), Guǎngzhōu (¥800), Hong Kong (Xiānggǎng; ¥1800), Kūnmíng (¥580), Shànghǎi (¥1600) and Xī'ān (¥1000).

International destinations include Seoul, Korea (Hànchéng; ¥2000), and Osaka, Japan (Dàbǎn; ¥3200).

BUS

Guìlín's **main bus station** (桂林汽车客运总站, Guìlín Qìchē Kèyùn Zǒngzhàn; 📞0773 386 2358; 65 Zhongshan Nanlu, 中山南路65号; 🚌3, 9, 10, 11, 16, 25, 51, 88, 91, 99) has regular buses to the following destinations:

Běihǎi ¥230, seven hours, one daily (11.30am)

Guǎngzhōu ¥140, 9½ hours, 10 daily

Huángyáo ¥61, five hours, two daily (9am and 1.30pm)

Nánníng ¥110 to ¥125, five hours, every 15 minutes

Sānjiāng ¥43, four hours, hourly

Shēnzhèn ¥250, 12 hours, two daily (6pm and 9.20pm)

Yángshuò ¥25, 1½ hours, every 15 to 20 minutes

The **North Bus Station** (桂林汽车客运北站, Guìlín Qìchē Běizhàn; 76 Beichen Lu, 北辰路76号; 🚌18, 32, 99, 100) has buses to Zīyuán (¥31, every 20 minutes, 6.40am to 5.50pm).

Buses to Lóngshèng and the Lóngjǐ Rice Terraces depart from the North Bus Station (¥34, two hours, four daily, 9am, 11.10am, 11.30am and 2.30pm) and **Qíntán Bus Station** (琴潭汽车站, Qíntán Qìchē Zhàn; 31 Cuizhu Lu, 翠竹路31号; 🚌2, 12, 26, 32, 85, 91) (¥34, two hours, every 40 minutes, 6.10am to 7pm).

TRAIN

Few trains start in Guìlín, which means it's often tough to find tickets, so get them a few days in advance. Most trains leave from Guìlín Station (桂林站; Guìlín Zhàn), but some may leave from Guìlín North Train Station (桂林北站; Guìlín Běizhàn), 9km north of the city centre.

Direct services include:

Běijīng West 1st/2nd class ¥1250/806, 10½ hours, two daily (10.35am and 12.07pm)

Chóngqìng ¥280, 20 hours, two daily (12.50pm and 1.13pm)

Guǎngzhōu 1st/2nd class ¥165/138, three hours, regular

Kūnmíng ¥280, 18½ to 24 hours, four daily (11.21am, 1.22pm, 3.50pm and 4.10pm)

Nánníng 1st/2nd class ¥130/108, three hours, regular

Shànghǎi G-class train 2nd/1st class ¥660/1049, 9½ hours, one daily (11.44am)

Xī'ān ¥367, 27 hours, one daily (7.10pm)

❶ Getting Around

TO/FROM THE AIRPORT

The airport is 30km west of the city. Half-hourly shuttle buses (¥20) run from the CAAC office between 6.30am and 9pm. From the airport, shuttle buses meet every arrival. A taxi costs about ¥120 (40 minutes).

BICYCLE

Guìlín's sights are all within cycling distance. Many hostels rent bicycles (about ¥20 per day). For decent bikes, head to **Ride Giant** (捷安特自行车, Jié'ǎntè Zìxíngchē; ☎ 0773 286 1286; 28 Dongjiang Lu, 东江路28号; per day ¥70, deposit ¥500; ◷ 9.30am-9pm).

BUS

Buses numbered 51 to 58 are all free but run very infrequently. Regular buses cost ¥1 to ¥2. The following are the most useful:

Bus 2 Runs past Elephant Trunk Hill and Folded Brocade Hill.

Bus 51 Starts at the train station and heads north along the length of Zhongshan Lu to the Bird Flower Market and beyond.

Bus 58 Goes to Elephant Trunk Hill, Seven Stars Park, Wave-Subduing Hill, Folded Brocade Hill and Reed Flute Cave.

WORTH A TRIP

LÍ RIVER TRIP

The popular Lí River trip from Guìlín to Yángshuò lasts about 4½ hours and includes a wonderfully scenic boat trip to Yángshuò, lunch and a bus ride back to Guìlín. Expect to pay ¥350 to ¥450 for a boat with an English-speaking guide. There's also the **Two Rivers Four Lakes** (二江四湖, Èr Jiāng Sì Hú) boat ride around Guìlín that does a loop of the Lí River and the city's lakes. Prices vary from ¥150 to ¥340 for 90 minutes, depending on the time of day (it costs more at night). Pretty much every Guìlín hotel and tourist information service centre can arrange these two tours.

Around Guìlín

Jiāngtóuzhōu Ancient Town 江头洲

The 1000-year-old village of **Jiāngtóuzhōu** (admission ¥20) is tucked away among farmland 32km north of Guìlín. There's an unmistakable rustic charm, with cobblestone alleyways and weathered homes from the Ming and Qing dynasties, where blocks of tofu are laid out to set in the courtyards. Its residents are descendants of the philosopher Zhou Dunyi (周敦颐), who is famed for his essay on virtue, 'Love of the Water-Lily'. The flower is a decorative motif throughout the village and inside the **ancestral hall**.

Jiāngtóuzhōu is a two- to three-hour bike ride from Guìlín. Alternatively, take an orange minibus on the stretch of Zhongshan Beilu near Guìlín North Train Station to Língchuān (灵川; ¥3, 40 minutes). Get off at Tǎnxià Lùkǒu (潭下路口), zip across the road and change to a bus to Jiǔwū (九屋; ¥4, 45 minutes), from where it's a 15-minute walk to the village. Buses stop running around 5.30pm.

Dàxū Ancient Town 大圩

☎ 0773 / POP 50,000

One of the four greatest ancient market towns in Guǎngxī, Dàxū (literally, 'Big Market') was founded in AD 200. The town's dusty streets run alongside the Lí River for 2km, flanked by one- and two-storey houses. Some of these are 'home offices' from which herbalists, barbers, cobblers and traditional craftspeople ply their trade. It's a leisurely place where doors are left open, children and chickens run freely, and corn is dried on the crooked banisters of an old stone bridge.

🛏 Sleeping & Eating

Guǎngchāng Museum MUSEUM, HISTORIC BUILDING
(广昌博物馆, Guǎngchāng Bówùguǎn; 66 Minzhu Lu) **FREE** The opulent residence and courtyards of Dàxū's wealthiest family, the Gaos (高), are lavishly embellished with ornate carvings and expensive classical furniture.

★ Ancient Town Fish Restaurant SEAFOOD $$
(古镇鱼餐厅, Gǔzhèn Yú Cāntīng; ☎ 0773 635 2299; 69 Minzhu Lu; dishes ¥30-65; ◷ 11.30am-3pm & 6-8.30pm) The kitchen of this excellent rustic place has cured pork hanging on white-tiled walls, fish swimming in tubs,

and baskets of vegetables plucked from their plot. Sometimes the staff will let you go into the kitchen and choose your meal. Look for the door with a red sign that says 古镇旅社 (Gǔzhèn Lǚshè). Go through the lobby into a courtyard and you'll see the restaurant.

❶ Getting There & Away

The town is 15km from Guìlín. Six buses (¥10, 40 minutes) per day depart for Dàxū Zhèn (大圩镇) from Guìlín's main bus station between 7.30am and 4pm. Buses to Dàxū Zhèn can be found through the stone lions just south of the bus station in Guìlín – walk through the corridor to the bus lot at the end.

Zīyuán 资源

📞 0773 / POP 167,000

About 107km north of Guìlín, Zīyuán County, built around the pristine Zī River, is a gateway to geological gems of Dānxiá (丹霞) topography, such as Bājiǎozhài National Geopark and Tiānmén Mountain. The town of Zīyuán is a good place to base yourself to explore these two sites.

Bājiǎozhài National Geopark (八角寨, Bājiǎozhài; Meixi Xiang Fúzhú Village, 梅溪乡, 福竹村; ¥80) is named after eight Dānxiá stone peaks that lie near the border with Húnán. Round, isolated, featuring ringlike troughs and leaning 45 degrees in the same direction, they resemble snails sunning themselves after the rain. The trail winds past cliffs, boulders, gorges and bamboo forests. On the way up to the car park, you'll pass a few farm restaurants. The chicken hotpot (土鸡火锅; tǔjī huǒguō), made with fresh free-range fowl and just-picked vegetables, is divine.

Tiānmén Mountain National Park (天门山景区, Tiānmén Shān Jǐngqū; adult/child ¥60/30, cable car one-way/return ¥60/120; ⏱9am-5pm, cable car 9.30am-4pm) is home to proud cliffs and sharp ravines as well as subtropical foliage, clusters of ash-brown dwellings and crumbling roadside shrines. There are multiple viewing spots along hiking trails in the park, including a U-shaped deck with a transparent floor. If you have time, boats are at hand to take you for a ride down the lovely Zī River.

For a good night's sleep, **Shéngyuán Hotel** (盛源大酒店, Shéngyuán Dàjiǔdiàn sheng; 📞0773 436 8988; http://glsydjd.com; 188 Chéngběi Kāifāqū, 城北开发区188号; s ¥330, tw ¥280-320, ste from ¥560; 🅿🌐🛜) in the northern area of the county is a very good choice. Rooms are spacious and the best ones overlook the river. The 8th floor is smoke-free.

Buses leave Guìlín's North Bus Station for Zīyuán every 20 minutes from 6.40am to 5.50pm. Tickets are between ¥31 and ¥40 for the three-hour ride.

A car directly from Guìlín to Tiānmén Mountain or Bājiǎozhài National Geopark will cost around ¥650 to ¥750.

From downtown Zīyuán, you can hire a car to Tiānmén Mountain, 30 minutes away, for around ¥140, or to Bājiǎozhài National Geopark, 45 minutes away, for slightly more. The driver will wait for you to hike, but take their mobile number in case you need a long time. If you do both places on the same day, it'll cost you over ¥200, but you'll need to start off early (say, at 7am) and spend no more than four hours at each destination.

Lóngjǐ Rice Terraces 龙脊梯田

📞 0773

This part of Guǎngxī is famous for its breathtaking vistas of terraced paddy fields cascading in swirls down into a valley. For hundreds of years, the paddy fields of Lóngjǐ Rice Terraces (Lóngjǐ Tītián) remained unknown to travellers, then everything changed in the 1990s when a photographer named Li Yashi (李亚石) moved here. His images of the scenery amazed the world and put Lóngjǐ (literally 'Dragon's Back') firmly on the tourist trail.

You'll find the most spectacular views around the villages of **Píng'ān** (平安), a Zhuang settlement; **Dàzhài** (大寨), a mesmerising Yao village; and **Tiántóuzhài** (田头寨), which sits slightly further above Dàzhài.

Being the earliest to open to tourism, Píng'ān has the best facilities and it's the closest point of access to the standout Nine Dragons & Five Tigers Viewing Point (p618) that looks down on breathtaking terraced field views. Tourism is picking up at Dàzhài and Tiántóuzhài to the east and a cable-car service has been added to Dàzhài.

At the time of writing, sections of the area had been reduced to a muddy quagmire with roads being built, but the main sights were undisturbed. Expect increased transport infrastructure to bring in even more crowds in future, however. A further area of terraced fields just to the southwest of Píng'ān has also been developed, the **Gǔzhuàngzhài Tītián** (古壮寨梯田).

The best time to visit Lóngjǐ is after the summer rains in May, after farmers have irrigated and the fields glisten with reflections. The fields turn golden just before the

October harvest, and snow-white in winter (December). Avoid early spring (March), when the mountains are often mist-shrouded; visitor numbers are way down.

◉ Sights & Activities

As hiking is a way of life here, bring a day pack and leave your luggage in Guìlín or in the main ticket office. Otherwise villagers will carry your bags for ¥50 apiece; there's a lot of hollering to provide this service.

You can take a number of **short walks** from each village to the fabulous viewing points, which are all clearly signposted. The three- to four-hour **trek** between the villages of Dàzhài, via Tiántóuzhài and Píng'ān is also highly recommended. However, get a local to guide you for around ¥100 or ask directions frequently along the way, as there are almost no signposts for this hike (astonishing considering the amount of money spent on new roads), and you will meet numerous sign-less forks in the path. Recent road construction has made it even more confusing (and muddy). To ask 'Is this the way to Píng'ān', show this to a local farmer: '去平安, 怎么走?' For Dàzhài, it's: '去大寨, 怎么走?' They will point the way. The path can be very slippery after rain, so take hiking boots with good grip – you can easily turn an ankle or take a fall.

Rice Terraces   LANDMARK
(龙脊梯田, Lóngjǐ Tītián; ¥100) These are the clear standouts in the area. Rising to 1000m, they are an amazing feat of farm engineering on hills dotted with minority villages. One of the most sublime and beautiful images rewards the climb up to the **Nine Dragons & Five Tigers Viewing Point** (九龙五虎观景点, Jiǔlóng Wǔhǔ Guānjǐngdiǎn) with its astonishing, curvaceous layers of terraces. It's around a 30-minute walk above Píng'ān. The oldest field is over 700 years old; you pass it just before making your ascent to Dàzhài.

🎎 Festivals & Events

Ghost Festival   CULTURAL
(鬼节, Guǐ Jié) During the Ghost Festival, celebrated on the eighth day of the fourth lunar month, the Yao and Zhuang eat 'rice of seven colours' (七彩饭; qīcǎi fàn), which consists of white glutinous rice, and rice dyed naturally with maple (black), amaranth (red), sweet vernal grass (yellow), and a kind of berry (blue), and, artificially, with purple and green dyes.

Clothes Drying Festival   CULTURAL
(晒衣节, Shàiyī Jié) One of the biggest Yao festivals is the Clothes Drying Festival, which falls on the sixth day of the sixth lunar month. On that day, the women lay out all their traditional costumes under the sun. This serves the dual purpose of disinfection and allowing the ladies to show off. If it rains, they take their fashion spread indoors, leaving the door open.

🛏 Sleeping & Eating

Nearly all guesthouses offer food, and most restaurants have English menus; dishes cost between ¥15 and ¥100.

Oil tea – fried tea leaves brewed and drunk with rice puffs and peanuts – is consumed for breakfast, as is egg in sweet wine (甜酒鸡蛋; tián jiǔ jīdàn), heated rice wine into which an egg is dropped. Another common dish is glutinous rice baked inside bamboo sticks (竹筒饭; zhútǒng fàn).

★ Lóngjǐ International Youth Hostel   HOSTEL $
(龙脊国际青年旅舍, Lóngjǐ Guójì Qīngnián Lǚshě; ☑ 0773 758 3265; yha-longji@qq.com; Píng'ān Village, 平安村; dm/tw/tr ¥40/128/168; ❄@🛜) One of the first accommodation options you find walking into Píng'ān, this thoroughly pleasant, friendly and amenable hostel has decent rooms in a kind of *Twin Peaks* wooden surrounds setting. Double rooms are comfortable and spacious enough, with views. The restaurant is also really good and the spacious bar is an excellent spot for drinking and chit-chat at night.

Dragon's Den Hostel   HOSTEL $
(大寨青年旅舍, Dàzhài Qīngnián Lǚshě; ☑ 0773 758 5780; www.dragonsdenhostel.com; Tiántóu Zhai, Dàzhài Village, 龙脊梯田大寨村田头摘; dm ¥40-45, tw & d ¥90-120; ❄❄🛜) With a cosy lounge and a children's library, this hostel has some rooms with sit-down toilets and air-conditioning; the rest have squatting latrines and the cool night breeze. Dorms are four- and five-bed rooms. It's a 40-minute climb from Dàzhài. When you see Mr Liao Cafe & Bar, turn right and go another 150m.

★ Panorama House Hotel   HOTEL $$
(全景楼大酒店, Quánjǐnglóu Dàjiǔdiàn; ☑ 136 1786 9898, 130 7764 6291, 0773 758 5688; www.quanjinglou.com; scenic spot no 1, Lóngjǐ Terrace, 龙脊金坑大寨瑶族梯田1号景观点; d & tw ¥880, tr & q ¥980, ste ¥1080-1888; ❄@🛜) This excellent 100-room brick-and-concrete hotel near

the summit of Dàzhài has a bird's-eye view of the fields. The rooms are sparkling, the restaurant is good (though pricey) and there are swings on the balconies. Ask for a room facing east, but rooms with views of the terraces are the priciest. Frequent discounts of around 60% or more.

★ **Lóngjǐ Holiday Hotel** INN $$
(龙脊假日酒店, Lóngjǐ Jiàrì Jiǔdiàn; ☏0773 758 3545, 134 5731 8219; www.ljjrjd.com; d/ste ¥200/520, ⊕③) This cosy place in Píng'ān is run by a pleasant Zhuang woman called Yanmei and her brother. Spacious tiled rooms sport sharp colour coordination, a display of Zhuang artefacts, pretty lights, sinks and showers, balconies and lovely views (especially on the upper floors). Stoves are in the pipeline. Yanmei also acts as a guide, charging around ¥300 for the walk to Dàzhài.

❶ Information

There's nowhere here to change money, so bring enough with you, especially if you are going on to Sānjiāng, which has the same problem.

❶ Getting There & Away

Hotels in Dàzhài and Tiántóuzhài arrange direct shuttle services from Dàzhài to Guìlín (10am, 1pm and 4pm), and from Guìlín to Dàzhài (8am, 10.30am and 2pm) for their guests. The price is usually ¥50 per person. They also take other passengers if seats are available. Reservations are a must. All hotels in Píng'ān provide a similar service.

For public transport from Guìlín, head to the city's North Bus Station (p615) or Qíntán Bus Station (p615). From there, take a bus to Lóngshèng (龙胜; ¥34, two hours, every 30 minutes, 7am to 7pm) and ask to get off at Hépíng (和平). From the road junction (or the ticket office three minutes' walk away), minibuses trundle between Lóngshèng and the rice terraces, stopping to pick up passengers to Dàzhài (¥10, one hour, every 30 minutes, 7am to 5pm) and Píng'ān (¥10, 30 minutes, every 20 minutes to one hour, 7am to 5pm). Buses go via Èrlóng Bridge (二龙桥; Èrlóng Qiáo). If you have walked from Píng'ān to Dàzhài and want to take the bus back to Píng'ān rather than head to Lóngshèng, you need to take a bus (¥12) first to Èrlóng Bridge, then another bus (¥8) to Píng'ān. The same applies in the other direction.

Guìlín's main bus station (p615) also has buses to Dàzhài and Lóngjǐ (Píng'ān; ¥50, three hours, 8.30am, 9am and 2pm). Renting a car from Guìlín to here is about ¥400.

Six buses run daily between Lóngshèng and Píng'ān (¥12, one hour, 7.30am, 9am, 11am, 1pm, 3pm and 5pm). Buses (¥10, 1½ hours, 8am to 5pm) also run direct hourly between Lóngshèng and Dàzhài.

To continue to Sānjiāng, catch a bus (¥22, regular) from Lóngshèng bus station. The bus runs scenically along the river to Sānjiāng.

Sānjiāng 三江

☑0772 / POP 367,707

Riverside Sānjiāng town is a rather nondescript place in itself, but is a convenient springboard to the ethereal Dong villages and their architectural wonders in Chéngyángqiáo Scenic Area.

The town is best treated as an arrival, overnighting and departure point, with high-speed trains to Guìlín and slower trains north into Húnán province.

★ **Drum Towers** TOWER
(鼓楼, Gǔlóu) A drum tower resembles a flamboyant, multieaved pagoda plonked on a rectangular pavilion; many are found in Dòng villages in the region. The taller ones are built entirely of cedar. Donate a few coins as you enter, and look up at the receding beams and the scalelike tiles. Some towers have a fire pit. Once the social and religious heart of the village, they're now colonised by old men watching TV and playing table tennis.

◉ Sights

★ **Chéngyáng Wind & Rain Bridge** BRIDGE
(程阳桥, Chéngyángqiáo; 林溪, Línxī; admission ¥80, incl with Chéngyángqiáo Scenic Area admission) Around 18km north of Sānjiāng, the grandest of over 100 nail-less wind-and-rain bridges in the area, this photogenic black-and-white structure (78m) was built from cedar and stone over 12 years in the early 1900s. It features towers with upturned eaves, pavilions where people gather to socialise or take shelter from the elements, and a sweeping corridor with handrails and benches.

Chéngyángqiáo Scenic Area AREA
(程阳桥景区, Chéngyángqiáo Jǐngqū; ¥80) Beyond the standout Chéngyáng Wind & Rain Bridge, the best way to take in this scenic area's natural and human-made beauty is by walking among the fields. Each hamlet has a distinctive-looking **drum tower** and a stage on which tables are set up for mahjong games. The homes are simple one- or two-storey cabins made of chocolate-toned cedar bark that exude an ancient grace

evocative of Kyoto. The Dong are known for their exquisite carpentry and each home is a celebration of that skill.

🛏 Sleeping & Eating

Most visitors aim to spend the night near the Chéngyáng Wind & Rain Bridge (p619). Sānjiāng itself has many hotels, especially along Furong Lu (芙蓉路), not far from the east bus station, but the town is not a particularly appealing place. It is handy, however, if you only want to take a day trip to the bridge.

Dòng Village Hotel INN $$
(程阳桥侗家宾馆, Chéngyángqiáo Dòngjiā Bīnguǎn; ☎0772 858 2421; www.donghotel.com; Chéngyángqiáo, 程阳桥; d/tr ¥200/250; 🖂❋🛜) This popular inn run by a friendly host, English-speaking Michael Yang, is excellently located right by the bridge. Rooms, connected by a creaking staircase, come with balconies, air-con and bathrooms. Pray for quiet neighbours – the walls are very thin. It's immediately on your left after the bridge crossing and has been a staple of visitors for years.

Sanjiang Hotel HOTEL $$
(三江饭店, Sānjiāng Fàndiàn; Furong Lu, 芙蓉路; d¥388-518, tr/ste ¥508/888; ❋🛜) Conveniently located in-between the east and west bus stations, this reasonably glossy three-star hotel has very clean, spacious and comfortable rooms. Staff are not that used to dealing with foreigners, but are friendly. The hotel has a lift and in-room wi-fi. In the off season, you can usually get a room for around ¥130.

Lánzhōu Lāmiàn NOODLES $
(兰州拉面; 46 Furong Lu, 芙蓉路46号; noodles from ¥7; ⏱6.30am-3am) This really popular noodle spot is often full of locals feasting on steaming bowls of beef noodles (牛肉拉面; niúròu lāmiàn); warm, filling and value for money. It's on the far side of the road from the Sānjiāng Hotel, towards the higher, southern end.

ℹ Information

With no Bank of China in town, there is nowhere to change money in Sānjiāng, so make sure you bring enough cash. As there is also nowhere to change money at the Lóngjǐ Rice Terraces, and many travellers will be coming from that direction, make sure you have enough money changed either in Guìlín or elsewhere.

ICBC (工商银行, Gōngshāng Yínháng; 22 Dongxiang Dadao, 侗乡大道22号) cannot change money, but it has a 24-hour ATM.

English-language skills are not strong at the **Tourist Office** (旅游服务中心, Lǚyóu Fúwù Zhōngxīn; ☎0772 861 6567; 19 Dongxiang Dadao, 侗乡大道19号; ⏱8am-6pm) but it is well equipped and helpful.

ℹ Getting There & Away

BUS

For Chéngyáng Bridge, take the half-hourly bus bound for Línxī (林溪) from Sānjiāng west bus station (¥31, 30 minutes, 7.30am to 5.30pm). If you miss the last bus, private minivans to Línxī wait on the main road outside the west bus station. The fare is the same but they won't leave until they're full.

Most buses go to/from Sānjiāng's east bus station (河东车站; hédōng chēzhàn), but buses to Chéngyáng Bridge go from the west bus station (河西车站; héxī chēzhàn), a 10-minute walk (about 500m, or a ¥4 pedicab ride) across the river. To reach the west bus station, turn right from the east bus station, right again over the river and right once more after you cross the river.

Buses from the east bus station include:

Běihǎi ¥200, nine hours, 9.50am

Chángshā ¥220, seven hours, 9pm

Guìlín ¥60, five hours, 8.30am, 9.35am, 2pm and 3.10pm

Lóngshèng ¥22, three hours, regular 7am to 5.55pm

Nánníng ¥160, seven hours, three daily

Apart from regular buses to Línxī (for Chéngyáng Bridge), the west bus station also has one bus a day to Guǎngzhōu (¥170, 3.20pm) and four buses (¥26) a day to Tōngdào across the border in Húnán province.

TRAIN

High-speed trains (¥27 to ¥34) from Guìlín arrive at and depart from the South Train Station (三江南站; Sānjiāng Nánzhàn), taking between 30 minutes and an hour, depending on which station in Guìlín they leave from. Heading north towards Húnán and Fènghuáng, you'll need to go to Sānjiāng Train Station (三江县站; Sānjiāng Xiàn Zhàn), a minute train station around 10km north of town. There is one train (¥36) per day from here to Huáihuà at 7.44pm. For a ¥5 commission, you can get train tickets from a booth opposite the Bird's Nest (三江侗乡鸟巢; Sānjiāng Dòngxiāng Niǎocháo) on Dongxiang Dadao, which is just beyond the tourist office.

ℹ Getting Around

Bus 1 (¥1) links the east and west bus stations. Sānjiāng Train Station is a ¥10 minivan ride away; a taxi will cost ¥50. Taxi flagfall is ¥5.

Yángshuò 阳朔

☑ 0773 / POP 308,296

Yángshuò is one of China's gold-ticket draws. The once-peaceful settlement is now a collage of Chinese tour groups, bewildered Westerners, pole-dancing bars, construction and the glue that binds any tourist hot spot together – touts. Come evening, Xijie is all thumping music and bristling with selfie-sticks, but go up a few flights to a hotel rooftop bar and behold the ethereal beauty of the surrounding karsts, their peaks lit up by searchlights.

Outside of town, which is the reason you will be here, the karst landscape becomes even more surreal and other-worldly. Take a bamboo-raft ride or cycle through the dreamy valleys and you'll see. And with the best hotels and guesthouses immersed in the surrounding countryside or plonked next to sublime river views, there is less reason to base yourself in Yángshuò town itself.

◉ Sights

The most accessible of Yángshuò's limestone peaks is **Bìlián Peak** (碧莲峰, Bìlián Fēng; ¥30), which overlooks Xijie and the Lí River, and can be climbed in half an hour. Look for the signboard that says 山水园. **Yángshuò Park** (阳朔公园; Yángshuò Gōngyuán) is a short walk west of Xijie and that's where you'll find **Man Hill** (西郎山; Xīláng Shān) 'bowing' to **Lady Hill** (小姑山; Xiǎogū Shān). Don't overlook going for a walk along the Lí River, to get away from the crowds and see what coming to Yángshuò is all about.

★ Lí Riverside Path RIVER
(Líjiāng Jiāngbīn Dào, 漓江江滨道; Binjiang Lu, 滨江路) When Xijie, the crowds and postcard hawkers get too much, head down the steps to the Lí River. Unfolding before you is a beautiful panorama of karst peaks, glittering river water and green bamboo. It's a stunning sight, and you can walk for a fair distance along the bank of the river, past folk practising taichi or playing with their children.

House of Xu Beihong MUSEUM
(徐悲鸿故居, Xú Bēihóng Gùjū; 5 Xianqian Jie, 县前街5号; ⊙8.30am-7pm) FREE This small shrine to the 20th-century artist Xu Beihong (famed most chiefly for his pictures of galloping horses) – in a small one-storey house where he once lived – is simple and understated, but makes a charming cultural addition to town. Photographs and paintings all have (occasionally misfiring) English captions.

🏃 Activities

Yángshuò is one of the hottest climbing destinations in Asia. There are eight major peaks in regular use, already providing more than 250 bolted climbs.

Bike Asia CYCLING
(☑0773 882 6521; www.bikeasia.com; 8 Guihua Lu, 桂花路8号; ⊙8.30am-6.30pm) Bike Asia has the best equipment and advice on trips. Bikes are ¥70 per day (deposit ¥300), including safety helmet and map. English-speaking guides (from ¥300 per day) are available.

Yángshuò Cooking School COOKING
(阳朔烹饪学校, Yángshuò Pēngrèn Xuéxiào; ☑137 8843 7286; Cháolóng Village) A classy cooking school worth checking out.

Insight Adventures Yángshuò CLIMBING
(☑0773 881 1033; www.insight-adventures.com; 12 Furong Lu, 芙蓉路12号; ⊙9am-9pm) Offers local advice for experienced climbers and fully guided, bolted climbs for beginners. Prices start at ¥350 per person for a half-day climb. Kayaking and other activities are also organised.

🛏 Sleeping

Yángshuò teems with hotels run by English-speaking staff, and virtually all provide wi-fi access. While the Xijie neighbourhood is stuffed with choices, quieter and more attractive lodgings lie on the outskirts.

For total peace and quiet and a glorious setting, opt for one of the accommodation choices in the Lí River area (p624).

Green Forest Hostel HOSTEL $
(瓦舍, Wǎshě; ☑0773 888 2686; greenforest_yangshuo@yahoo.com; 3rd fl, Zone A, Business St, Chéngzhōngchéng, Diecui Lu, 叠翠路, 城中城, 城南商业街A区3楼; dm/r ¥40/200; ❀@⛊) This hostel's attractiveness is highlighted by the rundown building it's in. Rooms are painted white with colourful accents and have earth-toned furnishings; communal areas are flooded in natural light. From the bus station, turn right and walk along Diecui Lu, past Guihua Lu. At the junction with Chengzhong Lu, turn right and look for 99 Shopping Centre (99超市).

Yángshuò Senior Leader Youth Hostel HOSTEL $
(阳朔老班长国际青年旅舍; Yángshuò Lǎobānzhǎng Guójì Qīngnián Lǚshè; ☑0773 691 9780; 36 Fuqian Xiang, Diecui Lu, 叠翠路, 府前巷36号; dm ¥45-50, d & tw ¥180; ❀❀@⛊) A

Yángshuò

Yángshuò

conveniently located hostel with friendly staff, basic rooms and a large, comfy and inviting lobby with a gurgling water feature in the corner. Note that the doubles have squat loos, but the twins have Western loos. The hostel is not far from the Sunshine 100 (阳光 100) and Huāróng Hotel (华荣大酒店). Step into the alley below the sign of Huāróng Hotel and you'll reach the hostel.

Rosewood Inn
HOTEL $$

(玫瑰木宾馆, Méiguī Mù Bīnguăn; ☑0773 881 3918; www.yangshuorosewood.com; 95 Guihua Lu, 桂花路95号; s ¥228, d ¥258-288, tr ¥388-488, ste ¥388-488; ❀@☎) Right by the water in the centre of town, but tucked away and out of the action, this decent, quite charming and comfortable choice has wood-panelled rooms, many with balcony (the cheapest of each type are without balcony). Service is very professional and friendly, making it a cut above the rest. Breakfast is an extra ¥41.

River View Hotel
HOTEL $$

(望江楼酒店, Wàngjiānglóu Jiŭdiàn; ☑0773 882 2688; www.riverview.com.cn; 11 Binjiang Lu, 滨江 路11号; r ¥360-680; ❀@☎) If you prefer staying downtown but want to avoid the crowds, this good-value hotel is a decent bet. The balcony rooms overlook the Lí River and are somewhat old-fashioned but decent and the restaurant on the ground floor is a good choice. The street below can be noisy, so tell the friendly staff you'd like a room on the 3rd or 4th floor.

Leisure Inn Yangshuo
HOTEL $$$

(阳朔丽怡假日酒店, Yángshuò Lìyí Jiàrì Jiŭdiàn; ☑0773 888 2999; www.leisureinn-yangshuo.com; 17 Diecui Lu, 叠翠路17号; r ¥1288-1388, ste ¥3288; ❀❀@☎) A good upmarket option in the Sunshine 100 (阳光100) block. The lobby has an outmoded, ethnic look but all 71 rooms feature subdued aesthetics and sleek modern lines that won a German design award. Do not be intimidated by the rack rates of the guest rooms – prices usually go down by half and include breakfast.

🍴 Eating

Local specialities include *tiánluóniàng* (田螺酿; stuffed snails) and *píjiǔ yú* (啤酒鱼; beer fish). The fish with the least bones are *jiàngǔyú* (剑骨鱼) and the bigger and cheaper ones *máogǔyú* (毛骨鱼). Almost all restaurants have English menus.

You can find anything from wood-fired pizza and chicken korma to full English breakfasts, frankfurters served by German chefs and outposts of US fast-food empires.

★ Echo Cafe
CAFE $

(2 Fuqian Jie, 府前街2号; mains from ¥30; ⊙9am-midnight) This lovely cafe is tucked a long way from the tourist maelstrom, despite being just around the corner from Xijie. Very relaxing and tranquil, guitars and ukuleles lie around randomly, awaiting musical fingers. Sounds are (ballpark) classic jazz ballads. Staff are sweet and a small library rounds it off. There's a tasty and changing German/Western menu too, and breakfasts (9am to midday). Great cheesecake.

Lucy's
INTERNATIONAL $

(露茜, Lùxī; 30 Guihua Lu, 桂花路30号; mains from ¥25; ⊙7am-midnight; 🛜) With graffiti-splattered walls, Lucy's is quite an institution. Western and Chinese food are done with equal aplomb – aim for one of the terrace seats upstairs overlooking the tourist traffic below. There's shepherd's pie (¥40), beer fish (¥88), sizzling beef platter (¥40), tuna spaghetti (¥35) and more, plus full English brekkies (¥38).

Lěngwá Shǎnxī Fēngwèiguǎn
SHANXI $

(愣娃陕西风味馆; 21 Diecui Lu, 叠翠路21号; mains from ¥10; ⊙8am-11pm) This small and simple Shǎnxī eatery specialises in the addictive *ròujiāmó* (肉夹馍; flat-bread buns filled with beef or pork and peppers) and *biángbiángmiàn* (flat Shǎnxī noodles; the character for 'biang' is the most complicated in the Chinese language, and impossible to reproduce here). One *ròujiāmó* is ¥10 and two are almost a meal; a bowl of *biángbiángmiàn* starts at ¥19. The friendly and affable owner is from Xī'ān and speaks English.

Dàcūnmén Night Market
MARKET $

(大村门夜市, Dàcūnmén Yèshì; Pantao Lu, 蟠桃路; ⊙5pm-late) This night market is a culture-filled slice of nontourist Yángshuò

life. Watch locals sniffing out the best spices, haggling over snails or tucking into a dog hotpot. It's a 30-minute walk from Xijie. After you pass the petrol station on Pantao Lu, look for the fire station on the left, behind which is the night market.

River View Hotel Restaurant
GUANGXI, WESTERN $$

(望江楼餐厅, Wàngjiānglóu Cāntīng; 11 Binjiang Lu, 滨江路11号; mains ¥20-80; ⊙8.30am-8.30pm; ▣🍴) Just a street removed from traffic-choked Diecui Lu, this place offers good food, quiet surrounds and attractive prices, with river views to boot. There's an English menu with pizzas and sandwiches, and a Chinese one with all the usual suspects, well executed.

🍷 Drinking & Nightlife

Yángshuò is stuffed with bars, but there are few of character and taste, and many are cheesy.

Several restaurants double as decent bars, and many hotels, hostels and guesthouses have relaxing bar areas. Just off Xijie is where German beer gardens sit alongside generic Western-style cafes.

★ Mojo Bar
BAR

(露天酒吧, Lùtiān Jiǔbā; 6th fl, Alshan Hotel, 18 Xijie, 西街18号阿里山大酒店六楼; ⊙7pm-3am; 🛜) Way above the throngs choking Xijie, Mojo Bar – on the 6th floor and roof of the Alshan Hotel – has the most amazing outdoor terrace with wraparound views of the *Avatar*-like karst landscape, set to Red Hot Chili Peppers. Inside it's pool, cheap beer (Tsingtao, ¥20) and rather cramped quarters; outside, on long summer evenings especially, it's astonishing views in all directions.

Find your way to No 18 Xijie, the Alshan Hotel, and take the lift to the 4th floor before walking up the last two flights to Mojo Bar.

☆ Entertainment

Impressions Liú Sānjiě
PERFORMING ARTS

(印象刘三姐, Yìnxiàng Liú Sānjiě; 📞0773 881 7783; tickets ¥200-680; ⊙7.30-8.30pm & 9.30-10.30pm) The busiest show in town is directed by filmmaker Zhang Yimou, who also directed acclaimed films such as *Raise the Red Lantern* and *House of Flying Daggers*. Six hundred performers take to the Lí River each night with 12 illuminated karst peaks serving as a backdrop. Book at your hotel for discounts and transport to/from the venue (1.5km from town).

ⓘ Information

Travel agencies are all over town. Backpacker-oriented cafes and most hotels can also often dispense good advice. Shop around for the best deals.

Bank of China (中国银行, Zhōngguó Yínháng; Xijie, 西街; ☺9am-5pm) Foreign exchange and 24-hour ATM for international cards.

People's Hospital (人民医院, Rénmín Yīyuàn; 26 Chengzhong Lu, 城中路26号) English-speaking doctors available.

Public Security Bureau (PSB, 公安局, Gōng'ānjú; Chengbei Lu, 城北路; ☺8am-noon & 3-6pm summer, 2.30-5.30pm winter) Has several fluent English speakers, but doesn't issue visa extensions. It's 100m east of People's Hospital.

ⓘ Getting There & Away

AIR

The closest airport is in Guìlín. Your hotel should be able to organise taxi rides directly to the airport (about ¥240, one hour).

BUS

Yángshuò has two bus stations: **Shímǎ South Bus Station** (汽车南站, Qìchē Nánzhàn; courtyard of the Agriculture Mechanisation Management Bureau, 321 Guodao, 国道321号, 农业机械化管理局) and **Dàcūnmén North Station** (汽车北站, Qìchē Běizhàn; fishery market next to Dàcūnmén Provincial Government Service Centre, Qingquan Lu, 大村门开发区清泉路,大村门县政务服务中心,水产批发市场处).

Direct bus links:

Guìlín ¥20, one hour, every 15 to 20 minutes (6.45am to 8.30pm), leaves when full

Guìlín Airport ¥70, 1½ hours, 8am, 10am, noon, 1.30pm, 3.30pm, 5.30pm, 7pm and 8.30pm

Nánníng ¥160, six hours, three daily (8.40am, 11.30am and 3.30pm)

Shēnzhèn ¥150 to ¥180, eight hours, seven daily (1.30am, 12.30pm, 1.30pm, 3pm, 8.30pm, 9.30pm and 10.30pm)

Xìngpíng ¥8, one hour, every 15 minutes (6.30am to 6pm)

Yángdī ¥9.50, one hour, every 20 minutes (7am to 6pm)

The bus from Guìlín to Huángyáo (¥61, 9am and 1.30pm) only stops in Yángshuò erratically, so check before purchasing tickets.

TRAIN

Yángshuò town itself has no train station, but there is a station called Yángshuò station servicing high-speed trains in Fànzèng Shān (饭甑山), near Xìngpíng, 14km away. Regular buses (¥20) connect the train station with Yángshuò, travelling via Xìngpíng. Trains include:

Guǎngzhōu 1st/2nd class ¥141/117, 2½ hours, five daily, 8.21am to 6.49pm

Guìlín 1st/2nd class ¥25/21, 30 minutes, seven daily, 9.03am to 7.19pm

Nánníng 1st/2nd class ¥157/131, 3½ hours, one daily, 9.03am

ⓘ Getting Around

Most places in town can be reached by pedicab for under ¥20. Bicycles can be rented at almost all hostels and from streetside outlets for ¥10 to ¥25 per day. A deposit of ¥200 to ¥500 is standard, but don't hand over your passport. For better-quality bikes, head to Bike Asia (p621).

Bike-rental operators will rent you an electric scooter (from ¥150 per day) or petrol scooter (from ¥200) without asking to see a driver's licence. Scooters can make the going easier, but be aware that if you don't have a Chinese driver's licence, you will probably not be insured (international driving licences are not accepted in China) and things could get complicated and costly in the event of an accident.

Bus 5 links the two bus stations (¥1); it also gets you to Xijie from either bus station (¥1).

Around Yángshuò

The countryside of Yángshuò and the region through which the Lí River (the body of water that connects Guìlín and Yángshuò) and its tributary waterways flow offer weeks of exploration by bike, boat, foot or any combination thereof. Scenes that inspired generations of Chinese painters are the standard here: wallowing water buffalo and farmers tending their crops against a backdrop of limestone peaks. Some of the villages come alive on **market days**, which operate on a three-, six- and nine-day monthly cycle. The Yùlóng River, the very pretty tributary of the Lí River, courses through this region, making for fantastic day trips, with riverside villages to explore, ancient settlements to stop by and verdant hills to climb.

◉ Sights & Activities

Moon Hill   HILL

(¥15) A 30-minute – extremely sweaty – climb up steps to the magnificent natural arch that adorns Moon Hill is rewarded with both lost calories and some exhilarating views of surrounding peaks and the tapestry of flat fields in the lowlands. Load up with liquids in hot weather, and be prepared to be pounced on by hawkers flogging water to anything that moves at the top. Moon Hill is easily reached by bike; just set off down Kangzhan Lu (抗战路), keep going and follow the signs.

Yùlóng River
RIVER

(遇龙河, Yùlóng Hé) The scenery along this small, quiet river about 6km southwest of Yángshuò is breathtaking. It is visited by hiring a boatman in Yángshuò for the lazy float up the river. Tell the boatman you want to visit the fairy-tale-like **Dragon Bridge** (遇龙桥; Yùlóng Qiáo), about 10km upstream from Yángshuò. This 600-year-old stone arched structure overhung with old gnarly trees is among Guǎngxī's largest and comes with crooked steps and leaning parapets.

Lóngtán Village
VILLAGE

(龙潭村, Lóngtán Cūn; admission ¥20) This fascinating village about 1.5km beyond Moon Hill is a treasure trove of traditional Qing-dynasty architecture. Beyond the initial, slightly cheesy scenic area at the beginning, you reach the village proper, where you can get lost in a maze of tight lanes. Look out for the old **Opium Den** (烟馆; Yānguǎn) at No 89 Longtan Cun, which didn't close till 1940, and note the village's carved upturned lintels, astonishingly regular brickwork and ample distribution of Cultural Revolution slogans.

🛏 Sleeping

Some of Yángshuò's best sleeping options lie scattered among the peaks and hills around the town, in the lush Lí River and Yùlóng River region, making it the area of choice to base yourself for either short or extended stays.

★ Giggling Tree
GUESTHOUSE $$

(📱 136 6786 6154; www.gigglingtree.com; Aǐshānmén Village, 矮山门村; dm ¥100, d ¥290-320, tw ¥290-320, tr ¥360-390, f ¥430-520; ❄ 🐾) Simply lovely rooms in a beautiful countryside setting is what's on offer at the Giggling Tree, run by Dutch owners Karst (perfect name) and Paulien. It's an old 23-room farmhouse, just 5km from Yángshuò, with mudbrick buildings, and magnificent scenery right on your doorstep. Rooms are delightful, even the three-bed dorms, with an abundance of polished wood and blue paint all round.

At night, you can hear a pin drop. Both Western and Chinese food is cooked up and you can rent bikes for ¥30 per day.

Phoenix Pagoda
Fonglou Retreat
BOUTIQUE HOTEL $$

(凤楼岁月, Fènglóu Suìyuè; 📱 0773 877 8458, 180 7730 5230; www.fonglou.com; 98 Fènglóu Village, Gāotián Town, 高田镇, 凤楼村98号; d & tw ¥320-380, f ¥560; 💺 ❄ @ 🐾) The 12 rooms here

Around Yángshuò

Around Yángshuò

🔴 Sights
1 Lóngtán Village.................................A3
2 Moon Hill...A3
3 Yùlóng River......................................A2

🛏 Sleeping
4 Giggling Tree....................................A3
5 Phoenix Pagoda Fonglou
   Retreat...A3
6 Secret Garden.................................A2
7 Tea Cozy Hotel................................A2

❌ Eating
8 Dàcūnmén Night Market..................A3

🎭 Entertainment
9 Impressions Liú Sānjiě....................B3

have wide balconies overlooking the hills, furniture made from local materials, wi-fi and no TV. Meals are served on the scenic rooftop patio. The Taiwanese owner Jerry has tips on hiking and biking. It's a ¥40 taxi ride from downtown Yángshuò.

★ Tea Cozy Hotel
BOUTIQUE HOTEL $$$

(水云阁, Shuǐyún Gé; 📱 0773 881 6158, 135 0783 9490; www.yangshuoteacozy.com; 212 Báishā Zhèn, Xiàtáng Village, 白沙镇夏棠村212号; r ¥580, ste ¥680-980; 💺 @ 🐾) What makes Tea

Cozy a true winner is not the 12 ethnic-style balcony rooms (though these are wonderful in themselves), but the exceptional service by the English-speaking staff. Also laudable are the culinary skills of the restaurant staff (mains ¥20 to ¥108). The hotel has three shuttle buses daily to Yángshuò (¥40) and back, the same price as a taxi.

★**Secret Garden** BOUTIQUE HOTEL **$$$**
(秘密花园酒店, Mìmì Huāyuán Jiǔdiàn; ☑0773 877 1932; www.yangshuosecretgarden.com; Jiùxiàn Village, 旧县村; r ¥468-498, ste ¥628-788; ✽@🖥) Middlesbrough-born South African designer Ian Hamlinton (nicknamed 'Crazy One' by the locals) has energetically and lovingly converted a cluster of Ming dynasty houses in the village of Jiùxiàn into a gorgeous Western-style boutique hotel with a choice selection of rooms. The Secret Garden was being expanded at the time of writing, and a restaurant was being added.

A taxi to Yángshuò from here costs ¥50; it takes about 20 minutes to half an hour by electric scooter.

✗ Eating

Some fine and occasionally outstanding restaurant choices can be found at many of the guesthouses, resorts and hotels that cater to outside visitors.

★**Luna** ITALIAN **$$**
(☑0773 877 8169; www.yangshuoguesthouse.com; 26 Moon Hill Village (Li Village), Gaotian Town, 月亮村 (历村) 26号, 高田镇; mains from ¥35) This fine rooftop restaurant experience is one of Yángshuò's best. The view of Moon Hill isn't quite as amazing as it used to be – thanks to a neighbour building a stack opposite – but it's still sublime. And the food remains topnotch: the *taglioni con gamberi e melanzana* (tagliolini with shrimp and eggplant) is lovely, but the whole menu's a winner. Romantic, delightful, highly appetising.

The pizza is fantastic too, and there's a good choice of vegetarian dishes. The attached Yangshuo Village Inn has delectable rooms too, if you need somewhere to kip after your fill. It's not easy to find, in a village called Li Village (历村; Lì Cūn), before you reach Gāotián Town.

Minibuses (¥2) run from Yángshuò to Gāotián. Before Gāotián, disembark at Li Village and it's a five-minute walk to the restaurant. A taxi one way from Yángshuò will cost around ¥30. If cycling to Moon Hill (p624), the restaurant is a short ride away.

❶ Getting There & Around

The region is best reached from Yángshuò by a combination of bus, bike and taxi. Bikes can be hired from rental operators along Xi Jie, especially towards the southern end, where you can also rent electric and petrol scooters. Buses to this region depart from Yángshuò; you can jump aboard them along Pantao Lu.

Except for visits to Xìngpíng (best visited by bus), the best way to explore this region is by bike, leisurely cycling through the flatlands of this karst region. Hiking is also an option and boating trips are available too.

Liúgōng 留公村
☑0773

The very quiet 400-year-old village of Liúgōng (Liúgōng Cūn), 13km from Yángshuò, was a trading hub on the Lí River during the Ming and Qing dynasties. Traces of its former affluence are visible in the handsome buildings (the walls of some still blush with slogans painted during the Cultural Revolution). You can stroll from the village to the hills behind it, where the only things punctuating the silence are cockerels and murmurs of the past.

⊙ Sights

Déyuè Building HISTORIC BUILDING
(得月楼, Déyuè Lóu) Once among Lí River's most beautiful buildings, Déyuè, with its ornate embellishments, stands weather-beaten by the river like a frail diva. The name literally means 'Obtain the Moon Building' and residents say it used to be an opera house – on performance nights music would reverberate over the moonlit water. An exquisite four-cornered pavilion sits on the rooftop.

🛏 Sleeping & Eating

Most visitors avail themselves of well known rural sleeping options around Yángshuò, such as the excellent Giggling Tree (p625) or the Secret Garden.

Liúgōng Gǔpú
Farmer Restaurant GUANGXI **$$**
(留公古朴农家饭, Liúgōng Gǔpú Nóngjiāfàn; ☑136 6946 2263, 0773 892 3581; mains ¥16-98; ⊙7am-late) All visitors to Liúgōng come here for fresh river fish, local fowl and homemade tofu. On national holidays, it's colonised by local tourists; book ahead. The restaurant also rents out kayaks (from ¥60 per day), but not if the river waters are too swollen with rain.

ⓘ Getting There & Away

To cycle or ride a scooter to Liúgōng, take Kangzhan Lu (抗战路) in Yángshuò until the roundabout. Bear left, passing traffic lights and entering the new Shima Lu (石马路). After crossing the bridge, you'll see Aishān Village (矮山村). At the junction, look for signage for Pǔyì (普益). Take the concrete road that heads in that direction. After a curve, continue for another 4km, passing other villages. At a road junction with small shops including a motorcycle repair shop, you'll see signage for Liúgōng Village. Another 5km on a concrete road brings you to a hill close to the roadside and then a rusty sign pointing to the village.

From the village pier, a 90-minute raft ride to Yángshuò generally costs ¥200 per person (¥260 for two).

Xìngpíng 兴坪

☑ 0773 / POP 43,000

Some say Xìngpíng is just like Yángshuò before the latter became a honeypot, for better or worse. This 1750-year-old town has loads of history and is certainly attractive; in fact, the landscape you see when you disembark from the raft is printed on the back of China's ¥20 banknote. Travellers come here for its yesteryear flavours; with the recent opening of nearby Yángshuò train station, however, it is set to get a lot busier.

⊙ Sights

Fish Village VILLAGE

(鱼村, Yúcūn; ¥10) You can hike the mountain behind Xìngpíng, past pomelo and orange groves, to sleepy Fish Village. Miraculously untouched during the Sino-Japanese War and the Cultural Revolution, the 400-year-old village has friendly residents and vernacular houses similar to those at Xìngpíng.

A bamboo raft back to Xìngpíng or Yángshuò costs ¥200 to ¥300.

Xìngpíng Ancient Stage HISTORIC SITE

(兴平古戏台, Xìngpíng Gǔ Xìtái; ⊗9am-5pm) FREE The highlight of Xìngpíng's old street is this well preserved and attractive Qing dynasty opera stage. You can see intricate carvings depicting operatic scenes and slash marks made by prop weaponry on the pillars. If you want to take pictures, an old man may collect a ¥1 donation from you. The trendy-looking **Master Cafe** is in the same compound.

⨼ Sleeping & Eatiing

Xìngpíng's bucolic setting makes it an excellent place to overnight and there's a great hostel here with dorm rooms as well as comfortable doubles, twins and family rooms.

★**This Old Place Youth Hostel** HOSTEL $

(老地方, Lǎo Dìfang; ☑0773 870 2887; www.top xingping.com; 5 Rongtan Lu, 榕潭街5号; dm ¥40-80, s ¥100-120, tw ¥130-200, q ¥180; ⊗cafe noon-9.30pm; ❋@≋) Set in a historic building, this hostel has a lovely backpacker vibe, with 12 solid rooms, and a supremely lounge-worthy living room with a wood-fire oven that cooks up delicious pizzas. Rooms are really pleasant; the south-facing ones in the new wing are the best. The hostel operators can suggest plenty of itineraries for guests.

Old Neighbourhood CHINESE $$

(老街坊餐吧, Lǎojiēfāng Cānbā; ☑137 3739 6512, 0773 870 1808; 12 Xinjie, 新街12号; dishes ¥20-120; ⊗8am-10.30pm) Old Neighbourhood's owner is a self-made cook from northeastern China who's lived in Guǎngdōng, so dishes from these and other regions all figure on the menu. Of particular note are the dumplings (饺子; jiǎozi) and the stuffed duck (莲子鸭; liánzǐ yā), which requires three hours' pre-ordering.

ⓘ Getting There & Away

High-speed trains connect Xìngpíng with Guìlín, Nánníng, Guǎngzhōu and other settlements via Yángshuò train station in the nearby settlement of Fànzèng Shān (饭甑山):

Guǎngzhōu 1st/2nd class ¥141/117, 2½ hours, five daily, 8.21am to 6.49pm

Guìlín 1st/2nd class ¥25/21, 30 minutes, seven daily, 9.03am to 7.19pm

Nánníng 1st/2nd class ¥157/131, 3½ hours, one daily, 9.03am

Regular buses head from the train station to Yángshuò, via Xìngpíng (¥5, 10 minutes). The bus continues to Yángshuò (¥15, 40 minutes).

Huángyáo 黄姚

☑ 0774 / POP 62,000

Huángyáo is one of China's most high-profile and picturesque villages, with many movies filmed here; *The Painted Veil*, starring Edward Norton, is possibly the most well known.

Bucolic charm permeates the lovingly preserved 900-year-old village, though Huángyáo struggles to cope with the influx of roving tour groups and housing them all. There's plenty on its eight streets to ensure the ¥100 entry fee is well spent, including two massive 500-year-old Chinese banyans that have wound their way up from the river's edge.

One of the village's most standout historical buildings, **Guōjiā Dàyuàn** (郭家大院; 44 An Dongjie, 安东街44号) is named after the Guo family that lived here.

🛏 Sleeping & Eating

To maximise its bucolic charms, spending the night in Huángyáo is an excellent idea and there's no shortage of accommodation options, some very comfortable and generally inexpensive.

Chance GUESTHOUSE $
(偶然间客栈, Ǒuránjiān Kèzhàn; 📞0774 672 2046; 38 Zhongxing Jie, 中兴街38号; d ¥100-260; ❋🛜) Scenically situated in an old brick building backing onto a hill, this place has a lovely traditional vibe, with a large choice of rooms and a bar.

★**Heterotopias Clan** BOUTIQUE HOTEL $$
(异托邦会馆, Yìtuōbāng Huìguǎn; 📞181 7679 6519; heterotopias@126.com; 49 Anle Jie, 安乐街49号; r ¥250-350; ❋❋@🛜) With its cultured, civilised air and eight elegant rooms, Heterotopias sits inside an old courtyard complex. The owners are intellectual types and the hotel's white walls and minimalist aesthetic showcase their literary collection and paintings by their artist friends to great effect. The wi-fi signal is not too good in some of the rooms.

Yuǎnfāngde Jiā INN $$
(远方的家; 📞133 7703 6002, 0774 672 2792; Yfdj13377036002@163.com; 94 Liyu Jie, 鲤鱼街94号; r ¥158, ste ¥288-358; ❋🛜) Two floors of small but adequate rooms connected by a creaky wooden staircase and run by friendly owners. It's on a busy street just before you reach Dàilóng Bridge (带龙桥; Dàilóng Qiáo).

★**Dàilóng Farmer Restaurant** GUANGXI $
(带龙桥龙家饭庄, Dàilóngqiáo Lóngjiā Fànzhuāng; 📞131 0054 9638; Zhongxing Jie, 中兴街; mains ¥15-80; ⏱11am-8pm) Rarely does a famous eatery (it's been featured countless times by the media) uphold its culinary excellence, and its boss, his modesty, so well. But that's precisely why patrons keep returning to feast on steamed spare ribs (豆豉蒸排骨; dòuchǐ zhēng páigǔ), stuffed tofu (豆腐酿; dòufu niàng) and other deliciousness on the river bank. The massively polite Mr Liang speaks English too. It's at the start of Dàilóng Bridge.

ℹ Getting There & Away

Two direct buses run daily from Guìlín (¥72, three hours, 9am and 1.30pm). The return buses from Huángyáo usually leave at 2pm and 8pm, though the service is erratic, meaning you may have to take a bus to Hèzhōu (贺州; ¥18, two hours) and change to a Guìlín service (¥62 to ¥80, 2½ to four hours). The last bus from Hèzhōu is at 5.10pm. You could also take a fast D-class train (1st/2nd class ¥69/57) from Hèzhōu to Guìlín. Joining a local tour from Yángshuò (arriving at 11am and departing at 4.30pm) costs around ¥198.

Nánníng 南宁

📞0771 / POP 7.1 MILLION

In many ways, Nánníng is a typical provincial capital with few sights of note, but many of its streets are lined with trees and shaded with a bountiful canopy of leaves, affording welcome shade. It's also a relaxing and friendly place to recharge your batteries before leaving for, or returning from, Vietnam. Nánníng's new metro system is helping to tame the town's distances.

◉ Sights

Guǎngxī Museum MUSEUM
(广西博物馆, Guǎngxī Bówùguǎn; cnr Minzu Dadao & Gucheng Lu, 民族大道古城路的路口; ⏱9am-4.30pm Tue-Sun; Ⓜ Minzu Guangchang) **FREE** This fairly interesting but very dated museum showcases Qing ceramics, art and calligraphy with Guǎngxī characteristics, and the customs of ethnic minorities. The collection of ancient copper drums is one of China's best. On the ground floor, the traditional **handicrafts shop** (广西传统工艺展示馆) has great souvenirs. The garden out back is a welcome highlight, with a reproduction **Wind and Rain Bridge**, where you can also dine.

🛏 Sleeping

Green Forest Hostel HOSTEL $
(瓦舍, Wǎshě; 📞0771 281 3977; greenforest_nanning@yahoo.com; 3rd fl, 3 Jiefang Lu, 解放路3号3楼, 近民生步行街; dm ¥50-60, d ¥138; ❋❋@🛜; Ⓜ Chaoyang Guangchang or Xinmin Lu) Located in an old and slightly distressed property, this hostel is located above a kindergarten (hence the paintings on the walls as you go up). Rooms are OK, but corridors are a bit musty and some rooms a tad damp. Get off the bus at Cháoyáng Sq (朝阳广场; Cháoyáng Guǎngchǎng), walk on for 10m, and you'll see the pedestrianised Minsheng Buxingjie.

Wànxīng Hotel HOTEL $$$
(万兴酒店, Wànxīng Jiǔdiàn; ☑ 0771 238 1000; www.nnwxhotel.com; unit 1, 42 Beining Jie, 北宁街 42-1号; d ¥438-788, tr/ste ¥888/1688; ❀ @ ☎) One of those seemingly characterless urban hotels that actually turn out to be very good. There's an uncluttered, marble-clad foyer overseen by very helpful staff, and rooms are comfortable, if unsurprising. Efficient and value for money; on the corner with Gonghé Lu.

✗ Eating & Drinking

Muslim Hotel CHINESE $
(清真饭店, Qīngzhēn Fàndiàn; ☑ 135 5848 3838; 25 Xinhua Lu, 新华路25号; noodles from ¥6.50, mains ¥30-80,; ⊘ 6.30am-8pm; Ⓜ Chaoyang Guangchang) If you want to sample some flavours from the other side of China, this Muslim eatery inside a green building serves cheap, generous and hearty noodles on the ground floor, and northwestern Chinese fare on the 1st floor.

★ Gānjiājiè Lemon Duck GUANGXI $$
(甘家界牌柠檬鸭, Gānjiājiè Pái Níngméngyā; ☑ 0771 585 5585; www.ganjiajie.com; 12-2 Yuanhu Lu, 园湖路12-2号; mains ¥30-70; ⊘ 10am-9.30pm; Ⓜ Macun) One of eight branches in town, the star here is the flavourful lemon duck (柠檬鸭; *níngméngyā*), a Nánníng dish that cooks the fowl with pickled lemon peel, ginger, garlic and chilli. You'd be quackers not to try it. Choose from two types of duck: we recommend the more tender cherry duck (樱桃谷鸭; *yīngtáo gǔyā*).

★ Āmóu Delicious Eats GUANGXI $$
(阿谋美食, Āmóu Měishí; Gucheng Lu, 古城路; mains from ¥25; ⊘ 11am-9pm; ❀; Ⓜ Minzu Guangchang) Unique and flavourful ethnic dishes served on a photogenic wind-and-rain bridge or in a dining room, both within the lovely garden of the Guǎngxī Museum. There's a huge range of ethnic food, from fried pork belly dipped in rice wine (么佬族乳香肉饼甜酒; *melāozú rǔxiāng ròubǐng tiánjiǔ*) to fragrant *máonán* beef (毛南香牛扣; *máonán xiāngníukòu*). There's a photo menu.

★ Queen's Head BAR
(22 Jiangbei Dadao, 江北大道22号; ⊘ 7pm-2am) With cider on tap (¥40), good cocktails, a London tube map on the wall, and posters of Big Ben, the London Eye and Union Jacks, this anglophone pub has a decent range of imported beers and a fun, likeable atmosphere. There's a big screen and a pool table. It's a cut above the other very samey competition along this (never-ending) road.

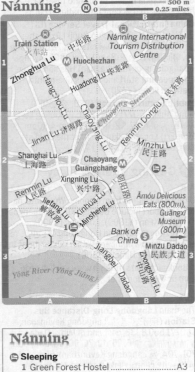

Nánníng

ⓔ Sleeping

ⓘ Information

ⓘ Transport

ⓘ Information

The useful *Street Map of Nanning* (南宁街道图; Nánníng Jiēdào Tú; ¥5), in English and Chinese, can be found at bookshops and kiosks around town.

Nánníng International Tourism Distribution Centre (南宁国际旅游集散中心, Nánníng Guójì Lǚyóu Jísàn Zhōngxīn; ☑ 0771 210 2362; 10 You'ai Nanlu, 友爱南路10号; ⊘ 7.30am-8.30pm; Ⓜ Huochezhan) A large distribution centre of travel information for domestic and international travellers.

Bank of China (中国银行, Zhōngguó Yínháng; Chaoyang Lu, 朝阳路; ⊘ 9am-5pm Mon-Fri; Ⓜ Chaoyang Guangchang) Changes travellers cheques and gives credit-card advances. Other

Bank of China branches around town have 24-hour ATMs that accept international cards.

China International Travel Service (CITS, 中国国际旅行社, Zhōngguó Guójì Lǚxíngshè; ☏ 0771 222 0000; www.cits.net; 72 Chaoyang Lu, 朝阳路72号; ⊙ 8am-11pm; ⊙ Chaoyang Guangchang or Huochezhan) Has some English-speaking staff and issues one-month Vietnam visas (¥420).

Public Security Bureau (PSB, 公安局, Gōng'ānjú; ☏ 0771 289 1260; 10 Xiuling Lu Xierli, 秀灵路西二里10号; ⊙ 9am-4.30pm Mon-Fri) Located 2km north of the train station, off Xiuling Lu (秀灵路).

ⓘ Getting There & Away

AIR

Direct daily flights from Nánníng Wúxū International Airport include Běijīng (¥1500), Shànghǎi (¥1700), Xī'ān (¥1800), Kūnmíng (¥900), Guǎngzhōu (¥730) and Hong Kong (¥1440). You can also fly to a number of other destinations in Asia, including Hanoi (¥1800).

Book air tickets through www.english.ctrip.com or www.elong.net.

BUS

The main **Lángdōng Long-Distance Bus Station** (琅东客运站, Lángdōng Kèyùnzhàn; ☏ 0771 550 8333; east end of Minzu Dadao, 民族大道东端; ⒨ 6, 25, 42, 76, 90, 98, 206, 603, 701, 704, Ⓜ Langdong Keyunzhan), 5km east of the city centre (linked on Line 1 of the new Nánníng metro), has high-speed, direct buses to pretty much everywhere, although you may be dropped at one of the other bus stations, also on the outskirts, when arriving. There's a downtown ticketing office on Chaoyang Lu near **CAAC** (CAAC, 中国民航, Zhōngguó Mínháng; ☏ 0771 243 1459; 82 Chaoyang Lu, 朝阳路82号; ⊙ 24hr). Destinations from Lángdōng Long-Distance Bus Station include:

Běihǎi ¥70, three hours, every 10 to 20 minutes (7.30am to 9.30pm)

Guǎngzhōu ¥140 to ¥210, nine hours, regular (8am to 11pm)

Guìlín ¥90 to ¥125, 4½ hours, every 15 to 30 minutes (8.20am to 10.45pm)

Píngxiáng ¥78 to ¥80, 2½ hours, regular (7.30am to 8.30pm)

Yángshuò ¥100 to ¥120, 3½ hours, three daily (10.10am, 3.40pm and 4.20pm)

There is one direct bus daily from Lángdōng Long-Distance Bus Station to Détiān Waterfall (Détiān Pùbù; ¥75, 3½ hours, 8.30am). Other daily routes include Chóngqìng, Chéngdū, Hǎinán Dǎo, Shànghǎi and Hong Kong (Xiānggǎng).

Buses for Yángměi leave from the Nánníngshì Huòyùn Xīzhàn (南宁市货运西站), just south of the corner of Daxue Lu and Luban Lu. Buses 4, 10, 24, 33, 34, 35 and 46 all pass by.

TRAIN

Nánníng has two train stations: the main train station at the centre of town and Nánníng East train station, where many high-speed trains stop and depart from.

Some daily services:

Běihǎi ¥58 to ¥70, 90 minutes, regular, 6.45am to 9.05pm

Běijīng West G-class train, 2nd/1st class ¥914/1380, 13 hours, two daily, 8am and 9.20am

Chéngdū ¥198, 27 hours, one daily (9.40pm)

Chóngqìng ¥164, 21½ hours, one daily (9.40am)

Guǎngzhōu South 1st/2nd class ¥203/169, four hours, three daily (8am, 11.50am and 6pm)

Guìlín ¥60 to ¥1180, 4½ hours to 6½ hours, over 20 daily

Hanoi soft sleeper ¥300, 10½ hours, one daily, 6.10pm

Shànghǎi G-class train 1st/2nd class ¥1179/768, 12 hours, one daily, 9.05am

Xī'ān ¥224, 30 hours, two daily (11.40am and 8.35pm)

Four daily trains go to Píngxiáng (¥30 to ¥33, four to six hours, 9.10am, 2.09pm, 2.50pm and 6.10pm) near the Vietnam border. Each one stops at Chóngzuǒ (¥18 to ¥20, two to three hours) and Níngmíng (¥26, 2½ to five hours), but only the slow one stops at Píngxiáng's north train station.

Booth 16 in the train station sells international tickets to Hanoi.

ⓘ BORDER CROSSING: GETTING TO VIETNAM FROM NÁNNÍNG

Six daily buses run to Hanoi (河内; Hénèi, Vietnam; ¥160, 7½ to eight hours) via Friendship Pass (友谊关; Yǒuyì Guān). Two departures (8am and 8.20am) leave from Nánníng International Tourism Distribution Centre, and four (8.40am, 9am, 10am and 1.40pm) leave from Lángdōng Long-Distance Bus Station.

Note that you'll have to get off and walk across the border at Friendship Pass before boarding another bus to Hanoi. There's also a daily train from Nánníng train station to Hanoi (soft sleeper ¥300, 10½ hours, 6.10pm). There are also four trains and regular buses daily to Píngxiáng.

Local hostels will help organise visas (for free – you pay for the visa only).

Getting Around

The airport shuttle bus (¥20, 40 minutes, 5.30am to 10.30pm) leaves every 30 minutes from outside the **Vienna Hotel** (维也纳酒店, Wéiyěnà Jiǔdiàn; 76 Chaoyang Lu, 朝阳路76号; M Chaoyang Guangchang or Huochezhan). Bus 301 (¥3) also runs to the airport from Chaoyang Guangchang (朝阳广场). A taxi to the airport is about ¥120.

Line 1 of the Nánníng metro links the train station with **Lángdōng Long-Distance Bus Station** in the east and Nánníng East train station. Two further lines are under construction.

Buses 6 and 213 run the length of Chaoyang Lu and Minzu Dadao until around 11pm (¥2 per ride). A taxi ride from Lángdōng bus station to downtown is around ¥40. Taxis start at ¥7 and short pedicab rides cost ¥5.

Yángměi 扬美

A former market town on the Yōng River (邕江; Yōng Jiāng), Yángměi (¥10) was founded a millennium ago and flourished in the 17th century, earning the nickname 'Little Nánníng'.

Spend a couple of hours wandering the cobbled streets, munching on fried fish (from ¥2), steamed rice rolls (¥4) and local starfruit (¥5 a *catty*) as you walk. The pace is slow and you're free to peep into the musty Ming and Qing dynasty homes.

Most of Yángměi's early inhabitants were migrants from Shāndōng, with a small percentage from Guǎngdōng. Hybridity is reflected in its buildings, which feature both the sturdy solemnity of Shāndōng vernacular architecture, and the penchant for embellishment of the softer southern style.

Buses for Yángměi leave from West Bus Station (南宁市货运西站; Nánníngshì Huóyùn Xīzhàn) near the corner of Daxue Lu (大学路) and Luban Lu (鲁班路) in the northeast of town. Take bus 604 from Minsheng Guangchang (民生广场); buses 4, 10, 24, 33, 34, 35 and 46 also pass by. Departures and returns are from 8.40am to 6pm (¥17, two hours, every 50 minutes). The last bus back from Yángměi leaves at 4pm, but gets packed so arrive early for a seat.

Běihǎi 北海

0779 / POP 1.5 MILLION

Běihǎi (literally 'North Sea') – called *baakhoi* in the local baíhuà dialect – is famed among Chinese tourists for its Silver Beach, dubbed 'number one beach on earth' in tourism brochures (it ain't). A far more charming and unique selling point, however, is the lovely and crumbling Old Quarter, a delightful vignette of colonnaded streets and colonial-era architecture. It's lovely in the right light, and with a fine cafe and hotel, the old town is the place to settle down for a day or two to ease into Běihǎi's lazy seaside rhythms. The volcanic island of Wéizhōu is a further draw, just 70 minutes away by boat.

Sights

Běihǎi's **old streets** (老街; *lǎojiē*) usually refer to Zhongshan Lu (中山路) and Zhuhai Lu (珠海路), once part of old Běihǎi's trading hub, which are now home to sleepy residences of the city's older population. Built a century ago, the streets spread from west to east and are flanked by recently restored 19th-century *qílóu* buildings (arcade houses) housing an alarming number of pearl shops.

Start your stroll at the western end of Zhuhai Lu. Look for the small white arch inscribed with the Chinese characters 升平街 (Shengping Jie), the road's former name. This street has been paved over and offers visitors an atmospheric walk.

Former British Consulate Building HISTORIC BUILDING
(英国领事馆旧址, Yīngguó Lǐngshìguǎn Jiùzhǐ; Beihai No 1 Middle School, 1 Beijing Lu, 北京路1号) Běihǎi's first consulate of a Western country is a whitewashed edifice built in 1885 that now sits inside the grounds of the Beihai No 1 Middle School. The building faces you as you stand in front of the school; the guard will let you in for a peek if you're nice.

Maruichi Drugstore HISTORIC BUILDING
(丸一药房, Wányī Yàofáng; 0779 203 9169; 104 Zhuhai Zhonglu, 珠海中路104号; 8.30-11.30am & 3-5.30pm) FREE This historic building was disguised as a pharmacy that allowed the Japanese to pursue espionage activities in the 1930s. Today, it serves as a tiny national security museum. No English captions.

Silver Beach BEACH
(银滩, Yíntān) FREE This 24km-long stretch of silvery-yellow sand with apparently clean water, about 8km south of the city centre, is an enjoyable spot. It's not as amazing and unparalleled as Chinese folklore attests, however. Take bus 3 (¥1.50) from town.

Sleeping

From the central bus station, cross Sichuan Lu (四川路) to reach Běihǎi's cheapest accommodation on Huoshaochuang Wuxiang

Běihǎi

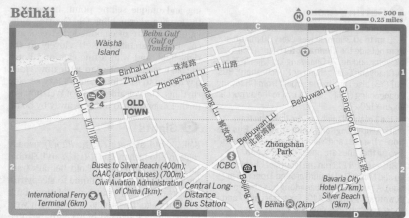

Běihǎi

◎ Sights
1 Former British Consulate
  Building C2

🛏 Sleeping
2 Backpacker Inn A1

🍴 Eating
3 Aunty Li's Shrimp Pancakes A1
4 Old Town Coffee, Bar &
  Restaurant A1

(火烧床五巷). This small alley off Beibuwan Xilu is jam-packed with *zhāodàisuǒ* (招待所), simple guesthouses offering doubles and twins from around ¥35, although some may not take foreigners.

★ Backpacker Inn INN $$
(老道精舍, Lǎodào Jīngshě; ☎0779 203 0605; www.backpacker-china.com; 165 Haizhu Xilu, 海珠西路165号; dm ¥46-68, d ¥178-208, ste ¥298-888; 🅰🛜) This cordial and welcoming place perched at the western end of atmospheric old-town street Zhuhai Lu has 13 fantastic rooms with oodles of space and upholstered bay windows that inspire relaxed reading with a good novel. The singer in the adjacent bar can get pretty vocal come evening, though, although the microphone is usually switched off quite early.

Bavaria City Hotel HOTEL $$$
(巴伐利亚酒店, Bāfáliyǎ Jiǔdiàn; ☎0779 223 7000; reservation@bavariahotel.net; 338 Xinan Dadao, Hǎichéng District, 海城区, 西南大道338号; r¥440, ste¥660-750; 😊🅰@🛜) A plush option in a new quarter close to the high-speed

train station (¥15 by cab to the old quarter or a 25-minute walk), Bavaria offers clean, bright and quiet rooms, with discounts usually in effect. You can flag down pedicabs outside the hotel, or the thoughtful staff will find you a taxi – just give them 10 minutes.

🍴 Eating

The old town is full of stalls selling steamed rice rolls (粉卷; *fěnjuǎn*) and shrimp pancakes (虾饼; *xiābǐng*). Overseas Town is not just a fun outing, it's your best bet for a reasonably priced seafood feast.

Aunty Li's Shrimp Pancakes GUANGXI $
(李姨虾饼店, Lǐyí Xiābǐng Diàn; 110 Zhuhai Lu, 珠海路110号; pancakes ¥4; ⊙8am-6pm) Nobody does the delicacy of dried shrimp pancakes (虾饼; *xiābǐng*) better than this hawker stall opposite Běihǎi Christ Church.

Old Town Coffee, Bar & Restaurant CAFE $
(老道咖啡, Lǎodào Kāfēi; ☎0779 203 1828; www.backpacker-china.com; 155 Zhuhai Lu, 珠海路155号; snacks ¥16-35, mains ¥25-60, drinks ¥28-45; ⊙9am-1.30am; 🛜) This charming and very efficiently staffed cafe, with distressed exposed brickwork and great coffees, has a ground floor that's open all day; the upper floors morph into a bar in the evenings, where singers croon nightly from 8pm. There are Western favourites (spaghetti, burgers, steak, sandwiches), but for us the curry in a bread bun stole the show (it's a meal in itself).

★ Overseas Town Restaurant SEAFOOD, VIETNAMESE $$
(侨港镇瘦佬大排档, Qiáogǎngzhèn Shòulǎo Dàpáidàng; ☎0779 388 2086; 7-8 Hongmian Lu, Overseas Town, 侨港镇, 红棉路7-8号; fish per

jīn ¥60-120, shrimp per jīn ¥60-150, clams per jīn from ¥30; ⊙ 10.30am-10.30pm) Take your pick from the seething tanks of aquatic life at the entrance and tell staff how you'd like it cooked; prices per *jīn* are all displayed on the glass. The pan-fried squid (香煎小鱿鱼; *xiāngjiān xiǎoyóuyú*) is exceptional, at ¥50 per *jīn*. There are also lion crabs (¥60 per *jīn*) and all manner of fish. Zero English, so hone your pointing skills.

If taking bus 5 to Qiaogang Market, walk along Qiaoxing Lu (侨兴路) right by where you disembark the bus and then turn right into Hongmian Lu. From Binhai Lu (滨海路), go west and turn left into Qiaobei Lu (侨北路). Walk to the end, turn right into Qiaoxing Lu (侨兴路), then left into Hongmian Lu.

🍷 Drinking & Nightlife

The best and most atmospheric part of town for a drink is along Zhuhai Lu. The Old Town Coffee, Bar & Restaurant is a great choice.

ℹ️ Information

ICBC (中国工商银行, Zhōngguó Gōngshāng Yínháng) Has a 24-hour ATM for international cards.

Public Security Bureau (PSB, 公安局, Gōng'ānjú; 213 Zhongshan Donglu, 中山东路213号; ⊙8am-noon & 2.30-5.30pm, 3-6pm summer) At the eastern end of the old town; can extend visas.

ℹ️ Getting There & Away

AIR

There are daily flights to Běijīng (¥1200) and Shànghǎi (¥1000). Běihǎi Fúchéng Airport is 21km northeast of the town centre.

BUS

There are two main bus stations: a Central Long-Distance Bus Station (北海和信客运中心, Běihǎi Héxìn Kèyùn Zhōngxīn; Beibuwan Zhonglu, 北部湾中路) and the newer, inconveniently located Nánzhū Bus Station (南珠汽车站, Nánzhū Qìchē Zhàn; cnr Beihai Dadao & Nanzhu Dadao, 北海大道南珠大道路口). Most buses drop you at the latter station. From Nánzhū bus station to Central Long Distance you'll need to take public bus 15 (¥1.50) to Beibuwan Lu or a taxi (¥25).

From the central bus station, bus 2 (¥1.50) goes to the train station.

Direct buses from the Central Long-Distance Bus Station run to Jiāngnán bus station in Nánníng (¥67, three hours, nine daily, 6am to 5.40pm), Guǎngzhōu (¥180, nine hours, five daily) and Hǎikǒu (¥138, four hours, 7.25am). From Nánzhū bus station there are regular buses to Nánníng Lángdòng long-distance bus station (¥70, every 10 minutes, 6am to 9.20pm), Guǎngzhōu (¥220, six daily) and Zhūhǎi (¥270). To reach Guìlín, you need to go first to Nánníng Lángdòng bus station and change for an onward bus.

TRAIN

Eighteen high-speed trains run daily from Nánníng train station and Nánníng East train station (¥70, 1½ hours, 6.45am to 9.05pm) to Běihǎi train station (北海站) on Zhanbei Lu (站北路).

LOCAL KNOWLEDGE

CHOW DOWN IN OVERSEAS TOWN

Běihǎi is the place to feast on fresh seafood – it's excellent and abundant. Yet at the most visible seafood eateries, especially those near Silver Beach, customers pay through the nose for a plate of squid.

This is because cab and pedicab drivers get a cut for bringing customers to these places – up to 50% of the bill! With that kind of incentive, some drivers will work hard to lure you to eateries that pay them. Insist on going elsewhere and they may feign ignorance of the location, or take you to their pet eatery and pretend it's the one you're after.

But there are exceptions to the rule. Seafood restaurants that don't overcharge can be found in Overseas Town (侨港镇; Qiáogǎng Zhèn), 4km away from Silver Beach. OT was established in 1979 to settle Vietnamese Chinese refugees who had arrived near the shores of Běihǎi. Most of the arrivals were fishermen who brought their unique mix of Chinese and Vietnamese culture to the area. There are no sights as such, but the pervasive Sino-Vietnamese atmosphere is quite unique. Note how written Vietnamese is abundantly used alongside Chinese on shop fronts.

Ask a driver to take you to Overseas Town (without mentioning a restaurant), then walk to your destination; alternatively, simply take bus 5 from Běibùwān Sq (北部湾广场; Běibùwān Guǎngchǎng), which runs direct to Qiáogǎng Shìchǎng (侨港市场; Qiáogǎng Market). The whole town is only 1.1 sq km.

In the other direction, regular high-speed trains run to Nánníng train station and Nánníng East train station (8.06am to 10pm) from Běihǎi. Tickets to onward destinations can be bought from the **train station ticket office** (☺8.10am-noon & 2-5pm) for a ¥5 fee.

ⓘ Getting Around

Airport shuttle buses (¥10, 30 minutes) leave from outside the **Civil Aviation Administration of China** (CAAC, 中国民航, Zhōngguó Mínháng; ☑0779 303 3757; Beibuwan Xilu, 北部湾西路; ☺8am-10pm) building a few hundred metres beyond Huoshaochuang Wuxiang, and connect with every flight. Flight tickets can also be bought here.

There are three-wheeled pedicabs and motorcycle taxis. You can get to most places in town, including to Silver Beach, for ¥5 to ¥20.

Wéizhōu Island   潿洲岛

☑0779 / POP 16,000

China's largest volcanic island, Wéizhōu Dǎo (6.5km long) makes for a relaxing day trip from Běihǎi, 124km away, if you like dormant volcanic scenery, water sports and religious architecture. You can pay for the entry ticket (¥115 per person) and buy a map (¥3) at the Běihǎi pier. Note, however, that the island's growing popularity with Chinese tourists has meant new surcharges and sometimes less-than-honest operators. With boats taking a mere 70 minutes, a day trip should suffice.

The main settlement of Nánwān Port (南湾港; Nánwān Gǎng) is 5km south of the pier.

◉ Sights & Activities

The waters around Wéizhōu contain some of the most diverse coral communities in the area; ask in Nánwān Port about motorboat rides and diving opportunities, though instructions will be in Chinese. If you're not into water sports, the beaches are skippable. On several of the beaches, you can hire sand buggies (沙滩车; shātānchē; ¥100 for 20 minutes).

★ **Wéizhōu Catholic Church**   CHURCH
(潿洲天主堂, Wéizhōu Tiānzhǔ Táng; Shèngtáng, 盛塘; ¥20) Quite an incredible sight, this church was built in 1835 with coral and volcanic rocks from the seabed in a neo-Gothic style. Quite formidable despite its modest size, the church was constructed by French missionaries for followers who had fled here to escape ethnic conflict in Guǎngdōng. It was damaged during the Cultural Revolu-

tion and rebuilt with donations from the wife of former premier Zhou Enlai, and a Catholic priest in Hong Kong. The admission charge is unfortunate, though.

Mouth of the Volcano   VOLCANO
(火山口, Huǒshān Kǒu) This breezy jaunt alongside the sea follows a long boardwalk that snakes past wave-sculpted caverns, sandy coves, rock pools, sea stacks, rock arches, crystal waters and animal shapes that were molten lava several millennia ago. It's a lovely expedition, despite the constant presence of Kenny G, and takes about 1½ hours. The volcano mouth is very small and a bit of a let-down, but the surrounding scenery is lovely.

🛏 Sleeping

Homestays (农家乐; nóngjiālè) on the island charge ¥60 to ¥80 per room. Choices are all rather samey; quite a few can be found in Nánwān Port, including the simple **Piggybar Hostel** (猪仔吧, Zhūzǎibā; ☑0779 601 3610; http://weibo.com/piggybar; Nánwān Port, 南湾港; dm ¥35-40, r ¥80-120), but there are several options near the pier as well.

ⓘ Getting There & Around

Tickets for boats to Wéizhōu Island can be purchased from the International Ferry Terminal (北海国际客运港; Běihǎi Guójì Kèyùngǎng) in Běihǎi. Fast boats (¥150 to ¥240) from Běihǎi to Wéizhōu Island leave at 8.30am, 11.30am and 3pm, taking just 70 minutes. Return boats from Wéizhōu Island to Běihǎi leave at 10.15am, 2pm and 5pm. There are more services on the weekend. Běihǎi's ferry terminal is on the road to Silver Beach (bus 3; ¥1.50).

Once on Wéizhōu Island, to get from the ferry pier to Nánwān Port, it's around ¥15 by pedicab. As the island is pretty large, consider hiring a pedicab (roughly ¥100 to ¥120 for four to five hours), a van (¥150) or a sightseeing cart (¥220), otherwise you will get quickly tired, especially in the heat (there is little shade). Drivers from the same operator may take turns chauffeuring you around, so make sure no one owes you change before you let them out of your sight. They should take you to five or six sights, before taking you back to the port.

Huāshān Cliff Murals   花山 岩画

The enigmatic **Huā Mountain Cliff Murals** (Huāshān Shíhuà; admission ¥80), 2000-year-old rock paintings of people and animals on sheer cliff faces, are the reason many people come to Guāngxī. The red-painted murals are believed to be the work of ancestors of the Zhuang, who refer to Huā Mountain as *pay laiz* – mountain with colourful paintings – but why they were painted remains a mystery. For an idea of scale, the largest of 1900 distinguishable images is 3m tall.

The crudely drawn figures are barefoot and shown in silhouette. Many have hands raised and knees bent, accompanied by pictures of drums and animals – features that suggest celebration of harvest or victory.

For several years now, conservation has kept portions of the cliff shrouded in scaffolding, as China continues its application for the site's inclusion on the UN World Heritage list.

The admission fee includes a two-hour boat ride on a spectacular section of the Zuǒ River (左江; Zuǒ Jiāng) past fallen cliff faces. The boat leaves at 10am and 2pm; outside these times, you can hire a private boat – it's ¥300 to ¥500 for 90 minutes to three hours, depending on the type of vehicle used.

The only way to see this ancient wonder is by boat from the village of Pānlóng (攀龙), commonly known as Huāshān Shānzhài (花山山寨). The cliffs are in Níngmíng (宁明), a county between Nánníng and Píngxiáng.

ⓘ Getting There & Away

Trains and buses that run between Nánníng and Píngxiáng stop at Níngmíng (宁明). From the train or bus station, pedicabs (¥30 to ¥50, 40 minutes) trundle to Huāshān Shānzhài.

Regular buses leave Níngmíng for Píngxiáng (¥13, one hour), Chóngzuǒ (¥22, 1½ hours) and Nánníng (¥70, three hours); the last buses leave at 6.30pm, 6pm and 7.50pm respectively.

Trains from Níngmíng to Píngxiáng leave at 12.30pm (¥9, one hour) and 7.28pm (¥9, 75 minutes). Trains to Chóngzuǒ (¥9, one hour) and Nánníng (¥26, three to four hours, 40 minutes) leave at 9.18am and 3.14pm.

Píngxiáng 凭祥

☑ 0771 / POP 110,000

Guāngxī's gateway to Vietnam (越南; Yuènán), Píngxiáng is a market town with a dusty, end-of-the-world feel. Everyone passing through is on their way to Vietnam, rather than visiting Píngxiáng specifically. In any case, there are no real sights of note and no reason to linger.

At the Chinese side of the Sino-Vietnamese border, **Friendship Pass Scenic Area** (友誼關景区, Yǒuyìguān Jǐngqū; ¥42; ⊙8am-8pm) is a quite attractive park sprinkled with old buildings, including a yellow French colonial number erected by the Qing government, and the virile-looking **Friendship Pass Tower**, rebuilt in 1957 on the original 2000-year-old site with battlements and ramparts.

You can find simple places on Beida Lu (北大路) behind the bus station, with air-con and wi-fi, ranging from ¥50 to ¥150. Look for the Chinese characters 宾馆 (bīnguǎn).

ⓘ GETTING TO/FROM VIETNAM FROM PÍNGXIÁNG

The Friendship Pass (友谊关; Yǒuyì Guān) border is located about 18km south of Píngxiáng on the Chinese side, and several kilometres from the obscure town of Dong Dang on the Vietnamese side; the nearest Vietnamese city (Liàngshān; Lang Son in Vietnamese) is 18km away. The border is open from 8am to 8pm Chinese time (China is one hour ahead of Vietnam), but some travellers have reported that passports aren't always stamped after around 4.30pm.

To get to the border crossing, take a pedicab or taxi (about ¥40) from Píngxiáng. From there it's a 600m walk to the Vietnamese border post. Onward transport to Hanoi, located 164km southwest of the border, is by bus or train via Lang Son.

If you're heading into China from Friendship Pass, catch a minibus to Píngxiáng bus station, from where there are regular onward buses to Nánníng and beyond. A word of caution: though train tickets to China are more expensive in Hanoi, it isn't advisable to walk across the border from Dong Dang and buy the ticket on the Chinese side. Dong Dang is several kilometres from Friendship Pass, and you'll need someone to take you by motorbike. If going by train, buy a ticket from Hanoi to Píngxiáng, and then in Píngxiáng, buy a ticket to Nánníng or beyond.

There are still reports of Lonely Planet's *China* being confiscated by border officials at Friendship Pass. We advise copying vital information and putting a cover over your guidebook just in case. Note that all bags are searched as you walk into the train station. Once you leave Píngxiáng, you won't have a problem.

Xiáng City Hotel (祥城国际大酒店, Xiángchéng Guójì Dàjiǔdiàn; ☑0771 802 2666; 2 Beida Lu, 北大路2号; r ¥260-300, ste ¥518; ❀⃝) is one of the more comfortable places to stay in Píngxiáng.

Turn right from the bus station's front entrance onto Yingxing Lu (银兴路) to find the Bank of China (中国银行; Zhōngguó Yínháng) and a couple of internet cafes (网吧; wǎngbā).

Regular buses depart from Píngxiáng bus station for Níngmíng (¥15, one hour) until 7pm, for Chóngzuǒ (¥34, one hour 20 minutes) until 6.40pm, and for Nánníng (¥78 to ¥80, three hours) until 8pm.

Trains leave for Níngmíng (¥9) and Nánníng (¥30 to ¥33, 3½ hours) from Píngxiáng Station (凭祥站; Píngxiáng Zhàn) from 6.20am. The train station is 3km south of the bus station and pedicabs (about ¥5) link the two.

Détiān Waterfall   德天瀑布

The picturesque Détiān Waterfall (Détiān Pùbù, Ban Gioc Waterfall; admission ¥80) belongs to the Chūnguī River (春归河, Chūnguīhé), which flows between China and Vietnam. The river is only 30m across in this upstream section, which means that people on both sides can see each other going about their business. It's not grand like Niagara Falls, but it is the largest falls spanning two countries in Asia, with the added buzz of being surrounded by karst peaks. The best months to see the waters in their full glory are between July and November.

The falls drop in three stages to create cascades and small pools. Swimming is not allowed, but bamboo rafts (¥30) will take you up to the spray. You can also legally cross the Vietnamese border at the 53rd merestone – tourists love doing selfies stepping into what's officially Vietnamese territory.

ⓘ Getting There & Away

There is only one direct bus from Nánníng's International Tourism Distribution Centre (¥75, 3½ hours, 7.40am), which stops en route at Lángdōng bus station (8.30am); otherwise you will have to take a bus (¥55, regular, 2½ hours) first to Dàxīn (大新) from Nánníng. At Dàxīn, switch to a bus headed to Détiān (德天; ¥20, two hours, hourly); a cab costs around ¥110.

The last bus leaves for Dàxīn at around 5.30pm. Regular buses run from Dàxīn to Nánníng until 8.30pm. The direct bus from the falls back to Nánníng leaves at 3.30pm.

Tōnglíng Grand Canyon   通灵大峡谷

Located in Bǎisè city (百色市), Jìngxī County (靖西县), the name Tōnglíng Grand Canyon (Tōnglíng Dàxiá Gǔ; ☑0771 618 0076; ¥90; ◷8am-5pm) means 'Connected to the Spirit World'. You will certainly feel spiritual as you descend narrow flights of stairs down to a large cavern, with flickering bulbs and the roar of an underground river. Emerging past the cave, you venture through a thick tropical forest into a series of wild gorges, and past vaulted cliffs with hanging stalactites and dramatic waterfalls that end in crystal pools framed by boulders.

You can walk around some of the waterfalls into the cool, other-worldly caves beyond. But you can't go near the tallest one, which has a drop of 170m and a splash of hundreds of metres in the summer.

From the canyon's exit, walk 30 minutes uphill to the entrance car park, where you can ask your driver to meet you. Alternatively, vans can take you there for ¥5.

ⓘ Getting There & Away

There are buses from Jìngxī south bus station that make the hour-long trip (¥10) to the canyon every 20 to 30 minutes until 7pm. Look for those headed for Húrùn town (湖润镇; Húrùnzhèn).

Buses (¥124) depart every 40 minutes between 8.50am and 6.50pm from Nánníng Lángdōng bus station for Jìngxī. Nánníng's Lángdōng bus station runs tour buses (¥55) to Dàxīn (大新) that stop at the canyon.

Lèyè   乐业

☑0776 / POP 157,000

Guǎngxī's highest county, Lèyè is perched on the western edge of the province, a fine springboard to the surrounding underground caves, primeval forests and natural sinkholes, and an opportunity to get off the beaten path to a less-visited part of the province.

⊙ Sights

Not a large place at all, peaceful Lèyè belongs to Bǎisè city (百色市), which also administers Jìngxī County (靖西县) where Tōnglíng Grand Canyon is located. Allow a day or two to visit the area's impressive sights.

You can buy a combo ticket (¥158) for the two sinkholes of Lèyè Geopark and the

Lotus Cave; just for the sinkholes (¥118); or for Dàshíwēi Sinkhole and the Lotus Cave (¥128).

⭐ **Lèyè Geopark**　　　　NATURE RESERVE
(乐业世界地质公园, Lèyè Shìjiè Dìzhì Gōngyuán; www.lfgeopark.com; ¥158; ⊙8.30am-5pm) There are 28 naturally formed and highly impressive sinkholes (天坑; *tiānkēng*) here, including six major ones; the remainder are large and medium-sized, with a handful of smaller sinkholes amid an environment of karst landforms, caves, underground rivers and dramatic geological features.

Luómèi Lotus Cave　　　　CAVE
(罗妹莲花洞, Luómèi Liánhuā Dòng; Tongle Lu, 同乐路; ¥80; ⊙8am-5pm) This 970m-long cave, once an underground river, shelters the world's largest collection of lotus-shaped limestone formations, illuminated by colourful lights (in a way that spoils their natural beauty). The cave is handily located 200m north of the bus station.

⭐ **Chuāndòng Sinkhole**　　　　CAVE
(穿洞天坑, Chuāndòng Tiānkēng; Lèyè Geopark, 乐业世界地质公园; admission ¥75; ⊙to 5.30pm) A two-hour hike takes you past limestone caves, primeval vegetation and an underground river in this sinkhole that reaches 312m in height. Trek to the sinkhole's bottom via an ethereal-looking cavern with a hole in its roof: on sunny days at noon, a shaft of light shines through the hole to illuminate the cavern floor.

There's no bus to Chuāndóng Sinkhole, but if you go to Dàshíwēi Sinkhole, the staff can arrange a driver to take you there and back to the city centre for ¥80 to ¥100 a car (seats four).

Dàshíwēi Sinkhole　　　　CAVE
(大石围天坑, Dàshíwēi Tiānkēng; Lèyè Geopark, 乐业世界地质公园; admission ¥98; ⊙8am-5.30pm) From the ticket office here, you're transferred to an electric cart for a 20-minute ride to what resembles a deep meteor crater; it's an astonishing sight. Follow the path to one of three viewing platforms at the top for cloud-level views of the surrounding karst ranges.

Every 20 to 30 minutes, between 8am and 4.30pm, a bus leaves Lèyè for Dàshíwēi Sinkhole. Catch it at a large temporary car park diagonally opposite the People's Hospital (人民医院; Rénmín Yīyuàn). The car park is accessible via a small alley. The 30-minute ride costs ¥4.30.

SKY PITS

Sinkholes, known as 天坑 (tiānkēng), literally 'sky pits' in Chinese, are depressions in the land caused by the collapse of the surface layer. This happens when bedrock made of a soluble substance such as limestone is eroded by underground water, forming caves that perforate the interior rock, which may eventually collapse inwards. Some sinkholes have openings into the caves below or to the underground rivers that have eroded its interior. Some are also carpeted by primeval forests that have sought purchase upon them.

🛏 Sleeping

There are several hotels where foreigners can stay, so you won't be stuck without a roof or bed for the night. Rooms start at around ¥75 and come with air-con and ensuite bathrooms. Xingle Lu is a good place to start looking.

City Comfort Inn　　　　HOTEL **$$**
(城市便捷酒店, Chéngshì Diànjié Jiǔdiàn; ☑0776 255 9888; unit 1, Bldg 4, Lètiān Gardens District, 乐天花园小区第4栋1单元; r ¥166-199) Small, bright and comfortable rooms in a small hotel next to Mínzú Middle School (民族中学).

❶ Getting There & Around

There are two daily buses from Nánníng Lángdōng bus station (¥120, six hours) at 10.10am and 7.20pm. The main station in Lèyè is on the southern end of Tongle Lu (同乐路) and the town is 1km north. The best way to get around is via pedicab – short rides cost about ¥8.

Détian's Húrùn Town Bus Station (湖润镇客运汽车站; Húrùnzhèn Kèyùn Qìchēzhàn) also runs buses to Jìngxī (靖西) every 20 minutes (¥10). Jìngxī has frequent buses to Bǎisè (¥60, 3½ hours).

Regular daily buses depart from Lèyè for:

Bǎisè (the regional hub where you can connect to southern destinations such as Dàxīn and Guǎngdōng) ¥60, three to four hours, 12.30pm to 8pm

Nánníng ¥120, six hours, twice daily

The easiest way to see the sights in Lèyè is to hire a pedicab for the day (¥200 to ¥250). Ask the driver: *Bāochē yìtiān yào duō shǎo?* 包车一天要多少? (How much is it to hire your car with chauffeur service for a day?).

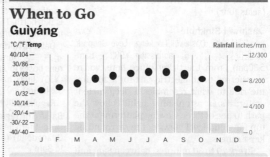

Guìzhōu

POP 35.1 MILLION

Why Go?

It's hard to call Guìzhōu (贵州) underrated as a travel destination when it's largely unknown to travellers outside China entirely – and what a travesty of justice. The province has two of the country's largest and most spectacular natural features – a waterfall and a cave – while outside the capital, Guìyáng, it's pretty much green hills and valleys, flowing rivers and limestone formations to the horizon. There's even a 'bamboo sea'.

Guìzhōu's people are as diverse as its environment. Around 37% of the province's population consists of more than 18 ethnic minorities. Flitting around the Dong and Miao villages in the east of the province is like an anthropological dream sequence. Nearby is the ancient riverside settlement of Zhènyuǎn, as striking as Guìlín to the south, where Chinese tourists chuckle into their hot-and-spicy sour fish soup that they still have it all to themselves.

Best Places to Eat

➡ Old Kaili Sour Fish Restaurant (p641)

➡ Sìhéyuàn (p641)

➡ Anshun Night Market (p653)

Best Places to Sleep

➡ Dàhéguān Hotel (p650)

➡ He House Art Hotel (p641)

➡ Indigo Lodge (p648)

➡ Double Tree Hilton (p652)

➡ River View Private Hotel (p658)

When to Go

Guìyáng

°C/°F Temp

Rainfall inches/mm

40/104 —
30/86 —
20/68 —
10/50 —
0/32 —
-10/14 —
-20/-4 —
-30/-22 —
-40/-40 —

— 12/300
— 8/200
— 4/100
— 0

J F M A M J J A S O N D

Jan Follow the birdsong to Cǎohǎi Lake, where birdwatchers flock each winter.

Jul & Aug Immerse yourself in the spray of 4000 waterfalls emerging from a bamboo forest.

Oct & Nov Toast the Miao New Year in the traditional villages around Kǎilǐ.

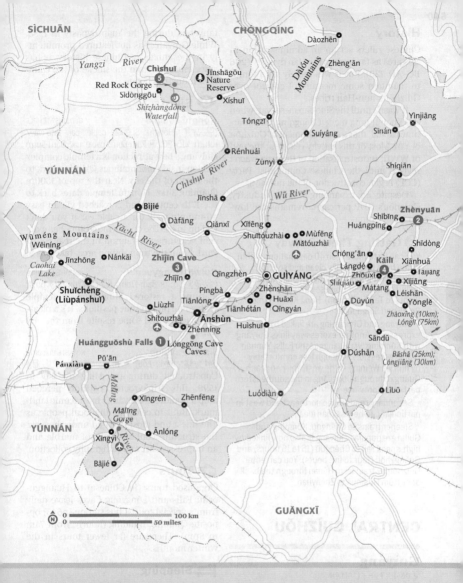

Guìzhōu Highlights

1 Huángguǒshù Falls
(p654) Rafting in the wash of
China's largest waterfall, and
hiking the nearby region.

2 Zhènyuǎn (p649) River-
cruising through a charming
2000-year-old settlement.

3 Zhījīn Cave (p654
Descending into the
spectacular largest cavern in
China.

4 Kǎilǐ (p646) Hopping
between the Miao villages
located around here.

5 Chìshuǐ (p657) Getting
way off the beaten track in
prehistoric fern forests.

6 Festivals (p644) Partying
with the locals at one of the
thousand-odd celebrations
held in Guìzhōu each year.

History

Chinese rulers set up an administration in this area as far back as the Han dynasty (206 BC–AD 220), but it was merely an attempt to maintain some measure of control over Guìzhōu's non-Han tribes.

It wasn't until the Sino-Japanese war, when the Kuomintang made Chóngqìng their wartime capital, that the development of Guìzhōu began. Most of this activity ceased at the end of WWII; industrialisation of the area wasn't revived until the Chinese Communist Party (CCP) began construction of the railways.

Despite an expanding mining industry, Guìzhōu's GDP per capita remains the lowest in all China.

ⓘ Getting There & Away

You can fly to more than 40 destinations within China from the squeaky clean and spacious Guìyáng Lóngdòngbǎo International Airport, including all major Chinese cities plus direct flights to Taipei (Taiwan), Hong Kong, Bangkok, Seoul and Singapore.

Guìyáng and Chóngqìng are linked by an expressway. Another expressway links Guìyáng with Kūnmíng, via Huángguǒshù Falls. Yúnnán is also accessible – though less comfortably – by bus via Wēiníng in the west. You can reach Guǎngxī through Cóngjiāng in the southeastern part of the province.

Secondary roads in the northeast and west in particular can be less than ideal.

Sleeper trains to Chéngdū, Kūnmíng and Guìlín are popular. Guìyáng is also now linked by high-speed rail to Chéngdū (15 to 16 hours) and Guǎngzhōu (four to five hours). You can enter Guìzhōu by train from Húnán through the back door from Huáihuà to Zhènyuǎn.

CENTRAL GUÌZHŌU

Guìyáng   贵阳

☑ 0851 / POP 3.1 MILLION

Guìyáng is an unpretentious, relatively youthful provincial capital under seemingly continual construction. While it may not leap out at the traveller, there are some interesting sights and affordable fine hotels, and the city's location makes it a perfect base for exploring the surrounding southern countryside, especially Huángguǒshù Falls, the ethnic villages around Kǎilǐ, and historic Zhènyuǎn.

The city passed through the hands of various warring states until it became es-

tablished during the Yuan dynasty in 1283. While Guìyáng has not featured prominently in the annals of Chinese history, it has since emerged from the smoke of the country's industrial boom.

◉ Sights

Hóngfú Temple   BUDDHIST TEMPLE

(弘福寺, Hóngfú Sì, ¥2, cable car one-way/return ¥15/20, ⊙ 7am-6pm, cable car 9am-5pm) Guìyáng's best attraction is a temple complex hidden inside mountainous Qiánlíng Park to the north of the city. Near the top of 1300m Qiánlíng Shān, Hóngfú Temple dates back to the 17th century and is reached via an easy 40-minute walk (or a cable car if you don't feel up to it). The on-site monastery has a decent vegetarian restaurant in the rear courtyard. From the train station area, take bus 2.

Cuìwēi Gōngyuán   BUDDHIST TEMPLE

(翠微公园; ⊙ 8am-11pm) FREE This city park features a restored Ming dynasty temple with some picturesque pavilions. It's a pleasant place to find some respite from the city noise.

Jiǎxiù Pavilion   NOTABLE BUILDING

(甲秀楼, Jiǎxiù Lóu; ⊙ 8.30am-6.30pm) FREE Constructed during the Ming dynasty in 1598, this triple-roofed pavilion perched atop a boulder is Guìyáng's most iconic landmark. Built to celebrate the local people as 'the finest and most talented under heaven', the structure contains slabs of marble and an impressive art and calligraphy collection.

☞ Tours

Organised tours (in Chinese) to Huángguǒshù Falls and Lónggōng Caves leave daily from a special tourist bus station (p643) opposite Qiánlíng Building (hourly, from 7am to 8pm). There are far fewer tours in the winter months.

⯞ Sleeping

Guìyáng has a few reasonable hostels, and a host of business hotels. The high-end places offer the best value, especially out in the new economic zone of Jīnyáng, 15km northwest of the centre.

Guìyáng Shu Hostel   HOSTEL $

(贵阳墅国际青年驿栈, Guìyáng Shù Guójì Qīngnián Yìzhàn; ☑ 181 9828 7383; 86 Wujin Lu, 乌金路 86号; dm ¥50) Quiet and friendly hostel run by a bilingual Singaporean expat has clean dorm rooms, spacious shared bathrooms and loads of useful information on travelling around the province. If coming from Guìyáng North train station, catch bus 261.

Hàntíng Express
HOTEL **$$**

(汉庭连锁酒店, Hàntíng Liánsuǒ Jiǔdiàn; ☑0851 855 1888; www.htinns.com; 372 Jiefang Lu, 解放路 372号; tw&d¥219-239; ✳@🛜) In a central but fairly uneventful part of town, this efficient chain hotel is a good-value 'overnighter' for singles. Rooms are spotless (if a little tight), and free coffee awaits guests in the lounge. Walk north up Zunyi Lu and turn left along Jiefang Lu; it's on the far side of the road.

★ He House Art Hotel
BOUTIQUE HOTEL **$$$**

(贵阳和舍艺术精品酒店, Guìyáng Héshè Yìshù Jīngpǐn Jiǔdiàn; ☑0851 682 5888; www.hehouse hotel.com; 219 Baoshanbei Lu, 宝山北路219号; d from ¥530; P✳🛜) Guìyáng's independent hotel scene has been lifted in one grand sweep by this large white gallery space in a converted building in the city's east. Open-plan rooms are oversized and crisply prepared with original artworks and bathroom amenities. Service is earnest but knowledgeable about the city. The on-site restaurant has a limited selection; breakfast buffet has a colourful continental variety.

✗ Eating

North of the train station and Jiefang Lu, Zunyi Xiang (遵义巷) is a lively and busy food street of hotpot, Sìchuān and Jiāchángcài restaurants, which all shut around 10pm.

Sìhéyuàn
GUIZHOU **$**

(四合院; ☑0851 682 5419; Qianling Lu, 黔灵路; mains from ¥15; ☺noon-9.30pm) Here's the quintessential local restaurant writ large, thanks to consistent Guìzhōu cuisine in an unpretentious setting. Hundreds of tables are squeezed in among the alleys off Zhonghua Beilu as diners feast year-round on the 200-plus spicy dishes on the menu. Just ask for recommendations. It's opposite the large red-crossed Protestant Church on Qianling Lu.

★ Old Kǎilǐ Sour Fish Restaurant
GUIZHOU **$$**

(老凯俚酸汤鱼, Lǎo Kǎilǐ Suāntāngyú; ☑0851 584 3665; 55 Shengfu Lu, 省府路55号; mains from ¥40; ☺11.30am-10pm) This local institution has two branches, but the one on Shengfu Lu has superior service and atmosphere (both have Miao waitstaff in traditional garb). Everyone comes for suāntāngyú (酸汤鱼; sour fish soup), a Miao delicacy and Guìzhōu's most famous dish. Choose a

fish from the tank and point to the vegetables you'd like; your soup is made to order. Delicious.

Tree Kitchen
GUIZHOU **$$**

(树厨, Shù Chú; ☑0851 582 6853; next door to Novotel Hotel, 诺富特酒店旁; dishes from ¥28; ☺10.30am-9.30pm) Next door to the Novotel is this homely restaurant set inside a courtyard of a former private residence. The modest menu considers the Western palate in dishes such as barbecued beef and leeks (火烧葱香牛肉; huǒshāo cōng xiāng niúròu) or the pork and sliced potato (软哨土豆片; ruǎnshào túdòupián).

🍷 Drinking & Nightlife

Highlands Coffee
CAFE

(高原咖啡, Gāoyuán Kāfēi; ☑0851 8582 6222; Bao'ai Lu & Liudong Jie, No 1 Street, 博爱路六洞街 1号; ☺10am-11pm) An American-owned and -operated coffee shop in the heart of the city may not sound like cause for celebration, but this is a delightful place with comfortable seating (inside and out), superb cheesecake and a serious brew. All staff speak some English.

Hobo's
BAR

(☑150 0851 2834; 11 Shangyu Jia Xiang, 上余家巷11号; ☺7pm-2am) The only cocktail bar in Guìyáng – no beer here. The bartenders were trained in Japan and really know their stuff. Reasonably priced drinks (cocktails from ¥45) and a fine collection of single malts, plus an amiable crowd. It's tucked down an alley off Qianlong Donglu's buzzing bar strip.

ℹ Information

Bank of China (中国银行, Zhōngguó Yínháng; cnr Wenchang Beilu & Yan'an Donglu, 文昌北路 六東路; ☺9am-5pm) Has an ATM and changes

GUIZHOU GUÌYÁNG

Guìyáng

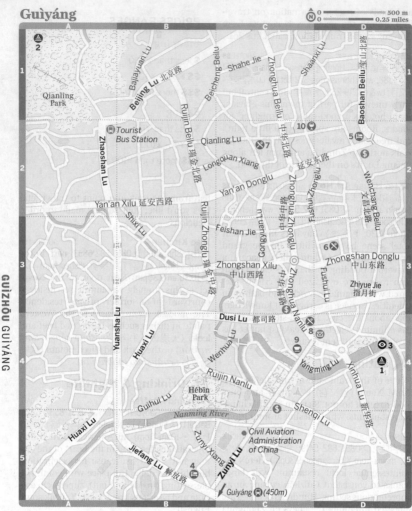

foreign currency. Other branches can be found near the corner of Dusi Lu and Zhonghua Nanlu (都司六中華 南路; ◎9am-5pm), and on Zunyi Lu (遵義路; ◎9am-5pm) near Renmin Sq.

Civil Aviation Administration of China (CAAC, 中国民航, Zhōngguó Mínháng; 264 Zunyi Lu, 遵義路264号; ◎8am-7pm) Buy airline tickets at this office. The airport bus also departs from here.

Public Security Bureau (PSB, 公安局, Gōng'ānjú; ☎0851 590 4509; Daying Lu, 大英路; ◎8.30am-noon & 2.30-5pm Mon-Fri) The staff don't see many foreigners here, but they seem pleasant enough.

🛈 Getting There & Around

AIR

Guìyáng Lóngdòngbǎo International Airport is around 10km east of the city. Destinations include:

Běijīng ¥1300, three hours, 24 daily
Shànghǎi ¥730, 2½ hours, 14 daily
Guǎngzhōu ¥649, 1½ hours, 11 daily
Chéngdū ¥690, 1¼ hours, 14 daily
Xī'ān ¥799, 1¾ hours, eight daily
Kūnmíng ¥355, 1¼ hours, eight daily
Hong Kong ¥910, 1½ hours, one daily

The Civil Aviation Administration of China (p642) office is around 1km north of the train

Guìyáng

⊙ **Sights**

1 Cuìwēi Gōngyuán D4
2 Hóngfú Temple A1
3 Jiàxiù Pavilion D4

🛏 **Sleeping**

4 Hànting Express B5
5 He House Art Hotel D2

🍴 **Eating**

6 Old Kaili Sour Fish Restaurant D3
7 Sìhéyuàn C2
8 Tree Kitchen C4

🍷 **Drinking & Nightlife**

9 Highlands Coffee C4
10 Hobo's C2

Chéngdū ¥238, 11 to 20 hours, seven daily (11.10am to 11.03pm)

Chóngqìng ¥130, nine to 12 hours, nine daily (7.10am to 10.50pm)

Kǎilǐ (hard seat) ¥59, 45 minutes

Kūnmíng ¥156, seven to 10 hours, 16 daily (4.20am to 11.59pm)

Zhènyuǎn (hard seat) ¥42, three to four hours, 14 daily (2.47am to 8.56pm)

The new **Guìyáng North train station** (贵阳火车北站, Guìyáng Huǒchē Běizhàn; Beizhan Jie, 北站街) has fast trains to the following destinations:

Guǎngzhōu (soft seat) ¥317, four to five hours, 23 daily

Shànghǎi Hóngqiáo (2nd-class seat) ¥735, nine hours, five daily

---

station, on the corner with Qingyun Lu; airport buses depart every 30 minutes from here (¥10, 20 minutes, 8am to 7pm).

A taxi from the airport will cost around ¥65.

BUS

The Jīnyáng long-distance bus station (金阳客运站; Jīnyáng kèyùnzhàn) is in the western suburbs on Jinyang Nanlu, 15km northwest of central Guìyáng. Take bus 219 (¥2, 6.30am to 10pm) from the train station; a taxi will cost ¥50. Destinations include the following:

Ānshùn ¥35, 1½ hours, every 20 minutes (7am to 9pm)

Huángguǒshù ¥58, 2½ hours, every 40 minutes (7.40am to 12.45pm)

Wēiníng ¥132, six hours, two daily (9am and 12.30pm)

For Kǎilǐ (¥60, 2½ hours, every 20 to 30 minutes, 7am to 9pm) and Cóngjiāng (¥150, seven hours, 9am, 11am and 3pm), head to the east bus station (东客运站; dōng kèyùnzhàn) on the eastern outskirts of town. Bus 229 (¥2) runs here from the train station. A taxi is about ¥30.

Tour buses to Huángguǒshù Falls and Lónggōng Caves depart from the Tourist Bus Station (旅游客运站, Lǚyóu Kèyùnzhàn).

TAXI

Taxi flag fall is ¥9; late at night it increases to ¥10.

TRAIN

Guìyáng's train station (贵阳火车站, Guìyáng Huǒchēzhàn) is useful for reaching Kǎilǐ, Ānshùn, Wēiníng and Zhènyuǎn. Destinations include the following (prices are for hard sleeper berths):

Ānshùn (hard seat) ¥16, 1½ hours, 27 daily (4.20am to 11.59pm)

Cǎohǎi (for Wēiníng; soft seat) ¥50, four to eight hours, six daily (7.50am to 4.54pm)

Qīngyán 青岩

📞 0851

With its winding, stone-flagged streets and restored city walls, **Qīngyán** (admission ¥80) makes a pleasant diversion from modern Guìyáng. A former Ming-era military outpost dating back to 1378, Qīngyán was once a traffic hub between the southwest provinces, leaving the village with Taoist temples and Buddhist monasteries rubbing up against Christian churches and menacing watchtowers.

Some of Qīngyán's places of worship are still active; make sure to visit the tranquil **Yíngxiáng Temple** (迎祥寺, Yíngxiáng Sì), on a side street populated by fortune tellers; also compare the current, minimalist **Catholic Church** (天主教堂, Tiānzhǔ Jiàotáng) with the now disused – but much more impressive – 19th-century original next door.

Note that you don't need the through ticket to see the major sights, but you do need it to access some places in town.

There are no places to stay inside the old town, but some options near the northern gate might save you heading back to the big city. One such place, **Qīngyán Yuèrán Wútóng Kèzhàn** (青岩悦然梧桐客栈, Qīngyán Yuèrán Wútóng Kèzhàn; 📞 157 2210 8809; d ¥150; 🅿❄🛜), is friendly, sufficiently clean and comfortable.

There are loads of cheap food stalls inside the city gates selling everything from pigfeet stew to fried tofu balls.

Qīngyán is about 30km south of Guìyáng and makes an easy day trip. Bus 210 runs here from the left-hand side of Hébīn Park (¥2, 1¼ hours, every 30 minutes from 6.30am). A taxi will cost around ¥100 one way.

EASTERN GUÌZHŌU

Kǎilǐ   凯里

♪ 0855 / POP 139,445

The largest city in eastern Guìzhōu, Kǎilǐ is a bustling industrial centre for the region with little to appeal to travellers. Still, it's a decent base – or at the very least a transit point – for planning your forays into the ever-popular ethnic minority villages in the gorgeous surrounding countryside.

◉ Sights

Jīnquánhú Park   PARK
(金泉湖公园, Jīnquánhú Gōngyuán) Known as the site of the Dongs' ceremonial **Drum Tower**, this park gets lively at festival time.

Minorities Museum   MUSEUM
(贵州民族博物馆, Guìzhōu Mínzú Bówùguǎn; Ningbo Lu, 宁波路; ⊙9am-4.30pm) FREE A small collection of local minority clothing and artefacts.

☆☆ Festivals & Events

Markets and festivals are one of Guìzhōu's major attractions, and the profusion of them around Kǎilǐ makes this sleepy town the best place to base yourself for exploring them.

☞ Tours

Wu Min, also known as Louisa, a local Miao woman, runs **treks** (☑158 8583 5852; wumin louisa@hotmail.com) to remote Miao and Dong villages that come highly recommended. She can also organise **homestays**, as well as arrange for visitors to study the Miao and Dong languages and learn local dances. She speaks good English.

⊨ Sleeping

Sīlāwéi Business Hotel   HOTEL $$
(斯拉威商务酒店, Sīlāwéi Shāngwù Jiǔdiàn; ☑0855 823 9111; 44 Yingpan Donglu, 营盘东路44号; d¥218; ⊛⊜) Another agreeable option close to the bus station, the Sīlāwéi is clean and boasts excellent bathrooms, including high-pressure showers. The price comes with a rather paltry breakfast.

C'est La Vie Hotel   HOTEL $$
(斯拉威酒店, Sī Lā Wēi Jiǔdiàn; ☑0855 823 9111; www.klslw.com; 44 Yingpan Donglu, 营盘东路44号; tw/d ¥228/248; ⊛⊜) Efficient staff, comfortable and sizeable rooms and a handy location close to the bus station make this one of the better choices in town, while the attached restaurant (with picture menu) is a solid and reasonably priced spot to eat.

Zòng Héng Hotel   HOTEL $$$
(纵横大酒店, Zònghéng Dàjiǔdiàn; ☑0855 869 8299; 5 Ningbo Lu, 宁波路5号; d from ¥588; P⊛⊜) A well established four-star hotel with questionable service, but the spacious, modern rooms make a good base for a family or small group. Carpets and communal areas are tired, but the restaurant cooks up delicious Chinese food.

✗ Eating

Savoury crepes, potato patties, barbecues, tofu grills, noodles, hotpot, *shuǐjiǎo* (boiled dumplings) and wonton soup overflow at reasonable prices at Kǎilǐ's street stalls. Look for *guōtiēdiàn* (锅贴店; dumpling snack restaurants) selling *guōtiē* (锅贴; fried dumplings) and Shànghǎi-style *xiǎolóngbāo*; there are several on Wenhua Beilu.

Also head to the bustling **night market** (夜市, Yèshì; off Beijing Donglu, 北京东路; ⊙5pm-2am), which has a wide range of barbecue places, as well as noodles and dumplings.

CELEBRATING WITH THE LOCALS, GUÌZHŌU-STYLE

Minority celebrations are lively events that can last for days at a time, and often include singing, dancing, horse racing and buffalo fighting.

One of the biggest is the **lúshēng festival**, held in either spring or autumn, depending on the village: a *lúshēng* is a reed instrument used by the Miao people. Other important festivals include the **Dragon Boat Festival**, the **hill-leaping festival** and the '**sharing the sister's meal' festival** (equivalent to Valentine's Day in the West). The **Miao New Year** is celebrated on the first four days of the 10th lunar month in Kǎilǐ, Guàdīng, Zhōuxī and other Miao areas.

All minority festivals follow the lunar calendar, so dates vary from year to year. They will also vary from village to village and shaman to shaman. **CITS** (p645) in Kǎilǐ can provide you with a list of local festivals.

Kǎilǐ

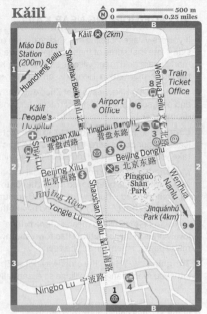

Liànghuānzhài Fish Soup Restaurant
CHINESE $

(快活林亮欢寨, Kuàihuó Línliànghuān Zhài; lhz. qcfs.com.cn; 98 Chengxi Lu, 城西路98号; soup ¥38-48; ⊙11am-10pm) The pick of the local sour soup venues gets the nod due to the high turnover of customers, the bubbly service and the sharp, tangy flavour. Take control of the chilli before someone else does! It's 2km west of the city centre.

ℹ Information

Bank of China (中国银行, Zhōngguó Yínháng; Shaoshan Nanlu, 韶山南路; ⊙9am-5pm) This main branch has all services and an ATM. A second branch on Beijing Donglu (中国银行, Zhōngguó Yínháng; Beijing Donglu, 北京东路; ⊙9am-5pm) will also change cash. Many other ATMs around town accept foreign cards.

Bóyǔ Internet Cafe (博宇网吧, Wǎngbā; Wenhua Beilu, 文化北路; per hr ¥3; ⊙24hr) One of a number of internet cafes on Wenhua Beilu. The staff here will normally log you in on one of their ID cards.

China International Travel Service (CITS, 中国国际旅行社, Zhōngguó Guójì Lǚxíngshè; ☑0855 822 2506; www.cits.net; 53 Yingpan Donglu, 营盘东路53号; ⊙9am-5.30pm) Tucked just behind Yingpan Donglu, CITS has the most up-to-date information on minority villages, festivals, markets and organised tours. Staff are helpful, with some English spoken.

Internet Cafe (网吧, Wǎngbā; cnr Wenhua Beilu & Beijing Donglu, 文化北路·; per hr ¥3; ⊙24hr) On the 2nd floor, with 400 computers and comfy chairs.

Kǎilǐ People's Hospital (凯里市第一人民医院, Kǎilǐshì Dìyī Rénmín Yīyuàn; 28 Yingpan Xilu, 营盘西路28号) The best place in town for medical care.

Public Security Bureau (PSB, 公安局, Gōng'ānjú; ☑0855 853 6113; Beijing Donglu, 北京东路; ⊙8.30-11.30am & 2.30-5.30pm Mon-Fri) Deals with all passport and visa enquiries.

ℹ Getting There & Away

AIR
For departures from Guìyáng Lóngdòngbǎo International Airport, airport buses (¥70, 2½ hours, 7am to 6pm) leave every 30 minutes from the **airport office** (☑0855 836 3868; 73 Jinjing Lu, 進京路73号; ⊙8am-7pm), where you can also check-in before your flight. You can also buy air tickets here.

BUS
Kǎilǐ's **long-distance bus station** (长途客运站, Chángtú Kèyùnzhàn; ☑0855 825 1025; Wenhua Beilu, 文化北路) has departures to most destinations.

Cóngjiāng ¥110, five hours, five daily (9am to 4pm)

Guìyáng ¥60, three hours, every 20 minutes (7am to 8pm)

Jǐnpíng (锦屏; for Lónglǐ) ¥91, four hours, 10 daily (8am to 4pm)

Léishān ¥14, 50 minutes, every 25 minutes (7.25am to 7pm)

Líping ¥137, five hours, eight daily (7.40am to 4.30pm)

VILLAGE-HOPPING NEAR KĂILĬ

If you are village-hopping into Guăngxī, plan on spending about a week on the Guìzhōu side. Note that some of these villages charge entrance fees. An extraordinary number of markets are held in the villages surrounding Kăilĭ. Check with the CITS (p645) in Kăilĭ for the latest information. Here are some lesser-known villages worth a visit:

Jītáng (基塘) Hike west out of Zhàoxīng from the bus station for an hour, up a steep hill and past some splendid rice terraces, and you're in friendly Jītáng, which has its own drum tower.

Lángdé (郎德) Superb extant Miao architecture and cobbled pathways naturally draw loads of tour buses here, but there's a terrific 15km trail along the Bālā River that will take you through several tourist-free Miao villages. About 20km outside Kăilĭ.

Mátáng (麻塘) 18km northwest of Kăilĭ is the home of the Gejia, renowned batik artisans. Mátáng has been dolled up a little for tourism – the inevitable performance square has materialised – but a worthwhile 30-minute walk from here brings you to the village of **Shílóngzhài** (石龙寨), populated by another sub-branch of the Miao called the Xijia.

Shíqiáo (石桥) Shíqiáo means 'stone bridge' and you'll know why when you spy the lovely ones in this beautiful Miao town southwest of Kăilĭ. Shíqiáo was famed for its handmade paper, which can still be seen.

Táng'ān (堂安) Head the other way out of Zhàoxīng through the fields and two hours later you reach Táng'ān, a village so essentially Dong it's been named a living museum.

Májiāng ¥17, one hour, hourly (8.20am to 5.50pm)

Róngjiāng ¥77 to ¥90, 4½ hours, every 40 minutes (7.20am to 6.20pm)

Xījiāng ¥15.50, 80 minutes, hourly (8.40am to 5.40pm)

Zhènyuǎn ¥35, two hours, six daily (8.30am to 4pm)

For Chóng'ān (¥13, one hour, every 20 minutes, 6.40am to 6pm) and Huángpíng (¥20, one hour, every 20 minutes, 6.40am to 6pm) head to the **Miáo Dū Bus Station** (苗都客运站; Miáo Dū Kèyùnzhàn) on Huangcheng Beilu.

TRAIN

The Kăilĭ high-speed railway opened in late 2015, significantly reducing the journey to Guìyáng (¥59, 45 minutes), Shànghǎi (¥694, eight hours) and Kūnmíng (¥315, eight to 10 hours).

Kăilĭ's train station is a couple of kilometres north of town. Regular trains run to Guìyáng (¥28, two to three hours), Zhènyuǎn (¥14, 1½ hours) and Huáihuà (¥21 to ¥42, four hours). A handy **train ticket office** (火车票代售处, Huǒchēpiào Dàishòuchù; ☑ 0855 381 7920; 38 Wenhua Beilu, 文化北路38号; ⊙ 8.30am-6.30pm) is on Wenhua Beilu.

❶ Getting Around

Bus fares cost ¥1 in Kăilĭ and almost all of the buses departing from the train station follow the same route: up Qingjiang Lu, past the long-distance bus station, along Beijing Donglu and down Shaoshan Nanlu to the Minorities Museum.

For the train station, take bus 2. Other local buses leave from the local stations (Map p645) on Shiyi Lu and Wenhua Nanlu.

Taxi flag fall is ¥6. A taxi to the train station from the centre of town will cost around ¥12.

Bāshā   岜沙

☑ 0855 / POP 2000

Visiting historic Bāshā is like stepping back in time to the Tang or Song eras. The local men wear period clothes with daggers secured to their belts and, when not farming, hunt with antique rifles. Meanwhile, the women parade in full Miao rig with their hair twisted in a curl on top of their heads.

A collection of six hamlets sprawls across a beautiful valley, with Chinese–English signs pointing the way to the various places of interest. The surrounding countryside is superb. You might also be able to arrange a hunting trip with the men.

Entrance to the village is ¥80 and there are two cultural performances each day for most of the year. Very modern Cóngjiāng (从江) is 7.5km away.

You can find very rudimentary rooms for ¥30, but there are a few decent options, too. Alternatively, you can spend the night in Cóngjiāng.

Family-run **Gǔfēngzhài Qīngnián Lǚguǎn** (古风寨青年旅馆; ☑ 138 8554 9720; dm

¥50, tw/d ¥128/168; @ 🛜) is the pick of the village. The views of the surrounding valley alone are worth the stay, but there's also real pride in the presentation of the modest private rooms and spotless dorms. Walk down the path to the left of the village square to find it.

Bashā has a couple of basic, but yummy *suāntāngyú* (酸汤鱼; sour fish soup) restaurants.

A few orange and grey minibuses run between Cóngjiāng and Bāshā early in the morning and late in the afternoon (¥5). Otherwise, you'll have to take a taxi (it's a very steep walk up to the village).

The return trip should cost ¥70; you'll need the driver to wait for you.

Léishān 雷山

🚄 0855

The village of Léishān is usually used as a transit point, but you can also head to 2178m **Léigōng Shān** (雷公山, Leigong Mountain; ¥100) for some hiking and to explore several charming settlements.

Several interesting villages near Léishān include the attractive Miao village of **Wūdōng** (乌东). Other nearby Miao settlements include **Páikǎ** (排卡; Páikǎ Miáozhài), around 3km south of Léishān, where *lúshēng* bamboo and reed musical instruments have been handmade for centuries.

There are no options to sleep here; try Xījiāng if you want the village experience, or head back to Kǎilǐ.

Your eating choices are limited to a few street stalls during the day.

From Kǎilǐ, there are numerous buses to Léishān (¥14, one hour).

Lónglǐ 隆里

🚄 0855

Stranded in splendid isolation amid fields and rice paddies near the Húnán border, Lónglǐ is a former garrison town populated by the descendants of Han soldiers sent to protect the empire from the pesky Miao. One of the province's 'eco-museums' – that is, a real-live village – it's fascinating for its extant architecture.

Enter Lónglǐ via the East Gate (Dōngmén) and take an hour's stroll to savour its warren of narrow cobblestone streets, mostly wooden houses, lovely courtyards, pavilions, temples and town walls. The sur-

rounding area is prime for exploration by bicycle, too.

A few basic guesthouses are located just outside the old town.

Lónglǐ Gǔchéng Jiǔdiàn (隆里古城酒店; 🚄 0855 718 0018, 136 3855 4888; tw ¥80) has basic rooms with squat toilets; it's located to the left of the East Gate entrance to Lónglǐ.

Coming from Kǎilǐ is rather arduous as there's no direct bus. You'll need to first take a bus to Jǐnpíng (锦屏; ¥91, two hours), then switch to another bus (¥16, 1½ hours, half-hourly or so from 7.30am to around 5pm) to Lónglǐ.

Xījiāng 西江

🚄 0855 / POPULATION 5000

Xījiāng tucked away in the undulating greenery of Léigōng Mountain west of the Báishuǐ River, is the largest Miao village in China at roughly 1200 wooden homes. Like many neighbouring Miao villages, the village is famous for its embroidery and silver ornaments (the Miao believe that silver can dispel evil spirits).

The town has upgraded to the next level of tourism whereby creature comforts and improving infrastructure come with the air-conditioned buses. The dances and clothing are stunning though, and a minute's walk in any direction takes you to lush paddies, wooden *diàojiǎolóu* (traditional handcrafted houses), water buffalo and seemingly year-round mist.

Entry to the village is ¥100.

🔘 Sights

When the sun obliges, Xījiāng is lovely. Head away from the village on paths that weave through rice paddies, sidestepping farmers and water buffalo, and recharge your soul in the surrounding hills. A lovely trek is the 50-minute hike past terraced fields and rice paddies over the hills to **Kāijué Miao Village** (开觉苗寨; Kāijué Miáozhài) and **Kāijué Waterfall** (开觉瀑布; Kāijué Pùbù) a bit further beyond.

There's also a three-day trek from Xījiāng to **Páiyáng** (排羊), a Miao village north of Xījiāng. This trail winds its way through some remote minority villages and lush scenery. You will probably find accommodation with locals en route, but you shouldn't expect it, so come prepared to sleep under the stars.

⌁ Sleeping & Eating

Many families in Xījiāng offer rooms from ¥50. There's also an increasing number of quality guesthouses.

There are a number of cheap and yummy restaurants run by local families here.

Miao Family Guesthouse GUESTHOUSE $
(苗寨人家, Miáo Zhài Rénjiā; ☑ 0855 334 8688; tw ¥188) This guesthouse has clean, comfortable rooms with hot water. It's across the river on the eastern side of Xījiāng.

998 HOSTEL $
(☑ 0855 334 871; dm/r ¥25/40) This bohemian residence is pretty and quiet (when the owner is not rocking the acoustic guitar), though bathrooms are a little scratchy. The communal landing with cushions is a fun place to meet other travellers.

Gǔzàngtóujiā INN $
(鼓藏头家; ☑ 136 3809 5568; r ¥50-100) Lean and fresh wooden rooms occupy a traditional building opposite the historic Gǔzàngtáng, an ancestral home which houses drums used in festivals. It's run by an old man who speaks nary a word of English. Call ahead and he'll meet you.

ⓘ Information

The tourist infrastructure runs to a performance square, English signposts, souvenir shops, an ATM taking foreign cards (sometimes) and even a few cafes with wi-fi. Head to the western side of the village for a more authentic experience. Come evening, when the day trippers have disappeared, the village reverts to a more traditional pace of life.

ⓘ Getting There & Around

From Kǎilǐ, buses run hourly between 8.40am and 5.40pm; there are hourly buses back to Kǎilǐ from 8.30am to 5.30pm. Alternatively, heading south and east towards Guǎngxī, there are regular buses to Léishān (¥11, 1½ hours, 6.30am to 5.40pm), from where you can head south towards Róngjiāng (榕江). There are also two buses a day to Guìyáng's east bus station (¥80, four hours, 9am and 3pm).

From the village's ticket office, buses (¥5) run to the village itself.

Zhàoxīng 肇兴
☑ 0855 / POP 4000

Zhàoxīng has emerged from its stunning natural seclusion as a drawcard for visitors looking to experience life in a Dong village.

The traditional wooden housing is overshadowed only by the 'wind and rain' bridges, reminiscent of a fantasy epic. Then there are the five drum towers that call forth generations of ritual and celebration.

Away from the main street, Zhàoxīng remains a working farming village, where most people still speak only their native Dong language and little has changed for generations.

Entry to the village is ¥100.

⌁ Sleeping & Eating

Any number of quasi-inns and guesthouses around the village offer rooms from ¥50.

The restaurants on the main street have English menus – which you might find helpful for decoding dishes, as they eat rat (老鼠肉; lǎoshǔ ròu) in this area.

Wàngjiāng Lóu Hostel GUESTHOUSE $
(望江楼客栈, Wàngjiānglóu Kèzhàn; ☑ 0855 613 0269; tw & d ¥100; ✳@☎) Family-run place by the river, with fresh and clean wooden rooms featuring hot showers and sit-down toilets.

Indigo Lodge LODGE $$
(☑ 139 7106 1291; d from ¥255; ✳☎) Indigo is indicative of the increasing professionalism of the Dong villages in catering to the travel community: hip, understated luxury; impeccable customer service (in English); and a real understanding of how to maximise your visit to the region. Lit up at night, it's a beauty. Expect copycat operations in the near future.

Zhàoxīng Bīnguǎn HOTEL $$
(肇兴宾馆; ☑ 0855 613 0899; tw & d ¥228-398; ✳☎) Spotless rooms with tiny but gleaming bathrooms. If it's not booked out by tour groups, you can usually score a 25% discount.

ⓘ Getting There & Away

Getting here from Kǎilǐ is a slog. First you have to travel by bus to Cóngjiāng (¥110, 4½ hours, five daily from 9am to 4pm) and then change for a bus to Zhàoxīng (¥19, two hours, 7.50am and 1pm). From Lípíng (黎平), there are five buses daily (¥25, 3½ hours, 8.20am to 2.50pm).

Heading out of Zhàoxīng, there are two morning buses (¥19, 7.30am and noon) to Cóngjiāng. If you're heading to Sānjiāng (三江) in Guǎngxī, you'll need to change buses in Lípíng (¥25, four daily, 7.20am, 9am, 10am, 1pm) or Cóngjiāng, where there are frequent buses to Guìlín (¥82), too.

GUIZHŌU ZHÀOXĪNG

Zhènyuǎn 镇远

📞 0855 / POP 60,000

Zhènyuǎn is the highlight for many visitors to southern China thanks to its unruffled charm, high density of historical sights, gorgeous locale by the Wǔyáng River (Wǔyáng Hé), and relative obscurity in the eyes of international travellers. (In some neighbouring provinces, places half as delightful draw twice the number of visitors.)

A former outpost on the trade route from Yúnnán to Húnán, Zhènyuǎn also features a great gorge cruise which makes a smart alternative to the bigger – and frankly less charming – Three Gorges option to the northeast.

👁 Sights

Sìfāngjǐng Xiàng — AREA
(四方井巷) Four old and well preserved alleys lead north away from the river: Sìfāngjǐng Xiàng, Fuxing Xiang, Renshou Xiang and Chongzikou Xiang. Wander along Sìfāngjǐng Xiàng and peek at its namesake **Sìfāngjǐng** (Four Directions Well), with its three deities overlooking the water, capped with red cloths. Note the magnificently made stone steps of this alley and the gorgeous old residences – a picture at night, when they're dressed with red lanterns.

Qīnglóng Dòng — TEMPLE, HISTORIC SITE
(青龙洞, Green Dragon Cave; ¥60; ⊙ 7.30am-6pm) Across the river from the old town, the epic vertical warren of temples, grottoes, corridors and caves of Qīnglóng Dòng rises up against **Zhōnghé Mountain** (Zhōnghé Shān; 中和山). Flooded with lights at night, it forms a sublime backdrop to the town. Put aside a good hour for exploration: it's a labyrinth and there's a lot to see, including some choice panoramas.

Tiānhòu Temple — BUDDHIST TEMPLE
(天后宫, Tiānhòu Gōng) This 'Temple of the Queen of Heaven' is a 16th-century temple complex on the north of the river, and the best preserved of a series built by Fujianese merchants.

Miáojiāng Great Wall — WALLS
(苗疆长城, Miáojiāng Chángchéng, Miao Border Great Wall; ¥30) There's an energetic half-hour climb above town, past the **Four Officials Temple** (四官殿, Sìguān Diàn) to the top of **Shípíng Shān** (石屏山), to the remains of this 16th-century wall built to protect Zhènyuǎn. Get up really early or leave it late in the day and you could get a jump on ticket collectors. Undulating across peaks, the wall is quite substantial and offers glorious views ranging over town.

Zhùshèng Bridge — BRIDGE
The most photographed sight in town, Zhènyuǎn's old bridge (祝圣桥; Zhùshèng Qiáo) is a gorgeous and robust span of arches topped with a three-storey pavilion, leading visitors across the water to Qīnglóng Dòng. It's an impressive sight. Views along the river from the bridge at night are serene, with Qīnglóng Dòng splendidly lit up.

Fire God Temple — TAOIST TEMPLE
(炎帝宫, Yándì Gōng) Small, obscured temple housing the fearsome deities Yandi and the Fire God himself.

City Walls — HISTORIC SITE
The old city walls on the south side of the Wǔyáng River have been restored and you can walk a considerable way along them towards the train station. In the other direction you'll reach a 14th-century arch, where lots of kids swim in summer.

Confucius Temple — CONFUCIAN TEMPLE
(文庙, Wénmiào; Shuncheng Jie, 顺城街) Now pretty much a block of flats from the 1960s, little remains of the Confucius Temple except for its main facade and the Lǐ Mén (Gate of Rites).

👉 Tours

River cruises (¥40 for 35 minutes, 8.30am to 9.30pm) are available here; buy tickets at the office next to Yùmén Wharf (p651), which is identifiable by the decorative arch.

Travel agents line Xinglong Jie; you should also be able to book tours around the area through your hotel.

🛏 Sleeping

There are rooms everywhere in the old town, with new guesthouses opening up steadily, often above restaurants. Don't expect any spoken English. Rooms south of the river get the amplified sound of trains rumbling by. Ask for discounts.

Déyīn Hotel — HOTEL $
(德音驿站, Déyīn Yìzhàn; 📞 0855 217 0888; 70 Xinzhong Jie, 新中街70号; tw & d ¥178-198; ❉ 🛜) Terrific value: modern rooms with soft mattresses, quality linen and stylish bathroom sinks. The top-floor rooms have river views.

Zhènyuǎn

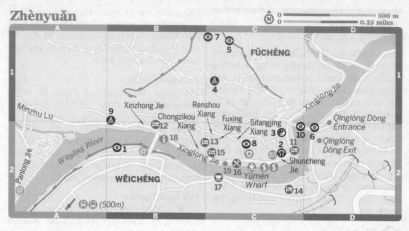

Tiānhòugōng Youth Hostel HOSTEL $
(镇远天后宫青年客栈, Zhènyuǎn Tiānhòugōng Qīngnián Kèzhàn; 天后宫, Tianhougong; dm ¥50) Set inside the grounds of Tiānhòu Temple, this small hostel is popular with local hikers. It has clean dormitories and, as expected, a very peaceful feel. There are some stairs to negotiate.

Jiāngnányuàn Inn INN $$
(江南苑客栈江, Jiāngnányuàn Kèzhàn; Zhou Jie, 周街; d from ¥288; P❋@🤶) A surprisingly stylish new hotel on the southern side of the river. Rooms have a distinctly Ming-era feel, with cool stone floors and simple wooden furniture and panelling. The beds are soft and the pillows are fluffy, which can be hard to find in these parts.

Liúfúlán Jiǔdiàn HOTEL $$
(刘胡兰酒店; ☎0855 572 0586; Xinglong Jie, 兴隆街; r ¥180-260; ❋@🤶) This excellent option overlooking the river has lovely wooden window frames and spacious terraces. Beware: no Western toilets.

★ Dàhéguān Hotel HOTEL $$$
(大河关客馆, Dàhéguān Bīnguǎn; ☎0855 571 0188; Shuncheng Jie, 顺城街; tw & d ¥380-680; ❋🤶) The faux-period wooden courtyard at the Dàhéguān passes the authenticity test well enough, but it's the corner location, classy finishing and luxurious beds that help make this the best hotel in town.

Héjiā Dàyuàn Kèzhàn HOTEL $$$
(何家大院客栈; ☎0855 572 3770; 8 Chongzikou Xiang, 冲子口巷8号; tw/d ¥388/428; ❋🤶) This traditional courtyard hotel has pleasant rooms in a lovely old property tucked up an alley leading away from the river. Discounts should be available.

🍴 Eating

Yǒngfúróng Inn CHINESE $
(永芙蓉客栈, Yǒngfúróng Kèzhàn; Xinglong Jie, 兴隆街; mains from ¥30) Busy restaurant overlooking the river, with some English spoken. Guìzhōu cuisine here can be made light on the chilli if requested. Rooms (from ¥180) are also available upstairs.

Gǔchéng Zhēngjiǎo DUMPLING $
(古城蒸饺; Xinglong Jie, 兴隆街; mains ¥9; ⊙noon-2am) Right next to Yùmén Wharf, this very simple restaurant does lovely *jiānjiǎo* (fried dumplings) and is a cheap place for a beer.

🍷 Drinking & Nightlife

Man Man's Little Space Café CAFE
(漫漫的小宇宙, Mànmàn dē Xiǎoyǔzhòu; 41 Zhou Dajie, 周大街41号) Amiable, easygoing place for a coffee or evening beer right by the river. Also does a few small Chinese dishes (from ¥18). Look for the yellow lantern.

ℹ Information

Agricultural Bank of China (农业银行, Nóngyè Yínháng; Xinglong Jie, 兴隆街; ⊙9am-5pm) ATM takes foreign cards; opposite Zhènyuǎn Museum.

Industrial & Commercial Bank of China (ICBC, 工商银行, Gōngshāng Yínháng; Xinglong Jie, 兴隆街; ⊙9am-5pm) ATM takes foreign cards.

Post Office (中国邮政; Xinglong Jie, 兴隆街; ⊙9am-6pm) You can book train tickets here (if more than three days in advance) for a commission (¥15).

Zhènyuǎn

Public Security Bureau (PSB, 公安局, Gōng'ānjú; Xinglong Jie, 兴隆街, ⊗8.30-11.30am & 2.30-5.30pm) Across from Yúmén Wharf.

Shénzhōu Internet Cafe (神舟网吧, Shénzhōu Wǎngbā; per hr ¥3; ⊗24hr) On the south side of the Xīndà Bridge, by the wall.

Zhènyuǎn Tourist & Information Centre (镇远旅游合询服务中心, Zhènyuǎn Lǚyóu Zīxún Fúwù Zhōngxīn; Xinzhong Jie, 新中街; ⊗8am-8pm) Good for maps of Zhènyuǎn (¥10).

⊙ Getting There & Away

The best way to reach Zhènyuǎn from Guìyáng is by train. Plunging into the far east of Guìzhōu from Kǎilǐ to Zhènyuǎn, the train traverses an astonishing panorama of surging peaks and hills densely cloaked with trees. The train station (huǒchēzhàn) is on the south of the river in the southwest of town, not far from Wǔyánghé Bridge (Wǔyánghé Dàqiáo). It's a good 20-minute walk to the old town from the train station, so either book your ticket out of Zhènyuǎn when you arrive or ask your hotel owner to book one for you (they will need to take your passport to do this, however). You can book tickets more than three days in advance at the post office (p650) for a commission (¥15). Trains from Zhènyuǎn include the following:

Ānshùn ¥54, 5½ hours, eight daily

Guìyáng ¥42, 3¾ hours, regular

Huáihuà ¥29, 2½ hours, regular

Kǎilǐ ¥15, 1¼ hours, regular

Yùpíng ¥13, one hour, regular

The bus station (chángtú qìchēzhàn) is opposite the train station. Bus services include:

Bàojīng ¥13, three daily (10.20am, 12.30pm and 3.20pm)

Kǎilǐ ¥21, six daily (8.30am to 4.30pm)

Tóngrén ¥55, two daily (11am and 3pm)

Yùmén Wharf (禹门码头, Yúmén Mǎtóu) Starting point for river cruises (¥40 for 35 minutes, 8.30am to 9.30pm).

⊙ Getting Around

A taxi to the old town from the train station costs ¥8, or else you can walk it in about 20 minutes. A **ferry** (¥1; ⊗6am-7.30pm) can punt you across the river.

Around Zhènyuǎn

Tiěxī Gorge   铁溪

A trip to the pleasant **Tiěxī Gorge** (admission ¥50) offers the chance to plunge along rocky trails shaded by overhanging trees. Don't miss the **Dragon Pool** (龙潭; Lóngtán) and **Jīguān Mountain** (鸡冠岭; Jīguān Lǐng). Food vendors are scattered along the 2½-hour walk to the mountain, ensuring you won't go hungry. Get here by buggy (¥6, 20 minutes) from the western end of Zhùshèng Bridge (p649) in Zhènyuǎn; vehicles depart when full. This is an excellent, intimate alternative to the Three Gorges.

Bàojīng   报京

Bàojīng is a Dong minority village with fine examples of diàojiǎolóu architecture. The village is also known for its **seed-sowing festival** (播种节; bōzhǒngjié) – held on the third day of the third lunar month, it's a lively celebration of dancing and courtship rituals.

Bàojīng is located 40km from Zhènyuǎn. Three buses (¥13, 10.20am, 12.30pm and

3.20pm) run there daily from Zhènyuǎn's bus station.

WESTERN GUÌZHŌU

Ānshùn   安顺

☑ 0853 / POP 765,310

Ānshùn is an unassuming provincial city which makes a convenient base for travel around western Guìzhōu. The prime attraction is Hóngshān Lake, especially when lit up at night; it's fringed by a gorgeous walking track leading up to two temples. Once a marvellous historical city ringed by a town wall, the city's heritage has largely vanished and now it's the surrounding sights that are the real draws. Shoppers can look out for batik, kitchen knives and the lethal Ānjiǔ brand of alcohol.

◉ Sights

Lóngwáng Miào   BUDDHIST TEMPLE
(龙王庙; ⊘ 7.30am-5.30pm) **FREE** A working Buddhist temple, just off Zhonghua Beilu.

Dōnglín Temple   BUDDHIST TEMPLE
(东林寺, Dōnglín Sì; 134 Gonghe Lu, 共和路134号; ⊘ 8am-5pm) **FREE** The resident Buddhist monks welcome visitors warmly to this temple, which was built in AD 1405 (during the Ming dynasty) and restored in 1668.

Fǔwén Miào   CONFUCIAN TEMPLE
(府文庙; ¥10; ⊘ 7.30am-midnight) Check out this charming Confucian temple in the north of town. It has some stunningly intricate cloud-scrolling carvings on the twin stone pillars before the main hall.

LOCAL SPECIALITIES

The speciality at Ānshùn's night market is barbecued fish (kǎoyú), while Uighur chefs feature snails sizzling up in woks and proudly displayed pigs' trotters. Another local speciality is qiáoliáng-fěn (乔凉粉), a spicy dish made from buckwheat noodles and preserved bean curd. A good on-the-run snack is chōng-chōng gāo (冲冲糕), a cake made from steamed sticky rice with sesame and walnut seeds and sliced wax gourd. Also look out for plates of fried potatoes, hawked at the roadside, which taste like chips; locals call them yángyì.

Túnpǔ Culture Museum   MUSEUM
(屯堡文化博物馆, Túnpǔ Wénhuà Bówùguǎn; through ticket ¥50; ⊘ 8am-6pm) Has exhibits relating to the history of the Túnpǔ settlements in the area, and is the required entry point to the Yúnfēng Bāzhài (p655) villages. To get here, take a bus (¥5, 40 minutes, every 25 minutes, 7am to 6pm) from Ānshùn's east bus station. The last bus from Yúnfēng Bāzhài to Ānshùn leaves at 6.20pm, passing through Běnzhài.

🛏 Sleeping

If your Chinese is up to it, try one of the guesthouses (lǚguǎn) around the train station for a cheap room. Otherwise, stay closer to the lake.

Liu's Express Inn   INN $
(利悠快捷酒店, Lìyōu Kuàijié Jiǔdiàn; ☑ 0859 338 8899; Qiánxīnán, 黔西南, Mǎlíng River Gorge; d ¥138; ❋🖙) If you choose to visit Mǎlíng River Gorge, this tidy, welcoming hotel located in the nearest town is a handy sleeping option.

Péngchéng Bīnguǎn   HOTEL $
(鹏程宾馆; ☑ 0853 372 2555; 10 Ma'anshan Lu; 马鞍山路10号; d ¥100-130; ❋🖙) A cut above its competitors close to the train station, it's less noisy, with modern, compact rooms and wi-fi. It's near the top of Maan Shan Lu. There's no English sign: look for four white characters on a yellow background.

Pearl Hotel   HOTEL $$
(珍珠飯店, Zhēnzhū Fàndiàn; 198 Xihang Lu, 西航路198号; tw from ¥248; ❋🖙) Large beds, fastidious cleaners and very friendly management put the Pearl above its rivals in the midrange category. Small desks and quality bathroom products are nice touches, too. Simple breakfast is included.

Xīxiùshān Bīnguǎn   HOTEL $$
(西秀山宾馆; ☑ 0853 333 7888; 63 Zhonghua Nanlu, 中华南路63号; s, d & tw ¥288-388; ❋🖙) A pleasant point of difference here is the variety of rooms across three buildings. Go for one near the garden courtyard, or nab a suite if you feel the need to stretch out. The premises are invariably spotless, though a few corners are starting to fade. Check the wi-fi in your room before committing.

Double Tree Hilton Ānshùn   HOTEL $$$
(安顺百灵希尔顿逸林酒店, Ānshùn Bǎilíng Xīěrdùn Yìlín Jiǔdiàn; ☑ 0853 3366 9666; www.doubletree3.hilton.com; 42 Hongshanhu Lu, 虹山湖路42号; d from ¥700; ❋@🖙❋) This gigan-

tic hotel towering over Hóngshān Lake like a grounded spaceship is the only high-end option in Ānshùn, so it's a good thing that it's quietly fabulous. Views from the plush lake rooms are stunning, especially at night, and the pool, gym and yoga studio are all first-class. The international breakfast buffet will fill you for the day.

✗ Eating

By far the best place to eat is the night market – the most happening spot in Ānshùn, with locals crowding out the many food tents and stalls that set up here. There are hotpot places on nearby Nan Shui Lu. The northern side of Hóngshān Lake has some charming small cafes that serve basic food.

Ānshùn Night Market   MARKET $
(安顺夜市, Ānshùn Yèshì; Gufu Jie, 顾府街; dishes from ¥10; ⊙ 5pm-late) Ānshùn's number-one attraction is this vibrant night market, where locals gather around plastic tables and in small restaurants to sample strange lake critters, skewers of vegetable and tofu, fresh *siwawa* (local pancakes), barbecued fish (烤鱼; *kǎoyú*), sizzling snails, pigs' trotters and fruit salad soaking in jelly soup. Electronic music blares in the entrance while everyone feasts and drinks stiff liquor.

Liúyìshǒu Kǎoyú   SEAFOOD $
(留一手烤鱼; Hongqi Lu, 红旗路; fish per jīn from ¥30; ⊙ 6pm-late) Packed during night-market hours – when the restaurant fills its premises on Hongqi Lu and spills onto tables flung out on Gufu Jie – this heaving eatery specialises in tasty grilled fish. It's best to dine as a group, as fish weights start at around three *jīn* (which is 1.8kg).

ℹ Information

Bank of China (中国银行, Zhōngguó Yínháng; cnr Tashan Xilu & Zhonghua Nanlu, 踏山西路·中華南路; ⊙ 9am-5pm) Offers all services and has an ATM. There are many other ATMs around town.

Post Office (中国邮政, Zhōngguó Yóuzhèng; cnr Zhonghua Nanlu & Tashan Donglu, 中華南路·踏山東路) Look for it tucked next to the China Telecom building.

ℹ Getting There & Away

BUS

The north bus station (客车北站; *kèchē běizhàn*) has buses (¥34, three hours, every 20 minutes, 7am to 6pm) to Zhījīn town (for Zhījīn Cave). Almost every other bus now leaves from the east

Ānshùn

bus station (东客运站; *dōng kèyùnzhàn*). Bus 16 (¥1) runs here from Zhonghua Nanlu opposite the Xīxiùshān Bīnguǎn; a taxi is ¥25 or ¥30.

Guìyáng ¥35, 1½ hours, every 20 minutes (7.10am to 7.10pm)

Huángguǒshù ¥20, one hour, every 20 minutes (7.20am to 7pm)

GUÌZHŌU ĀNSHÙN

Kūnmíng (sleeper) ¥150, 10 hours, four daily (9am, 10.40am, 1pm and 4pm)

Lónggōng Caves ¥10, 40 minutes, every 30 minutes (7.30am to 6pm)

Píngbà ¥15, 40 minutes, every 30 minutes (7.30am to 6.30pm)

Shuǐchéng ¥60, 3½ hours, every 50 minutes (8.20am to 4.40pm)

Wēiníng ¥90, five to six hours, one daily (10am)

Yúnfēng ¥5, 40 minutes, every 30 minutes (7.30am to 6pm)

TRAIN

Most trains from the train station (*huǒchēzhàn*) heading east stop in Guìyáng (¥15, 1½ hours, regular service). It is still hard to get sleeper reservations for trains from here; pick them up in Guìyáng instead. There's a train ticket office a few hundred metres north of the train station on Zhonghua Nanlu. Destinations include the following:

Cǎohǎi (for Wēiníng) ¥38, three to five hours, six daily

Guìyáng ¥16, 1½ hours, regular service

Kǎilǐ ¥44, four hours, 15 daily

Kūnmíng seat/sleeper ¥75/142, eight to 10 hours

Liùpánshuǐ ¥24, 2½ hours, regular

ⓘ Getting Around

Bus 1 zips around town from the train station and up Tashan Donglu. Bus 2 travels between the train station and the north bus station. Bus 16 runs from Zhonghua Nanlu to the east bus station. Buses cost ¥1.

Taxi flag fall is ¥6.

Around Ānshùn

Lónggōng Cave   龙宫洞

Even though the feeling is overwhelmingly tacky – think coloured lights, awkward commentary and boats full of tourists – there is something sublime about the water-borne **Lónggōng Cave** (Lónggōng Dòng, Dragon Palace; ¥150; ◎ 8.30am-5.30pm) expedition winding through 20 hills. There are add-on costs to be aware of, too: **Tiger Cave** (¥50) and the 'elevator ride' (¥50) between caves, both of which are kind of hard to avoid. Lónggōng is 23km south of Ānshùn and an easy day trip from there.

Local buses (¥10, 40 minutes) depart every 30 minutes from Ānshùn's east bus station from 7.30am. For the return trip, buses leave until about 5pm.

Zhījīn Cave   织金洞

At a monstrous 10km-long, **Zhījīn Cave** (织金洞, Zhījīn Dòng; ¥150; ◎ 8.30am-5.30pm) is the biggest cave in the country. A visit will satisfy everyone from hardcore spelunkers to wide-eyed tourists with a penchant for subterranean beauty. Pockets open up to 150m high to reveal Zhījīn's organic splendour twisting upward like a stone forest. Tickets to the cave, which is 15km outside Zhījīn and 125km north of Ānshùn, include a compulsory 2½-hour Chinese-only tour (minimum 10 people). The tour covers some 6km of the cave, up steep, slippery steps at times, and there are English captions at the main points along the way. Solo travellers visiting outside peak summer months or Chinese holidays should be prepared for what can be a tedious wait for enough people to roll up to form a group.

A long day trip from Ānshùn is possible, but you'll need to be on an early bus to Zhījīn (¥34, three hours, from 7am), from Ānshùn's north bus station. Once there, hop a taxi (¥4) to the local bus station on Yuping Jie and catch one of the minibuses that leave regularly for the cave entrance (¥8, 50 minutes). Returning from the caves, buses leave regularly; the last bus back to Ānshùn heads out of Zhījīn at 5.30pm.

From Guìyáng, regular buses (return ¥110, four hours, 6.30am to 5.20pm) depart every 30 minutes to Zhījīn from the long-distance bus station.

Huángguǒshù Falls   黄果树大瀑布

Hugely popular among domestic travellers for good reason, **Huángguǒshù Falls** (Huángguǒshù Dàpùbù, Yellow Fruit Tree Falls; Mar-Oct ¥180, Nov-Feb ¥160; ◎ 7.30am-6pm) are one of many cascades gushing around a pristine national park where sublime walking trails lead to stunning views. The 77.8m-tall, 81m-wide *dàpùbù* is understandably Guìzhōu's number-one natural attraction. From May to October in particular, these falls really rock the local landscape with their cacophony, while rainbows from the mist dance about **Rhinoceros Pool** below and colourful peacocks show off their dazzling plumage.

The cascades are actually part of a 450-sq-km cave and karst complex discovered when engineers explored the area in the 1980s to gauge the region's hydroelectric potential. Hiking here can get crowded on weekends, but it's well worth the occasional jostle.

YÚNFĒNG BĀZHÀI VILLAGES

Yúnfēng Bāzhài (云峰八寨) is a scattering of traditional villages about 20km northeast of Ānshùn. Introduced by the mildly interesting **Túnpǔ Culture Museum** (p652), which serves as the point of entry, the village of **Yúnshān** (云山), at the top of a steep set of steps leading up from the road (a 15-minute walk from the museum), is a gem. Hung with bright yellow dried corncobs and red lanterns, protected by a wall and a main gate and overlooked by the Yúnjiù Shān (Cloud Vulture Mountain), the settlement is a charming and unruffled portrait of rural Guìzhōu. At the heart of the almost deserted village stands a rickety **Money God Temple** (Cáishén Miào), opposite an ancient pavilion.

If you want to spend the night, a couple of *kèzhàn* (inns) can put you up in basic rooms for around ¥50. Whatever you do, don't miss the chance to walk up to **Yúnjiù Temple** (云鹫寺; Yúnjiù Sì) at the top of Yúnjiù Shān for some of the most extraordinary views in Guìzhōu. You can walk virtually all around the top of the temple for a sublime and unparalleled panorama of fields and peaks ranging off into the distance. In spring, flowering bright-yellow rapeseed plants (*yóucàihuā*) add vibrant splashes of colour.

From Yúnshān it's a 15-minute walk along the road to the village of **Bēnzhài** (本寨), also at the foot of Yúnjiù Shān. With its old pinched alleyways, high walls, carved wood lintels, stone lions and ancient courtyard residences, Bēnzhài is brim-full of history.

To reach Yúnfēng Bāzhài, take a bus (¥5, 40 minutes, every 25 minutes, 7am to 6pm) from Ānshùn's east bus station. The last bus from Yúnfēng Bāzhài to Ānshùn leaves at 6.20pm, passing through Bēnzhài. Coming from Tiānlóng, hop on a bus from the main road to Qīyǎnqiáo (七眼桥; ¥5, 20 minutes) and then take a motorbike (¥10) for the 10-minute journey to the museum and the villages.

Don't miss groping your way through the dripping natural corridor in the rock face of the 134m-long **Water Curtain Cave** (水帘洞; Shuǐlián Dòng), behind Huángguǒshù itself. Going underground into the colossal caves within the geological **Tiānxīng Qiáo Scenic Zone** (天星桥景区; Tiānxīng Qiáo Jǐngqū) is a quite awe-inspiring sideshow, especially if you do not have time for the Lónggōng or Zhījīn Caves.

To get around you'll really need to buy a ticket for one of the **sightseeing cars** (*guānguāngchē*; ¥50), located near the entrance, which can then be flagged down anywhere inside the park. It's an effective system as the cars are in fact registered taxis that link the main areas, including **Dǒupōtáng Waterfall**, **Lúosītān Waterfall**, Tiānxīng Qiáo Scenic Zone and the **Main Waterfall Scenic Zone**.

There are accommodation options everywhere in Huángguǒshù village, but there is little need to overnight here. The falls are an easy day trip from Ānshùn or, at a push, you can see them in a day trip from Guìyáng.

From Ānshùn, buses (¥20, one hour, 7am to 7pm) run every 30 minutes from the east bus station; buses back to Ānshùn run until 7pm. There are seven buses a day from Guìyáng to Huángguǒshù (¥55, 2½ hours, every 40 minutes from 7.40am to 12.45pm)

from the long-distance bus station on Jinyang Nanlu, the last bus returns to Guìyáng at 4pm.

Tiānlóng & Tiāntáishān   天龙、天台山

POP 5000

You only need around a couple of hours to explore this delightful village cut with a sparkling stream not far outside Ānshùn. **Tiānlóng** (天龙, ¥35, through ticket ¥50) is a well preserved Túnpǔ village, its settlements erected by Ming dynasty garrison troops posted here during the reign of Hongwu to help quell local uprisings and consolidate control. Coming from the middle and lower reaches of the Yangzi River, the soldiers brought their customs and language with them. Han descendants of these 14th-century soldiers live in Tiānlóng today. The local women are notable for their turquoise tops with embroidered hems; other local idiosyncrasies include distinct colloquialisms: the local expression for a thief is a *yèmāozi* (夜猫子, 'night cat').

Complementing its dry stonewalls and narrow alleyways, the architectural highlight of the village is the **Tiānlóng Xuétáng** (天龙学堂), an impressive and distinctive school building. The **Sānjiào Temple**

XĪNGYÌ

In the southwestern corner of the province lies the beautiful region of **Xīngyì**. The town itself is unremarkable, but take a taxi for 15km to the **Mǎlǐng River Bridge** (马岭河大桥; Mǎlǐng Hé) and you'll reach a feat of engineering running across a deep gorge where hiking paths criss-cross the river. From here you hike through the **Mǎlǐng River Gorge** (¥80) for 18km to **Wànfēnglín** (万峰林; Forest of Ten Thousand Peaks), where a magical karst mountain landscape awaits.

At Mǎlǐng River Gorge, you can stay at Liu's Express Inn (p652), while Wànfēnglín also has good accommodation.

(三教寺; Sānjiào Sì) is a creakingly dilapidated shrine dedicated to Taoism, Confucianism and Buddhism.

A well signed 30-minute walk will bring you to the forested mountain of **Tiāntaíshān** (天台山; ¥20). This forested mountain (1138m) has the astonishing temple of **Wǔlóng Sì** (伍龙寺) FREE at its summit. A refreshing hike through the trees takes you to the summit, where you can explore the various rooms of the temple. In a hall at the rear sits a lithe figure of Guanyin, illuminated by a guttering candle; a further hall displays exhibits relating to local **dìxì** theatre. Afterwards, climb to the Dàyuètái terrace to gaze out over the glorious countryside.

When descending from the temple keep an eye out for a small shrine along a narrow trail, where a statue of one of the 18 luóhàn (Buddhist statues) sits grumpily all alone. His skinny frame is the result of generosity in giving food to others; he also bestows good fortune on all. Further below rises a 21m-high and 500-year-old gingko tree festooned with ribbons, while other trails disappear into the trees.

Tiāntaíshān is a 30-minute walk from Tiānlóng; follow the signs.

A couple of *kèzhàn* in the village can put you up for the night for around ¥70 – a delightful option for a bucolic evening.

Short performances of *dìxì* – an ancient form of local drama – are regularly held in the Yǎnwǔtáng (演武堂) throughout the day.

Gorgeous-looking embroideries are on sale everywhere (bargain hard), while local women sit sewing small and exceptionally colourful embroidered shoes, in all sizes.

To reach Tiānlóng, hop on a bus for Píngbà (平坝; ¥15, 40 minutes, every 30 minutes, 7.30am to 6.30pm) from Ānshùn's east bus station; at the drop-off, change to the bus for Tiānlóng (¥4, 20 minutes).

Wēiníng 威宁

☑ 0857 / POP 58,500

On the historically significant trade route between north Yúnnán and Sìchuān, the small town of Wēiníng is now better known as the site of the wonderful Cǎohǎi Lake, which sits on its western edge and attracts birds and their human followers from across the global (the rare black-necked crane is the signature find).

Like much of the province, Wēiníng has remarkable ethnic diversity, including a large population of Muslim Hui. Seeing the fare and fashion on offer at the town's twice-weekly market is a worthy outing, especially if you don't have time to explore the villages further east.

◉ Sights

Cǎohǎi Lake LAKE, BIRD SANCTUARY
(草海湖, Cǎohǎi Hú, Grass Sea Lake) Guìzhōu's largest highland lake and southwest China's most significant wetland, Cǎohǎi Lake draws some 180 or so protected bird species, including black-necked cranes, black and white storks, golden and imperial eagles, white-tailed sea eagles, Eurasian cranes and white spoonbills. The prime time to see them is from November to March. Avoid the height of summer when the lake turns to mush.

The lake has a fragile history, having been drained during both the Great Leap Forward and the Cultural Revolution in hopes of producing farmland. It didn't work and the lake was refilled in 1980. Government tinkering with water levels in ensuing years impacted on the local environment and villagers' livelihoods; officials have since enlisted locals to help with the lake's protection in an effort to remedy both problems. The 20-sq-km freshwater wetland has been a national nature reserve since 1992, but many environmental problems remain, including excessive fishing by local villagers who rely on the region for their livelihoods.

Lovely trails explore much of the lake, but the best way to get a close-up view of the birds is to cruise around the lake on a punt. Buy tickets at the ticket office at the end of the path leading to the lake, rather than from the touts lurking nearby. A popular lunch stop is at **Lóngjiā** (龙家), but be mindful that the local fish are being threatened.

To get to the lake it's a 45-minute walk southwest of central Weining, or else a 10-minute taxi ride (¥6).

Sleeping & Eating

For budget rooms, try the bus station area and nearby Jianshe Donglu, where you should be able to net a room for around ¥100. There are few good choices near the lake itself.

With a large population of Hui, Muslim *yángròu fěn* (lamb rice noodles) and *niúròu fěn* (beef rice noodles) places are all over town, especially around the bus station area. A local delicacy is dragonfly larvae, consumed fried.

Black-Necked Crane Hotel HOTEL **$**
(黑颈鹤大酒店, Hēijǐng Hè Dàjiǔdiàn; opposite the Power Authority, Jianshe Donglu, 建设东路电力局对面; d ¥150; ✲✆) Centrally located near the bus station, rooms here are clean and sport some new furniture. The carpets are a little thin though, and the owners can be as hard to locate as the black-necked crane itself.

Cǎohǎi Jiàrì Jiǔdiàn HOTEL **$$**
(草海假日酒店; ☏0857 623 1881; Caohai Lu, 草海路; tw ¥358-388; ✲✆) The lakeside location is really the saving grace of this tired hotel, though rooms are large and management tries hard to accommodate. In summer (off-season for the twitchers), expect large discounts.

ℹ Information

Internet Cafe (per hr ¥3; ◷24hr) Internet cafe above the China Mobile shop opposite the bus station.

Punt Ticket Office (boat hire per 1/2/3hr ¥120/240/360; ◷8.30am-5.30pm) Buy tickets here for punts around Cǎohǎi Lake. Prices depend on the length of trip.

ℹ Getting There & Away

Wēiníng train station is 6km west of the town centre, connecting it to points east in Guìzhōu and Kūnmíng in Yúnnán. Sleeper tickets are hard to secure here, though. Note that the station's official name is Cǎohǎi (草海).

Wēiníng is a seven-hour bus ride from Guìyáng (¥132, 9am and 11am). You can also get here from Ānshùn's east bus station. First take a bus

to Shuǐchéng (水城; ¥60, 3½ hours, every 50 minutes from 8.20am to 4.40pm), then transfer to a Wēiníng-bound bus (¥35, two hours, hourly from 7.45am). Note that Shuǐchéng is also referred to as Liùpánshuǐ (六盘水).

Leaving Wēiníng, you can backtrack to Guìyáng, or take a bus south to Xuānwēi in Yúnnán (¥65, five to six hours, eight daily, 7.30am to 4pm), where you can transfer to a bus for Kūnmíng. From Wēiníng, there is also a daily direct bus to Kūnmíng (¥130, 10 hours, 12.30pm).

Alternatively, take a bus to Zhāotōng (¥45, three hours, three daily, 8.30am, 1.40pm and 3.30pm), from where you can hop over to Xīchāng in southern Sìchuān and connect with the Kūnmíng–Chéngdū train line.

Taxi flag fall is ¥6. Taxis charge a flat ¥15 to go to the train station.

NORTHERN GUÌZHŌU

Chìshuǐ　　　　赤水

☏0852 / POP 80,800

The northwestern tip of the province is centred on the handsome town of Chìshuǐ, which hugs the eponymous red-running river famed for its role in the salt trade. While the town proper is easily walked in an afternoon, just outside town are deep gorges and valleys flanked by towering cliffs hewn out of red sandstone – a World Heritage-listed feature known as *dānxiá* – and a profusion of waterfalls, as well as luxuriant bamboo and fern forests that date to the Jurassic era. Exploring this region will keep nature lovers busy for days.

The town sits on the east bank of the Chìshuǐ River (Chìshuǐ Hé). Cross the town's main bridge (Chìshuǐ Dàqiáo) to the other side and you're in Jiǔzhī (九支) in Sìchuān. The river was the site of many fabled crossings by the Red Army.

◉ Sights

It's hard to imagine a more dramatic landscape. The locals claim the region has 4000 waterfalls, and some are spectacular – everywhere you look they're gushing into the rivers that run red from the colour of the earth (Chìshuǐ means 'red water') and which cut through valleys and gorges covered in lush foliage. If that wasn't enough, there are huge forests of bamboo and alsophila plants – giant ferns that date back 200 million years and were once the food of dinosaurs.

To see the waterfalls at their fullest and loudest, come during the rainy season (May to October).

Jīnshāgōu Nature Reserve NATURE RESERVE
(金沙沟自然保护区, Jīnshāgōu Zìrán Bǎohùqū)
FREE This reserve was established to protect the alsophila ferns that grow in abundance here. Today, the prehistoric plants still dwarf visitors. It's also the site of a bamboo forest, known as the Bamboo Sea.

To get here, catch the buses heading to Jīnshāgōu village from Chìshuǐ's Lǚyóu Chēzhàn (¥12, one hour). From there, you'll have to negotiate with the locals for a motorbike or minibus ride to the park entrance, which is another 20 minutes away; expect to pay between ¥40 and ¥50 each way. Make sure to arrange a pick-up for your return, as very little transport hangs around the park.

Bamboo Sea NATURE RESERVE
(竹海, Zhúhǎi; ¥25; ◎8am-5pm) The sea barely parts for trekkers whose slippery soles pad along wooden pathways through towering green-bamboo forest. It's a heady experience, if only for the bug life near the forest floor. Come armed with repellent and water.

Sìdònggōu Valley VIEWPOINT
(四洞沟谷, Sìdònggōu Gǔ; ¥30; ◎8am-5pm) This 4.5km-long valley is forested with ancient ferns and dotted with gushing cataracts. Paths follow both sides of a river; gushing minifalls lead to four 'proper' waterfalls. The biggest and most impressive is the last, the 60m-high **White Dragon Pond Waterfall** (Báilóngtán Pùbù). You can even get really close to the falls here (you can even walk behind one). The circuit takes about three hours; there are also other trails leading off the main paths that intrepid hikers will enjoy.

Sìdònggōu is the most touristy of Chìshuǐ's sights, but still not overly crowded, even in summer. Buses run the 15km here from Chìshuǐ's bus station (¥8, 30 minutes) hourly from 7am, and return on the same schedule.

Buses to Sìdònggōu from Chìshuǐ also pass by the town of **Dàtóng** (大同), which has an attractive and historic old town (gǔzhèn) quarter.

Red Rock Gorge GORGE
(红石野谷, Hóngshí Yěgǔ; ¥30; ◎8am-5pm) This distinct, ochre sandstone gorge has long been a poster child for the province. Deep-blue waterfalls gush from between the dānxiá cliffs, also known as Yángjiāyán. Linger at sunset for a perfectly ethereal photograph.

Minibuses make the 16km journey here from the local bus station next door to the main bus station (¥6, 40 minutes, five daily from 8am to 4.30pm).

Shízhàngdòng Waterfall WATERFALL
(十丈洞瀑布, Shízhàngdòng Pùbù; ¥40; ◎8am-4pm) The undervisited understudy to the famous Huángguǒshù Falls in the south is a 76m-high beauty pummelling into the pools below. There are fewer restrictions on swimming here, but even if you stand 100m away, you will still get drenched if the wind is right.

It's about 40km from Chìshuǐ. Nine buses a day (¥13, 1½ hours) run here starting at 6.50am. The bus will drop you in Shízhàngdòng village, from where it's a short walk to the ticket office. From there, it's a 30- to 40-minute walk up a hard road to the turn-off to the waterfall, or you can ride there on a buggy (one-way/return ¥10/20).

Another, more pleasant walk, stretches to the falls on the other side of the river. Doing the complete circuit takes three to four hours. Try to visit before noon during the low season as a hydroelectric dam up-river slows the water after that time. The waterfall is also known as Chìshuǐ Waterfall (Chìshuǐ Dàpùbù).

🛏 Sleeping

Chìshuǐ has a range of modern, three-star hotels near the bus station, and some smarter options a short walk south.

Chìshuǐ Hotel HOTEL $
(赤水大酒店, Chìshuǐ Dàjiǔdiàn; ☑0852 282 1334; 106 Xinei Huanlu, 西内环路106号; tw & d ¥200; ❄@🛜) A little tired in the paint and plastering, but nonetheless a welcoming hotel with spacious rooms featuring English-language movies and strong internet connections. The beds are spine-aligningly firm.

River View Private Hotel HOTEL $$
(河景私人的酒店, Héjǐng Sīrénde Jiǔdiàn; ☑0852 2287 0888; 河滨路, Hebin Lu; d¥188-238; P❄🛜) Hustle through the shiny check-in and check out the murals in this (you guessed it) riverside hotel, which may be better suited to young lovers with cartoon dreams. Still, who doesn't love Super Mario on their wall? Especially when the floorboards, stylish interior design and quality

fittings surpass anything you'll find elsewhere in town.

Zhōngyuè Dàjiǔdiàn   HOTEL $$$
(中悦大酒店; ☑ 0852 282 3888; 22 Nanzheng Jie, 南正街22号; tw & d ¥628-768; ❀ @ ☎) When you crave the anonymity of a large hotel, this option will deliver discretion, soft carpets and powerful showers. There are discounts (30%) available, even in summer, but you will have to ask.

🍴 Eating

Popular restaurants are scattered in the area around Hebin Zhonglu, near the Chìshuǐ River, where there are also simple outdoor bars for an evening beer. The main drag of Renmin Xilu has hole-in-the-wall eateries serving noodle and rice dishes, dumplings and the ever-present pigs' trotters. There are also street-food stalls, supermarkets and a few hotpot places scattered along Renmin Beilu.

❶ Information

There's a branch of the **Industrial & Commercial Bank** (ICBC, 工商银行, Gōngshāng Yínháng; 红军大道, Hongjun Dadao; ◷ 9am-5pm) with an ATM on Hongjun Dadao, off Renmin Xilu. Another ATM on the corner of Renmin Xilu and Renmin Beilu should also take foreign cards.

Note that you cannot change money in either Chìshuǐ or Jiǔzhī, so bring extra cash with you or plan to use ATMs.

❶ Getting There & Away

Chìshuǐ's **bus station** (旅游车站; lǚyóu chēzhàn) is on Nan Jiao Lu on the riverfront opposite Sichuan, a ¥5 cab ride from Renmin Xilu. Buses for very local destinations leave from next door. Destinations include the following:

Chéngdu ¥127, five hours, three daily (7.50am, 9.30am and 3pm)

Chóngqìng ¥90, five hours, seven daily (6am to 5pm)

Guìyáng ¥168, 5½ hours, three daily (7.30am, 9.30am and 3pm)

Jīnshāgōu ¥12, 1½ hours, hourly (6am to 5pm)

Shízhàngdòng ¥12, 1½ hours, nine daily (6.50am to 4.30pm)

Sìdònggōu ¥8, 30 minutes, hourly (7am to 5pm)

Zūnyì ¥120, four hours, four daily (6.50am to 11.15am)

Taxi flag fall is ¥4.

❶ Getting Around

As sights are scattered, consider hiring a taxi or minibus to help you scoop them all up. Expect to pay ¥300 to ¥400 per day, depending on your bargaining skills.

SEAN PAVONE/SHUTTERSTOCK ©

XIA YUAN/GETTY IMAGES ©

1. Jīnshānlǐng Great Wall (p129)

This section of the Wall is fully restored, and its watchtowers include inscriptions in English explaining its history.

2. Pǔtuóshān (p284), Zhèjiāng

One of China's four sacred Buddhist mountains, this celebrated isle is home to many temples and pagodas.

3. Yùlóng River (p625), Guǎngxī

Float along the river and take in the beautiful scenery.

4. Bruce Lee statue by artist Cao Chong-en, Hong Kong

Stroll along Tsim Sha Tsui East Promenade (p511) for uninterrupted city views and tributes to stars of the Hong Kong film industry.

HELLO RF ZCOOL/SHUTTERSTOCK ©

1. Pǔdōng (p306), Shànghǎi
Pǔdōng has many high-rise observation decks, restaurants and bars, offering views over Shànghǎi.

2. Incense sticks
Incense is burned as an offering in many of China's Buddhist temples.

3. Naxi man, Yúnnán
The Naxi (p696) are descended from Tibetan Qiang tribes and have lived in Lìjiāng for around 1400 years.

4. West Lake (p265), Hángzhōu, Zhèjiāng
An example of classical beauty in China, West Lake is surrounded by faultless scenery.

MARK READ/LONELY PLANET ©

1. Cooking at an outdoor food stall, Yúnnán

Street-food stalls and markets offer an abundance of dishes to try.

2. National Centre for the Performing Arts (p110), Běijīng

This domed theatre, aka the 'Alien Egg', is an outstanding venue for classical music.

3. Shěnyáng (p169), Liáoníng

The provincial capital, Shěnyáng is home to an Imperial Palace and decent museums.

4. Forbidden City (p68), Běijīng

Yellow roof tiles are common features of the imperial style in traditional Chinese architecture.

Yúnnán

POP 47.13 MILLION

Best Places to Eat

➡ Duan's Kitchen (p687)
➡ Hungry Buddha (p692)
➡ Silent Holy Stones (p709)
➡ Tiāntiān Xiàn (p698)
➡ Yán Quán Nóngjiā (p691)

Best Places to Sleep

➡ Blossom Hill Joyland (p697)
➡ Fùjiā Liúfāngyuàn (p691)
➡ Jade Emu (p686)
➡ Lost Garden Guesthouse (p672)
➡ Nanshan Arts Hotel (p708)

Why Go?

Yúnnán (云南) is the most diverse province in all China, both in its extraordinary mix of peoples and in the splendour of its landscapes. That combination of superlative sights and many different ethnic groups has made Yúnnán *the* trendiest destination for China's exploding domestic tourist industry.

More than half of the country's minority groups reside here, providing a glimpse into China's hugely varied mix of humanity. Then there's the eye-catching contrasts of the land itself: dense jungle sliced by the Mekong River in the far south, soul-recharging glimpses of the sun over rice terraces in the southeastern regions, and snowcapped mountains as you edge towards Tibet.

With everything from laid-back villages and spa resorts to mountain treks and excellent cycling routes, Yúnnán appeals to all tastes. The roads are much better than they once were, so getting around is a breeze, but you'll need time to see it all – whatever time you've set aside for Yúnnán, double it.

When to Go
Kūnmíng

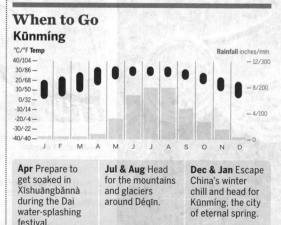

Apr Prepare to get soaked in Xīshuāngbǎnnà during the Dai water-splashing festival.

Jul & Aug Head for the mountains and glaciers around Déqīn.

Dec & Jan Escape China's winter chill and head for Kūnmíng, the city of eternal spring.

Yúnnán Highlights

① **Yuányáng Rice Terraces** (p680) Catching a magical sunrise or sunset at this awesome natural sight.

② **Tiger Leaping Gorge** (p701) Testing your legs and lungs on this famous trek.

③ **Déqīn** (p711) Marvelling at the peaks (and glacier) on the Yúnnán-Tibet border.

④ **Nuòdèng** (p690) Stepping off the tourist trail in this delightful ancient village.

⑤ **Xīshuāngbǎnnà** (p727) Hiking through the jungle to minority villages.

⑥ **Dàlǐ** (p684) Kicking back in the laidback cafes and bars.

⑦ **Lúgū Lake** (p704) Lazing around the shores of the lake.

⑧ **Shāxī** (p691) Seeing how time has stood still in this former Tea Horse Road oasis.

⑨ **Bīngzhōngluò** (p715) Getting way off the map in the remote Nù Jiāng Valley.

⑩ **Jiànshuǐ** (p678) Enjoying classic architecture and great barbecue

History

With its remote location, harsh terrain and diverse ethnic make-up, Yúnnán was once considered a backward place populated by barbarians.

The early Han emperors held tentative imperial power over the southwest and forged southern Silk Road trade routes to Myanmar (Burma). From the 7th to mid-13th centuries, though, two independent kingdoms, the Nanzhao and Dàlǐ, ruled and dominated the trade routes from China to India and Myanmar. It wasn't until the Mongols swept through that the southwest was integrated into the Chinese empire as Yúnnán. Even so, it remained an isolated frontier region, more closely aligned with Southeast Asia than China.

Today, Yúnnán is still a strategic jumping-off point to China's neighbours. Despite its geographical isolation, much of the province has modernised rapidly in recent years.

🛏 Sleeping

Yúnnán's busiest destinations – Kūnmíng, Dàlǐ, Lìjiāng and Shangri-la – offer the full range of accommodation options: hostels and guesthouses, budget and midrange places, and boutique and upmarket hotels. Smaller towns sometimes have guesthouses, but you are mostly reliant on standard budget and midrange hotels. In remote villages, homestays are the norm.

❶ Getting There & Around

Kūnmíng's newish airport is the fourth-largest and seventh-busiest in China and has daily flights to most cities, as well as to an increasing amount of international destinations. Lìjiāng is also well connected to a number of Chinese cities, while Dàlǐ and Jǐnghóng have many more flights than before.

PRICE RANGES

Sleeping

$ less than ¥200

$$ ¥200–¥350

$$$ more than ¥350

Eating

$ less than ¥40

$$ ¥40–¥60

$$$ more than ¥60

One adventurous route out of Yúnnán in the past was to travel down the Mekong by cargo boat from Jǐnghóng to northern Thailand. Recent security threats have put off most passengers, but it is still possible to hitch a ride.

Expressways link Kūnmíng with Dàlǐ, east to Guìzhōu and Guǎngxī, southwest past Bǎoshān to Ruìlì and past Jǐnghóng to the Laos border. An expressway is also being built from Kūnmíng to Hékǒu on the Vietnam border and beyond to Hanoi.

Railways link Yúnnán to Guìzhōu, Guǎngxī, Sìchuān and beyond. In Yúnnán itself, development of the railways has been slower than elsewhere, due mostly to topographical interference. The main route for travellers is the line from Kūnmíng to Dàlǐ and Lìjiāng.

CENTRAL YÚNNÁN

Central Yúnnán covers a big swath of land, including key destinations such as the capital Kūnmíng, long-time travellers favourite Dàlǐ, and the surrounding Ěrhǎi Lake and mountains of Cāng Shān, as well as the legendary rice terraces of Yuányáng, perhaps Yúnnán's finest photo opportunity. But central Yúnnán is also where you'll find some of the region's least visited highlights: the former Tea Horse Road caravan oasis of Shāxī, the ancient Bai village of Nuòdèng and the historic old towns of Jiànshuǐ and Wēishān, whose streets are lined with wooden houses, courtyard homes, temples and drum and bell towers.

With so many travellers passing through this region, the most visited places like Kūnmíng and Dàlǐ offer everything from hip hostels and boutique guesthouses to luxury hotels. But you'll find a growing number of sleeping options even in less well known places like Shāxī, or the villages set amid the rice terraces of Yuányáng. Expect to find family-run guesthouses, standard budget and midrange hotels and, occasionally, hostels in small towns and villages.

You'll find all of Yúnnán's wonderful food here, while Kūnmíng and Dàlǐ have an increasingly sophisticated choice of Western places too. Bai cuisine is on offer in Dàlǐ and the surrounding area, utilising strange and delicious vegetables, and is well worth trying, especially as it is less spicy than some of Yúnnán's other minority cooking. Jiànshuǐ is rightly famed for its superb barbecue and claypot dishes.

Kūnmíng and Xiàguān are the main transport hubs for central Yúnnán, both with airports, train stations and extensive bus connections. Kūnmíng's airport is one of the biggest in China and has many international flights and dozens of daily regional flights. You can also catch buses from Kūnmíng direct to Laos, or hop the train to Xiàguān for Dàlī. Xiàguān's airport serves destinations in Yúnnán, while its four bus stations provide onward transport to the rest of central Yúnnán and beyond. Xiàguān's train station has services northwest to Lìjiāng.

Kūnmíng 昆明

📞 0871 / POP 3.27 MILLION

Kunming has long been regarded as one of China's most liveable cities. Known as the 'Spring City' for its equable climate, it remains a very pleasant place to kick back for a few days. For visitors who haven't succumbed to the laid-back attitude displayed by the locals, there are plenty of temples and national parks nearby (including the legendary Stone Forest) to keep you busy.

Of course, like other Chinese cities, the face of Kūnmíng is constantly changing and most old neighbourhoods have been torn down to make way for shopping malls. And the traffic jams that were unknown a few years ago, are now a regular occurrence. Yet, the essentially easy-going nature of Kūnmíng is, thankfully, still the same.

History

The region of Kūnmíng has been inhabited for 2000 years, but it wasn't until WWII that the city really began to expand, when factories were established and refugees, fleeing from the Japanese, started to pour in from eastern China. As the end point of the famous Burma Road, a 1000km-long haul from Lashio in Myanmar, the city played a key role in the Sino-Japanese War. Renmin Xilu marks the tail end of the road.

After the war, the city returned to being overlooked and isolated. When China opened to the West, however, tourists noticed the province, and Kūnmíng used its gateway status to the rest of Yúnnán to become one of the loveliest cities in southwest China.

Now, as Běijīng looks to boost China's already significant economic presence in Southeast Asia, new transport routes south from Kūnmíng are being constructed. In particular, work has finally started on the long-touted high-speed railway designed to link Kūnmíng with Vientiane in Laos and Bangkok in Thailand. In the not-too-distant future, maybe as early as 2020, travellers will be able to jump on a train in Kūnmíng and arrive in Vientiane the same day.

⊙ Sights

Yuántōng Temple
BUDDHIST TEMPLE

(圆通寺, Yuántōng Sì; Yuantong Jie; ¥6; ⊙8am-5pm) This temple is the largest Buddhist complex in Kūnmíng and a draw for both pilgrims and locals. It's more than 1000 years old, but has been refurbished many times. To the rear, a hall has been added, with a statue of Sakyamuni, a gift from Thailand's king.

Green Lake Park
PARK

(翠湖公园, Cuìhú Gōngyuán; Cuihu Nanlu; ⊙6am-10pm) Come here to people-watch, practise taichi or just hang with the locals and stroll. The roads along the park are lined with wannabe trendy cafes, teahouses and shops. In November, everyone in the city awaits the return of the local favourites, red-beaked seagulls; it's a treat watching people, er, 'flock' to the park when the first one shows up.

Chuàng Kù
GALLERY

(创库艺术主题社区, Loft; 101 Xiba Lu) West of downtown in a disused factory area known as Chuàng Kù, you'll find a small number of galleries and cafes featuring modern Chinese artists and photographers. **Yuánshēng Art Space** (源生坊, Yuánshēngfáng; 📞0871 6419 5697; ⊙2.30-8.30pm Tue-Sun) is a gallery-bar-restaurant-theatre focusing on the province's ethnic groups. The cornerstone of sorts is TCG Nordica.

TCG Nordica
GALLERY

(诺地卡, Nuòdìkǎ; 📞0871 6411 4691; www.tcgnordica.com; 101 Xiba Lu; ⊙11am-9pm Mon-Fri, to 10pm Sat, closed Sun) TCG Nordica is best described as a gallery-exhibition hall-cultural centre. Live jazz and dance, art and photo exhibitions, an English corner on Monday's (a good opportunity to meet some locals) are all staged here and there's even a relaxing restaurant with Scandinavian and Chinese food (dishes from ¥15). Check out the website for the full slate of performances and events.

East Pagoda
PAGODA

(东寺塔, Dōngsì Tǎ; 63 Shulin Jie; ⊙9am-5pm) FREE Closed for renovations at the time of research, the East Pagoda is a Tang structure that was, according to Chinese sources, destroyed by an earthquake (Western ones say it was destroyed by the Muslim revolt in the mid-19th century). When it is open, it is a hang-out for senior citizens.

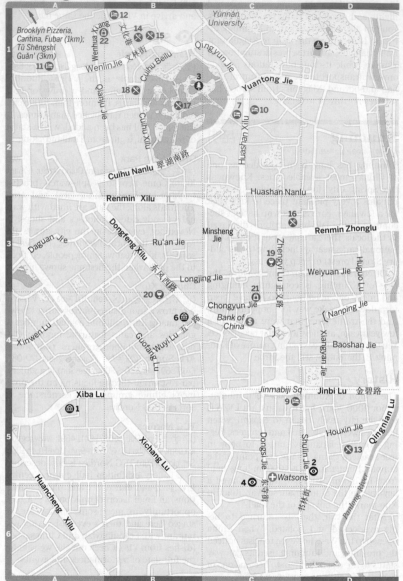

Yúnnán
Provincial Museum   MUSEUM
(云南省博物馆, Yúnnán Shěng Bówùguǎn; 118 Wuyi Lu; ⊗9am-4.30pm Tue-Sun) FREE Set inside a 1950s-era building, Yúnnán's provincial museum has been upgraded and its interior is sparkling throughout. There are reasonable exhibitions on Diān Chí (Dian Lake), prehistoric and early cultures, but the highlight is the section on Yúnnán's minorities, with excellent displays of ethnic costumes and musical instruments.

Kūnmíng

🛏 Sleeping

Some of the best hostels and guesthouses in all Yúnnán can be found in Kūnmíng, as well as budget, midrange and luxury hotels. Many are dotted around Green Lake Park and the surrounding area, which is a convenient central location. The cheapest places are close to the train station.

Kūnmíng Upland Youth Hostel HOSTEL $
(昆明倾城青年旅社, Kūnmíng Qīngchéng Qīngnián Lǚshè; ☎ 0871 6337 8910; uplandhostel@gmail.com; 92 Huashan Xilu, 华山西路92号; dm ¥41-46, s & d ¥132-204; @ 🖥) This place aims to impress with its sharp red and black decor, sizeable bar and inside and outdoor communal areas. Rooms have wood furnishings, and dorms come with big lockers and power outlets. It has English-speaking staff and a handy location near Green Lake. Bikes can be rented for ¥30 a day.

It's just off Huashan Xilu on a little alley called Dameiyuan Xiang (大梅园巷), near the back entrance of the landmark Green Lake Hotel.

West Pagoda PAGODA
(西寺塔, Xīsì Tǎ; Dongsi Jie; ⊙9am-5pm) FREE
Closed for renovations at the time of research, this Tang pagoda can't be climbed, nor is the temple complex open, but it is a good spot for people-watching with all manner of tea-drinking and mah-jong games going on.

Kūnmíng Ivies Will International Youth Hostel
HOSTEL $

(昆明爬山虎国际青年旅舍, Kūnmíng Páshānhǔ Guójì Qīngnián Lǚshě; ☑0871 6541 1919; www.ivies will.com; 24 Jindingshan Beilu, 金鼎山北路24号; dm ¥35-40, d ¥138; @ 🛜) This hostel caters mostly to local travellers, although some English is spoken. Dorms and rooms are big and comfortable and come with private bathrooms, there's a large communal area and there's even a basic gym. The drawback is that it is a ¥15 taxi ride from the centre of town. But buses 1, 83 and 168 all run here from the centre.

Hump Hostel
HOSTEL $

(驼峰客栈, Tuófēng Kèzhàn; ☑0871 6364 0359; www.thehumphostel.com; Jinmabiji Guangchang, Jinbi Lu, 金碧路金马碧鸡广场; dm ¥35-45, d with/without bathroom ¥165/90, tr ¥195; @ 🛜) Kūnmíng's liveliest hostel, in part because of its close proximity to many bars, karaoke joints and restaurants. Bring earplugs as all this activity could keep you up at night. The hostel itself has clean and big dorms (four to 10 beds); the private rooms (the cheapest lack windows) are sizeable, too, although the beds can be a bit hard.

Bike hire is ¥30 a day and the hostel's own bar and terrace are popular spots for late night carousing.

★ Lost Garden Guesthouse
GUESTHOUSE $$

(一丘田园客栈, Yīqiū Tiányuán Kèzhàn; ☑0871 6511 1127; www.lostgardenguesthouse.com; 7 Yiqiu Tian, 一丘田7号; dm ¥55-60, d ¥178-328; ❄@🛜) A relaxing oasis amid white-brick apartment blocks, this newly renovated boutique guesthouse has nouveau Dàlǐ decor with wood furniture, antiques, pleasant lounge and roof terrace. Rooms are spread across two adjoining buildings. It's tricky to locate: start by following the alley to the right of Green Lake Hotel, then take the first left and look for the sign pointing left.

Hàntíng Express
HOTEL $$

(汉庭快捷酒店, Hàntíng Kuàijié Jiǔdiàn; ☑400 8121 121; www.huazhu.com; 277 Beijing Lu, 北京路277号; tw/d ¥149/179; ❄🛜; S Tangzixiang) Handily located budget chain hotel with compact but modern and clean rooms. You won't hear any English spoken, but it's close to the subway, the train station and the centre of town. To get here, walk south of the Tangzixiang subway stop (line 2) for 200m.

Green Lake Hotel
HOTEL $$$

(翠湖宾馆, Cuìhú Bīnguǎn; ☑0871 6515 8888; www.greenlakehotel.com; 6 Cuihu Nanlu, 翠湖南路

6号; r from ¥2277; ❄❄@🛜❄) Proud but subdued, this gentle giant of Kūnmíng *hôtellerie* history has a fabulous location, opposite Green Park, and has kept up with modernity, doing so tastefully and with top-notch service. The panorama from the top floors is worth the price alone. Discounts of 50% are often available, and there are Chinese, Japanese and Western restaurants on-site.

Tè Yùn Hotel
HOTEL $$$

(特运酒店, Tè Yùn Jiǔdiàn; ☑0871 6809 0999; 40 Longxiang Jie, 龙翔街40号; d ¥688; ❄🛜) A Chinese-style midrange hotel with big rooms, decent beds and bathrooms and a useful location close to restaurants and bars. Routine 50% discounts make it an attractive choice. There's wi-fi throughout and the staff are helpful despite limited English.

Yúndà Bīnguǎn
HOTEL $$$

(云大宾馆, Yúnnán University Hotel; ☑0871 6503 4179; www.ynuhotel.com; Wenhua Xiang, 文化巷; d ¥188-788; ❄🛜) Conveniently close to the restaurant and bar hub of Wenhua Xiang and Wenlin Jie, the Yúndà's rooms are not exciting but do the job. The hotel is divided into two, with the cheaper rooms with hard beds in the wing across the road from the main entrance. Regular 40% discounts bring it into the midrange price category.

✗ Eating

Kūnmíng is a fine place to sample Yúnnán's most famous dish: 'across-the-bridge noodles' (过桥米线; *guòqiáo mǐxiàn*), but you'll find restaurants serving dishes from every corner of the province. For all manner of foreign restaurants, including Indian, Korean and Mexican, head to Wenhua Xiang. For self-catering, try Carrefour Supermarket, a branch of the popular French chain.

★ Yíng Jiāng Dǎi Wèi Yuán
YUNNAN $$

(盈江傣味园; ☑0871 6511 6788; 66 Cuihu Beilu, 翠湖北路66号; dishes from ¥20; ⏲11.30am-9pm) Popular with the locals, this bustling restaurant offers an authentic taste of the delicious, sour and spicy cuisine of the Dai minority from Xīshuāngbǎnnà in the deep south of Yúnnán, including such delicacies as bamboo worms (they taste better than they sound). Hefty portions and a pleasant location by Green Lake too. Picture menu.

Park Bar & Grill
INTERNATIONAL $$

(☑153 6817 1162; Shicui Cultural Centre, Green Lake Park, 翠湖公园拾翠文化中心; mains ¥40-80, breakfast from ¥30; ⏲9.30am-midnight, kitch-

ACROSS-THE-BRIDGE NOODLES

Yúnnán's best-known dish is 'across-the-bridge noodles' (过桥米线; *guòqiáo mǐxiàn*). You are provided with a bowl of very hot soup (stewed with chicken, duck and spare ribs) on which a thin layer of oil is floating, along with a side dish of raw pork slivers (in classier places this might be chicken or fish), vegetables and egg, and a bowl of rice noodles. Diners place all of the ingredients quickly into the soup bowl, where they are cooked by the steamy broth. Prices generally vary from ¥15 to ¥25, depending on the side dishes. It's usually worth getting these, because with only one or two condiments the soup lacks zest.

It is said the dish was created by a woman married to an imperial scholar. He decamped to an isolated island to study and she got creative with the hot meals she brought to him every day after crossing the bridge. This noodle dish was by far the most popular and christened 'across the bridge noodles' in honour of her daily commute.

en closes at 9pm); 🕏) With an enviable setting slap in the middle of Green Lake Park, this new place is drawing in both expats and flush locals. Solid menu of well cooked Western dishes, as well as a few Mexican favourites, and a good selection of foreign alcohol. There's a big outside area to eat at and they host DJ's, live music and film screenings too.

It's also good for a coffee during the day or a drink in the evening. You need to be inside the park by 10pm to get access late at night.

Tǔ Shēngshí Guǎn
YUNNAN $$
(土生食馆; ☑ 0871 6542 0010; District B, Jinding 1919, 15 Jindingshan Beilu, 金鼎山北路15号金鼎1919B区, dishes from ¥22; ⏰10am-9pm) Located on the ground-floor of a converted warehouse a couple of kilometres northwest of the city centre, this family-run place uses strictly organic ingredients for its selection of favourite local dishes. The veggies and homemade tofu are outstanding and the atmosphere relaxed; there's a small outside area. No English spoken, but there is an English menu.

As You Like
INTERNATIONAL $$
(有佳面包店, Yǒujiā Miànbāo Diàn; ☑ 0871 6541 1715; 5 Tianjundian Xiang, off Wenlin Jie, 文林街红豆园旁天君殿巷5号; salads from ¥15, pizzas from ¥32; ⏰11am-10.30pm Tue-Sun; 🕏🖊) Cute cubbyhole cafe/restaurant that's all vegetarian. Staff make excellent pizza, salads and sandwiches, all from local organic produce, as well as fine smoothies and there's a good range of Chinese teas. To find it, walk east on Wenlin Jie (coming from Wenhua Xiang) and take the first left up the narrow alley just before the school and follow it round.

1910 La Gare du Sud
YUNNAN $$
(昆明1910火车南站餐厅, Kūnmíng 1910 Huǒchē Nánzhàn Cāntīng; ☑ 0871 6316 9486; 8 Houxin Jie, 后新街8号; dishes from ¥15; ⏰11am-9pm) Of-

fering good-value Yúnnán specialities in a pleasant neo-colonial-style atmosphere, this place is a fave with both expats – it's the kind of place foreign students take their parents when they come to visit – and cashed-up locals. It's hidden down an alley off Chongshan Lu, south of Jinbi Lu. Call ahead for instructions on how to get here.

Hóng Dòu Yuán
YUNNAN $$
(红豆圆; ☑ 0871 6539 2020; 142 Wenlin Jie, 文林街142号; dishes from ¥15; ⏰11am-9pm) An old-school Chinese eatery, with a duck-your-head stairway, this is a real locals' hang-out on cosmopolitan Wenlin Jie. The food is excellent and will draw you back. Try regional specialities such as the *táozá rǔbǐng* (fried goat's cheese and Yúnnán ham) and *hang bái ròu* (peppery, tangy beef). Picture menu.

Cantina
ITALIAN $$
(意老夫子意大利餐厅, Yìlǎofūzi Yìdàlì Cāntīng; ☑ 138 4498 1890; 9 Hongshan Donglu, Backstreet Block, building 11-1, 虹山东路9号版筑翠园商铺11幢一层1号（麦当劳隔壁）; mains from ¥42; ⏰11am-11pm; 🕏) Big, light-filled, Italian-run venue set around an attractive central bar. There are 24 different types of pizza, as well as pasta and panini (from ¥28), steaks and excellent selections of cold meats and cheeses. Good wine list and it does daily lunch specials (from ¥49). It's inside the Banzhucuiyuan complex northwest of the centre. To find it, walk a little east of the McDonald's.

Humdinger
INTERNATIONAL $$
(玩啤, Wánpí; ☑ 0871 6360 1611; 111 Zhengyi Lu, 正义路111号; mains from ¥58; ⏰5.30pm-2.30am; 🕏) Despite the giant vats in which Humdinger's own beer brews, this place is much more of a restaurant than a bar. The western food – pizzas, ribs, burgers, steaks – is served up from an open kitchen

ONE-STOP SHOPPING

The **Flower & Bird Market** (花鸟市场, Huāniǎo Shìchǎng; Tongdao Jie; ⏰7am-8pm), also known as *lǎo jiē* (old street), has shrunk dramatically in recent years and is now ominously hemmed in by encroaching modernity. Nor are flowers and birds the main draw here any more, although there are still plenty of examples of both. Instead, strollers peruse stalls chock-full of jade and jewellery, curios, knick-knacks and clothing.

One block west of the intersection of Guanghua Jie and the pedestrian-only Zhengyi Lu sits **Fú Lín Táng** (福林堂), the city's oldest pharmacy, which has been dishing out the *sānqī* (the legendary Yúnnánese cure-all root mixed into tea; around ¥160 per gram) since 1857.

in an industrial-chic setting and the locals love it, packing it out every evening.

Brooklyn Pizzeria   PIZZA $$
(布鲁克林批萨店, Bùlǔkèlín Pīsàdiàn; 🖉0871 6533 3243; www.kunmingpizza.com; 6-8, Bldg 12 Banzhucuiyuan, 11 Hongshan Donglu, 虹山东路11号版筑翠园12栋6-8商铺; pizzas from ¥55; ⏰11.30am-10pm; 🐾) A big selection of stone-oven pizzas, as well as excellent New York–style grinder and Philly cheese steak sandwiches, are on offer here, plus lots of foreign beers. It's just northwest of the centre of town, in a rapidly expanding area of new restaurants and bars.

Tell your taxi to head for Banzhucuiyuan and then walk east from the McDonald's for 100m or so.

🍷 Drinking & Nightlife

Foreigners congregate in the bars on and around Wenhua Xiang and Banzhucuiyuan. Head to the Kūndū Night Market area and Jinmabiji Sq for Chinese-style clubs and bars.

Fubar   BAR
(139 Jianshe Lu, 建设路139号; beers from ¥20; ⏰6pm-late; 🐾) Kūnmíng's late-night crowd congregate at this friendly and suitably grungy bar, which closes only when the last customer has left (often when the sun is coming up). Decent selection of local and foreign alcohol, table football and a cool soundtrack. It's about 1km northwest of Wenlin Jie and close to Banzhucuiyuan.

Alei   BAR
(艾蕾酒廊, Àiléi Jiǔláng; 🖉0871 6836 9099; Bldg A1, Zhengyifang, 3 Qianwang Jie, 正义坊 A1栋 钱王街3号; cocktails from ¥50; ⏰5pm-2am; 🐾) The original of a growing number of Kūnmíng cocktail bars, Alei is a large, low-lit, modern space that has proved a hit with upwardly mobile locals. The bartenders know their trade and there's nightly live music.

Moondog   BAR
(月亮狗, Yuèliàng Gǒu; 138-5 Wacang Nanlu, 瓦仓南路138-5号; beers from ¥15; ⏰8pm-late; 🐾) A Chinese-run dive bar that attracts a mixed crowd of expats and locals. DJs most weekends and it shows the English football too.

🔒 Shopping

Yúnnán specialities are marble and batik from Dàlǐ, jade from Ruìlì, minority embroidery, musical instruments and spotted-brass utensils.

Yúnnánese tea is an excellent buy and comes in several varieties, from bowl-shaped bricks of smoked green tea called *tuóchá*, which have been around since at least Marco Polo's time, to leafy black tea that rivals some of India's best.

Mandarin Books & CDs   BOOKS
(五华书苑, Wǔhuá Shūyuàn; 🖉0871 6551 6579; 52 Wenhua Xiang; ⏰9am-10pm) Good spot for guidebooks, novels and a selection of travel writing in English and other languages, as well as books on Yúnnán itself.

ℹ Information

Most of the backpacker hotels and some of the cafes can assist with travel queries and they are usually the best places to get travel advice.

DANGERS & ANNOYANCES

Although Kūnmíng's reputation as one of China's safest cities was dented by a March 2014 attack on passengers at the train station by restive Uighurs that left 29 people dead, foreigners have little to fear here. As always, take special precautions against pickpockets at and around the train and long-distance bus stations. There have been a number of travellers who've been drugged and robbed on overnight sleeper buses.

MEDICAL SERVICES

Richland International Hospital (瑞奇德国际医院, Ruìqídé Guójì Yīyuàn; 🖉0871 6574 1988; Beijing Lu) Most of the doctors are Chinese but English is spoken here. Standards are generally good and prices are reasonable: consultations start from ¥30, then you pay for whatever treatment is required. It's on the bottom three floors

8675

of the Shàngdū International building; Yanchang Xian extension near Jinxing Flyover. A taxi ride from the city centre costs around ¥20.

Watsons (屈臣士; Qū Chén Shì; Dongsi Jie; ⊙9am-10pm) Western cosmetics and basic medicines. Other branches around town.

Yán'ān Hospital (延安医院; Yán'ān Yīyuàn; ☑0871 6321 1101; 1st fl, block 6, Renmin Donglu, 人民东路6号) Has a foreigners' clinic.

MONEY

Bank of China (中国银行, Zhōngguó Yínháng; 12 Dongfeng Xilu, 东风西路12号) changes foreign currency and travellers cheques. There is another branch on Renmin Donglu (⊙9am-5pm) that has all necessary services and an ATM.

PUBLIC SECURITY BUREAU

Public Security Bureau (PSB, 公安局, Gōng'ānjú; ☑0871 6301 7878; 399 Beijing Lu; ⊙8.30-11.30am & 1.30-4.30pm Mon-Fri) To visit the givers of visa extensions, head southeast off Government Sq (东风广场; Dōngfēng Guǎngchǎng) to the corner of Shangyi Jie and Beijing Lu. Another **office** (☑0871 6571 7001; Jinxing Lu; ⊙8.30am-11.30am, 1.30pm 4.30pm Mon-Fri) is off Erhuan Beilu in northern Kunming; take bus 3, 25 or 57.

POST

China Post (国际邮局, Zhōngguó Yóuzhèng; 223 Beijing Lu, 北京路223号; ⊙9am-6pm; ⓢTangzixiang) The main international office has poste restante and parcel service (per letter ¥3, ID required). It is also the city's Express Mail Service (LMS) and Western Union agent. Another branch on Dongfeng Donglu.

❶ Getting There & Away
AIR

Kūnmíng's airport is located 25km northeast of the city. It has direct services to/from North America, Europe and Australia. International flights to Asian cities include Bangkok (from ¥621), Hong Kong (from ¥560), Vientiane (from ¥1301), Yangon (from ¥1066) and Kuala Lumpur (from ¥627).

China Eastern Airlines (中国东方航空, Zhōngguó Dōngfāng Hāngkōng; 28 Tuodong Lu; ⊙8.30am-7.30pm) issues tickets for any Chinese airline but the office only offers discounts on certain flights.

Daily flights from Kūnmíng go to most major cities across China, including Běijīng (from ¥729), Guǎngzhōu (from ¥465) and Shànghǎi (from ¥564). There are regional services to Lhasa in Tibet (¥1960) and within Yúnnán, including Bǎoshān (from ¥538), Lìjiāng (from ¥320) and Xiàguān/Dàlǐ (from ¥350).

BUS

Kūnmíng's five bus stations are located on the outskirts of the city.

Buses departing the south bus station (彩云北路南客运站; cǎiyún běilù nán kèyùnzhàn):

Jiànshuǐ ¥81, 3½ hours, every 30 minutes (7.30am to 8.30pm)

Jǐnghóng ¥223 to ¥247, eight hours, every 30 minutes (8am to 10pm)

Yuányáng ¥139, seven hours, four daily (10.20am, 11am, 12.30pm and 6.30pm)

Buses departing the west bus station (马街西客运站; mǎjiē xī kèyùnzhàn):

Bǎoshān ¥167 to ¥233, nine hours, every hour (8.30am to 10pm)

Chǔxióng ¥55 to ¥58, two to three hours, every 10 minutes (7.10am to 7.10pm)

Dàlǐ ¥110 to ¥137, four to five hours, every 15 minutes (7.20am to 8.20pm)

Lìjiāng ¥184 to ¥217, nine hours, nine daily (9.30am to 8.30pm)

Ruìlì ¥273 to ¥300, 12 hours, eight daily (8.30am to 9pm)

Shangri-la ¥208 to ¥249, 12 hours, seven daily (8.30am to 8.30pm)

Téngchōng ¥230 to ¥289, 11 hours, ten daily (9am to 9pm)

> ### ❶ BORDER CROSSINGS: LAOS & VIETNAM
>
> #### Getting to Laos
>
> A daily bus from Kūnmíng to Vientiane (¥587) leaves from the south bus station, at 6.30pm, reaching its destination 30 hours later. Alternatively, take a bus to Móhān on the border with Laos; these depart at 12.20pm and 8pm, cost ¥272 to ¥301 and take about 10 hours.
>
> #### Getting To Vietnam
>
> Apart from getting on a plane, the only way to get to Vietnam from Kūnmíng for now is by bus. Two buses (11.40am and 7.30pm) run daily from Kūnmíng's east bus station to the border town of Hékǒu (¥147). Official proceedings at this border crossing can be frustrating (and officials have been known to confiscate Lonely Planet guides because they show Taiwan as a different country to China). Just keep your cool.
>
> On the Chinese side, the border checkpoint is technically open from 8am to 11pm but don't bank on anything after 6pm. Set your watch when you cross the border – the time in China is one hour later than in Vietnam. Visas are unobtainable at the border crossing.

YÚNNÁN KŪNMÍNG

Around Kūnmíng

⊙ 0 ___ 5 km
⊙ 0 ___ 2.5 miles

Around Kūnmíng

⊙ Sights

1 Bamboo Temple A1
2 Dragon Gate A2
3 Huátíng Temple A1
4 Tàihuá Temple A1
5 Yúnnán Nationalities Museum B1

ℹ Information

6 Vietnamese Consulate B1
7 Yán'ān Hospital B1

Buses departing the east bus station (白沙河东客运站; *báishāhé dōng kèyùnzhàn*):

Hékǒu ¥147, eight hours, two daily (11.40am and 7.30pm).

Shílín ¥38, two hours, every 30 minutes (7am to 7.30pm).

Allow plenty of time to get to the bus stations (60 to 90 minutes). Line 2 of the subway runs to the south bus station, as does bus 154 from the train station. Bus 80 runs to the west bus station from the train station, while bus 60 goes to the east bus station, which is also on the subway network. A taxi will cost ¥40 to ¥50.

TRAIN

You can buy train tickets up to 10 days in advance. The following prices are for hard-sleeper berths:

Běijīng ¥549.50 to ¥575

Chéngdū ¥251 to ¥272

Guǎngzhōu ¥351 to ¥378

Guìyáng ¥161 to ¥175

Liùpánshuǐ ¥108.50 to ¥128

Shànghǎi ¥496 to ¥533.50

Xī'ān ¥397 to ¥426

Within Yúnnán, 10 daily trains run to Dàlǐ (seat ¥49 to ¥64, hard sleeper ¥88 to ¥113, six to seven hours, 8.10am to 11.58pm). Book ahead, as it is a popular route.

Seven trains run daily to Lìjiāng (seat ¥89, hard sleeper ¥152 to ¥163, nine hours, 9.40am to 11.30pm).

ℹ Getting Around

TO/FROM THE AIRPORT

Airport buses (¥25) run to/from the airport every 30 minutes from nine different locations, the most convenient being the train station, north and west bus stations and the Kūnmíng Hotel. The buses start running from 5am or 6am, depending on the route. The subway will eventually extend to reach the airport.

Ignore the many unofficial taxi touts who will approach you after you exit customs. Always take an official cab. Taxis charge ¥70 to ¥100 into town, depending on traffic and where you are going, and a flat rate of ¥120 going to the airport.

BICYCLE

Hostels rent bikes for ¥30 per day, but Kūnmíng has lots of hills.

BUS

Bus 63 runs from the east bus station to the main train station. Bus 2 runs from the train station to Government Sq (Dongfeng Guangchang) and then past the west bus station. Fares range from ¥1 to ¥4. The main city buses have no conductors and require exact change.

TRAIN

Two subway lines are now operational in Kūnmíng, with four more under construction. Fares range from ¥2 to ¥6 and trains run approximately 6.30am to 11pm. For now, the most useful stops include the train station and south bus station, as well as Government Sq (Dongfeng Guangchang) in the centre of town.

Around Kūnmíng

There are some grand sights within a 15km radius of Kūnmíng, but getting to most of them is time-consuming and you'll find the majority of them extremely crowded (weekdays are best to avoid the crowds).

If you don't have much time, the Bamboo Temple and Xī Shān (Western Hills) are the most interesting. Both have decent transport connections. Diān Chí (Lake Dian) has terrific circular-tour possibilities of its own.

Bamboo Temple 筇竹寺

The serene **Bamboo temple** (Qióngzhú Sì; ¥10; ⊘ 8am-5pm, no photos allowed inside) is definitely one to be visited by sculptors as much as by those interested in temple collecting. Raised during the Tang dynasty, it was rebuilt in the 19th century by master Sichuanese sculptor Li Guangxiu and his apprentices, who fashioned 500 *luóhàn* (arhats or noble ones) in a fascinating mishmash of superb realism and head-scratching exaggerated surrealism.

Li and his mates pretty much went gonzo in their excruciating, eight-year attempt to perfectly represent human existence in statuary. How about the 70-odd surfing Buddhas, riding the waves on a variety of mounts – blue dogs, giant crabs, shrimp, turtles and unicorns? And this is cool: count the arhats one by one to the right until you reach your age – that is the one that best details your inner self.

So lifelike are the sculptures that they were considered in bad taste by Li Guangxiu's contemporaries (some of whom no doubt appeared in caricature), and upon the project's completion he disappeared into thin air.

The temple is about 12km northwest of Kūnmíng. Take bus 2 to Huáng tǔ pō, from where shared minivans (¥10 per person) run to the temple.

Diān Chí 滇池

The shoreline of Diān Chí (Lake Dian), located to the south of Kūnmíng, is dotted with settlements, farms and fishing enterprises. The lake is elongated – about 40km from north to south – and covers an area of 300 sq km. Plying the waters are *fānchuán* (pirate-sized junks with bamboo-battened canvas sails). The area around the lake is mainly for scenic touring and hiking, and there are some fabulous aerial views from the ridges at Dragon Gate in Xī Shān.

Xī Shān 西山

This cool, forested mountain range on the western side of Diān Chí makes for a great day trip from Kūnmíng. Xī Shān is full of walking trails (some very steep sections), temples, gates and lovely forests. But avoid the weekends when Kūnmíngers come here in droves.

Close to the top of the mountain is **Dragon Gate** (龙门, Lóng Mén; ¥40), a group of grottoes, sculptures, corridors and pavilions that were hacked from the cliff between 1781 and 1835 by a Taoist monk and co-workers, who must have been hanging up here by their fingertips.

At the foot of the climb, about 15km from Kūnmíng, is **Huátíng Temple** (华亭寺, Huátíng Sì; ¥25; ⊘ 8am-6pm), a country temple of the Nanzhao kingdom believed to have been constructed in the 11th century. It's one of the largest in the province and its numerous halls are decorated with arhats. A combined ¥25 ticket allows admission here and to **Tàihuá Temple** (太华寺, Tàihuá Sì; ¥25; ⊘ 8am-6pm).

Sānqīng Gé (三清阁), near the top of the mountain, was a summer villa of a Yuan dynasty prince, and was later turned into a temple dedicated to the three main Taoist deities (*sānqīng* refers to the highest level of Taoist 'enlightenment').

From near here you can catch a **chairlift** (one-way/return ¥25/40) if you want to skip the final ascent to the summit.

ℹ Getting There & Away

One day, Kūnmíng's metro system will extend out here. Until then, take bus 54 (¥2, 6am to 11pm) from the corner of Renmin Zhonglu and Zhengyi Lu in Kūnming to its terminus at Mián Shān Chē Chǎng (眠山车场), and then change to bus 6 (¥1, 6.30am to 8pm), which will take you to the foot of the hills. Buses run up Xī Shān itself to Sānqīng Gé (one-way/return ¥12.50/25, every 15 minutes, 8.10am to 6.10pm).

Returning, you could take the cable car across to Hǎigēng Park for ¥40. From here, take the 94 bus or a taxi for the 3km or so to the Yúnnán Nationalities Museum, where you can catch bus 44 (¥1, 40 minutes) to Kūnmíng's main train station.

Shílín 石林

📞 0871 / POP 87,955

A conglomeration of utterly bizarre but stunning karst geology and a hell of a lot of tourists, Shílín, about 120km southeast of Kūnmíng, is equal parts tourist trap and natural wonderland. A massive collection of grey limestone pillars split and eroded by wind and rainwater (the tallest reaches 30m high), the place was, according to legend, created by immortals who smashed a mountain into a labyrinth for lovers seeking privacy.

Yes, it's packed to the gills, every single rock is affixed with a cheesy poetic moniker, Sani women can be persistent in sales, and it's all pricey as hell. Yet, idyllic, secluded walks are within 2km of the centre and by sunset or moonlight Shílín becomes otherworldly. To avoid the crowds, arrive early and avoid weekends.

During the July/August **torch festival**, wrestling, bullfighting, singing and dancing are held at a natural outdoor amphitheatre by Hidden Lake, south of Shílín.

Shílín can easily be visited as a day trip from Kūnmíng, and it doesn't have much in the way of budget accommodation. But if you want to stay the night, the rooms at the **Shílín Hēisōngyán Jiǔdiàn** (石林黑松岩 酒店; ☑ 0871 6771 1088; tw ¥280; 🛜) are quiet and have good views over Shílín.

Sani song and dance evenings are organised when there are enough tourists. Shows normally start at around 8pm at a stage next to the minor stone forest but there are sometimes extra performances. There are also Sani performances at the same location during the day between 2pm and 3pm.

Buses to Shílín (¥38, two hours, every 30 minutes, 7am to 7.30pm) leave from Kūnmíng's east bus station.

Hēijǐng 黑井
☑ 0878

Time-warped Hēijǐng has been known for salt production for centuries and is still an important producer of the 'white gold', as well as home to a sizeable Hui Muslim community. Hēijǐng has retained much of its period architecture and is a great place to wander for a day or two, marvelling at the old gates, temples and shady narrow alleys. The village makes a fine stopping-off point if you want to take the route less travelled between Dàlǐ and Kūnmíng.

The ¥30 entry fee at the main gate (a couple of kilometres before the village) includes admission to **Dàlóng Cí** (大龙祠; the clan meeting hall) and **Gǔyán Fáng** (古盐坊; an old salt production facility). The latter offers brief descriptions of the history of salt production, although none in English. You can find it by walking east from the village for about 15 minutes. A few old salt wells can also be inspected, look out for the **Black Cow Well** (黑牛井; Hēiniú Jǐng), just south of Dàlóng Cí.

The best-known courtyard in town, **Wu Family Courtyard** (武家大院, Wǔjiā Dàyuàn; ☑ 0878 489 0358) was once owned by local salt magnate Wu Weiyang, who was summarily executed by communist forces in 1949. You can walk around the courtyard, or take tea here.

The rooms at **Wang Family Courtyard** (王家大院, Wángjiā Dàyuàn; ☑ 0878 489 0506; r ¥80; 🛜), a family-run guesthouse, are set around a pleasant courtyard. They're not huge and the bathrooms are simple (squat toilets), but it's a peaceful place and the courtyard is perfect for stargazing come nightfall.

The setting of new hotel **Wénmiào Zhuàngyuán Jiǔdiàn** (文庙状元酒店; ☑ 0878 604 3366; tw ¥368; 🏢 🛜) is historic – it is located inside the remains of the town's Confucious Temple, parts of which are still standing – but the hotel itself is a modern block with big, comfortable rooms and the best bathrooms in town.

ℹ️ Information

A small tourist information office near the first bridge can point the way to the various sites.

ℹ️ Getting There & Away

The best option to reach Hēijǐng is local train number 6162 (¥11.50, three hours), departing Kūnmíng at 7.10am and arriving at 10.10am. The train stops a couple of kilometres from the village but horse-drawn buggies and minivans (¥3 to ¥5 per person) meet the train to make the journey here. Going the other way, train 6161 departs at 1.34pm and reaches Kūnmíng at 5.30pm.

The alternative is to take the bus from Kūnmíng or Dàlǐ to the county capital **Chǔxióng** (楚雄). From Chǔxióng's main bus station, take a taxi (¥9) to the east bus station (东客运站; *dōng kèyùnzhàn*), where there are buses to Hēijǐng (¥19, 2½ hours) every hour between 9am and 3.50pm. From Hēijǐng, buses to Chǔxióng leave from outside the market at the end of the village from 6.40am to 2.30pm.

Jiànshuǐ 建水
☑ 0873 / POP 17,400

Jiànshuǐ is a charming town of old buildings (surrounded by a much larger modern city), an enormous Confucian temple, a cave laden with swallows, and some of the best steam-pot cooking and barbecue you'll find in Yúnnán. The architecture is constantly being 'facelifted', but still retains much of its distinct character, and the locals, who are a mix of Han, Hui and Yi, are friendly.

History

Known in ancient times as Bùtóu or Bādiàn (巴甸), Jiànshuǐ's history dates back to the Western Jin period, when it was under the auspices of the Ningzhou kingdom. It was handed around to other authorities until its most important days as part of the Tonghai Military Command of the Nanzhao kingdom. The Yuan dynasty established what would eventually become the contemporary town.

⊙ Sights

Classic architecture surrounds you here, and not just in the old-style back alleys. Virtually every main street has a historically significant traditional structure. The architecture is especially intriguing because of the obvious mixture of central plains and local styles. Many old buildings, despite official decrees positing them as state treasures, have been co-opted for other purposes and the trick – and the fun – is trying to find them.

You can buy a ¥133 **through ticket** (通票; *tōngpiào*) that gets you into the Confucian Temple, the Zhu Family Garden and Swallow's Cavern. It's on sale at any of those places.

Confucian Temple   CONFUCIAN TEMPLE
(文庙, Wénmiào; Lin'an Lu, 临安路; ¥60; ☉ 8am-6.30pm) Jiànshuǐ's most famous temple was modelled after the temple in Confucius' hometown of Qūfù (Shāndōng province) and finished in 1285; it covers 7.5 hectares and is the third-largest Confucian temple in China. (Some locals employ a flurry of Byzantine mathematics to prove it's the largest; either way, Xué Lake, around which it sits, uses the Chinese word for 'sea' in its name!)

Zhu Family Garden   HISTORIC SITE
(朱家花园, Zhūjiā Huāyuán; Hanlin Jie, 翰林街; ¥50; ☉ 8am-10pm) This spacious 20,000-sq-metre complex, a fascinating example of Qīng-era one upping-the-Joneses, comprises ancestral buildings, family homes, ponds and lovely gardens, and took 30 years to build. The Zhu family made its name through its mill and tavern, and dabbled in everything from tin in Gèjiù to opium in Hong Kong, eventually falling victim to the political chaos following the 1911 revolution.

Cháoyáng Gate   HISTORIC SITE
(朝阳搂, Cháoyáng Lóu; ¥20; ☉ 8am-10pm) Newly refurbished, Cháoyáng Gate is an imposing Ming edifice that guards the entrance to the old town. Modelled on the Yellow Crane Tower (p443) in Wǔhàn and the Yuèyáng Tower located at Dòngtíng Lake in Húnán, it bears more than a passing resemblance to the Gate of Heavenly Peace in Běijīng. You can climb to the second storey for moderate views.

🛏 Sleeping

There are guesthouses and inns scattered throughout the old town, as well as one hostel.

Typha Youth Hostel   HOSTEL $
(草芽青年旅舍, Cǎoyá Qīngnián Lǚshě; ☎ 0873 765 2451; yhajianshui@yahoo.com; 89 Ruyi Lane,

如意巷89号; 10-/4-bed dm ¥30/40, d ¥70-90; ❋@🏠) Under new management, this is a real hostel now with a cosy communal area, bike hire (¥30 per day) and sound travel advice: it's a good place to book a tour of the surrounding area. Dorms are clean and come with lockers, the private rooms are compact but OK.

To find it, walk 30m past the Confucian Temple and turn down an alley on the left-hand side of the road by 253 Lin'an Lu.

Lín'an Inn   INN $$
(临安客栈, Lín'an Kèzhàn; ☎ 0873 765 5866; linaninn@hotmail.com; 32 Hanlin Jie, 翰林街32号; d ¥228-328; ❋🏠) In a prime location in the heart of the old town and with well kept rooms, the biggest draw here is the great communal courtyard which is very pleasant for a beer in the evening. But the rooms are sizeable and well maintained too. It rents bikes for ¥30 per day and can get small discounts on the entry fees to the main sights.

🍴 Eating

Jiànshuǐ is legendary for its *qìguō* (汽锅), a stew often infused with medicinal herbs and served in earthenware pots. Expect to pay ¥40 to ¥50 per pot. Jiànshuǐ is also famous for barbecue (烧烤; *shāokǎo*), and you'll find many cubbyhole restaurants grilling away.

Ā́máo Qīngzhēn Shāokǎo   YUNNAN $
(阿毛清真烧烤; ☎ 134 0892 7657; Shuyuan Jie, 书院街; barbecue skewers from ¥2; ☉ 6pm-2am) This is the place to eat fine barbecue underneath the stars. Everything – fish, meat, veggies, tofu – is on display, so just pick and choose. It also does the coveted *mǐxiàn* (米线; rice noodles) from ¥7. It's tucked down an alley off Hanlin Jie close to the Zhu Family Garden: everyone knows it.

ℹ Getting There & Away

Jiànshuǐ has a couple of bus stations. The main one is 3km north of Cháoyáng Gate. For very local destinations, you need to head to the Hóng Yùn bus station (红运客运站, Hóng Yùn Kèyùnzhàn) a few minutes' walk west of the corner of Chaoyang Beilu and Beizheng Jie. A taxi from the main bus station to the old town is ¥7.

From the main station, there are buses continually leaving for Nánshà in Yuányáng (¥31, every 20 minutes, two to three hours, 6.30am to 6.40pm). For Xīnjiē and the rice terraces, there is one daily bus (¥43, three hours, 11.34am).

Frequent buses head to Kūnmíng (¥81, every 25 minutes, three to four hours, 7am to 9.30pm). There are two buses daily to Hékǒu (¥65, five

YÚNNÁN JIÀNSHUǏ

hours, 7.26am and 8.10am). Buses to Jǐnghóng (¥225, eight to nine hours) depart at 1pm and 4pm.

Swallow's Cavern   燕子洞

A freak of nature and ornithology, **Swallow's Cavern** (Yànzǐ Dòng; ¥80; ⊙ 9am-5pm) is halfway between Jiànshuǐ and Gèjiù. The karst formations (the largest in Asia) are a lure, but what you'll want to see are the hundreds of thousands of swallows flying around in spring and summer. The cave is split into two – one high and dry, the other low and wet. The higher cave is so large that a three-storey pavilion and a tree fit inside.

Plank walkways link up; the Lú River runs through the lower cave for about 8km and you can tour the caverns in 'dragon-boats'.

There's no direct bus, but the ones bound for Méngzì, Kāiyuán or Gèjiù which don't take the expressway pass the cavern (¥11, one hour).

Yuányáng Rice Terraces   元阳梯田

☎ 0873 / POP 22,700

Picture hilltop villages, the only things visible above rolling fog and cloud banks, an artist's palette of colours at sunrise and sunset, spirit-recharging treks through centuries-old rice-covered hills, with a few water buffalo eyeing you contentedly nearby. Yes, it's hard not to become indulgent when describing these *tītián* (梯田; rice terraces), hewn from the topography by the Hani throughout the centuries. They cover roughly 125 sq km and are one of Yúnnán's most stunning sights.

Yuányáng (元阳) is actually split into two: Nánshà, the new town, and Xīnjiē, the old town an hour's bus or minivan ride up a nearby hill. Either can be labelled Yuányáng, depending what map you use. Xīnjiē is the one you want, so make sure you get off there.

⊙ Sights

The terraces around dozens of outlying villages have their own special characteristics, often changing with the daylight. Bilingual maps are available at all hotels in town. Bear in mind that the *tītián* are at their most extraordinary in winter when they are flooded with water which the light bounces off in spectacular fashion. Avoid visiting at Chinese public holidays, when prices for minibuses go sky-high (¥600 and more per day).

A combined ¥100 ticket gets you access to Duōyīshù, Bádá, Quánfúzhuāng and Měngpǐn.

Duōyīshù Rice Terrace   HILL
(多依树梯田, Duōyīshù Tītián) Located about 25km from Xīnjiē, this rice terrace has the most awesome sunrises and, of all those at Yuányáng, is the one you should not miss.

Měngpǐn Rice Terrace   HILL
(勐品梯田, Měngpǐn Tītián) Among the rice terraces at Yuányáng, Měngpǐn, also known as Lǎohǔzuǐ (老虎嘴), is one of the most mesmerising places to watch the sunset.

Quánfúzhuāng Rice Terrace   HILL
(全福庄梯田, Quánfúzhuāng Tītián) Quánfúzhuāng is less-crowded than Duōyīshù and has easy access via trails.

Bàdá Rice Terrace   HILL
(坝达梯田, Bàdá Tītián) Bàdá is one of the finest rice terraces to catch a sunset.

🛏 Sleeping & Eating

Xīnjiē and Pǔgāolǎo are where most hotels and guesthouses are. Of the two places, Pǔgāolǎo is by far the nicer place to stay.

Almost all restaurants are concentrated in Xīnjiē. In Pǔgāolǎo, all guesthouses serve meals, although they can be pricey.

ⓘ Getting There & Away

Xīnjiē is the main transport hub for Yuányáng, with daily buses from the bus station to and from Kūnmíng, Jiànshuǐ and Hékǒu, as well as minivans to the surrounding villages. There are also many buses to the same destinations from Nánshà, an hour away from Xīnjiē by minivan.

While buses run to all the villages from the bus station, you are much better off arranging your own transport, or hooking up with other travellers to split the cost of a sunrise or sunset drive. Minivans and motor-rickshaws congregate around Yúntī Shùnjié Dàjiǔdiàn and on the street west of the bus station. Expect to pay ¥400 to ¥500 in peak season for a minivan. Less comfortable motor-rickshaws can be got for ¥250.

Xīnjiē   新街

☎ 0873 / POP 15,000

Xīnjiē is a bit grubby, but makes a useful base for exploring the Yuányáng Rice Terraces. The bus station is a minute's walk from Titian Sq, the town's hub.

🛏 Sleeping & Eating

You're not spoiled for choice here, with only a couple of budget and midrange hotels in the centre of town. There are a number of places around the bus station where rooms can be found for ¥40 and up.

Yǐngyǒuliàn Jiǔdiàn HOTEL $
(影友恋酒店; [☎] 159 8737 4367; caihuimei2006@ 163.com; r ¥33-80; [☎]) It's basic (the price is a clue), but some rooms have Western toilets and the wi-fi connection is strong. Owner Belinda speaks good English and is helpful when it comes to arranging transport to the outlying villages. To get here, walk up the road from the bus station for five minutes and it's on your left.

Yúntī Shùnjié Dàjiǔdiàn HOTEL $
(云梯顺捷大酒店; [☎] 0873 562 1588; Xīnjiē; d ¥188; [☎]) Just off Titian Sq and a few minutes from the bus station, this place is the best of the centrally located hotels with clean and compact rooms. Wi-fi, though, is only available in the lobby. Prices go up during festival periods.

🛍 Shopping

Window of Yuányáng ARTS & CRAFTS
([☎] 0873 562 3627) Do visit this place, down the steps from the main square (on the 2nd floor of a building on your right). Staff here work in sustainable economic development in local villages. Volunteers are very friendly and helpful. Great locally produced items are here too (not to mention coffee!).

❶ Information

Agricultural Bank of China (中国农业银行, Zhōngguó Nóngyè Yínháng) Has an ATM that sometimes takes foreign cards: don't rely on it. To find it, head down the stairs by the entrance to Yúntī Shùnjié Dàjiǔdiàn and walk on for a couple of minutes; it's on the left-hand side.

❶ Getting There & Away

There are four buses daily from Kūnmíng to Yuányáng (¥139, seven hours, 10.20am, 11am, 12.30pm and 6.30pm); these return at 9.05am, 12.30pm and 6.30pm (although the 12.30pm bus sometimes doesn't run in low season). Other destinations include Hékǒu (¥59, four hours, 7.30am and 10.10am) and Jiànshuǐ (¥44, three hours, one daily, 4.30pm). Note that many more buses run to Jiànshuǐ from nearby Nánshà. There are frequent minivans to Nánshà (¥10, one hour) from outside the bus station.

To forge on to Xīshuāngbǎnnà, catch any minivan to Nánshà, where there's a daily bus in high season (October to March) to Jǐnghóng at 3.30pm (¥178, eight hours). Otherwise, you have to backtrack to Jiànshuǐ and catch the twice-daily Jǐnghóng sleepers (¥225, 1pm and 4pm) from there.

From Xīnjiē, minivans leave when full to Duōyīshù's Pǔgāolǎo village for ¥15.

Yuányáng Rice Terraces

Map Distances
Xīnjiē to Nánshà 30km
Xīnjiē to Lóngshùbà 4km
Xīnjiē to Qīngkǒu 6km
Xīnjiē to Quánfúzhuāng 10km
Xīnjiē to Měngpǐn/Lǎohǔzuǐ .18km
Xīnjiē to Bǎdá 16km
Xīnjiē to Duōyīshù 25km

Pǔgāolǎo 普高老

[☎] 0873 / POP 780

Increasing numbers of travellers are now basing themselves in picturesque Pǔgāolǎo in Duōyīshù (多依树), a Hani village an hour by minivan from Xīnjiē. The rice terraces are all around you here and when not gazing out on them, you can experience something of traditional village life as you dodge the water buffalo, chickens and pigs that wander the stone paths of the village. It's a perfect place for catching the sunrise from the roof of your guesthouse.

🛏 Sleeping & Eating

There are a growing number of guesthouses in the village, ranging from the basic to the comfortable. Dorm beds can be got from ¥35 and up. Almost all places have roof terraces to watch the sunrise and sunset.

Belinda's Backpackers Guesthouse GUESTHOUSE $
(影友漫步客栈, Yǐngyǒumànbù Kèzhàn; [☎] 159 8737 4367; caihuimei2006@163.com; dm/d ¥35/120; [☎]) Like her operation in Xīnjiē, Belinda's guesthouse in Pǔgāolǎo is a little rough and ready, but the roof terrace offers solid views, the private rooms have Western toilets and Belinda's tours of the area – little-visited villages especially – get good feedback. It's at the top of the village, behind the K2 hostel.

K2 International Youth Hostel HOSTEL $
(K2国际青年旅舍, K2 Guójì Qīngnián Lǚshě; [☎] 137 6949 8158; k2yha@163.com; Pǔgāolǎo Village; dm ¥40, d ¥120-130; [☎]) The dorms here have good beds, but their bathrooms come with squat

toilets. Private rooms have Western toilets and are spartan but clean. The roof terrace here offers OK views. The hostel is at the top of the village, close to the parking area.

Timeless Hostel Yuanyang　　　HOSTEL **$**
(久居丽江客栈, Jiŭ Jū Yuányáng Kèzhàn; ✏️153 6837 6718; yuangyang.timeless@gmail.com; Pŭ-gāolǎo Village; dm/d ¥45/148; 🌐🏠) In the heart of the village, with fresh dorms and rooms, a roof terrace with decent views, an amenable communal area and English-speaking staff. Bikes can be hired for ¥30 per day and staff can offer advice on potential hiking routes, as well as organise transport to other villages.

ⓘ Getting There & Away

Minivans (¥15 per person, one hour) leave from outside Xīnjiē's bus station from 6.30am to 6pm. They return to Xīnjiē on the the same schedule and can be hailed on the main road.

Xiàguān　　　下关

📍 0872 / POP 367,122

Xiàguān, on the southwest shore of Ěrhǎi Lake (Ěrhǎi Hú), is a transport hub for travellers headed to Dàlǐ, a few kilometres further up the highway. Confusingly, Xiàguān is sometimes referred to as Dàlǐ (大理) on tickets, maps and buses.

There's no reason to stay in Xiàguān – you only need to come here to catch a bus or train (or to extend a visa). If you're waiting for a bus and need to eat, the roads by or close to the two main bus stations – Renmin Zhonglu and Nan Jian Lu – are jammed with restaurants all offering similar menus.

ⓘ Information

Bank of China (中国银行, Zhōngguó Yínháng; Jianshe Donglu; ⊙ 9am-5pm) Changes money and travellers cheques, and has an ATM that accepts all major credit cards.
Public Security Bureau (PSB, 公安局, Gōng'ānjú; ✏️ 0872 214 2149; Tai'an Lu; ⊙ 8-11am & 2-5pm Mon-Fri) Handles all visa extensions for Xiàguān and Dàlǐ. Take bus 8 from Dàlǐ and ask to get off at the Shi Ji Middle School (世纪中学; Shìjì Zhōngxué).

ⓘ Getting There & Away

AIR
Xiàguān's airport is 15km from the town centre. Buy air tickets online or at an agency in Old Dàlǐ. Seven flights leave daily for Kūnmíng (from ¥430) and one to Xīshuāngbǎnnà (from ¥510).

No public buses run to the airport; taxis will cost ¥50 from Xiàguān or ¥100 from Dàlǐ.

BUS
Xiàguān has four bus stations. The Dàlǐ express bus station (kuàisù kèyùnzhàn) is on Nan Jian Lu. The second main station used by travellers is the Xīngshèng bus station (also called the gǎo kuài kèyùnzhàn). To find it, turn left out of the the express bus station and walk up to the main road and then turn right and it's 200m ahead of you. The third station of interest is the north bus station (běi kèyùnzhàn) on Dali Lu, which is reached by bus 8 (¥2) or a ¥10 taxi ride.

Remember that when departing, the easiest way to Kūnmíng or Lìjiāng is to get a bus from Old Dàlǐ.

The following departures are from the Dàlǐ express bus station:
Chŭxióng ¥75, 2½ hours, every 40 minutes (7.40am to 6.40pm)
Fúgòng ¥128, eight hours, one daily (11.30am)
Kūnmíng ¥127, four to five hours, every 30 minutes (8am to 6pm)
Liùkù ¥88, five hours, hourly (7.20am to 3.20pm)
Mángshì (Lùxī) ¥127, six to eight hours, four daily (10am, 11.30am, 1pm and 7.30pm)
Ruìlì ¥161 to ¥185, eight hours, three daily (8.30am, 3pm and 7.30pm)
Yúnlóng (for Nuòdèng) ¥39, three hours, every 40 minutes (7.50am to 4.30pm)

The following departures are from the Xīngshèng bus station:
Bǎoshān ¥72, 2½ hours, every 40 minutes (7.50am to 7.20pm)
Kūnmíng ¥137, four to five hours, every 30 minutes (7.20am to 7.30pm)
Téngchōng ¥126, six hours, three daily (10am, 1pm and 2pm)
Wēishān ¥15, 1½ hours, every 20 to 30 minutes (6.30am to 6pm)

Departures from the north bus station include:
Jiànchuān (for Shāxī) ¥45, three hours, every 45 minutes (6.25am to 6.50pm)
Shangri-la ¥106, seven hours, every 30 minutes (6.30am to noon)

If you want to head to **Jīnghóng** (¥221, 15 hours, 8.20am, 9.40am and 11am), you need the east bus station (dōng kèyùnzhàn) by the train station, which also serves destinations on the east side of Ěrhǎi Lake such as Shuāngláng and Wāsè.

Buses to Old Dàlǐ (¥2, 35 minutes) leave from a number of locations. Bus 8 (¥2, 35 minutes) runs from Jianshe Lu, close to both the express and Xīngshèng bus stations, to a car park at the bottom of Yeyu Lu in Dàlǐ. Bus 4 runs from the centre of Xiàguān past Dàlǐ's West Gate. There is also an unnumbered bus (¥2, 35 minutes) that leaves from the train station and passes Dàlǐ's West Gate. If you want to be sure, ask for Dàlǐ gǔchéng (Dali old city).

Tickets for nearly all destinations can be booked in Dàlǐ and this is often the easiest way to do it as it will save you a trip to Xiàguān (although you will pay a service fee of ¥10 to ¥15).

TRAIN
There are nine trains daily from Kūnmíng's main train station (hard seat/sleeper ¥64/97, six to seven hours, 9.40am to 11.30pm). Returning to Kūnmíng, there are eight daily trains (10.04am to 11.39pm). There are eight trains daily to Lìjiāng (¥34 to ¥49, two to three hours, 4.37am to 5.38pm).

Wēishān　　　　　巍山

☑ 0872 / POP 20,700

Some 55km or so south of Xiàguān, Wēishān is the heart of a region populated by Hui and Yi. It was once the nucleus of the powerful Nanzhao kingdom, and from here the Hui rebel Du Wenxiu led an army in revolt against the Qing in the 19th century.

Today, it's an attractive and relaxed small town of narrow streets lined with traditional wooden houses, with drum and bell towers at strategic points and a lovely backdrop of the surrounding hills. It's still unspoiled and largely off the traveller map, but a few refugees from Dàlǐ have now begun moving here to open businesses. In the next few years, Wēishān is likely to develop fast as a tourist destination, so get here now before everyone else arrives.

◉ Sights

The town's central point is the unmistakable **Gǒngchǎng Tower** (拱辰楼; Gǒngchǎng Lóu) FREE. South from here you'll come first to **Xīnggǒng Tower** (星拱楼; Xīnggǒng Lóu) FREE, and then on the right-hand side of the street to **Mēnghuà Old Home** (蒙化老家, Mēnghuà Lǎojiā; ¥10; ⊙8.30am-9pm), the town's best-preserved slice of architecture. Make sure to check out the town's sizeable and well preserved **Confucius Temple** (文庙, Wénmiào; ⊙8am-7pm) FREE: turn right at Xīnggǒng Tower and follow West Street around to find it.

Wēibǎo Shān　　　　MOUNTAIN
(巍宝山, Wēibǎo Mountain; ¥60) Eminently worthy Wēibǎo Shān, about 10km south of Wēishān, has a relatively easy hike to its peak at around 2500m. During the Ming and Qing dynasties it was the zenith of Chi-

na's Taoism, and you'll find some superb Taoist murals; the most significant are at **Wénchāng Gōng** (文昌宫, Wénchāng Palace) and **Chángchún Cave** (长春洞, Chángchún Dòng). Birders in particular love the mountain; the entire county is a node on an international birding flyway.

There are no buses here. Head to the street running east of Gǒngchǎng Lóu in Wēishān to pick up a microvan to the mountain, or ask your hotel to arrange one. Expect to pay ¥80 to ¥100 for the round trip; you'll need the driver to wait for you.

⌁ Sleeping & Eating

A few hotels are scattered around the centre of town.

Línyè Bīnguǎn　　　　HOTEL $
(林业宾馆; ☑0872 612 0761; 24 Xi Xin Jie, 西新街24号; d¥100; ❀⌁) A hop, skip and a jump from Gǒngchǎng Lóu, with big and well kept rooms and a strong wi-fi connection. It's a ¥5 ride from the bus station in a motor-rickshaw.

Báilùyuán　　　　GUESTHOUSE $$$
(白露原; ☑157 527 98896; 19 Bei Jie, 北街19号; r ¥580; ⌁) Out front this is a lovely teahouse, which also serves coffee and juices, but out back you can stay in effectively what is your own little courtyard home, with a small garden and a very comfortable and tastefully decorated bedroom.

Yùfēng Cāntīng　　　　YUNNAN $$
(裕丰餐厅; Xixin Jie, 西新街; dishes from ¥10; ⊙8.30am-10pm) Excellent locals hang out, with fine veggies and tofu. There's no English menu, but everything is on display and the staff will do their best to help you out.

⍚ Drinking & Nightlife

Yàn Cafe　　　　CAFE
(焱咖啡, Yàn Kāfēi; ☑189 8707 0696; Bei Jie, 北街; coffee & tea from ¥20; ⊙11am-10.30pm; ⌁) Just down the street from Xīnggǒng Tower is this laid-back little cafe run by a former Dàlǐ resident and her musician husband. Proper coffee and tea, as well as fruit shakes and beer. For now, it's the only place in town like it.

❶ Getting There & Away

Xiàguān's Xīngshèng bus station has buses to Wēishān (¥15, 1½ hours, every 20 to 30 minutes, 6.30am to 6pm). They return to Xiàguān from 6.30am.

Dàlǐ 大理

📞 0872 / POP 40,000

Dàlǐ, the original backpacker hang-out in Yúnnán, was once *the* place to chill, with its stunning location sandwiched between mountains and Ěrhǎi Lake. Loafing here for a couple of weeks was an essential part of the Yúnnán experience.

In recent years, domestic tourists have discovered Dàlǐ in a big way and the scene has changed accordingly. Instead of dreadlocked Westerners, it's young Chinese who walk around with flowers in their hair. Still, Dàlǐ has not been overwhelmed by visitors like nearby Lìjiāng and remains a reasonably relaxed destination, with the local Bai population very much part of daily life.

Surrounding Dàlǐ there are fascinating possibilities for exploring, especially by bicycle and in the mountains above the lake, or you can do what travellers have done for years – eat, drink and make merry.

History

Dàlǐ lies on the western edge of Ěrhǎi Lake at an altitude of 1900m, with a backdrop of the imposing 4000m-tall Cāng Shān (Green Mountains). For much of the five centuries in which Yúnnán governed its own affairs, Dàlǐ was the centre of operations, and the old city retains a historical atmosphere that is hard to come by in other parts of China.

The main inhabitants of the region are the Bai, who number about 1.5 million and are thought to have settled the area some 3000 years ago. In the early 8th century they succeeded in defeating the Tang imperial army before establishing the Nanzhao kingdom, which lasted until the Mongol hordes arrived in the mid-13th century.

◎ Sights

Dàlǐ Catholic Church
CHURCH

(off Renmin Lu) It's worth checking out Dàlǐ's Catholic Church. Dating back to 1927, it's a unique mix of Bai-style architecture and classic European church design. Mass is held here every Sunday at 9.30am.

Three Pagodas
PAGODA

(三塔寺, Sān Tǎ Sì; ¥120; ⊙8.30am-6.30pm) Absolutely *the* symbol of the town and region, these pagodas, a 2km walk north of the north gate, are among the oldest standing structures in southwestern China. The tallest of the three, **Qiānxún Pagoda**, has 16 tiers that reach a height of 70m. It was originally erected in the mid-9th century by engineers from Xī'ān. It is flanked by two smaller 10-tiered pagodas, each of which is 42m high.

While the price is cheeky considering you can't go inside the pagodas, **Chóngshèng Temple** (Chóngshèng Sì) behind them has been restored and converted into a relatively worthy museum.

🕺 Activities

Climb Dàlǐ
CLIMBING

(📞131 5064 4701; www.climbdali.com; 20 Renmin Lu) This outfit runs active adventures around Dàlǐ, including rock climbing, mountaineering, kayaking and rafting trips. Contact Adam Kritzer.

🍲 Courses

Rice & Friends
COOKING

(📞151 2526 4065; www.riceandfriends.com) Recommended cooking school that includes trips to markets to purchase ingredients and tips on preparation, as well as cooking classes.

👉 Tours

China Minority Travel
CULTURAL

(📞138 8723 5264; chinaminoritytravel@gmail.com) Henriette, a Dutch expat, can offer a long list of trips, including tours to Muslim and Yi minority markets as well as through remote areas of Yúnnán and Guìzhōu.

Zouba Tours
BICYCLE TOUR, HIKING

(📞152 8814 5939; www.zoubatours.com) Bike tours and treks to the less-visited parts of Yúnnán.

Tibet Motorcycle Adventures
MOTORCYCLE TOUR

(📞151 8499 9452; www.tibetmoto.de) Motorbikes can be rented for ¥150 per day and tours (although not to Tibet) arranged. Contact Hendrik Heyne.

🎉 Festivals & Events

Third Moon Fair
CULTURAL

(三月节, Sānyuè Jié) Merrymaking – along with endless buying, selling and general horse-trading (but mostly partying) – takes place during the Third Moon Fair, which begins on the 15th day of the third lunar month (usually April) and ends on the 21st day.

Three Temples Festival
CULTURAL

(绕三灵, Ràosān Líng) The Three Temples Festival is held between the 23rd and 25th days of the fourth lunar month (usually May).

Dàlǐ

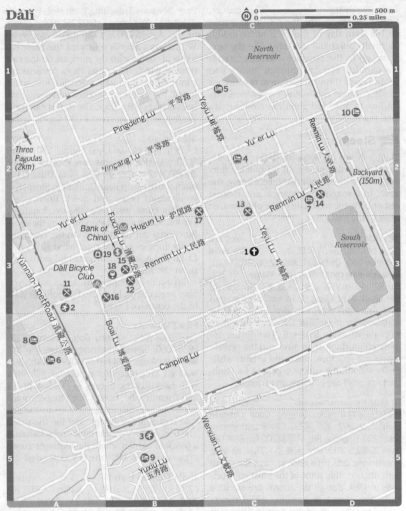

Dàlǐ

⊙ Sights
1 Dàlǐ Catholic Church...............................C3

⊕ Activities, Courses & Tours
2 Climb Dàlǐ...A3
3 Rice & Friends B5

🛏 Sleeping
4 Dàlǐ Spoor Youth Hostel.......................C2
5 Dragonfly Guesthouse C1
6 Five Elements A4
7 Four Seasons Travelling With Hotel D2
8 Jade Emu A4
9 Jim's Tibetan Hotel...............................B5
10 Sleepyfish Lodge D1

🍴 Eating
11 Birdbar Cafe A3
12 Cāng Ěr Chūn B3
13 Cháimǐduō C2
14 Duan's Kitchen.....................................D2
15 Good Panda B3
16 Lovely Lotus Delicious Vegetarian........B3
17 Serendipity B2

🍷 Drinking & Nightlife
18 Bad Monkey B3

🛍 Shopping
19 Mandarin Books & CDs..........................A3

Torch Festival
CULTURAL

(火把节, Huǒbǎ Jié) The Torch Festival is held on the 24th day of the sixth lunar month (normally July) and is likely to be the best photo op in the province. Flaming torches are paraded at night through homes and fields. Locals throw pine resin at the torches causing minor explosions everywhere. According to one local guesthouse owner, 'it's total madness'.

🛏 Sleeping

There's heaps of accommodation in Dàlǐ, but the popular places fill up quickly during peak summer months. Increasingly, the most in-demand guesthouses are located just outside the west gate of the old town, or close to the east gate.

★ Jade Emu
HOSTEL $

(金玉缘中澳国际青年旅舍, Jīnyùyuán Zhōng'ào Guójì Qīngnián Lǔshě; ☑ 0872 267 7311; www.jade-emu.com; West Gate Village, 西门村; dm ¥25-40, d ¥128-298; ❀@☎) Smack in the shadow of Cāng Shān and now spread over four buildings, the Jade Emu sets the standard for hostels in Dàlǐ and elsewhere with its attention to detail. The dorms are more comfortable than most and the private rooms are spacious, clean and bright, while the new boutique annexe is perfect for flashpackers. Staff are efficient and friendly.

Dragonfly Guesthouse
GUESTHOUSE $

(清亭国际青年旅舍, Qīngtíng Guójì Qīngnián Lǔshě; ☑ 0872 250 4255; www.dalidragonfly.com; 200 Pingdeng Rd, 平等路200号; 6-/4-bed dm ¥35/40, s ¥110/148; ❀@☎) This newish guesthouse gets rave reviews, and the dorm beds are certainly some of the most comfortable in Dàlǐ. But all the rooms are sizeable and have decent bathrooms, while there's a roof terrace with views towards the lake and mountains and a basic restaurant. It's 15 minutes' walk from the centre of town at the northern end of Yeyu Lu.

Dàlǐ Spoor Youth Hostel
HOSTEL $

(大理一步国际青年旅舍, Dàlǐ Shíbù Guójì Qīngnián Lǔshě; ☑ 0872 251 4476; yhaspoor@163.com; 121 Yeyu Lu, 叶榆路121号; dm ¥35-40, s ¥80, d ¥110-190; ❀@☎) The anonymous white exterior doesn't promise much, but there's an attractive garden courtyard here. The four-bed dorms are cramped, but the private rooms are a reasonable size and well maintained and the bathrooms OK. It sees mostly Chinese travellers, but some English is spoken.

Four Seasons Travelling With Hotel
HOTEL $

(四季客栈, Sìjì Kèzhàn; ☑ 0872 267 4507; 428 Renmin Lu, 人民路428号; s ¥58, d ¥138-248; ❀☎) With a large, interior courtyard, this place has a mix of rooms with the cheapest on the roof terrace, which offers fine views towards the surrounding mountains. Singles are small, but all the rooms are modern and some have beds raised off the floor. The staff speak some English and you can rent a bike for ¥20 a day.

Sleepyfish Lodge
HOSTEL $

(大理乐游客栈, Dàlǐ Lèyóu Kèzhàn; ☑ 0872 267 8040; www.sleepyfishlodge.com; Yu'er Lu, 玉洱路; dm ¥50, d ¥248-288; ☎) Well away from Dàlǐ's main tourist strip near Dongmen, Sleepyfish is all about peace and quiet. Rooms lack TVs, but come with balconies overlooking a garden and are a big step up from the more functional dorms. It's close to the east gate, down an alley off the right-hand side of Yu Er Lu just before the ornamental gate: signs point the way.

Bike-hire is available from ¥25 a day; you may need one as it's a good 20 minute walk to the centre of town.

Five Elements
HOSTEL $

(五行国际客栈, Wǔ Xíng Guójì Kèzhàn; ☑ 130 9985 0360; fiveelementsdali@gmail.com; 西门村, West Gate Village; 6-/4-bed dm ¥30/45, d ¥80-260; ❀@☎) This place has a popular following with backpackers, thanks to the low prices and friendly vibe. Dorms need more storage space but are reasonably sized, while the private rooms are a decent deal for the price. The best are very comfortable and set around a pleasant garden where the manager grows organic veggies. Bike hire is ¥30 per day.

Jim's Tibetan Hotel
HOTEL $$

(吉姆和平酒店, Jímǔ Hépíng Jiǔdiàn; ☑ 0872 267 7824; jimstibetanhotel@gmail.com; 13 Yuxiu Lu, 玉秀路13号; d ¥300-500; ❀☎) The rooms here are some of the most distinctive in Dàlǐ, coming with Tibetan motifs and packed with antique Chinese-style furniture, even if the bathrooms are looking their age now. There's also a garden, rooftop terrace, restaurant and bar. Travel services and tours can be booked, while bikes and scooters can be hired.

🍴 Eating

Bai food makes use of local flora and fauna – many of which are unrecognisable! Specialities include *rǔbǐng* (goat's cheese) and *ěr kuài* (饵块; toasted rice 'cakes'). Given the proximity of Ěrhǎi Lake, try *shāguō yú* (沙锅鱼), a claypot fish casserole/stew made from salted Ěrhǎi Lake carp – and, as a Bai touch, magnolia petals.

Lovely Lotus Delicious Vegetarian CHINESE $
(爱莲说素膳, Ài Lián Shuō Sùshàn; ☑ 0872 533 7737; B2, Jiulongju, west side of Fuxing Lu, 复兴路西侧九隆居B2号; buffet ¥20; ⏰ 11.30am-1.30pm & 6-8pm; ☑) No menu here; instead you choose from a tempting buffet of all-vegetarian dishes. It bustles at lunchtimes and there's a small outside area to eat at. It's just off Boai Lu on the right-hand side of a forecourt.

Good Panda YUNNAN $
(妙香园, Miàoxiāng Yuán, 81 Renmin Lu, 人民路81号; dishes from ¥18; ⏰ 9am-10pm) Surrounded by Western-style restaurants, this is a more local joint and a good introduction to classic Dàlǐ eats like sizzling beef (*tiěbǎn niúròu*) and crispy carp (*jiànchuān gānshāo yú*), plus Yúnnán-wide food and some Sìchuan dishes. There's a limited English menu, but some English is spoken and you can point at the vegetables that look best.

★ Duan's Kitchen YUNNAN $$
(小段厨房, Xiǎoduàn Chúfáng; ☑ 153 0872 7919; 12 Renmin Lu, 人民路12号; dishes from ¥38; ⏰ 11am-2pm & 5.30-9pm; ☑) Now so popular that you can expect to queue for a table, this place is set around a cosy and cute courtyard. The dishes are an interpretation of Bai cuisine rather than 100% the real deal, but the ingredients are absolutely local. It's at the far eastern end of Renmin Lu.

Serendipity AMERICAN $$
(大理美国小馆, Dàlǐ Měiguó Xiǎoguǎn; 53 Guangwu Lu, 广武路53号; mains from ¥38; ⏰ 8am-11.30pm; ☑) Busy, American-run diner with a traditional counter to sit around and a solid menu of properly cooked burgers, steaks, pasta and salad, as well as hefty, top-notch breakfasts. Some outdoor seating on an alley that is rather quieter than Dàlǐ's main drag.

Cāng Ěr Chūn YUNNAN $$
(苍洱春; 48 Renmin Lu, 人民路48号; dishes from ¥18; ⏰ 11am-11pm) A little more expensive than some other Bai restaurants and slightly brusque service, but the food is worthwhile and authentic: the locals like it. The *rǔbǐng* (乳饼; goat's cheese) is especially good here.

Birdbar Cafe JAPANESE $$
(鸟吧咖啡馆, Niǎoba Kāfēi Guǎn; ☑ 0872 250 1902; www.flightdiary.com; 20 Renmin Lu, 人民路20号; dishes from ¥28; ⏰ 9am-7pm Tue-Sun; ☑) There's a great, sun-filled upstairs area to lounge in over a coffee, tea or beer, while the menu mixes Western, Chinese and Japanese cuisine (all organic). The breakfasts are an especially good deal, as are the set meals (from ¥48).

Cháimǐduō INTERNATIONAL $$$
(柴米多; 204 Yeyu Lu, 叶榆路204号; mains & breakfast from ¥38, tapas from ¥18; ⏰ 9.30am-10pm; ☑☑) Iberian-Chinese fusion with a Spanish chef and all-organic ingredients sourced from their own farm outside Dàlǐ. All dishes are presented tapas-style. There's an open kitchen, artful, faux rustic design and a large outside area to eat in (good for the kids). It's more expensive than many places in town, but the food is consistently good.

🍷 Drinking & Nightlife

Backyard BAR
(后院酒吧, Hòuyuàn Jiǔbā; 27 Hongwu Lu, 洪武路27号; beers from ¥15; ⏰ 6pm-late, closed Thu; ☑) Dàlǐ's most laid-back and hidden away bar attracts locals and expats with a fine selection of foreign beers and alcohol and a bar set in a garden (hence the name). It shows live European football on the weekends, there's pool, table football and darts, and it serves the best chips and spaghetti bolognese in town.

MARKETS AROUND DÀLǏ

There's a market to go to nearly every day of the week. Every Monday at Shāpíng (沙坪), about 30km north of Dàlǐ, there is a colourful Bai market (Shāpíng Gǎnjí). From 10am to 2.30pm you can buy everything from food products and clothing to jewellery and local batik.

Regular buses to Shāpíng (¥11, one hour) leave from just outside the west gate. By bike, it will take about two hours at a good clip.

Markets also take place in Shuāngláng (双廊; Tuesday), Shābā (沙坝; Wednesday), Yòusuǒ (右所; Friday morning, the largest in Yúnnán) and Jiāngwěi (江尾; Saturday). Xīzhōu (喜州) and Zhōuchéng (州城) have daily morning and afternoon markets, respectively. Wāsè (挖色) has a popular market every five days with trading from 9am to 4.30pm. Thanks to the lack of boats, travellers now have to slog to Xiàguān's east bus station for buses to Wāsè (¥20).

Many guesthouses and hostels in Dàlǐ offer tours or can arrange transportation to these markets for around ¥150 for a half-day.

To find it, turn right at the east gate and walk along Hongwu Lu for 300m. It's down a small alley to the right of a motor repair shop. Look for the light.

Bad Monkey   BAR
(坏猴子, Huài Hóuzi; ☎136 8882 4871; 59 Renmin Lu, 人民路59号; beers from ¥15; ⊘9am-late; 🛜) The eternally happening, Brit-run Bad Monkey brews its own strong ales (from ¥30; the IPA packs a punch), has nightly live music and endless drink specials. There's also reasonable pub grub (pizzas, burgers and shepherd's pie) and Sunday roast for ¥55. A couple of doors down is a second Bad Monkey, which is more of a music venue than a bar.

🛍 Shopping

Dàlǐ is famous for its marble blue and white batik printed on cotton and silk. There are many clothes shops around Dàlǐ. Most can also make clothes to your specifications – which will come as a relief when you see how small some of the ready-made clothing is.

Maps and books can be found at **Mandarin Books & CDs** (五华书苑, Wǔhuá Shūyuàn; Huguo Lu, 护国路; ⊘9.30am-9.30pm).

ℹ Information

All hostels and guesthouses and many hotels offer travel advice, arrange tours and book tickets for onward travel. There are also numerous travel agencies and cafes that will book bus tickets and offer all manner of tours. They can be expensive unless you can get a group together.

Bank of China (中国银行, Zhōngguó Yínháng; Fuxing Lu, 复兴路) Changes cash and travellers cheques and has an ATM.

China Post (中国邮政, Zhōngguó Yóuzhèng; cnr Fuxing Lu & Huguo Lu, 复兴路护国路的路口; ⊘8am-8pm) Dàlǐ's main post office.

Public Security Bureau (PSB, 公安局; Gōng'ānjú; ☎0872 214 2149; Dàlǐ Rd; ⊘8-11am & 2-5pm Mon-Fri) Note that visas cannot be renewed in Dàlǐ; you have to go to Xiàguān.

ℹ Getting There & Away

The golden rule: almost all buses advertised to Dàlǐ actually go to Xiàguān. Coming from Lìjiāng and Shangri-la, Xiàguān-bound buses stop at the eastern end of Dàlǐ to let passengers off before continuing on to Xiàguān's north bus station.

From Kūnmíng's west bus station there are numerous buses to Dàlǐ (¥110 to ¥137, four to five hours, every 15 minutes from 7.20am to 8.20pm). Heading north, it's easiest to pick up a bus on the roads outside the west or east gates; buy your ticket in advance from your guesthouse or a travel agent and they'll make sure you get on

the right one. (You could hail one yourself to save a surcharge but you're not guaranteed a seat.)

From the old town (near the west gate) you can catch a 30-seat bus to Kūnmíng for ¥130; it runs seven times a day, departing 8.30am, 9.30am, 10.30am, 11.30am, 1.30pm, 2.30pm and 4.30pm. There are also frequent buses from the old town to Lìjiāng (¥85) and Shangri-la (¥117).

Buses run regularly to Shāpíng (¥11), Xǐzhōu (¥7) and other local destinations from outside the west gate.

ℹ Getting Around

From Dàlǐ, a taxi to Xiàguān airport takes 45 minutes and costs around ¥100; to Xiàguān's train station it costs ¥50.

Bikes are the best way to get around and can be hired at numerous places from ¥25 to ¥40 per day. Try **Dàlǐ Bicycle Club** (大理自行车俱乐部, Dàlǐ Zìxíngchē Jùlèbù; 41 Boai Lu; ⊘7.30am-8pm), which rents bikes and scooters.

Buses (¥2, 30 minutes, marked 大理) run between the old town and Xiàguān from as early as 6.30am; wait along the highway and flag one down. Bus 8 runs between Dàlǐ and central Xiàguān (¥2, 30 minutes), close to the express bus station and the Xīngshèng bus station. Bus 4 also travels between Dàlǐ and central Xiàguān (¥2, 30 minutes). There is also an unmarked bus that runs past the west gate to and from the train station every 15 minutes from 6.30am (¥2, 30 minutes).

Ěrhǎi Lake   洱海湖

Ěrhǎi Lake (Ěrhǎi Hú; 'Ear-Shaped' Lake) dominates the local psyche. The seventh-biggest freshwater lake in China, it sits at 1973m above sea level and covers 250 sq km; it's also dotted with villages to visit and surrounded by trails perfect for bike rides.

⊙ Sights

Cáicūn (才村), a pleasant little village east of Dàlǐ (¥1.50 on bus 2), is the nexus of lake transport. All boat travel is on 'official' vessels. Expect to pay ¥180 for a three-hour trip, although you can normally haggle that down to ¥120 in low season.

If you want to head to the east side of the lake, bargain for a boat to take you to Tiānjìng Gé (天镜阁), from where you can pick up a bus to Wāsè or Shuānglǎng. You should pay no more than ¥100.

On the east side of the lake, the beautiful waterside town of Shuānglǎng (双廊) is extremely popular with domestic tourists. The town is a labyrinth of winding old alleys and traditional homes sitting on a little peninsula that juts into the lake.

Dàlǐ & Ěrhǎi Lake

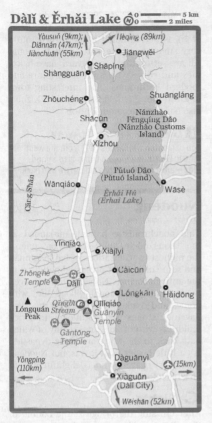

0   5 km
0   2 miles

Yóusuǒ (9km);
Diānnán (47km);
Jiànchuān (55km)

Héqìng (89km)

Jiāngwěi

Shāping

Shàngguān

Zhōuchéng

Shuāngláng

Shācūn

Nánzhào
Fēngqíng Dǎo
(Nánzhào Customs
Island)

Xīzhōu

Pǔtuó Dǎo
(Pǔtuó Island)

Wānqiáo

Ěrhǎi Hú
(Erhai Lake)

Wāsè

Cāng Shān

Yīnqiáo

Xiàjīyì

Zhōnghé
Temple

Dàlǐ

Cáicūn

Lóngkān

Hǎidōng

▲ Qīngbì
Lóngquán   Stream
Peak

Qīliqiáo
Guānyīn
Temple

Gǎntōng
Temple

Yǒngpíng
(110km)

Dàguānyì

Xiàguān
(Dàlǐ City)

(15km)

Wēishān (52km)

The other east-side highlight, close to Wāsè, is **Pǔtuó Dǎo** (普陀岛; Pǔtuó Island) and **Lesser Pǔtuó Temple** (小普陀寺, Xiǎopǔtuó Sì; Pǔtuó Island, 普陀岛), set on an extremely photogenic rocky outcrop.

Nánzhào Customs Island   ISLAND
(南诏风情岛, Nánzhào Fēngqíng Dǎo) This pleasant island has gardens, parks, a 17.5m-tall marble statue of Avalokiteshvara (Chenresig; aka Guanyin) and a hotel. Boats to the island cost ¥50, the price includes admission.

⚡ Activities

Roads encircle the lake so it is possible to do a loop (or partial loop) of the lake by mountain bike. A path goes from Cáicūn to Tǎo Yuán Port, which makes a great day trip (but most travellers turn around at Xīzhōu; 喜洲). Some hard-core cyclists continue right around the lake (the full loop is around 98km). The lack of boats means you're looking at an overnight stay or an extremely long ride in one day.

🛏 Sleeping

There are several guesthouses, as well as upmarket boutique hotels, in Cáicūn and Shuāngláng.

Sky & Sea Lodge   GUESTHOUSE $
(海地生活, Hǎidì Shēnghuó; ☑ 0872 246 1762; www.skysealodge.org; dm ¥40, d ¥120-1000; 🛜) Even the dorm at this peaceful lakeside hotel in Shuāngláng has decent views of Ěrhǎi Lake. Private rooms range from the functional to the swish, and most have balconies overlooking the lake. Friendly staff. You can't take a taxi there so you'll have to walk about 10 to 15 minutes through the village, ask locals to point the way.

Neverland   HOSTEL $
(牛背山国际青年旅舍, Niúbèishān Guójì Qīngnián Lǚshè; ☑ 0872 269 1677; Caicun Port, 才村码头; dm ¥35, d ¥108-228; ❄🛜) On the street leading to the boat dock, close to where the bus drops you off, this hostel caters mostly to Chinese travellers, but is friendly, and the light-filled, spacious rooms are decent value. There's a communal area and it offers Western and Chinese dishes.

❶ Getting There & Away

Bus 2 runs from Dàlǐ to Cáicūn, (¥1.50, 15 minutes), where you can pick up boats around Ěrhǎi Lake. Alternatively, head to Xiàguān's east bus station, where you can find regular buses to Shuāngláng and Wāsè and other destinations on the east side of the lake.

Cāng Shān   苍山

The range of gorgeous peaks known as Cāng Shān rises imposingly above Dàlǐ and offers the best legwork in the area. Most travellers head first for **Zhōnghé Temple** (中和寺, Zhōnghé Sì), on the side of **Zhōnghé Shān** (中和山, Zhōnghé Mountain; ¥40; ⏰ 8am-6pm). At the temple, be careful of imposter monks passing out incense and then demanding ¥200 for a blessing.

◉ Sights & Activities

You can hike up the mountain, a sweaty two to three hours for those in moderately good shape (but note the warning that there have been several reports of robbery of solo walkers). Keep your eyes peeled for the elusive red panda, a number of which have been spotted here recently. Walk about 200m north of the **chairlift** (苍山索道, Cāng Shān Suǒdào; return ¥60) base to the riverbed. Follow the left bank for about 50m and walk through the cemetery, then follow the path zigzagging under the chairlift. When you reach some stone steps, you know you are near the top. This is but one of several paths to the temple.

Branching out from either side of Zhōnghé Temple is a trail that winds along the face of the mountains, taking you in and out of steep, lush valleys and past streams and waterfalls. From the temple, it's a nice 11km walk south to **Gǎntōng Temple** (感通寺, Gǎntōng Sì), **Qīngbì Stream** (清碧溪, Qīngbì Xī) and/or **Guānyīn Temple** (观音堂, Guānyīn Táng), from where you can continue to the road and pick up a Dàlǐ-bound bus. The path, called **Jade Belt Road** (玉带路; Yùdài Lù), is paved and easily walkable.

There's also a **cable car** (感通寺索道, Gǎntōng Sì Suǒdào; one-way/return ¥50/80) between Qīngbì Stream and Gǎntōng Temple.

Alternatively, take the new **cable car** (洗马潭索道, Xǐmǎ Tán Suǒdào; return ¥280) up to the **Horse Washing Pond** (洗马潭, Xǐ Mǎ Tán), high in the mountain range, where Kublai Khan set up his base in the late 13th century. If you buy your ticket from your hostel, or online, you should get ¥50 off the price.

🛏 Sleeping

Higherland Inn INN
(高地旅馆, Gāodì Lǚguǎn; ☑0872 266 1599; www.higherlandinn.com; dm ¥30, d ¥80-120) Simple rooms, all with shared bathroom, high up in the Cāng Shān. There's also an artists studio here.

ℹ Information

On hikes around Cāng Shān there have been several reports of robbery of solo walkers. As ever, watch your bags and possessions when on buses and trains.

ℹ Getting There & Away

The starting point for Cāng Shān treks is walking distance from Dàlǐ.

Xīzhōu 喜洲
☑0872 / POP 2,500

A trip to the old town of Xīzhōu for a look at its well preserved Bai architecture is lovely, and some travellers now make it their base for exploring the area around Dàlǐ.

Although you're just a 30-minute bus ride from Dàlǐ, and there are places in the village where you can find beds for as little as ¥80, the **Linden Centre** (喜林苑,

Xǐ Lín Yuàn; ☑0872 245 2988; www.linden-centre.com; 5 Chengbei; d/ste incl breakfast ¥980/1480; @🛜), is a traditional home turned into a very smart boutique hotel with 16 rooms. All are set around a courtyard, have balconies and come with antique furniture and modern bathrooms. The interesting town of **Zhōuchéng** (州城), 7km north of Xīzhōu, also has basic accommodation.

ℹ Getting There & Away

You can catch a local bus (¥7) from the west gate in Dàlǐ, but a bicycle trip is also a good idea – although it's a long ride there and back.

Nuòdèng 诺邓
☑0872 / POP 1200

This anachronistic hamlet, oft-lauded as the 'thousand-year-old' village, has one of the highest concentrations of Bai in Yúnnán and some of the best preserved buildings in the entire province. Nuòdèng has managed to maintain traditional village life, with ponies and donkeys clomping up the steep flagstone streets past traditional mudbrick buildings with ornate gates, many of which date back to the Ming and Qing dynasties. It's a little busier than it was, but Nuòdèng is still very peaceful and a delightful place to kick back for a while.

⊙ Sights

After crossing the bridge at the bottom of the village you'll see one of the original **salt wells**, located inside a wooden shed. The town is built upon a steep hill and winding up through the alleys you'll reach an impressive **Confucian Temple** (孔庙; Kǒngmiào), which today serves as the village primary school (check out the detailed frescoes still visible on the ceiling). Further uphill is the picturesque 16th-century **Yuhuang Pavillion** (玉皇阁; Yùhuáng Gé).

Village life is centred on the small **market square**; a good place to catch some sun and gab with the local elders.

On the way to Nuòdèng village from Yúnlóng, the **Bi River** is forced by the surrounding hills into a serpentine roll that from above looks remarkably like a yin-yang symbol (Tàijítú; 太极图). You won't notice this natural phenomenon from ground level; you need to go up to a viewing platform on the nearby hill. The road to the pavilion is 7km of endless switchbacks, a tedious and tiring hike, or you could hire a rickshaw to take you there and back for ¥60 to ¥80.

YÚNNÁN XĪZHŌU

🛏 Sleeping

There are a few guesthouses in the village, but locals also advertise beds in their houses for as little as ¥30.

Fùjiǎ Liúfāngyuàn INN $
(复甲留方苑; ☑0872 572 3466; 502609@qq.com; dm ¥35, d ¥78-288; 🛜) Big rooms and sit-down toilets at this friendly, family-run guesthouse set around a lush garden of bougainvillea. The new annexe offers very comfortable rooms and a terrace that overlooks the village and is perfect for stargazing. It's right at the top of the village; call ahead and they'll come and meet you.

Luwo International Youth Hostel HOSTEL $
(驴窝驿国际青年旅舍; Lǘwōyì Guójì Qīngnián Lǚshě; ☑137 2507 3636; 674766748@qq.com; dm ¥35, d with/without bathroom ¥128/78; 🛜) This hostel at the top of the village – follow the signs – has sizeable rooms set around a large courtyard. Thin mattresses but everything is clean, there's a separate bar area and the staff speak some English.

🍴 Eating

★ **Yán Quán Nóngjiā** YUNNAN $$
(盐泉农家; ☑0872 552 5111; dishes from ¥20; ⏱11am-8pm) The one genuine restaurant in the village is also one of the most famous in Yúnnán, after being featured on the hit Chinese TV show *A Bite of China*. People come from far and wide to sample *huǒtuǐ* (火腿; ¥40), a slightly salty cured ham that is the local speciality. And it tastes great, as do the all-natural veggies and tofu. It's at the base of the village over a little bridge.

ℹ Getting There & Away

Buses (¥39, three hours, every 40 minutes from 7.50am to 4.30pm) leave from Xiàguān's express bus station to the sleepy county seat **Yúnlóng** (云龙), from where you can take a three-wheel rickshaw or minivan (¥30) the final 7km to Nuòdèng. Buses back to Xiàguān leave on a similar schedule; the final departure is at 4.30pm. At the time of writing there were no buses running to Lánpíng (兰坪), but if they start again you can change at Lánpíng for buses to Liùkù. There are also two daily buses to Kūnmíng (¥175 to ¥189; seven to eight hours, 9am and 10.30am).

Shāxī 沙溪
☑0872

The tiny hamlet of Shāxī, 120km northwest of Dàlǐ, is an evocative throwback to the days of the Tea Horse Road. (You can almost hear the clippety-clop of horses' hooves and shouts of traders.) It is one of only three surviving caravan oases that stretched from Yúnnán to India and is by far the best preserved – and the only one with a functioning **market** (Friday), when Bai and Yi villagers converge on the town. If you're here then, check out the animal trading down by the river.

The village's wooden houses, courtyards and narrow, winding streets make it a popular location for period Chinese movies and

---

THE TEA HORSE ROAD

Less well known than the Silk Road, but equally important in terms of trade and the movement of ideas, people and religions, the Tea Horse Road (茶马古道; Chámǎgǔdào) linked southwest China with India via Tibet. A series of caravan routes, rather than a single road, which also went through parts of Sìchuān, Myanmar (Burma), Laos and Nepal, the trails started deep in the jungle of Xīshuāngbǎnnà. They then headed north through Dàlǐ and Lìjiāng and into the thin air of the Himalayan mountains on the way to the Tibetan capital Lhasa, before turning south to India and Myanmar.

Although archaeological finds indicate that stretches of the different routes were in use thousands of years ago, the road really began life in the Tang dynasty (AD 618–907). An increased appetite for tea in Tibet led to an arrangement with the Chinese imperial court to barter Yúnnán tea for the prized horses ridden by Tibetan warriors. By the Song dynasty (AD 960–1279), 20,000 horses a year were coming down the road to China, while in 1661 alone some 1.5 million kilograms of tea headed to Tibet.

Sugar and salt were also carried by the caravans of horses, mules and yaks. Buddhist monks, Christian missionaries and foreign armies utilised the trails as well to move between Myanmar, India and China. In the 18th century the Chinese stopped trading for Tibetan horses and the road went into a slow decline. Its final glory days came during WWII, when it was a vital conduit for supplies from India for the Allied troops fighting the Japanese in China. The advent of peace and the communist takeover of 1949 put an end to the road.

TV shows, and there are ever-increasing numbers of domestic day trippers. However, this is still a wonderfully relaxed place where you can spend the night sitting by the river under a canopy of stars and listening to the frogs croaking in the rice paddies.

Sights

Sideng Jie (寺登街) is the ancient town street leading off the main road. It's about 300m downhill to the multifrescoed **Xìngjiào Sì** (兴教寺, Xìngjiào Temple; Shiji Guangchang, 市集广场; ¥20; ⊙9am-5pm), the only Ming dynasty Bai Buddhist temple. On the opposite side of the courtyard is the **Three Terraced Pavilion** (魁星阁, Kuíxīnggé; Shiji Guangchang, 市集广场; ¥20; ⊙9am-5pm), which has a prominent theatrical stage (古戏台; *gǔxìtái*), something of a rarity in rural Yúnnán. There is a small museum here, ask the guard at the temple for the key. The absolute highlight, however, is the **Ōuyáng Courtyard** (欧阳大院, Ōuyáng Dàyuàn; off Sideng Jie) **FREE**, a superb example of three-in-one Bai folk architecture in which one wall protected three yards/residences. Sadly, most of it is currently closed to the public, although you can poke your head inside for a quick look.

Exit the east gate and head south along the Huì River (惠江; Huì Jiāng) for five minutes, cross the ancient **Yùjīn Qiáo** (玉津桥; Yùjīn Bridge), and you're walking the same trail as the horse caravans. If you look hard enough, you'll still be able to see hoofprints etched into the rock, or so the locals claim. Ponies can be rented for ¥40 an hour by the river, if you want to ride part of the trail yourself.

Otherwise, the main activity around town is walking. The guesthouses in town have maps that can get you started and keep you busy for days.

Sleeping

Waiting for Shāxī   INN $
(沙溪古宇, Shāxī Gǔyǔ; ☑0872 472 1877; Beiguzong Xiang, 北古宗巷; r ¥120; ☎) The rooms aren't large at this traditional courtyard house, but they're comfortable enough with reasonable beds and are set around a small garden with a well. There's also a well stocked bar.

Horsepen 46   INN $
(马圈46客栈, Mǎjuàn Sìshíliù Kèzhàn; ☑0872 472 2299; www.horsepen46.com; 46 Sideng Jie, 寺登街46号; dm ¥30, r ¥80-120; @☎) In-demand

guesthouse with cute, compact rooms surrounding a sunny little courtyard. There's a laid-back traveller vibe here with daily communal dinners (¥25). There's also free laundry, bike hire (¥20 per day) and the helpful English-speaking staff can organise hikes in the area. It's tucked away to the right of the stage in the village square.

Old Theatre Inn   GUESTHOUSE $$$
(戏台会馆, Xìtái Huìguǎn; ☑0872 472 2296; reservations@shaxichina.com; Duànjiādēng Village, 段家登; r incl breakfast ¥520; @☎) This boutique guesthouse has been lovingly restored out of a 200-year-old Chinese theatre and inn. There are only five very comfortable rooms here, all with photogenic views towards the nearby mountains; book ahead. It's located 3km north of Shāxī; you can rent a bike here (¥20) to get around.

Eating

Lóngfèng Ruìyīng Qīngzhēn Fànguǎn   YUNNAN $
(龙凤瑞英清真饭馆; dishes from ¥10; ⊙7.30am-10pm) Excellent Huí-run restaurant on Shāxī's 'main' street. It's good for a noodle breakfast, or dinner. Try the *gānbā* (dried beef) or *zàn shuǐ kǔ cài*, a spinachlike vegetable that comes with a spicy dipping sauce. To find it, turn left at the top of Sideng Jie and walk for two minutes and look for the green sign with white characters.

★ **Hungry Buddha**   ITALIAN $$
(大嘴佛, Dàzuǐ Fó; www.soundinner.com; Sideng Jie, 寺登街; mains from ¥60; ⊙11am-9pm Tue-Sun; ☎♪) The most sophisticated eatery in town, and one of the most notable in all Yúnnán, with a mouth-watering, all-vegetarian menu utilising locally produced ingredients. Great homemade cheese, pasta and pizza, as well as a fine breakfast. Proper wine list too. There are only 10 spots at the wooden counter where you eat and watch your meal being prepared, so grab one early.

Getting There & Away

From Jiànchuān (剑川), minivans (¥13, 45 minutes) run to and from Shāxī. Moving on, you'll have to backtrack to Jiànchuān. There are buses every 20 to 30 minutes to Dàlǐ (¥39) between 6.30am and 6pm. To Lìjiāng (¥23, 1½ hours) there are buses at 9am, 10am, 11.30am, 1.30pm, 2.30pm and 3.30pm. Buses to Kūnmíng (¥168) leave at 9.30am and 6pm, and to Shangri-la (¥46) at 9am and 10am.

NORTHWEST YÚNNÁN

Northwest Yúnnán is a gorgeous blend of soaring mountains, pristine lakes and dizzyingly deep gorges and valleys. This is the part of Yúnnán to head to for epic treks: whether in the shadow of the 6000m peaks around Déqīn, or through the stunning Tiger Leaping Gorge. But the region is also home to the little-seen Nù Jiāng Valley, where Yúnnán meets both Tibet and Myanmar, and Lúgū Hú, a vast lake that straddles the Yúnnán–Sìchuān border and is home to the Mosuo people, the last matriarchal society in the world. If that wasn't enough, there are also the towns of Shangri-la, with its intriguing blend of Tibetan and Han Chinese culture, and Lìjiāng, a Unesco World Heritage Site that sucks in both domestic and foreign visitors.

The main towns in the region – Lìjiāng and Shangri-la – have a wide range of hostels, guesthouses and hotels that cater to every budget and taste. You'll also find many hostels and guesthouses in the popular trekking destinations around Déqīn, in Bīngzhōngluò in the Nù Jiāng Valley, Lúgū Hú and Tiger Leaping Gorge. Elsewhere, accommodation options tend to be standard budget or midrange hotels.

Lìjiāng and Shangri-la have the best restaurants in Northwest Yúnnán, with many Chinese and Western options. In Lìjiāng, make sure to try the cuisine of the local Naxi minority, while Shangri-la is a great place to sample Tibetan cooking. More remote destinations, such as around Déqīn and the Nù Jiāng Valley, have far fewer restaurants and many people eat in their guesthouses.

Lìjiāng and Shangri-la are the only places in Northwest Yúnnán with airports and train stations (although the railway isn't scheduled to reach Shangri-la until 2019), and from them you can connect to destinations across Yúnnán and beyond. But buses are the main way to get around this region and with roads winding through mountain passes, journey times can be long.

Lìjiāng 丽江

☏ 0888 / POP 40,000

How popular is this time-locked place? Lìjiāng's maze of cobbled streets, rickety (or rickety-looking, given gentrification) wooden buildings and gushing canals suck in over *eight million* people a year. So thick are the crowds in the narrow alleys that it can feel like they've all arrived at the same time.

JADE DRAGON SNOW MOUNTAIN 玉龙雪山

Also known as Mt Satseto, **Yùlóng Xuěshān** (Jade Dragon Snow Mountain; ¥135, plus Lijiang old town entrance ticket ¥80) soars to some 5500m. Its peak was first climbed in 1963 by a research team from Běijīng and now, at some 35km from Lìjiāng, it is regularly mobbed by hordes of Chinese tour groups and travellers, especially in the summer.

Buses from Lìjiāng arrive at a parking area where you can purchase tickets for the various cable cars and chairlifts that ascend the mountain. This is also where the **Impression Lijiang** (p699) show is held, a mega song-and-dance performance. Note that if you are going to the performance you will also have to pay the park admission fees. Close to the parking area is **Dry Sea Meadow** (干海子; Gànhǎizi), a good spot for photographing the mountain.

A **cable car** (¥180) ascends the mountain to an elevation of 4506m; from here you can walk up another 200m to a viewing point to see the glacier near the peak. It can often get chilly near the top so bring warm clothes. You will also have to pay ¥20 for the bus ticket to the base of the cable car.

Back down at the parking lot you can switch to a bus that goes to **Blue Moon Lake** (蓝月湖; Lányuè Hú) and **White Water River** (白水河; Báishuǐ Hé), where a walking trail leads along the river up to the lake (the round-trip walk takes about 90 minutes). The cable-car bus ticket is also good for the bus to the lake.

A 10-minute drive past Blue Moon Lake is **Yak Meadow** (牦牛坪; Máoniú Píng), where a **chairlift** (¥85, plus ¥20 bus ticket) pulls visitors up to an altitude of 3500m.

In summer, when crowds for the cable car are long (up to two hours' wait), most travellers just do the trip to the lake and Yak Meadow.

Minibuses (¥30) leave from opposite Lìjiāng's Mao Sq. Returning to Lìjiāng, buses leave fairly regularly but check with your driver to find out what time the last bus will depart.

Lìjiāng

YÚNNÁN LÌJIĀNG

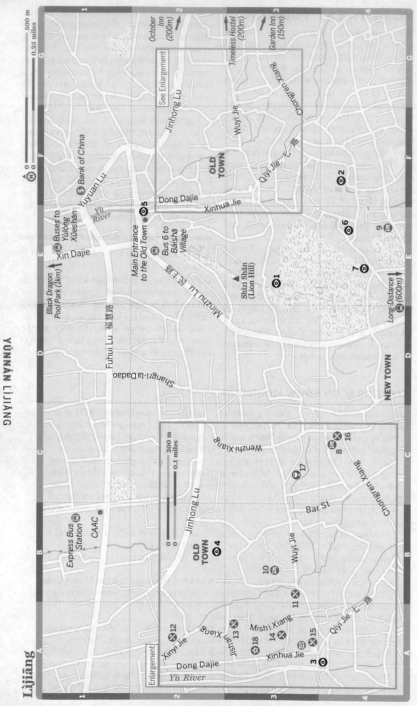

October Inn (200m)
Timeless Hostel (200m)
Garden Inn (150m)

Jinhong Lu
Wuyi Jie
Chongren Xiang
Qiyi Jie 七一路

See Enlargement

OLD TOWN

Bank of China
Yuyuan Lu
Buses to Yùlóng Xuěshān
Xin Dajie
Black Dragon Pool Park (1km)
Fuhui Lu 福慧路
Shangri-la Dadao

Dong Dajie
Xinhua Jie

Yù River
Main Entrance to the Old Town

Bus 6 to Báishā Village
Minzhu Lu 民主路
Shizi Shān (Lion Hill)

NEW TOWN

Long-Distance (600m)

Express Bus Station
CAAC

Jinhong Lu

OLD TOWN

200 m
0.1 miles

Wenzhi Xiang
Chongren Xiang
Bar St
Wuyi Jie

Dong Dajie
Yù River
Xinyi Jie
Jishan Xiang
Mishi Xiang
Xinhua Jie
Qiyi Jie 七一路

Enlargement

1
2
3
4
5
6
7
8
9
10
11
12
13
14
15
16
17
18

500 m
0.25 miles

Lìjiāng

But remember the 80/20 rule: 80% of the tourists will be in 20% of the places. Get up early enough and you can often beat the crowds. And when they do appear, that's the cue to hop on a bike and cycle out to one of the nearby villages.

⊙ Sights

Visitors to Lìjiāng's old town have long been required to buy a 'protection fee' ticket, allegedly for preservation projects, but now proof of payment is being enforced much more rigidly. The ticket is valid for 15 days and you'll need to hang onto it, as there are now ticket checks at the entrances leading into the old town. You will also need it to gain free entry to Black Dragon Pool, as well as to other sites such as Yùlóng Xuěshān (p693).

Old Town   HISTORIC SITE
(丽江古城, Lìjiāng Gǔchéng; ¥80) The old town is centred on the busy and touristy **Old Market Square** (四方街, Sìfang Jiē). The surrounding lanes are dissected by a web of artery-like canals that once brought the city's drinking water from Yuquan Spring, on the far outskirts of what is now Black Dragon Pool Park. Several wells and pools are still in use around town (but hard to find). Where there are three pools, these were designated into pools for drinking, washing clothes and washing vegetables.

A famous example of these is the **White Horse Dragon Pool** (白马龙潭, Báimǎlóng Tán) in the deep south of the old town, where you can still see the locals washing their veggies after buying them in the market.

Now acting as sentinel of sorts for the town, the **Looking at the Past Pavillion** (望古楼, Wànggǔ Lóu; incl in ¥80 old town entrance

ticket; ⊙8.30am-6pm) has a unique design using dozens of four-storey pillars – culled from northern Yúnnán old-growth forests.

A must-see is **Zhōngyì Market** (忠义市场, Zhōngyì Shìchǎng; Xianghe Lu, 祥和路; ⊙6am-5pm) where locals sell produce, copper items and livestock. If you are craving a slice of old Lìjiāng, this is where you'll find it.

Black Dragon Pool Park   PARK
(黑龙潭公园, Hēilóngtán Gōngyuán; Xin Dajie, 新大街; incl with town entrance ticket; ⊙7am-8pm) On the northern edge of town is the Black Dragon Pool Park; its view of Yùlóng Xuěshān (p693) is an obligatory photo shoot in southwestern China. The **Dōngbā Research Institute** (东巴文化研究室, Dōngbā Wénhuà Yánjiūshì; ⊙8am-5pm Mon-Fri) is part of a renovated complex on the hillside here. You can see Naxi cultural artefacts and scrolls featuring a unique pictograph script.

Trails lead up **Xiàng Shān** (Elephant Hill, 象山) to a dilapidated gazebo and then across a spiny ridge past a communications centre and back down the other side, making a nice morning hike, but note that there have been reports of solo women travellers being robbed in this area.

OLD TOWN, NEW TOWN

A Unesco World Heritage Site since 1997, Lìjiāng is a city of two halves: the old town and the very modern new town. The old town is where you'll be spending your time and it's a jumble of lanes that twist and turn. If you get lost (and most do), head upstream and you'll make your way back to the main square.

The **Museum of Naxi Dongba Culture** (纳西东巴文化博物馆, Nàxī Dōngbā Wénhuà Bówùguǎn; incl in ¥80 old town entrance ticket; ⊙8.30am-4.30pm) is at the park's northern entrance and is a decent introduction to traditional Naxi lifestyle and religion, complete with good English captions.

Note that the pool has dried up in recent years and without water some visitors are disappointed with this site; ask at your guesthouse first if the pool has water before deciding whether or not to visit.

Mu Family Mansion HISTORIC SITE
(木氏土司府, Mùshì Tǔsīfǔ; ¥60; ⊙8.30am-5.30pm) The former home of a Naxi chieftain, the Mu Family Mansion was heavily renovated (more like built from scratch) after the devastating earthquake that struck Lìjiāng in 1996. Mediocre captions do a poor job of introducing the Mu family but many travellers find the beautiful grounds reason enough to visit. Bizarrely, this sight is not covered by the old town entrance ticket.

👉 Tours

It is possible to see most of Lìjiāng's environs on your own, but a few agencies in Lìjiāng, such as Keith Lyons, offer half- or full-day tours, starting from ¥200, plus fees.

Keith Lyons TOUR
(☑137 6900 1439; keithalyons@gmail.com; per day from ¥200) Lìjiāng-based guide Keith Lyons runs tours and treks, specialising in the area outside Lìjiāng.

🎊 Festivals & Events

Fertility Festival CULTURAL
(⊙late Mar/early Apr) Held on the 13th day of the third moon, this festival sees Naxi people offering a sacrifice – normally a goat – to their patron saint Sānduǒ (三朵). The biggest celebration takes place at the Sānduǒ Temple (三朵寺; Sānduǒ Sì) on Yùlóng Xuěshān, where there's a big market and much revelry.

Torch Festival CULTURAL
(⊙Jul) The torch festival (Huǒbǎ Jié) is also celebrated by the Bai in the Dàlǐ region and the Yi all over the southwest. The origin of this festival can be traced back to the Nanzhao kingdom, when the wife of a man burned to death by the king eluded the romantic entreaties of the monarch by leaping into a fire.

These days, flaming torches are paraded through the streets to much merriment.

🛏 Sleeping

Rising rents mean that most guesthouses have relocated to just outside the old town, either north or south. Nevertheless, there are still well over a thousand places to stay in the old town, with more appearing all the time. Many have fewer than 10 rooms. In peak season (especially public holidays), prices double (or more).

October Inn GUESTHOUSE $
(汤姆家, Tāngmǔ Jiā; ☑139 8704 6967; www.october-inn.com; Xuantian Xiang, 玄天巷; 8-/4-bed dm ¥35/40, d & tw ¥120-160; 🖭) An intimate, secluded, increasingly popular guesthouse

THE NAXI

Lìjiāng has been the homeland of the 300,000-odd Naxi (纳西; pronounced 'na-see', also spelt Nakhi and Nahi) minority for about the last 1400 years. The Naxi descend from ethnically Tibetan Qiang tribes and lived until recently in matrilineal families. Since local rulers were always male it wasn't truly matriarchal, but women still seemed to run the show.

The Naxi matriarchs maintained their hold over the men with flexible arrangements for love affairs. The *azhu* (friend) system allowed a couple to become lovers without setting up joint residence. Both partners would continue to live in their respective homes; the boyfriend would spend the nights at his girlfriend's house but return to live and work at his mother's house during the day. Any children born to the couple belonged to the woman, who was responsible for bringing them up. The man provided support, but once the relationship was over, so was the support. Children lived with their mothers and no special effort was made to recognise paternity. Women inherited all property and disputes were adjudicated by female elders.

There are strong matriarchal influences in the Naxi language. Nouns enlarge their meaning when the word for 'female' is added; conversely, the addition of the word for 'male' will decrease the meaning. For example, 'stone' plus 'female' conveys the idea of a boulder; 'stone' plus 'male' conveys the idea of a pebble.

Useful phrases in Naxi are nuar lala (hello) and jiu bai sai (thank you).

with excellent, spacious dorms, a handful of private rooms – book ahead – and a cool roof terrace with great views. There are daily communal dinners (¥25) and bike hire is ¥30. It's a steep, 15-minute climb from the old town; call ahead and they'll pick you up when you arrive in Lìjiāng.

Timeless Hostel HOSTEL $
(久居丽江青年旅舍, Jiǔ Jū Lìjiāng Qīngnián Lǚshě; ☑0888 517 4626; lijiang.timeless@gmail.com; 63 Wenming Xiang, Wuyi Jie, Yishang, 义尚村五一街文明巷63号; dm/d ¥45/196; @☎) This amiable hostel at the quieter eastern end of Wuyi Jie has some of the best dorms in town: large with ensuite bathrooms and big lockers, as well as clean private rooms with shared balconies. All are set around a pleasant courtyard. The attached restaurant and bar are good for both meals and hanging out. Bike hire is ¥30.

Garden Inn GUESTHOUSE $
(丽江文庙国际客栈, Lìjiāng Wénmiào Guójì Kèzhàn; ☑151 0887 3494; www.mayhostel.wix.com/gardeninn; 7 Wenmiao Xiang, Beimen Jie, 文庙巷7号,北门街; dm ¥40, d ¥168-238; @☎) Now relocated higher up and just outside the old town (the views are better), this popular but peaceful hostel has compact, rather dark dorms, but they have their own bathrooms and the beds have proper mattresses. Private rooms are big with shared balconies and there's a roof terrace. There's a small communal area and the helpful staff can arrange tours.

It's up an alley just off Jinhong Lu, which the locals know as Bximen Jie. Call ahead and staff will come and get you.

Mama Naxi's Guesthouse GUESTHOUSE $
(妈妈纳西客栈, Māmā Nàxī Kèzhàn; ☑0888 510 0700; mamanaxi@hotmail.com; 22 Jixiang Lu, 吉祥路22号; 8-/6-bed dm ¥30/35, d ¥120-140; ☺@☎) Yet another long-time guesthouse driven out of the old town by rising rents, the new Mama Naxi is a rather swish place in a quiet residential compound close to the bus station. Dorms are spacious and the private rooms are comfortable, although it feels more like a hotel than a traditional guesthouse. It hosts daily communal dinners (¥25) and the staff remain friendly.

This is a good place to book tours to the surrounding area. Bike hire is ¥25 per day. It's difficult to find (no sign pointing the way), so call ahead and they will pick you up.

★**Blossom Hill Joyland** BOUTIQUE HOTEL $$$
(花间堂, Huājiān Táng; ☑4000 767 123; www.blossomhillinn.com; 55 Wenhua Xiang, Wuyi Jie, 五一

街文华巷55号; d ¥480-1280; ✳☎) There are only 18 rooms, all individually decorated in very tasteful and comfortable fashion, at this very popular boutique inn in the heart of the old town. Bathrooms are modern and large, while each room comes with its own collection of antiques and wood furnishings. Staff are helpful and there's a small common area with a library. It's essential to book ahead.

Intercontinental Lìjiāng HOTEL $$$
(丽江和府洲际度假酒店, Lìjiāng Héfǔ Zhōují Jiàrì Jiǔdiàn; ☑0888 558 8888; www.intercontinental.com; 276 Xianghe Lu, 祥和路276号; r ¥2200-4100; ✳@☎) The former Crowne Plaza is the best hotel in the old town, a magical space with lofty ceilings, little gardens and epic views of the Jade Dragon Mountain. The bathrooms are the finest in town, the beds huge and comfy. Other amenities include two restaurants, a swimming pool, day spa and children's play room. Discounts of 25% are sometimes available.

Zen Garden Hotel HOTEL $$$
(瑞和园酒店, Ruìhé Yuán Jiǔdiàn; ☑0888 518 9799; www.zengardenhotel.com; 36 Xingren Lane, Wuyi Jie, 五一街兴仁下段36号; r ¥500-2600; ☎) As befits its name, this is a serene, hushed establishment. Run by a Naxi teacher and decorated with help from her artist brother, the furniture and design in the communal areas are lovely, even if the cheapest rooms are a little plain for the price. Discounts of 30% are sometimes available.

✖ Eating

There are many, many eateries around the old town, and almost every menu will have both Chinese and Western dishes.

Bābā is the Lìjiāng local speciality – thick flatbreads of wheat, served plain or stuffed with meat, vegetables or sweets. There are always several 'Naxi' items on menus, including the famous 'Naxi omelette' and 'Naxi

Around Lìjiāng

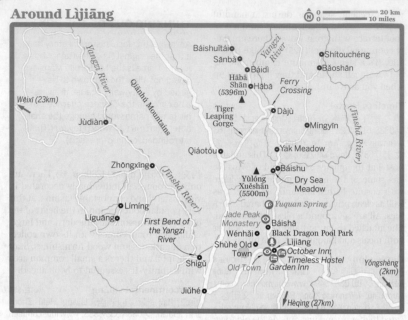

sandwich' (goat's cheese, tomato and fried egg between two pieces of local *bābā*). Try locally produced *qīng méi jiǔ* (a plum-based wine with a 500-year history) – it tastes like a semisweet sherry.

★ Tiāntiān Xiān   YUNNAN $

(天天鲜; ☑ 0888 518 4933; 47 Wangjiazhuang Xiang, Wuyi Jie, 五一街王家庄巷47号; dishes from ¥12; ☺ 11am-9pm) Locals flock here for the superb grilled fish and chicken and soybean-paste dishes (get here before 7pm or it will have run out). But all the Naxi specialities on offer are fantastic and great value. No English spoken, but there is an English menu. To find it, look for the three characters with 'Daily Fresh' written in English underneath them.

Sakura Good Food Square   YUNNAN $

(Yīnghuā Méishí Guángchǎng, Qiyi Jie, 樱花美食广场; snacks from ¥20; ☺ 10am-late; 🅰) Snackers should not miss the open-air food market where vendors sell appetising bite-size treats, some of which are native to Lìjiāng. Try the *Nàxī kǎo qiézi* (纳西烤茄子; Naxi grilled eggplant), served in a boat-shaped crust; *tǔ dòu bǐng* (土豆饼; Naxi potato pancake), and *Nàxī kǎolà cháng* (纳西烤腊肠; Naxi grilled, salty sausage) made with pork, fat and pepper.

Āmāyì Nàxī Snacks   YUNNAN $$

(阿妈意纳西饮食院, Āmāyì Nàxī Yínshí Yuàn; ☑ 0888 530 9588; Wuyi Jie, 五一街; dishes from ¥18; ☺ 11am-10pm) This calm courtyard restaurant offers a small but select and very authentic selection of Naxi cuisine. There are fantastic mushroom dishes, when in season, as well as *zhútǒng fàn* (rice packed in bamboo). It's down an alley off Wuyi Jie, close to the Stone Bridge.

Prague Cafe   CAFE $$

(布拉格咖啡馆, Bùlāgé Kāfēiguǎn; 80 Mishi Xiang, 密士巷80号; breakfast from ¥30, mains from ¥40; ☺ 8am-11pm; 🛜) Something of an oasis in the heart of the old town, with good coffee and tea, solid breakfasts and a selection of Western and Japanese dishes, as well as books to read. It serves alcohol too.

Lamu's House of Tibet   TIBETAN $$

(西藏屋西餐馆, Xīzàngwū Xīcāntíng; ☑ 0888 511 5776; 56 Xinyi Jie, 新义街56号; dishes from ¥20; ☺ 9.30am-10.30pm; 🛜) Friendly Lamu has been serving up smiles and hearty Tibetan and international fare for more than a decade. Ascend the little wooden staircase to the 2nd-floor dining area, a great spot for people-watching, and try the excellent Naxiburger, or choose from the selection of Tibetan dishes. There's also a good selection of paperback books to thumb through.

N's Kitchen INTERNATIONAL $$

(二楼小厨, Èrlóu Xiǎochú; ☑0888 512 0060; 17 Jishan Xiang, Xinyi Jie; breakfast from ¥20, mains from ¥28; ☺9am-10pm; ☎) Clamber up the steep stairs for one of the best breakfasts in town, a monster burger and fine Yúnnán coffee. It's a reliable source of travel info too and can arrange bus tickets.

🍷 Drinking & Nightlife

Stone the Crows BAR

(134-? Wenzhi Xiang, 文治巷134-2号; beers from ¥25; ☺6pm-late) Worth checking out is this foreign-owned, endearingly ramshackle bar with a good range of local and foreign beers and a mixed crowd of locals (many musicians who play in the nearby bars come here) and Westerners. There's a pool table and decent pub food: pizza, pies and burgers. It gets going later rather than earlier.

☆ Entertainment

Impression Lìjiāng DANCE

(tickets ¥230; ☺1pm daily) This big song and dance show, squarely aimed at local tour groups, takes place at the foot of Yùlóng Xuěshān.

Nàxī Orchestra LIVE MUSIC

(纳西古乐会, Nàxī Gǔyuè Huì; Nàxī Music Academy; Xinhua Jie, 新华街; tickets ¥120-160; ☺8pm) Attending a performance of this orchestra inside a beautiful building in the old town is a good way to spend an evening in Lìjiāng. Not only are all two dozen or so members Naxi, but they play a type of Taoist temple

music (known as *dòngjīng*) that has been lost elsewhere in China.

ℹ️ Information

Crowded, narrow streets are a pickpocket's heaven. Solo women travellers have been mugged when walking alone at night in isolated areas. Xiàng Shān (Elephant Hill) in Black Dragon Pool Park (Hēilóngtán Gōngyuán) has been the site of quite a few robberies. Pay admission at the entrance to the Old Town (p695).

Bank of China (中国银行, Zhōngguó Yínháng; Yuyuan Lu, 玉缘路; ☺9am-5pm) This branch has an ATM and is convenient for the old town. There are many ATMs in the old town too.

China Post (中国邮政, Zhōngguó Yóuzhèng; Minzhu Lu, 民主路; ☺8.30am-6pm) In the old town just north of Old Market Sq.

Public Security Bureau (PSB, 公安局, Gōng'ānjú; ☑0888 518 8437; 110 Taihe Jie, 110 Taihe Lu, 太和路110号; ☺8.30-11.30am & 2.30-5.30pm Mon-Fri) Come here for visa extensions. Located on the west side of the Government Building. A taxi here will cost ¥15 from the city centre.

ℹ️ Getting There & Away

AIR

Lìjiāng's airport is 28km east of town. Tickets can be booked at **CAAC** (中国民航, Zhōngguó Mínháng; cnr Fuhui Lu & Shangrila Dadao; ☺8.30am-9pm). Most hotels in the old town also offer an air-ticket booking service.

From Lìjiāng there are 13 daily flights to Kūnmíng (from ¥440), as well as daily flights to: Běijīng (¥1360), Chéngdū (¥710), Chóngqìng (¥590), Guǎngzhōu (¥970), Shànghǎi (¥1420), Shēnzhèn (¥1020), Xīshuāngbǎnnà (¥440)

MONASTERIES AROUND LÌJIĀNG

There are a number of monasteries around Lìjiāng, all Tibetan in origin and belonging to the Karmapa (Red Hat) sect. Most were extensively damaged during the Cultural Revolution and there's not much monastic activity nowadays.

Jade Peak Monastery (玉峰寺, Yùfēng Sì; ¥30) is on a hillside about 5km past Báishā. The last 3km of the track requires a steep climb. The monastery sits at the foot of Yùlóng Xuěshān (5500m) and was established in 1756. The monastery's main attraction nowadays is the Camellia Tree of 10,000 Blossoms (Wànduǒ Shānchá). Ten thousand might be something of an exaggeration, but locals claim that the tree produces at least 4000 blossoms between February and April. A monk on the grounds risked his life to keep the tree secretly watered during the Cultural Revolution.

Lìjiāng is also famed for its temple frescoes, most of which were painted during the 15th and 16th centuries by Tibetan, Naxi, Bai and Han artists; many were restored during the later Qing dynasty. They depict various Taoist, Chinese and Tibetan Buddhist themes and can be found on the interior walls of temples in the area. Remember, though, that the Cultural Revolution caused havoc around here so many are desecrated in various ways.

Frescoes can be found in Báishā and on the interior walls of Dàjué Palace (Dàjué Gōng) in the village of Lóngquán.

BUS

The main long-distance **bus station** (客运站; kèyùnzhàn) is south of the old town; to get here, take bus 8 or 11 (¥1; the latter is faster) from along Minzhu Lu.

Chéngdū ¥317, 24 hours, one daily (8am)

Jiànchuān ¥23, 1½ hours, five daily (8.20am, 11.30am, 1.30pm, 3.30pm and 5pm)

Kūnmíng ¥217, seven hours, seven buses daily (9am, 10am, 11am, 12.40pm, 4.30pm, 6pm and 8pm)

Lúgū Lake ¥100, eight hours, two daily (8.30am and 9am)

Nínglàng ¥49, five hours, five daily (8am, 8.30am, 9am, 9.30am and 11am)

Pānzhīhuā ¥88, eight hours, seven daily (7am, 7.30am, 8.30am, 9.30am, 11.30am, 4pm and 6pm)

Qiáotóu ¥22, 1½ hours, one daily (8.30am); Lìjiāng to Shangri-la buses also stop here.

Shangri-la ¥40 to ¥58, four hours, every 40 minutes (7.30am to 5pm)

Xiàguān ¥56 to ¥87, three hours, every 30 minutes (7.10am to 7pm)

Xīshuāngbǎnnà ¥242, 16 hours, one daily (7.30am)

In the north of town, the **express bus station** (高快客运站, Gāokuài kèyùnzhàn; Shangrila Dadao) is where many buses originate, but it's usually more convenient to catch your bus from the long-distance bus station.

TRAIN

There are seven trains daily to Dàlǐ (¥34 to ¥69, two to three hours, 8am to 9.50pm) and seven trains to Kūnmíng (hard sleeper ¥141, eight to nine hours, 8am to 11.50pm). The line will be extended to reach Shangri-la by 2019.

🛈 Getting Around

Buses to the airport (¥25) leave from outside the CAAC office (p699) from 6.30am to 10pm.

Bus 6 runs to Báishā Village from Minzhu Lu, close to the main entrance to the old town.

Buses to Yùlóng Xuěshān run from Mao Square, a few hundred metres north of the old town.

Bike hire is available at most hostels (¥30 per day). Taxi flagfall is ¥7 but taxis are not allowed into the old town.

Báishā 白沙

📞 0888

By far the most serene spot around Lìjiāng, Báishā is a small village near several old temples and makes a great day trip by bike from Lìjiāng. Alternatively, it's an ideal spot for lazing and cycling the surrounding area for a day or two.

Located on the plain north of Lìjiāng, Báishā was the capital of the Naxi kingdom until Kublai Khan made it part of his Yuan empire (1271–1368). Now, it's known as a centre of Naxi embroidery; you'll see examples of local handiwork throughout the village.

The 'star' attraction of Báishā is **Dr Ho Shi Xiu**, a legendary herbalist who was propelled to fame by the travel writer Bruce Chatwin when he mythologised him in a 1986 *New Yorker* story as the 'Taoist physician in the Jade Dragon Mountains of Lìjiāng'.

A sprightly 94 at the time of writing and still treating the ill every day with herbs collected from the nearby mountains, Dr Ho is very chatty (he speaks English, German and Japanese) and is happy to regale visitors with the secrets of good health and longevity. One result of his advanced years is that sometimes he delegates his 58-year-old son to speak to people. His 'surgery' is on Báishā's main street.

There are a couple of **frescoes** worth seeing in town and the surrounding area. The best can be found in Báishā's **Dàbǎojī Palace** (大宝积宫, Dàbǎojī Gōng; ¥30; ⊙ 8.30am-5.30pm), and at the neighbouring **Liúlí Temple** (琉璃殿; Liúlí Diàn) and **Dàdìng Gé** (大定阁). Note that you'll have to show the ¥80 Lìjiāng town entrance ticket to gain access to the Palace.

There are a few places to stay in the village. The laidback **Báishā There International Youth Hostel** (白沙那里青年旅舍, Báishā Nàlǐ Qīngnián Lǔshě; 📞 0888 534 0550; baishathere@hotmail.com; Sānyuán Village, 三元村; dm ¥35, d ¥168-248; @ 🛜) is a fine place for chilling out after the crowds. Dorms are bright, while the private rooms are spacious and comfortable. There's a cool communal area and a garden. Bike hire is ¥30 per day. It's down a lane off the street where Dr Ho's clinic is: look for the sign.

Me Let (米良, Mǐliáng; 📞 130 9744 0079; 14 Sānyuán Village, 三元村14号; breakfast ¥58; ⊙ 9.30am-6.30pm Mon-Sat; 🛜) is famous for its homemade plum juice, which also comes in an alcoholic version. The cafe, run by a transplanted Hong Konger, has a great garden to eat in. The all-day breakfast is hearty, and there's a small menu of Western dishes, as well as many coffees and teas (from ¥30) .

🛈 Getting There & Away

Báishā is a one-hour bike ride from Lijiāng. Otherwise, take bus 6 (¥1, 40 minutes) from Minzhu Lu, which drops you in the village. It returns to Lìjiāng regularly.

Shùhé Old Town 束河古城

☎ 0888 / POP 3000

Shùhé Old Town (Shùhé Gǔchéng) is attracting increasing numbers of travellers and day trippers due to the fact that it is marginally more tranquil than nearby Lìjiāng. A former staging post on the Tea Horse Road that's just 4km from Lìjiāng, Shùhé can be visited in a day, or makes a less frenetic alternative base for exploring the region.

Although there's little in the way of sights, the cobblestone alleys and streets south of its **main square** are picturesque and more peaceful at night than Lìjiāng. Head for the **original section of town**, which is sandwiched between the Jiǔdǐng and Qīnglóng Rivers and nestles beneath the foothills of Yùlóng Xuěshān. The first part of town, identified by a large Chinese-style gate, is actually completely new (though it looks old), built for the purposes of tourism in the early 2000s (this section of town is owned by a private company).

🛏 Sleeping & Eating

K2 International Youth Hostel HOSTEL $
(K2国际青年旅舍, K2 Guójì Qīngnián Lǔshě; ☎ 0888 513 0110; www.k2yha.com; 1 Guailiu Xiang, Kangpu Lu, 康普路拐柳巷1号; dm ¥35-50, d ¥158; @ 🛜) Big and busy hostel popular with Chinese travellers. Dorms are a little cramped, but there are two large communal areas and a decent cafe. Not much English spoken. To get here, don't enter the town's main gate, but take the road to the right, which leads on to Kangpu Lu after five minutes.

Sleepy Inn GUESTHOUSE $$
(丽舍客栈, Lìshè Kèzhàn; ☎ 0888 6401 0235; 8 Qinglong Lu, 青龙路8号; d ¥368; 🛜📶) A flashpacker hang-out, with large, well maintained, comfortable rooms set around a pleasant courtyard (they are regularly discounted by 50% in slack periods). Reach it by crossing the bridge over the Qīnglóng River and walking 100m west on Qinglong Lu. There's also a small swimming pool.

ℹ Getting There & Away

Getting to Shùhé from Lìjiāng is easy, with buses 5, 6 and 11 (all ¥1) running here, or within a 10-minute walk of the main gate. You can pick them up on Minzhu Lu.

Tiger Leaping Gorge 虎跳峡

☎ 0887

Gingerly stepping along a trail swept with scree to allow an old fellow with a donkey to pass; resting atop a rock, exhausted, looking up to see the fading sunlight dance between snow-shrouded peaks, then down to see the lingering rays dancing on the rippling waters a thousand metres away; feeling utterly exhilarated. That pretty much sums up **Tiger Leaping Gorge** (Hǔtiào Xiá, admission ¥65), the unmissable trek of southwest China.

One of the deepest gorges in the world, it measures 16km long and is a giddy 3900m from the waters of the Jīnshā River (Jīnshā Jiāng) to the snowcapped mountains of Hābā Shān (Hābā Mountain) to the west and Yùlóng Xuěshān to the east, and, despite the odd danger, it's gorgeous almost every single step of the way.

🏃 Activities

There are two trails: the higher and the lower; the latter follows the road and is best avoided, unless you enjoy being enveloped in clouds of dust from passing tour buses and 4WDs. While the scenery is stunning wherever you are in the gorge, it's absolutely sublime from the high trail. Make sure you don't get too distracted by all that beauty, though, and so miss the blue signs and red arrows that help you avoid getting lost on the trail.

At the time of writing, a new road was being tunnelled through part of the gorge, resulting in a diversion at the start of the high trail which makes the route an hour or so longer. From the Qiáotóu ticket office, it's seven hours to Běndìwān, nine hours to Middle Gorge (Tina's Guesthouse), or 10 hours to Walnut Garden. It's much more fun, and a lot less exhausting, to do the trek over two days. By stopping overnight at one of the many guesthouses along the way, you'll have the time to appreciate the magnificent vistas on offer at almost every turn of the trail.

YÚNNÁN'S BEST HIKES

Tiger Leaping Gorge

Nù Jiāng Valley (p713)

Xīshuāngbǎnnà (p727)

Yǔbēng & Kawa Karpo Hikes (p712)

Cāng Shān (p689)

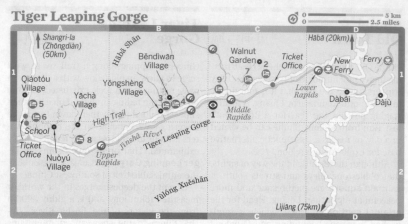

Tiger Leaping Gorge

Ponies can be hired (their owners will find you) to take you to the gorge's highest point for ¥200; it's not uncommon to see three generations of a family together, with the oldies on horseback and the young ones panting along on foot behind them.

The main hiking route along the higher road starts at Jane's Tibetan Guesthouse. Walk away from **Qiáotóu** (桥头), past the school, for five minutes or so, then head up the paved road branching to the left; there's a sign to guide you. After about 2.5km on the road, look for the blue sign pointing to the high trail diversion. The serious climbing starts straight away thanks to the diversion, with a steep ascent and then descent into **Nuòyú** (诺余) village.

The toughest section of the trek comes after Nuòyu, when the trail winds through the 28 agonising bends, or turns, that lead to the highest point of the gorge. Count on six hours at normal pace to get through here and to reach **Yáchà** (牙叉) village. It's a relatively straightforward walk on to **Běndiwān** (本地

湾). About 1½ hours on from here, you begin the descent to the road on slippery, poor, precarious paths. Watch your step here; if you twist an ankle, it's a long hop down.

After the path meets the road at Tina's Guesthouse, there's a good detour that leads down to the middle rapids and **Tiger Leaping Stone** (¥15), where a tiger is once said to have leapt across the Yangzi, thus giving the gorge its name. Locals charge ¥15 to go down the path and it's a two hour round trip. At the bottom of this insanely steep trail locals charge another ¥15 for one viewpoint but another spot is free. From one of the lower rest points another trail (¥15) heads downstream for a one-hour walk to **Walnut Garden** (核桃园).

Most hikers stop at Tina's, have lunch, and head back to Qiáotóu. Those continuing to Walnut Garden can take the trail along the river or use an alternative trail that keeps high where the path descends to Tina's, crosses a stream and a 'bamboo forest' before descending into Walnut Garden. If you are deciding where to spend the night, Walnut Garden is more attractive than Tina's.

🛏 Sleeping & Eating

There are numerous accommodation options along the trek through the gorge. In the unlikely event that everywhere is full, basic rooms will be available with a local. We've never heard of anyone who had to sleep rough in the gorge.

All the guesthouses double as restaurants and shops, where you can have meals, or pick up water and snacks. A few hardy vendors can be found along the high trail as far as Běndìwān, selling water, fruit, chocolate bars and, sometimes, the local herb.

Qiáotóu

Jane's Tibetan Guesthouse GUESTHOUSE $
(峡谷行客栈, Xiágǔ Xíng Kèzhàn; ☑0888 880 6570; janetibetgh@163.com; dm ¥35, d with/ without bathroom ¥120/70; 🛜) The rooms and dorms at this friendly place with a cosy communal area are basic, but this is still where many people start their trek. The breakfasts here make for good walking fuel and it has left-luggage facilities (¥5 a bag).

In the Gorge

Halfway Guesthouse GUESTHOUSE $
(中途客栈, Zhōngtú Kèzhàn; ☑131 7079 5128; Běndìwān; dm ¥40, d ¥120-300; 🛜) Once a simple home to a guy collecting medicinal herbs and his family, this is now a busy operation set around a courtyard and with a great roof terrace. The vistas here are awe-inspiring and perhaps the best of any lodging in the gorge; the view from the communal toilets alone is worth the price of a bed.

Come Inn GUESTHOUSE $
(下一客栈, Xiàyī Kèzhàn; ☑181 8385 3151; 641589921@qq.com; dm ¥45, d ¥160-280; 🛜) Big, well maintained dorms with bathrooms and sliding doors that open out onto a vast wooden terrace for super views are on offer at this newish guesthouse near the entrance to Běndìwān village. Private rooms are in tip-top condition. English spoken.

Chateau de Woody GUESTHOUSE $
(山白脸旅馆, Shānbáiliǎn Lǚguǎn; ☑139 8875 6901; sgrlwoody@163.com; dm ¥30, d ¥120-220; 🛜) This old-school gorge guesthouse has rooms with good views and modern bathrooms that are a decent deal. Across the road, the less-attractive modern extension has the cheapest rooms.

Tina's Guesthouse GUESTHOUSE $
(中峡旅店, Zhōngxiá Lǚdiàn; ☑0888 820 2258; tina 999@live.com; 8-/4-bcd dm ¥30/40, d ¥120-280; @🛜) Almost a package-holiday operation, with travellers funnelled to and from the gorge. Tina's lacks the charm of its competitors, but it's efficiently run, has plenty of beds and the location is perfect for those too knackered to make it to Walnut Garden. Pricier rooms have excellent views. There are daily buses from here to Lìjiāng and Shangri-la (¥55, 3.30pm).

Tea Horse Guesthouse GUESTHOUSE $
(茶马客栈, Chámǎ Kèzhàn; ☑139 8870 7922; dm ¥40, d ¥100-268; 🛜) Just after Yāchà village, this ever-expanding place has a reasonable restaurant – it makes a sensible lunch stop – as well as a small spa and massage parlour where aching limbs can be eased. The cheapest rooms share bathrooms, the most expensive are very big and have good beds, modern bathrooms and shared balconies.

Naxi Family Guesthouse GUESTHOUSE $
(纳西雅阁, Nàxī Kèzhàn; ☑139 8875 8424; dm ¥30, d ¥120-160; 🛜) Taking your time to spend a night here instead of double-timing it to Walnut Garden isn't a bad idea. It's an incredibly friendly, well run place (organic veggies and wines), set around a pleasant courtyard.

Sean's Spring Guesthouse GUESTHOUSE $$
(山泉客栈, Shānquán Kèzhàn; ☑0888 820 2223, 158 9436 7846; www.tigerleapinggorge.com; r ¥160-380, without bathroom ¥60-80; ☺🛜) One of the original guesthouses on the trail. The eponymous Sean is a true character, a good source of travel info and one of the few locals seriously concerned with the gorge's environmental well being. There are 28 rooms here, including a couple of cheapies, and the

---

ⓘ DANGERS OF THE TREK

The gorge hike is not to be taken lightly. Even for those in good physical shape, it's a workout and can certainly wreck the knees. The path constricts and crumbles and is alarmingly narrow in places, making it sometimes dangerous. When it's raining (especially in July and August), landslides and swollen waterfalls can block the paths, in particular on the low road. (The best time to come is May and the start of June, when the hills are afire with plant and flower life.)

A few people – including a handful of foreign travellers – have died in the gorge. During the past decade, there have also been cases of travellers being assaulted on the trail. It's safer in all ways not to do the hike alone.

Check with cafes and lodgings in Lìjiāng or Qiáotóu for trail and weather updates. Most have fairly detailed gorge maps; just remember they're not to scale and are occasionally out of date.

You can buy water along the way at the guesthouses on the route, but make sure to bring plenty of sunscreen and lip balm.

best have great views of Yùlóng Xuěshān. The meals are all-organic and tasty.

ℹ️ Getting There & Away

From Lìjiāng's long-distance bus station there is one direct bus a day to Qiáotóu at 8.30am (¥22, 1½ hours). Otherwise, catch any bus to Shangri-la (¥40, 1½ hours, every 40 minutes, 7.30am to 5pm) and get off at Qiáotóu.

Some travellers get a minivan (¥35) to the start of the walking track, organised through their guesthouse in Lìjiāng. The minivan can deliver extra luggage to the guesthouse of your choice (usually Tina's, p703, or Jane's, p703).

Returning to Lìjiāng from Qiáotóu, buses start passing through from Shangri-la at around 9.30am. The last one rolls through at around 8pm. The last bus to Shangri-la passes through at around 6.30pm. Tina's Guesthouse also organises one bus a day to both Lìjiāng and Shangri-la (both ¥55) at 3.30pm. You can also pick up a bus to Lìjiāng from Walnut Garden at 3.30pm (¥55).

There is one daily bus to Báishuǐtái from Lìjiāng at 9am (¥38, three hours). There is also one bus a day from Shangri-la to Báishuǐtái at 9.40am (¥24, three hours).

Tiger Leaping Gorge to Báishuǐtái

An adventurous add-on to the gorge trek is to continue north all the way to Hābā (哈巴) village and the limestone terraces of Báishuǐtái (p711). This turns it into a four-day trek from Qiáotóu and from here you can travel on to Shangri-la. From Walnut Garden to Hābā, via Jiāngbiān (江边), is a seven- to eight-hour walk. From here to the Yi village of Sānbà (三坝), close to Báishuǐtái, is about the same, following trails. You could just follow the road and hitch with the occasional truck or tractor, but it's longer and less scenic. The best way would be to hire a guide in Walnut Garden (¥400 per day for an English-speaker). A horse will cost ¥250 to ¥300 per day extra. The turn-off to Hābā starts 6km down the road from Walnut Garden, up the hill where you see 'Welcome to Tibet Guesthouse' painted on the retaining wall.

There are a number of guesthouses In Hābā. **Hābā Snow Mountain Inn** (哈巴雪山客栈, Hābā Xuěshān Kèzhàn; ☑ 0888 7886 6596; dm ¥30, d ¥80-150; 🛜) has old dorms and newer double rooms. The enthusiastic host can organise guides to lead you up to the base camp of **Hābā Mountain** (哈巴山, Hābā Shān), a two-day trek, or to **Black Lake** (黑海, Hēi Hǎi), a nine-hour round-trip hike. Note that

locals now charge a ¥200 'protection fee' per person for access to the mountain, supposedly going towards conservation efforts.

The daily bus to Sānbà passes Tina's Guesthouse (p703) around 1pm (¥40, three hours), but not if the road is blocked. One bus from Báishuǐtái to Shangri-la goes through Sānbà around noon (¥24, two hours). Minivans frequently ply these routes so flagging down a ride isn't too tough.

If you plan to hike the route alone, assume you'll need all provisions and equipment for extremes of weather. Ask for local advice before setting out.

Lúgū Lake   泸沽湖

☑ 0888

Straddling the remote Yúnnán–Sìchuān border, Lúgū Lake (Lúgū Hú) is an absolutely idyllic place, even with the rise in domestic tourism. The ascent to the lake, which sits at 2690m, is via a spectacular switchback road and the first sight of the 50-sq-km body of water, surrounded by lushly forested slopes, will take your breath away.

The best times to visit the lake are April to May, and September to October, when the weather is dry and mild. It's sometimes snowbound during the winter months.

👁 Sights & Activities

From Luòshuǐ and Lǐgé you can punt about with local Mosuo by dugout canoe – known by the Mosuo as 'pig troughs' (zhūcáo chuán). Expect to head for **Lǐwùbǐ Dǎo** (里务比岛), the largest island (and throw a stone into Sìchuān). The second-largest island is **Hēiwǎé Dǎo** (黑瓦俄岛). Boat-trip prices vary wildly. If you're in a group, it's ¥50 per person. But if it's a quiet time, you should be able to get a ride on your own for under ¥100.

Bikes (per day ¥30) and scooters (per day ¥80 to ¥100) can be hired along the lake shore at Luòshuǐ and Lǐgé. The lake is around 60km in circumference and you can travel around it by scooter in five hours or so. Strong cyclists will be able to circumnavigate it in a day (there are plenty of steep climbs).

Zhāměi Temple   MONASTERY
(扎美寺, Zhāměi Sì; Yǒngníng; admission by donation) This substantial Tibetan monastery at Yǒngníng village is worth a visit, although only a few lamas are in residence at any time. Admission is free, but a donation is expected. A private minivan costs ¥20 per person for the half-hour ride.

Mosuo Folk Custom Museum   MUSEUM
(摩梭民俗博物馆, Mósuō Mínzú Bówùguǎn;
Luòshuǐ; ¥60; ⊙8am-5pm) This museum in
Luòshuǐ is set within the traditional home of
a wealthy Mosuo family, and the obligatory
guide will explain how the matriarchal society functions. There is also an interesting
collection of photos taken by Joseph Rock
in the 1920s. The entrance fee is sometimes
discounted by 50%.

🛏 Sleeping

Hotels and guesthouses line the lakeside in
Luòshuǐ and Lǐgé, with basic rooms available from ¥80.

Lao Shay Youth Hostel   HOSTEL $
(老谢车马店, Lǎoxiè Chēmǎdiàn; ☑0888 588
1555; www.laoshay.com; Lǐgé; dm ¥40, s & d ¥88-
180; @🛜) Still the best spot for cheap digs
in Lǐgé, with a prime location smack in the
middle of the village. The best rooms have
balconies and lake views, the cheapest share
bathrooms. Dorms have lockers and are in
reasonable condition. Lackadaisical staff.
Bike hire is ¥30 per day.

Yǎsè Dába Lǚxíngzhě Zhījiā   HOTEL $$$
(雅瑟达伯旅行者之家; ☑0888 588 1196; ligemo
suo@126.com; Lǐgé; d ¥420-580; 🛜) Stuck out on
a little promontory at the edge of Lǐgé, all the
rooms here come with decent views, but the
ones on the 2nd floor are tremendous. They're
a little overpriced but the bathrooms are a cut
above the rest in the village. In the attached
restaurant, try Lúgū Lake fish (泸沽湖鱼;
Lúgū Hú yú) or sausage (香肠; *xiāngcháng*).

🍴 Eating

There are many restaurants that serve tra-
ditional Mosuo foods, including preserved
pig's fat and salted sour fish – the latter be-
ing somewhat tastier than the former. Most

popular of all is the fantastic barbecued
pork: you'll see the pigs being roasted out-
side. Lǐgé is the best place for barbecue.

Zhāxī Cāntīng   BARBECUE $$
(扎西餐厅; ☑0888 588 1055; Lǐgé; dishes from
¥30; ⊙5pm-midnight; 🛜) Lively restaurant
and barbecue joint that's good for the local
speciality, Mosuo pork (¥50). You'll see the
pigs being roasted whole outside, where you
can sit near the lake.

☆ Entertainment

Mosuo Dance Show   DANCE
(篝火晚会, Gōuhuǒ Wǎnhuì; Luòshuǐ; ¥30; ⊙8.20-
9.20pm) This nightly dance show sees group
dancing by many Mosuo women in traditional dress around a fire. The local name for it
translates as 'bonfire party', but don't expect
to see effigies of Guy Fawkes. It's very popular with domestic tourists and is held in a
forecourt off the street back from the lake.

🛈 Getting There & Away

Lìjiāng's express bus station has two direct buses a day to the lake (¥100, eight hours, 8.30am
and 9am), but buy your ticket at least one day in
advance as it's frequently sold out. Note too that
it often takes nine or ten hours to get to the lake
for various road-related reasons. Both the buses
pick up passengers at the main bus station (客
运站, *kèyùnzhàn*) as well.

For Lǐgé you'll have to change for a minibus in
Luòshuǐ (¥20 per person), or hire a bike.

Leaving Luòshuǐ, there are two daily buses
to Lìjiāng at 9.30am and 10am. Again, tickets
should be bought at least a day in advance. You
can also catch one of the regular minivans to
Nínglàng (宁蒗; ¥30, four hours), from where
there are five buses daily to Lìjiāng.

At the time of writing, no buses were running
to Xīchāng (西昌) in Sìchuān. But minivans make
the run (¥130, seven hours). Hostels can arrange
pick-ups.

VILLAGES AROUND LÙGŪ LAKE

Villages are scattered around the outskirts of the lake, with **Luòshuǐ** (洛水) the biggest
and most developed, and the one where the bus will drop you. As well as guesthouses,
restaurants and a few cafes with English menus and Western food, there are the inevitable souvenir shops and a number of bars with live music. Away from them, though, the
dominant night-time sound is the lapping of the lake.

Most travellers move quickly to **Lǐgé** (里格), 9km further up the road, tucked into a bay
on the northwestern shore of the lake. Although guesthouses make up most of the place,
along with restaurants serving succulent, but pricey, barbecue, the sights and nights here
are lovely. If you want a less touristy experience, then you need to keep village-hopping
around the lake to the Sìchuān side. At the moment, top votes for alternative locations are
Luòwǎ (洛瓦), **Wǔzhīluó** (五支罗) and **Zhào Jiā Wān** (赵家湾).

Shangri-la 香格里拉

0887 / POP 130,000

Shangri-la (Xiānggélǐlā), formerly known as Zhōngdiàn (中甸) and sometimes called 'Gyalthang' in Tibetan, is where you begin to breathe in the Tibetan world. That's if you can breathe at all, given its altitude (3200m). Travelling here allows you to experience an intriguing blend of Tibetan and Han Chinese culture.

Home to one of Yúnnán's most rewarding monasteries and surrounded by mountains, lakes and grassland, it's also the last stop in Yúnnán before a rough five- to six-day journey to Chéngdū via the Tibetan townships and rugged terrain of western Sìchuān.

The town is divided into two distinct sections: the larger modern side and the old quarter. A devastating fire in January 2014 sent much of the old town up in smoke, but it's now been almost completely rebuilt. Most of the places you'll visit in the new town are within walking distance of the old town, making getting around easy.

Plan your visit for between March or April and October. During winter, Shangri-la is still busy but it gets very cold indeed, although spectacular mountain views can be the reward for braving the frigid temperatures.

In mid- to late June, the town hosts a **horse-racing festival** that sees several days of dancing, singing, eating and, of course, horse racing. Accommodation is tight at this time.

◉ Sights

Shangri-la is a wonderful place for getting off the beaten track, with plenty of trekking and horse-riding opportunities, as well as little-visited monasteries and villages. However, the remote sights are difficult to reach independently given the lack of public transport.

One increasingly popular village is **Nírǔ** (尼汝), close to Pǔdácuò, which offers good hiking nearby. There are a couple of guesthouses in the village and a van from Shangri-la will cost ¥300.

Ganden Sumtseling Gompa   MONASTERY
(松赞林寺, Sōngzànlín Sì; ¥115; ⊘7am-7pm) About an hour's walk north of town is this 300-year-old Tibetan monastery complex with around 600 monks. Extensive rebuilding has robbed the monastery of some of its charm, but it remains the most important in southwest China and is definitely worth the visit. Bus 3 runs here from anywhere along Changzheng Lu (¥1). From the main gate where the tickets are sold you can catch a tourist bus to the monastery.

Zhùangjīn Tǒng   HISTORIC SITE
FREE This huge prayer wheel stands at 21m high and contains 100,000 small prayer wheels. At least six people are needed to make it spin.

Old Town   HISTORIC SITE
A few streets survived the January 2014 fire that reduced most of the old town to ashes, and these retain the mix of cobbled lanes and renovated wooden buildings that characterised Shangri-la's old town. Now, they have been joined by new 'old' wooden buildings that imitate them. Worth a visit is **Guīshān Sì** (龟山寺, Guīshān Temple), which is home to a handful of monks who conduct morning prayers.

Next to it is Zhùangjīn Tǒng. On the far side of Guīshān Sì is the **Shangri-la Thangka Academy** (唐卡学会, Tángkǎ Xuéhuì; 0887 888 1612; www.thangkaacademy.com; 31 Jinlong Jie, 金龙街31号), where young monks train in painting and Buddhist philosophy. The academy also offers classes for tourists, costing ¥100 per day, or you can stay at the academy to study for ¥200, including room and board.

Bǎijī Sì   BUDDHIST TEMPLE
(百鸡寺, 100 Chickens Temple) **FREE** For the best views over Shangri-la, head to this delightfully named and little-visited temple. The temple has a couple of monks inside and dozens of chickens wandering around outside. To get here, walk along the narrow paths behind Kersang's Relay Station, past the deserted temple, continue uphill and you'll see it on the left.

☞ Tours

Caravane Liotard   TOUR
(158 9436 7094; www.caravane-liotard.com) Named after a legendary French explorer, this French-run outfit specialises in tours along the former routes of the Tea Horse Road.

Haiwei Trails   TOUR
(139 8875 6540; www.haiweitrails.com) Has a good philosophy towards local sustainable tourism, and well over a decade of experience running treks and trips.

Khampa Caravan   TOUR
(康巴商道探险旅行社, Kāngbā Shāngdào Tànxiǎn Lǚxíngshè; 0887 828 8648; www.khampacaravan.com; Jinlong Jie, 金龙街; ⊘9am-noon & 2-5.30pm

Shangri-la

Shangri-la

Mon-Fri, 9am-noon Sat) Tibetan-run, this well established outfit organises some excellent treks and overland journeys, inside Tibet too, that get good feedback, as well as homestays with Tibetan families. The company also runs a lot of sustainable development programs within Tibetan communities. See www.shangrila association.org for more details.

🛏 Sleeping

A frenzy of construction followed the 2014 fire that devastated the old town and there's now a wide choice of guesthouses and hotels here again. Cheap digs (¥60 a room and up) can be found around the bus station.

Despite Shangri-la's often glacial night temperatures, most cheaper guesthouse and hotel rooms are not heated (although you will get an electric blanket). Many dorms in town are fairly basic too.

Desti Hostel HOSTEL $
(背包十年青年公园, Bēibāo Shínián Qīngnián Gōngyuán; ☑130 3860 8855; Chenni Village, 称尼村; dm ¥50-70, d ¥280-380; @🖈) Unusual and very flash new hostel located in a huge, converted Tibetan house in a village just outside town close to the grasslands and mountains. Tibetan-run, it has numerous communal ar-

eas, while dorms are heated and come with individual reading lights, USB sockets and comfy beds. Private rooms retain the original wood features of the former house.

But the real draw here is the chance to interact with the local villagers. You can herd yaks, help a Tibetan family farm before eating with them, study Tibetan and *thangka* painting, or ride horses or trek into the mountains. They offer free pick-up, and it's a 20-minute bike ride from town.

Tavern 47 GUESTHOUSE $
(仁和客栈, Rénhé Kèzhàn; ☑0887 888 1147; christinhe@hotmail.com; 47 Cuolang Jie, 措廊街 47号; dm ¥45, d with/without bathroom ¥150/100; ⊜@🖈) This hostel gets good feedback (book ahead) and the private rooms are distinctive, with Tibetan motifs and big, comfortable beds. Dorms are more basic, but there's a nice communal area with a big stove to keep warm by, a small garden and efficient staff, and Western, Korean and Naxi meals are available.

YÚNNÁN SHANGRI-LA

UP IN SMOKE

On 11 January 2014 much of Shangri-la's old town went up in flames, reducing the city's prime tourist attraction to a pile of smoking ashes.

The fire was caused by an electrical fault in a guesthouse. Once it took hold, the old town – a tightly packed warren of narrow, twisting lanes and wooden houses – had no chance. Some 260 buildings, including 40 guesthouses, were destroyed.

Thankfully, no one died in the inferno, a result of the fire services ordering an immediate evacuation of the area. Less impressive was the fact that their fire engines turned up without any water, resulting in them having to turn around and head to the nearest river to fill up.

For many locals, the fire was an accident waiting to happen. Ever since Chinese 'experts' announced in 1997 that the city of Shangri-la and the surrounding area was the fabled Shangri-la of James Hilton's best-selling 1933 novel *Lost Horizon*, the city had expanded at a pace that far outstripped its infrastructure.

Water shortages were common, while a lack of planning ensured the old town was nothing more than a fire trap, with locals opening shops, guesthouses and restaurants on top of each other to cash in on the tourism boom.

Hilton's novel – likely inspired by articles written by the famed northwest Yúnnán explorer Joseph Rock – tells the story of four travellers who are hijacked and taken to a mountain utopia whose residents can live for over 150 years. In contrast, the 'real' Shangri-la lasted a mere 17 years before it had to be reconstructed.

N's Kitchen & Lodge GUESTHOUSE $
(香格里拉藏地国际青年旅舍, Xiānggélǐlā Zàngdì Guójì Qīngnián Lǚshě; ☑ 0887 823 3870; nskitchen lodge@gmail.com; 24 Beimen Jie, 北门街24号; dm/d ¥40/150; @ 🛜) It does a fine yak burger, but N's is more of a lodge with compact dorms and private rooms set around a garden. There's a small roof terrace and movie room, as well as a pool table and travel advice.

Kersang's Relay Station INN $
(格桑藏驿, Gésāng Zàng Yì; ☑ 0887 822 3118; kersangs@yahoo.com; 1 Yamenlang, Jinlong Jie, 衙门廊1号、金龙街; dm ¥50, d ¥180-240; @ 🛜) This friendly, Tibetan-run place survived the 2014 fire by the skin of its teeth. Rooms are cosy with modern bathrooms and come with electric blankets. There's a cool terrace, communal lounge and pleasant staff. Call ahead, as it's not always open unless it has guests.

Kevin's Trekker Inn GUESTHOUSE $$
(龙门客栈, Lóngmén Kèzhàn; ☑ 0887 822 8178; www.kevintrekkerinn.com; 138 Dawa Lu, 达娃路138号; d ¥180-400; @ 🛜) Under new management, this guesthouse is still friendly and helpful. It has a cosy lounge and rooms that range from the cheap and boxy to the very comfortable, with good bathrooms and views over the newly rebuilt old town. It's located just off Dawa Lu behind the Long Xiang Inn.

★ **Nánshān Arts Hotel** BOUTIQUE HOTEL $$$
(南山艺术, Nánshān Yìshù; ☑ 0887 881 1222; 9 Cangfang Jie, 仓房街9号; d ¥428-1280; ❄🛜) Brand-new boutique hotel in the heart of the old town. Big rooms with high ceilings, large, comfortable beds, sofas and individual decoration. At night, spotlights indicate your residence, while each room gets a complimentary oxygen cylinder, just in case the altitude is getting to you. Best of all, the rooms are superwarm. Friendly staff and there's a cafe in the lobby.

Arro Khampa Hotel BOUTIQUE HOTEL $$$
(阿若康巴-南索达庄园, Aruòkāngbā Nánsuǒdá Zhuāngyuán; ☑ 0887 8881007; www.zinchospitality.com; 15 Jinlong Jie, 金龙街15号; d ¥980; ⊖🛜) Hushed boutique hotel with swish rooms set around a stone-flagged courtyard. Excellent beds and bathrooms, and the underfloor heating keeps everything toasty-warm. There's a restaurant offering Chinese and Tibetan dishes onsite. Efficient staff. Non-smoking too.

✗ Eating & Drinking

Shangri-la's numerous eating options include Tibetan, Chinese, Indian and Western food.

Rebgong TIBETAN $
(热贡艺人阁, Règòng Yìrén Gé; ☑ 182 8882 0252; Shangye Jie, 商业街; dishes from ¥15; ⏱ 11am-9.30pm; 🛜) Excellent joint for Tibetan eats, even if it is somewhat lacking in atmosphere – and always busy with locals. The house speciality is yak meat hotpot, and they do a small version for two people (¥88),

but the *mómo* (馍馍, Tibetan dumplings), which come in meat or veggie versions, or the spicy yak-meat pizza are good alternatives.

To find it, walk west of the big square underneath the giant prayer wheel, turn right on the first street you come to and it's about 100m ahead on the left-hand side.

★ **Silent Holy Stones**   TIBETAN $$
(静静的嘛呢石, Jìngjìngde Manishí; ☑ 0887 828 6627; 3 Zuobarui, 作巴瑞3号; dishes from ¥18; ⊙ 10am-11pm; 🖥) Re-opened after the 2014 fire in a new location and still a favourite spot for local Tibetans, this relaxed and welcoming place specialises in yak meat hotpots (from ¥148). Great *mómo* (馍馍, Tibetan dumplings) too, which come with a spicy dipping sauce, as well as a small selection of vegetable and mushroom dishes.

Compass   INTERNATIONAL $$
(舒灯库乐, Shūdēng kùlè; ☑ 0887 822 3638; 50 Shangye Jie, 商业街50号; mains from ¥40; ⊙ 8.30am-10pm Tue-Sun; 🖥) Bustling spot for a fine breakfast, and a popular hang-out for Western travellers. Salads, steaks, pasta and pizzas are all available, as well as a few generic Asian dishes. Great cakes and coffee and nonsmoking too. It's an ideal place to take a break from sightseeing.

Flying Tigers Cafe   INTERNATIONAL $$
(飞虎, Fēihǔ; ☑ 0887 828 6661; reservation@ flyingtigerscafe.com; 91 Jinlong Jie, 金龙街91号; mains from ¥40; ⊙ 11am-11pm Mon-Sat; 🖥) New, French-run bistro located in a converted courtyard house with the finest wine list in

town (from ¥30 a glass) and a small but select menu that utilises local ingredients: try the homemade mushroom ravioli or the yak burger. It's equally good for a daytime coffee or evening drink.

Noah's Cafe   INTERNATIONAL $$
(挪亚咖啡厅, Nuóyà Kāfēitīng; ☑ 139 8875 7634; Changzheng Lu, 长征路; dishes from ¥16; ⊙ 9am-10.30pm Tue-Sun; 🖥) It has been around a while in various guises, but Noah's remains a sound spot for its all-day breakfast (from ¥35) and is popular with the locals for its mix of Western and Chinese dishes. Decent coffee and its excellent stove means this is one of the warmest spots in town.

★ **Raven**   BAR
(乌鸦酒吧, Wūyā Jiǔbā; ☑ 0887 881 1663; 3/F, Bldg D8, Tancheng Wangjiao, 坛城旺角D8栋03号; beers from ¥20; ⊙ 11am-late; 🖥) Relocated since the 2014 fire, the Raven remains the best bar in town (and in northwest Yúnnán), with a huge range of beers and spirits. There's a big bar counter to sit around, sofas to sink into, New York–style pizzas (from ¥45), a pool table and decent sounds. It's a 10-minute walk from the old town, perched over a mini lake. Look for the raven sign.

🛍 **Shopping**

Dropenling   ARTS & CRAFTS
(卓番林, Zhuó Fāng Lín; ☑ 139 8871 8979; www. tibetcraft.com; 18 Cengfang Lu, 达娃路18号; ⊙ 2-9pm) Wide array of Tibetan handicrafts made by Tibetans in Tibet but designed for

---

JOSEPH ROCK

Yúnnán has always been a hunting ground for famous, foreign plant-hunters such as Joseph Rock (1884–1962). Rock lived in Lìjiāng between 1922 and 1949, becoming the world's leading expert on Naxi culture and local botany.

Born in Austria, the withdrawn autodidact taught himself eight languages, including Sanskrit. After becoming the world's foremost authority on Hawaiian flora, the US Department of Agriculture, Harvard University and later *National Geographic* (he was their famed 'man in China') sponsored Rock's trips to collect flora for medicinal research. He devoted much of his life to studying Naxi culture, which he feared was being extinguished by the dominant Han culture.

Rock sent more than 80,000 plant specimens from China – two were named after him – along with 1600 birds and 60 mammals. His caravans stretched for half a mile, and included dozens of servants, including a cook trained in Austrian cuisine, a portable darkroom, trains of pack horses, and hundreds of mercenaries for protection against bandits, not to mention the gold dinner service and collapsible bathtub.

Rock lived in Yùhú village (called Nguluko when he was there), outside Lìjiāng. Many of his possessions are now local family heirlooms.

The *Ancient Nakhi Kingdom of Southwest China* (1947) is Joseph Rock's definitive work. Immediately prior to his death, his Naxi dictionary was finally prepared for publishing.

Western tastes, including bags, cushions, toys and ornaments.

ℹ Information

Altitude sickness can be a problem here and most travellers need a couple of days to acclimatise.

Bank of China (中国银行, Zhōngguó Yínháng; Heping Lu) Has a 24-hour ATM and changes US dollars.

China Post (中国邮政, Zhōngguó Yóuzhèng) You can send mail overseas from here.

Public Security Bureau (PSB, 公安局, Gōng'ānjú; Kangzhu Dadao, 康珠大道; ⊗9am-noon & 2.30-5.30pm Mon-Fri) Shangri-la is an excellent place to extend your visa, the local police being both accommodating and friendly, although new regulations mean the process can take between three and seven days now. The PSB office is on the outskirts of town. Bus 2 (¥1) runs here from Changzheng Lu.

ℹ Getting There & Away

AIR

Shangri-la Airport is 5km from town and is sometimes referred to as Díqíng or Deqen – note that there is currently no airport at Déqīn.

There are five flights daily to Kūnmíng (¥850), one to Chéngdū (¥810), and a daily flight to Lhasa (¥2480) in peak season. Flights for other domestic destinations also leave from the airport but destinations change from week to week. You can enquire about your destination or buy tickets at **CAAC** (中国民航, Zhōngguó Mínháng; Wenming Jie). If booking online, you need to type in 'Diqing' for the airport name.

ℹ GETTING TO TIBET

At the time of writing, it was not possible to enter Tibet overland from Shangri-la, or anywhere in Yúnnán. If you're tempted to try and sneak in, then think again. There are many checkpoints operating on the road between Shangri-la and Lhasa; you will be caught, fined, detained, escorted to Chéngdū by the police and deported at your own expense. Any local person believed to have assisted you (for example by giving you a ride) will get into worse trouble.

It is possible to fly to Lhasa from Shangri-la, but flights are cheaper from elsewhere (Kūnmíng and Chéngdū), and you'll need to be part of an organised group with all the necessary permits. By far the best people to talk to about Tibet travel in Shangri-la are Khampa Caravan (p706).

BUS

Note that bus tickets may refer to either Shangri-la or Zhōngdiàn, but usually the former. Destinations from Shangri-la:

Bǎishuǐtái ¥24, three hours, one daily (9.40am)

Dàochéng ¥119, 11 hours, one daily (8am)

Déqīn ¥58, four hours, five daily (8.20am, 9.20am, 10.30am, 12.30pm and 2.30pm)

Dōngwàng ¥50, seven to eight hours, one daily (8am)

Kūnmíng ¥218 to ¥249, 10hours, five daily (8.30am, 9.30am, 2pm, 6pm and 7pm)

Lìjiāng ¥58 to ¥63, four hours, every 30 minutes (7.20am to 6pm)

Xiàguān ¥78 to ¥116, 6½ hours, every 30 minutes (7.30am to 12.30pm)

Xiāngchéng ¥85, eight hours, one daily (8am)

If you're up for the bus-hopping trek to Chéngdū in Sìchuān, you're looking at a minimum of three to four days' travel (often five to six) at some very high altitudes – you'll need warm clothes. Note that for political reasons this road may be closed at any time of the year (if the ticket seller at the bus says 'come back tomorrow', it's closed indefinitely for sure).

If you can get a ticket, the first stage of the trip is to Xiāngchéng in Sìchuān. From Xiāngchéng, your next destination is Lǐtáng, though if roads are bad you may be forced to stay overnight in Dàochéng. From Lǐtáng, it's on to Kāngdìng, from where you can make your way west towards Chéngdū.

Roads out of Shangri-la can be temporarily blocked by snow at any time from November to March. Bring a flexible itinerary.

TRAIN

A railway is being built from Lìjiāng to Shangri-la and is expected to be operational in 2019.

ℹ Getting Around

A taxi or minivan between the airport and Shangri-la will cost between ¥30 and ¥50. Otherwise, call your hotel to arrange a pick-up.

Bikes can be hired on and around Beimen Jie from ¥30 a day.

The bus station is 2km north of the old town, straight up Changzheng Lu. From outside the bus station, take local bus 1 (¥1) to the old town (古城, gǔchéng)

Around Shangri-la

Around Shangri-la are any number of sights: villages, mountains, meadows, ponds, *chörten* (Tibetan stupas), waiting to be explored.

Some Chinese travellers rave about **Wéixi** (维西), an area 80km southwest of Shangri-la sometimes known as 'The Rocky Mountains of Yúnnán' for their visual similarity to the mountain range in Colorado. There are four buses a day to Wéixi from Shangri-la's bus station at 8.30am, 10am, noon and 2pm (¥75, five hours); it's a bad road.

Emerald Pagoda Lake 碧塔海

Also known as Pǔdácuò (普达错), a Mandarinised-version of its Tibetan name, Emerald Pagoda Lake (Bìtǎ Hǎi; admission ¥258) is 25km east of Shangri-la The bus to Sānbà can drop you along the highway. From there, it's 8km down a trail (a half-hour by pony), and while the ticket price is laughably steep, there are other (free) trails to the lake. A bike is useful for finding them; taxis will drop you at the ticket office.

Pony trips can be arranged at the lake. An intriguing sight in summer are the comatose fish that float unconscious for several minutes in the lake after feasting on azalea petals.

The whopping entrance fee is also due to the inclusion of Shǔdū Hú, another lake approximately 10km to the north. The name means 'Place Where Milk is Found' in Tibetan because its pastures are reputedly the most fertile in northwestern Yúnnán.

Getting to the lake(s) is tricky. The easiest way is to go on a tour arranged by your hostel. Otherwise, catch the bus to Sānbà, get off at the turn-off and hitch. Getting back you can wait (sometimes interminably) for a bus or hike to one of the entrances or main road and look out for taxis – but there may be none. A taxi will cost around ¥300 to ¥400 for the return trip, including Shǔdū Hú.

Báishuǐtái 白水台

Báishuǐtái (admission ¥35) is a limestone deposit plateau 108km southeast of Shangri-la, with some breathtaking scenery and Tibetan villages en route. For good reason it has become probably the most popular backdoor route between Lìjiāng and Shangri-la. The terraces – think of those in Pamukkale in Turkey or Huánglóng in Sìchuān – are lovely, but can be tough to access if rainfall has made trails slippery.

A couple of guesthouses at the nearby towns of Báidì and Sānbà have rooms with beds from ¥50.

From Shangri-la there is one daily bus to Báishuǐtái at 9.40 am (¥24, three hours). One adventurous option is to hike or hitch all the way from Báishuǐtái to Tiger Leaping Gorge. A taxi from Shangri-la is ¥600.

Nàpà Hǎi 纳帕海

Some 7km northwest of Shangri-la you'll find the seasonal Nàpà Hǎi (Nàpà Lake; ¥60), surrounded by a large grassy meadow. Between September and March it attracts a myriad of rare species, including the black-necked crane. Outside of these months, the lake dries up and you can see large numbers of yaks and cattle grazing on the meadow.

Déqīn & Kawa Karpo 德钦、梅里雪山

Mellifluously named Déqīn (德钦) lies in some of the most ruggedly gorgeous scenery in China. Snugly cloud-high at an average altitude of 3550m, it rests in the near embrace of one of China's most magical mountains, Kawa Karpo (梅里雪山; Méilǐ Xuěshān). At 6740m, it is Yúnnán's highest peak and straddles the Yúnnán–Tibet border.

A true border town, Déqīn is one of Yúnnán's last outposts before Tibet, but from here you could also practically hike east to Sìchuān or southwest to Myanmar. Díqīng Prefecture was so isolated that it was never really controlled by anyone until the PLA (People's Liberation Army) arrived in force in 1957.

More than 80% of locals are Tibetan, though a dozen other minorities also live here, including one of the few settlements of non-Hui Muslims in China. The town itself, though, is unattractive and for travellers it is simply a staging post to the nearby mountains. Confusingly, Déqīn is the name of the city and county; both are incorporated by the Díqīng Tibetan Autonomous Prefecture (迪庆藏族自治州).

Once out into the mountains, Yùbēng village serves the needs of most travellers with guesthouses and restaurants.

◉ Sights

Entry to the sights requires buying an entrance ticket to Méilǐ Snow Mountain National Park (梅里雪山国家公园, Méilǐ Xuěshān Guó Jiā Gōng Yuǎn; ¥150-230). There are three ticket options: one includes three observation points and the glacier (¥228), another ticket is the same three observation points and Yùbēng village (¥230), and the third is just three observation points (¥150).

If you want to go to the glacier and Yùbēng village you should buy the full ticket. A student card nets a 50% discount.

Míngyǒng Glacier   GLACIER

(明永冰川, Míngyǒng Bīngchuān; ¥228) Tumbling off the side of Kawa Karpo peak is the 12km-long Míngyǒng Glacier. At over 13 sq km, it is not only the lowest glacier in China (around 2200m) but also an oddity – a monsoon marine glacier, which basically translates as having an ecosystem that couldn't possibly be more diverse: tundra, taiga, broadleaf forest and meadow.

The mountain has been a pilgrimage site for centuries and you'll still meet a few Tibetan pilgrims, some of whom circumambulate the mountain over seven days in autumn. Surrounding villages are known as 'heaven villages' because of the dense fog that hangs about in spring and summer.

The trail to the glacier leads up from Míngyǒng's central square. After 70 minutes of steady uphill walking you will reach the Tibetan **Tàizǐ Miào** (太子庙), a small temple where there are snack and drink stalls. A further 30 minutes along the trail is **Lotus Temple** (莲花庙; Liánhuā Miào), which offers fantastic views of the glacier framed by prayer flags and *chörten*. Horses can also be hired to go up to the glacier (¥200).

If you're coming from Yǔbēng, you could also hike to Míngyǒng from Xīdāng in around three hours if you hoof it.

Míngyǒng village consists of only a couple hotels, restaurants and shops. You can overnight in the newly renovated **Rénqín Hotel** (仁钦酒店, Rénqín Jiǔdiàn; ☑ 139 8871 4330; dm ¥35, d ¥120-160; ☎) which also serves meals.

From Déqīn, private minibuses to Míngyǒng leave regularly from the bridge near the market at the top end of town (¥20 per person), or you can hire your own for around ¥120.

The road from Déqīn descends into the dramatic Mekong Gorge. Six kilometres before Míngyǒng the road crosses the Mekong River and branches off to Xīdāng. Nearby is a small temple, the **Bǎishùlín Miào**, and a *chörten*. There is a checkpoint here where you will need to show your national park ticket.

Fēilái Sì   BUDDHIST TEMPLE

(飞来寺, Fēilái Temple; donation) Approximately 10km southwest of Déqīn is the small but interesting Tibetan Fēilái Temple (Fēilái Sì), or Naka Zhashi (or Trashi) Gompa in Tibetan, devoted to the spirit of Kawa Karpo. There's

YǓBĒNG & KAWA KARPO HIKES

The principal reason to visit Déqīn is the chance to hike to the foot of Kawa Karpo. The main destination is **Yǔbēng** (雨崩) village from where you can make day hikes to mountain meadows, lakes and the fabulous **Yǔbēng Waterfall** (雨崩神瀑; Yǔbēng Shénpù).

The five-hour, 18km trek to Yǔbēng starts at the **Xīdāng** (西当) hot spring, about 3km past Xīdāng village. The drive from Fēilái Sì to Xīdāng takes one hour and 40 minutes. There is a ¥5 entrance fee for Yǔbēng, but when you show your receipt at your guesthouse you'll get ¥5 off your bill.

Yǔbēng consists of two sections. You first arrive in 'Upper Yǔbēng', which contains most guesthouses, then the trail continues another 1km to 'Lower Yǔbēng'. Yǔbēng is busier than it was, so booking ahead at peak periods is a good idea. **Lobsang Trekker Lodge** (藏巴乐之家, Zàngbālè Zhījiā; ☑ 139 8879 7053; http://lobsangtrekkerlodge.webs.com; dm ¥30, d ¥150-200; ☎), in Upper Yǔbēng, is a popular place that offers meals, comfortable rooms and good traveller info. Also recommended is the **Interval Time Guesthouse** (间隔时光, Jiàngé Shíguāng; ☑ 180 0887 8300; Upper Yǔbēng; dm ¥25-40, d ¥150; ☎), which has knowledgable staff and decent food.

From Yǔbēng village, there are loads of treks. It's a three- to four-hour trip on foot or horseback to the waterfall. Or, you could head south to a picturesque lake (it's around 4350m high and not easy to find, so take a guide). Guides cost around ¥200 per day. Supplies (food and water) are pricey in Yǔbēng so stock up in Fēilái Sì.

Leaving the village, many travellers hike to **Nínóng** (尼农) village by the Mekong River, a five-hour downhill trek that includes a hairy one-hour section along a precarious, narrow path. If you are prone to vertigo, head back to Xīdāng instead. Vans run to Déqīn and Fēilái Sì from Nínóng for ¥25 per person or ¥200 for the whole van. If you are stuck, walk 6km to Xīdāng where there is more transport.

Then there's the legendary Kawa Karpo *kora*, a 12-day pilgrim circumambulation of Méilǐ Xuěshān. However, half of it is in the Tibetan Autonomous Region, so you'll need a permit to do it; and you'll definitely need a guide.

no charge but leave a donation. No photos are allowed inside the tiny hall.

Everyone comes here for the sublime **views** – particularly the sunrises – of the Méilǐ Xuěshān range, including 6740m Kawa Karpo (also known as Méilǐ Xuěshān or Tàizǐ Shān) and the even more beautiful peak to the south, 6054m Miacimu (神女; Shénnǚ in Chinese), whose spirit is the female counterpart of Kawa Karpo. Locals come here to burn juniper incense to the wrathful spirit of the mountain.

Sadly, the weather doesn't always cooperate, often shrouding the peaks in mist. October and November are the likeliest months for your sunrise photo op. A ticket office near the platform sells tickets for Fēilái Sì and other sites.

The 'town' is actually just an ugly, expanding strip of concrete shops, hotels and restaurants along the main road. Across the road, the government has unsportingly set up a wall, blocking the view of the mountains (just walk downhill 200m for the same view).

Most backpackers stay at **Feeling Village Youth Hostel** (觉色滇乡国际青年旅舍, Juésè Diānxiāng Guójì Qīngnián Lǚshè; ☑ 0887 841 6133; juesedianxiang@163.com; dm ¥25-35, d ¥100-120; ❀@⊛), which has cheerful English-speaking staff, simple but clean rooms with electric blankets and hot water in the evenings. It's set back from the main road; look for the sign turning right up the little alley at the bottom of the village.

On the main road, the **Zàng Jí Wáng Shāngwù Jiǔdiàn** (藏吉王商务酒店; ☑ 0887 302 2558; d ¥238-280; ⊛) has comfortable rooms with huge windows and spectacular mountain views. Prices are regularly discounted by 20%. **Restaurants** on the main road serve pricy Chinese and Western meals.

To get here from Déqīn a taxi will cost you ¥40, or take a minivan (¥10 per person).

🛏 Sleeping & Eating

The main places to stay are located in Yǔbēng village, which is divided into an upper and lower section. The majority of guesthouses can be found in 'Upper Yǔbēng', although there are a few in 'Lower Yǔbēng'. Thankfully, hot water and wi-fi are now standard.

Guesthouses double as restaurants in Yǔbēng.

❶ Getting There & Away

For Shangri-la, five daily buses leave from Déqīn's small bus station on the main street (¥58, four hours, 8.30am, 9.30am, 10.30am, 12.30pm and 4pm). There are also daily buses to Lìjiāng (¥114, eight hours, 7.30am), Kūnmíng (¥258, 16 hours, 1pm) and Xiàguān (¥148, 12 hours, 3pm).

A shared van from Fēilái Sì to Xīdāng will cost ¥20 per person or ¥180 for the whole van. You could also hike all the way from Fēilái Sì using local roads and paths. Another possibility is the bus from Déqīn to Xīdāng (¥20, 8.30am and 3pm), which stops in Fēilái Sì.

NÙ JIĀNG VALLEY 怒江大峡谷

The 320km-long Nù Jiāng Valley is one of Yúnnán's best-kept secrets. The Nù Jiāng (known as the 'Salween' in Myanmar; its name in Chinese means 'Raging River') is the second-longest river in Southeast Asia and a Unesco World Heritage Site.

Sandwiched between Gāolígòng Shān and Myanmar to the west, Tibet to the north and the imposing Bìluó Shān to the east, the gorge holds nearly a quarter of China's flora and fauna species, and half of China's endangered species. The valley also has an exotic mix of Han, Nu, Lisu, Drung and Tibetan nationalities, and even the odd Burmese trader. And it's simply stunning – all of it.

But like other parts of rural Yúnnán, change is coming to the Nù Jiāng Valley. The local government is touting investment opportunities in everything from truffle farms to stone quarries, and the main towns – Liùkù and Fúgòng especially – are booming, with new apartment blocks and shops appearing and Han migrants arriving in numbers.

Nevertheless, the Nù Jiāng remains one of only two rivers that have not been dammed in all China and the signs are that it will, thankfully, stay that way. And getting here remains a pain, which is a good thing in terms of keeping the valley as pristine as is possible in China. Travellers, though, should be prepared for roads that can be impassable due to heavy rain and/or landslides.

All traffic enters via Liùkù. From there, you trundle nine hours up the valley, marvelling at the scenery, and then head back the way you came.

Plans have been announced to blast a road from Gòngshān in the northern part of the valley to Déqīn, and another from the village of Bǐngzhōngluò even further north into Tibet. Given the immense topographical challenges, these schemes are a long way off. But you should make sure to get here before they happen.

Almost all hotels, guesthouses and hostels are confined to the main towns in the Nù Jiāng Valley – Liùkù, Fúgòng and Gòngshān – and the village of Bǐngzhōngluò. You can find bearable rooms from ¥80 and up.

Liùkù is the main transport hub for the Nù Jiāng Valley and you will have to go through there for buses heading into the valley.

Liùkù 六库

☎ 0886 / POP 184,835

Liùkù is the lively, pleasant capital of the prefecture. Divided by the Nù Jiāng River, it's the main transport hub of the region and growing fast, although it's of little intrinsic interest.

Sleeping & Eating

There are a handful of scruffy cheapies on Chuancheng Lu in the centre of town where rooms can be found from ¥80. Otherwise, most hotels are in the midrange bracket.

To eat, head to the riverbank, south of Renmin Lu, where lots of outdoor restaurants cook great barbecued fish.

Jīnyáng Bīnguǎn   HOTEL $
(金洋宾馆; ☎ 0886 381 0666; Chuancheng Lu, 穿城路; tw ¥138; ※ 🛈) This new place is a solid budget choice with big rooms and bathrooms, although the ones facing Chuancheng Lu can be noisy.

Nùjiāng Géruì Shāngwù Jiǔdiàn   HOTEL $$$
(怒江格瑞商务酒店; ☎ 0886 388 8885; 123 Chuancheng Lu, 穿城路123号; d ¥488; ※ 🛈) Routine discounts of 70% bring this place into the budget category. It has modern showers and large, comfortable rooms, although they can be a bit smoky. After crossing the bridge it's one block uphill from Renmin Lu.

Information

You will likely have to register your passport at a police checkpoint about 30 minutes before entering Liùkù.
Bank of China (中国银行, Zhōngguó Yínháng; 🕑 9am-5pm) Located uphill from the bus station.

Getting There & Away

The bus station is located south of the centre and across the river (a ¥15 taxi ride).
Bǎoshān ¥52, three to four hours, eight daily (8am to 4.30pm)
Bǐngzhōngluò ¥85, nine hours, one daily (8.20am)
Fúgòng ¥35, four hours, nine daily (7.20am to 4.20pm)
Gòngshān ¥78, eight hours, eight daily (7am to 1pm)
Kūnmíng ¥190 to ¥251, nine hours, seven daily (8.30am to 7pm)
Téngchōng ¥58, six hours, three daily (8am, 10am and 11am)
Xiàguān ¥88, four to five hours, 10 daily (8am to 7pm)

Fúgòng 福贡

☎ 0886 / POP 98,616

Hemmed in by steep cliffs on all sides, Fúgòng offers some of the best scenery in the Nù Jiāng Valley and has a large Lisu population. The town itself is unremarkable, although it is expanding rapidly (it has working ATMs now). Fúgòng is roughly halfway up the valley and the best place to break your journey if it's late.

Sleeping & Eating

All of Fúgòng's hotels are budget or midrange. There are no hostels here. The cheapest beds (from ¥50) can be found around the bus station.

Róngdū Shāngwù Jiǔdiàn   HOTEL $
(荣都商务酒店; ☎ 0886 889 4666; 2 Shiyue Jie, 石月街2号; tw ¥198; ※ 🛈) On the corner of the bus station street and the main drag, this new hotel offers clean, sizeable and modern rooms (sit-down toilets) and has a good wi-fi connection. Discounts of 50% are standard.

Zhèngzōng Chuānwèi Fàndiàn   YUNNAN $
(正宗川味饭店; Wenhua Lu, 文化路; dishes from ¥15; 🕑 9am-10pm) Almost all restaurants in Fúgòng offer the same selection of dishes, mostly on display so you can pick and choose. This one, despite its unprepossessing interior, sees a steady stream of locals and the food is tasty and clean. As ever in Yúnnán, the vegetables available are excellent.

Getting There & Away

There are twice-hourly buses to Liùkù (¥37, four hours) between 7.20am and 4.20pm. For Bǐngzhōngluò you'll have to wait for the bus from Liùkù to pass by, which happens around noon. Otherwise, buses to Gòngshān (¥35, nine daily) start running at 11am. Your best bet for a quick getaway to Gòngshān is take a shared minivan for ¥40. They start running from 7.30am and you'll find them outside the bus station.

There is also one daily bus to Kūnmíng (¥297, 2.30pm, 12 hours) and one to Xiàguān (¥128, 10.30am, eight hours).

Bǐngzhōngluò   丙中洛

☎ 0886 / POP 3000

The main reason to come to the Nù Jiāng Valley is to visit isolated, friendly Bǐngzhōngluò, a village set in a beautiful, wide and fertile bowl. Just 35km south of Tibet and close to Myanmar, it's a great base for hikes into the surrounding mountains and valleys. The area is at its best in spring and early autumn. Don't even think about coming in the winter.

🏃 Activities

Potential short hops include heading south along the main road for 2km to the impressive 'first bend' of the Nù Jiāng River, or north along a track more than 15km long that passes a 19th-century church and several villages (the road starts by heading downhill from Road to Tibet Guesthouse).

Longer three- or four-day treks include heading to the Tibetan village of **Dímáluò** (迪麻洛) and then onto the village of **Yǒngzhī** (永芝). From Yǒngzhī it's another two hours' walk to the main road from where you can hitch a ride to Déqīn. It is a demanding trek that can really only be done from late May until September as the 3800m pass is too difficult to cross in heavy snow.

👉 Tours

A guide is pretty much essential. Tibetan trek leader Aluo comes highly recommended. He's based at Road to Tibet Guesthouse, although he's often away on treks so email him or call him first on %139 8867 2792. Treks usually cost between ¥300 and ¥400 per day. Note that there are no villages en route to Yǒngzhī so you'll need to carry all your own food and sleep in basic huts along the way (porters can be hired for around ¥100 per day).

Another option is Peter, a Lemao guide, who offers treks for ¥380 a day. He speaks good English, although some travellers report he doesn't always deliver what he promises. You can find him at Nù Jiāng Baini Travel on the main street.

Nù Jiāng Baini Travel   TOUR
(☎ 139 8853 9641; yangindali@yahoo.co.uk) You can rent mountain bikes (¥80 per day), access the internet (¥8 per hour) and get travel information here. Treks can be arranged, with Peter the guide charging ¥380 per day.

🛏 Sleeping & Eating

There are a few guesthouses and hostels in Bǐngzhōngluò and a small selection of restaurants. All the guesthouses and hostels do meals.

Road to Tibet Guesthouse   GUESTHOUSE **$**
(☎ 0886 358 1168; aluo_luosang@hotmail.com; dm ¥35-45, d with/without bathroom ¥80-120; 🛜) Most backpackers end up at this place, located on the street heading downhill from the main road. Beds are hard but it's a clean place with some English spoken and they cook simple meals. The owner, Aluo, also has a basic guesthouse in his home village of Dímáluò, a good destination for a trek.

ℹ Information

All hotels in town have wi-fi and Peter has internet access at Nù Jiāng Baini Travel for ¥8 per hour.

ℹ Getting There & Away

There is one direct bus a day from Liùkù to Bǐngzhōngluò (¥85, nine hours, 8.20am). Or take any bus to Gòngshān (¥78, eight hours, nine daily, 7am to 1pm), where you can connect for regular buses to Bǐngzhōngluò (¥13, one hour).

Buses return from Bǐngzhōngluò to Liùkù from opposite Yù Dòng Bīnguǎn at 8am. Otherwise, take a bus to Gòngshān (¥13, one hour), where there are nine buses daily to Liùkù (¥79, eight hours, 7.30am to 12.10pm).

Dúlóng Valley   独龙江

Separated from the Nù Jiāng Valley by the high Gāolígòng Shān range and only reached by road in 1999, the Dúlóng Valley (Dúlóng Gǔ) is one of the remotest valleys in China and is home to the 5000-strong Dulong ethnic group. The Dúlóng River actually flows out of China into Myanmar, where it eventually joins the Irrawaddy.

There are a couple of basic hotels in the county capital Kǒngdāng (孔当) where you can find rooms from ¥80 to ¥100. Outside of Kǒngdāng, it might be possible to find a bed in a village (most are close to the main road), but bear in mind that the Dulong people are very shy and you'll hardly head any Mandarin, let alone English, here.

The main road in the valley itself is paved south towards the border with Myanmar (Burma) and north towards Tibet, but there are no hotels or restaurants outside Kǒngdāng. Strong cyclists will have a field day, but bring your own tent and food.

Although the road into the valley has been upgraded, no buses run here. Minivans make the four-hour, 96km trip infrequently (¥100 per person, or hire one for ¥600).

BĂOSHĀN REGION 保山

Scrunched up against Myanmar and bisected by the wild Nù Jiāng, the Bǎoshān region is a varied landscape that includes thick forests, dormant volcanoes and hot springs.

The eponymous capital is unremarkable; lovely Téngchōng (and its environs) is where it's at. The Téngchōng area is peppered with minority groups whose villages lie in and around the ancient fire mountains.

As early as the 4th and 5th centuries BC (two centuries before the northern routes through Central Asia were established), the Bǎoshān area was an important stop on the southern Silk Road – the Sìchuān–India route. The area did not come under Chinese control until the Han dynasty. In 1277 a huge battle was waged in the region between the 12,000 troops of Kublai Khan and 60,000 Burmese soldiers and their 2000 elephants. The Mongols won and went on to take Bagan.

Téngchōng County

Some highlights of this region are the traditional villages that are scattered between Téngchōng and Yúnfēng Shān (云峰山; Cloudy Peak Mountain). The relatively plentiful public transport along this route means that you can jump on and off minibuses to go exploring as the whim takes you. Otherwise, hire a taxi or minivan for a day tour for around ¥300.

Téngchōng 腾冲

☎ 0875 / POP 135,318

With 20 volcanoes in the vicinity, lots of hot springs and great trekking potential, there's plenty to explore in this neck of the woods. Téngchōng itself is a bit of an oddity – one of the few places in China that, though much of the old architecture has been demolished, remains a pleasant place to hang out, with oodles of green space (you can actually smell the flowers!) and a friendly populace.

◉ Sights

Much of the old-time architecture is now gone, but a few OK places for a random wander are still to be found. Téngchōng's proximity to Myanmar (Burma) means there are many jade and teak shops around town.

Láifēng Temple BUDDHIST TEMPLE
(来凤寺, Láifēng Sì) FREE Buddhist temple surrounded by lush pine forest.

Xiānle Tèmple BUDDHIST TEMPLE
(仙乐寺, Xiānlè Sì) FREE Buddhist temple in the west of town.

Diéshuǐ Waterfall WATERFALL
(叠水瀑布, Diéshuǐ Pùbù; ¥20) In the western suburbs of town, beside the Xiānlè Temple, this is a good place for a picnic. The area makes a nice destination for a bike ride and you could easily combine it with a trip to **Héshùn** (和顺), a picturesque village 4km outside Téngchōng.

Láifēng Shān National Forest Park PARK
(来凤山国家森林公园, Láifēng Shān Guójiā Sēnlín Gōngyuán; ◉ 8am-7pm) FREE On the western edge of town, walk through lush pine forests of this park to Láifēng Temple or make the sweaty hike up to the summit, where a pagoda offers fine views.

🛏 Sleeping & Eating

Xīnghuá Dàjiǔdiàn HOTEL $
(兴华大酒店; ☎ 0875 513 2688; 7 Tuanpo Xiaoqu, 团坡小区7号; d incl breakfast ¥120; ❀🛜) It's been around a while, and there are alarming, tiger-pattern carpets here, but the rooms themselves are clean and sizeable, if a little old-fashioned. The wi-fi connection is strong and the location is handy in what is a spread-out town.

Yudu Hotel HOTEL $$$
(玉都大酒店, Yùdū Dàjiǔdiàn; ☎ 0875 513 8666; 15 Tengyue Lu, 腾越路15号; d ¥978; ❀🛜) There are 130 rooms at this comfortable, professionally run place and they are routinely discounted by a whopping 70% to 80%, making them a great deal. Some come with computers, but all have decent bathrooms. Don't expect to hear any English, though. It's on the corner of Tengyue Lu and Guanghua Lu.

Héfēngyuán Cāntīng YUNNAN $$
(河风园餐厅; ☎ 0875 513 2758; opposite Aili Hotel, 爱丽酒店对面; dishes from ¥12; ◉ 11am-9pm) Eat outside in a large, pleasant courtyard at this busy place. Try the local cured ham, *huǒtuǐ* (火腿), a Téngchōng speciality, or choose from the wide range of fish, meat and veggies on display. No English spoken, but the staff are welcoming. It's right by the bridge over the river: look for the five red characters painted on the wall.

ℹ Information

Bank of China (中国银行, Zhōngguó Yínháng; cnr Fengshan Lu & Yingjiang Donglu) Has a 24-hour ATM and will change cash and travellers

Téngchōng

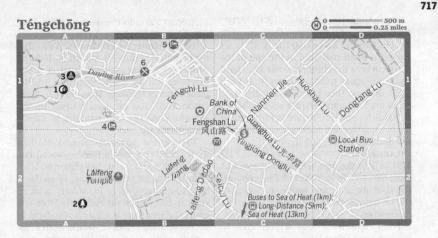

N 0 — 500 m
0 — 0.25 miles

cheques. There are other ATMs around town that take foreign cards too.

China Post (国际邮局, Zhōngguó Yóuzhèng; Fengshan Lu) You can send mail overseas from here.

Public Security Bureau (PSB, 公安局, Gōng'ānjú; ☏ 0875 513 1046; 20 Xiaxi Jie, 下西街20号; ◎ 8.30-11.30am & 2.30-5.30pm Mon-Fri) Come here for visa extensions.

ⓘ Getting There & Away

AIR
Téngchōng's airport, 12km south of town, has six flights daily to Kunming (from ¥580).

BUS
The city's long-distance bus station is in the south of town. A taxi to the centre of town is ¥15.

Bǎoshān ¥63, 2½ hours, every 40 minutes (8am to 7pm)

Kūnmíng ¥218 to ¥289, 10 hours, nine daily (9am to 8pm)

Lìjiāng ¥195, 10 hours, one daily (10.50am)

Liùkù ¥58, six hours, three daily (10am, 11am, noon)

Xiàguān ¥130, 5½ hours, four daily (10.30am, noon, 2pm and 7pm)

Téngchōng's local bus station (客运站, kèyùnzhàn) is on Dongfang Lu.

Mángshì ¥45, two to three hours, ten daily (8am to 4.30pm)

Ruìlì ¥80, four hours, nine daily (7.50am to 3.50pm)

Buses to local destinations north of Téngchōng, such as Mǎzhàn, Gùdòng, Ruìdiàn, Diántān or Zizhì, leave from the West Gate bus station, (西门客运站; Xīmén Kèyùnzhàn), which is really just a forecourt on the corner of Huoshan Lu and Guaijinlou Xiang in the northwest of town.

ⓘ Getting Around

Bus 2 runs from the town centre to the long-distance bus station (¥1), as well as passing the West Gate bus station. Bus 6 passes the local bus station on Dongfang Lu (¥1). Taxis charge ¥6 to hop around town. Minivans run to the airport from just south of the junction of Feicui Lu and Rehai Lu (¥30 per person).

Héshùn   和顺
☑ 0875 / POP 6,000

Southwest of Téngchōng, Héshùn has been set aside as a retirement village for overseas Chinese, but it's of much more interest as a traditional Chinese village with cobbled streets, even if there are an ever-increasing number of jade and jewellery shops here. But it's far from overwhelmed by day trippers and there are some great old buildings in the village, providing lots of photo opportunities.

The village has a small **museum** (博物馆; *bówùguǎn*) and a famous old **library** (图书馆; *túshūguǎn*), with 70,000 books, as well as a few interesting courtyard residences and temples. There's an ¥80 admission fee to get in to the village itself.

Mànbànpāi Kèzhàn (慢半拍客栈; ☑ 0875 515 0755; 1456160764@QQ.com; Cunjiawan, 寸家湾; 2-bed dm ¥50, d & tw ¥100-120; ❋ 🅰) is set around a small courtyard at the end of the village, where the cheaper rooms have hard beds and squat toilets, but are fine for a night or two. There's a pleasant 2nd-floor communal area and helpful staff, although no English is spoken. To find it, turn right at the banyan tree and waterwheel and head a few hundred metres uphill.

Lánnà Cafe (兰纳咖啡, Lánnà Kāfēi; ☑ 187 8750 1309; coffee from ¥28, breakfast from ¥30, mains from ¥38; ⏱ 9am-10pm; 🅰) is a chilled-out spot for a decent coffee. It also does OK breakfasts, as well as pasta, pizza and sandwiches.

From Téngchōng, bus 6 (¥1) goes to Héshùn from Feicui Lu.

Yúnfēng Shān 云峰山

A Taoist mountain dotted with 17th-century temples and monastic retreats, **Yúnfēng Shān** (admission ¥110, combined ticket including cable car ¥230) is 47km north of Téngchōng. It's possible to take a **cable car** (one-way/return ¥90/160), close to the top from where it's a 20-minute walk to **Dàxióng Bǎodiàn** (大雄宝殿), a temple at the summit. **Lǔzǔ Diàn** (鲁祖殿), the temple second from the top, serves up solid vegetarian food at lunchtime. It's a quick walk down but it can be hard on the knees. You can walk up the mountain in about 2½ hours.

To get to the mountain, go to the West Gate bus station in Téngchōng and catch a bus to Gùdōng (¥15), and then a microbus from there to the turn-off (¥10). From the turn-off you have to hitch, or you could take the lovely walk past the village of Héping (和平) to the pretty villages just before the mountain. From the parking lot a golf cart (¥5) takes you to the entrance. Hiring a vehicle from Téngchōng for the return trip will cost about ¥300 to ¥350.

Mǎzhàn Volcanoes

Téngchōng County is renowned for its volcanoes, and although they have been behaving themselves for many centuries, the seismic and geothermal activity in the area indicates that they won't always continue to do so. The closest volcano to Téngchōng is **Mǎ'ān Shān** (马鞍山; Saddle Mountain), around 5km to the northwest. It's just south of the main road to Yíngjiāng.

Around 22km to the north of town, near the village of **Mǎzhàn** (马战乡), is the most accessible cluster of **volcanoes** (¥40). The main central volcano is known as **Dàkōng Shān** (大空山; Big Empty Hill), which pretty much sums it up, and to the left of it is the black crater of **Hēikōng Shān** (黑空山; Black Empty Hill). You can haul yourself up the steps for views of the surrounding lava fields (long dormant).

To visit the volcanoes around Mǎzhàn from Téngchōng, take a Gùdōng-bound bus (¥15) from the West Gate bus station on Huoshan Lu and get off at Mǎzhàn, From there, it's a 10-minute walk to the volcano area, or you can take a motor-tricycle (¥5). Once you are in the area there is a fair bit of walking to get between the sights, or you can hitch rides.

Getting out to the villages around Téngchōng is a bit tricky. Catching buses part of the way and hiking is one possibility, hiring a taxi for the day (¥300) is another.

Sea of Heat 热海

A steamy cluster of hot springs, geysers and streams (but no actual sea), the **Sea of Heat** (Rèhǎi; ¥60, pool access ¥268; ⏱ 8am-9pm Apr-Oct, to 8pm Nov-Mar) is located about 12km southwest of Téngchōng. It's essentially an upmarket resort, with a few outdoor springs, a nice warm-water swimming pool along with indoor baths. You can wander the tree- and plant-lined stone paths admiring the geothermal activity. Some of the springs here reach temperatures of 102°C (don't swim in these ones!).

Note that it's possible to buy a combined ticket (¥100) for both the Sea of Heat and the Mǎzhàn volcanoes at **Yǎng Shēng Gé** (养生阁; ☑ 0875 586 9700; www.chinaspa.cn; d ¥1960, ste ¥3600-5600; ❋ 🅰).

Bus 2 (¥3) leaves Téngchōng for the Sea of Heat from Rehai Lu, 200m south of the junction with Feicui Lu.

DÉHÓNG PREFECTURE 德宏州

Déhóng Prefecture (Déhóng Zhōu and Jingpo Autonomous Prefecture) juts into Myanmar in the far west of Yúnnán. Once a backwater of backwaters, from the late 1980s the region saw tourists flock in to experience its raucous border atmosphere.

That's dimmed quite a bit and most Chinese tourists in Déhóng are here for the trade from Myanmar that comes through Ruìlì and Wǎndīng; Burmese jade is the most desired commodity and countless other items are spirited over the border.

Almost all travellers stay in Ruìlì, the capital of Déhóng, where there are many midrange and budget hotels, as well as one hostel. Expect discounts most of the time.

Ruìlì is a great place to sample Burmese food, with a number of restaurants offering it. You'll also find Dai dishes on many menus.

Ruìlì 瑞丽

🗓 0692 / POP 99,148

Back in the 1980s this border town was a notorious haven for drug and gem smugglers, prostitution and various other iniquities. The government cleaned it up in the late 1990s (on the surface anyway) and today you're more likely to stumble into a shopping mall than a den of thieves. Still, Ruìlì has an edge to it, thanks to its proximity to a notoriously anarchic region of Myanmar and a thriving gem market operated largely by Burmese traders. And with its palm-tree-lined streets, bicycle rickshaws and steamy climate, it has a distinctly laid-back, Southeast Asian feel.

The minority villages nearby are also good reason to come and it's worth getting a bicycle and heading out to explore. Another draw is Myanmar, just a few kilometres away. Though individual tourists are not allowed to cross freely, organising permits to take you through the sensitive border area is becoming easier.

⦿ Sights

Ruìlì Market
MARKET

(瑞丽市场, Ruìlì Shìchǎng; ⊗6am-6pm) This is one of the most colourful and fun markets in all Yúnnán; a real swirl of ethnicities, including Dai, Jingpo, Han and Burmese, as well as the odd Bangladeshi and Pakistani trader. Get here in the morning, when the stalls are lined with Burmese smokes, tofu wrapped in banana leaves, freshly made noodles, cosmetics and pharmaceuticals from Thailand, clothes – you name it. It's also a good place to grab lunch at one of the many snack stalls.

Jade Market
MARKET

(珠宝街, Zhūbǎo Jiē; ⊗8am-9pm) Ruìlì's ever-expanding jade market is great for people-watching and is the true centre of town in all senses. Burmese jade sellers run most of the shops here and for a while you may even forget you are still in China.

Ruìlì

🛏 Sleeping

There are many midrange and budget hotels in Ruìlì, as well as one hostel, with the cheapest rooms (from ¥100) available along Nanmao Jie.

Biānchéng Jiǔdiàn
HOTEL **$**

(边城酒店; ☑0692 415 6669; 85 Biancheng Jie, 边城街85号; d ¥138-328; ❋@🛜) This place in the centre of town has comfortable beds, power showers, good wi-fi and efficient staff (but little English spoken). The most expensive rooms are themed – think *Superman* decor – and have round beds. No English sign; look for the large, sand-coloured building close to the corner with Ruijiang Lu.

Irrawaddy International Youth Hostel
HOSTEL **$**

(伊洛瓦底国际青年旅舍, Yīluòwǎdǐ Guójì Qīngnián Lǚshě; ☑189 8824 3100; 7 Youyi Lu, 友谊路7号; dm ¥35-40, d ¥80-130; ❋🛜) This hostel located on a quiet, residential street in the north of town likes to fly under the radar: it's hard to find any English-language

MINORITY GROUPS

The most obvious minority groups in Déhóng are the Burmese (who are normally dressed in their traditional sarong-like *longyi*), Dai and Jingpo – known in Myanmar (Burma) as the Kachin – a minority group long engaged in armed struggle against the Myanmar government.

information about it. But the dorms and rooms are bright and reasonably well kept, the bathrooms have sit-down toilets, the staff are cheerful and speak a little English and there's a pleasant communal area and garden.

It's a 15-minute walk from Nanmao Jie, or a ¥8 taxi ride.

Míngruì Hotel   HOTEL $
(明瑞宾馆, Míngruì Bīnguǎn; ☑0692 410 8666; 98 Nanmao Jie, 南卯街98号; d ¥120; ❄🛜) Big, bright and clean rooms and a handy central location, although that means it can be noisy. Strong wi-fi connection. It's down an alley off the northern side of Nanmao Jie, close to the intersection with Xinan Lu.

Ruìlì Bīnguǎn   HOTEL $$$
(瑞丽宾馆; ☑0692 410 0888; 25 Jianshe Lu, 建设路25号; d ¥520; ❄🛜) This long-standing place, garishly painted orange and gold and close to the jade market, remains decent value with routine 50% discounts. The wood-panelled rooms aren't huge but they are comfortable and the staff are amenable: they can provide maps (¥10) of town and the surrounding area.

✗ Eating

You'll find a fair few Burmese restaurants in Ruìlì – try the area around the jade market – as well as ones serving Dai food. There are street stalls scattered all over town come nightfall, plus there's a night food market; just follow your nose.

★ Lántiān Xiǎochī   YUNNAN $
(蓝天小吃; Xin'an Lu, 新安路; dishes from ¥8; ☺7am-10pm) Fantastic, popular place for noodles at any time of day, but especially breakfast. It's also good for Burmese-style salads, fried rice dishes and fruit juices. No English menu, but there are pictures on the wall to choose from.

★ Bo Bo's Cold Drinks Shop   CAFE $
(步步冷饮店, Bùbù Lěngyǐndiàn; ☑0692 412 3643; Xinan Lu, 新安路; dishes from ¥10; ☺9am-midnight; 🛜) This Ruìlì institution is busy from early to late, with the Burmese waiters clad in their native, sarong-like *longyi* hustling as they serve up fantastic fruit juices, Burmese-style milky tea, ice cream and cakes. They also do simple but tasty rice and noodle dishes. Look for the English sign and climb the stairs to the large, 2nd floor covered terrace.

Myanmar Garden   BURMESE $
(缅甸园, Miǎndiàn Yuán; 73 Maohan Lu, 卯喊路 73号; dishes from ¥15; ☺10am-2am; 🛜) Great for authentic Burmese food like tea leaf and lime beef salads, as well as a smattering of northern Thai dishes. It's fine for coffee and juices as well, while a jug of chilled lager is ¥36. It's inside a forecourt just off Maohan Lu near the intersection with Xin'an Lu.

❶ Information

Bank of China (中国银行, Zhōngguó Yínháng; Nanmao Jie, 南卯街; ☺9am-4pm) Provides all the usual services and will cash travellers cheques for US dollars if you're headed to Myanmar.

China Post (国际邮局, Zhōngguó Yóuzhèng; cnr Mengmao Lu & Renmin Lu; ☺9am-6pm) You can send mail overseas from here.

Internet Cafe (网吧, Wǎngbā; cnr Nanmao Jie & Jiegang Lu; per hr ¥4; ☺24hr) At the time of writing, foreigners weren't allowed to use Ruìlì's internet cafes.

Public Security Bureau (PSB, 公安局, Gōng'ānjú; ☑0692 414 1281; Jianshe Lu; ☺8.30-11.30am & 2.30-5.30pm) Come here for visa extensions.

❶ Getting There & Away

An expressway from Bǎoshān to Ruìlì is close to completion and perhaps one day in the not-too-distant future there will be a high-speed rail link from Kūnmíng that will extend into Myanmar (Burma) via Ruìlì.

AIR
There are 18 daily flights from Mángshì to Kūnmíng (from ¥450). You can buy tickets at **China Eastern Airlines** (东方航空公司, Dōngfāng Hángkōng Gōngsī; ☑0692 411 1111; Renmin Lu; ☺8am-10pm).

BUS
The new **long-distance bus station** (长途客运站, chángtú kèyùn zhàn) is on the northeastern

outskirts of Ruìlì. Taxis charge a flat ¥15 to the centre of town.

Bǎoshān ¥93, six hours, every 50 minutes (8am to 5pm)

Jǐnghóng ¥410, 22 hours, one daily (10am)

Kūnmíng ¥295 to ¥331, 12 hours, five daily (8.30am, noon, 3pm, 6pm and 7.30pm)

Mángshì ¥36, two hours, every 30 minutes (7am to 7pm)

Téngchōng ¥82, four hours, every 40 minutes (7.20am to 1.20pm)

Xiàguān ¥161, nine hours, three daily (9am, 11am and 5pm)

Minivans and buses for local destinations cruise around town: flag them down on Nanmao Jie and Renmin Lu. Destinations include Wǎndīng (¥15), Zhāngfèng (¥15) and the village of Nóngdào (¥8).

🛈 Getting Around

Mángshì is a 1½-hour drive from Ruìlì. Shuttle taxis leave daily from the **China Eastern office**, three hours before scheduled flights (¥80).

The most interesting day trips require a bicycle. Ask at your accommodation about the best place to rent one.

A flat rate for a taxi ride inside the city should be ¥6, and is up for negotiation from there. There are also motorcycle taxis and cycle rickshaws.

Around Ruìlì

Most of the sights around Ruìlì can be explored by bicycle. It's worth making detours down the narrow paths leading off the main roads to visit minority villages. The people are friendly, and there are lots of photo opportunities.

The shortest ride is to turn left at the corner north of China Post and continue out of Ruìlì into the little village of **Měngmǎo**. There are half a dozen Shan temples scattered about; the fun is in finding them.

💿 Sights

Hǎnshā Zhuāng Temple   DAI TEMPLE

(喊沙奘寺, Hǎnshā Zhuāng Sì) **FREE** Hǎnshā Zhuāng Temple is an impressive wooden structure with a few resident monks. It's about 5km southwest of Ruìlì, set a little off the road. A green tourism sign marks the turn-off. The surrounding Dai village is interesting.

Léizhuāngxiāng   HISTORIC SITE

(雷装相) **FREE** Léizhuāngxiāng is Ruìlì's oldest stupa, dating back to the middle of the Tang dynasty. It's about 8km southwest of town.

Golden Duck Pagoda   PAGODA

(弄安金鸭塔, Nòng'ān Jīnyā Tǎ) **FREE** This pagoda is on the southwestern outskirts of Ruìlì on the main road. An attractive stupa set in a temple courtyard, it was established to mark the arrival of a pair of golden ducks that brought good fortune to what was previously an uninhabited marshy area.

Golden Pagoda   PAGODA

(姐勒金塔, Jiělè Jīntǎ) **FREE** A few kilometres to the east of Ruìlì on the road to Wǎndīng is the Golden Pagoda, a fine structure that dates back 200 years.

YÚNNÁN AROUND RUÌLÌ

VISITING JIĚGÀO

On land jutting into Myanmar (Burma), Jiěgào (姐告) is the main checkpoint for a steady stream of cross-border traffic. It's a bustling place, with plenty of traders doing last-minute shopping in the many shops and goods outlets. Tourists saunter right up to the border and snap photos in front of the large entry gate. It remains busy well into the night.

To get here, continue straight ahead from **Golden Duck Pagoda**, on the southwestern outskirts of town, cross the **China Myanmar Friendship Bridge** (中缅友谊桥; Zhōngmiǎn Yǒuyì Qiáo) over Ruìlì Jiāng and you will come to Jiěgào, about 7km from Ruìlì.

Shared red taxis (¥5) with signs for Jiěgào drive around the centre of Ruìlì from dawn until late at night.

Getting to Myanmar (Burma)

At the time of writing it was not possible for third-country nationals to travel across the border at Jiěgào. The only way to go is by air from Kūnmíng. Visas are available at the embassy in Běijīng or in Kūnmíng at the Myanmar Consulate (p1001). In Kūnmíng visas cost ¥235, take three days to process and are good for a maximum 28-day visit.

At the time of writing there were two daily nonstop flights from Kūnmíng to Yangon (from ¥1090) on Air China and China Eastern Airlines and one daily to Mandalay (from ¥1762).

XĪSHUĀNGBǍNNÀ REGION 西双版纳

North of Myanmar and Laos, Xīshuāng-bǎnnà is the Chinese approximation of the original Thai name of Sip Sawng Panna (12 Rice-Growing Districts). The Xīshuāngbǎn-nà region, better known as Bǎnnà, has become China's mini-Thailand, attracting tourists looking for sunshine, water-splashing festivals and epic jungle treks.

But Xīshuāngbǎnnà is big enough that it rarely feels overwhelmed by visitors and even the expanding capital, Jǐnghóng, remains reasonably laid-back.

Environment

Xīshuāngbǎnnà has myriad plant and animal species, although recent scientific studies have shown the tropical rainforest areas of Bǎnnà are now acutely endangered. The jungle areas that remain contain a handful of tigers, leopards and golden-haired monkeys. Elephant numbers have doubled to 250 since the early 1980s; the government now offers compensation to villagers whose crops have been destroyed by elephants, or who assist in wildlife conservation. In 1998 the government banned the hunting or processing of animals, but poaching is notoriously hard to control.

People

About one-third of the million-strong population of this region are Dai; another third or so are Han Chinese and the rest are a conglomerate of minorities that include the Hani, Lisu and Yao, as well as lesser-known hill tribes such as the Aini (a subgroup of the Hani), Jinuo, Bulang, Lahu and Wa.

Xīshuāngbǎnnà Dai Autonomous Prefecture, as it is known officially, is subdivided into the three counties of Jǐnghóng, Měng-hǎi and Měnglà.

Climate

The region has two seasons: wet and dry. The wet season is between June and August, when it rains ferociously, although not every day and only in short bursts. From September to February there is less rainfall, but thick fog descends during the late evening and doesn't lift until 10am or even later.

November to March sees temperatures average about 19°C. The hottest months of the year are from April to September, when you can expect an average of 25°C.

✹ Festivals & Events

During festivals, booking same-day airline tickets to Jǐnghóng can be extremely difficult. Hotels in Jǐnghóng town are booked solid and prices usually triple. Most people end up commuting from a nearby Dai village. Festivities take place all over Xīshuāng-bǎnnà, so you might be lucky further away from Jǐnghóng.

Water-Splashing Festival   CULTURAL

(☉ mid-Apr) Held at the same time as it is celebrated in Thailand and Laos, the three-day water-splashing festival washes away the dirt, sorrow and demons of the old year and brings in the happiness of the new. Jǐnghóng celebrates it from 13 to 15 April but dates in the surrounding villages vary. The actual splashing only occurs on the last day. Foreigners earn special attention, so prepare to be drenched all day.

Dǎntǎ Festival   CULTURAL

(赕塔节, Dǎntǎ Jié; ☉ Oct/Nov) This festival is held during a 10-day period in October or November, with temple ceremonies, rocket launches from special towers and hot-air balloons. The rockets, which often contain lucky amulets, blast into the sky; those who find the amulets are assured of good luck.

🛏 Sleeping & Eating

There are hotels and hostels aplenty in Jǐnghóng. Basic guesthouses are sometimes available in the villages, or locals will offer a bed. Make sure to pay for it: around ¥50 for a bed and meal is the going rate.

BǍNNÀ BORDER

At the time of writing, normally sleepy Bǎnnà was a hive of police activity, especially along the borders with Laos and Myanmar (Burma). The reason for this is the increase in the number of Uighurs – the restive Muslim ethnic minority group native to far-off Xīnjiāng Province – attempting to flee China across what are normally the country's most porous frontiers.

Any bus or car travelling close to the borders will be stopped at any number of checkpoints and the IDs of all passengers scrutinised. It is absolutely essential for all travellers to carry their passports with them when journeying around the border areas. The police will be unimpressed if you have no proof of who you are and where you are from.

Xīshuāngbǎnnà

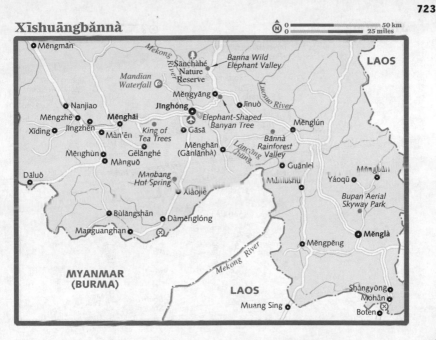

N 0 —— 50 km
0 —— 25 miles

Map labels: Mēngmǎn · Mekong · Mandian Waterfall · Sānchàhé Nature Reserve · Banna Wild Elephant Valley · LAOS · Nanjiao · Mēngyǎng · Jǐnghóng · Jīnuò · Luōsuǒ River · Mēngzhē · Měnghǎi · Elephant-Shaped Banyan Tree · Mēnglún · Xǐdīng · Jǐngzhēn · Màn'ēn · King of Tea Trees · Gǎsǎ · Láncāng Jiāng · Bānnà Rainforest Valley · Mēnghùn · Gēlǎnghé · Mēnghǎn (Gǎnlǎnhà) · Mànguǒ · Guǎnlěi · Yáoqū · Dàluò · Manbang Hot Spring · Xiǎojiē · Mānlushù · Bupan Aerial Skyway Park · Bùlǎngshān · Dàměnglóng · Mēngpēng · Mēnglà · Manguanghàn · MYANMAR (BURMA) · LAOS · Mekong River · Shàngyōng · Mòhàn · Muang Sing · Bōtèn

Bǎnnà is home to some of the best food in all China. Sour and spicy Dai food in particular is excellent, drawing on both Chinese and Southeast Asian influences. Dai dishes include barbecued fish, eel or beef cooked with lemongrass or served with peanut and tomato sauce. The region's fertile earth guarantees superb fruit and vegetables too.

ⓘ Getting There & Away

Jǐnghóng is the main transport hub for Xīshuāngbǎnnà, with air and bus connections to the rest of Yúnnán. Měnghǎi, about an hour west of Jǐnghóng by bus, is another key transport node for reaching many of Xīshuāngbǎnnà's outlying villages, including Xǐdīng, Mēnghùn and Jǐngzhēn. Frequent buses from Jǐnghóng's No 2 Bus Station travel to Měnghǎi's bus station, where you can pick up buses and minivans to the villages. You can also get direct buses from Jǐnghóng to destinations in Laos, including Luang Nam Tha and Luang Prabang, while there's also the possibility of hitching a ride on a cargo boat down the Mekong to northern Thailand. But there is still no overland access to Myanmar from here.

Jǐnghóng 景洪

⬛ 0691 / POP 205,523

Jǐnghóng – the 'City of Dawn' in local Dai language – is experiencing some serious investment. The once-sleepy capital of Xī-

shuāngbǎnnà Prefecture is expanding fast, with new apartment blocks sprawling down both sides of the Mekong River (known as the Láncāng in China) which bisects the city and ambitious developments sprouting on the city's outskirts.

The once underpopulated left bank of the Mekong is at the heart of the boom, meaning the city's axis is beginning to shift from its traditional centre on the right bank. Nevertheless, Jǐnghóng sees relatively few Western visitors and it remains laid-back despite the increasingly snarled traffic. And everything from the food to the weather has more in common with Southeast Asia than China.

⊙ Sights

Tropical Flower & Plants Garden GARDENS
(热带花卉园, Rèdài Huāhuìyuán; 99 Jinghong Xilu; ¥54; ⊙7.30am-6pm) This terrific botanic garden, west of the town centre, is one of Jǐnghóng's better attractions. Admission gets you into a series of gardens where you can view over 1000 different types of plant life.

🛏 Sleeping

Jǐnglán Kèzhàn HOTEL $
(景兰客栈; ⬛0691 212 5288; Off Menglong Lu, 勐龙路; d ¥120-150; ❄🛜) Tucked away in a forecourt off the end of Menglong Lu, this is a reliable and comfortable budget option,

Jĭnghóng

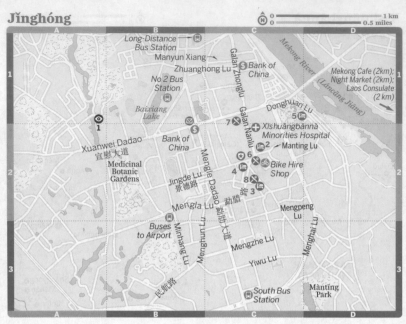

Jĭnghóng

Sights
1 Tropical Flower & Plants
  Garden..................................A1

Sleeping
2 Home Inn..................................C2
3 Jínglán Kèzhàn..........................C2
4 King Land Hotel.........................C2
5 Riverside International Hostel............C1

Eating
6 Bǎnnà Cafe..............................C2
7 Luó Luō Bīng Wū........................C1
8 Měiměi Café.............................C2

with decent beds and sizeable rooms, some of which have balconies. Good wi-fi and efficient staff, although you won't hear any English.

Riverside International Hostel   HOSTEL $
(西双版纳囍居国际青年旅舍, Xīshuāngbǎnnà Xǐjū Guójì Qīngnián Lǚshě; ☑0691 219 5611; wang xiang@sina.com; 15F, Bldg 1, Xishuang Shi'er Cheng (next to Green Eastern Hotel),西双十贰城国际公馆1栋15楼格林东方酒店旁; dm ¥40-45, d ¥238-299; ❈🛜) Despite its location in a new tower block, this is the best hostel in town. Private rooms are bright, fresh and large and many come with great Mekong River views. The dorms are spacious too and have little bal-

conies and lockers. There's a big communal area and helpful staff, even if you won't hear much English.

The hostel goes into hibernation during the rainy season, when it is crewed by a skeleton staff. To find it, look for the far two tower blocks beyond the performance square off Menghai Lu and head for the right-hand one.

Home Inn   HOTEL $
(如家酒店, Rújiā Jiǔdiàn; ☑0691 219 0688; homeinns069103@163.com; 2 Manting Lu, 曼听路 2号; d ¥149-179; ❈🛜) Not the most exotic of digs, but this chain hotel offers big, if a little gloomy, rooms, with modern bathrooms in a convenient central location. Some rooms can be smoky, so check them before you move in. Efficient staff.

King Land Hotel   HOTEL $$$
(鲸兰大酒店, Jínglán Jiǔdiàn; ☑0691 212 9999; 6 Jingde Lu, 景德路6号; d ¥490-1180; ❈🛜🏊) Sporting two enormous elephants at its entrance, this is one of Jĭnghóng's unmistakable landmarks. The rooms are a little plain and compact for the price, but this is the only four-star place with such a central location and a swimming pool. Rooms are routinely discounted by 20% out of season and they take Western credit cards.

✕ Eating

Dai dishes include grilled fish or beef cooked with lemon grass, or served with peanut and tomato sauce. The most authentic Dai restaurants are located on the outskirts of town and serve up big set-meal feasts, so get a group together. Ask at the Meimei Café for directions. In the centre, Menghai Lu, Mengpeng Lu and Menghun Lu all have decent Dai restaurants.

Jǐnghóng Night Market
MARKET $
(景洪夜市, Jǐnghóng Yeshi; Ganbai Jie, Shuishang Renjia, Ganzhuang Yichuangjiang, 甘庄四双景水上人家赶摆街; from ¥2; ⏲5pm-late) With Jǐnghóng's axis switching inexorably to the left bank of the river, this night market is increasingly popular with both locals and visitors. All manner of Dai and Yúnnán eats are on display, and you are close to the riverbank where Chinese-style bars are beginning to congregate. It's a ¥15 to ¥20 taxi ride from the centre of town.

Bǎnnà Cafe
INTERNATIONAL $
(版纳咖啡, Bǎnnà Kāfēi; ☎158 9430 9053; 1 Manting Lu, 曼听路1号; breakfast from ¥22, dishes from ¥20; ⏲9am-11.30pm; 🛜) A good place for breakfast, this friendly, Akha-owned cafe also has a small terrace that is ideal for a sundowner or late-evening libation while watching the world go by. Staff can also arrange treks and guides.

Luō Luō Bīng Wū
NOODLES $
(啰啰冰屋; ☎0691 213 1160; 96 Xuanwei Dadao, 宣威大道96号; dishes from ¥12; ⏲11am-1am) This buzzing local spot has Jǐnghóngers flocking here for the cheap and tasty rice noodle and fried rice dishes, as well as fruit juices, shakes and Taiwanese-style shaved-ice desserts that are perfect for cooling off. There's an open-air area out back.

★ Měiměi Café
INTERNATIONAL $$
(美美咖啡, Měiměi Kāfēi; ☎0691 216 1221; meimei-cafe.com; 107-108 Menglong Lu, 勐龙路107-108号; dishes from ¥18; ⏲8am-1am; 🛜) You'll find it and you'll eat here. This is the original of all the Western-style cafes in town and still the best, thanks to its menu of steaks, burgers, sandwiches, pizza and pasta, and foreigner-friendly Chinese and Thai dishes. Good range of local and foreign beers, plus proper coffee and juices. Owner Orchid is a great source of local info.

MINORITY GROUPS OF XĪSHUĀNGBǍNNÀ

The Dai (傣族) are Hinayana Buddhists (as opposed to China's majority Mahayana Buddhists) who first appeared 2000 years ago in the Yangzi Valley and were subsequently driven south to here by the Mongol invasion of the 13th century. The common dress for Dai women is a straw hat or towel-wrap headdress, a tight, short blouse in a bright colour, and a printed sarong with a belt of silver links. Some Dai men tattoo their bodies with animal designs, and betel-nut chewing is popular. The Dai language is quite similar to Lao and northern Thai dialects. Some Dai phrases include *douzao li* (hello), *yindi* (thank you) and *goihan* (goodbye).

The Jinuo people (基诺族), sometimes known as the Youle, were officially 'discovered' as a minority in 1979 and are among the smallest groups – numbering between 12,000 and 18,000. They call themselves 'those who respect the uncle' and are thought to possibly have descended from the Qiang. The women wear a white cowl, a cotton tunic with bright horizontal stripes and a tubular black skirt. Earlobe decoration is an elaborate custom among older women – the larger the hole and the more flowers it can contain, the more beautiful the woman is considered.

The Bulang people (布朗族) live mainly in the Bùlǎng, Xīdīng and Bādá mountains of Xīshuāngbǎnnà. They keep to the hills farming cotton, sugar cane and pǔ'ěr tea, one of Yúnnán's most famous exports. Men traditionally tattoo their arms, legs, chests and stomachs while women wear vibrant headdresses decorated with flowers.

The Hani (哈尼族), who are sometimes confused with the Akha, are closely related to the Yi as a part of the Tibeto-Burman group; the language is Sino-Tibetan but uses Han characters for the written form. They are mostly famed for their river-valley rice terraces, especially in the Red River valley, between the Āiláo and Wúliàng Shān, where they cultivate rice, corn and the occasional poppy. Hani women (especially the Aini, a subgroup of the Hani) wear headdresses of beads, feathers, coins and silver rings, some of which are decorated with French (Vietnamese), Burmese and Indian coins from the turn of the 20th century.

❶ BORDER CROSSING: GETTING TO THAILAND

In the past, it was possible to travel by cargo boat to Chiang Saen in northern Thailand; the journey took around 24 hours. Piracy and drug-related violence has largely put an end to that adventurous route south, though. But you can ask about hitching a ride on a cargo boat. They leave from Guānlěi (关累), about 75km southeast of Jǐnghóng. The Mekong Cafe (see below) can put you in touch with a boat captain. If you get a ride, expect to pay ¥800 to ¥1200 per person for the trip. Alternatively, head into Laos and then skip over the Thai border.

Mekong Cafe
INTERNATIONAL $$

(湄公咖啡, Méigōng Kāfēi; ☑ 0691 222 6588; mekongcafe@163.com; 1-1-1201, Ganbai Jie, Shuishang Renjia, Gaozhuang Xishuangjing, 告庄西双景水上人家赶街摆街1-1-1201号; dishes from ¥26; ☺ 9am-1am; 🛜) This long-standing presence has shifted to the other side of the river and now has a prime location on the riverbank, close to the night market (p725). It still serves up a wide-ranging mix of Western and Chinese food, as well as many foreign ales and decent wine. The attached travel agency specialises in eco-treks and is a reliable source of information and guides.

❶ Information

Very occasionally, we get reports from travellers who have been drugged and then robbed on the Kūnmíng–Jǐnghóng bus trip. Be friendly but aware, accept nothing, and never leave your stuff unattended when you hop off for a break.

Bank of China (中国银行, Zhōngguó Yínháng; Xuanwei Dadao) Changes travellers cheques and foreign currency, and has an ATM machine. There are other branches on Galan Zhonglu and Minhang Lu.

Bank of China (中国银行, Zhōngguó Yínháng) One of a number of branches around town.

China Post (国际邮局, Zhōngguó Yóuzhèng; cnr Mengle Dadao & Xuanwei Dadao; ☺ 9am-6pm) You can send mail overseas from here.

Public Security Bureau (PSB, 公安局, Gōng'ānjú; 13 Jingde Lu; ☺ 8-11.30am & 3-5.30pm Mon-Fri) Come here for visa extensions.

Xīshuāngbǎnnà Minorities Hospital (西双版纳民族医院, Xīshuāngbǎnnà Mínzú Yīyuàn; ☑ 0691 213 0123; Galan Nanlu) The best bet for having an English-speaker available.

❶ Getting There & Away

AIR

Jǐnghóng Airport is 5km south of the city.

There are around 40 daily flights to Kūnmíng (from ¥450) but in April (when the water-splashing festival is held) you'll still need to book tickets in advance to get in or out.

There are also daily flights to Dàlǐ (from ¥630) and Lìjiāng (¥450), as well as increasing numbers of flights that connect with cities across China via Kūnmíng. Lao Airlines has one direct flight a week from Jǐnghóng to Luang Prabang in Laos on Sunday (¥1264). At the time of writing, all flights from Jǐnghóng to Chiang Mai in Thailand were going via Kūnmíng. Travel agents all over town sell air tickets, or book online. Note that Jǐnghóng's airport is known as Xīshuāngbǎnnà.

BUS

The **long-distance bus station** (长途客运站, chángtú kèyùnzhàn; Minhang Lu) serves the following destinations and also has daily buses to Luang Nam Tha (¥70, five hours, 10.40am) and Huay Xai (¥150, eight hours, 6.50am) in Laos. Every other day, on even-numbered days, there is also a bus to Luang Prabang in Laos (¥180, 10 hours, 7.30am).

Jiànshuǐ ¥192 to ¥210, eight to nine hours, two daily (9.30am and 10.30am)

Kūnmíng ¥223 to ¥247, eight hours, six daily (8.30am, 10.30am, 12.30pm, 6.40pm, 8.10pm and 9.50pm)

Lìjiāng ¥257, 16 hours, one daily (9.30am)

Ruìlì ¥420, 22 hours, one daily (9am)

Xiàguān ¥210 to ¥230, 12 hours, two daily (8.30am and 10am)

If you want to explore Xīshuāngbǎnnà, go to the No 2 bus station (第二客运站, Dì'èr kèyùnzhàn), also known as the Bǎnnà bus station.

Gǎnlǎnbà ¥17, 40 minutes, every 20 minutes (7.40am to 7pm)

Měnghǎi ¥15 to ¥20, 50 minutes, every 20 minutes (7am to 7pm)

Měnglà ¥50, 2½ hours, every 30 minutes (6.30am to 5.20pm)

Měnglún ¥21, 1½ hours, every 20 minutes (7am to 7pm)

Měngyǎng ¥10, 40 minutes, every 30 minutes (8.30am to 6.30pm)

Sānchàhé ¥15, one hour, every 40 minutes (8am to 5pm)

Sīmáo ¥50, two hours, every 30 minutes (6.30am to 7.20pm)

For Měnghùn, take any bus to Měnghǎi and change there.

For buses to Dàměnglóng, head to the **south bus station** (客运南站, kèyùn nánzhàn; cnr Mengle Dadao & Menghai Lu), which also has departures to Kūnmíng.

If you want to get to the Yuányáng Rice Terraces, there is sometimes a direct bus from the long-distance bus station to Nánshà (¥178, seven to eight hours) in peak season (October to March), from where you can catch a minivan (¥10, one hour) to Xīnjiē. Otherwise, you'll have to catch the bus to Jiànshuǐ, where there is a daily bus to Xīnjiē and many more to Nánshà.

❶ Getting Around

Bus 1 (¥2) runs to the airport from a stop on Mengla Lu near the corner with Minhang Lu. A taxi will cost around ¥25 but expect to be hit up for more during festivals.

Jīnghóng is small enough that you can walk to most destinations, but a bike makes life easier and can be rented from some hostels for ¥30 a day or from the **bike hire shop** (per day ¥50; ☺9am-9pm) on Manting Lu.

Taxi flag fall is ¥8, but you may struggle to get drivers to use their meters.

Around Jīnghóng

Trekking (or travelling by bus) to the numerous minority villages is the draw here. You could spend weeks doing so, but even with limited time most destinations in Xīshuāngbǎnnà are only two or three hours away by bus. Note that to get to the most isolated villages, you'll often first have to take the bus to a primary (and uninteresting) village and stay overnight there, since only one bus per day – if that – travels to the tinier villages.

Market addicts can rejoice – it's an artist's palette of colours in outlying villages. The most popular markets are the Thursday market in Xīdìng and Měnghùn's Saturday market. Měngyǎng is another popular village destination, thanks to its famous elephant-shaped banyan tree.

Take note: it can feel like every second village begins with the prefix 'Meng' and it isn't unheard of for travellers to end up at the wrong village entirely because of communication problems. Have your destination written down in script before you head off.

Sānchàhé Nature Reserve (三岔河自然保护区, Sānchàhé Zìrán Bǎohùqū; ¥5), 48km north of Jīnghóng, is one of five enormous forest reserves in southern Yúnnán. It has an area of nearly 1.5 million hectares; seriously, treat it with respect – you get off-trail here, you won't be found.

Located in the reserve, **Bǎnnà Wild Elephant Valley** (版纳野象谷, Bǎnnà Yěxiànggǔ; ¥65) draws crowds eager to see the wild elephants indigenous to the area. The elephants are very retiring so you might not see any of them. You will see monkeys, though, and it's worth a visit if you want to see something of the local forest. A 2km-long **cable car** (one-way/return ¥50/70) runs over the tree

HIKING IN XĪSHUĀNGBǍNNÀ

Hikes around Xīshuāngbǎnnà used to be among the best in China – you'd be invited into a local's home to eat, sleep and drink *mǐjiǔ* (rice wine). Growing numbers of visitors have changed this in many places, while encroaching rubber and banana plantations – some wags now refer to the region as Xīshuāngbanana – are having an increasingly deleterious effect on the environment.

It's still possible to find villages that see very few foreigners and remain pristine, but they are remote. Don't expect to roll up in Jīnghóng and the next day to be in a village that hasn't seen a Westerner before. And don't automatically expect a welcome mat and a free lunch because you're a foreigner.

If you do get invited into someone's home, try and establish whether payment is expected. If it's not, leave an offering or modest gift (ask at the backpacker cafes to find out what's considered appropriate), even though the family may insist on nothing.

Also take care before heading out. It's a jungle out there, so go prepared, and make sure somebody knows where you are and when you should return. In the rainy season, you'll need to be equipped with proper hiking shoes and waterproof gear. At any time you'll need water purification tablets, bottled water or a water bottle able to hold boiled water, as well as snacks and sunscreen.

Seriously consider taking a guide. You won't hear much Mandarin on the trail, let alone any English. Expect to pay around ¥300 per day.

Both the Mekong Café (see far left) and the Bǎnnà Cafe (p725) in Jīnghóng can arrange treks and guides. The nearby Měiměi Café (p725) doesn't organise treks but does have lots of details in binders so you can find your own way.

tops from the main entrance into the heart of the park, as does an elevated walkway.

There is no accommodation in the park; it's best to stay in Jǐnghóng. There are 10 buses daily to Sānchàhé (¥15, one hour, 8am to 5pm).

If there are no roadworks, it is possible to cycle from Jǐnghóng to Měnghǎn in a brisk two hours or a leisurely three hours, but the traffic is heavy. You can rent a mountain bike from one of several bicycle shops along Manting Lu (¥30 per day).

Měnghǎn   勐罕

☑ 0691

Měnghǎn, or Gǎnlǎnbà (橄榄坝) as it's sometimes referred to, was once a grand destination – you'd bike here and chill. Sadly, much of the main attraction – the lovely, friendly, somnolent village itself – has basically been roped off as a quasi-minority theme park with tour buses and cacophonous dancing. That said, the environs of the village are still wondrous.

Dai Minority Park (傣族园, Dàizúyuán; ☑ 0691 250 4099; Manting Lu; ¥65) was once the part of town that everyone in this region came to experience – especially for its classic temples and Dai families hosting visitors in their traditional homes. Now, it's a 'theme park' where visitors can spend the night in villagers' homes and partake in water-splashing 'festivals' twice a day. Despite the artificial nature of it all, some people love the experience.

Restaurants inside the park are pricey and firmly aimed at tour groups. But you can also find restaurants on the road leading to the park.

Buses to Měnghǎn leave from Jǐnghóng's No 2 bus station (¥17, every 20 minutes, 7.40am to 7pm). From Měnghǎn's bus station, there are buses back to Jǐnghóng (¥17) every 20 minutes. The last bus leaves at 7.30pm. There's also one bus a day to Kūnmíng (¥255, nine hours, 6.30pm).

Měnglún   勐伦

☑ 0691

East of Měnghǎn, Měnglún is primarily known for being home to the **Tropical Plant Gardens** (热带植物园, Rèdài Zhíwùyuán; ¥104; ⏰ 7.30am-6pm) – the largest botanical gardens in all China. To get here, turn left out of the bus station and then take the first left. Follow the road downhill, cross the first intersection and the ticket office is 100m ahead, just before a footbridge across the Mekong.

Měnglún is an easy day trip from Jǐnghóng and there is no reason to stay here. But if you want to, there are a couple of basic hotels close to the bus station and the Gardens.

Chūnlín Bīnguǎn has simple but clean rooms – the cheapest have squat toilets. It's close to the Tropical Plant Gardens entrance.

From Jǐnghóng's No 2 bus station there are buses to Měnglún (¥21, 75 minutes, every 20 minutes, 7am to 7pm). From Měnglún, there are buses to Měnglà (¥25 to ¥29, two hours, every 20 minutes, 8am to 7pm) and Jǐnghóng (¥21, 75 minutes, every 20 minutes, 7.50am to 6pm).

Měnglà   勐腊

☑ 0691 / POP 84,625

Měnglà is the first (or last) main city for travellers headed to/from Laos. It's a fast-growing place set around one long main street, with palm-tree-lined side streets and

---

ℹ BORDER CROSSING: GETTING TO LAOS

On-the-spot visas for Laos can be obtained at the border. The price will depend on your nationality (generally US$35 to US$40). You can also pick one up at the Laotian Consulate (p1000) in Jǐnghóng, which is on the other side of the river on the edge of town. A taxi here will cost ¥15. The **Chinese checkpoint** (☑ 0691 812 2684; ⏰ 8am-5.30pm) is generally not much of an ordeal. Don't forget that Laos is an hour behind China.

Apart from the one bus from Měnglà to Luang Nam Tha in Laos, a daily bus also runs to Luang Nam Tha from Jǐnghóng (¥70, seven hours, 10.40am). Along with the daily bus to Vientiane from Kūnmíng (¥587, 30 hours, 6.30pm), it stops at Měnglà, but you're not guaranteed a seat.

No matter what anyone says, there should be no 'charge' to cross. Once your passport is stamped (double-check all stamps), you can jump on a motor-rickshaw to take you 3km into Laos for around ¥5. Whatever you do, go early – in case things wrap up early on either side. There are guesthouses on both the Chinese and Laos sides; people generally change money on the Laos side.

some garish orange-coloured buildings designed with local architecture in mind, but little in the way of sights.

With direct buses from Jǐnghóng to Luang Nam Tha, Huay Xai and Luang Prabang in Laos, as well as buses from Kūnmíng to Laos, there is no reason to stay in Měnglà. But there are many places along the main road in the centre of town where you can find a bed from ¥60 and up.

Buses run from Měnglà's main south bus station, about 2km south of the centre of town, to the following:

Jǐnghóng ¥50, every 30 minutes (6.30am to 6pm)
Kūnmíng ¥258, six daily, nine to 10 hours (9am to 8.30pm)
Luang Nam Tha ¥40, one daily, three hours (9am)
Měnglún ¥25 to ¥29, every 20 minutes (8am to 7pm)
Móhān ¥17, every 20 minutes (8am to 6pm)

Dàměnglóng 大勐龙

☑ 0691

About 55km south of Jǐnghóng and a few kilometres from the Myanmar border, Dàměnglóng (just the last two characters, 勐龙, 'Měnglóng', are written on buses) is undergoing a minirenaissance, like much of Xīshuāngbǎnnà, and its streets are now paved. But it's still a drowsy place and, a couple of pagodas apart, is really just a staging point for hikes to the surrounding minority villages. Bear in mind that rubber plantations have made the countryside here less pristine than it once was.

◉ Sights

White Bamboo Shoot Pagoda PAGODA
(曼飞龙塔, Mànfēilóng Tǎ; ¥30) Surrounded by jungle (watch out for stray snakes!), this pagoda dates back to 1204 and is Dàměnglóng's premier attraction. According to legend, the pagoda's temple was built on the location of a hallowed footprint left behind by the Sakyamuni Buddha, who is said to have visited Xīshuāngbǎnnà. If you have an interest in ancient footprints you can look for it in a niche below one of the nine stupas. The temple has been extensively renovated in recent years.

If you're in the area in late October or early November, check the precise dates of the Dǎn Tǎ Festival. At this time, White Bamboo Shoot Pagoda is host to hundreds of locals whose celebrations include dancing, rockets and fireworks, paper balloons and so on.

The pagoda is easy to get to: just walk back along the main road towards Jǐnghóng

for 2km until you reach a small village with a temple on your left. From here there's a path up the hill, it's about a 20-minute walk. A motor-rickshaw from Dàměnglóng is ¥10.

Black Pagoda PAGODA
(黑塔, Hēi Tǎ; FREE) Just above the centre of town is a Dai monastery with a steep path beside it leading up to the Black Pagoda – you'll notice it when entering Dàměnglóng. The pagoda itself is actually gold, not black. Take a stroll up and have a chat with the few monks in residence. The views of Dàměnglóng and surrounding countryside are more interesting than the temple itself.

🛏 Sleeping & Eating

There's no reason to stay in Dàměnglóng: it's either an easy day trip from Jǐnghóng, or just a place to catch a bus onto the jumping-off point for hikes into the countryside. But new hotels are opening up close to the bus station, where you can find a bed for ¥100 and up.

There are simple restaurants and Dai barbecue places scattered throughout the village. Try the ones close to the Black Pagoda.

ⓘ Getting There & Away

Buses to Dàměnglóng (¥17, 90 minutes, every 20 minutes, 6.30am to 6.30pm) leave from Jǐnghóng's south bus station. Remember, the 'Da' character (大) is sometimes not displayed. Buses for the return trip run on the same schedule.

Sìchuān

POP 80.8 MILLION

Best Places to Eat

➡ Chén Mápó Dòufu (p739)

➡ Taste of Tibet (p760)

➡ Chóngqìng Yúanlǎosì Old Hotpot (p739)

➡ Ā Bù Lǔ Zī (p779)

Best Places to Sleep

➡ Hóngchún Píng (p748)

➡ Ancient Hotel (p781)

➡ Dōngpō Tibetan Homestay (p762)

➡ Talam Khang Guesthouse (p764)

➡ Tiānyī Youth Hotel (p781)

Why Go?

It's fitting that an ancient form of opera and magic called *biànliǎn* (face-changing) originated here, for Sìchuān (四川) is a land of many guises.

Capital Chéngdū shows a modern face, but just beyond its bustling ring roads you'll find a more traditional landscape of mist-shrouded, sacred mountains, and a countryside scattered with ancient villages and cliffs of carved Buddhas. Central Sìchuān is also home to the giant panda, the most famous face in China. In the south, expect a veil of history and a muted beauty that sees far fewer travellers than the rest of the region.

To the north the visage changes again into a fairyland of alpine valleys and blue-green lakes. Sìchuān's Tibetan face appears as you venture west. This is Kham, one of the former Tibetan prefectures: a vast landscape of plateau grasslands and glacial mountains where Tibetan culture still thrives and you're certain to have your most challenging, yet most magical, experiences.

When to Go
Chéngdū

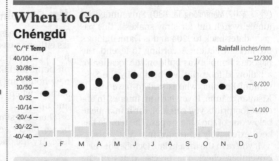

Mar-May Prime time for Chéngdū; not too humid, peach blossoms and little rain.

Jul & Aug In the west in the warm grasslands bloom in technicolour and festivals abound.

Sep & Oct Turquoise lakes to the north offer secluded camping amid autumn leaves.

History

Sìchuān's early history was turbulent. The region was the site of various breakaway kingdoms, ever skirmishing with central authority, but it was finally wrested under control and established as the capital of the Qin empire in the 3rd century BC. It was here that the kingdom of Shu (a name by which the province is still known) ruled as an independent state during the Three Kingdoms period (AD 220–80).

During the Warring States period (475–221 BC), local governor and famed engineer Li Bing managed to harness the flood-prone Mín River (岷江; Mín Jiāng) on the Chuānxī plain with his revolutionary weir system; the Dūjiāngyàn Irrigation Project still controls flooding, and supplies Chéngdū and 49 other provincial cities with water 2200 years after it was constructed. It's one of the reasons the Sìchuān basin is synonymous with fertile soil.

Another more recent factor was the efforts of Zhao Ziyang, the Party Secretary of Sìchuān in 1975. After the Great Leap Forward, when an estimated 10% of Sìchuān's population died of starvation, Ziyang became the driving force behind agricultural and economic reforms that restored farming output. He reinstated the 'Responsibility System', whereby plots of land were granted to farming families on the proviso that they sold a quota of crops to the state. Any additional profits or losses would be borne by the families. This household-focused approach was so successful that it became the national model. Sìchuān continues to be a major producer of the nation's grain, soybeans and pork.

Catastrophe struck the region on 12 May 2008, when the Wènchuān earthquake measuring 7.9 on the Richter scale hit the province's central region. Some sources reported it killed more than 88,000 people, as many as 10,000 of them school children, and left millions more injured or homeless. The trillion-yuan aid and rebuilding effort continues in the remote, mountainous areas. The main road linking Chéngdū with Jiǔzhàigōu took four years to reopen, and now travellers on that route will see brand-new villages rising from the rubble. In the areas surrounding the Wènchuān, the earthquake's epicentre, significant damage is still apparent nearly a decade on.

Language

Sichuanese is a Mandarin dialect, but with its fast clip, distinctive syntax and five tones instead of four, it can challenge standard Mandarin speakers. Two phrases easily understood are *yàodé* (pronounced 'yow-day', meaning 'yes' or 'OK') and *méidé* (pronounced 'may-day', meaning 'no').

Sìchuān's other major languages belong to the Tibeto-Burman family and are spoken by Tibetans and Yi minorities. Don't expect much help from standard phrasebooks. In western Sìchuān, Tibetan dialects vary from region to region or even town to town.

ⓘ Getting There & Around

Chéngdū serves as the province's transit hub. Smooth expressways to eastern and southern Sìchuān make for short trips to many destinations, but heading north or west is a different story; many roads are in poor shape or are under construction. Weather conditions are unpredictable at high elevations, and hazards ranging from landslides to overturned semis are common.

Chéngdū Shuāngliú International Airport is the largest airport in southwest China. Several small airports in Sìchuān's furthest corners are connected to it by one-hour flights — Jiǔzhàigōu in the north, Kāngdìng in the near west, Dàochéng-Yàdīng in the southwest, and Yùshù just across the western border with Qīnghǎi province – significantly cutting travel times to these otherwise remote destinations.

Trains head from Chéngdū to major cities across China, including to Lhasa via the famous high-altitude link. High-speed trains now connect Chéngdū to Qīngchéng Shān and Dūjiāngyàn in the north, Lè Shān and Éméi Shān in the south, and on to China's other provinces in every direction.

PRICE RANGES

Sleeping

The following price ranges refer to a double room. Unless otherwise stated, private bathroom is included in the price.

$ less than ¥100
$$ ¥100–¥400
$$$ more than ¥400

Eating

The following price ranges refer to a main course.

$ less than ¥30
$$ ¥30–¥50
$$$ more than ¥50

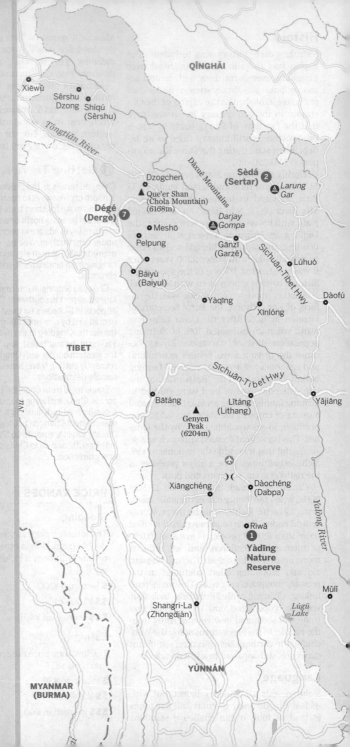

Sìchuān Highlights

1 **Yàdīng Nature Reserve** (p770) Making multiday pilgrimage treks around the stunning holy mountains.

2 **Larung Gar Five Sciences Buddhist Academy** (p766) Chatting with monks and nuns in training at Sèdá's massive Buddhist institution.

3 **Éméi Shān** (p746) Rising with the sun above the forested slopes at this cool, misty retreat.

4 **Giant Panda Breeding Research Base** (p734) Meeting China's cuddly national icon.

5 **Jiǔzhàigōu National Park** (p777) Camping in Jiǔzhàigōu's alpine valley through the park's ecotourism program.

6 **Grand Buddha** (p750) Peering over the toenails of the world's largest Buddha statue in Lè Shān.

7 **Bakong Scripture Printing Press** (p763) Observing the workings of a centuries-old monastic scripture press in Dégé.

8 **Four Sisters Mountain** (p745) Hiking at the foot of Sìchuān's second-highest mountain and taking in the panorama from the top of the Hǎizi Valley.

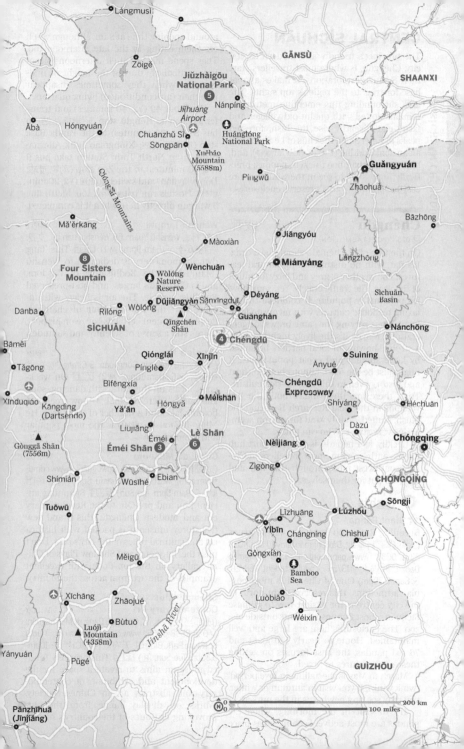

CENTRAL SÌCHUĀN

The province's friendly and modern capital city, Chéngdū, is where most travellers start their Sìchuān explorations. It makes a great base for trips to the region's top sights. The area surrounding this emerging metropolis remains dotted with quaint old villages and farmsteads. Nearby rise the lush, forested peaks of Éméi Shān, the cliffs of Lè Shān with an ancient Buddha (the world's largest), and, hidden in the bamboo thickets, pandas; practically impossible to see in the wild, they are easy to spot in the area's reserve enclosures.

Chéngdū 成都

♪ 028 / POP 14.42 MILLION

On the face of it, Chéngdū should be a drag. It's flat, with no distinguishing natural features. The weather is grey and hazy for much of the year. The traffic crawls. Yet, somehow, it's perennially popular. It could be the relaxing teahouse culture, with favourite local institutions serving the same brews for generations. Maybe it's the lively nightlife, with a strong showing of local partiers bolstered by large student and expat populations. It might just be the food, famous both for heat and history even in this cuisine-rich culture. Then there are the pandas, both the live versions in the local Research Base and the plush, stuffed, cuddly kind for sale on seemingly every street. Who can tell?

Luckily, as Chéngdū is the transport hub for the entire region, most travellers in China's southwest pass through this way and can find out for themselves.

◎ Sights

★Giant Panda Breeding Research Base   WILDLIFE RESERVE

(大熊猫繁育基地, Dàxióngmāo Fányù Jìdì; ♪028 8351 0033; www.panda.org.cn; 1375 Xiongmao Dadao, 熊猫大道1375号; adult/student ¥58/29; ◎8am-5.30pm) One of Chéngdū's most popular attractions, this reserve 18km north of the city centre is the easiest way to glimpse Sìchuān's most famous residents outside of a zoo. The enclosures here are large and well maintained. Home to nearly 120 giant and 76 red pandas, the base focuses on getting these shy creatures to breed.

March to May is the 'falling in love period' (wink wink). If you visit in autumn or winter, you may see tiny newborns in the nursery.

Try to visit in the morning, when the pandas are most active. Feeding takes place around opening time at 8am, although you'll see them eating in the late afternoon too. They spend most of their afternoons sleeping, particularly during the height of midsummer, when they sometimes disappear into their (air-conditioned) living quarters.

Catch bus 49 (¥2, 40 minutes) and transfer at Zhāojué Hénglù stop (昭觉横路站) to bus 87 (¥2, 20 minutes) to the Panda Base stop (熊猫基地站; Xióngmāo Jīdì). Alternatively, from North Train Station take bus 9 (¥2, 60 minutes) to the Zoo stop (动物园站; Dòngwùyuán) and switch to 198 (¥2, 20 minutes). Hostels run trips here, too. Metro line 3 will run directly here when it is completed.

Wénshū Temple   BUDDHIST TEMPLE

(文殊院, Wénshū Yuàn; 66 Wenshuyuan Lu, 文殊院路66号; ◎6am-9pm; M1) FREE This Tang dynasty monastery is dedicated to Wénshū (Manjushri), the Bodhisattva of Wisdom, and is Chéngdū's largest and best-preserved Buddhist temple. The air is heavy with incense and the low murmur of chanting; despite frequent crowds of worshippers, there's still a sense of serenity and solitude.

People's Park   PARK

(人民公园, Rénmín Gōngyuán; 9 Citang Jie, 祠堂街9号; ◎6.30am-10pm; M2) FREE On weekends, locals fill this park with dancing, song and taichi. There's a small, willow-tree-lined boating lake and a number of teahouses: Hè Míng Teahouse (p740) is the most popular and atmospheric.

Chéngdū Museum   MUSEUM

(成都博物馆, Chéngdū Bówùguǎn; www.cdmuseum.com; west side of Tiānfǔ Sq, 天府广场西侧; ◎9am-5pm Tue-Sun) FREE Spanning ancient Shu and pre-Qin to the Revolutionary era and modern Chéngdū, this brand-new five-storey museum is packed with historical and cultural relics of the city's past. Don't miss the 'Puppetry and Shadow Plays of China' gallery on the top floor, with excellent examples of the art from across the country.

Chéngdū Museum of Contemporary Art   GALLERY

(成都当代美术馆, Chéngdū Dāngdài Měishùguǎn; ♪028 8598 0055; www.chengdumoca.org; Tiānfǔ Software Park, Bldg C1, 天府软件园C1楼; ◎10am-5.30pm Tue-Sun; P) FREE This privately funded museum aims to create a space for the development and exhibition of contemporary and abstract art in Chinese society. Works on display range from thought-provoking critiques of the country's history to examinations of the interplay between nature and society, and make a visit well worth the trip out from central Chéngdu. Be sure to visit both wings of the museum, separated by a public garden space incorporated into the architecture of the museum itself.

Jīnshā Site Museum MUSEUM

(金沙遗址博物馆, Jīnshā Yízhǐ Bówùguǎn; www.jinshasitemuseum.com; 227 Qingyang Dadao, 青羊大道227号; ¥80; ⊙8am-5.30pm) In 2001 archaeologists made a historic discovery in Chéngdu's western suburbs: they unearthed a major site containing ruins of the 3000-year-old Shu kingdom. This excellent, expansive museum includes the excavation site and beautiful displays of many of the uncovered objects, which were created between 1200 and 600 BC.

Like the discoveries further outside the city at Sānxīngduī (p743), the 6000 or so relics here include both functional and decorative items, from pottery and tools to jade artefacts, stone carvings and ornate gold masks. A large number of elephant tusks were also unearthed here.

Take bus 901 from Xīnnánmén bus station, or metro line 2 to Yipintianxia (一品天下).

Wǔhóu Temple BUDDHIST TEMPLE

(武侯祠, Wǔhóu Cí; 231 Wuhouci Dajie, 武侯祠大街231号; adult/student ¥60/30; ⊙8am-8pm; ⓐ1, 21, 26) Located next to Nánjiāo Park and surrounded by mossy cypresses, this temple (rebuilt in 1672) honours several figures from the Three Kingdoms period, namely military strategist Zhuge Liang and Emperor Liu Bei (his tomb is here). Both were immortalised in the Chinese literature classic, *Romance of the Three Kingdoms (Sān Guó Yǎnyì)*.

Qīngyáng Temple TAOIST TEMPLE

(青羊宫, Qīngyáng Gōng; 9 Huanlu Xi Er Duan, 一环路西二段9号; ¥10; ⊙8am-6pm; ⓐ11, 27, 45) Located alongside **Culture Park** (文化公园, Wénhuà Gōngyuán; 9 Huanlu Xi Er Duan, 一环路西二段9号; ⊙6am-10pm; ⓐ) **FREE**, this is Chéngdu's oldest and most extensive Taoist temple. Qīngyáng (or Green Ram) Temple dates from the Zhou dynasty, although most of what you see is Qing. A highlight is the unusually squat, eight-sided pagoda, built without bolts or pegs. There's also a popular teahouse (¥10) inside, towards the back.

🛏 Sleeping

⭐**Loft Design Hostel** HOSTEL $

(四号工厂青年旅馆, Sìhào Gōngchǎng Qīngnián Lǚguǎn; ☑028 8626 5770; www.lofthostel.com; 4 Xiaotong Xiang, off Zhongtongren Lu, 中通仁路, 小桶巷4号; dm ¥50-60, s/d from ¥180/300; ⊛@🛜; ⓐ48, 54, 341) Chic boutique meets trendy hostel for grown-ups in this converted printing factory with its pretty cafe/bar, exposed brick and arty vibe. The front desk offers solid travel advice plus a decent cocktail selection. Dorms are small but the deluxe private rooms are spacious. The biggest downfalls: wi-fi is only in the common spaces and it's far from the metro.

Lazybones Backpacker Boutique Hostel HOSTEL $

(懒骨头青年旅舍, Lǎngǔtóu Qīngnián Lǚshè; ☑028 8669 5778; www.chengduhostel.com; 16 Yangshi Jie, 羊市街16号; dm ¥50, tw & d ¥189; ⊛@🛜) This friendly hostel can organise tours, whip up a Western breakfast, offer advice on the city, tell you about their free activities, or just leave you be to play with the house cat. If all that weren't enough, it's also just a few minutes from the Luomashi metro stop.

Nova Traveller's Lodge HOSTEL $

(成都乐浮国际青年旅舍, Chéngdu Lèfú Guójì Qīngnián Lǚshè; ☑028 8695 0016; www.dragontown.com.cn; 10 Taisheng Beilu, 太升北路10号; dm ¥45, standard/deluxe r ¥130/170; ⊛🛜) Clean, bright\ and quiet, and the staff here make the collection of good facilities into a truly excellent hostel. Standard private rooms are on the quite small side, so upgrade to one of the roomier deluxe rooms.

Cloud Atlas Hostel HOSTEL $

(云图国际青年旅舍, Yúntú Guójì Qīngnián Lǚshè; ☑028 8334 6767; cloudatlashostel@163.com; 288 Shuncheng Jie, 顺城街288号; dm ¥45-75, tw ¥150-240; ⊙⊛🛜) Excellent facilities, great coffee, lots of common space – this hostel has it all. It's large enough to feel a bit institutional on the dorm floors, but that just means there are tonnes of new friends to be made.

Chéngdu Dreams Travel Hostel HOSTEL $

(梦之旅国际青年旅舍, Mèngzhīlǚ Guójì Qīngnián Lǚshè; ☑028 8557 0315; www.dreams-travel.com/youthhostel/en; 242 Wuhouci Dajie, 武侯祠大街242号; dm ¥45-60, r ¥155-265; 🛜; ⓐ57) Across the street from Wǔhóu Temple, this backpacker joint has loads of common space and friendly, helpful staff. Our only complaint is that the bathrooms could use a good scrubbing.

Hello Chéngdu International Youth Hostel HOSTEL $

(老宋青年旅舍, Lǎosòng Qīngnián Lǚshè; ☑028 8335 5322, 028 8196 7573; www.gogosc.com; 211 Huanlu Bei 4 Duan, 一环路北四段211号; dm from

Chéngdū

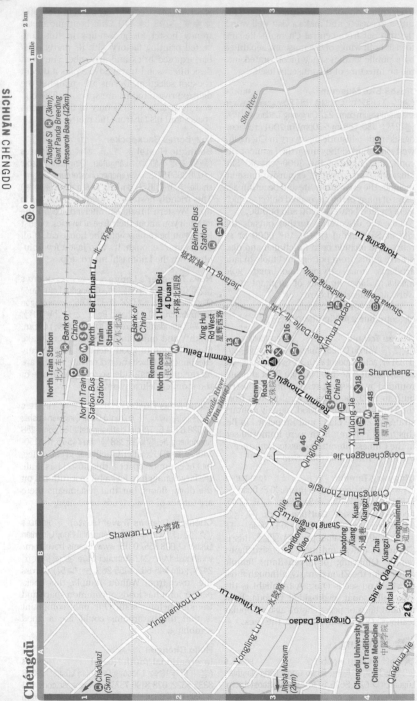

2 km
1 mile

Chadianzi (5km)

North Train Station 北火车站

Zhaojué Sì (3km); Giant Panda Breeding Research Base (12km)

Sha River

Bank of China

North Train Station Bus Station

Bei Erhuan Lu 北二环路

Bank of China

1 Huanlu Bei 4 Duan 环路北四段

Xing Hui Rd West 星辉西路

Jiezhi Lu 解放北路

Běimén Bus Station

Hongxing Lu

Shawan Lu 沙湾路

Yingmenkou Lu

Renmin North Road 人民北路

Renmin Beilu

Brocade River (Jin Jiang)

Wenwu Road 文殊院

Renmin Zhonglu

Bei Dajie 北大街

Xinhua Dadao

Taisheng Beilu

Shuwa Beijie

Shunchen

X'i Dajie

X'i Yulong Jie

Bank of China

Luomashi 骡马市

Dongchenggen Jie

Qingdao

Shang to Ren Lu 上人路

Changshun Zhongjie

Sandonga Qiao

Xi'an Lu

Xiaotong Xiang 小通巷

Kuan Xiangzi

Zhai Xiangzi

Changshun Zhongjie

Tonghuimen 通惠门

Shi'er Qiao

Qintai Lu

Qingyang Dadao

Xi Yihuan Lu 永陵路

Yongling Lu

Jinsha Museum (2km)

Chengdu University of Traditional Chinese Medicine 中医学院

Qinghua Jie

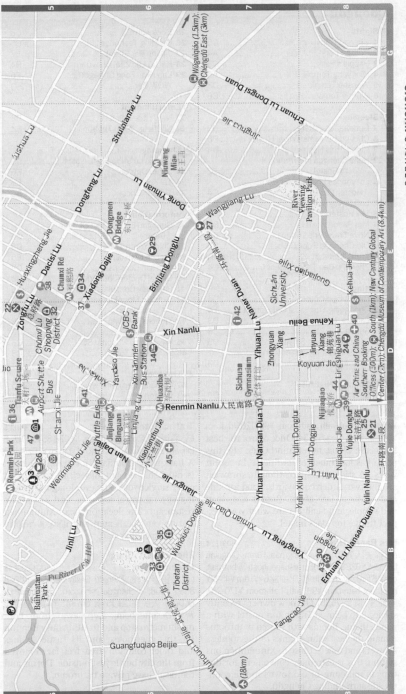

Wǔguiqiáo (1.5km);
Chéngdū East (3km)

Èrhuan Lu Dōngsì Duàn

Jīnghuá Jie

Shuǐjīnghé Lu

Dōngfeng Lu

Niuwang
Miao
牛王庙

Dōng Yīhuán Lu

River
Viewing
Pavilion Park

Wangliang Lu

Dacisi Lu

Chūnxī Rd
春熙路

Dōngmen
Bridge
东门大桥

Binjiang Dōnglu

Guojiāqiáo Xijie

Huaxīngzheng Jie

Zūshua Lu

Chūnxī Lù
Shopping
District

Xiadōng Dàjie

Sichuān
University

Kehua Jie

Zongfu Lù

38

31

34

29

27

Yíjinqiáo Lu

Yīhuán Lu Nánèr Duàn

Kehua Bēilù

ICBC
Bank

Xin Nánlu

42

40

Xīn Nánmén
Bus Station

Sichuan
Gymnasium
省体育馆

Zhongyuán
Xiàng

Jīnyuán
Xiàng
锦苑巷

Lin Eshiguan Lu

Air China and China
Southern Booking

Tianfu Square
天府广场

Airport Shuttle
Bus

Shaanxi Jie

Yanzǎo Jie

Xinkai Jie

Huaxiba
海椒市

Koyuan Jio

Nijiaqiáo
倪家桥

24

22

32

36

47

1

26

3

41

Renmin Park
人民公园

Jinjiang
Binguan
锦江宾馆

Linjiang Lu

Renmin Nánlu 人民南路

Nijiaqiáo Jie

39

44

21

25

South (1km); New Century Global
Center (3km); Chengdu Museum of Contemporary Art (8.4km)

Office (300m);

Yulin Dōnglu

Yulie Dōnglu
玉林东路

Wenmiaohòu Jie

Nan Dàjie
南大街

Xiaotiānzhu Jie
小天竺街

45

Yulin Dōngjie

Yulin Nánjie

Yulin Xilu

Yulin Lu

Jinli Lu

Bǎihuatán Park

Fu River (Fu Hé)

Wǔhòucí Dajie 武侯祠大街

Jiangxi Jie

Xīmian Qiáo Jie

Yongfeng Lu

Fangqin
Jie

Tibetan
District

35

6

8

33

Yulin Nánlu
三环路南二段

Èrhuan Lu Nánsan Duàn

43

30

Yīhuán Lu Nánsan Duàn

Guangfuqiáo Beijie

Wǔhòucí Dàjie 武侯祠大街

(18km)

Fangcao Jie

Chéngdū

¥40, s without/with bathroom ¥90/120, d from ¥140; ⊕ ❄ @ ⊛; ⊇ 28, 34) Once one of the best hostels in China, never mind Chéngdū, this place has lost much of its finesse in recent years. It's still a nice space, though, sprawled around two garden courtyards, good for kids and adults to laze about. Rooms are clean and simple, and facilities are what you'd expect from a top-class hostel.

Mrs Panda Hostel　　　　　　HOSTEL $
(熊猫夫人青年旅舍, Xióngmāo Fūrén Qīngnián Lǚshě; ☑ 028 8705 5315; mrspandahostel@hotmail.com; 6 Linjiang Zhonglu, 临江中路6号; dm ¥45-50, r without bathroom ¥90, with bathroom ¥170-210; ❄ @ ⊛; ⊇ 55, 76, 16) The new owners recently spruced up beloved Traffic Inn hostel with a panda theme. Rooms with shared bathrooms remain the best value thanks to the spotless showers and toilets. Close to Xīnnánmén bus station, this is extremely convenient for day trips to museums or old towns in the countryside surrounding Chéngdū.

Traffic Hotel　　　　　　HOTEL $
(交通饭店, Jiāotōng Fàndiàn; ☑ 028 8545 1017; 6 Linjiang Zhonglu, 临江中路6号; r from ¥80; P ⊛) A backpacker standard for ages, this hotel is old-fashioned but has clean rooms and every service you could ever imagine, including several travel agencies and an on-site restaurant. The location near Xīnnánmén station can't be beaten and it's got helpful English-speaking staff.

ZhengFu Cao Tang
Decent Inn　　　　　　GUESTHOUSE $$
(正福德馨客栈, Zhèngfú Déxīn Kèzhàn; ☑ 028 8666 4008; dxchengdu@sina.com; 5 Renmin Lu Er Duan, 人民路二段5号; dm ¥45, r ¥138; ❄ ⊛; Ⓜ 1) Despite being steps away from Loumashi metro stop and fronting busy Renmin Lu, this guesthouse and its rustic stylings and quiet common area feel far removed from the city bustle just outside. Dorms and rooms all have private bathroom.

BuddhaZen Hotel
HOTEL **$$$**

(圆和圆佛禅客栈, Yuánhéyuán Fúchán Kèzhàn, O 和O; ☎028 8692 9898; www.buddhazenhotel.com; B6-6 Wenshufang, 青羊区文殊坊B6-6号; incl breakfast s & d from ¥498, ste from ¥788; ✳@🛜; M1) Set in a tranquil courtyard building, this boutique hotel near Wénshū Temple blends traditional decor with modern comforts and a taste of Buddhist philosophy. You can ponder life sipping tea on your private balcony, circling the sand garden or soaking in a wooden tub at the spa. It's lovely here.

Old Chéngdū Book Club
HOTEL **$$$**

(成都书院, Chéngdū Shūyuàn; ☎028 8695 6688; www.oldchengduclub.com.cn; 28 Wuyuegong Jie, 五岳宫街28号; s/d/tr from ¥480/580/780; ✳@🛜) On Wénshū Temple's doorstep, the Ming-dynasty-style courtyard buildings and luxurious rooms of this hotel are decorated with lovely Chinese furnishings and artwork. It's worth upgrading to the bright and sumptuous rooms in the main building. Limited English spoken.

✖ Eating

Wénshū Temple Vegetarian Restaurant
VEGETARIAN **$**

(文殊院素宴厅, Wénshūyuàn Sùyàn Tīng; southeast cnr of Wénshū Temple, Wenshuyuan Lu, 文殊院路; dishes ¥12-48, tea from ¥68; ☺9.40am-9.30pm; 🍴) This excellent volunteer-staffed vegetarian restaurant and the atmospheric teahouse that surrounds it are on the Wénshū Temple's grounds. There's also a coffee shop in a separate pavilion in the first courtyard.

Lǎo Mā Rabbit Head
SICHUAN **$**

(老妈兔头, Lǎomā Tùtóu; ☎132 1902 5349; http://laomatutou.chengdu.edushi.com; 22 Jinsi Jie, 金丝22号; rabbit head ¥8, mains from ¥28; ☺8.30am-10pm) The menu has the full range of Sìchuān dishes, but it's only really worth the trip for the namesake: rabbit head (兔头; *tùtóu*). Order by the piece, kinda-spicy (五香; *wǔxiāng*) or pretty spicy (麻辣; *málà*). When it comes, dig in. Break open the jaw, split open the skull, and don't miss the best bits down in the cranial cavity.

Táng Sòng Food Street
STREET FOOD **$**

(春熙坊唐宋美食街, Chūnxīfāng Tángsòng Měishí Jiē; 29 Zongfu Lu, 总府路29号; mains from ¥12; ☺9.30am-10.30pm) This reconstructed ancient alleyway is jam-packed with tourists and Chéngdū favourites like *chāoshǒu* (抄手; wontons; ¥12) and *chuànchuàn xiāng* (串串香; the skewer version of the Chóngqìng hotpot; ¥2 to ¥4). Musical performances reverberate in the indoor space in the evening. Look for the wooden sign and doors near Lotte KTV. If you want to try traditional Sìchuān favourite *tùtóu* (兔头; rabbit head) head for Bāshǔ Shānhuò (巴蜀山货).

★ Chóngqìng
Yúanlǎosì Old Hotpot
HOTPOT **$$**

(重庆袁老四老火锅, Chóngqìng Yuánlǎosì Lǎohuǒguǒ; ☎028 8444 5220; 66 Mengzhuiwan Jie, 猛追湾街66号; pot ¥88, dishes from ¥10; ☺11am-10pm) Though it may seem like sacrilege to eat Chóngqìng-style hotpot in rival Chéngdū, this place is cleaner than most and the flavour and ingredient quality speak for themselves (plus the beer is cold).

Chén Mápó Dòufu
SICHUAN **$$**

(陈麻婆豆腐; ☎028 8674 3889; 197 Xi Yulong Jie, 西玉龙街197号; mains ¥22-58; ☺11.30am-2.30pm & 5.30-9pm) The plush flagship of this famous chain is a great place to experience *mápó dòufu* (麻婆豆腐; small/large ¥12/20) – soft, house bean curd with a fiery sauce of garlic, minced beef, fermented soybean, chilli oil and Sìchuān pepper. It's one of Sìchuān's most famous dishes and is this restaurant's specialty. Non-spicy choices, too.

Sultan
MIDDLE EASTERN **$$$**

(苏坦土耳其餐吧, Sūtǎn Tǔ'ěrqí Cānba; ☎028 8555 4780; 25-12 Fanghua Jie, 芳华街25号附12号; mains from ¥50; ☺noon-11pm; 🛜) Crowd-pleasing fare from the western reaches of the Silk Road, including lamb kebabs, hummus, house-made yoghurt, Turkish coffee, and warm naan. Hook into the free wi-fi outside on the patio, or into a sheesha pipe (¥50) in a private room piled with cushions.

🍷 Drinking & Nightlife

Sìchuān does teahouses better than anywhere else in China. In Chéngdū there are plenty of options for the harder stuff too, including raucous **Jiǔyǎn Bar Street** (九眼酒吧街, Jiǔyǎn Jiǔbā Jiē), a strip of bars and clubs on the Jǐn Jiāng, and the newly developed upscale bar/club/restaurant district at **Lan Kwai Fong** (兰桂坊, Lánguìfāng). For the latest on Chéngdū's nightlife, pick up copies of *Hello Chengdu* or *More Chengdu* (www.morechengdu.com), or check out www.gochengdoo.com/en.

★ Kǎi Lú Lǎo Zhái Cháyuán
TEAHOUSE

(庐恺老宅茶园; ☎180 3041 6632; 11 Kuan Xiangzi, 宽巷子11号; ☺10am-11pm; 🛜) For 200 years one of the city's most venerable teahouses has been tucked away in a peaceful courtyard behind a stone archway off frenetic Kuan

Alley, the distant hum of which is more than countered by the sound of zither music that plays in the background. These days there's wi-fi, but that seems to be about all that has changed. Tea from ¥38; snacks ¥12.

Hè Míng Teahouse
TEAHOUSE
(鹤鸣茶馆, Hèmíng Cháguǎn; People's Park, 人民公园; ⊙6am-9pm) Always lively, this century-old spot is most pleasant for whiling away an afternoon with a bottomless cup of tea (¥12 to ¥30). Neat tea-pouring performances happen on Saturdays from 2pm to 3pm. Ear cleanings (¥20) available daily.

Beer Nest
BAR
(啤酒窝酒吧, Píjiǔ Wō Jiǔbā; ☑151 0836 0121; info@thebeernest.com; 34-7 Jinxiu Li, 锦绣路34号附7号; ⊙2pm-late) Owned by a real-life Belgian brewing his own beer, this place is an instant favourite. There's a daily 'Buy-2-Get-1' Happy Hour (2pm to 8pm) and specials every day of the week, but Tuesday (three-beer sampler for ¥40), Thursday (beer pong 8pm to 11pm, free beer!) and Sunday (¥30 craft beers) are among the best. They can also get Tex-Mex delivered (¥15 to ¥38).

WOW Bar
BAR
(WOW酒吧, WOW Jiǔbā; ☑028 8525 2653; 2nd fl, 6 Taiping Nanxin Jie, 九眼桥太平南新街6号2楼; ⊙2pm-late) Anchoring the Jiǔyǎn Bar Street (p739), a free welcome cocktail and free beer till 10pm makes this place a no-brainer for starting a night out. If you're looking for a big Friday night, there's a weekly chugging contest, with the winner getting a bottle of vodka to take home. Drinks from ¥20.

Bookworm
CAFE
(老书虫, Lǎo Shūchóng; ☑028 8552 0177; www.chengdubookworm.com; 2 Yujie Dongjie, 28 Renmin Nanlu, 人民南路28号、玉洁东街2号; ⊙9am-1am) This hopping bookstore-cafe, like its branches in Běijīng and Sūzhōu, is a gathering place for expats and a pleasant spot for a beer or coffee (from ¥30). It also serves decent Western food (mains ¥35 to ¥95), but service can be painfully slow. You can buy or borrow from the English-language section, or stop by for author talks, live music and other events.

☆ Entertainment

Chéngdū is the birthplace of Sìchuān opera, which dates back more than 250 years. Besides glass-shattering songs, performances feature slapstick, martial arts, men singing as women, acrobatics and even fire breathing. An undoubted highlight is *biànliǎn* (变脸; face changing), where performers change character in a blink by swapping masks, manipulating face paint and other prestidigitation.

★ Shǔfēng Yǎyùn Teahouse
SÌCHUĀN OPERA
(蜀风雅韵, Shǔfēng Yǎyùn; ☑028 8776 4530; www.shufengyayun.net; inside Culture Park, 文化公园内面; tickets ¥140-500; ⊙ticket office 3-9.30pm, nightly shows 8-9.30pm) This famous century-old theatre and teahouse puts on excellent 1½-hour shows that include music, puppetry and Sìchuān opera's famed fire breathing and face changing. Come at around 7.15pm to watch performers putting on their elaborate make-up and costumes. For ¥50 to ¥100, kids (and adults) can try on garb and have a costume artist paint their face.

New Little Bar
LIVE MUSIC
(小酒馆芳沁店, Xiǎo Jiǔguǎn Fāngqìn Diàn; ☑028 8515 8790; http://site.douban.com/littlebar; 47 Yongfeng Lu & Fangqin Jie, 永丰路47号丰尚玉林商务港5楼,芳沁街; ⊙6pm-2am) This small pub-like venue is *the* place in Chéngdū to catch live local bands; they play most Fridays and Saturdays, and occasional weekdays, usually from 8pm. Live music carries a cover charge of around ¥15, depending on who's playing. Check online for the schedule.

🔒 Shopping

Fancy-pants shopping centres dot the city, with the highest concentration around the **Chūnxī Lù shopping district** (春熙路步行街, Chūnxīlù Bùxíngjiē; M 2) east of Tiānfǔ Sq. At the south end of town sprawls the **New Century Global Center** (新世纪环球中心, Xīn Shìjì Huánqiú Zhōngxīn; ☑028 6273 2888; 1700 Tianfu Bei Dadao, 天府北大道1700号; M 1 to Jincheng Square), the world's largest mall.

For traditional Tibetan shopping options, try the **shops** (藏族用品一条街, Zàngzú Yòngpǐn Yītiáo Jiē) in the Tibetan neighbourhood southeast of Wǔhóu Temple.

Outdoor enthusiasts gearing up for mountains trips should head to **Sanfo Outdoors** (三夫户外, Sānfū Hùwài; ☑028 8507 9586; www.sanfo.com; 243 Wuhouci Dajie, 武侯词大街243号; ⊙10am-8.30pm) or **Decathlon** (迪卡侬运动超市, Díkǎnóng Yùndòng Chāoshì; ☑028 8531 0388; 9 Zhanhua Lu, Gaoxin District, 高新区站华路9号; ⊙10am-10pm; M 1).

Tai Koo Li
SHOPPING CENTRE
(太古里, Tàigǔlǐ; M 2) An upscale extension of Chūnxī Lù with big international brand names in an ancient-style architectural zone, this is also one of the best places in town to fill up on foreign food and beer.

ⓘ Information

MEDICAL SERVICES

Global Doctor Chéngdū Clinic (环球医生, Huánqiú Yīshēng; ☑ 028 8528 3660, 24hr emergency 139 8225 6966; www.globaldoctor.com.au; 2nd fl, 9-11 Lippo Tower, 62 Kehua Beilu, 科华北路62号力宝大厦2层9-11号; ⊗ 9am-6pm Mon-Sat) English- and Chinese-speaking doctors and a 24-hour emergency line, and can even make house visits. Consultations cost ¥840; after-hours visits ¥1050; house calls ¥1700.

West China Hospital SCU (四川大学华西医院, Sìchuān Dàxué Huáxī Yīyuàn; ☑ 24hr emergency assistance in Chinese & English 028 8542 2761, for appointment 028 8542 2408; http://eng.cd120.com; 37 Guoxue Xiang, 国学巷37号; ☐ 1) This hospital complex is China's largest and is among the most well regarded. Foreigners should head for the International Hospital here, where doctors and some staff speak English. Note that some treatments without qualifying insurance may require a deposit.

MONEY

Bank of China (中国银行, Zhōngguó Yínháng; 35 Renmin Zhonglu, 2nd Section, 人民中路二段35号; ⊗ 8.30am-5.30pm Mon-Fri, to 5pm Sat & Sun) The bank's main Chéngdū branch changes money and travellers cheques, and offers cash advances on credit cards.

Bank of China (中国银行, Zhōngguó Yínháng; ⊗ 6.30am-11.30pm) Inside the entrance to the North Railway Station metro station.

PERMITS

Sìchuān Mountaineering Association (四川省登山户外运动协会, Sìchuānshěng Dengshan Hùwài Yùndòng Xiéhuì; ☑ 028 8543 8819; www.sma.gov.cn; 5th fl, 93 Xin Nanlu, 武侯区新南路93号亚华商厦5楼; ⊗ 9.30am-5pm) Permits generally take three days to process and cost from US$300 per site. You'll need to provide passports, proof of medical insurance and a clear itinerary. For popular but treacherous mountains such as Sìgūniáng (四姑娘), the association will arrange for a mandatory guide/liaison (from ¥300 per day). It can also assist with gear, meals and horses.

TRAVEL AGENCIES

Skip the gazillion Chinese travel agencies around town and head to the travel desks at one of Chéngdū's many excellent hostels, or try the following:

Tibetan Trekking (☑ 028 8597 6083, www.tibetantrekking.com, 47 Yongfeng Lu, Yulin Fengshang Room 1035, 47永丰路丰尚玉林商务港5楼, ⊗ 9am-noon & 2.30-5pm Mon-Fri)

Windhorse Tour (风马旅游, Fēngmǎ Lǚyóu, ☑ 028 8559 3923, www.windhorsetour.com, Ste 904, 21st fl, Bldg C, 1 Babao Lu, 八宝街1号万和苑C座904室; ⊗ 9am-6pm)

Extravagant Yak (☑ 028-8510 8093, www.extravagantyak.com, Unit #1117, 2 Gaosheng Qiao Donglu, Chéngdū)

VISAS

Chéngdū Entry & Exit Service Centre (成都市出入境接待中心, Chéngdūshì Chūrùjìng Jiēdài Zhōngxīn; ☑ 028 8640 7067; www.chengdu.gov.cn; 2 Renmin Xilu, 人民西路2号; ⊗ 9am-noon & 1-5pm Mon-Fri, to 4pm Sat) Visa extensions (in two working days), residence permits, and paperwork for lost passports are on the 3rd floor. It's in the building behind the Mao statue's right hand.

ⓘ Getting There & Away

AIR

You can fly directly to **Chéngdū Shuāngliú International Airport** (☑ 028 8520 5555; www.cdairport.com/front_en/index.jsp), 18km west of the city, from nearly any other major Chinese city in less than three hours. There are also direct international flights from Amsterdam, Bangkok, Doha, Frankfurt, Kathmandu, Kuala Lumpur, London, Melbourne, Mumbai, San Francisco, Seoul, Singapore, Tokyo and more.

Many travellers fly from here to Lhasa (¥892 to ¥1286; prepare for palpable oxygen deprivation). Flights to destinations within Sìchuān include Kāngdìng (¥470 to ¥923), Jiǔzhàigōu (¥830 to ¥1239) and Dàochéng-Yàdīng (¥701 to ¥1468), with Gānzī airport set to open in mid-2017.

Many hostels can book tickets, and the major Chinese airlines are also bookable online.

Air China Chéngdū Booking Office (国航世界中心, Guóháng Shìjiè Zhōngxīn; ☑ nationwide bookings 95583; 1 Hangkong Lu, 人民南路四段航空路1号; ⊗ 8.30am-5pm) By Tongzilin metro station, on the north side of Hangkong Lu.

China Eastern Airlines (中国东方航空公司, Zhōngguó Dōngfāng Hángkōng Gōngsī; ☑ 021 8615 5133; www.flychinaeastern.com; 6 Xiyu Jie, 西御街6号; ⊗ 9am-4.30pm) On the north side of Xiyu Jie, just to the west of Tiānfǔ Sq.

China Southern Airlines (中国南方航空, Zhōngguó Nánfāng Hángkōng; ☑ 028 8666 3618; www.csair.com; 15th fl, New Hope Tower, 45 Renmin Nanlu 4th Section, 人民南路四段45号新希望大厦15室; ⊗ 8.30am-5.30pm) Near Tongzilin metro station, just south of Hangkong Lu.

Dragon Air (港龍航空公司;, Gǎnglóng Hángkōng Gōngsī; ☑ 400 888 6628; www.dragonair.com; 5th fl, Sheraton Chengdu Lido Hotel, 15 Renmin Zhonglu, 1st Section, 人民中路1段15號天府麗都喜來登飯店5樓; ⊗ 9am-5pm Mon-Fri) Rather than visiting in person, it's possible to book tickets (in English) by phone from 7am to 11pm.

BUS

The main bus station for tourists is **Xīnnánmén** (新南门汽车站, Xīnnánmén Qìchēzhàn), officially the central tourist station; 旅游客运中心. Two other useful stations are **Běimén** (北门汽车站, Běimén Qìchēzhàn) and **Chádiànzi** (茶店子). Be prepared to be dropped at any one of these (and other) bus stations when arriving in Chéngdū. If you end up at Shíyángchǎng bus station (石羊场公交站), local bus 28 (¥2) connects it to Xīnnánmén and Běimén bus stations, as well as **North Train Station Bus Station** (火车北站汽车站, Huǒchē Běizhàn Qìchēzhàn). Limited buses also depart directly from the **airport bus station** (双流客运站).

Destinations from Xīnnánmén Station

Bamboo Sea ¥90 to ¥101, five hours, two daily (9.10am, 3.30pm)

Dānbā ¥141, eight hours, two daily (6.30am, 6.35am)

Émēi Shān ¥41, 2½ hours, every 20 minutes from 7.20am to 7.20pm

Hóngyǎ (for Liǔjiāng) ¥38, two hours, every 45 minutes from 7.40am to 5.40pm

Jiǔzhàigōu ¥138, 10 hours, four daily (7.20am, 8am, 9am, 10am). Extra morning buses run in July and August. Note: these buses pass Sōngpān (eight hours), but you may have to pay the full fare even if you get off at Sōngpān.

Kāngdìng ¥147, seven hours, one daily (9am)

Lè Shān ¥49, two hours, every 20 minutes from 7.20am to 7.35pm

Pínglè ¥20 to ¥24, two hours, six daily (8.20am to 3.30pm)

Sānxīngduī ¥50 return, two hours, one daily (9.30am)

Yǎ'ān (for Bìfēngxiá) ¥44, two hours, every 35 minutes from 7am to 7.30pm

Destinations from Chádiànzi Station

Lángzhōng ¥93, 3½ hours, every 30 minutes from 7.30am to 6.20pm

Yíbīn ¥103, four hours, six daily (7.20am to 5.40pm)

Zìgòng ¥84, 3½ hours, every 30 minutes from 7am to 7.20pm

Destinations from Chéngdū Shuāngliú International Airport

Lè Shān ¥54, two hours, about every two hours from 10.30am to 6.30pm

Yǎ'ān ¥49, two hours, three daily (11.20am, 2pm, 4.30pm)

Yíbīn ¥101, four hours, five daily (10.50am, 12.30pm, 2.30pm, 4.30pm, 7pm)

Zìgòng ¥82, 3½ hours, every hour from 11.20am to 5.20pm

TRAIN

Chéngdū's two main train stations are **Chéngdū North Train Station** (火车北站; huǒchē běizhàn) and the newer **Chéngdū East Train Station** (火车东站; huǒchē dōngzhàn), both of which connect directly to the metro.

Hotels, hostels and **China Youth Travel Agency** (CYTS, 中国青年旅行社, Zhōngguó Qīngnián Lǚxíngshè; 📞 028 6665 4311; www.cytstours.com; 283 Hongxing Lu, 红星路283号; ⊙9am-10pm) can book tickets, usually for a ¥5 fee.

Destinations from Chéngdū North Train Station

The **North Train Station ticket office** (火车北站售票处, Huǒchē Běizhàn Shòupiàochù; Huochezhan Guangchang, 火车站广场; ⊙24hr) is in the separate building on your right as you approach the station. Buy high-speed train tickets at the adjacent **intercity trains ticket office** (城际列车售票处, Chéngjì Lièchē Shòupiàochù; Huochezhan Guangchang, 火车站广场; ⊙9am-6pm Mon-Fri).

Émēi Town K/T seat ¥24, 2½ hours, five daily (7.21am to 2.57pm)

Kūnmíng K seat/hard sleeper ¥138/238, 18 to 22 hours, six daily (8.54am to 5.03pm)

Lhasa hard/soft sleeper ¥668/1062, 43 hours, one daily (2.48pm)

Qīngchéng Shān C seat ¥15, 45 minutes, four daily (6.48am, 8.49am, 4.41pm and 7.16pm)

Xī'ān seat/hard sleeper ¥112/194, 10 to 16 hours, 12 daily (7.36am to 10.16pm)

Yíbīn seat/hard sleeper ¥51/97, six to nine hours, six daily (8.54am to 10.02pm)

Zìgòng seat/hard sleeper ¥41/87, five to seven hours, five daily (8.54am to 10.02pm)

Destinations from Chéngdū East Train Station

Daily D/G-class trains depart from Chéngdū East Train Station for the following:

Chóngqìng 2nd/1st class ¥154/247, 1¾ hours, frequently (7.48am to 9.43pm)

Wǔhàn 2nd/1st class ¥355/425, 10 to 20 hours, seven daily (6.45am to 11.51pm)

Destinations from Chéngdū Shuāngliú International Airport

Sìchuān's newly completed high-speed train line stops at the airport (双流机场; Shuāngliú jīchǎng) on the way to two of the province's major tourist destinations:

Lè Shān 2nd/1st class ¥46/55, one hour, six daily (8.59am to 8.46pm)

Émēi Shān 2nd/1st class ¥56/68, one hour, six daily (8.59am to 8.46pm)

ℹ Getting Around

TO/FROM THE AIRPORT

From Chéngdū Shuāngliú International Airport, airport shuttle buses cover five routes, reaching all corners of the city. **Buses for Route 1** (机场班车, Jīchǎng Bānchē; www.cdairport.com/front_en/jt4.jsp; ⊙6am-10pm) are the most direct to the city centre, stopping in front of the Jīnjiāng Hotel on Renmin Nanlu, from where you

WORTH A TRIP

SĀNXĪNGDUĪ MUSEUM

The **Sānxīngduī Museum** (三星堆博物馆, Sānxīngduī Bówùguǎn; 028 565 1526; www.sxd.cn; 133 Xi'An Lu, Guǎnghàn, 广汉市西安路133号; ¥80, audioguide ¥10; 8.30am-6pm, last entry 5pm), 40km north of Chéngdū in Guǎnghàn (广汉), exhibits relics of the Shu kingdom, a cradle of Chinese civilisation dating from 1200 BC to 1100 BC. Some archaeologists regard these artefacts, which include stunningly crafted, angular and stylised bronze masks, as even more important than Xī'ān's Terracotta Warriors. Art and anthropology buffs will need at least a half day here, though budding archaeologists may be disappointed by the lack of access to the dig site itself.

Throughout the 20th century, farmers around Guǎnghàn continually unearthed intriguing pottery shards and dirt encrusted jade carvings when digging wells and tilling their fields. However, war and lack of funds prevented anyone from investigating these finds. Finally, in September 1986, archaeologists launched a full-scale excavation and made a startling discovery when they unearthed the site of a major city dating back to the Neolithic age in the upper reaches of the Yangzi River (Cháng Jiāng). It was previously believed that the oldest civilisations were concentrated around the Yellow River (Huáng Hé).

Buses to the site depart Chéngdū's Xīnnánmén bus station (¥50 return, one hour, 9.30am) and return from the museum around 3pm. Alternatively, buses from Chéngdū's Zhāojué Sì station (¥12, 1½ hours, 7am to 8pm) head to Guǎnghàn's tourist bus station (广汉客运中心) – transfer to local bus 10 (¥2, 6.30am to 8pm) for the remaining 10km to the site. A bus from the site back to Zhāojué Sì station leaves at 4.10pm, otherwise buses depart the tourist bus station for Xīnnánmén every 10 minutes (¥16, from 6.40am to 6.50pm).

can catch the metro. **Buses for Route 2** (机场大巴, Jīchǎng Dàbā; www.cdairport.com/front_en/jt4.jsp; ¥10; 6am-8pm) reach the South Train Station (which also has a metro connection), and then stops frequently along Renmin Lu to North Train Station. Route 5 connects with Chádiànzi bus station for western Sichuān departures.

A taxi will cost ¥70 to ¥90. Most guesthouses offer airport pick-up services for slightly more.

BICYCLE

Chéngdū is nice and flat, with designated biking lanes, although the traffic can be a strain for cyclists. Youth hostels rent out bikes for around ¥20 per day. Always lock up your bike.

BUS

You can get almost anywhere in Chéngdū by bus, as long as you can decipher the labyrinthine routes. Stops are marked in Chinese and English and some post route maps. Fares within the city are usually ¥2.

Useful routes:

Bus 1 City centre–Běimén bus station–Wǔhóu Temple

Bus 28 Shíyángchǎng bus station–Xīnnánmén bus station–Běimén bus station–Chéngdū North Train Station

Bus 16 Chéngdū North Train Station–Renmin Lu–Chéngdū South Train Station

Bus 82 Chádiànzi bus station–Jīnshā Site Museum (stop is 青羊大道口站)–Wǔhóu Temple–Xīnnánmén bus station

Bus 81 Mao statue–Qīngyáng Temple

Bus 69 Chéngdū North Train Station bus station–Zhāojué Sì bus station

Tourist Bus 87 Zhāojué Sì bus station–Giant Panda Breeding Research Base

Tourist Bus 60 Traffic Inn–Giant Panda Breeding Research Base

CAR & MOTORCYCLE

For trips west into Kham, groups might consider booking an SUV (越野车; yuèyě chē) with a driver. Given the high cost of gas and the challenging road conditions, rates are generally high, starting at ¥850 per day including tolls and petrol, but excluding food and sleeping costs for the driver. Add at least an additional ¥150 per day if the driver speaks English or Tibetan.

Most of Chéngdū's hotels and hostels can assist with finding a reliable, properly insured driver. Before embarking, settle on the itinerary, fee and what it covers, and what happens should the car break down or some other unpredictable, trip-altering problem arise.

METRO

Line 1 links Chéngdū North and South Train Stations, running the length of Renmin Lu and beyond. East–west Line 2 links Chéngdū East Train Station with the city centre, meeting Line 1 at Tiānfǔ Sq before continuing west to Chádiànzì bus station.

Line 3, which will run to the Giant Panda Breeding Research Base and Xīnnánmén bus station, and Line 4, for the new Chéngdū West Train Station, is slated for completion in 2017.

Rides cost ¥2 to ¥6 depending on the distance covered. Stations have bilingual signs, maps and ticket machines. The local public transit pass (天府通; Tiānfǔ tōng) is for sale at most metro stations, and also works for local buses.

AROUND CHÉNGDŪ

Dūjiāngyàn 都江堰

🎵 028 / POP 630,000

Two Unesco World Heritage sites in Dūjiāngyàn, 60km northwest of Chéngdū, make for very different glimpses into the history of Sìchuān. Qīngchéng Shān, most notably famous as the birthplace of Taoism, offers the chance to hike through misty forests past cascading waterfalls and ancient temples with views back down to the Chéngdū plains. The Dūjiāngyàn Irrigation System, the first in the world to control river flooding without the use of dams, is right in the thick of the modern city of Dūjiāngyàn; a look into how ancient engineering marvels still play a role in the life of modern China.

👁 Sights

Qīngchéng Shān TAOIST SITE
(青城山, Azure City Mountain; Dūjiāngyàn; Front Mountain adult ¥90, student/child/elderly ¥45, Back Mountain ¥20/10; ☺8am-5.30pm) Covered in lush, dripping forests, the sacred mountain of Qīngchéng Shān has been a Taoist spiritual centre for more than 2000 years. Its beautiful trails are lined with ginkgo, plum and palm, and there are caves, pavilions and centuries-old wooden temples to explore.

Visitors can experience two sides of the mountain. The main entrance is on the mountain's front side (前山; Qián Shān) and leads to paths that wind past 11 important Taoist sites. Those interested in hiking will prefer the back mountain (后山; Hòu Shān), accessed 40km northwest. In either case, to actually enjoy the views, avoid major holidays when masses of tourists arrive to pay tribute to their ancestors.

The trails at **Qián Shān** lead to a summit of only 1260m, a relatively easy climb – four hours up and down, even easier via the **cable car** (one-way/return ¥35/60). Snack stands are scattered along the mountain trails, and several of the major temples have small restaurants.

If you want to spend the night, a few temples on Qián Shān welcome guests. Most atmospheric is the fantastic Shàngqīng Temple (p744), a Qing-dynasty rebuild of the original Jin-dynasty temple in the middle of a forest near the top of the mountain, with guest rooms and a restaurant/teahouse attached. Alternatively, the **Tiānshī Cave Temple** (天师洞, Tiānshī Dòng; r from ¥128) has slightly less welcoming rooms, but is on a quieter stretch of the mountain.

Hòu Shān, the back of the mountain, has 20km of rugged pathways – expect a seven-hour round-trip hike to the 2128m summit, where you'll find **Báiyún Temple** (白云寺; Báiyún Sì); the cable cars at Jīnlī (one-way/return ¥30/55) and Báiyún (one-way/return ¥45/80) can shave a couple hours off the hike. You can find some guesthouses (山庄; shānzhuāng) at **Yòuyī Village** (又一村; Yòuyī Cūn), around halfway up the mountain's west side, of which **Jiāchún Villa** (佳派山庄, Jiāchún Shānzhuāng; 🎵155 2838 2949; Youyi Village, 又一村, Yòuyī Cūn; r from ¥100; ❀❀) is among the best.

Dūjiāngyàn Irrigation System HISTORIC SITE
(都江堰灌溉系统, Dūjiāngyàn Guàngài Xìtǒng; adult ¥90, student/child/elderly ¥45, shuttle to Yùlěi Pavilion ¥10; ☺8am-6pm) This Qin dynasty waterworks project (completed in 256 BC) is the oldest and only surviving non-dam irrigation system in the world. Still used to control water levels of the Mín Jiāng, this scenic area is studded with historic temples, forested hills, hilltop pagodas as well as coursing waters.

🛏 Sleeping

Shàngqīng Temple GUESTHOUSE $
(上清宫, Shàngqīng Gōng; d from ¥80; ❀) This Qing dynasty rebuild of the original Jin-dynasty temple is set in the forest near the top of the mountain; guest rooms are basic but comfortable but avoid the shared bathrooms. It has a restaurant (dishes ¥18 to ¥30) and a teahouse (tea from ¥10). No English menus, but there are a handful of photos to point at.

ℹ Getting There & Away

There are two high-speed rail routes from Chéngdū's North Train Station to the Dūjiāngyàn sites.

For the Dūjiāngyàn Irrigation System, take a train to Líduī Gōngyuán (离堆公园; ¥15, 33 minutes, 6.30am and 6.26pm). From there, walk out of the station to Dujiangyan Dadao (都江堰大道), turn left through the reconstructed city wall, and walk until the road ends at the site's entrance.

For Qīngchéng Shān, take the train to Qīngchéng Shān station (青城山; ¥15, 49 minutes, 6.48am, 4.20pm and 7.16pm). Pick up bus 101 (¥2, 10 minutes, every 15 minutes from 6.56am to 6.30pm) to the main gate (Qián Shān), or a tourist bus (中巴车; ¥25 return, 40 minutes) to Hòu Shān. Tourist buses leave when full and some pass the main gate en route, but only stop for passengers if there are empty seats.

Bus 101 (¥2, 40 minutes) also connects Qīngchéng Shān's train station and main gate with the Dūjiāngyàn Irrigation System.

The last trains back to Chéngdū depart at 12.33pm from Lídui Gōngyuàn and 10.18pm from Qīngchéng Shān.

Four Sisters Mountain 四姑娘山

☎ 0837 / POP 2893 / ELEV 3151M

Established as a national park in 1994 and declared a Unesco World Heritage Site in 2006, Four Sisters Mountain (Sìgūniang Shān) is famous among Chinese tourists as one of the most impressive natural areas of the entire country. At a magnificent 6250m the fourth of the Four Sisters, pyramid-shaped Yaomei Feng, comes in as the second-highest peak in all of Sìchuān.

Composed of three distinct valleys with a combined area of 450 sq km, the park has plenty of hiking and rock climbing for adventurous travellers looking to test their mettle. Anything beyond a day hike will require a permit and a local guide, but these peaks are well known among climbers and you may well see a group headed back down after a successful attempt.

Fall and spring are the high season, with great weather and stunning mountain views. Temperatures are most comfortable in summer, but there's also a good chance you'll be clouded in for days at a time by temperamental weather patterns. Winter is frigid, with snow on paths and night-time temps dropping to -15°C, but you'll have the parks mostly to yourself and benefit from reduced admission fees at each of the valleys from 1 December to 30 March.

◎ Sights

★ Hǎizi Valley　　　　NATIONAL PARK
(海子沟, Hǎizi Gōu; ¥60, student/off-season ¥40; ⊙ticket office 8am-4pm) Considered by many the most beautiful of the three valleys in the Four Sisters Mountain area, Hǎizi Valley's eponymous lakes and majestic views of the Four Sisters peaks make it hard to disagree. It's a steep walk for much of the way, so acclimatise in the other valleys first if possible. The entrance to the 19km-long valley is about 500m from the tourist centre, up an obvious staircase to the right of the building.

Shuāngqiáo Valley　　　NATIONAL PARK
(双桥沟, Shuāngqiáo Gōu; ¥80, student/off-season ¥50; ⊙ticket office 7.30am-3pm) The longest of the three main valleys in the area is also the most accessible to tourists, with a wooden boardwalk that runs for about 30km of the valley's 40km length and regular shuttle buses running throughout the day. Shuttle tickets are ¥70, not including the 7km transfer from Rìlóng, but if you want to get to the most impressive scenery at the far end of the valley it's the only way to do it in a day.

Chángpíng Valley　　　NATIONAL PARK
(长坪沟, Chángpíng Gōu; ¥70, student/off-season ¥50; ⊙ticket office 8am-4pm) While the first hour or so of the valley walk is on a wooden boardwalk, after that it's muddy trails through yak-filled pastures and dense forests all the way to the end. There's a shuttle (¥20) from the tourist centre to within the park just past Zhāngmu Village, but from there you'll need to be prepared to walk the rest of the way up the 29km valley trail.

🛏 Sleeping & Eating

A Lee Ben Hostel　　　　HOSTEL $
(阿里本青年旅舍, Ālǐběn Qīngnián Lǚshè; ☑180 9043 8688; www.aleeben.com; 49 Chángpíng Village, 长坪村49号; dm ¥30, d ¥120) With a common-room pool table, courtyard fountain, seemingly endless info on local sites and an English menu in the cafe this might just be a model hostel. Private rooms are comfortable after a day in the mountains, while dorms have all the little luxuries like lockers, private curtains and a large, clean shower.

Eight Treasures Restaurant　　TIBETAN $$
(八宝私房菜馆, Bābǎo Sīfáng Càiguǎn; Chángpíng Gujie, 长坪古街; dishes from ¥38) With meat sourced directly from the high-altitude grasslands for special dishes such as cowboy-style roast chicken and matsutake chicken stew, this is a good place to splash out for a celebratory meal after a long day of hiking.

❶ Information

Agricultural Bank of China ATM (⊙24hr) There's an Agricultural Bank of China ATM out front of the Four Sisters Mountain Tourist Centre.

Four Sisters Mountain Tourist Centre (四姑娘山游客中心, Sìgūniángshān Yóukè Zhōngxīn; ◎7.30am-5.30pm) Whether you're looking to buy tickets, pick up free maps (地图; *dìtú*) of the park, or have questions about exploring the three main valleys (only Chinese spoken); this is the place to do it. The building is at the eastern end of Rìlóng, at the entrance to the Chángpíng Valley.

Hùwài Zhōngxīn (户外中心; ◎9am-4.30pm) If you're hoping to camp or climb inside any of the valleys of the national park, this is the place to find your mandatory guide (from ¥300 per day). The office is on the road into Rìlóng, 500m past the Chángpíng Valley turn-off, on the right.

ⓘ Getting There & Away

A single daily bus to Chéngdū passes through Rìlóng between 8am and 9pm (¥140, seven to nine hours). Otherwise, arrange a seat in a shared vehicle (¥150) through your hostel.

In the other direction frequent minibuses head to Xiǎojīn (¥20, two hours, 7.30am to 4.40pm), from which a transfer to Dānbā is ¥30 (1½ hours).

Éméi Shān   峨眉山

☑ 0833 / POP 423,070

A cool, misty retreat from Sìchuān basin's heat, stunning Éméi Shān (3099m) is one of China's four sacred Buddhist Mountains (the others being Pǔtuó Shān, Wǔtái Shān and Jiǔhuá Shān). A farmer built the first Buddhist temple near Jīndǐng summit in the 1st century, marking Buddhism's arrival in the Eastern world. That temple stood until it was gutted by fire in 1972, and many of the more than 150 temples on the mountain suffered fires or looting over the centuries but around 30 have been maintained and restored in various degrees. Reconstructed in the 9th century, Wànnián Temple is the oldest surviving temple on the mountain.

Beyond its rich cultural heritage, the mountain also stands on the edge of the eastern Himalayan highlands and hosts a diverse range of plants and animals. Together with nearby Lè Shān, Éméi Shān is on Unesco's World Heritage list.

When to Go

The best time to visit is June to October, when the mist burns off by early afternoon. Epic crowds arrive in July and August. Avoid national holidays at all costs. Snowfall generally begins around November on the upper slopes. In winter you can rent crampons to deal with ice and snow and jackets (rental ¥30, ¥170 deposit) to stave off the cold. Expect rain and mist throughout the year.

Average temperatures:

	JAN	APR	JUL	OCT
Éméi town	7°C	21°C	26°C	17°C
Summit	-6°C	4°C	12°C	4°C

⊙ Sights & Activities

The entry ticket (adult ¥185/student and seniors ¥90, winter ¥110/55) gets you access to most sites on the mountain but does not include rides on the three buses to the main routes up or into a few of the temples.

Most rewarding is walking the whole way starting from Bàoguó Temple, but most opt to ride to Wànnián depot (for easy access to the cable car) or to Wǔxiàngǎng depot (an easy walk to poetic Qīngyīn Pavilion and other important sights). The Léidòngpíng bus drops off closest to the summit, just a few hours short of Jīndǐng Peak (or half an hour up to the upper cable car).

Regardless of your starting point, getting a feel for the place takes at least a full day, ideally two or three. Wander the wooden temples, meet the macaques demanding tribute for safe passage, then find shelter in a monastery guesthouse and wake up in time to welcome the sunrise. The early morning light refracting in the cool mist has been heralded since ancient times as Buddha's Halo, and the sea of clouds stretching out to the horizon is enough to make even the most jaded traveller feel a little bit closer to the heavens.

Bàoguó Temple   BUDDHIST MONASTERY
(报国寺, Bàoguó Sì; Emei Shan Lu; ¥8; ◎7am-7.30pm) Constructed in the 16th century, this temple (550m) features beautiful gardens of rare plants, as well as a 3.5m-high porcelain Buddha dating back to 1415, which is housed near the **Sutra Library**. This is not included in the Éméi Shān entrance ticket, but it also lies outside the scenic area so you won't need the ticket to visit.

Jiēyǐn Monastery   BUDDHIST MONASTERY
(接引寺, Jiēyǐn Sì) A large main hall and several smaller shrines mark the starting point of the final push to Jīndǐng Peak. To take the cable car to Jīndǐng, you'll have to walk up 1.5km from Léidòngpíng to here.

Jīndǐng Temple   BUDDHIST TEMPLE
(金顶寺, Jīndǐng Sì, Golden Summit) This magnificent temple is at the Golden Summit (Jīndǐng; 3077m), commonly referred to as

Émei Shān

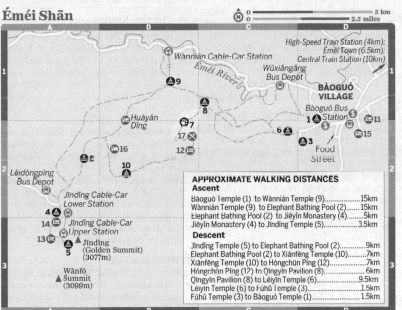

APPROXIMATE WALKING DISTANCES

Ascent

Bàoguó Temple (1) to Wànnián Temple (9)	15km
Wànnián Temple (9) to Elephant Bathing Pool (2)	15km
Elephant Bathing Pool (2) to Jiēyīn Monastery (4)	5km
Jiēyīn Monastery (4) to Jīndǐng Temple (5)	3.5km

Descent

Jīndǐng Temple (5) to Elephant Bathing Pool (2)	9km
Elephant Bathing Pool (2) to Xiānfēng Temple (10)	7km
Xiānfēng Temple (10) to Hóngchūn Píng (12)	7km
Hóngchūn Píng (12) to Qīngyīn Pavilion (8)	6km
Qīngyīn Pavilion (8) to Léiyīn Temple (6)	9.5km
Léiyīn Temple (6) to Fúhǔ Temple (3)	1.5km
Fúhǔ Temple (3) to Bàoguó Temple (1)	1.5km

Émei Shān

◎ Sights

1	Bàoguó Temple	D1
2	Elephant Bathing Pool	A2
3	Fúhǔ Temple	D2
4	Jiēyīn Monastery	A2
5	Jīndǐng Temple	A3
6	Léiyīn Temple	C2
7	Monkey Zone	B2
8	Qīngyīn Pavilion	C1
9	Wànnián Temple	B1
10	Xiānfēng Temple	B2

⊜ Sleeping

11	Happy Hotel	D1
12	Hóngchūn Píng	B2
13	Jīndǐng Dàjiǔdiàn	A3
14	Tuìtǐ Píng	A3
15	Teddy Bear Hotel	D2
16	Yùxiān Temple	B2

✪ Eating

17	Hard Wok Cafe	B2

the mountain's highest peak. This temple is a striking modern renovation, covered with glazed tiles and surrounded by white marble balustrades. In front, the prominent 48m-tall golden statue of multidimensional Samantabhadra (十方普贤; Shífāng Pǔxián) honours mountain protector Pǔxián, and was added in 2006. The views at sunset and sunrise, as golden light illuminates the clouds below, are a highlight of any visit to Émei.

Xiānfēng Temple BUDDHIST MONASTERY
(仙峰寺, Xiānfēng Sì) Somewhat off the beaten track on the long way round to the peak, this carefully tended monastery (1752m) is backed by rugged cliffs and surrounded by fantastic scenery. Entrance to the nearby Jiǔlǎo Cave is ¥10.

Wànnián Temple BUDDHIST MONASTERY
(万年寺, Wànnián Sì; ¥10) Reconstructed in the 9th century, Wànnián Temple (1020m) is the oldest surviving Émei temple. It's dedicated to the man on the white elephant, the Bodhisattva Pǔxián (also known as Samantabhadra), the Buddhist Lord of Truth and patron of the mountain. This 8.5m-high statue cast in copper and bronze dates from AD 980 and weighs an estimated 62,000kg. If you can manage to rub the elephant's hind leg, good luck will be cast upon you.

Monkey Zone WILDLIFE RESERVE
Between Qīngyīn Pavilion and Hóngchūn Píng (Venerable Trees Terrace), you will at some point encounter the mountain's infamous monkeys. Unfortunately, those before

you have teased this merry band into grab-by monsters. Rangers are usually on hand to help if things get out of hand, but avoid extended eye contact (a sign of aggression), put away any food and drinks when approaching and keep backpacks closed. Do not, under any circumstances, proceed through here carrying plastic bags by hand.

Elephant Bathing Pool   BUDDHIST MONASTERY
(洗象池, Xǐxiàng Chí) According to legend, Elephant Bathing Pool (2070m) is where Pǔxián flew his elephant in for a nice scrub, but today there's not much of a pool to speak of. Being almost at the crossroads of both major trails, the temple here is sometimes packed with pilgrims and often crowded with curious monkeys. Dorms are available for ¥50, but lock your doors and hide your valuables from those monkeys.

Qīngyīn Pavilion   BUDDHIST TEMPLE
(清音阁, Qīngyīn Gé) Named 'Pure Sound Pavilion' after the soothing sounds of the waters coursing around rock formations, this temple (710m) is built on an outcrop in the middle of a fast-flowing stream. Rest in one of the small pavilions here while you appreciate the natural 'music' of the water.

🛏 Sleeping

The tourist district in Émái town surrounds Bàoguó Temple and the travellers' bus station, where most people will spend a night on their way to and from the mountain. The real draw, though, is sleeping on the mountain itself, whether in one of the many basic temple-run guesthouses or the handful of standard hotels near the peak and bus stations.

🛏 On the Mountain

The majority of the temples on the mountain (with the notable exception of Jīndǐng Temple at the summit) offer dormitory-style accommodation with shared bathrooms but usually no showers, though they're not always cheap. Some also have guesthouse-quality private rooms with private bathrooms for a significant premium.

There are also standard hotels on the mountain, mostly by the **cable-car stations** (上金顶索道站, Shàng Jīndǐng Suǒdàozhàn; ascent ¥65, descent ¥55, return ¥120; ⏰ 6.30am-6.30pm). Jīndǐng Dàjiǔdiàn (p749) is to the right of the Jīndǐng cable-car exit and is a convenient launch pad for catching the sunrise. You can reach it on foot in about 10 hours up from the lower bus depots, or it's 15 minutes down from the summit.

★ Hóngchún Píng   MONASTERY $
(洪椿坪; ☎ 0833 509 9043; dm ¥50, tw ¥60-130; 🛜) The smartest temple accommodation on the mountain is at a comfortable 1120m, tucked away in a quiet stretch of forest. Rooms are simple, with wi-fi and shared bathrooms. Approximate walking times from base/summit are three/six hours. Friendly monks-in-residence and a contemplative location make this a great place to sleep if you're not aiming to summit for sunrise.

Tàizǐ Píng   MONASTERY $
(太子坪; dm ¥30-50, r ¥120) Blankets are musty and dorms could use a good cleaning, but this closest monastery to Jīndǐng Peak is predictably popular with backpackers. It's about 40 minutes from here up to the peak,

---

ÉMÉI SHĀN HIKING ROUTES

There are many combinations of paths, buses, cable cars and monastery rest stops on Émái Shān. Below are some possibilities. Estimated times exclude breaks, which you will certainly need after all those stairs.

One day Take the bus from Bàoguó station to Wànnián bus depot (45 minutes, ¥20), then hike to the Golden Summit (five hours) with the help of both **cable cars** (万年索道站, Wànnián Suǒdàozhàn; ascent ¥65, descent ¥45-55; ⏰ 6.30am-6.30pm). Catch a ride from Léidòngpíng bus depot (1½ hours, ¥50) back to Bàoguó Village.

Two days Take the bus from Bàoguó station to Wànnián bus depot, then hike to the summit (6½ hours). Sleep in a hotel at the peak or descend for a monastery, but either way make it back up to the top for sunrise. On the way down, turn right a short distance past Elephant Bathing Pool and take the more scenic path, via Xiānfēng Temple, to Wǔxiǎngǎng depot (eight hours) for a ride back to the village (30 minutes, round trip ¥40).

Three days Hoof it up and down the mountain (20 hours or more in total). To see all the sights the mountain has to offer, ascend via Wànnián Temple and descend via Xiānfēng Temple. (Perhaps make offerings to sore muscles at each – you'll be taking a break anyway.)

so set those alarms early. Dorms occasionally fill up and travellers have reported they don't accept guests in winter, so get here in time to pick a backup plan if you can't stay.

Huáyán Dǐng
MONASTERY $

(华严顶; dm ¥40) Though it sees quite a few visitors en route from Wànnián to Elephant Bathing Pool, very few decide to stay here. Views up to Jīndǐng Peak and a courtyard perfect for contemplation will make it compelling to some, though.

Yùxiān Temple
MONASTERY $

(遇仙寺, Yùxiān Sì; dm/tw from ¥40/240) At 1680m the views from this small temple are stunning, as is the quiet that descends when day trippers have stopped passing through. Choose from basic dorms to private twins. It is very remote here, which can either feel glorious or eerie, depending on your travel style. Approximate walking times from the base/summit are seven/three hours.

Jīndǐng Dàjiǔdiàn
HOTEL $$$

(金顶大酒店; ☑ 0833 509 8088; Jīndǐng, 金顶; r from ¥980; ✳ 🕸) One of the standard hotels on Émči Shān makes for a convenient base for catching both sunset and an early sunrise. Downhill to the right of the cable-car station at the Golden Summit, you can reach it on foot in about 10 hours from the base. Discounts of nearly 65% make it worth the splurge during off-seasons.

🏠 In Town

Stay in the tourist centre near **Bàoguó Bus Station** (报国车站, Bàoguó Chēzhàn), from where early-morning departures for the mountain bus depots are just steps away. There's a selection of hostels, hotels and high-end spas; you won't lack for choice except during the very busiest parts of the year.

3077 Hostel
HOSTEL $

(三零七七客栈, Sānlíngqīqī Kèzhàn; ☑ 0833 559 1698; Bàoguó tourist area, 报国寺景区; dm ¥35, r ¥160) With a hip bar to complement the clean and stylish rooms, this new hostel is one of the nicest in central Sìchuān. Turn left off the main street through the Bàoguó tourist area towards the large spa gateway; it's on the right just behind.

Happy Hotel
HOTEL $$

(幸福树酒店, Xìngfú Shù Jiǔdiàn; ☑ 400 823 0917; 31 Bàoguó Village, 4th group, 报国村4组31号; r incl breakfast from ¥148; 🅿 🕸) This straightforward, very tidy hotel also has a surprisingly good, reasonably priced Chinese restaurant (a rarity in Bàoguó Village). Some English spoken and there's bike rental, too.

Teddy Bear Hotel
HOSTEL $$

(玩具熊酒店, Wánjùxióng Jiǔdiàn; ☑ 0833 559 0135, manager 138 9068 1961; www.teddybear.com. cn; 43 Baoguo Lu, 报国路43号; dm ¥35, r ¥80-260; ✳ @ 🕸) If you can get past the theme (bears, bears, everywhere), this very clean backpacker hotel offers nice rooms and an English-speaking staff that provide solid, hostel-style travel services plus decent coffee and Western food. The left-luggage service is free, as are maps and pick-up from Émči town (call Andy, the manager). It's next to the bus station.

🍴 Eating

Hard Wok Cafe
CAFE $

(晓雨小餐店, Xiǎoyǔ Xiǎocāndiàn; ⏱ hours vary) As surprising as it is delightful, this tiny cliffside cafe reaches beyond the standard Sìchuān noodle menu to include *jiānbing* (煎饼; ¥25), something between a crêpe and a pancake. Apple and honey? Chocolate and banana? Mix and match to your stomach's content. It's about 15 minutes downhill from Hóngchún Píng.

ℹ️ Information

Agricultural Bank of China (农业银行, Nóngyè Yínháng; ⏱ 9am-5pm) Has a foreign-exchange desk (open 9am to 5pm) and a 24-hour foreign-card-friendly ATM.

China Construction Bank ATM (中国建设银行, Zhōngguó Jiànshè Yínháng; ⏱ 24hr) Attached to the Bàoguó bus station, this ATM accepts foreign cards.

ℹ️ Getting There & Away

The town of Émči (峨眉山市; Émči Shān Shì) is the transport hub and lies 6.5km east of the park entrance. Most buses terminate at Émči Shān central station (峨眉山客运中心; Émči Shān kèyùn zhōngxīn), directly opposite Émči Railway Station (峨眉山火车站; Émči Huǒchēzhàn). If you ask, some drivers will go all the way to the more convenient Bàoguó Village bus station (报国汽车站) – which confusingly is also known as the Émči Shān tourist bus station (峨眉山旅游客运中心; Émči Shān lǚyóu kèyùn zhōngxīn) – for ¥10 more. The newly finished High-Speed Train Station (高速列车站; Gāosù Lièchē Zhàn) is the closest to Bàoguó Village, around 4km away.

A taxi from Émči town to Bàoguó Village is about ¥25, or many guesthouses will pick you up if you arrange it with them in advance. Local bus 8 (¥1) connects the Émči town train station with the park entrance.

BUS

While it's not possible to travel directly to Bàoguó from most long-distance destinations, some long-distance buses do leave from Bàoguó:

Chéngdū South ¥50, 2½ hours, every two hours from 9am to 5pm

Chóngqìng ¥140, six hours, 8.30am

Lè Shān ¥11, 45 minutes, every 30 minutes from 8am to 5.30pm

Destinations from Éméi Shān central station include:

Hóngyǎ (for Liǔjiāng) ¥19, 1½ hours, frequently from 8am to 5pm

Kāngdìng ¥120, seven hours, one daily (9.50am)

Yǎ'ān ¥46, three hours, four daily (8.10am, 9.30am, 12.30pm, 2.20pm)

Yíbīn ¥75, four hours, four daily (7.10am, 10.30am, 12.50pm, 4.30pm)

Zìgòng ¥51, three hours, frequently 7.40am to 5.10pm

TRAIN

Chéngdū C/K&T ¥65/24, 1½ to 2¾ hours, 13 daily from 7.13am to 9.20pm

Kūnmíng K seat/hard sleeper ¥124/215, 15½ hours, one daily (4.02pm)

Lè Shān C ¥11, 15 minutes, seven daily from 7.13am to 9.06pm

Lè Shān 乐山

☑ 0833 / POP 1.12 MILLION

With fingernails larger than the average human, the world's largest ancient Buddha draws plenty of tourists to the relaxed riverside town of Lè Shān. This Unesco World Heritage Site is an easy day trip from Chéngdū or stopover en route to or from Éméi Shān, but the laid-back vibe and newly opened higher-quality accommodation options may convince you to linger.

◉ Sights

Grand Buddha　　　　BUDDHIST STATUE
(大佛, Dàfó; adult ¥90, students & seniors ¥45; ⊙7.30am-6.30pm Apr-early Oct, 8am-5.30pm early Oct-Mar) Lè Shān's serene, 1200-year-old Grand Buddha sits in repose, carved from a cliff face overlooking the confluence of three busy rivers: the Dàdù, Mín and Qīngyì. The Buddhist monk Haitong conceived the project in AD 713, hoping that Buddha would protect the boats and calm the lethal currents.

It was 90 years after Haitong's death that the project was completed, but afterwards the river waters obeyed. Believers credited Buddha's grace; others pointed to the construction process, in which piles of surplus rocks reshaped the rivers and changed the currents.

At 71m tall, he is indeed grand. His shoulders span 28m, and each of his big toes is 8.5m long. His ears are 7m. Their length symbolises wisdom and the conscious abandonment of materialism. It is said that heavy gold baubles left Siddartha's earlobes elongated even after he was no longer weighed down by material things. Inside the body, hidden from view, is a water-drainage system to prevent weathering, although he is showing his age and soil erosion is an ongoing problem.

To fully appreciate this Buddha's magnitude, get an up-close look at his head, then descend the steep, winding stairway for the lilliputian view. Avoid visiting on weekends and holidays, when traffic on the staircase can come to a complete standstill and queues can top two hours or more.

Afterwards, head up the path to Sū Yuán (苏园) just above the entry and exit area to the Buddha, a manicured garden around a cliffside teahouse (from ¥20) that's lovely when not hosting lunchtime tour groups.

Admission also includes access to a number of caves and temples on the grounds, though they are a decent hike from the main attraction. **Máhàoyá Tombs Museum** (麻浩崖墓博物馆, Máhàoyámù Bówùguǎn; ⊙7.30am-6.30pm Apr-early Oct, 8am-5.30pm early Oct-Mar) has a modest collection of tombs and burial artefacts dating from the Eastern Han dynasty (AD 25–220). **Wūyóu Temple** (乌尤寺, Wūyóu Sì; ⊙7.30am-6.30pm Apr-early Oct, 8am-5.30pm early Oct-Mar), like the Buddha, dates from the Tang dynasty, and has Ming and Qing renovations. This monastery contains calligraphy and artefacts, with the highlights in the Luóhàn Hall – 1000 terracotta *arhat* (Buddhist celestial beings, similar to angels) displaying an incredible variety of postures and facial expressions – no two are alike. Also inside is a fantastic statue of Avalokiteshvara (Guanyin), the Goddess of Mercy.

A separate park (not included in the Grand Buddha admission), the **Oriental Buddha Capital** (东方佛都, Dōngfāng Fódū; ☑0833 230 1177; ¥80; ⊙8am-6pm), houses a collection of 3000 Buddha statues and figurines from across Asia, including a 170m-long reclining Buddha, one of the world's longest. There is an entrance near the Grand Buddha's south gate; otherwise exit and take bus 3 or 13 (¥1) to the Oriental Buddha Capital (东方佛都; Dōngfāng Fódū)

Lè Shān

stop. The entrance is further than it looks on the park maps.

☞ Tours

Sightseeing Cruises BOATING
(游船, Yóuchuán; Lè Shān Dock, 乐山港; 20min round trip ¥70, kids under 12yr free; ☉7.30am to 6.30pm Apr-Oct, from 8am winter) Tour boats leave regularly from Lè Shān dock, passing by the cliffs for views of Dàfó, which reveal two guardians in the cliff side not visible from land. The ride is short and otherwise unexciting.

Mr Yang's Tours TOURS
(☐0833 211 2046, 159 8438 2528; 2nd fl, Apt 1, 186 Baita Jie, 白塔街186号二楼1间; per person ¥200) Affable Mr Yang has been guiding foreign tourists around Lè Shān since the 1970s. His hearing is going fast but his expertise is not. It's best to text message him to make arrangements. His signature half-day tour includes a calligraphy demonstration, an old-town stroll and a visit to a villager's home. Transport, lunch and his services as an English-speaking guide are included.

🛏 Sleeping

Ā Dīng Inn GUESTHOUSE $
(阿丁客栈, Ādīng Kèzhàn; ☐0833 211 3123; 134 Dong Dajie, 东大街134号; r¥88) Tucked down a small lane off Dongda Jie, this excellent little guesthouse's private rooms are attractively furnished and spotlessly clean. It's also just by bus stops for both the Grand Buddha and bus stations.

Jiāzhōu Hotel HOTEL $$
(嘉州宾馆, Jiāzhōu Bīnguǎn; ☐0833 213 9888; 85 Baita Jie, 白塔街85号; r incl breakfast from ¥360; ❋@☎) Rooms aren't as grand as the lobby suggests, but this place is more upmarket than most and makes for a comfortable stay. Even some of the cheaper rooms have river views.

🍴 Eating

Zhao Family Crispy Duck BARBECUE $
(赵记油烫甜皮鸭, Zhàojì Yóutàng Tiánpíyā; ☐0833 211 4196; 169 Xincun Jie & Renmin Nanlu, 新村街169号人民南路与新村街交界处; meals ¥20; ☉10am-6pm) Foodies flock to this tiny barbecue stand for its speciality – sweet, crispy roast duck (jīn; ¥22). The draw is the skin, which is best described as duck candy, a miraculously ungreasy bite of heaven. Eat it while it's hot – in the middle of the sidewalk with your bare hands, if necessary. Look for the sign 'Zhaoyazi, 赵鸭子'.

Zhanggong Qiao Jie MARKET $$

(张公桥街, Zhānggōng Qiáojiē; ⊘4pm-late) Zhanggong Qiao Jie's small night market is full of seafood restaurants that pull fish and more straight from tanks in front of the restaurant to throw into the pan. Dishes are priced by weight, so clarify a total cost before you place an order.

Drinking & Nightlife

Shelter Bar BAR

(栖堂酒吧, Xītáng Jiǔbā; ☑0833 242 3456; Binjiang Lu, north of Xuedao Jie, 滨江路南段乐山港万象楼; ⊘6.30pm-2am) European beers (and prices; from ¥48) are available here in an old-style pavilion overlooking the river.

❶ Information

Bank of China (中国银行, Zhōngguó Yínháng; ☑0833 213 2807; 16 Renmin Nanlu, 人民南路16号; ⊘9am-5pm) For all your money-changing and ATM needs.

China Post (中国邮政, Zhōngguó Yóuzhèng; 62 Yutang Jie, 玉堂街62号; ⊘9am-5.30pm)

People's Hospital (人民医院, Rénmín Yīyuàn; ☑0833 211 9310, after-hour emergencies 0833 211 9328; 222 Baita Jie, 白塔街222号) Has some English-speaking doctors. Pharmacies cluster around the entrance.

Public Security Bureau (PSB, 公安局, Gōng'ānjú; ☑0833 518 2555; http://lsscrj.gotoip1.com; 3rd fl, 548 Fenghuang Lu Zhongduan, 凤凰路中段548号3楼; ⊘9am-noon & 1-5pm Mon-Fri) Visa extensions the next working day. Take Bus 6 (¥1) from the centre.

❶ Getting There & Away

BUS

Lè Shān has three main bus stations, all within 5km of each other. Buses from Chéngdū's Xīnnánmén station usually arrive at **Xiàobà Bus Station** (肖坝旅游车站; Xiàobà Lǚyóu Chēzhàn), the main tourist station. The **Central Bus Station** (乐山客运中心车站; Lè Shān Kèyùn Zhōngxīn Chēzhàn) and **Liányùn Bus Station** (联运车站; Liányùn Chēzhàn) are also useful.

Note: if you're heading to Éméi Shān, it's better to use Xiàobà Bus Station, as buses from there go all the way to Bàoguó (¥11, 45 minutes, every 30 minutes from 7am to 5pm).

Other services from Xiàobà Bus Station include:

Chéngdū ¥45, two hours, every 30 minutes from 7am to 7pm

Chóngqìng ¥129, six hours, 10.40am

Éméi Town ¥8, 30 minutes, every 30 minutes from 7.30am to 6pm

Yǎ'ān ¥54, 2½ hours (9.50am, 2pm, 4.10pm)

Zìgòng ¥42, three hours, hourly from 8.30am to 5.10pm

TRAIN

High-speed trains depart Lèshān for Chéngdū's South and East Train Stations (¥54, 1¼ hours, 12 daily, 7.30am to 9.23pm) and Éméi Shān (¥11, 15 minutes, five daily, 8.38am to 9.36pm).

❶ Getting Around

Local buses cost ¥1. Some handy routes:

Bus 1 Xiàobà Bus Sstation–Jiāzhōu Hotel–town centre–Liányùn bus station

Bus 6 Xiàobà Bus Station–Renmin Nanlu–Public Security Bureau

Bus 8 Xiàobà Bus Station–town centre–Lè Shān dock

Bus 9 Central Bus Station–town centre–Lè Shān dock

Bus 13 Xiàobà Bus Station–town centre–Oriental Buddha Capital–Grand Buddha–Wūyóu Temple

Sightseeing cruises (p751) leave regularly from **Lè Shān dock** (乐山港, Lè Shān Gǎng), passing by the cliffs for views of Dàfó. The ride is short and otherwise unexciting.

Liǔjiāng 柳江

☑028 / POP 5164

The charming pastoral setting is the main attraction of Liǔjiāng, a riverside village nestled in central Sìchuān's countryside. The old town (古镇; gǔzhèn), with its narrow alleyways, wooden courtyard buildings and ancient banyan trees, straddles both sides of the Yángcūn River (杨村河; Yángcūn Hé) in a postcard-perfect scene. For now the reconstruction and sales tactics remain more palatable here than in other 'fixed-up' old towns, though the place is becoming popular with domestic tourists. This is a great spot for a picnic lunch or a dip in the river, but a half-day visit can easily turn into a lazy week in town before you know it.

There's some excellent walking to be done in the surrounding countryside. Look for wooden signboards in the old town with maps in Chinese of local walking trails. One option is the 3.5km uphill hike to **Hóujiā Shānzhài** (侯家山寨), marked by a wooden archway off the main driving road on the opposite side of the river from where the buses drop off. Once you've found that, follow the road up. Near the top is Tiàowàng Wǎwū, a renovated courtyard guesthouse.

Tiàowàng Wǎwū GUESTHOUSE $

(眺望瓦屋; ☑130 8838 1221; 4 Lianghe, 两河4号; r ¥88, meals ¥20-80) Near the top of Hóujiā Shānzhài is Tiàowàng Wǎwū, a renovated courtyard guesthouse with simple twin rooms and fabulous views, run by the friendly Liu family who've lived here for four generations. They'll pour you their homegrown tea and cook up noodle (面; *miàn*) or rice (饭; *fàn*) dishes made from their hillside gardens. A minibus from the old-town bus station is ¥30.

Wàngjiāng Kèzhàn GUESTHOUSE $$

(望江客栈; ☑ 139 9036 0876; 38 Liujiang Jie, 柳江街38号; r ¥150-200) Creaky wooden floorboards, simple, clean rooms with shared bathrooms, and river views make this central guesthouse a reason to linger in Liǔjiāng for a few nights. There's a pleasant terrace overlooking the river where you can have tea (from ¥20) or local food (mains ¥10 to ¥50). The riverside entrance is upriver from the plank bridge (板板桥), on the far bank from the bus station.

To reach Liǔjiāng, take a bus from Chéngdū's Xīnnánmén bus station to Hóngyǎ (洪雅; ¥60, 2½ hours, every 45 minutes from 7.40am to 5.40pm), then change for Liǔjiāng (¥10, 45 minutes, every 15 minutes from 8am to 6pm). The last bus from Hóngyǎ to Chéngdū is at 4pm. There are also regular buses from Hóngyǎ to Éméi Shān, Lè Shān and Yǎ'ān, but don't expect much after mid-afternoon.

Yǎ'ān   雅安

🗘 0835 / POP 1.53 MILLION

Chinese travellers head to Yǎ'ān as a hub for activities like picking tea leaves on the hills of Méngshān (蒙山) or watching sunrise from above the clouds at Bull's Back Mountain (牛背山; Niúbèishan), but for foreigners the primary draw is the Bīfēngxiá Panda Base. It's a treat to glimpse any one of the 1600 surviving pandas in the world, but with bustling Chéngdū 150km east, you can get a sense of their natural habitat here. Cubs in the 'panda kindergarten' climb high into the trees in their reasonably pleasant enclosures, while humans can hike along a forested river gorge with waterfalls and stunning scenery surrounding the main attraction.

◎ Sights

Yǎ'ān Bìfēngxiá Panda Base WILDLIFE RESERVE

(雅安碧峰峡大熊猫基地, Bīfēngxiá Dàxióngmāo Jīdī; ☑ 0835 231 8145; www.chinapanda.org.cn; ¥118, shuttle ¥15; ⏰ 8.30-11.30am & 1.30-4.30pm, kindergarten feeding 3.20pm) Yǎ'ān Bīfēngxiá Panda Base was established in prime forest in Yǎ'ān in 2003 for research purposes rath-

er than tourism, and its mission expanded in 2008 following the earthquake that severely damaged its sister reserve at Wòlóng. Bīfēngxiá is now home to 80 pandas, some of which may eventually be returned to the wild.

The panda centre is 3km away from the ticket office in the main car park where the minibus drops passengers. Pick up a map and store bags for free at the tourist information office. Turn left out of the ticket office then take the free lift (乘电梯, *chéngyúntī*; 8am to 7.30pm) down 50 storeys to the foot of the gorge for a 7.5km nature walk to the panda centre entrance. It takes about two hours to reach the centre via the concrete paths passing tall waterfalls, imaginatively named mountains, and a small collection of hanging coffins (悬棺; *xuánguān*) en route.

Skip the 'wildlife park' (read: zoo) near the tourist centre.

🛏 Sleeping

Qiáotóu Nóngjiālè GUESTHOUSE $

(桥头农家乐; ☑ 138 8243 7340; 200m uphill from Panda Base bus drop-off, 碧峰峡小西天前行200 米; r ¥80) This basic but friendly guesthouse inside the park is a good bet for those who would like to linger in the area. It's about 10 minutes up a small path from the entrance to the panda centre at the end of the gorge hike, or the same uphill by road from the shuttle stop.

ℹ Getting There & Away

Buses from Chéngdū's Xīnnánmén station (¥114) terminate at Yǎ'ān's Xīmén bus station (西门车站; Xīmén chēzhàn), but for Bīfēngxiá get off before this at the tourist bus station (旅游车站; lǚyóu chēzhàn) where minibuses (¥5, 45 minutes) wait to take you to the Panda Base. The last bus back to Chéngdū from the tourist bus station leaves at 6.30pm, or it's also possible to continue on to Qiónglái (邛崃; ¥26, one hour) for transfers to the historic town of **Pínglè** (平乐古镇, Pínglè Gǔzhèn).

From Yǎ'ān's Xīmén bus station, you can head on to various other destinations:

Éméi town ¥50, 2½ hours, four daily (8.30am, 10am, 12.10pm, 2pm)

Kāngdìng ¥100, 4½ hours, three daily (8am, 10am, 1pm)

Lè Shān ¥55, 2½ hours, seven daily from 8.30am to 6pm

A pedicab between Yǎ'ān's two bus stations costs ¥6. At the tourist bus station, the left-luggage office (9.30am to 6.30pm) holds bags for ¥1 per hour.

SOUTHERN SÌCHUĀN

Not often on the radar of foreign tourists, steamy southern Sìchuān is for those who enjoy digging into history and exploring the quiet side of nature. There are dinosaur fossils, ancient cliff-face hanging coffins, lush bamboo forests and ancient riverside villages to explore. It's also home to some stellar teahouses.

Zìgòng 自贡

📞 0813 / POP 1.26 MILLION

This intriguing riverside city has been an important centre of Chinese salt production for almost 2000 years. Remnants of that industry make up part of an unconventional list of sights that includes the world's deepest traditional salt and China's first dinosaur museum. Zìgòng is also a clear contender for the most atmospheric teahouses anywhere in Sìchuān, so there's plenty of opportunity to just put your feet up for a day.

◉ Sights

Dinosaur Museum　　　　MUSEUM
(恐龙馆, Kŏnglóng Guǎn; 📞 0813 580 1235; www.zdm.cn/en; 238 Dashan Pu, Da'an District, 大安区大山铺238号; adult ¥42, with 3D movie ¥77, student/child/elderly ¥22, with 3D movie ¥57; ⊗ 8.30am-5pm; 🚍 35) Built on top of the Dashanpu excavation site, which has one of the world's largest concentrations of dinosaur fossils, this specialised dinosaur museum, the first in China, has a fine collection of reassembled skeletons as well as partially excavated fossil pits.

The first publicised finds here were made in 1972. The huge numbers of fossils, mostly dating from the rarely seen early and middle Jurassic periods, baffled archaeologists at first. It is now believed that floods swept them here en masse. Budding palaeontologists will appreciate the *Huayangosaurus taibaii*, the most primitive and complete stegosaur ever discovered, as well as the incredibly rare skin fossil specimens on display. A kid-friendly movie screens at 10am, 11am, 2.30pm and 3.30pm daily.

Take bus 35 (¥1, 25 minutes) uphill from Róngguāng Business Hotel.

Shēnhǎi Salt Well　　　HISTORIC SITE
(桑海井, Shēnhǎi Jǐng; 📞 0813 510 6214; 289 Da'an Jie, 大安街289号; adult ¥22, student/child/elderly ¥11; ⊗ 8.30am-5.30pm) This fascinating museum is also a working salt mine. Its 1001m-deep artesian salt well was the world's

deepest well when it was built in 1835 and it remains the deepest salt well ever made using percussion drilling, a technique invented here and later applied throughout the world.

Many pieces of original equipment, including a 20m-high wooden derrick that towers above the tiny, 20cm-wide mouth of the well, are still intact. On the 2nd floor of the salt house, rows of cauldrons bubble away day and night over fires powered by natural gas, the mine's other product, until only fluffy white piles of glistening salt remain.

There are excellent English captions explaining the process, from how bamboo was once used to siphon brine from beneath the earth to how soy milk is added to clarify it. Bags of the salt (from ¥3.50) are sold from the window to the right when you exit.

Take bus 5 or 35 (¥1, six stops) uphill from the Róngguāng Business Hotel. Bus 35 continues to the Dinosaur Museum.

🛏 Sleeping & Eating

Róngguāng Business Hotel　　HOTEL $$
(荣光商务酒店, Róngguāng Shāngwù Jiǔdiàn; 📞 0813 211 9999; 25 Ziyou Lu, 自由路25号; r incl breakfast ¥98-258; ✳ @) Large clean rooms, friendly staff, free-to-use computers on the 4th floor, and a free buffet breakfast distinguish this hotel from the others in this prime location. Signage is poor though – look for the Chinese characters written on the door downhill from the Bank of China.

Take bus 1 or 35 from the bus station or bus 34 from the train station to the Shízì Kǒu (十字口) bus stop.

Xióngfēi Holiday Hotel　　HOTEL $$$
(雄飞假日酒店, Xióngfēi Jiàrì Jiǔdiàn; 📞 0813 211 8888; 193 Jiefang Lu, 解放路193号; r incl breakfast ¥960; ✳ @ 🛜) This large, upmarket hotel is within close reach of Zìgòng's riverside sights and the Shízì Kǒu (十字口) bus stop. While rack rates are high, discounts of nearly 80% put rooms within range of budget travellers.

Zìgòng Walking Street　　STREET FOOD $
(自贡商业步行街, Zìgòng Shāngyè Bùxíngjiē; ⊗ 7am-9pm) Lined with many shops, the highlights of this street are the small vendors who wheel their fresh noodles, dumplings and other tasty delights here to sell. It's uphill from the river, the first street on the right.

🍵 Drinking & Nightlife

★ **Wángyé Temple**　　TEAHOUSE
(王爷庙, Wángyé Miào; 3 Binjiang Lu, 滨江路3号; ⊗ 8.30am-11pm) Housed within the ochre

walls of a 100-year-old guild hall of boatmen and merchants, this lively teahouse (officially known as 临江茶楼; Línjiāng Chálóu) is one of the most atmospheric in Sìchuān. Tea costs ¥12 to ¥20.

Perched above the Fǔxī River, the teahouse sits on the opposite bank from the still-active Fǎzàng Temple (法藏寺; Fǎzàng Sì). The pair were built to ensure safe passage for boats transporting salt downstream. Everyone in the industry came here to make sacrifices to Wángyé, the protector of boatmen and sailors. Now locals gather here to banter, play cards and admire the river view. From the Shízì Kǒu (十字口) bus stop walk down to the river, turn left and follow the river for about 750m around a small bend.

ℹ Information

Bank of China (中国银行, Zhōngguó Yínháng; Ziyou Lu, 自由路; ⊙9am-5pm Mon-Fri) Has a 24-hour foreign-card-friendly ATM just across from the Shízì Kǒu (十字口) bus stop. The office is open business hours for currency exchange during the week.

ℹ Getting There & Around

To get to the hotels, walk out of the bus station, turn right and walk 200m to the first bus stop. Then take bus 1 or 35 (¥1) five stops to the Shízì Kǒu (十字口) stop. The hotels are across the road and down the hill. From the train station, which is at the east end of town, take bus 34 (¥1) to Bīnjiāng Lù (滨江路) bus stop. From there, walk back 200m and turn left up Ziyou Lu.

From Shízì Kǒu, bus 35 runs on to the Salt Well (six stops) and Dinosaur Museum (final stop) from 6.30am to 9.30pm. Additionally, bus 7 runs between these two points and the bus station.

BUS

Destinations from the main **bus station** (客运 总站, Kèyùn Zǒngzhàn; ☎0813 820 9777; 817 Dangui Dajie, 丹桂大街817号) include:

Chéngdū ¥84, 3½ hours, about every 20 minutes from 6.30am to 7.50pm

Chóngqìng ¥76, four hours, every half hour from 6.20am to 2.20pm

Éméi Shān ¥58, 3½ hours, four daily (9.10am, 11.50am, 2.10pm, 4pm)

Lè Shān ¥50, three hours, eight daily from 8.30am to 5.30pm

Yíbīn ¥27, one hour, every 30 minutes from 7.10am to 7pm

TRAIN

Chéngdū K ¥41, five hours, seven daily from 12.35am to 10.51am

Kūnmíng K seat/hard sleeper ¥119/207, 17 hours, three daily (2.52pm, 3.40pm, 4.13pm)

Yíbīn K ¥13, 1½ hours, six daily from 5.23am to 4.52pm

Yíbīn   宜宾

☑ 0831 / POP 4.47 MILLION

Where the Mín and Jīnshā converge to become the mighty Yangzi River, Yíbīn has stood as a town of great strategic military importance throughout history. Today it's a relatively modern midsized city, making it a convenient travel hub for trips to old town Lǐzhuāng, the Bamboo Sea and Luòbiǎo's hanging coffins.

The city is easily explored on foot. Turn right out of Jīngmào Hotel, and right again to reach the reconstructed **Shuǐ Dōng Mén** (水东门; East Water Gate), which has a teahouse on top of it (tea from ¥10, open 6am to 10pm). Further down and off to the right is a genuinely old city-wall **gateway**, plus remnants of the original **ancient city wall**, leading towards the **river confluence** and a modern public square where locals dance in the evening. Up to the right from the square are more city-wall remains with **Guānyīng Jiē Gǔmínjū** (冠英街古民居), a street of courtyard homes dating from the Qing dynasty.

In the middle of the action, **Jīngmào Hotel** (经贸宾馆, Jīngmào Bīnguǎn; ☎0831 613 7222; 108 Minzhu Lu, 民主路108号; tw ¥220; ❄@☎) is a no-frills but clean and serves its purpose. Discounts of up to 20% make it a bargain in this town.

ℹ Getting There & Away

BUS

Most travellers arrive at Gāokè bus station (高客 站; Gāokè zhàn). Departures from here include:

Chángníng ¥15, one hour, frequent services

Chéngdū ¥100, four hours, frequent services from 7.20am to 7pm

Chóngqìng ¥110, four hours, frequent services from 7.10am to 7pm

Gǒngxiàn ¥17, 1½ hours, frequent services

Lè Shān ¥62, four hours, hourly from 8.20am to 5.30pm

Zìgòng ¥28, one hour, frequent services from 7.30am to 7pm

Head across town to Nánkè bus station (南客站; Nánkè zhàn) for buses to Lǐzhuāng (¥4, 35 minutes, every 15 minutes from 6.15am to 7.30pm), the Bamboo Sea (¥22, 1½ hours, 9.30am) and Luòbiǎo (¥33, three hours, 2.05pm).

Travellers may find the nearby cities of Chángníng and Gǒngxiàn have more direct buses to the Bamboo Sea and Luòbiǎo.

TRAIN

Trains leaving from Yíbīn train station (火车站; huǒchē zhàn) include:

Chéngdū K ¥51, 6½ to 8½ hours, seven daily from 12.30am to 11.36pm

Kūnmíng K seat/hard sleeper ¥105/184, 12½ to 15½ hours, three daily (3.25pm, 5.13pm, 5.48pm)

Zìgòng K ¥13, 1½ hours, eight daily from 12.16am to 11.56pm

ℹ Getting Around

To get to the town centre from Gāokè bus station, take bus 22 (¥1, 15 minutes) into town and get off at the Xùfǔ Shāngchéng (叙府商城) stop on Renmin Lu (人民路). Turn right at the light; the Jīngmào Hotel will be on your left.

Bus 4 (¥1) connects Nánkè bus station with Gāokè bus station (45 minutes) via the Xùfǔ Shāngchéng stop (20 minutes) and train station (40 minutes).

Bus 11 (¥1) links the train station with Gāokè bus station (or it's a 10-minute walk between the two) and passes by the end of Renmin Lu.

Bamboo Sea　　　蜀南竹海

 0831 / POP 3000

Swaths of swaying bamboo, well marked walking trails and a handful of charming lakes and waterfalls make south Sìchuān's **Shǔnán Zhúhǎi National Park** (蜀南竹海国家公园, Shǔnán Zhúhǎi Guójiā Gōngyuán; ¥117) a worthwhile detour. There are more than 30 types of bamboo across this 120-sq-km national park and the scenery is gorgeous enough to have attracted many a TV and film director.

While the park is generally more optimised for travellers with vehicles than those on foot, the interconnected trails in the centre of the park, looping around still forest lakes and along temple-crowded cliff sides, make it worth the trip.

◉ Sights & Activities

The villages of Wànlǐng (万岭), at the west gate, and Wànlǐ (万里), near the east gate, are the main settlements inside the park. It's about 11km from one to the other if you follow the road the whole way.

Two cable cars (索道; suǒdào) ease the journey considerably, and are a great way to see the forest from another angle. The **Guānguāng cable car** (观光索道, Guānguāng Suǒdào; one-way/return ¥30/40; ⊙8am-5pm) near Wànlǐng takes you on a 25-minute ride over a stunning forest and past steep cliffs. There's a pleasant, one-hour walk along the

Mò Brook (墨溪; Mò Xī) that loops through the forest just past the cable-car entrance.

From the end of the Guānguāng cable car either follow the signs for a free lift to the **Dàxiágǔ cable car** (大峡谷索道, Dàxiágǔ Suǒdào; one-way/return ¥20/30; ⊙8.30am-5.30pm), a 10-minute ride traversing a dramatic gorge, or walk to the junction at Sānhé Jiè (三合界) where you can find a small selection of accommodation and food.

From both Dàxiágǔ or Sānhé Jiè your destination is the same: the trails that trace through the scenic area that includes a number of small lakes and caves with picturesque names like 'Sea within the Sea' (海中海) and 'Cave of the Immortals' (仙禹洞). Either way, at the end of the paths you'll need to retrace your steps or head back via the opposite route.

If you end up with extra time in Wànlǐng at the end of the day, the nearby **Forgotten Worries Valley** (忘忧谷; Wàngchén Gǔ) makes for a nice two-hour walk from the village and back past a number of progressively larger waterfalls.

🛏 Sleeping & Eating

Settle in a hotel in Wànlǐng, with the friendly Yang family's tidy, basic **Joan's Guesthouse** (晶鑫园农家乐, Jīngxīn Yuán Yíjiālè; ☐135 4771 7196; www.snzhjourney.com; West gate, 200m past the small bridge on Wànlǐng's main square, 小桥广场往观云亭方向前行200米左手边; r ¥120-160; ❋🤶) on the road above the village or at the **Chéngbīnlóu Jiǔdiàn** (承宾楼酒店; ☐0831 498 0104; Wànlǐng village square, 蜀南竹海小桥, 西大门前1公里; s/tw ¥220/280, discounted to ¥100/180; ❋🤶) on the main square.

All guesthouses and hotels serve food, which is generally pretty good. Around major junctions and sights in the park there are usually at least a couple of noodle shops, if not more formal restaurants. Try dishes with zhúsǔn (竹笋), tender bamboo shoots, and the various local fungi that propagate at their roots.

ℹ Getting There & Around

Buses into the park stop at the west gate to allow you to get off and buy your entrance ticket, before passing through Wànlǐng village and then terminating at Wànlǐ.

There are two direct buses from Wànlǐ to Yíbīn (¥22, two hours, 7am and 2pm). Both pass Wànlǐng (40 minutes) and, if you ask, will drop you at the junction for Chángníng (one hour), where you can change for Gōngxiàn to get to Luóbiǎo. Smaller local buses shuttle every 15 minutes between Wànlǐng and Chángníng (¥6, 7am to 6pm).

Motorbike taxis can take you between the two main villages (around ¥50, 45 minutes) if you decide not to walk.

WESTERN SÌCHUĀN

West of Chéngdū, green tea becomes butter tea, gentle rolling hills morph into jagged snowy peaks and the Mandarin *nǐ hǎo!* gives way to Tibetan *tashe deleg!*

This is the Garzê Tibetan Autonomous Prefecture, a territory that corresponds roughly with the Kham (in Chinese 康巴; Kāngbā), one of old Tibet's three traditional provinces. It is home to more than a dozen distinct Tibetan tribes, the largest being the Khampas, historically fierce warriors and horsemen.

Each season brings its own rugged beauty. In spring and summer many remote towns and monasteries can feel abandoned as villagers head out to harvest *byar rtswa dgun bu* (虫草; *chóngcǎo*) – cordyceps in English – a medicinal caterpillar fungus that grows on the alpine slopes and retails for outrageous amounts in lowland China and increasingly throughout the world.

Dangers & Annoyances

The roads in western Sìchuān are infamously bad, but many sections have been resurfaced in recent years and as a result travel times have been cut drastically. The occasional tumbled vehicle at the bottom of steep drops still attests to the danger of these highways, however, and with road work still ongoing in some areas it's not all smooth driving.

Health

At these elevations, altitude sickness and acute mountain sickness (AMS) are possible concerns, especially for those looking to get out into nature for long periods.

Western Sìchuān endures up to 200 freezing days per year, but sunny summer days can be blistering. This, combined with the high altitude, can leave new arrivals vulnerable to bad sunburn in addition to altitude sickness. Pack layers and take a couple of days to acclimatise when you arrive and as you continue to gain elevation.

ⓘ Getting There & Away

The recent completion of a number of high-altitude airports can cut travel times drastically, and more are on the way. Consider flying into Dàochéng and out of Qīnghǎi province's Yùshù, or in and out of Kāngdìng or the soon-to-open

ⓘ PERMITS

In 2009, after a dozen foreign climbers died on Sìchuān's mountains, the Chinese government began to enforce permit regulations. Officially, climbing any Sìchuān peak above 3500m requires registration through the **Sìchuān Mountaineering Association** (p741). When your plans involve more than a standard hike (for example, rock climbing, ice climbing, extended backpacking), you should at least register with the mountain's administrative office (管理) by the park's entrance gate. You may have to pay an environmental protection fee (from ¥150), and at popular but treacherous mountains such as **Sìgūniáng** (四姑娘), hire a guide (from ¥300 per day).

Gānzī airport. Flight prices can vary drastically depending on season and demand, so check Chinese booking sites such as **Ctrip** (http://english.ctrip.com/ChinaFlights) for current prices.

Most travellers will enter western Sìchuān overland, whether over the most common route from Chéngdū via Kāngdìng, or arduous backdoor routes from Yúnnán or Qīnghǎi provinces.

ⓘ Getting Around

In most cities throughout the region, one or two buses leave early each morning, with no more scheduled services throughout the day. To fill the gap, private drivers head to points throughout the province based on demand. You'll need to establish whether you want private hire – *bāochē* (包车) or a shared vehicle – *pīnchē* (拼车) – and if shared you'll usually need to wait around a while until the car fills up. Prices fluctuate based on demand and whim, and if you can't find a ride you're willing to pay for you may well need to try again the next morning.

Shared vehicles usually fill up quickly in the morning and more slowly as the day drags on. If possible, try to find a driver the day before and establish a departure time to guarantee yourself a seat.

Kāngdìng 康定

☏ 0836 / POP 110,000

Coming from the Chéngdū area, there are two main gateways into Tibetan Sìchuān. One is Dānbā, but far more popular is Kāngdìng (known in Tibetan as Dartsendo or Dardo), the capital of the Garzê Tibetan Autonomous Prefecture.

Set in a steep river valley at the confluence of the raging Zhéduō and Yǎlā Rivers (the Dar and Tse in Tibetan), Kāngdìng offers an easy introduction to Tibetan culture and elevations above 2500m while still putting visitors in range of mountains like snowcapped Gònggā Shān to the south, one of nearly two dozen peaks over 6000m within a few hours' drive.

This town has long stood as a trading centre between the Tibetan and Han, with sizeable Hui and Qiang minority populations also part of the mix; you'll find elements of all these cultures represented here. Golden-roofed monasteries, a city-centre mosque and several large churches attest to the diversity and harmony of the region.

◉ Sights & Activities

The mountains looming over Kāngdìng make for pleasant day hikes, while the less ambitious will appreciate a lazy ride up the Pǎomǎ Shān cable car (p758) or a soak in the **Èrdào Hot Springs** (二道桥温泉, Èrdàoqiáo Wēnquán; ☑0836 287 9111; Erdao Qiao, 二道桥; per hr ¥10-120; ☺7am-11pm) just outside of town.

Guōdá Shān   MOUNTAIN
(郭达山, Zhedra Rawo) Guōdá Shān looms large at the northern end of town and takes a full day to climb up and down. From the peak (1500m) you can take in the breathtaking glaciers to the south.

Gānzī Prefecture Tibetan Cultural Heritage Museum   MUSEUM
(自治州非物质文化遗产博物馆, Zìzhìzhōu Fēi Wùzhí Wénhuà Yíchǎn Bówùguǎn; ☑0836 2811 1312; 36 Xiangyang Jie, 向阳街36号; ¥30; ☺8.30am-5.30pm) By the Pǎomǎ Shān cable-car entrance, this bēng-kē-style (崩柯) structure (three-storey structures with split-log and packed-earth walls) houses exhibits surveying the Kham's rich heritage from the garb of regional tribes to thangka (sacred paintings), and a sky-burial horn fashioned from a teenage girl's femur.

Nánwú Sì   BUDDHIST TEMPLE
(南无寺, Lhamo Tse; Lucheng Nanlu, 炉城南路; ☺7am-9pm) FREE This temple belongs to the Gelugpa (Yellow Hat) sect of Tibetan Buddhism and is the most active monastery in the area. Walk south along the main road, cross the river and keep going for about 200m until you see a small sign ('南無村') for the monastery on your right. Follow the road straight uphill on a steep road to the gold-capped roofs.

Jīngāng Sì   BUDDHIST TEMPLE
(金刚寺, Dordrak Lhakang; Lucheng Nanlu, 炉城南路; ☺7am-9pm) FREE About 100m past Nánwú Sì along the main road is this 400-year-old Nyingma (Red Hat sect) monastery. The temple was undergoing major renovations at the time of research, but the main hall and some others were still accessible. Turn right from the main road into an archway labelled '金刚村'.

Gònggā Shān   MOUNTAIN
(贡嘎山, Minyak Konka) The trailhead for the five-day pilgrims' circuit of holy Gònggā Shān (7556m) is a half-hour drive from Kāngdìng. Many hostel staff can advise you on how to approach the trek, and rent out camping equipment. We recommend finding a guide with horses through Zhilam Hostel (p759).

Jiǔlián Shān   MOUNTAIN
(九连山) FREE With no concrete steps and free of charge, a two-hour climb up this natural hill brings you to a small grassland plateau (perfect for picnics) beyond which horses and yaks graze. Access it behind Zhilam Hostel (p759), which can provide maps for guests.

Guānyīn Sì   BUDDHIST TEMPLE
(观音寺; 9 Paomashan Donglu, 跑马山东路9号; ☺7am-6pm) FREE Looming over Kāngdìng on the lower slopes of Pǎomǎ Shān, above the three main halls of the temple is a path that leads on to several pagodas and another remote prayer hall. Continue following the same path to reach the scenic area around the **Pǎomǎ Sì** (跑马寺, Dentok Lhakang; ¥50; ☺8am-6pm).

Pǎomǎ Shān   MOUNTAIN
(跑马山, Dentok Rawo; ¥50; ☺8am-6pm) Pǎomǎ Shān is the famed mountain of the 'Kāngdìng Qíng Gē' ('Kangding Love Song'), one of China's most enduring folk songs, and will appeal the most to those who are familiar with the ditty. It's an easy ascent on foot or take the **cable car** (索道, Suǒdào; ☑0836 283 4680; 36 Xiangyang Jie, 向阳街36号; one-way/return adult ¥35/55, child ¥20/25; ☺9am-6.30pm) halfway up for excellent views of the town and surrounding peaks and valleys. You have to pay to go all the way up the stepped path, past ribbons of prayer flags and the Pǎomǎ Sì.

🎊 Festivals & Events

Circling the Mountain Festival   RELIGIOUS
(转山节, Zhuǎnshānjié) Kāngdìng's biggest annual festival takes place on Pǎomǎ Shān on the eighth day of the fourth lunar month

Kāngdìng (Dartsendo)

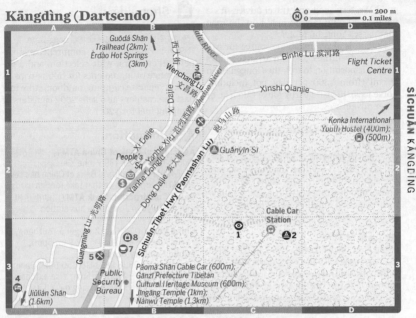

(normally in May) to commemorate the birthday of the Historical Buddha, Sakyamuni. White and blue Tibetan tents cover the hillside and there's wrestling, horse racing and visitors from all over western Sìchuān.

🛏 Sleeping

Konka International Youth Hostel   HOSTEL **$**
(贡嘎国际青年旅舍, Gònggā Guójì Qīngnián Lǚshě; ☑189 9048 1279, 0836 281 7788; 3rd fl, 59 Dongguan Yinle Guangchangjie, 东关音乐广场街 59号3楼; dm ¥35-40, s/d ¥150/170; @ 🛜) The most convenient option for bus travellers, with pleasant English-speaking staff offering all the usual services. They can also help arrange self-guided excursions into the mountains, even loaning out outdoor gear. From June through November, beds in rooftop tents go for ¥25. Lively communal dinners include vegetarian options (¥18 to ¥24 per person). Just 50m to the left of the bus station.

Dēngbā Hostel   HOSTEL **$**
(登巴国际青年旅舍, Dēngbā Guójì Qīngnián Lǚshě; ☑0836 287 7377; 88 Xi Dajie, 西大街88号; dm ¥35, r with shared bathroom ¥70; @ 🛜) Worn but welcoming hostel with small rooms off Xi Dajie, with free laundry a welcome surprise. Easiest access is through an alley at 16 Wenchang Lu (文昌路16号). Don't confuse this with the hostel of the same name near

Kāngdìng (Dartsendo)

🔴 Sights

🛏 Sleeping

✴ Eating

🍷 Drinking & Nightlife

🛍 Shopping

the bus station, which offers similar prices but not quality.

★ Zhilam Hostel   HOSTEL **$$**
(汇道客栈, Huìdào Kèzhàn; ☑0836 283 1100; www.zhilamhostel.com; 72 Baitukan Xiang, 白土坎巷72号; dm/r from ¥45/260; @ 🛜) Run by an American family, this fabulous, kid-friendly, hillside hostel is a comfortable base in Kāngdìng. It provides all manner of top-end hostel services, from camping-gear rental to

good Western food and travel advice. It's a winding 10-minute walk uphill on the road that passes Yōngzhū Motel.

Zhilam is also a reliable resource for wilderness adventures, and can arrange guides and transportation to trek the Gònggā Shān circuit (from ¥300 per day, not including horse fees), to visit nearby Muge Cuo lake or other adventures.

✕ Eating & Drinking

Mágē Miàn   NOODLES $
(麻哥面; 59 Yanhe Xilu, 沿河西路59号; noodles ¥10-13; ⏱ 24hr) A solid late-night option, with the speciality here *ma'gē miàn* (麻哥面) – house noodles topped with a spicy mince-meat sauce in small (一两; *yīliǎng*; ¥9) or large (二两; *èr liǎng*; ¥11) servings.

★ Taste of Tibet   TIBETAN $$
(葩姆名卡, Pāmǔ Línkǎ; ☎ 0836 699 9999; 13 Dong Dajie, 东大街13号; mains from ¥38; ⏱ 9am-midnight) This upscale joint offers a refined take on Tibetan fare in a rustic dining room decorated with a fine collection of traditional nomad tools and tapestries. The chef sources ingredients from the Kham – from Xīndūqiáo's fragrant barley (青稞) to tender yak (牦牛肉) from Shíqú.

Himalayan Coffee & Trading Co.   CAFE
(喜马拉帷咖啡, Xǐmǎyēwéi Kāfēi; ☎ 0836 281 8887; 54 Liuliu Cheng, 溜溜城54号, off Dong Dajie, 上东大街; ⏱ 7.30am-11pm; 🛜) The only spot for actual pour-over coffee (¥25) in all of the Kham, this cafe (food from ¥18) near the big yak sculpture is a veritable oasis for the caffeine-deprived. Wraps, pizzas, house-baked pastries, waffles and wi-fi satisfy other common traveller cravings – though at homeland prices. Even for nonsmokers the 'VIP' balcony out back makes for great people-watching over the street below.

LOAD UP WITH CASH

At the time of research it was impossible to change money or travellers cheques, get advances on credit cards or use ATMs with foreign bank cards anywhere in western Sìchuān apart from Kāngdìng. Larger towns such as Xīndūqiáo and Gānzī have a branch of the Agricultural Bank of China that theoretically accept foreign cards but in others, despite the Visa signs, expect rejection.

🛍 Shopping

Déhuì Supermarket   MARKET
(德惠超市, Déhuì Chāoshì; 96 Dong Dajie, 东大街96号; ⏱ 8am-10pm) A comprehensive supermarket with a wide selection, and a decent range of ingredients for hiking trips as well. A separate camping/outdoors store just past the cashiers also sells 230g canisters of camping fuel for ¥20.

ℹ Information

Agricultural Bank of China ATM (自动柜员机, Zìdòng Guìyuán Jī; 139 Yanhe Xilu, 沿河西路139号; ⏱ 24hr) Agricultural Bank of China has several ATMs around town that take foreign cards.

China Construction Bank ATM (自动柜员机, Zìdòng Guìyuán Jī; outside bus station, 车站外面; ⏱ 24hr)

China Post (中国邮政, Zhōngguó Yóuzhèng; 34 Yanhe Xilu, 沿河西路34号; ⏱ 9am-5pm)

Public Security Bureau (PSB, 公安局, Gōng'ānjú; ☎ 0836 281 1415; 150 Dong Dajie, 东大街150号; ⏱ 8.30am-5pm) Visa-extension service that takes five working days. First-time extensions only.

ℹ Getting There & Away

AIR

Kāngdìng Airport is 43km west of town and has daily flights to Chéngdū (¥750, 8.35am and 5.40pm), two weekly flights to Chóngqìng (¥940, 12.05pm Sunday and Thursday), and one per week to Dàochéng (¥442, 9.10am Wednesday).

Buy tickets online or from the **Flight Ticket Centre** (机场售票中心, Jīchǎng Shòupiào Zhōngxīn; ☎ 0836 287 1111; 28 Binhe Lu, inside the Airport Hotel, 滨河路28号; ⏱ 8.30am-5.30pm), which sometimes has tickets discounted by ¥100 or so. Pick up the airport shuttle (¥35, 1½ hours) at 6am in front of the Airport Hotel (also signed as the Xiang Yun Hotel – 翔云酒店 – from the street front). Shuttles from the airport (¥50) arrive here at around 11.30am.

BUS

Kāngdìng is a major transport hub in Sìchuān, and travellers can transfer from here to most of the province. The **bus station** is a 10-minute walk north from the centre of town (a taxi there is ¥7). Shared minibuses also leave from outside the bus station to most western Sìchuān destinations listed here, including to Tǎgōng (¥50 to ¥80) and Gānzī (around ¥200). Ask for either private hire (包车; *bāochē*) or a shared vehicle (拼车; *pīnchē*).

Báiyù ¥192, 20 hours, 6.45am (stops overnight in Gānzī; book the day before)

Chéngdū ¥111, eight hours, hourly from 6am to 4.30pm

Chóngqìng ¥240, 12 hours, 6.30am

Dānbā ¥55, three hours, two daily (7.30am, 2.30pm)

Dàochéng ¥124, 12 hours, two daily (both at 6am)

Éméi Shān ¥122, seven hours, 8am

Gānzī ¥121, 11 hours, 6.15am

Lè Shān ¥114, seven hours, 6am

Lǐtáng ¥97, eight hours, 6.30am

Sèdá ¥131, 12 hours, 6.15am

Tǎgōng ¥38, three hours, 7am

Xiāngchéng ¥174, 15 hours, 6am

Yǎ'ān ¥70, 4½ hours, about every hour from 6am to 4pm

Zìgòng ¥170, nine hours, 6am

ⓘ Getting Around

While Kāngdìng is quite walkable, infrequent local buses do connect the major sites in town.

Bus 2 (¥1) runs straight through town from the bus station to the Jīngāng and Nánwú temples.

Bus 3 (¥1) goes from the bus station along Xinshi Qianjie to Wenchang Lu before continuing for 3km to Èrdào Hot Springs. The terminus is a few stops beyond the springs, so ask the driver where to disembark.

Northern Garzê Prefecture

The famous Sìchuān–Tibet Hwy splits in two just west of Kāngdìng. The northern route is 300km longer than the southern route, and is generally less travelled. Following it, you'll traverse high-plateau grasslands and numerous Tibetan settlements, usually attached to a local monastery.

Come here prepared. Bring warm clothing; it can be frigid at these elevations even in midsummer, and snow is not unheard of. Bus services can be unreliable. At times the government closes all or part of the region (particularly Larung Gar and Yarchen Gar) to foreign travellers with no notice beyond an entrance checkpoint with a soldier saying you won't be allowed in. This is no place to be in a hurry.

The payoff, however, comes in visiting remote Tibetan towns and monasteries, many of which carry on traditions that have existed in the region for centuries. This was once the realm of great kingdoms and marauding nomads – traces of these still exist if you search hard enough.

ⓘ Getting There & Away

Making it to the other side of Chola Mountain (雀儿山; Què'ér Shān) requires negotiating a 5050m narrow pass, the highest this side of Lhasa, that takes you to Dégé and the border with the Tibet Autonomous Region (西藏; Xīzàng) – a no-go region unless you've secured the extremely rare permit to enter via Chamdo Prefecture.

You can continue on this route north into Qīnghǎi province via Shíqú and Yùshù. From Gānzī, you can hook back up with the southern route via Xīnlóng.

Remember that bus services can be unreliable in the region – this is not the place to be on a tight schedule.

Báiyù 白玉

📞 0836 / POP 6508 / ELEV 3090M

Those looking to get a small taste of the spectacle of Buddhist village life can do so at Pelyul Gompa, a monastery encircled by a swath of small white houses clinging to the mountainside above the modern town of Báiyù on the narrow floor of the gorge below. From the top of a large white stupa on the edge of the modern settlement, a panorama of gleaming monasteries and bright white houses opens up above.

⦿ Sights

Pelyul Gompa BUDDHIST MONASTERY

(白玉祖寺, Báiyù Zǔsì) FREE A remote settlement in the mountains of the former Tibetan province of Kham, here you can get a semblance of the spectacle of monastic life through a visit to Báiyù Sì (Baiyu; 3150m), a small monastery village of striking beauty. Wander the temples and observe the 200 monks living here, then explore the maze of lanes that wind among the red and white houses clinging to the hillside.

The original monastery, built in 1665, grew to be one of the six most influential monasteries of the Nyingma (Red Hat) sect. It has been restored and rebuilt several times, and at its height had more than 1000 monks before it was destroyed during the Cultural Revolution. The monastery was rebuilt in 1982 with a combination of private and government funds.

The monastery has a small printing operation in a building just uphill from the main halls. On the 2nd floor, you can watch carvers create delicate script in reverse as they cut away intricate designs out of small wooden blocks.

The monastery village infrastructure remains rudimentary; raw sewage flows onto the paths after rains. There are no restaurants or guesthouses, so head back down into the modern town below.

From the Báiyù bus station the temple is a 2km slog uphill through the lanes of the modern city, or accessible by car via a steep paved road on the northern edge of town.

🛏 Sleeping & Eating

Yǎruì Bīnguǎn   HOTEL $$
(雅瑞宾馆; ☎ 153 8766 7529; Binhe Lu, 滨河路; r ¥100-200) Yǎruì Bīnguǎn is on a quiet stretch of the riverfront. The rooms here (all with private bathroom) are clean and range from singles to triples. More expensive rooms include a large sitting area or overlook the river. From the traffic light, walk a few metres towards the river and turn right onto the promenade. It's a few doors down, on the 2nd floor.

Kǎwǎkàbù Zàngcān   TIBETAN $
(卡瓦卡布藏餐; ☎ 135 4146 9948; Hedong Shangjie, 河东上街; mains from ¥12; ⏱8am-11pm) Despite the lack of menus, ordering here is easy as the friendly Tibetan family drag you by the arm back into the kitchen for a look. Don't think too hard, though: the *momos* (牛肉包子; ¥2 each) are fantastic, among the best to be had anywhere in the Kham.

TIBET'S NO-GO REGIONS

Foreigners are forbidden from travelling individually overland from Sichuan into Tibet proper (西藏; Xīzàng) as Tibet's far eastern prefecture of Chamdo (昌都地区; Chāngdū Dìqū), which borders Sichuan, is usually off limits. During March (a time of holy celebrations and politically sensitive anniversaries), Tibet is often completely closed to foreigners. This closure has extended to Sichuan's Ābà and Gānzī Prefectures before as well, though not in recent years.

If the situation were to change, the town of Bātáng (due west of Lǐtáng) is a popular gateway into the province for locals in Southern Garzi Prefecture, while the stretch of highway between Dégé and Báiyù in the north of the prefecture has a score of bridges that enter Tibet via remote and rarely touristed rural regions.

Hostels keep up with the latest information, or check the China and Tibet branches of Lonely Planet's online forum, **Thorn Tree** (lonelyplanet.com/thorntree).

ℹ Getting There & Away

Buses depart from the new Báiyù station a 15-minute walk south of town for Kāngdìng (¥183, 18 hours, 6am) via Gānzī (¥80, 7½ hours).

Minibuses are the only options for Dégé (¥80, four hours), Lǐtáng (¥190, nine hours) and Yàqīng (¥50, three hours).

Dānbā   丹巴

☎ 0836 / POP 56,829 / ELEV 1893M

Dānbā (known as Rongtrak in Tibet; 1893m) straddles a dramatic gorge near the confluence of three rivers, and makes an interesting alternative to Kāngdìng as a gateway into or out of western Sichuan.

The town itself is not very exciting, but in the surrounding hills are clusters of picturesque Jiāróng Tibetan and Qiāng villages with ancient watchtowers and welcoming homestays.

◉ Sights

★ Zhōnglù   VILLAGE
(中路) Comparatively remote Zhōnglù, 13km from Dānbā, is a popular village for homestays and a good base for wandering through the countryside. Look for the old stone steps that climb above the village for fantastic views of the countryside and Zhōnglù's many watchtowers.

To get here, catch a minibus from a small parking lot across from 42 Sanchahe Nanlu (¥15, 25 minutes), about 10 minutes' walk from the hostels, or take a taxi (¥80). Minibuses return from the village to Dānbā until around 6pm.

Jiǎjū Zàngzhài   VILLAGE
(甲居藏寨; adult/student ¥50/25) Of all the pretty villages in the hills around here, Dānbā tourism's pride and joy is Jiǎjū, 12km northwest of town and perched at the top of a multi-switchback road that winds up a steep river gorge. With fruit trees, charming Tibetan stone houses and homestays, Jiǎjū's quaint architecture will pull in travellers for a half-day (or more) visit.

To get here, take a shared minivan (¥10) from the Bāměi end of Dānbā. A private taxi costs about ¥50 one way.

🛏 Sleeping

Dōngpō Tibetan Homestay   GUESTHOUSE $
(东坡藏家, Dōngpō Zángjiā; ☎ 135 5850 9707; Zhonglu Xiang, Kegenong Cun, 中路乡克格侬村; r incl meals without/with bathroom ¥80/100; P ☎) Spend a night or two in this converted

white-stone and crimson-timber homestead, the original structure of which dates back more than 700 years, so that you have time to partake in the multicourse meals (breakfast and dinner are included in room rates) and wander the surrounding countryside.

Zháxī Zhuōkāng
Backpackers Hostel · HOTEL $

(扎西卓康国际青年旅舍, Zháxī Zhuōkāng Guójì Qīngnián Lûshé; ☑139 9046 4961, 0836 352 1806; 35 Sanchahe Nanlu, 三岔河南路35号; dm ¥30-50, tw without/with bathroom ¥60/80; @ ⑦) This is traveller central in Dānbā proper; the friendly English-speaking management can arrange minibus rides and extended treks to natural springs and remote villages off the tourist map. Rooms are decidedly average but tidy, while the common area is recently renovated. It's a 25-minute walk from the bus station (keep the river on your left), or a ¥5 taxi ride.

① Getting There & Away

For Tǎgōng, take a minibus (¥65, three hours) from the west end of town, via Bāměi (¥40, two hours). Minibuses also head to Four Sisters Mountain (¥50, three hours) via Xiǎojīn (¥30, two hours). Bus destinations include:

Chéngdū ¥135, nine hours, two daily (6.30am, 10am)

Gānzī ¥101, nine hours, one daily (6.50am)

Kāngdìng ¥54, 3½ hours, two daily (6.30am, 3pm)

Dégé · 德格

☑ 0836 / POP 58,600 / ELEV 3334M

With roads improved and mountain tunnels nearly complete, once-remote Dégé (Derge) is no longer quite so cut off from the rest of western Sìchuān by the towering Chola Mountain (雀儿山; Què'ér Shān; 6168m).

While for now the road still climbs a rough dirt track over the 5050m-high Chola Pass, soon even this last hurdle to access will be circumvented by a tunnel scheduled to be finished in mid-2017.

Unless you've secured the rare permit to enter the Chamdo Prefecture of Tibet proper (西藏; Xīzàng), the main reason to make the arduous trek out here is to see Dégé's famous printing monastery, one of this region's premier sights.

◎ Sights

The Bakong Scripture Printing Press and Monastery is just above the centre of town, but further along the road uphill beyond it you'll reach the huge, reconstructed **Gonchen Monastery** (德格寺, Dégé Sì; Bagong Jie, 巴宫街; ⊙6am-8pm; FREE), which has stood here in various forms for over five centuries. High in the mountains to the south and east are several other monasteries that make for compelling day hikes, including Palpung Gompa, Dzongsar Gompa and Pewar Gompa.

★ Bakong Scripture Printing Press & Monastery · BUDDHIST MONASTERY, HISTORIC SITE

(德格印经院, Dégé Yìnjīngyuàn; www.degeparkhang.org; Bagong Jie, 巴宫街; ¥50; ⊙8.30-11.50am & 2-6pm) This fascinating 1792 monastery houses one of western Sìchuān's star attractions: an ongoing printing operation that still uses traditional woodblock printing methods and maintains more than 320,000 scripture plates, an astonishing 70% of Tibet's literary heritage. You aren't allowed to take photos of the library shelves or main hall, but ask the printers if it's OK to snap away as they meditatively fill customers' orders.

🛏 Sleeping & Eating

Fēnglíngdù
International Youth Hostel · GUESTHOUSE $

(风陵渡国际青年旅舍, Fēnglíngdù Guójì Qīngnián Lûshé; ☑150 0248 8791; 243 Chamashang Jie, 茶马上街243号; dm ¥30, r ¥150; ⑦) Travellers looking for a welcoming hostel vibe in Dégé need look no further. Lorna, the friendly owner from Liáoníng, speaks some English and keeps her rooms spick and span. It's on the highway from Mǎnígāngē. When entering town keep an eye out for the sign on the left about 300m in, or walk back about 20 minutes from the bus station.

Dégé Hotel · HOTEL $$

(德格宾馆, Dégé Bīnguǎn; ☑0836 822 6666; 11 Gesa'er Dajie, 格萨尔大街11号; r from ¥380; ❈⑦) This standard, reliable hotel is in a big building by the river near the bus station. All rooms have private baths and some even have nice mountain views. Turn left out of the bus station, cross the bridge, and follow the signs to turn right down the lane into the hotel courtyard. Rooms can be discounted to ¥190.

Kāngbā Zàngcān · TIBETAN $

(康巴藏餐; ☑139 9049 9806; Chamashang Jie, 茶马上街; dishes ¥15-40; ⊙9am-10pm) This Tibetan teahouse serves authentic Tibetan food, plus tea and beer. There's a picture menu, but if you're stumped try one of these

DON'T MISS

DARJAY GOMPA

One of the largest and most venerated monasteries in the prefecture; the reasoning behind the name 'Big Golden Temple' becomes apparent as soon as it appears on the horizon. There are two large halls surrounded by a small village. **Darjay Gompa** (大金寺, Dàjīn Sì) is 30km west of Gānzī on the road to Mǎnígāngē. It costs around ¥20 to get here from Gānzī in a shared minivan, at least ¥40 in a private taxi.

You may have to track down a monk to unlock (开门; *kāimén*) the temple halls. Keep an eye out for the fantastic sand mandalas the monks make from time to time.

A short walk from the Darjay Gompa is the **Talam Khang guesthouse and temple** (大金寺旅馆, Dàjīn Sì Lǚguǎn; ☑ 187 8366 2272; camping & dm ¥50, d/tw ¥100/200), with snow-capped mountains to one side, and rolling grasslands and a river to the other. To get here from Darjay Gompa, exit from the monastery's back gate and walk about 15 minutes along the dirt road. Walk towards the white stupa furthest on the left, keeping the grassland villages on your right. You'll see the temple as you come over the hill.

Tibetan favourites: yak-meat pie (牛肉饼; *niúròu bǐng*; ¥30), yak-meat *momos* (¥20), *tsampa* (¥10) and butter tea (from ¥15). Very little English is spoken. Turn left out of the bus station; it's across the intersection on the 2nd floor.

🍸 Drinking & Nightlife

Syokar Teahouse   TEAHOUSE
(萨噶茶, Sàgá Cháguǎn; ⊘9am-9pm; 🛜) The people-watching from this 2nd-floor teahouse overlooking the river is just as much a draw as the tea and Tibetan snacks (from ¥15) on the menu. It's the first building on the left just across the bridge to the Bakong Monastery.

ℹ️ Getting There & Away

Just one daily eastbound bus leaves from here at 6am, heading for Kāngdìng (¥206, 13 hours) via Mǎnígāngē (¥39, 2½ hours) and Gānzī (¥71, four hours). Otherwise there are minivans to Gānzī (¥80) and Mǎnígāngē (¥60).

Minibuses to Báiyù (¥90, two hours), though less reliably available, enable a loop back towards Gānzī via several small monastery towns; for the first hour or so of the trip the highway traces the Yangzi River border with Tibet and pays off in views towards the small hamlets and towering mountains just beyond.

Foreigners are not allowed to take public transport west from here into Tibet proper.

Gānzī   甘孜

☑ 0836 / POP 68,523 / ELEV 3475M

It's easy to spend a couple of days in the lively market town of Gānzī (Garzê) exploring the beautiful countryside, which is scattered with Tibetan villages and large monasteries surrounded by snowcapped mountains. Photo opportunities abound, especially from late July to October when the grassland is an impossible green accented with wildflowers.

👁️ Sights & Activities

From Gānzī, the terraced hillsides in every direction beckon to avid hikers. Head out in any direction for small village temples and stunning views of the snowy mountain peaks to the south.

For a range of day hikes to the feet of craggy mountains or to a number of temples scattered across rolling grasslands, head out to the Talam Khang Guesthouse for a few nights.

Garzê Gompa   BUDDHIST TEMPLE
(甘孜寺, Gānzī Sì; ¥10; ⊘approx 9am-6pm) North of the town's old Tibetan quarter is the region's largest monastery, dating back more than 500 years and glimmering with gold. Encased on the walls of the main hall are hundreds of small golden Sakyamunis. In a smaller hall down the hill to the west is an awe-inspiring statue of Jampa (Maitreya or Future Buddha) dressed in a giant silk robe, with a tooth of the historical Buddha embedded in the right big toe.

🛏️ Sleeping

Hóng Fú Guesthouse   GUESTHOUSE $
(鸿福旅馆, Hóngfú Lǚguǎn; ☑ 0836 752 5330, 135 5198 0898; 4th fl, 49 Chuanzang Lu, 川藏路49号四楼; per bed ¥40) In a traditional Tibetan wooden building on the main drag, Hóng Fú has one four-bed dorm just beside the family quarters and smallish twin rooms on a separate floor, all with shared toilets and one cramped shower. But, as the owners say, the hot springs are just up the road.

Turn left out of the bus station, take the first left and you'll soon see a sign on your right for Long Da Guesthouse (same prices; not as good). Walk towards that and you'll see Hóng Fú just beside it on the left.

Golden Yak Hotel
HOTEL $

(金牦牛酒店, Jīnmáoniú Jiǔdiàn; ☑ 0836 752 5188; 8 Dajin Tan, 打金滩8号; r without/with hot water ¥60/150) This dependable chain has branches at a number of bus stations in western Sìchuān. This particular one has a main building at the back of the bus station forecourt, with standard doubles discounted to ¥120, and a separate building across the forecourt housing enormous but slightly shabby twin rooms with bathrooms but no hot water.

Eating

Lake Mamosarovor Tibetan Restaurant
TIBETAN $

(玛旁雍措藏餐馆, Mǎpángyōngcuò Zàngcānguǎn; ☑ 150 8231 6818; Dong Dajie, 东大街; mains ¥15-50; ⊗ 8am-11.30pm; ☎) The friendly Tibetan family that run this restaurant serve a variety of authentic Tibetan dishes and a few local Sìchuān favourites, as well as a selection of tea styles from across the Tibetan cultural regions. It's a few doors down from the turn-off at Chuanzang Lu.

ℹ️ Getting There & Away

The new Gānzī Gesar Airport (50km north) is scheduled to be completed in 2017.

Scheduled bus services run to the following destinations:

Chéngdū ¥230, 18 hours, 6am

Dānbā ¥101, nine hours, 6.30am

Kāngdìng ¥134, 11 hours, two daily (both at 6.30am)

Tǎgōng ¥88, eight hours, 6.30am

Yǎ'ān ¥187, 14 hours, 6am

Minivans congregate outside the bus station and head to:

Dégé ¥160, six to seven hours

Lǐtáng ¥180, six to seven hours

Mǎnígāngē ¥50, two to three hours

Additionally, minibuses for two of the prefecture's largest monastic communities leave from a small parking lot on Chuanzang Lu just uphill from Qinghe Lu to:

Sèdá ¥60, four hours

Yàqīng ¥40, three to four hours

Mǎnígāngē
马尼干戈

☑ 0836 / POP 3850 / ELEV 2988M

There's not much going on in Mǎnígāngē (Manigango) itself, a small transit town halfway between Gānzī and Dégé. The surrounding hills do offer wonderful hiking opportunities, though, and the main draw in town (the magnificent Yilhun Lha-Tso lake) makes it well worth spending a full day in the area.

On hilltops to either side of Mǎnígāngē are the relatively new Yazisi and Lajiasi temples, the views from both of which also take in the mountains that ring the grasslands surrounding the city. The vast monastery and school Dzogchen Gompa (竹庆寺; Zhú Qìng Sì), an important seat of the Nyingma (Red Hat sect), is also within striking distance 58km north on the road to Yùnhù.

⊙ Sights

Yilhun Lha-tso
LAKE

(玉隆拉措, Yùlónglācuò; ¥30; ⊗ 7am-9pm) It is said King Gesar's beloved concubine Zhumu was so taken by these turquoise-blue waters that her heart fell in. This now-holy glacial lake, 8km southwest of Mǎnígāngē, is still awe inspiring. Follow a small dirt track around the north edge of the lake to a marshy plain at the far end, from which you can take in the spectacular views of peaks and glaciers from right up close. Locally, this area is also known as 新路海 (Xīnlù Hǎi).

The water is frigid and the surface freezes solid from September through March. Take it in by hiking among the *chörten* and *mani* stones, beneath snowcapped Chola Mountain to the west, whose melt-waters feed the lake. You can walk for a couple of hours up the foothills on the left side of the lake for more breathtaking views and possible glimpses of white-lipped deer (白唇鹿; *báichúnlù*).

You can also ride horses led by guides (from ¥100). Camping is frowned upon – though some self-sufficient travellers have slept in the caves without trouble. In summer you may also run into local monks setting up colourful tents.

To get here, take a Dégé-bound minibus (¥20 to ¥40), hitch a ride or hike (turn right out of Mǎnígāngē Páni Hotel and keep going for two hours). The lake is a 10-minute walk from the main road, along an easy track. Minivans (¥20) wait to take you back to Mǎnígāngē.

🛏️ Sleeping & Eating

Travellers' Teahouse
GUESTHOUSE $

(旅行茶坊, Lǚxíng Cháfáng; ☑ 183 8362 8666; r ¥60; ⊗ 11am-evening; ☎) This guesthouse on the 2nd floor opposite Mǎnígāngē Pani Hotel offers private rooms with one shared bath that are sparse but clean, while the teahouse facing the main street (tea from

¥10, open 11am to late) is perhaps the friendliest in town. Both have wi-fi.

Xuěchéng Lǚguǎn
GUESTHOUSE $$

(雪城旅馆; ☑158 8406 6202; per person ¥60) The clean single, double and triple rooms at this family-run guesthouse are all priced per person, and all share a handful of bathrooms. From the bottom of the T-junction, turn left and then almost immediately down a small street to the right; the guesthouse is just down on the left.

Xǐmǎlāyǎ Zàngcān
TIBETAN $

(喜马拉雅臧餐; dishes from ¥10; ⊙9am-10pm) This combined teahouse and restaurant serves up Tibetan favourites on the cheap. There's no menu, so if you get stuck order the momos (牛肉包子; niúròu bāozi) by the piece (¥1 each) and then grab a table by the window overlooking the streets below. It's at the bottom of the main street, across the T-junction, up a small staircase to the left.

❶ Getting There & Away

Buses depart from the parking lot of the **Mǎnígāngē Pani Hotel** (马尼干戈帕尼酒店, Mǎnígāngē Pàní Jiǔdiàn; ☑0836 822 2788; dm from ¥30, tw without/with bathroom ¥80/130; ☎) for Dégé (¥60, three hours, 4.30pm) and Gānzī (¥30, three hours, 7pm). Minibuses congregate at the east end of town at the crossroads of the main drag and the road north to Yùshù (S217). They head to Gānzī (¥50), Dégé (¥80) or Shíqú (¥80) when full.

Buses between other destinations no longer pass through the city now that a bypass road has been constructed on both sides, but it may be possible to find a seat on these from the main highway. A daily bus to Dégé (¥50, three to four hours) passes through Mǎnígāngē between 7am and 8.40am, but is often full. Going the other way, there are usually empty seats on the Gānzī-bound bus (¥50, three to four hours), which passes by at 7am to 8am. A bus from Gānzī to Shíqú (¥70, seven hours) also passes by here at around 8.30am.

Sèdá
色达

Sèdá (Sertar), home to the largest Buddhist academy in the world, offers an incredible glimpse into the life of monks and nuns.

Note that the area is occasionally closed to foreign travellers (including at the time of research), with the possibility of fines and compulsory trips to Chéngdū for those caught in the area. There are no official announcements of such closures, but check with other travellers in the area or tour agencies in Chéngdū for the latest updates.

Of all the Buddhist sights in western Sìchuān, there is none as striking as **Larung Gar Five Sciences Buddhist Academy** (喇荣五明佛学院, Lǎróng Wǔmíng Fó Xuéyuàn). The future of Tibetan Buddhism is contained here in this school, the largest of its kind in the world, cradled in a valley some 170km northeast of Gānzī. Some 10,000 students study here, dedicated for six to 13 years to serious monastic study.

There is a crowded strip of businesses just outside the monastery, but better options with wi-fi and 24-hour hot water overlook the walking street (步行街; Bùxíngjiē) in Sèdá Xiàn (色达县), 20km northwest. **Zàngyuán Bīngguǎn** (藏缘兵官; Buxing Jie, Sèdá County, 色达县步行街; r without/with bathroom ¥120/160; ☎) has a fantastic Tibetan teahouse downstairs. A gaggle of friendly ladies keep **Shūshì Bīngguǎn** (舒适兵馆; ☑0836 852 1850; Buxing Jie, Sèdá County, 色达县步行街; r without/with bathroom ¥158/248; ☎) particularly tidy. Your hotel may ask you to register in person at the PSB (公安局; Gōng'ānjú) on one end of the walking street.

Minibuses arrive and drop-off at the big parking lot halfway up the hill on the Larung Gar grounds. A ride to the Sèdá Xiàn walking street is about ¥10 with other passengers, ¥70 privately. Minibuses to and from Gānzī (¥70 to ¥100, 4½ hours) arrive and depart from here as well. From Sèdá Xiàn, regular buses to Chéngdū (¥239) and Kāngdìng (¥53) depart at around 6am from the east end of town, less than 1km from the walking street.

Tǎgōng
塔公

☑0836 / POP 8984 / ELEV 3718M

The Tibetan village of Tǎgōng (Lhagang) and its surrounding grasslands offer plenty of excuses to linger.

On the road from Kāngdìng is a sea of mani stones carved (and spray-painted) with ༀ་མ་ཎི་པདྨེ་ཧྰུྃ (om mani padme hum), the mantra of Buddha's path. Explore this terrain on horseback or foot, sip real yak-butter tea, then fall asleep in tents under the stars like a Tibetan nomad.

◉ Sights & Activities

Horse riding (per person per day for one/two/three people ¥415/390/360 with meals and homestay) and guided grassland hikes (per person per day ¥200) can be arranged through Khampa Cafe and Khampa Nomad Ecolodge for single-day/overnight trips (bespoke itineraries available).

You can hike into the grasslands on your own. One popular option is the two-hour hike south to Ser Gyergo (ask Khampa Cafe for directions).

Ser Gyergo Nunnery   BUDDHIST MONASTERY

(和平法会, Hépíng Fǎhuì) FREE Known locally as *ani gompa* ('nunnery' in Tibetan), Hépíng Fǎhuì is home to around 500 nuns and more than 100 monks. Lama Tsemper was a revered local hermit who spent much of his life meditating in a cave about two hours across the grasslands from Tǎgōng. Local nuns would bring him food and look after him, so when he requested a temple be built here just before his death in the 1980s it was decided that a nunnery be built too.

Lama Tsemper's remains are in a *chörten* inside the original cave; you may have to ask a nun to unlock the door to look inside. Below the cave is the temple and a huge *mani* wall as big as the temple itself, which has its own *kora* that attracts many pilgrims.

Getting to the nunnery is half the fun. Heading south out of town, turn left after about 40m into an alleyway beside a large yellow house. Follow the dirt track to the top of the hill, from which you can see the stupa-topped walls and shining gold roofs of the monastic college (*shedra*) in the distance. Trace the dirt track along a fence line until crossing a bridge, then head off through the grasslands on a pathless walk to the base of the *shedra*. Interact with the students of Hépíng Dàxué Fǎhuì (和平大学法会) and explore the new temple halls of the Mùyǎ Dàsì (木雅大寺) before continuing to the bottom of the hill to the left of the college towards Ser Gyergo Nunnery, where a small village surrounds the main temple halls.

Lhagang Monastery   BUDDHIST MONASTERY

(塔公寺, Tǎgōng Sì; Tagong Guangchang, 塔公广场; ¥20; ⊙5am-6pm) The story goes that when Princess Wencheng, the Chinese bride-to-be of Tibetan king Songtsen Gampo, was on her way to Lhasa in 640, a precious statue of Jowo Sakyamuni Buddha toppled off one of the carts in her entourage. A replica of the statue was carved on the spot where it landed and a temple built around it.

Golden Temple   BUDDHIST TEMPLE

(木雅金塔, Mùyǎ Jīntǎ; ¥20; ⊙6am-6pm) The glimmering roof and stupa-lined walls of this temple are set against the fantastic backdrop of the snowy mountains across the grasslands. Inside it's a more sedate affair, but the prayer-wheel-lined walls and central temple hall are worth a wander for those with spare time in town.

🛏 Sleeping

Jya Drolma & Gayla's Guesthouse   GUESTHOUSE $

(✆0836 286 6056; Tagong Guangchang, 塔公广场; dm ¥30, tw without bathroom ¥60; 🛜) Rooms here are a riot of golds, reds and blues, with elaborately painted ceilings and walls. There are common toilets on each floor and one shower with 24-hour hot water. Some basic English is spoken. From the entrance of Lhagang Monastery, walk to the back right corner of the square. Down a short alleyway is the guesthouse.

Khampa Cafe   GUESTHOUSE $$

(康巴咖啡, Kāngbā Kāfēi; ✆183 0287 9858; www.khampacafe.com; Tagong Guangchang, 塔公广场; r ¥100-200) A Czech/local couple run this popular guesthouse and cafe overlooking Tǎgōng's main square. There is just one shared bath, but the double and triple bedrooms are comfortable and clean. The top-floor cafe (open 8.30am to 11pm; dishes ¥15 to ¥90) is also the most popular hang-out in town, with a selection of Western and Tibetan dishes plus real coffee.

Khampa Nomad Ecolodge & Arts Center   LODGE $$$

(康巴牧民环保艺术客栈, Kāngbā Mùmín Huánbǎo Yìshù Kèzhàn; ✆136 8449 3301; www.definitely nomadic.com; r ¥400; 🛜) Tibetan/American couple Djarga and Angela have left Tǎgōng behind to open a new ecolodge out on the grasslands. With a sauna and hot tub in the works, this is a true luxury experience in the middle of rural Kham. Angela can advise on hiking routes and nomad homestays in the area, and rents tents and sleeping bags for ¥30 each.

From Tǎgōng the lodge is a 30-minute taxi ride (¥60; mention Angela and most local drivers know where to go) or a three-hour hike. Contact the lodge for details on either.

🍴 Eating

Rinchen Wangmu Tibetan Restaurant   TIBETAN $$

(仁青旺姆藏餐, Rénqīng Wàngmǔ Zàngcān; ✆139 9048 9067; across from Tagong Guangchang, 塔公广场马路对面; mains ¥20-80; ⊙8am-10pm) Run by a friendly Tibetan owner/chef, this Tibetan cafe just across from the main square is one of the tastiest in town (and one of the few with an English menu).

ℹ️ Getting There & Away

Buses pass through town en route to Gānzī (¥109, eight hours, 9am) and Kāngdìng (¥40, two hours, 9am). If these are full, minibuses leave from the main square to Lǐtáng (¥150, seven hours), Gānzī (¥100 to ¥150) and Kāngdìng (¥50 to ¥70).

For destinations north it's also possible to take a shared minivan to Bāměi (八美; ¥20, one hour), where you'll have your pick of minivans to places such as Dānbā (¥30, two hours) and Gānzī (¥50 to ¥70, seven hours).

For self-ride day trips, rent motorbikes in town (per day from ¥100).

Yàqīng 亚青

📞 0836 / POP 11,000 / ELEV 3975M

Centred around the Yarchen Gar Buddhist Institute and the massive community of monks and nuns that live here as students of the Dharma, Yàqīng offers an in-depth look into monastic life. The deeply spiritual atmosphere, combined with the privations those in residence endure, provides some evidence as to the importance of religion in the lives of the congregation.

Travel here is not for the squeamish, however, as living conditions are quite basic. Without running water, the residents of the improvised shelters that dominate the area make do with hauling buckets from taps near the temples for all their basic needs. Sanitation facilities are minimal, and during heavy rains the pit toilets on the outsides of the encampment often overflow and pour through the streets of the floodplain on which it is built.

⊙ Sights & Activities

Rolling grasslands dotted with small temples surround Yarchen Gar in every direction. From the encampment simply pick a direction and start walking, though be sure to pack food and water as facilities are sparse away from the one road.

⭐ Yarchen Gar
Buddhist Institute   BUDDHIST MONASTERY

(亚青邬金禅林, Yàqīng Wūjīn Chánlín; Yaqing Si, 亚青寺) **FREE** On a quiet bend of the Dzin-Chu River in the remote grasslands of Garzi Prefecture, this 10,000-strong Nyingma (Red Hat) community of nuns and monks living in improvised housing under the shadows of magnificent golden-roofed temples is rivalled only by the better-known Larung Gar Five Sciences Buddhist Academy (p766) to the north. The encampment is split

into a monks' residence to the east of the river and a much larger housing area for the 7000 nuns who live to the west (closed to visitors).

🛏️ Sleeping & Eating

Sleeping options are limited to the large **Yàqīng Hotel** (亚青宾馆, Yàqīng Bīnguǎn; 📞 178 2816 8966; Yaqing Si, 亚青寺; r ¥160) on the edge of town and a string of small guesthouses on the main road shortly before it reaches the river, of which **Jíxiáng Shàngjìn Bīnguǎn Cāntīng** (吉详上进宾馆餐厅; 📞 152 2884 2226; Yaqing Si, 亚青寺; dm ¥40-50, r ¥120) is by far the most pleasant.

A bunch of small restaurants are located at the entrance to Yàqīng, with another on the main road through town just before the bridge across the Dzin-Chu River to the nuns' quarters. Most sport the same set menu of vegetarian dishes (¥10 to ¥15), though **Yīpǐn Tiānxià** (一品天下; Yaqing Si entrance, 亚青寺车场; mains ¥10-15; ⊙ 6am-11pm) expands on this with other Sìchuān classics.

ℹ️ Getting There & Away

While regular minibuses depart from Gānzī to Yàqīng, arriving from elsewhere may necessitate a transfer (¥15) in the village of Á'Chá (啊察/呷村), from which it's a 17km (30-minute) trip.

One daily bus departs from the entrance of Yàqīng village between 7am and 8am for Gānzī (¥40, two to three hours). Additionally, minibuses congregate in the same area and leave when full, most reliably to Gānzī (¥45), Báiyù (¥50, two to three hours) and Dégé (¥100, four to five hours).

Southern Garzê Prefecture

Travelling through the southern reaches of western Sìchuān takes you through vast grasslands dotted with alpine lakes, shiny gold-roofed monasteries and temples, and grazing yaks with a background of snowy peaks that seem to reach to the sky.

Journeying along this 2140km route is slightly easier than taking the northern route, but it's still not for the faint-hearted; settlements are far and few and high altitude is a factor as much as ever. Warm clothing and sunscreen are a must. However, as the Kāngdìng–Lǐtáng–Xiāngchéng–Shangri-la journey has become a popular route into Yúnnán province, road conditions have vastly improved and so have the services available to travellers in the region.

The very new and very high Dàochéng-Yàdīng Airport puts everything in closer reach, but if you're opting for the one-hour flight from Chéngdū make sure you set aside a couple of days to acclimatise before tackling ambitious excursions.

Otherwise, it's a long overland journey from Chéngdū via high mountain passes and fertile river valleys, perhaps continuing on to Tibetan areas of Yúnnán.

Dàochéng 稻城

☑ 0836 / POP 32,300 / ELEV 3760M

Dàochéng (Dabpa) packs bags of rural charm despite the fact that its small town centre has been modernised. It makes a lovely base for exploring the magnificent Yàdīng Nature Reserve, but don't discount the appeal of Dàochéng itself. After Yàdīng, you can fill another couple of days here walking or cycling around boulder-strewn wetlands, hills and barley fields, all of it dotted with villages and Tibetan monasteries. Spring brings some of the clearest skies, while autumn is particularly beautiful as a blaze of red leaves and grass electrifies the landscape.

◉ Sights & Activities

Especially for travellers coming from lower elevations, it's worth exploring the areas around Dàochéng by foot or bicycle to get accustomed to altitude before tackling the hikes in Yàdīng Nature Reserve.

Back towards central Sìchuān on the road to Kāngdìng, the villages of Hóngcǎodì (红草地; 10km) and Sāngduī Zhèn (桑堆镇; 28km) are quiet and picturesque while the magnificent Benpo Monastery (邦普寺; Bāngpǔ Sì; 30km) is itself worth a half-day.

In the other direction, towards Yàdīng, the 15km road to Rèwū Temple (热乌寺, Rèwū Sì) passes through the Sèlā Grasslands (色拉草原; Sèlā Cǎoyuán) and several villages en route. Turn right for the temple onto a small dirt road just before the highway starts to ascend switchbacks out of the valley.

Rúbùzhákǎ Hot Springs HOT SPRINGS
(茹布查卡温泉, Rúbùzhákǎ Wēnquán; per person ¥30) The waters of Rúbùzhákǎ Hot Springs are believed to promote good health and long life, but even nonbelievers can appreciate the relaxing powers of soaking in 68°C pools after a long hike in the mountains. Turn left off Dàochéng's main road just beyond the city square, and the springs are about 3km outside of town on a small road to the right.

🛏 Sleeping & Eating

Dàochéng

International Youth Hostel HOSTEL $
(稻城国际青年旅舍, Dàochéng Guójì Qīngnián Lǚshě; ☑ 0836 572 7772; yourinn@gmail.com; across the XingFu bridge, 幸福桥头有间; dm/r ¥30/100) At the end of Dexi Lu across a small bridge, this new hostel in a small residential area can help with booking tickets and renting bikes, and the small cafe stays open from 7am to midnight.

Yàdīng Backpackers Hostel HOSTEL $
(亚丁人社区国际青年旅舍, Yàdīng Rén Shèqū Guójì Qīngnián Lǚshě; ☑ 139 2221 4940; www.yading.net; 58 Dexi Lu, 德西路58号; dm ¥30-50, tw ¥100; ☀ 🛜) Small rooms are set around the courtyard of a pretty Tibetan blockhouse (first right off Dexi Jie). English-speaking staff help arrange excursions, rides and luggage storage.

Snowy Tibetan Meal TIBETAN $
(雪域藏餐, Xuěchéng Zàngcān; ☑ 139 9048 8476; mains from ¥15; ☉ 7am 10pm) Sample Tibetan classics in this small family-run restaurant just outside the bus station. No English, but a photo menu on the walls helps smooth ordering along.

🍷 Drinking & Nightlife

Bù'èr Cafe CAFE
(不二咖啡, Bù'èr Kāfēi; ☑ 0836 572 6765; 48 Dexi Lu, 德西路48号; ☉ 10am-midnight; 🛜) This upstairs cafe in the midst of the guesthouses on Dexi Lu has the best coffee in town (¥28) and a relaxed atmosphere in which to spend time before or after trips to Yàdīng Nature Reserve. Along with the English menu, some English is spoken by the friendly staff.

ℹ Getting There & Away

Two buses leave daily at 6.10am, for which you can buy tickets from 2pm the day before. One goes to Chéngdū (¥288, 20 hours), via Lǐtáng (¥50, three hours), Kāngdìng (¥150, nine hours) and Yǎ'ān (¥237, 14 hours); the other goes southwest to Shangri-la (Zhōngdiàn; ¥140, 10 hours) in Yúnnán province, via Xiāngchéng (¥45, three hours).

Minibuses that gather across the street from the station are also popular for Lǐtáng and Xiāngchéng. Prices are negotiable, but expect to pay ¥20 or ¥30 more per seat than bus prices. For Yàdīng Nature Reserve (¥50, two hours) minibuses are the only option.

The new Dàochéng-Yàdīng Airport, 43km north, has several flights daily to Chéngdū (¥839, one hour) and thrice-weekly flights to Chóngqìng (¥1220, 12.15pm Tuesday, Thursday and Saturday). Minibuses (机场拼车; *jīchǎng pīnchē*) leave from near the town square (¥30, 50 minutes, around three hours before departures). Turn right out of the bus station, left before the square; buses leave from a parking lot just before the first intersection on the left.

Bicycle Rental (出租自行车, Chūzū Zìxíngchē; ☑ 187 8363 1507; 46 Dexi Lu, 德西路46号; per day bicycle/scooter ¥20/80; ☺ 7am-8pm) Full-day rentals of bicycles and electric scooters are available from this storefront on Dexi Lu between the guesthouses and main road.

Lĭtáng 理塘

☑ 0836 / POP 51,300 / ELEV 3886M

At a dizzying altitude of 3886m, Lĭtáng (Lithang) is one of the highest settlements on earth. Its scenery will certainly leave you breathless, and getting out to see it – whether on horse, motorcycle or foot – calls for spending at least a couple of days here.

For Tibetans, Lĭtáng occupies another exalted space as the birthplace of holy men,

---

YÀDĪNG NATURE RESERVE

The magnificent **Yàdīng Nature Reserve** (亚丁风景区, Yàdīng Fēngjǐngqū; ☑ 0836 572 2666; entry incl shuttle bus ¥270; ☺ 7.30am-5.40pm), 140km south of Dàochéng, centres around three sacred snowcapped mountains, a holy trinity encircled by forested valleys, crystal-clear rivers and glacier-fed lakes. These are, quite simply, some of the most stunning landscapes you'll ever see. There are opportunities to hike, ride and camp here.

Locals have worshipped these mountains for more than 800 years. The three peaks – Chenresig (compassion), Chana Dorje (power) and Jampelyang (wisdom) – represent bodhisattvas in Tibetan Buddhism. Even for nonbelievers, walking the 35km *kora* (转山; holy hike) around the highest peak, Chenresig (仙乃日; Xiānnǎirì), which tops out at 6032m, can be a hugely meaningful experience.

The clockwise circuit around Chenresig begins at **Lóngtóng Bà** (龙同坝) and takes at least 12 hours of serious hiking. To avoid one very long day, many use the campsites located about halfway, just below the first pass beyond Five-Colour Lake. You have to bring all your own gear and supplies. (Though you'll pass locals living in simple stone huts, under park rules they are not supposed to take you in.) Remember to keep the mountain on your right, and to always take the right-hand turn when there's a choice of paths. There is a longer, four-day, 110km hike that adds a circuit around 5958m **Chana Dorje** (夏郎多吉; Xiàláng Duōjí), which begins and ends at the same place as the *kora*.

These hiking trails are all around 4000m above sea level, so acclimatise properly and pack for a serious expedition before you set off. Guides are available for hire at Lóngtóng Bà.

If you don't have the time (or energy) for a full circuit, there are day-hike options that see far more visitors. Take the shuttle bus from the ticket office into the park, to the small settlement of Lóngtóng Bà. From here hike 3km to the 800-year-old **Chonggu Monastery** (冲古寺; Chōnggǔ Sì), where you can pick up **electric carts** (one-way/return ¥50/80, 6km, 20 minutes) into the **Luòróng Grassland** (洛绒牛场; Luòróng Niúchǎng), which offers incredible views of the trinity and is as far as most tourists go. The other direction, uphill from Chonggu Monastery, is a 40-minute uphill hike to **Zhuoma La** (卓玛拉; Zhuómǎ Lā). This small lake, just in the shadow of Chenresig's north face, is particularly impressive in spring when surrounded by blooming azalea flowers.

It's worth continuing another 5km (three hours) to **Milk Lake** (牛奶海; Niúnǎi Hǎi) and stunning **Five-Colour Lake** (五色海; Wǔsè Hǎi). You can also ride guided mules (one-way/return ¥200/300) for this segment, but keep in mind that even on four legs the round-trip journey takes 5½ hours on a steep, rocky trail. Riders must dismount multiple times to scramble alongside their ride for about a kilometre.

Take a shared minibus (per person ¥50, 2½ hours) from Dàochéng to the small town of Rìwǎ (日瓦), where you buy tickets for the reserve. The ticket includes a mandatory ¥120 shuttle-bus fee, so take the park shuttle bus the last 32km into the park (50 minutes); it stops first in Yàdīng village and then 3km later at Lóngtóng Bà.

There are guesthouses and places to eat in **Yàdīng village** (亚丁村). To get an early start on the *kora* sleep in a guesthouse in Yàdīng then catch the 7.30am shuttle the last few kilometres down to Lóngtóng Bà. Buses within the park run from the visitors centre between 7.20am and 5.40pm, and back from Lóngtóng Bà between 9am and 7.30pm.

The best times to visit the reserve are May to June and September to early October.

including the seventh and 10th Dalai Lamas and many revered lamas. Their birthplace and the town's large monastery, Chöde Gompa, draw devoted pilgrims from afar.

◉ Sights & Activities

Former Residence of the
7th Dalai Lama
BUDDHIST TEMPLE

(仁康古屋, Rénkāng Gǔwū; Renkang Gujie, off Genie Xilu, 仁康古街, 格桑西路; ◷visitors 8am-7pm) FREE Kelzang Gyatso (1708–57), the seventh Dalai Lama, was born in the basement of this house during a period of intense political struggle. He eventually grew into a visionary leader, and under his rule Tibet established a national archive, instituted civil-service training programs and formalised the Tibetan government structure. The house, built in the 16th century, is now Lǐtáng's best-preserved temple. While the building is officially open from 8am to 7pm, in practice hours are erratic.

Not all Tibetans shared the belief Gyatso was the reincarnate; to escape the ongoing civil war, the Dalai Lama was raised and educated largely in exile. Qing Emperor Kangxi issued a proclamation affirming his identity, and in 1720 sent his son and troops to install the Dalai Lama to power in Lhasa. Mongol uprisings, rebellions and several coups later, the Dalai Lama gained the support of the clergy and the people.

The main house is a series of rooms crowded with devotees lost in prayer, and displays of sacred relics of the Dalai Lama and the 13 other lamas born here. You may have to ask to see his actual birthplace, which is behind a door to the left of the entrance.

To get here, walk along Genie Xilu (格聂西路) after turning left past the China Post and just before King Gesar Sq (格萨尔广场; Gésà'ěr Guǎngchǎng Zhàn). Turn right onto Renkang Gujie (仁康古街) into the passage between No 72 and No 74 (marked by a number of large stones inscribed with Tibetan script).

White Temple Park
PARK, CHÖRTEN

(白塔公园, Báitǎ Gōngyuán; Baita Lu, 白塔路) FREE Circle the White Temple (白塔; Báitǎ) with worshippers as they recite mantras and spin the massive prayer wheels, or join the locals just hanging out in the surrounding park. Turn left out of the bus station and just keep walking. From the main intersection, it's another five minutes or so down Xingfu Xilu (幸福西路).

Chöde Gompa
BUDDHIST MONASTERY

(长青春科尔寺, Chángqīngchūn Kē'ěr Sì; ◷6am-11pm) FREE At the northern end of town, the large Chöde Gompa is a Tibetan monastery that was built for the third Dalai Lama. Inside is a statue of Sakyamuni, believed to have been carried from Lhasa by foot. Don't miss climbing onto the roof of the main hall on the far right for great views of the Tibetan homes leading up to the monastery, as well as the grasslands and mountains beyond. Monks climb up here to sound the *dungchen* (long horns).

To get here from the post office, turn left at the end of Tuanjie Lu, then take the first right and follow the road. Alternatively, bus 2 (¥2) terminates at the monastery. Pick it up at the King Gesar Sq stop (格萨尔广场站; Gésà'ěr Guǎngchǎng) one block north of the post office.

Hot Springs
HOT SPRINGS

(温泉, Wēnquán; per person from ¥20) About 6km west of the town centre behind a small temple. Skip the bathhouses right by the road; the better options are just up the hill.

🛏 Sleeping & Eating

Lǐtáng Summer
International Youth Hostel
HOSTEL $

(理塘的夏天国际青年旅舍, Lǐtáng de Xiàtiān Guójì Qīngnián Lǚshě; ☑180 1579 1574; litangsummer@gmail.com; 47 Ping'an Lu, 平安路47号; dm ¥35, r ¥140) This lively youth hostel has the most cheerful rooms in town with colourful, warm bedding and a service demeanour to match. Hike this mountain? Find this unmapped route? Make me breakfast (¥10)? They'll make it happen. Turn left out of the bus station, and then left again down Ping'an Lu (just before the building marked '308 Xingfu Donglu').

Tiānjīn Gǒubùlǐ Soup Dumplings
DUMPLING $

(天津狗不理灌汤包, Tiānjīn Gǒubùlǐ Guàntāngbāo; 264 Xingfu Donglu, 幸福东路264号; dumplings ¥1, mains ¥15; ◷6.30am-10pm) Don't be fooled by the diminutive size of this shop run by a family from Yúnnán province, because the large soup dumplings (汤包子; *tāngbāozi*) pack in quite a lot of taste. Be sure to ask for a dish of the spicy sauce served alongside main dishes, and at ¥1 per dumpling don't be afraid to order ambitiously.

Tiān Tiān Restaurant
SICHUAN $

(天天饮食, Tiāntiān Yǐnshí; ☑135 4146 7941; 126 Xingfu Donglu, 幸福东路126号; mains ¥15-35; ◷8am-9pm; 🖥) Long-standing travellers' haven run by the gregarious English-speaking chef, Mr Zheng, who can also offer expert travel advice. Food is high-quality Sìchuān fare, and the delicious potato pancakes (土豆饼; *tǔdòu bǐng;* ¥30) come from a family recipe that goes back several generations. Turn left out of the bus station and it's about 600m along on the left.

ⓘ Information

China Post (中国邮政, Zhōngguó Yóuzhèng; 110 Tuanjie Beilu, 团结北路110号; ⊙ 9.30am-noon & 2.30-5pm) Turn left out of the bus station, then right at the intersection of Xingfu Donglu (幸福东路).

Internet Cafe (网吧, Wǎngbā; 106 Tuanjie Beilu, 团结北路106号; per hr ¥5; ⊙ 8.30am-midnight) Next to the post office.

ⓘ Getting There & Away

It's normally easy to bag Kāngdìng or Xīndūqiáo bus tickets, but otherwise buses are often full by the time they reach Lǐtáng. Tickets to points west are only sold the day of departure, once it has been verified that space is available. Minivans (around ¥40 more expensive than buses) loiter outside the bus station to fill the void. The quickest way north to Gānzī (¥110, around five hours) is by minivan via Xīnlóng. No scheduled buses run this route directly.

Buses run to:

Bātáng ¥63, 3½ hours, around 3pm
Chéngdū ¥221, 20 hours, 9am; via **Yǎ'ān** ¥170, 16 hours
Dàochéng ¥48, four hours, around noon
Kāngdìng ¥93, eight hours, two daily (6.30am, 7am); via **Xīndūqiáo** ¥68, six hours
Xiāngchéng ¥79, five hours, two daily (both around noon)

Xiāngchéng   乡城

☑ 0836 / POP 55,000 / ELEVATION 2977M

The valley town of Xiāngchéng (Chaktreng) is a good spot to break your journey into or out of Yúnnán province if you can't bear it all in one go. It benefits from a microclimate that keeps temperatures here slightly warmer than everywhere else around it, making it a particularly comfortable stop, with a number of small villages nearby that make for pleasant wandering.

◉ Sights

Bsampeling Monastery   BUDDHIST MONASTERY
(桑披岭寺, Sāngpīlíng Sì; 27 Tongsha Xiang, 同沙巷27号; ¥15; ⊙ 5am-10.30pm) Originally established in 1669, this collection of

golden-roofed monastery buildings at the top end of town commands fine views of the surrounding hills. Be sure to take the stairs up to the 2nd and 3rd floors of the main structure for great close-up views of the large Buddha statues within and an excellent rooftop vantage over the town, respectively.

To reach the temple follow the main road left from the bus station. As the road curves to the right just outside of town, look for a number of small paths to the left that wind up to the temple area.

Seven Lakes   LAKE
(巴姆七湖, Bāmǔ Qīhú) According to locals, this string of seven small iridescent lakes strung along a mountain valley makes an excellent full-day trip from Xiāngchéng. It's around 25km on the road towards Dàochéng to the signposted turn-off for the lakes, and another several hours' walk to the top of the valley.

🛏 Sleeping

Xiāngchéng's main thoroughfare is lined with guesthouses and hostels, though there's very little to fill the gap between basic options and higher-end tour-group hotels. Of the few that exist, **Sīqīng Gémǎcāng** (思卿格玛苍; ☑ 0836 582 9520; behind bus station, 车站右侧二楼; r ¥150; 🖧) has some of the best-value rooms in town.

✕ Eating

The main road is dotted with restaurants offering similar menus of Sìchuān favourites. For a change of taste head up the small street to the left just before the town square – a northern Chinese couple cooks up their hometown-style of dumplings at **Hēilóngjiāng Dōngběi Jiǎozi** (黑龙江东北饺子; ☑ 182 8362 6582; 9 Sangpi Jie, 桑披街9号; dishes from ¥10; ⊙ 8.30am-9pm; 🖧).

ⓘ Getting There & Away

Two buses leave daily at 6am. One goes south into Yúnnán to Shangri-la (Zhōngdiàn; ¥88, eight hours); the other goes to Kāngdìng (¥147, 12 hours). Note that tickets to Lǐtáng are not sold on the Kāngdìng-bound bus, even though it's en route; take a shared minivan instead (¥90, 4½ hours).

A passing bus to Dàochéng (¥46, three hours, 2.30pm) sometimes has seats, otherwise a shared minivan to Dàochéng is around ¥70.

NORTHERN SÌCHUĀN

Hiking, or even camping, in Jiǔzhàigōu National Park or heading out on horseback around Sōngpān are how most travellers experience the carpets of alpine forest, swaths of grasslands, icy lakes and snow-topped mountains of northern Sìchuān. Looping around towards western Sìchuān and Dānbā, take time as well for the stunning valleys and panoramic peak-filled landscapes of Four Sisters Mountain en route.

The Road to Gānsù

Those heading north out of Sìchuān into Gānsù province will need to bus-hop their way from Sōngpān or Jiǔzhàigōu. First stop is **Zöigě** (若尔盖; Ruò'ěrgài), a small Tibetan town with a distinct frontier feel. The grasslands here burst into life with wildflowers in late summer, but otherwise there are few reasons to linger.

There are plenty of eating and accommodation options on Shuguang Jie, with **Shǔguāng Jiǔdiàn** (曙光酒店; ☑ 0837 229 2988; Shuguang Jie, 曙光街; r standard/deluxe ¥100/120; 🛜) among the best of the lot for those spending a night in between buses. Turn left out of the bus station and walk 100m.

Zöigě buses go to Sōngpān (¥49, three hours, 10am and 2.30pm) and Lángmùsì (郎木寺; ¥25, two hours, 2.30pm), an enchanting monastery town straddling the Sìchuān–Gānsù border from where it's possible to catch onward transport towards Lánzhōu. Buses can be sporadic, especially when snow renders roads impassable. Zöigě is at 3500m and temperatures can plummet suddenly.

Sōngpān   松潘

☑ 0837 / POP 67,972 / ELEV 3014M

Horse trekking into the woods and mountains is the main draw of the laid-back, historic town of Sōngpān, a holdover from its role as a major trading centre on the Tea Horse Road (茶马路, Chá Mǎ Lù). The hiking is also good, so there's a healthy backpacker population to swap travel tales with.

Much of the old town has been rebuilt in recent years, but architecturally it still holds much of its visual appeal and finding the touches of true history hidden throughout make it feel even more special. In midwinter (December to March) Sōngpān slows down and some businesses close; however, even in the cold, horse trekking is still possible.

👁 Sights

Sōngpān's partially rebuilt **city wall** may be less than 10 years old, but its **ancient gates** are original Ming dynasty structures dating back some 600 years. Note the horse carvings at the foot of the two south gates, half swallowed up by the ever-rising level of the road. The only original part of the **old wall** is by the rebuilt **West Gate** (西大门, Xī Dàmén; ⊙9am-6pm), which overlooks the town from its hillside perch far above.

Two wooden **covered bridges** (古松桥; Gǔsōng Qiáo and 映月桥; Yìng Yuè Qiáo), the bases of which are genuinely old, span the Min River. On the western side of the Yíngyuè Bridge is **Guānyīn Temple** (观音阁, Guānyīn Gé) FREE, a small temple near the start of a hillside trail that offers good views over Sōngpān en route to the West Gate.

Shàngníbā Monastery   BUDDHIST MONASTERY
(上泥巴寺, Shàngníbā Sì) FREE A two-hour hike or horse ride east over the hills from Sōngpān, this small Tibetan Buddhist monastery sits in a picturesque valley among small minority villages. One-day horse trips often head out here for a roughly five-hour round trip, including a stop for lunch.

North Gate   GATE
(北门, Běi Mén; ⊙9am-6pm) From just west of the North Gate, it's possible to ascend onto a small restored section of the city wall for ¥150.

🏃 Activities

One of the most popular ways to experience the alpine forests and lakes surrounding Sōngpān is by signing on for a horse trek. Many people rate this experience as a highlight of their travels in this region. Guides lead you through otherwise unseen territory to remote campsites aboard not-so-big, very tame horses. Food and gear are all provided.

One of the most popular routes is a three- or four-day trek through unspoilt scenery to **Ice Mountain** (雪宝顶; Xuěbǎodǐng), a spectacular peak. A three-day trek to **Qīcáng Valley** (七藏沟; Qīcáng Gōu), recently opened to camping, passes several technicolour lakes.

Rates are all-inclusive of gear, horses and two meals. Your guides take care of setting up tents and cooking, unless you want to.

> ### MONEY TIPS
> Note that banks in Northern Sichuan cannot change foreign currency, though ATMs do accept foreign cards.

Sōngpān

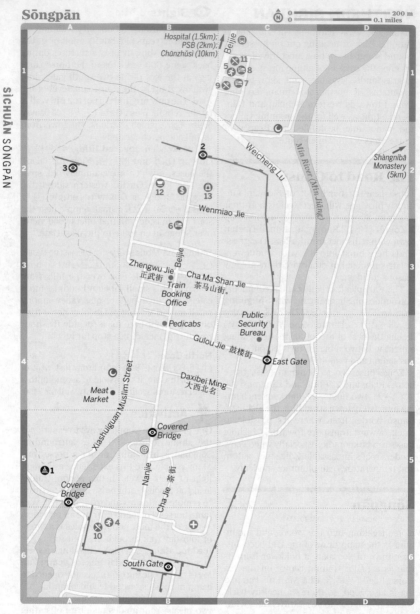

N
0 ———————— 200 m
0 ———————— 0.1 miles

Hospital (1.5km);
PSB (2km);
Chūnzhǔsì (10km)

Běijiē

Weicheng Lu

Mín River (Mín Jiāng)

Shàngníbā
Monastery
(5km)

Wenmiao Jie

Beijie

Zhengwu Jie
正武街

Cha Ma Shan Jie
茶马山街。

Train
Booking
Office

Pedicabs

Public
Security
Bureau

Gulou Jie 鼓楼街

East Gate

Daxibei Ming
大西北名

Xiashuiguan Muslim Street

Meat
Market

Covered
Bridge

@

Nanjie

Cha Jie 茶街

Covered
Bridge

South Gate

The only additional charges are park entry fees for some of the trips (you are told of these before you set out), and tips, should you be inclined.

The majority of travellers seem happy with their services, but we do sometimes receive reports of guides careless about environmental impact. Also, some travellers have had trouble getting refunds, particularly when the weather turned, which it often does. If you don't speak Chinese or Tibetan, we recommend booking through local and Chéngdū hostels, which will help you negotiate details such as the terms for a refund.

Sōngpān

The nearby hills are wonderfully good for hiking. One option is to hike around one hour up to the only remaining part of the original town wall, by the West Gate. There are three paths up: one starts beside the stream north of North Gate; another leads up the hill from the west end of Gulou Jie; while a third is accessed via Guānyīn Temple. Another option is to hike for about two hours to Shàngníbā Monastery in the eastern hills.

Qíqílè Mǎduì HORSE RIDING
(骑奇乐马队; ☑ 189 0904 3667, 0837 723 4138; www.517sp.net; Nanjie, Yingyue Xiang, 南街映月巷; per day per person from ¥220; ⊙ 8.30am-7pm) If you speak Chinese, you should enquire at this outfitter. They cover the usual local favourites and further afield to northerly Zöigê (若尔盖; Ruò'ergài; eight days) and southward to Hóng Yuán (红原; 10 days). Daily prices include food, tent rental and all other costs aside from admission to any national parks included in the route (which are outlined up front).

Shùnjiāng Horse Treks HORSE RIDING
(顺江旅游马队, Shùnjiāng Lǚyóu Mǎduì; ☑ 153 0904 6777, 0837 723 1064; Shunjiang Beilu, 顺江北路; per person per day all-inclusive ¥220-320) The most established union of guides in town has been leading tourists on horse treks for years. You can tailor trips from one to five days. Expect limited English-language skills. Guides take care of everything: you won't touch a tent pole or a cooking pot unless you want to. The only additional charge is entrance to the different sites and national parks visited on some trips.

However, in recent years we have received several complaints from readers about the company's overly aggressive attitude towards some guests when disputes about payment arise, and about the treatment of its horses. If you do decide to stay in their **guesthouse** (顺江自助旅馆, Shùnjiāng Zìzhù Lǚguǎn; ☑ 0837 723 1064, 139 0904 3501; Shunjiang Beilu, 顺江

北路; dm ¥30, r ¥120; 🛜) or go horse trekking with Shùnjiāng, make sure you are very clear about what you are getting, and for what price, before you commit to anything. For comparison you may want to also make enquiries with the less-established but well run Qíqílè Mǎduì, although they are less accustomed to dealing with foreign tourists.

🛏 Sleeping

Amdo Coffee House Inn HOTEL $$
(安多房子咖啡客栈, Ānduō Fángzi Kāfēi Kèzhàn; ☑ 139 9041 7006, English 135 1596 0964; Beijie, North Gate, 北街农行旁; s/d without bathroom from ¥200; 🛜) In a stylish wooden structure just inside the old town's north gate, this hip guesthouse packs in all the modern conveniences plus airport pick-up (¥120). Some rooms are small, so head downstairs to the wired cafe for real coffee (¥20) and a big window perfect for people-watching from 8am to 10pm. Room rates drop to ¥150 in low season.

Emma's Guesthouse GUESTHOUSE $$
(小欧洲青年旅舍, Xiǎo Ōuzhōu Qīngnián Lǚshě; ☑ 131 0837 2888, 0837 723 1088; emmachina@hotmail.com; Shunjiang Cun, 顺江村; dm ¥40-60, r ¥120-180, ste ¥200-300; 🛜) Knowledgable Emma runs this warm guesthouse, which is next to her family's wood-framed house down a quiet side street. The rooms are bright and clean with private bathrooms, and heaters and electric blankets for the cold months. Check in at Emma's Kitchen (p776).

🍴 Eating

Lǎo Wū Cháyuán TEAHOUSE $
(老屋茶园; ☑ 0837 723 3519; 15 Yingyue Jie, 映月街15号; tea from ¥5, dishes from ¥8; ⊙ 8am-11pm) Through an unassuming archway near the east end of Yìng Yuè Qiáo is this buzzing courtyard teahouse, a local favourite. The house special, spicy *liángfěn* (凉粉; ¥8), made of mung bean and potato starch, won

the prize for being the best in the region. The hours are a bit erratic in practice, but officially they're open from 8am to 11pm.

Song in the Mountain   CHINESE, WESTERN $

(山里子之歌川菜馆, Shānlizǐ Zhīgē Chuān Càiguǎn; ☑ 189 0904 3640; Shunjiang Beilu, 顺江北路; mains ¥18-45; ⊗ 8.30am-11.30pm; 🛜🍴) Run by the helpful Sarah Yang, this small restaurant serves a variety of simple but tasty Western and Chinese dishes at reasonable prices. Dozens of hand-written endorsements line the walls, testifying to its ongoing popularity with both local and foreign travellers.

Emma's Kitchen   CAFE, PIZZA $$

(小欧洲西咖啡餐厅, Xiǎo Ōuzhōu Xī Kāfēi Cāntīng; ☑ 131 0837 2888, 0837 723 1088; em-machina@hotmail.com; Shunjiang Beilu, 顺江北路; mains ¥18-58; ⊗ 8am-midnight; 🛜) Sōng-pān's main traveller hang-out is this laid-back cafe with wi-fi and fresh coffee (from ¥28), pizza and other Western fare, along with a range of Chinese dishes. Emma is exceedingly knowledgable and can sort out almost anything from laundry to tickets to picnic lunches for your horse trek, and leads on mountain-biking tours (from ¥220).

ALTITUDE SICKNESS

At elevations above 2800m altitude sickness and acute mountain sickness (AMS) are possible concerns that, while usually easily managed, can be fatal if left unattended.

It's important to give your body time to acclimatise as you proceed higher into the region, and to take heed of any signs of sickness as warnings to slow down and rest before proceeding any higher.

Early signs include:

➡ Headaches
➡ Trouble sleeping
➡ Nausea
➡ Shortness of breath

More serious warning signs:

➡ Confusion
➡ Difficulty walking
➡ Coughing up blood

If you or your travel partners experience any of these, particularly the more extreme signs of sickness, descend immediately to lower elevations and get medical help.

🍷 Drinking & Nightlife

Zūwū Heritage House   CAFE

(祖屋客栈, Zūwū Kèzhàn; ☑ 0837 723 1011; 45 Minshan Cun, 岷山村45号; ⊗ 8am-midnight; 🛜) Centred on a large tree-shaded courtyard, this combination teahouse/cafe/guesthouse is a chilled-out place to relax by day or a classy spot for a drink by night with drinks for all hours starting from around ¥20.

🔒 Shopping

Jīnmíngzhū Supermarket   MARKET

(金明珠购物中心, Jīnmíngzhū Gòuwùzhōngxīn; North Gate square, 北门广场; ⊗ 8.30am-9.30pm) At the foot of the square just inside the old town's North Gate, this supermarket is the best place in town to stock up on food for trips into the countryside.

ℹ Information

It is not currently possible to change foreign currency in Sōngpān. The ATMs at the **Agricultural Bank of China** (中国农业银行, Nóngyè Yínháng; Shunjiang Beilu, 顺江北路) accept Visa and MasterCard, though many travellers report problems accessing their foreign accounts.

Internet Cafe (沙巴克网吧, Shābākè Wǎngbā; old-town Nanjie, 古镇南街; per hr ¥10; ⊗ 24hr; 🛜) Upstairs off a side street on the southern foot of the central covered bridge. No English sign.

Public Security Bureau (PSB, 公安局, Gōng'ānjú; ☑ 0837 723 3778; East Gate square, 东门广场; ⊗ 8.30am-noon & 3-6pm) The PSB office can usually renew visas in one working day, though they may refer you to the new district (新区) main office (a ¥10 taxi ride) if the necessary personnel are not on hand. It's at the top of the square just inside the East Gate.

ℹ Getting There & Around

There's no public transport between Sōngpān and the nearby Jiǔhuáng Airport. A taxi should be around ¥100 (¥150 at night).

Buses leaving Sōngpān's **bus station** (汽车站, Qìchēzhàn) include:

Chéngdū ¥110, 8½ hours, four daily (6am, 6.30am, 7am, 12.30pm)
Dūjiāngyàn ¥107, 6½ hours, one daily (7.20am)
Huánglóng National Park ¥28, two hours, three daily (6am, 7am, 2pm)
Jiǔzhàigōu ¥40 to ¥46, 2½ hours, two daily (9am, 1pm)
Zöigê ¥50, three hours, one daily (6.20am)

While Sōngpān is not connected to China's rail network, the small **Train Booking Office** (售票处, Shòupiàochù; ⊗ 9am-5.30pm) in the heart of the old town can procure tickets for onward travel from ¥5 per booking.

Pedicabs wait on the west end of Gulou Jie (鼓楼街) to give rides, generally starting at ¥5.

Jiǔzhàigōu National Park 九寨沟风景名胜区

📞 0837 / POP 67,039 / ELEV 2175M

An enchanting Unesco World Heritage Site, **Jiǔzhàigōu National Park** (Jiǔzhàigōu Fēngjǐng Míngshèngqū; 📞 0837 773 9753; www.jiuzhai.com; incl bus adult/concession ¥310/200; ⊙7am 7pm May–mid-Nov, 8am-6pm mid-Nov–Apr, last tickets 4hr before closing) is one of Sìchuān's and even China's star attractions. More than two million people visit annually to gawk at its famous bluer-than-blue lakes, rushing waterfalls and deep woodlands backlit by snowy mountain ranges. The park's major sights are easily accessed on foot, via kilometres of well maintained boardwalk trails, or by bus. There are even opportunities to camp.

Jiǔzhàigōu means 'Nine Village Valley' and refers to the nine Tibetan villages scattered in the parklands. According to Tibetan legend, Jiǔzhàigōu was created when a jealous devil caused the goddess Wunosemo to drop her magic mirror, a present from her lover the warlord god, Dage. The mirror dropped to the ground and shattered into 114 shimmering turquoise lakes.

The best time to visit is September through to November, when you're most likely to have clear skies and (particularly in October) blazing autumn colours to contrast with the turquoise lakes. Summer is the busiest, and also rainiest, time. Spring can be cold but still pleasant, and winter, if you're prepared for frigid temperatures, brings dramatically frosted trees and frozen-in-place waterfalls, but also limited access to trails and an increased reliance on the park shuttle bus.

◉ Sights

It's still possible to get a glimpse of pristine nature for a moment or two at a time in this increasingly popular park, and even ballooning visitor numbers don't detract from the raw beauty of the sparkling lakes and rugged landscapes of the park's three main branches: the Zécháwā, Rìzé and Shùzhèng Valleys. Additionally, the restricted Zhārú Valley is open to those willing to pay a premium for an immersive ecotourism program.

Most travellers should visit the **Zécháwā Valley** (则查洼沟) first, since buses stop heading to the top around 2pm to 3pm. Ride for one hour and the full 18km to the foot of

Jiǔzhàigōu

◉ Activities, Courses & Tours
1 Ecotourism Program A2

😴 Sleeping
2 Angelie Hotel A1

🍴 Eating
3 Ā Bù Lǔ Zǐ...A2
4 Nuòrìlǎng Junction Tourist Service Center.....................................A4
5 Rúyìlínkǎ Càipǔ A1

ℹ Information
Agricultural Bank of China ATM .... (see 7)
6 Jiǔzhàigōu Park Entrance....................A2
7 Jiǔzhàigōu Visitors Centre A2

the 4350m length of **Long Lake** (长海; Cháng Hǎi), then walk back to **Five-Coloured Pool** (五彩池; Wǔcǎi Chí). It's possible to walk from here all the way back to the Nuòrìlǎng Junction (诺日朗中心站; Nuòrìlǎng Zhōngxīn

Zhàn) but travellers with limited time would be best advised to take the bus, especially during the low season when water levels are low in the rest of the lakes on this fork.

From Nuòrìlǎng Bus Station (p780), catch a shuttle for the roughly 19km ride to the **Primeval Forest** (原生森林; Yuánshēng Sēnlín) at the top of the **Rìzé Valley** (日则沟). Though not the most stunning section of the park, the 8km-long stretch of trail down from here to **Bamboo Arrow Lake** (箭竹海; Jiànzhú Hǎi) has some of the least-trodden trails. From here it's a short hike to **Panda Lake** (熊猫海; Xióngmāo Hǎi), **Five-Flower Lake** (五花海; Wǔhuā Hǎi) and **Pearl Shoals** (珍珠滩; Zhēnzhūtán); three of the park's most popular attractions for their crystal-clear water, variety of colours and, at the last, booming waterfalls with snowy peaks in the background. On the way keep an eye out for the path up to the **Tiger Mouth** (老虎嘴; Lǎohǔzuǐ), a cliff-top overlook of Five-Flower Lake that shows better than perhaps anywhere else in Jiǔzhàigōu the astounding array of colours that are possible in a single small lake.

It's around 3km from Pearl Shoals back to the **Nuòrìlǎng Junction and Waterfall** (诺日朗瀑布; Nuòrìlǎng Pùbù), and the top of the **Shùzhèng Valley** (树正沟). Most will skip the majority of this 14km valley, largely because buses tend to stop between 5pm and 6pm, after which the only option is to walk out or hire one of the very rare private vehicles as a taxi. There are a number of pretty lakes and three small Tibetan villages, however, and those with the legs to keep walking will find the paths largely free of visitors. Note that in some of the villages, especially **Shùzhèng** (树正寨), travellers may be approached by local families offering homestays from ¥100. This is officially against park regulations, and therefore is not recommended by Lonely Planet.

On the way out of the park, shuttles stop a few kilometres before the exit at **Zhārú Temple** (扎如寺; Zhārú Sì), a large Buddhist temple open to visitors from 2pm to 6pm, beyond which lies Zhārú Village and the restricted Zhārú Valley Ecotourism base. From the temple, it's a pleasant 15-minute walk back to the visitors centre.

Inside the park, overpriced snacks are available at any of the Tibetan villages and many of the shuttle-bus stops. For a full meal head to the pricey buffet of the **Nuòrìlǎng Junction Tourist Service Center** (诺日朗游客服务中心, Nuòrìlǎng Yóukè Fúwù Zhōngxīn; buffet from ¥68), or walk uphill about 400m to a row of small restaurants with mains from ¥18 to ¥58.

Seniors 70 and over and kids get in free but are required to purchase ¥10 visitor insurance. A ¥90 hop-on-hop-off bus fee is automatically included in admission for all visitors. During the low season (16 November to 31 March), admission tickets are valid for a second day of entry to the park.

HOW TO 'DO' JIǓZHÀIGŌU

Buy early Tickets are available from the visitors centre one day in advance, until 2pm. Drop by the park the afternoon before your visit and avoid the queues the next morning.

Start early Get to the park entrance just a few minutes after opening. The early jam will have cleared up, and you'll still avoid the crush of late-rising tour groups.

Go up first Since the most spectacular scenery is in the park's upper reaches, you'll see the highlights first if you take the bus to the top, then walk or ride down. Head first to either Long Lake or Grass Lake, work your way down to the Nuòrìlǎng junction, then go up the other fork. Later in the day you can see the lakes between Nuòrìlǎng and the entrance, or even double back to catch your first valley in a different light.

Get off the bus Trails run throughout the park; by walking, you'll steer clear of the biggest crowds – though they're by no means empty. The walking trails are generally on the opposite side of the lakes from the road, so you'll have more peace and quiet, too. If you have just a day, though, buses are required to see the entirety of both routes.

Pack a lunch Dining options inside the park are limited and expensive. If you bring your own food you can picnic far away from the masses and avoid spending any longer than necessary at the busiest points.

Take it easy Site elevations vary from 2140m to 3060m, which can be tough if you're not acclimatised. Ideally, spend a few nights in the region first to make the most of your time in the park.

🏃 Activities

As part of the park's **ecotourism experience** (九寨扎如沟生态旅游, Jiǔzhài Zhārú Gōu Zhēngtài Lǚyóu; ☏0837 773 7070, English 135 5148 2613; zharu.jiuzhai.com; 2nd fl, Heye Guesthouse, 荷叶迎宾馆二楼; 1/2/3 days from ¥560/1320/1960) visitors can hike and even camp inside the Zhārú Valley, just east of the main tourist areas. However, numbers are restricted and prices are high, so it won't be for everyone.

There are other great hikes all over this area, although not in the national park itself. One option is to hike around the hills near Zhuo Ma's Homestay, Zhuo Mǎ can advise you on good routes. She also arranges short horse treks (¥180, two hours) from the village.

🛏 Sleeping Eating

Angelie Hotel HOSTEL $

(三喜宾馆, Sānxǐ Bīnguǎn; ☏133 0904 3806; Péngfēng Village, 彭丰村; dm from ¥40, r from ¥200; ❋🛜) Angelie Hotel is equal parts hostel and hotel, and the friendly, English-speaking staff organise Huánglóng tours (¥120), cook Chinese and Western food, and book tickets – all the usual hostel stuff in a hotel-ish setting. Dorms offer incredible views of the mountains. From the park entrance cross the street, turn left and walk 400m.

★Zhuo Ma's Homestay HOMESTAY $$

(卓玛, Zhuómǎ; ☏135 6878 3012; www.zhuomajiuzhaigou.hostel.com; per person ¥200) A genuine Tibetan homestay, this pretty wood cabin in a tiny village about 10km from the main park has six simple rooms and a wonderfully accommodating family. There's a common bathroom with shower, and prices include three meals and pick-up from the bus station (otherwise it's around ¥60 in a taxi). There's also a new upscale ecolodge in the works.

Rúyìlínkǎ Càipǔ TIBETAN $

(如意林卡菜谱; ☏180 1577 8135; Péngfēng Village, 彭丰村; dishes ¥18-58; ⏱9am-11pm) Stop in for tasty Tibetan dishes (and beers) – the meat pie (牛肉烤饼; niúròukǎobǐng; ¥58) is extremely tasty, and large enough for breakfast leftovers in the park the next morning. To get here walk past Ā Bù Lǔ Zī away from the direction of the park; it's three alleys up, tucked away down on the right.

Ā Bù Lǔ Zī TIBETAN $$

(阿布氇孜藏餐, Ābù Lǔzī Fēngqíng Zàngcānba; ☏135 6878 3012; www.abuluzi.com; Péngfēng Village, 彭丰村; dishes from ¥39; ⏱11am-11pm) The fanciest Tibetan restaurant in Jiǔzhàigōu, this excellent establishment is run by the same family behind Zhuo Ma's Homestay (Zhuo Ma's brother, Ke Zhu, is a Lhasa- and Běijīng-trained chef). There's an extensive menu of delicious Tibetan dishes, and some Western ones as well. For a quick fix, there's an affiliated dumpling joint downstairs.

ℹ Information

A **China Construction Bank ATM** at the park entrance accepts foreign cards, as does the **Agricultural Bank of China ATM** (in Péngfēng Village), where you can also change cash.

The park has an informative multi-language website (www.jiuzhai.com). The **park entrance visitors centre** (沟口游客中心, Gōukǒu Yóukè Zhōngxīn; ⏱7am-2pm) is less helpful.

ℹ Getting There & Away

AIR

More than a dozen daily flights link Chéngdū with Jiǔzhàigōu Airport (officially, Jiǔhuáng Airport), which is actually in Chuānzhǔ Sì (川主寺), a small town closer to Sōngpān than Jiǔzhàigōu. Direct-flight routes in high season include Běijīng, Shànghǎi, Hángzhōu, Chóngqìng, Kūnmíng and Xī'ān.

Shuttle buses to Jiǔzhàigōu (¥50, 1½ hours) meet arriving flights and drop off at Mènghuàn Jiǔzhài parking lot (梦幻九寨停车场; Mènghuàn Jiǔzhài tíngchē chǎng), 4km west of the park entrance. A taxi from there costs about ¥10. Early arrivals also have the option of a shuttle to Jiǔzhàigōu via Huánglóng National Park (¥120, 1½ hours) with a four-hour stop for sightseeing before continuing on.

A taxi all the way from the airport is pricey during peak season – about ¥300 (over ¥500 after 11pm). Many hotels and hostels offer pick-up services for about the same price.

BUS

Jiǔzhàigōu Central Bus Station (九寨沟口汽车站, Jiǔzhàigōukǒu Qìchēzhàn) is just 2km east of the park entrance. Some buses arrive at Jiǔzhàigōu Xiàn's station (九寨沟县), 40km away. A taxi from Jiǔzhàigōu Xiàn to Péngfēng Village costs ¥40 to ¥100, depending on season and time of day.

Selected buses departing Jiǔzhàigōu Central Bus Station:

Chéngdū ¥140 to ¥155, 10 hours, 12 daily from 6.50am to 9.30am

Chóngqìng ¥250, 12 hours, one daily (7.30am)

Guǎngyuán ¥123, eight hours, one daily (6.30am)

Huánglóng National Park ¥48, three hours, two daily (7am, 7.30am)

Sōngpān ¥43, two hours, one daily (7.30am)

Note that you can travel to western Sìchuān, via Mǎ'ěrkāng (¥170, 8am) and Dānbā, without having to go via Chéngdū.

HUÁNGLÓNG NATIONAL PARK

A trip to **Huánglóng National Park** (黄龙景区, Huánglóng Jǐngqū; ☐ 0837 724 9166; www. huanglong.com; adult/student & senior ¥200/110, cable car ¥80; ⊙ 8am-5pm) is essentially a three- to four-hour, moderate hike up and down one small valley. However, the valley is stunning, with exquisite terraces of coloured limestone ponds in blues, greens, oranges, yellows and white. The best time to come from is June to October, ideally during mild July and August. Outside of this period, lack of water in the pools significantly reduces the visual impact of the park. At this elevation (3600m), always bring a jacket.

With smaller crowds than Jiǔzhàigōu, Huánglóng is certainly worth the trip in the right season. To see the whole park, walk 800m to the cable car (9am to 5pm), which drops you in a deep forest. The path leads you up a few kilometres to the start of the main sights, and then down again to the entrance – some 8km of long ascents and descents in all.

By the park entrance is a visitor centre with restaurant, teahouse and luggage check. Pack a picnic as bottled water costs ¥10 in the park. There are also a few expensive tour-group hotels nearby, but most people visit as a day trip from Sōngpān or Jiǔzhàigōu.

To get here, two daily buses depart Jiǔzhàigōu (¥48, three hours, 7am and 7.30am); travellers arriving on early-morning flights can take an airport shuttle (¥120, 1½ hours) directly to Huánglóng, where they will wait for four hours before departing for Jiǔzhàigōu. There's also one return bus to Jiǔzhàigōu (¥45, 3pm) and a minibus (¥120, departs when full) by the visitor centre. To get to Sōngpān, take the Jiǔzhàigōu bus and ask the driver to drop you at Chuānzhǔ Sì (川主寺; one hour), where you can catch a shared taxi to Sōngpān (¥60).

ⓘ Getting Around

Taxis ply the streets and don't use meters. Generally, rides within Péngfēng Village and to Jiǔzhàigōu Central Bus Station cost ¥10.

In Jiǔzhàigōu National Park, from **Nuòrìlǎng Bus Station** (诺日朗车站, Nuòrìlǎng Chēzhàn) catch a shuttle for the roughly 19km ride to the Primeval Forest (原生森林; Yuánshēng Sēnlín) at the top of the Rìzé Valley (日则沟).

Lángzhōng 阆中

☐ 0817 / POP 242,535

An endless sea of black-tile roofs with waves of swooping eaves, flagstone streets lined with tiny shops, and temples atop hills of mist overlooking the river. It's all here in the town of Lángzhōng, Sìchuān's capital city for 20 years during the Qing dynasty and now home to the province's largest grouping of extant traditional architecture.

◉ Sights

Imperial Examination Hall   HISTORIC BUILDING
(贡院, Gòng Yuàn; Xuedao Jie, 学道街; ¥55; ⊙ 8am-6.30pm) The best-preserved Qing-era imperial examination hall in China, with a number of in-character actors on hand to pose for photographs. On Xuedao Jie (学道街), which is parallel to Wumiao Jie, one block north.

Zhang Fei Temple   TEMPLE
(张飞庙, Zhāngfēi Miào; Xi Jie, 西街; ¥58; ⊙ 8am-6.30pm) This temple is the tomb of local boy Zhang Fei, a respected general during the kingdom of Shu and hero of the *Three Kingdoms* epics, who administered the kingdom from here until his murder in the year 221. It's on Xi Jie, a continuation of Wumiao Jie.

Feudal Government Office   HISTORIC BUILDING
(道台衙门, Dàotái Yámén; Xuedao Jie, 学道街; ¥40; ⊙ 8am-6.30pm) Dioramas inside this recreation of a Shu-era government office depict scenes of legal hearings, officials' lives and feudal-era prisons alongside captions (in limited English) describing the workings of the era's bureaucracy.

Jǐnpíng Park   MOUNTAIN
(锦屏山, Jǐnpíng Shān; ¥25; ⊙ 8am-6pm) Considered an essential element of the feng shui balance of ancient Lángzhōng and holy to Taoists, Jǐnpíng is dotted with pavilions, temples and caves. To get here, catch a ferry (¥3, from 8am to 6pm) across the river from the wharf just below the **Huáguāng Tower** (华光楼, Huáguāng Lóu; 21 Dadong Jie, 大东街21 号; ¥20; ⊙ 8am-6.30pm).

Jǐnpíng Gate   TOWER
(锦屏门, Jǐnpíng Mén; ⊙ 8am-6.30pm) FREE
Originally constructed in 1371 and renovated in 1767, the current version of Jǐnpíng Gate is a 2010 rebuild. Join art students sketching from the top in admiring the old town's slate rooftops from the concrete staircase just off Nan Jie, a street running parallel to Dadong Jie.

Zhōngtiān Tower

TOWER

(中天楼, Zhōngtiān Lóu; Wumiao Jie, 武庙街; ¥20; ⏰8am-6.30pm) For bird's-eye views of the city's rooftops and lanes, climb to the top of Zhōngtiān Lóu, a 2006 rebuild on the way to Zhang Fei Temple in the centre of the old town.

🛏 Sleeping & Eating

⭐ Tiānyī Youth Hotel

GUESTHOUSE $$

(天一青年旅舍, Tiānyī Qīngnián Lǚshě; ☎0817 622 5501; www.fshui.com; 100 Dadong Jie, 大东街 100号; r without bathroom ¥98-138, with bathroom ¥168-238; ❋@🛜) If you want to improve your geomancy, settle into this beautiful courtyard inn beside the Fēng Shuǐ Museum. The nice twin rooms are each inspired by a particular feng-shui element: earth, wood, fire, metal or water. The shared-bathroom twins and doubles are more simple, but are crisp and clean. Some have simple bedrolls (褥了; *rùzi*).

⭐ Ancient Hotel

HISTORIC HOTEL $$$

(杜家客栈, Dùjiā Kèzhàn; ☎0817 622 4436; 63 Xiaxin Jie, 下新街63号; r from ¥480; ❋@) The nicest rooms in this large wooden building with multiple courtyards are set around a back courtyard with an open-air stage (performances Friday and Saturday from 8pm to 10pm), and go for a discounted ¥295. Less-expensive rooms are slightly smaller and off the main courtyards, but share the same historical ambience (also discounted, to ¥148). Turn right off Dadong Jie just before Huáguāng Tower.

Chuānběi Liángfěn

SICHUAN $

(川北凉粉; ☎0817 622 6695; 90 Dadong Jie, 大东街90号; mains ¥7-38; ⏰8am-9pm) Outside the central old town just before the Fēng Shuǐ Museum, this busy restaurant is best known for the namesake bean-starch noodles, but the wide selection of Sìchuān-style favourites are all good.

ℹ Information

Bank of China ATM (中国银行, Zhōngguó Yínháng; cnr Dadong Jie & Neidong Jie, 大东街内东街的路口; ⏰24hr) At the top end of Dadong Jie; accepts foreign cards 24 hours and changes foreign currency from 9am to 5pm.

ℹ Getting There & Away

Buses from Chéngdū's Běimén bus station arrive at Lángzhōng's **main bus station** (七里客运中心汽车站, Qīlǐ kèyùn zhōngxīn qìchēzhàn), which also serves Dūjiāngyàn (¥115, four hours, 8am), Lè Shān (¥150, six hours, 9.30am), Yíbīn (¥148, six hours, 9.30am), and Chóngqìng (¥107, four hours, 8.30am, 10.50am and 3pm). Buses

return to Chéngdū (¥97, four hours, leaving frequently between 6.40am and 5.50pm).

Lángzhōng also has a smaller bus station, Bāshíjiǔ Duì (89队), which serves Guǎngyuán (¥57, 2½ hours, 8.20am, 9.50am and 2pm), from where you can catch trains north to Xī'ān or buses west to Jiǔzhàigōu.

From the Bāshíjiǔ Duì bus station, it's easiest just to walk to the old town. Turn left out of the station; after a couple of blocks turn right onto Tianshanggong Jie (天上宫街) and keep walking straight. Dadong Jie will be on your left. Wumiao Jie will be straight on through an ornamental archway.

ℹ Getting Around

Local bus 8 (¥2) connects the town's two bus stations via the old town. From Bāshíjiǔ Duì it's four stops (from the main station 10 stops) to the old-town stop at Yīqiáo Gǔchéng Rénkǒu (一桥古城人口). Walk up towards the Huáguāng Tower for Dadong Jie.

To explore the far side of the river, small boats (¥3) make the crossing irregularly from 8am to 6pm.

Guǎngyuán 广元

☎0839 / POP 2.54 MILLION

Those on their way to Xī'ān from Jiǔzhàigōu can take the most direct overland route via the midsized town of Guǎngyuán on the main Chéngdū–Xī'ān train line.

China's only female emperor, Wu Zetian, was born in Guǎngyuán during the Tang dynasty. **Huángzé Temple** (皇泽寺, Huángzé Sì; Zetian Nanlu, 则天南路; adult/student ¥50/25; ⏰8am-6pm), with its pavilions and 1000 carvings, is dedicated to her. Further north near the east bank of the Jiālíng River, **Qiānfú Cliff** (千佛崖摩崖造像, Qiānfú Yá Móyá Zàoxiàng; adult/student ¥50/25; ⏰8am-6pm) is a honeycomb of more than 7000 grotto carvings dating back 1500 years to the ancient cliff roads that linked Sìchuān to provinces further north.

If you need to stay the night, **Tiānzhào Hotel** (天罡马瑞卡酒店, Tiānzhào Mǎruìkǎ Jiǔdiàn; ☎0839 366 8888; 112 Jinlun Nanlu, 金轮南路112号; r from ¥148; 🅿❋@🛜) has smart rooms in a convenient spot. Turn right out of the train station; it's about two blocks on your right.

Bus services run to Chéngdū (¥111; four hrs; frequent, 9am to 9pm), Jiǔzhàigōu (¥106; 8½ hrs; two daily 6am & 10.20am), Lángzhōng (¥58; 2½ hrs; four daily – 10.30am, 11am, 2.50pm, 5.30pm) and Xī'ān (¥142; six hrs, two daily 10am, & 10.30am)

Destinations by train include Chéngdū (K; ¥47; five hrs; 20 daily from 12.06am to 11.36pm) and Xī'ān (K seat/sleeper ¥75/133; 10 hrs; nine daily, 2.22am to 11.01pm).

Chóngqìng

POP 30.17 MILLION

Best Places to Eat

➡ Zēng Lǎo Yāo Yú Zhuāng (p791)

➡ Mang Hot Pot (p790)

➡ Suzie's Pizza (p791)

Best Places to Sleep

➡ Travelling With Hostel (p789)

➡ Somerset (p789)

➡ Hóngyádòng Hotel (p790)

Why Go?

Chóngqìng (重庆) municipality may be a relatively recent creation, having been carved out of Sìchuān province in 1997, but with its eponymous city driving the economy of western China, it's now one of the most important regions in the whole country. And, despite its new name, the area it covers has played a significant role throughout Chinese history and remains a place of great natural beauty.

Thanks to the mighty Yangzi River (Cháng Jiāng), which powers its way through here, this region has long been one of strategic military importance. The river was responsible for creating one of China's greatest natural wonders, the magnificent Three Gorges.

Humans have left their indelible mark as well, with a panoply of ancient Buddhist sculptures, dozens of seemingly lost-in-time villages and, of course, the megalopolis that is Chóngqìng: one of the fastest-growing, buzzing cities in all China.

When to Go
Chóngqìng

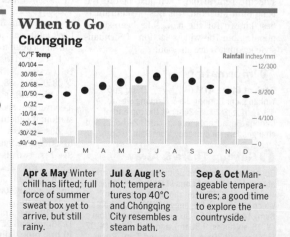

Apr & May Winter chill has lifted; full force of summer sweat box yet to arrive, but still rainy.

Jul & Aug It's hot; temperatures top 40°C and Chóngqìng City resembles a steam bath.

Sep & Oct Manageable temperatures; a good time to explore the countryside.

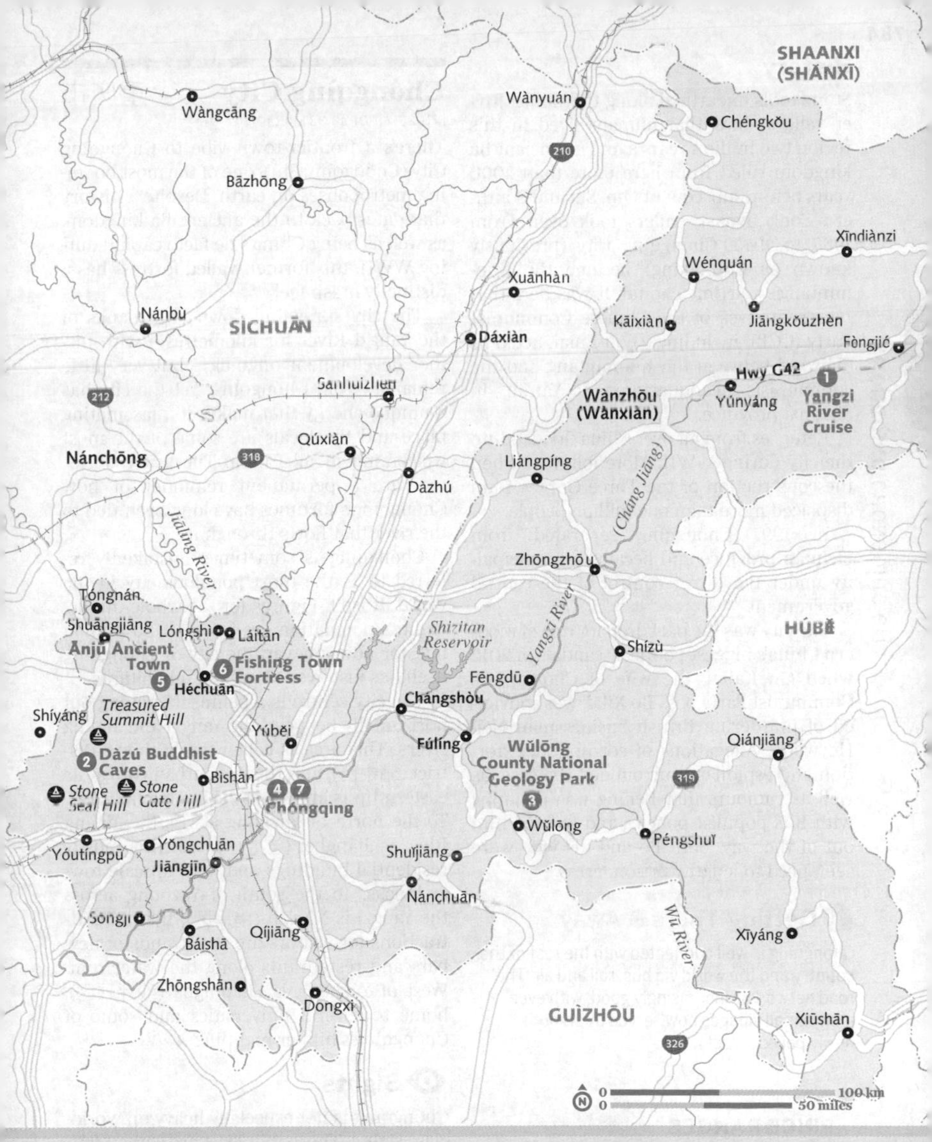
SHAANXI (SHĂNXĪ)
Wàngcāng
Wànyuán
Chéngkǒu
210
Bāzhōng
Xīndiànzi
Wénquán
Xuānhàn
Nánbù
SÌCHUĀN
Kāixiàn
Jiāngkǒuzhèn
Dáxiàn
Fèngjié
212
Sanhuizhen
Hwy G42
Yúnyáng
Wànzhōu (Wànxiàn)
1
Yangzi River Cruise
Qúxiàn
Nánchōng
318
Liángpíng
Dàzhú
(Cháng Jiāng)
Jiāling River
Zhōngzhōu
Yangzi River
Tóngnán
Shuāngjiāng
Lóngshì
Láitān
Ānjū Ancient Town
Shizitan Reservoir
Shízù
HÚBĚI
6
Fishing Town Fortress
5
Héchuān
Fēngdū
Treasured Summit Hill
Chángshòu
Shíyáng
Yúběi
Fúlíng
Qiánjiāng
2
Dàzú Buddhist Caves
Wǔlóng County National Geology Park
319
Stone Seal Hill
Stone Gate Hill
Bìshān
4
7
Chóngqìng
3
Wǔlóng
Péngshuǐ
Yóutíngpū
Yǒngchuān
Jiāngjīn
Shuǐjiāng
Nánchuān
Wū River
Sōngjì
Xīyáng
Báishā
Qíjiāng
Zhōngshān
Dongxi
GUÌZHŌU
Xiùshān
326
0 100 km
0 50 miles

Chóngqìng Highlights

1 Yangzi River Cruise (p51) Shifting down a gear or two as you float past the awe-inspiring Three Gorges.

2 Dàzú Buddhist Caves (p795) Gasping in wonder at the exquisite artwork of these ancient cliff carvings.

3 Wǔlóng County National Geology Park (p797) Exploring the wild waterfalls and karst formations of this mountain wilderness area.

4 Mang Hot Pot (p790) Tucking into the world's most mouth-numbing hotpot at this Chóngqìng favourite.

5 Ānjū Ancient Town (p798) Wandering the cobblestones of this exquisitely preserved Ming dynasty village.

6 Fishing Town Fortress (p794) Hiking the ruins of one of China's greatest battlefields.

7 Shāokǎo (p790) Pulling up a stool to enjoy these spicy meat, tofu and veggie skewers, one of Chóngqìng's greatest street snacks.

History

Stone tools unearthed along the Yangzi River valleys show that humans lived in this region two million years ago. The ancient Ba kingdom ruled from here more than 2000 years before subsequent Qin, Sui and Southern Song dynasty rulers took over. From 1938 to 1945, Chóngqìng City (previously known as Chungking) became the Kuomintang's wartime capital. It was here that representatives of the Chinese Communist Party (CCP), including Zhou Enlai, acted as 'liaisons' between the Kuomintang and the communists headquartered at Yán'ān, in Shaanxi province.

Refugees from all over China flooded into the city during WWII. More followed when the construction of the Three Gorges Dam displaced more than one million people.

In 1997 Chóngqìng separated from Sìchuān province and became a municipality under the direct control of the central government.

The city was the backdrop for one of modern China's biggest political scandals in 2012 when Gu Kailai, the wife of Chóngqìng's Communist Party boss Bo Xilai, was convicted of murdering British businessman Neil Heywood. Allegations of corruption, extortion and espionage surrounded the case, as well as rumours that Běijīng was unhappy with Bo's populist policies and wanted him out of the way. Both Bo and his wife were sentenced to lengthy prison terms.

ℹ Getting There & Away

Chóngqìng is well connected with the rest of the country and the world via bus, rail and air. The road network is increasingly good, with even many small villages now served by smooth, newly paved streets.

PRICE RANGES

Sleeping

$ less than ¥200

$$ ¥200–¥500

$$$ more than ¥500

Eating

$ less than ¥50

$$ ¥50–¥80

$$$ more than ¥80

Chóngqìng City 重庆市

🎧 023 / POP 13.33 MILLION

There's a frontier-town vibe to Chóngqìng City (Chóngqìng Shì), one of the most booming metropolises on earth. Despite a history that dates back to the ancient Ba kingdom, as well as being China's de facto capital during WWII, this former walled fortress has a distinctly brash feel.

The city sprawling down both banks of the Yangzi River for kilometres – with further development ongoing – but very little remains of old Chóngqìng. Yet the city has a unique energy that makes it a fascinating place and the locals are some of the most welcoming in all China. The gritty docks, too, are a permanent reminder of how Chóngqìng's fortunes have long been tied to the river that flows through it.

Chóngqìng is sometimes mistakenly referred to as the most populous city in the world. It isn't. Figures for the whole municipality's population are just over 30 million but, for now anyway, the city of Chóngqìng itself has just over 13 million inhabitants.

The city centre is a peninsula poking out horizontally between the Yangzi and Jiālíng rivers. This area is called the Yúzhōng District (渝中区), and the busy urban core at its eastern tip is known as Jiěfàngbēi (解放碑). To the north of Yúzhōng across the Jiālíng River is Jiāngběi (江北区), which is mostly residential buildings and new, upscale tower blocks. To the south of Yúzhōng across the Yangzi is Nán'àn (南岸区); the main attractions for visitors are the strands of new bars and restaurants along the waterfront. West of Yúzhōng is Shāpíngbà (沙坪坝区), home to several universities and some of Chóngqìng's hipper nightlife.

◉ Sights

Chóngqìng is not especially heavy on world-class sights. Those that exist are spread fairly evenly around the city.

Húguǎng Guild Hall MUSEUM
(湖广会馆, Húguǎng Huìguǎn; Map p786; 🎧023-6393 0287; Dongshuimen Zhengjie, 东水门正街; ¥30; ◉9am-5pm; ⓜXiaoshizi) You could spend several hours poking around the beautifully restored buildings in this gorgeous museum complex, which once served as a community headquarters for immigrants from the Hú (Húnán and Húběi) and Guǎng (Guǎngdōng and Guǎngxī) provinces, who arrived

Chóngqìng City

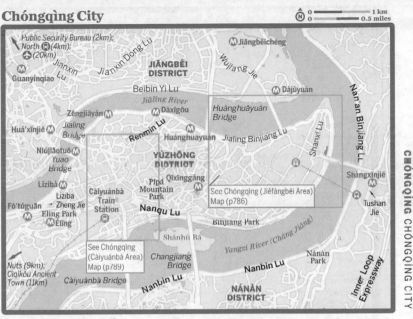

in Chóngqìng several hundred years ago. There are rooms filled with artwork and furniture, a temple, a teahouse and several stages for Chinese opera performances.

Luóhàn Temple
BUDDHIST TEMPLE

(罗汉寺, Luóhàn Sì; Map p786; Luohan Si Jie, 罗汉寺街; ¥10; ⊙7am-5pm; M Xiǎoshízi) Built around 1000 years ago, this still-active temple is now sandwiched between skyscrapers. A notable feature is the corridor flanked by intricate rock carvings found just after you enter the complex, but the main attraction here is **Arhat Hall** (罗汉堂; Luóhàn Táng), off to your right just after the corridor, which contains 500 terracotta arhats (a Buddhist term for those who have achieved enlightenment and who pass to nirvana at death).

Cíqìkǒu Ancient Town
OLD TOWN

(磁器口古镇, Cíqìkǒu Gǔzhèn; Shapingba; M Ciqikou, exit 1) The opportunity to snatch a glimpse of old Chóngqìng makes it worth riding out to Shapingba district, on the Jiālíng River west of the centre. Through the archway that is the entrance to the town, most of the buildings in this sprawling complex – many dating to the late Ming dynasty – have been restored. The main drag can feel like a carnival, complete with candied fruits and neon fairy wands for

sale, especially on weekends, but away from the central street, a living, working village remains.

You can easily lose yourself in its narrow lanes, peeking into homes and tiny storefronts. And there's plenty to eat here, both in the alleys and overlooking the river. It's also worth poking your head inside **Bǎolún Sì**, one of Cíqìkǒu's only remaining temples. Its main building is more than 1000 years old.

Hóngyá Cave
AREA

(洪崖洞, Hóngyá Dòng; Map p786; 56 Cangbai Lu, 沧白路56号; M Xiǎoshízi) Not a cave, but a theme-park-esque re-creation of the old stilt houses that once lined Chóngqìng's riverfronts, this 11-storey shopping, dining and entertainment complex anchors the city's tourism scene. Here, you can get a foot massage, buy a jade bracelet, eat a dinner of spicy skewers and down a beer at an international pub, all in one place. It's cheesy good fun, and at night, the lit-up complex is fairly spectacular.

Chóngqìng Ancient City Gates
RUINS

(古城门, Gǔchéngmén; Map p786) Sadly, only fragments remain of Chóngqìng's once-magnificent Ming dynasty city wall, which stretched 8km around the Jiěfàngbēi peninsula and was more than 30m tall in places.

Chóngqìng (Jiěfàngbēi Area)

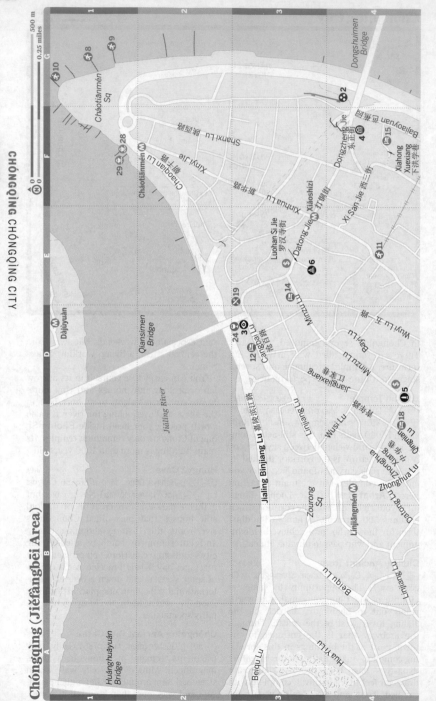

0.25 miles
500 m

Huánghuāyuán Bridge

Jiāling River

Qiánsīmén Bridge

Dàjùyuán

Jiāling Binjiāng Lu 嘉陵滨江路

Zòuróng Sq

Běiqū Lu

Huá Yī Lu

Běiqū Lu

Línjiāng Lu

Línjiāng Lu

Zhōnghuá Lu

Línjiāngmén

Dàtóng Lu

Zhōnghuá Lu

Wǔsī Lu

Mínzú Lu

Jiāngjiāxiàng

Qīngnián Lu 青年路

Xiāng 中华路

Zhōnghuá

Mínzú Lu

Bāyī Lu

Wǔyī Lu 五一路 北

Mínzú Lu

Cāngbái Lù 沧白路

Cāngbái Lu

Línjiāng Lu

Dàtóng Jiē

Xiǎoshízi

Xīnhuá Lu

Dǎtīng Jiē 打铜街

Luóhàn Sì Jiē 罗汉寺街

Xī Sān Jiē 西三街

Xī Sān Jiē

Xīnjiē Jiē

Chāotiānlù 储奇路

市中路

Shānxī Lu

Chāotiānmén

Cháoqián Lù 朝千路

Cháotiānmén Sq

Dōngzhèng Jiē
朱正街

Xiàhóng Xuéxiáng
下洪学巷

Bǎlíyuán

Dōngshuǐmén Bridge

2

4

15

6

19

14

3

24

12

5

18

11

10

8

9

28

29

Chóngqìng (Jiěfàngbēi Area)

Of the 17 gates that punctuated the wall before demolition began in 1927, two are still standing. The charming, moss-hewn **Dōngshuǐ Mén** (东水门; Map p786) is on a pathway beside the Yangtze River Hostel. Larger, and partly restored, is **Tōngyuán Mén** (通远门; Map p786; Ⓜ Qixinggang, exit 1), a short walk from Qīxīnggǎng metro station.

Three Gorges Museum
MUSEUM

(三峡博物馆, Sānxiá Bówùguǎn; Map p789; 236 Renmin Lu, Yuzhong; ⏰9am-4pm Tue-Sun; Ⓜ Zēngjiāyán, exit A) FREE This sleek museum showcases the history of settlement in the Chóngqìng region. There's the inevitable exhibition on the Three Gorges, including a model of the dam, as well as clothing and artwork relating to southwest China's minority groups. Some exhibits have better English captions than others.

Pípá Mountain Park
PARK

(枇杷山公园, Pípá Shān Gōngyuán; Map p789; 74 Pipa Shanzheng Jie, 枇杷山正街74号; ⏰6am-10pm) FREE For views of the city skyline, climb 345m Pípá Mountain Park, the highest point on the Chóngqìng peninsula. During the day, residents bring their songbirds to the park for air and group warbling.

🏃 Activities

While it is possible to cruise the Yangzi River in either direction, Chóngqìng is the most popular spot to start your trip along the river, mainly because of its proximity to the mighty Three Gorges. Both luxury and ordinary cruises depart daily and tickets for them are sold at travel agencies all over town. It's best to book a day or two ahead and, if possible, avoid Chinese public holidays when the boats get very crowded.

★ Rónghuì Hot Springs
HOT SPRINGS

(融汇温泉, Rónghuì Wēnquán; ☎023 6530 0378; www.cqrhwq.com; 171 Qingxi Lu, Shapingba, 沙坪坝区清溪路171号; entry ¥179; ⏰24hr; 🚼) The Chóngqìng area is famed for its hot springs, and Ronghui is the most popular and easily accessible hot spring spa inside the city limits. Visitors in swimsuits stroll the lushly landscaped grounds sampling dozens of spring-fed indoor and outdoor pools, some steeped with medicinal Chinese herbs, others luridly coloured and scented. Wandering pedicurists will be happy to service your tootsies as you lounge on a chaise or on the heated 'lava rock beds'. Massages start at ¥139 for 50 minutes.

There's a kid's water playground, but most families seem to just take the little ones right in the hot springs with them, inflatable duckies and all.

To get here, take the 224 bus from Shapingba station, or get a taxi to drop you off in front of the Radisson Blu next door. The Radisson is the best place to pick up a taxi after you're finished as well.

★ Yangzi River Cable Car
CABLE CAR

(长江索道, Chángjiāng Suǒdào; Map p786; Jiefang Donglu, 解放东路; one-way ¥10; ⏰7am-10pm; Ⓜ Xiǎoshízì, exit 5) A ride on the creaky old Yangzi River cable car is slightly disconcerting, but gives you a wonderful bird's-eye view of the murky waters and the cityscape beyond. It drops you off near the riverside bar and restaurant strip on Nan'an Binjiang Lu.

🛏 Sleeping

Chóngqìng has an enormous variety of sleeping options, from top-end international brands to backpacker hostels. Since the city attracts relatively few tourists, prices vary little throughout the year. Jiefangbei is the most central neighbourhood for sightseeing

---

CITY RIVER CRUISES

Chóngqìng looks best from the water, especially at night when the city flashes with neon. The so-called **two-river cruises** last for 60 to 90 minutes, leaving every afternoon (2pm to 3pm) and evening (7pm to 8pm) from Cháotiānmén Dock, and can be a fun way of getting an alternative view of this unique metropolis.

There are a number of boats offering the same service. The difference in prices reflects the quality and age of the boats. **Cháotiāngōng** (朝天宫, Cháotiāngōng; Map p786; Chaotianmen Guangchang, 朝天门广场; evening cruise ¥136), **Cháotiānmén** (朝天门, Cháotiānmén; Map p786; Chaotianmen Guangchang, 朝天门广场; evening cruise ¥158) and **Jīnbì Huánggōng** (金碧皇宫, Jīnbìhuánggōng; Map p786; Chaotianmen Guangchang, 朝天门广场; evening cruise ¥138) were the three most popular boats at time of research. Although there are cruises every day, not all boats run daily. The boats have no English signs and very little English is spoken. You can eat on board, although menus are in Chinese only and the food is pretty expensive (dishes ¥30 to ¥80). Prices listed are for evening cruises, which are much more popular (and more worthwhile). Expect to get tickets for as little as ¥40 to ¥50 for an afternoon cruise. Buy your tickets from the end of the jetty leading to the boat in question, or at any number of ticket sellers around town.

and eating; many of the best 'deals' on hotels found online mean you'll wind up in a far-flung business district.

★ Travelling With Hostel   HOSTEL $
(瓦舍, Wǎshě; Map p786; ☑ 023 6310 4270; 4th fl, Yuya Bldg, 7 Zhongxing Lu, 中兴路7号渝亚大厦4楼; r ¥64-95, tw/d/d with bath ¥280/290/325; ❇@🛜; M Jiàochǎngkǒu, exit 4) Still sometimes known by its former name, 'Green Forest Hostel', Travelling With is much nicer than its location, in a 4th-floor walk-up of a commercial building, might suggest. It's the only hostel in Chóngqìng with a relaxing social bar and common area, populated largely by young Chinese travellers. Friendly employees speak good English and are happy to help you book train tickets or tours. Rooms run the gamut from eight-person mixed dorms to doubles with private baths.

Deck 88 Hostel   HOSTEL $
(桃亭国际青年旅舍, Táotíng Guójì Qīngnián Lǚshě; Map p786; ☑ 023 6281 7796; 88 Jiahin Lu, 嘉滨路88号; dm/d ¥65/190-260; ❇@🛜; M Xiǎoshízi) This clean and pleasant hostel right on the riverfront sees more Chinese travellers than foreigners. Dorms are poky, but the private rooms are a decent deal for this part of town. Staff are friendly, although there's not much English spoken, and there's an amenable communal area with a bar.

To get here, take the lift at the Hóngyádòng complex on Cangbai Lu down to the ground floor, turn left and walk for 75m.

Sunrise Míngqīng Hostel   COURTYARD HOTEL $
(尚悦明清客栈, Shàngyuè Míngqīng Kèzhàn; Map p786; ☑023-6393 1295; www.cqsunrisemingqing.hostel.com; 23 Xiahong Xuexiang, down the steps from 26 Jiefang Donglu, 下洪学巷23号, 解放东路26对面; dm ¥69, tw & d from ¥300; ❇@🛜; M Xiǎoshízi) This renovated Qing dynasty courtyard hotel isn't a true hostel – there's no restaurant or cafe – but remains an atmospheric place to stay. Rooms are beautifully decorated but, like all courtyard places, they are dark and small, and guests complain about maintenance issues like broken bathroom lights. It can also be accessed by climbing the steep alley just to the west of Húguǎng Guild Hall.

Somerset   HOTEL $$
(盛捷解放碑服务公寓, Shèng Jié Jiěfāng Bēi Fúwù; Map p786; ☑ 023 8677 6888; www.somerset.com/en/china/chongqing/somerset_jiefangbei.html; 108 Minzu Road, 9F, Block B, Hejing Bldg, 民族路108号合景大厦B栋; ste from ¥500; ❇@🛜; M Xiǎoshízi) If you're staying in

Chóngqìng (Càiyuánbà Area)

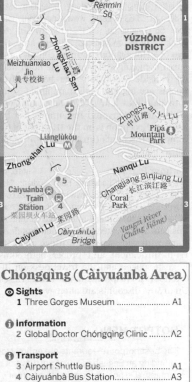

Chóngqìng (Càiyuánbà Area)

◎ Sights
1 Three Gorges Museum A1

ℹ Information
2 Global Doctor Chóngqìng Clinic A2

ℹ Transport
3 Airport Shuttle Bus............................. A1
4 Càiyuánbà Bus Station...................... A3
5 Escalator A3

Chóngqìng more than a day or two and hostels don't appeal, consider this welcoming suite hotel, perched high above the noise of Jiefangbei. Clean, spacious, modern suites, from studios to one- and two-bedroom apartments, come with kitchenettes and laundry machines. The large number of long-term international guests means there are communal activities, like Friday movie nights, not found in traditional hotels.

Xīnhuá Hotel   HOTEL $$
(新华酒店, Xīnhuá Jiǔdiàn; Map p786; ☑023 6355 7777; 9 Qingnian Lu, 青年路9号; tw from ¥828; ❇@🛜; M Jiàochǎngkǒu) This smallish, Chinese-style hotel has elegant, low-lit interior with spacious, well equipped rooms (TV, fridge, safe) but tiny bathrooms. Some English spoken. A stone's throw from

Liberation Monument so about as central as it gets. Routine 40% discounts make it a fair choice.

Hóngyádòng Hotel
HOTEL $$

(洪崖洞大酒店, Hóngyádòng Dàjiǔdiàn; Map p786; ☑023 6399 2888; www.hongyadong-hotel.com; 56 Cangbai Lu, 沧白路56号; tw & d from ¥650; ❄@☎; Ⓜ Xiǎoshízì) Sitting atop the massive Hóngyádòng tourism complex, this faux Chóngqìng stilt-house-style hotel hugs the cliffside overlooking the Jiālíng River. Rooms are big and well maintained, some with balconies and river views, and there are plenty of bars and restaurants just below you. Reception is on the 11th floor of the complex. Discounts (up to 30%) are generally available.

Harbour Plaza
HOTEL $$$

(重庆海逸酒店, Chóngqìng Hǎiyì Jiǔdiàn; Map p786; ☑023-6370 0888; www.harbour-plaza.com; Wuyi Lu, 五一路; tw & d from ¥888; ❄@☎☒; Ⓜ Jiàochǎngkǒu) Smart and large rooms at this centrally located and popular hotel. All come with wide-screen TV, fridge and safe. Wi-fi throughout and proper bathrooms. English spoken and the travel desk on the 3rd floor can help with Yangzi River cruises. Up to 50% discounts are often available.

🍴 Eating

Chóngqìng is all about hotpot (火锅; *huǒguō*): a fiery cauldron of head-burning *làjiāo* (辣椒; chillies) and mouth-numbing *huājiāo* (花椒; Sìchuān peppers) into which is dipped deliciously fresh ingredients, from vegetables and tofu to all types of fish and meat. It's a dish best sampled with a group. Indeed, hotpot restaurants tend to be among the liveliest you'll find.

As well as the local noodle dishes, another great thing to sample in Chóngqìng is *shāokǎo* (烧烤; barbecue skewers), the perfect point-and-eat street food. Just choose your skewers, hand them over and wait for them to come back spiced and grilled. Select from *dòufu pí* (豆腐皮; tofu skin), *xiǎo mántou* (小馒头; mini steamed rolls), *niángāo* (年糕; sticky rice cake), *qiézi* (茄子; eggplant/aubergine), and *jiǔcài* (韭菜; leek), among other ingredients.

Shāokǎo barbeque spots are found all over the city. Most *shāokǎo* places in Chóngqìng also do bowls of pigs brain (脑花; *nǎohuā*) as a side dish. We dare you.

Mang Hot Pot
HOTPOT $

(莽子老火锅, Mǎngzi Lǎo Huǒguō; Map p786; ☑023 6371 8492; Zhongxing Lu, 10 Wangyeshibao, 中兴路王爷石堡10号; dipping ingredients ¥6-26;

HOTPOT MENU

The best hotpot restaurants are entirely local affairs so you have about as much chance of finding an English menu as you have of being able to eat the thing without your nose running. (Do not underestimate a hotpot's bite. This part of China is renowned for fiery food, and it doesn't come spicier than hotpot.)

As with many dishes in Chóngqìng, the first thing to establish when ordering hotpot is how hot you want it – *bù là* (不辣; not spicy, but in Chóngqìng this will still be spicy), *wēi là* (微辣; mildly spicy), *zhōng là* (中辣; medium spicy), *zuì là* (最辣; very spicy) and *jiā má jiā là* (加麻加辣; extra, extra spicy).

Then you'll be given a menu checklist of raw ingredients that you will later cook in your pot. Here are some of our favourites for you to look out for on the menu:

➡ *yángròu juǎn* (羊肉卷; wafer-thin lamb slices)

➡ *féi niúròu* (肥牛肉; beef slices)

➡ *xiān máodǔ* (鲜毛肚; fresh tripe, usually lamb)

➡ *xiān yācháng* (鲜鸭肠; strips of duck intestine)

➡ *lǎo dòufu* (老豆腐; tofu slabs)

➡ *ǒu piàn* (藕片; slices of lotus root)

➡ *xiān huánghuā* (鲜黄花; chrysanthemum stalks)

➡ *tǔ dòu* (土豆; potato slices)

➡ *bǎi cài* (百菜; cabbage leaves)

➡ *mù'ěr* (木耳; mushroom)

➡ *kōngxīn cài;* (空心菜; water spinach)

CHÓNGQÌNG NOODLES

Chóngqìngers are particularly fond of noodles and you'll find noodle joints all over the region. They rarely have English menus or signs – just look for the character 面 (*miàn*; noodles) and you're good to go.

Specialities here include *xiǎomiàn* (小面) or *málà xiǎomiàn* (麻辣小面) – often eaten for breakfast despite being very spicy – and *liángmiàn* (凉面), which are delicious despite being served cold. Noodles in Chóngqìng are served by the *liǎng* (两; 50g). Two-*liǎng* (二两; *èr liǎng*) or three-*liǎng* (三两; *sān liǎng*) portions are most common. Expect to pay between ¥6 and ¥10 for a bowl. Remember: *wǒ néng chī làde* (I can handle spicy food); *bù yào tài là* (not too spicy, please).

Menu Decoder

➡ *málà xiǎomiàn* (麻辣小面; spicy noodles)

➡ *liángmiàn* (凉面; cold noodles)

➡ *niúròu miàn* (牛肉面; beef noodles)

➡ *jīdàn miàn* (鸡蛋面; egg noodles)

➡ *suānlà fěn* (酸辣粉; tangy glass noodles)

➡ *féicháng miàn* (肥肠面; pig intestine noodles)

🕙 11am-2am) A real locals' fave with some of the tastiest (and spiciest) hotpot in town. You sit on wooden benches around your table and bubbling broth. Expect to see male diners with their shirts off, beer bottles close to hand. It's just up the alley at the end of Qingnian Lu in the midst of the flower market on the left-hand side. There's a wooden sign with English and a picture of a man. No English menu, but the friendly staff will do their best to assist.

Liúyīshǒu Huǒguō   HOTPOT $
(刘一手火锅; Map p786; ☑023 6161 8555; 46 Cangbai Lu, 3rd fl, 沧白路46号南国丽景大厦3楼; dipping ingredients ¥5-34; 🕙10am-midnight; Ⓜ Xiaoshizi) The hotpot here is excellent, and the atmosphere is congenial, but the real attraction is the view, as you dine and gaze out across the Jiālíng River. You'll be pushed to find a river-view table at peak eating times, so perhaps come earlier or later than you'd usually eat. Take the lift to the right of Motel 168.

Zhào'er Huǒguō   HOTPOT $
(赵二火锅; Map p786; ☑023 6671 1569; 128 Jiefang Donglu, 3rd fl, 解放东路128号世纪龙门大厦三楼; dipping ingredients ¥4-36; 🕙 11am-2pm & 5.30pm-midnight) Highly popular, Zhào'er's hotpot is rightly lauded. There are various options: the nine-sectioned pot (九宫锅; *jiǔgōng guō*) allows you to separate the flavours of your raw ingredients (ideal if one of you is vegetarian), although the broth is shared; while the two-sectioned *yuān-yang guō* (鸳鸯锅) has a clear broth that is separated completely from the spicy one.

★ **Zēng Lǎo Yāo Yú Zhuāng**   HOTPOT $$
(曾老幺鱼庄; Map p786; ☑023 6392 4315; Changbin Lu, 长滨路; mains from ¥38-68; 🕙24hr) Outside, it's a seething mass of people crowded around tables. Inside, it's even more packed as you descend into a former bomb shelter – white-tiled walls and a rock roof. This Chóngqìng institution is a unique, utilitarian dining experience, with all stratum of society in search of the signature fish dish (鲫鱼; *jìyú*; carp) and the simply sublime spare ribs (排骨; *páigǔ*).

Xiǎo Bīn Lōu   SICHUAN $$
(小滨楼; Map p786; ☑023-6383 8858; Riyueguang Zhongxin Guangchang, 4th fl, 89 Minquan Lu, 民权路89号日月光中心广场4层; set menu ¥50-78; 🕙11.30am-2pm & 5.30-8.30pm) A gentle introduction to Chóngqìng cuisine, especially good for the spice-averse. Choose from a selection of small-sized dishes on display, or better still go for one of the set menus, either six or eight dishes. It's on the 4th floor of a semi-defunct-seeming shopping mall, but the interior is a spacious approximation of an old Chóngqìng eatery.

Suzie's Pizza   PIZZA $$
(苏蕊比, Sū Ruǐ Bǐ; ☑023 6531 2929; Three Gorges Sq, 12th fl UME Bldg, room 27 沙坪坝三峡广场玄地广场; pizza from ¥28-55; 🕙11am-10pm; Ⓜ Shapingba) English-speaking Suzie makes what many regard as the best pizza in town. The location, in a renovated apartment on the 12th floor of a residential tower, adds to the charm, as do the fake brick walls and

CHÓNGQÌNG'S STILT HOUSING

Once a striking feature of the Chóngqìng skyline, stilt houses (吊脚楼; *diàojiǎo lóu*) were in many ways the predecessor to the modern skyscraper; sprawling vertically rather than horizontally to save space. Their design also served to keep family units in close quarters despite the uneven terrain of hilly Chóngqìng. They were built on a bamboo or fir frame that was fitted into bore holes drilled into the mountain side, and their thin walls were stuffed with straw and coated with mud to allow for cooling ventilation in a city that swelters in summer.

Modernisation has turned stilt housing into a symbol of poverty and as a result it has all but disappeared in the city itself, with the last remaining stilt houses in the centre slated for demolition at the time of writing. But many survive in the villages around Chóngqìng municipality, with some fine examples in the alleyways of Sōnggài and especially by the river in Zhōngshān.

pictures of loyal customers chowing down on cheesy, gooey pies. To get here, enter the building lobby to the right of the McDonald's in Shapingba's Three Gorges Sq, and go to the second elevator lobby to get to the 12th floor.

🍷 Drinking & Nightlife

There are a string of riverside bars (酒吧; *jiǔbā*), cafes and restaurants on **Nan'an Binjiang Lu** (南岸滨江路); take the cable car over the Yangzi, then walk down to the river and turn left. From there, walk 15 minutes along the river or hop on any bus for one stop. Note: the cable car stops running at 10pm.

Dé Yǐ Shì Jiè (得以世界) is a public square surrounded by tacky bars, karaoke joints and the city's biggest nightclubs.

For traditional teahouses, head to Cíqìkǒu Ancient Town and look for signs for 茶园 (*cháyuán;* tea garden).

★ Cici Park   BAR
(西西公园, Xīxī Gōngyuán; Map p786; 1st fl Hongyadong, Jiabin Lu, 洪崖洞, 嘉滨路; beer from ¥15; ⏰5pm-late; Ⓜ Xiaoshizi) The most amenable bar in Chóngqìng, Cici's has a very chilled vibe and bohemian furnishings. Beers are affordable, mixers start at ¥30 and sometimes

there are DJs and live music. It attracts a mixed crowd of both locals and expats, some of whom like to roll their own cigarettes.

Cliff's Bar   BAR
(卡里佛咖啡吧, Kǎlǐfú Kāfēibā; Map p786; ☎13996296775; Hóngyá Cave, 10th fl, Jiefengbei, 洪崖洞10楼; ⏰5pm-2am; Ⓜ Xiǎoshízì) A party-happy mix of locals and foreigners down beers and cocktails at this convivial two-storey bar, on the 10th floor of the Hóngyá Cave (p785) complex. The dim interior is hung with international flags, and a rock band is usually jamming next to the bar.

Harp Irish Pub   BAR
(竖琴爱尔兰酒吧, Shùqín Ài'ěrlán Jiǔbā; ☎023-6880 0136; www.harpcq.com; Chóngqìng Tiāndì, 化龙桥重庆天地; draught beers from ¥35; ⏰2pm-2am; 📶) Not much to do with the Emerald Isle, but by far the best spot in town to catch live sport, especially the English Premier League, NBA and NFL. Strong selection of foreign brews and decent pub grub: fish and chips, pizzas, burgers and salads, as well as reasonable Mexican dishes. Also has a pool table and is nonsmoking.

It's located in a new complex of bars and restaurants a ¥25 taxi ride from the centre. There's another, smaller branch on the 9th floor of the Hóngyá Cave complex (p793).

☆ Entertainment

Nuts Live House   LIVE MUSIC
(坚果, Jiān Guǒ; Map p786; ☎133 5037 9029; https://site.douban.com/nutslivehouse/; Xinhua Rd, Deyi Fashion Mall, B1-21, 渝中区得意世界负一楼; beers from ¥15; ⏰7pm-2am; Ⓜ Jiàochǎngkǒu) Fabulous, below-ground club that's *the* place to catch live music. Local bands take to the stage every weekend, but it also hosts any act of note passing through town. Live music carries a ¥30 cover charge.

Chóngqìng Sìchuān Opera House   THEATRE
(重庆市川剧院, Chóngqìngshì Chuānjùyuàn; Map p786; ☎023-6371 0153; 76 Jintang Jie, 金汤街76号; tickets ¥20; ⏰2pm Sat) Holds a 2½-hour performance of Sìchuān opera every Saturday afternoon.

🛍 Shopping

For top-name brands, head to the glitzy shopping malls around the **Liberation Monument** (解放碑, Jiěfàngbēi; Map p786). For souvenirs, try the unashamedly touristy 3rd floor of Hóngyá Cave (p793), or head to Cíqìkǒu Ancient Town (p785).

Hóngyá Cave ARTS & CRAFTS
(洪崖洞, Hóngyádòng; Map p786; 沧白路56号; ⊙9am-10pm; ⓜXiǎoshízí) Built into the cliffs overlooking the Jiālíng, this massive complex is a Disney version of the tumbledown houses that once stood in its place. If you have just a day to try local food and pick up souvenirs, it's a fun place to wander around. The handicraft stalls are on the 3rd floor.

❶ Information

MEDICAL SERVICES

24-Hour Pharmacy (药店, Yàodiàn; Map p786; 63 Minquan Lu, 民权路63号; ⊙24hr; ⓜJiàochǎngkǒu) Western medicine, ground floor; Chinese medicine, 1st floor.

Global Doctor Chóngqìng Clinic (环球医生重庆诊所, Huánqiú Yīshēng Chóngqìng Zhěnsuǒ; Map p789; ☎023-8903 8837; Suite 701, 7th fl, Office Tower, Hilton Hotel, 139 Zhongshan Sanlu, 中山三路139号希尔顿酒店商务楼7层701室; ⊙9am-5pm Mon-Fri) A 24-hour emergency service is available by dialling the general clinic number.

MONEY

ATM (Map p786) ATM machine that takes foreign cards.

ICBC (Industrial & Commercial Bank of China, Gōngshāng Yínháng, 工商银行; Map p786; Minzu Lu, 民族路; ⊙9am-6pm; ⓜJiàochǎngkǒu) On Minzu Lu beside the Liberation Monument. Has a dedicated money-exchange facility.

HSBC (汇丰银行, Huìfēng Yínháng; Map p786; Minquan Lu, 民权路; ⊙9am-5pm Mon-Fri; ⓜJiàochǎngkǒu) Has a money-exchange facility.

POST & TELEPHONE

China Post (中国邮政, Zhōngguó Yóuzhèng; Map p786; Minquan Lu, 民权路; ⊙9am-6pm; ⓜJiaochangkou) You can top up your Chinese phone and buy SIM cards at the China Mobile store (open 9am to 9pm) on the 1st floor.

TRAVEL AGENCIES

Travelling With Hostel (壹院青年旅舍, Xīyuàn Qīngnián Lûshě, Yangtze River Hostel; Map p786; ☎023 6310 4208; 80 Changbin Lu, 朝天门长滨路80号; dm ¥35 50, tw & d ¥200; ❄@ⓢ; ⓜXiǎoshízí) Can arrange tours of all types and have better English-language speakers than the travel agencies and ticket offices around town. They charge minimal commission.

Harbour Plaza Travel Centre (海逸旅游中心, Hǎiyì Lûyóu Zhōngxīn; ☎023-6373 5664; 3rd fl, Harbour Plaza, Wuyi Lu; ⊙8am-10pm) Staff here are helpful, speak English and can book air tickets and arrange Three Gorges cruises.

PUBLIC SECURITY BUREAU

Public Security Bureau (PSB, 公安局, Gōng'ānjú; ☎023-6396 1994; 555 Huanglong Lu, 黄龙路555号; ⊙9am-noon & 2-5pm; ⓜTángjiā Yuànzi, exit 2) Extends visas. Accessed from Ziwei Zhilu (紫薇支路). Take metro Line 3 to Tángjiā Yuànzi (唐家院子). Leave from exit 2, go up the escalator, turn left then first right, then keep going until you see the large building with flags on your right (10 minutes).

❶ Getting There & Away

Chóngqìng is well connected to the rest of China via rail, bus and air. There are also numerous direct flights to other parts of Asia and beyond. If you don't speak Chinese, it's easiest to book rail and bus tickets at a hotel or travel centre, as there is no English spoken at the bus and train stations.

THE TOUGHEST PORTERS IN CHINA

Ever since the first Chóngqìngers couldn't bear the thought of carrying their buckets of water from the river up to their cliff-side homes, there's been a need for a special kind of porter. A porter who can lift more than his body weight and lug that load up and down hills all day long. A porter who can't use a trolley like in other cities, or a bike or a rickshaw, but instead works on foot using only the cheapest of tools: a bamboo pole – or 'bangbang' – and a length of rope.

Known as the Bangbang Army, these porters have been bearing the city's weights on their shoulders for hundreds of years, but their numbers really exploded in the 1990s when the government began resettling millions who lived along the Yangzi River. Many came from the countryside with little education and no relevant skills, and soon became part of the 100,000-strong workforce.

'Bangbang' porters earn around ¥50 per day to work in one of China's hottest, hilliest cities, lugging heavy loads up and down steep hills, although you'll also see them carrying people's shopping home on the subway.

Despite the wealth that's been pumped into the city in recent years (just look across the river at the Grand Theatre), the Bangbang Army continues to be an integral feature of Chóngqìng and porters are especially plentiful in the area close to the docks.

WORTH A TRIP

FISHING TOWN FORTRESS

Famed throughout China for being one of the great ancient battlefields, 700-year-old **Fishing Town Fortress** (钓鱼城, Diàoyú Chéng; ¥80; ⊙8.30am-6pm) is surrounded by rushing rivers on three sides and perched on top of a 300m-tall rocky mountain. This was the last stand of the Southern Song dynasty and famously, in the 13th century, the fortress withstood the mighty Mongol armies for an incredible 36 years, during which time an estimated 200 battles were fought here.

The fortress was protected by an 8km-long, 30m-tall double wall, punctuated with eight gate towers. Much of the outer wall and all the main gates remain today; some partly restored, others crumbling away. There is little here in terms of facilities (bring a picnic) but it's a fascinating and peaceful place to walk around; narrow stone pathways lead you through the forest, past Buddhist rock carvings, gravestones, bamboo groves, ponds, caves, the wall and its gateways and some fabulous lookout points. Sights not to miss include the serene, 11m-long, 1000-year-old **Sleeping Buddha** (卧佛; Wòfó), cut into the overhang of a cliff; **Hùguó Temple** (护国寺; Hùguó Sì), dating from the Tang dynasty, although largely rebuilt; and the **Imperial Cave** (黄洞; Huángdòng), an ancient drainage passage with steps leading down to it, clinging to the outside of the fort wall.

To reach the fortress, take a bus from Chóngqìng to Héchuān. Alternatively, numerous trains run from Chóngqìng North train station (¥12.50, 40 minutes) to Héchuān. There are no direct buses to the fortress. A taxi from the train station should be ¥25; from the bus station ¥10. The last bus back to Chóngqìng from Héchuān is at 6pm.

AIR

Chóngqìng's **Jiāngběi Airport** (重庆江北飞机场) is 25km north of the city centre, and connected to the metro system. As always, it's easiest to book online. Try www.ctrip.com or www.elong.net. Alternatively, buy tickets at the **China International Travel Service** (CITS, 中国国际旅行社, Zhōngguó Guójì Lüxíngshè; ☑ 023 6383 9777; www.cits.net; 8th fl, 151 Zourong Lu, 邹容路151号; ⊙9.30am-5.30pm Mon-Fri). Some English is spoken. Because of the high-speed rail link, there are no longer flights between Chóngqìng and Chéngdū. Direct flights include:

Běijīng (2½ hours, 12 daily)
Kūnmíng (70 minutes, 12 daily)
Shànghǎi (2½ hours, 12 daily)
Wǔhàn (90 minutes, nine daily)
Xī'ān (90 minutes, 10 daily)

BOAT

Chóngqìng is the starting point for hugely popular cruises down the Yangzi River through the magnificent Three Gorges.

Chóngqìng Ferry Port Ticket Hall (重庆港售票大厅, Chóngqìnggǎng Shòupiào Dàtīng; Map p786; Cháotiānmén Sq; ⊙7am-10pm; M Cháotiānmén) is the cheapest place to buy ordinary tourist boat tickets, and the only place that sells passenger ferry tickets. No English spoken.

BUS

Chóngqìng has several long-distance bus stations, but most buses use **Càiyuánbà Bus Station** (菜园坝汽车站, Càiyuánbà Qìchēzhàn; Map p789; M Lianglukou) beside the main (old) train station. There is no English spoken nor English signage, so you're best off buying tickets via an agency or a hostel. Destinations include:

Chéngdū 成都; Sìchuān ¥98, four hours, every hour, 6.30am to 8.30pm
Chìshuǐ 赤水; Guìzhōu (¥65 to ¥70, 4½ hours, six daily, 7.40am to 6.30pm
Dàzú 大足; ¥43, 2½ hours, every 30 minutes, 7am to 7pm
Héchuān 合川; ¥29, 90 minutes, every 30 minutes, 6.30am to 8.30pm
Sōnggài 松溉; ¥41, two hours, one daily, 1.20pm
Wànzhōu 万州; ¥111, 3½ hours, five daily from 8am to 5.30pm
Yíbīn 宜宾; Sìchuān ¥63 to ¥115, three to four hours, every 30 minutes, 6.45am to 8.30pm
Yǒngchuān 永川; ¥32, 90 minutes, every 20 minutes, 6.30am to 9.20pm

Buses for **Jiāngjīn** 江津; (¥24, 70 minutes, every 30 minutes, 7am to 9pm) and **Fèngjié** 奉节 (¥160, four to five hours, hourly, 7.30am to 8.30pm), where you can catch the Three Gorges ferry, leave from Lóngtóusì Bus Station (龙头寺汽车站; Lóngtóusì Qìchēzhàn), which is on metro Line 3 (station name: 龙头寺; Lóngtóusì).

For **Wǔlóng** 武隆; (¥60, three hours, every 40 minutes, 7.30am to 7.40pm), you need the Sìgōnglǐ Bus Station (四公里汽车站; Sìgōnglǐ Qìchēzhàn), which is on metro Line 3 (station name: 四公里; Sìgōnglǐ).

TRAIN

New, faster trains, including the D class 'bullet' train to and from Chéngdū, use Chóngqìng's new

North Station (重庆北站, Chóngqìng Běizhàn; Kunlun Dadao, 昆仑大道), but some others, such as the train to Kūnmíng, use the older train station at Càiyuánbà (菜园坝). There is no English in the stations, so if you don't speak Chinese try buying tickets ahead via an agency or hostel.

Destinations include:

Běijīng West 北京西; hard sleeper ¥393, 23 to 31 hours, five daily, 11.34am to 11.40pm

Chéngdū East 成都东; hard seat from ¥97, 1½ to two hours, 20 daily, 6.49am to 7.51pm

Guìlín 桂林; hard sleeper ¥270, 20 hours, one daily, 8.35pm

Kūnmíng 昆明; hard sleeper from ¥245, 18 to 19 hours, three daily, 9.24am, 2.12pm and 6.32pm

Shànghǎi 上海; hard sleeper from ¥510, 28 to 40 hours, three daily, 8.02am, 1.10pm and 4.29pm

Wǔhàn 武汉; hard sleeper from ¥260, 6½-7½ hours, three daily, 2.15pm, 6.18pm and 7.28pm

Xī'ān 西安; hard sleeper from ¥184, 10 to 11 hours, three daily, 10.05am, 12.45pm and 5.26pm

ℹ️ Getting Around

TO/FROM THE AIRPORT

Metro Line 3 goes from the airport (机场; jīchǎng) into town (¥4, 45 minutes, 6.22am to 10.30pm). Note, the metro is signposted as 'Light Rail' (轻轨; qīngguǐ) at the airport.

The **airport shuttle bus** (机场大巴, Jīchǎng Dàbā; Map p789; Shangqingsi Lu; ¥15, 45 min) meets all arriving planes and takes you to Meizhuanxiao Jie (美专校街), a small road off Zhongshan Sanlu (中山三路), via a couple of stops in the north of the city. Bus 461 goes from Zhongshan Sanlu to Cháotiānmén (朝天门). To get to the metro, turn left onto Zhongshan Sanlu and go straight over the large roundabout. Niújiǎotuó (牛角沱) station will be on your left.

Shuttle buses going to the airport run from 6am to 8pm.

A taxi is ¥55 to ¥70.

BUS

Local bus fares are ¥1 or ¥2. Useful routes:

Bus 105 North Train Station–Línjiāngmén (near Liberation Monument)

Bus 120 Cháotiānmén–Càiyuánbà Train Station

Bus 141 North Train Station–Cháotiānmén

Bus 419 North Train Station–Càiyuánbà Train Station

Bus 461 Cháotiānmén–Zhongshan Sanlu (for airport bus)

Bus 462 Zhongshan Sanlu (airport bus)–Liberation Monument

METRO

Chóngqìng's part-underground, part-overground metro system has four lines and links the Jiěfàngbēi peninsula with many parts of the city, including the airport and the two train stations. Fares are ¥2 to ¥10 and trains run 6.30am to 11.30pm. Signs are mostly bilingual and the electronic ticket-selling kiosks have an English option.

The metro station for Càiyuánbà Train Station is called Liǎnglùkǒu (两路口) and is accessed via one of the world's longest escalators (大扶梯, dà fútī; Map p789; ¥2).

TAXI

Taxi flag fall is ¥10. A taxi from Jiěfàngbēi to Shapingba should cost around ¥45.

Dàzú Buddhist Caves 大足石窟

The superb rock carvings of Dàzú (Dàzú Shíkū) are a Unesco World Heritage Site and one of China's four great Buddhist cave-sculpture sites, along with those at Dūnhuáng, Luòyáng and Dàtóng. The Dàzú sculptures are the most recent of the four, but the artwork here is arguably the best and in better condition.

Scattered over roughly 40 sites are thousands of cliff carvings and statues (with Buddhist, Taoist and Confucian influences), dating from the Tang dynasty (9th century) to the Song dynasty (13th century). The main groupings are at Treasured Summit Hill and North Hill.

👁 Sights

Treasured Summit Hill   ARCHAEOLOGICAL SITE
(宝顶山, Bǎodǐng Shān; ¥135, combination ticket with North Hill ¥170; ⊙8.30am-6pm) If you only have time for one Dàzú stop, make it this, the largest and most impressive of the sites. Of all the stunning sculptures here, which are believed to have been carved between 1174 and 1252, the centrepiece is a 31m-long, 5m-high reclining Buddha depicted entering nirvana, with the torso sunk into the cliff face. Next to the Buddha, protected by a temple, is a mesmerising gold Avalokiteshvara (or Guanyin, the Goddess of Mercy).

Treasured Summit Hill differs from other cave sites in that it incorporates some of the area's natural features – a sculpture next to the reclining Buddha, for example, makes use of an underground spring. At the time of writing, some of the sculptures were undergoing renovation.

The site is about 15km northeast of Dàzú town and is accessed by buses (¥3, 20 minutes, every 30 minutes, until 7pm) that leave from Dōngguānzhàn bus stop. Dàzú has two bus stations; old and new. Buses from Chóngqìng drop you at Dàzú's old bus station (老站; *lǎozhàn*). Buses from Chéngdū drop you at Dàzú's new bus station (新站; *xīnzhàn*). From either, take bus 101 (¥1) or a taxi (¥7) to get to Dōngguānzhàn bus stop.

Once at the site, it's a shadeless 25-minute walk from where the bus drops you off to the entrance to the sculptures. Buses returning from Treasured Summit Hill run until 6pm.

North Hill   ARCHAEOLOGICAL SITE

(北山, Běi Shān; ¥90, combination ticket with Treasured Hill Summit ¥170; ⊙8.30am-6pm) This site, originally a military camp, contains some of the region's earliest carvings. The dark niches hold several hundred statues. Some are in poor condition, but it is still well worth a visit. The pleasant, forested North Hill is about a 30-minute hike – including many steps – from Dàzú town; turn left out of the old bus station and keep asking the way. It's ¥20 in a taxi.

Buddha Vairocana Cave   CAVE

(毗卢洞, Pílú Dòng) The truly adventurous might like to catch a bus to the tiny town of Shíyáng (石羊), which has a little-seen collection of Song dynasty Buddhist rock carvings.

Buses to Shíyáng, in Sìchuān province, leave from Dàzú's old bus station. When you get there, keep asking for Pílú Dòng (毗卢洞); it's walking distance. From Shíyáng, you can continue by bus to Chéngdū.

Stone Gate Hill &
Stone Seal Hill   ARCHAEOLOGICAL SITE

If you're really into Buddhist rock carvings, try to get out to the rarely visited sculptures at **Stone Gate Hill** (石门山; Shímén Shān), 19km southeast of Dàzú, or those at **Stone Seal Hill** (石篆山; Shízhuàn Shān), 20km southwest of town. You'll have to take a taxi.

South Hill   ARCHAEOLOGICAL SITE

(南山, Nán Shān; ¥20; ⊙8.30am-6pm) This modest site really only has one set of carvings, but makes a nice appetiser before you delve into the main courses at North Hill and Treasured Summit Hill. It's behind the old bus station and takes around 15 minutes to walk to. It's ¥10 in a taxi.

🛏 Sleeping & Eating

Dàzú is usually visited as a day trip from Chóngqìng. If you plan to stay overnight, there are several hotels in Dàzú city, though many don't accept foreigners.

Bring snacks, as there's little to eat at most of the sites, though Treasured Summit Hill has a row of vendors hawking street food. Group tours of the area will include a lunch stop. Dàzú city itself has plenty of restaurants.

ℹ Getting There & Away

Buses from Dàzú old station:

Chóngqìng ¥43, 2½ hours, every 30 minutes, 6.30am to 6.30pm

Shíyáng ¥12, one hour, every 40 minutes, 7.20am to 5.40pm

Yǒngchuān, for Sōnggài (¥22, 90 minutes, every 30 minutes, 7.10am to 5.40pm)

Buses from Dàzú new station:

Chéngdū ¥102, four hours, five daily, 7.15am to 9.50pm

Lèshān ¥102, 4½ hours, one daily, 7.20am

Zìgòng ¥52, 3½ hours, two daily, 8am and 1.30pm

Láitán   涞滩古镇

📋 023

The main attraction in Láitán (Láitán Gǔzhèn), an ancient walled village overlooking the Qú River, is the towering **Láitán Buddha**, one of the largest in China, carved into a hillside and surrounded by more than 1000 ministatues.

Allow time to wander around the village, which is more than 1000 years old, checking out the small shops and eateries. Láitán *mǐjiǔ* (米酒; rice wine) is a local speciality.

Although it is possible to visit Láitán as a day trip from Chóngqìng, some people might like to stay the night within the village walls at one of several informal local guesthouses – ask around for information.

From Chóngqìng, change buses at Héchuān. You'll be dropped at the town centre bus station, called *kèyùn zǒngzhàn* (客运总站). Turn right out of this station and take local bus 202 (¥1) to the larger bus station on the edge of town, called *kèyùn zhōngxīn zhàn* (客运中心站); it's the last stop. From there, there are three direct buses to Láitán (¥10, 50 minutes, 10.10am, 1.35pm and 4.10pm) as well as regular buses to Lóngshì (¥9.50, 45 minutes). From Lóngshì, minibuses (¥2, five minutes) leave for Láitán from outside the bus station.

The last buses back to Chóngqìng from Héchuān are 6pm (from *kèyùn zǒngzhàn*) and 6.30pm (from *kèyùn zhōngxīn zhàn*).

Zhōngshān 中山

📷 023

Chóngqìng's once-ubiquitous stilt houses have all but disappeared from the city itself, but visit the gorgeous riverside village of Zhōngshān and you'll find plenty of them to gawp at. The old town (古镇; *gǔzhèn*) is essentially one long street lined with wooden homes on stilts above the riverbank. Walk down to the river and look up at the houses to see their support structures. You can also hike along the other side of the river.

There are a few simple local guesthouses in town (rooms ¥30 to ¥100). Look for signs saying 住宿 (*zhùsù*; lodgings). Most are small but clean and the more expensive rooms have their own bathrooms and cracking river views.

Several local restaurants and guesthouses will cook up a meal for you. Look for *gǔzhèn lǎolàròu* (古镇老腊肉; cured pork fried with green chillies; ¥35), *héshuǐ dòufu* (河水豆腐; river water tofu; ¥7) and *yě cài* (野菜, a type of spinach grown in the hills here; literally 'wild veg'; ¥10).

Zhào Shìkè (赵世客; 📱 138 8320 9407; r ¥30-80) is a friendly, family-run place. The best rooms have river views and tiny private bathrooms.

Most residents have turned their front rooms into storefronts. While some hawk souvenir trinkets, others sell locally made products such as chilli sauce or jugs of rice wine. Popular snacks include squares of smoked tofu (烟熏豆腐; *yānxūn dòufu*; ¥2) and sweet doughy rice cakes filled with ground nuts.

To get here from Chóngqìng, change buses at Jiāngjīn (江津), from where buses leave for Zhōngshān (¥15, one hour 45 minutes, roughly every 30 minutes from 6.30am to 4.45pm. The last bus back to Jiāngjīn is at 4.20pm. The last bus from Jiāngjīn back to Chóngqìng is at 7pm. You can also head south into Guìzhōu province from Jiāngjīn, via Zūnyì (遵义; ¥107, 3½ hours, 8.40am and 2pm), or north to the caves at Dàzú (大足; ¥51, two hours, 7.30am and 2.10pm).

Wǔlóng 武隆喀斯特

📷 023 / POP 351,000 (WǓLÓNG COUNTY)

Head three or so hours southeast of Chóngqìng City and you enter Wǔlóng (*Wǔlóng Kāsītè*), a dramatic landscape where deep ravines cut through the thickly-forested hills, while waterfalls plunge into mighty rivers, and jagged limestone karst formations rise up towards the sky. Mostly off the map for foreign travellers, the Wǔlóng County National Geology Park is a fantastic place to experience this wild scenery.

◉ Sights

Wǔlóng County National Geology Park   PARK
(武隆国家地质公园, Wǔlóng Guójiā Dìzhí Gōngyuán) 🏞 About 20km from the town of Wǔlóng, this fairy-tale landscape of river-run gorges, karst peaks, natural bridges and mossy caves lies deep within the mountains about three hours from Chóngqìng. The park has three main areas: Three Natural Bridges, Qingkou Tiankeng Scenic Area and Furong Cave. Most visitors come to Wǔlóng via organised tours from Chóngqìng, which usually stop at the Three Natural Bridges area, home to three magnificent natural bridges you can gaze at from beneath.

Travelling here independently is difficult; the easiest way is to hire a car and driver. If you do, you'll be able to visit some of the more far-flung areas, including the spectacular (and spectacularly neon-lit) Furong Cave.

Three Natural Bridges   NATURAL FEATURE
(天生三桥, Tiānshēng Sān Qiáo; ¥135) Towering above huge, hollowed-out karst formations, these natural bridges (you don't walk across them) are the highest in the world and utterly unique; you won't see anything like them anywhere else on the planet. A wander through the mossy, green gorge floor beneath the bridges takes about two hours. A vertiginous glass elevators takes you into the gorge; once down, sedan-chair carriers will try to offer you a lift and electric trams whisk the hiking-averse up the hill back to the bus terminal.

Furong Cave   CAVE
(芙蓉洞; ¥120; ⊙8am-5pm) This vast karst cavern is hung with dripping stalactites and lined with surreal rock formations, all lit up with multicoloured stage lights. Follow a guide along the raised pathway for some 2km, passing stone 'waterfalls' and rocks shaped like dragons or Buddhas.

From the Wǔlóng bus station, shuttle buses run to Furong Cave, or you can take a taxi. Admission prices are lower in winter.

Lóngshuǐ Gorge   CANYON
(龙水峡, Lóngshuǐ Xiá) A tall glass elevator lowers you to the floor of this deep gorge, created by the flow of an ancient river. It takes an hour or two to wander the length of the canyon,

exploring dripping caves and traversing elevated pathways over milky green waters. Numerous waterfalls along the rocky gorge walls mean you can expect to get a little damp.

🛏 Sleeping

Though most people visit as a day trip, there are a number of hotels in Wǔlóng city, and many more under construction.

Yúzhū Garden Hotel   HOTEL $
(武隆瑜珠花園酒店, Yúzhū Huāyuán Jiǔdiàn; ☑ 023 7779 9888; www.yuzhugardenhotel.com; 16 Furong Xi Lu, 芙蓉西路16號, Wǔlóng; r from ¥300) If you're planning on staying overnight in Wǔlóng town, this international-style riverfront hotel is your best bet. Despite luxury trappings, Western guests complain of hard beds, though that's par for the course in this part of the world. It has a Chinese restaurant, and is an easy walk from other restaurants and a market.

ℹ Getting There & Away

Visiting the park as an independent traveller is difficult. While there are regular buses to the unremarkable town of Wǔlóng from Chóngqìng's Sìgōnglǐ Bus Station, the park is 22km northeast of there and you'll need a taxi to reach it. You'll also require private transport to get around the park, which is massive. Each site also has a separate (and pricey) admission ticket, while the restaurants and hotels scattered around the park are expensive.

The best way to visit is on a day tour. Expect to pay ¥350 to ¥400 (bring your passport), which will include transport, lunch and admission to the Three Natural Bridges and at least one other site, usually Lóngshuǐ Canyon. Travelling With Hostel (p793) in Chóngqìng can arrange tours.

Ānjū Ancient Town   安居古镇
☑ 023

First established in 588 AD, Ānjū Ancient Town (Ānjū Gǔzhèn) is a riverfront village of beautifully preserved Ming and Qing dynasty buildings, and once an important centre of culture and scholarship. Today, the village traffics in its own history. Designated an official 'ancient town', its main streets have been refurbished and opened to tourism. Still, you're unlikely to see many non-Chinese faces, and on weekdays you're unlikely to see many other travellers at all. Beyond the city's preserved heart are ancient crumbling lanes where chickens roam, old ladies carry bundles on their backs and the smell of homemade noodles perfumes the air.

Although it is located within the borders of Sìchuān, Ānjū is generally reached from Chóngqìng.

◉ Sights

Ānjū City Temple   HISTORIC BUILDING
This pagoda-style temple overlooking the river is Ānjū's main worship site. It was under construction at the time of research, but still worth a visit for a gander at its dusty deities and the views over the water.

Whampoa Military Academy   HISTORIC BUILDING
Part of the Republic of China's army academy was relocated to Ānjū in 1938. Many of the commanders who fought the Japanese in WWII were trained here. Today you can visit the old stone barracks.

Huguang Guild Hall   HISTORIC BUILDING
(South St; ¥20) This sprawling guild hall features regular dance performances on its stage. Further towards the back are a number of rooms furnished with elaborately carved wedding beds and other period furniture.

Ānjū City Gates   HISTORIC SITE
Ānjū has nine city gates dating back to the Ming dynasty. One of the most spectacular and easily located is the South Gate, directly uphill behind the tourist office.

🛏 Sleeping & Eating

Ānjū boasts some half-dozen inns, including several in reconstructed historical buildings. No English is spoken. Expect to pay between ¥100 and ¥150 a night.

Restaurants throughout Ānjū serve regional specialities like eel stewed with chilli and spicy cold rabbit, as well as more familiar fare like hotpot, noodles, twice-cooked pork (古镇老腊肉; gǔzhèn lǎo làròu) and 'river water' tofu (河水豆腐; héshuǐ dòufu).

Lung Ying Inn   INN $
(迎龙客栈, Yínglóng Kèzhàn; ☑ 023 4585 2888; Xijie, 西街; r from ¥98) Overlooking the river, this two-story stone hotel has fairly modern rooms and a quiet lobby with windows open to the water.

ℹ Getting There & Away

To get to Ānjū, take a bus to Tóngliáng (铜梁), which takes about 90 minutes and costs ¥30. From here, take a taxi to Ānjū (about ¥20). Hiring a car to take you to Ānjū for the day will set you back about ¥800.

Xīnjiāng

POP 22.9 MILLION

Best Places to Eat

→ Altun Orda (p817)

→ Ōu'ěr Dáxīkè Night Market (p817)

→ Miss Chen's Pizza House (p811)

→ Marco's Dream Cafe (p826)

→ Rendezvous (p805)

Best Places to Sleep

→ Dap Hostel (p808)

→ Zabay Guest House (p812)

→ Doppa Youth Hostel (p831)

→ Turpan Silk Road Lodge (p808)

→ K2 Youth Hostel (p822)

Why Go?

China's largest province, Xīnjiāng (新疆) is the homeland of the Muslim Uighurs and a fast-changing region where ancient and modern grind up against each other in surprising ways. High-speed railways crothere ss the Martian landscapes linking cities in hours rather than days, and the regional capital Ürümqi is a forest of high-rise apartments and glass skyscrapers; while in parts of the Silk Road oases of Kashgar, Hotan and Turpan, life goes as it has for centuries, based around the mosque, the tea house and the bazaar.

Despite the enormous military and police presence here due to several years of ethnic unrest, Xīnjiāng is increasingly attracting visitors for its extraordinary natural beauty and fascinating Central Asian history and culture. In short, a visit to Chinese Turkestan makes for an exploration of China's past and its unsettled multicultural present, or simply a journey into some of the most sublime landscapes on earth.

When to Go
Ürümqi

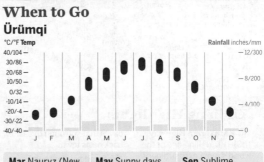

Mar Nauryz (New Year) festivals are held in Kazakh and Kyrgyz villages.

May Sunny days and cool breezes make this one of the best times to visit Xīnjiāng.

Sep Sublime autumnal colours at Kanas Lake and Hémù.

History

By the end of the 2nd century BC, the expanding Han dynasty had pushed its borders west into what is now Xīnjiāng. Military garrisons protected the fledgling trade routes, as silk flowed out of the empire in return for the strong Ferghana horses needed to fight nomadic incursions from the north. Chinese imperial rule waxed and waned over the centuries, shrinking after the collapse of the Han and reasserting itself during the 7th-century Tang, though central control was tenuous at best. A Uighur kingdom based at Khocho thrived from the 8th century and oversaw the Central Asian people's transformation from nomads to farmers and from Manichaeans to Buddhists.

It was during Kharakhanid rule in the 10th to 12th centuries that Islam took hold in Xīnjiāng. In 1219, Ili (modern Yīníng), Hotan and Kashgar fell to the Mongols and their various successors controlled the whole of Central

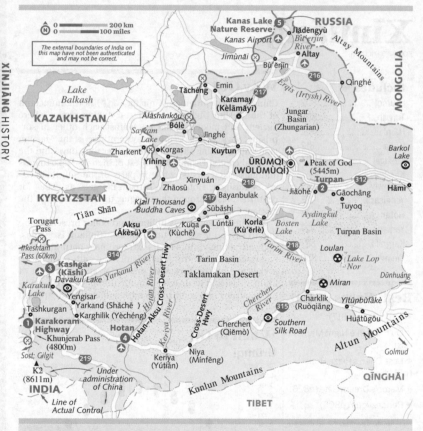

Xīnjiāng Highlights

1 Karakoram Highway (p819) Travelling one of the world's most extraordinary road journeys.

2 Turpan (p808) Exploring ancient ruins, mountain landscapes and Buddhist caves that surround this laid-back oasis town.

3 Sunday livestock market (p814) Witnessing Central Asia at its most authentic in Kashgar.

4 Sunday Market (p825)

Choosing between silk, spices, jade and carpets at Hotan's excellent bazaar.

5 Kanas Lake Nature Reserve (p830) Heading into Xīnjiāng's remote north to see magnificent mountain scenery.

Asia until the mid-18th century, when the Manchu army marched into Kashgar.

In 1865, a Kokandi officer named Yaqub Beg seized Kashgaria, proclaimed a short-lived independent Turkestan, and made diplomatic contacts with Britain and Russia. The Manchu army eventually returned and two decades later Kashgaria was formally incorporated into China's newly created Xīnjiāng (New Frontier) province. With the fall of the Qing dynasty in 1911, Xīnjiāng came under the chaotic and violent rule of a succession of Muslim and Chinese warlords, over whom the Kuomintang (the Nationalist Party) had very little control. In the 1930s and 1940s there was an attempt in both Kashgar and Ili to establish an independent state of Eastern Turkestan, but both were short-lived.

Since 1949, the Chinese government's main social goal in Xīnjiāng has been to keep a lid on ethnic separatism, dilute local culture, and flood the region with Han Chinese. Economically, the 'Develop the West' campaign has used the region's oil resources to ramp up the local economy. But this has led to an increase in Han settlers, which has exacerbated ethnic tensions. In a telling statistic, Uighurs once composed 90% of Xīnjiāng's population; today they make up less than 50%. But despite the unease and resentment of the native population, Xīnjiāng remained peaceful throughout the 1990s and early 2000s, even as China began to open up to the outside world.

However, in 2008, street protests and bomb attacks rocked the province, and in 2009 communal violence between Han and Uighur civilians in central Ürümqi led to around 200 deaths and 1700 injuries, according to Chinese police reports. Protests, riots and terrorist acts have continued to simmer ever since, though 2014 was a recent high watermark, with a knife attack at a train station in Kūnmíng that killed 29 and injured 143 being blamed on Uighur separatists. The next month, two attackers stabbed people at the Ürümqi train station before setting off vest explosives. A few weeks later, a suicide car and bomb attack on a market in Ürümqi ended with 31 killed and 90 injured. As a direct result, the Chinese authorities launched a huge security crackdown, the results of which can still be seen on any street corner in the province. Hundreds of Uighurs were sentenced to long jail terms and dozens were executed.

The current situation remains tense. As long as Uighur resentment continues to be fuelled by what they view as economic marginalisation, cultural restrictions, ethnic discrimination and outright oppression, violence looks likely to remain a threat in the restive province, though as travellers are highly unlikely to be caught up in this, there is no reason to avoid travelling to Xīnjiāng.

Climate

Xīnjiāng's climate is one of extremes Turpan is the hottest spot in the country – temperatures of 54°C have been recorded in the summer months – while the Tarim and Jungar Basins aren't much cooler. Spring (April and May) has much better temperatures, though frequent sandstorms can sometimes obscure the landscape. Winters (November to March) see the mercury plummet below 0°C throughout the province, although March is a good time to catch some festivals. Late May, June, September and (especially) October are the best times to visit.

Language

Uighur, the traditional language of Xīnjiāng, is part of the Turkic language family and is thus fairly similar to other regional languages, including Uzbek, Kazakh and Kyrgyz. While previously written using Latin letters, it is nowadays written using the Arabic alphabet. Learning a few words and phrases will mean the world to Uighur people you meet on your travels.

In general, the Han Chinese in Xīnjiāng don't speak Uighur, though there is a growing number of exceptions to this rule among the younger generation, as both languages are now compulsory in schools. Many Uighurs can't – or won't – speak Mandarin, and even fewer can read Chinese characters proficiently.

English is spoken by almost nobody, even in the hotel industry. Basic Chinese, a Chinese phrasebook or judicious use of Google

XĪNJIĀNG HISTORY

PRICE RANGES

Sleeping

$ less than ¥150

$$ ¥150–300

$$$ more than ¥300

Eating

$ less than ¥30 (for a main course)

$$ ¥30–50

$$$ more than ¥50

Translate are your only hope at communication in most cases.

ⓘ Getting There & Away

You can fly between Xīnjiāng and most of the larger Chinese cities, as well as to several Central Asian capitals and a couple of cities further afield, including Moscow, Tehran, Dubai, Seoul and Istanbul.

There are overland border crossings with Pakistan (Khunjerab Pass), Kyrgyzstan (Irkeshtam and Torugart Passes) and Kazakhstan (Korgas, Ālāshānkǒu, Tǎchéng and Jímùnǎi). The Qolma Pass to Tajikistan remains closed to foreign travel, sadly. All of these border crossings are by bus, except Ālāshānkǒu, China's only rail link to Central Asia. A new high-speed railway line to Pakistan is under construction.

Heading back into mainland China, the obvious route is the train line following the Silk Road through Gānsù. More rugged approaches are the mountain roads from Charklik to Qīnghǎi, and Karghilik to Ali (Tibet).

ⓘ Getting Around

Xīnjiāng is enormous (slightly bigger than Iran), and getting around usually takes time, money or both. The bus is the standard way to get around, and while bus journeys are cheap, new laws forbidding drivers to drive overnight and constant document checks along the way have increased travel times over the past few years. Buses are often sleepers, which means you're on either the top (cheaper) or bottom (pricier) bunk, arranged in three lines down the middle of the bus. On-board entertainment usually includes kung fu–film marathons cranked to the hilt. Shared taxis run along many of the bus routes, taking up to half as long, and costing twice as much as buses. Shared taxis only depart when full.

In 2015, the brand new Ürümqi–Lánzhōu high-speed railway line opened, massively cutting travel times within Eastern Xīnjiāng. In the west

of the province, train journeys are not nearly as fast, but they're a lot of fun, with overnight sleepers being the norm – a great way to meet locals.

Flying around the province can save a lot of time and tickets are often discounted by up to 60%. Be aware that flights can sometimes be cancelled for lack of passengers or due to bad weather, but if you have more money than time, this is a good way to claw some back.

CENTRAL XĪNJIĀNG

Bound by deserts and mountain ranges, much of present-day Central Xīnjiāng would have been completely familiar to Silk Road traders on the Northern Route to Kashgar. Today the largest and most important city in the region is Xīnjiāng's capital, Ürümqi, though for travellers the ancient cities around Turpan, the Tianshan mountains, and the Buddha caves of Kuqa are the bigger draws.

Ürümqi   乌鲁木齐

☑ 0991 / POP 3.1 MILLION

In Xīnjiāng's capital, Ürümqi (Wūlǔmùqí), high-rise apartments form a modern skyline that will soon dash any thoughts of spotting wandering camels and ancient caravanserais. The vast majority of its inhabitants are Han Chinese, and the city is one of the least typical of Xīnjiāng, though glimpses of the distant Tiān Shān mountains provide a taste of the extraordinary landscapes awaiting you elsewhere.

As a fast-growing Central Asian hub, the city does business with traders from Běijīng to Baku and plays host to an exotic mix of people. Indeed, it's hard to imagine where else in the world you'll see Chinese, Arabic,

---

DANGERS & ANNOYANCES

Due to the unrest and terrorism that has been a rare – but recurring – feature of life in Xīnjiāng since 2008, and which most recently peaked again in 2014, the province today has a very visible military and police presence, which can unnerve some. Foreigners are actually of little or no interest to these patrols, whose main function is to deter any public protest in the cities, and to check the passports of anyone travelling by train or bus. It's essential that you carry your passport with you at all times; you're simply asking for trouble otherwise. The main annoyance for travellers is the sheer amount of time that just getting into a train station can take, or the number of stops a long-distance bus is obliged to make, during which Chinese citizens will be required to disembark to have their IDs scanned. As foreign passports cannot be scanned in this way, you may or may not be required to disembark yourself; await instructions at each checkpoint. Note that you may not bring cigarette lighters, scissors or anything that could potentially be used as a weapon, however seemingly innocuous, onto any bus or train.

Latin and Cyrillic script so commonly side-by-side. This truly is Central Asia.

Ürümqi is not a historic city, but its museum is excellent and there are some atmospheric Uighur districts. Most travellers pass through the provincial capital at some point, and many find their stay to be surprisingly enjoyable.

⊙ Sights & Activities

★ Xīnjiāng

Autonomous Region Museum   MUSEUM
(新疆自治区博物馆, Xīnjiāng Zìzhìqū Bówùguǎn; 132 Xībei Lu; ⊙10am-6pm Tue-Sun) **FREE** Xīnjiāng's massive provincial museum is a must for Silk Road aficionados. The highlight is the locally famous 'Loulan Beauty', the first of half a dozen 3800-year-old desert-mummified bodies of Xīnjiāng's erstwhile Indo-European inhabitants. Other exhibits include some amazing silks, decorative arts, pottery and sculpture, a collection of white jade and an introduction to the traditions of each of the province's minorities. From the Hóngshān Intersection, take bus 7 for four stops and ask to get off at the museum (bówùguǎn).

Hóngshān Park   PARK
(红山公园, Hóngshān Gōngyuán; ¥10; ⊙dawn-dusk) More of an amusement park than a natural wonder, Hóngshān Park is nevertheless a great place to stroll and enjoy the good city views, particularly from the 18th-century hilltop pagoda, which has become something of a city icon. The main southern entrance is to the north of the Xīdàqiáo Intersection – it can be hard to find your way in elsewhere, as the park is fenced off with totalitarian relish.

People's Park   PARK
(人民公园, Rénmín Gōngyuán; ⊙7.30am-dusk) A green oasis with manicured grounds and a ceremonial pagoda in its centre, around which visitors may paddle little boats in the summer months. Like most parks here, its perimeters are sealed with high fences and razor wire: enter either via the park's north or south entrance.

★ Altus Expeditions   ADVENTURE
(⊉0991 230 0257; www.altus-expeditions.com) This American-run, Ürümqi-based adventure travel company offers tours all over Xīnjiāng, and specialises in cycling trips, for which it has a fleet of top-of-the-line mountain bikes. Expect physically challenging but safety-conscious adventure packages. Bespoke tours can also be arranged, and the owners know Xīnjiāng better than almost anyone else.

WHICH TIME IS IT?

All of China officially runs on Běijīng time (Běijīng shíjiān). Xīnjiāng, several time zones removed from Běijīng, however, unofficially runs duelling clocks: while the Chinese tend to stick to the official Běijīng time, the locals set their clocks to unofficial Xīnjiāng time (Xīnjiāng shíjiān), two hours behind Běijīng time. Thus 9am Běijīng time is 7am Xīnjiāng time. Most government-run services, such as banks, post offices, bus stations and airlines, run on Běijīng time, generally operating from 10am to 1.30pm and from 4pm to 8pm to cater to the time difference. Uighurs will often automatically use Xīnjiāng time – a political statement as much as anything else – so always double check which clock they're using when making plans!

🛏 Sleeping

White Birch
International Youth Hostel   HOSTEL $
(白桦林国际青年旅舍, Báihuàlín Guójì Qīngnián Lǚshě; ⊉0991 488 1428; jiangtao.xj@foxmail.com; 186 Nanhu Nanlu, 南湖南路186号; dm ¥40-60, d ¥160; @🖥🛜) There's usually at least one English-speaking staff member at this hostel who can help with local tips and onward transport. The hostel is a bit out of the centre but rooms are fine, if sparse, and there's laundry and a nearby park. It's the most popular spot for international backpackers, and as such it's the best place to meet other travellers. Email for bus directions or to arrange a pick-up from the airport.

Màitián International Youth Hostel HOSTEL $
(麦田国际青年旅舍, Màitián Guójì Qīngnián Lǚshě; ⊉139 9988 3785, 0991 459 1488; 726 Youhao Nanlu, 友好南路726号; dm ¥45-60, r ¥160; @🛜) On the east side of the Parkson Shopping Mall, the excellently located Màitián has simple doubles and dorms, some with private bathrooms, and a chilled out, brightly decorated common area and bar. The cheapest dorms share decent bathrooms and all the rooms get a regular cleaning. Book ahead in summer. The friendly staff speak almost no English.

Jǐnjiāng Inn   HOTEL $$
(锦江之星, Jǐnjiāng Zhīxīng; ⊉0991 281 5000; 93 Hongqi Lu; r incl breakfast ¥249; ❄🛜) This small and rather under-the-radar place is nevertheless a real find – it's in the heart of

Ürümqi

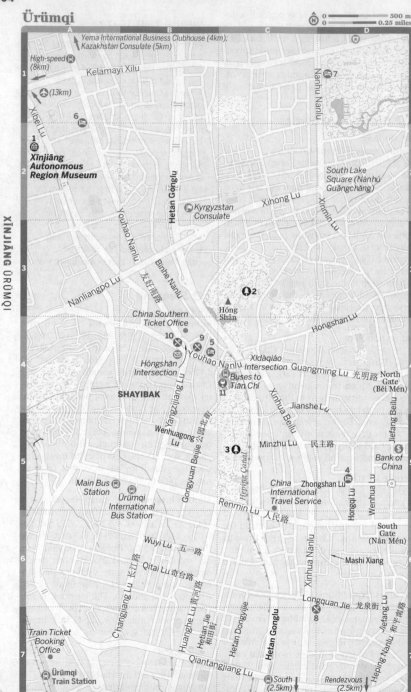

Yema International Business Clubhouse (4km);
Kazakhstan Consulate (5km)

0   500 m
0   0.25 miles

High-speed
(8km)

Kelamayi Xilu

(13km)

Xibei Lu

6

Nanhu Nanlu

7

1
**Xīnjiāng
Autonomous
Region Museum**

South Lake
Square (Nánhú
Guǎngchǎng)

Hetan Gonglu

Youhao Nanlu

Kyrgyzstan
Consulate

Xihong Lu

Xinmin Lu

Nanliangpo Lu

Binhe Nanlu

友好南路

China Southern
Ticket Office

2

Hóng
Shān

Hongshan Lu

10
9 5

Youhao Nanlu

**Hóngshān
Intersection**

Xīdàqiáo
Intersection   Guangming Lu   光明路   North
Gate
(Běi Mén)

SHAYIBAK

Buses to
Tiān Chí

11

Xinhua Beilu

Jianshe Lu

Jiefang Beilu

Yangzijiang Lu

Gongyuan Beijie 公园北街

Wenhuagong
Lu

Heping Canal

3

Minzhu Lu   民主路

Bank of
China

4
Zhongshan Lu

China
International
Travel Service

Hongqi Lu

Wenhua Lu

Main Bus
Station

Ürümqi
International
Bus Station

Renmin Lu   人民路

South
Gate
(Nán Mén)

Wuyi Lu   五一路

Qitai Lu 奇台路

Xinhua Nanlu

Mashi Xiang

Changjiang Lu 长江路

Huanghe Lu 黄河路

Hetan Jie 和田街

Hetan Dongyilie

Longquan Jie   龙泉街

8

Heping Nanlu 和平南路

Jiefang Nanlu

Train Ticket
Booking
Office

Ürümqi
Train Station

Qiantangjiang Lu

Hetan Gonglu

South
(2.5km)

Rendezvous
(2.5km)

XĪNJIĀNG ÜRÜMQI

Ürümqi and has spotless (if rather functional) minimalist rooms that come with TVs, kettles and bright red furniture. In fact, for this price, it's streets ahead of most of the other midrange accommodation options. Some English is spoken.

Sheraton Ürümqi Hotel　LUXURY HOTEL **$$$**
(喜来登乌鲁木齐酒店, Xǐláidēng Wūlǔmùqí Jiǔdiàn; ✆0991 699 9999, www.starwoodhotels.com; 669 Youhao Beilu; r from ¥607; ❀❄@
🛜🍴🛏) There is no shortage of luxury accommodation in Ürümqi these days, but all in all, the Sheraton's offerings are the best in town. The property has a prime location on the city's best shopping street and is actually quite affordable given its excellent facilities, English-speaking staff and high service standards. Rooms are big, well appointed and stylishly furnished.

✗ Eating

Ürümqi has the greatest variety of cuisine available in Xīnjiāng, whether it be the ad hoc Uighur street food that takes over entire neighbourhoods in the evenings, or the more formal restaurants offering cuisine from all regions of China and beyond.

Xīqí　NOODLES **$**
(西岐; Lanxiuyuan Xijie, 揽秀园西街; mains ¥15-22; ☺24hr) This fantastic place in the heart of the city is busy with hungry diners all day and night. The fare is simple but delicious: choose from a variety of steaming bowls of spicy noodles and delicious meat-filled buns. Point at what you want at the counter, pay and take your number and grab a booth.

Tous Les Jours　CAFE, BAKERY **$**
(多乐之日, Duōlè Zhī Rì; Youhao Nanlu, 友好南路, Parkson Shopping Mall; cakes from ¥5; ☺10am-10pm; 🛜) This excellent bakery serves up an impressive selection of baked goods, including croissants, fresh bread and cakes, and

does real coffee, fresh juice and a number of other things that might seem like a dream come true after weeks of Chinese hotel breakfasts. There are several other outlets around town, but this one is the handiest.

Rendezvous　INTERNATIONAL **$$**
(瑞都西餐厅, Ruìdōuxī Cāntīng; ✆0991 255 5003; 960 Yan'an Lu, 延安路960号; mains ¥32-65; ☺11am-10.30pm; 🛜) Well worth travelling out a little way for, this American-run cafe offers a welcome change of pace from Ürümqi's other dining options, with pizza, sandwiches, Tex-Mex and real coffee on the menu, not to mention an English menu, English-speaking staff and wi-fi. It's in the neighbourhood around the Russian market; take a cab.

Emin　UIGHUR **$$**
(✆0991 888 8462; Longquan Jie; meals ¥15-50; ☺8am-midnight) This is a great spot to try Uighur food if you fancy something more formal than a kebab stand. There's a pictorial menu to help you decide between various beef and lamb dishes; take a seat in the red-velvet chairs and enjoy the Uighur tea.

♡ Drinking & Nightlife

Fubar　BAR
(福吧, Fúbā; 40 Gongyuan Beijie, 公园北街40号; beer ¥25-35, mains ¥40-80; ☺7pm-4am; 🛜) This well known, long-running expat watering hole has a good selection of imported beers, and classic pub grub such as pizzas and burgers. It's popular with a crowd of young expat teachers and volunteers, making this a good place to get the up-to-date information about goings on in and around Ürümqi. There's a pool table and views into the People's Park.

ⓘ Information

Bank of China (中国银行, Zhōngguó Yínháng; cnr Jiefang Beilu & Dongfeng Lu; ☺10am-6.30pm Mon-Fri, 11am-3.30pm Sat & Sun) Can handle most transactions and has an ATM.

XĪNJIĀNG ÜRÜMQI

China International Travel Service (CITS, 中国国际旅行社, Zhōngguó Guójì Lǚxíngshè; ☑ 0991 282 1428; www.xinjiangtour.com; 16th fl, 33 Renmin Lu; ⏰ 10am-7.30pm Mon-Fri) This office runs tours around the province and can supply a driver and English-speaking guide.

China Post (中国邮政, Zhōngguó Yóuzhèng; Hóngshān Intersection; ⏰ 10am-10pm) The main branch handles all international parcels.

Public Security Bureau (PSB, 公安局, Gōng'ānjú; ☑ 0991 281 0452, ext 3456; Kelamayi Donglu; ⏰ 10am-1.30pm & 4-6pm Mon-Fri) You should be able to renew a visa here but processing times can be as long as three weeks, so it's really a last resort. It's far better to come to Xīnjiāng with plenty of time left on your visa for your travels.

🛈 Getting There & Away

AIR

Ūrūmqi Diwopu International Airport is a big domestic and international hub, and its international destinations include Almaty (Kazakhstan), Bishkek (Kyrgyzstan), Baku (Azerbaijan), Tbilisi (Georgia), Istanbul (Turkey), Islamabad (Pakistan), Seoul (South Korea), Dubai (UAE), Moscow (Russia), Dushanbe (Tajikistan), Tashkent (Uzbekistan) and Tehran (Iran). Some of these flights are seasonal, however, and schedules change with great regularity.

You can get to Ūrūmqi by direct flights from almost anywhere in China. Destinations within Xīnjiāng include Altay (Ālètài), Hotan (Hétián), Kashgar (Kāshí), Kuqa (Kùchē) and Tǎchéng and Yīníng. China Southern has the most flights to and around Xīnjiāng, with a central booking office in the **Southern Airlines Pearl International Hotel** (南方航空收票处, Nánfāng Hángkōng Shòupiàochù; www.global.csair.com; 576 Youhao Nanlu).

BUS

There are two long-distance bus stations in Ūrūmqi, one of which serves northern destinations, the other serves destinations to the south.

The main bus station (碾子沟长途汽车站, Niànzigōu Chángtú Qìchēzhàn; Heilongjiang Lu) has sleeper buses to the following:

Bù'ěrjīn ¥178 to ¥188, 13 hours, three daily (11am, 8pm and 8.30pm)

Hāmì ¥150 to ¥160, 10 hours, two daily (1pm and 8pm)

Yīníng ¥193 to ¥203, 10 to 13 hours, almost hourly (8am to 9pm)

BRT bus 1 runs from the train station to Hóngshān, passing Heilongjiang Lu on the way. Bus 44 or 906 pass directly in front of the bus station.

The south bus station (南郊客运站, Nánjiāo kèyùnzhàn; Xinhua Nanlu) has frequent departures to the following:

Cherchen ¥323 to ¥343, 22 to 24 hours, daily at 7pm

Hotan ¥370 to ¥390, 24 hours, hourly from 2pm, last bus at 8.30pm

Kashgar ¥260 to ¥280, 24 hours, 10 buses per day between 10.40am and 8pm

🛈 BORDER CROSSING: GETTING TO KAZAKHSTAN

Now that Kazakhstan no longer requires visas for most visitors, it's far easier to get onboard the daily 7pm bus to Almaty (upper/lower bunk ¥440/460, 24 hours) departing from **Ūrūmqi International Bus Station** (乌鲁木齐国际运输汽车站, Wūlǔmùqí Guójì Yùnshū Qìchēzhàn; ☑ 0991 587 8637; Heilongjiang Lu), next to the main bus station. Be at the bus station no later than 6pm and expect hold-ups lasting several hours at the Korgas customs post. A longer but more pleasant trip is to break the journey in Yīníng.

Trains currently depart Ūrūmqi twice weekly for Almaty, Kazakhstan (K9795, via Ālāshānkǒu), on Monday and Saturday at midnight. The journey takes a slow 33 hours, six of which are spent at Chinese and Kazakh customs. Hard/soft sleepers cost ¥892/1020.

There is also a Thursday service (9797) to the Kazakh capital of Astana leaving at midnight. Hard/soft sleepers cost ¥892/1094.

Tickets can only be purchased in the lobby of the Yà'ōu Jiǔdiàn (next to the train station), at the **booking office** (往阿拉木图火车票售票处, Wǎng Ālāmùtú Huǒchēpiào Shòupiàochù; ⏰ 10am-1pm & 3.30-6pm Mon, Wed, Thu & Sat). The booking office regulations are worth noting: on Monday you can buy same-day train tickets; Wednesday and Thursday you can buy tickets for the next Saturday and Monday; Saturday you buy same-day tickets and tickets for next Monday.

If you are unlucky enough to need a visa for Kazakhstan (most Westerners can travel there visa-free these days), you can apply for a 30-day tourist visa at the Kazakhstan Consulate (p1000) in Ūrūmqi. Visas take five days to be issued, cost US$25 and you need one passport photo and copy of your passport and China visa. Visas generally specify your entry date into Kazakhstan. If possible, apply for a visa in Běijīng or your home country.

Kuqa ¥150 to ¥215, 12 to 13 hours, every 30 minutes in the afternoon only

Turpan ¥45, 2½ hours, every 20 minutes

A seat in a shared taxi to Turpan costs ¥85 and takes around two hours; drivers can be found outside the bus station.

Bus 51 or 7 will get you to the south bus station from Hóngshān Intersection. BRT bus 3 will get you here from the South Lake Square (via People's Sq).

Tourists **buses to Tiān Chí** (return ¥50) leave from the northern end of People's Park.

TRAIN

Ürümqi's giant, super-modern **High-Speed Railway Station** (Shayibake 沙依巴克区) opened in mid-2016, and is now where all high-speed services to the city depart and arrive. The high-speed line stretches all the way to Lánzhōu, from where it's possible to connect to the rest of the Chinese high-speed rail network. Travel times have plummeted and rail travel in the region has never been so comfortable or convenient. Destinations from here include multiple daily services to Turpan (1st/2nd class ¥74/49, one hour), Hāmì (1st/2nd class ¥196/164, three hours) and Lánzhōu (1st/2nd class ¥626/514, 11 hours).

Ürümqi South (乌鲁木齐南站; Yashan Beilu), the city's old train station, handles all non-high-speed services to and from the regional capital, including services to the south of Xīnjiāng, as well as international connections to Kazakhstan.

Both stations are surrounded by an incredible number of security points, passport checks, ticket controls and X-ray points – even by local standards. Do give yourself plenty of time to get to either station before catching your train.

The following regular train routes depart from Ürümqi South, with hard/soft sleeper ticket prices:

Běijīng ¥566/915, 31½ to 39½ hours, two daily

Hotan ¥316/553, 25 hours, one daily

Kashgar ¥303/494 16¾ to 24½ hours, four daily

Kuqa ¥194/285, eight to 12½ hours, six daily

Yīníng ¥132/237, 6½ to 10 hours, six daily

ⓘ Getting Around

The airport is 16km northwest of the centre; a taxi to central Ürümqi costs about ¥40 to ¥50. Avoid the touts inside the terminal and head for the official taxi stand outside, where drivers will automatically use a meter. An airport bus (¥10) runs straight south through town via Hóngshān Intersection to the train station every 30 minutes. In the city centre, an airport shuttle (¥15, free for China Southern passengers) leaves from the Southern Airlines Pearl International Hotel every 30 minutes starting at 7.30am. You'll need to arrive at least 10 minutes earlier to get a seat.

A subway system was under construction at the time of writing and was proving massively disruptive to traffic in the city. Its first line is expected to open in 2019, and will connect the airport to the city centre and then to the south bus station.

The fastest and most useful buses are the BRT (Bus Rapid Transit) expresses, which have their very own bus lanes. Sadly they're very hard for travellers to use as maps and signage are posted only in Chinese and Uighur. BRT 1 runs from the railway station to Hóngshān Intersection and then north up Beijing Nanlu. BRT 3 runs from the south bus station to People's Sq and the South Lake Sq. Fares are a flat ¥1, drop a ¥1 note into the box at the ticket gates.

Other useful buses (¥1, pay the driver as you board, no change given) include bus 7, which runs up Xinhua Lu from the south bus station through the Xīdàqiáo and Hóngshān Intersections, and bus 52 from the train station to Hóngshān Intersection.

Taxis are everywhere and cost a standard ¥10 per journey for the first few kilometres, rising quickly after that.

Tiān Chí   天池

The rugged Tiān Shān range was well known to travellers along the northern Silk Road, who had to traverse its southern edge if they had any hope of making progress. Modern travellers have it far easier and plan trips into the mountains for fun, especially to stunning Tiān Chí (Heaven Lake ¥100). This high-altitude lake is extremely popular (to the point that many old Xīnjiāng hands stay away in despair at the all-encompassing nature of mass Chinese tourism here), but you can still escape the worst of the crowds, who either stick to the paved paths on the northern end or ride overpriced boats across the lake. Stay overnight to get a few hours of quiet in the morning before the tour buses arrive.

Two thousand metres up in the Tiān Shān range is Tiān Chí, a small, long, steely-blue lake nestled below the view-grabbing 5445m **Peak of God** (博格达峰; Bógédá Fēng). Scattered across the alpine pine and spruce-covered slopes are Kazakh yurts and lots of sheep. It was a paradise described in Vikram Seth's wonderful travelogue *From Heaven Lake*; and still is for some.

In late May, Kazakhs set up yurts around the lake for tourists at ¥50 to ¥80 per person in a shared yurt for up to 10 people; English-speaking **Rashit** (☏138 9964 1550; twin ¥150, with meals ¥200) is a popular host for backpackers and can arrange for a car to pick you up at the ticket booth. The yurt owners sometimes require ID, so make sure to bring your passport. Alternatively, you can camp at the lake but do so away from the main areas.

Regardless of the temperature in Ürümqi, take warm clothes and rain gear, as the weather at the lake can be unpredictable.

ℹ Getting There & Around

Tourist buses to the Tiān Chí main gate leave Ürümqi at 9am from the north gate of People's Park, and return around 7pm. Buy your ticket from **Xinjiang Xinda Travel** (☑ 181 6791 8556, 0991 5566 0035; round trip ¥50) inside the small pagoda next to the entrance to the park.

Buses stop at major hotels on the way out of the city to pick up passengers before leaving town. In the low season they may not run at all. The return fare is ¥50 and the trip takes about 2½ hours. Expect to stop at several awful tourist shopping traps along the way, to the delight of your fellow travellers. As there is no alternative transport option, unless you hire a driver, you have little choice but to use this service.

From the main gate (where you purchase a ticket), all travellers must take the park's own bus (¥90, every 10 to 15 minutes) for the 30-minute ride to another parking lot, which itself is still 1km before the lake. You can walk from the final lot or take a shuttle (¥10).

Turpan　吐鲁番

☑ 0995 / POP 650,000

Turpan (Tǔlǔfān) is China's Death Valley. At 154m below sea level, it's the second-lowest depression in the world and the hottest spot in China. In July and August, temperatures soar above 40°C and even 50°C, forcing the local population to sleep on their roofs and visiting tourists into a state of semi-torpor.

Despite the heat, the ground water and fertile soil of the Turpan depression has made it a veritable oasis in the desert, evidenced by the nearby centuries-old remains of ancient cities, imperial garrisons and Buddhist caves. The city itself has a mellow vibe to it, and recovering from a day's sightseeing over a cold Xīnjiāng beer under the grape vines on a warm summer evening is one of the joys of travelling through the province.

◉ Sights

Turpan Museum　　　　　　　　MUSEUM
(吐鲁番博物馆; Tǔlǔfān Bówùguǎn; Laocheng Donglu, 老城东路; ⊙10am-7pm Tue-Sun) FREE Xīnjiāng's second-largest museum houses a rich collection of relics recovered from archaeological sites across the Turpan Basin, including a superb collection of dinosaur fossils, dinosaur eggs and various species

of ancient rhino. Upstairs there's a ghoulish gallery of local mummies. Pop in here before signing up for a regional tour; the photos of nearby sites at the entrance might help you decide which ones to visit. Despite the free entry, you'll need to collect a ticket downstairs. No thongs (flip-flops) allowed.

Emin Minaret　　　　　　　　ISLAMIC SITE
(额敏塔, Émǐn Tǎ; ¥45; ⊙9am-8pm) Built to honour Turpan general Emin Hoja, this splendid 44m-high mud-brick structure is the tallest minaret in China. Also known as Sūgōng Tǎ after Emin's son Suleiman, who oversaw its construction (1777–78), its bowling-pin shape is decorated with an interesting mix of geometrical and floral patterns: the former reflect traditional Islamic design, the latter Chinese. You can no longer climb the interior steps of the minaret, but the rest of the grounds, including the adjacent mosque, are open.

🛏 Sleeping

⭐**Dap Hostel**　　　　　　　　HOSTEL $
(吐鲁番达卜青年旅舍, Tǔlǔfān Dábo Qīngnián Lǚshě; ☑ 0995 626 3193, 186 9951 3631; Lane 8 off Shahezi Lu, 砂河子路8巷; dm ¥35-45, d/q ¥120/180; ❀⊛) Set in an atmospheric and traditional-style Uighur house whose courtyard boasts carpet-covered beds for socialising on, a small garden and a plenty of other cosy nooks and crannies, the Dap Hostel is the best budget option in town. The dorms are spacious and spotless, and all share clean bathrooms and toilets. Laundry is available and staff speak English.

Tǔlǔfān Bīnguǎn　　　　　　　HOTEL $$
(吐鲁番宾馆; ☑ 152 9944 4128, 0995 856 9000; tlfbg@126.com; 2 Qingnian Nanlu, 青年南路2号; s/d incl breakfast ¥120/180; ❀⊛) This rather aged place is nevertheless good value, and the wonderfully eccentric Arabian Nights–style lobby certainly has its own curiosity value. Things get significantly less ornate once you head to the rooms, which are rather musty and have springy mattresses that will pattern your skin. On the plus side, it has a great central location.

⭐**Turpan Silk Road Lodge**　BOUTIQUE HOTEL $$$
(吐鲁番市丝绸之路公寓, Tǔlǔfānshì Sīchóu Zhīlù Gōngyù; ☑ 136 3997 6886, 0995 856 8333; www.silkroadlodges.com; Munar Lu, 木纳尔路; r with breakfast ¥680; ⊙Apr-Oct; ❀@⊛) To call it boutique might be a slight stretch, but the Silk Road is definitely one of the most atmospheric and charming accommodation options in Xīnjiāng. Though the rooms fea-

ture a rather flat international-chain-hotel design, the rooftop views over the surrounding vineyards and low rising desert hills make this a unique and peaceful retreat.

✕ Eating

Gaochang Lu Night Market   MARKET $

(高昌路夜市, Gāochāng Lù Yèshì; Gaochang Lu; dishes from ¥10; ⊗7pm-midnight) Come dusk, dozens of stalls set up shop by the fountains to the west of the main central square. Grab a cold beer and choose from fried fish, *shaguo* (沙果; casseroles), goat's feet soup and cumin-scented kebabs. This is a wonderfully atmospheric and deeply Uighur experience.

Kadinas Taamliri   UIGHUR $$

(凯蒂娜美食; ☑ 0995 856 8722; Bezeklik Lu, 柏孜克里克路; mains ¥20-60) This excellent Uighur place is popular with local families coming for a feast, and has a photo menu that runs the gamut of Uighur cooking, from multiple ways to cook lamb to delicious 'Uighur pizza'.

ⓘ Information

Bank of China (中国银行, Zhōngguó Yínháng; Laocheng Xilu; ⊗9.30am-12.30pm & 4.30-7.30pm) Changes cash and has an ATM.

Public Security Bureau (PSB, 公安局; Gōng'ānjú; Gaochang Lu) North of the city centre; will likely refer you to the capital for visa extensions.

ⓘ Getting There & Away

Turpan is now connected to Ürümqi and elsewhere in China by the new high-speed railway, whose brand new train station, Turpan North Station (吐鲁番北站, Tǔlǔfān Běi Zhàn), is 12km northwest of the city centre. A taxi from the city centre costs ¥30, or you can take bus 202 (¥1). From here, several trains a day go to Ürümqi (1st/2nd class ¥74/49, one hour) and Hāmì (1st/2nd class ¥137/121, two hours).

The old train station, simply known as Turpan, is actually at Dàhéyán (大河沿), a whopping 54km north of Turpan. Count on paying ¥100 for a taxi here, or take a shared taxi (¥20 per person), which go to and from Turpan's **long-distance bus station** (长途汽车站, Chángtú Qìchēzhàn; Chun Shu Lu, 椿树路). From Turpan station, older and far slower rolling stock trundles to Ürümqi and Hāmì, though as journey times are more than twice as long and tickets bizarrely more expensive than on the high-speed line, there's little reason to use this station to get to either city. However, you'll have to use this station for direct train connections to Kuqa (hard/soft sleeper ¥132/248, 6½ to 10½ hours), Kashgar (hard/soft sleeper ¥298/476, 15 to 22 hours) and Hotan (hard/soft sleeper ¥330/535, 23 hours).

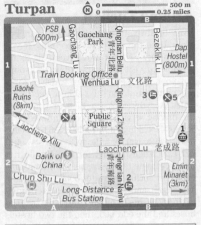

Turpan

⊙ Sights

1 Turpan Museum..................................B2

⊜ Sleeping

2 Tǔlǔfān Bīnguǎn...............................B2
3 Turpan White Camel Youth Hostel.....B1

✕ Eating

4 Gaochang Lu Night Market A2
5 Kadinas Taamliri B1

You can buy tickets for trains from either station in Turpan at the **train booking office** (火车售票处, Huǒchē Shòupiàochù; Qingnian Beilu; commission ¥5; ⊗9am-1pm & 3.30-8pm), located in the city centre.

Buses to Ürümqi (¥45, 3½ hours) run every 20 minutes from 8.10am to 8.30pm. A bus to Hāmì (¥89, six hours) departs daily at 10.30am. There is currently no bus service to Kashgar, but there is a 5pm sleeper bus that goes to Kuqa (¥170, nine hours) and then to Hotan (¥280, 24 hours). Change in Kuqa for Kashgar. For Dūnhuáng (¥182, 12 hours) in Gānsù, take the afternoon sleeper bus, which originates in Ürümqi and normally arrives in Turpan around 4pm. It's best to buy your ticket for this service a day beforehand, and the route has an unpredictable timetable.

ⓘ Getting Around

Public transport around Turpan is by taxi (flag fall at ¥5), minibus or bicycle. Bicycles (about ¥5 per hour), available from Dap Hostel and **White Camel Youth Hostel** (吐鲁番白驼青年旅舍, Tǔlǔfān Bái Tuó Qīngnián Lǚshě; ☑ 0995 866 0556, 156 0995 5676; www.turpanwhitecamel. hostel.com; 55 Bezeklik Lu), are convenient for getting around the city and visiting the sights a little further from the centre.

Around Turpan

Most of Turpan's best sights are scattered around the the city in all directions. If you have plenty of time and several days, it's possible to visit some by public transport, but your best bet is to hire a driver for a day or two and you'll be able to see pretty much everything. We can highly recommend the driving services and local knowledge of English-speaking **Tahir** (☑150 2626 1388; tahirtour8@yahoo.com). A full-day tour costs ¥480 per car. When packing for the day, do not underestimate the desert heat: essential survival gear includes a water bottle, sunscreen, sunglasses and a hat. If you're determined to do the sights as much as possible by local buses and the odd taxi, then the two hostels in Turpan can both give reliable information.

The small Uighur village of **Astana** contains this ancient imperial cemetery, chiefly of interest for the mummies you normally see in museums in the exact positions in which they were discovered. However, as just one of the three subterranean **graves** (阿斯塔那古墓区, Āsītǎnà Gǔmùqū; Astana; ¥40; ⊙9.30am-8pm summer, 10.30am-6pm winter) you can visit on the walking tour contains mummies, it may well seem an expensive visit. The most interesting finds are now in museums in Ürümqi and Turpan. There's a colourful Friday bazaar in the village.

Some travellers enjoy the **Karez System** (坎儿井, Kǎn'ěrjǐng; ¥40), a museum dedicated to the uniquely Central Asian-style irrigation system that includes hundreds of kilometres of above and underground canals, wells and reservoirs, much of it still working.

Near the Bezeklik Caves and Tuyoq are the **Flaming Mountains** (火焰山, Huǒyàn Shān; ¥40), which appear at midday like multicoloured tongues of fire. The Flaming Mountains were immortalised in the classic Chinese novel *Journey to the West*, in which Sun Wukong (the Monkey King) used his magic fan to extinguish the blaze. There's no need to pay the entry fee at the touristy official viewpoint, as you can see the mountains anywhere on the dramatic drives to the Bezeklik Cave Complex, Gāochāng and Tuyoq.

Jiāohé Ruins   交河故城

Also called Yarkhoto, **Jiāohé** (Jiāohé Gù Chéng; admission ¥70) was established by the Chinese as a garrison town during the Han dynasty. It's one of the world's largest (6500 residents once lived here), oldest (1600 years old) and best-preserved ancient cities, inspiring with its scale, setting and palpable historical atmosphere. Get an overview of the site at the central governor's complex, then continue along the main road past a large monastery to a 'stupa grove' with a 10m-tall pagoda surrounded by 100 smaller pagoda bases.

While far busier than the Gāochāng ruins these are definitely the most impressive of the two, mainly due to the sheer number of surviving structures and the dramatic location, on a hillside with views in all directions. The ruins are 8km west of Turpan and can easily be visited by public transport. Take bus 101 (¥1) to its terminal station Yǎer Xiāng (亚尔乡) and then a minibus (¥2) or taxi (¥15). It's also possible to cycle here from Turpan.

Tuyoq   吐峪沟

Set in a green valley fringed by the Flaming Mountains, the mud-brick village of **Tuyoq** (Tǔyùgōu; admission ¥30) offers a fascinating glimpse of traditional Uighur life and architecture. It has been a pilgrimage site for Muslims for centuries, as on the hillside above is the Hojamu Tomb, a *mazar* (a tomb of a saint or holy), said to hold the first Uighur to convert to Islam. The *mazar* is not open to non-Muslims. The rest of the village is great for strolling.

Gāochāng   高昌故城

Dating from the 1st century, **Gāochāng** (Gāochāng Gù Chéng; ¥30) rose to power during the Tang dynasty in the 7th century. Also known as Khocho, or sometimes Karakhoja, Gāochāng became the Uighur capital in AD 850 and was a major staging post on the Silk Road until it burnt in the 14th century. Though the earthen city walls, once 12m thick, are clearly visible, not much else is left standing other than a large Buddhist monastery in the southwest. Its 30km from Turpan.

Bezeklik Cave Complex   柏孜克里克千佛洞

The **Bezeklik Cave Complex** (Bózīkèlǐkè Qiānfó Dòng; admission ¥40), which dates from the 6th to 14th century, has a fine location in a mesmerising desert landscape. Bezeklik means 'Place of Paintings' in Uighur and the murals painted in the 11th century represented a high point in Uighur Buddhist art. Sadly, German, Japanese and British teams removed most of the site's distinctive cave art in the early 20th century, and only a few caves can be entered today. However, the location is gorgeous and well worth the trip.

Hāmì 哈密

📞 0902 / POP 472,000

Hāmì (Kumul in the Uighur language), with its famously sweet melons, was a much-anticipated stop on the Silk Road for ancient travellers. It's still worth a break today, with its green and well kept city centre and a few interesting sights that can keep you busy for a day if you're travelling between Turpan and Dūnhuáng.

The main sights are located near the main bus station and 5km south of the train station; a taxi between the two is about ¥10.

◎ Sights

★ Hāmì Kings Mausoleum TOMB
(哈密王陵, Hāmì Wánglíng; Huancheng Lu, 环城路; adult/student ¥40/20; ⊙9am-8pm Apr-Sep, 10am-7pm Oct-Mar) The chief reason to visit Hāmì is for this wonderfully serene complex of tombs containing the nine generations of Hāmì kings who ruled the region from 1697 to 1930. The blue- and green-tiled main tomb is the resting place of the seventh king, Muhammed Bixir, with family members and government ministers housed in Mongolian-style buildings to the side. Facing it is the rather garish facade of the Etigar mosque, which has a wonderful colonnaded interior.

Barkol Lake LAKE
(巴里坤湖, Bālǐkūn Hú) If the summer heat of Hāmì is unbearable, take a day trip out to the cooler climes of Barkol Lake (Bālǐkūn Hú), on the north side of the Tiān Shān. Kazakh herders set up their yurts here in summer and offer horse riding for ¥10 per hour. Sadly it's not possible to swim, but the bucolic setting and views are well worth the trip.

To reach the yurts, first take a bus from Hāmì's central bus station to Bālǐkūn town (¥25, three hours, hourly between 8.30am and 5.30pm). From Bālǐkūn it's 16km to the yurts. A return taxi starts at ¥50. Along the route from Hāmì, keep an eye out for the remains of ancient beacon towers slowly disintegrating by the roadside.

Hāmì Museum MUSEUM
(哈密博物馆, Hāmì Bówùguǎn; Huancheng Lu, 环城路; ⊙9.30am-7pm Tue-Sun) FREE Across from the Hāmì Kings Mausoleum, this mildly interesting three-floor museum spotlights mummies and dinosaurs found in the region, including several impressively preserved fossilised nests of dinosaur eggs, and, for a reason we were unable to glean, an enormous display of plastic food. Sadly there's almost no English signage.

🛏 Sleeping & Eating

Hāmì Hotel HOTEL $$
(哈密宾馆, Hāmì Bīnguǎn; 📞0902 223 9206; www.hamihotel.com; 4 Yingbin Lu, 迎宾路4号; r ¥228-988; ❄@�) This enormous hotel complex is Hāmì's tourist mainstay. Set in verdant grounds in the centre of town, it's focused on a fancy high rise building with a lobby worthy of a five-star hotel. Upstairs, the rooms don't quite live up to that promise, but they are spacious and modern. The cheaper rooms are in the smaller blocks in the grounds.

There are four restaurants here, as well as a cafe (Fashion Drink) in the lobby that does espresso and baked goods.

★ Miss Chen's Pizza House PIZZA $$$
(陈小姐的披萨小屋, Chén Xiǎojiě de Pīsà Xiǎowū; 📞0902 726 7521; Qianjin Donglu, 前进东路; pizza ¥50-100; ⊙10am-11pm; �) A young and friendly English-speaking team run this pizza joint, in perhaps the least likely culinary find in Hāmì. The pizzas (on an English-language menu) are handmade, and include the delicious Pannodo (basil, garlic, onion and pepper). From the train station, turn left onto the main road and Miss Chen's is 1.3km away, on your left. There's an English sign.

ℹ Information

A **Bank of China** (中国银行, Zhōngguó Yínháng; Guangchang Beilu) is located just north of the main square (Shídài Guǎngchǎng).

ℹ Getting There & Around

Hāmì is now on the high-speed rail network, connecting it with Ürümqi (1st/2nd class ¥196/164, three hours) and Turpan (1st/2nd class ¥137/121, two hours). For some ticket sites you'll need to use Hāmì's other name, Kumul.

Long-distance buses depart from the **south bus station** (南郊客运站; nánjiāo kèyùnzhàn), located 200m east of the Hāmì Kings Mausoleum. For services to Dūnhuáng, try to buy a ticket one day in advance.

Dūnhuáng ¥78, irregular times, usually one or two buses a day originating from Ürümqi

Turpan ¥89, six hours, 9.30am

Ürümqi ¥90 to ¥105, nine hours, three daily

Local bus number 3 (¥1) runs from outside the train station through the centre of the city to the south bus station via the Hāmì Hotel and the museums.

Kuqa 库车

📞 0997 / POP 76,000

The ancient town of Kuqa (Kùchē), once a major centre of Buddhism and now a largely Han Chinese–dominated modern city, is worth a stopover between Ürümqi and Kashgar for its bazaar, old town and some interesting excursions to the surrounding desert ruins.

The once thriving city-state, known as Qiuci, Kuqa was famed in Tang-era China for its music and dancers. Kumarajiva (AD 344–413), the first great translator of Buddhist sutras from Sanskrit into Chinese, was born here to an Indian father and Kuqean princess, before later being abducted to central China to manage translations of the Buddhist canon. When the 7th-century monk Xuan Zang passed through nearby Subashi, he recorded that two enormous 30m-high Buddha statues flanked Kuqa's western gate, and that the nearby monasteries housed more than 5000 monks.

👁 Sights

Sunday Bazaar   MARKET
(老成巴扎, Lǎochéng Bāzā; ⏰ 8am-4pm Sun) Every Sunday, a large bazaar is held next to the bridge over the Kuqa River on Renmin Lu, which leads into the Uighur Old Town – about 2.5km west of the modern town. The market is no rival to Kashgar's, but you won't find any tour buses here. A small livestock market also takes place here on Fridays.

Rasta Mosque   MOSQUE
(热斯坦清真寺, Rèsītǎn Qīngzhēn Sì; Rasta Lu, 热斯坦路) The charmingly painted Rasta Mosque, about 2.5km west of the modern town, draws a throng of worshippers at Friday lunchtime. The rest of the time it's quietly neglected and you're welcome to wander into its courtyard.

Maulana Ashiddin Mazar   TOMB
(默拉纳额什丁麻扎, Mòlānà Éshídīng Mázā; Wenhua Donglu, 文化东路; ⏰ 8am-dusk) FREE This timeless green-tiled mosque and tomb of a 13th-century Arabian missionary is surrounded by a sea of graves and overflows with worshippers at Friday lunchtime prayers. It's a 10-minute walk from central Kuga, along mulberry tree–lined Wenhua Lu.

Great Mosque   MOSQUE
(清真大寺, Qīngzhēn Dàsì; off Paha Tabaza Lu, 帕哈塔巴扎路; ¥15) Kuqa's Great Mosque, rebuilt in 1932 on the site of a 16th-century original, is the second largest in Xīnjiāng. (The largest

is the Id Kah Mosque (p814) in Kashgar.) It's a wonderfully quiet and meditative space, with a huge and ornately painted colonnaded prayer hall that makes for a pleasant refuge from the heat of the day. There's a small museum with a gift shop on the premises, too, which is mainly worth peeking into for its interesting old-town views.

🛏 Sleeping

⭐ Zabay Guest House   HOSTEL $
(📞 180 9587 9669, 0997 777 8525; 450 Tianshan Donglu, 天山东路450号; dm ¥45-60 r ¥168-198; @ 🛜) It's quite extraordinary to find this great hostel in fairly remote Kuqa. Run by a young, friendly English-speaking team, it's inside a converted warehouse in a courtyard and is stylishly designed with concrete floors and a minimalist air. The private rooms are all themed, and include a prison cell and a traditional Uighur home, and all rooms have private bathrooms.

The hostel is 4km east of the town centre on the south side of Tianshan Donglu between Changan Lu and Changjiang Lu, and there was no sign when we visited. Taxi drivers will know the nearby Bingsansi gas station: ask for Bīngsānsì Jiāyóu Zhàn (兵三司加油站).

Bǎiyuè Boutique Hotel   BOUTIQUE HOTEL $$
(柏悦精品酒店, Bǎiyuè Jīngpǐn Jiǔdiàn; 📞 0997 799 5111; Wuyi Nanlu, 五一南路; r incl breakfast from ¥268; ❄ 🛜) This recently opened hotel projects a very Chinese vision of what a boutique hotel should be: specifically lots of marble, LEDs and enormous dark-wood and leather-upholstered beds. Decor is full-on but pretty clean, with large bathrooms, flatscreen TVs and a central location. Staff are fairly clueless but mean well.

Kùchē Bīnguǎn   HOTEL $$
(库车宾馆, 📞 0997 712 2901; 04-1 Jiefang Beilu, 解放北路04-1号; tw incl breakfast from ¥190; ❄ 🛜) Kuqa's main tourist hotel has ageing rooms with springy beds, but is otherwise a perfectly decent place to stay. The included breakfast is surprisingly good, and the hotel is centrally located.

🍴 Eating

⭐ Uchar Darvaza Bazaar   MARKET $
(乌恰农贸市场, Wūqià Nónghuò Shìchǎng; meals from ¥20; ⏰ 10am-1am) The best place in Kuga for Uighur food is this street at the junction of Tianshan Zhonglu and Youyi Lu. Kebabs, noodles and samsas (baked mutton pies) are all served hot and fresh, though our fa-

vourites are the chicken kebabs served with sombrero-sized local naan. Some stalls start to close at 9pm, others only set up from 10pm.

Xīntián Cafe
BAKERY $

(心甜咖啡, Xīntián Kāfēi; cnr Wuyi Zhonglu & Tianshan Zhonglu, 五一中路天山中路的路口; pastries from ¥5; ☺10am-10.30pm; 🛜) This bakery is a great breakfast option, and offers a range of pastries, cakes and sandwiches, as well as good coffee. Upstairs there's a cosy seating area where there are even waffles pizza, chicken wings and steaks on the menu. Look for the 'Heart Sweet Coffee' sign.

Chóngqìng Lǎotàipó Tāntān Miàn
NOODLES $

(重庆老太婆摊摊面; Wuyi Nanlu, 五一南路; mains ¥15-20; ☺8.30am-1am) This cheap and cheerful noodle bar serves up a range of simple dishes in the Chóngqìng style (read: very spicy). It has a pictorial menu, friendly staff and cheap, cold beer, a rarity in these parts.

ℹ Information

Bank of China (中国银行, Zhōngguó Yínháng; 25 Wenhua Lu; ☺9.30am-6.30pm Mon-Fri) One of several Banks of China along Wenhua Lu. Has an ATM. Travellers cheques are not accepted.

ℹ Getting There & Around

The small airport, 35km west of the city, has four daily flights to Ūrümqi (from ¥360, one hour) on China Southern and Tiānjīn Airlines. A taxi there costs around ¥30.

The **bus station** (☎0997 712 2379; Tianshan Zhonglu) has a variety of sleepers heading east. There is currently no direct bus service to Kashgar; you'll need to take a bus to Aksu and change there, or take a direct train.

Aksu ¥66, four hours, hourly; connect here for regular buses to Kashgar (¥128, six hours)
Hotan ¥171, 10 hours, noon and 3.30pm
Ūrümqi ¥180 to ¥200, 14 hours, seven daily (one at noon, the others in the evening)

The train station is southeast of the centre. A taxi costs ¥10.
Kashgar hard/soft sleeper ¥164/239, 8½ to 12 hours, four daily
Ūrümqi hard/soft sleeper ¥194/285, nine to 14 hours, six daily

Taxi rides are a standard ¥5 per trip within the town centre, with pedicabs, tractors and donkey carts around half this.

Around Kuqa

Seventy-five kilometres northwest of Kuqa, **Kizil Thousand Buddha Caves** (克孜尔千佛洞, Kèzī'ěr Qiānfó Dòng; ¥70; ☺10.30am-7pm) is the largest Buddhist cave-art site in Xīnjiāng. One of the main reasons to come here is for the incredible landscapes you see along the way: bleak and empty jagged mountains on either side of the road make for haunting views. The site itself is impressive, although sadly only a handful of the 236 caves can be visited and the once dazzling wall art has been largely destroyed by 'archaeologists' and religious zealots.

The interior murals date from the 3rd to the 8th centuries and, as ancient Kuqa was an ethnically diverse place, artisans were inspired by Afghan, Persian and Indian motifs and styles. The heavy use of blue pigment in middle-period murals is a Persian influence, for example, with only the last phase showing any Chinese influence. Each cave is generally built the same way, with two chambers and a central vaulted roof. The roof contains murals of the Buddha's past lives (so-called Jātaka tales) and, unique to Kizil, the pictures are framed in diamond-shaped patterns. Several caves were stripped bare by German archaeologist Albert Von le Coq in the early 20th century, only for the treasures to be destroyed during WWII – as you will hear if you take a free guided tour (in Chinese only). Note the richly decorated roof of Cave 8, where the Buddha's golden robes have been systematically removed over the centuries.

Private transfer is the only way to get here, and a return taxi will cost around ¥250 and takes 90 minutes each way. Most people combine the trip with one to Sūbāshí, even though you have to return to Kuqa between the two sights. Reckon on paying ¥350 for both.

Sūbāshí (苏巴什故城; ¥25; ☺10am-8pm) was a Buddhist complex that thrived from the 3rd to 13th centuries. It's less visited than other ancient cities in Xīnjiāng, but with its starkly beautiful desert setting, it's worth the trip – Sūbāshí is a 23km trip northeast of Kuqa. There are a number of buildings that you visit, though the best preserved one is the pagoda on the far side of the ruins (the main path takes you there), where brickwork and some decoration can still be seen.

Most people just go to the western complex, with its large central vihara (monastery) and two pagodas, but the dramatic eastern complex across the Kuqa River is worth the hike, though it was being renovated at the time of research. A return taxi to Sūbāshí costs about ¥100; you'll need to pay extra waiting time if you want to visit the eastern ruins.

XĪNJIĀNG KUQA

SOUTHWEST XĪNJIĀNG – KASHGARIA

The Uighurs' heartland is the southwest of Xīnjiāng, known as Kashgaria, the rough but mellifluous-sounding historical name for the western Tarim Basin. Consisting of a ring of oases lined with poplar trees, it was a major Silk Road hub and has bristled with activity for more than 2000 years, with the weekly bazaars remaining the centre of life here to this day.

The centre of the region is undoubtedly the ancient city of Kashgar, one of the absolute highlights of any visit to Xīnjiāng. Another highlight is the breathtaking scenery along the Karakoram Hwy between Kashgar and remote Tashkurgan: neither should be missed.

Kashgar   喀什

📞 0998 / POP 400,000

Locked away in the westernmost corner of China, closer to Tehran and Damascus than to Běijīng, Kashgar (Kāshí) has been the epicentre of regional trade and cultural exchange for more than two millennia.

In recent years, modernity has swept through Kashgar, bringing waves of Han migrant workers and huge swathes of the old city have been bulldozed in the name of 'progress'. Only a tiny section of the 'real' Old Town remains today, and is unlikely to survive for much longer.

Yet, in the face of these changes, the spirit of Kashgar lives on. Uighur craftsmen and artisans still hammer and chisel away as they have done for centuries, traders haggle over deals in the boisterous bazaars and donkey carts still trundle their way through the narrow alleyways. Do not miss the city's Sunday livestock market, which remains a fascinating sight, no matter how many tour buses roll up.

◉ Sights

★ Sunday Livestock Market   MARKET
(动物市场, Dòngwù Shìchǎng, Mal Bazaar; ⊗8am-6pm Sun) No visit to Kashgar is complete without a trip to the Livestock Market, which takes place once a week on Sunday. The day begins with Uighur farmers and herders trekking into the city from nearby villages. By lunchtime, just about every saleable sheep, camel, horse, cow and donkey within 50km has been squeezed through the bazaar gates. It's dusty, smelly and crowded, and most people find it wonderful, though some visitors may find the treatment of the animals upsetting.

Trading at the market is swift and boisterous between the old traders; animals are carefully inspected and haggling is done with finger motions. Keep an ear out for the phrase 'Bosh-bosh!' ('Coming through!') or you risk being ploughed over by a cartload of fat-tailed sheep.

A taxi here costs ¥25 to ¥30; it's a good idea to pay it to wait for your return. Alternatively take bus number 13 or 23 from the Sunday Bazaar. Tour buses usually arrive in the morning, so consider an early afternoon visit, or come first thing for good light and fewer crowds. A few simple stalls offer delicious hot samsa (lamb meat buns) if you get peckish.

★ Grand Sunday Bazaar   MARKET
(大巴扎, Dàbāzhā, Yengi Bazaar; Aizirete Lu, 艾孜热特路; ⊗daily) Kashgar's main bazaar is open every day but really kicks it up a gear on Sunday. Step through the jam-packed entrance and allow your five senses to guide you through the market; spices and teas are an obvious highlight, as are silk, doppa (traditional Uighur hats) and carpets, all of which can be seen in abundance. Of the variety, here locals joke that only chicken milk cannot be found amid this mercantile chaos.

Kashgar Old Town   OLD TOWN
(喀什老城区, Kāshí Lǎo Chéngqū) The Old Town is the soul of Kashgar, and as such the Chinese government has spent much of the past two decades knocking it down block by block and building a modern, soulless replacement. Yet it's still possible to see some of the remaining alleyways: check out the neighbourhood near Donghai Lake in the eastern part of the city. Around Jiefang Lu there are also alleys lined with Uighur workshops and adobe houses that have withstood the passage of time.

Abakh Hoja Mausoleum   TOMB
(香妃墓, Xiāngfēimù, Abakh Hoja Maziri, Afaq Khoja Mausoleum; ¥30; ⊗dawn-dusk) On the north-eastern outskirts of town is the Abakh Hoja Mausoleum, a 3-hectare complex built by the Khoja family who ruled the region in the 17th and 18th centuries. Widely considered the holiest Muslim site in Xīnjiāng, it's a major pilgrimage destination and a beautiful piece of Islamic architecture well worth a visit.

Id Kah Mosque   MOSQUE
(艾提尕尔清真寺, Ài Tígǎ'ěr Qīngzhēn Sì; Id Kah Sq; ¥45; ⊗dawn-dusk outside of prayer times) The yellow-tiled Id Kah Mosque, which dates from 1442, is the spiritual and physical heart of the city. Enormous (it's the largest mosque in Xīnjiāng), its courtyard and gardens can hold

Kashgar

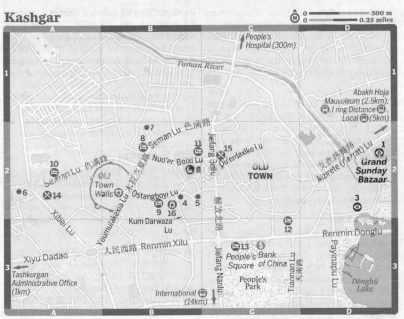

Kashgar

20,000 people during the annual Qurban Baiyram. Also known as Eid, celebrations fall in June for the next few years. Non-Muslims may enter, but not during prayer time. Dress modestly, including a headscarf for women. Take off your shoes if entering carpeted areas and be discreet when taking photos.

☞ Tours

Popular tours include four-day treks around Muztagh Ata, overnighting in tents, yurts or villages, as well as overnight camel tours into the dunes fringing the Taklamakan Desert around Davakul Lake or Yarkand. For a real challenge, consider cycling the Karakoram Hwy: normally travellers get a lift to Tashkurgan with their bikes and then cycle back down to Kashgar over three days.

★ **Thirsty Camel Tours**   TOUR
(☏ 135 7933 6273, 189 9909 3311; www.travelkash gar.com; Tianyuan International Hotel, 8 Renmin Donglu) Run by the charming and friendly, English-speaking Abdul Waheed, Thirsty

Camel Tours offers a full range of excursions in and around Kashgar, and specialises in trips into the Taklamakan Desert and along the Southern Silk Road. Abdul has years of experience in the local tourist industry and brings enormous good cheer to any trip.

Uighur Tours   TOURS
(☎0998 298 0770, 133 9977 3311; www.kashgar tours.com; 144 Seman Lu, Chini Bagh Royal Hotel) English-speaking Ali Tash runs this highly recommended agency offering tours and travel between Kashgar and Xī'ān along the Northern Silk Road (via Turpan), as well as trips to Muztagh Ata that don't require the punishingly expensive permits. Bike hire in Kashgar can also be arranged.

Old Road Tours   TOURS
(☎0998 220 4012, 138 9913 2103; www.oldroad tours.com; 337 Seman Lu) One of the best (as well as the priciest) of the local agencies, Old Road Tours has been run for more than 15 years by fluent-English-speaking Abdul Wahab and operates out of the Seman Hotel. The agency can arrange tours throughout Xīnjiāng, including trekking at Muztagh Ata, homestays in Turpan and Yīníng and multi-day camel tours in the Taklamakan desert.

Ablimit 'Elvis' Ghopor   TOURS
(☎138 9913 6195; elvisablimit@yahoo.com) Local English-speaking Uighur-carpet dealer Elvis organises city-wide cultural trips, with a special emphasis on Uighur classical music and the Kashgar carpet market. He also offers tours and treks to Karakul and the Taklamakan Desert. He doesn't have an office as such; find him at the Ostangboyi Ancient Tea House near Id Kah Mosque.

Kashgar Tourist Service Centre   TOURS
(☎0998 283 1196, 158 0904 2877; kashgar7@ hotmail.com; Ostangboyi Lu; ◷10am-8pm) This travel agency offers a range of services including facilities for tour groups in Kashgar. It is also of interest to independent travellers, as it can offer bespoke tour services, including English-speaking guides and drivers to destinations all over Kashgaria, as well as renting pricey bikes (¥80 per day). The cafe here has excellent coffee and walnut cake.

🛏 Sleeping

Despite being Xīnjiāng's biggest tourist draw, Kashgar's accommodation options remain fairly mediocre, especially in the mid-range category. There are now a number of well run hostels, however, so budget travellers are well catered for, at least.

★ Kashgar Old Town Youth Hostel HOSTEL $
(喀什老城青年旅舍, Kāshí Lǎochéng Qīngnián Lǚshě; ☎152 7610 6605, 0998 282 3262; www. pamirinn.com; 233 Ostangboyi Lu, 吾斯塘博依路233号; dm ¥35-50, d ¥120-150; @🛜) Nestled in the old city, this atmospheric place is set around a courtyard where overlanders hang out on *shyrdaks* (Kyrgyz-style felt carpets), swapping stories and travel info. The rooms are bare, the toilets simple and the beds rock hard, but the English-speaking staff are very friendly, can organise local tours and there's cheap laundry and reliable hot water.

KKH Breeze Hostel   HOSTEL $
(微风青年旅舍, Wéifēng Qīngnián Lǚshě; ☎180 9955 4185, 0998 259 0151; mobilelife@sina.com; 268 Seman Lu, Block 6, Kangmei Xiaoqu; dm ¥40-50, d/tw/q ¥140/140/200; 🛜) Expertly run by

---

SHIPTON'S ARCH

Extraordinary **Shipton's Arch** (Tushuk Tagh; ¥45; ◷9am-9pm Apr-Oct, 11am-6.30pm Nov-Mar) is a natural rock arch (the rather prosaic Uighur name means simply 'mountain with a hole in it') is one of the tallest on earth. The first Westerner to describe it was Eric Shipton, the last British consul-general in Kashgar, during his visit to the region in 1947. Successive expeditions attempted to find it without success until a team from *National Geographic* rediscovered the arch in 2000. Located 80km northwest of Kashgar, it's a half-day excursion from Kashgar.

The first part of the trip involves an hour's drive towards the Irkeshtam Pass, followed by another 20km ride and then a 45-minute hike through a sublimely lunar landscape, hemmed in on all sides by sheer cliffs. At times you'll be scrambling through the narrowest part of the gorge over small ladders and staircases, until your final ascent to the arch itself, which takes you up a long wooden staircase. Kashgar-based tour operators can arrange a day trip with guide for ¥600 to ¥800, or you can simply take a taxi and walk from the car park yourself, as the route is well signposted. Bring sturdy shoes, a sun hat and water. For the best light and the smallest crowds, go early in the morning or late in the afternoon.

English-speaking Rita and her husband, this new addition to Kashgar's hostel scene is outside the Old Town and inside an apartment block, which at least makes for an unusual set up. Dorms and private rooms are all spotless, and each has its own bathroom. There's a common room, communal kitchen and a pleasant garden area outside.

Pamir Youth Hostel HOSTEL $

(喀什帕米尔青年旅舍, Kāshí Pàmǐ'ěr Qīngnián Lǚshě; ☑ 180 9985 1967, 0998 282 3376; www.pamirhostel.com/en; 3f Id Kah Bazaar District 7, Section A, dm ¥40-50, d ¥140, 🌐🌐) With an outdoor terrace that overlooks the beautiful Id Kah Mosque, this hostel has quickly become a popular base for exploring the city and its historical surroundings. Dorm rooms are basic but include individual lockers and free wi-fi. To find Pamir look for the green dome just north of the mosque.

★ Super 8 Hotel HOTEL $$

(速8酒店, Sùbā Jiǔdiàn; ☑ 0998 259 1555, 186 9981 3007; www.super8.com.cn; Kazanqlyabel Lu; r ¥258-328; 🌐🌐) Ironically, it's a new Chinese-run hotel that gets our vote as the best midrange place to stay in Kashgar's Old Town. This low-slung new build has a faux-traditional facade but thoroughly modern, clean and spacious rooms with decent bathrooms and working wireless. No English is spoken, but big discounts are available outside peak season, and there's no traffic noise.

Tiānyuán International Hotel HOTEL $$

(天缘国际酒店, Tiānyuán Guójì Jiǔdiàn; ☑ 0998 280 2266, 0998 280 1111; 8 Renmin Donglu; r from ¥180) This smart place overlooking the Old Town (p814) and the city's main square is one of Kashgar's better midrange hotels. The rooms are clean and well maintained, there's a decent breakfast and staff – while they speak no English – are welcoming.

🍴 Eating

Kashgar is one of the best places in Xīnjiāng to try the full gamut of Uighur food. There are two excellent night markets and an incredible bazaar, and street food is available on almost every corner of the expansive Old Town.

★ Õu'ěr Dáxīkè Night Market UIGHUR $

(欧尔达稀克夜市, Õu'ěr Dáxīkè Yèshì; Ou'er Daxike Lu; meals from ¥10; ⊙ 6pm-2am) Across from the Id Kah Mosque, this photogenic night market is a great place to sample local fare. Among the goodies are fried fish, chickpeas, kebabs, fried dumplings known as *hoshan*

and bubbling vats of goat's-head soup. Top off a meal with a glass of pomegranate juice or freshly churned vanilla ice cream.

★ Altun Orda UIGHUR $$

(金噢尔达饮食, Jīn'ào'ěrdà Yǐnshí; Xibei Lu; dishes ¥15-175; ⊙ 8am-midnight) Easily Kashgar's most memorable and atmospheric restaurant, Altun Orda is a sumptuously decorated place famous for its roast mutton, sweet pumpkin dumplings, meat pies and raisin and almond pastries. Though the restaurant has been on the tourist radar for some time – as the English iPad menus demonstrate – you'll still usually be an object of curiosity amid a sea of Uighur families.

Eden Cafe UIGHUR, TURKISH $$

(一甸咖啡, Yīdiàn Kāfēi; ☑ 0998 266 5555; 148 Seman Lu, Eden Hotel; mains ¥36-78; ⊙ 10.30am-2am) This lavishly decorated restaurant inside the **Eden Hotel** (海尔巴格大饭店, Hǎiěr bāgé Dàfàndiàn; ☑ 0998 266 4444; r from ¥160; ❄🌐) is one of Kashgar's best, and it oozes atmosphere and is always full of locals. The menu is photographic, though there's no English, and the food is full of Turkish and Uighur standards as well as a few Chinese and international dishes. There's no alcohol but they serve up real coffee.

🍸 Drinking & Nightlife

★ Ostangboyi Ancient Tea House TEAHOUSE

(吾斯塘博依老茶馆, Wúsītángbóyī Lǎo Cháguǎn; Ostangboyi Lu; ⊙ 10am-10pm) The last traditional Uighur teahouse in Kashgar, this is a wonderfully atmospheric place to come for a drink. While it's certainly the preserve of Uighur Old Town elders, the crowd here are quite used to tourists dropping by, and even have an English tea menu.

🛍 Shopping

For serious shopping go to the Old Town, ready to bargain. Kum Darwaza Lu is a good starting point. The Grand Bazaar has a decent selection but prices tend to be higher. Hats, teapot sets, copper- and brassware, kebab skewers and Uighur knives are among the best souvenirs.

Grand Sunday Bazaar MARKET

(大巴扎, Dàbāzhā; Aizirete Lu; ⊙ daily) Most carpet dealers display their wares at the Market pavilion. The rugs here are made of everything from silk to synthetics and finding traditional designs can be difficult – go with a local if possible. The brightly coloured felt Kyrgyz-style *shyrdaks* are a good buy.

Ahmed Carpet Shop   HOMEWARES

(📞0998 283 1557; 49 Kum Darwaza Lu; ⊙10am-8pm) Ahmed and his son run this Old Town carpet shop, offering a good selection of antique and new carpets from across Central Asia.

ℹ Dangers & Annoyances

Kashgar is the most conservative corner of Xīnjiāng and though the wearing of the veil has been banned by the Chinese government since 2014, it is wise for women travellers to dress as would be appropriate in any Muslim country, covering arms and legs.

Some visitors have lost money or passports to pickpockets at the Sunday Market, so keep yours tucked away.

ℹ Information

Kashgar has a wide availability of ATMs, though many still do not accept international cards. Try ATMs around the junction of Renmin Xilu and Jiefang Beilu, as well as around Renmin Guangchang.

Bank of China (中国银行, Zhōngguó Yínháng; Renmin Guangchang; ⊙9.30am-1.30pm & 4-7pm) Changes travellers cheques and cash and has a 24-hour ATM. You can also sell yuan back into US dollars at the foreign-exchange desk if you have exchange receipts; this is a good idea if you are headed to Pakistan, as the bank hours in Tashkurgan are erratic.

People's Hospital (人民医院, Rénmín Yīyuàn; Jiefang Beilu) North of the river. Kashgar's biggest hospital.

Public Security Bureau (PSB, 公安局, Gōng'ānjú; 111 Youmulakexia Lu; ⊙9.30am-1.30pm & 4-8pm) At the time of writing, the Kashgar PSB was issuing one-month visa ex-

---

ℹ BORDER CROSSINGS

To Kyrgyzstan

There are two passes into Kyrgyzstan: the Torugart Pass, which leads to Naryn and then Bishkek in the north; and the Irkeshtam Pass, which goes to Osh in the south.

Going through the Irkeshtam Pass and on to Osh is straightforward, with a sleeper bus leaving Kashgar's international bus station at 9am on Monday and Thursday. You can also hire a car through a Kashgar agency, though no special permits or guides are needed for this route.

Crossing the Torugart Pass requires more red tape, for which you will need a travel agency's help. You will also need to have arranged transport on the Kyrgyz side, which travel agents can arrange with their contacts in Naryn or Bishkek. The pass is open year-round to foreigners, though taxis cannot go here; only cars with permits allowing them to make the journey may pass.

Most travellers no longer need a visa to enter Kyrgyzstan, so the red tape is at least simplified in this respect.

To Pakistan

Trips from Kashgar to Sost are done in two stages – there is no direct bus. Take one of the two daily buses to Tashkurgan from Kashgar's local bus station, and then stay overnight at Tashkurgan, before continuing at 9.30am the following morning for the bus to Sost (which runs only Monday to Friday, as the pass is closed at weekends).

Officially, the border opens daily between 1 April and 1 December. However, the border can open late or close early depending on conditions at the Khunjerab Pass, and is always closed on Saturdays and Sundays. The Chinese customs and immigration formalities are done at just beyond Tashkurgan (3km down the road towards Pakistan). Then it's 126km to the last checkpost at Khunjerab Pass, the actual border, where your documents are checked again before you head into Pakistan. Pakistan immigration formalities are performed at Sost. Pakistani visas are no longer available to tourists on arrival (and visas are difficult to get in Běijīng), so the safest option is to arrive in China with a visa obtained in your home country. Check the current situation as this could change.

To Tajikistan

The 4362m Qolma (Kulma) Pass linking Kashgar with Murghab (via Tashkurgan) opened in 2004 to local traders, but sadly remains closed to foreign travellers, even if you already have a Tajik visa.

tensions in one day. Simply come here at least a day before your visa expires with a hotel receipt and ¥180 and leave your passport overnight for processing. This information is vulnerable to change, however, so check out the most recent situation with a Kashgar travel agency.

ℹ Getting There & Away

AIR

Also known as Kashi Airport, Kashgar's busy airport has more than a dozen daily flights to and from Ürümqi (from ¥550, two hours).

BUS

All of Kashgar's bus stations have changed location in recent years. The long-distance and local bus stations are next to each other near the train station, around 7km northwest of the Old Town, while the international bus station is 14km south of the Old Town.

The **long-distance bus station** (地区客运站, Dìqū Kèyùnzhàn; Jiefang Beilu) handles buses to the north of the region, including the following services:

Kuqa ¥147 to ¥160, 12 hours, 7pm
Turpan ¥235 to ¥255, 22 hours, hourly between 10am and 7.30pm
Ürümqi ¥265 to ¥285, 24 hours, hourly between 10am and 7.30pm

Note that all Ürümqi and Turpan buses go through Kuqa, but a ticket to Kuqa on these services is far pricier (¥255) as you have to buy a ticket to Turpan, so you're far better off using the cheaper 7pm service that terminates in Kuqa.

Buses heading south use the **local bus station** (公共汽车站, Gōnggòng Qìchē Zhàn; Jiefang Bellu, Guangzhou New City), which is located next door to the long-distance bus station. Destinations from here:

Hotan ¥153 to ¥200, seven to 10 hours, every 1½ hours
Karghilik ¥93 to ¥118, four hours, frequent
Tashkurgan ¥89 to ¥119, six hours, two per day (10am and noon)
Yarkand ¥68 to ¥88, three hours, frequent
Yengisar ¥28, 1½ hours, frequent

Buses to Kyrgyzstan depart from the **international bus station** (国际汽车站, Guójì Qìchēzhàn; ☑ 138 9914 0624, 138 9916 8559):
Bishkek ¥285, nine hours, Monday at 10.30am
Osh ¥275, eight hours, Monday and Thursday at 8am

Bus 20 connects the Old Town to all three bus stations.

An alternative to taking a bus to Tashkurgan is to take a faster shared taxi, which leaves when full from the **Tashkurgan Administration Office** (塔什库尔干办事处, Tǎshíkù'ěrgān Bànshìchù; 166 Xiyu Dadao Lu, 西域大道166号).

TRAIN

Kashgar's **train station** (喀什火车站, Kāshí Huǒchē Zhàn; Tianshan Donglu) is 7km northeast of the Old Town, and there are regular connections to the rest of the region, including the following destinations:

Hotan hard/soft sleeper ¥53/118, six to eight hours, one to two daily
Ürümqi hard/soft sleeper ¥303/494 16¾ to 24½ hours, four daily

Hotan trains also serve Yengisar (two hours), Yarkand (four hours), and Karghilik (5½ hours).

ℹ Getting Around

The airport is 13km northeast of the town centre. A taxi costs ¥15 to ¥20 but drivers often ask for double this. Insist on a meter being used, and avoid the touts in the arrivals hall. Bus 2 (¥1) goes directly to the airport from People's Sq and Id Kah Mosque, from where it's an easy walk to most hotels.

Bikes are a popular way to get around Kashgar, and can be rented from Kashgar Old Town Youth Hostel (p816), Uighur Tours (p816), Kashgar Tourist Service Centre (p816) and Kashgar Pamir Youth Hostel (p817). Expect to pay between ¥40 and ¥80 per day.

Useful bus routes are numbers 2 (Jiefang Lu north to the international bus station and the airport), 9 (international bus station to the Chini Bagh Hotel and Sèmǎn Bīnguǎn), 20 (China Post to Abakh Hoja Tomb) and 28 (Id Kah Mosque to the train station). Place a ¥1 note (change is not given) into the plastic box when you board.

Taxis can be found easily, and drivers use their meters almost without fail. Flag fall is ¥5, and nowhere in town should cost more than ¥15.

Karakoram Highway 中巴公路

The Karakoram Hwy (KKH; Zhōngbā Gōnglù) over the Khunjerab Pass (4800m) is one of the world's most spectacular roads and China's gateway to Pakistan. For centuries this route was used by caravans plodding down the Silk Road. Khunjerab means 'valley of blood' as local bandits used to take advantage of the terrain to slaughter merchants and plunder their wares. Today, it's a far more welcoming place, not to mention an easier journey, with a new road and a high-speed rail link to Pakistan under construction at the time of writing. Whatever you do in Xīnjiāng, do not miss this incredible journey.

The main (and practically the only) town between Kashgar and Pakistan is Tashkurgan, a surprisingly modern and sprawling town with a devastatingly beautiful mountain setting. This is where the bus journey to Pakistan begins, and it's also as far as most travellers not entering Pakistan itself are able to go.

Kashgar to Tashkurgan

Travelling up the KKH to Tashkurgan is a highlight of Kashgaria and of China as a whole. The journey begins with a one-hour drive through the Kashgar oasis to **Upal** (乌帕尔; Wùpà'ěr), where most vehicles stop for breakfast, especially during the interesting Monday market. The renovated **Tomb of Mahmud Kashgari** (¥30), a beloved local 11th-century scholar, traveller and writer, is a potential excursion but it's far from unmissable. The tomb is about 2.5km from the market on the edge of Upal hill.

Two hours from Kashgar, you enter the canyon of the Ghez River (Ghez Darya in Uighur), with its dramatic claret-red sandstone walls. Ghez itself is a major checkpoint; photographing soldiers or buildings is strictly prohibited. At the top of the canyon, 3½ hours above the plain, you pop out into a huge wet plateau ringed with mountains of sand, part of the Sarikol Pamir, and aptly called Kumtagh (Sand Mountain) by locals.

Soon Kongur Mountain (Gōnggé'ěr Shān; 7719m) rises up on the left side of the road, followed by heavily glaciered Muztagh Ata (慕士塔格峰; Mùshìtǎgé Fēng; 7546m). The main stopping point for views is **Karakul Lake**, a glittering mirror of glacial peaks 194km from Kashgar. From here you can hike into the hills or circumnavigate the lake.

The journey climbs to a pass offering fine views, then meanders through high mountain pastures dotted with grazing camels and yaks, before passing the turn-off to the Qolma Pass (currently closed to foreigners), which leads into neighbouring Tajikistan. The final major town on the Chinese side is **Tashkurgan** at 3600m. You could easily kill a couple of hours wandering the streets and visiting the small museum at the **Folk Culture Centre** (¥30; ☉ 10am-5pm) at the central crossroads (marked by the eagle statue).

On the outskirts of town, close to the river, is Tashkurgan Fort, the 1400-year-old stone (*tash*) fortifications (*kurgan*) of which give the town its name. The ruins were one of the filming locations for the movie *The Kite Runner*. The boggy valley below is dotted with Tajik yurts in summer and offers some spectacular views back towards the fort from a touristy boardwalk that rises above the waterlogged valley floor.

Some travellers head up to the Khunjerab Pass for a photo opportunity on the ac-

THE SILK ROAD

Nomadic trading routes across Asia and Europe had existed for thousands of years but what we now call the Silk Road, an intercontinental network connecting the East and West, began to take shape in the 2nd century BC. At the time, the Mediterranean had already been linked to Central Asia by Alexander the Great (and his Roman successors), and China, in its need to defend itself from marauding Xiongnu, was about to do its part.

In 138 BC, the Emperor Wudi sent envoy Zhang Qian to negotiate an alliance with the Yuezhi, a Central Asian people being driven west by the Xiongnu. On his return (after much hardship which included being kidnapped twice), Zhang piqued the emperor's interest with tales of wealthy neighbouring kingdoms, powerful horses, and trade of Chinese goods, including silk, that had already reached these regions. Over the next two centuries, the Han experienced endless setbacks as they sought to defeat the Xiongnu and secure safe passage from Gānsù through Xīnjiāng, but eventually formal trade with Central Asia was established.

Owing as much to continuous political instability as geographical challenges, there was never any one route that goods travelled along, much less a road; the name Silk Road was coined in 1877 by German geographer Ferdinand von Richtofen. The loose, fragile and often dangerous network of ancient times had its Chinese start in Cháng'ān (modern Xī'ān) and from there proceeded up the Héxī Corridor to Dūnhuáng. At this great oasis town it split north and south to circumvent the unforgiving Taklamakan Desert. The routes then met again at Kashgar, where they once more split to cross the high, snowy Pamirs, Karakorum and Tiān Shān Mountains to connect with Samarkand (and eventually Iran and Constantinople), India and the Russian Volga.

Despite the distances that goods could reach, almost all trade was small scale and local: large caravan teams were rare unless travelling as official envoys, and goods were seldom

tual Pakistan–China border. Note that you need a border permit (available in Kashgar) and a guide, which most tour agencies can arrange. Travelling into Pakistan itself is perfectly possible if you have a valid visa, though always check in Kashagr or Islamabad whether the pass is open before you set out.

Sights & Activities

Within China, many travellers head up the highway at least to Tashkurgan. It's possible to do a day trip to Karakul Lake and back but it's much better to spend a night or two up in these gorgeous mountains either camping and trekking or just in a hotel in Tashkurgan. Some travellers also hire bikes in Kashgar: get a lift up to Tashkurgan and cycle back for an exciting three-day journey.

Tashkurgan Fort   FORT
(石头城, Shítóuchéng; ¥30) The 1400-year old stone (*tash*) fortifications (*kurgan*) of this fort give the town of Tashkurgan on the Karakorum Hwy its name. The ruins were one of the filming locations for the movie *The Kite Runner*. The boggy valley below is dotted with Tajik yurts in summer (as well as a network of walkways for tourists) and offers some spectacular views.

Bulungkol Lake   LAKE
(布伦库勒湖, Bùlúnkùlēi Hú) This absolute wonder of nature is the first of the big plate-glass lakes you meet as you head up to Tashkurgan on the Karakoram Hwy. Backed by sublime sand mountains and often without a single ripple in its waters, it's an astonishing sight on a calm day, when the landscape is perfectly mirrored in the lake. It's currently totally deserted, though it looked like some form of construction was beginning when we were there, suggesting that mass tourism can't be far away.

Karakul Lake   LAKE
(喀拉库勒湖, Kālākùlēi Hú) This extraordinarily beautiful lake sits below the soaring snow-capped peak of Mt Muztaghata (7509m) and has a couple of small Kyrgyz settlements along its western shore. Famed for its perfect plate-glass reflections of the surrounding mountains, it's a popular overnight stop between Kashgar and Tashkurgan where travellers can stay in traditional yurts or stone huts as guests of local families. This is best organised through a travel agency.

Sleeping & Eating

Unless you plan to do an expedition, your hotel choices are limited to the decent selection

carried more than a few hundred kilometres by any one group. An average day's journey was 15km to 20km and traders often made lengthy stops at oasis towns to plan their next stage.

In addition to silk, which was often used as currency, goods included spices, nuts, fruit, metals, leather products, chemicals, glass, paper, precious gems, gold, ivory, porcelain and exotic animals, including the powerful Ferghana horse much prized by the Chinese. It was the exchange of ideas, technology and culture, however, that is the true legacy of the Silk Road.

Buddhism entered China via the Silk Road, and later allowed Chinese monks to travel to Gandhara and India for direct study and the gathering of primary texts. In copying Buddhist cave art, which originated in India, the Chinese created some of the finest examples in locations such as Mogao and Kizil. Going in the other direction, fine Chinese tri-coloured pottery had influence across Central Asia, the Middle East and Europe.

The heyday of Silk Road trade began in the 6th century under the stable but militarily strong Tang dynasty. Cháng'ān became one of the most cosmopolitan capitals in the world, with an estimated 5000 foreigners, including Indians, Turks, Iranians, Japanese and Koreans permanently settled there. Trade declined and then stabilised under Mongolian rule of China, but by the 14th century, sea routes were supplanting the slow and still dangerous overland routes. By the 16th century, the Silk Road network had reverted to obscure local trading and never recovered its former importance.

In June 2014, at the behest of China, Kazakhstan and Kyrgyzstan, Unesco listed the 5000km Tiān Shān Corridor of the Silk Road as World Heritage. The designation highlights not just the obvious pagodas, palaces, cave art and remains of the Great Wall (including beacon towers and forts), but also the caravanserai and way stations that provided relief and lodging for traders. Hopefully in the coming years the listing will encourage more conservation and research and not be seen as a license for unfettered tourist development.

in Tashkurgan – which now includes a youth hostel – and some fairly unappealing yurts and stone huts on the shore of Karakul Lake.

Tashkurgan has plenty of simple eating options and some decent shopping at the town bazaar. Elsewhere on the Karakoram Hwy you will need to take supplies.

★ **K2 Youth Hostel**   HOSTEL $
(凯途国际青年旅舍, Kǎitú Guójì Qīngnián Lǚshě; ☑ 0998 349 2266, 182 9965 1555; kyyh@qq.com; Tashkurgan; dm ¥30-60, d/tr ¥120/200; @ 🛜) Housed in a huge warehouse space overlooking Tashkurgan's busy main pedestrian shopping street, this friendly hostel is run by a young English-speaking team who offer a warm welcome and lots of travel advice. There's a pool table, bar, roof terrace and plenty of public space. Rooms are big, minimalist and great value, though the whole place can get swamped in high season.

Look for the 'Kute Hostel' sign.

Crown Inn   HOTEL $$$
(皇冠大酒店, Huángguān Dàjiǔdiàn; ☑ 0998 342 2888; enquiries1@crowninntashkorgan.com; 23 Pami'er Lu, Tashkurgan; d/tw ¥488/468; ❄ 🛜) This friendly and modern Singaporean-run hotel offers comfortable, bright rooms centred on a pebble garden courtyard. Rooms are bright, if somewhat sparse, and some have excellent views. It's in the centre of Tashkurgan and its restaurant is also the best in town.

ℹ ADVANCE PLANNING

There are almost no settlements on the road between Kashgar and Tashkurgan, so be sure to take everything you need, including warm clothing, food and drink. If you take a bus, be aware that anything stowed on the bus roof will be unavailable during the journey. Check the state of the highway well ahead of time, as heavy snows and landslides can close it at almost any time. If you plan to continue into Pakistan, it's essential to have a Pakistani visa already in your passport. To get past the first checkpoint at Ghez, you'll need to have a permit: these can be arranged by any travel agency in Kashgar, they're free and you'll just need to submit a copy of your passport's photo page to allow them to get the permit, which is issued on the spot.

ℹ Permits

Foreigners need a permit from a travel agent to get past the checkpoint at Ghez. The Khunjerab Pass is open Monday to Friday from 1 April to 1 December, though these dates can change at any time due to weather conditions. Note that foreigners are not allowed to travel any significant distance off the KKH (including the area beyond the city limits of Tashkurgan) without special permits, which limits trekking options if you're not using the services of a travel agency.

ℹ Getting There & Around

From Kashgar, two daily buses run to Tashkurgan from the local bus station (p819), leaving at 10am and noon (¥89, six to eight hours). Shared taxis (¥150, six hours) also depart from Kashgar's Tashkurgan Administration Office (p819), in the west of town. They leave when full.

From Tashkurgan, there are two daily buses to Kashgar at 9.30am and 11.30am, and there's occasionally a third bus at 12.30pm. There is also a daily bus from Tashkurgan to Sost in Pakistan (¥225, eight hours) at 9.30am. It's best to buy your ticket for both services the day before you travel, or at least head to the bus station early in the morning to do so.

From Kashgar, it's 118km to the Ghez checkpoint, 194km to Karakul Lake, 283km to Tashkurgan and 380km to the Pakistani border.

In Tashkurgan, cabs buzz you around town for a flat fare of ¥5, rising to ¥10 if you need to go just outside the town itself.

SOUTHERN SILK ROAD

The Silk Road east of Kashgar splits into two threads in the face of the Taklamakan Desert, the second-largest sandy desert in the world. The northern thread follows the modern road and railway to Kuqa and Turpan. The southern road charts a more remote course between desert sands and the towering Pamir and Kunlun mountain ranges.

This off-the-grid journey takes you far into the Uighur heartland, as well as deep into the ancient multi-ethnic heritage of the region. You're as likely to come across a centuries-old tiled mosque as the ruins of a Buddhist pagoda from the 4th century.

It's possible to visit the southern towns as a multiday trip from Kashgar before crossing the Taklamakan Desert to Ürümqi, or as part of a rugged backdoor route into Tibet or Qīnghǎi.

Yengisar 英吉沙

The tiny town of **Yengisar** (Yīngjíshā) is synonymous with knife production. A lesser-known but more sensitive fact is it's the birthplace of the Uighur's icon of nationalism, Isa Yusuf Alptekin (1901–95), the leader of the First East Turkestan Republic in Kashgar, who died in exile in Istanbul. Neither of these facts are particularly popular with the Chinese government, and the town has suffered badly in the past few years and feels today like a rather sad backwater.

There are dozens of knife shops here, most of them strung along the highway; ask for the 'knife factories' (小刀厂; *xiǎodāochǎng* in Chinese; *pichak chilik karakhana* in Uighur). Traditionally each worker makes the blade, handle and inlays by hand, using only the most basic tools, though many knives on sale here are now factory produced and brought in from elsewhere, so be sure you're buying a real handmade knife if you decide to stop here. Another thing to consider is that knives are prohibited in luggage on buses, trains and planes (even in the hold), so you'll have to ship them home – ask the vendors about this, as they're used to arranging this as part of a knife sale.

It's currently not possible for foreigners to stay the night in Yengisar, so you'll have to limit your visit to a day trip, or to a quick stop by bus between Kashgar and Yarkand.

Buses pass through the town regularly en route between Yarkand (¥30, 1½ hours) and Kashgar (¥15, 1½ hours). To get to the knife sellers from the main bus station, hop in a taxi (¥5) for the 3km trip. They are right on the main road, so you'll pass right by them on the journey to or from Yarkand, and can simply ask the driver to let you out there.

Charklik 若羌

Charklik (Ruòqiāng) may be a soulless, modern Chinese town, but intrepid history buffs may find themselves heading here as there are several ancient city ruins nearby. The most famous is remote Lóulán (楼兰), located some 260km northeast of Charklik, but you'll probably have to join a very pricey group tour to visit as permits can run into the thousands of dollars. The ruined fortress and stupa of Miran (米兰) is closer, located just 7km southeast of the modern town of Miran (which is 85km northwest of Charklik). Permits here are more reasonable, being a few hundred rénmínbì for a group. Con-

tact **CITS** (www.xinjiangtour.com) in Ürümqi for help with the paperwork.

At the time of writing, no hotels in town were accepting foreigners, though this may change, and arrangements can certainly be made by CITS or other travel agencies.

From Charklik, you can complete the Taklamakan loop by taking one of several daily buses to Korla (¥128, four hours). Alternatively, you can continue east over the mountains to Golmud in Qīnghǎi on a daily sleeper bus (¥332, 18 hours). There's also a 7am bus each day that heads along the Southern Silk Road to Hotan (¥210, 13 hours).

Cherchen 且末

🌐 0996 / POP 53,000

Emerging from any direction into the dusty oasis town of Cherchen (Qiěmò) is an unforgettable experience, as you'll have had to pass through hundreds of kilometres of desert just to get here. Indeed, the town itself is struggling against being swallowed up by the massive Taklamakan Desert to its north, and dust storms and hazy days are common here.

The predominantly Uighur town is fairly unremarkable, but pleasant enough, with a couple of interesting sights nearby that are worth stopping off for if you're passing through. As a foreigner you'll be an object of great curiosity here, including to the police, who may well stop and photograph you.

◉ Sights

To visit the main sights outside Cherchen, go first to the Cherchen Museum, as one of the staff members will have to go with you to unlock the gates. This is a free service and you'll only be charged for the entry tickets, though you'll also need to pay for the return taxi, which should be ¥50.

Cherchen Museum MUSEUM
(且末县博物馆, Qiěmò Xiàn Bówùguǎn; ◉9.30am-1.30pm & 4-7.30pm) **FREE** Relics from Cherchen's main sights are on display at this regional museum, alongside displays ranging from yetis to the travels of explorer Sven Hedin. Sadly there's almost no labelling in English. It's in the northwest of town: the second of three buildings along the south side of the huge government square.

Zaghunluq Ancient Mummy Tomb TOMB
(扎滚鲁克古墓群景点, Zāgǔnlǔkè Gǔmùqún Jǐngdiǎn; ¥30; ◉9.30am-1.30pm & 4-7.30pm) This 2600-year-old tomb contains 13 naturally

mummified Mongol bodies, still sporting shreds of colourful clothing. What's particularly interesting here is that unlike the mummies on display in the various regional museums, you get a real sense of how the bodies were buried, including the depth, which makes it amazing they were ever found. The site is a further 4km west of the Toghraklek Manor, on the edge of the desert.

Toghraklek Manor   HISTORIC BUILDING
(托乎拉克庄园, Tuōhūlākè Zhuāngyuán; ¥20; ⊙9.30am-1.30pm & 4-7.30pm) The main sight in Cherchen itself is this fine example of early-20th-century Kashgarian architecture, built in 1911 for a local warlord. The compound has half a dozen rooms, with carved walls, bamboo ceilings and bright carpets, though sadly none of the original furniture remains and the whole site requires quite a bit of imagination to evoke Cherchen a century ago. It's 2.5km west of town.

🛏 Sleeping & Eating

Hóngzǎo Shāngwù Bīnguǎn   HOTEL $
(红枣商务宾馆; ☑0996 761 1888; Aita Lu, 埃塔路; r ¥100-120; 🕸@🛜) Slightly worn though spacious rooms are on offer at this place next to the bazaar, though some bathrooms are cleaner than others, and many of them are afflicted by Chinese toilet aroma. The better rooms come with computers and desks, though wireless is limited to the lobby only. There's no English spoken and staff seem utterly overwhelmed by foreigners.

Elkut   UIGHUR $$
(爱乐美食, Àiyuè Měishí; Aita Lu, 埃塔路; mains ¥20-50; ⊙10am-midnight) This friendly and clean Uighur restaurant is about the best you can hope for in a town like Cherchen. The photo menu takes in all the Uighur classics though the gregarious staff may well insist on preparing their signature local lamb dish for you as their honoured guest. Take a seat under the chandelier and enjoy!

ℹ Getting There & Around

There are sleeper buses to Ürümqi every evening (¥320 to ¥340, 20 hours, including a five-hour sleeping stop for the driver) and a 10am and 7pm bus to Korla (¥160 to ¥180, six hours); both of these go via the Cross-Desert Hwy.

The bus to Hotan (¥163 to ¥183, 10 hours) leaves daily at 10am, while at the same time another daily bus heads 350km east to Charklik at 10am (¥61, four hours).

A taxi from Cherchen bus station to the centre of town costs ¥5.

Hotan   和田
☑0903 / POP 322,000

An ancient Silk Road city with a long and illustrious history, Hotan (Hétián) is nevertheless moving quickly and relentlessly into the modern age. Indeed, today it can be hard at first to imagine that this was once the focal point of the ancient kingdom of Khotan (224 BC to AD 1006), or that later it became an important junction of the southern Silk Road from where trade routes led into India.

But get off the busy main avenues and enter the fabulous bazaar or wonderfully varied night market and you'll quickly get a sense of this important Uighur city's history and culture. The main reason to come here today is to explore several ancient sites around the city, or simply to shop for jade, silk, carpets and all manner of other things at Hotan's various markets.

History

New religions first entered Xīnjiāng (and China) through Hotan, and as with Buddhism (which arrived around 84 BC), they became well established. In fact, the Khotan Kingdom was a centre for Buddhist translation and study, and famous Chinese monks such as Faxian and Xuan Zang who passed through in the 5th and 7th centuries, respectively, commented favourably on the wealth and size of Khotan's Buddhist community. In 1006, Khotan was conquered by the Muslim Karakhanids and slowly Islam became the dominant cultural force. In the 13th century, Marco Polo visited and reported that the entire population followed the new religion.

Hotan has also long been known as the epicentre of the central Asian and Chinese jade trade. Locally unearthed jade artefacts have been dated to around 5000 BC and it is believed that Hotan attracted Chinese traders along the Jade Road even before they headed westward to open up the Silk Road. In the 5th century AD, the Hotanese were also the first non-Han to learn the secret of Chinese silk making, and later established themselves as the region's foremost carpet weavers.

⦿ Sights

Beijing Xilu is the main east–west axis running past the enormous, heavily guarded main square (Tuánjié Guǎngchǎng), with its paternalistic statue of Mao shaking hands with a Uighur craftsman.

Hotan

⭐ **Hotan Sunday Market** MARKET
(星期天市场, Xīngqítiān Shìchǎng; Taibei Donglu,
台北东路; ⊙dawn-dusk) Hotan's most popular
attraction is its weekly Sunday market. The
covered market bustles every day of the week,
but on Sundays it swamps the northeast part
of town, reaching fever pitch between noon
and 2pm Xīnjiāng time. The most interesting
parts are the *doppi* (skullcap) bazaar, the colourful *atlas* (tie-dyed, handwoven silk) cloth
to the right of the main entrance and the *gil-
im* (carpet) bazaar, across the road. Nearby
Juma Lu (加买路) is filled with traditional
medicine and spice shops.

Rawaq Stupa ARCHAEOLOGICAL SITE
(Rawak Stupa; ¥200; ⊙10am-6pm) This 9m-tall
ruin is the largest of the southern Silk Road
Buddhist stupas yet discovered. Built between the 3rd and 5th centuries for a wealthy
Khotanese monastery, it might have been visited by the Chinese monk Faxian in AD 401
on his way to India. It was certainly explored
by archaeologist Aurel Stein, who excavated
the site in 1901, and declared it a magnificent
ruin. Stein's original work also uncovered 91
large Buddhist statues (now all sadly gone).

Rawaq is about 50km north of Hotan and
it's best to go with a guide who knows the site,
as taxi drivers have been known to get lost.

Mazar of Imam Asim TOMB
FREE A few kilometres beyond Jíyà lies the
tomb complex of Imam Asim (Tomb of Four
Imams). It's a popular pilgrimage site, particularly during May, and you'll likely see
groups of Uighurs praying and chanting at
the desert shrine, which is slowly being en-
gulfed by the Taklamakan Desert. Buses to

Hotan

⊙ **Top Sights**
1 Hotan Sunday Market D1

🛏 **Sleeping**
2 Happy Hotan Hotel C1
3 West Lake Yín Dù International
Hotel B2
4 Yudu Hotel...................................... B2

❌ **Eating**
5 Marco Dream Cafe Bakery C2
6 Marco's Dream Cafe.........................C2

the town of Jíyà drop you 3km from the site,
from where you should be able to hire a motorised cart to take you to the site.

Melikawat Ruins RUINS
(玛利克瓦特古城, Mǎlìkèwǎtè Gǔchéng; ¥20;
⊙dawn-dusk) The deserts around Hotan are
peppered with the faint remains of abandoned cities. The most interesting are those
of Melikawat, 25km south of town, a Tang
dynasty settlement with wind-eroded walls,
Buddhist stupas and the remains of pottery
kilns. Some scholars believe Melikawat was
a capital city of the Yutian state (206 BC to
AD 907), an Indo-European civilisation that
thrived during the height of the Silk Road.
A taxi should cost about ¥100 to Melikawat.

🛏 Sleeping

Happy Hotan Hotel HOTEL $
(和田幸福宾馆, Hétián Xìngfú Bīnguǎn; ☑0903
202 4804; 59 Taibei Lu; r ¥100; 🛜) One of many
budget hotels around the main bus station,
Happy Hotan Hotel has a courtyard location

with a surprisingly charming, brightly painted courtyard. Sadly the charm ends there, and rooms are simple cells, though each has a bathroom. Turn right out of the bus station and it's just down the road.

Yudu Hotel
HOTEL $$

(玉都大酒店 Yùdū Dàjiǔdiàn; ☑0903 202 3456, 0903 202 2888; 11 Guangchang Xilu, 广场西路11号; r from ¥238; ✴🛜) The three-star 'Jade Capital' is the best value in town, and offers spacious, clean and modern rooms, with a useful location on the west side of the main square. There's working in-room wi-fi (for the most part), decent bathrooms and the front-desk staff speak a modicum of English. Rooms facing the square can be loud, however.

West Lake Yín Dū International Hotel
HOTEL $$$

(西湖银都国际酒店, Xīhú Yíndū Guójì Jiǔdiàn; ☑0908 252 9999, 0903 252 2222; 111 Tanaiyi Donglu; r incl breakfast ¥358; ✴🛜) This plush and excellently located hotel is generally considered to be the best Hotan has to offer. Rooms are big, with desks, fridges and glass-walled bathrooms. Breakfast is a plentiful buffet affair served in the ground-floor restaurant, while there's also an enormous choice of eating options in the immediate vicinity.

✕ Eating

Hotan has some excellent eating options, including one of the most traveller-friendly cafes in Xīnjiāng. Don't miss the excellent night market.

Uighur Night Market
MARKET $

(维族人夜市, Wéizúrén Yèshì; Nan Huan Lu & Ta'naiyi Nanlu, 南环路塔乃依南路的路口; meals from ¥20; ⊙7pm-midnight) Recently moved to its own purpose-built area about 1km due south of the main square, Hotan's night market is one of the liveliest and busiest in Xīnjiāng. Come here once darkness falls to grab such goodies as *tonur kebab* (whole roast sheep) and *chuchvara* (meat dumplings in broth), topped off with sweet *tangzaza* (sticky rice with syrup and yoghurt).

Marco's Dream Cafe
CAFE $$

(马克驿站, Mǎkè Yìzhàn; off Jianshe Lu, 建设路; mains ¥30-50; ⊙1.30-9.30pm Tue-Sun; 🛜) This Malaysian-run place serves a welcome range of Western and Asian dishes, including delicious curried chicken and steaks, while the friendly English-speaking owners can provide excellent travel advice. It's hidden in a courtyard beyond a red gate entrance, though the

owners warn they may have to move again soon: check their more permanent **bakery** (Mǎkè Yìzhàn; Kunlun Xiaoqu, Bldg 8, Door 12, 昆仑小区8号楼12号门面; pizza from ¥30; ⊙1.30-9.30pm Tue-Sat; 🛜) if you can't find this one.

🛍 Shopping

Hotan is one of the best shopping destinations in Xīnjiāng, and boasts a huge bazaar, as well as numerous jade, silk and carpet outlets. For jade, check out the stores around the northern end of the main square. Carpets and silk are sold along Taibei Donglu, between Wenhua Lu and the Sunday Market.

ℹ️ Information

Bank of China (中国银行, Zhōngguó Yínháng; cnr Urumqi Nanlu & Aqiale Lu; ⊙9.30am-1.30pm & 4-8pm Mon-Fri) Cashes travellers cheques, and has a 24-hour ATM in the southwest of town.

Southern Silk Road Tour (☑137 7929 1939; www.southernsilkroadtour.com) Local English-speaking guide Kurbanjan runs private tours along the southern Silk Road. Contact him by phone or email (he currently has no office) to get a quote for whatever you want to do, be it a one-day city tour of Hotan to multi-day camel treks in the desert.

ℹ️ Getting There & Away

AIR

There are about a dozen daily flights between Hotan and Ürümqi (from ¥750 one way) on various airlines including China Southern, Tianjin Airlines, Shanghai Airlines and Air China. The airport is 10km southwest of town.

BUS & CAR

There are two bus stations in Hotan. The **main bus station** (客运站, Kèyùnzhàn; Taibei Xilu) serves the following destinations:

Kashgar ¥128 to ¥145, seven to 10 hours, at 9.30am, 11.30am, 2pm and also stop at Karghilik (¥58 to ¥78, five hours) and Yarkand (¥77 to ¥90, six hours)

Kuqa ¥167 to ¥187, eight hours, two daily at 2pm and 8pm

Ürümqi ¥270 to ¥340, 25 hours, daily at 4.30pm and 9pm. Sleeper buses head straight across the desert on one of two cross-desert highways.

Shared taxis also run from outside the bus station to Karghilik (¥100), Yarkand (¥130) and Kashgar (¥200).

The **east bus station** (东郊客运站, Dōngjiāo Kèyùnzhàn), 2km east of downtown, has buses to/from the following:

Cherchen ¥124 to ¥160, 10 hours

Niya ¥63, four hours

Shared taxis run to all the same destinations from each bus station, and depart as soon as they're full.

TRAIN

Hotan is connected to the main Xīnjiāng railway line, though high-speed trains do not yet reach the city, meaning that journeys are slow, and considerably indirect if you're heading beyond Kashgar. The vast **train station** (和田火车站, Hétián Huǒchē Zhàn) is 5.5km north of the city centre. Sample prices:

Kashgar hard seat/sleeper ¥53/118, six to eight hours, one to two daily

Ürümqi hard/soft sleeper ¥350/586, 29 hours, one daily at 12.12pm

ⓘ Getting Around

Metered taxis start at ¥5 within town; figure on ¥15 to the train station and ¥30 to the airport. Buses criss-cross the city and cost a flat fare of ¥1.

Yarkand 莎车

♫ 0998 / POP 82,500

At the end of a major trade route from British India, over the Karakoram Pass from Leh, Yarkand (Shāchē) was for centuries an important caravan town and regional centre for the trade in cashmere wool. Today this very dusty, traditional and conservative town is a transport hub and little else, though scratch the thoroughly modern surface and you'll find the remains of a thriving Uighur Old Town and an impressive collection of mosques and mausoleums.

Be aware that Yarkand was the site of a still opaque violent protest on 28 July 2014, which led to 96 official deaths; the WUC (World Uyghur Congress) claim it was more than 2000. Security is tight here, though it's quite OK for foreigners visit.

Yarkand's main sights are clustered around its charming central 18th-century **mosque** (阿勒屯清真寺, Ālètún Qīngzhēn Sì) FREE. The surrounding sprawling cemetery is home to several other impressive shrines, with white flags marking the graves of *pir* (holy men). There are normally groups of elderly Uighurs praying here. The complex sits on a large square that was being totally redone on our last visit.

To escape modern Yarkand's uninspiring grid system, take a walk in the **Old Town** to the east of the Altun Mosque, where craftsmen still work their wares with ball-peen hammers and grindstones, several work-

shops churn out traditional Uighur instruments and horses and carts rule the streets. To get here, take the dirt lane headed east, just south of the Altun Sq, and keep going. Eventually you'll link up with Laocheng Lu and can return west back to the New Town.

Only a handful of hotels in Yarkand currently accept foreigners, and these are concentrated in and around Xincheng Lu.

Délóng Hotel (德隆大酒店, Délóng Dà Jiǔdiàn; ✆ 0998 852 5588; Qinai Bage Lu, 其乃巴格路; r ¥200; ✿ ⊚) is the only hotel in town that seems totally happy lodging foreigners. The plush and even rather stylish lobby leads to two floors of well sized and well maintained rooms that come with desks and flat-screen TVs. The bathrooms are on the stinky and aged side, though. It's near the junction of Qinai Bage Lu and Xinsheng Lu.

For meals, excellent **Turkan** (图尔康咖啡馆, Túěrkāng Kāfēi Guǎn, Gulebage Lu, 古勒巴格路, mains ¥28-68, ⊙ 10am-11pm) restaurant is easy to spot: look for the large 'Tea Coffee' sign in English on the awning. Inside it's a well appointed place with white-gloved waiters rushing dishes from a pictorial menu to the well heeled guests seated in gold and velvet chairs. As well as Uighur dishes, you can enjoy pizza (of a sort) and even a cappuccino. To find it, turn left out of the bus station.

ⓘ Getting There & Around

Buses leave half-hourly to Kashgar (¥46, 3½ hours), Yengisar (¥36, 1½ hours) and Karghilik (¥13, 1½ hours). There are four buses daily to Hotan (¥58, five hours), and six leave for Ürümqi (¥320 to ¥360, 25 hours). Faster shared taxis also depart when full to Kashgar, Yengisar and Karghilik.

Modern Yarkand is split into a Chinese New Town and a Uighur Old Town to its east. Take a right upon exiting the bus station to get to the main avenue. Once there, take another right and flag down any public bus, which will take you to the Old Town and the Altun Mosque complex nearby.

Karghilik 叶城

♫ 0998 / POP 383,664

Karghilik (Yèchéng) is an extremely dusty and unappealing Uighur town of importance to travellers only as the springboard to the fantastically remote Hwy 219, the Xīnjiāng–Tibet highway that leads to Ngari (Ali) in far western Tibet. There's absolutely nothing to detain you here, though travellers heading into Tibet may need to overnight here at a push.

The main attraction in town is the 15th-century **Friday Mosque** (Jama Masjid) and the surrounding adobe-walled backstreets of the Old Town.

Jiāotōng Bīnguǎn (交通宾馆; ☑ 0998 728 5540; 1 Jiatong Lu, 交通路1号; r ¥150; ❇ ⓢ) is right next to the bus station, which means it's both handy and central, as well as noisy and chaotic. Rooms are fine, though aged and pretty basic. Ask for a room in the quieter and cleaner back block. Turn left out of the bus station and look for the sign in English saying Communication Guest House.

NORTHERN XĪNJIĀNG

The north of Xīnjiāng is both geographically and culturally very different from the rest of the province; here thick evergreen forests, rushing rivers and isolated mountain ranges are home to Tuvan and Kazakh nomads, and while the Han Chinese population is growing, as it is throughout Xīnjiāng, you'll still find markedly different landscapes and people here. The entire north of Xīnjiāng was closed to foreigners until the 1990s, due to the proximity of the sensitive Russian, Mongolian and Kazakhstan borders, but today the region is growing fast as both a tourist and trade centre.

Bù'ěrjīn　布尔津

☑ 0906 / POP 70,000

Bù'ěrjīn, also known as Burqin, is 620km north of Ürümqi, and marks the end of the desert-like Jungar Basin and the beginning of the lusher sub-Siberian birch forests and mountains to the north. The town's population is mainly Kazakh, but there are also Russians, Han, Uighurs and Tuvans.

The town itself is clean and friendly, and has clear architectural influences from nearby Russia. There's little to see and do, but it's a pleasant place to start or end a journey to the magnificent Kanas Lake Nature Reserve.

If you have some time to kill, stroll to the southern limits of town to the Erqis (Irtysh) River, where dozens of stone *balbals* (Turkic grave markers) line the river embankment. From here the river flows eventually into the Arctic Ocean, the only major river in China to do so. In summer you'll be confronted with swarms of biting insects around dusk, so stock up on insect repellent.

🛏 Sleeping & Eating

Bù'ěrjīn has many hotels, though only a handful accept foreigners. Rates peak between July and September and are heavily discounted at other times. Budget travellers may want to check out the **Pigeonhouse Youth Hostel** (鸽子窝客栈, Gēziwō Kèzhàn; ☑ 180 4073 1030, 0906 651 8651; 17 Meilifeng Beilu, 美丽峰北路17号; dm ¥80), which was due to reopen in 2016 after a hiatus of several years.

Burqin Tourist Hotel　　　　HOTEL **$$**
(布尔津旅游宾馆, Bù'ěrjīn Lûyóu Bīnguǎn; ☑ 0906 652 1325, 0906 651 0099; 4 Wolongwan Xilu, 卧龙湾西路4号; d ¥270-488; ❇ ⓢ) Burqin's main hotel is centrally located and has a choice of two-, three- and four-star blocks. The biggest and best block has spacious and wellmaintained rooms and is superb value outside of high season, when huge discounts mean you can get a good room for as little as ¥120. Prices rise from late May to September.

Bù'ěrjīn Night Market　　　MARKET **$**
(河提夜市, Hétí Yèshì; Hebin Lu; mains from ¥10; ⏱ 7pm-midnight May-Sep) Specialising in grilled fish, fresh yoghurt and *kvas* (a yeasty brew popular in Russia), this riverside night market makes for very atmospheric dining, even if the whole riverside development has been a little Disneyfied. To find it, walk south on Youyifeng Lu and keep going until the street dead ends: it's on the right.

ℹ Getting There & Away

There's no airport in Bù'ěrjīn itself, but Altay, 1½ hours away, has an airport with several year-round daily flights to Ürümqi (from ¥690, but far more expensive in the summer months due to high demand). There is no bus service from Altay Airport to Bù'ěrjīn, you'll either need to head into Altay itself and take a bus from the bus station to Bù'ěrjīn, or take a taxi (¥250) to Bù'ěrjīn directly from the airport.

There are two buses a day from Bù'ěrjīn to Ürümqi, one leaving at 10am (¥183, 10 hours) and one leaving at 7pm (¥183, 12 hours). Hourly buses run to Altay (Ālètài; ¥24, 1½ hours) between 10am and 7pm.

Four daily buses run to Jímùnǎi (¥23, two hours) on the border with Kazakhstan. They depart at noon, 1pm, 4pm and 6pm.

Fast shared taxis run from outside the bus station to Ürümqi (¥250 per seat) and Altay (¥40 per seat).

There is no train station in Bù'ěrjīn. The closest station is Běitún (北屯), from where you have to catch a shared taxi or bus the final 90km. Make sure to buy your return train tickets in advance.

Kanas Lake　　　哈纳斯湖

Stunning Kanas Lake (Hānàsī Hú) is a long finger of water surrounded by soaring mountain peaks nestled in the southernmost reaches of the Siberian taiga ecosystem, pinched in between Mongolia, Russia and Kazakhstan. Most of the local inhabitants are Kazakh or Tuvan, though Chinese tourists (and the occasional foreigner) descend on the place in droves during the summer months. With a little effort it's just about possible to escape the crowds, but as facilities grow and domestic travel increases, it gets harder every year. Many visitors come hoping for a cameo by the Kanas Lake Monster, China's Nessie, who has long figured in scary stories around yurt campfires. She appears every year or two, bringing journalists and conspiracy hounds in her wake.

The whole area is only easily accessible from April to October, with ice and snow

UIGHUR FOOD

Uighur cuisine includes all the trusty Central Asian standbys, such as kebabs, *polo* (pilau rice) and *chuchura* (dumplings), but has benefited from Chinese influence to make it the most enjoyable region of Central Asia in which to eat.

Uighurs boast endless varieties of *laghman* (pulled noodles; *lāmiàn* in Chinese), though the usual topping is a combination of mutton, peppers, tomatoes, eggplant and garlic shoots. *Suoman* are torn noodle squares fried with tomatoes, peppers, garlic and meat, and *suoman goshsiz* are the vegetarian variety. *Suoman* can be quite spicy, so ask for *lazasiz* (without peppers) if you prefer a milder version. *Dapanji* (literally 'big plate chicken') is a local speciality that is now a common dish all over China: it's a chicken stew that also contains red peppers, onions, potatoes, chilli, garlic, ginger and sometimes Sichuan peppers, and is most commonly served with noodles. The pieces of chicken contain bones, however, so eat carefully!

Kebabs are another staple and are generally of a much better standard than the *shashlyk* of the Central Asian republics, though locals prize the fattiest cuts of meat far more than the leaner chunks, which means that some visitors will prefer to ask specifically for no fat. *Jiger* (liver) kebabs are ideal for this. *Tonor* kebabs are larger and baked in an oven *tonor* (tandoori) style. True kebab connoisseurs insist on *kovurgah kebab* or *bel kebab*, made from rib and waist meat respectively. Most are flavoured with *zir* (cumin), and then wrapped in bread and squeezed, releasing the juice onto the bread.

Naan (bread) is another favourite staple and irresistible when straight out of the oven and sprinkled with poppy seeds, sesame seeds or fennel. Most Uighur restaurants serve small cartons of delicious *ketik* (yoghurt) to accompany your meal.

Other snacks include *serik ash* (yellow, meatless noodles), *nokot* (chickpeas), *pintang* (meat and vegetable soup) and *gang pan* (rice with vegetables and meat). *Opke* is a broth of bobbing goats' heads and coiled, stuffed intestines, while *laohu cai* (tiger salad) is the region's most popular salad, a mix of raw onions, red pepper, green chillies and tomato.

Samsas (baked mutton dumplings) are available everywhere, but the meat-to-fat ratio varies wildly. Hotan and Kashgar offer huge meat pies called *daman* or *gosh girde*.

For dessert, try *morozhenoe* (vanilla ice cream churned in iced wooden barrels), *kharsen meghriz* (fried dough balls filled with sugar, raisins and walnuts, also known as *chiker koimak*) or *dogh* (sometimes known as *doghap*), a delicious mix of shaved ice, syrup, yoghurt and iced water. As with all ice-based food, try this at your own risk. *Tangzaza* are triangles of glutinous rice wrapped in bamboo leaves covered in syrup.

Anyone with a sweet tooth should look for carts selling *matang* (walnut fruit loaf) and *sokmak*, a delicious paste of walnuts, raisins, almonds and sugar, sold by the 500g jar (¥20 to ¥30) at honey and nut stalls. It's fine to ask for a free sample.

Xīnjiāng is justly famous for its fruit, whether it be *uruk* (apricots), *uzum* (grapes), *tawuz* (watermelon), *khoghun* (sweet melon) or *yimish* (raisins). The best grapes come from Turpan; the sweetest melons from Hāmì. Markets groan with the stuff from July to September.

Meals are washed down with *kok chai* (green tea), often laced with nutmeg or rose petals. The one local beer worth going out of your way for is bottled Xīnjiāng Black Beer, a dark lager-style brew, though note that most Uighur restaurants will not serve alcohol of any sort – you'll often need to go to a Chinese-run establishment if you want a drink.

KANAS VILLAGE

You can also explore Kanas Village itself, which is full of log houses and has several affordable noodle restaurants for a lunch stop. Other activities include water-rafting trips (¥200) and horse rides (per hour ¥40 to ¥60).

It's even possible to take an overnight **horse trek** to Hémù, via Karakol (Black Lake, or Héi Hú). Check with AHA International Youth Hostel.

making transport difficult at other times. The gorgeous autumn colours peak around mid-September.

About 160km from Bù'ěrjīn, the road comes to an end at Jiǎdēngyù, basically a collection of hotels near the entrance to the **Kanas Lake Nature Reserve** (喀纳斯湖自然保护区, Kānàsī Hú Zìrán Bǎohùqū; ¥110). Buy an entrance ticket and board a tourist bus (¥100, unlimited rides, May to October only), which carries you 16km up the canyon to the tourist base. You'll need to have your passport to sign in at the park entrance.

At the tourist base, which is dominated by an ugly visitor complex, you can change buses to take you the final 2km to Kanas Lake. From the final stop it's a five-minute walk to the lake. At the lakeshore you can take a speedboat ride, walk the long lakeshore boardwalk or head downstream from the dock along the river, or hike to the lookout point **Guānyú Pavilion** (观鱼亭; Guānyú Tíng; 2030m), which takes a couple of hours each way from the lake itself – most people take a taxi to the access road and then walk up (around 45 minutes) to save time. The views from the top are incredible.

It's quite possible to do a day trip to Kanas from either Bù'ěrjīn or Altay if you pay for a driver for the day. If you want to spend more time here, there are homestays and hotels at Jiǎdēngyù, and in the park at the tourist base and in Kanas Village. There are plenty of eating options available at the tourist facilities in Jiǎdēngyù and in smaller, privately run noodle restaurants in Kanas Village. Hikers and campers should bring food with them.

ⓘ Getting There & Away

Kanas airport (KJI) – also confusingly known as Bù'ěrjīn airport, despite being nowhere near Bù'ěrjīn – is 50km south of the reserve. It has between one and four daily flights to and from Ürümqi (from ¥950, one hour) between June and September. From here, taxis will take you the rest of the way to the reserve (¥100, 30 minutes). At other times, you'll need to fly into Altay airport, which has year-round connections to Ürümqi.

There is no public bus to the main gate at Jiǎdēngyù from Bù'ěrjīn.

Shared taxis do run from Bù'ěrjīn and Jiǎdēngyù, though outside summer it may be hard to find a ride. Taxi drivers will look for you at Bù'ěrjīn's bus station.

ⓘ Getting Around

Inside the park in high season, you're limited to the tourist bus that regularly connects the park entrance, Jiǎdēngyù and Kanas Village, following the main road along the Kanas River. There are frequent stops along the way where you can get out for photo opportunities. Early and late in the season (April, May, September and October), private drivers are normally permitted to enter the park. In peak summer, your only alternative is the few taxis that have permission to operate in the park.

Hémù 禾木

This gorgeous little Tuvan village is an alternative place to base yourself when you visit Kanas Lake. It's 70km southeast of the lake, but far less crowded come the summer months. May and June are great times to visit, when the blossom is thick on the trees, while September is a riot of autumnal colours.

Stay at the **AHA International Youth Hostel** (阿哈国际青年旅社, Āhā Guójì Qīngnián Lǚshè; ☑187 9904 3039, 1380 995 5505; ahaty@hotmail.com; Bahaba Village; dm/d ¥100/250; ☐), a rustic wood-cabin hostel and comfortable base for exploring the village and mountains.

Buses to Hémù leave from Jiǎdēngyù but are sporadic.

Yīníng 伊宁

☑0999 / POP 450,000

Located on the historic border between the Chinese and Russian empires, Yīníng (Yili or Gulja) has long been subject to a tug-of-war between the two sides. The city was occupied by Russian troops between 1872 and 1881, and in 1962 there were major Sino–Soviet clashes along the Ili River (Yīlí Hé). There are no unmissable sights here but it's a pleasant, little-visited stop en route to Sayram Lake, or a good place to break an overland journey to Kazakhstan.

In 2014, the stadium in Yīníng was the site of a mass trial in which 55 Uighurs were charged with terrorist activities. At least one death sentence was handed down. A similar mass trial was held in 1997 and is the subject of Nick Holdstead's book *The Tree That Bleeds*.

◎ Sights

Shǎnxī Mosque   MOSQUE
(陕西大寺, Shǎnxī Dàsì; Shengli Nan Lu) A couple of blocks southeast of the People's Sq is the Uighur Old Town and the impressive 260-year-old mosque, which looks far more like a piece of traditional Chinese architecture than a Muslim place of worship. All around the mosque you'll find workshops making traditional-style leather Uighur boots and other locally produced accessories for sale.

🛏 Sleeping & Eating

Just to the south of town is a line of open-air restaurants where you can sit and watch the mighty Ili River (Ili Daria in Uighur, Yīlí Hé in Chinese) slide by over a bottle of honey-flavoured *kvass* (a fermented drink made from rye bread).

★ Doppa Youth Hostel   HOSTEL $
(朵帕青年旅舍, Duǒpà Qīngnián Lǚshè; ☑186 9995 5027, 0999 898 8823; doppahostel@163.com; 5 Alley 9, Li Guang Lu; dm ¥35-50, s/d ¥80/100; 🛜) This excellent hostel is housed in a charming old mansion and has tons of Uighur atmosphere, friendly English-speaking staff and a charming gazebo in the courtyard that is great for hanging out. The gender-segregated dorms and one private room share the communal bathrooms and squat toilets, while extras include laundry (¥10 per load), bike rental and a book exchange.

The hostel is on the northern edge of a bizarre set of concentric streets that form a giant hexagon, which at least makes it easy to find on any mapping app. It's a 10-minute walk from the bus station: turn left onto the main road and then turn left onto Gongren Lu, then take the third left and keep going until you find the hostel on your right.

Xīnjiāng Yìzhàn Hostel   HOSTEL $
(伊栈国际青年旅舍, Yìzhàn Guójì Qīngnián Lǚshè; ☑182 9996 3623; Xijiuxiang, off Liqun Lu; dm ¥35-60, d ¥138; 🌐🛜) This unexpected find is a little tricky to locate; it's down a small side street off Liqun Lu. However, it's well worth the effort, whether you're looking for a hostel or a more comfortable midrange experience. The friendly, English-speaking staff can help with local tips, and the dorms and private rooms are all spotless and all have their own bathrooms.

Zǐxiānggě Coffee Club   INTERNATIONAL $$
(紫香舸咖啡馆, Zǐxiānggě Kāfēi Guǎn; Yīlí Bīnguǎn, 8 Yangbin Lu, 迎宾路8号伊犁宾馆; mains ¥20-70; ⊙10am-4am; 🛜) Within the grounds of the enormous Yīlí Bīnguǎn (伊犁宾馆; ☑0999 802 3799; 8 Yingbin Lu, 迎宾路8号; r ¥180-680; 🌐🛜), this surprisingly lavish multiroom restaurant specialises in coffee and tea, but also has a small Western menu serving up pizza, steaks and even a club sandwich, alongside a selection of Chinese dishes. There's also a full drinks list, making this a good evening option as well. Staff are super-friendly and love foreigners.

ℹ Getting There & Away

The main bus station (长途客运站; *chángtú kèyùnzhàn*) is 3km from the centre at the northwest end of Jiefang Lu, the main thoroughfare through town. There are approximately hourly buses to Ürümqi (¥150 to ¥190, nine to 12 hours) from 8.30am to 2pm, and three evening sleepers. There are also half-hourly buses to Bólè (博乐) for Sayram Lake (¥60, four hours, from 10.50am to 4.50pm). Buses also run every 30 minutes for the Kazakh border at Korgas (¥19 to ¥23, 30 minutes), from where it's possible to connect to Almaty once you cross the border, though at the time of writing there was no direct bus service to Almaty from Yīníng. There are also direct buses to Kuqa (¥210 to ¥230, 4pm, 12 to 14 hours) and Kashgar (¥330 to ¥360, 20 to 23 hours, 2pm and 4pm).

The train station is 8km northwest of the city centre. There are seven daily trains to Ürümqi (hard/soft sleeper from ¥80/¥130, 6½ to 11 hours).

The airport is 5km north of town. There are a dozen daily flights to Ürümqi (from ¥400) with China Southern, Shandong Airlines, Tiānjīn Airlines and China Eastern Airlines.

Sayram Lake   塞里木湖

Vast **Sayram Lake** (Sàilǐmù Hú), 120km north of Yīníng and 90km west of Bólè, is an excellent spot to get a taste of the Tiān Shān range (Tengri Tagh in Kazakh). The lake is especially colourful during June and July, when the alpine flowers are in full bloom. In the height of summer, there are Kazakh yurts scattered around the lake willing to take boarders.

By bus, Sayram Lake is two hours from Bólè or three hours from Yīníng; any bus passing between the two cities can drop you by the lake. Coming from Yīníng, the last section of road is a spectacular series of mountain bridges and tunnels.

Gānsù

POP 25.9 MILLION

Best Places to Eat

➡ Mǎzilù Beef Noodles (p836)

➡ Nirvana Restaurant & Bar (p842)

➡ Zhāixīng Gé (p856)

➡ Zhengning Lu Night Market (p836)

➡ Happy Homemade Yunnan Taste (p847)

Best Places to Sleep

➡ Nirvana Hotel (p842)

➡ Silk Road Dūnhuáng Hotel (p855)

➡ Bean Sprout Hostel (p850)

➡ Boke Youth Hostel (p846)

Why Go?

Synonymous with the Silk Road, the slender province of Gānsù (甘肃) flows east to west along the Héxī Corridor, the gap through which goods and ideas once streamed between China and Central Asia. The constant flow of commerce left Buddhist statues, beacon towers, forts, chunks of the Great Wall and ancient trading towns in its wake.

Gānsù offers an entrancingly rich cultural and geographic diversity. Historians immerse themselves in Silk Road lore, art aficionados swoon before the wealth of Buddhist paintings and sculptures, while adventurers hike through desert rockland, ascend sand dunes and tread along high-mountain paths well worn by Tibetan nomads. The ethnic diversity is equally astonishing: throughout the province, the local Hui Muslims act as though the Silk Road lives on; in Xiàhé and Lángmùsì a pronounced Tibetan disposition holds sway, while other minority groups such as the Bao'an and Dongxiang join in the colourful minority patchwork.

When to Go
Lánzhōu

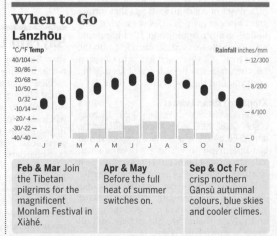

Feb & Mar Join the Tibetan pilgrims for the magnificent Monlam Festival in Xiàhé.

Apr & May Before the full heat of summer switches on.

Sep & Oct For crisp northern Gānsù autumnal colours, blue skies and cooler climes.

History

Although the Qin dynasty had a toehold on eastern Gānsù, the first significant push west along the Héxī Corridor came with the Han dynasty. An imperial envoy, Zhang Qian (Chang Ch'ien), was dispatched to seek trading partners and returned with detailed reports of Central Asia and the route that would become known as the Silk Road. The Han extended the Great Wall through the Héxī Corridor, expanding their empire in the process. As trade along the Silk Road

Gānsù Highlights

1 Mògāo Grottoes (p858)
Viewing one of the most important Buddhist sites on the Silk Road.

2 Bǐnglíng Sì (p837)
Gazing up at the giant Buddha carved into a desert cliff at this remote temple.

3 Zhāngyè Dānxiá National Geopark (p851)
Photographing the rainbow of desert colours on these Martian-like hills.

4 Màijī Shān Grottoes (p862) Ascending nerve-rattling catwalks for a peek inside these Buddhist caves.

5 Singing Sands Mountain (p860)
Stargazing over dunes with a glass of Mogao wine in hand.

6 Labrang Monastery (p839) Going with the Tibetan flow around the kora at Gānsù's most important monastery.

7 Lángmùsì (p845) Hiking to your heart's content around this chilled-out Amdo town.

8 Jiāyùguān Fort (p852) Feeling the Gobi wind in your hair standing on the ramparts of this ancient mud fortress.

9 Yǎdān National Park (p860) Witnessing the setting sun melt over eerie desert rock formations.

grew, so did the small way stations set up along its route; these grew into towns and cities that form the major population centres of modern Gānsù. The stream of traders from lands east and west also left their mark in the incredible diversity of modern Gānsù. The Buddhist grottoes at Mògāo, Màijī Shān and elsewhere are testament to the great flourishing of religious and artistic schools along the Silk Road.

The mixing of cultures in Gānsù eventually led to serious tensions, which culminated in the Muslim rebellions of 1862 to 1877. The conflict left millions dead and virtually wiped out Gānsù's Muslim population. Ethnic tensions have never fully left the province as the pro-Tibetan demonstrations in Xiàhé in 2008 and 2012 illustrate.

Though remote from the investment banks and manufacturing hubs along the east coast of China, Gānsù is not a poor province. Gross Domestic Product has been growing at a higher rate than the already blistering national average and massive investments in wind energy are fuelling the transformation of both the natural and urban landscapes.

Climate

Gānsù rarely sees any rain outside of the southern regions, and dust storms can whip up, particularly in the spring. Winters are nippy from November to March. Summer temperatures in the desert regions can top 40°C. It's important to keep well hydrated and pack adequate skin protection.

❶ Getting There & Away

Lánzhōu airport has flights around the country; other airports such as Dūnhuáng, Jiāyùguān and outside Xiàhé only have a handful of flights to major cities, with fewer flights in the winter.

PRICE RANGES

Sleeping
Price indicators for a double room:

$ less than ¥150

$$ ¥150 to ¥500

$$$ more than ¥500

Eating
Price indicators per meal:

$ less than ¥30

$$ ¥30 to ¥80

$$$ more than ¥80

❶ Getting Around

Both trains and buses are handy for connecting the province's Silk Road sights, and the addition of a new high-speed rail linking Lánzhōu with Ürümqi in Xīnjiāng has cut the time between cities significantly. In southern Gānsù you are largely at the mercy of buses, though upgrades to highways in recent years have cut travel times significantly.

LÁNZHŌU 兰州

☑ 0931 / POP 3.61 MILLION

At China's cartographic bullseye, Lánzhōu marks the halfway point for overlanders trekking across the country. Growing up on a strategic stretch of the Yellow River (黄河; Huáng Hé), and sitting between competing Chinese and Central Asian empires, Gānsù's elongated capital city frequently changed hands, reflected today in its mix of ethnic groups and cultures. These days, Lánzhōu is perhaps most well known for its favourite food – Lánzhōu beef noodles (牛肉拉面; *niúròu lāmiàn*) – and with several excellent night markets, this is an excellent place to sample the delights of Chinese Silk Road fare. Lánzhōu's reputation as being hazy and traffic-choked is also changing with the building of a new metro, which should be open by the time you read this.

◉ Sights

Sandwiched between mountains, the city sprawls in an east–west concrete melange for over 20km along the banks of the Yellow River. There are some attractive neighbourhoods along the northwest, and a pleasant riverside promenade, but travellers moving onward to other places in Gānsù may find themselves spending a lot of time around the train station, where there is an assortment of hotels and eateries.

White Pagoda Temple　　　BUDDHIST SITE
(白塔寺, Báitǎ Sì; White Pagoda Park, Binhe Zhonglu, 白塔山公园宾河中路; ⊙7am-8pm) FREE This temple, built during the Yuan dynasty (1206–1368) for a fallen Tibetan monk, stands on a hilltop in **White Pagoda Park** (Báitǎ Shān Gōngyuán) on the northern bank of the Yellow River and provides excellent city and river views on a clear day.

Enter from a gate on the north side of **Zhōngshān Bridge** (Zhōngshān Qiáo, 中山桥; Zhongshan Lu, 中山路) and walk up the stairs or catch the cable car (p838) on the south side a few blocks to the east.

Lánzhōu

Lánzhōu

⊙ Sights
1 White Cloud Temple................................A1
2 White Pagoda Temple.............................A1
3 Zhōngshān Bridge A1

🛏 Sleeping
4 JI Hotel D4
5 JJ Sun Hotel..D2

⊗ Eating
6 Mǎzilù Beef Noodles................................B1
7 Néngrénjù D3
8 Zhengning Lu Night Market.................B2

⊕ Drinking & Nightlife
9 Sunny Coffee B1

⊕ Information
10 Western Travel Agency D2

⊕ Transport
11 Gānsù Airport Booking Office...............D2
12 Lánzhōu East Bus Station.....................D3
13 Lánzhōu Long-Distance Bus
    Station D4
14 Tiānshuǐ Bus Station.............................D4
15 Upper Cable Car Station A1
16 Yellow River Cable Car...........................A1

Gānsù Provincial Museum   MUSEUM
(甘肃省博物馆, Gānsù Shěng Bówùguǎn; ☎0931
233 9131; www.gansumuseum.com; 3 Xijin Xilu, 西
津西路3号; ⊙9am-5pm Tue-Sun) FREE This
museum has an intriguing collection of Silk
Road artefacts with English descriptions,
including inscribed Han dynasty wooden

tablets used to relay messages along the Silk
Road, and dinosaur skeletons.

The graceful Eastern Han (25 BC–AD
220) bronze horse galloping upon the back
of a swallow is known as the 'Flying Horse
of Wǔwēi'. Unearthed at Léitái near Wǔwēi,
it has been proudly reproduced across

northwestern China. Bring your passport for admission.

Take bus 1 (¥1, 40 mins) here from Lán-zhōu train station.

White Cloud Temple TAOIST TEMPLE
(白云观, Báiyún Guān; Binhe Zhonglu, 宾河中路; ¥10; ⊘7am-6.30pm) Founded in the 8th century, this largely rebuilt Taoist temple features five halls and was among the most important Quanzhen-order temples during the Qing dynasty.

🛏 Sleeping

Lánzhōu can be a frustrating place to book accommodation, especially if you're travelling on a budget. Many budget hostels and midrange places are off limits to foreigners, including some nationwide chains. Often, places billed as hostels are actually private apartments that have been fitted out with bunk beds. There is a useful branch of **Jǐnjiāng Inn** (锦江之星; Jǐnjiāng Zhīxīng) on Tianshui Nanlu if you get stuck.

JI Hotel HOTEL $$
(全季酒店兰州天水南路店, Quánjì Jiǔdiàn; ☏0931 889 4999; 161 Tianshui Nanlu, 天水南路161号; tw/d ¥408/417; ❇@🛜) Bright and clean business hotel with Ikea-style furnishings and soft beds. Enjoys a handy location a five-minute walk from the train station.

JJ Sun Hotel HOTEL $$$
(锦江阳光酒店, Jǐnjiāng Yángguāng Jiǔdiàn; ☏0931 880 5511; 589 Donggang Xilu, 东岗西路589号; tw/d ¥459/590; ❇@) This four-star choice has well groomed, spacious and affordable rooms. There's a pleasant wood-panelled restaurant on the 2nd floor. It has a handy location across from the airport shuttle bus stop. Discounts of 40% are usual.

🍴 Eating

Lánzhōu is famous for its *niúròu lāmiàn* (牛肉拉面), beef soup with hand-pulled noodles and a spicy topping. There are plenty of places to try the dish, including on Huochezhan Xilu (left as you exit the train station) and Dazhong Xiang near the Zhōngshān Bridge (p834). These streets are also lined with restaurants serving dumplings and noodle dishes. Most have picture menus.

★Mǎzilù Beef Noodles NOODLES $
(马子禄牛肉面, Mǎzilù Niúròu Miàn; ☏0931 845 0505; 86 Dazhong Xiang, 大众巷86号; noodles ¥7; ⊘6.30am-2.30pm) In business since 1954, this place has locals flocking here for steaming

bowls of the city's most well known export: spicy hand-pulled noodles (拉面; *lāmiàn*). Join the queue inside the door and ask for *niúròu miàn* (牛肉面). You'll be given a ticket, which you take to the kitchen counter where chefs will prepare your noodles fresh. Grab chopsticks from machines at the ticket counter.

Go early, as noodles are traditionally a breakfast food in Lánzhōu.

Zhengning Lu Night Market MARKET $
(正宁路小吃夜市, Zhèngníng Lù Xiǎochī Yèshì; Zhengning Lu, 正宁路; lamb sticks ¥1) One of Lánzhōu's best night markets, this small pedestrian street is lined with vendors on both sides cooking up all manner of Silk Road delights. The mix of Hui, Han and Uighur stalls offer everything from goat's head soup to steamed snails, *ròujiābǐng* (肉夹饼; mutton served inside a 'pocket' of flat bread), lamb dishes seasoned with cumin, *dàpán jī* (大盘鸡; large plate of spicy chicken, noodles and potatoes), dumplings, spare-rib noodles and more.

Néngrénjù HOTPOT $$
(能仁聚; 216 Tianshui Nanlu, 天水南路216号; hotpot from ¥35; ⊘11am-10pm) At this Běijīng-style *shùan yángròu* (涮羊肉; traditional lamb hotpot) restaurant, the pot of broth costs ¥25, after which you can add sliced mutton (¥30), greens (¥10) and various other dishes. The restaurant is about 100m past the intersection with Minzhu Lu.

🍷 Drinking & Nightlife

Much of Lánzhōu's nightlife is centred on its night markets, which heave with people especially at weekends. Vendors ply the markets with bottles of the local beer and spirits.

Several permanently docked 'beer boats' line the banks of the Yellow River near Zhōngshān Bridge (p834). These open-air boats are pleasant places to while away an afternoon or evening supping on a Huang He beer on its eponymous river.

Sunny Coffee COFFEE, BAR
(桑昵的咖啡, Sāngnìde Kāfēi; Dazhong Xiang, 大众巷; coffee ¥26, beer ¥45; ⊘11am-10pm; 🛜) This cafe-bar serves coffees, juices and imported Belgian beers, and has free wi-fi. The live-in kitty is very friendly.

ℹ Information

Bank of China (中国银行, Zhōngguó Yínháng; 525 Tianshui Nanlu, 天水南路525号; ⊘9am-5pm) Has a 24-hour ATM.

THE BUDDHA CAVES OF BǏNGLÍNG SÌ

With its relative inaccessibility, **Bǐngling Sì** (炳灵寺; ☑ 0930 887 9057; ¥50; ☉ 8am-6pm, closed Dec-Mar) is one of the few Buddhist grottoes in China to have survived the tumultuous 20th century unscathed. Which is a good thing, as during a period spanning 1600 years, sculptors dangling from ropes carved 183 niches and sculptures into the porous rock of steep canyon walls. The cave art can't compare to Dūnhuáng, but the setting, few tourists and the remarkable terraced landscapes you pass getting here make Bǐngling Sì unmissable.

Today the cliffs are isolated by the waters of the Liújiāxiá Reservoir (刘家峡水库; Liújiāxiá Shuǐkù) on the Yellow River and hemmed in by a ring of dramatic rock citadels.

The star is the 27m-high **seated statue of Maitroya**, the future Buddha, but some of the smaller, sway-hipped Bodhisattvas and guardians, bearing an obvious Indian influence, are equally exquisite.

As you loop around past the Maitreya cave, consider hiking 2.5km further up the impressive canyon to a small **Tibetan monastery**. There might also be 4WDs running the route.

You can visit Bǐngling Sì as a day trip from Lánzhōu or en route to Xiàhé via Línxià. Take a boat or taxi from the town of Liújiāxiá. Frequent buses from Lánzhōu's west bus station (¥20, 2½ hours) run to Liújiāxiá bus station. From there, you will need to take a 10-minute taxi (¥6) to the boat ticket office at the dam (大坝; dàbà). Try to catch the earliest buses possible from Lánzhōu (starting at 7am) to avoid getting stuck on the way back. The last return bus to Lánzhōu leaves at 6.30pm.

A covered speedboat (seating nine people) costs ¥700 for the one-hour journey. The boat ticket office will refuse to make the trip unless the boat is full, so independent travellers may have to wait for a small group to form; expect to pay around ¥150 per person in this case. In summer, you should have no trouble finding a seat, but in shoulder season, you may find yourself stranded.

Surprisingly, the much more scenic route to the caves is by hiring a private car (¥250 return). Out of Liújiāxiá, the road runs high into the rugged hills above the reservoir, and for 90 minutes you will twist and turn, dip and rise through a wonderland of corn-growing terraces laddering and layering every slope, mound, outcrop and ravine. The final descent to the green-blue reservoir, with its craggy backdrop, is sublime. Driver touts ply the bus station in Liújiāxiá; bargain hard for a good deal.

If heading to Línxià after the grottoes, there are frequent buses (¥21, three hours) from the station at Liújiāxiá.

You can also opt to stay overnight in Liújiāxiá for a less rushed experience. The **Dorsett Hotel** (临夏刘家峡帝豪大酒店, Línxià Liújiāxiá Dìháo Dà Jiǔdiàn; 169 Huanghe Lu, Liújiāxiá, 黄河路169號, 刘家峡; tw/d ¥233/250; ❈ @ ☎) at the north end of town is a good option with huge rooms overlooking the Yellow River.

China Post (中国邮政, Zhōngguó Yóuzhèng; 381 Huochezhan Donglu, 火车站东路381号; ☉ 9am-5pm) Look for the green China Post sign to your right as you exit the train station.

ICBC (工商银行, Gōngshāng Yínháng; 475 Dingxi Nanlu, 定西南路475号) Twenty-four-hour ATM

Public Security Bureau (PSB, 公安局, Gōng'ānjú; ☑ 0931 871 8610; 482 Wudu Lu; ☉ 8.30-11.30am & 2.30-5.30pm Mon-Fri)

Western Travel Agency (西部旅行社, Xībù Lǚxíngshè; ☑ 0931 882 0529; 486 Donggang Xilu; ☉ 8am-6pm) On the 2nd floor of the west wing of Lánzhōu Fàndiàn. Offers tours around Lánzhōu (as far south as Xiàhé) and ticket bookings.

🛈 Getting There & Away

AIR

Lánzhōu Zhōngchuān Airport has flights to Běijīng (¥1460), Dūnhuáng (¥1466), Jiāyùguān (¥1576), Kūnmíng (¥1902), Shànghǎi (¥1750) and Xī'ān (¥480).

Gānsù Airport Booking Office (甘肃机场集团售票中心, Gānsù Jīchǎng Jítuán Shòupiào Zhōngxīn; ☑ 0931 888 9666; 616 Donggang Xilu, 东岗西路616号; ☉ 9am-6pm) can book all air tickets at discounted prices.

BUS

Lánzhōu has several bus stations, all with departures for Xīníng. The **main long-distance bus station** (兰州汽车站, Lánzhōu Qìchē Zhàn; 129 Pingliang Lu, 平凉路129号) is just a ticket office, outside which you catch a shuttle bus 30 minutes before departure for the **east bus station** (汽车东站, Qìchē Dōngzhàn; ☑ 0931 841 8411; 276 Pingliang Lu, 平凉路276号). Most bus journeys back into Lánzhōu end up at the east bus station; if you want to rough it on a sleeper to Zhāngyè or Jiāyùguān, buy a ticket directly at that station.

Journeys to and from the south of Gānsù, including to Xiàhé, go through the south bus station (汽车南站; qìchē nánzhàn). A taxi to the train station costs ¥45 and takes 45 minutes, or take bus 111 (¥1).

Services from the main long-distance bus station:

Píngliáng ¥125, five hours, hourly (7am to 6pm)

Tiānshuǐ ¥84, four hours, every 30 minutes (7am to 6pm)

Xīníng ¥59, three hours, every 30 minutes (7.10am to 8.10pm)

Yínchuān ¥124, six hours, seven per day (7am to 8pm)

The following services depart from the south bus station. Frustratingly tickets can only be purchased there, though can be bought just before departure:

Hézuò ¥74, four hours, every 25 minutes (7am to 4.30pm)

Línxià ¥39, three hours, every 30 minutes (7am to 7.30pm)

Xiàhé ¥75, four hours, five daily (7.30am, 8.30am, 9.30am, 2pm, 3pm)

Note: there is no direct bus from Lánzhōu to Lángmùsì. Go to Hézuò and change.

The west bus station (汽车西站; qìchē xīzhàn) has frequent departures to Liújiāxiá (¥19.50, 2½ hours, 7am to 6pm), useful if you are heading to Bǐnglíng Sì (p837).

Hidden off Tianshui Nanlu, the **Tiānshuǐ bus station** (天水汽车站, Tiānshuǐ Qìchēzhàn; Tianshui Nanlu, 天水南路) has buses for eastern Gānsù, including Luòmén (¥55, four hours, hourly). To find the station, look for a large WC sign and turn right into the narrow alley.

TRAIN

Lánzhōu is the major rail link for trains heading to and from western China. The city has two train stations: the centrally located Lánzhōu station (兰州火车站; Lánzhōu huǒchē zhàn) and Lánzhōu west railway station (兰州火车西站; Lánzhōu huǒchē xīzhàn). Both stations serve the Lánzhōu–Xīnjiāng high-speed rail line and airport trains, though the most frequent departures go from Lánzhōu Station.

In high season buy your onward tickets at least a couple of days in advance to guarantee a sleeper berth. For Dūnhuáng, double-check whether you are getting a train to the town itself or Liǔyuán, which is 180km away.

From Lánzhōu Station, there are frequent trains to the following:

Dūnhuáng Hard/soft sleeper ¥276/430, 13 to 15 hours, two daily direct to Dūnhuáng at 5.25pm and 5.50pm; the rest go to Liǔyuán

Jiāyùguān 1st/2nd-class seat ¥215/258, four hours; hard/soft sleeper ¥193/297, seven to 10 hours

Ürümqi Hard/soft sleeper ¥418/659, 19 to 24 hours

Wǔwēi Hard/soft seat ¥47/72, 3½ hours

Xī'ān Hard/soft sleeper ¥184/283, eight to nine hours

Zhāngyè 1st/2nd-class seat ¥180/150, three hours

Zhōngwèi Seat/soft sleeper ¥47/159, five to six hours

From Lánzhōu West Railway Station, there are trains to the following:

Jiāyùguān South 1st/2nd-class seat ¥258/215, 4½ hours

Ürümqi South 1st/2nd-class seat ¥658/549, 11½ hours

Xīníng 1st/2nd-class seat ¥70/58, one to 1½ hours

Zhāngyè West 1st/2nd-class seat ¥180/150, 2½ to 3½ hours

ℹ Getting Around

Lánzhōu Zhōngchuān Airport is 70km north of the city. Airport shuttle buses (¥30, one hour) leave hourly from 5.30am to 7pm in front of the **Gānsù Airport Booking Office** (p837) on Donggang Xilu, near the **JJ Sun Hotel** (p836). A taxi costs around ¥150.

A high-speed intercity rail line opened in 2015 connecting the airport with Lánzhōu's main railway station (40 to 50 minutes, ¥21.50 to ¥26) and Lánzhōu west railway station (30 to 40 minutes, ¥18.50 to ¥22), where you can get high-speed rail connections to Zhāngyè and Jiāyùguān.

Public buses cost ¥1; taxis are ¥7 for the first 3km. There is no bus from the train station to the south bus station, so you are better off taking a taxi for ¥35 for 45 minutes.

A cable car runs from the **Yellow River Cable Car Station** (黄河索道, Huánghé Suǒdào; down/up/return adult ¥25/35/45, child ¥10/15/20; ☑ 34) to the **Upper Cable Car Station** (黄河索道上站, Huánghé Suǒdào Shàngzhàn) for easy access to White Pagoda Temple (link).

USEFUL BUS ROUTES

Buses 1 and 6 From the train station to the west bus station via Xiguan Shizi.

Bus 111 From Zhongshan Lu (at the Xiguan Shizi stop; 去汽车南站的111路公交车) to the south bus station.

Buses 7 and 10 From the train station up the length of Tianshui Nanlu before heading west and east, respectively.

SOUTHERN GĀNSÙ

Mountainous and largely verdant, the southern part of Gānsù is a sight to behold. The Tibetan-inhabited areas around Xiàhé and Lángmùsì are the principal enticements here – perfect stopovers for overlanders heading to or from Sìchuān or destinations in their own right. Southwest of Lánzhōu, the inspiring vistas of the Yellow River and the Buddhist grottoes of Bǐnglíng Sì, carved out of dusty desert cliffs, remain some of the best-kept secrets in the country.

❶ Getting There & Away

Southern Gānsù is not served by train, so transport radiates south from Lánzhōu by bus. The most popular destinations are generally within two to four hours of the capital, and the ever-expanding road network in the area means that connections are easy to come by.

Xiàhé   夏河

📇 0941 / POP 80,000

The alluring monastic town of Xiàhé attracts an astonishing band of visitors: backpack-laden students, insatiable wanderers, shaven-headed Buddhist nuns, Tibetan pilgrims in their most colourful finery, camera-toting tour groups and dusty, itinerant beggars. Most visitors are rural Tibetans, whose purpose is to pray, prostrate themselves and seek spiritual fulfilment at holy Labrang Monastery, around which Xiàhé has grown up.

In an arid mountain valley at 2920m above sea level, Xiàhé has a certain rhythm about it and visitors quickly tap into its fluid motions. The rising sun sends pilgrims out to circle the 3km *kora* (pilgrim path) that rings the monastery. Crimson-clad monks shuffle into the temples to chant morning prayers. It's easy to get swept up in the action, but some of the best moments come as you set your own pace, wandering about town or in the splendid encircling mountains.

◉ Sights

Xiàhé stretches northeast to southwest in a narrow valley along the eponymous Xià River (Xià Hé; 夏河). Labrang Monastery marks the division between Xiàhé's mainly Han Chinese and Hui Muslim eastern quarter (where you'll find the bus station and a swath of Han-style shops and restaurants) and the older, low-rise Tibetan village to the west.

Labrang Monastery covers much of Xiàhé and a ticket to the monastery covers the main buildings on a guided tour. Several other buildings have their own admission fees, and tickets for those can be purchased at small ticket offices or from attendants at the entrances. In general, opening hours for the monastery's buildings are 8am to 5pm, although you can wander the grounds from very early in the morning, and many pilgrims begin walking the *kora* before dawn.

★**Labrang Monastery**   BUDDHIST TEMPLE
(拉卜楞寺, Lābǔléng Sì; Renmin Xilu, 人民西路; tour ¥40) With its succession of squeaking prayer wheels (3km in total), hawks circling overhead and the throb of Tibetan long-horns resonating from the surrounding hills, Labrang is a monastery town unto itself. Many of the chapel halls are illuminated in a yellow glow by yak-butter lamps, their strong-smelling fuel scooped out from voluminous tubs. Even if Tibet is not on your itinerary, the monastery sufficiently conveys the mystique of its devout persuasions, leaving indelible impressions of a deeply sacred domain.

In addition to the chapels, residences, golden-roofed temple halls and living quarters for the monks, Labrang is also home to six *tratsang* (monastic colleges or institutes), exploring esoteric Buddhism, theology, medicine, astrology and law.

Labrang Monastery was founded in 1709 by Ngagóng Tsúndé (È'angzōngzhé in Chinese), the first-generation Jamyang (a line of reincarnated Rinpoches or living Buddhas ranking third in importance after the Dalai and Panchen lamas), from nearby Gānjiā. The monastery is one of the six major Tibetan monasteries of the Gelugpa order (Yellow Hat sect of Tibetan Buddhism). The others are Ganden (p922), Sera (p923) and Drepung (p922) monasteries near Lhasa; Tashilhunpo Monastery (p926) in Shigatse; and Kumbum Monastery (p900) near Xīníng in Qīnghǎi.

TRADITIONAL MEDICINE

Among the six tratsang (colleges) of **Labrang Monastery**, the Institute of Medicine is renowned throughout the Tibetan world. Many Tibetans and pilgrims come here to be seen by monastic doctors, and there are numerous small clinics around town that treat the ill and infirm. If you wish to be seen by a monastic doctor, it's best to ask advice from your guesthouse, or enquire at the Nirvana Hotel (p842).

Xiàhé

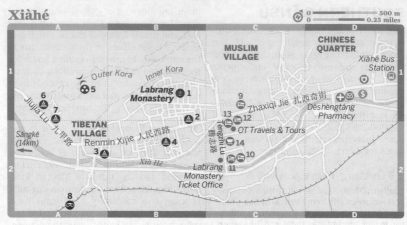

Xiàhé

At its peak, Labrang housed nearly 4000 monks, but their ranks greatly declined during the Cultural Revolution. Modern Labrang is again such a popular destination for young disciples that numbers are currently capped at 1800 monks with about 1600 currently in residence, drawn from Qīnghǎi, Gānsù, Sìchuān and Inner Mongolia.

➔ Main Buildings

The only way to visit the interior of the most important buildings is on a tour (no photos allowed inside buildings), which generally includes the Institute of Medicine, the Manjushri Temple, the Serkung (Golden Temple) and the main Prayer Hall (Grand Sutra Hall), plus a museum of relics and yak-butter sculptures. English-language **tours** (per person ¥40) leave the monastery's **ticket office** (售票处; *shòupiàochù*) around 10.15am and 3.15pm most days, and although they give plenty to see, they can feel a bit rushed. Outside those times you can latch on to a Chinese tour, with little lost even if you don't understand the language, but be aware you must purchase the ¥40 ticket to gain entrance to any of the buildings' interiors. Even better is to show up at around 6am or 7am, when the monks come out to pray and chant. At dusk the hillside resonates with the throaty sound of sutras being chanted behind the wooden doors.

➔ Inner Kora

The rest of the Labrang can be explored by walking the inner kora (pilgrim path). Although many of the temple halls are padlocked shut, there are a couple of separate smaller chapels you can visit, though they can often be closed for unexplained reasons. Some charge admission. Among the most popular are the three-storey Barkhang, the Hall of Hayagriva with its enchanting murals, and the golden **Gòngtáng Pagoda** (贡唐宝塔, Gòngtáng Bǎotǎ, Gòngtáng Chörten; admission ¥20), which offers incredible views over the whole monastery from its roof.

Access to the rest of the monastery area is free, and you can easily spend several hours just walking around and soaking up the atmosphere in the endless maze of mud-packed walls. The Tibetan greeting in the local Amdo dialect is *Cho day mo?* ('How do you do?') – a great icebreaker.

The best morning views of the monastery come from the **Thangka Display Terrace** `FREE`, a popular picnic spot, or the forested hills south of the main town.

➡ **Hall of Hayagriva**

(马头明士殿, Matóu Míngwáng Diàn, Hall of Horse-head Buddha; ¥10) A repository of vivid and bright murals, the hall encapsulates a startlingly fierce 12m-high effigy of Hayagriva – a wrathful manifestation of the usually calm Avalokiteshvara (Guanyin) – with six arms and three faces. The hall is down a side lane almost directly across from the lane to the Barkhang.

➡ **Barkhang**

(Printing Temple; ¥10) The three-storey Barkhang serves as the monastery's (p839) traditional printing temple. With rows upon rows of more than 20,000 wood blocks for printing, it's well worth a visit, and photos are allowed. The Barkhang is off the main road down a small side lane. The temple typically closes for lunch for a couple of hours around noon.

Ngakpa Gompa   BUDDHIST SITE

(红教寺, Hóngjiào Sì; Tibetan Village, 九甲村; ¥5) Visit this small Nyingmapa (Red Hat) school monastery to catch a glimpse of lay monks who wear striking red and white robes and have long, braided hair. No entry to actual school.

Nunnery   BUDDHIST SITE

(尼姑庵, Nígū'ān, Ani Gompa; Tibetan Village, 九甲村; ¥10) This nunnery is on the hill above the Tibetan part of Xiàhé. The outer *kora* (pilgrim path) begins just to the left of here.

☞ Tours

Guided tours of the surrounding area can be arranged by OT Travels & Tours (p843), the couple who run Nirvana Hotel (p842) and the staff at Snowy Mountain Cafe (p842). Most guesthouses in town can also help with day trip arrangements.

✦ Festivals & Events

Festivals are central to the calendar for both the devotional monks and the nomads who stream into town from the grasslands in multicoloured splendour. Tibetans use a lunar calendar, so dates for individual festivals vary from year to year.

Monlam Festival   RELIGIOUS

(Great Prayer Festival) This festival starts three days after the Tibetan New Year, which is usually in February or early March, with significant days accompanied by spectacular processions and prayer assemblies. Monlam Festival finishes with a creative display of monk-sculpted butter lanterns lighting up the 15th evening (and full moon) of the New Year.

☰ Sleeping

Xiàhé has long been a traveller's destination, and is loaded with small guesthouses, inns and hotels catering to a variety of budgets. Most are located at the west end of Renmin Xilu/Zhaxiqi Jie near the entrance to Labrang Monastery.

GĀNSÙ XIÀHÉ

WALK LIKE A TIBETAN

Following the 3km **inner kora** (pilgrim path) encircling Labrang Monastery is perhaps the best approach to grasping the giant temple's layout, scale and significance. The *kora* is lined with long rows of squeaking prayer wheels, whitewashed *chörtens* (Tibetan stupas) and chapels. Tibetan pilgrims with beads in their hands and sunhats on their heads, old folk, mothers with babies and children, shabby nomads and curious visitors walk in meditative fashion clockwise along the path (called *zhuǎnjìngdào*, 'scripture-turning way' in Chinese), rotating prayer wheels as they go. Look also for the tiny meditation cells on the northern hillside.

For a short hike, the more strenuous **outer kora** takes about an hour and climbs high above the monastery. To reach the start, head past the monastery's western edge. About one block into the Tibetan village look for a large signpost (in Tibetan but it's the only one around) on the right. Follow the alley up to the right, and make your way to the ridge, where you wind steeply uphill to a collection of prayer flags and the ruins of a **hermitage**. The views of the monastery open up as you go along. At the end of the ridge there's a steep descent into town.

A lot of hotels here utilise solar gain to power their hot-water supplies, so showering in the evening offers the best chance for scalding hot water in many places.

Overseas Tibetan Hotel
HOTEL $

(华侨饭店, Huáqiáo Fàndiàn; ☎0941 712 2642; www.overseastibetanhotel.com; 77 Renmin Xijie, 人民西街77号; dm ¥50, d ¥200-300; ☎) A well run and bustling place with wi-fi that reaches every corner, and solar powered hot water. The modern doubles have clean enclosed showers, flat-screen TVs and cushy, thick mattresses. Discounts of 20% in quiet periods.

It's owned by Losang, an energetic, likeable Tibetan with faultless English and in touch with the wants of travellers. Services include bike rental (¥20 per day), laundry, the OT Travels & Tours travel agency and the **Everest Cafe** with Western set breakfasts with yak yoghurt (¥30).

Tara Guesthouse
GUESTHOUSE $

(卓玛旅社, Zhuōmǎ Lǚshè; ☎0941 712 1274; 268 Yagetang, 雅鸽搪268号; dm ¥40, d ¥320, s/tw per bed without bathroom ¥85/100; ☎) This long-established budget place is run by monks from Sìchuān and has extremely frugal dorms, small *kàng* rooms (shared shower) and doubles with private bathrooms. English is spoken at the front desk.

Labrang Red Rock International Hostel
HOSTEL $

(拉卜楞红石国际青年旅馆, Lābǔléng Hóngshí Guójì Qīngnián Lǚguǎn; ☎0941 712 3698; 253 Yagetang, 雅鸽搪253号; dm/d ¥50/150; @☎) This Tibetan-themed, quiet hostel has pine-wood rooms, solar-powered hot showers, a restaurant-bar, and a beautiful display of *thangka* (Tibetan Buddhist paintings). Doubles are clean with futon-style beds, and YHA cardholders get a discount.

★ Nirvana Hotel
HOTEL $$

(德古园, Dégǔyuán; ☎0941 718 1702; www.nirvana-hotel.net; 247 Yagetang, 雅鸽搪247号; d ¥300; ☻✳@☎) ✎ Run by a friendly, English-speaking Tibetan-Dutch couple, Nirvana's cosy rooms are decorated tastefully in traditional Tibetan style, with giant, comfy beds. Small details make its slightly higher prices worthwhile: international plug boards, free coffee/tea/bottled water and toiletries. The bonus of having Nirvana's popular bar-restaurant downstairs and the friendliness of the proprietors make this a haven in this part of China.

Labrang Baoma Hotel
HOTEL $$

(拉卜楞宝马宾馆, Lābǔléng Bǎomǎ Bīnguǎn; ☎0941 712 1078; Zhaxiqi Jie, 扎西奇街; dm ¥35, r from ¥480; @) Pleasant and vibrantly colourful hotel with Tibetan-style courtyard and comfortable doubles with private bathroom. Discounts of 50% are common.

✗ Eating

For those who can't make it to Tibet, Xiàhé provides an opportunity to develop an appetite for the flavours of the Land of Snows, whether it's *mómo* (dumplings), *tsampa* (a porridge of roasted barley flour), yak-milk yoghurt or throat-warming glasses of the local barley-based firewater (*chang* in Tibetan, *qīngkèjiǔ*, 青稞酒 in Chinese).

★ Nirvana Restaurant & Bar
TIBETAN, WESTERN $

(德古园, Dégǔyuán; ☎0941 718 1702; 247 Yagetang, 雅鸽搪247号; dishes ¥15-35; ⊘9am-9pm; ✳☎) ✎ This lovely, bright restaurant serves Tibetan and Western dishes, such as the popular yak stew with potatoes (¥20), pizza and fresh espresso. The welcoming, casual vibe makes leaving Nirvana difficult, as does the long booze menu, which includes all the standards plus big bottles of locally brewed craft beer (¥45) and homemade 'cowboy barley wine'.

Snowy Mountain Cafe
TIBETAN, WESTERN $

(雪山餐厅, Xuěshān Cāntīng; ☎151 0940 8910; Renmin Xilu, 人民西路; ⊘9am-10pm; ☎) This chilled-out spot caters to travellers with a menu of Tibetan, Chinese and Western staples, as well as a full-service bar. Try the Tibetan-style noodles (¥20) or yak steak (¥70). There's also a nice Western breakfast menu, including a set menu of eggs, toast, yoghurt and tea/coffee (¥30).

Tara Restaurant
TIBETAN

(268 Yagetang, 雅鸽搪268号) This restaurant on the ground floor of Tara Guesthouse serves some of the best *mómo* (¥15) in town and is popular with monks for the many vegetarian options.

⬤ Drinking & Nightlife

Norden Cafe
CAFE

(诺尔丹咖啡, Nuò'ěrdān Kāfēi; Tengzhi Lu, 腾志路; tea ¥15; ☎) Traveller-friendly cafe with warm pine-wood interior serving homemade cakes, soups and burgers, plus excellent tea and coffee. Lovely big window seats overlook Labrang Monastery's ticket office (p840).

🛍 Shopping

Xiàhé is an excellent place to look for Tibetan handicrafts, from cowboy hats and Tibetan trilbies, to *chuba* (Tibetan cloaks), monk's boots, strings of prayer flag or *thangka* (Tibetan sacred art) paintings. Stacks of handicraft shops line Zhaxiqi Jie east of the monastery, and some painting shops are found off the southern *kora* (pilgrim path) alongside the river.

ℹ Information

Xiàhé is located at nearly 3000m in altitude, and some travellers experience mild altitude sickness when they arrive. The most common complaints are headache, fatigue and dizziness. Take care not to overexert yourself, especially for the first 24 hours while you acclimatise.

China Post (中国邮政, Zhōngguó Yóuzhèng; 8 Renmin Xijie; ⊙8am-6pm)

Déshèngtáng Pharmacy (德盛堂药店, Déshèngtáng Yàodiàn; 14 Renmin Xijie; ⊙9.30am-9pm) Western, Chinese and Tibetan medicine; just west of China Post.

ICBC (工商银行, Gōngshāng Yínháng; 98 Nanxiahe Jie, 南下河街98号; ⊙8.30am-4pm) Has an ATM and changes US dollars.

OT Travels & Tours (☑ 0941 712 2642; www.overseastibetanhotel.com/TravelAgency.htm; 77 Renmin Xijie, 人民西街77号; ⊙8am-9pm) This travel agency based at the **Overseas Tibetan Hotel** (see far left) can arrange cars and English-speaking guides to nearby sights, and also specialises in overland tours from Lánzhōu, Xīníng and Chéngdū to Xiàhé.

ℹ Getting There & Away

Trains don't run to Xiàhé, but it's regularly serviced by bus. Most travellers head on to either Lánzhōu or Sichuān; the road less travelled takes you over the mountains to Tóngrén in Qīnghǎi.

AIR

Gānnán Xiàhé Airport (甘南夏河机场; Gānnán Xiàhé Jīchǎng), 65km south of Xiàhé, opened in late 2013 with flights to a number of cities, including Xī'ān (¥500), Běijīng (¥1330), Shànghǎi (¥1400) and Chéngdū (¥600). Book flights online in English at ctrip.com.

LÍNXIÀ AND ITS MINORITY COMMUNITIES

Línxià (临夏; population 202,500) is a centre of Chinese Islam settled by ancient Silk Road Muslims and now populated by their descendants. At one time known as Hézhōu (河州), the city's strategic location at the junction of the Silk Road and several north–south trade routes meant it was, for centuries, an important commercial centre. These crossing roads brought Muslim teachers from Central Asia and further afield, some of whom stayed and went on to turn Línxià into an important centre for Chinese Islamic scholarship, particularly Sufism. The city itself is occasionally used by travellers (and monks) to break up the trip between Xiàhé and Lánzhōu or Qīnghǎi. Línxià is home to more than 80 mosques and *gōngběi* (拱北; Sufi master's shrine complexes) dotted all over town.

Spilling over a ridge high above Línxià and home to both Hui and Dongxiang minorities, the little market town of **Suǒnánbà** (锁南坝; population 12,000) has a single street that's a hive of activity, with locals trading livestock and occasional shepherds shooing flocks about.

The town is sometimes also called Dōngxiāng (东乡) after the surrounding county. The Dongxiang people speak an Altaic language and are believed to be descendants of 13th-century immigrants from Central Asia, moved forcibly to China after Kublai Khan's Middle East conquest.

Dàhéjiā (大河家; population 4500), with sweeping views over the Yellow River, towering red cliffs and (in summer) verdant green terraces, is a kaleidoscope of colour. The surrounding area is home to a significant population of Bao'an (保安族), Muslims who speak a Mongolic language. The Bao'an are famed for producing knives and share cultural traits with the Hui and Dongxiang. Their Mongol roots come out during summer festivals, when it is possible to see displays of wrestling and horse riding.

To Suǒnánbà, frequent minibuses (¥7, one hour) head up on the pleasant journey past terraced fields from Línxià's east bus station.

You can visit Dàhéjiā when travelling on the road between Línxià and Xīníng. Most buses between the two will stop here. From Línxià you can also catch a frequent minibus (¥25, three hours) from the station (城郊汽车站; *chéngjiāo qìchē zhàn*) on the outskirts of town.

BUS

The following bus services depart from Xiàhé:

Hézuò ¥25, 1½ hours, every 30 minutes (6.10am to 5.20pm)

Lángmùsì ¥84, 3½ hours, one daily (7.40am)

Lánzhōu ¥76, 3½ hours, five daily (6.30am, 7.30am, 8.30am, 12.50pm and 2.30 pm)

Línxià ¥31, two hours, every 30 minutes (7am to 5pm)

Tóngrén ¥41, Three hours, one daily (7.30am)

Xīníng ¥78, six hours, one daily (6.10am)

If you can't get a direct ticket to/from Lánzhōu, take a bus to Línxià or Hézuò and change there. If heading to Xīníng, note that buses run there every 40 minutes from Tóngrén.

ℹ Getting Around

There is no airport bus, but OT Travels & Tours (p843) can arrange a private taxi to the airport for ¥400. The journey takes an hour.

Xiàhé is easily walkable. A number of hotels and restaurants rent out bikes for ¥30 per day. Taxis cost ¥1 to ¥2 per seat for a short trip around town, including to the bus station and Labrang Monastery. Leaving the bus station, turn right for a 1km walk to the monastery and main part of town.

Around Xiàhé

Gānjiā Grassland   甘加草原

The **Gānjiā Grasslands** (Gānjiā Cǎoyuán), 34km from Xiàhé, aren't as pretty as those at nearby Sāngkē, but there is more to explore. From Xiàhé a bumpy road crosses the Naren-Ka pass (impassable after long rains) before quickly descending into wide grasslands dotted with herds of sheep and backed by ever-more dramatic mountain scenery.

Past Gānjiā Xiàn village, a side road climbs 12km to **Nekhang**, a cave complex where pilgrims lower themselves down ropes and ladders into two sacred underground chambers. A Dutch traveller fell to his death here in 2006, and to prevent the same fate we advise avoiding this place.

Just up the road from the caves is **Trakkar Gompa** (白石崖寺, Báishíyá Sì; admission ¥30), a monastery of 90 monks set against a stunning backdrop of vertical rock formations. From Trakkar it's a short drive to the 2000-year-old Han dynasty village of **Bājiǎo** (八角, Karnang; ¥25). The remarkable 12-sided walls here still shelter a small living community. From the village it's a short 5km diversion to the renovated **Tseway Gompa**

(佐海寺, Zuǒhǎi Sì; ¥30), one of the few Bön monasteries in Gānsù. Make sure you circumnavigate any holy site counterclockwise in the Bön fashion. There are great views of Bājiǎo from the ridge behind the monastery.

A four- to five-hour return trip to the Gānjiā Grasslands costs around ¥180 for a taxi from Xiàhé. An English-speaking driver and guide costs ¥450 for the full return trip and can be arranged at Snowy Mountain Cafe (p842).

Sāngkē Grasslands   桑科草原

Expanses of open grassland dotted with Tibetans and their grazing yak herds highlight a trip to the Sāngkē Grasslands (Sāngkē Cǎoyuán), 14km from Xiàhé. Development has turned the area into a small circus, complete with touristy horse rides and fake yurts, but there is good hiking in the nearby hills and you can keep going to more distant and pristine grasslands in the direction of Amchog.

You can cycle to Sāngkē from Xiàhé in about one hour. A taxi costs ¥50 return, or ¥250 for an English-speaking guide and driver; enquire at Snowy Mountain Cafe (p842). The grasslands are lushest in summer.

Hézuò   合作

✆ 0941 / POP 90,000

The regional capital of Gānnán (甘南) prefecture, Hézuò mainly serves as a transit point for travellers plying the overland route between Gānsù and Sìchuān provinces. The city is also the site of the incredible Milarepa Palace, a bewitching Tibetan temple ranging spectacularly over nine floors.

Hézuò is a fairly compact town, with a large public square (文化广场; Wénhuà Guǎngchǎng) roughly halfway between the two bus stations.

Milarepa Palace Buddhist Temple   BUDDHIST TEMPLE

(九层佛阁, Sekhar Gutok, Jiǔcéng Fógé; ¥20; ⊙7am-6pm) About 2km from the bus station along the main road towards Xiàhé is this towering temple, ringed by prayer wheels. Resembling a boutique hotel, Milarepa is odd in the Tibetan world in that different spiritual leaders from varying sects are worshipped on each floor. The town's main monastery, **Tso Gompa** (合作寺, Hézuò Sì, Hézuò Monastery; Nawulu, 那吾路; ⊙8am-6pm) **FREE**, is next door. A taxi here costs ¥2 to ¥3 from the central main bus station.

With Xiàhé just an hour to the north, there is little reason to stay overnight here, and the cheaper hotels often don't accept foreigners. If you get stuck, head for **Butter Lamp Holiday Hotel** (合作酥油燈假日酒店, Hézuò Sūyóudēng Jiàrì Jiǔdiàn; ☑0941 591 1999; 25 Zhuoni Donglu, 卓尼東路25號; d ¥417; @☎) right next to the main bus station.

There are restaurants around the public square, and also around the bus stations.

You'll find banks with ATMs around the public square (文化广场; Wénhuà Guǎngchǎng).

ⓘ Getting There & Away

Hézuò is where buses from Zöigě (Ruò'ěrgài), in Sìchuān, and Lángmùsì and Xiàhé meet. Though there is no train station here; you can book tickets for other destinations at the **train booking office** just outside the central bus station on Zhuoni Donglu (卓尼东路).

Services from the central bus station (长途汽车站; chángtú qìchēzhàn):

Lánzhōu ¥74, four hours, every 30 minutes

Línxià ¥30, 1½ hours, every 30 minutes

Xiàhé ¥15, One hour, every 30 minutes (7am to 4pm)

From the **south bus station** (汽车南站; qìchē nánzhàn):

Lángmùsì ¥50, three hours, three daily (6.30am, 10.20am and noon)

Zöigě ¥78, 3½ hours, one daily (7.30am)

ⓘ Getting Around

Most taxi rides around town cost ¥2. To get between the two bus stations take a taxi or bus 1 (¥1).

Lángmùsì   郎木寺

☑0941 / ELEVATION 3325M / POP 4500

Straddling the border between Sìchuān and Gānsù is Lángmùsì (Taktsang Lhamo in Tibetan), an expanding and modernising alpine Amdo Tibetan village nestled among steep grassy meadows, evergreen forests of slender pine trees, crumbling stupas, piles of *mani* stones, and snow-clad peaks. Lángmùsì is a delightful place surrounded by countless red and white monastery buildings, flapping prayer flags, and the mesmerising sound of monks chanting at twilight.

The White Dragon River (白龙江; Báilóng Jiāng) divides the town in two, and the Sìchuān side has quickly become the far more comfortable part to stay in. From where the bus drops you off, most of the

---

GĀNJIĀ GRASSLANDS TO DÁLĬJIĀ MOUNTAIN

It's possible to hike over several days from the Gānjiā Grasslands to 4636m-high **Dálĭjiā Mountain** (达里加山; Dálĭjiā Shān), but you will need to be well equipped. Summer is the best season for such treks as you have more daylight hours, wildflowers and warmer weather. There are also treks between Tibetan villages and around **Dàowéi Tibetan Village** (道帏藏族乡; Dàowéi Zàngzú Xiāng; also called Guru).

OT Travels & Tours (p843) in Xiàhé can advise on these and other trips and arrange a car for four people for ¥500 per day and an English-speaking guide (for another ¥400); it can also arrange fun camping trips for overnighting on the grasslands

budget accommodation and restaurant options lie along this main street or just beside, with the Kerti Gompa up a small street on the left and Serti Gompa on a hillside to the right beyond the river.

◉ Sights

Kerti Gompa   BUDDHIST MONASTERY
(格尔蒂寺, Gé'ěrgài Sì; ¥30; ⊙6.30am-8pm) Rising up on the Sìchuān side of White Dragon River is this monastery – otherwise dubbed the Sìchuān Monastery – built in 1413, home to around 700 monks and composed of six temples and colleges. Try catching a glimpse of student monks in class by visiting the monastery in the morning and late afternoon. The admission is valid for two days.

Serti Gompa   BUDDHIST MONASTERY
(赛赤寺, Sàichì Sì; ¥30; ⊙6am-7.30pm) This small monastery (simply referred to as the Gānsù Monastery) with golden- and silver-roofed halls dates from 1748 and stands on the Gānsù side of White Dragon River. The views are lovely from the uppermost temple building, looking back down into Lángmùsì town and along the White Dragon River.

✲ Festivals & Events

If you're in the area in late July, head out to Mǎqǔ (玛曲) to see the **annual horse races**. The exact dates change each year, so try contacting Lángmùsì Tibetan Horse Trekking (p846) for details on when they're being held. Măqŭ is 67km west of Lángmùsì. Traveller cafes and hotels in Lángmùsì can arrange transport to the town.

🏃 Activities

Hiking

Bountiful hiking opportunities radiate in almost every direction. For all-day or overnight treks, including to Huágàishén Shān (华盖神山; 4200m), all the horse-trekking companies and most of the hostels in town can arrange a local guide.

Southwest of Kerti Gompa is **Namo Gorge** (纳摩峡谷; Nàmó Xiágŭ), which makes for an excellent two- to three-hour (return) hike. The gorge contains several sacred grottoes, one dedicated to the Tibetan goddess Palden Lhamo, the other a stone-tablet-labelled **Fairy Cave** (仙女洞; Xiānnŭ Dòng), where monks sometimes chant inside, which gives the town its Tibetan name (*lángmù* means 'fairy'). Cross rickety bridges flung over the gushing stream, trek past piles of *mani* stones and prayer flags, and hike on into a splendid ravine. After about 30 minutes of clambering over rocks you reach a grassy plain surrounded by towering peaks.

A popular trek is the hike along the White Dragon River to the **river's source** (白龙江源头; Báilóng Jiāng Yuántóu), where domestic hikers go in search of *chóngcăo* (虫草), a coveted herb used in Chinese medicine.

Another lovely walk heads out over the hills along a narrow paved road from the stupa at Serti Gompa (you must pay admission to pass through) to the small village of **Jíkēhé Cūn** (吉科合村). This hike can be combined with the hike to the White Dragon River source. When you reach the village, simply follow the loop and then head down a dirt path towards the valley below. Watch out for local dogs.

For glorious views over Lángmùsì, trek up the coxcomb-like **Red Stone Mountain** (红石崖; Hóngshí Yá). To start, turn right one street back (heading out of Lángmùsì) from the intersection where the bus drops off.

Horse Trekking

The mountain trails around Lángmùsì offer spectacular riding opportunities. There are two outfits in town offering similar one- to four-day treks overnighting at nomads' tents and with the option of climbing nearby peaks along the way. Both companies have English-speaking staff and are good sources of travel information.

Lángmùsì
Tibetan Horse Trekking   HORSE RIDING, CYCLING
(☎0941 667 1504; www.langmusi.net; ⊗8am-10pm) This established, officially licensed outfit offers horse hire per day for ¥300 for a single traveller; ¥220 for two or more. In addition to guides, food and sleeping bags, trips include a package on nomad culture. If nobody's in the office, ask inside the Black Tent Cafe across the road.

Can also help with bike tours and rents bikes (¥60 to ¥80 per day).

Wind Horse Trekking   HORSE RIDING
(郎木寺白戊马队, Lángmùsì Báiwù Măduì; ☎151 0944 1588; ⊗8am-8pm) Offers horse-riding packages starting at ¥180 per day (bring your own sleeping bag). Opposite the China Telecom office on Lángmùsì's main road. Often closed outside of high season.

Cycling

For serious cyclists, Lángmùsì is worth exploring on two wheels. The many dirt tracks snaking into the hills, Red Stone Mountain and the source of the White Dragon River all make for steep pedaling. Lángmùsì Tibetan Horse Trekking can help with bike tours and also rents bikes (¥60 to ¥80 per day).

🛏 Sleeping

As Lángmùsì grows in popularity with domestic travellers, large tour-group hotels continue to spring up at a surprising pace. A number of good hostels are scattered through town as well, most of which can offer food or advice and a comfortable atmosphere for weary travellers.

Boke Youth Hostel   HOSTEL $
(泊客青年旅舍, Bókè Qīngnián Lǚshè; ☎188 0666 1900; dm/s & d ¥30/60; ❀🖭) This new addition to the Lángmùsì hostel scene offers large and clean dorms or small but cosy private rooms, along with a glassed-in patio where food is served. Head back from the bus drop-off towards the highway; it's on the left inside a courtyard just a bit past the China Post office.

Tibetan Barley Youth Hostel   HOSTEL $
(藏地青稞国际青年旅舍, Zàngdé Qīngkē Guójì Qīngnián Lǚshè; ☎134 3879 8688; http://weibo.com/tibetanbarley; Sangqu Riverside, Muslim Village, 回民村桑曲河畔; dm ¥35-40, d/tw with shower from ¥100; ❀🖭) This hostel has clean, colourful rooms (though dorms can feel a bit cramped), and a homely bar-lounge with Chinese meals and cushion seating. To get

here go straight ahead from the bus drop-off, turn left down a small riverfront path just before the bridge; the hostel is on the left.

Comanager Yezi speaks good French and English, is full of travel information, can arrange tours and has even drawn a useful Lángmùsì map.

Yŏng Zhōng Hotel   HOTEL $$
(永忠宾馆, Yŏngzhōng Bīnguǎn; ☑0941 667 1032; downhill from Kerti Gompa, 农村信用社隔壁; tw ¥180-220; ❋ ⚛) On the Sìchuān side of town is this pleasant family-run hotel with small, bright, modern rooms with air-con and 24-hour hot water. On street level keep an eye out for the shoe shop through which you access the hotel. Expect discounts of 45%.

Lángmùsì Hotel   HOTEL $$$
(朗木寺大酒店, Lángmùsì Dà Jiŭdiàn; ☑0941 667 1555; langmusihotel@yahoo.com.cn; across from the entrance to Kerti Gompa, 格尔盖寺大门对面; d/tr ¥680/700; ❋ @ ⚛) This friendly four-storey hotel is the most upscale in Lángmùsì and offers pleasant, clean and spacious rooms in either standard or Tibetan styling. It's on the road towards Kerti Gompa, just across from the ticket booth. Discounts of up to 30%.

✗ Eating

Happy Homemade Yunnan Taste   YUNNAN $
(源自原位, Yuánzì Yuánwèi; dishes ¥12 45, ⚇ 9am-10pm; ⚛) The Yunnanese folk at this family-run restaurant are infectiously happy. Sample the strong homemade *báijiŭ* (Chinese spirit) and you might be too. Popular with travellers for the *guòqiáo mĭxiàn* (Yunnanese hotpot) and huge servings of classics such as *yúxiāng qiézi* (red-pepper stewed eggplant). Located on the road to Kerti Gompa just up from the turn, and open late in summer.

Hangzhou Dumplings   DUMPLING $
(杭州小笼包, Hángzhōu Xiǎolóngbāo; ☑152 5754 5988; downhill from Kerti Gompa, 信用社斜对面; dishes ¥15-45; ⚇ 7am-10pm, later in Jul & Aug; ⚛) This friendly family-run restaurant offers a wide range of Chinese dishes and top-quality dumplings. There is an English menu, but note that many of the prices are out of date so you'll need to compare to the regular menu to confirm.

Black Tent Cafe   TIBETAN $$
(黑帐篷咖啡, Hēi Zhàngpeng Kāfēi; dishes ¥28-50; ⚇8am-10pm; ⚛) Friendly service, a Tibetan-style interior, rooftop seating, proper

coffee (from ¥25), and a good menu offering numerous Western and some Tibetan dishes are some of the highlights of this 2nd-floor cafe run by the folks at Lángmùsì Tibetan Horse Trekking. The cafe is one door up the side street from the intersection where the bus drops passengers off.

☕ Drinking & Nightlife

Bear's House   CAFE
(熊窝客栈, Xióngwo Kèzhàn; ☑153 4677 6632; ⚇9.30am-11pm; ⚛) This 2nd-floor cafe overlooking the main street of Lángmùsì sells coffee (¥20), tea (¥15), and breakfast/snacks (¥15) in a cosy cafe setting with English menus. Guest rooms are in the works as well, but were not complete at the time of writing. On the main street halfway through town.

Bái Mǎ Méi Duŏ   BAR
(白玛梅朵主—客栈; ☑182 0941 8882; ⚇7am-midnight; ⚛) Though it also features coffee from ¥35 and a mix of Western and Sichuanese dishes (¥28 to ¥68), this newcomer is most notable as the closest thing to a nightlife scene in Lángmùsì. Beer from ¥15 and tea from ¥25; located on the main road at the turn to Kerti Gompa.

ℹ Information

There's nowhere to change money and no ATMs that accept foreign cards, so get plenty of cash before you arrive in Lángmùsì.

China Post (中国邮政, Zhōngguó Yóuzhèng; ⚇10am-4pm) On the main road through town, back towards the highway and away from the bus drop-off.

Public Security Bureau (PSB, 公安局, Gōng'ānjú) Around 1km from the centre of town, towards the main highway. Does not handle visa extensions; for this, you'll need to go to Hézuò or Línxià.

ℹ Getting There & Away

There's one daily bus to Zöigé (Ruò'ěrgài; ¥25, 2½ hours) at 7am, which arrives with time to connect with the bus to Sōngpān. There are two to three daily buses to Hézuò (¥50, three hours), departing at 6.30am (summer only), 7.20am and noon. Take the only direct bus to Xiàhé (¥72, 3½ hours) at 2pm, or change in Hézuò for frequent buses to Xiàhé and Lánzhōu.

Guesthouses may be able to coordinate a seat to Chuānzhŭsì or Jiŭzhàigōu on the bus that passes by on the main highway at around 2.20pm, otherwise you'll have to change in Hézuò.

For the latest scheduling info see www.langmusi.net.

GĀNSÙ LÁNGMÙSÌ

HÉXĪ CORRIDOR 河西走廊

Bound by the Qílián Shān range to the south and the Mǎzōng (Horse's Mane) and Lóngshǒu (Dragon's Head) mountains to the north, the narrow Héxī Corridor (Héxī Zǒuláng) is the crux around which the province is formed. This valley was once the sole western passage in and out of the Middle Kingdom.

ℹ Getting There & Around

The Héxī Corridor is connected to the rest of Gansu and eastern China by high-speed rail and modern highways. Cities along the route have airports, though most travellers opt to fly in/out of either Lánzhōu or Dūnhuáng and travel by train within the province.

The Lánzhōu–Xīnjiāng High Speed Railway was completed in November 2013 and whisks passengers up the valley via Xīníng in Qīnghǎi. The slower Y667 train (hard/soft/deluxe sleeper ¥276/430/911, 13 hours) is a dedicated tourist train that departs Lánzhōu for Dūnhuáng at 5.50pm and offers freshly cooked meals on board, sparkling clean facilities and multi-lingual announcements. Deluxe sleepers have two beds and a private bathroom.

Wǔwēi 武威

📱 0935 / POP 1.81 MILLION

Wǔwēi stands at the strategic eastern end of the Héxī Corridor. It was from here, two millennia ago, that the emperors of China launched their expeditionary forces into the unknown west, eventually leading them to Jiāyùguān and beyond. Temples, tombs and traditional gates hint at Wǔwēi's Silk Road past, while the rapidly modernising city has some pleasant squares and pedestrian streets.

◉ Sights

Wǔwēi has a few pleasant temples and pagodas to explore, but most travellers base themselves here to explore the Tiāntīshān Grottoes, located 57km southeast of town.

Wǔwēi is compact enough that with the exception of Hǎizàng Temple you can walk to all the sights in an afternoon. Most travellers base themselves in the southern part of town near the rebuilt South Gate (南门). The city's main square, Wénhuà Guǎngchǎng (文化广场), is about 1km directly north of the gate on Bei Dajie. Mingqing Fanggu Wenhua Jie (or simply Mingqing Jie) extends east from the gate and is an attractive street lined with restaurants, coffee shops and a KTV or two.

Hǎizàng Temple   BUDDHIST TEMPLE
(海藏寺, Hǎizàng Sì; Liangzhou District, Jinsha Township, 凉州区金沙乡; ⊙9am-5pm) FREE A fascinating active monastery with a minute pavilion to the right of the entrance containing a well whose 'magic waters' (神水; shénshuǐ) are said to connect by subterranean streams to a Holy Lake (圣湖; Shènghú) in the Potala Palace in Lhasa. Drinking the water is said to cure myriad ailments. Bus 5 (¥2) towards Hǎizàng Gōngyuán (海藏公园) or a taxi (¥10) will take you the short trip outside town to Hǎizàng Park entrance (¥2); the temple is out back.

Kumarajiva Pagoda   BUDDHIST PAGODA
(罗什寺, Luóshí Sì; 66 Bei Dajie, 北大街66号; ⊙8am-6pm) FREE This 12-storey pagoda dates from AD 488 and is surrounded by a tranquil complex of both unpainted and colourful wooden temples with old folk gossiping under trees. Dedicated to Kumarajiva, the great translator of Buddhist sutras (who lived here for 17 years and whose tongue was buried beneath the pagoda), the original 17th-century structures were toppled during a great earthquake in 1927 and rebuilt.

It's located 400m north of Wǔwēi's main square.

Léitái Tomb & Park   TOMB, BUDDHIST
(雷台公园, Léitái Gōngyuán; Leitai Donglu, 雷台东路; ¥45; ⊙9am-5pm) The pride and joy of the city, the bronze Flying Horse of Wǔwēi (飞马; Fēimǎ) was discovered here in 1969 and is the unofficial symbol of Gānsù. It was found in a secret tomb beneath this temple, built on top of steep earthen ramparts. The Flying Horse is now displayed in the Gānsù Provincial Museum (p835).

The site is 1.2km north of Wǔwēi; turn right at Leitai Donglu. Note that you'll need your passport to enter.

🛏 Sleeping & Eating

Wǔwēi is not a city that will wow with its spectacular accommodation options, but there are plenty of clean, comfortable hotels scattered around town.

Zǐyúngé Hotel   HOTEL $$
(紫云阁酒店, Zǐyúngé Jiǔdiàn; 📱0935 225 3888; east of Changmen Guangchang, 南城门广场东侧; d/tr ¥137/172; ▓@🛜) This international-style hotel has spacious, comfortable rooms with showers, though the decor is showing a bit

of age. The best thing about the hotel is its convenient location just east of Wǔwēi's South Gate. Wi-fi only in lobby.

Yúnxiáng International Hotel　HOTEL
(云翔国际酒店; Yúnxiáng Guójì Jiǔdiàn; Beiguan Donglu, 北关东路云翔升字; d/ste incl breakfast ¥240/530; ❄ @) Clean international hotel with comfy-if-generic features and furnishings. Rooms have spacious bathrooms and there is a restaurant serving the Chinese-style buffet breakfast included in the room price.

Liángzhōu Market　MARKET, HAWKER $
(凉州市场, Liángzhōu Shìchǎng; Pedestrian St, 步行街; dishes ¥7-20) This warren of covered pedestrian streets packs in dozens of snack stands, hawker stalls and small, hole-in-the-wall restaurants in a blaze of garish neon signs. Lots of easy foods on a budget, from simple fried noodles (炒面; *chǎomiàn*) to barbecue, dumplings and hot pot.

❶ Information

Bank of China (中国银行, Zhōngguó Yínháng; 21 Xidajie, nr West Gate of Buxingjie, 西大街21号步行街西口) West end of Pedestrian St (步行商业街; Buxing Shangye Jie); can change money.

❶ Getting There & Away

Express buses to cities in the Héxī Corridor run from the main bus station (快客站; kuài kè zhàn) on Nanguan Xilu, though trains are faster and cheaper still.

There are two train stations in Wǔwēi: the old station, located at the south end of Jianshe Lu (建设路) and the newer Wǔwēi south station (武威南站; Wǔwēi Nánzhàn). Both have similarly frequent departures to the main cities in Gānsù, though direct trains to Dūnhuáng only run from Wǔwēi Station.

Jiāyùguān Hard seat/sleeper ¥69/139, 4½ to six hours, every 20 to 30 minutes

Lánzhōu Hard/soft seat ¥47/72, 3½ hours, every 20 to 30 minutes

Zhāngyè Hard/soft seat ¥41/61, two to three hours, every 20 to 30 minutes

Zhōngwèi (Níngxià) Seat/hard sleeper ¥41/98, three to four hours, nine daily

To pre-purchase tickets, cross the square opposite the Confucius Temple (cnr of Xin Qingnianxiang & Wenmiaolu; 新青年巷文庙路) to the **train booking office** (火车票代售点).

From Wuwei Station only:

Dūnhuáng Hard/soft sleeper ¥219/339, 10 hours (three per day directly to Dūnhuáng at 9.02pm, 9.35pm and 1.15am; other trains drop you off at Liǔyuán)

❶ Getting Around

Taxi rides around town are around ¥4 to ¥7. To reach the main train station from Wénhuà Guǎngchǎng, take buses 1 and 2 (¥1) or a taxi (¥10).

It's quite typical for taxi drivers in Wǔwēi to stop and pick up other passengers for an additional fare. Be sure to agree your fare with the driver before you set off, or ask to use the meter.

Around Wǔwēi

It's hard to appreciate how massive the 15m-high Shakyamuni Buddha statue at **Tiāntīshān Grottoes** (天梯山石窟, Tiāntīshān Shíkū; Dēngshān Village, 灯山村, ¥30; ⊙8.30am-6.30pm) is until you are at its truck-sized feet and peering up at its outstretched hand emerging from the cliff face. These 1600-year-old carvings stand majestically in the open air, not hidden in dark caves, so snap away.

There are 17 caves here containing ancient murals (tigers, black dragons), along with some scroll paintings. Only one is open to the public, however, as many suffered devastation after a large earthquake in 1927. In 1959 many of the relics from lower caves were moved to Gānsù Provincial Museum (p835) to make way for the construction of a reservoir. The Buddha is the real star, his enormous feet protected from the reservoir's flood by a giant, half-moon dam around which you can walk to see him from varying vantages. Two sets of stairs also lead to the dam floor, allowing worshippers to descend and light incense.

Transportation to Tiāntīshān is irregular. The best way to get here is to hire a private driver or taxi in Wǔwēi (¥200, half-day). Some through buses go from Wǔwēi bus station; you'll have to ask for the Tiāntīshān minibus (¥12, 3½ hours, every 30 minutes). You'll be dropped off along the main highway, from where it's a 20-minute walk to the grottoes; however, the return journey can be very problematic, with no regular buses or services from the grottoes themselves.

Zhāngyè　张掖

✔ 0936 / POP 1.19 MILLION

Smack-dab in the middle of the Héxī Corridor, the chilled-out city of Zhāngyè has a relaxed atmosphere that belies its historical status as an outpost connecting Central Asia to the Chinese empire via the Silk Road.

Marco Polo is said to have spent a year here around 1274 – he provided a detailed description of Zhāngyè (by its historical name, Campichu) in *The Travels of Marco Polo*. Even the name Zhāngyè alludes to its Silk Road importance: 张掖 is a shortening of '张国臂掖，以通西域', which translates as 'Extending the arm of the nation to its Western Realm'.

Today, Zhāngyè is a useful base from which to explore the otherwordly landscapes of the Dānxiá Geopark and the ancient cliff temples at Mǎtí Sì. In town, one of Asia's largest reclining Buddhas is ensconced in a beautifully preserved wooden temple, which, according to legend, was the birthplace of Mongol warrior Kublai Khan.

◉ Sights

Zhāngyè is roughly divided into Xi (West), Dong (East), Nan (South) and Bei (North) Dajie, depending on which direction its two main streets radiate from the drum tower. Jianfu Jie intersects with Xi Dajie a few blocks from the drum tower and heading north takes you to a pleasant eating street, while Nan Dajie leads (more or less) to the Giant Buddha Temple and Wooden Pagoda.

★ Giant Buddha Temple   BUDDHIST SITE
(大佛寺, Dàfó Sì; ☏ 0936 821 9671; www.zydfs. com; Dafo Xiang, off Minzhu Xijie, 大佛寺巷; ¥41; ⊙ 8.30am-6pm) Originally dating to 1098 (Western Xia dynasty), this lovely temple contains an astonishing 35m-long sleeping Buddha – China's largest of this variety and among the biggest wooden reclining Buddhas in Asia – surrounded by mouldering clay arhats (Buddhists who have achieved enlightenment) and Qing dynasty murals.

This is one of the few wooden structures from this era still standing in China and there is a wealth of traditional symbols to examine. Even the unrestored exterior is fascinating and there's an impressive white **clay stupa** (土塔; *tǔtǎ*) dating from the Ming dynasty. The former Princesses Wencheng hall towards the back of the temple now contains an **exhibition** showcasing Buddhist artefacts, and there is also a display of golden sutras associated with the temple.

The **Shanxi Guild Hall** at the northeast corner of the temple is also worth a look. Dating to 1724, this Qing era complex was used as a meeting place and includes rare intact wooden stage and platform viewing areas.

From the drum tower, head south on Nan Dajie about 1km.

Xīlái Wooden Pagoda   PAGODA
(西来寺, Xīlái Sì; cnr Minzhu Xijie & Xianfu Jie, 民主西街县府街的路口; ¥50; ⊙ 8am-6pm) Zhāngyè's main square is dominated by this nine-tiered brick and wooden pagoda. Though first built during the Northern Zhou dynasty (AD 557–588), the present 27.4m structure is a thorough reconstruction from 1926. Admission buys you a ticket to the top, which offers views over the city.

Though official closing hours are listed as 6pm, some travellers have reported the pagoda as being open during the evening.

🛏 Sleeping & Eating

Mingqing Jie (明清街) is an alley of faux-Qing architecture lined with dozens of clean, friendly restaurants with picture menus. To find it, head 300m west of the drum tower along Xi Dajie. Local specialities include *lǎoshǔfěn* (老鼠粉; rice-flour noodles) and *cuōyúmiàn* (搓鱼面; twisted fish noodles), so named because they are hand-twisted into oblong pointed shapes resembling small fish.

★ Bean Sprout Hostel   HOSTEL $
(豆芽旅舍, Dòuyá Lǘshě; ☏ 185 1634 0930; 113 Changshou Jie, 长寿街113号; dm ¥105; ❀✴@🛜) This adorable hostel run by a Chinese couple features dorms and family rooms set around a Qing dynasty–styled indoor courtyard with tables, lanterns and greenery. There is not a whiff about the place, everything is bright and spotlessly clean, and the couple are extremely passionate about Zhāngyè and helping travellers. The central location is the icing on the cake.

They can book tours or arrange private cars to Mǎtí Sì (p852) and Dānxiá National Geopark, as well as onward train tickets. Unfortunately, no English is spoken, but the friendliness of the owners overcomes that; they'll go out of their way to make sure you're looked after.

Huáyì Snack Square   MARKET, HAWKER $
(华谊小吃广场, Huáyì Xiǎochī Guǎngchǎng; Dong Dajie, 东大街; ⊙ 10am-10pm) This pedestrianised market has dozens of snack stalls and small restaurants, many selling local specialities and Chinese standards, hand-pulled noodles (拉面; *lāmiàn*) and dried fruits and vegetables. This is also a good place to try the local speciality *cuōyúmiàn* (搓鱼面; twisted fish noodles).

ℹ Information

There's an internet cafe on the southwest corner of the drum-tower intersection. Hotels, hostels, KFC and coffee shops have free wi-fi.

Bank of China (中国银行, Zhōngguó Yínháng; 388 Dong Dajie, 东大街388号; ⊗ 8.30am-noon & 2.30-5pm Mon-Fri) Has a 24-hour ATM

ℹ Getting There & Away

BUS

Zhāngyè has three bus stations, in the south, east and west. The **west bus station** (汽车西站; qìchē xīzhàn) has the most frequent departures. Destinations include Xīníng, Golmud, Jiāyùguān, Lánzhōu, Dūnhuáng and Wǔwēi, though it's faster, cheaper and far easier to take a train.

TRAIN

In 2015 Zhāngyè became an important stop along the newly opened high-speed rail line that connects Lánzhōu and Ürümqi in Xīnjiāng. High-speed trains now depart from Zhāngyè west railway station (张掖西站; Zhāngyè Xīzhàn) for Lánzhōu via Xīníng in Qīnghǎi province. Services include the following:

Jiāyùguān South Hard/soft seat ¥66/79, 1½ hours, every 30 minutes

Lánzhōu West Hard/soft seat ¥150/180, three hours, every 30 minutes

Ürümqi Hard/soft seat ¥399/479, eight hours, every 45 minutes

Xīníng Hard/soft seat ¥92/110, two hours, every 45 minutes

Slower departures for Wǔwēi and destinations further east go from Zhāngyè Railway Station, locally known as *lǎozhàn* (老站; old station), including the following:

Dūnhuáng Hard/soft sleeper ¥145/223, 7½ hours, two daily (12.29am and 4.05am); day trains all go to Liǔyuán or Liǔyuán on the high-speed line

Wǔwēi Seat/hard sleeper ¥41/98, 2½ to 3 hours, every 20 to 30 minutes

There is a **train booking office** (火车票代售点, Huǒchēpiào Dàishòu Diǎn; 12 Oushi Jie, 欧式街 12号; ⊗ 8am-6pm). To get there walk west of the drum tower and turn right (north) at Oushi Jie.

ℹ Getting Around

A taxi from any of the bus stations to the hotels costs ¥4 to ¥5. Bus 4 runs past the west bus station from Dong or Xi Dajie.

The old train station is 7km northeast of the city centre, and a taxi will cost ¥10, or take bus 1 (¥1). The west railway station is 3.5km from the centre of town. Shared taxis depart from in front of the station for ¥10 per person.

Around Zhāngyè

The swirling orange, yellow, white and brown lunar landscape of **Zhāngyè Dānxiá National Geopark** (张掖丹霞国家地质公园, Zhāngyè Dānxiá Guójiā Dìzhí Gōngyuán; ¥60; ⊗ 6am-8pm) is the result of sandstone and mineral deposits that have eroded into odd shapes over the course of millennia. These 'rainbow mountains' have been quietly drawing photographers for the last few years.

Infrastructure was installed inside the park after it was named a national geopark in 2011, making it – for better or worse – very accessible to tourists. Wooden stairs and platforms allow visitors to reach the tops of the hills without damaging the delicate landscape and offer stunning views over the coloured strata.

The park opens early for a reason: the best time to visit (and photograph) this magnificent landscape is at sunrise on a clear day. From Zhāngyè, a taxi to both Mǎtí Sì (p852) and Dānxiá will cost around ¥350, or a taxi here only about ¥150. Once here, a hop-on, hop-off bus shuttles visitors to various stops inside the park, and you are welcome to take your time at the various scenic platforms.

Mǎtí Xiāng 马蹄乡
☑ 0936

Carved into the cliff sides in foothills of the grand Qílián Mountains (Qílián Shān), the venerable Buddhist grottoes of Mǎtí Sì (p852) make for a fine short getaway from the hectic small towns along the Héxī Corridor. The tiny tourist village of Mǎtí Xiāng serves as a gateway to the temples. There's excellent hiking in the nearby hills, and a small range of very simple accommodation and food from May to September. Come in July to see the mountain valleys carpeted in blue wildflowers.

There are several good day hikes around Mǎtí Sì, including the five-hour loop through pine forest and talus fields to the **Línsōng Waterfall** (临松瀑布; Línsōng Pùbù) and back down past **Sword Split Stone** (剑劈石; Jiànpīshí). For unrivalled panoramas, take the steep ascent of the ridge starting across from the white chörten (Tibetan stupa) just above the village at Sānshísāntiān Shíkū (三十三天石窟).

Mǎtí Sì   CAVE, BUDDHIST SITE

(马蹄寺; ¥74; ⊙8.30am-5.30pm) Mǎtí Sì translates as 'Horse Hoof Monastery', a reference to when a heavenly horse left a hoof imprint in a grotto. Between the 5th and 14th centuries a series of caves were almost as miraculously built in sheer sandstone cliffs and filled with carvings, temples and meditation rooms. The caves are reached via twisting staircases, balconies, narrow passages and platforms that will leave your head spinning.

The grottoes are not in one area but spread over several sections. The most accessible are the **Thousand Buddhas Caves** (千佛洞石窟; Qiān Fó Dòng Shíkū) just past the entrance gate to the scenic area. Within this complex is the **Pǔguāng Temple**, where you'll find the relic of the horse hoof imprint. The **Mǎtí Sì North Caves** (马蹄寺北石窟; Mǎtí Sì Běi Shíkū) are above the village (2km up the road from the Thousand Buddhas Caves) and feature the more dizzying platforms as well as a large grotto with a tall golden Buddha.

Mǎtí Sì is 65km north of Zhāngyè, and one or both of the main caves may be closed outside of April to September.

If you're adequately prepared for camping, some overnight trips are possible. The tiny village also has several basic guesthouses (tw ¥60).

ℹ️ Getting There & Away

Buses leave every 30 minutes from Zhāngyè's south bus station for the crossroads village of Mǎtí Hé (马蹄河; ¥10, 1½ hours, 6.40am to 5.40pm), from where you can catch a minibus or taxi (¥30) for the final 7km or so.

Direct buses to Mǎtí Sì depart from Zhāngyè's south bus station hourly throughout the morning from May to September. The last bus back to Mǎtí Hé or Zhāngyè leaves before 5pm. Check with locals on the exact time.

A return taxi from Zhāngyè will cost around ¥160, and for this price the driver will also shuttle you around to the various temple sites at Mǎtí Sì.

Jiāyùguān   嘉峪关

☎ 0937 / POP 231,000

You approach Jiāyùguān through the forbidding lunar landscape of north Gānsù. It's a fitting setting, as Jiāyùguān marks the symbolic end of the Great Wall, the western gateway of China proper and, for imperial Chinese, the beginning of the back of beyond. One of the defining points of the Silk Road, a Ming dynasty fort was erected here in 1372 and Jiāyùguān came to be colloquially known as the 'mouth' of China, while the narrow Héxī Corridor, leading back towards the *nèidì* (inner lands), was dubbed the 'throat'.

You'll need plenty of imagination to conjure up visions of the Silk Road, as modern Jiāyùguān is a city of straight roads, identikit blocks and manufacturing. But the Jiāyùguān Fort is an essential part of Silk Road lore and most certainly worth a visit.

◎ Sights

With the exception of the Wèijìn Tombs, all the sites are covered by purchasing a through ticket (通票; *tōngpiào*) to the Jiāyùguān Fort; admission fees quoted for individual sites are for entry without admission to the fort. Through tickets can be purchased at any of the three sites.

★ Jiāyùguān Fort   FORT

(嘉峪关城楼, Jiāyùguān Chénglóu; Guancheng Nanlu, 关城南路; ¥120; ⊙8.30am-8pm, to 6pm in winter) One of the classic images of western China, this fort once guarded the narrow pass between the snowcapped Qílián Shān peaks and the Hēi Shān (Black Mountains) of the Mǎzōng Shān range.

Built in 1372, it was named the 'Impregnable Defile Under Heaven'. Although the Han Chinese often controlled territory far beyond here, this was the last major stronghold of imperial China – the end of their 'civilised world', beyond which lay only desert demons and the barbarian armies of Central Asia.

Towards the eastern end of the fort is the **Gate of Enlightenment** (光化楼; Guānghuá Lóu) and on the west side is the **Gate of Conciliation** (柔远楼; Róuyuǎn Lóu), from where exiled poets, ministers, criminals and soldiers would have ridden off into oblivion. Each gate dates from 1506 and has 17m-high towers with upturned flying eaves and double gates that would have been used to trap invading armies. On the inside are horse lanes leading up to the top of the inner ramparts.

The fort received major refurbishments in 2015, brightening up wood with coats of paint and reinforcing foundations and cracked walls.

Near the fort entrance gate is the excellent Jiāyùguān Museum of the Great Wall, which has some interesting exhibits about the Wall and its history in this part of China.

Overhanging Great Wall HISTORIC SITE

(悬壁长城, Xuánbì Chángchéng; ¥21, incl in through ticket to Jiāyùguān Fort; ⊙ 8.30am-8pm, to 6pm winter) Running north from Jiāyùguān Fort, this section of the Great Wall is believed to have been first constructed in 1539, though it was reconstructed in 1987. It's quite an energetic hike up the equivalent of 55 flights of stairs to excellent views of the desert and the glittering snow-capped peaks in the distance, though views are a little mired by Jiāyùguān's increasingly polluted air. The Wall is about 9km north of the fort.

Jiāyùguān Museum of the Great Wall MUSEUM

(嘉峪关长城博物馆, Jiāyùguān Chángchéng Bówùguǎn; Jiāyùguān Fort; incl in through ticket to Jiāyùguān Fort; ⊙ 8.30am-6pm) **FREE** Located inside Jiāyùguān Fort, this excellent museum contains photos, artefacts, maps, Silk Road exhibits and models to show just how the fort and the Great Wall of China influenced the history of the Hexi Corridor and China as a whole.

Wèijìn Tombs TOMB

(新城魏晋壁画墓, Xīnchéng Wèijìn Bìhuàmù; ¥35; ⊙ 8.30am-8pm) These tombs date from approximately AD 220–420 (the Wei and Western Jin periods) and contain extraordinarily fresh brick wall paintings (some ineptly retouched) depicting scenes of everyday life, from making tea to picking mulberries for silk production. There are thousands of tombs in the desert 20km east of Jiāyùguān, but only one is currently open to visitors, that of a husband and wife.

There is a small museum that's also worth a look; it's the only area where photos are permitted. A taxi here from central Jiāyùguān will cost around ¥70. If you pay a little more (¥100), the driver will also take you to nearby Yěmáwān Cūn (野麻湾村), the crumbling remains of a former walled village about 10km from the tombs.

First Beacon Platform of the Great Wall HISTORIC SITE

(长城第一墩, Chángchéng Dìyī Dūn; ¥22, incl in through ticket to Jiāyùguān Fort; ⊙ 8.30am-8pm, to 6pm winter) Atop a 56m-high cliff overlooking the Tǎolài River south of Jiāyùguān, a crumbling pile of packed earth is all that remains of this beacon platform, believed to be the first signalling tower along the western front of the Great Wall. Views over the river and bare gorge below are impressive and

you can walk alongside attached vestiges of adobe Ming-era Great Wall.

A sightseeing trolley (¥12) shuttles visitors 3km from the ticket office to the **subterranean viewing platform**, labelled the 'Underground Valley'. Inside, an excellent exhibition on the beacon platform, the fort and the history of the Wall in this area provides some context. Views of the beacon platform can be had from a see-through **cantilever bridge** at the back of the exhibit hall.

🛏 Sleeping

Jiāyùguān's hotel landscape is rather bland, with a number of just-fine business- or international-style hotels lining its main streets. There is a very clean, friendly outlet of the popular Jǐnjiāng Inn (锦江之星; Jǐnjiāng Zhīxīng) chain on Lanxin Lu.

Shèngjīng Holiday Hotel HOTEL **$$**

(盛景假日酒店, Shèngjīng Jiàrì Jiǔdiàn; ☑ 0937 637 8666; 78 Xinhua Beilu, 新華北路78號; d from ¥207; ✴@🛰) Excellent midrange option built in 2015. Enjoys a handy location on Xinhua Beilu in the centre of town and has bright, clean rooms with modern facilities. Good discounts if you book online.

Jiāyùguān Hotel
HOTEL $$$

(嘉峪关宾馆, Jiāyùguān Bīnguǎn; ☑0937 620 1588; 1 Xinhua Beilu, 新华北路1号; d/tw from ¥669/768; ✳@☎) Rooms here are modern with heavy accents on the brown woods and faux marble. Most include a Chinese breakfast and computers with broadband. Other services include a restaurant serving Western-style food, a spa, travel agent and attentive staff, some who speak English. Conveniently located on the pleasant tree-lined shopping boulevard of Xinhua Zhonglu. Discounts of 30% to 60% are common.

✖ Eating

Much of Jiāyùguān's dining scene centres on its two main small-foods markets. For breakfast ask or look around for small shops selling *bāozi* (包子; steamed meat- or veg-filled buns) and *dòujiāng* (豆浆; soya milk). At lunch, small stands line the entryways to Jiāyùguān Fort and the Overhanging Great Wall selling noodles and *ròujiāmó* (肉夾饃; pulled-pork sandwich).

Jìngtiě Market
MARKET $

(镇铁小吃城, Jìngtiě Xiǎochīchéng; Xinhua Zhonglu, 新华中路; ☉10am-10pm) At this busy market load up on lamb kebabs, *ròujiāmó* (肉夹馍; pork sandwiches), beef noodles, roast duck and more. There are a handful of small restaurants on the north side of the market that offer sit-down meals.

Yuànzhōngyuàn Restaurant
SICHUAN $$

(苑中苑酒店, Yuànzhōngyuàn Jiǔdiàn; Jingtie Xilu, 镇铁西路; dishes ¥15-50; ☉9am-9pm) Directly across from the bus station on the far side of a small park is this pleasant Sìchuān restaurant. Try its *gōngbǎo jīdīng* (宫保鸡丁; spicy chicken and peanuts), *tiěbǎn dòufu* (铁板豆腐; fried tofu) or a *yúxiāng ròusī* (鱼香肉丝; stir-fried pork and vegetable strips).

ⓘ Information

Bank of China (中国银行, Zhōngguó Yínháng; 42 Xinhua Zhonglu, 新华中路42号; ☉9.30am-5.30pm Mon-Fri, 10am-4pm Sat & Sun) Has an ATM and can change money. It's south of Lanxin Xilu intersection.

China Post (中国邮政, Zhōngguó Yóuzhèng; Xinhua Zhonglu, 新华中路; ☉8am-6pm) Doubles as a train ticket booking office.

ICBC (工商银行, Gōngshāng Yínháng; 1493 Xinhua Zhonglu, 新华中路1493号) Has a 24-hour ATM.

People's No 1 Hospital (第一人民医院, Dìyī Rénmín Yīyuàn; 26 Xinhua Zhonglu) This hospital can only be used by Chinese nationals.

ⓘ Getting There & Away

Jiāyùguān has an airport with flights to Běijīng, Shànghǎi and Lánzhōu, but most people arrive by bus or train.

Jiāyùguān's **bus station** (嘉峪关汽车站, Jiāyùguān Qìchēzhàn; 312 Lanxin Xilu, 兰新西路312号) is by a busy four-way junction on Lanxin Xilu, next to the main budget hotels. It is cheaper and quicker to take a train, but bus destinations include Dūnhuáng, Lánzhōu, Wǔwēi and Zhāngyè.

Jiāyùguān has two train stations. The main train station (嘉峪关站; Jiāyùguān Zhàn) is southwest of the town centre. Bus 1 runs here from Xinhua Zhonglu (¥1). A taxi costs ¥10.

Jiāyùguān south station (嘉峪关南站; Jiāyùguān Nánzhàn) serves the high-speed rail line that connects Lánzhōu to Xīnjiāng. It is located 8km southeast of the town centre. A taxi costs ¥30.

Direct trains to Dūnhuáng are labelled as such. Beware of the more frequently scheduled trains to Liǔyuán – a lengthy 180km away from Dūnhuáng. Train tickets can be booked in town at the post office on Xinhua Zhonglu.

Dūnhuáng Seat/hard sleeper ¥53/112, five hours

Lánzhōu Seat/hard sleeper ¥98/201, six to eight hours; high-speed 2nd-class seat ¥215, five hours

Ürümqi Hard/soft sleeper ¥287/449, ten to 14 hours; high-speed 2nd-class seat ¥336, 6½ hours

Wǔwēi Seat/hard sleeper ¥69/139, four to six hours

Zhāngyè Seat/hard sleeper ¥38/95, two to three hours; high-speed 2nd-class seat ¥66, 1½ hours

ⓘ Getting Around

A taxi to the airport (25 minutes) costs ¥50. Bus 1 (¥2) runs from the train station to the bus station.

A taxi to all the sights in the area, which are all outside town, is likely to cost ¥240, or ¥60 per sight. A taxi just to the sites covered by the **Jiāyùguān Fort** (p852) ticket will cost ¥180. Touts ply the train and bus stations offering rides; bargain hard. Alternatively, most hotels can arrange a taxi to pick you up, which takes the hassle out of having to bargain for the price.

Dūnhuáng 敦煌

☑ 0937 / POP 186,000

The fertile Dūnhuáng oasis has for millennia been a refuge for weary Silk Road travellers. Most visitors stayed long enough only to swap a camel; but some stayed, building the forts, towers and cave temples that are scattered over the surrounding area. These sites, along with some dwarfing sand dunes and desertscapes, make Dūnhuáng a magnificent place to visit.

Despite its remoteness, Dūnhuáng's per capita income is among the highest in China, thanks to a push into wind and solar energy production. The town is thoroughly modern, but has maintained its distinctive desert-sanctuary ambience – with clean, tree-lined streets, slow-moving traffic, bustling markets, budget hotels, cafes and souvenir shops.

Though relatively small, it's a great walking town with wide footpaths and narrow alleys opening up into squares, markets and the lives of ordinary citizens. The riverside is worth a visit if only to see if you are brave enough to cross to the platforms in the middle of the stream.

◉ Sights

Dūnhuáng Museum   MUSEUM
(敦煌博物馆, Dūnhuáng Bówùguǎn; ☑ 0937 882 2981; Mingshan Lu; ⊙ 8am-6pm) FREE Outside of town on the road to Singing Sands Dune (p860) is this sparkling museum that takes you on an artefact-rich journey through the Dūnhuáng area (from prehistoric to Qing dynasty times) via hallways designed to make you feel as if you were in a cave. You can easily walk here in 15 minutes from the centre of town. Bring your passport for admission.

☞ Tours

Ask at any hostel or Charley Johng's Cafe (p856) for tourist info; they can also help with tours, from camel treks to overnight camping excursions and day trips. Bus tours (¥100) that include visits to Yǎdān National Park (p860) and Jade Gate Pass (p861) and Sun Pass (p861) depart daily from Dūnhuáng and can also be arranged at Charley Johng's. Be aware you'll have to pay for admission to each site separately during the tour.

Sleeping

Competition among Dūnhuáng's hotels is fierce, and you should get significant discounts (50% or more) outside of summer.

There are a dozen or so smaller business-type hotels along Mingshan Lu and Yangguan Zhonglu. They tend to be around ¥200 in the off season and ¥300 to ¥400 in the height of summer.

Shāzhōuyì
International Youth Hostel   HOSTEL $
(敦煌沙州驿国际青年旅舍, Dūnhuáng Shāzhōuyì Guójì Qīngnián Lǚshě; ☑ 0937 880 8800; 8 Qilian Lu, 祁连路8号, 北辰市场对面; dm/tw/d ¥50/60/158; P ❂ ❄ ⊚) This hostel is plant- and light-filled, inviting you to lounge and plan one of the offered tours. Dorm beds are comfy with modern shared bathrooms. Doubles are bright and spacious. The street is traffic heavy but has cheap eats, with the Shāzhōu Night Market (p857) a 10-minute walk away through a leafy park. English spoken. It runs a free shuttle bus from the train station.

Mògāo Hotel   HOTEL $$
(莫高宾馆, Mògāo Bīnguǎn; ☑ 0937 885 1777; 248 Mingshan Beilu, 鸣山路12号; s/d from ¥225/250; ❂ @ ⊚) With its excellent location near restaurants and shops, this is one of the better options for the single traveller who wants a private room. Rooms are decidedly Chinese style but comfy. In the off season the singles go for around ¥150.

Silk Road Dūnhuáng Hotel   HOTEL $$$
(敦煌山庄, Dūnhuáng Shānzhuāng; ☑ 0937 888 2088; www.dunhuangresort.com; Dunyue Lu, 敦月路; tw ¥560-1080, d ¥660-1200; ❂ @ ⊚) This four-star resort is tastefully designed with Central Asian rugs, a cool stone floor and Chinese antiques. The hotel's rooftop restaurant has without doubt the best outdoor perch in Dūnhuáng with an amazing view of Singing Sands Dune (p860). It's located south of town on the road to the dunes; a taxi costs ¥10, or take minibus 3 (¥2). Discounts of 20% to 40%.

✕ Eating

Dūnhuáng's local speciality is donkey-meat noodles (驴肉黄面; lǘròu huángmiàn), though these days this is more of a novelty dish than everyday food. You'll still find restaurants all over town offering the dish, which consists of roasted, sliced donkey meat served cold over warm egg noodles.

GĀNSÙ DŪNHUÁNG

Dūnhuáng

Dūnhuáng

🛏 Sleeping
1 Mògāo Hotel B3
2 Shāzhōuyì International Youth
   Hostel A1

🍴 Eating
3 Charley Johng's Cafe B4
4 Shāzhōu Night Market D2

🍷 Drinking & Nightlife
5 Brown Sugar Cafe................................D3
6 Memory Box Cafe D2

🎭 Entertainment
   Dūnhuáng Goddess.....................(see 7)
7 Dūnhuáng Theatre...............................C2

There are restaurants large and small all over Dūnhuáng, many with English or picture menus. For *niúròu miàn* (牛肉面; beef noodles) head to any of a number of restaurants along Xiyu Lu. The night market is the most popular spot for eats in the city.

Charley Johng's Cafe BREAKFAST, CHINESE $
(风味餐馆, Fēngwèi Cānguǎn; ☑ 0937 388 2411; Mingshan Lu, 名山路; dishes ¥6-36; ⊙ 8am-10pm; 🛜) Tasty Western-style breakfasts, including scrambled eggs, muesli with yoghurt, and pancakes, are available all day either à la carte or as a set. There are also sandwiches, and a host of Chinese dishes such as stir-fries and dumplings. It also arranges daily tours to surrounding sights, including Yǎdān National Park (p860), and is a good source of traveller information. English spoken.

★ Zhāixīng Gé CHINESE, INTERNATIONAL $$
(摘星阁, Silk Road Dūnhuáng Hotel; Dunyue Lu, 敦月路; dishes ¥18-38; ⊙ 7am-1pm & 4.30pm-midnight) Part of the Silk Road Dūnhuáng Hotel, this rooftop restaurant is ideal for a meal (the Western buffet breakfast is excellent)

or a sundowner gazing out over the golden sand dunes. Dishes do not cost much more than places in town. Try the Uighur bread or the surprisingly good thick-crust pizza.

Shāzhōu Night Market
MARKET $$

(沙洲夜市, Shāzhōu Yèshì; btwn Yangguan Donglu & Xiyu Lu; ☺morning-late) Extending from Yangguan Lu south to Xiyu, this market is both a place to eat and to socialise, night and day. Off Yanguang Donglu are dozens of well organised stalls with English signs: expect Sichuan, Korean noodles, dumplings, claypot, barbecue including *ròujiāmó* (肉夹馍; pulled-pork sandwich) and Lánzhōu noodles. Also look out for cooling cups of *xìngpíshuǐ* (杏皮水; apricot juice; ¥5).

There is also an open-air seating area nearby with singing, music bands and roast lamb by the platter or skewer. Along with the seated areas along Fanggu Shangye Yitao Jie, this is the most expensive place to eat barbecued meat. For a better deal try the alleys radiating east.

🍷 Drinking & Nightlife

The streets around Shāzhōu Night Market, particularly the ones near Dūnhuáng Mosque, have cafes that also serve as bars in the evening. In summer the Silk Road Dūnhuáng Hotel (p855) hosts a beer garden at the entrance to the grounds, while its stylish rooftop Zhǎixīng Gé offers peerless views over the desert to go with a beer or a glass of local ice wine.

Memory Box Cafe
CAFE, BAR

(时光盒子咖啡馆, Shíguāng Hézi Kāfēi Guǎn; ☑0937 881 9911; room 106a, 7th Bldg, Fengqing City; juice ¥25, beer ¥15) This comfy cafe serves a range of drinks and Chinese and Western snacks, including Illy coffee and some imported beers. It also has a few nice seats out front in warmer weather.

Silk Road Beer Town
BEER GARDEN

(丝路酒坊, Sīlù Jiǔfáng; Silk Road Dūnhuáng Hotel, Dunyue Lu, 敦煌山庄敦月路; ☺12.30-4pm & 6pm-1am) An airy covered beer garden in front of the Silk Road Dūnhuáng Hotel (p855) serving up cheap, cold bottles of Tsingtao (¥15) and heaping portions of fried noodles (炒面; *chǎomiàn*) and other Chinese dishes.

Brown Sugar Cafe
CAFE

(黑糖咖啡, Hēitáng Kāfēi; ☑0937 881 7111; 28 Tianma Jie, 天马街28号; tea ¥25-38, bottle of wine ¥78-198; ☺1pm-midnight; 🛜) This friendly cafe mixes modern with crafty decor and cafe

classics with a Dūnhuáng twist. Try a cup of fresh-leaf Chinese tea to balance out a sweet black-rice muffin. Things turn smoky at night when fashionable locals come to sip beer and Mògāo wine.

☆ Entertainment

There are often night-time opera and other music performances in the square near the mosque.

Dūnhuáng Theatre (敦煌大剧院, Dūnhuáng Dàjùyuàn; Yangguan Zhonglu, 阳关中路) hosts **Dūnhuáng Goddess** (敦煌神女, Dūnhuáng Shénnǚ; ticket ¥220; ☺8.30pm), an 80-minute acrobatic dramatisation of stories on the walls of the Mògāo Grottoes. English subtitles are provided.

ℹ Information

Wi-fi is widely available in cafes and hotel rooms, and there are internet cafes on the main streets if you get stuck.

Bank of China (中国银行, Zhōngguó Yínháng; Yangguan Zhonglu, 阳关中路; ☺8am-noon & 2-6pm Mon-Fri) Has a 24-hour ATM.

China Post (中国邮政, Zhōngguó Yóuzhèng; Yangguan Donglu, 阳关中路; ☺8.30am-6pm daily) Sells stamps and delivers packages internationally.

Fēitiān Travel Service (飞天旅行社, Fēitiān Lǚxíngshè, Fēitiān Bīnguǎn; ☑138 3070 6288, 0937 885 2318; 551 Mingshan Lu, 鸣山路551号) Can arrange tours to **Mògāo Grottoes** (p858), local day trips and car rental.

Mògāo Grottoes Reservation and Ticket Center (莫高窟参观预约售票中心, Mògāo Kū Cānguān Yùyuē Shòupiào Zhōngxīn; Yangguan Dadao, 阳关大道迎宾花园北区15号楼102号)

Public Security Bureau (PSB, 公安局, Gōng'ānjú; ☑0937 886 2071; Yangguan Zhonglu, 阳关中路; ☺8am-noon & 3-6.30pm Mon-Fri) Two days needed for visa extension.

ℹ Getting There & Away

AIR

Apart from November to March, when there are only flights to/from Lánzhōu and Xī'ān, there are regular flights to/from Běijīng, Lánzhōu, Shànghǎi, Ūrümqi and Xī'ān.

Seats can be booked at the air ticket office in the lobby of the Yóuzhèng Bīnguǎn hotel (邮政宾馆), on Yangguan Donglu west of China Post.

BUS

From Dūnhuáng's **bus station** (长途汽车站, Zhǎngtú Qìchēzhàn; ☑0937 885 3746; Xiyu Lu; ☺7am-8pm daily), you can catch buses to Jiāyùguān and Lánzhōu (though trains are cheaper and faster), as well as the following:

Golmud ¥99, nine hours, two daily (9am and 7.30pm)

Liǔyuán (柳园) ¥20, three hours, eight per day (7.30am to 6.30pm)

Ürümqi ¥198, 14 hours, one daily (7pm), sleeper. May stop in Turpan.

TRAIN

Dūnhuáng's station is 10km east of town, but for some destinations, such as Běijīng West and Ürümqi, you'll have to leave from Liǔyuán Station, a crazy 180km away.

Jiāyùguān Seat/hard sleeper ¥53/112, 4½ hours, seven daily

Lánzhōu Hard/soft sleeper ¥141/276, 14 hours, three daily (9.12am, 6.55pm and 8.07pm); more trains leave from Liǔyuán Station

Turpan (from Liǔyuán Station) Hard/soft sleeper ¥93/184, six to eight hours; high-speed trains go to Turpan North

Ürümqi (from Liǔyuán Station) Hard/soft sleeper/high-speed 2nd-class seat ¥112/219/247, five to nine hours; high-speed trains leave from Liǔyuán South

Tickets can be booked at the **train booking office** (火车票发售点, Huǒchē Piào Fāshòu Diǎn; Tianma Jie, 天马街; ⊙8am-noon & 1-4pm, to 8pm summer) south of the mosque.

If you are heading to Liǔyuán Station (for trains to Ürümqi and high-speed rail), catch a bus or shared taxi (per person ¥45) from the front of the bus station (p857). Give yourself at least three hours to get to Liǔyuán Station (including waiting for the taxi to fill up with other passengers).

ⓘ Getting Around

The airport is 13km east of town; a taxi to/from the airport costs ¥40 and takes 20 minutes.

The train station is 14km from the centre of town, on the same road as the airport. Bus 1 runs to the train station from the **bus stop** (Mingshan Lu) from 7.30am to 9pm.

You can rent bikes from travellers' cafes for ¥5 per hour.

Taxis around town start at ¥5.

Around Dūnhuáng

Most people visit the Mògāo Grottoes in the morning, followed by the Singing Sands Dune in the late afternoon to catch the sunset. Note that it can be 40°C in the desert during the summer so go prepared with water, a sunhat and snacks.

Mògāo Grottoes 莫高窟

The **Mògāo Grottoes** (Mògāo Kū; www.mgk. org.cn/index.htm; low/high season ¥120/220; ⊙8am-6pm May-Oct, 9am-5.30pm Nov-Apr) are considered one of the most important collections of Buddhist art in the world. At its peak during the Tang dynasty (618–907), the site housed 18 monasteries, more than 1400 monks and nuns, and countless artists, translators and calligraphers.

Tours by excellent English-speaking guides at 9am, noon and 2.30pm are included in the admission price, and you should be able to arrange tours in other languages as

---

SILK ROAD RAIDERS

In 1900, the self-appointed guardian of the **Mògāo Grottoes**, Wang Yuanlu, discovered a hidden library filled with tens of thousands of immaculately preserved manuscripts and paintings, dating as far back as AD 406.

It's hard to describe the exact magnitude of the discovery, but stuffed into the tiny cave were texts in rare Central Asian languages, military reports, music scores, medical prescriptions, Confucian and Taoist classics, and Buddhist sutras copied by some of the greatest names in Chinese calligraphy – not to mention the oldest printed book in existence, the *Diamond Sutra* (AD 868). In short, it was an incalculable amount of original source material regarding Chinese, Central Asian and Buddhist history.

Word of the discovery quickly spread and Wang Yuanlu, suddenly the most popular bloke in town, was courted by rival archaeologists Aurel Stein and Paul Pelliot, among others. Following much pressure to sell the cache, Wang Yuanlu finally relented and parted with an enormous hoard of treasure. On his watch close to 20,000 of the cave's priceless manuscripts were whisked off to Europe for the paltry sum of £220.

Today, Chinese intellectuals bitter at the sacking of the caves deride Stein, Pelliot and others for making off with what they consider to be national treasures. Defenders of the explorers point out that had the items been left alone, there is a chance they could have been lost during the ensuing civil war or the Cultural Revolution.

well. Many of the guides are students or researchers at the Dūnhuáng Academy, which administers the caves.

In 2015 the Mògāo Grottoes site saw a huge upgrade, with a state-of-the-art visitor centre built just a few kilometres outside of central Dūnhuáng. Admission includes two 30-minute films, one on the history of the area and the Silk Road, and one that allows close-up computer-generated views of cave interiors not normally open to visitors in an IMAX-style theatre. From here, visitors are shuttled to the caves 15km down the road in dedicated coaches.

Of the 492 caves, 20 'open' caves are rotated fairly regularly. Entrance is strictly controlled – it's impossible to visit them independently. In addition to the two films, the general admission ticket includes a roughly two-hour tour of 10 caves, including the famous **Hidden Library Cave** (cave 17), the two **big Buddhas**, 34.5m and 26m tall, and a related exhibit containing rare fragments of manuscripts in classical Uighur and Manichean.

Photography is prohibited inside the caves. If it's raining or snowing or there's a sand storm, the site will be closed.

Tickets must be purchased in advance either online at the caves' official website (Chinese ID card needed at the time of writing) or from the Mògāo Grottoes Reservation and Ticket Center (p857), a separate booking office where staff speak English. Note that tickets are not sold at the main visitor centre.

History

Wealthy traders and important officials were the primary donors responsible for creating new caves, as caravans made the long detour past Mògāo to pray or give thanks for a safe journey through the treacherous wastelands to the west. The traditional date ascribed to the founding of the first cave is AD 366.

The caves fell into disuse for about 500 years after the collapse of the Yuan dynasty and were largely forgotten until the early 20th century, when they were 'rediscovered' by a string of foreign explorers.

Northern Wei, Western Wei & Northern Zhou Caves

These, the earliest of the Mògāo Caves, are distinctly Indian in style and iconography. All contain a central pillar, representing a stupa (symbolically containing the ashes of the Buddha), which the devout would circle in prayer. Paint was derived from malachite (green), cinnabar (red) and lapis lazuli

TICKETS TO THE GROTTOES

Though you used to be able to buy tickets to the Mògāo Grottoes directly at the entrance, the sight's popularity and relative ease of accessibility in recent years has meant that advance purchase is necessary. You can buy tickets online up to 14 days in advance at www.mgk.org. cn, although at the time of writing, this was Chinese-language only. Alternately, go to the **Mògāo Grottoes Reservation and Ticket Center** (p857) in Dūnhuáng when you arrive. Most hotels and hostels in Dūnhuáng can also book tickets, but may levy a surcharge.

(blue), expensive minerals imported from Central Asia.

The art of this period is characterised by its attempt to depict the spirituality of those who had transcended the material world through their asceticism. The Wei statues are slim, ethereal figures with finely chiselled features and comparatively large heads. The northern Zhou figures have ghostly white eyes.

Sui Caves

The Sui dynasty (AD 581–618) was short lived and very much a transition between the Wei and Tang periods. This can be seen in the Sui caves at Mògāo: the graceful Indian curves in the Buddha and Bodhisattva figures start to give way to the more rigid style of Chinese sculpture.

The Sui dynasty began when a general of Chinese or mixed Chinese–Tuoba origin usurped the throne of the northern Zhou dynasty and reunited northern and southern China for the first time in 360 years.

Tang Caves

The Tang dynasty (AD 618–907) was Mògāo's high point. Painting and sculpture techniques became much more refined, and some important aesthetic developments, notably the sex change (from male to female) of Guanyin and the flying apsaras (Buddhist celestial beings), took place. The beautiful murals depicting the Buddhist Western Paradise offer rare insights into the court life, music, dress and architecture of Tang China.

Some 230 caves were carved during the religiously diverse Tang dynasty, including two impressive grottoes containing enormous, seated Buddha figures. Originally open to the elements, the statue of Maitreya in cave 96 (believed to represent Empress Wu Zetian, who used Buddhism to consolidate her power) is a towering 34.5m tall, making it the world's third-largest Buddha. The Buddhas were carved from the top down using scaffolding, the anchor holes of which are still visible.

Post-Tang Caves

Following the Tang dynasty, the economy around Dūnhuáng went into decline, and the luxury and vigour typical of Tang painting began to be replaced by simpler drawing techniques and flatter figures. The mysterious Western Xia kingdom, which controlled most of Gānsù from 983 to 1227, made a number of additions to the caves at Mògāo and began to introduce Tibetan influences.

🛈 Getting There & Away

The Mògāo Grottoes are 25km (30 minutes) southeast of Dūnhuáng, but tours start and end at the visitor centre, about 5km from Mingshan Lu near the train station. A green minibus (one way ¥3) leaves for the visitor centre every 30 minutes from 8am to 5pm from outside the Silk Road Hotel (丝路宾馆; Sīlù Bīnguǎn). A taxi costs ¥15 one-way, and taxis generally wait outside the visitor centre, so it's easy to find one on the way back.

Singing Sands Dune   鸣沙山

Six kilometres south of Dūnhuáng at **Singing Sands Dune** (Míngshā Shān; ¥120; ⊙6am-7.30pm), the desert meets the oasis in most spectacular fashion. From the sheer scale of the dunes, it's easy to see how Dūnhuáng gained its moniker 'Shāzhōu' (Town of Sand). The view across the undulating desert and green poplar trees below is awesome.

You can bike to the dunes in 20 minutes from the centre of Dūnhuáng. Bus 3 (¥2) shuttles between Shazhou Lu and Mingshan Lu and the dunes from 7.30am to 9pm. A taxi costs ¥20 one way.

The climb to the top of the dunes – the highest peak swells to 1715m – is sweaty work, but worth it. Rent a pair of bright-orange shoe protectors (防沙靴; fángshā-xuē; ¥15) or just shake your shoes out later.

At the base of the colossal dunes is a famous pond, **Crescent Moon Lake** (月牙泉; Yuèyáquán). The dunes are a no-holds-barred tourist playpen, with dune buggies, 'dune surfing' (sand sledding), paragliding and even microlighting. But it's not hard to hike away to enjoy the sandy spectacle in peace.

Tickets are good for three days' entry. To avail of this, you must ask the security staff at the gate as you exit – they will take your fingerprint so only you can use the ticket again.

Hostels in Dūnhuáng offer overnight camel treks to the dunes from ¥400 per person. There are also five- to eight-day expeditions out to the Jade Gate Pass, Liǔyuán and even as far as Lop Nor in the deserts of Xīnjiāng.

Yúlín Grottoes   榆林窟

About 180km south of Dūnhuáng, the 40-plus caves of the **Yúlín Grottoes** (Yúlín Kū; ¥40; ⊙8.30am-6pm) face each other across a narrow canyon. It's intriguing to observe the original carved interior tunnels that formerly connected the caves. The interior art spans a 1500-year period, from the Northern Wei to the Qing dynasty. Many show a distinctive Tibetan influence.

The only way to get out here is to hire a driver (¥400) for the half-day. Excellent English guides are available on-site for ¥15.

While the art at the Mògāo Grottoes (p858) is considered higher quality, the frescoes here are better preserved; there is little of the oxidation and thickening of painted lines so prevalent at Mògāo.

Yǎdān National Park   雅丹国家地质公园

The weird, eroded desert landscape of **Yǎdān National Park** (Yǎdān Guójiā Dìzhì Gōngyuán; admission ¥120; ⊙8am-5.30pm) is 180km northwest of Dūnhuáng, in the middle of the Gobi Desert's awesome nothingness. A former lake bed that eroded in spectacular fashion some 12,000 years ago, the strange rock formations provided the backdrop to the last scenes of Zhang Yimou's film *Hero*. Tours (included in the price) are confined to group minibuses (with regular photo stops) to preserve the natural surrounds, but the desert landscape here is so dramatic you will still feel like you're at the ends of the earth.

To get to Yǎdān you have to pass through (and buy a ticket to) the Jade Gate Pass and Sun Pass. The best way to get here is take one of two daily **minibus tours** (¥100 per person): the first departs at 7am and can be booked through Charley Johng's Cafe (p856); the other leaves at 12.30pm and is organised through the Shazhouyi International Youth Hostel (p855). Tour prices don't include entrance fees to the individual sights. The 10- to 12-hour tours include a stop at the Jade Gate and Sun Passes and the **Western Thousand Buddha Caves** (西千佛洞, Xī Qiānfó Dòng; ¥40; ⊙8.30am-5pm).

Jade Gate Pass HISTORIC SITE

(玉门关, Yùmén Guān & 阳关, Yáng Guān; Jade Gate ¥60, South Pass ¥40) The Jade Gate Pass, 78km west of Dūnhuáng, was originally a military station. Together with Sun Pass, it formed part of the Han dynasty series of beacon towers that extended to the garrison town of Lóula'n in Xīnjiāng. Admission includes entry to a section of Han dynasty **Great Wall** (101 BC), impressive for its antiquity and lack of restoration; and the ruined city walls of **Hécāng Chéng**, 15km down a side road.

For caravans travelling westward, the Jade Gate marked the beginning of the northern route to Turpan and was one of the last outposts that travellers and banished criminals saw before leaving the Chinese empire. The Jade Gate derived its name from the important traffic in Khotanese jade that thrived along the Silk Road, which passed through here.

Tours that take in the Jade Gate Pass and Sun Pass, usually in combination with Yǎdān National Park, can be arranged at Charley Johng's Cafe (p856).

Sun Pass HISTORIC SITE

(阳关, Yángguān; ¥50; ⊙8am-8pm) This Han dynasty military post was one of the two most important gates marking the end of the Chinese empire along the ancient Silk Road. Today, a dusty museum chronicles some of the site's artefacts, but the real draw is the crumbling beacon tower atop Dundun Hill, where a modern viewing platform offers generous vistas of the surrounding Taklamakan Desert.

EASTERN GĀNSÙ

Tiānshuǐ 天水

☎0938 / POP 3.26 MILLION

Tiānshuǐ's splendid Buddhist caves at nearby Màijī Shān entice a consistent flow of visitors. Though the city is not a draw in and of itself, it is a pleasant place to spend the night on the way to or from Màijī Shān and has enough dining and sleeping options to keep you occupied on your way through. The city has recently started to develop a waterside promenade along the Wei River that promises to become a very pleasant place for a stroll or evening beer.

Modern Tiānshuǐ is actually two very separate districts 15km apart: there is the railhead sprawl, known as Màijī Qū (麦积区; formerly Běidào), and the central commercial area to the west, known as Qínzhōu Qū (秦州区), where you'll arrive if coming in by bus. The two sections are lashed together by a long freeway that runs along the river.

Sights

Tiānshuǐ's main draw is Màijī Shān (p862), in the hills 35km south of town. Within walking distance of the Tiānshuǐ Dàjiǔdiàn hotel on the Qínzhōu side of town are two temples worth checking out if you have time to kill.

Fúxī Temple BUDDHIST TEMPLE

(伏羲庙, Fúxī Miào; off Jiefang Lu, Qínzhōu, 秦州区解放路; ¥40; ⊙8am-5.40pm) This Ming dynasty temple was founded in 1483 in honour of Fúxī, the father and emperor of all Chinese people. The Tiānshuǐ resident's seminaked statue is in the main hall, along with traditional symbols such as bats, dragons and peonies. The hall ceiling's original paintings of the 64 hexagrams (varying combinations of the eight trigrams used in the *I Ching*) have uncanny similarities to computer binary language. It's worth visiting just for the 1000-year-old cypress tree in the tranquil gardens.

Sleeping & Eating

If your aim is to get to Màijī Shān early, your best bet is to stay in Màijī Qū, the area around the railway station, which has a couple of decent Chinese-style business hotels. For better dining and nightlife options, opt to stay in Qínzhōu Qū.

In Qínzhōu Qū, you'll find good claypot, Sìchuān and noodle snack stalls, as well as fruit and nut sellers, around Tiānshuǐ Dàjiǔdiàn.

Tasty *ròujiāmó* (肉夹馍) and other fine snack food in **Màijī Qū** fill Erma Lu, a pedestrian street two blocks directly south of the train station.

Tiānshuǐ Dàjiǔdiàn HOTEL $

(☎0938 828 9999; 1 Qinzhou Dazhong Nanlu; r ¥130; ❄@📶) This popular hotel is a solid choice in Qínzhōu district. The bus to Màijī Shān is just 200m south and restaurants abound. Standard rooms with private bathrooms are usually discounted up to 40%.

It's just opposite the main square, Zhōngxīn Guǎngchǎng.

Tiānshuǐ Garden Hotel   HOTEL $$

(天水花园酒店, Tiānshuǐ Huāyuán Jiǔdiàn; ☑152 4937 3206; 1 Longchang Xilu, Màijī Qū, 麦积区隆昌西路1号; d ¥238; ❀@☎) This hotel is very handily located directly across from the train station. It's modern and clean, though the furnishings are showing a bit of wear and tear. The bus to Màijī Shān Grottoes departs from the stop on Longchang Lu just east of Bubei Lu.

Běidào Qīngzhēn
Lǎozìhào Niúròu Miànguǎn   NOODLES

(北道清真老字号牛肉面馆; Shangbu Lu Pedestrian St, 商埠路步行街; dishes ¥4-12; ☺7am-10pm) Get a ticket from the kiosk out front and collect your beef noodles (*niúròu miàn;* ¥7) from the kitchen window inside. The noodles are excellent, infused with dollops of scarlet-red chilli oil. For extra meat, ask for *jiāròu niúròumiàn* (加肉牛肉面; ¥10). There's no English sign, but it's the green-and-white place roughly opposite a small branch of ICBC bank.

❶ Information

Bank of China (中国银行, Zhōngguó Yínháng; Longchang Lu; ☺8.30am-noon & 2.30-5.30pm) Has Forex and an ATM.

❶ Getting There & Away

BUS

Buses leave from the long-distance bus station in Qínzhōu for the following destinations:

Huīxiàn ¥35, three hours, hourly (7.20am to 6pm)

Lánzhōu ¥74, four hours, every 20 minutes (7.20am to 7pm)

Línxià ¥99, seven hours, one daily (6.30am)

Luòmén ¥25, two hours, three daily (7am, 11am and 2.30pm)

Píngliáng ¥65, five hours, hourly (7am to 3pm)

TRAIN

Tiānshuǐ is on the Xī'ān–Lánzhōu rail line; there are dozens of daily trains in each direction.

Bǎojī Hard seat/soft sleeper ¥24/79, 2½ hours

Dìngxī Hard seat/soft sleeper ¥28/142, two to four hours

Lánzhōu Hard seat/soft sleeper ¥52/169, four hours

Xī'ān Hard seat/soft sleeper ¥51/165, five hours

❶ Getting Around

Taxis shuttle passengers between Qínzhōu Qū (from both the city bus station 200m south of **Tiānshuǐ Dàjiǔdiàn** hoand also from the long-distance bus station) and the train station in Màijī Qū. It costs ¥10 per person (¥40 for the whole taxi). Alternatively, take the much slower bus 1 or 6 (¥3, 40 minutes).

Around Tiānshuǐ

Set among wild, green mountains southeast of Tiānshuǐ, the grottoes of **Màijī Shān** (麦积山石窟, Màijīshān Shíkū; admission ¥90; ☺9am-5pm) hold some of the most famous Buddhist rock carvings along the Silk Road. The cliff sides of Màijī Shān are covered with 221 caves holding more than 7800 sculptures carved principally during the Northern Wei and Zhou dynasties (AD 386–581). The rock face rises in a steep ascent, with the hundreds of grottoes connected by a series of constructed walkways clinging to the sheer cliff.

Within the hard-to-miss Sui dynasty trinity of Buddha and two Bodhisattvas is the largest statue on the mountain: the cave's central effigy of Buddha tops out at 15.7m. During restoration works on the statue in the late 1980s, a handwritten copy of the Sutra of Golden Light was discovered within the Buddha's fan.

Vertigo-inducing catwalks and steep spiral stairways cling to the cliff face, affording close-ups of the art. It's not certain just how the artists managed to clamber so high; one theory is that they created piles from blocks of wood reaching to the top of the mountain before moving down, gradually removing them as they descended.

A considerable amount of pigment still clings to many of the statues – a lot of which are actually made of clay rather than being hewn from rock – although you frequently have to climb up steps to peer at them through tight mesh grills with little natural illumination. Much, though, is clearly visible and most of the more impressive sculptures decorate the upper walkways, especially at cave 4.

At the time of writing, a new visitors centre was being constructed at the base of the mountain to replace the crescent of noodle stalls that previously served as the only refreshments on the mountain.

An English-speaking guide charges ¥50 for up to a group of five. It may be possible to view normally closed caves (such as cave 133) for an extra fee of ¥500 per group.

The admission ticket includes entry to **Ruìyìng Monastery** (瑞应寺; *Ruìyìng Sì*), at the base of the mountain, which acts as a small museum of selected statues. Across from the monastery is the start of a trail to a **botanic garden** (植物园; *zhíwùyuán*), which allows for a short cut back to the entrance gate through the forest. If you don't want to walk the 2km up the road from the ticket office to the cliff, ask for tickets for the **sightseeing trolley** (观光车; *guānguāng chē*; ¥15) when buying your entrance ticket.

You can also climb **Xiāngjī Shān** (香积山). For the trailhead, head back towards the visitor centre where the sightseeing bus drops you off and look for a sign down a side road to the left.

To reach Màijī Shān, take bus 34 (¥5 one way, one hour, every 15 minutes) from the bus shelter across from Tiānshuǐ Railway Station. It terminates at the Màijī Shān ticketing office.

Píngliáng 平凉

📞0933 / POP 2.06 MILLION

A booming, midsized Chinese city, Píngliáng is a logical base for visits to the nearby holy mountain of Kōngtóng Shān, which, according to Taoist legend, is where the Yellow Emperor came to meet the avatar Guangchengzi.

Kōngtóng Shān (崆峒山; high/low season ¥120/60; ⊗8am-5pm), 11km west of Píngliáng, is one of the 12 principal peaks in the Taoist universe. It was first mentioned by the philosopher Zhuangzi (399–295 BC), and illustrious visitors have included none other than the Yellow Emperor. Numerous paths lead over the hilltop past dozens of picturesque (though entirely restored) temples to the summit at over 2100m. While the mountain is an enchanting place to hike, those looking for genuine historical artefacts or ambience will be disappointed.

From the north gate visitor centre (pick up a free map here to orient yourself) catch a bus to Zhōngtái (¥32) or Xiāngshān (¥48); both are essentially small visitor areas on the mountain with paths radiating out to lookouts and temples. A taxi from Píngliáng to Kōngtóng Shān will cost ¥30, or you can

catch bus 16 (¥1) on Xi Dajie and then transfer to bus 13 (¥2) when you reach Kongtong Dadao. Bus 13 drops you off right in front of the main visitor centre before continuing on to the East Gate. At the end of your visit you can walk down from Zhōngtái to the East Gate and catch bus 13 back to town.

Accommodation in Píngliáng is limited to just-fine Chinese-style hotels. The top hotel in town is **Píngliáng Hotel** (平凉宾馆, Píngliáng Bīnguǎn; 📞0933 821 9485; 86 Xi Dajie, 西大街86号; tw/d ¥216/250; 圈@𝄢). has a grandiose marble lobby and spacious rooms with modern furnishings in subtle colours. Expect discounts up to 40%.

For meals, look for the Sìzhōng Alley market (四中巷市场; Sìzhōng Xiàng Shìchǎng), just off the main street (Xi Dajie). There are numerous restaurants here, and more food stalls serving noodles, spicy hotpot and barbecued meats, as well as fresh fruit.

🛈 Getting There & Away

BUS

The following services depart from Píngliáng's main bus station, in the western part of town on Lai Yuan Lu:

Gùyuán ¥24, 1½ hours, frequent

Lánzhōu ¥105, five hours, hourly (6.30am to 5.30pm)

Tiānshuǐ ¥65, seven hours, one daily (9am)

Xī'ān ¥88, six hours, every 40 minutes (6.20am to 6pm)

For Tiānshuǐ there are more frequent departures from the east bus station (qìchē dōngzhàn).

TRAIN

The train station is in the northeastern part of town. It's better to take a bus to Xī'ān as trains either leave or arrive at very inconvenient hours.

Lánzhōu Seat/hard sleeper ¥49/109, 11½ hours, one daily leaving at 9.53pm

Xī'ān Hard seat/soft sleeper ¥53/172, five to six hours

Bǎojī Hard seat/soft sleeper ¥33/134, four hours

🛈 Getting Around

Bus 1 (¥2) runs from the train station to Xi Dajie. A taxi costs ¥10. From Xi Dajie to the bus station costs ¥4 or take bus 16 (¥1).

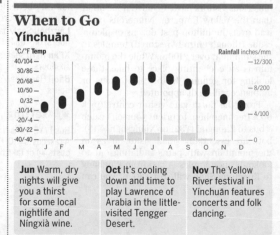

Níngxià

POP 6.4 MILLION

Best Places to Eat

➜ Xiānhè Lóu (p868)

➜ Xiǎochī Night Market (p874)

➜ Dà Mǎ Jiǎozi Guǎn (p868)

➜ Quánjùdé (p869)

Best Places to Sleep

➜ Yinchuan Hotel (p868)

➜ Holiday Inn (p868)

➜ Zhōngwèi Dàjiǔdiàn (p871)

Why Go?

With its raw landscape of dusty plains and stark mountains, sliced in two by the Yellow River (Huáng Hé), there's a distinct *Grapes of Wrath* feel to Níngxià (宁夏). Outside the cities is a timeless landscape where farmers till the hard yellow earth just like their ancestors did.

Yet Níngxià was once the frontline between the empires of the Mongols and the Han Chinese and there's a host of historic sites here, ranging from little-seen Buddhist statues to the royal tombs of long-past dynasties, as well as ancient rock carvings that predate the emperors. And as the homeland of the Muslim Hui ethnic minority, Níngxià is culturally unique, too.

Then there's the chance to camp out under the desert sky, or float down the Yellow River on a traditional raft. But best of all, Níngxià sees few foreign visitors so it seems like you have the place all to yourself.

When to Go
Yínchuān

Jun Warm, dry nights will give you a thirst for some local nightlife and Níngxià wine.

Oct It's cooling down and time to play Lawrence of Arabia in the little-visited Tengger Desert.

Nov The Yellow River festival in Yínchuān features concerts and folk dancing.

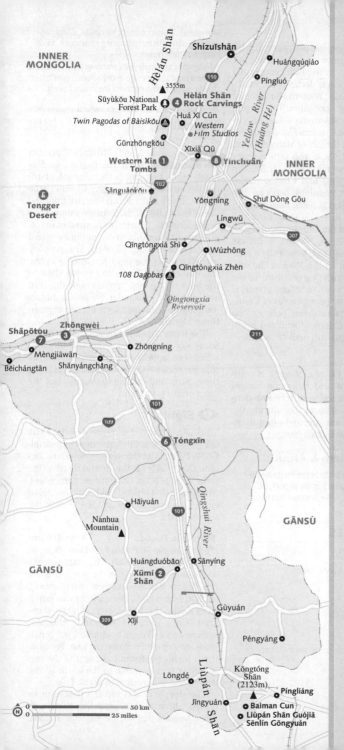

Níngxià Highlights

1 Western Xia Tombs (p867) Visiting these imperial tombs outside Yínchuān, a rare reminder of a long-vanished culture.

2 Xūmí Shān (p873) Exploring these little-visited Buddhist grottoes with their hundreds of statues.

3 Gāo Temple (p870) Being startled by the unsettling statuary in the riveting Arhat Hall.

4 Hèlán Shān Rock Carvings (p870) Admiring unique rock carvings that date back thousands of years.

5 Tengger Desert (p872) Hopping on a camel to trek into the dunes for an overnight stay.

6 Great Mosque (p874) Getting way off the beaten track at this marvellous Ming-era complex in Tóngxīn.

7 Shāpōtóu (p871) Rafting down the Yellow River or sliding down the sand dunes at this desert playground.

8 Hǎibǎo Pagoda (p866) Taking in the beautiful lines of this unusually styled Buddhist tower.

History

Níngxià had been on the periphery of Chinese empires ever since the Qin dynasty, but it took centre stage in the 10th century AD when the Tangut people declared the establishment of the Xixia (Western Xia) empire in the face of Song opposition. The empire was composed of modern-day Gānsù, Níngxià, Shaanxi and western Inner Mongolia, but it soon collapsed in the face of Mongol might.

The Mongol retreat in the 14th century left a void that was filled by both Muslim traders from the west and Chinese farmers from the east. Tensions between the two resulted in Níngxià being caught up in the great Muslim Rebellion that convulsed northwest China in the mid-19th century.

Once part of Gānsù, Níngxià is China's smallest province, although technically it is an autonomous region for the Muslim Hui ethnic minority, who make up one-third of the population, rather than an official province. It remains one of the poorest areas of China, with a sharp economic divide between the more fertile, Han Chinese–dominated north and the parched, sparsely populated south.

Climate

Part of the Loess Plateau, Níngxià is composed primarily of arid mountain ranges and highlands in a region of very low rainfall. Summer temperatures soar during the day, while winters are long and often freezing; spring is lovely, though blustery.

ⓘ Getting There & Around

Níngxià's capital Yínchuān is the major flight hub, although Zhōngwèi has an airport, as does Bayanhot (for connections within Inner Mongolia). Trains connect Yínchuān, Zhōngwèi and Gùyuán with neighbouring provinces, as do long-distance buses.

Níngxià is so small you can cross it by vehicle it in a few hours. Buses go everywhere, sometimes slowly, while trains connect the major towns.

Yínchuān 银川

📞 0951 / POP 750,000

In the sun-parched land of Níngxià, Yínchuān has managed to thrive. The Tangut founders wisely chose this spot as their capital, planting the city between a source of water (the Yellow River) and a natural barrier from the Gobi Desert (the Hèlán Shān mountains).

Modern-day Yínchuān is predominantly Han, although its many mosques reveal its status as the capital of the Hui peoples' homeland. But the most interesting sights, the Western Xia Tombs and Hèlán Shān to the west of the city, predate both the Han and the Hui. Yínchuān is also a handy jumping-off point for longer trips to western Inner Mongolia.

The name Yínchuān means 'Silver River'. Some say it comes from the alkaline land which can appear white, while others say that it's because the Yellow River is clear in these parts and can appear bright, but the exact origin is obscure.

◉ Sights

Yínchuān is divided into three parts. Xīxià Qū (西夏区; New City), the new industrialised section, is on the western outskirts. Jīnfèng Qū (金凤区) is the central district (the train station is on Jīnfèng's western edge). Xìngqìng Qū (兴庆区; Old City) is 12km east of the train station and has most of the town's sights.

★ **Hǎibǎo Pagoda**   BUDDHIST PAGODA
(海宝塔, Hǎibǎo Tǎ; Hǎibǎo Park, Minzu Beijie, 民族北街的海宝公园; ¥10) This fantastically well preserved pagoda in the north of town is a beauty. Its cross-shaped (from above), straight-edged and tapering form was exquisitely built. The pagoda was slightly damaged during the 2008 Sìchuān earthquake, so sadly can no longer be climbed, but repair work may reopen it down the line. For now, it is a highly photogenic element of the surrounding temple, while to the south lie the waters and willow trees of South Lake.

The steeple is also rather unusual in its design, although it is similar to the town's other famous pagoda, Chéngtiānsì Pagoda.

PRICE RANGES

Eating
Price ranges for a main course:

$ less than ¥30

$$ ¥30–¥50

$$$ more than ¥50

Sleeping
Prices for a double room with shower or bathroom:

$ less than ¥250

$$ ¥250–¥400

$$$ more than ¥400

Yínchuān

Also known as North Pagoda (北塔; Běitǎ) and at one time also called the Black Pagoda, the structure was possibly originally built in the 5th century (although the exact date is unknown), before being toppled by an earthquake in 1739. It was then rebuilt in its current form in 1771. Take bus 29 from the Drum Tower, then enter by the east gate which will take you to the pagoda (and the lovely lakeside park it is located in).

Western Xià Tombs   HISTORIC SITE
(西夏王陵, Xīxià Wánglíng; ¥60; ⊙8am-5.30pm, to 6pm summer) The Western Xia Tombs, which resemble giant beehives, are Níngxià's most celebrated sight. The first tombs were built a millennium ago by Li Yuanhao, the founder of the Western Xia dynasty. There are nine imperial tombs, plus 200 lesser tombs, in an area of 50 sq km – there are electric carts if you're not up for walking. The tomb you'll see belongs to Li Yuanhao; it's a 23m-tall tomb originally constructed as an octagonal seven-storey wooden pagoda. All that remains is the large earthen core. Permits, usually organised through local tour operators, are required to visit other tombs in the area.

The examples of Buddhist art in the good site museum (8am to 5.30pm) offer a rare glimpse into the ephemeral Western Xia culture, and point to clear artistic influences from neighbouring Tibet and Central Asia. There are also many fascinating artefacts excavated from Li Yuanhao's tomb.

The tombs are 33km west of Yínchuān. A return taxi costs from around ¥150 (including waiting time). Regular buses (¥12, every 30 minutes, 7am to 7pm) run past the tombs from the bus station next to the Nánguān

Mosque (南关清真寺; Nánguān Qīngzhēnsì), not far from South Gate Square (南门广场; Nánmén Guǎngchǎng); you will need to tell the driver you want to get off at the tombs. From the South Gate, you could also take bus 2 or 4 to its terminus in Xīxià Qū and then take a van (around ¥40 each way) from there. As the site is on the road towards Bayanhot, you can get off any bus heading that way.

Chéngtiānsì Pagoda   BUDDHIST PAGODA
(承天寺塔, Chéngtiānsì Tǎ; Jinning Nanjie; ¥5, climb pagoda ¥20; ⊙9am-5pm Tue-Sun, to 5.30pm summer) Climb the 13 storeys of steep, narrow stairs of this brick pagoda topped with a green spire for 360-degree views of Yínchuān. The pagoda is also known as Xī Tǎ (西塔; West Pagoda) and dates back almost 1000 years to the Western Xia dynasty, though it has been rebuilt several times since, especially after it toppled during the great Níngxià earthquake of 1738; the current pagoda dates to 1820. Buses 9, 10, 24 and 25 all reach the temple.

Yínchuān

◎ Sights

⊜ Sleeping

⊗ Eating

♢ Drinking & Nightlife

NÍNGXIÀ YÍNCHUĀN

WORTH A TRIP

108 DAGOBAS

An unusual arrangement of Tibetan-style Buddhist dagobas, or stupas, **108 Dagobas** (一百零八塔, Yìbǎilíngbā Tǎ; ¥60) is 83km south of Yínchuān, not far from the town of Qīngtóngxiá (青铜峡). The 12 rows of (much renovated) brick vaselike structures date from the Yuan dynasty and are arranged in a large triangular constellation on the banks of the Yellow River.

Take a bus (¥25, 2½ hours) from Yínchuān long-distance bus station to Qīngtóngxiá and then take bus 2 to the Qīngtóngxiá Hydroelectric Station (青铜峡水电站; Qīngtóngxiá Shuǐdiànzhàn) and take a boat (included in the admission ticket) to the far bank.

Nánxūn Mén   GATE

(南薰门, Nánxūn Mén; Nanxun Dongjie, 南薰东街) The sole surviving gate of the old town wall, Nánxūn Mén looks south out onto Nanmen Sq (南门广场; Nánmén Guǎngchǎng) from its position east of Nanxun Dongjie. The two viewing platforms were added in the 1970s, making a faithful duplication in miniature of Běijīng's Gate of Heavenly Peace – Tiān'ānmén, which looks over Tiān'ānmén Sq. Mao's portrait was added, to perfect the copy.

Shuǐ Dòng Gōu   ARCHAEOLOGICAL SITE

(水洞沟; ☉8am-6pm) This archaeological site, 25km east of Yínchuān, right on the border with Inner Mongolia, has been turned into something of an adventure theme park. The site is divided into two parts; the first is a **museum** that resembles Jabba the Hutt's bunker and which contains the Palaeolithic-era relics first uncovered here in 1923.

From there, it's a golf-cart ride to an unrestored section of the **Great Wall** dating back to the Ming dynasty. Then it's a walk, boat trip, donkey- and camel-cart ride to a **fortress** with an elaborate network of underground tunnels once used by Chinese soldiers defending the Wall. The renovated tunnels include trap doors, false passages and booby traps.

The catch is that the admission price to Shuǐ Dòng Gōu only lets you into the site itself. Everything else – the museum, fort and all transport – costs extra, making this an expensive day out. Unless you fancy an 8km walk around the complex, the cheapest way to

do it is to buy the through ticket (通票, tōngpiào) for ¥130. Standard admission costs ¥60.

Buses run from Yínchuān's southern bus terminal past Shuǐ Dòng Gōu (¥12, 40 minutes, eight daily) from 7.30am to 5.30pm. To return, wait by the highway and flag down any passing Yínchuān-bound bus.

🛏 Sleeping

There are several decent choices in Xìngqìng Qū in all price brackets. This is the part of town to base yourself in, for history, character and tourist amenities.

★ Yínchuān Hotel   HOTEL $

(银川宾馆, Yínchuān Bīnguǎn; ☑0951 603 7666; 28 Yuhuangge Nanjie, 玉皇阁南街28号; d ¥138-238; ⊛) Yes, it's an old-school clunker. Yes, a pompous grand classical portico greets you. Yes, a vast dusty chandelier hangs from its capacious lobby ceiling. But this place has lovely staff and the rooms are huge, and a bargain. For ¥138 you acquire a colossal room with swirly carpet, flat-screen TV, shower room and more-than-acceptable beds.

Holiday Inn   HOTEL $$$

(假日酒店, Jiàrì Jiǔdiàn; ☑0951 7800 000; www.holidayinn.com.cn; 141 Jiefang Xijie, 解放西街141号; d ¥600-2488, ste ¥2488-4888; ⊛✳⊛⊠) This newish hotel at the Yínchuān International Trade Centre is excellent, offering a range of stylish amenities, professional service, comfortable, well equipped contemporary rooms and a choice of smart dining options, as well as a smooth bar. The inviting 18m swimming pool is a further draw.

🍴 Eating

★ Xiānhè Lóu   CHINESE $

(仙鹤楼; 204 Xinhua Dongjie, 新华东街204号; dishes from ¥15; ☉24hr) This fantastic, cavernous place opens round the clock, serving both big spenders and budget-seekers. You could splash out on the pricey fish dishes or the gorgeous *kǎoyángpái* (烤羊排; barbecued ribs; ¥108) from the picture menu, but a half *jīn* of fried lamb dumplings (羊肉煎饺; *yángròu jiānjiǎo*; ¥28) makes for a filling meal for one, arriving with a crimson soy sauce and chilli dip.

Dà Mā Jiǎozi Guǎn   DUMPLING $

(大妈饺子馆; 32 Jiefang Dongjie, 解放东街32号; dumplings per half jīn from ¥15; ☉11am-9.30pm; ⊛) This popular place is dedicated to Chinese dumplings which come by the *jīn*, but you can order a half or quarter *jīn*, and there are all sorts of beef, prawn and vegie options as well as pot-stickers (锅贴; *guōtiē*) – delicious fried dumplings, too. Plenty of other soups, meat, fish and noodle dishes also available in the large, glossy photo (English) menu.

★ **Quánjùdé** PEKING DUCK $$
(全聚德; Jiefang Dongjie, 解放东街; half-duck ¥76; ⊙11am-10pm) If you pine for Peking duck, Quánjùdé steps up to the plate. For ¥76 you get half a duck, a meal for one, served with cucumber, scallions and hoisin sauce. Purists maintain that the best Peking duck is served within earshot of the Forbidden City, but as a Běijīng institution, Quánjùdé is a close second.

The picture menu is Chinese only, but you can ask either for a whole duck (一只烤鸭; *yìzhī kǎoyā*) or a half duck (半只烤鸭; *bànzhī kǎoyā*). The chef carves it for you at your table, as in Běijīng.

🍸 Drinking & Nightlife

Liángyuán Bar BAR
(凉缘酒吧; 127 Wenhua Dongjie, 文化东街127号; beer from ¥25; ⊙10.30am-1am; 🛜) This pretty standard, rock-steady bar has been dishing up drinks and live music since 1998. It's a seasoned spot with cratered and scratched tables, Tiffany lampshades and a range of Belgian brews plus other cheaper brands. The live band kicks off at around 9.30pm, with Bob Marley, Coldplay and other anthemic numbers bringing on sporadic applause.

ℹ️ Information

All hotels and a fair few restaurants have wi-fi.
Bank of China (中国银行, Zhōngguó Yínháng; 170 Jiefang Xijie, 解放西街170号; ⊙8am-noon & 2.30-6pm) You can change travellers cheques and use the 24-hour ATM at this main branch. Other branches change cash only.
China Comfort International Travel Service (CCT, 康辉旅游, Kānghuī Lǚyóu; ☏0951 504 5678; 317 Jiefang Xijie, 解放西街317号; ⊙8.30am-noon & 2.30-6pm Mon-Fri) Organises desert trips, rafting and permits for Éjìnà Qí (Inner Mongolia). It's located 2km west along a road running from the Drum Tower to just before the Fenghuangjie intersection.
China Post (中国邮政, Zhōngguó Yóuzhèng; cnr Jiefang Xijie & Minzu Beijie, 解放西街民族北街的路口; ⊙9am-5pm Mon-Fri) Handily located post office.
Public Security Bureau (PSB, 公安局, Gōng'ānjú; 472 Beijing Donglu; ⊙8.30am-noon & 2.30-6.30pm Mon-Fri) For visa extensions. It's on a busy intersection near a hospital, a large park and schools. Take bus 3 from the Drum Tower.

ℹ️ Getting There & Away

AIR
Yínchuān Hedong International Airport (银川河东国际机场; Yínchuān Hédōng Guójì Jīchǎng) is located by the Yellow River, 24km southeast of the Drum Tower and Xīngqìng Qū. Flights connect Yínchuān with Běijīng (¥900), Chéngdū (¥1100), Guǎngzhōu (¥1150), Shànghǎi (¥900), Ūrūmqi (¥1080) and Xī'ān (¥380). Buy tickets at www.ctrip.com or www.elong.net.

BUS
The main **South Bus Station** (银川汽车站; Yínchuān qìchēzhàn) is 5km south of Nanmen Sq on the road to Zhōngwèi. Departures run to the following destinations:

Bayanhot ¥30, two to three hours, every 40 minutes (7.20am to 6pm)
Gùyuán ¥68 to ¥90, five hours, every 20 minutes (6.15am to 6.54pm)
Lánzhōu ¥140, six hours, every 45 minutes (7.20am to 5.05pm)
Xī'ān ¥181, eight to 10 hours, six daily (8.30am to 7pm), last three are sleepers
Yán'ān ¥136, 5¼ hours, four daily (8.50am to 2.10pm)
Zhōngwèi (¥35), two hours, every 30 minutes (7.35am to 6.15pm)

Some buses north to Inner Mongolia also go from the **northern (tourism) bus station** (北门车站; *běimén chēzhàn*). Bus 316 (¥1) trundles between it and the main bus station.

From the southern terminal the express buses (*kuàikè*) to Zhōngwèi and Gùyuán are far quicker than the local buses that stop at every village along the way.

TRAIN
Yínchuān is on the Lánzhōu–Běijīng railway line, which runs via Hohhot (11 hours) and Dàtóng (13½ hours) before reaching Běijīng (21 hours). If you're heading for Lánzhōu, the handy overnight K9679 train (hard/soft sleeper ¥130/194, seven to nine hours) leaves at 10.40pm, arriving at around 7am. For Xī'ān, the K1615 (hard/soft sleeper ¥230/351, 15½ hours) leaves Yínchuān at 7.05pm, arriving in Xī'ān at 7.20am.

The train station is in Xīxià Qū, about 12km west of the Xìngqìng Qū centre. Book sleeper tickets well in advance. A **train ticket booking office** (⊙8am-noon & 1-7pm) is at the South Bus Station.

ℹ️ Getting Around

The airport is 25km from the Xìngqìng Qū (Old City) centre; buses (¥20, 30 minutes, hourly 6am to 6pm) arrive and leave from in front of the Civil Aviation Administration of China office on Changcheng Donglu, just south of Nanmen Sq. A taxi to/from the airport costs around ¥60.

Between 6am and 11.30pm green BRT bus 1 (¥1) runs from the southern bus terminal (from the bus shelter in the middle of the road) to Nanmen Sq (10 minutes) in Xìngqìng Qū, via Nanmen Sq and along Jiefang Jie and on to the train station in Xīxià Qū (40 to 50 minutes). Buses 45 (¥1, 6.40am to 8pm) and 521 (¥1, 7am to 10.30pm) also run from the train station to Nanmen Sq.

Taxis cost ¥7 for the first 3km. A taxi between the train station and Xìngqìng Qū costs ¥20 to ¥30. A taxi to the South Bus Station from Nanmen Sq is ¥12.

Hèlán Shān 贺兰山

📞 0951

The rugged Hèlán mountains (Hèlán Shān) have long proved an effective barrier against both nomadic invaders and the harsh Gobi winds. They were the preferred burial site for Xixia monarchs, and the foothills are today peppered with graves and honorific temples.

The most significant sight in Hèlán Shān are the ancient **rock carvings** (贺兰山岩画, Hèlánshān Shíhuà; ¥70; ⊗ 8am-6.30pm), thought to date back 10,000 years. Over 2000 pictographs depict animals, hunting scenes and faces, including one (so local guides like to claim) of an alien, and they are the last remnants of the early nomadic tribes who lived in the steppes north of China. Admission includes entry to a museum on ancient rock art and a ride in a golf cart to the valley containing the rock carvings.

Don't miss the image of the Rastafarian-like sun god (climb the steps up the hill on the far side of the valley). Bus Y2 (游二路; ¥15, two hours) goes to the Rock Carvings from Xinyue Sq (新月广场; Xīnyuè Guǎngchǎng) in Yínchuān; get off at the last stop. The last bus back to town is at 3.30pm.

Sūyùkǒu National Forest Park (苏峪口国家森林公园, Sūyùkǒu Guójiā Sēnlín Gōngyuán; ¥60; ⊗ 7am-5pm) is a good place to start exploring the Hèlán mountains. You can hike up the trails from the car park or take the cable car (up/down ¥50/30) straight up to cool pine-covered hills. Bus Y2 (游二路; ¥15, two hours) goes to the Sūyùkǒu National Forest Park from Xinyue Sq (新月广场; Xīnyuè Guǎngchǎng) in Yínchuān; get off at the second-last stop. The last bus back to town is at 3.30pm.

Most visitors come to Hèlán Shān on a day-trip excursion from Yínchuān. It's best to stock up with snacks and bring your own food as the area is not well supplied with restaurants, and food can be both expensive and not particularly varied.

❶ Getting There & Around

Bus Y2 (游二路; ¥15, two hours) goes to the Hèlánshān Rock Carvings from Xinyue Sq (新月广场; Xīnyuè Guǎchǎng) in Yínchuān; the bus also stops at the Sūyùkǒu National Forest Park, the stop prior to the Hèlánshān Rock Carvings. Alternatively, you can hire a taxi to take you to and around the Hèlán Shān area. You can hire a minibus from the train station for ¥200 return to do a loop of the sights. You could combine that with a visit to the Western Xia Tombs for around ¥300.

There is no public transport around the Hèlán mountains, although bus Y2 will take you from the Hèlánshān Rock Carvings to Sūyùkǒu National Forest Park and vice versa.

Zhōngwèi 中卫

📞 0955 / POP 1 MILLION

With its wide streets and relaxed feel, Zhōngwèi – 167km to the southwest of Yínchuān – easily wins the prize for Níngxià's best looking, most laid-back and friendliest city. It's an ideal base for a trip up the Yellow River or further afield into the Tengger Desert.

◉ Sights

Gāo Temple TEMPLE
(高庙, Gāo Miào; Gulou Beijie, 鼓楼北街; ¥30; ⊗ 7.30am-7pm) Gāo Temple means 'High Temple', and this is one of the most extraordinary temples in China, where the three faiths of Buddhism, Confucianism and Taoism are revered, although Buddhist deities are clearly in the ascendancy. Do check out the unnerving **Arhat Hall** (罗汉堂; Luóhàn Táng), which contains 500 arhat, many in grotesque and unsettling guises and postures, including one whose arm shoots through the ceiling. The drawcard oddity is the **Dì Gōng** (地宫), a former bomb shelter and labyrinth converted into a Buddhist hell.

The eerie, dimly lit tunnels contain numerous scenes of the damned having their tongues cut out, being sawed in half, eyes poked out or stoked in the fires of hell, while their screams echo all around. The ceiling is very low, so prepare to crouch your way through. Look for the signs to 'The Infernal'.

The name of the temple becomes clear after you exit the **Hall of Heavenly Kings** (天王殿; Tiānwáng Diàn) to climb some seriously steep steps to the halls high above.

After your climb, you are greeted by woodwork in a blaze of gold, blue, green and vermilion paint. At the time of research, the temple halls on the upper floors at the top of the steps were closed. To the rear, a reclining Buddha lies supine in most relaxed fashion within the **Sleeping Buddha Hall** (卧佛殿; Wòfó Diàn), while other side halls are dedicated to Guanyin and other Bodhisattvas as a host of obscure Taoist deities peek out from smoky shrine niches in the walls.

Shāpōtóu
DESERT

(沙坡头; winter/summer ¥65/100; ⏰7am-6pm) The desert playground of Shāpōtóu, 17km west of Zhōngwèi, lies on the fringes of the Tengger Desert at the dramatic convergence of sand dunes, the Yellow River and lush farmlands. It's based around the Shāpōtóu Desert Research Centre, which was founded in 1956 to battle the ever-worsening problem of desertification in China's northwest.

These days, though, Shāpōtóu is more of an amusement park. The main office is more of a massive service centre, with a post office and a large number of shops. You can zipline (¥80) on a wire across the Yellow River, go sand-sledding (¥30), camel riding (¥60 to ¥100) or bungee jumping (¥160).

It's also a good place to raft the churning Yellow River. The traditional mode of transport on the river for centuries was the *yángpí fázi* (leather raft), made from sheep or cattle skins soaked in oil and brine and then inflated. From Shāpōtóu you can roar upstream on a speedboat and return on a traditional raft. Prices range from ¥80 to ¥240, depending on how far you go. You can also combine the boat/raft ride with a camel ride (¥110). If you want to flee the crowds for the sands, off-road buggies (¥300 to ¥1500) are available for rent, taking up to three passengers. Tourist buses wheel visitors around (¥10 to ¥15) from point to point.

Shāpō Shānzhuāng is a basic but comfortable hotel near the dunes. Meals are available.

Bus 2 (¥5, 45 minutes) from the bus station (客运总站; *kèyùn zǒngzhàn*) runs between Zhōngwèi and Shāpōtóu from 7.30am to 6.30pm. You can also pick it up on Changcheng Xijie about 200m past the Gāo Temple on the opposite side of the road. Taxis cost ¥30 each way.

🛏 Sleeping

Quite a few hotels in Zhōngwèi won't accept foreigners. If your Chinese is up to it, you can try your luck with the cheap guesthous-

Zhōngwèi

◉ Sights
1 Gāo Temple A1

🛏 Sleeping
2 North by Northwest Hostel A1
3 Zhōngwèi Dàjiǔdiàn B1

🍴 Eating
4 Zhōngwèi Shāngchéng Night Market A2

ⓘ Transport
5 Train Ticket Office A2

es that line the east side of People's Sq and its environs, but we don't guarantee success.

North by Northwest Hostel
HOSTEL $

(西北偏北青年旅舍, Xīběi Piānběi Qīngnián-lǚshè; ☎0955 763 5060; 453190353@qq.com; 87 Xinglong Beijie, 兴隆北街87号; dm ¥40-50, d/tr ¥150/180; ❈🐾) This is Zhōngwèi's only hostel, but rooms and shower rooms really need some TLC as things are coming apart at the seams. The murals, mosaic-like washbasins and homemade Zhōngwèi postcards create an art-school vibe and the jovial young staff are extremely helpful, have a go with English and offer Shāpōtóu and desert tours.

★ Zhōngwèi Dàjiǔdiàn
HOTEL $$

(中卫大酒店; ☎0955 702 5555; 66 Gulou Beijie, 鼓楼北街66号; d & tw ¥429-498, f ¥598, ste ¥698, all incl breakfast; ❈🐾) This smart hotel has large and comfortable rooms with decent-sized beds and attractive rosewood furniture. Discounts are available outside peak season, bringing room prices down most

WORTH A TRIP

TENGGER DESERT

If you fancy playing Lawrence of Arabia, make a trip out to the Tengger Desert (腾格里沙漠; Ténggélǐ Shāmò), a mystical landscape of shifting sand dunes and the occasional herd of two-humped camels. Shāpōtóu (p871) lies on the southern fringe, but it's definitely worth heading deeper into the desert to avoid the crowds. The sun is fierce out here, so you'll need a hat, sunglasses and plenty of water. Nights are cool, so bring a warm layer.

Níngxià Desert Travel Service (see right) in Zhōngwèi offers overnight camel treks through the desert, with a visit to the Great Wall by car, for ¥500 per person per day for a group of four. The price includes transport, food and guide. Ask your guide to bring along a sand sled for a sunset surfing session. Drinking beers around the campfire under a starry sky tops off the experience. The desert trek can be combined with a rafting trip down the Yellow River.

of the time to the ¥198 mark, making it a bargain.

✕ Eating

Zhōngwèi Shāngchéng
Night Market   MARKET **$**
(中卫商城夜市, Zhōngwèi Shāngchéng Yèshì; off Xinglong Nanjie, 兴隆南街旁边; dishes ¥10-20; ⊙4pm-4am) A Dante's Inferno of flaming woks and grills, the night market is made up of countless stalls in the alleys running left off Xinglong Nanjie (which is lined with Chinese-style bars). There are tonnes of cheap eats. Two favourites to check out are *ròujiāmó* (肉夹馍; fried pork or beef stuffed in bread, sometimes with green peppers and cumin) and *shāguō* (砂锅; mini hotpot), as well as the ever-present pulled noodles (拉面; *lāmiàn*).

❶ Information

Bank of China (中国银行, Zhōngguó Yínháng; cnr Gulou Beijie & Gulou Dongjie, 鼓楼北街鼓楼东街的路口; ⊙9am-5pm) One of many around town.

China Post (中国邮政, Zhōngguó Yóuzhèng; Gulou Xijie, 古楼西街) Right at the heart of town.

Níngxià Desert Travel Service (宁夏沙漠旅行社, Níngxià Shāmò Lǚxíngshè; ☑0955 702 7776, 186 0955 9777) Professional outfit for camel and rafting trips. A five-night desert camping trip starts at around ¥1480. Contact Billy, the English-speaking manager.

Public Security Bureau (PSB, 公安局, Gōng'ānjú; ☑0955 706 7520; Ping'an Donglu, 平安东路; ⊙8.30am-noon & 2.30-5pm) Around 3.5km south of the Drum Tower. For visa extensions you have to go to Yínchuān.

❶ Getting There & Away

BUS

The long-distance bus station (汽车客运总站; qìchē kèyùn zǒngzhàn) is 2.5km east of the Drum Tower, along Gulou Dongjie. Take bus 2, which runs to the train station, or a taxi (¥7, 10 minutes). Destinations include the following:

Gùyuán ¥70, four hours, two daily (10.10am and 2.30pm); express bus (快车, kuàichē)

Tóngxīn ¥26, two hours, five daily (from 9am)

Yínchuān ¥35 to ¥53, 2½ hours, every 45 minutes (7.20am to 6pm); express bus

Buses to Xī'ān (¥180, eight hours, 6pm) run every other day from in front of the train station.

TRAIN

You can reach Yínchuān in 2½ hours (¥25, regular), though you'll be dropped off closer to the city centre in Yínchuān if you take the bus. It's 5½ hours to Lánzhōu (hard seat/hard sleeper ¥47/101, nine daily) and 12½ hours to Xī'ān (hard/soft sleeper ¥169/253, five daily). For Gùyuán (¥33, 3½ hours, nine daily) take the Xī'ān train. A **train ticket office** (火车票代售点, Huǒchēpiào Dàishòudiǎn; cnr Yingli Nanjie & Gulou Xijie, 应理南街鼓楼西街路口) can be found in the west of town.

❶ Getting Around

Bus 2 (¥5) runs to Shāpōtóu from the main bus station, running along Changcheng Lu, taking 45 minutes. The first bus departs at 7am and the last bus returns at 6pm.

Gùyuán   固原
☑0954 / POP 1.2 MILLION

An expanding but still small and historic city that dates to the 6th century, Gùyuán makes a convenient base for exploring little-visited southern Níngxià. Largely populated by easygoing Hui Muslims and a large Han community, the city sees few foreigners, so expect some attention from the locals. An important but abandoned and neglected vestige of the town's history is its City Wall.

⊙ Sights

Xūmí Shān
CAVE

(须弥山; ¥50; ◷8am-5pm) These magnificent Buddhist grottoes (Xūmí is the Chinese transliteration of the Sanskrit *sumeru*, or Buddhist paradise) some 50km northwest of Gùyuán are southern Níngxià's must-see sight. Cut into the five adjacent sandstone hills are 132 caves housing a collection of over 300 Buddhist statues dating back 1400 years, from the Northern Wei to the Sui and Tang dynasties. Cave 5 contains the largest statue, a colossal Maitreya (future Buddha), standing 20.6m high.

Further uphill, the finest statues are protected by the **Yuánguāng Temple** (圆光寺; Yuánguāng Sì; caves 45 and 46; 6th century) and the **Xiàngguó Temple** (相国寺; Xiàngguó Sì; cave 51; 7th century), where you can walk around the interior and examine the artwork up close – amazingly, the pigment on several of the statues is still visible in places, despite the obvious weathering.

To reach the caves, buses run from Wenhua Xilu, by the two big hospitals opposite the Xiǎochī night market, to Sānyíng (三营; ¥7, one hour), from where you'll need to take a taxi for the 40km return trip (¥100 including waiting time) to Xūmí Shān.

Liùpán Shān Guójiā Sēnlín Gōngyuán
PARK

(六盘山国家森林公园, Liùpán Mountain National Forest Park; ☑0954 564 8319; ¥65; ◷7am-6pm) Those on the trail of Genghis Khan will want to visit southern Níngxià's Liùpán Shān, where some maintain the great man died in 1227. Legend attests that the Mongol emperor fell ill and came here to ingest medicinal plants native to the area, but perished on its slopes (though it's much more likely he died elsewhere). The mountain is now a protected area.

A walking trail leads 3km up a side valley to a waterfall. About 5km further up the main valley is a clearing with some stone troughs and tables that locals say was used by the Mongols during their stay.

To get here, take a bus from Gùyuán's main bus station to Jīngyuán (泾源; ¥16, one hour) and then hire a taxi for the final 18km to the reserve (¥80 return). A return taxi from Gùyuán will cost around ¥200.

Gùyuán City Wall
HISTORIC SITE

(固原城墙, Gùyuán Chéngqiáng; Kaicheng Lu, 开城路) Largely demolished during the tenure of Mao Zedong, Gùyuán's city wall has mostly vanished, but you can explore its earthen remnants between the two gates of Hépíng Mén (和平门) and Jìngshuò Mén (靖朔门). Just around the corner from Jìngshuò Mén, it's possible to climb atop the earthen city wall (for free) and walk along to Hépíng Mén for around 300m to 400m. The crumbling ramparts are in a state of neglect, but are interesting to explore and afford views over town.

Gùyuán Museum
MUSEUM

(固原博物馆, Gùyuán Bówùguǎn; 133 Xicheng Lu, 西城路133号; ◷9am-5.30pm Tue Sun, to 6.30pm summer) For such an out-of-the-way place, Gùyuán's museum is rather good, with Neolithic-era artefacts, Tangut ceramics and some fine figurines from the Northern Wei dynasty. Decent English captions, too. At the time of writing, the museum was shut for a complete refurbishment.

City God Temple
TAOIST SITE

(城隍庙, Chénghuáng Miào; 37 Zhengfu Donglu, 政府东路37号) A rare vestige of old Gùyuán is this smoky and dusty, single-hall affair, with colourful banners flapping in the breeze outside and the City God enthroned within.

🛏 Sleeping

Gùyuán has several decent and affordable hotels that accept foreigners located close to each other not far from Xiǎochī Night Market (p874).

Liùpánshān Bīnguǎn
HOTEL $

(六盘山宾馆; ☑0954 202 1666; 35 Zhongshan Nanjie, 中山南街35号; s ¥158, d ¥146-166, ste ¥580; ❊⊚) The rooms at this long-standing hotel are not the freshest, but they are decent and quiet, and staff, although not used to dealing with foreigners, are helpful. Wi-fi reception in some rooms is rather weak, but regular discounts make it cheap.

Délóng Business Hotel
HOTEL $$

(德龙商务酒店, Délóng Shāngwù Jiǔdiàn; ☑0954 286 3918; 109 Wenhua Donglu, 文化东路109号; s ¥138, d ¥148-298, ste ¥388; ❊⊚) Friendly, helpful staff and good-sized rooms with modern bathrooms make this the pick of the hotels along Wenhua Donglu, and puts you within walking distance of some good dining choices. Go through the drive-in alley to the reception block at the rear.

🍴 Eating & Drinking

The streets empty around about 10pm in Gùyuán, but you can sink a beer till late and watch the locals coming and going at the Xiǎochī Night Market (p874).

Xiǎochī Night Market MARKET $

(小吃城, Xiǎochī Chéng; 44 Wenhua Donglu, 文化东路44号; dishes from ¥11; ⊙noon-dawn)
This alley of food stalls runs till the break of dawn and specialises in delicious *shāguō* (砂锅; mini hotpot), as well as *shāokǎo* (barbecue) kebabs and noodles. Dishes are on display, so you can pick and choose. It's down a covered arcade off Wenhua Donglu, directly opposite two big hospitals; look for No 44. Most places are Hui-run, but most serve beer too.

ℹ️ Information

Make sure to bring cash; precious few ATMs in this part of the world accept foreign cards.

China Post (中国邮政, Zhōngguó Yóuzhèng; 6 Zhongshan Nanjie, 中山南街6号; ⊙8am-6pm) Opposite the Liùpánshān Bīnguǎn (p873).

ℹ️ Getting There & Away

AIR

Gùyuán Liùpánshān Airport (固原六盘山机场, Gùyuán Liùpánshān Jīchǎng) is just under 9km from town, with flights to Yínchuān, Xī'ān, Chóngqìng and Shànghǎi.

BUS

The **long-distance bus station** (固原汽车站, Gùyuán Qìchēzhàn; ☎ 0954 266 2905) is about 4km west of central Gùyuán's hotels and museum. No buses connect with town; a taxi costs ¥7. There are frequent buses to Tóngxīn (¥26 to ¥33, 1½ hours), Xī'ān (¥120, six hours) and Yínchuān (¥70 to ¥90, four hours), as well as the following destinations:

Lánzhōu ¥100, nine hours, two daily (8am and 3.30pm)

Tiānshuǐ ¥85, seven hours, two daily (6.30am and 10.40am)

Zhōngwèi ¥70, 2½ hours, two daily (10.10am and 3pm)

TRAIN

Gùyuán is on the Zhōngwèi–Bǎojī railway line. Sleeper tickets are near impossible to get and the majority of trains depart in the middle of the night. To get to the train station, on Guxi Lu in the northwest of town around 4km away from the Liùpánshān Bīnguǎn, take bus 1 or a taxi (¥5).

Lánzhōu Seat ¥43 to ¥75, hard sleeper ¥91, 9½ hours, two daily (11.03pm and 11.30pm)

Xī'ān Hard/soft sleeper ¥118/175, six to nine hours, four daily (12.51am, 3.08am, 3.56am and 11.58pm)

Yínchuān Seat/hard sleeper ¥54/108, six hours, six daily (1.25am to 10.34pm)

The **Train Ticket Booking Office** (火车售票处, Huǒchē Shòupiàochù; 6 Zhongshan Nanjie, 中山南街6号; ⊙8am-noon & 2-4pm) is at the post office on Zhongshan Nanjie.

ℹ️ Getting Around

Bus 1 travels between the long-distance bus station and the train station.

Tóngxīn 同心

☎ 0953 / POP 400,000

South of Zhōngwèi, the Han Chinese-dominated cities of northern Níngxià give way to the Hui heartland. Journeying here takes you deep into rural Níngxià, through villages of mud-brick houses where the minarets of the numerous mosques tower over the endless cornfields.

Tóngxīn has a very strong Muslim feel. There are always students in residence at the mosque training to be imams and they will greet you with a *salaam alaikum* and show you around. Tóngxīn is also one of the few places in China outside of southern Xīnjiāng where you'll see women in veils and covered from head to toe in black.

Of all the mosques in Níngxià, the most hallowed is the **Great Mosque** (清真大寺, Qīngzhēn Dà Sì; ¥15). Dating back to the 14th century (although the present mosque was built in 1573 and then renovated in 1791), it was the only one of Níngxià's 1000-odd mosques to avoid the ravages of the Cultural Revolution. As such, it's a near-perfect example of Ming- and Qing-era temple architecture. Not until you get up close and notice the crescents that top the pagoda roofs does it become apparent that it's a mosque.

Most travellers visit Tóngxīn as a day trip from Zhōngwèi, but if you get stuck here, try the **Huí Chūn Bīnguǎn** (回春宾馆; ☎0953 803 1888; Yinping Xijie, 银平西街; d¥138; ❀) opposite the bus station.

As a largely Muslim town, the opportunities for drinking and nightlife are limited in Tóngxīn. It's best to head to Zhōngwèi or Yínchuān for a knees-up.

ℹ️ Getting There & Away

There are frequent express buses between Tóngxīn and Yínchuān (¥52, three hours), making a long day trip possible. The last bus back to Yínchuān leaves at 4pm. You could also visit from Zhōngwèi (¥26, 2½ hours), or stop for a couple of hours if you are heading further south to Gùyuán (¥26, two hours).

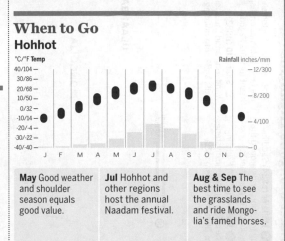

Inner Mongolia

POP 24.7 MILLION

Best Places to Eat

➡ Grandma (p880)

➡ Xiānbáichéng Gǔtāng Hélè Miàn (p880)

➡ Nana's Cafe (p880)

➡ Jīnchuān Dòuhuāzhuāng (p885)

Best Places to Sleep

➡ Inner Mongolia Hotel (p879)

➡ Alxa Guesthouse (p890)

➡ Shangri-La (p886)

➡ Shangri-La Hotel (p880)

Why Go?

Mongolia. The name alone stirs up visions of nomadic herders, thundering horses and, of course, the warrior-emperor Genghis Khan.

Travellers heading north of the Great Wall might half expect to see the Mongol hordes galloping through the vast grasslands. The reality is rather different: 21st-century Inner Mongolia (内蒙古; Nèi Měnggǔ) is a wholly different place from Mongolia itself. The more-visited south of the province is industrialised, prosperous and very much within the realm of China's modern economic miracle. Having said that, Inner Mongolia is more than nine times the size of England and the Mongolia of your dreams can be found off the tourist route, amid the shimmering sand dunes of the Badain Jaran Desert or the vast grasslands in the north. Some effort is required to reach these areas, but the spectacular scenery can make it an unforgettable journey.

When to Go
Hohhot

May Good weather and shoulder season equals good value.	**Jul** Hohhot and other regions host the annual Naadam festival.
Aug & Sep The best time to see the grasslands and ride Mongolia's famed horses.	

Inner Mongolia Highlights

1 Hǎilā'ěr (p884) Saddling up for a horse ride around the Hūlúnbèi'ěr grasslands.

2 Hohhot (p877) Exploring the colourful esoteric mysteries of Tibetan Buddhism at Dà Zhào, and being astonished by the tantric statues on display at beautiful Wǔtǎ Pagoda.

3 Shàngdū (p882) Wandering amid the ancient walls and contemplating the vanished wonders of Kublai Khan's pleasure dome.

4 Énhé (p886) Finding some peace and sampling the local milk and produce at this laid-back farming town.

5 Badain Jaran Desert (p889) Mounting a camel and setting off in search of the desert's massive dunes.

6 Shí Wéi (p887) Mingling with Chinese-speaking ethnic Russians at this unique village near the Russian border.

7 Bayanhot (p888) Discovering Alashan culture and west Inner Mongolia's heritage at the Alashan Museum.

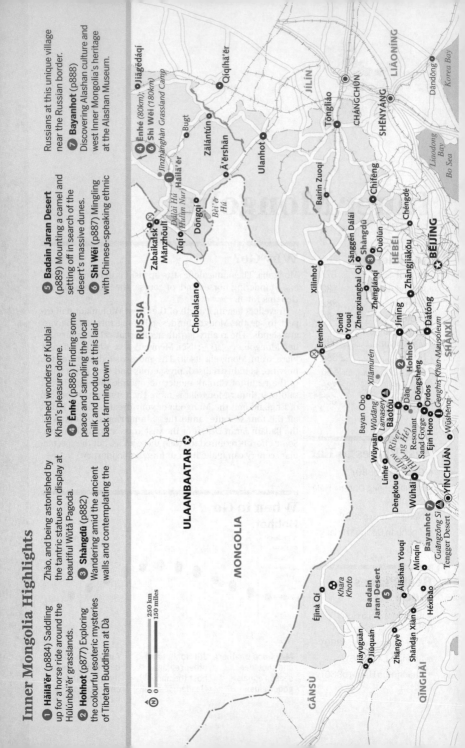

History

The nomadic tribes of the northern steppes have always been at odds with the agrarian Han Chinese, so much so that the Great Wall was built to keep them out. But it acted more like a speed bump than an actual barrier to the Mongol hordes.

Genghis Khan and grandson Kublai rumbled through in the 13th century, and after conquering southern China in 1279 Kublai Khan became the first emperor of the Yuan dynasty. But by the end of the 14th century the Mongol empire had collapsed, and the Mongols again became a collection of disorganised roaming tribes. It was not until the 18th century that the Qing emperors finally gained full control of the region.

A divide-and-conquer policy by the Qing led to the creation of an 'Inner' and 'Outer' Mongolia. The Qing opened up Inner Mongolia to Han farmers, and waves of migrants came to cultivate the land. Outer Mongolia was spared this policy and, with backing from the USSR, it gained full independence in 1921.

Now Mongolians make up only 15% of Inner Mongolia's population. Most of the other 85% are Han Chinese, with a smattering of Hui, Manchu, Daur and Ewenki.

Inner Mongolia's economy boomed in recent years thanks to extensive mining of both coal and rare earth minerals. That growth came at great environmental cost. The mines swallowed up pastureland at alarming rates and desertification has been the root cause of the dust storms that envelop Běijīng each spring. Only the far north of the region, where the economy is largely based on cattle ranching and tourism, has escaped heavy industrialisation.

Climate

Siberian blizzards and cold air currents rake the Mongolian plains from November to March. June to August brings pleasant temperatures, but the west is scorching hot during the day.

The best time to visit is between July and September, particularly to see the grasslands, which are green only in summer. Make sure you bring warm, windproof clothing, as even in midsummer it's often windy, and evening temperatures can dip to 10°C or below.

Language

The Mongolian language is part of the Altaic linguistic family, which includes the Central Asian Turkic languages and the now defunct Manchurian. Although the vertical Mongolian script (written left to right) adorns street signs, almost everyone speaks standard Mandarin.

ⓘ Getting There & Around

Inner Mongolia borders Mongolia and Russia. There are border crossings at Erenhot (Mongolia) and Mǎnzhōulǐ (Russia), which are stopovers on the Trans-Mongolian and Trans-Manchurian Railways, respectively. To Mongolia, you can also catch a local train to Erenhot, cross the border and take another local train to Ulaanbaatar (with the appropriate visa). Possible air connections include Hohhot to Ulaanbaatar or Hǎilā'ěr to Ulaanbaatar and Choibalsan (eastern Mongolia). The far west of Inner Mongolia has opened up to air travel with the opening of airports at Éjìnà Qí, Ālāshàn Yòuqí and Bayanhot, making transport to the region far easier.

Trains and long-distance buses reach Hohhot, Bāotóu and other large towns from neighbouring provinces.

Inner Mongolia is vast and stupendously long from east to west, so you may find yourself flying at least once, especially when accessing the northeast of the province and the far west. Otherwise you'll be relying on a mixture of trains and long-distance buses. The far west of Inner Mongolia has no rail line, so you'll have to either fly or take long-distance buses.

Hohhot 呼和浩特

☑ 0471 / POP 2.86 MILLION

Founded by Altan Khan in the 16th century, the good-looking capital of Inner Mongolia is an increasingly prosperous city. Hohhot (known in Mandarin as Hūhéhàotè) means 'Blue City' in Mongolian, a reference to

PRICE RANGES

Sleeping
Prices for a double room with shower or bathroom:
$ less than ¥200
$$ ¥200–¥400
$$$ more than ¥400

Eating
Price ranges for a main course:
$ less than ¥30
$$ ¥30–¥50
$$$ more than ¥50

the arching blue skies over the grasslands. Streets are attractively tree-lined (although the roads are traffic-snarled) and there are some truly astonishing Tibetan Buddhist temples in town – more than enough to keep you busy for a day or two before heading to the hinterlands. Helpfully, most of the sights congregate in the same part of town, making sightseeing a doddle. Note that the cumbersome name of the city is often colloquially shortened to 呼市 (Hūshì).

◎ Sights

★ Dà Zhào
(大召; Danan Jie, 大南街; ¥35; ⊙ 8am-7pm) MONASTERY
This spectacular Tibetan Buddhist temple is the oldest and largest temple in the city. Also called 'Immeasurable Temple' (无量寺; Wúliàng Sì) in Chinese, the complex was originally built in the 16th century and much enhanced in the following century. A very sacred place and a fascinating introduction to the mysterious ways of Tibetan Buddhism, Dà Zhào attracts pilgrims from across the land, who prostrate themselves fully in prayer on boards in front of the magnificent altars through the temple.

Look for the amazing-looking and blue-faced **Medicine Buddha** (药师佛; Yàoshī Fó) seated in his namesake hall and garbed in the most astonishing fashion. Also seek out the many-armed golden deity in the esoteric **Mìzōng Hùfǎ Hall** (密宗护法殿; Mìzōng Hùfǎ Diàn), the central tantric deity within the **Shènglè Jīngāng Hall** (胜乐金刚殿; Shènglè Jīngāng Diàn) and the huge jade Buddha residing in the **Jade Buddha Hall** (玉佛殿; Yùfó Diàn). The temple is also home to a 2.55m silver effigy of Sakyamuni, contained within the **Buddha Hall** (佛堂; Fótáng). In other halls, pilgrims walk in clockwise fashion around altars, twirling prayer wheels, lost in prayer.

The plaza south of the temple is popular with kite-flyers and is great for people-watching. There's an attractive decorative archway and a vast statue of Altan Khan (1507–82), the Mongol founder of the city and ruler who began building the temple.

★ Wǔtǎ Pagoda
(五塔寺, Wǔtǎ Sì; Wutasi Houjie, 五塔寺后街; ¥35; ⊙ 8am-6pm) Rising up at the rear of the Five Pagoda Temple, this striking, Indian-influenced, five-tiered pagoda was completed in 1732. Its main claim to fame is the Mongolian **star chart** around the back (protected behind glass), though the engraving PAGODA

of the Diamond Sutra (in Sanskrit, Tibetan and Mongolian), extending around the entire base of the structure, is in much better condition. Another fascinating aspect of the temple is the 'Temple Culture Exhibition of Hohhot' Hall, containing a mesmerising array of **tantric statues**.

Guanyin Temple
BUDDHIST SITE
(观音寺, Guānyīn Sì; E'erduosi Dajie, 鄂尔多斯大街) FREE Its colossal halls capped in saffron tiles visible from a huge distance away, this massive temple is dedicated to the Goddess of Mercy, Guanyin. The colossal **statue** of the 1000-arm Guanyin within the **Yuántōng Treasure Hall Bǎodiàn** (圆通宝殿; Yuántōng Bǎodiàn) is simply staggering. The head of the three-faced statue wears a tower of several heads on top. Within the **Great Treasure Hall** are vast seated effigies of the past, present and future Buddhas as well as the 18 *luóhàn* (arhats).

Xílìtú Zhào
MONASTERY
(席力图召; Da'nan Jie, 大南街; ¥30; ⊙ 7.30am-6.30pm) Across from the Dà Zhào temple is this simple, peaceful monastery, which is also known as Xiǎo Zhào or Yánshòu Temple (延寿寺; Yánshòu Sì). The temple is the official residence of Hohhot's 11th Living Buddha (he actually works elsewhere). Monks chant at 9am and 3pm.

Inner Mongolia Museum
MUSEUM
(内蒙古博物院, Nèi Měnggǔ Bówùyuàn; Xinhua Dongdajie, 新华东大街; ⊙ 9am-5.30pm Tue-Sun) FREE This massive museum in the northeastern section of town has a distinctive sloping roof supposed to resemble the vast steppes of Mongolia. It's one of the better provincial museums, with a focus on Mongolian culture, from an excellent dinosaur exhibition to Genghis Khan and the space age (English captions are less than space age, though). Take bus 3 from Xinhua Dajie or pay ¥15 for a taxi.

⁂ Festivals & Events

Naadam
CULTURAL, SPORTS
The week-long summer festival known as Naadam (literally meaning 'Games' in Mongolian) is the most famous knees-up in Inner Mongolia, featuring traditional Mongolian sports such as archery, wrestling and horse racing. The competitions and festivities takes place at Gegentala and at various grassland areas in early July when the grass is green. Book local tours at your accommodation.

Hohhot

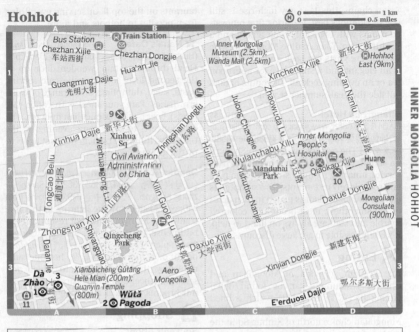

Hohhot

⦿ **Top Sights**
1 Dà Zhào A3
2 Wŭtă Pagoda B3

⦿ **Sights**
3 Xílítú Zhào A3

🛏 **Sleeping**
4 Āndá Guesthouse D2
5 Inner Mongolia Hotel C2

6 Jīnjiāng Inn B1
7 Shangri-La Hotel B3

✕ **Eating**
8 Dàndàn Tóngguŏshuàn D2
9 Grandma B1
10 Nana's Cafe D2

🛍 **Shopping**
11 Souvenir Shops A3

🛏 Sleeping

Hohhot is pretty well provided with hotels at the top end, but at the budget end things look fairly miserable. Your best bet for lower midrange accommodation is in express chain hotels, such as Jīnjiāng Inn.

Āndá Guesthouse   HOSTEL **$**
(安达旅馆, Āndá Lûguǎn; ☎0471 691 8039, 159 475 19807; www.andaguesthouse.com; middle section of Qiaokao Xijie, 桥靠西街中段; dm/d with shared bathroom ¥60/180; @🛜) This rather average place thrust down a charmless alley has compact five-bed dorms and uncomfortable, cluttered doubles. The bathrooms could be cleaner, but there's a small lounge, kitchen facilities and a cute courtyard. Staff are eager to show off Mongolian culture and

organise trips to the grasslands, as well as to the Kubuqi Desert and Naadam. With little competition, it's set in its ways.

Jīnjiāng Inn   HOTEL **$$**
(锦江之星, Jīnjiāng Zhīxīng; ☎0471 666 8111; www.jinjianginns.com; 6 Xinhua Dajie, 新华大街 6号; s ¥169-239, d ¥249; ✳@🛜) This large, pleasant and snappy branch of the ultra-efficient chain hotel is located in a tower, with very clean if somewhat characterless rooms. The hotel has a very decent restaurant attached; breakfast is an extra ¥18.

Inner Mongolia Hotel   HOTEL **$$$**
(内蒙古饭店, Nèi Měnggǔ Fàndiàn; ☎0471 693 8888; www.nmghotel.com; Wulanchabu Xilu, 乌兰察布西路; r from ¥1480; ✳@🛜✖) Despite competition from upmarket Western and

Asian chains, this 14-storey high-rise is still one of Hohhot's best, featuring fine renovated rooms with big comfy beds, a pool and a health centre. You can dine Mongolian-style in concrete yurts out back and the cafe-bar is an elegant and restful place for afternoon tea or an evening cocktail. Discounts of 60% outside the peak summer season.

Shangri-La Hotel HOTEL $$$
(☑0471 336 6888; www.shangri-la.com; 5 Xilin Guo-le Nanlu, 锡林郭勒南路5号; d ¥1388, ste ¥4588; ❀❅🌐🏊) The exemplary, 365-room Shangri-La should really tick all your boxes: five-star service, amazing rooms, a stunning 25m pool and some lovely restaurants. It's a sumptuous choice: the lobby floor is plated in lush acres of the smoothest, most beautifully coloured marble and staff are always on hand to help. It's often possible to get large discounts.

✖ Eating

An excellent selection of Mongolian and Chinese restaurants can be found down Huang Jie (黄街; Yellow St), which is lined with about 40 small eateries. A standout Mongolian choice north of Xinhua Sq in the centre of town is Grandma.

★ Grandma MONGOLIAN $
(格日勒阿妈, Gérilè Āmā; ☑0471 333 0055; www.gerileama.com; Xilin Guole Beilu, 锡林郭勒北路; mains from ¥12; ⏰7am-2pm & 5-9pm; 🌐) Overlooked by a portrait of Genghis Khan, diners love this colourful, fun and vibrant upstairs restaurant that does a roaring trade. There's a huge variety of Mongolian specialities to choose from, including sweet cheese (¥10), camel meat pie (¥12), cheese mooncakes (¥12), roast lamb ribs (¥68 per *jīn*), steamed lamb and veggie dumplings (¥7 per portion) and handmade yoghurt (¥12).

★ Xiānbáichéng
Gǔtāng Hélè Miàn NOODLES $
(鲜百诚骨汤饸饹面; cnr Wutasi Nanjie & Wutasi Xijie, 五塔寺南街五塔寺西街的路口; noodles from ¥10; ⏰24hr) This place does huge, filling and scrumptious bowls of delicious and appetising buckwheat noodles, with large chunks of beef or pork and free cold Chinese vegetable dishes by the counter. There's also cheap beer.

Wanda Mall FOOD HALL $
(万达广场, Wàndá Guǎngchǎng; Xinhua Dongda-jie, 新华东大街; dishes from ¥15; ⏰10am-10pm) The glossy Wanda mall, diagonally opposite the museum, has a clutch of Chinese res-taurants on the top floor serving everything from noodles to hotpots and more.

★ Nana's Cafe INTERNATIONAL, MONGOLIAN $$
(Huang Jie, 黄街; dishes from ¥24; ⏰10am-2pm) Head through a blue wooden door up to the second level for this cute cafe serving pasta, salad, dumplings and a range of Western dishes. Pair your meal with coffee (big mugs), beer or salty Mongolian milk tea. The cafe converts to a bar come evening. At the time of writing, the owners were set to occupy the ground floor too.

Dàndàn Tóngguōshuàn MONGOLIAN, HOTPOT $$
(旦旦铜锅涮; ☑0471 662 1062; 9 Sanshiwu-zhong Xiangnei, 三十五中巷内9号; mains from ¥40; ⏰6.30am-11pm) The lighting in this fine traditional Mongolian hotpot restaurant is a bit intense, but the menu's sure-fire. Choose from spicy (辣; *là*) or mild (清淡; *qīngdàn*) broth, or a *yuānyāng* (鸳鸯; hot one side, non-spicy the other) pot into which you scald your beef and lamb strips and piles of mushrooms, potatoes and other veggies.

🛍 Shopping

Souvenir Shops GIFTS & SOUVENIRS
(表记店铺, Biǎojì Diànpù) Opposite Dà Zhào (p878) monastery, this Qing-era-look street is packed with stalls selling Mongolian tat, jade and Buddhist and Mao memorabilia.

ℹ Information

Bank of China (中国银行, Zhōngguó Yínháng; Xinhua Dajie, 新华大街; ⏰9am-5pm Mon-Sat) Has a 24-hour ATM.

China Post (中国邮政, Zhōngguó Yóuzhèng; Chezhan Dongjie, 车站东街)

Exit-Entry Administration Bureau (出入境管理处, Chūrùjìng Guǎnlǐchù; ☑0471 669 9318; www.hhhtga.gov.cn; 1 Chileichuan Dajie, 敕勒川大街1号; ⏰8.30am-noon & 2.30-5pm Mon-Fri) For visa extensions and other enquiries. The foreign-affairs bureau is to the left of the main building, outside the gated compound.

Inner Mongolia People's Hospital (内蒙古自治区人民医院; ☑0471 662 0000; www.nmgyy.cn; 20 Zhaowuda Lu, 昭乌达路20号)

ℹ Getting There & Away

AIR

Hohhot Baita International Airport is 15km east of the city. Daily flight destinations (routes are reduced in winter) include Běijīng (¥500), Xī'an (¥800), Hǎila'ěr (¥1300), Mǎnzhōulǐ (¥1000) and Shànghǎi (¥1350). Book flights on www.elong.net or www.ctrip.com, or go to (or contact) the **Civil Aviation Administration of China** (中国民航

公司, CAAC, Zhōngguó Mínháng Gōngsī; ☑0471 696 4103; Xilin Guole Lu, 锡林郭勒路) office.

BUS

Hohhot's **main bus station** (长途汽车站, chángtú qìchēzhàn; ☑0471 696 5969) is next door to Hohhot Train Station.

Bāotóu ¥40, two hours, every 30 minutes (7am to 7pm)

Běijīng ¥150, six to eight hours, 8.30am, 10.10am, 1.30pm, 3.50pm and 5pm

Dàtóng ¥80, four hours, hourly (7.20am to 4.30pm)

Dōngshèng ¥65, three hours, every 30 minutes (6.30am to 7.25pm)

Erenhot (Èrlián) ¥95, five hours, 8am, 8.20am, 8.50am, 12.30pm and 1.30pm

Liángchéng ¥35, two hours, hourly (7.10am to 5.20pm)

TRAIN

Hohhot has two train stations: Hohhot Train Station (呼和浩特火车站; Hūhéhàotè Huǒchēzhàn) and Hohhot East Train Station (呼和浩特东站; Hūhéhàotè Dōngzhàn), around 9km to the east. Most useful trains leave from Hohhot Train Station. Sleeper tickets are hard to come by in July

and August; hotel travel desks can book them for a ¥30 commission. From Hohhot, trains go to the following destinations:

Bāotóu ¥22 to 25, two hours, regular

Běijīng hard seat/hard sleeper ¥75/142, six to 11 hours, regular

Dàtóng seat ¥37 to ¥44, three to four hours, 12 daily

Erenhot (Èrlián) hard seat ¥54, hard/soft sleeper ¥146/222, 8½ hours, 9.58am and 11.52pm

Xilinhot seat/hard sleeper ¥91/169, 9½ hours, 7.20pm and 9.14pm

Yínchuān seat/hard sleeper ¥93/174, 10 hours, three daily

❶ Getting Around

The **airport bus** (机场巴士, Jīchǎng Bāshì; ¥15; ⏱5.30am–last flight) (¥15, 40 mins) runs from 5.30am to the last flight. Between 10am and 10pm, the bus runs every half an hour, less regularly outside those hours. There are three lines, but the most useful route for travellers is line 1, which runs in a loop along Xinhua Dongjie, then north to the train station before heading east along Beiyuan Dongjie (北垣东街) back to the airport. You can pick it up at the train station.

---

❶ BORDER CROSSINGS: GETTING TO MONGOLIA

Two direct trains run between Běijīng and Ulaanbaatar, the Mongolian capital, on Wednesday and Saturday at 11.22am. The trains are the Chinese-owned K3 (hard/soft sleeper/deluxe ¥1222/1723/1884, 30 hours) and the Mongolian-owned K23 (hard/deluxe sleeper ¥1259/1849). You need to buy tickets from CITS (China International Travel Service) in Běijīng, not from the train station. The same train stops in Erenhot (二连浩特; Èrliánhàotè; hard sleeper ¥130, 10½ hours), at the Mongolian border. Erenhot is listed on Chinese train timetables as Èrlián (二连).

There are also five daily buses from Hohhot to Erenhot (¥95, six hours), leaving between 8am and 1.30pm; as they depart more regularly, buses are more practical than the train, although the overnight train at 11.52pm is very useful. From Erenhot you can catch a jeep across the border (about ¥60) and continue to Ulaanbaatar on the daily 5.50pm local train.

A train also runs from Hohhot to Ulaanbaatar on Monday and Friday, leaving at 10.50pm and taking 30 hours. Two trains run from Hohhot to Erenhot: the 6856 (hard seat ¥54) departs at 9.58am and arrives in Erenhot at 6.28pm; the overnight T4202 (hard/soft sleeper ¥146/222) from Bāotóu leaves Hohhot at 11.52pm, pulling into Erenhot at 6.40am.

To fly from Hohhot to Ulaanbaatar, you need to go via Beijing, where Air China (¥2500) and **Aero Mongolia** (Map p879; ¥1630) have flights to Ulaanbaatar. Book online at www.ctrip.com. Flights can be reduced in winter.

For a Mongolian visa, go to the **Mongolian Consulate** (p1000) in Hohhot. The 30-day visa costs ¥260 and takes four days to process. A rush visa (¥495) can be obtained the following day. US citizens do not need a visa to visit Mongolia for visits of up to 90 days; for citizens of Israel, it's 30 days visa-free. To find the consulate, travel east on Daxue Dongjie, turn left on Dongying Nanjie and look for the consulate 200m on the left. Go early.

There is also a consulate in **Erenhot** (p1000). To find the consulate from the bus station, walk half a block east to the T-junction and head left. Walk north along this road (Youyi Lu) for 10 minutes until you see the red, blue and yellow Mongolian flags on your left. A 30-day rush tourist visa (¥495) can be obtained the next day.

Lines 2 and 3 run into town via Hohhot East Train Station. A taxi to the airport will cost ¥50 (flag fall ¥6).

Useful bus routes include bus 1, which runs from the Train Station to the old part of the city past Zhongshan Xilu, and bus 33, which runs east on Xinhua Dajie from the Train Station. Buses 19 (¥1) and 83 (¥1) run to the East Train Station.

Around Hohhot

In the middle of the fields, 7km east of the airport (about 22km from Hohhot), is **Bái Tǎ** (白塔, White Pagoda, ¥35), a striking seven-storey tower built during the Liao dynasty. A steep, double-barrelled staircase leads to a small shrine room at the top. Few travellers come here, so you will feel like you have the place to yourself.

About 90km north of Hohhot, the grassland area of **Xīlāmùrén** (希拉穆仁, Xīlāmùrén; ¥80) caters largely to the burgeoning domestic market, with dozens of faux concrete yurt camps and a commercialised feel in pockets that robs some of it of a true wilderness experience. But it's a huge area, so you can eke out that true grassland feel if you explore. Go in summer, otherwise the grass will be brown and patchy. Activities are provided by horse rides; meals (principally lamb) are available, but are pricey.

For a really authentic Mongolian grassland experience, Āndá Guesthouse (p879) in Hohhot will set you up at the home of a local family, where you get to pick your own dried cow dung to light a campfire! Day trips start from ¥290 (including one meal) or ¥390 for an overnight trip (including three meals). Horse riding is an extra ¥100 per hour. The guesthouse also offers multiday tours which cover Bái Tǎ, Wǔdāng Lamasery, the Kùbùqí desert and sections of the Great Wall at Liángchéng.

Shàngdū 上都

☑ 0479 / POP 83,000 (ZHÈNGLÁNQÍ)

The 'very fine marble palace' described by explorer Marco Polo and eulogised and immortalised by poet Samuel Taylor Coleridge as a 'stately pleasure-dome' is today little more than a vast prairie with vague remnants of its once mighty walls, but it continues to have an allure that is far greater than the sum of its remaining parts.

Today Xanadu, or Shàngdū as it was actually called, is accessed via the small gateway town of Zhènglánqí (正蓝旗).

Conceived by Kublai Khan, grandson of Genghis and the first Yuan emperor, Shàngdū's lifespan as the summer capital was relatively brief. Construction of the city started in 1252 and lasted four years, serving as Kublai Khan's summer palace away from his palace in Zhongdu (Khanbaliq), the Yuan dynasty capital in today's Běijīng. Shàngdū was overrun and destroyed by Ming forces in 1369.

Shàngdū actually consisted of three distinct cities: the outer city, the imperial city and the palace city. All that is visible now are the outer and inner walls, which are ticketed (admission ¥30). The site was listed as a Unesco World Heritage site in June 2012.

From the yurt where you buy your ticket, it's another 1.5km to the outer walls (a golf buggy will take you for ¥10 or you can rent a bicycle for ¥10). From there, you can walk another 500m to the inner ramparts. Paths through the wildflower-covered grassland that has swallowed up the city offer the chance for pleasant strolls and reflective musings on the vagaries of history.

Xanadu Museum
MUSEUM

(上都博物馆, Shàngdū Bówùguǎn; ¥20; ⊙8am-5pm Tue-Sun) Zhènglánqí's Xanadu Museum is very important to visit for the scale models that give a realistic impression of the sheer ambition of Shàngdū, as well as for relics from the site, including ceramics, statues and decorative and structural pieces of the original palace, which crucially put the ancient complex into context.

🛏 Sleeping & Eating

Jiādì Shāngwù Bīnguǎn
HOTEL $

(佳帝商务宾馆; Shangdu Dajie, 上都大街; tw ¥200; 🕾) This modern business-style hotel towards the west end of Shangdu Dajie has clean and OK rooms. Expect to get reasonable discounts.

188 Liánsuǒ Bīnguǎn
HOTEL $$

(188 连锁宾馆; ☑0479 423 9188; Jinlianchuan Dajie, 金莲川大街; r¥188-588; 🖧🕾) This fresh place has very clean and spacious rooms in a building right next to the bus station.

ℹ Information

On Shangdu Dajie, you'll find a branch of the ICBC bank with a 24-hour ATM that takes foreign cards; it's near the corner with Zhiyou Hutong. At the time of writing there was no Bank of China in town, so make sure you bring enough cash.

ℹ Getting There & Away

Although Shàngdū signifies distant wonders in the Western imagination, in truth it's not that isolated (275km northwest of Běijīng). But it does feel remote, partly because of the huge empty prairie it sits in, and also because getting here requires some effort. Hohhot's bus station has buses to Zhènglánqí (¥132, six to seven hours, 7am and 2pm), also just known as Lánqí (蓝旗). From Zhènglánqí it's about a 20km taxi ride (¥170 return) to Shàngdū. Buses return to Hohhot at 7am and 12.30pm.

Bāotóu   包头

📅 0472 / POP 2.73 MILLION

The largest city in Inner Mongolia, booming Bāotóu is no oil painting, sprawling across more than 20km of dusty landscape, much of it an industrialised smear. However, if you're heading to the Wǔdāng Lamasery and Genghis Khan's Mausoleum, you may find yourself passing through and maybe stopping for a night.

◎ Sights

Wǔdāng Lamasery   BUDDHIST SITE

(五当召, Wǔdāng Zhào; ¥45; ⊙8.30am-4.30pm) Lying on the pilgrim route from Tibet to Outer Mongolia and established in 1749, at its height this handsome monastery was the largest monastery in Inner Mongolia, housing 1200 monks belonging to the Gelugpa sect of Tibetan Buddhism. Numbers are down to around 60 resident monks today, but Wǔdāng's numerous buildings, occupied by local villagers, are a reminder of its former importance. Climb the steps leading up the hill opposite the car park for views of the complex and the prayer-flag-draped landscape.

A little compound beside the public toilet has basic beds (¥50, no showers) and home-cooked meals if you wish to stay the night.

Wǔdāng monastery is 67km northeast of Bāotóu. Direct buses (¥20, 1½ hours) depart from the bus parking lot in front of Bāotóu East Railway Station at 9am and 3.20pm. Buses return at 7am and 1pm. It's better to get the 9am bus as sometimes the afternoon bus does not run. Alternatively, bus 7 (¥10, one hour), from the same parking lot, goes to Shíguǎi (石拐), 40km from Bāotóu, every 20 minutes between 7.15am and 5.30pm. From Shíguǎi you can hire a taxi for the final 30-minute journey to the monastery (one-way/return ¥50/100). A taxi from Bāotóu East Railway Station to the monastery and back is around ¥300.

🛏 Sleeping & Eating

The older eastern district (Dōnghé) is a convenient place to stay; if you're arriving by train make sure to get off at the Bāotóu East Railway Station (包头东站; Bāotóu Dōngzhàn) and not the west station. The modern western district (Kūnqū) is 25km away and where most residents now work and stay.

Head to Nanmenwai Dajie for a selection of restaurants within walking distance of the Bāotóu East Railway Station and a short hop in a cab (¥7) from the east bus station.

Xīhú Fàndiàn   HOTEL $$

(西湖饭店, West Lake Hotel; ☎0472 414 4444; 10 Nanmenwai Dajie, 南门外大街10号; d from ¥288; ✸@🛜) A five-minute walk from the east train station, this friendly place was renovated in 2014 and has plenty of clean, comfortable rooms with modern bathrooms. You can usually get a room for around ¥190.

ℹ Getting There & Away

AIR

Flights connect Bāotóu with Běijīng (¥750), Shànghǎi (¥990) and other cities. Buy tickets at www.ctrip.net. The airport is 2km south of Bāotóu East Railway Station. A taxi to the airport is ¥15, but ¥30 in the other direction.

BUS

When arriving in Bāotóu, ask if the bus stops at Dōnghé (东河) or Kūnqū (昆区). If it's the latter bus station (昆区汽车站; Kūnqū Qìchēzhàn), you will need to get off in between and take a bus (K10; ¥2.50) or a taxi (¥35) to head to the eastern Dōnghé district. The following buses leave from the main bus station (包头汽车总站; Bāotóu Qìchē Zǒngzhàn) in Dōnghé:

Dōngshèng ¥34, two hours, every 20 to 30 minutes (8am to 7pm)

Hohhot ¥40 to ¥45, three hours, every 30 minutes (7.30am to 5pm)

Yán'ān (Shaanxi) ¥156, eight hours, 3pm

Yúlín (Shaanxi) ¥95, five hours, eight daily (6.30am to 4.30pm)

TRAIN

Frequent trains between Hohhot and Bāotóu (¥25, two hours) stop at both the east and west stations. The following trains depart from the east station.

Běijīng hard/soft sleeper ¥175/264, 8½ to 13 hours, 12 daily

Lánzhōu hard/soft sleeper ¥230/351, 15 to 17 hours, four daily

Tàiyuán hard/soft sleeper ¥174/263, 10 to 12 hours, three daily

Yínchuān hard/soft sleeper ¥136/204, six hours, 10 daily

Genghis Khan Mausoleum 成吉思汗陵园

Located 130km south of Bāotóu in the middle of nowhere is the **Genghis Khan Mausoleum** (Chéngjí Sīhàn Língyuán; ¥120, with museum entry ¥150; ⏰8am-6pm), China's tribute to the great Mongol warlord. Unfortunately, old Genghis Khan (成吉思汗; Chéngjí Sīhàn) is not buried here (his resting place has never been found). Instead, the mausoleum's existence is justified by an old Mongol tradition of worshipping Genghis Khan's personal effects, including his saddle, bow and other items. Kublai Khan established the cult and handed over care for the objects to the Darhats, a Mongol clan.

Darhat elders kept the relics inside eight white tents, which could be moved in times of warfare. In the early 1950s, the government decided to build a permanent site for the relics and constructed this impressive triple-domed building, in the traditional Mongolian style. By then, most of the relics had been lost or stolen (everything you'll see here is a replica). But even today, some of the guards at the site still claim descent from the Darhat clan. The ¥150 ticket includes entry to a museum with information on Genghis and Monglian culture.

From Bāotóu there is currently only one bus (¥47, two hours, 9.10am) to Chénglíng (成陵) from the main bus station in Dōnghé. You'll then have to catch a taxi (¥15) the final 7km to the mausoleum. All buses from Bāotóu to Yúlín pass by Chénglíng, so that is an option (same in the other direction, if you are coming from north Shǎnxī).

GENGHIS' GRAVE

The great Genghis left stern instructions that his burial place be kept secret. Legend has it that the slaves who built his tomb were massacred afterwards by soldiers, who were then subsequently killed themselves to prevent anyone knowing the location of his grave. Archaeologists hunting for Genghis' final resting place have been further hampered by a reputed curse that has supposedly struck some down. Most historians assume that after his death (and no one knows where that occurred) in 1227, Genghis' body was taken back to Mongolia and buried near his birthplace in Khentii Aimag close to the Onon River.

There are 11 trains (hard seat ¥18, 80 minutes) per day from Bāotóu to Dōngshèng West train station, 60km from the tomb. There are also regular buses (¥34, two hours, every 20 to 30 minutes, 8am to 7pm) from Bāotóu to Dōngshèng.

To move on, take a cab back to a small tourist village (with shops, hotels and restaurants) to flag down any Dōngshèng-bound bus at the roundabout. Buses should pass by regularly till about 4pm. From Dōngshèng (东胜) you can connect to Bāotōu (¥34), Hohhot (¥65, four hours, hourly) and other regional destinations as well as Yúlín in north Shǎnxī province.

At the roundabout, there are also share taxis to Ejin Horo Qi (伊金霍洛旗; Yījīn Huòluò Qí; ¥15 per person), known as 'Yī Qí', where you can get a bus to Hohhot (¥70, 4½ hours, last bus 3pm).

Hǎilā'ěr 海拉尔

☎ 0470 / POP 350,000

Northern Inner Mongolia's largest city, Hǎilā'ěr is a busy, rather ordinary place. Don't fret, the city isn't the draw: surrounding the town range the expansive Hūlúnbèi'ěr Grasslands, a vast prairie that begins just outside the city and rolls northwards towards the Russian and Mongolian borders, seemingly forever. Superbly lush and deeply verdent come July and August, the grasslands are a fantastic sight and *the* place in Inner Mongolia to saddle up a horse.

The immediate area around Hǎilā'ěr sees several inevitably touristy yurt camps where you can eat, listen to traditional music and sometimes stay the night. Although they're not places where Mongolians actually live, you can still learn a bit about Mongolian culture, and the wide-open grasslands are a gorgeous setting.

For a more authentic experience, travel further away, although staying with local families in the grasslands is not easy to organise unless you speak some Mandarin (or Mongolian).

⊙ Sights

Ewenki Museum MUSEUM
(鄂温克博物馆, Èwēnkè Bówùguǎn; Youji Jie, 友谊街; ⏰8.30-11.30am & 2.30-5.30pm) FREE
Roughly 20,000 Ewenki people live in northern Inner Mongolia, most of them in the Hūlúnbèi'ěr Grasslands surrounding Hǎilā'ěr. Glimpse some of their history and culture at

this modern museum. Traditionally herders, hunters and farmers, the Ewenki are one of the few peoples in China to raise reindeer. You can see a *chum*, a wig-wam style portable dwelling that the Ewenki traditionally used.

The museum is on the southeastern edge of town. Regular minibuses (¥4, 15 minutes) run here from Buxing Jie beside the Busen shopping centre.

☞ Tours

North of Hǎilā'ěr are few permanent settlements, just the yurts of herders with their flocks of sheep and cows and strings of Mongolian ponies set in some of the greenest grasslands you will ever see. Closer to the Russian border, the rolling prairie becomes more wooded, as spindly white pine trees appear. Bring along binoculars if you want to have a closer look at the Russian villages across the border.

If you speak Chinese, you can hire a private car for ¥500 per day to take in the sights around Hǎilā'ěr. Contact **Mr Liu** (刘师父, Liú Shīfù, ☑159 4775 3673). During busier seasons, he can find Chinese travellers to carpool (拼车, *pīnchē*) with. He has set itineraries that cover Ēnhé, Shì Wěi and Mǎnzhōulǐ.

☆☆ Festivals & Events

Naadam CULTURAL, SPORTS
The Hǎilā'ěr Naadam (sports festival) is held annually in July on the grasslands just north of town. You'll see plenty of exciting wrestling, horse racing and archery. The city is, however, flooded with tour groups from across China at this time, making it difficult to find a room, and hotel prices double.

▙ Sleeping & Eating

Jīnzhànghàn Grassland Camp GER $
(金帐汗草原, Jīnzhànghàn Cǎoyuán; ☑133 2700 0919; ☺Jun-early Oct) Set along a winding river about 40km north of Hǎilā'ěr, this grasslands camp has a spectacular setting, even if it is aimed at tourists. You can pass an hour or so looking around and sipping milk tea, spend the day horse riding (per hour ¥200) or hiking, or come for an evening of dinner, singing and dancing.

If you want to stay the night, the yurts are ¥100 per person. There's no indoor plumbing, but there is a communal toilet hut. To get here, you'll have to hire a taxi from Hǎilā'ěr (about ¥300 return) or join one of the Chinese group tours (sign up at your hotel or at the booth at the Hǎilā'ěr train station).

About 2km before the main camp there are a couple of unsigned family-run camps. Prices for food, accommodation and horse rental are about half what you pay at Jīnzhànghàn, but they are rather less organised. To skip the tourist-run camps, push further north through the grasslands towards Ēnhé and Shì Wěi.

Jīnchuān Dòuhuāzhuāng HOTPOT $$$
(金川豆花庄; ☑0470 834 6555; Xi Dajie, 西大街; meals from ¥70; ☺10am-11pm) This big, bustling and fantastic hotpot restaurant is packed with locals; choose from a wide selection of meat, seafood and veggie options, as well as choosing between spicy (辣; *là*) or mild (清淡; *qīngdàn*) broth. There's no English or picture menu, but the waitresses will help you out. It's on the corner of Xi Dajie and Bei Xiejie, not far from the intersection with Zhongyang Dajie.

❶ Information

Bank of China (中国银行, Zhōngguó Yínháng; cnr Xingan Donglu & Zhongyang Dajie, 兴安东路中央大街的路口; ☺9am-5pm Mon-Sat) Next door to Bèi'ěr Dàjiǔdiàn in the centre of town.

Public Security Bureau (PSB, Gōng'ānjú; Alihe Lu, 阿里河路) Opposite CITS in the Hédōng district on the east side of the river.

❶ Getting There & Away

AIR

Hūlúnbèi'ěr Hǎilā'ěr Airport (呼伦贝尔海拉尔机场, Hūlúnbèi'ěr Hǎilā'ěr Jīchǎng) Direct daily flights to Běijīng (¥1140, two hours), Hohhot (¥1150, 2¼ hours) and Shànghǎi (¥1860, 3½ hours). Go to www.elong.net or www.ctrip.com to book flights.

Hunnu Air (☑+976 7000 1111; www.hunnuair. com) Flies to Ulaanbaatar (from ¥900) in Mongolia every Thursday and Sunday. The airline also flies from Hǎilā'ěr to eastern Choibalsan in eastern Mongolia. Book tickets online.

BUS

The **Long-Distance Bus Station** (长途车站, Chángtú Chēzhàn) in the Hédōng district has buses to the following destinations:
Lābùdálín ¥38, two hours, half-hourly (7am to 5.30pm)
Mǎnzhōulǐ ¥45, three hours, hourly (7.20am to 5pm)

TRAIN

Ten daily trains go to Mǎnzhōulǐ (hard seat ¥29, two to three hours). There are also daily trains between Hǎilā'ěr and Hā'ěrbīn (hard/soft sleeper ¥178/273, 10 to 14 hours), Qíqíhā'ěr (seat/

hard sleeper ¥72/136, eight hours, six daily) and Běijīng (hard/soft sleeper ¥377/582, 28 hours).

The train station is in the northwestern part of town. A taxi to the city centre is ¥7.

ℹ Getting Around

Airport buses (¥5) connect to all flights and depart from the train station roughly 1½ hours before departure. A taxi to the airport from town costs ¥30.

Buses 1, 3, 7 and 9 run from the train station past Bèi'ěr Dàjiǔdiàn (Bèi'ěr Hotel). Bus 18 runs from the Long-Distance Bus Station in Hédōng to the train station, while taxis charge ¥12. Taxi fares start at ¥6.

Ēnhé 恩和

The small township of Ēnhé, located 70km north of Lābùdálín en route to Shì Wěi, is one of the area's unsung villages brimming with an unhurried and authentic atmosphere. Surrounded by hills and acres of lush grass, the village only recently opened to tourism, so a low-key vibe survives. Many residents are of Chinese-Russian origin; some could easily pass for Russians. Here, herders milk their cows outside their properties when they aren't taking them out to pasture. Sample boiled milk at your accommodation.

Horse rides start at around ¥60 (a bargain in Inner Mongolia!). You can hire bikes (¥10 per hour) – an excellent way to get about – or go for hikes. The mosquitoes are totally killer in summer so bring plenty of repellent.

There's a handful of places you can stay in the village, but in terms of accessibility, travel info and affordability, the Ēnhé Grasslands International Hostel (呼伦贝尔恩和牧场国际青年旅舍, Hūlúnbèi'ěr Ēnhé Mùchǎng Guójì Qīngnián Lǚshě; ☑ 0470 694 2277; www.yhachina.com; dm ¥45-50, d & tw ¥100-240, tr ¥240, q ¥260; 🛜) is a good choice. Many hotels shut up shop during the winter months, opening again in spring.

Several small restaurants can be found in the village for barbecues, steamed bread and noodles. Some of the hotels can cook up dishes too, but for more choice, head back to Lābùdálín or Hǎilā'ěr.

ℹ Getting There & Away

To get here from Hǎilā'ěr, you need to travel first to Lābùdálín (拉布达林; ¥40, two hours, half hourly 7am to 5.30pm). Lābùdálín (sometimes called É'ěrgǔnà) has two daily direct buses (¥27, two hours), at 12.10am and 2.30pm. Buses return to Lābùdálín in the morning at 8.30am and 9.30am.

Shì Wěi–bound buses also stop on the main road leading to Ēnhé, from where it's a 1.5km walk into town. You can flag onward buses to Shì Wěi from the main road at around 11.15am and 5.15pm.

Mǎnzhōulǐ 满洲里

☑ 0470 / POP 300,000

This laissez-faire border city, where the Trans-Siberian Railway crosses from China to Russia, is a pastel-painted boomtown of shops, hotels and restaurants catering to the Russian market. Unless you look Asian, expect shopkeepers to greet you in Russian. Mǎnzhōulǐ is modernising at lightning speed, but a few Russian-style log houses still line Yīdào Jie.

Mǎnzhōulǐ is small enough to get around on foot. From the train station to the town centre, it's a 10-minute walk. Turn right immediately as you exit the station, then right again to cross the footbridge. You'll come off the bridge near the corner of Yidao Jie and Zhongsu Lu.

◉ Sights

Hūlún Lake LAKE
(呼伦湖, Hūlún Hú; ¥30) Occupying an enormous 2339 sq km and one of China's largest freshwater lakes, Hūlún Lake, called Dalai Nuur (Ocean Lake) in Mongolian, unexpectedly pops out of the grasslands like a colossal inland sea. You can hire a horse (¥100 per 30 minutes) or a quad bike (¥100 per 20 minutes), take a boat ride (¥10 per 20 minutes) or simply stroll along the rocky lakeshore, taking in its magnificence. The lake is 39km southeast of Mǎnzhōulǐ.

The only way to get to the lake is by hiring a taxi. Expect to pay about ¥200 return, including a visit to the nearby Russian Doll Park.

🛏 Sleeping

Fēngzéyuán Lǚdiàn GUESTHOUSE $
(丰泽源旅店; ☑ 139 4709 3443, 0470 225 4099; Yidao Jie, 一道街; tw ¥200; @ 🛜) Located inside a restored Russian log cabin (painted yellow and green), this friendly guesthouse offers large, clean and affordable rooms. Coming off the pedestrian bridge from the train station, it's the first building in front of you, next to the statue of Zhou Enlai. Prices fall to ¥50 during the slow season.

Shangri-La HOTEL $$$
(香格里拉大酒店, Xiānggélǐlā Dàjiǔdiàn; ☑ 0470 396 8888; www.shangri-la.com; 99 Liudao Jie, 六道街99号; d ¥1388, ste ¥4588; ⊕ ✳ @ 🛜 ✕) A by-

word for quality, style and professionalism across Asia, the luxurious Shangri-La is an excellent choice. Very comfortable rooms offer views over the surrounding grasslands, and there are Chinese and open-kitchen international restaurants, a 20m swimming pool and a spa. Prices are often discounted to around ¥850.

✕ Eating

There are plenty of restaurants (*pectopah* in Russian) in town. For a smart choice of Chinese and international dining, the Shangri-La is a very good choice.

Bèijiā'ěr Hú Xī Cāntīng RUSSIAN $$
(贝加尔湖西餐厅; 23 Zhongsu Lu, near Wudao Jie, 中苏路23号; dishes from ¥30; ⏰24hr) The name of the restaurant translates as 'Lake Baikal Western Restaurant', giving some indication of its target audience. Rub shoulders with Russians who come for robust Chinese-style Russian dishes such as borscht and steaks set to a Russian soundtrack. The set meals are the way to go, letting you sample the best dishes; paired with cold draft beer, they work wonders. There's a picture menu available.

ⓘ Information

China International Travel Service (CITS, 中国 国际旅行社, Zhōngguó Guójì Lǚxíngshè, ☑0470 622 8319; 二道街35号; ⏰8-11.30am & 2-4pm Mon-Fri) Sells train tickets for Chinese cities and one-day tours to the local sights, but not good for tourist information. Located on the 1st floor of Guójì Fàndiàn (国际饭店; International Hotel).
China Post (中国邮政, Zhōngguó Yóuzhèng; cnr Haiguan Jie & Sidao Jie, 海关街四道街路口; ⏰9am-5pm) Slightly south of the intersection, on the west side of Haiguan Lu.
Industrial & Commercial Bank of China (ICBC, 工商银行, Gōngshāng Yínháng; cnr Yidao Jie & Zhongsu Lu, 一道街中苏路的路口) On the southeast corner of Yidao Jie and Zhongsu Lu.
Public Security Bureau (PSB, 公安局, Gōng'ānjú; cnr Sandao Jie & Shulin Lu, 三道街树林路的路口)

ⓘ Getting There & Around

Mǎnzhōulǐ Xijiāo Airport (满洲里西郊机场, Mǎnzhōulǐ Xijiāo Jīchǎng) is on the edge of town, around 9km away. There are daily flights to Běijīng (¥1150, 2¼ hours) and, in summer, to Hohhot (¥1150, 2½ hours) and Shànghǎi.
Hunnu Air (www.hunnuair.com) flies internationally twice a week to Ulaanbaatar (2½ hours).
There are 10 buses a day to Hǎilā'ěr (¥45, three hours, 6.30am to 5.30pm) from the **Interna-**

tional Bus Station (国际汽车站, Guójì Qìchē Zhàn; ☑0470 622 0358; Yidao Jie, 一道街).

You can reach Mǎnzhōulǐ by train from Hǎilā'ěr (¥26 to ¥29, 2½ hours, 10 daily), Hā'ěrbīn (hard/soft sleeper ¥230/351, 13 to 17 hours, six daily) and Qíqíhā'ěr (hard/soft sleeper ¥163/252, 11 hours). Two trains per day also roll to Běijīng (hard/soft sleeper ¥444/684, 32 hours, 9.18pm and 11.29pm) and one very slow train goes to Hohhot (hard/soft sleeper ¥488/752, 40 hours, 4.10pm).

Taxis charge ¥10 for most trips around town. A taxi to the airport will take about 15 minutes (¥40).

Shì Wěi 室韦
☑0470 / POP 1800

A small Russian-style town of log cabins located right on the É'ěrgǔnà River, which marks the border with Russia, Shì Wěi is deep within the glorious grasslands. Shì Wěi itself is no longer the backwater it once was and the commercial summer tourist season gets busy with domestic visitors, although very few foreigners make it up here, especially out of season. But it's fun to ride a horse along the riverbank (¥40 per half-hour) while gazing at the Russian village on the opposite bank, or sitting down to some Russian food. Look for wooden stages on both sides of the river: each country used to host performances for their neighbours! Taking the backcountry roads here, through the elm forests, is another attraction.

Spring and autumn see fewer visitors, but summer sees the grasslands at their greenest best, while winter is so cold activity slows to a glacial crawl and you can barely move.

For a closer look at Russia, you can walk to the **Friendship Bridge** (友谊桥, Yǒuyì Qiáo; ¥20; 8am-5pm). Chinese tourists pose for photos at the foot of the bridge connecting the two countries before wandering down to a hut to buy Russian chocolate and souvenirs. Taxis can take you to **Línjiāng** (临江) – a less touristy border village with a lovely natural setting – for ¥100 return. You can also find accommodation in Línjiāng but will need to head back to Shì Wěi if you want to get the bus back to Lābùdálín.

Sleeping & Eating

In Shì Wěi, families have turned their homes into guesthouses and/or restaurants, often named after families. As these are the principal source of income for local families, they are not hard to find. You can get a room for around ¥100 to ¥300.

In the evening barbecue stalls set up along the main drag and in most of the adjacent lanes. Restaurants are run by local families, and guesthouse owners can generally cook up meals for guests.

Zhuóyàzhījiā   GUESTHOUSE **$**
(卓雅之家; ☑150 4701 7557; d & tw ¥100) Neat doubles and courtyard river views can be had for ¥100 at Zhuóyàzhījiā. From the bus drop-off, walk ahead towards the town square and turn left on the last lane. The house is 100m to the right.

Getting There & Away

From Hǎilā'ěr, first travel to Lābùdálín (拉布达林; ¥38, two hours, half-hourly 7am to 5.30pm), and from there there are two daily direct buses to Shì Wěi (¥44, four hours), at 9.30am and 3.30pm. Buses return to Lābùdálín at 8am and 1pm but make sure you buy your ticket in advance to secure a seat.

Bayanhot   阿拉善左旗
☑0483 / POP 140,000

In the far west of Inner Mongolia, Bayanhot (Ālāshàn Zuǒqí; also called 巴彦浩特; Bāyànhàotè) is most easily reached by land from Yínchuān in Níngxià. If coming from Níngxià, it can serve as a handy one-stop introduction to Mongol culture, its language, food and the vast deserts and high blue skies of far western Inner Mongolia. The town is also the gateway to the fantastic temple Guǎngzōng Sì and has a crop of interesting sights of its own, including the excellent, modern museum and the traditional architecture of the Qīnwáng Fǔ. Despite the absence of railways, the airport links Bayanhot with Ālāshàn Yòuqí (for the Badain Jaran Desert) and Éjìnà Qí (for Khara Khoto) in Inner Mongolia, so access from further afield has been greatly simplified.

Sights

Qīnwáng Fǔ   HISTORIC BUILDING
(亲王府; 9am-6pm) FREE This fabulous courtyard palace is the former home of the local prince, the Alashan Qin Wang. A well restored, Qing-era complex of buildings and courtyards, the palace has photos of the last prince (1903–68) and his family, plus some of their personal effects, but it's the splendid traditional layout and architecture that steals the show.

Alashan Museum   MUSEUM
(阿拉善博物馆, Ālāshàn Bówùguǎn; Ande Jie, 安德街; 9am-6pm) FREE This stunning museum, rehoused in 2011, affords a fascinating insight into Alashan and Mongolian culture. English captions are sporadic, which is a shame, but there's a wealth of objects to explore. The Dinosaur gallery on the 1st floor is very professional, but the upstairs galleries are exemplary, with displays of Mongolian clothing, saddles and Buddhist instruments, as well as a range of sacred masks and a *thangka*. There's also a gallery on ancient stone carvings and a model of Khara Khoto in its heyday.

There's also an aerial photo of today's Khara Khoto, for comparison. The museum itself is a recent, forward-thinking construction, in keeping with its location in a very modern-looking new area that was clearly designed to put the town on the map. The museum has free wi-fi. Taxis from the long-distance bus station will take you here for around ¥10.

Guǎngzōng Sì   MONASTERY
(广宗寺; ¥80; 8am-6pm) Once one of the most magnificent monasteries in Inner Mongolia, Guǎngzōng Sì has a stunning setting in the mountains 38km south of Bayanhot. At its height, some 2000 monks lived here. So important was the monastery that the main prayer hall, Gandan Danjaling Sum, contains the remains of the sixth Dalai Lama inside the golden stupa that dominates it.

Tragically, the monastery was demolished during the Cultural Revolution; a 1957 photo in the main prayer hall gives you an idea of how big it once was. The temples have since been rebuilt, but in the last couple of years a hotel, yurt restaurants and a supremely

INNER MONGOLIA'S FAR WEST

The golden deserts, shimmering lakes and ruined cities of western Inner Mongolia are fantastic places for adventures far from the beaten track. With new airports in the three major towns across the region now providing links to Hohhot and Xī'ān, the Badain Jaran Desert and ancient town of Khara Khoto are far more accessible than before.

One destination is **Khara Khoto** (Black City; 黑城; Hēichéng; ¥10; ⊙8am-7pm), a ruined Tangut city was built in 1032 and captured by Genghis Khan in 1226 (his last great battle). Khara Khoto continued to thrive under Mongol occupation, but in 1372 an upstart Ming battalion starved the city of its water source, killing everyone inside. Six hundred years of dust storms nearly buried Khara Khoto, until the Russian explorer PK Kozlov excavated and mapped the site, recovering hundreds of Tangut ore texts (now kept at the Institute of Oriental Manuscripts in St Petersburg). Located about 25km southeast of Éjìnà Qí (额济纳旗), the allure here is the remoteness of the site and surrounding natural beauty. A great time to visit is late September to early October when the poplar trees are changing colours; but be warned that every hotel room in Éjìnà Qí will be booked out at this time.

The second tourist drawcard in these parts is the remote but stunning **Badain Jaran Desert** (巴丹吉林沙漠; Bādānjílín Shāmò), a mysterious 49,000-sq-km landscape of desert lakes, Buddhist temples and towering dunes. The dunes here are among the tallest in the world, some topping 460m (taller than the Empire State Building). The tallest are static with a solid core, and do not move. Home to spring-fed lakes, the desert actually sprawls across not just Inner Mongolia, but Ningxià and Gānsù provinces too. **Badanjilin Travel Service** (巴丹吉林旅行社; Bādānjílín Lǚxíngshè; ☑0483 602 4888; www.badanjilin.net), in town, organises camel treks (from ¥120 per hour), tours to desert lakes with English-speaking guides (from ¥1000), as well as overnight expeditions. It can also organise a car to Khara Khoto for ¥1600 return. Chéngdū-based Navo Tours (www.navo-tour.com) runs 4WD tours here (three days of which is in the desert) starting from Lánzhōu with English-speaking guides. The closest town in the region, Ālāshàn Yòuqí (阿拉善右旗; also known as Badanjilin), is a 30-minute drive from the dunes.

All three towns in the region are well supplied with restaurants, but Bayanhot has the best selection. In Ālāshàn Yòuqí, **Jinsha Holiday Hotel** (金沙假日大酒店; Jīnshā Jiàrì Dàjiǔdiàn; ☑0483 602 6666; Badanjilin Nanlu, 巴丹吉林南路; d from ¥220, ste ¥500; ⚐) is a reasonable option. As you need a permit to travel to Éjìnà Qí, you will be asked for that at any hotel you wish to stay at, but not all hotels accept foreigners, so it's perhaps best to visit the town as a day trip.

This part of Inner Mongolia is highly militarised (China's space city is nearby) and travel permits are required for the road between Jiǔquán and Éjìnà Qí, as well as Khara Khoto itself and Ālāshàn Yòuqí and the Badain Jaran Desert. Travel agents need at least three days to organise the necessary permits, but it can take as long as a week.

Getting There & Around

You can fly around the region's three airports, which is the fastest approach. The smallest airport is Alxa Right Banner Badanjilin Airport (阿拉善右旗巴丹吉林机场; Ālāshàn Yòuqí Bādānjílín Jīchǎng) at Ālāshàn Yòuqí, which only has flights to the other two Alxa League airports.

You can access the region overland by bus either to Bayanhot from Bāotóu or from Yínchuān, the latter being far closer, with regular buses only taking two to three hours to reach Bayanhot. There are daily buses from Ālāshàn Yòuqí to Bayanhot (¥121, six to eight hours) and Éjìnà Qí (¥106, six hours).

The closest rail links are in Gānsù province. Two daily buses (¥24, 90 minutes) travel between Ālāshàn Yòuqí and Shāndān Xiàn (山丹县) in Gānsù province, from where you can take trains to Lánzhōu, Dūnhuáng and Urumqi. Two daily buses (¥39, 2½ hours) also leave Ālāshàn Yòuqí for Zhāngyè in Gānsù province. Other buses from Ālāshàn Yòuqí include two daily departures to Héxībǎo (河西堡; ¥34, three hours), also in Gānsù province, and Mínqín (民勤; ¥39, three hours), from where you can connect with long-distance buses onwards and outwards.

tacky shopping street have been added to the complex to entice domestic tour groups here.

There are good walking trails in the mountains behind the complex; take the path to the right of the main temple and follow it for one hour to a grassy plateau with fantastic views.

From Bayanhot, a taxi to the monastery and back is around ¥150, but the driver may not want to wait for long (in this case he will naturally charge more). If going on to Yínchuān (your taxi driver can drop you at the highway where you can stop any Yínchuān-bound bus), look out for the crumbling, yet still mighty, remains of the Great Wall at Sānguānkǒu (三关口). Some sections are up to 10m high and 3m wide.

Yánfú Sì
BUDDHIST TEMPLE

(延福寺; ⊘8am-noon & 3-6pm) FREE The original Mongol town of Bayanhot was centred on this 18th-century temple. Completed in 1742, it once housed 200 lamas; around 30 are resident here now. The **Hall of the Three Buddhas** is an authentic and dusty shrine housing its namesake trinity of Buddha in various incarnations, while the **Money God Temple**, in one of the side halls, sees the shining Money God himself, flanked by ferocious Tibetan Buddhist deities, gazing out over flickering, burning wicks suspended in oil.

Catholic Church
CHURCH

(天主教堂, Tiānzhǔ Jiàotáng; ⊘7am-noon & 2.30-6pm) This twin-spired, brick-built church is quite a sight as you head towards town from the long-distance bus station. Of relatively recent construction, it's a welcoming place with a pure white interior and paintings depicting the Stations of the Cross on the walls; 10 wall radiators keep it cosy in winter. Built for what must be a sizeable congregation, the church has a small side chapel too, with Christian literature in Chinese scattered about.

The gate may appear shut, but you can slide the bolt and walk in.

🛏 Sleeping & Eating

Hotels are dotted around town, with some usefully located right by the long-distance bus station. You'll end up spending around ¥80 to ¥100 for a cramped room at the grotty, smaller places, so you may as well spend another ¥40 to ¥80 for a far nicer room in the smarter choices.

The restaurant centre of Bayanhot focuses on the roads around New Century Sq (新世纪广场; Xīnshìjì Guǎngchǎng), especially along Yabrai Lu (雅布赖路) and Hoxud Lu

(和硕特路), where you can find noodle and lamb restaurants, plus fast-food outlets.

Āndá Jiàrì Jiǔdiàn
HOTEL $$

(安达假日酒店, Āndá Holiday Hotel; ☑0483 877 0999; Tuerhute Beilu, next to long distance bus station, 土尔扈特北路汽车站旁边; r incl breakfast ¥170-400; ⊛❋⊜) This classy hotel is excellently located for that early-morning bus to Bāotóu or Ālāshān Yòuqí. Rooms are bright, spacious and quiet and excellent discounts regularly bring the cheapest rooms down to around ¥140.

Alxa Guesthouse
HOTEL $$$

(阿拉善宾馆, Ālāshàn Bīnguǎn; ☑0483 221 1889; www.alsbg.com; 42 Hoxud Lu, 和硕特路42号; ⊛❋⊜) Opened in 2012, this smart and sparkling four-star hotel is the best in town, with very swish and comfortable rooms in the main block. Cheaper rooms are located in the other buildings, with discounts of around 40% in effect most of the time. The airport bus leaves from the main gate.

🔒 Shopping

Bayanhot means 'Rich City' in Mongolian and there's a thriving jade trade here. Numerous shops deal in it and there's a small market in front of the Qīnwáng Fǔ. Bargain hard if you're in a buying mood.

ℹ Getting There & Around

Bayanhot is served by **Alxa Left Banner Bayanhot Airport** (阿拉善左旗巴彦浩特机场, Ālāshàn Zuǒqí Bāyànhàotè Jīchǎng), to the southwest of town, which opened in 2013. Joy Air flights connect Bayanhot with Xī'ān and Okay Airways flies to Ālāshàn Yòuqí, Éjìnà Qí and Hohhot. Snow can scupper flights, so be prepared for delays.

Buses depart every 40 minutes from Yínchuān's south bus station for Bayanhot (¥30, two to three hours) between 7.20am and 6pm (you could stop off at the Western Xia Tombs). In the other direction, the first bus leaves Bayanhot at 6.20am, the last departs at 6.05pm. If you want to travel further west into Inner Mongolia from Bayanhot there are three buses in the morning to Éjìnà Qí (¥140, eight hours), at 8am, 9am and 9.20am. One daily bus goes to Ālāshàn Yòuqí (阿拉善右旗; ¥121, six to eight hours) at 7.10am. There is a bus to Bāotóu (¥131, eight to nine hours) at 7.10am, a sleeper to Hohhot at 4pm (¥176) and one bus per day to Dōngshèng (¥131) at 9.30am.

Regular shuttle buses connect the airport with the Měnggǔ Bīnguǎn (蒙古宾馆; Mongolia Hotel) in town. The long-distance bus station is on the outskirts of town, a ¥2 trip from the centre. Taxis are ¥2 to ¥5 to most short-haul destinations in town; taxis always stop regularly to pick up multiple passengers.

Qīnghǎi

POP 5.6 MILLION

Best Monasteries & Temples

➡ Kumbum Monastery
(p900)

➡ Yòuníng Monastery (p898)

➡ Lóngwù Sì (p902)

➡ Princess Wencheng
Temple (p905)

Best Natural Sights

➡ Nangchen County (p906)

➡ Qīnghǎi Lake & Chákǎ Salt
Lake (p899)

➡ Kanbula National Park
(p901)

➡ Mt Amnye Machen (p907)

➡ Zhālíng & Èlíng Lakes
(p908)

Why Go?

Big, bold and beautifully barren, Qīnghǎi (青海), larger than any country in the EU, occupies a vast swath of the north-eastern chunk of the Tibetan Plateau. As far as Tibetans are concerned, this is Amdo, one of old Tibet's three tradition-al provinces. Much of what you'll experience here will feel more Tibetan than Chinese; there are monasteries galore, yaks by the thousands and nomads camped out across high-altitude grasslands.

Rough-and-ready Qīnghǎi, which means 'Blue Sea' in Chinese, is classic off-the-beaten-track territory, often with a last frontier feel to it. Travelling here can be a little incon-venient, though China's rapid development plans have be-gun to touch the province, with huge highways and new rail lines under construction. Despite that, Qīnghǎi still delivers a heavy dose of solitude among middle of-nowhere high-plateau vistas, Martian-like red mountains, mouth-watering cuisine and encounters with remote communities of China's ethnic minorities.

When to Go

Xīníng

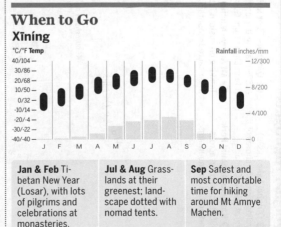

| | Jan & Feb Ti-betan New Year (Losar), with lots of pilgrims and celebrations at monasteries. | Jul & Aug Grass-lands at their greenest; land-scape dotted with nomad tents. | Sep Safest and most comfortable time for hiking around Mt Amnye Machen. |

Qīnghǎi Highlights

1 **Qīnghǎi Lake** (p899) Cycling along the shores of the largest lake in China.

2 **Kanbula National Park** (p901) Scrambling across Martian-like red mountains.

3 **Qīnghǎi–Tibet Railway** (p899) Taking the iconic train ride to Lhasa from Golmud.

4 **Mt Amnye Machen** (p907) Trekking on eastern Tibet's most sacred mountain.

5 **Tóngrén** (p902) Buying a Tibetan *thangka* (scroll painting) straight from the artist's easel.

6 **Princess Wencheng Temple** (p905) Walking through a web of prayer flags around the hills beside Yùshù.

7 **Guìdé** (p903) Turning the world's largest prayer wheel near the walled Old Town.

8 **Source of the Yellow River** (p908) Venturing across the Qīnghǎi–Tibet plateau to the source of China's most important river.

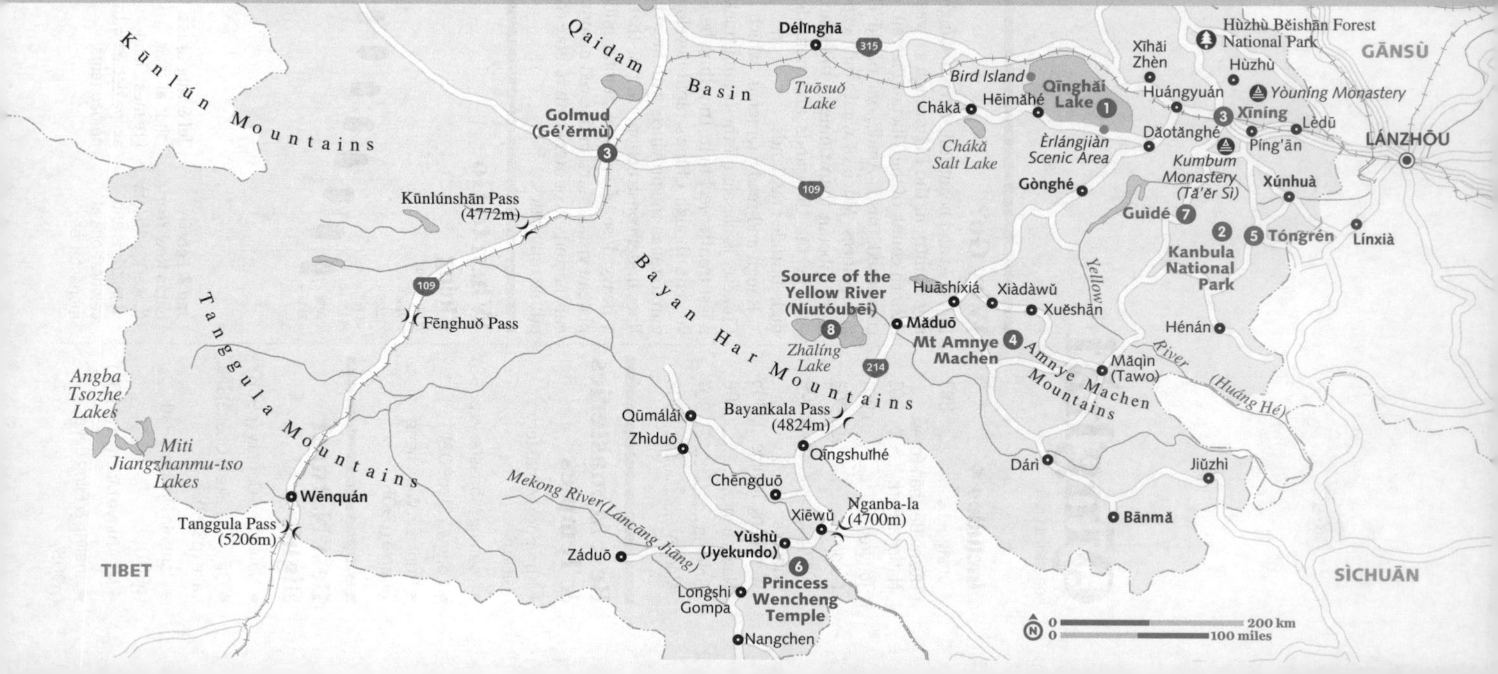

History

The northern Silk Road passed through what is now Qīnghǎi province, and in 121 BC the Han dynasty established a military base near modern Xīníng to counter Tibetan raids on trading caravans.

During the Yarlung dynasty, a time of Tibetan power expansion, Qīnghǎi was brought under Lhasa's control. After the collapse of the dynasty in AD 842, local rulers filled the ensuing power vacuum, some nominally acting as vassals of Song dynasty emperors.

In the 13th century, all of Qīnghǎi was incorporated into the Yuan empire under Genghis Khan. During this time, the Tǔ began to move into the area around Hùzhù, followed a century or so later by the Salar Muslims into Xúnhuà.

After the fall of the Yuan dynasty, local Mongol rulers and the Dalai Lamas in Lhasa wrestled for power. The Qing emperors restored the region to full Chinese control, setting it up as a prefecture with more or less the same boundaries as today. As in the past, however, they left administrative control in the hands of local elites.

Qīnghǎi became a province of China in 1928 during the republican era, though at the time it was under the de facto control of the Muslim Ma clan. When the People's Republic of China was established in 1949, Qīnghǎi retained its provincial borders and capital city, Xīníng.

In the late 1950s an area near Qīnghǎi Lake (青海湖; Qīnghǎi Hú) became the centre of China's nuclear weapons research program. During the next 40 years, at least 30 tests were held at a secret base, the Qīnghǎi Mine.

In April 2010, Yùshù, a Tibetan town in remote southwest Qīnghǎi, was devastated by a 7.1-magnitude earthquake. Thousands died – some say tens of thousands – but the rebuilding effort was swift and Yùshù's main centre reopened as a tourist destination in early 2014.

Today, the province is experiencing rapid growth (not unlike the rest of China). It's not uncommon to see large apartment blocks under construction in the capital Xīníng and even in provincial towns. Highways are being constructed to connect places like Mt Amnye Machen to the rest of the province.

ⓘ Entry & Exit Formalities

As with everything in China, things change rapidly in Qīnghǎi and areas that may be open to travellers one week could be closed or require permits the next. It's always best to check once

you arrive before heading to a new destination. The Xīníng Public Security Bureau (p897) has updated lists.

ⓘ Getting There & Around

Off-the-beaten-track overland routes include south into Sìchuān, at Aba or Shíqú, and north into Gānsù or Xīnjiāng from Golmud (check before going as foreigners travelling this way may need a special permit). Routes southwest into Tibet are even more remote and are usually closed to foreigners altogether, and some areas north of Qīnghǎi Lake have been closed to foreigners for years.

Most people arrive by train, usually into Xīníng, but after that train lines are limited, so long-distance buses are the best way to get around. In more remote areas you'll often have no option but to hire a private car and driver.

Xīníng 西宁

☑ 0971 / POP 2.2 MILLION

Situated on the eastern edge of the Tibetan Plateau, this lively provincial capital makes a good base from which to dive into the surrounding sights and on to the more remote regions of Qīnghǎi and beyond. Though many travellers use Xīníng as a jumping-off or landing point from the Qīnghǎi–Tibet Railway, it's also a wonderful place to explore the province's varied cultures – Muslim (Huí, Salar and Uighur), Tibetan and Han Chinese – especially the dynamite culinary mix that these groups bring together.

⊙ Sights

★ **Tibetan Culture & Medicine Museum** MUSEUM
(藏文化博物馆, Zàng Wénhuà Bówùguǎn; ☑ 0971 531 7881; www.tibetanculturemuseum.org; 36 Jing'er Rd, 经二路36号; ¥60; ⊙9am-6pm

May-Sep, to 5pm Oct-Apr; 🖥1) Exhibitions at this museum focus on traditional Tibetan medicine, astronomy and science, as well as traditional Tibetan life, homes and costumes. The highlight is a 618m-long *thangka* (Tibetan sacred art) scroll – the world's longest – which charts most of Tibetan history. Completed in 1997, it's not an ancient relic, but it is unbelievably long. It took 400 artists four years to complete and is displayed in a maze-like exhibition hall.

The museum is located on the far northwest side of Xīníng. Bus 1 (¥1, 35 minutes) goes here from Dong Dajie (stop at 新乐花园). A taxi costs about ¥20 from the city.

Dōngguān Grand Mosque   MOSQUE
(清真大寺, Qīngzhēn Dàsì; 25 Dongguan Dajie, 东关大街25号; ⊙7am-8pm) FREE About one-third of Xīníng's population is Muslim and there are more than 80 mosques across the city. It's not the prettiest, but in fact, it's one of the largest mosques in China. Friday lunchtime prayers regularly attract 50,000 worshippers, who spill out onto the streets before and afterwards. And during Ramadan as many as 300,000 come here to pray, with police closing off the streets to traffic.

Nánchán Sì   BUDDHIST SITE
(南禅寺; 93 Nanshan Lu, 南山路93号) Stood atop Phoenix Mountain, this Buddhist temple is the southern counterpart to Běichán Sì (北禅寺; ⊙8am-4pm) FREE, overlooking Xīníng from the south. The temple was built during the Northern Song dynasty (960–1127) and is the oldest Chan (Chinese Zen) Buddhist temple in Qīnghǎi province. It's a quiet spot that leads to good views of the city.

Xīníng City Wall   RUINS
(西宁城墙, Xīníng Chéngqiáng; Kunlun Zhonglu, 昆仑中路) FREE One or two isolated sections of Xīníng's old city wall still remain, the most accessible being this short stretch within a park on Kunlun Zhonglu. The wall was originally built in 1385, but different

---

ⓘ FULL HOUSE

Scoring a hotel room in Xīníng and popular tourist spots during the summer months can be surprisingly difficult, especially for foreigners as not all places will accept them. Book your room or dorm bed as early as possible, preferably one week in advance, especially in July and August.

---

portions were erected, repaired or left to crumble over subsequent centuries. The wall's remains, an overgrown dirt embankment beside a busy road, aren't all that impressive; however, the tiered pathways that wind through the park make for a pleasant stroll in good weather.

🛏 Sleeping

Xīníng has a wealth of sleeping options and its first foreign five-star hotel, the Sofitel, opened here west of town in 2015.

City Nomad Youth Hostel   HOSTEL $
(2605844103@qq.com; 11th fl, Unit 3, Bldg 6, Nanshan Lu, Jianxin Longyuan Pinnacle Lane Commune, 南山路建新巷陇原叠翠小区6号楼3单元11楼; dm ¥45-50, d without bathroom ¥120; 🔊; 🖥31) Xīníng's newest hostel is run by friendly, English-speaking Tashi. Located in a tatty high-rise slightly south of town, City Nomad is nonetheless a good spot to base yourself. Tibetan decor spruces up the place and rooms are cosy and clean, and there's a good stream of international travellers. Note that there's *only* one shower. Bookings by email only.

The best way to get here is via taxi (¥15) or take bus 31 from the railway station and get off at the Tibetan Medicine Hospital (藏医院) stop, walk back 25m to Jianxìn Xiang (建新巷) and up the road 150m till you see a gated complex on the right. Look for the first blue building on the left and find doorway 3. You can get also bus tickets from a China Post office just to the left of the compound as you exit. As a former guide, Tashi also helps with Tibetan visas and local travel plans.

Qīnghǎi Sāngzhū Youth Hostel   HOSTEL $
(青海桑珠国际青年旅舍, Qīnghǎi Sāngzhū Guójì Qīngnián Lǘshè; 📞189 9704 0278; szhostel@163.com; 94 Huzhu Zhonglu, 互助中路94号; dm/d ¥55/130; @🔊; 🖥32, 33) A spacious hostel with a big lounge decorated with Tibetan artwork. The rooms have comfortable beds and bathrooms are decent too. It's more popular with Chinese backpackers, though some English is spoken. There's traveller information posted on the walls. It's a 2.5km east of the train station, however, so you'll need to take a bus (32 or 33) or taxi to get anywhere.

Sanwant Hotel Xining   HOTEL $$$
(西宁神旺大酒店, Xīníng Shénwàng Dà Jiǔdiàn; 📞0971 820 1111; http://sanwant-xining.hotel.com.tw; 79 Changjiang Lu, 长江路79号; s/d ¥680/780; P🏵@🔊) If you're looking to splash out a little, this international hotel does the trick, with clean rooms, English-speaking staff

QĪNGHǍI EATS

Qīnghǎi's cuisine is rather unique. Influenced by its mix of ethnic populations – Muslim (Huí, Salar and Uighur), Tibetan and Han Chinese – the food you'll eat here is hearty fare with an emphasis on breads, dumplings and lots of lamb. The following are Qīnghǎi staples. To sample, head to the **Mǎzhōng Snack Centre** (马忠美食城, Mǎzhōng Měishíchéng; 11-16 Mojia Jie, 莫家街11-16号; noodles ¥10-18, dishes from ¥25) or **Shuǐjǐng Xiàng** (水井巷; Shuijing Xiang) in Xīníng, where all the options are laid out for the taking.

Miànpiàn (面片) Literally translated as 'noodle slices,' this dish consists of small, flat squares of noodles cooked in a light broth with greens, fresh tomato and sometimes egg and bits of meat. This is a favourite local snack and you'll see small restaurants all over the province with blinking signs boasting the Chinese characters for miànpiàn.

Kǎobǐng (烤饼) These thick bread buns are baked and then further roasted over coal fire and lightly dusted with spicy chilli powder, garlic salt and spices. Order in Muslim restaurants or procure from street vendors, who roast them over coal after dark.

Mómo (馍馍) Tibetan-style dumplings similar to Chinese bāozi (steamed meat buns), typically filled with savoury lamb mince and served with spiced chilli oil. An alternate version is served in hot broth.

Yak milk yoghurt (牦牛酸奶, máoniú suānnǎi) Whether love or hate, visitors usually have a strong reaction to this Tibetan-style yoghurt made from yak's milk. Shops and vendors all over Qīnghǎi sell small portions in plastic cups or bowls, usually served with a sprinkling of rock sugar to balance the tartness. It's a wonderfully fresh dessert or snack. Locals also claim it helps combat altitude sickness.

and a tour desk that can arrange excursions in the area. Rooms are of an international standard, with private bathrooms (and tubs), though like many international hotels in this part of China, the decor is a bit dated. Breakfast included.

✖ Eating

Xīníng has a great range of food, especially Tibetan and Hui Muslim cuisines. For Muslim food head to Dongguan Dajie, near the Grand Mosque, or the northern stretch of Nanxiaojie. Most malls have a food court on the upper floors with easy point-and-choose options.

Elite's Bar & Grill   INTERNATIONAL $
(☑ 138 9747 2199; Qiyi Lu, 七一路; dishes ¥30-80, drinks from ¥20; ⊘ noon-midnight) If you have a hankering for Western food, Elite's extensive menu should do the job. Massive burgers, pulled pork, steaks, salads...Elite's serves it all up. There's a good wine and beer list at decent prices, too. Located 150m east of the Xīníng Bīnguǎn (西宁宾馆).

Ah Ma La   TIBETAN $$
(阿妈啦; 120 Nanshan Donglu, 南山东路120号; dishes ¥15-150; ⊘ 10am-10.30pm) Delish Tibetan food, tacky decor, English-speaking Tibetan boss, picture menu. That pretty much sums

up the Ah Ma La experience. Slide into a booth seat and order up authentic Tibetan dishes such as yak tongue and mómo (馍馍; dumplings) and wash it down with Lhasa beer. The restaurant is along Nanshan Donglu, opposite the Tibetan Hospital.

🍺 Drinking & Nightlife

Open-air beer gardens line both sides of the Nánchuān River between Kunlun Zhonglu and Xiguan Jie, most of which are open from the afternoon till early evening serving big bottles of local beer and snacks.

For a more mellow evening, there's a growing set of cafes, music bars and pubs along Xiadu Dajie between Nanxiao Jie and Huayuan Nanjie near Greenhouse.

★1/2 Sugar   BAR
(Bàn Táng Qù, 半糖趣; Qiyi Lu, Xindadi Huayuan, 七一路 新大地花园; beer from ¥30, coffee from ¥26; ⊘ 1pm-1am; 🛜) Xīníng just upped its hipster game with an unlikely (but cool) craft brewery and cafe. Sitting in a purpose-built complex off a small alley behind Qiyi Jie, knowledgeable staff can recommend and let you sample draft beer from all over China, including their in-house IPA. A large international craft-beer selection is available at reasonable prices.

Xíning

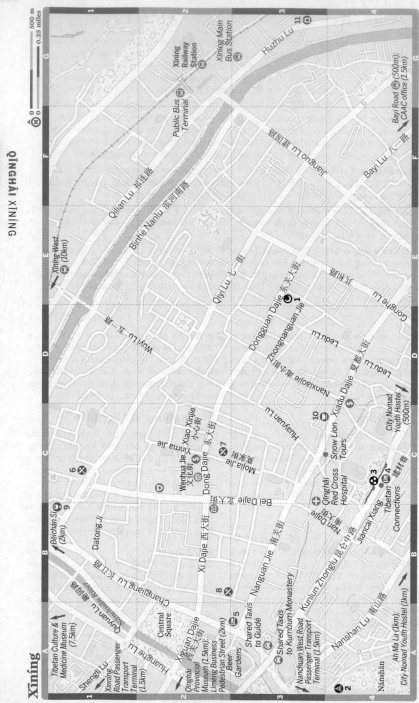

500 m
0.25 miles

Tibetan Culture & Medicine Museum (7.5km)

Xīníng Road Passenger Transport Terminal (1.5km)

Qīnghǎi Provincial Museum (1.5km); Límèng Business Pedestrian Street (2km)

Běichán Sì (2km)

Xīníng West (10km)

Xīníng Railway Station

Xīníng Main Bus Station

Public Bus Terminal

Bāyī Road (500m); CAAC office (1.5km)

Qílián Lù 祁连路

Bīnhé Nánlù 滨河南路

Huzhù Lù

Jiànguó Lù 建国路

Bāyī Lù 一八路

Gōngbeí Lù

Lèdū Lù

Lèdū Lù Xiàdū Dàjiē 夏都大街

Dōngguān Dàjiē 东关大街

Zhōngshānguān Jiē

Nánxiàojiē 南小街

Huáyuán Lù

Qīyī Lù 七一街

Wǔyī Lù

Snow Lion Tours

City Nomad Youth Hostel (500m)

Qīnghǎi Red Cross Hospital

Tibetan Connections

Jiànccái Xiàng

Nán Dàjiē

Kūnlún Zhōnglù 昆仑中路

Nánchuān West Road Passenger Transport Terminal (1.5km)

Shared Taxis to Kumbum Monastery

Nánguān Jiē

Xī Dàjiē 西大街

Běi Dàjiē 北大街

Dōng Dàjiē

Wénhuà Jiē 文化街

Xiǎo Xīnjiē 小心街

Mòjiā Jiē

Shared Taxis to Guìdé

Chánglǐáng Lù 长江路

Datong Ji

Central Square

Huángshí Lù

Nánshān Lù 南山路

Nánshān

Ah Ma La (1km); City Nomad Youth Hostel (3km)

Qūyuán Lù Nánshan River

Xīníng

An ever-expanding menu of Western faves such as burgers and pizza is worth a look at and there's great coffee if beer isn't your thing.

To find the place, walk 200m west from Xīníng Bīnguǎn (西宁宾馆) and turn right into the first unmarked alley and right again into an open compound. The bar is in a grey-bricked complex on the left.

Greenhouse CAFE
(古林坊咖啡, Gǔlínfáng Kāfēi; ☑ 0971 820 2710; 222-22 Xiadu Dajie, 夏都大街222-22号; coffee from ¥25, food ¥33-80; ⊙8:30am midnight; 🛜) Rustic split-level wood interior with smoothies and some of the best coffee in town. You can also munch on pizzas, burgers and sandwiches to a mellow music selection. The building facade was under construction at the time of research.

Liméng Business Pedestrian Street BAR STREET
(Liméng Shāngyèxiàng Bùxíngjiē, 力盟商业步行街; off Wusi Dajie) There's a cluster of decent bars (some with live music) near a 'new' pedestrian street in 3.5km west of town. You'll also find Western cafes such as Starbucks, a couple of malls and a range of modern chain restaurants. It's a ¥10 taxi ride from town and sits between Wusi Dajie and Xiguan Dajie .

🛍 Shopping

Xīníng Tibetan Market MARKET
(西藏市场, Xīzàng Shìchǎng; Xiǎoshāngpǐn Shìchǎng, Huzhu Lu, 互助路小商品市场; ⊙9am-5pm) The four floors of this market are chock-full of Tibetan goods and you'll see groups of monks stopping in to stock up on various Buddhist knick-knacks and attire. A few shops specialise in Tibetan Buddhist music (and instruments), and there are numerous places to score a statue of a Buddha or Bodhisattva or a string of prayer flags.

ℹ Information

Free wi-fi is available in plenty of places.

Tiāntángniǎo Internet (天堂鸟网络, Tiāntángniǎo wǎngluò; Dong Dajie; per hr ¥2-3.50; ⊙24hr) is a basic internet cafe popular with the local gamers.

Bank of China (中国银行, Zhōngguó Yínháng; 22 Dong Dajie, 东大街22号; ⊙9am-5pm Mon-Fri, 10am-4pm Sat & Sun) Has a number of large branches around town that exchange cash and have foreign-friendly ATMs.

ICBC ATM (工商银行, Gōngshāng Yínháng; 55 Nanxiaojie, 南小街55号) Has ATMs that accept foreign cards.

Mystic Tibet Tours (☑182 0971 5464; http://mystictibettours.com; Suite 2082, 24 Bayi Rd, 24号八一路2082室) Excellent agency run by English speaking Tibetan guide Gonkho. Organises tours around Amdo including Amnye Machen. Located 10km east of town. Your best bet is to email or call Gonkho in advance.

Post Office (中国邮政, Zhōngguó Yóuzhèng; cnr Xi Dajie & Bei Dajie, 西大街北大街的路口; ⊙8.30am-6pm)

Public Security Bureau (PSB, 公安局, Gōng'ānjú; 35 Bei Dajie, 北大街35号; ⊙8.30-11.30am & 2.30-5.30pm Mon-Fri) Can extend visas.

Qīnghǎi Red Cross Hospital (青海红十字医院, Qīnghǎi Hóngshízì Yīyuàn; ☑0971 824 7545; Nan Dajie) English-speaking doctors available. Outpatients (门诊部; ménzhěn bù) has a 24-hour pharmacy (药店; yàodiàn).

Snow Lion Tours (☑0971 816 3350; www.snowliontours.com; Office 408, Xiadu Dasha Bldg, Xiadu Dajie, 夏都大厦,夏都大街; ⊙9am-6pm) Run by a knowledgeable English-speaking Tibetan, Wangden; arranges treks, camping with nomads and Tibet permits.

Tibetan Connections (☑189 9720 0974; www.tibetanconnections.com; 12th fl, Bldg 5, International Village Apartments, 2-32 Jiancai Xiang, Guoji Cun Gong Yu, 建材巷国际村公寓5号楼12楼1209室) This Tibetan-run tour company focuses on remoter parts of Amdo and Kham but can arrange trips into Tibet. Prices may be a little higher than local travel agencies

WORTH A TRIP

YÒUNÍNG MONASTERY

Well known throughout the Tibetan world, **Yòuníng Monastery** (佑宁寺, Yòuníng Sì; ☉8am-6pm), a 17th-century hillside monastery in the Hùzhù Tǔzú (互助土族) Autonomous County, is considered one of the greats of the Gelugpa order. The monastery lies at the edge of a forested valley, and many chapels perch wondrously on the sides of a cliff face. Give yourself a couple of hours to explore the entire picturesque area.

Famous for its academies of medicine and astrology, its scholars and its living Buddhas (*tulku*), Yòuníng Monastery (*Rgolung* in Tibetan) was instrumental in solidifying Gelugpa dominance over the Amdo region. The monastery was founded by the Mongolian 4th Dalai Lama, and over time became a religious centre for the local Tǔ (themselves a distant Mongolian people). At its height, over 7000 monks resided here; these days there are probably fewer than 200, all of whom are Tǔ. Expansion works continue in the main complex. Three kilometres up the road from the main complex is a small *kora* that takes you up a smaller temple and up the surrounding hills.

A daily bus (¥12, 90 minutes, 10.30am) departs from Bayi Road Bus Station. Otherwise, take a bus to Píng'ān (¥8, 40 minutes) from Xīníng's Public Bus Terminal. From there, you'll need to hire a taxi (one-way/return ¥70/100, 30 minutes), Alternately, if you have a group, you could hire a private car or taxi (return ¥400) from Xīníng. The monastery is about 25km north of Píng'ān.

but staff speak English and are good to deal with. The agency is located below the Lete Youth Hostel on the 12th floor.

❶ Getting There & Away

AIR

The airport is 27km east of the city. There are daily flights to Běijīng (¥1250), Chéngdū (¥990), Shànghǎi (¥1800), Yùshù (¥1500), Golmud (¥1350), Tiānjīn (¥950) and Xī'ān (¥650). There are now daily direct flights to Lhasa (¥1330).

The **Civil Aviation Administration of China** (CAAC, 中国民航, Zhōngguó Mínháng; ☑0971 813 3333; 32 Bayi Xilu; ☉8.30am-5.30pm) has a booking office on Bayi Lu near the Bayi Road bus station. Shuttle buses (¥21, 35 minutes) leave hourly from there, the main bus station and from outside the Qīnghǎi Bīnguǎn (青海宾馆), just west of town across the river (¥10 taxi ride from town).

BUS

Xīníng has way too many bus stations for a city of its size. Most leave from the **Xīníng Main Bus Station** (西宁客运车站, Xīníng Kèyùn Chēzhàn; 200m east of the main train station) beside the main railway station, but some buses leave from from one of the other three (!) stations.

From Xining Main Bus Station, there are buses to the following:

Bird Island ¥66, 4½ hours, 7.45am

Chákǎ ¥60, five hours, five daily (8am, 9.45am, 11am, 12.35pm, 3.30pm)

Golmud ¥165, 15 hours, four daily (2pm, 5pm, 5.30pm, 6pm)

Hēimǎhé ¥44, four hours, two daily (8.30am, 9.30am)

Hùzhù Běishān National Forest Park ¥30, four hours, two daily (noon, 2pm)

Kanbula National Park ¥23, 2½ hours, 10.30am and every 30 minutes from noon to 5pm

Kumbum Monastery ¥6, 45 minutes, every 20 minutes from 7am to 6.30pm

Lánzhōu ¥65, three hours, hourly from 7.20am to 6.30pm

Línxià ¥61, five hours, hourly from 7.15am to 10.15am

Qīnghǎi Lake ¥34, three hours, hourly from 8am to 6pm

Tóngrén ¥31, four hours, every 40 minutes from 7.30am to 5.30pm

Xīhǎi Zhèn ¥25, 2½ hours, every 25 minutes from 7.30am to 5.30pm

Yùshù Seat/sleeper ¥191/211, 15 hours, hourly from 11am to 6pm

Of the other three stations:

Bayi Road Bus Station (八一路汽车站, Bāyī Lù Qìchē Zhàn; cnr Bayi Lu & Huangzhong Lu, 八一路和湟中路路口) runs buses to Tóngrén (¥35, four hours, every 30 minutes from 7.30am to 5pm) and Yòuníng Temple (¥12, 70 minutes, 10.30am)

Nanchuan West Road Passenger Transport Terminal (南川西路客运站, Nánchuān Xīlù Kèyùn Zhàn; 4 Nanchuan Xilu, 南川西路4号) has buses to Guìdé (¥26, two hours, every 20 minutes from 7.35am to 5.30pm) and Mǎduō (¥100, eight hours, 8am)

Public Bus Terminal (公脚车站, Gōngjiāo Chēzhàn) has a bus to Píng'ān (¥5, two hours, every five minutes) and also connects with terminal station for local buses.

The **Xinning Road Passenger Transport Terminal** (新宁路客运站, Xīnníng Lù Kèyùn

Zhàn; Xinning Lu, 新宁路), 2.5km northwest of the city, is the least useful station. There are buses from here to Lèdū (¥21, one hour, every 15 minutes from 7am to 6.45pm).

TRAIN

The Xīníng Railway Station (火车站; Huǒchē Zhàn) reopened in September 2015, with new high-speed rail services passing through here between Lánzhōu in Gānsù province and Ürümqi in Xīnjiāng. Regional trains also start/stop at Xīníng West Railway Station (西火车站; Xī Huǒchē Zhàn), about 10km west of the city centre.

Lhasa-bound trains pass through Xīníng (hard/soft sleeper ¥500/800, 22 hours) on their way towards the now world famous Qīnghǎi–Tibet Railway stretch of China's rail network. Make sure to have all your Tibet papers in order and get tickets way in advance.

Other destinations from Xīníng:

Běijīng Hard/soft sleeper ¥288/500, 18 to 24 hours

Chéngdū Hard/soft sleeper ¥332/478, 25 hours

Golmud Seat/hard sleeper ¥114/220, eight to 11 hours

Lánzhōu Seat ¥40, 2½ hours

Xī'ān Seat/hard sleeper ¥115/230, 10 to 14 hours

❶ Getting Around

City buses cost ¥1 per ride. A handy route is bus 1, which runs from **Bayi Road Bus Station** along Dongguan Dajie before heading north to the nearby Tibetan Culture Museum, a 45-minute ride.

Taxis are easy to flag and cost ¥8 for the first 3km and ¥1.40 per kilometre thereafter. Ignore the touts at stations.

While it's best to catch buses from the stations, some travellers prefer to take a shared taxi/minibus to **Guìdé** (per person ¥70; ⊙ leaves when full,) or **Kumbum Monastery** (per person ¥10; ⊙ leaves when full); for both destinations you can find drivers near or in the parking space under the bridge at the corner of Kunlun Zhonglu and Changjiang Lu.

Around Xīníng

Qīnghǎi Lake 青海湖

China's largest lake, Qīnghǎi Lake (Qīnghǎi Hú; Lake Kokonor; elevation 3600m) is nearly six times the size of Singapore and a huge draw for large tour groups. While it can be maddeningly difficult to get to the actual shoreline, views of the lake backdropped by mountains still make the trek out worthwhile.

Plenty of Chinese tourists come in for whistle-stop one- or two-day guided tours, but the lake is now popular with more adventurous sorts who rent bikes for a more leisurely circuit around the lake. If the latter appeals, head to Xīhǎi Zhèn (西海镇) where you can rent good-quality bikes and gear.

Avoid the lake on the weekends and public holidays when traffic slows to a crawl. Sights are organised by proximity to Xīníng.

⊙ Sights

Chákǎ Salt Lake LAKE

Located 25km west of the main lake past Heimǎhé, **Chákǎ Salt Lake** (茶卡盐湖; Chákǎ Yánhú; ¥50) is a popular side trip for a stunning optical illusion that occurs between noon and 4pm daily. On a clear day, you can capture amazing photographs of skies and people mirrored onto the lake's surface.

In order to get the best portraits on the lake, wear something bright (yellow, blue and red are great). Black and grey colours are hipster cool but they don't show up very well in images.

A daily train (¥62.50, five hours, 8.25am) from Xīníng to Chákǎ drops you just at the tourist entrance of the lake. It returns at 5.30pm so you could do the salt lake as a long day trip if you aren't coming from the main lake. Buses from Xīníng (¥60, five hours, 8am, 9.25am and noon) drop you at the Chákǎ town, 2km from the lake, where waiting taxis will take you the rest of the way for ¥30.

From Heimǎhé, you can flag down a bus to Chákǎ (roughly noon and 1.25pm) or hire a private car (¥320 return).

Bird Island ISLAND

(鸟岛, Niǎo Dǎo; ¥115) This island (now in fact a peninsula) on China's largest lake is the breeding ground for thousands of wild geese, gulls, cormorants, sandpipers, extremely rare black-necked cranes and other bird species. Perhaps the most interesting are the bar-headed geese that migrate over the Himalaya to spend winter on the Indian plains, and have been spotted flying at altitudes of 10,000m.

The island is located on the western side of the lake, about 300km from Xīníng. The best time to visit is from March to late May, when migratory birds have stopped over to nest.

A daily bus (¥66, five hours, 7.45am) leaves from Xīníng's main bus station. From Heimǎhé, you can flag down a bus to Bird Island (roughly 11.45am) or hire a private car (¥340 return).

🛏 Sleeping

Qīnghǎi Hú Jīshí

Guójì Qīngnián Lǚshè HOSTEL $
(青海湖奇石国际青年旅舍; ☏0974 851 9313;
dm ¥50-70, d ¥180-220; 🛜) Handy hostel with
clean rooms, located at the eastern end of
the main street in Heīmǎhé. It's nothing
special but you can find other travellers for
shared trips to Bird Island (¥80 per person
or ¥340 per car) and Chákǎ Salt Lake (¥80
per person or ¥320 per car). Staff also organise a driver to take you to the shore for
sunrise (¥25 per person).

ℹ Getting There & Away

One way to see the sights around Qīnghǎi Lake
is by hiring a private car and driver (¥500 to
¥600 per day). Alternately, all-inclusive overnight stays and multiday trips can be organised
through travel agencies in Xīníng. Touts abound
at every bus station in Xīníng; bargain hard and
you could score a great deal on a shared taxi.

Alternatively, you can take a bus from the
Xīníng bus station to Xīhǎi Zhèn (西海镇), from
where you can rent bikes to tour the lake.

If you want to do the lake via public transport,
there's a new daily train service that goes from
Xīníng to Chákǎ (¥62.50, 8.25am, five hours). If you
take this route, you can work your way back towards
Xīníng across two days by taking a bus back and
stopping along Heīmǎhé (黑马河), zipping up to
Bird Island and then looping back down to Èrláng-
jiàn Scenic Area and then back to Xīníng.

Xīhǎi Zhèn

🕿 0970 / POP 12,000

A tidy little town, 43km east of Qīnghǎi
Lake, Xīhǎi Zhèn is where travellers come
to rent bicycles for a tour round the lake.
There's not much to see in town, so plan
on getting here early, picking up your bikes,
grabbing supplies and then hitting the road.

Xīhǎi Zhèn is small and easy to get around
on foot. With more than 20 bicycle-rental
stores, you're spoilt for choice.

Bike rental ranges from ¥80 to ¥180, depending on the model. All are solid brand-
name bikes and rental includes panniers,
helmet, tool kit and spares. The sun gets
really harsh so be sure to bring sunscreen,
long-sleeved riding gear, sunglasses and a
face bandana.

The full circuit round the lake is 360km
and takes four days but you can drop your
bikes off at various stops along the lake if
you don't fancy riding all the way. Ask the
store where you drop them off. Stores can
also suggest itineraries and offer discounted

accommodation with hotel partners around
the lake.

Qīnghǎi Hú Zìxíngchē Jìbīnguǎn CYCLING
(青海湖自行车骑宾管; ☏138 9710 9209, 0970
864 2113; www.qhhzxc.cn; Menyuan Lu; bike rental
per day ¥80-180; ⊙8am-6pm) The town's largest bicycle-rental store has the best selection
of models (including one they designed
themselves) and all the gear you'll need for
a tour around the lake. Staff are friendly
and can help with planning your journey
although English is limited.

From the bus station, head east and after 100m make a right at the T-intersection.
This store is behind a gate: you can't miss it.

Hǎiběi Bīnguǎn HOTEL $$
(海北宾馆; ☏0970 864 2648; 17 Yintan Lu; d
¥158-258; 🛜) If you happen to get stuck in
town for the night, this is the only hotel that
accepts foreigners. The cheaper rooms in
the older wing are a little dated but clean,
while the pricier rooms feature flat-screen
TVs and fresher fittings.

The main bus station is on the east end of
Yuanzi Lu (原子路). There are regular buses to
Xīníng (¥25, two hours) from 7.30am to 5pm.

Kumbum Monastery   塔尔寺

One of the great monasteries of the Gelugpa
(Yellow Hat) sect of Tibetan Buddhism, **Kum-
bum Monastery** (Tǎ'ěr Sì; ¥80; ⊙8.30am-6pm)
was built in 1577 on hallowed ground – the
birthplace of Tsongkhapa, founder of the sect.
It's of enormous historical significance, and
hundreds of monks still live here but, perhaps
because it's such a big tourist draw, the atmos-
phere can feel a bit overrun. The artwork and
architecture, however, remain impressive.

Nine temples are open, each with its own
characteristics. The most important is the
Grand Hall of Golden Tiles (大金瓦殿; Dà-
jīnwǎ Diàn), where an 11m-high *chörten* (Ti-
betan stupa) marks the spot of Tsongkhapa's
birth. You'll see pilgrims walking circuits
of the building and prostrating outside the
entrance. Also worth seeking out is the
Yak Butter Scripture Temple (酥油画馆;
Sūyóuhuà Guǎn), which houses sculptures
of human figures, animals and landscapes
carved out of yak butter.

Kumbum is located 27km from Xīníng in
the town of Huángzhōng. Buses (¥6, 35 min-
utes) leave every 20 minutes from the Xīníng
Main Bus Station (p898) starting at 7am. Get
off at the last stop and walk up the hill to the
monastery. The last bus back is at 7pm.

> **WORTH A TRIP**
>
> ## KANBULA NATIONAL PARK
>
> The desert scenery outside of Tóngrén comes to a pinnacle in **Kanbula National Park** (坎布拉国家森林公园, Kǎnbùlā Guójiā Sēnlín Gōngyuán; incl bus & boat tour ¥240; ⊙ 8am-6pm), where flaming-red mountains meet the turquoise waters of a reservoir created by the damming of the Yellow River. A nervous-sweat-inducing road snakes up through the park's peaks, past sleepy Tibetan villages and colourful prayer flags waving high on the wind.
>
> Alas, the park no longer allows private cars unless you're a) coming from Guìdé or b) in a local car. This means you're either shunted on a pricey but decent fixed bus-and-boat tour (roughly three hours) or you can skip the entrance fee and fully experience the park, including plenty of photo stops, by going with a local taxi driver (¥100 if you find at least one other person to share with).
>
> Otherwise, find a private driver to bring you here from Guìdé (¥400 per day). To get here from Xīníng, take the 10.30am bus to Kanbula from the main bus station. You'll be dropped 7km from the park entrance. Taxis will take you there for ¥10. The last bus returns at 4.30pm or so so make sure you get out early otherwise you'll have to stay the night where the bus drops you or hitch back.

Hùzhù Běishān Forest National Park 互助北山 国际森林公园

📞 0972 / POP 11,149

Here is proof, should you need it, that Qīnghǎi has incredibly diverse landscapes: an alpine forest located 100km north of Xīníng with an elevation that spans 2200m to 4000m. Within are farming communities, mountain goats, family restaurants, birch forests, waterfalls, lakes and plenty of hiking opportunities. The **Hùzhù Běishān national park** (Hùzhù Běishān Guójiā Sēnlín Gōngyuán; ¥82, incl mandatory transport ticket) is popular with Xīníng folk seeking a weekend retreat.

Your ticket includes access to a tourist car that zips across several stops and you can hop on and off anywhere within the park. Some of the more interesting sites includes a couple of waterfalls (瀑布; *pùbù*) where you can soak your feet, and the Sleeping Buddha (睡佛; Shuìfó), a rock that looks like, well, a sleeping Buddha. If you're game, you can hike 7km up to the tiny Heavenly Lake (Tianchí; 天池) at 3000m elevation. Hiking opportunities abound: join grazing goats and look out for chubby marmots.

You can do homestays with locals (¥100) or stay at the Cáilúnduō Sēnlín Nóngzhuāng, a lodge with dorm beds and private rooms.

A sprawling lodge, **Cáilúnduō Sēnlín Nóngzhuāng** (才伦多森林农庄; 📞 155 9722 9788; cailunduo@sina.com; dm/d ¥60/260, family ¥100 per bed; P 🎐 🎎) was built by a local who made good as an interior designer in Wúhàn before settling with his family back here.

The eclectic compound houses 19 comfortable rooms, a BBQ patio, riverside pagodas (for 'daydreaming') and a restaurant wing. While short on English, the owners are high on service. Sample the in-house brewed highland barley *báijiǔ* (clear liquor) and pick local dishes (from ¥15) such as yak and wild mushrooms from an English menu. Get the tourist car to drop you off at Cáilúnduō (才伦多), 4km from the main gate. There are some good trails behind the lodge that lead up the back mountain for good views.

From Xīníng, there's a daily 9.45am bus (¥28.50, four hours) from the main bus station. It may stop in the town of Hùzhù for 45 minutes so don't panic. Coming back, there's a 4pm bus that returns to Xīníng.

Tóngrén 同仁

📞 0973 / POP 308,583

Tóngrén (Rebkong in Tibetan) is set on the slopes of the wide and fertile Gu-chu river valley. For several centuries now, the villages outside the monastery town of Tóngrén have been famous for producing some of the Tibetan world's best *thangkas* (scroll paintings) and painted statues, so much so that an entire school of Tibetan art is named after the town. Visiting Wútún Sì monastery not only gives you a chance to meet the artists, but also to purchase a painting or two, fresh off the easel.

The local populace is a mix of Tibetans and Tǔ. Aside from the monasteries, the valley and surrounding hills are easily explored on foot.

◎ Sights

Wútún Sì MONASTERY

(吾屯寺; per monastery ¥30) This two-monastery complex is the place to head if you're interested in Tibetan art. The **Upper (Yango) Monastery** (吾屯上寺; Wútún Shàngsì) is closest to Tóngrén, while the **Lower (Mango) Monastery** (吾屯下寺; Wútún Xiàsì) is larger and may offer the chance to see monks painting. The monks will show you around and you can usually ask to see a showroom or workshop. The resident artists are no amateurs – commissions for their *thangka* come in all the way from Lhasa.

Artwork is usually of an exceptionally high quality, but expect to pay hundreds of rénmínbì for the smallest painting, thousands for a poster-sized one and tens or even hundreds of thousands for the largest pieces. There are a handful of showrooms outside the Lower Monastery where you can browse and buy.

The Lower Monastery is easily recognisable by eight large *chörten* out front and a new triple Buddha statue. While there, check out the 100-year-old **Jampa Lhakhang** (Jampa Temple) and the newer chapels dedicated to Chenresig and Tsongkhapa.

The Upper Monastery includes a massive modern *chörten* as well as the old *dukhang* (assembly hall) and the new chapel dedicated to Maitreya (Shampa in Amdo dialect). The interior murals painted by local artists are superb.

To get here, take a minibus (¥3 per seat) from the intersection just uphill from Tóngrén bus station ticket office or a taxi (¥15). Hail a minibus on its way back to town to avoid a dusty walk back.

Gomar Gompa BUDDHIST MONASTERY

(郭麻日寺, Guōmárì Sì; ¥10; ⊙8am-6pm) Across the Gu-chu river valley from Wútún Sì is this mysterious 400-year-old monastery that resembles a medieval walled village. There are 130 monks in residence living in white-washed mud-walled courtyards and there are a few temples you can visit. The huge *chörten* (Tibetan stupa) outside the monastery entrance was built in the 1980s and is the biggest in Amdo. You can climb it, but remember to always walk clockwise. There are photos of the 14th Dalai Lama at the top.

To get here, turn left down a side road as you pass the westernmost of the eight *chörten* outside Wútún Sì's Lower Monastery. Follow the road 1km across the river and turn right at the end on a main road. Then head up

the track towards the giant *chörten*. Further up the valley is **Gasar Gompa**, marked by its own distinctive eight *chörtens*. Note that women may not be allowed into the Gomar Gompa or Gasar Gompa.

Lóngwù Sì MONASTERY

(隆务寺, Rongwo Gonchen Gompa; Dehelong Nanlu, 德合隆南路; ¥60; ⊙8am-6pm) Tóngrén's main monastery is a huge and rambling maze of renovated chapels and monks' residences, dating from 1301. It's well worth a wander, and you'll need one or two hours to see everything. Your ticket includes entry into six main halls, although you may be able to take a peek inside others, too.

🛏 Sleeping

Hēpíng Bīnguǎn HOTEL $

(和平宾馆; ☎0973 872 4188; Maixiu Lu, 麦秀路; d from ¥120) Offers large clean rooms overlooking a car park. Good value for money, and the cheerful family owners will often offer discounts.

★ **Rebgong Norbang Travel Inn** HOTEL $$

(热贡诺尔邦旅游客栈, Règòng Nuò'ěrbāng Lǚyóu Kèzhàn; ☎0973 872 6999, 138 9753 5393; www.nuoerbang.com; Xuelian Donglu, 雪莲东路; d ¥188-300, ste ¥400-500; [P][@][⊛]) The Norbang is a surprisingly good choice in Tóngrén and offers fantastic value with its 'almost' boutique-hotel stylings. Forgo the generic Western-style rooms, and pay a little extra to bunk in a traditional Tibetan-style room with wooden platform beds and sparkling private bathrooms. Breakfast is ¥10 extra.

🍴 Eating

Restaurants come and go quickly here. There are a variety of options along Jiānzhā Lù (尖扎路) including noodles, hotpot and more. Déhélóng Nánlù (德合隆南路) leading to the Lóngwù Sì is also filled with food and other interesting stores.

Língzhūmā Zàng Cāntīng TIBETAN $$

(岭珠妈藏餐厅; ☎138 939 6688; Tiewu Xiao Qu, Regong Gongyu Yi Lou, 铁吾小区热贡公寓一楼; dishes ¥20-120; ⊙10am-10pm) There's construction going on next door but this brand-new Tibetan restaurant located across the bridge in the eastern portion of town delivers the goods. Walk past a row of prayer wheels, slide into a booth seat and chose from a range of delicious dishes including *momos* (Tibetan-style dumplings), yak meat and more. Yes, there's Lhasa beer too. A taxi from town costs ¥5.

ℹ Information

China Construction Bank ATM (建设银行,
Jiànshè Yínháng; 47 Zhongshan Lu, 中山路47
号) Foreign-card friendly.

ℹ Getting There & Around

The scenery on the road from Xīníng is awesome, as it follows a tributary of the Yellow River
through steep-sided gorges. There are regular
daily buses to Xīníng (¥40, four hours). A freeway
is being constructed and when complete should
cut driving time by an hour. For Xiàhé (¥28, three
hours, 8am) and Línxià (¥45, four hours, 8am)
try to buy your ticket one day in advance.

The city is easy to get around on foot but taxis
cost ¥5 for most trips if you get lazy.

Guìdé 贵德

♪ 0974 / POP 101,771

As the Yellow River (黄河; Huáng Hé) flows
down from the Tibetan Plateau it makes a
series of sharp bends, powering its way past
ancient Guìdé, where the water turns turquoise. The river, popular with Chinese tourists, was to provide a tourism lifeline to the
town and the government's plans began with
the old town (古城; gǔchéng), still largely enclosed within its crumbling 10m-high mud
walls. Buildings were knocked down, and
faux new-old ones were built – but the prom-
ised tourism boom never quite got there.

Guìdé, stuck in limbo between boom town
and old town, is the perfect epitome of modern China. Walk past the slick facade in the
old town and you'll find crumbling ruins and
residents clinging on to life in packed earth-
en houses. It's the space between the old and
new which makes Guìdé so intriguing. Wandering along the remains of the Qing dynasty
walls through the lanes behind the old town
towards the Yellow River offers a glimpse at
China that will no longer be here in the next
couple of years. So get here while you can.

◉ Sights

★**Guìdé National Geological Park** PARK
(贵德国家地质公园, Guìdé Guójiā Dìzhì
Gōngyuán; 101 Provincial Rd, 省道101; ¥100; ▣11)
In the stunning multicoloured clay scenery
of Dānxiá Canyon (丹霞峡谷; Dānxiá Xiágǔ),
this geopark offers walking trails in among
red and orange hills that have eroded into
other-worldly shapes. Set against the contrasting blue Qīnghǎi skies and teal waters
of the Yellow River, this is a lovely spot to
spend an afternoon wandering and taking

photos, or exploring the peculiar geology of
this part of the Tibetan Plateau.

There's a museum with decent signs and
maps in English, and well kept paths allow
for easy access to the geological formations,
making this an easy walk rather than a
back-country hike. Admission includes a
Chinese-speaking guide (which you can
politely decline) and you can also save ¥20
by declining the tourist electric car (观光
车; Guānguāng Chē). Once inside, there are
opportunities to go off-piste and clamber up
the dirt mounds between canyons but do
take care as you're on your own. The park
also has the Tōngtiānxiá (通天峡) trail that's
under renovation at the time of research but
once open will take you to the top of one of
the peaks for views of the Yellow River.

The park is located about 20km north of
Guìdé. A taxi will cost around ¥40 or you can
wait at the exit gate of the bus station and
get on a bus heading towards Xīníng and
tell the driver you're stopping here. Coming
from Xīníng, the bus to Guìdé can also drop
you off. Local bus 11 stops here.

China Fortune Wheel BUDDHIST SITE
(中华福运轮, Zhōnghuá Fúyùnlún; Nanbinhe Lu,
南滨河路; ¥80; ◉8.30am-6pm) This enormous, gold-plated Tibetan prayer wheel is
turned with the aid of rushing water from
the Yellow River (along with some elbow
grease). The prayer wheel is 27m tall, 10m in
diameter and weighs 200 tonnes, earning it
a spot in the *Guinness World Records* as the
world's largest prayer wheel.

Inside the wheel are 200 copies of the
Kangyur text, and the base contains a large
prayer hall. Near the wheel is a museum of
Tibetan artefacts.

The wheel is located in a dedicated
park along the Yellow River, which can be
reached on foot by following Huanghe Nanlu behind Yùhuáng Pavilion and turning left
at the large suspension bridge (itself a great
spot for catching sunset over the river). You
can rent bikes in the old town or at the start
of Nanbinhe Lu (from ¥15 per hour) to cycle
along the Yellow River.

⌂ Sleeping

Qīnghǎi Guìdé Hot Spring Hotel HOTEL $$
(温泉宾馆, Wēnquán Bīnguǎn; ♪0974 855 3534;
355 Yingbin Lu, 迎宾路355号; d/ste ¥200/550;
❀@◉❀) While the hotel is starting to
show its age, it's a decent choice for foreign-
ers, with clean rooms, a heated pool (¥50
per use), spa and pleasant garden grounds.

There are no hot springs on-site; instead the hotel claims to have piped water from the springs into its pool and taps. Located 1km west of the bus station.

Peninsular Holiday Inn   HOTEL $$$
(半岛假日酒店, Bàndǎo Jiàrì Jiǔdiàn; ☑ 0974 855 8555; 64 Nan Dajie, 南大街64号; d ¥388; ☎) Centrally located on Nan Dajie leading up to the old town, the Peninsular is a brand-new hotel with large rooms, comfy beds (they're not your usual hard Chinese mattresses), sparkling Western-style bathrooms and friendly staff. Discounts bring doubles down to ¥228. Rates include breakfast.

ℹ Information

China Construction Bank ATM (建设银行, Jiànshè Yínháng; 14 Yingbin Xilu, 迎宾西路) Accepts foreign cards.

ℹ Getting There & Around

There are regular buses to Xīníng (¥26, two hours) and several other destinations around Qīnghǎi. Bus 11 (¥5) goes to the Guìdé National Geological Park.

The old town is 1.5km from the bus station. Turn left out of the station on Yingbin Xilu, then left again along Nan Dajie and past the old town gate to arrive at Bei Dajie. Taxis and three-wheel motorised rickshaws ply the streets of Guìdé. Most short trips cost ¥5 to ¥10.

Yùshù   玉树

☑ 0976 / POP 380,000 / ELEVATION 3681M

Until the spring of 2010, Yùshù (Jyekundo is the name of the town while Yùshù is the prefecture) and its surrounding areas gained popularity as one of Qīnghǎi's best adventure-travel destinations. All that changed on 14 April 2010, when a 7.1-magnitutude earthquake struck, killing 2698 people (although some believe the true figure across the whole region to be more like 20,000).

After the earthquake most of Jyekundo's buildings were pulled down and an army of construction workers arrived to rebuild the city. A shiny new town centre built in Tibetan-style architecture (with a modern Chinese twist) was officially reopened in 2014. Jyekundo is slowly bouncing back: it's a great launching pad for the grasslands, mountain passes, monasteries, rivers and diversity of flora and fauna nearby.

Yùshù still has a long way to go, but with improved infrastructure and support from the government, the future looks bright.

◉ Sights

Seng-ze Gyanak Mani Wall   BUDDHIST SITE
(新寨嘉那嘛呢石堆, Xīnzhài Jiānà Mání Shíduī; Xīnzhài Village) FREE Completely rebuilt after suffering extensive damage in the 2010 earthquake, this site is thought to be the world's largest *mani* wall (piles of stones with Buddhist mantras carved or painted on them). Founded in 1715, the *mani* comprises an estimated 2.5 billion mantras, piled one on top of the other over hundreds of square meters. It's an astonishing sight that (literally) grows as you circumambulate the wall with the pilgrims.

While seemingly touristy, the *mani* wall is an important religious site for locals, many of whom visit daily. All the *mani* stones are quarried from the hillside opposite and it's common practice for locals to purchase the locally carved stones to add to the wall. Simple ones cost between ¥1 and ¥10 while massive slabs with prayer chants cost well over ¥10,000. The earthquake unearthed *mani* stones used by the Chinese for building works: these were repatriated to the pile! A taxi from the town centre costs ¥10 or it's a 2km walk east.

Drogon Gompa   BUDDHIST MONASTERY
(歇武寺, Xiēwǔ Sì; ⊙ 8am-6pm) This Sakyapaschool monastery includes the scary *gönkhang* (protector temple). Set atop a hill, it is adorned with snarling stuffed wolves and tantric masks. Only men may enter the temple.

Jyekundo Dondrubling Monastery   MONASTERY
(结古寺, Jié Gǔsì; ⊙ 8am-6pm) FREE First built in 1398, the Jyekundo Dondrubling Monastery suffered heavy damage from the 2010 earthquake (the main prayer hall was completely destroyed and a number of resident monks were killed). The monastery has since been rebuilt and it's dramatically located in a ridge perched above town.

It takes about 25 minutes to walk the 1.5km from town, or a taxi costs ¥20. When walking up the hill, stick to the road as the pathway is home to some aggressive wild dogs. Rabies shots are not fun.

✹ Festivals & Events

Horse Festival   CULTURAL
(Yùshù Sàimǎ Jié, 玉树赛马节; ⊙ late Jul) Yùshù's spectacular three-day horse festival features traditional horse and yak races, Tibetan wrestling, archery, shooting and dance. The festival is held at different parts

of the county each year, with a mega, multi-county affair occurring every four to five years. Check the latest before you make this part of your itinerary.

🛏 Sleeping

Yùshù has been rebuilt and hotels abound. Competition has meant that prices are reasonable, though quality, and wi-fi access, might differ. A hostel is slated to open soon, so do check if you want a budget option.

Pearl Business Hotel   HOTEL $$
(明珠商务宾馆, Míngzhū Shāngwù Bīnguǎn; ☑ 0976 881 1177; 33 Qionglong Lu, 琼龙路33号; d ¥280; 📶) This hotel has an intimate feel with all the regular amenities and bright, clean bathrooms. There's 24-hour hot water and rooms come with hairdryers and high-speed broadband connection. Prices are negotiable, so ask to see a room first.

★ Gesar Palace Hotel   HOTEL $$$
(Yùshù Gésàěr Wángfǔ Fàndiàn, 玉树格萨尔土府饭店; ☑ 0976 882 1999; Minzhu Lu, 民主路; d ¥500-1000; 📶🅿) Located 100m west of the town square, and towering overs the local buildings, is the town's best hotel. Traditional Tibetan decor greets you in the cavernous lobby. Rooms feature comfortable beds, tasteful dark-wood panels and modern toilets. Service is rough round the edges, but the comfort levels makes it a good choice. Discounts bring rooms down to ¥290. Includes breakfast.

ℹ Information

Gesartour (☑ 139 0976 9192; www.gesartour. com) The best way to see the region is via a private vehicle, and English-speaking Tibetan manager Tsebrtim can organise a bunch of different options based on your interests. You'll get a great wealth of regional and Tibetan knowledge from Tsebrtim and his guides.

ℹ Getting There & Away

AIR
Yùshù Bātáng Airport is 25km south of town. There are pricey daily flights to Xīníng (¥1500), with continuing service to Xī'ān (¥1800). There are also flights to Chéngdū (¥1140, four flights a week) and Lhasa (¥2000, four flights a week) with plans for a direct service from Běijīng in the near future.

BUS
Yùshù's rebuilt **long-distance bus terminal** (玉树长途客运站, Yùshù Chángtú Kèyùn Zhàn; Xihang Lu, 西航路), in combination with a new stretch of highway connecting it to Xīníng (seat/

sleeper ¥191/211, 8am, 9am, noon, 1pm, 4pm, 5pm, 5.30pm, 6pm), reduces travel time to just 12 hours.

Buses for Chéngdū (¥500) go from the **Yùshù Provincial Bus Station** (玉树州客运公司, Yùshù Zhōu Kèyùn Gōngsī; Xīnzhài Village, 新寨村) in Xīnzhài (新寨) Village, 2km east of town.

Long-distance minibuses depart from outside the long-distance bus terminal, bound for Nangchen (¥50, three to four hours) but leaving only when full. Vehicles also depart when full for Gānzī (¥170, five to seven hours) in Sìchuān. Ask around for other destinations. Minibuses for other parts of Qīnghǎi, including Nangchen, also leave from another minivan square located on Shuangyong Jie (双拥街), 550m north of the long-distance bus terminal.

ℹ Getting Around

A taxi to the airport is ¥50. Airport buses meet flights and cost ¥20 into town. Local bus routes 2, 3 and 4 (¥1) connect the main areas of town via three stations: Zhā Xīkē (扎西科), Fó Xuéyuàn (佛学院) and Xī Háng (西杭). You need to hail the bus for it to stop, and they run infrequently. Taxis are prevalent and fares start at ¥10, rising steeply if you head anywhere out of town.

Princess Wencheng Temple　文成公主庙

A small but busy temple, 15km south of Yùshù, **Princess Wencheng Temple** (Wénchéng Gōngzhǔ Miào; ⊗8am-6pm) FREE is dedicated to the Tang dynasty Chinese Princess Wencheng, who was instrumental in converting her husband and Tibetan king, Songtsen Gampo, to Buddhism in the 7th century. The temple marks the spot where the princess (and possibly the king) paused for a month en route from Xī'ān to Lhasa.

Said to be the oldest Buddhist temple in Qīnghǎi, the inner chapel has a rock carving (supposedly self-arising) of Vairocana (Nampa Namse in Tibetan), the Buddha of primordial wisdom, which allegedly dates from the 8th century. To the left is a statue of King Songtsen Gampo.

The temple, which suffered minor damage from the 2010 Yùshù earthquake, is small, and few linger in it for long. Look around the surrounding rock faces for old rock and scripture carvings. Do allow time to explore the nearby hills. Here a sprawling spider's web of blue, red, yellow, white and pink prayer flags runs up the slopes, down the slopes and over the ravine, covering every inch of land.

A steep trail (a popular *kora* route for pilgrims) ascends from the end of the row of eight *chörtens* (Tibetan stupas) to the left of the temple. At the end of the trail head up the grassy side valley for some great hiking and stunning open views.

Private minibuses (¥200 return) depart from outside the long-distance bus terminal in Yùshù, or a taxi costs about ¥100 return.

Nangchen   囊谦

♫ 0976 / POP 3630M

The scenic county of Nangchen (Nángqiān), a former Tibetan kingdom, is the end of the line for most travellers. The drive from Yùshù to the dusty little county capital of Sharda (香达镇; Xiāngdá Zhèn; 3630m), colloquially referred to as Nangchen, takes you past some incredibly diverse landscapes filled with mountains, valleys, monasteries, rushing rivers and a plethora of animals and flora. You'll be tempted to stop the driver to take photos along every bend in the road.

Further south is the Qīnghǎi–Tibet border, with roads to Riwoche and Chamdo, but foreigners aren't allowed access. As you approach Nangchen, you'll pass through the 'new' town, 90% of whose buildings are unoccupied. Everything happens in the old town where the bus drops you.

◉ Sights

Gading Gompa   BUDDHIST MONASTERY
(嘎丁寺, Gādīng Sì; ⊙8am-6pm) Nestled on a piece of land within a horseshoe bend in the Dzichu River, Gading makes for one of the most stunning photos you could take in the region. The monastery itself is nothing special, but hike up the hill opposite for views across both sides of the valley. When you're done, pitch a tent and have a picnic along the river. Gading Gompa is 15km from Nangchen. A car will cost ¥350 return.

Dana Gompa   BUDDHIST MONASTERY
(达那寺, Dánǎ Sì; ⊙8am-6pm) The stunning Dana Monastery is remote and the road out from Nangchen takes you across a valley towards 4000m elevation. Once there, you'll find the province's largest nunnery. Getting out here is expensive and drivers will ask ¥1200 for the 320km return journey. It can be included on a tour itinerary.

Gar Gompa   BUDDHIST MONASTERY
(尕尔寺, Gǎ'ěr Sì; ⊙8am-6pm) Nestled on the ridge of a forested mountain about 70km south of Nangchen is this picturesque monastery. Wildlife is prevalent in the area, including blue sheep and monkeys. It's a popular spot for birdwatchers. A taxi from Nangchen costs about ¥550 return.

🛏 Sleeping & Eating

Hotels are pricey for the poor standards on offer, and not all accept foreigners.

Dōngfāng Bīnguǎn   HOTEL $
(东方宾馆, Dōngfāng Bīnguǎn; ☑152 9702 5483; Xiangda Nanjie, 香达南街; d ¥150; 🛜) With clean bathrooms and hot showers, this Salar-run hotel has bright rooms with fresh linens and heating in the winter. Located in an unfinished-looking concrete block as you head 100m south down Xiangda Nanjie.

Travellers report that sometimes this hotel has issues registering foreigners. Your best bet is to ask when you arrive.

Yǎzhuó Shāngwù Bīnguǎn   HOTEL $$
(雅卓商务宾馆; ☑0976 887 5555; Xiangda Donglu, 香达东路; d ¥288; 🛜) Clean, decent option with Western toilets, wi-fi and breakfast. Off-season rates drop to ¥180. Located on the main road 100m east before the bus station. Rates include breakfast.

Zhēngqì Niúròu Miàn Guǎn   NOODLES $
(蒸汽牛肉面馆; Xiangda Dongjie, 香达东街; dishes ¥12-20; ⊙9am-9pm) A popular and cheap place for Muslim-style noodles. Try the *zhá jiàng miàn* (炸酱面), a dish consisting of hearty meat noodles topped with minced beef. Located roughly 200m west of the main bus station. There's another branch on Xiangda Nanjie near Dōngfāng Bīnguǎn.

❶ Information

Most hotels now have wi-fi.

Agricultural Bank of China (农业银行, Nóngyè Yínháng; Xiangda Dongjie, 香达东街) ATM accepts foreign cards.

❶ Getting There & Around

From Nangchen bus station on the main road, one daily bus goes to Xīníng (¥264, 15 to 18 hours) departing at 10am. Book at least one day in advance.

To reach Yùshù (¥50, three hours), most locals travel by shared minibuses, which assemble on the main road outside Nangchen's bus station.

Nangchen itself is a dusty town where you're likely to see stray dogs trotting beside cows on the main street. You'll need to hire a taxi to see many of the sights around town, or contact Gesartour (p905) in Yùshù for a trip out here via the back roads. The route takes twice as long to travel but offers plenty of picturesque stops, including a hike up to the hills behind Gādīng Sì (嘎丁寺) where you can take Instagram-worthy snaps of the monastery sitting on a piece of land in a horseshoe bend along the Dzichu River.

Golmud 格尔木

📞 0979 / POP 200,000 / ELEVATION 2800M

For three decades Golmud (Gé'ěrmù) faithfully served overlanders as the last jumping-off point before Lhasa. Bedraggled backpackers hung around the city's truck depot trying to negotiate a lift to the 'Roof of the World'. But since the completion of the Qīnghǎi–Tibet Railway, this lonesome backwater has become even less important, as most Tibet-bound travellers board the train elsewhere and blow right through town. Today it's mostly of use to travellers trying to get between Lhasa and Dūnhuáng (in Gānsù) or Huātǔgōu (en route to Xīnjiāng).

🛏 Sleeping & Eating

There are plenty of hotels in Golmud un-fortunately only a few accept foreigners.

Dōngfāng Hotel HOTEL $
(东方宾馆, Dōngfāng Bīnguǎn; 📞 0979 841 0011; 7 Bayi Zhonglu, 八一中路7号; d ¥98-118; 📶) This centrally located hotel has decent rooms rough round the edges. Some of the larger rooms come with floor-to-ceiling windows overlooking noisy Hédōng Market (河东市场; Hédōng Shìchǎng) and the main street. It's a ¥6 taxi ride from the train station.

⭐ **Qíjì Shǒugōng Miànpiàn Fāng** HUI MUSLIM $
(祁记手工面片坊; Bayi Zhonglu; noodles ¥13-15, dishes ¥5-50; ⏰ 9am-10.30pm) An unexpected gem, this noodle joint has both style that wouldn't look out of place in Běijīng and substance by way of delicious handmade *miànpiàn* (面片; noodle slices). With its almost-Scandi decor and friendly service,

---

HIKING ON MT AMNYE MACHEN

The 6282m peak of Machen Kangri, or **Mt Amnye Machen** (阿尼玛卿, Ānímǎqīng), is Amdo's most sacred mountain – it's eastern Tibet's equivalent to Mt Kailash in western Tibet. Tibetan pilgrims travel for weeks to circumambulate the peak, believing it to be home to the protector deity Machen Pomra. The circuit's sacred geography and wild mountain scenery make it a fantastic, adventurous trekking destination.

Unfortunately, much of the route is suffering the effects of a major road project that will see elevated bridges and asphalt highways passing through the Amnye Machen region. This means that you may spend much of the route covered in dust billowing in the wake of heavy vehicles. The construction is slated to be completed in 2017/18 (depending on which section you're in). It's best to check before you go.

The full circuit takes around 11 days (including transport to/from Xīníng), though tourists often limit themselves to a half circuit. Several monasteries lie alongside the route. With almost all of the route above 4000m, and the highest pass hitting 4600m, it's essential to acclimatise before setting off, preferably by spending a night or two at the nearby Mǎduō (玛多; 4290m). The best months to trek are May to October, though be prepared for snow early and late in the season.

Since local public transport is almost nonexistent, most trekkers go on an organised tour. Expect to pay around US$180 per person per day, all-inclusive in a group, and double or triple that if you are going solo. During the construction period, the tour agencies listed in the Xīníng section take trekkers on an alternate (non-pilgrimage) route through the less disturbed parts of Mt Amnye Machen.

If you do want to try venturing out on your own, take the bus to Huāshíxiá (花石峡) or Mǎduō and then hitch or hire a shared minivan (¥300 to ¥400 per person) to Xiàdàwǔ (下大吾). Mǎduō is slightly further away but it has better amenities and you can pack in an excursion to the Source of the Yellow River (p908).

In Xiàdàwǔ the starting point for the *kora* (holy hike) path is at Guru Gompa (格日寺; Gěrì Sì), and from here follow the road east. After three days the road peters out near Xuěshān (雪山), from where you can hitch a ride to Mǎqìn. If you intend to continue past Xuěshān you'll need to ask a local to show you the *kora* path. In Xiàdàwǔ, a guide costs ¥150 to ¥200 per day, and it's about the same price for a packhorse or yak. You'll need to be fully sufficient and bring a tent, sleeping bag etc.

it's not hard to return here for noodles, *suānnǎi* (酸奶; yoghurt), cold dishes and other chunkier meat options displayed in a glass case.

ⓘ Information

Agricultural Bank of China (农业银行, Nóngyè Yínháng; Bayi Zhonglu) Has a 24-hour ATM that accepts foreign cards.

Bank of China (中国银行, Zhōngguó Yínháng; cnr Kunlun Lu & Chaidamu Lu; ⊙9am-5pm Mon-Fri, 10am-4.30pm Sat & Sun) Changes cash. Foreign-friendly ATM.

CAAC (机场售票处, Jīchǎng Shòupiàochù; ☑24hr booking line 0979 842 3333; ⊙8.30am-6pm) Can help book onward flights.

China Post (中国邮政, Zhōngguó Yóuzhèng; 38 Yingbing Lu; ⊙9am-5.30pm Mon-Fri) Located 100m north of the main train station.

China Travel Service (CTS, 中国旅行社, Zhōngguó Lǚxíngshè; ☑0979 725 8858; 3rd fl, 46 Kunlun Zhonglu Wumao Dasha, 昆仑中路46号物贸大厦3层; ⊙8.30am-6pm Mon-Fri) The only place in town that can arrange Tibet permits, though it takes seven to 10 days. Best used as a last resort. Limited English.

Public Security Bureau (PSB, 公安局, Gōng'ānjú; 6 Chaidamu Dong Lu; ⊙8am-noon & 2.30-5pm Mon-Fri) Can extend visas.

ⓘ Getting There & Away

Golmud's airport is 15km west of town. Daily flights go to Xīníng (¥1500), Xī'ān (¥1500) and Běijīng (¥3500).

There are buses to a number of destinations in Qīnghǎi and neighbouring provinces from Golmud's **main bus station** (格尔木长途车站, Gé'ěrmù Chángtú Chēzhàn; ☑0979 845 3688; 23 Jiangyuan Nanlu, 江源南路23号) including Dūnhuáng (¥115, 10 hours, 9am and 11am), Huǎtǔgōu (¥106, six hours, 10am and 11am) and Xīníng (¥140, 11 to 14 hours, 4pm, 5pm, 6pm). There is also a bus to Charklik (Ruòqiāng; ¥228, 12 hours, 11am) in Xīnjiāng.

Trains to Lhasa (hard sleeper ¥375, 14 hours) depart from **Golmud Railway Station** (格尔木火车站, Gé'ěrmù Huǒchē Zhàn; ☑0979 722 2222; Yingbin Lu, 迎宾路) late in the night or past midnight; you'll need your Tibet permit to be in order to board. Trains also go to Xīníng (hard sleeper ¥208, eight to 10 hours).

ⓘ Getting Around

A taxi to/from Golmud Airport costs ¥50.

Local taxis start at ¥6 for 3km and ¥1.30 per kilometer thereafter.

Mǎduō · 玛多

☑0975 / POP 10.750 / ELEVATION 4290M

Mǎduō is a burgeoning town now popular as a launch pad for visits to Zhālíng and Èlíng Lakes, purportedly the source of the Yellow River. The town isn't much more than two streets but there are a couple of good hotels and eating options. Remember this area is over 4000m high so altitude sickness is a real risk. Consider coming from Yùshù (3680m) rather than Xīníng (2275m) so you don't have to ascend too much in one go. Temperatures in Mǎduō can drop to near zero even in summer so come prepared.

Zhālíng & Èlíng Lakes (扎陵湖和鄂陵湖, Zhālíng Hú Hé Èlíng Hú; Níutóubēi, 牛头碑; ¥80) are the widely accepted source of the Yellow River, and most Chinese tourists drive or hire a vehicle to take them to **níutóubēi** (牛头碑), an engraved stone tablet that marks the 'source'. There's nowhere to stay or eat, so most people visit as a day trip from Mǎduō. SUVs or minivans will take you to the lake and back for ¥800 to ¥1000 per vehicle (four to five hours return). It's possible to camp here in the summer, but you'll need to be completely self-sufficient. You'll find drivers through your hotel or hanging around the main T-intersection in town. If you want to get to the very-hard-to-find true source of the Yellow River you'll need a two-day round trip from Mǎduō (sleeping in the 4WD or camping) that includes some hiking and will cost around ¥3000 per vehicle, assuming you can find a driver willing to take you. You can also get here via an itinerary organised by one of the tour agencies in Xīníng or Yùshù.

There are several hotels in Mǎduō, but only the pricier ones accept foreigners. **Língguó Shāngwù Bīnguǎn** (岭国商务宾馆; ☑0975 834 8888; opposite the Wenhua Guangchang, 文化广场对面; d ¥388; ☎) is a clean, centrally located hotel with Western toilets, 24-hour hot water and heating. Discounts bring prices down to ¥210.

When heading to Mǎduō, you'll likely be dropped off at the intersection leading into town. It's a 3km walk in or you can hitch or try to flag a taxi (¥10). There's a daily bus to Xīníng at 7.30am. You can also hit the main intersection to flag down passing buses to Xīníng or Yùshù.

Tibet

POP 3.2 MILLION

Best Places to Eat

➡ Sumptuous Tibetan Restaurant (p928)

➡ Lhasa Namaste Restaurant (p920)

➡ Third Eye Restaurant (p928)

Best Places to Sleep

➡ Kyichu Hotel (p918)

➡ Yeti Hotel (p926)

➡ Gang Gyan Orchard Hotel (p926)

Why Go?

For many people, the highlights of Tibet will be of a spiritual nature: magnificent monasteries, prayer halls of chanting monks, and remote cliffside retreats. Tibet's pilgrims – from local grandmothers murmuring mantras in temples to hardcore visitors walking or prostrating themselves around Mt Kailash – are an essential part of this appeal. Tibet has a level of devotion and faith that seems to belong to an earlier age. It's fascinating, inspiring and endlessly photogenic.

Tibet's other big draw is the elemental beauty of the highest plateau on earth. Geography here is on a humbling scale and every view is lit with spectacular mountain light. Your trip will take you past glittering turquoise lakes, across huge plains dotted with yaks and nomads' tents, and over high passes draped with colourful prayer flags. Hike past the ruins of remote hermitages, stare open-mouthed at the north face of Everest or make an epic overland trip along some of the world's wildest roads. The scope for adventure is limited only by your ability to get permits.

When to Go
Lhasa

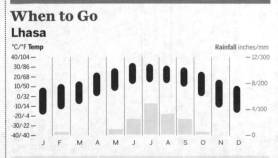

May–Sep The warmest weather makes travel, trekking and transport easiest.

Apr & Oct–Nov The slightly colder weather means fewer travellers and a better range of vehicles.

Dec–Feb Very few people visit Tibet in winter, so you'll have key attractions largely to yourself.

Tibet Highlights

1. **Lhasa** (p915) Rubbing shoulders with Tibetan pilgrims in this holy city
2. **Gyantse Kumbum** (p925) Marvelling at the murals of angels and demons in the 108 chapels of this architectural wonder
3. **Mt Kailash** (p931) Erasing the sins of a lifetime on the three-day pilgrim circuit
4. **Everest Base Camp** (p929) Catching sunrise from a yak-wool tent or monastery guesthouse.
5. **Qīnghǎi–Tibet Railway** (p923) Riding the planet's highest rails across the roof of the world
6. **Samye Monastery** (p924) Exploring the mandala-shaped chapels and stupas at Tibet's first monastery
7. **Friendship Highway** (p931) Hiring a vehicle for the week-long trip along one of Asia's great road trips

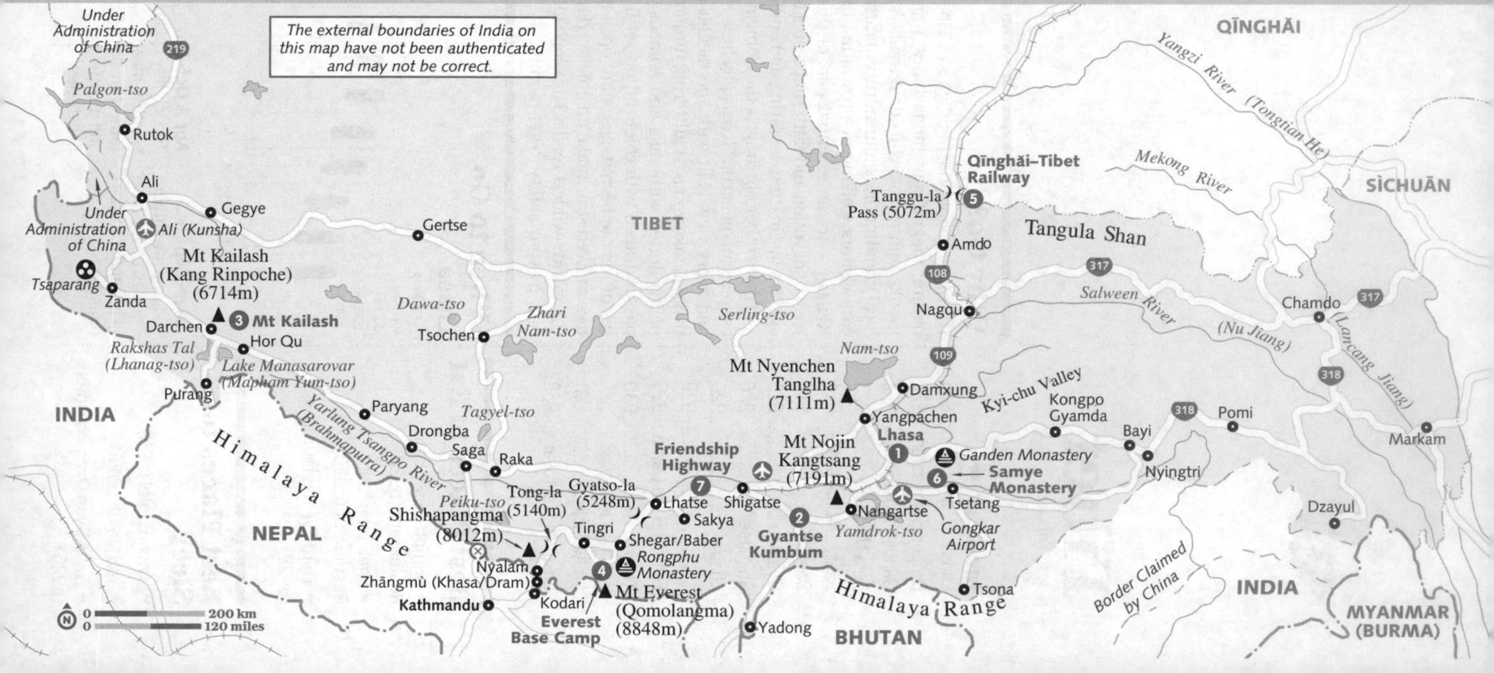

The external boundaries of India on this map have not been authenticated and may not be correct.
Under Administration of China
Palgon-tso
Rutok
Ali
Gegye
Ali (Kunsha)
Tsaparang
Zanda
Mt Kailash (Kang Rinpoche) (6714m)
Mt Kailash
Darchen
Hor Qu
Rakshas Tal (Lhanag-tso)
Lake Manasarovar (Mapham Yum-tso)
Purang
INDIA
Gertse
Dawa-tso
Tsochen
Zhari Nam-tso
TIBET
Serling-tso
Paryang
Tagyel-tso
Drongba
Saga
Raka
Yarlung Tsangpo River (Brahmaputra)
Himalaya Range
NEPAL
Peiku-tso
Shishapangma (8012m)
Tong-la (5140m)
Gyatso-la (5248m)
Tingri
Nyalam
Zhāngmù (Khasa/Dram)
Kathmandu
Kodari
Everest Base Camp
Shegar/Baber
Rongphu Monastery
Mt Everest (Qomolangma) (8848m)
Lhatse
Sakya
Friendship Highway
Shigatse
Gyantse Kumbum
Mt Nojin Kangtsang (7191m)
Yamdrok-tso
Nangartse
Yadong
BHUTAN
Tsona
Gongkar Airport
Tsetang
Samye Monastery
Ganden Monastery
Lhasa
Yangpachen
Mt Nyenchen Tanglha (7111m)
Nam-tso
Damxung
Kyi-chu Valley
Kongpo Gyamda
Bayi
Nyingtri
Pomi
Nagqu
Amdo
Tanggu-la Pass (5072m)
Qīnghǎi–Tibet Railway
Tangula Shan
Salween River
(Nu Jiang)
Mekong River
Yangzi River (Tongtian He)
QĪNGHĂI
SÌCHUĀN
Chamdo
(Lancang Jiang)
Markam
Dzayul
Border Claimed by China
INDIA
MYANMAR (BURMA)
219
108
109
317
318
0 200 km
0 120 miles

History

Recorded Tibetan history began in the 7th century AD, when the Tibetan armies began to assemble a great empire. Under King Songtsen Gampo, the Tibetans occupied Nepal and collected tribute from parts of Yúnnán. Shortly afterwards, the Tibetan armies moved north and took control of the Silk Road and the great trade centre of Kashgar, even sacking the imperial Chinese city of Cháng'ān (present-day Xī'ān).

Tibetan expansion came to an abrupt halt in 842 with the assassination of anti-Buddhist King Langdarma, the region subsequently broke into independent feuding principalities. The increasing influence of Buddhism ensured that the Tibetan armies would never again leave their high plateau.

By the 7th century, Buddhism had spread through Tibet, though it had taken on a unique form, as it adopted many of the rituals of Bön (the indigenous pre-Buddhist belief system of Tibet). The prayer flags, pilgrimage circuits and sacred landscapes you'll see across modern Tibet all have their roots in the animist religion of Bön.

From the 13th century, power politics began to play an increasing role in religion. In 1641 the Gelugpa ('Yellow Hat' order) used the support of Mongol troops to crush the Sakyapa, their rivals. It was also during this time of partisan struggle that the Gelugpa leader adopted the title of Dalai Lama (Ocean of Wisdom), given to him by the Mongols. From here on out, religion and politics in Tibet became inextricably entwined and both were presided over by the Dalai Lama.

With the fall of the Qing dynasty in 1911, Tibet entered a period of de facto independence that was to last until 1950. In this year a resurgent communist China invaded Tibet, claiming it was 'liberating' more than one million Tibetans from feudal serfdom and bringing it back into the fold of the motherland.

Increasing popular unrest in response to Chinese land reform resulted in a full-blown revolt in 1959, which was crushed by the People's Liberation Army (PLA). Amid popular rumours of a Chinese plot to kidnap him, the Dalai Lama fled to India. He was followed by an exodus of 80,000 of Tibet's best and brightest, who now represent the Tibetan government-in-exile from Dharamsala, India.

The Dalai Lama, who has referred to China's policies on migration as 'cultural genocide', is resigned to pushing for autonomy rather than independence, though even that concession has borne little fruit. The Chinese, for their part, seem to be waiting for him to die, positioning themselves to control the future politics of reincarnation. The Dalai Lama's tireless insistence on a non-violent solution to the Tibet problem led to him winning the Nobel Peace Prize in 1989, but despite global sympathy for the Tibetan cause, few nations are willing to raise the issue and place new business deals with China's rising economic superpower at risk.

The Chinese are truly baffled by what they perceive as the continuing ingratitude of the Tibetans. They claim that Tibet pre-1950 was a place of abject poverty and feudal exploitation. China, they say, has brought roads, schools, hospitals, airports, factories and rising incomes.

Many Tibetans, however, cannot forgive the destruction in the 1950s and 1960s of hundreds of monasteries and shrines, the restrictions on religious expression, the continued heavy military presence, economic exploitation and their obvious second class status within their own land. Riots and protests in the spring of 2008 brought this simmering dissatisfaction out into the open, as Lhasa erupted into full-scale riots and protests spread to other Tibetan areas in Gānsù, Sìchuān and Qīnghǎi provinces. The Chinese response was predictable: arrest, imprisonment and an increased police presence in many monasteries. The increasing desperation felt by many Tibetans has led

PRICE RANGES

Sleeping

The following price ranges refer to a standard double room before discounts. Unless otherwise stated, breakfast is not included.

$ less than ¥200

$$ ¥200–400

$$$ more than ¥400

Eating

The following price ranges refer to a standard dish in Chinese restaurants or a main course in Western restaurants. There are no additional taxes, though some higher-end places may add a service charge.

$ less than ¥30

$$ ¥30–80

$$$ more than ¥80

TIBET TRAVEL RESTRICTIONS

Travel to the Tibet Autonomous Region (TAR) is radically different from travel to the rest of China; a valid Chinese visa is not enough to visit Tibet. You'll also need several permits, foremost of which is a **Tibet Tourism Bureau** (TTB, ☎ 0891-683 4315, http://en.xzta.gov.cn) permit, and to get these you have to book a tour. At a minimum you will need to hire a guide for your entire stay and transport for any travel outside Lhasa.

Travel regulations to Tibet are constantly in flux, dependent largely on political events in Lhasa and Běijīng. Don't be surprised if the permit system is radically different from how we describe it. In fact, expect it. One of the best places for updated information is the dedicated Tibet page of Lonely Planet's Thorn Tree, at lonelyplanet.com/thorntree. Other good sources of permit information are the websites www.thelandofsnows.com and www.tibetpermit.org. The latter is run by an agency in Sìchuān but is generally reliable on permit matters.

Start your tour planning two months in advance. Agencies need two to four weeks to arrange permits. All of the rules have exceptions and by the time you have finished reading the below list of tips and fine print, many of them will probably have changed:

➡ A valid Chinese visa and a Tibet Tourism Bureau (TTB) permit are required to enter Tibet.

➡ To get these permits you need to prebook an itinerary, a guide for your entire stay and transport for outside Lhasa with an agency, pay a deposit, send a scan of your passport information pages and Chinese visa; and, if flying to Lhasa, arrange an address in China (usually that of a hotel, guesthouse or local agency) to receive your posted TTB permit, all before travelling to Tibet.

➡ TTB permits are not issued in March due to the anniversary of several politically sensitive dates.

➡ You need a TTB permit to board a train or plane to Lhasa. You will need to arrange an itinerary through a travel agent before arriving in Tibet.

➡ You need travel permits to travel outside Lhasa prefecture and you can currently only get these by hiring transportation and a guide. Foreigners are not allowed to take public transport outside Lhasa.

➡ If you enter Tibet from Nepal, you will have to travel on a short-term group visa available in Kathmandu, which is hard to extend and can make it tricky to continue into the rest of China.

➡ In Lhasa budget travellers can hire a guide without transport and just take taxis around town. You can also travel to Shigatse by train without the need for vehicle hire.

➡ TTB permits generally take three days to process and are not available during weekends. The actual permit is a sheet of paper listing the names and passport numbers of all group members.

➡ If you are planning to arrive in Lhasa on a flight or dates that differ from those of your travel companions, your agency may have to issue a separate TTB permit for the time you are by yourself. When you meet your friends you'll then join the main permit. There doesn't seem to be a problem getting on a flight with one or two group members not present.

➡ You will likely have to wire or transfer a deposit to your travel agency's Bank of China account in Lhasa, though some agencies accept PayPal. You will pay the balance in cash in Lhasa. Check with the agency.

Alien's Travel Permits & Military Permits

Once you have a visa and have managed to wangle a TTB permit, you might think you're home and dry. Think again. Your agency will need to arrange an alien's travel permit for most of your travels outside Lhasa.

Travel permits are *not* needed for Lhasa or places just outside the city such as Ganden Monastery, but most other areas do technically require permits. Permits are most easily arranged in the regional capital, so for Ngari (western Tibet) you'll have to budget an hour in Shigatse, and possibly also Ali or Darchen, for your guide to process the permit. Agencies can only arrange a travel permit for those on a tour with them.

Sensitive border areas – such as Mt Kailash, the road to Kashgar and the Nyingtri region of eastern Tibet – also require a military permit and a foreign-affairs permit. For remote places such as the Yarlung Tsangpo gorges in southeastern Tibet, the roads through Lhoka south of Gyantse or for any border area, you will likely not be able to get permits even if you book a tour. Regions can close at short notice. The entire Chamdo prefecture has been closed since 2010, effectively blocking overland trips from Sìchuān and Yúnnán. You'll have to check to see if this has changed.

You should give your agency a week to 10 days to arrange your permits, and three weeks if military or other permits are required. The authorities generally won't issue permits more than 15 days in advance. Local Public Security Bureau (PSB) officers often make the ultimate decision on whether you can visit a site, so you'll need a certain flexibility if you're headed off the beaten track.

Tour Agencies in Tibet

In general, Tibetan tour agencies are not as professional as agencies in neighbouring Nepal or Dhutan. The following companies in Lhasa are experienced in arranging customised trips.

For good information on responsible tour companies and ecotourism initiatives in Tibet, visit www.tibetecotravel.com and www.tibetgreenmap.

Explore Tibet (📱 158 8909 0408, 0891-632 9441; www.tibetexploretour.com; 4-5 House, Namsel No 3, Doudi Rd) Contact Jamphel.

Namchen Tours (Map p919; 📱 0891-633 0823; www.tibetnamchen.com; 2 Barkhor North St) At Barkhor Namchen Guest House. Contact Dhoko.

Road to Tibet (📱 133 0898 1522; www.roadtotibet.com; Jinzhu Xilu 8-5) Contact Woeser Phel.

Shigatse Travels (Map p919; 📱 0891-633 0489; www.shigatsetravels.com; Yak Hotel, 100 Beijing Donglu) Top-end tours from a large agency that uses European trip managers.

Spinn Café (Map p919; 📱 136 5952 3997; www.cafespinn.com; 135 Beijing Donglu) Contact Kong/Pazu.

Tibet Highland Tours (Map p919; 📱 0891-634 8144, 139 0898 5060; www.tibethighland tours.com; Danjielin Lu) Contact Tenzin or Dechen.

Tibet Roof of World International Travel (Map p919; 📱 0891-679 1995; www.budgettibet tour.com; Kailash Hotel, 143 Beijing Donglu) Offers scheduled budget tours across Tibet.

Tibet Songtsan International Travel Company (Map p919; 📱 0891-636 4414; www.songtsan travel.com; 2nd fl, Barkhor Sq; 📶) Run by Tenzin, this up-and-coming outfit is eager to serve new clients.

Tibet Tsolha Garbo Travel (📱 139 0891 5618, 0891-633 3871; www.dmigmar.wix.com/tibet -tsolha-garbo) Contact David Migmar or Sonam Yergye.

Tibet Wind Horse Adventure (Map p916; 📱 0891-683 3009; www.windhorsetibet.com; B32 Shenzheng Huayuan, Sera Beilu) Top-end trips, strong on trekking and rafting.

Tibetan Guide (📱 136 2898 0074; www.tibetanguide.com) Contact Mima Dhondup.

Visit Tibet Travel and Tours (📱 028-8325 7742; www.visittibet.com; Jiaji Lu) Can arrange Nepal add-ons.

Tour Agencies Elsewhere in China

Access Tibet (www.accesstibettour.com; Room 8110, Lhasa Chaoyang Grand Hotel, 81 Beijing Xilu) Chéngdū-based agency with an office in Lhasa.

Extravagant Yak (p741) Foreign-owned company in Chéngdū that runs tours in both Tibet and Tibetan areas of surrounding provinces.

Khampa Caravan (p706) Overland trips from Yúnnán to Lhasa when possible, with an emphasis on sustainable tourism and local communities. Contact Dakpa in Shangri-La.

Leo Hostel (广聚园宾馆, Guǎngjùyuán Bīnguǎn; 📱 010 6303 3318, 010 6303 1595; www.leohostel.com; 52 Dazhalan Xijie, 大栅栏西街 52号; 🚇 Line 2 to Qianmen, exit B or C) Popular hostel in Běijīng that books tours through an agency in Tibet.

Mix Hostel (📱 028 8322 2271; www.mixhostel.com) In Chéngdū. Books standard tours and can help find other backpackers to share the cost.

Snow Lion Tours (p897) In Xīníng. Contact Wangden Tsering.

Tibetan Connections (p897) In Xīníng. Focuses on remoter parts of Amdo and Kham but can arrange trips into Tibet. Prices may be a little higher but staff members are good to deal with.

Tibetan Trekking (p741) In Chéngdū. Contact Gao Liqiang for treks and 4WD trips, especially in Tibetan areas of western Sichuān.

Wild China (Map p92; 📱 010-6465 6602; www.wildchina.com; Room 803, Oriental Place, 9 Dongfang Donglu, North Dongsanhuan Rd, 东三环北路东方东路9号东方国际大厦803室; ⏰ 9am-6pm Mon-Fri; 🚇 Line 10 to Liangmaqiao, exit B) In Běijīng. Professionally run and top-end private trips.

to a spate of self-immolations by Tibetans across the region, including two in Lhasa's Barkhor Circuit in 2012.

As immigration and breakneck modernisation continue, the government is gambling that economic advances will diffuse the Tibetans' religious and political aspirations. It's a policy that has so far been successful in the rest of China. Whether it will work in Tibet remains to be seen.

Climate

Most of Tibet is a high-altitude desert plateau at more than 4000m. Days in summer (June to September) are warm, sunny and generally dry, but temperatures drop quickly after dark. It's always cool above 4000m and often freezing at night, though thanks to the Himalayan rain shadow there is surprisingly little snow in the Land of Snows. Sunlight is very strong at these altitudes, so bring plenty of high-factor sunscreen and lip balm.

Language

Most urban Tibetans speak Mandarin in addition to Tibetan. Even in the countryside you can get by with basic Mandarin in most restaurants and hotels, since they are normally run by Mandarin-speaking Han or Hui Chinese. That said, Tibetans are extremely pleased when foreign visitors at least greet them in Tibetan, so it's well worth learning a few phrases.

❶ Getting There & Away

For most international travellers, getting to Tibet will involve at least two legs: first to a gateway city such as Kathmandu (Nepal) or Chéngdū (China) and then into Tibet.

The most popular options from the gateway towns into Tibet are as follows: flights from Kathmandu, Chéngdū, Kūnmíng, Xī'ān or Běijīng; the train link from Qīnghǎi to Lhasa; or the overland drive from Kathmandu to Lhasa along the Friendship Hwy.

At the time of writing, bureaucratic obstacles to entering Tibet from China were many and involved signing up for a preplanned and prepaid tour. The situation from Nepal is even trickier because of ever-changing group-visa requirements. Political events, both domestic and international, can mean that regulations for entry into Tibet change overnight. Nerves of steel are definitely useful when arranging flights and permits. Always check on the latest developments before booking flights.

AIR

There are no direct long-haul flights to Tibet. You will probably have to stop over in Kathmandu,

Chéngdū, Guǎngzhōu or Běijīng, even if you are making a beeline for Lhasa, especially considering you need to to pick up your permit in your chosen gateway city before heading to Lhasa.

LAND

Many individual travellers make their way to Tibet as part of a grand overland trip through China, Nepal, India and onwards. In many ways, land travel to Tibet is the best way to go, not only for the scenery en route but also because it can help spread the altitude gain over a few days.

All overland trips inside the Tibet Autonomous Region have to be organised tours with vehicle rental and a guide.

Train

Trains to Lhasa leave from Běijīng, Chéngdū, Shànghǎi, Xīníng and Guǎngzhōu daily, and every other day from Chóngqìng (via Xī'ān) and Lánzhōu, to link with the Chéngdū and Xīníng trains, respectively. A twice-daily train service from Lhasa to Shigatse started in late 2014. Future extensions will include lines from Lhasa to Tsetang and the eastern region of Kongpo, to the Nepal border and from Golmud to Dūnhuáng in Gānsù province.

All current trains cross the Tibetan plateau during daylight, guaranteeing you great views. From Golmud, the train climbs through desert into the jagged caramel-coloured mountains of Nánshānkǒu (Southern Pass), passing what feels like a stone's throw from the impressive glaciers beside Yùzhū Fēng (Jade Pearl Peak; 6178m). Other highlights include the tunnel through the 4776m Kunlun Pass, where you can see the prayer flags at the top of the pass, and Tsonak Lake (4608m), 9½ hours from Golmud near Amdo, claimed to be the highest freshwater lake in the world. Keep your eyes peeled throughout the journey for antelopes, foxes and wild asses, plus the occasional nomad. The train crosses into Tibet over the 5072m Tanggu-la (Tánggǔlā Shānkǒu) Pass, the line's high point.

❶ Getting Around

Tibet's transport infrastructure has developed rapidly in recent years. Most of the main highways are now paved. Airports are springing up on the plateau and the railway line is slowly extending beyond Lhasa. In 2011 Tibet's Metok county was the very last of China's 2100 counties to be connected by road.

Bus Lots of services, but foreigners are currently not allowed to take buses or shared taxis in Tibet.

Car The only way to travel around Tibet at the moment, since foreign travellers have to hire private transport as part of their obligatory tour.

Train Great for getting to and from Tibet but of limited use inside Tibet, unless you are just taking a short trip from Lhasa to Shigatse and back.

LHASA

ལྷ་ས་ 拉萨

☑ 0891 / ELEV 3650M / POP 257,000

The centre of the Tibetan Buddhist world for over a millennium, Lhasa (Lāsà; literally the 'Place of the Gods') remains largely a city of wonders. Your first view of the red and white Potala Palace soaring above the Holy City raises goosebumps and the charming whitewashed old Tibetan quarter continues to preserve the essence of traditional Tibetan life. It is here in the Jokhang, an other-worldly mix of flickering butter lamps, wafting incense and prostrating pilgrims, and the encircling Barkhor pilgrim circuit, that most visitors first fall in love with Tibet.

These days the booming boulevards of the modern Chinese city threaten to overwhelm the winding alleyways and temples of the Tibetan old town, but it is in the latter that you should focus your time. If possible, budget a week to acclimatise, see the sights and roam the fascinating back streets before heading off on a grand overland adventure.

◉ Sights & Activities

For Tibetan pilgrims the principal points of orientation in Lhasa are the city's three *koras* (pilgrim circuits): the Nangkhor, which encircles the inner precincts of the Jokhang; the Barkhor circuit; and the Lingkhor (Maps p916 and p919). Remember always to go clockwise.

★ Potala Palace
PALACE

(ཕོ་བྲང་, 布达拉宫, Bùdálā Gōng; Map p916; May-Oct ¥200, Nov-Apr ¥100; ⊙9.30am-3pm Nov-Apr, 9am-3.30pm May-Oct, interior chapels close 4.30pm) The magnificent Potala Palace, once the seat of the Tibetan government and the winter residence of the Dalai Lamas, is Lhasa's cardinal landmark. Your first sight of its towering, fortress-like walls is a moment you'll remember for years. An architectural wonder even by modern standards, the palace rises 13 storeys from 130m-high Marpo Ri (Red Hill) and contains more than 1000 rooms. Pilgrims and tourists alike shuffle open-mouthed through the three storeys, past the dozens of magnificent chapels, golden stupas and prayer halls.

The first recorded use of the site was in the 7th century AD, when King Songtsen Gampo built a palace here. Construction of the present structure began during the reign of the fifth Dalai Lama in 1645 and took more than 50 years to complete. It is impressive enough to have caused Chinese premier Zhou Enlai to send his own troops to protect it from the Red Guards during the Cultural Revolution.

The layout of the Potala Palace includes the rooftop White Palace (Map p916; the eastern part of the building), used for the living quarters of the Dalai Lama, and the central Red Palace (Map p916), used for religious functions. The most stunning chapels of the Red Palace house the jewel-bedecked golden chörten (Tibetan stupa) tombs of several previous Dalai Lamas.

Tickets for the Potala are limited and your guide will need to book a time slot several days in advance. Arrive at the palace an hour or so before your allotted time. After a security check (no water or lighters allowed), follow the other visitors to the stairs up into the palace. Halfway up you'll pass the ticket booth, where you'll buy your ticket. Note that if you arrive later than the time on your voucher (or if you forget your voucher) you can be refused a ticket. Photography isn't allowed inside the chapels.

★ Jokhang Temple
BUDDHIST TEMPLE

(ཇོ་ཁང་, 大昭寺, Dàzhāo Sì; Map p919; ¥85; ⊙8.30-6.30pm, most chapels closed after noon) The 1300-year-old Jokhang Temple is the spiritual heart of Tibet: the continuous waves of awestruck pilgrims prostrating themselves outside are a testament to its timeless allure. The central golden Buddha image here is the most revered in all of Tibet.

The Jokhang was originally built to house an image of Buddha brought to Tibet by King Songtsen Gampo's Nepalese wife. However, another image, the Jowa Sakyamuni, was later moved here by the king's other wife (the Chinese Princess Wencheng), and it is this image that gives the Jokhang both its name and its spiritual potency: Jokhang means 'chapel of the Jowo'.

The two-storeyed Jokhang is best visited in the morning, though the crowds of yak-butter-spooning pilgrims can be thick. Access is possible in the afternoon through a side entrance, but only the ground-floor chapels can be viewed (and then only through a grille) and there are no pilgrims.

★ Barkhor Circuit
PILGRIMAGE

(བར་འཁོར་, 八廓, Bākuò; Map p919) FREE It's impossible not to be swept up in the wondrous tide of humanity that is the Barkhor, a kora (pilgrim circuit) that winds clockwise around the periphery of the Jokhang Temple. You'll swear it possesses some spiritual centrifugal force, as every time you approach within 50m, you somehow get sucked right in and gladly wind up making the whole circuit again! It's the place to start exploring

Lhasa

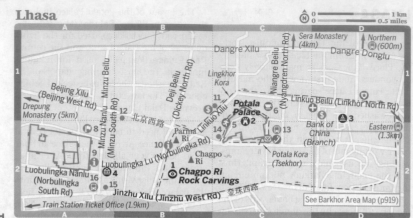

Lhasa

Lhasa and the last spot you'll want to see before you bid the city farewell.

★ **Chagpo Ri Rock Carvings** HISTORIC SITE
(药王山, Yàowáng Shān; Map p916; Deji Zhonglu; ¥10; ☉ dawn-dusk) This hidden corner of Lhasa features more than 5000 painted rock carvings that were created at the back of Chagpo Ri over the course of a millennium. Throughout the day, pilgrims perform full-body prostrations in front of the images, while stone carvers at the far end of the courtyard contribute to a large chörten built entirely of the carvers' mani stones. The best way to visit the area is as part of the Lingkhor pilgrim route).

Barkhor Square SQUARE
(八角广场, Bājiǎo Guǎngchǎng; Map p919) For your first visit to the Barkhor, enter from Barkhor Sq, a large plaza that was cleared in 1985. The square has been a focus for violent political protest on several occasions, notably in 1998 (when a Dutch tourist was shot in the shoulder) and most recently in 2008. The square is now bordered by metal detectors, riot-squad vehicles, fire-extinguisher teams (to prevent self-immolations) and rooftop surveillance. Despite the stream of selfie-taking tourists, the atmosphere is one of occupation or siege.

Tibet Museum MUSEUM
ཞབ་ལྗོངས་ལྷོ་ཁང་ , 西藏博物馆, Xīzàng Bówùguǎn; Map p916; Minzu Nanlu; ☉ 9.30am-5.30pm Tue-Sun) FREE This museum has some interesting exhibits and heavy Communist Party propaganda. Starting with the prehistory of Tibet, the multiple halls cover everything

from weapons and musical instruments to folk handicrafts and fine ancient thangkas (Tibetan sacred art). A useful handheld audio self-touring device (¥10) is available if you bring your passport as a deposit.

👉 Tours

Higher Ground Treks & Tours   TOUR
(☎0891-686 5352; higherground_treks_tours@yahoo.com; 75 Beijing Zhonglu) The head of this trekking agency, Karma Khampa, was once a manager at the long-standing Tibet International Sports Travel.

✱✱ Festivals & Events

Losar Festival   RELIGIOUS
(☉Feb) New Year celebrations take place in the first week of the first lunar month, with performances of Tibetan opera, prayer ceremonies at the Jokhang and Nechung Monastery, and the streets thronged with Tibetans dressed in their finest.

Saga Dawa   RELIGIOUS
(☉May or Jun) The 15th day (full moon) of the fourth lunar month sees huge numbers of pilgrims walking and prostrating along the Lingkhor and Barkhor pilgrim circuits. Follow the locals' cue and change ¥10 into a wad of one-máo notes to hand out as alms during the walk.

Drepung Festival   RELIGIOUS
(☉Jul) The 30th day of the sixth lunar month is celebrated with the hanging at dawn of a huge thangka at Drepung Monastery. Lamas and monks perform opera in the main courtyard.

Shötun Festival   RELIGIOUS
(☉Aug) The first week of the seventh lunar month sees the unveiling of a giant thangka at Drepung Monastery; festivities then move down to Sera and to the Norbulingka for performances of *lhamo* (Tibetan opera) and some epic picnics.

Tsongkhapa Festival   RELIGIOUS
(☉Dec) Much respect is shown to Tsongkhapa, the founder of the Gelugpa order, on the anniversary of his death on the 25th day of the 10th lunar month. Check for processions and monk dances at the monasteries at Ganden, Sera and Drepung.

🛏 Sleeping

The Tibetan eastern end of town is easily the most interesting place to be based, with accommodation options in all budgets. There are dozens of shiny, characterless Chinese-style hotels scattered around other parts of town. You might find yourself in one of these if you arrive on a tour or book a hotel online. Note that most of the budget places don't accept reservations.

Banak Shol   HOTEL **$**
(八郎学宾馆, Dālángxué Dīnguǎn; Map p010; ☎0891-632 3829; 8 Beijing Donglu; dm ¥50, d/tr without bathroom ¥100/150, d with bathroom ¥150-160; 🛜) It's a mixed picture at this backpacker stalwart. The newest triple rooms without

TIBET LHASA

LHASA IN...

Two Days

On arrival in Lhasa you need at least two days to adjust to the altitude; you can expect to be tired and headachey most of the time. We recommend adding an extra day and taking the first day very easy.

Start at **Barkhor Square** (p916), finding your legs on a relaxed stroll around the **Barkhor circuit** (p915) before visiting the **Jokhang** (p915). Grab lunch at nearby **Snowland Restaurant** (p920) or **Lhasa Kitchen** (p918). In the afternoon head to **Sera Monastery** (p923) to catch the monks debating. If your headache's gone, round off the day with a cold Lhasa Beer at **Dunya** (Map p919; 100 Beijing Donglu; beer ¥15; ☉3-11pm) or on the roof of **Shambhala Palace** (p918).

On day two visit the **Potala Palace** (p915) at your allotted time and then spend the afternoon losing yourself in the fascinating old town.

Four Days

With four days you could leave the Potala until day three, and add on a stroll around the **Potala kora** (Map p916), grabbing some sweet te a in a teahouse en route. On day four leave the city on a day trip out to **Ganden Monastery** (p922), visiting the hermitage caves of **Drak Yerpa** (བྲག་ཡེར་པ, 扎叶巴寺, Zhā Yèbā Sì; ¥30) on the way back. Try to budget some time for handicraft shopping at **Dropenling** (p920).

bathroom are spacious, fresh and carpeted, and the shared shower blocks are sparkling. The recently renovated Chinese-style standard rooms with bathroom are normally the cheapest such options in town. Avoid the older roadside doubles and singles, though, as these are still small, noisy and overpriced.

Bike Hostel
HOSTEL $

(风马飞扬旅舍, Fēngmǎ Fēiyáng Lǚshě; Map p919; ☑0891-679 0250; www.tibetbike.com; dm ¥33-50, d without/with bathroom ¥120/180; 🛜) This tidy courtyard hostel (north of Beijing Donglu behind the Yak Hotel) is a decent budget option, especially if you speak some Chinese and want to connect with the many overland Chinese cyclists here. The en-suite rooms are bright, modern and good value, and the dorms come with shared hot showers and free washing-machine access.

Dōngcuò International Youth Hostel
HOSTEL $

(东措国际青年旅馆, Dōngcuò Guójì Qīngnián Lǚshè; Map p919; ☑0891-627 3388; yhalhasa@ hotmail.com; 10 Beijing Donglu; dm ¥30-55, s/d/ tr with bathroom ¥120/140/180, r without bathroom ¥80-120; @🛜) Lhasa's best Chinese-run hostel attracts mainly Chinese backpackers, though a few foreign travellers find their way here. Rooms are smallish but well maintained, with wooden floors and crisp white sheets, but the beloved graffiti-covered walls add to the slightly grim, institutional feel. Bike rental (¥30) and a laundry service are bonuses. Prices rise in July and August.

★Yak Hotel
HOTEL $$

(亚宾馆, Yà Bīnguǎn; Map p919; ☑0891-630 0195; 100 Beijing Donglu; dm ¥50, d ¥240-650, r VIP ¥880; 🛇@🛜) The ever-popular Yak has matured in recent years from backpacker hang-out to tour-group favourite, eschewing the cramped dorm rooms (there are three left) for a range of comfortable en-suite rooms. Reservations are recommended through your agency (online booking websites are currently unreliable). The 5th-floor breakfast bar offers great views of the Potala. Walk-in discounts of 40% are standard.

Tashi Choeta Tibetan Folk Hotel
HOTEL $$

(扎西曲塔风情酒店, Zhāxī Qūtǎ Fēngqíng Jiǔdiàn; Map p919; ☑139 8998 5865; 🛇@🛜) This new hotel (opened in 2016) has a great location on the edge of the old town, with 58 comfortable Tibetan-style rooms ranged around a sunny atrium. The superior rooms are more spacious; all are set around a cen-

tral courtyard restaurant. Prices were not fixed at the time of research.

★Kyichu Hotel
HOTEL $$$

(吉曲饭店, Jíqǔ Fàndiàn; Map p919; ☑0891-633 1541; www.lhasakyichuhotel.com; 18 Beijing Donglu; r standard/deluxe from ¥480/580; 🛇@🛜) The renovated Kyichu is a friendly and well run choice that's very popular with repeat travellers to Tibet. Rooms are comfortable and pleasant, with wooden floors, underfloor heating, Tibetan carpets and private bathrooms, but the real selling points are the location, the excellent service and – that rarest of Lhasa commodities – a peaceful garden courtyard (with espresso coffee). Reservations recommended.

★Shambhala Palace
BOUTIQUE HOTEL $$$

(香巴拉宫, Xiāngbālā Gōng; Map p919; ☑0891-630 7779; www.shambhalaserai.com; 16 Taibeng Gang; r incl breakfast ¥480-720; 🛇closed mid-Jan–end Apr; @🛜) This quiet 17-room hotel is hidden deep in the old town, offering stylish rooms, a spacious rooftop and good service. Avoid the smallest rooms, though. Manager Nyima Tashi is particularly helpful. Low-season discounts of 20% are available.

★House of Shambhala
BOUTIQUE HOTEL $$$

(桌玛拉宫, Zhuōmǎlā Gōng; Map p919; ☑0891-632 6533; www.shambhalaserai.com; 7 Jiri Erxiang, 吉日二巷7号; d incl breakfast ¥490-980; 🛇closed mid-Jan–end Apr; @) Hidden in the old town in a historic Tibetan building, the romantic, boutique-style Shambhala mixes the neighbourhood's earthy charm with buckets of style and a great rooftop lounge, making it perfect for couples who prefer atmosphere over mod cons.

✕ Eating

The best Tibetan, Nepali and Western restaurants are in the Tibetan quarter around Barkhor Sq. Almost all places offer decent breakfasts, perhaps the best being at **Lhasa Kitchen** (拉萨厨房, Lāsà Chúfáng; Map p919; 3 Danjielin Lu; mains ¥20-30, Nepali sets ¥35; 🛇9am-11pm) and Snowland (p920). Most eateries serve lunch and dinner, but you will struggle to find a meal after about 10pm. For the flashiest Chinese restaurants you'll have to head to the western districts.

Father Vegetarian Restaurant
TIBETAN $

(父亲素食厨房, Fùqīn Sùshí Chúfáng; Map p919; mains ¥17-40; 🛇11am-9.30pm; 🍴) This hole-in-the wall ('Yebche Gartse Suertob' in Tibetan) is a good place to get a cheap and authentic

Barkhor Area

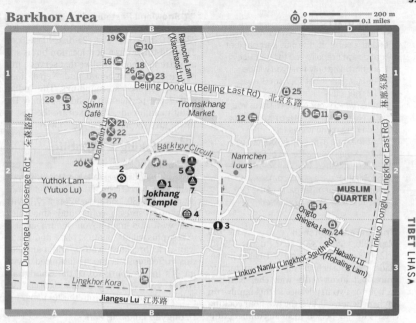

Barkhor Area

vegetarian lunch. There's no English menu, so consider going with your Tibetan guide. The combo dishes with rice are good value at ¥10 and the Tibetan-style fried mush-rooms (臧式炒蘑菇, *zāngshì chǎomógu*) and dry hotpot (干锅, *gànguō*) dishes are particularly recommended.

TIBET LHASA

ⓘ PERMITS

Lhasa is currently the only part of Tibet that doesn't require you to hire pricey transport. The only time you will be asked for your Tibet Tourism Bureau (TTB) permit is when you check into a hotel, which your guide will help you with. No other permits are required for the city or surroundings.

At the time of research you had to visit the main monasteries of Drepung, Sera and Ganden and Jokhang Temple and Potala Palace in the company of your guide, but other parts of the city were fine to explore by yourself.

Tibetan Family Kitchen   TIBETAN $
(Map p919; ☎138 8901 5053; dishes ¥15-40; ☉12:30-9pm; 🛜) For a taste of Tibetan home-made recipes such as yak meat in tomato sauce, put in an order with chef Namdon an hour or two in advance at this family-run kitchen. Better still, take the two-hour cooking class (¥100 per person, including dinner), during which you can learn to make authentic *momos* (dumplings) and Amdo-style noodles.

Seyzhong Nongze Bösey Restaurant   TIBETAN $
(金臧特宝藏餐, Jīnzàng Tèbǎo Zāngcāan; Map p916; Ramoche Lam; dishes ¥15-35) Super-convenient if you're visiting the next-door **Ramoche Temple** (ﲮﲮﲮﲮ, 小昭寺, Xiǎozhāo Sì; Map p916; ¥20; ☉7.30am-8pm), this pleasant upstairs Amdo Tibetan restaurant offers great views over the street below from the low Tibetan-style tables. Try the set meal of *shemdre* (meat, rice and curried potatoes) for ¥25 or choose something more adventurous from the photo menu, such as the sizzling beef and peppers or the tiger-skin chillies (虎皮青椒; *hǔpíqīngjiāo*).

⭐**Lhasa Namaste Restaurant**   INTERNATIONAL, NEPALI $$
(拉萨娜玛瑟德餐厅, Lāsà Nàmǎsèdé Cāntīng; Map p919; 11 Lugu Wu Xiang; mains ¥25-50; ☉11am-9:30pm) It's worth battling the labyrinthine old-town backstreets to get to this Nepali-run restaurant, with a charming location in the garden courtyard of the **Trichang Labrang Hotel** (志江拉让宾馆, Chìjiāng Làràng Bīnguǎn; Map p919). The rewards are some of Lhasa's tastiest curries, as well as sizzlers, yak burgers and cakes. Arrive before 6pm to get a table and leave a popcorn trail to find your way back again.

⭐**Snowland Restaurant**   INTERNATIONAL $$
(雪域餐厅, Xuěyù Cāntīng; Map p919; ☎0891-633 7323; 8 Danjielin Lu; dishes ¥25-70; ☉10am-10pm) This old-timer has a new location but is still an extremely popular place that serves a mix of excellent Continental and Nepali food in very civilised surroundings. The Indian dishes are particularly good, especially the giant naan breads. The cakes are the best in town; give the lemon pie our fond regards.

🍷 Drinking & Nightlife

⭐**Summit Café**   CAFE
(顶峰咖啡店, Dǐngfēng Kāfēidiàn; Map p919; www.thetibetsummitcafe.com; 1 Danjielin Lu; coffee ¥22-30, mains ¥50-80; ☉8:30am-9:30pm; 🛜) With authentic espresso coffee and smoothies, free wi-fi and melt-in-your-mouth cheesecakes, plus salads, paninis, pizza and American-style breakfast waffles and pancakes, this coffeehouse is mocha-flavoured nirvana. It's in the courtyard of the **Shangbala Hotel** (香巴拉酒店, Xiāngbālā Jiǔdiàn; Map p919), a stone's throw from the Jokhang.

Dzongyab Lukhang Park Teahouse East   TEAHOUSE
(龙王潭风经情茶园, Lóngwángtán Fēngqíng Cháyuán; Map p916; tea ¥4) One of two good teahouse restaurants in pleasant Dzongyab Lukhang Park. Grab a thermos of sweet tea or try a cheap lunch of *shemdre* (meat and curried potatoes; mains ¥15 to ¥20).

🛍 Shopping

⭐**Dropenling**   ARTS & CRAFTS
(桌番林, Zhuōfānlín; Map p919; ☎0891-633 0558; www.tibetcraft.com; 11 Chaktsalgang Lam; ☉10am-8pm) 🌿 This impressive nonprofit enterprise aims to bolster traditional Tibetan handicrafts in the face of rising Chinese and Nepali imports. Products are unique and of high quality, and they are made using traditional techniques (natural dyes, wool not acrylic etc) updated with contemporary designs. Ask about the 90-minute artisan walking tour of Lhasa's old town (¥30 per person).

Outlook Outdoor Equipment   SPORTS & OUTDOORS
(达塞远景户外装备, Biànsài Yuǎnjǐng Hùwài Zhuāngbèi; Map p919; ☎0891-633 8990; 11 Beijing Donglu) This trekking shop has a dwindling selection of Western-quality sleeping bags (¥350 to ¥600), Gore-Tex jackets, and tents, plus imported knick-knacks such as altimeters, trekking socks and Primus cook sets. A limited amount of gear is also available for rent.

❶ Information

DANGERS & ANNOYANCES

If you fly straight into Lhasa, remember to take things easy for your first day or two: it's not uncommon to feel breathless, suffer from headaches and sleep poorly because of the altitude. Don't attempt the steps up to the Potala for the first few days and drink lots of fluids.

Chinese armed-police posts and riot-squad teams currently occupy every street corner in the old town. Most Tibetans ignore them, but you should take care not to photograph any military posts or armed patrols.

EMERGENCY NUMBERS

Ambulance ☑120
Fire ☑119
Police ☑11

INTERNET ACCESS

Most public internet cafes won't accept foreigners without a local identity card. Almost all hotels and some cafes offer free wi-fi to patrons.

MEDICAL SERVICES

120 Emergency Centre (急救中心, Jíjiù Zhōngxīn; Map p916; ☑ 0891-633 2462; 16 Linkuo Beilu) Part of People's Hospital. Consultations cost around ¥150.

Tibet Military Hospital (西藏军区总医院, Xīzàng Jūnqū Zǒngyīyuàn; ☑ 0891-625 3120; Niangre Beilu) Travellers who have received medical attention confirm that this place is the best option (if you have an option).

MONEY

Bank of China (Main Office; 中国银行, Zhōngguó Yínháng; Map p916, Linkuo Xilu; ⊙9am 1pm & 3:30-6:30pm Mon-Fri, 10:30am-4pm Sat & Sun) West of the Potala, this is the only place to arrange a credit-card advance (3% commission) or a bank transfer. The ATMs outside the building are open 24 hours.

Bank of China (Branch; 中国银行, Zhōngguó Yínháng; Map p919; Beijing Donglu; ⊙24hr) Fully automated, with a currency-exchange machine that's converts cash relatively quickly. Bring your cleanest notes, as the machine can be fussy. ATMs dispense cash 24 hours a day.

Bank of China (Branch; Map p916; Duosenge Lu; ⊙ 9:30am-5:30pm Mon-Fri, 10:30am-4pm Sat & Sun) If you actually need to talk to a human to change money, this bank branch is the closest to the Tibetan old town.

POST

China Post (中国邮政, Zhōngguó Yóuzhèng; Map p916; 33 Beijing Donglu; ⊙9am-6pm) Counter number three sells stamps. Express Mail Service (EMS) is also here. Leave parcels unsealed until you get here, as staff will want to check the contents for customs clearance.

TELEPHONE

China Mobile (中国移动通信, Zhōngguó Yídòng Tōngxìn; Map p916; ⊙9am-6pm Mon-Sat) This is the best place to get a local SIM card for your mobile phone. Choose from data, calls or a mixture of both. It's a fairly complicated procedure and you'll likely need a local ID card, so go with your guide. Expect to pay around ¥100 for a month of data.

VISAS

Lhasa City PSB (PSB, 拉萨市公安局, Lāsà Shì Gōng'ānjú; Map p916; ☑ 0891-624 8154; 17 Linkuo Beilu; ⊙9am-12:30pm & 3:30 6pm Mon-Fri) Visa extensions of up to a week are very rarely given; if they are they will only be granted a day or two before your visa expires and only through your tour agency.

Nepalese Consulate-General (p1001) Issues visas in 24 hours. The current fee for a 15-/30-/90-day visa is ¥175/280/700. Bring a visa photo. Chinese tourists have to get their visas here; foreigners will find it easier to obtain visas on the spot at the Nepalese border.

❶ Getting There & Away

While there are a number of ways to get to Lhasa, the most popular routes are by air from Chéngdū (in Sìchuan), by train from Xīníng, and overland or by air from Kathmandu.

AIR

Flying *out* of Lhasa is considerably easier than flying in. No permits are necessary – just turn up at the **Civil Aviation Authority of China office** (Map p916) and buy a ticket. In August and around national holidays, you'd be wise to book your ticket at least a week in advance. At other times you'll generally get a 30% discount off the full fare.

To book a ticket you'll need to complete a form, get a reservation and then pay the cashier (cash only). Sample full fares include ¥1680 to Chéngdū, ¥3260 to Běijīng (only some flights are direct) and ¥1900 to Xīníng.

BUS & MINIBUS

At the time of research foreigners were not allowed to take bus services around Tibet and had to arrange their own transport and so the bus station will not sell you a ticket. Should this change, there are buses from the Western Bus Station to Shigatse, Tsetang and Nagchu (Năqū), plus a daily service to Gyantse and beyond.

TRAIN

There are daily trains to/from Běijīng, Xī'ān, Shànghǎi and Guǎngzhōu and four daily to/from Xī'níng or Lánzhōu, and every other day to/from Chéngdū and Chóngqìng. The train station is 4km southwest of town.

A daily train service to Shigatse started in late 2014. Fares for the three-hour trip cost around ¥41 for a hard seat or ¥120/176 for a hard/soft sleeper. Train Z8801 departs Lhasa at 8.30am, returning from Shigatse at 6.40pm. Train Z8803 departs Lhasa at 3.20pm, returning from Shigatse at 12.05pm. If your tour agency can secure tickets you may be able to add Shigatse onto a Lhasa trip without having to fork out for pricey vehicle hire.

You can buy train tickets up to two months in advance at the Lhasa train station ticket office or the more centrally located **city ticket office** (火车票代售处, Huǒchēpiào Dàishòuchù; Map p916; Beijing Donglu; commission ¥5; ⊙8am-5:30pm). You'll need your passport. Note that it's generally much easier to get tickets *from* Lhasa than *to* Lhasa.

A taxi to/from the station costs around ¥30.

❶ Getting Around

For those travellers based in the Tibetan quarter of Lhasa, most of the major inner-city sights are within fairly easy walking distance. For sights such as the Norbulingka over in the west of town, it's better to jump in a taxi.

TO & FROM THE AIRPORT
Modern Gongkar airport is 66km from Lhasa, via the new expressway and Gālá Shān tunnel.

Airport buses (Map p916; ☑ 0891-682 7727; Niangre Beilu) leave up to 10 times a day (¥30, 1¼ hours) between 7:30am and 1pm from beside the CAAC building and are timed to meet flights. From the airport, buses wait for flights outside the terminal building. Some agencies will let their tourists travel by airport bus as long as they buy a return ticket for the guide. Buy tickets on the bus.

A taxi to the airport costs ¥200.

BICYCLE
Bicycles are a reasonably good way to get around Lhasa once you have acclimatised to the altitude. Traffic has become surprisingly busy in recent years, so take care.

Bike Hostel (p918) rents mountain bikes for ¥25 per day with a ¥600 deposit and is a meeting place for long-distance Chinese cyclists.

Bicycle theft is a problem in Lhasa, so be sure to park your bike in designated areas. A lock and chain are essential.

BUS
Buses (¥1) are frequent on Beijing Donglu, and if you need to get up to western Lhasa this is the cheapest way to do it.

PEDICAB
There is no shortage of pedicabs, but they require endless haggling and are only really useful for short trips (around ¥5). At least most are Tibetan-owned. *Always* fix the price before getting in.

TAXI
Taxis charge a standard fare of ¥10 for the first 3km (then ¥2 per subsequent kilometre), resulting in a ¥10 ride within the city centre.

AROUND LHASA

Drepung Monastery འབྲས་སྤུངས་ 哲蚌寺

Along with Sera and Ganden Monasteries, **Drepung Monastery** (Zhébàng Sì; ¥60; ⊙9:30am-5:30pm, smaller chapels close at 3pm) functioned as one of the three 'pillars of the Tibetan state', and it was purportedly the largest monastery in the world, with around 7000 resident monks at its peak. Drepung means 'rice heap', a reference to the white buildings dotting the hillside. The 1½-hour kora (pilgrim circuit) around the 15th-century monastery, 8km west of Lhasa, is among the highlights of a trip to the city.

The kings of Tsang and the Mongols savaged the place regularly, though, oddly, the Red Guards pretty much left it alone during the Cultural Revolution. With concerted rebuilding, Drepung once again resembles a monastic village and around 600 monks reside here. At lunchtime you can see the novices bringing in buckets of tsampa (roasted-barley flour) and yak-butter tea. In the afternoons you can often see Tibetan-style religious debating (lots of hand slapping and gesticulating). The best way to visit the monastery is to follow the pilgrim groups or the yellow signs. Nearby **Nechung Monastery**, a 10-minute walk downhill, was once the home of the Tibetan state oracle and is worth a visit for its blood-curdling murals.

The **Monastery Restaurant** (mains ¥7-12; ⊙10am-3pm) near the bus stop serves reviving sweet tea by the glass or thermos (¥7), as well as bowls of *shemdre* (meat and curried potatoes) and vegetable *momos* (dumplings).

Bus 25 (¥1) runs from Beijing Donglu to the foot of the Drepung hill, from where minivans (¥2) run up to the monastery. Most tourists take a taxi from the Barkhor area for around ¥40. There is a ¥10 to ¥20 charge per chapel for photography.

Ganden Monastery དགའ་ལྡན་ 甘丹寺
ELEV 4300M

Just 50km northeast of Lhasa, **Ganden Monastery** (Gāndān Sì; ¥50; ⊙dawn-dusk) was the first Gelugpa monastery and has been the main seat of this major Buddhist order ever since. If you only have time for one monastery excursion outside Lhasa, Ganden is the best choice. With its stupendous views of the surrounding Kyi-chu Valley and its fascinat-

---

THE WORLD'S HIGHEST TRAIN RIDE

There's no doubt the Qīnghǎi–Tibet train line is an engineering marvel. Topping out at 5072m, it is the world's highest railway, snatching the title from a Peruvian line. The statistics speak for themselves: 86% of the line is above 4000m, and half the track lies on permafrost, requiring a cooling system of pipes driven into the ground to keep it frozen year-round to avoid a rail-buckling summer thaw. Construction of the line involved building 160km of bridges and elevated track, seven tunnels (including the world's highest) and 24 hyperbaric chambers, the latter to treat altitude-sick workers.

Aside from environmental concerns, Tibetans are deeply worried about the cultural and political impact of the train. The trains unload thousands of Chinese tourists and immigrants into Lhasa every day, and connecting China's rail network to the only province in China lacking a rail link has forged Tibet and China together. A similar thing happened with the 1999 railway line to Kashgar in Xīnjiāng.

The authorities stress the economic benefits of the line: highly subsidised, it has decreased transport costs for imports by up to 75%. But Tibetans remain economically marginalised. More than 90% of the 100,000 workers employed to build the line came from other provinces and few, if any, Tibetan staff members work on the trains. The US$4.1 billion cost of building the line is greater than the amount Běijīng has spent on hospitals and schools in Tibet over the past 50 years.

---

ing kora (pilgrim circuit), Ganden makes for an experience unlike those at the other major Gelugpa monasteries in the Lhasa area.

Ganden means 'joyous' in Tibetan and is the name of the Western Paradise (also known as Tushita) that is home to Jampa, the Future Buddha. There is a certain irony in this because, of all the great monasteries of Tibet, Ganden suffered most at the hands of the Red Guards, possibly because of its political influence. Ganden is also the start of the popular wilderness trek to Samye Monastery (p925).

The **Ganden Kora** is simply stunning and should not be missed. There are superb views over the Kyi-chu Valley along the way and there are usually large numbers of pilgrims and monks offering prayers, rubbing holy rocks and prostrating themselves along the path. There are two parts to the walk: the high kora and the low kora. The high kora climbs Angkor Ri south of Ganden and then drops down the ridge to join up with the low kora.

Tourists are generally not allowed to stay overnight at Ganden, but there is a guesthouse here, so check with your tour agency.

The simple **Monastery Guesthouse** (dm ¥20-45, d without bathroom ¥200) at Ganden was once used by trekkers headed to Samye, but it currently doesn't accept foreigners. If this changes, the better-quality double rooms are above the well stocked monastery shop just up from the car park.

The **monastery restaurant** (dishes ¥10-20) has thugpa (Tibetan noodles) and some fried-vegetable dishes. Head for the nicer upper-storey hall.

Pilgrim buses run to a stop at Ganden in the early morning from a block west of Barkhor Sq, but tourists are currently not allowed to take them. The road from Lhasa follows a new highway east, from which a paved road switchbacks the steep final 12km to the monastery.

On the way back to Lhasa, pilgrims traditionally stop for a visit at Sanga Monastery, set at the foot of the ruined Dagtse Dzong (or Dechen Dzong; *dzong* means fort).

A 4WD for a day trip to Ganden currently costs around ¥500.

Sera Monastery   སེ་ར་དགོན་པ 色拉寺

About 5km north of Lhasa, **Sera Monastery** (Sèlā Sì; ¥50; ⊙9am-5pm; ₪22, 23) was founded in 1419 by a disciple of Tsongkhapa as one of Lhasa's two great Gelugpa monasteries. About 600 monks are now in residence, down from an original population of around 5000. The half-dozen main colleges feature spectacular prayer halls and chapels. Equally interesting is the monk debating that takes place from 3pm to 5pm in a garden near the assembly hall. Don't miss the fine, hour-long kora (pilgrim circuit) around the exterior of the monastery.

Chapels start to close at 3pm, so it makes sense to see the monastery chapels before heading to the debating.

From Sera Monastery it's possible to take a taxi northwest for a couple of kilometres to little-visited **Pabonka Monastery** (ཕ་བོང་

ཁ་དགོན་པ་, 帕邦喀寺, Pàbāngkā Sì; ◎dawn-dusk; **FREE**. Built in the 7th century by King Songtsen Gampo, this is one of the most ancient Buddhist sites in the Lhasa region.

The simple **restaurant** (dishes ¥3-8; ◎10am-3pm) serves up cheap noodles and thermoses of sweet, milky tea in its back garden.

Sera is only a half-hour bicycle ride from the Barkhor area of Lhasa, or take bus 20 from Beijing Donglu, or bus 25 or minibus 2 from Niangre Lu, to a stop at the monastery. A taxi (¥20) is the easiest option.

Ü   དབུས་

Ü (དབུས་) is Tibet's heartland and has almost all the landscapes you'll find across the plateau, from sand dunes and meandering rivers to soaring peaks and juniper forests. Due to its proximity to Lhasa, Ü is the first taste of rural Tibet that most visitors experience, and you can get off the beaten track surprisingly quickly here. Fine walking opportunities abound, from day hikes and monastery koras (pilgrim circuits) to overnight treks.

Ü is the traditional power centre of Tibet, and home to its oldest buildings and most historic monasteries. The big sights, such as Samye, are unmissable, but consider also heading to lesser-visited places such as the Drak and Ön Valleys, or to smaller monasteries like Dranang and Gongkar Chöde. Make it to these hidden gems and you'll feel as though you have Tibet all to yourself.

Samye Monastery   བསམ་ཡས་དགོན་པ་ 桑耶寺

About 170km southeast of Lhasa, on the north bank of the Yarlung Tsangpo (Brahmaputra) River is Samye Monastery (Sāngyē Sì), the first monastery in Tibet. Founded in 775 by King Trisong Detsen, Samye is famed not just for its pivotal history but for its unique mandala design: the main hall, or **Ütse** (¥40; ◎7.30am-5.30pm), represents Mt Meru, the centre of the universe, while the outer temples represent the oceans, continents, subcontinents and other features of the Buddhist cosmology.

Simple accommodation is available at the **Monastery Guesthouse** (桑耶寺宾馆, Sāngyésì Bīnguǎn; ☑0893-783 6666; d without bathroom ¥160, d/tr ¥240/300), outside the monastery walls, with comfortable doubles

and a hot-water shower. The monastery restaurant serves good *momos* (dumplings) and Chinese dishes with bags of local atmosphere. The **Friendship Snowland Restaurant** (雪域同胞旅馆, Xuěyù Tóngbāo Lǚguǎn, Gangjong Pönda Sarkhang; meals ¥16-50; ◎8.30am-11pm), outside the east gate, serves better Chinese and Tibetan dishes, banana pancakes and milky tea. Dorm rooms (¥50) with real (not foam) mattresses are available upstairs. There are several other decent accommodation options nearby, including the friendly **Tashi Guesthouse** (扎西旅馆, Zhāxī Lǚguǎn; ☑189 8993 7883; dm/r ¥60/120).

If you are heading to Everest Base Camp or the Nepali border, a visit here will only add one day to your itinerary. You may have to detour briefly to the nearby town of Tsetang (泽当; Zédāng) for your guide to pick up a required travel permit.

The Yarlung Tsangpo Valley is easily accessible and most places are within a three-hour drive of Lhasa on good roads. A rail spur line is currently under construction from Lhasa to Tsetang but will take a few years to complete.

SOUTHERN NGARI

The tarmacking of the 500km section of road from Saga to Hor Qu is now completed, which means driving times from Lhasa to Mt Kailash have been reduced to as little as three days. It is important that you don't rush, however, but take time to acclimatise.

Even if you're coming from Lhatse, consider adding three days or so to your itinerary and continuing along the Friendship Hwy to visit Everest Base Camp and Tingri and enjoy the stunning lake views of Peiku-tso.

Saga

☑0892 / ELEV 4610M

The sprawling truck-stop town of Saga (Sàgá), on the banks of the Yarlung Tsangpo river, is the last town of any size on the southern route and a logical overnight stop on the way to Mt Kailash. It's the only place until Darchen that has reliable electricity. There's little to see in town – most people use the time to wash up, check emails and stock up on supplies.

Saga is a full day's drive from Shigatse or Darchen. Closer destinations include Lhatse (306km) and Paryang (246km).

TSANG   གཙང

For most travellers, the former province of Tsang is either the first or last place they experience in Tibet, and the setting for two of Asia's great mountain drives: out to far western Tibet and across the Himalaya to Nepal. The great overland trip across Tibet – from Lhasa along the Friendship Hwy to the Nepali border via Gyantse, Shigatse and Mt Everest Base Camp – goes straight through Tsang, linking most of the highlights of the region on one irresistible route. Along the way are fantastic day walks, several multiday treks, an adventurous detour to the base of Mt Everest and a scattering of ancient Tibetan monasteries and historic towns. Dozens of smaller monasteries just off the highway offer adventurers plenty of scope to get off the beaten track and experience an older Tibet.

ℹ Permits

As with the rest of Tibet, you need permits to visit Tsang and for this you will need to travel with an organised tour with a guide and transport. Your guide will most likely need to register and get an alien's travel permit while in Shigatse.

Special trekking permits are needed if you plan to trek in the Everest region beyond Base Camp. Trekking permits for Camp III (also known as Advanced Base Camp or ABC) are issued by the China Tibet Mountain Association. Trekkers will need help from an agency to get the permits.

ℹ Getting There & Around

Public transport runs along the Northern Friendship Hwy to the Nepal border but foreigners are not allowed to take it. The Qīnghǎi–Tibet railway extension from Lhasa to Shigatse opened in 2014 and Shigatse now has its own airport with direct flights to Chéngdū.

Gyantse   རྒྱལ་རྩེ 江孜

📞 0892 / ELEV 3980M / POP 15,000

Lying on a historic trade route between India and Tibet, Gyantse (Jiāngzī) has long been a crucial link for traders and pilgrims journeying across the Himalayan plateau. It was once considered Tibet's third city, behind Lhasa and Shigatse, but in recent decades has been eclipsed by fast-growing Chinese-dominated towns like Bāyī and Tsetang. Perhaps that's a good thing, as Gyantse has managed to hang onto its small-town charm and laid-back atmosphere.

Gyantse's greatest sight is the Gyantse Kumbum, the largest chörten remaining in Tibet and one of its architectural wonders, but there's plenty more to see. With good hotels and restaurants, Gyantse is the town in Tibet that most warrants an extra day to explore little-visited nearby monasteries or wander the town's charming back streets.

👁 Sights

★ Gyantse Kumbum   BUDDHIST STUPA

(འབུམ་སྐུ་འབུམ, 江孜千佛塔, Jiāngzī Qiānfótǎ; incl with Pelkor Chöde Monastery) Commissioned by a Gyantse prince in 1427 and sitting inside the Pelkor Chöde complex, the Gyantse Kumbum is the town's foremost attraction. The 32m-high chörten, with its white layers trimmed with decorative stripes and its crown-like golden dome, is awe-inspiring. But the inside is no less impressive, and in what seems an endless series of tiny chapels you'll find painting after exquisite painting (*kumbum* means '100,000 images').

Pelkor Chöde Monastery   BUDDHIST MONASTERY

(白居寺, Báijū Sì; ¥60; ⊙9am-6:30pm, some chapels closed 1-3pm) The high red-walled compound in the far north of town houses Pelkor Chöde Monastery, founded in 1418. The main assembly hall is the main attraction but there are several other chapels to see. There's a small but visible population of 80 monks and a steady stream of prostrating, praying, donation-offering pilgrims doing the rounds almost any time of the day.

Gyantse Dzong   FORT

(江孜宗, Jiāngzī Zōng; 📞0892-817 2116; ¥30; ⊙9:30am-6:30pm) The main reason to make the 20-minute climb to the top of the Gyantse Dzong is for the fabulous views of the Pelkor Chöde Monastery and Gyantse's whitewashed old town below. Most visitors drive up halfway to the top but there is also footpath access via a gate just north of the main roundabout in town.

🎊 Festivals & Events

Dhama Festival   CULTURAL

If you happen to be in Tibet in mid-July, you can catch Gyantse's three-day Dhama Festival, featuring 19 local villages trying to outdo each other in horse races, yak races, wrestling and traditional dances. Accommodation is tight in Gyantse during the festival, but you could easily commute from Shigatse, 90 minutes away.

🛏 Sleeping & Eating

Gyantse is a popular stop for tours and has a good range of accommodation and food along north–south Yingxiong Nanlu.

⭐**Yeti Hotel** HOTEL $$

(雅迪花园酒店, Yǎdí Huāyuán Jiǔdiàn; ☑0892-817 5555; www.yetihoteltibet.com; 11 Weiguo Lu; d incl breakfast ¥328; ✸@🛜) The revamped three-star Yeti is easily the best midrange option in Gyantse, with 24-hour hot water, clean carpeted rooms, quality mattresses and reliable wi-fi, so make sure you reserve in advance. The cafe and excellent lobby restaurant serve everything from yak steak to pizza, alongside one of Tibet's best buffet breakfasts.

Jiànzàng Hotel HOTEL $$

(建藏饭店, Jiànzàng Fàndiàn; ☑0892-817 3720; jianzanghotel@yahoo.com.cn; 14 Yingxiong Nanlu, 英雄南路14号; dm ¥60, d with breakfast ¥260; 🛜) The Jiànzàng offers decent rooms in a quiet new courtyard block with ensuite rooms and 24-hour hot water. The budget triples and quads come with an ensuite squat toilet and hot showers down the hall. The 2nd-floor Tibetan-style restaurant is a cosy option for breakfast or a thermos of tea.

Tashi Restaurant NEPALI, INTERNATIONAL $$

(扎西餐厅, Zhāxī Cāntīng; Yingxiong Nanlu; mains ¥30-50; ⊙7:30am-11pm; 🖉) This Nepali-run place (a branch of Tashi in Shigatse) whips up tasty and filling curries, pizza and yak sizzlers. It also has the best range of Western breakfasts. The decor is Tibetan but the Indian movies and Nepali music give it a head-waggling subcontinental vibe.

ⓘ Information

Agricultural Bank of China (中国农业银行, Zhōngguó Nóngyè Yínháng; Weiguo Lu; ⊙9:30am-12:30pm & 3:30-6pm Mon-Fri, 11am-2pm Sat & Sun) At the time of research, the ATM here was not accepting foreign cards or changing cash, so you'll have to go to Shigatse to access your money.

ⓘ Getting There & Around

Minibuses and taxis shuttle the 90km between Gyantse and Shigatse but don't take foreigners. The drive to Shigatse takes around 90 minutes, but allow half a day with stops en route.

All of Gyantse's sights can be reached comfortably on foot, but there are rickshaws and even taxis if you need them. Negotiate all prices before you head out.

Shigatse གཞིས་ཀ་རྩེ 日喀则

☑0892 / ELEV 3840M / POP 80,000

Tibet's second-largest town and the traditional capital of Tsang province, Shigatse (Rìkāzé) is a modern, sprawling city, with wide boulevards humming with traffic. As you drive in across the plains, the site of the Potala-lookalike Shigatse Dzong, high on a hilltop overlooking the town, will probably fire your imagination, but the fort is empty and most of what you see dates from a 2007 reconstruction. It is the Tashilhunpo Monastery, to the west of town, that is the real draw.

History

As the traditional capital of the central Tsang region, Shigatse was long a rival with Lhasa for political control of the country. The Tsang kings and later governors exercised their power from the imposing heights of the (recently rebuilt) Shigatse Dzong. Since the time of the Mongol sponsorship of the Gelugpa order, Shigatse has been the seat of the Panchen Lamas, the second-highest-ranking lamas in Tibet. Their centre was and remains the Tashilhunpo Monastery.

⊙ Sights

Tashilhunpo Monastery BUDDHIST MONASTERY

(བཀྲ་ཤིས་ལྷུན་པོ, 扎什伦布寺, Zhāshílúnbù Sì; ¥80; ⊙9am-7:30pm) One of the few monasteries in Tibet to weather the stormy seas of the Cultural Revolution, Tashilhunpo remains relatively unscathed. It is a real pleasure to explore the busy cobbled lanes twisting around the aged buildings. Covering 70,000 sq metres, the monastery is now the largest functioning religious institution in Tibet and one of its great monastic sights. The huge golden statue of the Future Buddha is the largest gilded statue in the world. Buy your tickets by the southern entrance.

🎉 Festivals & Events

Tashilhunpo Monastery Festival CULTURAL

During the second week of the fifth lunar month (around June/July), Tashilhunpo Monastery becomes the scene of a three-day festival, featuring masked dances, the creation of a sand mandala and the unveiling of a huge thangka.

🛏 Sleeping

Shigatse has a good range of decent hotels, most with flush toilets and 24-hour hot water.

⭐**Gang Gyan Orchard Hotel** HOTEL $

(日喀则刚坚宾馆, Rìkāzé Gāngjiān Bīnguǎn; ☑0892-882 0777; 77 Zhufeng Lu; dm ¥50, d with bathroom ¥200; ✸🛜) This hotel offers modern, Western-style rooms with comfortable

TIBET SHIGATSE

Shigatse

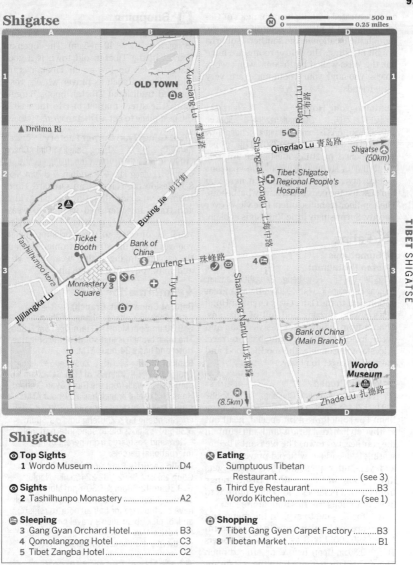

| 0 | | 500 m |
| 0 | | 0.25 miles |

Shigatse

◎ Top Sights
1 Wordo Museum D4

◎ Sights
2 Tashilhunpo Monastery A2

🛏 Sleeping
3 Gang Gyan Orchard Hotel.................... B3
4 Qomolangzong Hotel C3
5 Tibet Zangba Hotel............................... C2

✗ Eating
Sumptuous Tibetan
    Restaurant .... (see 3)
6 Third Eye Restaurant........................... B3
Wordo Kitchen................................. (see 1)

🛍 Shopping
7 Tibet Gang Gyen Carpet Factory B3
8 Tibetan Market B1

TIBET SHIGATSE

beds and clean, hot-water bathrooms. Best of all is the convenient location, right across from Tashilhunpo Monastery, less than 100m from the Tashilhunpo kora and next to two of Shigatse's best restaurants. Ask for a room overlooking the interior courtyard as these are much quieter.

Tibet Zangba Hotel   HOTEL $$
(臧巴大酒店, Zāngbā Dàjiǔdiàn; ☏0892-866 7888; 9 Renbu Lu; d/tr ¥240/340; ❄🛜) This

three-star Tibetan place is a good choice. The rooms are fresh, modern and carpeted, with contemporary bathrooms and lots of Tibetan touches, including a good Tibetan restaurant. Side rooms are quietest.

Gesar Hotel   HOTEL $$$
(格萨尔酒店, Gésà'ěr Jiǔdiàn; ☏0892-880 0088; Longjiang Lu; r standard/deluxe incl breakfast ¥380/480; ❄@🛜) This new four-star giant has clean and modern Tibetan-style rooms,

each decorated with its own thangka of Gesar Ling, and a pleasant rooftop teahouse, though the location in the southern suburbs is a bit of a drag. The deluxe rooms are huge but the glass-walled bathrooms won't work unless you and your room-mate are very close friends.

Qomolangzong Hotel HOTEL $$$
(乔穆朗宗酒店, Qiáomùlǎngzōng Jiǔdiàn; ☑0892-866 6333; cnr Shanghai Zhonglu & Zhufeng Lu; d incl breakfast ¥780) This plush hotel opened in 2015, offering an impressive lobby of stone and wood, and spacious Tibetan-style rooms, though even here you can't escape the occasional stinky bathroom. The top-floor teahouse offers fine views over the city. Surprisingly little English is spoken.

✗ Eating

★ Sumptuous Tibetan Restaurant TIBETAN $
(丰盛藏式餐厅, Fēngshèng Zàngshì Cāntīng; Zhufeng Lu; mains ¥15-50; ⏰10am-11pm) A great option next to the Gang Gyan Orchard Hotel that's always buzzing and full of Tibetans. Choose from comfy Tibetan-style seats and decor inside or the pleasant back terrace. Prices are reasonable, the food is good and the waiters eager to please.

★ Wordo Kitchen TIBETAN $$
(吾尔朵厨房, Wú'ěrduǒ Chúfáng; ☑0892-882 3994; 8 Zhade Donglu; mains ¥15-70; ⏰9:30am-11pm) For something a bit special, head out to this stylish restaurant and museum in the southeast of town. The pleasant Tibetan seating is decorated with old prayer wheels, and yak-butter pots and live music gets things going in the evenings. Dishes range from curried potatoes and potato *momos* to more ambitious yak ribs and lamb's leg.

Ask for Kelsang to explain the menu and make sure you head upstairs to the **museum** (☑139 8992 0067; ¥20, for restaurant customers ¥15; ⏰9:30am-11pm) before or after dinner. There are plans to move both the restaurant and museum to south Shigatse in 2018.

★ Third Eye Restaurant NEPALI $$
(雪莲餐厅, Xuělián Cāntīng; ☑0892-883 8898; Zhufeng Lu; dishes ¥25-50; ⏰9am-10pm) A Nepali-run place that is popular with both locals and tourists. Watch as locals sip *thugpa* while travellers treat their taste buds to the city's best Indian curries and sizzlers. The chicken tikka masala and the yak steak are both excellent. It's upstairs, next to the Gang Gyan Orchard Hotel.

🛍 Shopping

Tibetan Market ARTS & CRAFTS
(Bangjiakong Lu; ⏰10am-6pm) The open-air market in the Tibetan old town is a good place to pick up low-grade Tibetan crafts and souvenirs, such as prayer wheels, rosaries and traditional Tibetan boots. Bargain hard. The street market just to the east is the best place to get a Tibetan *chuba* (cloak).

Tibet Gang Gyen Carpet Factory CARPETS
(西藏刚坚地毯厂, Xīzàng Gāngjiān Dìtǎn Chǎng; ☑139 0892 1399; www.tibetgang-gyencarpet.com; 9 Zhufeng Lu; ⏰9am-1pm & 3-7pm Mon-Sat) Beside the Gang Gyan Orchard Hotel, 100m down a side alley, this workshop hires and trains impoverished women to weave high-quality wool carpets. Upon arrival you'll be directed to the workshop, where you can watch the 80 or so women work on the carpets, singing as they weave, dye, trim and spin; you're free to take photos.

ℹ Information

Bank of China (Main Branch) (中国银行, Zhōngguó Yínháng; Shanghai Zhonglu; ⏰9:30am-6pm Mon-Fri, 11am-4pm Sat & Sun) The main branch is just south of the Shigatse Hotel and has a 24-hour ATM.

Bank of China (中国银行, Zhōngguó Yínháng; Zhufeng Lu; ⏰9:30am-6pm Mon-Sat, 10am-6pm Sun) A short walk from the Gang Gyan Orchard Hotel, this useful branch has a 24-hour ATM.

China Post (中国邮政, Zhōngguó Yóuzhèng; cnr Shandong Lu & Zhufeng Lu; ⏰9:30am-6:30pm) It's possible to send international letters and postcards from here, but not international parcels.

Public Security Bureau (PSB, 公安局, Gōng'ānjú; ☑0892-882 2240; Jilin Nanlu; ⏰9:30am-12:30pm & 3:30-6pm Mon-Fri, 10am-1:30pm Sat & Sun) Your guide will likely have to stop here for half an hour to register and/or pick up an alien's travel permit for the Friendship Hwy or western Tibet. It's in the southern suburbs, near the Gesar Hotel.

ℹ Getting There & Away

Tibet Airlines operates four flights a week from Shigatse's Peace Airport to Chéngdū (¥1880).

Minibuses, buses and taxis travel from Shigatse to Lhasa and run in the morning to Sakya (4 hours), Lhatse (5 hours) and Gyantse (1½ hours), but foreign tourists aren't allowed to take them.

The 250km train spur line from Lhasa to Shigatse opened in late 2014 and foreigners can now theoretically take these trains as part of their guided tour. It's certainly a lot faster given the number of checkposts currently in place on the Lhasa–Shigatse road.

Train Z8804 departs Shigatse at 12:05pm, while train Z8802 departs at 6:40pm. Both services run daily and take just under three hours. A hard-seat ticket costs ¥41, while a seat in soft sleeper costs from ¥170. The station is about 10km south of town on the road to Gyantse.

Lhatse ལྷ་རྩེ་ 拉孜

☑ 0892 / ELEV 3950M

Approximately 150km southwest of Shigatse and some 30km west of the Sakya turn-off, the modern town of Lhatse (Lāzī) is a convenient overnight stop for travellers headed to western Tibet. Lhatse is more or less a one-street town with a small square near the centre. The 3km-long main street runs east–west and used to be part of the Friendship Hwy, but this has now been diverted to the north. Passing traffic will mostly be heading to Everest Base Camp, the Tibet–Nepal border or the turn-off for western Tibet, about 6km out of town past a major checkpoint.

If you have time to kill you could visit the renovated Changmoche Monastery at the western end of town.

Daily morning minibuses (five hours) run between Shigatse and Lhatse and a couple of buses a day pass through en route to Shegar and Saga, although tourists cannot take these services. Lhatse is 50km from Sakya and 150km from Shigatse.

Sakya ས་སྐྱ་ 萨迦

☑ 0892 / ELEV 4320M

A detour to visit the small town of Sakya (Sàjiā) is pretty much de rigueur for any trip down the Friendship Hwy. The town is southeast of Shigatse, about 25km off the Southern Friendship Hwy, accessed via a paved road through a pretty farming valley. The draw is Sakya Monastery, which ranks as one of the most atmospheric, impressive and unique monasteries in Tibet. Moreover, Sakya occupies a pivotal place in Tibetan history.

In recent years Sakya village has transformed from a village into a town and the area around the monastery has been developed by a private company to include a huge parking lot and a hefty new entry fee, but Sakya still feels somewhat off the grid.

The immense, grey, thick-walled **Sakya Monastery** (萨迦寺, Sàjiā Sì; ¥180; ⊙9am-6pm) is one of Tibet's most impressive constructed sights, and one of the largest monasteries. Established in 1268, it was designed

defensively, with watchtowers on each corner of its high walls. Inside, the dimly lit hall exudes a sanctity and is on a scale that few others can rival. As usual, morning is the best time to visit as most chapels are closed from 1:30pm to 3:30pm.

The renovated rooms at **Manasarovar Sakya Hotel** (神湖萨迦宾馆, Shénhú Sàjiā Bīnguǎn; ☑0892-824 2555; 1 Gesang Xilu; d/tr ¥220/280; 🌐) are spacious and comfortable, with hot-water bathrooms and electric blankets, making it the best value in town.

Sakya's newest hotel, **Yuan Mansion Hotel** (元府大酒店, Yuánfǔ Dàjiǔdiàn; ☑0892-824 2222; Gesang Xilu; d ¥480; 🌐🌐) is run by the next-door Manasarovar Sakya Hotel and is similar, but boasts newer bathrooms and better furniture.

Overlooking the main street, **Sakya Farmer's Taste Restaurant** (萨迦农民美食厅, Sàjiā Nóngmín Měishítīng; ☑0892-824 2221; dishes ¥20-35) has a cosy atmosphere amid Tibetan decor. The waiters are friendly and will help explain the various Tibetan and Chinese dishes available. The food is tasty but portions are small.

Sakya is 25km off the Friendship Hwy. En route you'll pass the impressive ridgetop Tonggar Choede Monastery. Just 5km before Sakya at Chonkhor Lhunpo village is the Ogyen Lhakhang, where local farmers go to get blessings from relics said to be able to prevent hailstorms.

Everest Base Camp ཇོ་མོ་གླང་མའི་རྒྱབ་ཁས་འོག 珠峰基地营

For foreign travellers, Everest Base Camp has become one of the most popular destinations in Tibet, offering the chance to gaze on the magnificent north face of the world's tallest peak, Mt Everest (珠穆朗玛峰; Zhūmùlǎngmǎ Fēng; 8848m). The Tibetan approach provides far better vistas than those on the Nepali side, and access is a lot easier as a road runs all the way to base camp.

Everest's Tibetan name is generally rendered as Qomolangma, and some 27,000 sq km of territory around Everest's Tibetan face have been designated as the Qomolangma Nature Preserve.

Most visitors are content with early morning views of the mountain from Rongphu Monastery and the viewpoint above Everest Base Camp, though we recommend throwing in some explorations on foot and then exiting the region via the little-used dirt road to Old Tingri.

Endowed with springs, **Everest Base Camp** (Zhūfēng Jīdìyíng, EBC, 5150m) was first used by the 1924 British Everest expedition. Tourists are not allowed to visit the expedition tents a few hundred metres away, but you can clamber up the small hill festooned with prayer flags for great views of the star attraction. Be prepared for plenty of crowds and selfie sticks.

Although religious centres have existed in the region since around the 8th century, **Rongphu Monastery** (绒布寺, Róngbù Sì; ¥25, 4980m) is now the main Buddhist centre in the valley. While not of great antiquity, Rongphu can at least lay claim to being the highest monastery in Tibet and, thus, the world. It's worth walking the short kora path around the monastery's exterior walls. The monastery and its large chörten make for a superb photograph with Everest thrusting its head skyward in the background.

The monastery-run **guesthouse** (绒布寺招待所, Róngbù Sì Zhāodàisuǒ; ☑ 136 2892 1359; dm ¥60, tw without bathroom ¥200) is probably the most comfortable place to stay at Everest. The private rooms with proper beds and stone walls tend to be warmer than the tent camp and there's certainly more privacy. Best value are the beds in a four-bed room. All rooms share the pit toilets.

ⓘ Permits

Apart from the normal Tibet travel permits, you need to buy an entry ticket for the Qomolangma Nature Preserve to visit the Everest region, either at the main turn-off from the Friendship Hwy or in Old Tingri. The ticket costs ¥400 per vehicle plus ¥180 per passenger. Your guide (but not driver) will also need a ticket. Make sure you are clear with your agency about whether this cost is included in your trip (it usually isn't).

Your passport and PSB permit will be scrutinised at the checkpoint 6km west of Shegar, where you'll have to walk through the passport check. Queues can be long, especially after lunch.

Your ticket will be checked again just before Rongphu Monastery. If you are driving in from Tingri, you'll go to the checkpoint at Lungchang. A military checkpost at Rongphu will also want to check your permits.

ⓘ Getting There & Away

There is no public transport to Everest Base Camp. It's either trek in or come with your own vehicle. From Chay it's 91km to Base Camp; from Tingri it's around 70km on an unpaved road.

Tingri

☑ 0892 / ELEV 4330M

The village of Tingri (Dìngrì or Tingri Gankar) comprises a gritty kilometre-long strip of restaurants, guesthouses and truck-repair workshops lining the Friendship Hwy. Sometimes called Old Tingri, it overlooks a sweeping plain bordered by towering Himalayan peaks (including Everest) and is a common overnight stop for tours heading to or from the Nepali border. On clear days there are stunning views of Cho Oyu from Tingri; if you can't make it to Everest Base Camp, at least pause here and take in the Himalayan eye candy.

It is possible to trek between Everest Base Camp and Tingri, though the route now follows a dirt road.

Kangar Hotel (岗嘎宾馆, Gǎnggā Bīnguǎn; ☑ 0892-826 5777; www.tibetshangrila.com/hotel.html; d/tr ¥260/360; ☎) on the east end of town is well run, offering comfortable rooms, a fine sunroof sitting area, a modern restaurant and great views of the mountains. Water pressure can be iffy upstairs so ask the staff to adjust the pump when you want a shower. Probably your best bet in town.

The best place in town for a meal, **Base Camp Restaurant** (大本营餐厅, Dàběnyíng Cāntīng; dishes ¥30-50; ☉ 11am-10pm) is a pleasant Tibetan-style restaurant attached to Héhū Bīnguǎn, boasting traditional furniture, helpful staff and tasty Chinese and Tibetan dishes. Prices are reasonable for Tingri.

Entry tickets to Qomolangma Nature Preserve are available at the **ticket office** (☑ 156 9262 6148) within the compound of the **Snow Leopard Guesthouse** (雪豹客栈, Xuěbào Kèzhàn; ☑ 0892-826 2711; d/tr ¥250/320).

From Tingri down to Zhāngmù on the Nepal border it's an easy half-day drive of just under 200km. If you are coming the other way, you should break the trip into two days to aid acclimatisation. The highest point along the paved road is the Tong-la pass (5140m), 95km from Tingri, from where you can see a horizon of 8000m Himalayan peaks.

FAR WEST NGARI

Tibet's far wild west has few permanent settlers but is nevertheless a lodestone to a billion pilgrims from three major religions (Buddhism, Hinduism and Jainism). They are drawn to the twin spiritual power places of Mt Kailash and Lake Manasarovar, two of

FRIENDSHIP HIGHWAY (NEPAL TO TIBET)

The 1000km-or-so stretch of road between Kathmandu and Lhasa is without a doubt one of the most spectacular in the world. There are currently two routes from Kathmandu. The oldest route is via the border crossing at Kodari (1873m) and Zhāngmù (2250m), but this section was badly affected by Nepal's 2015 earthquake and remains closed to international traffic.

The main Nepal–Tibet border crossing has shifted to Rasuwa at the meeting of Nepal's Langtang region and Tibet's Kyirong Valley. Chinese travellers have been using the border crossing for a few years now, but it was only opened to foreigners in 2016. It's a spectacular route that allows you to combine a trek in Nepal's Langtang region with a visit to lovely Peiku-tso on the Tibetan side. The section of road on the Tibetan side is paved, but the Nepali road is slow going, especially during the monsoon months from June to September.

The closure of the border at Kodari means that Zhāngmù and Nyalam (3750m), where travellers used to spend their first night, are now virtual ghost towns. The two routes join just north of the La Lung-la (4845m) on the Friendship Hwy and continue to Tingri.

It is essential to watch out for the effects of altitude sickness during the early stages of this trip. If you intend to head up to Everest Base Camp (5150m), you really need to slip in a rest day at Tingri or Kyirong. China is 2¼ hours ahead of Nepali time.

the most legendary and far-flung destinations in the world.

This part of Ngari is a huge, expansive realm of salt lakes, Martian-style deserts, grassy steppes and snowcapped mountains. It's a mesmerising landscape, but it's also intensely remote: a few tents and herds of yaks may be all the signs of human existence you'll come across in half a day's drive.

Darchen & Mt Kailash 塔钦、冈仁波齐峰

📋 0897 / ELEV 4670M

Sacred Mt Kailash (ﾀﾞﾝﾎﾞﾝﾎﾟ; Kang Rinpoche, or 'Precious Jewel of Snow' in Tibetan; 冈仁波齐峰; Gāngrénbōqí Fēng in Chinese) dominates the landscape of western Tibet with the sheer awesomeness of its four-sided summit, just as it dominates the mythology of a billion people. The mountain has been a lodestone to pilgrims and adventurous travellers for centuries, but until recently very few had set eyes on it. This is changing fast.

Nestled in the foothills at the base of Mt Kailash, the small town of Darchen (ﾀﾞﾝﾁﾞﾝ; 塔钦; Tǎqīn) is the starting point of the sacred mountain's famous kora (pilgrim circuit). It is a rapidly expanding settlement of hotel compounds, tourist restaurants and pilgrim shops. Almost everyone spends a night here before setting off on the kora, and many spend a second night after the trek, taking advantage of the facilities to grab a hot shower and check their emails. On the

kora you can use your cell phone's 3G connection to go online.

Darchen is 3km north of the main Ali–Saga road, about 12km from Barkha, 107km north of Purang, 330km southeast of Ali and a lonely 1200km from Lhasa.

🏃 Activities

The main reason anyone comes to Darchen is to to make the three-day walk around the Mt Kailash kora, but there are also a couple of good acclimatisation hikes around town.

The age-old path around Mt Kailash is one of the world's great pilgrimage routes and completely encircles Asia's holiest mountain. With a 5630m pass to conquer, this kora is a test of both the mind and the spirit.

There's some gorgeous mountain scenery along this trek, including close-ups of the majestic pyramidal Mt Kailash, but just as rewarding is the chance to see and meet your fellow pilgrims, many of whom have travelled hundreds of kilometres on foot to get here. Apart from local Tibetans, there are normally dozens of Hindus on the kora during the main pilgrim season (June to September). Most ride horses, with yak teams carrying their supplies. There are also plenty of Chinese tourists.

The route around Mt Kailash is a simple one: you start by crossing a plain, then head up a wide river valley, climb up and over the 5630m Drölma-la, head down another river valley, and finally cross the original plain to the starting point. It's so straightforward and so perfect a natural circuit that it's easy to see how it has been a pilgrim favourite for thousands of years.

The Mt Kailash trekking season runs from mid-May until mid-October, but trekkers should always be prepared for changeable weather. Snow may be encountered on the Drölma-la at any time of year and the temperature will often drop well below freezing at night. The pass tends to be snowed in from early November to early April.

The kora is becoming more and more popular. A tent and your own food are always a nice luxury, but there is now accommodation and simple food at Dira-puk and Zutul-puk. Guides can even book you a room here in advance. Bottled water, beer, instant noodles and tea are available every few hours at teahouse tents. Natural water sources abound, but you should bring the means of water purification. A dirt road now encircles two-thirds of the kora, but traffic is light and it's fairly easy to avoid.

Horses, yaks and porters are all available for hire in Darchen, the gateway town to the kora. Big groups often hire yaks to carry their supplies, but yaks will only travel in pairs or herds, so you have to hire at least two. Horses are an easier option but are surprisingly expensive because they are in great demand by Indian pilgrims. Most hikers carry their own gear or get by with the services of a local porter (¥210 per day for a minimum of three days). All guides and pack animals have to be arranged through a central **office** (岗仁波齐牛马运输服务中心, Gǎngrén Bōqí Niúmǎ Yùnshū Fúwù Zhōngxīn; ☑porters 139 8907 5383, yaks & horses 136 3897 3593) in Darchen.

Your guide will register your group with the **PSB** (公安局, Gōng'ānjú; ☑0897-260 7018; ⊙24hr) in Darchen. The entrance fee to Mt Kailash is ¥150 per person and is paid at a large entry gate before you arrive in Darchen.

⚜ Festivals & Events

Saga Dawa RELIGIOUS
(⊙May or Jun) The festival of Saga Dawa marks the enlightenment of Sakyamuni, and occurs on the full-moon day of the fourth Tibetan month. In the Kailash region the highlight is the raising of the Tarboche prayer pole in the morning. Monks circumambulate the pole in elaborate costumes, with horns blowing. After the pole has been raised, about 1pm, everyone sets off on their kora.

🛏 Sleeping & Eating

Most travellers spend a night in Darchen before the kora. Many guesthouses offer basic accommodation (no running water, outdoor pit toilets). Bigger places can be fully booked with large groups of Indian pilgrims during the summer months of June, July and August.

Supplies on the Mt Kailash kora are limited to instant noodles and beer, so stock up on snacks in Darchen's supermarkets before heading off.

One of the best options in Darchen, **Kailash & Holy Lake Guest House** (神山圣湖宾馆, Shénshān Shènghú Bīnguǎn; ☑136 2891 8072; dm ¥50, d ¥200-240) is the first hotel you come to as you enter town from the south. It's far from perfect – check the plumbing before accepting a room – but the hot water is pretty reliable and rooms are spacious.

Markham Teahouse (芒康藏餐, Mángkāng Zàngcān; dishes ¥15-30) is a cosy and friendly Tibetan teahouse whose comfy sofas beckon for sweet tea, breakfast omelettes, noodles and fried dishes, all easy to order on a picture menu. It's on the upper floor, above a shop, on the southwestern corner of Darchen's central crossroad.

Lake Manasarovar
མ་ཕམ་མཚོ་
玛旁雄错
ELEV 4560M

Sacred Lake Manasarovar (Mapham Yumtso, or Victorious Lake, in Tibetan; Mǎpáng Xióngcuò, in Chinese) is the most venerated of Tibet's many lakes and one of its most beautiful. With its sapphire-blue waters, sandy shoreline and snowcapped-mountain backdrop, Manasarovar is immediately appealing, and a welcome change from the often forbidding terrain of Mt Kailash.

Most visitors base themselves at picturesque **Chiu village**, site of Chiu Monastery, on the northwestern shore of the lake. Indian pilgrims often drive around the lake, immersing themselves in the sacred waters at some point. You'll also see Tibetan pilgrims walking the four-day kora path around the lake. The lake area has a one-time admission fee of ¥150 per person (the Mt Kailash fee does not cover this).

Chiu, at the northwestern corner of the lake, is 15km south of Barkha junction, from where it is 22km west to Darchen or 22km east to Hor Qu. The only way to get around is to have your own transport or hike around the lake.

Understand China

China Today

A highly idiosyncratic mix of can-do entrepreneurs, inward-looking Buddhists, textbook Marxists, overnight millionaires, the out-of-pocket, leather-faced farmers, unflagging migrant workers and round-the-clock McJobbers, China today is as multifaceted as its challenges are diverse. From the outside, China's autocratic decision-making may suggest national uniformity, but things are actually more in a state of controlled, and not so controlled, chaos.

Best on Film

Still Life (Jia Zhangke; 2005) Bleak and hauntingly beautiful portrayal of a family devastated by the construction of the Three Gorges Dam.

Raise the Red Lantern (Zhang Yimou; 1991) Exquisitely fashioned tragedy from the sumptuous palette of the Fifth Generation.

In the Mood for Love (Wong Kar-Wai; 2000) Seductive, stylishly costumed and slow-burning Hong Kong romance.

Best in Print

Country Driving: A Chinese Road Trip (Peter Hessler) Hessler's amusing and insightful journey at the wheel around the highways and byways of China.

Tiger Head, Snake Tails (Jonathan Fenby) Compelling account of contemporary China's myriad challenges and contradictions.

Diary of a Madman & Other Stories (Lu Xun) Astonishing tales from the father of modern Chinese fiction.

The Economy: Speed-bump or Cul-de-sac?

China's eye-watering growth appears to be nearing the end of its blinding three-decade run, although experts remain divided over long-term implications for its US$11 trillion economy. Confrontingly high levels of debt, chronic overcapacity in manufacturing, a constellation of real-estate bubbles dotted around the land and a stock market prone to sudden dives, mean the days of easy, double-digit growth have given way to more sober forecasts. The economy may not be coming off the rails, but China's ambitious proposals in its current five-year plan could take a bruising, including its commitment to hugely expand social security and feed the country's large and demanding military budget. The latter expenditure is perhaps most crucial, to satisfy a growing domestic appetite for a strong nation when rivalries within the region and with the US are at their keenest. While a bust is perhaps unlikely, China may need to prepare for a period of middle-income blues with fewer jobs, reduced expectations and the days of double-digit growth a thing of the past.

China goes Travelling

China's crashing stock market seems to have done little to stop the Chinese from joining the top league of travelling nations for the first time in their tumultuous and predominantly inward-looking recent history. So while the world goes to China, China is increasingly going to the world. In 2015 a record 120 million (a bit less than the population of Mexico) outbound visitors left China. In the same year, Chinese arrivals to the UK were up by 40% in the first nine months of 2015. Chinese travellers spent a staggering US$215 billion abroad in 2015 (more than the GDP of Portugal), up 53% on the previous 12 months, while Chinese tourism is predicted to account for 14% of worldwide tourism revenue by 2020. Relaxed visa rulings from several nations, including the US and UK, have helped get Chinese feet into their outbound travelling shoes. It doesn't quite mean you'll find China deserted when you get there – the Chinese are more actively travelling around their home nation too: Běijīng is hoping that domestic travellers will outlay ¥5.5 trillion on travel around China by 2020.

Troubled Waters & Restive Borderlands

China's dazzling economic trajectory over the last three decades has been watched with awe by the West and increasing consternation by the Middle Kingdom's neighbours. By virtue of its sheer size and population, a dominant China will ruffle some East Asian feathers. The long-festering dispute between China and Vietnam, the Philippines and other nations over the control of waters, islands, reefs, atolls and rocky outcrops of the Paracel (Xīshā) and Spratly (Nánshā) Islands in the South China Sea worsened in recent years when China unilaterally began reclaiming land around, and building on, contested reefs. China has attempted to enforce a 12-nautical-mile exclusion zone around these reefs, which has been tested by the US Navy conducting 'freedom of navigation' exercises. The possibility of miscalculation, that could lead to conflict, has never been greater. Meanwhile, the seemingly intractable spat over the contested and uninhabited Diàoyú Islands (Senkaku Islands to the Japanese) continues to sour relations between China and Japan. While keeping an eye on maritime issues, at home President Xi Jīnpíng has had to deal with unrest in Xīnjiāng province, where Uighur disquiet has prompted an increasingly harsh security clampdown from Běijīng, which may threaten to inflame sentiments further.

POPULATION: **1.37 BILLION**

AREA: **9.6 MILLION SQ KM**

GDP (PPP): **$19.51 TRILLION**

LABOUR FORCE: **804 MILLION**

HIGHEST POINT: **MT EVEREST (8848M ABOVE SEA LEVEL)**

if China were 100 people

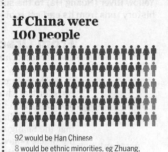

92 would be Han Chinese
8 would be ethnic minorities, eg Zhuang, Manchu, Uighur

belief systems
(% of population)

52 unaffiliated
22 folk religion
18 Buddhist
5 Christian
2 Muslim
1 other

population per sq km

CHINA　RUSSIA　USA

👤 ≈ 9 people

History

The epic sweep of China's history can suggest prolonged epochs of peace occasionally convulsed by sudden breakup, internecine division or external attack, yet for much of its history China has been in conflict either internally or with outsiders. The Middle Kingdom's size and shape may have continuously changed – from tiny beginnings by the Yellow River (Huáng Hé) to the subcontinent of today – but an uninterrupted thread of history runs from its earliest roots to the full flowering of Chinese civilisation.

From Oracle Bones to Confucius

The earliest 'Chinese' dynasty, the Shang, was long considered apocryphal. However, archaeological evidence – cattle bones and turtle shells in Hénán covered in mysterious scratches, recognised by a scholar as an early form of Chinese writing – proved that a society known as the Shang developed in central China from around 1766 BC. The area it controlled was tiny – perhaps 200km across – but Chinese historians have argued that the Shang was the first Chinese dynasty. By using Chinese writing on 'oracle bones', the dynasty marked its connection with the Chinese civilisation of the present day.

Sometime between 1050 and 1045 BC, a neighbouring group known as the Zhou conquered Shang territory. The Zhou was one of many states competing for power in the next few hundred years but developments during this period created some of the key sources of Chinese culture that would last till the present day. A constant theme of the first millennium BC was conflict, particularly the periods known as the 'Spring and Autumn' (722–481 BC) and 'Warring States' (475–221 BC).

The Chinese world in the 5th century BC was both warlike and intellectually fertile, in a way similar to ancient Greece during the same period. From this disorder emerged the thinking of Confucius (551–479 BC), whose system of thought and ethics underpinned Chinese culture for 2500 years. Confucius dispensed lessons in personal behaviour and statecraft, advocating an ordered and ethical society obedient towards hierarchies and inclined towards ritual. Confucius' desire for an ordered and ethical world was a far cry from the warfare of his times.

Ancient
Icons
....

Army of
Terracotta
Warriors (p391)
....

The Great Wall
(p124)
....

Forbidden City
(p68)
....

Mògāo Grottoes
(p858)

TIMELINE	c 4000 BC	c 1700 BC	c 600 BC
	The first known settlements appear along the Yellow River (Huáng Hé). The river remains a central cultural reference point for the Chinese throughout history.	Craftsmen of the Shang dynasty master the production of bronzeware (in the form of ritual vessels) in one of the first examples of multiple production in history.	Laotzu (Laozi), founder of Taoism, is supposedly born. The folk religion of Taoism goes on to coexist with later arrivals such as Buddhism, a reflection of Chinese religion's syncretic, rather than exclusive, nature.

Early Empires

The Warring States period ended decisively in 221 BC. The Qin kingdom conquered other states in the central Chinese region and Qin Shi Huang proclaimed himself emperor. The first in a line of dynastic rulers that would last until 1912, later histories portrayed Qin Shi Huang as particularly cruel and tyrannical, but the distinction is dubious: the ensuing Han dynasty (206 BC–AD 220) adopted many of the short-lived Qin's practices of government. Qin Shi Huang oversaw vast public works projects, including walls built by some 300,000 men, connecting defences into what would become the Great Wall. He unified the currency, measurements and written language, providing the basis for a cohesive state.

Establishing a trend that would echo through Chinese history, a peasant, Liu Bang (256–195 BC), rose up and conquered China, founding the Han dynasty. The dynasty is so important that the name Hàn (汉 漢) still refers to ethnic Chinese and their language (汉语; Hanyu; 'language of the Han'). Critical to the centralisation of power, Emperor Wu (140–87 BC) institutionalised Confucian norms in government. Promoting merit as well as order, he was the first leader to experiment with examinations for entry into the bureaucracy, but his dynasty was plagued by economic troubles, as estate owners controlled more and more land. Indeed, the issue of land ownership would be a constant problem throughout Chinese history to today. Endemic economic problems and the inability to exercise control over a growing empire, coupled with social unrest that included an uprising by Taoists (known as the Yellow Turbans) led to the collapse and downfall of the Han. Upheaval would become a constant refrain in later Chinese dynasties.

Han trade along the Silk Road demonstrated clearly that China was fundamentally a Eurasian power in its relations with neighbouring peoples. To the north, the Xiongnu (a name given to various nomadic tribes of Central Asia) posed the greatest threat to China. Diplomatic links were also formed with Central Asian tribes, and the great Chinese explorer Zhang Qian provided the authorities with information on the possibilities of trade and alliances in northern India. During the same period, Chinese influence percolated into areas that would later become known as Vietnam and Korea.

Evidence from Han tombs suggests that a popular item of cuisine was a thick vegetable and meat stew, and that flavour enhancers such as soy sauce and honey were also used.

Disunity Restored

Between the early 3rd and late 6th centuries AD, north China witnessed a succession of rival kingdoms vying for power while a potent division formed between north and south. Riven by warfare, the north succumbed to non-Chinese rule, most successfully by the northern Wei dynasty (386–534), founded by the Tuoba, a northern people who embraced Buddhism and left behind some of China's finest Buddhist art, including the famous caves outside Dūnhuáng. A succession of rival

551 BC	214 BC	c 100 BC	c 100 BC
The birth of Confucius. Collected in *The Analects,* his ideas of an ethical, ordered society that operated through hierarchy and self-development would dominate Chinese culture until the early 20th century.	Emperor Qin indentures thousands of labourers to link existing city walls into one Great Wall, made of tamped earth. The brick cladding of the bastion dates from the much later Ming dynasty.	The Silk Road between China and the Middle East takes Chinese goods to places as far flung as Rome.	Buddhism first arrives in China from India. This religious system ends up thoroughly assimilated into Chinese culture and is now more powerful in China than in its country of origin.

regimes followed until nobleman Yang Jian (d 604) reunified China under the fleeting Sui dynasty (581–618). His son Sui Yangdi contributed greatly to the unification of south and north through construction of the Grand Canal, which was later extended and remained China's most important communication route between south and north until the late 19th century. After instigating three unsuccessful incursions onto Korean soil, resulting in disastrous military setbacks, Sui Yangdi faced revolt and was assassinated in 618 by one of his high officials.

So far, some 7000 soldiers in the famous Terracotta Army have been found near Xī'ān. The great tomb of the first emperor still remains unexcavated, although it is thought to have been looted soon after it was built.

The Tang: China Looks West

Tang rule (618–907) was an outward-looking time, when China embraced the culture of its neighbours – marriage to Central Asian people or wearing Indian-influenced clothes was part of the era's cosmopolitan élan – and distant nations that reached China via the Silk Road. The Chinese nostalgically regard the Tang as their cultural zenith and Chinatowns around the world are called Tángrénjiē (Tang People Streets). The output of the Tang poets is still regarded as China's finest, as is Tang sculpture, while its legal code became a standard for the whole East Asian region.

The Tang was founded by the Sui general Li Yuan, his achievements consolidated by his son Taizong (r 626–49). Cháng'ān (modern Xī'ān) became the world's most dazzling capital, with its own cosmopolitan foreign quarter, a population of a million, a market where merchants from as far away as Persia mingled with locals, and an astonishing city wall that eventually enveloped 83 sq km. The city exemplified the Tang devotion to Buddhism, with some 91 temples recorded in the city in 722, but a tolerance of and even absorption with foreign cultures allowed alien faiths a foothold, including Nestorian Christianity, Manichaeism, Islam, Judaism and Zoroastrianism.

Taizong was succeeded by a unique figure: Chinese history's sole reigning woman emperor, Wu Zetian (r 690–705). Under her leadership

RUINS

Many of China's historical artefacts may be in a state of perpetual ruin, but some vestiges get top-billing:

Ruins of the Church of St Paul in Macau (p537) China's most sublime architectural wreck.

Jiànkòu Great Wall (p127) No other section of the Great Wall does the tumble-down look in such dramatic fashion.

Great Fountain Ruins (p97) Sublime tangle of Jesuit-designed stonework

Shàngdū (p882; Xanadu) A vivid imagination is required to conjure up impressions of Kublai Khan's pleasure palace.

AD 755–763	874	c 1000	1215
An Lushan rebels against the Tang court. Although his rebellion is subdued, the court cedes immense military and fiscal power to provincial leaders, a recurring problem through Chinese history.	The Huang Chao rebellion breaks out, which helps reduce the Tang empire to chaos and leads to the fall of the capital in 907.	The major premodern inventions – paper, printing, gunpowder, the compass – are commonly used in China. The economy begins to commercialise and create a countrywide market system.	Genghis Khan conquers Běijīng as part of his creation of a massive Eurasian empire under Mongol rule. The Mongols overstretch themselves, however, and neglect good governance.

the empire reached its greatest extent, spreading well north of the Great Wall and far west into inner Asia. Her strong promotion of Buddhism, however, alienated her from the Confucian officials and in 705 she was forced to abdicate in favour of Xuanzong, who would preside over the greatest disaster in the Tang's history: the rebellion of An Lushan.

Xuanzong appointed minorities from the frontiers as generals, in the belief that they were so far removed from the political system and society that they would not harbour ideas of rebellion. Nevertheless, it was An Lushan, a general of Sogdian-Turkic parentage, who took advantage of his command in north China to make a bid for imperial power. The fighting lasted from 755 to 763, and although An Lushan was defeated, the Tang's control over China was destroyed forever. It had ceded huge amounts of military and tax-collecting power to provincial leaders to enable them to defeat the rebels, and in doing so dissipated its own power. A permanent change in the relationship between the government and the provinces formed; prior to 755, the government had an idea of who owned what land throughout the empire, but after that date the central government's control was permanently weakened. Even today, the dilemma has not been fully resolved.

In its last century, the Tang withdrew from its former openness, turning more strongly to Confucianism, while Buddhism was outlawed by Emperor Wuzong from 842 to 845. The ban was later modified, but Buddhism never regained its previous power and prestige. The Tang decline was a descent into imperial frailty, growing insurgencies, upheaval and chaos.

The Song: Conflict & Prosperity

Further disunity – the fragmentary-sounding Five Dynasties or Ten Kingdoms period – followed the fall of the Tang until the northern Song dynasty (960–1127) was established. The Song dynasty existed in a state of constant conflict with its northern neighbours. The northern Song was a rather small empire coexisting with the non-Chinese Liao dynasty (which controlled a belt of Chinese territory south of the Great Wall that then marked China's northern border) and less happily with the western Xia, another non-Chinese power that pressed hard on the northwestern provinces. In 1126 the Song lost its capital, Kāifēng, to a third non-Chinese people, the Jurchen (previously an ally against the Liao). The Song was driven to its southern capital of Hángzhōu for the period of the southern Song (1127–1279), yet the period was culturally rich and economically prosperous.

The full institution of a system of examinations for entry into the Chinese bureaucracy was brought to fruition during the Song. At a time when brute force decided who was in control in much of medieval Europe, young Chinese men sat tests on the Confucian classics, obtaining office if successful (most were not). The system was heavily biased towards the rich, but was remarkable in its rationalisation of authority. The

The features of the largest Buddhist statue in the Ancestor Worshipping Cave at the Lóngmén Grottoes outside Luòyáng were supposedly based on Tang female emperor Wu Zetian, a famous champion of Buddhism.

1286	1298–99	1368	1406
The Grand Canal is extended to Běijīng. Over time, the canal becomes a major artery for the transport of grain, salt and other important commodities between north and south China.	Marco Polo pens his famous account of his travels to China. Inconsistencies in his story have led some scholars to doubt whether he ever went to China at all.	Zhu Yuanzhang founds the Ming dynasty and tries to impose a rigid Confucian social order on the entire population. However, China is now too commercialised for the policy to work.	Ming Emperor Yongle begins construction of the 800 buildings of the Forbidden City. This complex, along with much of the Great Wall, shows the style and size of late-imperial architecture.

classical texts set for the examinations became central to the transmission of a sense of elite Chinese culture, even though in later centuries the system's rigidity failed to adapt to social and intellectual change.

China's economy prospered during the Song rule, as cash crops and handicraft products became far more central to the economy, and a genuinely China-wide market emerged, which would become even stronger during the Ming and Qing dynasties. Sciences and arts also flourished under the Song, with intellectual and technical advances across many disciplines. Kāifēng emerged as a centre of politics, commerce and culture.

The cultural quirk of foot binding appears to have emerged during the Song dynasty. It is still unknown how the custom of binding up a girl's feet in cloths so that they would never grow larger than the size of a fist began, yet for much of the next few centuries, it became a Chinese social norm.

Qing emperor Kangxi sponsored a vast encyclopedia of Chinese culture, which is still read by scholars today.

Mongols to Ming

The fall of the Song reinforced notions of China's Eurasian location and growing external threats. Genghis Khan (1167–1227) was beginning his rise to power, turning his gaze on China; he took Běijīng in 1215, destroying and rebuilding it; his successors seized Hángzhōu, the southern Song capital, in 1276. The court fled and, in 1279, southern Song resistance finally crumbled. Kublai Khan, grandson of Genghis, now reigned over all of China as emperor of the Yuan dynasty. Under Kublai, the entire population was divided into categories of Han, Mongol and foreigner,

DIRTY FOREIGN MUD

Although trade in opium had been banned in China by imperial decree at the end of the 18th century, the *cohong* (local merchants' guild) in Guǎngzhōu helped ensure that the trade continued, and fortunes were amassed on both sides. When the British East India Company lost its monopoly on China trade in 1834, opium imports increased to 40,000 chests a year.

In 1839 the Qing government sent Imperial Commissioner Lin Zexu to stamp out the opium trade once and for all. Lin successfully blockaded the British in Guǎngzhōu and publicly burned the 'foreign mud' in Hǔmén. Furious, the British sent an expeditionary force of 4000 men from the Royal Navy to exact reparations and secure favourable trade arrangements.

What would become known as the First Opium War began in June 1840 when British forces besieged Guǎngzhōu and forced the Chinese to cede five ports to the British. With the strategic city of Nanking (Nánjīng) under immediate threat, the Chinese were forced to accept Britain's terms in the Treaty of Nanking.

The treaty abolished the monopoly system of trade, opened the 'treaty ports' to British residents and foreign trade, exempted British nationals from all Chinese laws and ceded the island of Hong Kong to the British. The treaty, signed in August 1842, set the scope and character of the unequal relationship between China and the West for the next half-century.

1557	1644	1689	1823
The Portuguese establish a permanent trade base in Macau, the first of the European outposts that will eventually lead to imperialist dominance of China until the mid-19th century.	Běijīng falls to peasant rebel Li Zicheng and the last Ming emperor Chongzhen hangs himself in Jǐngshān Park; the Qing dynasty is established.	The Treaty of Nerchinsk is signed, delineating the border between China and Russia: this is the first modern border agreement in Chinese history, as well as the longest lasting.	The British are swapping roughly 7000 chests of opium annually – with about 140lb of opium per chest, enough to supply one million addicts – compared with 1000 chests in 1773.

with the top administrative posts reserved for Mongols, even though the examination system was revived in 1315. The latter decision unexpectedly strengthened the role of local landed elites: since elite Chinese could not advance in the bureaucracy, they decided to spend more time tending their large estates instead. Another innovation was the introduction of paper money, although overprinting created a problem with inflation.

The Mongols ultimately proved less adept at governance than warfare, their empire succumbing to rebellion and eventual vanquishment within a century. Ruling as Ming emperor Hongwu, Zhu Yuanzhang established his capital in Nánjīng, but by the early 15th century the court had begun to move back to Běijīng, where a hugely ambitious reconstruction project was inaugurated by Emperor Yongle (r 1403–24), building the Forbidden City and devising the layout of the city we see today.

Although the Ming tried to impose a traditional social structure in which people stuck to hereditary occupations, the era was in fact one of great commercial growth and social change. Women became subject to stricter social norms (for instance, widow remarriage was frowned upon) but female literacy also grew. Publishing, via woodblock technology, burgeoned and the novel appeared.

Emperor Yongle, having usurped power from his nephew, was keen to establish his own legitimacy. In 1405 he launched the first of seven great maritime expeditions. Led by the eunuch general Zheng He (1371–1433), the fleet consisted of more than 60 large vessels and 255 smaller ones, carrying nearly 28,000 men. The fourth and fifth expeditions departed in 1413 and 1417, and travelled as far as the present Middle East. The great achievement of these voyages was to bring tribute missions to the capital, including two embassies from Egypt. Yet ultimately, they were a dead end, motivated by Yongle's vanity to outdo his father, not for the purpose of conquest nor the establishment of a settled trade network. The emperors who succeeded Yongle had little interest in continuing the voyages, and China dropped anchor on its global maritime explorations.

The Great Wall was re-engineered and clad in brick while ships also arrived from Europe, presaging an overseas threat that would develop from entirely different directions. Traders were quickly followed by missionaries, and the Jesuits, led by the formidable Matteo Ricci, made their way inland and established a presence at court. Ricci learned fluent Chinese and spent years agonising over how Christian tenets could be made attractive in a Confucian society with distinctive norms. The Portuguese presence linked China directly to trade with the New World, which had opened up in the 16th century. New crops, such as potatoes, maize, cotton and tobacco, were introduced, further stimulating the commercial economy. Merchants often lived opulent lives, building fine private gardens (as in Sūzhōu) and buying delicate flowers and fruits.

Two Nestorian monks smuggled silkworms out of China in 550 AD, divulging the method of silk production to the outside world.

1839	1842	1856	1882
The Qing official Lin Zexu demands that British traders at Guǎngzhōu hand over 20,000 chests of opium, leading the British to provoke the First Opium War in retaliation.	The Treaty of Nánjīng concludes the First Opium War. China is forced to hand over Hong Kong Island to the British and open up five Chinese ports to foreign trade.	Hong Xiuquan claims to be Jesus' younger brother and starts the Taiping uprising. With the Nian and Muslim uprisings, the Taiping greatly undermines the authority of the Qing dynasty.	Shànghǎi is electrified by the British-founded Shanghai Electric Company. Shànghǎi's first electricity-producing plant generates 654kw and the Bund is illuminated by electric light the following year.

The Ming was eventually undermined by internal power struggles. Natural disasters, including drought and famine, combined with a menace from the north: the Manchu, a nomadic warlike people, who saw the turmoil within China and invaded.

The Qing: the Path to Dynastic Dissolution

After conquering just a small part of China and assuming control in the disarray, the Manchu named their new dynasty the Qing (1644–1911). Once ensconced in the (now torched) Forbidden City, the Manchu realised they needed to adapt their nomadic way of life to suit the agricultural civilisation of China. Threats from inner Asia were neutralised by incorporating the Qing homeland of Manchuria into the empire, as well as that of the Mongols, whom they had subordinated. Like the Mongols before them, the conquering Manchu found themselves in charge of a civilisation whose government they had defeated, but whose cultural power far exceeded their own. The result was quite contradictory: on the one hand, Qing rulers took great pains to win the allegiance of high officials and cultural figures by displaying a familiarity and respect for traditional Chinese culture; on the other hand, the Manchu rulers made strong efforts to remain distinct. They enforced strict rules of social separation between the Han and Manchu, and tried to maintain – not always very successfully – a culture that reminded the Manchu of their nomadic warrior past. The Qing flourished most greatly under three emperors who ruled for a total of 135 years: Kangxi, Yongzheng and Qianlong.

Ban Zhao was the most famous female scholar in early China. Dating from the late 1st century AD, her work *Lessons for Women* advocated chastity and modesty as favoured female qualities.

Much of the map of China that we know today derives from the Qing period. Territorial expansion and expeditions to regions of Central Asia spread Chinese power and culture further than ever. The expansion of the 18th century was fuelled by economic and social changes. The discovery of the New World by Europeans in the 15th century led to a new global market in American food crops, such as chillies and sweet potatoes, allowing food crops to be grown in more barren regions, where wheat

---

OLD TOWNS & VILLAGES

For strong shades of historic China, head for the following old towns (古镇; *gǔzhèn*):

Píngyáo (p371) The best preserved of China's ancient walled towns.

Fènghuáng (p486) Exquisite riverside setting, pagodas, temples, covered bridges and ancient city wall.

Hóngcūn (p407) Gorgeous Huīzhōu village embedded in the lovely Ānhuī countryside.

Shāxī (p691) Flee modern China along Yúnnán's ancient Tea-Horse Road.

Zhènyuǎn (p649) Peaks, temples and age-old alleys in this riverside Guìzhōu town.

1898	1898	1900	1904–05
Emperor Guangxu permits major reforms, including new rights for women, but is thwarted by the Dowager Empress Cixi, who has many reformers arrested and executed.	The New Territories adjoining Kowloon in Hong Kong are leased to the British for 99 years, eventually returning, along with the rest of Hong Kong, in 1997.	The Hanlin Academy in Běijīng – centre of Chinese learning and literature – is accidentally torched by Chinese troops during the Boxer Rebellion, destroying its priceless collection of books.	The Russo-Japanese War is fought entirely on Chinese territory. The victory of Japan is the first triumph by an Asian power over a European one.

and rice had not flourished. In the 18th century, the Chinese population doubled from around 150 million to 300 million people.

Historians now take very seriously the idea that in the 18th century China was among the most advanced economies in the world. The impact of imperialism would help commence China's slide down the table, but the seeds of decay had been sown long before the Opium Wars of the 1840s. Put simply, as China's size expanded, its state remained too small. China's dynasty failed to expand the size of government to cope with the new realities of a larger China.

War & Reform

For the Manchu, the single most devastating incident was not either of the Opium Wars, but the far more destructive anti-Qing Taiping Rebellion of 1850–64, an insurgency motivated partly by a foreign credo (Christianity). Established by Hakka leader Hong Xiuquan, the Heavenly Kingdom of Great Peace (Taiping Tianguo) banned opium and intermingling between the sexes, made moves to redistribute property and was fiercely anti-Manchu. The Qing eventually reconquered the Taiping capital at Nánjīng, but upwards of 20 million Chinese died in the uprising.

The events that finally toppled the dynasty, however, came in rapid succession. Foreign imperialist incursions continued and Western powers nibbled away at China's coastline; Shànghǎi, Qīngdǎo, Tiānjīn, Gǔlàng Yǔ, Shàntóu, Yāntái, Wēihǎi, Níngbō and Běihǎi would all either fall under semicolonial rule or enclose foreign concessions. Hong Kong was a British colony and Macau was administered by the Portuguese. Attempts at self-strengthening – involving attempts to produce armaments and Western-style military technology – were dealt a brutal blow by the Sino-Japanese War of 1894–95. Fought over control of Korea, it ended with the humiliating destruction of the new Qing navy. Not only was Chinese influence in Korea lost, but Taiwan was ceded to Japan.

Japan itself was a powerful Asian example of reform. In 1868 Japan's rulers, unnerved by ever greater foreign encroachment, had overthrown the centuries-old system of the Shōgun, who acted as regent for the emperor. An all-out program of modernisation, including a new army, constitution, educational system and railway network was launched, all of which gave Chinese reformers a lot to ponder.

One of the boldest proposals for change, which drew heavily on the Japanese model, was the program put forward in 1898 by reformers including the political thinker Kang Youwei (1858–1927). However, in September 1898 the reforms were abruptly halted, as the Dowager Empress Cixi, fearful of a coup, placed the emperor under house arrest and executed several of the leading advocates of change. Two years later, Cixi made a decision that helped to seal the Qing's fate. In 1900 north China was convulsed

During the Cultural Revolution, some 2.2 billion Chairman Mao badges were cast. Read *Mao's Last Revolution* (2006) by Roderick MacFarquhar and Michael Schoenhals for the history; see Zhang Yimou's film *To Live* (1994) to understand the emotions.

1905	1908	1911	1912
Major reforms in the late Qing dynasty include the abolition of the 1000-year-long tradition of examinations in the Confucian classics to enter the Chinese bureaucracy.	Two-year-old Puyi ascends the throne as China's last emperor. Local elites and new classes such as businessmen no longer support the dynasty, leading to its ultimate downfall.	Revolution spreads across China as local governments withdraw support for the dynasty, and instead support a republic under the presidency of Sun Yatsen (fundraising in the US at the time).	Yuan Shikai, leader of China's most powerful regional army, goes to the Qing court to announce that the game is up: on 12 February the last emperor, six-year-old Puyi, abdicates.

by attacks from a group of peasant rebels whose martial arts techniques led them to be labelled the Boxers, and who sought to expel foreigners and kill Chinese Christian converts. In a major misjudgement, the dynasty declared its support for the Boxers in June. Eventually, a multinational foreign army forced its way into China and defeated the uprising which had besieged the foreign Legation Quarter in Běijīng. The imperial powers then demanded huge financial reparations from the Qing. In 1902 the dynasty reacted by implementing the Xinzheng (New Governance) reforms. This set of reforms, now half-forgotten in contemporary China, looks remarkably progressive, even against the standards of the present day.

The Cantonese revolutionary Sun Yatsen (1866–1925) remains one of the few modern historical figures respected in both China and Taiwan. Sun and his Revolutionary League made multiple attempts to undermine Qing rule in the late 19th century, raising sponsorship and support from a wide-ranging combination of the Chinese diaspora, the newly emergent middle class and traditional secret societies. In practice, his own attempts to end Qing rule were unsuccessful, but his reputation as a patriotic figure dedicated to a modern republic gained him high prestige among many of the emerging middle-class elites in China, though much less among the key military leaders.

The end of the Qing dynasty arrived swiftly. Throughout China's southwest, popular resentment against the dynasty had been fuelled by reports that railway rights in the region were being sold to foreigners. A local uprising in the city of Wǔhàn in October 1911 was discovered early, leading the rebels to take over command in the city and hastily declare independence from the Qing dynasty. Within a space of days, then weeks, most of China's provinces did likewise. Provincial assemblies across China declared themselves in favour of a republic, with Sun Yatsen (who was not even in China at the time) as their candidate for president.

One product of the new freedom of the 1980s was a revived Chinese film industry. *Red Sorghum*, the first film directed by Zhang Yimou, was a searingly erotic film of a type that had not been seen since 1949.

The Republic: Instability & Ideas

The Republic of China lasted less than 40 years on the mainland (1912–1949) and continues to be regarded as a dark chapter in modern Chinese history, when the country was under threat from what many described as 'imperialism from without and warlordism from within'. Yet there was also breathing room for new ideas and culture. In terms of freedom of speech and cultural production, the era of the republic was a far richer time than any subsequent time in Chinese history. Yet the period was certainly marked by repeated disasters, similar to the almost contemporaneous Weimar Republic in Germany.

Sun Yatsen returned to China and only briefly served as president, before having to make way for militarist leader Yuan Shikai. In 1912 China held its first general election, and it was Sun's newly established Kuo-

1915	1916	1925	1926
Japan makes the '21 demands', which would give it massive political, economic and trading rights in parts of China. Europe's attention is distracted by WWI.	Yuan Shikai tries to declare himself emperor. He is forced to withdraw and remain president, but dies of uraemia later that year. China splits into areas ruled by rival militarists.	The shooting of striking factory workers on 30 May in Shànghǎi by foreign-controlled police inflames nationalist passions, giving hope to the Kuomintang party, now regrouping in Guǎngzhōu.	The Northern Expedition: Kuomintang and communists unite under Soviet advice to bring together China by force, then establish a Kuomintang government.

mintang (Nationalist; Guómíndǎng, literally 'Party of the National People') party that emerged as the largest grouping. Parliamentary democracy did not last long, as the Kuomintang itself was outlawed by Yuan, and Sun had to flee into exile in Japan. However, after Yuan's death in 1916, the country split into rival regions ruled by militarist warlord-leaders. Supposedly 'national' governments in Běijīng often controlled only parts of northern or eastern China and had no real claim to control over the rest of the country. Also, in reality, the foreign powers still had control over much of China's domestic and international situation. Britain, France, the US and the other Western powers showed little desire to lose those rights, such as extraterritoriality and tariff control.

Shànghǎi became the focal point for the contradictions of Chinese modernity. By the early 20th century, Shànghǎi was a wonder not just of China, but of the world, with skyscrapers, art deco apartment blocks, neon lights, women (and men) in outrageous new fashions, and a vibrant, commercially minded, take-no-prisoners atmosphere. The racism that accompanied imperialism was visible every day, as Europeans kept themselves separate from the Chinese. Yet the glamour of modernity was undeniable, as workers flocked from rural areas to the city, and Chinese intellectuals sought out French fashion, British architecture and American movies. In the prewar period, Shànghǎi had more millionaires than anywhere else in China, yet its inequalities and squalor also inspired the first congress of the Chinese Communist Party (CCP) in 1921.

The militarist government that held power in Běijīng in 1917 provided 96,000 Chinese who served on the Western Front in Europe, not as soldiers but digging trenches and doing hard manual labour. This involvement in WWI led to one of the most important events in China's modern history: the student demonstrations of 4 May 1919.

Double-dealing by the Western Allies and Chinese politicians who had made secret deals with Japan led to an unwelcome discovery for the Chinese diplomats at the Paris Peace Conference in 1919. Germany had been defeated, but its Chinese territories – such as Qīngdǎo – were not to be returned to China but would instead go to Japan. Five days later, on 4 May 1919, some 3000 students gathered in central Běijīng, in front of the Gate of Heavenly Peace, and then marched to the house of a Chinese government minister closely associated with Japan. Once there, they broke in and destroyed the house. Over in a few hours, the event immediately found a place in modern Chinese folklore.

The student demonstration came to symbolise a much wider shift in Chinese society and politics. The May Fourth Movement, as it became known, was associated closely with the New Culture, underpinned by the electrifying ideas of 'Mr Science' and 'Mr Democracy'. In literature, a May Fourth generation of authors wrote works attacking the Confucianism

HISTORY THE REPUBLIC: INSTABILITY & IDEAS

Top History Books

The City of Heavenly Tranquillity: Beijing in the History of China (Jasper Becker; 2009)

The Penguin History of Modern China: The Fall and Rise of a Great Power 1850–2008 (Jonathan Fenby; 2008)

China, A History (John Keay; 2008)

1927	1930s	1930	1931
The Kuomintang leader Chiang Kaishek turns on the communists in Shànghǎi and Guǎngzhōu, having thousands killed and forcing the communists to turn to a rural-based strategy.	Cosmopolitan Shànghǎi is the world's fifth-largest city (the largest in the Far East), supporting a polyglot population of four million people.	Chiang's Kuomintang government achieves 'tariff autonomy': for the first time in nearly 90 years, China regains the power to tax imports freely, an essential part of fiscal stability.	Japan invades Manchuria (northeast China), provoking an international crisis and forcing Chiang to consider anti-Japanese, as well as anticommunist, strategies.

that they felt had brought China to its current crisis, and explored new issues of sexuality and self-development. The CCP, later mastermind of the world's largest peasant revolution, was created in the intellectual turmoil of the movement, many of its founding figures associated with Peking University, such as Chen Duxiu (dean of humanities), Li Dazhao (head librarian) and the young Mao Zedong, a mere library assistant.

The Northern Expedition

After years of vainly seeking international support for his cause, Sun Yat-sen found allies in the newly formed Soviet Russia. The Soviets ordered the fledgling CCP to ally itself with the much larger 'bourgeois' party, the Kuomintang. Their alliance was attractive to Sun: the Soviets would provide political training, military assistance and finance. From their base in Guăngzhōu, the Kuomintang and CCP trained together from 1923, in preparation for their mission to reunite China.

Sun died of cancer in 1925. The succession battle in the party coincided with a surge in antiforeign feeling that accompanied the May Thirtieth Incident when 13 labour demonstrators were killed by British police in Shànghăi on 30 May 1925. Under Soviet advice, the Kuomintang and CCP prepared for their 'Northern Expedition', the big 1926 push north that was supposed to finally unite China. In 1926–27, the Soviet-trained National Revolutionary Army made its way slowly north, fighting, bribing or persuading its opponents into accepting Kuomintang control. The most powerful military figure turned out to be an officer from Zhèjiāng named Chiang Kaishek (1887–1975). Trained in Moscow, Chiang moved steadily forward and finally captured the great prize, Shànghăi, in March 1927. However, a horrific surprise was in store for his communist allies. The Soviet advisers had not impressed Chiang and he was increasingly convinced that the communists aimed to use their cooperation with the Kuomintang to seize control themselves. Instead, Chiang struck first. Using local thugs and soldiers, Chiang organised a lightning strike by rounding up CCP activists and union leaders in Shànghăi and killing thousands of them.

Kuomintang Rule

Chiang Kaishek's Kuomintang government officially came to power in 1928 through a combination of military force and popular support. Marked by corruption, it suppressed political dissent with great ruthlessness. Yet Chiang's government also kick-started a major industrialisation effort, greatly augmented China's transport infrastructure and successfully renegotiated what many Chinese called 'unequal treaties' with Western powers. In its first two years, the Kuomintang doubled the length of highways in China and increased the number of students studying engineering. The government never really controlled more than a

Ping pong (*pīngpāngqiú*) may be China's national sport (*guóqiú*), but it was invented as an after-dinner game by British Victorians who named it wiff-waff and first used a ball made from champagne corks.

1932	1935	1937	1938
War breaks out in the streets of Shànghăi in February–March, a sign that conflict between the two great powers of East Asia, China and Japan, may soon be coming.	Mao Zedong begins his rise to paramount power at the conference at Zūnyì, held in the middle of the Long March to the northwest, on the run from the Kuomintang.	The Japanese and Chinese clash at Wanping, near Bĕijīng, on 7 July, sparking the conflict that the Chinese call the 'War of Resistance', which only ends in 1945.	Former prime minister Wang Jingwei announces he has gone over to Japan. He later inaugurates a 'restored' Kuomintang government with Japan holding the whip hand over government.

few (very important) provinces in the east, however, and China remained significantly disunited. Regional militarists continued to control much of western China; the Japanese invaded and occupied Manchuria in 1931; and the communists re-established themselves in the northwest.

In 1934 Chiang Kaishek launched his own ideological counterargument to communism: the New Life Movement. This was supposed to be a complete spiritual renewal of the nation, through a modernised version of traditional Confucian values, such as propriety, righteousness and loyalty. The New Life Movement demanded that the renewed citizens of the nation must wear frugal but clean clothes, consume products made in China rather than seek luxurious foreign goods, and behave in a hygienic manner. Yet Chiang's ideology never had much success. Against a background of massive agricultural and fiscal crisis, prescriptions about what to wear and how to behave lacked popular appeal.

The new policies did relatively little to change everyday life for the population in the countryside, where more than 80% of China's people lived. Some rural reforms were undertaken, including the establishment of rural cooperatives, but their effects were small. The Nationalist Party also found itself unable to collect taxes in an honest and transparent fashion.

The Long March

The communists had not stood still and after Chiang's treachery, most of what remained of the CCP fled to the countryside. A major centre of activity was the communist stronghold in impoverished Jiāngxī province, where the party began to try out systems of government that would eventually bring them to power. However, by 1934, Chiang's previously ineffective 'extermination campaigns' were making the CCP's position in Jiāngxī untenable, as the Red Army found itself increasingly encircled by Nationalist troops. The CCP commenced its Long March, travelling over 6400km. Four thousand of the original 80,000 communists who set out eventually arrived, exhausted, in Shaanxi (Shǎnxī) province in the northwest, far out of the reach of the Kuomintang. It seemed possible that within a matter of months, however, Chiang would attack again and wipe them out.

The approach of war saved the CCP. There was growing public discontent at Chiang Kaishek's seeming unwillingness to fight the Japanese. In fact, this perception was unfair. The Kuomintang had undertaken retraining of key regiments in the army under German advice, and also started to plan for a wartime economy from 1931, spurred on by the Japanese invasion of Manchuria. However, events came to a head in December 1936, when the Chinese militarist leader of Manchuria (General Zhang Xueliang) and the CCP kidnapped Chiang. As a condition of his release, Chiang agreed to an openly declared United Front: the Kuomintang and communists would put aside their differences and join forces against Japan.

The ghostly shadows of Cultural Revolution slogans can be hard to find in large and modern cities, but are quite a common sight in rural destinations such as the towns of Píngyáo and Fènghuáng and small historic villages across China.

In the 18th century, the Chinese used an early form of vaccination against smallpox that required not an injection, but instead the blowing of serum up the patient's nose.

1939	1941	1941	1943
On 3–4 May Japanese carpet bombing devastates the temporary Chinese capital of Chóngqìng. From 1938 to 1943, Chóngqìng is one of the world's most heavily bombed cities.	In the base area at Yán'ān (Shaanxi), the 'Rectification' program begins, remoulding the Communist Party into an ideology shaped principally by Mao Zedong.	The Japanese attack the US at Pearl Harbor. China becomes a formal ally of the US, USSR and Britain in WWII, but is treated as a secondary partner at best.	Chiang Kaishek negotiates an agreement with the Allies that, when Japan is defeated, Western imperial privileges in China will end forever, marking the twilight of Western imperialist power in China.

War & the Kuomintang

China's status as a major participant in WWII is often overlooked or forgotten in the West. The Japanese invasion of China, which began in 1937, was merciless, with the notorious Nánjīng Massacre (also known as the Rape of Nánjīng) just one of a series of war crimes committed by the Japanese Army during its conquest of eastern China. The government had to operate in exile from the far southwestern hinterland of China, as its area of greatest strength and prosperity, China's eastern seaboard, was lost to Japanese occupation.

In China itself, it is now acknowledged that both the Kuomintang and the communists had important roles to play in defeating Japan. Chiang, not Mao, was the internationally acknowledged leader of China during this period, and despite his government's multitude of flaws, he maintained resistance to the end. However, his government was also increasingly trapped, having retreated to Sìchuān province and a temporary capital at Chóngqìng. Safe from land attack by Japan, the city still found itself under siege, subjected to some of the heaviest bombing in the war. From 1940, supply routes were cut off as the road to Burma was closed by Britain, under pressure from Japan, and Vichy France closed connections to Vietnam. Although the US and Britain brought China on board as an ally against Japan after Pearl Harbor on 7 December 1941, the Allied 'Europe First' strategy meant that China was always treated as a secondary theatre of war. Chiang Kaishek's corruption and leadership qualities were heavily criticised, and while these accusations were not groundless, without Chinese Kuomintang armies (which kept one million Japanese troops bogged down in China for eight years), the Allies' war in the Pacific would have been far harder. The communists had an important role as guerrilla fighters, but did far less fighting in battle than the Kuomintang.

The real winners from WWII, however, were the communists. They undertook important guerrilla campaigns against the Japanese across northern and eastern China, but the really key changes were taking place in the bleak, dusty hill country centred on the small town of Yán'ān, capital of the CCP's largest stronghold. The 'Yán'ān way' that developed in those years solidified many CCP policies: land reform involving redistribution of land to the peasants, lower taxes, a self-sufficient economy, ideological education and, underpinning it all, the CCP's military force, the Red Army. By the end of the war with Japan, the communist areas had expanded massively, with some 900,000 troops in the Red Army, and party membership at a new high of 1.2 million.

Above all, the war with Japan had helped the communists come back from the brink of the disaster they had faced at the end of the Long March. The Kuomintang and communists then plunged into civil war in

The oldest surviving brick pagoda in China is the Sōngyuè Pagoda, on Sōng Shān in Hénán province, dating to the early sixth century.

1946	1949	1950	1957
Communists and the Kuomintang fail to form a coalition government, plunging China back into civil war. Communist organisation, morale and ideology all prove key to the communist victory.	Mao Zedong stands on top of the Gate of Heavenly Peace in Běijīng on 1 October, and announces the formation of the Peoples Republic of China (PRC), saying 'The Chinese people have stood up'.	China joins the Korean War, helping Mao to consolidate his regime with mass campaigns that inspire (or terrify) the population.	A brief period of liberalisation under the 'Hundred Flowers Movement'. However, criticisms of the regime lead Mao to crack down and imprison or exile thousands of dissidents.

1946 and after three long years the CCP won. On 1 October 1949 in Běijīng, Mao declared the establishment of the People's Republic of China.

Chiang Kaishek fled to the island of Formosa (Taiwan), which China had regained from Japan after WWII. He took with him China's gold reserves and the remains of his air force and navy, and set up the Republic of China (ROC), naming his new capital Taipei (台北, Táiběi).

Mao's China

Mao's China desired, above all, to exercise ideological control over its population. It called itself 'New China', with the idea that the whole citizenry, down to the remotest peasants, should find a role in the new politics and society. The success of Mao's military and political tactics also meant that the country was, for the first time since the 19th century, united under a strong central government.

Most Westerners – and Western influences – were swiftly removed from the country. The US refused to recognise the new state at all. However, China had decided, in Mao's phrase, to 'lean to one side' and ally itself with the Soviet Union in the still-emerging Cold War. The 1950s marked the high point of Soviet influence on Chinese politics and culture. However, the decade also saw rising tension between the Chinese and the Soviets, fuelled in part by Khrushchev's condemnation of Stalin (which Mao took, in part, as a criticism of his own cult of personality). Sino-Soviet differences were aggravated with the withdrawal of Soviet technical assistance from China, and reached a peak with intense border clashes during 1969. Relations remained frosty until the 1980s.

Mao's experiences had convinced him that only violent change could shake up the relationship between landlords and their tenants, or capitalists and their employees, in a China that was still highly traditional. The first year of the regime saw some 40% of the land redistributed to poor peasants. At the same time, some one million or so people condemned

The first railroad in China was the Woosung Railway, which opened in 1876, running between Shànghǎi and Wusong; it operated for less than a year before being dismantled and shipped to Taiwan.

FOREIGN CONCESSIONS & COLONIES

China's coastline is dotted with a string of foreign concession towns that ooze both charm and the sensations of 19th- and early-20th-century grandeur.

Shànghǎi (p299) Shànghǎi's most stylish concession goes to the French.

Gǔlàng Yǔ (p344) Charming colonial remains on a beautiful island setting in Xiàmén.

Qīngdǎo (p220) Wander the German district for cobbled streets and Teutonic architecture.

Hong Kong (p499) Outstanding ex-colonial cachet on the Guǎngdōng coast.

Macau (p536) An unforgettable cocktail of Cantonese and Portuguese flavour.

Shāmiàn Island (p560) Gentrified and leafy lozenge of Guǎngzhōu sand.

1958	1962	1966	1972
The Taiwan Straits Crisis. Mao's government fires missiles near islands under the control of Taiwan in an attempt to prevent rapprochement between the US and USSR in the Cold War.	The Great Leap Forward causes mass starvation. Politburo members Liu Shaoqi and Deng Xiaoping reintroduce limited market reforms, which lead to their condemnation during the Cultural Revolution.	The Cultural Revolution breaks out, and Red Guards demonstrate in cities across China. The movement is marked by violence as a catalyst for transforming society.	US President Richard Nixon visits China, marking a major rapprochement during the Cold War, and the start of full diplomatic relations between the two countries.

as 'landlords' were persecuted and killed. The joy of liberation was real for many Chinese, but campaigns of terror were also real and the early 1950s was no golden age.

As relations with the Soviets broke down in the mid-1950s, the CCP leaders' thoughts turned to economic self-sufficiency. Mao, supported by Politburo colleagues, proposed the policy known as the Great Leap Forward (Dàyuèjìn), a highly ambitious plan to harness the power of socialist economics to boost production of steel, coal and electricity. Agriculture was to reach an ever-higher level of collectivisation. Family structures were broken up as communal dining halls were established: people were urged to eat their fill, as the new agricultural methods would ensure plenty for all, year after year.

However, the Great Leap Forward was a horrific failure. Its lack of economic realism caused a massive famine that killed tens of millions; historian Frank Dikötter posits a minimum figure of 45 million deaths in his *Mao's Great Famine* (2010), a figure greater than the total number of casualties in WWI. Yang Jisheng's *Tombstone: The Great Chinese Famine, 1958–1962* (2012) conservatively estimates there were 36 million deaths. Yet the return to a semimarket economy in 1962, after the Leap had comprehensively ended, did not dampen Mao's enthusiasm for revolutionary renewal. This led to the last and most fanatical of the campaigns that marked Mao's China: the Cultural Revolution of 1966–76.

> The Tang saw the first major rise to power of eunuchs (*huànguān*). Often from ethnic minority groups, they were brought to the capital and given positions within the imperial palace. In many dynasties they had real influence.

Cultural Revolution

Mao had become increasingly concerned that post-Leap China was slipping into 'economism' – a complacent satisfaction with rising standards of living that would blunt people's revolutionary fervour. Mao was particularly concerned that the young generation might grow up with a dimmed spirit of revolution. Mao decided upon a massive campaign of ideological renewal, in which he would attack his own party.

Still the dominant figure in the CCP, Mao used his prestige to undermine his own colleagues. In summer of 1966 prominent posters in large, hand-written characters appeared at prominent sites, including Peking University, demanding that figures such as Liu Shaoqi (president of the PRC) and Deng Xiaoping (senior Politburo member) must be condemned as 'takers of the capitalist road'. Top leaders suddenly disappeared from sight, only to be replaced by unknowns, such as Mao's wife Jiang Qing and her associates, later dubbed the 'Gang of Four'. Meanwhile, an all-pervasive cult of Mao's personality took over. One million youths at a time, known as Red Guards, would flock to hear Mao in Tiān'ānmén Sq. Posters and pictures of Mao were everywhere. The Red Guards were not ashamed to admit that their tactics were violent. Immense violence permeated throughout society: teachers, intellectuals and landlords were killed in their thousands.

1973	1976	1980	1988
Deng Xiaoping returns to power as deputy premier. The modernising faction in the party fights with the Gang of Four, who support the continuing Cultural Revolution.	Mao Zedong dies, aged 83. The Gang of Four are arrested by his successor and put on trial, where they are blamed for all the disasters of the Cultural Revolution.	The one-child policy is enforced. The state adopts it as a means of reducing the population, but at the same time imposes unprecedented control over the personal liberty of women.	The daring series *River Elegy (Héshāng)* is broadcast on national TV. It is a devastating indictment of dictatorship and Mao's rule in particular, and is banned in China after 1989.

While Mao initiated and supported the Cultural Revolution, it was also genuinely popular among many young people (who had less to lose and more to gain). Police authority effectively disappeared, creative activity came to a virtual standstill and academic research was grounded.

The Cultural Revolution could not last. Worried by the increasing violence, the army forced the Red Guards off the streets in 1969. The early 1970s saw a remarkable rapprochement between the US and China: the former was desperate to extricate itself from the quagmire of the Vietnam War; the latter terrified of an attack from the now-hostile USSR. Secretive diplomatic manoeuvres led, eventually, to the official visit of US President Richard Nixon to China in 1972, which began the reopening of China to the West. Slowly, the Cultural Revolution began to cool down, but its brutal legacy survives today. Many of those guilty of murder and violence re-entered society with little or no judgement while today's CCP discourages open analysis and debate of the 'decade of chaos'.

Paul French's *Midnight in Peking* (2012) is a gripping true-crime murder mystery examining the death of Pamela Werner in 1937 Peking.

Reform

Mao died in 1976, to be succeeded by the little-known Hua Guofeng (1921–2008). Within two years, Hua had been outmanoeuvred by the greatest survivor of 20th-century Chinese politics, Deng Xiaoping. Deng had been purged twice during the Cultural Revolution, but after Mao's death he was able to reach supreme leadership in the CCP with a radical program. In particular, Deng recognised that the Cultural Revolution had been highly damaging economically to China. Deng enlisted a policy slogan originally invented by Mao's prime minister, Zhou Enlai – the 'Four Modernisations'. The party's task would be to set China on the right path in agriculture, industry, national defence, and science and technology.

Two of China's oldest wooden buildings can be found in two temples in the environs of Wǔtái Shān: the main hall (8th century) of Nánchán Sì and one of the halls (9th century) of Fóguāng Sì.

To make this policy work, many of the assumptions of the Mao era were abandoned. The first highly symbolic move of the 'reform era' was the breaking down of the collective farms. Farmers were able to sell a proportion of their crops on the free market, and urban and rural areas were also encouraged to establish small local enterprises. 'To get rich is glorious,' Deng declared, adding, 'it doesn't matter if some areas get rich first'. As part of this encouragement of entrepreneurship, Deng designated four areas on China's coast as Special Economic Zones (SEZs), which would be particularly attractive to foreign investors.

Politics was kept on a much shorter rein than the economy, however. Deng was relaxed about a certain amount of ideological impurity, but some other members of the leadership were concerned by the materialism in reform-era China. They supported campaigns of 'antispiritual pollution', in which influences from the capitalist world were condemned. Yet inevitably the overall movement seemed to be towards a freer, market-oriented society. The new freedoms that the urban middle classes enjoyed created

1989	1997	2001	2004
Hundreds of civilians are killed by Chinese troops in the streets around Tiān'ānmén Sq. No official reassessment has been made, but rumours persist of deep internal conflict within the party.	Hong Kong is returned to the People's Republic of China. Widespread fears that China will interfere directly in its government prove wrong, but its politics become more sensitive to Běijīng.	China joins the World Trade Organization, giving it a seat at the top table that decides global norms on economics and finance.	The world's first commercially operating Maglev train begins scorching a trail across Shànghǎi's Pǔdōng District, reaching a top speed of 431km/hr.

the appetite for more. After student protests demanding further opening up of the party in 1985–86, the prime minister (and relative liberal) Hu Yaobang was forced to resign in 1987 and take responsibility for allowing social forces to get out of control. He was replaced as general secretary by Zhao Ziyang, who was more conservative politically, although an economic reformer. In April 1989 Hu Yaobang died, and students around China used the occasion of his death to organise protests against the continuing role of the CCP in public life. At Peking University, the breeding ground of the May Fourth demonstrations of 1919, students declared the need for 'science and democracy', the modernising watchwords of 80 years earlier, to be revived.

In spring 1989 Tiān'ānmén Sq was the scene of an unprecedented demonstration. At its height, nearly a million Chinese workers and students, in a rare cross-class alliance, filled the space in front of the Gate of Heavenly Peace, with the CCP profoundly embarrassed to have the world's media record such events. By June 1989 the numbers in the square had dwindled to only thousands, but those who remained showed no signs of moving. Martial law was imposed and on the night of 3 June and early hours of 4 June, tanks and armoured personnel carriers were sent in. The death toll in Běijīng has never been officially confirmed, but it seems likely to have been in the high hundreds or even more. Hundreds of people associated with the movement were arrested, imprisoned or forced to flee to the West.

For some three years, China's politics were almost frozen, but in 1992 Deng made his last grand public gesture. That year, he undertook what Chinese political insiders called his 'southern tour', or *nánxún*. By visiting Shēnzhèn, Deng indicated that the economic policies of reform were not going to be abandoned. The massive growth rates that the Chinese economy has posted ever since have justified his decision. Deng also made another significant choice: grooming Jiang Zemin – the mayor of Shànghǎi, who had peacefully dissolved demonstrations in Shànghǎi in a way that the authorities in Běijīng had not – as his successor by appointing him as general secretary of the party in 1989.

Deng died in 1997, the same year that Hong Kong returned to China under a 'one country, two systems' agreement with the UK, which would maintain the ex-British colony's independence in all aspects except defence and foreign affairs for the next 50 years. Macau followed suit two years later. Faced with a multitude of social problems brought on by inequalities spawned by the Deng years, President Jiang Zemin, with Zhu Rongji as premier, sought to bring economic stability to China while strengthening the centralised power of the state and putting off much-needed political reforms. Faced with a protest of up to 10,000 Falun Gong adherents outside Běijīng's Zhōngnánhǎi in April 1999, Jiang branded the movement a cult and sought its eradication through imprisonment and detention, backed by a draconian propaganda campaign.

Toilet paper was first used in China as early as the 6th century AD, when it was employed by the wealthy and privileged for sanitary purposes.

Traditionally the dragon (*lóng*) was associated with the emperor and the male principle while the phoenix (*fènghuáng*) was a symbol of the empress and the female principle.

2006	2008	2008	2008
The Three Gorges Dam is completed. Significant parts of the landscape of western China are lost beneath the waters, but energy is also provided for the expanding Chinese economy.	Běijīng hosts the 2008 Summer Olympic Games and Paralympics. The Games go smoothly and are widely considered to be a great success in burnishing China's image overseas.	Violent riots in Lhasa, Tibet, again put the uneasy region centre stage. Protests spread to other Tibetan areas in Gānsù, Sìchuān and Qīnghǎi provinces.	A huge 8.0-magnitude earthquake convulses Sìchuān province, leaving 87,000 dead or missing and rendering millions homeless.

21st Century China

Jiang Zemin was succeeded in 2002 by President Hu Jintao, who made further efforts to tame growing regional inequality and the poverty scarring rural areas. China's lopsided development continued, however, despite an ambitious program to develop the western regions. By 2009, an in-flow of US$325 billion had dramatically boosted GDP per capita in the western regions but a colossal prosperity gap survived and significant environmental challenges persisted.

The question of political reform found itself shelved, partly because economic growth was bringing prosperity to so many, albeit unevenly. Property prices – especially in the richer eastern coastal provinces – were rocketing and the export and investment-driven economy was thriving. For many, the first decade of the 21st century was marked by spectacular riches for some – the number of dollar billionaires doubled in just two years and property prices began moving dramatically beyond the reach of the less fortunate, while bringing wealth to the more fortunate. This coincided with the greatest migration of workers to the cities the world has ever seen. China responded to the credit crunch of 2007 and the downturn in Western economies with a stimulus package of US$586 billion between 2008 and 2009. Property and infrastructure construction enjoyed spectacular growth, buffering China from the worst effects of the global recession, but the export sector contracted as demand dried up overseas. A barrage of restrictions on buying second properties attempted to flush speculators from the market and tame price rises. These policies partially worked but millions of flats across China lay empty – bought by investors happy to see prices rise – and entire ghost towns (such as Ordos in Inner Mongolia, built on the back of the coal rush) had already risen from the ground.

Vice president from 2008, Xi Jinping replaced Hu Jintao as president in 2013. Pledging to root out corruption, Xi also sought to instigate reforms, including the abolition of both the one-child policy and the *láo jiào* (re-education through labour) system. These reforms were matched by a growing zeal for internet and social media controls and a domestic security budget that sucked in more capital than national defence.

Xi Jinping inherited a China that was a tremendous success story, but one beset with problems. Despite resilient and ambitious planning (massive expansion of the high-speed rail network, a space program setting itself bold targets, some of the world's tallest buildings), the Chinese economy remained fundamentally imbalanced, with an excess reliance on the export market. Political reform found itself even more on the back burner as economic considerations took centre stage and storm clouds gathered above the competing claims over the reefs, shoals and islands of the South China Sea.

Best History Museums

Hong Kong Museum of History (p513)

Shànghǎi History Museum (p307)

Macau Museum (p539)

Shaanxi History Museum (p383)

2009	2012	2014	2015
July riots in Ürümqi leave hundreds dead as interethnic violence flares between Uighurs and Han Chinese. Běijīng floods the region with soldiers and implements a 10-month internet blackout.	After the heaviest rainfall in 60 years, Běijīng is inundated with epic summer floods; 77 people are killed by the floodwaters and 65,000 evacuated.	Malaysia Airlines Flight 370 disappears while flying from Kuala Lumpur to Běijīng, with 152 Chinese passengers on board (of a total of 239 people).	Satellite imagery reveals that China has been rapidly constructing an airfield at Fiery Cross Reef in the Spratly (Nánshā) Islands, part of territory also claimed by Vietnam, the Philippines and Taiwan.

People of China

The stamping ground of roughly one-fifth of humanity, China is often regarded as being largely homogenous, at least from a remote Western perspective. This is probably because Han Chinese – the majority ethnic type in this energetic and bustling nation – constitute over nine-tenths of the population. But like Chinese cuisine, and of course the nation's mystifying linguistic Babel, you only have to travel a bit further and turn a few more corners to come face to face with a surprising hodgepodge of ethnicities.

> The Naxi created a written language more than 1000 years ago using an extraordinary system of pictographs – the only hieroglyphic language still in use today.

Ethnicity

Han Chinese

Han Chinese (汉族; Hànzú) – the predominant clan among China's 56 recognised ethnic groups – make up the lion's share of China's people, 92% of the total figure. When we think of China – from its writing system to its visual arts, calligraphy, history, literature, language and politics – we tend to associate it with Han culture.

Distributed throughout China, the Han Chinese are however predominantly concentrated along the Yellow River, Yangzi River and Pearl River basins. Taking their name from the Han dynasty, the Han Chinese themselves are not markedly homogenous. China was ruled by non-Han Altaic (Turk, Tungusic or Mongolian) invaders for long periods, most demonstrably during the Yuan dynasty (Mongols) and the long Qing dynasty (Manchu), but also under the Jin, the Liao and other eras. This Altaic influence is more evident in northern Chinese with their larger and broader frames and rounder faces, compared to their slighter and thinner southern Han Chinese counterparts, who are physically more similar to the southeast Asian type. Shànghǎi Chinese for example are notably more southern in appearance; with their rounder faces, Běijīng Chinese are quite typically northern Chinese. With mass migration and increased frequency of marriage between Chinese from different parts of the land, these physical differences are likely to diminish slightly over time.

The Han Chinese display further stark differences in their rich panoply of dialects, which fragments China into a frequently baffling linguistic mosaic, although the promotion of Mandarin has blurred this considerably. The common written form of Chinese using characters (汉字; Hànzi – or 'characters of the Han'), however, binds all dialects together.

Overseas Chinese frequently refer to people of Chinese blood from China or abroad as Huárén (华人; 'people of China'. Conversely, foreigners are always called lǎowài ('outsiders' or 'foreigners'); the term is constantly used and does not respect geography – Chinese visitors overseas refer to local people as lǎowài, despite they themselves in context being lǎowài. Very rarely, Westerners may be called yángrén (洋人; 'people of the ocean'), although down south you might encounter the slurs guǐlǎo ('foreign devils') and hēiguǐ ('black devil'; for black people).

The Non-Han Chinese

A glance at the map of China reveals that the core heartland regions of Han China are central fragments of modern-day China's huge expanse. The colossal regions of Tibet, Qīnghǎi, Xīnjiāng, Inner Mongolia and the three provinces of the northeast (Manchuria – Hēilóngjiāng, Jílín and Liáoníng) are all historically non-Han regions, some areas of which remain essentially non-Han today.

Many of these regions are peopled by some of the remaining 8% of the population: China's 55 other ethnic minorities, known collectively as *shǎoshù mínzú* (少数民族; minority nationals). The largest minority groups in China include the Zhuang (壮族; Zhuàng zú), Manchu (满族; Mǎn zú), Miao (苗族; Miáo zú), Uighur (维吾尔族; Wéiwú'ěr zú), Yi (彝族; Yí zú), Tujia (土家族; Tǔjiā zú), Tibetan (藏族; Zàng zú), Hui (回族; Huízú), Mongolian (蒙古族; Ménggǔ zú), Buyi (布依族; Bùyī zú), Dong (侗族; Dòng zú), Yao (瑶族; Yáo zú), Korean (朝鲜族; Cháoxiǎn zú), Bai (白族; Bái zú), Hani (哈尼族; Hāní zú), Li (黎族; Lí zú), Kazak (哈萨克族; Hāsàkè zú) and Dai (傣族; Dǎi zú). Population sizes differ dramatically, from the sizeable Zhuang in Guǎngxī to small numbers of Menba (门巴族; Ménbā zú) in Tibet. Ethnic labelling can be quite fluid: the roundhouse-building Hakka (客家; Kèjiā) were once regarded as a separate minority, but are today considered Han Chinese. Ethnic groups also tell us a lot about the historic movement of peoples around China: the Bonan minority, found in small numbers in a few counties of Qīnghǎi and Gānsù, are largely Muslim but show marked Tibetan influence and are said to be descended from Mongol troops once stationed in Qīnghǎi during the Yuan dynasty.

China's minorities tend to cluster along border regions, in the northwest, the west, the southwest, the north and northeast of China, but are also distributed throughout the country. Some groups are found in just one area (such as the Hani in Yúnnán); others, such as the Muslim Hui, live all over China. Wedged into the southwest corner of China between Tibet, Myanmar (Burma), Vietnam and Laos, fecund Yúnnán province alone is home to more than 20 ethnic groups, making it one of the most ethnically diverse provinces in the country.

Despite Manchu culture once ruling over China during the Qing dynasty (1644–1911), possibly fewer than 50 native speakers of the Manchu language survive today, although the closely related Xibo language is spoken by around 20,000 descendants of Xibo tribes resettled in Xīnjiāng in China's northwest in the 18th century.

The Chinese Character

Shaped by Confucian principles, the Chinese are thoughtful and discreet, subtle but also pragmatic. Conservative and rather introverted, they favour dark clothing over bright or loud colours while their body language is usually reserved and undemonstrative, yet attentive.

The Chinese can be both delightful and mystifyingly contradictory. One moment they will give their seat to an elderly person on the bus or help someone who is lost, and the next moment they will entirely ignore an old lady who has been knocked over by a motorbike.

Particularly diligent, the Chinese are inured to the kind of hours that may prompt a workers' insurrection elsewhere. This is partly due to a traditional culture of hard work but is also a response to insufficient social-security safety nets and an anxiety regarding economic and political uncertainties. The Chinese impressively save much of what they earn, emphasising the virtue of prudence. Despite this restraint, however, wastefulness can be breathtaking when 'face' is involved: mountains of food are often left on restaurant dining tables, particularly if important guests are present. Chinese people are deeply generous. Don't be surprised if a person you have just met on a train invites you for a meal in the dining carriage; they will almost certainly insist on paying, grabbing the bill from the waiter at blinding speed while resisting attempts to help out.

For an idea of local urban salaries, a chef or wait-staff in a Shànghǎi restaurant can expect to earn between ¥2500 and ¥3500 (about US$380 to US$535) per month.

David Eimer's *The Emperor Far Away: Travels at the Edge of China* (Bloomsbury, 2014) is a riveting journey through China's periphery, from the deserts of Xīnjiāng and the mountains of Tibet, to the tropical jungles of Xīshuāngbǎnnà and the frozen wastes of far northern Hēilóngjiāng.

The Chinese are also an exceptionally dignified people. They are proud of their civilisation and history, their written language and their inventions and achievements. This pride rarely comes across as arrogance, however, and can be streaked with a lack of self-assurance. The Chinese may, for example, be very gratified by China's new-found world status, but may squirm at the mention of food safety or pollution.

The modern Chinese character has been shaped by recent political realities, and while Chinese people have always been reserved and circumspect, in today's China they can appear even more prudent. Impressive mental gymnastics are performed to detour contentious domestic political issues, which can make the mainland Chinese appear complicated, despite their reputation for being straightforward.

China's 'One-Child Policy'

The 'one-child policy' (in effect a misnomer) was railroaded into effect in 1979 in a bid to keep China's population to one billion by the year 2000 (a target it failed to meet); the population is expected to peak at around 1.5 billion in 2028. In a momentous reversal, in 2015 it was announced that the policy would be abolished and in January 2016 the regulation was officially amended to a two-child policy.

China has almost 90 cities with populations of five to 10 million people and more than 170 cities with between one and five million people.

The policy was harshly implemented at first but rural revolt led to a softer stance; nonetheless, it generated much bad feeling between local officials and the rural population. All non-Han minorities were exempt from the one-child policy; Han Chinese parents who were both single children could have a second child and this was later expanded to all couples if at least one of them was a single child. Rural families were allowed to have two children if the first child was a girl, but some had upwards of three or four kids. Additional children often resulted in fines, with families having to shoulder the cost of education themselves, without government assistance. Official stated policy opposed forced abortion or sterilisation, but allegations of coercion continued as local officials strived to meet population targets. In 2014 the film director Zhang Yimou was fined US$1.2m for breaking the one-child policy.

Families who abided by the one-child policy often went to horrifying lengths to ensure their child was male, with female infanticide, abortion and abandonment becoming commonplace, resulting in an imbalance of the sexes – in 2010, 118 boys were born for every 100 girls. By 2020, potentially around 35 million Chinese men may be unable to find spouses.

As women could have a second child abroad, this also led to large numbers of mainland women giving birth in Hong Kong (where the child also qualified for Hong Kong citizenship). The Hong Kong government eventually used legislation to curb this phenomenon, dubbed 'birth tourism', as government figures revealed that almost half of babies born in the territory in 2010 were born to mainland parents. In 2013, the Hong Kong government prohibited mainland women from visiting Hong Kong to give birth, unless their husband is from the territory.

CHINA'S DEMOGRAPHICS

Population: 1.37 billion

Birth rate: 12.49 births per thousand people

People over 65: 10%

Urbanisation rate: 3.05%

Male to female ratio: 1.17 : 1 (under 15s)

Life expectancy: 75.4 years

Another consequence of the one-child policy has been a rapidly ageing population, with over a quarter of the populace predicted to be over the age of 65 by 2050. The 2016 abolition of the one-child policy has sought to adjust these imbalances, but some analysts argue it has come too late.

Women in China

Equality & Emancipation

Growing up in a Confucian culture, women in China traditionally encountered great prejudice and acquired a far lowlier social status to men. The most notorious expression of female subservience was foot binding, which became a widespread practice in the Song dynasty. Female resistance to male-dominated society could sometimes produce inventive solutions, however: discouraged from reading and writing, women in Jiāngyǒng county (Húnán) once used their own invented syllabic script (partly based on Chinese) called *nǚshū* (女书) to write letters to each other (which men found incomprehensible).

Women in today's China officially share complete equality with men; however, as with other nations that profess sexual equality, the reality is often far different. Chinese women do not enjoy strong political representation and the CCP remains a largely patriarchal organisation. Iconic political leaders from the early days of the CCP were men and the influential echelons of the party persist as a largely male domain. Only a handful of the scientists celebrated in a photographic mural at Shànghǎi's Science and Technology Museum are women.

The Communist Party after 1949 tried to outlaw old customs and put women on equal footing with men. It abolished arranged marriages and encouraged women to get an education and join the workforce. Women were allowed to keep their maiden name upon marriage and leave their property to their children. In its quest for equality during this period however, the Communist Party seemed to 'desexualise' women, fashioning instead a kind of idealised worker/mother/peasant paradigm.

Chinese Women Today

High-profile, successful Chinese women are very much in the public eye, but the relative lack of career opportunities for females in other fields also suggests a continuing bias against women in employment.

Women's improved social status today has meant that more women are putting off marriage until their late 20s or early 30s, choosing instead to focus on education and career opportunities. This has been enhanced by the rapid rise in house prices, further encouraging women to leave marriage (and having children) till a later age.

Some Chinese women are making strong efforts to protect the rights of women in China, receiving international attention in the process. In 2010 the Simone de Beauvoir prize for women's freedom was awarded to Guo Jianmei, a Chinese lawyer and human rights activist, and film-maker and professor Ai Xiaoming. Guo Jianmei also received the International Women of Courage Award in 2011. In a sign of growing confidence among the female workforce, a young Běijīng woman won the first ever gender discrimination lawsuit in China in 2014.

Rural Women in China

Urban women are far more optimistic and freer, while women from rural areas, where traditional beliefs are at their strongest, fight an uphill battle against discrimination. Rural Chinese mores are heavily biased against females, where a marked preference for baby boys still exists. This results in an ever greater shift of Chinese women to the city from rural areas. China's women are more likely to commit suicide than men; the suicide rate for rural Chinese women is around five times the urban rate.

The colossal Yangzi River Bridge in Nánjīng has surpassed the San Francisco Golden Gate Bridge as the most used suicide site in the world.

Religion & Philosophy

Ideas have always possessed an extraordinary potency and vitality in China. The 19th-century Taiping Rebellion fused Christianity with revolutionary principles of social organisation, almost sweeping away the Qing dynasty in the process and leaving 20 million dead. The momentary incandescence of the Boxer Rebellion drew upon a volatile cocktail of martial-arts practices and superstition, blended with xenophobia, while the chaos of the Cultural Revolution further suggests what may happen in China when ideas assume the full supremacy they seek.

Anyone interested in Tibetan Buddhism will find Inner Mongolia easier to reach than Tibet; the province is home to many important and historic Lamaseries, including Dà Zhào in Hohhot, Wŭdāng Lamasery and Guǎng-zōng Sì.

Religion Today

The Chinese Communist Party (CCP) today remains fearful of ideas and beliefs that challenge its authority. Proselytising is not permitted, religious organisation is regulated and monitored, while organisations such as Falun Gong (a quasi-Buddhist health system) and the Church of Almighty God (a radical Christian group) can be deemed cults and banned outright. Despite constraints, worship and religious practice is generally permitted and China's spiritual world provides a vivid and colourful backdrop to contemporary Chinese life.

China has always had a pluralistic religious culture, and although statistics in China are a slippery fish, an estimated 400 million Chinese today adhere to a particular faith, in varying degrees of devotion. The CCP made strident efforts after 1949 to supplant religious worship with the secular philosophy of communism but since the abandonment of principles of Marxist-Leninist collectivism, this policy has significantly waned.

Religion in China is enjoying an upswing as people return to faith for spiritual solace at a time of change, dislocation and uncertainty. The poor and destitute may turn to worship as they feel abandoned by communism and the safety nets it once assured. Yet the educated and prosperous are similarly turning to religious belief for a sense of guidance and direction in a land many Chinese suspect has become morally bereft.

Religious belief in China has traditionally been marked by tolerance. Although the faiths are quite distinct, some convergence exists between Buddhism, Taoism and Confucianism, and you may discover shrines where all three faiths are worshipped. Guanyin, the Buddhist Goddess of Mercy, finds her equivalent in Tianhou (Mazu), the Taoist goddess and protector of fisher folk, and the two goddesses can seem almost interchangeable. Other symbioses exist: elements of Taoism and Buddhism can be discerned in the thinking of some Chinese Christians, while the Virgin Mary finds a familiar toehold in the Chinese psyche owing to her resemblance, in bearing and sympathetic message, to Guanyin.

Buddhism

Although not an indigenous faith, Buddhism (佛教; Fójiào) is the religion most deeply associated with China and Tibet. Although Buddhism's authority has long ebbed, the faith still exercises a powerful sway over China's spiritual inclinations. Many Chinese may not be regular temple-goers but they harbour an interest in Buddhism; they may merely be 'cultural Buddhists', with a strong affection for Buddhist civilisation.

Chinese towns with any history usually have several Buddhist temples, but the number is well down on pre-1949 figures. The small Héběi town of Zhèngdìng, for example, has four Buddhist temples, but at one time had eight. Běijīng once had hundreds, compared to the 20 or so you can find today.

Some of China's greatest surviving artistic achievements are Buddhist in inspiration. The largest and most ancient repository of Chinese, Central Asian and Tibetan Buddhist artwork can be found at the Mogao Grottoes in Gānsù, while the carved Buddhist caves at both Lóngmén and Yúngāng are spectacular pieces of religious and creative heritage. To witness Buddhism at its most devout, consider a trip to Tibet.

Origins

Founded in ancient India around the 5th century BC, Buddhism teaches that all of life is suffering, and that the cause of this anguish is desire, itself rooted in sensation and attachment. Suffering can only be overcome by following the eightfold path, a set of guidelines for moral behaviour, meditation and wisdom. Those who have freed themselves from suffering and the wheel of rebirth are said to have attained nirvana or enlightenment. The term Buddha generally refers to the historical founder of Buddhism, Siddhartha Gautama, but is also sometimes used to denote those who have achieved enlightenment.

Siddhartha Gautama left no writings; the sutras that make up the Buddhist canon were compiled many years after his death.

Buddhism in China

Like other faiths such as Christianity, Nestorianism, Islam and Judaism, Buddhism originally reached China via the Silk Road. The earliest recorded Buddhist temple in China proper dates back to the 1st century AD, but it was not until the 4th century, when a period of warlordism coupled with nomadic invasions plunged the country into disarray, that Buddhism gained mass appeal. Buddhism's sudden growth during this period is often attributed to its sophisticated ideas concerning the afterlife (such as karma and reincarnation), a dimension unaddressed by either Confucianism or Taoism. At a time when existence was especially precarious, spiritual transcendence was understandably popular.

As Buddhism converged with Taoist philosophy (through terminology used in translation) and popular religion (through practice), it went on to develop into something distinct from the original Indian tradition. The most famous example is the esoteric Chan school (Zen in Japanese),

> Author of *Titus Groan* and *Gormenghast*, Mervyn Peake was born in Lúshān in 1911, the son of Ernest Cromwell Peake, a missionary doctor from the London Missionary Society.

FALUN GONG

Falun Gong – a practice that merges elements of qìgōng-style regulated breathing and standing exercises with Buddhist teachings, fashioning a quasi-religious creed in the process – literally means 'Practice of the Dharma Wheel'. Riding a wave of interest in qìgōng systems in the 1990s, Falun Gong claimed as many as 100 million adherents in China by 1999. The technique was banned in the same year after over 10,000 practitioners stood in silent demonstration outside Zhōngnánhǎi in Běijīng, following protests in Tiānjīn when a local magazine published an article critical of Falun Gong. The authorities had been unnerved by the movement's audacity and organisational depth, construing Falun Gong as a threat to the primacy of the Chinese Communist Party (CCP). The movement was branded a cult (*xiéjiào*) and a robust, media-wide propaganda campaign was launched against practitioners, forcing many to undergo 're-education' in prison and labour camps. After the ban, the authorities treated Falun Gong believers harshly and reports surfaced of adherents dying in custody. Falun Gong remains an outlawed movement in China to this day.

which originated sometime in the 5th or 6th century, and focused on attaining enlightenment through meditation. Chan was novel not only in its unorthodox teaching methods, but also because it made enlightenment possible for laypeople outside the monastic system. It rose to prominence during the Tang and Song dynasties, after which the centre of practice moved to Japan. Other major Buddhist sects in China include Tiantai (based on the teachings of the Lotus Sutra) and Pure Land, a faith-based teaching that requires simple devotion, such as reciting the Amitabha Buddha's name, in order to gain rebirth in paradise. Today, Pure Land Buddhism is the most common.

Confucius Institutes around the world aim to promote Chinese language and culture internationally, while simultaneously developing its economic and cultural influences abroad.

Buddhist Schools

Regardless of its various forms, most Buddhism in China belongs to the Mahayana school, which holds that since all existence is one, the fate of the individual is linked to the fate of others. Thus, Bodhisattvas – those who have already achieved enlightenment but have chosen to remain on earth – continue to work for the liberation of all other sentient beings. The most popular Bodhisattva is Guanyin, the Goddess of Mercy.

Ethnic Tibetans and Mongols within China practise a unique form of Mahayana Buddhism known as Tibetan or Tantric Buddhism (Lǎma Jiào). Tibetan Buddhism, sometimes called Vajrayana or 'Thunderbolt Vehicle', has been practised since the early 7th century AD and is influenced by Tibet's pre-Buddhist Bon religion, which relied on priests or shamans to placate spirits, gods and demons. Generally speaking, it is much more mystical than other forms of Buddhism, relying heavily on *mudras* (ritual postures), mantras (sacred speech), yantras (sacred art) and esoteric initiation rites. Priests called lamas are believed to be reincarnations of highly evolved beings; the Dalai Lama is the supreme patriarch of Tibetan Buddhism.

GUANYIN

The boundlessly compassionate countenance of Guanyin, the Buddhist Goddess of Mercy, can be encountered in temples across China. The goddess (more strictly a Bodhisattva or a Buddha-to-be) goes under a variety of aliases: Guanshiyin (literally 'Observing the Cries of the World') is her formal name, but she is also called Guanzizai, Guanyin Dashi and Guanyin Pusa, or, in Sanskrit, Avalokiteshvara. Known as Kannon in Japan, Guanyam in Cantonese and Quan Am in Vietnam, Guanyin shoulders the grief of the world and dispenses mercy and compassion. Christians will note a semblance to the Virgin Mary in the aura surrounding the goddess, which at least partially explains why Christianity has found a slot in the Chinese consciousness.

In Tibetan Buddhism, her earthly presence manifests itself in the Dalai Lama, and her home is the Potala Palace in Lhasa. In China, her abode is the island of Pǔtuóshān in Zhèjiāng province, the first two syllables of which derive from the name of her palace in Lhasa.

In temples throughout China, Guanyin is often found at the very rear of the main hall, facing north (most of the other divinities, apart from Weituo, face south). She typically has her own little shrine and stands on the head of a big fish, holding a lotus in her hand. On other occasions, she has her own hall, often towards the rear of the temple.

The goddess (who in earlier dynasties appeared to be male rather than female) is often surrounded by little effigies of the *luóhàn* (or arhat; those freed from the cycle of rebirth), who scamper about; the Guānyīn Pavilion outside Dàlǐ is a good example of this. Guanyin also appears in a variety of forms, often with just two arms, but frequently in multiarmed form (as at the Pǔníng Temple in Chéngdé). The 11-faced Guanyin, the fierce and wrathful horse-head Guanyin (a Tibetan Buddhist incarnation), the Songzi Guanyin (literally 'Offering Son Guanyin') and the Dripping Water Guanyin are just some of her myriad manifestations. In standing form, she has traditionally been a favourite subject for *déhuà* (white-glazed porcelain) figures, which are typically very elegant.

Taoism

A home-grown philosophy-cum-religion, Taoism (道教; Dàojiào) is also perhaps the hardest of all China's faiths to grasp. Controversial, paradoxical, and – like the Tao itself – impossible to pin down, it is a natural counterpoint to rigid Confucianist order and responsibility.

Taoism predates Buddhism in China and much of its religious culture connects to a distant animism and shamanism, despite the purity of its philosophical school. In its earliest and simplest form, Taoism draws from *The Classic of the Way and Its Power* (Taote Jing; Dàodé Jīng), penned by the sagacious Laotzu (Laozi; c 580–500 BC), who left his writings with the gatekeeper of a pass as he headed west on the back of an ox. Some Chinese believe his wanderings took him to a distant land in the west where he became Buddha.

The Classic of the Way and Its Power is a work of astonishing insight and sublime beauty. Devoid of a godlike being or deity, Laotzu's writings instead endeavour to address the unknowable and indescribable principle of the universe, which he calls Dao (道; dào; 'the Way'). Dao is the way or method by which the universe operates, so it can be understood to be a universal or cosmic principle.

The opening lines of *The Classic of the Way and Its Power* confess, however, that the treatise may fail in its task: 道可道非常道, 名可名非常名; 'The way that can be spoken of is not the real way, the name that can be named is not the true name.' Despite this disclaimer, the 5000-character book, completed in terse classical Chinese, somehow communicates the nebulous power and authority of 'the Way'. The book remains the seminal text, and Taoist purists see little need to look beyond its revelations.

One of Taoism's most beguiling precepts, *wúwéi* (inaction) champions the allowing of things to naturally occur without interference. The principle is enthusiastically pursued by students of Taiji Quan, Wuji Quan and other soft martial arts who seek to equal nothingness in their bid to lead an opponent to defeat himself.

Confucianism

The very core of Chinese society for the past two millennia, Confucianism (儒家思想; Rújiā Sīxiǎng) is a humanist philosophy that strives for social harmony and the common good. In China, its influence can be seen in everything from the emphasis on education and respect for elders to the patriarchal role of the government.

Confucianism is based upon the teachings of Confucius (p216) (Kongzi), a 6th-century BC philosopher who lived during a period of constant warfare and social upheaval. While Confucianism changed considerably throughout the centuries, some of the principal ideas remained the same – namely an emphasis on five basic hierarchical relationships: father-son, ruler-subject, husband-wife, elder-younger, and friend-friend. Confucius believed that if each individual carried out his or her proper role in society (a son served his father respectfully while a father provided for his son, a subject served his ruler respectfully while a ruler provided for his subject, and so on) social order would be achieved. Confucius' disciples later gathered his ideas in the form of short aphorisms and conversations, forming the work known as *The Analects* (Lúnyǔ).

Early Confucian philosophy was further developed by Mencius (Mèngzǐ) and Xunzi, both of whom provided a theoretical and practical foundation for many of Confucius' moral concepts. In the 2nd century BC, Confucianism became the official ideology of the Han dynasty, thereby gaining mainstream acceptance for the first time. This was of major importance and resulted in the formation of an educated elite that served both the government as bureaucrats and the common people as

Beyond Tibet, China has four sacred Buddhist mountains, each one the home of a specific Bodhisattva. The two most famous mountains are Wǔtái Shān and Éméi Shān, respectively ruled over by Wenshu and Puxiang.

China's oldest surviving Buddhist temple is the White Horse Temple in Luòyáng; other more ancient Buddhist temples may well have existed but have since vanished.

exemplars of moral action. During the rule of the Tang dynasty an official examination system was created, which, in theory, made the imperial government a true meritocracy. However, this also contributed to an ossification of Confucianism, as the ideology grew increasingly mired in the weight of its own tradition, focusing exclusively on a core set of texts.

Nonetheless, influential figures sporadically reinterpreted the philosophy – in particular Zhu Xi (1130–1200), who brought in elements of Buddhism and Taoism to create Neo Confucianism (Lǐxué or Dàoxué) – and it remained a dominant social force up until the 1911 Revolution toppled the imperial bureaucracy. In the 20th century, modernist writers and intellectuals decried Confucian thought as an obstacle to modernisation and Mao further levelled the sage in his denunciation of 'the Four Olds'. But feudal faults notwithstanding, Confucius' social ethics recently resurfaced in government propaganda where they lent authority to the leadership's emphasis on 'harmony' (héxié).

An inspiring read, *God is Red: The Secret Story of How Christianity Survived and Flourished in Communist China* (2011) by Liao Yiwu, himself not a Christian, relates his encounters with Christians in contemporary China, set against a background of persecution and surging growth for the faith.

Christianity

The explosion of interest in Christianity (基督教; Jīdūjiào) in China over recent years is unprecedented except for the wholesale conversions that accompanied the tumultuous rebellion of the pseudo-Christian Taiping in the 19th century.

Christianity first arrived in China with the Nestorians, a sect from ancient Persia that split with the Byzantine Church in 431 AD, who arrived in China via the Silk Road in the 7th century. A celebrated tablet – the Nestorian Tablet – in Xī'ān records their arrival. Much later, in the 16th century, the Jesuits arrived and were popular figures at the imperial court, although they made few converts.

Large numbers of Catholic and Protestant missionaries established themselves in the 19th century, but left after the establishment of the People's Republic of China in 1949. One missionary, James Hudson Taylor from Barnsley in England, immersed himself in Chinese culture and is credited with helping to convert 18,000 Chinese Christians and building 600 churches during his 50 years in 19th-century China.

THE CHURCH OF ALMIGHTY GOD

An unhealthy by-product of the recent explosion of interest in Christianity in China and the widespread number of unofficial 'house churches' has been the emergence of Christian heresies with large numbers of devoted followers. Chief among these is The Church of Almighty God, which teaches that a Chinese woman named Yang Xiangbin is the second Christ.

After being blacklisted in 2000, Yang Xiangbin and the founder of the cult, Zhao Weishan, fled to the US. It was only when some followers killed a 37-year-old woman in a branch of McDonald's in Shāndōng, after she refused to give them her mobile phone number, that the organisation came to greater public attention.

Directly opposed to the Chinese Communist Party (CCP), which it terms the Great Red Dragon, the organisation continues to aggressively recruit adherents in China, although its members live a largely underground and secretive existence.

Sharing features with the revolutionary Taiping, who believed that their leader Hong Xiuquan was the Son of God, the Church of Almighty God fuses elements of Christian belief with other faiths that contradict mainstream Christianity. The group also encourages members to turn away from their families and devote themselves to the church; however, it is the church's opposition to the CCP that singled itself out for a nationwide ban.

Promoting itself via website and also known as Eastern Lightning, the church is one of 14 religious groups identified as cults by Chinese authorities. Strongly worded propaganda posters warning of the cult can be seen in churches and on notice boards across China.

In today's China, Christianity is a burgeoning faith perhaps uniquely placed to expand due to its industrious work ethic, associations with first-world nations and its emphasis on human rights and charitable work.

Some estimates point to 100 million Christians in China. However, the exact population is hard to calculate as many groups – outside the four official Christian organisations – lead a strict underground existence (in what are called 'house churches') out of fear of a political clampdown.

Churches (教堂; *jiàotáng*) are not hard to find and most towns will have at least one. Cities like Shànghǎi, Běijīng, Dàtóng, Tàiyuán and Qīngdǎo (and many other large towns) have cathedrals, most of them dating to the 19th and early 20th centuries.

In signs of greater official unease at the spread of Christianity, authorities in Wēnzhōu – a city in Zhèjiāng province known as 'China's Jerusalem' – demolished churches, threatened others with demolition and removed large crosses from some church spires in 2014. Officials argued they were enforcing building laws but Christian locals saw the moves as a deliberate attempt to undermine their faith.

Běijīng has also recently ratcheted up efforts to suppress fringe Christian groups such as the Church of Almighty God, an anti-Communist Party apocalyptic church which was designated a cult. Over a thousand members of the Church of Almighty God were arrested over a three-month period in 2014.

Islam

Islam (伊斯兰教; Yīsīlán Jiào) in China dates to the 7th century, when it was first brought to China by Arab and Persian traders along the Silk Road. Later, during the Mongol Yuan dynasty, maritime trade increased, bringing new waves of merchants to China's coastal regions, particularly the port cities of Guǎngzhōu and Quánzhōu. The descendants of these groups – now scattered across the country – gradually integrated into Han culture, and are today distinguished primarily by their religion. In Chinese, they are referred to as the Hui.

Other Muslim groups include the Uighurs, Kazaks, Kyrgyz, Tajiks and Uzbeks, who live principally in the border areas of the northwest. It is estimated that 1.5% to 3% of Chinese today are Muslim.

Animism

A small percentage of China's population is animist, a primordial religious belief akin to shamanism. Animists see the world as a living being, with rocks, trees, mountains and people all containing spirits that need to live in harmony. If this harmony is disrupted, restoration of this balance is attempted by a shaman who is empowered to mediate between the human and spirit world. Animism is most widely believed by minority groups and exists in a multitude of forms, some of which have been influenced by Buddhism and other religions.

Communism & Maoism

Ironically (or perhaps intentionally), Mao Zedong, while struggling to uproot feudal superstition and religious belief, sprung to godlike status in China via a personality cult. By weakening the power of deities, Mao found himself substituting those very gods his political power had diminished. In the China of today, Mao retains a semideified aura.

Communism sits awkwardly with the economic trajectory of China over the past 30 years. Once a philosophy forged in the white-hot crucible of civil war, revolution and the patriotic fervour to create a nation free from foreign interference, communism had largely run its credible course by the 1960s. By the death of Mao Zedong in 1976, the political philosophy had repeatedly brought the nation to catastrophe, with the

RELIGION & PHILOSOPHY ISLAM

During the Cultural Revolution, many Christian churches around China served as warehouses or factories, a utilitarian function that actually helped preserve many of them. They were gradually rehabilitated in the 1980s.

Believing he was the son of God and brother of Jesus Christ, Hakka rebel Hong Xiuquan led the bloody and tumultuous pseudo-Christian Taiping Rebellion against the Qing dynasty from 1856 to 1864.

Hundred Flowers Movement, the Great Leap Forward and the disastrous violence of the Cultural Revolution.

Communism remains the official guiding principle of the CCP. However, young communist aspirants are far less likely to be ideologues than pragmatists seeking to advance within the party structure. Many argue that communism has become an adjunct to the survival of the CCP.

Chinese Communism owes something to Confucianism. Confucius' philosophy embraces the affairs of man and human society and the relationship between rulers and the ruled, rather than the supernatural world. Establishing a rigid framework for human conduct, the culture of Confucianism was easily requisitioned by communists seeking to establish authority over society.

With the collapse of the Soviet Union in 1989, Běijīng became aware of the dangers of popular power and sought to maintain the coherence and strength of the state. This has meant that the CCP still seeks to impose itself firmly on the consciousness of Chinese people through patriotic education, propaganda, censorship, nationalism and a strong nation.

Communism also holds considerable nostalgic value for elderly Chinese who bemoan the erosion of values in modern-day China and pine for the days when they felt more secure and society was more egalitarian. Chairman Mao's portrait still hangs in abundance across China, from drum towers in Guǎngxī province to restaurants in Běijīng, testament to a generation of Chinese who still revere the communist leader.

Until his spectacular fall from power in 2012, Chinese politician and Chóngqìng party chief Bo Xilai launched popular Maoist-style 'red culture' campaigns in Chóngqìng, which included the singing of revolutionary songs and the mass-texting of quotes from Mao's *Little Red Book*. President Xi Jinping has also faced accusations of attempting to build a personality cult, allowing himself to be nicknamed Xi Dada (Big Daddy Xi), a kind of perennially good, sympathetic and paternal figurehead for the nation, with his citizens' best interests always at heart.

Nationalism

In today's China, '-isms' (主义; *zhǔyì* or 'doctrines') are often frowned upon. Any *zhǔyì* may suggest a personal focus that the CCP would prefer people channel into hard work instead. 'Intellectualism' is considered suspect as it may ask difficult questions. 'Idealism' is deemed nonpragmatic and potentially destructive, as Maoism showed.

China's one-party state has reduced thinking across the spectrum via propaganda and censorship, dumbing down an educational system that emphasises patriotic education. This in turn, however, helped spawn another '-ism': nationalism.

Nationalism is not restricted to Chinese youth but it is this generation – with no experience of the Cultural Revolution's terrifying excesses – which most closely identifies with its message. The *fēnqīng* (angry youth) have been swept along with China's rise; while they are no lovers of the CCP, they yearn for a stronger China that can stand up to 'foreign interference' and dictate its own terms.

The CCP actively encourages strong patriotism, but is nervous about its transformation into aggressive nationalism and the potential for disturbance. Much nationalism in the PRC has little to do with the CCP but everything to do with China; while the CCP has struggled at length to identify itself with China's civilisation and core values, it has been only partially successful. With China's tendency to get quickly swept along by passions, nationalism is an often unseen but quite potent force, most visibly flaring up into the periodic anti-Japanese demonstrations that can convulse large towns and cities.

One of China's most historic mosques is the Great Mosque in Tóngxīn in Níngxià, which dates to the Ming dynasty and survived the destruction of the Cultural Revolution.

Kāifēng in Hénán province is home to the largest community of Jews in China. The religious beliefs and customs of Judaism (犹太教; Yóutài Jiào) have died out, yet the descendants of the original Jews still consider themselves Jewish.

Chinese Cuisine

Cooking plays a central role in both Chinese society and the national psyche. When Chinese people meet, a common greeting is *'Nǐ chīfàn le ma?'* ('Have you eaten yet?'). Work, play, romance, business and family all revolve around food. The catalysts for all manner of enjoyment, meals are occasions for pleasure and entertainment, to clinch deals, strike up new friendships and rekindle old ones. To fully explore this tasty domain on home soil, all you need is a visa, a pair of chopsticks, an explorative palate and a passion for the unusual and unexpected.

Real Chinese Food

Because the nation so skilfully exported its cuisine abroad, your very first impressions of China were probably via your taste buds. Chinatowns the world over teem with the aromas of Chinese cuisine, ferried overseas by China's versatile and hard-working cooks; Sundays often see diners flocking to them for 'yum cha' and feasts of dim sum. Chinese food is indeed a wholesome and succulent point of contact between an immigrant Chinese population and everyone else.

But what you see – and taste – abroad is usually just a wafer-thin slice of a very hefty and wholesome pie. Chinese cuisine in the West is lifted from the cookbook of an emigrant community that originated mainly from China's southern seaboard. In a similar vein, the sing-song melodies of Cantonese were the most familiar of China's languages in Chinatowns, even though the dialect finds little traction in China beyond Hong Kong, Macau, Guǎngdōng, parts of Guǎngxī and KTV parlours nationwide. So although you may be hard-pressed to avoid dim sum and *cha siu* in your local Chinatown, finding more 'obscure' specialities from elsewhere in China may still be a challenge, or an expensive proposition. The 'Peking duck' at your local restaurant, for example, may be at best a distant relative of the fowl fired up over fruit-tree wood in the ovens of Běijīng *kǎoyādiàn* (Peking duck restaurants).

To get an idea of the size of its diverse menu, remember that China is not that much smaller than Europe. Just as Europe is a patchwork of different nation states, languages, cultural traditions and climates, China is also a smorgasbord of dialects, languages, ethnic minorities and extreme geographic and climatic differences, despite the common Han Chinese cultural glue. The sheer size of the land, the strength of local culture, and differences in geography and altitude mean there can be little in common between the cuisines of Xīnjiāng and Tibet, even though they are adjacent to each other. Following your nose (and palate) around China is one of the exciting ways to journey the land, so pack a sense of culinary adventure along with your travelling boots!

Regional Cuisines

The evolution of China's wide-ranging regional cuisines has been influenced by the climate, the distribution of crop and animal varieties, the type of terrain, proximity to the sea, the influence of neighbouring nations and the import of ingredients and flavours. Naturally seafood is prevalent in coastal regions of China, while in Inner Mongolia and Xīnjiāng there is a dependence on meat such as beef and lamb.

Another crucial ingredient is history. The flight of the Song court south of the Yangzi River (Cháng Jiāng) from northern Jurchen invaders in the 12th century helped develop China's major regional cuisines. This process was further influenced by urbanisation, itself made possible by the commercialisation of agriculture and food distribution; this led to the emergence of the restaurant industry and the further consolidation of regional schools. Further impetus came from the merchants and bureaucrats who travelled the land, and from improved transport options such as the Grand Canal, which allowed for shipping ingredients and recipes between Běijīng in the north and Hángzhōu further south.

Many Chinese regions lay claim to their own culinary conventions, which may overlap and cross-pollinate each other. The cooking traditions of China's ethnic minorities aside, Han cooking has traditionally been divided into eight schools (中华八大菜系; zhōnghuá bādàcàixì): **Chuān** (川; Sìchuān cuisine); **Huī** (徽; Ānhuī cuisine); **Lǔ** (鲁; Shāndōng cuisine); **Mǐn** (闽; Fújiàn cuisine); **Sū** (苏; Jiāngsū cuisine); **Xiāng** (湘; Húnán cuisine); **Yuè** (粤; Cantonese/Guǎngdōng cuisine); **Zhè** (浙; Zhèjiāng cuisine). Although each school is independent and well defined, it is possible to group these eight culinary traditions into northern, southern, western and eastern cooking.

A common philosophy lies at the heart of Chinese cooking, whatever the school. Most vegetables and fruits are *yīn* foods, generally moist and soft, possessing a cooling effect while nurturing the feminine aspect. *Yáng* foods – fried, spicy or with red meat – are warming and nourish the masculine side. Any meal should harmonise flavours and achieve a balance between cooling and warming foods.

Northern Chinese Cooking

With Shāndōng (鲁菜; *lǔcài*) – the oldest of the eight regional schools of cooking – at its heart, northern cooking also embraces Běijīng, northeastern (Manchurian) and Shānxī cuisine, creating the most time-honoured and most central form of Chinese cooking.

In the dry northern Chinese wheat belt, an accent falls on millet, sorghum, maize, barley and wheat rather than rice (which requires lush irrigation by water to cultivate). Particularly well suited to the harsh and hardy winter climate, northern cooking is rich and wholesome (northerners partially attribute their taller size, compared to southern Chinese, to its effects). Filling breads – such as *mántou* (馒头) or *bǐng* (饼; flat breads) – are steamed, baked or fried, while noodles may form the basis of any northern meal. (The ubiquitous availability of rice means it can always be found, however.) Northern cuisine is frequently quite salty, and appetising dumplings (铰子; *jiǎozi*) are widely eaten – usually boiled and sometimes fried.

As Běijīng was the principal capital through the Yuan, Ming and Qing dynasties, Imperial cooking is a chief characteristic of the northern school. Peking duck is Běijīng's signature dish, served with typical northern ingredients – pancakes, spring onions and fermented bean paste. You can find it all over China, but it's only true to form in the capital, roasted in ovens fired up with fruit-tree wood.

With China ruled from 1644 to 1911 by non-Han Manchurians, the influence of northeast cuisine *(dōngběi cài)* has naturally permeated northern cooking, dispensing a legacy of rich and hearty stews, dense breads, preserved foods and dumplings.

Meat roasting is also more common in the north than in other parts of China. Meats in northern China are braised until falling off the bone, or slathered with spices and barbecued until smoky. Pungent garlic, chives

Search www.
bbcgoodfood.com
for a mouth-
watering selec-
tion of Chinese
recipes and full
instructions on
throwing together
some classic and
lesser-known
dishes from
around China.

and spring onions are used with abandon and also employed raw. Also from the northwest is the Muslim Uighur cuisine.

The nomadic and carnivorous diet of the Mongolians also infiltrates northern cooking, most noticeably in the Mongolian hotpot and the Mongolian barbecue. Milk from nomadic herds of cattle, goats and horses has also crept into northern cuisine – as yoghurts *(suānnǎi)*, for example. Some hallmark northern dishes:

PINYIN	SCRIPT	ENGLISH
Běijīng kǎoyā	北京烤鸭	Peking duck
jiāo zhá yángròu	焦炸羊肉	deep fried mutton
jiǎozi	饺子	dumplings
mántou	馒头	steamed buns
qīng xiāng shāo jī	清香烧鸡	chicken wrapped in lotus leaf
ròu bāozi	肉包子	steamed meat buns
sān měi dòufu	三美豆腐	sliced bean curd (tofu) with Chinese cabbage
shuàn yángròu	涮羊肉	lamb hotpot
sì xǐ wánzi	四喜丸子	steamed and fried pork, shrimp and bamboo shoot balls
yuán bào lǐ jí	芫爆里脊	stir-fried pork tenderloin with coriander
zào liū sān bái	糟溜三白	stir-fried chicken, fish and bamboo shoots

Southern Chinese Cooking

The southern Chinese – particularly the Cantonese – historically spearheaded successive waves of immigration overseas, leaving aromatic constellations of Chinatowns around the world. Consequently, Westerners most often associate this school of cooking with China.

Typified by Cantonese (粤菜; *yuècài*) cooking, southern cooking lacks the richness and saltiness of northern cooking and instead coaxes more subtle aromas to the surface. The Cantonese astutely believe that good cooking does not require much flavouring, for it is the *xiān* (natural freshness) of the ingredients that marks a truly high-grade dish. Hence the near-obsessive attention paid to the freshness of ingredients in southern cuisine.

The hallmark Cantonese dish is dim sum (点心; Mandarin: *diǎnxīn)*. Yum cha (literally 'drink tea') – another name for dim sum dining – in Guǎngzhōu and Hong Kong can be enjoyed on any day of the week. Dishes, often in steamers, are wheeled around on trolleys so you can see what's available to order. Well known dim sum dishes include *guōtiē* (a kind of fried dumpling), *shāomài* (a kind of open pork dumpling), *chāshāobāo* (pork-filled bun) and *chūnjuǎn* (spring rolls). The extravagantly named *fèngzhuǎ* (phoenix claw) is the ever-popular steamed chicken's feet. *Xiǎolóngbāo* (steamed dumplings) are often sold in dim sum restaurants but are traditionally from Shànghǎi.

Local esteem for Cantonese food is evident in a popular Chinese saying: 'Be born in Sūzhōu, live in Hángzhōu, eat in Guǎngzhōu and die in Líuzhōu'. (Sūzhōu was famed for its good-looking people, Hángzhōu was a lovely place to live in, Guǎngzhōu was the best place to eat while Liǔzhōu was famed for the wood of its coffins!)

Fújiàn (闽菜; *mǐncài*) cuisine is another important southern cooking style, with its emphasis on light flavours and, due to the province's proximity to the East China Sea, seafood.

You will be charged for a wrapped-up packet of a hand-cleaning wipe or tissues if you open it at your restaurant table; if you don't use it, it should not appear on your bill.

Hakka cuisine from the disparate and migratory Hakka people (Kè-jiāzú) is another feature of southern Chinese cooking, as is the food of Cháozhōu in eastern Guǎngdōng.

Rice is the primary staple of southern cuisine. Sparkling paddy fields glitter across the south; the humid climate, plentiful rainfall and well irrigated land means that rice has been farmed here since the Chinese first populated the region during the Han dynasty (206 BC–AD 220). Some southern-school dishes:

PINYIN	SCRIPT	ENGLISH
bái zhuó xiā	白灼虾	blanched prawns with shredded scallions
dōngjiāng yánjú jī	东江盐焗鸡	salt-baked chicken
gālí jī	咖喱鸡	curried chicken
háoyóu niúròu	蚝油牛肉	beef with oyster sauce
kǎo rǔzhū	烤乳猪	crispy suckling pig
mì zhī chāshāo	密汁叉烧	roast pork with honey
shé ròu	蛇肉	snake
tángcù lǐjǐ/gǔlǎo ròu	糖醋里脊/咕老肉	sweet-and-sour pork fillets
tángcù páigǔ	糖醋排骨	sweet-and-sour spare ribs

Western Chinese Cooking

The cuisine of landlocked western China, a region heavily dappled with ethnic shades and contrasting cultures, welcomes the diner to the more scarlet end of the culinary spectrum. The trademark ingredient of the western school is the fiercely hot red chilli, a potent firecracker of an ingredient that floods dishes with an all-pervading spiciness. Aniseed, coriander, garlic and peppercorns are thrown in for good measure to add extra pungency and bite.

The standout cuisine of the western school is fiery Sìchuān (川菜; chuāncài) food, one of China's eight regional cooking styles, renowned for its eye-watering peppery aromas. One of the things that differentiates Sìchuān cooking from other spicy cuisines is the use of 'flower pepper' (huājiāo), a numbing, peppercorn-like herb that floods the mouth with an anaesthetising fragrance in a culinary effect termed málà (numb and hot). A Sìchuān dish you can find cooked up by chefs across China is the delicious sour cabbage fish soup (酸菜鱼; suāncàiyú), which features wholesome fish chunks in a spicy broth. The Chóngqìng hotpot is a force to be reckoned with but must be approached with a stiff upper lip (and copious amounts of liquid refreshment). If you want a hotpot pitched between spicy and mild, select a yuanyang hotpot (yuānyáng huǒguō), a vessel divided yin-yang style into two different compartments for two different soup bases. Sìchuān restaurants are everywhere in China: swarming around train stations, squeezed away down food streets or squished into street markets with wobbly stools and rickety tables parked out front.

Another of China's eight regional schools of cooking, dishes from Húnán (湘菜; xiāngcài) are similarly pungent, with a heavy reliance on chilli. Unlike Sìchuān food, flower pepper is not employed and instead spicy flavours are often sharper, fiercer and more to the fore. Meat, particularly in Húnán, is marinated, pickled or otherwise processed before cooking, which is generally by stir- or flash-frying.

Cuisine in Tibet includes tsampa (porridge of roasted barley flour), bö cha (yak-butter tea), momos (dumplings with vegetables or yak meat), thugpa (noodles with meat), thenthuk (fried noodle squares) as well as shemdre (rice, potato and yak-meat curry).

Spanish traders in the early Qing dynasty first introduced the red chilli pepper to China. Not only a spice, chillies are also a rich source of vitamins A and C.

Some western-school dishes:

PINYIN	SCRIPT	ENGLISH
bàngbàng jī	棒棒鸡	shredded chicken in a hot pepper and sesame sauce
Chóngqìng huǒguō	重庆火锅	Chóngqìng hotpot
dāndan miàn	担担面	spicy noodles
gānshāo yán lǐ	干烧岩鲤	stewed carp with ham and hot-and-sweet sauce
huíguō ròu	回锅肉	boiled and stir-fried pork with salty-and-hot sauce
málà dòufu	麻辣豆腐	spicy tofu
Máoshì Hóngshāoròu	毛氏红烧肉	Mao family braised pork
shuǐ zhǔ niúròu	水煮牛肉	spicy fried and boiled beef
shuǐzhǔyú	水煮鱼	fried and boiled fish, garlic sprouts and celery
suāncàiyú	酸菜鱼	sour-cabbage fish soup
yú xiāng ròusī	鱼香肉丝	fish-flavour pork strips
zhàcài ròusī	榨菜肉丝	stir-fried pork or beef tenderloin with tuber mustard

Eastern Chinese Cooking

The eastern school of Chinese cuisine derives from a fertile region of China, slashed by waterways and canals, glistening with lakes, fringed by a long coastline and nourished by a subtropical climate. Jiāngsū province itself is the home of Jiāngsū (苏菜; *sūcài*) cuisine – one of the core regions of the eastern school – and is famed as the 'Land of Fish and Rice', a tribute to its abundance of food and produce. The region has been historically prosperous, and in today's export economy the eastern provinces are among China's wealthiest. This combination of riches and bountiful food has created a culture of epicurism and gastronomic enjoyment.

South of Jiāngsū, Zhèjiāng (浙菜; *zhècài*) cuisine is another cornerstone of Eastern cooking. The Song dynasty saw the blossoming of the restaurant industry here; in Hángzhōu, the southern Song-dynasty capital, restaurants and teahouses accounted for two-thirds of the city's business during a splendidly rich cultural era. One of Hángzhōu's most famous dishes, *dōngpō ròu* (named after the celebrated poet and governor of Hángzhōu, Su Dongpo), was invented during this era.

Generally more oily and sweeter than other Chinese schools, the eastern school revels in fish and seafood, reflecting its geographical proximity to major rivers and the sea. Fish is usually *qīngzhēng* (清蒸; steamed) but can be stir-fried, pan-fried or grilled. Hairy crabs (*dàxháxiè*) are a Shànghǎi speciality between October and December. Eaten with soy, ginger and vinegar and downed with warm Shàoxīng wine, the best crabs come from Yangcheng Lake. The crab is believed to increase the body's *yīn* (coldness), so *yáng* (warmth) is added by imbibing lukewarm rice wine with it. It is also usual to eat male and female crabs together.

As with Cantonese food, freshness is a key ingredient in the cuisine, and sauces and seasonings are only employed to augment essential flavours. Stir-frying and steaming are also used, the latter with Shànghǎi's famous *xiǎolóngbāo*, steamer buns filled with nuggets of pork or crab swimming in a scalding meat broth. Learning how to devour these carefully without the meat juice squirting everywhere and scalding the roof of your mouth (or blinding your neighbour) requires some practice.

With a lightness of flavour, Ānhuī (徽菜; *huīcài*) cuisine – one of China's eight principle culinary traditions and firmly in the eastern cooking sphere – puts less emphasis on seafood. Braising and stewing of vegetables and wildlife from its mountainous habitats is a pronounced feature of this regional cuisine.

China's best soy sauce is also produced in the eastern provinces, and the technique of braising meat using soy sauce, sugar and spices was perfected here. Meat cooked in this manner takes on a dark mauve hue auspiciously described as 'red', a colour associated with good fortune.

Famous dishes from the eastern school:

PINYIN	SCRIPT	ENGLISH
gōngbào jīdīng	宫爆鸡丁	spicy chicken with peanuts, aka *kung pao* chicken
háoyóu niúròu	蚝油牛肉	beef with oyster sauce
hóngshāo páigǔ	红烧排骨	red-braised spare ribs
hóngshāo qiézi	红烧茄子	red-cooked aubergine
hóngshāo yú	红烧鱼	red-braised fish
huǒguō	火锅	hotpot
húntùn tāng	馄饨汤	wonton soup
jiācháng dòufu	家常豆腐	'homestyle' tofu
jiǎozi	饺子	dumplings
jīdànmiàn	鸡蛋面	noodles and egg
qīngjiāo ròupiàn	青椒肉片	pork and green peppers
shāguō dòufu	沙锅豆腐	bean-curd (tofu) casserole
suānlàtāng	酸辣汤	hot-and-sour soup
tiěbǎn niúròu	铁板牛肉	sizzling beef platter
xīhóngshì chǎojīdàn	西红柿炒鸡蛋	fried egg and tomato
xīhóngshì jīdàntāng	西红柿鸡蛋汤	egg and tomato soup
xīhóngshì niúròu	西红柿牛肉	beef and tomato
yúxiāng qiézi	鱼香茄子	fish-flavoured aubergine

Home-Style Dishes

Besides China's regional cuisines, there is a tasty variety of *jiāchángcài* (homestyle) dishes you will see all over the land, cooked up in restaurants and along food streets.

Notable *jiāchángcài* dishes:

PINYIN	SCRIPT	ENGLISH
jiāng cōng chǎo xiè	姜葱炒蟹	stir-fried crab with ginger and scallions
mìzhī xūnyú	蜜汁熏鱼	honey-smoked carp
níng shì shànyú	宁式鳝鱼	stir-fried eel with onion
qiézhī yúkuài	茄汁鱼块	fish fillet in tomato sauce
qīng zhēng guìyú	清蒸鳜鱼	steamed Mandarin fish
sōngzǐ guìyú	松子鳜鱼	Mandarin fish with pine nuts
suānlà yóuyú	酸辣鱿鱼	hot-and-sour squid
xiǎolóngbāo	小笼包	steamer buns
yóubào xiārén	油爆虾仁	fried shrimp
zhá hēi lǐyú	炸黑鲤鱼	fried black carp
zhá yúwán	炸鱼丸	fish balls

Dining Ins & Outs

Table Manners

Chinese meal-times are generally relaxed affairs with no strict rules of etiquette. Meals can commence in a Confucian vein before spiralling into total Taoist mayhem, fuelled by incessant toasts with *báijiǔ* (a white spirit) or beer and furious smoking by the men.

Meals typically unfold with one person ordering on behalf of a group. When a group dines, a selection of dishes is ordered for everyone to share rather than individual diners ordering a dish just for themselves. As they arrive, dishes are placed communally in the centre of the table or on a lazy Susan, which may be revolved by the host so that the principal guest gets first choice of whatever dish arrives. It is common practice and not impolite (unless moody!) to use your own chopsticks to serve yourself straight from each dish. Soup may appear midway through the meal or at the end. Rice often arrives at the end of the meal; if you would like it earlier, just ask. Chinese diners will often slurp their noodles quite noisily, which is not considered to be impolite.

It is good form to fill your neighbours' tea cups or beer glasses when they are empty. To serve yourself tea or any other drink without serving others first is bad form; appreciation to the pourer is indicated by gently tapping the middle finger on the table. When your teapot needs a refill, signal this to the waiter by simply taking the lid off the pot.

It's best to wait until someone announces a toast before drinking your beer; if you want to get a quick shot in, propose a toast to the host. The Chinese do in fact toast each other much more than in the West – often each time they drink. A formal toast is conducted by raising your glass in both hands in the direction of the toastee and crying out *gānbēi* (literally, 'dry the glass') which is the cue to drain your glass in one hit – this can be quite a challenge if your drink is 65% *báijiǔ*. Your glass will be rapidly refilled to the top after you drain it, in preparation for the next toast.

Smokers can light up during the meal, unless they are in the non-smoking area of a restaurant. Depending on the restaurant, smokers may smoke through the entire meal. If you are a smoker, ensure you hand around your cigarettes to others, which is standard procedure.

Don't use your chopsticks to point or gesticulate – and never stick your chopsticks upright in bowls of rice (it's a portent of death).

Last but not least, don't insist on paying for the bill if someone else is tenaciously determined to pay – usually the person who invited you to dinner. By all means offer to pay, but then raise your hands in mock surrender when resistance is met: to pay for a meal when another person is determined to do it is to make them lose face.

Chinese toothpick etiquette is similar to that found in other Asian nations: one hand excavates with the toothpick, while the other hand shields the mouth.

Desserts & Sweets

The Chinese do not generally eat dessert, but fruit – typically watermelon *(xīguā)* or oranges *(chéng)* – often concludes a meal. Ice cream can be ordered in some places, but in general sweet desserts *(tiánpǐn)* are consumed as snacks and are seldom available in restaurants.

Breakfast

Breakfast in China is generally light, simple and over and done with quickly. The meal may consist of merely a bowl of rice porridge (粥; *zhōu*) or its watery cousin, rice gruel (稀饭; *xīfàn*). Pickles, boiled eggs, steamed buns, fried peanuts and deep-fried dough sticks (油条; *yóutiáo)* are also popular, washed down with warm soybean milk. Breakfast at your Chinese hotel may consist of some or all of these.

Coffee is rarely drunk at breakfast time, unless the family is modern, urban and middle-class, but it's easy to find in cafes, especially in large towns. Sliced bread (面包; *miànbāo*) was once rare but is increasingly common, as is butter (黄油; *huángyóu*).

Drinks

Tea

An old Chinese saying identifies tea as one of the seven basic necessities of life, along with firewood, oil, rice, salt, soy sauce and vinegar. The Chinese were the first to cultivate tea, and the art of brewing and drinking it has been popular since Tang times (AD 618–907). Tea is to the Chinese what fine wine is to the French: a beloved beverage savoured for its fine aroma, distinctive flavour and pleasing aftertaste.

China has three main types of tea: green tea *(lǜ chá)*, black tea *(hóng chá)* and *wūlóng* (a semifermented tea, halfway between black and green tea). In addition, there are other variations, including jasmine *(cháshuǐ)* and chrysanthemum *(júhuā chá)*. Some famous regional teas of China are Fújiàn's *tiě guānyīn*, *pǔ'ěrh* from Yúnnán and Zhèjiāng's *lóngjǐng* tea. Eight-treasure tea *(bābǎo chá)* consists of rock sugar, dates, nuts and tea combined in a cup; it makes a delicious treat.

Beer

If tea is the most popular drink in China, then beer (啤酒; *píjiǔ*) is surely second. Many towns and cities have their own brewery and label, although a remarkable feat of socialist standardisation ensures a striking similarity in flavour and strength. You can drink bath tubs of the stuff and still navigate a straight line. If you want your beer cold, ask for *liáng de* (凉的); if you want it truly arctic, call for *bīngzhèn de* (冰镇的).

The best-known beer is Tsingtao, made with Láo Shān mineral water, which lends it a sparkling quality. It was originally a German beer, since the town of Qīngdǎo (formerly spelt 'Tsingtao') was once a German concession; the Chinese inherited the brewery, which dates to 1903, along with Bavarian brewing methods. Several foreign beers are also brewed in China and there's a growing market for craft brews in the wealthier cities. If you crave variety, many of the bars we list should have a selection of foreign imported beers; prices will be high, however.

Wine

Surging demand for imported wines has seen China remain the world's largest consumer of red wine in recent years. Expensive French reds *(hóngjiǔ)* are treasured in a fashionable market that was only finding its feet a mere 17 years ago. Wine has become the drink of choice among an increasingly sophisticated business class eager to appear discerning and flamboyant. Unfortunately this also means you can pay way over the odds at restaurants in Shànghǎi or Běijīng for imported wines. White wine consumption in China is increasingly associated with female drinkers.

China has also cultivated vines and produced wine for an estimated 4000 years, and Chinese wines are generally cheaper than imports from abroad. The provinces of Xīnjiāng and Níngxià, in the distant northwest of China, are famous for their vineyards.

Spirits

Many Chinese 'wines' are in fact spirits. Maotai, a favourite, is a very expensive spirit called *báijiǔ* made from sorghum and used for toasts at banquets. The cheap alternative is Erguotou, distilled in Běijīng but available all over China; look out for the Red Star (Hongxing) brand. *Báijiǔ* ranges from milder forms to around 65% proof. Milder rice wine is intended mainly for cooking but can be drunk warm like sake.

It is quite common for banquets and dinners in China to finish abruptly, as everyone stands up and walks away in unison with little delay.

Arts & Architecture

China is custodian of one of the world's richest cultural and artistic legacies. Until the 20th century, China's arts were deeply conservative and resistant to change but revolutions in technique and content over the last century fashioned a dramatic transformation. Despite this evolution, China's arts – whatever the period – embrace a common aesthetic that embodies the very soul and lifeblood of the nation.

Aesthetics

In reflection of the Chinese character, Chinese aesthetics have traditionally been marked by restraint and understatement, a preference for oblique references over direct explanation, vagueness in place of specificity and an avoidance of the obvious in place of a fondness for the veiled and subtle. Traditional Chinese aesthetics sought to cultivate a more reserved artistic impulse, principles that compellingly find their way into virtually every Chinese art form, from painting to sculpture, ceramics, calligraphy, film, poetry, literature and beyond.

As one of the central strands of the world's oldest civilisation, China's aesthetic traditions are tightly woven into Chinese cultural identity. For millennia, Chinese aesthetics were highly traditionalist and, despite coming under the influence of occupiers from the Mongols to the Europeans, defiantly conservative. It was not until the fall of the Qing dynasty in 1911 and the appearance of the New Culture Movement that China's great artistic traditions began to rapidly transform. In literature the stranglehold of classical Chinese loosened to allow breathing space for *báihuà* (colloquial Chinese) and a progressive new aesthetic started to flower, ultimately leading to revolutions in all of the arts, from poetry to painting, theatre and music.

It is hard to square China's great aesthetic traditions with the devastation inflicted upon them since 1949. Confucius advocated the edifying role of music and poetry in shaping human lives, but 5th-century philosopher Mozi was less enamoured with them, seeing music and other arts as extravagant and wasteful. The communists took this a stage further, enlisting the arts as props in their propaganda campaigns, and permitting the vandalism and destruction of much traditional architecture and heritage. Many of China's traditional skills (such as martial arts lineages) and crafts either died out or went into decline during the Cultural Revolution. Many of the arts have yet to recover fully from this deterioration, even though opening up and reform prompted a vast influx of foreign artistic concepts.

Calligraphy

Although calligraphy (书法; *shūfǎ*) has a place among most languages that employ alphabets, the art of calligraphy in China is taken to unusual heights of intricacy and beauty in a language that is alphabet-free and essentially composed of images.

To fully appreciate how perfectly suited written Chinese is for calligraphy, it is vital to grasp how written Chinese works. A word in English represents a sound alone; a written character in Chinese combines both sound and a picture. Indeed, the sound element of a Chinese character – when present – is often auxiliary to the illustration of a visual image, even if that image is abstract.

Furthermore, although some Chinese characters were simplified in the 1950s as part of a literacy drive, most characters have remained unchanged for thousands of years. As characters are essentially images, they inadequately reflect changes in spoken Chinese over time. A phonetic written language such as English can alter over the centuries to reflect changes in the sound of the language (so the written language changes). Being pictographic, Chinese cannot easily do this, so while the spoken language has transformed over the centuries, the written language has remained more static. Indeed, any changes to traditional written Chinese characters would result in changes to the pronunciation of how they are read.

This helps explain why Chinese calligraphy is the trickiest of China's arts to comprehend for Western visitors, unless they have a sound understanding of written Chinese. The beauty of a Chinese character may be partially appreciated by a Western audience, but for a full understanding it is also essential to understand the meaning of the character (or characters).

There are five main calligraphic scripts – seal script, clerical script, semicursive script, cursive script and standard script – each of which reflects the style of writing of a specific era. Seal script, the oldest and most complex, was the official writing system during the Qin dynasty and has been employed ever since in the carving of the seals and name chops (stamps carved from stone) that are used to stamp documents. Expert calligraphers have a preference for using full-form characters (*fántǐzì*) rather than their simplified variants (*jiǎntǐzì*).

Painting

Traditional Painting

Unlike Chinese calligraphy, no 'insider' knowledge is required for a full appreciation of traditional Chinese painting. Despite its symbolism, obscure references and occasionally abstruse philosophical allusions, Chinese painting is highly accessible. For this reason, traditional Chinese paintings – especially landscapes – have long been treasured in the West for their beauty.

As described in Xie He's 6th-century-AD treatise, the *Six Principles of Painting*, the chief aim of Chinese painting is to capture the innate essence or spirit (*qì*) of a subject and endow it with vitality. The brush line, varying in thickness and tone, was the second principle (referred to as the 'bone method') and is the defining technique of Chinese painting. Traditionally, it was imagined that brushwork quality could reveal the artist's moral character. As a general rule, painters were less concerned with achieving outward resemblance (that was the third principle) than with conveying intrinsic qualities.

Early painters dwelled on the human figure and moral teachings, while also conjuring up scenes from everyday life. By the time of the Tang dynasty, a new genre, known as landscape painting, had begun to flower. Reaching full bloom during the Song and Yuan dynasties, landscape painting meditated on the surrounding environment. Towering mountains, ethereal mists, open spaces, trees and rivers, and light and dark were all exquisitely presented in ink washes on silk. Landscape paintings attempted to capture the metaphysical and the absolute, drawing the viewer into a particular realm where the philosophies of Taoism and Buddhism found expression. Humanity is typically a small and almost

The five fundamental brushstrokes necessary to master calligraphy can be found in the character 永, which means eternal or forever.

insignificant subtext to the performance. The dreamlike painting sought to draw the viewer in rather than impose itself on them.

On a technical level, the success of landscapes depended on the artists' skill in capturing light and atmosphere. Blank, open spaces devoid of colour create light-filled voids, contrasting with the darkness of mountain folds and forests, filling the painting with *qì* and vaporous vitality. Specific emotions are not aroused but instead nebulous sensations permeate. Painting and classical poetry often went hand in hand, best exemplified by the work of Tang-dynasty poet/artist Wang Wei (699–759).

Modern Art
Socialist Realism

After 1949, classical Chinese techniques were abandoned and foreign artistic techniques imported wholesale. Washes on silk were replaced with oil on canvas and China's traditional obsession with the mysterious and ineffable made way for concrete attention to detail and realism.

By 1970 Chinese artists had aspired to master the skills of socialist realism, a vibrant communist-endorsed style that drew from European neoclassical art, the lifelike canvases of Jacques-Louis David and the output of Soviet Union painters. The style had virtually nothing to do with traditional Chinese painting techniques. Saturated with political symbolism and propaganda, the blunt artistic style was manufactured on an industrial scale (and frequently on industrial themes).

The entire trajectory of Chinese painting – which had evolved in glacial increments over the centuries – had been redirected virtually overnight. Vaporous landscapes were substituted with hard-edged panoramas. Traditional Taoist and Buddhist philosophy was overturned and humans became the master of nature and often the most dominant theme. Dreamy vistas were out; smoke stacks, red tractors and muscled peasants were in.

Propaganda Art

Another art form that found a fertile environment during the Mao era was the propaganda poster. Mass-produced from the 1950s onwards and replicated in their thousands through tourist markets across China today, the colourful Chinese propaganda poster was a further instrument of social control in a nation where aesthetics had become subservient to communist orthodoxy.

With a prolific range of themes from chubby, well fed Chinese babies to the Korean War, the virtues of physical education, the suppression of counter-revolutionary activity and paeans to the achievements of the Great Leap Forward or China as an earthly paradise, propaganda posters were ubiquitous. The golden age of poster production ran through to the 1980s, only declining during Deng Xiaoping's tenure and the opening up of China to the West.

The success of visual propaganda lay in its appeal to a large body of illiterate or semiliterate peasants. The idealism, revolutionary romanticism and vivid colouring of Chinese propaganda art brought hope and vibrancy to a time that was actually often colourless and drab, while adding certainty to an era of great hardship and struggle.

Post-Mao

It was only with the death of Mao Zedong in September 1976 that the shadow of the Cultural Revolution – when Chinese aesthetics were conditioned by the threat of violence – began its retreat and the individual artistic temperament was allowed to thrive afresh.

The most abstract calligraphic form is grass or cursive script (*cǎoshū*), a highly fluid style of penmanship which even Chinese people have difficulty reading.

Chinese individuals and companies are also purchasing non-Chinese art masterpieces. In 2015 Claude Monet's *Bassin aux nymphéas, les rosiers* sold for $20.4m at auction to the Dalian Wanda Group.

ARTS & ARCHITECTURE PAINTING

Painters such as Luo Zhongli employed the realist techniques gleaned from China's art academies to depict the harsh realities etched in the faces of contemporary peasants. Others escaped the suffocating confines of socialist realism to navigate new horizons. A voracious appetite for Western art brought with it fresh concepts and ideas, while the ambiguity of precise meaning in the fine arts offered a degree of protection from state censors.

One group of artists, the Stars, found retrospective inspiration in Picasso and German Expressionism. The ephemeral group had a lasting impact on the development of Chinese art in the 1980s and 1990s, paving the way for the New Wave movement that emerged in 1985. New Wave artists were greatly influenced by Western art, especially the iconoclastic Marcel Duchamp. In true nihilist style, the New Wave artist Huang Yongping destroyed his works at exhibitions, in an effort to escape from the notion of 'art'. Political realities became instant subject matter as performance artists wrapped themselves in plastic or tape to symbolise the repressive realities of modern-day China.

In 2011 an ink and brush painting by artist Qi Baishi (1864–1957) sold for ¥425 million (US$65 million) at auction.

Beyond Tiān'ānmén

The Tiān'ānmén Square protests in 1989 fostered a deep-seated cynicism that permeated artworks with loss, loneliness and social isolation. An exodus of artists to the West commenced. This period also coincided with an upsurge in the art market as investors increasingly turned to artworks and money began to slosh about.

Much post-1989 Chinese art dwelled obsessively on contemporary socioeconomic realities, with consumer culture, materialism, urbanisation and social change a repetitive focus. More universal themes became apparent, however, as the art scene matured. Meanwhile, many artists who left China in the 1990s have returned, setting up private studios and galleries. Government censorship remains, but artists are branching out into other areas and moving away from overtly political content and China-specific concerns.

Cynical realists Fang Lijun and Yue Minjun fashioned grotesque portraits that conveyed hollowness and mock joviality, tinged with despair. Born in the late 1950s, Wang Guangyi took pop art as a template for his ironic pieces, fused with propaganda art techniques from the Cultural Revolution.

BEST MUSEUMS & ART GALLERIES

Shànghǎi Museum (p294) An outstanding collection of traditional Chinese art and antiquities.

Poly Art Museum (p78) Inspiring displays of traditional bronzes and Buddhist statues.

Rockbund Art Museum (p295) Forward-thinking museum of contemporary art, just off the Bund.

M50 (p303) Contemporary art in a converted Shànghǎi industrial zone.

798 Art District (p87) Běijīng's premier art zone, housed in a former factory.

Propaganda Poster Art Centre (p302) Shànghǎi treasure trove of propaganda art from the communist golden age.

AFA (Art for All Society) (p538) Nonprofit gallery promoting the best in contemporary Macau art.

ShanghART (p303) Impressive warehouse-sized Shànghǎi gallery dedicated to contemporary Chinese artists.

China Sculpture Museum (p361) Set within the restored walls of Dàtóng, this cavernous museum has a huge collection of contemporary pieces.

Born just before the Cultural Revolution in 1964 and heavily influenced by German expressionism, Zeng Fanzhi explored the notions of alienation and isolation – themes commonly explored by Chinese artists during this period – in his *Mask* series from the 1990s. Introspection is a hallmark of Zeng's oeuvre. In 2008 Christie's in Hong Kong sold Zeng Fanzhi's painting *Mask Series 1996 No. 6* (featuring masked members of China's communist youth organisation, the Young Pioneers) for US$9.7 million, which is the highest price yet paid for a modern Chinese artwork.

Also born in the early 1960s, Zhang Dali is another artist who gave expression to social change and the gulf between rich and poor, especially the circumstances of the immigrant worker underclass in Běijīng.

Contemporary Directions

Most artists of note and aspiration gravitate to Běijīng (or Shànghǎi perhaps) to work. Today's China provides a huge wellspring of subject matter for artists, tempered by the reality of political censorship and the constraints of taboo. Themes that can seem tame in the West may assume a special power in China, so works can rely upon their context for potency and effect.

Ai Weiwei, who enjoys great international fame partly due to his disobedient stand, best exemplifies the dangerous overlap between artistic self-expression, dissent and conflict with the authorities. Arrested in 2011 and charged with tax evasion, Ai Weiwei gained further publicity for his temporary *Sunflower Seeds* exhibition at the Tate Modern in London.

Working collaboratively as Birdhead, Shànghǎi analogue photographers Ji Weiyu and Song Tao record the social dynamics and architectural habitat of their home city in thoughtful compositions. Běijīng-born Ma Qiusha works in video, photography, painting and installations on themes of a deeply personal nature. In her video work *From No.4 Pingyuanli to No.4 Tianqiaobeili*, the artist removes a bloody razor blade from her mouth after narrating her experiences as a young artist in China. Born in 1982, Ran Huang works largely in film but across a spectrum of media, conveying themes of absurdity, the irrational and conceptual. Shànghǎi artist Shi Zhiying explores ideas of a more traditional hue in her sublime oil-paint depictions on large canvases of landscapes and religious and cultural objects. Also from Shànghǎi, Xu Zhen works with provocative images to unsettle and challenge the viewer. Xu's *Fearless* (2012), a large mixed-media work on canvas, is a powerful maelstrom of symbolism and the fragments of cultural identity. Xīnjiāng-born Zhao Zhao – once an assistant to Ai Weiwei – communicates provocative sentiments in his work, exploring ideas of freedom and themes of a nonconformist nature.

Ceramics

China's very first vessels – dating back more than 8000 years – were simple handcrafted earthenware pottery, primarily used for religious purposes. The invention of the pottery wheel during the late Neolithic period, however, led to a dramatic technological and artistic leap.

Over the centuries, Chinese potters perfected their craft, introducing many new and exciting styles and techniques. The spellbinding artwork of the Terracotta Warriors in Xī'ān reveals a highly developed level of technical skill achieved by Qin-dynasty craftsmen. Periods of artistic evolution, during the cosmopolitan Tang dynasty, for example, prompted further stylistic advances. The Tang dynasty 'three-colour ware' is a much-admired type of ceramic from this period, noted for its vivid yellow, green and white glaze. Demand for lovely blue-green celadons grew in countries as distant as Egypt and Persia.

Major art festivals include Běijīng's 798 International Art Festival, China International Gallery Exposition and Běijīng Biennale, the Shànghǎi Biennale, Guǎngzhōu Triennial and Hong Kong's one-day Clockenflap festival.

A dark and Gothic image in the West, the bat is commonly used in Chinese porcelain, wood designs, textiles and artwork as it is considered a good luck omen.

ARTS & ARCHITECTURE CERAMICS

The Yuan dynasty saw the first development of China's standout 'blue and white' (qīnghuā) porcelain. Cobalt-blue paint from Persia was applied as an underglaze directly to white porcelain with a brush, the vessel then covered with another transparent glaze and fired. This technique was perfected during the Ming dynasty and such ceramics became hugely popular all over the world, eventually acquiring the name 'China-ware', whether produced in China or not.

Although many kilns were established in China, the most famous was at Jǐngdézhèn in Jiāngxī province, where royal porcelain was fired.

During the Qing dynasty, porcelain techniques were further refined and developed, showing superb craftsmanship and ingenuity. British and European consumers dominated the export market, displaying an insatiable appetite for Chinese vases and bowls decorated with flowers and landscapes. Stunning monochromatic ware is another hallmark of the Qing, especially the ox-blood vases, imperial yellow bowls and enamel-decorated porcelain. The Qing is also notable for its elaborate and highly decorative wares.

In 2010 a Qing dynasty Chinese vase sold for £53.1 million after being discovered in the attic of a house in north-west London and put up for auction.

Jǐngdézhèn remains an excellent place to visit ceramic workshops and purchase various types of ceramic wares, from Mao statues to traditional glazed urns. The Shànghǎi Museum has a premier collection of porcelain, while several independent retailers in Běijīng, Shànghǎi and Hong Kong also sell more modish and creative pieces. Spin (p330), in particular, sells a highly creative selection of contemporary ceramic designs.

In recent years wealthy Chinese collectors have embarked on a lavish spending spree, buying back China's ceramic heritage in the international auction markets, with staggering prices paid for pieces.

Sculpture

The earliest sculpture in China dates to the Zhou and Shang dynasties, when small clay and wooden figures were commonly placed in tombs to protect the dead and guide them on their way to heaven.

With the arrival of Buddhism, sculpture turned towards spiritual figures and themes, with sculptors frequently enrolled in huge carving projects for the worship of Sakyamuni. Influences also arrived along the Silk Road from abroad, bringing styles from as far afield as Greece and Persia, via India. The magnificent Buddhist caves at Yúngāng in Shānxī province, for example, date back to the 5th century and betray a noticeable Indian influence.

Chisellers also began work on the Lóngmén Grottoes in Hénán province at the end of the 5th century. The earliest effigies are similar in style to those at Yúngāng, revealing further Indian influences and an other-worldliness in their facial expressions. Later cave sculptures at Lóngmén were completed during the Tang dynasty and display a more Chinese style.

The most superlative examples are at the Mògāo Grottoes at Dūnhuáng in Gānsù province, where well preserved Indian and Central Asian–style sculptures, particularly of the Tang dynasty, carry overtly Chinese characteristics – many statues feature long, fluid bodies and have warmer, more refined facial features.

The Shànghǎi Museum has a splendid collection of Buddhist sculpture, as does Capital Museum and the Poly Art Museum, both in Běijīng.

Beyond China's grottoes, other mesmerising Chinese sculpture hides away in temples across China. The colossal statue of Guanyin in Pǔníng Temple in Chéngdé is a staggering sight, carved from five different types of wood and towering over 22m in height. Shuānglín Temple outside Píngyáo in Shānxī province is famed for its astonishing collection of painted statues from the Song and Yuan dynasties.

Literature

Classic Novels

Until the early 20th century, classical literature (古文; *gǔwén*) had been the principal form of writing in China for thousands of years. A breed of purely literary writing, classical Chinese employed a stripped-down form of written Chinese that did not reflect the way people actually spoke or thought. Its grammar differed from the syntax of spoken Chinese and it employed numerous obscure Chinese characters.

Classical Chinese maintained divisions between educated and uneducated Chinese, putting literature beyond the reach of the common person and fashioning a cliquey lingua franca for Confucian officials, scholars and the crudite elite.

Classical novels evolved from the popular folk talon and dramas that entertained the lower classes. During the Ming dynasty they were penned in a semivernacular (or 'vulgar') language, and are often irreverently funny and full of action-packed fights.

Probably the best-known novel outside China is *Journey to the West* (Xīyóu Jì) – more commonly known as *Monkey*. Written in the 16th century, it follows the misadventures of a cowardly Buddhist monk (Tripitaka; a stand-in for the real-life pilgrim Xuan Zang) and his companions – a rebellious monkey, lecherous pig-man and exiled monster-immortal – on a pilgrimage to India.

The 14th century novel *The Water Margin/Outlaws of the Marsh/All Men are Brothers* (Shuǐhǔ Zhuàn) is, on the surface, an excellent tale of honourable bandits and corrupt officials along the lines of Robin Hood. On a deeper level, though, it is a reminder to Confucian officials of their right to rebel when faced with a morally suspect government (at least one emperor officially banned it).

Written by Cao Xueqin and one of the most famous tales in Chinese literature, the *Dream of the Red Mansions* (Hónglóu Mèng) is an elaborate 18th-century novel penned in a vernacular, semiclassical form of Chinese. Also known as *The Story of the Stone*, the lavish tale relates the decline of an aristocratic family, affording a captivating overview of the mores and manners of upperclass Qing society.

Classical Poetry

The earliest collection of Chinese poetry is the *Book of Songs* (Shījīng), which includes over 300 poems dating back to the 6th century BC, gathered together by royal musicians who lived in the many feudal states clustered along the banks of the Yellow River during the Zhou dynasty. Centred on themes of love, marriage, war, agriculture, hunting and sacrifice, the poems were originally meant to be sung.

China's greatest early poet is Qu Yuan, who lived during the Warring States period (475–221 BC) and is known for his romantic, lyrical poetry.

The Tang dynasty is considered to be the golden age of Chinese poetry, when two of China's greatest poets – Li Bai and Du Fu – lived and created some of the most beautiful and moving poems in classical Chinese. The most famous of these poems are gathered into an anthology called *300 Tang Poems*. During the Song dynasty, a lyric form of poetry called *cí* emerged, expressing feelings of passion and desire. Su Shi (Su Dongpo) is the most famous poet from this period.

Modern Literature

Early 20th-Century Writing

Classical Chinese maintained its authority over literary minds until the early 20th century, when it came under the influence of the West. Torch-bearing author Lu Xun wrote his short story *Diary of a Madman*

The *I Ching* (*Yijing*; Book of Changes) is the oldest Chinese text and is used for divination. It is comprised of 64 hexagrams, composed of broken and continuous lines, that represent a balance of opposites (yin and yang), the inevitability of change and the evolution of events.

The Book and the Sword by Jin Yong/Louis Cha (2004) is China's most celebrated martial-arts novelist's first book. The martial-arts genre (*wǔxiá xiǎoshuō*) is a direct descendant of the classical novel.

in 1918. It was revolutionary stuff. Apart from the opening paragraph which is composed in classical Chinese, Lu's seminal and shocking fable is cast entirely in colloquial Chinese.

For Lu Xun to write his short story in colloquial Chinese was explosive: readers were finally able to read language as it was spoken. *Diary of a Madman* is a haunting and unsettling work and from this moment on, mainstream Chinese literature would be written as it was thought and spoken: Chinese writing had been instantly revolutionised.

Other notable contemporaries of Lu Xun include Ba Jin (*Family;* 1931), Mao Dun (*Midnight;* 1933), Běijīng author Lao She (*Rickshaw Boy/Camel Xiangzi;* 1936) and the modernist playwright Cao Yu (*Thunderstorm*).

Contemporary Writing

A growing number of contemporary voices have been translated into English, but far more exist in Chinese only. The provocative Nobel Prize–winning Mo Yan (*Life and Death are Wearing Me Out;* 2008), Yu Hua (*To Live;* 1992) and Su Tong (*Rice;* 1995) have written momentous historical novels set in the 20th century; all are excellent, though their raw, harrowing subject matter is not for the faint of heart.

Zhu Wen mocks the get-rich movement in his brilliantly funny short stories, published in English as *I Love Dollars and Other Stories of China* (2007). It's a vivid and comic portrayal of the absurdities of everyday China.

'Hooligan author' Wang Shuo (*Please Don't Call Me Human;* 2000) is one of China's best-selling authors with his political satires and convincing depictions of urban slackers. Alai (*Red Poppies;* 2002), an ethnic Tibetan, made waves by writing in Chinese about early 20th-century Tibetan Sìchuān – whatever your politics, it's both insightful and a page-turner. Refused entry into China, exiled author Ma Jian writes more politically critical work; his 2001 novel *Red Dust* was a Kerouacian tale of wandering China as a spiritual pollutant in the 1980s. Banned in China, his 2008 novel *Beijing Coma* is set against the Tiān'ānmén demonstrations of 1989, and their aftermath. China's most renowned dissident writer, Gao Xingjian, won the Nobel Prize for Literature in 2000 for his novel *Soul Mountain,* an account of his travels along the Yangzi after being misdiagnosed with lung cancer. All of his work has been banned in the People's Republic of China (PRC) since 1989.

Controversial blogger Han Han (http://blog.sina.com.cn/twocold) catapulted himself into the literary spotlight with his novel *Triple Door,* a searing critique of China's education system. His successful 2010 roadtrip novel *1988: I Want to Talk with the World* only served to grow his already massive fan base and establish him as spokesman of a generation.

Candy (2003) by Mian Mian is a hip take on modern Shànghǎi life, penned by a former heroin addict musing on complicated sexual affairs, suicide and drug addiction in Shēnzhèn and Shànghǎi. It's applauded for its urban underground tone, but sensational more for its framing of post-adolescent themes in contemporary China. *Years of Red Dust: Stories of Shanghai* (2010) by Qiu Xiaolong contains 23 short stories in the context of momentous historic events affecting the city and the inhabitants of Red Dust Lane.

In his novel *Banished,* poet, essayist, short-story writer and blogger Han Dong reaches to his own experiences during the Cultural Revolution for inspiration. Winner of the Man Asian Literary Prize in 2010, Bi Feiyu's *Three Sisters* is a poignant tale of rural China during the political chaos of the early 1970s. In *Northern Girls,* Sheng Kcyi illuminates the prejudices and bigotries of modern Chinese society in her story of a Chinese girl arriving as an immigrant worker in Shēnzhèn. *The Fat Years* (2009) by Chan Koonchung is a science-fiction novel set in a near-future

Published by the Chinese University of Hong Kong Research Centre for Translation, *Renditions* (www.cuhk.edu.hk/rct/renditions/index.html) is an excellent journal of Chinese literature in English translation, covering works from classical Chinese to modern writing.

totalitarian China where the month of February 2011 has gone missing from official records.

For a taste of contemporary Chinese short-story writing with both English and Chinese, buy a copy of *Short Stories in Chinese: New Penguin Parallel Text* (2012). *The Picador Book of Contemporary Chinese Fiction* (2006) brings together a range of different contemporary voices and themes into one accessible book.

Film

Early Cinema
The moving image in the Middle Kingdom dates to 1896, when Spaniard Galen Bocca unveiled a film projector and blew the socks off wide-eyed crowds in a Shànghǎi teahouse. Shànghǎi's cosmopolitan verve and exotic looks would make it the capital of China's film industry, but China's very first movie – *Conquering Jun Mountain* (an excerpt from a piece of Běijīng opera) – was actually filmed in Běijīng in 1905.

Shànghǎi opened its first cinema in 1908. In those days, cinema owners would cannily run the film for a few minutes, stop it and collect money from the audience before allowing the film to continue. The golden age of Shànghǎi film-making came in the 1930s when the city had over 140 film companies. Its apogee arrived in 1937 with the release of *Street Angel*, a powerful drama about two sisters who flee the Japanese in northeast China and end up as prostitutes in Shànghǎi; and *Crossroads*, a clever comedy about four unemployed graduates. Japanese control of China eventually brought the industry to a standstill and sent many film-makers packing.

Communist Decline
China's film industry was stymied after the Communist Revolution, which sent film-makers scurrying to Hong Kong and Taiwan, where they played key roles in building up the local film industries that flourished there. Cinematic production in China was co-opted to glorify communism and generate patriotic propaganda. The days of the Cultural Revolution (1966–76) were particularly dark. Between 1966 and 1972, just eight movies were made on the mainland, as the film industry was effectively shut down.

Resurgence
It wasn't until two years after the death of Mao Zedong, in September 1978, that China's premier film school – the Běijīng Film Academy – reopened. Its first intake of students included Zhang Yimou, Chen Kaige and Tian Zhuangzhuang, who are considered masterminds of the celebrated 'Fifth Generation'.

The cinematic output of the Fifth Generation signalled an escape from the dour, colourless and proletarian Mao era, and a second glittering golden age of Chinese film-making arrived in the 1980s and 1990s with their lush and lavish tragedies. A bleak but beautifully shot tale of a Chinese Communist Party cadre who travels to a remote village in Shaanxi province to collect folk songs, Chen Kaige's *Yellow Earth* aroused little interest in China but proved a sensation when released in the West in 1985.

It was followed by Zhang's *Red Sorghum*, which introduced Gong Li and Jiang Wen to the world. Gong became the poster girl of Chinese cinema in the 1990s and the first international movie star to emerge from the mainland. Jiang, the Marlon Brando of Chinese film, has proved both a durable leading man and an innovative, controversial director of award-winning films such as *In the Heat of the Sun* and *Devils on the Doorstep*.

Rich, seminal works such as *Farewell My Concubine* (1993; Chen Kaige) and *Raise the Red Lantern* (1991; Zhang Yimou) were garlanded

Wolf Totem (2009) by Jiang Rong is an astonishing look at life on the grasslands of Inner Mongolia during the Cultural Revolution and the impact of modern culture on an ancient way of life.

with praise, receiving standing ovations and winning major film awards. Their directors were the darlings of Cannes; Western cinema-goers were entranced. Many Chinese cinema-goers also admired their artistry, but some saw Fifth Generation output as pandering to the Western market.

In 1993 Tian Zhuangzhuang made the brilliant *The Blue Kite*. A heart-breaking account of the life of one Běijīng family during the Cultural Revolution, it so enraged the censors that Tian was banned from making films for a decade.

Each generation charts its own course and the ensuing Sixth Generation – graduating from the Běijīng Film Academy post–Tiān'ānmén Square protests – was no different.

Sixth Generation film directors eschewed the luxurious beauty of their forebears, and sought to capture the angst and grit of modern urban Chinese life. Their independent, low-budget works put an entirely different and more cynical spin on mainland Chinese film-making, but their darker subject matter and harsh film style (frequently in black and white) left many Western viewers cold.

Independent film-making found an influential precedent with Zhang Yuan's 1990 debut *Mama*. Zhang is also acclaimed for his candid and gritty documentary-style *Beijing Bastards* (1993).

Meanwhile, *The Days*, directed by Wang Xiaoshui, follows a couple drifting apart in the wake of the Tiān'ānmén Square protests. Wang also directed the excellent *Beijing Bicycle* (2001), inspired by De Sica's *Bicycle Thieves*.

Architecture
Traditional Architecture

Four principal styles governed traditional Chinese architecture: imperial, religious, residential and recreational. The imperial style was naturally the most grandiose, overseeing the design of buildings employed by successive dynastic rulers; the religious style was employed for the construction of temples, monasteries and pagodas; while the residential and recreational styles took care of the design of houses and private gardens.

The 2010 remake of *The Karate Kid*, starring Jackie Chan, is set in Běijīng and authentically conveys the city despite having nothing to do with karate.

Whatever the style, Chinese buildings traditionally followed a similar basic ground plan, consisting of a symmetrical layout oriented around a central axis – ideally running north–south to conform with basic feng shui (风水; *fēngshuǐ*) dictates and to maximise sunshine – with an enclosed courtyard (院; *yuàn*) flanked by buildings on all sides.

In many aspects, imperial palaces are glorified courtyard homes (south-facing, a sequence of courtyards, side halls and perhaps a garden at the rear) completed on a different scale. Apart from the size, the main dissimilarity would be guard towers on the walls and possibly a moat, imperial yellow roof tiles, ornate dragon carvings (signifying the emperor), the repetitive use of the number nine and the presence of temples.

Religious Architecture

Chinese Buddhist, Taoist and Confucian temples tend to follow a strict, schematic pattern. All temples are laid out on a north–south axis in a series of halls, with the main door of each hall facing south.

With their sequence of halls and buildings interspersed with breezy open-air courtyards, Chinese temples are very different from Christian churches. The roofless courtyards allow the weather to permeate within the temple and permits *qì* (气; spirit) to circulate, dispersing stale air and allowing incense to be burned.

Buddhist Temples

Once you have cracked the logic of Buddhist temples, you will see how most temples conform to a basic pattern. The first hall and portal to the temple is generally the Hall of Heavenly Kings (天王殿; Tiānwáng Diàn), where a sedentary, central statue of the tubby Bodhisattva Maitreya is flanked by the stern and often ferocious Four Heavenly Kings. Behind is the first courtyard, where the Drum Tower (鼓楼; Gǔlóu) and Bell Tower (钟楼; Zhōnglóu) may rise to the east and west, and smoking braziers may be positioned.

The main hall is often the Great Treasure Hall (大雄宝殿; Dàxióng-bǎo Diàn) sheltering glittering statues of the past, present and future Buddhas, seated in a row. This is the main focal point for worshippers at the temple. On the east and west interior wall of the hall are often 18 *luóhàn* (arhat – a Buddhist who has achieved enlightenment) in two lines, either as statues or paintings. In some temples, they gather in a throng of 500, housed in a separate hall, usually called the Luohan Hall (罗汉殿; Luóhàn Diàn). A statue of Guanyin (the Goddess of Mercy) frequently stands at the rear of the main hall, facing north, atop a fish's head or a rocky outcrop. The goddess may also have her own hall and occasionally presents herself with a huge fan of arms, in her 'Thousand Arm' incarnation – the awesome effigy of Guanyin in the Mahayana Hall at Pǔníng Temple in Chéngdé is the supreme example.

The rear hall may be where the sutras (Buddhist scriptures) were once stored, in which case it will be called the Sutra Storing Building. A pagoda may rise above the main halls or may be the only surviving fragment of an otherwise destroyed temple. Conceived to house the remains of Buddha and later other Buddhist relics, sutras, religious artefacts and documents, a pagoda (塔; tǎ) may rise above the temple.

Many Buddhist temples also have a vegetarian restaurant in one of the halls that has been converted for use as a canteen, which may be open to the public, serving meat-free, affordable food.

Taoist Temples

Taoist shrines are not as plentiful and are generally more nether-worldly than Buddhist shrines, although the basic layout echoes Buddhist temples. They are decorated with a distinct set of motifs, including the *bāguà* (八卦; eight trigrams) formations, reflected in eight-sided pavilions and halls, and the Taiji yin/yang (*yīn/yáng*) diagram. Effigies of Laotzu, the Jade Emperor and other characters popularly associated with Taoist myth, such as the Eight Immortals, Guandi and the God of Wealth, are customary.

Taoist door gods, similar to those in Buddhist temples, often guard temple entrances; the main hall is usually called the Hall of the Three Clear Ones (三清殿; Sānqīng Diàn), devoted to a triumvirate of Taoist deities. Pagodas are generally absent.

BATTLE OF THE BUDDHAS

China's largest ancient Buddha gazes out over the confluence of the waters of the Dàdù River and the Mín River at Lèshān in Sìchuān. When the even bigger Buddha at Bamyan in Afghanistan was demolished by the Taliban, the Lèshān Buddha enjoyed instantaneous promotion to the top spot as the world's largest. The Buddha in the Great Buddha Temple at Zhāngyè in Gānsù province may not take it lying down, though: he is China's largest 'housed reclining Buddha'. Chinese children once climbed inside him to scamper about within his cavernous tummy.

Lounging around in second place is the reclining Buddha in the Mògāo Grottoes, China's second largest. The vast (and modern) reclining Buddha at Lèshān is a whopping 170m long and the world's largest 'alfresco' reclining Buddha. Bristling with limbs, the Thousand Arm Guanyin statue in the Pǔníng Temple's Mahayana Hall in Chéngdé also stands up to be counted: she's the largest wooden statue in China (and possibly the world). Not to be outdone, Hong Kong fights for its niche with the Tian Tan Buddha Statue, the world's 'largest outdoor seated bronze Buddha statue'.

Taoist monks (and nuns) are easily distinguished from their shaven-headed Buddhist confrères by their long hair, twisted into topknots, straight trousers and squarish jackets.

Confucian Temples

Unless they have vanished or been destroyed, Confucian temples can be found in the old town district of ancient settlements throughout China and are typically very quiet havens of peace and far less visited than Buddhist or Taoist temples. The largest Confucian temple in China is at Qūfù in Shāndōng, Confucius' birthplace.

Confucian temples are called either Kǒng Miào (孔庙) or Wén Miào (文庙) in Chinese and bristle with stelae celebrating local scholars, some supported on the backs of *bìxì* (mythical tortoiselike dragons). A statue of Kongzi (Confucius) usually resides in the main hall (大成殿; Dàchéng Diàn), overseeing rows of dusty musical instruments and flanked by disciples and philosophers.

A mythical animal, the *qílín*, is commonly seen at Confucian temples. The *qílín* was a chimera that only appeared on earth in times of harmony.

Discovered by amateur astronomer William Kwong Yu Yeung in 2001, the main belt asteroid '83598 Aiweiwei' was named after Chinese artist Ai Weiwei in 2001.

Modern Architecture

Architecturally speaking, anything goes in today's China. You only have to look at the Pǔdōng skyline to discover a melange of competing designs, some dramatic, inspiring and novel, others rash. The display represents a nation brimming with confidence, zeal and money.

If modern architecture in China is regarded as anything post-1949, then China has ridden a roller-coaster ride of styles and fashions. In Běijīng, stand between the Great Hall of the People (1959) and the National Centre for the Performing Arts (2008) and weigh up how far China travelled in 50 years. Interestingly, neither building has clear Chinese motifs. The same applies to the form of Běijīng's CCTV Building, where a continuous loop through horizontal and vertical planes required some audacious engineering.

The coastal areas are an architect's dreamland – no design is too outrageous, zoning laws have been scrapped, and the labour force is large and inexpensive. Planning permission can be simple to arrange – often all it requires is sufficient *guānxì* (connections). Even the once cash-strapped interior provinces are getting in on the act. Opened in Chéngdū in 2013, the staggeringly large New Century Global Center is the world's largest free-standing building: big enough to swallow up 20 Sydney Opera Houses!

Many of the top names in international architecture – IM Pei, Rem Koolhaas, Norman Foster, Kengo Kuma, Jean-Marie Charpentier, Herzog & de Meuron – have all designed at least one building in China in the past decade. Other impressive examples of modern architecture include the National Stadium (aka the 'Bird's Nest'), the National Aquatics Center (aka the 'Water Cube') and Běijīng South train station, all in Běijīng; and the art deco–esque Jīnmào Tower, the towering Shànghǎi World Financial Center, Tomorrow Square and the Shànghǎi Tower in Shànghǎi. In Guǎngzhōu, the Zaha Hadid–designed Guǎngzhōu Opera House is an astonishing contemporary creation, both inside and out. In Hong Kong, the glittering 2 International Finance Center on Hong Kong Island and the International Commerce Center in Kowloon are each prodigious examples of modern skyscraper architecture.

For something rather different, Jīnhuá Architecture Park, a project of artist Ai Weiwei, is an abandoned, overgrown, mouldering yet thought-provoking collection of modern memorial pavilions (designed by such names as Herzog & de Meuron), slowly returning to nature. They can be found in Jīnhuá, Zhèjiāng province.

China's Landscapes

The world's third-largest country – on a par size-wise with the USA – China swallows up an immense 9.5 million sq km, only surpassed in area by Russia and Canada. So whatever floats your boat – verdant bamboo forests, sapphire Himalayan lakes, towering sand dunes, sublime mountain gorges, huge glaciers or sandy beaches – China's landscapes offer simply jaw-dropping diversity.

The Land

Straddling natural environments as diverse as subarctic tundra in the north and tropical rainforests in the south, this massive land embraces the world's highest mountain range and one of its hottest deserts in the west, to the steamy, typhoon-lashed coastline of the South China Sea. Fragmenting this epic landscape is a colossal web of waterways, including one of the world's mightiest rivers – the Yangzi (长江; Cháng Jiāng).

Mountains

China has a largely mountainous and hilly topography, commencing in precipitous fashion in the vast and sparsely populated Qīnghǎi–Tibetan plateau in the west and levelling out gradually towards the fertile, well watered, populous and wealthy provinces of eastern China.

This mountainous disposition sculpts so many of China's scenic high lights: from the glittering Dragon's Backbone Rice Terraces of Guǎngxī to the incomparable stature of Mt Everest, the stunning beauty of Jiǔzhàigōu National Park in Sìchuān, the ethereal peaks of misty Huángshān in Ānhuī, the vertiginous inclines of Huá Shān in Shaanxi (Shǎnxī), the sublime karst geology of Yángshuò in Guǎngxī and the volcanic drama of Heaven Lake in Jílín.

Averaging 4500m above sea level, the Qīnghǎi–Tibetan region's highest peaks thrust up into the Himalayan mountain range along its southern rim. The Himalayas, on average about 6000m above sea level, include 40 peaks rising dizzyingly to 7000m or more. Also known as the planet's 'third pole', this is where the world's highest peak, Mt Everest – called Zhūmùlǎngmǎfēng by the Chinese – thrusts up jaggedly from the Tibet–Nepal border.

This vast high-altitude region (Tibet alone constitutes one-eighth of China's landmass) is home to an astonishing 37,000 glaciers, the third-largest mass of ice on the planet after the Arctic and Antarctic. This enormous body of frozen water ensures that the Qīnghǎi–Tibetan region is the source of many of China's largest rivers, including the Yellow (Huáng Hé), Mekong (Láncāng Jiāng) and Salween (Nù Jiāng) Rivers and, of course, the mighty Yangzi, all of whose headwaters are fed by snowmelt from here. Global warming is inevitably eating into this glacial volume, although experts argue over how quickly they are melting.

This mountain geology further corrugates the rest of China, continuously rippling the land into spectacular mountain ranges. There's the breathtaking 2500km-long Kunlun range, the mighty Karakoram mountains on the border with Pakistan, the Tiān Shān range in Xīnjiāng, the

China has earmarked a staggering US$140 billion for an ambitious program of wind farms; ranging from Xīnjiāng province to Jiāngsū province in the east, the huge wind farms are due for completion in 2020.

Tanggula range on the Qīnghǎi–Tibetan plateau, the Qinling mountains and the Greater Khingan range (Daxingan Ling) in the northeast.

Deserts

China's Bayan Obo Mining District in Inner Mongolia produces roughly half of the world's rare earth metals, elements essential for the production of mobile phones, high-definition TVs, computers, wind turbines and other products.

China contains head-spinningly huge – and growing – desert regions that occupy almost one-fifth of the country's landmass, largely in its mighty northwest. These are inhospitably sandy and rocky expanses where summers are staggeringly hot and winters bone-numbingly cold, but as destinations, the visuals can be sublime. North towards Kazakhstan and Kyrgyzstan from the plateaus of Tibet and Qīnghǎi is Xīnjiāng's Tarim Basin, the largest inland basin in the world. This is the location of the mercilessly thirsty Taklamakan Desert – China's largest desert and the world's second-largest mass of sand after the Sahara Desert. Many visitors to Xīnjiāng will experience this huge expanse during their travels or can arrange camel-trekking tours and expeditions through its vast sand dunes. China's biggest shifting salt lake, Lop Nur (the site of China's nuclear bomb tests) is also here.

The Silk Road into China steered its epic course through this entire region, ferrying caravans of camels laden with merchandise, languages, philosophies, customs and peoples from the far-flung lands of the Middle East. The harsh environment shares many topographical features in common with the neighbouring nations of Afghanistan, Kyrgyzstan and Kazakhstan, and is almost the exact opposite of China's lush and well watered southern provinces. But despite the scorching aridity of China's northwestern desert regions, their mountains (the mighty Tiān Shān, Altai, Pamir and Kunlun ranges) contain vast supplies of water, largely in the form of snow and ice.

Northeast of the Tarim Basin is Ürümqi, the world's furthest city from the sea. The Tarim Basin is bordered to the north by the lofty Tiān Shān range – home to the mountain lake of Tiān Chí – and to the west by the mighty Pamirs, which border Pakistan. Also in Xīnjiāng is China's hot spot, the Turpan Basin. Known as the 'Oasis of Fire' and 'China's Death Valley', it gets into the record books as China's lowest-lying region and the world's second-deepest depression after the Dead Sea in Israel.

China's most famous desert is, of course, the Gobi, although most of it lies outside the country's borders. In little-visited Western Inner Mongolia, the awesome Badain Jaran Desert offers travellers spectacular journeys among remote desert lakes and colossal, stationary sand dunes over 460m in height; further west lie the famous grasslands and steppes of Inner Mongolia.

Rivers & Plains

At about 5460km long and the second-longest river in China, the Yellow River (黄河;Huáng Hé) is touted as the birthplace of Chinese civilisation and has been fundamental in the development of Chinese society. The mythical architect of China's rivers, the Great Yu, apocryphally noted 'Whoever controls the Yellow River controls China'. From its source in Qīnghǎi, the river runs through North China, meandering past or near many famous towns, including Lánzhōu, Yínchuān, Bāotóu, Hánchéng, Jìnchéng, Lùoyáng, Zhèngzhōu, Kāifēng and Jǐ'nán in Shāndōng, before exiting China north of Dōngyíng (although the watercourse often runs dry nowadays before it reaches the sea).

The Yangzi (the 'Long River') is one of the longest rivers in the world (and China's longest). Its watershed of almost 2 million sq km – 20% of China's landmass – supports 400 million people. Dropping from its source high on the Tibetan plateau, it runs for 6300km to the sea, of which the last few hundred kilometres is across virtually flat alluvial plains. In the course of its sweeping journey, the river (and its tributaries) fashions many of China's scenic spectacles, including Tiger Leaping Gorge and the Three Gorges, and cuts through a string of huge and historic cities, including Chóngqìng, Wǔhàn and Nánjīng, before surging into the East China Sea north of Shànghǎi. As a transport route, the river is limited, but the Three Gorges cruise is China's most celebrated river journey. The waterborne journey along the Lí River between Guìlín and Yángshuò in Guǎngxī is China's other major riverine experience.

Fields & Agriculture

China's hills and mountains may surround travellers with a dramatic backdrop, but they are a massive agricultural headache for farmers. Small plots of land are eked out in patchworks of land between hillsides or rescued from mountain cliffs and ravines, in the demanding effort to feed 20% of the world's population with just 10% of its arable land.

As only 15% of China's land can be cultivated, hillside gradients and inclines are valiantly levelled off, wherever possible, into bands of productive terraced fields. Stunning examples of rice terraces – beautiful in the right light – can be admired at the Yuányáng Rice Terraces in Yúnnán and the Dragon's Backbone Rice Terraces in Guǎngxī.

Wildlife

China's vast size, diverse topography and climatic disparities support an astonishing range of habitats for animal life. The Tibetan plateau alone is the habitat of over 500 species of birds, while half of the animal species in the northern hemisphere exist in China.

It is unlikely you will see many of these creatures in their natural habitat unless you are a specialist, or have a lot of time, patience, persistence, determination and luck. If you go looking for large animals in the wild on the off chance, your chances of glimpsing one are virtually nil. But there are plenty of pristine reserves within relatively easy reach of travellers' destinations such as Chéngdū and Xī'an and even if you don't get the chance to see animals, the scenery is terrific. Try Yàdīng Nature Reserve in Sìchuan, Mèngdá Nature Reserve in Qīnghǎi, Sānchàhé Nature Reserve in Yúnnán, Fànjìngshān in Guìzhōu, Shénnóngjià in Húběi, Wǔzhǐshān in Hǎinán, Kanas Lake Nature Reserve in Xīnjiāng and Chángbái Shān, China's largest nature reserve, in Jílín.

Mammals

China's towering mountain ranges form natural refuges for wildlife, many of which are now protected in parks and reserves that have escaped the depredations of loggers and dam-builders. The barren high plains of the Tibetan plateau are home to several large animals, such as

In 2010, six of China's *dānxiá* (eroded reddish sandstone rock), karst-like geological formations, were included in Unesco's World Heritage List. The list includes Chishuǐ in Guìzhōu province. The rocks can also be seen outside Zhāngyè in Gānsù.

TOP BOOKS ON CHINA'S ENVIRONMENT

➡ *When a Billion Chinese Jump* (2010) Jonathan Watts' sober and engaging study of China's environmental issues.

➡ *China's Environmental Challenges* (2012) Judith Shapiro's excellent primer for understanding China's manifold environmental problems.

➡ *The River Runs Black: The Environmental Challenge to China's Future* (2010; 2nd edition) Elizabeth Economy's frightening look at the unhappy marriage between breakneck economic production and environmental degradation.

➡ *The China Price: The True Cost of Chinese Competitive Advantage* (2008) Alexandra Harney's telling glimpse behind the figures of China's economic rise.

➡ *China's Water Crisis* (2004) Ma Jun rolls up his sleeves to fathom China's water woes.

the *chiru* (Tibetan antelope), Tibetan wild ass, wild sheep and goats, and wolves. In theory, many of these animals are protected but in practice poaching and hunting still threaten their survival.

The beautiful and retiring snow leopard, which normally inhabits the highest parts of the most remote mountain ranges, sports a luxuriant coat of fur against the cold. It preys on mammals as large as mountain goats, but is unfortunately persecuted for allegedly killing livestock.

The Himalayan foothills of western Sìchuān support the greatest diversity of mammals in China. Aside from giant pandas, other mammals found in this region include the panda's small cousin – the raccoon-like red panda – as well as Asiatic black bears and leopards. Among the grazers are golden takin, a large goatlike antelope with a yellowish coat and a reputation for being cantankerous, argali sheep and various deer species, including the diminutive mouse deer.

The sparsely populated northeastern provinces abutting Siberia are inhabited by reindeer, moose, bears, sables and Manchurian tigers.

Overall, China is unusually well endowed with big and small cats. The world's largest tiger, the Manchurian tiger (dōngběihǔ) – also known as the Siberian tiger – only numbers a few hundred in the wild, its remote habitat being one of its principal saviours. Three species of leopard can be found, including the beautiful clouded leopard of tropical rainforests, plus several species of small cat, such as the Asiatic golden cat and a rare endemic species, the Chinese mountain cat.

Rainforests are famous for their diversity of wildlife, and the tropical south of Yúnnán province is one of the richest in China. These forests support Indo-Chinese tigers and herds of Asiatic elephants.

The wild mammals you are most likely to see are several species of monkey. The large and precocious Père David's macaque is common at Éméi Shān in Sìchuān, where bands often intimidate people into handing over their picnics; macaques can also be seen on Hǎinán's Monkey Island. Several other monkey species are rare and endangered, including the beautiful golden monkey of Fànjìngshān and the snub-nosed monkey of the Yúnnán rainforests. But by far the most endangered is the Hǎinán gibbon, numbering just a few dozen individuals on Hǎinán Island.

The giant panda (*xióngmāo* – literally 'bear cat') is western Sìchuān's most famous denizen, but the animal's solitary nature makes it elusive for observation in the wild, and even today, after decades of intensive research and total protection in dedicated reserves, sightings are rare. A notoriously fickle breeder (the female is only on heat for a handful of days each spring), there are approximately 1600 pandas in the Chinese wilds according to World Wildlife Fund. Interestingly, the panda has the digestive tract of a carnivore (like other bears), but has become accustomed to exclusively eating bamboo shoots and leaves. However, the panda's digestive tract is unable to efficiently break down plant matter so the mammal needs to consume huge amounts to compensate and spends much of its time eating, clearing one area of bamboo before moving on to another region. The easiest way to see pandas outside of zoos is at the Giant Panda Breeding Research Base, just outside Chéngdū or at the Yǎ'ān Bìfēngxiá Panda Base, also in Sìchuān.

Chángqīng Nature Reserve in Shaanxi province is well worth a visit for its relatively unspoilt montane forest and the chance to see giant pandas in the wild. Find out more at www.cqpanda.com.

Birds

Most of the wildlife you'll see in China will be birds, and with more than 1300 species recorded, including about 100 endemic or near-endemic species, China offers some fantastic birdwatching opportunities. Spring is usually the best time, when deciduous foliage buds, migrants return from their wintering grounds and nesting gets into full swing. BirdLife International (www.birdlife.org/datazone/country/china), the worldwide bird conservation organisation, recognises 14 Endemic Bird

Areas (EBAs) in China, either wholly within the country or shared with neighbouring countries.

Although the range of birds is huge, China is a centre of endemicity for several species and these are usually the ones that visiting birders will seek out. Most famous are the pheasant family, of which China boasts 62 species, including many endemic or near-endemic species.

Other families well represented in China include the laughing thrushes, with 36 species; parrotbills, which are almost confined to China and its near neighbours; and many members of the jay family. The crested ibis is a pinkish bird that feeds on invertebrates in the rice paddies, and was once found from central China to Japan.

Among China's more famous large birds are cranes, and nine of the world's 11 species have been recorded here. In Jiāngxī province, on the lower Yangzi, a vast series of shallow lakes and lagoons was formed by stranded overflow from Yangzi flooding. The largest of these is Póyáng Lake, although it is only a few metres deep and drains during winter. Vast numbers of waterfowl and other birds inhabit these swamps year-round, including ducks, geese, herons and egrets. Although it is difficult to reach and infrastructure for birdwatchers is practically nonexistent, birders are increasingly drawn to the area in winter, when many of the lakes dry up and attract flocks of up to five crane species, including the endangered, pure white Siberian crane.

Recommended destinations include Zhālóng Nature Reserve, one of several vast wetlands in Hēilóngjiāng province. Visit in summer to see breeding storks, cranes and flocks of wildfowl before they fly south for the winter. Běidàihé, on the coast of the Bohai Sea, is well known for migratory birds. Other breeding grounds and wetlands include Qīnghǎi Hú in Qīnghǎi, Cǎohǎi Lake in Guìzhōu, Jiǔzhàigōu in Sìchuān and Mai Po Marsh in Hong Kong. For the last, the Hong Kong Bird Watching Society (www.hkbws.org.hk) organises regular outings and publishes a newsletter in English.

Most birdwatchers and bird tours head straight for Sìchuān, which offers superb birding at sites such as Wòlóng. Here, several spectacular pheasants, including golden, blood and kalij pheasants, live on the steep forested hillsides surrounding the main road. As the road climbs up, higher-altitude species such as eared pheasants and the spectacular Chinese monal may be seen. Alpine meadows host smaller birds, and the rocky scree slopes at the pass hold partridges, the beautiful grandala and the mighty lammergeier (bearded vulture), with a 2m wingspan.

Parts of China are now well established on the itineraries of global ecotour companies. Bird Tour Asia (www.birdtourasia.com) has popular tours to Sìchuān, Tibet, Qīnghǎi, eastern China and southeast China, and also provides custom tours.

Plants

China is home to more than 32,000 species of seed plant and 2500 species of forest tree, plus an extraordinary plant diversity that includes some famous 'living fossils' – a diversity so great that Jílín province in the semifrigid north and Hǎinán province in the tropical south share few plant species.

Apart from rice, the plant probably most often associated with China and Chinese culture is bamboo, of which China boasts some 300 species. Bamboos grow in many parts of China, but bamboo forests were once so extensive that they enabled the evolution of the giant panda, which eats virtually nothing else, and a suite of small mammals, birds and insects that live in bamboo thickets. Most of these useful species are found in the subtropical areas south of the Yangzi, and the best surviving thickets are in southwestern provinces such as Sìchuān.

The dawn redwood (*Metasequoia*), a towering (growing up to 60m) and elegant fine-needled deciduous Chinese tree, dates to the Jurassic era. Once considered long extinct, a single example was discovered in 1941 in a Sichuān village, followed three years later by the discovery of further trees.

Many plants commonly cultivated in Western gardens today originated in China, among them the ginkgo tree, a famous 'living fossil' whose unmistakable imprint has been found in 270-million-year-old rocks.

Deciduous forests cover mid-altitudes in the mountains, and are characterised by oaks, hemlocks and aspens, with a leafy understorey that springs to life after the winter snows have melted. Among the more famous blooms of the understorey are rhododendrons and azaleas, and many species of each grow naturally in China's mountain ranges. Best viewed in spring, some species flower right through summer; one of the best places to see them is at Sìchuān's Wòlóng Nature Reserve.

A growing number of international wildlife travel outfits arrange botanical expeditions to China, including Naturetrek (www.naturetrek.co.uk), which arranges tours to Yúnnán, Sìchuān and the Tibetan plateau.

China Dialogue (www.chinadialogue.net) is a resourceful dual-language website that seeks to promote debate on China's immense environmental challenges.

Endangered Species

Almost every large mammal you can think of in China has crept onto the endangered species list, as well as many 'lower' animals. The snow leopard, Indo-Chinese tiger, chiru antelope, crested ibis, Asiatic elephant, red-crowned crane and black-crowned crane are all endangered.

Deforestation, pollution, hunting and trapping for fur, body parts and sport are all culprits. The Convention on International Trade in Endangered Species of Wild Fauna and Flora (CITES) records legal trade in live reptiles and parrots, and high numbers of reptile and wildcat skins. The number of such products collected or sold unofficially is anyone's guess.

Despite the threats, a number of rare animal species cling to survival in the wild. Notable among them are the Chinese alligator in Ānhuī, the

SOUTH–NORTH WATER DIVERSION PROJECT

Water is the lifeblood of economic and agricultural growth, but as China only has around 7% of the world's water resources (with almost 20% of its population), the liquid is an increasingly precious resource.

A region of low rainfall, northern China faces a worsening water crisis. Farmers are draining aquifers that have taken thousands of years to accumulate, while industry in China uses three to 10 times more water per unit of production than developed nations. To combat the water crisis, the Chinese Communist Party (CCP) embarked on the construction of the US$81 billion South–North Water Diversion Project, a vast network of pumping stations, canals and aqueducts (as well as a tunnel under the Yellow River) lashing north and south via three routes. The ambition is to divert 3.8 million Olympic swimming pools' worth of water annually from the Yangzi River to the parched regions of China's north. The first stage began operating in 2013 and water began flowing along the second stage at the end of 2014. Calculations, however, suggest that by 2020 only 5% of Běijīng's water requirements will be met by the diverted water.

There are also concerns that pollution in the Yangzi River waters will become progressively concentrated as water is extracted, while Yangzi cities such as Nánjīng and Wǔhàn are increasingly uneasy that they will be left with a water shortfall. Alarm has also arisen at the pollution in channels – including the Grand Canal, which links Hángzhōu with north China – earmarked to take the diverted waters. There are worries that these polluted reaches are almost untreatable, making elements of the project unviable. In 2016, it was revealed that lakes along the Yangzi River were drying up, with a 40% drop of water inflows into Dòngtíng Lake being reported.

Critics also argue that the project, which will involve the mass relocation of hundreds of thousands of people, will not address the fundamental issue of China's water woes – the absence of policies for the sustainable use of water as a precious resource. Pricing is also a central issue. In regions where water is an increasingly scarce resource, the liquid is still very cheap, which encourages further wastefulness.

giant salamander in the fast-running waters of the Yangzi and Yellow Rivers, the Yangzi River dolphin in the lower and middle reaches of the river (although there have been no sightings since 2002), and the pink dolphin of the Hong Kong islands of Sha Chau and Lung Kwu Chau. The giant panda is confined to the fauna-rich valleys and ranges of Sìchuān.

Intensive monoculture farmland cultivation, the reclaiming of wetlands, river damming, industrial and rural waste, and desertification are reducing unprotected forest areas and making the survival of many of these species increasingly precarious. Although there are laws against killing or capturing rare wildlife, their struggle for survival is further complicated as many remain on the most wanted lists for traditional Chinese medicine and dinner delicacies.

The Environment

China may be vast, but with two-thirds of the land mountain, desert or uncultivable, the remaining third is overwhelmed by the people of the world's most populous nation. For the first time in its history, China's city dwellers outnumbered rural residents in 2011, with an urbanisation rate set to increase to 65% by 2050. The speed of development – and the sheer volume of poured concrete – is staggering. During the next 15 years, China is expected to build urban areas equal in size to 10 New York Cities and a staggering one billion Chinese could be urban residents by 2030.

Beyond urban areas, deforestation and overgrazing have accelerated the desertification of vast areas of China, particularly in the western provinces. Deserts now cover almost one-fifth of the country and China's dustbowl is the world's largest, swallowing up 200 sq km of arable land every month. Over 400 million Chinese people are affected by China's encroaching deserts while each spring sees vast dust storms sweeping across north China, scouring cities such as Běijīng and Xī'ān, turning the skies red and depositing several hundred thousand tonnes of grit, bringing traffic to a standstill and pushing face masks to their limits.

A Greener China?

China is painfully aware of its accelerated desertification, growing water shortages, shrinking glaciers, acidic rain, contaminated rivers, caustic urban air and polluted soil. The government is keenly committed, on a policy level, to the development of greener and cleaner energy sources. China's leaders are also seeking to devise a more sustainable and less wasteful economic model for the nation's future development.

There is evidence of ambitious and bold thinking: in 2010 China announced it would pour billions into developing electric and hybrid vehicles (although the goal of 30% of car sales going to electric vehicles seemed wildly optimistic); Běijīng committed itself to overtaking Europe in renewable energy investment by 2020; wind farm construction (in Gānsù, for example) continues apace; and China leads the world in the production of solar cells. Coal use is also declining: in 2015, China imported 30% less and consumed 3.7% less coal, aiming to shut 1000 mines in 2016. Some analysts say China has already surpassed 'peak coal', but two-thirds of China's power still comes from the fossil fuel.

Public protests – sometimes violent – against polluting industries have proliferated in recent years across China and have scored a number of notable victories, including the 2012 demonstrations in Shífāng (Sìchuān), which led to the cancellation of a planned US$1.6 billion copper smelting facility. A 2013 survey in China revealed that 78% of people would demonstrate if polluting industries were constructed near their homes. Much of the agitation is the result of health concerns as cancer is now the leading cause of death in China, with 7500 deaths per day as a result of the disease (lung cancer being the most prevalent form).

The World Health Organization estimates that air pollution causes more than 1.4 million fatalities per year in China, while around 300 million rural Chinese do not have access to safe drinking water.

Over 1.2 million tonnes of transparent plastic sheeting is used annually by China's farmers to reduce water loss from evaporation, but much of the plastic is later ploughed into the earth, polluting the soil and decreasing crop yields.

Martial Arts of China

Unlike Western fighting arts – Savate, kickboxing etc – Chinese martial arts are deeply impregnated with religious and philosophical values. And, some might add, a morsel or two of magic. Many eminent exponents of *gōngfū* – better known in the West as kung-fu – were devout monks or religious recluses who drew inspiration from Buddhism and Taoism and sought a mystical communion with the natural world. These were not leisurely pursuits but were closely entangled with the meaning and purpose of life.

Fújiàn White Crane is a southern Chinese fighting style invented by a woman called Fang Qiniang who based the art's forms and strategy of attack and defence on careful observatoin of the bird's movements.

Styles & Schools

China lays claim to a bewildering range of martial arts styles, from the flamboyant and showy, inspired by the movements of animals (some legendary) or insects (such as Praying Mantis Boxing) to schools more empirically built upon the science of human movement (eg Wing Chun). On the outer fringes lie the esoteric arts, abounding with metaphysical feats, arcane practices and closely guarded techniques.

Many fighting styles were once secretively handed down for generations within families and it is only relatively recently that outsiders have been accepted as students. Some schools, especially the more obscure styles, have been driven to extinction partly due to their exclusivity and clandestine traditions.

Some styles also found themselves divided into competing factions, each laying claim to the original teachings and techniques. Such styles may exist in a state of schism, while other styles have become part of the mainstream; the southern Chinese martial art of Wing Chun in particular has become globally recognised, largely due to its associations with Bruce Lee.

Unlike Korean and Japanese arts such as taekwondo or karate-do, there is frequently no international regulatory body that oversees the syllabus, tournaments or grading requirements for China's individual martial arts. Consequently, students of China's myriad martial arts may be rather unsure of what level they have attained. It is often down to the individual teacher to decide what to teach students, and how quickly.

Hard School

Although there is considerable blurring between the two camps, Chinese martial arts are often distinguished between hard and soft schools. Typically aligned with Buddhism, the hard or 'external' (外家; *wàijiā*) school tends to be more vigorous, athletic and concerned with the development of power. Many of these styles are related to Shàolín Boxing and the Shàolín Temple in Hénán province.

Shàolín Boxing is forever associated with Bodhidharma, an ascetic Indian Buddhist monk who visited the Shàolín Temple and added a series of breathing and physical exercises to the Shàolín monks' sedentary meditations. The Shàolín monks' legendary endeavours and fearsome physical skills became known throughout China and beyond. Famous external schools include Báiméi Quán (White Eyebrow Boxing) and Cháng Quán (Long Boxing).

Soft School

Usually inspired by Taoism, the soft or 'internal' Chinese school (内家; *nèijiā*) develops pliancy and softness as a weapon against hard force. Taichi (Tàijí Quán) is the best known soft school, famed for its slow and lithe movements and an emphasis on cultivating *qì* (energy). Attacks are met with yielding movements that smother the attacking force and lead the aggressor off balance. The road to taichi mastery is a long and difficult one, involving a re-education of physical movement and suppression of one's instinct to tense up when threatened. Other soft schools include the circular moves of Bāguà Zhăng and the linear boxing patterns of Xíngyì Quán, based on five basic punches – each linked to one of the five elements of Chinese philosophy – and the movements of 12 animals.

Forms

Most students of Chinese martial arts – hard or soft – learn forms (套路; *tàolu*), a series of movements linked together into a pattern, which embody the principal punches and kicks of the style. In essence, forms are unwritten compendiums of the style, to ensure passage from one generation to the next. The number and complexity of forms varies from style to style: taichi may only have one form, although it may be very lengthy (the long form of the Yang style takes around 20 minutes to perform). Five Ancestors Boxing has dozens of forms, while Wing Chun only has three empty-hand forms.

Qìgōng

Closely linked to both the hard and especially the soft martial-arts schools is the practice of *qìgōng*, a technique for cultivating and circulating *qì* (energy) around the body. *Qì* can be developed for use in fighting to protect the body, as a source of power or for curative and health-giving purposes.

Qì can be developed in a number of ways – by standing still in fixed postures or with gentle exercises, meditation and measured breathing techniques. Taichi itself is a moving form of *qìgōng* cultivation while at the harder end of the spectrum a host of *qìgōng* exercises aim to make specific parts of the body impervious to attack.

Bāguà Zhăng

One of the more esoteric and obscure of the soft Taoist martial arts, Bāguà Zhăng (八卦掌; Eight Trigram Boxing, also known as Pa-kua) is also one of the most intriguing. The Bāguà Zhăng student wheels around in a circle, rapidly changing direction and speed, occasionally thrusting out a palm strike.

The linear movements and five punches of the internal Chinese martial art Body-Mind Boxing (Xíngyì Quán) possibly evolved from spear-fighting techniques.

Zhang Sanfeng, the founder of taichi, was supposedly able to walk more than 1000 *li* (around 560km) a day; others say he lived for more than 200 years!

COURSES, BOOKS & FILMS

Often misinterpreted, *gōngfū* (kungfu) teaches an approach to life that stresses patience, endurance, magnanimity and humility. Courses can be found in abundance across China, from Běijīng, Hong Kong, Shànghǎi, Wǔdāng Shān in Húběi to the Shàolín Temple in Hénán.

John F Gilbey's *The Way of a Warrior* is a tongue-in-cheek, expertly written and riveting account of the Oriental fighting arts and their mysteries. *Meditations on Violence: A Comparison of Martial Arts Training & Real World Violence* by Sgt Rory Miller is a graphic, illuminating and down-to-earth book on violence and its consequences.

For metaphysical pointers, soft-school adherents can dip into Laotzu's terse but inspiring *The Classic of the Way and Its Power*. For spectacular (if implausible) Wing Chun moves and mayhem, watch *Ip Man* (2008), starring the indefatigable Donnie Yen.

Bāguà Zhǎng draws its inspiration from the trigrams (an arrangement of three broken and unbroken lines) of the classic *Book of Changes* (*Yì-jīng* or *I Ching*), the ancient oracle used for divination. The trigrams are typically arranged in circular form and it is this pattern that is traced out by the Bāguà Zhǎng exponent. Training commences by just walking the circle so the student gradually becomes infused with its patterns and rhythms.

A hallmark of the style is the exclusive use of the palm, not the fist, as the principal weapon. This may seem curious and perhaps even ineffectual, but in fact the palm can transmit a lot of power – consider a thrusting palm strike to the chin, for example. The palm is also better protected than the fist as it is cushioned by muscle. The fist also has to transfer its power through a multitude of bones that need to be correctly aligned to avoid damage while the palm sits at the end of the wrist. Imagine hitting a brick wall as hard as you can with your palm (and then picture doing it with your fist!).

The student must become proficient in the subterfuge, evasion, speed and unpredictability that are hallmarks of Bāguà Zhǎng. Force is generally not met with force, but deflected by the circular movements cultivated in students through their meditations upon the circle. Circular forms – arcing, twisting, twining and spinning – are the mainstay of all movements, radiating from the waist.

Despite being dated by historians to the 19th century, Bāguà Zhǎng is quite probably a very ancient art. Beneath the Taoist overlay, the movements and patterns of the art suggest a possibly animistic or shamanistic origin, which gives the art its timeless rhythms.

Wing Chun

Conceived by a Buddhist nun from the Shàolín Temple called Ng Mui, who taught her skills to a young girl called Wing Chun (詠春), this is a fast and dynamic system of fighting that promises quick results for novices. Wing Chun (Yǒng Chūn) was the style that taught Bruce Lee how to move and, although he ultimately moved away from it to develop his own style, Wing Chun had an enormous influence on the Hong Kong fighter and actor.

Wing Chun emphasises speed over strength and evasion, rapid strikes and low kicks are its hallmark techniques. Forms are simple and direct, dispensing with the pretty flourishes that clutter other styles.

The art can perhaps best be described as scientific. There are none of the animal forms that make other styles so exciting and mysterious. Instead, Wing Chun is built around its centre line theory, which draws an imaginary line down the human body and centres all attacks and blocks along that line. The line runs through the sensitive regions: eyes, nose, mouth, throat, heart, solar plexus and groin and any blow on these points is debilitating and dangerous.

The three empty hand forms – which look bizarre to non-initiates – train arm and leg movements that both attack and defend this line. None of the blocks stray beyond the width of the shoulders, as this is the limit of possible attacks, and punches follow the same theory. Punches are delivered with great speed in a straight line, along the shortest distance between puncher and punched. All of this gives Wing Chun its distinctive simplicity.

A two-person training routine called *chi sau* (sticky hands) teaches the student how to be soft and relaxed in response to attacks, as pliancy generates more speed. Weapons in the Wing Chun arsenal include the lethal twin Wing Chun butterfly knives and an extremely long pole, which requires considerable strength to handle with skill.

Praying Mantis master Fan Yook Tung once killed two stampeding bulls with an iron-palm technique.

Iron Shirt (*tiěshān*) is an external *gōngfū* (kungfu) *qìgōng* training exercise that circulates and concentrates the *qì* (energy) in certain areas to protect the body from impacts during a fight.

Survival Guide

Directory A–Z

Accommodation

China's accommodation choices are impressive but enormously varied. Top-tier cities have a rich variety of sleeping options; other towns can have a poor supply, despite being inundated with visitors. Rural destinations are largely a patchwork of homesteads and hostels, with the occasional boutique-style choice in big-ticket villages.

Homestays In rural locations, you can often find double rooms in converted houses, with meals provided.

Hostels Exist across China in growing numbers, usually offering dorm beds and double rooms and dispensing useful travel advice.

Hotels From two-star affairs with very limited English and simple rooms to international-level, five-star towers and heritage hotels.

Booking

Booking online can help you secure a room and obtain a good price, but remember you should be able to bargain down the price of your room at hotel reception (except at youth hostels and the cheapest hotels) or over the phone. To secure accommodation, always plan ahead and book your room in advance during the high season. Airports at major cities often have hotel-booking counters that offer discounted rates.

Ctrip (www.english.ctrip.com) Excellent hotel booking, air and train ticketing website, with English helpline. Useful app available.

Elong (www.elong.net) Hotel and air ticket booking, with English helpline.

Lonely Planet (lonelyplanet.com/china/hotels) Recommendations and bookings.

Travel Zen (www.travelzen.com) Air tickets and hotel bookings; Chinese-only website. English helpline.

It's worth noting that major online booking websites sometimes errantly list and make bookable Chinese hotels that do not, in fact, accept Western travellers. Ctrip and Elong seem to be the most reliable booking sites for Westerners.

Rooms & Prices

Accommodation is divided by price category, identified by the symbols **$** (budget), **$$** (midrange) or **$$$** (top end); accommodation prices vary across China, so regional budget breakdowns may differ. We list the rack rate, which generally reflects the most it would cost. However, at most times of the year discounts are in effect, which can range from 10% to 60% off.

Rooms come with private bathroom or shower room, unless otherwise stated. Rooms are generally easy to procure, but reserve ahead in popular tourist towns (such as Hángzhōu), especially on weekends.

Most rooms in China fall into the following categories:

Double rooms (双人房、标准间; *shuāng rén fáng* or *biāozhǔn jiān*) In most cases, these are twins, ie with two beds.

One-bed rooms/singles (单间; *dānjiān*) This is usually a room with one double-sized bed (only rarely a single bed).

Large-bed rooms (大床房; *dàchuáng fáng*) Larger than a one-bed room, with a big double bed.

Suites (套房; *tàofáng*) Available at most midrange and top-end hotels.

Dorms (多人房; *duōrénfáng*) Usually available at youth hostels (and at a few hotels).

Business rooms (商务房; *shāngwù fáng*) Usually equipped with computers.

BOOK YOUR STAY ONLINE

For more accommodation reviews by Lonely Planet authors, check out http://lonelyplanet.com/hotels/. You'll find independent reviews, as well as recommendations on the best places to stay. Best of all, you can book online.

Traveller Restrictions

The majority of hotels in China still do not have the authorisation to accept foreigners as guests. This can be a source of frustration when you find yourself steered towards pricier midrange and top-end lodgings.

To see if a hotel accepts foreign guests, ask: *zhège bīnguǎn shōu wàiguórén ma?* (这个宾馆收外国人吗?).

Checking In & Out

At check-in you will need your passport; a registration form will ask what type of visa you have. For most travellers, the visa will be L (travel visa). A deposit (押金; *yājīn*) is required at most hotels; this will be paid either with cash or by providing your credit card details. International credit cards are generally only accepted at midrange hotels or chain express hotels and top-end accommodation; always have cash just in case. If you pay your deposit in cash, you will be given a receipt and the deposit will be returned to you when you check out. Ask for a discount on a deposit, especially if it is higher than one night's stay.

You usually have to check out by noon. If you check out between noon and 6pm you will be charged 50% of the room price; after 6pm you have to pay for another full night.

Camping

There are few places where you can legally camp and as most of China's flat land is put to agricultural use, you will largely be limited to remote, hilly regions. Camping is more feasible in wilder and less populated parts of west China.

In certain destinations with camping possibilities, travel agencies and hotels will arrange overnight camping trips or multiday treks, in which case camping equipment will be supplied. Camping on the Great Wall is technically ille-gal, but the watchtowers are often used for pitching tents or rolling out a sleeping bag (if you do, make sure to clean up after yourself and take care of the Wall).

Courtyard Hotels

Largely confined to Běijīng, courtyard hotels have rapidly mushroomed. Arranged around traditional *sìhéyuàn* (courtyards), rooms are on ground level. Courtyard hotels are charming and romantic, but are often expensive and rooms are small, in keeping with the dimensions of courtyard residences. Facilities will be limited, so don't expect a swimming pool, gym or subterranean garage.

Budget Business Chain Hotels

Dotted around much of China, budget business chain hotels can sometimes be a decent alternative to old-school two- and three-star hotels, with rooms around the ¥180 to ¥300 mark. In recent years, however, their once-pristine facilities have sometimes come to resemble the threadbare clunkers they aimed to replace. Still, their sheer ubiquity means you can usually find accommodation (but look at the rooms first). They often have membership/loyalty schemes, or online deals, which make rooms cheaper.

Although most of these branches accept foreigners, the odd branch does not. Chains include:

Home Inn (www.homeinns.com) Includes the Motel 168 chain.

Jǐnjiāng Inn (www.jinjianginns.com)

Guesthouses

The cheapest of the cheap are China's ubiquitous guesthouses (招待所; *zhāodàisuǒ*), often found clustering near train or bus stations (from where touts will take you) but also dotted around cities and towns. Not all guest-houses accept foreigners and Chinese skills may be crucial in securing a room. Rooms (doubles, twins, triples, quads) are primitive and grey, with tiled floors and possibly a shower room or shabby bathroom; showers may be communal. Other terms for guesthouses:

➜ 旅店 (*lǚdiàn*)

➜ 旅馆 (*lǚguǎn*)

➜ 有房 (*yǒufáng*) means 'rooms available'

➜ 今日有房 (*jīnrì yǒufáng*) means 'rooms available today'

➜ 住宿 (*zhùsù*) means 'accommodation'.

Homesteads

In more rural destinations, small towns and villages, you should be able to find a homestead (农家; *nóngjiā*) with a small number of rooms in the region of ¥50. Bargaining is possible; you will not need to register. The owner will be more than happy to cook up meals for you as well. Showers and toilets are generally communal.

Hostels

If you're looking for efficiently run budget accommodation, turn to China's youth hostel sector. **Hostelling International** (www.yhachina.com) hostels are generally well run; other private youth hostels scattered around China are unaffiliated and standards at these may be variable. Book ahead in popular towns as rooms can go fast.

Superb for meeting like-minded travellers, youth hostels are typically staffed by youthful English-speakers who are also well informed on local sightseeing and transport. The foreigner-friendly vibe in youth hostels stands in marked contrast to many Chinese hotels. Double rooms in youth hostels are frequently better than midrange equivalents and often just as comfortable and better located; these places may be cheaper (but not always), or can arrange better-value tours. Many offer wi-fi, while most have at least one internet terminal (either free, free for 30 minutes or roughly ¥5 to ¥10 per hour). Laundry, book-lending, kitchen facilities, bike rental, lockers, and a noticeboard, bar and cafe should all be available, as well as possibly a pool, ping pong, movies, game consoles and other forms of entertainment. Soap, shower gel and toothpaste are generally not provided, although you can purchase them at reception.

Dorms usually cost between ¥40 and ¥55 (with discounts of around ¥5 for members). They typically come with bunk beds but may have standard beds. Most dorms won't have ensuite showers, though some do; they should have air-con. Many hostels also have doubles, singles, twins and sometimes even family rooms; prices vary but are often around ¥150 to ¥250 for a double (again, with discounts for members). Hostels can arrange ticketing or help you book a room in another affiliated youth hostel.

Book ahead – online if possible – as rooms are frequently booked out, especially at weekends or the busy holiday periods. In popular destinations, hostels may charge elevated rates on Friday and Saturday.

Hotels

Hotels vary wildly in quality within the same budget bracket. The star rating system employed in China can also be misleading: hotels may be awarded four or five stars when they are patently a star lower in ranking. The best rule of thumb is to choose the newest hotel in each category, as renovations can be rare. Deficiencies may not be immediately apparent, so explore and inspect the overall quality of the hotel – viewing the room up front pays dividends.

China has few independent hotels of real distinction,

so it's generally advisable to select chain hotels that offer a proven standard of international excellence. Shangri-La, Marriott, Hilton, St Regis, Ritz-Carlton, Marco Polo and Hyatt all have a presence in China and can generally be relied upon for high standards of service and comfort.

Note the following:

➡ English skills are often poor, even in some five-star hotels.

➡ Most rooms are twins rather than doubles, so be clear if you specifically want a double.

➡ Virtually all hotel rooms, whatever the price bracket, will have air-con and a TV.

➡ Very cheap rooms may have neither telephone nor internet access.

➡ Wi-fi is generally ubiquitous in hostels and midrange and top-end hotels (but might be available only in the lobby).

➡ Late-night telephone calls or calling cards from 'masseurs' and prostitutes are still common in budget and lower midrange hotels.

➡ All hotel rooms are subject to a 10% or 15% service charge, though the price quoted usually is the final price and includes this.

➡ Practically all hotels will change money for guests, and most midrange and top-end hotels accept credit cards.

➡ A Western breakfast may be available (certainly at four-star establishments).

➡ The Chinese method of designating floors is the same as that used in the USA, but different from, say, in Australia. What would be the ground floor in Australia is the 1st floor in China.

➡ The number '4' is considered unlucky in China and the number '8' lucky. So you may find that your room on the 4th floor (or any level) starts with the number '8', even though it isn't on the 8th floor.

In China, there are several words for 'hotel':

➡ bīnguǎn (宾馆)

➡ dàfàndiàn (大饭店)

➡ dàjiǔdiàn (大酒店)

➡ fàndiàn (饭店)

➡ jiǔdiàn (酒店).

Customs Regulations

Chinese customs generally pay tourists little attention. 'Green channels' and 'red channels' at the airport are clearly marked. You are not allowed to import or export illegal drugs, or animals and plants (including seeds). Pirated DVDs and CDs are illegal exports from China – if found they will be confiscated. You can take Chinese medicine up to a value of ¥300 when you depart China. Duty free, you're allowed to import:

➡ 400 cigarettes (or the equivalent in tobacco products)

➡ 1.5L of alcohol

➡ 50g of gold or silver. Also note:

➡ Importation of fresh fruit and cold cuts is prohibited.

➡ There are no restrictions on foreign currency, but you should declare cash exceeding US$5000 or in another currency.

Objects considered antiques require a certificate and a red seal to clear customs when leaving China. Anything made before 1949 is considered an antique, and if it was made before 1795 it cannot legally be taken out of the country. To get the proper certificate and red seal, your antiques must be inspected by the **State Administration of Cultural Heritage** (Guójiā Wénwù Jú; 📞010 5679 2211; www.sach.gov.cn; 83 Beiheyan Dajie; ⏰8.30am-5pm; 🚇Lines 6, 8 to Nanluoguxiang, exit B or Line 5 to Zhangzizhonglu, exit D) in Běijīng.

Discount Cards

Seniors over the age of 65 are frequently eligible for discounts and 70-and-overs get free admission, so make sure you take your passport when visiting sights as proof of age.

An **International Student Identity Card** (ISIC; www.isic.org; GBP £12/USD $25) can offer half-price discounts at many sights, but you may have to insist – and you may have as much luck with your home country's student card.

Electricity

There are three types of plugs used in China – three-pronged angled pins, two flat pins (the most common) or two narrow round pins. Electricity is 220 volts, 50 cycles AC.

220V/50Hz

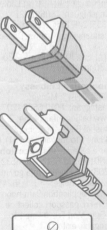

220V/50Hz

Embassies & Consulates

Embassies are located in Běijīng, with consulates scattered around the country. There are three main embassy areas in Běijīng: Jiànguóménwài, Sānlǐtún and Liàngmǎqiáo. Embassies are open from 9am to noon and 1.30pm to 4pm Monday to Friday, but visa departments are often only open in the morning. For visas, you need to phone to make an appointment.

Australian Embassy
(澳大利亚大使馆; Àodàlìyà Dàshǐguǎn; ☑010 5140 4111; www.china.embassy.gov.au; 21 Dongzhimenwai Dajie; 东直门外大街21号; ☺9am-noon & 2-3.30pm Mon-Fri; Ⓢ Line 2 to Dongzhimen, exit B)

Australian Consulates
Hong Kong (☑852 2827 8881; http://hongkong.china.embassy.gov.au; 23rd fl, Harbour Centre, 25 Harbour Rd, Wan Chai; ☺9am-5pm Mon-Fri; Ⓜ Wan Chai, exit C)

Shànghǎi (澳大利亚领事馆, Àodàlìyà Lǐngshìguǎn; Map p317; ☑021 2215 5200; www.shanghai.china.embassy.gov.au; 22nd fl, CITIC Sq, 1168 West Nanjing Rd; 南京西路1168号 22楼; ☺8.30am-5pm Mon-Fri; Ⓜ Line 2, 12, 13 to West Nanjing Rd)

Guǎngzhōu (澳大利亚驻广州总领事馆; Àodàlìyàzhùguǎng Zhōuzhōng Lǐngshìguǎn;☑020 3814 0111; 12th fl, Development Centre, 3 Linjiang Dadao)

Canadian Embassy
(加拿大大使馆; Jiānádà Dàshǐguǎn;☑010 5139 4000; www.china.gc.ca; 19 Dongzhimenwai Dajie; 东直门外大街19号; ☺8.30-11am Mon-Fri & 1.30-3pm Tue & Thu; Ⓢ Line 2 to Dongzhimen, exit B)

Canadian Consulates
Hong Kong (☑852 3719 4700; 5th fl, Tower 3, Exchange Square, 8 Connaught Place, Central; Ⓜ Central, exit A)

Shànghǎi (加拿大领事馆, Jiānádà Lǐngshìguǎn; Map p317; ☑021-3279 2800; www.shanghai.gc.ca; 8th fl, 1788 West Nanjing Rd; 南京西路1788号8楼; ☺8.30am-noon & 1-5pm; Ⓜ Line 2, 7 to Jing'an Temple)

Chóngqìng (☑023-6373 8007; Suite 1705, 17th fl, Metropolitan Tower, 68 Zourong Lu)

Guǎngzhōu (☑020 8611 6100; Suite 801, China Hotel Office Tower, Liuhua Lu)

French Embassy
(法国驻华大使馆; Fǎguó Zhùhuá Dàshǐguǎn;☑010 8531 2000; www.ambafrance-cn.org; 60 Tianze Lu; 天泽路60号; Ⓢ Line 10 to Liangmaqiao, exit B)

French Consulates
Hong Kong (☑852 3196 6100; www.consulfrance-hongkong.org; 26th fl, Tower II, Admiralty Centre, 18 Harcourt Rd, Admiralty; Ⓜ Admiralty, exit C2)

Shànghǎi (法国领事馆; Fǎguó Lǐngshìguǎn;☑021 6010 6050; www.consulfrance-shanghai.org; 8th fl, Bldg A, Soho Zhongshan Plaza, 1055 West Zhongshan Rd; 中山西路1055号中山广场A座18楼; ☺8.15am-12.15pm Mon, 8.45am-12.15pm Tue-Fri)

Chéngdū (法国驻成都总领事馆; Fǎguózhù Chéngdūzōng Lǐngshìguǎn;☑028 6666 6060; www.ambafrance-cn.

org/-Chengdu-Consulat-; 30th fl, Times Plaza, 2 Zongfu Lu; 总府路2号时代广场30楼; 🕐9am-5pm)

Shěnyáng (☎024 2319 0000; 34 Nanshisan Weilu; 南十三纬路34号)

Guǎngzhōu (☎020 2829 2000; Rm 810, 8th fl, Main Tower, Guǎngdōng International Hotel, 339 Huanshi Donglu)

Wǔhàn (☎027 6579 7900; rooms 1701-1708, New World International Trade Center, 568 Jianshe Dadao; 建设大道568号)

German Embassy
(德国大使馆; Déguó dàshǐguǎn; ☎010 8532 9000; www.china.diplo.de; 17 Dongzhimenwai Dajie; 东直门外大街17号; [S]Line 2 to Dongzhimen, exit B)

German Consulates
Hong Kong (☎852 2105 8788; www.hongkong.diplo.de; 21st fl, United Centre, 95 Queensway, Admiralty; [M]Admiralty, exit C2)

Shànghǎi (德国领事馆; Déguó Lǐngshìguǎn; Map p304;☎021 3401 0106; www.shanghai.diplo.de; 181 Yongfu Rd; 永福路181号)

Chéngdū (德国领事馆; Déguó Lǐngshìguǎn;☎028 8528 0800, emergency only 137 3060 0952; www.chengdu.diplo.de; 25th fl, Western Tower, 19 Renmin Nanlu 4th Section; 人民南路4段19号威斯顿联邦大厦25层; 🕐9am-5pm)

Guǎngzhōu (☎020 2829 2000; Rm 810, 8th fl, Main Tower, Guǎngdōng International Hotel, 339 Huanshi Donglu)

Indian Embassy
(印度大使馆; Yìndù Dàshǐguǎn; ☎010 8531 2500; www.indianembassy.org.cn; 5 Liangmaqiao Beijie; 亮马桥北街5号; 🕐visa office 9.30-10.30am Mon-Fri; [S]Line 10 to Liangmaqiao, exit B)

Indian Consulates
Hong Kong (☎852 3970 9900; www.cgihk.gov.in; Unit A, 16th fl, United Centre, 95 Queensway, Admiralty; 🕐9am-5.30pm Mon-Fri)

Irish Embassy
Běijīng (爱尔兰大使馆; Ài'ěrlán Dàshǐguǎn;☎010 8531 6200; www.irishembassy.cn; 3 Ritan Donglu; 日坛东路3号; 🕐9am-12.30pm & 2-5pm Mon-Fri; [S]Line 1 to Yonganli, exit A1)

Irish Consulates
Hong Kong (☎852 2527 4897; www.dfa.ie/irish-consulate/hong-kong; 33 Des Voeux Rd Central, Sheung Wan; 🕐10am-noon & 2.30-4.30pm Mon-Fri; [M]Central)

Shànghǎi (爱尔兰领事馆, Ài'ěrlán Lǐngshìguǎn; Map p317;☎021 6010 1360; www.embassyofireland.cn; 700a Shànghǎi Centre, 1376 West Nanjing Rd; 南京西路1376号700a室; 🕐9.30am-4.30pm Mon-Fri; [M]Line 2, 7 to Jing'an Temple; Line 2, 12, 13 to West Nanjing Rd)

Japanese Embassy
(日本大使馆; Rìběn Dàshǐguǎn; ☎010 8531 9800; www.cn.emb-japan.go.jp; 1 Liangmaqiaodong Jie; 亮马桥东街1号; 🕐9-11.30am & 1-4.30pm; [S]Line 10 to Liangmaqiao, exit B)

Japanese Consulates
Hong Kong (☎852 2522 1184; www.hk.emb-japan.go.jp; 46-47th fl, 1 Exchange Sq, 8 Connaught Pl, Central; [M]Central, exit D1)

Shànghǎi (日本领事馆; Rìběn Lǐngshìguǎn;☎021 5257 4766; www.shanghai.cn.emb-japan.go.jp; 8 Wanshan Rd; 万山路8号; 🕐9am-12.30pm & 1.30-5.30pm Mon-Fri)

Qīngdǎo (☎0532 8090 0001; 59 Xianggang Donglu; 🕐9-11am & 1.30-4pm)

Kazakhstan Embassy
(哈萨克斯坦使馆; Hāsàkè Sītǎn Shǐguǎn;☎010 6532 6182; www.kazembassy.cn; 9 Sanlitun Dongliujie; [S]Line 10 to Liangmaqiao, exit B)

Kazakhstan Consulate
Ürümqi (哈萨克斯坦共和国驻; Hāsàkè Sītǎn Gònghéguó Zhù; ☎0991 369 1444; 216 Kunming Lu; 🕐9am-1pm Mon-Fri)

Kyrgyzstan Embassy
(☎010 6468 1348; www.kyrgyzstanembassy.net; 18 Xiaoyun Lu, 10/11 H District, King's Garden Villas; 霄云路18号京润水上花园别墅H区10/11; 🕐applications 9-11am Mon, Wed, Fri; [S]Sanyuanqiao)

Kyrgyzstan Consulate
Ürümqi (吉尔吉斯斯坦共和国驻; Jí'ěrjísī Sītǎn Gònghéguó Zhù; 38 Hetan Beilu; 🕐noon-2pm Mon-Fri)

Laotian Embassy
(老挝大使馆; Lǎowō Dàshǐguǎn;☎010 6532 1224; laoemcn@public.east.cn.net; 11 Sanlitun Dongsijie; 三里屯东二街11号; [S]Line 10 to Agricultural Exhibition Center, exit D2)

Laotian Consulates
Hong Kong (☎852 2544 1186; 14th fl, Arion Commercial Centre, 2-12 Queen's Rd West, Sheung Wan)

Kūnmíng (老挝领事馆; Lǎowō Lǐngshìguǎn;☎0871 6316 8916; Ground fl, Kūnmíng Diplomat Compound, 6800 Caiyun Beilu; 彩云北路6800号)

Jǐnghóng (老挝领事馆; Lǎowō Lǐngshìguǎn; ☎0691 221 9355; 2/F, Bldg 2, Gaozhuang Xishuangjing, Xuanwei Dadao; 宣慰大道，告庄西双景综合楼2楼; 🕐8.30-11.30am & 2.30-4.30pm Mon-Fri)

Mongolian Embassy
(蒙古大使馆; Ménggǔ Dàshǐguǎn;☎010 6532 1203; www.beijing.mfa.gov.mn; 2 Xiushui Beijie; 秀水北街2号; [S]Line 1 to Yonganli, exit A1). It has a separate **visa section** (☎010 6532 6512, 010 6532 1203; www.beijing.mfa.gov.mn; 2 Xiushui Beijie; 秀水北街2号; 🕐visa application 9am-noon Mon-Fri, passport collection 4-5pm Mon-Fri; [S]Line 1 to Yonganli, exit A1).

Mongolian Consulates
Hohhot (蒙古领事馆; Měnggǔ Lǐngshìguǎn;☎0471 492 3819, 0471 468 5161; Unit 1, Bldg 5, Wulan Residential Area, Sai Han District; 赛罕区乌兰小区五号楼一单元; 🕐9am-noon Mon, Tue & Thu)

Erenhot (蒙古领事馆; Měnggǔ Lǐngshìguǎn;☎0479 753 9200, 0479 753 9201; 1206 Youyi Lu, Erenhot; 友谊路1206号,; 🕐9am-noon & 3-5pm Mon-Fri).

Myanmar Embassy

(缅甸大使馆; Miǎndiàn Dàshǐguǎn; ☎010 6532 0359; www.myanmarembassy.com/english; 6 Dongzhimenwai Dajie; 东直门外大街6号; ⓢLine 10 to Agricultural Exhibition Center, exit D2)

Myanmar Consulate

Kūnmíng (缅甸领事馆; Miǎndiàn Lǐngshǐguǎn; ☎0871 6816 2804; www.mcgkunming.org; 99 Yingbin Lu, Guāndù District Consular Zone; 官渡区昆明外国领馆区迎宾路99号 (世纪金源大酒店劳), ⓗ9am-noon Mon-Fri)

Nepalese Embassy

(尼泊尔大使馆; Níbó'ěr Dàshǐguǎn; ☎010 6532 1795; www.nepalembassy.org.cn; 1 Sanlitun Xiliujie; 三里屯西六街1号; ⓗ10am-noon & 3-4pm Mon-Fri; ⓢLine 10 to Agricultural Exhibition Center or Liangmaqiao, exit D)

Nepalese Consulate

Hong Kong (☎852 2369 7813; 715 China Aerospace Tower, Concordia Plaza, 1 Science Museum Rd, Tsim Sha Tsui; ⓜHung Hom, exit D1)

Lhasa (尼泊尔领事馆, Níbó'ěr Iǐngshǐguǎn; ☎0891-681 5744; www.nepalembassy.org.cn; 13 Luobulingka Beilu; ⓗ10am-noon Mon-Fri).

Netherlands Embassy

(荷兰大使馆; Hélán Dàshǐguǎn; ☎010 8532 0200; http://china.nlembassy.org/; 4 Liangmahe Nanlu; 亮马河南路4号; ⓗ9am-12.30pm & 2-5.30pm Mon-Fri; ⓢLine 10 to Liangmaqiao, exit B)

Netherlands Consulates

Hong Kong (☎852 2599 9200; http://hongkong.nlconsulate.org; Room 2402B, 24th fl, 23 Harbour Rd, Great Eagle Centre)

Shànghǎi (荷兰领事馆; Hélán Lǐngshǐguǎn; ☎021 2208 7288; http://china.nlembassy.org; 10th fl, Tower B, Dawning Center, 500 Hongbaoshi Rd; 红宝石路500号中银中心东塔10楼; ⓗ9am-noon & 1-5.30pm Mon-Fri)

Guǎngzhōu (☎020 3813 2200; http://china.nlembassy.org; Teem Tower, 208 Tianhe Lu)

New Zealand Embassy

(新西兰大使馆; Xīnxīlán Dàshǐguǎn; ☎010 8531 2700; www.mfat.govt.nz; 3 Sanlitun Dongsanjie, 三里屯东三街3号; ⓗ8.30am-5pm Mon-Fri; ⓢLine 10 to Agricultural Exhibition Center, exit D2),

New Zealand Consulates

Hong Kong (☎852 2525 5044; www.eit.ac.nz; Room 6501, 65th fl, Central Plaza, 18 Harbour Rd, Wan Chai; ⓗ8.30am-1pm, 2-5pm Mon-Fri; ⓜWan Chai, exit C)

Shànghǎi (新西兰领事馆; Xīnxīlán Lǐngshǐguǎn; ☎021 5407 5858; www.nzembassy.com; 2801-2802A & 2806B-2810, 5 Corporate Ave, 150 Hubin Rd; 湖滨150号; ⓗ8.30am-noon & 1-5pm Mon-Fri)

Guǎngzhōu (☎020 8667 0253; Rm 1055, China Hotel Office Tower, Liuhua Lu)

North Korean Embassy

(北朝鲜驻华大使馆; Běi Cháoxiǎn Zhùhuá shǐguǎn; ☎010 6532 1186; 11 Ritan Beilu; 日坛北路11号; ⓢLine 6 to Dongdaqiao, exit D)

North Korean Consulate

Shěnyáng (☎024 8685 2742; 37 Beiling Dajie, 北陵大街37号)

Pakistan Embassy

(巴基斯坦大使馆; Bājīsītǎn Dàshǐguǎn; ☎010 6532 6660; www.pakbj.org.pk; 1 Dongzhimenwai Dajie; 东直门外大街1号; ⓗ9.30-11.45am Mon-Fri; ⓢLine 10 to Agricultural Exhibition Center, exit A)

Pakistan Consulate

Chéngdū (巴基斯坦领事馆; Bājīsītǎn Lǐngshǐguǎn; ☎028 8526 8316; parepchengdu@mofa.gov.pk; 7 Xinguanghua Jie, One Aerospace Center, Ste 2306; 新光华街7号航天科技大厦2306室; ⓗ9am-noon Mon & Thu)

Russian Embassy

(俄罗斯大使馆; Èluósī Dàshǐguǎn; ☎010 6532 1381, visa section 2-6pm Mon-Fri 010 6532 1267; www.russia.org.cn; 4 Dongzhimen Beizhongjie; 东直门内大街东直门北中街4号, off Dongzhimennei Dajie; ⓗ9.30-11.30am Mon-Fri; ⓢLines 2, 13 to Dongzhimen, exit A)

South Korean Embassy

(南韩大使馆; Nánhán Dàshǐguǎn; ☎010-8531 0700; www.chn.mofat.go.kr; North Lu, 7 Liangmaqiao Lu; 北京市朝阳区亮马桥北小街7号; ⓢLine 10 to Liangmaqiao, exit B)

South Korean Consulates

Shěnyáng (☎024 2385 3388; 37 Nanshisan Weilu; 南十三纬路31号)

Qīngdǎo (☎0532 8897 6001; 88 Chunyang Lu; 春阳路88号; ⓗ9am-noon Mon-Fri summer, 9am-5pm Mon-Fri winter)

Thai Embassy

(泰国大使馆; Tàiguó Dàshǐguǎn; ☎010 6532 1749; www.thaiembbeij.org; 40 Guanghua Lu; 光华路40号; ⓗ8.30am-noon & 2-5.30pm; ⓢLines 1, 2 to Jianguomen, exit B)

Thai Consulates

Shànghǎi (泰国领事馆; Tàiwángguó Lǐngshǐguǎn; ☎021 5260 9899; www.thaishanghai.com; 18 Wanshan Rd; 万山路18号; ⓗvisa office 9.30-11.30am Mon-Fri; ⓜYili Rd)

Kūnmíng (泰国领事馆; Tàiguó Lǐngshǐguǎn; ☎0871 6316 8916; 18th fl, Shuncheng Twin Tower, East Building, Dongfeng Xilu; 东风西路顺城东塔18楼; ⓗ9am-11.30pm Mon-Fri)

UK Embassy

(联合王国大使馆; Liánhé Wángguó Dàshǐguǎn; ☎010 5192 4000; www.gov.uk; 11 Guanghua Lu; 光华路11号; ⓗ9am-noon Mon, Tue, Thu & Fri; ⓢLine 1 to Yonganli, exit A1)

UK Consulates

Hong Kong (☎852 2901 3000; www.gov.uk/government/world/hong-kong; 1 Supreme Court Rd, Admiralty; ⓗ8.30am-5.15pm Mon-Fri; ⓜAdmiralty, exit F)

Shànghǎi (英国领事馆; Yīngguó Lǐngshǐguǎn; Map p317; ☎021 3279 2000; http://ukinchina.fco.gov.uk; 17th fl Garden Sq, 968 West Beijing Rd; 京西路968号花园广场17号; ⓗ8.30am-5.30pm Mon-Fri, consular service 9am-noon & 2-4pm Mon, Wed & Thu, 9am-noon Tue & Fri; ⓜLine 2, 7 to Jing'an Temple; Line 2, 12, 13 to West Nanjing Rd)

Chóngqìng (☑023-6369 1500; Suite 2801, 28th fl, Metropolitan Tower, 68 Zourong Lu)

Guǎngzhōu (☑020 8314 3000, emergency 010 5192 4000; 2nd fl, Main Tower, Guǎngdōng International Hotel, 339 Huanshi Donglu)

US Embassy

(美国大使馆; Měiguó Dàshǐguǎn;☑010 8531 3300; http://beijing.usembassy-china. org.cn; 55 Anjialou Lu, off Liangmaqiao Lu; 亮马桥安家楼路55号; ⓢLine 10 to Liangmaqiao, exit B)

US Consulates

Hong Kong (☑852 2523 9011; 26 Garden Rd, Central; ⓂCentral, exit J2)

Shànghǎi (美国领事馆, Měiguó Lǐngshìguǎn; Map p317; ☑after-hour emergency for US citizens 021 3217 4650; http:// shanghai.usembassy-china.org. cn; 8th fl, Westgate Tower, 1038 West Nanjing Rd; 南京西路1038 号8楼; ⏱8.15-11.30am & 1.15-2.30pm Mon-Fri; ⓂLine 2, 12, 13 to West Nanjing Rd, exit 1)

Chéngdū (美国领事; Měiguó Lǐngshìguǎn;☑028 8558 3992; http://chengdu.usembassy-china.org.cn; 4 Lingshiguan Lu; 领事馆路4号; ⏱1-4pm Tue, Thu, Fri)

Guǎngzhōu (☑020 3814 5000; Huaxia Lu, Zhūjiāng New Town, Tiānhé District)

Shěnyáng (☑024 2322 1198; 52 Shisi Weilu; 十四纬路52号)

Vietnamese Embassy

(越南大使馆; Yuènán Dàshǐguǎn;☑010 6532 1155; http://vnemba.org.cn; 32 Guanghua Lu; 光华路32号; ⓢLine 1 to Yonganli, exit A1)

Vietnamese Consulates

Hong Kong (☑852 2591 4517, 852 2835 9318; www.mofa.gov. vn; 15th fl, Great Smart Tower, 230 Wan Chai Rd, Wan Chai; ⏱9am-5.30pm Mon-Fri; ⓂWan Chai, exit A3)

Kūnmíng (越南领事馆; Yuènán Lǐngshìguǎn;☑0871 6352 2669; 507, Hongta Mansion, 155 Beijing Lu; 北京路155号红塔大厦507室)

Food & Drink

Unless otherwise noted, the following eating price ranges used in this guide are for mains.

Běijīng
$ Up to ¥40
$$ ¥40–100
$$$ over ¥100

Shànghǎi
$ Up to ¥60
$$ ¥60–160
$$$ over ¥160

Hong Kong (prices for a two-course meal with drinks)
$ Up to HK$200
$$ HK$200–500
$$$ over HK$500

Macau (prices for a two-course meal with drinks)
$ Up to MOP$200
$$ MOP$200–400
$$$ Over MOP$400

GLBTIQ Travellers

Greater tolerance exists in the big cities than in the more conservative countryside, but even in urban areas, gay and lesbian public displays of affection can raise an eyebrow. You will often see Chinese friends of the same sex holding hands or putting their arms around each other, but this usually has no sexual connotation. There are gay bars and clubs in the major cities, but it is far more common for people to socialise on apps. A same-sex couple staying in a hotel room with only one bed will rarely attract any resistance or comments (at least not to their faces).

Dànlán (淡蓝; www.danlan.org) Chinese-only news and lifestyle.

Spartacus International Gay Guide (www.spartacusworld. com/en) Best-selling guide for gay travellers; also available as an iPhone App.

Utopia (www.utopia-asia.com/ tipschin.htm) Tips on travelling in China and a complete listing of gay bars nationwide.

Internet Access

Wi-fi accessibility in hotels, cafes, restaurants and bars is generally good. The best option is to bring a wi-fi equipped smartphone, tablet or laptop or use your hotel computer or broadband internet connection. Chain restaurants and cafes with free wi-fi often still require a Chinese phone number to receive a login code.

The Chinese authorities remain mistrustful of the internet, and censorship is heavy-handed. Around 10% of websites are blocked; the list is constantly changing but includes sites and apps such as Facebook, Twitter, Instagram, Google-owned sites (YouTube, Google Maps, Gmail, Google Drive), Dropbox and Telegram, so plan ahead. Google's search function is blocked, but a limited Chinese version of Yahoo and Bing are accessible. Newspapers such as the *New York Times* are also blocked, as is Bloomberg, though the *Guardian* is allowed.

Users can gain access to blocked websites by using a VPN (Virtual Private Network) service such as VyperVPN (www.goldenfrog.com). Be aware that they can be slow, and often are blocked themselves so must be installed before arriving in China – and not all even work in China.

Many internet cafes only accept customers with Chinese ID, thus barring foreigners. In large cities and towns, the area around the train station generally has internet cafes.

The internet icon in hotel reviews indicates the presence of an internet cafe or a terminal where you can get online; wi-fi areas are indicated with a wi-fi icon.

Legal Matters

China does not officially recognise dual nationality or the foreign citizenship of children born in China if one of the parents is a PRC national. If you have Chinese and another nationality you may, in theory, not be allowed to visit China on your foreign passport. In practice, Chinese authorities are not switched-on enough to know if you own two passports, and should accept you on a foreign passport. Dual-nationality citizens who enter China on a Chinese passport are subject to Chinese laws and are legally not allowed consular help. If over 16 years of age, carry your passport with you at all times as a form of ID.

Gambling is officially illegal in mainland China, as is distributing religious material.

China takes a particularly dim view of opium and all its derivatives; trafficking in more than 50g of heroin can lead to the death penalty. Foreign passport holders have been executed in China for drug offences. The Chinese criminal justice system does not ensure a fair trial and defendants are not presumed innocent until proven guilty. If arrested, most foreign citizens have the right to contact their embassy.

Money

ATMs

Bank of China and the Industrial & Commercial Bank of China (ICBC) 24-hour ATMs are plentiful, and you can use Visa, MasterCard, Cirrus, Maestro Plus and American Express to withdraw cash. All ATMs accepting international cards have dual-language ability. The network is largely found in sizeable towns and cities.

The exchange rate on ATM withdrawals is similar to that for credit cards, but there is a maximum daily withdrawal amount. Note that banks can charge a withdrawal fee for using the ATM network of another bank, so check with your bank before trav-

elling. Bank of Nanjing ATMs waive the withdrawal fee for members of the Global ATM Alliance (ask your bank).

If you plan on staying in China for a few weeks or more, it is advisable to open an account at a bank with a nationwide network of ATMs, such as Bank of China or ICBC. HSBC and Citibank ATMs are available in larger cities. Keep your ATM receipts so you can exchange your yuan when you leave China.

To have money wired from abroad, visit Western Union or Moneygram (www.money-gram.com).

Credit Cards

In large tourist towns, credit cards are relatively straightforward to use, but don't expect to be able to use them everywhere, and always carry enough cash. The exception is in Hong Kong, where international credit cards are accepted almost everywhere (although some shops may try to add a surcharge to offset the commission charged by credit companies, which can range from 2.5% to 7%). Check to see if your credit card company charges a foreign transaction fee (usually between 1% and 3%) for purchases in China.

Where they are accepted, credit cards often deliver a slightly better exchange rate than banks. Money can also be withdrawn at certain ATMs in large cities on credit cards such as Visa, MasterCard and Amex.

Electronic Payments

Paying for purchases with a smartphone app or a phone itself has become a common practice in the larger cities in China, particularly in large stores and chains. Plenty of convenience stores, fast-food restaurants, cafes, ride-sharing cars and online stores accept electronic payments from digital wallets paid through apps such as WeChat and Alipay.

For a visitor, the only accessible system that allows

foreign cards is Apple Pay, accepted where you see the Apple Pay or QuickPass logos. Payments are made by holding your compatible device against the payment machine and verifying with your fingerprint.

Ride-sharing service Uber also works in China in the major cities without a Chinese bank card.

Currency

The Chinese currency is the rénmínbì (RMB), or 'people's money'. The basic unit of RMB is the yuán (元; ¥), which is divided into 10 jiǎo (角), which is again divided into 10 fēn (分). Colloquially, the yuán is referred to as kuài and jiǎo as máo (毛). The fēn has so little value these days that it is rarely used.

The Bank of China issues RMB bills in denominations of ¥1, ¥2, ¥5, ¥10, ¥20, ¥50 and ¥100. Coins come in denominations of ¥1, 5 jiǎo, 1 jiǎo and 5 fēn. Paper versions of the coins remain in circulation.

Hong Kong's currency is the Hong Kong dollar (HK$). The Hong Kong dollar is divided into 100 cents. Bills are issued in denominations of HK$10, HK$20, HK$50, HK$100, HK$500 and HK$1000. Copper coins are worth 50c, 20c and 10c, while the $5, $2 and $1 coins are silver and the $10 coin is nickel and bronze. The Hong Kong dollar is pegged to the US dollar at a rate of US$1 to HK$7.80, though it is allowed to fluctuate a little.

Macau's currency is the pataca (MOP$), which is divided into 100 avos. Bills are issued in denominations of MOP$10, MOP$20, MOP$50, MOP$100, MOP$500 and MOP$1000. There are copper coins worth 10, 20 and 50 avos and silver-coloured MOP$1, MOP$2, MOP$5 and MOP$10 coins. The pataca is pegged to the Hong Kong dollar at a rate of MOP$103.20 to HK$100. In effect, the two currencies are interchangeable and Hong Kong dollars, including coins, are accepted in Macau. Chinese rénmínbì is also accepted in many places in Macau at one-to-one. You can't spend patacas anywhere else, however, so use them before you leave Macau. Prices quoted are in yuán unless otherwise stated.

Money Changers

It's best to wait till you reach China to exchange money as the exchange rate will be better. Foreign currency and travellers cheques can be changed at border crossings, international airports, branches of the Bank of China, tourist hotels and some large department stores; hours of operation for foreign exchange counters are 8am to 7pm (later at hotels). Top-end hotels will generally change money for hotel guests only. The official rate is given almost everywhere and the exchange charge is standardised, so there is little need to shop around for the best deal.

Australian, Canadian, US, UK, Hong Kong and Japanese currencies and the euro can be changed in China. In some backwaters, it may be hard to change lesser-known currencies; US dollars are still the easiest to change. Lhasa has ATM-style currency exchange machines that can change cash in several currencies into rénmínbì 24 hours a day, with your passport.

Keep at least a few of your exchange receipts. You will need them if you want to exchange any remaining RMB you have at the end of your trip.

Taxes & Refunds

When shoppping, tax is already included on the displayed prices. Nearly all of the major cities offer a tax refund for foreign tourists on purchases made in the previous 90 days; the list of provinces keeps expanding.

The 11% tax is refunded at the airport and all items must leave China with you. Goods have a minimum purchase of ¥500 from the one store.

Tipping

Restaurants Tipping is never expected at cheap, and many midrange, restaurants. In general there is no need to tip if a service charge has already been added, so check your bill for one.

Hotels Porters may expect a tip.

Taxis Drivers do not expect tips.

Travellers Cheques

With the prevalence of ATMs across China, travellers cheques are not as useful as they once were and cannot be used everywhere, so always ensure you carry enough ready cash. You should have no problem cashing travellers cheques at tourist hotels, but they are of little use in budget hotels and restaurants. Most hotels will only cash the cheques of guests. If cashing them at banks, aim for larger banks such as the Bank of China or ICBC.

Stick to the major companies such as Thomas Cook, Amex and Visa. In big cities travellers cheques are accepted in almost any currency, but in smaller destinations, it's best to stick to big currencies such as US dollars or UK pounds. Keep your exchange receipts so you can change your money back to its original currency when you leave.

Opening Hours

China officially has a five-day working week; Saturday and Sunday are public holidays.

Banks Open Monday to Friday 9am to 5pm (or 6pm); may close for two hours in the afternoon. Many also open Saturday and maybe Sunday. Same for offices and government departments.

Bars Open in the late afternoon, shutting around midnight or later.

Post offices Generally open daily.

Restaurants Open from around 10.30am to 11pm; some shut from 2pm until 5pm or 6pm.

Shops Open daily 10am to 10pm. Same for department stores and shopping malls.

Post

The international postal service is generally efficient, and airmail letters and postcards will probably take between five and 10 days to reach their destinations. Domestic post is swift – perhaps one or two days from Guǎngzhōu to Běijīng. Intracity post may be delivered the same day it's sent.

China Post operates an express mail service (EMS) that is fast, reliable and ensures that the package is sent by registered post. Not all branches of China Post have EMS.

Major tourist hotels have branch post offices where you can send letters, packets and parcels. Even at cheap hotels you can usually post letters from the front desk. Larger parcels may need to be sent from the town's main post office.

In major cities, private carriers such as **United Parcel Service** (☑800 820 8388; www.ups.com), **DHL** (Dūnháo; ☑800 810 8000; www.cn.dhl. com), **Federal Express** (Liánbāng Kuàidì; ☑800 988 1888; http://fedex.com/cn) and **TNT Skypak** (☑800 820 9868; www.tnt.com) have a pick-up service as well as drop-off centres; call their offices for details.

If you are sending items abroad, take them unpacked with you to the post office to be inspected; an appropriate box or envelope will be found for you. Most post offices offer materials for packaging (including padded envelopes, boxes and heavy brown paper), for which you'll be charged. Don't take your own packaging as it will probably be refused. You will also need to show your passport or other ID.

Public Holidays

The People's Republic of China has a number of national holidays. Some of the following are nominal holidays that do not result in leave. It's not a great idea to arrive in China or go travelling during the big holiday periods as hotel prices reach their maximum and transport can become very tricky. It is also possible to contact a hotel and ask when large conferences occur in the area.

New Year's Day 1 January

Chinese New Year 16 February 2018, 5 February 2019; a week-long holiday for most.

International Women's Day 8 March

Tomb Sweeping Festival First weekend in April; a popular three-day holiday period.

International Labour Day 1 May; for many it's a three-day holiday.

Youth Day 4 May

International Children's Day 1 June

Dragon Boat Festival 30 May 2017, 18 June 2018, 7 June 2019

Birthday of the Chinese Communist Party 1 July

Anniversary of the Founding of the People's Liberation Army 1 August

Mid-Autumn Festival 4 October 2017, 24 September 2018, 13 September 2019

National Day 1 October; the big one – a week-long holiday.

Safe Travel
Loss Reports
If something of yours is stolen, report it immediately to the nearest Foreign Affairs Branch of the Public Security Bureau (PSB; 公安局; Gōng'ānjú). Staff will ask you to fill in a loss report before investigating the case.

A loss report is crucial so you can claim compensation if you have travel insurance. Be prepared to spend many hours, perhaps even several days, organising it. Make a copy of your passport in case of loss or theft.

Transport
Traffic accidents are the major cause of death in China for people aged between 15 and 45, and the World Health Organization (WHO) estimates there are 600 traffic deaths per day. On long-distance buses, you may find there are no seatbelts, or that the seatbelts are virtually unusable through neglect or are inextricably stuffed beneath the seat. Outside of the big cities, taxis are unlikely to have rear seatbelts fitted.

Your greatest danger in China will almost certainly be crossing the road, so develop 360-degree vision and a sixth sense. Electric cars and 'hoverboards' can approach quite silently. Crossing only when it is safe to do so could keep you perched at the side of the road in perpetuity, but don't imitate the local tendency to cross without looking. Note that cars frequently turn on red lights in China, so the green 'walk now' figure does not always mean it is safe to cross.

Telephone
Nearly everybody in China has a mobile phone (you may be judged on your model). Landlines and calling cards are rare. Some hotels will give you unlimited local or national calls.

Mobile Phones
If you have the right phone (eg Blackberry, iPhone, Android), you can use **Skype** (www.skype.com), **Viber** (www.viber.com) and **Whatsapp** (www.whatsapp.com) to make either very cheap or free calls with wi-fi access, even if your phone is network-locked or you have no phone credit. Communication through Chinese app **WeChat** (微信; Wēixìn; www.wechat.com), which boasts half a billion users, is standard practice between both friends and small businesses and is not considered unprofessional. (Note that although Chinese also use the word 'app', they spell it out as 'a-p-p'.)

Consider buying a data SIM card plan in China for constant network access away from wi-fi hot spots; plans start at under ¥70 for 500MB of data and 200 minutes of China calls per month. You will be warned about cancelling this service before leaving the country to avoid a hefty bill should you return. For this reason and the language barrier, it can be more convenient (if more expensive) to pick up a SIM card on arrival at an airport in the major cities. Though more expensive, **3G Solutions** (www.3gsolutions.com.cn) offers a range of mobile data and voice packages with pre-booking online, and will have the SIM card delivered

GOVERNMENT TRAVEL ADVICE
The following government websites offer travel advisories and information on current hot spots:

Australian Department of Foreign Affairs & Trade (www.smarttraveller.gov.au)

British Foreign & Commonwealth Office (www.gov.uk/foreign-travel-advice)

Canadian Department of Foreign Affairs & International Trade (http://travel.gc.ca/travelling/advisories)

New Zealand Ministry of Foreign Affairs and Trade (www.safetravel.govt.nz)

US State Department (http://travel.state.gov)

to your accommodation on the day you arrive in China.

If you want to get a SIM card independently, China Unicom offers the most reliable service with the greatest coverage. China Mobile or China Unicom outlets can sell you a standard prepaid SIM card, which cost from ¥60 to ¥100 and include ¥50 of credit. (You'll be given a choice of phone numbers. Choose a number without the unlucky number 4, if you don't want to irk Chinese colleagues.)

Top up prepaid credti by buying a credit-charging card (充值卡; *chōngzhí kǎ*) from outlets. Cards ar e also available from newspaper kiosks and shops displaying the China Mobile sign.

Buying a mobile phone in China is also an option as they are generally inexpensive. Make sure the phone uses W-CDMA, which works on China Unicom and most carriers around the world, and not TD-SCDMA, which works only on China Mobile and not international carriers.

Cafes, restaurants and bars in larger towns and cities frequently offer wi-fi. Consider investing in a USB portable power bank for charging your phone and other devices while on the road.

Landlines

If making a domestic call, look out for very cheap public phones at newspaper stands (报刊亭; *bàokāntíng*) and hole-in-the-wall shops (小卖部; *xiǎomàibù*); you make your call and then pay the owner. Domestic and international long-distance phone calls can also be made from main telecommunications offices and 'phone bars' (话吧; *huàbā*). Cardless international calls are expensive and it's far cheaper to use an internet phone (IP) card.

Public telephone booths are rarely used now in China but may serve as wi-fi hot spots (as in Shànghǎi).

Time

The 24-hour clock is commonly used in China. Despite China's breadth, there is one single time zone in China: UTC+8. (You can also find UTC+6 used in Tibet and Xīnjiāng, though it is not official.)

Tourist Information

Tourist information continues to improve, with modern booths with pamphlets springing up even in smaller cities. The quality of spoken English can be hit-and-miss, though. Visit the China National Tourist Office website (www.cnto.org).

Travellers with Disabilities

China is not easy to navigate for travellers with limited mobility, but travel in a wheelchair is possible in the large cities at top-end accommodation (with lots of preparation and pre-booking). Even still, expect plenty of stares.

Download Lonely Planet's free *Accessible Travel* guide from http://lptravel.to/AccessibleTravel.

Visas

Applying for Visas
FOR CHINA

Apart from visa-free visits to Hong Kong and Macau and useful 72-hour visa-free transit stays (for visitors from 51 nations) to Běijīng, Shànghǎi (144-hour visa-free transit), Guǎngzhōu, Xī'ān, Guìlín, Chéngdū, Chóngqìng, Dàlián and Shěnyáng, among others, you will need a visa to visit China. Citizens from Japan, Singapore, Brunei, San Marino, Mauritius, the Seychelles and the Bahamas do not require a visa to visit China. There remain a few restricted areas in China that require an additional

permit from the PSB. Permits are also required for travel to Tibet, a region that the authorities can suddenly bar foreigners from entering.

Your passport must be valid for at least six months after the expiry date of your visa (nine months for a double-entry visa) and you'll need at least one entire blank page in your passport for the visa. For children under the age of 18, a parent must sign the application on their behalf.

At the time of writing, applicants were required to provide the following:

➡ a copy of flight confirmation showing onward/return travel

➡ for double-entry visas, flight confirmation showing all dates of entry and exit

➡ if staying at a hotel in China, confirmation from the hotel (this can be cancelled later if you stay elsewhere and often just showing the first night is enough)

➡ if staying with friends or relatives, a copy of the information page of their passport, a copy of their China visa and a letter of invitation from them.

At the time of writing, prices for a standard single-entry 30-day visa were as follows:

➡ UK£85 for UK citizens

➡ US$140 for US citizens

➡ US$40 for other nationals.

Double-entry visas:

➡ UK£85 for UK citizens

➡ US$140 for US citizens

➡ US$60 for other nationals.

Six-month multiple-entry visas:

➡ UK£85 for UK citizens

➡ US$140 for US citizens

➡ US$80 for other nationals.

A standard, 30-day single-entry visa can be issued in four to five working days. In many countries, the visa service has been outsourced from the Chinese embassy to a compulsory Chinese Visa Application Service Centre (www.visaforchina.org), which levies an extra administration fee. In the case of the UK, a single-entry visa costs UK£85, but the standard administration charge levied by the centre is an additional UK£66 (three-day express UK£78, postal service UK£90). In some countries there is more than one service centre nationwide.

A standard 30-day visa is activated on the date you enter China, and must be used within three months of the date of issue. Travel visas of 60 days and 90 days are harder to get but possible just by applying. To stay longer, you can extend your visa in China.

Visa applications require a completed application form (available from the embassy, visa application service centre or downloaded from its website) and at least one photo (normally 51mm x 51mm). You generally pay for your visa when you collect it.

A visa mailed to you will take up to three weeks. In the US and Canada, mailed visa applications have to go via a visa agent, at extra cost. In the US, many people use the **China Visa Service Center** (☑in the US 800 799 6560; www.mychinavisa.com), which offers prompt service. The procedure takes around 10 to 14 days. CIBT (www.uk.cibt.com) offers a global network and a fast and efficient turnaround.

Hong Kong is a good place to pick up a China visa. **China Travel Service** (CTS; 中国旅行社; Zhōngguó Lǚxíngshè) will be able to obtain one for you, or you can apply directly to the **Visa Office of the People's Republic of China** (☑10-11am & 3-4pm Mon-Fri 852 3413 2424, recorded info 852 3413 2300; www.fmcoprc.gov.hk; 7th fl, Lower Block, China Resources Centre, 26 Harbour Rd, Wan Chai; ⊙9am-noon & 2-5pm Mon-Fri; Ⓜ Wan Chai, exit A3). American and UK passport holders must pay

considerably more for their visas. You must supply two photos. Prices for China visas in Hong Kong are as follows:

Standard visa One-/two-/three-day processing time HK$500/400/200

Double-entry visa One-/two-/three-day processing time HK$600/500/300

Multiple-entry six-month visa One-/two-/three-day processing time HK$800/700/500

Multiple-entry one-, two- or three-year visa One-/two-/three-day processing time HK$1100/1000/800.

You can buy a five-day, Shēnzhèn-only visa (¥168 for most nationalities, ¥469 for Brits; cash only) at the **Luóhú border** (Lo Wu; 9am-10.30pm), **Huánggǎng** (9am-1pm & 2.30-5pm) and **Shékǒu** (8.45am-12.30pm & 2.30-5.30pm). US citizens must buy a visa in advance in Macau or Hong Kong.

VISA-FREE TRANSITS

Citizens from 51 nations (including the US, Australia, Canada, France, Brazil and the UK) can stay in Běijīng for 72 hours without a visa as long as they are in transit to other destinations outside China, have a third-country visa and an air ticket out of Běijīng. Similarly, citizens from the same nations can also transit through Chángshā, Chéngdū, Chóngqìng, Dàlián, Guǎngzhōu, Guìlín, Harbin, Kūnmíng, Qīngdǎo, Shěnyáng, Tiānjīn, Wǔhàn, Xiàmén and Xī'ān for 72 hours visa-free, with the same conditions. Visitors on such three-day stays are not allowed to leave the transit city, with the exception of Chángshā, Chéngdū, Guǎngzhōu and Qīngdǎo, where visitors are given more movement and are not allowed to leave the transit province. Dàlián and Shěnyáng also allow movement between the two cities.

Similarly, citizens of the 51 nations arriving in Shànghǎi, Nánjīng or Hángzhōu can now stay even longer (144 hours) without a visa. An added benefit is that visitors on such six-day stays can move between Shànghǎi, and Zhèjiāng and Jiāngsū provinces – regardless of the transit city of entry. Also, visitors may enter by ports and train stations as well as by air.

For visa-free transit:

➡ You must inform your airline at check-in.

➡ Upon arrival, look for the dedicated immigration counter.

➡ Your transit time is calculated from just after midnight, so you may actually be permitted a little over 72 or 144 hours.

➡ If not staying at a hotel, you must register with a local police station within 24 hours.

➡ Hong Kong, Macau and Taiwan are eligible third countries.

➡ Visitors on the 72-hour visa-free transit must leave the country from the airport of entry.

Check your eligibility as the rules change quickly and new cities are being added.

Hǎinán has a complicated, 15-day visa-free policy for tour groups of five or more citizens of 21 countries. See this website for details: http://en.visithainan.gov.cn.

Three-day visas are also available at the **Macau–Zhūhǎi border** (¥168 for most nationalities, ¥469 for British, US citizens excluded; 8.30am to 12.15pm, 1pm to 6.15pm & 7pm to 10.30pm). US citizens have to buy a visa in advance from Hong Kong or Macau.

Be aware that political events can suddenly make visas more difficult to procure or renew.

When asked about your itinerary on the application form, list standard tourist destinations; if you are considering going to Tibet or western Xīnjiāng, just leave it off the form. The list you give is not binding. Those working in media or journalism may want to profess a different occupation; otherwise, a visa may be refused or a shorter length of stay may be given.

FOR HONG KONG

At the time of writing, most visitors to Hong Kong, including citizens of the EU, Australia, New Zealand, the USA and Canada, could enter and stay for 90 days without a visa. British passport holders get 180 days, while South Africans get 30 days. If you require a visa, apply at a Chinese embassy or consulate before arriving. If you visit Hong Kong from China, you will need a double-entry, multiple-entry or new visa to re-enter China.

FOR MACAU

Most travellers, including citizens of the EU, Australia, New Zealand, the USA, Canada and South Africa, can enter Macau without a visa for between 30 and 90 days. British passport holders get 180 days. Most other nationalities can get a 30-day visa on arrival, which will cost MOP$100/50/200 per adult/child under 12/family. If you're visiting Macau from China and plan to re-enter China, you will need to be on a multiple- or double-entry visa.

Visa Extensions
FOR CHINA

The Foreign Affairs Branch of the local Public Security Bureau (PSB) deals with visa extensions.

First-time extensions of 30 days are usually easy to obtain on single-entry tourist visas, but must be done at least seven days before your visa expires; a further extension of a month may be possible, but you may only get another week. Travellers report generous extensions in provincial towns, but don't bank on this. Popping across to Hong Kong to apply for a new tourist visa is another option.

Extensions to single-entry visas vary in price, depending on your nationality. At the time of writing, US travellers paid ¥185, Canadians ¥165, UK citizens ¥160 and Australians ¥100. Expect to wait up to seven days for your visa extension to be processed.

The penalty for overstaying your visa in China is up to ¥500 per day, and you may even be banned from returning to China for up to 10 years if you overstay by more than 11 days. Some travellers have reported having trouble with officials who read the 'valid until' date on their visa incorrectly. For a one-month travel (L) visa, the 'valid until' date is the date by which you must enter the country, not the date on which your visa expires.

FOR HONG KONG

For tourist-visa extensions, inquire at the **Hong Kong Immigration Department** (☑852 2824 6111; www.immd.gov.hk; 2nd fl, Immigration Tower, 7 Gloucester Rd, Wan Chai; ⏰8.45am-4.30pm Mon-Fri, 9-11.30am Sat; MWan Chai, exit C). Extensions (HK$160) are not readily granted unless there are extenuating circumstances, such as illness.

FOR MACAU

You can obtain a single one-month extension from the **Macau Immigration Department** (☑853 2872 5488; ground fl, Travessa da Amizade; ⏰9am-5pm Mon-Fri).

VISA TYPES

There are 12 visa categories (most travellers will get an L visa).

TYPE	ENGLISH NAME	CHINESE NAME
C	Flight attendant	乘务; *chéngwù*
D	Resident	定居; *dìngjū*
F	Business or student	访问; *fǎngwèn*
G	Transit	过境; *guòjìng*
J1	Journalist (more than six months)	记者1; *jìzhě 1*
J2	Journalist (less than six months)	记者2; *jìzhě 2*
L	Travel	旅行; *lǚxíng*
M	Commercial and trade	贸易; *màoyì*
Q1	Family visits (more than six months)	亲属1; *qīnshǔ 1*
Q2	Family visits (less than six months)	亲属2; *qīnshǔ 2*
R	Talents/needed skills	人才; *réncái*
S1	Visits to foreign relatives/private (more than six months)	私人1; *sīrén 1*
S2	Visits to foreign relatives/private (less than six months)	私人2; *sīrén 2*
X1	Student (more than six months)	学习1; *xuéxí 1*
X2	Student (less than six months)	学习2; *xuéxí 2*
Z	Working	工作; *gōngzuò*

Transport

GETTING THERE & AWAY

Entering China

No particular difficulties exist for travellers entering China. Chinese immigration officers are scrupulous and highly bureaucratic, but not overly officious. The main requirements are a passport that's valid for travel for six months after the expiry date of your visa, and a visa. Travellers arriving in China will receive a health declaration form and an arrivals form to complete.

Air

Airports & Airlines

Hong Kong, Běijīng and Shànghǎi are China's principal international air gateways; Báiyún International Airport in Guǎngzhōu is of lesser, but growing, importance.

Báiyún International Airport (白云国际机场; CAN; Báiyún Guójì Jīchǎng; ☑020 3606 6999;

www.gbiac.net) In Guǎngzhōu; receiving an increasing number of international flights.

Capital Airport (北京首都国际机场; Běijīng Shǒudū Guójì Jīchǎng; PEK; ☑010 6454 1100; www.en.bcia.com.cn) Běijīng's international airport; three terminals.

Hong Kong International Airport (HKG; ☑852 2181 8888; www.hkairport.com) On an island off the northern coast of Lantau and connected to the mainland by several spans.

Hóngqiáo Airport (SHA; 虹桥国际机场; Hóngqiáo Guójì Jīchǎng; ☑021 5260 4620, flight information 021 6268 8899; www.shairport.com) In Shànghǎi's west; domestic flights, some international connections.

Pǔdōng International Airport (PVG; 浦东国际机场; Pǔdōng Guójì Jīchǎng; ☑021 6834 7575, flight information 96990; www.shairport.com) In Shànghǎi's east; international flights.

China doesn't have one single national airline, but large airlines that operate

both domestic and international flights. The largest are **Air China** (www.airchina.com); **China Eastern Airlines** (www.ce-air.com), based in Shànghǎi; and **China Southern Airlines** (www.cs-air.com), based in Guǎngzhōu. They fly to China from the US, Europe, Australia/New Zealand and other parts of Asia. Benefits can include a generous checked luggage allowance, and sometimes a night's accommodation when stopping over on the way to other destinations – great for visa-free travel. Multiple international carriers also fly to China along similar routes.

Some smaller airlines that offer international flights to China include:

AirAsia (www.airasia.com)

Asiana Airlines (www.flyasiana.com)

Dragon Air (www.dragonair.com)

Tiger Airways (www.tigerairways.com)

Vietnam Airlines (www.vietnamair.com.vn)

CLIMATE CHANGE & TRAVEL

Every form of transport that relies on carbon-based fuel generates CO_2, the main cause of human-induced climate change. Modern travel is dependent on aeroplanes, which might use less fuel per kilometre per person than most cars but travel much greater distances. The altitude at which aircraft emit gases (including CO_2) and particles also contributes to their climate change impact. Many websites offer 'carbon calculators' that allow people to estimate the carbon emissions generated by their journey and, for those who wish to do so, to offset the impact of the greenhouse gases emitted with contributions to portfolios of climate-friendly initiatives throughout the world. Lonely Planet offsets the carbon footprint of all staff and author travel.

Tickets

The cheapest tickets to Hong Kong and China exist on price comparison websites or in discount agencies in Chinatowns around the world. Budget and student-travel agents offer cheap tickets, but the real bargains are with agents that deal with the Chinese, who regularly return home. Airfares to China peak between June and September.

The cheapest flights to China are with airlines requiring a stopover such as Air France to Běijīng via Paris, or Malaysia Airlines to Běijīng via Kuala Lumpur.

The best direct ticket deals are available from China's international carriers, such as China Eastern Airlines, Air China or China Southern Airlines.

Land

China shares borders with Afghanistan, Bhutan, India, Kazakhstan, Kyrgyzstan, Laos, Mongolia, Myanmar (Burma), Nepal, North Korea, Pakistan, Russia, Tajikistan and Vietnam; the borders with Afghanistan, Bhutan and India are closed. There are also official border crossings between China and its special administrative regions, Hong Kong and Macau.

Lonely Planet *China* guides may be confiscated by officials, primarily at the Vietnam–China border.

Kazakhstan

Border crossings from Ürümqi to Kazakhstan are via border posts at Korgas, Ālāshànkǒu, Tāchéng and Jímùnǎi. Ensure you have a valid Kazakhstan visa (obtainable, at the time of writing, in Ürümqi, or from Běijīng) or China visa.

Apart from Ālāshànkǒu, which links China and Kazakhstan via train, all other border crossings are by bus; you can generally get a bike over, however. Two trains weekly (32 hours) run between Ürümqi and Almaty, and one train per week runs to Astana.

Remember that borders open and close frequently due to changes in government policy; additionally, many are only open when the weather permits. It's always best to check with the **Public Security Bureau** (PSB; Gōng'ānjú) in Ürümqi for the official line.

Kyrgyzstan

There are two routes between China and Kyrgyzstan: one between Kashgar and Osh, via the Irkeshtam Pass; and one between Kashgar and Bishkek, via the dramatic 3752m Torugart Pass.

Laos

From the Měnglà district in China's southern Yúnnán province, you can enter Laos via Boten in Luang Nam Tha province (from Móhàn on the China side), while a daily bus runs between Vientiane and Kūnmíng and also from Jǐnghóng to Luang Nam Tha in Laos.

On-the-spot visas for Laos are available at the border, the price of which depends on your nationality (although you cannot get a China visa here).

Mongolia

From Běijīng, the Trans-Mongolian Railway trains and the K23 train run to Ulaanbaatar. There are also trains and regular buses between Hohhot and the border town of Erenhot (Èrlián). Mongolian visas on the Chinese side can be acquired in Běijīng, Hohhot or Erenhot.

Myanmar (Burma)

The famous Burma Road runs from Kūnmíng in Yúnnán province to the Burmese city of Lashio. The road is open to travellers carrying permits for the region north of Lashio, although you can legally cross the border in only one direction – from the Chinese side (Jiēgào) into Myanmar. However, at the time of writing the border was not open to foreign travellers and flying in from Kūnmíng was the only option. Myanmar visas can only be arranged in Kūnmíng or Běijīng.

Nepal

The 865km road connecting Lhasa with Kathmandu is known as the Friendship Highway, currently only traversable for foreign travellers by rented vehicle. It's a spectacular trip across the Tibetan plateau, the highest point being Gyatso-la Pass (5248m).

Visas for Nepal can be obtained in Lhasa, or at the border at Kodari.

When travelling from Nepal to Tibet, foreigners still have to arrange transport through tour agencies in Kathmandu. Access to Tibet can, however, be restricted for months at a time without warning.

North Korea

Visas for North Korea are not especially hard to arrange, although it is not possible to travel independently so

---

INTERNATIONAL TRAIN ROUTES

In addition to the Trans-Siberian and Trans-Mongolian rail services, the following routes can be travelled by train:

➡ Hung Hom station in Kowloon (Jiǔlóng; Hong Kong; www.mtr.com.hk) to Guǎngzhōu, Shànghǎi, Běijīng

➡ Pyongyang (North Korea) to Běijīng

➡ Almaty (Kazakhstan) to Ürümqi

➡ Astana (Kazakhstan) to Ürümqi

➡ Běijīng to Ulaanbaatar (Mongolia)

➡ Běijīng to Hanoi (Vietnam)

A good resource is the website **The Man in Seat Sixty-One** (www.seat61.com).

you will need to be on a pre-planned tour. Those interested in travelling to North Korea on tours from Běijīng should contact Nicholas Bonner or Simon Cockerell at **Koryo Tours** (Map p92; 🖉 Běijīng 010 6416 7544; www.koryogroup.com; 27 Beisanlitun Nan; Ⓢ Line 2 to Dongsi Shitiao, exit C, or Line 10 to Tuanjiehu, exit A).

Four international express trains (K27 and K28) run between Běijīng train station and Pyongyang.

Pakistan

The exciting trip on the Kar-akoram Hwy, said to be the world's highest public international highway, is an excellent way to get to or from Chinese Central Asia. There are buses from Kashgar for the two-day trip to the Pakistani town of Sost via Tashkurgan when the pass is open. Pakistani visas are no longer available to tourists on arrival (and visas are difficult to get in Běijīng), so the safest option is to arrive in China with a visa obtained in your home country. Check the current situation as this could change.

Russia

The train from Harbin East to Vladivostok is no longer running, but you can take the train to Suífēnhé and take an onward connection there.

The Trans-Mongolian (via Erenhot) and Trans-Manchurian (via Harbin) branches of the Trans-Siberian Railway run from Běijīng to Moscow.

There are also border crossings 9km from Mǎn-zhōulǐ and at Hēihé.

Tajikistan

At the time of writing, the Qolma (Kulma) Pass, linking Kashgar with Murghab, was only rarely open to foreign travellers.

Vietnam

Visas are unobtainable at border crossings; Vietnam visas can be acquired in Běijīng, Kūnmíng, Hong Kong and Nánníng. China visas can be obtained in Hanoi.

Sea Routes

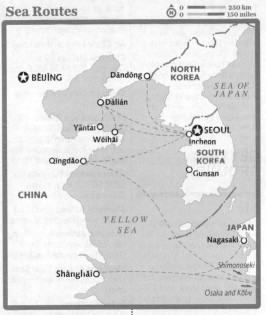

FRIENDSHIP PASS

China's busiest border with Vietnam is at the obscure Vietnamese town of Dong Dang, 164km northeast of Hanoi. The closest Chinese town to the border is Píngxiáng in Guǎngxī province, about 10km north of the actual border gate.

Seven Hanoi-bound buses run from Nánníng via the Friendship Pass; twice-weekly trains (T5 and T6) connect Běijīng and Hanoi (via Nánníng), while a daily train (T8701 and T8702) links Hanoi with Nánníng.

HÉKŎU

The Hékŏu–Lao Cai border crossing is 468km from Kūn-míng and 294km from Hanoi. At the time of writing, the only way to reach Vietnam via Hékŏu was by bus from Kūnmíng.

MONG CAI

A third, but little-known border crossing is at Mong Cai in the northeast corner of Vietnam, just opposite the Chinese city of Dōngxīng and around 200km south of Nánníng.

River

At the time of writing, fast ferries from Jǐnghóng in Yún-nan to Chiang Saen in Thailand had been suspended.

Sea

Japan

There are weekly ferries between Osaka and Kōbe and Shànghǎi. There are also twice-weekly boats from Qīngdǎo to Shimonoseki. The weekly ferry from the Tiānjīn International Cruise Home Port to Kōbe (神户; Shénhù) had been suspended indefinitely at the time of writing.

Check in two hours before departure for international sailings.

South Korea

International ferries connect the South Korean port of Incheon with Wēihǎi, Qīngdǎo, Yāntái, Dàlián and Dāndōng. Tickets can be bought cheaply at the pier, or from China International Travel Service (CITS; Zhōngguó Guójì Lǚxíng-shè) for a very steep premium.

Taiwan

Daily ferries ply the route between Xiàmén and Kinmen Island in Taiwan, from where you can fly to other major cities in Taiwan. You can also catch a ferry from Fúzhōu's Máwěi ferry terminal to Taiwan's archipelago of Matzu, from where there are boats to Keelung and flights to other cities in Taiwan.

GETTING AROUND

Air

China's air network is extensive and growing. The civil aviation fleet is expected to triple in size over the next two decades, up to 70 new airports were planned for construction in recent years alone and 100 more were to be expanded or upgraded. Air safety and quality have improved considerably, but the speed of change generates its own problems: a serious shortage of qualified personnel to fly planes means China needed a reported 18,000 new pilots by 2015. When deciding between flying and using high-speed rail, note that flight delays in China are the worst in the world (according to FlightStats), while trains almost always leave on time.

Planes vary in style and comfort. You may get a hot meal, or just a small piece of cake and an airline souvenir.

Shuttle buses usually run from Civil Aviation Administration of China (CAAC; Zhōngguó Mínháng) offices in towns and cities throughout China to the airport, often running via other stops. For domestic flights, arrive at the airport one hour before departure.

Remember to keep your baggage receipt on your ticket as you'll need to show it when collecting your luggage.

Airlines in China

The CAAC is the civil aviation authority for numerous airlines. Some listed here also have subsidiary airlines. Not all Chinese airline websites have English-language capability.

Air China (www.airchina.com)

Chengdu Airlines (✈in Chengdu 028 6666 8888; www.chengduair.cc)

China Eastern Airlines (www.ce-air.com)

China Southern Airlines (✈in Guǎngzhōu 4006 695 539; www.csair.com/en) Serves a web of air routes, including Běijīng, Shànghǎi, Xī'ān and Tiānjīn.

Hainan Airlines (✈in Hǎinán 0898 95339; www.hainan airlines.com)

Shandong Airlines (✈400 60 96777; www.shandongair.com.cn)

Shanghai Airlines (✈in Shànghǎi 95530; www.ceair.com) Owned by China Eastern Airlines.

Shenzhen Airlines (✈in Shēnzhèn 95080; www.shenzhenair.com)

Sichuan Airlines (✈in Chéngdū 4008 300 999; www.scal.com.cn)

Spring Airlines (✈in Shànghǎi 021 95524; www.china-sss.com) Has connections between Shànghǎi and tourist destinations such as Qīngdǎo, Guìlín, Xiàmén and Sānyà.

Tianjin Airlines (✈in Tiānjīn 950710; www.tianjin-air.com)

Tibet Airlines (✈4008 0891 88; www.tibetairlines.com.cn; ⊗7am-9pm) Domestic connections all over China from Lhasa.

Tickets

Except during major festivals and holidays, tickets are easy to purchase, with an oversupply of airline seats. Purchase tickets from branches of the CAAC nationwide, airline offices, travel agents or the travel desk of your hotel; travel agents will usually offer a better discount than airline offices. Discounts are common, except when flying into large cities such as Shànghǎi and Běijīng on the weekend, when the full fare can be the norm. Fares are calculated according to one-way travel, with return tickets simply costing twice the single fare. If flying from Hong Kong or Macau to mainland China, note that these are classified as international flights; it is much cheaper to travel overland into Shēnzhèn, Zhūhǎi or Guǎngzhōu and fly from there.

You can use credit cards at most CAAC offices and travel agents. Departure tax is included in the ticket price.

Ctrip Excellent hotel booking, air and train ticketing website, with English helpline. Useful app available.

Elong Hotel and air ticket booking, with English helpline.

Travel Zen Air tickets and hotel bookings. Chinese-only website.

Bicycle

Bikes (自行车; zìxíngchē) are an excellent method for getting around China's cities and tourist sights. They can also be invaluable for exploring the countryside and surrounding towns.

Hire

Hángzhōu has the world's largest bicycle-share network, with docking stations dotted around the town; however, its success (and foreigner-friendly ease of use) has only been fitfully replicated elsewhere in China. Generally, the best places to try are youth hostels, which rent out bicycles – as do many hotels, although the latter are more expensive.

Bikes can be hired by the day or by the hour; it is also possible to hire for more than one day. Rental rates vary depending on where you find yourself, but rates start at around ¥10 to ¥15 per day in cities such as Běijīng.

Touring

Cycling through China allows you to go when you want, to see what you want and at your own pace. It can also be an extremely cheap, as well as a highly authentic, way to see the land.

You will have virtually unlimited freedom of movement but, considering the size of China, you will need to combine your cycling days with trips by train, bus, boat, taxi or even planes, especially if you want to avoid particularly steep regions, or areas where the roads are poor or the climate is cold.

A basic packing list for cyclists includes a good repair kit, sunscreen, waterproofs, fluorescent strips and camping equipment. Ensure you have adequate clothing, as many routes will be taking you to considerable altitude. Road maps in Chinese are essential for asking locals for directions.

BikeChina (www.bikechina.com) arranges tours and is a good source of information for cyclists coming to China.

Boat

Boat services within China are limited, especially with the growth of high-speed rail and expressways. They're most common in coastal areas, where you are likely to use a boat to reach offshore islands such as Pǔtuóshān or Hǎinán, or the islands off Hong Kong. The Yāntái–Dàlián ferry will probably survive because it saves hundreds of kilometres of overland travel, although a super-long undersea tunnel is in on the drawing board.

The best-known river trip is the three-day ride along the Yangzi (Cháng Jiāng) from Chóngqìng to Yichang. The Lí River (Lí Jiāng) trip from Guìlín to Yángshuò is popular.

Hong Kong employs an out-and-out navy of vessels that connects with the territory's myriad islands, and a number of boats run between the territory and other parts of China, including Macau, Zhūhǎi, Shékǒu (for Shēnzhèn) and Zhōngshān.

Boat tickets can be purchased from passenger ferry terminals or through travel agents.

Bus

Long-distance bus (长途公共汽车; *chángtú gōnggòng qìchē*) services are extensive

and reach places you cannot reach by train; with the increasing number of intercity highways, journeys are getting quicker.

Buses & Stations

Routes between large cities sport larger, cleaner and more comfortable fleets of private buses, some equipped with toilets and hostesses handing out snacks and mineral water; shorter and more far-flung routes still rely on rattling minibuses into which as many fares as possible are crammed. Buses often wait until they fill up before leaving, or (exasperatingly) trawl the streets looking for fares.

Sleeper buses (卧铺客车; *wòpù kèchē*) ply popular long-haul routes, costing around double the price of a normal bus service. Bunks can be short, however, and there have been several fatal fires in recent years.

Bus journey times should be used as a rough guide only. You can estimate times for bus journeys on nonhighway routes by calculating the distance against a speed of 25km per hour.

All cities and most towns have one or more long-distance bus stations (长途汽车站; *chángtú qìchēzhàn*), generally located in relation to the direction the bus heads in. Most bus stations have a left-luggage counter. In many cities, the train station forecourt doubles as a bus station.

Tickets

Tickets are getting more expensive as fuel prices increase, but are cheaper and easier to get than train tickets; turn up at the bus station and buy your ticket on the spot. The earlier you buy, the closer to the front of the bus you will sit, although you may not be able to buy tickets prior to your day of travel. At the time of writing, ID was required for the purchase of bus tickets in restive Xīnjiāng.

Tickets can be hard to procure during national holiday periods.

Dangers & Annoyances

Breakdowns can be a hassle, and some rural roads and provincial routes (especially in the southwest, Tibet and the northwest) remain in bad condition. Precipitous drops, pot holes, dangerous road surfaces and reckless drivers mean accidents remain common. Long-distance journeys can also be cramped and noisy, with Hong Kong films and cacophonous karaoke looped on overhead TVs, and drivers continuously leaning on the horn – taking a music player is crucial for one's sanity. Note the following when travelling by bus:

➡ Seat belts are a rarity in many provinces.

➡ Take plenty of warm clothes on buses to high-altitude destinations in winter. A breakdown in frozen conditions can prove lethal for those unprepared.

➡ Take a lot of extra water on routes across areas such as the Taklamakan Desert.

Car & Motorcycle

Hiring a car in China has always been complicated or impossible for foreign visitors and in mainland China is currently limited to Běijīng and Shànghǎi, cities that both have frequently gridlocked roads. Throw in the dangers, complexity of Chinese roads for first-time users and the costs of driving in China and it makes more sense to use the subway/metro system and taxis. Hiring a car with a driver from your hotel is possible, but it's generally far cheaper and more convenient to hire a taxi for the day instead.

Driving Licences

To drive in Hong Kong and Macau, you will need an International Driving Permit. Foreigners can drive motorcycles if they are residents in China and have an official Chinese motorcycle licence. International Driving Permits are not accepted in China.

Hire

Běijīng Capital Airport has a Vehicle Administration Office where you can have a temporary three-month driving licence issued (an international driver's licence is insufficient). This will involve checking your driving licence and a simple medical exam (including an eyesight test).

You will need this licence before you can hire a car from Hertz, which has branches at Capital Airport. There are also branches in both central Běijīng and Shànghǎi. Hire cars from Hertz start from ¥230 per day (up to 150km per day; ¥20,000 deposit). Avis also has a growing network around China, with car rental starting from ¥200 per day (¥5000 deposit).

Road Rules

Cars in China drive on the right-hand side of the road. Even skilled drivers will be unprepared for China's roads: in the cities, cars lunge from all angles and chaos abounds.

Local Transport

Long-distance transport in China is good, but local transport is less efficient, except for cities with metro systems. The choice of local transport is diverse but vehicles can be slow and overburdened, and the network confusing for visitors. Hiring a car is often impractical, while hiring a bike can be inadequate. Unless the town is small, walking is often too tiring. On the plus side, local transport is cheap, taxis are usually ubiquitous and affordable, and clean and efficient metro systems continue to rapidly expand in large tourist towns.

Bus

With extensive networks, buses are an excellent way to get around town, but foreign travellers rarely use them. Ascending a bus, point to your destination on a map and the conductor (seated near the door) will sell you the right ticket. The conductor will usually tell you where to disembark, provided they remember. In conductor-less buses, you put money for your fare into a slot near the driver as you embark.

➜ Fares are very cheap (usually ¥1 to ¥2) but buses may be packed.

➜ In cities such as Běijīng, Shànghǎi and Hong Kong, a locally purchased transport card can be used on buses.

➜ Navigation is tricky for non-Chinese speakers as bus routes at bus stops are generally listed in Chinese.

➜ In Běijīng, Shànghǎi and other tourist towns, stops will be announced in English.

➜ Always have change ready if there is no conductor.

➜ Buses with snowflake motifs are air-conditioned.

➜ Disembark from the back door.

Subway, Metro & Light Rail

Going underground or using light rail is fast, efficient and cheap; most networks are either very new or relatively recent and can be found in a rapidly growing number of cities, including Běijīng, Chéngdū, Chóngqìng, Dàlián, Guǎngzhōu, Hángzhōu, Hong Kong, Kūnmíng, Shànghǎi, Shěnyáng, Shēnzhèn, Sūzhōu, Tiānjīn, Wǔhàn and Xī'ān.

Taxi

Taxis (出租汽车; *chūzū qìchē*) are cheap and easy to find. Taxi rates per kilometre are clearly marked on a sticker on the rear side window of the taxi; flag-fall varies from city to city, and depends upon the size and quality of the vehicle. Most taxis have meters but they may only be switched on in larger towns and cities. If the meter is not used (on an excursion out of town, for example, or when hiring a taxi

for the day or half-day), negotiate a price before you set off and write the fare down. If you want the meter used, ask for *dǎbiǎo* (打表). Also ask for a receipt (发票; *fāpiào*); if you leave something in the taxi, you can have the taxi located by its vehicle number printed on the receipt.

Some more tips:

➜ Congregation points include train and long-distance bus stations, but usually you can just flag taxis down.

➜ Taxi drivers rarely speak any English – have your destination written down in characters.

➜ If you have communication problems, consider using your mobile to phone your hotel for staff to interpret.

➜ You can hire taxis on a daily or half-day basis, often at reasonable rates (always bargain).

➜ To use the same driver again, ask for his or her card (名片; *míngpiàn*).

➜ In many provinces, taxis often cover long-distance bus routes. They generally charge around 30% to 50% more but are much faster. You'll need to wait for four passengers.

Other Local Transport

A variety of ramshackle transport options exist across China; always agree on a price in advance (and preferably have it written down).

➜ Motor pedicabs are enclosed three-wheeled vehicles (often the same price as taxis).

➜ Pedicabs are pedal-powered versions of motor pedicabs.

➜ Motorbike riders also offer lifts in some towns for what should be half the price of a regular taxi. You must wear a helmet – the driver will provide one.

Train

For information on train travel, see the China by Train chapter, p1015.

China by Train

Trains are the best way to travel long distance around China in reasonable speed and comfort. They are also adventurous, exciting, fun, practical and efficient, and ticket prices are reasonable to boot. Colossal investment over recent years has put high-speed rail at the heart of China's rapid modernisation drive. You really don't have to be a trainspotter to find China's railways a riveting subculture; as a plus you'll get to meet the Chinese people at their most relaxed and sociable.

CHINA'S TRAIN NETWORK

One of the world's most extensive rail networks, passenger railways penetrate every province in China and high-speed connections are suddenly everywhere. In line with China's frantic economic development and the pressures of transporting 1.4 billion people across the world's third-largest nation, expansion of China's rail network over the past decade has been mind-boggling.

The network currently totals over 103,000km in length. In China, thousands of kilometres of track are laid every year and new express trains have been zipping across the land since 2007, shrinking once daunting distances. State-of-the-art train stations are ceaselessly appearing, many to serve

high-speed links. You can climb aboard a train in Běijīng or Shànghǎi and alight in Tibet's capital (although ticket scarcity for trains into Lhasa means it's easier to fly in and take the train out); lines are poking further into Tibet, with a line to Shigatse. The time to get to Yánjí (near the South Korean border) from Chángchūn in northeast China has recently been slashed by hours. The highly anticipated Xī'ān–Chéngdū line will hopefully open by 2018 and will cut travel times from 13 hours to under three.

With the advent of high-speed D, G and C class express trains, getting between major cities is increasingly a breeze (albeit far more expensive than regular fast trains). High-speed rail has put the squeeze on numerous domestic air routes and the punctuality of trains sees far fewer delays than air travel. Useful high-speed links that have opened in recent years have connected Běijīng and Xī'ān, Lánzhōu and Ürümqi, and Tiānjīn and Bǎoding; there is even talk of extending links through Central Asia and Turkey to Bulgaria. Down south, China is planning a high-speed link from Kūnmíng in Yúnnán to Singapore, via Laos, Thailand and Malaysia.

TRAIN TRAVEL

Trains are generally highly punctual in China and are usually a safe way to travel.

Train stations are often conveniently close to the centre of town. Travelling on sleeper berths at night means you can frequently arrive at your destination first thing in the morning, saving a night's hotel accommodation. Think ahead, get your tickets early and you can sleep your way around a lot of China.

On entering a large, old-style station (such as Běijīng West Train Station), you will have to find the correct waiting room number, displayed on an illuminated screen as you walk in. Modern stations (such as Shànghǎi Hóngqiáo Train Station) are more straightforward and intelligently designed, without waiting rooms; instead your platform number will appear on the screen.

Trolleys of food and drink are wheeled along carriages during the trip, but prices are high and the selection is limited. You can also load up on mineral water and snacks at stations, where hawkers sell items from platform stalls. Long-distance trains should have a canteen carriage (餐厅车厢; cāntīng chēxiāng); they are sometimes open through the night.

In each class of sleeper, linen is clean and changed for each journey; beds are generally bedbug-free.

If taking a sleeper train, you will generally be required to exchange your paper ticket for a plastic or metal card with your bunk number on it.

REGULAR TRAINS

TYPE	PINYIN	CHINESE	TOP SPEED
Z class (express)	*zhídá*	直达	160km/h
T class	*tèkuài*	特快	140km/h
K class	*kuàisù*	快速	120km/h

The conductor then knows when you are due to disembark, and will awake you in time to return your ticket to you. Some tips:

➡ Don't wait to board your train until the last minute, as queues outside the train station entrance can be long.

➡ You are required to pass your bags through a security scanner at the entrance.

➡ Keep passports handy when entering a station as checks will match the name on your ticket with the name on your passport.

➡ Keep your ticket handy after disembarking the train as there can be checks when exiting the platform and ticket-fed turnstiles in newer stations.

➡ On a nonsleeper, ask a member of staff or a fellow passenger to tell you when your station arrives.

TRAIN TYPES

Chinese train numbers are usually (but not always) prefixed by a letter, designating the category of train.

The fastest, most luxurious and expensive intercity trains are the streamlined, high-speed C, D and G trains, which rapidly shuttle between major cities.

D class trains were the first high-speed trains to appear and breathlessly glide around China at high speed, offering substantial comfort and regular services. Their temperature-regulated 1st-class carriages have mobile and laptop chargers; seats are two abreast with ample legroom and TVs. Second-class carriages have five seats in two rows. G class trains are faster than D class trains, but have limited luggage space.

Less fast express classes include the overnight Z class trains, and the older and more basic T and K class trains.

TICKETS

It is possible to upgrade (补票; *bǔpiào*) your ticket once aboard your train. If you have a standing ticket, for example, find the conductor and upgrade to a hard seat, soft seat or hard sleeper (if there are any available).

Soft Sleeper

Soft sleepers are a very comfortable way to travel and work perfectly as mobile hotels; tickets cost much more than hard-sleeper tickets and often sell out, however, so book early. Soft sleepers vary between trains and the best are on the more recent D and Z class trains. All Z class trains are soft-sleeper trains, with very comfortable, up-to-date berths. A few T class trains offer two-berth compartments, with toilet.

Tickets for upper berths are slightly cheaper than for lower berths. Expect to share with total strangers. If you are asleep, an attendant will wake you to prepare you to disembark so you will have plenty of time to ready your things. Available on some lines, two-bed deluxe soft sleepers usually have a toilet and sink. VIP sleepers, essentially three-bed compartments which one person can book in its entirety, are available on the Kūnmíng–Lìjiāng route. Soft sleeper carriages contain:

➡ four air-conditioned bunks (upper and lower) in a closed compartment

➡ bedding on each berth and a lockable door to the carriage corridor

➡ meals, flat-screen TVs and power sockets on some routes

➡ a small table and stowing space for your bags

➡ a hot-water flask for drinking (plain or for tea) or instant noodles, filled by an attendant (one per compartment).

Hard Sleeper

Hard sleepers are available on slower and less modern T, K and N class trains, as well as trains without a letter prefix. As with soft sleepers, they serve very nicely as an overnight hotel.

HIGH-SPEED TRAINS

TYPE	PINYIN	CHINESE	TOP SPEED
C class	*chéngjì*	城际	350km/h
D class	*dòngchē*	动车	250km/h
G class	*gāotiě*	高铁	350km/h

There is a small price difference between the numbered berths, with the lowest bunk (下铺; *xiàpù*) the most expensive and the highest bunk (上铺; *shàngpù*) the cheapest. The middle bunk (中铺; *zhōngpù*) is a good choice, as all and sundry invade the lower berth to use it as a seat during the day, while the top one has little headroom and puts you near the speakers. As with soft sleepers, an attendant will wake you in advance of your station.

Hard-sleeper tickets are the most difficult to buy; you almost always need to buy these a few days in advance. Expect:

➡ doorless compartments with half a dozen bunks in three tiers

➡ sheets, pillows and blankets on each berth

➡ a no-smoking policy

➡ lights and speakers out at around 10pm

➡ a hot-water flask, filled by an attendant (one per compartment)

➡ trolleys passing by selling food and drink

Seats

Soft-seat class is more comfortable but not nearly as common as hard-seat class. First-class (一等; *yīděng*) and 2nd-class (二等; *èrděng*) soft seats are available in D, C and G class high-speed trains. G class trains also offer business class and/or VIP seats, which include a hot meal and added comfort. High-speed trains are truly nonsmoking, unlike other trains, which allow smoking between carriages, inevitably carrying through into the carriages.

First-class comes with TVs, mobile phone and laptop charging points, and seats arranged two abreast. Second-class soft seats are also very comfortable; staff are very courteous throughout. Overcrowding is not permitted and power points are available. On older trains, soft-seat carriages are often double-decker, and are not as plush as the faster and more modern high-speed express trains.

Hard-seat class is not available on the faster and

CHINA TRAIN ROUTES

ROUTE	DURATION	FARE (SEAT/SLEEPER)
Běijīng West–Xī'ān North	5½-6hr	2nd/1st ¥516/825
Běijīng West–Guìlín	10½hr	2nd/1st class ¥806/1250
Běijīng–Dàtóng	6¼hr	Hard seat/sleeper ¥54/113
Běijīng South–Hángzhōu	5hr	2nd/1st class ¥540/909
Běijīng West–Kūnmíng	34hr	Hard seat/sleeper ¥317/575
Běijīng West–Lhasa	41hr	Hard/soft sleeper ¥815/1200
Běijīng South–Qīngdǎo	4½hr	2nd/1st class ¥314/474
Běijīng South–Shànghǎi Hóngqiáo	5½hr	2nd/1st class ¥553/933
Běijīng South–Tiānjīn	33min	2nd/1st class ¥54/65
Shànghǎi Hóngqiáo–Hángzhōu	1hr	2nd/1st class ¥77/117
Shànghǎi Hóngqiáo–Shēnzhèn North	10½-11½hr	Hard seat/sleeper ¥479/597
Shànghǎi–Lhasa	48hr	Hard seat/sleeper ¥403/896
Shànghǎi Hóngqiáo–Nánjīng South	1½hr	2nd/1st class ¥135/230
Shànghǎi Hóngqiáo–Wǔhàn	5-6hr	2nd/1st class ¥302/426
Shànghǎi Hóngqiáo–Xiàmén North	6½-8hr	2nd/1st class ¥331/416
Shànghǎi–Xī'ān North	11hr	2nd-class seat/soft sleeper ¥338/834
Píngyáo–Xī'ān North	3hr	2nd/1st class ¥150/188
Shēnzhèn North–Guìlín North	3hr	2nd/1st class ¥212/265
Kūnmíng–Lìjiāng	7-10hr	Hard/soft sleeper ¥152/245
Kūnmíng–Chéngdū	17½hr	Hard seat/sleeper ¥139/270
Kūnmíng–Guìlín	19hr	Hard seat/sleeper ¥153/296
Ürümqi–Kashgar	17hr	Hard/soft sleeper ¥344/537
Wǔhàn–Guǎngzhōu South	4hr	2nd/1st class ¥464/739
Xī'ān North–Luòyáng Lóngmén	2hr	2nd/1st class ¥175/280
Běijīng West–Píngyáo	4hr	2nd/1st class ¥183/255

plusher C, D and G class trains, and is only found on T and K class trains and trains without a number prefix; a handful of Z class trains have hard seats. Hard-seat class generally has padded seats, but it's hard on your sanity: often unclean and noisy, and painful on the long haul.

Since hard seat is the only class most locals can afford, it's packed to the gills.

You should get a ticket with an assigned seat number; if seats have sold out, ask for a standing ticket, which gets you on the train, where you may find a seat or can upgrade. Otherwise you will have to stand in the carriage or between carriages (with the smokers).

Buying Tickets

The Achilles heel of China's overburdened rail system, buying tickets can be a pain.

Most tickets are one-way only, with prices calculated per kilometre and adjustments made depending on class of train, availability of air-con, type of sleeper and bunk positioning.

Tips on buying tickets:

➡ Never aim to get a sleeper ticket on the day of travel – plan and purchase ahead.

➡ Most tickets can be booked 18 days in advance when booking in person at ticket offices and 20 days when booking online.

➡ Buying tickets for hard-seat carriages at short notice is usually no hassle, but it may be a standing ticket rather than a numbered seat.

➡ Tickets can be purchased only with cash or bank cards that are part of the Chinese UnionPay network.

➡ You will need your passport when buying a ticket (the number is printed on your ticket). Your name will also appear on tickets bought online.

➡ All automated ticket machines (eg at Shànghǎi Train Station) require Chinese ID – your passport will not work.

➡ Buying tickets around the Chinese New Year and the 1 May and 1 October holiday periods can be very difficult.

➡ Tickets on many routes (such as to Lhasa) can be very hard to get in July and August; consider flying to distant destinations.

➡ Expect to queue for up to 30 minutes for a ticket at the station; offices outside of the station are often less busy.

➡ Avoid black-market tickets: your passport number must be on the ticket.

➡ Refunds for lost train tickets involve purchasing a new ticket and getting a refund at the other end once it has been proved no one occupied your seat.

➡ If you miss your D or G class train, you will be allowed to take the next available train on the same day only at no charge. For all other trains, your ticket is forfeited (unless your connecting train was late).

➡ Booking tickets on apps lets you avoid missing out. A fee of ¥20 to ¥40 applies, and tickets still need to

be picked up from a ticket collection window (often with a queue) at any train station.

Ticket Offices & Buying Online

Ticket offices (售票厅; shòupiàotīng) at train stations are usually to one side of the main train station entrance. Automated ticket machines operate on some routes but never accept foreign passports as ID. At large stations there should be a window staffed by someone with basic English skills.

Alternatively, independent train ticket offices usually exist elsewhere in town, where tickets can be purchased for a ¥5 commission without the same kind of queues; we list these where possible. Larger post offices may also sell train tickets. Your hotel will also be able to rustle up a ticket for you for a commission, and so can a travel agent.

It's cheaper to buy your ticket at the station, but tickets can be bought online at the following (China DIY Travel is the cheapest) and collected from any train before travel:

China DIY Travel (www.china -diy-travel.com; 6 Chaoyang Park Nanlu; 朝阳公园南路6号; commission per ticket $10)

China Trip Advisor (www. chinatripadvisor.com)

Ctrip (www.english.ctrip.com)

You can also find English-language train timetables on these websites.

TRAIN TICKETS

TICKET TYPE	PINYIN	CHINESE
soft sleeper	ruǎnwò	软卧
hard sleeper	yìngwò	硬卧
soft seat	ruǎnzuò	软座
hard seat	yìngzuò	硬座
standing ticket	wúzuò or zhànpiào	无座\站票

For trains from Hong Kong to Shànghǎi, Guǎngzhōu or Běijīng, tickets can be ordered online at no mark-up from KCRC (www.mtr.com.hk); however, for Běijīng or Shànghǎi a faster alternative is the high-speed trains from Shēnzhèn to Shànghǎi (D train) and Běijīng (G train), which take around 10 hours compared to 20 to 24 hours for departures from Hong Kong.

To get a refund (退票; *tuìpiào*) on an unused ticket, look for the marked windows at large train stations, where you can get from 80 to 95% of your ticket value back, depending on how many days prior to the departure date you cancel.

TRAVELLING THE TRANS-SIBERIAN RAILWAY

Rolling out of Europe and into Asia, through eight time zones and over 9289km of taiga, steppe and desert, the Trans-Siberian Railway and its connecting routes constitute one of the most famous and most romantic of the world's great train journeys.

There are, in fact, three railways. The 'true' **Trans-Siberian** line runs from Moscow to Vladivostok. But the routes traditionally referred to as the Trans-Siberian Railway are the two branches that veer off the main line in eastern Siberia for Běijīng.

Since the first option excludes China, most readers of this guide will be choosing between the **Trans-Mongolian** and the **Trans-Manchurian** railway lines. The Trans-Mongolian route (Běijīng to Moscow; 7865km) is faster, but requires an additional visa and another border crossing – on the plus side, you also get to see some of the Mongolian countryside. The Trans-Manchurian route is longer (Běijīng to Moscow; 9025km).

Trans-Mongolian Railway

Trains offer deluxe two-berth compartments (with shared shower), 1st-class four-berth compartments and 2nd-class four-berth compartments. Tickets for 2nd class/1st class/deluxe cost from around ¥3496/5114/5064 to Moscow, ¥1222/1723/1883 to Ulaanbaatar and ¥2559/3734/4052 to Novosibirsk. Ticket prices are cheaper if you travel in a group. The K23 service departs on Sunday (2nd/1st class ¥1259/1849, 11.22am, 30 hours) and terminates at Ulaanbaatar on Monday.

From Běijīng Train K3 leaves Běijīng Train Station on its five-day journey to Moscow at 11.22am every Tuesday, passing through Dàtóng, Ulaanbaatar and Novosibirsk before arriving in Moscow the following Monday at 1.58pm.

From Moscow Train K4 leaves at 9.35pm on Tuesday, arriving in Běijīng Train Station the following Monday at 2.04pm. Departure and arrival times may fluctuate slightly.

Trans-Manchurian Railway

Trains have 1st-class two-berth compartments and 2nd-class four-berth compartments; prices are similar to those on the Trans-Mongolian Railway.

From Běijīng Train K19 departs Běijīng Train Station at 11pm on Saturday, arriving in Moscow (via Manzhōulǐ) the following Friday at 5.58pm.

From Moscow Train K20 leaves Moscow at 11.58pm on Saturday, arriving at Běijīng Train Station the following Friday at 5.32am. Departure and arrival times may fluctuate.

Buying Tickets

Book well in advance (especially in summer); in Běijīng tickets can be conveniently purchased and booked in advance in central Běijīng from **CITS** (China International Travel Service; 中国国际旅行社; Zhōngguó Guójì Lǚxíngshè; ☎010 6512 0507; 9 Jianguomennei Dajie, Běijīng International Hotel, Dōngchéng; 🕒9am-noon & 1.30-5pm Mon-Fri, 9am-noon Sat; [S]Lines 1, 2 to Jianguomen, exit A), for a ¥50 mark-up. Tickets can also be booked with a mark-up through **China DIY Travel** (www.china-diy-travel.com; 6 Chaoyang Park Nanlu; 朝阳公园南路6号; commission per ticket $10).

Visas

Travellers will need Russian and Mongolian visas for the Trans-Mongolian Railway, as well as a Chinese visa. These can often be arranged along with your ticket by travel agents such as **China International Travel Service** (CITS; www.cits.net).

Health

China is a reasonably healthy country to travel in, but some health issues should be noted. Pre-existing medical conditions and accidental injury (especially traffic accidents) account for most life-threatening problems, but becoming ill in some way is not unusual. Outside of the major cities, medical care is often inadequate, and food and waterborne diseases are common. Malaria is still present in some parts of the country; altitude sickness can be a problem, particularly in Tibet.

In case of accident or illness, it's best just to get a taxi and go to hospital directly.

The following advice is a general guide only and does not replace the advice of a doctor trained in travel medicine.

Before You Go

Health Insurance

➡ Even if you are fit and healthy, don't travel without health insurance – accidents happen.

➡ Declare any existing medical conditions you have (the insurance company *will* check if your problem is pre-existing and will not cover you if it is undeclared).

➡ You may require extra cover for adventure activities such as rock climbing or skiing.

➡ If you're uninsured, emergency evacuation is expensive; bills of more than US$100,000 are not uncommon.

➡ Ensure you keep all documentation related to any medical expenses you incur.

Vaccinations

Specialised travel-medicine clinics stock all available vaccines and can give specific recommendations for your trip. The doctors will consider your vaccination history, the length of your trip, activities you may undertake and underlying medical conditions, such as pregnancy.

➡ Visit a doctor six to eight weeks before departure, as most vaccines don't produce immunity until at least two weeks after they're given.

➡ Ask your doctor for an International Certificate of Vaccination (otherwise known as the 'yellow booklet'), listing all vaccinations received.

➡ The only vaccine required by international regulations is yellow fever.
Proof of vaccination against yellow fever is only required if you have visited a country in the yellow-fever zone within the six days prior to entering China. If you are travelling to China directly from South America or Africa, check with a travel clinic as to whether you need a yellow-fever vaccination.

RECOMMENDED VACCINATIONS

The World Health Organization (WHO) recommends the following vaccinations for travellers to China:

Adult diphtheria and tetanus (ADT) Single booster recommended if you've not received one in the previous 10 years. Side effects include a sore arm and fever. An ADT vaccine that immunises against pertussis (whooping cough) is also available and may be recommended by your doctor.

Hepatitis A Provides almost 100% protection for up to a year; a booster after 12 months provides at least another 20 years' protection. Mild side effects such as a headache and sore arm occur in 5% to 10% of people.

Hepatitis B Now considered routine for most travellers. Given as three shots over six months; a rapid schedule is also available. There is also a combined vaccination with hepatitis A. Side effects are mild and uncommon, usually a headache and sore arm. Lifetime protection results in 95% of people.

Measles, mumps and rubella (MMR) Two doses of MMR is recommended unless you have had the diseases. Occasionally a rash and a flu-like illness can develop a week after receiving the vaccine. Many adults under 40 require a booster.

Typhoid Recommended unless your trip is less than a week. The vaccine offers around 70% protection, lasts for two to three years and comes as a single shot. Tablets are also available; however, the injection is usually recommended as it has fewer side effects. A sore arm and fever may occur. A vaccine combining hepatitis A and typhoid in a single shot is now available.

Varicella If you haven't had chickenpox, discuss this vaccination with your doctor.

The following immunisations are recommended for travellers spending more than one month in the country or those at special risk:

Influenza A single shot lasts one year and is recommended for those over 65 years of age or with underlying medical conditions such as heart or lung disease.

Japanese B encephalitis A series of three injections with a booster after two years. Recommended if spending more than one month in rural areas in the summer months, or more than three months in the country.

Pneumonia A single injection with a booster after five years is recommended for all travellers over 65 years of age or with underlying medical conditions that compromise immunity, such as heart or lung disease, cancer or HIV.

Rabies Three injections in all. A booster after one year will then provide 10 years' protection. Side effects are rare – occasionally a headache and sore arm.

Tuberculosis A complex issue. High-risk adult long-term travellers are usually recommended to have a TB skin test before and after travel, rather than vaccination. Only one vaccine is given in a lifetime. Children under five spending more than three months in China should be vaccinated.

Pregnant women and children should receive advice from a doctor who specialises in travel medicine.

Medical Checklist

Recommended items for a personal medical kit:

➡ Antibacterial cream, eg mucipirocin

➡ Antibiotics for diarrhoea, including norfloxacin, ciprofloxacin or azithromycin for bacterial diarrhoea; or tinidazole for giardia or amoebic dysentery

➡ Antibiotics for skin infections, eg amoxicillin/clavulanate or cephalexin

➡ Antifungal cream, eg clotrimazole

➡ Antihistamine, eg cetirizine for daytime and promethazine for night-time

➡ Anti-inflammatory, eg ibuprofen

➡ Antiseptic, eg Betadine

➡ Antispasmodic for stomach cramps, eg Buscopan

➡ Decongestant, eg pseudoephedrine

➡ Diamox if going to high altitudes

➡ Elastoplasts, bandages, gauze, thermometer (but not mercury), sterile needles and syringes, safety pins and tweezers

➡ Indigestion tablets, such as Quick Eze or Mylanta

➡ Insect repellent containing DEET

➡ Iodine tablets to purify water (unless you're pregnant or have a thyroid problem)

➡ Laxative, eg coloxyl

➡ Oral-rehydration solution (eg Gastrolyte) for diarrhoea, diarrhoea 'stopper' (eg loperamide)

and antinausea medication (eg prochlorperazine)

➡ Paracetamol

➡ Permethrin to impregnate clothing and mosquito nets

➡ Steroid cream for rashes, eg 1% to 2% hydrocortisone

➡ Sunscreen

➡ Thrush (vaginal yeast infection) treatment, eg clotrimazole pessaries or Diflucan tablet

➡ Urinary infection treatment, eg Ural

Websites

Centers for Disease Control & Prevention (www.cdc.gov)

Lonely Planet (www.lonelyplanet.com)

MD Travel Health (www.mdtravelhealth.com) Provides complete travel-health recommendations for every country; updated daily.

World Health Organization (www.who.int/ith) Publishes the excellent *International Travel & Health*, revised annually and available online.

Further Reading

➡ *Healthy Travel – Asia & India* (Lonely Planet) Handy pocket size, packed with useful information.

➡ *Traveller's Health* by Dr Richard Dawood.

➡ *Travelling Well* (www.travellingwell.com.au) by Dr Deborah Mills.

HEALTH ADVISORIES

It's usually a good idea to consult your government's travel advisory website for health warnings before departure (if one is available).

Australia (www.dfat.gov.au/travel)

Canada (www.travelhealth.gc.ca)

New Zealand (www.safetravel.govt.nz)

UK (www.gov.uk/foreign-travel-advice) Search for travel in the site index.

USA (www.cdc.gov/travel)

Tips for Taking Medications to China

➡ Pack medications in their original, clearly labelled containers.

➡ If you take any regular medication, bring double your needs in case of loss or theft.

➡ Take a signed and dated letter from your physician describing your medical conditions and medications (using generic names).

➡ If carrying syringes or needles, ensure you have a physician's letter documenting their medical necessity. If you have a heart condition, bring a copy of your ECG taken just prior to travelling.

➡ Get your teeth checked before you travel.

➡ If you wear glasses, take a spare pair and your prescription.
In China you can buy some medications over the counter without a doctor's prescription, but not all, and in general it is not advisable to buy medications locally without a doctor's advice. Fake medications and poorly stored or out-of-date drugs are also common, so try to bring your own.

In China

Availability & Cost of Health Care

Good clinics catering to travellers can be found in major cities. They are more expensive than local facilities but you may feel more comfortable dealing with a Western-trained doctor who speaks your language. These clinics usually have a good understanding of the best local hospital facilities and close contacts with insurance companies should you need evacuation. As a rough idea of cost, the private section of a large hospital in Běijīng dedicated to foreigners will charge about ¥500 up-

front for a consultation, plus another ¥500 for an X-ray. Waiting times are roughly an hour for each step.

If you think you may have a serious disease, especially malaria, do not waste time – get to the nearest quality facility. To find the nearest reliable medical facility, contact your insurance company or your embassy. Hospitals are listed in the Information sections for cities and towns.

Infectious Diseases

DENGUE

This mosquito-borne disease occurs in some parts of southern China. There is no vaccine so avoid mosquito bites – the dengue-carrying mosquito bites day and night, so use insect-avoidance measures at all times. Symptoms include high fever, severe headache and body ache. Some people develop a rash and diarrhoea. There is no specific treatment – just rest and paracetamol. Do not take aspirin.

HEPATITIS A

A problem throughout China, this food- and waterborne virus infects the liver, causing jaundice (yellow skin and eyes), nausea and lethargy. There is no specific treatment for hepatitis A; you just need to allow time for the liver to heal. All travellers to China should be vaccinated.

HEPATITIS B

The only sexually transmitted disease that can be prevented by vaccination, hepatitis B is spread by contact with infected body fluids. The long-term consequences can include liver cancer and cirrhosis. All travellers to China should be vaccinated.

JAPANESE ENCEPHALITIS

Formerly known as 'Japanese B encephalitis', this is a rare disease in travellers; however, vaccination is recommended if you're in rural areas for more than a month during summer months, or

if spending more than three months in the country. No treatment is available; one-third of infected people die, another third suffer permanent brain damage.

MALARIA

Malaria has been nearly eradicated in China; it is not generally a risk for visitors to the cities and most tourist areas. It is found mainly in rural areas in the southwestern region bordering Myanmar, Laos and Vietnam, principally Hǎinán, Yúnnán and Guǎngxī. More limited risk exists in the remote rural areas of Fújiàn, Guǎngdōng, Guìzhōu and Sìchuān. Generally, medication is only advised if you are visiting rural Hǎinán, Yúnnán or Guǎngxī.

To prevent malaria:

➡ Avoid mosquitoes and take antimalarial medications (most people who catch malaria are taking inadequate or no antimalarial medication).

➡ Use an insect repellent containing DEET on exposed skin (natural repellents such as citronella can be effective, but require more frequent application than products containing DEET).

➡ Sleep under a mosquito net impregnated with permethrin.

➡ Choose accommodation with screens and fans (if it's not air-conditioned).

➡ Impregnate clothing with permethrin in high-risk areas.

➡ Wear long sleeves and trousers in light colours.

➡ Use mosquito coils.

➡ Spray your room with insect repellent before going out for your evening meal.

RABIES

An increasingly common problem in China, this fatal disease is spread by the bite or lick of an infected animal, most commonly a dog. Seek medical advice immediately after any animal bite and commence post-exposure treatment. The pretravel vaccination means the post-bite treatment is greatly simplified.

If an animal bites you:

➡ Gently wash the wound with soap and water, and apply an iodine-based antiseptic.

➡ If you are not prevaccinated, you will need to receive rabies immunoglobulin as soon as possible, followed by a series of five vaccines over the next month. Those who have been prevaccinated require only two shots of vaccine after a bite.

➡ Contact your insurance company to locate the nearest clinic stocking rabies immunoglobulin and vaccine. Immunoglobulin is often unavailable outside of major centres, but it's crucial that you get to a clinic that has immunoglobulin as soon as possible if you have had a bite that has broken the skin.

SCHISTOSOMIASIS (BILHARZIA)

This disease occurs in the central Yangzi River (Cháng Jiāng) basin, carried in water by minute worms that infect certain varieties of freshwater snail found in rivers, streams, lakes and, particularly, behind dams. The infection often causes no symptoms until the disease is well established (several months to years after exposure); any resulting damage to internal organs is irreversible. Effective treatment is available.

➡ Avoid swimming or bathing in fresh water where bilharzia is present.

➡ A blood test is the most reliable way to diagnose the disease, but the test will not show positive until weeks after exposure.

TYPHOID

Typhoid is a serious bacterial infection spread via food and water. Symptoms include headaches, a high and slowly progressive fever, perhaps accompanied by a dry cough and stomach pain. Vaccination is not 100% effective, so still be careful what you eat and drink. All travellers spending more than a week in China should be vaccinated against typhoid.

Traveller's Diarrhoea

Between 30% and 50% of visitors will suffer from traveller's diarrhoea within two weeks of starting their trip. In most cases, the ailment is caused by bacteria and responds promptly to treatment with antibiotics.

Treatment consists of staying hydrated; rehydration solutions such as Gastrolyte are best. Antibiotics such as norfloxacin, ciprofloxacin or azithromycin will kill the bacteria quickly. Loperamide is just a 'stopper' and doesn't cure the problem; it can be helpful, however, for long bus rides. Don't take loperamide if you have a fever, or blood in your stools. Seek medical attention if you do not respond to an appropriate antibiotic.

➡ Eat only at busy restaurants with a high turnover of customers.

➡ Eat only freshly cooked food.

➡ Avoid food that has been sitting around in buffets.

➡ Peel all fruit, cook vegetables and soak salads in iodine water for at least 20 minutes.

➡ Drink only bottled mineral water.

AMOEBIC DYSENTERY

Amoebic dysentery is actually rare in travellers and is over-diagnosed. Symptoms are similar to bacterial diarrhoea – fever, bloody diarrhoea and generally feeling unwell. Always seek reliable medical care if you have blood in your diarrhoea. Treatment involves two drugs: tinidazole or metronidazole to kill the parasite in your gut, and then a second drug to kill the cysts. If amoebic dysentery is left untreated, complications such as liver or gut abscesses can occur.

GIARDIASIS

Giardiasis is a parasite relatively common in travellers. Symptoms include nausea, bloating, excess gas, fatigue and intermittent diarrhoea. 'Eggy' burps are often attributed solely to giardia, but are not specific to the parasite. Giardiasis will eventually go away if left untreated, but this can take months. The treatment of choice is tinidazole, with metronidazole a second option.

INTESTINAL WORMS

These parasites are most common in rural, tropical areas. Some may be ingested in food such as undercooked meat (eg tapeworms) and some enter through your skin (eg hookworms). Consider having a stool test when you return home.

Environmental Hazards

AIR POLLUTION

Air pollution is a significant and worsening problem in many Chinese cities. People with underlying respiratory conditions should seek advice from their doctor prior to travel to ensure they have adequate medications in case their condition worsens. Take treatments such as throat lozenges, and cough and cold tablets.

ALTITUDE SICKNESS

There are bus journeys in Tibet, Qīnghǎi and Xīnjiāng where the road goes above 5000m. Acclimatising to such extreme elevations takes several weeks at least, but most travellers come up from sea level very fast – a bad move! Acute mountain sickness (AMS) results from a rapid ascent to altitudes above 2700m. It usually commences within 24 to 48 hours of arriving at altitude, and symptoms include headache, nausea, fatigue and loss of appetite (feeling much like a hangover).

If you have altitude sickness, the cardinal rule is that you must not go higher as you are sure to get sicker and could develop one of the more severe and potentially deadly forms of the disease: high-altitude pulmonary oedema (HAPE) and high-altitude cerebral oedema (HACE). Both are medical emergencies and, as there are no rescue facilities similar to those in the Nepal Himalaya, prevention is the best policy.

AMS can be prevented by 'graded ascent'; it is recommended that once you are above 3000m you ascend a maximum of 300m daily with an extra rest day every 1000m. You can also use a medication called Diamox as a prevention or treatment for AMS, but you should discuss this first with a doctor experienced in altitude medicine.

Diamox should not be taken by people with a sulphur drug allergy.

If you have altitude sickness, rest where you are for a day or two until your symptoms resolve. You can then carry on, but ensure you follow the graded-ascent guidelines. If symptoms get worse, descend immediately before you are faced with a life-threatening situation. There is no way of predicting who will suffer from AMS, but certain factors predispose you to it: rapid ascent, carrying a heavy load, and having a seemingly minor illness such as a chest infection or diarrhoea. Make sure you drink at least 3L of noncaffeinated drinks daily to stay well hydrated.

HEAT EXHAUSTION

Dehydration or salt deficiency can cause heat exhaustion. Take time to acclimatise to high temperatures, drink

sufficient liquids and avoid physically demanding activity.

Salt deficiency is characterised by fatigue, lethargy, headaches, giddiness and muscle cramps; salt tablets may help, but adding extra salt to your food is better.

HYPOTHERMIA

Be particularly aware of the dangers of trekking at high altitudes or simply taking a long bus trip over mountains. In Tibet it can go from being mildly warm to blisteringly cold in minutes – blizzards can appear from nowhere.

Progress from very cold to dangerously cold can be rapid due to a combination of wind, wet clothing, fatigue and hunger, even if the air temperature is above freezing. Dress in layers; silk, wool and some artificial fibres are all good insulating materials. A hat is important, as a lot of heat is lost through the head. A strong, waterproof outer layer (and a space blanket for emergencies) is essential. Carry basic supplies, including food containing simple sugars, and fluid to drink.

Symptoms of hypothermia are exhaustion, numb skin (particularly the toes and fingers), shivering, slurred speech, irrational or violent behaviour, lethargy, stumbling, dizzy spells, muscle cramps and violent bursts of energy.

To treat mild hypothermia, first get the person out of the wind and/or rain, remove their clothing if it's wet, and replace it with dry, warm clothing. Give them hot liquids – not alcohol – and high-calorie, easily digestible food. Early recognition and treatment of mild hypothermia is the only way to prevent severe hypothermia, a critical condition that requires medical attention.

INSECT BITES & STINGS

Bedbugs don't carry disease but their bites are very itchy. Treat the itch with an antihistamine.

WATER

In general, you should never drink the tap water in China, even in five-star hotels. Boiling water makes it safe to drink, but you might still prefer to buy bottled water for the taste or mineral make-up.

Follow these tips to avoid becoming ill:

➡ Never drink unboiled tap water.

➡ Water fountains at the major airports are clearly marked if they are safe to drink from.

➡ Bottled water is generally safe – check that the seal is intact at purchase.

➡ Avoid ice.

➡ Avoid fresh juices – they may have been watered down.

➡ Boiling water is the most efficient method of purifying water.

➡ At very high altitudes, boil water for an extra minute as water bubbles at a lower temperature.

➡ The best chemical purifier is iodine. It should not be used by pregnant women or those with thyroid problems.

➡ Water filters should also filter out viruses. Ensure your filter has a chemical barrier such as iodine and a pore size of less than 4 microns.

Lice inhabit various parts of the human body, most commonly the head and pubic areas. Transmission is via close contact with an affected person. Lice can be difficult to treat, but electric lice combs/detectors can be effective (pick one up before travelling); otherwise you may need numerous applications of an antilice shampoo such as permethrin. Pubic lice (crab lice) are usually contracted from sexual contact.

Ticks are contracted by walking in rural areas, and are commonly found behind the ears, on the belly and in armpits. If you have had a tick bite and experience symptoms such as a rash, fever or muscle aches, see a doctor. Doxycycline prevents some tick-borne diseases.

Women's Health

Pregnant women should receive specialised advice before travelling. The ideal time to travel is in the second trimester (between 14 and 28 weeks), when the risk of pregnancy-related problems is at its lowest and pregnant women generally feel at their best. During the first trimester, miscarriage is a risk; in the third trimester, complications such as premature labour and high blood pressure are possible. Travel with a companion and carry a list of quality medical facilities for your destination, ensuring you continue your standard antenatal care at these facilities. Avoid rural areas with poor transport and medical facilities. Above all, ensure travel insurance covers all pregnancy-related possibilities, including premature labour.

Malaria is a high-risk disease in pregnancy. The World Health Organization recommends that pregnant women do not travel to areas with chloroquine-resistant malaria.

Traveller's diarrhoea can quickly lead to dehydration and result in inadequate blood flow to the placenta. Many drugs used to treat various diarrhoea bugs are not recommended in pregnancy. Azithromycin is considered safe.

Heat, humidity and antibiotics can all contribute to thrush. Treatment is with antifungal creams and pessaries such as clotrimazole. A practical alternative is a single tablet of fluconazole (Diflucan). Urinary tract infections can be precipitated by dehydration or long bus journeys without toilet stops; bring suitable antibiotics.

Supplies of sanitary products may not be readily available in rural areas. Birth-control options may be limited, so bring adequate supplies of your own form of contraception.

Language

Discounting its many ethnic minority languages, China has eight major dialect groups: Pǔtōnghuà (Mandarin), Yue (Cantonese), Wu (Shanghainese), Minbei (Fuzhou), Minnan (Hokkien-Taiwanese), Xiang, Gan and Hakka. These dialects also divide into subdialects.

It's the language spoken in Běijīng that is considered the official language of China. It's usually referred to as Mandarin, but the Chinese themselves call it Pǔtōnghuà (meaning 'common speech'). Pǔtōnghuà is variously referred to as Hànyǔ (the Han language), Guóyǔ (the national language) or Zhōngwén or Zhōngguóhuà (Chinese). With the exception of the western and southernmost provinces, most of the population speaks Mandarin (although it may be spoken there with a regional accent). In this chapter, we have included Mandarin, Cantonese, Tibetan, Uighur and Mongolian.

MANDARIN

Writing

Chinese is often referred to as a language of pictographs. Many of the basic Chinese characters are in fact highly stylised pictures of what they represent, but around 90% are compounds of a 'meaning' element and a 'sound' element.

A well educated, contemporary Chinese person might use between 6000 and 8000 characters. To read a Chinese newspaper you need to know 2000 to 3000 characters, but 1200 to 1500 would be enough to get the gist.

Theoretically, all Chinese dialects share the same written system. In practice, Cantonese adds about 3000 specialised characters of its own and many of the dialects don't have a written form at all.

WANT MORE?

For in-depth language information and handy phrases, check out Lonely Planet's *China Phrasebook*. You'll find it at **shop.lonelyplanet.com**

Pinyin & Pronunciation

In 1958 the Chinese adopted pinyin, a system of writing their language using the Roman alphabet. The original idea was to eventually do away with Chinese characters. However, tradition dies hard, and the idea was abandoned.

Pinyin is often used on shop fronts, street signs and advertising billboards. Don't expect all Chinese people to be able to use pinyin, however. In the countryside and the smaller towns you may not see a single pinyin sign anywhere, so unless you speak and read Chinese you'll need a phrasebook with Chinese characters.

Below we've provided pinyin alongside the Mandarin script.

Vowels

a	as in 'father'
ai	as in 'aisle'
ao	as the 'ow' in 'cow'
e	as in 'her' (without 'r' sound)
ei	as in 'weigh'
i	as the 'ee' in 'meet' (or like a light 'r' as in 'Grrr!' after c, ch, r, s, sh, z or zh)
ian	as the word 'yen'
ie	as the English word 'yeah'
o	as in 'or' (without 'r' sound)
ou	as the 'oa' in 'boat'
u	as in 'flute'
ui	as the word 'way'
uo	like a 'w' followed by 'o'
yu/ü	like 'ee' with lips pursed

Consonants

c	as the 'ts' in 'bits'
ch	as in 'chop', but with the tongue curled up and back
h	as in 'hay', but articulated from further back in the throat
q	as the 'ch' in 'cheese'
sh	as in 'ship', but with the tongue curled up and back
x	as the 'sh' in 'ship'
z	as the 'ds' in 'suds'
zh	as the 'j' in 'judge' but with the tongue curled up and back

The only consonants that occur at the end of a syllable are n, ng and r.

In pinyin, apostrophes are occasionally used to separate syllables in order to prevent ambiguity, eg the word píng'ān can be written with an apostrophe after the 'g' to prevent it being pronounced as pín'gān.

Tones

Mandarin is a language with a large number of words with the same pronunciation but a different meaning. What distinguishes these homophones (as these words are called) is their 'tonal quality – the raising and the lowering of pitch on certain syllables. Mandarin has four tones – high, rising, falling-rising and falling, plus a fifth 'neutral' tone that you can all but ignore. Tones are important for distinguishing meaning of words – eg the word ma has four different meanings according to tone, as shown below. Tones are indicated in pinyin by the following accent marks on vowels:

high tone	mā (mother)
rising tone	má (hemp, numb)
falling-rising tone	mǎ (horse)
falling tone	mà (scold, swear)

Basics

When asking a question it is polite to start with qǐng wèn – literally, 'May I ask?'

Hello.	你好。	Nǐhǎo.
Goodbye.	再见。	Zàijiàn.
How are you?	你好吗？	Nǐhǎo ma?
Fine. And you?	好。你呢？	Hǎo. Nǐ ne?
Excuse me. (to get attention)	劳驾。	Láojià.
(to get past)	借光。	Jièguāng.
Sorry.	对不起。	Duìbùqǐ.
Yes./No.	是。/不是。	Shì./Bùshì.
Please ...	请……	Qǐng ...
Thank you.	谢谢你。	Xièxie nǐ.
You're welcome.	不客气。	Bù kèqi.

What's your name?
你叫什么名字？ Nǐ jiào shénme míngzi?

My name is ...
我叫…… Wǒ jiào ...

Do you speak English?
你会说英文吗？ Nǐ huìshuō Yīngwén ma?

I don't understand.
我不明白。 Wǒ bù míngbái.

KEY PATTERNS – MANDARIN

To get by in Mandarin, mix and match these simple patterns with words of your choice:

How much is (the deposit)?
(押金)多少？ (Yājīn) duōshǎo?

Do you have (a room)?
有没有(房)？ Yǒuméiyǒu (fáng)?

Is there (heating)?
有(暖气)吗？ Yǒu (nuǎnqì) ma?

I'd like (that one).
我要(那个)。 Wǒ yào (nàge)

Please give me (the menu).
请给我(菜单)。 Qǐng gěiwǒ (càidān).

Can I (sit here)?
我能(坐这儿)吗？ Wǒ néng (zuòzhèr) ma?

I need (a can opener).
我想要(一个 Wǒ xiǎngyào (yīge
开罐器)。 kāiguàn qì).

Do we need (a guide)?
需要(向导)吗？ Xūyào (xiàngdǎo) ma?

I have (a reservation).
我有(预订)。 Wǒ yǒu (yùdìng).

I'm (a doctor).
我(是医生)。 Wǒ (shì yīshēng).

Accommodation

Do you have a single/double room?
有没有(单人/ Yǒuméiyǒu (dānrén/
套)房？ tào) fáng?

How much is it per night/person?
每天/人多少钱？ Měi tiān/rén duōshǎo qián?

campsite	露营地	lùyíngdì
guesthouse	宾馆	bīnguǎn
hostel	招待所	zhāodàisuǒ
hotel	酒店	jiǔdiàn
reception	总台	zǒng tái
air-con	空调	kōngtiáo
bathroom	浴室	yùshì
blanket	被子	bèizi
bed	床	chuáng
cot	张婴儿床	zhāng yīng'ér chuáng
hair dryer	吹风机	chuīfēngjī
safe	保险箱	bǎoxiǎnxiāng
sheet	床单	chuángdān
towel	毛巾	máojīn
window	窗	chuāng

SIGNS – MANDARIN

入口	Rùkǒu	**Entrance**
出口	Chūkǒu	**Exit**
问讯处	Wènxùnchù	**Information**
开	Kāi	**Open**
关	Guān	**Closed**
禁止	Jìnzhǐ	**Prohibited**
厕所	Cèsuǒ	**Toilets**
男	Nán	**Men**
女	Nǚ	**Women**

Directions

Where's (a bank)?
(银行) 在哪儿? (Yínháng) zài nǎr?

What's the address?
地址在哪儿? Dìzhǐ zài nǎr?

Could you write the address, please?
能不能请你 Néngbुनéng qǐng nǐ
把地址写下来? bǎ dìzhǐ xiě xiàlái?

Can you show me where it is on the map?
请帮我找它在 Qǐng bāngwǒ zhǎo tā zài
地图上的位置。 dìtú shàng de wèizhi.

Go straight ahead.
一直走。 Yīzhí zǒu.

Turn left.
左转。 Zuǒ zhuǎn.

Turn right.
右转。 Yòu zhuǎn.

at the traffic lights	在红绿灯	zài hónglǜdēng
behind	背面	bèimiàn
far	远	yuǎn
in front of ...	……的前面	... de qiánmian
near	近	jìn
next to	旁边	pángbiān
on the corner	拐角	guǎijiǎo
opposite	对面	duìmiàn

Eating & Drinking

What would you recommend?
有什么菜可以 Yǒu shénme cài kěyǐ
推荐的? tuījiàn de?

What's in that dish?
这道菜用什么 Zhèdào cài yòng shénme
东西做的? dōngxi zuòde?

That was delicious.
真好吃。 Zhēn hǎochī.

The bill, please!
买单! Mǎidān!

Cheers! 干杯! Gānbēi!

I'd like to reserve a table for ...
我想预订 Wǒ xiǎng yùdìng
一张…… yīzhāng ...
的桌子。 de zhuōzi.
(eight) o'clock (八) 点钟 (bā) diǎn zhōng
(two) people (两个) 人 (liǎngge) rén

I don't eat ... 我不吃…… Wǒ bùchī ...
fish 鱼 yú
nuts 果仁 guǒrén
poultry 家禽 jiāqín
red meat 牛羊肉 niúyángròu

Key Words

appetisers	凉菜	liángcài
bar	酒吧	jiǔbā
bottle	瓶子	píngzi
bowl	碗	wǎn
breakfast	早饭	zǎofàn
cafe	咖啡屋	kāfēiwū
chidren's menu	儿童菜单	értóng càidān
(too) cold	(太)凉	(tài) liáng
dinner	晚饭	wǎnfàn
dish (food)	盘	pán
food	食品	shípǐn
fork	叉子	chāzi
glass	杯子	bēizi
halal	清真	qīngzhēn
highchair	高凳	gāodèng
hot (warm)	热	rè
knife	刀	dāo
kosher	犹太	yóutài
local specialties	地方小吃	dìfāng xiǎochī
lunch	午饭	wǔfàn
main courses	主菜	zhǔ cài
market	菜市	càishì
menu (in English)	(英文)菜单	(Yīngwén) càidān
plate	碟子	diézi
restaurant	餐馆	cānguǎn
(too) spicy	(太)辣	(tài) là
spoon	勺	sháo
vegetarian food	素食食品	sùshí shípín

Meat & Fish

beef	牛肉	niúròu
chicken	鸡肉	jīròu
duck	鸭	yā

fish	鱼	yú
lamb	羊肉	yángròu
pork	猪肉	zhūròu
seafood	海鲜	hǎixiān

Fruit & Vegetables

apple	苹果	píngguǒ
banana	香蕉	xiāngjiāo
bok choy	小白菜	xiǎo báicài
carrot	胡萝卜	húluóbo
celery	芹菜	qíncài
cucumber	黄瓜	huánggguā
fruit	水果	shuǐguǒ
grape	葡萄	pútáo
green beans	扁豆	biǎndòu
guava	石榴	shíliu
longan	龙眼	lóngyǎn
lychee	荔枝	lìzhī
mango	芒果	mángguǒ
mushroom	蘑菇	mógū
onion	洋葱	yáng cōng
orange	橙子	chéngzi
pear	梨	lí
pineapple	凤梨	fènglí
plum	梅子	méizi
potato	土豆	tǔdòu
radish	萝卜	luóbo
spring onion	小葱	xiǎo cōng
sweet potato	地瓜	dìguā
vegetable	蔬菜	shūcài
watermelon	西瓜	xīguā

Other

bread	面包	miànbāo
butter	黄油	huángyóu
egg	蛋	dàn
herbs/spices	香料	xiāngliào
pepper	胡椒粉	hújiāo fěn

salt	盐	yán
soy sauce	酱油	jiàngyóu
sugar	砂糖	shātáng
tofu	豆腐	dòufu
vinegar	醋	cù
vegetable oil	菜油	càiyóu

Drinks

beer	啤酒	píjiǔ
Chinese spirits	白酒	báijiǔ
coffee	咖啡	kāfēi
(orange) juice	(橙)汁	(chéng) zhī
milk	牛奶	niúnǎi
mineral water	矿泉水	kuàngquán shuǐ
red wine	红葡萄酒	hóng pútáo jiǔ
rice wine	米酒	mǐjiǔ
soft drink	汽水	qìshuǐ
tea	茶	chá
(boiled) water	(开)水	(kāi) shuǐ
white wine	白葡萄酒	bái pútáo jiǔ
yoghurt	酸奶	suānnǎi

Emergencies

Help!	救命!	Jiùmìng!
I'm lost.	我迷路了。	Wǒ mílù le.
Go away!	走开!	Zǒukāi!
There's been an accident. 出事了。		Chūshì le.
Call a doctor! 请叫医生来!		Qǐng jiào yīshēng lái!
Call the police! 请叫警察!		Qǐng jiào jǐngchá!
I'm ill. 我生病了。		Wǒ shēngbìng le.
It hurts here. 这里痛。		Zhèlǐ tòng.
Where are the toilets? 厕所在哪儿?		Cèsuǒ zài nǎr?

QUESTION WORDS – MANDARIN

How	怎么	Zěnme
What	什么	Shénme
When	什么时候	Shénme shíhòu
Where	哪儿	Nǎr
Which	哪个	Nǎge
Who	谁	Shuí
Why	为什么	Wèishénme

Shopping & Services

I'd like to buy ... 我想买……		Wǒ xiǎng mǎi ...
I'm just looking. 我先看看。		Wǒ xiān kànkan.
Can I look at it? 我能看看吗?		Wǒ néng kànkan ma?
I don't like it. 我不喜欢。		Wǒ bù xǐhuan.

NUMBERS – MANDARIN

1	一	yī
2	二/两	èr/liǎng
3	三	sān
4	四	sì
5	五	wǔ
6	六	liù
7	七	qī
8	八	bā
9	九	jiǔ
10	十	shí
20	二十	èrshí
30	三十	sānshí
40	四十	sìshí
50	五十	wǔshí
60	六十	liùshí
70	七十	qīshí
80	八十	bāshí
90	九十	jiǔshí
100	一百	yībǎi
1000	一千	yīqiān

How much is it?
多少钱？ Duōshǎo qián?

That's too expensive.
太贵了。 Tàiguì le.

Can you lower the price?
能便宜一点吗？ Néng piányi yīdiǎn ma?

There's a mistake in the bill.
帐单上 Zhàngdān shàng
有问题。 yǒu wèntí.

ATM	自动取款机	zìdòng qǔkuǎn jī
credit card	信用卡	xìnyòng kǎ
internet cafe	网吧	wǎngbā
post office	邮局	yóujú
tourist office	旅行店	lǚxíng diàn

Time & Dates

What time is it?
现在几点钟？ Xiànzài jǐdiǎn zhōng?

It's (10) o'clock.
（十）点钟。 (Shí) diǎn zhōng.

Half past (10).
（十）点三十分。 (Shí) diǎn sānshífēn.

morning	早上	zǎoshang
afternoon	下午	xiàwǔ
evening	晚上	wǎnshàng

yesterday	昨天	zuótiān
today	今天	jīntiān
tomorrow	明天	míngtiān
Monday	星期一	xīngqī yī
Tuesday	星期二	xīngqī èr
Wednesday	星期三	xīngqī sān
Thursday	星期四	xīngqī sì
Friday	星期五	xīngqī wǔ
Saturday	星期六	xīngqī liù
Sunday	星期天	xīngqī tiān
January	一月	yīyuè
February	二月	èryuè
March	三月	sānyuè
April	四月	sìyuè
May	五月	wǔyuè
June	六月	liùyuè
July	七月	qīyuè
August	八月	bāyuè
September	九月	jiǔyuè
October	十月	shíyuè
November	十一月	shíyīyuè
December	十二月	shí'èryuè

Transport

boat	船	chuán
bus (city)	大巴	dàbā
bus (intercity)	长途车	chángtú chē
plane	飞机	fēijī
taxi	出租车	chūzū chē
train	火车	huǒchē
tram	电车	diànchē

Buses & Trains

I want to go to …
我要去…… Wǒ yào qù …

Does it stop at (Harbin)?
在（哈尔滨）能下 Zài (Hǎ'ěrbīn) néng xià
车吗？ chē ma?

At what time does it leave?
几点钟出发？ Jǐdiǎnzhōng chūfā?

At what time does it get to (Hángzhōu)?
几点钟到 Jǐdiànzhōng dào
（杭州）？ (Hángzhōu)?

Can you tell me when we get to (Hángzhōu)?
到了（杭州） Dàole (Hángzhōu)
请叫我，好吗？ qǐng jiào wǒ, hǎoma?

I want to get off here.
我想这儿下车。 Wǒ xiǎng zhèr xiàchē.

When's the ... (bus)?	·····(车) 几点走?	... (chē) jǐdiǎn zǒu?
first	首趟	shǒutàng
last	末趟	mòtàng
next	下一趟	xià yītàng
A ... ticket to (Dàlián).	一张到 (大连)的 ······票。	Yīzhāng dào (Dàlián) de ... piào.
1st-class	头等	tóuděng
2nd-class	二等	èrděng
one-way	单程	dānchéng
return	双程	shuāngchéng
aisle seat	走廊的 座位	zǒuláng de zuòwèi
cancelled	取消	qǔxiāo
delayed	晚点	wǎndiǎn
platform	站台	zhàntái
ticket office	售票处	shòupiàochù
timetable	时刻表	shíkè biǎo
train station	火车站	huǒchēzhàn
window seat	窗户的 座位	chuānghu de zuòwèi

Taxis

I'd like a taxi to depart at (9am)
我要订一辆出租车，
(早上9点钟)出发。
Wǒ yào dìng yīliàng chūzū
chē. (zǎoshàng jiǔ diǎn
zhōng) chūfā.

I'd like a taxi now.
我要订一辆出租车，
现在。
Wǒ yào dìng yīliàng chūzū
chē, xiànzài.

I'd like a taxi tomorrow
我要订一辆出租车，
明天。
Wǒ yào dìng yīliàng chūzū
chē, míngtiān.

Where's the taxi rank?
在哪里打出租车？
Zài nǎli dǎ chūzū chē?

Is this taxi free?
这出租车有人吗？
Zhè chūzū chē yǒurén ma?

Please put the meter on.
请打表。
Qǐng dǎbiǎo.

How much is it (to this address)?
(到这个地址)
多少钱？
(Dào zhège dìzhǐ)
duōshǎo qián?

Please take me to (this address).
请带我到
(这个地址)。
Qǐng dàiwǒ dào
(zhège dìzhǐ).

Cycling

bicycle pump	打气筒	dǎqìtóng
child seat	婴儿座	yīng'érzuò
helmet	头盔	tóukuī

CANTONESE

Cantonese is the most widely used Chinese language in Hong Kong, Macau, Guǎngdōng, parts of Guǎngxī and the surrounding region. Cantonese speakers use Chinese characters, but pronounce many of them differently from a Mandarin speaker. Also, Cantonese adds about 3000 characters of its own to the character set. Several systems of Romanisation for Cantonese script exist, and no single one has emerged as an official standard. In this chapter we use Lonely Planet's pronunciation guide, designed for maximum accuracy with minimum complexity.

Pronunciation

In Cantonese, the ng sound can appear at the start of a word. Words ending with the consonant sounds p, t, and k are clipped. Many speakers, particularly young people, replace the n with an l at the start of a word – eg náy (you) often sounds like láy. Where relevant, our pronunciation guide reflects this change.

The vowels are pronounced as follows: a as the 'u' in 'but', ai as in 'aisle' (short), au as the 'ou' in 'out', ay as in 'pay', eu as the 'er' in 'fern', eui as eu followed by i, ew as in 'blew' (short, with lips tightened), i as the 'ee' in 'deep', iu as the 'yu' in 'yuletide', o as in 'go', oy as in 'boy', u as in 'put', ui as in French oui.

Tones in Cantonese fall on vowels (a, e, i, o, u) and on n. The same word pronounced with different tones can have a different meaning eg gwàt (dig up) vs gwàt (bones). There are six tones, divided into high- and low-pitch groups. High-pitch tones involve tightening the vocal muscles to get a higher note, while lower-pitch tones are made by relaxing the vocal chords to get a lower note. Tones are indicated with the following accent marks: à (high), á (high rising), à (low falling), á (low rising), a (low), a (level – no accent mark).

Basics

Hello.	哈佬。	hàa·ló
Goodbye.	再見。	joy·gin
How are you?	你幾好 啊嗎？	láy gáy hó à maa
Fine.	幾好。	gáy hó
Excuse me.	對唔住。	deui·ǹg·jew
Sorry.	對唔住。	deui·ǹg·jew
Yes./No.	係。/不係。	hai/ǹg·hai
Please ...	唔該······	ǹg·gòy ...
Thank you.	多謝	dàw·je

What's your name?
你叫乜嘢名？
láy giu màt·yé méng aa

My name is ...
我叫⋯⋯ — ngáw giu ...

Do you speak English?
你識唔識講
英文啊？ — láy sìk·ǹg·sìk gáwng
ying·mán aa

I don't understand.
我唔明 。 — ngáw ǹg mìng

Accommodation

campsite	營地	yìng·dạy
guesthouse	賓館	bàn·gún
hostel	招待所	jiù·dọy·sáw
hotel	酒店	jáu·dịm
Do you have	有冇⋯⋯	yáu·mó ...
a ... room?	房？	fáwng
double	雙人	sèung·yạn
single	單人	dàan·yạn
How much is it	一⋯⋯幾多	yàt ... gáy·dàw
per ...?	錢？	chín
night	晚	mạan
person	個人	gaw yạn

Directions

Where's ...?	⋯⋯喺邊度？	... hái bìn·dọ
What's the address?	地址係？	dạy·jí hại
left	左邊	jáw·bìn
on the corner	十字路口	sạp·jị·lọ·háu
right	右邊	yạu·bìn
straight ahead	前面	chịn·mịn
traffic lights	紅綠燈	hùng·lụk·dàng

Eating & Drinking

What would you recommend?
有乜嘢好介紹？ — yáu màt·yé hó gaai·siụ

That was delicious.
真好味 。 — jàn hó·mạy

I'd like the bill, please.
唔該我要埋單 。 — ǹg·gòy ngáw yiu mạai·dàan

Cheers!
乾杯！ — gàwn·buì

I'd like to	我想	ngáw séung
book a	訂張檯	deng jèung tóy
table for ...	⋯⋯嘅 。	... ge
(eight) o'clock	(八) 點鐘	(bàat) dím·jùng
(two) people	(兩) 位	(léung) ái

NUMBERS – CANTONESE

1	一	yàt
2	二	yị
3	三	sàam
4	四	say
5	五	ńg
6	六	lụk
7	七	chàt
8	八	baat
9	九	gáu
10	十	sạp
20	二十	yị·sạp
30	三十	sàam·sạp
40	四十	say·sạp
50	五十	ńg·sạp
60	六十	lụk·sạp
70	七十	chàt·sạp
80	八十	baat·sạp
90	九十	gáu·sạp
100	一百	yàt·baak
1000	一千	yàt·chìn

bar	酒吧	jáu·bàa
bottle	樽	jèun
breakfast	早餐	jó·chàan
cafe	咖啡屋	gaa·fè·ngùk
dinner	晚飯	mạan·fạan
fork	叉	chàa
glass	杯	buì
knife	刀	dò
lunch	午餐	ńg·chàan
market	街市 (HK)	gàai·sí
	市場 (China)	sí·chèung
plate	碟	díp
restaurant	酒樓	jáu·lạu
spoon	羹	gàng

Emergencies

Help!	救命！	gau·mẹng
I'm lost.	我蕩失路 。	ngáw dạwng·sàk·lọ
Go away!	走開！	jáu·hòy

Call a doctor!
快啲叫醫生！ — faai·dì giu yì·sàng

Call the police!
快啲叫警察！ — faai·dì giu gíng·chaat

I'm sick.
我病咗 。 — ngáw bẹng·jáw

Shopping & Services

I'd like to buy ...
我想買…… ngáw séung máai ...

How much is it?
幾多錢? gáy·dàw chín

That's too expensive.
太貴啦 。 taai gwai laa

There's a mistake in the bill.
帳單錯咗 。 jeung·dàan chaw jáw

internet cafe	網吧	máwng·bàa
post office	郵局	yàu gúk
tourist office	旅行社	léui·hàng·sé

Time & Dates

What time is it?	而家 幾點鐘 ?	yì·gàa gáy·dím·jùng
It's (10) o'clock.	(十)點鐘 。	(sap)·dím·jùng
Half past (10).	(十)點半 。	(sap)·dím bun

morning	朝早	jiù·jó
afternoon	下晝	haa·jau
evening	夜晚	ye·máan
yesterday	寢日	kàm·yat
today	今日	gàm·yat
tomorrow	听日	tìng·yat

Transport

boat	船	sèwn
bus	巴士 (HK)	bàa·sí
	公共	gùng·gung
	汽車 (China)	hay·chè
train	火車	fáw·chè

A ... ticket to (Panyu).	一張去 (番禺)嘅 ……飛 。	yàt jèung heui (pùn·yèw) ge ... fày
1st-class	頭等	tàu·dáng
2nd-class	二等	yi·dáng
one-way	單程	dàan·chìng
return	雙程	sèung·chìng

At what time does it leave?
幾點鐘出發 ? gáy·dím jùng chèut·faa

Does it stop at ...?
會唔會喺……停呀 ? wuí·ǹg·wuí hái ... tìng aa

At what time does it get to ...?
幾點鐘到…… ? gáy·dím jùng do ...

TIBETAN

Tibetan is spoken by around six million people, mainly in Tibet. In urban areas almost all Tibetans also speak Mandarin.

Most sounds in Tibetan are similar to those found in English, so if you read our coloured pronunciation guides as if they were English, you'll be understood. Note that â is pronounced as the 'a' in 'ago', ö as the 'er' in 'her', and ü as the 'u' in 'flute' but with a raised tongue. A vowel followed by n, m or ng indicates a nasalised sound (pronounced 'through the nose'). A consonant followed by h is aspirated (accompanied by a puff of air).

There are no direct equivalents of English 'yes' and 'no' in Tibetan. Although it may not be completely correct, you'll be understood if you use la ong for 'yes' and la men for 'no'.

Hello.	བཀྲ་ཤིས་བདེ་ལེགས།	ta·shi de·lek
Goodbye. (if staying)	ག་ལེར་ཕེབས།	ka·lee pay
(if leaving)	ག་ལེར་བཞུགས།	ka·lee shu
Excuse me.	དགོངས་དག	gong·da
Sorry.	དགོངས་དག	gong·da
Please.	ཐུགས་རྗེ་གཟིགས།	tu·jay·sig
Thank you.	ཐུགས་རྗེ་ཆེ།	tu·jay·chay

How are you?
ཁྱེད་རང་སྐུ་གཟུགས། kay·râng ku·su
བདེ་པོ་ཡིན་པས། de·po yin·bay

Fine. And you?
བདེ་པོ་ཡིན། ཁྱེད་རང་ཡང་ de·bo·yin kay·râng·yâng
སྐུ་གཟུགས་བདེ་པོ་ཡིན་པས། ku·su de·po yin·bay

What's your name?
ཁྱེད་རང་གི་མཚན་ལ། kay·râng·gi tsen·là
ག་རེ་རེད། kâ·ray·ray

My name is ...
ངའི་མིང་ལ ... རེད། ngay·ming·la ... ray

Do you speak English?
ཁྱེད་རང་དབྱིན་ཇི་སྐད་ kay·râng in·ji·kay
ཤེས་ཀྱི་ཡོད་པས། shing·gi yö·bay

I don't understand.
ཧ་གོ་མ་སོང་། ha ko ma·song

How much is it?
གོང་ཚད་རེད། gong kâ·tsay ray

Where is ...?
... ག་པར་ཡོད་རེད། ... ka·bah yö·ray

UIGHUR

Uighur is spoken all over Xīnjiāng. In China, Uighur is written in Arabic script. The phrases in this chapter reflect the Kashgar dialect.

In our pronunciation guides, stressed syllables are indicated with italics. Most consonant sounds in Uighur are the same as in English, though note that h is pronounced with a puff of air. The vowels are pronounced as follows: a as in 'hat', aa as the 'a' in 'father', ee as in 'sleep' (produced back in the throat), o as in 'go', ŏ as the 'e' in 'her' (pronounced with rounded lips), u as in 'put', and ü as the 'i' in 'bit' (with the lips rounded and pushed forward). Stressed syllables are in italics.

Basics

Hello.	ئەسسالامۇ	as·saa·laa·mu
	ئەلەيكۇم.	a·lay·kom
Goodbye.	خەير ـ خوش.	hayr·hosh
Excuse me.	كۆرۈڭچەك كە	ka·chü·rüng ga
	قانداق	kaan·daak
	باردۇ؟	baar·i·du
Sorry.	كۆرۈڭچەك.	ka·chü·rüng
Yes.	ھەنە.	ee·a·a
No.	ياق.	yaak
Please.	مەرھەممەمەت.	ma·ree·am·mat
Thank you.	رەخمەت سىزگە.	rah·mat siz·ga
How are you?		
قانداق		kaan·daak
ئەھۋالىڭىز؟		a·ee·vaa·li·ngiz
Fine. And you?		
ياخشى، سىزچۇ؟		yaah·shi siz·chu
What's your name?		
سىزنىڭ		siz·ning
ئىسمىڭىز نىمە؟		is·mi·ngiz ni·ma
My name is ...		
مېنىڭ ئىسمىم ...		mi·ning is·mim ...
Do you speak English?		
سىز ئىنگگىلىزچە		siz ing·gi·lis·ka
بىلەمسىز؟		bi·lam·siz
I don't understand.		
چۈشەنمەدىم.		man chu·shan·mi·dim
How much is it?		
قانچە پۇل؟		kaan·cha pool
Where is ...?		
... نەدە؟		... na·da

MONGOLIAN

Mongolian has an estimated 10 million speakers. The standard Mongolian in the Inner Mongolia Autonomous Region of China is based on the Chahar dialect and written using a cursive script in vertical lines (ie from top to bottom), read from left to right. So if you want to ask a local to read the script in this section, just turn the book 90 degrees clockwise. Our coloured pronunciation guides, however, should simply be read the same way you read English.

Most consonant sounds in Mongolian are the same as in English, though note that r in Mongolian is a hard, trilled sound, kh is a throaty sound like the 'ch' in the Scottish loch, and z is pronounced as the 'ds' in 'lads'. As for the vowels, ē is pronounced as in 'there', ô as in 'alone', ŏ as 'e' with rounded lips, öö as a slightly longer ŏ, u as in 'cut' and ŭ as in 'good'.

Stressed syllables are in italics.

Basics

Hello.	sēn bēn nô
Goodbye.	ba·yur·tē
Excuse me./Sorry.	ôch·lē·rē
Yes.	teem
No.	oo·gway
Thank you.	ba·yur·laa
How are you?	sēn bēn nô
Fine. And you?	sēn sēn / sēn nô
What's your name?	tan·nē al·dur
My name is ...	min·nee nur ...
Do you speak English?	ta ang·gul hul mu·tun nô
I don't understand.	bee oil·og·sun·gway
How much is it?	hut·tee jôs vē
Where's ...?	... haa bēkh vē

GLOSSARY

apsara – Buddhist celestial being

arhat – Buddhist, especially a monk, who has achieved enlightenment and passes to nirvana at death

běi – north; the other points of the compass are *dōng* (east), *nán* (south) and *xī* (west)

biānjiè – border

biéshù – villa

bīnguǎn – hotel

bìxì – mythical tortoiselike dragon

Bodhisattva – one who is worthy of nirvana and remains on earth to help others attain enlightenment

Bon – pre-Buddhist indigenous faith of Tibet

bówùguǎn – museum

CAAC – Civil Aviation Administration of China

cadre – Chinese government bureaucrat

cāntīng – restaurant

cǎoyuán – grasslands

CCP – Chinese Communist Party

chau – land mass

chéngshì – city

chí – lake, pool

chop – carved name seal that acts as a signature

chörten – Tibetan *stupa*

CITS – China International Travel Service

cūn – village

dàdào – boulevard

dàfàndiàn – large hotel

dàjiē – avenue

dàjiǔdiàn – large hotel

dǎo – island

dàpùbù – large waterfall

dàqiáo – large bridge

dàshà – hotel, building

dàxué – university

déhuà – white-glazed porcelain

dìtiě – subway

dōng – east; the other points of the compass are *běi* (north), *nán* (south) and *xī* (west)

dòng – cave

dòngwùyuán – zoo

fàndiàn – hotel, restaurant

fēng – peak

fēngjǐngqū – scenic area

gé – pavilion, temple

gompa – monastery

gōng – palace

gōngyuán – park

gōu – gorge, valley

guān – pass

gùjū – house, home, residence

hǎi – sea

hǎitān – beach

Hakka – Chinese ethnic group

Han – China's main ethnic group

hé – river

hú – lake

huáqiáo – overseas Chinese

Hui – ethnic Chinese Muslims

huǒchēzhàn – train station

huǒshān – volcano

hútòng – a narrow alleyway

jiāng – river

jiǎo – unit of *renminbi*; 10 jiǎo equals 1 *yuán*

jiàotáng – church

jīchǎng – airport

jiē – street

jié – festival

jīn – unit of weight; 1 *jīn* equals 600g

jīngjù – Beijing opera

jìniànbēi – memorial

jìniànguǎn – memorial hall

jiǔdiàn – hotel

jū – residence, home

junk – originally referred to Chinese fishing and war vessels with square sails; now applies to various types of boating craft

kang – raised sleeping platform

KCR – Kowloon–Canton Railway

kora – pilgrim circuit

Kuomintang – Chiang Kaishek's Nationalist Party; now one of Taiwan's major political parties

lama – a Buddhist priest of the Tantric or Lamaist school; a title bestowed on monks of particularly high spiritual attainment

lǐlòng – Shànghǎi alleyway

lín – forest

líng – tomb

lìshǐ – history

lóu – tower

LRT – Light Rail Transit

lù – road

lǚguǎn – guesthouse

luóhàn – Buddhist, especially a monk, who has achieved enlightenment and passes to nirvana at death; see also *arhat*

mahjong – popular Chinese game for four people; played with engraved tiles

mǎtou – dock

mén – gate

ménpiào – entrance ticket

Miao – ethnic group living in Guìzhōu

miào – temple

MTR – Mass Transit Railway

mù – tomb

nán – south; the other points of the compass are *běi* (north), *dōng* (east) and *xī* (west)

páilou – decorative archway

pinyin – the official system for transliterating Chinese script into roman characters

PLA – People's Liberation Army

Politburo – the 25-member supreme policy-making authority of the Chinese Communist Party

PRC – People's Republic of China

PSB – Public Security Bureau; the arm of the police force set up to deal with foreigners

pùbù – waterfall

qì – life force

qiáo – bridge

qìchēzhàn – bus station

rénmín – people, people's

renminbi – literally 'people's money'; the formal name for the currency of China, the basic unit of which is the *yuán*; shortened to RMB

sampan – small motorised launch

sānlún mótuōchē – motor tricycle

sānlúnchē – pedal-powered tricycle

SAR – Special Administrative Region

sēnlín – forest

shān – mountain

shāngdiàn – shop, store

shěng – province, provincial

shi – city

shí – rock

shìchǎng – market

shíkū – grotto

shíkùmén – literally 'stone-gate house'; type of 19th-century Shànghǎi residence

shòupiàochù – ticket office

shuǐkù – reservoir

sì – temple, monastery

sìhéyuàn – traditional courtyard house

stupa – usually used as reliquaries for the cremated remains of important *lamas*

tǎ – pagoda

thangka – Tibetan sacred art

tíng – pavilion

wān – bay

wǎngbā – internet café

wēnquán – hot springs

xī – west; the other points of the compass are *dōng* (east), *běi* (north) and *nán* (south)

xī – small stream, brook

xiá – gorge

xiàn – county

xuěshān – snow mountain

yá – cliff

yán – rock or crag

yóujú – post office

yuán – basic unit of *renminbi*

yuán – garden

zhào – lamasery

zhāodàisuǒ – guesthouse

zhíwùyuán – botanic gardens

zhōng – middle

Zhōngguó – China

zìrán bǎohùqū – nature reserve

Behind the Scenes

SEND US YOUR FEEDBACK

We love to hear from travellers – your comments keep us on our toes and help make our books better. Our well travelled team reads every word on what you loved or loathed about this book. Although we cannot reply individually to your submissions, we always guarantee that your feedback goes straight to the appropriate authors, in time for the next edition. Each person who sends us information is thanked in the next edition – the most useful submissions are rewarded with a selection of digital PDF chapters.

Visit **lonelyplanet.com/contact** to submit your updates and suggestions or to ask for help. Our award-winning website also features inspirational travel stories, news and discussions.

Note: We may edit, reproduce and incorporate your comments in Lonely Planet products such as guidebooks, websites and digital products, so let us know if you don't want your comments reproduced or your name acknowledged. For a copy of our privacy policy visit lonelyplanet.com/privacy.

OUR READERS

Many thanks to the travellers who used the last edition and wrote to us with helpful hints, useful advice and interesting anecdotes:

A Alexander Luijt, Alexandra Coley, Alistair Hayes, Andrew Smith, Anne Agersted **B** Brian Favell **C** Cedric Schelfhaut, Charlotte Toolan, Chris Purslow, Christoph Messmer, Ciriaco Vicente-Mazariegos, Constantin Berger **D** Daniel Gauthier, David Evans, Donald Ross **E** Erik Ainley **F** Ferry Quast, Frans van Eijk **G** Gabriele Corsetti, Geoff Crowhurst, Georg Fernkorn **J** James Lindsay, Jérôme Andrey, Jim Wilcox, Johannes Voit, John Hobkinson, Jon Wisloff, Julien Chapuis, Juul Scheffers **K** Katherine Perez, Kathleen Vennens, Kellie Simms **L** Laurence Markens **M** Massimiliano Ammannito, Mateusz Poślednik, Mathias Herr, Michele Martin, Michelle Josselyn **P** Paolo Priotto **R** Ralph Pringsheim, Raul Cruz Sierra, Rebecca Lagomarsino, Richard Barnett, Rita Selke, Ron Crawford, Ron Perrier **S** Sandy Dance, Sara Santambrogio, Scott Mills, Shohei Takashiro, Stijn Eeckhaut, Susanne Badertscher **T** Tom de Bruin, Tricia Fort **W** Wouter Kolkman **Y** Yana Yout, Yu Hongyuan **Z** Zy Zhang

WRITER THANKS

Damian Harper

Much gratitude to Xiao Xue, Mr Zhang, Jason, Li Chengyuan, Grace, Kathy with the perfect English, Margaux, Alvin, Dai Min, Ann Harper, Ba and Ma, the lovely couple who befriended and helped me on the bus outside Datong and all the countless offers of help and guidance from one of the friendliest nations on this planet. Thanks to all of you.

Piera Chen

Thanks to the Lonely Planet team, and to my friends Janine Cheung and Yuen Ching-sum for their generous assistance. Thanks also to my husband Sze Pang-cheung and daughter Clio for their patience and wonderful support.

Megan Eaves

Many thanks to my incredible China writers, especially Damian Harper and Phillip Tang for taking on giant chunks of research. Vega Liu and Coco Guan at LPCN. Gratitude to the Fujianese monks who rescued me when I was stranded at Tiantishan. As always, Dave Carroll, Jen Carey and Tom Hall, who continue to trust me to run off to China for three weeks and actually come back to the office. And Bill, who forever supports my random need to just go be by myself in the desert for awhile.

David Eimer

Special gratitude goes to Emi Yang for her invaluable assistance. Thanks also to Cathy and Lijuan in Jinghong for their inside knowledge, as well as to Megan Eaves at Lonely Planet. As ever, thanks to the many people along the way who passed on tips, whether knowingly or unwittingly.

Helen Elfer

A huge 谢谢 to everyone I met on this trip who patiently answered questions and offered advice, also to friends past and present who made my time in China so memorable. Particular gratitude to bona fide China Hands Casey and Mike Hall for all sorts of logistical, technical and moral support, plus heaps of fun. And finally thanks to Orlando for coming along for the ride, to China and in general.

Daisy Harper

For time and effort, big thanks as ever to Margaux, Alvin too, Dai Ruibin, Liu Meina, Jamie Chen, Li Jiaqi, Sun Rong and Jackie Zhang. I am also very grateful to my husband and to Jiafu and Jiale, all ever helpful and patient. Thanks also to everyone else I bumped in to along the way who made my job that bit easier.

Trent Holden

First up a massive thanks to Megan Eaves for commissioning me on Beijing. A massive honour indeed to cover a city of this magnitude. Also wanted to say a big thank you to fellow LP colleagues based in the Beijing office, including Vega Liu for all your great tips, beers and assistance along the way, and Guan 'Coco' Yuanyuan for letting me use the office as a temporary workspace – a big help! A shout out to everyone who I shared a beer with, and the tips on places to check out. As always lots of love to my girlfriend Kate Morgan, and all my family and friends in Melbourne and London.

Stephen Lioy

Makiko, for being a patient partner in travel and life – no matter how long the trips become. Jason, for being a steadfast and reliable friend. See you on the trail soon, I hope. Alina, for being an endless source of information. See you in five more years or so? Becky (of teaandprayerflags.com), for being a far more engaged and invested traveller of Tibetan regions than me, and for making sure that those who follow have the deepest experience possible.

Shawn Low

Thanks goes to Jamin Lobsang, Tashi and Tsebtim for showing me the parts of the world you love and know so well. I also depended on the kindness of strangers: for tips, rides and company. To Megan for sending me back to China and to Wyn-Lyn for your constant support!

Tom Masters

Enormous thanks to the people who helped me research this tough destination. Particularly effusive gratitude to Jacob Schickler, who joined me on the road to take pictures for two superb weeks, and whose library of work on Xinjiang is simply superb. I've decided not to thank anyone personally inside Xinjiang here, due to the political sensitivities there, but a big shout out to the tour guides, hostel employees, intrepid taxi drivers and bloggers I met on my travels, you know who you are!

Emily Matchar

Thanks to Megan Eaves and the rest of the LP team for their terrific work. Thanks to Mao Mao for her excellent hot pot suggestions. Thanks to the staff of Travelling With hostel in Chongqing for all their help and advice. And thanks to my husband, Jamin Asay, for accompanying me on this exploration of the hilly terrain and ultra-spicy food of this part of China.

Bradley Mayhew

Thanks to Tenzin and Dechen at Tibet Highland Tours for their help, and to guides Jamyang and Lobsang for their patience. *Tashi delek* to Sandra Braunfels for coming along on yet another Kailash trek. Cheers also to Jamin York and Sonam Jamphel.

Rebecca Milner

I'm indebted to Frank, Marian, Nikki, Ping and so many others whose small kindnesses were deeply felt. Chris P: your advice was so helpful. Megan: this was such an amazing experience, thank you! M&D: none of this would have been possible without you, in so many ways. C, your support means the world to me.

Kate Morgan

Thanks to Destination Editor, Megan Eaves, for commissioning me for this great project. Big thanks to Pat Rogers and Chris Rogers for some excellent Shànghǎi suggestions, and thanks very much to my parents Heather and Gary for all of their support. Most important thank you goes to my favourite person and travel partner, Trent, for always being there for me and for all the laughs along the way.

Tom Spurling

To Lucy, for following me around the world. To Oliver and Poppy, for keeping our spirits up when we just wanted to go home. To Marcus, for the Jiangxi shuffle and for supporting my television career. To Mo Laoshi, for the local wisdom. To Megan, for the stellar opportunity. And to all the citizens of the PRC, for the sincere enthusiasm towards a traveller who was too busy not getting lost at times to pay you sufficient attention.

Phillip Tang

I'm incredibly grateful to 邹嘉 in Shěnyáng not only for hospitality, but for your viciously good knowledge. Big thanks to Megan Eaves, Nigel Chin and Ali Lemer for keen eyes and

guidance. Thanks to all the Chinese people for warmth in their towns – Jimmy in Guǎngzhōu, Wayne in Méizhōu, 小民in Yánjí, Ted in Wǔdàlián Chí and borderlands, and especially Gorden in Cháozhōu. Reflective thanks to family in Guǎngzhōu.

ACKNOWLEDGEMENTS

Climate map data adapted from Peel MC, Finlayson BL & McMahon TA (2007) 'Updated World Map of the Köppen-Geiger Climate Classification', *Hydrology and Earth System Sciences*, 11, pp1633–44.

Cover photograph: Chinese Traditional Opera, Julian W/Shutterstock ©

Illustrations: pp72–3 and pp300-1 by Michael Weldon.

BEHIND THE SCENES

THIS BOOK

This 15th edition of Lonely Planet's *China* guidebook was researched and written by Damian Harper, Piera Chen, Megan Eaves, David Eimer, Helen Elfer, Daisy Harper, Trent Holden, Stephen Lioy, Shawn Low, Tom Masters, Emily Matchar, Bradley Mayhew, Rebecca Milner, Kate Morgan, Christopher Pitts, Tom Spurling and Phillip Tang. This guidebook was produced by the following:

Destination Editor
Megan Eaves

Product Editors
Kate Chapman, Catherine Naghten

Senior Cartographer
Julie Sheridan

Book Designer Mazzy Prinsep

Assisting Editors
Sarah Bailey, Judith Bamber, Michelle Bennett, Carolyn Boicos, Nigel Chin, Grace Dobell, Andrea Dobbin, Bruce Evans, Samantha Forge, Carly Hall, Paul Harding, Gabby Innes, Helen Koehne, Kellie Langdon, Ali Lemer, Anne Mason, Kate Mathews, Anne Mulvaney, Lauren O'Connell, Charlotte Orr, Susan Paterson, Vicky Smith, Tracy Whitmey,

Amanda Williamson, Simon Williamson

Cartographers
Hunor Csutoros, Julie Dodkins, James Leversha

Cover Researcher
Naomi Parker

Thanks to Jane Atkin, Joe Bindloss, Cheree Broughton, Jennifer Carey, David Carroll, Neill Coen, Daniel Corbett, Coco Guan, Gemma Graham, Jane Grisman, Corey Hutchison, Andi Jones, Lauren Keith, Indra Kilfoyle, Chris LeeAck, Vega Liu, Claire Naylor, Karyn Noble, Laura Noiret, Tom O'Malley, Ellie Simpson, Nav Sushil, Dora Whitaker

Index

Map Legend

Sights

- Beach
- Bird Sanctuary
- Buddhist
- Castle/Palace
- Christian
- Confucian
- Hindu
- Islamic
- Jain
- Jewish
- Monument
- Museum/Gallery/Historic Building
- Ruin
- Shinto
- Sikh
- Taoist
- Winery/Vineyard
- Zoo/Wildlife Sanctuary
- Other Sight

Activities, Courses & Tours

- Bodysurfing
- Diving
- Canoeing/Kayaking
- Course/Tour
- Sento Hot Baths/Onsen
- Skiing
- Snorkelling
- Surfing
- Swimming/Pool
- Walking
- Windsurfing
- Other Activity

Sleeping

- Sleeping
- Camping

Eating

- Eating

Drinking & Nightlife

- Drinking & Nightlife
- Cafe

Entertainment

- Entertainment

Shopping

- Shopping

Information

- Bank
- Embassy/Consulate
- Hospital/Medical
- Internet
- Police
- Post Office
- Telephone
- Toilet
- Tourist Information
- Other Information

Geographic

- Beach
- Gate
- Hut/Shelter
- Lighthouse
- Lookout
- Mountain/Volcano
- Oasis
- Park
- Pass
- Picnic Area
- Waterfall

Population

- Capital (National)
- Capital (State/Province)
- City/Large Town
- Town/Village

Transport

- Airport
- Border crossing
- Bus
- Cable car/Funicular
- Cycling
- Ferry
- Metro/MRT/MTR station
- Monorail
- Parking
- Petrol station
- Skytrain/Subway station
- Taxi
- Train station/Railway
- Tram
- Underground station
- Other Transport

Note: Not all symbols displayed above appear on the maps in this book

Routes

- Tollway
- Freeway
- Primary
- Secondary
- Tertiary
- Lane
- Unsealed road
- Road under construction
- Plaza/Mall
- Steps
- Tunnel
- Pedestrian overpass
- Walking Tour
- Walking Tour detour
- Path/Walking Trail

Boundaries

- International
- State/Province
- Disputed
- Regional/Suburb
- Marine Park
- Cliff
- Wall

Hydrography

- River, Creek
- Intermittent River
- Canal
- Water
- Dry/Salt/Intermittent Lake
- Reef

Areas

- Airport/Runway
- Beach/Desert
- Cemetery (Christian)
- Cemetery (Other)
- Glacier
- Mudflat
- Park/Forest
- Sight (Building)
- Sportsground
- Swamp/Mangrove

Bradley Mayhew
Tibet

Bradley has been writing guidebooks for 20 years now. He started travelling while studying Chinese at Oxford University, and has since focused his expertise on China, Tibet, the Himalaya and Central Asia. He is the co-author of Lonely Planet guides to Tibet, Nepal, Trekking in the Nepal Himalaya, Bhutan, Central Asia and many others. Bradley has also fronted two TV series for Arte and SWR, one retracing the route of Marco Polo via Turkey, Iran, Afghanistan, Central Asia and China, and the other trekking Europe's 10 most scenic long-distance trails.

Rebecca Milner
Ānhuī, Zhèjiāng, Hǎinán

California born and longtime Tokyo-resident (14 years and counting!), Rebecca has co-written Lonely Planet guides to Tokyo, Japan, Korea and China. Her freelance writing covering travel, food and culture has been published in the *Guardian*, the *Independent*, the *Sunday Times Travel Magazine*, the *Japan Times* and more. After spending the better part of her twenties working to travel – doing odd jobs in Tokyo to make money so she could spend months at a time backpacking around Asia – Rebecca was fortunate enough to turn the tables in 2010, joining the Lonely Planet team of freelance writers.

Kate Morgan
Shànghǎi

Having lived and travelled extensively in North Asia, Kate was very keen for the chance to get back to explore Shànghǎi. Days were spent shooting up to the top of Pǔdōng skyscrapers, hunting out the best boutiques in the French Concession, tracing Jewish history in Hóngkǒu, taste-testing oolong tea and dining on dumplings...not a bad day's work. Kate has worked for Lonely Planet for over a decade now on destinations including Japan, India, Melbourne and Zimbabwe.

Christopher Pitts
Hénán, Héběi, Tiānjīn

Chris started off his university years studying classical Chinese poetry before a week in 1990s Shànghǎi (en route to school in Kūnmíng) abruptly changed his focus to the idiosyncracies of modern China. Several years in Asia memorising Chinese characters got him hooked, and he returns whenever he can to immerse himself in what is surely one of the world's most fascinating languages. He's written for Lonely Planet China since 2004. Visit him online at www.christopherpitts.net.

Tom Spurling
Fújiàn, Húběi, Jiāngxī, Guìzhōu

Tom is an Australian guidebook author and high school teacher currently based in Hong Kong in search of the long-lost expatriate package. He's worked on 13 Lonely Planet titles, including *Japan*, *China*, *Central America*, *Turkey*, *India*, *South Africa* and *Australia*. When not chasing his tail, he enjoys tucking it under his crossed legs for minutes on end.

Phillip Tang
Guǎngdōng, Hēilóngjiāng, Liáoníng, Jílín

Phillip grew up on typically Australian pho and fish'n'chips. A degree in Latin-American and Chinese cultures launched him into travel and writing about it for Lonely Planet's *Canada*, *China*, *Japan*, *Korea*, *Mexico*, *Peru* and *Vietnam* guides. Phillip has made his home in Sydney, Melbourne, London and Mexico City. His travels include most countries in Europe, much of Asia and Latin America, as well as the greatest hits of North America. Phillip writes about travel and the people there, who just call it living. He likes smelling fresh mint in a market in a new town and imagining a parallel life there. More pics and words: philliptang.co.uk. Phillip also wrote the Survival Guide chapters.

Helen Elfer
Hángzhōu, Shànghǎi

Helen made Shanghai her home between 2007-10, so she was delighted to be able to return and contribute to the latest Lonely Planet *China* and *Shanghai* guides. After a two-year stint in Abu Dhabi, she moved back to London, working as a travel writer for various newspapers and magazines. She's currently Lonely Planet's Destination Editor for the Middle East and North Africa.

Daisy Harper
Shāndōng, Jiāngsū

Born in the Shāndōng town of Qīngdǎo, Daisy grew up in China before going to university in Beijing to study English and then moving to the UK to pursue a career as a journalist and travel writer. A native speaker of Chinese, She has concentrated her energies on China travel, exploring and further fathoming her home country, working on four editions of Lonely Planet China to date.

Trent Holden
Běijīng

A Geelong-based writer, located just outside Melbourne, Trent has worked for Lonely Planet since 2005. He's covered 30 plus guidebooks across Asia, Africa and Australia. With a penchant for megacities, Trent's in his element when assigned to cover a nation's capital – the more chaotic the better – to unearth cool bars, art, street food and underground subculture. On the flipside he also writes books to idyllic tropical islands across Asia, in between going on safari to national parks in Africa and the subcontinent. When not travelling, Trent works as a freelance editor, reviewer and spending all his money catching live gigs.

Stephen Lioy
Sìchuān

Stephen is a photographer, writer, hiker, and travel blogger based in Central Asia. A 'once in a lifetime' Eurotrip and post-university move to China set the stage for what would eventually become a semi-nomadic lifestyle based on sharing his experiences with would-be travellers and helping provide that initial push out of comfort zones and into all that the planet has to offer.

Shawn Low
Qīnghǎi

After many hot, sticky and sweaty years in Singapore, Shawn made for the cooler but more temperamental climes of Melbourne in 2001. He found his way into Lonely Planet as a book editor in 2006. Since then, he's done two stints as a commissioning editor and has constantly (sometimes successfully) flirted with the Lonely Planet TV. Shawn has penned a dozen LP guides and recently co-founded a London-based travel startup Firef.ly.

Tom Masters
Xīnjiāng

Tom has been travelling in China since 2004, having begun teaching himself Mandarin in his bedroom aged 14 during a bout of Sinophilia from which he's never quite recovered. Tom has written many books about off-the-beaten track destinations for Lonely Planet, including as a regular author on the *Central Asia* guide, which made him an obvious choice to cover Xīnjiāng for this book. Tom lives in Berlin and can be found online at www.tommasters.net

Emily Matchar
Chóngqìng, the Yangzi, Hong Kong

A native of Chapel Hill, North Carolina, Emily first caught Relapsing Travel Fever during a high-school semester abroad in Argentina. To date, Emily has contributed to some two dozen Lonely Planet guides. She also writes about culture, travel, politics and food for the *New York Times*, the *Washington Post*, the *New Republic*, the *Atlantic, Men's Journal, Outside, Gourmet* and many more. When she's not busy rating Memphis barbecue joints, wandering around night markets in Laos, or tramping in New Zealand, she can be found chowing down on dumplings in her adopted city of Hong Kong.

OUR STORY

A beat-up old car, a few dollars in the pocket and a sense of adventure. In 1972 that's all Tony and Maureen Wheeler needed for the trip of a lifetime – across Europe and Asia overland to Australia. It took several months, and at the end – broke but inspired – they sat at their kitchen table writing and stapling together their first travel guide, *Across Asia on the Cheap*. Within a week they'd sold 1500 copies. Lonely Planet was born.

Today, Lonely Planet has offices in Franklin, London, Melbourne, Oakland, Dublin, Beijing and Delhi, with more than 600 staff and writers. We share Tony's belief that 'a great guidebook should do three things: inform, educate and amuse'.

OUR WRITERS

Damian Harper
Guǎngxī, Húnán, Shaanxi, Shānxī, Inner Mongolia, Níngxià

Ten years of British boarding school gave Damian every incentive to explore new horizons beyond home. A degree in History of Art at Leeds University followed in 1995 and a few years later Damian applied to work on the Lonely Planet China guide. Since then, Damian has served as coordinating author on seven editions of the guide and has co-authored multiple editions of the *Beijing* and *Shanghai* city guides, *Malaysia, Singapore and Brunei, Vietnam, Thailand, London, Great Britain* and *Ireland;* Damian also wrote the 1st edition of *Shanghai Encounter* and *Best of Shanghai* and co-wrote *China's Southwest* (3rd edition) and two Hong Kong titles.

Damian also wrote the Understand and Planning chapters.

Piera Chen
Hong Kong

When not on the road, Piera divides her time between hometown Hong Kong, Taiwan and Vancouver. She has authored more than a dozen travel guides and contributed to as many travel-related titles. Piera has a BA in Literature from Pomona College. Her early life was peppered with trips to Taiwan, China and Southeast Asia, but it was during her first trip to Europe that dawn broke. She remembers being fresh off a flight, looking around her in Rome, thinking, 'I want to be doing this every day.' And she has.

Megan Eaves
Gānsù

Megan is Lonely Planet's North Asia Destination Editor and her writing has appeared in Lonely Planet's guidebooks to China and South Korea. Having lived everywhere from her home state of New Mexico to eastern China and Prague, she's now based in Lonely Planet's London office, where she's the resident beer nerd and dumpling addict. If lost, she is likely to be found stargazing in a desert somewhere.

David Eimer
Yúnnán, Běijīng

David has been a journalist and writer ever since abandoning the idea of a law career in 1990. After spells working in his native London and in Los Angeles, he moved to Beijing in 2005, where he contributed to a variety of newspapers and magazines in the UK. Since then, he has travelled and lived across China and in numerous cities in Southeast Asia, including Bangkok, Phnom Penh and Yangon. He has been covering China, Myanmar and Thailand for Lonely Planet since 2006.

OVER PAGE MORE WRITERS

Published by Lonely Planet Global Limited
CRN 554153
15th edition – June 2017
ISBN 978 1 78657 522 7
© Lonely Planet 2017 Photographs © as indicated 2017
10 9 8 7 6 5 4 3 2 1
Printed in Singapore